thimblerig . . . Ixion offspring . . . water ouzel

And hundreds more esoteric/obscure clues are listed in this fascinating, easy-to-use dictionary. But this book is much more—it's also a veritable fount of fascinating facts. Where else could you find the countries that make up the ABC powers . . . an Arndt piece . . . Andy Gump's wife . . . the former name of Annapolis . . . without even getting out of the A's!

A masterpiece of compilation, **The New Comprehensive A-Z Crossword Dictionary** is a practical and invaluable reference book that is sure to become the crossword puzzle and wordgame freak's indispensable aid!

"Most puzzle dictionaries can be more of a riddle than the puzzle you are seeking to solve. One of the attractions of this dictionary is the alphabetical arrangement, a practical method which enables the puzzle fan to go directly to subject words on the basis of the barest clue." *Charles Preston*, Puzzle Editor, *The National Observer* and Compiler, *Crosswords for the Connoisseur*.

The New Comprehensive A-Z Crossword Dictionary

Compiled by Redentor Ma. Tuazon
and Edy Garcia Schaffer

AVON BOOKS  NEW YORK

AVON BOOKS
A division of
The Hearst Corporation
105 Madison Avenue
New York, New York 10016

Copyright © 1973 by Redentor Ma. Tuazon
Published by arrangement with Grosset & Dunlap, Inc.
Library of Congress Catalog Card Number: 72-79971
ISBN: 0-380-00168-3

First Avon Books Printing: November 1974

AVON TRADEMARK REG. U.S. PAT. OFF. AND IN OTHER COUNTRIES, MARCA
REGISTRADA, HECHO EN U.S.A.

Printed in the U.S.A.

K–R 30 29

To Bobby, Lynn and Ruby, whose mother's unfailing support and encouragement enabled me to finish this book.

Also to Rafael L. Dizon, Sr., Auditor, Central Bank of the Philippines, and Blas F. Ople, Philippine Secretary of Labor, for timely aid.

Redentor Ma. Tuazon

THE NEW COMPREHENSIVE
A-Z
CROSSWORD
DICTIONARY

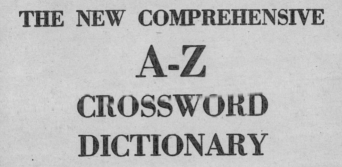

About the Authors

Redentor Ma. Tuazon, a Philippine native, was about twelve years old when he first saw a crossword puzzle. That was back in 1923. He immediately became a devoted enthusiast and began collecting puzzle clues into notebooks. *The New Comprehensive A-Z Crossword Dictionary* is the result of those painstakingly kept notebooks, compiled over almost fifty years. Mr. Tuazon has been Director of Public Relations for the Boy Scouts of the Philippines, Public Information Officer of the Philippine National Red Cross and a newspaper reporter for the *Manila Daily Bulletin*. Now retired, he lives in Quezon City, Philippines.

Edy Garcia Schaffer was Mr. Tuazon's valuable co-researcher during many of the later years this dictionary was compiled. Mrs. Schaffer now resides in California.

Foreword

The authors and the publishers want you to know that no effort has been spared to bring to you, the serious word puzzle fan, the most comprehensive and useful crossword dictionary available on the market today.

The compiling, assembling and cross-referencing of the material for this compendium of clues and solutions took almost half a century. In recent years, special attention has been paid to updating clues, adding current material and making sure that the puzzle addict is fully equipped to do battle with today's clever and wily crossword puzzle constructors.

In the setting of the text, no less than three different types have been used so as to proffer an easy-to-read-and-understand page. Individual and initial entries are set in a clean boldface type. Subentries are indented and set in an unobtrusive lightface. (If a subentry, however, has a further indented subentry, the column's head reverts to boldface to catch the eye.) All solution words appear in small caps. A bold type runninghead allows quick location of clue words in this completely alphabetized work.

The following page lists the abbeviations used in this book. Though necessary to make manageable a work of these proportions, they have been used sparingly in the interest of readability.

The authors and the publishers hope that they have succeeded in putting together a volume that will take its place on shelves alongside more serious reference works and see practical and pleasurable use for years to come.

Listing of Abbreviations Used

abbr.	abbreviation
Austral.	Australian
Brit.	British
colloq.	colloquial
comb. form	combining form
Eng.	English
Fr.	French
Ger.	German
Gr.	Greek
Ital.	Italian
Lat.	Latin
Mex.	Mexican
myth.	mythology
N.	North
Russ.	Russian
S.	South
Scot.	Scottish
sl.	slang
Sp.	Spanish
U.S.	United States

A

A, Greek .... ALPHA
   Hebrew .... ALEPH
aa .... LAVA
aardvark .... ANTEATER,
              ANTBEAR
   eating place .... ANTHILL,
            FORMICARY
Aaron's ally .... HUR
   brother .... MOSES
   death mount ...... HOR
   miracle worker ..... ROD
   rod .... MULLEIN
   sister .... MIRIAM
   son ..... NADAD, ABIHU
aba .... ROBE, GARMENT
abaca .... LINAGA, LUPIS,
        HEMP, FIRER
   product .... ROPE
aback, taken .... SURPRISED,
     STARTLED, CONFUSED,
      DISCONCERTED
Abaddon .. HELL, ABYSS, SATAN
   angel .... APOLLYON
abaft .... ASTERN, AFT,
      BEHIND, REAR
abalone .... ORMER, SNAIL,
   EARSHELL, ASSEIR, MOLLUSK
abandon .... LEAVE, DISCARD,
  FORSAKE, DESERT, ABDICATE
abandoned .... DESOLATE,
   DERELICT, FORSAKEN, LEFT
abandonment .... DESERTION,
   DESOLATION, DEFECTION
à bas .... DOWN
abase ...... DEMEAN, LOWER,
  HUMBLE, DEGRADE, DISHONOR
abasement .... SHAME,
  HUMILIATION, DEGRADATION
abash ... EMBARRASS, SHAME,
  CONFOUND, DISCOMFIT,
  DISCONCERT, CONFUSE
abate ...... SUBSIDE, LESSEN,
  DECREASE, DIMINISH,
  LOOSEN, WANE, QUASH, EASE
abatement .... LETUP,
  REDUCTION, EASEMENT
abatis .... BARRICADE
abattoir .. SLAUGHTERHOUSE,
      SHAMBLES
abb ... . YARN, WOOL

abba .... FATHER
abbe ... ABBOT, MONK, PRIEST
   domain .... ABBACY,
       MONASTERY
abbess .... AMMA
   domain ...... CONVENT,
       NUNNERY
   who loved Abelard .....
       HELOISE
abbey .. CONVENT, MONASTERY
   head ..... ABBOT, ABBESS
   of an .... ABBATIAL
abbot ... ABBE, ABBAS, COARB,
      HEGUMEN
   assistant .... PRIOR
   hero .... ROLLO
abbreviate .... SHORTEN,
    CONTRACT, CUT
ABC power ..... ARGENTINA,
    BRAZIL, CHILE
abdicate .. RENOUNCE, RESIGN,
      SURRENDER
abdication .... DEMISSION
abdomen ... BELLY, STOMACH,
    PAUNCH, VENTER
   of the .... ALVINE
abdominal .... VENTRAL
   limb, crustacean ......
      PLEOPOD
   pain .... COLIC,
   COLLYWOBBLES, PYROSIS
   region .... PUBES
   swelling .... BLOAT
abduct .... KIDNAP
   slang .... SNATCH,
      SHANGHAI
Abdul the Bul Bul ..... AMIR
Abel's brother .... CAIN
   parent .... ADAM, EVE
Abelard's love ...... HELOISE
abele .... POPLAR, PINE
aberration ...... DEVIATION,
   DERANGEMENT, DELIRIUM
abet ... EGG, FOMENT, INCITE,
    AID, HELP, SECOND
abeyance .... SUSPENSION,
      PENDENCY
abhor .. DETEST, HATE, LOATHE
abhorrence .... AVERSION,
  ODIUM, HATRED, DETESTATION

1

abide .... DWELL, LIVE, STAY, REMAIN, (A)WAIT, TARRY

abiding ... ENDURING, LASTING

Abie's loved one .... ROSE

abigail .... MAID

Abigail's husband ..... NABAL, DAVID

Abijah's son .... ASA

ability .... FLAIR, POWER, PROWESS, TALENT, CALIBER, FACULTY

to borrow .... CREDIT

to feel ..... (A)ESTHESIA, SENSATION

to read and write .... LITERACY

abject .... BASE, PITIFUL, WRETCHED, SERVILE

abjectly afraid .... CRAVEN

abjure ... RECANT, REPUDIATE, DENY, RENOUNCE, DISAVOW

ablaze .... AFLAME, AFIRE, BURNING, EAGER, EXCITED

able .... HABILE, ADEPT, SKILLFUL, SKILLED, COMPETENT, QUALIFIED

to pay .... SOLVENT

to read and write .... LITERATE

to reason .... SANE

willing and .. READY, SET

ablegate .... ENVOY

abluent .... DETERGENT, SOAP

ablution .... BATH(ING), WASHING, CLEANSING

abnegation .... DENIAL

Abner epithet/character ... LIL

abnormal .... IRREGULAR, UNNATURAL, ODD

eye condition .... MYOPIA

Abo .... TURKO

abode ...... NEST, HABITAT, RESIDENCE, HABITATION, HOME

of animals ... LAIR, DEN, WARREN, HUTCH, STY

of birds ..... NIDE, NEST, AERIE, COTE, AVIARY

of gods ...... ASGARD, OLYMPUS

of humans ..... MIGARD

of paradise .... EDEN

of sinner's soul ... LIMBO, PURGATORY

of the dead ..... ARALU, ORCUS, HADES, SHEOL, PARADISE, NIRVANA

of the Muses .... PARNASSUS

abolish .... ANNUL, CANCEL, REPEAL, REVOKE, DISCARD

aboma .... SNAKE, BOA

abominable .... VILE, LOATHSOME, DETESTABLE, HATEFUL, HEINOUS

Snowman .... YETI

abominate ... DETEST, LOATHE, EXECRATE, HATE

abomination .... PLAGUE, AVERSION, HATRED, LOATHING

aboriginal .... NATAL, FIRST, INDIGENOUS

weapon .... WADDY, BOOMERANG, NULLA, BLOWPIPE, WO(O)MERA

aborigine ... NATIVE, INDIGENE

world boxing champ .... (LIONEL) ROSE

abort ...... CHECK, THWART

abortion .... MISCARRIAGE

illegal .... FETICIDE, ABORTICIDE

abortive .... FRUITLESS, UNSUCCESSFUL

abound .... TEEM, SWARM

abounding .... RIFE, PLENTIFUL, TEEMING

suffix .... FUL, ULANT

about .... OF, ANENT, RE, REGARDING, CIRCA, ALMOST, CONCERNING

face: colloq. ... REVERSAL, SOM(M)ERSAULT, TURNABOUT

above .. : OVER, ALOFT, HIGHER, ATOP, UPON, PAST, SUPRA

board ..... LEGIT, OPEN, HONEST, FAIR, BLAMELESS

poetic .... O'ER

prefix ..... SUPER, SUPRA

reproach ..... INNOCENT, BLAMELESS, PURE

the ear .... EPIOTIC

zero .... PLUS

abra .... DEFILE, PASS

abracadabra .... SPELL, JARGON, GIBBERISH

abrade ... RUB, CHAFE, GRATE, RASP, SCRAPE, WEAR, ERODE

abrading tool .... FILE, RASP

abrading material .... EMERY, CORUNDUM, SAND(PAPER), ERODENT

Abraham's birthplace ..... UR
    brother .... HARAN
    father .... TERAH
    grandfather ..... NAHOR
    nephew .... LOT
    son ..... ISAAC, MEDAN,
        SHUAH, ISHMAEL
    wife ..... SARAH, SARAI
abramis ... BREAM, CARP, FISH
abrasion ...... SCRAPE, BRUISE
abrasive ... EMERY, BORT(Z),
    ERODENT, QUARTZ,
    SAND(PAPER), TRIPOLI
abraxas ... CHARM, GEM, STONE
abri ...... SHELTER, DUGOUT
abridge ... SHORTEN, CURTAIL,
    EDIT, DIGEST
abridgment .... SUMMARY,
    SYNOPSIS, DIGEST, EPITOME,
    COMPEND(IUM)
abroad .... OUTDOORS,
    OVERSEAS, AWAY
abrogate .... ANNUL, CANCEL,
    REPEAL, ABOLISH, RESCIND
abrogation ...... RESCISSION,
    CASSATION, ABOLITION
abrupt ... STEEP, RUDE, HASTY,
    BRUSQUE, CURT, GRUFF,
    SUDDEN, UNEXPECTED
abruptly ... SPANG, SUDDENLY
Absalom's captain/cousin ....
    AMASA
    father .... DAVID
    sister .... TAMAR
    slayer .... JOAB
abscess ...... PUSTULE, BOIL,
    FESTER, ULCER
    on gums ..... GUMBOIL
abscond ...... ELOPE, FLEE,
    DECAMP, LEVANT, ESCAPE,
    ELOINE
absence, leave of ..... EXEAT,
    PERMIT, FURLOUGH
    of feeling .... INSENSATE,
    COLD, NUMB
    of hair .... ACOMIA,
    ALOPECIA
    of motion .. REST, INERTIA
    of shame .... BRAZEN
    of taste .... AGEUSIA
absent ..... AWAY, OUT, GONE
    minded .... LOST,
    ABSORBED, DISTRAIT,
    PREOCCUPIED
    without leave ..... AWOL

absentee, a kind of ....
    MALINGERER, TRUANT
absinthe ... GENIPI, LIQUEUR,
    WORMWOOD
absolute ...... UTTER, TOTAL,
    SHEER, PLENARY, WHOLE,
    CERTAIN, DEFINITE, PURE,
    VERY, STARK
    independence ...... ALOD
    rule .... AUTARCHY,
    DESPOTISM
    ruler ..... DESPOT, TSAR,
    SULTAN, SHAH, CZAR
    superlative .... ELATIVE,
    ULTRA
absolutely .... SIMPLY,
    CERTAINLY, UTTERLY
absolution .... REMISSION,
    PARDON, FORGIVENESS,
    CLEARANCE
absolve ...... PARDON, REMIT,
    ACQUIT, CLEAR, FREE,
    EXONERATE
    in law .... VESTED
    sin .... SHRIVE
absorb ..... ENGROSS, SUCK,
    ENGULF, DRINK, SWALLOW,
    ASSIMILATE
absorbed ... (W)RAPT, ENRAPT,
    LOST, ENGROSSED,
    ASSIMILATED
absorbent .... BIBULOUS
    material .... SPONGE,
    BLOTTER, GAUZE
abstain .... REFRAIN,
    DESIST, FORBEAR, DENY
    from .... ESCHEW
    from eating .... FAST
abstainer of a kind ....
    TEETOTALER, DRY
abstemious ...... TEMPERATE,
    MODERATE, SOBER
absterge ... PURGE, CLEAN(SE),
    WIPE
abstinence .. SELF-RESTRAINT,
    SELF-DENIAL
    from alcoholic drinks ....
    TEETOTALISM, SOBRIETY
    sexual .... CHASTITY,
    CONTINENCE, CELIBACY
    total ...... TEMPERANCE
abstract ...... REMOVE, BRIEF,
    STEAL, PRECIS, COMPEND,
    EPITOME, SUMMARY, RESUME,
    DIGEST
    being .... ENS, ESSE

abstraction .... NOTION, PREOCCUPATION

abstruse ... DEEP, RECONDITE, ESOTERIC, SUBTLE, HIDDEN

absurd .... RIDICULOUS, SILLY, NONSENSICAL, INEPT, FOOLISH, PREPOSTEROUS

slang ... COCKEYED, RICH

absurdity .... NONSENSE, FOOLISHNESS

abundance ...... PLENITUDE, RIFE, EXUBERANCE, WEALTH, GALORE, STORE

abundant .. AMPLE, PLENTIFUL, TEEMING, AFFLUENT, RIFE

abuse ..... REVILE, MISTREAT, RAIL, MISUSE, VIOLATE, SCOLD, MALTREAT(MENT)

a confidence .... BETRAY

abut .... ADJOIN, BORDER

abysm .... ABYSS

abysmal .... FATHOMLESS, IMMEASURABLE

abyss .... CHASM, GULF, HOLE, PIT, DEPTH

Babylonian mythology .. APSU

below Hades .. TARTARUS

Abyssinia ... ETHIOPIA, AXUM

Abyssinian .... KAF(F)A, ETHIOPIAN

banana .... ENSETE

capital .... ADDIS ABABA

city ..... HARAR, ADOWA

coin/money ..... TALARI, GIRSH, BESA

dialect ..... GEEZ, GHESE

district .... HARAR

division ...... SHOA, TIGRE

drink ..... BOUSA, MESE

emperor .... NEGUS, SELASSIE, MENELIK

fly .... ZIMB

grain/plant .... TEFF

Hamite ..... AGAO, BEJA, AFAR(A)

herb .... RAMTIL

lake .... TSANA, DEMBEA

language .... SAHO, GEEZ, AMHARIC, AGOW

liquid measure .... KUBA

money .... BESA, TALARI

mountain .... AMBA

ox ..... GALLA, SANGA

primate .... ABUNA

prince .... RAS

river ..... MOFER, MAREB, ABAI

rock salt money ... EMOL

tree .... KOSO, CUSSO

tribe .... AFAR

tribesman .... SHOA

wolf .... KABERU

weight ..... AKET, ALADA, KASM, NATR

acacia ...... LOCUST, BABUL, SHRUB, MIMOSA, SHITTAH, MYALL, WATTLE

astringent ..... CATECHU

academe .... GROVE

academic .... CLASSIC, SCHOLASTIC, SCHOLARLY, PEDANTIC, SPECULATIVE

achievement .... DEGREE, DOCTORATE

costume appendage ..... LIRIPIPE

degree, kind of .... LICENTIATE

paper .... THESIS

Acadia .... NOVA SCOTIA

acaleph .... JELLYFISH, SEA NETTLE

acarid .... MITE, TICK, ARACHNID

acaudal/acaudate ... TAILLESS

accede ..... CONSENT, AGREE

accelerant .... CATALYST

accelerate ... SPEED, HASTEN, RACE, STEP-UP

accelerator ... THROTTLE, GUN

accent .. TONE, STRESS, BROGUE, ICTUS, EMPHASIS, MARK

accenting syllable ...... ARSIS

accentuate .... STRESS, EMPHASIZE, HEIGHTEN

accept ..... ADMIT, SWALLOW, ALLOW, RECEIVE, GRANT

as true .... CREDIT, ADMIT

accepted standard ..... NORM, TYPE, MODEL, PAR

access ...... ENTREE, ENTRY, INCREASE, ADMISSION, APPROACH

accessible .... OPEN, APPROACHABLE

accessory .... ADJUNCT, APPURTENANT, ACCOMPLICE, ADDITIONAL, EXTRA

accident ... CASUALTY, MISHAP

accidental ...... FORTUITOUS, CASUAL, ADVENTITIOUS

accipiter ... HAWK, EAGLE, OWL

acclaim ...... LAUD, PRAISE, APPLAUD, HAIL

acclamation .... SHOUT, CRY, PRAISE, PLAUDIT

word of .... OLE, BRAVO, BANZAI, MABUHAY, RAH, HAIL, AVE, HEIL

acclimate ..... ENURE, INURE, ACCUSTOM

acclivity .... SLOPE, TALUS

accolade .... AWARD, HONOR, PRAISE, EMBRACE

accommodate ... LEND, ADAPT, OBLIGE, GRANT, ADJUST, RECONCILE, LODGE

accommodation ... LODGING, LOAN, BERTH, FAVOR

accompaniment .... VAMP

accompany .... JOIN, ESCORT, CONVOY, CHAPERON(E)

accomplish .... EFFECT, ACHIEVE, FILL UP, DO

accomplished ...... SKILLED, SKILLFUL, PROFICIENT, POLISHED

accomplishment .... ACHIEVEMENT, DEED, SKILL, TALENT

accord .... UNITY, GIVE, CONCERT, UNISON, HARMONY

according to ...... PER, ALLA, PURSUANT

good form ... DE RIGUEUR

law/rule ..... LEGAL(LY), LEGITIMATE, DE REGLE, FORMAL

morals .... ETHICAL

usage .... CUSTOMARY

accordion-like instrument .... CONCERTINA, MELODEON

accost .... HAIL, GREET, CALL, ADDRESS, SALUTE

account .... STATEMENT, EXPLAIN, COMPUTE, STORY, SCORE, TAB, SAKE, REPORT

entry ...... ITEM, CREDIT, DEBIT

accounting ..... BOOKKEEPING

form .... LEDGER

accouter ...... DRESS, EQUIP, ARRAY, OUTFIT

accouterment ... TRAPPING(S), HABILIMENT

accredit .... APPOINT, DEPUTE, AUTHORIZE, CERTIFY

Accra is its capital .... GHANA

accrue .... ENSUE, RESULT, INCREASE, ACCUMULATE, ISSUE

accumulate ... AMASS, ACCRUE, COLLECT, GATHER

accumulation ... HOARD, FUND, COLLECTION, HEAP, PILE

accuracy .... PRECISION, FAITHFULNESS

of reproduction .... FIDELITY

accusation ..... CHARGE, RAP, BLAME, ARRAIGNMENT, INDICTMENT

accuse ...... CHARGE, BLAME, INDICT, ARRAIGN, IMPEACH

accustom ...... INURE, ENURE, HABITUATE, TOUGHEN, ACCLIMATE

accustomed ... INURED, WONT, USED, USUAL, HABITUATED

ace ..... STAR, HERO, ONE(R), EXPERT, TIB, ONESPOT

of clubs .... BASTO

queen combination ..... TENACE

to ten in poker .... STRAIGHT

to ten, same suit .... (ROYAL) FLUSH

acephalous .... HEADLESS, LEADERLESS

acerate .... NEEDLELIKE

acerb .... TART, BITTER, SHARP, ACID, HARSH

acerbate .... EMBITTER, VEX, IRRITATE

aces, two .... AMBSACE, AMESACE

acetic acid .... ACETATE, VINEGAR, ESTER

acetone ... ACETOL, KEYSTONE

acetose .... ACID, SOUR

acetum .... VINEGAR

acetylene .... TOLANE, ETHIN(E)

ache ... PAIN, YEARN, THROB, PINE

Acheron ...... HADES, RIVER

tributary ...... COCYTUS

achieve .... ATTAIN, WIN, REALIZE, ACCOMPLISH, REACH

achievement .... FEAT, EXPLOIT, ACCOMPLISHMENT, ATTAINMENT

Achilles . . . . PELIDES
   adviser . . . . NESTOR
   captive . . . . BRISEIS
   parent . . . PELEUS, THETIS
   slayer . . . . PARIS
   teacher . . . . CHIRON
   victim . . . . HECTOR
   vulnerable spot . . . . HEEL
   warriors . . . . MYRMIDONS
   woman captive . . . BRISEIS
achira . . . . CANNA
achromatic substance . . . LININ
acicular . . . . . . SPINY, BRISTLY
acid . . . . . SOUR, TART, SHARP,
   BITING, ACERB
   base indicator . . . . LITMUS
   etching . . . . MORDANT
   kind of . . . . AMINO, BORIC,
   SALYCIC, NITRIC, OLEATE
   neutralizer . . . . . . ALKALI
   nicotinic . . . . NIACIN
   slang . . . . LSD
   tanning . . . . . . CATECHIN
acidity . . . . . ACOR, ACERBITY,
   SOURNESS
acidulous . . . . TART
acinus . . . . RASPBERRY
ack-ack fire . . . . FLAK
   gun . . . . POMPOM
acknowledge . . . . . OWN, ADMIT,
   AVOW, SIGN, RECOGNIZE,
   CONFESS
acknowledgment . . . . . CREDIT
   of liability . . . . COGNOVIT
acle . . . . IRONWOOD
acme . . . . . . APEX, PINNACLE,
   SUMMIT, TOP
acolyte . . . . ALTARBOY,
   THURIFER
acolyte's garb . . . . COTTA
acomia . . . . BALDNESS
aconite . . . . ATIS, MONKSWOOD,
   WOLFSBANE
acor . . . . ACIDITY
acorn . . . . NUT, CAMATA,
   FRUIT, OVEST, MAST
   barnacle . . . . SCUTA
   cup . . . . VALONIA
   shaped . . . . BALANOID
acoustic equipment . . . . SIRENE
   vase . . . . ECHEA
acoustics . . . . PHONICS
acquaint . . . . APPRISE, INFORM,
   TELL, FAMILIARIZE
acquainted . . . . KNOWN,
   FAMILIAR, (CON)VERSANT

acquiesce . . . . AGREE, ACCEDE,
   ASSENT, CONSENT
acquire . . . . GAIN, OBTAIN,
   REAP, EARN, GET
   in advance . . . . PREEMPT
   knowledge . . . . . . LEARN
acquired knowledge . . . .
   EDUCATION
acquisitiveness . . . . GREED,
   AVARICE
acquit . . . . ABSOLVE,
   EXCUSE, CLEAR, FREE,
   EXCULPATE
acquittance . . . . RELEASE,
   CLEARANCE
acre, ¼ of . . . . ROOD
acres, 2.47 . . . . HECTARE
acrid . . . SHARP, SOUR, BITING,
   PUNGENT, BITTER, HARSH,
   MORDACIOUS
acrimonious . . . . BITTER,
   STINGING, CAUSTIC, HARSH
acrimony . . . . ASPERITY
acrobat . . . . GYMNAST,
   TUMBLER, DAREDEVIL,
   AERIALIST, STUNTMAN
   high-wire . . . . . AERIALIST
   of India . . . . NAT
   tights of . . . . . FLESHINGS
acrobat's equipment . . . . BARS,
   TIGHTWIRE, TIGHTROPE,
   POLE, TRAMPOLINE
   forte . . . . STUNTS,
   SOM(M)ERSAULTS
   net . . . . TRAMPOLINE
   risk . . . . FALL, SLIP
   wear . . . . LEOTARD,
   TIGHTS, FLESHINGS
acrogen . . . . FERN
acrolith . . . . STATUE
acropolis . . . . CADMEA,
   CITADEL, HILL, LARISSA
across . . . . . . OVER, TRAVERSE,
   ATHWART, ASTRADDLE,
   ASTRIDE
   combining form . . . . TRA,
   TRANS, DIA
acrostic . . . AGLA, TELESTIC(H)
act . . . . . . DEED, FEAT, EMOTE,
   PERFORM, EDICT, BEHAVE
   according to rules . . . .
   CONFORM
   helpful . . . . . GOOD TURN
   like . . . . SIMULATE
   of prudence . . . . CAUTION
   over . . . . EMOTE

prima donna's .... TANTRUM
silly .... CLOWN
up .... PRISS
with exaggeration .. HAM, EMOTE
acting by turns ...... ALTERN
pertaining to ....
HISTRIONIC, THESPIAN
trophy .... OSCAR, TONY
action ...... DEED, LAWSUIT, ACTIVITY, COMBAT, BEHAVIOR
melodramatic ... HEROICS
put into .... ACTUATE, ACTIVATE
to outwit another .. PLOY
to recover ...... TROVER, REPLEVIN
where it is .... .. ARENA, STAGE, TABLE, DIAMOND, COURT, OVAL, SCENE, STADIUM, (COCK)PIT
with ridiculous end ..... FIASCO
word .... VERB
activate .... SPARK
activator .... CATALYST
active ... SPRY, ABOUT, AGILE, LIVELY, BRISK, WORKING, BUSY, MOVING, ASTIR
place .... HIVE, HUB
activity .... OPERATION, STIR, ACTION
actor .... STAR, THESPIAN, MIME, HISTRIO(N), PLAYER, PERFORMER, MUMMER
last words of .... TAG
many-faced ...... MUNI, (LON) CHANEY
minor role .... WALK-ON
mythical .... SPELVIN
of a thousand faces .....
(LON) CHANEY
overacting .... MUGGER
second-rate .... HAM, BARNSTORMER
veteran .... TROUPER
with speaking part ......
SUPER
actors' aid .... (PRESS)AGENT, STANDIN, DRESSER, PROMPTER, ZANIES
apers .... ZANIES
association ... AEA, AAAA
group .... CAST, TROUPE

hint to .... CUE
improvisation ... AD LIB
in dramatics .. AMATEURS
offstage place ....
GREEN ROOM
part .... ROLE, LEAD, STAR(RING), VILLAIN, COMIC
pest .... HECKLER
actress (see actor) ...... DIVA, STAR
"blond bombshell" .....
HARLOW
from Brooklyn ....
(MAE) WEST
role sometimes .. INGENUE
with "it" .. (CLARA) BOW
with "oomph" . ...
(ANN) SHERIDAN
actual .... REAL, FACTUAL, TRUE, VERITABLE, DE FACTO
being .... ESSE
actuality ...... FACT, TRUTH, VERITY, REALITY
actually .... REALLY, IN FACT
actuate .... ROUSE, MOVE, INCITE, STIR, MOTIVATE, ACTIVATE
acuate .... POINTED
acuity .... EDGE, WIT, KEENNESS
acumen .... INSIGHT, KEENNESS, SHREWDNESS
acute .... CUTE, SHREWD, SEVERE, CRITICAL, SHARP
A.D., part of ... ANNO, DOMINI
ad .... ADVERTISEMENT, NOTICE, INSERTION
in tennis .... ADVANTAGE
infinitum .. WITHOUT END, ENDLESSLY, FOREVER
interim ..... MEANTIME, TEMPORARY, MEANWHILE
lib .... IMPROVISE, EXTEMPORIZE, ASIDE
sum .... PRESENT
type of ..... CLASSIFIED, DISPLAY, COVER, INSIDE, COLOR(ED)
verbum ..... VERBATIM, LITERAL
verse .... JINGLE
adage .... SAW, MAXIM, PROVERB, SAYING
subject ...... TIME, TIDE
adagio .... SLOW, BALLET(DANCE)

Adam-and-Eve ..... ORCHID, PUTTYROOT
Smith is pseudonym of .. GOODMAN
Adam's mate of legend ...... LILITH
needle .... YUCCA
second mate/rib .... EVE
son ....ABEL, CAIN, SETH
adamant ... HARD, FIRM, SET, IMMOVABLE
Adamite .... NUDIST
adapt ..... ADJUST, CONFORM, FIT, SUIT, ORIENT
add carbon dioxide ... CHARGE
dash of liquor ...... LACE
details ..... EMBROIDER, ELABORATE
member to a board ...... COOPT
on ...... AFFIX, ATTACH
spirits .... LACE
sugar .... SWEETEN
up .... TOTAL, SUM, TOT, TALLY, JIBE
up to .... MEAN, SIGNIFY
adda .... LIZARD
addax .... ANTELOPE
added to .... PLUS
addendum .... ADDITION, APPENDIX
adder ..... ASP, SNAKE, VIPER, REPTILE
addict .... USER, DEVOTEE
slang .... BUG, FIEND
addicted .... PRONE
addiction ...... WONT, HABIT, INCLINATION
adding machine ... TOTALIZER
Addis Ababa is capital of ....
ABYSSINIA, ETHIOPIA
Addison, poet ... CLIO, JOSEPH
addition .... ADDENDUM, ALSO, ELSE, AND, ADDEND
to a bill .... RIDER
to a building .... ELL, ANNEX
to a letter .... PS, POSTSCRIPT, NOTA BENE
additional name ...... ALIAS, PSEUDONYM
pay .... BONUS, TIP
addle .... MUDDLE(D), CONFUSE(D), EMPTY
addlebrained ..... MUDDLED, STUPID

addlepated ... STUPID, IDIOTIC
address .... SPEECH, TALK, ACCOST, BEARING, GREET, TACT
army .... APO
navy .... FPO
President's .... WHITE HOUSE
Secretary of Defense .... PENTAGON
to someone ... DEDICATE
adduce .... CITE, INFER, QUOTE, ADVANCE
adeem ..... REVOKE, CANCEL
Adelina, singer .... PATTI
Adenauer's sobriquet .... (DER) ALTE
adept .... ACE, SKILLED, EXPERT, DEFT, PROFICIENT
adequate .... EQUAL, SUFFICIENT, SUITABLE, ACCEPTABLE
Adhem _____ ..... (BEN) ABOU
adhere .... CLING, STICK, CLEAVE, GLUE
adherent .... FOLLOWER, DISCIPLE, ZEALOT, VOTARY, ITE, IST, DEVOTEE, STICKING, RETAINER, PARTISAN
adhesive .... GLUE, PASTE, PLASTER, STICKY, GUM
adhibit .... APPLY, ADMIT
adieu .... GOODBY(E), FAREWELL, TATA
adios: Sp. .... GOODBY(E), FAREWELL
adipose ...... OBESE, FAT(TY)
adit ...... ENTRANCE, ACCESS, STULM
adjacent .... CONTIGUOUS, NEAR, ADJOINING
adjective .... ADNOUN
ending .... ENT, IAL, INE, ITE, IST, ISH, OUS
adjoin .... TOUCH, ABUT
adjourn .... CEASE, END, PROROGUE, SUSPEND, RETIRE, RECESS
adjudge .... CONDEMN, DECIDE, SENTENCE, SETTLE, AWARD, DEEM
unfit .... CONDEMN, DISQUALIFY, RULE OUT
adjudicate .... TRY, HEAR, DECIDE
adjunct .... APPENDAGE

adjust .... FIX, ADAPT,
ATTUNE, ORIENT, FIT, SUIT
adjutant .... AIDE, HELPER,
ALLY, ASSISTANT
bird .... MARABOU,
ARGALA, HURGILA
ad-lib .... EXTEMPORIZE,
IMPROVISE, ASIDE
adman .... COPYWRITER,
HUCKSTER, SPIEL, BARKER
Admetus' wife ..... ALCESTIS
administer .... MANAGE, GIVE,
CONDUCT, GOVERN,
HUSBAND, DEAL
administration .... RULE,
MANAGEMENT, REGIME(N)
administrative body ... JUNTA,
JUNTO, BOARD
admiral of fame .... BYRD,
NELSON, KING, DEWEY,
HALSEY, FARRAGUT
winged ..... BUTTERFLY
admire ...... ESTEEM, REGARD
admissible, in law .... LIE
admission .... ENTREE,
ACCESS, ACKNOWLEDGMENT,
CONCESSION, CONFESSION
ticket: sl. .... DUCAT
admit .... FESS, ALLOW, OWN,
PROFESS, CONCEDE, RECEIVE,
INTROMIT
admitted fact .... DATUM,
TRUTH, TRUISM
admixture .... BLEND,
COMPOUND, ALLOY
admonish .... ADVISE, WARN,
REPROVE, CHIDE, CAUTION,
SERMON(IZE)
adnoun .... ADJECTIVE
admonisher .... MONITOR,
ADVISOR, MENTOR
admonition .... ADVICE,
WARNING, REPRIMAND
first word of, sometimes ..
DON'T
ado .... FUSS, STIR,
POTHER, BUSTLE, TO-DO
adobe .... CLAY, BRICK, DOBY
adolescence .... YOUTH,
TEENS, TEENAGE, NONAGE
adolescent, designating one ...
BOBBYSOXER, HIPPIE,
TEENAGER
Adonais, per Shelley ... KEATS
Adonis' slayer .... ARES
adopt .... ESPOUSE,

TAKE ON, CHOOSE
adore ..... WORSHIP, IDOLIZE,
REVERE, DOTE
adorn .... DECORATE,
GRACE, ORNAMENT,
BEAUTIFY, EMBELLISH,
(BE)DECK, DRESS, DIGHT
with diamonds ... BEGEM
with rich clothing ....
CAPARISON
adorner .... DECORATOR,
EMBELLISHER
adrenal hormone ... CORTISONE
Adriana's servant ...... LUCE
Adriatic city .... TRIESTE
island .... LAGOSTA
peninsula .... ISTRIA
port ... . FIUME,
TRIESTE, RIJEKA, RIMINI
resort .... LIDO
seaport .... VALONA,
AVLONA
wind .... BORA
adrift ...... DERELICT, LOST,
ASEA, AFLOAT, UNTIED, LOOSE
adroit .... HABILE, SKILLFUL,
ADEPT, CLEVER, DEFT, NEAT
adularia .... MOONSTONE,
FELDSPAR
adulate ..... FLATTER, PRAISE
adulation, object of .... HERO,
STAR, CONQUEROR,
WINNER, VICTOR
adulator, kind of ....
SYCOPHANT, BOOTLICKER,
COURTIER, YESMAN, FAWNER,
FLATTERER, TOADY,
FAN
adulterant, common .. WATER,
FIZZ
adulterate .... DEBASE,
DEFILE, DENATURE,
CORRUPT, ADMIX
adulterated .... IMPURE
adult .... GROWN(UP),
MATURE, OF AGE
person ... MAN, WOMAN
insect .... IMAGO
tadpole .... FROG
wriggler .... MOSQUITO
adust .... BURNT, SCORCHED,
PARCHED
advance .... MARCH,
PROGRESS, LEND, PROMOTE,
LATEN
money .... (IM)PREST

payment ... ANTE, ARLES
slowly ..... CREEP, INCH
to prospector ....
        GRUBSTAKE
unit .... VAN(GUARD)
word .... TIP, WARNING
advanced .... FAR(GONE)
advancement ..... PROGRESS,
    PROMOTION, IMPROVEMENT
advantage ..... EDGE, PROFIT,
    ODDS, USE, BENEFIT, GAIN
kind of, in tennis .....
        AD IN, AD OUT
take ..... TRICK, CHEAT,
        ABUSE
advent .... COMING, ARRIVAL,
        APPROACH
adventitious .... CASUAL,
    ACCIDENTAL, EPISODIC
lung sound .... RALE
adventure .... GEST(E),
    QUEST, ENTERPRISE,
        ESCAPADE
adventurer ...... SPECULATOR,
    FORTUNE HUNTER,
        PICAROON
of old .... KNIGHT,
    FREEBOOTER, MERCENARY
adventurous .... RASH
adversary ...... ENEMY, FOE,
    OPPONENT, PROTAGONIST
adverse .... HOSTILE, OPPOSED,
    UNFAVORABLE, INIMICAL
criticism: sl. .. PAN(NING)
opinion .... CENSURE
reaction, show of ... HOOT
    HISS, BOO, RASPBERRY,
        SCOWL, POUT
adversity .... MISFORTUNE,
    POVERTY, CALAMITY
advertisement .... AD,
    INSERTION, NOTICE, ORBIT,
    HANDBILL, BLURB,
    BILLBOARD, NEON,
        COMMERCIAL
abbreviation ... AD, ADVT
book jacket ..... BLURB
interpolate .... PLUG
make-up ...... LAYOUT
slang .... PLUG, DODGER
advertiser .... PLUGGER,
    SPIELER, HAWKER
kind of .... BARKER
to an ad agency ....
        ACCOUNT
advertising client ... ACCOUNT

colloquial .... BALLYHOO
contract ...... ACCOUNT
handbill: sl. ..... DODGER
man: colloq. ....
        HUCKSTER
medium .... NEWSPAPER,
    RADIO, TV, BROCHURE,
    BILLBOARD, FLYER, MARQUEE
on book jacket .... BLURB
poster .... BILL
praise in .... PUFFERY
statuette .... CLIO
text .... COPY
advice ...... COUNSEL, REDE,
    REPORT, MESSAGE, AVISO,
        ADMONITION
in 1835 .... GO WEST
to stockholders in 1933...
        SELL, UNLOAD
advise .... INFORM, TELL,
    APPRISE, CAUTION, ACQUAINT
and ____ ...... CONSENT
adviser .... MONITOR,
    COUNSELOR, MENTOR,
        NESTOR, EGERIA
advisory .... HORTATIVE
on weather .... WARNING
advocate .... LAWYER,
    APOLOGIST, ABETTOR,
    DEFENDER, PLEAD(ER),
        ESPOUSE
of majority rule ....
        DEMOCRAT
adytum .... SANCTUARY,
    SHRINE, SANCTUM
adz ..... AX(E), CUTTING TOOL
Aeetes' daughter ..... MEDEA
Aegean gulf/sea ..... SAROS
inhabitant ..... SAMIOTE,
        LELEGE
island .... MELOS, SAMOS,
    TENOS, IOS, NIO, PATMOS,
    MYTILENE, LESBOS
river .... STRUMA
Aegeon's wife .... AEMILIA
Aegir's wife .... RAN
aegis .... SHIELD,
    AUSPICES, SPONSORSHIP
Aello .... HARPY
Aeneas follower .... ACHATES
great grandson .... BRUT
parent .... ANCHISES,
        VENUS
son .... ASCANIUS
wife .... CREUSA

Aeneid author .... VERGIL, VIRGIL
  first word of ..... ARMA
Aeolian lyricist ..... SAPPHO
Aeolus' daughter ... HALCYONE
aeonian .... ETERNAL
aerial .... IMAGINARY, UNREAL, ANTENNA
  battle .... DOGFIGHT
  bomb: sl. .. BREADBASKET, EGG
  bombardment .... BLITZ
  bombing, describing one .. SATURATION, CARPET
  car suspended from cables TELPHER
  navigation aid .. TELERAN
  stunt .... AEROBATIC, LOOP, BARREL, ROLL, LOOP-THE-LOOP
aerialist .... ACROBAT, WIREWALKER, BALANCER
aerobatics ..... STUNTS, LOOP, ROLL, IMMELMANN TURN
aerolite .... METEORITE
aeronaut ... AVIATOR, AIRMAN, PILOT, SPACEMAN
aeronautics .... AVIATION
aerostat .... BALLOON, BLIMP, DIRIGIBLE, ZEPPELIN
aerugo ..... RUST, VERDIGRIS
aes .... BRONZE, COIN
Aesculapius' teacher .. CHIRON
Aesir ..... LOKI, ODIN, THOR, FREYA, WODEN, BALDER
Aesop ..... FABULIST, WRITER
  story .... FABLE
aesthete .... DILETTANTE, CONNOISSEUR, VIRTUOSO
aesthetic .... ARTISTIC
aestival .... SUMMER
aestivate, opposed to .... HIBERNATE
Aether's father ...... EREBUS
Aetolian prince .... TYDEUS
afar .... AWAY, OFF, DISTANT, HAMITE
affable .... POLITE, AMIABLE, SUAVE
affair ...... BUSINESS, AMOUR, MATTER, ROMANCE
  of honor, usually .. DUEL
  of high school juniors ... PROM
  of seniors .... HOP
affect ...... PRETEND, FEIGN,

POSE, INFLUENCE, TOUCH, MOVE, IMPRESS, SWAY
affectation .... PRETENSE, PRETENSION, POSE, AIR
  of elegance ... FRIPPERY
affected .... FEIGNED, FALLAL, POSEY, AFFLICTED, MOVED, HISTRIONIC
  elegance ...... FROUFROU
affection .... FONDNESS, DISEASE, LOVE, FEELING
affectionate ... FOND, WARM, TENDER, LOVING
afferent .... SENSORY
affiance .... TRUST, BETROTH, ENGAGE, PLEDGE, FLIGHT
affiant ... DEPONENT, TESTATOR
affidavit addendum .... JURAT
  maker ...... DEPONENT, TESTATOR
  taker .... NOTARY
affiliate ..... JOIN, ASSOCIATE, MEMBER
affinity ...... RELATION(SHIP), ATTRACTION, KINSHIP, CONNECTION
affirm .... ASSERT, AVER, AVOW, SWEAR, POSIT, VOUCH, RATIFY
affirmation ... CONFIRMATION, DECLARATION, ASSERTION
affirmative .... POSITIVE, YES, YEA, AMEN, AYE
affix .... APPEND, ATTACH, FASTEN, SEAL, STAMP
afflatus .... INSPIRATION
afflict ... DISTRESS, TRY, VEX, TROUBLE, PAIN, GRIPE
affliction ..... WOE, DISTRESS, TRIAL, AILMENT, SCOURGE, PAIN, SUFFERING, MISFORTUNE
affluence .... WEALTH, RICHES, ABUNDANCE, OPULENCE
afflux .... FLOW
afford .... SPARE, GIVE, YIELD, SUPPLY, ENABLE
affray .... MELEE, BRAWL, FIGHT, RIOT
affront ..... INSULT, OFFEND, SLIGHT, DISPLEASE, SNUB
affright .... SCARE, ALARM, DAUNT, TERRIFY, HORRIFY
affy ...... BETROTH, ESPOUSE
Afghan(istan) ...... PATHAN, DURANI, HOUND, BLANKET,

SHAWL

ameer .... SHERE
capital .... KABUL
carpet .... BUKHARA
city .... HERAT
coin .... AMANIA
garment .... CHADRI
king .... SHAH, ZAHIR
language ...... PASHTO,
PUSHTU
nomad .... KUCHI
parliament ....
WOLESI JIRGA
pony .... YABU
prime minister ... YUSUF
prince ..... AMEER, AMIR
range ...... HINDU KUSH
river .... HARIRUD
rug .... BUKHARA
ruler .... SHER SHAH
title .... KHAN
town ...... FERAH, HERAT,
KUNDUZ, KANDAHAR
tribe .... ULUS, SAFI
tribesman ...... PATHAN
valley .... WAKHAN
aficionado .... FAN, DEVOTEE,
ENTHUSIAST
aflame .... ABLAZE, GLOWING,
BURNING
afloat ...... ASEA, CURRENT,
IN CIRCULATION, SEABORNE,
AIRBORNE
afoot ..... ABROAD, MOVING,
ASTIR
aforesaid .... PRIOR,
ANTECEDENT
aforethought ..... PREPENSE,
PREMEDITATED
afraid ..... SCARED, FEARFUL,
FRIGHTENED, TIMOROUS,
TERRIFIED
afresh .... ANEW, AGAIN
afreet .... JINNEE, DEMON,
JINNI
Africa's ancient name .. LIBYA
African .... NEGRO, NEGROID,
BLACK
antelope .... ASSE, ELAND,
GEMSBOK, KOB, ORIBI,
KUDU, IMPALA, BLESBOK,
BLESBUCK, ADDAX, PEELE,
BUBAL(IS), BUSHBUCK,
BOS(C)HBOK, BONGO, GNU,
BONTEBOK, KOODOO,
DUIKER(BOK)

ape .... BABOON
aunt .... TANTA
bass .... IYO
bat ...... HAMMERHEAD
bird .... TURAKOO,
UMBER, UMBRETTE, COLY,
LORY, LOURI
boss .... BAAS
burrowing animal ......
SURICATE, GERBIL(LE)
bushman ..... NEGRILLO
bustard ... KORI, PAAUW
caffeine tree .. KOLA, COLA
camp .... BOMA
cape .... RAS
capital .... DAKAR,
ALGIERS, ADDIS ABABA,
ANKARA, BOMA, ACCRA,
LAGOS, BERBERA, CAIRO
carnivore .... CANNIBAL,
LION, RATEL, HYENA
catfish .... SHAL
charm .... GRIGRI
civet .... NANDINE
city ...... ORAN, DAKAR,
TUNIS, HERAT, RABAT,
TRIPOLI, ALGIERS,
CASABLANCA, CAIRO,
ANKARA
coin ...... PESA, TOQUE,
GIRSH, TALARI, RIAL, OKIA
colonist .... BOER
cony .... DAS, DASSIE
corn .... MEALIE
council ... INDABA, BAAD
country .... EGYPT,
ALGERIA, ETHIOPIA, CONGO,
GHANA, MALI, NIGERIA,
SOMALIA, TUNISIA, GABON,
UGANDA, TOGO, LIBERIA,
ZAMBIA, KENYA, GUINEA,
IVORY COAST, MALAWI
dance .... N'GOMA
desert .... SAHARA,
KALAHARI
dialect .... TAAL
disease .... NENTA
district ... RAND, NYASSA
dog .... BASENJI
drink .... OMEIRES
explorer .... AKELEY
ferryboat .... PONT
fish .... CHARACIN
fly .... KIVU, TSETSE
fox .... ASSE, CAAMA
garment ... TOBE, KAROSS

gazelle ..... ADMI, ARIEL, CORA, NORA
giraffe-like animal ...... OKAPI
gold district ...... RAND
gorge .... KLOOF
grass .... ESPARTO, ALFA, FUNDI
grass country ... VELD(T)
grivet .... WAAG
harp .... NANGA
hartebeest .... TORA
headland .... RAS
hemp .... IFE
hill .... KOP
hog .... BOSCHVARK
hornbill .... TOCK
horse disease ..... SURRA
Hottentot .... NAMA
hunting party .... SAFARI
hut .... KRAAL
iris .... IXIA
jackal .... DIEB
lake .... NYAS(S)A, T(S)ANA, VICTORIA, CHAD
language ... TAAL, BANTU
lemur .... MACACO
lily ... ALOE, AGAPANTHUS
master .... BAAS
mint plant ...... COLEUS
money (shell) ... COWRIE, COWRY
monkey .... GRIVET, COLOBUS, MACAQUE, MONA, BASENJI, GUENON
Moslem .... BERBER
mountain .... ATLAS, CAMERON, KILIMANJARO
mountain pass .... NEK
musical instrument ..... NANGA
native ...... ASHA, ZULU, DAMARA, ASHANTI, FULAH, MAUMAU, KOPI, IBO, WATU(T)SI
nut tree .... COLA
palm ...... DOOM, DOUM
peasant .... KOPI
pigmy .... HOTTENTOT, NEGRILLO, ITA
pirate .... ALGERINE
plant .... IXIA, ALOE, CALABAR, COLEUS
plateau .... KAROO
poisonous tree .... SASSY
port ...... ORAN, DAKAR

Portuguese colony ...... ANGOLA
pygmy ...... [see pigmy]
race .... SOMALI
region .... CONGO, NUBIA, SUDAN, SOUDAN
rhinoceros ..... KEITLOA
river ...... GABON, NILE, CALABAR, UMO, SENEGAL, TANA, UELE, CONGO, NIGER, ABBA, SHARI, VAAL, BIA UBANGI, BENIN, ORANGE, GABUM, CHARI
rug .... KAROSS
ruminant .... CAMEL
scrub .... RITO
seaport .... TUNIS, CASABLANCA, ORAN, DAKAR
sect .... ABELITE
snake ... ELAP, CERASTES
soldier .. ASKARI, SPAHI
songbird .... LINNET
sorcery .... OBI
spear .... ASSAGAI, ASSEGAI
squirrel .... XERUS
stockade ... BOMA, KRAAL
stork .... ARGALA, MARABOU
tableland .... KAROO
"telegraph" ... TOM TOM
title .... SIDI, AGA, AGHA, NEGUS, RAS
tree .... COLA, ARTAR, BAOBAB, TARFA, KOLA, AKEE, BAKU, SHEA, SASSY, MOLI, SAMANDURA, COPAIBA
tribal conference .... PALAVER
tribe ... BONI, KABONGA, BANTU, KREPI, KUA, GOGO, MAKA, ZULU, KAFFIR, TIBU, ABO, KALI, DOMA, ALUR, NUBA, AKAN, HABE, KETU, VACA, WARI
trip .... TREK, SAFARI
U.N. president .... (MONGI) SLIM
valley .... WADI, KLOOF
village ..... DORP, STAD, KRAAL
weasel .... ZORIL(A)
weasel-like animal ...... ICHNEUMON

whip .... KOORBASH
wild cat .... SERVAL
wild hog .... BOSCHVARK,
WART(HOG), BOAR
wild sheep ...... UDAD,
AOUDAD, ARUI
wind .... SIMOOM,
SIMOON, SAMIEL
witchcraft ... OBEAH, OBI
wolf .... AARD
wood .... TEAK,
EBONY
worm .... LOA
Afrikaans ...... BOER, TAAL
aft .... ABAFT, (A)STERN
after ... LATER, NEXT, BEHIND
a while .... ANON,
SHORTLY, LATER
dinner treat .... CORDIAL
expenses .... NET
the style of .... A LA
afterbirth .... SECUNDINE
aftermath ..... CONSEQUENCE,
ROWEN, RESULT, SEQUEL
afternoon nap .... SIESTA
party .... TEA
show .... MATINEE
afterpiece ..... EXODE, EPODE
of a sort .... ENCORE
aftersong .... EPODE
afterthought .... REGRET,
REMORSE, RECONSIDERATION
in letter ..... POSTSCRIPT
afterward .... LATER,
SUBSEQUENTLY
Agag's slayer .... SAMUEL
again .... ANEW, ENCORE,
MORE, BESIDES
appear/happen ... RECUR
do/say .... REPEAT
against .... CON, ANTI,
CONTRA, VERSUS
a person/thing ....
UNFRIENDLY, HOSTILE
a thing, in law .... IN REM
morals .... WICKED,
OBSCENE, UNETHICAL,
ILLICIT
prefix .... ANTI, CONTRA
the current ... UPSTREAM
the law .... ILLEGAL,
ILLICIT
the state .. TREASON(OUS),
SEDITIOUS
agalite .... TALC
agalloch wood .... ALOE,

AGAR, GAROO
agallochum ..... AGAL, AGAR,
ALOE
agama .... LIZARD,
CHAMELEON
Agamemnon rescued her .....
BRISEIS
Agamemnon's brother ....
MENELAUS
children ..... IPHIGENIA,
ELECTRA, ORESTES
father .... ATREUS
agamic .... ASEXUAL
Agana is capital of ..... GUAM
agaric .... FUNGUS,
MUSHROOM, TOADSTOOL
agate .... MARBLE, ONYX,
ACHATE, RUBY, QUARTZ,
TYPE
agave .... AMOLE, ISTLE,
PITA, SISAL, ALOE, DATIL,
MAGUEY, PULQUE,
HENEQUEN
juice drink ..... PULQUE,
MESCAL
age ..... MELLOW, EON, ERA,
CENTURY, RIPEN, YEARS,
MATURE, TIME, EPOCH,
LIFETIME
designating one ... IRON,
STONE, BRONZE, ATOMIC,
GOLDEN, TEEN(S),
ADOLESCENCE, PUBERTY,
OLD
of moon on June 1st ....
EPACT
old ... SENESCE, SENILITY
pertaining to an ... ERAL,
EVAL, INNOCENCE, HEYDAY
same .... COEVAL
aged .... OLD(EN), ANILE,
SENILE, RIPE
agee .... ASKEW, AWRY
Agena .... ATLAS
agency .... MEANS, HAND,
MEDIUM
news .... UPI, AP,
REUTERS, TASS, DOMEI,
MENA, NCNA, HAVAS
agendum .... RITUAL
Agenor's daughter .... EUROPA
agent ...... FACTOR, FACIENT,
DEPUTY, ENVOY, EMISSARY,
REPRESENTATIVE, PROXY,
MIDDLEMAN, PROCTOR,
BROKER

foreign firm .... COMPRADOR
insurance .... UNDERWRITER
007 .... BOND
007 movie .. GOLDFINGER, THUNDERBALL, DR. NO
undercover .... SPY
undercover work .... ESPIONAGE
agglomerate .... MASS, LUMP, HEAP, CLUSTER, GATHER
aggrandize .... INCREASE
aggravate .... WORSEN, INTENSIFY
aggregate ...... TOTAL, MASS, SUM, GATHER
fruit of strawberry ...... ETAERIO
aggress .... ATTACK, INVADE, PROVOKE
aggressive .... MILITANT, ASSERTIVE, PUSHING
aggressor .... ATTACKER, ASSAILANT, PROVOKER, INVADER, OFFENDER
aggrieve ...... SLIGHT, OFFEND, INJURE, WRONG
aghast .... AMAZED, STUNNED, APPALLED, TERRIFIED, HORRIFIED
agialid .... BITO
agile .... NIMBLE, SPRY, LISSOM(E), ACTIVE, QUICK
aging .... SENESCENT
agio .... PREMIUM, FEE, EXCHANGE, DISCOUNT
agitate .... STIR, ALARM, CHURN, ROUSE, EXCITE, DISTURB, FLUSTER, ROLL, WORRY, F(E)AZE, FEEZE
agitation .... RUMPUS, DITHER, TUMULT, POTHER, TURMOIL, FLURRY
state of .... SEETHING, STORMY, TUMULTUOUS, BOILING, AGOG
agitator ...... RABBLE-ROUSER, PROVOKER, INCITER, DEMAGOG(UE), PROVOCATEUR, FIREBRAND, ANARCHIST, INCENDIARY
Aglaia .... GRACE
aglet .... LACE, SPANGLE, TAG

agley .... AWRY
aglow .... ALIT, SHINING, RADIANT
agnail .... HANGNAIL
agname .... NICKNAME, PET NAME, MONICKER
agnate ...... KIN, RELATIVE, ALLIED
agnomen .... (NICK)NAME
agnostic .... ATHEIST, SKEPTIC, CYNIC, NESCIENT
Agnus Dei .... PRAYER, LAMB
ago ...... PAST, ERST, GONE, SINCE
agog .... EAGER, EXPECTANT, ASTIR
agonize .... SUFFER, STRAIN, TORTURE, RACK, STRUGGLE
agonizing struggle .... THROES
agony ...... PAIN, THROE(S), ANGUISH, DISTRESS, SUFFERING, PASSION
"agony ____" of newspaper .. COLUMN
agora .... ASSEMBLY, MARKETPLACE
coin .... OBOL
agouti .... PACA, RODENT
Agra's pride ..... TAJ MAHAL
Agram .... ZAGREB
agree .... JIBE, CONCUR, MATCH, TALLY, ASSENT, COINCIDE, CORRESPOND, APPROVE
agreeable .... PLEASING, SUITABLE, PLEASANT, WILLING, AMENABLE
odor .... AROMA, PERFUME, FRAGRANCE, SCENT
taste .... SAVORY, SWEET, TOOTHSOME, PALATABLE
agreeableness of letter .... EUTONY
agreement .... PACT, TREATY, CARTEL, ACCORD, DEAL, MISE, ENTENTE, CONCORD, CONTRACT, COVENANT
in opinion ... CONSENSUS
with conditions .. ESCROW
agrestic ..... RURAL, RUSTIC, PASTORAL, CRUDE
agricultural ...... AGRARIAN
overseer .... AGRONOME

worker .... PEASANT, OKIE, RYOT
agriculture, goddess of ......
CERES, DEMETER
Agrippa's temple .. PANTHEON
Agrippina's son .... NERO
agua .... TOAD, WATER
ague .... FEVER, CHILL
Ahab's cabin boy .... PIP
daughter ...... ATHALIE
father .... OMRI
ship .... PEQUOD, WHALER
Ahasuerus' minister .. HAMAN
wife .... ESTHER
ahead .... LEADING, FORWARD, FRONT, BEFORE
forge .... PROGRESS, ADVANCE, LEAD
ahem sound .... COUGH
ahuehuete .... CYPRESS
ai .... SLOTH
aid .... ASSIST, HELP, SUCCOR, ABET, FURTHER
Aida's lover ..... R(H)ADAMES
rival .... AMNERIS
aide .... ASSISTANT, ADJUTANT, SUBALTERN, LIEUTENANT
memoire .. MEMORANDUM
aiglet .... POINT, TAG
ail .... PAIN, BOTHER
aileron part .... TAB
ailing .... SICK, ILL
ailment .... ILLNESS, DISEASE, MALADY
minor .... PIP
aim .... INTENT, PURPOSE, END, GOAL, AMBITION, ASPIRE, POINT, OBJECT(IVE), TARGET, SIGHT
aimless .... DESULTORY, HAPHAZARD, FUTILE, POINTLESS
scribble .... DOODLE
wanderer of sorts ....
NOMAD, TRAMP, JEW, ROVER
ain .... OWN
air .... ARIA, MEIN, TUNE, MANNER, CARRIAGE, SONG, ATMOSPHERE, MELODY
apparatus ..... AERATOR, FAN, BLOWER, SCUBA
bends .... AEROEMBOLISM
boundary .... FRONT

castle ..... (DAY)DREAM, AUTISM, FANTASY, REVERIE
combining form ....
AER(I), AERO
current ... EDDY, STREAM
currents, rising ....
ANABATIC
expose to ...... AERATE
fear of ..... AEROPHOBIA
fill with .... AERATE, GAS UP
filled film of liquid .....
BUBBLE
force girl ... WASP, WREN
fresh .... OZONE
friction ...... WINDAGE
gauge ...... AEROMETER
group ...... WING, RAF, USAF, ESCADRILLE
hero .... ACE
in motion ...... WIND, BREEZE, ZEPHYR
in violent agitation .....
WHIRLWIND, STORM, TORNADO, CYCLONE, TEMPEST
mail, via ..... PAR AVION
navigation officer ....
AVIGATOR
navigation system ....
SHORAN, TELERAN
of .... AERIAL
open .... ALFRESCO
passage .... FLUE, NOSTRIL, VENT(IDUCT)
pertaining to .... AURAL, AERIAL
pipe .. VENTIDUCT, FLUE
plant .... ORCHID, EPIPHYTE
poisonous ..... MIASMA, MALARIA
pure .... OZONE
race marker ..... PYLON
spirit ..... SYLPH, ARIEL
stream producer ....
BELLOWS, FAN, PROPELLER
tight .... HERMETIC
unwholesome .. MALARIA, MIASMA
upper ..... OZONE, ETHER
aircraft .... AIRPLANE, DIRIGIBLE, GLIDER, ZEPPELIN, AUTOGIRO, HELICOPTER

abrupt climb . . . .
    CHANDELLE
air from propeller . . . . . .
    SLIPSTREAM, DOWN-WASH
altitude controller . . . . . .
    BALLAST
altitude indicator . . . .
    ALTIMETER, STATOSCOPE
attack with gunfire . . . . . .
    STRAFE
battle . . . . DOGFIGHT
body . . . . FUSELAGE
bombs . . . . EGGS
carried by another . . . . . .
    PICKABACK
carrier . . . . FLAT-TOP,
    AMERICA, ENTERPRISE
climb, sudden . . . . ZOOM
commercial . . . . . . LINER
delivery of sold . . . FERRY
designer . . . . . SIKORSKY,
    FOKKER
detector . . . . RADAR
dome . . . . BLISTER
enclosed part . . . NACELLE
engine cover . . . COWLING
engineless . . . . . GLIDER,
    SAILPLANE
flapping . . . . . . FLUTTER,
    ORTHOPTER, ORNITHOPTER
flight . . . HOP, BARNSTORM
flight record . . . . LOG
formation . . . . ECHELON,
    FLIGHT
front . . . . NOSE
fuel, antiknock . . . .
    TRIPTANE
group . . . ECHELON, WING,
    SQUADRON, ESCADRILLE
gun turret shield . . . .
    BLISTER, DOME
heavier than air . . . .
    AERODYNE
idle propeller of . . . .
    FEATHER
landing position . . . .
    PANCAKE
landing/take-off strip . . .
    RUNWAY
launcher on ship . . . .
    CATAPULT
lever . . . . (JOY)STICK
maneuver on ground . . . .
    TAXI
manufacturer . . . BOEING,

DOUGLAS, LOCKHEED,
    CESSNA
military scouting . . . .
    GRASSHOPPER
movable flap . . . . . . GILL,
    AILERON, RUDDER
navigation aid . . . .
    SHORAN, LORAN, TELERAN,
    BEACON
notice to pilots . . . NOTAM
obsolete . . . . CANARD
opening for missile . . . . .
    BOMB BAY
pilotless . . . . DRONE,
    GLIDER
pilot's place . . . COCKPIT
position finder . . . LORAN
propeller . . . . SCREW
recovery from a dive . . . .
    PULLOUT
runner for landing . . SKID
shed/shelter . . . HANGAR,
    SHED, AIRDROME,
    AERODROME
small . . . . FLIVVER
squadron . . . ESCADRILLE
stabilizer . . . . FIN,
    EMPENNAGE, AIRFOIL
struts arrangement . . . . . .
    CABANE
stunts . . . . . AEROBATICS,
    (BARREL) ROLL,
    LOOP(-THE-LOOP),
    SPIN, IMMELMAN(TURN)
tail part . . . . FIN,
    RUDDER, STABILIZER,
    ELEVATOR
towed target . . . . DROGUE
throttle . . . . GUN
trip . . . . FLIGHT, HOP
turn . . . . BANK,
    BARREL ROLL, LOOP
twisting force . . . TORQUE
type . . . . FIGHTER,
    BOMBER, JET, AMPHIBIAN,
    TWOSEATER, MONOPLANE,
    COMMERCIAL, LINER
war . . . . FIGHTER,
    BOMBER, MIG, SABREJET,
    SUPERFORT, STUKA,
    SPITFIRE, SPAD, ZERO
water landing gear . . . . . .
    PONTOON
window . . . . . BOMB BAY
wing section for
   banking . . . . AILERON

wing support .... STRUT, CABANE
airdrome .... HANGAR, AIRPORT
airedale .... TERRIER
airfoil .... PLANE, TAB
airing .... OUTING, VENTILATION, REVEALING, EXPRESSION
airmail, by .... PAR AVION
airman ...... AVIATOR, PILOT, BARNSTORMER
  mythological .... ICARUS
  non-flying .... KIWI
  would-be .... DODO
airplane (see aircraft) .... AIRCRAFT, PLANE, AERO, AVION
airport .... (AIR)DROME, AERODROME
  marker .... PYLON
  part .... APRON, RUNWAY, TOWER
  paving .... TARMAC
air-raid shelter .... ABRI, BUNKER, DUGOUT
airs, given to .... PRISSY, SNOOTY
airship ..... AERO, BALLOON, BLIMP, DIRIGIBLE, ZEPPELIN
  gas-using .... BALLOON, BLIMP, DIRIGIBLE, ZEPPELIN
airtight .... HERMETIC
airy .... GAY, ETHEREAL, LIGHT, JAUNTY, BREEZY
aisle ..... CORRIDOR, ALLEY, PASSAGEWAY, NAVE
  tread the middle .. MARRY
  treader of the middle ... BRIDE(GROOM)
ait ...... ISLE(T), HOLM, EYOT
Aix-la-Chapelle ..... AACHEN
Ajaccio is capital of .. CORSICA
Ajax, father of ...... TELEMON
  the ____ .... LESS
akin .... SIB, AGNATE, GERMANE, LIKE, RELATED
Al Smith character ...... JEFF, MUTT
ala .... WING
  mode .... STYLISH, FASHIONABLE
  mort .... MORTALLY, MELANCHOLY
Alabama capital .... MONTGOMERY

city ... SELMA, ANNISTON, DECATUR, MOBILE, PELL
county .... LAMAR, LEE
  nickname .... COTTON STATE, YELLOWHAMMER
  state flower ... CAMELLIA
alackaday .... ALAS
alacrity .... WILLINGNESS, READINESS, QUICKNESS, CELERITY
Aladdin's servant ..... GENIE, JINNI
alamandite .... GARNET
alameda ... PROMENADE, WALK
alamo .... POPLAR
  hero ... BOWIE, CROCKETT
  in Texas .... MISSION, SHRINE
Alamogordo county .... OTERO
Alan, author .... PATON
aland .... DOG
alange .. DREARY, DRAB, DULL
alantin .... INULIN
alar .... WINGED, WINGLIKE, WINGSHAPED, PTERO
Alaric's men .... GOTHS
alarm .... SCARE, PANIC, SIREN, AROUSE, CALL, WARN(ING)
  bell .... TOCSIN
  poetic .... ALARUM
  system for short ... DEWS
  whistle .... SIREN(E), BLAST, FOGHORN
alas .... ALACK(ADAY), WOE (IS ME)
Alaska capital .... JUNEAU
  former capital .... SITKA
Alaskan auk .... ARRIES
  bear .... KODIAK
  blizzard .... PURGA
  cape .... NOME
  city .... NOME, ANCHORAGE, SITKA, JUNEAU, GADSDEN
  garment .... PARKA
  glacier .... MUIR
  highway .... ALCAN
  Indian .... TLINGIT, TLINKIT
  inlet .... COOK
  island .... ADAK, ATKA, ATTU, ALEUTIANS, PRIBILOF, KODIAK
  mining town ...... NOME

monument ...... KATMAI
mountain .... ADA,
    FAIRWEATHER
native .... ALEUT,
    ESKIMO, DENE
peak .... MCKINLEY
peninsula .... KENAI,
    UNGA, SEWARD
river .. YUKON, TANANA
seaport ..... KETCHIKAN
town .... FAIRBANKS,
    NOME
valley ...... MATANUSKA
vehicle .... SLED
volcano .... KATMAI
alb .... VESTMENT, ROBE
alba .... AUBADE, SONG
albacore .... TUNNY,
    BONITO, FISH, MACKEREL
Albanese, soprano ..... LICIA
Albanian .... GHEG
capital .... TIRANA
city ... SCUTARI, VALONA
coin ..... LEK, QUINTAR
dialect .. TOSK, CHAM, GEG
king .... ZOG
river .. DRIN, ARTA, MATIA
seaport .... SCUTARI,
    VALONA, AVLONA
soldier .... PALIKAR
spy .... CICERO
Albany is capital of ....
    NEW YORK
albatross .... GONY, NELLY,
    MALLEMUCK
Albee's Alice .... TINY
albeit ... ALTHOUGH, EVEN IF
Alberta scenery .... BANFF
albinism .... ALPHOSIS
Albion .... ENGLAND
    adjective for .. PERFIDIOUS
albite .... FELDSPAR
album .... SCRAPBOOK
albumen .... GLAIR
alburnum .... SAPWOOD
alcaide ..... JAILER, WARDEN
Alcestis' husband ... ADMETUS
alchemical .... HERMETIC
alchemist, pioneer .... THOTH
alchemy, work on .. ALMAGEST
alchitran .... TAR, PITCH
Alcides .... HERCULES
Alcinous' gardens ..... SCHERIA
alcohol ... INTOXICANT, SPIRITS
crystal .... TALITOL
ingredient ...... ETHYL,

    AMYL, METHYL
solid .... STEROL
alcoholic .... DRUNKARD,
    DIPSOMANIAC
drink .... GIN, RUM,
    MEAD, POSSET, WINE, TOT
drink from rice/molasses
    ARRACK, SAKE
haunt of ...... SKIDROW
liquor .... TIPPLE,
    MESCAL
liquor, craving for ......
    THIRST
liquor from wine ....
    BRANDY
liquor, fruit ..... BRANDY
liquor smuggler ....
    RUMRUNNER
liquor to an Indian .....
    FIREWATER
sugar .... TROSSE
Alcoran .... KORAN
Alcott heroine .... AMY, BETH,
    JO, MEG
alcove .... RECESS, NOOK,
    ORIEL, BOWER, BAY, NICHE
Alda, Frances ...... SOPRANO,
    DIVA
aldehyde, liquid ..... CITRAL
alder .... SAGE ROSE,
    ALNUS, ARN
ale ... BEER, ALEGAR, LAGER,
    PORTER, FLIP, BOCK, MOM,
    STOUT, YILL, STINGO,
    NOG(G)
flavor .... HOPS
ingredient .... MALT,
    YEAST, HOPS
measure ...... NOGGIN,
    PINT, GILL
mug .... TOBY, STEIN
strong .... NAPPY,
    STINGO
sour .... ALEGAR
vinegar .... ALEGAR
alec .... (FISH)SAUCE
Alecto .... FURY
alee, opposite of .. AWEATHER,
    STOSS
alegar ... VINEGAR, (SOUR)ALE
alehouse .... SALOON,
    TAVERN, INN, PUB
alembic .... RETORT, STILL,
    DISTILLER
Alençon is capital of .... ORNE
    product .... LACE

Aleppo native .... SYRIAN
alert .... AWAKE, AWARE,
KEEN, WARNING, VIGILANT,
READY, GLEG
Aleut .... UNUNGUN
Aleutian fish ..... GREENLING
isle ... ADAK, ATTU, ATKA
alewife ...... FISH, WALLEYE,
POMPANO, HERRING
Alexander ____ ...... POPE,
FLEMING, SEROV, KING,
ARCHIPELAGO, THE GREAT
Alexander the Great's battlesite
GRANICUS
conquest .... ISSUS,
ARBELA, PARTHIA
general ...... ANTIPATER
Alexandria, patriarch ... PAPA
Alexandrian courtesan .. THAIS
mathematician ....
PTOLEMY
theologian .... ARIUS
writer .... ORIGEN
alfalfa .... LUCERN(E), PEA,
FODDER, MEDIC, SATIVA
alforja .... SADDLEBAG
alfresco .... OUTDOOR(S),
OUTSIDE
alga .... NORI, DIATOM,
SEAWEED, SCUM, DESMID,
ANABAENA, CONFERVA,
SPYROGYRA, NOSTOC
filament ...... TRICHOMA
algae genus .... ALARIA
like .... ALGOID
algarroba ...... CAROB, TREE,
(HONEY) MESQUITE, CALDEN,
LOCUST
Algeria, Roman name ....
POMARIA
Algerian capital .... ALGIERS
cavalryman ...... SPAHI
city ...... ORAN, ALGIERS
city section ...... CASBAH
governor .... DEY
grass .... ESPARTO
guerilla chieftain .. ZBIRI
infantryman ..... TURCO
minority group .. BERBERS
native .... BERBER,
KABYLE
native quarter .. KASBAH,
CASBAH
port ...... ORAN, BONE,
ALGIERS
president .... BELLA,

BOUMEDIENNE
ruler .... BEY
soldier .... SPAHI,
SPAHEE, TURCO
weight .... ROTL
algesis .... ACHE, PAIN
algia, as suffix .... PAIN
algid .... COLD, CHILLY
algolagnia .... SADISM,
MASOCHISM
Algonquian Indian ..... CREE,
LENAPE, OTTAWA, MIAMI,
SAC, SHAWNEE,
ARAPAHO(E)
friend .... NETOP
Indian money ....
SE(A)WAN, SEAWANT
algor .... CHILL
algum .... ALMUG,
SANDALWOOD
Ali Baba ...... WOODCUTTER
brother of ...... CASSIM
helper of ..... MORGIANA
word(s) of ....
(OPEN) SESAME
alias .... PSEUDONYM,
OTHERWISE KNOWN, HANDLE
letters before ...... AKA
alibi .... PLEA, EXCUSE
alible .... NUTRITIVE,
NOURISHING
Alice's cat .... DINAH
alidade .... DIOPTER
alien .... FOREIGN(ER),
STRANGER, ADVERSE,
METIC, OUTSIDER,
EMIGRE(E), OUTLANDER
alienate ... ESTRANGE, WEAN,
TRANSFER, DISAFFECT
alienist .... PSYCHIATRIST
alight .... DISMOUNT,
STEP DOWN, ROOST, LAND
align .... TRUE, ALINE,
STRAIGHTEN
alignment .... LINAGE
alike .... SIMILAR, AKIN,
SAME, MATCHED
combining form ..... ISO
aliment ... FOOD, NOURISHMENT
alimentary canal .... ENTERON
motion ..... PERISTALSIS
aliped creature .... BAT
alit .... AGLOW, LANDED,
DISMOUNTED, RADIANT
alive .... QUICK
alkali ...... LYE, SALT, SODA,

SALTWORT, POTASH,
ANTACID
alkaline .... LIME, OXIDE
solution .... LYE
alkaloid .... ARICIN,
CAFFEIN(E), ESERINE,
ARABINE, CODEINE,
DITAMIN, SINAPIN,
CAPSAICIN, QUININ(E),
MESCALINE, BERBERIN(E),
MORPHINE
bean .... ESERIN
hemlock ...... CONIN(E)
mushroom .. MUSCARINE
poison(ous) .... CURARE,
CONIN, MUSCARIN(E),
BRUCIN(E), TROPIN(E),
THEBAINE
sedative ..... CODEIN(E)
tea .... THEINE
alkanet .... ANCHUSA,
BUGLOSS, DYE
alkene .... OLEFIN
all ..... WHOLE, EVERY(ONE),
ANY, TOTAL(ITY), ENTIRE
around .... VERSATILE
combining form .... PAN,
OMNI
creating .... OMNIFIC
fours .... SEVEN UP
in .... TIRED, WEARY,
FATIGUED
in Latin .... TOTO
in music .... TUTTI
powerful ... OMNIPOTENT
religions, believer in ....
OMNIST
right ..... HONEST, GOOD
Saints' Day, observance ..
HALLOWMASS, HALLOWEEN
seed .... KNOTWEED,
GOOSEFOOT
seed herb ..... RADIOLA
allan .... GULL
allanite ..... ORTHITE, CERINE
allay ... CALM, EASE, RELIEVE,
ASSUAGE, ASSURE, QUIET,
MOLLIFY, SLAKE, ALLEVIATE
allegation ..... PLEA, CLAIM,
AVERMENT, EXCUSE, ALIBI
allege ... CLAIM, ASSERT, STATE
alleged electric force ... ELOD
force ...... OD, ODYLE
Allegheny city .... OLEAN
allegiance .... FEALTY,
LOYALTY, DEVOTION

allegorical .... PARABOLIC
allegory .... PARABLE, FABLE
Allen, ____ .. FRED, STEVE, IRA,
ETHAN
allergic reaction .... BASH,
SNEEZE, COLD
skin condition .... HIVES
to firearms ..... GUNSHY
allergy .... SENSITIVENESS
medicine for .. BENADRYL
alleviate .... LIGHTEN,
MITIGATE, EASE, ALLAY,
LESSEN
alleviation .... RELIEF
alley ... LANE, MIB, PASSAGE,
STREET, TAW, WALK, MARBLE
blind .... CULDESAC,
DEADEND
closed at one end ....
DEADEND
allheal ..... PLANT, VALERIAN
alliance ..... LEAGUE, UNION,
CONFEDERACY
of nations ... UN, NATO,
SEATO, OAS, AXIS, BIG FIVE
of parties ... COALITION
allied .... AKIN, SIMILAR,
RELATED, UNITED,
ASSOCIATED, JOINED
alligator ... CAYMAN, CAIMAN,
SAURIAN, LIZARD, LEATHER
pear .... AVOCADO
allium .... ONION, GARLIC,
LEEK
allocate ...... METE, ASSIGN,
GRANT, GIVE, DISTRIBUTE,
ALLOT, ASSIGN, SHARE
allot .... ALLOCATE,
ASSIGN, SHARE, APPORTION,
METE
allotment ...... SHARE, QUOTA,
PORTION, RATION
allow .... PERMIT, LET,
ADMIT, PROVIDE, OPINE,
TOLERATE
free use .... LEND
to become known .. LEAK
allowable variance ....
TOLERANCE
allowance .... SUPPORT,
REDUCTION, RATION,
TOLERATION
depreciation .... AGIO
food ... CORODY, RATION
loss of weight .... DRAFT
small .... PITTANCE

waste ..... TRET, DRAFT
weight .... TARE
alloy ...... METAL, MIXTURE,
AMALGAM
aluminum .. DURALUMIN,
ALNICO
black .... NIELLO
cheap jewelry ....
TOMBAC(K), TOMBAK
copper-nickel-zinc ......
ALBATA, ELECTRUM
copper-tin ...... BRONZE
copper-tin-zinc .. OROIDE
copper-zinc ...... BRASS
gold-like ...... AROIDE,
ORMOLU
gold-silver .... ASEM,
ELECTRUM
iron-carbon ...... STEEL
lead-tin .... TERNE,
PEWTER
mercury ..... AMALGAM
nickel-steel .... INVAR
non-ferrous .... TULA
pewter-like .... BIDRI
sulfur .... NIELLO
three-metal ... TERNARY
tin-copper-antimony ....
BABBIT, BRITANNIA
tin-copper-lead .. PEWTER
tin-zinc .... OROIDE
used in cheap jewelry ...
OROIDE, TOMBAC, TOMBAK,
TOMBACK
with aluminum ....
CALORIZE
yellow .... AICH
alloyed .... SPURIOUS,
SHAM, MIXED, BASE,
INSINCERE
allspice ...... PIMENTO, BERRY
allude ...... REFER, MENTION,
CITE
allure ...... ENTICE, ATTRACT,
BAIT, FASCINATION, TEMPT,
TOLE
allurement ..... FASCINATION,
CHARM, ENTICEMENT
allusion ..... HINT, INKLING,
REFERENCE
allusive ...... METAPHORICAL
alluvial clay .... ADOBE
deposit .... MUD, SILT,
PLACER
fan .... DELTA
matter .... GEEST

alluvion .... FLOOD, SILT
ally .... JOIN, ASSOCIATE,
HELPER
alma ...... ALME(H), DANGER
almain .... GERMAN
almanac .... CALENDAR,
YEARBOOK
astronomical ....
EPHEMERIS
almandine ... SPINEL, GARNET
almighty .... OMNIPOTENT,
ALL-POWERFUL
almond ..... TREE, LIGHT TAN,
AMYGDALA, BADAM,
KANARI
emulsion ...... ORGEAT
eyed .... SLANT-EYED
flavored liquor .. RATAFIA
oil .... AMARIN
shaped ..... AMYGDALOID
almost .... NEARLY
alms .... DOLE, CHARITY
box .... ARCA
distributor .... ALMONER
almshouse ...... POORHOUSE,
BEADHOUSE
almuce .... HEADDRESS,
TIPPET, AMICE
alnus .... ALDER
alod .... ALODIUM,
ESTATE, FREEHOLD
aloe ..... AGAVE, LILY, DRUG,
MAGUEY
derivative .... ALOIN
aloft ...... UP, IN THE AIR,
ASOAR, OVERHEAD
aloha ...... LOVE, GREETING,
FAREWELL, GOODBYE,
WELCOME
alone ...... SOLITARY, SOLO,
ONLY, SOLE, SINGLE
on stage ... SOLA, SOLUS
along .... LENGTHWISE,
BESIDE, ON
the way .... ENROUTE
aloof ..... APART, RESERVED,
DISTANT, COLD
alopecia .... BALDNESS
aloud .... AUDIBLE
alow .... BELOW, UNDER
alp .... MOUNTAIN, PEAK
alpaca ...... WOOL, CLOTH,
RUMINANT
like animal ... GUANACO,
VICUNA, LLAMA

alpha ..... START, STAR, FIRST, DENEB
  rays .... BETA
alphabet .... RUDIMENTS, PRIMER
  character .... OGAM, RUNE, LETTER
  Kashmir .... SARADA
  teacher ... ABECEDARIAN
alphabetical list, kind of .....
  CATALOG(UE), CONCORDANCE
Alpine animal .... IBEX, CHAMOIS
  dress .... DIRNDL
  goat ..... IBEX, STEINBOK
  herdsman .... SENN
  house/hut ...... CHALET
  pass ..... (MONT)CENIS, COL, SIMPLON
  primrose ... AURICULA
  river .... RHONE
  wind .... FOEHN, BISE, BORA
Alps .... TIROL, TYROL, MATTERHORN, BLANC, NERNINA, JUNGFRAU
already .... PREVIOUSLY
Alsatian ...... WHITEFRIARS, POLICE DOG
alsike ...... CLOVER, FODDER
also .... LIKEWISE, TOO, BESIDES, AND
  known as ... ALIAS, AKA
  ran .... LOSER
alt .... ISLE(T)
Altair .... STAR
altar .... TABLE, STAND
  area around ... CHANCEL
  boy .... THURIFER, ACOLYTE
  carpet .... PEDALE
  cloth ... DOSSAL, DOSSEL, PALL, HAPLOMA, CORPORAL, VESPERAL
  constellation ...... ARA
  curtain .... RIDDEL
  enclosure .... BEMA
  end of the church .. APSE
  endowed ..... CHANTRY
  offering ...... ALTARAGE, EUCHARIST
  part .... PREDELLA, PISCINA
  piece .... TRIPTYCH
  rail .... SEPTUM
  screen/veil .... REREDOS,

ANTEPENDIUM
shelf ... GRADIN, RETABLE
slab/top .... MENSA
table .... CREDENCE
altazimuth of astronomer .... ABA
alter ... ADAPT, VARY, CHANGE, MUTATE, MODIFY, PERMUTE
  ego .... SIDEKICK, FRIEND, STOOGE
alteration .... CHANGE, REVISION
altercation .... QUARREL, DISPUTE, ARGUMENT, SPAT
alternate .... ROTATE, OTHER, SUBSTITUTE, STAND-IN
alternative ...... CHOICE, OR, EITHER, AND/OR, OPTION
althorn .... SAXHORN
although .... EVEN IF, IN SPITE OF, WHILE
altogether ... IN ALL, WHOLLY, QUITE
altitude barometer .. OROMETER
Altona .... HAMBURG
altruist, one kind of .... SAMARITAN
  opposite of ..... EGOIST
alum .... ASTRINGENT, EMETIC, SALT
aluminum compound .... TERMITE, BAUXITE
  ore .... BAUXITE
  oxide .... ALUMINA, CORUNDUM, RUBY, TOPAZ
alumnus .... GRAD(UATE)
alveary .... (BEE)HIVE
alveolar .... GINGIVAL
alveolate ..... HONEYCOMBED, HOLEY
always .... AY, E'ER, INVARIABLY, (FOR)EVER
alyssum .... MADWORT
ama .... CUP, VESSEL
amadou .... PUNK, STYPTIC, TINDER
amah .... NURSE(MAID), SERVANT, AYAH
amain .... FORCEFULLY, HASTILY, MIGHTILY
Amakusa port .... AMUTA
Amalekite king .... AGAG
amalgam .... ALLOY, MIXTURE, BLEND, COMBINATION

amalgamate .... MIX, BLEND, FUSE, MERGE, COMBINE
amalgamating pan ...... TINA
amanuensis ...... SECRETARY, SCRIVENER
amaranth .... PIGWEED, TUMBLEWEED, FLOWER
amaranthine ..... DEATHLESS, UNFADING
amaryllis .... AGAVE, SHEPHERDESS, BULB, PLANT, BELLADONNA
mass .... HEAP, GATHER, COLLECT, PILE, ACCUMULATE
Amata's daughter ... LAVINIA, LATINIA
amateur .... DILETTANTE, TYRO, NOVICE, DABBLER, DUB, GREENHORN, NEOPHYTE
athlete's goal .. OLYMPICS
boxing championship .... GOLDEN GLOVES
colloquial ... SIMON PURE
opposite of .... PRO(FESSIONAL), EXPERT
painter .... DABBLER
radio operator ..... HAM
thief, sometime .... SHOPLIFTER
amateurish .... CLUMSY, INEPT, AWKWARD
Amati ...... VIOLIN, NICOLO
amative .... AMOROUS, EROTIC, LOVING
amatol .... EXPLOSIVE
amaze .... SURPRISE, ASTONISH, STUN
amazed .... AGHAST, PUTOUT, AWED
amazing event ..... MIRACLE
trick .... MAGIC, SLEIGHT OF HAND
Amazon ...... RIVER, WOMAN, ANT, PARROT, VIRAGO
cetacean .... INIA
estuary/mouth ..... PARA
fish .... LEPIDOSIREN
part of .... SOLIMOES
tributary .... APA, TAPAJOZ, JURUA, JAVARI, JAVARY, JAPURA
valley Indian .. TAPUYAN
ambagious .... DEVIOUS, CIRCUITOUS

ambary .... FIBER, NALITA, PLANT
ambassador .... ENVOY, DIPLOMAT, MINISTER, AGENT, EMISSARY
papal ... NUNCIO, LEGATE
amber .... RESIN, YELLOW
fish .... MEDREGAL
like .... AMBEROID, AMBROID
ambergris .... SECRETION, PERFUMERY
ambi: comb. form ..... BOTH
ambience .... MILIEU, ENVIRONS
ambiguous .... INDEFINITE, UNCERTAIN, VAGUE, OBSCURE, DELPHIC
ambit ...... CIRCUIT, SCOPE, LIMITS, BOUNDS
ambition .... GOAL, END, DESIRE, ASPIRATION
amble: sl. .... MOSEY
ambling horse .... PADNAG
ambo .... PULPIT, STAND, LECTERN
Ambracian Gulf .... ARTA
ambrosia .... RAGWEED, BEEHEAD, NECTAR
ambrosial .... DELICIOUS, FRAGRANT
drink .... AMRITA
ambry .... CUPBOARD, LOCKER, CLOSET, NICHE, PANTRY
ambsace ...... DOUBLE ACES, BAD LUCK, TWO ACES
ambulance chaser, so-called .. SHYSTER
ambulant .... WALKING, ON FOOT
seller .... PEDDLER
ambulator ...... PEDOMETER
ambush ...... TRAP, WAYLAY, AMBUSCADE
ameliorate .... IMPROVE, BETTER, RELIEVE, ALLEVIATE
amen ...... VERILY, SO BE IT, APPROVAL
amenable .... OBEDIENT, AGREEABLE, RECEPTIVE, PERVIOUS
to reason .... BROADMINDED, OPEN-MIND(ED)

amend .... ALTER, REVISE, IMPROVE, CHANGE, MODIFY

amendment ..... CORRECTION, REVISION, CHANGE

    tricky .... RIDER, JOKER

amends .... PAYMENT, ATONEMENT, REDRESS

amenities, observance of the .. PUNCTILIO

amenity .... COURTESY, CIVILITY

ament .... IDIOT, SPIKE, CATKIN, CHAT, CATTAIL

amerce .... PUNISH, FINE, PENALIZE

America, reputed discoverer .. (AMERIGO) VESPUCCI, ERIC, VOTAN

American (see U.S.) .... YANK(EE), AMERICANO, GRINGO

    aborigine ...... INDIAN

    admiral .... CARNEY, FARRAGUT, HALSEY, KING, SIMS, NIMITZ, KINKAID, DEWEY

    aircraft carrier .... ENTERPRISE, AMERICA

    antelope ...... BLESBOK, SASSABY

    anthologist .... UNTERMEYER

    archeologist .. ANDREWS

    artist ..... KENT, FLAG WEST, PEALE, HOME.., HICKS, COPLEY, CADMUS, INNESS, BENTON

    astronaut ...... WHITE, SCHIRRA, BORMAN, LOVELL, STAFFORD, COLLINS, ALDRIN

    author ..... ASCH, AMES, HERSEY, YERBY, HARTE, BAUM, FERBER, LORING, WYLIE, POE, TARKINGTON, HEMINGWAY, SPILLANE, GARDNER

    badger ...... CARCAJOU

    balladeer ..... GUTHRIE

    balsam .... TOLU

    battle scene, Phillipines .. BATAAN, CORREGIDOR, MANILA BAY

    beauty .... ROSE

    bingo .... LOTTO

    bird ..... GUAN, TOWHEE, RHEA, JUNCO, GROUSE, ROBIN, STARLING, BOBOLINK, SPARROW

    bishop .... SHEEN

    cactus .... CEREUS

    capitalist .... ASTOR, BARUCH

    capital lobbyist .... RAINMAKER

    cardinal .... CUSHING, SPELLMAN, BRENNAN

    caricaturist .... NAST

    cartoonist .... CAPP, FISHER, DISNEY, ARNO, NAST, HERBLOCK, CONRAD, SANDERS, OLIPHANT, MAULDIN, HESSE, DARCY

    choreographer .. ROKINE

    coin .... DIME, NICKEL, QUARTER, CENT, EAGLE

    columbo ...... GENTIAN

    commodore ..... PERRY

    composer ...... BERLIN, PORTER, COPLAND, PAINE, NEVIN, IVES, KERN

    Confederate soldier ..... REB(EL), BUTTERNUT

    contralto .... ANDERSON

    critic .... AYRES, HALE

    dinosaur .... BRONTOSAURUS

    dramatist ...... BARRY, WILLIAMS, ODETS, CROUSE, HART

    diplomat ...... HARRIMAN, LODGE, DULLES, BOHLEN, GREW

    dog .... ALCO

    duck ...... BUFFLEHEAD

    editor ...... BOK, LUCE, MENCKEN, WALLACE, GREELY, DANA

    educator ...... CONANT, HUME, FISK, HUTCHINS, MANN, KIRK

    elk .... WAPITI

    evangelist ..... GRAHAM

    evergreen ..... FIR, PINE

    explorer .... PEARY, BYRD, LEWIS, FREMONT, CLARK

    fashion designer .. STARR, CHARLES

    feminist .... CATT, PAUL, STONE, STANTON

    financier .... ASTOR,

MORGAN, BARUCH, GOULD
finch ..... JUNCO, SISKIN
flag .... OLD GLORY
flycatcher ...... PHOEBE
fowl ...... WYANDOTTE
frontier scout ... HICKOK
frontiersman ... CARSON,
CROCKETT, BOONE
fur merchant .... ASTOR
game .... POKER,
BASEBALL, FOOTBALL,
BASKETBALL
general .... LEE, GRANT,
RENO, BRADLEY,
MACARTHUR, OTIS, MEADE,
SCOTT, ORD, EISENHOWER,
STILWELL, POPE,
BURNSIDE, BUELL
general of the army ....
PERSHING, MACARTHUR,
EISENHOWER
geologist .... DANA
girl of 1890's .... GIBSON
grapes .... NIAGARA
Great White Father ... .
PRESIDENT
guitarist ...... GUTHRIE
historian .... BAILEY,
HYMAN, ROBINSON,
SCHLESINGER
horse .... BRONCO,
PINTO, MUSTANG
humorist ..... ADE, NYE,
COBB, ROGERS, NASH,
BENCHLEY, TWAIN,
LARDNER
illustrator ...... FLAGG,
ROCKWELL, NEWELL
imaginary town ....
PODUNK
Indian .. HOPI, UTE, SIOUX,
ARIKARA, MIAMI, SENECA,
PECOS, KIOWA, APACHE,
PIMA, LENAPE, BILOXI,
CROW, OTOE, OSAGE,
PAWNEE, UINTA, LUMMI,
POMO
and Negro descent ....
SAMBO, GRIFF(E)
ax .... TOMAHAWK
baby .... PAPOOSE
beads ...... WAMPUM
dwelling ...... TEPEE,
WIGWAM, LODGE
greeting .... NETOP
grunt .... UGH

language .... NA-DENE
peace offering ... PIPE
pipe .... CALUMET
pony .... CAYUSE,
PINTO
trophy .... SCALP
woman's husband ....
SQUAWMAN
inventor .... MORSE,
HOWE, EDISON, OTIS,
FULTON, WHITNEY
ivy .... WOODVINE
isthmus .... PANAMA
Japanese .... NISEI,
ISSEI, KIBEI
journalist ...... BROWN,
REID, BIGELOW, GUNTHER
jurist .... TANEY,
MARSHALL, COOLEY,
MOORE, CARDOZO, TAFT,
PAINE, LANDIS
jute .... MALLOW
keno ..... BINGO, LOTTO
larch .... TAMARACK
lawyer ... DARROW, PAINE
leopard .... JAGUAR
lexicographer .. WEBSTER
light wood ...... BALSA
lion ..... COUGAR, PUMA
lizard ... ANOLE, BASILISK
lotto ...... KENO, BINGO
lynx .... BOBCAT
mammal .... OTTER,
OPOSSUM
Marine .. LEATHERNECK,
GYRENE
Mexican name for ......
GRINGO
monetary unit .. DOLLAR
money market ....
WALL STREET
monkey .... TEETEE,
SAPAJOU, TITI, CAPUCHIN
national military cemetery
ARLINGTON
national military park ...
SHILOH
naturalist .... SETON,
BAIRD, AUDUBON, MUIR
nature writer ..... BEEBE
naval historian .. MAHAN
navy enlisted man ......
BLUEJACKET
navy gripe session .. MAST
newspaper publisher ....
SCRIPPS, FIELDS, HEARST

night hawk .... PISK
nightshade ... POKEHEED,
HENBANE, BELLADONNA
novelist ...... FAULKNER,
BALDWIN, FERBER, STEELE
nutmeg .... CALABASH
operatic singer ... PRICE,
FARRAR, CALLAS, STEVENS,
ALDA
orator ..... BRYAN, OTIS,
HENRY
painter .... SARGENT,
BENTON, INNESS, LUKS,
BELLOWS, RYDER, CURRY,
HOMER, PETERS, SLOAN
painter of animals ......
SETON
paper money ....
GREENBACK, LONG GREEN
patriot ... HALE, REVERE,
RUSS, ALLEN, OTIS, HENRY,
PAINE
"patron saint" ....
TAMMANY
philanthropist ....
CARNEGIE, HEARST, FORD,
RIIS, BARTON, CHANNING,
ROCKEFELLER
philosopher ... DURANT
pianist .... DUCHIN,
CLIBURN, LEVANT
pioneer .... BOONE
pirate .... KIDD
playwright ... SAROYAN,
WILLIAMS, MILLER, ODETS,
KAUFMAN, ASCH
plover .... KILLDEER
poet .... POE, BENET,
ELIOT, FROST, SANDBURG,
LANIER, NASH, AUDEN,
GUEST, TATE, WHITTIER,
LINDSAY
poetess .... MILLAY,
STEIN, LOWELL
political scientist ......
MACGREGOR, ROSSITER,
NEUSTADT
portraitist .... PEALE
President .. WASHINGTON,
ADAMS, JEFFERSON,
MADISON, MONROE,
JACKSON, VAN BUREN,
HARRISON, TYLER, POLK,
TAYLOR, FILLMORE, PIERCE,
BUCHANAN, LINCOLN,
JOHNSON, GRANT, HAYES,
GARFIELD, ARTHUR,
CLEVELAND, MCKINLEY,
ROOSEVELT, TAFT, WILSON,
HARDING, COOLIDGE,
HOOVER, TRUMAN,
EISENHOWER, KENNEDY,
JOHNSON, NIXON
president's wife ....
FIRST LADY
prime minister of England
CHURCHILL
professor of drama ......
BAKER
publisher ... MCCORMICK,
HEARST, HOWARD, FIELD,
NEWHOUSE, OCHS, COWLES,
LUCE, KNIGHT
quail .... COLIN
railroad magnate ....
HARRIMAN, REA
rebel soldier .. BUTTERNUT
Red Cross organizer ....
BARTON
reformer .... RIIS
Revolution soldier ......
BUCKSKIN
river .... MISSISSIPPI,
OHIO, RAPIDAN, HUDSON,
WABASH, COLUMBIA
rodent .... RABBIT,
SQUIRREL, BEAVER
sculptor .... SMITH,
PROCTOR, CALDER
shipyard ...... GROTON
shrub ... CHICO, WAHOO
singer .... HORNE,
PRESLEY, MARTIN, BAEZ,
PRICE, GARLAND, TUCKER,
PAGE, LANZA, STEVENS,
EDDY
soldier .... YANKEE,
DOGFACE, DOUGHBOY, GI,
SAD SACK
songbird ..... GREENLET
songwriter ..... PORTER,
RODGERS, BERLIN
soprano .... CALLAS,
PONS, STEBER, ALDA,
MUNSEL, STEVENS, SILLS
statesman ...... DULLES,
BARUCH, BAKER, LODGE,
BLAINE, JAY, STIMSON,
STEVENSON, ACHESON,
BENTON, LOGAN
suffragist .... CATT
surgeon .... MAYO,

PARRAN

thrush .... WAGTAIL
tree .... CALABASH,
   MAPLE, OAK, REDWOOD,
   PINE, SYCAMORE, ELM,
   ASH, BUTTONWOOD
volcano .... SHASTA,
   LASSEN
weather phenomenon ...
   SMOG, SMAZE, POGONIP
widgeon ...... BALDPATE
wild sheep .... BIGHORN,
   ARGALI
winter fog ..... POGONIP
wolf .... COYOTE
woman governor, first ...
   ROSS
wood, light ...... BALSA
writer ...... CALDWELL,
   MICHENER, MEAD, PYLE,
   SAROYAN, HARTE
writer in Yiddish ... ASCH
writer of fables ..... ADE
yew .... HEMLOCK
Amerind .... REDSKIN,
   INDIAN, ESKIMO, CREE
symbol .... XAT
amethyst .... QUARTZ,
   CORUNDUM, PURPLE,
   VIOLET
ami(e): Fr. .... FRIEND
amiable ..... AFFABLE, GENIAL
amicable .... PEACEFUL,
   FRIENDLY
amice .... COWL, TIPPET,
   ALMUCE, CAPE, HOOD
amid(st) ...... AMONG, MIDST
amidine .... STARCH
Amiens river .... SOMME
amigo .... FRIEND
amino acid .... PROLIN(E),
   LACTAM, LEUCINE, LYSINE
amiss ...... WRONG, FAULTY
amity .... FRIENDSHIP,
   GOODWILL
Amman is capital of .. JORDAN
ammo .... AMMUNITION
Ammon ...... ZEUS, JUPITER
ammonia compound .. AMIN(E),
   DIAMINE
   in water solution ....
   HARTSHORN
ammoniac ...... GUM RESIN,
   STIMULANT, CEMENT
ammunition .... AMMO, SHOT,
   MEANS, SHELLS, BULLETS,

GRENADES

carrier .... CAISSON
amnesia .... FUGUE
amnesty .... PARDON
amok .... KILLER,
   BERSERK, AMUCK
amole ..... SOAP, ROOT, AGAVE
among .... AMID(ST),
   IN, MID(ST)
amor .... LOVE, EROS
amoretto .... CUPID
amorous .... LOVING,
   EROTIC, SPOONY
amorous look .... OGLE, LEER
amorphous .... FORMLESS,
   SHAPELESS
amort .... LIFELESS,
   SPIRITLESS
Amos' partner .... ANDY
amount caught .... HAUL,
   CATCH
   lost by waste ....
   DECREMENT
   of boastful words ....
   MOUTHFUL
   of gossip .... EARFUL
   of stake in gambling ....
   MISE
   offered at auction ... BID
   possessed .... RATAL
   produced ...... OUTPUT
   used ...... CONSUMPTION
amour propre ..... SELF LOVE
ampere .... WEBER
ampersand .... AND
amphetamine .. METHEDRINE
amphibian ... ANURAN, FROG,
   TOAD, NEWT, BATRACHIA,
   SALAMANDER
   order ... ANURAN, BUFO
   tailed .... CAUDATE
   tank .... ALLIGATOR
   tree .... HYLA
   young .... TADPOLE
amphibious carnivore .. MINK,
   OTTER, SEAL
   vehicle .... AMTRAC,
   DUCK
amphibole .... ASBESTOS,
   MINERAL, EDENITE,
   URALITE, TREMOLITE
Amphion's wife .... NIOBE
amphioxus .... LANCELET
amphipod .... SAND FLEA,
   SHRIMP, CRUSTACEAN
amphitheater .... ARENA,

GALLERY, BOWL
entrance ..... VOMITORY
natural .... CIRQUE
amphora ..... JAR, URN, VASE
ample .... SPACIOUS,
ROOMY, ABUNDANT, FULL
poetic .... ENOW
amplification factor ...... MU
amplify ... EXPAND, INCREASE,
ELABORATE
amplifying device .... MASER,
LASER
amputate ..... LOP, CUT OFF
Amu Darya .... OXUS
amuck .... BERSERK,
BARESARK
amulet .... CHARM,
TALISMAN, PERIAPT
Philippine ....
ANTING ANTING
Amun-Re's wife .... MUT
Amundsen, explorer .. ROALD
Amur tributary .... SUNGARI,
USSURI, ARGUN
amuse .... DIVERT,
ENTERTAIN, BEGUILE,
HUMOR
amusement .... FUN,
DIVERSION, SPORT, GAME
amusing ...... DROLL, RISIBLE,
FUNNY
amygdala .... ALMOND,
TONSIL
Amy's sister ... MEG, BETH, JO
an ... ANYONE, EACH, ONE, PER
ana ..... COLLECTION, DATA,
MEMOIR, ANECDOTES, BITS
anabaena .... ALGA
anaconda .... BOA,
CONSTRICTOR, SNAKE
anadem .... WREATH, GARLAND
anadromous ..... EMPORIUM
an(a)esthetic .... GAS, OPIATE,
SEDATIVE, ANALGESIC
anagram .... GAME, REBUS,
LOGOGRIPH
game ...... LOGOMACHY
analgesic .... OPIATE,
AN(A)ESTHETIC
analogy .... LIKENESS,
COMPARISON
analyst, ore .... ASSAYER
analyze .... EXAMINE,
ASSAY, DISSECT
grammatically .... PARSE
anamnesis .... REMEMBRANCE

Ananias .... LIAR
wife of .... SAPPHIRA
anarchic .... LAWLESS
anarchist .... TERRORIST,
AGITATOR, REBEL, NIHILIST,
RED
anarchy .... DISORDER,
VIOLENCE
anasarca .... EDEMA,
DROPSY
anathema .... DAMNED,
CURSE
anathemize ...... (AC)CURSE,
DAMN, BAN
Anatole ____ novelist .. FRANCE
Anatolia ...... ASIA MINOR
Anatolian capital ... ANKARA
goddess .... MA
anatomical model, of an .....
CLASTIC
model of human body ..
MANIKIN
walls .... SEPTA
anatomy .... SCIENCE,
SKELETON, STRUCTURE
dealing with muscles .....
MYOLOGY
of animals ..... ZOOTOMY
of regions ... TOPOLOGY
ancestor .... ELDER,
FOR(E)BEAR, FAMILY,
STOCK, SIRE
Irish .... MIL, MILED
ancestral ..... AVITAL, AVAL
spirits .... LARES, MANES
ancestry .... FAMILY,
LINEAGE, PEDIGREE
Anchises' son ......(A)ENEAS
anchor ... FIX, KEDGE, MOOR,
TIE, BERTH, CAT, HOOK,
BOWER
chain .... CABLE
fluke .... BILL
heaviest of a ship ....
BOWER
lift .... CAT, WEIGH
lifting device .. CAPSTAN,
WINDLASS
man .... ENDMAN
part ... ARM, FLUKE, RING,
CROWN, SHANK, STOCK,
PALM
place of ...... CATHEAD
slightly raised .... ATRIP
small .... KEDGE,
GRAPNEL, KILLICK,

KILLOCK
tackle .... CAT
anchorage .... MOORAGE,
RADE, MARINA, DOCKAGE,
(ROAD)STEAD, HARBOR
anchoret .... RECLUSE,
ASCETIC, EREMITE
anchorite .... HERMIT,
RECLUSE
opposed to .. C(O)ENOBITE
anchovy .... HERRING, SPRAT
sauce .... ALEC
anchusa .... ALKANET,
BUGLOSS
ancient .... ANTIQUE,
OLD(EN), AGED, PRIMEVAL,
ELD, ARCHAIC, HOARY
Alexandrian writer ......
ORIGEN
alphabetical character ...
RUNE
Briton ...... CELT, PICT
Chinese .... SERES
city .... THEBES,
CORINTH, NICAEA, NINEVEH,
TYRE, EUS
country .... ELAM,
GAUL, MEDEA, EOLIS, ARAM
court .... EYRE, LEET
drink .... MORAT
Egyptian king .. RAMESES,
PHARAOH
Egyptian scrolls .. PAPYRI
Greek invader .. DORIAN
language .... LATIN,
SANSKRIT, GREEK
lyre .... ASOR
manuscript ..... CODEX
Mariner's victim ....
ALBATROSS
musical instrument .....
ASOR, CITHARA, LUTE, REBEC
Persian .... MEDE
priests .... MAGI
sword .... ESTOC
tax .... CRO
temple .... NAOS
times .... YORE
warship ...... GALLEON,
BIREME, GALLEY,
LONG SHIP
weapon .... DAG,
SPEAR, PIKE, MACE, SLING,
HALBERD, ARQUEBUS
wicked city ..... SODOM,
GOMORRAH, BABYLON

ancillary ...... SUBORDINATE,
HELPER, AUXILIARY,
SERVANT
ancon ...... ELBOW, CONSOLE
and .... ALSO, MOREOVER,
PLUS, AS WELL AS, TOO,
AMPERSAND
others .... ET AL
so on/so forth ....
ETC(ETERA), USW
Andalusian .... SPANIARD,
SPANISH, LEGHORN
port .... CADIZ
province .... JAEN
Andean .... PAMPERO
Andersen, Christian ... HANS
Anderson, singer .... MARIAN
writer ...... MAXWELL,
SHERWOOD
Andes .... MOUNTAIN
camel-like animal ....
GUANACO, LLAMA,
VICUNA, ALPACA
deer .... PUDU
grass .... ICHU
mountain ...... SORATA,
CHIMBORAZO, POTOSI,
HUILA, MISTI, ILLAMPU,
HUASCARAN, COTOPAXI
peak .... ACONCAGUA
plain ... PARAMO, LLANO
plateau .... PUNA
rodent ..... CHINCHILLA
ruminant ...... LLAMA,
GUANACO, ALPACA
volcano ...... OMATE,
MISTI, CHIMBORAZO
wind .... PAMPERO
andiron ....(FIRE)DOG,
HESSIAN
Andre, John, for example ....
SPY
Andrew .... APOSTLE
androgen ...... HORMONE
Andromache's husband ......
HECTOR
Andromeda's husband ....
PERSEUS
androsterone ...... HORMONE
Andy Gump's wife ...... MIN
Andy's partner .... AMOS
anecdotage ..... TALES, ANA
anecdotes, expert in ....
RACONTEUR
anele .... ANOINT, OIL
anemia .... CHLOROSIS

anemic .... PALE, BLOODLESS,
WAN, COLORLESS
anemone .... PLANT,
WINDFLOWER, ANIMAL,
POLYP, ACTINIA, SNOWDROP
anent .... REGARDING,
ABOUT, CONCERNING, INRE
anes .... ONCE
anesthesia .... NUMBNESS
anesthetic .... ETHER,
PROCAINE, OPIATE,
CARVACROL, COCAIN(E),
STOVAIN(E)
anet .... DILL(SEED)
anew .... AGAIN, AFRESH
do .... REPEAT,
RESUME
angel .... CHERUB,
SERAPH(IM), MESSENGER,
SPIRIT, SERAF
fallen .... LUCIFER
fish .... SHARK
gold-digger's ....
SUGAR DADDY
loyal .... MICHAEL
of bottomless pit ....
APOLLYON
of Broadway, etc. ......
SUGAR DADDY, FINANCIER
of death .... AZRAEL,
SAMUEL, DANITE
of music .... ISRAFIL
rebel .... AZAZEL,
LUCIFER
Angeli, actress .... PIER
angelic .... CHERUBIC,
SAINTLY
messenger ..... GABRIEL
Angelica .... ARCHANGEL
angels collectively ....
HIERARCHY
ngelus .... PRAYER,
VESPER
anger .... IRE, DANDER,
RILE, ENRAGE, INDIGNATION,
WRATH, INCENSE
fit of .... TEMPER, RAGE,
PIQUE, TANTRUM, CHOLER,
TIFF
give vent to .... RAGE,
FUME
angina .... CROUP
Angkor relics .... RUINS,
TEMPLES
temple ruins ..... BAYON
Wat (or Vat) .... TEMPLE

angle ...... SLANT, ANCON,
CORNER, ASPECT, POINT,
FISH, TRICK, RADIAN
branch .... AXIL
formed by aircraft .. YAW
forming no ..... AGONIC
in geology .... HADE
leafstalk .... AXIL
measuring device ......
GONIOMETER
outside .... CANT
pipe .... TEE
trench .... ZIG
with no .... AGONIC
angler .... FISHER(MAN),
SCHEMER, TRICKSTER
angler's basket ...... CREEL
delight .... BITE, STRIKE
need .... BAIT, ROD,
CREEL, LINE, HOOK
Angleterre .... LACE
Anglian kingdom ..... DEIRA
Anglican anthem .... AGNUS DEI
Anglo-Indian empire founder ..
CLIVE
kingdom .... KENT
nurse ...... AMAH, AYAH
title of address ..... BABU
troop .... RESSALA
man, rich ...... NAWAB,
NABOB
woman, rich ... BEGUM
Anglo-Saxon .... ENGLISH
armor .... HAUBERK
assembly .... GEMOT(E)
coin .... ORA, SCEAT
consonant...... ETH, EDH
court .... GEMOT(E)
folk hero .... BEOWULF
freeman .... THANE
hunter's attendant ......
GILLY, GILLIE
king .... EDGAR
king's council .... WITAN
kingdom .... MERCIA,
ESSEX
lord's attendant .. THANE,
THEGN
noble/prince .. ATHELING
slave .... ESNE
warrior ... THEGN, THANE
Angola capital ..... LUANDA
port .... LUANDA,
LOBITO
Angora .... ANKARA, CAT,
GOAT, RABBIT

goat .... CHAMAL
goat fabric ..... MOHAIR
angostura .... BOLIVAR,
    BARK, TONIC, FLAVOR
angry .... INDIGNANT,
    SORE, IRATE, CROSS, MAD,
        HOT, WROTH
creature ..... SOREHEAD,
    WET HEN, AMOK, AMUCK,
        BERSERK
    look .... GLOWER,
        SCOWL, GLARE
anguillid .... EEL
anguine .... SNAKELIKE
anguish .... PAIN, AGONY,
    DOLOR, PANG, DISTRESS
angular .... CORNERED,
    GAUNT, BONY
    opposite of ..... AGONIC
anhydrous ..... DRY, PARCHED
ani .... CUCKOO
anil .... SHRUB, INDIGO
anile .... CRONE,
    INFIRM, WEAK
aniline, dye/red ....
    FUCHSIN, MAGENTA
anima ...... PRINCIPLE, SOUL
animal ...... BEAST, BESTIAL,
    SENSUAL, GROSS
    anatomy ..... ZOOTOMY
ant-eating .... ECHIDNA,
    AARDVARK, TAMANDUA,
    PANGOLIN, ANTBÉAR
antlered .... STAG,
    CARIBOU, ELK, MOOSE,
        (REIN)DEER
aquatic .... SEAL, OTTER,
    WHALE, SEACOW,
        WALRUS, MINK
arboreal ...... TARSIER,
    SQUIRREL, KOALA, UNAU,
        AI, SLOTH
armor ...... ARMATURE,
    CARAPACE, SHELL, PLATE
"armored" .. ARMADILLO
baggage carrier ....
    SUMPTER
body .... SOMA
bone-like covering ......
    CARAPACE
born prematurely .. SLINK
breast .... BRISKET,
    THORAX
bristly .... HOG, BOAR,
    PORCUPINE
burrowing ..... WOMBAT,

ARMADILLO, BADGER,
RATEL, BROCK, MOLE,
MARMOT, GROUNDHOG,
    GOPHER
castrated ... STAG, CAPON,
    OX, STEER, GELDING,
        BARROW
cat family .... FELID,
    FELINE
clumsy .... JUMBO
coat ...... PELAGE, FUR,
    WOOL, HAIR, PELT
collection ....:. ZOO,
    MENAGERIE
coop .... HUTCH
dam builder ..... OTTER
decay poison ....
    PTOMAIN(E)
disease .... ROT,
    ANTHRAX, GID, STAGGERS
doctor ... VET(ERINARIAN)
enclosure ... PEN, CAGE,
    CORRAL
fat ...... SUET, TALLOW,
    GREASE, LARD
fierce .... OUTLAW
flying .... BAT, LEMUR
food ... FORAGE, FODDER
footless .... APOD
footprint .... PUG
game-killer ..... VERMIN
giraffe-like .... OKAPI
handler .... TAMER,
    TRAINER
hibernating ...... BEAR,
    WOODCHUCK
hide .... FELL, PELT
homing instinct ....
    ORIENTATION
hornless .... POLLARD
humped .... CAMEL,
    ZEBU, DROMEDARY,
        BISON
imaginary ...... SNARK
inferior: sl. ...... PLUG
innards ...... HA(R)SLET
large ...... PACHYDERM,
    RHINO, ELEPHANT,
        BEHEMOTH
lean, scrawny ..... SCRAG
leopard-like ... CHEETAH
life in a region ... FAUNA
life, study of ... ZOOLOGY
like an .... THEROID
living inside another ....
    ENTEZOON

magnetism .. MESMERISM
male .. BUCK, BULL, JACK
marsupial .... KOALA,
TAIT, WOMBAT, KANGAROO,
(O)POSSUM, PHALANGER
microscopic .... ROTIFER
mixed breed .. MONGREL,
MULE, HYBRID
mouth opening .. RICTUS
multi-celled ... METAZOA
multi-segmented ....
CENTIPEDE
mythical .... GRIFFIN,
GRIFFON
neck hair .... MANE
"necklace" .... TORQUES
nipple .... DUG
of an .... ZOOID
of mixed parentage .:...
HYBRID, MONGREL
one-celled ...... MONAD,
PROTIS, PROTOZOAN,
RHIZOPOD, STENTOR
one-horned ....
RHINO(CEROS), UNICORN,
BADAK
pack .... SUMPTER
passage .... BURROW,
TUNNEL
pen .... STY, HUTCH,
CORRAL
Peruvian .... ALPACA,
LLAMA
pet .... CAT, POODLE,
DOG, CADE, COSSET
pictures painter ....
LANDSEER
plant life .... BIOTA,
BIOS
pound .... PINFOLD
scent .... FOIL
sexual excitement .. HEAT,
RUT, ESTRUS
shelter .... BURROW,
TUNNEL
skin .... PELT, FUR,
HIDE, FELL
skin dealer .. FELLMONGER
skin disease ..... MANGE
simplest form of ....
AM(O)EBA
snouted ... COATI, TAPIR
spiny .... PORCUPINE
spot on face of ... BLAZE
spotted .... PIEBALD,

DAPPLE(D)
starch .... GLYCOGEN
stomach ... CRAW, MAW
stories, collection of ....
BESTIARY
striped .... TIGER,
ZEBRA, QUAGGA
tanned hide of .... CROP
ten-footed .... DECAPOD
thigh .... HAM
trail .... SLOT, SPOOR,
SPUR, PUG, FOIL
trainer ..... LEHR (LEW)
trap .... DEADFALL
tusked .... WARTHOG,
WALRUS, ELEPHANT
uncontrollable .. OUTLAW
vital organs ...... PLUCK
weasel family .... PEKAN
web-footed ..... BEAVER,
PLATYPUS, DUCKBILL
with no nervous system ..
ACRITA
with pouch for young ....
KOALA, (KANGA)ROO
young ..... JOEY, COLT,
CUB, FOAL, PIGLET, CALF,
HEIFER, BULLOCK, BUNNY
animalcule .... ROTIFER
animals born at one time ....
FALL, LITTER
brood of young ... TEAM
carrying their young ....
MARSUPIAL
collectively .... ZOOLOGY
driven together .. COFFLE,
HERD
male of some ..... BULL,
BUCK, TOM, STAG, BOAR
molt of some ... EXUVIAE
painter of .... BONHEUR,
SETON
tied together .... COFFLE
animate .... QUICKEN,
INSPIRE, STIMULATE,
(EN)LIVEN, VIVIFY
animated-cartoon producer ...
DISNEY, LANTZ
bird .... WOODPECKER
character ...... MAGOO,
POPEYE
dog .... PLUTO
duck .... DONALD
person .... ORIG
animating principle ..... SOUL

animation .... VIVACITY, LIFE, BRIO, PEP, SPIRIT
anime .... RESIN, COPAL
animosity .... HATRED, ILL WILL, RANCOR, HOSTILITY, SPITE, ANIMUS, ENMITY, GRUDGE
animus .... GRUDGE, ANIMOSITY, SPIRIT, MIND, PASSION
anion, opposite of .... CATION
anise ...... ANET, DILL(SEED), FLAVOR
anisette .... CORDIAL
Ankara .... ANGORA
    is capital of ..... TURKEY, ANATOLIA
ankh ... CROSS, CRUX, ANSATA
ankle .... TALUS, TARSI, CUIT, JOINT, TARSUS
    bone .... TALUS, ASTRAGALUS
    iron .... BASIL
    joint protuberance ...... MALLEOLUS
    pertaining to .... TARSAL, TALARIC
anklet .... SOCK, FETTER, CHAIN, BANGLE
anlace .... DAGGER
anlage .... PROTON
anna .... COIN
    ½ of .... PICE
    16 of them ...... RUPEE
"Annabel Lee" author .... POE
annals .... HISTORY, CHRONICLES, RECORD
Annamese ...... MONGOL(IAN)
    capital .... HUE
    coin .... QUAN
    measure ...... TAO, SAO, GON, MAU
Annapolis, former name .... ANNE ARUNDEL
    institution .... ACADEMY, USNA
    student .... CADET, MIDSHIPMAN
annatto .... DYE
anneal .... TEMPER, BAKE, GLAZE, FUSE, FIRE
annealing oven .... LEER, KILN
annelid ...... WORM, LEECH, CHAETOPOD
annex .... ELL, WING, ATTACH(MENT), CONNECT

Annie Oakley .... PASS, (FREE)TICKET
annihilate .... DESTROY, DEMOLISH, EXTERMINATE
anniversary, 100th .... CENTENNIAL
anno ____ .... DOMINI, MUNDI, REGNI
annotate .... GLOSS
annotation ... NOTE, COMMENT, REFERENCE, FOOTNOTE, APOSTIL, GLOSSARY
announce .... DECLARE, PROCLAIM, HERALD, STATE
announcement ...... NOTICE, BLURB, BULLETIN, ORBIT, AD
    printed .... CARD
annoy .... FASH, IRK, VEX, TRY, TEASE, MOLEST, DISTURB, PESTER, GRATE, (BE)DEVIL
annoyance ...... HARASSMENT, VEXATION
    expression of ...... BAH, OH MY, GLOWER, GRIMACE, SCOWL
annoyer .... PEST, HARASSER, HECKLER
    camp .... GNAT
annual .... YEARLY, YEARBOOK, ETESIAN
    bean .... URD
    headache of a sort ...... INCOME TAX
    income .... RENTES
    movie award ..... OSCAR
    plant .... OKRA
    prize ... NOBEL, PULITZER
    produce .... CROP
    TV award .... EMMY
annually .... YEARLY, PER YEAR
annuity .... INCOME, TONTINE, RENTE
annul .... INVALIDATE, VOID, CANCEL, UNDO, REVOKE, RECALL, VACATE, QUASH
    in law .... QUASH
annular .... RINGLIKE, ROUND
    die .... DOD
annulate .... RINGED
annulet, in heraldry ..... VIRE

annum .... YEAR
annunciate .... ANNOUNCE
anodyne .... OPIATE,
   SEDATIVE, DRUG, SOOTHER,
               BALM
anoint .... OIL, ENOIL, ANELE,
   BLESS, CONSECRATE
anomalous .... ODD,
   IRREGULAR, ABNORMAL
anon .... SOON, SHORTLY,
   THENCE, IMMEDIATELY,
          ANONYMOUS
anonym ... PSEUDONYM, ALIAS
anonymous .... NAMELESS,
   UNKNOWN, INNOMINATE
anorak .... JACKET
   garment like ..... PARKA
another .... DIFFERENT,
   ADDITIONAL, ELSE
   set of clothes ... CHANGE
ansate .... HANDLED
anschluss .... UNION
anserine .... GOOSELIKE,
   FOOLISH, STUPID
answer .... REPLY,
   RESPOND, RESPONSE,
   REJOIN(DER), DEFENSE
   in kind .... RETORT
   purpose .... SERVE,
         DO, SATISFY
   unfavorable .... REBUFF
ant .... PISMIRE, EMMET,
   TERMITE, ANAY, AMAZON
   bear .... AARDVARK
   black .... KELEP
   combining form ....
          MYRMECO
   cow .... APHID
   eater .... AARDVARK,
   ECHIDNA, TAMANDU(A),
     PANGOLIN, MANIS
   genus .... FORMICA
   kind of .... SOLDIER
   nest .... FORMICARY,
           HILL
   thrush .... PITTA
anta .... PIER, COLUMN,
         PILASTER
antacid .... ALKALI,
        MAGNESIA
antagonism .... ENMITY,
   HOSTILITY, ANIMUS
antagonist .... RIVAL, FOE,
   OPPONENT, ADVERSARY
antagonistic .... HOSTILE,
   OPPOSED, UNFRIENDLY

Antarctic _____ ...... OCEAN,
   CONTINENT, CIRCLE, SEA,
           ZONE
   bird .... PENGUIN
   explorer ..... BYRD, ROSS,
         AMUNDSEN
   icebreaker .... ATKA
   sea ...... WEDDEL, ROSS
Antares ..... RED STAR, MARS
antbear .... AARDVARK
ante .... PAY, STAKE,
   RAISE, PONY, PRICE
   as prefix ... BEFORE, PRIOR
   bellum .... PRE-WAR
antebrachium .... FOREARM
antecedence ...... PRIORITY,
       PRECEDENCE
antecedent ... . PRIOR,
   ANCESTOR, PRECEDING
antecedents .... ANCESTRY
antechamber ..... ANTEROOM,
     WAITING ROOM
antedate .... PREDATE,
        PRECEDE
antelope .... NILGAI, SASIN,
   SAIGA, BEIRA, OTEROP,
   CHIRU, GOA, GAZELLE,
   TAKIN, ELAND, BUBALINE,
     BUBALIS, CHAMOIS
   African .... IMPALA,
   ASSE, KOB, GNU, KUDU,
   TORA, ELAND, ORIBI,
   STEINBOK, WANTO,
   KONZE, ADDAX, BONGO,
   GEMSBOK, KOODOO,
   DIKDIK, NAGOR,
   DUIKER(BOK), SASSABY,
       ORYX
   American ..... BLESBOK,
       SASSABY
   ancient .... PYGARG
   female .... DOE
   goat ... SEROW, CHAMOIS
   Himalayan ..... CHIRU,
       GORAL
   like .... BOVID
   male .... BUCK
   pygmy .... ORIBI
   red .... PALLA(H),
      REEDEBOK
   sheep-like .... SAIGA
   striped .... OTEROP,
       BONGO
   tawny .... ORIBI
   young .... KID

antenna .... AERIAL, PALP, FEELER, ANTENNULE
part of .... LEAD IN
anterior .... PRIOR, PREVIOUS, EARLIER, FRONT, PRECEDING
anteroom .... WAITING ROOM, ANTECHAMBER, LOBBY
anthelion .... HALO, AUREOLE
anthem .... SONG, MOTET, AGNUS DEI
anther .... STAMEN
anthesis .... BLOOM
anthocyanin .... PIGMENT
anthologist .... COMPILER
anthology ...... COLLECTION, ANA, POTPOURRI, COLLECTANEA, COMPILATION
anthozoan ..... POLYP, CORAL, ANEMONE
anthracite .... COAL
pieces/refuse ..... CULM
anthrax .... BOIL, CARBUNCLE, PUSTULE
anthropoid .... APE, MANLIKE, GORILLA, GIBBON, CHIMPANZEE, ORANG(UTAN), LAR, MONKEY, SIMIAN, TROGLODYTE
anthropophagi ... CANNIBALS
anti .... CON, AGAINST, OPPOSED, OPPOSER, HOSTILE
knock fuel .... TRIPTANE
knock fuel ingredient ... BROMINE
labor union contract .... YELLOW DOG
antiaircraft artillery .... ACK-ACK, POMPOM
cannon .... BOFORS
gunfire ... FLAK, ACK-ACK
missile .... NIKE
target aiming device .... PREDICTOR
antiar ... UPAS, TREE, POISON
antibiotic .... PENICILLIN, STREPTO(MYCIN), AUREOMYCIN
antibody dissolving bacteria, etc. .... LYSIN(E)
antic .... DIDO, CAPER, PRANK, CLOWN
anticipate ..... EXPECT, HOPE, FORESEE

anticipating ...... PROLEPSIS
anticlimax .... DROP, DESCENT, DECREASE
antidote ..... REMEDY, SODA, SERUM, TREACLE
for madness .... CHRYSOLITE
Antigone's parent .. OEDIPUS, JOCASTA
sister .... ISMENE
uncle .... CREON
antihemophilic factor ...... GLOBULIN
Antilles, _____ .... GREATER, LESSER
island .... CUBA
native ..... CARIB(BEAN)
antimacassar .... TIDY
antimalaria remedy .... ATABRIN(E), ATEBRIN, QUININE
antimony .... STIBIUM, REGULUS
source .... STIBNITE
Antiope's son ...... AMPHION
antipasto .... APPETIZER, RELISH
antipathy .... DISLIKE, AVERSION, REPUGNANCE, DISTASTE
antiphon ...... HYMN, PSALM
antipodean ...... AUSTRALIAN
antipodes .... OPPOSITES
antiquate .... OUTDATE
antiquated ... OLD, OBSOLETE, PASSE, OUT OF DATE, ARCHAIC, FOSSIL
antique .... ANCIENT, RELIC, OLD
antiques, where usually found MUSEUM, CURIO SHOP
antiquity .... PAST, YORE, PALEOLOGY, ELD
antiseptic .... ALCOHOL, LISTERINE, IODIN(E), EUSOL, LYSOL, SALOL, CRESOL, EGOL, EUPAD, CHLORINE, ARNICA, ARGYROL, CATECHOL, FORMALIN, TACHIOL, PICROL, BORIC, RETINOL, CARVACROL
surgery pioneer .. LISTER
antisubmarine vessel .... CORVET(TE)

antitoxin ....•..•... SERUM,
         ANTIVENIN
antler .... HORN
    branch .... PRONG,
        BEZ, BAY, BROW
    furry skin ...... VELVET
    main shaft .... BEAM
    part of .... PALM
    point ..... PRONG, TINE
    unbranched ...... SPIKE,
        DAG(UE)
antlered animal .... STAG,
    ELK, MOOSE, CARIBOU,
    (REIN)DEER
antlers of stag .... ATTIRE
antlion larva ..... DOODLEBUG
antra .... SINUSES
antre .... CAVE, CAVERN
antrum .... CAVERN
ants, pertaining to ... FORMIC
anurous .... TAILLESS,
    ACAUDAL, ACAUDATE
amphibian .... TOAD,
    FROG
Anu's husband .... ANAT
Anubis .... HERMES
anvil ..... INCUS, BLOCK, JAW,
    TEEST, STITHY
    block .... STOCK
    City .... NOME
    user ..... (BLACK)SMITH
anxiety .... WORRY,
    MISGIVING, CARE, CONCERN
anxious .... UNEASY,
    TENSE, EAGER
any .... ALL, SOME,
    WHICHEVER
anything ..... AT ALL, AUGHT
    badly matched ... CENTO
    of least value .... PLACK,
    TRIFLE
    of value .... ASSET
    small .... PINHEAD
    that stirs .... FILLIP
aoristic .... INDEFINITE
aorta .... ARTERY,
    BLOOD VESSEL
aoudad .... SHEEP, ARUI
apace .... FAST, SWIFT(LY),
    SPEEDY
Apache ...... INDIAN, THUG,
    GANGSTER, DANCE
    chief .... GERONIMO,
    COCHISE
ap(p)anage ..... DEPENDENCY,
    SUPPORT, ADJUNCT,

    PERQUISITE
apart .... ASIDE, AWAY,
    SEPARATE, SPLIT
    prefix .... DIS
apartment ...... ROOM, SUITE,
    FLAT, DUPLEX
    for women ...... HAREM
    house, English .. MANSION
    without elevator ....
    WALK-UP
apathetic .... INDIFFERENT,
    LISTLESS, UNMOVED, COLD
apathy .... INDIFFERENCE,
    COOLNESS, DISINTEREST
ape ...... MONKEY, GORILLA,
    ORANG(UTAN), GIBBON,
    KRA, COPY, IMITATE,
    PRIMATE, SIMIAN,
    SIAMANG
    kind of ..... MIME, MIMIC,
    CLOWN, JESTER
    sound .... CHATTER
apeman .... ALALUS
    of fiction .... TARZAN
Apennines people .... SABINES
aper .... MIMIC, MIME,
    IMITATOR
apercu .... GLANCE,
    INSIGHT, DIGEST
aperient .... LAXATIVE
aperitif .... DRINK,
    APPETIZER, COCKTAIL
    wine .... DUBONNET
aperture ..... VENT, ORIFICE,
    HOLE, SLOT, GAP, STOMA,
    OPENING
apery .... MIMICRY
apes .... SIMIA
apetalous .... PETALLESS
apex .... TIP, PEAK,
    VERTEX, CLIMAX, ZENITH,
    SUMMIT, PINIAL
    covering .... EPI
    of elbow .... ANCON
    rounded .... RETUSE
aphasia .... ALALIA
aphid .... INSECT, LOUSE
    sucking tube .... NECTARY
aphorism ...... SAW, MAXIM,
    ADAGE, SAYING, PROVERB,
    AXIOM
aphrodisiac .... ERINGO,
    ERYNGO
Aphrodite .... VENUS,
    URANIA, GODDESS,
    BUTTERFLY

Aphrodite's love .... ADONIS, ARES
mother .... DIONE
priestess .... HERO
son .... EROS
temple site ..... PAPHOS
aphta .... THRUSH
apian .... BEELIKE
apiculture .... BEEKEEPING
apiece .... EACH, PER
apish .... SILLY, IMITATIVE, AFFECTED
aplomb .... ASSURANCE, POISE, AIR, FLAMBOYANCE
fellow of .... COXCOMB, FOP, DANDY, BLUFFER, DUDE, ORATOR, BRAGGART, (PEA)COCK
apnea .... ASPHYXIA
apocalypse .... BOOK, REVELATIONS, PROPHECY
apocope .... ELISION
apocopate ... ELIDE, SHORTEN
apocryphal .... SPURIOUS, COUNTERFEIT
book ..... ESDRA, TOBIT
apodal .... FOOTLESS
apogee .... CLIMAX
Apollo ... SUNGOD, PHOEBUS, HELIOS
astronaut ...... LOVELL, ANDERS, BORMAN, ALDRIN, COLLINS
birthplace .... DELOS
festival .... DELIA
giant killed by .... OTUS
instrument .... LUTE, LYRE, BOW
mother ... LETO, LATONA
oracle .... DELOS
oracle site ...... DELPHI
priest .... ABARIS, CALCHAS
serpent slain by .. PYTHON
sister .... ARTEMIS, DIANA
son .... ION, IAMUS
spring sacred to .... CASTALIA
temple site .... DELOS
twin .... ARTEMIS
vale .... TEMPE
Apollyon ..... ANGEL, DEVIL, SATAN
apologia .... APOLOGY, EXCUSE, EXPLANATION

apologue .... FABLE, ALLEGORY
apomixis .... APOGAMY
apoplectic with ____ ... RAGE
apoplexy .... PARALYSIS
aport ...... LEFT(SIDE), NEAR
apostasy .... BETRAYAL, DESERTION
apostate .... RENEGADE, DESERTER, RECREANT, TURNCOAT
apostil .... ANNOTATION, FOOTNOTE
apostle .... DISCIPLE, PREACHER, MISSIONARY
Biblical ...... ANDREW, BARTHOLOMEW, JAMES, JUDE (THADDEUS), PHILIP, SIMON, PETER (SIMONPETER), PAUL, JUDE (LEBBAEUS), JUDAS (ISCARIOT), MATTHEW, (LEVI), JOHN, THOMAS (DIDYMUS), MATTHIAS
of the Franks ..... REMI
of the Indians .... ELIOT
of the Goths .... ULFILAS
thirteenth .... MATTHIAS
Apostles John and James .... BOANERGES
teaching of .... DIDACHE
apostolic .... PAPAL
see ..... BISHOPRIC, ROME
apothecary .... DRUGGIST
measure .... MINIM, DRAM, OUNCE, PINT, GALLON
weight .... GRAIN, SCRUPLE, DRAM, OUNCE, POUND
apothegm .... SAYING, MAXIM, APHORISM, ADAGE, DICTUM, AXIOM
apotheosize .... DEIFY, GLORIFY, IDEALIZE
Appalachian range .. RAMAPO
appal(l) .... HORRIFY, SHOCK, DISMAY, AWE, STUN, ASTONISH, FRIGHTEN
appanage .... PREQUISITE, SUPPORT, DEPENDENCY, ENDOWMENT
apparatus .... DEVICE, MACHINE, GEAR, INSTRUMENT, TACKLE, GADGET

air blowing ... BELLOWS
air cooling .... FAN
artificial respiration .....
PULMOTOR
beauty shop ....
(HAIR)DRIER
binding .... BALER
blacksmith's ..... FORGE
dentist's ..... DRILL
doctor's ... STETHOSCOPE
for bacterial cultures ....
INCUBATOR
hauling/hoisting ....
WINDLASS, WINCH, CRANE,
FORKLIFT
machine shop .... LATHE
under-water breathing ...
AQUALUNG, SNORKEL,
SCUBA
water drawing .... PUMP
weaver's .... LOOM
apparel .... GARMENT,
CLOTHING, DRESS, ATTIRE,
RAIMENT
apparent .... VISIBLE,
EVIDENT, OBVIOUS,
PLAIN, PATENT, CLEAR,
OVERT
apparently .... SEEMINGLY,
EVIDENTLY
apparition .... GHOST,
PHANTOM, SPECTER,
SPECTRE, WRAITH, EIDOLON
of living person ... FETCH
appassionata ... IMPASSIONED,
PASSIONATE
appeal ..... CALL, PRAY, SUE,
PROTEST, PLEAD, PETITION,
ATTRACTION
sex: sl. ...... OOMPH, IT
appear .... SEEM, LOOK,
LOOM, EMERGE
appearance .. AIR, MIEN, LOOK,
SHOW, SEMBLANCE, PRESENCE
appease .... CALM, SOOTH,
PLACATE, ALLAY, PACIFY,
BELIEVE, SATISFY,
MOLLIFY
appeasement, kind of .... SOP
appellation .... NAME, TITLE,
DESIGNATION, NAMING
append ... ADD, AFFIX, ATTACH
appendage ... LEG, TAIL, ARM,
ADJUNCT, LIMB
crab .... ANTENNA,

FEELER
fish .... FIN, BARBEL
leaf .... STIPULE
lobster .... PALP(US)
grain .... AWN, BEARD
threadlike ...... CIRRUS
appendix .... ADDENDUM,
OUTGROWTH, CODICIL
appertain ... BELONG, RELATE
appetence .... CRAVING,
APPETITE, DESIRE
appetite ... DESIRE, CRAVING,
APPETENCE, STOMACH
for alcoholic drink ......
DIPSOMANIA
for food .... HUNGER
for something ... TOOTH,
TASTE
for water .... THIRST
huge ...... GARGANTUAN
insatiable .... GREED,
VORACITY
pertaining to ... ORECTIC
appetizer .... CANAPE,
ANTIPASTO, TIDBIT
drink .... COCKTAIL,
DUBONNET, APERITIF
appetizing .... SAVORY,
DELICIOUS, TASTY
applaud ..... CHEER, PRAISE,
COMMEND, LAUD, EXTOL,
GIVE A HAND
applauder .... CHEERER,
ROOTER, FAN, CLAPPER
applauders' group ....
CHEERING SQUAD, CLAQUE
applause .... APPROVAL,
PRAISE, COMMENDATION,
HAND, ECLAT
round of ...... OVATION
word of .... HEAR,
MABUHAY, OLE, BANZAI
apple .... POME, PIPPIN,
GOLDEN, LOVE, SORB,
DELICIOUS, COSTARD,
RUSSET, CRAB, WINESAP,
MAY, GREENING, GRIMES,
GRAVENSTEIN, PEARMAIN,
QUEENING, JONATHAN
acid .... MALIC
butter .... JAM
center .... CORE
crushed pulp .... POMACE
custard .... ANONA
disease .... STIPPEN
elongated ...... CODLING

fall variety .... FAMEUSE, WEALTHY
fermented drink ... CIDER
for backing ...... BIFFIN
fried .... ROLPENS
inferior ..... CODLIN(G)
juice .... CIDER
kin ...... TOMATO, POME, QUINCE
love .... TOMATO
of the eye .... PET, FAVORITE
Persian .... PEACH
pie, deep-dish .... PANDOWDY
pudding ... BROWN BETTY
pulp .... POMACE
red .... MCINTOSH
red winter ..... BALDWIN
Russian ..... ASTRACHAN
sauce: colloq. .... NONSENSE, HOKUM
seed/stone .... PIP, PYRENE
seller .... COSTER
shaped fruit .... QUINCE
tosser: myth. ...... ERIS
tree .... SORB, SAPODILLA, WILDING
unripe .... CODLIN
variety .... NON(E)SUCH
worm .... MOTH
apples, pert. to .... MALIC
applesauce .... DESSERT, RELISH
colloquial ... NONSENSE, HOKUM, BALONEY
applethorne .... EPIGENE
appliance, electrical .... IRON, RANGE, OVEN, MIXER, DISHWASHER, TOASTER, REFRIGERATOR
applicable .... RELEVANT, PERTINENT
application .... REQUEST, FORM, DILIGENCE, RELEVANCE, USE, REMEDY
applied decoration .... GESSO, OIL, APPLIQUE, PAINT
science .... TECHNOLOGY
apply ..... EMPLOY, USE, PUT, PLACE, DEVOTE, REQUEST
force ..... EXERT, PRESS
friction .... RUB, GRATE, RASP
pressure ..... INFLUENCE, COERCE
appoggiatura ... GRACE NOTE, THANK YOU
appoint ...... NAME, ASSIGN, NOMINATE, DETAIL, CHOOSE, DESIGNATE, COMMISSION
as agent .... DEPUTE, DELEGATE
to benefice ..... COLLATE
appointment .... TRYST, DATE, NOMINATION, ENGAGEMENT, SET, FURNITURE, EMPLOYMENT
apportion .. METE, DEAL, ALLOT, DIVIDE, DISTRIBUTE
apposite ..... RELEVANT, APT, APPROPRIATE, PROPER
appraisal .... EVALUATION, RATING, ESTIMATE
appraise .... ASSESS, RATE, VALUATE, JUDGE, ASSAY
appraiser .... ASSESSOR, RATER
appreciable ..... NOTICEABLE, PERCEPTIBLE
appreciate ..... VALUE, ENJOY, ESTEEM, UNDERSTAND, NOTICE
apprehend .... ARREST, PERCEIVE, UNDERSTAND, NAB, HOLD, HENT
apprehension .... ALARM, PERCEPTION, ARREST, FEAR, ANXIETY, CAPTURE
apprehensive .... UNEASY, ANXIOUS, WORRIED, FEARFUL
apprentice .... TRAINEE, LEARNER, NOVICE, BEGINNER, DEVIL
apprenticeship contract ...... INDENTURE
approach ..... NEAR, ACCESS, COME, APPROXIMATE, OVERTURE
stealthily .... STALK
approbation ..... APPROVAL, SANCTION, FAVOR
appropriate .... STEAL, SUITABLE, FIT, PROPER, APT, BECOMING, MEET, PREEMPT, ADOPT, APPOSITE, GERMANE, POCKET

improperly ..... USURP,
STEAL
approval ..... ENDORSEMENT,
SANCTION
    kind of .... IMPRIMATUR
    sign of .... NOD
    word of .. OK(AY), SHOOT
approve .... SANCTION,
CONFIRM, ENDORSE,
CERTIFY, PASS, RATIFY
approving mention ....
ACCOLADE, CITATION
approximate .... NEAR, CLOSE,
APPROACH
approximately .... ABOUT,
NEARLY, ROUGHLY
appurtenance ...... ADJUNCT
appurtenant ..... PERTINENT,
GERMANE
apronaceous .... SANDY
apres .... AFTER
apricot .... FRUIT, TREE,
DRUPE, ANSU, UME
    cordial .... PERSICO
April Dancer's colleague .....
NOEL
apron .... PINAFORE,
SHIELD, BELT
    child's ...... BISHOP, BIB
    painter's .... SMOCK
apropos ..... RELEVANT, APT,
OPPORTUNELY, PAT,
FITTING, BY THE WAY
apse ...... APSIS, PROJECTION
    dome cover ..... CONCHA
apt .... APPROPRIATE,
FITTING, RELEVANT,
PRONE, INCLINED, QUICK,
LIKELY, DEFT, CLEVER
apteral .... WINGLESS
apteryx .... KIWI, MOA,
BIRD, ROA
aptitude .... INCLINATION,
BENT, FLAIR, TALENT,
ABILITY, KNACK, GIFT
aptly chosen ...... FELICITOUS
Apulia's capital .... BARI
aqua .... WATER, LIQUID,
SOLUTION
    fortis ...... NITRIC ACID
    vitae .... ALCOHOL,
BRANDY, LIQUOR
aquamarine .... BERYL,
PIGMENT, (BLUISH)GREEN
aquarium ..... (WATER)TANK
    fish .... GUPPY

plant .... FANWORT
    small .... FISHBOWL
aquatic animal .... OTTER,
BEAVER, NEWT, MINK
    bird .... FLAMINGO,
GOOSE, GULL, DUCK, COOT,
AUK, LOON, GREBE,
PENGUIN, SWAN, SCAUP,
PELICAN
    entertainment ....
AQUACADE
    mammal ..... MANATEE,
SEACOW, WHALE, SEAL,
OTTER, DUGONG, MINK
    movie character ....
FLIPPER
    performer .... SEAL,
FLIPPER, DIVER,
DOLPHIN
    vertebrate .... FISH
aqueduct .... PIPE, CONDUIT,
CANAL, PASSAGE
    of Sylvius .... ITER
aqueous .... WATERY
    solution .... JAVEL
Aquila .... EAGLE,
CONSTELLATION
    star .... ALTAIR
ara .... ALTAR,
CONSTELLATION, MACAW
Arab .... SEMITE, TATAR,
GAMIN, BEDOUIN,
HORSE, WAIF, URCHIN,
SARACEN, ANSAR
Arabia .... SAUDI,
PENINSULA
    poetic .... ARABY
Arabian abode .... DAR
    antelope .... ADDAX
    ape .... BABOON
    beverage .... LEBAN,
BOZA, BOSA(H)
    bird of fable .... ROC
    camel ...... DROMEDARY
    capital .... SAN'A
    chief ..... SAYID, SHERIF
    chieftain ... AMIR, EMIR,
AMEER, EMEER, REIS,
SHEIK(H)
    chieftain's domain ......
EMIRATE
    city .... ADEN, BEDA,
CHAFRA, BERA, DAMAR,
SAN'A, MEDINA, RIYADH,
JIDDA, JEDDA
    cloth .... ABA

coffee .... MOCHA
coin .... TALARI
country .... YEMEN,
    JORDAN, SAUDI ARABIA,
    IRAN, IRAQ, KUWAIT
demon .... EBLIS, GENIE,
    JINN(I), AFREET
dervish of story .... AGIB
desert ... SAHARA, NEFUD
drink ... LEBAN, BOSA(H),
    BOZA
dromedary ..... BELOOL,
    HEJEEN
evil spirit ...... AFREET,
    AFRIT(E)
father .... ABOU, ABU
garment ... ABA, HAI(C)K
gazelle .... ARIEL
gulf .... ADEN, OMAN
head cord .... AGAL
jasmine .... BELA
javelin .... JER(R)ID,
    JER(R)EED
judge .... CADI
kingdom .... SABA,
    SHEBA, JORDAN
laborer .... FELLAH
leather .... MOCHA
letter .... BA, GAF, KAF,
    MIM, ALIF, THA, JIM, KHA,
    DAL, LAM, NUN, DAD, YA,
    WAW, DHAL
magistrate .... CADI
measure .... COVIDO,
    ARDEB
measure, grain .. TOMAN,
    SAA
mock battle ... JER(R)ID,
    JER(R)EED
monarchy .... YEMEN
Moslem .... WAHABI
nomad .... SLEB
oasis .... DOUMA
palm .... DOUM
peasant .... FELLAH
peninsula .... SINAI,
    ADEN
prince .... SHERIF
ruler ...... EMIR, EMEER,
    SULTAN, SHEIK(H)
sacred territory .. HARAM
sailboat .... DHOW
Scripture ..... ALCORAN
Sea river .... INDUS
seaport ... ADEN, MOCHA
sheikhdom .... KUWAIT

spirit .... JINN(I),
    AFREET, AFRIT
state ..... YEMEN, OMAN
sultanate .... OMAN
sword .... SCIMITAR
system of numerals .....
    ALGORISM
tambourine ...... DAIRA,
    DAIRE, TAAR
teacher .... ULEMA
tent village ...... DOUAR
tribal chief ..... SHEIK(H)
veil .... YASMAK
wagon .... ARABA
weight .... DIRHEM
wind .... SIMOOM,
    SAMIEL
woman's veil ... YASMAK
Arabic acid ...... ARABIN
letter ..... DAL, AYN, KAF,
    KHA, MIM, THA, WAW,
    ZAY, ALIF, DHAL, GHAYN
arabinose ... PENTOSE, SUGAR
arable .... TILLABLE
araceous .... AROID
plant .... LILY, TARO,
    CABBAGE, ARUM
Arachne .... SPIDER
arachnid .... MITE, SPIDER,
    SCORPION, TICK, ACARID
segment .... TELSON,
    SOMITE
arachnoid, space below ......
    CISTERNA
structure .... WEB
arado .... LAND
Aram .... SYRIA
arbalest .... CROSSBOW
Arbela .... ERBIL
arbiter .... JUDGE,
    ARBITRATOR, MEDIATOR,
    OVERMAN
archaic ...... DAYSMAN
baseball ...... UMP(IRE)
boxing, basketball ......
    REF(EREE)
fashion .... STYLIST,
    DIOR, BALMAIN
arbitrary .... CAPRICIOUS,
    DESPOTIC, DICTATORIAL,
    WHIMSICAL
arbitrator .... JUDGE,
    ARBITER, MIDDLEMAN,
    OVERMAN
arbor ..... BOWER, PERGOLA,
    TREE, SHAFT, BEAM,

SPINDLE, AXLE, TRELLIS
vitae .... THUJA
Arboreal .... TREE-LIKE,
DENDRAL
amphibian .... TREETOAD
creature .. SLOTH, UNAU,
AI, KOALA, SQUIRREL,
TARSIER, COLUGO
arbutus .... MAYFLOWER,
PLANT, SHRUB
arc ..... CURVE, ARCH, BOW
chord .... SINE
of 90 degrees .. QUADRANT
sky .... RAINBOW
arcade .... PORTICO,
ARCATURE, GALLERY,
PIAZZA
Arcadian .... PEACEFUL,
PASTORAL, RUSTIC,
BUCOLIC, SHEPHERD
princess .... AUGE
Arcady .... ARCADIA
arcane ...... SECRET, HIDDEN
arcanum ... SECRET, MYSTERY,
ELIXIR, REMEDY
arcature .... ARCADE
arch .... CHIEF, MAIN,
PRINCIPAL, CURVE, SLY,
CRAFTY, CLEVER, HANCE,
FORNIX, ARC
as combining form .....
RULER
curve inside ... INTRADOS
fiend ..... DEVIL, SATAN
lower part ..... IMPOST,
SPRINGER
of bridge .... SPAN
of heaven .... COPE
of spears over shoulders
YOKE
over eye .....(EYE)BROW
pointed .... OGIVE, OGEE
side of .... HAUNCH
underside .... SOFFIT
archaic .... ANCIENT, OLD,
ANTIQUATED
command .... HEST
archangel ..... SATAN, URIEL,
ANGELICA, MICHAEL,
RAPHAEL
archbishop .... PRIMATE,
METROPOLITAN
of Canterbury ....
CRANMER, ANSELM, BECKET
subordinate of ....
SUFFRAGAN

ARCTIC, GULF 43

archbishopric ..... APOSTOLIC,
SEE
arched .... CURVED,
VAULTED, COPED
passageway .... ARCADE
way .... CLOISTER
archeological find in 1887 ....
SIDON
archeologist's concern .. RUINS
archer .... BOWMAN,
CONSTELLATION
angel .... CUPID
buff ...... TOXOPHILITE
of story .... ROBIN HOOD,
(WILLIAM) TELL
of the sky ... SAGITTARIUS
protective hand .. BRACER
target ..... CLOUT, ROVER
archer, or .... SAGITTARY
arches, row of .... ARCUATION
archetype .... MODEL, IDEAL,
PROTOTYPE, EXAMPLE
archil .... LICHEN, DYE
archimage .... MAGICIAN,
WIZARD
archipelago .... COLON, SULU,
MALAY, PAUMOTO,
BISMARCK, TUAMOTU
architect .... DESIGNER,
BUILDER, CREATOR
architectural .... TECTONIC
column ...... PILASTER
concave molding ....
CAVETTO
design .... SPANDREL
drawing .... EPURE
ornament ...... CORBEIL,
DENTIL
pier .... ANTA
type ..... DORIC, IONIC,
GOTHIC, MAYAN
archly ..... PERTLY, SAUCILY
archon ... MAGISTRATE, RULER
Arctic .... COLD, FRIGID,
OVERSHOE, POLAR,
NORTH(ERN)
base ...... THULE, ETAH
bird .... AUK, ROTCH(E),
DOVEKIE, DOVEKEY, JUNCO,
GUILLEMOT
dog ... MALEMUTE, SAMO,
SAMOYEDE
explorer ... PEARY, ERIC,
KANE, RAB
goose .... BRANT
gulf .... OB

gull .... XEMA,
   BURGOMASTER
home ..... IGLU, IGLOO
jacket ... ANORAK, PARKA
native .... ESKIMO
pinniped .... SEAL
plain .... TUNDRA
seagull ..... KITTIWAKE
tribesman .... LAPP
wasteland ..... TUNDRA
arcuate .... CURVED, ARCHED
arcubalist ..... CROSSBOWMAN
Arden, ____ .... ENOCH, EVE,
   ELIZABETH
ardent.......... PASSIONATE,
   EAGER, ENTHUSIASTIC,
   FERVENT, WARM
partisan ...... DEVOTEE,
   FANATIC
spirits ..... GIN, WHISKY,
   LIQUOR
ardor .... FIRE, ZEAL, VERVE,
   ELAN, FERVOR, PASSION,
   HEAT
arduous .... LABORIOUS,
   ENERGETIC, DIFFICULT,
   HARD
area .... SCOPE, RANGE,
   EXTENT, DISTRICT, REGION
around moving body ....
   PERIPTER
between leaf veins ......
   AREOLA
measure of .... ARE,
   ACRE, DECARE, HECTARE,
   CENTIAR(E)
on bird's bill .... CERE
small ..... CLOSE, AREOLA
areaway ...... YARD, COURT,
   PASSAGE
areca .... BETEL, PALM
arena .... FIELD, RING,
   SPHERE, BULLRING, STADIUM,
   OVAL, PIT, LISTS
kind of ..... (COCK)PIT,
   GRIDIRON, DIAMOND,
   COURT
arenaceous .... SANDY
arenose .... SANDY
areo, as combining form .....
   MARS
areola ...... SPACE, HOLLOW
Ares .... MARS
parent ..... ZEUS, HERA
sister .... ERIS
arete .... RIDGE, CREST,

   ARISTA
Arethusa .... NYMPH, ORCHID
argal .... ERGO, HENCE,
   THEREFORE, TARTAR,
   SHEEP, ARGALI
argala .... STORK,
   MARABOU, ADJUTANT
argali ..... SHEEP, BIGHORN,
   AOUDAD
argent .... SILVER(Y)
Argentina's capital ....
   BUENOS AIRES
Argentine armadillo .. PELUDO
city .... SALTA,
   AVELLANEDA, CORDOBA,
   CORRIENTE, TUCUMAN
crested bird .... SERIEMA
Indian .... PAMPEAN
plain .... PAMPAS
port .... LA PLATA,
   ROSARIO
president .... ILLIA,
   ONGANIA, PERON
region ...... PATAGONIA
river .... BERMEJO,
   PARANA, SALADO
seaport ...... LA PLATA
"sleeping beauty" ......
   (MARIA) TELLO
timber tree .... TALA
wage earner ....
   DESCAMISADO
argil .... CLAY
Argo ... SHIP, CONSTELLATION
argol .... TARTAR
Argolis native .... AGIVE
vale of .... NEMEA
Argonaut .... JASON,
   ACASTUS, MELEAGER
of the gold rush ....
   FORTY-NINER
ship .... ARGO
argosy ... SHIP, FLEET, VESSEL
argot ..... JARGON, SLANG,
   LINGO, CANT, DIALECT,
   PATOIS
argue ..... REASON, DISPUTE,
   OBJECT, DEBATE, DISCUSS,
   CONTEND, JAW, WRANGLE
for argument's sake .....
   ARGUFY
in court .... PLEAD, PRAY
price/terms ... HAGGLE,
   HIGGLE, BARGAIN
argument .... DEBATE,
   DISCUSSION, HASSLE,

TOPIC, POLEMIC
about words ....
    LOGOMACHY
kind of .... PRO, CON,
    RHUBARB
to justify .... DEFENSE
argumentation ... DIALECTICS
argumentative .. CONTENTIOUS,
    COMBATIVE, POLEMICAL,
    ERISTICAL
Argus .... GIANT,
    WATCHMAN
eyed .... VIGILANT,
    OBSERVANT
aria .... SONG, SOLO,
    AIR, MELODY
brilliant flourish ....
    CADENZA
like an .... ARIOSO
arias .... SOLI
Ariadne's father ...... MINOS
love .... THESEUS
arid .... DRY, BARREN,
    UNFERTILE, JEJUNE,
    STERILE, TORRID,
    ANHYDROUS
region .... DESERT
region, U.S. .. DUST BOWL
ariel ...... SPIRIT, SATELLITE,
    GAZELLE
Ariel's master ..... PROSPERO
Aries ... RAM, CONSTELLATION
arietta .... MELODY, ARIA,
    AIR, SONG
arikara .... REE
ariose .... MELODIC,
    SONGLIKE
arioso .... MELODIOUS
composer .... BACH
arise .... GET UP, ASCEND,
    EMANATE, ISSUE,
    ORIGINATE
arista .... AWN, BEARD,
    BRISTLE
aristocracy .... ELITE,
    NOBILITY, OLIGARCHY
aristocrat .... NOBLEMAN,
    HIGH BORN, SNOB
Athenian/Greek ....
    EUPATRID
Roman ..... PATRICIAN
Russian .... BOYAR
Spanish .... HIDALGO,
    GRANDEE
aristocratic .... PATRICIAN

aristocrats collectively ....
    NOBLESSE, NOBILITY
Aristotle .... STAGIRITE
birthplace ...... STAGIRA
follower ... PERIPATETIC
logic .... DEDUCTIVE,
    SYLLOGISM
teacher of .... PLATO
arithmetic, common .. LOGISTIC
arivederci .... GOODBY,
    SO LONG
Arizona capital .... PHOENIX
city .... TUCSON,
    YUMA, MESA
Cochise county seat ....
    BISBEE
county .... PINAL
desert .. .. PAINTED
Indian ...... HOPI, HANO,
    MOQUI, TEWA, PIMA, YUMA,
    APACHE, PAIUTE
nut .... PINON
river .... GILA
state flower ... SAGUARO,
    CACTUS
state nickname ....
    SUNSET LAND, APACHE
tourist's sight ....
    GRAND CANYON
ark .... BOAT, REFUGE
animals/birds .... PAIRS
builder ..... NOAH, NOE
landing place ....
    (MT) ARARAT
porter .... BEN
Arkansas capital ....
    LITTLE ROCK
county ..... IZARD, YELL
nickname ... BEAR STATE
river .... WASHITA
state flower ....
    APPLE BLOSSOM
arles .... ANTE, PREPAYMENT,
    TOKEN, EARNEST
arm .... LIMB, FORTIFY,
    FURNISH, TENTACLE,
    BRANCH, WEAPON
badge .... BRASSARD
band .... BRACER
bone ... HUMERUS, ULNA
bone, pert. to ... ULNAR
cover .... SLEEVE
extendible .. PANTOGRAPH
hole .... SCYE
in-arm .... OXTER
joint ..... ELBOW, WRIST

length of .... REACH
like .... BRACHIAL
of the sea .... BAY,
   FIRTH, FIORD, INLET, FJORD
pertaining to .. BRACHIAL
shield .... BUCKLER
armada .... FLEET
armadillo .... APAR(A),
   PEBA, TATOU, POYOU
  Argentine ...... PELUDO
  shell .... CARAPACE
  6-banded ...... PELUDO
  3-banded .... APAR,
   MATACO
  12-banded ..... TATOUAY
Armageddon .. (LAST) BATTLE
  author .... URIS
  maybe .... MEGIDDO
armament ...... WEAPONRY,
   ARMS, EQUIPMENT,
   ORDNANCE
  factory ... KRUPP, SKODA
armature .... ARMOR
armband, protective .. BRACER
armchair .... FAUTEUIL
armed band .... POSSE
  conflict .... WAR, BATTLE
  escort .... CONVOY,
   BODYGUARD
  fleet .... NAVY
  galley .... AESC
  guard .... SENTINEL,
   SENTRY
Armenia's capital .... ERIVAN
  mountain ...... ARARAT
armet .... HELMET
armhole .... SCYE
armiger ..... ARMOR BEARER,
   SQUIRE
armistice .... TRUCE,
   CEASE-FIRE
armlet .... BANGLE
armoire .... CUPBOARD,
   CABINET
armor .... MAIL, SHIELD,
   BARD(E), PLATE
  arm .... BRASSARD,
   PALLETTE, BRASSART
  back .... CUIRASS
  bearer .... ARMIGER,
   SQUIRE
  body ...... TACE, CULET,
   CUIRASS, SURCOAT
   LORICA, TASSE
  breast .... CUIRASS
  chain .... MAIL

clamp .... AGRAFFE
elbow to shoulder ......
   BRASSARD
foot .... SOLLERET
hand .... GAUNTLET
head ... VISOR, BASINET,
   BEAVER, HAUBERK,
  SCONCE, ARMET, HELMET
hook .... AGRAFFE
horse .. BARD(E), TESTIERE
jacket .... JUPON, GIPON
joint .... GUSSET
leg .... JAMB(E), GREAVE
neck .... GORGET
plate ..... LAME, MASCLE
rings ...... BRIGANDINE
snail's .... SHELL
shirt cover ... CAMISADO
shoulder ...... AILETTE,
   PAULDRON
thigh .... TASSET, CUISH,
   TUILE, CUISSE
throat .... GORGET
tunic ... GIPON, JUPON
turtle's ...... CARAPACE
unworn ..... BARESARK
armored animal .. ARMADILLO
person of old ... KNIGHT
ship .... IRONCLAD,
   MONITOR, MERRIMAC
vehicle .... TANK
armorial .... HERALDIC
bearings/ensigns ......
   HERALDRY
armory .... HERALDRY,
   ARSENAL
orator's .... WORDS,
   CLICHES
armpit .... AXILLA, ALA,
   OXTER
swelling .... BUBO
arms .... WEAPONS, INSIGNIA,
   WARFARE
creature with eight ......
   OCTOPOD, OCTOPUS
of the night, so-called ...
   DARKNESS
army .. HOST, TROOPS, HORDE,
  ARMED FORCES, LEGION
car .... JEEP
caterer .... SUTLER
chaplain .... PADRE
engineer .... SAPPER
follower .... SUTLER
front of ... VAN(GUARD)
group .... CORPS,

REGIMENT, BRIGADE, SQUAD, PLATOON
insignia of rank ... STAR, EAGLE, LEAF, BAR, STRIPE
mascot .... MULE
meal .... MESS, CHOW
mounted sentinel ....
VEDETTE, VIDETTE
of the .... MILITARY
priest .... CHAPLAIN, PADRE
rank .... GENERAL, COLONEL, CAPTAIN, LIEUTENANT, SERGEANT, CORPORAL, PRIVATE, MAJOR
vehicle ... AMTRAC, JEEP, TANK, WEAPONS CARRIER
Arndt (Felix) piece ..... NOLA
arnica ... ANTISEPTIC, PLANT
Arnold (Matthew) character ..
SOHRAB, RUSTUM
aroid ..... ARUM, ARACEOUS, TARO, TANIA
aroma ... ODOR, FRAGRANCE, SMELL, SAVOR, FLAVOR
aromatic ... SPICY, PUNGENT, FRAGRANT, SAVORY, ODOROUS
bark .... ANGOSTURA, CASCARILLA
berry .... CUBEB
beverage .... COFFEE
condiment .... SPICE
fruit .... NUTMEG
gum .... MYRRH, ARALIA, BALM, BALSAM
herb ...... MINT, ANISE, THYME, CARAWAY, FLEAWORT
leaves ..... LAUREL, BAY, BUCHU
liquid .... BAYRUM
oil .... BALM
ointment .... NARD
plant ...... WORMWOOD, ARTEMISIA, NARD, BASIL, TANSY, MINT, SAGE, CARUM, ANGELICA
resin ... COPAIBA, COPALM
root .... GINSENG
seed .... ANISE, DILL, CUM(M)IN, GUAIAC, FENNEL
smoke .... FUME
spice ... CLOVE, NUTMEG, MACE

tree .... BALSAM, FIRPINE
weed .... TANSY
wood .... CEDAR, BASSWOOD
Arouet's nickname ..... ZOZO
around ..... NEARBY, ABOUT, CLOSE TO, CIRCA
arouse .... STIR, FIRE, EXCITE, ANIMATE, INCITE, SPUR, FAN, INFLAME, FOMENT, PIQUE
arpeggio .... ROULADE
arraign ..... INDICT, ACCUSE, CHARGE
arrange .... PREPARE, FIX, SORT, CLASSIFY, ADJUST, ADAPT, MARSHAL
by twos .. .. PAIR, MATE
for battle .... DEPLOY
for reference ...... FILE
in advance .... PLAN, PREPARE
in files .... STACK
in threes ...... TERNATE
methodically ...... FILE
the hair .... COMB, DRESS
arrangement ... PREPARATION, PLAN, AGREEMENT, ORDER, SET-UP, ADAPTATION, SETTLEMENT
arrant .... NOTORIOUS, UNMITIGATED, OUT AND OUT, BOLD
arras .... TAPESTRY
array ...... ATTIRE, MARSHAL, ORDER, DECK, DRESS, FINERY, TURN-OUT
arrear .... BACKLOG
arrest .... STEM, CHECK, HALT, STOP, HOLD, SEIZE, NAB, NICK
slang .... PINCH
writ .... CAPIAS
arrival, scheduled: abbr. .. ETA
arrive ... REACH, ATTAIN, COME
arrogance ..... HAUGHTINESS, PRIDE, HUBRIS
arrogant ...... OVERBEARING, PROUD, HAUGHTY, CAVALIER, COCKY, LOFTY
arrow ... SHAFT, DART, BOLT, SAGITTA
ancient .... QUARREL
barb .... FLUKE
blunt .... BUTT, SHAFT
body of .... STELE

case .... QUIVER
crossbow .... BOLT
feather .... VANE
feather-fitter .... PLUMIER
feathered .... VIRE
like .... SAGITTAL
notch for bowstring .....
          NOCK
poetic .... REED
poison .... CURARE,
    UPAS, INEE, ANTIAR(IN)
put feather on ... FLETCH,
          FLEDGE
user ... BOWMAN, ARCHER
arrowroot ... CANNA, TAPIOCA,
    PIA, ARARAO, ARUM
arrows, quiverful of ... SHEAF
Arrowsmith, Mrs. ..... LEORA
arrowwood .... WAHOO,
    VIBURNUM, DOGWOOD
arrowworm .... SAGITTA
arroyo .... WADI, GULLY,
    RIVULET, STREAMBED,
          PIT, HONDO
arse .... BUTTOCKS, RUMP
arsenal .... ARMORY
Arsene, Monsieur ..... LUPIN
arsenic sulfide ..... REALGAR
    powder ...... SALVARSAN
arsis .... UPBEAT, ICTUS
arsonist .... PYROMANIAC,
    FIREBUG, INCENDIARY
art .... SKILL, ARTIFICE,
    CRAFT, TRICK, PAINTING,
    MUSIC, DRAMA, DANCE
exhibition .... SALON
gallery ..... FREER, TATE,
          SALON
Latin .... ARS
movement of 1920's .....
          DADA
objects .... VIRTU, VERTU
of argumentation ....
          DIALECTICS
of bookbinding ....
          BIBLIOPEGY
of carving/engraving ....
          GLYPTICS
of devising dances ......
          CHORE(O)GRAPHY
of discourse .. RHETORIC
of disputation ... ERISTIC
of dwarfing trees/plants ..
          BONSAI
of horsemanship ....
          MANEGE

of mapping ....
          CHOROGRAPHY
of motion pictures ......
          CINEMATICS
of public speaking ......
          ELOCUTION
of teaching ... DIDACTIC
style ... GENRE, DADA,
    CUBISM, IMPRESSIONISM,
          ARABESQUE
work, inferior ....
          POTBOILER
artal, singular of ...... ROTL
artel .... COOPERATIVE
Artemis ...... DIANA, DELIA,
    PHOEBE, GODDESS
birthplace .... DELOS
mother ... LETO, LATONA
twin .... APOLLO
victim .... ORION
artemisia .... WORMWOOD
artery .... AORTA,
    BLOOD VESSEL, STREET
neck .... CAROTID
pulse .... ICTUS
artful .... WILY, CRAFTY,
    CUNNING, DECEITFUL,
    ADROIT, POLITIC, SLY
arthritis ... GOUT, DROP, CLOT
treatment ... CORTISONE,
    ACTH, VERATRIA,
          VERATRIN(E)
arthropod .... ARACHNID,
    CRUSTACEAN, INSECT,
    MYRIAPOD, MILLEPEDE
segmented part .. SOMITE,
          TELSON
arthropoda .... PHYLA
arthrotome .... SCALPEL
Arthur (see King Arthur)
Arthur Conan _____ .... DOYLE
character ....
          SHERLOCK (HOLMES)
title .... SIR
Arthurian enchantress ....
          VIVIAN
tales compiler .. MALORY,
          LOOMIS
artichoke .... PLANT,
    SUNFLOWER, TUBER,
    CYNARA, CHOROGI
kin .... CARDOON
leaf stalks ...... CHARD
article .... AN, THE, ESSAY,
    ITEM, REPORT, THING,
          PAPER

in a document ... CLAUSE
of faith/belief ... CREED, CREDO
of personal property .... CHATTEL
articles, miscellaneous .... RUMMAGE
of excellence .. IMPERIALS
of virtu .... CURIO, BIBELOT
sold together ..... TIE-IN
articulate .... JOINTED, ENUNCIATE, EXPRESSIVE, VOICE
articulated joint ...... HINGE
speech sound ..... LENIS
artifice .... STRATEGEM, CRAFT, RUSE, GUILE, WILE, DODGE, DEVICE, TRICK(ERY)
artificial .... POSTICHE, SIMULATED, SYNTHETIC, SHAM, COUNTERFEIT
bait ...... LURE, DECOY
butter .... OLEO, MARGARINE
fly ..... COACHMAN, DUN, DOCTOR, NYMPH
foodstuff .... ERSATZ
ivory .... IVORIDE
jewelry .... PASTE
language .... IDO, ESPERANTO
respiration apparatus ... PULMOTOR
smile of a sort ... SIMPER
teeth .... DENTURE
waterway .... CANAL
artillery .... GUNNERY, ORDNANCE
abbreviation .... ORD
antiaircraft ... ACK ACK, POMPOM
fire angle measurement .. MIL
man .... GUNNER, CANNONER, LASCAR
type of .... MOBILE, MOUNTED
wagon .... CAMION, CAISSON
artisan .... ARTIST, CRAFTSMAN, TRADESMAN
artist .... PERFORMER, PAINTER, MINIATURIST, ETCHER, DANCER, PORTRAITIST, PIANIST,

SCULPTOR
abbreviation on painting PNXT
unconventional .... BOHEMIAN
artistic style .... GUSTO
artist's colony .... TAOS, LATIN QUARTER, GREENWICH
copy .... TRACING
frock .... SMOCK
medium .... OIL, CANVAS, PASTEL, TEMPERA, MARBLE, CLAY, BRONZE
milieu .... STUDIO, ATELIER
mixing board .. PALETTE
name on painting ...... DELINEAVIT
stand .... EASEL
artless ...... NAIVE, CLUMSY, CRUDE, SIMPLE, NATURAL, INGENUOUS
woman/girl ... INGENUE
artlessness .... NAIVETE, INNOCENCE, SIMPLICITY
arts and ___ .... CRAFTS, SCIENCES, LETTERS
votary .... ESTHETE, CONNOISSEUR, PATRON
arum ..... TARO, LILY, AROID, CALLA, CALADIUM
aruspex ... SOOTHSAYER, SEER
Aryan .... MEDE, SLAV
god .... AGNI
language ...... SANSKRIT
as .... THUS, WHILE, BECAUSE, THOUGH, QUA
if .... QUASI
soon as .... ONCE
usual: music ..... SOLITO
written: music ...... STA
"As You Like It" character .. ROSALIND, JACQUES
asafetida .... RESIN, FERULA, LASER
asarum .... PLANT, GINGER
asbestos .... SILICATE, AMPHIBOLE, BOARD
ASCAP member ..... AUTHOR
ascarid .... ROUNDWORM, HOOKWORM, (PIN)WORM
ascend ...... CLIMB, (A)RISE, SOAR, SCALE
ascendancy ..... DOMINATION, MASTERY, RISE, PREDOMINANCE

ascent ..... RISE, ACCLIVITY,
SLOPE, STIPE
ascertain .... LEARN, VERIFY,
SEE, DETERMINE
ascertainment ... ASSURANCE
ascetic .... AUSTERE, HERMIT,
ESSENE, RECLUSE,
MONASTIC, YOGA, FAKIR,
STOIC, EREMITE, MONK,
STYLITE
Asch name .... SHOLEM,
SHOLOM
asci .... SPORE SAC
ascidian .... TUNICATE
Ascot ...... SCARF, (NECK)TIE
ascribe .... ATTRIBUTE,
IMPUTE, CREDIT, ASSIGN
ascus .... (SPORE)SAC
aseptic .... STERILE
asexual .... SEXLESS,
NEUTER, AGAMIC
reproduction .... FISSION
Asgard, bridge to .... BIFROST
watchman of .. HEIMDALL
ash ..... TREE, WOOD, EMBER,
POWDER, RESIDUE, PALLOR,
ARTAR
can .... DUSTBIN
can: sl. ... DEPTH BOMB,
DEPTH CHARGE
fruit .... SAMARA,
KEY, MAPLE
gray .... CINEREOUS
mountain .... ROWAN
pertaining to .. CINERARY
solution .... LYE
tree juice .... MANNA
Wednesday to Easter ....
LENT
Ashanti capital ...... KUMASI
ashen ..... PALE, WHITE, WAN,
GRAY, PALLID, LIVID
Asher's daughter ...... SERAH
mother .... ZILPAH
son .... ISUI, BERIAH
ashes, pert. to ..... CINERARY
ashlar .... BEAM, PLAN
Ashtoreth .... ASTARTE,
ISHTAR
ashy .... PALE, LIVID
Asia Minor .... ANATOLIA
bishop ... (ST) NICHOLAS
city ...... MYRA, ANTIOCH,
TYRE, GAZA, TROY,
NICAEA, ISSUS, EPHESUS,
CHALCEDON, SARDIS

country .... CARIA,
CILICIA, LYCIA, MYSIA,
LYDIA, PISIDIA,
PHRYGIA
district ... IONIA, TROAD
Greek city ..... MILETUS
island .... SAMOS
kingdom .... PONTUS
mountain .... IDA
people .... HITTITES
province ...... GALATIA,
LYCAONIA
region .... EOLIS, TROAS
river ...... CAICUS, IRIS,
GRANICUS
sheep .... BROADTAIL,
KARAKUL
tree .... SYCAMORE
Asiatic ancient people .. SERES
ass .... ONAGER
bean .... SOY(A)
bird .... MINA,
MYNA(H), PITTA
cat .... OUNCE,
SIAMESE, TIGER
cattle .... ZEBU
civet .... ZIBET(H)
coin, Annam ...... QUAN
coin, China ... LI, TAEL,
TIAO, YUAN
coin, India ... ANNA, PIE,
HOON, PICE, FELS, RUPEE,
TARA
coin, Iran ... PUL, POUL,
RIAL, DARIC, DINAR,
MOHUR, LARI
coin, Iraq .... DINAR
coin, Malaya .... TRA(H)
coin, Nepal ..... MOHAR
coin, Siam/Thailand ....
BAHT, TICAL, ANNA
country ... ANNAM, IRAQ,
IRAN, BURMA, CHINA,
VIETNAM, KOREA, SYRIA,
THAILAND (SIAM), SIKKIM,
NEPAL, MALAYSIA,
SINGAPORE, INDIA,
PAKISTAN, LAOS,
CAMBODIA, TIBET, ARABIA
country. ancient .. MEDEA,
EOLIA, ELAM, ACCAD
cow .... ZO(H), ZOBO
deer .... AXIS,
SAMBAR, SASIN
desert .... GOBI
disease .... BERIBERI

fiber .... RAMIE, HEMP
finch .... SISKIN
gangster .... DACOIT
gazelle ...... AHU, CORA,
    ARIEL
ginger ...... CARDAMOM,
    CARDAMUM
goat antelope .... SEROW
grass ...... CITRONELLA
grassland ...... MAIDAN
herb .... CARDAMOM,
    CARDAMUM
hog .... BABIRUSA
isthmus .... KRA
kingdom ... ELAM, IRAN,
    IRAQ, SIAM, NEPAL,
    AN(N)AM, KOREA
lake ...... BAIKAL, ARAL
lemur ... LORIS, MACACO
medicine man ... SHAMAN
millet .... DARI
monkey .... MACAQUE
mountain .... ALTAI
native .... MONGOL,
    TA(R)TAR, AN(N)AMESE,
    SIAMESE, TIBETAN, TAI,
    CHINESE, KOREAN,
    INNUIT, YUIT, HUN
nomad .... TATAR
palm .... ARECA, BETEL,
    NIPA
peninsula .... KOREA,
    MALAY
perennial plant ... RAMIE
plague .... CHOLERA
plain .... CHOL
plant ... RAMIE, SESAME,
    TAMPALA, ODAL, GINSENG,
    HEMP
port .... AMOY,
    HAIPHONG, SAIGON,
    SHANGHAI, MACAO
river .... MEKONG,
    AMUR, YALU, YANGTZE,
    YELLOW, OXUS, ILI, LENA,
    ONON, PEARL, INDUS
rodent .... MARMOT,
    PIKA, CONY
ruminant .... YAK, ZEBU
sardine .... LOUR
sea ... CHINA, ARAL, AZOL
sheep .... ARGALI
shrub ... TEA, THEA, TCHE
storm .... TYPHOON
snowstorm ...... BURAN
tea .... CHA, PEKOE,
    OOLONG
thug .... DACOIT
trade wind .... MONSOON
tree .... TEAK, ACLE,
    SIRIS, BANYAN, DITA, NARRA
tribe .... TAI, UZBEG,
    TATAR
weight .... TAEL, CATTY
wild hog ..... BABIRUSA,
    BOAR
wild sheep ..... ARGALI,
    RASSE
aside .... AWAY, APART
set .... TABLE
stage .. AD LIB, WHISPER
asinine ...... IDIOTIC, STUPID,
    SILLY, NUTTY, INANE
ask .. ... DEMAND, INQUIRE,
    INVITE, QUESTION, QUIZ,
    SOLICIT, BEG
for a handout ... TOUCH
for a loan: sl. .... BRACE
askew ... AWRY, ALOP, AGEE,
    ASLANT
asleep .... DOZING,
    DORMANT, DEAD, INACTIVE,
    NAPPING
at the ____ ..... SWITCH
Asmara is capital of .. ERITREA
asor .... LYRE
asp ... VIPER, SNAKE, URAEUS
on headdress .... URAEUS
asparagus tip .... SPEAR
aspect .... VIEW, LOOK,
    PHASE, OUTLOOK, MIEN,
    APPEARANCE
general .... FACIES
aspen .... POPLAR,
    FLUTTERING, TREMBLING,
    QUIVERING
asper .... COIN
asperation .... SLUR
asperity .... HARSHNESS,
    ROUGHNESS, SHARPNESS,
    RIGOR
asperse ...... SLANDER, LIBEL,
    VILIFY, SLUR, REVILE
aspersion .... INNUENDO,
    SLANDER, SLUR
asphalt .... BITUMEN,
    GILSONITE, UINTAITE
like mineral ... ALBERTITE
asphyxia ... APNEA, ACROTISM
aspic ...... JELLY, LAVENDER,
    RELISH, MOLD

aspirant .... CONTENDER, CANDIDATE
aspiration .... BREATH, AMBITION, DESIRE, GOAL
aspire .... HOPE, LONG, SEEK, BREATHE
aspirin .... TABLET
ass .... DONKEY, BURRO, DOLT, FOOL, SIMPLETON, ONAGER
   female .... JENNY
   hybrid .... ZEBRASS
   male .... JACK
   young .... FOAL
assa .... CAAMA
assagai ...... SPEAR, JAVELIN
assai .... PALM, DRINK
assail ..... SET UPON, ATTACK, ASSAULT, BESET
assailant .... ATTACKER, AGGRESSOR
Assamese capital .. SHILLONG
   dialect .... LHOTA
   Mongol .... GARO, NAGA
   shrub .... TEA
   silkworm .... ERI(A)
   tribe .... AKA, NAGA, AHOM, GARO
assassin .... MURDERER, KILLER, BRAVO, SLAYER, THUG
   Abel's .... CAIN
   Biblical .... CAIN
   character ..... SMEARER, SLANDERER, DEFAMER, ROORBACH
   Garfield's ..... GUITEAU
   Kennedy's ..... OSWALD
   Lincoln's .... BOOTH
   origin of word .. HASHISM
assassinate .... KILL, MURDER, SLAY
assault ..... ONSET, ATTACK, CHARGE, RAPE
   and battery .... BEATING
   prolonged .... SIEGE
   prolonged verbal ...... TIRADE
assaulter .... MUGGER
assay .... TEST, ANALYZE, ANALYSIS, APPRAISE
assaying cup .... CUPEL, TEST
asse .... FOX, ANTELOPE
assemblage ... CONGREGATION, MEETING, GATHERING
assemble ..... (FOR)GATHER,

COLLECT, FIT, MUSTER
assembly .... GATHERING, MEETING, SESSION, AUDIENCE, HUSTINGS, RALLY
assent .... CONSENT, COMPLY, AGREE(MENT), CONCUR(RENCE)
   show .... NOD
   sign of .. NOD, THUMBS UP
   word of .... AMEN, OKAY, YES
assert .... AVER, STATE, SAY, DECLARE, AFFIRM
   as a fact .... POSIT, CLAIM, ALLEGE
   formally ..... ALLEGATE
   positively .... SWEAR
assess ...... APPRAISE, RATE, TAX, LEVY, FINE, DUN
assessment ... RATAL, WORTH, ESTIMATE, TAX, VALUATION, APPRAISAL
assessor .... JUDGE, APPRAISER, RATER
asset .... PROPERTY, POSSESSION, ADVANTAGE, ESTATE, RESOURCE
   personal ...... BEAUTY, WIT, TACT, CHARM, CHARISMA
assets and liabilities .. ESTATE
asseverate .... STATE, ASSERT, AVER
assiduous .... DILIGENT, BUSY
assign .... DESIGNATE, APPOINT, TRANSFER, ALLOT, RELEGATE
   cause/reason .... ATTRIBUTE, ASCRIBE
   parts in play ...... CAST
assignation .... TRYST, RENDEZVOUS, APPOINTMENT
assimilate .... ABSORB, DIGEST, INCORPORATE
   facts .... LEARN
assimilation of learning ...... EDUCATION
assist .... HELP, AID, SUPPORT, ATTEND
assistance ... HELP, HAND, AID
   in kind ..... ALMS, DOLE
   to disaster victims ...... RELIEF

assistant .... AIDE, DEPUTY
  chairman at public dinner
                CROUPIER
  first, of a sort ....
             RIGHT HAND
  of bishop .. COADJUTOR,
              VERGER
  pastor .... CURATE
  to an abbot ...... PRIOR
assize ..... COURT, SESSIONS,
        INQUEST, OYER
associate .... ALLY,
  COLLEAGUE, CRONY,
  CONNECT, JOIN, PARTNER,
            CONFRERE
  in crime .... ACCOMPLICE
  with others ..... HOBNOB
association .... SOCIETY,
  LEAGUE, ORGANIZATION
  business firms' .. CARTEL
  football .... SOCCER
  merchants' ...... HANSE
  mutual aid ...... ARTEL
  mutual protection ......
              GUILD
  oldest in membership ...
              DEAN
  scholars', etc. .. ACADEMY
  workers' .... UNION
assoil .... ATONE, PARDON,
             ABSOLVE
assonance .... PUN
assort ...... CLASSIFY, MATCH,
         HARMONIZE
assorted .... VARIOUS,
  MISCELLANEOUS, CLASSIFIED
assortment ... VARIETY, OLIO,
         COLLECTION
  of types .... FONTS
assuage ..... ALLAY, PACIFY,
  CALM, RELIEVE, MITIGATE
assume .... INFER, FEIGN,
  SUPPOSE, UNDERTAKE,
  PRETEND, AFFECT,
  SIMULATE, ARROGATE
  a part .... IMPERSONATE,
             ACT
  an attitude .... POSE
  as a fact .... POSIT
  another's personality ....
        IMPERSONATE
  control ..... TAKE OVER
  without right ..... USURP
assumed character ..... ROLE
  identity for disguise .....
         INCOGNITO

name .... ALIAS,
        PSEUDONYM
  personality ....
       IMPERSONATION
assumer of other personality ...
        IMPOSTOR
assumption .... PRETENSE,
       PRESUMPTION
assurance ...... CONFIDENCE,
  CERTAINTY, GUARANTEE
assuredly .... CERTAINLY,
       DECIDEDLY
assurgent .... RISING
Assyrian .... AMORITE,
       S(H)EMITE
  capital .... NINEVEH
  chief deity ..... AS(S)UR,
       AS(S)HUR
  city ...... ARBELA, HARA,
      OPIS, AKKAD
  god ..... ASHUR, AS(S)UR,
  ANAT, IRA, NINIB, TAMMUS,
  NABO, NUSKU, HADAD, SIN
  goddess ...... IS(H)TAR,
  ALLATU, NANA, SARPANIT
  king ... PUL, SARGON (II)
  mountain ...... ZAGROS
  pyramid ..... ZIGGURAT,
       ZIKURAT
  queen .... SEMIRAMIS
  river ...... ZAB, ADHIAN
  warrior .... SARGON
  weight .... COLA
Astaire, ____ ... FRED, ADELE
  dancing partner .... RITA
Astarte .... ISHTAR,
      ASHTORETH
astatic .... UNSTEADY,
      UNSTABLE
aster ... FLOWER, TANGLEFOOT,
  DAISY, OXEYE, TANSY,
      ZINNIA
asterisk .... STAR
astern ..... BACKWARD, AFT,
  ABAFT, REAR, BAFT
asteroid .... STARLIKE, EROS,
  CERES, STARFISH, PALLAS
asthenic .... FEEBLE
asthma medicine ... GRINDELIA
asthmatic breath .... WHEEZE
astigmatism ...... AMETROPIA
astir .... MOVING, ABOUT,
  AGOG, AWAKE
Astolat maid .... ELAINE
astonish .... AMAZE,
  SURPRISE, ASTOUND

Astor, Lady ....(NANCY), LANGHORNE
astound .... AMAZE, BEWILDER
astrachan .... APPLE
astrakhan ..... APPLE, PELT, KARAKUL, CLOTH
astraddle .... ASTRIDE
Astraea .... VIRGO
astragal(us) .... ANKLEBONE, TALUS
astral ..... STELLAR, STARRY, ASTER, LAMP
astray ..... LOST, OFF COURSE, AMISS
astride .... ASTRADDLE
astringent .... ALUM, STYPTIC(AL), HARSH, SEVERE, TANNIN, STERN, COTO, CASHOO, CATECHU
fruit .... SLOE
gum .... KINO
material .... CATECHU
resin .... MASTIC
root .... BISTORT
salt .... ALUM
astrolabe .... ALIDAD(E)
astrologer .... STARGAZER, ASTRONOMER
ancient .... MAGUS, CHALDEAN
French .. NOSTRADAMUS
legendary ...... MERLIN
astrological .... CHALDEAN
diagram .... SCHEME
belief .... SIDERISM
astrology, work on .. ALMAGEST
astromonk .... BONNY
astronaut .... SPACEMAN, MOONMAN
American ..... SHEPARD, WHITE, BORMAN, SCHIRRA, BEAN, CONRAD, LOVELL, STAFFORD, EISELE, GORDON, ALDRIN
Russian ...... KOMAROV, GAGARIN
astronautic activity ....LUNAR PROBE
vehicle .... SPUTNIK, MARINER, APOLLO, SURVEYOR
astronomer .... BRAHE, METON, PTOLEMY, STARGAZER
astronomical ... LARGE, HUGE, URANIC
almanac ..... EPHEMERIS
arc .... AZIMUTH
cloud .... NEBULA
cycle .... SAROS
instrument ..... ORRERY
intersecting points ......NODES
measure ... APSIS, PARSEC
phenomenon .... PULSAR, QUASAR
shadow .... UMBRA, PENUMBRA
astronomy, work on ....ALMAGEST
astute ..... SHREWD, CRAFTY, KEEN, WILY, CANNY
Astyanax's parent .. HECTOR, ANDROMACHE
Asuncion is capital of ......PARAGUAY
asunder .. APART, SEPARATED
Aswan .... DAM, SYENE
asylum .... RETREAT, HAVEN, REFUGE, SANCTUARY, HOME, SHELTER
describing a kind of ....POLITICAL
inmate .... LUNATIC, REFUGEE
at .... NEAR, BY, ON
all .... ANY, AUGHT
all times .. EVER, ALWAYS
an angle ... ATILT, ALIST
full length ... FLAT(LING)
hand .... PRESENT, HERE, NEAR(BY)
home ..... IN, RECEIVING
large ...... LOOSE, FREE, ABROAD
last .... FINALLY, ULTIMATELY, ENFIN
not time .... NEVER
odds .... HOSTILE
once .... RIGHT NOW, PRONTO, IMMEDIATELY
that time .... THEN
the age of ...... AET(AT)
the same time ... COEVAL
variance ...... DIFFERENT
atabal .... (KETTLE)DRUM, TABOR
Atahualpa .... INCA, KING
Atalanta's victor .. HIPPOMENES
ataman .... COSSACK
atap .... NIPA, PALM

Ataturk, Kemal ...... MUSTAFA
Ate .... AVENGER
atelier ... STUDIO, WORKSHOP
    worker .... PAINTER,
        ARTIST, MODEL
athanasia ..... IMMORTALITY
atheist .... AGNOSTIC,
    INFIDEL, FREE-THINKER,
    NONBELIEVER
atheling .... NOBLE(MAN),
    PRINCE
Athena .... MINERVA,
    PALLAS, NIKE
    shield .... (A)EGIS
    title of .... ALEA
Athenian .... ATTIC
    aristocrat ..... EUPATRID
    astronomer ...... METON
    citadel ...... ACROPOLIS
    clan .... OBE
    coin .... CHALCUS
    courtesan .... THAIS
    demagogue ...... CLEON
    general ... CLEON, CIMON,
    ARISTIDES, MILTIADES,
    NICIAS
    judge .... DICAST
    juryman .... DICAST
    law-giver .... SOLON
    magistrate ..... ARCHON
    market .... AGORA
    money .... OBOL
    political subdivision .....
    PHYLE
    room ... ADYTUM, CELLA
    ruler .... ARCHON
    sculptor .... PHIDIAS
    seaport .... PIRAEUS
    statesman .... ARISTIDES,
    PERICLES, CIMON
    temple ...... NIKE, ZEUS,
    PARTHENON
    tribunal .... AREOPAGUS
Athens founder ..... CECROPS
athirst .... EAGER, AVID,
    PARCHED
athlete's crown ..... LAUREL
    dream ... CHAMPIONSHIP,
    OLYMPICS
    foot .... RINGWORM
    jump .... BROAD
    jump with pole ... VAULT
    speed event ...... DASH,
    SPRINT
    throw .... JAVELIN,
    DISCUS, PASS

trainer .... GYMNAST,
    HANDLER, COACH
athletic .... BRAWNY
    contest, 5 events ....
    PENTATHLON
    contest, 10 events ....
    DECATHLON
    exercises .. CALISTHENICS,
    GYMNASTIC(S)
    field ..... OVAL, DIAMOND,
    COURT, STADIUM
    group ...... TEAM, FIVE,
    NINE, CREW, ELEVEN
    prize ..... AGON, MEDAL,
    TROPHY
athletics ...... SPORTS, GAMES,
    EXERCISES, GYMNASTICS
athodyd .... RAMJET
atingle ...... EXCITED, AGOG
atis .... CONITE
Atlanta is capital of .. GEORGIA
atlantes .... TELAMON
Atlantic coast fish ... TAUTOG,
    RED DRUM
    tributary ...... MIN(H)O,
    SENEGAL
Atlas' daughter .... CALYPSO,
    HYAD(E), MAIA, PLEIAD
    name .... AGENA
    wife .... PLEIONE
Atli .... KING, HUN
    wife .... GUDRUN
atman .... EGO, SOUL
atmosphere .. AIR, TONE, AURA
    in some cities ..... SMOG,
    SMAZE
atmospheric condition ....
    CLIMATE, WEATHER
    gas .... ARGON
    phenomenon .... STORM,
    TEMPEST, CYCLONE,
    TORNADO, TYPHOON,
    HAIL, RAINBOW
    pressure .... BARIC
atoll .... (CORAL) ISLAND,
    BIKINI
    pool .... LAGOON
atom .... JOT, PARTICLE,
    IOTA, MONAD, ION, PROTON
    bomb target .. HIROSHIMA
    part .... PROTON, ION
    smasher ... SYNCHROTON
    smashing .... FISSION
    with valence of two .....
    DYAD

atomic .... MOLECULAR, MINUTE
   particle ..... NEUTRINO, ELECTRON, PROTON, NEUTRON
   physicist .... UREY, RABI, COMPTON, MILLIKAN, FERMI, BOHR
   submarine ...... SKATE, NAUTILUS, TRITON, SCORPION
atomize ... SPRAY, PULVERIZE
atomizer .... SPRAYER
atomy ...... DWARF, PYGMY, SKELETON, PIGMY
atone ...... EXPIATE, AMEND, REDEEM, ASSOIL
atonement ..... REPARATION, REDRESS, REDEMPTION
atonic sound .... SURD
atoning .... PIACULAR, EXPIATORY
atrabilious .... MOROSE
Atreus' brother ..... THYESTES
   parent .... PELOPS
   son .... AGAMEMNON, MENELAUS
atrium ...... COURT, ROOM, HALL, ENTRANCE
atrocious .... CRUEL, BRUTAL, ABOMINABLE, BAD, HEINOUS
atrocity .... BRUTALITY, OUTRAGE, BARBARITY
   a physical ...... FREAK, DWARF, GNOME, MONSTER
   visual .... EYESORE
atrophy of horse's muscles ... SWEENY
Atropos .... FATE, WEIRD
attach .... ADD, AFFIX, APPEND, CONNECT, JOIN, TIE, SEIZE, TACK
attaché .... DIPLOMAT
attached .... FOND, DEVOTED, APPENDED
   to branch .... SESSILE
attack ..... ASSAIL, ASSAULT, OFFENSIVE, ONSLAUGHT, ONSET, POUNCE, SIC
   artillery ..... CANNONADE
   diversionary ..... FEINT
   for quick victory .... BLITZ(KRIEG)
   in words/writing .. SQUIB, LAMPOON, LASH, BASTE
   kind of .... SNEAK, SURPRISE, VERBAL, BLITZ(KRIEG), BLIND, TACTICAL, STRATEGIC
   prolonged .... SIEGE
reputation ..... DEFAME, SLANDER, LIBEL, MALIGN
signal .... WARISON
swift, overwhelming ..... BLITZ(KRIEG)
swift, surprise ..... RAID
violent, intense .... ONSLAUGHT
warning of ...... ALERT, ALARM
attacker .... ASSAILANT, AGGRESSOR, OFFENDER, INVADER, RAIDER
attain .... ACHIEVE, EARN, GAIN, REACH, WIN
attainment .... SKILL, ACCOMPLISHMENT, ACHIEVEMENT, LEARNING, SUCCESS
attaint ... CONVICT, DISGRACE, DISHONOR, ATTAINDER, CONDEMN, CORRUPT
attar .... OIL, PERFUME, (ROSE)EXTRACT
attempt ... TRY, ESSAY, STAB, ENDEAVOR, ATTACK
   in Scottish ...... ETTLE
attend ... SERVE, ACCOMPANY, HEED, ESCORT
attendance ...... TURN-OUT, GATHERING, HOUSE
   describing some ... FULL, FULL-HOUSE, STANDING ROOM, SRO
   full .... PLENARY
attendant .... SERVER, CONCOMITANT, SERVANT, RETAINER, SERVITOR
   bridegroom's ... BESTMAN
   fact ..... CIRCUMSTANCE
   hunter's .... GILLIE, GILLY, GUNBEARER
   knight's .... SQUIRE
   on horseback .. OUTRIDER
   patient's .... NURSE
   personal .... VALET
   queen's .... CONSORT
attendants, group of .... RETINUE, ENTOURAGE, TRAIN, COURT
attended by all ...... PLENARY
attent .... HEEDFUL

attention .... EAR, HEED,
NOTICE, CONSIDERATION
getting sound ..... AHEM,
COUGH, PSST, PST, SST,
WHISTLE, YELL
holding ...... GRIPPING
order of ...... PRIORITY
attentive .... OBSERVANT,
ALERT, DEVOTED,
THOUGHTFUL
attenuate .... DILUTE, RAREFY,
LESSEN, WEAKEN
attest ...... VOUCH, CERTIFY,
AFFIRM, DEMONSTRATE
in earnest ...... SWEAR
attestation, formal/solemn ...
OATH
sign of official ..... SEAL,
SIGNATURE
attic ... GARRET, (COCK)LOFT,
ATHENIAN, MANSARD
bird ...... NIGHTINGALE
part of .... DORMER
salt .... WIT
Attica, capital of .... ATHENS
king .... CECROPS
native ...., METIC
township .... DEME
valley ... . ICARIA
Attican .... ATHENIAN
Attila .... HUN, KING,
ETZEL, ATLI
adjective for ... SCOURGE
attire .... GARB, ARRAY,
CLOTHES, FINERY, DRESS,
RIG, RAIMENT
man's complete .... SUIT
stag's .... ANTLERS
winter's .... SNOW
woman's .... GOWN
Attis' love .... CYBELE
attitude .... DISPOSITION,
OPINION, POSTURE,
MOOD, FEELING
strike an .... POSE
attract .... DRAW, LURE,
CHARM, FASCINATE,
CAPTIVATE
attractive .... FETCHING,
ALLURING, PRETTY,
ENGAGING, CUTE
girl, describing one .....
CURVACEOUS, SEXY, PINUP,
WHISTLEBAIT
girl's body: sl. .... CHASSIS
powerfully ... MAGNETIC

price to buyer .... CHEAP,
BARGAIN, CUTRATE
very .... STUNNING
attribute .... ASSIGN,
ASCRIBE, QUALITY, IMPUTE
attribution ...... IMPUTATION
attrition .... EROSION,
REPENTANCE
battle of .... SIEGE
attune .... HARMONIZE,
RECONCILE
to the times .. MODERNIZE,
UP-DATE
au .... COLD
courant .... UP-TO-DATE
fait .... EXPERT
naturel .... NAKED
revoir .... GOODBY
aubade .... MATIN, ALBA
counterpart .. SERENADE
auberge .... INN, HOSTEL(RY)
auburn ...... BROWN, TITIAN
auction .... SELL, SALE,
VENDUE, ROUP
price .... BID, UPSET
auctioneer's hammer .. GAVEL,
MALLET
platform .... BLOCK
word ..... SOLD, GOING
audacious ... SAUCY, DARING,
RECKLESS, BOLD, INSOLENT
audacity .... TEMERITY,
DARING, INSOLENCE,
IMPUDENCE, CRUST, CHEEK,
BRASS, GALL
audience .... ASSEMBLY,
HEARING, RECEPTION
INTERVIEW
kind of ...... AUDITION
official .... DURBAR
part of, sometimes ......
STANDEES
audio-visual aid .... FILM,
SLIDE, TAPE, MOCK-UP
audiphone ..... HEARING AID
audition .... HEARING,
TRY-OUT, TEST
auditor .... HEARER,
LISTENER, CPA
auditory .... OTIC, AURAL,
AURICULAR
Audubon, John ....
ORNITHOLOGIST,
NATURALIST, PAINTER
auf wiedersehen ..... GOODBY
Augean ..... STABLE, FILTHY

auger, groove of .... POD
    relative ..... AWL, DRILL,
    BORER, GIMLET, WIMBLE
augment ..... ENLARGE, ADD,
    INCREASE, EKE
augur ...... BODE, PORTEND,
    PROPHET, SOOTHSAYER,
    AUSPEX
augury ...... OMEN, PORTENT,
    PROPHECY, SIGN
august .... IMPOSING,
    MAGNIFICENT, GRAND,
    SUBLIME
    body, so-called .. SENATE,
    CONGRESS, SUPREME COURT
    first .... LAMMAS
Augustan .... CLASSICAL,
    ELEGANT
    Age writer .... OVID
Augustinian .... FRIAR
Augustus title ...... PRINCEPS
    wife .... LIVIA
auk ... ALCA, MURRE, PUFFIN,
    DOVEKIE, DOVEKEY,
    ROTCH(E)
    family .... ALCIDINE
    genus .... ALLE
    small .... ROTCH(E)
aulic .... COURTLY, SUAVE
aunt: Fr. .... TANTE
    S. African .... TANTA
    Spanish .... TIA
Auntie of stage/movies .. MAME
aura .... EMANATION,
    ATMOSPHERE
    of splendor ..... NIMBUS
aural ...... OTIC, AURICULAR
aureate .... GOLDEN,
    GILDED, ORNATE
aureole .... HALO, GLORY,
    CORONA
auric .... GOLDEN
    acid salt .... AURATE
auricle .... EAR, PINNA
auricular .... OTIC, AURAL
Auriga .... WAGONER
aurist .... OTOLOGIST
    instrument .. OTOSCOPE
aurochs ..... BISON, URUS, OX
Aurora .... EOS, DAWN,
    BOREALIS, AUSTRALIS
auroral ... BRIGHT, RADIANT,
    ROSEATE, EOAN
aurum .... GOLD, AU
auscultation ...... LISTENING
Ausonia .... ITALY

auspex .... AUGUR,
    SOOTHSAYER, SEER
auspice(s) .... OMEN,
    DIVINATION, PROPHECY,
    PATRONAGE, EGIS
auspicious .... FAVORABLE,
    PROPITIOUS, SUCCESSFUL
    start in a theater ....
    FULL HOUSE, SRO SIGN
    start of a speech ......
    LAUGHTER, APPLAUSE
austere .... STERN, HARSH,
    SEVERE, ASCETIC,
    RIGOROUS
austral .... SOUTHERLY,
    SOUTHERN
Australian .... AUSSIE,
    ANTIPODEAN, ANZAC
    aborigine ...... MAORI,
    MARA, MYALL, BUSHMAN
    aborigine weapon ......
    NULLA, WO(O)MERA,
    BOOMERANG
    acacia ... MYALL, WATTLE
    anteater ...... ECHIDNA
    arboreal animal .. KOALA
    badger .... WOMBAT,
    BANDICOOT
    bear-like animal .. KOALA
    bee .... KARBI
    beef-wood .... BELAR
    bird .... PARDALOTE,
    LEIPOA, ARA, ARARA,
    LOWAN, MALLEE, LORY,
    EM(E)U, LORIKEET, MEGAPOD
    boomerang ..... KILEY,
    KYLIE
    brushwood ..... MALLEE
    bushman .... ABO
    bushranger ....
    HIGHWAYMAN
    cane .... WADDY
    cape .... HONE, YORK,
    HOWE
    capital ..... CANBERRA
    cat-like animal ....
    LINSANG
    cedar .... TOON(A)
    chick .... SHEILA
    city .... PERTH,
    BRISBANE, MANLY
    ADELAIDE, BALLARAT
    SYDNEY, BENDIGO
    clover .... NARDOO
    club of aborigines ......
    WADDY

cockatoo .... GALAH
cry .... COOEE, COOEY,
            CODER
dasyure .... YABBI
Davis Cup player ... ROY,
  EMERSON, ROCHE, STOLLE,
      HOAD, NEWCOMBE
desert .... NULLARBAR
explorer ..... BASS, COOK
eucalyptus ...... MALLEE
festival .... CORROBORI,
            CORROBOREE
fish ..... BARRAMUNDA,
            MADO
fish with lungs ....
            CERATODUS
flycatcher ..... FANTAIL
gale .... BUSTER
goldfish .... FANTAIL
grass ......,, SPINIFEX
gum tree .... TUART,
            KAR(R)I
harrier/hawk .... KAHU
highwayman ....
            BUSHRANGER
hinterland ..... OUTBACK
horse .... WALER,
  BRUMBY, BRUMBIE,
            WARRAGAL
hut ...... MIMI, MIAM(IA)
island .... TASMANIA
kangaroo ..... WALLABY,
      WOLABA, WOLARU
kingfisher ..... HALCYON
lake .... EYRE, FROME
laughing bird ....
            KOOKABURRA,
      DACELO, GIGAS
lizard .... GOANNA,
            MOLOCH
marsupial .... KOALA,
  YABBI, WOMBAT, TAIT,
  PHALANGER, KANGAROO,
  BANDICOOT, DASYURE
measure of capacity .....
            ARNA
mining refuse .. MULLOCK
mole .... PLATYPUS
mountain .... BLUE
mountain range ....
            FLINDERS
native ... MAORI, MARA,
  MYALL, BUSHMAN, ABO
ostrich .... EM(E)U
oven .... UMU
parrot ...... COCKATEEL,

COCKATOO, PARAKEET,
BUDGERIGAR, ROSELLA,
      GALAH, CORELLA
peninsula .... EYRE
pepper .... KAVA
pigeon .... WONGA
pine .... DAMMAR
plant .... WARATAN
prime minister .... HOLT,
            GORTON
"puritan" ..... WOWSER
river .... SWAN, DARLING,
            MURRAY
sea mile .... NAUT
seaport .... SYDNEY,
  BRISBANE, DARWIN,
            PERTH
shark .... MAKO
shield .... MULGA
shrub .... CORREA
soldier .... ANZAC
spear-throwing device ...
            WO(O)MERA
territory .. .. PAPUA
traveler ,...... SWAGMAN
tree ...... BILLA, BELAR,
  PENDA, QUADANG,
  QUANDONG, ACACIA,
  MYALL, TODART, BOREE,
            MARARA
tree-dwelling animal ....
            KOALA
walking stick ... WADDY
wild dog .... DINGO
wild horse ..... BRUMBIES
wilderness ..... OUTBACK
Austria: Ger. ... OSTERREICH
Austrian amphibian .... OLM
  capital .... VIENNA
  chancellor ..... DOLLFUSS
  city .... GRAZ, WEIN,
            VIENNA, LINZ
  coin ... DUCAT, FLORIN,
      HELLER, GROSCHEN,
  KRONE, KREU(T)ZER,
      GULDEN, GUILDER
  composer ...... MOZART,
            STRAUSS
  country dance .. LANDLER
  folk dance ...... DREHER
  grass .... MARRAM
  hunter ... JAGER, YAGER
  liquid measure .... FASS
  monetary unit ... KRONE,
            CROWN
  name prefix .... VON

physicist .... MACH
province .... STYRIA
psychiatrist ..... ADLER,
    FREUD
rifleman .. JAGER, YAGER
river .... MUR, ENNS,
    DANUBE, DRAVE, RAAB,
    RABA, ISER, DRAU
ruling family .. HABSBURG
ski champ ...... SAILER,
    SCHRANZ
soprano .... JERITZA
violinist .... KREISLER,
    MORINI
writer .... KAFKA
autarchy .... DESPOTISM
authentic .... GENUINE,
    ORIGINAL, REAL,
    VERITABLE, TRUE
authenticate ... SEAL, ATTEST
author .... ORIGINATOR,
    CREATOR, WRITER, FATHER
concern of ....
    PLOT, STYLE
of many works ....
    POLYGRAPH
unknown ....
    ANON(YMOUS)
authoritative .... MAGISTRAL,
    OFFICIAL
rule of law .. ORDINANCE
authority .... POWER,
    INFLUENCE, LICENSE,
    FORCE
letter of ... BREVE, BILLET
point as .... CITE, QUOTE
authorization .... FIAT,
    MANDATE, BILLET, LICENSE
authorize .... LICENSE,
    EMPOWER, COMMISSION,
    ACCREDIT, DEPUTE,
    PERMIT, ALLOW,
    GIVE LEAVE
auto (see automobile) .... CAR,
    MOTORCAR, AUTOMOBILE
clean .... SIMONIZE
colloquial .... BUS
court .... MOTEL
explosion ..... BACKFIRE
for hire ... CAB, TAXI(CAB)
obsolete .... REO,
    PACKARD, MODEL T,
    FLIVVER
old ..... JALOPY, CRATE,
    FLIVVER
old style .... LANDAU,

CABRIOLET, VICTORIA
panel ...... DASHBOARD
prefix .... MANU
racing champion .. CLARK
shelter ... BARN, GARAGE,
    CARPORT
super-charged: colloq. ...
    HOTROD
type ..... SEDAN, COUPE,
    BERLIN(E), ROADSTER,
    HARDTOP, CONVERTIBLE,
    TUDOR
autobiography .... MEMOIR
autochthon .... NATIVE,
    ABORIGINE, INDIGENE
autocrat .... DESPOT,
    DICTATOR, TSAR, MOGUL,
    CAESAR
automat .... RESTAURANT
automatic .... SPONTANEOUS,
    PISTOL
action, kind of ..... TIC,
    REFLEX
coal stoker ..... HOPPER
clothes cleaner ....
    LAUNDROMAT
automaton ... ROBOT, GOLEM,
    ANDROID
automobile (see auto) ....
    (MOTOR)CAR, BUS
accessory ..... MUFFLER
baggage compartment ...
    BOOT
body .... BERLIN(E),
    TONNEAU
canvas-topped ....
    CONVERTIBLE
decrepit .... FLIVVER,
    CRATE
fast .... CLIPPER
framework ..... CHASSIS
furnishings .... TRIM
hood .... BONNET
lamp .... HEADLIGHT
like a coupe .. CABRIOLET
model .... V-EIGHT
mudguard ...... FENDER
operator .... DRIVER
panel ...... DASHBOARD
shelter .... CARPORT,
    GARAGE
speed .... HIGH, LOW
starter .... IGNITION
supercharged: sl. ....
    HOTROD
two-door .... COUPE

with folding top .... CABRIOLET
autopsy ...... POST-MORTEM, NECROPSY
autumn .... FALL
flower .... ASTER
auxiliary .... SUBSTITUTE, SUB, SUBSIDIARY, COADJUTOR, ASSISTANT, HELPER
avail ... USE, PROFIT, UTILIZE
available .... HANDY, ACCESSIBLE, ON HAND, READY, FREE, OPEN
money .... CASH
avalanche .... LAWINE, (LAND)SLIDE
Avalon .... ISLE, AVILION
avant garde ...... VANGUARD
avarice .... GREED, CUPIDITY
avaricious .... GREEDY, MISERLY, GRASPING, GRIPPLE
avast .... STOP, CEASE
avaunt ...... BEGONE, AROINT
ave .... HAIL, GREETING, FAREWELL, SALUTATION
avena .... OAT, GRASS
avenge .... RETALIATE, REVENGE, PUNISH, REQUITE
avenger .... ATE, NEMESIS
avenging spirit .... FURY, ALECTO, MEGAERA, TISIPHONE, ATE
avenue .... ROADWAY, DRIVE, PROMENADE, STREET, THOROUGHFARE, MALL
of trees .... ARCADE
aver .... ASSERT, AFFIRM, DECLARE
average ...... MEAN, USUAL, ORDINARY, NORM(AL), MEDIAN
averse ... LOATH, RELUCTANT, UNWILLING, AGAINST
aversion .... DISLIKE, ANTIPATHY, REPUGNANCE, REVULSION
avert ...... PREVENT, WARD, AVOID, THWART, PARRY, FRUSTRATE
a blow .... DUCK
a draft .... DODGE
a thrust .... PARRY
Avesta language .... ZEND

aviary .... BIRD(S)CAGE, VOLERY
aviate .... FLY
aviator .... PILOT, FLYER, AIRMAN
free lance .. BARNSTORMER
hazard ...... BLACKOUT
signal .... CONTACT
with five kills ...... ACE
aviatrix, famous .... (AMELIA) EARHART
avid ... EAGER, GREEDY, KEEN
avifauna .... ORNIS
Avilion .... AVALON
avion .... AIRPLANE
avis indica .... APUS
aviso ...... NOTICE, ADVICE, INFORMATION, BOAT
avital .... ANCESTRAL
avocado .... PEAR
Mexican .... COYO
avocation ... HOBBY, PASTIME
avocet .... STILT, PLOVER, COOT, STORK, GODWIT
avoid .... SHUN, SHIRK, ESCAPE, SIDESTEP
blow .... DUCK
commitment ..... HEDGE, HEM AND HAW
conscription .... DODGE
person ... DUCK, DODGE
work .... MALINGER, SHIRK, GOLDBRICK, DUCK
avoidance ...... ANNULMENT, SHUNNING
of battle .... FABIAN
avoirdupois .... WEIGHT, HEAVINESS, EMBONPOINT
$1\frac{1}{3}$ pounds .... CATTY
avouch ...... AVOW, AFFIRM, GUARANTEE
avow .... DECLARE, AVER, ADMIT, CONFESS, ACKNOWLEDGE
awa .... MILKFISH, KAVA
Scottish .... AWAY
await ... EXPECT, BIDE, ATTEND
awake ...... ROUSE, ACTIVE, ALERT, ACTIVATE, STIR
award .... ADJUDGE, GRANT, DECISION, PRIZE, MEDAL
journalism/literature .... PULITZER
kind of .... BOOBY PRIZE
movie .... OSCAR
peace/medicine ... NOBEL

TV .... EMMY
aware .... CONSCIOUS, COGNIZANT, ON TO, SENSIBLE, HIP
awash ..... FLOATING, AFLOAT
away ..... GONE, OFF, ABSENT, OUT, ABROAD
from mouth .... ABORAL
from wind .... ALEE
prefix .... AB
awe .... FEAR, REVERENCE, VENERATION, DREAD
aweather .... WINDWARD
opposite of .... ALEE
awesome .... FEARFUL, TERRIBLE
awful .... APPALLING, DREADFUL, TERRIBLE
awfully ... VERY, EXTREMELY
awkward ..... CLUMSY, INEPT, UNWIELDY, GAUCHE, MALADROIT
age .... ADOLESCENCE
boat ..... ARK, DROGHER
person .... LOUT, RUSTIC, GAWK, SIMPLETON, FOOZLE, GALOOT, DUFFER
stroke .... FOOZLE
awl .... BODKIN, GIMLET, AUGER, ELSIN
for picking typeset ...... BODKIN
shaped ...... SUBULATE
type of ..... PEG, SEWING
with chisel head .... BRADAWL
awn .... BEARD, ARISTA, BARB, FIBER
awned .... ARISTATE
awning .... CANVAS, SHELTER, MARQUEE, SUNSHADE
of bed/door .... CANOPY
Roman .... VELARIUM
awry .... ASKEW, AMISS, AGEE, AGLEY, CROOKED, TIPSY
ax(e) .... ADZ, HATCHET
bonehead .. TOMAHAWK

cut of .... KERF
head, prehistoric .. CELT
Indian ..... TOMAHAWK
like tool .... ADZ(E)
stone .... TOMAHAWK
axil .... ANGLE, ALA
axilla .... ARMPIT
axillary .... ALAR
axiom .... MAXIM, PRINCIPLE
axis deer .... CHITAL
member .... JAPAN, ITALY, GERMANY, REICH
axle ... SPINDLE, ARBOR, ROD
bearing .... HOTBOX
ayah ..... AMAH, NURSEMAID
ay(e) .... YES, YEA, EVER, ALWAYS, ALAS
aye-aye .... LEMUR
ayuntamiento ..... CITY HALL, TOWN HALL
azalea .... LAUREL
Azerbaijan's capital .. TABRIZ, BAKU
azo, as combining form ...... NITROGEN
Azores island .... FLORES, PICO, FAYAL, TERCEIRA
port .... HORTA
volcano .... PICO
azote .... NITROGEN
azoth .... QUICKSILVER, MERCURY
azothic .... NITRIC
Aztec .... NAHUATLAN
country .... AZTLAN
emperor ... MONTEZUMA
god .... XIPE, EECATL
hero .... NATA
language ... NAHUATL
spear .... ATLATL
temple .... TEOPAN
azure .... (SKY)BLUE, CERULEAN, CELESTE, CYANIC
azygous .... ODD, SINGLE, MATELESS
azym .... BREAD

B

B .... SHOT, SECONDARY, BISHOP
girl .... BARGIRL, BARMAID
Greek .... BETA
Hebrew .... BETH

in chemistry ...... BORON
in chess .... BISHOP
letter ..... BE, BEE, BETA
picture (movies): sl. ..... QUICKIE
ba .... SOUL

in chemistry .... BARIUM
baa .... BLEAT
    bleater .... SHEEP, LAMB
Baal .... (SUN)GOD, IDOL
Baalist .... IDOLATER
Bab .... BABUDDIN
babbitt .... PHILISTINE,
        BUSINESSMAN
babble .... PRATTLE, BLAB,
    MURMUR, BLAT, PRATE,
        JABBER
babe ..... BABY, INFANT, GIRL
    Ruth's forte ... HOMERUN
Babel .... TOWER, TUMULT,
        CONFUSION, JARGON
baby's breath .... MADDER,
    HYACINTH, PLANT,
        GYPSOPHILA
babirusa .... HOG
baboo .... CLERK, SIR, TITLE
baboon .... APE, CHACMA,
        (MAN)DRILL
babu .... SIR, TITLE
babul .... ACACIA
babushka .... KERCHIEF,
        SCARF
baby .... PAMPER,
    CODDLE, INFANT, YOUNG,
    CHILD, GIRL, CHRISOM
    ailment .... CROUP
    bathing tub .. BATHINETTE
    bed .... CRADLE
    bedroom ..... NURSERY
    boot .... BOOTEE
    breechcloth ..... DIAPER
    cap .... BONNET, BIGGIN
    carriage .... PRAM,
        PERAMBULATOR, BUGGY,
        STROLLER, GO-CART
    cloth .... DIAPER,
        LAYETTE, CREEPER
    diaper .... NAPKIN
    food .... PAP
    grand .... PIANO
    head's soft spot ....
        FONTANEL(LE)
    Indian .... PAPOOSE
    Italian .... BAMBINO
    jacket .... SACQUE, SACK
    outfit .... LAYETTE
    pacifier .... NIPPLE,
        TEETHING RING
    pants .... SOAKERS
    powder .... TALC
    premature ..... PREEMIE
    robe, baptismal ....

CHRISOM
    shoes .... BOOTEES
    sitter ...... AMAH, AYAH,
        AUNT, NURSE
    sitter's problem ... BRAT,
        CRYBABY
    sound ..... CROW, MEWL
    Spanish ..... NINA, NINO,
        NENA
    talk .... DADA, LISP,
        BABBLE
    teething toy ..... CORAL,
        PACIFIER
    toy .... BAUBLE
    word .... DADA
Babylonia .... SHINOR,
        SHINAR
    founder ...... SEMIRAMIS
Babylonian .... WICKED
    abode of dead ... ARALU
    canal .... JESUF
    chief god ... ANU, ENKI,
        BEL, HEA
    chief goddess .. IS(H)TAR
    city ... AKKAD, CUNAXA
    deity ... ALALU, HEA, BEL,
        MERODACH, ANU
    division ... SUMER, ELAM,
        NITUK
    god .... NABU, NEBO,
    RAMMAN, ZU, ADDU, ADAD,
        TAMMUZ, UTUG, DAGAN,
        SIRIS, SHAMASH, ANU, EA,
        NANNAR, UTU, NINIB, BEL,
        ENLIL, MARDUK, ANSHAR
    goddess .. NINA, NANA(I),
        AYA, ERUA, ISHTAR, GULA,
        BAU, ARURU
    hero .... ETANA
    monarch .... ALOROS
    numeral .... SAR(OS)
    people .... SUMERIAN
    priestess .... ENTUM
    river .... TIGRIS
    storm god .... ADAD
    temple ...... BEL, ISTAR
    tower .... ZIGGURAT
    weight .... MINA
bac .... VAT, CISTERN
baccarat .... CHEMIN DE FER
baccate .... PULPY
bacchanal ... ORGY, CAROUSER
    cry .... EVOE
bacchante .... M(A)ENAD,
        CAROUSER
Bacchus ..... GOD, DIONYSUS

devotee .... SATYR, BACCHANT, M(A)ENAD

son .... COMUS

Bach's composition ... ARIOSO

bachelor .... GRADUATE, SINGLE, CELIBATE

bachelor's button .... CORNFLOWER, KNAPWEED, TANSY

party .... STAG

back .... AID, REAR, REVERSE, SPONSOR, ABET, SUPPORT, HIND, SECOND, ENDORSE, TUB, TERGUM, DORSUM, TERGAL

ache .... LUMBAGO

and fill .... ZIGZAG

at the .... RETRAL

book's .... SPINE

call .... REVOKE, WITHDRAW

country ... HINTERLAND

cramp .... CRICK

door .... POSTERN, UNDERHAND, SURREPTITIOUS, CLANDESTINE

down/out ... WITHDRAW, YIELD

entrance .... POSTERN

flow .... EBB, RECEDE

gate .... POSTERN

in zoology ..... TERGUM

lying on .... SUPINE

near the .... RETRAL

of animal ...... DORSUM, RIDGE

of head .... POLL

of insects ...... NOTUM

of neck ... NAPE, NUCHA, SCRUFF, SCRAG

of skull ..... OCCIPITAL, NION

pain .... STITCH

part .... DERRIERE

part: comb. form .. NOTO

pertaining to the .... DORSAL, TERGAL

scratcher .... TOADY

seat, carriage ... DICKEY, RUMBLE

seat driver: colloq... WIFE

take word ..... RECENT, RETRACT

talk: colloq. ...... SASS, RETORT, LIP

toward .... RETRAL

wound .... STAB

backache .... LUMBAGO

backbite .... SLANDER, MALIGN, VILIFY

backbone ...... SPINE, RIDGE, COURAGE, VERTEBRA

having ...... VERTEBRATE

of animal .... CHINE

of fish .... GRATE

backbreaking ...... HEAVY, TIRING, DIFFICULT, STRENUOUS

backdoor .... SECRET, CLANDESTINE

backdrop .... SETTING, SCENE(RY)

backer .... PATRON, SPONSOR

stage show ...... ANGEL, SUGAR DADDY

backfire .... EXPLOSION, BOOMERANG

backgammon .... TRIC(K)TRAC(K)

exposed man ..... BLOT

game series ..... RUBBER

backhanded ..... SARCASTIC, EQUIVOCAL, INSINCERE

backhouse .... PRIVY

backless .... SPINELESS

dress .... DECOLLETE

person .... YELLOW, COWARD

seat .... STOOL, OTTOMAN

backlog .... RESERVE, ACCUMULATION

backside ... RUMP, BUTTOCKS

backslide .... RELAPSE

backtrack .... RETREAT

backward ..... REVERSE, SHY, BASHFUL, SLOW, RETARDED

backwater .... BAYOU

channel ..... BILLABONG

backwoodsman ...... RUSTIC, HILLBILLY

bacon, bring home the .. WIN, SUCCEED

coating .... RIND

cut .... RASHER

side of .. FLITCH, GAMMON

strip .... LARDO(O)N

bacteria culture .... AGAR, STRAIN

destroyer .... LYSIN, BACTERICIDE, ALEXIN

free of .... ASEPTIC

mass of .... CLUMP
organ of locomotion ....
             FLAGELLUM
s-shaped .... VIBRIO
bacterium .... FUNGUS,
             BACILLUS
bacteriologist's wire .... OESE
Bactria .... BALKH
bactrian .... CAMEL
bad ... EVIL, UNFIT, WICKED,
  DISAGREEABLE, HARMFUL,
  SPOILED, INFERIOR, ILL,
             BASE
  blood .... ENMITY,
             RESENTMENT
  breath .... HALITOSIS
  combining form ... MAL
  girl ...... TRAMP, HUSSY
  habit .... VICE
  humor ..... TIFF, TEMPER
  Land mountain .. BUTTE
  liquor: colloq. .... BOUSE
  luck ...... MISFORTUNE,
  MISHAP, WANION, AMBSACE,
  AMESACE, CESS, HOODOO
  luck man .. JONAS, JONAH
  mannered person .. GOOP,
             BOOR, LOUT
  prefix .... CACO, MAL(O),
             MIS
  smell .... STENCH,
  MEPHITIS, REEK
  smell of oil/fats .. RANCID
  smelling ..... MEPHITIC,
             MALADOROUS
  sport .... CRYBABY
  temper .... BILE, SPLEEN
  temper sign .... TANTRUM
  tempered .... GRUFF,
  DORTY, TESTY, IRRITABLE,
  WASPISH, CRANKY, CRUSTY,
  SURLY, SPLENETIC,
  GRUMPY, SNAPPISH,
             GRUMPISH
  tempered person .. FURY,
  SHREW, VIRAGO, HOTHEAD
  woman .... FLOOZY,
  FLOOZIE, QUEAN, TRAMP,
             WHORE, TART
badak .... RHINO
badge .... EMBLEM, PIN,
             SIGN, MARK
  Japanese .... MON
  of braid .... CORDON
  of honor .... MEDAL
  of ribbon .... CORDON

on arm ...... BRASSARD
on hat ...... COCKADE
badger .... NAG, TORMENT,
  PESTER, HECKLE, HARRY,
             TEASE, BROCK
  animal ...... WOMBAT,
  BANDICOOT, BROCK,
             HAWKER
  Canadian ... CARCAJOU
  European .... BROCK
  genus .... MELES
  honey .... RATEL
  Java .... TELEDU
  like animal .... MARMOT,
             PAHMI
  State .... WISCONSIN
badinage .... CHATTER,
             BANTER, TALK
badlands .... WASTE
badly .... ILLY, POORLY
  colloquial ..... GREATLY,
             MUCH
badminton ... (COURT) GAME,
             DRINK
  cork ..... SHUTTLECOCK
  racket ..... BATTLEDORE
Baedeker .... GUIDEBOOK
Baffin's discovery .... SEA,
             ISLAND
baffle .... BALK, PUZZLE,
  ELUDE, CONFOUND,
  NONPLUS, BEWILDER,
  FRUSTRATE, FOIL,
  MYSTIFY, THWART, CONFUSE
baffling .... INSCRUTABLE,
             ELUSIVE
  problem .... POSER,
  DILEMMA, PUZZLE,
             MYSTERY
  question .... RIDDLE,
  ENIGMA, PUZZLE,
             CONUNDRUM
bag .... SAC, POUCH, POKE,
  LUGGAGE, SATCHEL,
  SUITCASE, PURSE,
  UDDER, CAPTURE, SEIZE,
             CYST
  floating ...... BALLOON
  for books, papers, etc. ...
             BRIEFCASE
  grain .... SACK
  kind of .... DUFFEL
  making material ....
  SACKING, JUTE, BURLAP,
             FLAX, HEMP
  slang .. WOMAN, CAPTURE

sleeping .... SACK
toilette .... MUSETTE
with perfumed powder...
.... SACHET
bagasse ...... (CANE) REFUSE,
.... MEGASS(E)
bagatelle .... TRIFLE
baggage .... LUGGAGE
boy .... PORTER
car .... FOURGON
carrier ...... HAM(M)AL,
.... PORTER, REDCAP
slang .... WOMAN, SAUCY,
.... GIRL
wagon .... FOURGON
baggie ...... BELLY, STOMACH
bagging material .... JUTE,
.... HEMP, FLAX, BURLAP
baggy .... PUFFED, UNPRESSED
bagman: Eng. ..... SALESMAN
bagnio .... BATHHOUSE,
.... BROTHEL, PRISON, CABANA
Bagnold .... ENID
bagpipe .... MUSETTE,
.... DRONE, DOODLESACK,
.... LOURE
drone .... BOURDON
flute .... CHANTER
music .... PIBROCH
part .... CHANTER
play .... SKIRL
sound .... SKIRL
bagworm .... LARVA,
.... CATERPILLAR
bah! ... ROT, TUT, PSHAW, FIE,
.... NUTS
Bahama Islands ..... ABACO,
.... ANDROS, ELEUTHERA,
.... BIMINI
capital .... NASSAU
premier .... PINDLING
Bahia ..... (SAO) SALVADOR
Bahrein Islands capital ......
.... MANAMA, MANAMEH
bail .... BOND, RELEASE,
.... BUCKET, PALISADES, FREE,
.... SCOOP, FORTIFICATION,
.... LADE
one who needs ....
.... DETAINEE, PRISONER
out .... PARACHUTE,
.... JUMP, RELEASE
bailiff .... TIPSTAFF,
.... REEVE, OVERSEER, STEWARD
bailiwick ...... FIELD, SPHERE,
.... HOMEGROUND, DOMAIN,

.... JURISDICTION
bairn .... CHILD, SON,
.... DAUGHTER
bait .... LURE, TORMENT,
.... TEMPT, BADGER, RIDE,
.... HECKLE, DECOY, TRAP,
.... HECTOR, ENTICE(MENT),
.... GUDGEON
drop .... DIP, DAP
fish .... CHUM, LURE
take .... BITE
baize .... DRAPE, CLOTH,
.... DOMETT
bake .... FIRE, ROAST, COOK,
.... DRY UP, BROIL, ANNEAL
with crumbs ... SCALLOP,
.... ESCALOP
baked clay .... TILE
dishes, etc. ... CROCKERY
pot .... OLLA
baker bird .... HORNERO
baker's dozen ..... THIRTEEN
itch .... RASH,
.... PSORIASIS
job .... KNEAD
kneading trough .. BRAKE
material .... FLOUR,
.... YEAST, LEAVEN
shovel .... PEEL
tool .... PEEL
workshop .... YALE
baking chamber ...... OAST,
.... OVEN, KILN
dish .... RAMEKIN,
.... RAMEQUIN, CASSEROLE,
.... SCALLOP
pit: Hawaiian ...... IMU
soda .... SALERATUS
baksheesh .... ALMS, TIP,
.... GRATUITY
Balaam's beast .... ASS
bal ____ ... TABARIN, MASQUE
balalaika .... GUITAR
balance ...... EVEN, OFFSET,
.... SCALES, LIBRA, REMAINDER,
.... POISE, SYMMETRY,
.... EQUILIBRIUM
crossbar of .... BEAM
of sales .... ATRY
state of .... EQUIPOISE
weighing .... STEELYARD
balancer .... ACROBAT,
.... TIGHTROPE WALKER,
.... WIRE WALKER
of books ... ACCOUNTANT
balancing weight .... BALLAST

balas .... SPINEL
balata gum .... CHICLE
Balboa's ocean ...... PACIFIC
balcony .... TERRACE,
GALLERY, GAZEBO
bald .... BARE, PLAIN,
FRANK, BLUNT, HAIRLESS,
GLABROUS
headed man ... PILGARLIC
baldachin .... BROCADE,
CANOPY
Balder, giant victim of .. LOKI
parent ..... ODIN, FRIGG
slayer of .... HODUR,
HODER
wife .... NANNA
balderdash .... NONSENSE,
PALAVER, RIGMAROLE
baldness .... ALOPECIA,
ACOMIA, CALVITIES
baldpate .... WIDGEON
cover ..... TOUPEE, WIG
baldric .... BELT
Baldwin .... APPLE
cousin .... WINESAP
bale .... PACKAGE,
BUNDLE, DISASTER,
SORROW, BAIL, WOE
Balearic Island .... MAJORCA,
MINORCA, MENORCA
capital .... PALMA
language ...... CATALAN
baleen .... WHALEBONE
balefire ...... BONFIRE, PYRE
baleful .... SINISTER,
EVIL, DEADLY
baler .... BUNDLER, TIER
Bali holy day .... NJEPI
balk .... JIB, OBSTRUCT,
SHY, BLUNDER, ERROR,
THWART, FOIL, STOP
Balkan ..... SERB(IAN), SLAV,
BULGAR(IAN), SLOVENE
balker, congenital .... ASS,
DONKEY, MULE
Balkh .... BACTRIA
balky .... CONTRARY,
RESTIVE, OBSTINATE,
STUBBORN
ball .... GLOBE, IVORY,
DANCE, SPHERE, PLANET,
BULLET
and chain .... WIFE
batted high .... FLY
game .... KENO, SOCCER,
TENNIS, BASEBALL,

BOWLING, CRICKET,
RUGBY, BOWL, LACROSSE
hit for practice .. FUNGO
low .... LINER
metal, athletics ....
SHOTPUT, HAMMER
of electrical discharge ...
CORPOSANT
of meat/rice ..... PINDA
of perfume mixture .....
POMANDER
of yarn/thread .... CLEW
on the .... ALERT,
EFFICIENT
play .... COOPERATE
rope missile ..... BOLA(S)
sign displayer ...
PAWNSHOP
swing bat at ...... SWAT
thread .... .CLEW
throwing device ... TRAP
tiny .... GLOBULE
up .... CONFUSE, MUDDLE
yarn .... CLEW
ballad .... SONG, POEM, LAY,
DERRY, CALYPSO, CHANSON
hero .... LOCHINVAR
monger ...... POETASTER
singer .... MINSTREL,
TROUBADOUR
stanza, rhyme of .. ABCB
word .... DERRY
ballast .... STABILIZE(R)
ballerina .... DANSEUSE,
TOE DANCER
descriptive word for a ...
ASOLUTA, PRIMA
famous ..... FONTEYN,
TALLCHIEF, MARKOVA,
ULANOVA, SHEARER, RASCH
finale .... TWIRL,
PIROUETTE
forte .... TOEDANCE,
PIROUETTE
ballet .... ADAGIO,
CHOREOGRAPH, MASQUE,
DANCE, BEZANT
dance solo ..... PAS SEUL
dancer ...... BALLERINA,
DANSEUSE, CORYPHEE,
FIGURANT
dancer's buoyancy ......
BALON
dancer's skirt ..... TUTU
director .... IMPRESARIO
famous ..... SWAN LAKE

jump .... JETE, ENTRECHAT
number ..... TOE DANCE
number between acts .... INTERMEZZO
Petipa's ..... RAYMONDA
posture ..... ARABESQUE
step ..... PAS, GLISSADE
turn .... PIROUETTE, FOUETTE
wear ..... TUTU, TIGHTS, LEOTARD
ballista .... CATAPULT
ballistic missile launching .... BLAST-OFF
launching place .... PAD
storage place ...... SILO
warhead ...... PAYLOAD
balloon .... AEROSTAT, INFLATE, RUBBERBAG, BAG, SWELL
altitude controller ...... BALLAST
bag .... ENVELOPE
ballast ...... DRAGROPE
basket .... NACELLE, CAR
cabin .... GONDOLA
car .... NACELLE, BASKET
covering ..... ENVELOPE
gas .... HELIUM, HYDROGEN
mooring line .. DRAGROPE
pilot .... AERONAUT
shape of ...... SAUSAGE, ROUND
trial .... FEELER, TEST
vine .... HEARTSEED
ballot .... VOTING, TICKET, VOTE(S), SLATE
straw .... POLL
ballroom dance ...... WALTZ, REDOWA
balls tosser .... JUGGLER
ballyhoo ..... TALK, UPROAR, PROPAGANDA, ADVERTISE, PLUG, TOUT
balm .... BALSAM, OINTMENT, OIL, SALVE, FRAGRANCE, SOOTH, UNGUENT, RESIN, ANODYNE
for divorce ..... ALIMONY
for injury .... DAMAGES
of Gilead ...... BALSAM, POPLAR, FIR, OINTMENT, OIL
Balmoral .... PETTICOAT, CAP, CASTLE
balmy .... FRAGRANT, SOOTHING, SOFT, MOONY, CRAZY, FOOLISH, IDIOTIC, MILD
balneal .... BATH(ING)
baloney ..... NONSENSE, ROT, BUNCOMBE, BUNK, BOLOGNA
balsa .... WOOD, RAFT, TREE, CORKWOOD
like wood .... BONGO
balsam .... RESIN, BALM, GUM, TOLU, IMPATIENS, FIR, COPAIBA, LIQUIDAMBAR
gum resin ..... STORAX, BALM
Swiss .... RIGA
tree .... TOLU
Balt .... ESTH
Baltic gulf .... RIGA
island ...... ALSEN, DAGO, OS(S)EL
port .... KIEL, RIGA, STETTIN, MEMEL, REVAL
river .... ODER
Sea city .. LIBAU, LIEBAJA
seaport .... ROSTOCK
state .... LATVIA, LITHUANIA, ESTONIA, FINLAND
Baltimore oriole ... HANGBIRD, GOLDENROBIN, HANGNEST
stove .... LATROBE
Balto-Slav .... LETT
Baluchistan capital ... QUETTA
grain .... JOWAR
mountain .... HALA
race .... BRAHOES
river .... BOLAN, MOOLA
ruler .... KHAN, SIRDAR
town .... BEYLA, DADUR
tribe .... REKI
tribesman .... MARI
balustrade ..... BAN(N)ISTER, RAILING
Balzac's father ...... GORIOT
bambino: Ital. .... CHILD, BABY(BOY)
bamboo .... CANE, GRASS, REED, TONKIN
like .... REEDY
shoot pickle .... ACHAR
stalk .... REED

bamboozle .... TRICK, CHEAT,
PUZZLE, BUFFALO
ban .... FORBID, PROHIBIT,
CURSE, TABU, TABOO,
GOVERNOR, PROCLAMATION
Bana, daughter of .... USHA
banal .... TRITE, CORNY,
HACKNEYED, STALE, TRIVIAL
banality .... PLATITUDE,
CLICHÉ
banana .... ENSETE, MUSA,
PESANG, FEI
bunch/cluster .... HAND
disease .... MOSAIC
like fruit ...... PLANTAIN
of the .... MUSACEOUS
oil: sl. .... NONSENSE
Philippine ...., SAGING,
LATUNDAN
plant .... MUSA, PESANG
band .... BELT, STRIP,
COPULA, BINDING, COLLAR,
COMPANY, TAPE, FILLET,
GATHER, GROUP, GIRDLE,
FASCIA
across escutcheon .. FESS
brain .... LIGULA
deputized .... POSSE
head ... CORONET, AGAL
ecclesiastical .. ORPHREY
leader .... JAMES, SHAW,
VALLEE, CUGAT, WHITEMAN,
CHORAGUS
leaders .... CHORAGI
mourning .... WEED
narrow .... STRIA(E),
TAPE
of soldiers ..... COHORT
of stone on wall ....
CORDON
ornamental .... CORONET
priest's arm .... FANO(N),
FANUM, PHANO
sheriff's .... POSSE
wheel .... RIGGER
bandage ..... STUPE, LIGATE,
LIGATURE, SWATH(E),
GAUZE, SPICA
in surgery ...... FASCIA
shaped .... LIGULATE
used as compress .. DOSSIL
bandanna .... (HAND)KERCHIEF
bandeau ...... (HAIR)RIBBON,
BRASSIERE
banderilla .... DART
banderole ... FLAG, PENNANT,

STREAMER, BANNEROL
bandicoot ..... RAT, BADGER
bandit .... BRIGAND,
HIGHWAYMAN, ROBBER,
LADRONE
more than one .. BANDITTI
banditry .... BRIGANDAGE
bandleader .... CHORAGUS
bandmaster .... SOUSA,
CONDUCTOR
bandog .... MASTIFF,
BLOODHOUND, WATCHDOG
bandoline .... POMADE
bandore .... PANDORA,
PANDORE
bandwagon riders ... WINNERS
bandy ....,, EXCHANGE,
GIVE-AND-TAKE, CLUB,
CHAFFER, BOWED
legs .... BOWED
some are .... LEGS
bane .... POISON, RUIN, CURSE
baneful .... VENOMOUS,
DEADLY, PERNICIOUS,
RUINOUS, BAD
Banff National Park Lake ....
LOUISE
bang .... SLAM, BEAT,
STRIKE, CLOSE, EXPLOSION
slang .... PLEASURE,
ENJOYMENT
up ..... BRUISE, DAMAGE.
Bangalore, where it is ....
MYSORE
banged-up .... EXCELLENT,
WELL DONE, A-ONE
bangs ...... HAIRCUT, HAIRDO
Bangkok, capital of ....
THAILAND, SIAM
coin ... BAHT, ATT, TICAL
language .... THAI
river .... MENAM
twin city .... DHONBURI
bangle .... BRACELET,
ARMLET, ANKLET
banian .... MERCHANT, SHIRT
banish .... EXILE, DISMISS,
PROSCRIBE, RELEGATE,
EXPATRIATE, DEPORT
banister .... BALUSTER,
BALUSTRADE, HANDRAIL
banjo .... SAMISEN
string sound .... TWANG,
TUM
bank .... RELY, DEPEND,
RIDGE, SHOAL, SHORE

clerk .... TELLER
employee ...... RUNNER
kind of .... BLOOD, EYE,
    POOL, DOMESTIC, PIGGY
note .... BILL
river .... RIPA
river, pert. to .. RIPARIAN
teller's window .. WICKET
vole .... MOUSE
bankbook .... PASSBOOK
banker ... LAMONT, MORGAN,
    GIANNINI, SHROFF,
    ROTHSCHILD
banking game .... FARO
bankroll .... WAD
    colloquial ... CAPITALIZE
bankrupt .... INSOLVENT,
    FAILURE, PENNILESS, BROKE
    abbreviation ...... BKPT
banner .... ENSIGN, FLAG,
    BANDEROLE, FOREMOST,
    LEADING, BLAZON, PENNON,
    STREAMER, GONFALON
    headline ..... STREAMER
bannock .... CAKE
banquet ..... FEAST, DINNER,
    MEAL
    rich, luxurious ....
    LUCULLAN
banquette .. SIDEWALK, BENCH
banshee .... SPIRIT
bant .... DIET
bantam .... SMALL, PINT-SIZE,
    FOWL, MIDGET
    publication ... VESTBOOK,
    POCKETBOOK, TABLOID
banteng .... OX, TSINE
banter ... TEASE, PERSIFLAGE,
    RAILLERY, BADINAGE,
    JEST, CHAFF, JOSH,
    PLEASANTRY
bantling ... YOUNGSTER, BRAT
Bantu .... KAF(F)IR, JAGA
    Congo .... RUA, WARUA,
    BAKALAI
    language ..... ILA, SUTO,
    RONGA
    lion .... SIMBA
    nation .... GOGO
    native ..... ZULU, YAKU,
    BASUTO, DUALA, SWAZI
    speaking people ....
    BECHUANA
    tribe ...... PONDO, RORI,
    RAVI
banzai ... CHARGE, GREETING,

CHEER, CRY
baobab .... FIBER, TREE
    leaves, dried/powdered ..
    LALO
baptism ...... PURIFICATION,
    RITE, INITIATION,
    NAMING
    for example .. SACRAMENT
    of fire ..... TEST, ORDEAL
baptismal basin .... FONT,
    LAVER, BAPTISTERY
    cloth .... CHRISOM
    oil .... CHRISM
    robe .... CHRISOM
    water .... LAVER
baptize ...... CHRISTEN, DIP,
    PURIFY, CLEANSE,
    INITIATE, NAME
bar ..... LAWYERS, BARRIER,
    COUNTER, STRIPE, PUB,
    DRAMSHOP, OBSTRUCT,
    BISTRO, EXCLUDE, ESTOP,
    OPPOSE, WINESHOP,
    TAPROOM, TAPHOUSE
    chisel-pointed .. SPUDDER
    dividing .... MULLION
    door .... STANG
    employee .... B-GIRL,
    TAPSTER
    for holding hair ....
    BARRETTE
    for mining .... GAD
    habitue .... BARFLY
    iron ingot .... BLOOM
    legally .... ESTOP
    of —— .... SOAP,
    CHOCOLATE, METAL, JUSTICE
    of justice .... COURT
    of loom .... EASER
    pin .... BROOCH
    room .... TAPROOM,
    SALOON
    sinister .... BATON
    slang .... GIN MILL
    soap frame .... SESS
    square metal .... BILLET
    supporting .... FID
    used with fulcrum ......
    LEVER
    woman employee ......
    B-GIRL
Bara, actress .... THEDA
barb .... BRISTLE, AWN,
    STING, SHARPNESS, JAG,
    FLUE, FLUKE, PIGEON,
    HORSE, SPINE

of feather ... HARL, HERL
of wit .... STING
small .... BARBULE,
    BARBEL
Barbados fish .... GUPPY
  native ... BARBADIAN, BIM
barbarian ... BRUTE, SAVAGE,
    BEAST, PRIMITIVE, HUN,
    VANDAL, GOTH(IC)
barbarism .... SOLECISM
barbarity .... CRUELTY,
    BRUTALITY
barbarized term/word ....
    CORRUPTION
barbarous .... GOTHIC,
    BRUTAL, CRUEL, PRIMITIVE
Barbary ape .... MAGOT
  horse .... BARB
  state .... MOROCCO,
    ALGIERS, TUNIS, TRIPOLI
barbate ... BEARDED, AWNED
barbecue ..... ROAST, BROIL,
    BURGOO, COOK OUT
  bar .... SPIT, SKEWER
  site ... PATIO, BACKYARD
barbed ... STINGING, CUTTING,
    HOOKED, UNCINATE
  dart .... BANDERILLA
  missile .... ARROW,
    DART, HARPOON, SPEAR
  point .... FLUE
  spear .... GAFF
  tool .... HOOK
  wire blaster .. BANGALORE
  wire obstacle .. ABAT(T)IS
barbel ... BARB, FISH, BARBULE
  fish .... WATTLE
  fish with ...... CATFISH,
    MULLET
barber ... TONSOR, SHAVE(R),
    HAIRCUTTER
  of Seville .... FIGARO
  work .... TONSORIAL
barber's call .... NEXT
barbet .... POODLE, BIRD
barbital .... VERONAL, DRUG
barbiturate .... SEDATIVE
  slang .... DOWNIES,
    UPPIES
"Barcarolle" composer ......
    CHOPIN
bard .... POET, RUNER,
    VERSIFIER, MINSTREL,
    DRUID, SCOP
  of Avon ... SHAKESPEARE
bard's river .... AVON

bare .... NAKED, EXPOSE,
    STARK, DIVULGE, STRIP,
    MERE, NUDE, BARREN
  faced .... SHAMELESS,
    OPEN, UNCONCEALED,
    BRAZEN
  foot ... UNSHOD, SHOELESS
  foot pilgrim, car-buyer ..
    SUCKER
  footed .... DISCALCED
  headed .... HATLESS,
    UNCOVERED
  naked .... DENUDE
  rock, standing .... SCAR
barely .... HARDLY, MERELY,
    SCARCELY, MEAGERLY,
    SCANTILY
bargain . CONTRACT, HIGGLE,
    DICKER, CHEAP, HAGGLE,
    TRADE, BARTER, DEAL, BUY
  closed .... DEAL
  colloquial .... DEAL
  hunter .... SHOPPER
  place .... BASEMENT
  strike a .... AGREE
bargainer's delight .... SALES,
    CUTRATES, BUYS,
    DISCOUNT, REBATE
  favorite spot .. BASEMENT
barge .... BOAT, COLLIDE,
    WHERRY, KEEL, LIGHTER,
    SCOW, PUNT, CASCO
  heavy .... HOY
  in .... ENTER
  load of coal .... KEEL
  river .... GONDOLA
baric .... BAROMETER
barilla .... SALTWORT
barite .... SPAR
barium monoxide ... BARYTA
  oxide .... BARYTA
  sulphate .... BARITE
bark .... SNAP, TAN, BARQUE,
    (SAIL)BOAT, TREE SKIN,
    YAP, YELP, CORTEX, BAY,
    BRUISE, RIND, WOOF
  aromatic ... CASCARILLA
  bitter ...... ANGOSTURA,
    NIEPA, NIOTA,
    CHINCHONA
  buckthorn ..... CASCARA
  cloth .... TAPA
  drug from ... BEBEERINE
  fiber .... BAST
  flavoring .... SASSAFRAS
  fragrant .... CANELLA

inner .... BAST, LIBER
laxative ..... BEARWOOD
louse ..... APHID, APHIS
medicinal .. CHINCHONA,
    COTO, PEREIRA
mulberry .... TAPA
of pain/fear ...... YELP
pertaining to .. CORTICAL
remover .... SPUDDER
shrill .... YELP, YIP
soap .... QUILLAI
spice/tonic .... CANELLA
stripper .... SPUDDER
tree .... RIND, NIEPA
barkeeper ...... BARTENDER,
    PUBLICAN, TAPSTER
barker .... TOUT, SPIELER
aide of .... SHILL
talk of .... PATTER, SPIEL
barking .... LATRANT
barley ... BIGG, BERE, TSAMBA,
    CEREAL, GRASS
beard .... AWN
Indian .... PAPOOSE
liquor .... WHISK(E)Y
meal cake ..... BANNOCK
steeped .... MALT
water .... PTISAN
barm .... YEAST
barman .... BARTENDER,
    TAPSTER
barmy: Brit. sl. .... SILLY,
    IDIOTIC
barn ..... SHED, MEW, STABLE
bar .... BAIL
bird .... OWL
compartment ...... BAY
cow .... BYRE
gallery .... LOFT
owl .... TYTO
part for hay/grain .....
    (HAY)LOFT, (HAY)MOW
pole .... BAIL
barnacle .... SHELLFISH,
    GOOSE, CIRRIPED
Bill: sl. ... TAR, SAILOR
of a sort .... BUR(R)
barnacles: Brit. colloq. ....
    EYEGLASSES
barnstorm .... CAMPAIGN
Barnum .... SHOWMAN,
    PHINEAS
elephant .... JUMBO
midget ..... TOM THUMB
specialty .... CIRCUS
barnyard denizen .. ROOSTER,

COCK, TURKEY, HEN, COW,
    GOAT
pest .... FOX, WEASEL
sound .... MOO, BLEAT,
    CROW, CACKLE, BAA
barometer .... ANEROID,
    OROMETER, STATOSCOPE
barometric .... BARIC
line .... ISOBAR
baron .... MAGNATE,
    NOBLEMAN, SIRLOIN,
    CAPITALIST
dwelling of .... HALL
heir apparent of .. MASTER
wife of .... LADY
"Baron Munchausen" .. PEARL
compiler .... RASPE
baronet's addition to name ...
    BART
baronial ..... GRAND, SHOWY
barony, Japanese .... HAN
baroque ... ROCOCO, ORNATE
barque ...... BARK, SAILBOAT,
    VESSEL
barracks .... CASERN,
    ETAPE, GARRISON
barracuda .... SPET, SENNET,
    PICUDA
barrage ..... DRUMFIRE, DAM,
    BARRIER, BOMBARD
barramunda ..... CERATODUS
barranca ..... RAVINE, GORGE
barrel ...... CYLINDER, CASK,
    TIERCE, BUTT, SPEED UP,
    KEG, KILDERKIN, CASK
cork .... BUNG
groove .... CROZE
house ..... SALOON, BAR,
    TAVERN
like container .... DRUM
maker .... COOPER
one part .... FIRKIN
part .... STAVE, HOOP
rim ...... CHIMB, CHIME,
    CHINE
stave .... LAG
staves, set .... SHOOK
stopper .... BUNG
worker .... COOPER,
    HOOPER
barrelful .... CASK
barren ...... STERILE, EMPTY,
    DEVOID, EFFETE, BORING,
    UNFRUITFUL, JEJUNE, ARID,
    STARK
land .... DESERT,

USAR, DUSTBOWL
barret .... CAP, BIRETTA
barrette .... BAR, CLASP
barricade .... BARRIER,
     CONSTRUCT, ABAT(T)IS,
     PALISADE, OBSTACLE,
     ROADBLOCK, STOCKADE
Barrie (James) play ....
                    MARY ROSE
barrier .... OBSTRUCTION,
     OBSTACLE, WALL, SCREEN
  of logs .... BOOM
  of stakes ...... PALISADE,
                    STOCKADE
  river .... BOOM
barrio .... SUBURB
  chief .... DAT(T)O
barrister .... LAWYER,
     ATTORNEY, COUNSELOR
  head wear .... WIG
barrow .... HANDCART,
     TRUCK, HILL, MOUND,
     TUMULUS, PIG, CITY
  type of .... HAND, WHEEL
Barrymore, _____ ..... ETHEL,
     JOHN, LIONEL, MAURICE
Bart .... BARONET
bartender .... BARMAN,
     BARKEEP(ER), TAPSTER,
                    MIXER
barter .... SWAP, TRADE,
     EXCHANGE, TRUCK
bartizan .... TURRET
Bartlett .... PEAR
Baruch, statesman .. BERNARD
barytron ... MESOTRON, MESON
bas bleu ...... BLUE-STOCKING
basal .... BASIC,
              FUNDAMENTAL
basalt .... ROCK, POTTERY
  source ... . LAVA
basaltic rock .... WHIN,
     TRAP, GREENSTONE
bascule .... SEESAW
base ..... FOUNDATION, BED,
     BASIS, HEADQUARTERS,
     ROOT, IGNOBLE, MENIAL,
     IMPURE, MEAN, ABJECT,
     VILE, FELON
  architectural ..... SOCLE,
                    PLINTH
  attached to ..... SESSILE
  baseball ..... SACK, BAG
  coal tar .... ANILINE
  hit in baseball ... SINGLE,
                    TWO-BAGGER

of bird's bill ...... CERE
of column .... PEDESTAL,
              DADO, PLINTH
root .... RADIX
baseball abbreviation .... RBI
  backstop .... CAGE
  base .... SACK, PLATE
  batting practice .. FUNGO
  bungler in .... MUFF
  catcher .... RECEIVER
  catcher-pitcher
    combination .. BATTERY
  club/team .... METS,
     WHITESOX, CARDINALS,
     TWINS, SENATORS, TIGERS,
     GIANTS, YANKEES, ORIOLES,
     INDIANS, DODGERS,
     ATHLETICS, PHILLIES,
     PIRATES, ANGELS, BRAVES,
     ASTROS, PADRES, REDSOX
  commissioner ....
     CHANDLER, LANDIS, FRICK,
                    KUHN
  curve .... HOOK
  event .... SERIES
  field dispute .. RHUBARB
  ground .... DIAMOND
  "Hall of Fame" name ...
     SISLER, DIMAGGIO, COBB,
                    RUTH
  hit .... CLOUT
  mistake .... ERROR
  name ..... (CONNIE)MACK
  pitch ..... SLIDER, CURVE,
     DROP BALL, SPITBALL
  pitch aimed at batter's
    head ..... BEANBALL
  pitcher's fault ..... BALK
  pitcher's stand .. MOUND,
                    SLAB, BOX
  play .... ASSIST,
     SQUEEZE, DOUBLE, PUT-OUT
  player of fame ... RUTH,
     COBB, DIMAGGIO, DEAN,
     MARIS, MANTLE, MAYS,
     KOUFAX, REESE, SPAHN,
     AARON, ROBINSON
  player's miss at bat .. FAN,
                    STRIKEOUT
  player's shelter .. DUGOUT
  Rule 8.02's concern ....
                    SPITBALL
  stadium .... PARK
  team .... NINE
  VIP .... UMP(IRE),
     PITCHER, COMMISSIONER

baseball's Dean ..... DIZZY, DAFFY
　　Hank Henry ..... AARON
　　Koufax ... SANDY, LEFTY
　　Mel .... OTT
　　"Preacher" .... ROE
　　Ruth .... BABE
　　Sparky .... LYLE
　　"The Lip" ....
　　　　　　　DUROCHER (LEO)
　　Yogi .... BERRA
baseborn .... BASTARD, ILLEGITIMATE
based on 10 .... DECIMAL
baseless .... UNFOUNDED, SUPPORTED
　　report/rumor ... CANARD, HOAX
bash .... SMASH, STRIKE, PARTY, SPREE
Bashan King .... OG
Bashaw's title .... AGHA, PASHA, AGA, KEMAL, PACHA
bashful .... SHY, COY, SHEEPISH, RETIRING, TIMID
Bashful of fairy tale .. DWARF
Bashkir's capital .... UFA
basic .... FUNDAMENTAL, ESSENTIAL, PRIMARY, ELEMENTAL
　　law ..... CONSTITUTION, CHARTER
　　part .... ROOT, CORNERSTONE
　　rule .... CANON, PRINCIPLE, LAW
basics .... ABC(S)
basidiomycete ... MUSHROOM, RUST, SMUT, PUFFBALL, FUNGUS
basil .... PLANT, HERB
basilica .... COURTROOM, TEMPLE, LATERAN, PALACE
　　part of .... APSE
basilisk .... COCKATRICE, LIZARD
basin .... BOWL, SINK, POND, RESERVOIR, BAY, LAVER, FONT, STOUP, PAN, DOCK
　　altar .... PISCINA
　　holy water ...... STOUP, FONT, ASPER SORIUM, STOOP
　　in geology .... TALA
　　ornamental .... CUVETTE
basinet ...... BASNET, HELMET
basis ..... BASE, FOUNDATION

　　of argument ... PREMISE
bask ...... EXPOSE, SUN, BEAT,
basket .... POT, HAMPER, GABION, DOSSER, SCUTTLE, PANNIER, CAUL
　　abbreviation .... BKT
　　baby .... BASSINET
　　balloon ... CAR, NACELLE
　　coal ..... CORF, SCUTTLE
　　fiber .... RAFFIA
　　figs ...... CABAS, TAPNET, FRAIL
　　fish ..... CREEL, WICKER
　　fruits .... POTTLE, PUNNET, CALATHUS, SCUTTLE
　　grains .... SCUTTLE
　　hop-picker's .... BIN
　　material .... OSIER, WILLOW, RUSH, RAFFIA, REED, WICKER, WOOD, RATTAN, SPLINT
　　official papers .. HANAFER
　　ore .... CORF
　　pack animal ..... DOSSER, PANNIER
　　pelotari's .... CESTA
　　raisins .... FRAIL
　　rummy .... CANASTA
　　sculptured .... CORBEIL
　　symbol of abundance ... CALATHUS
　　vegetables ..... SCUTTLE
　　wicker .... HANAFER, BASSINET, CORF
basketball basket ...... CAGE
　　maneuver ...... DRIBBLE, LAY-UP, FREEZE, PRESS
　　player .... CAGER, GUARD, CENTER, FORWARD
　　team .... FIVE, QUINT(ET)
basking shark ...... SAILFISH
basnet .... BASINET
basque ..... BLOUSE, BODICE, TUNIC
Basque .... IBERIAN
　　cap .... BERET
　　game .... PELOTA
　　land .... EUZKADI
　　pelota player .. PELOTARI
　　province .... BISCAY, ALVA, VISCAYA, SOULE, NAVARRA, LABOURD, GUIPUZCOA
Basra native .... IRAQI
bass .... BAST, CHUB

black .... CHUB
double .... VIOL
double-reed ... BASSOON,
    OBOE
European .... BRASSE
horn .... TUBA
like fish .... SNAPPER
sea .... JEWFISH
stop of organ .. BOURDON
viol .... CONTRABASS
voice .... DRONE
wind instrument ....
    HELICON
basset .... DOG, HOUND
horn .... CLARINET
bassinet .... (BABY)BED,
    BASKET, CRADLE
bassoon ... OBOE, WOODWIND
basswood .... LINDEN,
    LIME(TREE), WAHOO
bast .... PHLOEM, RAMIE,
    BARK, BASS, FIBER
fiber .... CATENA
like .... LIBRIFORM
bastard .... SHAM, INFERIOR,
    BYBLOW, COUNTERFEIT,
    ILLEGITIMATE, MISBEGOT(TEN)
    wing of bird ..... ALULA
baste .... SEW, MOISTEN,
    STRIKE, BEAT, ABUSE,
    THRASH, TACK
bastille .... PRISON,
    FORTRESS, TOWER
bastinado .... ROD, STICK,
    CUDGEL
bastion ... BULWARK, DEFENSE
Basutoland capital ... MASERU
bat ... CLUB, STICK, CUDGEL,
    CHUNK, VAMPIRE, WINK,
    NOCTULE, BLINK,
    HAMMERHEAD
an eye ..... WINK, BLINK
blood-sucking .. VAMPIRE
colloquial .... SPREE,
    SPEED, BLOW, WINK, BLINK,
    FLUTTER
flying .... KALONG
for .... DEFEND,
    ADVOCATE
hold on .... GRIP
like .... ALIPED
like fish ...... GURNARD,
    GURNET, (STING)RAY
manure .... GUANO
mining .... SHALE
pingpong .... PADDLE

tennis .... RACKET,
    RACQUET
wing-footed .... ALIPED
batch ...... LOT, SET, GROUP
bate ...... REDUCE, DIMINISH,
    SOAK
bateau .... BOAT
batfish ... GURNARD, DIABOLO,
    STINGRAY, SKATE, RAY,
    STINGAREE
bath .... ABLUTION, WASH,
    SOAK, STEEP
kind of .... TURKISH,
    SAUNA, MILK, SHOWER
therapeutic .. WET PACK
tub .... TOSH
Bath's river .... AVON
bathe ... WASH, WET, MOISTEN,
    LAVE, SUFFUSE
bathhouse .... BAGNIO,
    CABANA, SAUNA
bathing, of .... BALNEAL
suit .... BIKINI
batho: as prefix .... DEPTH
batholite .... GRANITE
bathos .... ANTICLIMAX
bathroom .... TOILET
fixture .... TUB
baths .... THERMAE
Bathsheba's husband .. DAVID,
    URIA(H)
mother .... SHEBA
son .... SOLOMON
bathtub .... TOSH
Bathurst is capital of .. GAMBIA
batiste .... LINEN, MUSLIN,
    CAMBRAI
batman .... SERVANT
baton .... ROD, STAFF, STICK,
    WAND, TRUNCHEON
fairy's .... WAND
jester's .... BAUBLE
race .... RELAY
wielder ... CONDUCTOR,
    TOSCANINI, BEECHAM,
    SOUSA, MAJOR(ETTE),
    MAGICIAN
batrachian ...... AMPHIBIANS,
    TOAD, FROG
batten .... THRIVE, OVERFEED,
    WOODSTRIP, FASTEN
batter ... BEAT, POUND, RAM,
    BATSMAN
cake .... CRUMPET,
    WAFFLE, PANCAKE,
    FLAPJACK

battering machine ...... RAM
   ram of ship .... BEAK
battery ...... BEATING, CELL
   compartment ...... CELL
   floating .... PRAM
   material .... ACID
   part .... ANODE,
     CATHODE, PLATE
   partner of ...... ASSAULT
   plate .... GRID
batting, manner of .... FUNGO
   order .... LINEUP
battle .... FIGHT, CONTEST,
   WAR, COMBAT, CONFLICT
   area .... ARENA, RING,
   NO-MAN'S-LAND, SECTOR
   avoidance .... FABIAN
   ax .... TOMAHAWK,
   HATCHET, TWIBIL(L),
     GISARME
   ax: sl. .... SHREW,
   VIRAGO, NAG, AMAZON
   cry .... BANZAI,
   TO HORSE, (WAR)WHOOP
   dress .... ARMOR
   formation .... PHALANX,
   HERSE, ARRAY, ECHELON
   of Hastings site .. SENLAR
   of the ___ ...... SEXES
   of wits ...... REPARTEE,
     BANTER
   of words ...... DEBATE,
     ARGUMENT
   plane .... FIGHTER,
   BOMBER, SPITFIRE,
   SABREJET, SPAD, ZERO
   relic ...... SCAR, TROPHY
   royal .... MELEE,
   FEEE-FOR-ALL, BRAWL,
     RUMBLE
   scarred fighter ....
     VET(ERAN)
   trophy of Indian .. SCALP
   victim .... CASUALTY
battledore .... PADDLE,
     RACKET
battlement .... RAMPART,
     BASTION
   part of .... MERLON,
   EMBRASURE, CRENEL(LE)
Battles of 1429 ...... ORLEANS
battleship ...... GALLEON,
   MAN O'WAR, DESTROYER,
   DREADNAUGHT, CRUISER
   gun turret ..... CUPOLA
   slang .... WAGON

battue ...... HUNT, MASSACRE
batty .... CRAZY, ECCENTRIC,
     INSANE
bauble .... TRINKET,
   GIMCRACK, GEWGAW, TOY,
   TRIVIA, BEAD, DOODAD
baudekin .... BALDACHIN,
     BROCADE
baudrons: Scot. .... CAT
Bauhaus school founder ......
     GROPIUS
Bavaria, capital of ... MUNICH
   German name ... BAYERN
Bavarian city .... HOF,
   BAYREUTH, NUREMBERG
   river .... ILLER, ISAR,
     MAIN, EGER
   weight .... GRAN
bawbee ... COIN, HALF PENNY
bawd .... PROCURESS
bawdy .... INDECENT,
     OBSCENE
   house .... BROTHEL,
     BAGNIO
bawl .... HOWL, SHOUT,
   BELLOW, YELL, WEEP, CRY
   colloquial ...... SCOLD,
   REPRIMAND, REPROVE
bay ..... COVE, BIGHT, BARK,
   HOWL, INLET, WING, HORSE,
     ULULATE
   bring to ... CORNER, TREE
   color .... ROAN
   horse .... ROAN, BAYARD
   keep at .... HOLD(OFF)
   name of ... VOE, MANILA,
   BISCAY, BAFFIN, CAMPECHE
   of Biscay city/resort ....
     BIARRITZ
   of Biscay river .... LOIRE
   State ... MASSACHUSETTS
   sweet .... BREWSTER
   tree .... LAUREL
   window .... ORIEL,
   MIRADOR, PAUNCH,
     (POT)BELLY
bayard ..... HORSE, KNIGHT,
Bayern .... BAVARIA
Baylor eleven .... BEARS
bayou .... BACKWATER,
   EVERGLADES, INLET, CREEK
bazaar .... SHOP, FAIR
   church/club .. SALE, FAIR
bbl. .... BARREL
bdl. .... BUNDLE
be ...... ARE, EXIST, OCCUR,

HAPPEN, BELONG

a match .... COPE
a success .... CLICK
at habitually .... HAUNT, FREQUENT
of use .... AVAIL, UTILE, SERVICEABLE
on one's guard .. BEWARE
overly fond ...... DOTE, ADORE
silent, in music .. TACE(T)
still ...... QUIET, HUSH, SHUT-UP, SSH
your age ...... BEHAVE
beach .... SHORE, STRAND, GROUND, COAST, SANDS
bath house ..... CABANA
bird .... SANDERLING
fixture ...... LIFESAVER, LIFEGUARD, SUNBATHER
Florida .... POMPANO
on the: colloq. .... UNEMPLOYED
panhandler .... BEACHCOMBER
pest .... SANDFLY
walk ..... BOARDWALK, ESPLANADE
wave over ..... COMBER
beacon .... SIGNAL FIRE, LIGHTHOUSE, PHAROS, BEAM
light .... CRESSET
on summit ...... PIKE
Beaconsfield, Earl of .... DISRAELI
bead .... DROP, BUBBLE, GLOBULE
draw one on ...... AIM
for trimming dresses .... BUGLE
gun muzzle's ..... SIGHT
money .... PEAG
beaded moisture .... DEW
beadhouse .... ALMSHOUSE
beading .... GADROON
beadle .... MESSENGER, MACE-BEARER
of fiction ...... BUMBLE
beads .... NECKLACE
Indian .... WAMPUM, PEAG(E)
of perspiration ... SWEAT
prayer .... ROSARY, CHAPLET
trimming dress ... BUGLE
beadsman .... PRAYER,

BEGGAR

beagle .... DOG, HOUND
beak .... BILL, NEB, NIB, ROSTRUM
like process ..... ROSTEL
ship's ...... RAM, SPERON
slang .... NOSE, SNOUT
trim with .... PREEN
beaked .... HOOKED, AQUILINE
beaker .... CUP, GOBLET
beam .... RAY, SIGNAL, SMILE, RAY, ASHLAR, DIRECT, RAFTER, RADIATE, SHINE, CROSSBAR, SCANTLING
architectural .. TEMPLET, TEMPLATE
on the .... ALERT, KEEN, RIGHT
off the .... WRONG, AMISS, LOST
supporting ..... GIRDER
tie .... BALK
underside .... SOFFIT
beaming .... RADIANT, SMILING, HAPPY
beamy ..... BROAD, MASSIVE, JOYOUS, BRIGHT
bean ... SEED, ARBOR, SOY(A), LEGUME, CALABAR, GOA, LIMA, TONKA, PINTO
dish .... SUCCOTASH
flour .... FARINA
fly .... MIDAS
kidney .... HARICOT, FRIJOL(E)
like plant ..... SAINFOIN
lima .... HABA
locust .... CAROB
meal .... FARINA
Mexican ...... FRIJOL(E)
mottled .... PINTO
oil .... CASTOR
poisonous ..... CALABAR
sauce .... SOY
seed ...... SOY, PULSE
slang .... HEAD, BRAIN, MIND
soy .... SOJA
stalk/stem .... HA(U)LM
yonka .... GUAIAC
tree ... CAROB, CATALPA
used for counting ...... BEANO
versatile .... SOY(A)
white .... PEA

beanie .... (SKULL)CAP
beano .... BINGO
beany .... CAP
bear .... ENDURE, CARRY,
    SHOW, STAND, TRANSPORT,
    BRUIN, TOTE, WEAR, SUFFER,
    SUSTAIN, TOLERATE
  brown .... URSUS
  down ...... PRESS, PUSH
  down on .... CHARGE
  honey .... KINKAJOU
  in mind ..... REMEMBER
  like .... URSINE,
    URSIFORM
  like animal ..... KOALA,
    PANDA
  out ... CONFIRM, SUPPORT
  sky .... URSA
  squeeze of a .... HUG
  Syrian .... DUBB
  variety .... BROWN,
    BLACK, GRIZZLY, POLAR,
    HONEY
  which was a nymph .....
    CALLISTO
  with .... TOLERATE,
    PUT UP, ENDURE
  witness .... ATTEST,
    TESTIFY
  woolly .... WOOBUT,
    CATERPILLAR
  young ..... CUB, WHELP
bearberry ..... HOLLY, SHRUB
bearcat .... PANDA, CIVET
beard ...... WHISKERS, BARB,
    BARBEL, DEFY, BURNSIDES,
    GOATEE, IMPERIAL
  disease of the ... SYCOSIS
  grain ..... AWN, ARISTA
  hairlike .... CRINITE
  pointed .... GOATEE,
    VANDYKE
  red .... BARBAROSSA
  short growth ... STUBBLE
  the lion ... TAME, SUBDUE
bearded .... ARISTATE,
    BARBATE, AWNED, GOATEED
  butter .... GOA
  grass .... RYE
  seal .... MAKLUK
beardless .... YOUNG, CALLOW
bearer in India ...... SIRDAR
  of the world: myth. .....
    ATLAS
bearing .... MIEN, AIR,
    RELATION, CARRIAGE,

    MANNER, DEMEANOR,
    PRESENCE, CARRYING
  twins .... BIPAROUS
  writer's name .. ONYMOUS
bearish .... RUDE, ROUGH,
    CROSS, SURLY
bear's breech ..... ACANTHUS,
    SHRUB
  foot .... HELLEBORE
  skin .... (FOR)CAP
bearwood .... CASCARA
beast .... BRUTE, ANIMAL,
    QUADRUPED
  huge .... BEHEMOTH,
    MONSTER, MASTODON
  in French .... BETE
  like .... THEROID
  of burden ...... BURRO,
    ASS, CARABAO, CAMEL,
    MULE, LLAMA, DONKEY,
    YAK, ONAGER
  of prey ..... LION, TIGER,
    WOLVERINE
beastly .... BESTIAL,
    THEROID, BRUTAL,
    DISGUSTING
  British colloq. .... VERY
beat .... CANE, CADENCE,
    FLAIL, TROUNCE, POMMEL,
    PULSE, RHYTHM, DRUB,
    POUND, FLOG, WHIP, MIX,
    DEFEAT, FORGE, THRASH,
    PUMMEL, LAMBASTE
  back .... REPEL, REPULSE
  colloquial ...... WHALE,
    LARRUP, SHELLACK
  dead ... CHEAT, WELSHER
  group member .. BEATNIK
  in foil .... FOLIATE
  in journalism .... SCOOP,
    ASSIGNMENT
  into plate ..... MALLEATE
  it! .... SCRAM, SCAT,
    SHOO
  off ..... REPEL, REPULSE
  on the .... ATEMPO,
    IN TUNE, ATTUNED
  police .... ROUND
  repeatedly ..... CLOBBER
  slang .... TIRED,
    EXHAUSTED, PASTE, LAM
  sole of feet with stick ...
    BASTINADO
  soundly .... ROUT, DRUB,
    OVERWHELM, WALLOP
  thin .... MALLEATE

to softness .... MASH
up ..... THRASH, MAUL
with stick .... DRUB,
    CUDGEL, BASTINADO, CLUB
with whip ... FLOG, LASH
beatable .... VINCIBLE,
    VULNERABLE
beaten path .... TRAIL
beatific .... JOYFUL, BLISSFUL
beatify .... BLESS
beating .... DEFEAT,
    PULSATION, PUNISHMENT
    of person .... BATTERY
    underbrush to flush game
        BATTING, BATTUE
Beatles, former manager of ..
    EPSTEIN
    one of the ...... RINGO,
        LENNON
beatnik .... HEPCAT, HIPSTER
Beatrice's lover .... DANTE
beau ... DANDY, SWEETHEART,
    SUITOR, LOVER, FOP,
    FELLOW
    colloquial ..... BF, SPARK
    Brummell .. DANDY, FOP
    geste .... GALLANTRY
    ideal .... NERO
    monde's center ... SALON
beaut .... LULU
beautician ...... MANICURIST,
    COIFFURIST, HAIRDRESSER
beautiful .. PRETTY, HANDSOME,
    COMELY, FAIR, LOVELY
    eyes .... TULIPS
    girl: sl. .... LULU
    island .... FORMOSA
    slang .... SHARP
    woman .... PERI, HELEN,
        VENUS, HOURI, NYMPH
beauty, a .... ACE, LULU,
    PERFECT, HOURI, VENUS,
    HELEN
    reigning .... BELLE
    of form, etc. ..... GRACE
    parlor dye .... HENNA
    parlor specialty ... SET,
    WAVE, PERMANENT,
    MASSAGE, DYE, MANICURE
    parlor worker .. MASSEUR,
    MANICURIST, PEDICURIST
    shop .... SALON
    spot ...... MOLE, PATCH
beaver .... ANIMAL,
    (SILK)HAT, FUR
    den of .... LODGE

describing one ... EAGER
    eager ... DOER, HUSTLER
    fur hat .... CASTOR
    like animal .... NUTRIA,
        COYPU
    of armor .... CASTOR
    oily substance ....
        CASTOR(EUM)
    skin .... PLEW
    State .... OREGON
bebop .... JAZZ
because .... SINCE, INASMUCH
beche-de-mer ...... TREPANG,
    SEACUCUMBER
beck ...... STREAM, SUMMON,
    BECKON, NOD
    partner of ...... CALL
beckon ...... SUMMON, CALL
becloud .... DARKEN,
    CONFUSE, MUDDLE
become ...... BEFIT, SUIT,
    CHANGE, DEVELOP, GROW
    cheese-like .... CASEFY
    different .... CHANGE
    dull .... PALL, BORE,
        HEBETATE
    extinct .... DIE
    forfeit .... LAPSE
    less stern ...... RELENT,
        SOFTEN, THAW
    red in face ...... FLUSH,
        BLUSH, COLOR
    shabby ...... GO TO SEED
    void for cause .... LAPSE
    well .... HEAL
bed .... PALLET, BOTTOM,
    BUNK, KIP, STRATUM, SACK
    and board ... HOME, KEEP
    awning .... CANOPY
    baby's ... CRIB, CRADLE
    British slang ...... DOSS
    built-in ... BERTH, BUNK
    canopy .... TESTER
    clothes .... PILLOWS,
    BLANKETS, SHEETS, LINEN
    coils .... SPRINGS
    cover(ing) .... PUFF,
    TESTER, COVERLET,
    QUILT, (BED)SPREAD
    curtain/drapery ....
        VALANCE
    frame .... STEAD
    hanging ..... HAMMOCK
    kind of ... ROSES, OYSTER
    maker ... CHAMBERMAID
    of roses: colloq. ....

LUXURY, EASE
ore .... REEF
pest .... BEDBUG
river .... CHANNEL
slang ... BAG, DOSS, SACK
small .... COT, BASSINET,
PALLET
straw .... PALLET
stream .... DONGA,
ARROYO, WADI
type .... HAMMOCK,
BERTH, BUNK,
MATRIMONIAL
bedaub ...... SMEAR, SMUDGE,
PAINT
bedbug ..... CHINCH, CIMEX,
VERMIN
bedding, straw/hay/leaves ...
LITTER
Bede, _____ .. ADAM, VENERABLE
bedeck .... ADORN, TRIM,
EMBELLISH
bedevil .... HARASS, PLAGUE,
PESTER, WORRY, TORMENT
bedew .... MOISTEN
bedfellow .... ASSOCIATE,
CO-WORKER, COMPANION
bedlam .... CONFUSION,
UPROAR, MADHOUSE,
TURMOIL
Bedloe island .... LIBERTY
bedmate ..... WIFE, HUSBAND
Bedouin .... ARAB, NOMAD,
WANDERER, BERBER, RIFF
headband cord .... AGAL
tribe .... AMALEKITE
bedraggled .... UNKEMPT,
UNTIDY, UNCOMBED
bedroom .... CUBICLE,
CABIN, CHAMBER
caretaker .. CHAMBERMAID
bedside character ... DOCTOR,
NURSE, (BABY)SITTER
manners, describing .....
GENTLE, SOOTHING,
REASSURING
bedstead .... CHARPOY,
CHARPAI, FOURPOSTER
bedtime story: colloq. .. YARN,
FAIRY TALE, EXPLANATION
bee .... APIS, SOCIAL,
MEETING, ANDRENID,
HYMENOPTER
balm .... PLANT,
(OSWEGO) TEA
bird .... FLYCATCHER

birling ＮＮＮＮＮ ROLEO
built structure ....
HONEYCOMB
caulking substance ......
PROPOLIS
colony .... HIVE
eater .... KINGBIRD
family .... APIDAE
female .... QUEEN
girl named after ....
MELISSA
glue .... PROPOLIS
hive .... SKEP
house .... APIARY, HIVE,
SKEP
keeper .... APIARIAN,
APIARIST
keeping ..... APICULTURE
killer .... ROBBERFLY
kind of .... SPELLING,
SEWING, DRONE, WORKER,
QUEEN
like .... APIAN
male .... DRONE
martin .... KINGBIRD
nest-building ... CARDER
nose of .... LOR
of the .... APIAN
plant .... BALM, CLOVER,
SPIDERFLOWER
pollen brush of ... SCOPA
scientific study of ....
APIOLOGY
secretion .... WAX
sound ..... BUZZ, HUM,
DRONE
tree .. LINDEN, BASSWOOD
wax .... CEROTIC
beebread .... AMBROSIA
beech .... NUT, WOOD,
TREE, ROBLE
beechnuts .... MAST
beef ... COW, OX, BULL, STEER
braised ..... POT ROAST
cattle breed .. GALLOWAY,
ANGUS
colloquial/slang ....
MUSCLE, BRAWN,
COMPLAIN(T), GRIPE
corned .... BULLY
cut .... RIB, CHUCK,
SHANK, SEY, LOIN, ROAST,
BRISKET, STEAK, SIRLOIN
dish .... MIROTON,
PASTRAMI
double sirloin ... BARON

dried .... CHARQUI,
BUCCAN
eater: Eng. ..... YEOMAN
food for explorers ......
PEM(M)ICAN
nearest shoulder .. CLOD
rolled .... PASTRAMI
State .... NEBRASKA
stew .... GOULASH,
POT-AU-FEU
tea .... BROTH
tinned .... BULLY
up .... STRENGTHEN,
FATTEN
beehead .... AMBROSIA
beehive .... SKEP, BEEGUM,
APIARY
State .... UTAH
beekeeper .... APIARIST,
SKEPPER, APIARIAN
beefwood .... TOA
beefy .... BRAWNY, FLESHY,
MUSCULAR
Beelzebub ..... DEVIL, SATAN
beer ...... ALE, LAGER, SUDS,
BOCK, KVAS(S), MALT,
WEISS, PORTER, STOUT
cask .... TUN, KEG,
PUNCHEON
cup .... STEIN, MUG,
TOBY, SEIDEL
flavor ...... MULL, HOPS
foam ..... BEAD, FROTH,
HEAD
glass .... SCHOONER
house .... SALOON,
TAVERN, INN
ingredient .. MALT, HOPS,
YEAST
inventor ..... GAMBRINUS
make .... BREW
material ... MALT, MASH,
MEAL, HOPS
mug ...... SEIDEL, STEIN
party .... WASSAIL
plant ... HOPS, BREWERY
shop ...... PUB, TAVERN,
FARO, INN, SALOON
slang .... SUDS
sour .... KVAS(S)
spiced/sweetened .. FLIP
strong .... STINGO, MUM
sweeten and flavor ......
MULL
weak .... SWIPES
beery .... DRUNKEN,

TIPSY, MAUDLIN
bees, feeding on .. APIVOROUS
pertaining to ..... APIAN
study of ...... APIOLOGY
beet .... PLANT, ROOT,
CHARD, MANGEL
crushed ..... MEGASS(E)
sugar .... SUCROSE,
SACCHAROSE
Beethoven's birthplace .. BONN
composition ... MINUET,
MISSA SOLEMNIS
forte .... SONATA
opera .... FIDELIO
teacher .... NEEFE,
HAYDN
3rd symphony .... EROICA
beetle .... SCARAB, DOR,
ELATER(ID), MELOE, WEEVIL,
CLUB, CURCULIO, EARWIG,
SNAPPER, MALLET,
SKIPJACK, SAWYER,
WHIRLIGIG
blister .... MELOID
browed ...... FROWNING,
SCOWLING
click ...... ELATER, DOR,
SNAPPER
dung ..... COCKCHAFER
fruit-eater ... FIG-EATER,
JUNE BUG
gaudy .... LADYBUG,
LADYBIRD
grain .... CADELLE
grapevine .... THRIP
ground .... AMARA
head .... BLOCKHEAD,
NITWIT
larva .... BEEWOLF,
CADELLE, GRUB, GRUGRU
like charm ..... SCARAB
like insect ..... EARWIG
order of .... COLEOPTERA
sacred to Egyptians .....
SCARAB
snouted ..... CURCULIO
tree .... GIRDLER
wing cover ...... SHARD,
ELYTRON
with club-shaped feelers
CLAVICORN
wood .... SAWYER
beetling ..... OVERHANGING,
PROJECTING
befall ...... HAPPEN, OCCUR,
PASS, HAP

befit .... SUIT, BECOME
befitting .... PROPER,
    SUITABLE, APPROPRIATE
befog .... BLUR, OBSCURE,
    CONFUSE
befool .... TRICK, DUPE,
    DECEIVE
before .... ERE, PREVIOUS,
    PRECEDING, FORMERLY,
    PRIOR
    all others .... FIRST
    long .... SOON, ANON,
    SHORTLY, PRESENTLY
    prefix .... PRE, ANTE
befoul .... DIRTY, SOIL
befuddle .... CONFUSE,
    STUPEFY
beg .... IMPLORE, BESEECH,
    ASK, ENTREAT, IMPORTUNE,
    PRAY, PLEAD, PANHANDLE,
    MOOCH
    off ... ASK OUT, DECLINE,
    EXCUSE
    the question .... EVADE
beget .... SIRE, FATHER,
    PRODUCE, PROCREATE
beggar .... RASCAL, DERVISH,
    FAKIR, PANHANDLER,
    LAZZARONE, MENDICANT,
    LAZAR, PLEADER, RANDY,
    SCHNORRER
    equipment of ... TINCUP
    gift to .. HANDOUT, ALMS
    roving ..... GANGREL,
    GABERLUNZIE, FAKIR
    speech of .... CANT
beggarly .... MEAN, PETTY
beggars' lice .... BUR(R),
    CLEAVERS
    patron saint ...... GILES
begging, practice of ....
    MENDICANCY, MENDICITY
begin .... OPEN, START,
    INITIATE, COMMENCE,
    ORIGINATE
beginner ...... TYRO, NOVICE,
    NEOPHYTE, APPRENTICE
    GREENHORN, PUPIL
beginning .... ONSET, ORIGIN,
    GERM, BIRTH, GENESIS,
    OUTSET
begone! .... SCAT, SCRAM,
    AVAUNT, SHOO, AROINT
begrime .... SOIL, DIRTY,
    SMUDGE, SMEAR
begrudge ..... GRUMBLE, ENVY

beguile .... DECEIVE, DELUDE,
    VAMP, CHARM, AMUSE,
    COZEN, MISLEAD, LURE
beguilements .... ARTS
begum, Indian ..... PRINCESS
Beguin .... BEGHARD
behalf .... INTEREST, SIDE,
    SAKE
behave ... CONDUCT, DEPORT,
    COMPORT, ACT
    foolishly .... FRIBBLE
behavior .... CONDUCT,
    MANNERS, ACTION,
    ACTUATION
    in polite society ....
    ETIQUETTE
    science of ..... ETHOLOGY
behead .... DECAPITATE,
    DECOLLATE
behemoth .... BEAST,
    HIPPO(POTAMUS), ELEPHANT
behest ..... ORDER, BIDDING,
    COMMAND
behind .... ABAFT, LATE,
    ASTERN, (A)REAR
    colloquial ..... BUTTOCKS
    time(s) .... PASSE,
    OUTMODED, LATE, OVERDUE,
    TARDY
behold! .... SEE, LO, VOILA
    Latin .... ECCE
beholden .... INDEBTED,
    OBLIGED
behoove .... INCUMBENT
beige .... ECRU, GRAYISH TAN
being .... LIFE, EXISTENCE,
    CREATURE, ENTITY
    abstract ...... ENS, ENTIA
    actual .... ESSE
    essential .... ENS
    individual .... MONAD
Beirut is capital of .. LEBANON
bejewel .... BEGEM
Bela Lugosi's pet .... BAT
belabor .... BEAT, WHIP,
    ATTACK, POUND
belated .... TARDY
belay ... SECURE, HOLD, STOP
belaying cleat ...... BOLLARD,
    KEVEL
belch ...... EMIT, ERUCT(ATE),
    VOMIT, BURP
beldam .... HAG, CRONE,
    ALECTO, MEGAER, ERINYES
beleaguer .... BESIEGE,
    SURROUND

beleaguerment .... SEIGE
Belem is capital of ..... PARA
belemite ..... THUNDERSTONE
belfry .... BELL TOWER
   dweller .... BAT
Belgian .... WALLOON,
     FLEMING, FLEMISH
   canal .... YSER
   capital .... BRUSSELS
   city ...... MONS, GHENT,
     LOUVAIN, MALINES,
     TOURNAI, ARLON, YPRES,
     SPA, ALOST, JEMAPPES,
     ROULERS, HUY, LIEGE,
     BRUGES
   commune .... TAMINES,
     NAMUR, JETTE, VORST, SPA,
     LEDE, ROUX, ANS, ATH,
     NIEL
   Congo river ...... UELE
   currency unit ..... BELGA
   dog .... SCHIPPERKE
   fascist party .... REX
   hare .... LEPORID
   king, former .. BAUDOUIN,
     ALBERT, LEOPOLD
   marble ... RANCE, RANSE
   police .... GENDARME
   port .... OSTEND
   possession, former ......
     CONGO
   province .... LIEGE,
     NAMUR, LIMBOURGE
   queen .... ASTRID
   reclaimed land ... POLDER
   resort ...... SPA, OSTEND
   river .... LYS, YSER,
     SENNE, MEUSE, SAMBRE,
     SCHELDE, OISE
   rodent .... LEPORID
   seaport .... OSTEND,
     ZEBRUGGE
   statesman .... SPAAK
   textile center .... GHENT
   town .... YPRES
   violinist .... YSAYE
   watering place ..... SPA
Belgrade .... BEOGRAD
   is capital of .. YUGOSLAVIA
Belial .... ANGEL, SATAN
belie .... DENY, DISPROVE,
   DISGUISE
belief .... CONVICTION,
   FAITH, TRUST, OPINION,
   CREED, ISM, DOCTRINE,
   CREDENCE

based on .... DOXIC
beyond ..... INCREDIBLE
in ghosts ..... EODOLISM
in one god ...... THEISM
beliefs, set of .. CREDO, CREED
believe .... SUPPOSE, EXPECT,
   TRUST, ASSUME, CREDIT
believer .... IST, DEIST
   easy .... GULLIBLE,
     CREDULOUS
   in god ..... THEIST, DEIST
   in spirits .... ANIMIST
   of all religions ... OMNIST
believing .... CREANT
belittle .... SLIGHT,
   DEPRECIATE, DISPARAGE,
   DEMEAN, KNOCK
Belize is capital of ....
   HONDURAS
bell .... CAMPANA,
   CARILLON, GONG, BELLOW,
   ROAR
   alarm .... TOCSIN
   call to prayer ... ANGELUS
   clapper .... TONGUE
   flower ..... CAMPANULA,
     RAMPION
   jar .... CLOCHE
   man .... RINGER,
     (TOWN)CRIER
   ring by hammer .. CHIME
   ringer .... SEXTON
   ringing device .... CHIME
   striker .... HAMMER,
     CLAPPER
   sound ...... DONG, PEAL,
     TING, CLANG, RING,
   TING-A-LING, KNELL, TOLL
   shaped glass jar .. CLOCHE
   tongue .... CLAPPER
   tower .... BELFRY,
     COMPANILE
   town in story .... ADANO
belladonna .... NIGHTSHADE,
   MANICON
   alkaloid .... ATROPIN(E)
   drug .... ATROPIN(E)
   lily .... AMARYLLIS
bellboy ..... PAGE, BELLHOP,
   BUTTONS
   call to .... FRONT
   colloquial ...... BUTTONS
belle .... BEAUTY
   of the West ...... STARR
belles-lettres ..... LITERATURE

bellhop . . . . BELLBOY,
 CALLBOY, BUTTONS
  call . . . . FRONT, BELL
bellicose . . . . HOSTILE,
 WARLIKE, BELLIGERENT
belligerence . . . . WAR,
 BELLICOSITY
belligerent . . . . WARLIKE,
 BELLICOSE, PUGNACIOUS,
 PROTAGONIST, CONTENTIOUS,
 AGGRESSIVE, QUARRELSOME
  right of a . . . . ANGARY
Bellini . . . . PAINTER
  pupil . . . . TITIAN
  son . . . . GENTILE,
 GIOVANNI
Bellini's (Vincenzo) opera . . . .
 NORMA
Bellona's brother . . . . MARS
bellow . . . . ROAR, WAIL, BELL
bellows . . . . BLOWER
bells, set of . . . . CARILLON,
 CHIME(S)
bellwether . . . . SHEEP, LEADER
belly . . . . . ABDOMEN, BAGGIE,
 WOMB, STOMACH, BULGE,
 WAME, VENTER
  laugh . . . . GUFFAW,
 ROAR, CHORTLE
  near/on the . . . . VENTRAL
  protruding . . . . . PAUNCH,
 BAY WINDOW
bellyache: colloq. . . . . . GRIPE,
 COMPLAIN
bellyband . . . . . . GIRTH, CINCH
bellybutton . . . . NAVEL
bellyful . . . . SURFEIT
belong . . . . APPERTAIN,
 PERTAIN
belonging to certain people . . .
 NATIVE, ENDEMIC,
 INDIGENOUS
belongings . . . . POSSESSION,
 PROPERTY, CHATTEL
beloved . . . . DARLING, LIEF
  physician . . . . LUKE
below . . . . (BE)NEATH,
 (UNDER)NEATH, ALOW
  combining form . . HYP(O)
  the belt . . . . FOUL
belt . . . . BAND, GIRDLE, AREA,
 BLOW, CUFF, CORDON,
 SASH, STRAP, CESTUS, OBI,
 BALDRIC, CINGULUM,
 CINCTURE, ZOSTER
  below the . . FOUL, UNFAIR

  case . . . . HOLSTER
  fancy . . . . SASH
  imaginary, heavenly . . . . .
 ZODIAC
  tighten . . . . . ECONOMIZE,
 RETRENCH
  sword . . . . BALDRIC
Beltane . . . . MAYDAY
beluga . . . . STURGEON,
 DOLPHIN, WHALE,
 WHITEFISH
  roe/eggs . . . . CAVIAR
belvedere . . . . SUMMERHOUSE,
 GALLERY, PAVILION
bema . . . . PLATFORM,
 CHANCEL
bemoan . . . . LAMENT,
 DEPLORE, WAIL,
bemuse . . . . MUDDLE,
 CONFUSE, STUPEFY
ben . . . . . SON, PEAK, PARLOR
  relative . . . . IBN
bench . . . . SEAT, GALLERY,
 SETTEE, WORKTABLE,
 COURT, EXEDRA, PEW
  judges' . . . . BANC
  in sports . . . . . . SIDELINE
  the . . . . JUDICIARY
  tool . . . . VISE
bend . . . . CROOK, CROFT,
 FLEX(URE), ARCH, BOW,
 STOOP, YIELD, WALE, KINK
  and bob . . . . NID
  as of light, heat . . . .
 REFRACT
  back . . . . REFLEX
  in adoration . . . . . . KNEEL
  in stream . . . . HOOK
  in timber . . . . SNY
  inward . . . . . INTROVERT
  knee in worship . . . .
 GENUFLECT
  light wave . . . . . . REFRACT
  sinister . . . . BATON
  the arm . . . . FLEX
bender . . . . SPREE, ORGY,
 WASSAIL
bending . . . BIGHT, FLECTION,
 FLEXION
bends, having two . . . . . BIFLEX
  the . . . . CRAMPS
bendy . . . . OKRA
bene . . . . (WILD)HOG,
 PRAYER, BOON
  vale . . . . FAREWELL
beneath . . . . . . BELOW, UNDER

combining form .. HYP(O)
benedict, former ... BACHELOR,
CELIBATE
Benedictine .... LIQUEUR,
MONK, NUN
benediction .... BLESSING,
INVOCATION, GRACE,
BENISON
benefaction .... BOON
benefactor .... PATRON
benefic .... KINDLY,
CHARITABLE
benefice, appoint to a ....
COLLATE
first income of .... ANNAT
holder ... APPROPRIATOR
of a sort ...... SINECURE
revenue ...... ANNAT(E)S
temporary .. COMMENDAM
beneficial .... BENIGN
benefit ...... FAVOR, PROFIT,
AVAIL, SAKE, HELP
benevolent .... KIND, HUMANE,
CHARITABLE
order .... ELKS
Bengal bison .... GAUR
capital .... CALCUTTA
city .... PATNA
cotton .... ADATI
grass .... MILLET
groom .... SAICE
light .... FIREWORK
native .... BENGALI,
KOL, BANIAN
benighted .... LOST
benign .... KIND(LY),
FAVORABLE, BENEFICIAL
benison .... BLESSING,
BENEDICTION
benjamin .... GUM, BENZOIN,
FAVORITE SON
Benjamin's father ..... JACOB
son ...... ROSH, ARD, EHI
Benjamin Franklin's musical
instrument ....
HARMONICA
benne .... SESAME
bennet ... VALERIAN, HEMLOCK
bent .... INCLINATION,
GRASS, TASTE, CROOKED,
SET, CURVED, BOUND,
FLAIR, APTITUDE,
PROPENSITY
backward ..... RETRORSE
like a knee .. GENICULATE
Bentley's sleuth .... TRENT

benumb .... HEBETATE
benzedrine .... INHALANT,
STIMULANT
benzene .... BENZOL,
SOLVENT
Beograd .... BELGRADE
Beowulf, monster slain by ....
GRENDEL
bequeath .. WILL, HAND DOWN,
ENDOW, LEAVE
bequest .... LEGACY,
INHERITANCE, HERITAGE,
ENDOWMENT
berate ...... SCOLD, REBUKE,
UPBRAID
Berber .... MOSLEM, RIFF,
HAMITE, TUAREG, KABYLE
chief .... CAID
dialect .... TUAREG
hermit .... MARABOUT
tribe .... RIFF, DAZA
tribesman ..... KABYLE
berceuse .... LULLABY
bereave ...... DEPRIVE, STRIP,
ROB
bereavement .... LOSS,
DEPRIVATION
expression of ....
CONDOLENCE
bereft ..... LORN, DEPRIVED,
LONELY
beret .... CAP, BIRETTA
berg .... ICE
bergamot .... PEAR,
HORSEMINT, MONARDA
Bergen's Mortimer .... SNERD
Berger, singer .... ERNA
Bergerac's sore point ... NOSE
Bergman, Miss ...... INGRID
beriberi .... DROPSY
Japanese .... KAKKE
medicine ..... THIAMIN(E)
Bering Sea river ...... YUKON
Berkshire .... HOG
county seat ..... READING
race course ..... ASCOT
Berlin ..... CARRIAGE, CITY,
CAPITAL, SONGWRITER
district .... SPANDAU
hit .... REMEMBER
prison .... SPANDAU
river .... SPREE
sight .... WALL
songwriter ...... IRVING
berm .... LEDGE, TERRACE
Bermuda capital ... HAMILTON

arrowroot ...... ARARAO
grass ...... DOOB, DOUB
product .... ONION
to pleasure seekers .....
    PLAYGROUND
Bern is capital of ....
    SWITZERLAND
Bernese Alps mountain ......
    WETTERHORN
bernicle .... GOOSE
berry ...... TOMATO, GRAPE,
    BANANA, CURRANT, BOCCA,
    ACINUS, ALLSPICE,
    MADRONA
    branch .... CANE
    cigarette .... CUBEB
    combining form ... BACCI
    fragrant .... MYRTLE
    grape .... ACINUS
    like .... BACCATE
    slang .... DOLLAR
bersagliere .... RIFLEMAN,
    SHARPSHOOTER
berserk .... AMOK, AMUCK,
    BARESARK
berseem .... CLOVER
Bert ____ ..... LAHR, PARKS
berth .... ANCHORAGE,
    BED, BUNK, PLACE
    Pullman car ..... LOWER,
    UPPER
Bertha .... COLLAR
    "Big" .... CANNON
beryl .... EMERALD,
    AQUAMARINE, MINERAL,
    MORGANITE
beseech ...... PRAY, ENTREAT,
    PLEAD, IMPLORE, BEG,
    SOLICIT
beset ...... ATTACK, HARRY,
    HARASS, STUD, PESTER,
    OBSESS
beshow .... SABLEFISH
beshrew: archaic ..... CURSE
beside ..... NEAR, CLOSE, BY
    prefix .... PARA, PAR
    oneself ... MAD, ANGRY,
    SORE
besides ..... MOREOVER, ELSE,
    EXCEPT, ALSO, TOO
besiege .... OVERWHELM,
    BESET, CROWD, HARASS,
    BELEAGUER, INVEST
besiegers' explosive ... PETARD
    protective cover ......
    MANT(E)LET

besmirch .... STAIN, TARNISH,
    SULLY, SOIL, DIRTY, DEFAME
besom .... BROOM
bespangle .... STUD,
    DECORATE, STAR
bespatter ...... SOIL, SMEAR,
    SPLASH
bespeak ..... RESERVE, SHOW
Bessemer process product ....
    STEEL
best .... EXCELLENT, UTMOST,
    DEFEAT, OUTWIT
    colloquial .... TOPFLIGHT
    combining form .. ARISTO
    man at wedding .....
    PARANYMPH
    part ...... ELITE, CREAM,
    MEAT, FLOWER
    seller .... HIT
bestial .... BRUTISH, BRUTAL,
    SAVAGE, VILE, ANIMAL
bestiary book author .. BORGES
bestow .... GIVE, AWARD,
    CONFER, DEVOTE
bestrew .... SCATTER
bestride .... STRADDLE
bet .... WAGER, STAKE,
    PROPOSITION, GAMBLE,
    PARLAY
    against card dealer .....
    PUNT
    colloquial ... CANDIDATE,
    ENTRY
    fail to pay .... WELSH
    in an election ....
    CANDIDATE
    in roulette .... BAS
    sure win ..... IN THE BAG
    to win in horse race ....
    ON THE NOSE
    without odds ...... ITOI
    you! .... CERTAINLY,
    YES INDEED
betake .... GO, JOURNEY,
    REPAIR
Betancourt .... MONK, CURATE
bete noire .... OUTCAST,
    PARIAH, LEPER, BUGBEAR
    of nursery .... CROUP
betel ..... SIRI, PEPPER, PLANT
    leaf .... BUYO, PAN
    nut ..... SERI, CATECHU
    palm ... ARECA, PINANG
    pepper ..... ITMO, IKMO
Betelgeuse .... STAR
bethel ...... CHURCH, CHAPEL

betide ..... HAPPEN, BEFALL, OCCUR
betimes .... EARLY, QUICKLY, PROMPTLY, SOON
betoken .... DENOTE, FORESHOW, AUGUR, INDICATE
beton .... CONCRETE
betray .... DECEIVE, REVEAL, SELL, VICTIMIZE
betrayal .... PERFIDY
betrayer .... TRAITOR, SEDUCER, DECEIVER
Biblical .... JUDAS (ISCARIOT)
betroth .... AFFIANCE, ENGAGE, PLIGHT, AFFY
betrothed person ..... FIANCE, FIANCEE
Betsy: sl. .... GUN, GAT, EQUALIZER
better .... IMPROVE, OUTDO, AMEND, SURPASS
half: colloq. .... WIFE
looking .... CUTER, HANDSOMER
betting system ...... PARLAY, PARI-MUTUEL
another way: colloq. .... ROLL
loser's ... MARTINGAL(E)
between .... MIDDLE, INTERMEDIATE, BETWIXT
in law .... MESNE
meals treat .. SNACK, SODA
prefix ... INTER, DIA, META
betwixt and between .. MIDDLE
Bevan's nickname .... NYE
bevel ... EDGE, BEZEL, SLANT, CANT
out .... REAM
ship timber ...... SNAPE
to join ..... MITER, MITRE
beveled angle/surface .. SPLAY
beverage ..... DRINK, COFFEE, ADE, ALE, TEA, SOUR, WINE, TOKAY, SAKE, MATE, KAVA, BOZA, LEBAN, NOG(G), EGGNOG
add liquor to ...... LACE
almond flavored .... RATAFIA
beer-lemonade .. SHANDY
brandy, sugar, spice ..... TODDY
carbonated ... POP, SODA

Christmas ..... EGGNOG
fermented .. SAKE, MEAD
from leaves .... TEA
from meat extract ...... BEEF TEA
from molasses ..... RUM
fruit (crushed) ... SMASH
hot milk .... POSSET
palm sap .... TODDY
sour ... LIME, LEMONADE
vermouth, etc. ... BRONX
wine .... VERMOUTH, NEGUS, BISHOP
with anise ...... KUMMEL
beverages, place for .... CELLAR(ET), BAR
bevy .... FLOCK, COVEY
bewail ..... MOURN, LAMENT, COMPLAIN, GRIEVE, DEPLORE
beware ...... GUARD, WATCH
bewilder ... PUZZLE, MYSTIFY, CONFUSE, STUMP, PERPLEX, DAZE
bewildering .... MAZY
bewitch .... ENCHANT, FASCINATE, CHARM, HEX, ENTRANCE
bewitchment .... SPELL
bey .... DEY, GOVERNOR
Beyoglu .... PERA
beyond .... PAST, YONDER, EXCEEDING, LATER
combining form .. ULTRA, META, SUR, PARA
compare ...... PEERLESS
reach ... UNATTAINABLE, INACCESSIBLE
Beyrouth .... BEIRUT
bezant .... COIN, BALLET
bezel .... FACET, FLANGE, TEMPLATE, RIM
bhang .... HEMP
Bhutan capital (summer) ...... TASHI-CHHO
capital (winter) .... PUNAKHA
people .... BHOTIYA
pine .... KAIL
ruler ...... MAHARAJA(H)
Bialystok .... BELOSTOK
Biafran leader ...... OJUKWU
biannual .... BIENNIAL, SEMIANNUAL
bias .. PARTIALITY, PREJUDICE, INFLUENCE, TENDENCY
biased ... PARTIAL, ONE-SIDED,

UNFAIR, NARROW-MINDED,
PREJUDICED

person . . . . BIGOT

bib . . . DRINK, IMBIBE, TIPPLE,
APRON, NAPKIN, DICKEY

and tucker . . . . . CLOTHES

companion of . . . TUCKER

bibb . . . . BIBCOCK

bibber . . . . . . DRINKER, TOPER,
TIPPLER

bibcock . . . . BIBB, FAUCET

bibelot . . CURIO, BRIC-A-BRAC,
VIRTU, ARTIFACT, VERTU

Bible books of New Testament
MATTHEW, MARK, LUKE,
JOHN, ACTS, ROMANS,
CORINTHIANS, GALATIANS,
EPHESIANS, PHILIPPIANS,
COLOSSIANS, TIMOTHY,
THESSALONIANS, TITUS,
PHILEMON, HEBREWS,
JAMES, PETER, JUDE,
REVELATION

books of Old Testament
GENESIS, EXODUS,
LEVITICUS, NUMBERS,
JOSHUA, JUDGES, RUTH,
DEUTERONOMY, SAMUEL,
KINGS, CHRONICLES,
EZRA, ESTHER,
JOB, PSALMS, PROVERBS,
ISAIAH, AMOS, JEREMIAH,
LAMENTATIONS, EZEKIEL,
DANIEL, JOEL, HOSEA,
OBADIAH, JONAH, MICAH,
NAHUM, HAGGAI,
ZECHARIAH, MALACHI,
NEHEMIAH, ZEPHANIAH

reading . . . . PSALM

the . . . . HOLY WRIT,
SCRIPTURES

translator . . . . . ULFILA(S)

version . . . . . . VULGATE,
PESHITO, DOUAY,
APOCRYPHA, DOUAI

biblical . . . . SCRIPTURAL

armies . . . . SABAOTH

ascetic order . . . . . ESSENE

boat . . . . ARK

character . . . BOAZ, ESAU,
EZRA, NOAH, AMOS,
HEROD, HAGAR,
AARON, NAOMI, RUTH,
PILATE, ABEL, CAIN, JONAH,
ELIAS, ENOS, HAMAN, PELEG,
LEAH, JOSIAH, TOBIT, LABAN

charioteer . . . . JEHU

city . . . . . GOLM, BABEL,
DAN, AVEN, EKRON, RESEN,
GATH, GAZA, SODOM,
HEBRON, ZOAR

coin . . . TALENT, SHEKEL

cony . . . . HYRAX

country . . . . CANAAN,
CHALDEA, EDOM, SHEBA,
SEIR, PUL, ENON, SEBA

curser . . . . BALAAM

desert . . . . PARAN

expression . . . . SELAH

flight . . . . EXODUS

food . . . . MANNA

giant . . . . GOLIATH, ANAK,
ENIM

gift-bearer(s) . . . . . MAGI,
GASPAR, MELCHOR

Hades . . . . SHEOL

hill . . . . ZION

hosts . . . . SABAOTH

hunter . . . ESAU, NIMROD

judge . . . . HEROD, ELI,
GIDEON, ELON, SOLOMON

king . . . SAUL, OMRI, OG,
AGAG, ASA, AHAB, HEROD,
BERA, NADAB, ELAH, AMON

kingdom . . . ELAM, MOAB,
SAMARIA, SHEBA

land . . . . . NOD, GOSHEN,
EDOM, TOB

language . . . . ARAMIC

length measure . . . . . REED

liar . . . . ANANIAS,
SAPPHIRA

lion . . . . ARI

lyrelike instrument . . . . . .
SACKBUT

mass migration . . EXODUS

measure . . . OMER, CUBIT,
EPHA(H), SHEKEL, KOR,
GERAH, BEKA

merchant . . . . TUBAL

mount . . . . . . ABLA, HOR,
EBAL, NAIN, PEOR, HOREB,
NEBO, SIER, SINAI, TABOR,
ARARAT, GILEAD, OLIVET

name . . . . . . ARAM, AROM,
EBAL, EBED, GADDI, ONO,
ANIM, REBA, ASOM, IVAH,
REBA, AMASA, AHIRA,
ABIAM, MAGOG, ISHMAEL,
VASHTI, UR, MERAB, HELI,
IRAD, IRA, ELAH

ornament . . . . URIM

passage used .... TEXT
patriarch ... ADAM, ENOS,
NOAH, SETH, SHEM, ABRAM,
JOB, ISAAC, JACOB, PELEG,
TERAH, LAMECH, JARED,
REU
place .... ENDOR, ENON,
SHILOH, JORDAN
place of torment ....
GEHENNA
pool .... SILOAM
precious stone .. JACINTH,
LIGURE
priest .... ELI, LEVI,
AARON, ANNAS
promised land .. CANAAN
prophet ... AMOS, EZRA,
JOEL, HOSEA, JONAH,
MICAH, MOSES, ELISHA,
ISAIAH, DANIEL,
JEREMIAH, EZEKIEL
queen .... SHEBA,
ESTHER, VASHTI
rich man .... DIVES
river ..... JORDAN, NILE,
ABANA, ARNON
sacred objects .... URIM
scribe .... BARUCH
serpent ..... NEHUSHTAN
sheep-owner ..... NABAL
shepherd .... ABEL
skipper .... NOAH
spice .... STACTE
spring .... AIN, ESEC,
SILOAM
spy .... CALEB
stopping place ... MARAH
tax collector ... MATTHEW
temptress .... EVE,
DELILAH
thief .... BARABBAS
timber .... ALMUG
tower ...... BABEL, EDAR
town ..... ENDOR, CANA,
NAIN, BETHEL
tree ...... ALGUM, ALMUG
tribe .... AMON
valley .... NEMEA,
BACA, SIDDIM, ELAH
verb ending .... ETH
vineyard owner .. NABOTH
wanderer .... CAIN
weed .... TARE
well ..... AIN, ESEK, ESEC
wild ox .... REEM
wise men ...... MAGI

word .... SELAH,
MENE, RACA
bibliographer's abbr. ... OBED
bibliotheca .... LIBRARY,
CATALOG(UE)
bibulous .... DRUNK,
ABSORBENT, ALCOHOLIC
festival .... ALE,
BACCHANALIA
party .... WASSAIL
person .... SOT,
TIPPLER, DRUNKARD,
BACCHANT, TOPER
bicarbonate ... SODA, BICARB
bice .... PIGMENT, BLUE,
VERDITER
bicephalous .... TWO-HEADED
bicker .... CAVIL, ARGUE,
WRANGLE, QUARREL,
SQUABBLE, GURGLE, DISPUTE
bicuspid .... TOOTH
bicycle .... BIKE, VELOCIPEDE
rider's seat ..... SADDLE
two-seater ...... TANDEM
bid .... TENDER, ASK,
COMMAND, OFFER
OVERTURE
in bridge .. DECLARATION
return .... RECALL
bidarka .... CANOE
bidding .... COMMAND,
REQUEST, SUMMONS,
INVITATION, (BE)HEST
biddy .... HEN, CHICKEN
bide .... STAY, CONTINUE,
WAIT, DWELL, RESIDE
bield .... SHELTER
bienvenue .... WELCOME
bier ... COFFIN, CATAFALQUE,
PYRE, FERETORY, HEARSE,
LITTER
bifacial ... TWO-FACED, JANUS
biff ... CUFF, HIT, STRIKE, BOX
biffin .... APPLES
bifid .... FORKED, CLEFTED
bifurcate .... FORKED,
BRANCHED
big .... LARGE, LOUD,
IMPRESSIVE, POMPOUS,
HUGE, NOBLE, SIZABLE,
MAN-SIZE
and clumsy .. LUBBER(LY),
HULKING
and strong ...... BURLY,
BRAWNY, HUSKY
Ben .... CLOCK

Ben's place ...... TOWER, LONDON
Bertha .... CANNON
Bertha, where cast ...... ESSEN
casino .... TEN
Dipper ..... URSA MAJOR
Five member, WWI ..... JAPAN, ITALY, FRANCE
Five member, WWII .... CHINA, FRANCE, RUSSIA
Horn .... MOUNTAIN, RIVER
house: sl. .... PRISON
shot: sl. .... BIGWIG, BRASS, VIP, FATCAT
show: sl. .... THREE RING CIRCUS
teethed .... MACRODONT
toe .... HALLUX
toe ailment .... GOUT, BURSITIS
top .... CIRCUS, TENT(ROOF)
tree .... SEQUOIA, REDWOOD
with child .... PREGNANT
bighead .... CONCEIT, EGOTISM
biggin: Brit. ..... CAP, HOOD
bighorn ...... SHEEP, ARGALI
bight ... LOOP, GULF, CORNER, HOLLOW, FORK, CURVE, BAY
bignonia tree ..... CALABASH
bigot .... ZEALOT
bigwig: colloq. ..... TOPBRASS, VIP, FATCAT
Oriental .... AGA
Bihar's capital .... PATNA
bijou ...... TRINKET, JEWEL
bike: colloq. .... BICYCLE
Bikini .... ATOLL
on the beach .. SWIMSUIT
bilateral .... RECIPRÓCAL, TWO-SIDED
bilbo ..... SHACKLES, RAPIER
bile ... GALL, CHOLER, ANGER, BITTERNESS, TEMPER
black ...... MELANCHOLY
combining form .... CHOL(O), CHOLE
yellow .... CHOLER
bilestone .... GALLSTONE
bilge .... BULGE, SWELL
slang .... NONSENSE
bilingual .... DIGLOT

bilious ...... CROSS, LIVERISH, BITTER, BAD-TEMPERED, GREEN
bilk .... SWINDLE(R), DEFRAUD, CHEAT(ER), DECEIVE, GYP
bill .... DUN, NÉB, BEAK, TAB, STATEMENT, POSTER, HALBERD, LIST, ROAR, BELLOW, WILLIAM
and coo .... KISS, PET
fill the ..... QUALIFY, SUIT
five-dollar .... VEE
foot the .... PAY
joker in a .... RIDER
of exchange ..... DRAFT
of exchange dealer ...... CAMBIST
of fare .... MENU, CARTE
of lading ... CARGO LIST
of Rights .... MAGNA CHARTA
part of .... NEB, CERE
pass thru mutual aid .... LOGROLL
stroke with ...... PECK, PREEN
one dollar .... BUCK
two dollar ...... DEUCE
ten dollar .... SAWBUCK, TENNER
100 dollar ...... C-NOTE, CENTURY
1000 dollar ...... GRAND
billboard .... SIGNBOARD, HOARDING, POSTER
billet .... QUARTER(S), LODGING, POSITION
doux ..... (LOVE)LETTER
billfish .... GAR, SKIPPER, SAILFISH, SPEARFISH
billfold .... WALLET, CASE, POCKETBOOK
billhead .... LETTERHEAD
billiards ball .... IVORY
red ball ..... CARAMBOLA
shot ..... CAROM, MASSE
stick .... CUE
billing .... LISTING, DUNNING
billingsgate lingo ...... FOUL, VULGAR, ABUSIVE
billion .... MILLIARD
billow ... WAVE, SHELL, BORE, EAGRE, SURGE, ROLL
billy ...... CLUB, TRUNCHEON, STICK, CAN, KETTLE

billycock .... HAT, DERBY
bilsted ..... TREE, SWEET GUM
Bimini legend ....
    FOUNTAIN OF YOUTH
bimonthly .... BIMENSAL
bin .... BOX, RECEPTACLE
    fish .... KENCH
    fodder .... CRATCH
    for ship's coal, fuel oil ...
    BUNKER
    storage .... HUTCH
binal .... TWOFOLD
binate .... DOUBLE
binaural .... STEREO
bind ..... TIE, ATTACH, TAPE,
    ROPE, HOLD, GIRD, SECURE
    matrimonially .. MARRY,
    WED
    mouth .... GAG
    together by rope ... FRAP
    wound .... BANDAGE
binder ... BAND, CORD, ROPE,
    BALER
binding .... OBLIGATORY,
    BANDAGE, BAND
    device .... CONTRACT
    machine .... BALER
    substance .... TAR,
    GLUE, PASTE
bindle stiff ..... HOBO, TRAMP
bine .... STEM, HOP
binge .... SPREE, BENDER,
    LARK, ORGY, WASSAIL
bingo ... LOTTO, BEANO, KENO
binocle .... TELESCOPE,
    FIELD GLASS, OPERA GLASS
biocatalyst .... VITAMIN,
    HORMONE
biographical sketch .. PROFILE
biography .... LIFE STORY,
    MEMOIR
biological .... BIOTIC(AL)
    change .... MUTATION
    division .... GENERA
    factor .... GENE
    group .... SPECIES
    reproductive cell ......
    GAMETE
biology, branch of ....
    GENETICS
    of behavior .. ETHOLOGY
Bion .... POET
    opposed to ... MORPHON
bionomics .... ECOLOGY
biped ...... MAN, TWO-FOOTED
birch .... BETULA,

HORNBEAM, IRONWOOD,
HAZELNUT, WHIP, BIRK,
    CANE, ALDER
bird .... FLYER, CROW,
DOVE, PARROT, MYNA, RAIL,
    SHRIKE, KIWI, SWAN
    adjutant .... STORK,
    MARABOU, ARGALA
    African .... COLY, LORY,
    LOURI, TURAKOO, UMBER,
    UMBRETTE
    air route .... FLYWAY
    albatross .... NELLY
    American .... JUNCO,
    TOWHEE, RHEA
    Andean .... CONDOR
    apteryx .... IAO, KIWI
    aquatic .... LOON, AUK,
    GOOSE, DUCK, PELICAN,
    SWAN, GULL, SCAUP,
    PENGUIN
    Arctic .... FULMAR,
    XEMA, LONGSPUR
    Asiatic ..... MINA, MYNA,
    PITTA, PITA
    attack ... POUNCE, SWOOP
    auk family ..... PUFFIN,
    ALCA, DOVEKIE, ROTCH(E)
    Australian ... EMU, KOEL,
    COOEE, EMEW, PARDALOTE,
    ARARA, ARA, KAHU,
    LEIPOA, COCKATOO
    baker .... HORNERO
    bastard wing ..... ALULA
    beach ...... SANDERLING
    beak ... LORA, NEB, NIB,
    BILL
    beak part ..... MANDIBLE
    beaky .... TOUCAN
    bell .... MAKO
    big-footed ..... MEGAPOD
    bill .... NEB, BEAK
    bittern .... HERON
    black ...... CROW, ANI,
    RAVEN, ROOK, MERL(E),
    AMSEL, OUSEL, THRUSH,
    GRACKLE
    blue .... JAY, IRENA
    blue-footed .... TITI
    bobolink ...... ORTALAN
    bobwhite .... QUAIL,
    COLIN, PARTRIDGE
    Brazilian ..... CARIAMA,
    SERIEMA, TOUCAN
    bright-colored .. HOOPOE,
    TOURACO, TOUCAN

bristle-billed ..... BARBET
broad-billed .... SCAUP,
DUCK, SPOONBILL
brood ..... COVEY, NIDE
butcher .... SHRIKE
call .... PIPE
caress .... BILL
carrion .... VULTURE,
URUBU, CROW
catcher .... FOWLER
catching at night ....
BATFOWL
chameleonic ....
PTARMIGAN
chatterer .... JAY,
(MAG)PIE, WAXWING,
WHEAT-EATER, STONECHAT,
COTINGA
class of .... AVES
claw-winged ....
HOA(C)TZIN
cockateel .... PARROT
cockatoo .... ARARA
colin .... BOBWHITE
"collar" .. RUFF, TORQUES
colloquial ...... PERSON
colored beak .... PUFFIN
cormorant ..... GUANAY
corvine .... CROW, DAW,
RAVEN
courlan .... JACAMAR,
TINAMOU
crane ...... DEMOISELLE,
SERIEMA
craw .... MAW
crest ... TUFT, CALOT(TE),
COP, HOOD
crested ...... QUE(T)ZAL,
COCKATOO, BLUEJAY,
HOA(C)TZIN
crocodile ... TROCHILUS
crop ...... CRAW, MAW
crow .... CHOUGH,
CORBIE, CORBY
crow-like ...... MAGPIE,
CORVINE, ROOK
cry .... CAW, SHRIEK,
ROAR, WEEP, BELLOW
cuckoo ...... KOEL, ANI,
ANO
disease .... GAPES
diving ..... AUK, GREBE,
DUCKER, DIDAPPER, LOON,
SMEW, ALCIDINE, PUFFIN,
LOOM, OSPREY
dodo .... GEESE

dog .... POINTER, SETTER
duck family ....
MERGANSER, SMEW
duck-like ... COOT, GOOSE
dunlin .... STIB,
SANDPIPER
eagle, sea .... ERN(E)
eagle's nest ...... AERIE,
EYRIE
East Indies ..... SHAMA,
BESRA, PEREGRINE,
REDPOOL, SHAHIN
Egyptian sacred .... IBIS
emu-like .... CASSOWARY
European .... REED,
OUSEL, GLEDE, TEREK,
SEDGE, AMSEL, REDSTART,
WOODCOCK
extinct ..... DODO, MOA,
MAMO, GREAT AUK,
NOTORNIS
eye tissue ...... PECTEN
fabulous .. ROC, PHOENIX
falcon .... MERLIN,
SAKER, TERCEL, BESRA,
PEREGRINE, REDPOOL
feather .... PENNA
feather-legged ... GROUSE
feather under the wing ..
AXILLAR
feathers .... PLUMAGE
feathers near mouth .....
VIBRISSA
feet for perching ....
ENSESSO
fighting ...... AMADAVAT
finch ... SISKIN, TOWHEE,
MORO, SERIN, BUNTING,
CANARY, CARDINAL,
LINNET, SPARROW
finch-like .... GROSBEAK,
CHEWINK
fish-eating .... ERN,
KINGFISHER, OSPREY,
GOOSANDER, LOON,
MERGANSER
fish-hawk ...... OSPREY
flightless .... DODO, MOA,
OSTRICH, PENGUIN, KAGU,
KIWI, AUK, CASSOWARY,
RATITE, APTERYX, WEKA,
RHEA, EM(E)U, NOTORNIS
flock ...... CONVEY, POD
fluid spraying .. HOUBARA
flycatcher .... OSCINE,
PEWEE, KINGBIRD, PHOEBE

footless: heraldry .... MARTLET
for food .... CAPON
forelimb .... WING
fork-tailed ...... PETREL
frigate .... IWA
fruit-eating ..... TOUCAN, PARROT
fulmar .... NELLY
game bird ...... GROUSE, SNIPE, TURNIX
game-killer ..... VERMIN
gluttonous ... CORMORANT
goatsucker ... GUACHARO
gold finch ...... REDCAP
goose .... GANDER
greedy .... CORMORANT
grouse .... BLACKCOCK, GORCOCK
guan .... ORTALIS
gull-like .... TERN, JAEGER, SKUA
gull, pert. to .... LARINE
gull, sea ..... KITTIWAKE, MEW, TERN
harsh-voiced ... MACAW
Hawaiian ... MAMO, IWA, IIWI, OOAA, ALALA
hawk ...... CARACARA, GOSHAWK, KITE, EYAS, KAHU
hawk-like .... OSPREY
heron ...... EGRET, IBIS, BITTERN, SOCO
hind toe .... HALLUX
homing instinct .... ORIENTATION
honey-eating .... TUI, MANUAO, MOHO, IAO
hood-like crest .... CALOT(TE)
house ..... COTE, AVIARY, NEST, NIDE, VOLERY
humming ..... COLIBRI, SYLPH, TROCHILUS, AVE
hunter .... FOWLER
hunting .... FALCON, HAWK
Indian ...... AMADAVIT, SHAMA, SARUS, ARGALA, JACANA
insectivorous ..... VIREO, TODY, HARRIER
jackdaw ...... COR, KAE, DAW

jay-like .... PIET, MOTMOT
killing of .... AVACIDE
kite .... GLEDE
lake .... LOON
lamellirostral .... DUCK, SWAN, GOOSE
lapwing .... WEEP, PEWIT, PLOVER
laughing .. LOON, DACELO GIGAS, KOOKABURRA
large .... EMU, OSTRICH, GUAN, MOA, KITE, JABIRU
large-footed ... MEGAPOD
Latin for .... AVIS
leaf-walker ..... JACANA
leg outgrowth ..... SPUR, CALCAR
leg strap .... JESS
life .... ORNIS
like in appearance ...... ORNITHOID
limicoline ...... AVOCET
long-billed .. NUTHATCH, CREEPER
long-legged ..... AGAMI, STILT, HERON, BUSTARD, EGRET, CRANE, WADER, FLAMINGO, SERIEMA, IBIS
long-necked ...... SWAN, FLAMINGO, CRANE, HERON, EGRET
loon-like .... GREBE
love-making .... BILL AND COO
lyre .... MENURA
magpie .... PIET
male ... COCK, ROOSTER, TOM, GOBBLER, GANDER, BANTAM
marsh .... STILT, RAIL, SORA, BITTERN, COOT, GALLINULE
martin .... MARTLET
meadow .... LARK, BOBOLINK
migratory ...... PLOVER, WHEATEATER, KNOT, SANDPIPER, BOBOLINK, WHIN, WOODCOCK
mina .... STARLING
morepork .... RURU
mound-building .. LEIPOA, MEGAPOD
mouth opening .. RICTUS
mythical ... ROC, PHOENIX
nail of .... CLAW

national .... EAGLE
nest-collector .. OOLOGIST
nocturnal .... OWL,
GOATSUCKER, GUACHARO
noisy .... BLUEJAY
non-flying (see flightless bird)
non-passerine ... HOOPOE,
TODY, KINGFISHER,
HORNBILL
note ..... TWEET, CHIRP,
PIPE
ocean .... FULMAR,
PETREL, ALBATROSS,
MALEMUCK
of Jove .... EAGLE
of Paradise .... APUS
of peace .... DOVE
of prey .... EAGLE,
BUZZARD, ACCIPETER,
GLEDE, ERN(E), HAWK,
KITE, OWL, KESTREL,
ELANET, GOSHAWK,
VULTURE
one-year-old .. ANNOTINE
orange-colored .. ORIOLE
order of .... RASORES
oscine .... CROW,
TANAGER, VIREO, CHAT,
ORIOLE, LARK, SHRIKE,
BUNTING
ostrich-like ..... EM(E)U,
RATITE, RHEA, TINAMOU
owl: Samoan ...... LULU
parakeet .... BUDGIE
parrot .... KAKAM,
KAKAPOS, KEA, COCKATOO,
LORY
parson .... POE, TUI
partridge .... SEESEE,
BOBTAIL, QUAIL
partridge-like .. TINAMOU,
TINAMIDA
passerine ..... SPARROW,
PITA, STARLING, TANAGER
patch on throat .. GORGET
pelican-like ...... SOLAN
perching .... LARK,
BUNTING, SHRIKE, FINCH,
OSCINE
Persian .... BULBUL
pertaining to .... AVIAN,
ORNITHIC, AVINE
Peruvian .... GUANAY
petrel ..... TITI, FULMAR
pewee .... PHOEBE

phoebe ... PEWIT, PEWEE
plover-like .... LAPWING,
KILLDEER
protuberance ..... SPUR,
CALCAR
quail .... BOBWHITE,
PARTRIDGE
queer: colloq. ....
ECCENTRIC, IDIOT(IC),
LOCO
rail .... CRAKE, MOHO,
SORA, COOT, GALLINULE,
SCOTER, SULTANA
rail-like .... COURLAN
rain .... PLOVER
razor-billed .... AUK,
MURRE
rear young ..... FLEDGE
red-eyed .... VIREO
reed .... BOBOLINK
ring-dove .... CUSHAT
robber .... SKUA,
JA(E)GER, DAW
ruffed .... SANDPIPER,
REEVE, GROUSE, PIGEON,
PARTRIDGE
running, swift .. COURSER
sacred .... IBIS
Samoan ..... IAO, LULU
sandpiper .. REEVE, KNOT,
DUNLIN, GREENSHANK
scaup duck .. BLACKHEAD
screamer .... CHAJA
sea ..... ERN(E), GANNET,
GULL, MURRE(LET), SCAUP,
ALBATROSS, TERN, PETREL,
PUFFIN, SCOTER, SKUA,
JAEGER, CORMORANT
seed-eating ...... JUNCO,
GROSBEAK, CHICKADEE,
CANARY, FINCH, CARDINAL,
SPARROW, BUNTING
sheep-killer .... KEA
shore .... AVOCET, SORA,
STILT, WILLET, RAIL, SNIPE,
PLOVER, SANDPIPER,
PRATINCOLE
short-tailed ...... BREVE,
PLOVER
singing .... OSCINE
skin around eye ... ORBIT
small .... TIT, PIPIT,
WREN, TODY, TITMOUSE,
BLUET, CHICKADEE, COSTA,
BIRDIE, FINCH, SYLPH,
PEWEE, VIREO, TOMTIT,

SERIN, VERDIN, COLIBRI,
MANAKIN, SAPPHO
snake .... ANHINGA
snipe .... CURLEW,
DOWITCHER, GODWIT
snipe-like ...... WILLET
song ..... LARK, SHAMA,
BOBOLINK, ROBIN, LINNET,
PIPE, BLUEBIRD, OUZEL
sorrel .... OCA
sound ..... COO, CHIRP,
PEEP, TWEET, SHRIEK,
CROW, HONK, ROAR,
BELLOW, CAW, WEEP,
CHATTER, SCREECH,
TIRALEE, WHOOP, TWITTER,
QUACK
South American ....
TOUCAN, GUAN, WARRIOR,
JACANA, SYLPH, TURCO,
SERIEMA, JACU, TINAMOU,
GUACHARO
space on head ..... LORE
sparrow .... TOWHEE,
BUNTING, PEABODY
starling .... MINA,
MYNA, MINAH
stib .... DUNLIN
stitch .... IHI
stupid .... NODDY,
GOOSE, DODO
swallow .... MARTLET
swallow-like ....
HIRUNDINE, MARTIN, SWIFT
swan .... WHOOPER
swimming .... SWAN,
DUCK, GREBE, LOON,
PHALAROPE
symbolic .... EAGLE,
OWL, STORK, DOVE
tail feathers ..... TRAIN,
RECTRIX
tail hump ... UROPYGIUM
talking .... PARROT,
MINA, MYNA(H)
thief ...... DAW, SKUA,
JA(E)GER, ROOK
three-toed .... STILT,
TURNIX
thrush .... THROSTLE
titmouse ..... BLUECAP,
VERDIN, CHICKADEE
toe .... HALLUX
top of its head ... PILEUM
towhee ...... CHEWINK,
SPARROW

trill .... TIRALEE
tropical ... ANI, BARBET,
JACANA, TROGON,
JACAMAR, TOUCAN, JABIRU
trumpeter .... AGAMI,
(BLACK)SWAN
turkey ... TOM, GOBBLER
turkey-like ... CURASSOW
unfledged .... SQUAB
vulture .... URUBU,
CONDOR
wading .... COOT,
CURLEW, HERON, IBIS,
JACANA, RAIL, WILLET,
CRANE, SORA, AVOCET,
STORK, FLAMINGO,
GALLINULE, STILT, EGRET,
UMBER, BOATBILL, JABIRU,
KILLDEER, SNIPE, UMBRETTE
wag-tail .... PIPIT
warbler ..... REDSTART,
TROCHILUS, BLACKPOLL,
CHICKADEE
water .... HYACINTH,
PELICAN
water-carrier .. ALBATROSS
weaver ... MUNIA, TAHA
web-footed ...... DUCK,
LOON, GOOSE, COOT, AUK
whiskered ...... BULBUL
white-plumed ... EGRET,
SHRIKE
white-tailed ..... ERN(E)
whooper .... SWAN
wing .... PINION
wing-outgrowth ....
CALCAR
wing quills .... FLAG
wing part .... ALULA,
CALCAR, SPUR
with changing color .....
PTARMIGAN
with irregular flight .....
LAPWING, PEWIT
with scalelike feathers ...
PENGUIN
woman .... AVIATRIX
woodpigeon .. RINGDOVE
yellowhammer ... FINCH,
CUCKOO, FLICKER
young ..... FLEDGLING,
OWLET, EAGLET, EYAS,
CHICK, GOSLING, NESTLING
birds .... AVES
breeding place ....
ROOKERY, HERONRY

care of ..... AVICULTURE
eggs, study of ... OOLOGY
flight south ... MIGRATION
foot plant .... FERN,
      TREFOIL, VIOLET
of a region .... ORNIS
of singing .... OSCINE
pertaining to .... AVIAN,
      AVINE, ORNITHIC
raising of ... AVICULTURE
reservation .. SANCTUARY
study of ... ORNITHOLOGY
biretta .... BARRET, CAP,
      BER(R)ET(T)A
birk .... BIRCH
birl .... REVOLVE, WHIRR,
      SPIN
birling .... LOGROLLING
bee .... ROLEO
object of ...... BALANCE
what lumberjacks use for
      LOGS
birr .... ENERGY, FORCE,
      ONRUSH, SPEECH
birth .... NATIVITY,
   GENESIS, ORIGIN, DESCENT,
      BEGINNING
before .... PRENATAL
control advocate ....
      SANGER
control device ....
   CONTRACEPTIVE, PILL
Jesus' .... NATIVITY
of high .... NOBLE
of one's .... NATAL
of two .... BIPAROUS
pains .... LABOR
rate .... NATALITY
root .... TRILLIUM
birthmark ... MOLE, N(A)EVUS
birthright .... HERITAGE,
   INHERITANCE, PATRIMONY
birthstone, January ... GARNET
February ..... AMETHYST
March .... JASPER,
   AQUAMARINE, BLOODSTONE
April .... DIAMOND
May ... EMERALD, AGATE
June .. PEARL, MOONSTONE
July .... ONYX, RUBY
August ...... SARDONYX,
      CARNELIAN
September .... SAPPHIRE
October .... OPAL
November ..... TOPAZ
December ... TURQUOISE,

ZIRCON
birthwort .... CLEMATITE,
      ARISTOLOCHIA
bis ...... TWICE, REPEAT, BI,
      ENCORE
Biscay .... BASQUE
island .... YEU
biscuit ..... WAFER, CRACKER,
   COOKY, SNAP, SCONE,
   POPOVER, RUSK, PANAL,
   BUN, RATAFEE, SIMNEL,
   ZWIEBACK, MACAROON
in ceramics ...... BISQUE
knotted .... PRETZEL
sweetened .... RUSK
bisect .... DIVIDE, FORK
bishop .... PRELATE,
   CHESSMAN, PONTIFF,
      EPARCH
in chess .... ALFIN
of Rome .... POPE
vestment ..... DALMATIC
weed ..... AMMI, GOUT
bishop's assistant ....
   COAD(JUTOR), VERGER
cap ...... HURA, MITRE,
   MITER, MITERWORT
deputy .... VICAR
first year's revenue ......
      ANNAT
lap cloth ...... GREMIAL
letter .... PASTORAL
robe .... CHIMER(E),
      CHIMAR
seat .... BEMA,
   CATHEDRA, SEE
see .... EPISCOPATE
skullcap .... ZUCCHETTO
staff .... CROSIER,
   CROZIER, CROOK
staff bearer ..... VERGER
throne .... CATHEDRA
title ..... PRIMATE, ABBA
vestment .... ROCHET,
   GREMIAL, COPE, SURPLICE
bishopric .... SEE, DIOCESE
bishops collectively ....
      EPISCOPACY
bison .... BUFFALO,
   AUROCHS, BOVINE
crossed with cattle ......
      CATALO
bisque ..... SOUP, ICE CREAM,
      BISCUIT
bissextile .... LEAP YEAR
bistort .... ASTRINGENT

bistro .... WINESHOP, BAR,
 NIGHTCLUB, RESTAURANT,
 CAFE
 habitue .... BARFLY
bit ..... CHECK, CURB, SPECK,
 PIECE, COIN, MOMENT,
 SMALL, BLADE, NIPPED,
 MOTE, WHIT, MORSEL,
 GOBBET
 by bit ...... GRADUALLY
 colloquial ...... STITCH
 holder .... BRACE
 least .... WHIT
 of comic business ... GAG
 of gossip .... TIDBIT
 player .... EXTRA
 small .... NIP
bitch .... SHREW, BRACH
 of Buchenwald ....
  (ILSE) KOCH
 slang .... COMPLAIN,
  BOTCH, SPOIL
bite ... STING, GRIP, CORRODE,
 MOUTHFUL, HOLD, NIP,
 SNACK, MORSEL, NIBBLE
 bit by bit .. GNAW, CHEW,
  MASTICATE
 colloquial .... LUNCH
 down hard ...... CHAMP
 impatiently .... FRET
 off .... CROP
 sharply ..... KNAP, SNAP
 suddenly .... SNAP
 the dust ..... LOSE, FALL
biting .... CUTTING,
 MORDACIOUS, STINGING,
 SHARP, CAUSTIC, NIPPY
Bitolj .... MONASTIR
bits .... ANA
bitstock .... BRACE
bitt .... DECK POST
bitte .... PLEASE
bitter .... ACERB, ACRID,
 GRIEVOUS, HARSH, SEVERE,
 VIRULENT, PAINFUL
 apple ...... COLOCYNTH
 bark .... ANGOSTURA
 cassava product ....
  TAPIOCA
 combining form .. PICRO
 compound .... AMARINE
 cynic .... TIMON
 drug .... ALOE
 feeling .. ACRIMONY,
  HATE, GRUDGE, RANCOR
 flavoring agent .. ASARUM

 herb .... ALOE
 liquid from brine ....
  BITTERN
 nut .... KOLA
 plant substance ... ALUM,
  LUPULIN, ALOIN
 vetch .... ERS
bittern .... SOCO, BIRD
bitterness .... ILL WILL,
 RANCOR, HATE, ACERBITY,
 VILE
bitters: Fr. .... AIGRE
bitterweed .... RAGWEED
bitumen .... PITCH,
 ASPHALT, MALTHA
bivalent .... DIATOMIC
bivalve ...... MOLLUSK, CLAM,
 MUSSEL, SCALLOP, OYSTER,
 QUAHOG, PIDDOCK
bivouac ..... ENCAMP(MENT),
 ETAPE, CAMP
bizarre .... ODD, GROTESQUE,
 QUEER, FANTASTIC, OUTRÉ,
 LURID
Bizet opera .... CARMEN
blab ..... CHATTER, PRATTLE,
 GOSSIP
blabber ..... GOSSIP(MONGER),
 TATTLER
black ..... EBON, SABLE, JET,
 INKY, WICKED, RAVEN,
 COLLY, JET(TY)
 alder .... WINTERBERRY,
  SHRUB
 alloy .... NIELLO
 and-blue .... BRUISED,
  LIVID
 and-tan .... TERRIER,
  DOG, RAT TERRIER
 and-white .... WRITING,
  PRINT, PHOTOGRAPH
 art ..... MAGIC, SORCERY
 bass .... (GAME)FISH
 beer .... DANTZIC
 bile, having .... MOROSE,
  MELANCHOLY
 bird .... CROW, DAW,
  RAVEN
 bread ingredient .... RYE
 buck .... SASIN
 chimney product .. SOOT
 coal .... ATROUS
 coffee .... CAFE NOIR
 combining form ... ATRO,
  MELAN(O)
 country ..... MIDLANDS

cuckoo .... ANI
Death .... (BUBONIC)
                    PLAGUE
diamonds .... COAL
Earth area .... OREL
eye: colloq. ...... SHAME,
    SHINER, DISHONOR, MOUSE
eyed nymph ..... HOURI
eyed pea ...... COWPEA
eyed Susan .... KETMIE,
    (YELLOW) DAISY,
                RUDBECKIA
fever .... KALA-AZAR
fin snapper .... SESI
flag .... JOLLY ROGER
Forest ... SCHWARZWALD
Friar .... DOMINICAN
garnet .... MELANITE
gold .... OIL
gum .... TUPELO, NYSSA,
                PEPPERIDGE
hair and eyes ....
                BRUNET(TE)
Hand .... CAMMORA,
    MAF(F)IA, BLACKMAILERS
haw .... VIBURNUM,
                SHEEPBERRY
hole .... DUNGEON
ink item .... ASSET
knot .... FUNGUS
lead .... GRAPHITE
letter .... UNLUCKY,
                UNFORTUNATE
letter type ..... CAXTON
lustrous .... RAVEN
magic .... SORCERY,
    WITCHCRAFT, VOODOO
make .... NIGRIFY
Maria .. (POLICE)WAGON,
    PATROL WAGON,
                PADDY WAGON
mark .... DISREPUTE
mineral ..... IRIDE, JET,
                    COAL
Monk ..... BENEDICTINE
nightshade .... MOREL
pepper ...... SEASONING
Plague .... BUBONIC
Power leader ... BROWN,
    NEWTON, CARMICHAEL
Prince .... EDWARD
race .... NEGRO
rhinoceros ..... BORELE
Rod .... USHER
rot .... FUNGUS
rust .... FUNGUS

saltwort .... GLAUX
Sea .... EUXINE
Sea city .... ODESSA,
                    YALTA
Sea empire .. TREBIZOND
Sea fish .... HAUSEN
Sea inlet .... AZOV
Sea, of the ...... PONTIC
Sea peninsula ... CRIMEA
Sea port .... VARNA,
                ANAPA, ODESSA
Sea resort .... YALTA
sheep: colloq. ....
    PRODIGAL, BAD ONE
Shirt .... FASCIST, NAZI
silver ...... STEPHANITE
snake .... RACER
suit cards .... SPADES,
                    CLUBS
swan .... TRUMPETER
tea .... BOHEA
tern .... DARR
tie .... BOW,
        (DINNER)JACKET
very .... JETTY
vomit ... YELLOW FEVER
water .... PYROSIS
widow .... SPIDER
wood .... EBONY
blackamoor .... NEGRO
Blackbeard .... PIRATE,
        TEACH, PRIVATEER
blackbeetle ..... COCKROACH
blackberry ... BRAMBLE, BUSH,
                    VINE
blackbird ...... RAVEN, ANI,
    MERL(E), CROW, GRACKLE,
        COWBIRD, THRUSH,
    STARLING, JACKDAW
    European .. OUSEL, OUZEL
blackboard .... SLATE
blackboy .. GRASS TREE, PLANT
blackcap ... BIRD, CHICKADEE,
                RASPBERRY
blackcock .... GROUSE
blackdamp .... GAS
blacken .... JAPAN, SMEAR,
    TAR, INK, SLANDER,
        DARKEN, NIGRIFY,
            DENIGRATE, SOIL
blackened with soot .. COLLIED
blackface ...... BOLD, NEGRO,
                MINSTREL
Blackfeet .... INDIAN
blackfellow: Austral. .. MAORI
blackfin snapper .... SESI

blackfish .... TAUTOG, WHALE, SWART

blackguard .... SCOUNDREL, CAD, VILLAIN, VULGAR, ABUSIVE

blackhead .... DUCK, PIMPLE, PLUG, COMEDO

blackheart .... CHERRY

blackhearted .... WICKED, MALEVOLENT, CRUEL

blacking .... SHOE POLISH

blackjack .... BLUDGEON, MUG, OAK, CARD GAME, TWENTY-ONE

blackleg .... FUNGUS
   British .. STRIKEBREAKER, SCAB, GAMBLER, CROOK, CHEAT

blacklist .... OSTRACIZE

blackly .... ANGRILY, GLOOMILY, MENACINGLY

blackmail .... TRIBUTE, EXTORTION, COERCE, CHANTAGE

blackmailer .... VAMPIRE, MAF(F)IA, CAMMORA

blackness .... NIGRITUDE

blackout .... PASS OUT
   kind of .... FAINT, SWOON
   news ...... CENSORSHIP

blackpoll .... WARBLER, CHICKADEE, REDSTART

blacksmith ... FARRIER, LOHAR
   block .... ANVIL
   chisel .... HARDY
   furnace .... FORGE
   shop .... SMITHY, STITHY
   tool .... FULLER

blacksnake .. RACER, COLUBER

blacktail .... MULEDEER
   fish .... DASSY

blackthorn .. SLOE, HAW, CANE

blacktop ...... TAR, ASPHALT

blackwood ...... BITI, EBONY

blackwort ...... COMFREY

bladder .... BAG, AIR SAC, VESICA
   combining form .. VISICO
   deposit .... CALCULUS

bladdernose .. (HOODED) SEAL

bladderworm ...... HYDATID, CYSTICERCUS

blade ... VANE, RUNNER, LEAF, OAR, SWORD(SMAN),

TOLEDO
   grass .... SPEAR
   in botany .... LAMINA
   leaf .... LAMINA
   sword .... TOLEDO, DAMASCUS

bladebone .... SCAPULA

blah: sl. ..... NONSENSE, ROT

blain ...... BLISTER, PUSTULE, SORE, BULLA

Blake's symbol .... ZOA

blame .... ACCUSE, RAP, CONDEMN, FAULT, CENSURE, CRITICIZE, ACCUSATION, REPROACH

blamed: colloq. ..... DAMNED

blameless .... SPOTLESS, CLEAN, INNOCENT

blanch ..... WHITEN, BLEACH, SCALD, PALE, ETIOLATE

blancmange .... FLUMMERY

bland .... SUAVE, SMOOTH, SOOTHING, MILD, TEMPERATE, SOFT, GENTLE, AFFABLE

blandation .... FLATTERY, BLARNEY

blandish .... FLATTER, CAJOLE, COAX

blank ...... MARKLESS, EMPTY, WHITE, BARREN, UNWRITTEN
   check of a sort ... CARTE BLANCHE
   draw a ...... FAIL, LOSE, ZERO
   in baseball .... SHUTOUT
   in printing .... QUAD
   look ...... POKER FACE
   look, describing one .... VACANT
   sheet in book ... FLYLEAF
   space ..... HIATUS, GAP, VOID

blanket .... COVER, SHEET, OVERSPREAD, AFGHAN
   authority .... FULL POWER(S)
   horse .... MANTA
   Mexican .... SERAPE
   worn as cloak .. PONCHO

blankety-blank .... DAMNED, EXPLETIVE

blare .... BLAZON
   trumpet's ..... FANFARE, TANTARA

blarney .... FLATTERY, WHEEDLE, COAX, SOFT TALK, FLAM

blase .... BORED, WEARY, SATED, SATIATED

blaspheme .... PROFANE, CURSE, REVILE

blasphemous ..... IRREVERENT

blasphemy ...... PROFANITY, IRREVERENCE

blast ..... GUST, EXPLOSION, EXPLODE, BLOW-UP, ATTACK, ERUPTION, SEAR, BLIGHT

furnace .... FORGE, SMELTER

furnace part ...... BOSH, TROMPE, TUYERE, MANTLE

of horn .... TOOT

off step ... COUNT DOWN

sluice .... SOW

blastie: Scot. .... DWARF

blat ..... BLEAT, BLURT, BLAB

blatant .... BOISTEROUS, NOISY, FLASHY, SHOWY, GAUDY, VOCIFEROUS, LOUDMOUTHED

blather .... NONSENSE, FOOLISH TALK

blaubok .... ANTELOPE, ETAAC

blaze ... FLARE, FLAME, FIRE, OUTBURST, FLASH, SHINE

away .... SHOOT, (RAPID)FIRE

on animal's face ... SPOT

star .... NOVA

blazer .... JACKET

blazes, go to ..... BE DAMNED, HELL

blazing star .... COMET, TORCH LILY

blazon .... COAT OF ARMS, DISPLAY, PROCLAIM, EMBLEM, BLARE

bleach .... WHITEN, BLANCH, ETIOLATE, CHLORE, DECOLORIZE

by sunning .... INSOLATE

bleaching powder .. CHLORIDE

vat .... KEIR, KIER

bleak .... TREELESS, BARE, STARK, PALE, COLD, DESOLATE, RAW, GLOOMY, DREAR

blear .... MISTY, BLURRED, BLUR, DIM

eyed .... RHEUMY, DULL-WITTED, TEARY

bleat .... BLAT, MAA, BAA, WHINE

bleater .... SHEEP, LAMB, CRYBABY, GOAT, CALF, WHINER

bleb .... BLISTER, VESICLE, BUBBLE, BULLA

bleed .... SUFFER, OOZE, EXTORT, SUCK

certain way ...... LEECH

white ...... IMPOVERISH

bleeder .. LEECH, HEMOPHILIAC

bleeding, stoppage of .... HEMOSTASIS

stopper ...... HEMOSTAT

uncontrollable .... HEMOPHILIA

bleffert .... SQUALL

blemish ..... DEFECT, FAULT, STAIN, FLAW, MAR, BLOT, MACULATE, TARNISH

cloth .... AMPER

on reputation .. DISHONOR

skin .... NEVUS, NAEVUS, SCAR

blench ...... SHRINK, QUAIL, FLINCH, WHITEN, PALE

blend .... MERGE, FUSE, HARMONIZE, MIX(TURE), MELD

colors .... FONDU

blende ..... SPHALERITE, ORE

blenny .... GUNNEL, SHANNY

blesbok .... ANTELOPE, NUNNI

bless .... HALLOW, CONSECRATE, BEATIFY, ENDOW, GLORIFY, SANCTIFY

against evil ...... SAIN

blessed ...... HOLY, SACRED, BLISSFUL, BEATIFIED

event .... BIRTH

French .... SACRE

Sacrament ... EUCHARIST

blessing .... BENEDICTION, GRACE, APPROVAL, BOON, SAIN, BENISON

at meal .... GRACE

blet .... FRUIT DECAY

blight .... DESTROY, FRUSTRATE, SEAR, RUST, SMUT, MILDEW, NIP, BLAST, RUIN

blighter: Brit. sl. ..... RASCAL, FELLOW, CHAP
blighty: Brit. sl. .... ENGLAND, HOME
blimp: colloq. .... AIRSHIP
blind .... EYELESS, SIGHTLESS, DAZZLE, SEEL, SHUTTER, COVER, RECKLESS
a hawk .... SEEL
alley .... DEADEND, IMPASSE, CUL-DE-SAC
as a ___ .... BAT
bargain ... PIG-IN-A-POKE
daters .... STRANGERS
dolphin .... SUSU
fear .... PANIC
flower-girl .... NIDIA
god ...... HODER, HUTH
impulse .... ATE
love, usually .... INFATUATION
pig: sl. ...... SPEAKEASY
shot .... HIT OR MISS
slang: .... DRUNK
spot .... SCOTOMA
spot: colloq. .. WEAKNESS, IGNORANCE
staggers ... GID, MEGRIM, VERTIGO
tiger: sl. ..... SPEAKEASY
blindage .... CAMOUFLAGE
blinder .... BLINKER, SEEL, WINKER
blinders .... GOGGLES
blindfold .... HOODWINK, MISLEAD, SEEL
blinding light .... GLARE
blindman: Sp. .... CIEGO
blindness .. CECITY, TYPHLOSIS
blindpig .... SPEAKEASY
blinds .... PERSIENNES
blindstory .... GALLERY
blindworm .... ORVET
blink ...... TWINKLE, WINK, IGNORE, BAT, FLUTTER, NICTATE
blinker .... BLINDER, EYE
bliss .... JOY, RAPTURE, ECSTASY, FELICITY
blissful ..... ELYSIAN, JOYOUS
blister ... BULLA, BLEB, BLAIN, VESICATE, VESICLE
beetle ...... SPANISH FLY
causing ...... VESICANT
cloth .... YAW

on neck ..... MALANDERS
blistering agent ... SPISPASTIC, VESICANT
blithe ...... GAY, CHEERFUL, AIRY, MERRY, CHEERFUL
spirit, Shakespearean ... ARIEL
blitz ..... ATTACK, DESTROY, OVERWHELM
blitzkrieg of a sort ..... COUP, COUP D'ETAT, COUP DE MAIN
blizzard .... SNOWSTORM, WINDSTORM
in Alaska .... PURGA
blk. .... BLACK, BLOCK, BULK
bloat .... SWELL, PUFF, DRUNKARD
bloated .... TURGID
blob .... SPLOTCH, DROP, SPLASH
block .... MOLD, OCCLUDE, SPRAG, IMPEDE, HINDER, STONEWALL, DAM
casks' .... QUOIN
for nails on wall .... NOG
go to the ... UP FOR SALE, AUCTION
hawser .... BITT
house .... FORT
ice .... SERAC
mechanical ..... PULLEY
metal .... NUT
of type metal ..... QUAD
of wood .... NOG, DEADEYE, CHUMP
set against wheel ... TRIG
small .... TESSERA
up .... BLOCKADE, STEM, OBSTRUCT, DAM, CHOKE, CLOG
wedge-shaped .... QUOIN
blockade .... ISOLATE, BOTTLE-UP, ROADBLOCK
runner of a sort .... SMUGGLER, CONTRABANDIST
blockhead ..... IDIOT, STOCK, ASS, FOOL, NITWIT, MUTT, NUMSKULL
blocky .... STOCKY, CHUNKY
bloke: sl. .... FELLOW, OAF
blond(e) .... FLAXEN(HAIRED), LACE, WOMAN, TOWHEAD
kind of .... PEROXIDE, PLATINUM
Blonde Bombshell of movies .. HARLOW

blood .... GORE, LIFE, LIFE-FLUID, LINEAGE, KINSHIP, PEDIGREE
accumulation in body .... CONGESTION
bad .... ANIMOSITY, ANGEL, ANTAGONISM
bath ... MASSACRE, PURGE
cancer .... LEUKEMIA
cell .... MONOCYTE
clot ..... GRUME, CRUOR, GORE
clot formation .... THROMBOSIS
clotted .... GORE
carrying .. SANGUIFEROUS
clotting remedy .... HISTONE
color ... RED, SANGUINE
colored .... HEMATIC
coloring matter .. CRUOR, HEMOGLOBIN
combining form .. HEMA, HEM(O), HEMATO, SANGUI, HEMAT, HAEMATO, HAEMO
condition ...... LITHEMIA
congestion .. HYPEREMIA
corpuscle ... MACROYTE, MICROCYTE
corpuscle structure ...... STROMA
coughing ... HEMOPTYSIS
covered/filled with ...... HEMATOSE, GORY
disease ...... LEUKEMIA
emulsion .... CHYLE
escaping from its vessel .. HEMORRHAGE
excess of ..... PLETHORA
feud .... VENDETTA
flow, stoppage of .. STASIS
flowing from wound .... CRUOR, GORE
fluid part of .... PLASMA
formation .... HEMATOSIS
from wound ...... GORE
having to do with ...... H(A)EMIC, H(A)EMAL
kin ..... GENS, RELATIVE
like .... HEMATOID, HEMOID
money .... CRO, WER(E)GILD
movement .... CIRCULATION
of gods .... ICHOR

of the .... HEMIC
oxygen-carrier .... HEMOGLOBIN
particles in .. CORPUSCLES
pertaining to ... HEMATIC
poisoning .. SEPTICEMIA, PY(A)EMIA, SAPR(A)EMIA, SEPSIS, TOXEMIA, COPR(A)EMIA
pressure drug .... ADRENALIN, HISTAMINE
pressure hormone ...... ADRENALIN
pressure instrument ..... MANOMETER
pudding .... SAUSAGE
red .... CRIMSON, SANGUINE
relation .. KIN, RELATIVE, FAMILY, SIB
shed from wound .. GORE
solvent .... LYSIN(E)
spitting .... HEMOPTYSIS
stream foreign matter ... CLOT, (AIR)BUBBLE, EMBOLUS
study of ... HEMATOLOGY
substance in .... OPSONIN
sucker ... LEECH, VAMPIRE
sucking insect .... CONENOSE, TABANID, HORSEFLY, GADFLY, MOSQUITO, FLEA, LOUSE, BEDBUG
sucking monster .. LAMIA
thirsty one .... LEECH, VAMPIRE, LOMIA
transferred to another person ... TRANSFUSION
vessel ... AORTA, ARTERY, VEIN, CAPILLARY
vessel, dilated .... VARIX
vessel obstruction ...... EMBOLISM
vessels network .... RETE
watery part of ... SERUM, SERA
with reduced corpuscles.. AN(A)EMIA
bloodbath .... PURGE, MASSACRE
bloodcurdling .... FRIGHTFUL, TERRIBLE, HORRIFYING, DREADFUL
blooded ..... THOROUGHBRED

bloodhound .... SLEUTH,
HUNTING DOG, MANHUNTER
bloodied .... GORY
bloodily .... SAVAGELY,
CRUELLY
bloodless ... PALE, AN(A)EMIC
bloodletting ...... LEECHING,
BLEEDING, BLOODSHED
art of ..... PHLEBOTOMY
bloodline .... LINEAGE,
PEDIGREE, DESCENT,
ANCESTRY
bloodroot .... PUCCOON,
POPPY, SANGUINARIA
bloodshed .... KILLING,
SLAUGHTER, CARNAGE
much .... GORY
bloodshot .... RED
bloodstone ..... BIRTHSTONE,
HELIOTROPE, HEMATITE
bloodsucker .... LEECH, TICK,
MITE, VAMPIRE, EXTORTER,
PARASITE, FLEA, DEERFLY
bloodthirsty .... CRUEL,
MURDEROUS, PITILESS,
SANGUINARY
bloody .... GORY, CRIMSON
Brit. slang ..... CURSED,
DAMNED, VERY
bloom ..... FLOWER, BLOSSOM,
PRIME, FLOURISH
life's .... HEYDAY
bloomers .... TROUSERS
bloomery ... FURNACE, FORGE,
HEARTH
blooming .... THRIVING,
FLOURISHING
colloquial .... UTTER,
CONFOUNDED
too early .... RATH(E)
blossom ..... FLOWER, BLOOM,
FLOURISH
blot .... STAIN, SPOT,
DISGRACE, EXPUNGE, SULLY,
MACKLE
in printing ..... MACKLE
out ..... ERASE, DELETE,
DESTROY, WIPE OFF
blotch .... STAIN, SMEAR,
MARK, MACULA, MOTTLE
blotter .... RECORD
usual keeper of .. POLICE
blotto: sl. .... DRUNK,
UNCONSCIOUS
blouse .... MIDDY, WAIST
Korean silk ..... CHIMA

under pinafore .. GUIMPE
with tight waist .. BASQUE
blow ..... SWAT, THUD, PUFF,
STORM, SHOCK, BRAG,
BUFF, BLAST, MISFORTUNE,
WALLOP, HUFF
colloq. ... SPEND, TREAT,
FETE
dull-sounding ..... DUNT
for blow ... TIT FOR TAT,
RETALIATION
gently .... WAFT
horn ....' TOOT
horn: colloq. ..... BRAG,
BOAST
hot and cold .... WAVER,
HESITATE, VACILLATE
in: colloq. .... ARRIVE
off ..... ERUPT, EXPLODE,
TALK, RANT
off chaff .... WINNOW
on the head ... NOB, CONK
on the knuckles ..... RAP
one's top off: colloq. ...
EXPLODE, RAVE, RAGE
over .... PASS, COOL,
DISSIPATE
resounding ..... WHACK
Scottish ... BLAW, DEVEL
sharp and quick ... CLIP
slang ..... SCRAM, LEAVE,
FLEE
stormily ...... BLUSTER
unexpected ....
SNEAKPUNCH, BOLT
up .... EXPLODE,
ENLARGE, INFLATE, ERUPT
whistle ... TOOT, BLAST,
SIREN
with club .... DRUB,
CUDGEL
with fist: sl. .. POKE, PASTE
blower .... BELLOWS, FAN
blowgun .... SPRAYER,
SUMPITAN
missile .... DART, PELLET
blowhole .... BREATHER,
FLUE, SPIRACLE
of whale ...... SPIRACLE
blowing mammal .... WHALE
blowoff: sl. .... BOASTER
blowout .... PARTY, BANQUET,
CELEBRATION, TREAT, FEAST
one result of a .. FLAT TIRE
blowpipe .... BLOWGUN

blowup: colloq. ... EXPLOSION, OUTBURST

blowy .... WINDY, GUSTY, BLUSTERY

blowzy ... SLOVENLY, FROWZY
woman .... SLATTERN, SLUT

blubber .... CRY, WEEP, (WHALE)FAT
piece of .... LIPPER
strip .... FLENSE

blucher ... (HALF)BOOT, SHOE

bludgeon ..... CLUB, COERCE, BULLY, CUDGEL, BAT

blue .... ANIL, COBALT, LIVID, GLOOMY, SAD, AZURE, PERSE, SMALT, CELESTE
back .... TROUT
bird .... JAY
blood ..... ARISTOCRAT, NOBLE, NOBILITY, ROYALTY, (SOCIAL)REGISTER
chip .... STOCK
chips: colloq. ....
VALUABLE, EXCELLENT
combining form ... CYAN
days .... MONDAYS
deep ..... ULTRAMARINE
devils .... DELIRIUM
dyestuff .... WOAD, INDIGO, ANIL
Eagle of New Deal .. NRA
fin ...... TUNA, HERRING
flag ...... IRIS, FLOWER
flower .... LARKSPUR
gas .... OZONE
grass .... POA
grayish .... SLATE, BICE, TEAL, PERSE, AZURINE
Grotto home ..... CAPRI
jeans .... LEVIS, DENIMS
mineral .... IOLITE
Nile country .. ETHIOPIA
peacock .... PAON
pencil ...... EDIT, CUT, CORRECT
pigment ... BICE, SMALT
pill .... LAXATIVE
pointer shark ..... MAKO
print .... CYANOTYPE
racer .... SNAKE
river, so-called .. DANUBE
ribbon .... FIRST(PRIZE), AWARD, BADGE, DECORATION
shade ..... ALICE, AZURE

star .... VEGA
the .... SKY, SEA
wing teal .... GARGANEY

Bluebeard, latest ... LANDRU
Bluebeard's wife ..... FATIMA

bluebell .... HYACINTH, HAREBELL, COWSLIP

bluebonnet .. SCOTS(MAN), CAP, LUPINE

bluebottle .... BLOWFLY, FLY, CORNFLOWER
bly larva .... GENTLE

bluecap .... TITMOUSE
bluecoat .... POLICEMAN
bluegill .... SUNFISH
Bluegrass State ... KENTUCKY
bluejack .... VITRIOL
bluejacket .... SOLDIER, SAILOR, ENLISTED MAN

bluenose: colloq. .... PURITAN, NOVA-SCOTIAN

bluepoint .... OYSTER
blueprint .... CYANOTYPE
blues .... DOLDRUMS, MEGRIM, DUMPS
bluestone .... VITRIOL
bluet .... INNOCENCE
blueweed .... BUGLOSS
blueprint ..... PLAN, OUTLINE
bluish gray .... CESIOUS, MERL(E), PEARL, SLATE, BICE
green ..... AQUAMARINE
red .... MALLOW
white metallic element ...
ZINC

bluff ...... MISLEAD, BLUSTER, BLUNT, BRAVADO, BRUSQUE, SCARE, BAMBOOZLE, FOURFLUSH(ER)
in poker .... RAISE, COUNTER-RAISE
rounded .... MORRO

bluffer ... FOURFLUSHER, LIAR, IMPOSTOR

bluing material ...... INDIGO
bluish green .... AQUA

blunder .... STUMBLE, FLOUNDER, ERR(OR), MISTAKE, BUNGLE, SLIP, GAFFE
in social etiquette ....
FAUX PAS, SOLECISM

stupid: sl. .... BONER
blunderbore .... OGRE
blunderbuss .... GUN

blunt .... CURT, TERSE, DULL,
BLUFF, OBTUSE, BRUSQUE,
OUTSPOKEN, GRUFF, OBTUND
arrow .... BUTTSHAFT
end .... CHUMP
end of hammer .... POLL
headed bullet ... DUMDUM
refusal .... REBUFF
blur ...... BLOT, STAIN, DIM,
HAZE, MACULATE, MACKLE
on film/photo ...... FOG
blurb .... ANNOUNCEMENT,
AD(VERTISEMENT)
blurt .... BLABBER
blush .... REDDEN, FLUSH,
COLOR
at first .... INITIALLY,
OFFHAND
cause of .. DISCOMFITURE,
EMBARRASSMENT, ANGER,
SHAME
bluster ... BULLY, THREATEN,
STORM, RANT, BRAVADO
blustering .... SWASH
blustery ..... WINDY, GUSTY
blvd. .... BOULEVARD
bo: slang ... HOBO, VAGRANT,
TRAMP
tree .... PIPAL
boa .... ANACONDA,
CONSTRICTOR, PYTHON,
SCARF, SNAKE
ringed .... ABOMA
boar ..... HOG, PIG, BARROW,
SUS, SWINE
flesh, picked .... BRAWN
for example ..... TUSKER
tooth .... TUSK
board ....:... PLANT, TABLE,
FOOD, COUNCIL, CLOSE UP,
GET ON, PLANCH(E)
and lodging .... KEEP
artist's .... PALETTE
for holding mortar ......
HAWK
from sugarcane residue ..
CELOTEX
game .... DARTS,
BACKGAMMON, PA(R)CHISI,
CHECKERS, CHESS
member ...... TRUSTEE,
DIRECTOR, REGENT
boarding house ... DORMITORY,
DORM, PENSION
house lodger ..... GUEST
school pupil ...... SCUM

boards, the ... STAGE, THEATER
boarish .... SWINISH
boast ... BRAG, VAUNT, CROW,
GASCONADE
empty .... BLUFF
boaster .... BRAGGART,
BRAGGADOCIO, BLOWOFF
of one's patriotism ....
JINGO
boastful .... THRASONICAL
air .... BRAVADO,
SWAGGER
talk .... GASCONADE,
BRAG, GAS, FANFARONADE
walk ... STRUT, SWAGGER
boasting ..... BRAGGADOCIO,
RODOMONTADE
boat ....., ... STEAMER,
WATERCRAFT, GIG, VESSEL,
TUB, SHIP
African .... DHOW
American river ... CANOE
ancient .... BIREME,
TRIREME, CORACLE,
GALLEY, GALLEON
awkward ..... DROGHER,
ARK
basin .... MARINA
Bolivian .... BALSA
Canadian .... BATEAU
canoe-like ...... PIROGUE
captain .... SKIPPER
captain of story ... AHAB,
NEMO, BLIGH
Ceylon/E. Indies .. DONI,
DHONI, DINGEY
Chinese .... SAMPAN,
JUNK
clumsy ..... TUB, HULK,
ARK, DROGHER, HOOKER
dispatch ... AVISO, OOLAK
Dutch Indies ... PRAAM,
HOOKER
Egyptian ...... SANDAL,
BARIS
English .... COBLE
Eskimo .... UMIAK,
KAYAK, KYAK, OOMIAK,
BIDARKA, BIDARKEE
ferry .... BAC
fishing .... DOGGER,
TRAWLER, COBLE, CORACLE,
SMACK, DORY
flatbottomed ..... DORY,
PUNT, COBLE, BARGE,
PONTOON, BATEAU, KEEL

for gathering shellfish ...
DREDGER
freight .... WHERRY,
LIGHTER, BARGE, SCOW,
TRAMP
French ..... CARAVELLE
front .. PROW, FORE, BOW
helm .... TILLER
Indian .. DHOW, MASOOLA
Indian river ... ALMADIA
Italian .... GONDOLA
landing .... LST
Levantine .... SAIC,
XEBEC, BUM, KETCH
mail .... PACKET
Malayan ... PROA, PRAU,
PAHI, PRAO, PRAH, TOUP
marker .... BUOY
Mediterranean .. SET(T)EE
merchant .... ARGOSY
Netherlands ... BILANDER
Nile river ...... SANDAL
North Sea ...... DOGGER
of classified words ......
THESAURUS, DICTIONARY,
GLOSSARY
old ..... HOOKER, HULK
on vessel .... JOLLY,
PINNACE
on warship ..... DINGHY,
LAUNCH
Philippine .... CASCO,
BANCA, BATEL
pole-propelled ... PUNT,
CASCO, GONDOLA
propeller .... OAR, POLE,
SCULL, PADDLE, POLE,
SAIL
race .... REGATTA
racing ... SCULL, SHELL,
YACHT
raft .... CATAMARAN
rear end of .. AFT, STERN
river ... BARGE, WHERRY,
SAMPAN, FERRY, PACKET,
CANOE
row .... DINGHY,
WHERRY, SKIFF, COBLE,
SHELL
rudder ... TILLER, WHEEL
sail .... SKIFF, SMACK
scout .... VEDETTE,
VIDETTE
shallow, small ... COCKLE
shaped ..... NAVICULAR,
SCAPHOID

shaped ornament .... NEF
ship's ... PINNACE, YAWL
sink deliberately ....
SCUTTLE
small ... DINGHY, DORY,
SHALLOP, COG, SKIFF,
COCKLE, JIGGER
slow .... DROGHER,
BUCKET, ARK, TRAMP
steering part .... WHEEL,
RUDDER, TILLER
tender .... HOY
tiller .... WHEEL,
RUDDER
timber .... KEEL
towing .... TUG
three-oared .... RANDAN
two-masted ... PIRAGUA,
PIROGUE, DOGGER
boating ... ROWING, SAILING,
CRUISING
boatman .... OARSMAN, POLER,
GONDOLIER, PADDLER,
VOYAGEUR
on Styx .... CHARON
boats, small fleet of .. FLOTILLA
boatswain .... BOSUN
whistle .... PIPE
Boaz' son .... OBED
wife .... RUTH
bob .... RAP, CURTSY,
PENDANT, HAIRCUT, FLOAT,
SLED, DOCK, REFRAIN,
SHILLING
bait .... DIB
British slang ... SHILLING
bobbery .... ROW, HUBBUB
bobbin ... REEL, SPOOL, PIRN,
PIN
lace .... CLUNY
of weaver's shuttle .. PIRN
bobbins holder ...... SPINDLE,
CREEL
bobby .... POLICEMAN
soxer: colloq. ....
TEENAGER
station of a ...... POINT
bobcat .... LYNX, WILDCAT
bobolink .... ORTALAN,
SONGBIRD, SORA, RICEBIRD
bobsled .... TOBOGGAN
bobwhite .... COLIN,
PARTRIDGE, QUAIL
bocaccio ...... ROCKFISH, COD
bocca .... BERRY

Boccaccio's work ....
DECAMERON
Boche .... GERMAN,
SQUAREHEAD, HUN, JERRY
bock .... BEER
bode .... PRESAGE, OMEN,
AUGUR, PORTEND
bodega: Sp. .... CELLAR,
WAREHOUSE
bodice .... VEST, BASQUE,
CHOLI, WAIST, CORSAGE
front piece .... JABOT
posy .... CORSAGE
bodily .... SOMATIC
bodkin .... HAIRPIN,
NEEDLE, DAGGER, STILETTO,
EYELETEER
body ... SOMA, TRUNK, TORSO,
CORPSE, PERSON, CARCASS
animal ..,, ... SOMA
appetite .... LUST
beautiful, adjective for ..
SEXY
coldness .... CHILL
combining form ....
SOMAT(O)
dead .... CORSE, CORPSE,
CADAVER, CARCASS
duct .... MEATUS
heavenly .... SUN, STAR,
PLANET, MOON, COMET
injury .... TRAUMA
internal organs ... VITALS,
INNARDS
joint ...... KNEE, ELBOW,
WRIST
main .... TRUNK, TORSO
odor: colloq. .... BO
of advisers .... CABINET
of assistants ..... STAFF
of horse .... BARREL
of laws .... CODE
of learning .... LORE
of men .... POSSE, ARMY,
TROOP
of nobility ..... PEERAGE
of retainers ... RETINUE,
ENTOURAGE, SUITE
of the .... SOMATIC,
CORPOR(E)AL
of troops ..... COMPANY
of vertebra .... CENTRUM
of writing .... TEXT
opening ...... FORAMEN
orbiting around planet ..
SATELLITE

orbiting around sun ....
PLANET
pertaining to the ......
CORPOREAL
plant .... SOMA
politic .... WEAL, STATE
servant .... VALET
slang .... CHASSIS
trunk of .... TORSO
weakness .... DEBILITY
bodyguard .... ESCORT,
PROTECTOR
slang .... TORPEDO
Boeotia's capital ..... THEBES
Boer dialect .... TAAL
general .... BOTHA,
HERTZOG
statesman ..... HERTZOG
War town besieged .....
MAFEKING
troops ...... COMMANDO
Boers' victim ..... MATABELE
bog .... QUAG, MIRE, FEN,
MARSH, OOZE, QUAGMIRE,
SWAMP, MUSKEG
orchid .... CALYPSO
peat .... MOSS
product .... PEAT
trotter ...... IRISH(MAN)
bogey .... BUGABOO, BOGY,
BUGBEAR, BOGIE, PAR
bogged down ...... STALLED
boggle .... EQUIVOCATE,
BUNGLE, BOTCH, SCRUPLE,
HESITATE
boggy .... MIRY, SWAMPY,
MARSHY, QUAGGY
tract .... MORASS
bogie: Brit. .... CART, TRUCK
bogus .... SPURIOUS,
COUNTERFEIT, SHAM
bogy .... (HOB)GOBLIN,
BUGBEAR, BOGIE, BUGABOO
bohea .... (BLACK) TEA
Bohemia .... CECHY
Bohemian .... GYPSY,
ARTIST, DILETTANTE, ARTY
city .... PRAHA, PILSEN
composer ...... MAHLER
dance .... TALIAN,
POLKA, REDOWA
garnet .... PYROPE
general ... ZIZKA, ZISKA
Girl .... ARLINE
hotsprings site ....
CARLSBAD, KARLSBAD

martyr .... HUS(S)
mountain .... ERZ
patron saint ....
     WENCESLAUS
reformer .... HUS(S)
river ... ISER, EGER, OHRE
town .... CARLSBAD
Bohr, physicist .... NIELS
boil .... SEETHE, CHURN,
     BUBBLE, SIMMER, STEW,
     ANGER, PUSTULE, STY,
     ANTHRAX, CARBUNCLE,
     FURUNCLE
eyelid .... STY
slow ..... SIMMER, STEW
boiled rice: Philippines ....
     KANIN
rice with meat, spiced ....
     PILAU
shirt: sl. .... BRAGGART,
     POPINJAY
boiler .... COPPER,
     CA(U)LDRON
coating inside of .. SCALE
covering ..... LAG(GING)
safety device ....
     HYDROSTAT
tend .... STOKE
vent .... TUE
boiling point ...... HIGH-TEST
boisterous .... ROUGH,
     VIOLENT, TURBULENT,
     VOCIFEROUS, JINK(S)
bola: Span. .... BALL
bolar .... CLAYEY
bold ...... DARING, FEARLESS,
     FRESH, BRAVE, AUDACIOUS,
     PROMINENT
and resolute ..... HARDY
faced .... FORWARD,
     IMPUDENT, SAUCY, PERT
front .... BLUFF
girl .... TOMBOY, HOYDEN
bole ..... TRUNK, CLAY, TREE
bolero .... DANCE, VEST
composer of ...... RAVEL
boletus .... TOADSTOOL
bolide .... METEOR,
     FIREBALL
Bolivar .... COIN,
     (THE) LIBERATOR
Bolivian boat.......... BALSA
capital .... LA PAZ
capital, nominal .. SUCRE
city .... ORURO
Indian .... URO, ITEN,

     AYMARA
lake .... POOPO
llama .... ALPACA
money ...... BOLIVIANO,
     TOMINE
mountain ...... POTOSI,
     SORATA, ILLAMPU
plains ... GRAND CHACO
river ..... BENI, MAMORE,
     MADEIRA, IVARI, PIRAY
seat of government .....
     LA PAZ
boll .... POD, CAPSULE
weevil .... PICUDO,
     BEETLE
bollard ... COLT, HORSE, BEAM
bollix: sl. ... BUNGLE, BOTCH
bolo .... MACHETE, KNIFE
bologna .... SAUSAGE
slang .... BALONEY
Bolshevik ... LENIN, TROTSKY
secret police ...... OGPU,
     NKVD
bolster .... CUSHION, PAD,
     PILLOW, PROP, SUPPORT
bolt .... ARROW, COTTER,
     SHAFT, RIVET, PAWL, ROLL,
     LIGHTNING, ROD, DECAMP,
     DEFECT, RUN, PIN, PINTLE
fastener .... NUT
pivot .... PINTLE
turner .... SPANNER
bolter .... SIEVE, SIFTER,
     DEFECTOR, DESERTER,
     RUNAWAY
bolthead ..... FLASH, ALEMBIC
bolus .... PILL, LUMP, MASS
boma .... BOA, PYTHON
bomb ...... MISSILE, ATTACK,
     EXPLOSIVE, GRENADE,
     ATOM, SHELL, TEAR
aerial: sl. .. BREADBASKET,
     EGG
defective .... DUD
kind of .... TEAR,
     INCENDIARY, ATOM,
     HYDROGEN, MOLOTOV
pit .... CRATER
powerful .. BLOCKBUSTER
shelter .... DUGOUT,
     ABRI, BUNKER
small .... GRENADE
sound on way ... WHINE,
     BUZZ
underwater ....
     DEPTHCHARGE, ASHCAN

bombard ..... SHELL, BATTER, STRAFE
bombardment ..... BARRAGE, DRUMFIRE, CANNONADE, SHELLFIRE
bombardon .... BASSOON, TUBA, ORGAN, OBOE
bombast .... RANT, BLUSTER, FUSTIAN
bombastic .... TURGID, POMPOUS, TUMID, FLOWERY, OROTUND, GRANDIOSE, FLAMBOYANT, PLETHORIC
style .... TUMID
Bombay city ... POONA, SURAT
native .... MARATHA, MAHRATTA
bomber .... AIR-RAIDER, LIBERATOR
approach of ...,   . RUN
crewman ...... GUNNER, NAVIGATOR, BOMBARDIER
famed ...... ENOLA GAY
German .... STUKA
gunner's place in ....
TURRET
bombing, describing a kind of CARPET, SATURATION, STRATEGIC
raid starting place ....
SHANGRI-LA
victim .... EVACUEE, REFUGEE
bombproof shelter .. CASEMATE, BUNKER, DUGOUT
bombshell, sort of .. SCANDAL, SENSATION
bombycid ... MOTH, EGGER, IO
bombyx ... ERI(A), SILKWORM
bon ami ...,,. ...... FRIEND
mot .... WITTICISM, QUIP, (APT)SAYING
vivant .... GOURMET, EPICURE, GOURMAND
bona fide .... AUTHENTIC, FEAL, GENUINE
fides .... HONESTY, GOOD FAITH
bonanza .... PROSPERITY, WINDFALL, MINE
Bonaparte .... EMPEROR, CORSICAN, NAPOLEON, LUCIEN, JEROME, LOUIS
bonbon ... CANDY, SUGARPLUM
bonbonniere ..... CANDYBOX
bond ..... TIE, VOW, PLEDGE,

LINK, COVENANT, GUARANTEE, DUTY, AGREEMENT, SLAVE
marriage .... KNOT
part of .... COUPON
bondage .... SERFDOM, SLAVERY, SERVITUDE, YOKE
bondman ... SERF, ESNE, SLAVE, VASSAL, CHURL, CARL, VILLEIN
bondsman ... SURETY, SLAVE, ESNE, HELOT
bone .... OS, DICE, CUBE, SKULL, STERNUM, RIB, FEMUR, VERTEBRA, CLAVICLE, SCAPULA
ankle .... TARSUS
arched .... RIB
arm ,, ULNA HUMERUS
break .... FRACTURE
breast , ... STERNUM
canals, of .... HAVERSIAN
cavity ... ANTRUM, SINUS
change to .... OSSIFY
cheek .... MALAR
colloquial .... DICE
combining form ....
OSTE(O)
decay .... CARIES, OSITE
disease ...... RACHITIS, RICKETS
ear ...... ANVIL, INCUS, TYMPANIC, HAMMER, STAPES
elevation, knoblike ......
TUBERCLE
face .... MAXILLA
finger .... PHALANGE
flat .... BLADE
forelimb ..... HUMERUS
formation .... OSTOSIS
growth on .... EXOTOSIS
inflammation .. OSTEITIS
joint inflammation ......
ARTHRITIS
leg ..... FEMUR, PATELLA, TIBIA, FIBULA
like .... OSTEOID, OSSEOUS
marrow, of the ....
MYELOID
of contention, literally ...
WOMAN
of leg ..... FIBULA, TIBIA
of sorts .... FUNNY
of sternum ..... STERNAL
of thigh .... FEMUR

of wrist .... CARPUS, CARPAL(E)
opening .... FORAMEN
organic basis .... OSSEIN
pelvic .... ILIUM
pertaining to .... OSTEAL
sac between joints .... BURSA
scraper .... XYSTER
skull .... PARIETAL, TEMPORAL, FRONTAL, MANDIBULA
small .... OSSICLE
spine .... SACRUM, VERTEBRA
tissue .... MARROW
turn into .... OSSIFY
U-shaped .... HYOID
boner ...... ERROR, BLUNDER, GOOF
bonehead ..... FOOL, NITWIT, DOLT
boneless fish/meat ... FIL(L)ET
bones .... OSSA, DICE
  as in song .... DRY
  combining form .... OSTE(O)
  container for .. OSSUARY
boneset .... AGUEWEED
bonfire .... BALEFIRE
  kind of .... CAMPFIRE
bongo ..... ANTELOPE, DRUM
bonhomie .... PLEASANT, AFFABLE, GOOD NATURE
boniface .... INNKEEPER, LANDLORD, HOST
Bonin Island ..... OGASAWARA
bonito .... FISH, MACKEREL
bonne .... MAIDSERVANT, NURSEMAID
  foi: Fr. .... HONESTY
bonnet ..... CAP, HEADDRESS, HAT, POKE, HOOD
  folding .... CALECHE, CALASH
  projecting rim ..... BRIM
  woman's .... CAPOTE
bonnie/bonny .... BEAUTIFUL, HANDSOME, PRETTY, FINE
bonnyclabber ....
    (CURDLED) MILK
bonus .... GIFT, BOUNTY, PREMIUM, DIVIDEND, TIP
bony ... SCLEROUS, SCRAGGY, ANGULAR, OSTEAL, THIN, EMACIATED, OSSEAN,

OSSEOUS
part of nose ..... BRIDGE
plate/scale .... SCUTE
tissue inflammation .....
    OSTEITIS
bonze .... MONK
boo .... HOOT, JEER, HISS
boob: sl. .. FOOL, IDIOT, DUNCE
booboo .... SNAFU
booby .... NITWIT
  prize scores ...... LOWS
  trap .... PITFALL
  trap, lethal .... MINE
boodle .... CROWD, MOB, BRIBE, LOOT
boohoo ...... WEEP(ING), CRY
boojum .... SNARK
book .... PRIMER, TEXT, READER, REGISTER, RECORD, ENTER, SCHEDULE, TOME, ENGAGE, VOLUME, LIBER
  about saints ... PASSIONAL
  announcement ... BLURB
  Bible ...... SCRIPTURES
  back of .... SPINE
  blank sheet of .. FLYLEAF
  case for ... FOREL, FORRIL
  circulating agency ......
    LIBRARY
  collection .. BIBLIOTHECA, LIBRARY
  collector ... BIBLIOPHILE
  combining form .. BIBLIO
  cover fastener ..... HASP
  division .... CHAPTER
  end .... FINIS
  first page ... FRONTISPIECE
  foreign exchange ....
    CAMBIST
  installment ..... FASCICLE
  introduction ... ISAGOGE, PREFACE, FOREWORD
  jacket ad .... BLURB
  large ... TOME, VOLUME, FOLIO
  leaf .... PAGE
  leaf turned down ....
    DOG-EAR
  left-hand page ... VERSO
  lining .... DOUBLURE
  make-up .... FORMAT, LAYOUT
  map .... ATLAS
  marginal comment ......
    MARGENT

of account ..... LEDGER
of charts, etc. ..... ATLAS
of church service forms ..
    ORDINAL, ORDINARY
of devotions .... MISSAL
of feasts .... ORDO
of fiction .... NOVEL
of gospel .... MARK
of hours .... HORA(E)
of Jewish law ... TALMUD
of knowledge ....
    (EN)CYCLOPEDIA
of listings ... DIRECTORY
of loose leaves ... CAHIER
of nobility ... PEERAGE
of psalms ... PSALTER(Y)
of public records .. LIBER
of rolled script ... SCROLL
of synonyms/antonyms ..
    THESAURUS
of stories of same author
    OMNIBUS
on nobles ..... PEERAGE
on plants .... HERBAL
on saints' lives ....
    HAGIOLOGY
on strange subjects ......
    CURIOSA
operatic ...... LIBRETTO
page size ... DUODECIMO
palm .... TARA, TALIERA
paper cover ..... JACKET
part .... FLYLEAF,
    FRONTISPIECE, PREFACE,
    FOREWORD, GLOSSARY,
    CHAPTER, PAGE, JACKET,
    COVER
sampler .... BROWSER
school .... TEXT
section ..... LEAF, PAGE,
    CHAPTER
shape and size ... FORMAT
shelves, set of .... STACK
size .... QUARTO
technical description of ..
    COLLATION
the .... BIBLE
title page .. FRONTISPIECE
unbound .... PAMPHLET
boogie-woogie .... JAZZ
bookbinding .... BIBLIOPEGY
material ..... BUCKRAM,
SUPER, MOROCCO, VELLUM,
    SKIVER
style ... . GROLIER
bookie: sl. .... BET TAKER

booking .... ENGAGEMENT
bookish .... LITERARY,
    PEDANTIC, STODGY,
    SCHOLARLY, ERUDITE,
    LEARNED
bookkeeper .... ACCOUNTANT
book of .... LEDGER
mentor of ..... AUDITOR
bookkeeping book ... LEDGER
column ... DEBIT, CREDIT
item .... RENTAL,
    INTEREST, INCOME,
    DISBURSEMENTS, PROFIT,
    LOSS
booklet .... PAPERBACK,
    BANTAM, POCKETBOOK
unstitched ..... FOLDER
bookmaker ...... PUBLISHER,
    COMPILER
slang .... BOOKIE
bookmakers collectively .. RING
bookplate .... EX LIBRIS
books .... LIBRI
collection of .... LIBRARY
bookseller .... BIBLIOPOLE,
    STATIONER
catalogue of ....
    BIBLIOTHECA
bookselling ...... BIBLIOPOLY
bookstall .... NEWS-STAND
bookstore reading .. BROWSING
boom .... RESOUND, SPAR,
    SPRIT, JIB, BARRIER,
    ROAR, FLOURISH,
    PROSPERITY, BOOST,
    GROW
Boomer State ..... OKLAHOMA
boomerang .... KILEY, KYLIE
in a way ..... REBOUND,
    RICOCHET, KICKBACK,
    BACKFIRE
boon .... BLESSING, BENEFIT,
    FAVOR, REQUEST,
    MERRY, PLEASANT,
    GAY, BENE
boondocks ..... WILDERNESS,
    HINTERLAND
Boone, _____ .... PAT, DANIEL
boor ...... OAF, LOUT, CHURL,
    CLOD, CLOWN,
    PLEASANT, TYKE,
    CHUFF
boorish .... RUDE, AWKWARD,
    UNCOUTH, ILL-MANNERED
boost: colloq. ...... PUSH UP,
    LIFT, RAISE, INCREASE

booster .. SHOPLIFTER, ROOTER
boot ..... BUSKIN, GALOSH(E),
STOGIE, STOG(E)Y, KICK,
DISMISS, RECRUIT,
PAC(K), BROGAN
   Eskimo .... KAMIK
   kind of .... ZIPPER
   named after German
     fieldmarshal .. BLUCHER
   of Europe, so-called .....
        ITALY
   part of .... VAMP
   slang ...... DISCHARGE,
        DISMISS
   to .... BESIDES,
        IN ADDITION
   brightest star .. ARCTURUS
Bootes .... HERDSMAN
bootblack .... SHOESHINER
booth .... STALL, SHED,
KIOSK(O), STAND
   Oriental market ... SOOK
bootlace .... LACET
   tip .... AGLET
bootleg .... SMUGGLE
   whisky maker ....
        MOONSHINER
bootlegger ..... MOONSHINER,
SMUGGLER, RUMRUNNER
bootlegger's ware ..... ALKY,
POTEEN, MOONSHINE, WHISKY
bootless ... HOPELESS, USELESS,
VAIN, FUTILE
bootlick .... FLATTER, FAWN,
PANDER
bootlicker ... YESMAN, TOADY,
SYCOPHANT
boots .... SHOES
   and saddles .. BUGLE CALL
   high, waterproof ....
        WADERS
booty .... LOOT, PRIZE,
SPOILS, SWAG, PELF
booze ..... LIQUOR, WHISKY,
DRINK
bop .... JAZZ
   slang .... BLOW, STRIKE,
PUNCH
borax .... TINCAL, FLUX
Bordeaux ..... CLARET, WIND
bordel(lo) .... BROTHEL
border ..... EDGE, SIDE, RIM,
FRONTIER, FRINGE, BRIM,
BRINK, RAND, LIMBUS,
MARGE
   customs gate ... BARRIER

   design .... GUILLOCHE
   land in dispute ... MARCH
   on .... ABUT
   on stamps ..... TRESSURE
   raise and ridge .... MILL
   river ..... YALU, MEKONG
   wall .... DADO
bordered .... FLANKED,
HEMMED
borderland disputed .. MARCH
borderline .... INDEFINITE,
DOUBTFUL
bore .... TIRE, DRILL, WEARY,
HOLE, CALIBER, EAGRE,
WAVE, ENDURED
   gun ... GAUGE, CALIBER,
CALIBRE, CHASE
   mine shaft ..... TREPAN
   river .... EAGRE
   slang .... DRAG
boreal .... NORTHERN,
NORTHWIND
bored .... BLASE, FED UP
boredelaise .... SAUCE
boredom .... ENNUI, TEDIUM
   sign of .... YAWN
borele .... RHINO(CEROS)
borer ... AWL, AUGER, GIMLET,
DRILL, BEETLE
Borge's (Victor) forte .. PIANO
Borges' (Jorge) forte ....
BESTIARY
Borgia, ___ .... CESARE,
LUCREZIA
boric acid salts ...... BORATE
boring ... TIRESOME, TEDIOUS,
DULL
   tool .... AWL, DRILL,
AUGER, WIMBLE, GIMLET,
JUMPER
borings .... CHIPS
born .... NEE
being .... NASCENT
borne .... CARRIED
Borneo .... KALIMANTAN
   apartment ... LONGHOUSE
   ape .... ORANG
   burrowing animal ....
TELEDU
   capital .... BRUNEI
   hornbill ...... KENYALANG
   mountain ... KINABALU
   native .... DYAK
   pepper plant .... ARA
   port .... MIRI, JESSELTON
   squirrel .... PENTAIL

tribe ..... DAYAK, IBAN, KAYAN, KENYAH, DELABIT, MELANAUS
Borodin's prince ...... IGOR
boron and one other element ... BORIDE
borough ...... BURG, TOWN
citizen .... BURGESS
borrow .... BRACE
bort ..... DIAMOND, ABRASIVE
borzoi ... DOG, WOLFHOUND
bos(s) .... BEEF, COW
bosc .... PEAR
boscage .... GROVE, SHRUBBERY, THICKET
bosh: colloq. ..... NONSENSE, ROT
bosk .... GROVE, THICKET
bos'n .... BOATSWAIN
bosom ..... BREAST, INTIMATE, MIDST
Bosporus rowboat .... CAIQUE
boss ...... MASTER, SACHEM, FOREMAN, EMPLOYER, CHIEF, KNOB, STUD
on shield .... UMBO
bossy .... DOMINEERING, STUDDED
Boston ... CARD GAME, WALTZ
basketball team .. CELTICS
Brahmin .... SNOB
city near .... MALDEN
name .... CABOT, FILENE, LOWELL
symbol of ..... CODFISH
Bostonian .... HUBBITE
bosun .... BOATSWAIN
bot(t) .... LARVA, MAGGOT
botanical angle .... AXIL
sac .... THECA
botanist ..... MENDEL, BROWN
botany .... PHYTOLOGY
botch ... FLUB, BUNGLE, FAIL, MESS, SPOIL, GOOF, MUFF, FUMBLE, LOUSE(UP)
both .... TOGETHER, EQUALLY, ALIKE
prefix .... AMBI
bother ...... ANNOY, WORRY, MOLEST, TROUBLE, PESTER, FUSS, ADO, AIL
Bothnia .... ALAND
botryose .... RACEMOSE
bottle .... VIAL, PHIAL, CARAFE, DECANTER, CARBOY, COSTREL, FLASK,

CRUET, FLAGON, MAGNUM
containing garden ...... TERRARIUM
earthenware ... DEMIJOHN
for acids .... CARBOY
for condiments .. CASTER, CRUET
for liquids ..... CARBOY
hit the .... BOOZE
indentation at bottom ... KICK
medicine .... TENREC
perfume .... FLACON
shaped vessel .... FLASK
stopper .... CORK
top .... CAP, CROWN
two-quart .... MAGNUM
vinegar .... CRUET
water .... CARAFE, DECANTER
bottleneck .... HINDRANCE, SNAG
bottlenose .... PORPOISE, DOLPHIN
bottom ..... BED, BASE, ROOT, SHIP, SOURCE, LOWEST, LAST
colloquial ..... BUTTOCKS
of ship .... KEEL
bottomless ...... ABYSMAL
pit/gulf ... ABYSS, HELL, UNDERWORLD, ABADDON
bottoms .... HOLM
boudoir .... BOWER, DRESSING ROOM
bouffant ...... PUFFED, FULL
bouffe .... COMIC OPERA
bough ... BRANCH, TWIG, LIMB
of tree .... RAMAGE
boughpot .... JARDINIERE, BOUQUET, BOWPOT
bougie .... WAX, CANDLE
bouillon .... BROTH, CUBE
Boulder Dam designer .... SAVAGE
boulevard ... STREET, AVENUE, CONCOURSE, PROMENADE
boullabaisse...CHOWDER, SOUP
Boumedienne, Algerian
president .... HOUARI
bounce ...... BUMP, THUMP, BOUND, EXPEL, DISMISS, SPRING, JUMP, REBOUND, DASH, SPIRIT
British ..... IMPUDENCE, BLUSTER

on water surface .... DAP
slang ..... SPIRIT, DASH,
DISMISS
bouncing ... LUSTY, HEALTHY,
BUXOM, BIG
bound .... LEAP, SWORN,
PLEDGED, JUMP, TIED,
DESTINED, OBLIGED,
HEADED
horse's .. VAULT, CURVET
boundaries, mark off ....
DEMARCATE
boundary .... BORDER,
BUTTING, VERGE, LIMIT,
METE, MERE, LINE, AMBIT
common .. CONTERMINAL,
CONTERMINOUS
combining form .... ORI
outer .... PERIMETER
bounden .... OBLIGATORY,
INDEBTED, OBLIGED
bounder .... CAD, BOOR,
SCOUNDREL
Bounding Main .. (OPEN)SEA,
OCEAN
boundless .... VAST, INFINITE,
UNLIMITED
bounds .. AMBIT, SCOPE, LIMITS
out of ...... OFF LIMITS,
PROHIBITED
bounteous .... GENEROUS,
ABUNDANT, PLENTIFUL,
AMPLE
bounty .... BONUS, TIP,
REWARD, PREMIUM,
ALLOWANCE, GENEROSITY,
LARGESSE
bouquet .... CORSAGE, AROMA,
SPRAY, FRAGRANCE,
NOSEGAY, ODOR, SCENT,
POSY
Bourbon ...... REACTIONARY,
REUNION, WHISKY
bourg .... TOWN, VILLAGE
bourgeois ...... SHOPKEEPER,
MIDDLECLASS, SMUG
RESPECTABLE, COMMONPLACE
bourgeoisie .... CAPITALISTS,
MIDDLECLASS
bourn(e) ..... BROOK, STREAM,
DOMAIN, GOAL, OBJECTIVE
bourse .... (STOCK)EXCHANGE
bouse .... LIQUOR, BOOZE,
HOIST, DRINK, CAROUSE
boutique .... STORE, SHOP
Bovary, Mme. .... EMMA

bovid .... OX, CATTLE, SHEEP,
GOAT, ANTELOPE
bovine .... OX, SLOW, STOLID,
PATIENT, BULL, TAURINE,
CATTLE, COW
Asiatic .... YAK
Celebes .... ANOA
male .... BULL, STEER
tuberculosis ..... GRAPE
bow .... STOOP, SUBMIT,
CURVE, NOD, YIELD
and arrow art .. ARCHERY
maker .... BOWYER
of eyeglasses .... BRIDGE
of ship ..... PROW, FORE
of woman's dress ....
BUSTLE
of wood .... YEW
Oriental .... SALAAM
ornamental/ribbon .....
KNOT
shaped .... ARCUATE
bowdlerize ..... EXPURGATE,
PURIFY
bowed .... ARCHED, BENT,
SURRENDERED
bowel .... INTESTINE, GUT,
ENTRAIL, INTERIOR, COLON
movement stimulant ....
CATHARTIC, LAXATIVE
pains .... GRIPES
bowels .... GUTS
clearer .... LAXATIVE,
PURGATIVE, CATHARTIC
purge of ...... CATHARSIS
bower ...... ARBOR, RETREAT,
COTTAGE, ANCHOR, ALCOVE,
PERGOLA
bowery ... FARM, PLANTATION,
LEAFY
"Bowery Boys" member ......
GORCEY
bowfin .... MUDFISH, AMIA,
DOGFISH, GANOID
bowhead .... WHALE
bowie .... HUNTING KNIFE
bowl .... STADIUM, CUP,
ROLL, DISH, BASIN, CRATER
drinking .... MAZER,
MAZARD
flower .... JARDINIERE
for pounding substance ..
MORTAR
name of U.S. athletic ....
ORANGE, SUGAR, SUN,
ROSE, COTTON, TANGERINE

over .... OVERWHELM,
ASTONISH, STAGGER
punch .... MONTEITH
sound ...... BOOLA, RAH,
BOO, YELL, CHEERS
toilet .... CLOACA
bowleg ...... VARUS, TALIPES
bowler .... DERBY, KEGLER
bowling .... TENPINS,
DUCKPINS
alley .... LANE
alley track ..... RUNWAY
center mark ...... JACK
first-ball target .. KINGPIN
game division .... FRAME
green .... RINK
seven/ten pins ....
CORNERS
term ... SPARE, STRIKE,
BREAK
widest split .. GOALPOSTS
bowls .... TENPINS, NINEPINS,
SKITTLES
bowman ... ARCHER, OARSMAN
bowse .... DRINK
bowstring .... CORD, GARROTE
sound .... TWANG
bowwow .... BARK
box ... CASE, BIN, SPAR, CHEST,
CARTON, CUFF, BIFF
cash ..... REGISTER, TILL
fish .... KENCH
for fodder .... CRIB
for money .... KIST
for relics .... RELIQUARY
for tea, etc. ... CANISTER
like sleigh .... PUNG
of explosives ... CAISSON
office receipts: colloq. ...
TAKE
office window ... WICKET
score item ... RUNS, HITS,
ERRORS
seat .... LOGE
small .... CASKET
specimen coins .. PYX, PIX
strong .... SAFE
tea ... CANISTER, CADDY
tool .... KIT, CHEST
boxcar, in dice ..... TWELVE,
CRAP
boxer .... PUG(ILIST),
PRIZEFIGHTER, DOG,
RINGSTER
colloquial .. MITTSLINGER,
BEAKBUSTER, BRUISER,

PUG, MAULER
boxer's arm length ... REACH
hands: colloq. .... MITTS
savior, sometimes .. GONG
second .... HANDLER
trade mark ....
CAULIFLOWER EARS
trainer .... HANDLER
boxing bouts collectively .....
CARD
champion ... CLAY, BAER,
CARNERA, DEMPSEY,
LOUIS, TUNNEY, WILLARD,
VILLA, WALCOTT, ORTIZ,
CORBETT, HARADA, COKES,
GRIFFITH, SCHMELING
decision ... DRAW, TKO,
KO, NO CONTEST
glove .... CESTUS
match ..... SETTO, BOUT,
GO, FISTICUFFS
of .... FISTIC
official .... REF(EREE)
period .... ROUND
pertaining to ..... FISTIC
pre-bout need .. WEIGH-IN
promoter ....
(TEX) RICHARD
science of .... FISTICUFFS
wrestling contest ....
PANCRATIUM
boxwood ..... SERON, SHRUB,
TREE
boy .... LAD, YOUTH,
MAN-CHILD, YOUNGSTER,
STRIPLING, SPRIG, TAD,
NIPPER, GOSOON
age of .... PUBERTY
assistant .... JACK
attendant .... PAGE
colloquial .... BUB,
SON(NY), SHAVER, KID,
BUSTER
friend: colloq. ..... BEAU,
LOVER, SWEETHEART
ESCORT
Scottish ..... GALLAN(T)
Boy Scout assembly ....
JAMBOREE, CAMPOREE
daily object .. GOOD TURN
founder .. BADEN-POWELL
gathering .... JAMBOREE,
CAMPOREE
group .... TROOP,
PATROL, DEN, PACK
hiking gear .. HAVERSACK

motto ..... BE PREPARED
new .... TENDERFOOT
popular image of ....
    DO-GOODER
boycott, in a way .. OSTRACIZE,
    STRIKE
Boz, pseudonym ..... DICKENS
BPOE .... ELKS
bra .... BRASSIERE
Brabant's capital ... BRUSSELS
    princess .... ELSA
brabble .... QUARREL,
    SQUABBLE, CHATTER
brace ... BIND, TIGHTEN, PROP,
    STIMULATE, BIT, PAIR,
    COUPLE, FASTENER,
    BITSTOCK, SPLINT
bracelet ... ARMIL, WRISTLET,
    BAND, CHAIN, BANGLE,
    HANDCUFF
bracer ... STIMULANT, TONIC,
    DRINK
braces .... GALLUSES
    Brit. slang .. SUSPENDERS
brachial .... ARMLIKE
brachyuran .... CRAB,
    CRUSTACEAN
bracing .... INVIGORATING,
    REFRESHING
bracken .... BRAKE, FERN
bracket ... CONSOLE, CORBEL,
    CLASSIFICATION, GROUP,
    ANCON
brackish ...... SALTY, BRINY,
    NAUSEOUS
bract .. GLUME, SPATHE, PALEA
    cluster .... COMA
    grass .... GLUME
brad ..... (WIRE)NAIL, SPRIG
brae: Scot. ... BANK, HILLSIDE
brag .... BOAST(ER),
    BRAGGART, VAUNT,
    GASCONADE, CROW
braggadocio ...... BRAGGART,
    BOASTING
braggart .... BOASTER,
    BRAGGER
    slang .... BLOW
Bragi's parent .. ODIN, FRIGGA
Brahma ... CREATOR, CATTLE,
    FOWL
Brahman bull .... ZEBU
    rule .... SUTRA, SUTTA
    title .... AYA
    wiseman .... PUNDIT
Brahmin: Hindu ..... PRIEST

braid ... TRESS, BAND, PLAIT,
    QUEUE, LACET, PLAT
    decoration ..... CORDON
    of gold thread .. GALLOON
    trimming ..... RICKRACK,
    GALLOON, SOUTACHE
    zigzag .... RICKRACK
braided material ..... SENNIT
brain .... MIND, INTELLECT
    action ..... CEREBRATION,
    COGITATION
    canal .... ITER
    child: colloq. .. IDEA, PLAN
    colloquial .. GRAY MATTER
    covering .... MATER
    disease .... PARESIS,
    APHASIA, KURU
    fever ..... ENCEPHALITIS
    "food" .... FISH
    groove .... SULCUS
    layer of gray matter .....
    CORTEX
    membrane .. PIA(MATER),
    DURA(MATER), ARACHNOID,
    EPENDYMA
    of the .... CEREBRAL,
    CEREBRIC
    opening .... PYLA
    part .... CEREBRUM,
    CEREBELLUM, MEDULLA
    passage .... ITER
    pertaining to the ....
    CEREBRAL
    ridge ..... HIPPOCAMPUS
    storm: colloq. ....
    (BRIGHT) IDEA, INSPIRATION,
    PLAN, CEREBRATION
    structure of nerve fibers ..
    FORNIS
    surgery ...... LOBOTOMY
    tissue .... TELA
    truster: sl. ..... EGGHEAD,
    ADVISER, EXPERT
    tumor .... GLIOMA
brainless ... STUPID, FOOLISH,
    IDIOTIC
brainpan ... CRANIUM, SKULL
brains .... INTELLIGENCE,
    INTELLECT
    colloquial/slang ....
    MASTERMIND, IDEAMAN,
    KNOWHOW
brainwash ..... INDOCTRINATE
brainy .... INTELLIGENT,
    SHARP, SMART, WISE,
    INTELLECTUAL

brake .... FERN, BRACKEN,
KNEADER, HARROW,
SLOWDOWN, CLUMP,
THICKET, CURB
for woman's tongue .....
BRANKS
part .... SHOE
Bram Stoker's thriller ....
DRACULA
bramble .... RASPBERRY,
DEWBERRY, BLACKBERRY,
SHRUB, BRIER
brambling .... FINCH
brambly ... PRICKLY, THORNY
bran .... HUSK, SKIN
meal, etc., mixture ......
MASH
branch ... DOUGH, TWIG, LIMB,
BROOK, RIVULET, OFFSHOOT,
DIVISION, RAMIFY, ARM,
RAMUS, FURCATE, SPRIG,
FURCATION
angle .... AXIL
in biology .... RAMUS
like .... RAMOUS
of family .... STIRPS
of learning ...... ART(S),
SCIENCE, DISCIPLINE,
OLOGY
off ...... FORK, DIVERGE
railroad ... SPUR, SIDING
trim .... LOP
branched ... RAMOSE, RAMOUS,
RAMIFORM
branches, bearing many ......
RAMOSE
branchiae .... GILLS
branching ..... ARBORESCENT
brand ... MARK, STIGMA(TIZE),
LABEL, TRADEMARK, STAMP,
SEAR, DISGRACE
goose .... BRANT
new .... UNUSED, FRESH
brandish ...... WAVE, SHAKE,
FLOURISH, SWING
brandling ... WORM, FISHBAIT
brandy ...... MARK, COGNAC,
AQUA VITAE
and soda .... PEG
cordial .... ROSOLIO
branks .... BIT, BRIDLE
brant .... GOOSE
brantail .... REDSTART, BIRD
brash .... RASH, HASTY,
BRITTLE, INSOLENT,

FRAGILE, IMPUDENT,
SHOWER, PYROSIS
Brasilia is capital of ... BRAZIL
designer of ... NIEMEYER
brass .... METAL, ALLOY
as imitation gold ....
ORMOLU
colloquial ... IMPUDENCE
color .... AENEOUS
combining form ....
CHALCO
knuckles ... BLACKJACK
like alloy .... LATTEN
mythical man of ... TALOS
plate, kind of .... CYMBAL
slang .... MONEY
tacks .... FACTS,
PARTICULARS
brassard ... CABBAGE, TURNIP,
BROCCOLI, COLE
brassica .... CABBAGE, TURNIP,
BROCCOLI, COLE
brassie, for example ......
GULF CLUB
brassiere ... BANDEAU, UPLIFT
slang .... FALSY
brassworker .... BRASIER
brassy .... IMPUDENT, LOUD,
INSOLENT, SHOWY, BOLD
brat ...... IMP, CHILD, RAG,
CLOTH, BANTLING
brattice .... PARAPET,
BREASTWORK
brattle ...... RATTLE, CLATTER,
SCAMPER
brave ... COURAGEOUS, BOLD,
PLUCKY, VALIANT, MANLY,
HEROIC, DEFY, STOUT
front, usually .... BLUFF
Indian .... WARRIOR
bravery .... VALOR
bravo .... WELL DONE,
EXCELLENT, OLE,
VERY GOOD, ASSASSIN,
DESPERADO, CHEER, EUGE
bravado ..... BLUSTER, BLUFF
bravura ... DASH, TECHNIQUE,
BRILLIANCE
braw .... FINE, EXCELLENT
brawl .... MELEE, FRAY, RIOT,
ROW, FREE-FOR-ALL,
UPROAR, BROIL, FRACAS
brawler .... HECTOR,
HOOLIGAN, HOODLUM
brawn .... MUSCLE(S),
STRENGTH

colloquial .... BEEF
brawny .... MUSCULAR,
    STRONG, STRAPPING
bray ..... HEEHAW, GUFFAW,
    LAUGH, TRITURATE,
    SPREAD, CRUSH, POUND
brayer, in printing .... ROLLER
braze .... SOLDER
brazen ..... IMPUDENT, BOLD,
    SHAMELESS, HARSH
brazier and grill ..... HIBACHI
Brazilian aborigine ... CARIB,
    ANDOA, AMIRANHA
    armadillo .... TATOUAY,
        TATU
    bird ...... ARA, AGAMI,
        SERIEMA, JABIRU
    "Black Pearl" ..... PELE
    capital .... BRASILIA
    capital, former ...... RIO
    cape .... FRIO
    city .... RIO, CUYABA,
        MACEIO, MANAOS,
        BELEM, PARA, CEARA,
        FORTALEZA
    coin .... CENTAVO,
        MOIDORE, (MIL)REI
    crested bird .... SERIEMA
    dance .... SAMBA
    drink .... ASSAI
    estate .... PAZENDA
    estuary .... PARA
    fiber .... IMBE
    footballer .... PELE,
        TOSTAO
    forest ... MATTA, MATTO
    heron .... SOCO
    holly .... MATE
    Indian ... ARARA, CARIB,
        TUPI, GUANA, ZAPARO,
        MURA, PURU, ACROA,
        TAPUYAN
    ipecac .... EVEA
    island .... MARAJO
    killers .... JAGUNCOS
    long-legged bird ....
        SERIEMA
    macaw .... ARARA
    measure, dry ..... MOIO
    measure, liquid .... PIPA
    medicinal plant ....
        AYAPANA
    money .... (MIL)REI,
        CONTO, CRUZEIRO
    mountain ... CORCOVADO
    nut ..... PARA, COQUILLA

    orchid .... DICHEA
    palm .... ASSAI,
        PIAS(S)AVA, BABASSU,
        JUPATI, CARNAUBA
    parrot .... ARA(RA),
        MACAW, TIRBA
    plant .... MANIHOT,
        MANIOC
    port ...... RECIFE, PARA,
        BELEM, NATAL, PELOTAS,
        BAHIA, CEARA
    quartz .... CACO
    river ...... APA, JAPURA,
        JAVARY, MADEIRA,
        TAPAJOZ, PARA,
        PUTUMAYO, ARAGUAYA,
        IGUASSU, PARNARIBA,
        PARANA, JAVARI, JURUA,
        ICA, ACARA, ACAMEA
    rubber tree ... ULE, HULE,
        SERINGA
    seaport ... NATAL, SANTOS
    state ... CEARA, PARANA,
        PARA, BAHIA
    stork .... JABIRU
    tapir .... ANTA
    tea plant .... MATE
    title of respect ..... DOM
    tree .... APA, ANDA,
        MURURE, ARAROBA
    tree bark ...... PEREIRA
    tree powder .... ARAROBA
    waterfall ...... IGUASSU
    weight ... ONCA, ARROBA
    wood .... BRASIL, SATINE
breach ..... GAP, RIFT, BREAK,
    HERNIA, RUPTURE,
    BREAKTHROUGH, OPENING
    of etiquette ... SOLECISM,
        FAUX PAS, IMPROPRIETY
    of the peace ...... RIOT,
        BRAWL
    of relations .... RENT
    of trust .... BETRAYAL
bread ... LOAF, GLUTEN, FOOD,
    PONE, RUSK, CRUST, AZYM,
    MUFFIN, BROTCHEN
    and-butter .. LIVELIHOOD,
        YOUTHFUL, COMMONPLACE,
        EVERYDAY
    and-butter letter ....
        GRACENOTE
    blessed ... EULOGIA, HOST
    boiled and flavored .....
        CUSH, PANADA
break .... EAT, DINE

crisp coating .... CRUST, RIND
dough .... SPONGE
Eucharist .... HOST
from heaven ..... MANNA
garnish .... SIPPET
hard .... HARDTACK
Hebrew .... AZYM
in one baking ... BATCH
ingredient .... FLOUR, YEAST, LEAVEN
maker .... BAKER
part ..... CRUST, CRUMB, RIND
roll .... BAGEL
St. John's .... CAROB
soaked in beef broth .....
BREWIS
soaked in milk ..... SOP
soaked in soup/gravy ...
SIPPET
spread .... OLEO, MARGARINE, BUTTER, JAM, JELLY
sweet, raised ..... RUSK
toasted/fried ... SIPPET
unleavened ... HARDTACK
white .... MANCHET
breadbasket ...... GRANARY
slang ... BELLY, STOMACH, (AERIAL)BOMB
breadfruit .... RIMA(S)
like tree .... JACK
breadwinner: colloq. .. DADDY, PAPA, EARNER
break ...... GAP, C(A)ESURA, PAUSE, HIATUS, BUST, SNAP, RUPTURE, SMASH, CRACK, SHATTER, DEMOTE, RUIN, FRACTURE, SURPASS, DISCLOSE, QUARREL
away .... ESCAPE, SEPARATE, BOLT
colloquial ...... ESCAPE
down .... ANALYZE, ITEMIZE, CRUSH, DEMOLISH, GIVE WAY
from habit .... WEAN
in .... TRAIN, INTERRUPT, INTRUDE, ENTER
in rock strata .... FAULT
in the dike .... CREVASSE
into parts ..... DIFFRACT
of day .... DAWN, MORN, DAYBREAK
off ..... STOP, SEPARATE, SEVER
off connection ... SECEDE
out ...... ERUPT, ESCAPE
moral principle ..... SIN
popular to workers ....
COFFEE, REST
religious law .... SIN
through .... PIERCE
thru eggshell .... PIP
up .... DISPERSE, SEPARATE
up marriage .... DIVORCE
breakable .... BRITTLE, FRAGILE
breakbone fever ..... DENGUE
breakdown .... COLLAPSE, FAILURE, CRACKUP
breaker .... WAVE, KEG, COMBER, EAGRE
breakers .... SURF
breakfast and lunch .. BRUNCH
food .... OATMEAL, CEREAL, FARINA
last .... DEJEUNER
nook .... ALCOVE
breaking of waves .... BREACH
breakneck .. FAST, DANGEROUS
breakthrough .... BREACH, INFILTRATION
breakup .... COLLAPSE, DISPERSION, SEPARATION, END, STOPPAGE, DISBAND(MENT)
breakwater ...... MOLE, PIER, JETTY, DIKE, BULWARK
bream ..... SPAROID, PORGY, CHAD, SUNFISH, ABRAMIS
Japanese .... TAI
breast .... BOSOM, BUST, CHEST, OPPOSE, PETTO
animal's .... BRISKET
feed ..... SUCKLE, NURSE
inflammation .. MASTITIS
meat cut .... BRISKET
of the .... PECTORAL
plate .... CUIRASS
shaped .... MASTOID
surgical removal of .....
MASTECTOMY
breastbone .... STERNUM
flat .... RATITE
of the .... STERNAL
breastpin .... BROOCH
breastplate .... URIM, PLASTRON, (A)EGIS
breastwork .... REDOUBT,

BARRICADE, BARRIER, BRATTICE

breath ... ODOR, WHIFF, PUFF, LIFE, AIR, WHISPER, HALITUS, RESPIRATION, MOMENT

asthmatic ...... WHEEZE

bad .... HALITOSIS

catch one's .... GASP, PANT, PAUSE, GULP

forced noisily .... SNORT

odorous ..... HALITOSIS

of life .... PNEUMA

of wind .... FLATUS

out of .... WINDED

save one's ..... SHUT UP, STOP, REST

sweetener .... LOZENGE, CACHOU

taking ...... THRILLING, EXCITING

whistling .... WHEEZE

breathe .... INHALE, EXHALE, MURMUR, RESPIRE, BLOW

hard .. PANT, HEAVE, GASP

in .... SUCK, INHALE

noisily .... HAZZLE, HASSEL, SNORE

one's last .... DIE

out .... EXHALE, SUSPIRE

out noisily .... SNORT, SNORE

tentatively, as it were .... SNIFF

with whistling sound .... WHEEZE

breather .. NOSE, NARES, GILL

of fish .... GILL

of whale ... BLOWHOLE, SPIRACLE

slang ..... REST, PAUSE, BREAK

breathing ...... RESPIRATION, LIVING, ALIVE

abnormal .... HYPERPNEA

device ..... RESPIRATOR

device, under water ..... SNORKEL

difficult .... DYSPNEA, DYSPNOEA

harsh ..... RALE, SNORE

hole ..... SPIRACLE, NOSE

rapid .... HYPERPNEA

smooth .... LENE

sound ..... RALE, SNORE, STRIDOR, RHONEUS

space: colloq. .... ROOM, REST, RESPITE

breathless ... DEAD, GASPING, PANTING, STIFLING

bree: Scot. .... BROTH

breech ...... BUTTOCKS, RUMP

loading rifle .. CHASSEPOT

breechblock signature, ballistics .... IDENTIFICATION

breechcloth ..... LOIN(CLOTH)

Polynesian .... MALO

breechclout .... G-STRING

breeches .... TROUSERS, TRUNKS, SLOPS

riding .... JODHPURS

Scot. .... TREWS

too big for one's .... SWELL-HEAD(ED), PROUD, OVERBEARING

breed .... HATCH, RAISE, ORIGINATE, REPRODUCE, RACE, STOCK, KIND, REAR

cattle .... DEVON

breeding ...... UPBRINGING, REARING

place ...... NIDUS, NEST, STUD FARM, ROOKERY

breeze ..... GENTLE WIND, AIR, ZEPHYR

colloquial .. COMMOTION, DISTURBANCE

refreshing ...... CALLER

slight .... BREATH, ZEPHYR

water rippling .... CAT'S PAW

breezing horse in a race ...... EASY WINNER

breezy .... LIVELY, CAREFREE, BRISK, AIRY

Bremen's river .... WESER

Brenner ____ .... PASS

Breslau river ..... OSAR, ODER

Breton .... CELT

breve .... BILLET, ORDER, WRIT, LETTER

brevet .... COMMISSION

breviary ... PORTAS, COMPEND

brevity .... BRIEFNESS, CONCISENESS, TERSENESS, SHORTNESS

is the soul of ____ .. WIT

of expression .. LACONISM

brew .. ALE, BEER, TEA, PUNCH, PLOT, CONCOCT, LAGER

brewer's ferment ..... LOB(B)
    grain .... BARLEY
    tub .... KEEVE
    yeast .... BARM
    vat .... TUN
brewery .... DISTILLERY
    refuse ...... LEES, DREGS,
                 DRAFF
brewing, one .... GYLE
brewis .... (BEEF)BROTH,
                  BREAD
Briareus, what it had many of
                  HANDS
bribe ... SOP, BOODLE, SUBORN
    collector ...... BAGMAN
    money .... SLUSH(FUND),
                 BOODLE
    slang .... SQUARE,
          GREASE, PAYOLA
bric-a-brac ... KNICKKNACK,
    CURIO, BIBELOT, VIRTU
brick ..... BLOCK, NOG, TILE,
              (A)DOBE
    burned partly ..... BAT,
         BUR(R), CLINKER
    carrier .... HOD
    colloquial .. FINE FELLOW
    compressed coal dust ....
             BRIQUET
    cracked .... CHUFF
    hard .... CLINKER
    making material .. MARL,
               PUG
    masonry ..... NOGGING
    pile .... HACK
    refuse .... SAMEL
    sun dried .... ADOBE
    trough for .... HOD
    worker .... MASON
bricklayer .... MASON
    helper of .... HODMAN
    tool of .... TROWEL
bricks, pile of .... HACK
brickwork .... MASONRY
bricole .... CATAPULT
bridal ... WEDDING, MARITAL
    path .... AISLE
    wreath .... SPIREA, SHRUB
Bridalveil .... WATERFALL
bride .... BETROTHED
    in needle-work .... LOOP,
                  TIE
bridesmaid ...... PARANYMPH
bridewell .. GAOL, JAIL, PRISON
bridge .... SPAN, PONTOON,

BAILEY, CARD GAME,
CANTILEVER, VIADUCT,
               RIALTO
bid .... SLAM
builder .... EADS
calls .... BIDS
card game ..... AUCTION,
            CONTRACT
card game position .....
NORTH, EAST, SOUTH, WEST
declaration .... BID
defeat .... SET
expert .... GOREN
floating .... PONTOON
game series ..... RUBBER
hand without trumps ....
              CHICANE
holding .... TENACE
Midgard to Asgard ......
            BIFROST
move/maneuver .. FINESSE
"no game" .... NIL
of bow instrument ......
          PONTICELLO
of musical instrument ...
           MAGAS
over gorge, etc. .. VIADUCT
part .... TRESTLE, SPAN,
      GIRDER, WALK
pathway ..... CATWALK
railroad .... TRESTLE
support .... TRUSS,
GIRDER, ABUTMENT, PIER,
           PONTOON
term ... SLAM, GOBY, BID,
PASS, TENACE, BOOK, RUFF,
            NIL
to Paradise .... ALSIRAT
tricks .... BOOK
type .... BASCULE, DRAW,
         SUSPENSION
bridle .... HARNESS,
    RESTRAIN, CURB, REIN
    part ... HEADSTALL, BIT,
      REINS, NOSE BAND
    wise animal ..... HORSE
brief ... SHORT, TERSE, CURT,
    PITHY, CONCISE, SUMMARY
    biography .... VITA
    case .... BAG, PORTFOLIO
    in expression .. LACONIC,
    TERSE, BLUNT, CURT
    in law .... BREVE
    note .... JOT, MEMO
    sleep .... NAP, DOZE,
             SNOOZE

summary ..... EPITOME, RESUME, GIST, FILL-IN
telegraphic message ..... FLASH
time .... MOMENT, SECOND, FLASH
briefly ..... IN SUM, IN SHORT, MOMENTARILY
briefs .... UNDERSHORTS
brier ... BUSH, BRAMBLE, PIPE, HEATH, THORN
briery ..... PRICKLY, THORNY, SPINY
brig .... SHIP, PRISON, GUARDHOUSE
brigade need .... BUCKET
brigadier general, rank below .. COLONEL
brigand ..... BANDIT, PIRATE, HIGHWAYMAN, LADRONE
bright .... SHINING, CHEERFUL, LIVELY, QUICK, CLEVER, LUSTROUS, LUMINOUS, SMART, RELUCENT, ROSY, ROSEATE
and cheerful .... SUNNY
colored bird ... TANAGER, ORIOLE
colored fish ...... OPAH, WRASSE, CATALINA
combining form .. HELI(O)
idea: colloq. .... BRAINSTORM, INSPIRATION, BRAINCHILD
saying .... BON MOT, WITTICISM
star .... NOVA
youngster ..... PRODIGY
youngster: slang .... WHIZ KID
Bright's disease .... NEPHRITIS
brighten .... GLADDEN, CHEER(UP), FURBISH, POLISH
brightness .... LUMINOSITY, SHEEN, LUSTER, RADIANCE, GLOSS
brill .... FLATFISH, TURBOT
brilliance .... SPLENDOR, GLITTER, ECLAT
brilliant .... VIVID, PRISMATIC, GAY, EMINENT, TALENTED, GEM, MAGNIFICENT
array .... GALAXY
facet of .... CULET

gathering .... SALON
stroke/strategem ... COUP
tennis stroke .... ACE
brim ... EDGE, RIM, BRINK, LIP
of bonnet .... POKE
of cap .... BILL
brimless cap ...... TAM, FEZ, BIRETTA, BARRET, BERET
brimmer .... BUMPER
brimming ... FULL, SUFFUSED
brimstone .... SULPHUR, SULFUR
brindled .... TABBY
brine ..... SEA, OCEAN, TEARS, SALT WATER, SOUSE
shrimp .... ARTEMIA
to salt residue ... BITTERN
bring .... FETCH, PRESENT
about ..... ACCOMPLISH, CAUSE
around ..... CONVINCE, PERSUADE
back ... RETURN, RESTORE
down .... LOWER
foot down ...... STAMP
forth .... ENGENDER, EAN, PRODUCE, SPAWN
forth young ..... HATCH, YEAN, WHELP
forward .... SHOW, INTRODUCE, CARRY OVER
home the bacon: colloq... WIN, EARN
in ...... IMPORT, ARREST, CAPTURE
in as price .... FETCH
into court ..... ARRAIGN, SUE, HALE
on oneself .... INCUR
out .... REVEAL, EXPOSE, DISPLAY, PUBLISH, INTRODUCE
to .... REVIVE
to bay ... TREE, CORNER
to bear .... EXERT, PRESS
to completion .. FINALIZE, FINISH
to light .... UNEARTH, DISCLOSE, REVEAL
to mind ... REMIND, RECALL, REMEMBER, RECOLLECT
to naught .... UNDO, NULLIFY, DESTROY, RUIN
to standstill .. STALEMATE, STALL

together ..... ASSEMBLE,
GATHER, AMASS
up .... REAR, INTRODUCE,
BROACH
up the _____ .... REAR
upon oneself ..... INCUR
bringer of bad luck ..... JINX
bringing to central point ......
AFFERENT
brink .... EDGE, VERGE
brinkmanship, exponent of ....
DULLES
briny .... SALTY
deep .... SEA, OCEAN
brio .... ANIMATION, ZEST,
VIVACITY
brioche .... ROLL
briquet .... BRICK
brisk .. LIVELY, ZIPPY, SHARP,
SPRY, ACTIVE, ENERGETIC
in music .... ALLEGRO
brisket ... BREAST, MEAT CUT
brisling .... SPRAT, FISH,
SARDINE
bristle ..... HAIR, TRICHOME,
STIFFEN, SETA, CHAETA
combining form ... SETI
hooked .... BARB
like growth ...... AWN,
ARISTA, BARBEL, SETA
pertaining to ..... SETAL
ruffed animal ..... BOAR
shaped .... SETIFORM
surgical .... SETON
bristles, covered with .. HISPID
having .... SETOSE,
STRIGOSE, SETACEOUS
tuft of .... PAPPUS
bristletail ...... THYSANURAN
bristling ..... ECHINATE, IRATE
bristly ..... HORRENT, HAIRY,
HIRSUTE, SHAGGY,
SETOSE, HISPID, PRICKLY,
SCOPATE, ACICULAR
animal ...... PORCUPINE,
HOG, BOAR
Bristol paper ..... PASTEBOARD
Britain ... BRITANNIA, ALBION
ancients ... PICT, SILURES
mythical king ..... BRAN,
BRUT
part of .... WALES,
ENGLAND, SCOTLAND
B'rith, _____ .... BNAI
British .... BRITON, ENGLISH,
BLIGHTY, SAXON, LIMEY

ache .... STOUND
active .... NIPPY
actor ... OLIVIER, EVANS,
MARSHALL, AHERNE,
RATHBONE, ARLISS,
COWARD, GRANGER
actress .... NEAGLE,
GARSON, KERR, OBERON,
GWYN, ANDREWS
admiral .... BEATTY,
NELSON
airforce .... RAF
ale .... NOG(G)
altogether .... JOLLY
anger .... WAX
apartment house ....
MANSION
architect ... ADAM, WREN,
SCOTT
armor bearer .... SQUIRE,
ARMIGER
army bugle call .... POST
army fur hat ..... BUSBY
army staff officer: sl. .....
BRASSHAT
assurer ... UNDERWRITER
author ..... MEE, MORE,
ARLEN, SHUTE, CAINE,
BACON, LANDOR, ROGET,
WAUGH, OPIE, AUSTEN,
DEFOE, ELIOT, READE,
BARRIE, BELLOC, MILNE,
STERNE, DORAN
authoress ...... BRONTE,
AUSTEN, ELIOT, WAUGH
baby carriage ..... PRAM
baby hood ..... BIGGIN
bagman ...... SALESMAN
bailiff ... REEVE, STEWARD
ballerina ..... FONTEYN
bar .... PUB
bard, ancient ...... SCOP
barge .... WHERRY
baseball-like game ......
ROUNDERS
basket .... CORF
bathe .... TUB
beak ...... MAGISTRATE,
SCHOOLMASTER
bed .... DOSS
beer .... SWIPES
bit .... SPOT
blackbird ...... THRUSH
boat, ancient .. CORACLE
boatman .... BARGEE

book on the aristocracy .. BRETT'S
borough .... BURGH, LEEDS
bottoms .... HOLM
boy .... NIPPER
boys' school ...... ETON, RUGBY
brandy soda .... PEG
bread .... MANCHET
bulrush .... CATTAIL
bunk .... DOSS
buttercup ... CROWTREE
buttocks: sl. ...... BUM
canal laborer .... NAVVY
captain's boat ... GALLEY
car name .... ROVER, AUSTIN
carbine .... STEN
card game .... PATIENCE
card sharp .... BLACKLEG
carol singer ...... WAIT
cascade .... LADORE
cash: sl. .... RHINO
cask .... KILDERKIN
cat-boat .... UNA
cathedral city ...... ELY, YORK, TRURO
cavalry ...... YEOMANRY
certainly .... RATHER
channel .... SOLENT
Channel isle .... WIGHT
Channel, river to .. SEINE, RANCE, ORNE, SOMME
chap .... COVE
chase .... CHEVY
chemist ...... FARADAY
chief, ancient ...... PENDRAGON
cheese .... STILTON
china .... SPODE
cigarette: sl. .... GASPER
circuit court ...... EYRE
city .... COVENTRY, LEEDS, BATH, LONDON, MANCHESTER, DOVER, HASTINGS, YORK, ELY
clown .... GRIMALDI
cluster .... PLUMP
coachman ...... JARVEY
coal carrier .... CORF
coin ... GEORGE, SOVRAN, SOV(EREIGN), GUINEA, PENNY, FARTHING, PENCE, SHILLING
coin, old ..... CAROLUS,

GROAT, ANGEL
college ... ETON, BALLIOL
college servant ..... GYP
college steward .... MANCIPLE
colonial official .... PROCONSUL
Columbia capital .... VICTORIA
Columbia Indian .. HAIDA
comedian .... TOOLE
composer .... ARNE, ELGAR, DELIUS, COATES
conductor .... BEECHAM, BARBIROLI, SARGENT
conservative party .. TORY
coronation rite .... UNCTION
country festival .... ALE
country gentleman ...... SQUIRE
county ... SHIRE, SUSSEX, DORSET, ESSEX, WILTS, SURREY, HANTS, KENT, YORK, OXON, DERBY, BUCKS, CORNWALL
courage .... PECKER
court ...... LEET, EYRE, SOC, HUSTINGS
cow .... RUNT
crazy .... POTTY
crook .... BLACKLEG
crow .... BRAN
crown jewel .. KOHINOOR, KOHINUR
cue ball .... MASSE
dance, ancient ... MORRIS
dandy .... TOFF, (BEAU)BRUMMEL
dealer .... MONGER
derby hat ...... BOWLER
dessert .... FLAN
diarist ... EVELYN, PEPYS, BURNEY
diplomat .. EDEN, LLOYD
divine ..... INGE, DONNE
dramatist .. SHAW, READE, PINERO, TOBIN, PEELE, SITWELL, MARLOWE
drunk: sl. ..... SCREWED
dump truck ..... TIPPER
dupe .... MUGGINS
dynasty ... STUART, TUDOR
early conqueror .. HORSA, HENGIST, NORMANS
elevator .... LIFT

emblem .... ROSE
emperor of India ....
                    PADISHAU
entry .... CLOSE
essayist ...... LAMB, ELIA
estuary .... HUMBER
exam for honors .. TRIPOS
explorer ... SCOTT, ROSS,
    STANLEY, CABOT, HUDSON,
    RALEIGH, STEELE, LANG,
        BAFFIN, BURTON,
            FROBISHER
expression .... ISAY,
        BULLY, CHEERIO
fashion model .. TWIGGY
fell ... MOOR, HILL, DOWN
fellow .... COVE
field marshal ..... HAIG
field marshal at Arlington
                    DILL
financier ...... GRESHAM,
                    RHODES
first overlord ... EGBERT
fishing boat ..... COBLE,
                    HOOKER
flashlight .... TORCH
food .... TUCK
fool .... MUGGINS
foolish ...... SPOON(E)Y
forest .... ARDEN,
                SHERWOOD
fox hunter .... PINK
franchise .... SOC
free tenant ...... DRENG
freeman .... THANE,
        CHURL, CEORL
gambler who cheats .....
                BLACKLEG
gasoline .... PETROL
general ...... BRADDOCK
geologist .... LYELL
good-by .... PIPPIP
good time .... BASH
government .. WHITEHALL
grove .... SPINNEY
Guiana's capital ....
                GEORGETOWN
gum .... DEXTRIN
gumshoe: sl. .... TEC
gun ...... ENFIELD, STEN
hackney driver .. JARVEY
hamlet .... DORP
handball .... FIVES
handbook on peers ......
                    BRETT'S
hare .... PUSS

hawker .... CHAPMAN
hayfork .... PIKEL
head .... CONK
headland .... NAZE
hedgerow .... REW
highball .... STINGER
highwayman .... TURPIN
historian .... BEDE,
    ACTON, GIBBON, GROTE
holm .... BOTTOMS
Honduras' capital/seaport
                    BELIZE
hooligan .... SPIV
horse .... PRAD, GARRON,
                    SCREW
horse dealer ..... COPER
house-dress ... OVERALL
humorist .... STERNE
hunt .... CHEVY
hunting cry ...... CHEVY,
                    YOICKS
hunting dog ... LURCHER
hut .... NISSEN
hymnodist ...... NEALE,
                    LYTE
ID mark .. BROAD ARROW
India emperor ....
                    PADISHAH
India, founder of ... IVAN
Indian coin .... ANNA
Indian monetary unit ...
                RUPEE, ANNA
Indian nursemaid ....
                AYAH, AMAH
Indian province ... SIND,
                    ASSAM
informer ..... NARK, SPY,
                    NOSE
innkeeper ..... PUBLICAN
island in Atlantic ....
                ASCENSION
island in Indian Ocean ...
                MAURITIUS
island near Borneo ......
                    LABUAN
isle ... ELY, MAN, IRELAND
king ... EDWARD, GEORGE,
    JAMES, HAL, HAROLD
king, ancient ....
            A(E)THELSTAN
king, legendary ... BRUT,
    KNUT, ARTHUR, LUD,
    CANUTE, BELI, BRAN
labor strike(r) ....
                TURN-OUT
laborer ... PROLE, NAVVY

landowner ...... SQUIRE, THANE
language, ancient .... CYMRIC
lecturer .... READER
legislator .... COMMONER
legislature .. PARLIAMENT
lexicographer .. FOWLER, GOWERS
liberal party ...... WHIG
loan money .... PREST
lodgings .... DIGS
lunch .... TIFFIN
machine-gun ..... BREN
mail .... POST
malt liquor .... PORTER
marine: sl. ...... JOLLY
mark on gov't property .. BROAD ARROW
martyr .... ALBAN
meal .... (HIGH) TEA
measure .... ELL
measure, former ... INCH
measure, liquid .... KILDERKIN
mendicant order .. FRIARS
merry-making .... RANT
military police .. REDCAP
military school .... SANDHURST
mine wagon .... ROLLEY, CORF
minister of state ... PITT, PEEL, WALPOLE
mint box .... PYX
miser .... SCREW
model .... TWIGGY
molasses ...... TREACLE
money ...... STERLING, POUND, PENCE, SHILLING, FARTHING
money advanced to enlisted men .... PREST
money: sl. .... RHINO
monk .... B(A)EDA
monk historian .... BEDE
mop .... MALKIN
murderer .... ARAM
naturalist ...... SLOANE
navigator .... DRAKE
navy enlisted man .... BLUEJACKET
nimble .... NIPPY
noble ...... DUKE, EARL, LORD, BARON, PRINCE, VISCOUNT

nonsense! ...... HAVERS
North America .. CANADA
novelist .. READE, RAMEE, ARTHUR, CRONIN, CAINE, MACHEN, BRONTE, HUXLEY, STERNE, DICKENS
nurse .... SISTER
oak .... ROBUR
oatmeal pudding .. MUSH
odd .... RUM
officer's servant .. BATMAN
orator ... PITT, WILLIAM, BURKE
order .... GARTER
ore carrier .... CORF
outcry of blame ..DIRDUM
outlet .... POINT
ox .... RUNT
Pacific protectorate ..... TONGA
pain .... STOUND
painter .... ORPEN, TURNER, CONSTABLE, ROMNEY, PAYNTER, OPIE
parish official .. OVERSEER
parliament member ..... BURGESS
parliamentary record .... HANSARD
party ..... TORY, WHIG, LABOR
passageway ..... SMOOT, CLOSE
path .... PAD
patron saint .. (ST)GEORGE
peddler .... CHAPMAN
people, ancient ... ICENI
petrol ... GAS, GASOLINE
petty .... POTTY
philosopher .... RUSSELL, BACON, HUME, JOAD, SPENCER
physician .... ROSS
physicist .... FARADAY
pianist .... BAUER
pickpocket .... PRIG
playwright .... SHAW, PEELE
pluck .... PECKER
pocket .... SACK
poet .... AUDEN, HUGH, GRAY, KEATS, SPENCER, BLAKE, MASEFIELD, AUSTIN, BYRON, SITWELL, DONNE, ELIOT, LANG
poet, earliest .. CAEDMON,

SCOP

poet laureate ....
    MASEFIELD, CIBBER,
    AUSTIN, DAY-LEWIS
poetess .... SITWELL,
    BROWNING
policeman ...... BOBBY,
    PEELER
policeman's station .....
    POINT
political party ..... TORY,
    CONSERVATIVE, LABOR
political philosopher ....
    BURKE
Pope .... ADRIAN(IV)
port ...... HULL, DOVER,
    POOLE, LIVERPOOL,
    PRESTON, COWES, BRISTOL
pot herb .... CLARY
pottery/porcelain .. SPODE
prefab shelter ... NISSEN
prig .. THIEF, PICKPOCKET
prime minister .. WILSON,
    ASQUITH, CHURCHILL,
    PITT, BALDWIN, PEEL,
    ATTLEE, BALFOUR, HOME,
    LAW, MACMILLAN, CANNING
prime minister called
    Ironside .... PITT
prime minister with the
    cigar .... CHURCHILL
prime minister with the
    umbrella ....
    CHAMBERLAIN
prince .... ANDREW,
    CHARLES
princess ..... MARGARET,
    ANNE, URSULA
printer .... CAXTON
printing type ...... RUBY
prison ..... DARTMOOR,
    LEADS
prison: sl. ... QUOD, QUAD
property tax ...... RATE
psychologist ...... ELLIS
publisher .. BEAVERBROOK
pudding .... MUSH,
    ROLY-POLY
pupil: sl. .... SCUM
Quaker .... PENN
queen .... ANNE, MARY,
    ELIZABETH, VICTORIA
queen, ancient ....
    BOADICEA
queer .... RUM
quick .... NIPPY

race course ...... ASCOT,
    EPSOM(DOWNS)
RAF fighter .. SPITFIRE
rage .... WAX
raincoat ... WATERPROOF
range .... KITCHENER
ratable .... TAXABLE
Reformation leader .....
    SEYMOUR
reformer .... SPENCE
resort ...... BLACKPOOL,
    BATH, MARGATE
retail store .. WAREHOUSE
river ..... AVON, MERSEY,
    THAMES, ALN, CAM, WYE,
    EXE, URE, OUSE, TEES, AIRE,
    TEE, TRENT, TYNE, USK,
    NENE, NEN, SEVERN, DEE,
    YARE
river lowland .. BOTTOMS,
    HOLM
road .... PAD
rock singer ....
    (MICK) JAGGER
routine .... ROTA
royal family ..... TUDOR,
    STUART
royal guard officer .. EXON
royal house ..... TUDOR,
    YORK, HANOVER, WINDSOR,
    STUART
royal household official ..
    GROOM
royal stables ...... MEWS
rubbish! .... HAVERS
ruler, early .. EGBERT, OFFA
ruling family .. WINDSOR,
    TUDOR
sailor .... LIMEY
saint .... ALBAN, AARON
salary .... SCREW
salesman ...... BAGMAN
saloon-keeper .. PUBLICAN
sandhill .... DENE
scarecrow ...... MALKIN
school boy servant .. FAG
school, prep ..... ETON,
    HARROW, RUGBY
school teacher ... MASTER,
    MISTRESS
schoolmaster ..... ARAM,
    BEAK
scientist .... DARWIN
seaman ...... RATING
seaport.. .BOOTLE, DOVER,
MARGATE, GRIMSBY, WHITBY

sedan .... SALOON
sentimental ...... SOPPY
serf ..... ESNE, THRALL
sergeant-at-law cap .....
.... BIGGIN
sheriff's aid ... BULLDOG
sidewalk artist ....
.... SCREEVER
silly .... SPOON(E)Y
slaughterhouse ....
.... KNACKER
sleep: sl. .... DOSS
smart .... STOUND
smack .... HOOKER
smock .... OVERALL
snarl .... GIRN
social event ...... ASCOT
socialist .... FABIAN
soldier .. REDCOAT, LIMEY,
TOMMY, ATKINS
soldier's furlough/leave ..
.... BLIGHTY
solitaire .... PATIENCE
songbird .... BULBUL,
BULLFINCH
spa ..... BATH, MARGATE
spark .... SPUNK
spot .... BIT
spy .. ANDRE, NOSE, NARK
stage .... PLATEAU
statesman .. PITT, BURKE,
GREY, HOARE, EDEN, CLIVE
steal .... PRIG
stool pigeon: sl. ... NARK
stove .... KITCHENER
strange .... RUM
streetcar .... TRAM
student, senior ....
.... PREPOS(I)TOR
surgeon .... LISTER
swell dresser .... TOFF
symbol .... (JOHN) BULL
tax ... SESS, GELD, EXCISE
tea .... ELM
tent .... MARQUEE
thanks .... TAS
theologian ..... ALCUIN
theorist .... LASKI
thicket .... SPINNEY
thief .... PRIG
tin mine ..... STANNARY
title ..... DUKE, PRINCE,
BARON, EARL
toast .... CHEERS
tobacco bit ...... SCREW
tourist .... TRIPPER

trader .... MONGER
traveler .... TRIPPER
trout .... SEWIN, SEWEN
truck .... LORRY
tutor .... MASTER
25 pounds: sl. ..... PONY
unit of measure ... STACK
university disciplinarian ..
.... BULLDOG
university official ....
.... BEADLE
university student ....
.... SOPHISTER
very .... JOLLY
village ... BOURG, ARAWE,
DORP
wage earner ..... PROLE
waiter .... POTMAN
warrior .... CNUT
Wave .... WREN
weight ..... STONE, MAST,
KEEL
weight for wool ..... TOD
whisky-soda ... STINGER
willow herb ... ROSEBAY
with the umbrella ......
.... CHAMBERLAIN
woman politician ....
(LADY) ASTOR
woman servant .. SLAVEY
woman, slovenly ....
.... MALKIN
wood pigeon ... CULVER
woodland area ... WEALD
work horse ... GARRAN
World War I commander
.... HAIG
wrap .... RUG
Briton, early .. ANGLE, JUTE,
PICT, CELT, ICENI
Brittany .... BRETAGNE,
ARMORICA
brittle .... CRISP, FRAGILE,
CRACKLY, BRASH
Brno name ..... (JOSIP) TITO
bro. .... BROTHER
broach ..... BRING UP, AWL,
CHISEL, RIMER, HOLE, REAMER,
SPIT, SKEWER, INTRODUCE
broad ...... WIDE, SPACIOUS,
EXTENSIVE, GENERAL, CLEAR
band: heraldry ..... FESS
slang .... WOMAN
broadbill ...... SCAUP, DUCK,
SPOONBILL, GAPER, RAYA

broadbrim: colloq. .... FRIEND, QUAKER, HAT

broadcast .. SPREAD, SCATTER, TELECAST, SOW

broadcasting system .... NBC, CBS, ABC

broadcloth .... PIMA

broaden .... WIDEN, EXPAND, SPREAD

broadleaf .... TOBACCO

broadminded ...... TOLERANT, LIBERAL, UNDERSTANDING

broadside ..... ABUSE, SALVO, ATTACK

broadsword ..... CLAYMORE, CUTLASS, BILL, GLA(I)VE

broadtail ... SHEEP, KARAKUL, ASTRAKHAN

Broadway character ... ANGEL, SUGAR DADDY, PRESS AGENT, HOOFER

girls, former .... FLORADORA

impresario .... MERRICK

(nick)name .... FLO ZIEGFELD, COHAN, BILLY ROSE

restauranteur .... SARDI

square .... HERALD

venture ... PLAY, REVUE, MUSICAL(E)

Brobdingnagian .... GIANT, GIGANTIC

brocade .... BALDACHIN, BAUDEKIN, BROCHE

gold .... KINCOB

Japanese ...... NISHIKI

broccoli .... CAULIFLOWER

brochette .... SKEWER

brochure .... PAMPHLET

brock .... BADGER

brocket .... DEER, PITA, SPITTER

brogan ... BROGUE, BOOT, SHOE

brogue .... ACCENT, PRONUNCIATION, SHOE

Scotch .... TRICK, DECEPTION

broil .... ROAST, BARBECUE, BRAWL, GRILL, BAKE, BRAISE

broiled meat ...... BARBECUE

broiler ..... CHICKEN, CAPON, PAN, GRIDIRON

broke: sl. .... PENNILESS, BANKRUPT

broken .... TAMED, SPLINTERED, VIOLATED, INTERRUPTED, SMASHED

colloquial .... DISMISSED

down ... RUINED, USELESS, CHATTERED, DECREPIT

grain husk .... BRAN

ice .... BRASH

mass of clouds .... RACK

piece .... FRAGMENT

pieces of pottery ...... SHARDS

pieces of masonry ...... RUBBLE

spike of grain .... CHOB

stone debris .... RUBBLE

wind .... HEAVES

broker ..... AGENT, FACTOR, MIDDLEMAN

business of .... AGIOTAGE

order to ..... BUY, SELL, UNLOAD

real estate ..... REALTOR

brokerage .... AGIO

fee .... BROKAGE

Brom Bones' lack ...... HEAD

broma .... COCOA

bromide .... SEDATIVE, PLATITUDE, SOP

bromine .... HALOGEN

bronchial tube ..... TRACHEA, WINDPIPE

bronchitis remedy .... GRINDELIA

bronc(h)o ...... HORSE, PONY, MUSTANG

buster .. COWBOY, TAMER

Bronte biographer ..... GERIN

brother ...... BRANWELL

family's native village ... HAWORTH

husband of Charlotte .... NICHOLLS

pseudonym of Anne ..... ACTON BELL

pseudonym of Charlotte ..... CURRER BELL

pseudonym of Emily .... ELLIS BELL

work .... JANE EYRE, WUTHERING HEIGHTS

bronto as combining form ..... THUNDER, HUGENESS

brontosaurus ...... DINOSAUR

Bronx ... BOROUGH, COCKTAIL

cheerer's feeling .... DERISION, DISGUST, SCORN

bronze .... ALLOY, TAN, COPPER, AENEOUS, LATTEN
   coating/crust of .. PATINA
   coin .... AES
   component ..... COPPER (AND) TIN
   "gold" .... ORMOLU, VERMEIL
   green coating .... VERD, PATINA VERDIGRIS, ANTIQUE
   Roman .... AES
   tool .... CELT
broo: Scot. ..... BROTH, BREE
brooch ... PIN, OUCH, CLASP, CLIP, CAMEO
brood .... MOPE, THINK, COGITATE, HATCH, PONDER, SULK, HOVER, SIT, FLOCK
   of birds .... COVEY
   of chicks .... CLUTCH
   of family .... CHILDREN
   of eaglets .... AERIE
   of goats/sheep ... FLOCK
   of pheasants ...... NIDE
   of sucks/pigs ..... TEAM
brooder ...... HEN, WORRIER
brooding hen's sound .. CLUCK, CACKLE
brook .... STREAM, BEAR, RILL(ET), RIVULET, RUNNEL, ENDURE, GILL
brooklime .... VERONICA
Brooklyn Dodgers' nickname SUPERBAS
   institute .... PRATT
   island .... CONEY
brookweed ...... PIMPERNEL
broom ...... BRUSH, SWEEP, SHRUB, BESOM, CLEANER, WHISK
   grass/material .. ZACATON
   plant .... BESOM
broomcorn grain ...... HIRSE
broth ...... SOUP, CONSOMME, POTAGE, BROO, BREE, GRUEL
   cabbage/greens ... KALE
brothel .... BORDEL(LO), BAGNIO, WASTE, KIP, BAWDYHOUSE
   keeper .... BAWD, PROCURESS, MADAM
brother .... FRA, FRIAR, FRATER, PEER, FELLOW, MONK
   colloquial ... BROD, BUB
brotherhood .... ELKS, SODALITY, ORDER, FRATERNITY, ASSOCIATION, UNION
brotherly .... FRATERNAL
brougham .... CARRIAGE, AUTOMOBILE, LIMOUSINE
brought up ... BRED, REARED, BROACHED, INTRODUCED
   by hand .... CADE
brouhaha .... UPROAR, COMMOTION, HUBBUB, STIR
brow ...... FOREHEAD, BRAE, EYEBROW, EDGE
browbeat ...... BULLY, INTIMATE, BAMBOOZLE, HECTOR
brown ... TAN, SEPIA, UMBER, BISTER, RUSSET, SORREL, SIENNA, TOAST, ROAST, DUN, BEIGE
   actress .... VANESSA
   apple .... RUSSET
   betty ... (APPLE)PUDDING
   coal .... LIGNITE
   dark .... BURNET
   kiwi .... ROA
   light .... PONGEE
   paper .... KRAFT
   pigment .... BISTER, BISTRE, UMBER
   reddish .... AUBURN
   seaweed .... KELP
   Shirt ... NAZI, HITLERITE
   shoes .... TANS
   skinned people .... MALAY(IANS), FILIPINOS, INDONS
   study .... REVERIE
   thrasher ..... SONGBIRD
   yellow .... PABLO
brownie .... ELF, GOBLIN, GIRL SCOUT, CAKE, GNOME, NIS, PIXIE, KOBOLD, CAMERA
Browning's home in Italy ..... ASOLO
brownish .... DUN
   purple .... PUCE
   red .... TERRA-COTTA, RUFOUS, MAROON
   yellow .... TAWNY, BUFF
brownout .. DIMOUT, DIMMING
brownstone front ..... STOOP, FACADE
   sign ..... ROOMS, TO LET
browntail .... MOTH
browse .... NIBBLE, GRAZE, FEED, GLANCE

Broz, Josip .... TITO
brucine .... ALKALOID
bruin .... BEAR
bruise ...... CONTUSE, CRUSH,
    DISCOLORATION, JAM
    application for .. ARNICA
bruiser .... BOXER, BULLY
bruising implement ... PESTLE
bruit .... CLAMOR, RUMOR,
    SPREAD, GOSSIP, TELL,
    REPORT
brumal .... WINTRY, SLEETY,
    HIEMAL
brume ..... FOG, MIST, VAPOR
brummagem: colloq. ...CHEAP,
    GAUDY, FAKE
brumous .... FOGGY, MISTY
Brunhild's husband ....
    GUNTHER, GUNNAR
Brunn .... BRNO
Brunnhilde (see Brynhild) .....
    VALKYRIE
    fate of .... SLEEP
    mother of .... ERDA
    savior .... SIEGFRIED
brunt .... IMPACT, SHOCK
brush .... TOUCH, CLEAN,
    POLISH, PAINT, FITCH,
    GRAZE, SKIRMISH, BROSSE,
    DUSTER, BROOM, SWEEP
    aside .... IGNORE,
    SWEEP(OUT)
    for sweeping ..... BROOM
    lightly .... SCUFF
    like .... SCOPULATE
    material .... ZACATON
    off .... DISMISS(AL), SNUB
    up ... NEATEN, CLEAN UP
brushwood .... COPSE,
    COPPICE, SCRUB, BRAKE
    fence .... WEIR
brushwork .... PAINTING
brushy ..... BRISTLY, BUSHY
brusque ..... ABRUPT, BLUNT,
    CURT, SHORT, BLUFF, GRUFF
Brussels carpet ..... TOURNAI
    is capital of ..... BELGIUM
    sprouts .... CABBAGE
brut .... DRY
brutal ..... SAVAGE, CRUEL,
    COARSE, RUDE, FERAL,
    FERINE
    behavior .... BARBARISM
    soldier .... PANDOUR
brute .... INSENSATE, STUPID,
    BEAST, ANIMAL, GROSS

Brynhild's brother-in-law .....
    SIGURD
    husband ...... GUNNAR,
    GUNTHER
    mother .... ERDA
    sister-in-law ... GUDRUN,
    GUTHRUN
bryophyte .. MOSS, LIVERWORT
bryozoan ..... POLYP, HYDRA,
    CORAL, SEAPEN,
    SEA ANEMONE, POLYZOAN
Brythonic sea-god .... LER
bskt. .... BASKET
bub: colloq. ... BROTHER, BOY
bubaline .... ANTELOPES,
    HARTEBEESTS
bubble ...... BLEB, GLOBULE,
    BEAD, BOIL, FOAM
    air .... BLEB
    Archaic .... CHEAT,
    SWINDLE
    fragrantly .... PERK
    maker .... GUM
    over .. OVERFLOW, EXULT
    up .... BOIL
    with excitement/joy .....
    GUSH
bubbler of a sort ... FOUNTAIN,
    BROOK
bubbling .... FIZZY,
    EFFERVESCENT
bubbles, full of ..... HUBBLY
bubonic plague carrier ... FLEA,
    RAT
buccal .... MALAR
buccaneer .... PIRATE,
    SEA ROBBER, CORSAIR, GRILL
    ancient .... VIKING
Bucephalus ..... (WAR)HORSE,
    STEED
Buceresti .... BUCHAREST
Bucharest, capital of ....
    ROMANIA
buck .... DEER, GOAT,
    SAWHORSE, DANDY
    and wing ..... TAPDANCE
    antler of ..... ADVANCER
    black .... SASIN
    colloquial .... RESIST
    four-year old ...... SORE
    Indian .... SASIN
    novelist .... PEARL
    red .... PALLAH
    slang .... DOLLAR
    up: colloq. .. CHEER(UP),
    BRACE(UP)

water .... KOB
young ... INDIAN, NEGRO, LAD
buckaroo .... COWBOY
bucket .... PAIL, SKEEL, BAIL, CANNIKIN
butter .... KIT
coal ..... SCUTTLE, TUB
fish .... KIT
handle .... BAIL
kick the .... DIE
make of a .... OAKEN
mining .... TUB
Scot. .... STOUP
Buckeye State .... OHIO
buckish .... FOPPISH
buckle ... CLASP, CATCH, JOIN, GRAPPLE, WARP, KINK, OUCH
ancient .... FIBULA
under ... YIELD, SUBMIT, COLLAPSE, GIVE IN
buckler .. (ARM)SHIELD, TARGE
bucko .... BULLY
buckra, in Africa .. WHITEMAN
buckthorn .. CASCARA, WAHOO
buckwheat tree .. TITI, TEETEE
weed ...... DOCK, JUNK, TARE, LOCO
bucolic .... ARCADIAN, RURAL, RUSTIC, AGRESTIC, PASTORAL, GEOPONIC
sound ... MOO, LOW, BAA, BLEAT, CROW, CACKLE
bud ... BULB(IL), PULLULATE, (S)CION, GEMMA, BURGEON, SPROUT, GERM
dried .... CLOVE
Fisher's creation .. MUTT, JEFF, CICERO
for grafting ..... (S)CION
large and compact .. HEAD
like outgrowth ... GEMMA
nip in the .. CHECK, STOP
of society .... DEB
on a flower stalk .. BULBIL
potato .... EYE
scale .... CATAPHYLL
variation .... SPORT
Budapest is capital of .... HUNGARY
Buddha .... GAUTAMA, FO
cousin of ...... ANANDA
Japanese ... AMIDA, AMITA
mother of .... MAYA
tree of .... PIPAL

Buddhism, fate in .... KARMA
form of .... LAMAISM
founder of .... GAUTAMA
hatred .... DOSA
perfect blessedness ...... NIRVANA
religious language .. PALI
Buddhist angel .... DEVA
column .... LAT
church ... TERA, PAGODA
dialect .... PALI
fate .... KARMA
festival .... BON
final release .... NIRVANA
gateway .... TORAN
hell .... NARAKA
holy city ... LHASA, LASSA
holy man .... MAHATMA
language .... PALI
lierature .... SUTRA
monastery .... TERA
monk .... TALAPOIN, BONZE, BO, LAMA
mound .... STUPA
novice .... GOYIN
paradise .... JODO
pillar .... LAT
priest .... LAMA, BONZE, MAHATMA, BO
religious observances .... DHARMA
saint .... AR(A)HAT
scripture .. SUTRA, SUTTA
sect, Japanese ...... ZEN
shrine .... DAGOBA, STUPA, TOPE
Siamese .... LAO
temple .... PAGODA, VIHARA
title of respect .... MAHATMA
buddle ..... TROUGH, DRAIN
buddy ..... COMPANION, PAL, COMRADE, BOY, CRONY
British slang ..... CULLY
budge .... MOVE, FUR, LAMBSKIN, POMPOUS
budgerigar .... PARAKEET, BUDGIE
budget ... BAG, POUCH, STOCK, SCHEDULE, APPROPRIATION
anything ..... APPORTION
plan .... INSTALLMENT
buds, pickled .... CAPERS
put forth ...... SPROUT, SHOOT, BURGEON

bueno: Sp. . . . GOOD, VERY WELL
Buenos Aires is capital of . . . .
   ARGENTINA
buenos días: Sp. . . . .
   GOOD MORNING, GOOD DAY,
   GREETING
buff . . . . LEATHER, POLISH,
   SPINDLE, BLOW
   colloquial . . . . DEVOTEE,
   FAN, AFICIONADO
buffalo . . . . OX, BISON
   Bill . . . . CODY
   bird . . . . COWBIRD
   bug . . . . BEETLE
   Celebes . . . . ANOA
   crossed with cattle . . . . .
   CAT(T)ALO
   female . . . . COW
   hybrid . . . . CAT(T)ALO
   Philippine . . . . CARABAO,
   TIMARAW, TIMARAU
   skin . . . . BUFF
   slang . . BAMBOOZLE, BULLY
   S. African . . . . NIARE
buffer . . . . CUSHION,
   SOCK ABSORBER
buffet . . . . . CREDENZA, BLOW,
   PUNCH, SLAP, COUNTER,
   TOSS, TABLE, SIDEBOARD
   meals . . . . SPREADS
buffeted: poetic . . . . TOST
bufflehead . . . . . BUTTERBALL,
   DUCK
buffo . . . . COMIC,
   OPERA SINGER, CLOWN
   voice of a . . . . BASS
buffoon . . . . CLOWN,
   PRANKSTER, DROLL, ZANY,
   JESTER, MIME(R),
   (MERRY) ANDREW,
   FOOL, HARLEQUIN,
   PUNCHINELLO
buffoonery . . . . . . CLOWNING,
   DROLLERY
bufo: Latin . . . . TOAD
bug . . . . . . CONENOSE, CIMEX,
   GERM, ANNOY, HOBGOBLIN,
   BEETLE, INSECT
   living on other insects . . .
   ASSASSIN
   river . . . . NAREW
   slang . . . . . . MICROPHONE,
   ADDICT, DEFECT, ANGER,
   ANNOY
   with sucking beak . . . .
   ASSASSIN

with built-in light . . . .
   FIREFLY
bugaboo . . . . . . MUMBO JUMBO,
   BUGBEAR, SCARECROW
   African . . . GOGO, BOGIE
bugbear . . . (HOB)GOBLIN, BOGY
   of a kind . . . . OGRE
bugger . . . . . SODOMITE, CHAP,
   FELLOW
buggy . . . . PRAM,
   PERAMBULATOR, CARRIAGE,
   CHAISE, SHAY
bughouse: sl. . . . . . NUTHOUSE,
   INSANE, CRAZY
bugle . . . . HORN, PLANT, READ
   call . . . . RETREAT,
   TANTARA, TAT(T)OO,
   TAPS, REVEILLE, ASSEMBLY
   carabao horn . . TAMBULI
   note . . . . TIRALEE
   signal . . . . TATTOO
   yellow . . . . IVA
bugloss . . . . ANCHUSA
bugs: sl. . . . . . INSANE, CRAZY
buhr . . . . WHETSTONE
build . . . . REAR, ERECT,
   CONSTRUCT, RAISE,
   STATURE, PHYSIQUE
   up: colloq. . . . PUBLICITY,
   PRAISE, PLUG
builder's knot . . CLOVEHITCH
building . . . . EDIFICE,
   STRUCTURE, PILE
   caretaker . . . . . . JANITOR
   crowded . . . . . . WARREN
   behind a big one . . . .
   BACKHOUSE
   external corner of . . . .
   QUOIN
   for bowling . . . . . ALLEYS
   for exhibits . . . PAVILION
   for famous dead persons
   PANTHEON
   for fodder . . . . SILO
   for fruit-growing . . . .
   GRAPERY
   for gambling . . . CASINO
   for grains . . . . GRANARY,
   ELEVATOR
   for musical performances
   OPERA HOUSE,
   AUDITORIUM
   inscription on . . EPIGRAPH
   material . . . . ADOBE,
   MORTAR, CONCRETE,
   WOOD, STONE, STAFF

projecting ornament .... GARGOYLE
projection .... BAY
round .... ROTUNDA
site ..... LOT, STEADING
wing ... ELL, ANNEX, BAY
built-in bed .... BUNK, BERTH
Bukhara product .... RUG
bulb .... BUD, ONION, HYACINTH, GARLIC, LEEK, SEGO
edible .... CAMAS(S)
glass .... AMPOULE
like root ..... TUBEROSE
like stem, plant with ..... CORM, TUBER, CROCUS
lily .... CAMAS, SEGO
lily, dried ...... SQUILL
plant ...... SEGO, TULIP
segment .... CLOVE
bulbous plant .... GARLIC, TUBEROSE
bulbul .... SONGBIRD, NIGHTINGALE
Bulgarian ... SLAV, CHUVASH
capital .... SOFIA
coin ... LEV, LEW, DINAR, STOTINKA
czar/tsar ... ... BORIS
king .... SIMEON
moslem .... POMAK
queen ...... MARGARITA
seaport .... VARNA
weight .... OKA, OKE
bulge .... SWELLING, PROTRUDE, FLARE, PROTUBERANCE, PROJECTION
of belly: sl. .... BAY WINDOW
of skull .... INION
bulging ..... GIBBOUS, TUMID, TOROUS, TOROSE
bulimia, in medicine .. HUNGER
bulk ..... SIZE, MASS, VOLUME, TOTAL, WHOLE, MAJORITY
bulkhead .... WALL, EMBANKMENT
bulky .... LARGE, MASSIVE, BIG, MASSY, HEFTY
bull ..... TORO, TAURUS, MALE, SEAL, LIE
castrated ..... BULLOCK
cry .... BELLOW
John .... ENGLAND
of/like a ..... TAURIN(E)
of Hercules .... CRETAN
of myth ..... MINATOUR
sacred: Egyptian ... APIS
slang .... NONSENSE, POLICEMAN, COP
young ... STOT, BULLOCK
bull's eye, circle next to ...... INNER
bulla ...... BLISTER, VESICLE, BLAIN, BLEB, PUSTULE
bullace .... PLUM, TREE
bullbat .... NIGHTHAWK
bulldog .... PUG, MASTIFF, REVOLVER
color .... BRINDLE
soft-nosed .... DUMDUM
trait .... COURAGE, STUBBORNNESS, TENACITY
bulldogging place ..... RODEO
"Bulldogs" .... ELIS
bulldoze .... COERCE, BROWBEAT, FORCE, BULLY, FRIGHTEN
bullet ... PELLET, SHOT, SLUG, MISSILE, BALL
charge container .... CARTRIDGE
kind of .... DUMDUM, TRACER
metal covering .. JACKET
size .... CALIBER
bulletin .... STATEMENT, PUBLICATION, NEWS(LETTER), REPORT
kind of .... WEATHER, MEDICAL
bulletproof shield .... MANT(E)LET
bullfight cheer .... OLE
bullfighter ..... MATADOR, TOREADOR, PICADOR
assistant .... PICADOR
mantle .... CAPA
on foot .... TORERO
queue of .... COLETA
bullfighting dart .... BANDERILLA
participant .... BANDERILLERO
bullfinch .. SONGBIRD, HEDGE OLP, REDBIRD
bullfrog's cry .... BOOM
bullhead ...... FISH, CATFISH, SCULPIN
bullheaded .... STUBBORN, HEADSTRONG
animal, of a sort ... MULE

bullion before coinage .. INGOT,
    BAR, GOLD, SILVER, BILLOT
bullock ..... OX, STEER, STIRK
bully ... BUCKO, PIMP, THUG,
    BRUISER, CORNED BEEF,
    HUFF, BROWBEAT, HECTOR,
    BULLDOZE, BAMBOOZLE
colloquial ... FINE, GOOD,
    WELL DONE
    tree .... BALATA
bulrush ...... PAPYRUS, TULE
    British .... CATTAIL
bulwark ...... EARTHWORK,
    WALL, RAMPART,
    BREAKWATER, SCONCE,
    DEFENSE, PROTECTION
bum .... IDLER, LOAFER,
    SPREE, SPONGER, LOAF,
    BOAT
    a ride ..... HITCH(HIKE)
    ambulant ..... VAGRANT
    British slang .. BUTTOCKS
    check, describing one ....
    BOUNCING
bumble .... BLUNDER
bumblebee .... DOR
bump .... COLLIDE, JOLT,
    SWELLING, LUMP, JOSTLE
    off: sl. .... MURDER, KILL
    slang .... REPLACE
bumper ... LARGE, ABUNDANT,
    TOAST, BRIMMER
    auto .... GUARD
bum(p)kin ...... LOUT, YOKEL,
    CLOD, RUBE, YAHOO
    ship's .... BOOM, SPAR
bumpkins .... CAVES
bumptious ...... CONCEITED,
    ARROGANT, PUSHING
bumpy ..... ROUGH, JOLTING,
    JERKY
bun .... ROLL, LOAF, KNOT
bunch ...... CYME, CLUSTER,
    TUFT, COLLECTION, LOT,
    BUNDLE
    grass .... STIPA
    of branches ...... COMA
    of grapes ..... BOTRYOID
    of sheaves ...... SHOCK,
    SHOOK
    small .... WISP
bunchberry .... DOGWOOD
bunco: colloq. ...... SWINDLE,
    CHEAT
buncombe .... HUMBUG,
    BOMBAST, BUNK,

TWADDLE, MALARKEY
bund .. LEAGUE, CONFEDERATION
    Oriental .... QUAY,
    EMBANKMENT
bundle ... PACKAGE, PARCEL,
    BUNCH, BALE, PACK, SHEAF,
    TRUSS
    of fibers .... FASCICLE
    of hay .... WASE
    of joy: colloq. ..... BABY
    of rods .... FASCES
    of sticks/twigs ... FAGOT,
    FASCINE
    of straw .... WASE
    small .... FASCICLE
    of sheaves of grain ......
    STOOK
bundling device .... BALER
bung .... CORK, STOPPER,
    CLOSE
    slang ... BRUISE, DAMAGE
bungalow .... COTTAGE
bungle .... BOTCH, LOUSE(UP),
    SPOIL, MESS, MUFF, FOOZLE,
    FUMBLE
    a golf stroke .... DUB
    a play .... MUFF
    slang .... BOLLIX
bungling .... MALADROIT
bunion .... BURSITIS
bunk ...... BED, COT, BERTH,
    SLEEP
    British slang ...... DOSS
    slang .... HOKUM,
    BUNCOMBE, NONSENSE,
    TWADDLE, HOOEY
bunker .... BIN, TANK,
    SANDTRAP
bunko ...... CHEAT, SWINDLE
bunny .... RABBIT
    playboy's .... HOSTESS
    tail .... SCUT
    time .... EASTER
bunt ...... SHOVE, BAT, SMUT
    with horn: Brit. ... BUTT,
    STRIKE
bunting .... FLAGS, BIRD,
    ORTOLAN, ETAMINE, FINCH
    migratory ... DICKCISSEL
Bunyan's ox .... BABE
buoy .. DAN, FLOAT, MAKEFAST
    for mooring boat ....
    DOLPHIN
    type .... CAN, NUN,
    WHISTLE, BELL, SPAR
    up ... ENCOURAGE, BOOST

buoyancy ... GAIETY, LEVITY,
FLOTAGE, RESILIENCE,
CHEERFULNESS
bur .... SEEDCASE, WEED
buran .... WINDSTORM
burble ...... GURGLE, BUBBLE
burbot ... LING, MARIA, CUSK
burd: obsolete .... LADY
burden .... LOAD, OPPRESS,
ONUS, CUMBER,
WEIGH DOWN, INCUBUS
bearer .... AMASA, ATLAS,
PORTER
beast of ..... MULE, ASS,
BURRO, CAMEL, DONKEY
squaw's .... PAPOOSE
burdensome .... HEAVY,
OPPRESSIVE, ONEROUS
burdock .... BURR, CLITE,
COCKLEBUR
bureau .... DRESSER, DESK,
CHEST, OFFICE, CHIFFONIER,
HIGHBOY
top cover .... SCARF
bureaucracy ...... OFFICIALS,
OFFICIALDOM
petty ...... BEADLEDOM
bureaucratic failing: colloq. ...
RED TAPE
burg ... TOWN, CITY, VILLAGE
lord of .... BURGRAVE
burgeon .... SPROUT, BUD
burgess .... CITIZEN, FREEMAN
burgess' invention ..... GOOP
burgh ..... BOROUGH, TOWN
burglar .. THIEF, ROBBER, YEGG
hazard of .... ALARM BELL
loot of .... SWAG
burgomaster ... MAYOR, GULL
burgonet ... HELMET, MORION
burgoo .... PORRIDGE, GRUEL,
SCUP, BARBECUE
Burgundy wine ...... CHABLIS
kingdom of .... ARLES
burial .... INTERMENT,
SEPULTURE, INHUMATION
box ..... CASKET, COFFIN,
BIER
clothes ..... CERECLOTH,
CEREMENT, SHROUD
ground for the poor .....
POTTER'S FIELD
heap/mound .. TUMULUS,
BARROW
pertaining to ... FUNERAL,
FUNERARY

pile .... PYRE
place .. TOMB, CATACOMB,
SEPULCHER, CRYPT,
CEMETERY, GRAVE(YARD)
vault .... SEPULTURE
burin .... GRAVER
like tool .... CHISEL
burke .... MURDER,
SUFFOCATE, SUPPRESS
Burke's subject ..... PEERAGE
Burkitt's tumor .. LYMPHOMA
burl .... KNOT, VENEER
burlesque .... PARODY,
CARICATURE, COMEDY,
VAUDEVILLE
number .... STRIP TEASE,
SKIT
burley .... TOBACCO
burly .... MUSCULAR, HUSKY,
GROSS
Burma Road's other name ....
(THE) HUMP
terminus .... LASHIO
Burmese Buddhist ..... MON,
PROME
capital .... RANGOON
capital, former ..... AVA
chief .... BO(H)
city .... MANDALAY,
RANGOON, MAULMAIN,
MOULMEIN
dagger .... DOW, DAH
demon .... NAT
district .... PROME
division .... PEGU,
ARAKAN, YEU
ethnic group ...... MONS,
CHINS, KARENS, NAGAS,
KACHINS
gibbon .... LAR
garment .... LONGYI
gate .... TORAN
girl .... MIMA
governor .. WOON, WUN
hill .... NAGA, CHIN,
KACHIN
hillman .... LAI
knife ... KAH, KHAO, DOW
language .... LAI, PEGU,
CHIN, KUKI, WA, KACHIN
measure ..... DHA, SEIT,
BYEE
Mongol .... LAI
monk .... BO
mountain range ....
ARAKAN

musical instrument ......
TORAN, TURR
native ... PEGUAN, KADU,
KUKI, LAI, WA, WAS
pagoda .... PHAYA
peasant .... TAO
premier .... U NU
river ...... IRRAWADDY,
TAPING
robber .... DACOIT
sarong .... LONGYI
shelter .... ZAYAT
shrimp .... NAPEE
spirit .... NAT
town .... LASHIO
tree .... ACLE
tribe .... TAI, SHAN
weight ..... VIS(S), RUAY,
KYAT, TICAL
burn .... FIRE, SCORCH, GLOW,
SEAR, CHAR
down .... RAZE
hair ends .... SINGE
incense .... CENSE
mark .... ESCHAR
mark of sun ...... TAN,
SUNTAN
mark with hot iron ...
BRAND
nap of cloth ...... SINGE
Scot. .... STREAM
slightly .... SINGE
the midnight oil ......
LUCUBRATE, BONE, CRAM
the road .... RACE,
SPEED(UP), BARREL
to stop infection ......
CAUTERIZE
unsteadily ..... FLICKER
up: colloq. ..... ANGER,
ENRAGE, IRRITATE
with hot fluid .... SCALD
with hot iron/needle ....
CAUTERIZE, BRAND
without flame ....
SMO(U)LDER
burned up: sl. ... SORE, ANGRY
burner .... BUNSEN,
CREMATORY, INCINERATOR,
ARGAND
burning ..... AFIRE, AFLAME,
ABLAZE, EAGER, FEVERISH
bush .... WAHOO,
FRAXINELLA
coal container .. BRASIER,
BRAZIER

glass .... LENS
malicious .... ARSON
process .... COMBUSTION
sensation ... CAUSALGIA,
HEAT
stick .... BRAND
woodpile outdoors ......
BONFIRE
burnish ...... POLISH, GLOSS,
SHINE, FURBISH
an error/fault .... GLOSS
Burns' sweetheart ....
(HIGHLAND) MARY
burnsides .... WHISKERS,
BEARD, MUTTON CHOPS
burnt .... ADUST
sugar .... CARAMEL
burp: sl. .... BELCH
burr .... SEEDCASE,
ROUGH EDGE, DRILL, POD
plant/weed ... BURDOCK,
COCKLEBUR, THISTLE,
TEASEL
Burr's daughter .... THEO
burro .... DONKEY, ASS
female .... MARE
burrow ... HOLE, TUNNEL, DIG
burrowing animal ....
ARMADILLO, BADGER,
HARE, WOMBAT, MOLE,
BROCK, RATEL, GOPHER,
GERBIL(LE), TELEDU
crustacean ... SQUILL(A)
mammal of S. Africa ....
SURICATE
mollusk .... PIDDOCK
rodent .... VOLE
tortoise .... GOPHER
burry .... PRICKLY
bursa .... SAC, POUCH
inflammation of a .....
BURSITIS
bursal .... FISCAL
bursar .... TREASURER
burse .... PURSE
Scot. ..... SCHOLARSHIP
bursitis .... BUNION
burst .... EXPLODE,
BREAK OPEN, BULGE,
RUPTURE, BUST, BREACH,
SPLIT, SALVO
forth .... ERUPT
of anger .... HUFF
of cheers ..... OVATION,
APPLAUSE, SALVO
of energy .. SPURT, RALLY

open .... POP
pod, open ..... DEHISCE
sudden .... GUST
bursting tire .... BLOW-OUT
Burundi capital .. BUJUMBURA
　king ....
　　(MWAMI) MWAMBUTSA
native .... WATUSI,
　　BAHUTU
tribe .... BAHUTU,
　　WATUTSI
bury .... INTER, INHUME,
　INURN, SINK, IMMERSE,
　　SEPULCHER
　the hatchet ... RECONCILE
　to hoard/hide ... CACHE
bus ... (MOTOR)COACH, JITNEY
　colloquial ....
　AUTO(MOBILE), FAMILY CAR
　for excursion ....
　　CHARABANC
busby .... HAT
　wearer .... HUSSAR
bush .... SHRUB, BRIER,
　THICKET, TAIL, TOD
　burning .... WAHOO
　league .... MINORS
　leaguer .. SECOND RATER
bushbuck .... ANTELOPE
bushel, in tailoring ... ALTER,
　　MEND
　$\frac{1}{8}$ of .... GALLON
　$\frac{1}{4}$ of .... PECK
bushelman .... TAILOR
bushels, 11⅔ .... HOMER
　32 or 36 ...... CHALDRON
bushes, stunted ...... SCRUB
bushing .... LINING
bushman ... PIGMY, NEGRILLO
bushmaster .... VIPER, SNAKE
bushranger .... HIGHWAYMAN
bushwhacker ....
　　(BACK)WOODSMAN,
　GUERRILLA, RAIDER
bushy clump .... TOD
　tail .... BRUSH
business .... PROFESSION,
　OCCUPATION, AFFAIR,
　COMMERCE, TRADE,
　　STORE
　agent .... SYNDIC,
　COMPRADOR, SALESMAN
　association ... SYNDICATE
　cartel .... TRUST,
　　MONOPOLY
　connection ..... CONTACT

cycle, part of ..... BOOM,
　SLUMP, PROSPERITY,
　　DEPRESSION
　establishment ..... FIRM,
　COMPANY, STORE
　event .... MERGER,
　RECESSION, SLUMP, BOOM,
　STRIKE, DEAL
　firm .... HOUSE
　location .... STAND, SITE
　monopoly ..... CARTEL,
　　CORNER
　schedule .... AGENDA
　secrets, spy on .... KEEK
　slump .... RECESSION,
　　DEPRESSION
　solicitor .... RUNNER,
　　BARKER
　transaction .... DEAL
　upsurge .... BOOM
businessman ...... MERCHANT,
　　TRADER
　conventional ... BABBITT
　Latin of .... INRE
　one kind of ....
　　ENTREPRENEUR
busk .... READY, OUTFIT
buskin .... BOOT, DRAMA
busline, end of ..... TERMINUS
buss .... KISS
　colloquial .. PECK, SMACK
bust .... BOSOM, BREAST,
　BREAK, BURST
　form/shape ..... TAILLE
　slang ... SPREE, FAILURE,
　HIT, PUNCH, DEMOTE, BLOW
bustard ... BIRD, OTIS, TARDA
buster of a kind ....
　　TRUST BREAKER
　slang .... BOY
bustle .... TO-DO, ADO,
　POTHER, STIR, HURRY
　colloquial ..... HOOPLA
　companion of ... HUSTLE
　of woman's dress ......
　　PADDING, BOW
busy .... DILIGENT,
　ASSIDUOUS, ACTIVE,
　INDUSTRIOUS, OCCUPY
　creature .... ANT, BEE,
　　OTTER
　place .... HIVE
　sound .... HUM
busybody .... MEDDLER,
　GOSSIP, SNOOP(ER),
　　QUIDNUNC

but .... EXCEPT, SAVE, YET,
STILL, HOWEVER, MERELY
Scottish .... OUTER,
OUTSIDE, OUTER ROOM
butcher .... MEAT-SELLER,
KILL, SLAUGHTER
bird .... SHRIKE
hook of ...... GAMBREL,
GAFF
meat cutter ..... CLEAVER
shop of .... SHAMBLES
butler .... MAJORDOMO,
STEWARD, MAITRE D'HOTEL
concern of ...... CELLAR,
PANTRY, SILVER(WARE)
butt .... TARGET, BARREL,
CASK, FISH, ABUT, TUP
in ... MEDDLE, INTERFERE,
INTERVENE, INTRUDE
of cigar(ette) ..... STUB
of criticism usually ....
SCAPEGOAT
of goat .... RAM
of joke, figuratively .....
GOAT
of tree .... STUMP
of whip .... CROP
slang ..... CIGARET(TE),
BUTTOCKS
butte .... HILL, MESA
butter .... SPREAD, OIL,
FLATTER(Y), GHEE
and-eggs .... PLANT,
TOADFLAX
and-flour mix ..... ROUX
bucket .... KIT
buffalo milk .... GHEE
color for .... ANATTO,
AN(N)ATTO
India ...... GHEE, GHI
like ... OLEO, MARGARINE,
BUTYRACEOUS, BUTTERINE
lump .... PAT
making contrivance .....
CHURN
piece of .... PAT
roll .... BRIOCHE
substitute .. MARGARINE,
OLEO, BUTTERINE, SUINE
tree .... SHEA
tub .. CHURN, FIRKIN, KIT
butterball .... BUFFLEHEAD
slang ...... FATSO, FATTY
butterbean .... LIMA
buttercup ...... GOLDILOCKS,
CROWTOE

buttered crumbs/crust ....
GRATIN
butterfish .... GUNNEL
butterflies, order of ....
LEPIDOPTERA
butterfly .... ADMIRAL,
FRITILLARY, VANESSA, IO,
GRAYLING, SATYR, KIHO,
SWALLOWTAIL, SKIPPER,
VICEROY, MONARCH,
TROILUS, NYMPHALID
admiral ...... ATALANTA
combining form .. CALIGO
fish ...... BLENNY, PARU
large .... IDALIA
larva ..... CATERPILLAR
lily .... SEGO
named after goddess ....
APHRODITE, DIANA
peacock .... IO
proboscis .... LINGUA
small .... BLUE
tongue-like organ ....
LINGUA
butternut .... SOUARI
buttery .... STOREROOM,
PANTRY, SPENCE
butting animal ... GOAT, RAM,
CARABAO
buttinsky .... MEDDLER
buttocks ..... RUMP, BREECH,
ARSE, DERRIERE,
FUNDAMENT, BEHIND,
BUTT, PRAT, ASS, NATES,
BUM, SEAT, POSTERIOR
button .... EMBLEM, KNOB,
FASTEN, STUD, KNOP
cover .... FLY, FLAP
fencing sword ..... FOIL
the lips .... SHUT UP
buttonhole ..... HOLD, DETAIN
flower .... GARDENIA
buttons .... BELLBOY,
(HOTEL)PAGE
and .... BOWS
buttonwood .... SYCAMORE
buttress ...... SUPPORT, PROP,
PIER, REINFORCE, BOLSTER,
STAY
butts and bounds ....
BOUNDARIES
buxom ..... PLUMP, COMELY,
OBEDIENT, HEALTHY, JOLLY
buy .... PURCHASE,
BRIBE, BARGAIN

at one's risk .... CAVEAT EMPTOR
back .... REDEEM
good: colloq. .... CHEAP, BARGAIN
off .... BRIBE
buyer .... PURCHASER, CONSUMER, VENDEE, EMPTOR
and seller ...... DEALER, JOBBER
of office ..... BARRATER
of old horses .. KNACKER
buyers' strike ...... BOYCOTT
buying to gain monopoly .... COEMPTION
buzz ... HUM, GOSSIP, SIGNAL, DRONE, WHIRR
bomb: Ger. V1
colloquial .... TELEPHONE
buzzard ...... HAWK, BUTEO, HARRIER, FALCON, TESA, OSPREY, COCKCHAFER, DUCKHAWK
honey .... BEEHAWK
moor .... HARPY
turkey ... VULTURE, JOHN
buzzer signal .... CALL
buzzing sound ... DRONE, HUM
by.......... PER, NEAR, AT, BESIDE, THROUGH, ASIDE
and by ... SOON, SHORTLY, ANON
birth .... NEE, NATAL
blow .... BASTARD
hand .... PERSONAL
hand: prefix ..... MANU
pass ...... AVOID, SHUNT, DETOUR

right .... DEJURE
the day .... PERDIEM
way of .... VIA
word of mouth .... ORAL, VERBAL, PAROL
work .... SIDELINE, HOBBY, AVOCATION
byblow .... BASTARD
bye ...... RUN, INCIDENTAL, ODD MAN
bye .... GOODBY
Byelorussian city .... MOGILEV
bygone .... PAST
byname .... SURNAME, NICKNAME
byplay .... ADLIB
byre .... COWBARN
Byron, name of .... NOEL
poem by .... BEPPO
Byronic ... ROMANTIC, PROUD, CYNICAL, IRONIC
byssus .... FLAX, LINEN
bystander .... ONLOOKER
bystreet .... ALLEY
byway ..... ALLEY, SIDEROAD, SIDESTREET
byword .... PROVERB, PROVERBIAL
Byzantine coin ...... BEZANT
emperor .... ALEXIUS, HERACLIUS
emperor's scepter .... FERULA
empress .... ZOE
logothete, so-called ..... (WOODROW) WILSON
works of art ...... ICONS
Byzantium capital .. ISTANBUL, CONSTANTINOPLE

C

C, Greek .... GAMMA
letter .... CEE
mark under .... CEDILLA
Roman numeral .... HUNDRED, 100
symbol for ... CONSTANT
Ca, in chemistry ... CALCIUM
Caaba .... SHRINE
site .... MECCA
caama .... ASSE, FOX
cab .... TAXI, HACK, HANSOM, CARRIAGE, FIACRE, CALASH
driver .. HACK, CABETTE
CAB subjects ..... AIRLINES

cabal .... PLOT, FACTION, INTRIGUE, JUNTO, CLIQUE, JUNTA
cabala .. OCCULTISM, MYSTERY
cabalist .... MYSTIC
cabalistic ... SECRET, MYSTIC
caballero .... GENTLEMAN, CAVALIER, KNIGHT, HORSEMAN
cabana ... BATHHOUSE, CABIN, HUT, COTTAGE, BAGNIO
cabaret .... BARROOM, RESTAURANT, HONKY-TONK
cabbage ... SAVOY, OXHEART,

KOHLRABI, COLE(WORT),
KALE, KAIL, CAULIFLOWER
broth .... KALE
fermented .. SAUERKRAUT
garden .... KALEYARD
plant like .... COLE
salad/shredded ... SLAW
tree .... YABA
cabby ... TAXI-DRIVER, HACK
caber .... POLE, BEAM
cabin .. COTTAGE, HUT, SHACK,
CABANA, SHED, LOGHOUSE
balloon/dirigible ....
GONDOLA
ship's main ..... SALON
Swiss .... CHALET
cabinet ...... CASE, PRIVATE,
SECRET, CONSOLE, ALMIRAH,
BUHL, ARMOIRE
composition ... ADVISERS
describing one .. KITCHEN
for wines, etc. .. CELLARET
wood .... ROSEWOOD,
CEDAR, KOA, WALNUT
cable .. ROPE, CHAIN, MESSAGE,
WIRE
car ...... TELFER, ELPHER
old .... JUNK
used as brace ..... STAY
cabob .... (ROAST) MEAT
holder .... SPIT, SKEWER
cabochon .... STONE
caboodle ...... LOT, GROUP
companion of ..... KIT
caboose .... CAB
ship's .. GALLEY, KITCHEN
cabrilla ... GROUPER, FISH,
REDHIND
cacao alkaloid .. THEOBROMINE
product .... COCOA,
CHOCOLATE
seed powder .... BROMA
cachalot ...... SPERM, WHALE,
PHYSETER
cache ..... CONCEAL, HOARD,
STORE, SECRETE
cachet .... CAPSULE, SEAL,
STAMP
cachou ... LOZENGE, CATECHU
cacique ...... LORD, PRINCE,
ORIOLE, CHIEF, TROUPIAL
cackle ..... LAUGH, CHATTER,
PRATTLE, CLACK
cackler .... HEN, GOOSE
cacoethes ..... ITCH, MANIA
cacophonous .... DISCORDANT

cactus ..... CHOLLA, CEREUS,
PRICKLY PEAR, MESCAL,
SAGUARO, PEYOTE, NOPAL,
OPUNTIA
fruit ...... COCHAL, FIG
like plant ...... SPURGE,
EUPHORBIA, STAPELIA
plant .... TUNA
plant process ..... SPINE
spineless .... CHAUTE
cad ... BOUNDER, SCOUNDREL,
HEEL, MUCKER
cadaver ... COR(P)SE, CARCASS,
BODY, REMAINS
preserved .... MUMMY
slang .... STIFF
cadaverous .... PALE, GAUNT,
GHASTLY
caddis worm .... CADEW
caddish .. ILL-BRED, LOUTISH
caddy .... (TEA)BOX
Caddoan Indian .... REE,
PAWNEE
cade .... JUNIPER
cadence .... MODULATION,
CADENZA, LILT, METER, BEAT,
INFLECTION, RHYTHM
recite in .... CHIME
cadet .... STUDENT, SON
designating one ... PLEBE,
DODO, MILITARY, AIR,
NAVAL
mark against .. DEMERIT
naval ...... MIDSHIPMAN,
MIDDY
cadge .. BEG, PEDDLE, MOOCH,
SPONGE
cadgy ..... LEWD, WANTON,
MERRY
cadi .... JUDGE, MAGISTRATE
Cadmean-like victory ....
PYRRHIC
Cadmus' daughter .. SEMELE,
INO
parent .... AGENOR
sister .... EUROPA
wife .... HARMONIA
cadre .... FRAMEWORK,
NUCLEUS, CELL
caduceus .... STAFF, SCEPTER,
WAND
bearer .. MERCURY, HERMES
Caen river .... ORNE
Caesar .... SALAD, SID,
EMPEROR, DICTATOR,
JULIUS

augur who warned ..... SPURINNA
assassin of .... CASSIUS, BRUTUS, CASCA
love of .... SERVILIA
mistress of ...... EUNOE, CLEO(PATRA)
Pompey battle site ..... THAPSUS
wife .... POMPEIA
Caesarian operation .... HYSTEROTOMY
Caesars, one of the ... JULIUS, AUGUSTUS, TIBERIUS, GAIUS, CLAUDIUS, NERO, GALBA, OTHO, VITELLIUS, VESPASIAN, TITUS, DOMITIAN
caesura .. REST, BREAK, PAUSE
cafe .... COFFEE, SALOON, CABARET, DIVAN, ESTAMINET, BISTRO, RESTAURANT
card .... MENU
owner ... RESTAURATEUR
society member .... PLAYBOY
caffein source .. COFFEE, COLA, KOLA, TEA
tea .... THEIN(E)
caftan .... ROBE
cage ..... CONFINE, PEN, GIG, JAIL
elevator .... CAR
hauling .... MEW
hawks' .... MEW
poultry .... COOP
occupant .... BIRD, PET, ANIMAL, PRISONER, TELLER, CASHIER
cagey .. SLY, TRICKY, CUNNING
cahier .... NOTEBOOK, REPORT
cahoots, in .... LEAGUE, PARTNERSHIP, CONNIVANCE, CONSPIRACY
caiman .... ALLIGATOR
Cain .... MURDERER
brother of .... ABEL
descendant of .... JUBAL
land of .... NOD
parent of .... ADAM, EVE
son of .... ENOCH
caique ... ROWBOAT, SAILBOAT
caird ...... TINKER, VAGRANT, GYPSY
cairngorm .... QUARTZ
Cairene .... EGYPTIAN
Cairo is capital of .... EGYPT

shopping district .... MOUSSKY
caisson .... WAGON, BOX, CHEST, TUMBREL, TUMBRIL
content of .. AMMUNITION, EXPLOSIVES, AMMO
disease .... BENDS
man in a ...... SANDHOG
occasional use of .... HEARSE
caitiff .. EVIL, MEAN, CRAVEN, POLTROON
cajeput .... LAUREL
cajole ...... FLATTER, COAX, WHEEDLE, BLANDISH
cajolery .... PALAVER
cake ...... HARDEN, CIMBAL, RUSK, TORTE, MERINGUE
barley meal ... BANNOCK
batter .... CRUMPET, CRULLER, FRITTER
chocolate ..... BROWNIE
corn .... PONE
covering ..... MERINGUE, FROSTING, ICING
fish .... PATTY
in pipe bowl ... DOTTLE
kind of ... BATTER, LAYER
meat .... PATTY
oatmeal .... BANNOCK
porous .... SPONGE
pressed tobacco ... PLUG
ring-shaped .. DOUGHNUT
rum .... BABA
seed .... WIG
small ...... COOKY, BUN
takes the .. WINS, EXCELS, OVERDONE
tea .... SCONE
thin ... JUMBLE, WAFER, FARL
without flour .... TORTE
cakes and ale, life of .... HEDONISM
cakewalk .... DANCE, STEP, STRUT
calabash ...... GOURD, SHELL
calaber ...... FUR, SQUIRREL
calaboose .. JAIL, PRISON, GAOL
Calais' English neighbor ..... DOVER
calamary .... SQUID
calamine .... OINTMENT
calamitous .. FATAL, TRAGIC, DISASTROUS
calamity ... MISERY, REVERSE,

WOE, DISASTER,
CATASTROPHE, BLOW
calamus .. QUILL, PALM(TREE),
SWEET FLAG
calcar .... SPUR
calced .... SHOD
calcine ...... BURN, OXIDIZE
calcined metal/residue .. CALX
calcium carbonate .. CALCITE,
TUFA, CALICHE
carbonate, of ....
CALCAREOUS
crust .... SINTER
gypsum .... PLASTER
oxide ...... (QUICK)LIME
phosphate .... APATITE
sulphate ...... GYPSUM,
PLASTER, HEPAR
calculate .. COUNT, COMPUTE,
ESTIMATE, RECKON, FIGURE,
THINK, SUPPOSE, GUESS
calculating ...... CUNNING,
SHREWD, CAUTIOUS
device ... ABACUS, TABLE,
COMPUTER
calculation, of ..... LOGISTIC
calculi, of .... LITHIC
calculus .... (GALL)STONE,
GRAVEL
combining form .. LITHO
Calcutta is capital of .. BENGAL
calderite .... GARNET
caldron ...... BOILER, KETTLE
Caleb's companion ... JOSHUA
Caledonia .... SCOTLAND
calefy .... WARM, HEAT
calendar ..... REGISTER, LIST,
SCHEDULE, ALMANAC,
DOCKET, MENOLOGY
church .... ORDO
of business .... AGENDA
calender ... DERVISH, MANGLE
calenture .... FEVER
calesa .... CALASH, CALECHE,
CAB
calf .... BOSS
cry .... BL(E)AT
for slaughter ... FATLING
front .... SHIN
hide .... KIP
leather .... ELK
leg .... SURAL
like a .... VITULINE
meat .... VEAL
motherless ... MAVERICK,
DOGIE, DOGY

skin .... KIP
skin parchment .. VELLUM
stray ... DOGIE, MAVERICK
suckling .... BOB
unbranded ... MAVERICK
Caliban's master .. PROSPERO
mother .... SYCORAX
caliber ...... BORE, QUALITY,
ABILITY, GAUGE, METTLE
calico ...... (COTTON)CLOTH,
DOWLAS
East Indies ..... SALLOO
horse .. PINTO, PIEBALD,
PONY
loin cloth .. LAVA-LAVA
printing .... LAPIS, TEER
printing material ....
TRAGACANTH, LACTARENE
California ...... EL DORADO
army base .... ORD
bay .... MONTEREY
bulrush .... TULE
cape ...... MENDOCINO
capital .... SACRAMENTO
capital, former ....
MONTEREY
city .... ALAMEDA,
PALOMAR, MORAGA, NAPA,
CHINO, LODI, POMONA,
FRESNO, GLENDALE,
LONGBEACH, LYNWOOD,
VALLEJO, BUENA PARK,
DOWNY, PALO ALTO,
PASADENA, TORRANCE
college ...... NAIROBI
county ..... NAPA, KERN,
LAKE, MONO, YOLO
fish .. CABEZON, GRUNION
gold rusher .. ARGONAUT
grape picker .. BRACERO
grape pickers' strike ....
HUELGA
herb .... AMOLE
holly .... TOYON
Indian ... PAIUTE, HUPA
kingfish .... OPAH,
PINTADO, WHITING
lake .... TAHOE, BUENA,
OWENS
laurel ...... CAJEPUT,
CAJUPUT, MYRTLE
motto .... EUREKA
mountain ..... PALOMAR,
SIERRAS, MUIR
mountain peak .. SHASTA
nickname ...... GOLDEN

oak ..... ROBLE, ENCINA
observatory ... PALOMAR
pass .... SONORA
pioneer .... SUTTER
river .... TRINITY,
SACRAMENTO
rockfish .... RE(I)NA
shrub .. SALAL, KUMQUAT
state flower ... (GOLDEN)
POPPY
town .. ASTI, MONTEREY
valley .... YOSEMITE
volcano .... SHASTA
Caligula .... BOOTIKIN
caliph .... IMAM, ALI, OMAR,
OMMIAD
calisthenics .... GYMNASTICS,
EXERCISES
system ...... DEL SARTE
calix .... CUP, CHALICE
calk .... CHINSE, SEAL, CLOSE,
STOP
calker .... STAVER
calking material .. OAKUM, TAR
call .. DUB, CRY, DIAL, SHOUT,
ANNOUNCE, SUMMON,
CONVOKE, (TELE)PHONE,
NAME, PAGE, VISIT, RING
army .... DRAFT
auction .... BID
baseball ..... OUT, SAFE,
STRIKE
boy .... PAGE, BELLHOP
creditor's .... DUN
down .. SCOLD, REBUKE,
UPBRAID
for .... DEMAND, ASK
for aid .... APPEAL
for hogs .... SOOK
for repetition .... ENCORE
forth .. EVOKE, SUMMON,
ELICIT, EXCITE
girl .. PROSTITUTE, HOSTESS
greeting ..... HAIL, AVE
hotel lobby ...... PAGE
in .... SUMMON
in poker .... SEE
in question .... IMPUGN
off .... CANCEL
on ...... SEE, VISIT, TAP
out .... SHOUT, SUMMON,
ANNOUNCE
prayer ..... ADAN, AZAN
to account .... ARRAIGN,
CHARGE
to arms, medieval .. BAN

to attract attention .....
HEY, PSST, HIST
to mind .... REMINISCE,
REMEMBER, RECALL
to witness ...... OBTEST
together ..... CONVOKE,
ASSEMBLE
up .... (TELE)PHONE,
SUMMON, DIAL, RING UP
within ... CLOSE, NEARBY
calla .... ARUM, LILY
callboy ..... BELLHOP, PAGE,
BUTTONS
called .... YCLEPT, NAMED
caller .... VISITOR, GUEST
from minaret .. MUEZZIN
midnight .... CRIER
persistent .... DUTY
calligrapher .... COPYIST,
PENMAN
calligraphy .. HANDWRITING,
SCRIPT
calling ... METIER, VOCATION,
PROFESSION, OCCUPATION,
PURSUIT, TRADE, MISSION
Calliope .... MUSE
Callisto .... NYMPH,
CONSTELLATION
callous ... UNFEELING, HARD,
PITILESS, HARD-BOILED,
TOUGH
growth .... CORN
render ... HARDEN, SEAR,
NUMB
calloused .... HORNY
callow .... IMMATURE,
UNFLEDGED, YOUNG, GREEN
person .... YOUTH
callus, horse's ..... CHESTNUT
on toe .... CORN
calm .. SOBER, PACIFY, PACIFIC,
IMPASSIVE, COOL, LULL,
ABATE, PLACATE, STILL,
SERENE, SMOOTH, SOOTHE,
ALLAY
before the _____ ... STORM
calmness, mental/emotional ..
ATARAXIA
calmative ... OPIATE, SEDATIVE,
DRUG, BALM
calomel .. POWDER, CATHARTIC
caloric ...... HEAT, THERMAL
calorie .... THERM(E)
counter .. DIETER, MILADY
counter's standby ....
CYCLAMATE, SACCHARIN

calories, count(ing) .... DIET(ING)
    pertaining to .. THERM(AL)
calotte .. (SKULL)CAP, CREST
Calpurnia's husband ....
          (JULIUS) CAESAR
caltrop .... THISTLE
calumet .... (PEACE)PIPE
    user of .. INDIAN, REDSKIN
calumniate .. MALIGN, ASPERSE,
    SLUR, LIBEL, SLANDER,
          DEFAME
calumny ..... SLANDER, LIBEL
Calvary ..... ARAM, SKULL
Calve, soprano .... EMMA,
          ROQUER
Calvinist of Toulouse .. CALAS
Calvinist(ic) .... GENEVAN,
    GENEVESE, DOGMATIC
calvities .... BALDNESS
Calydonian boar killer ....
          MELEAGER
Calypso ..... NYMPH, ORCHID,
    FLOWER, DANCE, BALLAD,
         SONG, MUSIC
    island of ...... OGYGIA
calypster .... ALULA
calyx leaf ..... SEPAL, PETAL
cam .... TAPPET, TRIPPET,
    COG(WHEEL), CATCH,
    TRIPPER, WIPER
    wheel projection .. LOBE
camaraderie .... COMRADESHIP
camalig .... GRANARY,
    WAREHOUSE, HUT
camarilla .... CABAL, CLIQUE
camass .. LOBELIA, QUAMASH
Cambodia ...... CAMBODGE,
          CAMBOJA
    capital ...... PNOM PENH
    capital, ancient .. ANGKOR
    city .... ANGKOR
    lake .... TONLE SAP
    native of .... KHMER
    neighbor .... LAOS,
    VIETNAM, THAILAND
    premier .... NOL
    river .... MEKONG
    ruins .... ANGKOR
    seaport .... KAMPOT
    skirt .... SAMPORT
cambogia ...... (GUM)RESIN
cambrai ..... BATISTE, LINEN
cambric ... PERCALE, COTTON,
    LINEN, LAWN

Cambridge U. college servant
          GYP
    exam for honors .. TRIPOS
    head/fellow ...... DON
    student ... SIZAR, SIZER,
          OPTIME
came about ..... HAPPENED,
          AROSE
    down ...... DESCENDED,
          (A)LIT
camel .. DELOUL, RUMINANT,
    ARABIAN, GUANACO,
    DROMEDARY, BELOOL,
    HEJEEN, BACTRIAN
    back breaker ... STRAW
    driver .... SARWAN
    feature .... HUMP
    hair cloth .. ABA, CAMLET,
    CAMLOT, CASHMERE
    hair robe .... ABA
    keeper .... OBIL
    like animal ..... LLAMA,
          GUANACO
    load .... FARDEL
    milk, fermented ....
    KOUMIS(S), KUMISS
    rawhide ...... SHAGREEN
    seat on .... HOUDAH,
          HOWDAH
    ship of the ____ .. DESERT
camellia .... JAPONICA
camelopard .... GIRAFFE
Camelot's source of fame ....
    ARTHUR, ROUND TABLE,
          KNIGHTS
    lady .... ENID
    sport ..... TILT, JOUST,
          TOURNEY
Camenas .... NYMPHS
cameo ..... ANAGLYPH, GEM,
          CARVING
    cutting tool ..... SPADE
    opposed to .... INTAGLIO
    stone .... ONYX
camera .. POLAROID, LUCIDA,
    BROWNIE, BOX, CHAMBER,
          KODAK
    film protector ....
          CARTRIDGE
    holder .... TRIPOD
    kind of .... CANDID
    opening ...... APERTURE
    part ..... FINDER, LENS,
          SHUTTER
    platform .... DOLLY
    portable .... KODAK

shot .... STILL
stand .... TRIPOD
camerlingo ... CHAMBERLAIN,
CARDINAL
Cameroon capital .. YAOUNDE
native .... ABO
Camille author ..... DUMAS
role actress ..... GARBO
camion ..... WAGON, TRUCK,
DRAY
camise .... SHIRT, SMOCK
camisole .... JACKET
camlet ...... PONCHO, CLOTH
camomile .... MAYWEED
Camorra .. (SECRET) SOCIETY
like group ..... MAF(F)IA
member's specialty .....
MURDER, TERRORISM,
EXTORTION, BLACKMAIL
camouflage ..... DECEPTION,
DISGUISE
expert .... CAMOUFLEUR
camouflaging material ....
SMOKE, PAINT, LEAVES
camp ...... BIVOUAC, ETAPE,
TABOR
barricaded by wagons ...
LA(A)GER
besiegers' ..... LEAGUER
facility .. LATRINE, TENT
follower .... SUTLER,
VIVANDIERE, DOXY
kind of .... INTERNMENT,
CONCENTRATION
military .... BASE
out .... MAROON
pertaining to .. CASTRAL
privy/toilet ... LATRINE
campagna .... PLAIN
campaign .. CRUSADE, DRIVE,
BARNSTORM
against an idea .. JIHAD
goal .... ELECTION
matters .... ISSUES
motive .... CAUSE
campanile ..... (BELL)TOWER,
BELFRY
campanula ...... HAREBELL,
RAMPION
camper's kit/equipment .....
DUFFLE, DUFFEL
campesino .... PEASANT
camphol .... BORNEOL
camphor-like ...... BORNEOL
oil .... SAFROL(E)
campo .... PLAIN

campstool-shaped chair ......
CURULE
campus .. QUAD, FIELD, YARD
building .... GYM, DORM
group .. FRAT, SORORITY
VIP .... DEAN, ATHLETE,
PREXY
can ... CONSERVE, CONTAINER,
PAIL, TIN, JUG
slang .... PRISON,
BUTTOCKS, TOILET,
DISMISS, DISCHARGE
Canada, Lower ..... QUEBEC
Canadian .... CANUCK
airport .... GANDER
boatman .... VOYAGEUR
capital .... OTTAWA
city .... LEVIS, BANFF
crookneck .... CUSHAW
canal .... WELLAND
emblem .... MAPLE
farmer ...... HABITAN(T)
folk singer .. LIGHTFOOT
football .... ROUGE
game .... LACROSSE
game preserve .. JASPER
gannet .... MARGOT
gold field .... KLONDIKE
goose .... OUTARDE
grape .... ISABELA
humorist ...... LEACOCK
Indian .... CREE, SIOUX,
MICMAC
lake ...... TESLIN, CREE,
LOUISE
land measure .. ARPENT
lynx .. CARCAJOU, PISHU
mountain ...... LEWIS,
LUCANIA
national park .. JASPER,
YOHO, BANFF
official .... REEVE
park ..... BANFF, JASPER
peak .... LOGAN
peninsula .... GASPE
policeman ..... MOUNTIE
porcupine ...... URSON
prime minister ....
TRUDEAU, PEARSON,
LAURIER
province ..... ALBERTA,
ONTARIO, QUEBEC,
MANITOBA, YUKON,
NOVA SCOTIA, NORTHWEST
provincial capital ....
TORONTO, EDMONTON,

QUEBEC, HALIFAX, REGINA,
VICTORIA, WINNIPEG,
ST. JOHNS
resort .... GASPE
river ... OTTAWA, YUKON,
NELSON, BATEAU, LIARD,
MACKENZIE
rodent .... LEMMING
scenic region .... GASPE
settler ...... SOURDOUGH
squaw .... MAHALA
summer resort ... BANFF
territory .... YUKON
town president .. REEVE
woodsman ... VOYAGEUR
canaille .... MOB, RABBLE,
RIFFRAFF
canal ..... WATERWAY, ERIE,
CONDUIT, SUEZ, WELLAND,
PANAMA, KIEL, PASSAGE,
ACEQUIA
bank .... BERM(E)
boat .... GONDOLA
boat tower .... MULE
ear .... SCALA
enclosed part ..... LOCK
from mouth to anus ....
ALIMENTARY, ENTERON
in anatomy/zoology ....
DUCT, TUBE, VAS
lock gate .... WICKET
Suez: colloq. ...... SOO
worker .... NAVVY
zone seaport .... BALBOA
zone town ..... GATUN,
ANCON
canape ..... DIVAN, COUCH,
APPETIZER
spread .. CAVIAR, CHEESE,
SARDINE
canard .... RUMOR, HOAX,
DUCK, HUMBUG, AIRPLANE
Canary ..;.... DANCE, WINE,
MADEIRA, SONGBIRD, ROLLER,
FINCH
hybrid .... MULE
island .... PALMA,
TENERIF(FE)
island mount .... TEIDE,
TEYDE
island seaport ....
LAS PALMAS
island wine ...... SACK
kin .... SERIN
seed .... ALPIST
yellow .... MELINE

canasta play/score .... MELD
Canaveral, Cape .. KENNEDY
Canberra is capital of ....
AUSTRALIA
cancel .. ANNUL, ERASE, REMIT,
RESCIND, REVOKE, RECALL
deletion made .... STET
in printing ... DELE(TE),
KILL
cancellation mark on mail ....
CACHET, STAMP
cancer .. CARCINOMA, TUMOR,
SCIRRHUS, LEUKEMIA, CRAB
describing .... BENIGN,
MALIGNANT
like .... CANCROID
non-malignant .. BENIGN
of the jaw .... LYMPHONA
producing substance......
CARCINOGEN
surgery .... MASTECTOMY
treatment ..... RADIUM,
RADON
candelabrum .. CANDLESTICK,
CANDELABRA
candent .... GLOWING,
(WHITE)HOT
candescent .... GLOWING
Candia .. CRETE, HERAKLEION
candid. ...... OPEN, HONEST,
IMPARTIAL, FRANK,
OUTSPOKEN, GUILELESS,
BLUNT
"Candida" author .... SHAW
candidate .. NOMINEE, ASPIRANT
for graduation .. SENIOR
for knighthood .. ESQUIRE
kind of ...... OFFICIAL,
REBEL, INDEPENDENT
candidates' list ..... TICKET,
SLATE, BALLOT
platform ...... HUSTINGS
staple ...... PROMISES,
PLEDGES
winning score ....
MAJORITY, PLURALITY
candied .... GLACE
fruit .... COMFIT,
SWEETMEAT
rind .... CITRON
candies, imitation of ....
CONFETTI
Candiot .... CRETAN
candle ... DIP, TAPER, CIERGE,
SERGE, RUSH, GLIM
holder .. SCONCE, HEARST,

CANDELABRA, CHANDELIER,
  GIRANDOLE
lighter .... TAPER
maker .... CHANDLER
material .... CARNAUBA,
  WAX, TALLOW, WICK,
  OZOCERITE
part .... WICK, SNAST
seller .... CHANDLER
slang .... GLIM
spike .... PRICKET
wax .... TAPER, BOUGIE,
  CARNAUBA
wick's end .... SNUFF
candlelight .... EVENING,
  TWILIGHT
candlenut .... AMA
candlestick .. PRICKET, CRUSIE,
  LAMPAD, SCONCE
  branched ... GIRANDOLE,
  CANDELABRA, JESSE,
  CANDELABRUM
  ornamental .. FLAMBEAU,
  LUSTRE
  shelf .... GRADIN(E)
candlewick's charred end ....
  SNUFF
candor ...... SINCERITY,
  FRANKNESS
candy .. BONBON, LOLLYPOP,
  COMFIT, SWEETMEAT, SWEET,
  DRAGEE, KISS, LOZENGE
  chewy .. CARAMEL, TAFFY,
  TOFFEE, TOFFY
  crisp .... BRITTLE
  filler .... FONDANT
  flavor .... LIME
  fudge-like ... PANOCHA,
  PENUCHE
  gelatinous ... JELLYBEAN
  hard: sl. ... JAWBREAKER
  jelly-like .... PASTE
  nutty .. PRALINE, NOUGAT
  on a stick .... LOLLIPOP,
  LOLLYPOP
  piece .. DROP, LOLLYPOP,
  WAFER, GOODY
  pull .... PARTY
  seller .... BUCHER
  soft .... FUDGE
candytuft .... MUSTARD
cane .... BEAT, STEM,
  (WALKING)STICK, FLOG,
  FLAY, RAT(T)AN, HICKORY,
  WADDY
  flogging .... SWISH

like a ..... FERULACEOUS
metal cap .... SHOE,
  PERRULE
plant .... BAMBOO,
  RATTAN
strip .... SPLINT
sugar .... SACROSE,
  SACCHAROSE
walking .... MALACCA
canella .... CINNAMON
Canfield (D.) play .... SOLO
cangue-like device ... PILLORY
canicula .. DOG STAR, SIRIUS
canine (see dog) .. DOG, WOLF,
  JACKAL, FOX
  disease .. RABIES, MANGE,
  DISTEMPER
  mongrel .... CUR, TYKE
  tooth ...... TUSH, FANG,
  LANIARY
canister .... BOX, CAN
canker .. INFECT, ROT, DECAY,
  SORE
canna .... ACHIRA
cannabin .... RESIN
cannabis .... HEMP, HASHISH
canned .... PRESERVED, TINNED
  beef .... BULLY
  food toxin ..... BOTULIN
  food poisoning ....
  BOTULISM
  slang .... DISMISSED,
  CASHIERED
Cannes .... RESORT
cannibal .... SAVAGE,
  MAN-EATER, CARNIVORE
  human food of ....
  LONG PIG
cannikin .. CUP, CAN, BUCKET,
  PAIL
cannon .. MORTAR, HOWITZER,
  (CRACK)GUN, ORDNANCE
  ball .... MISSILE,
  PROJECTILE
  collectively ... ARTILLERY
  dummy .... QUAKER
  firing material ....
  LANIARD, LANYARD,
  LINSTOCK
  fodder, so-called ....
  SOLDIERS
  harness for men ....
  BRICOLE
  in billiards ..... CAROM
  kick of .... RECOIL

mounted .... JINGAL, GINGAL
old ...... DRAKE, ASPIC, CULVERIN, FALCON
pivot .... TRUNNION
oriental .... LANTAKA
platform .... TERREPLEIN
shot .... PROJECTILE
cannonade .... BOMBARDMENT, BARRAGE, SALVO
cannoneer .... GUNNER, ARTILLERYMAN
cannonry .... ARTILLERY, ORDNANCE
cannular .... TUBULAR
canny .. CAREFUL, CAUTIOUS, WARY, SHREWD
canoe .... BOAT, DUGOUT, PITPAN
African .... BONGO, ALMADIA
air chamber .. SPONSON
dugout .... PIRAGUA, PIROGUE
Arctic .... KAYAK
Eskimo .. KAYAK, KAIAK, UMIAK, BIDARKA
Hawaii .... WAAPA
Malabar .... TONEE
Malay .... PROA, PAHI, PRAU, PRAH(O)
Maori .... WAKA
Philippine ..... BANCA, BANKA, CASCO
propeller .. PADDLE, POLE
with outrigger/sail ...... PROA
canon .... RULE, LAW, CRITERION
in music .... ROUND
law expert .... DECRETIST
of the Mass prayer ..... MEMENTO
canonical .... AUTHORITATIVE, ACCEPTED
hour ..... PRIME, SEXT, COMPLIN, NONES, VESPERS, LAUDS, MATIN, TIERCE
law, Moslem .... SHERI
canonicals ...... ALB, COPE, STOLE, AMICE, SURPLICE, MANIPLE
canonize ..... SAINT, GLORIFY, DEIFY
canonized person .... SAINT
canons, group of ... CHAPTER

canopy .. COPE, AWNING, CIEL, DAIS, TILT, COVER
altar ...... BALDACHIN, CIBORIUM
bed/tomb ...... TESTER
boat/cart .... TILT
support .... BAIL
canorous ...... MELODIOUS, MUSICAL, CLEAR
cant .... DIALECT, ARGOT, LINGO, TRITE, SLANG, PATOIS, JARGON, TILT, TOSS, TURN, SLANT, PATTER
hook .... PEAV(E)Y
cantabile .... SONGLIKE
cantaloup(e) .. (MUSK)MELON
cantankerous ...... ORNERY, BAD-TEMPERED, CONTENTIOUS, PERVERSE, QUARRELSOME
fellow .... CURMUDGEON
cantata .... VOCAL SOLOS, CHORUSES, ARIA, PASTORAL
dramatic/pastoral ...... SERENATA
canteen .... POST EXCHANGE, SHOP, PX, FLASK
canter .. LOPE, GALLOP, GAIT
Canterbury, archbishop of ... DUNSTAN
bell .... CAMPANULA
Tales' author .. CHAUCER
Tales' heroine .... GRISELDA
Tales' inn ...... TABARD
cantharides ...... IRRITANT, STIMULANT
cantharis .... FLY
canticle .. ODE, CHANT, PSALM, HYMN, BRAVURA, SONG
canticles .... SONG OF SONGS
cantina .... SALOON
cantle .... PIECE, SLICE
canto .... PASSUS, STANZA
Archaic .... FIT
obsolete .. SONG, BALLAD
Canton .. DISTRICT, QUARTER, BILLET, QUADRANS
capital of .. KWANGTUNG
city ...... KWANGCHOW
flannel .... NAP
river .... PEARL
river island ...... MACAO
cantor .... PRECENTOR, CHAZ(Z)AN
cantrip .... (MAGIC)SPELL, PRANK

cantus ...... SONG, MELODY
Canuck .... CANADIAN
canvas ..... SAIL(S), TENT(S),
    PAINTING, CLOTH, DUCK
  boat .... CANOE
  cover .... TILT, AWNING
  like fabric .... WIGAN
  shelter .... TENT
  ship's .. JIB, FOREROYAL,
    STUDDING, MIZZEN,
    SPANKER
  waterproofed ....
    TARP(AULIN)
canvasback .... DUCK
  relative .... SCAUP,
    REDHEAD
canvass ... SOLICIT, EXAMINE,
    DISCUSS
  voters .... ELECTIONEER,
    POLL, SURVEY
canyon ..... VALLEY, RAVINE
  entrance .... JAWS
  mouth .... ABRA
  wall .... CLIFF
canzone ... MADRIGAL, POEM
canzonet ... SONG, MATIN(S),
    CENTO, LILT
caoutchouc .... RUBBER,
    ELATERITE
  source ...... CEARA, ULE,
    LATEX
cap .... HEADGEAR, COVER,
  COIL, COIF, FEZ, TAM,
  SURPASS, BERET, BEANY
  a-pie .... ENTIRELY,
    HEAD TO FOOT
  academic .. MORTARBOARD
  and bells wearer ....
    (COURT) JESTER
  bottle .. CAPSULE, CROWN
  brim .... VISOR
  brimless .... CALOT(TE),
  PILEUS, BERET, TAM,
  BALMORAL, TARBOOSH,
  FEZ, BIRETTA
  child's .... BIGGIN
  children's ..... BONNET
  close/fitting ...... COIF,
    TOQUE
  decoration ... COCKADE,
  POMPON, FEATHER
  ecclesiastical ... BARRET,
    BERET, BIRET(TA)
  jester's ..... COCKSCOMB
  Jewish priest's .. MITER,
    MITRE

  kind of .. MORTARBOARD,
    PERCUSSION
  knitted .... THRUM
  lawyer's .... COIF
  military ..... PERSHING,
  BUSBY, SHAKO, KEPI,
  HAVELOCK
  mushroom's ..... PILEUS
  Oriental .. CALPAC, FEZ,
    TURBAN, KALPAK
  part .. BRIM, VISOR, BILL
  Scottish ...... BALMORAL,
    TAM
  shaped .... PILEATE
  sheepskin ...... CALPAC,
    KALPAK
  skull ..... COIF, PILEUS,
    CALOT(TE)
  slang .... LID
  square .... BIRETTA
  tube .... CAPSULE
  turned up front ....
    COCKUP
  visor .... BILL
  winter .... TUQUE
  with flap ..... MONTERO
capable .... COMPETENT,
  SKILLED, EFFICIENT, ABLE
  of defense .... TENABLE
  of following advice .....
    AMENABLE
  of motion ...... MOTILE
capacious .. AMPLE, SPACIOUS,
    ROOMY
capacitor .... CONDENSER
capacity .. CONTENT, VOLUME,
  APTITUDE, POSITION, STATUS,
    FUNCTION
  for feeling ... SENTIENCE
caparison .... OUTFIT,
  TRAP(PINGS)
cape .... HEADLAND,
  PROMONTORY, MANTLE, NESS,
  TALMA, MANTILLA,
  FORELAND, MANTELET,
  MANTA
  cod food fish .... CERO
  cotton .... MANTA
  Dutch ..... AFRIKAANS,
    TAAL
  ecclesiastical ... AMICE,
    COPE
  fur .. PALATINE, ERMINE,
  PELERINE, COLLARET(TE)
  hanging part ... TIPPET

hooded .. AMICE, ALMUCE, MOZ(Z)ETTA
land's .... RAS
like garment .. DOLMAN
Mexican .... SERAPE
muslin .... FICHU
papal ... ORALE, FANON, FANUM, PHANO
sleeveless ..... INVERNESS
3-cornered ...... FICHU
vestment resembling .... COPE
Cape Verde Islands capital ... PRAIA
native .... SERER
Capek (Karel) character ... ROBOT
play .... RUR
capelin .... SMELT
Capella .... GOAT, STAR, KID
caper ... ANTIC, DIDO, JUMP, FRISK, GAMBOL, CAPRIOLE, CURLICUE, LEAP, TITTUP, ROLLICK, OATCAKE
capillary .. HAIRLIKE, MINUTE
action .... ATTRACTION, REPULSION
capital ... RESOURCES, CHIEF, PRINCIPAL, ASSETS, METROPOLIS
business .... STOCK
colloquial .. FIRST RATE, EXCELLENT
make .... EXPLOIT
letter ...... UPPER-CASE, INITIAL, MAJUSCULE
punishment .... DEATH, EXECUTION, HANGING
ship .... BATTLESHIP, CRUISER, DREADNAUGHT
capitalist .... BARON
capitate ...... HEAD-SHAPED
capitulary .... ORDINANCES
capitulate .... SURRENDER, YIELD, SUBMIT
capon .... ROOSTER, CHICKEN
caporal .... TOBACCO
capote .. BONNET, TOP, COVER, HOOD
capouch .... HOOD, CAPUCHE
capra .... SHE-GOAT
Capri .... ISLE
capriccio ..... PRANK, WHIM
caprice .... WHIM(SY), FANCY, VAGARY, FREAK, HUMORESQUE
capricious ...... WHIMSICAL,

ECCENTRIC, ERRATIC, FLIGHTY, MOONISH, FANCY, HOITY-TOITY, FANTASY, WAYWARD, FICKLE
Capricorn .... GOAT, CONSTELLATION
capriole .... CAPER, LEAP
capsize .... KEEL, TIP, OVERTURN, UPSET, TURN TURTLE
capsicum ... PEPPER, CAYENNE, PAPRIKA, PAPRICA
capstan ..... WINDLASS, WHIM
drum .... RUNDLE
top .... DRUMHEAD
capsule .... CAP, SEAL, CONTAINER, POD, PILL, WAFER, CACHET, AMPULE
egg .... OVISAC
plant .... BOLL
spore .... THECA
captain ..... CHIEF, LEAD(ER), HEAD
Absalom's ...... AMASA
allowance of ... PRIMAGE
boat of the .... GIG
Cook's discovery .... SANDWICH(ISLAND)
dialectic .... CAP'N
in a restaurant .... HEADWAITER
of ship, fiction ... AHAB, NEMO, BLIGH, QUEEG
ship's .. SKIPPER, MASTER
caption .. LEGEND, HEADING, (SUB)TITLE
subject of .... PICTURE, EXHIBIT
captious ... TRICKY, CRITICAL, FAULT-FINDING
captivate .. ENAMOR, CHARM, FASCINATE, ATTRACT, ENTHRALL, ENCHANT
captive .... PRISONER
bail of .... RANSOM
burden of .... YOKE
captivity ..... IMPRISONMENT, BONDAGE
capture ... BAG, CATCH, NAB, NET, SEIZE, COP, SEIZURE
captured object ...... PRIZE
capuche .... HOOD, CAPOUCH
Capuchin ..... MONK, CLOAK, MONKEY, SAPAJOU
monkey .... SAI
caput .... HEAD, DOOMED

capybara ..... RODENT, CAVY, HOG

car ..... SEDAN, AUTOMOBILE, CAGE

  baggage ..... FOURGON

  balloon .... NACELLE

  battered .... HEAP

  bubble of .... BLISTER

  checkup, repair .... OVERHAUL

  closed .... SEDAN

  compartment ... TRUNK

  decrepit .. CRATE, JALOPY, HEAP

  dome .... BLISTER

  for hire .. TAXICAB, CAB, TAXI

  hyped-up ..... MACH(I), MUSTANG, HOTROD

  in a building .. ELEVATOR, LIFT

  kind of .... USED, SECONDHAND, MOTOR, RACER, UTILITY, RAILROAD, TOWN, ARMORED, CLOSED, SEDAN, COUPE

  mine .... HUTCH

  old-make .. REO, T-MODEL

  part .. FENDER, RADIATOR, TIRE, WINDSHIELD, WHEEL, HEADLIGHT, BUMPER, MUFFLER

  suspended .... TELPHER, TELFER, MONORAIL, ELEVATOR, LIFT

  tassle .... TOGGLE

  touring .... PHAETON

  train's last ..... CABOOSE

  versatile .... JEEP

carabao .... BUFFALO, TAMARAW, TAMARAU

  horn bugle .... TAMBULI

carabineer ..... CAVALRYMAN, HORSEMAN

carabinieri .... POLICE

caracal .... LYNX, FUR

caracara .... HAWK, FALCON

Caracas is capital of .... VENEZUELA

  coin .... BOLIVAR

carack .... GALLEON

caracole ...... TURN, WHEEL

caracul .... SHEEP, FUR

carafe ... BOTTLE, DECANTER

caramel ...... (BURNT)SUGAR, CANDY

carangoid ... FISH, CAVALLA, CERO, POMPANO, YELLOWTAIL, YELLOWJACK

carapace .... LORICA, SHELL

  animal with .... TURTLE, TORTOISE, ARMADILLO, CRAB, TERRAPIN

  material .... CHITIN

  under part of .. PLASTRON

caravan .... VAN, TRAIN

  Arabian .... CAFILA

  of a kind .... SAFARI

  stopping place .... CARAVANSARY, SERAI, OASIS

caravansary ... KHAN, SERAI, IMARET, INN

caravel .... BEETLE, SHIP, VESSEL

  of history ... NINA, PINTA

caraway .... SEED, PLANT

  cooky ...... SEED CAKE

carbide, tungsten .. CARBOLOY

carbine ..... MUSKET, RIFLE, ESCOPET, STEN

  firearm resembling ...... PETRONEL

carbohydrate ...... STARCH, SUGAR, CELLULOSE, PECTIN, LICHENIN, LEVULIN

  suffix .... OSE

carbolic acid .... PHENOL

carbon ... LEAD, SOOT, COKE, CRAYON

  combine chemically with .. CARBURET

  copy: colloq. .... LOOK ALIKE, (SPITTING)IMAGE, DUPLICATE

  iron alloy ..... PEARLITE

  pencil .... CHARCOAL

  precious/pure .. DIAMOND

  product .... SOOT

carbonado ... MEAT, DIAMOND, SLASH, HACK

carbonate of lime .... STALAGMITE, STALACTITE, CALCITE

carborundum ..... ABRASIVE, EMERY

  tool .... GRINDSTONE

carboy .... BOTTLE

carbuncle .. PIMPLE, ANTHRAX

carburetant .... GASOLINE, BENZENE

carcajou ... WOLVERINE, LYNX,
    BADGER, COUGAR
carcass .. BODY, FRAMEWORK,
    SKELETON
carcinoma surgery ....
    MASTECTOMY
card .. ACE, PASTEBOARD, LIST,
  DEUCE, JACK, KING, TREY,
KNAVE, COMB, BRUSH, CARTE,
    PAM
  cheat .... SHARPER,
    BLACKLEG
  combination ... TENACE,
    MELD
  dealer .... TALLIER
  dealer's leftovers ....
    STOCK, TALON
  file .... CATALOG(UE)
  fortune-telling .., TAROT
  French .... CARTE
  game ... BACCARAT, LOO,
  FARO, MONTE, WHIST,
  SOLITAIRE, MUGGINS,
  BEZIQUE, CRIBBAGE,
  HEARTS, PEDRO, CASINO,
  SLAPJACK, FANTAN,
  CANASTA, BRIDGE,
  PINOCHLE, NULLO,
  POKER, ECARTE, BRAG,
  QUADRILLE, SEVEN-UP
  game "adviser" ....
    KIBITZER
  game dealer ... TALLIER
  game extra hand ....
    KITTY, WIDOW
  game for one .. SOLITAIRE
  game for two ... PIQUET,
  COONCAN, CONQUIAN
  game holding .... HAND
  game like bridge .. VINT
  game like rummy ....
  CONQUIAN, COONCAN
  game shuffler .... DEALER
  game, solitaire ....
    CANFIELD
  game, 3-hand ..... SKAT
  game win ... GIN, VOLE,
    SLAM
  games, authority on ....
    HOYLE
  holding .. HAND, TENACE
  in faro .... SODA
  kind of .... COMPASS,
  CALLING, POST(AL),
  WEDDING, PLAYING,
  PASTE, BUSINESS

  playing .... PASTEBOARD
  sharp .... BLACKLEG
  suit, same ...... FLUSH
  three-spot .... TREY
  two-spot .... DEUCE
  with four spots .. QUATRE
  wool ..... TEASE, COMB,
    ROVE
cardamom ...... HERB, SEED,
    GINGER
cardboard box ..... CARTON
cardialgin ...... HEARTBURN
cardigan ... JACKET, SWEATER,
  WAMPUS, WAM(M)US
cardinal .. CHIEF, PRINCIPAL,
FUNDAMENTAL, BIRD, CLOAK,
  RED, PIVOTAL, FINCH
  American ...... REDBIRD
  chair of .... THRONE
  is one .... PRINCE
  office of .... DATARIA,
    PURPLE
  rank of .... PURPLE
  sign of rank .. RED HAT
  skullcap of .. ZUCCHETTO
  title of honor .. EMINENCE
  vestment .... DALMATIC
cardinals' meeting room .....
    CONCLAVE
carding machine cylinder .....
    SWIFT
cards, fortune-telling ....
    TAROTS
  held .... HAND
  highest .... HONORS
  left after dealing ....
  TALON, CAT, STOCK
care ...... WORRY, ANXIETY,
CUSTODY, CHARGE, MIND,
  CONCERN, CAUTION,
  TUTELAGE
  for ..... PROVIDE, LOVE,
  (AT)TEND, NURSE, MIND
  of the aged .. MEDICARE
careen .... TIP, LURCH, LIST,
  LEAN, TILT, HEEL
career .... LIFEWORK,
PROFESSION, OCCUPATION,
  VOCATION
careful ..... WARY, PRUDENT,
DISCREET, CAUTIOUS, CHARY,
  FINICAL, METICULOUS
careless .... ARTLESS,
NEGLIGENT, LAX, SLIPSHOD,
  SLOPPY
caress ..... FONDLE, DANDLE,

EMBRACE, KISS, CUDDLE, BILL, PET
bear's .... HUG
bird's .... PECK, BILL
dove's .. BILL (AND COO)
Scottish ... DAUT, DAWT
slang .... NECK
caretaker .... CUSTODIAN, KEEPER
apartment .. CONCIERGE
house of .... LODGE
museum/library .... CURATOR
of government, temporary .... REGENT
property .... TRUSTEE
careworn .. HAGGARD, WEARY
cargo ...... FREIGHT, LOAD, PORTAGE, LADING
boat ... OILER, TANKER, SCOW, TRADER, FREIGHTER
cast overboard ship ..... JETSAM
from wrecked ship ..... FLOTSAM
hot ...... CONTRABAND
put on .... LADE, LOAD
ship's .... BULK
space in ship ..... HOLD
carhop ..... WAITRESS, WAITER
Carib .... GALIBI, INDIAN
Caribbean island .... ARUBA, AVES, BONAIRE
port .... COLON
caribe .... PIRAYA
caribou .... REINDEER
Algonquian ... KALEBOO
male .... STAG
caricature .... PARODY, TRAVESTY, SATIRE, DISTORTION, BURLESQUE, TAKE-OFF
means of expression .... CARTOON, LAMPOON, BURLESQUE
caricaturist ..... CARTOONIST, SATIRIST
carinate .... KEEL-SHAPED
carillon .... PEAL
cariole ..... CART, CARRIAGE
cark .... WORRY, ANNOY
carl ...... CHURL, BONDMAN, VILLEIN
carline .. HAG, WITCH, WOMAN
Carlton's (hotel) partner ..... RITZ

Carmelite .... (WHITE)FRIAR
"Carmen" composer .... BIZET
Carmichael (Hoagy) songhit .. STARDUST
carminative seeds .. CARAWAY
carmine ...... CRIMSON, RED
carnage .... SLAUGHTER, MASSACRE, BLOODSHED, BUTCHERY
carnal .... SENSUAL, SEXUAL, BODILY, FLESHY, MUNDANE, WORLDLY
carnation .. DIANTHUS, PINK, RED, FLOWER, PICOTEE
carnauba .... PALM
product .... WAX
carnelian .... QUARTZ, CHALCEDONY
carnival .... GALA, FESTIVAL, FESTIVITY, MERRYMAKING, FAIR, EXHIBITION
character ..... BARKER, SHILL, GRIFTER
famous .... MARDI GRAS
feature ...... CONFETTI, PARADE, PAGEANT, SIDESHOWS, RIDES
gambling operator ...... GRIFTER
hawker's spot ... PITCH
carnivore ...... MINK, URSUS, OTTER, DOG, PUMA, WOLF, LION, SEAL, (POLE)CAT, FOUMART, BEAR, TIGER, GENET, HYENA, RATEL, SERVAL
diet ...... MEAT, FLESH
opposed to .. HERBIVORE
carnivorous insect ... MANTIS
reptile .... TUATARA, CROCODILE, MONITOR
carnotite .. MINERAL, URANIUM
carob ... LOCUST, POD, TREE, ALGAROBA
carol .... TRILL, SING
Christmas .... NOEL
singer .... WAIT
Caroline, dimunitive of ...... CARRIE
island .. PALU, TRUK, YAP
Carolinian .... TARHEEL
carom .. RICOCHET, REBOUND
carotid .... ARTERY
carousal ...... BINGE, SPREE, ORGY, REVELRY, WASSAIL, TEAR

carouse .. BOUSE, SPREE, REVEL
carousel ... MERRY-GO-ROUND,
    WHIRLIGIG, LILIOM
carp ...... CRITICIZE, CAVIL,
    BLEAK, TENCH, LOACH
  Japanese .... KOI
  kin .... MINNOW
  like fish .... DACE,
    GOLDFISH, IDE
  minnow .... SHINER
  red-eye .... RUDD
carpal joint .... KNEE
Carpatho-Ukraine .. RUTHENIA
carpel .... ACHENE
carpels, united ...... PISTIL
carpenter .. WRIGHT, JOINER,
    WOODWORKER, ANT
  joint of .. MITER, MORTISE
  tool of .... CHISEL, PLANE,
    BEVEL, SAW, ADZE
carpet .... MAT, COVER, RUG,
    TAPETE, TAPIS, MOQUETTE,
    FOOTCLOTH, WILTON
  Afghan .... HERAT
  city ..... TOURNAI, AGRA
  India .... AGRA
  material .... DRUGGET,
    MOQUETTE
  on the .... CHARGED,
    ACCUSED
  Persian .... KALI
carpetbagger .. ADVENTURER,
    POLITICIAN, PROMOTER
carping .. CAPTIOUS, CRITICAL
carport .... GARAGE
carpus .... WRIST
  bone .... CARPAL(E)
carrack ... GALLEON, VESSEL
carrageen ...... IRISH, MOSS,
    SEAWEED
carreta .... CART
carriage .... POISE, BEARING,
    CONVEYANCE, CARIOLE, GIG,
    CHAISE, VOITURE, SULKY,
    LANDAU, PHAETON, SHAY,
    AIR, SURREY, PORTANCE, RIG,
    ROCKAWAY, STANHOPE
  attendant .... FLUNKEY,
    OUTRUNNER, OUTRIDER
  baby ... PERAMBULATOR,
    BUGGY, GO-CART, PRAM,
    CLARENCE
  berlin(e) .... BAROUCHE
  closed .... COUPE
  dog .... DALMATIAN
  driver ..... HACK(MAN),

    COACH(MAN)
  driver's seat .. DICK(E)Y
  folding top ... CALASH,
    CALECHE, PHAETON
  for hire .... FIACRE,
    HANSOM, HACK
  for state occasions ......
    CAROCHE
  four-wheeled ....
    DEARBORN, LANDAU,
    CLARENCE, BERLIN(E),
    PHAETON, BAROUCHE,
    BUCKBOARD, TARANTAS,
    CHAISE, VICTORIA
  French .... FIACRE
  hackney .... FLY
  hood .... CAPOTE
  Java .... SADO
  low-wheeled .. TARANTAS,
    CALASH
  luggage space .. RUMBLE
  man-drawn .. JINRIKSHA,
    RICKSHA(W)
  one-horse .... TRAP,
    CARRYALL, CARIOLE, SHAY,
    CHAISE, CALESIN
  Philippine ..... CALESA,
    CARROMATA, TARTANILLA,
    CALESIN
  pole ..... THILL, SHAFT
  Russian ... TARANTAS(S),
    TROIKA
  seat .... RUMBLE
  servant's seat in ....
    DICKEY, RUMBLE
  single-seat ... STANHOPE
  top .... CAPOTE
  two-wheeled ..... SULKY,
    TRAP, TILBURY, CURRICLE,
    CALESA, CALECHE, CALASH,
    CHAISE, HERDIC
  with collapsible top .....
    CHAISE, CALASH, CALECHE,
    BRITSKA
  with liveried attendants ..
    EQUIPAGE
carried .... TRANSPORTED,
    BORNE, TOTED, SWAYED
  away .... RAPT,
    OVERWHELMED
carrier .. REDCAP, MESSENGER,
    PORTER, BEARER, TOTER,
    PORTER
  air .... AIRPLANE
  armor .. ARMIGER, SQUIRE
  bad luck .... JINX

coal/brick/mortar ... HOD, CORF
in a depot ..... PORTER
of disease virus .. VECTOR
Oriental .... HAMAL
Spanish ..... CARGADOR
water .... BHEESTEE
carrion ... FILTHY, DECAYING, ROTTEN
crow .... VULTURE
Carroll (Lewis) heroine ...... ALICE
forte .... PARODY
carron oil .... LINIMENT
carrot ...... FENNEL, PLANT
like plant ...... PARSNIP
oil tube .... VITTA
carroty .. ORANGE, RED-HAIRED
car(r)ousel ... TOURNAMENT, MERRY-GO-ROUND, WHIRLIGIG
carry .. TRANSPORT, CONVEY, LEAD, WIN, TRANSMIT, CART, SWAY, LUG, BEAR, TOTE, SUSTAIN, FETCH
across water .... FERRY
away .... EXCITE
off .... ABDUCT, KIDNAP
on ... CONTINUE, WAGE, CONDUCT, PROSECUTE
on person .... WEAR
out ...... ACCOMPLISH, EFFECT, OBEY, EXECUTE
over .... POSTPONE
too far .... OVERDO
weight .... COUNT
carryall .... BAG, BASKET, CARRIAGE
kind of .... BUS
carrying away .... EFFERENT
unborn child ....
PREGNANT, ENCEINTE
Carson City is capital of ..... NEVADA
cart ..... WAIN, VAN, LORRY, CARRY, WAGON, HAUL, DRAY, CARIOLE, BOGY, TRUNDLE
ammunition ... TUMBREL, TUMBRIL, CAISSON
hand .... PRAM
racing .... CHARIOT
carte ... MENU, BILL OF FARE, QUART(E), CARD
blanche of a sort ....
BLANK CHECK

cartel .... CHALLENGE, AGREEMENT, MONOPOLY
of a sort .... TRUST, SYNDICATE
Carter Dickson pseudonym ... CARR
Carthage, capital of ....
CARALIS
destroyer of .... ROMANS, SCIPIO
foe of .... CATO
founder of .... DIDO
god of .... MOLOCH
goddess .... TANIT
of .... PUNIC
queen of .... DIDO
Roman idea of ....
TREACHEROUS, FAITHLESS
wars of .... PUNIC
Carthaginian conqueror .....
HANNIBAL
general ..... HAMILCAR, HANNIBAL, HASDRUBAL
Carthusian .. EREMITE, MONK, NUN
order founder ....
(SAINT) BRUNO
cartilage .... PLAIT, GRISTLE
combining form ....
CHONDRO
dog tongue's .... LYTTA
cartograph ..... MAP, CHART, PLAT
cartographer ..... MERCATOR
cartographical half .... HEMI
carton .... (CARDBOARD) BOX
cartoon .... DRAWING, COMIC STRIP, SKETCH
kind of .... CARICATURE, EDITORIAL
vocals .... BALLOONS
cartoonist .... DRAWER, SKETCHER, (DAVID) LOW, (PETER) ARNO, ADDAMS, CAPP, DISNEY, NAST, KIRBY, SOGLOW, OLIPHANT, SCHULTZ
cartoons .... STRIPS
cartridge .... SHOT, SHELL
box .... CARTOUCH(E)
container .... CLIP
cartwheel .. HAT, HANDSPRING
slang .... COIN
caruncle .... COMB, WATTLE, GILL
Caruso, opera singer .. ENRICO

carvacrol .... ANTISEPTIC, ANESTHETIC
carve ...... CUT, (EN)GRAVE, CHISEL, SLICE, INCISE, SCULPT
carved ..... GRAVEN, GLYPHIC
  figure .... GLYPH
  gem .... CAMEO
  image .... STATUE
carver .... SCULPTOR, GRAVER
carving .... SCULPTURE
  art .... GLYPTICS
  in low relief .... ANAGLYPHY
  stone .... CAMEO
  tool .... CHISEL
Cary Grant .. (ARCHIE) LEACH
casaba .... (MUSK)MELON
  fruit like ... CANTALOUPE
Casal's (Pablo) instrument ... CELLO
cascade .. WATERFALL, LINN, SHOWER, FALL
cascara .... BUCKTHORN, BEARWOOD, WAHOO
case ...... MATTER, INSTANCE, AFFAIR, EXAMPLE, SITUATION, EVENT, CAPSULE, CONTAINER, CRATE, SHEATH, BOX, QUESTION, LOOK OVER
  armadillo's ... CARAPACE
  auto tire .... SHOE
  book .... FOREL
  bullet .... CARTRIDGE
  chalice linen ..... BURSE
  egg .... SHELL
  for arnica ...... BRUISE
  for liquor bottles .... CELLARET
  fruit .... RIND
  grammatical .... DATIVE, NOMINATIVE, ABLATIVE, ACCUSATIVE, GENITIVE
  hospital .... PATIENT
  in any .... ANYHOW
  in: sl. .... DIE
  insect larva's .. INDUSIUM
  of explosives ... PETARD
  pea .... POD
  portrait .... LOCKET
  pupa .... COCOON
  sausage ..... INTESTINE
  seed .... POD
  ship .... HULL
  slang .... LOOK OVER, EXAMINE

small ... CAPSULE, ETUI, ETWEE, PYXIS
toilet ... ETUI, COMPACT, ETWEE
trial site .... VENUE
turtle .... CARAPACE
casein preparation .... LACTARENE
  synthetic fabric .... LANITAL
casemate .... ENCLOSURE
  describing a .... SHELLPROOF, ARMORED
casement ... WINDOW, FRAME
casern .... BARRACKS
cash .. (READY) MONEY, COINS, DILS, CURRENCY, SPECIE
  advance .. IMPREST, ARLES
  box ..... TILL, REGISTER
  note .... VOUCHER
  note of sorts .... IOU
  on delivery .... COD
  ready .... TILL
  receipts/payments handler ...... CASHIER, TELLER
  register sign ... NO SALE
cashaw .... CUSHAW, SQUASH
cashbook .... LEDGER
cashew .... ANACARD, PISTACHIO, MANGO
  French ...... (A)CAJOU
  oil .... CARDOL
cashier .. TELLER, DISCHARGE, DISCARD, BURSAR, PURSER, DISMISS
cashmere ... WOOL, KASHMIR
cashoo .... CATECHU
Cashin, dress designer .... BONNIE
casing .... HULL, COVER, SHEATH(ING), FRAME
casino ...... SUMMERHOUSE, CARD GAME
cask ..... KEG, BARREL, VAT, TUN, BARECA, TIERCE, BUTT, FIRKIN, PUNCHEON
  bulge .... BILGE
  content measurer .... GA(U)GER
  cork .... BUNG
  forty-two-gallon .. TIERCE
  four-gallon .... TUB
  groove .... CROZE
  maker .. COOPER, HOOPER
  rim ..... CHIMB, CHIME, CHINE

small .... RUN(D)LET
stave .... LAG
staves, set ...... SHOOK
stopper .... BUNG
casket .. BOX, CHEST, COFFIN,
PIX
carrier ..... PALLBEARER
for sacred relics .. CIST,
KIST, RELIQUARY
for valuables .... COFFER
Caspary (Vera) play .. LAURA
Caspian Sea fish .. STURGEON,
BELUGA
tributary .. URAL, VOLGA,
KURA
casque .... HELMET
cassaba .... (MUSK)MELON
Cassandra .... SEERESS,
PROPHETESS
descriptive of ..... LIAR
parent of .... PRIAM,
HECUBA
cassava .... JUCA, MANIOC,
MANIHOT
product .... STARCH,
BREAD, TAPIOCA
casserite .... TINSTONE
casserole .... STEW, RAGOUT,
DISH, (SAUCE) PAN,
(FRYING) PAN
dish .... GRATIN
cassia ...... CINNAMON, BARK
cathartic drug ... SENNA
cassimere .... CASHMERE,
CLOTH
Cassini, designer ...... OLEG
Cassiopeia's chair .... STARS,
CONSTELLATION
daughter ... ANDROMEDA
husband .... CEPHEUS
cassock .. VESTMENT, SOUTANE,
CLERGYMAN
belt .... SURCINGLE
cassowary ..... BIRD, RATITE
bird like ...... OSTRICH,
RHEA, EMU
cast .. FLING, THROW, HURL,
SHED, MOLD, TOSS, FOUND
about ... SEARCH, LOOK,
DEVISE
amorous glances .. OGLE
aside .... DISCARD,
ABANDON
away .... DISCARD
ballot .... VOTE
blame on ...... REFLECT

down ... REJECT, DISOWN,
HURL
founded ...... FUSIL(E)
horn .... MEW
in printing .. STEREOTYPE,
ELECTROTYPE
iron ...... HARD, RIGID
metal mass .. PIG, INGOT
of characters .. PERSONAE
off .... EXUVIATE, SHED,
DISCARD, SLOUGH
off by animal .... MOLT
out .. EXPEL, EJECT, EVICT
thing ..... VOTE, BALLOT,
BAIT, DICE, FLY, NET,
ANCHOR
up .... VOMIT
with matrix ...... MOLD
Castalia .... SPRING
castanea .... CHESTNUT
castaway ... WAIF, OUTCAST,
PARIAH
a kind of .... LEPER
merchants' .... TELI
shipwreck's ... DERELICT
caste .. SOCIAL SYSTEM, CLASS
castellan .... WARDEN,
GOVERNOR, CHATELAIN
caster ...... CRUET, ROLLER,
BOTTLE, STAND, TRUNDLE,
TRUCKLE
castigate .. CHASTISE, REBUKE,
PUNISH, CRITICIZE
Castile .... SOAP
designating part of .....
NUEVA, VIEJA
province .... AVILA
river .... EBRO
casting mold .... DIE, MATRICE
place .... FOUNDRY
castle .... STRONGHOLD,
CHESSPIECE, ROOK, KEEP,
HOME
attackers' explosive .....
PETARD
court .... BAILEY
ditch .... MOAT
entrance ...... POSTERN
French .... CHATEAU
governor/warden ....
CASTELLAN
in the air .... DAYDREAM,
REVERIE
keep .... DONJON
keeper ...... CASTELLAN,
CHATELAIN

lady of the .. CHATELAINE
open space ...... WARD
tower .... DONJON,
BARRICAN, KEEP
underground cell ....
DUNGEON
VIP ..... KING, KNIGHT
wall .... BAIL(EY)
warden ...... CONSTABLE
Castles' dance .... WALK,
BUNNY HUG
castoff .... DISCHARGED,
DISOWNED, ABANDONED,
SHED
Castor .. CRUET, BEAVER, HAT,
BEAN, STAR
and Pollux .... GEMINI,
TWIN, DIOSCURI
bean protein ..... RICIN
father of .... ZEUS
killer of .... IDAS
mother of .... LEDA
oil poison .... RICIN
silk .... ERI(A)
twin brother of .. POLLUX
castrate .. EMASCULATE, GELD,
MUTILATE, CAPONIZE,
UNMAN, SPAY, STERILIZE,
ALTER
castrated .... GIBBED
animal .. NEUTER, STAG,
GIB
boar .... HOG
bull .... OX
cat .... GIB
cattle .... STEER
horse .... GELDING
man .... EUNUCH
pig .... BARROW
rooster/cock ..... CAPON
sheep .... WETHER
casual .... CHANCE, IDLE,
OFFHAND, INCIDENTAL,
AIMLESS, CURSORY, RANDOM,
PASSING
casualty .. ACCIDENT, VICTIM,
FATALITY
casuist .... QUIBBLER
alleged .... JESUIT
of a sort .... SOPHIST
casuistic .... SPECIOUS
casus .... HAPPENING, EVENT,
CASE
belli result .... WAR
cat .. FELINE, TIGER, ANGORA,
LION, COUGAR, LEOPARD,

PUMA, CIVET, GENET(TE),
FELID, BAUDRONS, LYNX,
MALKIN, MAWKIN, OCELOT,
MARGAY, PANTHER, PUSS(Y)
brier .... SMILAX
castrated ...... GIB(BED)
colloquial .. KITTY, PUSSY
domestic .... MANX
drinking way of .... LAP
epithet ...... BAUDRONS
eyed animal ...... LYNX
family ...... FELI(DAE),
FELINE
female .... TABBY,
GRIMALKIN, QUEEN
grinning, proverbial ....
CHESHIRE
like animal .... ZIBET(H),
GENET(TE), LINSANG
mice-hunting .... MOUSER
move like a .. PUSSYFOOT
musk-yielding .... CIVET
nap .... DOZE
o-nine-tails .... WHIP
of the .... FELINE
pet ... SIAMESE, PERSIAN,
MALTESE, ANGORA
ring-tailed ...... SERVAL
sound .... PURR, ROAR,
MIAOW, MIAUL, MEW,
MEOW, CATERWAUL
spotted ...... JAGUAR,
SERVAL, MARGAY, OCELOT
striped .... TIGER
young .... KITTEN
cat's-eye .... GEM, QUARTZ,
CHATOYANT, CHRYSOBERYL
paw .. PAD, DUPE, TOOL,
STOOGE, PAWN, KNOT
whisker(s) .. VIBRISSA(E)
cata, as prefix ...... DOWN,
AWAY, AGAINST, THROUGH,
BACKWARD
catachresis, victim of ....
(MRS.) MALAPROP
cataclysm ... FLOOD, DELUGE,
DISASTER, UPHEAVAL
kind of .... WAR,
EARTHQUAKE
catacomb .. CRYPT, CEMETERY,
LOCULUS
catafalque .... BIER
catalase .... ENZYME
catalo ...... BUFFALO, BISON,
BOVINE
catalogue ..... LIST, RECORD,

SCHEDULE, REGISTER, CLASSIFY, ROLL, INDEX

bookseller's .... BIBLIOTHECA

box .... CARD FILE

of goods, etc. .... INVENTORY

of saints ..... HAGIOLOGY

official .... CANON

Catalonian poet-musician .... TROUBADOR

catalyst .... ACTIVATOR, REAGENT

catamaran ..... RAFT, BALSA, BOAT, FLOAT

catamenia .... MENSTRUATION

catamite .... PUNK

catamount ... PUMA, COUGAR, LYNX

cataplasm .... POULTICE

catapult ..... BRICOLE, HURL, ONAGER, BALLISTA, TREBUCHET

kin of ...... MANGONEL

projectile .... PELLET

cataract .... (WATER)FALL, DELUGE, DOWNPOUR, LINN, CASCADE

catarrh .... RHEUM, COLD

cigarette for ...... CUBEB

nasal .... CORYZA

catastasis .... EXORDIUM

catastrophe .. RUIN, DISASTER, MISFORTUNE, CALAMITY

in geology ... CATACLYSM

Catawba ...... GRAPE, WINE

catch ..... NAB, SEIZE, HOOK, CAPTURE, NAIL, RATCHET, TRAP, PAWL

breath ..... GASP, PANT

fish .... HAUL

in a bill .. RIDER, JOKER

of clock .... DETENT

on .... GET IT, CLICK, UNDERSTAND

phrase .... SLOGAN, WARCRY, MOTTO

releaser .. PAWL, TRIPPER, DETENT

sight of ...... ESPY, SPOT, DESCRY

up .... OVERTAKE, OVERHAUL

with the ____ .... GOODS

catchall .. (RAG)BAG, BASKET, HANDBAG, ET AL, ETC(ETERA)

one kind of ..... ATTIC, CLOSET

catcher ..... CAPTOR, NABBER

catching .... CONTAGIOUS, INFECTIOUS, ATTRACTIVE, FETCHING

catchment, kind of ...... RESERVOIR, CISTERN

catchpenny .... CHEAP, WORTHLESS

catchpole ..... TAXGATHERER, CHICKEN CHASER

catchup ... KETCHUP, CATSUP

catchword ..... SLOGAN, CUE, MOTTO

catchy ...... TRICKY, FITFUL, DECEIVING

cate ..... DELICACY, DAINTY

catechism .... HANDBOOK

catechu ... CASHOO, GAMBLER, CUTCH

like gum .... KINO

catechumen .... PUPIL

categorical .... ABSOLUTE, POSITIVE, DIRECT, EXPLICIT

category ... DIVISION, SPECIES, CLASS, GENRE

catena .... CHAIN

cater .... PANDER, SERVE, PURVEY, PROVIDE

cornered .. DIAGONAL(LY)

cateran .... ROBBER

caterer, army .... SUTLER

kind of ..... PANDERER, PROCURER, PIMP

caterpillar ..... LARVA, WERI, WOOLLYBEAR, SLUG, CUTWORM, WOOBUT, LOOPER, WEBWORM

disease .... WILT

hair .... SETA

treaded vehicle ... TANK, HALF-TRACK, AMTRAC, TRACTOR, CAT

caterwaul .... MIAUL, HOWL, SCREECH, WAIL, SCREAM

catfish .... TANDAN, (BULL)POUT, BULLHEAD, DORAD, SILURID, SCULPIN, SHAL

electric .... RAAD

Row resident ... PORGY, BESS

catgut ..... CATLING, VIOLIN, WHIPCORD

cathartic .... CALOMEL,

CASTOR OIL, LAXATIVE, PURGING, ALOIN, GAMBOGS, ALOE, EVACUANT, EMETIC, CASSIA, PHYSIC
drug .... SENNA
from flax .... LININ
resin .... SCAMMONY
Cathay .... CHINA
cathedra .... THRONE, SEE
cathedral .... AUTHORITATIVE, OFFICIAL, DUOMO, MINSTER
city .... ELY, AMIENS, CHARTRES, R(H)EIMS
clergyman ...... CANON
famous ..... NOTRE DAME
passage .... SLYPE
presiding official ... DEAN
private land of ... CLOSE
Cather, novelist ...... SIBERT, WILLA
Catherine, mother of 3 kings .. MEDICI
Catherine the Great .. TSARINA
favorite ...... POTEMKIN
Catholic .... UNIVERSAL, LIBERAL
lay society .... SODALITY
tribunal .... ROTA
tribunal member .... AUDITOR
catholicon .... PANACEA, CURE-ALL, ELIXIR
cation .... ION
catkin ... AMENT(A), CATTAIL, PUSSY, CHAT
tree ..... BIRCH, WILLOW, POPLAR
catlike .. NOISELESS, STEALTHY
animal .... LINSANG
catling ...... CATGUT, KNIFE
catnap .... DOZE
catnip .... NEP
catouse .... UPROAR
catsup ..... KETCHUP, SAUCE, CATCHUP
Catt, American suffragist .... CARRIE
cattail .... CATKIN, TULE, (BUL)RUSH, DODD, REED(MACE), RAUPO
cattiness .... MEANNESS
cattle .. BOVINE, KINE, BOVID, OXEN, NOWT
beef ... STEER, HOLSTEIN
black .... KERRY
boat .... TARTAN

breed .... DEVON, KERRY, DURHAM, LONGHORN
castrated .... STEER
catcher .... HAYWARD
catching rope ..... BOLA
crossed with bison/buffalo CAT(T)ALO
dairy .. KERRY, GUERNSEY
dealer .... DROVER
dewlap .... JOWL
disease ...... BOTS, GID, STAGGERS, ANTHRAX, NAGANA, GARGET, TEXAS FEVER, LUMPY JAW, LOCO, MURRAIN, MEASLES, SCOURS, SHAKES
dwarf .... DEVON, NIATA
dysentery .... SCOURS
enclosure ...... RODEO, KRAAL, CORRAL
epidemic ... RINDERPEST
farm ... RANCH, ESTANCIA
farm manager ... RANCHER
fat .... SUET, TALLOW
feed for hire ...... GIST
feed from linseed .... OIL CAKE
fodder .... FARRAGO
foot of .... HOOF
frenzied run .. STAMPEDE
grazing land .... RANGE, PASTURE
herdsman ..... VAQUERO
hybrid ...... CAT(T)ALO
nervous ailment .... STAGGERS
parasitic larva .. WARBLE
pen .... KRAAL, CORRAL, YARD
plague ...... RINDERPEST
polled .... MUL(L)EY
ranch .... ESTANCIA
ranch man .... COWBOY, VAQUERO
raiser .... STOCKMAN, RANCHER
round-up ..... WRANGLE, RODEO
short-horned ... DURHAM
stall .... CRIB
stealer .... RUSTLER
stealing ..... RUSTLING
tender .... COWHEAD, VAQUERO
tormentor .... GNAT
urine .... STALE

vertigo .... MEGRIM
cattleman .. RANCHER, DROVER, HERDER
catty .... MEAN, SPITEFUL, MALICIOUS
catwalk .... PATHWAY, PLATFORM, BRIDGE
Caucasian .. IRANIAN, ARYAN, TATAR, WHITE MAN
   carpet ..... KUBA, BAKU
   goat .... TUR
   language .... GEORGIAN, SEMITIC, CIRCASSIAN
   race .... SEMITE
   rug .... BAKU
Caucasus inhabitant .... OSSET(IAN)
   region .... OSSETIA
   river .... KUBAN
   wild goat .... TUR
caucho tree .... ULE
caucus .... MEETING, CONFAB
caudad, opposed to .... CEPHALAD
caudal appendage ...... TAIL
caudillo .... LEADER, COMMANDER
   El .... FRANCO
caudle .... DRINK, GRUEL
caul .... VEIL
cauld .... COLD
cauldron ... KETTLE, COPPER, POT
caulicle .... STEM
cauliflower .... CABBAGE, BROCCOLI
   eared one .. BOXER, PUG
   row character ... BOXER, PUG
caulis .... STEM, STALK
caulk .. STOP UP, SEAL, CHINSE
caulking material ...... TAR, OAKUM
causal connective ..... SINCE, THEREFORE, FOR
cause ...... REASON, MOTIVE, GROUND, MOVEMENT, EFFECT, INDUCE, OCCASION
   bad luck .... HEX, JINX
   celebre, usual .... CASE, TRIAL, SCANDAL
   for divorce .. GROUND(S)
   for war ..... CASUS BELLI
   in law ...... (LAW) SUIT
   impelling ... MAINSPRING
   spasm .... CONVULSE

to arch .... ROACH
to do unwillingly .... COERCE, PRESS
to fight .... EMBROIL
to happen ...... BRING, EFFECTUATE
causerie .... PLEAD, PARLEY, DEBATE, CHAT, DISPUTE, TALK
causes, science of .... (A)ETIOLOGY
causeuse .. SOFA, TETE-A-TETE
causeway .... ROAD, CAUSEY
causing abortion ... ECBOLIC
   disaster .... MALEFIC
   no pain ..... INDOLENT
   sneezing ...... ERRHINE
caustic .. CORROSIVE, CUTTING, SNAPPISH, VITRIOLIC, MORDACIOUS, SARDONIC, MORDANT, BITING, TART, STINGING, LIME, SARCASTIC
   agent .. ERODENT, ACID, LYE
   solution .... LYE
   substance, burn with .... CAUTERIZE
   temper .. SNAPPISH, TESTY
cauterant .... MOXA
cauterize .. BURN, SEAR, CHAR
cauterizing agent ...... MOXA
cautery .... MOXA
caution .... WARN(ING), BAIL, PRUDENCE, CARE, ALERT, ADMONITION, ADMONISH
cautious ..... WARY, CHARY, CAREFUL, CIRCUMSPECT, WARE
   general .... FABIUS
cavalcade .... PARADE, PROCESSION, PAGEANT
cavalier .... KNIGHT, GENTLEMAN, GAY, ARROGANT, PROUD
cavalla ... CARANGOID, HORES, CERO, FISH
cavalry .... TROOPS, HORSE
   attack obstacle .... CALTRAP, CALTROP
   command ... TO HORSE, DISMOUNT, CHARGE
   commander .. HIPPARCH
   flag .... CORNET
   horse .. TROOPER, WALER
   men's hazard .. CALTRAP, CALTROP
   soldier .. LANCE(R), SPAHI

standard ..... LABARUM
sword .... SABER
unit .... SQUADRON
cavalryman .... DRAGOON,
 TROOP(ER), LANCER
Algerian .... SPAHI
French .... CARABINEER,
 CARABINIER, CHASSEUR
German .... U(H)LAN
horse .... WALER
Hungarian/Croatian ....
 HUSSAR
mount of Algerian ......
 CAMEL
Russian .... COSSACK
Turkish .. SPAHI, SPAHEE
weapon of ..... LANCE,
 SABRE
cavatina ..... SUNG, MELODY
cave .. DEN, HOLLOW, CRYPT,
GROT(TO), ANTRE, ANTRUM,
 LAIR
dweller ... TROGLODYTE,
BAT, BEAR, LION, HERMIT,
 TROLL
dwelling .... SPEL(A)BAN
explorer .... SPELUNKER
formation .. STALACTITE,
 STALAGMITE
in ...... COLLAPSE, SINK,
 YIELD, SUBMIT
man ...... TROGLODYTE,
 HERMIT
man-made ...... CRYPT
man's time .. STONE AGE
of a .... SPELEAN
poetic ..... GROT, ANTRE
caveat .... WARNING, NOTICE
Cavell, nurse .... EDITH
cavern ...... GROT(TO), LAIR,
 ANTRE
Hebrides Island ....
 FINGAL'S CAVE
caves, inhabiting ... SPELEAN
science of .. SPELEOLOGY
caviar .... RELISH, ROE
connoisseur ... GOURMET,
 RUSSIAN, GOURMAND
fish .. STERLET, STURGEON
material .... (FISH)EGGS,
 ROE
source of ..... STERLET,
SALMON, STURGEON, SHAD
cavil .. CARP, QUIBBLE, OBJECT,
 BICKER
cavities, full of ... CAVERNOUS

cavity ...... ANTRUM, HOLE,
HOLLOW, CELL, PIT, SINUS,
 FOSSA, FOLLICLE
animal tissue .. LOCULUS
combining form ....
 C(O)ELE
crystal-lined ... GEODIC
crystal-lined rock ....
GEODE, VOOG, VUGG, VUGH
embryonic .. COELOM(E)
eye .... ORBIT
heart .... ATRIUM
honeycomb .... CELL,
 ALVEOLUS
in anatomy ..... FOSSA,
BURSA, ANTRUM, LACUNA,
 SINUS, ALVEOLUS
in biology ...... LACUNA
in zoology ..... CLOACA,
 ALVEOLUS
membrane ..... VESICLE
nose ... ANTRUM, SINUS
of abdominal .. COELIAC
opening/outlet .. ORIFICE
plant tissue .... LOCULUS
stone with crystal-lined ..
 GEODE
cavort .. CAPER, PRANCE, LEAP
cavy .... RODENT, PACA,
 CAPYBARA, GUINEA PIG
caw sounder ... CROW, RAVEN
Cawdor castle site .... NAIRN
cay .... (CORAL)REEF,
 (SAND)BANK, KEY
cayenne ... PEPPER, CAPSICUM,
 CHILIES, CANARY
cayman .... ALLIGATOR, YAKI
cayuse .... PONY
cowpoke's .... HOSS
Ceara .... FORTALEZA
cease ..... END, DESIST, STOP,
DISCONTINUE, REFRAIN, QUIT
nautical .... AVAST
ceaseless .... CONTINUAL,
 ENDLESS, CONTINUOUS
Cechy .... BOHEMIA
Cecrops .. KING, MAN-DRAGON
daughter of ...... HERSE
cecum .... POUCH
cedar .... JUNIPER, THUJA,
WOOD, SAVIN(E), TOON(A),
 DEODAR, CONIFER
Himalayan ..... DEODAR
cedarbird .... WAXWING
cede ..... GRANT, TRANSFER,
 YIELD

Cedric .... (WAR) CHIEF
   ward of .... ROWENA
cedula .. CERTIFICATE, PERMIT
ceiba .. KAPOK, SILK-COTTON
ceil .... LINE, COVER
ceiling, decorated ... PLAFOND
   division .... TRAVE
   hit the: colloq. ... RAGE,
                        ERUPT
   mine .... ASTEL
   of sunken panels ......
                        LACUNAR
   picture .... MURAL
   plasterwork ....
                        PARGET(ING)
   rounded .. CUPOLA, DOME
   section .... PANEL
Celaeno .... HARPY
celandine .... PILEWORT
celanese .... RAYON
Celebes .... SULAWESI
   city .... MACASSAR
   ox .... ANOA
celebrant at mass ..... PRIEST
celebrate .... SOLEMNIZE,
   COMMEMORATE, OBSERVE, FETE
   in song .... CAROL
celebrated .. OBSERVED, NOTED,
       FAMOUS, RENOWN,
       SOLEMNIZED, EMINENT
celebration, gala ..... FIESTA
   with much drinking ....
       CAROUSAL, WASSAIL
celebrities' meeting place .....
                        SALON
celebrity .. IDOL, LION, FAME,
       RENOWN, STAR, HERO
   treat like a ..... LIONIZE
celerity .... QUICKNESS,
   DISPATCH, HASTE, SPEED,
                        SWIFTNESS
celery ... PLANT, VEGETABLE,
                        SMALLAGE
   like plant .... UDO
celesta for example ....
                        IDIOPHONE
celeste .... BLUE, AZURE
celestial .. HEAVENLY, DIVINE,
   URANIC, HOLY, ETHEREAL,
       SUPERNAL, OLYMPIAN
   being ... ANGEL, CHERUB,
                        SERAPH
   body .. SUN, STAR, MOON,
                        COMET
   circle .... COLURE, HALO
   empire .... CHINA

   happiness .... BLISS,
                        ECSTASY
   phenomenon .... COMET,
       ECLIPSE, RAINBOW
   slang .... CHINAMAN
   vault .... EMPYREAN
celibacy ..... BACHELORHOOD,
                        SINGLE LIFE
celibate .. BACHELOR, SINGLE,
                        UNMARRIED
   former .... BENEDICT
   one kind of ...... MONK,
                        PRIEST
cell ... EGG, GERM, CONVENT,
   MONASTERY, CADRE, BATTERY
   cavity .... VACUOLE
   center .... NUCLEUS
   combining form ... CYTO,
                        CYTE
   destruction .. (CYTO)LYSIS
   division .... SPIREME,
                        (A)MITOSIS
   formation .. CYTOGENESIS
   formed by two gametes ..
                        ZYGOTE
   framework ..... STROMA
   honeycomb ... ALVEOLUS
   nerve .... NEURON(E)
   nucleus ...... MESOPLAST
   small .. CELLULE, PAPILLA
   stinging .... NEMATOCYST
   study of the .. CYTOLOGY
   wall .... PARIES
   wall rib .... RAPHE
cella .... NAOS, TEMPLE
cellar .. WINE-STOCK, PANTRY,
                        STOREROOM
   location of .... BASEMENT
   man in charge of ....
                        BUTLER
   room .... VAULT
   wine .... VAULT, BUTTERY
celled structure ..... PRISON,
   CONVENT, MONASTERY,
                        HONEYCOMB
cells, consisting of ....
       LOCULAR, CELLULAR
   change in ... CATAPLASIA
   form into .... CELLULATE
   mass of .... MORULA
   ovum-formed mass of ...
                        MORULA
   union of .... ZYGOSIS
   water-conducting .....
                        TRACHEID

cellular .... ALVEOLATE, LOCULAR
celluloid : colloq. .... (MOVIE) FILM, MOVIES
cellulose fiber .... RAYON, CELANESE
   wrapping material ...... CELLOPHANE
Celt ... BRETON, IRISH, GAEL, WELSH, SCOT, CHISEL
Celtic .... ERSE, IRISH
   chief's heir ...... TANIST
   dart .... COLP
   god .... AENGUS, LER
   island of paradise ...... AVALON
   judge .... DRUID
   king .... BELI
   language .... WELSH, BRETON, MANX, CYMRIC
   lord .... TANIST
   people of Wales .... CYMRIC
   priest .... DRUID
   religious order ... DRUID
   sea god .... LER
   sea robber ...... FOMOR
cement .. GLUE, JOIN, SOLDER, MALTHA, MASTIC
   ingredient .. LIME, CLAY, WATER
   like substance .... PASTE, GLUE
   material .... MARL
   mixture .... MORTAR, SLURRY, PUTTY
   patch with ...... SLUSH
   pipe joints .... LUTE
   sealing .... LUTE
   smoothing tool .. TROWEL
   wall .... STUCCO
cemetery .... GRAVEYARD, BONEYARD, ACROPOLIS, NECROPOLIS, GOD'S ACRE
   underground .... CATACOMB(S)
cenobite .... MONK, RECLUSE, ESSENE
   dwelling ..... CONVENT, MONASTERY
   opposed to .. ANCHORITE
cenotaph ... TOMB, MONUMENT
cense .... THURIFY
censer .... THURIBLE
censor .. CRITIC, FAULTFINDER, REVIEWER

   kind of .... EDITOR
   tool of movie .. SCISSORS
censorious .... CRITICAL
censorship of speech .... GAG
   movie scenes ...... CUTS
censure .... CHIDE, LASH, CONDEMN(ATION), ASPERSE, DECRY, CRITICIZE, BLAME, IMPEACH, RAP, OBLOQUY
census, literally .... HEAD COUNTING, NOSE COUNTING
   taker ...... ENUMERATOR
cent ... COIN, COPPER, PENNY
   one hundred of them ... DOLLAR
   one tenth of ...... MILL
   per .... HUNDRED
   twenty-five of them ..... QUARTER
centaur ..... CHIRON, NESSUS, SAGITTARY
   father of .... IXION
   killed by Hercules ...... NESSUS
centavo .... COIN, CENTIMO
centenary .... CENTURY
center .... CORE, MID, FOCUS, HUB, PIVOT, NUCLEUS, MIDDLE, HEART
   at, in or near .. CENTRIC
   farthest from .... DISTAL
   having common .... CONCENTRIC
   line of verse .... CESURA
   moving from .... CENTRIFUGAL
   moving toward .... CENTRIPETAL
   nearest the ... PROXIMAL
   non-revolving .... DEAD POINT
   of activity .... HIVE, HUB, GANGLION, FOCUS
   of attention ...... FOCUS
   of attraction .. CYNOSURE
   of command .... HEADQUARTERS
   of energy/force .... GANGLION
   of mass ...... CENTROID
   of operations .. THEATER
   of target .... BULL'S-EYE, EYE
   toward .... MESIAL
   wheel's .... HUB

centerpiece .. EPERGNE, DOILY
centesimal ...... HUNDREDTH
   unit .... GRADE
centesimo, 100 of them .. LIRA,
           BALBOA, PESO
centiare, 100 of them .... ARE
centimes, five .... SOU
   100 .... FRANC
centipede .... MYRIAPOD,
      CHILOPOD, EARWIG,
         ARTHROPOD
   legs, front pair .. FANGS
   relative ...... MILLIPEDE
cento .... PATCHWORK
central .... BASIC, PRINCIPAL,
   HUB, CHIEF, FOCAL, MAIN,
           MID(DLE)
Central African capital ......
           BANGUI
   president .... DACKO,
           BOKASSA
Central American bird ......
   CACIQUE, CURASSOW, URUBU,
   ATRATA, JUNCO, MANAKIN,
          QUE(T)ZAL
   city .... BAMBARI,
          BERBERATI
   country .. (EL)SALVADOR,
   GUATEMALA, NICARAGUA,
   COSTA RICA, PANAMA,
        HONDURAS
   ethnic group .... BANDA,
      AZANDE, MBAKA
   fiber plant .... MAGUEY,
      HENEQUEN
   hat .... JIPIJAPA
   monkey ..... MARMOSET
   parrot .. MACAW, AMAZON
   plant .... JIPIJAPA
   president .... DACKO,
      BOKASSA, ROBLES,
      LOPEZ(ARELLANO),
      SOMOZA, TREJOS,
      SANCHEZ, MENDEZ
   rodent .... PACA, AGOUTI
   sash .... TOBE
   stinging ant ..... KELEP
   tortoise .... HICATEE
   tree ...... EBO(E), AMATE
   vulture .. URUBU, ATRATA
   wildcat .. EYRA, MARGAY
central and guiding .... POLAR
   figure ...... STAR, HERO,
      HEROINE
   line .... AXIS
   mark of target ....

        BULL'S-EYE
   part .... CORE, NUCLEUS
   point(s) ... FOCUS, FOCI,
      PIVOT, NODE
centrifugal force, cause of ...
       INERTIA
   in physiology .. EFFERENT
centripetal, in physiology ....
       AFFERENT
century ..... AGE, HUNDRED,
      SIECLE
   plant (fiber) ..... AGAVE,
   ALOE, TEQUILA, PITA,
      MAGUEY
ceorl ...... FREEMAN, CHURL
cephalad, opposed to ....
      CAUDAD
cephalopod .... MOLLUSK,
   OCTOPUS, CUTTLE(FISH),
      SQUID
Cepheus' daughter ....
      ANDROMEDA
   wife .... CASSIOPEIA
ceraceous .... WAXY, WAXLIKE
Ceram .... SERANG
ceramic .... FICTILE
   mixes .... FRITS
   pigment ..... SMALTINE
   plaque .... TILE
ceramics, of .... FICTILE
   product ...... POTTERY,
   EARTHENWARE, TILE,
      PORCELAIN
ceramist .... POTTER
cerate ...... WAX, OINTMENT,
      SALVE
ceratodus ..... BARRAMUNDA
ceratin product ... HAIR, NAIL,
      HORN, CORN
ceratoid/ceratose ..... HORNY
cerberus .... DOG
   concern of .... HADES
   descriptive of ....
      THREE-HEADED
cere .... WAX, MEMBRANE
cereal .... GRAIN, GRASS
   flour .... FARINA
   food .... RICE, OATMEAL,
      HOMINY, SAMP
   grain .. OAT, RYE, MILLET,
   WHEAT, CORN, MAIZE
   grass ..... RYE, WHEAT,
   RAGGY, MILLET, OAT,
      RAG(G)I, RAGGEE
   ground .. HOMINY, GRITS
   husk .... BRAN

meal .... FARINA
spike .... EAR, COB
stem ... STALK, HA(U)LM
cerebral .... INTELLECTUAL
vitamin, so-called ... LSD
cerebrate .. THINK, COGITATE,
PONDER
cerebrum, cortex of .. MANTLE
cerecloth .. SHROUD, CEREMENT
ceremonial .. RITUAL, FORMAL
bow .... CURTSY, SALAAM
dance .... PAVAN(E)
drink .... TOAST
entrance/exit signal .....
SENNET
procession ..... PARADE,
CAVALCADE, CORTEGE
trumpet call .... SENNET
ceremonious .. FORMAL, PRIM
act ..... SALUTE, SALAAM,
FLOURISH
display .... FANFARE
leave-taking .. CONGE(E)
motion .... FLOURISH
show of homage ....
KOWTOW, SALAAM
ceremony .. FORMALITY, RITE,
RITUAL, POMP
hypocritical ... MUMMERY
Ceres .... DEMETER, PLANET,
ASTEROID, GODDESS
parent of .. OPS, SATURN
cereus .... CACTUS
Cerigo Island ...... KYTHERA
cerise .... RED
cerium dioxide .... CERIA
silicate .... CERITE
cero .... CAVALLA
combining form .... WAX
fish resembling ....
MACKEREL
certain ..... FIXED, APODITIC,
SURE, TRUE, RELIABLE,
POSITIVE
certainly .. SURELY, OF COURSE
archaic .... IWIS
certainty .... CERTITUDE,
ASSURANCE
certificate, graduation ....
DIPLOMA
money .... SCRIP
Spanish .... CEDULA
certification ... ATTESTATION,
OK
certify ...... VOUCH, VERIFY,

DEPOSE, ASSURE, TESTIFY,
NOTARIZE, ATTEST
certitude .... ASSURANCE,
CERTAINTY
cerulean .. AZURE, (SKY) BLUE
cerumen .... EARWAX
ceruse .... (WHITE)LEAD,
COSMETIC
Cervantes, author ... MIGUEL
cervine .. DEER, STAG, CERVID
Cesare, basso .... SIEPI
cespitose .. MATTED, TURF-LIKE
cess ...... TAX, ASSESSMENT
cessation .. END, STOP(PAGE),
PAUSE, CEASING, LET-UP,
SURCEASE
of activity, temporary ...
LULL, BREAK, RESPITE
of war, temporary ......
TRUCE, CEASEFIRE
cession ... YIELDING, CEDING
cessionary .... ASSIGNEE
cesspool .... SUMP
cestode .... TAPEWORM
cestus .... GIRDLE, BELT
cesura .... PAUSE
cetacean ..... DOLPHIN, INIA,
GRAMPUS, WHALE, PORPOISE,
SUSU
Arctic ..... NARWHAL(E),
NARWAL
tusked .... NARWHAL
Cetus .... WHALE,
CONSTELLATION
Ceylon .... SINHALA
Ceylon(ese) .... TAMIL,
SIN(G)HALESE, CINGALESE
aborigine .... VEDDA(H),
TODA
ape .... MAHA
Buddhist temple site ....
KANDY
capital .... COLOMBO
city .... KANDY
export .... TEA
fortress town .... GALLE
garment .... SARONG
grass ... PATANA, CHENA
hill dweller .... TODA
language .. TELUGU, PALI,
MALAYALAM, KANARESE,
TAMIL, INDIO
lotus .... NELUMBO
monkey .... LANGUR,
WANDEROO, MAHA, TOQUE
moss ... AGAR, GULAMAN

moss derivative .... ALEC
native .... SIN(G)HALESE,
DRAVIDIAN, CINGALESE,
VEDDA(H), TODA, TAMIL
palm ;......... TALIPOT
policeman .... PEON
rat .... BANDICOOT
seaport .. GALLE, JAFFNA
snake ...... ANACONDA
strait .... PALK
tea .... PEKOE
temple site ...... KANDY
trading vessel .. D(H)ONI
tree .... PALMYRA
water lily ...... NELUMBO
CGS, part of .. CENTIMETER,
GRAM, SECOND
unit .... ERG, DYNE
cha .... TEA
chablis .... WINE
chabouk .... HORSEWHIP
chacma .... BABOON
Chad .... BREAM
capital of ... FORT LAMY
city .... MOUNDOU
ethnic group .... MASSA,
SARA, KANEMBOU
president .. TOMBALBAYE
chaeta .. SETA, SPINE, BRISTLE
chaetopod .... ANNELID
chafe ..... ANNOY, IRRITATE,
RUB, EXCORIATE, GALL,
ABRADE
at the bit .... FRET
chafer ..... BEETLE, SCARAB,
ROSE BUG
chaff ...... BANTER, TEASING,
HUSK, BRAN
like .... ACEROSE
like bract .... PALEA
mixed with .... ACEROSE
chaffer ..... HIGGLE, BANDY,
HAGGLE, BARGAIN(ING)
chaffinch .... (SONG) BIRD
chaffy ... WORTHLESS, ACEROSE
chafing .... GALLING
result of ... SORE, FROTH
chagrin ..... MORTIFICATION,
DISCOMFITURE
chain ..... FETTER, SHACKLE,
CATENA, IRON, LINKWORK
ball and .... WIFE
decorative .. CHATELAINE
form into a .. CATENATE
mail .. HAUBERK, BYRNIE
mail, like ...... ARMURE

mountain .. CORDILLERA,
RANGE
of reasoning ....
CONSECUTION
part .... LINK
pulling .... TUG
smoker for example ....
ADDICT
TV-radio .... NETWORK
chair .... SEAT, OFFICE,
POSITION, BENCH, CENTER,
PLACE, ROCKER
arrangement .... SEATING
back part .... SPLAT
backless .... STOOL,
OTTOMAN
bar connecting legs .....
ROUND
bowlegged ..... CURULE
cover .... TIDY
covered .... SEDAN
litter-like .... KAGO
making material .. SPLAT
of authority ..... THRONE
on elephant's back .....
HOWDAH, HOUDAH
on poles .... SEDAN
part .. SEAT, RUNG, ARM,
SPLAT, LEG, BOTTOM,
ROUND
portable .. SEDAN, LITTER,
PALANQUIN
state .... THRONE
take the .... PRESIDE
chaise .... CARRIAGE, BUGGY,
SHAY, SHANDRYDAN
longue .... CHAIR
chalaza .... TREAD
chalcedony .. QUARTZ, ONYX,
JASPER, CARNELIAN, AGATE,
(CHRYSO)PRASE, CAT'S-EYE,
SARD(INE), CHERT
Chaldean .... ASTROLOGER,
SORCERER
astronomical cycle .....
SAROS
capital .... BABYLON
city .... UR
chalet .. HUT, CABIN, COTTAGE
chalice .... AMA, GOBLET, CUP,
GRAIL, CALIX
cloth .... PALL
flower .... DAFFODIL
chalk .... LIMESTONE, TALLY,
CRAYON, CALCITE, WHITING
composition .. SEASHELLS

linseed oil mixture ......
PUTTY
up .... SCORE
chalkstone .... TOPHUS
chalky silicate .... TALC
challenge .... DEMAND,
EXCEPTION, QUESTION, DARE,
DEFY
  as false .... IMPUGN
  hurled ..... DEFI, GAGE
  means of .... SLAP, GAGE
  to duel .... CARTEL
  written .... CARTEL
challenging .... DEFIANT,
BELLICOSE, BELLIGERENT
Cham .... KHAN
chamber .... (BED)ROOM,
COUNCIL, CAMERA,
CAMARILLA
  for dead .... VAULT
  judge's .... CAMERA
  of a .... CAMERAL
  pot .... JORDAN
  underground .... VAULT
chambered creature of poetry..
NAUTILUS
chamberlain .... STEWARD,
TREASURER
  Oriental potentate's .....
EUNUCH
chambers, legislature of two ..
BICAMERAL
chambray .... GINGHAM
chameleon .... LIZARD,
LACERT(IL)IAN
  like .... FICKLE,
CHANGEABLE
  like creature ..... AGAMA
chamfer ..... BEVEL, GROOVE,
FLUTING
chamois .. ANTELOPE, AOUDAD,
SHAMMY
  animal like ...... GORAL,
KLIPSPRINGER
  habitat .... ALPS
champ ...... CHEW, MUNCH
  colloquial ... CHAMPION
champagne .... WINE
  bottle .... JEROBOAM
  brand .... POMMERY
  capital of ...... TROYES
  for example ..... FIZ(Z)
  of teas, so-called .....
DARJEELING
champignon ..... MUSHROOM
champion .... ADVOCATE,

PALADIN, ESPOUSE, WINNER,
DEFEND(ER), PROTECTOR
auto racing ...... MOSS,
CLARK
boxer .... CLAY, HARADA,
DEMPSEY, LOUIS, GRIFFITH,
ELORDE, VILLA
golf .. NICKLAUS, PALMER,
HOGAN, PLAYER, SNEAD,
JONES
heroic .... PALADIN,
KNIGHT
marathon .... BIKILA
pole vault ..... SEAGREN,
BIZZARRO
soccer football ..... PELE
tennis .... NEWCOMBE,
ASHE, TILDEN, HOAD, KING,
GONZALES, SANTANA,
LAVER
wrestling .... TAKTI
yacht racing .. INTREPID
chance ... CASUAL, FORTUITY,
HAP, RISK, GAMBLE, LUCK,
RANDOM, HAZARD
  betting .... ODDS
  big .... OPPORTUNITY
  by ..... ACCIDENTAL(LY)
  goddess of ..... TYCHE,
FORTUNA
  on ... MEET, ENCOUNTER
chancel .... SACRARIUM
  part ..... BEMA, RAILING
  part surrounded by .....
ALTAR
  screen .... JUBE
  seats .... SEDILIA
chances .... ODDS
chancre .. SORE, LESION, ULCER
chandelier .... CORONA,
GASELIER, LUSTER
  pendant .... LUSTER
change .... ADAPT, ALTER,
AMEND, MODIFY, MUTATE,
VARY, SWITCH, MUTATION
  color .... FADE
  course ..... HAUL, TACK,
VEER
  current flow .... RECTIFY
  direction ... CANT, TACK,
TURN, VEER, DEVIATE
  in form, nature ....
MUTATION
  in linguistics ... UMLAUT
  in religion .. CONVERSION
  into liquid .... LIQUEFY

into steel ..... ACIERATE
of mind, feeling .... CAPRICE
opinion .... HAUL
party ...... DEFECT, BOLT
policy ...... DEMARCHE, TACK
residence .... MOVE
sentence ..... COMMUTE
small .... COINS
tack .... JIBE
to direct current .... RECTIFY
changeable .... FICKLE, CAPRICIOUS, MOBILE, PROTEAN, MUTABLE, VOLATILE, FLUID
person ...... CHAMELEON
changeling ..... DOLT, IDIOT, CHILD, TURNCOAT, OAF
Changsa is capital of .. HUNAN
channel ..... STRAIT, COURSE, MEDIUM, CHUTE, RUNNEL, RUNWAY, NECK, KILL, SHOOT
artificial .. FLUME, CANAL, SLUICE(WAY)
between cliffs ...... GAT
cutting sandbank .... SWASH
direct .... PIPELINE
English .... (THE) SOLENT
entrance .... CHOPS
excess water .. SPILLWAY
fence .... WEIR
inland .... GAT
island .... JERSEY, ALDERNEY, GUERNSEY, SARK
Island, official ... JURAT
marker .... BUOY
narrow .... STRIA
obstruction ...... WEIR
of unpredictable currents EURIPUS
principal .... ARTERY
vertical .... GLYPH
water ...... RACE(WAY)
channeled .... GROOVED, FLUTED, COURSED, ROUTED
channels .... MEDIA
chanson ...... SONG, BALLAD, LYRIC
chant .... SINGSONG, MELODY, INTONE, INTONATION
poetic .... WARBLE
chantage .... BLACKMAIL

chanterelle .... MUSHROOM
chanteuse .... SINGER
chantey ...... (SAILOR) SONG
chanticleer ... ROOSTER, COCK
chantilly .... LACE
chantry ..... ALTAR, CHAPEL
chaos .... DISORDER, CONFUSION, MESS
Archaic .. ABYSS, CHASM
in language ...... BABEL
in printing .... PI
chaotic .... MUDDLED, DISORDERLY
chap .. JAW, CHEEK, BUGGER, ROUGHEN, KIBE, SKATE, GUY
colloquial .... MAN, BOY, FELLOW
chapeau .... HAT, HEADGEAR
chapel ... CHANTRY, GALILEE, VESTRY
clergyman ... CHAPLAIN
Egyptian mortuary's .... MASTABA(H)
medieval church .... GALILEE
private .... ORATORY
sailors' .... BETHEL
small .... ORATORY, CHANTRY
Vatican .... SISTINE
chaperon .... DUEN(N)A, ACCOMPANY, ESCORT
strict .... DRAGON
chaplain .... CLERGYMAN, PADRE, ORDINARY
chaplet ... WREATH, GARLAND
poetic .... ANADEM
chapman .. TRADER, DEALER, PEDDLER, HAWKER
chaps .. CHOPS, CHAPAREJOS, CHEEK, JAW
of hound .... FLEWS
chapter .... EPISODE, SECTION, LOCAL
fraternity .... LODGE
of a .... CAPITULAR
char .... BURN (UP), SCORCH, CINDERS, TROUT
charabanc .... BUS
character .... CODE, CIPHER, KIND, NATURE, ROLE, TRAIT, REPUTE
ancient alphabetical .... OGHAM, RUNE
assassination .. SLANDER, LIBEL

element in .... ETHOS
giver .... TONER
ill-tempered ... VINEGAR
in .... APPROPRIATE
in a play .... ACTOR
musical ..... CLEF, REST,
NOTE
odd .. ECCENTRIC, CRANK
of community ... ETHOS
police ...... CRIMINAL,
LAW-BREAKER,
MALEFACTOR
quality of ...... METTLE
representing a word .....
LOGOGRAM
sour .... VINEGAR
strength of .... GRISTLE
characteristic .... TRAIT,
TYPICAL, DISTINCTIVE,
PECULIARITY
expression .... IDIOM
marks .... INDICIA
taste .... FLAVOR
characters, drama/play ......
PERSONAE
of slums .... DEAD-END
characterize .. DESCRIBE, MARK
charade .... PUZZLE,
WORD GAME
charcoal .. CARBON, LIGNITE,
BONEBLACK
burning brazier ....
HIBACHI
combining form ....
CARB(O)
pencil .... FUSAIN
powdered ...... POUNCE
residue .... BREEZE
use of .... FILTER
chard ...... LEAFSTALK, BEET
chare .... CHORE
charge .... INDICT(MENT),
DEBIT, PRICE, INSTRUCT,
ATTRIBUTE, COMMAND, FEE,
ACCUSATION, COST, IMPUTE,
RUSH, DASH
in court .... ARRAIGN
kind of .... CAVALRY
mail .... POSTAGE
of the Light ___ ....
BRIGADE
on property .. LIEN, TAX
restaurant/tavern ....
COVER, CORKAGE, TIP
road .... TOLL
school .... TUITION

solemnly .... ADJURE
to expense/loss ... DEBIT
to experience ....
WRITE OFF
with crime ...... INDICT
charged .... FRAUGHT
particle .... ION
water .... SODA
charger ... STEED, WARHORSE
Archaic ...... PLATTER,
DESTRIER
chariot .. ESSED(E), QUADRIGA
race .... AGON
race course ....
HIPPODROME
race site, ancient ....
CIRCUS, COLOSSEUM
charioteer .... WAGONER
constellation .... AURIGA
furious .... JEHU
of fiction ..... BEN HUR
charisma ... CHARM, APPEAL,
GIFT, GRACE
Charisse, dancer .... CYD
charitable institution .. MISSION
charity .. ALMS, BENEVOLENCE,
BENEFACTION, DOLE
fair .... KERMIS, KERMESS
sale .... RUMMAGE,
BAZA(A)R
charivari .... SERENADE
charlatan .. IMPOSTOR, QUACK,
EMPIRIC, FAKER, PHON(E)Y,
SCIOLIST
Charlemagne .. CARLO MAGNO,
EMPEROR
father of .... PEPIN
(THE SHORT)
gift to Rinaldo .. BAYARD
grandfather of ... MARTEL
knight(s) of ... PALADIN,
DOUZEPERS, TWELVE
nephew of .... ORLANDO,
ROLAND
peer ... OLIVER, ROLAND,
ORLANDO
soubriquet .. (THE) GREAT
Charles Dickens' pseudonym ..
BOZ
Charles' Wain ... BIG DIPPER,
URSA MAJOR, AURIGA
charleyhorse .... CRAMP
charlock ... MUSTARD, WEED
charlotte .. PUDDING, DESSERT,
LOTTA, LOTTIE, LOTTY
charm ... ENAMOR, ENCHANT,

INCANTATION, FASCINATE, ATTRACT, GRACE, FETISH, SPELL

African .... OBEAH, OBI, JUJU

against evil/injury ...... AMULET

bracelet disc ... BANGLE

good luck .... TALISMAN

jewel .... SCARAB

magic .... JUJU

charmer .... MAGICIAN, ENCHANTER, SORCERER, EXORCIST

female .... SIREN

of German legend ...... LORELEI

charming .... WINSOME, WINNING

charnel house .... OSSUARY, TOMB

of a sort ...... PANTHEON, MORTUARY

Charon .... FERRYMAN

fee .... OBOL

river .... STYX

charpoy (charpai) .. BEDSTEAD, COT

charqui .... BEEF

char(r) .... TROUT

chart ... MAP, LAYOUT, PLOT, GRAPH, OUTLINE

charter ...... HIRE, FRANCHISE, LEASE

fundamental .... CONSTITUTION

Charteris (Leslie) detective ... (THE) SAINT

forte of ..... WHODUNITS

Chartres river .... EURE

Chartreuse .... LIQUEUR

chary .. CAREFUL, CAUTIOUS, SHY

Charybdis .... WHIRLPOOL

rock opposite ... SCYLLA

chase ..... PURSUE, FOLLOW, CHEVY, FRET, HUNT, PURSUIT, ENGRAVE

continually ..... HOUND

object of .... HARE, FOX, RAINBOW, ESCAPEE, GAME

the .... VENERY

chaser ...... HUNTER, DRINK, CHISEL, GRAVER, WASH

ambulance ..... SHYSTER

chasing tool .. CHISEL, TRACER

chasm .. GAP, ABYSS, HIATUS, RIFT

in a glacier ... CREVASSE

chasseur .... HUNTER, HUNTSMAN, SERVANT

chassis .... FRAME

slang .... BODY

chaste ..... PURE, VIRTUOUS, MODEST, VESTAL, DECENT

woman .... VIRGIN

chatelaine .... PIN, CLASP

chasten ... PUNISH, CHASTISE, SUBDUE, HUMBLE

chastise ..... SPANK, PUNISH

physically ... WHIP, FLOG

verbally .. SCOLD, BERATE

chastity .... CELIBACY, VIRGINITY, DECENCY

vower of .. MONK, NUN, PRIEST, VESTAL

chat ... TALK, CONVERSATION, CONVERSE

colloquial ...... CONFAB

French .... CAUSERIE

friendly ... COZE, COSE

hippie's slang ..... RAP

of maple ...... SAMARA

of plantain .... SPIKE

of willow .... AMENT, CATKIN

chateau .... CASTLE

entrance .... PORTE

mistress of .. CHATELAINE

chatelain .... CASTELLAN

chatelaine .. CHAIN, BROOCH, ETUI

chatoyant ... GEM, CAT'S-EYE

chattel .... CHOSE, GOODS

Archaic .... SLAVE

chatter .... BLAB, PRATE, CACKLE, CLACK, PRATTLE, BABBLE, GAS, GIBBER

Aussie colloq. .. YABBER

colloquial .... GAB

gossipy .... TATTLE

incoherent ...... JABBER

slang .... CHIN

unintelligible ... GIBBER

chatterbox .... MAGPIE, JAY

chatterer, bird .. MAGPIE, COTINGA, WAXWING, JAY, PIET

Chaucer, poet .... GEOFFREY

pilgrim .... REEVE

songs .... CHAUNTS

title .... DAN

work ....
CANTERBURY TALES
chauffer ...... STOVE, HEATER
chauffeur .... DRIVER
chaussure ... FOOTWEAR, SHOE,
BOOT, SLIPPER
chauvinist .... JINGO
chazan .... CANTOR
cheap .. COMMON, INEXPENSIVE,
MEAN, PICAYUNE, RAFFISH
and showy ..... TINHORN
colloquial .. BRUMMAGEN,
DIME-A-DOZEN
in Spanish ...... BARATO
jewelry .... TRINKET
jewelry peddler .. DUFFER
price .... BARGAIN
race horse ...... PLATER
slang .... TWO-BIT
cheapest theater seats ....
GALLERY
cheapskate .... MISER,
TIGHTWAD, PIKER, NIGGARD
cheat .... SWINDLE(R), SHAM,
FOIL, (DE)FRAUD, GYP, BILK,
COZE, GAFF, HUMBUG, FUB,
FOB, FINAGLE, NICK,
WELSH(ER), MUMP
colloquial .... DIDDLE,
CHISEL, BUNCO
by fraud .... FLEECE
easy to ...... GULLIBLE
in schoolwork .... CRIB
slang ..... MUMP, STICK,
CLIP
through trickery ....
COZEN, GOUGE
cheated, person easily .. GULL,
DUPE
cheater in school ... CRIBBER
mean .... JACKAL
cheaters: sl. .... FALSIES,
(EYE)GLASSES
chebec .... FLYCATCHER
Checchi, Signora ...... DUSE
check ..... NIP, RESTRAIN(T),
CURB, CONTROL, REIN,
VERIFY, REBUFF, ASCERTAIN
accounts .... AUDIT
bad ...... RUBBER, KITE
bleeding .. STANCH, STEM
colloquial .... CORRECT,
RIGHT
completely .... STOP
describing bad one .....
RUBBER, BOUNCING

flow ..... STEM, STANCH,
DAM
growth/development ....
NIP, STUNT
in .... REGISTER, REPORT
infection by burning ....
CAUTERIZE
mark .... TICK
out place ...... COUNTER
rain .... STUB
restaurant .... TAB, CHIT
speed .... BRAKE
up .... PROBE
checker .... CASHIER, DICE
Archaic .... CHESSBOARD
checkerberry .. WINTERGREEN
checkered .... VARIED,
TATTERSALL
cloth .... PLAID, TARTAN
checkers ... GAME, DRAUGHTS
checking block .... SPRAG
checkmate ...... FRUSTRATE,
STYMIE, BAFFLE, DEFEAT,
CORNER, STOP
Cheddar .... CHEESE
cheddite .... EXPLOSIVE
cheek ..... JOWL, TEMERITY,
JAW, CHOP, CHAP
by jowl .... CLOSE,
FAMILIAR, INTIMATE
bone .... MALAR
colloquial .. SAUCE, GALL,
INSOLENCE, NERVE, BRASH,
SAUCINESS, IMPUDENCE
glow of .... BLOOM
hair growth ... SIDEBURN
hollow .... DIMPLE
muscle .... BUCCINATOR
of the .. MALAR, BUCCAL,
GENAL, JUGAL
pouch .... ALFORJA
to cheek .... CLOSE,
CHUMMY
tongue in .... INSINCERE
cheeks and mouth .... CHOPS
cheeky: colloq. ...... SAUCY
cheep .... CHIRP, PEEP
cheer .. GLADDEN, COMFORT,
APPLAUD, ROOT, INCITE,
ELATE, ENCOURAGE,
(EN)LIVEN
approving ..... ATTABOY
bullring .... OLE
college .... RAH
English .... HEAR
French .... VIVE

Italian .... VIVA, BRAVO
Japanese .... BANZAI
kind of .... BRONX
Mexican .... VIVA
Nazi .... HEIL
Philippine ..... MABUHAY
Spanish .... OLE
up .. (EN)LIVEN, COMFORT
cheerer .... ROOTER, FAN
cheerful .... JOLLY, BLITHE,
GAY, MERRY, RIANT, SUNNY
cheerfully bright ..... SUNNY
cheerio: Brit. .... HELLO,
GOODBYE
cheerless ...... DRAB, DREARY,
SAD
cheery .... GAY, LIVELY
cheese ..... MYSOST, STILTON,
SAPSAGO
and toast dish .. RABBIT,
RAREBIT
basis of .... CASEIN
American .... BRIE
Belgian ... LIMBURG(ER)
brick ...... LIMBURG(ER)
crust .... GRATIN
dish .. SOUFFLE, FONDUE,
RAREBIT
drying frame ..... HACK
Dutch .. EDAM, COTTAGE
English .... STILTON,
CHEDDAR
enthusiast ...... MOUSE
French .... CAMEMBERT,
BRIE, ROQUEFORT
from curds ...... GOUDA
goat's/ewe's milk ....
ROQUEFORT
Italian .... PARMESAN
like .... CASEOUS
making substance ......
RENNET
place for drying .. HACK
Scottish .... KEBBOCK
Swiss .... COTTAGE,
SAPSAGO, GRUYERE
tang .... NIP
whole milk ..... DUNLOP
cheesecake: sl. ...... PIN-UP
cheesy .... CASEOUS
slang .... INFERIOR, POOR
cheetah .... GUEPARD
chef .... (CHIEF) COOK
Chek(h)ov, writer ..... ANTON
chela ..... CLAW, PINC(H)ERS
India .. NOVICE, DISCIPLE

cheloid .... TUMOR
chelonian .. TORTOISE, TURTLE
chemical catalyst ... REAGENT
change ...... REACTION
combining capacity .....
VALENCE
compound ..... AMIDE,
AMINE, ESTER, BORIDE,
CERIA, IODINE, ISOMER,
TOULENE, ELATERIN
compounds, describing ..
LABILE
element .... ARGON,
HALOGEN
element 43 ... MASURIUM
ink remover ....
ERADICATOR
prefix ..... OXA, AMIDO,
ACETO, AMINO
radical ... TOLYL, BUTYL
reaction ..... CATALYSIS
reagent ...... CATALYST,
CATALYSER
salt .. SAL, IODATE, ESTER,
NITRE, BORATE
substance .... LININ
suffix .. OSE, YLENE, ANE,
YL, OLIC
unit ...... TITER, TITRE
word ending ... OL, INE,
ENOL
chemin de fer .... RAILROAD,
BACCARAT
chemise ...... CYMAR, SARK,
LINGERIE, SLIP
colloquial ..... UNDIES,
SHIMMY
chemisette .... TUCKER
chemist .... ANALYST,
PHARMACIST, DRUGGIST
flask of ...... BOLTHEAD
pot of .... ALUDEL
chemistry, suffix in ...... OLE,
ENE, INE
Chemulpo .. INCHON, JINSEN
chenille .... CORD, DOG
Chenpao to Russians ....
DAMANSKY
Cheops .... KHUFU
edifice built by ....
PYRAMID
cherish .... NURTURE,
APPRECIATE, VALUE, ADORE,
FOSTER, PRIZE, TREASURE
companion in marriage
vow ..... LOVE, OBEY

Cherokee sage .... SEQUOYAH
cheroot .... CIGAR
cherry .... MARASCA, DRUPE,
    OXHEART, MORELLO,
    BIGAROON, AMARELLE,
    CAPULIN, BLACKHEART,
    RUDDY
    disease .... BLACKKNOT
    product ...... PIE, JAM
    red .... CERISE
    sour .... EGRIOT
    stone .... NUTLET
    sweet/wild ... MAZZARD,
    GEAN, BIGAROON
cherrystone .. CLAM, QUAHOG,
    NUTLET
chersonese .... PENINSULA
cherub .... ANGEL, AMOR,
    SERAPH
cherubic .... ANGELIC
chess castle .... ROOK
    certain defeat in ....
    CHECKMATE
    champion .. BOTVINNIK,
    SPASSKY, CAPABLANCA,
    PETROSIAN, FISHER
    corner piece ...... ROOK
    expert .... HOYLE
    opening .... GAMBIT,
    CHASSE
    piece ..... PAWN, ROOK,
    CASTLE, KING, QUEEN,
    BISHOP, KNIGHT
    sacrifice .... GAMBIT
    term ...... CHECKMATE,
    EN PASSANT
chest .... TREASURY, BOX,
    BUREAU, LOCKER, ARCA,
    BOSOM, THORAX, KIST,
    COFFERS
    a kind of ..... CAMPHOR,
    MEDICINE, TOOL,
    COMMUNITY
    animal .... BRISKET
    bone .... RIB
    cavity membrane ....
    PLEURA
    clothes .... TRUNK
    combining form ....
    STETH(O)
    for money/valuables ....
    COFFER, CASKET
    for storage ..... HUTCH
    for supplies ... WANIGAN
    human .... THORAX

located on the ....
    PECTORAL
of drawers .. CHIFFONIER,
    COMMODE, TALLBOY,
    HIGHBOY, LOWBOY
of sacred utensils .. CIST
sacred ...... ARCA, ARK
Scottish .... KIST
small .... CASKET
sound .... RALE
tool .... KIT
vibration ..... FREMITUS
Chesterfield .. SOFA, TOPCOAT,
    LORD
Chesterfieldian ...... SUAVE,
    ELEGANT, URBANE
chessman .... PAWN
chestnut ...... HORSE, TREE,
    MARRON, BUCKEYE, MAST,
    OLDIE
    Chinese .... LING
    colloquial .. JOKE, CLICHE
    Polynesian ...... RATA
    preserved in syrup ....
    MARRONS
    tree .... CHINCAPIN,
    CHINQUAPIN
    water .... LING
chevalier ... GALLANT, NOBLE
    Archaic .... KNIGHT
Chevlot .... OVINE, SHEEP
chevron .... BAR, STRIPE
    shape .... VEE
    symbol of ...... SERVICE,
    RANK
chevrotain ... NAPU, DEERLET
chevy .... HUNT, CHASE, FRET
chew .... MASTICATE, GRIND,
    CHAMP, GNAW, MUNCH, CUD,
    (S)CRUNCH, MANDUCATE,
    MUMBLE
    cud .... RUMINATE
    inability to ... AMOSESIS
    leaf to .... BETEL
chewing gum ingredient .....
    CHICLE, MASTIC
    gum tree .... SAPODILLA
    tobacco piece ..... PLUG
chewink ..... TOWHEE, FINCH
chewy confection .. CARAMEL,
    GUM
Chiang Kai-shek .... GISSIMO
    party of .. KUOMINTANG
    wife of .... MEI-LING
Chianti .... (RED) WINE
Chiapas, capital of .. TUXTLA

chiaus: Turkish ... EMISSARY, SERGEANT
chibouk ..... (TOBACCO) PIPE
chic .... SMART, STYLISH, ELEGANT, FASHIONABLE, JAUNTY
Chicago .... WINDY CITY
   airport .... O'HARE
   ball team .... WHITESOX
   business/theater area ... LOOP
   feature ..... STOCKYARDS
   football team .... BEARS
   personage .... SANDBURG
   "Wall Street" .. LA SALLE
chicalote .... POPPY
chicane .... TRICK(ERY)
chicanery .... TRICKERY, DECEPTION
chick .. PEEPER, CHILD, SHEILA
   pea .... PLANT, GRAM, FODDER
chickadee .. TITMOUSE, BIRD, TOMTIT
chickaree .... SQUIRREL
chicken .... FOWL, BIDDY, SHANGHAI, HAMBURG
   breast, cause of .... RICKETS
   breed .... (WHITE) LEGHORN, PLYMOUTH, CANTONESE, SULTAN, JAVA, MINORCA
   castrated .... CAPON
   chaser ...... CATCHPOLE
   dish ...... GALANTINE
   feed: sl. .. COINS, CHEAP, NEGLIGIBLE, PIDDLING, DIMES, PEANUTS
   female .... HEN
   five-toed .... HOUDAN
   hearted .... COWARDLY, TIMID, YELLOW
   livered .... TIMID, COWARDLY, YELLOW
   male .... ROOSTER, COCK
   meat course .. GALANTINE
   pen/cage .... COOP, RUNWAY
   pox .... VARICELLA
   resting place ... PERCH, ROOST
   slang .. TIMID, COWARDLY
   small .... BANTAM
   snake .... BOBA
   sound .... CACKLE
   young ... FRYER, CHICK, POULT, PEEPER
chickens, collectively .... POULTRY
   enclosure for ... RUNWAY
chickweed .... ALSINE, SPURR(E)Y, STITCHWORT, ALSONE
chicle .... SAPOTA
   product .. CHEWING GUM, BALATA
   source ..... SAPODILLA
chico .. SHRUB, GREASEWOOD
chicory .... ENDIVE, SUCCORY
   use for .... COFFEE
chide ...... SCOLD, UPBRAID, REBUKE, BERATE, BLAME, REPROVE
chief .. LEADER, ARCH, HEAD, PRINCIPAL, MAIN, FOREMOST, CAPTAIN, STELLAR, PREMIER
   actor .. STAR, LEAD, HERO
   barrio ...... DATO, DATU
   Canaan .... SISERA
   character .... HERO
   colloquial .... BOSS
   commander-in .... CINC
   commodity ..... STAPLE
   Cossack ...... ATAMAN, HETMAN
   excellence ...... FORTE, STRONG, POINT, TALENT
   executive ... PRESIDENT
   Indian ...... TECUMSEH, GERONIMO, COCHISE, SACHEM, BRANT, POWHATAN, SITTING BULL
   ingredient .... BASE
   Italian .... DUCE
   Justice, U.S. ... WARREN, MARSHALL, TANEY
   Moslem .... REIS
   of foreign mission ...... AMBASSADOR, NUNCIO
   of state ...... PRESIDENT, KING
   of workmen ... FOREMAN, OVERSEER
   official .... PREMIER, PRIME MINISTER
   product .... STAPLE
   singer .... CANTOR
   Spanish .... JEFE
chiefly ..... MAINLY, MOSTLY, ESPECIALLY
chieftain .... LEADER

Scandinavian ..... JARL
Indian .... SACHEM
political .... BOSS
chield .... YOUTH
chiffon .... SILK
chigger .... FLEA, CHIGOE, LARVA
chigoe .... LARVA, FLEA, CHIGGER
Chihli .... HOPEI
Chihuahua .... (TOY)DOG
chilblain .... SORE, KIBE
child .... BABY, INFANT, TAD, PRODUCT, TOT, BABE, MOPPET, ISSUE, CHIT, KIDDY, KIDDIE
    abnormal .... OAF
    bastard ...... BY-BLOW
    bad-tempered ....
        CHANGELING
    beggar's employer ......
        PADRONE
    bib .... DICKEY
    cap of .... BIGGIN
    colloquial .. TYKE, TIKE, TODDLER, CHIT, CHICK, LAMBKIN
    combining form ....
        P(A)EDO
    dirty, ragged ....
        RAGAMUFFIN
    feet of ...... PETTITOES
    game of ...... PEEKABOO
    hand of .... PUD
    homeless .... WAIF
    hood of .... BIGGIN
    impudent .... BRAT
    like .... NAIVE
    little .... MOPPET
    milk source .. WET NURSE
    mischievous .. ELF, BRAT, LIMB, IMP, JACKANAPES
    murder of .. PROLICIDE, FILICIDE
    noble born ..... CHILDE
    of .... FILIAL
    of light and day, so-called
        EROS
    of mixed blood .. MUSTEE, MESTEE, MESTIZO, HALF-BREED, MULATTO, HALF-CASTE, GRIFFE
    of the street ...... ARAB, WAIF, GAMIN
    of the Sun .... INCA
    Philippine .. BATA, ANAK

pinafore .. DICKEY, TIER, SLIP
playroom ..... NURSERY
pretty .... DOLL
ragged ..... RAGAMUFFIN
relation to parent ......
    FILIATION
savings bank of ....
    SAVE-ALL
Scottish .... BAIRN
spoiled .. COCKNEY, BRAT
substitute .. CHANGELING
teacher/trainer ....
    GOVERNESS
toy of ...... PEG TOP
ugly .... CHANGELING
undershirt ..... WAIST
unruly .... BRAT
unweaned .... SUCKLING
walk of .... TODDLE, WADDLE, PADDLE
childbearing ... PARTURATION
    primitive custom ....
        COUVADE
childbirth .... DELIVERY, PARTURATION
    confinement ... LYING-IN
    discharge after .. LOCHIA
    pains .. TRAVAIL, LABOR
childhood writings, etc. ......
    JUVENALIA
childing .... PREGNANT
childish ... IMMATURE, SILLY, ASININE, FOOLISH, PUERILE, INFANTILE, ANILE
    state due to age ....
        DOTAGE
    walk .. TODDLE, WADDLE
childhood disease .... MUMPS
childlike .... INNOCENT, TRUSTING, NAIVE, NAIF
    adult .... MORON, IDIOT
    speech .... LISP
children .... PROGENY, OFFSPRING
    book for ..... JUVENILE
    colloquial ... (SMALL)FRY
    of family ...... BROOD, FLOCK
    of heaven and earth, alleged .... TITANS
    of Israel .... JEWS, HEBREWS
    of the mist ... NIBELUNG
    study of ..... PEDOLOGY
    without .... NONPAROUS

children's book author ......
    MILNE, OUIDA, RAMEE
  book, doll in ....
    GOLLIWOG
  disease .... RICKETS,
    MUMPS, RACHITIS
  game .. TAG, JACKSTONE
  doctor ...... PEDIATRIST,
    PEDIATRICIAN
  jacket .... PALETOT
  mouth disease .. APHTHA,
    THRUSH
  patron saint ....
    SANTA (CLAUS)
  pinafore .... TIER
  playroom ...... NURSERY
  playsuit .... ROMPERS
  wasting condition ......
    MARASMUS
Chile, meaning of ..... SNOW
Chilean aborigine ...... INCA
  beech tree ...... ROBLE
  capital .... SANTIAGO
  city/town .... SANTIAGO,
    VALPARAISO, ARICA,
    CONCEPCION, LOTA, TALCA,
    VINA DEL MAR, IQUIQUE,
    ANGOL, ANTOFAGASTA
  coastal wind ..... SURES
  coin ... COLON, CENTAVO,
    ESCUDO
  court dance ..... CUECA
  deer .... PUDU
  department ..... ARICA
  desert .... ATACAMA
  evergreen .... MAQUI
  island .... HOSTE
  language ...... SPANISH
  monetary unit .. ESCUDO
  mountain ..... JUNCAL,
    MAIPU, ANDES
  palm tree ..... COQUITO
  pianist .... ARAU
  president ..... ALLENDE
  province ...... ATACAMA,
    TACNA, MAULE, TARAPACA
  region ...... PATAGONIA
  river .... BUENO, BIOBIO,
    LOA, ITATA
  saltpeter .... NITER
  seaport ... ARICA, LOTA
  shrub .... MAQUI
  tree .... PELU, RAULI,
    ROBLE, ULMO, QUILLAI
  volcano .... ANTUCO,
    CALBUCO

  wind .... SURES
chili con ____ .... CARNE
  flavored dish ....
    ENCHILADA
chiliad .... THOUSAND
chill .. COOL, DEPRESS, FROST,
  DISPIRIT, COLD(NESS), AGUE,
    ALGOR
chilling device .... ICER,
    REFRIGERATOR
  material .... ICE
chills and fever ...... AGUE,
    MALARIA
chilly ... COLD, RAW, ALGID,
    BLEAK
chilopod .... CENTIPEDE
chimar .... ROBE
chimb .... RIM
chime .. HARMONY, RIM, BELL,
    PEAL
  in ... INTERRUPT, AGREE,
    JOIN
chimer .... ROBE
chimera ... FANCY, MONSTER
  desert traveler's ... OASIS,
    WATER
  sailor's .... LAND
chimerical ...... IMAGINARY,
  FANTASTIC, VISIONARY
chimney ..... (SMOKE)STACK,
    TEWEL, FUNNEL
  bird .... SWIFT, SWALLOW
  carbon .... SOOT
  corner .... FIRESIDE,
    INGLE(NOOK)
  cover ..... MITER, COWL,
    MITRE
  lining .... PARGET
  of volcano .... VENT
  piece ... MANTEL, PAREL
  pipe .... FLUE
  pot .... TALLBOY
  screen .... BONNET
  swallow .... SWIFT
chimpanzee ..... APE, JOCKO,
    TROGLODYTE
  relative .... GORILLA,
  ORANGUTAN, GIBBON
chin flesh .... GILL
  hairy growth ... GOATEE,
    BEARD
  hollow .... DIMPLE
  pertaining to .... GENIAL,
    MENTAL
  slang .. CHATTER, TALK,
    GAB

China ...... CATHAY, SPODE
    capital .... PEKING
    made with clay ... BONE
chinaware ..... PORCELAIN,
    DRESDEN, DISHES, CROCKERY
chincapin .... CHESTNUT
chinch .... BEDBUG
chinche .... SKUNK
chinchilla ..... RODENT, FUR
    relative ...... VISCACHA
chine ..... BACKBONE, SPINE,
    RAVINE, RIDGE, SILK
Chinese .... SINIC, ORIENTAL,
    MIAO, SERIC
    A-bomb site ... LOP NOR
    alimentary paste ....
    WANTON, WONTON
    American dish ....
    CHOWMEIN, CHOP SUEY,
    SUBGUM
    arithmetical device .....
    ABACUS
    aromatic root .. GINSENG
    art/customs expert .....
    SINOLOGUE
    artichoke ..... CHOROGI
    association .... TONG
    autumn .... CH'IU
    bamboo stick .. WHANGEE
    bean .... ADSUKI
    boat .... JUNK, SAMPAN,
    TONGKANG
    brand on goods .. CHOP
    Buddhism .... FOISM
    Buddhist monk/priest ...
    LAMA
    bugaboo .. YELLOW PERIL
    capital .... PEKING
    capital, former ....
    CHUNGKING
    card game .... FAN TAN
    Caucasian tribesman ..
    LOLO
    cauterizing agent .. MOXA
    characters in Japanese ..
    MANA
    chestnut .... LING
    city ..... SIAN, CANTON,
    PEKING, SOCHE, CHEFOO,
    SHANGHAI, TIENTSIN,
    WUHAN, SHUFU, TSINAN,
    MUKDEN, FATSHAN,
    NINGPO, NANKING,
    SWATOW, SOOCHOW,
    PEIPING, HANKOW,
    JEHOL, KOTIEN,

    MINHOW, KALGAN,
    KHOTAN, FOOCHOW,
    ICHANG, KWEILIN,
    YENAN, WUSIH, WUHU
    club .... TONG
    coat .... MANDARIN
    coin .. TAEL, LIANG, TIAO,
    YUAN, LI
    coin with hole .... CASH
    combining form .. CHINO,
    SINO
    Communist leader ......
    MAO, CHOU, PING, PIAO
    custom peculiar to ......
    SINICISM
    dependency ...... TIBET
    dialect .. ... CANTONESE,
    PEKIN(G)ESE
    dialect, official ......
    MANDARIN
    dictator .... MAO
    (TSE-TUNG)
    dog .. CHOW, PEKIN(G)ESE
    duck eggs, preserved ....
    PIDAN
    dynasty .. MANCHU, WEI,
    CHOU, YIN, MONGOL, HSIA,
    T'ANG, MING, SUNG, HAN,
    SHANG, LIAO, TA CHING
    dynasty, first ..... HSIA
    dynasty, last ... MANCHU
    eating implement ....
    CHOPSTICKS
    emperor ...... KUBLAI,
    HUANG
    emperor, last .... PU-YI
    empress .... HOU
    empress, last ... TZU-HSI
    eyes describing ....
    ALMOND, SLIT
    factory .... HONG
    feudal state .... WEI
    fiber plant ...... RAMIE
    fish .... TREPANG
    flute .... TCHE
    fruit .... LOQUAT
    gambling game ....
    FAN-TAN
    game with tiles ....
    MAHJONG(G)
    gateway .... PAILOU
    gelatin .... AGAR
    glue .... AGAR
    god .... JOSS, SHEN
    gong .... TAM-TAM,
    TOM-TOM

grape .... WAMPEE
guild .... TONG
hairdo .... PIGTAIL
Han city ...... HANKOW,
    HANYANG, WUCHANG
harbor craft .... SAMPAN
herb .. GINGER, GINSENG
ideograph .... KANJI
idol .... JOSS
import duties .. HAIKWAN
incense ..... JOSS STICK
indigo .... ISATIS
invention ... GUNPOWDER
island .. TAIWAN, AMOY,
    MATSU, FORMOSA, QUEMOY
kingdom, old ...... WEI
laborer .... COOLIE
lake .... POYANG,
    KOKO NOR
language .... SHAN,
    MANDARIN
language/customs,
    study of .... SINOLOGY
license .... CHOP
lord of lower world ....
    YENLO
magnolia .... YULAN
Manchu dynasty ....
    TA CHING
mandarin's residence ....
    YAMEN
measure .. CHANG, TSUN,
    CHIH, LI
medicinal herb ....
    GINSENG
metropolis ...... WUHAN
mile LI
military academy ....
    WHAMPOA
monetary unit ... YUAN
money ...... TAEL, SYCEE
Mongol ...... MANCHU
Mongol dynasty .. YUAN
Mongol dynasty
    founder....... KUBLAI
monk .... BONZE, LAMA
mountain ...... LUSHAN
Nationalist party ....
    KUOMINTANG
noodles .... MEIN
nuclear center ....
    LOP NOR, LANCHOW
numeral, 1 to 10 ... YIH,
    URH, SAN, SZE, WOO, LUH,
    TSIEH, PA, KEW, SHIH
nurse .... AMAH

official .... MANDARIN,
    KUAN, KWAN
official seal ...... CHOP
oil tree .... TUNG
omelet .... FOOYONG
orange .... MANDARIN
ounce .... TAEL
pagoda .... TAA
pear .... PYRUS
peninsula ..... LIAOTUNG
peony .... MOUTAN
permit .... CHOP
philosopher ....
    CONFUCIUS, YUTANG,
    MENCIUS, MENG-TSE
phoenix ... FENG, HUANG
pickles ..... CHOWCHOW
pine .... MATSU
plant .. GINSENG, MOXA,
    RAMIE
poet .... LI PO
political party .... TONG,
    KUOMINTANG
porcelain material ......
    PETUNTSE
port .. CANTON, TIENTSIN,
    AMOY, ICHANG, SHANGHAI
pottery .... MING
pound .... CATTY
president .. SUN (YAT-SEN)
priest .... LAMA
principle .... YIN, YANG
province .. HOPEI, CHIHLI,
    SHAN(G)TUNG, HUNAN,
    SHANSI, KIANGSI,
    SINKIANG, HONAN,
    CHINGHAI, CHEKIANG,
    SHENSI, KANSU, YUNNAN,
    KWANGSI, HOPEH,
    HUPEH, HUPEI
provincial tax .... LIKIN
punishment .... CANGUE
puzzle .... TANGRAM
race designation ....
    YELLOW
rebellion of 1900 .. BOXER
religion .... TAOISM,
    BUDDHISM
river ..... YUAN, PEARL,
    HAN, ILI, LIAO, TARIM,
    WEI, SIKIANG, YUEN
river boat ...... SAMPAN
sacred tree ... WU TUNG
salutation .... KOWTOW
satin .... PEKIN
sauce .... SOY

sea cucumber .. TREPANG
seal .... CHOP
seaport .... DAIREN,
    TSINGTAO
season .... CH'UN, HSIA,
    CH'IU, TUNG
secret society ..... TONG
sedge .... MATI
servant .... AMAH
shark fins .... YU CHI
silk .. PONGEE, PEKIN,
    SHA, SHANTUNG, TUSSER,
    TUSSA(H)
silkworm .. SINA, TASAR
silver ingot ...... SYCEE
silver money ..... SYCEE
sky .... TIEN
slang .... CHINK
soapberry ..... LICHEE,
    LITCHI
society ..... BOXER, HUI,
    TONG
son .... TAI
soup material .. TREPANG,
    BIRD'S NEST
spring .... CH'UN
squash .... CUSHAW,
    CASHAW
stamp .... CHOP
statesman .... KOO
string money ...... TIAO
summer .... HSIA
tax .... LIKIN
tea ...... CHA, OOLONG,
    CONGO(U), TSIA, BOHEA,
    HYSON, SOUCHONG
team work ... GUNG HO
temple ..... JOSSHOUSE,
    TAA, PAGODA
trading boat ....
    TONGKANG
treaty port .... AMOY,
    SHANGHAI
tree .... GINK(G)O,
    WUTUNG, LOQUAT
truth .... TAO
unicorn ... CHILLIN, LIN
walking stick .. WHANGEE
warehouse .... HONG
wax .... PELA
weight .. CATTY, PICUL,
    TAEL, LI, HAO, FAN
wine vessel ...... TSUN
winter .... TUNG
wood oil .... TUNG
work together ....

    GUNG HO
wormwood .... MOXA
yellow .... SIL
chink .. FISSURE, RIMA, CRACK,
    SLIT, CRANNY, CREVICE
    filler .... GROUT
    slang .... CHINESE
chinks, full of ...... RIMOSE,
    RIMOUS
chinky .... RIMOUS
Chinook ..... WIND, INDIAN,
    SALMON
    Indian .... FLATHEAD
    powwow .... WAWA
    lily/bulb ...... QUAMASH
chinquapin ..... (CHEST)NUT,
    TREE
chinse .... CLOSE, CALK
chintz .... CLOTH
chip ...... NICK, CUT, CHOP,
    SLICE, SCRAP, BIT, FLAKE
    in .... CONTRIBUTE
    of stone .. SPALL, GALLET
    off the old block ....
    SON(NY), JUNIOR
    on one's shoulder ......
    GRUDGE, RANCOR
chipmunk .. SQUIRREL, CHIPPY,
    TRACKEE
    cheek pouch .. ALFORJA
chippendale furniture leg .....
    CABRIOLE
chipper .... PERT, LIVELY,
    CHISEL, ADZ, CHIRP, TWITTER
    colloquial ...... BABBLE,
    CHATTER
Chippewa .. OJIBWA(Y), INDIAN
chippy .. SPARROW, CHIPMUNK,
    PROSTITUTE
chirk .... LIVELY, CHEERFUL
chiro, as combining form ....
    HAND
chirographer .... PENMAN
chiromancer .... PALMIST
Chiron .... CENTAUR
    forte of ...... MEDICINE
    pupil of ...... ACHILLES,
    HERCULES
chiropodist .... PEDICURE
    advice of .... FOOTBATH
chiropter .... ALIPED, BAT
chirp .. CHEEP, PEEP, TWITTER,
    TWEET
chirper .... NESTLING,
    FLEDGLING, BIRD, CICADA
chirrup .... CHIRP, TWEET

chisel .. CUT, GOUGE, ENGRAVE,
BURIN, HARDY, SCULP(T),
BROACH, FIRMER, GRAVER,
CHASER, TOOLER
 bar .... SPUDDER
 broad-faced ..... DROVE
 colloquial ...... CHEAT,
SWINDLE
 mason's .... POMMEL
 part .... TANG
 polishing .... SLICK
 primitive/stone .... CELT
 stonemason's .. QUARREL
chiseled profile .... CLASSICAL,
ROMAN
chiseler .... SWINDLER,
CHEAT(ER)
chit .... NOTE, SHOOT, SPROUT
 colloquial .... TAB, IOU,
CHILD, GIRL
 of a kind ..... VOUCHER,
MEMO
chitchat .... TALK, GOSSIP
chiton .. MOLLUSK, GARMENT,
LIMPET
chitter ..... TWITTER, SHIVER
chive .... ONION, FLAVOR,
GARLIC
chiv(v)y .... HARRY, HUNT,
CHASE, FRET
chlamys .... MANTLE, CLOAK
Chloe and others .... AUNTS
 love of .... DAPHNIS
chloride .... MURIATE
chlorine ... BROMINE, IODINE,
HALOGEN
chloroform, for one ....
ANESTHETIC, SOLVENT
chlorophyll .... ETIOLIN
chock .... BLOCK, WEDGE,
CLEAT, TRIG, SPRAG
chockablock .... CROWDED
chocolate .... DRINK, CANDY
 cake .... BROWNIE
 candy filling .. FONDANT
 flavored .... MOCHA
 mixer .... MOLINET
 powder .... COCOA
 source .... CACAO
 tree .... CACAO
choice .... PREFERENCE,
SELECTION, ELITE, CREAM
 between two evils ......
DILEMMA
 food .... DELICACY
 make a .... OPT

 morsel .... TIDBIT
 object .... PLUM
 of words ...... DICTION
 other ...... ALTERNATIVE
 part ...... CREAM, MEAT,
MARROW
choir boys' collar ...... ETON
 leader .... CHORAGUS
 leader's aide ....
SUCCENTOR
 of a .... CHORAL
 place in church .... LOFT,
GALLERY
 section ..... ALTO, TENOR
 vestment .... COTTA,
SURPLICE
choke .. SMOTHER, SUFFOCATE,
STIFLE, THROTTLE
 by squeezing throat .....
STRANGLE
 by stuffing mouth .. GAG
 to death .... BURKE
 up .... CLOG
 with iron collar ....
GARROTE
choked up: colloq. ....
SPEECHLESS
choker .. NECKLACE, NECKTIE,
FUR(PIECE), COLLAR
cholecyst .... (GALL)BLADDER
choler ...... BILE, RAGE, IRE,
ANGER, FIT, WRATH
cholera bacillus ...... COMMA
 type of ..... NOSTRAS,
INFANTUM, MORBUS
choleric ... IRASCIBLE, ANGRY,
IRATE, TESTY, IRRITABLE
cholesterol product ....
GALLSTONE
cholla .... CACTUS
chololith .... GALLSTONE
Chomo-lungma ..... EVEREST
chondroma .... TUMOR
choose .. SELECT, CULL, PICK,
OPT, PREFER, WALE
 for office .... ELECT
 your ___ ... EXIT, WILD,
PARTNER
choosing, right of .... OPTION
choosy .... FASTIDIOUS, FUSSY
chop .. CUT, LOP, AXE, CHEEK,
HEW, JAW, DICE, FELL, HACK,
MINCE
 chop-chop .... QUICKLY,
AT ONCE

in China, India .. PERMIT,
SEAL, LICENSE
stroke, in tennis .. SLICE
tool ..... AX(E), CLEAVER
chophouse, Chinese ....
CUSTOMHOUSE, RESTAURANT
specialty .... STEAK
Chopin's (Frederic) country ..
POLAND
love ..... (GEORGE) SAND
chopine .... SHOE, PATTEN
chopper .... AX(E)
meat .... CLEAVER
slang .... HELICOPTER
chopping blows with hand ....
KARATE
chops .... JAWS, JOWL, MOUTH
choral music ...... ORATORIO,
CANTATA
chord ...., .. STRING
dissonance .... WOLF
5-tone .... TRIAND
chordate .... VERTEBRATE
example of a ...... MAN
chore .... CHARE, TASK,
(ODD)JOB, STINT
choreographer of note ....
ANTON, BALANCHINE
choreography ...... DANCING,
BALLET
chorine .... CHORUS GIRL,
STEPPER
chorister's garment .. CASSOCK
chorography .... MAP
choroid membrane .. TAPETUM
chortle ..... CHUCKLE, SNORT
chorus .... UNISON, REFRAIN
girl: colloq. ... CHORINE
leader .... CHORAGUS
of a ... CHORAL, CHORIC
of song .... BURDEN,
REFRAIN
chose .... CHATTEL
Chosen .... KOREA
Chou ____, Chinese bigwig ...
EN-LAI
chough .... CROW
chouse .. CHEAT, SWINDLE(R),
DUPE
chow ...... DOG, FOOD, MEAL
chowchow .... PICKLES, OLIO,
MIXED, ASSORTED
chowder ingredient .... CLAM
christen ..... BAPTIZE, NAME
Christian ... DECENT, HUMAN
abbreviation ..... XTIAN

bishop of the Goths ....
ULFILA(S)
church .. ORANT, BASILICA
church as a whole ......
CATHOLIC
church of Egypt .. COPT
church, the .... HERITAGE
love feast .... AGAPE
non .... PAYNIM, PAGAN,
HEATHEN
Oriental .... UNIAT
pulpit .... AMBO
religion founder .. JESUS
Science founder .. BAKER
Science healer ....
PRACTITIONER
theologian ..... ORIGEN
traitor .... TRADITOR
Christiania .... OSLO
was capital of .. NORWAY
Christians, all ...... CHURCH
Christmas .... YULE(TIDE), NOEL
abbreviation ..... XMAS
bonanza .... GIFTS
cake .... SIMNEL
carol ...... NOEL, NOWEL
crib .... CRECHE
day .... NATIVITY
decorative item ....
MISTLETOE
drink .... EGGNOG
favorite figure ....
SANTA (CLAUS)
fruitcake .... SIMNEL
gift container .. STOCKING
masked funster ....
MUMMER
mock-up of Nativity ....
CRECHE
musician .... WAIT
pantomime .... MUMMER,
GUISER
season ...... YULE(TIDE)
song ...... CAROL, NOEL
street singer ...... WAIT,
CAROLER
time entertainment .....
PANTOMIME
tree .... HOLLY, PINE
vehicle .... SLED, SLEIGH
chromosome load .... GENES
chronic .... RECURRING,
HABITUAL, CONFIRMED
chronicle .... ACCOUNT,
HISTORY, RECORD, DIARY,
ANNAL(S)

chronicler . . . . HISTORIAN, ANNALIST, RECORDER
chronometer . . . . WATCH
chrysalis . . . . . PUPA, COCOON
chrysanthemum . . MUM, KIKU, POMPON, DAISY, COSTMARY, MARGUERITE
   badge: Jap. . . . . MON
chrysolite . . PERIDOT, OLIVINE
chub . . . . (BLACK) BASS
chubby . . . . . ROTUND, PLUMP
chuck . . . . TOSS, THROW, DISCARD
   slang . . . . FOOD
chuckle . . . . . LAUGH, CLUCK, GIGGLE
chucklehead . . . . DOLT, IDIOT
chuckleheaded . . . . . . STUPID
chuddar . . . . SHAWL
Chudskoe lake . . . . PEIPUS
chuff . . . BRICK, BOOR, CHURL
chum . . . . ROOMMATE, FRIEND, CRONY, PAL
   in fishing . . . . BAIT
chummy . . . . INTIMATE, FRIENDLY
chump . . . . BOOB, FOOL
chunk . . . . . . PORTION, PIECE, GOBBET, HUNCH, BAT
chunky . . CORPULENT, STOUT, THICKSET, STOCKY, SQUAT
church . . DENOMINATION, SECT, TEMPLE, CHAPEL, BETHEL, KIRK, FOLD, FANE, MINSTER
   altar offerings . . . . ALTARAGE
   archaic . . . . FANE
   basin . . . . LAVABO, FONT, PISCINA, STOUP
   bell/ringer . . . . . SEXTON
   bell tower . . . . . . BELFRY
   bench . . . . PEW
   benefice . . . . LIVING
   benefice, holding of . . . . . INCUMBENCY
   benefit sale . . . . . BAZAAR
   bishop's . . . . CATHEDRAL
   body of . . . . NAVE
   Buddhist . . . . PAGODA
   building . . . . ECCLESIA
   calendar . . . . ORDO
   caretaker . . . . . . SEXTON, VERGER
   chancel . . . . BEMA
   cathedral . . . . . . MINSTER
   chandelier . . . . . CORONA

chapel . . . . CHANTRY, ORATORY
ceremony . . (HIGH) MASS, TE DEUM
choir leader . . CHORAGUS, CHORISTER, PRECENTOR
contribution to . . TITHE
council . . . . SYNOD, CONSISTORY
court . . . . . ROTA, CLASSIS, CONSISTORY
cup . . . . CHALICE
dignitary . . POPE, DEAN, LEGATE, NUNCIO, PRELATE, CARDINAL, PRIMATE, BISHOP
director . . . . PRECENTOR, CHORAGUS
dish . . . . PATEN
dissenter . . . . APOSTATE, SECTARY
district . . PARISH, DIOCESE
division in a . . . . SCHISM
doorkeeper . . . . OSTIARY
elder . . . . PRESBYTER
endowment to a . . . . PATRIMONY
festival . . . . EASTER
fund-raising sale . . . . BAZA(A)R
gallery . . . . . . JUBE, LOFT
governing group . . . . CLASSIS
government . . HIERARCHY
grave-digger . . . . SEXTON
grounds . . . . PRECINCT
guard . . . . OSTIARY
head . . . . PONTIFF
jurisdiction . . OBEDIENCE
land . . . . GLEBE
law . . . . CANON
lay leader . . . . ELDER
leader . . . . HIERARCH
lectern . . . . AMBO
living . . . . BENEFICE
loft . . . . JUBE
main part . . . . NAVE
members . . . . ECCLESIA, FOLD, FLOCK
monastery's . . . MINSTER
morning service . . LAUD, MATIN
Moslem . . . . MOSQUE
of Latter Day Saints . . . . MORMON
office . . . . BENEFICE

office, sale of .... SIMONY
officer ...... PRESBYTER,
   SACRIST(AN), SEXTON,
BEADLE, ORDINARY, ELDER,
   VERGER
part .... APSE, PEW,
STEEPLE, TRANSEPT, ALTAR,
CHANCEL, SACRISTY, BEMA,
   ORATORY, VESTRY
place for shrines ....
   FERETORY
poetic .... FANE
porch .. GALILEE, PARVIS
practice of peace ....
   IRENICS
property .... GLEBE
reader .... LECTOR
reading stand .... AMBO,
   LECTERN
recess .. .. APSE
revenue ...... BENEFICE,
   TITHE
rite .... BAPTISM,
COMMUNION, BENEDICTION,
   MASS
Roman .... BASILICA
room for sacred vessels ..
   VESTRY, SACRISTY
sale of offices, etc. ......
   SIMONY, BARRATRY
sanctuary ... SACRARIUM
Scottish .... KIRK
screen ..... ICONASTASIS
seamen's .... BETHEL
seat .... PEW, STALL
seat for clergy .. SEDILIA
separation from .. SCHISM
service .. TE DEUM, MASS,
   NONES, LAUD
service clothes ....
   CANONICALS
service invocation ......
   BENEDICTION
service reader ... LECTOR
service reading .. LECTION
shrine's place .. FERETORY
singers' group .... CHOIR
tax .... TITHE
tower .. STEEPLE, BELFRY
tower top .... SPIRE
tribunal .... ROTA
vault .... CRYPT
vestibule ..... NARTHEX
vestment room ....
   SACRISTY, VESTRY
washbowl ...... LAVABO

wine cup ...... CHALICE
woman assistant ....
   DEACONESS
yard .... PARVIS
Churchill Downs event ....
   DERBY, RACE
Churchill's (W.) daughter ....
   SARAH
   forte .... PROSE
   lady .... CLEMENTINE
   nickname ...... WINNIE
   son .... RANDOLPH
   son-in-law ..... SOAMES
   trademark ...... CIGAR,
      VEE SIGN
churchman .. MINISTER, PRIEST,
ECCLESIASTIC, ELDER, PASTOR,
CARDINAL, BISHOP, CLERGY
churchyard .... PARVIS
churl ...... DOOR, OAF, HIND,
   PEASANT, LOUT, CEORL,
   KNAVE, FREEMAN, VILLEIN,
      CARL(E)
churlish ...... RUSTIC, SURLY,
   BOORISH, DOUR, SULLEN
churn ..... STIR, BEAT, SHAKE
   rotator .... DASHER
chute ... WATERFALL, RAPIDS,
   TROUGH, RUNWAY,
   ROLLWAY, SHOOT, SLIDE
   for logs .... FLUME
chutney .... RELISH
Chuvash .... BULGARIAN
cibol .... ONION
ciborium .. CUP, PYX, CANOPY
cicada .... LOCUST
   vibrating membrane of ..
      TIMBAL
cicatricle .... TREAD
cicatrix .... SCAR
Cicero ...... MARCUS, TULLY
   target of ...... CATILINE
cicerone .. DRAGOMAN, GUIDE
Cid .... LEADER
   play, author of ....
      CORNEILLE
   name of .... RUY,
      (RODRIGO) DIAZ
   sword of .... COLADA
cider .... (APPLE) JUICE,
   VINEGAR, SYTHER, PERKIN
   pear juice .... PERRY
   spiced/sweetened .. FLIP
   sweeten .... MULL
ci-devant ..... FORMER, LATE,
      RECENT

cigar ..... HAVANA, LONDRES, SMOKE, CULEBRA, CORONA, COLORADO, CHEROOT, TOBACCO, PANATEL(L)A, MANILA, TOBY, WEED, CLARO, PERFECTO
box .... HUMIDOR
butt .... STUB, SNIPE
cheap .. STOGIE, STOG(E)Y, TOBY
descriptive of a .... MADURO
Philippine .... MANILA
puff .... DRAG
self-lighting .. LOCOFOCO
Spanish .. CIGARRO, PURO
stub .... BUTT
cigarette, berry ...... CUBEB
brand .... SALEM, CAMEL, PALL MALL, PIEDMONT, KENT, MARLBORO, WINSTON, TRUE, CHESTER(FIELD)
butt .... STUB, SNIPE
ingredient .... TOBACCO
kind of .... FILTER
lighter .... VESUVIAN
marijuana ...... REEFER
material .... MAKINGS
non-tobacco .... REEFER, CUBEB, MARIJUANA
piece .... STICK
product .. NICOTINE, TAR
puff .... DRAG
slang .... FAG, BUTT, GASPER, NAIL
smoke cleaner ... FILTER
smoke cooler .. MENTHOL
smoking aid ...... PIPE
stub .... BUTT
cigarfish .... SCAD
cilia .... EYELASHES
cilice .... HAIRCLOTH
cilium .... EYELASH
cimex .... BEDBUG
Cimmerian .... DARK, BLACK, GLOOMY
cinch .... GIRTH, FASTEN
slang ...... SURE THING
cinchona .. BARK, TREE, QUILL
alkaloid ...... QUININE, QUINIDINE
Cincinnati ball club .... REDS, REDLEGS
family .... TAFT(S)

cincture ... . BELT, ENCLOSURE, GIRDLE, WAISTBAND
cinder .... SLAG, ASH(ES)
like lava .... SCORIA
sifter .... RIDDLE
Cinderella of Pop ... HOPKIN
cinema ..... MOVIE, THEATER, MOTION PICTURE
cinerarium .... URN
cinerator .... CREMATORY, FURNACE
cingulum .... BELT, GIRDLE
cinnabar ..... ORE, PIGMENT, VERMILION, SINOPLE
cinnamon .... SPICE, BARK, CANELLA
adulterant .... CASSIA
roll .... QUILL
stone .. GARNET, ESSONITE
cinquefoil .... CLOVER, FIVE-FINGER, POTENTILLA
cion ..... GRAFT, SHOOT, BUD
Cipango .... JAPAN
cipher .... NONENTITY, CODE, NAUGHT, MONOGRAM, ZERO, OUGHT
system .... CODE
cipolin .... MARBLE
circa .... ABOUT
Circe .... ENCHANTRESS, TEMPTRESS
home of .... ABABA
circle .... COTERIE, CIRQUE, GROUP, ORBIT, LOOP, RING, CLIQUE, WHIRL, ZODIAC
angle/arc .... RADIAN
describing one .. VICIOUS
half a ...... HEMICYCLE
imaginary celestial ...... COLURE
of guards ...... CORDON
of light .. CORONA, NIMB, HALO
part .... ARC, SECTOR, RADIUS, SECANT
poetic .... RONDURE
quarter section .. OVOLO, QUADRANT
circuit .... AMBIT, LAP, TOUR, CYCLE, DISTRICT, ORBIT, LOOP
court .... EYRE
in radio .... HOOKUP
judges' .... EYRE
track .... LAP
circuitous .... DEVIOUS, ROUNDABOUT

circular .... ROUND, BILL,
ADVERTISEMENT
   band .... RING, HOOP
   course ...... RACETRACK,
OVAL
   cross section ... TERETE
   figure/line .... RING
   form .... GYRE
   letter, papal ....
ENCYCLICAL
   motion .... EDDY,
GYRATION, SPIN, GYRE
   plate ... DISH, DISC, DISK
   saw .... EDGER
   space .... CIRQUE
   step .... AMBIT
   turn .... LOOP
   wall of dome .... DRUM
circulate .... SPREAD,
MOVE AROUND, DIFFUSE
circumference .... PERIPHERY,
AMBIT, GIRTH
circumlocution ..... AMBAGE,
PERIPHRASE, VERBIAGE,
PERIPHRASIS
circumnavigator, first ....
MAGELLAN
circumscribe ...... ENCIRCLE,
CONFINE, ENCOMPASS, LIMIT
circumspect .... WARY,
CAUTIOUS, CAREFUL,
PRUDENT
circumspection .... PRUDENCE
circumstance .. STATE, DETAIL,
CONDITION, FACT
circumvent ... SKIRT, OUTWIT
circus ...... ARENA, CIRQUE,
(TENT) SHOW
   animal ..... LION, BEAR,
ELEPHANT, SEAL
   arena .... RING,
HIPPODROME
   colloquial ..... BIG TOP
   director .... RINGMASTER
   horse .... GRAY
   laborer ...... ROUSTER,
ROUSTABOUT
   minor attraction ....
SIDE SHOW
   name, bigtime ....
RINGLING, BARNUM, BAILEY
   net ...... TRAMPOLIN(E)
   perennial .... CLOWN
   performer .. FLEA, SEAL,
EQUESTRIEN(NE), CLOWN,
UNICYCLIST, AERIALIST,

TUMBLER, ACROBAT
   ring cover .... TANBARK
   swing .... TRAPEZE
   vehicle .... CARAVAN
cirque .... CIRCLE, RING,
AMPHITHEATER, CIRCUS
cirriped .... BARNACLE,
CRUSTACEAN
cirrus .... FEELERS, TENDRIL,
CLOUDS
   cloud ...... MARE'S-TAIL
cirsoid ..... VARICOSE, VARIX
cisco .. (WHITE)FISH, HERRING
cist .... TOMB, CHEST
cistern .... (RAIN) TANK, BAC,
VAT
   in anatomy .. SAC, CAVITY
   natural ...... RESERVOIR
citadel .... FORT, CASTLE,
REFUGE, TOWER,
STRONGHOLD, FORTRESS,
ACROPOLIS
   of justice, so-called .....
COURT
   Russian ...... KREMLIN
cital .... SUMMONS
citation .... SUMMONS,
QUOTATION, REFERENCE
   favorable .... ACCOLADE
cite .... SUMMON, QUOTE,
MENTION, CALL
cithern .... CITOLE
cities, between .. INTERURBAN
citified: colloq. .... URBAN
citizen .. NATIVE, INHABITANT,
FREEMAN, BURGESS, RESIDENT,
SUBJECT, NATIONAL,
DENIZEN
   army .... MILITIA
   French .... CITOYEN
   of the world ....
COSMOPOLITE
citizens, assembly of ....
ECCLESIA
   of .... CIVIC, CIVIL
citole .... CITHERN
citron .. LEMON, LIME, ETROG
citrus drink .... (LEMON)ADE,
(ORANGE)ADE, (LIME)ADE
citrus fruit .. MANDARIN, LIME,
GRAPEFRUIT, BERGAMOT,
LEMON, ORANGE, CITRON
   disease .... PSOROSIS
   membrane .... RAG
   oil .... BERGAMOT
   skin .... ZEST

city ... TOWN, MUNICIPALITY
   bishop's .... SEE
   business section ....
              DOWNTOWN
   cathedral ... YORK, ELY,
       R(H)EIMS, CHARTRES
   colloquial ... BURG, BURH
   district .... WARD
   father ...... ALDERMAN,
            COUNCILOR
   fellow: sl. .... DUDE
   gangster ... PLUG-UGLY
   great ...... MEGALOPOLIS
   hall .... AYUNTAMIENTO
   heavenly .... SION, ZION
   main ...... METROPOLIS
   of a ...... CIVIC, URBAN,
            MUNICIPAL
   of Angels .... BANGKOK
   of Bridges ...... BRUGES
   of Kings .... LIMA
   of lights .... PARIS
   of masts .... LONDON
   of Pillars .... IREM
   of Refuge ...... MEDINA
   of Saints .... MONTREAL
   of Seven Hills .... ROME
   of sin .... SODOM,
      GOMORRAH, BABYLON
   of the dead .. NECROPOLIS
   of the Gods ... ASGARD
   of the leaning tower ....
              PISA
   of the Rhine ..... MAINZ
   of vice .... BABYLON
   official .... MAYOR,
     COUNCILOR, ALDERMAN
   on the sea .... PORT
   Pearl of the Orient .....
            MANILA
   pertaining to .... CIVIC,
            URBAN
   square .... PARK
   state .... VATICAN,
          SINGAPORE
   subdivision ...... WARD,
          PRECINCT
   vice center .. TENDERLOIN
   wicked ...... BABYLON,
      SODOM, GOMORRAH
civet .... FUR, CAT, NANDINE,
    RASSE, FOSSA, DEDES,
      MUSANG, ZIBET
   like animal .. GENET(TE),
         SURICATE
   odor .... MUSK(LIKE)

   of the .... VIVERINE
civil ...... POLITE, URBANE,
    COURTEOUS, TEMPORAL
   magistrate ..... SYNDIC
   marriage performer .....
            JUDGE
   wrong .... TORT
Civil War admiral ....
           FARRAGUT
   battlefield ... ANTIETAM,
    GETTYSBURG, SHILOH,
     ATLANTA, BULL RUN
   before the .. ANTEBELLUM
   cartoonist .... NAST
   general .... FREMONT,
    GRANT, LEE, HOOD, POPE,
    SHERMAN, SCOTT, BUELL,
    HOOKER, EWELL, MEADE,
     SHERIDAN, BRAGG,
       MCCLELLAN
   soldier ... YANKEE, REB
   vet .... GAR
   volunteer ..... ZOUAVE
civilian .... NONMILITARY,
           CIV(V)IES
   clothes .... MUFTI
civilization .... CULTURE
   cradle of .... ASIA
civilize .... EDUCATE, REFINE
clabber ...... MILK, CURDLE
clack .. BLAB, PRATE, CHATTER
clad .... DRESSED, ROBED,
      CLOTHED, ATTIRED
claim .. RIGHT, TITLE, ASSERT,
          ALLEGE
   legal .... DEMAND, LIEN
   mining .... STAKE
   on property ...... LIEN
   without right .. ARROGATE
claimant, kind of .. PRETENDER
clairvoyance .... INSIGHT
clairvoyant .... SEER
clam .... MOLLUSK, MYA
   hard-shell .... QUAHOG,
         QUAHAUG
   joint of .... HINGE
   killer .... WINKLE
   razor .... SOLEN
   shell .... TEST, SHUCK
   shell opening .... GAPE
   soft-shell ..... STEAMER
   young ...... LITTLENECK
clamant ...... NOISY, URGENT
clambake ... PICNIC, OUTING,
         COOKOUT
clamber ...... CLIMB, SCALE

clamor .. RIOT, NOISE, UPROAR,
    OUTCRY, DIN, YAMMER
clamorous .... NOISY,
    VOCIFEROUS, LOUD
clamp .... VISE, FASTENER
    like device ...... CHUCK
clan ..... TRIBE, SET, CLIQUE,
    FAMILY, GENS
    leader ...... CHIEFTAIN,
      TANIST, THANE
    of a .... GENTILE
    pattern .... TARTAN
    quarrel .... FEUD
    symbol .... TOTEM
clandestine .. SECRET, FURTIVE,
    HIDDEN, UNDERHAND,
    SURREPTITIOUS
    meeting, usually .. TRYST,
      RENDEZVOUS
clang ..... DING, RING, PEAL
clangor .. PEAL, JANGLE, DIN
clannish .... TRIBAL
clans, quarrel between .. FEUD
clap .... SLAP, BLOW
clapboard .... SIDING
clapper, bell .... TONGUE
claptrap ..... DRIVEL, BOSH,
    HEROICS, HOKUM
clare .... MINT
clarence .... CARRIAGE
claret ...... WINE, BORDEAU
clarify .. EXPLAIN, ELUCIDATE,
    PURIFY, CLEAR, DEFINE,
    EXPOUND
    lard .... RENDER
clarinet .... REED
    forerunner .. CHALUMEAU
    socket .... BIRN
clarinetist, bandleader ....
    (ARTIE) SHAW
clarion .... TRUMPET
clarity .. CLEARNESS, LUCIDITY
claro .... CIGAR
clarry .... MINT
clash ..... COLLIDE, CONFLICT,
    DISAGREE
clasp ...... EMBRACE, TASSEL,
    HUG, HASP, HOOK, BUCKLE,
    FASTENING, ENFOLD, CINCH,
    FIBULA, OUCH
    hair .... BARRETTE
    ornamental .... BROOCH
class ...... KIND, CASTE, ILK,
    CATEGORY, ORDER, SPECIES,
    KIDNEY
    first .... BEST

of animal/plant .. GENUS
of ruling deities ....
    THEARCHY
scientific .... GENUS,
    GENERA
slang ...... EXCELLENCE,
    QUALITY
classical language .... LATIN,
    GREEK
    music ...... CONCERTO,
    SYMPHONY, SONATA
    non .. MODERN, POPULAR,
    ROMANTIC
classics annotator .. SCHOLIAST
classification .... LABEL
    of diseases .... NOSOLOGY
    science of .... TAXONOMY
classified (information) ......
    SECRET
classify .... LIST, SORT,
    CATALOGUE, TYPE, LABEL,
    RATE
classis .... ROTA
classy ..... ELEGANT, STYLISH
clatter .... HUBBUB, RATTLE,
    BRATTLE, HURTLE
claudicant .... LAME, LIMPING
clavichord .... SPINET
clavicle .... COLLARBONE
clavier .... KEYBOARD
    common .... PIANO
claviform .... CLAVATE,
    CLUB-SHAPED
claw ...... SCRATCH, TALON,
    UNGUIS, UNGULA, HOOK,
    POUNCE, NAIL, NIPPER
    having/like a ... UNGUAL
    like process .... CALCAR
    of crustacean ... CHELA,
    PINCER
    pincer-like .. CHELIFORM
    retract .... SHEATHE
claws .... UNCI
clay .... LOESS, ARGIL, MARL,
    LOAM, LATERITE, LUTE,
    SAGGER, SAGGAR,
    LITHOMARGE, KAOLIN(E),
    FIGULINE
    baked ... ADOBE, BRICK,
    TILE, BOLE
    case .. SAGGER, SAGGAR,
    SEGGAR
    chunk .... BAT
    clump of .... CLOD
    desert .... ADOBE
    earthy ... OCHER, OCHRE

formation .... SHALE
granite .... PETUNTSE
layer .... SLOAM
like .... BOLAR
lump .... BAT
mixture .. LOAM, PUDDLE,
CEMENT
molded .... PUG
ore-bearing ..... OCHER,
OCHRE
paste .... PATE
pertaining to .... BOLAR
pigeon .... TARGET
pigeon shoot .... SKEET
plastic .... PUG
porcelain ...... KAOLIN,
PASTE
potter's .... ARGIL,
FIGULINE, PASTE
rock .... MUDSTONE
sieve .... LAUN
thinned .... SLIP
tobacco pipe ... DUDEEN
wad .... BAT
water mixture ... SLURRY
white .... PETUNTSE
clayey ...... BOLAR, LUTOSE
cement .... LUTE
soil .... MARL, LOAM,
MALM, LOESS, BOLE
claymore .... (BROAD) SWORD
clean ...... PURE, ABSTERGE,
SINLESS, UNSOILED, SPOTLESS
and draw fowl ... DRESS
breast, make a .. CONFESS
by rubbing ...... SCOUR,
SCRUB
clothes .... LAUNDER
copy .... LEGIBLE,
READABLE
hands .... INNOCENT
of impurities .... PURGE,
PURIFY
ship's bottom .. BREAM,
GRAVE
slate ...... TABULA RASA
up .... FINISH
with abrasive ... SCRAPE,
SCOUR
with broom ..... SWEEP
with mop .... SWAB
cleaner ..... SOAP, SWEEPER,
CHARWOMAN
cleaning cloth .... RAG
powder ... PUMICE, ARIEL

cleanse .... PURGE, DETERGE,
PURIFY
cleansing substance ....
ABSTERGENT, SOAP, BORAX,
DETERGENT, PURGATIVE,
ARIEL
clear .... APPARENT, OBVIOUS,
CLARIFY, LIMPID, LUCULENT,
RID, EVIDENT, LIQUID,
(PEL)LUCID, HURDLE, FREE
conscience ... INNOCENT
cut .... DISTINCT, SHARP,
TRENCHANT
day .... SUNNY
of charges ..... ABSOLVE,
ACQUIT, EXONERATE
out .. LEAVE, DEPART, GO,
DECAMP
perfectly .. LUCID, LIMPID
profit .... NET
sky .... ETHER
the way! ..... GANGWAY
throat audibly ... HAWK,
HEM
title .... UNENCUMBERED
to the mind ... PALPABLE
up .. EXPLAIN, CLARIFY,
STRAIGHTEN
clearance .... MARGIN,
ADJUSTMENT
sale .... RUMMAGE
cleareyed .... PERCEPTIVE
clearing, wood ...... GLADE
cleat .. KEVEL, BATTEN, PITON
make secure around ....
BELAY
cleavage .... CLEFT, RIFT,
DIVISION, FISSION, GULF
cleave .. SPLIT, DIVIDE, SEVER,
REND, RIVE, CLING, SUNDER
cleaver .... FROE, FROW,
CHOPPER
sky .... LIGHTNING
cleek .... HOOK
cleft ... SPLIT, DIVIDED, GAP,
FISSURE, RIFT, SCISSURE,
FORKED
easily .... FISSILE
Clemenceau's soubriquet .....
TIGRE, TIGER
clemency .... GRACE, MERCY,
LENIENCY
Clemens' pen name ....
(MARK) TWAIN
clement ..... MILD, LENIENT,
MERCIFUL

clench .... CLINCH, GRIP
clenched hand .... FIST
Cleopatra's domain .. EGYPT,
                     NILE
    killer .... ASP
    lover .... ANTONY,
          (JULIUS) CAESAR
    maid .... IRAS
    Needle .... OBELISK
    river .... NILE
    son .... CAESARION
clepe .... CALL, NAME
clepsydra ... (WATER)CLOCK,
           WATERGLASS
clergy ... CLOTH, FIRST ESTATE,
           MINISTRY
clergyman .. MINISTER, PRIEST,
    CURATE, CLERIC, ABBE,
    PARSON, PASTOR, CANON,
          DIVINE
    and author ...... SHEEN
    church service vestment ..
          CANONICALS
    colloquial ..... DOMINIE
    degree of .... STB
    position/garment ....
         CASSOCK, FROCK
    residence of .... MANSE,
    PARSONAGE, RECTORY
    salary of ...... PREBEND
    with the military ....
       CHAPLAIN, PADRE
clerical cap .... BIRETTA
    collar .. RABATO, REBATO
    vestment ... AMICE, ALB,
    SURPLICE, FANON, ORALE
clerisy .... INTELLECTUALS
clerk .... SALESMAN,
    OFFICE WORKER, SCRIBE,
         SCRIVENER
"Clerk's Tale" heroine ......
         GRISELDA
Cleveland waterfront ... ERIE
clever .... ADEPT, ADROIT,
    TALENTED, BRIGHT, CUTE,
    CUNNING, SMART, HABILE,
         SLICK
    as a fox .... VULPINE
    remark: sl. ...... NIFTY,
         CRACK
    retort .. REPARTEE, SALLY,
    BON MOT, RIPOST(E),
         WITTICISM
cleverly done/said .... NEAT
clew .... THREAD, CLUB, KEY,
         TIP, BALL

cliche ... BANALITY, PLATITUDE
click .. PAWL, CATCH, AGREE,
    SUCCEED, PALLET, SNICK
    beetle .. ELATER, DOR(R)
clicking sound .... TICK
client .. DEPENDENT, CUSTOMER
    without ...... BRIEFLESS
clientele .... PATRONAGE,
    PATRONS, TRADE, CUSTOMERS
cliff .. ESCARPMENT, PRECIPICE,
         BLUFF
    debris .... TALUS
    edge .... BROW
    fissure .... CHINE
    fissure for climbing ....
         CHIMNEY
    rock pile .... TALUS
cliffs, channel between .. GAT
    line of .... PALISADES
climacteric .... CRUCIAL
    woman's .... MENOPAUSE
climate ...... SKY, WEATHER
    study of ... METEOROLOGY
climax ...... SUMMIT, ACME,
    CULMINATION, APOGEE
climb .. ASCEND, MOUNT, RISE,
    ASCENT, SCALE, CLAMBER
    a rope/pole .... SHIN
    down .... DESCEND
climbers .... VINES
    social .... PARVENU
climbing .... SCALING
    adapted for .. SCANSORIAL
    by attachment ....
         SCANDENT
    iron ..... CRAMPON, SPUR
    means of ...... LADDER
    palm .... RATTAN
    plant process ... TENDRIL
    vine .. IVY, BINE, BRYONY,
    LIANA, LIANE, HOP, PEA
    wall by ladder ....
         ESCALADE
clime ... CLIMATE, REALM,
    REGION, COUNTRY
clinch ... FASTEN, NAIL, GRIP,
    GRAPPLE, HUG, CLOSE
    argument .... SETTLE
    breaker .... REFEREE
    nautical ... KNOT, NOOSE,
         CLENCH
    slang .... EMBRACE
cling .... ADHERE, STICK,
         COHERE
clingfish ..... REMORA, TESTAR
clinic .... DISPENSARY

clink ..... PRISON, JAIL, RING
clinker .... SLAG, BRICK
  built .... LAPSTRAKE
clinking sound ...... TINKLE
clinquant .... TINSEL(ED)
"Clinton's ditch" ....
                ERIE (CANAL)
Clio's field .... HISTORY
clip ..... CUT, FASTEN, GRIP,
                MOW, SCAR
  colloquial .... PACE, HIT,
        PUNCH, SPEED, CHEAT,
                SWINDLE
  ornamental .... BROOCH
  Scottish .... COLL
clipper ...... SHIP, AIRPLANE,
                SHEARER
  barber's ...... SCISSORS
clippings .... SCRAPS
clique ...... CIRCLE, COTERIE,
        SET, RING, FACTION
  advisers' .... CAMARILLA,
                CABAL
cloaca .... SEWER, PRIVY
cloak ... DISGUISE, GARMENT,
        CONCEAL, MANTUA, WRAP,
        CHLAMYS, PALL, GREGO
  and-dagger group .. CIA,
                OSS, OGPU
  blanket-like ... PONCHO,
                SERAPE
  fur-lined .... PELISSE
  hood of .... COWL
  hooded .... CAPOTE,
        BURNOOSE, BURNOUS,
        CAMAIL, CARDINAL
  over armor ... SURCOAT,
                TABARD
  room .. VESTIARY, CLOSET
  short ...... MANT(E)LET,
        GREGO, MANTILLA
  Spanish .. MANTA, CAPA
  used as raincoat ....
                PONCHO
  woman's ..... MANTEAU,
                CARDINAL
clobber .... BEAT, HIT, MAUL,
                DEFEAT
cloche ..... (GLASS) JAR, HAT
clock .... TIME(PIECE),
                HOROLOGE
  face of .... DIAL
  inhabitant ..... CUCKOO
  London's famed ....
                BIG BEN
  part .. CHIME, PENDULUM,

        HAND, PALLET, CLICK,
                PAWL
  shaped .... NEF
  sound ...... TICK(TOCK),
                CHIME
  water .... CLEPSYDRA
  work device ....
                METRONOME
clocklike .. PRECISE, REGULAR
clockwise .... SUNWISE
clod .... DOLT, LUMP, EARTH,
        SOIL, GALOSH(E)
clodhopper .. PLOWMAN, BOOR,
                SHOE
clodpate .. BLOCKHEAD, FOOL
clodpoll .. BLOCKHEAD, DOLT
clog ... SABOT, SHOE, IMPEDE,
        BLOCK, PATTEN, DANCE,
        HAMPER, CHOKE, CHOPINE
cloisonne finish ..... ENAMEL
cloister ..... NUNNERY, STOA,
        ABBEY, MONASTERY, CONVENT,
                PRIORY, FRIARY
  dweller .... MONK, NUN,
        ABBOT, ABBESS
cloistered .... SECLUDED,
                RETIRED
close ... SHUT(IN), CONCLUDE,
        FINISH, COMPACT, FINALE,
        END, SEAL, LOCK, OCCLUDE,
        INTIMATE, NIGH, SULTRY,
                STINGY
  British .. ENTRY, PASSAGE
  building ...... PADLOCK
  by ...... (A)NEAR, NIGH
  conclusively .... CLINCH
  down/up .... STOP
  fist .... CLENCH
  fitting .... (SKIN)TIGHT,
                SNUG
  hermetically .... SEAL
  in ...... SURROUND
  in music .... CODA
  mouthed ..... TACITURN
  mouthed one ..... CLAM
  of day .... EVENTIDE
  poetic .... ANEAR, NIGH
  tightly ...... SEAL, CORK
  to the wind .... LUFF
  violently .... SLAM
closed at one end ..... BLIND
closefisted .. STINGY, MISERLY,
                NIGGARD
closet .... TOILET, CUPBOARD,
        ROOM, CUDDY, PRIVY,
        AMBRY, LOCKER

closing passage in music ......
  CODA
word .... AMEN
closure .... CONCLUSION, END,
  CLOTURE, STOPPAGE
clot .... GRUME, COAGULATE,
  CRUOR, JELL, GOUT
  preventing substance ....
  HEPARIN
cloth ...... FABRIC, DRAPERY,
  BRAT, SERGE, TWEED, DENIM,
  MUSLIN, TABARET, TRICOT,
  TEXTILE, TWILL, GOODS,
  RATTEEN, WOOF
  altar .... PALL, VESPERAL
  baptismal ...... CHRISOM
  bark .... TAPA
  buff-colored ... NANKIN,
  NANKEEN
  calico .... DOWLAS
  camel's hair .... ABA,
  CAMLET
  chalice .... PALL
  checkered .... PLAID,
  TARTAN
  corded .... DIMITY,
  BENGALI
  cotton ... MUSLIN, JEAN,
  MANTA, CALICO, DRILL,
  CHINTZ, NANKEEN,
  HOLLAND, GINGHAM,
  CHINO, DENIM, CANVAS,
  CRASH, MADRAS
  cover ...... DRAPE, TILT
  cretonne .... TOILE
  crinkled .. CRAPE, CREPE
  curtain .... TAPIS
  damask-like .... LAMPAS
  dealer .... DRAPER,
  CLOTHIER
  diagonal weave .. TWILL
  dressing .. STUPE, GAUZE
  drying .... TOWEL
  drying frame ... TENTER
  edge .... SELVAGE
  end part of .... FAG
  equal to 2¼ inches .. NAIL
  fiber .... COTTON, RAMIE,
  LINEN, FLAX, NAP, SILK
  figured ...... BROCADE,
  BROCATEL(LE)
  finishing machine ....
  BEETLE, CALENDER
  flaxen .... LINEN
  flaw .... RIP, TEAR, SNAG
  floor covering ...... RUG

for face sweat ....
  VERONICA, SUDARIUM
for sheets, pillowcases ...
  MUSLIN
frieze-like ...... RATTEEN
gauzy .. BAREGE, ILLUSION
glazed .... CHINTZ,
  JACONET
glossy ... SATIN, SATEEN,
  SILK, LUSTRING,
  LUTESTRING, CALAMANCO
goat's hair .... ABA
gold ... CYPRUS, CYPRESS
hairy surface .... NAP
handwoven .. TAPESTRY
hanging in folds ....
  DRAPERY
heavy .... MACE
hemp .... CANVAS
jute .... GUNNY
knot .... BURL
lightweight .... DELAINE
linen ...... DRILL, TOILE,
  DOWLAS, HOLLAND
loin .... LAVA-LAVA
make of .... WOVEN,
  KNITTED, PRESSED
maker .... DRAPER
making spy ...... KERK
material ...... COTTON,
  WOOL, SILK, HAIR, RAYON,
  SKIN, FIBER, FLAX
measure .... ELL, NAIL
medicated .... STUPE
metallic .... LAME
mix-colored .... MOTLEY
mulberry bark ..... TAPA
mummy .... BYSSUS
nautical .. CANVAS, SAIL
needlework ..... CANVAS
ornamentally designed ..
  LAMPAS
penitent's ... SACKCLOTH
plaid .... TARTAN
plush-like ...... BOLIVIA
powder .... SACHET
rib .... CORD
ribbed .... CORDUROY
ridge .... RIB
sample .... SWATCH
selvage .... LIST
sheer .... TOILE
silk .. CHIFFON, SARCENET,
  LUSTRING, LEVANTINE,
  CHARMEUSE

soft .... SATIN, SILK, GOSSAMER
stiffening .... WIGAN
strip .... LIST
strips for decoration .... BUNTING
surface .... NAP
symbol of penitence .... SACKCLOTH
synthetic .... RAYON, DACRON, NYLON
table .... NAPKIN
tapestry .... TAPIS
texture .... WALE
the .... CLERGY
to wrap dead person in .. CEREMENT, SHROUD, BYSSUS
triangular .... GORE
twilled .... JEAN, SERGE, DENIM, CHINO, PLAID, LEVANTINE
umbrella .... GLORIA
upholstering .... BROCATEL(LE), TABARET
veil .... BAREGE
velvet-like ...... PANNE
wall hanging .. TAPESTRY
waste .... RAG
waterproof ... GOSSAMER
waxed .... CEREMENT
wiping .. NAPKIN, TOWEL
with decorative pictures .. TAPESTRY
with diagonal weave .... DRILL
with raised design ...... BROCADE, BROCHE
with satin strips .... TABARET
with uncut loops .. TERRY
wool(en) .... SEE "WOOL(EN)"
worn like a scarf .. STOLE
clothe .. DRESS, GARB, INVEST, ROBE, RIG
clothed .... CLAD, INVESTED
clothes ..... RAIMENT, DRESS, APPAREL, ATTIRE, TOGGERY
basket .... HAMPER
bride's ...... TROUSSEAU
cheap .... SLOPS
chest .. BUREAU, DRESSER
closet .... WARDROBE
collection of .... WARDROBE, ENSEMBLE

colloquial .. TOGS, DUDS, RAGS
fancier ..... DUDE, FOP, DANDY
gaudy .... FRIPPERY
moth .... TINEA
party ..... (GLAD)RAGS
pertaining to .. VESTIARY
place for ...... CLOSET, BUREAU, DRESSER, WARDROBE
powder .... SACHET
press .... IRON, ARMOIRE
ragged .... TATTERS
set of .. SUIT, ENSEMBLE
splendid .... REGALIA
stand ...... TREE, RACK
to be washed .. LAUNDRY
work .. DENIM, COVERALL, JEANS, SMOCK, DUNGAREES, APRON
clotheshorse: colloq. .... FOP, DANDY, COXCOMB, DUDE
famed .. (BEAU) BRUMMEL
clothespress .... ARMOIRE
clothing ... RAIMENT, ATTIRE
of men's .... SARTORIAL
ready-made ...... SLOPS
store .... TOGGERY
Clotho .... FATE, WEIRD
clotting protein ... GLOBULIN
cloture .... CLOSURE, CLOSING
cloud .... DARKEN, OBSCURE, SULLY
combining form .. NEPHO
composition ..... DUST, SMOKE, STEAM, GAS
formation ...... CIRRUS, CUMULUS, STRATUS, NIMBUS
like mass .... COMA, NEBULA
of dust/smoke/gas .. MIST
photo of .... NEPHOGRAM
surrounding gods .... NIMBUS
cloudburst .. RAIN, DOWNPOUR
cloudless .... BRIGHT, CLEAR, SUNNY
clouds, fleecy .... CIRRUS
broken mass of .... (W)RACK
combining form .. NEPHO
cumulus .... WOOLPACK
in the .... IMPRACTICAL, FANCIFUL

study of .... NEPHOLOGY
wind-driven .... SCUD
cloudy .. NUBILOUS, OVERCAST,
DIM, HAZY, LOWERING,
NEBULOUS, TURBID
clough ...... RAVINE, GORGE
clout ..... SWAT, RAP, BLOW,
KNOCK, HIT, CUFF, SLAP
clove .. SPICE, BUD, CARNATION
cloven .. CLEFT, SPLIT, DIVIDED
footed .... DEVILISH,
SATANIC, FISSIPED
hoofed ...... BISULCATE
clover .... TREFOIL, NARDOO,
SHAMROCK, LADINO, BERSEEM,
ALSIKE, MELILOT, MEDIC,
ALFALFA, FOUR-LEAF
plan resembling .. MEDIC
clown .. BOOR, BUFFOON, LOUT,
ZANY, APER, JESTER, COMIC,
BUFFO, MIME, CUTUP,
HARLEQUIN, PUNCHINELLO
forte of a ....
(TOM)FOOLERY, JOKES,
TRICKS, ANTICS
garment of .... MOTLEY
of a sort: sl. ..... CUTUP
Shakespearean play .....
FESTE, LAVACHE
woman .... BUFFA
clownish ..... BOORISH, RUDE,
CLUMSY
cloy .. SURFEIT, SATIATE, PALL,
SATE, GLUT
cloying .... LUSCIOUS
club .....'... STICK, CUDGEL,
TRUNCHEON, MAUL, BAT
aborigine's ...... WADDY
armor-breaking ... MACE
baseball .... BAT
benefit sale .... BAZAAR,
RUMMAGE
billiards ..... MACE, CUE
college ...... SORORITY,
FRAT(ERNITY)
for beating cloth ......
BEETLE
for sandtraps .... WEDGE
golf ...... CLEEK, IRON,
DRIVER, PUTTER
hockey .... BANDY
hold on .... GRIP
local division .. CHAPTER
manager ...... STEWARD
metal-headed .... MACE
military service ..... USO

moss .... LYCOPOD
policeman's ...... BILLY,
TRUNCHEON
polo .... MALLET
service .... KIWANIS,
ROTARY, LIONS, JAYCEES
shaped .... CLAVATE,
CLAVIFORM
social .... COTERIE,
SORORITY
women's ...... SOROSIS,
ZONTA, SORORITY
wooden .... MAUL
clubfoot .... TALIPES
clubfooted .... TALIPED
clubman .. ROTARIAN, JAYCEE,
LION, KIWANIAN
clucking sound ...... CLACK
clue .... CLEW, TIP, HINT,
POINTER
clumber ...... DOG, SPANIEL
clump .... MASS, CLUSTER,
THICKET
bushy .... TOD
of bushes .... SHAW
of earth .... CLOD
of ivy, etc. .... TOD
of trees .. BOSK, MOTT(E),
TUFT
clumps, growing in .. CEPITOSE
clumsy .... AWKWARD, INEPT,
INELEGANT, GAUCHE,
OAFISH, UNGAINLY, GAWKY,
LUMPY, MALADROIT
and stupid ..... LOUTISH
boat ... ARK, DROGHER,
BARGE
person .... OAF, JUMBO,
LUBBER, OX, LUMMOX
player .... DUB
thing .... JUMBO
worker .... COBBLER,
DABSTER, DABBLER,
BUNGLER
Cluny product .... LACE
clupeid .. HERRING, SARDINE,
SHAD
cluster .... BUNCH, CLUMP,
TUFT, SORUS, GLOMERATION,
KNOT
arranged in ... AGMINATE
banana .... HAND
bracts .... COMA
compact .... GLOMERULE
fibers .... FASCICLE

flowers .. CYMB, RACEME, PANICLE
fruits .... BUNCH
leaves .... FASCICLE
of seven stars .. PLEIADES
of shrubs .... CLUMP
of spore cases .... SORUS
of trees .... CLUMP
clustered .... GLOMERATE
clusters, growing in ....
.... ACERVATE
clutch .. GRASP, SNATCH, SEIZE, GRIP, HOLD
clutches ... POWER, CONTROL, GRIP
clutter ..... JUMBLE, LITTER, BUSTLE, LUMBER
clyster .... ENEMA
Clytemnestra's husband .....
.... AGAMEMNON
lover .... AEGISTHUS
mother .... LEDA
son .... ORESTES
coach .. CARRIAGE, BUS, TUTOR
athletic .... TRAINER
dog .... DALMATIAN
for hire .. HACK, HANSOM, FIACRE
for state occasions ......
.... CAROCHE
four-horse drawn ....
.... TALLYHO
roof/top of ... IMPERIAL
coachman ..... DRIVER, LURE, HACK, JEHU, FLY
coaction .... FORCE, COERCION, COMPULSION
coagulate .... CURDLE, CAKE, CLOT, CONGEAL, JELL, SET, CRUD
coagulated mass ...... CLOT
coagulating substance ......
RENNET, RENNIN, STYPTIC, COAGULIN, PRECIPITIN
coagulation, blood ..... CLOT, THROMBOSIS
coal .... CARBON, COKE, ANTHRACITE, BITUMINOUS, LIGNITE
barge load of ..... KEEL
bin .... BUNKER
box .... HOD, BIN, DAN, SCUTTLE
bucket .... SCUTTLE
burner .... BRASIER

container of live ....
.... BRAZIER
deposit .... SEAM
digger .. PITMAN, COLLIER
distillate .... TAR
dust .. CULM, DUFF, SMUT, ASH, SLACK
feeder .... STOKER
glowing piece of .. EMBER, GLEED
grade of ..... WALLSEND
hod .... SCUTTLE
impurities ..... CLINKER, CULM
leavings .... SLACK
like substance .... JET
live ...... EMBER, GLEED
lump/mass .... COB
measure .... CHALDRON, PEA
mine ..... COLLIERY, PIT
bed .... WINNING
carrier .... TUB, TRAM
gas .... METHANE, FIREDAMP
roof prop ..... SPRAG
shaft ... PIT, WINNING
wagon .... CORF
miner .. COLLIER, PITMAN
miner's consumption ....
.... ANTHRACOSIS
oil .... KEROSENE, PETROLEUM
partially burned ....
.... CINDER
pieced .... LUMP
region ..... SAAR, RUHR
screening device ....
.... TROMMEL
scuttle .... HOD
ship .... COLLIER
shovel .... SCOOP
sieve .... TROMMEL
size of .. PEA, EGG, NUT, WALLSEND
stoker .... HOPPER
tar compound ....
.... SACCHARIN
tar derivative .. TOLUENE, PITCH, CRESOL, BITUMEN, CREOSOTE, TOLUOL(E)
tar dye .. EOSIN, ALIZARIN
truck .... CORF
wagon ..... CORF, TRAM
waste .. CULM, CLINKER
coalesce .. MIX, MERGE, UNITE

coalescence .. MERGER, UNION
coalfish .... POLLACK, CUDDY
coalition .. UNION, ALLIANCE, FUSION, MERGER, ENTENTE
coals, rake over the .... CRITICIZE, CENSURE
coarse .. CRUDE, INDELICATE, RIBALD, ROUGH, GROSS, VULGAR, OBSCENE, CRASS, HARSH, LOWBRED
   cloth .. DENIM, BURLAP, SCRIM, JUTE, LENO
   corn meal .... SAMP, HOMINY
   fiber .... TOW
   flour .... MEAL
   hominy ... GRITS, SAMP
   lace .... MACRAME
   meal .... GROUT
coast .. (SEA) SHORE, SEASIDE, GLIDE, BEACH, RIVAGE
   Guard boat ..... CUTTER
   Guard girl .... SPAR
   line curve .... BIGHT
   of the .... LITTORAL
   on aircraft ... VOLPLANE
coastal .... LITTORAL
coaster ... SLED, TOBOGGAN
coasting vehicle ...... SLED, TOBOGGAN, SKI, SURFBOARD
coat .... JACKET, LAYER, COVERING, GARMENT, PLATE, TOG, KIRTLE
   animal ...... FUR, SKIN, WOOL
   arm-pinning .... STRAIGHTJACKET
   close-fitting .... COATEE, NEW MARKET
   daytime ...... CUTAWAY
   double-breasted .... REEFER, MACKINAW
   formal .. CUTAWAY, TAILS
   fur-lined .... PELISSE
   icy ... RIME, (HOAR)FROST
   kind of ... TRENCH, TOP, DUSTER
   leather .... JACK
   long .... REDINGOTE
   long-sleeved ... KAFTAN, CAFTAN
   loose .... SACK, PALETOT
   madman's .... STRAITJACKET
   of a mammal .. PELAGE, HAIR, FUR

of alloy .... PATINA
of armor .. BRIGANDINE
of arms .... BLAZON, SHIELD, CREST, HERALDRY
of arms band .... BATON, TRESSURE
of arms edge .. BORDURE
of gold ..... GILD, GILT
of icing .... GLACE
of mail .... ARMOR, HAUBERK, BYRNIE
of metal .... PLATE
person in white .. DOCTOR
slang .... TOG
sleeveless .... JACK
slit .... VENT
soldier's .... TUNIC
thin .... VENEER
waterproof .... SLICKER, MACKINTOSH
with aluminum .... CALORIZE
with brass .... BRAZE
with gold ... GILD, GILT
with metal .... PLATE
with tar .... PAY
woman's .... REDINGOTE, REEFER, DOLMAN
worn as armor .... GAMBESON
coati-like animal .. RACCOON
coating ..... COVERING, FILM, VENEER
   boiler's inside ...... FUR
   for photographic plates .. COLLODION
   for wounds .. COLLODION
   fruit .... BLOOM
   glossy .. ENAMEL, GLAZE
   icy ... SLEET, (HOAR)FROST
   metal ... PATINA, PATINE
   on ceiling ...... PARGET
   on copper, bronze ...... PATINA, PATINE
   on eyes .... GLAZE
   pottery .. GLAZE, ENAMEL
   wall .... PARGET
coax .... CAJOLE, WHEEDLE, PERSUADE, TEASE, BLARNEY, BLANDISH
cob .... SWAN, HORSE, (SEA)GULL
   coal .... COBBLES
cobalt .... BLUE
Cobb, baseball player ..... TY
cobble .. PAVE, MEND, PATCH

cobbler .... SOLER,
(SHOE)MENDER, CRISPIN
 block of .... LAST
 tool of .... AWL
coble .... ROWBOAT,
(FISHING)BOAT
cobra .. SNAKE, NAGA, VIPER,
MAMBA, ELAPINE
 fighter ...... MONGOOSE
 headdress ...... URAEUS
cobweb ..... GOSSAMER, TRAP
 describing a .... FLIMSY,
GAUZY, FILMY
 material .... FIBROID
Coca, comedienne .. IMOGENE
Coca-Cola product ..... TAB,
FRESCA
cocaine .... NARCOTIC,
ALKALOID, ANESTHETIC
 addict .... SNOWBIRD
 slang .... SNOW
 source .... COCA, CUCA
Cochin-China capital ....
SAIGON
cochineal .... DYE
 pigment .... LAKE
cochleate .... SPIRAL
cock ...... ROOSTER, CROW,
LEADER, FAUCET, TAP
 -a-hoop ..... CONCEITED,
ELATED
 -and-bull story ....
CANARD, HOAX, YARN
 comb of ..... CARUNCLE
 fighting .... HEELER
 young .... COCKEREL
cockade ..... KNOT, ROSETTE
cockateel .... PARROT
cockatoo .... PARROT, ARARA
cockatrice .... SERPENT,
BASILISK
cockboat ...... COG, TENDER
cockchafer ..... DOR, BEETLE,
BUZZARD
cockcrow ..... DAWN, MORN
cocker .... SPANIEL, PAMPER,
CODDLE, PET, FONDLE
cockerel .... ROOSTER
cockeyed: sl. ..... CROOKED,
AWRY, ABSURD, SCREWY,
DRUNK
cockfight .... SPAR
cockiness .... CONCEIT
cockle ... DARNEL, WRINKLE,
WEED, SHELLFISH, BOAT,
PUCKER

cocklebur ... ... BURDOCK,
RAGWEED
cockloft ...... ATTIC, GARRET
cockney .... EGG, CHILD,
DIALECT
 famous ...... HORNSBY
cockpit .... ARENA, CABIN
 occupant .... PILOT
 of Europe, so-called ....
BELGIUM
cockroach .... WATERBUG
cockscomb .. CAP, FOP, DANDY
cockspur ...... (HAW)THORN
cocktail .... DRINK, MARTINI,
APPETIZER, BRONX,
MANHATTAN
 fruit .... MACEDOINE
 ingredient ...... BITTERS
 lethal .... MOLOTOV
 measure .... SPLIT
 mixer ... ... BARTENDER,
SHAKER
 room .... LOUNGE
 rum .. DAIQUIRI, ZOMBI(E)
 tidbit .... OLIVE
 with legs .... HORSE
cocky ..... CONCEITED, VAIN,
SAUCY
coco ... ... PALM(TREE)
cocoa .... CHOCOLATE, BROMA
 bean, crushed ...... NIBS
coconut .... PALM
 husk fiber .... COIR
 liquid .... MILK
 meat, dried .. COPRA(H),
COPPERAH
 oil source ...... COPRA
cocoon .... POD, CASE, THECA
 covering .... FLOSS
 fiber .... SILK
 in zoology .... FOLLICLE
 occupant .... PUPA
 silkworm .... CLEW
Cocos Islands ..... KEELING
cod .... LING, BURBOT,
BOCACCIO, CUSK, GADID,
GLASHAN, WHITING
 Archaic .... BAG
 fishing bait .. CAP(E)LIN
 kin .... HAKE
COD, part of ..... CASH, ON,
DELIVERY, COLLECT
coda .... FINALE
coddle .... PET, PAMPER,
PARBOIL, SPOONFEED, BABY

code .. SALIC, CODEX, CIPHER, LAW
  church .... CANON
  emperor's .... NAPOLEON
  message in .... CRYPTOGRAM
  moral .... ETHICS
  of a kind ..... PASSWORD
  of laws .... HAMMURABI
  word, GI's radio .. ABLE, BAKER, ROGER
codfish .... TORSK, CUSK, GADOID, GLASHAN, BURBOT, LING, GADID
  young .... SCROD
codger .. FELLOW, ECCENTRIC, MISER, CHURL
codicil ..... APPENDIX, RIDER
codling ...... SCROD, APPLE
Cody, American plainsman ... (BUFFALO) BILL
coelenterate .... HYDRA, JELLYFISH, ANEMONE, ACALEPH(E)
  larva of .... PLANULA
coenurus .... LARVA
  host of .... SHEEP
coerce ...... COMPEL, FORCE, CONSTRAIN, COW
  colloquial .... BULLDOZE, BULLY
coercion .... COMPULSION, DURESS
  slang ... HEAT, PRESSURE
coercive indoctrination .... BRAINWASHING
coetaneous .... COEVAL
Coeur d'Alene Indian .... SALISHAN
  de Lion .... RICHARD (I)
coeval ...... CONTEMPORARY, COETANEOUS
coffee .. JAVA, MOCHA, SHRUB, CAFE, BRAZIL, SUMATRA, MADDER
  alcoholic addition .. LACE
  alkaloid ..... CAFFEIN(E)
  bean .... NIBS
  box .... CANISTER
  break .. RESPITE, TIME-OFF
  brewer ..... URN, SILEX
  cake .... KUCHEN
  can .... CANISTER
  cup .... DEMITASSE
  cup stand .... ZARF
  extract .... CAFFEIN(E)

  grinder .... MILL
  house .... CAFE
  making container .. URN, SILEX, PERCOLATOR
  mixture ...... SUCCORY, CHICORY
  plantation ...... FINCA
  pot .. URN, DRIPOLATOR, BIGGIN, PERCOLATOR
  room .... DIVAN
  substitute ..... CHICORY, SUCCORY
  tree .... CHICOT
coffer ... CHEST, STRONGBOX, LOCK, ARK
coffers .... TREASURY, FUNDS, CHEST
coffin .. CASKET, (BURIAL) BOX, BIER, LITTER
  carrier .... PALLBEARER, HEARSE, CAISSON
  cover .... PALL
  nail: sl. ..... CIGARETTE
  stand .. CATAFALQUE, BIER
  stone .... SARCOPHAGUS
cog .... GEAR, TOOTH, WHEEL, (COCK)BOAT, PAWL, SWINDLE, CHEAT
cogent .... CONVINCING, COMPELLING, VALID
cogitate ... THINK, CONSIDER, PONDER, MULL, CEREBRATE, CHEW
cognac .... BRANDY
cognate .... RELATED, AKIN
cognition .... NOESIS, PERCEPTION
cognizance .... NOTICE, PERCEPTION
cognizant .... ON TO, AWARE, HEP
cognize .... KNOW, PERCEIVE, NOTICE
cognomen ...... (SUR)NAME, NICKNAME
cognoscente ... CONNOISSEUR
cogon .... GRASS
cogwheel ...... GEAR, PINION
Cohan's song .... OVER THERE
coheir .... PARCENER
cohere ...... ADHERE, STICK
coherent .... CONSISTENT
cohort .... ALLY, BAND
  one third of ... MANIPLE
cohune .... PALM
coif .... (SKULL)CAP

coiffeur .... HAIRDRESSER
coiffure .. HAIRDO, HEADDRESS
    pad .... RAT
    quickie .... WIG, TOUPEE
    style .... CHAR
coign .... CORNER
coil .. WIND, CURL, CONVOLVE,
    TWIST; LOOP, WHORL, FAKE
    cable/rope .... FAKE
    in a ball .... CLEW
    yarn .... SKEIN
coiled .. CONVOLUTE, TORTILE,
    SPIRY, HELICOID
coiling creature .. SNAKE, BOA,
    CONSTRICTOR, PYTHON
coin .. MINT, INVENT, DEVISE,
    SPECIE
    Abyssinian .. GIRSH, BESA
    Afghanistan ... AMANIA
    Albanian .. LEK, QUINTAR
    American (U.S.) .. CENT,
    DIME, DOLLAR, EAGLE,
    NICKEL, QUARTER
    Anglo-Saxon ...... ORA,
    SCEAT
    Annam .... QUAN
    Arabian .... TALARI
    Argentine ..... CENTAVO
    Austrian .... DUCAT,
    KRONE, GULDEN
    back of .... VERSO
    Biblical .... TALENT,
    SHEKEL
    box .... PYX, PIX
    Brazilian ..... (MIL)REI,
    MOIDORE, CENTAVO
    Bulgarian .. DINAR, LEV,
    LEW, STOTINKA
    Chilean .... COLON,
    ESCUDO, CENTAVO, PESO
    Chinese ... TIAO, LIANG,
    TAEL
    coating .... BLOOM
    collector .. NUMISMATIST
    Colombian .... PESO
    Costa Rican ..... COLON
    counterfeit ... RAP, SLUG
    cross-figured ....
    KREU(T)ZER
    cut edges of .... NIG
    Czech .. DUCAT, KRONEN
    Danish .... ORA, KRONE,
    CROWN, ORAS
    design .... INCUSE
    drop .... SLOT
    Dutch .. GULDEN, STIVER,

    GUILDER, FLORIN
    Dutch East Indies .. DUIT
    Ecuadorian ..... SUCRE
    edge .... NIG
    Egyptian ...... PIASTRE,
    PIASTER
    El Salvador ..... COLON
    English .. GROAT, PENCE,
    GUINEA, UNITE, ORA,
    TESTON, CAROLUS,
    FLORIN
    Ethiopian ...... TALARI
    expert .... NUMISMATIST
    French ..... ECU, LOUIS,
    BESANT, SOU, PISTOLE
    front of .... OBVERSE
    German .. KRONE, MARK,
    T(H)ALER
    Greek .. OBOL, DRACHMA
    Hebrew .. GERAH, SHEKEL
    hole .... SLOT
    Hungarian .... PENGO,
    GARA, FORINT, FILLER
    Icelandic ...... AURAR,
    KRONA
    imitation .... SLUG
    India ...... ANNA, PICE,
    RUPEE, PIE
    into money .. MONETIZE,
    MINT
    Iranian .... RIAL, DARIC,
    DINAR, MOHUR, PAHLAVI
    Iraqi .... DINAR
    Italian .... LIRA, SCUDO,
    SOLDO
    Japanese .. RIN, SEN, YEN
    Jewish .. GERAH, SHEKEL
    large ...... CARTWHEEL
    Latvian .... LAT(U)
    Lithuanian ..... LIT(AS),
    RUBLE
    making metal ..... FLAN
    metal .. FLAN, PLANCHET
    metallic .... SPECIE
    Mexican ...... CUARTO,
    CENTAVO, PESO
    money .... MINT
    Moroccan .... RIAL
    Nepalese .... MOHAR
    Norwegian ..... KRONE,
    ORE, CROWN
    Oman .... GAZ, GOZ
    Oriental .... DINAR
    Persian .. DINAR, DARIC
    Peruvian .... CENTAVO,
    SOL, DINERO, PESETA

pewter .... TRA
plant .... MINT
Polish ... DUCAT, ZLOTY
Portuguese ..... (MIL)REI
reverse side ...... VERSO
ridges .... KNURL
Roman ... SOLIDUS, AES,
    SESTERCE, DENARIUS
Rumanian .... LEU, LEY
Russian .... RUBLE,
    CHERVONETS, KOPE(C)K
Scandinavian ... KRONAR
Serbian .... DINAR
shaped ..... NUMMULAR
Sicilian .... SCUDO
side .... OBVERSE, VERSO
slang .... INVENT
small value ... PICAYUNE,
    MITE
South American ....
    CONDOR
space for date, etc. .....
    EXERGUE
Spanish .. PESETA, REAL,
    PESO, DOBLA, DURO,
    PISTOLE
Spanish colonial ....
    PISTAREEN
Swedish .... KRONA, ORE,
    KRONER
Swiss ...... FRANC, BATZ
tester .... SHROFF
Thailand .... ATT, BAHT,
    CATTY, TICAL
tin .... TRA
Turkish .... LIRA, ASPER,
    ALTUN, PIASTER, PIASTRE
Venetian .... DUCAT
Venezuelan .... PESO
Yugoslav .... DINAR
coincide .... AGREE
coiner of words .. NEOLOGIST
coins, collection of ....
    NUMISMATICS
  collector of ....
    NUMISMATIST
  pertaining to ....
    NUMISMATICS
  roll of .... ROULEAU
  small .... CHANGE
  sound of .... JINGLE
  study of .. NUMISMATICS
coke .... COAL, FUEL
  measure .... CHALDRON
  residue .... BREEZE
  slang .... COCAIN(E)

col .... GAP, PASS
colander .... PAN, SIEVE,
    STRAINER
Colchis princess ..... MEDEA
cold .. BLEAK, CATARRH, ICY,
    ALGID, RHEUM, GELID,
    MARBLY, CHILLY
  blooded ...... CALLOUS,
    PITILESS
  blooded creature .. FISH
  congeal by ..... FREEZE
  dish .... SALAD, SLAW
  extremely .... GELID,
    FRIGID
  head .... CORYZA
  hearted .... UNKIND
  leave out in the . SNUB,
    IGNORE, NEGLECT,
    ABANDON
  Scottish .... CAULD
  season .... WINTER
  shoulder .. SNUB, REBUFF,
    BRUSH-OFF
  sore .... HERPES, LABIALIS
  steel .... BLADE, SWORD
  stinging .... NIP
  tableland .... PUNA
  very .. FRIGID, FREEZING,
    GELID, HYPERBOREAN
  War weapon ....
    PROPAGANDA
  weather wear .. ANORAK,
    PARKA, EARMUFFS,
    EARFLAPS
coldness of body ...... CHILL
cole ... CABBAGE, RAPE, KALE
coleopter .... BEETLE, WEEVIL
coleslaw .... SALAD
colewort .... KALE, CABBAGE,
    COLLARD
colic .... ILEUS
  stone .... JADE
colima .... IRONWOOD
colin ...... BOBWHITE, QUAIL
coliseum .... STADIUM
collaborator .... LAVAL,
    QUISLING
  what he gives enemy ....
    AID, COMFORT
collage of a sort ..... MOSAIC
collapse ... CAVE IN, FALL IN,
    FAIL, BREAKDOWN, FOLD UP,
    DEFLATE, SLUMP
collapsible hat .... GIBUS
collar .. NECKWEAR, CAPTURE,

RUFF, PARRAL, PARREL, GORGET, CARCANET
ancient metal ... TORQUE
bird with feathered ..... GROUSE, PARTRIDGE
bird's .... FLANGE
bone .... CLAVICLE
clerical .... RABATO
colloquial ...... CHOKER
detachable ...... TUCKER
English schoolboy's .... ETON
fastener .... STUD
frilled .... RUFF
high .... FRAISE
ornamental .. CARCANET
pleated/frilled ..... RUFF
projecting ..... FLANGE
strangling .... GAROTTE, GARROTE
turned down ... RABATO, FALL
woman's ...... BERTHA, DICKEY
collard .... KALE
collared .... TORQUATE
collate ... COMPILE, COMPARE
collateral .... PARALLEL
collation .... MEAL, TEA
colleague .... ASSOCIATE, CONFRERE
collect .... PRAYER, COMPILE, GATHER, ASSEMBLE, AMASS, ACCUMULATE, REAP, GARNER, SCRAPE
grain leftovers .. GLEAN
collectanea ...... ANTHOLOGY, CORPUS
collected .... COOL, CALM, SERENE, AMASSED
collection ... GROUP, BUNCH, REPERTORY, HEAP, LUMP, KIT, PACK, GALAXY, BEVY
a .... SET
anecdotes .... ANA
animal fables .. BESTIARY
animals .... MENAGERIE, ZOO, HERD, DROVE
art works ...... GALLERY
assorted .. MISCELLANEA, MISCELLANY
books .... LIBRARY, BIBLIOTHECA
Brahman maxims .... SUTRA

bridal clothes .... TROUSSEAU
coins ...... NUMISMATICS
commentaries .... GLOSSARY
documents ...... PAPERS
dried plants .. HERBARIUM
essays ...... SYMPOSIUM
explanatory notes ...... GLOSSARY
facts .... ANA, DATA
information about person DOSSIER
large .... RAFT, RAFF
laws .... CORPUS, JURIS, CODE
literary ...... ANALECTA, ANALECTS
logs on river .... DRIVE
Norse poetry ..... EDDA
of writings ..... PAPERS
operas, songs, etc. ...... REPERTOIRE
opinions .... SYMPOSIUM
paintings ...... GALLERY
piano pieces ... GRADUS
poems, etc... ANTHOLOGY
postage stamps ...... PHILATELY
prayers for mass .. MISSAL
precious ..... TREASURE
reminiscences .. MEMOIRS, ANA
saints' lives .... HAGIOLOGY, LEGENDARY
sayings .... ANA
statues .... GALLERY
things .... CONGERIES
tools .... KIT
types .... PI(E)
collective bargaining result ... CONTRACT
farm .... KOL(K)HOZ
security group ... NATO, SEATO
collectivism ...... SOCIALISM
collector, art ...... VIRTUOSO
bank .... RUNNER
birds' eggs .... OOLOGIST
book .... BIBLIOPHILE
coin ...... NUMISMATIST
curios .... VIRTUOSO
excise tax ..... GA(U)GER
fare .... CONDUCTOR
gem .... LAPIDARY
item for a .... CURIO,

RELIC, BIBELOT, MASTER, FIRST ISSUE
jokes .... CERF
Munchausen's tales ..... RASPE
phonograph record ..... DISCOPHILE
plants ...... HERBALIST
shell .... CONCHOLOGIST
stamp ..... PHILATELIST
colleen .... GIRL, LASS
college .. UNIVERSITY, SCHOOL, ACADEMY
athletic team ... VARSITY
building ...... LAB, GYM, DORM(ITORY)
campus .... QUAD
cheer .. YELL, RAH(RAH)
cheerleader: Japan ..... OENDAN
course: abbr. .... ANAT, MATH, ECON, TRIG, BIOL, BOT, ARCH, MED, ZOOL, ENG
dance .... HOP, PROM
dining hall .. REFECTORY
exams .... MIDTERMS
fellow .... DON
freshman .... FROSH
get-together ... REUNION
girl .... COED
graduate(s) .. ALUMNUS, ALUMNI
grounds .. QUAD(RANGLE), CAMPUS
group .... FRAT(ERNITY), SORORITY
half year ..... SEMESTER
hall .... AULA
honor society .... ARISTA
league symbol .... IVY(LEAF)
lecturer ..... PRELECTOR
living quarters .... DORM(ITORY), HALL
of attendance .... ALMA MATER
official .. DEAN, REGENT, REGISTRAR, PROVOST
optional subject .... ELECTIVE
organization .... FRATERNITY, SORORITY, CLUB
permit for absence ...... EXEAT

president .... PREXY
publication .... ANNUAL, YEARBOOK
rank .... DEGREE
scholars' .... ULEMA
servant .... GYP
student ..... FRESHMAN, SOPHOMORE, JUNIOR, SENIOR
students' revelry .... GAUDEAMUS
teacher ..... PROF(ESSOR)
treasurer ...... BURSAR
colleges' sports group .... IVY LEAGUE
collegiate .... VARSITY
collide .... CLASH, CRASH, HURTLE, BUMP
collie .... (SHEEP) DOG
of book ..... LASSIE, LAD
of movies ...... LASSIE
collier .... (COAL)MINER, PITMAN, SHIP, TENDER
colliery .... (COAL)MINE
tunnel .... ADIT
collinsia .... FIGWORT
collision .... SMASHUP
force of .... IMPACT
colloidal dispersion in fluid ... SOL
collop .... PIECE, SLICE
colloquial .. CONVERSATIONAL
affirmative ... YEP, YEAH
colloquialism .. IDIOM, SLANG, PATOIS
"Colloquies" author .... ERASMUS
colloquy ..... CONVERSATION, PARLEY, CONFERENCE
collude .... CONSPIRE
colly .. BLACKEN, SOOT, GRIME
collyrium .... EYEWASH, EYEWATER
collywobbles .... COLIC
colocynth ...... VINE, BITTER, APPLE
cologne ...... TOILET WATER
Colombia, capital of ...... BOGOTA
city .. CARTAGENA, CALI, PASTO, MEDELLIN
Indian .... MIRANA
mountain .... HUILA
river ...... MAGDALENA, CAUCA, JAPURA
volcano .... PASTO

colon, surgical removal of .... COLECTOMY
colonel's command ....
        REGIMENT
  insigne .... EAGLE
  navy counterpart ....
        CAPTAIN
colonial senate member ......
        DECURION
colonist ... SETTLER, PLANTER
  Indian greeting to ......
        NETOP
colonize .... SETTLE
colonizing insect ... ANT, BEE
colonnade .... GALLERY,
        PORTICO
colony .... PLANTATION,
        SETTLEMENT
  bees .... SWARM
  of insects .... NEST
colophony .... ROSIN
color .... BLUSH, FLUSH, DYE,
  PIGMENT, PAINT, STAIN, HUE,
    BICE, SEPIA, BLUE, RED,
  WHITE, YELLOW, GREEN,
  EBONY, COBALT, CORAL,
        TINCT
  animal .. ROAN, TAWNY,
    DAPPLE, FAWN, TAUPE,
        BRINDLE, PINTO
  band .... FASCIA
  blindness .... DALTONISM
  change ... BLUSH, FLUSH
  changing substance .....
        ALTERANT
  combining form ....
        CHROMAT(O)
  expert .... DYER
  fixer .... FIXATIVE,
        MORDANT
  fixer, in dyeing .... BASE
  flesh .... INCARNATE
  for French victory ......
        MAGENTA
  gradation .. TINT, SHADE
  in music .... TIMBRE
  intensity .... CHROMA
  lack of .... PALLOR
  lacking .... ALBINO
  lightly ...... TINGE, TINT
  lose .... FADE, PALE
  neutral .... GREGE
  pale .... PASTEL
  patch of .... FLECK
  pertaining to ....
        CHROMATIC

  primary/prismatic .. RED,
    ORANGE, GREEN, VIOLET,
    YELLOW, BLUE, INDIGO
  purity of .... CHROMA
  small amount of .. TINGE,
        TINT
  splash .... BLOB
  streak .... FLECK, LACE
  with red ocher ....
        RADDLE, REDDLE
Colorado capital ..... DENVER
  city .. ALAMOSA, LAMAR,
    PUEBLO, AURORA,
        BOULDER
  county .. LARIMER, OTERO
  feature .... MESA
  Indian ... ARAPAHOE, UTE
  mountain ...... RATON,
  OWEN, ANTERO, SAGUACHE,
        SAWATCH
  nickname .... ROVER,
        CENTENNIAL
  park .... ESTES
  peak ...... ESTES, EOLUS
  phenomenon ... RAINBOW
  Pittsburgh of ... PUEBLO
  resort .... MANITOU
  river ...... GILA, LARAMIE
  River lake .... MEAD
  state flower .. COLUMBINE
colored chalk .... PASTEL,
        CRAYON
  glass .... SMALTO
  highly .... PRISMAL
  many .... PRISMATIC
colorful bird .... TANAGER
  life, describing a .....
        CHECKERED
  spectacle .. PAGEANT(RY),
        EXTRAVAGANZA
coloring matter .. DYE, STAIN,
    PIGMENT, MORIN, RUDDLE
  for crayon ...... PASTEL
colorless .... WAN
  combining form .. LEUKO
  person .... ALBINO,
        NONENTITY
colors, artist's ...... PALETTE
  having three ... TRICHOIC
  the .... FLAG
colossal .... HUGE, GIGANTIC,
    ENORMOUS, LARGE
  beast .... BEHEMOTH,
    LEVIATHAN, WHALE
Colossi of Memnon, actually ..
        AMUNHOTEP

colossus ...... STATUE, GIANT
   sculptor of the .. CHARES
colt .... HORSE, REVOLVER,
           BOLLARD, FOAL
   revolver: sl. ....
       PEACEMAKER, HOG-LEG
coltish .... FRISKY
columbary .... DOVECOTE
Columbia eleven ...... LIONS
   River catch .... SALMON
columbine .... AQUILEGIA
columbite .... DIANITE
columbium .... NIOBIUM
columbo .... GENTIAN
Columbus' birthplace .. GENOA
   discovery ..... AMERICA,
       CUBA, COSTA RICA
   navigator of ... PINZON
   ship ...... NINA, PINTA,
        SANTA MARIA
   starting point .... PALOS
column .... PILLAR, PILASTER,
           SHAFT
   base .... PLINTH
   Buddhist .... LAT
   capital of .... CHAPTER
   convex swelling .. ENTASIS
   designating a ..... IONIC,
           DORIC
   figure, female .. CARYATID
   figure, male .. TELAMON,
         ATLANTES
   ornament .... GRIFFE
   shaft .... SCAPE
   square .... ANTA, PIER
   substitute for ....
       ATLANTES, ATLAS
   support of ...... BASE,
       PEDESTAL, PLINTH
   top of .... CAPITAL
columnist ...... WINCHELL,
   LIPPMANN, WESTON,
      PEARSON, ALSOP
columns, row of .. PERISTYLE,
      COLONNADE
colza .. COLE(SEED), RAPESEED
coma ... STUPOR, CATALEPSY,
        TRANCE
   having a ..... COMATOSE
comate, in botany .... HAIRY,
        TUFTED
comatose .... TORPID
comb .... CARUNCLE
   horse .... CURRY
   like implement .. RIPPER

   of fowl ..... CARUNCLE,
          CREST
   the hair .... DRESS
   wool ...... TEASE, CARD
combat ...... BATTLE, FIGHT,
   STOUR, STRIFE, JOUST, TILT,
        DUEL
   challenge to ..... CARTEL
   end of mortal .... DEATH
   mortal .... AMORT
   operation ...... MISSION
   place .... LISTS
   to decide issue .. DERAIGN
   troops .... CAVALRY,
       INFANTRY
   with lances .. JOUST, TILT
combatant .... FIGHTER
combative ...... PUGNACIOUS,
   QUARRELSOME, MILITANT
comber .... WAVE
combination .. ALLOY, BLEND,
   AMALGAM, MIXTURE, UNION
combine .... UNITE, JOIN,
   MERGE(R), COMPOUND
   kind of .... SYNDICATE,
       COALITION
   resources .... POOL
combining form for:
   alike .... ISO
   among .... INTER
   another .... HETERO
   angle .... GONIO
   asunder .... DICH(O)
   bad .... CAC(O), MAL
   below .... INFERO
   between .... INTER
   bile .... CHOL(O), CHOLE
   body fluid .... SERO
   both .... AMBI
   brass .... CHALCO
   bright .... HELI(O)
   bristles .... CHAET(O)
   broad .... EURY, PLAT(Y)
   cartilage ...... CHONDRO
   cavity .... C(O)ELE
   cell .... CYTE
   circular .... CYCL(O)
   cold .... CRY(O)
   color .... CHROMAT(O)
   copper .... CUPRI
   corpse .... NECR(O)
   curl .... CIRRI
   cutter .... TOMB
   death .... NECR(O)
   depth .... BATHO
   different ...... HETER(O)

digit .... DACTYL(O)
double .... DIPL(O)
drawing .... GRAPHO
dreadful .... DINO
dung .... COPR(O)
earth .... GEO
end .... TEL(O)
English .... ANGLO
entire .... HOLO
equal .. ISO, EQUI, PARI
external .... ECT(O)
eye defect .... OPIA
far .... TELE
fatty .... LIP(O)
feather .... PTERO
feces .... COPR(O)
feet .... PED(E), PEDI
female .. GYN(O), GYNOUS
fermentation ..... ZYMO
fever .... FEBRI
fine .... LEPT(O)
finger .... DACTYL(O)
firm .... STERE(O)
fish .... PISCI
flat .... PLAT(Y)
flesh .... SARC(O)
flow .... RHEO
foot ...... PED(E), PED(I)
freezing .... CRY(O)
French .... GALLO
fruit .... CARP(O)
fungus .... MYC(O)
gall ..... CHOL(O), CHOLE
gaseous .... AERI
glass .... HYALO
grain .... GRANI
gyrating .... GYRO
hair .... CHAET(O)
hand .. CHIRO, CHEIRO
hatred .... MIS(O)
height .... HYPSO
hidden .... CRYPT(O)
hide .... DERMAT(O)
horn .. CERAT(O), KERATO
horse .... HIPPO
hundred .... CENTI,
                HECT(O)
identical .... ISO
inner .... END(O)
insect(s) .... ENTOMO
inside .... INTRA, INTRO
intestine ...... ENTER(O)
iron .... FERRO
latest .... CENE, NEO
liking .... PHIL(E)
lime .... CALCI

lip .... CHIL(O)
little .... MICR(O)
liver .... HEPAT(O)
male/man ...... ANDR(O)
many .... POLY
Mars .... AREO
masculine ..... ANDR(O)
milky .... GALACT(O)
minute .... MICR(O)
moon .... LUNI
moving .... KINETO
much .... POLY
nitrogen .... AZO
one and a half .. SESQUI
one tenth of ...... DECI
other .... HETER(O)
outside .... ECT(O)
people .... ETHN(O)
personal .... IDIO
pointed .... STYL(O)
poor .... CAC(O)
prickly .... ECHIN(O)
race .... ETHN(O)
radiant .... HELI(O)
red .... ERYTHR(O)
rib(s) .... COST(O)
secondary → . DEUTER(O),
                DEUT(O)
secret .... CRYPT(O)
self .... AUTO
seven .. SEPTEM, HEPT(A)
shaft .... SCAPI
sham .... PSEUD(O)
sharp .... STYL(O)
short .... BRACHY
similar .... ISO
simple .... HAPL(O)
single .... HAPL(O)
skin .... DERMAT(O),
                DERM(O)
sleep .... HYPN(O)
slender .... LEPT(O)
small .... MICR(O)
solid .... STERE(O)
spiny .... ECHIN(O)
spiral .. GYRO, HELIC(O)
stalk .... SCAPI
stationary .... STAT
stomach ...... GASTR(O)
stone .. LITH, LITE, LYTE
sun .... HELI(O)
swelling .... CELE
tallow .... SEBI
teeth .. ODONT(O), DENT(I)
ten .... DEC(A)
terrible .... DINO

thin .... LEPT(O)
tissue .... HIST(O)
tooth .. DENTI, ODONT(O)
transparent .... HYAL(O)
tree .. DENDRO, DENDR(I),
    DENDRON
tumor .... CELE
twin .... DIPL(O)
two .... DIPL(O)
universe .... COSM(O)
water .... HYDR(O)
wave .... CYMO
wax .... CERO, SEBI
weight .... BARO
whole .... HOLO
wing .... PTERO
within .. END(O), INTRA,
    INTRO
woman .... GYN(E)O,
    GYNOUS
wood .... HYL(O)
wool .... LANI
world .... COSM(O)
worship .... LATRY
writing .... GRAPHO
yellow(ish) .... LUTEO
combustible .... IMFLAMMABLE,
    EXCITABLE, FIERY
combustion ... BURNING, FIRE
come .... ARRIVE, APPEAR,
    OCCUR, RESULT
about ... OCCUR, HAPPEN
across .... GIVE, PAY UP,
    MEET
afterwards .... ENSUE
around .. REVIVE, YIELD,
    VISIT
back .... RETURN, RECUR
before .... PRECEDE
between .... DIVIDE,
    INTERVENE
by .... GAIN, ACQUIRE
down .... ALIGHT, LAND
forth .... APPROACH,
    EMERSE
forward .... VOLUNTEER,
    ADVANCE
into ... INHERIT, ACQUIRE
into view .. LOOM, PEER,
    PEEP
on! .... HURRY(UP)
ons .... LURES, BAITS
out .... EMERGE
out even .... DRAW, TIE
to grips with ... TANGLE
to mind .... OCCUR

to pass .. HAPPEN, OCCUR'
    TRANSPIRE
to rest .... SETTLE
to terms .... AGREE
to view .. APPEAR, LOOM
together ...... GATHER
up .... ARISE
up to .... EQUAL
upon .. CHANCE, MEET
comeback .... RETORT,
    REPARTEE, REJOINDER,
    RIPOSTE
comedian .... BUFFO, COMIC,
    ZANY, JESTER, PIERROT
circus .... CLOWN
deadpan .... KEATON
foil of .. .. STOOGE,
    STRAIGHTMAN
forte ...... JOKES, GAGS,
    CRACKS, TOMFOOLERY,
    HORSEPLAY
missile of .... PIE
of note .... (BOB) HOPE,
    (ED)WYNN, FERNANDEL,
    (JERRY) LEWIS,
    (JACK) BENNY, (BUSTER)
    KEATON, (RED) SKELTON,
    (STAN) LAUREL, (OLIVER)
    HARDY, (BERT) LAHR
comedienne .. (FANNY) BRICE,
    (ZAZU) PITTS,
    (LUCY) BALL
comedo .... BLACKHEAD
comedy .. FARCE, SLAPSTICK,
    BURLESQUE, HORSEPLAY
character ...... PIERROT,
    ZANY
symbol .... SOCK
comely .... HANDSOME,
    DECOROUS, PRETTY, FAIR,
    GAINLY
woman .... BUXOM
comensal .... INQUILINE
comestible(s) ...... EATABLE,
    EDIBLE, VICTUAL, FOOD
comet .... BIELA'S, HALLEY'S,
    HOLMES', SWIFT'S, ALCOCK'S
envelope .... COMA
head's part .... NUCLEUS
nucleus and coma ......
    HEAD
part .... TAIL, TRAIN
comeuppance: sl. ....
    PUNISHMENT
comfit .... CONFECTION,
    PRALINE, CANDY, SWEETMEAT

comfort .. CONSOLE, SOOTHE, SOLACE, EASE
comfortable .... SNUG, COSE, COZY
  chair .... ROCKER
comic .... COMEDIAN, FUNNY, HUMOROUS, AMUSING, DROLL, LAUGHABLE
  afterpiece .... EXODE
  element in play .. HOKUM
  opera .. BOUFFE, BUFFO, BUFFA
  relief .. SKIT, AFTERPIECE
  strip .... CARTOONS
  strip brat .. HANS, FRITZ
  strip character ....
    MILQUETOAST, LULU, SLUGGO, NANCY, MUTT, JEFF, (LIL) ABNER, (ETTA) KETT, JIGGS
  strip vocals .. BALLOON(S)
  theatrical sketch ... SKIT
  with wooden sword .....
    HARLEQUIN
comical ...... FUNNY, DROLL, HUMOROUS, ZANY
  very .... KILLING
coming .. ADVENT, APPROACH
  early in the day ....
    RATH(E)
  from outside .. ENTHETIC, EXTRANEOUS
  of tide .... FLUX
  out party .... DEBUT
  to an end ... MORIBUND
comity .... COURTESY, POLITENESS
comma .... PAUSE, MARK
  shaped organism ....
    VIBRIO
command .. DICTATE, CHARGE, DIRECT, BID(DING), BEHEST, ORDER, ENJOIN
  authoritative .. MANDATE
  level of .... ECHELON
  market .... CORNER, MONOPOLIZE
  station .... POST
  to helmsman ... STEADY
  to horse .... GEE, WHOA, HAW
  to huskies .... MUSH
commander .... LEADER
  Egyptian .... SIRDAR
  in-chief, U.S. ....
    PRESIDENT

  of 1000 men: Roman ....
    CHILIARCH
  rod/staff of ..... WARDER
commanding .... DOMINATING, IMPRESSIVE
commandment ..... PRECEPT, ORDER, LAW
  in Judaism .... MITZVAH
Commandments, the Ten ....
    DECALOG(UE)
commando .... RAIDER
  assignment .... MISSION
  specialty .... SABOTAGE, RAID, DEMOLITION
comme il faut ...... PROPER, FITTING
commemorate .... CELEBRATE, OBSERVE
commemorative ... MEMORIAL
  piece .... MEDAL
commence .... BEGIN, START, OPEN
commencement .... START, BEGINNING
  address .... VALEDICTORY
  exercise .... GRADUATION
commend ..... EXTOL, LAUD, ENTRUST, PRAISE, CITE
commensurate ....
    PROPORTIONATE, EVEN
comment ...... ANNOTATION, REMARK, TALK, DESCANT
  adverse ...... CRITICISM
  at bottom of page .....
    FOOTNOTE
  derisive .... JEER
  favorable .. PRAISE, RAVE
  marginal ...... MARGENT
  on disapprovingly ......
    ANIMADVERT
commentary .... MEMOIR, REMARK, OBSERVATION, CRITIQUE
commentator .... CRITIC, ANNOTATOR
  newspaper ...... EDITOR, COLUMNIST
commerce .. TRADE, BUSINESS, TRAFFIC
commercial ...... MERCANTILE
  agent .... CONSUL
  paper, worthless .... KITE
  spy .... KEEK
comminate ...... CURSE, BAN
commingle .... BLEND, (INTER)MIX

comminute ～～～ PULVERIZE, GRIND, MILL, CRUSH

comminution, product of ～～～ POWDER, TALC, DUST

commiseration ～～～～～ PITY, EMPATHY, COMPASSION

commissary ～ DEPUTY, STORE, CANTEEN

colloquial ～～～～～ PX

commission ～～～～～～ ORDER, EMPOWER, AUTHORITY, DOING, AUTHORIZE

grafter's ～～～ KICKBACK

slang ～～～～ RAKE-OFF

commissure ～～～ JOINT, SEAM

commit ～～～ CONSIGN, BIND, ENGAGE, ENTRUST

in mind ～～～～ MEMORIZE

perjury ～～～～ FORSWEAR

to paper ～～～～ RECORD

commitment ～～～～～ PLEDGE, PROMISE, UNDERTAKING

commix ～～～～～ BLEND

commode ～～ CHEST, BUREAU, CHIFFONIER, WASHSTAND, TOILET

commodious ～～～～ ROOMY, SPACIOUS

commodity ～ WARE, ARTICLE, STAPLE

control of ～～ OLIGOPOLY

common ～～～ PUBLIC, USUAL, GENERAL, LOW, AVERAGE, ORDINARY, MUTUAL

arithmetic ～～～ LOGISTIC

carrier ～～～ BUS, TRAIN, COACH

footing ～～～～～ PAR

people ～～～～ MASSES, POPULACE, DEMOS, PLEBS, PLEBE, FOLKS, HOI-POLLOI

people, of the ～～～～～ GRASS ROOTS

run ～～～～～～ RUCK

saying ～～ SAW, ADAGE, PROVERB

sense ～ SAVVY, GUMPTION

talk ～ RUMOR, HEARSAY, GOSSIP

to both sexes ～ EPICENE

commoner ～～～ LOWBORN, ROTURIER

commonly accepted ～～～～ VULGATE

supposed ～～ PUTATIVE

commonplace ～～～ ORDINARY, USUAL, TRITE, PROSAIC, BANAL, HUMDRUM, BOURGEOIS

expression ～～ BROMIDE, CLICHE, PLATITUDE, TRUISM

commonsense ～～～～ SAVVY, GUMPTION

commotion ～ TURMOIL, STIR, TO-DO, HUBBUB, ADO, BROUHAHA, FUSS, POTHER, UPROAR, SHINDY, FLURRY, MUSS

commove ～～～～～ EXCITE

communal ～～～～～ PUBLIC

marriage ～～ HETAERISM

commune ～～ CONVERSE, MIR, KIBBUTZ, ANS, ATH, EDE, EPE

communicable ～ CONTAGIOUS

communicate ～～～ IMPART, TRANSMIT

communication ～～～～～ INFORMATION, MESSAGE

form of ～～～～ SIGNAL, LETTER, TALK, ORAL, CODE

means of ～～ TELEPHONE, TELEGRAPH, RADIO, WORD, SIGN, CABLE

communications satellite ～～ TELSTAR

signal set ～～～～ CODE

communicative ～～ TALKATIVE

communion ～～～～ SHARING

cloth ～～～～ CORPORAL

cup ～～～～～～ AMA

Holy ～～～ EUCHARIST, SACRAMENT

plate ～～～～～ PATEN

table ～～～～ CREDENCE

communique ～～ STATEMENT, BULLETIN

communism, exponent of ～～ MARX, ENGELS

Communist curtain ～～ IRON, BAMBOO

Party member ～～～～～ COMRADE

policy body ～ POLITBURO

spy ～ BURGESS, MACLEAN, PHILBY

youth league ～ COMSOMOL

community ～ PUBLIC, SOCIETY, SIMILARITY, TOWN

of creatures ～～ COLONY

of Greek monks/hermits

.... SKETE
of peasants: Russ. .. MIR
commutator ...... RHEOTROPE
commute .. EXCHANGE, TRAVEL
Comoro Islands capital ......
            MORONI
  island .... MAYOTTE
comose .... HAIRY
compact .... BRIEF, TERSE,
  DENSE, SOLID, AGREEMENT,
            THICK, SERRIED
  between nations ....
            TREATY
  mass .... WAD
companion .... COMRADE,
  ASSOCIATE, MATE, FERE
  at meals .... COMMENSAL
  close .. COMRADE, BUDDY
  colloquial .... SIDEKICK
  constant .... ALTER EGO,
            SHADOW
  of back .... FORTH
  of bill .... COO
  of black .. WHITE, BLUE
  of blue .... RED, WHITE
  of bolts .... NUTS
  of bread ...... BUTTER
  of cease .... DESIST
  of fits .... STARTS
  of hook ... CROOK, LINE,
            SINKER
  of huff .... PUFF
  of kit .... CABOODLE
  of mortise ...... TENON
  of oro .... PLATA
  of snick .... SNEE
  of stars .... STRIPES
  of Tom .... DICK, HARRY
  of turn .... TOSS
  of wrack .... RUIN
companionway .. STAIR, WALK
companionship ...... SOCIETY
company .... SOCIETY, BAND,
            FIRM, TROOP
  amusing .... CAST
  colloquial .... GUEST(S),
            VISITOR(S)
  commander ... CAPTAIN
  French .... CIE
  of hunters ...... SAFARI
  of players ..... TROUPE,
            TEAM
  of soldiers ..... TROOPS
  of ten soldiers ....
            DECURION
  of travelers ... CARAVAN,

            CARAVANSARY
  part .... SEPARATE
comparable .... SIMILAR
compare .... COLLATE,
            CONTRAST, LIKEN
  beyond ...... PEERLESS,
            NONPAREIL
  critically ...... COLLATE
compartment .. STALL, BOOTH,
            LOCKER
  grain/hay .... BAY
  in aircraft ..... CAPSULE
  small/sleeping .. CUBICLE
compass .. UNDERSTAND, GAIN,
  SCOPE, SURROUND, REACH
  beam .... TRAMMEL
  cardinal point .... EAST,
  NORTH, WEST, SOUTH
  case .... BINNACLE
  dial .... CARD
  face of .... DIAL
  plant .... ROSINWEED
  point .... QUARTER,
            R(H)UMB
  sight .... VANE
  zero of .... NORTH
compassion .... PITY, MERCY,
            GRACE, EMPATHY
compatible ...... CONGRUOUS
compeer ... EQUAL, COMRADE
compel .. FORCE, CONSTRAIN,
  OBLIGE, DRIVE, INTIMIDATE,
            COERCE
compelling .... COGENT
  influence .... PRESSURE,
            DURESS
compend .... BREVIARY
compendium ...... SUMMARY,
  DIGEST, SYLLABUS, PRECIS
compensation ...... PAY, FEE
  for loss ..... INDEMNITY,
            DAMAGES
  for service ..... SALARY,
            WAGE, STIPEND
compete ...... CONTEND, VIE
competence .. SKILL, ABILITY,
            CAPACITY
competent ... CAPABLE, ABLE,
            FIT
  mentally .... SANE
competition .... RIVALRY,
  STRIFE, MATCH, CONTEST,
            OPPOSITION
competitor ..... (COR)RIVAL,
  CONTENDER, ENTRANT, ENTRY
Compiegne river ...... OISE

compilation .... COLLECTION,
                     SELECTION
   of anecdotes .. MEMOIRS
   of stories, poems ....
                     ANTHOLOGY
compiler ...... ANTHOLOGIST,
   ENCYCLOPEDIST, CERF, RILEY,
                     GLOSSARIST
   Arthurian tales .. MALORY
   English words ... ROGET
   population data ....
                     CENSUS TAKER
   quotations .... BARTLETT
complain ..... GRIPE, ACCUSE,
   CARP, GROUSE, BEEF,
   GRUMBLE, BELLYACHE,
   CRAB, KICK, YAMMER
complainer, habitual .. GROUSE
complainant ...... ACCUSER,
   PLAINTIFF, LITIGANT
complaining ...... QUERULOUS
   cry .... WHINE
complaint .... GRIEVANCE,
   CLAMOR, SQUAWK, GROUSE,
   AILMENT, ILLNESS, CHARGE,
   PROTEST, KICK, WHINE
   muttered ..... MURMUR
   part of ...... GRAVAMEN
complaisant ...... OBLIGING,
                     POLITE
complete ...... FULL, ENTIRE,
   WHOLE, TOTAL, INTACT,
   OUTRIGHT, RANK, UTTER
   attendance .... PLENARY
   disorder .... CHAOS
   entity .... INTEGER
   consumption ....
                     EXHAUSTION
   not .... PARTIAL
completed ..... DONE, ENDED,
   FINISHED, OVER
completely .... UTTERLY
   occupied .... RAPT,
   ENGROSSED, BUSY
   united .... SOLIDARY
complex .... INTRICATE,
   INVOLVED, MIXED UP,
                     NETWORK
   get .... THICKEN
   kind of .... INFERIORITY,
                     OEDIPUS
complexion .... TEMPERAMENT,
   COLOR, ASPECT
complexity ...... INTRICACY
compliant .... SUBMISSIVE,
   OBEDIENT, WEAK, TRACTABLE

complicated ...... INVOLVED,
   COMPLEX, KNOTTY
complication ... MESS, NODUS,
                     SNAG
compliment .. PRAISE, TOAST,
   CONGRATULATE, LAUD
   exaggerated ... FLATTERY
   kind of .... LEFT-HANDED
complot .... CONSPIRE,
                     CONSPIRACY
comply .... OBEY, ACCEDE
compo .... PLASTER, MORTAR
component .. PART, ELEMENT,
   INGREDIENT, CONSTITUENT,
                     UNIT
   of atom .... PROTON
comport .... BEHAVE, ACT
comportment ...... CONDUCT,
                     BEHAVIOR
compos mentis .... SANE
   non .... MAD, CRAZY,
                     INSANE
compose .... CONSTITUTE,
   FRAME, CREATE, ADJUST,
                     WRITE
   differences ... RECONCILE
   in printing .... TYPE
composed .... COOL, WROTE,
                     CALM
composer ...... SONGWRITER,
   DEBUSSY, PUCCINI, HAYDN,
   CHOPIN, BACH, TUNESMITH,
   HARMONIST, WEBER, BIZET,
                     RAVEL, WAGNER
   great .... MAESTRO
   in printing shop ....
   TYPESETTER, LINOTYPIST
   of marches ...... SOUSA
   of poems .... BARD,
   RHYMER, VERSIFIER
   opera .. BIZET, WAGNER,
   VERDI, LEHAR, DONIZETTI
   of Thais ...... MASSENET
composers' group ..... ASCAP
composite .... COMPOUND,
                     INTEGRAL
composition ⇁ ESSAY, THEME,
                     OPUS
   artistic .... PIECE
   for nine instruments ....
                     NONET
   for organ ..... TOCCATA
   for piano ..... BALLADE,
   STUDE, TOCCATA
   for practice ..... ETUDE
   for seven ... SEPTET(TE)

for three ~ ~ ~ ~ ~ TRIO
for two .... ~ DUET
hodgepodge musical ~ ~
    MEDLEY, CENTO
musical .. OPUS, SONATA,
    CONCERTO, ORATORIO,
    ETUDE, MOTET,
    RONDO, SUITE,
    FANTASIA, SERENADE,
    NOCTURNE
operatic . ~ ~ ~ ~ ~ SCENA
sacred ... ~ .. ~ ~ ~ MOTET
compositor ~ ~ ~ LINOTYPIST,
    TYPESETTER
guide of ~ ~ ~ ~ ~ JIGGER
compost heap part ~ .. ~ HUMUS
composure .... CALMNESS,
    EQUANIMITY, POISE, AIR,
    SANG-FROID
compound ~ .. ~ COMBINE, MIX,
    CONCOCT
  carbon ~ ~ ~ ~ CARBIDE
  of silica ~ ~ ~ ~ GLASS
  raceme .... PANICLE
  words' separation of parts
    TMESIS
comprador ~ ~ ~ ~ ~ BUYER
comprehend ~ ... UNDERSTAND,
    INCLUDE, GRASP, SEE
comprehensible .... ~
    INTELLIGIBLE, EXOTERIC
comprehension .... ~ GRASP
  thru intellect .... NOESIS
compress ... PAD, CONTRACT,
    DOSSIL, WRING, SQUEEZE
comprise .. INCLUDE, CONTAIN
compromise . ~ TRIM, ADJUST,
    ENDANGER
compulsion .. FORCE, DURESS,
    CONSTRAINT, COACTION
compulsive craze,
  obsession, etc. ~ MANIA
  petty thievery .... ~ ~
    KLEPTOMANIA
compulsory ~ ~ ~ ~ COERCIVE,
    OBLIGATORY, MANDATORY
  military service .. DRAFT,
    CONSCRIPTION, LEVY
compunction ...... PENITENCE,
    SCRUPLE, QUALM, REMORSE
compurgation ~ .. ~ CLEARANCE
computation ... CALCULATION
compute ~ .. RECKON, FIGURE,
    CALCULATE
computer, type of ~ .. ANALOG,
    DIGITAL, IBM

computerize ~ ~ ~ AUTOMATE
computing device .... ~ ~ .. ~
    COMPTOMETER, ABACUS,
    SLIDE RULE
comrade ~ ~ ~ ~ FRIEND, PAL,
    COMPANION, PARTNER,
    BUDDY, TOVARISCH, FRATER,
    KAMERAD
comte ~ ~ ~ ~ ~ ~ ~ ~ COUNT
con ~ ~ . STUDY, READ, ANTI,
    AGAINST, PERUSE
  amore ~ ~ ~ . TENDERLY,
    WITH LOVE
  man ~ SWINDLER, SHILL,
    GRIFTER, STEEPER
  over ~ ~ ~ ~ ~ ~ ~ SCAN
  slang ~ ~ ~ . CONFIDENCE,
    SWINDLE
  vessel ~ ~ ~ ~ ~ ~ . STEER
concatenate ... ~ ~ ~ LINK(ED)
concave molding ~ . CAVETTO,
    SCOTIA
conceal ~ ~ ~ ~ HIDE, SECRETE,
    CLOAK
  goods ~ CACHE, HOARD,
    ELOI(G)N
  in law ~ ~ ~ ~ ~ ELOIN
concealed ... ~ ~ CLANDESTINE,
    HIDDEN, COVERT, PERDUE
  sharpshooter ~ ~ SNIPER
concealment, attack from ~ ~
  AMBUSH, AMBUSCADE, SNIPE
concede ~ ~ ~ ~ YIELD, GRANT,
    ADMIT
conceit ~ ~ ~ ~ VANITY, PRIDE,
    EGO(ISM), TYMPANY
  colloquial ~ ~ BIGHEAD
conceited .. VAIN(GLORIOUS),
    PROUD, EGO(T)ISTIC,
    STUCK-UP
  person ~ ~ ~ ~ PEACOCK,
    EGO(T)IST
conceive ~ ~ ~ . THINK, IDEATE,
    IMAGINE
concenter ~ CONVERGE, FOCUS
concentrate .. FOCUS, COLLECT
concentration camp, German ~
    STALAG, DACHAU
concept .. ~ ~ ~ IDEA, NOTION
conception ~ ~ ~ ~ IDEA, HENT,
    IDEATION
  product of ~ ~ EMBRYO,
    BRAINCHILD
concern ~ ... ~ AFFAIR, CARE,
    WORRY, SOLICITUDE,
    LOOKOUT

concerned .. UNEASY, ANXIOUS
concerning .... ABOUT, ANENT,
INRE
concert .... CONCORD
hall .... AUDITORIUM,
ODEUM
in .... TOGETHER
master's instrument .....
VIOLIN
organizer .... IMPRESARIO
outdoor platform ....
BANDSHELL
concertina kin ... ACCORDION
concession ... GRANT, RIGHT,
PRIVILEGE, FRANCHISE
kind of .... SOP
conch .... SHELL
concha .... APSE
Conchobar's intended ....
DEIRDRE
concierge ..... DOORKEEPER,
JANITOR, CARETAKER
conciliate .. PLACATE, PACIFY,
APPEASE, SOOTHE, MOLLIFY
conciliatory theology ....
IRENICS
concise — BRIEF, TERSE, PITHY,
SUCCINCT, LACONIC
conclave .... MEETING
conclude .... CLOSE, END,
DEDUCE, INFER, FINISH,
TERMINATE
a speech ...... PERORATE
concluding passage in music ..
CODA, STRETTO, STRETTA,
FINALE
conclusion .... OUTCOME, END,
RESULT, DECISION, JUDGMENT,
FINIS(H), FINDING
in .... LASTLY
judge's .... FINDING
conclusive ... DECISIVE, FINAL
blow: sl. .. SOCKDOLOGER,
HAYMAKER
point .... CLINCHER
concoct .. DEVISE, PLAN, BREW,
HATCH, MIX, COOK-UP,
COMPOUND
concoction, liquid ... COFFEE,
TEA, COCKTAIL
concomitant .... ATTENDANT
concord .. ONENESS, HARMONY,
GRAPE, UNISON, TREATY
concordant ..... HARMONIOUS
concordat .... COMPACT,

COVENANT, AGREEMENT,
ENTENTE
concourse .. CROWD, THRONG
concrete ..... REAL, ACTUAL,
SPECIFIC, BETON
being .... ENS
concubinage ..... HETAERISM,
HETAIRISM
concubine in harem .. ODALISK,
ODALISQUE
concupiscence .... LUST
concur ...... ACCEDE, AGREE,
ASSENT, CONSENT, COINCIDE
concurrence .... ACCORD,
AGREEMENT
concussion .. SHOCK, SHAKING
condemn ... CENSURE, DOOM,
CONVICT, DENOUNCE, DECRY
condemnation ...... DECRIAL
condemned heretic's garment
.... SANBENITO
condense .... COMPRESS,
CONTRACT, ABRIDGE,
INSPISSATE
condensed form .... CAPSULE
moisture .... DEW
condenser .... CAPACITOR
condescend .... DEIGN, STOOP
condescending .. PATRONIZING,
HOITY-TOITY
condign .. DESERVED, FITTING,
SUITABLE
condiment .. SPICE, VINEGAR,
SEASONING, RELISH, SAUCE,
MACE, MUSTARD, PEPPER,
PAPRIKA, PAPRICA
bottle/container ....
CASTER, CRUST
condition ..... IF, PROVISION,
STATE, STATUS, ACCUSTOM,
CASE, FIG, FETTLE
contract ... STIPULATION,
TERM, PROVISO
of body .... HEALTH
of decline ... DECADENCE
of great vitality .. STHENIA
of oblivion ...... LIMBO
of payment ..... TERMS
of servitude .. BONDAGE,
SLAVERY
of stupor .... COMA,
NARCOSIS
conditional surrender ....
CAPITULATION
HUDDLE, CAUCUS, PARLEY,
JUNTA

conditions of possession .... TENURE
condole .... COMMISERATE
condone .... FORGIVE, OVERLOOK, PARDON
condor .... VULTURE
conduce .... TEND, LEAD, CONTRIBUTE
conduct ..... WAGE, BEHAVIOR, ESCORT, MANAGE
in polite society .... ETIQUETTE
under guard .... CONVOY, ESCORT
conductor ..... GUIDE, LEADER, MAESTRO
orchestra .... TOSCANINI, BEECHAM, BERNSTEIN, BARBIROLLI, MEHTA, BOULEZ, ORMANDY
platform of ...... PODIUM
stick .... BATON
tourists' ...... CICERONE, GUIDE, DRAGOMAN
woman .... QUACH
conduit .... MAIN, PIPE, SEWER, DRAIN
cone .... STROBILE
bearing tree ... PINE, FIR, SPRUCE, CYPRESS, PINASTER, LARCH, CEDAR, YEW, CONIFER, JUNIPER, ZAMIA
seed-bearing ... STROBIL(E)
shaped .... CONOID, PINEAL, CONIC(AL), TURBINATE
shaped paper container ... CORNUCOPIA
shaped pile ...... COCK
shaped yarn roll .... COP
spiral .... HELIX
conepate .... SKUNK
coney ...... RODENT, RABBIT, DAMAN, HYRAX
confab ...... TALK, CHAT, POWWOW
confection .... PRALINE, BONBON, CONFITURE, SWEETMEAT, COMFIT
almond .... NOUGAT, MARZIPAN, MARCHPANE
cold .... ICE CREAM
flavor .... VANILLA
sugar .... CANDY
Turkish .... HALVAH

confederacy ...... ALLIANCE
confederate .... ACCOMPLICE, ALLY
general .... LEE, BRAGG, HAMPTON, LONGSTREET
president .... DAVIS
soldier, Civil War .. REB
confederation .... BUND
confer ... BESTOW, CONVERSE, AWARD, ENDOW
privately .... COLLOGUE
conference .... MEETING, CONFAB, PALAVER, POWWOW, Indian .... POWWOW
private .... HUDDLE, CAUCUS, TETE-A-TETE
site of 1945 ...... YALTA
site of 1943 ...... CAIRO, TEHERAN
conferred, thing ..... HONOR, FAVOR, TITLE, RIGHT, DEGREE
conferring respect ....
HONORIFIC
confess .. ADMIT, OWN, AVOW
slang ..... SING, SQUEAL, PEACH
confession ...... ADMISSION, REVELATION, AVOWAL
of faith .. CREED, CREDO
"Confessions" author ....
ROUSSEAU
confetti .. CANDIES, PAPER BITS
confidant .... FRIEND
confide ...... ENTRUST, TELL
confidence .... TRUST, SECRET, ASSURANCE
game .... SWINDLE, THIMBLERIG, SHELL GAME, BUNCO, BUNKO
game item .. SEED, CUP, NUTSHELL
man .... CON, SWINDLER, STEERER, SHILL, GRIFTER
show of .... BRAVADO
confident ... ASSURED, SURE, CERTAIN, BOLD, SECURE
confidential ...... ESOTERIC, SECRET, PRIVATE
advisers' group ....
CAMARILLA, CABAL
disclosure/warning .....
TIP-OFF
confiding .... TRUSTFUL
confine ..... RESTRICT, LIMIT, IMMURE, BOX, PEN, CAGE, FETTER, HEM

to a place ..... LOCALIZE
confined .... PENT(UP)
  in circulation .... CLOSE
confinement, place of ....
  PRISON, HOSPITAL, ASYLUM
  cause of .... ILLNESS,
  CONVICTION
confirm .... VERIFY, VALIDATE,
  RATIFY, ATTEST,
  SUBSTANTIATE
confirmation .. RITE, EVIDENCE,
  VERIFICATION, SACRAMENT
confirmed ...... INVETERATE,
  ARRANT, CHRONIC, HABITUAL
confiscate .... SEIZE, ESCHEAT
  APPROPRIATE,
confiture .. PRESERVE, CANDY,
  SWEETMEAT,
conflict .... CLASH, DISCORD,
  STRUGGLE, CONTEST, FIGHT,
  STOUR, STRIFE, JAR
  armed .... WAR
  of characters in drama ..
  AGON
confluence .... CROWD
conform ..... ADAPT, AGREE
conforming to morals ....
  ETHICAL
conformist .... ASSENTER
  kind of .... YESMAN
confound .. STUMP, CONFUSE,
  BEWILDER, PUZZLE
confraternity .. BROTHERHOOD
confrere .... COLLEAGUE,
  ASSOCIATE
confront .. FACE, STAND, MEET
confuse .... DISCONCERT,
  PUZZLE, FLUMMOX, ABASH,
  PERPLEX, FLABBERGAST,
  BEWILDER, CONFOUND
confused .. ADDLED, HAYWIRE,
  MUZZY
confusion .... CHAOS, MESS,
  DISORDER, DISARRAY,
  JUMBLE, MOIL, MUDDLE,
  RUCKUS, WELTER, TANGLE,
  MIX-UP
  of tongues .... BABEL
  sudden .... FLURRY
conge .. DISMISSAL, FAREWELL
congeal .... GEL, FREEZE, SET,
  SOLIDIFY, JELL, CURDLE
congealed water (vapor) .. ICE,
  SNOW
congealer, wound ... COMFREY
congenial .. BOON, FRIENDLY,
AGREEABLE
congenital .. INBORN, INNATE,
  CONNATE
  mark .... MOLE
conger .... EEL
  trap .... EELPOT
congeries .... HEAP, PILE,
  COLLECTION
congest .... OVERCROWD
Congo .. EEL, TEA, DYE, RIVER
  capital ... BRAZZAVILLE,
  KINSHASA
  city ...... POINTE-NOIRE,
  KISANGANI
  dwarf .... AKKA, ACHUAS
  ethnic group ... BAI ALI,
  BAVILI, BATEKE, HAMITE,
  BANTU
  language .... BANTU,
  SWAHILI, LINGALA
  peanut .... NGUBA
  premier .... ADOULA,
  LUMUMBA, TSHOMBE
  president .... KASAVUBU,
  YOULOU, MOBUTU
  province .. KWILU, KIVA,
  KATANGA
  red .... SALT
  river tributary .. UBANGI
  tribesman .... SIMBA
congou .... TEA
congratulate .... FELICITATE,
  HAIL, SALUTE, COMMEND
congratulatory ... GRATULANT
congregate .... COLLECT,
  GATHER, ASSEMBLE
congregation ...... ASSEMBLY,
  ASSEMBLAGE, FLOCK, FOLD,
  PARISH
congress .. MEETING, ASSEMBLY,
  LEGISLATURE
  attendant .... PAGE
  concern of ...... BILLS,
  RESOLUTIONS, BUDGET
  time off .... RECESS
congressman not reelected ....
  LAMEDUCK
congruence ...... AGREEMENT
congruity .. FITNESS, HARMONY
congruous .... FIT(TING),
  SUITABLE
conic section .... CURVE,
  ELLIPSE, PARABOLA
conical roll of yarn ..... COP
conifer .... PINE, CEDAR,
SPRUCE, YEW, FIR, LARCH

coniferous forest ...... TAIGA
conium .... HEMLOCK
conjecture .... SURMISE,
    GUESS(WORK), THEORY
conjoin ..... UNITE, CONNECT
conjoint .... UNITED
conjugal ..... MATRIMONIAL,
    CONNUBIAL, MARITAL
conjugate ..... UNITE, COUPLE
conjugation .... SYNGAMY
conjunction ..... UNION, AND,
    COINCIDENCE, OR, BUT, SINCE
    in biology ...... ZYGOSIS
conjunctivitis ..... TRACHOMA
conjuration .. MAGIC, SORCERY
conjure .... SUMMON, INVOKE,
    CALL UPON
conjuror ... MAGICIAN, MAGE,
    SORCERER, WARLOCK,
    WIZARD
    stick of .... WAND, ROD
    words of .. HOCUS-POCUS
conk .... KNOCK
    British slang ...... NOSE,
    HEAD, BLOW
    out .... FAIL
connate .... INBORN, INNATE,
    CONGENITAL
connect ...... JOIN, COUPLE,
    ASSOCIATE, LINK
    secretly .... TAP
Connecticut, capital of ......
    HARTFORD
    city .... DANBURY,
    STAMFORD, MERIDEN,
    HARTFORD
    nickname ...... NUTMEG
    official, borough ....
    WARDEN
    state flower ....
    (MOUNTAIN) LAUREL
    town .... LYME, HAMDEN,
    GREENWICH
connecting body of water ....
    STRAIT
    part .... LINK
    pipe .... TEE
    strip of land ... ISTHMUS
connection .... UNION,
    RELATION, CONTACT,
    NEXUS, KINSHIP
connective .... SYNDETIC
    tissue ... TENDON, FASCIA
    word .... AND, (N)OR,
    (N)EITHER

Connelly, playwright ....
    MARC(US)
Connie Mack's ballpark .....
    SHIBE
conning tower adjunct ....
    PERISCOPE
conniption .... TANTRUM
connive .... CONSPIRE,
    COOPERATE
connoisseur ...... (A)ESTHETE,
    CO(G)NOSCENTE, JUDGE
    art .... VIRTUOSO
    fine foods/drinks ....
    GO(U)RMAND, GOURMET,
    EPICURE
connubial .... CONJUGAL,
    MARITAL
conquer .... OVERCOME,
    DEFEAT, SUBDUE,
    VANQUISH, SUBJUGATE
conquerable .... VINCIBLE
conqueror .... VICTOR
conquistador .... CORTEZ,
    PIZARRO, CONQUEROR
Conrad (Joseph) character ...
    SEAMAN, MARINER, LENA,
    AXEL
    novel .... VICTORY
consanguinity ...... KINSHIP,
    AFFINITY
conscience, twinge of ....
    SCRUPLE, QUALM, REMORSE
conscientious objector ....
    CONCHY
conscious ... (A)WARE, AWAKE,
    COGNIZANT, SENTIENT
consciousness, lose ....
    PASS OUT, FAINT, SWOON
conscript .... ENROLL,
    DRAFT(EE), FORCE,
    RECRUIT, MUSTER, LEVY
conscripted person .. DRAFTEE
consecrate .. DEVOTE, ANOINT,
    DEDICATE, HALLOW, BLESS,
    SANCTIFY
consecrated bread ....
    SACRAMENT
    Host's receptacle ....
    MONSTRANCE
    oil .... CHRISM
consecration .... BLESSING
    of the bread ... SACRING
consecutive ...... SUCCESSIVE
consensus ...... AGREEMENT,
    OPINION, SYMPOSIUM

consent ..... AGREE, CONCUR, ACCEDE, AGREEMENT
consenting .... WILLING
consequence ...... RESULT, EFFECT, OUTCOME, IMPORTANCE, SEQUEL
person of ..... BIGSHOT, BIGWIG, NABOB, TYCOON, VIP
consequently .. THUS, HENCE, THEREFORE, ERGO
conservative ..... MODERATE, PRUDENT, RIGHT(IST), REACTIONARY, TORY, STANDPAT
person .... FOG(E)Y
conservatory .. MUSIC SCHOOL, GREENHOUSE
conserve .... SAVE(UP)
fruit .... JAM
consider ..... HEED, PONDER, STUDY, WEIGH, ENTERTAIN
kindly .... FAVOR
considerable .. MUCH, LARGE, GREAT DEAL
colloquial ...... PRETTY, TIDY, GOODLY
consideration .... ESTEEM, REFLECTION, FEE
consign .. ENTRUST, RELEGATE, DELIVER
to hell .. DAMN, CONDEMN
consistency .... FIRMNESS, HARMONY, AGREEMENT
consistent .... UNIFORM, COHERENT
consisting of 100 degrees ..... CENTIGRADE
consolation .... SOLACE, COMFORT, SOP
console .... COMFORT, CHEER, BRACKET, ANCON
like bracket .... CORBEL
the bereaved ... CONDOLE
consolidate ... UNITE, MERGE, COMBINE, STRENGTHEN, STABILIZE
consomme ..... SOUP, BROTH
consonant, aspirated ... SURD
hard .... FORTIS
unaspirated ...... LENE
voiceless .... ATONIC
consonantal sound ... SPIRANT
consort ...... SPOUSE, MATE, HUSBAND, WIFE

Queen Juliana's .... BERNHARD
Queen Victoria's .... ALBERT
Siva's .... DEVI
conspicuous .... OBVIOUS, NOTICEABLE, SALIENT, OVERT
success ..... ECLAT, HIT
conspiracy .. PLOT, INTRIGUE, CONNIVANCE, CABAL
to defraud ...... COVIN
conspire .... (COM)PLOT, COLLUDE, CONNIVE, SCHEME
constable .. WARDEN, BAILIFF, POLICE(MAN), BULL, TIPSTAFF
constabulary .. (STATE)POLICE
constancy ..... CONSISTENCY, STEADINESS
constant .... CONTINUAL, FAITHFUL, CHRONIC, LOYAL, STEADY, STABLE
visitor ..... FREQUENTER
Constantinople ... ISTANBUL, ISTAMBOUL
foreign quarter ... PERA, BEYOGLU
inn .... IMARET, SERAI, CARAVANSARY
constellate .... CLUSTER
constellation ...... CLUSTER, GATHERING, NORMA
altar .... ARA
arrow .... SAGITTA
balance .... LIBRA
bear .... URSA
bird of paradise ... APUS
box .... PYXIS
brightest star ...... COR
bull .... TAURUS
centaur .... SAGITTARIUS
charioteer ...... AURIGA
crab .... CANCER
crane .... GRUS
cross .... CRUX
dog .... CANIS
dragon .... DRACO
eagle .... AQUILA
equatorial .... CETUS, ORION
fish .... PISCES
fly .... MUSCA
foot .... RIGEL
goat .... CAPRICORN
hare .... LEPUS
harp .... LYRA
hunter .... ORION

in the Zodiac .... ARIES, TAURUS, GEMINI, CANCER, LEO, VIRGO, LIBRA, SCORPIO, SAGITTARIUS, CAPRICORN(US), AQUARIUS, PISCES

lion .... LEO

Northern ...... SAGITTA, CYGNUS, AURIGA, BOOTES, PERSEUS, DRACO, DELPHINUS, CASSIOPEIA, LEO MINOR, LYRA, POLARIS, CEPHEUS, PEGASUS, ARIES, SERPENS, AQUILA, HERCULES, ANDROMEDA, LACERTA, HYDRA, VULPECULA, URSA, SCUTUM

painter .... PICTOR

peacock .... PAVO

ram .... ARIES

raven .... CORVUS

scales .... LIBRA

scorpion .... SCORPIO, SCORPIUS

serpent .... HYDRA

snake .... SERPENS

Southern .. ARA, ORION, CANIS, LUPUS, PICTOR, LEPUS, CETUS, CIRCINUS, DORADO, CRUX, CRATER, FORNAX, CENTAURUS, INDUS, VELA, PAVO, TUCANA, ERIDANUS, GRUS, HYDRUS, MENSA, MONOCEROS, NORMA, PHOENIX, APUS, MUSCA, ANTLIA, CAELUM, CARINA, PUPPIS, OCTANS, PYXIS, SEXTANS, VOLANS, SCULPTOR, CORVUS, COLUMBA

swan .... CYGNUS

twins .... GEMINI

veil .... VELA

water carrier .. AQUARIUS

whale .... CETUS

wolf .... LUPUS

woman .... VIRGO

consternation .... DISMAY, ALARM, TERROR, AMAZEMENT

constipated .... COSTIVE

constituent .... ELECTOR, COMPONENT, ELEMENT, INTEGRANT

constitution ...... STRUCTURE, COMPOSITION, MAKE-UP, BASIC LAW, CHARTER

addition to .. AMENDMENT

composition of .... ARTICLES, BY-LAWS, PREAMBLE

constitutional .... BASIC, ESSENTIAL, ORGANIC

colloquial .... WALK, EXERCISE

constrain ... FORCE, COMPEL, OBLIGE, IMPEL

constraint ..... COMPULSION, COERCION, REPRESSION

constrict .... CONTRACT, SQUEEZE, COMPRESS

constriction of duct, etc. ...... STENOSIS

constrictor .. BOA, ANACONDA, PYTHON, SPHINCTER, CRUSHER

construct ..... ERECT, BUILD, FORM, DEVISE, MAKE

construction ...... BUILDING, STRUCTURE, INTERPRETATION

battalion member ...... SEABEE

constructive .... POSITIVE, HELPFUL

arts .... TECTONICS

construe .. EXPLAIN, ANALYZE, PARSE, READ, INFER, INTERPRET

consuetude ... HABIT, CUSTOM, USAGE

consul's authority .... EXEQUATUR

consult ... CONFER, REFER TO

consultant, common .... DOCTOR, LAWYER, ENGINEER, EXPERT, TECHNICIAN

consume ..... EAT, DESTROY, USE UP, WASTE

consumer .... USER, EATER

goods .. FOOD, CLOTHING

opposed to .. PRODUCER

consummate .. END, COMPLETE, PERFECT, FINISH

is what some are ...... ARTISTS, LIARS

skill .... FINESSE

consummation .... OUTCOME, FULFILLMENT

consumption ... WASTE, USE, DESTRUCTION

lung ... ... TABES, PHTHISIS,
    TUBERCULOSIS
consumptive ... ... HECTIC,
    LUNGER
contact ... ... TOUCH, MEET,
    CONNECTION, TACTION
    in physical .. CONTIGUOUS
contagion ... POISON, MEASLES,
    INFECTION, (SMALL)POX,
    VECTION
contagious ... ... CATCHING,
    INFECTIOUS, COMMUNICABLE
contain ... ... HOLD, ENCLOSE,
    EMBODY, CHECK
container ... ... TIN, JAR, PAIL,
    BOX, CRATE, CAN, BAG,
    POUCH, KEG, BASKET
    cardboard ... ... CARTON
    dose of medicine ... ...
        CAPSULE
    animal food ... ... TROUGH
    burning oil ... ... CRESSET
    documents ... ... HANAPER
    for relics ... ... RELIQUARY,
        CUSTODIAL
    for the sacred host ... ...
        TABERNACLE
    glass ... ... CARBOY
    half-gallon ... ... POTTLE
    material for making ...
        OSIER, JUTE, FLAX, TIN,
        ALUMINUM, PLASTIC,
        BURLAP, STAVE
    metal ... ... COPPER
    of assorted things ... ...
        HANDBAG, ATTIC,
        CATCHALL
    oil ... ... AMPULLA
    pasteboard ... ... CARTON
    perforated ... ... DREDGER
    sealed ... ... CAN, TIN,
        ENVELOPE
    water ... TROUGH, TANK,
        CISTERN, RESERVOIR
    wine ... ... AMPULLA
containing defects ... FAULTY
    perforations ... ...
        FENESTRATE
contaminate ... ... POLLUTE,
    TAINT, DEFILE, SULLY,
    CORRUPT, SPOIL
contaminator, air ... ... SMOG,
    SMAZE
conte ... ... TALE, SHORT STORY
contemn ... ... DESPISE, SCORN
contemplate ... GAZE AT, MUSE,
    CONSIDER, MEDITATE
contemporaneous ... COEVAL,
    SIMULTANEOUS, CURRENT
contemporary ... ... COEVAL,
    COETANEOUS
contempt ... ... DISDAIN, SCORN
    show of ... SNIFF, SNEER,
        SNORT, FLEER
contemptible ... ... MEAN, BASE,
    VILE, LOW, ABJECT, PALTRY,
    SCURVY, LOW(DOWN)
    fellow ... ... HEEL, RASCAL,
        BLOKE, SCOUNDREL,
        CULLION, SKATE, CAD
contend ... ... FIGHT, ARGUE,
    COPE, COMPETE, VIE
contender ... ... COMPETITOR,
    CONTESTANT, RIVAL
contending parties ... ... SIDES,
    OPPONENTS, PROTAGONISTS
contendre, _____ (not contested)
    NOLO
content ... SATISFIED, CAPACITY
contention ... ... ARGUMENT,
    DISPUTE, STRIFE
    in words only ... ...
        LOGOMACHY
contest ... TOURNAMENT, AGON,
    DISPUTE, FIGHT, TOURNEY
    armed ... ... WAR
    boxing ... ... BOUT
    endurance ... MARATHON
    for two, armed ... DUEL
    in court ... ... LITIGATION,
        LITIGATE
    in law ... ... LITIGATE
    judges ... ... PANEL, JURY
    long distance ... ...
        MARATHON
    of knights ... TOURNEY,
        TILT, JOUST, DUEL
    participant ... ... ENTRY,
        ENTRANT
    second placer ... ...
        RUNNER UP
    winner ... ... CHAMPION
    with lances .. JOUST, TILT
contestant .. ENTRY, ENTRANT,
    COMPETITOR, CONTENDER
mercenary ... ... POTHUNTER
contestants as a whole .. FIELD
contiguous ... NEXT, ADJACENT,
    TOUCHING
continence ... ... MODERATION
continent ... ... TEMPERATE,
    CHASTE, MAINLAND, AFRICA,

ASIA, AUSTRALIA, EUROPE, NORTH AMERICA, SOUTH AMERICA
hypothetical .. CASCADIA, LEMURIA
icy .... ANTARCTICA
legendary .... ATLANTIS
Continental Congress president HANCOCK
contingency ..... POSSIBILITY, CHANCE, EVENT, EMERGENCY
contingent ...... DEPENDENT, FORTUITOUS, PROVISORY, GROUP, SUBJECT
continual .... CONSTANT, INCESSANT
change/movement ...... FLUX(ION)
continually ..... REPEATEDLY, CONSTANTLY, NEVER-ENDING
continuance in time .... DURATION
continuation ...... SEQUEL, RESUMPTION
continue .. PERSIST, KEEP-UP, GO ON, STAY, LAST
obsolete .... DURE
tediously .... DRAG
continued story/movie .... SERIAL
continuous ...... UNBROKEN, NONSTOP
series .... STREAM
contort .... TWIST, DEFORM, WARP
contortionist ...... HOUDINI
contour .... (OUT)LINE
of head .... PROFILE
of region .. TOPOGRAPHY
contra .... OPPOSITE
contraband .... HOT GOODS
of a sort .... BOOTLEG
contrabandist .... SMUGGLER, (RUM)RUNNER
contrabass .... VIOL(ONE)
contract .. INCUR, (COM)PACT, NARROW, AGREEMENT, SHRINK, FLEX
betrothal .... HANDFAST
bridge bid .... SLAM
brow(s) .... KNIT, FROWN
illegal labor .... YELLOW DOG
of agency .... MANDATE
rental .... LEASE
work .... INDENTURE

contraction of muscles .... SPASM, CRAMPS
contradict ..... DENY, BELIE, REBUT, REFUTE, GAINSAY
contradiction ...... DENIAL, INCONSISTENCY
in terms ...... ANTILOGY
contraption .... GADGET, CONTRIVANCE
contrary ... BALKY, OPPOSED, OBSTINATE, PERVERSE, REVERSE, WRY
to rules .... FOUL
contrast .... COMPARE
contravene .... OPPOSE, DISAGREE, VIOLATE
contribute .... GIVE, DONATE
contribution .. DONATION, GIFT
form of .... CASH, KIND
small .... MITE
to the Pope .... (PETER'S) PENCE
contrite .. REPENTANT, SORRY, REGRETFUL, PENITENT
contrition .... PENITENCE, REMORSE
contrivance ... CONTRAPTION, INVENTION, DEVICE, GADGET, GIMMICK
contrive .... DEVISE, PLAN, SCHEME
control .... DIRECT, MANAGE, RESTRAIN(T), CHECK, RULE, GRASP, GRIP, MASTERY
firm, severe .. IRON HAND
controversial ..... DEBATABLE, MOOT, ERISTIC(AL), POLEMIC(AL)
area .... SAAR, RUHR, KASHMIR, SABAH, CHACO, DAMANSKY
city .... DANZIG
theorist .... DARWIN
theory ...... EVOLUTION
controversialist ...... ERISTIC
controversy .... DEBATE, DISPUTE, QUARREL
controvert .... DISCUSS, DENY, DISPUTE, ARGUE, DEBATE, OPPUGN
contumacious .... INSUBORDINATE, DISOBEDIENT
contumely .... INSOLENCE, RUDENESS
contusion .... BRUISE, INJURY

conundrum .. RIDDLE, PUZZLE, QUESTION, ENIGMA, MYSTERY

convalescent, diet of .. GRUEL, SOUP, LIQUIDS

convene .. ASSEMBLE, SIT, CALL, SUMMON, MEET, CONVOKE

convenience .... ADVANTAGE, COMFORT, ACCOMMODATION, FACILITY

convenient .. HANDY, EXPEDIENT

convent .... NUNNERY, MONASTERY, CLOISTER

  cubicle .... CELL

  dining hall .. REFECTORY

  head .... SUPERIOR

  inmate .. CENOBITE, NUN, MONK

  member, new .... NEOPHYTE

convention ...... ASSEMBLY, CUSTOM, USAGE

  man .... DELEGATE

conventional .... CUSTOMARY, USUAL, SET, BOURGEOIS, ORTHODOX

  act .... FORMALITY

  measure of length .. PACE

conversant .... FAMILIAR, HEP

conversation .... CHAT, DIALOGUE, COLLOQUY

  between two .. DUOLOGUE

  private ..... TETE-A-TETE

  witty .... REPARTEE

conversational comeback .... RETORT, RIPOSTE

  event .... GABFEST

  expert of a sort .... WIT

  form of writing .... COLLOQUY

  style, writing in .... CAUSERIE

converse .... TALK, OPPOSITE, COMMUNE, CHAT

convert ...... (EX)CHANGE, TRANSFORM, PROSELYTE

  fat into soap .. SAPONIZE, SAPONIFY

  into money .... REALIZE, LIQUIDATE

  new .. NOVICE, NEOPHYTE

convertible into cash .. LIQUID

  vehicle .... LANDAU

convertite .... MAGDALEN

convex curve .... CAMBER

  molding .. OVOLO, TORUS, TORE, ASTRAGAL

swelling in column ...... ENTASIS

convey .. CEDE, CARRY, DEAD, TRANSPORT, TRANSMIT, TRANSFER, BRING

  beyond jurisdiction ...... ELOIN

  by deed .... REMISE

conveyance .. CARRIAGE, CAR, CARRIER, VEHICLE, CESSION

  for dead .... HEARSE

  instrument .... DEED

conveying away from center .. EFFERENT

  toward center .. AFFERENT

conveyor basket/car ... TRAM

convict ...., FELON, CONDEMN, PRISONER, CULPRIT

  privileged ...... TRUSTY

  slang .... TERMER, LIFER, LOSER, JAILBIRD, LAG

convicts, squad of .... GANG

conviction .. OPINION, BELIEF

convince .... PERSUADE

convincing .. VALID, COGENT, PERSUASIVE

convivial .. GAY, BOON, JOVIAL, FESTIVE, SOCIABLE, JOLLY, MERRY

  drinking ...... BOWL, WASSAIL

convocation ...... ASSEMBLY

convoke .... CALL, CONVENE, ASSEMBLE

convolute .... COIL

convoy .. ESCORT, ACCOMPANY, CONDUCT

convulse .... SHAKE, AGITATE

convulsion .... SPASM, FIT, UPHEAVAL, PAROXYSM

  attacks of .. ECLAMPSIA

  of rage, etc. .. PAROXYSM

cony .. DAMAN, HYRAX, DUPE, PIKA, RABBIT, FUR, DAS(SIE), GANAM

coo ...... CURR, MURMUR

  companion of .... BILL

cooer .. DOVE, PIGEON, LOVER

cooing sound .... CURR

cook by dry heat ...... BAKE

  chief .... CHEF

  colloquial ...... FALSIFY

  galley of .... CUDDY

  gently .... CODDLE

  in cream ...... SHIR(R)

  in oil/fat .... FRY

in oven .... BAKE, ROAST
specialty of .... POTPIE,
    POT ROAST
up ... CONCOCT, DEVISE,
    PLOT
cook's domain aboard ship ...
    GALLEY, CUDDY
cookbook item ...... RECIPE
cooked meat shop ....
    DELICATESSEN
   partially .... RARE
cookhouse, ship's .... GALLEY
cookies .'. SNAPS, BUNS, CAKES,
    MACAROON
cooking aid ... . SPICE,
    CONDIMENT
   art of ... . CULINARY,
    CUISINE
   directions .... RECIPE
   formula .... RECIPE
   glassware .... PYREX
   means of .. BOILING,
FRYING, BAKING, ROASTING
   odor .... NIDOR
   outfit .... KITCHEN
   pot .... OLLA
   stove .... RANGE
   style .... CUISINE
   vessel .... PAN
cooky ..... MACAROON, BUN,
   (GINGER)SNAP, JUMBLE,
   LADYFINGER, HERMIT
cool ... COMPOSED, CALM, FAN,
    QUENCH
   calm and .... COLLECTED
   color ...... BLUE, GREEN,
    GRAY
   hot liquid .... KEEL
   make .... CHILL, ICE
cooled .... FRAPPE
cooler: sl. ...... JAIL, CLINK
Coolidge Dam river .... GILA
   alma mater .... AMHERST
coolie .... LABORER
   woman ...... CHANGAR
coomb .... RAVINE
coon .... RACCOON
coop ..... COTE, HUTCH, PEN
   fly the .. ESCAPE, DECAMP,
    ABSCOND
cooper .. HOOPER, CASKMAKER
   actor ..... GARY, JACKIE
   Mohican hero of ....
    UNCAS
cooperate ... ... HELP

secretly ... . CONNIVE,
    COLLUDE
coordinate ... . HARMONIZE,
    ADJUST
Coorg's capital .... MERCARA
coot ... SCOTER, FOOL, DUCK,
   SIMPLETON, AVOCET,
   SHUFFLER, MUDHEN,
   NOTORNIS, WATERHEN
cootie .... LOUSE
cop .... TOP, CREST, HEAD
   club of .... BILLY, STICK,
   TRUNCHEON
   slang .. POLICEMAN, SEIZE,
   STEAL, BULL, FLATFOOT
copaiba .... RESIN, TUPI
copal .... RESIN, ANIME
copalm .... RESIN, TREE
cope .... VESTMENT, CANOPY,
   VAULT, SKY, CONTEND
Copenhagen is capital of .....
    DENMARK
copier .... IMITATOR
copious ...... PROFUSE, LUSH,
   PLENTIFUL, AMPLE
Copland, composer ... AARON
copper .... COIN, METAL, AES,
   CA(U)LDRON, CUPRUM
   alchemist's .... VENUS
   alloy .. AROIDE, TOMBAK,
    TOMBAC(K)
   alloy coin .... CASH
   and tin alloy .... ORMOLU
   coating .... PATINA,
   VERDIGRIS, VERD ANTIQUE
   coin .... PENNY
   color ... REDDISH BROWN
   combining form ....
    CHALCO
   gilded .... VERMEIL
   nickel .... NICCOLITE
   nickel, zinc alloy ....
    ALBATA
   ore .... CUPRITE,
    CHALCOCITE
   skin .... INDIAN
   sulphate .... VITRIOL
   tin, zinc alloy .. OROIDE
   zinc alloy .... PINCHBECK
copperah .... COPRA
copperhead .... SNAKE,
   NORTHERNER, VIPER
coppice ...... COPSE, THICKET
copra .... COPPERAH
copse ..... COPPICE, THICKET,
BOSCAGE, BOSK, HOLT, SHAW

Coptic bishop's title .... ABBA
copula .... BAND, LINK
copy .... MODEL, DUPLICATE,
    FACSIMILE, IMITATE, APE,
    ECTYPE, RESCRIPT
    closely .... MIMIC
    court record .... ESTREAT
    document's .... TENOR
    of original ...... REPLICA
    photographic ....
        PHOTOSTAT, PRINT
    read .... EDIT
copycat ..... APER, IMITATOR,
    MIMIC
copyist .... TRANSCRIBER,
    COPIER, SCRIVENER
copyread .... EDIT
copyright .... PATENT
coquet .. FLIRT, DALLY, TRIFLE
coquette .... FLIRT
coquina .. LIMESTONE
coquito .... PALM
cora .... GAZELLE
coracle ..... BOAT, CURRACH,
    CURRAGH
coral ...... POLYP, RED, ROE,
    SPAWN, ZOOID, POLYPITE
    cavity .... CALICLE
    formation .. REEF, SHELF,
    ATOLL
    group .... MADREPORE
    island .. KEY, ATOLL, REEF
    lobster's .... ROE
    part .... STOLON
    reef ...... CAY, KEY,
    MADREPORE
    source .... POLYPS
corbel ..... BRACKET, CONSOLE,
    ANCON
corbeling .... SQUINCH
corbie .... CROW, RAVEN
Corcyra .... CORFU
cord ... STRING, ROPE, TWINE,
    FUNICLE
    braided .... SENNIT
    cable end's ... MARLINE
    cattle catching .... BOLA
    drapery .... TORSADE
    head .... AGAL
    knob/lump .... KNOT
    rope end's ..... MARLINE
    strangling .... GAROTTE,
    GARROTE
    tip .... TAG, A(I)GLET
    trimming .... CHENILLE
    umbilical .... FUNICULUS

cordage fiber .. AGAVE, SISAL,
    FERU, HEMP, IMBE, MAGUEY,
    JUTE, ABACA, COIR, ISTLE
    grass .... ESPARTO
corded cloth .... REP, POPLIN,
    CORDUROY
Cordelia's father .... LEAR
    sister .... REGAN
cordelle .... TASSEL
cordial .... LIQUEUR, GENIAL,
    ROSOLIO, RATAFIA, HEARTY,
    AMIABLE, ANISETTE,
    HIPPOCRAS, MARASCHINO
    apricot .... PERSICO
cordierite .... IOLITE
cordite .... EXPLOSIVE
cordon .. CIRCLE, BRAID, RING,
    CORD, RIBBON, BELT
corduroy .... FUSTIAN
    ridge .... WALE
core .... HEART, CENTER
    bone/feather ..... PITH
    corn ear .... COD
coreopsis .... TICKSEED
corf ... BASKET, MINEWAGON,
    TRUCK
corfu ... CORCYRA, KERKYRA
corium ..... DERMA, DERMIS,
    SKIN, CUTIS
Corinthian capital's scroll ...
    VOLUTE
    volute .... HELIX
cork .... TAP, PLUG, STOPPER,
    BARK, STOPPLE, BUNG, SPILE
    barrel's .... BUNG
    bottle .... SHIVE
    change into ... SUBERIZE
    county port ...... COBH
    famous feature of ......
    BLARNEY STONE
    helmet ..... TOPI, TOPEE
    like .... SUBEROSE
    noise .... POP
    of a .... SUBERIC,
    SUBEREOUS
    shallow .... SHIVE
    waxy substance .....
    SUBERIN(E)
corker .. LIE, LULU, CLINCHER
corking .... EXCELLENT
corkwood .... BALSA
corm .... BULB, TUBER
    plant with ... GLADIOLUS,
    CROCUS
cormorant ... BIRD, GREEDY,

GLUTTON(OUS), SHAG, GUANAY, GORMAW

corn .. KERNEL, MAIZE, GRAIN, CALLUS, SALT, PAPILLOMA, FLINT, PICKLE

and beans dish .... SUCCOTASH

belt (per J. Luzzatto) ... BOURBON

bin .... CRIB

bread .. PONE, TORTILLA

cake .... TORTILLA

covering .... HUSK

crake .. RAIL, DAKER HEN

flour .... PINOLE

flower .... BLUENOSE

green ear ...... TUCKET

ground .. HOMINY, GRITS, MEAL, FLOUR

grower .... IOWAN

hair .... TASSEL

hulled .... HOMINY

husk .... SHUCK

imperfect .... NUBBIN

Indian .... MAIZE

lily .... IXIA

liquor .... WHISK(E)Y

meal ...... MASA, SAMP, HOMINY

meal, baked/fried ...... HOECAKE

meal bread/cake .... DODGER, PONE

meal dish ..... SCRAPPLE

meal dough .... HUSH PUPPY

meal mush .... ATOLE

meal porridge .... MUSH, STIRABOUT, POLENTA

meal pudding .... MUSH

mill .... QUERN

porridge .... SAMP

slang .... MUSH

small .... NUBBIN

stalk .... STOVER

state .... IOWA

stump ...... STUBBLE

toe .... CALLUS

variety .... FLINT

cornea inflammation .... KERATITIS

leucoma of the .... WALLEYE

opacity on ..... NEBULA, LEUCOMA

corned .... SALTED

beef .... BULLY

beef connoisseur .. JIGGS

beef's partner .. CABBAGE

cornel .... DOGWOOD

Cornelia Otis ____ .. SKINNER

corneous .. HORNY, HORNLIKE

corner .. BIGHT, REGION, TRAP, ANGLE, COIGN, NOOK, NICHE, TREE

angle .... CANT

chimney .... INGLENOOK

cozy .... NOOK, ALCOVE

fireplace .... INGLENOOK

of building .... CANT, QUOIN

of sail .... CLEW

projecting .... COIGN(E)

support .... CORBELING, LINTEL, ARCH, SQUINCH

cornerstone ... FOUNDATION, COIGN(E), QUOIN

cornet .... CAVALRY FLAG

Cornhusker state .. NEBRASKA

cornice .... MOLDING

projection .... DRIP, CORONA

support .... ANCON

corniculate .... HORNED

Cornish patron saint .. COLIN

town .... ST. IVES

cornu(copia) .... HORN

Cornwall county seat .... BODMIN

islands .... SCILLY

corny .... TRITE, BANAL, SENTIMENTAL, MUSHY

corolla ... PETALS, PERIANTH, LIGULE

cuplike part .... CORONA

heraldic .... GALEA

corollary, a ...... INFERENCE, DEDUCTION

geometrical ...... PORISM

corona .. AURA, HALO, CROWN, AUREOLE, CIGAR

Australis .... WREATH

coronach .. DIRGE, THRENODY

coronal ..... CROWN, DIADEM, GARLAND

coronet ..... ANADEM, CROWN, DIADEM, TIARA

wearer .... DUKE

corporal .. BODILY, PERSONAL

famous ...... NAPOLEON

for short .... NCO

infamous .... HITLER

Little — — —. NAPOLEON
punishment .. FLOGGING,
WHIPPING
rank after —. SERGEANT
tobacco of .... COPORAL
corporate — UNITED, COMMON,
JOINT
corporation manager .. SYNDIC
corporeal .. SOMAL, MATERIAL,
PHYSICAL, BODILY, SOMATIC
corpse — — CADAVER, CARCASS,
CARCASE, LICH
animated ..... ZOMBI(E)
dissection — NECROTOMY
embalmed ..... MUMMY
platform for — — —. BIER
prefix ... — — —. NECR(O)
slang — — — — ...... STIFF
corpsman — — — — .... MEDIC
corpulent .... FAT, OBESE,
FLESHY, STOUT, GROSS, PURSY
corpuscles, lack of red .. — — —
AN(A)EMIA
corral —. ROUND UP, POUND,
PEN, STOCK(ADE)
correct ... — — —. CURE, PROPER,
ACCURATE, PRIM, RIGHT,
EDIT, EMEND
one's fault ...... REFORM
correctional house ... — — — —
BRIDEWELL, REFORMATORY
correlative — (N)EITHER, (N)OR
correspond — MATCH, AGREE,
EQUAL, SUIT, TALLY, WRITE,
COINCIDE
correspondence .. AGREEMENT,
COMMUNICATION
kind of — — — BUSINESS,
OFFICIAL
correspondent, kind of ...... —
PENPAL, STRINGER, FOREIGN
corrida cry .... OLE
corridor — PASSAGEWAY, AISLE,
GALLERY, HALL(WAY)
corrival ... — —.. COMPETITOR
corroborant — — — —.. TONIC
corroborate — — — — SUPPORT,
CONFIRM
corrode .. WEAR AWAY, RUST,
EAT INTO, ERODE, GNAW
corroded — — — .... CARIOUS
corrosive ... ACID, MORDANT,
CAUSTIC, ESCHAROTIC
corrugate — . FURROW, PLEAT
WRINKLE
corrugated — — — — RUGATE,

RUGOUS, RUGOSE
corrupt — ROTTEN, SPOIL, EVIL,
VITIATE, VENAL, DEBASE,
DEFILE, PERVERT, INFECT
morally — — .... PUTRID
one way — BRIBE, SUBORN
official — — — —. GRAFTER
corruption, trace of — —. TAINT
corsage — BOUQUET, BODICE,
NOSEGAY
corsair — — — — FREEBOOTER,
PRIVATEER, PIRATE
ship — — — — — — XEBEC
corselet — LORICA, CUIRASS
corset — — —. BODICE, LORICA,
LORLEA
bone — — — — — BUSK
stiffener — — STAY, BUSK,
WHALEBONE
Corsican capital — — AJACCIO
famous ... — — NAPOLEON
seaport ... — — — BASTIA
sheep — ...... MOUFLON
cortege — — —. TRAIN, RETINUE,
PROCESSION
cortex — — — — BARK, RIND
corundum ..... RUBY, TOPAZ,
AMETHYST, SAPPHIRE, EMERY
coruscate .. SPARKLE, GLITTER
corvine bird — RAVEN, CROW,
ROOK
Corvus — — — — — — RAVEN
coryza — — — COLD, CATARRH
sign of — SNIFFLE, SNEEZE
cos — — — — COAN, LETTUCE,
ROMAINE
cosher — — — — — — PAMPER
cosmetic — — — ...... CERUSE
base for — — ... LANOLIN(E)
cheek/lip ... — — ROUGE
eyelid/eyelash — — — — —
MASCARA, KOHL
hair — — — — — HENNA
paste — — .... PACK
skin ... — — — LOTION
use/decorate with — — —
PAINT
cosmetics: sl. — — ... WARPAINT
cosmic — — GRANDIOSE, VAST
cycle ... — — — — — EON
ray particle ...... MESON
cosmography, branch of ... — —
GEOGRAPHY, ASTRONOMY,
GEOLOGY
cosmonaut ...... ASTRONAUT,
SPACEMAN, ROCKETMAN

American .... SHEPARD, COLLINS, ALDRIN, BORMAN, BEAN
Russian ...... GAGARIN, KOMAROV
cosmos .... UNIVERSE, REALM, EARTH, GLOBE, HARMONY, ORDER, WORLD, THISTLE
god of the ..... VARUNA
opposed to ...... CHAOS
Cossack ...... CAVALRYMAN, RUSSIAN, TATAR
chief .. ATAMAN, HETMAN
fame of the .... HORSEMANSHIP
whip .... KNOUT
cosset .. PET, PAMPER, FONDLE, LAMB
cost .... PRICE, SACRIFICE
colloquial ..... DAMAGE
exceeding contract price . OVERRUN
costa .... RIB
Costa Rica capital .. SAN JOSE
coin .... COLON
discoverer of .. COLUMBUS
mountain .... IRAZU
port .... LIMON
president .... TREJOS
costard .... HEAD, APPLE
costly ...... EXPENSIVE, DEAR, PRECIOUS
costmary .. CHRYSANTHEMUM
costrel ...... FLASK, BOTTLE
costume .... DRESS, HABIT, GET-UP
colloquial ..... RIG, TOG
jewelry .... TRINKET, GEWGAW, BAUBLE, BROOCH
jewelry material .... STRASS, PASTE, OROIDE, ORMOLU
masquerade .... DOMINO
matching parts .... ENSEMBLE
riding .... HABIT
silk material .... SENDAL
wear one in fun .... MUM(M)
cot ← BED, SHELTER, CHARPAI, CHARPOY
poetic .... COTTAGE
cote .... SHELTER, SHED
coterie ← CIRCLE, CLIQUE, SET, CAMARILLA, JUNTO
cotillion ←.......... DANCE

cotinga .... CHATTERER
Cotswold .... SHEEP
cotta .... SURPLICE
cottage .... CASINO, CHALET, VILLA, CABANA, BUNGALOW, HUT, BOWER
cheese ...... SMEARCASE
cotter .... BOLT, WEDGE
pin .... FORELOCK
cotton ..... THREAD, CLOTH, JEAN, MADRAS, PIMA, ROVE, NAINSOOK, JACONET, MALLOW
and wool cloth .... SATINET(TE), LINSEY
batting fibers ... LINTERS
Bengal .... ADATI
canvaslike .... WIGAN
cleaning machine .... WILLOW, GIN, LINTER
cloth .... KHAKI, CHINO, CRASH, CHINTZ, CALICO, ETAMINE, GALATEA, NANKEEN, NANKIN, PIMA, MULL, DUCKS, MANTA, MADRAS, REPP, REP(S), OXFORD, SEERSUCKER, MUSLIN, JEAN, GRENADINE, ORGANDY
cloth, canvaslike ...... WIGAN
cloth for curtains, etc. .. SCRIM, DIMITY, LAWN
cloth for handkerchiefs, blouse, etc. .... LAWN
cloth for linings .... PERCALINE, SILESIA
cloth for sheets .... PERCALE, MUSLIN
cloth, glazed .. JACONET, CHINTZ
cloth, glossy .... SATEEN
comb .... CARD
fiber .... LINT(ER), BATTING
fiber knot .... NEP
gauze .... LENO
gum tree ...... TUPELO
machine ... GIN, BALER, MULE, LINTER, WILLOW(ER)
measure .... HANK, LEA
pad .... SPONGE
pod .... BOLL
seed cleaner .... LINTER, GIN
seed fiber .... LINTER

sheer .... VOILE
spinning wheel ....
      CHARK(H)A
stainer .... BUG
State .... ALABAMA
thread .... LISLE
tuft .... LOCK
twilled .... JEAN, DENIM,
      CHINO
twisted .... ROVE
waste .... FLOCK
with glazed/water finish .
      PERCALINE
cottonmouth .... SNAKE
cottontail .... HARE, LEVERET,
      RABBIT
cottonwood .. ALAMO, POPLAR
cottony ..... FLUFFY, DOWNY
couch .. DIVAN, LAIR, CANAPE,
   DAVENPORT, SETTEE, SOFA,
   STATE, SQUAB, LOUNGE,
    RECLINE, OTTOMAN
hanging ...... HAMMOCK
like chair ....
     CHAISE LONGUE
poetic .... BED
to carry wounded ......
      LITTER
cougar ..... PUMA, PANTHER,
   CATAMOUNT, CARCAJOU,
     PAINTER
cough .... TUSSIS, HACK
  candy .... HOARHOUND,
     HOREHOUND
  drop .... LOZENGE,
    TROCHE, PASTILLE
  medicine .... GRINDELIA
  of a .... TUSSIVE, TUSSAL
  sound like a .... HICCUP
  to attract attention .....
      AHEM
  up .... HAND OVER, EJECT
  whooping .... PERTUSSIS
coughing up pus ..... VOMICA
coulee .. RAVINE, GULCH, LAVA
couloir ...... GORGE, GULLY
coulter .... (PLOW)SHARE
council ...... BOARD, JUNTA
  African tribe's .. INDABA
  chamber .... CAMARILLA,
    DIVAN, CABINET
  church .... SYNOD,
     CONSISTORY
  of deacons .. CONSISTORY
  table .... BOARD

counsel ..... ADVICE, ADVISE,
      REDE
  legal .... LAWYER
counselor .. ADVISER, LAWYER,
      MENTOR
  woman .... EGERIA
count .. TALLY, RELY, RECKON,
  ADD, (E)NUMERATE, FIGURE
  down purpose ....
   BLAST-OFF, LAUNCHING
  French .... COMTE
  German .... GRAF
  in .... INCLUDE
  in law .... CHARGE
  of Monte Cristo ....
      DANTES
  of population ..., CENSUS
  of Vienna ...... DAUPHIN
  out .... DISREGARD, OMIT
  palatine ..... PALSGRAVE
countenance ..... ABET, FACE,
    VISAGE, SUPPORT
counter ...... OPPOSITE, BAR,
   COMPUTER, BUFFET,
     CONTRARY
  in cards .... MILLE
  irritant .... SALVE,
  DEMULCENT, OINTMENT,
  CALAMINE, MOXA, SETON,
   LOTION, MUSTARD
  kind of .... GEIGER
  sale .... RETAIL
counteract ...... NEUTRALIZE
counterbalance ... EQUIPOISE
counterfeit .. FALSE, FORGE(D),
  POSTICHE, IMITATION, SHAM,
   BOGUS, PHON(E)Y
  coin .... SLUG
countermand ...... CANCEL,
   OVERRULE, REVOKE,
    CALL BACK
counterpane ...... COVERLET
counterpart ..... COPY, LIKE,
  DUPLICATE, TWIN, REPLICA,
     PARALLEL
counterpoint .... DESCANT
  of ...... CONTRAPUNTAL
countersign ...... PASSWORD
countersink .... REAM
counterweight .... TARE
countess' title of respect ......
      LADY
counting frame .... ABAC(US)
  sheep purpose ... SLEEP
  ten purpose .. COOL OFF,
      STALL

countless .... MYRIAD
countrified .. RUSTIC, RURAL,
    CORNFED, HODDEN
country .... REGION, LAND,
    REALM
  ancient .. ILLYRIA, PERSIA
  bumpkin .. HICK, RUBE,
    YOKEL, RUSTIC, CHURL,
    YAHOO
  dance .... REEL, HAY
  dance: Brit. ... COVERLEY
  fellow .... CORYDON
  French .... PAYS
  gallant .... SWAIN
  gentleman .... COVERLEY,
    ESQUIRE
  girl .... PHILLIS, PHYLLIS,
    WENCH
  house ..... VILLA, CASINO,
    HACIENDA
  house, of a .... VILLATIC
  in law .... PAIS
  in the city .. RUS IN URBE
  lad .... SWAIN
  live in the ... RUSTICATE
  middle region ....
    MIDLAND, INTERIOR,
    INLAND
  of fable ..... EL DORADO
  of the .... RURAL
  on 38th parallel .. KOREA
  open, flat ... CHAMPAIGN
  open, wild ...... WEALD
  poetical .... CLIME
  social .. BEE, BARNDANCE
  Spanish .... PAIS
  ways .... PATHS
countryman .... RUSTIC,
    COMPATRIOT
  Spanish .... PAISANO
countryside, of the .. BUCOLIC
county .. SHIRE, DISTRICT, AMT
  law officer ..... SHERIFF
coup .... BLOW,
    (MASTER) STROKE
  d' _____ .... ETAT
  de grace ... DEATH BLOW
  de grace dagger ....
    MISERICORD(E)
  reporter's .. SCOOP, BEAT
couple .... DUO, PAIR, BRACE,
    LINK, DUAD, YOKE, FEW,
    SEVERAL, TWO (SOME)
coupled .. GEMINATED, LINKED,
    PAIRED, TEAMED
"Couples" author .... UPDIKE

couplet .... DISTICH
coupling for electric fixtures ..
    HICKEY
courage ...... PLUCK, HEART,
    GUTS, NERVE, GALL, FACE,
    CHEEK, VALOR, METTLE, GRIT,
    SPUNK, SAND, FORTITUDE
  loss of .... COLDFEET
  pretended .... BRAVADO
  symbol of ..... BULLDOG
courageous .... BRAVE, SANDY,
    STOUT, SPUNKY
courier ..... MESSENGER, POST,
    ESTAFETTE
courlan .... LIMPKIN
course ... PATH, WAY, ROUTE,
    DIRECTION, LANGLAUF,
    PROCESS, DISH
  athletics .... GYMNASTICS
  meal .... VIAND, SALAD,
    ENTREE, DISH
  of action .. PROCEDURE,
    PROCEEDING, TACK
  of official papers ....
    CHANNELS
  of study ... CURRICULUM,
    LESSONS
  of travel ..... ITINERARY,
    ROUTE
court ... WOO, ASSIZE, BENCH,
    PERISTYLE, ROMANCE,
    TRIBUNAL, SPARK
  action .... SUIT
  aggressively ...... RUSH
  assembly .... LEVEE
  case .... CAUSE
  castle's .... BAILEY
  central .... ATRIUM
  challenge .... RECUSE
  church .... CONSISTORY,
    ROTA
  crier .... BEADLE
  crier's call .. OYEZ, OYES
  criminal .... ASSIZE
  decree .... ARRET
  enclosed .... PARVIS
  entrance .... ATRIUM
  equity ...... CHANCERY
  favorite ...... GRACIOSO
  game .... TENNIS,
    HANDBALL, BASKETBALL,
    BADMINTON, SQUASH
  hearing .... OYER
  inner .... PATIO
  jurisdiction .... SOKE
  manorial .... LEET

martial defendant ...... MUTINEER, AWOL, TRAITOR, DESERTER
martial in the field ..... DRUMHEAD
messenger ...... BEADLE
minutes .... ACTA
of a .... AULIC
of justice ... BAR, BENCH
of law .... FORUM
official ...... ATTORNEY, BAILIFF, FISCAL, REFEREE, DA
order .... WRIT, ARRET, MANDAMUS, SUBPOENA
order extract ... ESTREAT
panel .... JURY
pertaining to .... AULIC
proceeding...., . TRIAL, HEARING
ruling, plea for .. MOTION
session .. ASSIZE, HEARING
summons .... CITATION, SUBPOENA
writ .... OYER, SUBPOENA, SUMMONS
yard .... PATIO
courteous .... URBANE, CIVIL, POLITE
regard .... RESPECT, DEFERENCE
courtesan .. PROSTITUTE, THAIS
courtesy .. FAVOR, POLITENESS
courtly ..... SUAVE, ELEGANT, POLISHED, AULIC
courtship ..... WOOING, SUIT, PLIGHT
dance .... CUECA
of Miles _____ .. STANDISH
result of, usually .... WEDDING, MARRIAGE
courtyard .... PATIO, QUADRANGLE
sunken ...... AREAWAY
cousin .... COS
couteau .... DAGGER
couturier ...... DRESSMAKER, STYLIST
fabric of .... SOIE, LAME
famed .. DIOR, BALMAIN, ST. LAURENT, GIVENCHY, NORELL, MAINBOCHER, GERNREICH, BALENCIAGA
cove ...... HOLE, BAY, INLET, NOOK

British .. FELLOW, CHAP, BOY
covenant .. AGREEMENT, PACT, TESTAMENT, BOND
Coventry, goddess of .. GODIVA
cover ... TOP, LID, CAP, HIDE, COAT, SHEATHE, ENVELOP(E), ROOF, CANOPY, WHELM
bottle ...... CROWN, CAP
break .... EMERGE
detachable ...... BINDER
face .... VEIL, MASK
girl ..... PIN UP, MODEL
hard ..... SHELL, PLATE, CARAPACE
inner surface .. LINE, PAD
lap .... RUG
log .. PUTTEE, CHAUSSES, LEGGING
nipa .... THATCH
ornamental ...... SHAM
pie's ...... CRUST, RIND
protective ...... ARMOR, SHELL, CARAPACE
superficial ...... VENEER
thickly .... SMOTHER
thin .... VENEER
thinly .... SKIM
top wall .. CEIL, COPING, CAPSTONE
under .. HIDDEN, SECRET
up ...... CONCEAL, HIDE
with asphalt ...... PAVE
with cloth .... DRAPE
with feathers ... FLEDGE
with jewels ...... BEGEM
with plaster .... CEIL
with trappings .... CAPARISON
coverage, insurance ..... RISK
covered colonnade .... STOA
entrance .... PORCH
garden ...... HOTHOUSE
portico .... GALLERY
vehicle .... VAN
wagon .... SCHOONER, CONESTOGA
walk ...... STOA, MALL, CLOISTER, PORTICO, ARCADE, GALLERY
with blood ... HEMATOSE, GORY
with bristles .... HISPID
with fine feathers ...... DOWNY

with flakes .... SCURFY,
LEPIDOTE
with hair .... PILOSE,
HISPID, TOMENTOSE
with leaves ..... FOLIOSE
covering .. SHEATHE, TEGUMEN,
INTEGUMENT, TEGMEN
for concealment ....
CAMOUFLAGE, BLINDAGE
gloomy .... PALL
glossy .... SHEEN
material .... PATCH
membrane of ovary .....
TUNICA
of clouds ..... OVERCAST
protective ...... LORICA,
ARMOR, SHELL, MAIL
shiny .... SHEEN
teeth .... DENTINE
coverlet .. BEDSPREAD, QUILT,
COUNTERPANE, PALL
covert .. SECRET, CONCEALED,
VEILED, HIDDEN
covet .... DESIRE, CRAVE, ENVY
covetous .... GREEDY,
AVARICIOUS
covey .. FLOCK, BROOD, BEVY
cow ..... DAUNT, (OVER)AWE,
BOVINE, BULLY, KINE,
THREATEN, VACA, BEEF, BOSS,
CRUMMIE, CRUMMY
ad .... ELSIE
barn ..... STABLE, BYRE
breed ..... ANGUS, KERRY,
JERSEY
call .... MOO, LOW
cud .... RUMEN
dewlap of .... LAPPET
dialectic .... CRITTER,
CRITTUR
fat ...... TALLOW, SUET
fish .... TORO
genus .... BOS
gland .... UDDER
headed deity .... ISIS
hornless ..... MUL(L)EY
killer .... WASP
mammary gland .. UDDER
milking .... MILCH
pilot .... PINTANO
polled .... MUL(L)EY
sea .. MANATEE, DUGONG
sound ..... LOW, MOO
tuberculosis of ... GRAPE
udder inflammation .....
GARGET

unbranded ... MAVERICK
young .... HEIFER, CALF,
STIRK
coward ..... CRAVEN, SNEAK,
POLTROON, DASTARD
colloquial ..... YELLOW,
CHICKEN
descriptive of a ....
YELLOW
(Noel) show ....
BITTER-SWEET
(Noel) song ...... NINA
cowardice, symbol of ......
WHITE FEATHER
cowardly ...... CRAVEN,
DASTARDLY
animal ...... HY(A)ENA
knight of story ....
FALSTAFF
person .. CUR, POLTROON,
CAITIFF
slang .. CHICKEN, YELLOW
cowbird .... TROUPIAL
cowboy .... BUCKAROO,
VAQUERO, HERDER, LLANERO,
RANCHER, WRANGLER,
BRONCOBUSTER, BUCKAYRO
Australian .. STOCKMAN,
RINGER
bed .... BUNK
big day of ...... RODEO,
ROUNDUP
breeches .... CHAPS
concern of ...... CATTLE
friend of ..... PARD(NER)
habitat .. RANGE, RANCH,
PAMPAS
jacket .... CHAQUETA
kind of ...... PUNCHER
original ...... PECOS BILL
overalls .... LEVIS
pampas .... GAUCHO
rope ..... LASSO, REATA,
RIATA, LARIAT
saddlebag ...... ALFORJA
show .... RODEO
South American ......
GAUCHO
trousers ...... CHAPS,
CHAPARAJOS
cowcatcher ...... FENDER
cower ...... CRINGE, QUAIL,
SHRINK, CROUCH
cowering thru fear .... FUNK
Cowes, sight in ...... YACHTS

cowfish — .... TORO, MANATEE,
DUGONG, GRAMPUS
cowl ... HOOD, CLOAK, AMICE
like headdress .. ALMUCE,
COUS
cowpox .... VACCINIA
cows .... KINE
roundup of .. WRANGLE
cowslip .... BLUEBELL,
MAYFLOWER
coxa .... HIP
coxcomb ..... DANDY, DUDE,
POP, TOFF
coy — — .. BASHFUL, DEMURE,
TIMID, RETIRING, SHY,
DIFFIDENT
coyo .... AVOCADO
coyote .... WOLF
coypu ...... RODENT, NUTRIA
coze .... CHAT, TALK
cozen ...... DECEIVE, CHEAT,
TRICK
cozy —.. SNUG, COMFORTABLE,
HOM(E)Y
retreat .. NEST, NOOK, DEN
crab .. SHELLFISH, NAG, CARP,
MALACOSTRACAN
apple .... SCRAB
claw .... CHELA, NIPPER
PINC(H)ER
constellation .... CANCER
feeler .... ANTENNA
front of .... METOPE
kind of .... FIDDLER
king — .. — ..... LIMULUS,
LIMULOID
larva .... ZOEA
like a .... CANCROID
mantis .... SQUILLA
Scottish .... PARTAN
shell .... TEST
upper shell of ....
CARAPACE
walk of — — ..... SIDLE,
SIDEWISE
crabbed .... CRAMP
crabfish .... GRAMPLE
crack ... BREAK, SPLIT, SNAP,
CREVICE, CHINK, FIRST RATE
CHAP, RIFT, JOKE, FRACTURE,
QUIP
deep .... CREVASSE
filler .... GROUT
glacier .... CREVASSE
open .... CHAP
seal .... CA(U)LK

up ... COLLAPSE, CRASH,
BREAK DOWN
crackbrained .... NUTTY,
CRAZY, INSANE, IDIOTIC
cracked wheat/oats .. GROATS
cracker .. BISCUIT, WAFER,
SALTINE
crackerjack .... NAILER
crackers, dish of ... PANADA
crackle .... CREPITATE
cracklings .. SCRAPS, GREAVES
crackly .... CRISP
cracknel .... GREAVES
crackpot .... CRANK, NUT
cracks, full of — — CHOPPY,
CHAPPED
cracksman .. BURGLAR, YEGG
cradle . ... CRATE, CRIB
in mining ...... ROCKER
period .... INFANCY
song .... LULLABY
craft .... ART, TRADE, SKILL,
TALENT, GUILE, OCCUPATION,
CUNNING, ARTIFICE
air .... AIRPLANE,
HELICOPTER, DIRIGIBLE
union of old .... GUILD
water — — — BOAT, SHIP,
VESSEL
craftsman — ARTIST, ARTISAN,
ARTIFICER
chief .... — MAESTRO
metal .... SMITH
crafty .. SLY, CUNNING, WILY,
ARTFUL, FOXY, FELINE,
INSIDIOUS
crag .. CLIFF, TOR, PRECIPICE
crake .... RAIL
cram .... BONE, PACK, STUFF,
TUCK
cramp .... HAMPER
neck ...... KINK, CRICK
crampfish .... TORPEDO
crampon .. GRAPLIN, GRAPNEL
cranberry disease ...... SCALD
crane .... HERON, STORK,
DEMOISELLE, RUBBERNECK
arm .... JIB
framework ..... GANTRY
genus .... GRUS
Ichabod, rival of ......
(BROM) BONES
like bird .... CHUNGA,
SERIEMA
pertaining to .... GRUINE
relative .... BUSTARD

ship's .... DAVIT
sound .... CLANG
cranesbill .... GERANIUM
cranial nerve .... VAGUS
cranium .... SKULL
crank .... WHIM, TWIST,
CAPRICE
case reservoir ... OILPAN
colloquial ... CRACKPOT,
QUEER, ECCENTRIC
cranky .... CROSS, IRRITABLE,
QUEER, GROUCHY
cranny ...... CREVICE, CHINK
crap, in dice ...... BOXCAR
shooter's "four" ....
CATER, JOE
crape .... WEED, WEEPER
crapehanger ...... PESSIMIST
crappie .... SUNFISH
craps throw .... DIE
crash .. FALL, COLLIDE, BREAK,
COLLAPSE, SMASH
crass — GROSS, STUPID, CRUDE,
COARSE
Cratchit's job .... CLERK
crate .. BASKET, HAMPER, BOX
slang .... JALOPY
crater .... PIT, CAVITY, HOLE,
CALDERA
lunar .... LINNE
one with ...... VOLCANO
cravat ..... SCARF, (NECK)TIE,
ASCOT, OVERLAY
fabric .... REP
hangman's ...... NOOSE
ornament ..... STICKPIN
crave — BEG, HANKER, YEARN,
COVET
craven .... COWARD(LY)
person ...... POLTROON,
CAITIFF
craving .. APPETITE, HUNGER,
APPETENCE, MANIA, OBSESSION
craw .... CROP, MAW
crawl .. CREEP, SLITHER, INCH,
GROVEL
crawler ...... BABY, WORM,
REPTILE
crawling ... REPENT, REPTANT
crayfish egg .... BERRY
segment ...... METAMERE
crayon — CHARCOAL, CHALK,
PASTEL
pastel .... PASTILLE
picture .... PASTEL

craze .. FUROR, FASHION, FAD,
MANIA
women's style ....
MINISKIRT, PANTSUIT
crazed ... INSANE, DEMENTED,
MAD(DENED)
crazy ... INSANE, MAD, DAFT,
WACKY, CRACKED, DOTTY,
LOCO, BUGS, NUTS, POTTY,
CUCKOO, KOOKY, KOOKIE,
LOONY, LUNY
person .... MANIAC
to kill — — AMUCK, AMOK,
BERSERK
creak — — — SQUEAK, SCROOP,
GRATE
cream .. ELITE, BEST, COSMETIC
color .... ECRU
French .... CREME
separator ... CENTRIFUGE
creamy white ... IVORY, MILKY
crease ... RIDGE, FOLD, MUSS,
WRINKLE, RUCK, RIMPLE,
RUMPLE, RUCK, RUGA
creased .... RUGATE
create .... MAKE, ORIGINATE,
PRODUCE
creation .. INVENTION, COSMOS,
GENESIS
God's ...... UNIVERSE
creative .... INVENTIVE
writing — FICTION, NOVEL,
POEM, POETRY
creator, the .... GOD
creature, small, imaginary ...
GREMLIN
creche figure .. JOSEPH, MARY,
INFANT, LAMB, MAGI,
SHEPHERD
part .... MANGER
crecopia .... MYTH
credence ...... BELIEF,
CREDENTIAL
credential — — CERTIFICATE,
CREDENCE
credenza .... BUFFET
credible .... RELIABLE,
PLAUSIBLE, BELIEVABLE,
LIKELY
credit .. BELIEVE, ATTRIBUTE,
ASCRIBE, TRUST, HONOR,
REBATE
British .... TICK
card organization ....
DINER'S(CLUB)
for achievement .. KUDOS

creditor .. .. LENDER,
NOTE HOLDER
avaricious ..... USURER,
LOAN SHARK
exacting ...... SHYLOCK
credo .. BELIEF, CREED, TENET
credulous .... GULLIBLE
creed, one such .... NICENE
political ...... ISM, DOXY
creek ...... INLET, BAY, RIA,
INDIAN, STREAM, BAYOU, KILL
creel .... BASKET
user .. .. FISHERMAN,
ANGLER
creep .. .. CRINGE, FAWN,
CRAWL, SLINK, SLITHER
slang .... DRIP
creeper .. VINE, IVY, SNAKE
creeping .... REPENT, REPTANT
charlie, for one ... WEED
plant .. VINE, BINE, LIANA
creeps, the .... FEAR,
REPUGNANCE, REVULSION
creepy .. .. EERIE, CRAWLY
creese ... KRIS, CRIS, DAGGER
cremate .. BURN, INCINERATE
crematory .... CINERATOR
Cremona .. .. AMATI, VIOLIN,
STRAD(IVARIUS)
river .... ADDA
violin maker .. GUARNERI,
AMATI
crenate .. .. SCALLOPED,
NOTCHED
crenel .... EMBRASURE
Creole ancestry .. .. SPANISH,
FRENCH
and Indian .... MESTIZO
milieu .... NEW ORLEANS
patois ... GUMBO, GOMBO
rice cake .... CALA
state .... LOUISIANA
creosol .... ANTISEPTIC
crepe suzette .. .. .. PANCAKE,
FLAPJACK
crepitate .. CRACKLE, RATTLE
crepuscle .... DUSK, TWILIGHT
crescent .... SEMILUNAR,
DEMILUNE, MENISCUS
moons .... MENISCI
of a ...... BICORN, HORN
point of .... CUSP
shape figure ...... LUNE,
LUNULE, LUNULA,
MENISCUS
shaped .. LUNATE, LUNE,

BICORN, LUNULAR
(SEMI)LUNAR
cress .. .. SALAD, HERB
cresset .... LANTERN
crest ..... CAP, HELMET, TOP,
CROWN, RIDGE, PEAK
cock's .. COMB, CARUNCLE
mountain .... ARETE
of bird/fowl ..... COMB,
CALOT(TE), CARUNCLE
wave's .... COMB
crested .. CROWNED, PILEATE,
CRISTATE
crestfallen .... DEJECTED
Cretan ... CANDIAN, MINOAN
Crete .... CANDIA
born painter/sculptor .
EL GRECO, DOMENICO
capital/seaport ... CANEA
city .. KNOSSOS, KHANIA
guard of .... TALOS
king .... MINOS
mountain .... IDA
mythical beast ......
MINOTAUR
mythical structure ......
LABYRINTH
princess ...... ARIADNE
cretin .... IDIOT
cretonne .... TOILE
crevasse .... CHASM, FISSURE
crevice .... CHINK, CLEFT,
FISSURE
crevices, full of ..... RIMOSE
crew .. GANG, COMPANY, MOB,
CROWD, TEAM
of ship .. .. COMPLEMENT
relief .... RELAY
crewel .... YARN
crib .... RACK, TROUGH, BIN,
STALL, MANGER, PLAGIARIZE,
PONY
baby's .... CRADLE
colloquial .... STEAL
content of ...... FODDER
in writing ... PLAGIARISM
cribbage .... CARD GAME
game lost .... LURCH
score ...... PEGS, NOBS
crick .... CRAMP, KINK
cricket .. GRASSHOPPER, GRIG,
FOOTSTOOL, HOOP
bowled ball .... YORKER
club .. .. BAT
colloquial .... FAIR PLAY

equipment .. BALL, BAT, WICKET
inning unplayed .... WICKET
like insect .. .. .. LOCUST
score .. .. BYE
sound .. .. CHIRP
team .. .. ELEVEN
term .. .. (TICE)BYE
crier .... MUEZZIN
crime .... SIN, WRONGDOING, FELONY, GUILT, MISDEED, MALEFACTION
against king .... LESE MAJESTE
high .. .. TREASON
major .. .. FELONY
syndicate .. COSA NOSTRA, MAFIA
syndicate member .. .. .. MAFIOSO
where committed .. VENUE
Crimea Conference (1945) site YALTA
Crimean city .. .. SEVASTOPOL, YALTA
lamb's fur .. . CRIMMER, KRIMMER
river .. .. ALMA
sea .... AZOF
seaport .. YALTA, KERCH
strait .... KERCH
criminal .. IMMORAL, CONVICT, FELON, CULPRIT, YEGG, MALEFACTOR, OUTLAW, MISCREANT, MALFEASANT
act .... JOB
colloquial ...... LOSER
conditional release of ... PROBATION
dangerous .. . DESPERADO
habitual .. .. RECIDIVIST, ROUNDER
lawyer: sl. .. MOUTHPIECE
mark of a ...... STIGMA
unreconstructed .. .. .. RECIDIVIST
criminals collectively ...... FELONRY
crimp .. PLEAT, WAVE, CURL, CRINKLE, FOLD, FLUTE, GOFFER
crimple .. .. WRINKLE
crimson ...... RED, CARMINE, BLOODY, MADDER
Crimson's rival .. .. YALE

cringe .. .. QUAIL, COWER, SHRINK, CROUCH
crinkled paper/cloth ... CREPE
crinkly .... WAVY
crinoid .... SEA LILY
crinoline .... PETTICOAT, (HOOP)SKIRT
cripple .. LAME, DISABLE, MAIM, HAMSTRING
a horse .... HOCK
walking aid .. .. CRUTCH, CANE
cripples .... (THE) HALT
patron saint of ...... (ST.) GILES
crisis .. .. .. TURNING POINT, EMERGENCY
of disease ..... SOLUTION
crisp ...... WAVY, ANIMATED, BRITTLE, CURT, CRUMP
biscuit ... CRACKER, SNAP
crisper .. .. CURLER
cristate .... CRESTED
criterion .. RULE, TEST, NORM, STANDARD, CANON
critic .. .... SLATER, CARPER, FAULTFINDER, CENSOR, REVIEWER
disapproval of a .. .. .. PAN(NING)
inferior .. .. .. CRITICASTER
literary ...... REVIEWER
"missile" of, literally .. .. TOMATO, EGG
uninhibited .. .. .. BOOER, HISSER
work of .. .. REVIEW(ER), CRITIQUE
critical .... CAPTIOUS, ACUTE, DECISIVE, CENSORIOUS, EXIGENT
analysis .. .. EXEGESIS
mark .... OBELUS
moment .. CRUX, CRISIS, ZERO HOUR
situation .. .. .. CLUTCH
writing .... LAMPOON, SATIRE
criticism .. REVIEW, DESCANT, CRITIQUE
abusive ...... DIATRIBE
adverse: colloq. .... PAN
criticize .... FLAY, BLAME, CENSURE, DENOUNCE, SLASH, SLAM, SLATE, DAMN,

CONDEMN, ANIMADVERT, SCORE, OPPUGN
  colloquial .. PAN, ROAST, RAKE
critique .... REVIEW, EPICRISIS COMMENTARY
croak ..... CROUP, GRUMBLE
  slang .... DIE
croaker ...... FROG, RAVEN, CROW, SQUETEAGUE
croaking .... RAUCOUS
Croat .... SLAV
Croatian capital .... ZAGREB
  soldier .... PANDOUR
croc .... CROCODILE
crochet .... KNIT(TING), KINK
crock .. SMUT, SOOT, POT, JAR, SHARD, POTSHERD
crockery ..... CHINA(WARE), POTS, JARS, DISHES
Crockett, frontiersman ...... DAVID, DAVEY
  place of heroism .... ALAMO
crocodile .. REPTILE, SAURIAN, YACARE
  bird .... PLOVER, TROCHILUS
  for short .... CROC
  India .. GAVIAL, MUGGER, MUGGAR, MUGGUR
  relative .... CAYMAN, CAIMAN, ALLIGATOR
  Malaysia ...... MUGGAR, MUGGER, MUGGUR
  Philippine .... BUAYA
  River .... LIMPOPO
  teeth picker .. TROCHILUS
crocus .... IRIS
  bulb .... CORM
  color .... SAFFRON
croft .... FARM
cromlech .... DOLMEN, TOMB, MONUMENT, MEGALITH
Cromwell (Oliver), army of .. IRONSIDES
  soubriquet ... IRONSIDES
  title ... LORD PROTECTOR
  victory site ..... NASEBY
crone ...... HAG, BELDAM(E), CARLINE, ANILE, WITCH
Cronus ...... TITAN, SATURN
  parent .... URANUS, GAEA
  sister of .... TETHYS
  son of .... ZEUS
crony .... PAL, CHUM

Cronyn, actor .... HUME
crook ... BEND, HOOK, CURVE
  bishop's .... CROSIER
  branch's .... KNEE
  colloquial ...... THIEF, SWINDLER, CHEAT(ER)
  in tree branch .... KNEE
crooked ...... AGEE, CURVED, ASKEW, DISHONEST, TIPSY, AWRY, BENT, TORTUOUS
  slang .... COCKEYED
crop .. GIZZARD, CRAW, MAW, CLIP, PRODUCE
  animal feed ..... FODDER
  riding .... WHIP
  up again .... RECUR
cropper .. FAILURE, TUMBLER, FARMER
croquet .... ROQUE
  handicap .... BISQUE
  kind of .... ROQUE
  wicket .... ARCH
croquette .... CUTLET
Crosby, ____ .... BING, BOB, GARY
  crooner's soubriquet .... (THE) GROANER
crosier .... STAFF, CROOK, PASTORAL
cross .... ROOD, TESTY, EDGY, SURLY, INTERSECT, CRANKY, SPAN, FRACTIOUS, LIVERIZE, HYBRIDIZE, CRUCIFIX
  bar .... RUNG
  bearer .... CRUCIFER
  breed .... HYBRIDIZE
  by wading .... FORD
  carrier .... CRUCIFER
  church .... ROOD
  country runner .... HARRIER
  country skiing .... LANGLAUF
  current ..... RIP(TIDE)
  cut .... SAWN
  decoration ... VICTORIA, IRON
  Egyptian .... ANKH
  examination, of .... ELENCTIC
  examine .. INTERROGATE, GRILL
  eye(d) ..... STRABISMUS, SQUINT, STRABISMAL
  fertilization .. XENOGAMY

horizontal beam .... TRANSOM
in heraldry .... CRUX
off .... CANCEL
out ... DELE(TE), CANCEL
question ...... EXAMINE
river .... FORD
shaped .... CRUCIAL, CRUCIFORM
Southern .... CRUX
stroke .... SERIF
crossbar .... RUNG
crossbeam .... TRAVE, TREVE, TRANSOM
crossbill genus .... LOXIA
crossbow .... ARBALEST
missile .. BOLT, QUARREL
crossbreed .... HYBRID, MONGREL
crossed .. THWARTED, OPPOSED, FRUSTRATED
star .. ILLFATED, TRAGIC
crossette .... ANCON
crosspiece ...... RUNG, SPAR, CLEAT, TRANSOM, LINTEL, SILL
crossruff in whist ..... SEESAW
crossthreads .... WOOF
crosswise .... TRANSVERSE
crotchet ..... HOOK, CAPRICE
half of a .... QUAVER
crotchety person ..... CRANK, CURMUDGEON, GROUCH
croton bug ...... COCKROACH
crouch .... BOW, CRINGE, COWER, STOOP
crouching position .... SQUAT
croup .... CATARRH, ANGINA, CRUPPER
horse's .... RUMP
crouse .... BOLD, PERT
crouton .... SIPPET
crow .... CRAKE, (JACK)DAW, CAW, BOAST, EXULT, BRAG, ROOK, CHOUGH, NUTCRACKER
constellation .... CORVUS
cry .... CAW
eat .... RECANT
hooded ...... GRAYBACK
Indian .... SIOUX
kin .... JAY
like a .... CORVINE
like bird .. ORIOLE, ROOK, RAVEN
of .... CORVINE

crow's-nest .... LOOKOUT
crowbar .. PRY, LEVER, JIMMY, JEMMY
crowd ...... HORDE, CLIQUE, PRESS, JAM, FLOCK, CRAM, THRONG, MOB, SHOVE, DROVE, CONCOURSE, SWARM, GATHERING
busy .... HIVE
close together .. HUDDLE, HERD
every which way ... MILL
fancier ..... ACTOR, DIP
moving .... SWARM
crower ...... COCK, ROOSTER, BABY, BOASTER
crowfoot flower ...... PEONY
crown .... DIADEM, TREE TOP, CREST
bottle .... CAP
cock's .... COMB
Egyptian .... ATEF
head's .... POLL
in botany ...... CORONA
in zoology ...... CREST
jewel .... TIARA
prince ....
    HEIR (APPARENT), DAUPHIN
Prince, English .... CHARLES
Prince, Japanese .... AKIHITO
slang .... CONK
small .... CORONET
crowtoe .... BUTTERCUP
crucial .... SEVERE, DECISIVE, CRITICAL
point .... CRUX, CRISIS
crucible ...... CRUSET, TEST, TRIAL, FIREPOT, MELTING POT
crucifix .... CROSS, ROOD
crucifixion, place of Jesus' ... CALVARY
crude .... ROUGH, RAW, BARE, COARSE, UNREFINED, AGRESTIC, UNCOUTH, LOWBRED
metal .... ORE
Scottish .... RANDY
sugar .... MELADA, PANOCHA
cruel ...... BRUTAL, PITILESS, HEARTLESS, MEAN, BESTIAL, SAVAGE, HARSH
ruler ... DESPOT, TYRANT

cruet ... ... VIAL, CASTER,
AMPULLA, CASTOR
cruller ... DOUGHNUT, DONUT,
(FRIED)CAKE
crumb ... BIT, SCRAP, PARTICLE,
ORT
ore ... ... SPALL
crumble ... ... DISINTEGRATE,
DECAY, MO(U)LDER
easy to ... ... FRIABLE
crummy ... ... LOW, INFERIOR,
SHABBY
crumple ... CRUSH, WRINKLE,
RUCK, COLLAPSE, BUCKLE
crunch ... ... CHEW, CHAMP,
MUNCH
cruor ... ... BLOOD, GORE
crus ... ... SHANK
crusade ... ... CAMPAIGN,
MOVEMENT, MISSION
Moslem ... JIHAD, JEHAD
crusader ... ... REFORMER,
TEMPLAR, PILGRIM, TANCRED
crusaders' foe ... ... SALADIN,
SARACENS
leader ... ... TANCRED
objective ... ... REFORM(S)
port ... ... ACRE
crush ... GRIND, BRAY, MASH,
SUBDUE, SUPPRESS, PRESS,
QUASH, BRUISE, JAM,
(OVER)WHELM, TRITURATE,
SQUASH, SQUEEZE
colloquial ... ...
INFATUATION, LOVE
to softness ... ... MASH
underfoot ... ... TRAMPLE
with mortar, pestle ... ...
BRUISE
with teeth ... ... CHEW
crushed sugarcane refuse ... ...
BAGASSE, MEGASS(E)
crust ... ... SCAB, BREAD, LOAF,
RIND
fruit-filled ... DUMPLING
metal ... ... PATINA
slang ... ... AUDACITY,
INSOLENCE
crustacean ... LOBSTER, CRAB,
SHRIMP, LIMULUS, PRAWN,
COPEPOD, ISOPOD,
PAGURID, SCHIZOPOD,
PAGURIAN
burrowing ... ... SQUILLA,
MANTIS CRAB
claw ... ... CHELA

covering ... ... SHELL
eggs ... ... ROE, CORAL
feeler ... ... ANTENNA
horny substance ... CHITIN
limb of ... ... PLEOPOD
parasitic ... ... CIRRIPED,
BARNACLE
segment ... ... SOMITE,
TELSON
skin secretion ... ... CHITIN
spawn ... ... ROE, CORAL
10-legged ... ... PRAWN,
MACRURAN, LOBSTER,
SHRIMP, DECAPOD
walking and swimming ... ...
AMPHIPOD, SANDFLEA,
SHRIMP
crusty ... ... HARSH, SURLY,
ILL-TEMPERED
spot ... ... SCAB
crutch ... ... PROP, SUPPORT
crux ... ... PUZZLE, CROSS
ansata ... ... ANKH
cry ... ... SHOUT, SOB, BEG,
EXCLAIM, ENTREATY,
CLAMOR, WEEP, PULE,
YELP, WAIL
animal's ... ... BRAY
Australian ... ... COOEE,
COOBY
baby ... ... MEWL
companion of ... ... HUB
harsh, loud ... ... SQUAWK
high-pitched/shrill ... ...
SQUEAL, SQUALL
hunter's ... ... TALLYHO
like crazy ... ... BAWL
mournful ... ... YOWL
of Bacchantes ... ... EVOE
of calf ... ... BLEAT
of child ... MEWL, PULE,
WHIMPER
of disapproval ... ... BOO,
HISS, CATCALL, HOOT
of goat ... ... BLEAT
of pain ... ... OUCH
of surrender, 1918 ... ...
KAMERAD
out ... ... ULULATE, YELL,
EXCLAIM
party ... ... SHIBBOLETH,
WATCHWORD, SLOGAN
to the hounds ... YOICKS
crybaby ... ... POOR LOSER,
POOR SPORT
crypt ... ... VAULT

cryptic ..... SECRET, OCCULT,
OBSCURE, ENIGMATIC
cryptogram .... CODE, CIPHER
crystal .... CLEAR, GLASS,
HEMITROPE
clear .... LUCID
gazer .... SEER
crystalline .... PELLUCID
alcohol ... CALCIFEROL
alkaloid ...... ATROPINE,
AMARINE
and granular ....
SACCHAROID
biblical ...... BDELLIUM
compound ... BORAZON,
SERINE, CATECHOL,
CELESTINE
lined stone ...... GEODE
moisture .... DEW
resin .... CANNABIN
salt .... BORAX
substance ... CARBAZOLE,
UREA
crystallite ..... JELL, SOLIDIFY,
(TAKE)FORM
crystallize .... JELL
crystallized sugar/syrup .....
CANDY
ctenophores .... NUDA
cub ...... NOVICE, BEGINNER,
LIONET
kind of ...... REPORTER
Scout group .... DEN
Cuba, U.S. base in ....
GUANTANAMO
cubage .... VOLUME
Cuban .... HABANERO
bearded one ....
(FIDEL) CASTRO
capital .... HAVANA
castle .... MORRO
chess champ ....
CAPABLANCA
cigar .... HAVANA
city .. MARIANO, HOLGUIN,
CAMAGUEY
dance .... R(H)UMBA,
HABANERA
dictator ...... BATISTA,
CASTRO
discoverer ... COLUMBUS
drum .... BONGO
food fish ...... PINTADO
measure .... TAREA
monetary unit ..... PESO
music .... MAMBO

palm leaf .... CHIP
premier .... CASTRO
president .... DORTICOS,
MACHADO
province .... ORIENTE
rum .... BACARDI
seaport .... MANZANILLO,
MATANZAS
secret police ..... PORRA
snake .... JUBA
tempest .... BAYAMO
tobacco .... VUELTA
cubbyhole of a sort .... DEN
cube .... DIE, DICE
cubeb ..... BERRY, CIGARETTE
cubic capacity, ship's ....
TONNAGE
content ...... CUBATURE,
VOLUME
decimeter .. LITER, LITRE
foot per second ... CUSEC
meter .... STERE
cubicle .. DEN, BEDROOM, CELL,
COMPARTMENT
cuckoo .... ANI, BIRD, GOWK,
KOEL, TOURACO
of the ..... CUCULIFORM
slang ..... CRAZY, SILLY,
FOOLISH
cuckoopint .... ARUM
cucullate .. COWLED, HOODED
cucumber .... GHERKIN, PEPO,
GOURD, PICKLE
cool as a .. CALM, POISED,
COMPOSED
pickled .... MANGO
relish .... PICKLES
Spanish .... PEPINO
cucurbit ...... GOURD, FLASK
cucurbitaceous herb .. GOURD,
SQUASH, MELON, CUCUMBER
cud .... RUMEN, CHEW
chew the .... RUMINATE,
PONDER
chewer's stomach ......
PAUNCH, RUMEN
chewing animal ... COW,
RUMINANT, CATTLE,
BUFFALO, BISON, DEER,
CAMEL, GOAT, LLAMA,
GIRAFFE, CARABAO
variant of .... QUID
cudbear .... DYE, LICHEN
cuddle .... HUG, CARESS,
EMBRACE, SNUGGLE, NESTLE,
CURL UP

cuddy .... CUPBOARD, CLOSET
    Scottish ...... DONKEY,
                    COALFISH
cudgel .... CLUB, SHILLALAH,
    DRUB, STICK, TRUNCHEON,
           BASTINADO, BAT
    one's brains ...... RACK
cudgels, take up the .. DEFEND
cue .. HINT, SIGNAL, ROD, TIP,
                  TAIL
    actor's ..... CATCHWORD
    bridge of .... JIGGER
    in music .... PRESA
    of hair .. PIGTAIL, QUEUE,
                BRAID
    substitute, billiards .....
                MACE
cuff .. BOX, SLAP, BIFF, BELT,
    CLOUT, WRISTBAND
Cugat, bandleader ... XAVIER
cuirass .. BREASTPLATE, MAIL,
    LORIC(A), ARMOR, CORSELET,
           LORLEA
cuisine .... KITCHEN
    of the .... CULINARY
cuisinier .... CHEF, COOK
cul-de-sac ...... BLIND ALLEY
Culbertson, card expert .. ELY
culex pipiens ..... MOSQUITO
cull ...... SELECT, PICK OUT,
               GLEAN
cullis .... GUTTER
cully .... DUPE
    British: sl. ... PAL, BUDDY
culm ... COAL, DUST, HA(U)LM
culminating point .. HIGH TIDE,
               CRISIS
culmination .... ACME, CLIMAX
    sun's ...... NOON, ZENITH
culpa .... FAULT, GUILT
culpability .... GUILT
culprit .. OFFENDER, CRIMINAL
cult .... SECT, FAD, ISM
    artistic .... DADA
    naked .... NUDISM
cultivate .. GROW, FARM, TILL,
    FOSTER, DEVELOP, NURSE
cultivated .. REFINED, TILLED,
    CULTURED, HIGHBROW
    land ...... ARADA, FARM
    plot .... GARDEN
cultivation of soil .. CULTURE,
               TILTH
cultivator .... TILLER
cultural studies ...... ARTS

culture .. CIVILIZATION, ARTS,
    REFINEMENT, POLISH
    medium .... AGAR
cultured person .... LADY,
    GENTLEMAN, SCHOLAR
culver .... DOVE, PIGEON
culvert .. WATERWAY, DRAIN
    opening .... INLET
cum .... WITH
cumber .... HINDER, HAMPER,
          BURDEN, LOAD
cumbersome .. HEAVY, CLUMSY
cumin .... ANISE
cummer .... GODMOTHER
cummerbund .... SASH
cumshaw .... GRATUITY, TIP
cunner .. GILTHEAD
cunning .. CLEVER, SLY, WILY,
    ARTFUL, CRAFT(Y), FOXY,
            GUILE
    as a fox .... VULPINE
cuon .... DHOLE
cup .. BOWL, CHALICE, CALIX,
    CANNIKIN, BEAKER
    assaying .... CUPEL, TEST
    ceremonial ...... AMA
    drinking .. MUG, GOBLET,
        TASS, TANKARD,
        NOGGIN, CRUSE,
        STOUP, CYLIX,
        RUMMER, TAZZA
    druggist's ...... BEAKER
    flower .... CALYX
    gem-cutting .... DOP
    holder .... ZARF
    knight's quest ... GRAIL
    like .... CALICULAR
    like spoon ...... LADLE
    like vessel .. CUPEL, TEST
    metal .... PANNIKIN
    of tea: Brit. colloq. .....
    HOBBY, AVOCATION
    sports championship ....
    DAVIS, RYDER,
    WIGHTMAN, AMERICA'S
    to measure liquid ....
              JIGGER
    wine .... BEAKER
cupbearer of the gods .... HEBE,
          GANYMEDE
cupboard .. ARMOIRE, CUDDY,
    AMBRY, CLOSET, CABINET
Cupid .... EROS, AMOR
    infant .... AMORETTO,
          AMORINO
    mother of .... VENUS

sweetheart of ... PSYCHE
title of .... DAN
cupidity ..... AVARICE, GREED
cupola .... DOME
  battleship's ..... TURRET
cuprous oxide ... CHALCOCITE
cuprum .... COPPER
cur .... MONGREL, TIKE, TYKE,
                            MUTT
curable .... MEDICABLE
curacao, orange-flavored .....
                       COINTREAU
curare .... POISON, URARI,
  OURALI, WOURALI, WOORALI,
                            URALI
curate .. CLERGYMAN, PRIEST
curative ...... THERAPEUTIC,
  SANATIVE, SANATORY,
  HEALING, REMEDIAL
curator .... GUARDIAN
  concern of ... ARCHIVES,
    MUSEUM, LIBRARY,
                         RELICS
curb .. CHECK, REIN, RESTRAIN,
                        MARKET
  colloquial .... LID
  for woman's tongue ....
                        BRANKS
  market item ...... STOCK,
                          BOND
curbing inward ...... ADUNC
curch .... KERCHIEF
curculio .... BEETLE
curcuma .. TURMERIC, GINGER
curd .... CASEIN
  soybean ... TAHO, TOFU,
                         TOKUA
curdle .... COAGULATE,
  CLABBER, CONGEAL
curdled milk ...... CLABBER
curdling material ... RENNET,
                        RENNIN
curds with cream .... JUNKET
cure .... HEAL, REMEDY,
  THERAPY, PRESERVE
  all .... ELIXIR, PANACEA,
    CATHOLICON, NOSTRUM
  by salting .... CORN
  French .... PRIEST
  kind of .... REST, WATER
curfew feature .. LIGHTS OUT
  man ...... TOWN(CRIER)
curia official, Catholic ....
                        DATARY
curio(s) ..... BIBELOT, VIRTU
  collector ..... VIRTUOSO

curiosa .... NOVELTIES
curious .... ODD, PRYING,
  INQUISITIVE, NOS(E)Y
  one .. PRY, SNOOP(ER),
    BUSYBODY, CAT
curl .. COIL, RINGLET, FRIZ(ZLE)
  hair .... MARCEL
  snugly ...... ENSCONCE,
                        CUDDLE
  the lip .... SNEER
curled ...... CRISPATE, SPIRY,
                        CRIMPED
  lip .... SNEER
curlew .... SNIPE, WHAUP,
                        GODWIT
  bird resembling ....
                        WHIMBREL
"Curlew River" character ....
                        FERRYMAN
curlicue .... FLOURISH, CURVE
curling iron .... CRISPER
  mark/target .... TEE
  match .... BONSPIEL
  place .... RINK
curlpaper .... PAPILLOTE
curly .... KINKY, WAVY
curmudgeon .... CRAB
curn .... GRAIN, FEW
curr .... MURMUR, COO
currach .... CORACLE
currant ...... GRAPE, BERRY,
  SHRUB, RISSEL
  syrup .... CASSIS
currency ...... CIRCULATION,
  PREVALENCE, MONEY, CASH
  value of .... VALUTA
current .... GOING(ON), TIDE,
  IN VOGUE, STREAM
  air .... DRAFT
  beneath surf ....
                        UNDERTOW
  combining form .. RHEO
  expenses .... OVERHEAD
  opposite ...... SETBACK
currently .. NOW, PRESENTLY,
  AT PRESENT
currier .... COMBER
Currier and Ives ..... PRINTS
curry .... STEW, BEAT, COMB,
  DRESS, FLOG, DRUB
  favor .... FAWN, FLATTER
  ingredient .... CUMIN
curse ..... DAMN, ANATHEMA,
  BAN, OATH, REVILE,
  IMPRECATION, EXECRATE,
  SWEAR, BANE, SWEARWORD,

MARANATHA, MALISON,
MALEDICTION

Archaic ... ... WANION,
MALISON

colloquial ... ... CUSS

cursed .. EVIL, WICKED, ODIOUS

curser, Biblical ... . BALAAM

cursillo founder ... ... HERVAS

cursive ... ... RUNNING

cursory ... ... RANDOM, CASUAL,
SUPERFICIAL

look .. GLANCE, GLIMPSE

curt ... ... BLUFF, BRIEF, TERSE,
BLUNT, SHORT, BRUSQUE

dismissal ... ... CONGE

curtail ... .. REDUCE, SHORTEN

curtain ... ... DRAPE, SCREEN,
COVER, VALANCE,
VEILING

behind stage ... BACKDROP

Cold War ... ... IRON,
BAMBOO

color ... ... ECRU

holder ... ... ROD

material .. GAUZE, SCRIM,
NINON, TAPIS, LENO,
GRENADINE

of gun fire ... ... BARRAGE

raiser ... ... SKIT,
PRELIMINARY

rod band ... ... CORNICE

sash ... ... TIEBACK

shade ... ... ECRU

woman's apartment ... ...
PURDAH

curtains: sl. ... ... END, DEATH

curtsy .. SALUTATION, SALUTE,
BOB, LOUT

curvature ... ... ARC(H)

curve ... ... ARC, BEND, OGEE,
ARCH, SINUS, FLEXURE,
HYPERBOLA

baseball pitch ... ... HOOK

double ... ... ESS

handwriting .. CURLICUE,
FLOURISH

inward ... ... INFLECT

mark over vowel .. BREVE

of a column ... .. ENTASIS

of river ... ... BEND

path of missile ... ...
TRAJECTORY

pitcher's ... ... HOOK

plane ... ... PARABOLA

S-shaped ... ... OGEE

curved ... ARCUATE, ARCHED,

BENT, ADUNC, FALACTE,
FALCIFORM

in ... ... CONCAVE

molding ... ... OGEE

out ... ... CONVEX

plank, ship's ... ... SNY

surface of arch ... ...
EXTRADOS

sword ... ... SCIMITAR

curves, having two ... BIFLEX

curvet ... ... LEAP, FROLIC,
GAMBOL, VAULT

curving inward ... ... ADUNC

cushat ... ... (WOOD)PIGEON,
(RING)DOVE

cushaw ... ... SQUASH

cushion .. PILLOW, PAD, MAT,
ABSORB, HASSOCK, BOLSTER,
SQUAB

Cush's father ... ... HAM

son ... ... NIMROD

cushy: sl. ... ... EASY

cusk ... ... BURBOT

relative ... ... COD

cusp of moon ... ... HORN

cuspid ... ... TOOTH, FANG

cuspidor ... ... SPITTOON

cussed: colloq. ... STUBBORN,
SWORE

custard ... ... PIE

apple ... ... PA(W)PAW

cake ... ... ECLAIR

dish ... ... FLAN

like dish ... ... TIMBALE

Custer's battle site ... ...
LITTLE BIG HORN

nemesis .. SITTING BULL

custodian ... ... CARETAKER,
CONCIERGE, KEEPER, CUSTOS,
GUARDIAN, JANITOR,
WARDEN, WARDER

museum ... ... CURATOR

of funds ... ... TREASURER

of minors ... GUARDIAN

custody ... ... CHARGE, CARE,
GUARDIANSHIP, TRUST,
WARDSHIP

take into ... ... ARREST,
DETAIN, HOLD

custom ... ... HABIT, USAGE,
WONT, PRACTICE, PRAXIS

built .. MADE-TO-ORDER

with force of law ... ...
MORES, MOS

customary .. WONTED, USUAL,
HABITUAL, RULE

extras .... ETCETERAS
requirement .. FORMALITY
usage .... MODE
customer .... PATRON, BUYER,
               USER
credit record .. PASSBOOK
present to a ....
            LAGN(I)APPE
customers .. TRADE, CLIENTELE
customs .... MORES
charge .... IMPOST, DUTY
collector: biblical ....
               MATTHEW
municipal ...... OCTROI
official ...... SURVEYOR
cut .. SHEAR, LOP, SEVER, SAW,
      SNIP, NIP, KERF, DOCK,
           TRENCH, HEW
across .... TRANSECT,
           INTERSECT
beef .... CHUCK
blubber .... FLENSE
and dried .... DULL,
      BORING, ROUTINE
close .. SHAVE, CROP, CLIP
colloquial .... SNUB,
           IGNORE
companion of .... DRIED
crop .... REAP
crudely .... HACKLE,
           HAGGLE
dead: colloq. ..... SNUB,
      COLD SHOULDER,
           REBUFF
deep .... GASH
down ...... FELL, MOW
down trees .... LUMBER
edge of coin ...... NIG
ends .. SHEAR, TRIM, LOP
expenses .... ECONOMIZE,
           RETRENCH
glass .... CRYSTAL
grass .... MOW
hair .... BARBER
horse's tail .... DOCK
in .... INTERRUPT
in cubes .... DICE
in half ... BISECT, HALVE
into ...... INCISE, LANCE
into small pieces ....
      MINCE, DICE, HASH
leather .... SKIVE
lengthwise .... SLIT
meat .... CARVE
neck .... BEHEAD,
           DECAPITATE

notch ..... NICK, SNICK
of ax .... KERF
of meat ...... SPARERIB,
      SIRLOIN, CHINE, LOIN,
      T-BONE, CHOP, CHUCK,
           STEAK
off .... BOB, DOCK, CLIP,
      POLL, KERF, LOP,
      ROACH, INTERCEPT,
           INTERRUPT
off head .... DECAPITATE
off piece/slice ... CANTLE
off wool ... SHEAR, POLL
out ...... EXCISE, ELIDE,
      EXCIDE, EXSCIND,
           EXSECT
out disk .... TREPAN
rind .... PARE, PEEL
roast .... CARVE
roughly .. HACKLE, HACK
saw-toothed edge .. PINK
short .. BOB, CROP, STOP,
           POLL, CLIP
skin .... PARE, PEEL
slang .... SHARE
slight .... NICK, SNICK
spiral grooves .... RIFLE
thin ...... SLICE, SLIVER,
           SKIVE
thru water .... PLOUGH,
           PLOW
to pieces .. SHRED, MINCE
to requirement .. TAILOR
V-shaped .... NOTCH
way thru .... PLOW
with axe ... HACK, HEW,
           CHOP
with scissors ...... SNIP
with sweeping stroke ....
           SLASH
cutaneous .... DERMAL
cutch .... CATECHU
cute .... CLEVER, SHARP,
      SHREWD, PRETTY
cuticle ...... EPIDERMIS, SKIN
cutis .... DERMA, DERMIS,
           CORIUM
cutlass ...... (BROAD)SWORD,
           CURTLE AX
cutlery item .. KNIFE, SPOON,
           FORK
cutlet, veal .... SCHNITZEL
cutout pattern ...... STENCIL
cutpurse .. THIEF, PICKPOCKET
cutter .. VESSEL, SLED, YACHT,
      SLEIGH, SLOOP

leaf .... ANT
of life's thread .. ATROPOS
of precious stones ......
.... LAPIDARY
cutthroat — — ASSASSIN, THUG
.... MURDERER
cutting .... TART, EDGED,
SHARP, INCISIVE, (S)CION,
KERF, TRENCHANT, KEEN
British .... CLIPPING
edge .... LIP
off last letter of word ...
.... APOCOPE
off vowel .... ELISION
part of tool .... BIT
remarks ...... RAP, DIG,
INSULT, SARCASM
tool .... AX(E), BOLO,
MACHETE, ADZ(E),
RAZOR, KNIFE, BUR,
SHEARS, MOWER,
SCISSORS, SICKLE,
SCYTHE, SAW
tool, engraver's .. BURIN,
GRAVER, CHISEL,
CHASER
tool holder ...... ARBOR
tool seller .... CUTLER
tools .... CUTLERY
tooth .... INCISOR
cuttlefish — — SEPIA, SQUID,
BELEMNITE
bone .... POUNCE
ejecting organ .. SIPHON
fluid/secretion ..... INK
fossil — — THUNDERSTONE,
BELEMNITE
kin .... SPIRULA
cutup .... PRANKSTER, CLOWN
Cuzco Indian .... INCA
location of .... PERU
Cy Young awardee .. MCLAIN,
GIBSON, SEAVER
cyanic .... BLUE
cyanotype .... BLUEPRINT
Cybele .... RHEA
beloved of .... ATTIS
Cyclades ... IOS, MILO, NAXOS,
PAROS, TINOS, DELOS, ZEA,
KEOS, MELOS
cycle .... AGE, SAROS
of 15 years ... INDICTION
of heavenly body .. ORBIT
of years .... EPOCH, EON
cycloid .... CIRCULAR
cyclone .... TORNADO,

HURRICANE, WINDSTORM,
TWISTER
Cyclops .... GIANT
Odysseus' captor ......
.... POLYPHEMUS
cyclostome — — — LAMPREY,
HAGFISH
cyesis — — — — GESTATION,
PREGNANCY
cygnet .... SWAN
Cygnus .... SWAN,
CONSTELLATION
star in .... DENEB
cylinder ...... TUBE, BARREL
covering .... LAG(GING)
in a cylinder ..... PISTON
part .... PISTON
spiral .... HELIX
water marker ....
.... DANDY ROLL(ER)
cylindrical .. TOROSE, TOROUS,
TERETE
cyma ...... MOLDING, GOLA
cymar .... CHEMISE
cymbals .... TAL, ZEL
cyme .... PHLOX
Cymric ..... WELSH, BRETON,
CELTIC
cynic, look of — LEER, SNEER,
COLD
of sorts .... SKEPTIC
cynosure .... POLESTAR,
LODESTAR, NORTH STAR
Cynthia ...... LUNA, MOON,
ARTEMIS, DIANA
diminutive of .... CINDY
cypress .. TREE, CLOTH, SATIN,
SILK
cyprinoid ... CARP, GOLDFISH,
BARBEL, IDE, DACE, CHUB
Cyprus, capital of .. NICOSIA,
LIMASSOL
city ... SALAMIS, PAPHOS,
FAMUGUSTA
leader .... MAKARIOS
union with Greece ......
.... ENOSIS
Cyrano's shame — — NOSE
Cyrenaica .... BARCA
capital .... CYRENE
Cytherea .. VENUS, APHRODITE
cyst .. SAC, WEN, POUCH, BAG,
VESICLE
with worm larvae ....
.... HYDATID

czar .... TSAR, EMPEROR,
DESPOT, NICHOLAS
daughter of .. CZAREVNA,
TSAREVNA
heir of ..... CZAREVITCH
wife of .... CZARINA,
TSARINA, CZARITZA
Czechoslovakian .... SLOVAK,
BOHEMIAN, MORAVIAN, SLAV,
SILESIAN
brandy ...... SLIVOVITZ
capital .. PRAGUE (PRAHA)
castle .... HRADCANY
city ...... BRNO, PILSEN,
BUDWEIS, BRUNN,
BRATISLAVA, OSTRAVA,
KOSICE, OLOMOUC
coin ← DUCAT, KRONEN,
HELLER, KORUNA
composer ....
(RUDOLF) FRIML,
SMETANA, JANACEK

folk hero ..... SCHWEIK
hero .... (JAN)HUS
historian ...... PALACKY
leader .. DUBCHEK, HUSAK
monetary unit .. KORUNA
munition works .. SKODA
news agency .... CETEKA
patriot ...... MASARYK,
STEFANIK
premier .... LENART,
CERNI(C)K
president .... NOVOTNY,
BENES, MASARYK,
GOTTWALD, SVOBODA
public square ....
WENCESLAS
rail center ...... ZILINA
region .. CECHY, BOHEMIA
river .. ISER, IPOLY, OHRE,
MOLDAU, VLTAVA,
MORAVA, EGER
steel works ...... SKODA
town .← CARLSBAD, LIDICE

D

D, Greek .... DELTA
Hebrew ..... DALETH,
DALEDH
letter .... DEE, DELTA
dab .... PECK, PAT, TAP,
FLATFISH, FLOUNDER,
TOUCH, STRIKE, PAINT
colloquial ...... EXPERT
dabble .... DIP, WET
in .... SMATTER
dabbler ...... DILETTANTE,
AMATEUR, TYRO, DUFFER
dabchick .... GREBE, DUCKER,
DIDAPPER, DIPPER,
HELL-DIVER
dabster ..... EXPERT, DABBLER
dace .... CARP
dachshund .... DOG
dacoit ...... ROBBER, BANDIT
dacron .... FIBER
dactyl, in zoology ... FINGER,
TOE
dactylogram .... FINGERPRINT
dad .... FATHER
daddy ..... FATHER, DAD, POP,
PAPPY
longlegs .... CRANE, FLY,
SPINNER, HARVESTMAN
dado .... DIE, WAINSCOT,
SOLIDUM

daedal .... INGENIOUS,
INTRICATE, ELABORATE,
VARIED
Daedalus' son .... ICARUS
victim/nephew .. TALOS
daemon .... DEVIL
daffodil .... NARCISSUS
plant resembling ....
JONQUIL
Daffy, baseball player .. DEAN
colloquial ...... CRAZY,
SILLY, IDIOTIC,
FOOLISH
daft .... SILLY, FOOLISH,
INSANE, IDIOTIC
dagger .... DIRK, BODKIN,
PONIARD, SNEE,
STILETTO, CREESE,
SKEAN
attached to gun ....
BAYONET
Burmese .... DAH
double .... DIESIS
handle .... HILT, HAFT
hilt .... DUDGEON
mark, in printing ....
DIESIS, OBELUS
Malay ..... KRIS, CRIS(S)
medieval ...... ANLACE
of mercy .. MISERICORD(E)

signs in printing ... OBELI
stroke ..... LUNGE, STAB,
          THRUST, STOCCADO
two-edged ..... COUTEAU
wound .... STAB
Dahomey capital ....
          PORTO NOVO
chief of state ..... SOGLO
city .... COTONOU
ethnic group ...... FON,
     ADJA, BORIBA, MAHI,
          YORUBA
native .... FON
seaport ...... WHIDAH
Dai Nippon .... JAPAN
daily .... NEWSPAPER,
     DIURNAL, EVERYDAY,
          QUOTIDIAN, PER DIEM
delivery ..... MAIL, MILK
dozen ...... EXERCISES,
          CONSTITUTIONAL
fare .... DIET
feature article ... COLUMN
newspaper ..... JOURNAL
record .... DIARY,
          JOURNAL
daimio .... NOBLEMAN
retainer of ..... SAMURAI
dainties .. DELICACIES, TIDBITS
dainty .... FINE, NICE,
     FASTIDIOUS, DELICATE,
     MIGNON, CHOICE, TAFFETA
archaic .... CATE
daiquiri .... COCKTAIL
ingredient .... RUM, LIME
Dairen .... TALIEN, DALNY
dairy .... LACTARY,
          LACTARIUM
cattle .... JERSEY
farm area   MILKSHED
maid ...... DEY, GOWAN
product .... BUTTER,
          CHEESE, MILK
shop .... CREAMERY
dais ...... PODIUM, PLATFORM,
     ROSTRUM, STAGE,
     ESTRADE, TRIBUNE
daisy .... OXEYE, SHASTA,
     CHRYSANTHEMUM,
     GOWAN, MARGUERITE
cutter, baseball ....
          GROUNDER
English .... GOWAN
dak .... MAIL
Dakar, capital of ... SENEGAL
Daker hen ..... CORN CRAKE

Dakota Indian .... SIOUX, REE
dale .... DELL, DINGLE,
          GLEN, VALE, VALLEY
Dali, painter ..... SURREALIST,
          SALVADOR
dalles .... RAPIDS
dalliance .... FLIRTATION
dally ...... LOITER, TRIFLE,
          FLIRT, TOY
Dalmatian .... DOG, SLAV
decor .... SPOTS
dog's name .... SPOT
dam ..... BARRAGE, BARRIER,
     MILLPOND, KEEP BACK,
          STEM, DIKE
archaic .... MOTHER
builder, animal ... OTTER
designer .... SAVAGE
Egyptian .... ASWAN,
          SADD
horse .... MARE
in the U.S. ..... HOOVER,
     SHASTA, BOULDER,
          COULEE
river .... WEIR
damage ...... LOSS, INJURE,
          INJURY, HARM
colloquial .... COST,
          EXPENSE
slang .... BUNG
suit .... TROVER
damages, claim for ... TROVER
daman .... HYRAX, CONY,
          CONEY, MAMMAL
Damansky to the Chinese .....
          CHEN PAO
Damascene .... PLUM
Damascus caliph .... OMMIAD
is capital of ..... SYRIA
damask .... ROSE, LINEN,
          STEEL
for hangings ... DORNICK
for vestments, etc. ......
          DORNICK, DORNOCK
like cloth ...... LAMPAS
dame .... LADY, MATRON
equivalent title of .... SIR
slang .... GIRL, WOMAN,
          GAL
dammar .... RESIN
damn ...... CONDEMN, CURSE,
          DOOM
damnation .... PERDITION
damned .... OUTRAGEOUS
dialectic .... TARNATION,
          TARNAL

Damocles, word associated with
SWORD
damoiselle ..... DAMSEL, MISS
Damon and ——— .... PYTHIAS
damp .... HUMID, DANK,
MOIST, WET(NESS)
   become .... JIG
dampen .... DEPRESS, WET,
DISHEARTEN, MOISTEN
damsel .... GIRL, MAIDEN
   fly .... DRAGONFLY
damson .... PLUM
Dan ...... MASTER, SIR, BUOY
   Cupid .... EROS
Dane .... JUTLANDER
dance .... BALL, CLOG,
CAPER, BALLET, JIG, POLKA,
HOOF, GALOP, TRIPPING
   attendance ..... WAIT ON
   Bohemian ..... REDOWA
   child on knee ... DANDLE
   college ...... HOP, PROM
   colloquial ...... SHINDIG,
DRAG
   country ..... REEL, BARN,
ALTHEA, LANDLER, HAY
   crazed person ....
TARANTIST
   Cuban .... R(H)UMBA,
CONGA, HABANERA
   English .... MORRIS
   folk .... DREHER, HORA
   for two .... TANGO,
WALTZ, FOXTROT
   French ... BAL, MINUET,
FARANDOLA, RIGADOON,
GAVOT, GALLIARD
   hall ...... CABARET, GAFF,
CASINO
   hall girl .... HOSTESS
   Hawaiian .. HULA (HULA)
   Hungarian ..... CZARDAS
   Israeli .... HORA
   Italian .... COURANTE
   kind of .... FOXTROT, TOE,
WALTZ, BALLET, TAP,
BELLY
   lively .... REEL, JUBA,
FANDANGO, GALOP,
COURANTE, CONGA,
GALLOPADE,
COTILLION, HORNPIPE,
TAMBOURIN, CORANTO,
FLING, SALTARELLO
   made to castanets ......
BOLERO, FLAMENCO

   modern .... SHAG, FRUG,
ROCK N'ROLL
   music .... VALSE, WALTZ,
FOXTROT, TANGO,
RAGTIME
   Negro .... JUBA
   of death ....
DANSE MACABRE
   of 1930 .... SHAG
   of 1929 .... CHARLESTON
   old .... PAVAN(E),
PAVIN, CAROLE
   on knee .... DANDLE
   Polish .... POLONAISE
   polka like .. MAZ(O)URKA
   sailor's ...... HORNPIPE
   school ...... PROM, HOP
   Scottish .... REEL
   slang .... HOOF
   slow, graceful ... ADAGIO,
MINUET
   South American ....
TANGO, CARIOCA
   Southwest ...... BAILE
   Spanish ..... FANDANGO,
FLAMENCO, BOLERO, TANGO
   square ...... DOSADOS,
LANC(I)ERS, HOEDOWN
   stately .... MINUET,
SARABAND
   step .... CURTSY, PAS,
GLISSADE, CHASSE, SHAG
   triple time .... JIG
   two-fourth time ... GALOP
   Virginia .... REEL
   war .... PYRRHIC
   watcher ... WALLFLOWER
   white-tie .... FORMAL
   with castanets ....
FLAMENCO, BOLERO
   with handclapping .. JUBA
   with high kicking ......
CANCAN
   with wooden shoes .....
CLOG
dancer ...... ALME(H), ALMA,
CHORINE, DANSEUSE,
ASTAIRE, CASTLE, ZORINA,
STEPPER
   ballet ..... DANSEUSE,
FIGURANT, BALLERINA,
CORYPHEE, FONTEYN,
SHEARER, PAVLOVA,
RASCH, ULANOVA, NUREYEV
   co-worker of ..... COMET
   concern of .... RHYTHM,

CHOREOGRAPHY, STEPS
dress of .... TUTU
jazz music .... JITTERBUG
kind of ...... TOE, BELLY,
TAP, BALLET, TANGO,
FLAMENCO, APACHE,
STRIPTEASE
professional ..... HOOFER
shoe of .... CLOG
swing .... HEPCAT
tap .... HOOFER
wear of ...... LEOTARD,
TUTU, TIGHTS
dancing ...... CHOREOGRAPHY,
SALTANT, SALTATION
craze for .... TARENTISM,
TARANTISM
girl, Egyptian ....
ALMD(H), ALMA
girl, India .... BAYADERE,
BAYADEER, ALME(H)
girl, Japanese .... GEISHA
girls .... CHORINE
horses .... LIPPIZAN
kind of .... TOE, BELLY,
TAP
master ...... MURRAY,
ASTAIRE
muse of .... TERPSICHORE
partner, professional ....
GIGOLO
place also .... CASINO
shoes .... PUMPS
dandelion .... WEED,
KOK-SAGYZ
stalk .... SCAPE
tuft .... PUFFBALL
dander ...... ANGER, TEMPER,
IRE
dandify .... SPRUCE, DRESS UP
dandle .... FONDLE, DANCE,
PET, CARESS
dandruff .... FURFUR, SCURF
dandy .... PRIG, COXCOMB,
TOFF, NATTY, BUCK,
FOP, DUDE, BEAU
fever .... DENGUE
roll impression ....
WATER MARK
slang .... FIRST CLASS,
FINE, JOHNNY, JOHNNIE
dandyish .... BUCKISH
danger ...... PERIL, HAZARD,
JEOPARDY, RISK
hidden .... PITFALL
signal .. RED, ALARM, SIREN

dangerous .... PERILOUS,
UNSAFE, CRITICAL, RISKY
dangle .... LOLL, HANG
dangling .... ALOP
Daniel ____ ...... BOONE,
WEBSTER
Danish .... DANE
astronomer ...... BRAHE
capital .... COPENHAGEN
cheese ..... DANBO, ELBO,
FYNBO, TYBO, MOLBO,
MARIBO, BRIE, MYCELLA,
CAMEMBERT
chieftain .... JARL
coin .... RIGSDALER,
KRONE
composer ..... NIELSEN
district .... AMT
duchy .... HOLSTEIN
"farmer prince" .. INGOLF
historian .... SAXO
horse .... ZAIN
island ..... AERO, FAROE,
LOLLAND, GREENLAND,
ALS, FUNEN, FYN,
SEELAND
king .... CANUTE, CNUT,
FREDERIK, WALDEMAR,
KNUT
king, Shakespearean ....
HAMLET
land measure ... MORGEN
legislature .... RIGSDAG,
FOLKETING
monetary unit .... KRONE
native .... DANE
navigator ...... BERING
noble .... JARL
novelist .... NEXO
parliament .... RIGSDAG
peninsula ...... JUTLAND
physicist .... BOHR,
OERSTED
pianist .... BORGE
queen .... INGRID
seaport ...... HELSINGOR,
AARHUS
toast .... SKOAL
weight .... LOD
dank ...... DAMP, MOIST,
WET, HUMID
"Danse ____" ...... MACABRE
danseuse .... DANCER,
BALLERINA, CORYPHEE,
FIGURANT
Dante's beloved ..... BEATRICE

deathplace ..... RAVENNA
work .... INFERNO,
    DIVINE COMEDY
Danube city ...... LINZ, ULM
in German ...... DONAU
in Hungarian ..... DUNA
in Romanian .. DUNAREA
river .... ULM, SAVA,
    SAU, MORAVA, ISAR
Danzig .... GDANSK
dap .... DIP, BOUNCE, DIB,
    SKIP
Daphne ..... NYMPH, LAUREL,
    SHRUB
Dapnis' lover .... CHLOE
dapper ...... NEAT, SPRUCE,
    SMART, TRIM, NATTY
dapple .... MOTTLED, SPOTTED,
    PIEBALD, FLECK(ED),
    PIED
poetic .... FREAK
Dar es Salaam is capital of ....
    TANZANIA
darb .... DILLY, DART
Darcy's forte .... PRIDE
Dardan .... TROJAN
Dardanelles ..... HELLESPONT,
    STRAIT
dare .... RISK, VENTURE,
    FACE, DEFY, DAST,
    CHALLENGE, OPPOSE,
    DEFI
daredevil .... STUNTMAN,
    RECKLESS, BOLD,
    FOOLHARDY
Darien ...... GULF, ISTHMUS
daring .... BOLD, INTREPID,
    BRAVE, RISQUE, HARDY,
    ICARIAN
action ...... DERRING-DO
Darius scene of defeat .. ISSUS
dark .... EVIL, SINISTER,
    BLACK, DIM, EBON,
    HIDDEN, DUSKY, MIRK,
    RAYLESS, SABLE,
    TENEBROUS, MURK(Y),
    TENEBRIFIC
and dull .... SOMBER,
    SOMBRE
area of vision ... SCOTOMA
brown ...... BRUNET(TE),
    SEPIA, BISTRE, BISTER
complexion ..... BRUNET,
    SWARTHY
Continent .... AFRICA
haired .... MELANOUS

horse: colloq. .... SLEEPER,
    LONG-SHOT
hue ..... SOMBRE, SWART
in the .... IGNORANT,
    UNAWARE
marking in marble ......
    CLOUD
portending rain ....
    LOWERING
red .... LAKY
skinned ...... MELANOUS,
    SWARTHY
skinned person ... DAGO,
    WOP
wood .... EBONY
darkey .... NEGRO
darkness .... NIGHT
combining form .. SCOTO
darling ...... FAVORITE, PET,
    BELOVED, CHERI(E),
    MINIKIN
colloquial ...... DEARIE,
    DEARY, TOOTS
darn .... MEND
colloquial .... DAMN
darnel .... COCKLE, WEED,
    TARE
darning needle ... DRAGONFLY
dart ...... FLIT, DASH, SCOOT,
    MISSILE, ARROW,
    BARB, BOLT, SPURT
darter .... SNAKEBIRD
darts, bullfighter's ....
    BANDERILLA
Dartmoor ...... GAOL, PRISON
Darwinian theory ....
    EVOLUTION, PANGENESIS
dash .... SMASH, SPLASH,
    WRITE, VERVE, BIT,
    ELAN, ARDOR, DART,
    SPRINT, THROW
against .... LASH
colloquial .... DAM
mark .... HYPHEN
opposed to .... DOT
dashboard .... PANEL
dasheen ...... SPROUTS, TARO
dasher .... DOLLY
of a churn ..... PLUNGER
dashing ..... SHOWY, SPIRITED
manner .... PANACHE,
    DEVIL-MAY-CARE
dastard ...... COWARD, CAD,
    CRAVEN, POLTROON
dastardly .... COWARDLY,
    MEAN

dasyure ‥‥‥‥‥ MARSUPIAL
data ‥‥‥‥ FACTS, FIGURES
   computer's ‥‥‥‥ INPUT
date ‥‥‥‥‥ APPOINTMENT,
   PERIOD, FRUIT, CALENDS,
   TRYST, RENDEZVOUS
   abbreviation ‥‥‥ APPT
   approximate ‥‥‥ CIRCA
   fruit like ‥‥‥‥ JUJUBE
   go on a ‥‥‥‥ STEP OUT
   plum ‥‥‥‥‥ KAKI,
   PERSIMMON
   out of ‥‥‥‥ PASSE,
   OLD-FASHIONED
   sugar ‥‥‥‥‥ GHOOR
   tree ‥‥‥‥‥‥ PALM
   up to ‥‥‥‥‥ MODERN,
   FASHIONABLE, AS YET,
   UNTIL NOW
dated ‥‥‥‥ OLD-FASHIONED,
   PASSE, DECLASSE
datum plane example ‥‥‥‥
   SEA LEVEL
datura ‥‥‥‥‥‥ JIMSON
daub ‥‥‥‥ PLASTER, SMEAR,
   PAINT, GREASE,
   SLUBBER
daughter ‥‥‥‥ FILLE, HIJA
daughter(s) of Atlas and Pieione
   PLEIAD(ES)
daunt ‥‥‥‥‥ DISMAY, COW,
   INTIMIDATE, AWE, FAZE
dauntless ‥‥‥ BRAVE, INTREPID
davenport ‥‥‥‥ COUCH, SOFA,
   DESK
David's (King) captain ‥ JOAB
   commander ‥‥‥ AMASA,
   JOAB
   daughter ‥‥‥‥ TAMAR
   father ‥‥‥‥‥ JESSE
   rebuker ‥‥‥‥ NATHAN
   son ‥‥‥‥‥ SOLOMON
   wife ‥‥‥‥ BATHSHEBA
Davidoff's subject ‥‥‥ CIGARS
Davis, actress ‥‥‥‥ BETTE
Davis, Jr. ‥‥‥‥‥ SAMMY
davit ‥‥‥‥‥‥ CRANE
Davy Jones' seabottom ‥‥‥
   LOCKER
daw ‥‥‥‥‥‥ CROW
dawdle ‥‥‥‥ LOITER, IDLE,
   LOAF, LINGER,
   PIDDLE, PUTTER, POTTER
dawn ‥‥‥‥ DAYBREAK,
   SUNRISE, AURORA,
   MORN, SUNUP

goddess of ‥‥‥‥ EOS
herald of ‥‥‥‥ COCK,
   ROOSTER, LARK
pertaining to ‥‥‥ EOAN
to noon ‥‥‥‥ MORNING
to sunset ‥‥‥ DAYTIME
day ‥‥‥‥ AGE, EPOCH, ERA
and night of equal length
   ‥‥‥‥‥‥ EQUINOX
bed ‥‥‥‥ SOFA, COUCH
before ‥‥‥‥‥ EVE
every ‥‥‥‥‥ DAILY
in court ‥‥‥‥ HEARING,
   CHANCE, OPPORTUNITY
Latin ‥‥‥‥‥ DIES
letter ‥‥‥‥ TELEGRAM
march ‥‥‥ ‥‥‥ ETAPE
of greatest vigor ‥‥‥‥
   HEYDAY
Roman ‥‥‥ IDES, NONES
scholar ‥‥‥‥ EXTERN
star ‥‥‥‥‥‥ SUN
daybook ‥‥‥‥‥ DIARY,
   JOURNAL
daybreak ‥‥ DAWN, SUNRISE,
   AURORA, MORN
daydream ‥‥‥‥ REVERY,
   REVERIE, FANCY
daydreaming ‥‥‥‥ AUTISM,
   REVERIE
dayfly ‥‥‥‥‥ MAY FLY
daylight ‥‥‥ DAWN, PUBLICITY
   slang ‥‥‥‥‥ EYES
dayspring ‥‥‥‥‥ DAWN
daytime, pertaining to ‥‥‥‥
   DIURNAL
days, describing youthful ‥‥‥
   SALAD
Dayton suburb ‥‥‥ KETTERING
daze ‥‥‥‥ STUPEFY, TRANCE,
   DAZZLE, STUN,
   BEWILDER(MENT)
dazzle ‥‥‥‥ BLIND, IMPRESS
dazzling ‥‥‥‥‥ BLINDING,
   PRISMATIC
   momentarily ‥‥‥‥‥
   METEORIC
DDT ‥‥‥‥‥ INSECTICIDE,
   PESTICIDE
de facto ‥‥‥ ACTUAL, IN FACT
   jure ‥‥‥‥‥ BY RIGHT
   luxe ‥‥‥‥‥ ELEGANT,
   SUMPTUOUS
deacon ‥‥‥‥‥ CLERGYMAN,
   ADULTERATE
   clergyman above ‥ PRIEST

deactivate .... DEMOBILIZE
dead ..... DECEASED, LIFELESS,
(A)MORT, INANIMATE,
DEPARTED, EXTINCT
animal pretending to be ..
POSSUM
beat: colloquial ....
TIRED, EXHAUSTED
beat, slang ..... SPONGE,
WELSHER, LOAFER
bodies on battlefield ....
CARNAGE
body .... CADAVER,
CORPSE, CARCASS,
CARCASE, CORPUS,
STIFF, LICH
calm .... DOLDRUMS
combining form ... SAPRO
end .... IMPASSE
End Kids' member .....
GORCEY
end place .... SLUM,
GHETTO
flesh .... CARRION
hand .... MORTMAIN
heat .... TIE
house .... CHARNEL,
OSSARIUM, MORTUARY
pan .... POKERFACE
pan comedian ....
KEATON
person .... DECEDENT,
DECEASED
point .... CENTER
recently .... LATE
Sea find .... SCROLLS
Sea kingdom ...... MOAB
Sea river .... JORDAN
Sea scrolls location .....
QUMRAN
set .... DETERMINED,
FIRM
species .... EXTINCT
when delivered ....
STILLBORN
word preceding name of ..
LATE
deaden .... DULL, NUMB,
DAMPEN, OBTUND
sound .... MUFFLE, MUTE
deadener, pain ...... OPIATE,
AN(A)ESTHETIC, ANALGESIC,
DEMEROL
deadline .... TIME LIMIT
deadlock .... STALEMATE,
IMPASSE, STANDSTILL

jury .... HANG
deadly ...... FATAL, MORTAL,
LETHAL, DANGEROUS,
FERAL, BANEFUL,
VIRULENT, VITAL
Archaic .... FELL
enemy .... NEMESIS
plant ...... NIGHTSHADE,
BELLADONNA
poison ... STRYCHNINE(E)
sin .... PRIDE, LUST,
ANGER, COVETOUSNESS,
GLUTTONY, ENVY, SLOTH
snake ...... COBRA, ASP
to both sides ....
INTERNECINE
deadpan .... MASK
deaf ... UNHEARING, HEEDLESS
and _____ .... DUMB
deafen .... SOUNDPROOF
Scottish .... DEAVE
deafening .... NOISY
deal ...... DISTRIBUTE, SALE,
TRADE, FIR WOOD, GIVE,
ADMINISTER, NEGOTIATE,
TREAT
colloquial .... BARGAIN,
AGREEMENT
crookedly ...... PALTER
give-and-take ....
(HORSE)TRADE
out .... DOLE, ISSUE
dealer .... DISTRIBUTOR,
BUYER, SELLER, TRADER,
CHAPMAN, MONGER
cattle .... DROVER
cloth .... CLOTHIER,
DRAPER, MERCER
cutting tools .... CUTLER
foodstuff .... GROCER
gem .... LAPIDARY
in bonds ....
(STOCK)BROKER
in houses/lots .. REALTOR
in skins .... FURRIER
right of .... PONE
scrap .... JUNKMAN,
RAGMAN
dealings ...... TRANSACTIONS,
RELATIONS
dean .... DOYEN
baseball player ....
DIZZY, DAFFY
ecclesiastical .... PREFECT
feminine ...... DOYENNE
of a .... DECANAL

residence of .... DEANERY
deanery .... DECANAL
dear ...... BELOVED, COSTLY,
DARLING, EXPENSIVE
slang .... TOOTS
dearie .... DARLING
dearth ..... PAUCITY, FAMINE,
SCARCITY, LACK
death ...... DEMISE, PASSING,
DECEASE, MORT
by burning ..... SUTTEE
by hanging .... ROPE
causing .... FATAL,
LETHAL, MORTAL
combining form ....
NECR(O)
cup .... MUSHROOM
herald of ..... DANSHER,
BANSHIE
march .... DIRGE
march scene .... BATAAN
mercy ...... EUTHANASIA
near .... DYING
noise .... RATTLE
notice ...... OBIT(UARY),
NECROLOGY
of .... LETHAL, MORTUARY
painless, easy ....
EUTHANASIA
put to ...... KILL, HANG,
EXECUTE, SLAY
rate .... MORTALITY
rattle .... RALE
ring announcing .. TOLL,
KNELL
symbol .... SKULL
toll .... KNELL
view of .... THANATOPSIS
deathblow .... COUP DE GRACE
deathless .... IMMORTAL
deathlessness ..... ATHANASIA
death's-head .... SKULL
deathsman ...... EXECUTIONER
deathwatch ..... VIGIL, BEETLE
deave .... DEAFEN
deb .... DEBUTANTE, BUD
debacle ...... ROUT, DISASTER
debar ...... HINDER, EXCLUDE
debark .... LAND, UNLOAD,
ALIGHT
debase ..... CORRUPT, DEFILE,
DEGRADE, DEMEAN,
LOWER, PERVERT,
VITIATE, PROFANE
liquid .... DILUTE
metal .... ALLOY

morally .... DEPRAVE,
DEBAUCH
debatable .... MOOT,
CONTROVERSIAL
debate ..... ARGUE, DISPUTE,
CAUSERIE, CANVASS,
DISCUSS, REASON,
PALAVER, PLEAD
ending device .. CLOTURE
pertaining to ... FORENSIC
debauch .... CORRUPT,
DEPRAVE, DEBASE, ORGY
prolonged .. HELLBENDER
debauchee ...... RAKE, SATYR,
ROUE, LIBERTINE,
LECHER
debilitate .... WEAKEN,
ENERVATE, ENFEEBLE
debilitated .... RUN-DOWN
debility .... ATONY
debit .... CHARGE
debonair .... GENIAL, GAY,
SUAVE, URBANE
debouch .... EMERGE
debris ...... RUBBLE, RUBBISH,
SCREE, RUINS, DETRITUS,
TRASH, LITTER
tree prunings ..... BRASH
debt .... LIABILITY, ACCOUNT,
OBLIGATION
evader .... DEADBEAT
in theology .... SIN
note .... IOU
overdue .... ARREAR
relating to .... DEBIT
debtor .... OWER
debtor's prison .... FLEET
debunk ..... EXPOSE, UNMASK,
REFUTE
Debussy, composer ....
ACHILLE CLAUDE
composition ..... REVERIE
debut .... INTRODUCTION,
PRESENTATION
debutant(e) ...... BUD, DEB
ball .... COTILLION
delight of ..... STAGLINE
party for .... COMING OUT
decade ..... TEN, DECENNIUM
decadence ... DECLINE, DECAY,
DETERIORATION
decalogue, part of ....
COMMANDMENT
Decameron tales author ......
BOCCACCIO
decamp .... BOLT, FLEE,

ABSCOND, RUN AWAY, VAMO(O)SE, CLEAR OUT

decanal .... DEANERY

decant ..... POUR, ELUTRIATE

decanter .... CARAFE

stand .... TANTALUS

decapitate .... BEHEAD, DECOLLATE

decapitation ...... EXECUTION

decapod .... CRAB, SQUID, LOBSTER, SHRIMP, PRAWN

decay .... ROT, SPOIL, DECOMPOSE, PUTREFY, GANGRENE

bone .... CARIES

dental .... CARIES

fruit .... BLET, ROT

slow, crumbling .... MO(U)LDER

teeth .... CARIES

decayed .... PUTRID, ROTTEN, CARIOUS

in botany .... DOTY

in fruit .... BLET

decaying .... ROTTING

combining form ... SAPRO

dead body ..... CARRION

from age .... DOTING

vegetable matter ... DUFF

decease .... DEATH, DIE, DEMISE

deceased .... DECEDENT, DEAD, DEPARTED, LATE

deceit ..... LIE, WILE, FRAUD, COZENAGE, DECEPTION, IMPOSTURE, GUILE

archaic .... COVIN

deceitful .... FALSE, DISHONEST, DECEPTIVE, ARTFUL, WILY, TRICKY, CRAFTY

face .... MASK

sight .... MIRAGE, ILLUSION, HALLUCINATION

words .... LIES

deceive ...... DUPE, MISLEAD, DELUDE, LIE, HOODWINK, BEGUILE, FOOL, BETRAY, SPOOF, FOB, FUB, COZEN, ENTRAP

by flattery .... FLAM

deceiver .... BETRAYER, LIAR, FAKER, IMPOSTOR

decelerate .... SLOW DOWN

December decoration .... MISTLETOE, TINSEL

perennial .... SNOW

symbol ... SANTA (CLAUS)

28th........ CHILDERMAS

decenary .... TITHING

decency .... PROPRIETY, GOOD TASTE, DECORUM

decennium .... DECADE

decent ..... CHASTE, MODEST, RESPECTABLE, FAIR, PROPER, KIND

decentralize .... DISPERSE

deception .... LIE, FRAUD, HOAX, IMPOSTURE, CHICANERY, JAPE, TRICKERY, SPOOF, RUSE, FLIMFLAM

deceptive .... ILLUSORY, TRICKY, AMBIGUOUS, MISLEADING, DELUSIVE

trick .... FLAM

decide .... SETTLE, JUDGE, RESOLVE, CONCLUDE

issue by combat .... DERAIGN

judicially ...... ADJUDGE

decided ...... DEFINITE, SET, CLEAR CUT, SETTLED

decidedly .... CERTAINLY, DEFINITELY

decider of right or wrong ..... CASUIST

deciding game when tied .... RUN-OFF

vote .... CASTING

deciduous .... TEMPORARY

opposed to ... EVERGREEN

decimal ...... TENTH, DENARY

point .... DOT

point system inventor ... STEVIN

system of counting ... ALGORISM

decimate .... SLAUGHTER, MASSACRE

decipher ...... READ, DECODE, TRANSLATE

decipherable .... LEGIBLE, READABLE

decision .... JUDGMENT, SENTENCE, VERDICT, DECREE

await .... PEND

good for the future ..... PRECEDENT

decisive .... CONCLUSIVE,
       FINAL, FATEFUL
  argument ..... CLINCHER
  point/moment .. CLIMAX
    CRISIS, CRUCIAL,
    ZERO HOUR
deck .... ADORN, TRIM,
    CLOTHE, PLATFORM,
    COVER, ARRAY
  hand .... SAILOR,
    ROUSTABOUT
  hit the ..... GET UP, RISE
  lowest .... ORLOP
  on ..... READY, ON HAND
  out .... (BE)DIZEN,
    ARRAY, ADORN,
    CAPARISON
  Scottish .... DINK
  ship's ..... ORLOP, POOP
declaim .... ORATE, RANT,
    RECITE, PERORATE
declaimer .... RANTER,
    ORATOR
declamation ...... HARANGUE,
    ORATORY, ORATION
declaration ...... STATEMENT,
    PROCLAMATION
  in bridge .... BID
  of aims .... CHARTER,
    MANIFESTO
Declaration of Independence
  signer .... HANCOCK, WYTHE
declare ..... ASSERT, ALLEGE,
    PROFESS, AVER, STATE,
    PUBLISH
  guilty .... CONDEMN
  in cards .... MELD
  innocent .... ACQUIT,
    CLEAR
  untrue .... DENY
declasse .... DATED, PASSE
decline ...... SPURN, ABATE,
    REFUSE, SLUMP, WANE,
    DIP, EBB, REJECT
declivity .... SLOPE, SCARP
decoct ..... EXTRACT, DISTILL
decoction .... TISANE, PTISAN,
    TEA
decode .... DECIPHER
decollate .... BEHEAD,
    DECAPITATE
decollete .... LOW-CUT,
    LOW-NECKED
decolorize .... BLEACH
decompose ...... DECAY, ROT,
    PUTREFY, SPOIL

decomposed .... PUTRID
decompression sickness ......
    BENDS
decontaminate .... PURIFY,
    CLEAR
decontrol ..... FREE, LIBERATE
decor .... DECORATION
decorate .... TRIM, DECK,
    DRESS, ADORN,
    EMBELLISH
  in showy way ....
    BEDIZEN
  with jewels ...... BEGEM,
    ENCRUST
decorated wall .... DADO
decoration ..... ADORNMENT,
    TRIMMING, RIBBON,
    ORNAMENT
  as sign of honor ....
    MEDAL, BADGE
  furniture .... BUHL
  hat .... COCKADE
  military ... PURPLE HEART
  style of .... ROCOCO
decorative ...... ORNAMENTAL
  anklet/armlet ... BANGLE
  band .... SASH
  border design ....
    GUILLOCHE
  braid .... CORDON
  curve .... ESCALOP,
    SCALLOP
  garland .... FESTOON
  line in writing .. FLOURISH
  plant .... HERB
  ribbon .... RIBAND,
    CORDON
  stroke .... TAG, FLOURISH
decorous ...... PRIM, PROPER,
    DIGNIFIED
  person .... PRIG
decorticate ...... STRIP, PARE,
    PEEL, BARK
decorum .... DECENCY,
    PROPRIETY, DIGNITY,
    ETIQUETTE
decoy .... LURE, BAIT,
    ENTICE, PLANT, BLIND
  barker's .... SHILL
  dog .... TOLLER
  gambler's .... SHILL,
    CAPPER
  object of .... GAME
  police ..... STOOLPIGEON
  songbird, use .... CAJOLE

decrease ...... ABATE, LESSEN, DIMINISH, REDUCE, TAPER
decree .. ORDER, LAW, ARRET, ACT, DECISION, EDICT, ORDAIN, MANDATE, FIAT, DECIDE, FIRMAN, CANON, RESCRIPT
   by judicial sentence ..... DECERN
   by the Pope .. DECRETAL
   judicial .... WRIT
   Moslem ruler's .... IRADE
   of outlawry .... BAN
   papal .... BULL
   Russian .... UKASE
decrees, collection of papal ... DECRETAL
decrement .... WASTE, LOSS
   opposed to ... INCREMENT
decrepit .... OLD, WEAK, BROKEN DOWN WORN
   airplane .... CRATE
   automobile ..... JALOPY, CRATE
decresent .... WANING
decretal .... DECREE
decrier .... DEPLORER
decry .... CENSURE, CONDEMN, DISPARAGE, DISCREDIT, DENOUNCE
decumbent .... TRAILING, PROSTRATE, PRONE
   opposed to ..... SUPINE
decuple .... TENFOLD
dedicate ..... DEVOTE, APPLY, INSCRIBE
dedication ...... INSCRIPTION, ENVOY, ENVOI
deduce .... INFER, CONCLUDE, DERIVE
deduct .... SUBTRACT
deductible tax item .... EXPENSES, DONATIONS
deduction .... INFERENCE
   for loss of weight .... DRAFT
   for waste .... DRAFT
   kind of .... TARE
   opposed to .. INDUCTION
   union dues ...... CHECKOFF
deed ...... ACT, FEAT, ACTION, GEST(E), EXPLOIT
   in ...... REALLY, IN FACT
   kind of .... SALE, TRANSFER
   ownership .... TITLE

deeds .... ACTA
   of chivalry .... ERRANTRY
deejay's concern .... DISKS
deem ...... CONSIDER, JUDGE, BELIEVE
deep .... ABSTRUSE, WISE, PROFOUND, OCEAN
   bow .... OBEISANCE, SALAAM
   crack .... CREVASSE
   dish, covered .... TUREEN
   dish, fruit pie .. COBBLER
   dish pudding .... PANDOWDY
   gorge .... GULLY, RAVINE
   hole .... PIT
   low .... CURTSY, NOD
   red .... CARNATION
   seated .... ROOTED
   sleep .... SOPOR, STUPOR, LETHARGY
   sound .... RUMBLE, BOOM
   the .... SEA, OCEAN
   valley .... CANYON, CANON
deepfreeze ..... REFRIGERATOR
deeply .... INLY
deepset .... CAVERNOUS
deer .... WHITETAIL, ROE, RUMINANT, BROCKET, MUNTJAK, MUNTJAC
   American ..... CARIBOU, WAPITI, MOOSE
   Andean .... PUDU
   antler .... TAG
   antler branch ..... POINT
   antler shaft .... BEAM
   antler, type ...... RUSINE
   Asiatic .... ROE, SAMBAR, SAMBUR, AHU
   axis .... CHITAL
   barking .... KAKAR
   entrails .... UMBLES
   feeding place ...... YARD
   female ...... DOE, HIND, ROE
   flesh .... VENISON
   foot .... HOOF
   forest cover .... VERT
   genus .... RUSA
   green cover ...... VERT
   hart .... STAG
   hog .... AXIS, RUSA
   horn .... ANTLER
   hornless .... POLLARD

horn's second branch ...
    BEZ ANTLER
large .... MOOSE, ELK,
    REINDEER, CARIBOU
like a .... CERVINE
like giraffe .... OKAPI
male .... (ROE)BUCK,
    STAG, HART
maned .... RUSA, SAMBAR
moose-like .... ELK
mouse .... NAPUS
mouse-like .. CHEVROTAIN
mule .... BLACKTAIL
of a .... CERVINE
of India ..... AXIS, RUSA
Persian .... MARAL
red ..... ELAPHINE, HART,
    STAG
secretion .... MUSK
sexual excitement .. RUT,
    ESTRUS
short tail of .... SCUT
small ..... MUNTJAC, ROE,
    NAPUS, BROCKET,
    CHEVROTAIN
spotted .... CHITAL
tail .... FLAG, SCUT
Tibet .... SHOU
track .... SLOT
three-year-old ..... SOREL
two-year-old ....
    BROCK(ET), TEG, PRICKET
vital organs .... NUMBLES,
    NOMBLES, HUMBLE PIE
young .... FAWN, SPITTER
deerlet .... NAPU, CHEVROTAIN
deerlike .... CERVINE
deface ...... MAR, MUTILATE,
    DISFIGURE
defalcate .... EMBEZZLE
defamation ... LIBEL, SLANDER,
    CALUMNY
defamatory .... LIBELOUS
    remarks .... MUD
defame ..... LIBEL, SLANDER,
    CALUMNIATE, MALIGN,
    VILIFY
default ..... FORFEIT, FAILURE,
    WELSH
defaulter .... EMBEZZLER
    DEFALCATOR
defeat .... WIN, BEAT,
    OVERCOME, REVERSE,
    BEST, WORST, LICK,
    LOSS, WHIP, TROUNCE
by small margin .... NOSE

chess .... MATE
decisively ...... CLOBBER,
    DRUB, WALLOP, ROUT
disorderly .... ROUT
easy to .... PUSHOVER
incumbent .... UNSEAT
overwhelming .... ROUT,
    SHELLACKING, MASSACRE,
    LACING
scoreless .... WHITEWASH
soundly .... DRUB, LACE,
    SKUNK
two ways ..... WHIPSAW
unexpectedly ..... UPSET
defeated: slang .... KAPUT
defeatist, kind of.... PESSIMIST
defecate ..... PURIFY, REFINE,
    EXCRETE
defect .... SHORTCOMING,
    BOLT, IMPERFECTION,
    BLEMISH, FLAW, FAULT,
    SNAG, FLEE, DEMERIT,
    SPOT, FAILING
in fabric .... SCOB
in machine .... BUG
in weave .... SCOB
labial .... HAIRLIP
slang .... BUG
defection .... DESERTION
defective .... FAULTY, FLAWED,
    IMPERFECT, MANQUE
bomb .... DUD
defector ...... BOLTER, RAT,
    TURNCOAT, RENEGADE
defend ..... GUARD, PROTECT,
    JUSTIFY, SHIELD
defendable .... TENABLE
defendant .... ACCUSED,
    CULPRIT
opposed to ... PLAINTIFF,
    COMPLAINANT
place of .... DOCK
plea of .... NOLO
statement of .... PLEA
who refuses to plead ....
    MUTE
defender .... CHAMPION,
    PROTECTOR, ADVOCATE
defense .... JUSTIFICATION,
    PROTECTION, BULWARK
defendant's .... ALIBI
kind of .... ORAL, LEGAL,
    ATTACK
line: Ger. .... LIMES
means of .... ARMOR,
    ABATIS, SPINE, SHELL,

PALISADE, SMOKESCREEN,
BARRICADE, MUNIMENT
defenseless .... HELPLESS
defensible .... TENABLE,
JUSTIFIABLE
defensive covering .... ARMOR,
MAIL, SHIELD, EGIS, HELMET
ditch .... MOAT
embankment ....
EARTHWORK, GABIONADE
structure .... FORT,
STOCKADE, ABATIS
outwork ..... FORTALICE
wall .... BULWARK
defer ...... DELAY, POSTPONE,
PEND, YIELD, SHELVE
deference .... RESPECT,
YIELDING, OBEISANCE
deferment .... DELAY
defi .... CHALLENGE, DARE,
CARTEL
defiance .... CHALLENGE,
RESISTANCE
defiant .... CHALLENGING,
BELLIGERENT
confidence .... BRAVADO
one .... REB, REBEL,
CHALLENGER
deficiency .... SHORTAGE,
LACK, DEFECT, DEFICIT,
WANT, ULLAGE
disease .... BERIBERI,
DROPSY, RICKETS, SCURVY,
PELLAGRA
in supply ..... SHORTAGE
of oxygen in body ......
ANOXIA
deficient .... DEFECTIVE,
INCOMPLETE, WANTING,
SHORT
deficit ...... SHORTAGE, LACK
defile ...... TAINT, POLLUTE,
CORRUPT, PASS, SULLY,
DIRTY, VALLEY, PROFANE
define ...... OUTLINE, EXPLAIN
definite ... EXPLICIT, CERTAIN,
POSITIVE
definitive ..... FINAL, DECISIVE,
CONCLUSIVE
deflate .... COLLAPSE
deflated tire .... FLAT
deflect .... BEND, TURN,
SWERVE, DIVERT, FEND
Defoe, novelist ...... DANIEL
character ...... CRUSOE,
FRIDAY

deform .... CONTORT, WARP,
MISSHAPE
deformed person ....
HUNCHBACK, CRIPPLE,
FREAK
deformity, back...... HUNCH,
HUMP
buccal .... HARELIP
foot ..... TALIPES, VARUS,
CLUBFOOT
of lower limbs ....
BOWLEGS, VARUS
defraud ...... SWINDLE, GYP,
CHEAT, BILK, COZEN,
STICK, NICK
defray ...... PAY, COVER COST
defrost .... MELT, DEICE
deft ...... SKILLFUL, ADROIT,
DEXTEROUS, CLEVER, APT
defunct ...... EXTINCT, DEAD
defy .... DARE, RESIST, OPPOSE,
CHALLENGE, FLOUT
degrade .... ABASE, HUMILIATE,
DEBASE, HUMBLE,
DEMEAN
degraded .... DISGRACED,
SHAMED
degrading .... MENIAL
degree .... STEP, STAGE, RANK,
PEG
of occurrence ....
INCIDENCE
suffix .... NESS
to a .... SOMEWHAT
dehydrate ...... DRY, PARCH
deictic ...... DEMONSTRATIVE
opposed to .... ELENCTIC
deific .... GODLIKE
deiform ..... DIVINE, GODLIKE
deify .... IDEALIZE, ADORE,
WORSHIP, EXALT,
APOTHEOSIZE
deign .... CONDESCEND, STOOP
deil: Scot. .... DEVIL
Deirdre's guardian ....
CONCHOBAR
deity .... GOD(HOOD), GODDESS
Buddhist .... DEVA
Japanese .... AMIDA,
AMITA
minor .... DEMIGOD
of music/poetry ....
APOLLO
of flocks .... FAUN
secondary ..... DEMIURGE
underworld ...... OSIRIS

woodland .... FAUN, PAN,
SATYR, ZEPHYRUS
deject ...... SADDEN, DEPRESS
dejected .... SAD, DOWNCAST,
CRESTFALLEN, DEPRESSED
dejection, lowest point ....
NADIR
dejeuner .... BREAKFAST,
LUNCHEON
delate: Scot. .... ACCUSE,
DENOUNCE, ANNOUNCE
delator .... INFORMER
Delaware ...... LENI, LENAPE,
GRAPE
Bay discoverer ....
HUDSON
capital .... DOVER
city .... ELSMERE,
NEWARK, MILFORD,
TRENTON
Indian .... LANAPE
River city ..... TRENTON
settlers .... SWEDES
delay .... SLOW, HINDER,
DEFER(MENT), IMPEDE,
DETAIN, STALL,
RETARD, LINGER, PEND
in law .... MORA, LACHES
inexcusable ..... LACHES
delaying action .... STALL
in Congress ... FILIBUSTER
in law .... MORATORY
dele .... DELETE, REMOVE,
ERASE
delectable .... YUMMY
delectation .... DELIGHT,
AMUSEMENT
delegate .... DEPUTE, DEPUTY,
REPRESENTATIVE, ENVOY,
DEPUTIZE
kind of .... ACCREDITED,
ALTERNATE
unofficial ..... OBSERVER
delete ...... ERASE, EXPUNGE,
DELE, CROSS OUT
deleterious .... HARMFUL, BAD,
PERNICIOUS
deletion of word's last letter ..
APOCOPE
cancel .... STET
Delia .... ARTEMIS
deliberate .... PONDER,
PREMEDITATED, UNHURRIED,
SLOW, CONSIDER, KNOWING
discourtesy .... SNUB,
REBUFF, CUT

Delibes, composer .... LEO
ballet .... NAILA
opera .... LAKME
delicacy .... FRAILTY,
FINENESS, FINESSE,
CAVIAR, CATE, TIDBIT,
KICKSAW
of performance ....
FINESSE
delicate ..... DAINTY, TENDER,
EXQUISITE, FRAIL, NICE,
FINE(SPUN), FRAGILE,
TICKLISH, TAFFETA
delicately pretty ..... DAINTY,
MIGNON
delicatessen ...... FOODSHOP
delicious .... DELIGHTFUL,
AMBROSIAL, SWEET,
TASTY, APPETIZING,
LUSCIOUS
fruit .... APPLE
delict .... OFFENSE,
MISDEMEANOR
delight ...... ENTRANCE, JOY,
PLEASE, PLEASURE
delightful .... PLEASING,
CHARMING
Delilah ... TEMPTRESS, HARLOT
victim of .... SAMSON
delimit .... DEMARCATE
delineate ...... DRAW, DEPICT,
DESCRIBE, OUTLINE
delineation .... SKETCH,
PORTRAIT, DRAWING
delinquency ... GUILT, MISDEED
record/report ...... GIG
delinquent .... GUILTY,
OVERDUE
a .... JUVENILE
alleged other .... PARENT
likely home of ....
REFORMATORY, BOYS'
TOWN
deliquesce .... MELT
delirious .... EXCITED, RAVING
delirium ...... MANIA, FRENZY
tremens .... JIMJAMS
delitescent ... LATENT, HIDDEN,
INACTIVE
deliver .... FREE, RESCUE,
SAVE, HAND OVER, RID,
UTTER, TRANSFER, DISTRIBUTE
goods for sale ... CONSIGN
prematurely ..... SLINK
sermon .... PREACH

deliverance .. RESCUE, RELEASE, OPINION

deliverer .... LIBERATOR, REDEEMER, COURIER

delivery .... TRANSFER, DISTRIBUTION, CHILDBIRTH, UTTERANCE, PARTURITION

boy .... JUMPER

of property ...... LIVERY

dell .... VALE, GLEN, DALE, VALLEY, RAVINE, DINGLE, SLACK

dells .... RAPIDS

Delmar, novelist .... VINA

Delos inhabitant ...... DELIAN

Delphic .... ORACULAR

priestess .... PYTHIA, PYTHONESS

seer .... ORACLE

delphinium .... LARKSPUR

delude .... MISLEAD, DUPE, BEGUILE, DECEIVE, KID

deluge ..... FLOOD, INUNDATE, INUNDATION, CATACLYSM, CATARACT

of words .... SPATE

delul ..... CAMEL, DROMEDARY

delusion .... MIRAGE, ILLUSION, VISION, FANCY, PARANOIA

of grandeur .... MEGALOMANIA

delve ...... DIG, INVESTIGATE, SEARCH, FATHOM, PROBE

demagogue ... RABBLE ROUSER, MOUNTEBANK, AGITATOR, QUACK

demand ...... REQUIRE, CLAIM, EXACT, CRY, NEED

final .... ULTIMATUM

for identification .... CHALLENGE

in .... SOUGHT

noisy .... CLAMOR

payment of debt .... DUN

repetition .... ENCORE

demandant .... PLAINTIFF

demanding .... CLAIMANT, EXACTING, CLAMOROUS, EXIGENT

demarcate .... DELIMIT

demarcation .... LINE

deme .... TOWNSHIP

demean ..... DEGRADE, ABASE, HUMBLE

demeanor ...... MANNER, AIR, CONDUCT, BEARING, MIEN, CARRIAGE, PORTANCE

having dignified .... PORTLY

dement .... DERANGE

demented ...... MAD, CRAZY, INSANE, FLIGHTY, LOONY, LUNY, LOCO

dementia .... INSANITY

demerit .... FAULT, DEFECT

slang .... GIG

demerol .... ANALGESIC, DRUG, SEDATIVE

demesne ..... DOMAIN, REALM, REGION

Demeter .... CERES

demigod .... HERO, DEITY, IDOL

demilune .... CRESCENT

demise ...... DEATH, DECEASE, BEQUEST

demit ...... RESIGN, ABDICATE

demitasse ...... (COFFEE) CUP

demobilize .... DISBAND, DISMISS

democracy, a ...... REPUBLIC

world's largest .... INDIA

world's smallest SAN MARINO

Democrat, any ..... LOCOFOCO

Democratic Party faction .... LOCOFOCO

demode ...... OLD-FASHIONED, PASSE

demographic item ..... BIRTH, DEATHS, MARRIAGES

demoiselle .... CRANE, DAMSEL, DRAGONFLY

demolish ...... RAZE, DESTROY

demon .... FIEND, DEVIL, OGRE, ANITO, D(A)EDAL, GHOUL, NAT

Arabian ... AFREET, EBLIS, JINN(I), GENIE, AFRIT, DAITYA

female .... LAMIA

little .... IMP

demoness .... LILITH, SUCCUBA, SUCCUBUS

demoniac .... DEVILISH, FRANTIC

demons, abode of all PANDEMONIUM

demonstrable ...... APODICTIC

demonstrate .... PROVE, SHOW, EVINCE, EXHIBIT

demonstrative .. ILLUSTRATIVE, D(E)ICTIC

in grammar .... D(E)ICTIC
demoralize ...... DISHEARTEN,
CONFUSE, WEAKEN,
DISCOURAGE
demos .... PEOPLE, DEME,
MASSES, POPULACE
demote ..... DEGRADE, LOWER
opposed to ..... PROMOTE
slang ...... BUST, BREAK
demotics .... SOCIOLOGY
Dempsey, Jack, soubriquet ...
(MANASSA) MAULER
demulcent .. SOOTHING, SALVE,
OINTMENT
demur ..... OBJECT, HESITATE,
PROTEST
demure ...... PRIM, COY, SHY,
SEDATE, MODEST, MIM,
SOBER
demurrer .... OBJECTION,
OBJECTOR
den ...... DIVE, STUDY, LAIR,
CAVE, ROOM, HAUNT,
RETREAT, HANGOUT
secret .... MEW, HIDEOUT
wild animal's .... LODGE,
LAIR
denarii, 12 .... SOLIDUS
denary .... DECIMAL, TENFOLD
dendritic .... TREELIKE
dendroid .... TREELIKE
dene .... DUNE
dengue .... DANDY FEVER
denial .... REFUSAL,
ABSTINENCE, REPUDIATION
in diplomacy ... DEMENTI
official .... DEMENTI
opposed to ....
COMPLIANCE,
AFFIRMATIVE
statement of ....
DENEGATION
denier .... DISOWNER,
DISCLAIMER, COIN
denigrate .... BLACKEN,
DEFAME
denim ...... (COTTON) CLOTH
use for .... (C)OVERALLS,
UNIFORMS
denizen .... INHABITANT,
CIT(IZEN), OCCUPANT
Denmark (see Danish)
island .... FALSTER
Dennis __ .... DAY
Dennis the ____ .... MENACE

denominate ..... NAME, TITLE,
CALL
denomination .... CLASS, SECT,
NAME
denominational .... SECTARIAN
denote ...... MARK, INDICATE,
SIGNIFY, MEAN
denouement .... OUTCOME
denounce ..... ASSAIL, ACCUSE,
EXCORIATE, CONDEMN,
CRITICIZE, DECRY
dense .... THICK, STUPID,
PACKED, POPULOUS,
CLOSE, GROSS
growth of trees ....
FOREST, WOODS, JUNGLE
dent .... DINT, HOLLOW
dental drill .... BURR
paste .... DENTIFRICE,
ZIRCATE
dentate ... SERRATE, TOOTHED,
NOTCHED
dented .... TOOTHED
denticle .... TOOTH
dentine .... IVORY
dentist: colloq. ....
TOOTH PULLER
drill of .... BURR
pincers of ...... FORCEPS
dentistry .... ODONTOLOGY
dentifrice .... ZIRCATE
denture .... PLATE, TEETH,
BRIDGE
denude .... STRIP
denunciation .... ACCUSATION,
THREAT, DIATRIBE
Denver is capital of ....
COLORADO
deny .... NEGATE, ABJURE,
GAINSAY, REFUSE, DISAVOW,
CONTRADICT, DISOWN,
REPUDIATE, FORSWEAR
denying .... DENEGATION
deodar .... CEDAR
deodorant ..... MUM, PASTILLE
deontology .... ETHICS
depart ...... GO (AWAY), DIE,
SET OUT, LEAVE
from script ...... AD LIB
secretly .... DECAMP,
ABSCOND
slang .... MOSEY
departed .... PAST, LEFT,
(BY)GONE
the .... DEAD

department store, designating a
    FIVE-AND-TEN
    stairway ..... ESCALATOR
departure .... DEVIATION,
    LEAVING, DEATH, EXIT
    mass .... EXODUS
    of Israelites from Egypt ..
        EXODUS
depend .... RELY, BANK
dependable .... RELIABLE
dependency .... COLONY,
    AP(P)ANAGE
dependent .... CONTINGENT,
    SUBORDINATE, WARD,
    SUBJECT, PENSIONARY
    kind of .... SATELLITE
depict .... PICTURE, PAINT,
    PORTRAY, DRAW, RENDER
    in words ..... DELINEATE,
        DESCRIBE
depilate .... SHAVE, PLUCK
depilation .... ELECTROLYSIS
deplete ...... EXHAUST, DRAIN
deplorable .... GRIEVOUS
deplore .... LAMENT, BEWAIL,
    RUE, DECRY
deploy .... SPREAD (OUT)
deplume .... PLUCK
depone ...... TESTIFY, DEPOSE
deponent's statement ....
    AFFIDAVIT, TESTIMONY
deport ...... BANISH, BEHAVE,
    EXPEL, EXILE
deportment .... BEHAVIOR,
    BEARING, CONDUCT
depose ...... TESTIFY, REMOVE,
    OUST, DEPONE, DETHRONE
deposit, alluvial ...... DELTA,
    GEEST
    body .... CALCULUS
    clayey .... MARL
    geyser .... SINTER
    glacial .... MORAINE,
        PLACER
    mineral .... LODE
    on teeth .... TARTAR
    sediment .... SILT
    waste .... SLUDGE
    water-borne ..... PLACER
    wine cask ...... TARTAR
depositary .... TRUSTEE, BANK,
    SAFE, VAULT
deposition .... TESTIMONY
    form of .... AFFIDAVIT
depot .... STOREHOUSE,

WAREHOUSE, STATION,
    ENTREPOT
    arms .. ARMORY, ARSENAL
    French .... GARE
    military ...... MAGAZINE,
        ARSENAL
deprave .... DEBASE, PERVERT,
    DEBAUCH
depraved ..... EVIL, CORRUPT,
    VILE, PUTRID, DISSOLUTE
depravity .... TURPITUDE
deprecate ... DEPLORE, BEWAIL
depreciate .... DISPARAGE,
    BELITTLE, LESSEN
    money officially .. DECRY
depredate ..... PLUNDER, ROB,
    PILLAGE
depress ..... SADDEN, LOWER,
    DAMPEN, DISHEARTEN,
    DEJECT
depressant .... SEDATIVE
depressed .... DEJECTED, BLUE,
    FLATTENED, SAD, GLUM,
        MOODY
depression .... SADNESS, DENT,
    HOLLOW
    between hills ...... GLEN
    between mountains .. COL
    in economics .. RECESSION
    small .... FOVEA
deprivation ...... LOSS, DENIAL
deprive .... DISPOSSESS, DIVEST,
    TAKE (AWAY)
    of ownership ....
        EXPROPRIATE
    of power to reproduce ...
        GELD, CASTRATE,
            STERILIZE,
            EMASCULATE
    of sunlight ..... ETIOLATE
deprived ..... (BE)REFT, SHORN
depth ... LOWNESS, OCEAN, SEA
    bomb .... ASHCAN
    charge .... ASHCAN
    combining form .. BATHO
    of water displaced by ship
        .... DRAFT
depurate .... PURIFY
deputation ...... DELEGATION
depute .... APPOINT, SEND,
    DELEGATE
deputies' group .... POSSE
deputy ... AGENT, (DE)LEGATE,
    SURROGATE, PROXY,
    ENVOY, VICAR,
VICEREGENT, LIEUTENANT

Der Alte .... ADENAUER, SCHRANZ
Fuehrer .... HITLER
deracinate .... UPROOT
derange .... UPSET, DISORDER, MESS UP
deranged ...... INSANE, CRAZY
Derby .... HAT, BOWLER, HORSE RACE
English colloquial ...... BILLYCOCK
site .... EPSOM, KENTUCKY
winner ..... KAUAI KING, CITATION, BUCKPASSER, ZEV, TWENTY GRAND, WAR ADMIRAL, ASSAULT, WHIRLAWAY, SWAPS, TIM TAM, SECRETARIAT
derelict .... FLOTSAM, WRECK, TRAMP, FORSAKEN, REMISS, CASTAWAY
deride ...... RIDICULE, SCORN, JEER, MOCK, GIBE, SCOFF, TAUNT
derisive .... SCORNFUL, CONTEMPTUOUS
cry ..... CATCALL, HOOT, BOO, HISS, RAZZ
derivation .... DESCENT
word .... ETYMOLOGY
derive ...... DRAW, (D)EDUCE, INFER, GET
derived from oil .... OLEIC
derm, as suffix .... SKIN, COVERING
dermatoid .... SKINLIKE
dermis .... SKIN, CUTIS
dernier ...... LAST, FINAL
cri .... LAST WORD, LATEST(STYLE)
derogate .... DECRY, DETRACT, DISPARAGE
derogatory .... ADVERSE, CRITICAL, DETRACTING
remark .... SLUR
derrick .... CRANE, STEEVE, HOIST, RIG, DAVIT
part of ..... BOOM, SPAR, BEAM, PULLEY, JIB
derriere ...... REAR, BEHIND, BUTTOCKS
derringer .... PISTOL, GUN
derris extraction ... ROTENONE
derry .... BALLAD
dervish .... FAKIR, BEGGAR
headgear .... TAJ

Moslem .... SADITE
practice ...... WHIRLING, HOWLING
wandering .... CALENDER
Des Moines is capital of ..... IOWA
descant .... MELODY, SING, COMMENT
descend .... COME DOWN, STEP DOWN
descendant .... SCION, OFFSPRING, PROGENY, BREED
female .... DAUGHTER
male .... SON
descent .... DERIVATION, BIRTH, EXTRACTION, ORIGIN, DECLINE, FALL, LINEAGE
sudden, swift .... SWOOP, POUNCE
describe ...... DEPICT, PAINT, PICTURE, LIMN, LABEL
exactly .... DEFINE
grammatically .... PARSE
graphically .... PORTRAY
description ..... KIND, SORT
descriptive name/title .... EPITHET
word .... LABEL
descry .... ESPY, SEE, KEN, DETECT, SIGHT, SPOT
Desdemona's husband .... OTHELLO
slanderer .... IAGO
desecrate .... PROFANE, DEFILE, VIOLATE, POLLUTE
desecration .... SACRILEGE
deseret .... HONEYBEE
desert ...... ABANDON, LEAVE, FORSAKE, WASTE, MERIT, QUIT, COLORADO
African .... SAHARA, KALAHARI
Arabian .... NEFUD, DAHNA
Asiatic .... GOBI, SHAMO, THAR, KARA KUM, QARA QUM
Australian ... NULLABAR, GIBSON
animal .... CAMEL
Arctic .... TUNDRA
Chilean .... ATACAMA
China .... TAKLA MAKAN

dweller ...... ARAB(IAN), BEDOUIN
dwelling .... TENT
fertile spot .... OASIS
Fox .... ROMMEL
horse .... ARAB
India .... THAR
Iran .... LUT
like .... ARID
Mongolian .... GOBI
pertaining to .... EREMIC
plant .... CACTUS, AGAVE, OCOTILLO
plant, tree like .... SOTOL
Russian ...... KIZIL DUM
shrub .... RETEM
train .... CARAVAN, CARAVANSARY
Turkestan ... KARA KUM, KIZIL KUM
U.S. .... MOHAVE, PAINTED (DESERT)
valley .... BOLSON
wind .... SIMOOM, SIROCCO, SIMOON
deserted .... DESOLATE, SOLITARY, ABANDONED, FORLORN
by owner ...... DERELICT
deserter ... RENEGADE, BOLTER, TURNCOAT, RUNAGATE, APOSTATE, RUNAWAY, RATTER, FUGITIVE
army .... AWOL
describing a .... RAT
desertion .... DEFECTION, ABANDONMENT
deserts .... DUE
deserve .... EARN, MERIT
deserved reward/punishment .. DESERT(S)
deservedly .... JUSTLY
deserving ...... MERITORIOUS
punishment .... GUILTY, CULPABLE
desiccant .... DRIER
desiccate .... DRY
desiccated coconut meat ...... COPRA
design .... IDEA, PATTERN, CONTRIVE, PURPOSE, SCHEME, AIM, PLAN
having .... FIGURED
highlight .... MOTIF
on a page ..... VIGNETTE
ornamental ..... DEVICE

sinister, usually .... PLOT
designate ...... MARK, ASSIGN, ENTITLE, SPECIFY, NAME, APPOINT
designation .... APPOINTMENT
designer .... STYLIST
designing .... ARTFUL, CRAFTY, SCHEMING
desil .... DEIL
desinence .... SUFFIX
desirable part ... MEAT, CREAM
desire .... WISH, CRAVE, WILL, WANT, COVET
characterized by .... ORECTIC
for sleep .... NARCOLEPSY
overwhelming .... ESTRUS
seat of .... LIVER
strong .... HUNGER
weakest .... VELLEITY
desirous .... FAIN
desist .... STOP, ABSTAIN, CEASE, FORBEAR
desk .... TABLE, PULPIT, POST, ROLLTOP
for prayer ..... PRIE DIEU
reading .. LECTERN, AMBO
use of .... WRITING, DRAWING, READING
writing ..... DAVENPORT, ESCRITOIRE, SECRETARY
desman .... MUSK
desmid .... ALGA
desolate ...... BLEAK, LONELY, SOLITARY, DESERTED, (FOR)LORN, FORSAKEN, STARK
desolation ...... WASTE, RUIN, MISERY
despair .... MISERY, DESPERATION, DESPOND
desperado ... BRAVO, OUTLAW, CRIMINAL
hunters .... POSSE
desperate ... HOPELESS, RASH, RECKLESS
appeal .... SOS
criminal .... BRAVO, DESPERADO
despicable .... CONTEMPTIBLE, CONDEMNABLE, VILE, LOW-DOWN
person ..... CAD, SKUNK, SCOUNDREL, COWARD
slang .... SCALY
despise ...... SCORN, DISDAIN,

CONTEMN, HATE, ABHOR,
DETEST
despite ... NOTWITHSTANDING,
INSULT, MALICE,
(AL)THOUGH
despoil .... ROB, RUIN,
PILLAGE, PLUNDER,
LOOT, RAVAGE
despoiled: archaic ...... REFT
despond .... DESPAIR
despondency ...... DEJECTION,
DESPAIR
despot .... AUTOCRAT,
DICTATOR, TYRANT,
CZAR, TSAR
Persian .... SATRAP
despotic ruler .... TSAR, SHAH,
CZAR
despotism .... TYRANNY,
AUTOCRACY, AUTARCHY
despumate .... SKIM
desquamate .... PEEL (OFF)
dessert ..... FLAN, SWEET, ICE,
MOUSSE, PARFAIT,
SILLABUB, SUNDAE
fruit juices .... FRAPPE
fruit, gelatin ....
CHARLOTTE
item ...... PUDDING, PIE,
ICE CREAM, FRUITS
kind of .... SASS
melon .... BOMBE
milk and starchy substance
BLANC MANGE
rum .... BABA
spongecake ...... TRIFLE
desserts .... DUE
destiny ..... FATE, LOT, DOOM
Oriental .... KISMET
destitute .... POOR, NEEDY,
DEVOID, LACKING
destitution .... POVERTY, NEED,
PENURY
destrier ..... CHARGER, STEED,
WARHORSE
destroy .... RAZE, RUIN,
WRECK, ERADICATE,
SACK, SLAY, RAVAGE,
LAY WASTE, OBLITERATE
by fire .... GUT
entirely .... EXTERMINATE
machinery to force
agreement .... RATTEN
slowly .... ERODE, WASTE
destroyer, crop ...... BLIGHT,
DROUGHT, LOCUST

historical .... ATTILA
kind of .... VANDAL
of monster ...... HERMES,
ST. GEORGE
of vermin ....
EXTERMINATOR
of wood .... TERMITE
destruction ..... HAVOC, RUIN,
WRECKAGE, WRACK
by fire .... HOLOCAUST
malicious .... VANDALISM
mass .... SLAUGHTER,
MASSACRE, DECIMATION,
GENOCIDE
of nation ..... GENOCIDE
widespread .. HOLOCAUST
destructive insect ..... LOCUST,
TERMITE, MOTH
liquid .... ACID
natural phenomenon ....
STORM, TORNADO,
TYPHOON, EARTHQUAKE,
CYCLONE
to metal .... RUST
destructor .... FURNACE,
INCINERATOR
desuetude .... DISUSE
desultory .... RANDOM,
HAPHAZARD, AIMLESS,
EXCURSIVE
detach ...... SEVER, SEPARATE,
UNFASTEN
detached .... ALOOF, SEPARATE,
INDIFFERENT
in music ...... SPICCATO
detachment .... UNIT,
ALOOFNESS, ISOLATION
detail ..... PARTICULAR, ITEM,
ASSIGN(MENT), SPECIFY
attentive to .. METICULOUS
detailed .... ITEMIZED,
ELABORATE, ASSIGNED
account .... EXPLICATION
explanation .. EXPOSITION
list .... ENUMERATION,
DIRECTORY, INVENTORY,
ROSTER
details, small and unimportant
MINUTIAE
detain .... HOLD, DELAY,
CONFINE
ship in port ..... INTERN
detect .... DISCOVER, SPOT,
SENSE, ESPY, DESCRY
detecting device ...... RADAR,

BUG, DOWSER, SONAR, ANTENNA, FEELER, TENTACLE

detection ... DISCOVERY, ESPIAL

detective ...... SLEUTH, TEC, DICK, OPERATIVE, HAWKSHAW, GUMSHOE, SPOTTER

Conan Doyle's .. HOLMES

describing one .. SHADOW, PRIVATE EYE, TAIL

of fiction/movie .. TRENT, NERO, CHAN, MOTO, HOLMES, DRAKE, POIROT, SAINT

orchid-loving ...... NERO

story .... MAIGRET

story character .... CORONER, SHERIFF, GOON, HATCHETMAN, INFORMER

detector of sorts .... BUG, ANTENNA, FEELER, NOSE, SONAR, RADAR

detent ... CATCH, CLICK, PAWL

detente .... COOLING OFF

of a sort .... RAPPROCHEMENT

deter .. DISCOURAGE, PREVENT

deterge .... CLEAN(SE)

detergent .... ABLUENT, CLEANSER, SAPONIN, SOAP, ARIEL

deteriorate .. DECAY, CORRUPT, DEBASE, WORSEN, DEPRECIATE

determinant .... CAUSE

determinate .... FIXED, DEFINITE, SPECIFIC

determination .... WILL

determine .... JUDGE, DECIDE, DEFINE, ASCERTAIN

issue by combat .... DERAIGN

quotient .... DIVIDE

worth of ..... EVALUATE, APPRAISE

determined .... SET, RESOLUTE, FIRM, DEAD SET

deterrent of a kind ..... FEAR, SHAME, DOUBT

war .... A-BOMB

detest .... DISLIKE, ABHOR, HATE, LOATHE, EXECRATE

detestable .... ODIOUS, HATEFUL, EXECRABLE

person ...... BOOR, LOUT, COWARD, POLTROON

detestation .. HATRED, DISLIKE, LOATHING

dethrone .... DEPOSE

dethronement, object of ...... KING, EMPEROR, CHAMPION

detonate .... EXPLODE, FULMINATE

detonating device ...... FUSE, PERCUSSION, CAP, PIN, TRIGGER

object ..... FIRECRACKER, SQUIB, BOMB, GRENADE, BULLET, SHELL, DYNAMITE

detour ..... TURN, DEVIATION, DIVERT

detract .... DEROGATE, DISPARAGE, TAKE AWAY, DEPRECIATE

d'etre, ____ .... RAISON

detriment ..... HARM, INJURY, DAMAGE

detritus .... DEBRIS

Detroit (Michigan) product ... AUTOMOBILE, CAR

of Italy .... TURIN

suburb .... ECORSE

deuce .... TWO (SPOT)

Deus .... GOD

deus ex ____ ...... MACHINA

Deutschland .... GERMANY

devastate ...... SACK, RAVAGE, DESTROY, LAY WASTE, RAZE, LEVEL

devastation ..... HAVOC, RUIN, DESTRUCTION

devel .... BLOW

develop .... GROW, EVOLVE, RIPEN, ELABORATE

development .... EVENT, GROWTH, PROGRESS

of fetus .... FETATION, PREGNANCY

Devi .... SAKTI, MAYA

consort of .... SIVA

father of .... HIMAVAT

deviate ...... STRAY, DIVERGE, SHEER

from course .... DETOUR, YAW, VEER, SWERVE

from main topic .... DIGRESS

device .... PLAN, SCHEME, HICK(E)Y, TRICK, INVENTION, DESIGN, GADGET

air moistening .. HUMIDOR

any: sl. .... DINGUS

deceptive ...... GIMMICK
for catching criminals/fish
DRAGNET
for hearing sound ....
STETHOSCOPE
for holding stone in jewel
cutting .... DIAL
for raising bucket ....
WINDLASS
for secret listening .. BUG
gripping .... VISE, CLAMP
ingenious .... GADGET
light wave amplifying ....
LASER
measuring .... TAPE,
RULE(R)
secret .... GIMMICK
sound amplifying ....
MASER
time beating ....
METRONOME
to check vibration ......
DAMPER
tone muffling .... PEDAL,
MUTE
trick .... GIMMICK
devil .... DEMON, SATAN,
BELIAL, AZAZEL, LUCIFER,
FIEND, SHAITAN, MAHOUND,
OLD NICK, OLD HARRY,
SCRATCH
dog .... MARINE,
LEATHERNECK
little .... IMP, BRAT
may-care ... INSOUCIANT,
RECKLESS
Moslem .... SHAITAN
of the .... DIABOLIC
worshipper .... DIABOLIST
devilfish .... RAY, MANTA,
OCTOPUS, SKATE, SEABAT
devilish .... INFERNAL,
WICKED, CRUEL,
DIABOLIC(AL), DEMONIAC
devilkin .... IMP
devil's bones .... DICE
name ...... NICK, SATAN,
LUCIFER
deviltry .... MISCHIEF
devious .... ROUNDABOUT,
CROOKED, WINDING,
CIRCUITOUS, TORTUOUS
dcvise .... PLAN, WILL,
CONCOCT, INVENT,
SCHEME, CONTRIVE, GIFT
devised, not .... INTESTATE

devisor .... TESTATOR
devitalize .... WEAKEN, SAP
devotee .... FAN, BUFF, ZEALOT,
AFICIONADO
of beauty .... (A)ESTHETE,
CONNOISSEUR
of the fine arts ....
DILETTANTE
devoid ... DESTITUTE, LACKING
devoir .... DUTY
devolve .... PASS (ON)
devote .... CONSECRATE,
DEDICATE, APPLY
devoted ..... LOYAL, FAITHFUL
devotee ..... ZEALOT, IST, FAN,
FOLLOWER, VOTARY,
PARTISAN, BUFF
devotion .... PIETY, FEALTY,
ZEAL, LOYALTY,
ARDOR, FIDELITY
nine-day .... NOVENA
devotions .... PRAYERS
devour .... EAT, CONSUME,
DESTROY
greedily .... WOLF, GORGE
devout .... PIOUS, EARNEST,
RELIGIOUS
devoutness .... PIETY
dew .... MOISTURE
frozen .... RIME,
(HOAR)FROST
dewclaw .... DIGIT
dewlap .... JOWL, WATTLE,
PALEA, LAPPET
DEWS, part of ..... DISTANT,
EARLY, WARNING, SYSTEM
dextcr .... RIGHT-HAND
opposed to ..... SINISTER
dexterity ...... KNACK, SKILL,
ADROITNESS, CLEVERNESS
special .... CRAFT
dexterous .... HANDY, ADROIT,
SKILLFUL, ADEPT, ADROIT
dextral ...... RIGHT(HANDED)
dextrose .... SUGAR, GLUCOSE
dhole .... CUON
di, as prefix .... TWICE,
DOUBLE, TWOFOLD
dia, as prefix .... ACROSS,
THROUGH
diabetes remedy ..... INSULIN
diabetics' bread ..... GLUTEN
remedy .... INSULIN
diablerie .... SORCERY,
MISCHIEF, DEVIL(T)RY

diabolic .... SATANIC, DEVILISH, FIENDISH, WICKED, INFERNAL

diabolism .... SORCERY

diacritical mark .... TILDE, UMLAUT, DIERESIS

diadem .... CROWN, TIARA, HEADBAND

diagnose .... EXAMINE

diagnostic in medicine .... SYMPTOM, DIACRITIC

rap .... PERCUSS

diagonal .... OBLIQUE, SLANTING

line .... BIAS

line between words ..... VIRGULE

diagram ..... SKETCH, CHART, DRAWING, GRAPH, PLAN, PLOT, SCHEMA, SCHEME

dial .... TUNE IN, CALL

compass .... CARD

miner's .... COMPASS

dialect .... LANGUE, IDIOM, LINGO, SPEECH, SLANG, ARGOT, CANT, PATOIS, VERNACULAR, JARGON, TONGUE

dialects, mixture of .... LINGUA FRANCA

dialectician .... LOGICIAN

dialectics .... ARGUMENTATION

dialogue ...... CONVERSATION, INTERLOCUTION

dialogues of Buddha .... SUTRA

diamagnetic substance .... BISMUTH, ZINC

diameter ... WIDTH, THICKNESS

measuring device .... CALIPER

of tube/gun .... CALIBER, BORE

diametrical .... DIRECT, CONTRARY, OPPOSITE

diamond .... STONE, GEM, PLAYGROUND, LOZENGE

base .... CULET

base, baseball ...... SACK

center, ancient .... GOLCONDA

circular, flat .... RONDEL

crystal .... MACLE

cup .... DOP, DOBB

cut .... FACET, BRIOLETTE

drill .... CARBONADO

facet .... CULET

holder .... DOP

in baseball ...... INFIELD

industrial use .. ABRASIVE, DRILLING, CUTTING

inferior .... BORT

native .... CARBON

official, baseball .... UMP(IRE)

perfect .... PARAGON

rough .... BRAIT

shaped armor plate ..... MASCLE

figure .. LOZENGE, MASCLE

shaped pattern ... DIAPER

slang ..... ICE, SPARKLER

State .... DELAWARE

synthetic ..... FABULITE

twin crystal ...... MACLE

diamondback ... SNAKE, MOTH, TERRAPIN, RATTLER

diamonds or hearts .... RED SUIT

Diana .... DELIA, ARTEMIS

parent of .... JUPITER. LATONA

poetic .... MOON

dianthus .... CARNATION

diapason .... (ORGAN)STOP, TUNING FORK

diaper .. TOWEL, NAPKIN, DIDY

diaphanous ...... SHEER, THIN, TRANSPARENT, GAUZY, TRANSLUCENT

diaphoresis .... SWEAT, PERSPIRATION

diaphragm .... MIDRIFF

pertaining to.... PHRENIC

sound .... HICCUP, HICCOUGH

diarist .... PEPYS, BURNEY, NICOLSON, JOURNALIST

diarrhea .... LIENTERY

medicine ..... PAREGORIC

diary ...... RECORD, DIURNAL, JOURNAL, DAYBOOK, EPHEMERIS

ship's .... LOG(BOOK)

diastase .... ENZYME, AMYLASE

diatomic .... BIVALENT

shell .... FRUSTULE

diatonic, opposed to .... CHROMATIC

scale .... GAMUT

diatribe ...... DENUNCIATION,
PHILIPPIC, TIRADE
Diaz, Mexican president .....
PORFIRIO
Rodrigo .... (EL) CID
dib .... BOB, DIP, DAP
dibble .... DIB, DAP
dice .... BONES, CUT, CRAP,
CHOP, CUBE, GAME,
CHECKER, IVORY
cater of .... FOUR
five on .... CINQUE
game .... NOVUM,
HAZARD
game losing throw .. CRAP
six in .... SICE
spot .... PIP
term .... COMB, NATURAL,
CRAPS, AMBSACE, ELEVEN
three spots .... TREY
throw .... DIE, CHAPS,
ROLL, RAILROAD, BOXCAR,
CATER, JOE
throw natural ..... SEVEN
trick .... COG
diced .... CUBED
dichroite .... IOLITE
Dick: sl. .... DETECTIVE
Dickens (Charles) beadle .....
(MR.) BUMBLE
character ... ROSA, DORA,
DORRIT, PICKWICK,
GAMP, TIM, FAGIN,
(OLIVER) TWIST, HEEP,
(JENNY) WREN, PIP,
BUMBLE
colloquial .... DEVIL,
DEUCE
hero .... CARTON
pen name .... BOZ
pickpocket .... FAGIN
dicker ..... BARTER, BARGAIN,
TRADE
dickey .... BIB, PINAFORE,
DONKEY, COLLAR,
PLASTRON, (BACK)SEAT,
RUMBLE
dicotyledon .... EXOGEN
dictate .... COMMAND, ORDER,
BID
dictator ... DESPOT, AUTOCRAT,
TYRANT
propaganda of... BIG LIE
dictatorial ... BOSSY, DESPOTIC,
IMPERIOUS, ARBITRARY
diction .... ENUNCIATION

poor .... CACOLOGY
dictionary .... LEXICON,
THESAURUS
prosody .... GRADUS
dictum .... SAYING, SAY-SO,
PRONOUNCEMENT
didactic .... PEDANTIC
didactics .... PEDAGOGY
didapper .... GREBE, DABCHICK
diddle ...... CHEAT, SWINDLE,
JIGGLE
Diderot, Fr. philosopher ......
DENIS
dido .... ANTIC, PRANK, CAPER
love of .... AENEAS
realm of .... CARTHAGE
didy .... DIAPER
didymous ...... TWIN, DOUBLE
die ...... DADO, DICE, MATRIX,
MOLD, STAMP, CUBE,
PERISH, EXPIRE, SUCCUMB,
DECEASE, PASS AWAY,
CROAK
due to cold .. WINTERKILL
diehard .... STUBBORN
dieresis .... UMLAUT
Dies Irae .... HYMN,
JUDGMENT DAY
diet .... ASSEMBLY, FAST,
(DAILY)FARE
course of ...... REGIMEN
faulty .... DISTROPHY
old style .... BANT
dietetics .... SITOLOGY
differ .... EXCEPT, TAKE ISSUE,
VARY, DISAGREE, DISSENT
difference ..... DISAGREEMENT,
DISPUTE, QUARREL,
VARIANCE
lunar and solar year ....
EPACT
different .... ELSE, OTHER,
DIVERSE(R), (AN)OTHER,
UNLIKE
ones .... OTHERS
difficult .... HARD
problem .... POSER,
DILEMMA, GORDIAN(KNOT)
to please .... QUEASY
difficulty .... SNAG, JAM,
HARDSHIP, FIX, TROUBLE,
PROBLEM, PICKLE, SCRAPE,
RIGOR, STRAITS
without solution ......
STALEMATE
diffident ...... COY, TIMID, SHY

diffuse ...... WORDY, SPREAD, SCATTER, RADIATE, PERMEATE

diffusion .... SPREADING, DISSEMINATION

thru a membrane .... OSMOSIS

dig .... DELVE, JAB, EXCAVATE, UNEARTH, PROD, POKE, NUDGE, SPUD

colloquial ... TAUNT, JEER

for metal .... MINE

out .... GOUGE, MINE, SCOOP, EXHUME

slang ...... UNDERSTAND, SEE

up .... DELVE

with snout ... ROOT, ROUT

digest ... ABSTRACT, SUMMARY, ASSIMILATE, SYNOPSIS, SUMMARIZE, APERCU

the .... PANDECT

digestion, good ...... EUPEPSIA

impaired ..... DYSPEPSIA

of .... PEPTIC

digestive enzyme ...... PEPSIN, PAPAIN

digger ..... MINER, TRENCHER, SAPPER, SPADER, HOER, SANDHOG

digging tool ...... SPADE, HOE, TROWEL, PICKAX(E), MATTOCK, SPUD

dight .... ADORN, EQUIP

digit .... FINGER, TOE, CIPHER, NUMBER, INTEGER

useless .... DEWCLAW

digital infection .... FELON

digitalis .... FOXGLOVE

digits .... HALLUCES

diglot .... BILINGUAL

dignified .... DECOROUS, STATELY, SEDATE

grace/richness .... ELEGANCE

dignify ..... HONOR, ENNOBLE, EXALT

dignitary .... PERSONAGE

dignity ..... NOBILITY, HONOR, STATELINESS, DECORUM, MAJESTY

steeped in .... STAID, DECOROUS, PRIM, PRIGGISH

digress ..... RAMBLE, DEVIATE, DIVAGATE

digressions of a sort ... ASIDES, AD LIBS

dik-dik .... ANTELOPE

dike ...... DITCH, LEVEE, DAM, CAUSEWAY, EMBANKMENT

break in a ..... CREVASSE

protective mat .... MATTRESS

dilantin, users of .. EPILEPTICS

dilapidated .... BROKEN DOWN, RUINED, RAMSHACKLE, RUN-DOWN, RATTY

dilapidation .... RUIN

dilate ...... SWELL, EXPAND, WIDEN, DISTEND

dilation .... ENLARGEMENT, EXPANSION

cause of eyes' .... SURPRISE, WONDER, INCREDULITY

heart's .... DIASTOLE

pupil's .... MYDRIASIS

dilatory .... DELAYING

tactic in Congress ...... FILIBUSTER

dilemma ...... PREDICAMENT, FIX, JAM

horn of .... ALTERNATIVE, CHOICE

play's .... NODE

dilettante .... TRIFLER, AMATEUR, DABBLER, (A)ESTHETE

of a sort .... AFICIONADO, BOHEMIAN

diligence .... STAGECOACH, APPLICATION, INDUSTRY, PERSEVERANCE

diligent .... ACTIVE, SEDULOUS, HARDWORKING, BUSY

dill(seed) .... ANET, ANISE

dilly .... BARB

colloquial .. BEAUT, LULU

dillydally ..... LOITER, TRIFLE, HESITATE, VACILLATE, WAVER

diluent .... SOLVENT

dilute .... WATER, THIN

diluted .... THIN, WASHY

diluting substance .... DILUENT

dim ..... VAGUE, DARK, FAINT, UNCLEAR, OBSCURE, DULL, MIRK(Y), MURK(Y)

dime .... TEN CENTS, COIN

novel detective .... (NICK) CARTER

dime-a-dozen .... CHEAP

dimension ..... EXTENT, SCOPE,
MEASUREMENT, SIZE,
BREADTH

dimensions, of three .... CUBIC

diminish ..... REDUCE, LESSEN,
(A)BATE, DECREASE,
PETER, TAPER, WANE

diminutive ...... PETITE, WEE,
TINY, SMALL,
MINIKIN

  animal .... RUNT

  fowl .... BANTAM

  suffix .... KIN, ETTE, ULE,
IE, LET, LING

dimple .... HOLLOW, FOSSETTE

dimwit .. IDIOT, SIMPLETON, SAP

din .... NOISE, UPROAR

dinar .... COIN

dindle .... TINGLE, THRILL,
VIBRATE

diner .... RESTAURANT

ding .... RING

dingbat......... STONE, STICK

dinghy .... (ROW)BOAT,
SHALLOP, SABOT

dingle .... DALE, DELL,
VALLEY, GLEN

dingus .... DEVICE, GADGET

dingy .... GRIMY, DISMAL,
SHABBY

dining alcove .... DINETTE

  car .... DINER

  hall .... REFECTORY, MESS

  room .... GRILL, DINETTE

  table .... BOARD

  table companion ....
MESSMATE

  table ornament ....
EPERGNE

dink .... TRIM, DECK

dinkey .... TROLLEY,
LOCOMOTIVE

dinky .... SMALL

dinner course .... ENTREE

  jacket .... TUX(EDO)

  of .... PRANDIAL

  treat .... POTROAST

  wagon .... TEACART

  with toasting, etc. .....
BANQUET

dinosaur .... DIPLODOCUS,
ORNITHOPOD, SAURIAN,
SAUROPOD

dint .... FORCE, EXERTION,
DENT

diocese .... SEE, BISHOPRIC,
EPARCHY

Diomedes' father ..... TYDEUS

Dionysus' attendant ....
NYMPH, M(A)ENAD

  son .... PRIAPUS

  staff .... THYRSUS

diopter .... ALIDADE

Dioscuri ..... TWINS, CASTOR,
POLLUX

dip ...... IMMERSE, SINK, DAP,
CANDLE, LADE

  a doughnut .... DUNK

  bait .... DAP, DIB(BLE)

  in liquid ...... (IM)MERSE,
DOUSE

  lightly .... DIB, DAP

  slang .... PICKPOCKET

  the colors .... SALUTE

diplo, as combining form .....
TWO, TWIN, DOUBLE

diploma .... CHARTER,
CERTIFICATE

  colloquial .... SHEEPSKIN

diplomacy .... TACT

  way of .... PROTOCOL

diplomat ..... ENVOY, LEGATE,
AMBASSADOR, MINISTER,
CONSUL

  papal .... NUNCIO

diplomatic .... POLITIC,
TACTFUL, ARTFUL,
SUAVE

  agreements ... PROTOCOL

  ceremonial forms ....
PROTOCOL

  change of policy ....
DEMARCHE

  corps, dean of .... DOYEN

  denial .... DEMENTI

  dispatch container .....
POUCH

  immunity .... DIPPLE

  paper .... MEMORIAL

  privilege ..... IMMUNITY

  staff member .... ATTACHE

diplopia ...... DOUBLE VISION

dipody .... SYZYGY, VERSE,
DIMETER

dipper .... SCOOP, PIGGIN,
URSA, GREBE, LADLE

dipsomaniac ..... DRUNKARD,
SOT, TOPER

dipsomaniacs, society of ......
ANONYMOUS

dipterous insect .... GNAT, HOUSEFLY, MOSQUITO

dire ...... FEARFUL, TERRIBLE, DREADFUL, HORRIBLE

direct ...... STRAIGHT, FRANK, CONDUCT, MANAGE, IMMEDIATE, FIRST HAND

   attention to .... REFER

   hit .... BULL'S EYE, ON TARGET

   proceedings .... PRESIDE

direction ..... COURSE, ORDER, ADDRESS, GUIDANCE, TREND, MANAGEMENT

   without fixed ... AIMLESS, MEANDERING, ERRATIC

directions, in all ...... ABOUT

directive .... ORDER, INSTRUCTION

directly .... SOON, INSTANTLY, AS SOON AS

   colloquial .... SPANG

   opposite ... DIAMETRICAL

director .... SUPERVISOR, MANAGER

   in music .... CONDUCTOR

directory .... REGISTER

   enter in .... LIST

dirge .... HYMN, MASS, THRENODY, CORONACH, LAMENT, GRIEF, SONG, EPICEDIUM

   for dead .... REQUIEM

dirigible .... BALLOON, BLIMP, ZEPPELIN

   bag/covering .. ENVELOPE

   cabin .... GONDOLA

   gas .... HELIUM

   pilot .... AERONAUT

diriment .... NULLIFYING, VOIDING

dirk ...... DAGGER, PONIARD, SNEE

dirl .... TINGLE, VIBRATE

dirt ...... FILTH, SOIL, GRIME, GOSSIP, MUCK

dirty .... FOUL, UNCLEAN, OBSCENE, FILTHY, DEFILE, POLLUTE, SORDID

Dis .... PLUTO, HADES, UNDERWORLD, ORCUS

disability .... INCAPACITY

disable .... CRIPPLE, MAIM, DISQUALIFY, LAME, HAMSTRING

disadvantage ..... DRAWBACK, HANDICAP, DETRIMENT

disaffect .. ESTRANGE, ALIENATE

disagee .... DIFFER, DISPUTE

disagreeable .... CROSS, UNPLEASANT, OFFENSIVE

   situation .... SCRAPE, FIX, JAM, SCOUR

   smell .... FETOR

disagreement .... DISPUTE, DIFFERENCE, QUARREL

   result of couple's .... DIVORCE, SEPARATION, SPAT

disallow .... REJECT, DENY

disappear ... VANISH, GO, PASS, EVANESCE, FLEE, ESCAPE

disappoint ... FAIL, LET DOWN, DISPLEASE

disappointment .... LET DOWN

disapproval .... REJECTION, DISLIKE

   show of ...... BOO, HISS, SNEER, SNORT, HOOT

disapprove .... REJECT, TURN DOWN, CONDEMN, DENY

disarrange ...... MUSS, MIXUP, RUMPLE, MESS, UNSETTLE

disarray ... UPSET, CONFUSION, DISORDER

disarticulate ...... AMPUTATE, DISJOINT

disaster ...... EVIL, CALAMITY, MISFORTUNE

   sudden and great .... DEBACLE

disavow .... ABJURE, DISCLAIM, DISOWN, REPUDIATE, DENY

disband .. BREAK UP, DISPERSE, DEMOBILIZE, SCATTER

disbar .... EXCLUDE

disbelief in God ..... ATHEISM

disbeliever .. SKEPTIC, DOUBTER

disburse ...... EXPEND, SPEND, PAY OUT

disc ...... DISH, PLATE, PATEN

discalced .... BAREFOOTED

discard ..... SCRAP, SHED, RID, JUNK, DROP, CAST OFF, CHUCK

   card from hand .. THROW

discarded cargo ...... JETSAM

discern ...... SEE, PERCEIVE, NOTICE

   beforehand ..... FORESEE

discerning .. ASTUTE, SHREWD, APPRECIATIVE, SAGACIOUS, SAPIENT

discernment ..... TASTE, SENSE, ACUMEN, APPRECIATION, UNDERSTANDING, FLAIR, KNACK

discharge .. RELIEVE, EMISSION, RELEASE, UNLOAD, FREE, DISMISS, EMIT, FIRE, FLUXION, SACK, CASHIER

a debt .... QUIT

morbid .... GLEET

of pus ..... SANIES, ISSUE

projectile .... FIRE

pus .... MATURATE, SUPPURATE

disciple .... PUPIL, ADHERENT, FOLLOWER, APOSTLE

India .... CHELA

disciplinarian ..... MARTINET, STICKLER

British university .... BULLDOG

stick of a .... FERULE

disciplinary mark .... DEMERIT

discipline .... TRAIN, CONTROL, PUNISH, DRILL

fellow student ..... HAZE

disclaim ..... DISAVOW, DENY, DISOWN, REPUDIATE

disclaimer .... DENIAL

disclose .... REVEAL, TELL, OPEN, BARE, DIVULGE

disclosure .... REVELATION, EXPOSE

confidential ..... TIP-OFF

discolor .... STAIN

discolored by bruise .... LIVID

discomfit .... CONFUSE, UPSET, DISCONCERT, JAR, EMBARRASS, ABASH, RUFFLE

discomfort .... ACHE, DISTRESS, UNEASINESS, PAIN

physical .... MALAISE

discommode .. INCONVENIENCE, DISTURB

discompose ... UPSET, AGITATE, DISTURB, DISCONCERT, RUFFLE

disconcert .... ABASH, RATTLE, DISTURB, UPSET, JAR, EMBARRASS, CONFUSE, FLABBERGAST, F(E)AZE, FEEZE

disconnect .... UNCOUPLE, SEPARATE, DETACH, SEVER

disconsolate .... SAD, GLOOMY

discontent, feeling of .... DYSPHORIA

discontented one .... WHINER, GRIPER

discontinue .... STOP, QUIT, HALT, CEASE, SUSPEND

discord .... DISSENSION, CONFLICT, CLASH, DIN

discordant .... JARRING, DISSONANT, HARSH, CACOPHONOUS

ringing .... JANGLE

discotheque .... CAFE

discount ..... REBATE, AGIO, SUBTRACT, SET ASIDE, DEDUCT(ION)

discourage ... DETER, DAMPEN, DISHEARTEN, DEPRESS, DEMORALIZE, DAUNT

discourse ...... CONVERSATION, TALK, LECTURE, SERMON, TREATISE, DISSERT(ATION), HOMILY, DESCANT

art of .... RHETORIC

combining form .. LOG(O)

discourteous .. RUDE, IMPOLITE

discover ...... LEARN, DETECT, FIND(OUT), ESPY, DESCRY

discovery .. DETECTION, ESPIAL, FIND(ING)

discredit ... DISGRACE, DOUBT, DISHONOR, DISPARAGE, SLUR

discreet ... PRUDENT, CAREFUL

discrepancy ... GAP, VARIANCE, DIFFERENCE

discrete ... SEPARATE, DISTINCT

discretion .... PRUDENCE, OPTION, JUDGMENT

discriminate ... DIFFERENTIATE, SECERN, DISTINGUISH, DEMARCATE

discrimination .. DISCERNMENT, TASTE, PERCEPTION

discursive .... PROLIX

discus .... DISK, QUOIT

thrower's statue .... DISCOBOLUS

discuss ...... DISPUTE, DISSERT, DELIBERATE, DEBATE, ARGUE

in detail .... CANVASS

discussed publicly .. NOTORIOUS

discussion ..... DELIBERATION, DEBATE
   group .... FORUM, PANEL, SEMINAR
   heated ... HASSLE, HASSEL, RHUBARB
   secret: sl. .... HUDDLE
disdain .... SNEER, DESPISE, CONTEMPT, SCORN, SPURN
disdainful one ...... SNEERER, SCORNER, SNOB
disease ..... ILLNESS, AILMENT, MALADY, AFFECTION, DISORDER
   animal .... ANTHRAX, MANGE, GID, SPAVIN, NAGANA
   bone .... RACHITIS, RICKETS
   carried by mosquito ..... MALARIA
   carried by tsetse .... NAGANA
   carrier ...... TSETSE, RAT, MOSQUITO, ANOPHELES, FLY, VECTOR
   cause of .... GERM, MICROBE, BACILLUS, VIRUS, PATHOGEN
   causing .... PECCANT, MORBIFIC
   combining form .. NOS(O)
   contagious ..... MEASLES, TUBERCULOSIS, PLAGUE, PESTILENCE
   chronic tropical ... SPRUE
   cranberry .... SCALD
   deficiency .... PELLAGRA, BERIBERI, RICKETS, SCURVY, MARASMUS, KWASHIORKOR
   dust-caused .... SILICOSIS
   epidemic .... PESTILENCE, PLAGUE, BUBONIC
   eye .... CATARACT
   fowl .... PIP, ROUP
   from Anopheles mosquito MALARIA
   germ killer .. ANTIBIOTIC, ANTIBODY
   gradual end of ..... LYSIS
   imaginary .... CRUD
   indigenous ..... ENDEMIC
   infectious ..... MALARIA, NAGANA, FAVUS
   intestinal ...... CHOLERA

   leading to ..... MORBIFIC
   liver .... CIRRHOSIS, PORPHYRIA
   malignant ...... PLAGUE, PESTILENCE, TUMOR, CANCER, FEVER
   muscles ...... MYOPATHY
   nervous .. PELLAGRA, TIC, CHOREA, EPILEPSY
   of .... MORBID
   of beard .... SYCOSIS
   of chills and fever .. AGUE, MALARIA
   of hip .... COXALGIA
   of horses .... SPAVIN, GLANDERS, LAMPERS, LAMPAS
   of kings so-called ...... HEMOPHILIA
   of rye .... ERGOT
   of wheat .... RUST
   origin of ...... ETIOLOGY
   passage into body ...... ATRIUM
   pig .... BULL NOSE
   plant .... SMUT
   poultry .... ROUP, PIP
   recurrence of ... RELAPSE
   recurring ...... CHRONIC
   scratchy .... ITCH
   sheep .... ROT, GID
   skin ..... ECZEMA, TINEA, RINGWORM, TETTER, ACNE, LUPUS
   source .... NIDUS
   spreader .... CARRIER
   study of causes .... ETIOLOGY
   swine .... GARGET
   tropical .... YAWS, SPRUE
   virus .... FLU, COLD, RUBELLA, INFLUENZA, VARIOLA, RABIES, POX, VIROSIS, MEASLES, VARICELLA
   warning symptom ...... PRODROME
   wasting .... TABES, CONSUMPTION
diseased .... SICK, ILL, MORBID, PATHIC
   beggar .... LEPER, LAZAR
diseases, classification of ..... NOSOLOGY
disembark .... DETRAIN, LAND
disembodied spirit ...... SOUL

disembowel ...... EVISCERATE,
GUT, DRAW
disembowelment, suicide by ...
HARAKIRI
disenchant .... DISILLUSION
disencumber .... RID, RELIEVE,
FREE
disengage ..... DETACH, FREE,
UNFASTEN, RELEASE
disentangle .... RAVEL,
EXTRICATE
disfigure ...... DEFACE, SCAR,
DEFORM, MAR, UGLIFY,
MUTILATE, MANGLE
disfigurement .. BLEMISH, SCAR
disgorge .... VOMIT, EMPTY
disgrace .... BLOT, ODIUM,
INFAMY, IGNOMINY,
OBLOQUY, SHAME,
DISHONOR, SCANDAL
disgraceful .... INDIGN
disgruntle .... DISPLEASE
disgruntled one .... SOREHEAD,
CRYBABY, AX-GRINDER
disguise .. MASK, CAMOUFLAGE,
CLOAK, VEIL
assumed ..... INCOGNITO
in .... INCOGNITO
wearer .... MUMMER
disgust .... DISTASTE,
REPUGNANCE
disgusting .. FULSOME, ODIOUS,
LOUSY
matter .... FILTH
dish .. PLATE, PLATTER, PATEN,
VIAND, COURSE, RAMEKIN,
RAMEQUIN, SAUCER, TUREEN
between courses ....
ENTREE, ENTREMETS
boiled bread/cracker ....
PANADA
candy .... COMPOTE,
COMPOTIER
cheese .... RAREBIT
choice .... VIAND
colloquial ...... SERVING,
TREAT, FOOD
cooking .... BLAZER
eggs, cheese, etc ....
SOUFFLE
fancy .... KICKSHAW
for cookies, etc. ....
EPERGNE
for cooking ... CASSEROLE
for cooking over coal ...
BLAZER

for evaporating liquid ....
CAPSULE
fruit .... COMPOTE,
COMPOTIER, EPERGNE
highly spiced ...... OLIO
Hungarian ..... GOULASH
main .... ENTREE
maize and pepper ....
TAMALE
make of a ... PORCELAIN,
GLASS, PLASTIC, METAL,
EARTHENWARE
meat ..... STEW, RAGOUT
Mexican ....
CHILI CON CARNE, TAMALE
served before the roast ...
ENTREE
serving .. NAPPY, NAPPIE,
TRAY
soup .... TUREEN
tasty .... MORSEL
type ..... SAUCER, PLATE,
BOWL, CUP
vegetable .... SALAD
dishearten .. DAUNT, DEJECT,
DISCOURAGE, DAMPEN
dishes .... WARE
dishevel .... TOUSLE, MUSS,
RUMPLE
disheveled .... BLOWZY,
UNKEMPT
dishonest ... DECEITFUL, LYING
card player .... SHARPER,
CHEAT, BLACKLEG
lawyer .... PETTIFOGGER,
SHYSTER
person ... LIAR, CHEATER,
STEALER, DECEIVER
dishonor .... SHAME, DISGRACE,
DISCREDIT, ABUSE
dishonorable .... BASE
disillusion .... DISENCHANT
disinclined .. AVERSE, AGAINST,
UNWILLING, RELUCTANT
disinfect .... STERILIZE,
FUMIGATE
disinfectant ... LYSOL, CRESOL,
CHLORINE, IODINE
disingenuous ... SLY, INSINCERE
disintegrate .... DECAY,
CRUMBLE, BREAKUP,
ERODE, MELT
by acid .... CORRODE
by water/wind .... ERODE
disinter .... EXHUME, DIG UP

disinterested .... UNBIASED, IMPARTIAL

disjoint .... DISLOCATE, DISMEMBER

disk ... PATEN, PATINA, PLATE
 bright surrounding saints
 .... NIMBUS
 for breaking soil .... HARROW
 gem-cutting .... LAP
 hockey .... PUCK
 ice hockey .... PUCK
 jockey ..... ANNOUNCER, DEEJAY
 like ..... DISCOID, DISCAL
 metal .... PATEN
 obsolete .... DISCUS
 on radio/telephone ..... DIAL
 phonograph .... RECORD
 poker .... CHIP
 sealing .... WAFER
 shaped .... DISCOID
 throwing device .... TRAP
 to seal joints .... GASKET

dislike .... ANTIPATHY, AVERSION, DISTASTE
 intense .... HATRED, DETESTATION

dislocate .... SPLAY, UPSET, DISARRANGE, LUXATE, DISJOINT

dislodge ...... EJECT, REMOVE

disloyal .... FAITHLESS, UNFAITHFUL, RECREANT
 person, kind of ....
 TRAITOR, TURNCOAT, RENEGADE, INGRATE

dismal .... DREARY, DINGY, BLEAK

dismantle .... STRIP

dismay ...... DAUNT, TERRIFY, DISCONCERT, ALARM, ABASH, APPAL(L)

dismember .... DISJOINT

dismiss ...... REMOVE, DEMIT, EXPEL, CASHIER, OUST, DISCHARGE, FIRE
 archaic .... DEMIT
 colloquial ... SACK, BOOT, BRUSH OFF
 from command .. CASHIER
 in disgrace ...... CASHIER
 troops ...... DEMOBILIZE

dismissal ... OUSTER, REMOVAL, MITTIMUS

curt .... CONGE

dismount .. ALIGHT, GET DOWN, STEP DOWN

Disney, movie producer .....
 WALT
 artist ...... CARTOONIST, ANIMATOR
 dog .... PLUTO
 duck .... DONALD, DAISY
 duckling .. HUEY, DEWEY, LOUIE
 goldfish .... CLEO
 middle name of .... ELIAS
 mouse .. MICKEY, MINNIE
 pachyderm ...... DUMBO
 puppet .... PINOCCHIO

disobedient ... INSUBORDINATE

disorder .. CONFUSION, JUMBLE, CLUTTER, RIOT, MESS, CHAOS, UPSET, MUSS, LITTER
 vague: sl. .... CRUD

disorderly ... CHAOTIC, MESSY, RIOTOUS, UNRULY, UNTIDY, PELLMELL
 flight ... ROUT, STAMPEDE

disorganized .... DISORDERLY, HAYWIRE

disown ...... DISCLAIM, DENY, DISAVOW, REPUDIATE

disparage ... PEJORATE, DECRY, DEMEAN, DEPRECIATE, BELITTLE, LESSEN, SLUR, DISCREDIT, VILIPEND

disparaging remark ... SMEAR, SLUR, ASPERSION

disparate .. UNLIKE, DIFFERENT

dispassionate ..... FAIR, CALM, COOL

dispatch ... NEWS STORY, KILL, SEND(OFF), SPEED, HASTE, MESSAGE, POST
 bearer .... COURIER, MESSENGER
 boat .... AVISO

dispel ...... DISPERSE, SCATTER

dispensary .... CLINIC, INFIRMARY

dispensation ... DISTRIBUTION, EXEMPTION, MANAGEMENT

dispense ... EXCUSE, DEAL OUT, DISTRIBUTE

dispenser of alms ... ALMONER

disperse .... SCATTER

displace .... DISCHARGE, SUPPLANT, SUPERSEDE

displaced person .... DP,
    EVACUEE, REFUGEE
display .... EXHIBIT(ION),
    SHOW (OFF), UNFOLD,
    REVEAL, EXPOSE, SPORT
  brilliant .... RIOT, POMP,
    SPECTACLE, PARADE
  case .... COUNTER
  empty .... PAGEANT
  frame ..... EASEL, SHELF,
    SHELVE
  means of ..... SHOWCASE,
    (FASHION) SHOW
  of temper ..... TANTRUM
  ostentatiously .. FLAUNT,
    PARADE
  pretentious: colloq. .....
    SPREAD
  showy .... FANFARE,
    SPLURGE, BLAZON
  superficial .... VENEER
displease ...... ROIL, OFFEND,
    VEX, PIQUE, ANNOY,
    ANGER, MIFF
disport .... PLAY, FROLIC
dispose .... POSIT
  of .... SETTLE, SELL,
    GIVE AWAY, LIQUIDATE
disposed ...... APT, INCLINED,
    PRONE, BENT, WILLING,
    MINDED
  to agree ...... AMENABLE
  to fight .... BELLIGERENT,
    PUGNACIOUS
disposition ...... BENT, MOOD,
    ARRANGEMENT, TENDENCY,
    TEMPER(AMENT), MORALE,
    NATURE
  of mean .... ORNERY
  sour ... TESTY, GROUCHY,
    CRANKY, VINEGARY
dispossess ...... DIVEST, OUST,
    EJECT, DEPRIVE, EVICT,
    EXPROPRIATE
disproof .... REFUTATION
disprove ... GAINSAY, CONFUTE,
    REFUTE, REBUT
disputable .... MOOT
  at law .... LITIGIOUS
disputant .... ERISTIC
disputation .. DEBATE, POLEMIC
  art of .. POLEMICS, ERISTIC
disputatious .... CONTENTIOUS
dispute ...... ARGUE, DEBATE,
    CONTEST, CAUSERIE,
    BICKER, QUARREL, DOUBT,

    SQUABBLE, DOUBT, DISCUSS,
    ARGUMENT, FLITE, POLEMICS
  angrily ...... ALTERCATE
  beyond .... SETTLED
  noisy .. FRACAS, WRANGLE
  petty .... SPAT
disputer ... ARGUER, DEBATER,
    OPPOSER, DISSENTER
disqualified ...... INELIGIBLE
disqualify .... RULE OUT
disquiet ...... UNEASE, FRET,
    ANXIETY, UNREST
disquisition .... DISCOURSE
disregard .. IGNORE, OVERRIDE,
    OVERRULE
disregarding rule .... PECCANT
disreputable .... SHADY,
    UNSAVORY, ODOROUS,
    RAFFISH
  shrewish woman ....
    HARRIDAN, DEMIREP
disrespectful .. RUDE, IMPOLITE
disrupt .. REND, BREAK APART,
    SPLIT
dissatisfied (one) ....
    MALCONTENT
dissatisfy .... DISPLEASE
dissect .... CUT APART
dissemble .... FEIGN, PRETEND,
    SIMULATE, LIE
dissembler, alleged ..... JESUIT
disseminate ..... SPREAD, SOW,
    SCATTER, PROPAGATE,
    STREW
  by word of mouth ......
    BROADCAST
  through the press ....
    PUBLICIZE
  through the radio ....
    BROADCAST
  through TV .... TELECAST
dissension .. DISCORD, QUARREL
dissent .... DISAGREE, PROTEST
dissenter ... PROTESTANT, ANTI,
    OPPOSER, OBJECTOR,
    SECTARY
dissepiment .... SEPTUM
dissert .... ARGUE
dissertation .. THESIS, TREATISE,
    DISCOURSE, PAPER
dissident .... ANTI, REBEL,
    OPPOSER, INTRANSIGENT,
    MALCONTENT
disservice .... INJURY
dissimilar .... DIFFERENT,
    DISPARATE, UNLIKE

dissipate ... DISPEL, SQUANDER, SPEND, WASTE
dissipated man ... ROUE, RAKE, DEBAUCHEE
dissociate .... SEPARATE, DISENGAGE
dissolute .... LAX, PROFLIGATE, RAKISH, LICENTIOUS
   person ...... RAKE, ROUE
dissolution .... DIALYSIS
   combining form ... LYSIS
dissolve .... LIQUEFY, MELT, THAW
   and wash away ... LEACH
dissolved substance .... SOLUTE
dissonance from violin group .. WOLF
dissonant .... ATONAL
dissuade .... DEHORT
   opposed to ... PERSUADE, EXHORT
distaff ...... WOMAN, WOMEN
distal .... TERMINAL
   opposed to ..... PROXIMAL
distance .... REMOTENESS
   around .. CIRCUMFERENCE
   between ends ...... SPAN
   from equator .. LATITUDE
   in radio .... DX
   in the .... AFAR
   shortest .... BEELINE, STRAIGHTLINE
   three miles ...... LEAGUE
   traveled recorder .... ODOGRAPH
distant ..... AWAY, RESERVED, ALOOF, REMOTE, A(FAR), OFF
   past .... EARLY
   prefix .... TEL(E)
distaste .... DISLIKE, AVERSION
distemper ..... DISEASE, PAINT, DISORDER
distend ...... DILATE, EXPAND, STRETCH, INFLATE, SWELL
distended .... TURGID
   condition ..... TYMPANY
distich .... COUPLET
distill .... DRIP, TRICKLE, DECOCT, BREW
   several times .. COHOBATE
distillery ..... BREWERY, STILL
   mash .... SLOPS
   waste .... POTASH
distilling apparatus .. ALEMBIC, STILL
   refuse .... TAILING

   vessel .. RETORT, MATRASS
distinct .... DIFFERENT, CLEAR, SEPARATE, PLAIN
   part .... FEATURE
distinction .... HONOR
distinctive air .... AURA, ATMOSPHERE
   nature .... FLAVOR, TRAIT
   taste ..... SAVOR, PALATE
distinctly .... CLEARLY
distinguish ..... DISCRIMINATE, DISCERN, KNOW, LABEL, DIFFERENTIATE, SECERN
distinguished .... FAMOUS, EMINENT
   man .... DON
distinguishing feature .. TRAIT, CHARACTERISTIC
distort .... DEFORM, TWIST, MISREPRESENT, WARP
distorted ...... WRY, WARPED
distortion, ludicrous .... TRAVESTY
distract ..... DIVERT, CONFUSE, HARASS
distraction ...... AMUSEMENT, DIVERSION
   frenzied .... TIZZY
distraint .... POIND
distraught ..... CRAZED, MAD, CONFUSED, HARASSED
distress ...... AGONY, AFFLICT, TROUBLE, PAIN, GRIEF, GRIPE, UPSET, STRAITS
   signal ...... SOS, MAYDAY
distribute .. DOLE, METE, ALLOT
   cards .... DEAL
distributor .... DEALER
district .. AREA, ZONE, CIRCUIT, SECTOR, WARD, PRECINCT
distrust .... DOUBT, SUSPICION
disturb .... ANNOY, PESTER, AGITATE, PERTURB, ROIL, MOLEST, FEEZE, F(E)AZE, UPSET
disturbance .... DISORDER, COMMOTION, HUBBUB, RUMPUS, UPROAR
disunion ... SCHISM, BREAK-UP, SEPARATION, DISCORD
disunite .. SEPARATE, BREAK UP
disuse .... DESUETUDE
ditch .. CHANNEL, DIKE, FOSS(E)
   a suitor .... JILT
   castle .... MOAT
   digger .... TRENCHER

filling sticks ..... FASCINE
for defense ...... TRENCH
road .... GUTTER
slang ... DESERT, DISCARD
dither, in a ... EXCITED, AGOG
dithyramb ..... SONG, SPEECH,
POEM, ODE, HYMN
dittany .... MINT, FRAXINELLA
ditto ... SAME, LIKEWISE, COPY
ditty .... SONG, REFRAIN
diuretic ..... URETIC, URINARY
stimulant .. CANTHARIDES
diurnal ...... DAILY, JOURNAL,
DIARY
opposed to .. NOCTURNAL
diva .... PRIMA DONNA, SINGER
forte of ..... ARIA, OPERA
divagate .... DIGRESS
divan ..... CAFE, SOFA, COUCH,
SETTEE, CANAPE, OTTOMAN,
LOUNGE
divaricate .... FORK, BRANCH
dive .... PLUNGE, DEN,
HONKY-TONK
bomber .... STUKA
colloquial .... SALOON
fancy .... SWAN, GAINER,
BACKFLIP
into water .... SUBMERGE
diver, breathing aid of .. SCUBA
from airplane ....
PARACHUTIST
gear of .... FLIPPERS,
AQUALUNG, SPEARGUN,
(PARA)CHUTE
diverge .... DIFFER, VARY,
DEVIATE
divergent strabismus ....
WALLEYE
divergence .... VARIANCE
divers ...... VARIOUS, SUNDRY
diverse .... VARIED, DIFFERENT,
SEVERAL
prefix .... POLY
diversify .... VARY
diversion .... AMUSEMENT,
PASTIME, DISTRACTION
diversionary tactic ...... FEINT
divert ...... AMUSE, ESTRANGE,
DISTRACT, DEFLECT,
ENTERTAIN
divertissement ..... DIVERSION,
ENTR'ACTE, INTERMEZZO,
BALLET
divest ...... STRIP, DISPOSSESS,
DEPRIVE

divide ..... SUNDER, SEPARATE,
BISECT, SPLIT, APPORTION,
ALIENATE, HALVE, TRANSECT
grammatically ....
PUNCTUATE
into feet .... SCAN
into four parts .. QUARTER
into layers ...... FOLIATE
into three ...... TRISECT
into two ..... BISECT, HALF
voting area ....
GERRYMANDER
divided .... CLEFT
into 100 degrees ....
CENTIGRADE
dividend .... BONUS
dividing line .... SOLIDUS
wall .... SEPTUM
divination .... AUGURY,
PROPHECY, NUMEROLOGY,
HYDROMANCY
by communication with
the dead ....
NECROMANCY
by figures .... GEOMANCY
by lots .... SORTILEGE
by the stars .. ASTROLOGY
combining form .. MANCY
having powers of ....
MANTIC
pertaining to .... FATIDIC
powers of .... MANTIC
divine .. HOLY, SACRED, GUESS,
GODLIKE, CONJECTURE,
SUPERNAL
bread .... MANNA
Comedy author ... DANTE
Comedy setting .... HELL,
PURGATORY, PARADISE
communication .. ORACLE
favor ... GRACE, BLESSING
food .... MANNA
intervention ... THEURGY
love .... AGAPE
presence ...... SHEKINAH
punishment ..... PLAGUE
spirit .... GHOST
tree .... DEVA
word .... LOGOS
work .... MIRACLE
diviner ...... SEER, CONJUROR
divining rod .... WAND
search water with ......
DOWSE
user .... AARON
diving aid .... AQUALUNG

apparatus .. BATHYSCAPH
bell inventor .... EADS
bird .... LOON, GREBE,
DUCKER
boat .... SUBMARINE
hazard .... BENDS
divinity ...... DEITY, NUMEN,
THEOLOGY, CANDY,
GOD(HEAD), GODHOOD
division ...... PART, SECTION,
SEPARATION, FISSION,
PARTITION, SCISSION,
SCHISM
book .... CHAPTER
cell .... MITOSIS
city .... ZONE, WARD,
PRECINCT
game .... HALF, SET,
INNING, QUARTER,
CHUKKER
in a group .... SCHISM
mankind .... RACE
mark of .... OBELUS
opera .... SCENA
play .... ACT, SCENE
poem ... CANTO, STANZA,
VERSE
race .... LAP, HEAT
road .... LANE
society .... CASTE
religious .... SCHISM
result of .... QUOTIENT
divorce allowance ... ALIMONY
ground for ... ADULTERY,
MENTAL CRUELTY,
INCOMPATIBILITY
suit defendant ....
CORRESPONDENT
suit subject .... ALIMONY,
SETTLEMENT
divorcee .... FEME SOLE
divorcee's alimony .. ESTOVERS
divot .... TURF
divulge ... TELL, REVEAL, SPILL,
DISCLOSE
divvy: sl. ..... SHARE, PORTION
Dixie-land ...... (THE) SOUTH
suffix used with .... CRAT
dixit, ____ .... IPSE
Dixon's partner .... MASON
dizen .... DECK
dizziness .. VERTIGO, GIDDINESS
attack of .... FAINT
dizzy .... GIDDY, GROGGY,
VERTIGINOUS

colloquial .... SILLY,
FOOLISH
of baseball fame ... DEAN
person: colloq. .... DAME
djebel .... HILL
do ..... CARRY OUT, PERFORM
alone .... SOLO
away with .... KILL,
ABOLISH
in .... KILL, SLAY
it-yourself set ...... KIT
make .... EKE
over ...... REDECORATE
superficially ..... DABBLE
without ... SPARE, FOREGO
dobbin .... HORSE
dobson fly .... SIALID(AN)
doby: colloq. .... ADOBE
doc ...... DOCTOR, DOCUMENT
docile ...... GENTLE, PLIANT,
TRACTABLE, OBEDIENT,
TAME
dock .... JETTY, PIER, CLIP,
BOB, WHARF, BANG, QUAY,
LAND
area .... MARINA
post .... BOLLARD
worker ...... STEVEDORE,
LONGSHOREMAN, LUMPER
docked tail .... BOB
docket .... AGENDA, LABEL,
TICKET
docking space .... SLIP
doctor .. SURGEON, PHYSICIAN,
OSTEOPATH, CHIROPRACTOR,
MEDICINEMAN, TAMPER,
FALSIFY, TREAT
assistant of ... INTERN(E),
NURSE
colloquial ... MEDICO, VET
fake .... QUACK
herb .... QUACK
hospital .... INTERN
inquest .... CORONER
kind of ... QUACK, WITCH
Moslem .. HAKEEM, HAKIM
of animals ....
VET(ERINARIAN)
of foot/hand diseases ...
CHIROPODIST
teeth .... DENTIST
doctors' association ..... AMA
rap .... PERCUSS
doctrinaire .... VISIONARY,
DICTATORIAL
doctrine ...... BELIEF, DOGMA,

CULT, ISM, THEORY, TENET,
    PRINCIPLE, PRECEPT
mystical .... CABALA
of salvation ... LEGALISM
religious .. DOGMA, DOXY,
    CREED
widespread ...... GOSPEL
doctrines to be believed ....
    CREDENDA
document .. PAPER, CONTRACT,
    DEED
    container ...... HANAPER
    draft .... PROTOCOL
    formal .... INSTRUMENT
    handwritten by signer ....
    HOLOGRAPH
    legal .... WRIT
    part of .... SEAL
    ribbon of .... LAPEL
    written .... SCRIPT
documents, collection of .....
    PAPERS
dodder ...... SHAKE, TREMBLE,
    TOTTER
doddering person ..... DOTARD
Dodecanese island ... COS, KOS,
    PATMOS, RHODES, COAN,
    LERO, SIMI, CASO
dodge ... EVADE, RUSE, PARRY,
    DUCK
dodger ...... EVADER, ELUDER,
    RASCAL
Dodgers' (baseball) "preacher"
    ROE
dodo in flying school ... CADET
doe .... DEER
    in its 2nd year ...... TEG
doff .... REMOVE, GET RID,
    TAKE OFF, VAIL
dog ...... FOLLOW, CLUMBER,
    CANINE, TYKE, PUG,
    HOUND, HUNT, DANE,
    SLUT, SPANIEL, BOXER,
    LAP, BEAGLE, CHENILLE,
    MASTIFF, RATTER
    Alaskan ..... MALEMUTE,
    MALAMUTE, MALEMIUT
    Arctic .... HUSKY,
    MALEMUTE
    ape .... BABOON
    Australian .... DINGO
    Chinese breed .... CHOW,
    PEKIN(G)ESE
    chops .... FLEWS
    coach .... DALMATIAN
    collar ring .... TERRET

combining form ... CYNO
command to ...... MUSH
constellation ...... CANIS
cry .... HOWL
cur .... TYKE
curly-haired .... POODLE,
    BARBET
disease ...... DISTEMPER,
    RABIES, MANGE
drinking way of ..... LAP
eat-dog affair .. RAT RACE
Eskimo .... HUSKY
face of .... MASK
family .... CANIDAE
FDR's .... FALA
female ..... BITCH, SLUT,
    BRACH(ET)
fennel .... HOGWEED,
    MAYWEED
ferocious ...... BANDOG,
    BLOODHOUND
foxhound-like .. HARRIER
genus .... CANIS
German ...... SHEPHERD
gone! ...... DARN, DAMN
greyhound ...... SALUKI
guard of the underworld
    CERBERUS
hair on neck ... HACKLES
hell .... CERBERUS
hound .... BEAGLE,
    BRACH(ET)
house .... KENNEL
howl of .. ULULATION, BAY
hunting .... BASSET,
    RETRIEVER, BRACH(ET),
    POINTER, SETTER,
    BEAGLE, HARRIER
hybrid ... CUR, MONGREL
in meteorology ....
    PARHELION
large .... MASTIFF
LBJ's .... YUKI
like animal ...... JACKAL
long-bodied ....
    DACHSHUND
loss of scent ...... FAULT
mongrel ...... TYKE, CUR
mongrel in White House
    YUKI
movie ...... ASTA, LASSIE,
    RIN TIN TIN, KELLY, NEIL
mythological .. CERBERUS
name of ..... ASTA, FALA,
    LASSIE, FIDO, ROVER,
    SPOTTY

neck hair ...... HACKLES
of hell .... CERBERUS
on India .... DHOLE
of mixed breed ..... CUR, MONGREL
pack .... KENNEL
parasite .... HEARTWORM
pet .... LAP, PEKINESE, POMERANIAN, CHIHUAHUA
Philippine .... ASO
police ... DANE, ALSATIAN
pound ... MONGREL, CUR, STRAY
pug-nosed ... PEKIN(G)ESE
rabbit/hare hunter ...... HARRIER
racing .... WHIPPET
Russian .... SAMOYED
short-legged .... BEAGLE
Siberian .... SAMOYED
slang .... POOCH
sled .... HUSKY
small .... ALCO, CHIHUAHUA, POMERANIAN, PUG, BEAGLE, WHIFFET, POM
"space" .... LAIKA
spaniel .... COCKER
Star ... SIRIUS, CANICULA, PROCYON
Star, of the ...... SOTHIC
swift .... WHIPPET
tail of .... FLAG
tailless ...... SCHIPPERKE
team leader .. OUTRUNNER
television .. LASSIE, CLEO, LAD-A-DOG
terrier ..... SCHNAUZER, SEALYHAM
tongue cartilage .. LYTTA
tooth ..... FANG, CUSPID, LANIARY
toy ..... POM, PEKE, PUG, CHIHUAHUA
three-headed .. CERBERUS
Wales .... SEALYHAM
wild ..... DINGO, JACKAL, TANATE, DHOLE
wire-haired .... GRIFFON, GRIFFIN, PINSCHER, SCHNAUZER
with foxlike head .. CORGI
young ... PUP(PY), WHELP
dogcart .... TRAP

dogface: sl. .... G.I., INFANTRYMAN
dogfish .... BOWFIN, SHARK
skin .... SHAGREEN
dogged .... STUBBORN
dogger .... BOAT
doggerel .... JINGLE, VERSE
dogie .... CALF, MAVERICK
dogma ..... DOCTRINE, TENET, BELIEF, ISM
dogmatic .... DICTATORIAL
principle .... DICTA
saying .... DICTUM
dogmatist, a .... CALVINIST
dogs: sl. .... FEET
dogwood ...... CORNEL, OSIER, ASSEGAI, ASSAGAI, CORNUS, TUPELO
doilies .... NAPERY
doily .... MAT, NAPKIN
doited: Scot. .. SENILE, FOOLISH
doldrums ..... CALM, TEDIUM, LISTLESSNESS, BLUES, DUMPS
dole .. ALMS, DISTRIBUTE, METE
archaic .. SORROW, DOLOR
out .... RATION, METE
doleful .... DISMAL, SAD, MOURNFUL, LUGUBRIOUS
dolerite .... BASALT
doll ..... CHILD, TOY, PUPPET, MARIONETTE, MAUMET, MAMMET
real .... LULU
slang ...... GIRL, WOMAN
dollar bill, five: sl. .. FIN, FIVER
bill, one: sl. .... BUCK
bill, 100: sl. ... CENTURY, C-NOTE
bill, 1000: sl. ..... GRAND
bill, ten: sl. ... SAWBUCK, TENNER
bill, two: sl. ...... DEUCE
coin part .. NICKEL, DIME, CENT, QUARTER, EAGLE
coin: sl. ..... CARTWHEEL
Mexican .... PESO
quarter: sl. ... TWO BITS
slang .. SIMOLEON, BERRY, BUCK, PLUNK
Spanish .... DURO
dolly .... DASHER, LOCOMOTIVE
Indian .... TRAY
Varden ..... TROUT, HAT
what it holds ..... RIVET
dolman .. ROBE, JACKET, COAT, WRAP, MANTLE

dolmen stone ...... MEGALITH
Dolomites peak .. MARMOLADA
dolor .. SORROW, GRIEF, PANG,
            ANGUISH, AGONY
dolorous .... SAD
dolphin .... INIA, SOOSOO,
      PORPOISE, BELUGA, SUSU,
         BUOY, CETACEAN
   frolic of .... GAMBOL
   musician saved by ......
              ORION
   Spanish .... DORADO
   striker .... SPAR,
          MARTINGAL(E)
   whale .... ORC
dolt ...... CLOD, DUNCE, OAF,
     FOOL, ZANY, BLOCKHEAD,
      NUMSKULL, NITWIT,
      NINNY, HALFWIT, SAP
domain ...... REALM, DEMESNE,
     DEMENE, ESTATE, FIELD,
      SPHERE, BAILIWICK
   poetic .... BOURN(E)
dome .... ROOF, CUPOLA
   apse's .... CONCHA
   building/hall with ......
           ROTUNDA
   poetic .... MANSION
   slang .... HEAD
   with cupola ...... TOPE
Domenico, painter .. EL GRECO
domestic ... ENCHORIAL, TAME,
     NATIVE, ENCHORIC,
     SERVANT, MENIAL,
     LOCAL, SLAVEY
   animal: dialectic ....
       CRITTER, CRITTUR
   establishment ... MENAGE,
     HOUSEHOLD, DOMICILE
   fowl .. DORKING, POULTRY
   servant ..... (HOUSE)MAID
   type of .... SLEEP-IN
   worker .. SERVANT, COOK,
       MAID, BUTLER
domesticate ... TAME, CIVILIZE,
          BREAK
domicile ...... HOME, MENAGE,
    RESIDENCE, HOUSE(HOLD)
dominance .... CONTROL,
    MASTERY, SUPREMACY
dominant .... RULING,
   PREVAILING, PRE-EMINENT,
       IN CONTROL
dominate .... RULE, CONTROL,
     MASTER, HECTOR
dominated .... RIDDEN

domineer .. LORD OVER, BULLY
   husband .... HENPECK
Dominican .... FRIAR
dominie .... PASTOR,
   SCHOOLMASTER, CLERGYMAN
dominion ..... DOMAIN, SWAY,
     RULE, REIGN, REALM,
   EMPERY, EMPIRE, LORDSHIP
domino .. CLOAK, (HALF) MASK,
         TILE, LUMP
   spot .... PIP
   with four spots .. QUATRE
   variant .... MUGGINS
dominoes not dealt .... STOCK
don .... WEAR, PUT ON, INVEST
   Cambridge college ......
     HEAD, TUTOR, FELLOW
   Juan ... . RAKE,
         PHILANDERER
   Juan, greatest ....
     (ANTOINE) DUBOIS
   Juan's mother ...... INEZ
   opposed to .... DOFF
   Quixote, author ....
         CERVANTES
   Quixote's horse ....
         ROSINANTE
   Quixote's ladylove ......
         DULCINEA
   river .... DUNA
   Spanish .... GENTLEMAN,
         NOBLEMAN
dona .... LADY, MADAM
Donar, god of thunder .. THOR
donate ..... GIVE, CONTRIBUTE
Donau river .. DUNAREA, DUNA,
         DANUBE
done for ...... KAPUT, KILLED
   with .... OVER
   with hands ..... MANUAL
Donetsk .... STALINO
donjon .... TOWER, KEEP,
         DUNGEON
donkey ..... BURRO, DICK(E)Y,
   ONAGER, JENNET, CUDDY,
       (JACK)ASS
   and horse offspring .....
       HINNY, MULE
   animal like a ... QUAGGA
   cry .... BRAY
   female .... MARE
   male .... JACK
   man rebuked by ....
         BALAAM
   pet name of .... MOKE
   young .... COLT, FOAL

donna: Ital. .... LADY, MADAM
donnybrook .... FREE-FOR-ALL
donor .... GIVER
doodad ... BAUBLE, GIMCRACK,
GADGET, TRINKET, GEWGAW
doodle ..... DAWDLE, SCRAWL
doodlebug .... LARVA
doodlesack .... BAGPIPE
doohickey ... DINGUS, DEVICE,
GADGET, DINGBAT
doom .. DESTINY, FATE, DEATH,
CONDEMN
doomed .. KAPUT, CONDEMNED,
FATED
to death .... FEY
to eternal punishment ...
DAMNED
Doone, heroine .... LORNA
husband of .... RIDD
door .... PASSAGE, ACCESS,
PORTAL, ENTRY, WICKET
back .... POSTERN
catch .... LATCH
cover .. CANOPY, AWNING
crosspiece .... LINTEL,
TRANSOM
fastener .... LATCH, HASP
frame piece .... TILE
frame(work) .... GRATE,
GRATING, SASH
grating .... GRILLE
handle .... KNOB
joint .... HINGE
knocker .... RAPPER
lock .... LATCH
lower half of .... HATCH
part .. STILE, SILL, LINTEL,
PANEL, KNOB, LATCH,
HASP, JAMB, RAIL
rooflike projection ......
CANOPY
doorkeeper .. PORTER, OSTIARY,
CONCIERGE, USHER
Masonic .... TILER
doorman .... CONCIERGE,
JANITOR, PORTER
doorsill .... THRESHOLD
doorway .. PORTAL, ENTRANCE
curtain .... PORTIERE
drapery .... LAMBREQUIN
out .... EXIT
sidepost ...... JAMB(E)
dope .... DRUG, NARCOTIC
addict .... FIEND, JUNKIE,
JUNKY
seller .... PUSHER

slang ..... INFORMATION,
FIGURE OUT, STUPID, INFO,
LOW-DOWN
dor .... BEETLE, BUMBLEBEE
dorado .... DOLPHIN
dorbeetle .... COCKCHAFER
Dorcas .... TABITHA
Doric cornice block .. MUTULE
droplike ornaments .....
GUTTA
Dorlcote Mill site ...... FLOSS
dormancy .... TORPOR
dormant ...... ASLEEP, QUIET,
STILL, INACTIVE, TORPID,
LATENT, QUIESCENT, RESTING
dormer .. LUTHERN, SKYLIGHT,
WINDOW
dormitory ... BOARDINGHOUSE,
HALL
dormouse ..... LEROT, RODENT
dornick ..... DAMASK, STONE
dorp .... VILLAGE, HAMLET
dorsal .... BACK, TERGAL
opposed to ..... VENTRAL
dorsum .... TERGUM, BACK
dorty .... SULLEN
dory .... (FISHING)BOAT
dos-a-dos .... SOFA, SEAT
Dos Passos' trilogy ...... USA
dose .... POTION
doss .... BED, BUNK, SLEEP
dosser .... PANNIER
dossier .... RECORD, FILE
dossil .. TENT, PLEDGET, STUPE,
COMPRESS
dot .. POINT, SPOT, IOTA, MARK,
PERIOD, DOWRY,
STIPPLE, SPECK
dotage .... SENILITY
dotard .... OCTOGENARIAN
describing a ...... SENILE
dote .... ADORE
doting ...... DECAYING, FOND
dotted .... MOTTLED, DAPPLE,
STIPPLED, PIED
in heraldry .... SEME
dotterel .... DUPE, GULL,
PLOVER
dotty .... FEEBLE, CRAZY
double ...... BINATE, DUPLEX,
TWIN, TWOFOLD, PAIRED,
DUAL, TWICE, DUPLE
aces .. AMBSACE, AMESACE
bass .... VIOLONE
chromosome ...... DYAD

cross: sl. .... TREACHERY, BETRAY, CHEAT
curve .... ESS
dagger mark ...... DIESIS
dealer .... CHEATER
dealing ...... DUPLICITY
decker: colloq. .... SANDWICH
door part .... SWING
faced .... INSINCERE
faced god .... JANUS
faced person .... HYPOCRITE
meaning .... EQUIVOQUE, EQUIVOKE
moldboard plow ... LISTER
on the .... QUICKLY
prefix .... DI(S)
reed instrument ... OBOE, SHAWM, BASSOON
ripper/runner ...... SLED
ring .... GEMEL
sirloin beef ...... BARON
talk .... GIBBERISH
tongued ...... DECEITFUL
tongued creature .. SNAKE
tooth .... MOLAR
tripod .... CAT
up .... CLENCH, FOLD
vision .... DIPLOPIA
doublet .... POURPOINT
doubletree .... CROSSBAR
doubly .... TWICE
doubt .... FEAR, UNCERTAINTY, MISTRUST
beyond .. SURE, CERTAIN
cause/feel ...... MISGIVE
doubter ..... SKEPTIC, THOMAS
doubtful .... UNSURE, DUBIOUS
doubting Thomas .... SKEPTIC
douce: Scot. .... PLEASANT
douceur .... TIP, BRIBE
dough .... PASTE, BATTER
dry strip of ..... NOODLE
fermenting ...... LEAVEN
slang .... MONEY
toughener ...... GLUTEN
doughboy ..... INFANTRYMAN, DUMPLING
doughnut ... CRULLER, DONUT, FRIEDCAKE
colloquial .... SINKER
doughty .... BOLD, BRAVE, VALIANT
doughy .... PASTY, SOFT
doum .... PALM

dour .... STERN, SEVERE, GRIM, SULLEN
Douro .... DUERO
douse .... EXTINGUISH, DUCK, HIT, DRENCH
dove ... NUN, CULVER, PIGEON
describing a ..... GENTLE
genus .... COLUMBA
kind of .... HOMING, POUTER, TUMBLER
like .... COLUMBINE
make sound of .. MOURN, COO
shelter .... COTE, COLUMBARY
symbol ..... HOLY SPIRIT, PEACE
dovecote .... COLUMBARY
dovekie ...... AUK, ROTCH(E), GUILLEMOT, ALLE
Dover is capital of .. DELAWARE
dovetail .... JOINT, FIT
dowager .... WIDOW
dowdy .... SLOVENLY, SHABBY, FRUMP, TACKY
woman .... FRUMP
dowel .... PIN
like ...... TENON, PINTLE
dower ...... BEQUEST, TALENT, INHERITANCE, GIFT, ENDOW, DOWRY
dowlas .... LINEN, CALICO
down ..... FLOOR, BELOW, ILL, FEATHERS, HAIR, FLUFF, FUR, PILE, FELL
a mound like ..... DUNE
and out .... HELPLESS, HOPELESS
combining form .. CAT(A), KATA, CATH
covered with ...... PUBESCENT, LANUGINOSE, LANUGINOUS
duck's .... EIDER
east .... MAINE, NEW ENGLAND
facing .. PRONE, PRONATE
feather .... PLUMULE
in baseball .... (PUT)OUT
in the mouth .... SAD
loose particles of ... FUZZ
plant .... VILLUS
prefix ..... CAT(A), KATA, CATH

source of .... EIDER
Under ...... AUSTRALIA,
  NEW ZEALAND, ANZAC
downcast ..... DEJECTED, SAD,
  GLOOMY
downfall .. RUIN, LABEFACTION
downhearted .. SAD, DEJECTED,
  DESPONDENT
downhill, go ,........ DECLINE
downpour ...... RAIN(STORM),
  SPATE, TORRENT,
  SHOWER
downright ... BLUNT, UTTERLY,
  ABSOLUTE, PLAIN, FRANK,
  SHEER, STARK
Downs, the .... ROADSTEAD
downtrodden ...... OPPRESSED
downy .... FLUFFY, FUZZY,
  NAPPY, VILLOUS, FLOSSY,
  FEATHERY, SERICEOUS
feather .... PLUMULE
growth ... LANUGO, MOLD
mass .... FLUE
surface/fiber .... NAP
dowry .... GIFT, TALENT,
  ENDOWMENT
of a .... DOTAL
doxology .... KADDISH
first word .... GLORIA
doxy ... DOCTRINE, ISM, CREED
slang ..... HUSSY, WENCH
doyen .... DEAN
doze ..... (CAT)NAP, DROWSE,
  SNOOZE, SLEEP
dozen .... TWELVE
baker's .... THIRTEEN
long .... THIRTEEN
dozy ...... SLEEPY, DROWSY
Dr. No's nemesis .... BOND
drab .... DULL, SLUT,
  LACKLUSTER
drabbet .... LINEN
drach .... DRAM
drachma .... COIN
1/100 of .... LEPTON
drachmas (1,700) in 1949 ......
  DOLLAR
Draco .... DRAGON
Draconian ..... CRUEL, SEVERE
draff .... DREGS, LEES, REFUSE,
  SEDIMENT
draft ..... SKETCH, CONSCRIPT,
  DRAWING, POTATION,
  DRINK(ING), TASS, CHECK,
  DRAIN, POTION

animal ... OX, ELEPHANT,
  CARABAO, MULE
animal and its vehicle ...
  TEAM
card burner ... OBJECTOR,
  DODGER
deep .... SWIG
military service .. IMPRESS
draftee .. CONSCRIPT, RECRUIT
drafts .... CHECKERS
draftsman .... SCRIVENER
drag .... HAUL, HALE, LUG,
  TOW, TUG, DREDGE,
  CONTINUE, TRAIL, PULL,
  SWEEP, GRAPNEL
feet .... SCUFF(LE)
slang .. INFLUENCE, PUFF,
  DANCE
dragee .... CANDY, PILL
draggletail ... SLUT, SLATTERN
dragnet .... TRAWL, WEB
dragoman ...... INTERPRETER,
  CICERONE, GUIDE
dragon .. MONSTER, FIREDRAKE
archaic .. SNAKE, SERPENT,
  DRAKE
breath of .... FIRE
deb's .... DUENNA
giant .... FAFNIR
Greek .... LADON
in astronomy .... DRACO
mythical .... BASILISK
slayer ...... (ST.)GEORGE,
  CADMUS
two-legged ...... WIVERN
dragoon .... CAVALRYMAN,
  HARASS
drain .... EMPTY, SEWER,
  EXHAUST, DEPLETE,
  BUDDLE, FILTER, DRAW OFF,
  PIPE, DRAFT
liquid from ... TAP, SAP
open ... KENNEL, GUTTER
road .... CULVERT
drainage hole ...... CESSPOOL,
  SUMP
pit .... SUMP
drake .... DUCK, CANNON,
  MAY FLY, MALLARD
archaic .... DRAGON
dram .. NIP, SLUG, SIP, DRINK,
  DRAFT
in assaying ..... CENTNER
drama .... (STAGE)PLAY,
  BUSKIN
climax ..... CATASTROPHE

colloquial .... LEGIT
comic scenes ..... RELIEF
conflict of character .....
            AGON
Japanese .... KABUKI
main character ....
            PROTAGONIST
opening .... PROTASIS
outdoor .... PAGEANT
pertaining to ... THESPIAN
staging place ... THEATER
tragic .... BUSKIN
wordless ..... PANTOMIME
dramatic ..... VIVID, EXCITING
art .... THEATER
impersonator .... DISEUSE
dramatics ... HISTRIONICS
dramatis personae ...... CAST,
            CHARACTERS
dramatist ...... PLAYWRIGHT
dramshop .... BAR, SALOON
drape .. CURTAIN, BAIZE, FOLD
draper .... CLOTHIER
drapery ... ARRAS, CURTAIN,
     CLOTH, FABRIC, TEXTILE,
            VALANCE
bed .... CANOPY
cloth ... MOREEN, MADRAS
cord .. TORSADE, TIEBACK
material ...... VELOURS,
            VELURE
shelf/door/window .....
            LAMBREQUIN
drapes .... CURTAIN
drastic .... SEVERE, HARSH,
            EXTREME
drat .... EXPLETIVE
draught .... DRAFT
draughts: Brit. ...... CHECKERS
Dravidian ... TELEGU, TELUGU
draw .. DRAFT, LIMN, TIE, TUG,
     STALEMATE, DEPICT,
     DELINEATE, DRAG, PULL,
     SKETCH, HAUL, ATTRACT,
     DISEMBOWEL, EXTRACT
after .... TOW
as conclusion .... INFER,
            DEDUCE
at a cigar(ette) ..... PUFF,
            DRAG
away ..... DIVERT, DRAFT
back .... RECOIL, RECEDE,
            QUAIL
back in fear .... QUAIL,
       COWER, CRINGE
close ... APPROACH, NEAR

forth ..... ELICIT, EDUCE,
            EVOKE
in dots .... STIPPLE
lots .... CAST
off ...... DRAFT, SIPHON
off from dregs ..... RACK
out .... PROTRACT,
     CONTINUE, PROLONG,
     LENGTHEN, EXTRACT
sap .... BLEED
tight ..... TAUTEN, TENSE,
            FRAP
to scale ...... PROTRACT
drawback ... DEFECT, REFUND,
     REBATE, SHORTCOMING
drawbridge .... BASCULE,
            PONTLEVIS
drawer .... DRAFTSMAN
for money .... TILL
handle of .... KNOB
drawers .... SHORTS
women's .... PANTIES,
        PANTALET(TE)S
drawing ..... DESIGN, SKETCH,
     DIAGRAM, LOTTERY,
            TRACTION
architectural ..... EPURES
carbon pencil ....
            CHARCOAL
charcoal .... FUSAIN
in dots .... STIPPLE
of load/vehicle ... DRAFT
on walls, etc. .. GRAFFITO
paper .... ATLAS
power .... PULL
room .... PARLOR, SALON,
            SALA
with crayons ....
            CALCOGRAPHY
with lead-pointed
instrument ....
            PLUMBAGO
drawn ...... TIRED, HAGGARD,
     EVEN, TENSE, TAUT
out .... LENGTHY
dray .... CART
dread .... AWE, FEAR
dreaded disease ...... CANCER,
     CHOLERA, TUBERCULOSIS,
     LEUKEMIA, SMALLPOX
dreadful ..... DIRE, AWESOME,
     TERRIBLE, HORRID, HIDEOUS
dreadfully: colloq. ..... VERY,
            EXTREMELY
dreadnaught ..... BATTLESHIP,
            WARSHIP

dream .. FANCY, VISION, HOPE, ILLUSION, FANTASY

day .... REVERIE

French .... REVE

goal .... IDEAL

up ... CONCEIVE, IMAGINE

world .... UTOPIA

dreamer .. FANTAST, VISIONARY

dreamland .... SLEEP

dreams, forecast based on ....
ONEIROMANCY

interpret .... REDE

interpretation of ....
ONEIROLOGY

interpreter ....
ONEIROCRITIC

dreamy .... FANCIFUL, VISIONARY, IMPRACTICAL, VAGUE, MISTY

from dope smoking .. KEF

person .... POET, IDEALIST

dreary .... DISMAL, DULL, GLOOMY, CHEERLESS

Scottish .... DREE

dredge ... SIFT, DEEPEN, DRAG, SPRINKLE

bucket ...... CLAMSHELL

shovel .... SCOOP

dree .... ENDURE, DREARY, TEDIOUS, SUFFER

dregs ... RESIDUE, SILT, DRAFF, MAGMA, LEES, REFUSE, SEDIMENT, SCUM, FECES, GROUT

Dreiser (Theodore) character ..
CARRIE

drench ...... SOP, WET, SOAK, SATURATE, SOUSE, DOUSE

drenched ...... ASOP, SOAKED, WET, SOPPING

Dresden .... PORCELAIN, CHINAWARE

dress .. ATTIRE, DECK, CLOTHE, FROCK, GARB, DECORATE, ACCOUTERMENTS, ADORN, TRIM, APPAREL, RAIMENT, RIG

a horse .... CURRY

by rubbing .... DUB

characteristic .... LIVERY

colloquial .... TOG(S), FIG

designer .... STYLIST

down .... SCOLD, REPRIMAND

external ... COAT, CLOAK, CAPE

fashion designer ....
NORELL, GALANOS, SARMI, BALMAIN, BLASS CASHIN, BEENE, TIFFEAU, GERNREICH

feathers .... PREEN

formal .. GOWN, TUXEDO, CUTAWAY

flax .... TED

gaudily .... BEDIZEN

hat .... SHAKO

in fine array ...... DINK

leather ..... CURRY, TAN, DUB

man's full .... TAILS

manner of .... GUISE

material .. VOILE, MUSLIN, SILK, PONGEE, WOOL

odd .... TOG

ornamental slit .... SLASH

pertaining to .. SARTORIAL

riding .... HABIT

showily .... FIG

spangle .... SEQUIN

stone .... NIG

style, men's ...... NEHRU

style, women's ....
MINISKIRT, SEE-THROUGH, TOPLESS, PANTSUIT, MUU-MUU, PALAZZO, CHEONGSAM

suit .... TUX(EDO)

to the ___ ...... NINES

trimming .. RUCHE, GIMP, PIPING

up ..... DANDIFY, PRANK, PRIMP, PRINK, PRUNE

with beak .... PREEN

with tails .... CUTAWAY

dressed ...... CLOTHED, CLAD, GARBED, ARRAYED

shabbily .... POK(E)Y, DOWDY

smartly .... CHIC

to ___ .... KILL

to the ___ .... NINES

dresser ... BUREAU, CUPBOARD, CHEST

flashy .... SPIFF

of another person ......
VALET

stylish .. TOFF, DUDE, FOP, DANDY

dressing .... SAUCE, STUFFING, PLEDGET

down .... SCOLDING

gown ... KIMONO, CAMISE, CAMISOLE, ROBE
medicated .... STUPE
soil .... MANURE
table ..... TOILET, VANITY
wound ...... BANDAGE, DOSSIL, STUPE, LINT
dressmaker .... MODISTE, SEAMSTRESS, COUTURIER(E), TAILOR, SARTOR
dressmaking term ...... GORE, FACE, HEM
dressy ..... STYLISH, ELEGANT, CHIC
Dreyfus' champion .... (EMILE) ZOLA
dribble ...... TRICKLE, DROOL, SLAVER, DROP
in basketball .... BOUNCE
in football .... KICKS
dried coconut meat .... COPRA
flower bud .... CLOVE
grape .... RAISIN
grass .... HAY
orchid tuber ...... SALEP
plum .... PRUNE
up .... SERE
drier ...... DESICCATOR, KILN, OVEN, OAST, BLOWER, DESSICANT
natural .... SUN, FIRE
drift .... TENOR, INTENT, PILE, TREND, TENDENCY, INCLINATION, MEANING
ice : ...... SLUDGE, FLOE
in mining ...... HEADING
in nautical usage .... SAG
drifter .. HOBO, TRAMP, CLOUD, DERELICT, NOMAD, VAGABOND
drill ...... AWL, BORE, PIERCE, AUGER, BABOON, TRAIN, CLOTH, GIMLET, PRACTICE, DISCIPLINE
dentist's .... BURR
hall .... ARMORY
team .... SQUAD
drilling equipment ...... RIG
machinery support .. DERRICK
drink ..... SWALLOW, ABSORB, RICKEY, IMBIBE, QUAFF, TIFF, POTATION, LAP, TIPPLE, BOUSE, TEA, BEVERAGE, TODDY, ADE, ALE, BIB, AMRITA, DRAFT

a certain way .... LAP
addicted to alcoholic .... BIBULOUS
admiral's .... GROG
agave juice ...... PULQUE
alcoholic ...... LIBATION, RUM, GROG, GIN, SAKE, PEG, WHISKY, MEAD, BRANDY, BOOZE, TOT, LIQUOR, SWIZZLE
ancient .... MEAD, MORAT
another's health ... TOAST
appetizer ..... COCKTAIL, BRACER
aromatic .. COFFEE, JULEP
barley .... PTISAN
beer and lemonade ..... SHANDY
beerlike, sour .... KVAS(S)
before meal ..... APERITIF
brandy .... COGNAC, SANGAREE
brandy and soda .... PEG
Brazilian .... ASSAI
Christmas .... NOG
claret, soda and sugar ... BADMINTON
cocktail .... MARTINI, HIGHBALL
cold ..... JULEP, COBBLER
crushed fruit ..... SMASH
deep .... SWILL
drug a .... HOCUS
East Indies .. NIPA, SOMA, TODDY
effervescent .... FIZ(Z)
excessively .. TOPE, BOUSE
fermented .... MEAD, ALE, BEER, RUM, SAKE, PERRY
for invalids ..... CAUDLE
for fermented molasses .. RUM
for fermented rice .. SAKE
fruit juice .. BRANDY, ADE
gin .... RICKEY
granting immortality .... AMRITA
greedily .... SWILL, GULP, GUZZLE
habitually .. TIPPLE, TOPE
heartily/heavily .... CAROUSE
honey ..... MORAT, MEAD
hot .... TODDY
iced ..... COBBLER, SLING
in great gulps ..... SWIG

in large quantities ...... QUAFF, SWILL
insipid ...... WISH-WASH
Japanese alcoholic .. SAKE
Mexican .... TEQUILA
mint, etc. .. JULEP, SMASH
mixed ... COCKTAIL, NOG, HIGHBALL
named after admiral .... GROG
of beverage with shaved ice .... FRAPPE
of forgetfulness .... NEPENTHE
of poison/medicine ..... POTION
of rum .... GROG, BUMBO
of sarsaparilla sirup ..... MEAD
of spiced, sugared gruel .. CAUDLE
of the gods ..... NECTAR
palm .... TUBA, NIPA
rice .... SAKE
Russian .... VODKA
short .... DRAM
single .... SLUG, SHOT
slang .. OCEAN, SEA, LUSH
slowly .... SIP, NURSE
sly .... NIP
small .. DRAM, SIP, SNORT, SNIFTER, TIFF, (S)NIP
soft .... ADE, POP
spiced ..... BISHOP, FLIP, PUNCH
spiced ale ...... WASSAIL
stimulant .... BRACER
stirring stick ... MUDDLER
sweet sap .... TODDY
sweetened .. POSSET, FLIP, BISHOP, ORGEAT, NEGUS, PUNCH
teenage ... SODA, MALTED
to .... TOAST, SALUTE
to excess ... TOPE, SWILL, CAROUSE
together .... HOBNOB
weak .... WISH-WASH
whisky-soda ... HIGHBALL
wine and honey .... OENOMEL
wine, spices and water .. SANGAREE
drinkable .... POTABLE
drinker .. TOPER, SOT, IMBIBER, TIPPLER, TOSSPOT, BIBBER

insatiable alcoholic ..... DIPSOMANIAC
drinking .... TIFFIN, POTATION
bout .... WASSAIL, SPREE, COMPOTATION, BENDER, BAT
bowl ... MAZER, MAZARD, JORUM
convivial .... BOWL, WASSAIL
cup ..... RUMMER, TOBY, BEAKER, TASS, NOGGIN, MUG, TANKARD, STEIN
excessive ..... POTATION, WASSAIL, CRAPULOUS, CRAPULENT
fountain ...... BUBBLER, SCUTTLEBUTT
glass .. TUMBLER, GOBLET, RUMMER
mug, leather .... JACK
party .. CAROUSAL, ORGY, WASSAIL
salutation ..... WASSAIL, TOAST
song .... WASSAIL
spree ..... BOUSE, BOOZE, CAROUSAL, WASSAIL, BENDER
toast .. MABUHAY, PROSIT, SALUD, SKOAL
drip .... TRICKLE, LEAK, DROP, SEEP
slang .... CREEP
dripping .... ASOP, TRICKLING
drive ... AVENUE, URGE, GOAD, FORCE, IMPEL, RIDE, PROPEL, PRESSURE, FEEZE, PROD, CAMPAIGN, PUSH, ENERGY, RUSH, CHARGE
away .... SHOO
back .... REPEL, REPULSE, REBUFF
colloquial .... HUSTLE
from cover ...... FLUSH
head first ..... BUTT, RAM
in offering .. FOOD, DRINK, MOVIE
in waiter ...... CARHOP
nail obliquely .... TOE
out .... ROUT, ROUST
out by incantation ...... EXORCISE
reformer's ..... CRUSADE
tree-lined .... AVENUE

drivel .... DROOL, SLOBBER,
TWADDLE, SALIVA,
NONSENSE, MAUNDER, SLUSH
driven obliquely .... TOED
driver .. JEHU, WHIP, MOTORIST,
CHAUFFEUR, MOTORMAN
animal .... MAHOUT,
MULETEER, SKINNER
backseat, usual .. WIFE(Y)
camel .... SARWAN
carriage ..... COACHMAN,
HACK
coach .... JARVEY
elephant .... MAHOUT
gear of ... CRASH HELMET
kind of .... PILE, MALLET,
HAMMER, TAMP
mule .... MULETEER
reckless .... JEHU
seat of .... BOX
slave ...... TASKMASTER,
MARTINET
driving, a .... DRIFT
ambition ...... GET-UP
desire .... OBSESSION
force, human .... LIBIDO
line .... REIN
drizzle .... MIZZLE, RAIN
drogher .... SAILBOAT
droghiere .... GROCER
droit .... (LEGAL) RIGHT
droll .. BUFFOON, COMIC, JESTER,
AMUSING, WAG, ODD,
HUMOROUS
drome, as suffix .... RUNNING,
RACECOURSE
dromedary ... DELUL, MEHARI,
CAMEL
dromon(d) .... SHIP
drone .... HUM, IDLER,
(HONEY)BEE, LOAF(ER),
AIRPLANE, BAGPIPE
drool .... DRIVEL, SLAVER,
SLOBBER, TWADDLE,
NONSENSE
droop ..... LOP, WEAKEN, SAG,
NUTATE, WILT, FLAG,
PEAK, LANGUISH, LOLL
drooping .... NUTANT, LOPPY,
LANGUID, SLOUCH
on one side .... ALOP
drop ...... BLOB, FALL, OMIT,
GUTTA, GLOBULE, DECREASE,
SLUMP, GOUT, DISMISS,
LOWER, PLOP, FLUNK,
FLUMP, PLUMP

below surface ...... SINK
fish line .... DAP
gently .... DAP, DIP, PLOP
heavily .... FLUMP
in trickles .... DRIP
one .... MINIM
sharp .... NOSE DIVE
straight down .. PLUMMET
sudden ..... SLUMP, DIVE,
CRASH
viscous substance .. BLOB
droplike ornaments .... GUTTA
dropout, for one ..... QUITTER
dropper .... PIPET(TE)
droppings .... DUNG, MANURE,
GUANO
dropsical .... EDEMIC
dropsy ... (U)EDEMA, BERIBERI,
ANASARCA
drosophila ...... (FRUIT)FLY
dross .... SCORIA, SCUM, SLAG,
WASTE, REFUSE, RUBBISH
drought .... DRYNESS
plant .... XEROPHYTE,
GUAR, CACTUS
droughty .... DRY, ARID
drove .... CROWD, FLOCK,
HORDE, HERD
composition of .. CATTLE,
HOGS, SHEEP
drover .... CATTLE DEALER
drown ..... INUNDATE, FLOOD,
DEADEN, MUFFLE
drowning, execution by ......
NOYADE
drowse ...... DOZE, NOD, NAP
drowsiness ...... OSCITANCY,
LETHARGY
drowsy .... SLEEPY,
HEAVY-LIDDED, LETHARGIC
from using drug ..... KEF
drub .. BEAT, CUDGEL, THRASH,
DEFEAT
drubbing .... DEFEAT
drudge ... PLOD, HOUSEKEEPER,
SLAVE, TOIL(ER), CHORE,
MOIL, GRUB, SCRUB
literary .... HACK
drudgery .. FAG, MOIL, CHORE,
TASKWORK, RUT, GRIND,
SWEAT
drug ..... COCAIN(E), HEROIN,
OPIUM, MARIJUANA,
NARCOTIC, MEDICINE,
STUPEFY, HOCUS

addict .... JUNKIE,
   HOPHEAD, SNOWBIRD
bitter .... QUASSIA
causing vomit .... EMETIC
cocain .... COKE
compressed form ......
   TABLOID
eye .. NEOMYCIN, MYOTIC,
   MYDRIATIC
for addicts ... METHADON
for blood pressure ......
   ADRENALIN
for drying .... DESSICANT
for epileptic attacks .....
   DILANTIN
for forgetfulness ....
   NEPENTHE
for perspiration ....
   BONESET
grinder .... MULLER
heroin: sl. .... SMACK
intoxicating .... PEYOTE
laxative .... ALOE
LSD: sl. .... ACID
marijuana: sl. .... POT
plant ...... ALOE, POPPY
slang .... DOPE
"speed" .... LSD,
   METHEDRINE,
   AMPHETAMINE
drugget .... RUG, MAT
druggist .... PHARMACIST,
   CHEMIST
  container of ... GALLIPOT
drugs, action of ..... SYNERGY
drugstore ...... APOTHECARY,
   PHARMACY
  soap .... SAPO
drum .. TUM, TAMBOUR, BONGO,
   TAMBOURIN(E), TYMPAN
  beat ..... DUB, RUBADUB,
   RATAPLAN
  call ...... TATTOO, DIAN
  capstan's .... RUNDLE
  continuously .... TATTOO
  hand ... TIMBREL, TABOR,
   TAMBOURINE
  head .... TYMPANUM
  jungle .... TOMTOM
  like a .... TYMPANIC
  long .... TAMBOURIN
  low continuous beating of
   RUFFLE
  major's rod ...... BATON
  Moorish .... ATABAL
  of a .... TYMPANIC

  Oriental .... TOMTOM
  played with hands ......
   BONGO
  played with stick ....
   TABORIN(E)
  player .... TYMPANIST
  primitive ...... TOM-TOM,
   TAM-TAM
  signal ... CHAMADE, TAPS,
   TATTOO
  small .. TABORET, TABOUR,
   TABORIN(E), TABRET
  sound ...... ROLL, BEAT
  string across ...... SNARE
  with fingers ...... THRUM
drumbeat ...... DUB, TATTOO,
   FLAM, RATAPLAN, RUFFLE,
   RUB-A-DUB-DUB
  continuous .... ROLL,
   RUFFLE
drumfire .... BARRAGE
drumfish .... WHITING
drumlin .... HILL, RIDGE
drummer .... SALESMAN
  famed .... (GENE) KRUPA
  kind of ...... SALESMAN
drumming, continuous ......
   TATTOO
drunk(ard) ..... INTOXICATED,
   INEBRIATE(D), TIPSY,
   BOUSY, BOOZY,
   BIBULOUS, GROGGY, TIGHT,
   BLIND, COCKEYED, FRIED,
   STEWED, HIGH, BLOAT,
   RUMMY, DIPSOMANIAC,
   SOT, TOSSPOT, TOPER,
   BLOTTO, WALLEYED,
   LOADED, NAPPY, SOAK,
   PLASTERED, TIPPLER, SOUSE,
   POTTED, BARFLY, MALTY,
   ROUNDER
drunken .... SOUSED, BACCHIC,
   INTOXICATED
  carouser ... BACCHANT(E)
  celebration .... JAG
  party ...... BACCHANAL,
   WASSAIL
  spree .... BINGE, SOAK
drunkenness .... INTOXICATION
drupe ..... APRICOT, CHERRY,
   PLUM
drupelet ..... TRYMA, ACINUS,
   NUTLET
drupelets, fruit of many ......
   (BLACK)BERRY, LOGANBERRY,
   RASPBERRY, GRAPE

dry .. SERE, BRUT, DEHYDRATE,
ARID, DULL, BORING,
WITHERED, MATTER-OF-FACT,
(DE)SICCATE, JEJUNE,
ANHYDROUS
as wine ...... SEC, BRUT
cleaning solvent ....
GASOLINE, NAPHTHA,
BENZINE
colloquial ....
PROHIBITIONIST
combining form ... XERO
fly .... LURE
French .... SEC
goods dealer .... DRAPER
lake basin .... PLAYA
moderately ..... SUBARID
opposed to .... WET
run .... REHEARSAL
spell .... DROUGHT
story, describing .. JEJUNE
throat .... HUSKY
to .... BLOT, SUN
tongue, sign of ... THIRST
up ..... WITHER, PARCH,
WIZEN
with cloth/mop .... WIPE
with heat .... SUN, BAKE,
TORREFY, TORRIFY
dryad .... NYMPH
dryer .... BLOWER, DESICCANT,
SUN, OAST, KILN
dryfly .... LURE
drying cloth .... TOWEL
machine .... TEDDER
drying, spread for ...... TED
dryness from lack of rain ....
DROU(G)HT
of skin/eyeball .. XEROSIS
DST, part of ..... DAYLIGHT,
SAVING, TIME
Du Barry's title ..... MADAME,
COMTESSE
duad ..... DUAL, TWO, PAIR
COUPLE
dual ...... DOUBLE, TWOFOLD
channel audio .... STEREO
dualism, element of .... MIND,
MATTER, GOOD, EVIL,
PHYSICAL, SPIRITUAL
dub ... POKE, THRUST, KNIGHT,
DUFFER, HIT, (NICK)NAME,
DRUMBEAT
dubiety .... UNCERTAINTY
dubious ...... SHADY, VAGUE,
SKEPTICAL, DOUBTFUL,

QUESTIONABLE, LEERY
dubitation .... DOUBT
Dublin is capital of .. IRELAND
ducal .... DUKEDOM
ducat: sl. .. (ADMISSION) TICKET
duce: Ital. ..... LEADER, CHIEF
Italian .... MUSSOLINI
Duchess of Windsor ....
(WALLIS) WARFIELD
title of respect .... GRACE
duck .... AVOID, BUFFLEHEAD,
CLOTH, BIRD, DOUSE,
TERN, SMEE, PINTAIL, EIDER,
MALLARD, DODGE, PEKIN,
COOT, SCO(O)TER
Asiatic .... MANDARIN
colloquial ...... DARLING
color on wing ....
SPECULUM
cry of .... QUACK
decoyer .... TOLLER
diving .. REDHEAD, SMEW,
MERGANSER, POCHARD
downy .... EIDER
fabric .... COTTON, LINEN
fish-eating .. MERGANSER,
GOOSANDER
foot membrane ..... WEB
genus ...... ANSER, ANAS
handsome ... WOODLUCK
Hawaiian .... NENE
hawk .. FALCON, HARRIER
hunter's screen .... BLIND
large .... MUSCOVY
like .... COOT
lure .... DECOY
male .... DRAKE
merganser .... SMEW
non-quacking .. MUSCOVY
pintail .... SMEE
river .... TEAL
sea .. EIDER, SCAUP, COOT,
SCO(O)TER
shooting boat ..... SKAG
slang ..... PERSON, QUEER
small .... SMEW
use of man-made .. DECOY
walk .... WADDLE
wild .... MALLARD,
CANVASBACK, SHELDRAKE,
SCAUP, DRAKE, WIDGEON,
GADWALL, GOLDEN-EYE
young .... DUCKLING
duckbill .... PLATYPUS,
MONOTREME
ducker ..... DABCHICK, GREBE

duckpins .... BOWLING
ducks, brood of .... TEAM
duct ...... CANAL, PIPE, TUBE,
    CHANNEL, CONDUIT, VAS
  body .... MEATUS
  narrowing of ... STENOSIS
ductile ..... TENSILE, ELASTIC,
    PLASTIC, PLIANT, PLIABLE,
    TRACTILE
ductless gland, of a .. THYROID,
    ADRENAL, PITUITARY,
    ENDOCRINE
  glandlike body .. THYMUS
ducts, of or having .. VASCULAR
dud .... FLOP, FAILURE
duddy: Scot. .... RAGGED
dude .. COXCOMB, FOP, DANDY
  one kind of ..... TOURIST
  ranch's use ...... RESORT
dudeen .... (TOBACCO)PIPE
Dudevant, Baronne ....
    (GEORGE) SAND
dudgeon ... RESENTMENT, HILT,
    · PIQUE, ANGER
duds .... CLOTHES, TRAPPINGS
due ... DEBT, RIGHT, PAYABLE,
    OWING, FITTING, PROPER
  one's .... DES(S)ERTS
duel .... CONTEST, COMBAT
  challenge .... CARTEL
  mock .... TILT, JOUST
  principal of famous .....
    BURR, HAMILTON
  victim of ..... HAMILTON
dueling code/art ..... DUELLO
  position ...... EN GARDE
duenna .... CHAPERON,
    GOVERNESS
Duero .... DOURO
dues .... FEE, TAX
duet .... DUO
duff ... PUDDING, (COAL)DUST,
    SLACK
duffel .... BAG
duffer .... PEDDLER, DUB,
    FUMBLER
dug .... NIPPLE, TEAT
dugong .... COWFISH, SEACOW,
    HALICORE, MANATEE
dugout .. BOAT, CANOE, BANCA,
    PIROGUE, (BOMB)SHELTER,
    FOXHOLE, PIRAGUA
  French .... ABRI
  India .... DONGA
duke, of a .... DUCAL
  son eldest, of .. MARQUIS

title of respect .... GRACE
wife of .... DUCHESS
dukedom .... DUCHY
dukes: sl. .... FISTS, HANDS
dulcet .... SWEET, MELODIOUS,
    ARIOSO, ORGAN STOP
dulcimer ...... CITOLE, SITAR,
    PSALTERY, HARP
Dulcinea .... SWEETHEART
dull .. STODGY, STUPID, TEDIOUS,
    BORING, SLACK, INSIPID,
  VAPID, BLUNT, LACKLUSTER,
  DRAB, JEJUNE, PROSY, FLAT,
  FISHY, MAT(TE), CRASS,
  GROSS, OBTUSE, LOGY,
  HUMDRUM, HEBETATE
  and fat .... JEJUNE
  color ...... MATTE, DUN,
    TERNE, DRAB
  edge/point .... BLUNT
  finish .... MAT(TE)
  grayish brown ..... DUN
  make .... OBTUND, BLUNT
  mentally .... STUPID
  period ..... SLACK, LULL,
    SLUMP
  person, describing one ...
    BORE, DULLARD, DUNCE
  sound .... THUD
dullard .... DUNCE, OAF, LOUT,
    BOOR, SIMPLETON, DOLT,
    NUMSKULL
dulse .... SEAWEED
duly .... PROPERLY, FITTINGLY,
    AS DUE
Dumas character .... ARAMIS,
  PORTHOS, ATHOS, BONIFACE,
    D'ARTAGNAN
  novel .... CAMILLE
dumb .... MUTE, SILENT,
    RETICENT
  clucks .... OXEN
  clucks, per J. Luzzatto ..
    OXES
  colloquial .... STUPID
  show figure ..... PUPPET,
  MARIONETTE, PANTOMIME
  waiter .... ELEVATOR
dumbbell ..... MORON, IDIOT
dum(b)found .... AMAZE,
    ASTONISH
dumdum .... BULLET
dummy .... STRAWMAN, DUPE,
  MUTE, MANNEQUIN, TOOL
  cannon .... QUAKER
  colloquial .... FRONT

field .... SCARECROW
in railroading ....
          LOCOMOTIVE
kind of ..... FIGUREHEAD
ventriloquist's .... SNERD
dump ..... LUMP, UNLOAD,
   EMPTY OUT, CHUCK, PILE,
              HEAP
   archaic ..... TUNE, SONG
dumpling .... PIE
   boiled .... DOUGHBOY
dumps, the .... BLUES, GLOOM,
             DOLDRUMS
dumpy .. SQUAT, MELANCHOLY,
              PUDGY
dun ..... ASK, ARTIFICIAL FLY,
     MAY FLY, BROWN
Duna, in German ..... DVINA
   in Hungarian .. DANUBE
   in Russian .... DON
Duncan, dancer ..... ISADORA
dunce .. COOT, OAF, NUMSKULL,
   DOLT, NANNY, SIMPLETON,
             MORON
dunderhead .... DUNCE, DOLT,
    IDIOT, NUMSKULL
dune ...... HILL, RIDGE, DENE
dung .. DROPPING(S), MANURE,
   FILTH, EXCREMENT, ORDURE
   beetle .. CHAFER, SCARAB,
             DOR
   piece .... CHIP
dungeon .... DUNJON, PRISON,
    TOWER, OUBLIETTE
dungy .... FILTHY
dunk .... DIP, SOUSE
dunker .... SOPPER
dunlin .... SANDPIPER
dunnage .... BAGGAGE
Dunne, actress .... IRENE
dunnite .... EXPLOSIVE
duo .... DUET, PAIR
   as combining form ......
          TWO, DOUBLE
duomo .... CATHEDRAL
dupe .... CHEAT, FOOL, TRICK,
   VICTIM, GULL, CON(E)Y,
   GREENHORN, HOCUS,
   MUGGINS, HUMBUG
   kind of .. TOOL, CATSPAW,
         DUMMY
   rare .... CULLY
duple ..... DOUBLE, TWOFOLD
duplex ... APARTMENT, HOUSE,
         DOUBLE
duplicate ..... COPY, REPLICA,

    DOUBLE, FACSIMILE
   copy .... ESTREAT
duplicating machine ... RONEO,
   (XEROX) COPIER, MIMEOGRAPH,
         MULTIGRAPH
duplication .... COPY, REPLICA
duplicity .. FRAUD, DECEPTION,
   DOUBLE-DEALING, FALSENESS
durable ..... STABLE, LASTING
   stage performer ....
         (MAE) WEST,
     (MARLENE) DIETRICH
duramen .... HEARTWOOD
durance .... IMPRISONMENT
duration .. PERIOD, TIME, TERM
durbar: India ..... RECEPTION,
     AUDIENCE, HALL
dure .... LAST, ENDURE
duress .... IMPRISONMENT,
   CONSTRAINT, COERCION,
        COMPULSION
during .... PENDING
durmast .... OAK
duro: Sp. ...... PESO, DOLLAR
Duroc-Jersey .... HOG
Durocher, baseball manager ..
       (THE)LIP, LEO
durra ...... SORGHUM, MILLET
durum .... WHEAT, FLOUR
Duse, actress ..... ELEONORA,
         CHECCHI
   burial place ...... ASOLO
dusk ...... GLOOM, TWILIGHT,
   EVENFALL, GLOAMING,
   CREPUSCLE, NIGHTFALL
dusky ..... DARK, SWART(HY),
         TAWNY
dust .... POLLEN, EARTH,
   POWDER, SPRINKLE, ASH,
         STOUR
   bite the .... LOSE
   British ... ASHES, RUBBISH
   filter .... INHALER
   lick the .... LOSE, GROVEL
   of flower .... POLLEN
   slang .... MONEY
   windblown .... STOUR
dustbin .... ASHCAN
duster .. COAT, BRUSH, WIPER,
    RAG, WIND, BROOM
dusting powder .... TALC
Dutch (see Netherlands)
   admiral .... RUYTER
   Antilles .... ARUBA
   apple, fried .... ROLPENS
   astronomer .... HUYGENS

beef .... HUTSPOT
botanist .... VRIES
cheese ..... EDAM, GOUDA
city .... EDE
coin .... DOIT, STIVER
colonist .... BOER
colonizer ...... PATROON
cupboard .... KAS
dialect in Africa ... TAAL,
    AFRIKAANS
donkey .... EZEL
East Indies island ......
    TIMOR, JAVA
engraver .... LEYDEN
farm .... BOWERY
fishing boat ..... HOOKER
Guiana .... SURINAM
gypsy .... BAZIGAR
Hottentot breed ....
    GRIQUA
housewife ..... VROU(W)
humanist ...... ERASMUS
measure .... AAM, ANKER
metal .... TOMBAC
mistress, in S. Afr. .. NOI
Mrs. .... VROUW
navigator .... TASMAN
New Guinea negrito ....
    TAPIRO
news agency ..... ANETA
painter ..... HALS, STEEN,
    REMBRANDT, LELY, GOGH,
    BORCH, CUYP, MEER,
    LEYDEN
philosopher .... SPINOZA
physicist ...... HUYGENS,
    LORENTZ
river .... MAAS
settler's farm ... BOWERY
ship .... GAL(L)IOT,
    GALLOT
slang .... GERMAN
South African statesman
    KRUGER
South African ..... BOER
statesman ...... GROTIUS
theologian ..... ERASMUS,
    JANSEN
title of address .... HEER,
    MYNHEER
town .... STAD
uncle .... OOM
vessel, flatbottomed .....
    FLYBOAT
village .... DOORN
West Indies .... ANTILLES

woman .... FROU(W),
    VROUW
Dutchman ...... HOLLANDER,
    MYNHEER
slang .... GERMAN
dutiful .... OBEDIENT
duty ...... TASK, EXCISE, TAX,
    RESPONSIBILITY, TOLL,
    IMPOST, OBLIGATION
burdensome .... ONUS
turn of .... TRICK
duumvir .... MAGISTRATE
Dvina river .. DAUGAVA, DUNA
Dvorak, composer .... ANTON
symphony .. NEW WORLD
dwarf ...... ATOMY, MANIKIN,
    BANTAM, MANAKIN, RUNT,
    MIDGET, STUNT, OUTSHINE,
    HOMUNCULUS
African/Asiatic .. PYGMY,
    PIGMY
animal .... RUNT
antelope .... ORIBI
cattle ..... NIATA, DEVON
chestnut .... CHINQUAPIN
kind of .... FREAK, GRIG,
    ELF, GNOME, PEE WEE
like .... GNOMISH
misshapen .... GNOME
Norse mythology ......
    ANDVARI
Philippine ..... NEGRITO,
    AETA
plant .... ALYSSUM
Scandinavian folklore ...
    TROLL
Scottish .... BLASTIE
shrub/tree ...... BONSAI
storybook .. TOM THUMB,
    LILLIPUTIAN, DOPEY, DOC,
    BASHFUL
underground ..... GNOME
dwarfish deer .... CHEVROTAIN
dog .... CHIHUAHUA
horse .... PONY
dwarfism .... NANSOMA
dwarfs, fairy tale ... BASHFUL,
    DOC, DOPEY, GRUMPY,
    HAPPY, SLEEPY,
    SNEEZY
king of .... ALBERICH
dwell ... (A)BIDE, LIVE, LODGE,
    RESIDE
on .... HARP
dweller .... TENANT, RESIDENT,
    INHABITANT

dwelling ... RESIDENCE, HOUSE, ABODE, HOME
house .... TENEMENT
instant .... PREFAB
bear's .... CAVE, DEN
bird's .... NEST
high .... AERIE, EYRIE
imposing ...... MANSION
lion's .... LAIR, DEN
miserable .... HOVEL
mobile .... TRAILER
on artificial island ...... CRANNOG
on wheels ...... TRAILER
place, kind of .... FLAT, APARTMENT
royal .... PALACE
rude .... HOVEL, HUT
slum .... TENEMENT
dwindle ... SHRINK, LESSEN, DIMINISH, PETER, DECREASE, ABATE
DX, in radio .... DISTANT, DISTANCE
dyad ....,.... PAIR
Dyak blowgun ..... SUMPITAN
knife .... PARANG
dye .. COLOR, STAIN, TINT, HUE, BRASIL, FUCUS, CASHOO, ANNATTO, WELD, TAINT
aniline .... MAGENTA, FUCHSIN, SAFRANINE
azo .... CROCEIN(E)
base ... ANILINE, FLAVONE
blue ...... WOAD, PASTEL
butter coloring . ANNATTO
coal tar .... EOSIN, MAUVE
from whelks ..... MUREX
gum .... KINO
hair .... HENNA
Hindu .... ALTA
indigo ...... ANIL, ISATIN
ingredient .. ALAZARIN(E), TANNIN
insect body's .... KERMES
lichen .... ARCHIL
mustard plant .... WOAD
orange .... MANDARIN
plant .... CHAY, ANIL, SUMAC(H), ALKANET, ANCHUSA, BUGLOSS, PUCCOON, AMIL, BLOODROOT
purple .. MUREX, ARCHIL, ORCHAL, ORCHIL, TURNSOLE

red ..... EOSIN(E), AURIN, COCHINEAL, CERISE, RHODAMINE, ALKANET, ANCHUSA, MADDER, KERMES, FUCHSIN, SOLFERINO
reddish-brown .... HEMAT(E)IN
source .... LICHEN, CUDBEAR
substance .... TANNIN
synthetic .... RHODAMINE
yellow .... FUSTIC
dyeing astringent .... GAMBIER
color fixer .... MORDANT
liquid container .... VAT
method .... BAT(T)IK
solution .... VAT
substance .... MORDANT
dyer ...... STAINER, COLORIST
dyestuff .. CATECHU, MAGENTA, ANIL, INDIGO, WOAD, CASHOO
dyeweed .... WOODWAXEN
dying .... MORIBUND
dyke .... DAM, DIKE
dyna as combining form ...... POWER
dynamic .... ENERGETIC, VIGOROUS
opposed to ...... STATIC, ORGANIC
dynamics .. KINETICS, STATICS, FORCES
dynamite .... EXPLOSIVE
kind of .... TNT
ingredient .... NITROGLYCERIN(E)
inventor of .... NOBEL
dynamo .... GENERATOR, MAGNETO
combining form .. POWER
part .... STATOR, COMMUTATOR, ARMATURE, WINDING, BRUSH
dynast .... RULER
dynasty, Chinese .. MING, SUNG
dys as prefix .... ILL, BAD
dysgenic, opposed to .... EUGENIC
dyspepsia .... INDIGESTION
medicine .... HYDRASTINE
dyspeptic .. GLOOMY, GROUCHY
dysphoria .... ANXIETY, DISCONTENT, DISCOMFORT
Dzhugashvili .... STALIN

E

E, Greek .... EPSILON
each ...... PER, EVERY(ONE),
APIECE, ALL, ANA
Eads (James) invention ......
DIVING BELL
eager .... FAIN, AGOG,
ARDENT, AVID, KEEN,
ANXIOUS, AFIRE, IMPATIENT,
EARNEST, DESIROUS
eagle .. BIRD, COIN, ACCIPITER
beaked .... AQUILINE
biblical .... GIER
brood .... AERIE
constellation .... AQUILA
double-crested ... HARPY
family .... FALCON
Latin .... AQUILA
like/of an ..... AQUILINE
like bird .... VULTURE,
CONDOR
nest of .... AERIE, EYRIE,
AERY
passenger of ..... ETANA
sea .... ERN(E)
young ..... EYRIE, EYRY,
AIGLETTE
eaglestone .... ETITE
eagre ... BORE, (TIDAL) WAVE
Eamon de Valera .... DEV
eanling .... LAMB, KID
ear .... HEARING, LUG
anvil .... INCUS
auricle .... PINNA,
PAVILION
bone ... STAPES, STIRRUP,
INCUS, ANVIL, HAMMER,
TEGMEN, AMBOS, OCCICLE
canal .... SCALA
cartilage .... HELIX
cavity .... COCHLEA,
UTRICLE, SACCULE
doctor ...... OTOLOGIST,
AURIST
drum .... TYMPANUM
external ...... AURICLE,
CONCHA, PINNA
give ...... LISTEN, HEED,
HEARKEN
gland below .... PAROTID
hammer .... MALLEUS
hollow .... CONCHA
in Latin .... AURIS
inflammation .... OTITIS
inner .... LABYRINTH

instrument .... OTOSCOPE
labyrinth ...... SACCULE
lend an .... LIST(EN),
HEED, HEARKEN
like part .... LUG
lobe ...... EARLAP, LUG,
ALA, LAPPET
middle ...... TYMPANUM
near the ...... PAROTIC,
PAROTID
of corn .... MEALIE
of grain ..... SPIKE, SPICA
opening ...... FENESTRA
outer rim .... HELIX
pain .... OTALGIA
part .... LOBE, AURICLE,
PINNA, COCHLEA,
TYMPANUM, ANVIL,
HAMMER, STIRRUP
pertaining to ..... AURIC,
OTIC, AURAL
play by the ... IMPROVISE
prefix .... OTO
projection .. LUG, TRAGUS
science of the .. OTOLOGY
secretion .... WAX,
CERUMEN
shaped .... AURIFORM
shaped mollusk .. ORMER,
ABALONE
shell .... ABALONE,
MOLLUSK, ORMER
specialist .... AURIST,
OTOLOGIST
stirrup-shaped bone .....
STAPES
wax .... CERUMEN
wheat .... SPICA
earache .... OTALGIA
eardrum .... TYMPANUM
of the .... TYMPANIC
prominence ...... UMBO
eared .... AURICULATE
seal .... OTARY
earful ..... SCOLDING, NEWS,
GOSSIP
earl .... NOBLEMAN
Biggers' sleuth ....
(CHARLIE) CHAN
deputy of an .. VISCOUNT
wife of .... COUNTESS
earliest .... PREMIER
early .... FORWARD
bird's victim ...... WORM

in the day/season .... RATH(E)

earmark ...... BRAND, SIGN, IDENTIFY, RESERVE

earn ...... MERIT, GAIN, WIN
   difficultly .... EKE

earnest .... ASSURANCE, SERIOUS, AVID, SINCERE, FERVENT, EAGER, TOKEN, PLEDGE

   money .... HANDSEL, ARLES, TOKEN, ADVANCE

earnings ... WAGES, SALARIES, PROFITS

earphone .... RECEIVER

earpiece .... FLAP

earring .... GIRANDOLE, HOOP, PENDANT

ears .... ANTENNA
   all .. .... ATTENTIVE
   having two ... BINAURAL

earsplitting .... LOUD, DEAFENING

earth ... LAND, DIRT, GLOBE, TERRA, DUST, TERRENE, GROUND, UNIVERSE, WORLD
   combining form .... GEO
   crust ...... LITHOSPHERE
   deposit ..... MARL, SILT
   division .... ZONE
   down to ..... REALISTIC, PRACTICAL
   eating of ..... GEOPHAGY
   goddess ...... DEMETER, SEMELE, ERDA, CERES
   greenish ... TERRE-VERTE
   hypothetical figure ..... GEOID
   inhabitant ... TELLURIAN
   line .... EQUATOR
   lump of .... CLOD
   of the .... TELLURIAN
   pertaining to the .... GEOGRAPHICAL, TERRENE
   pigment .... UMBEL
   poetic ...... VALE, MARL
   satellite ..... EXPLORER, ATLAS, PIONEER, MIDAS, ECHO, TIROS, MARINER, SPUTNIK, LUNIK, SKYLAB, VOSTOK
   tamping implement ..... BEETLE
   volcanic .... TRASS
   white ...... TERRE ALBA,

GYPSUM, KAOLIN, MAGNESIA

earth's treasure guardian ..... GNOME

earthborn ...... LOW, HUMAN, MORTAL, VULGAR

earthdrake .... DRAGON

earthen cup .... MUG
   jar .... OLLA

earthenware .... DELFT, POTTERY, PORCELAIN, CROCK(ERY), JUG, POT
   cooking ...... CASSEROLE
   jar .... CROCK
   maker .... POTTER
   making material .... PUG
   pertaining to ... CERAMIC
   pot .... PIPKIN
   unglazed .. TERRA COTTA
   water container .... GOGLET, GURGLET

earthly .... WORLDLY, TEMPORAL, SECULAR, MUNDANE, TERRESTRIAL, TERRENE, TELLURIAN, TELLURIC
   not .... CELESTIAL, ETHEREAL
   opposed to .... SPIRITUAL

earthnut .... TUBER, POD, PEANUT, TRUFFLE, FUNGUS

earthquake ... SEISM, TEMBLOR, TREMOR
   combining form .... S(E)ISMO
   focus of ..... EPICENTER
   over center of disturbance EPIFOCAL
   pertaining to ... SEISMAL, SEISMIC
   recorder .... RICHTER
   slight .... MICROSEISM
   starting point .... FOCUS

earthquakes, pertaining to .... SEISMIC
   phenomena of .. SEISMISM
   study of ..... SEISMOLOGY

earthwork .... TUMP, FORTIFICATION, DIKE, MOUND, AGGER, VALLATION

earthworm .... ESS
   like an ... LUMBRICOID

earthy ..... NATURAL, SIMPLE, COARSE, GROSS, TEMPORAL, TERRENE
   pigment .... SIENNA

earwax .... CERUMEN
earwig ... CENTIPEDE, BEETLE
ease ...... RELIEVE, COMFORT,
POISE, FACILITY, REST,
LEISURE, LOOSEN, PALLIATE
take one's .... RELAX
easel .... CANVAS HOLDER
easement ... RELIEF, COMFORT
in law .... SERVITUDE
easily .... DEXTEROUSLY,
BY FAR, READILY
affected .... SENSITIVE
angered .... IRACUND,
IRASCIBLE, IRRITABLE,
TESTY
bent ... FLEXIBLE, LIMBER,
PLIANT
broken .... FRAGILE
cheated .... GULLIBLE,
CREDULOUS
frightened .... SCARY
handled ... TAME, GENTLE
mixed .... MISCIBLE
offended .... TOUCHY,
SENSITIVE
remembered ... CATCHY
set on fire .... FIERY,
FLAMMABLE
tempted .... FRAIL
tricked .... GULLIBLE,
CREDULOUS
easiness .... FACILITY
east ... ORIENT, LEVANT, ASIA
East Indies .... INDONESIA
animal, small .... TARSIER
ape .... GIBBON
arboreal mammal ....
COLUGO
bark .... NIEPA
bird ... LORIKEET, ARGUS
boatman .... SERANG
calico .... SALLOO
cat-like animal .. LINSANG
cedar ..... TOON, DEODAR
cereal grass ..... RAGEE,
RAG(G)
chief .... RAJA(H)
civet .... MUSANG
coin .... CASH
cuckoo .... KOEL
deer .... MUNTJAC
dye .... CHAY
elephant driver .. MAHOUT
fiber (plant) .. JUTE, SUNN
fish .... DORAB

fruit ... DURIAN, DURION,
MANGOSTEEN
garment .... SARONG
grass ... GLAGA, VETIVER
harvest .... RABO
hemp .... SUNN
herb ... SESAME, ROSELLE,
PIA, CHOY, CHAY, SOLA,
GINGER
honeybee .... DINGAR
island ... BALI, SUMATRA
lemur .... COLUGO
litter .... DOOLEE,
DOOLI(E), DOOL(E)Y
mail .... DAK
medicinal root .. ZEDOARY
mint plant ...... COLEUS
monkey ...... ENTELLUS
musical instrument .....
RUANA, BINA
myrtle .... CAJEPUT,
CAJUPUT
oil plant .... BENNE,
SESAME
palm tree ...... TALIPOT
parrot .... COCKATOO
peacock-like bird .....
ARGUS
perfume .... PATCHOULI
persimmon ...... GA(U)B
plant ... DERRIS, COLEUS,
SESAME, BEN(NE), CHAY,
AMBARY, JUTE, TURMERIC,
SUNN, AMIL, PATCHOULI
prince .... RAJA(H)
rat .... KOK
relish .... PICALILI
root .... CHOY, CHAY
sailor .... LASCAR
sauce .... CURRY
seaweed product ....
AGAR-AGAR
shrub .... CUBEB
snake .... KUPPER
spice .... CINNAMON
squirrel .... TAGUAN
tree .... CAJUPUT,
CALAMANDER, TOON,
CHAULMOOGRA, TEAK,
JACK, DEODAR, POON, SAJ,
CINCHONA, BANYAN,
ACANA, SIRIS, MEE,
SAPANWOOD, PINEY,
KAMALA
vessel .... PATAMAR
warrior .... SINGH

weight .... CATTY
wood ...... TOON, TEAK,
   LIGNALOES, KOKRA, ENG
Easter .... PASCH(A)
   feast of .... PASCH
   fruitcake .... SIMNEL
   Island .... RAPANUI
   of .... PASCHAL
   souvenirs ..... BUNNIES,
      EGGS
   third Sunday after ......
      JUBILATE
eastern .... ORIENTAL,
      ASIATIC
   Christian .... UNIAT
   Orthodox church prayers
      EKTENE
   Orthodox church monk ..
      CALOYER
   palace .... SERAI,
      SERAGLIO
   ruler .... EMEER, EMIR
easy .... SOFT, FACILE,
      MODERATE, SMOOTH,
      SIMPLE, EFFORTLESS
   chair .... ROCKER
   course: sl. .... PIPE
   gait ...... LOPE, CANTER
   job .... SNAP, SINECURE,
      CINCH
   mark ...... DUPE, GULL,
      PUSHOVER
   opposed to ..... TIGHT,
      HARD
   slang .... CUSHY
   take it ..... RELAX, REST
   to convince ... GULLIBLE,
      CREDULOUS
   to understand ....
      PELLUCID, SIMPLE
eat ... SUP, GNAW, CONSUME,
      DINE, GRUB
   away ... GNAW, CORRODE,
      CANKER, ERODE, FRET
   greedily .... DEVOUR,
      GORGE, GAMP, WOLF,
      GOBBLE, GULP, GUTTLE,
      GORMANDIZE
   immoderately ..... GLUT,
      GORGE
   into .... CORRODE
   one's word ... RETRACT,
      RECANT
eatable ... ESCULENT, EDIBLE,
      FOOD, COMESTIBLE

eater, heavy ... TRENCHERMAN,
      GLUTTON
eating capacity, huge ....
      EDACITY
   implement .... CUTLERY,
      CHOPSTICK
   hall ... MESS, REFECTORY
   of .... DIETARY
   place ... AUTOMAT, DINER,
      CAFE, RESTAURANT
   regulated .... DIET,
      REGIMEN
eats: colloq. .... FOOD, MEALS
eau .... DEVIE, WATER
   de vie .... BRANDY
   designating one kind ....
      COLOGNE, JAVELLE
eaves, trough under ... GUTTER
eavesdrop .... LISTEN
Eban, Israeli diplomat .. ABBA
ebb .... SUBSIDE, RECEDE,
      DECLINE, FLOW BACK,
      REFLUX, WANE
   and flow .... TIDE
   tide .... NEAP
   tide, opposed to .. FLOOD
ebbing .... REFLUX,
      REFLUENT, REFLUENCE
Eber's father .... MILED
Eblis .... SATAN
ebon .... BLACK, DARK
ebonite .... VULCANITE
ebonize .... BLACKEN
ebony .... WOOD, BLACK
ebullience .... ELAN,
      EXUBERANCE
ebullient .... BUBBLING,
      BOILING, EXUBERANT
ecarte .... CARD GAME
ecce .... LO, SEE, BEHOLD
eccentric .... ODD, OUTRE,
      OFF CENTER, CAPRICIOUS
      PECULIAR, QUEER,
      CRANK(Y), W(H)ACKY
   person ..... NUT, GEEZER
   slang ... KOOKIE, KOOKY,
      BATTY
   wheel part .... CAM
eccentricity .... ODDITY,
      IDIOSYNCRASY, KINK
Ecclesiastes, book of ......
      KOHELETH
ecclesiastic .... PRIEST,
      CLERGYMAN, PRELATE, FRA
ecclesiastical attendant ......
      ACOLYTE

benefice .... GLEBE
cape .... ORALE,
         MOZ(Z)ETTA
council .... SYNOD
court ..... CLASSIS, ROTA
dean .... PREFECT
headdress .... MITER,
         BIRETTA
hood .... AMICE
office, trading of ....
         BARRATRY
proceedings ...... ACTA
residence .... MANSE,
         ABBEY, PRIORY
seat .... SEDILE
skullcap .... BIRETTA
vestment .... AMICE,
     ALB, STOLE, ORALE, COPE
eccrinology, subject of ....
     SECRETION, EXCRETION
ecdysis .... MO(U)LT
echidna .... ANTEATER,
         MONOTREME
echinate .... BRISTLY,
        SPINY, PRICKLY
  animal ..... PORCUPINE,
         HEDGEHOG
echinoderm .... STARFISH,
     SEA URCHIN, TREPANG
echinus .... SEA URCHIN
echo ...... REPEAT, RESOUND,
     OREAD, NYMPH,
     REVERBERATE, PARROT
echoing .... RESOUNDING,
        RESONANT
eclair .... PASTRY
eclat ... RENOWN, SPLENDOR,
     PRAISE, ACCLAIM, FAME,
     NOTORIETY, GLORY
eclectic .... CHOOSING
eclipse ... OBSCURE, SURPASS,
     STAIN, DARKEN,
     OVERSHADOW, SURPASS
  kind of .... LUNAR,
     TOTAL, PARTIAL, SOLAR,
     STELLAR
  part .... PENUMBRA
eclogue .... POEM, PASTORAL,
        IDYL(L)
ecole .... SCHOOL
economic policy, kind of .....
     AUTARKY
  system .... COMMUNISM,
     CAPITALISM
economical .... THRIFTY,
     FRUGAL, SPARING

economize .... SCRIMP, SAVE,
     RETRENCH, SKIMP
ecru .... TAN, YELLOW, BEIGE
ecstasy ... RAPTURE, BLISS, JOY
ectad, opposed to ..... ENTAD
ectoparasite .... REMORA,
     LEECH
ectype .... COPY
ecu .... COIN, SHIELD
Ecuador, capital of .... QUITO
  city/town ...... AMATO,
     CUENCA, IBARRA, LOJA,
     MANTO, NAPO
  Indian .... CARA,
     KECHUA, QUECHUA
  monetary unit .... SUCRE
  mountain ..... COTOPAXI
  province .... ORO
  seaport .... MANTA,
     GUAYAQUIL
  volcano ..... ANTISANA,
     COTOPAXI, CHIMBORAZO
ecumenical .... UNIVERSAL,
     GENERAL
  council site .... TRENT
eczema ...... HERPES, TETTER
  horse's ... MAL(L)ANDERS
edacious .... VORACIOUS,
  DEVOURING, CONSUMING,
     RAVENOUS
edacity .... GREED, VORACITY
eddo .... TARO, ROOT
eddy .... SWIRL, VORTEX,
    WHIRLPOOL, BORE,
     (WHIRL)WIND
edema ... DROPSY, ANASARCA
edemic .... SWOLLEN,
     EDEMATOUS
Eden .... HEAVEN, PARADISE,
     GARDEN
  resident ...... EVE, ADAM
  river .... PISON
edentate ... TOOTHLESS, SLOTH,
    ANTEATER, ECHIDNA,
     AARDVARK
edge .... BRIM, PICOT,
  VERGE, MARGE, RIM, MARGIN,
    BLADE, LEDGE, SKIRT,
    BRINK, BORDER, SIDLE
  beveled .... CANT
  cliff's .... BROW
  colloquial ... ADVANTAGE
  crater's .... LIP
  garment's .... HEM
  hat's .... BRIM
  keen ...... ZEST, SHARP

on ... IMPATIENT, EAGER, IRRITABLE
roof's .... EAVE
tool .... CHISEL
with loops .. PURL, PICOT
edged .... CUTTING, KEEN, SHARP
object ... SWORD, RAZOR, BLADE, SABER, KNIFE, BOLO, CUTLASS, AX(E)
rough .... EROSE
edgewise, move .... SIDLE
walker .... CRAB
edging ..... RUCHE, TATTING, FRINGE, TRIMMING, PICOT, LIMBUS
edgy ...... NERVOUS, TENSE, IRRITABLE
edible .... COMESTIBLE, ESCULENT, EATABLE, FOOD
bulb .... CAMAS(S), QUAMASH
fungus ... MOREL, CEPE, MUSHROOM
grain .... CEREAL
plant .... VEGETABLE
root ..... YAM, CASSAVA, TARO, GARLIC, CARROT, BEET, MANIOC
seed ..... BEAN, PEANUT, PEA, LENTIL, PINON
shoot .... UDO, BAMBOO
tuber ...... TARO, YAM, OCA, POTATO, SALEP
edict .... DECREE, FIAT, MANDATE, PROCLAMATION
Pope's .... BULL
sultan's .... IRADE
tsar's .... UKASE
edifice .... BUILDING
edify ... INSTRUCT, ENNOBLE
Edinburgh is capital of .... SCOTLAND
poetic .... EDINA
Edirne .... ADRIANOPLE
Edison, inventor .... THOMAS (ALVA)
edit.. ...... REVISE, CORRECT, REDACT
edition ...... ISSUE, NUMBER, COPY, PRINTING
collector's ...... FIRST
early morning newspaper .... BULLDOG
six versions ... HEXAPLA
special .... EXTRA

editor .... REDACTOR, JOURNALIST
editorial .... ARTICLE, COMMENT, OPINION
main .... LEADER
Edmonton is capital of .... ALBERTA
Edna Ferber novel ... SO BIG, SARATOGA
Edo .... TOKYO
Edom ..... ESAU, IDUM(A)EA
mountain .... HOR
Edson de Arantes Nacimento .. PELE, NEGRAO
educate ...... TRAIN, TEACH, INSTRUCT
educated .... LITERATE, LEARNED
education .... TRAINING, KNOWLEDGE, TEACHING
educational institution ...... COLLEGE, SCHOOL, ACADEMY, SEMINARY, UNIVERSITY, CONSERVATORY
group .... NEA
educator ... TUTOR, MENTOR, TEACHER, PROFESSOR, INSTRUCTOR
educe ...... ELICIT, DEDUCE, INFER, EXTRACT, EVOKE, DRAW, EVOLVE
Edward Kennedy Ellington ... DUKE
specialty .... JAZZ
eel .... MORAY, LAMPREY, CARAPO, GRIG, ANGUILLID
fish for .... SNIGGLE
fried ...... SPITCHCOCK
young ... ELVER, CONGER
eelpout .... BURBOT, LING
eelworm .... NEMA
eely .... SLIPPERY, ELUSIVE
eerie (eery) .... UNCANNY, WEIRD, MACABRE, ELDRITCH
efface ...... EXPUNGE, ERASE, ODIC, RUB OUT, BLOT OUT, OBLITERATE, WIPE OUT, BLUR
effect ..... ACHIEVE, RESULT, EFFICACY, TENOR, MEANING, IMPRESSION, ACCOMPLISH, OUTCOME, ISSUE
in .... VIRTUALLY, ACTUALLY

effective .... ACTIVE, EFFICIENT, OPERATIVE
effects .... PROPERTY, BELONGINGS
effectual ... VALID, EFFECTIVE
effectuate ...... ACCOMPLISH
effeminate .... UNMANLY, WEAK, SOFT, WOMANISH, FEMININE, LYDIAN
   boy ..... SISSY, MILKSOP
   person, in a way ... FOP, DANDY
effendi ... SIR, MASTER, TITLE
effervesce ..... BUBBLE, BOIL, FOAM, FIZZ, FROTH, SPARKLE
effervescence ..... VIVACITY, EXUBERANCE, FOAMING, LIVELINESS, EBULLIENCE
effervescent ...... BUBBLING, FIZZY
effete .... BARREN, ARID, STERILE, SPENT, EXHAUSTED, WORN OUT
efficacious .... EFFECTIVE
efficient .... COMPETENT, CAPABLE, ABLE, EFFECTIVE
effigy .... ICON, LIKENESS, STATUE, PORTRAIT, IMAGE
   fate of, sometimes ...... HANGED, BURNED
effloresce .... FLOWER, BLOSSOM (OUT)
effluence .... EMANATION
effluvia .... RAIN
effluvium ..... AURA, VAPOR, ODOR, REEK, FLATUS, MIASM(A)
efflux .... OUTFLOW
effluxion .... EMANATION, STREAM
effort ... NISUS, TRY, EXERTION, ENDEAVOR, PAINS, ATTEMPT, CONATUS
effortless .... EASY
effrontery ..... BRASS, CHEEK, GALL, TEMERITY, IMPUDENCE, PRESUMPTION, GUTS
effulge .... SHINE
effulgence ... GLORY, LUSTER, RADIANCE, SPLENDOR
effuse .... SPREAD
effusive .... EXUBERANT, OVERFLOWING, GUSHY, DEMONSTRATIVE, GUSHING

eft .... LIZARD, NEWT
eftsoon: archaic ...... AGAIN, FORTHWITH, OFTEN
e.g., part of .... EXEMPLI, GRATIA
egad .... EXPLETIVE, OATH
Egeria ...... NYMPH, ADVISER
egest ... DISCHARGE, EXCRETE
egesta .... FECES, SWEAT, PERSPIRATION
egg ..... OVUM, URGE, INCITE
   capsule .... OVISAC, OOTHECA
   case .... OVISAC
   collector ..... OOLOGIST
   combining form .... OO, OVI
   constituent .... YOLK, GLAIR, ALBUMEN
   dish ...... OMELET(TE)
   drink .... NOG(G)
   fertilized ..... OOSPERM, OOSPORE
   immature .... OOCYTE
   insect .... NIT
   laying animals .. OVIPARA
   laying mammal .... PLATYPUS, DUCKBILL, ECHIDNA, MONOTREME, ANTEATER
   lobster .... BERRY
   louse .... NIT
   mollusk's ..... OOTHECA
   on ... PROD, GOAD, URGE, SPUR
   part .... YOLK, SHELL
   protoplasm .... ARCHIBLAST
   relish .... CAVIAR(E)
   shaped ... OVATE, OVOID, OVAL, OVIFORM, OBOVOID
   shaped, longitudinal section ...... OBOVATE
   slang .... PERSON
   small .... OVULE
   tester .... CANDLER
   unfertilized .... OOSPHERE
   white ... GLAIR, ALBUMEN
   yolk .... VITELLUS, VITELLINE
   yolk pigment ... LUTEIN
   yolk substance .. LECITHIN
egger ...... MOTH, BOMBYCID
egghead ...... INTELLECTUAL
eggheads collectively .... CLERISY

eggs .. URGES, NIT, OVA, PRODS
   fish .... ROE, BERRIES
   nest of .... CLUTCH
eggshell color ... ECRU, IVORY
egis .... SHIELD, BREASTPLATE,
    AUSPICES, SPONSORSHIP,
        PROTECTION
eglantine .... SWEETBRIER
ego ... ATMAN, SELF, CONCEIT
egocentric ... SELF-CENTERED
egoism .... CONCEIT,
    SELFISHNESS, VANITY
   opposed to ... ALTRUISM
egoist, opposite of ... ALTRUIST
egotism ..... PRIDE, VANITY,
        BIGHEAD
egregious .... FLAGRANT,
    BAD, GROSS, PRECIOUS
egress .... OUTLET, EXIT,
    WAY OUT, EMERGENCY
egret .... HERON, PLUME
Egypt .... MIZRAIM
Egyptian .... NILOT, COPT
   alloy .... ASEM
   amulet .... MENAT
   antelope .... BUBALIS
   ape: myth. .... AANI
   archaeologist .... RAZEK,
       SALEH, SAAD
   Asiatic conquerors ......
       HYKSOS
   asp on headdress ....
       URAEUS
   astronomer ... IMHOTEP
   boat .... FELUCCA
   bird .... IBIS, TROCHILUS
   bull: myth. .... APIS
   capital .... CAIRO
   capital, ancient ....
      AMARNA, TANIS, SAIS,
       MEMPHIS
   captain ...... RAIS, REIS
   captor of Jerusalem .....
      SALADIN
   Christian .... COPT
   city ... ASWAN, DUMYAT,
     TANTA, DAMIETTA,
    FA(I)YUM, TANIS, ZOAN,
    FAYUM, SYENE, THEBES,
    HELIOPOLIS, EL GIZA
   cobra .... HAJE, URAEUS
   coin .... BEDIDLIK,
      PIASTRE
   commander ..... SIRDAR
   conquerors ... LYBIANS,
    NUBIANS, PTOLEMY,

    NAPOLEON, AMRU
   cosmetic .... KOHL
   cowheaded goddess ....
      HATHOR
   creator god .... ATUM
   crocodile god .... SOBEK
   cross ..... ANKH, CRUX,
      ANSATA
   dancing girl ... ALMA(H),
    ALME(H), GHAWAZI
   dead body, preserved ....
      MUMMY
   desert .... SKETIS
   division ...... PATHROS,
    MAZOR, FAIYUM
   dry measure ..... ARDEB
   dynasty .... NARMER,
   MENES, CHEOPS, PEPI, UNAS,
    AHMOSE, SETI, RAMSES,
    NECHO, DARIUS, PTOLEMY
   dynasty founder ....
      MENES
elf .... OUPHE
embalmed dead body ....
      MUMMY
fabled monster .. SPHINX
falcon-headed god ......
    HORUS, MENTU
fertile land ..... GOSHEN
gate .... PYLON
god ..... SETH, ANUBIS,
  HORUS, GEB, ATEN, MNEVIS,
  THOTH, ATMU, WAPUET,
  KHENSU, AMEN-RA, MIN,
     HAPI
god bearer of the ankh ...
     PTAH
god judge of the dead ...
     OSIRIS
god-king ...... RAMSES,
   KHAFRE, THUTMOSE,
   SENUSERT, PEPI,
    MENKAURE
god of creation .... PTAH
god of evil .... SET(H)
god of lower world ......
    SERAPIS
god of medicine ....
    IMHOTEP
god of pleasure ..... BES
goddess ...... BAST, NUT,
  (H)ATHOR, SESHAT, DOR,
  MAAT, SATI, ISIS, APET,
    MUT, SEKHET
governor ... BEY, MUDIR
hairstyle ...... SIDELOCK

hare-like animal .. HYRAX
hawk-headed god .... RA
heart .... HATI
heaven ..... AARU, AALU,
LALU
high priest ..... RANOFER
ibis-headed god .. THOTH
jackal-headed god ......
WAPUET
khedive's domain ....
DAIRA
king .... PTOLEMY,
MENES, CHEOPS, TUT, FUAD,
FAROUK
king of underworld .....
OSIRIS
laborer .... FELLAH
language .... COPTIC
lighthouse ...... PHAROS
lizard .... ADDA
lord of sky .... HORUS
lute .... NABLA
magician .... IMHOTEP
measure .... ARDES
money ..... MINA, PIASTRE,
TALENT, DRACHMA
money of account .. ASPER
month ..... APAP, TOTH,
MECHIR, MESORE
monument figure ....
CARTOUCH(E)
moon god .... THOTH
mortuary chapel ....
MASTABA(H)
mouse .... JERBOA
mullet .... BOURI
mummy cloth ... BYSSUS
native .... NILOT
oasis .... DAKHLA
obsolete .... GYPSY
opium .... THEBAINE
party .... WAFD
patron of artists .. PTAH
peasant .... FELLAH
peninsula ...... PHAROS,
SINAT
Pharaoh .... RAM(E)SES,
AKHENATON
phoenix .... BENU
police .... GHAFIR
port .... SAID
pound .... ROTL
premier .... SAAD
queen ..... CLEOPATRA,
NEFERTARI, NEFERTITI,
HATSHEPSUT

queen of gods ...... SATI
Rameses ..... PHARAOH
rattle .... SISTRUM
reed .... PAPYRUS
relic, kind of ... MUMMY
river .... NILE
rock .... PORPHYRY
royal tomb .... PYRAMID
ruler .... KHEDIVE,
MAMELUKE, PHARAOH
sacred beetle ... SCARAB
sacred bird ... IBIS, BENU
sacred bull .... APIS
scribe .... ANI
seaport .... PORT SAID
serpent: myth. .... APEPI
"shepherd kings" ....
HYKSOS
singing girl ...... ALMA,
GHAWAZI
site of ruins ..... LUXOR,
AMARNA, KARNAK, THEBES,
SAKKARA, ABYDOS
skink .... ADDA
slave-soldier .. MAMELUKE
snake .... ASP
solar deity .... SHU
solar disk .... ATEN
soul .... KA
spirit .... HAPI
statue, kind of ... SPHINX
structure .... PYLON,
PYRAMID
sultan .... SALADIN
sun .... ATEN
sun god ...... RA, AMON,
HORUS, AMEN-RA
sycamore fig tree .. DAROO
symbol of fertility ....
SERAPIS
symbol of life .... ANKH
tambourin .... RIKK
Tanis .... ZOAN
temple gate ...... PYLON
temple site ..... KARNAK
Thebes .... LUXOR
thorn ..... BABUL, KIKAR
title ..... CALIPH, PASHA
tomb .... MASTABA(H)
tree .... SYCAMORE
unit of currency .. GERSH,
PIASTRE
verbal shrug .. MA'ALESH
viceroy .... KHEDIVE
waterway .... SUEZ
weight ...... OCHA, KET,

KANTAR, MINA, OKA, OKE, KAT

whip .... KURBASH
wind .... K(H)AMSIN, KHAMSEEN
woman pharaoh .... HATSHEPSUT
woman singer .... (OM)KALTHUM
writing form .. DEMOTIC, HIERATIC, HIEROGLYPHIC
writing material .... PAPYRUS
Zeus .... AMMON
Egyptologist ... EMERY, LAUER, NIMS, EADY
eider ...... DOWN, (SEA)DUCK
eidolon .... IMAGE, ICON, PHANTOM
eight ball, behind the .... FIX, DILEMMA, PREDICAMENT, SPOT
  combining form .. OCT(O), OCT(A)
  group of .... OCTAD, OCTET(TE), OCTAVE, OCTONARY
  hundred forty yards of cotton .... HANK
  multiply by ... OCTUPLE
  of .... OCTONARY
  performers ... OCTET(TE)
  series of .... OCTAD
  sided figure ... OCTAGON
  stringed instrument ..... OCTACHORD
eighteen XVIII
eightfold .... OCTUPLE
eighth day, every .... OCTAN
  note .... QUAVER
  part of circle .... OCTANT
eighty .... FOURSCORE
Einstein's birthplace ..... ULM
Eire legislature .... DAIL
  president .... HYDE
  river .... SHANNON
Eisenhower, Gen. .... IKE, DWIGHT
  middle name ..... DAVID
  wife of ... MAMIE (DOUD)
ejaculate .... EXCLAIM, DISCHARGE, EJECT
eject ...... EMIT, EXPEL, EVICT, OUST, DISLODGE, VOID, DISMISS, ERUPT, SPEW,

SQUIRT, EJACULATE, CAST OUT
ejecta .... REFUSE
eke .... ADD, INCREASE,
  out .... SUPPLEMENT
el .... WING, EXTENSION, RAILWAY, THE
Cid ..... (RODRIGO) DIAZ, RUY
Salvador coin ... COLON
elaborate .. DETAILED, ORNATE, PAINSTAKING, FANCY, EXPATIATE
  decoration ...... FINERY
elaborately made ... EXQUISITE
Elam's capital .... SUSA, SHUSHAN
clan ... ARDOR, VIGOR, DASH, SPIRIT
eland .... ANTELOPE
elanet .... HAWK, KITE
elapine .... COBRA, MAMBA
elapse ... DIE, PASS, SLIP (BY), EXPIRE
elastic .... FLEXIBLE, SPRINGY, SUPPLE, RESILIENT, BUOYANT, ADAPTABLE
  band/strap ..... GARTER
  wood .... YEW
elasticity .... RESILIENCE
  muscular .... TONUS
elate .... EXALT, GLADDEN
elated ..... GLEEFUL, JOYFUL
elater .... (CLICK) BEETLE, DOR
Elba's important inhabitant ... NAPOLEON
Elbe .... LABE
  city on the ..... MEISSEN
  tributary ..... EGER, ISER, OHRE, MOLDAU
elbow ...... CROWD, ANCON, NUDGE, BEND, JOINT, JOSTLE, SHOVE
  jab with the ..... NUDGE
  of the .... ULNAR
elder ...... IVA, SIRE, SENIOR, ANCIENT, ANCESTOR, EARLIER, FORMER
  church .... PRESBYTER
elder statesman .. GENRO, ITO
elderly ...... OLD, VETERAN, AGED, SENILE
eldest ... FIRST-BORN, SENIOR, AINE

Eldorado's riches ...... GOLD, DIAMONDS
eldritch .... EERIE, EERY, WEIRD, GHASTLY
Eleanor, diminutive of NORA, ELLA, NELL
variant .... ELINOR
Eleanora ____, actress ... DUSE
elecampane roots ..... INULA
elect .... CHOOSE, ELITE, CHOSEN, SELECT, OPT
election .... POLL
casualty ..... LAME DUCK
platform ..... HUSTINGS, PLANK
proceedings ... HUSTINGS
report .... RETURNS
tour .... STUMP
electioneer .... STUMP
elective .... OPTIONAL, ELECTORAL
elector .... VOTER, ELISOR
Electra .... PLEIAD
brother of ..... ORESTES
parent of .... CLYTEMNESTRA, AGAMEMNON
electric .... MAGNETIC, EXCITING
bell part ..... ARMATURE
bulb .... GLOBE
catfish .... RAAD
chair .... HOT SEAT
circuit .... LOOP
circuit switch .... TOGGLE
company employe ...... READER
current regulator .... RHEOSTAT
engine for towing .. MULE
generator ...... DYNAMO
insulating material ...... EBONITE
light .... BULB, LAMP
light bulb ...... MAZDA, GLOBE
particle ... ... (AN)ION, CATION
potential .... TENSION
railway, underground ... SUBWAY, METRO
ray .... NUMBFISH, TORPEDO
unit ... AMP(ERE), DYNE, ELOD, OHM, VOLT, WATT, REL, FARAD, PERM

wires tube ..... RACEWAY
electrical appliance ... RANGE, (FLAT)IRON, TOASTER, FRYPAN, BLENDER
atom .... ELECTRON
circuit regulator .... BOOSTER
failure .... SHORT
force .... ELOD
particle .... CATION, (AN)ION
phenomenon .... ARC
system .... WIRING
terminal ... ELECTRODE, ANODE
unit ...... VOLT, JOULE, WATT
unit of measurement ....
FARAD, BARAD, FARADAY, REL
electrician .... WIRE MAN
electricity: sl. .... JUICE
unit of ... AMPERE, OHM, MHO
electrified particle .... ION
electrify ..... THRILL, EXCITE, SHOCK
electrode .. ANODE, CATHODE, GRID, THERMION
electrograph .... WIRE PHOTO
electromagnet ...... SOLENOID
electromotive force ....
PRESSURE, TENSION, VOLT(AGE)
electron .... MESON
tube .... TRIODE, STROBOTRON, KLYSTRON
electronic "brain" ....
CALCULATOR, COMPUTER
detector ... RADAR, SONAR
device .... MASER, LASER
electrum .... ALLOY
eleemosynary ... CHARITABLE, FREE, GRATUITOUS
elegance ...... GRACE, POLISH, REFINEMENT, LUXE
affected/excessive ....
FROUFROU
of manners .... PANACHE
elegant .... DIGNIFIED, DE LUXE, REFINED, FINE, COURTLY, POSH, PLUSH, SUPERB, GENTEEL, POLISHED, FLOSSY
elegiac ...... SAD, PLAINTIVE, MOURNFUL

elegist .... GRAY, SHELLEY
elegy .... DIRGE, NENIA,
REQUIEM
Shelley's .... ADONAIS
eleme .... FIG
element ... COMPONENT, PART,
INGREDIENT, FACTOR,
SILICON
an ...... EARTH, AIR, FIRE,
WATER
inert gas .... NEON
number 10 .... NEON
of air .... ARGON
similar to another ....
ISOTOPE
with valence six .. HEXAD
with valence two .. DYAD
worthless .... SCUM
elemental .... PRIMARY,
SIMPLE, HYPOSTATIC
elementary .... PRIMARY,
BASIC, PRIMAL, SIMPLE
elemi .... RESIN, ANIME
elenctic .... REFUTING
opposed to ... D(E)ICTIC
elephant .... PACHYDERM,
HATHI, JUMBO, TUSKER
boy .... SABU
driver .... MAHOUT
extinct ...... MASTODON,
MAMMOTH
female .... COW
frenzy of .... MUST
goad .... ANKUS
keeper .... MAHOUT
male .... BULL
maverick .... ROGUE
nose .... SNOUT
outlaw .... ROGUE
seat on ...... HOWDAH,
HOUDAH
sound .... TRUMPET,
BELLOW
tooth .... TUSK
tower on .... CASTLE
trap .... KEDDAH,
KHEDAH
tusk .... IVORY
white .... ALBINO
young .... CALF
elephants ear ...... BEGONIA,
TARO
elevate ... RAISE, LIFT, EXALT
elevated .... LOFTY, EDIFYING,
HIGH
railway ... EL, MONORAIL

roadway ..... OVERPASS
elevating muscle ..... LEVATOR
elevation .. EMINENCE, HEIGHT,
ALTITUDE, PLATEAU, MOUNT
elevator .... WAREHOUSE,
GRANARY, HOIST
aircraft .... AIRFOIL
British .... LIFT
car .... CAGE
kind of ... DUMB-WAITER
passage for ...... SHAFT
pawnbroker's ..... SPOUT
elf ...... GNOME, HOB, IMP,
GOBLIN, PERI, PUCK, FAY,
NIX, SPRITE, PIXY, BROWNIE,
FAIRY, PIXIE
elfin .... FEY
shelter ...... TOADSTOOL
Eli .... HIGH PRIEST
pupil of .... SAMUEL
Elia .... LAMB
elicit ...... EDUCE, EXTRACT,
DRAW, EVOKE, FETCH
elide .... SUPPRESS, SLUR,
LEAVE OUT, OMIT
eligibility .... QUALIFICATION,
ACCEPTANCE
eligible .... COMPETENT, FIT,
QUALIFIED, SUITABLE
eliminate .... RID, REMOVE,
OMIT, EXPEL, ERASE,
EXCRETE, EXCLUDE
Elijah ... ELIA, ELIAS, PROPHET
diminutive .... LIGE
successor of ..... ELISHA
Eliot, George .... EVANS
hero ..... MARNER, BEDE
heroine ..... ROMOLA
Elisheba's husband ... AARON
elision ... SYNCOPE, OMISSION
victim of .... VOWEL,
SYLLABLE
elite ... SELECT, PICK, CREAM
assemblage ..... GALAXY,
SALON
elixir ... PANACEA, CURE-ALL,
ARCANUM, NOSTRUM,
CATHOLICON
Elizabeth _____ ......TAYLOR
diminutive of ... LIZ(ZIE),
LISSET(T)E, BETH, BETTY
Elizabeth I adviser ..... CECIL
parent .... BOLEYN,
HENRY (VIII)
tutor .... ASCHAM

elk .... MOOSE, SAMBAR,
WAPITI, ALCE, LOSH
    male .... BULL
ell .... WING, EXTENSION
Elfen's lake .... KATRINE
Ellice Islands' old name ......
    LAGOON
ellipse .... CURVE, OVATE
ellipsoidal .... OVAL
elliptical ...... OVAL, OVATE,
OVOID, OBLONG
elm .... WAHOO
    fruit .... SAMARA
Elman, violinist ..... MISCHA
Elmo's (St.) fire .. CORPOSANT
Elohim .... GOD
elongate .... STRETCH,
LENGTHEN, EXTEND
elongated .... PROLATE,
OBLONG
    combining form ....
    MACR(O)
elope .... RUN AWAY, ESCAPE,
ABSCOND
elopers, usual .... LOVERS
eloquent .... ORATORICAL,
FLUENT, EXPRESSIVE,
ARTICULATE
else .... OTHER(WISE),
DIFFERENT, IF NOT, BESIDES
elt .... PORKER
elucidate .... CLEAR,
CLARIFY, EXPLAIN
elude .... SHUN, AVOID,
EVADE, ESCAPE, BAFFLE,
DODGE
elusive .... EVASIVE, EELY,
BAFFLING, SLIPPERY
eleuthera yield ... CASCARILLA
elsin .... AWL
elusion ... EVASION, AVOIDANCE
elusive ... SLIPPERY, BAFFLING
    thing ..... FUGITIVE, EEL
elutriate .... DECANT, PURIFY
elver .... CONGER, EEL
Elwin, anthropologist ....
VERRIER
Ely's famed building ....
CATHEDRAL
Elysian ..... HAPPY, BLISSFUL
Elysium .... PARADISE, EDEN
em: colloq. .... THEM
    half an .... EN
emaciated .... THIN, BONY,
GAUNT, SKINNY, WASTED
emaciation ... TABES, WASTE,

ATROPHY, MARASMUS
emanate .... ISSUE, RISE,
COMB FORTH, EMIT
emanation(s) .... NITON,
VAPOR, EFFLUX,
EXHALATION, AURA(E)
    flower ... AROMA, SCENT
    invisible ... AURA, VAPOR
    subtle .... AURA
emancipate ... FREE, MANUMIT,
RELEASE, LIBERATE
emancipation .. MANUMISSION
emasculate .... CASTRATE,
WEAKEN, GELD, STERILIZE
embalm .. PRESERVE, MUMMIFY
embalmed body ..... MUMMY
embalming fluid ... FORMALIN
embankment ... DIKE, LEVEE,
DAM, BUND, STAITH
    castle .... RAMPART
    protective mat ....
MATTRESS
embar .... ARREST, STOP,
CONFINE
embargo .... RESTRAINT,
RESTRICTION
embark .... ENGAGE
embarrass ...... DISCONCERT,
FLUSTER, ABASH,
DISCOMFIT, FAZE
    a speaker ...... GRAVEL,
HECKLE
embarrassed .... QUEASY
embarrassing situation ....
SCRAPE
embarrassment ..... PUDENCY
embassy ... LEGATION, MISSION
    official .... ATTACHE
embellish ...... PINK, ADORN,
GILD, EMBOSS, EMBROIDER,
POLISH, DECK, DECORATE,
TOUCH UP, ORNAMENT
embellishment .... FILLIP,
TRAPPING, ADORNMENT
ember ... ASH, CINDER, SPARK,
GLEED, IZLE, COAL
embezzle .. STEAL, DEFALCATE,
PECULATE
embezzlement .... THEFT
embezzler .... PECULATOR
embitter .... ACERBATE,
ENVENOM, FESTER, RANKLE
emblaze .... KINDLE
emblazon .... ADORN, EXTOL,
DECORATE
emblem (see symbol) .. BADGE,

SYMBOL, SIGN, INSIGNE
authority .... MACE,
ENSIGN, BADGE, FASCES,
GAVEL, CROWN
Christianity's .... CROSS
clan .... TOTEM
heraldic .... DEVICE
international .. RED CROSS
national .... FLAG
of royalty ...... PURPLE
shield .... IMPRESA
Turkish .... CRESCENT
U.S.A. .... EAGLE
emblematic .. HIEROGLYPH(IC)
embodiment ...... AVATAR,
EPITOME, INCARNATION,
IMAGE
embody ...,... INCORPORATE,
INCARNATE
embolden .... ENCOURAGE
embolism .... INTERCALATION
embonpoint ..... CORPULENCE,
STOUTNESS
embowel ...,..... EVISCERATE
embrace ...... CARESS, HUG,
INCLUDE, ENCLASP, ENFOLD,
ADOPT, ENCLOSE, COMPRISE,
INARM, CUDDLE
affectionate ... BEARHUG
slang .... CLINCH
embracer .... ARM
embrasure ...... CRENEL(LE)
embrocation .... LOTION,
LINIMENT
embroider ...,.. TAT, DECORATE,
PURL, ORNAMENT,
EMBELLISH, EXAGGERATE,
COUCH
embroidery ...,... LACEWORK,
NEEDLEWORK
design ...., BREDE
frame ....,.. TABO(U)RET,
TAMBOUR
loop .... PICOT
piece of .... BREDE
embroil ...,. MIX UP, MUDDLE,
INVOLVE, ENTANGLE
embrown .... TAN
embrue .... WET
embryo .... CELL, GERM
developed ..... FETUS
food for ..... ENDOSPERM
outer cells ..... EPIBLAST
membrane ..... AMNION
middle layer .. MESODERM,
MESOBLAST

emend ...... CORRECT, EDIT,
REVISE
emerald ...... BERYL, GREEN,
STONE, SMARAGD
Isle ...... IRELAND, ERIN
emerge .... ISSUE, RISE
emergence .... EGRESS
emergency man ....
PINCH-HITTER,
TROUBLE-SHOOTER
situation ...... CLUTCH
treatment ..... FIRST AID
emeritus .... RETIRED
emery .... CORUNDUM,
ABRASIVE
use for .... GRINDING,
POLISHING, BRASIVE
emesis .... VOMITING
emetic .... ALUM, ALOIN,
CATHARTIC, EVACUANT,
IPECAC, EXPECTORANT,
VOMIT
plant .... TURPETH
emetine .... EXPECTORANT
source .... IPECAC
emigrant ..... EMIGRE, ALIEN
emigre, kind of ..... REFUGEE,
EVACUER
Emil ____, author ... LUDWIG
Emile Herzog's pen name ....
MAUROIS
Zola book .... NANA
eminence .... DIGNITY,
REPUTE, FAME, NOTE
eminent .... RENOWNED,
EXALTED, DISTINGUISHED,
FAMOUS, NOTED
emir's domain .... EMIRATE
emissary .. AGENT, MESSENGER,
ENVOY, (DE)LEGATE
emission .... DISCHARGE,
ISSUANCE
of urine, involuntary ....
ENURESIS
emit .... ERUCT, EXHALE,
DISCHARGE, ISSUE, REEK
air .... BLOW
Emma ____, poet ... LAZARUS
emmet .... ANT, PISMIRE
Emmy .... STATUETTE,
AWARD
brother of .... OSCAR
emodin shade .... ORANGE
emolument ... GAIN, SALARY,
WAGE(S), FEE(S), STIPEND
emote .... ACT, PERFORM

emotion ...... PATHOS, ENVY, PASSION, FEELING, ANGER, FEAR, LOVE, HATE
   seat of ... SPLEEN, LIVER
   strong .. FLAME, PASSION
   turn of .... CAPRICE
emotional excitement .... HYSTERIA
   illness .... PSYCHOSE, NEUROSE
emotionless ...... UNFEELING, STOICAL, NUMB, DEAF, INSENSATE
emperor .... PADISHAH, IMPERATOR, BUTTERFLY, DESPOT, AUTOCRAT, CAESAR
   Constantine's standard .. LABARUM
   decree of ...... RESCRIPT
   German .... KAISER
   Japanese ...... MIKADO, TENNO
   Russian .... CZAR, TSAR
   sovereignty of ... EMPERY, EMPIRE
emphasis ... STRESS, WEIGHT, ACCENT
emphasize .... STRESS
emphatic .... FORCIBLE, STRIKING
   speech .... BIRR
emphysema .... HEAVES
empire ..... DOMINION, REALM
   state .... NEW YORK
empiric .... CHARLATAN, QUACK, MOUNTEBANK
employ .... HIRE, USE, AVAIL, OCCUPY, DEVOTE, ENGAGE, PLACE
employees .... PERSONNEL
employer .... HIRER, BOSS, USER
employment .... WORK, OCCUPATION, JOB, PROFESSION, EXERCISE
   contract, illegal .... YELLOW-DOG
emporium ..... STORE, MART, MARKET(PLACE)
empower .... ENABLE, AUTHORIZE, DEPUTE, PERMIT, VEST
empress .... ZITA
emprize .... DARING, PROWESS
emptiness .... VACUITY

empty .... IDLE, INANE, BLANK, DEPLETE, (DE)VOID, VACUOUS, DRAIN, VACANT, BARE, WORTHLESS, VAIN, TEEM, LACKING, WITHOUT, FLUSH
   colloquial ..... HUNGRY
   headed ... SILLY, STUPID
   of thought ..... VACANT
   talk .... FUDGE
   wind from sail .... SPILL
empyema .... PUS
empyreal .... CELESTIAL, SUBLIME, HEAVENLY
empyrean ...... ETHER, SKY, FIRMAMENT
EMs .... RANKS
emu-like bird .... OSTRICH, CASSOWARY
emulate ..... COMPETE, RIVAL, VIE, APE, EQUAL
emulsifier .... GELATIN, GUM ARABIC
emunctory ... LUNGS, KIDNEYS, SKIN
enable .... EMPOWER
enact .... ORDAIN, DECREE, PORTRAY, PASS, ACT OUT, LEGISLATE, PERFORM, PLAY
enactment .... DECREE, LEGISLATION, PASSAGE, EDICT, LAW, ORDINANCE
enamel ... COATING, LACQUER, PAINT, VARNISH, GLAZE, NAIL POLISH, SMALTO
enamelware .... LIMOGES, CLOISONNE, CERAMICS, PORCELAIN, DISHES, UTENSILS
enamor ... CAPTIVATE, CHARM
encamp ..... BIVOUAC, TENT, PITCH
enceinte .... PREGNANT
enchain .... FETTER, BIND
enchant ... BEWITCH, CHARM, ATTRACT, DELIGHT, ENTHRAL(L)
enchanting .... MAGIC
enchantment ... CHARM, SPELL
enchantress ... SIREN, WITCH, SORCERESS, MEDEA, HAG
   in Odyssey .... CIRCE
enchiridion .... HANDBOOK
enchorial ... NATIVE, POPULAR
encina .... (LIVE) OAK
encircle .... GIRD, RING,

CORDON, ENCOMPASS,
ENLACE, ENVIRON,
WREATHE, GIRT, SURROUND,
HEM
encircling, an ..... CINCTURE
enclasp ...... EMBRACE, HUG
enclave .... GOA
enclose .... HEM, FENCE (IN),
SURROUND, ENCYST,
ENVIRON
enclosed area .... CORRAL,
RING, STOCKADE, SEPT,
YARD, COMPOUND
part of aircraft .. NACELLE
space .... COMPOUND
enclosing line .... VERGE
membrane ...... TUNICA
enclosure ... STOCKADE, YARD,
PEN, CAGE, FENCE, WALL,
CORRAL, COTE, WRAPPER,
ENVELOPE, COCOON, COOP,
CINCTURE, TERRARIUM
animal .... VIVARIUM,
TERRARIUM
cattle ... CORRAL, KRAAL,
ATAJO
for grazing ...... WALK
for stray animals ....
POUND
in water .... CRAWL
of wagons for defense ...
CORRAL
race track .... PADDOCK
encomiast .... EULOGIST
encomium .... TRIBUTE,
PANEGYRIC, PRAISE,
ELOGE, EULOGY,
COMMENDATION
encompass .... ENCIRCLE,
SURROUND, INCLUDE, RING,
GIRD
encore .... AGAIN, OVER,
REPETITION, BIS, REPEAT
encounter -- MEET, COME UPON,
BATTLE, FIGHT
encourage ..... ABET, BOOST,
EMBOLDEN, HEARTEN,
FOSTER, CHEER
encroach .... INVADE,
TRESPASS, INTRUDE,
IMPINGE
encroachment ..... INTRUSION
encumber ..... LOAD, SADDLE,
BURDEN, HAMPER
encumbrance .... BURDEN
in law ..... CLAIM, LIEN

kind of ...... MORTGAGE
encyclopedist ..... COMPILER,
DIDEROT, D'ALEMBERT
end .... AIM, FINALE, CLOSE,
TAIL, FINIS(H),
CONCLUSION, TIP, PURPOSE,
LAST, OBJECT, RESULT,
UPSHOT, STOP, TERMINATE,
OMEGA, SAKE
combining form .. TEL(O)
in music ...,...... FINE
thick .... BUTT
toward an .... TELIC
up .... LAND
endanger .... IMPERIL,
JEOPARDIZE
endearment .. .... CARESS,
AFFECTION
endeavor ..... STRIVE, ESSAY,
VIE, NISUS, TRY, ATTEMPT,
EFFORT
endemic .... INDIGENOUS,
NATIVE
ending .... CONCLUSION,
FINIS(H), FINALE
have same ....
CONTERMINAL
in grammar ... DESINENCE
endive ... CHICORY, ESCAROLE
endless .... ETERN(AL),
INFINITE, LASTING,
PERPETUAL, INTERMINABLE
endmost ..... LAST, FARTHEST
endocrine .... GLAND
designating one ....
ADRENAL, THYROID,
PITUITARY
endogamy .... INBREEDING
endoparasite ..... HOOKWORM,
ENDAMEBA
endorse .... SANCTION,
APPROVE, BACK
endorsement .. VISA, BACKING
endow .... VEST, BESTOW,
BEQUEATH, ENDUE
endowment ...... GIFT, BOON,
GRANT, TALENT, BEQUEST,
(WITH)STAND, DONATION
for graduate student .....
FELLOWSHIP
natural .. DOWER, DOWRY
endue .... DIGEST, CLOTHE,
COVER, ENDOW, DOWER
endurable .... TOLERABLE
endurance ...... FORTITUDE,
STAMINA, PATIENCE

endure .... BEAR, LAST, LIVE,
    BROOK, HOLD OUT, STAND,
    UNDERGO, TOLERATE,
    CONTINUE
enduring .... LASTING,
    PERMANENT
endways .... UPRIGHT,
    LENGTHWISE
Endymion .... SHEPHERD
    lover of .... SELENE
enema .... CLYSTER
enemy .... FOE, RIVAL,
    ADVERSARY, OPPONENT,
    ANTAGONIST
    alien detained .. INTERNEE
energetic .... ACTIVE,
    FORCEFUL, LIVE
    activity .... EXERTION
    one .... DYNAMO,
    HUSTLER, GO-GETTER
energize ... FORTIFY, ACTIVATE
energy ...... PEP, VIGOR, ERG,
    VIM, STEAM, BIRR, FORCE,
    ZIP
    and initiative ....
    ENTERPRISE
    luminous .... LIGHT
    measure of .... ENTROPY
    potential .... ERGAL
    slang .... STINGO
    unit of ...... ERG, JOULE
enervate ...... DRAIN, WEAKEN,
    SAP, DEBILITATE
enfeeble .... WEAKEN
enfilade ..... BARRAGE, RAKE,
    GUNFIRE
enfin ...... AT LAST, FINALLY
enfold .... EMBRACE, ENLACE,
    WRAP
enforce ...... COMPEL, IMPOSE
enfranchise .. FREE, LIBERATE,
    EMANCIPATE
engage .... BIND, PLEDGE,
    BETROTH, HIRE, EMPLOY,
    RESERVE, AFFIANCE, BOOK,
    MESH, OCCUPY, UNDERTAKE
engaged .... BUSY, OCCUPIED,
    BETROTHED
engagement .... DATE,
    APPOINTMENT, TROTH
engaging .... SAPID, WINSOME
engender ...... BEGET, BREED,
    CAUSE, PRODUCE,
    GENERATE, PROMOTE
engine ...... MOTOR, MOGUL,
    TURBINE, LOCOMOTIVE,

    APPARATUS, MACHINE,
    GIN, DIESEL
    compressed air .. RAMJET
    cylinder .... PISTON
    exhaust noise ..... CHUG
    of war .... ONAGER,
    CATAPULT, RAM,
    MANGONEL,
    TREBUCHET
    on wheels ... LOCOMOTIVE
    platform .... WALK
    puff .... PANT
engineer's aid .... STOKER,
    OILER
    place .... CAB
engineless airplane .... GLIDER
England (see British) ....
    ANGLIA, ALBION, EGBERT
    personified ... JOHN BULL
English ... ANGLE, ANGLICAN,
    SILURES
    East India company ship
    INDIAMAN
Englishman .... SASSENACH,
    LIMEY
engram .... TRACE
engrave ... CHISEL, CUT, ETCH,
    CHASE, CARVE, INCISE,
    HATCH
engraver ... ETCHER, CHASER,
    LAPIDARY
    mark of ...... REMARQUE
    tool of .... BURIN
engraving .... PRINT, CUT
    art of .... GLYPTICS,
    GLYPTOGRAPHY
    by dots .... STIPPLE
    means of ...... GRAVURE
    method ...... MEZZOTINT
    on metal ....
    CHALCOGRAPHY
    pertaining to ... GLYPTIC
    process ...... CEROTYPE,
    ELECTROTYPE
    stone .... INTAGLIO
    tool ..... STYLE, CHISEL,
    BURIN
    wood .... XYLOGRAPH
engross ..... ABSORB, OCCUPY
engrossed .... RAPT, ABSORBED
engulf .... (OVER)WHELM,
    SWALLOW
enhance .... INCREASE,
    AUGMENT, INTENSIFY,
    HEIGHTEN
Enid .... BAGNOLD

husband of: legendary ...
GERAINT
enigma ...... REBUS, PUZZLE,
RIDDLE, MYSTERY,
CONUNDRUM
enigmatic .... OBSCURE,
BAFFLING, INSCRUTABLE,
MYSTIC(AL), CRYPTIC
person .... SPHINX
saying .... PARABLE
enisle ... (SET) APART, ISOLATE
enjoin ...... URGE, (FOR)BID,
DIRECT, ORDER, EXHORT
enjoy with others ..... SHARE
enjoyment .... PLEASURE,
RELISH, GRATIFICATION,
GUSTO, ZEST, FUN
enlarge .... DILATE, EXPAND,
INCREASE, DISTEND,
MAGNIFY, BLOW UP,
EXPATIATE, REAM
hole/bore .... REAM
on .... EXPATIATE,
ELABORATE
enlarged thyroid gland ......
GOITER
picture: colloq. ... BLOWUP
enlarger .... REAMER
enlighten ... INFORM, CLARIFY,
ILLUMINE
enlist ...... ENROLL, RECRUIT,
JOIN(UP), VOLUNTEER
enlistment, compulsory ......
DRAFT, LEVY,
CONSCRIPTION
period .... HITCH
enliven .... ANIMATE,
REFRESH, BRIGHTEN
enmesh .... KNOT, SNARL,
(EN)TANGLE, ENGAGE
enmity .... HATRED,
ANTAGONISM, ANIMOSITY,
ANIMUS, RANCOR, FEUD,
DISCORD, HOSTILITY,
MALICE
ennead .... NINE
ennoble ...... DIGNIFY, EXALT
ennui ... LANGUOR, BOREDOM,
WEARINESS
enormous ...... HUGE, VAST,
IMMENSE, GIGANTIC,
MAMMOTH
animal ...... MASTODON,
BEHEMOTH
number .... GOOGOL
Enos' cousin .... ENOCH

father .... SETH
grandparent .. EVE, ADAM
uncle .... ABEL, CAIN
enough ... QUITE, SUFFICIENT,
ADEQUATE
archaic .... ENOW
enrage .... ANGER, INFURIATE,
INCENSE
enrapture .. DELIGHT, RAVISH,
ENTRANCE, ENCHANT
enrich .... LARD
enroll ...... ENLIST, JOIN UP,
ENTER, IMPANEL, INSCRIBE,
RECORD, REGISTER
enroot ..... IMPLANT, EMBED
ens .... BEING, ENTITY,
EXISTENCE
ensconce ...... HIDE, CONCEAL,
SHELTER
ensemble .... SUIT
ensiform .... XIPHOID
ensign .... FLAG, BANNER,
ORIFLAMME, STANDARD,
GONFALON
ensilage ... FODDER, STORAGE
ensile .... STORE
enslave .... DOMINATE,
SUBJUGATE, ENTHRAL(L)
enslavement .... BONDAGE
ensnare ... SNIGGLE, TREPAN,
TRICK, (EN)TRAP, NET
ensue ...... FOLLOW, RESULT,
SUPERVENE
entablature, part of .. CORNICE,
ATLANTES, FRIEZE,
ARCHITRAVE
support .... ATLAS,
ATLANTES, COLUMN
entail .. INVOLVE, NECESSITATE
entangle .... WEB, ENLACE,
MAT, ENMESH, ENSNARE,
FOUL, RAVEL, MESH,
EMBROIL, COMPLICATE,
CONFUSE, KNOT
entanglement .... KNOT
Entebbe is capital of .. UGANDA
entellus .... MONKEY
entente .... AGREEMENT,
UNDERSTANDING
enter .... RECORD, START,
ENROLL, INSERT, PIERCE,
INSERT, JOIN, POST
clumsily .... BARGE
into conflict ... ENGAGE,
WAR, AGGRESS
enteric fever .... TYPHOID

enterprise ..... UNDERTAKING, PROJECT, VENTURE, GUMPTION

entertain ... DIVERT, REGALE, AMUSE, TREAT, FETE, CONSIDER

entertainer ... COMIC, AMUSER, DISEUSE, HOST(ESS), ARTISTE

entertaining .... AMUSING, HOSPITABLE

entertainment ... AMUSEMENT, HOSPITALITY, FETE
between acts ....
INTERLUDE, INTERMEZZO, RELIEF

enthrall .... ENSLAVE, ENCHANT, CAPTIVATE, FASCINATE

enthrone .... SEAT, EXALT

enthuse .... RAVE, REVEL

enthusiasm ... ARDOR, VERVE, PEP, SPIRIT, CRAZE, MANIA, ZEAL, ELAN, FERVOR, PASSION

enthusiast .... IST, ZEALOT, BUG, AFICIONADO, FAN, BUFF, DEVOTEE, FANATIC, ADDICT

enthusiastic ..... AVID, WARM, HOT, EAGER, ARDENT, RABID, KEEN
appreciation ..... GUSTO

entice .... BAIT, TEMPT, CAJOLE, LURE, ATTRACT, COAX, INVEIGH, TOLE, INVEIGLE

enticer ..... SEDUCER, DECOY, TEMPTRESS

entire ..... LIVELONG, TOTAL, ALL, WHOLE, COMPLETE
combining form .. HOLO
prefix .... HOLO
range .... GAMUT

entirely .... UTTERLY

entitle .... NAME, DUB, CALL, QUALIFY

entity ..... THING, UNIT, ENS, BEING, EXISTENCE

entoblast .... ENDODERM

entomb .... BURY, INTER, INURN

entomo, as prefix .. INSECT(S)

entourage .... ATTENDANTS, ROUT, RETINUE, TRAIN

entozoon .... PARASITE, TAPEWORM, HOOKWORM

entr'acte ...... INTERMISSION, INTERLUDE

entrails ... INTESTINES, GUTS, VISCERA, INNARDS, BOWELS, OFFAL, UMBLES

entrance ...... PORTAL, ADIT, GATE, DELIGHT, CHARM, DEBUT, INGRESS, ENCHANT, DOOR, ADMISSION, GATE
back .... POSTERN
court .... ATRIUM
hall ..... LOBBY, FOYER, ATRIUM
with evil intent ... ENTRY

entrant .. ENTRY, CONTESTANT, COMPETITOR

entrants collectively .... FIELD

entreat ... BESEECH, IMPLORE, PRAY, BEG, PLEAD

entreaty ...... PRAYER, PLEA, SUPPLICATION

entrechat .... LEAP, JUMP

entree .... ADMISSION, ACCESS, DISH

entrench .... TRESPASS, ENCROACH, INFRINGE, SECURE

entrepot .... DEPOT, WAREHOUSE, STOREHOUSE

entrepreneur ...... PROMOTER

entresol .... MEZZANINE

entrust .... CONFIDE, TURN OVER, CONSIGN

entry ...... POST, ENTRANCE, DOOR, INGRESS, ACCESS
British .... CLOSE
illegal ...... INTRUSION, TRESPASS
in ledger ... ITEM, DEBIT, CREDIT, RENT(AL), INTEREST
permit .... VISA, PASS, PRATIQUE

entwine .... (EN)LACE, WEAVE, TWIST

enumerate .... COUNT, TICK OFF, NUMBER

enumeration .... CENSUS, LIST

enumerator, kind of ....
NOSE COUNTER

enunciate ...... UTTER, STATE, ANNOUNCE, DECLARE, PROCLAIM

enunciation .... DICTION

enure ... HARDEN, ACCUSTOM, HABITUATE

enuresis .... URINATION
envelop ..... SHROUD, COVER,
    HIDE, CONCEAL, ENFOLD,
    WRAP, INVEST
envelope ...... CASE, SHROUD,
    WRAPPER, COVER(ING),
    SHEATHE
    fetus .... CAUL
    silky .... COCOON
    turtle's ...... CARAPACE,
    SHELL
envenom ... POISON, EMBITTER
environ .... PURLIEU,
    OUTSKIRT, ENCIRCLE,
    ENCLOSE, SURROUND,
    LOCALE
environment .... HABITAT,
    AMBIENCE, MILIEU, SETTING
environs .... PRECINCTS,
    VICINITY, SUBURBS,
    NEIGHBORHOOD,
    SURROUNDING, PERIPHERY,
    PURLIEU
envoy .... LEGATE,
    AMBASSADOR, MESSENGER,
    AGENT, EMISSARY
    originally ... DEDICATION,
    POSTSCRIPT
    papal .... NUNCIO
envy .... COVET, (BE)GRUDGE,
    JEALOUSY, SPITE
enzyme .... DIASTASE,
    MUTASE, RENNIN, CASEASE,
    ASE, MALTASE, CATALASE,
    OLEASE, EREPSIN, AMYLASE,
    OXIDASE, INVERTASE,
    INULASE, PECTASE,
    PROTEASE, RENNET,
    ZYMASE, ZYME
    action of .... ZYMOLYSIS
    blood .... THROMBIN
    digestive ...... TRYPSIN,
    PEPSIN(E), LIPASE
    in saliva .... PTYALIN
    in yeast .... LACTASE
    producing ... ZYMOLYSIS
    protein-splitting .. PAPAIN
eolith .... AX
eon ...... AGE, EPOCH, OLAM
eonic .... ERAL
Eos .... GODDESS, AURORA,
    DAWN
eosin .... NOPALIN, DYE
eparch ... GOVERNOR, BISHOP
eparchy .... DIOCESE
epaulet .... KNOT

epee .... SWORD
epergne ... CENTERPIECE, DISH
ephah, one tenth of ..... OMER
ephemera .... MAY FLY
ephemeral ...... TRANSITORY,
    TRANSIENT, EVANESCENT,
    MOMENTARY
ephemeris .... ALMANAC,
    DIARY, CALENDAR
ephemeron .... MAY FLY
epic ...... POEM, EPOS, SAGA,
    GRAND, HEROIC, MAJESTIC
    events, series of .... EPOS
    poem .... EPOPEE,
    (A)ENEID, ILIAD,
    ODYSSEY, BEOWULF, EPOS
    poetry .... EPOPEE,
    EPOPOEIA, EPOS
epicarp .... HUSK, RIND
epicedium .... DIRGE
epicene .... NEUTER
epicrisis ... CRITIQUE, REVIEW,
    CRITICISM
epicure .. GOURMET, SYBARITE,
    GOURMAND, GASTRONOME
    of a kind ..... GLUTTON
epicurean .... APICIAN,
    LUXURIOUS, SENSUOUS
epicurism ...... GASTRONOMY,
    HEDONISM
epidemic .... PLAGUE,
    WIDESPREAD
    among plants ....
    EPIPHYTOTIC
epidermal tissue .... KERATIN
epidermis .... CUTICLE, SKIN,
    BARK, INTEGUMENT,
    SCARFSKIN
epigram .... ADAGE, MOT,
    SAYING, POEM, MONOSTICH
epigraph .... INSCRIPTION,
    MOTTO, QUOTATION
epilepsy ...... CATALEPSY, FIT,
    SEIZURE
    attack of ... GRAND MAL,
    PETIT MAL
epileptic attack, feeling before
    AURA
    treatment ...... DILANTIN
Epimetheus .... TITAN
    brother ..... PROMETHEUS
    wife .... PANDORA
epinephrin(e) ..... ADRENALIN,
    HORMONE
epinette .... LARCH

epiphyte .... ORCHID, MOSS, LICHEN, FUNGUS
episcopacy .... BISHOPS
episcopal minister .. PRESBYTER
see .... CATHEDRA
episcopate .... SEE
episode .... INCIDENT, INSTALLMENT, EVENT
epispastic .... VISICANT
episperm .... TESTA
epistaxis .... NOSEBLEED
epistle .... LETTER, NOTE, BILLET(DOUX), MISSIVE
epitaph .... INSCRIPTION, HIC JACET, HERE LIES
epithem .... POULTICE
epithet .... AGNOMEN, (BY)NAME, OATH, MISNOMER
for Alexander ....
(THE) GREAT
Clemenceau .... TIGER
Eric .... (THE) RED
Ivan ... (THE) TERRIBLE
Jackson ... STONEWALL
Pitt .... IRONSIDE
epitome ...... BRIEF, DIGEST, ABSTRACT, SUMMARY, GIST
epoch .. EON, AGE, ERA, PERIOD
epode .... (LYRIC) POEM, AFTERSONG
epopee .... EPIC (POEM), EPOS
epoptic .... MYSTIC
epos .... EPIC
Epsom ____ .. DOWNS, SALT(S)
event .... DERBY
equable ... TRANQUIL, EVEN, STEADY, UNIFORM, SERENE
equal .... EVEN, TIE, PARALLEL, RIVAL, SAME, (COM)PEER, ALIKE, MATCH
angled figure ..... ISOGON
combining form .... ISO, PARI, EQUI
distribution of weight ...
EQUIPOISE
footing .... PAR
make ... . EQUATE
quantity .... IDENTIC
Rights party .. LOCOFOCO
without ..... NONPAREIL, PEERLESS
equalitarian of a kind
DEMOCRAT
equality .... PARITY
French .... EGALITE

of laws .... ISONOMY
of rights, laws .. ISONOMY
state .... WYOMING
equanimity .... POISE, COMPOSURE, SERENITY, SANG-FROID
colloquial .... COOL
equator crosser ... SHELLBACK
equatorial .... TORRID, TROPICAL, SUBSOLAR
Equatorial Guinea capital ....
BATA
native .... BUBI, FANG
president ...... MACIAS
equestrian .... HORSEMAN, RIDER
order of knights .. EQUITES
equilateral figure .... RHOMB, TRIANGLE
equilibrist .... BALANCER, ROPE WALKER
equilibrium ...... (EQUI)POISE
lacking .... ASTASIA
equine .... HORSE
cry .... NEIGH, WHINNY
disease ...... FARCY, GLANDERS, LAMPAS, LAMPERS, SPAVIN
equip .... RIG, GIRD, FIT, TRAIN, FURNISH, DIGHT
for military service ......
ACCOUTER, ACCOUTRE
equipage .... CARRIAGE, RETINUE, TRAIN, FOLLOWING, TURN-OUT
equipment .... GEAR, OUTFIT, RIG, TURN-OUT, TACKLE
equipoise .... BALANCE, EQUILIBRIUM
equisetum .... HORSETAIL
equitable .. HONEST, FAIR, JUST
equitant .... OVERLAPPING
equitation ..... RIDE, MANEGE, HORSEMANSHIP
equity .... JUSTICE, FAIR
Equity initials .... AEA
member .... ACTOR, ACTRESS, PLAYER
equivalent .... TANTAMOUNT
equivocal .... ENIGMATIC, UNCERTAIN, DOUBTFUL, UNDECIDED, AMBIGUOUS, MISLEADING, EVASIVE
equivocate .... FENCE, PALTER, LIE, HEDGE, EVADE
equivoke .... PUN, AMBIGUITY

era ... AGE, EON, TIME, EPOCH, PERIOD

eradicate ... EPILATE, ANNUL, (UP)ROOT, DESTROY, WIPE OUT, EXTERMINATE

erase ..... DELE(TE), EFFACE, EXPUNGE, OBLITERATE, CANCEL

slang ..... KILL, RUB OUT

erased, can't be ... INDELIBLE

eraser .... RUBBER

Erbil .... ARBELA

ere .... RATHER, BEFORE, IN TIME, SOONER THAN

Erebus, place after ... HADES

erect .... REAR, RAISE, UPRIGHT, VERTICAL, BUILD, PITCH, CONSTRUCT, STIFF, ASSEMBLE

erelong .... ANON, SOON

eremite ..... HERMIT, RECLUSE

erenow .... HERETOFORE

ergo ..... HENCE, THEREFORE

ergon .... WORK, ERG

ergot .... FUNGUS

of rye .... SPUR

eri .... SILKWORM

eria .... BOMBYX

erica .... HEATH(ER)

Erie port .... SANDUSKY

Erin .... EIRE, HIBERNIA, IRELAND, IERNE, OLD SOD

erinaceous animal .. HEDGEHOG

Erinyes .... MEGAERA, TISIPHONE, FURIES, ALECTO, EUMENIDES

eristic .... DISPUTANT, ARGUMENTATIVE, CONTROVERSIAL

Eritrea's capital ..... ASMARA

seaport .... MASSAUA, MASSAWA

ermine ... STOAT, WEASEL, FUR

fur ... MINIVER, MINEVER

ern .... (SEA)EAGLE

erode .... EAT INTO, DISINTEGRATE

erodent .... CAUSTIC

"Eroica" composer ... LISZT

Eros ..... CUPID, AMOR, GOD

erose .... GNAWED, IRREGULAR, UNEVEN

erosion .... CORROSION

erotic ... AMATIVE, AMOROUS, AMATORY, SEXY, PAPHIAN, LESBIAN

err ... TRIP, SLIP, SIN, BLUNDER

errand .... MISSION

boy ..... PAGE, BELLHOP, CADDIE, RUNNER, BUTTONS

errant .... WANDERING, ITINERANT, WRONG, TRUANT

erratic .... VAGRANT, IRREGULAR, QUEER, ECCENTRIC, WAYWARD, UNSTEADY, CAPRICIOUS

erring .... SINNING

erroneous .... WRONG, MISTAKEN, FALSE

error ...... ERRATUM, LAPSE, SIN, SLIP, GAFFE, GOOF, FALLACY, LAPSUS, BONER, MISCUE, MISTAKE, BLUNDER, FAULT, WRONGDOING, FAUX PAS

in etiquette ... FAUX PAS

in naming .... MISNOMER

error(s) in printing .. ERRATUM, ERRATA

ersatz .... SUBSTITUTE, ARTIFICIAL

Erse ..... CELT, GAEL, GAELIC

erst ... FORMERLY, LONG AGO, FIRST

erstwhile ...... FORMER, ONCE

erubescent .... REDDISH, BLUSHING

eruct .... BELCH

erudite .... LEARNED, SCHOLARLY, WISE

person .... PUNDIT

erudition ..... WISDOM, LORE, LEARNING, SCHOLARSHIP

erupt ...... EJECT, EXPLODE, BURST, EMIT

eruption ... RASH, OUTBURST, EXPLOSION, OUTBREAK

eryngo .... SEA HOLLY

erysipelas ... ROSE, WILDFIRE

Esau .... EDOM

brother .... JACOB

descendant of .. EDOMITE

father-in-law ..... ELON

grandson ...... AMALEK

parent ... ISAAC, REBEKAH

wife .... ADAH

escadrille .... SQUADRON

escalade .... SCALE

escalate .... EXPAND

escalator .... STAIRWAY

escalop .... MOLLUSK

escapade ...... CAPER, DIDO, PRANK, ADVENTURE
escape ... ELOPE, EVADE, FLEE, AVOID, LAM, LEAK, DISAPPEAR, KEEP AWAY, ELUDE, VENT, GET AWAY
   narrow .... CLOSE SHAVE
escapee .... RUNAWAY
escargot .... SNAIL
escarole .... ENDIVE
escarpment ...... SLOPE, CLIFF
eschalot .... SHALLOT, ONION, SCALLION
eschar(a) ... SCAB, BRYOZOAN
escharotic .... CAUSTIC, CORROSIVE
eschatology subject ... DEATH, RESURRECTION, IMMORTALITY, JUDGMENT
escheat .... CONFISCATE
eschew .... AVOID, SHUN
escort .... ACCOMPANY, RETINUE, (E)SQUIRE, BEAU, CONDUCT, CHAPERON(E)
   armed .... CONVOY
   kind of .... BODYGUARD, USHER, CONVOY, OUTRIDER
   lady's .... CAVALIER, CABALLERO
   woman .... DUENNA, CHAPERONE
escritoire ... . DESK, SECRETARY, TABLE
escrow .... BOND, DEED, AGREEMENT, CONTRACT
escudo .... COIN
   1/100 of .... CENTAVO
esculent .... EDIBLE, EATABLE, COMESTIBLE
escutcheon ...... ARMS, CREST, SHIELD
   band .... FESS(E)
   center .... FESSPOINT
   point on .... NOMBRIL
   vertical stripe ... PALLET
   voided .... ORLE
Esdras .... APOCRYPHA, EZRA, NEHEMIAH
esker (eskar) .... OS, OSAR, RIDGE
Eskimo .... ALASKAN, ALEUT, INNUIT, ESQUIMAU, ITA, YUIT, HUSKY
   boat ..... UMIAK, OOMIAC
   boot .... MUKLUK

canoe .... KAYAK, BIDARKA, OOMIAK, BAIDAR
dog ... HUSKY, MALEMUTE
garment .... PARKA, TEMIAK
house ..... IGLOO, IGLU, TOPEK
jacket .... ANORAK
knife .... ULU
language .... HUSKY
medicine man .. ANGEKOK
memorial post ...... XAT
settlement .... ETAH
esne .... SERF, SLAVE
esophagus .... GULLET, WEASAND, GULA
   pain ...... CARDIALGIA
   rod for clearing .... PROBANG
esoteric .... PRIVATE, CONFIDENTIAL, MYSTIC, ARCANE, OCCULT
   doctrine .... CABALA
   opposed to ... EXOTERIC
espalier .... TRELLIS, LATTICE, PALISADE
España .... SPAIN
esparto .... GRASS
especial .... PARTICULAR, EXCEPTIONAL, OUTSTANDING
Esperanto .... IDO
   deviser ...... ZAMENHOF
espionage .... SPYING
esplanade ..... WALK, GLACIS, ROADWAY
espousal .... BETROTHAL, MARRIAGE, WEDDING, ADVOCACY
espouse ..... MARRY, ADOPT, ADVOCATE, ABET, AFFY
esprit de corps ...... MORALE, SPIRIT, CAMARADERIE
espy .... SPOT, DESCRY, SIGHT, SEE
Esquimau .... ESKIMO
esquire ...... SHIELDBEARER, ATTENDANT, ESCORT, GENTLEMAN
ess .... CURVE
essay .... TOY, ATTEMPT, THEME, PAPER, TRACT, TREATISE, THESIS
esse .... ESSENCE, BEING, EXISTENCE
essence ..... ATTAR, GIST, ENS, PITH, NATURE, CORE,

KERNEL, ESSE, PERFUME, INBEING, FLAVOR, EXTRACT of anything ...... JUICE
Essene ...... MYSTIC, ASCETIC
essential .... INHERENT, INTRINSIC, HYPOSTATIC, BASIC, NECESSARY, VITAL, MUST, BASAL, REQUISITE, INDISPENSABLE
element .... PART
oil .... ESSENCE
oil liquid ...... CINEOLE
part ..... PITH, MEMBER
thing .... KEY
Essex city .... ILFORD
essonite .... GARNET
establish .... FOUND, FIX, SETTLE, INSTITUTE, PROVE, VERIFY, SET
securely ..... ENTRENCH, PLANT, EMBED, RIVET
established value .... PAR
establishment, domestic ...... MENAGE
estafet .... COURIER
estaminet .... CAFE
estancia .... RANCH(O)
estate .... ASSETS, PLANTATION, CAPITAL, HACIENDA, ALOD, DEMESNE, PROPERTY
country .... HACIENDA
first .... CLERGY
fourth .... PRESS, JOURNALISM
holder .... TERMOR
in expectancy .... REMAINDER
landed .. DOMAIN, MANOR
overseer .... BAILIFF
second .... NOBILITY
Spanish-America ...... ESTANCIA
third ...... BOURGEOISIE
under feudal lord .. FIEF, FEOD
esteem ...... ADMIRE, HONOR, PRIDE, VALUE, PRIZE, RESPECT, REGARD, APPRECIATE
ester .... OLEATE, SILICATE, STEARIN, ACETIN, IODIDE, MALATE, PICRATE
esthesia .... SENSATE
esthete .... CONNOISSEUR
esthetic .... ARTISTIC

esthetics .... ARTS
estimate .... MEASURE, APPRAISE, GAUGE, CALCULATE, EVALUATE
in advance ... FORECAST
estivate .... SUMMER
opposed to ... HIBERNATE
Estonia, capital of ... TALLINN
city of ... TARTU, YUREV
Estonian island .... OESEL
monetary unit .... KROON
estop .... PREVENT, BAR, OBSTRUCT
estovers .... NECESSARIES
allowed divorcee .... ALIMONY
estrange ... ALIENATE, WEAN, DIVERT, SEPARATE, DISAFFECT
estray .... WAIF
estrol ..... HORMONE, THEELOL
estrone ... THEELIN, HORMONE
estrus .... FRENZY, HEAT
estuary .... RIA, LOCH, FRITH, BAY, FIRTH, INLET, FIORD
tidal wave .. EAGRE, BORE
esurient ... GREEDY, HUNGRY, VORACIOUS
et .... AND
al .... OTHERS
etagere .... WHATNOT
etamine .... CLOTH, VOILE
Etanin .... DRACONIS
etape .... STOREHOUSE, ENCAMPMENT
Etats _____ UNIS
etch .... CUT, ENGRAVE, CHISEL
etching acid .... MORDANT
Eteocles, brother of .... POLYNICES
kingdom .... THEBES
parent of ...... JOCASTA, OEDIPUS
eternal .... AGELESS, (A)EONIAN, EVERLASTING, TIMELESS, FOREVER, PERPETUAL
City .... ROME
The .... GOD
eternity .... (A)EON, TIME, INFINITY, IMMORTALITY, OLAM
etesian .... PERIODIC, ANNUAL, SEASONAL
Ethan Frome's wife .... ZEENA
Ethanim .... TISHRI

Ethel ——, performer .... MERMAN, BARRYMORE
ether .... AIR, SKY, SPACE
   compound .... ESTER
   use of ..... ANESTHETIC, SOLVENT
ethereal ..... .AIRY, DELICATE, HEAVENLY, CELESTIAL, SUPERNAL
   fluid .... ICHOR
   salt .... ESTER
ethical ... VIRTUOUS, MORAL, RIGHT
ethics ...., MORALS
Ethiopia .... ABYSSINIA
   Biblical ..... CUSH, KUSH
   capital .... ADDIS ABABA
Ethiopian ántelope ... DIKDIK
   ape .... GELADA
   Black Jews ..... FALASHA
   capital, ancient .. MEROE
   city .... ADOWA, ADUA, HAR(R)AR
   coin .... TALARI
   cotton toga ..... SHAMMA
   district .. AMHARA, HARAR
   fly .... ZIMB
   Hamite ... GALLA, AFAR
   Hamitic tribe member ... FALASHA
   ibex .... SAOL, WALIE
   king ... NEGUS, MEMNON
   kingdom, former .... AMHARA
   lake ... T(S)ANA, DEMBEA
   language ...... AMHARIC, GEEZ
   native .... NEGRO
   prince .... RAS
   province ... SHOA, TIGRE
   queen .... CANDACE
   river ...... OMO, ATBARA, TANA
   seaport .... MASSAUA
   table-mountain ... AMBA
   title ...... RAS, NEGUS
   tribesman ..... FALASHA
   walled city ..... GONDAR
   wolf .... KABERU
ethnarch .... GOVERNOR
ethnic ...... HEATHEN, RACIAL
   group ...... FOLK, RACE
ethologist .... LORENZ
ethos ...... CHARACTERISTICS
   opposed to ..... PATHOS
ethyl .... GASOLINE

alcohol .... ETHANOL
   derivative .... ETHER
etiolate ..... BLANCH, BLEACH
etiquette .... DECORUM, PROPRIETY
   breach of ..... SOLECISM, FAUX PAS
   required by ... DE RIGUER
Etna .... VOLCANO, LAMP
Eton .... TOWN, SCHOOL
   article of wear .. COLLAR, JACKET, COAT
   rival of .... HARROW
   student .... OPPIDAN
Etruscan god .... LAR(ES), PENATES, TINIA, TURMS
   goddess ... UNI, MENFRA, TURAN
   king .... PORSENA
   Minerva .... MENFRA
Etta of comic strips .... KETT
etude .... STUDY
etui .... CASE
etwee .... CASE
etymological .... LITERAL
etymon .... RADIX, ROOT
Etzel .... ATTILA
eucalyptol .... CINEOLE
eucalyptus .... MALLEE, YATE, IRONBARK
Eucharist .... EULOGIA, HOUSEL, SACRAMENT
   box .... PIX, PYX
   bread ... HOST, OBLATION, WAFER
   cloth .... FANON
   to dying person .... VIATICUM
   vessel .... PATEN, AMA
   wafer .... HOST
   wine of the ... OBLATION
eucharistic plate ...... PATEN
   service .... LITURGY
   vestment ..... MANIPLE, FANON
Euclid ...... MATHEMATICIAN
   forte of .... GEOMETRY
   work on geometry ...... ELEMENTS
eudaemonia ...... HAPPINESS
euge .... BRAVO
eugenics, pioneer in ,. GALTON
   subject of .... RACES, BREEDS
eulogia .... EUCHARIST

eulogistic .... ELOGE,
LAUDATORY, MAGNIFIC
eulogize ...... EXTOL, LAUD,
PRAISE
eulogy .... ENCOMIUM,
PANEGYRIC, TRIBUTE,
PRAISE, ELOGE
Eumenides .... FURIES,
ERINYES
eunuch .... CHAMBERLAIN,
GELDING
euphemism for hell ..... HECK
euphonium, like .... TUBA
euphony ..... MELODY, METER
euphorbia .... SPURGE,
POINSETTIA
euphoria ...... COMPLACENCY,
SMUGNESS
Euphrosyne .... JOY
euphuism .... BOMBAST
Eurasian in India ... FERINGI,
FERINGHEE
range .... URAL
eureka .... AHA, SEE,
EXCLAMATION
state .... CALIFORNIA
euripus .... STRAIT, CHANNEL
Europa's father ..... OGENOR
lover .... ZEUS
European ..... LAPP, FRENCH,
BOHUNK, FRANK, DANE,
FINN, LETT, BALT
antelope ...... CHAMOIS
apple tree ...... SORB
aromatic herb ....
FLEAWORT
ash tree juice .... MANNA
beetle .... DORBUG,
COCKCHAFER
bellflower ..... RAMPION
bird ... HOOPOE, TURNIX,
REEDLING, ROLLER,
WHIMBREL
bison .... AUROCHS
blackbird .... MERLE,
OUSEL, OUZEL
blenny .... SHANNY
brantail ...... REDSTART
buttercup .. GOLDILOCKS
butterfly ... RED ADMIRAL
canal .... KIEL
carp .... BLEAK
catfish .... SILURID
cavalryman ... U(H)LAN,
HUSSAR
cereal grass ..... MILLET

chestnut .... MARRON
chicken .... HAMBURG
coal region .... SAAR
commercial weight ......
CENTNER
country, ancient ....
HELVETIA
crow .... CHOUGH,
NUTCRACKER
deer ..... FALLOW, STAG
diving duck ... POCHARD
dog .... GRIFFON
dormouse .... LEROT
dotterel .... PLOVER
duck ... WIDGEON, SMEW,
POCHARD
falcon .... HOBBY,
LANNER(ET), MERLIN
finch ...... SERIN, SISKIN
fish .... RUDD, BOCE,
BARBEL, PLAICE, GUDGEON
flatfish .... BRILL
fly .... FRIT
food fish ... SAUREL, SCAD
food seed .... LUPINE
gamebird ...... TURNIX
garlic .... MOLY
grosbeak ..... HAWFINCH
hawk .... PUTTOCK
haybird ...... BLACKCAP
health resort .... BADEN,
EMS
herb ..... LOVAGE, RUTA,
ELECAMPANE, TARRAGON
herring .... SPRAT
holly .... ACEBO
in India .... FERINGI
iris .... ORRIS
juniper .... CADE
kite .... GLED(E)
lake ..... ONEGA, GENEVA
mignonette ...... WELD,
WOLD
mint .... CLAR(R)Y,
CLARE, HYSSOP
news agency ...... HAVAS
nomad .... LAPP
oak .... HOLM, DURMAST
oriole .... LORIOT
pea .... LICORICE
plant .... ALFILARIA,
COMFREY, LAVENDER,
LICORICE
plover ...... DOTT(E)REL
polecat .... FITCH,
FOUMART

principality ... MONACO, ORANGE, WALACHIA
range .... URAL
ratlike animal .. HAMSTER
ray .... THORNBACK
redstart ...... BRANTAIL
river .... ISAR
robin .... RUDDOCK
rodent .... DORMOUSE
rose tree .... MEDLAR
shad .... ALOSE
shark .... TOPE
shore bird ... WHIMBREL
shrub ...... MEZEREON, OLEASTER
slang .... BOHUNK
smelt .... SPARLING
songbird ...... LINNET, OUSEL, REDWING, THROSTLE, THRUSH, WHITETHROAT, MAVIS
squirrel .... SUSLIK
sumac .... TEREBINTH
swallow ...... MARTLET, MARTIN
thrush ... OUSEL, MISSEL, MAVIS, FIELDFARE
tree .... DURMAST, HOLM
vulture ... LAMMERGEI(E)R
water bird ... GARGANEY
wheat .... SPELT
wild duck ... WI(D)GEON, SHELDRAKE
wild goose .... GRAYLAG, GREYLAG
woodpigeon ... CUSHAT, RINGDOVE
wormwood .. SANTONICA
Eustachian tube ..... SYRINX, SALPINX
euthenics subject ..... RACES, BREEDS
evacuant .... CATHARTIC, EMETIC
evacuate .... VOID, EMIT, (RE)MOVE, WITHDRAW, EMPTY
evacuee .... REFUGEE
evade .... AVOID, ESCAPE, ELUDE, DODGE, GEE
payment .... BILK
work .. SHIRK, MALINGER, GOLDBRICK
evaginate .... EVERT
evaluate ... APPRAISE, ASSAY, GAUGE, ESTIMATE, RATE, ASSESS
evanesce ...... FADE, VANISH, DISAPPEAR
evanescent ...... EPHEMERAL, TRANSIENT, FLEETING
evangel .... GOSPEL
evangelist ... MARK, MATTHEW, LUKE, JOHN, PREACHER, REVIVALIST, MISSIONARY
Mormon .... PATRIARCH
"Evangeline" locale .... GRAND PRE
Evans, Mary Ann ..... ELIOT
evaporate ...... DRY, VANISH
evaporating quickly .. VOLATILE
evasion .... ELUSION, EQUIVOCATION, SALVO, SUBTERFUGE
evasive ..... TRICKY, ELUSIVE, EQUIVOCAL, SHIFTY
eve .... EVENING
of festival .... VIGIL
even ... EQUABLE, PLANE, TIED, LEVEL, FLAT, SMOOTH, UNIFORM, CALM, SERENE, STILL, TOSSUP, STEADY, PLACID
if .... THO(UGH)
minded ...... EQUABLE, PLACID
slang .... HUNKY
evenfall ..... TWILIGHT, DUSK
evenhanded .... FAIR, IMPARTIAL, JUST
evening .... DUSK, GLOAMING
affair .... SOIREE
dress .... TUXEDO
glory .... SUNSET
love song ..... SERENADE
of .... VESPERTINE
poetic .... EVE
prayer .... VESPER(S), EVENSONG
service .... VESPER
star ..... VENUS, MOON, HESPER(US), VESPER
evensong .... VESPERS
event .... INCIDENT, OCCURRENCE, RESULT, HAPPENING, CASUS, OCCASION
causing war .. CASUS BELLI
of June 1953 .... CORONATION
eventful .... MOMENTOUS

eventide .... VESPER, DUSK, TWILIGHT
eventual ... FINAL, ULTIMATE
eventuality ..... CONTINGENCY
eventually .... FINALLY, ULTIMATELY
eventuate ..... RESULT, TURN, HAPPEN
ever ... ALWAYS, REPEATEDLY, AYE
Everest conqueror .. HILLARY, TENZING
    peak .... LHOTSE
    rival ...... ANNAPURNA
everglade ...... SWAMPLAND
    denizen .... (ALLI)GATOR
evergreen ... SPRUCE, CASHEW, CAROB, YEW, CEDAR, TITI, CALABA, BALSAM, MADRONA, PINE, FIR, CONIFER, DEODAR, OLIVE
    bean .... CAROB
    genus .... ABIES
    giant .... REDWOOD, SEQUOIA
    herb .... GALAX
    oak .... ILEX, HOLM
    opposed to .. DECIDUOUS
    shrub .... OLEANDER, ROSEMARY
    tree .... HEMLOCK
    tree bark .... CASSIA
    tree fruit .... CONE
everlasting .... AGELONG, ETERNAL, ETERN(E), ETERNITY, DURABLE
every .... EACH, ALL
    combining form .... PANT(O)
everyday ... USUAL, COMMON, DAILY
everything .... ALL
everywhere ... HIGH AND LOW, UBIQUE
    combining form ... OMNI
evict .... OUST, EJECT, EXPEL, REMOVE
evidence .... INDICATION, SIGN, PROOF
evident .... APPARENT, CLEAR, MANIFEST, OBVIOUS, PLAIN, PALPABLE, PATENT
evil .... WICKED, BAD, SIN, DEPRAVITY, BASE, VILE, MAL, MALEFIC(ENT)
    act .... CRIME

child .... IMP
    combining form .... MAL
    deed .... SIN
    doer .... MISCREANT, CRIMINAL, MALEFACTOR
    eye .... JINX, WHAMMY
    for evil .... RETALIATION
    habit .... VICE
    intent ... DOLUS, MALICE
    minded .... MALICIOUS, WICKED, SALACIOUS, PRURIENT
    motivation ..... MALICE, SPITE
    person .... CAITIFF
    smelling .. MALODOROUS, STINKING
    spirit, taken by .... POSSESSED
    spirit, woman ..... HAG
    wishing ..... MALIGNANT
evince ... INDICATE, MANIFEST, SHOW
eviscerate ... DISEMBOWEL, GUT
evitable .... AVOIDABLE
evocation .... SUMMONS, CALLING
evoke .... EDUCE, CALL, REMIND, RECALL, ELICIT, DRAW, SUMMON
evolution ..... DEVELOPMENT, GROWTH, MUTATION
    theorist on ..... DARWIN, LAMARK
evolutionary development of plant/animal ... PHYLOGENY
evolve ... UNFOLD, WORKOUT, DEVELOP, DERIVE
ewe .... SHEEP
    mate of .... RAM
    necked animal ... HORSE
    udder inflammation ..... GARGET
ewer .... PITCHER, JUG
ex ____ ... CATHEDRA, PARTE
    libris .... BOOKPLATE
    parte .... ONE-SIDED
    preposition ... WITHOUT
exacerbate ... EMBITTER, IRK, ANNOY, IRRITATE
exact .... LITERAL, LEVY, BLEED, STRICT, ACCURATE, CORRECT, PRECISE, DEMAND, SEVERE, EXTORT
    copy .... DUPLICATE
    moment .... POINT

money .... LUG
thoroughly ... RIGOROUS
exaction ... EXTORTION, TAX,
TOLL
ancient .... TRIBUTE
exactitude .... ACCURACY,
PRECISION
exaggerate .... EMBROIDER,
OVERSTATE, MAGNIFY
tendency to ... MYTHOMIA
exaggerated .... OUTRE
comedy .... FARCE
pious feeling .... PIETISM
praise .... PUFFERY,
FLATTERY
exaggeration ....
OVERSTATEMENT
for effect ... HYPERBOLE
exalt ...... ELEVATE, EXTOL,
RAISE, PRAISE, GLORIFY,
ELATE
exaltation .. ELATION, RAPTURE
exalted .... SUBLIME, HIGH,
NOBLE, STRONG, TIPSY
examination ...... SCRUTINY,
INQUIRY, INSPECTION,
TEST(ING), QUIZ, TRIAL
of dead body .. AUTOPSY,
NECROPSY
examine .... TRY, TEST,
EXPLORE, SCRUTINIZE,
INSPECT
accounts .... AUDIT
by touching ... PALPATE
examiner .... CENSOR,
INSPECTOR, EYER, TESTER
example ... PARADIGM, MODEL,
CASE, SAMPLE, INSTANCE,
PATTERN, SPECIMEN
examples, set of ...... PRAXIS
exasperate .... INFURIATE,
INCENSE, IRK, ENRAGE,
TRY, IRRITATE, ANNOY,
VEX, ANGER
exasperation .... DISGUST
excaudate .... TAILLESS
excavate .... DIG, UNEARTH,
HOLLOW OUT, DREDGE,
EXHUME, HOE, SCOOP
excavation .... MINE, PIT,
HOLE, HOLLOW, STOPE
mining .... STOPE
excavator .... DREDGE(R),
DIGGER, SCOOP(ER)
exceed ... SURPASS, OUTDO,
EXCEL, OUTREACH

exceedingly .... UNCO
excel .... BEST, OUTDO, STAR,
EXCEED, SURPASS,
TRANSCEND
excellence .... MERIT,
SUPERIORITY, VIRTU(E),
GOODNESS
excellent .... CAPITAL, AONE,
RARE, PEACHY, TOPS,
OUTSTANDING, SUPERB,
RIPPING, SUPER
except ...... SAVE, BUT, BAR,
EXCLUDE, OMIT, OBJECT
exception .... EXCLUSION,
OMISSION, OBJECTION,
RESERVATION, CHALLENGE
in law .... SAVING
take .... DEMUR, RESENT,
OBJECT
exceptional .... ESPECIAL,
OUTSTANDING, UNUSUAL
excerpt ..... EXTRACT, QUOTE,
PASSAGE, SELECT
excess ... (SUR)PLUS, NIMIETY,
PLETHORA, OVER(AGE),
INTEMPERANCE, EXTRA,
SURFEIT
of solar over lunar year ..
EPACT
excessive .... UNDUE,
IMMODERATE, EXTRAVAGANT,
EXORBITANT, INORDINATE,
ULTRA
affection .... DOTAGE
combining form .. HYPER
demand ..... EXACTION,
EXTORTION
in belief .... RABID
joy .... RAPTURE,
EXALTATION
saliva secretion ....
PTYALISM
zeal .... FANATICISM
excessively .... UNDULY,
EXTREMELY, OVERLY
fond .... DOTING
exchange .. BANDY, COMMUTE,
SWAP, TRADE, BARTER,
TRUCK, SWITCH, RIALTO
business ... AGIO, BONDS,
SHARES, CURRENCY
discount .... AGIO
fee .... AGIO
medium .... SYCEE
of shots .... GUNPLAY
premium .... AGIO

Scottish .... NIFFER
stock .... BOURSE
visit .... GAM
exchequer ... FISC, TREASURY,
FUNDS, FINANCES
excide .... CUT OUT, REMOVE,
EXCISE
excise .... TOLL, DUTY,
CUT OUT, IMPOST, REMOVE,
EXSCIND, TAX
tax collector .. GA(U)GER
excitable .... FIERY, HOT
excite ... STARTLE, TITILLATE,
FLUSTER, PIQUE, STIR(UP),
(A)ROUSE, PROVOKE,
AGITATE, ROIL
interest/curiosity ....
INTRIGUE
excited .... ASTIR, AGOG,
(A)DITHER, HET UP,
AGITATED
greatly .... FRANTIC,
FRENZIED
state .... FEY
exciting .... ELECTRIC
excitement ..... FUROR, TIZZY,
FEVER, STIR, HEAT, FLUTTER
pleasurable .... KICK
reducer .... SEDATIVE
exclaim .. EJACULATE, CRY OUT
exclamation ... OUTCRY, POOH,
AH, ALAS, BAH, FIE, PUGH,
SHUCKS, RATS, NUTS,
PSHAW, OH MY, GEE, GOSH
German ..... ACH, HOCH
of joy .... WHOOPEE
of pain ..... YOW, OUCH
of praise ...... HOSANNA,
ADORATION
of triumph ..... EUREKA
point .... SCREAMER
to attract attention .. HEY
exclave, example of .. PRUSSIA
exclude ...... OMIT, EXCEPT,
EXPEL, ELIMINATE,
(DE)BAR, REJECT, BAR
by general consent ......
OSTRACIZE
exclusive .... SOLE, SINGLE,
POSH, ONLY, SELECT
control ..... MONOPOLY
of .... EX
set .... ELITE
excommunicate .... BAN,
CONDEMN, DAMN
excommunication .. EXCISION,

CONDEMNATION, BAN,
ANATHEMA
excoriate ..... ABRADE, FLAY,
CHAFE, DENOUNCE
excoriation ... SORE, ABRASION
excrement .... FECES, REFUSE,
MANURE, DUNG
excrescence .... STUD,
OUTGROWTH, APPENDAGE,
WART
example of .. FINGERNAIL,
BUNION, HAIR
excreta .... URINE, SWEAT
excrete .... EGEST, EXUDE
excretion .... SWEAT,
PERSPIRATION, URINE
excruciate . TORTURE, PAIN,
TORMENT, AGONIZE
exculpate .... ACQUIT, CLEAR,
EXONERATE, ABSOLVE
excursion ...... JAUNT, TOUR,
SIDE TRIP, OUTING, JUNKET
coach ...... CHARABANC
excursive .... RAMBLING,
WANDERING
excusable .... VENIAL
excuse .... ALIBI, PLEA,
PRETEXT, OVERLOOK,
JUSTIFY, ABSOLVE,
APOLOGY, RELEASE, SALVO
for absence ..... ESSOIN
partial ..... EXTENUATION
execrable .... DETESTABLE,
HATEFUL, ABOMINABLE
execrate .... DETEST, CURSE,
HATE, LOATHE, ABHOR
execute .... HANG, DO,
PERFORM, FULFILL, KILL
unlawfully ...... LYNCH
execution by burning .. STAKE
by drowning .... NOYADE
by hanging ..... HALTER,
SWING, STRETCH
executioner ...... HANGMAN,
HEADSMAN, DEATHSMAN,
HANGER
gangland's ....
HATCHETMAN
Executive Mansion ....
WHITE HOUSE
exegesis .... EXPLANATION
exemplar ... MODEL, PATTERN,
EXAMPLE, (ARCHE)TYPE,
SPECIMEN
exempt .... IMMUNE, FREE,
EXCUSE(D), RELEASE

exemption from punishment .. IMPUNITY, IMMUNITY
temporary .... GRACE
exequies .... FUNERAL, OBSEQUIES
exercise .... USE, EMPLOY(MENT), PRACTICE, PROBLEM, TRAIN, DRILL, PRAXIS, LESSON, EXERT, PERPLEX, WORRY, HARASS
exercises, athletic .... CALISTHENICS
set of .... PRAXIS
trained .... MANEGE
exert .... EXERCISE
exertion .... EFFORT
exeunt .... EXIT
exfoliate ..... CAST OFF, PEEL
exhalation ... HALITUS, AURA, FUME, BREATH, EXPIRATION, EVAPORATION, EMANATION
exhale ... EXPIRE, EVAPORATE, BREATHE OUT
exhaust .... TIRE, FAG, DRAIN, DEPLETE, USE UP, SPEND
exhausted ..... TIRED, DONE, SPENT, USED UP, ALL IN, EFFETE
exhibit .... STAGE, SHOW, DISPLAY, PRESENTATION, EXPOSE
in law ...... DOCUMENT, EVIDENCE, PROOF
exhibition ..... PRESENTATION, DISPLAY, FAIR
international ....
EXPOSITION
of art works ...... SALON
place ... GALLERY, SALON
exhilarate ... ELATE, ENLIVEN, ANIMATE, STIMULATE
exhilaration ..... ANIMATION, LIVELINESS
exhort .... URGE, PROD, EGG, ADMONISH
exhume .... DISINTER, UNEARTH, DIG OUT
exigency .... NEED, URGENCY, EMERGENCY, DEMAND
exigent .... URGENT, CRITICAL, EXACTING, PRESSING
exiguous ... SMALL, MEAGER, LITTLE, SCANTY
exile ..... RELEGATE, DEPORT, EXPATRIATE, BANISH(MENT)

exist .... (A)LIVE, BE, IS
existence ... ESSE, BEING, ENS, LIFE, LIVING
coming into ... NASCENT
existent ..... ALIVE, PRESENT
existing ...... REAL, EXTANT, ALIVE
exit .... EGRESS, ISSUE, OUTLET, DEPART(URE), WAY OUT, LEAVE
exocarp .... RIND
exodus ..... HEGIRA, FLIGHT, DEPARTURE, EMIGRATION
hero .... ARI
leader .... MOSES
scene .... RED SEA
exogen .... DICOTYLEDON
exogenous .... ENTHETIC
exonerate .... ACQUIT, CLEAR, EXCULPATE, ABSOLVE
exorbitant .... EXCESSIVE, IMMODERATE, UNDUE
interest .... USURY
exorcism .... EXPULSION
exordial ...... INTRODUCTORY
exordium .... PROEM, OVERTURE, OPENING, BEGINNING
exoteric .... EXTERNAL, POPULAR, PUBLIC
opposed to .... ESOTERIC
exotic ...... ALIEN, FOREIGN, IMPORTED, STRANGE
expand .... INFLATE, INTUMESCE, DILATE, FLAN, ENLARGE, SWELL, DISTEND
expanse .... SEA, OCEAN, BREADTH, AREA, REACH, SPREAD
expatiate .. ENLARGE, DESCANT, ELABORATE
expatriate ..... EXILE, BANISH
expect ... HOPE, ANTICIPATE, PRESUME, AWAIT
expectation .... HOPE, ANTICIPATION, PROSPECT, OUTLOOK
expecting .... PREGNANT
expectorant .. EMETIN(E), EMETIC
expectorate .... SPIT
expedient ...... CONVENIENT, ADVISABLE, POLITIC
expedite ...... EASY, HASTEN, FACILITATE, SPEED(UP), HURRY
expediter: colloq. ... TICKLER

expedition .... CRUSADE,
SAFARI, SPEED, DISPATCH,
TRIP, MARCH
heroic .... QUEST
hunting .... SAFARI
military .... ANABASIS
purpose .. EXPLORATION,
BATTLE, HUNT(ING)
religious ...... CRUSADE
expeditious .... PROMPT,
SPEEDY
expel ..... EJECT, DRIVE OUT
from country .... EXILE,
BANISH, DEPORT,
EXPATRIATE
expend .... USE, CONSUME,
SPEND
expendable ..... REPLACEABLE
expenditure .. OUTGO, OUTLAY
expense .... COST, FEE,
CHARGE, SACRIFICE
colloquial ..... DAMAGE
expensive ..... COSTLY, DEAR
experience .... FEEL, UNDERGO
trying .... ORDEAL
experiment ...... TEST, TRIAL,
TRY
experimental .... TENTATIVE,
TESTING
workshop ....
LAB(ORATORY)
expert ... ACE, VIRTUOSO, PRO,
SKILLFUL, DEFT, ADEPT,
MASTER, DAB(STER), SHARP
in canon law .. DISCRETIST
on anecdotes/stories ....
RACONTEUR
on coins .... SHROFF
expiate ...... ATONE, REPAIR,
SATISFY
expiation ...... ATONEMENT,
AMENDS, REPARATION
place of ..... PURGATORY
expiatory .... PIACULAR
expire ...... DIE, PERISH, END,
STOP, CEASE, TERMINATE
explain .... EXPLICATE, DEFINE,
CLEAR, ELUCIDATE,
CLARIFY, EXPOUND,
INTERPRET
explanation .. INTERPRETATION,
CLARIFICATION,
ELUCIDATION
of Biblical passage ......
EXEGESIS
explanatory .... EXEGETIC

expletive ...... OATH, CURSE,
EXCLAMATION
explicate .... EXPLAIN
explicit ... DEFINITE, EXPRESS,
EXACT, PRECISE, SPECIFIC,
CLEAR
explode .... POP, BURST,
DISCREDIT, DETONATE,
BLOW UP, FIRE, CRUMP
exploding meteor ..... BOLIDE,
BOLIS
exploit ... ACT, FEAT, GEST(E),
PROMOTE, DEED, HEROISM,
ACTION, UTILIZE
explore .... INVESTIGATE,
EXAMINE, PROBE
explorer ... ERIC, RAE, BYRD,
AMUNDSEN, BALBOA,
DE SOTO, CORTES, PERRY,
LEWIS
explosion .... BLOWUP,
DETONATION, OUTBURST
explosive ... DYNAMITE, TNT,
MINE, GUNPOWDER,
CORDITE, SOUP, TONITE,
BOMB, DUNNITE, LIGNOSE,
CHEDDITE, ROBURITE,
LYDDITE, AMYTOL, PETARD
charge, part of ....
WARHEAD
sound ..... DETONATION,
CHUG, POP, BOOM, CLAP
explosives box ...... CAISSON
material .... CELLULOSE
storage place .. MAGAZINE
exponent ... SYMBOL, EXAMPLE,
ADVOCATE
in mathematics ... INDEX
expose ...... BARE, DISCLOSE,
REVEAL, UNMASK, DISPLAY,
EXHIBIT, SHOW
as false .... EXPLODE,
DEBUNK
to danger .... IMPERIL
exposition .... EXHIBITION,
SHOW, FAIR
expository .... EXEGETIC,
EXPLANATORY
expostulate .... OBJECT,
REMONSTRATE, PROTEST
exposure .... AIRING
expound .... EXPLAIN,
ELUCIDATE, CLARIFY,
INTERPRET
express ...... STATE, REVEAL,

SIGNIFY, EXPLICIT, UTTER,
EXTORT

dissatisfaction ....
COMPLAIN, GRIPE, BEEF,
HOOT

in numbers ... EVALUATE

expression .... TERM,
REPRESENTATION,
LOCUTION, SAYING,
ARTICULATION

local .... IDIOM

of contempt ...... SNIFF,
SNORT, GRUNT, SNEER

of reproach .... FIE

of sympathy ....
CONDOLENCE

expressionless mien ....
DEADPAN, POKERFACE

expressive .... ELOQUENT

action ....GESTURE

expressly .... DEFINITELY,
PLAINLY, ESPECIALLY,
EXPLICITLY

expropriate ...... DISPOSSESS

expulsion ... EJECTION, OUSTER

kind of .... DEPORTATION

expunge ... DELE(TE), EFFACE,
ERASE, CANCEL, WIPE(OUT)

expurgate ... CENSOR, PURGE,
CLEANSE, PURIFY

exquisite .... DELICATE,
FASTIDIOUS, RARE

exsanguine .... ANEMIC

exscind .... EXCISE, CUT(OUT)

exsert ... THRUST, PROTRUDE

exsiccate .... DRY, PARCH

extant .... EXISTING

extemporaneous ... OFFHAND,
IMPROMPTU, IMPROVISED

extemporize ...... IMPROVISE

extend .... PROTRACT,
OUTREACH, RENEW,
STRETCH, JUT, CONTINUE,
PROLONG, SPREAD

across .... SPAN

extension .... RENEWAL,
ADDITION, CONTINUATION

building ...... ELL, WING

extent ...... LENGTH, SCOPE,
COVERAGE, MAGNITUDE,
LATITUDE

of precedence ..... LEAD

extenuate .... WEAKEN,
LESSEN, DIMINISH,
MITIGATE, PALLIATE

exterior ... ECTAL, EXTRINSIC,

OUTER, OUTSIDE, FOREIGN,
EXTERNAL

toward the .... ECTAD

exterminate ...... EXTIRPATE,
ERADICATE, DESTROY,
ANNIHILATE

extermination, mass ....
GENOCIDE

external ... OUTER, EXOTERIC,
EXTERIOR, SUPERFICIAL

combining form .. ECT(O)

covering ... HIDE, PELT,
COAT, SKIN, CRUST,
SHEATHE

cover of flower ....
PERIANTH

world .... NONEGO

extinct ...... EXTINGUISHED,
DEAD, DEFUNCT,
NON-EXISTENT

animal .... MASTODON

bird .... DODO, MOA,
MAMO, KIWI

elephant ..... MAMMOTH

elephantlike animal .....
DINOTHERE

mammal ... GLYPTODONT

ox .... URUS

reptile .... DINOSAUR,
DINOCERAS

extinguish .... PUT OUT,
DESTROY, SMOTHER,
QUENCH, ECLIPSE, DOUSE,
DOWSE, SNUFF

in law .... NULLIFY

extirpate .... EXSCIND,
DESTROY, ABOLISH, RAZE,
UPROOT, ERADICATE

extol ... PRAISE, LAUD, EXALT,
GLORIFY

extort .. WRING, MILK, SCREW,
EXTRACT, EXACT, WREST,
SQUEEZE, BLEED, MULCT

extortioner ..... BLACKMAILER

extra ... SPARE, ODD, EXCESS,
SURPLUS, ADDITIONAL, OVER

actor .... SUPER,
SUPERNUMERARY,
FIGURANT(E)

pay .... BONUS

Scottish .... ORRA

extract .... DISTIL, ELICIT,
ESTREAT, EXCERPT,
PULL OUT, QUOTATION,
WRING, EDUCE, EVOKE,
EXTORT, ATTAR, DRAW

by boiling ..... DECOCT
by dissolving .... LEACH
forcibly ..... EVULSE
from balsam ... TOLUENE
of court record .. ESTREAT
extraction .... LINEAGE,
   ORIGIN, BIRTH, DESCENT
extracurricular activity ......
   DEBATING, DRAMATICS,
   ATHLETICS
extradite .... REPATRIATE
extraneous ... EXOTIC, OUTER,
   FOREIGN, EXTRINSIC,
   ALIEN
extraordinary ...... UNIQUE,
   GREAT, UNUSUAL,
   EXCEPTIONAL, UNCO,
   REMARKABLE, MARVELOUS
extrasensory perception ... ESP
extravagant .... BAROQUE,
   PROFUSE, EXCESSIVE,
   EXORBITANT, WASTEFUL,
   LAVISH, PRODIGAL, ULTRA
spending .... LAVISH
extravaganza ..... SPECTACLE,
   REVUE
extreme ... RADICAL, ULTRA,
   SEVERE, SUPERLATIVE,
   FINAL, EXCESSIVE,
   IMMODERATE, DRASTIC,
   RANK, LAST
limit .... OUTRANCE
opposed to .... MEAN
unction ..... SACRAMENT
unction, give ..... ANELE
extremely ...... VERY, UNCO,
   HIGHLY
fine .... SUPERB
wicked .... HEINOUS
extremist .... RADICAL,
   NIHILIST
extremity .... POLE, TIP, TOE,
   END, DYING
extremities .... LIMBS
extricate ...... RELEASE, FREE
extrinsic ...... EXTRANEOUS,
   FOREIGN, ALIEN
extrude ...... EXPEL, PROJECT
extrusive .... VOLCANIC
exuberant .... EFFUSIVE,
   LAVISH
exudate, plant ... GUM, RESIN,
   LAC
exudation .... SUDOR,
   EMANATION, SWEAT,
   PERSPIRATION, RESIN, GUM

exude .... EMIT, REEK,
   DISCHARGE, FLOW, OOZE
water .... WEEP
exult ..... REJOICE, GLORIFY,
   JUBILATE, GLORY
exultant .... JUBILANT
exults ..... CROWS, REJOICES,
   GLORIES
exuviae .... MOLTS, SHELLS
exuviate ..... MOLT, CAST OFF
eyas .... HAWK, NESTLING
eye ... OPTIC, OCELLUS, OGLE,
   BUD, ORB, GLIM, SIGHT,
   VISION, GLANCE, LOOK, SEE
bean's ..... HILUM, HILA
black ... SHINER, MOUSE
bruise under .... MOUSE
cavity .... ORBIT
coating .... GLAZE
colloquial .... OPTIC
combining form ....
   OCUL(O)
contraction of pupil ....
   MYOSIS
cover ... . PATCH
defect .... DIPLOPIA,
   MYOPIA, OXYOPIA
dirt .... MOTE
discharge .... RHEUM
disease ...... GLAUCOMA,
   CATARACT
disorder .... SQUINT,
   STRABISMUS
doctor .... OCULIST,
   OPHTHALMOLOGIST
dropper .... PIPETTE
filler .... BEAUTY
filling ...... BEAUTIFUL
film .... GLAZE
for-an-eye .. TIT FOR TAT,
   TALION
for only one.. MONOCULAR
German .... AUGE
glass .... PINCENEZ,
   MONOCLE, LENS,
   SPECTACLES, LORGNETTE,
   LORGNON
glass maker/seller ......
   OPTICIAN
inflammation ...... STY,
   IRITIS
instrument .. ORTHOSCOPE
lashes .... CILIA
layer .... UVEA
magic ... RADAR, SONAR
membrane .... IRIS

of the .... OPTIC, OCULAR
opening .... PUPIL
part ...... UVEA, RETINA,
    LENS, CHOROID, PUPIL,
    CORNEA, HUMOR
pus .... HYPOPYON
shield .... PATCH,
    BLINDER, VISOR, BLINKER
simple .... OCELLUS
slang ... PEEPER, WINKER
socket .... ORBIT
Spanish .... OJO
thing with ...... POTATO,
    STORM, NEEDLE, TARGET,
    HURRICANE
wash .... EYEMO, MURINE
worm .... LOA
eyeball dryness ..... XEROSIS
    outer coat ..... CORNEA
eyebrow .... BREE
    cosmetic ..... MASCARA
    marker .... PENCIL
    Spanish .... CEJA
eyebrows, space between .....
    GLABELLA
eyedrop drug .... ESERINE,
    MURINE
eyeful .... ATTRACTIVE,
    STRIKING
eyeglasses .... PINCE NEZ,
    SPECS, MONOCLE,
    LORGNETTE, SPECTACLES,
    HARLEQUIN
    maker/seller of ....
        OPTICIAN
    slang .... CHEATERS
eyelash ..... CILIUM, WINKER
    cosmetic ..... MASCARA
eyelashes .... CILIA
    of .... CILIARY
eyeless .... BLIND
"Eyeless In Gaza" author ....
    HUXLEY
eyelet ... GROMMET, GRUMMET,

PEEPHOLE, LOOPHOLE,
    OCELLUS
making tool ... BODKIN,
    STILETTO
eyeleteer ... BODKIN, STILETTO
eyelid, corner of ... CANTHUS
    cosmetic .... KOHL
    drooping .... PTOSIS
    inflammation .... STY,
        BLEPHARITIS
eyes: colloq. ...... SPARKLERS
    cover the ...... SEEL,
        BLINDFOLD, HOODWINK
    deep-set .... CAVERNOUS
    slang .... DAYLIGHT
    describing some ....
        DEEPSET, GREEN, SOULFUL,
        DOE, EVIL, SHIFTY,
        SQUINT(Y)
    inflammation ...... STY,
        HAW
    of the .... OCULAR
    poetic .... ORBS
    slang .... LAMPS
    swelling .... MOUS(I)E
    third .... HAW
    tissue .... TARSUS
    trouble ...... TRICHOMA
eyelids, of the ..... PALPEBRAL
eyesight .... VISION
    by .... OCULAR
eyesore .... UGLY
eyetooth ..... CUSPID, FANG,
        CANINE
eyewash .... COLLYRIUM,
    EXCUSE, MURINE, EYEMO,
    NONSENSE, FLATTERY
eyewink ...... INSTANT, HINT,
        SIGNAL
eyot .... AIT, ILE, ISLE(T)
eyra .... WILD CAT
eyre .... TOUR, CIRCUIT
eyrie .... NEST, EAGLET
Ezida frequenter .... NEBO
Ezra, book about .... ESDRAS

F

F, letter .... EF
fabaceous plant .... PEA
Fabian strategy ...... DELAY,
    AVOIDANCE
Fabius, soubriquet ....
    CUNCTATOR, (THE) DELAYER
    victim of ..... HANNIBAL
fable ... LEGEND, APOLOG(UE),

MYTH, FALSEHOOD, FICTION,
    ALLEGORY, PARABLE, STORY
    writer .... (A)ESOP,
    MORALIST, ADE, PHAEDRUS
fabled being .... TROLL,
    GNOME, DWARF, MINOTAUR,
    SIREN, OGRE, TITAN,
    CENTAUR

bird .... ROC
fish .... MAH
fables have one .... MORAL,
  LESSON
fabric .... DRAPERY, FELT,
  SATEEN, SOIE, ORLON,
  STRUCTURE, CREPE, LENO,
  ETOILE, TULLE, VOILE,
  SILK, ATLAS, FAILLE,
  NINON, TEXTURE, CLOTH,
  RAYON, MOIRE, MOHAIR,
  CANVAS, TAPA, WOOF, WEB,
  RAS
  Angora .... MOHAIR,
    CAMLET
  carpet .... MOQUETTE
  coarse ... ORLON, CRASH,
    MAT, DOWLAS, RATINE
  corded .... REP(P),
    PIQUE, PADUASOY, REPS
  cotton .... MOREEN,
    PENANG, PIQUE, MADRAS,
    DENIM, SCRIM, CALICO,
    NANKIN, NANKEEN,
    CRETON(NE), MULL,
    MANTA, LENO
  cravat/tie .... REP
  creased ...... KORATRON
  crinkled .... CREPE,
    CRAPE
  curtain ..... NET, SCRIM
  drapery .... MOREEN
  edge .... SELVAGE
  felt-like .... BAIZE
  filling .... WEFT
  floor cover ..... CARPET
  glazed .... CAMBRIC
  glossy .... SATIN, ETOILE
  heavy .... BROCADE
  kind of ... KNIT, PRINT,
    WOOLEN, WORSTED
  knitted .... TRICOT
  hempen .... BURLAP
  light wool ..... ALPACA
  linen .... SCRIM, DOWLAS
  lining ... FLEECE, SATEEN
  metallic .... LAME
  mourning .... CRAPE,
    ALMA
  napped .... FLEECE
  net ..... TULLE, MALINE
  plaid .... TARTAN
  printed .... PERCALE,
    CHALLIS, BAT(T)IK
  protector ..... CAMPHOR
  puckered .... PLISSE

reversible ...... DAMASK
rib .... WALE
ribbed ... TWILL, PIQUE,
  REP(P), CORD, REPS
rugs .... CHENILLE
satin ..... ETOILE, PEKIN
sheer .... ORGANZA,
  GAUZE, VOILE, BATISTE
shiny .... SATEEN,
  POPLIN, SILK
silk ..... SURAH, FAILLE,
  PONGEE, SAMITE, TOBINE
silk and gold .... SAMITE
stiff .... WIGAN
stretcher .... TENTER
striped ...... GALATEA,
  DORIA, MADRAS, ZENANA,
  DO(O)REA, BAYADEER,
  BAYADERE
towel .... TERRY
twilled .... SERGE
upholstery .... BROCATEL,
  MOREEN
velvet-like .... TERRY
wastes .... MUNGO
watered silk ..... MOIRE
wavy patterned ... MOIRE
wax-coated ... BAT(T)IK
window shades ....
  HOLLAND
woolen ... BEIGE, ALPACA,
  SERGE, MERINO, VICUNA,
  TAMIS, TARTAN,
  ESTAMIN(E), ETAMINE
worsted .... SERGE,
  ETAMINE
woven silk ..... TRICOT
fabricate ... CONCOCT, COIN,
  DEVISE, INVENT, MAKE(UP),
  CONSTRUCT, LIE
fabrication ...... LIE, WEB,
  DECEIT, MANUFACTURE,
  FALSEHOOD
fabricator .... FORGER,
  INVENTOR, LIAR, MAKER
fabrics dealer .... MERCER
fabulist .... (A)ESOP, ADE,
  LIAR, GRIMM, LA FONTAINE
fabulous .... MYTHICAL,
  IMAGINARY, LEGENDARY,
  INCREDIBLE
  animal ...... UNICORN,
    CENTAUR
  bankers ... ROTHSCHILD
  monster .... CHIMERA
  place .... EL DORADO

serpent .... BASILISK, COCKATRICE
tale .... LEGEND
facade .... FRONT, FACE
main ...... FRONTISPIECE
face .... MEET, ANSWER, (CON)FRONT, FACADE, VISAGE, COUNTENANCE,
card ...... KING, QUEEN, JACK
coin's .... HEAD
colloquial ... AUDACITY, MUG, MAP, PUSS, SNOOT
crease ...... WRINKLE, LINE
down .... LIE, PRONE
expressionless .... DEAD PAN, POKER
gem's .... FACET
guard ... BEAVER, VISOR
hair .... BEARD
obsolete .... MAZARD
of rock ...... BROW, CLIFF
powder .... TALCUM
slang .... PAN, PUSS, KISSER, PHIZ, MAP, MUG
spot .... FRECKLE
to face .... VIS-A-VIS, TETE-A-TETE
value .... PAR
with stone .... REVET
facet .... BEZEL, CULET, PHASE, COLLET, BEZIL, FLANGE
facetious ... COMICAL, DROLL, WITTY, JOCOSE, JOCULAR
person ...... HUMORIST, WAG, JESTER
facial adornment .... GOATEE, MUSTACHIO, BEARD, VANDYKE, MUSTACHE, IMPERIAL
expression ...... SMILE, GRIMACE, POUT, LEER, GRIN, PHIZ, SMIRK, SCOWL
facile .... EASY, FLUENT, AFFABLE, DEFT, ADROIT
facilitate .... FURTHER, HELP, QUICKEN
facility .... MEANS, EASE, DEXTERITY, FLUENCY, SKILL, CONVENIENCE, KNACK
facing ... LINING, TRIMMING, FORNENT, TOWARD
glacier .... STOSS
inward .... INTRORSE

facsimile .... COPY, LIKENESS, REPLICA, REPRODUCTION
fact ... FIAT, DATUM, TRUTH, REALITY, ACTUALITY
of knowing .... KNOWLEDGE
state as a ... POSIT, AVER
faction ... BLOC, JUNTO, SIDE, CLIQUE, CABAL
factional .... PARTISAN
division .... SCHISM, SPLIT, SPLINTER
factious .... CONTENTIOUS, PARTISAN
factitious .... ARTIFICIAL, FORCED
factor ...... AGENT, BROKER, ELEMENT, GENE
biological .... GENE
Scottish ...... STEWARD, BAILIFF
factory ...... PLANT, MILL
country ...... HACIENDA
factotum .... SERVANT, AGENT, HANDYMAN
facts .... DATA, LOW-DOWN
factual .... REAL, ACTUAL
facultative ...... CONTINGENT, OPTIONAL
faculty .... TALENT, SENSE, POWER, ABILITY, KNACK, APTITUDE
of apt expression .... FELICITY
fad .... CRAZE, HOBBY, FASHION, MODE, STYLE, MEGRIM
fade .... PEAK, WILT, LANGUISH, WITHER, DIM, DROOP, WANE, DIE(OUT)
from sight ... EVANESCE, DISAPPEAR
out ...... END, DISSOLVE
faded ... DULL, WORN, DRAB
fading .... FUGITIVE
fado .... FOLKSONG
"Faerie Queen" ... MAB, UNA
character ...... AMORET, ALMA, TALUS, ACRASIA
Fafnir's brother ...... REGIN
slayer .... SIGURD
fag .... EXHAUST, SLAVE, TIRE, DRUDGE(RY), FATIGUE, HOMOSEXUAL, WEARY

end .... RUCK, STUB, REMNANT, RUMP
slang .... CIGARETTE
fagaceous plant ... BEECH, OAK
fagot ... SEW, FASCINE, ESCINE
faience .... POTTERY, PORCELAIN
fail .... PETER, EBB, COLLAPSE, MISCARRY, DEFAULT, MISS, FIZZLE, FLOP, FLUNK
  as a motor ... CONK OUT
  in duty .... SHIRK, REMISS
  in health ..... LANGUISH
  to catch ... FUMBLE, MUFF
  to follow suit ..... RENIG, RENEGE, FAINAIGUE
failing .... DEFECT, FAULT, WEAKNESS
failure .... DUD, FIASCO, OMISSION, BUST, FLOP, TURKEY
  complete ..... WASHOUT, FIASCO
  to pay .... DEFAULT
  to prosecute ... DEFAULT
fain ...... GLAD(LY), READY, EAGER
faineant .... OTIOSE, LAZY, IDLE
faint .... WAN, DIM, SWOON, WEAK, FEEBLE, TIMID, UNCLEAR, SWOUND
fainthearted .... TIMID, COWARDLY
fainting .... SYNCOPATION
  fit ..... SYNCOPE, SWOON
fair .... EVEN, JUST, COMELY, CLEAR, FESTIVAL, KERMIS, CARNIVAL, BAZA(A)R, EXHIBITION, IMPARTIAL, LOVELY, BEAUTIFUL, UNBIASED, DECENT, SO-SO, BLOND, EXPOSITION
  haired .... FAVORITE, BLOND(E), PET
  place ..... STALL, BOOTH, PAVILION
  portion .... CHUNK
  sex .... WOMAN
  spoken .... POLITE, BLAND
  to middling ... PASSABLE, SO-SO
Fairbanks native .... ALASKAN

fairies' queen ... MAB, TITANIA, UNA
fairy ...... LEPRECHAUN, ELF, PIXIE, PIXY, SPRITE, ELVE, FAY, PERI, TINKERBELL
  air .... SYLPH
  fort .... SHEE, LIS(S)
  king .... OBERON
  lake dweller .... MORGAN(LE FAY)
  like .... ELFIN
  queen ... TITANIA, UNA, MAB
  story .... MARCHEN, ALLEGORY, FABLE, TALE, MYTH, LIE
  tale character .. SANDMAN
  wood .... NYMPH
faith ... BELIEF, CREED, TROTH, DOXY, RELIGION, TRUST, LOYALTY, CULT, DOGMA
  archaic .... FAY
  article of .... TENET
  bad .... DUPLICITY, DISHONESTY
  good .... SINCERITY
  healer, kind of ... QUACK
  matters of ... CREDENDA
  of .... PISTIC
faithful ...... FAST, DEVOTED, LOYAL, HONEST, STA(U)NCH, CONSTANT, RELIABLE, EXACT, TRUE, TRIED
  friend .... ACHATES, DAMON, PYTHIAS
  poetic .... LEAL
faithless ... FALSE, DISLOYAL, PERFIDIOUS, TRAITOROUS
faitour .... ROGUE
fake .... CHEAT, TRICK, PHONEY, SHAM, COUNTERFEIT, FRAUD, COIL
  attack .... FEINT
  colloquial .. BRUMMAGEN
faker ..... SWINDLER, FRAUD, QUACK
  kind of ..... MALINGERER
fakir .... MENDICANT, MONK, YOGI, SWAMI, BEGGAR
falbala ..... FRILL, FLOUNCE, FURBELOW, RUFFLE
falcate .... CURVED, HOOKED
falchion .... SWORD
falcon ..... HAWK, CANNON, LANNER(ET), PEREGRINE,

MERLIN, LUGGER,
WINDHOVER, SAKER
Asian .... LAGGAR
close eyes of .... SEEL
E. Indian .... BESRA
European .... SAKER,
KESTREL, HOBBY
eye-blinder .. SEEL, HOOD
female .... LANNAR
headed deity .... RA,
MENT(U)
India ... SHAHIN, LAGGER
leg-strap .... JESS
male .... TERCEL,
LANNERET
peregrine .. DUCK HAWK
repair wing of ...... IMP
small .... MERLIN,
KESTREL
swoop of .... SOUSE
use of .... HUNTING
falconer .... HAWKER
falconer's decoy .... LURE
falconry .... HAWKING
falderal .... NONSENSE,
TRIFLE, GEWGAW
fall ..... DROP, SLIP, LITTER,
SPILL, PLOP, RUIN,
CASCADE, PLUNGE,
AUTUMN, SLUMP, DESCEND,
TUMBLE, PLUMMET,
COLLAPSE, TOPPLE, PLUNK
back ... RECEDE, RETREAT,
RELAPSE
behind .... LAG
forward .... TOPPLE
guy: sl. .... PATSY,
SCAPEGOAT, DUPE
headlong .... PITCH
in .... AGREE
in drops .... DRIP,
DRIB(BLE), TRICKLE
in line .... FILE
out ..... QUARREL, SHED
through .... FAIL
to .... START
to pieces ..... CRUMBLE,
DISINTEGRATE
fallacious ..... ERRONEOUS,
DECEPTIVE
notion .... IDOLISM
fallacy .... ERROR, IDOLA,
IDOLUM, DECEPTION,
MISTAKE
fallal ...... FINERY, FRIPPERY

fallen .. DROPPED, PROSTRATE,
DEGRADED, DEAD
falling .... CADENT
out .... QUARREL
over .... TOPPLE
sickness ...... EPILEPSY
star .... METEOR
Fallopian tube ...... OVIDUCT,
SALPINX
fallout particles .... SLEET,
SNOW
fallow deer .... TEG, DAMA
false .... SPURIOUS, UNTRUE,
MENDACIOUS, PSEUDO,
SHAM, FORGED, INCORRECT,
FAKE, BOGUS, WRONG,
MISTAKEN, ARTIFICIAL,
FAITHLESS
belief .... DELUSION
entry .... RINGER
excuse ...... SUBTERFUGE
face .... MASK
friend ... TRAITOR, JUDAS,
IAGO
front ..... BLUFF, DUMMY
god ...... BAAL, IDOL
hair .... PERUKE,
(PERI)WIG, TOUPEE
jewelry .... PASTE
move ...... MISSTEP, SLIP
name ... ANONYM, ALIAS
prefix .... PSEUDO
pretense ... AFFECTATION
reasoning ...... IDOLISM
report ... CANARD, HOAX
seed cover .... ARILLODE
show ..... MASQUERADE
show, make ...... FEIGN
show to be ..... DEBUNK,
DISPROVE
step ..... TRIP, STUMBLE
story ... CANARD, HOAX,
FUDGE
swearing ...... PURJURY
teeth .... DENTURE
wing .... ALULA
witness .. PERJURER, LIAR
falsehood ... LIE, TALE, FLAM,
FABLE, CANARD, INVENTION,
PERJURY, DECEPTION,
LYING, FIB
falsies: colloq. .... PADS
falsify .... FORGE, FAKE,
(BE)LIE, GARBLE, DISTORT,
ALTER
Falstaff's man .... PETO

falter .... HAW, WAVER,
TOTTER, STUMBLE,
STAMMER, FLINCH, HESITATE
fama .... RUMOR
fame ...... KUDOS, RENOWN,
GLORY, REPUTE,
REPUTATION, NAME, ECLAT
kind of ...... NOTORIETY
famed .. EMINENT, NOTORIOUS,
REPUTED, CELEBRATED
Fameuse .... APPLE
familiar ..... CLOSE, INTIMATE,
FRIENDLY, COMMON,
ORDINARY, BOLD, VERSANT
saying ..... SAW, ADAGE,
MOT, MOTTO, TAG
familiarize .... ACQUAINT
families, quarrel between .....
FEUD
family .... LINE, HOUSEHOLD,
STIRPS, TRIBE, CLAN, KIN,
RACE, LINEAGE, STOCK,
KINSFOLK, ILK, BREED
ancient ... ESTE, MEDICI,
DORIA
branch ..... STIRPS, STEM
car .... SEDAN
car: colloq. .... BUS
diagram .... TREE
famous ... ESTE, SOONG,
ROTHSCHILD, MEDICI,
KENNEDY
life .... FIRESIDE
meal .... POTLUCK
name .... SURNAME,
COGNOMEN, PATRONYMIC
next door .... NEIGHBOR
pertaining to ... LINEAGE,
FAMILIAL, DOMESTIC
tree .... PEDIGREE
famine .. STARVATION, HUNGER
famish .... STARVE
famous ..... NOTED, EMINENT,
CELEBRATED, NOTORIOUS,
RENOWNED
aunt .... MAME
friend .. DAMON, PYTHIAS
murderer .... CAIN,
BOOTH, ARAM, OSWALD
trio member ..... ATHOS,
ARAMIS, PORTHOS
fan ... COOL, FOMENT, VOTARY,
EXCITE, AFICIONADO, BLOW,
ROOTER, BUFF, ZEALOT,
DEVOTEE
form .... PLICATE

of leaves .... TALIPOT
oriental ..... PUNKA(H)
palm .... PALMETTO
Pope's ...... FLABELLUM
shaped ..... FLABELLATE
fanatic .... BIGOT, NUT,
ZEALOT, PHRENETIC,
PARTISAN, RABID, JINGO
murderous ...... THUG,
AMOK, BERSERK
fanatical .... RABID, RADICAL
fanaticism ...... ZEAL(OTRY)
fancied .... IMAGINED,
IMAGINARY
fear ... BUGABOO, BOG(E)Y
fancier, kind of ....
CONNOISSEUR, GOURMET,
GOURMAND
fanciful .... IMAGINATIVE,
WHIMSICAL, ODD,
IMAGINARY, QUAINT,
UNREAL
fancy ..... DREAM, DELUSION,
FAD, IDEA, MEGRIM,
ILLUSION, NOTION, WHIM,
VISION, WEEN, CAPRICE,
CHIMERA
dive ..... SWAN, GAINER,
ISANDER
foolish .... CHIMERA
fandango ... . DANCE
fane .... TEMPLE, SANCTUARY,
CHURCH, SHRINE
fanfare ... TANTARA, FLOURISH
fanfaron .... BRAGGART
fang .... CUSPID, CLAW,
TALON, TUSK, CANINE TOOTH
fanlight .... TRANSOM
Fannie ____, writer ... HURST
fanny: sl. .... BUTTOCKS
fanon ...... MANIPLE, ORALE,
VANE
fantail .... PIGEON, GOLDFISH
fantasia .... MEDLEY
fantast .. VISIONARY, DREAMER
fantastic ...... OUTLANDISH,
UNREAL, BIZARRE,
GROTESQUE, ODD,
ECCENTRIC
imitation ...... PARODY,
TRAVESTY
style ... OUTRE, BAROQUE,
ROCOCO
fantasy ..... DREAM, FANCY,
ILLUSION, CAPRICE,
PHANTASM

far .... REMOTE, DISTANT,
ADVANCED, AWAY
and near ... EVERYWHERE
and wide .... ABROAD
apart .... DISPARATE
combining form .... TELE
cry .... LONG WAY
down .... DEEP
go .... LAST LONG
off ..... DISTANT, REMOTE

farce .... COMEDY, SKIT,
TRAVESTY, MOCKERY,
PARODY, EXODE,
BURLESQUE, MIME

farceur ... JOKER, HUMORIST,
WAG, CLOWN

farcical .. FUNNY, LUDICROUS,
RIDICULOUS, ABSURD

farcy .... GLANDERS

fardel .... BURDEN, PACK,
BUNDLE

fare ..... FOOD, DIET, MENU,
PAY, RESULT, GET ON,
PASSENGER

farewell .... CONGE, VALE,
ADIOS, GOODBY, PARTING,
LAST, AVE, VALEDICTION
appearance .. SWANSONG
drink ..... STIRRUP CUP
French .... ADIEU
Hawaiian .... ALOHA
Japanese ..... SAYONARA
Latin .... AVE
Spanish .... ADIOS

farfetched .... FORCED,
STRAINED, REMOTE

farflung .... REMOTE

farina ... FLOUR, MEAL, STARCH

farinaceous .... STARCHY,
MEALY
drink .... PTISAN

farinose .... MEALY

farm .... TORP, GRANGE,
HACIENDA, CULTIVATE,
RANCH, BARTON, TILL
building .... BARN, SILO,
SHED
grazing .... RANCH(O)
implement .... HARROW,
FLAIL, PLOW
kind of ... DAIRY, OYSTER
machine .... REAPER,
CHURN, TRACTOR,
SCARIFIER, TEDDER
of a .... VILLATIC
small .... CROFT

Spanish ..... HACIENDA
Swedish .... TORP
tenant .... COTTER,
CROFTER
worked by renter .. CROFT
worker .... HIND,
CAMPESINO, ORRAMAN,
PLOWMAN
yard .... BARTON

farmer ..... PLANTER, RYOT,
SOWER, GRANGER, TILLER,
HUSBANDMAN, PEASANT,
CROPPER, HABITAN(T)
migrant .... OKIE
peasant .... CROFTER
Philippine ... MAGSASAKA
Russian .... KULAK
S. African ... BOER, WERF

farmhouse, land nearest ......
INFIELD

farming .... HUSBANDRY,
AGRICULTURE

farmyard .... BARTON

faro card .... SODA
form of .... MONTE

Faroes whirlwinds .... OES

farrago .... JUMBLE, MEDLEY,
MIXTURE

Farrar, soprano .. GERALDINE

farrier .... BLACKSMITH,
VETERINARY

farrow .... LITTER, PIG

farseeing .... PROVIDENT

farsighted ... HYPERMETROPIC

farsightedness ... HYPEROPIA

farther .... REMOTER
India .... INDO-CHINA

farthest .... ENDMOST,
ULTIMATE
back .... HINDMOST, REAR

fasces carrier .... LICTOR

fascia .... STRIP, BAND(AGE),
FILLET

fascicle .... CLUSTER

fascinate .... ALLURE,
CAPTIVATE, ENCHANT,
ATTRACT, CHARM, INTRIGUE,
BEWITCH

fascination .. CHARM, ALLURE,
ENCHANTMENT

Fascist .... NAZI, FALANGIST
leader ..... MUSSO(LINI),
FRANCO, HITLER, RAS
mayor .... PODESTA
organization in Spain ....
FALANGE

theoretician ..... PARETO
fash: Scot. ..... VEX, ANNOY, TROUBLE
fashion ... RAGE, VOGUE, CUT, FAD, STYLE, CRAZE, KIND, SORT, MODE, MANNER, MOLD, SHAPE, DESIGN
designer .. SCHIAPARELLI, ST. LAURENT, GIVENCHY, BALENCIAGA, NORELL, BALMAIN, DIOR, MAINBOCHER, GALITZINE, GERNREICH
figure .... MODEL, MODISTE, DESIGNER, TAILOR, CUTTER
model .... TWIGGY
news .... HEMLINE, NECKLINE, MINI, MAXI
plate .. BEAU(BRUMMELL), DANDY, DUDE
fashionable ... RITZY, TONEY, NEW, SMART, SLEEK, CHIC, STYLISH, POSH, ALAMODE, KNOBBY
gathering ...... SALON
society .... BONTON
Fashoda, Sudan town .. KODOK
fast .... APACE, FIRM, RAMADAN, SECURE, TANTIVY, PRESTO, DEVOTED, FIRM, SPEEDY, SWIFT, RAPID, FLEET, HASTY, QUICK
combining form .. TACHY
fasten .... TETHER, ROPE, ATTACH, CONNECT, FIX, TIE, BATTEN, RIVET, LASH
boat .... BERTH
firmly ...... RIVET, NAIL, SECURE, CHAIN, INFIX
nautical .. BATTEN, BELAY
fastener ... PEG, CLAMP, SNAP, STRAP, PIN, HASP, CLASP, STAPLE, CLEAT, CLIP, BITT
slide .... ZIPPER
wire .... STAPLE
wood .... PEG, NOG, PIN
fastening .... BOLT, LOCK, BUTTON, HOOK, CLASP, LATCH, TACH(E)
fastidious .... PRECISE, CRITICAL, NICE, QUEASY, REFINED, DAINTY, FINICAL, FINICKY, FUSSY, PER(S)NICKETY

fastigiate .... CONELIKE
fasting period .... LENT, RAMADAN, RAMAZAN
fastness .... STRONGHOLD
fat ...... OILY, PORTLY, SUET, ESTER, STOUT, PORKY, PUDGY, DUMPY, PUFFY, OBESE, PINGUID, GROSS, PURSY, FLESHY, PLUMP, CORPULENT, THICK, TALLOW
and squat .... FUBSY
animal .... ADIPOSE, GREASE, TALLOW, LARD, ALEPS
beef .... SUET
chance: sl. .... HOPELESS
chew the ..... CHAT, GAB
combining form .... STEAT(O)
decomposition of .... LIPOLYSIS
hog .... LARD
in butter .... OLEO
like .... LIPAROID, LIPOID, LIPIDE, UNGUINOUS, STEARIC
liquid part .... OLEIN
lot .... NOTHING
of .... UNGUINOUS, STEARIC, ADIPIC
refuse .... SLUSH
roasting meat .. DRIPPING
solid part of .. STEARIN(E)
Tuesday ... MARDI GRAS
wool ... SUINT, LANOLIN
yielding tree .... SHEA
Fata Morgana .... MIRAGE, FAIRY
fatal .... VITAL, FUNEST, FATEFUL, LETHAL, RUINOUS, DEADLY, MORTAL, FERAL
fatality .... DEATH, DEADLINESS, CASUALTY
fate .... DOOM, DESTINY, KISMET, LOT
Buddhism/Hinduism .... KARMA
mythological .. ATROPOS, CLOTHO, LACHESIS, PARCA
twist of .... IRONY
fated .... DOOMED, FEY, ORDAINED, DESTINED
fateful .... PROPHETIC, DECISIVE, OMINOUS, DIRE

Fates, one of the ..... PARCA, CLOTHO, ATROPOS, LACHESIS, NONA, MORTA, DECUMA

  whichever one ... WEIRD

fathead ...... DUNCE, IDIOT, STUPID

fatheaded .... DULL, OBTUSE, STUPID

father ..... SIRE, PAPA, ABBA, PARENT, PROTECTOR, ANCESTOR, FOREBEAR, CREATOR, BEGET, PRIEST, PATER

  Arabic ...... ABU, ABOU

  brother of .... UNCLE

  colloquial ..... OLDMAN, DAD, PA, POP, PAPPY

  combining form .. PATRO, PATRI

  dialectic .... PAW

  disciples' .... ZEBEDEE

  French .... PERE

  Hebrew .... ABBA

  of all .... JUBAL

  of American football .... CAMP

  of gods .... ZEUS

  of History ... HERODOTUS

  of Medicine .... HIPPOCRATES

  of Waters .... MISSISSIPPI

  pertaining to a .. AGNATE, PATERNAL

  relative on side of .... AGNATE

  Spanish ... PADRE, PAPA

  superior .... ABBOT

fatherhood ...... PATERNITY

fatherless .... ORBATE

fathom ...... DELVE, PROBE, PLUMB, SOUND

  one fourth of .. QUARTER

fatigue ... WEARY, FAG, JADE, WEARINESS, EXHAUST, TIRE, BORE

  clothes .... DENIM

Fatima descendant .. SAY(Y)ID

  descended from .... FATIMID, FATIMITE

  father of ..... MOHAMMED

  husband of ... BLUEBEARD

  sister ..... ANNE, JINNAH

  step-brother .... ALI

fatling ..... CALF, LAMB, KID, PIG

fats, solvent for ...... ETHER

fatten .... BATTEN, ENRICH

  land .... FERTILIZE

fatty .... GREASY, OILY, ADIPOSE, LIPAROID, ALIPHATIC

  acid ... ADIPIC, VALERIC

  combining form .. LIP(O)

  comedian ..... ARBUCKLE

  secretion of gland .... SEBUM

  substance from sheep's wool .... SUINT

  tumor .... LIPOMA

fatuity ...... FOLLY, IDIOCY, STUPIDITY, IMBECILITY

fatuous ..... SAPPY, IDIOTIC, SILLY, FOOLISH, INANE, ASININE

faubourg .... SUBURB

fauces ..... GULLET, THROAT

faucet .... BIBB, TAP, (BIB)COCK SPIGOT, PETCOCK, STOPCOCK

fault .... CAVIL, LAPSE, MISTAKE, WEAKNESS, LACK, FLAW, FAILING, DEFECT, ERROR, MISDEED, IMPERFECTION

  amusing .... FOIBLE

  antonym of ..... VIRTUE

  find ..... CARP, CENSURE, COMPLAIN, NAG, CAVIL

  finder .... NAG(GER), CENSOR, SCOLD(ER), CRITIC, KNOCKER

  finding .... CRITICAL, CAPTIOUS, CARPING, QUERULOUS

  moral .... VICE

  slight .... PECCADILLO

faultfinder .... KNOCKER, NAG(GER), CRITIC, MOMUS

faultless ..... IDEAL, PERFECT, MODEL, PARAGON, IMPECCABLE

faulty .... PECCANT

faun .... SATYR, DEITY

Fauntleroy .... CEDRIC, ERROL

  mother of ..... DEAREST

Faunus .... PAN

  son .... ACIS

Faure, essayist .... ELIE

"Faust," composer of .... GOUNOD

  poem, writer of .. GOETHE

fauteuil .... ARMCHAIR

faux pas ..... ERROR, MISSTEP,
SOCIAL BLUNDER, GAFFE,
BONER, SLIP

faveolate .... CELLED,
HONEYCOMBED, ALVEOLATE

favonian .... GENTLE

favor ..... LETTER, RESEMBLE,
LIKING, LEAVE, GRACE,
LEAN, HELP, NOTE, BOON

favorable .... AUSPICIOUS,
PRO, PROPITIOUS

in astrology ...... TRINE

most .... OPTIMUM

opinion .... ESTEEM

favored ... TALENTED, GIFTED

favoring .... PRO, FOR

favorite .... PET, PREFERRED,
MINION, DEAR

activity .... HOBBY

activity: Brit. ....
CUP OF TEA

son .... BENJAMIN

favoritism .... NEPOTISM

favors from public office .. PAP

fawn ...... CRINGE, FLATTER,
DEER, GROVEL, DOE

fawning .... SERVILE

fay .. ELF, JOIN, FAIRY, SPRITE

archaic .... FAITH

faze .... ANNOY, DAUNT,
DISTURB, AGITATE, WORRY,
DISCONCERT, EMBARRASS

FBI director, former .. HOOVER

FDR's burial place ....
HYDE PARK

fe .... IRON

fealty ... LOYALTY, FIDELITY,
ALLEGIANCE, DUTY

fear .... AWE, PANIC,
MISGIVING, FRIGHT,
APPREHENSION, DISMAY,
PHOBIA

excessive .... PHOBIA

frantic, unreasoning .....
PANIC

from sudden danger .....
ALARM

intensely .... DREAD

of animals .. ZOOPHOBIA

of becoming insane .....
LYSSOPHOBIA

of being alone ....
MONOPHOBIA

of being poisoned ....
TOXIPHOBIA

of fire ..... PYROPHOBIA

of food ..... SITOPHOBIA

of heights .. ACROPHOBIA

of lightning .. TROPHOBIA

of pain .... ALGOPHOBIA

of law .... METUS

of strangers .. XENOPHOBIA

overwhelming .. TERROR

sudden, shocking ......
FRIGHT, CHILL

fearful .... NERVOUS, DIRE,
AFRAID, TERRIFYING,
TREPID, PAVID

fearless .... BRAVE, BOLD,
DARING, HEROIC, IMPAVID,
INTREPID

fearsome .... DREADFUL,
FRIGHTFUL, TIMID,
TIMOROUS

one .... OGRE

feasible ... POSSIBLE, LIKELY,
PRACTICABLE

feast .... FESTIVAL,
BANQUET, REGALE, FETE

after harvest .... FOY

day: comb. form ... MAS

describing one ....
LUCULLAN

for departing person ....
FOY

Hawaiian .... LUAU

list .... ORDO

of Lots .... PURIM

of the Nativity .... YULE

outdoor .... PICNIC

feastless day .... FERIA

feat ..... DEED, EXPLOIT, ACT,
STUNT, ACCOMPLISHMENT

feather .... PENNA, PINNA,
PLUMAGE, PLUME, QUILL,
PINION, DOWN

arrow ... FLETCH, FLEDGE

barb .... HARL, HERL

cloak .... MAMO

combining form .. PENNI

fine .... EGRET

grass .... STIPA

helmet .... PANACHE

like .... PINNATE,
PLUMOSE, PENNIFORM

neckwear .... BOA

part of ..... VANE, WEB

prefix .... PTERO

quill .... BARREL,
CALAMUS

resembling a .. PINNATE, PLUMATE
shaft .... SCAPE
shed: archaic ..... MEW, MOLT
small .... PLUMULE, PLUMELET
submarine's ...... WAKE
under wing ..... AXILIAR
vane of .... VEXILLUM
wing .... PINION
featherbed .... MATTRESS
featherbrained .... IDIOT, FOOLISH, SIMPLE, SILLY, FRIVOLOUS
feathered .... PENNATED, PLUMOSE, PLUMY, FLEDGED, PLUMED, WINGED
neckpiece ... . BOA
featherer of arrows .. PLUMIER
featherless .... CALLOW
feathers .... DOWN, PLUMAGE
adorn with ... (IM)PLUME
bunch of .... TUFT
bird's wing ..... ALULA, COVERTS
for flying ...... REMIGES
grow .... FLEDGE
plume of ..... PANACHE
pull out the ... DEPLUME, PLUCK
quill ... CALAMI, BARRELS, COVERTS
smooth the ...... PLUME
soft ...... DOWN, EIDER
tail .... RECTRIX
trim the .... PREEN
featherweight .... LIGHT, TRIVIAL, NONENTITY, BOXER, WRESTLER
feathery .... DOWNY, FLUFFY
feature .... PART, CHARACTERISTIC, TRAIT, MOTIF, FORM
double .... CHIN
salient ...... HIGHLIGHT, MOTIF
feaze .... UNRAVEL, FAZE, FEEZE
febrile .... FEVERISH
feces ..... DREGS, SEDIMENT, EGESTA
feckless ..... WEAK, CARELESS
feculence ...... FILTH, DREGS
feculent .... FILTHY, FOUL
fecund ... FERTILE, FRUITFUL,

PROLIFIC, PRODUCTIVE
fecundate .... POLLINATE
fecundity .... FERTILITY
fed up: sl. .... BORED, DISGUSTED, SURFEITED
fedayeen leader .... HABASH, ARAFAT
federate .... UNITE
federation .... ALLIANCE, LEAGUE, UNION
fedora .... HAT
author of play ... SARDOU
fee ...... FIEF, HONORARIUM, TIP, AGIO, DUES, TOLL, CHARGE, GRATUITY, FEOD
for settling accounts .....
EXCHANGE
hold in ... OWN, POSSESS
lawyer's ...... RETAINER
feeble .... DOTTY, PUNY, WASHY, WEAK, FRAIL, FLABBY, FLACCID, RICKETY
minded .... DOTTY
mindedness ... AMENTIA
minded person ....
IMBECILE, IDIOT, MORON, DOTARD, AMENT, HALF-WIT, DOLT, FOOL
feed .... OATS, EAT, NOURISH, SUBSIST, PROVIDE, BROWSE, COSHER
animal .... FORAGE, FODDER
breast .... NURSE
cattle .... AGIST
colloquial ... MEAL, CHOW
fuel to .... STOKE
well at other's expense ...
BATTEN
feeder .... TRIBUTARY, SUBSIDIARY
of furnace ...... STOKER
of lines .... STOOGE, STRAIGHTMAN
feeding box .... TROUGH, MANGER
feel ..... PALP, SENSE, SUFFER, TOUCH
ability to ... (A)ESTHESIA
able to .... PASSIBLE, SENSIBLE
about .... GROPE
absence .... MISS
like .... INCLINED
out .... SOUND
regret ..... RUE, REPENT

feeler .... TENTACLE,
PALP(US), RADUEL,
ANTENNA, SMELLER
   kind of .... TRIAL
BALLOON, CIRRUS
   small .... ANTENNULE
feelers, having .... LONGICORN
feeling .... SENSITIVITY,
SENSATION, AWARENESS,
EMOTION, PITY, OPINION,
PREMONITION, PASSION,
SENTIMENT, SENTIENCE
   affect the .... MOVE
   capable of .... SENTIENT
   impatient .... RESTIVE
   of illbeing .... DYSPHORIA
   of regret ..... REMORSE,
REPENTANCE
   of weariness ..... ENNUI,
LASSITUDE
   of wellbeing ... EUPHORIA
   show .... EMOTE, REACT
   strong .... HEAT
   sudden, violent .. SPASM
   turn of .... CAPRICE,
WHIM
feet, care of .... PODIATRY
   combining form .. PED(E),
PED(I)
   having .... PEDATE
   having many ....
MULTIPED(E)
   having three .. TRIPEDAL,
TRIPODIC, TRIPODAL
   of two syllables ... IAMBI
   pertaining to the .. PODAL,
PEDARY, PEDAL
   pig's .... PETTITOES
   slang .... DOGS
   three .... YARD
   verse of two .... DIPODY
   without .... APOD
feeze ..... DISTURB, AGITATE,
DRIVE, DISCONCERT
feign .... FAKE, DISSEMBLE,
INVENT, FABRICATE,
PRETEND, SIMULATE, ACT,
ASSUME
   sickness ...... MALINGER
feigned .... FICTIVE, SIMULAR
feint ...... BLIND, DIVERSION,
SHAM, PRETENSE
   in fencing .... APPEL
feldspar .... ANORTHITE,
ALBITE, ADULARIA,
MOONSTONE, KAOLIN,

ODINITE, SILICATE,
LABRADORITE
felicitate .... BLESS,
CONGRATULATE
felicitous .... APPROPRIATE
felicity .... BLISS, HAPPINESS
felid .... CAT, FELINE
feline .... OUNCE, TIGER,
CRAFTY, SLY, JAGUAR,
PUSS, CAT(LIKE), LEOPARD,
LION, PUMA, PANTHER,
LYNX
fell ...... TERRIBLE, CRUEL,
CUTDOWN, FIERCE, PELT
   archaic .... DEADLY
   British ..... HILL, MOOR,
DOWN
   of animal ... SKIN, HIDE,
PELT
fellah: Egyptian ... PEASANT,
LABORER
feller: sl. .... FELLOW
felling .... HAG
fellow (see person/man) ......
CHAP, EGG, PARTNER,
ASSOCIATE, PEER, MATE,
BUGGER, SIRRAH, BLOKE,
CORYDON, JACK,
TRUMP
   archaic .... SIRRAH
   big, clumsy ...... LOOBY
   British: colloq. ... CULLY
   brutish .... YAHOO
   clumsy ... LOUT, LOOBY,
OAF
   colloquial .... MAN, BOY,
BEAU, SUITOR, GUY
   conceited ..... COXCOMB
   contemptible ...... CAD,
SCAB, BLOKE, SCOUNDREL
   countryman ....
COMPATRIOT
   feeling .... SYMPATHY
   fine .... TRUMP
   flashy .... SPORT
   little .... BUB
   member ...... CONFRERE,
ASSOCIATE, COLLEAGUE
   nicknamed Hi ... HIRAM
   queer ... GEEZER, CODGER
   Scottish .... WAT,
CALLAN(T)
   slang ..... FELLER, BOZO,
GUY, HOMBRE, GINK
   stupid ..... LUG, LOOBY,

OAF, GANDER, CLOD,
LOGGERHEAD

traveler ... SYMPATHIZER

unprincipled ....
SCAPEGRACE

worthless ... CAD, SCAMP,
ROGUE, RASCAL

young .. CHAP, BLADE,
CALLAN(T), SPRIG

fellowship .... SODALITY,
BROTHERHOOD, COMPANY,
ENDOWMENT

felly .... CRUELLY,
WHEEL RIM, DEADLY

felo-de-se .... SUICIDE

felon .... VILLAIN, CRIMINAL,
BASE, WICKED, CON,
WHITLOW

felonious .... BASE, CRIMINAL

felony ...... CRIME, MURDER,
ARSON, RAPE

felt .... SENSED, FABRIC

obliged ..... COMPELLED,
HAD TO

felucca .... SHIP

felwort ... GENTIAN, MULLEIN

female ..... GIRL, FEMININE,
WOMAN(LY)

animal ..... JENNY, SOW,
JILL, BITCH, DAM, COW,
SHE, VIXEN

animal's teat .... DUG

buffalo .... ARNEE

camel .... NAGA

cat .... TABBY

change of life ....
MENOPAUSE, CLIMATERIC

combining form ....GYNE

deer .... DOE, ROE, HIND

demon .... HAG

dog .... BITCH, SLUT

donkey .... JENNET

elephant .... COW

ferret .... JILL

figure, sculptured ....
ORANT, CARYATID

fox .... VIXEN

gossip .... TABBY

insect .... GYNE

kangaroo .... GIN

mythical .... FURY

pig .... SOW, GILT

praying figure ... ORANT

prophet .... SEERESS,
CASSANDRA

rabbit .... DOE

reproductive organ ......
OVARY

ruff .... REEVE, REE

sandpiper .... REE

servant ... MAID, WENCH

sex .... DISTAFF

sex hormone ... ESTRIOL,
ESTRONE

sheep .... EWE

slave ..... ODALISK, DASI

sovereign .... QUEEN,
EMPRESS

warrior .... AMAZON

wolf .... BITCH

feme .... WIFE

sole ... SPINSTER, WIDOW

feminine .... PETTICOAT,
FEMALE, WOMANLY,
EFFEMINATE

suffix ...... ETTE, STRESS,
INE, ESS, TRIX

femininity ...... MULIEBRITY

femme .... WOMAN, WIFE

fatale ... LORELEI, SIREN,
MATA HARI, DELILAH

femur .... THIGH(BONE)

fen ... MORASS, MOOR, MARSH,
SWAMP, BOG

fence .... PALE, BARRIER,
PARRY, EVADE, PALISADE,
RAIL(ING), ENCLOSE,
DEFENSE, SWORDPLAY,
RADDLE

construction site ....
HOARDING

crossing .... STILE

material ... TITE, PICKET,
PALE

of shrubs .... HEDGE

of stakes ...... PALISADE

of woven work .. WATTLE,
RADDLE

part .... PALING,
BARBED WIRE

stake ...... PALE, PICKET

step .... STILE

sunken .... (H)AHA

temporary ..... HURDLE,
HOARDING

to .... SCRIME

fenced enclosure for cattle/
sheep .... KRAAL

grounds ..... CURTILAGE

fencer .... SWORDSMAN

cry of .... SASA, HAI,
ON GUARD

opening position ....
EN GARDE
fencing attack ...... REPRISE
breastplate ... PLASTROM
dummy for .... PEL
foil guard ...... BUTTON
leap .... VOLT
mask .... HELMET
movement .... APPEL
point .... FOIL
position .... CARTE,
TIERCE, SECONDE,
SEPTIME, SIXTE,
QUARTE, QUINTE
score .... PUNTO
stroke ..... BUTT, APPEL,
LUNGE, RIPOSTE
sword ..... EPEE, RAPIER,
FOIL
term .... TIERCE,
EN GARDE, TOUCHE,
SECONDE
thrust .... REPRISE, BUTT,
REMISE, LUNGE,
RIPOSTE PUNTO
fend .... AVERT, WARD, SHIFT,
RESIST, PARRY
off ...... REPEL, REPULSE
fender .... MUDGUARD,
COWCATCHER
fenestra .. WINDOW, OPENING
fennec .... FOX
fennel .... ANISE, HERB
fenny .... BOGGY
feod .... FEE, FIEF
feracious .... FRUITFUL
feral .... DEADLY, FERINE,
UNTAMED, WILD, SAVAGE,
BRUTAL, FATAL
Ferber (Edna) heroine ....
SELINA
novel .... SO BIG
Ferde, composer ...... GROPE
fer de lance .... SNAKE
Ferdinand .... BULL, TORO
fere ...... COMPANION, MATE,
PEER, WIFE, HUSBAND
feretory .... SHRINE, BIER
feria .... FESTIVAL, HOLIDAYS
ferine .... FERAL, WILD
fermata .... PAUSE, HOLD
ferment ... FRET, SACCHARIZE,
YEAST, LEAVEN, BREW,
BACTERIA, (EN)ZYME,
AGITATION, UNREST,
COMMOTION, SEETHE

fermented drink ... ALE, BEER,
MEAD, SAKE, WINE, KUMISS
fermentation .... ZYMOSIS
chemistry of ... ZYMURGY
fermenting agent ..... YEAST,
ENZYME, LEAVEN
fern .... WOODSIA, BRACKEN,
MULEWORT, BRAKE,
MAIDENHAIR, MOONWORT
coarse .... BRAKE
edible .... TARA
filaments .... RHIZOID
flowering ...... OSMUND
leaf .... FROND
like plant ...... ACROGEN
patches .... SORI
perennial stemmed ......
ACROGEN
petiole .... STIPE
rootstock .... ROI
seed .... SPORE
spore .... SORUS
ferocious .... SAVAGE, FERAL,
BEASTLY, FIERCE, WILD
Ferrer, actor .... JOSE
ferret ...... WEASEL, SEARCH,
INVESTIGATE
female .... JILL
like animal ...... TAYRA,
MONGOOS(E)
ferric oxide, anhydrous ......
HEMATITE
powder .... ROUGE
ferrotype .... TINTYPE
ferrous sulfate .... COPPERAS
ferrule ... TIP, RING, BUSHING
ferrum .... IRON
ferry ...... PONT, TRANSPORT,
CROSS
ferryboat ...... BAC, TENDER,
PONT
ferryman .... CHARON
fertile ... PINGUID, FRUITFUL,
FECUND, RANK, FAT,
PROLIFIC, PRODUCTIVE
area .... OASIS
become .... BATTEN
land's surface ... TOPSOIL
fertilize .... ENRICH,
POLLINATE, FRUCTIFY
fertilizer ... COMPOST, MARL,
MANURE, AMMONITE,
GUANO, ALINIT
ferule ...... STICK, TIP, ROD,
RULER, HERB, SCEPTER
fervency ...... ARDOR, ZEAL

fervent .... HOT, EARNEST, ARDENT, PASSIONATE, GLOWING

fervid .... FIERY, HOT, BURNING, FERVENT, IMPASSIONED, INTENSE

fervor ... ZEST, ARDOR, ZEAL, PASSION

Fescennine .... OBSCENE, VULGAR

fescue .. GRASS, STICK, STRAW

festal .... GALA, JOYOUS, GAY

fester .... RANKLE, PUSTULE, ULCERATE, ABSCESS, SUPPURATE, DECAY, EMBITTER

festering condition .... ULCER

festival .... FAIR, ALE, FIESTA, FEAST, FERIA, FETE, GALA, CARNIVAL, CELEBRATION, MERRYMAKING

Apollo .... DELIA

Dutch .... KERMIS

Greek ...... DELIA, AGON

New Orleans .... MARDI GRAS

paper shower .. CONFETTI

religious .... FIESTA

festive .... GAY, MERRY, JOYOUS, JOVIAL

festivity .... JOY, PARTY, MIRTH, GAIETY, REVELRY

festoon ... GARLAND, WREATH, LEI

feta .... CHEESE

fetation .... PREGNANCY

fetch ... GET, RETRIEVE, BRING, PRODUCE, ELICIT, INFER, WRAITH, CHARM, SELL FOR

fetching .... ATTRACTIVE, CHARMING

fete .... ENTERTAIN(MENT), FESTIVAL

feterita .... SORGHUM

fetial .... PRIESTS

fetid .... OLID, RANCID, STINKING, ODOROUS, RANK, FOUL, PUTRID

fetiparous animal .... MARSUPIAL, KANGAROO, BANDICOOT, OPOSSUM, WOMBAT

fetish .... JUJU, AMULET, TALISMAN, WEAKNESS, CHARM, ANITO, VOODOO, OBEAH, GRIGRI, TOTEM

fetlock .... TUFT

fetor .... STENCH, STINK

fetter ... CHAIN, BOND, IRON, GYVE, SHACKLE, HAMPER, HOBBLE, MANACLE, HANDCUFF

fettle .... TRIM, STATE, CONDITION

fetus, hair of ...... LANUGO

malformed ... TERATISM

membrane .... CHORION, CAUL

premature birth of ...... MISCARRIAGE

feu .... FEE

feud ... QUARREL, VENDETTA, FEE, FIEF, FEOD, STRIFE

feudal .... FEOD

baron .... THANE

benefice .... FIEF, FEU

estate .... FEU, FIEF

estate head .... LORD

jurisdiction ... SOC, SOKE

land .... BENEFICE, FEOD

lord .... SEIGNEUR

retainers .... MEINIE, MEINY

service .... AVERA

slave .... SERF

tax .... TALLAGE, TAIL(L)AGE

tenant .... SOCAGER, VASSAL, COTTER

tenant's payment .... HERIOT

title .... BARON, EARL

feudatory ...... FIEF, VASSAL

fever .... AGUE, PYREXIA, CAUMA, BRUCELLOSIS, HEAT

blister ..... COLD (SORE), HERPES

causing .... PYRETIC

characterized by ...... FEBRILE

chill .... ALGOR, AGUE

intermittent ..... OCTAN, QUARTAN, TERTIAN

kind of .... DENGUE, MALARIA, DANDY, BREAKBONE, TROPICAL, JUNGLE, YELLOWJACK, TERTIAN, QUINTAN, QUARTAN

pertaining to ... PYRETIC

recurring .... QUOTIDIAN

reducer .... FEBRIFUGE, ANTIPYRETIC, PIPERINE
sore .... HERPES
tropical ...... CALENTURE, DENGUE
undulant .... MALTA
fevered .... HECTIC
feverish ...... FEBRILE, PYRETIC, HECTIC
few .... CURN
and far between ... SPARSE
the .... MINORITY
fewer .... LESS
fewest .... LEAST
fey .... FATED, DOOMED
fez-like cap .... TURBAN, TARBOOSH
wearer .... SHRINER, EGYPTIAN
fiacre ...... CARRIAGE, CAB
fiance .... BETROTHED
fiasco ...... FAILURE, WASHOUT, FIZZLE, TURKEY
fiat .... SANCTION, DECREE, ORDER
fib .... LIE
fibber .... LIAR
fiber .... NATURE, QUALITY, FILAMENT, FUNICLE, DATIL
bark .... TAPA
century plant .... PITA, AGAVE
cleaning tool .... HATCHEL
coconut .... COIR
combing .... CARDING
cordage .... HEMP, ABACA, MAGUEY, SISAL, IMBE, PIÑA, FILASSE, AMBARY, AMBARI, RAFFIA, SUNN
East Indies plant ... RAMIE
knot .... NEP
palm .... ERUC
phloegm .... BAST
plant ...... COTTON, ISTLE, FLAX, IXLE, MAGUEY, ALOE, RAMIE, SISAL, HEMP, ABACA, AMBARY
roll of .... SLUB
small .... FIBRIL
strand .... YARN
synthetic .... DACRON, ORLON
tree .... BASS, BAST, BAOBAB
waste .... NOIL, FLOSS

wool .... STAPLE, PILE
woven fabric ... MAT(TING)
fibers, fine .... FUZZ
to clean .... SCUTCH
twist .... ROVE
fibril .... FILAMENT, ROOT HAIR
fibrin .... GLUTEN
fibrous texture ...... DESMOID
fibula .... PIN, CLASP, BUCKLE, BONE
of the .... PERONEAL
fichu .... CAPE, LACE
fickle .... VOLATILE, FLIGHTY, GIDDY, MOONISH, INCONSTANT, CAPRICIOUS, CHANGEABLE
girl ...... FLIRT, COQUETTE
fico .... TRIFLE, SNAP, FIG
fictile .... PLASTIC, CERAMIC
fiction ...... TALE, YARN, NOVEL
kingdom of .... OZ
fictitious .... FALSE, FABULOUS, MYTHICAL, ASSUMED, IMAGINARY, UNREAL
name .... ALIAS, JOHN DOE
story .... PIGMENT
fictive .... SHAM, FEIGNED, IMAGINARY
fid .... BAR, PIN
fiddle .... VIOLIN, KIT, VIOL, FIDGET, GIGA
bow of .... ARCO
faddle .... FUSS, NONSENSE
fit as a .... HALE
fiddledeedee .... NONSENSE
fiddler .... VIOLINIST
crab .... UCA
fiddlestick .... TRIFLE
fiddlesticks .... NONSENSE
fiddling .... PETTY, USELESS, TRIFLING
"Fidelio" character .... LENORE, FLORESTAN
fidelity ...... LOYALTY, FEALTY, FAITHFULNESS, DEVOTION, ALLEGIANCE
fidget ...... FRET, FIDDLE, JITTER
fidgety .... RESTIVE, UNEASY, NERVOUS, RESTLESS
fie .... SHAME
fief .... FEE, FEUD, FEOD, BENEFICE
give or sell .... FEOFF
holder .... FEOFFEE

person granting ....
FEOFFER, FEOFFOR

field .... ACRE, GLEBE,
PLAIN, SAVANNA
border .... RAND
combat .... ARENA
enclosed ... AGER, CROFT
glacial ...... NEVE, FIRN
glass .... BINOCLE
grassy ..... LEA, PASTURE
hospital ..... AMBULANCE
mouse .... VOLE
of honor ....
BATTLEGROUND
of work .... METIER,
CAREER, LINE
officer .. COLONEL, MAJOR
open .... CAMPUS
tent .... MARQUEE
unplowed strip ... RAND
fieldfare .... THRUSH
fiend ..... SHAITAN, SHEITAN,
DEMON, DEVIL, ADDICT,
SATAN
fiendish .... HELLISH,
DEMONIC, CRUEL, WICKED,
DEVILISH
fierce .... WILD, SAVAGE,
VIOLENT, INTENSE, LUPINE,
FEROCIOUS
fiery ..ARDENT, INFLAMMABLE,
HOT, IGNEOUS, SPIRITED,
EXCITABLE, GLARING, RED,
SULTRY
fiesta ... GALA, FETE, FESTIVAL,
FERIA, HOLIDAY,
CELEBRATION
fife .... FLUTE
Fifth Avenue jewelry shop ....
CARTIER
columnist ....
COLLABORATOR,
QUISLING
finger ..... PINKY, PINKIE
fiftieth anniversary .. JUBILEE
fifty-fifty ...... EQUAL, EVEN
fig ...... TRIFLING, BIT, FICO,
DRESS, SHAPE, RETUND,
SYCONIUM, ELEME
basket .... CABAS
don't care a ....
INDIFFERENT
dried .... CARICA
Italian .... FICO
like .... CARICOUS
marigold .... SAMH

parrot .... LORILET
Smyrna ... ELEME, ELEMI
tree .... UPAS, PIPAL,
BO TREE
figeater ... BEETLE, JUNE BUG
fight .... ROW, SCRAP, STRIFE,
FRAY, TUSSLE, WARFARE,
CONTEST, QUARREL,
STRUGGLE, CONTEND,
OPPOSE, COMBAT, CONFLICT,
BATTLE, BRUSH, MELEE,
RUN-IN
close quarters ....
HAND TO HAND
colloquial .... MIX-UP
desire to .... ANIMUS
fond of .... SCRAPPY
free-for-all ...... MELEE,
RIOT, RUMBLE
program .... CARD
with feet and fists ....
SAVATE
fighter .... PUGILIST
frenzied .... AMOK,
AMUCK, BARESARK
kind of ...... AIRPLANE
Fighting Bob, soubriquet .....
EVANS
chance of a sort ... ODDS
policy ...... MILITANCY
figment of the mind .. FANTASM,
PHANTASM(A)
figuline .... STATUE, CLAY,
POTTERY, PORCELAIN
figurant ... (BALLET)DANCER,
SUPERNUMERARY, EXTRA
figuration .... ADORNING,
SHAPING, FORM(ING),
APPEARANCE
figurative .... ALLEGORIC(AL),
SYMBOLIC, METAPHORICAL
language ...... IMAGERY,
TROPE
not .... LITERAL
figure ... SYMBOL, DIGIT, FORM,
DIAGRAM, PICTURE,
RECKON, IMAGINE,
COMPUTE, SOLID
architectural .. CARYATID,
TELAMON
carved .... GLYPHIC
crescent shaped ... LUNE,
LUNULA
8-sided .... OCTAGON,
OCTANGLE
equal-angled .... ISOGON

4-sided ...... TETRAGON,
QUADRANGLE, SQUARE
of speech .... TROPE,
SIMILE, LITOTES,
HYPERBOLE,
HENDIADYS, ZEUGMA,
OXYMORON, METAPHOR,
METONYMY, IMAGERY
on ...... RELY, DEPEND
ornamental ..... DEVICE
out ... SOLVE, COMPUTE,
UNDERSTAND, REASON,
DOPE
oval .... ELLIPSE
part of human ..... BUST,
TORSO, TRUNK
10-sided ... DECAGON(AL)
up .... ADD, TOTAL,
COMPUTE
used as support ... ATLAS,
TELEMON, CARYATID,
ATLANTES
figurehead .... DUMMY
figures .... DATA, STATISTICS,
ADDS UP
figurine .... STATUETTE,
TANAGRA
well-known ..... OSCAR,
EMMY
figurines, Gr. town known for ..
TANAGRA
figwort .... MULLE(I)N,
FOXGLOVE, SNAPDRAGON
Fiji island .... VITI
capital .... SUVA
chestnut .... RATA
dependency .... ROTUMA
tree .... BURI
filament ...... STRAND, HERL,
HAIR, THREAD, FIBER,
FILUM, HARL(E)
spun .... YARN
filature .... REEL
filbert .... HAZEL(NUT)
filch .... NIM, PURLOIN,
PILFER, STEAL, ROB
file ...... DOSSIER, ROW, RASP,
CARLET, ENTER, RECORD,
CABINET, FOLDER
flat .... QUANNET
rough .... RASP
filet .... NET, LACE
filial duty ...... HONOR, OBEY
filibeg .... KILT
filibuster .... FREEBOOTER,
ADVENTURER, MERCENARY

filigree .... LACE
filings .... SCRAPINGS
Filipino (see Philippines) ....
MORO, TAGALOG
aborigine ...... NEGRITO
boat .... BATEL
canoe .... BANCA
canoe, big .... CASCO
child .... BATA
food staple .... RICE
knife .... BOLO, ITAK
language .... TAGALOG,
ENGLISH, SPANISH
Muslim leader .... DATO,
DATU, HADJI
native ... MORO, NEGRITO,
IGOROT, ATA, IFUGAO,
ITA
nursemaid .... YAYA
peasant ... TAO, KASAMA
sailboat .... KUMPIT
soldier .... KAWAL
fill .... PAD, STUFF, SATE,
OCCUPY, PLUG, SUPPLY,
PERVADE, LOAD
in .... SUBSTITUTE, BRIEF
to excess .... HEAP,
CONGEST
with hate ..... EMBITTER,
ENVENOM
with wrath ..... INCENSE
fille ... GIRL, MAID, SPINSTER,
DAUGHTER
de joie ..... PROSTITUTE
filled gold .... BRASS
to capacity ...... SATED,
CHOCKFUL
filler .... SHIM, STUFFING
fillet .... RIBBON, BONE, BAND,
STRIP, FACIA, LABEL,
T(A)ENIA
architectural .. ORLE, ORLO
hair ...... SNOOD, BAND
narrow .... ANADEM,
ORIE, STRIA
filling .... WOOF
dentist's ...... AMALGAM,
GOLD
material .... PUTTY
fillip .... EXCITE, TAP, TONIC,
STIMULUS, SNAP
fillister .... GROOVE
filly .... FOAL, MARE
colloquial .... GIRL,
WOMAN
film .... COATING, MOVIE,

PHOTOGRAPH, NEGATIVE, SHOOT
green .... PATINA
part .... REEL
filmy .... GAUZY, HAZY, BLURRED
cloth .... GOSSAMER
filose .... THREADLIKE, FILAMENTOUS
fils .... SON, YOUTH
English equivalent ...... JUNIOR
filter ...... PERCOLATE, SIEVE, SIFT, COLATURE, OOZE, STRAIN, FILTRATE
screen .... RESEAU
substance ... SAND, FELT, CHARCOAL
through .... SEEP
filth .... SQUALOR, MUCK, DIRT, LUCRE, FECULENCE, OBSCENITY, INDECENCY, ORDURE
filthy ..... FOUL, LUCRE, RICH, DIRTY, SQUALID
animal .... PIG
smelly place ... CESSPOOL, STY
filtrate .... STRAIN, FILTER
fin .... FLIPPER, PINNA, PINNULE, VEE, FIVER
de ____ .... SIECLE
describing one .. DORSAL, VENTRAL, CAUDAL
footed animal .. PINNIPED
in aeronautics .. AIRFOIL, RUDDER
slang .... HAND
finagle ...... CHEAT, RENEGE, WANGLE
final ... DERNIER, END, TELIC, LAST, DECIDING, CONCLUSIVE, ULTIMATE
discharge ...... QUIETUS
judgment .... DOOM
finale .... CODA, END, SWAN SONG, CONCLUSION
finally ...... AT LAST, EN FIN, IN THE END, EVENTUALLY
finances ... PURSE, ACCOUNTS, FUNDS
financial .... PECUNIARY, MONETARY, FISCAL
gain, unexpected ...... WINDFALL
financially sound ... SOLVENT

financier ...–..... CAPITALIST, BANKER, TYCOON
finback ...... WHALE, GRASO, RORQUAL, RAZORBACK
finch ...... REDPOOL, SISKIN, CANARY, SPINK, CHEWINK, GROSBEAK, SERIN, SONGBIRD, MORO, BUNTING, CARDINAL, SPARROW, OSCINE
African ..... MORO, FINK
American ..... CHEWINK, TOWHEE, LINNET, BURION, JUNCO
canary-like ...... SERIN
kin .... CARDINAL
like bird ...... TANAGER
small .... SERIN
yellow .... SERIN
find ...... DISCOVER, LEARN, DECIDE
fault ...–..... BEEF, CARP, COMPLAIN
out ...... LEARN, SOLVE
finding .... DISCOVERY, CONCLUSION
fine .... AMERCE, BULLY, SCONCE, EXCELLENT, THIN, KEEN, SUBTLE, MULCT
and ____ ...... DANDY
arts .... PAINTING, SCULPTURE, CERAMICS, MUSIC, DANCING, LITERATURE
arts buff ..... DILETTANTE
bearing .... BEL AIR
drawn .... SUBTLE
feather .... EGRET
for misconduct .. SCONCE
gravel .... SAND
in law .... CRO
line of letter ...... SERIF
point .... NICETY
porcelain ...... LIMOGES
powder ..... SOOT, DUST
rain .... DRIZZLE
record of .... ESTREAT
thread .... LISLE
fineness .... DELICACY, RARITY, TENUITY
finery .... DECORATION, FRILL, FRIPPERY, FALDERAL, REGALIA, GAUD(ERY)
useless .... FALLAL
finespun .... DELICATE, FRAGILE, SUBTLE

finesse ..... SKILL, CUNNING, CRAFT, ART
finest part .... FLOWER
Fingal's Cave island .. STAFFA
finger .... DIGIT, STEAL, HANDLE, DACTYL(US), TOUCH
  covering/sheath .... COT
  cymbals ..... CASTANETS
  fifth/smallest .... PINKIE, PINKY
  fore .... INDEX, POINTER
  game .... MORA
  hole of instrument ...... VENTAGE
  infection .... AGNAIL, FELON, WHITLOW
  joint .... KNUCKLE
  like .... DIGITATE
  little .... PINKIE
  middle .... MEDIUS
  nail half-moon .. LUNULE
  pertaining to ... DIGITAL
  protective cover .. STALL, COT
  ring .... HOOF
  slang .... IDENTIFY, POINT TO, INDICATE
  snap of .... FILLIP
  stall .... COT
  stroke .... FLIP
fingerless glove .... MITT
fingerling ... PARR, FISH, FRY, SAMLET
fingernail, care of .. MANICURE
  mark .... LUNULE
fingerprint ... DACTYLOGRAM
  mark .... ARCH, LUNULE, WHORL, LOOP
fingers, membrane uniting .... WEB(BING)
finial .... APEX, PEAK, TIP, SUMMIT, EPI
finical .... PRUDISH, METICULOUS, FASTIDIOUS, FUSSY, PARTICULAR, EXACTING
finicky ... PRECISE, OVERNICE
finis ...... END, CONCLUSION
finish ..... END, ACCOMPLISH, POLISH, STOP, TERMINATE, PERFECTION, CLOSE
  colloquial .... KILL
  dull .... MATTE
  line .... TAPE, WIRE
  off ...... DESTROY, KILL

finished, for short ...... THRU
finisher ..... REAMER, EDGER, SOCKDOLAGER
finishing school product ..... LADY
  tool ..... REAMER, LATHE
fink .... SPY, STRIKEBREAKER, INFORMER
Finland .... SUOMI
finnan haddie ...... HADDOCK
Finnish .... SUOMI
  bath(house) ..... SAUNA
  canto .... RUNE
  capital .... HELSINKI
  city ... TURKU, TAMPERE
  coin ..... MARKKA, PENNI
  composer .... SIBELIUS
  dialect .... KARELIAN
  epic poem ... KALEVALA
  field marshal .... MANNERHEIM
  god .... JUMALA
  inlet .... FIORD
  island .... ALAND
  lake ..... ENARA, ENARE, SAIMA
  language .... SUOMI
  monetary unit .. MARKKA
  native .... LAPP, LAPLANDER, KARELIAN
  poem .... RUNE
  seaport .... ABO, TURKU
finnikin .... PIGEON
Finno-Ugric language .. LAPP, FINNISH, ESTONIAN, MAGYAR, HUNGARIAN
Finns .... SUOMI
fiord .... INLET
fipple .... PLUG
fir ...... BALSAM, EVERGREEN
  board wood .... DEAL
  pole .... UFER
fire ... KINDLE, HURL, DISMISS, INGLE, IGNITE, ARDOR, BURN, EXCITE, (IN)FLAME, ANNEAL
  alarm ...... BELL, SIREN, WHISTLE, PYROSTAT
  artillery .... BARRAGE, SALVO
  away .... START
  back .... REREDOS
  basket ... CRESSET, GRATE
  big, destructive .... CONFLAGRATION
  catching .... IGNITION

clay ..... BRICK, SAGGER
combining form .. PYRO, IGNI
cracker .... PETARD
damp .... METHANE
Dance composer .... DE FALLA
department head .... MARSHAL
feeder .... STOKER
god ...... VULCAN, AGNI, SIVA, KAMA
irons ... POKER, SHOVEL, TONGS
of .... IGNEOUS
opal .... GIRASOL(E)
pot .... CRUCIBLE
principle of .. PHLOGISTON
produced by ... IGNEOUS
put out .... DOUSE
stir up .... STOKE
worshiper .. PYROLATER, PARSEE, GHEBRE, GHEBER, PARSI
firearm (see gun) ..... PISTOL, RIFLE, DERRINGER, REVOLVER, GUN, GAT, PETRONEL, IRON
barrel's end .... MUZZLE
charge .... LOAD
hammer .... COCK
firearms protective coating .... COSMOLINE
fireball ..... METEOR, BOLIDE
firebrand .... AGITATOR, HOTHEAD
firebug .... ARSONIST, INCENDIARY, PYROMANIAC
firecracker .... PETARD
box for .... MARROON
broken .... SQUIB
fired clay .... TILE, BRICK
firedamp ..... METHANE, GAS
firedog .... ANDIRON
firedrake .... DRAGON
firefly .... BUG, BEETLE, GLOWWORM
lighting substance ...... LUCIFERIN
fireman ...... STOKER, VAMP, HAGBUT, HACKBUT
hat of .... HELMET
Firenze .... FLORENCE
fireplace ..... INGLE, GRATE, HEARTH
guard .... FENDER

ledge .... HOB
log holder ..... FIREDOG, ANDIRON
part ...... MANTEL, SPIT, HOB, JAMB(E), CHIMNEY, SHELF
screen .... FENDER
Spanish .... FOGON
tool .... TONGS
fireplug .... HYDRANT
fireside ...... HEARTH, HOME
firewater ...... WHISKY, RUM
firewood ... FAG(G)OT, BARIN, BILLET
fireworks ... PETARD, RIPRAP, PYROTECHNICS, ROCKETS, GERB(E)
cluster ...... GIRANDOLE
hissing ... SQUIB, FIZGIGS
material .... REALGAR
firkin .... TUB
firm .... FIXED, HARD, SOLID, RESOLUTE, FINAL, STEADY, STIFF, COMPANY, STA(U)NCH
firmament ..... HEAVEN, SKY, VAULT, ARCH
revolving ..... PINWHEEL, TOURBILLION
firman ..... DECREE, SANCTION
firmer .... CHISEL
firmly set ..... ROOTED, FIXED, EMBEDDED, PINNED, RIVETED
united .... SOLID
firmness, lacking .... FLABBY, LOOSE, LAX, LIMP, SOFT
firn .... SNOW, NEVE, ICE
first ...... INITIAL, ORIGINAL, MAIDEN, CHIEF, FOREMOST, EARLIEST, PRINCIPAL
abbreviation ...... ORIG.
appearance ...... DEBUT, MAIDEN
born ...... HEIR, OLDEST, EIGNE
cause .... SOURCE
circumnavigator .... MAGELLAN
class ... QUALITY, AONE, TOPS, DANDY
day of Quakers .. SUNDAY
day of Roman month ... CALENDS
estate .... CLERGY
finger .... INDEX
game .... OPENER

in rank .... PREMIER
in time .... PRIMAL
Lady's husband ....
         PRESIDENT
letter .... INITIAL
move .... OVERTURE,
         INITIATIVE
night .... PREMIERE
nighter ...... REVIEWER,
         CRITIC
officer: nautical ... MATE
performance ... PREMIERE
Pope .... PETER
prefix .... PROTO
principles .... ABCS
rate ... SUPER, ACE, AONE,
         ONER, TOPS,
         EXCELLENT, NOBBY,
         TOPFLIGHT, CAPITAL,
         TOPNOTCH
rate: Anglo-Indian ......
         PUCKA, PUKKA
sergeant ...... TOPKICK
showing ...... PREMIERE
sight ..... PRIMA FACIE
space traveler .. GAGARIN
speech, describing ......
         MAIDEN
stage .... INCIPIENCE
valuable .... EDITION
year's revenue of benefice
         ANNAT
year student ..... FROSH,
         FRESHMAN, PLEB(E)
year West Pointer .. PLEBE
firsthand .... ORIGINAL,
         DIRECT, BRAND NEW
firth .... KYLE, ARM, INLET,
         ESTUARY, FIORD
fisc .... TREASURY, EXCHEQUER
fiscal .... FINANCIAL,
         PROSECUTOR, BURSAL
fish ...... ANGLE, BRAINFOOD,
         TROLL, TRAWL, SABALO,
         GAR, RAY, BASS, SHAD,
         OPAH, LING, CHUB, HAKE,
         CARP, DACE, DARTER,
         SCROD, PERCH, SNAPPER,
         TARPON, EELPOUT, WRASSE,
         STURGEON, SCULPIN,
         MACKEREL, BULLHEAD,
         LARROID
African ...... CHARACIN
air bladder .... MAW
air-swallowing .. PUFFER,
         SWELLFISH, GLOBEFISH

appendage .... FIN,
         FLIPPER, BARBEL
aquarium .... MOLLY,
         SWORDTAIL
ascending river ....
         ANADROM
Atlantic .... TAUTOG
bait ..... LIMPET, HOLA,
         LURE, SHINER, CHUM,
         CAP(E)LIN, LUGWORM,
         MENBRADEN, MINNOW
ball .... RISSOLE
barbel .... WATTLE
barracuda .... SPET
basket .... WEEL, CREEL,
         CAWI
batlike ... GURNARD,
         GURNET, (STING)RAY
beaked .... SAURY
beard .... BARB(EL)
bin for salting .... KENCH
boat ... COBLE, TRAWLER,
         WHALER, DORY
boneless .... FIL(L)ET
bony .... TELEOST
box .... KENCH
bright-colored ... OPAH,
         WRASSE, PINTANO,
         COWPILOT, DRAGONET,
         MORAY, MOLLY
bucket .... KIT
burbot ...... LING, CUSK,
         EELPOUT
butter .... GUNNEL
butterfly .... PARU,
         BLENNY
capelin .... SMELT
carangoid .... CAVALLA,
         YELLOWTAIL, POMPANO,
         YELLOWJACK
caribe .... PIRAYA,
         PIRANHA
carp family ..... ROACH,
         BLEAK, IDE, LOACH,
         MINNOW, DACE, CHUB,
         TENCH, REDFIN, ROUD,
         RUD(D)
cat .... RAAD
catch .... HAUL
char(r) .... TROUT
chopped .... CHUM
cigar .... SCAD
cleaner .... SCALER
climbing ...... ANABAS
clinging ...... REMORA,
         TESTAR

coal .... POLLACK,
          POLLOCK
cod family .... CUSK,
    GADID, BACALAO,
    HADDOCK, POLLACK,
    HAKE, LING, BURBOT
combining form ... PISCI
COW .... MANATEE
    DUGONG, GRAMPUS
crab and fiddler .... UCA
creature: legendary .....
    MERMAN, MERMAID
Cuban .... DIABLO
cure .... BLOAT
cusk .... BURBOT
cuttle ...... SEPIA, SQUID
cyprinoid ...... BARBEL,
    CARP, LOACH, ROUD,
    BREAM, DACE,
    GOLDFISH, BLEAK,
    ORF(E)
deep sea .... WEEVER
delicacy .... ROE
devil ...... MANTA, RAY,
    SKATE
dog .... SHARK, BOWFIN
dolphin .... INIA,
    CETACEAN, PORPOISE
drying frame ..... HACK
East Indies ...... DORAB,
    GOURAMI
eating ...... PISCIVOROUS
eating animal .... OTTER,
    SEAL
eating bird ..... OSPREY,
    PELICAN, ERN(E)
eating fish ..... ANGLER
edible ...... BASS, TROUT,
    DORY, BRISLING,
    HADDOCK, LOACH,
    SPRAT, BARRACUDA,
    PIKE, MACKEREL,
    TAUTOG, IDE,
    ARAPAIMA, WRASSE,
    COD
eel .... CONGER,
    LAMPREY, ELVER,
    MORAY, LING
eel-like .... APOD
eelpout .... BURBOT
eel-shaped .. LEPIDOSIREN
eggs .... ROE, SPAWN
eggs relish .... CAVIAR(E)
elasmobranch .. SAWFISH,
    RAY, MANTA, SKATE,
    SHARK

elongated .... EEL, PIKE,
    GAR
European ...... BARBEL,
    PLAICE, BRISLING,
    BREAM, UMBER,
    WRASSE, BRASSE,
    BLEAK, SENNET,
    TENCH, DACE, SPRAT
eyed on head's top ......
    STARGAZER
fabled .... MAH
feeler .... BARBEL
fence ..... WEIR, CRAWL,
fierce .... PIKE, PIRANHA,
    BARRACUDA, BLENNY,
    PICKEREL, SEABASS,
    SHARK
flat .. TURBOT, FLOUNDER,
    SKATE, DAB, BRILL,
    PLAICE, HALIBUT,
    BUTT, SOLE, RAY,
    FLUKE
Florida .... TARPON,
    BONACI
flying .... SAURY,
    GURNARD
food ... SNAPPER, JUREL,
    POLLACK, MORAY,
    TUNA, SCUP, HAKE,
    CERO, CARP, GROUPER,
    MULLET, COD, LING,
    PLAICE, POMPANO,
    SMELT, SARDINE, SHAD,
    TROUT, BONITO
fork-tailed .. CARANGOID,
    CAVALLA, POMPANO,
    JUREL
fresh-water ..... ANABAS,
    IDE, DACE, CRAPPIE,
    BASS, TENCH, LOACH,
    DARTER, REDEYE,
    ARAPAIMA
frog .... ANGLER
from boat .... TROLL
full of: poetic ..... FINNY
game .... MARLIN,
    TARPON, SWORDFISH,
    SALMON, TROUT,
    (BLACK)BASS
ganoid .... GAR,
    BOWFIN, STURGEON
garth .... WEIR
genus .... AMIA
gig .... SPEAR, HOOK
gobioid .... GOBY
goby-like ..... DRAGONET

grampus .... ORC, DOLPHIN
grasping-tailed ....
    HIPPOCAMPUS
green ... SHANNY, PLAICE
grouper ..... (SEA)BASS, MERO
grunting ..... CROAKER, PIGFISH, GURNARD
gurnard family ....
    SEA ROBIN
Hawaiian .... AKU
hawk .... OSPREY
head of .... JOWL
herring .... CISCO, MENHADEN, SPRAT, PILCHARD, PILCHER, CLUPE(O)ID, SARDINE, ANCHOVY, TARPON, OLDWIFE
herring-like ...... SHAD, ALEWIFE
herring, young .... BRIT
hook .... GAFF, GIG
illegally .... POACH
Japanese ..... TAI, FUGU
jelly .... MEDUSA, ACALEPH
jew ...... MERO, TARPON, (SEA)BASS
jurel .... RUNNER
king .... OPAH, WHITING, PINTADO
lacking pelvic fins .. APOD
lake .... POLLAN
land-walking ... ANABAS
largest freshwater ....
    ARAPAIMA
like animal ... LANCELET
line ...... SNELL, TROT, TROLL, TRAWL
line cork .... BOB
ling .... BURBOT
little .. MINNOW, SARDINE, SMELT
lizard .... ULAE
loach .... SMERLIN
long-beaked ..... SAURY, GAR
lure .... SPINNER
mackerel .. TUNA, TUNNY, ALBACORE, BONITO
mackerel-like ..... CERO, TINKER
male .... MILTER
man-eating ...... SHARK

marine ... SCUP, BONITO, WRASSE, CUSK, LING, TARPON, ROBALO, BLENNY, MENHADEN
maskonge .... PIKE
measure .... MEASE
meat, broiled ....
    CARBONADO
migration .... RUN
milk .... SABALO
mollusk ...... OCTOPUS, SQUID
mucous coating ... SLIME
mythological .... MAH
nest-building .... ACARA
net .... SEINE, TRAWL, FYKE, GILL, FLUE, FLEW
New Zealand .... IHI
ocean bed ...... WEEVER
of .... PISCINE, PISCATORY, PISCATORIAL
organ of touch ... BARBEL
parasite .... REMORA
parrot ..... LANIA, LORO
pen ...... CRAWL, WEIR
perch family .... RUFF(E)
perch-like ...... ANABAS, DARTER, CABRILLA
pertaining to ... PISCINE, PISCATORY, FINNY, TELEOST
pickle .... ALEC
piece .... FIL(L)ET
pike .... LUCE, PICKEREL
pike-like .... GAR, BARRACUDA, ROBALO
place for drying ... HACK
pond .... PISCINA
poor .... SIMP
porgy .... SCUP, TAI
Polynesian .... ISDA
porpoise ..... DOLPHIN, INIA, CETACEAN
primitive ... COELACANTH
ray ...... MANTA, SKATE
red-eyed .... RUDD
relish .... BOTARGO
reproductive glands .....
    MILT
resembling ..... PISCINE
river ascending .. SALMON, SHAD, ANADROM
rock .... RE(I)NA, BASS, GROUPER, COD
runner .... JUREL

Russian .... STERLET,
STURGEON
salmon, young .... PARR,
SAMLET
salmonoid .. NAMAYCUSH,
TROUT, STEELHEAD
salt-water ... DORY, SHAD,
TUNA, CYCLOTOME,
HAKE
salting box ...... KENCH
sardine ..... PILCHARD,
HERRING, SPRAT,
CLUPEID
sardine-like ... BRISLING,
ANCHOVY, CISCO
sauce ... ALEC, ANCHOVY
saurel .... SCAD
scabbard .... HIKU
scad .... SAUREL
scale .... GANOID
scaleless .... BULLHEAD,
SCULPIN, CATFISH
sculpin family .. CABEZON,
BULLHEAD
sea .... TUNA, SAURY,
SCULPIN
sergeant .... ROBALO
shad-like .... ALEWIFE
shark ..... MAKO, TOPE,
ANGELFISH
shark family .. CHIMAERA
shark's pilot .... REMORA
shell ... CLAM, ABALONE,
WHELK, LIMPET, SLUG,
SCALLOP, OCTOPUS
sign of zodiac .... PISCES
silver-bellied .. MACKEREL
silvery .... PINTADO,
MULLET, SMELT, OPAH
skeleton ... ARETE, ARISTA
slimy .... BLENNY
small .... FRY, ID(E),
SMELT, FINGERLING,
DARTER, SPELT,
MINNOW, DACE, SPRAT,
SAMLET
smelt .... CAP(E)LIN
snouted ... SAURY, GAR,
BOARFISH, PORPOISE,
DOLPHIN, PICKEREL,
STURGEON
South American ....
CARIBE, ARAPAIMA,
PIRANHA, PIRAYA
spawning movement ....

CATADROMOUS,
ANADROMOUS
spear ..... GIG, LEISTER
sperm .... MILT, ROE
spiny ... GOBY, SCULPIN
spotted .... OPAH
stewed ..... MATELOT(TE)
story .... YARN,
EXAGGERATION
sturgeon .... STERLET,
BELUGA
sucking .... REMORA,
HAMMERHEAD
swimming bladder ......
SOUND
tank ... STEW, AQUARIUM
teleost .... EEL
that recently spawned ...
SHOTTEN
to .... ANGLE, TROLL
toad .... SAPO
trap ..... KELONG, WEIR,
TRAWL, EELPOT,
HATCH, FYKE, CRAWL,
SEINE, GILL, CREEL
tropical ... BARRACUDA,
SARGO, SALEMA,
ROBALO, SNAPPER
trout .... CHAR(R)
tub .... KIT
ugly-looking .... CATFISH
unicorn .... UNIE
upholding universe .. MAH
voracious ...... CARIBE,
SHARK, PIRANHA,
CATFISH
wahoo .... ONO
wall-eyed ..... BLOWFISH
West Indies ..... TESTAR
whale ...... CETACEAN,
CACHALOT, NARWHAL,
GRAMPUS, ORC(A)
whisker .... BARBEL
whiskered ..... CATFISH
whiting ..... MENHADEN,
HAKE
with a spoon ...... SPIN
with lungs/gills ....
CERATODUS, DIPNOAN,
BARRAMUNDA
with staring eyes ... PIKE,
PERCH, POLLACK,
ALEWIFE
with sucking mouth .....
LAMPREY, CYCLOSTOME,
HAGFISH, REMORA

with suction disk ... GOBY
with whiplike tail ......
    SKATE, STINGAREE,
    (STING)RAY
young .... BRIT, ALEVIN,
    FRY, PARR, FINGERLING,
    ELVER, SAMLET
fishbait .... LUGWORM, CHUM
fishbowl .... AQUARIUM
fisher ...... WEJACK, PEKAN,
    MARTEN, SEAL
fisherman .... WALTON, EELER,
    ANGLER, PISCATOR
  basket .... CREEL
  line of .... SNELL
fisherman's bend .... KNOT
  hut .... SKEO
fishes, characteristic of ......
    ICHTHYIC
fishgig .... SPEAR
fishhook ... GAFF, DRAIL, GIG
  line .... SNELL
fishing .... ANGLING
  bait .... DRAKE, MAYFLY
  basket .... CREEL
  boat ... DORY, TRAWLER,
    SMACK, CORACLE,
    DOGGER, SHARPIE
  device .... EELPOT
  float .... BOB
  fly .... HACKLE
  fly, artificial .... NYMPH
  fly trimmer .... HERL
  ground ...... FISHERY,
    PISCINA, PISCARY,
    POUND
  line float .... BOB
  line with hooks ....
    BOULTER
  net .... FLUE, FLEW,
    SEINE, FYKE, TRAWL,
    GILL, TRAMMEL
  pertaining to ....
    PISCATORIAL
  place ... PISCARY, POUND
  pole ...... ROD, TONKIN
  reel .... PIRN
  right .... PISCARY
  season, feast after ... FOY
  smack .... DOGGER
  spear ... HARPOON, GAFF
fishline leader .... SNELL
fishnet sagging part ..... BUNT
fishpond .... WEIR
fishskin disease .. ICHTHYOSIS
fishwife .... NAG(GER)

fishworm: Jap. ..... ANISAKIS
fishy .... FUNNY, INCREDIBLE,
    SHADY, DOUBTFUL, DULL,
    SUSPICIOUS
fission .... SCISSION
fissure ... RIFT, CRACK, SPLIT,
    CLEFT, CRANNY, RENT,
    CHINK, CREVICE, RIME
  in glacier ..... CREVASSE
fissures, full of ...... RIMOUS,
    RIMOSE
fist .... NIEVE
  blow .... PUNCH, PASTE
  fight .... MILL
fistic .... PUGILISTIC, BOXING
fisticuffs ..... BOUT, PUNCHED,
    SETTO, BOXING
fists: sl. .... DUKES
fistula .... CAVITY, PIPE, TUBE
fistulous .... TUBULAR
fit ...... APT, SPASM, ADAPT,
    MEET, TRIG, ELIGIBLE,
    KOSHER, KASHER,
    SUIT(ABLE), EQUIP, PAT,
    ATTACK, APOPLEXY,
    PAROXYSM, CONVULSION,
    PROPER, RIGHT, READY
  arrow on string ... NOCK
  closely/exactly ..... FAY
  for cultivation .. ARABLE
  gamecock with spurs ....
    HEEL
  of shivers .... AGUE
  of temper ... ANGER, IRE,
    OUTBURST, HUFF, RAGE,
    TANTRUM, TIFF,
    CONNIPTION, MIFF, PIQUE
  out _____ EQUIP
  to be ___ .... TIED
  to drink .... POTABLE
  to eat .... EDIBLE,
    EATABLE, ESCULENT,
    KOSHER
  to live in ..... HABITABLE
  to requirement ... TAILOR
  to work .... ABLE
  together .... MESH
fitchew .... POLECAT
fitful .... IRREGULAR,
    SPASMODIC
fitly .... DULY, SUITABLY,
    SPASMODIC
fitness ... APTNESS, PROPRIETY
fits and ___ .... STARTS
fitting ... APT, MEET, PROPER
fittingly .... DULY

fittings .... FIXTURES, DECORATIONS, FURNISHINGS
Fitzgerald, singer ...... ELLA
Fiume .... RIJEKA
Five Civilized Nations member CHEROKEE, CREEK, CHOCTAW, CHICKASAW, SEMINOLE
   cent coin .... NICKEL, JITNEY
   collection of .... QUINTUPLET
   combining form .... PENT(A)
   consisting of .... QUINTUPLE
   day duel protagonist .... ROLAND, OLIVER
   dollar bill ..... FIN, VEE, FIVER
   finger .... OXLIP, CINQUEFOIL, STARFISH, POTENTILLA
   fold .... QUINTUPLE
   group of .... PENTAD
   hundred, card game ..... EUCHRE
   in cards .... PEDRO
   lined nonsensical poem .. LIMERICK
   Nations member .... CAYUGAS, ONEIDAS, MOHAWKS, SENECAS, ONONDAGAS, TUSCARORAS
   of trumps in 7-up .. PEDRO
   on the dice ..... CINQUE
   set of .... QUINARY, QUINTET(TE)
   sided figure ... PENTAGON
   year period ... LUSTRUM, PENTAD
fiver .... FIN
fives .... HANDBALL
fix ...... (A)MEND, SPOT, SET, DEFINE, RIVET, REPAIR, DILEMMA, LIMIT, FASTEN, ESTABLISH, FREEZE
   colloquial .... PREDICAMENT, SCRAPE, SPOT, DILEMMA
   in memory .... CON, REMEMBER
   jewel in setting .. MOUNT
fixation .... OBSESSION, PREOCCUPATION
fixative .... MORDANT

fixed ..... FIRM, IMMOVABLE, RIGID, SET, RESOLUTE, STATIONARY, STABILE
   charge item ...... RENT, INTEREST, TAX
fixings .... ACCESSORIES
fixture hanging from ceiling ... CHANDELIER
fixtures .... FITTINGS, FURNITURE
fizgig .... FIREWORK, FLIRT
fizz ...... DRINK, CHAMPAGNE
fizzle ...... FIASCO, FLOP, FAIL
fizzwater .... SODA
fizzy .... BUBBLING, EFFERVESCENT
fjeld .... PLATEAU
fjord .... INLET
   passage .... GAT
flabbergast .... SURPRISE, ASTONISH, STUN, ABASH, DISCONCERT
flabellum .... FAN
flabby ...... FLACCID, WEAK, FEEBLE
flaccid ... LIMP, WEAK, FLABBY
flacon .... FLASK
flag ..... GONFALON, ENSIGN, WEAKEN, BUNTING, BLACKJACK, SIGN, BANNER, DROOP, TIRE, COLORS, STANDARD, GUIDON
   background ...... FIELD
   bearer .... CORNET
   cloth .... BUNTING
   corner .... CANTON
   deer's .... TAIL
   flower .... IRIS
   identifying ...... BURGEE
   little .... PENNANT, BANDEROLE, BANNERET, BANNEROL
   military .... GUIDON, ENSIGN
   officer .... ADMIRAL, CAPTAIN
   over tomb .. BANDEROL(E)
   pirate's .... ROGER
   plant .... IRIS
   pole ...... STAFF, SHAFT
   position .... FANION
   rope .... HALYARD
   ship's .... BURGEE
   signal .... ENSIGN
   swallow-tailed .... BURGEE, PENNON

sweet .... CALAMUS
triangular ...... PENNON,
        BURGEE
flagellant .... ALBI
flagellate .... WHIP, FLOG
flagellum .... WHIP, SHOOT,
        RUNNER
flageolet ... FLUTE, RECORDER,
        PIPE
flagitious .... HEINOUS,
        WICKED, VILE
flagon ... JUG, EWER, CARAFE,
        STOUR, STOUP
flagrant .... EGREGIOUS,
OUTRAGEOUS, SCANDALOUS,
NOTORIOUS, GLARING,
        GROSS, RANK
flagrante delicto ....
        RED HANDED
flagship official launch .. BARGE
flags collectively .... BUNTING
flagstone .... SLAB, BRICK
Flaherty movie film ... MOANA
flail ..... THRESH, WHIP, BEAT
    part .... SWIP(P)LE,
        SWINGLE
flair .... BENT, TALENT,
APTITUDE, KNACK, ABILITY,
        DISCERNMENT
flak .... ACK-ACK
flake ... CHIP, SPALL, LAMINA,
CARNATION, RACK, SCALE,
        FLECK
flakes, covered with .. LEPIDOTE
flaky ...... SCALY, SQUAMOSE
flam ..... HUMBUG, BLARNEY,
LIE, TRICK, DECEPTION
flambeau ... CRESSET, TORCH,
        CANDLESTICK
flamboyance ...... PANACHE
flamboyant .... ORNATE,
SHOWY, FLOWERY,
        BOMBASTIC
flame ..... BEAM, BLAZE, FIRE,
        SPUNK
    long, narrow .... TONGUE
    slang .... SWEETHEART
flamen .... PRIEST
flamenco dancer .... GRECO
flan .... TART, BLANK
Flanders battlesite .... YPRES
    native .... FLEMING
    river .... YSER
flanerie .... LOAFING
flaneur ... STROLLER, LOAFER,

TRIFLER, ROAMER,
        GADABOUT
flank .... SIDE, LOIN
    combining form ....
        LAPAR(O)
flannel .... LANA
flannelmouth .... CATFISH
flannels: colloq. .. UNDERWEAR
flap ...... TAB, SWING, SLAP,
BEAT, FLUTTER, FLY,
LAPPET, WHIP, SLAT
    airplane ...... AILERON,
        AIRFOIL
    of flesh .. GILL, WATTLE,
        DEWLAP
    vigorously .... SLAT
    wings .... FLICKER
flapjack .... PANCAKE,
        GRIDDLECAKE
flapper .... FIN
flare .... BLAZE, FUZEE,
FLICKER, GLARE, FLECK,
FLASH, BULGE, OUTBURST
    signal .... FUSEE
flaring .... LURID, GAUDY
    edge .... FLANGE
flash .... GLINT, GLEAM,
GLIMMER, SPARK, FLARE,
SPARKLE, BLAZE, MOMENT,
SCINTILLATE, GLITTER
    of lightning .... BOLT
    out .... EFFULGE
flasher .... BEACON
flashy .... GAUDY, SHOWY,
        RAFFISH
flask ..... CANTEEN, MATARA,
CRUSE, COSTREL, CARAFE,
THERMOS, MATRASS,
CUCURBITE, FLAGON,
        FLACON
flat ..... LEVEL, APARTMENT,
EVEN, TABULAR, SUITE,
INSIPID, PLANE, STALE,
VAPID, ABSOLUTE, DULL
    and circular .... DISCUS
    and even ... HORIZONTAL
    boat ...... DORY, SCOW,
        BARGE, PUNT, RAFT
    bottle .... FLASK
    bottom boat ..... BARGE,
        SCOW, PUNT, BATEAU,
        DORY
    canopy .... TESTER
    colloquial ... PENNILESS,
        BROKE
    dish .... PLATTER

fish ... SKATE, SOLE, DAB, RAY, TURBOT, FLOUNDER, FLUKE
headed Indian .. CHINOOK
headed nail .... TACK
hill .... MESA
land .... PLAIN
nosed .... SNUB, PUG, SIMOUS
on one's back ... SUPINE
stick .... FERULE
stone .... SLAB
surface .... AREA, TABULAR, PLANE, PLAIN
taste .... INSIPID
flatboat .... BARGE, PUNT, SCOW
flatfish ..... FLOUNDER, SOLE, HALIBUT, FLUKE, BUT(T), BRILL, TURBOT, PLAICE, RAY, (SAND)DAB
flatfoot: sl. ...... POLICEMAN, COP
Flathead ... CHINOOK, SALISH
flatiron .... SADIRON
flatten .... KNOCK DOWN, LEVEL OFF, PROSTRATE
flatter .... PRAISE, PLEASE, COMPLIMENT, TOADY, FAWN, BLANDISH, ADULATE, OIL
flatterer, servile .. FLUNK(E)Y, TOADY, SYCOPHANT, COURTIER, LICKSPIT(TLE)
flattery .... SOFT SOAP, BLARNEY, PALAVER, TAFFY, BLANDISHMENT, FLUMMERY, SUGAR
flattop: sl. .... (AIRCRAFT)CARRIER
flatulence .... VANITY, GAS
flatulent .... POMPOUS, VAIN, WINDY
flatus .... GAS, PUFF
flatwork ..... SHEETS, NAPKIN
flatworm .... TREMATODE, FLUKE
Flaubert heroine ...... EMMA
novelist .... GUSTAVE
flaunt .... FLUTTER, WAVE, SHOW(OFF), DISPLAY
flavescent .... YELLOWISH
flavin .... PIGMENT
flavor .... SMACK, SAUCE, AROMA, ODOR, SMELL, GUST, SAPOR, SAVOR, SALT, TASTE,

ESSENCE, RELISH, TANG, LACE, SEASON
drinks .... MULL
keeping substance ...... ESSENCE
of .... SAPOROUS
spicy .... GINGER
with spice .... MULL
flavoring .. EXTRACT, LICORICE, ESSENCE, VANILLIN, VANILLA
bulb .... SHALLOT
plant ...... ANISE, MINT, LAUREL, LEEK, BASIL, SAGE
root .... LICORICE
seed ... ANISE, CARAWAY
flavorless .... VAPID
flavorsome .... SAPID
flaw .... CRACK, BLEMISH, DEFECT, FAULT, ERROR
flawless ... PERFECT, POLISHED
flax .... LINEN, FIBER, BYSSUS
capsule .... BOLL
clean and dress .. HECKLE
cloth .... CANVAS, SACKING, STUPE
comber ...... HATCHEL, HACKLE, CARD
dresser .... HATCHEL, HECKLE
fabric .... LINEN
fiber .... TOW, SILVER
filament .... HARL
husk .... SHIVE
like .... TOWY
pod .... BOLL
prepare .... RET
refuse of .... HARDS, HURDS, TOW
remove seeds from ...... RIPPLE
seed .... LINSEED
soak .... RET
weed .... TOADFLY
flaxen color .... GOLDEN, BLOND(E)
flaxseed .... LINSEED
flay .... EXCORIATE, BEAT, CANE, WHIP, SCOLD, CRITICIZE, ROB, FLEECE, PILLAGE
flea .... JIGGER, CHIGOE, REDBUG, CHIGGER

bitten .... DECREPIT,
WRETCHED
fleam ... LANCET, PHLEBOTOME
fleawort .... HERB, PLANTAIN
fleche .... SPIRE
fleck ... SPOT, SPECK, FREAK,
PARTICLE, FLAKE, SPECKLE
flection ... BEND(ING), FLEXING
"Fledermaus" character ......
ADELE
fledgling .... NESTLING
flee ... SKIP, DECAMP, ELOPE,
RUN, BOLT, DESERT, LAM,
ABSCOND, VANISH
fleece ...... FELL, PILE, ABB,
FLAY, MULCT, WOOL,
CHEAT, SWINDLE, STEAL,
SHEAR
cloth .... HODDEN
fleeced .... SHORN
fleecy .... LANIFEROUS
fleer ..... GIBE, MOCK, SNEER,
RUNAGATE, RUNAWAY,
JEER, SCOFF
fleet ..... FLOTILLA, MARINE,
RAPID, FAST, NAVY, FLIT,
FLY, SWIFT
commander's vessel .....
FLAGSHIP
front of .... VAN
merchant .... ARGOSY
small .... FLOTILLA
Spanish .... ARMADA
unit .... SQUADRON
fleeting .... TRANSIENT,
EPHEMERAL, TRANSITORY
Flemish geographer ....
MERCATOR
mathematician .. STEVIN
painter ...... MEMLING,
RUBENS, VANDYKE,
VAN DYCK
flense .... SKIN
flesh .... MEAT, MANKIND
become .... CARNIFY
calf .... VEAL
cattle .... BEEF
deer .... VENISON
eating ... CARNIVOROUS,
CANNIBAL(ISTIC),
CARNIVORE
eating plant .. CARNIVORE
eating raw .. OMAPHAGIA
fly .... BLOWFLY
fold of .... COLLOP
game animal ... VENISON

of dead body ... CARRION
outgrowth ... CARUNCLE,
COMB, WATTLE
pertaining to .. SARCOUS,
CARNAL
sheep .... MUTTON
swine .... PORK
fleshings .... TIGHTS
fleshly .. CARNAL, CORPOREAL,
SENSUAL
fleshpot .... LUXURY
fleshy ..... FAT, OBESE, PLUMP,
ADIPOSE, PULPY, STOUT
fruit .... APPLE, QUINCE,
DRUPE, BERRY,
TOMATO, BANANA,
PEAR, POME,
SARCOCARP, CHERRY,
PLUM
fleur-de-lis ... COAT-OF-ARMS,
IRIS, LILY
flex .... BEND, CURVE,
CONTRACT
flexible ...... SUPPLE, LITHE,
LIMBER, TENSILE, DUCTILE,
LISSOM(E), PLIANT,
TRACTABLE, ELASTIC,
PLASTIC
flexile .... MOBILE, PLIANT
flexing .... FLECTION
flexor .... MUSCLE
flexure .... FOLD, CURVE,
BEND(ING)
flibbertigibbet .. CHATTERBOX
flick ...... FLIP, SNAP, DASH,
STREAK, FLUTTER, FLECK
"Flicka" creator ..... OHARA
flicker ...... YELLOWHAMMER,
FLUTTER, FLAP, BLAZE,
WOODPECKER
dialect ..... HIGH-HOLE,
WOODPECKER
flickering .... LAMBENT
flick: sl. .... MOTION PICTURE,
MOVIE, FILM
flier ..... WINGMAN, AVIATOR,
STEP, HANDBILL
on an eagle ...... ETANA
slang .... GAMBLE,
SPECULATION
flight ...... EXODUS, HEGIRA,
HEJIRA, VOLITATION,
FLEEING, MIGRATION
capable of .... VOLITANT
disorderly .... ROUT
hasty .... SCUTTLE

headlong .... LAM,
    STAMPEDE
organ .... WING
short .... HOP
slang .... LAM
type of ... TEST, NONSTOP,
    MAIDEN, SOLO
flightless bird .... RATITE,
    CASSOWARY, OSTRICH,
WEKA, EMU, RHEA, PENGUIN,
KIWI, APTERYX, MOA, DODO
flighty ... FICKLE, FRIVOLOUS,
    BARMY, FANCIFUL,
    HOITY-TOITY, GIDDY,
    CAPRICIOUS
one .... BIRDBRAIN
flimflam ..... TRICK, HUMBUG,
NONSENSE, HOCUS, RUBBISH
flimsy .... FRAGILE, FRAIL,
    TRIVIAL, THIN, SHEER,
    WEAK, SLIGHT, TENUOUS
flinch .... QUAIL, WINCE,
    RECOIL, COWER, BLENCH,
        CRINGE
flinder ... FRAGMENT, SPLINTER
fling ... TOSS, HURL, THROW,
    CAST, EMIT, RUSH, DASH,
        SLING
flint ... SILICA, CORN, CHERT,
    QUARTZ, SILEX
rock like ... HORNSTONE
flintlock .... MUSKET
Flint's outfit .... ZOWIE
flip ... TOSS, FILLIP, JERK, TAP,
    DRINK, PERT, SAUCY,
    FLIPPANT, SNAP
flippancy .... LEVITY
flippant ... GLIB, PERT, SAUCY,
    SASSY, AIRY
flipper .... FIN, PADDLE
relative .... PAW
slang .... HAND
flippered mammal .... SEAL,
    WALRUS
flirt ..... COQUET(TE), TRIFLE,
    PLAY, TOY, DALLY, VAMP
in the theater ....
        SOUBRETTE
male .... WOLF
flirting .... DALLIANCE
flit .... HOVER, FLUTTER, FLY,
        DART
flittermouse .... BAT
flivver .... AUTO(MOBILE),
    AIRPLANE, FAIL, CRATE
float ...... BUOY, BOB, RIDE,

RAFT, CORK, WAFT,
PONTOON, DRIFT, SELL
fishing line ..... DOBBER,
        BOB
floating .... NATANT, ADRIFT,
        AWASH
debris .... FLOTAGE
ice .... FLOE, BERG,
    GROWLERS, CLUMPERS
island ingredient ... EGGS
leaf .... LILYPAD
plant .... WATERLILY
power of .... FLOTAGE
wreckage ..... FLOTSAM
flocculent .. FLUFFY, WOOLLY
flock .... SWARM, DROVE,
    PACK, HERD, CROWD,
    BROOD, CONGREGATION,
        GROUP
of a .... GAGGLE
of birds .... COVEY,
        BEVY, POD
of cattle ... HERD, DROVE
of partridges/quail ......
        COVEY
of seals .... POD
of sheep ... HERD, DROVE,
        FOLD
of whales .... POD
pertaining to a ....
        GREGARIOUS
wild fowl .... SKEIN
flog .... LARRUP, LASH, TAN,
    FLAGELLATE, SHELLACK,
    LAM, SWISH, HIDE, BEAT,
    WHIP, TROUNCE
flogging rod .. SWISH, SWITCH
whip ...... CHAB(O)UK,
        KURBASH
flood ... CATARACT, TORRENT,
    SPATE, SWAMP, INUNDATE,
    INUNDATION, OVERFLOW,
    DELUGE, OUTPOURING
gate ..... SLUICE, HATCH
great .... DELUGE,
        CATACLYSM
light .... KLIEG
tidal .... EAGRE
flooded condition ..... SPATE
floor .... PLANCH(E),
    KNOCK DOWN, STORY,
        PUZZLE, DALLE
above street floor ....
    ENTRESOL, MEZZANINE
chateau .... ETAGE

cover ..... RUG, CARPET, LINOLEUM, MAT(TING)
covering, fabric for ..... DRUGGET
raised border .. COAMING
floorcloth .... LINOLEUM
flooring chip/slab .... DALLE, TERRAZZO, PARQUET
floorleader .... WHIP
flop .... DROP, FALL, FAIL
colloquial ...... FAILURE
slang .... SLEEP
flora .... PLANTS
and fauna .... BIOTA
floral arrangement, art of .... IKEBANA
envelope ..... PERIANTH
leaf ...... SEPAL, BRACT
Florence .. FIRENZE, FIORENZA
Florentine friar ..... SERVITE
name .... MEDICI
painter .. CIMABUE, LIPPI, SARTO
florid .... ORNATE, FLOWERY, TAFFETA, RUDDY, ROSY, GAUDY, SHOWY
style .... ARABESQUE, ROCOCO
Florida bay .... TAMPA
bird .... LIMPKIN, COURLAN
cape .... SABLE
capital of .. TALLAHASSEE
city .... OCALA, NAPLES, TAMPA, ORLANDO, MIAMI, HIALEAH, PALATKA, LAKELAND
fish ...... TETARD, MERO, BONACI, PINTADO, CABRILLA, SALEMA
grouper .... BONACI
Indian .... SEMINOLE
perchlike fish .. CABRILLA
plant .... COONTIE
resort .... MIAMI, PALM BEACH
river .... S(U)WANEE
sapodilla .... BUSTIC
seaport ..... PENSACOLA, TAMPA
scenic road .... TAMIAMI
tortoise .... GOPHER
tree .... BUSTIC
wood oil .... TUNG
florist's specialty ... CORSAGE, BOUQUET

floss .... SLEAVE, SILK
flossy ...... FLUFFY, DOWNY, FANCY, ELEGANT, LA-DI-DA
flotage .... FLOTSAM
Flotow opera ...... MART(H)A
flotsam ... FLOTAGE, FLOATAGE
and jetsam ... VAGRANTS, DRIFTERS
flounce .... FALBALA, JERK, TWIST, RUFFLE, FURBELOW
flounder .. SOLE, DAB, TURBOT, FLUKE, PLAICE, WALLOW, WALLOP, TOSS, FLATFISH, HALIBUT
flour .... FARINA, DURUM, BUCKWHEAT
bean .... PINOLE
boiled, thick .. FLUMMERY
cereal .... FARINA
corn .... PINOLE
making product .... SEMOLINA
mixture .... PASTE, DOUGH, ROUX
pudding .... DUFF
sieve .... BOLTER
Spanish .... HARINA
flourish ..... BRANDISH, WAVE, ROULADE, TWIRL, PROSPER, FLAUNT, TANTARA, BOOM, SWING, THRIVE, FANFARE, SUCCEED
in an aria ..... CADENZA
in music .... ROULADE
in signature ..... PARAPH
in writing .... TAG
flout ..... MOCK, JEER, SCOFF, FLEER
flow ... RISE, FLUX, RUN, OOZE, SPOUT, ISSUE, WELL, STREAM, GLIDE, CURRENT
against/along ..... LAVE
and spread .... FLUSH
back ...... EBB, RECEDE, REGORGE
combining form .. RHEO
in drops .... DRIBBLE
of tide ...... EBB, FLUX, NEAP, RISE
out ...... POUR, EXUDE, ISSUE, SPILL, STREAM
stop ..... STANCH, STEM
that can ...... FLUID
through .... SEEP
flower ...... BLOSSOM, BLOOM, MAGNOLIA

amaranth ..... PIGWEED
annual .... ASTER
arrangement .. VERTICIL,
    IKEBANA
aster ...... TANGLEFOOT
balsam ...... IMPATIENS
bell-shaped ... HYACINTH
bending downward .....
    CERNUOUS
biennial ..... FOXGLOVE
bloom .... ANTHESIS
blue .... VIOLET,
    HYDRANGEA
bract .... PALEA
bud .... BULBIL, KNOT
buds for seasoning .....
    CAPERS
butterfly-like ....
    MARIPOSA(LILY)
children, so-called ......
    HIPPIES
cluster ... UMBEL, CYME,
    CORYMB, PANICLE,
    CAPITULUM, LILAC,
    TRUSS, THYRSUS,
    RACEME
cover of .... SPATHE
cormus ..... GLADIOLUS,
    CROCUS
covering .... CALYPTRA,
    SPATHE
cowslip ..... MARIGOLD,
    PRIMROSE
cup-shaped ..... CHALICE
daisy .... OX-EYE
Dutch .... TULIP
envelope ...... PERIANTH
erica .... HEATH
ericaceous ...... LAUREL,
    AZALEA
extract .... AT(T)AR
fadeless ..... AMARANTH,
    EVERLASTING
fall .... ASTER
field ..... DAISY, GOWAN
form of .... PELORIA
fragrant .... ROSE,
    HONEYSUCKLE,
    HYACINTH, AZALEA,
    LILAC, JASMIN(E),
    JESSAMINE
full bloomed .. ANTHESIS
garden .... ROSARY,
    GREENERY
genus ..... ROSA, HEATH
goddess .... FLORA

growing, art of ....
    HORTICULTURE
having only one ....
    MONANTHOUS
head .... PANICLE,
    CAPITULUM
heath .... AZALEA
honeysuckle .... ELDER,
    CLOVER
imaginary ... AMARANTH
iris ...... ORRIS, ORRICE
leaf ...... BRACT, PALEA,
    SEPAL, COROLLA
like .... ANTHOID
like animal .... ANEMONE
like ornament .. ROSETTE
lily .... LOTUS, SEGO,
    CALLA, MARIPOSA
marigold ...... COWSLIP
moon .... ACHETE
musk-odored ....
    MOSCHATEL
nightblooming .. CEREUS
nightshade ... HENBANE,
    BELLADONNA
of .... FLORAL
of forgetfulness ... LOTUS
orchid .... ARETHUSA,
    WALING-WALING
pansy .... HEARTSEASE
part ...... STEM, STYLE,
    POLLEN, ANTHER,
    BRACT, PISTIL, SEPAL,
    PETAL, OVULE, STAMEN,
    SPADIX, AMENT,
    CALYX, COROLLA,
    OVARY, STIGMA
perennial ...... DAHLIA,
    AMARANTH
petals .... COROLLA
pigweed ..... AMARANTH
pink .... TITI, RHODORA,
    ELDER, HYDRANGEA
pistil .... CARPEL
plot .... BED
pollen-bearing part .....
    STAMEN
primrose ...... COWSLIP
receptacled ...... TORUS,
    THALAMUS
red .... MARIGOLD,
    CAMELLIA, OXALIS
rootstock ...... TARO,
    ORRIS, ORRICE
rose of Sharon .. ALTHEA
seed .... OVULE

seed bearing part .. PISTIL
sex cells .... POLLEN
shaped .... FLEURON
small .... FLORET
spike ... SPICULE, SPICA, MIGNONETTE, AMENT, CATKIN
spring .... TULIP, HYACINTH
stalk .... PETIOLE, PEDUNCLE
stalk bud/bulb ... BULBIL
stand .... EPERGNE, JARDINIERE
sun prone .. HELIOTROPE
support .... PEDUNCLE
symbol of luxury .... ORCHID
syringa .... LILAC
tanglefoot .... ASTER
the .... ELITE
three-petaled .... ORCHID
turban-like ...... TULIP
unfading .... AMARANTH, EVERLASTING
velvety .... PANSY
waterlily .... LOTUS
white ..... TITI, CROCUS, CAMELLIA, OXALIS, LILAC, GENTIAN, ELDER, HYDRANGEA, TRILLIUM
wild .... THISTLE
wind .... ANEMONE
windowbox .... PETUNIA
wood sorrel ..... OXALIS
yellow .... BENNET, GOWAN, MARIGOLD, COWSLIP
flowering grass .... STIPA
herb .... HEPATICA
more than once a season REMONTANT
plant ..... FERN, AVENS, ARUM, CANNA, YUCCA, POINSETTIA, LOBELIA, ROSE, VALERIAN, GERANIUM, SPIREA, LUPIN(E), ORCHID
shrub ... LILAC, SUMAC, AZALEA, SPIREA
vine .... WISTERIA
flowerless plant .... AGAMOUS, FERN, LICHEN, GENTIAN
flowers, bunch of ... BOUQUET, CORSAGE, POSY, NOSEGAY

in a spathe ...... SPADIX
of .... FLORAL
on woman's shoulder .... CORSAGE
sculptured ..... CORBEIL
flowery .... BOMBASTIC, FLAMBOYANT, ORNATE
girl .... ROSA
flowing ... (AF)FLUX, CURSIVE, EMANATING, FLUXION
and ebbing .... TIDAL
back .... REFLUX, REFLUENT
out .... EFFLUX
together ...... CONFLUX, CONFLUENCE
flown ..... EXCITED, FLUSHED
flu .... INFLUENZA
drug for .... SYMMETREL, AMANTADINE
flub .... ERROR, FAILURE
fluctuant .... VARYING, UNDULATING
fluctuate .... SWING, VEER, VARY
flue .... CHIMNEY, PIPE, FUNNEL, SHAFT, FLUKE, FLUFF
dust .... POTASH
fluency .... ELOQUENCE, GLIBNESS
fluent ... FACILE, EXPRESSIVE, ELOQUENT, GLIB
fluff ... ERROR, BONER, FLUE, DOWN, LINT, FLOSS, NAP
fluffy .... FLOSSY, LINTY, DOWNY, FEATHERY, FLOCCULENT
fluid .... SERUM, LIQUID, GAS, SAP, MOBILE, PLASTIC
aeriform .... GAS
body ...... LYMPH, BILE
colloidal system ..... SOL
life-saving ...... BLOOD
matter .... FLUX
rock .... LAVA
fluke ..... BARB, TREMATODE, CLEEK, HOOK, FLOUNDER, FLATFISH, (FLAT)WORM, FLUE
flume ..... CHANNEL, CHUTE, TROUGH, GORGE, RAVINE, SLUICE, SHUTE
flummery .... OATMEAL, CUSTARD, FLATTERY

flummox: sl. ...... CONFUSE, PERPLEX
flump .... DROP
flunk ..... GIVE UP, RETREAT, FAIL(URE)
flunk(e)y .... TOADY, YES-MAN, FOOTMAN
flunks at Annapolis ... BILGES
fluorite .... JADE
flurry .... STIR, HURRY, ADO, GUST, COMMOTION, CONFUSION, AGITATION
flush ..... BLUSH, REDDEN, GLOW, EXCITE, LAVISH, PROFUSE, FULL, EMPTY, EXHILARATE
  with water ...... WASH
flushed .... RED, AGLOW, FLORID, RUDDY, HECTIC
fluster ..... POTHER, FUDDLE, CONFUSE, EXCITE, UNSETTLE, EMBARRASS
flute .... PIPE, GROOVE, PIPING, FIFE, PICCOLO
  ancient .... HEMIOPE, TIBIA
  bagpipe ...... CHANTER
  Chinese .... (T)CHE
  early form ... RECORDER
  India .... MATALAN
  like instrument ....
    FLAGEOLET
  player ...... TOOTLER, FL(A)UTIST
  stop .... VENTAGE
fluted .... SULCATE
fluting .... GROOVE(S), GAUFFER, GOFFER
  architectural .. GODROON, GADROON
  wavelike .... STRIGIL
flutter .. WAVE(R), TREMBLE, QUIVER, PALPITATE, BUSTLE, HOVER, FLIP, FLICKER, FLIT, FLAP, VIBRATE, FLY
  of eyes .... BLINK
flux ...... FLOW(ING), PURGE, SOLDER, ROSIN, BORAX, FUSE
fluxion .... FLOWING, DISCHARGE
fly ...... MUSCA, SOAR, SCUD, WING, FLEE, FLAP, AVIATE, FLIT, HOVER, FLUTTER, GNAT, MOSQUITO, MIDGE, WHIR, TACHINA

able to .... VOLANT, VOLITANT
  African .... TSETSE
  after game .... RAKE
  agaric ...... MUSHROOM, AMANITA
  amanita ..... MUSHROOM
  artificial ... HARL, HERL, CAHILL, DUN, ZULU, HACKLE
  at .... ATTACK
  before the wind .... SCUD
  block .... PULLEY
  bloodsucking .. TABANID, GADFLY
  case .... ELYTRON
  catcher .. PEEWEE, PEWIT, PHOEBE, TODY
  close to the ground ......
    HEDGEHOP
  experimental ....
    DROSOPHILA
  hit .... SWAT
  insect resembling ....
    CICADA
  Latin .... MUSCA
  let .... THROW
  of the .... MUSCID
  sheet .... PAMPHLET
  slang ..... SHARP, AGILE, NIMBLE
  small ..... MITE, PUNKIE
  to and fro .... VOLITANT
  wheel .... WHORL
  wing cover ... ELYTRON, ELYTRUM
flyaway .... STREAMING, FLIGHTY, ESCAPEE
flyblow ... LARVA, SPOIL, TAINT
flycatcher .. PEEWEE, KINGBIRD, PHOEBE, TODY, ALDER, CHEBEC, FANTAIL, PEWIT
flyer of myth .... ICARUS
flyer's stunt ..... LOOP, ROLL
flying .... VOLANT, VOLITANT
  act of .... VOLITATION
  air mattress ... PARAFOIL
  colors .... VICTORY, SUCCESS
  Dutchman ..... SAILOR, SHIP
  Dutchman maid ... SENTA
  Finn .... NURMI
  fish ... SAURY, GURNARD, GURNET
  Fortress .... BOMBER

fox .... BAT, KALONG
gurnard .... GURNET
island, fictional .. LAPUTA
jib .... SAIL
lemur .... COLUGO
lizard's skin fold ....
PARACHUTE,
PATAGIUM
machine .... AERO,
(AIR)PLANE, AIRCRAFT
marsupial ... PHALANGER
saucer, for short .... UFO
signal .... ROGER
spindrift .... SCUD
squirrel's skin fold ......
PATAGIUM
water .... SPRAY
Flynn, actor .... ERROL
flyspeck .... DOT, SPOT
flywheel .... WHORL, WHARVE
foal .... FILLY, COLT
foam ... SCUM, LATHER, YEAST,
FROTH, SPUME, SUD(S),
BUBBLE, FIZZ
of ..... SPUMY, SPUMOUS
poetic .... SEA
foaming .... NAPPY
foamy ..... SPUMOUS, FROTHY
yeast .... BARN
fob .... CHEAT, TRICK,
(WATCH)POCKET, DECEIVE,
PENDANT
off .... FOIST, PALM
focal point ..... EPICENTER,
CYNOSURE, HUB
focus .... CONCENTRATE,
SPOTLIGHT
in ..... CLEAR, DISTINCT
fodder .... BERSEEM,
PROVENDER, SILAGE, OATS,
GRASS, ALFALFA, VETCH,
ALFILARIA, RAPE,
CORNSTALK, HAY, STRAW,
FORAGE, ALSIKE
bin .... CRATCH
grain .... KAFFIR
pertaining to .... FORAGE
pit .... SILO
plant .. GRAM, CHICKPEA,
CLOVER, ALSIKE,
ALFALFA, STOVER,
SAINFOIN
preservation ... ENSILAGE
rack .... CRATCH
storage place ...... SILO
straw .... STOVER

tower .... SILO
tree pod .... CAROB
trough .... MANGER
foe .... ENEMY, RIVAL,
ADVERSARY, OPPONENT
of shams ... ICONOCLAST
fog .... HAZE, BRUME, MURK,
VAPOR, CONFUSE, MIST
and smoke .... SMOG
fog(e)y .... MOSSBACK
fogeyish .... FUSTY
foggy ... CLOUDY, BRUMOUS,
NUBILOUS, MISTY, MURKY,
DIM, CONFUSED
foghorn .... SIREN(E)
foible .... FAULT, WEAKNESS,
FRAILTY
opposed to ...... FORTE
foil .... BALK, STOOGE,
BAFFLE, EPEE, FRUSTRATE,
THWART, STUMP
comedian's ..... STOOGE,
STRAIGHTMAN
foilsman .... FENCER
foist .... PALM(OFF), FOB
Fokine, choreographer ......
MICHEL
fold .... CRIMP, LAP, PLY,
WRAP, CLASP, RUCK, REEF,
RUGA, DRAPE, PLAIT,
FLOCK, PLEAT, EMBRACE,
FLEXURE, ENVELOP, CREASE,
LAYER, PLICA(TION)
animal's throat .. DEWLAP
coat .... LAPEL
mark .... CREASE
sail .... REEF
sheep .... PEN
skin .... PLICA
slang .... FAIL
stitched .... TUCK
up .... FAIL, CLOSE,
COLLAPSE
folded .... DOUBLED,
PLEATED, PLICATE, RUGATE
folder .... PAMPHLET,
BOOKLET, LEAFLET
folding bed .... COT
hood .... CALASH
leaves, plant with ......
MIMOSA
foliage .... LEAVES, LEAFAGE,
UMBRAGE
mass of .... SPRAY,
BOUQUET
folio ... PAGE, BOOK, NUMBER

foliose .... LEAFY
folium .... LOOP
folk .... PEOPLE, RACE,
NATION, TRIBE, PERSONS,
KOLO
dance .... HORA, MORRIS,
DREHER
tale .... MARCHEN
tale tiny hero ....
TOM THUMB
folklore .... LEGEND, BELIEFS,
SAYINGS
character .... OGRE,
DWARF, FAIRY, TROLL,
GIANT, SANDMAN
folksinger .... IVES, BAEZ
folksong .... LULLABY
folkways .... MORES
follicle .... SAC, CAVITY,
GLAND, POD, CAPSULE,
COCOON
follies .... REVUE
follow ... HEED, ENSUE, CHASE,
PURSUE, TAG, ATTEND,
ACCOMPANY, IMITATE,
RESULT, OBEY, TRAIL, TAIL,
TRACK
continually .... DOG,
HOUND
stealthily .... TAIL,
SHADOW, STAG
follower .... PARTISAN,
VOTARY, HENCHMAN, IST,
ITE, BUFF, ADHERENT, FAN,
MINION, SUPPORTER,
DISCIPLE, SERVITOR
faithful .... FRIDAY,
MYRMIDON
kind of .... SERVANT,
ATTENDANT, SATELLITE,
HANGER-ON
followers, group of ..... CULT
following .... TRADE,
EQUIPAGE, ENSUING,
RETINUE, SECT, AFTER
this .... HEREAFTER,
HENCEFORTH
folly .... FOOLISHNESS,
FATUITY, LUNACY
foment ...... BREW, AROUSE,
INSTIGATE, INCITE, ABET,
SPUR
fond .... ATTACHED, TENDER,
LOVING, AFFECTIONATE,
DOTING
of arguing .. DISPUTATIVE

of fighting .. COMBATIVE,
PUGNACIOUS
of, foolishly ... UXORIOUS,
DOTING
of luxury, etc. ....
EPICUREAN
fondant .... CANDY
fondle ... COSSET, PET, CARESS,
STROKE, DANDLE
fondling .... PET, FOOL,
NINNY, SIMPLETON
fondness ..... TASTE, LIKING,
PENCHANT, FLAIR
font .... BOWL, BASIN,
FOUNTAIN, SPRING, ORIGIN,
LAVER, STOUP, SOURCE, STOOP
rite .... BAPTISM
fontal .... ORIGINAL,
BAPTISMAL
fontanel(le) .... OPENING,
OUTLET
food .... NOURISHMENT,
NUTRIMENT, ALIMENT,
FARE, VICTUAL, PABALUM,
DIET, VIAND, MESS,
REFECTION, COMESTIBLE,
TABLE, BOARD, PEMMICAN
allowance ..... CORODY,
RATION
and shelter ...... KEEP,
BOARD
animal .... FORAGE,
FODDER
being digested ... CHYME
between meals ... SNACK
bits .... SCRAPS, ORTS
cereal ..... OAT, WHEAT,
RICE, CORN
chewed, solid ... BROMA
choice: archaic .... CATE
colloquial ...... CHOW,
GRUB, EATS
dealer .... GROCER
desire for ...... HUNGER
diet ..... REGIMEN, FARE
disk-shaped ..... PATTY
drying platform ... FLAKE
fancy .... KICKSAW
fish ..... TROUT, SHAD,
BASS, SALMON, SARDINE,
SCROD, TUNA, CERO,
COD, MACKEREL, PERCH
from heaven ... MANNA
Hawaiian .... POI
liquid .... SLOP, BROTH,
SOUP

look for ..... SCAVENGE
Maori .... KAI
need for .... HUNGER
non-flesh .... MAIGRE
of the gods ... AMBROSIA,
AMRITA
place for .... LARDER,
PANTRY, SPENCE,
SPENSE, CUPBOARD
plant ..... TARO, MANIOC,
CASSAVA
poisoning .... BOTULISM,
PTOMAIN(E)
provider .... CATERER
rack .... FLAKE
regimen .... DIET
scrap .... ORT
served .... HELPING
shavings .... CHIPS
shop .... DELICATESSEN
slang ...... CHOW, EATS,
GRUB, CHUCK
slices .... CHIPS
soft .... PAP, FLUMMERY
solid in medicine .. BROMA
spoiler ... YEAST, MOLD,
ENZYME, BACTERIA
stock of ..... PROVISIONS,
VICTUAL
supplier .... CATERER
supply place .... LARDER
foods, study of ... SITOLOGY,
DIETETICS
fool .... IDIOT, CLOWN, SIMP,
OAF, DUPE, ZANY, DOTARD,
DUNCE, NINNY, JAPE,
SAP(HEAD), GABY,
SIMPLETON, CHUMP, BOOB,
JESTER, DECEIVE, TRICK,
ASS, DOLT, MUGGINS,
MOONCALF, NOODLE,
NODDY
around .... TRIFLE
hen .... GROUSE
play the .... CLOWN
professional ..... JESTER
foolhardy .. ICARIAN, DARING,
BOLD, RASH, RECKLESS,
BRASH
person .... DAREDEVIL
foolish .... SILLY, BALMY,
ANSERINE, SAPPY, ABSURD,
RIDICULOUS, UNWISE, DAFT,
ASININE, IMPRUDENT, INANE,
PUERILE, SILAGE, ZANY,
LUNATIC, CUCKOO

action ... (TOM)FOOLERY,
FOLLY
affection .... DOTAGE
blunder .... HOWLER
fancy .... CHIMERA
from overdrinking ......
SCOTTISH
from old age ... DOITED,
SENILE
talk ...... FLAPDOODLE,
BABBLE, CHATTER
undertaking .... FOLLY
foolishly loving .... FOND
foolishness .... FOLLY,
NONSENSE, FATUITY,
LUNACY
fool's bauble .... MAROTTE
gold .... PYRITE
foot ... HOOF, BASE, BOTTOM,
WALK, TREAD
animal ...... PAW, PAD
and-mouth disease ......
MURRAIN
child's .... TOOTSY
colloquial ...... PAY, PEG
combining form .. PED(I),
PED(E), POD(E)
deformity ...... TALIPES
disease .... PODAGRA,
GOUT
disorders, specialist in ...
PODIATRIST
lever ... PEDAL, TREADLE
like part .... PES
loose .... FREE,
WANDERING
of 4 syllables ....
TETRABRACH
on .... STANDING
part ... INCH, SOLE, SHIN,
ARCH, TOE
pedal .... TREADLE
pertaining to a .... PEDAL
poetic .... ANAPEST,
IAMB(IC), SPONDEE,
DACTYL
prefix .... PED
race ...... STEEPLECHASE
shaped .... PEDIFORM
soldier ... INFANTRYMAN,
KERN(E)
soldier's coat ..... JACK
sole of .... VOLAR,
THENAR, PLANTAR
sore .... CHILBLAIN
study of ...... PODIATRY

swelling .... BUNION
three-syllable ... ANAPEST
traveler .... HIKER,
TRAMP, PEDESTRIAN
with .... PEDATE
woman's .... TOOTSY
football ...... ELEVEN, RUGBY
association ..... SOCCER
colloquial ..... PIGSKIN
conference ..... BIG TEN
field .... GRID(IRON)
name in .... ROCKNE,
STAGG, THORPE
official .... LINEMAN
player .... UNITAS,
NAMATH, BLANDA,
GABRIEL, OJ, TITTLE
position .... END,
GUARD, TACKLE,
CENTER, KICKER
score ..... TOUCHDOWN
slang .... GRID
team .... JETS, RAMS,
DOLPHINS, CHIEFS,
COLTS, PACKERS,
BROWNS, COWBOYS,
VIKINGS
term ...... PUNT, PASS,
CUTBACK, HUDDLE
footboy .... PAGE
footcloth ...... RUG, CARPET
footed, large ..... MEGAPOD
single .... MONOPODE
footfall ...... TREAD, STEP
foothold, for example ....
BEACHHEAD, LODG(E)MENT
footing ...... BASIS, POSITION,
FOOTHOLD, TOEHOLD
footless .... APOD(AL)
footlights .... THEATER,
STAGE, KLIEG, FLOAT(S)
footlike .... PEDATE
footloose ..... FREE, ROVING
footman .... FLUNK(E)Y,
LACKEY, PEON
footnote .... COMMENTARY,
REFERENCE, APOSTIL,
ANNOTATION
marker ...... ASTERISK,
OBELUS
footpad .... HIGHWAYMAN,
ROBBER, HOLDUPPER, THUG,
BRIGAND, BANDIT
footprint .... CLUE, PAD, STEP,
TRACK, TREAD, PUG
animal .... PUG

combining form .. ICHNO
mold ... MOULAGE, CAST
study of .... ICHNOLOGY
footrest .... STOOL, OTTOMAN
foots ...... DREGS, SEDIMENT
footstalk ... SHANK, PEDICEL
footstep sound ... PAD, CLUM
footstool .... OTTOMAN,
CRICKET, HASSOCK
footway ..... SIDEWALK, PATH
ship .... CATWALK
footwear ...... SHOES, SPATS,
SABOTS, RUBBERS, CLOGS,
SKATES, BOOTS, SLIPPERS
foozle .... BUNGLE
fop .... DUDE, DANDY,
COXCOMB, POPINJAY,
JOHNNIE, JOHNNY
foppish ... BUCKISH, LADIDA,
LADEDA
for .... PRO, IN FAVOR
aye ...... ALWAYS, EVER
each ...... PER, EVERY
example ...... VIDE, E.G.
fear that .... LEST
shame .... FIE
the most part ... MAINLY,
LARGELY
the time being ....
PRO TEM, NONCE,
MEANWHILE
this reason ...... HENCE,
THEREFORE
forage .... FOOD, PROG,
FODDER, FEED, RAVAGE,
PLUNDER, MARAUD
crop ... MILO, SORGHUM
plant ... ALFALFA,
LUCERN(E), ALSIKE,
GUAR
foramen ...... OPENING, PORE,
MEATUS
foray .... RAID, MARAUD,
INROAD, PILLAGE, PLUNDER
forbear .. ANCESTOR, ABSTAIN,
PARENT, ENDURE,
TOLERATE, AVOID, REFRAIN
forbearance ..... RESTRAINT,
PATIENCE, TOLERANCE
forbearing .... TOLERANT,
PATIENT
forbears, of ..... ANCESTRAL,
AVITAL
Forbes, novelist ...... ESTHER
forbid .... TABOO, STOP, BAN,
INHIBIT, PREVENT,

INTERDICT, ENJOIN,
PROSCRIBE, PROHIBIT, VETO
forbidden ..... TABU, TABOO,
BANNED, VERBOTEN
city .... LHASA, LASSA
fruit .... APPLE
forbidding ...... STERN, GRIM,
UGLY, REPELLANT,
DISAGREEABLE
force .... DURESS, ODYL,
COMPEL, DINT, STRAIN,
COERCE, CONSTRAIN, IMPEL,
DRIVE, IMPETUS, STRENGTH,
POWER, VIGOR, ENERGY,
BIRR, VIS, SINEW
armed .... POSSE
back ... REPEL, REPULSE
by .... AMAIN
colloquial .... STEAM
down ... DETRUDE, RAM
driving ..... MAINSPRING
hypothetical .... OD,
ODYLE, OG, ELOD
into service .... LEVY,
COMMANDEER, DRAFT,
CONSCRIPT
Latin .... VIS
military ... ARMY, NAVY
of blow .. IMPACT, BRUNT
of expression/feeling ....
EMPHASIS
one's way in .... MUSCLE
out .... EXCLUDE, OUST,
ROUT, EJECT, EVICT,
EXPEL
rotating .... TORQUE
side of .... FLANK
unit of .... DYNE
forced .... COMPULSORY
journey .... FLIGHT,
HEGIRA
labor .... CORVEE
forceful .. COGENT, EFFECTIVE,
VIGOROUS, STRONG,
ENERGETIC, STOUT
forceps ..... TONGS, PINCERS,
NIPPER
forcible .... VIOLENT
ford .... CROSS, WADE
fore, opposite of .... AFT
forearm bone .... ULNA
forebode .... PREDICT,
PORTEND, FORETELL
foreboding ... AUGURY, DARK,
OMINOUS, OMEN
PRESENTIMENT, PORTENT

forecast ... FORESEE, PREDICT,
PROPHESY, PROGNOSIS,
PREVISE
forecaster .... SEER, DOPESTER
racetrack ...... TIPSTER,
TOUT
forefather ..... PROGENITOR,
ANCESTOR
forefinger ... INDEX, POINTER
forefoot .... PAW
part of .... MANUS
forefront ...... VAN(GUARD),
FOREMOST
forego ...... WAIVE, ABSTAIN
foregoing .... ABOVE,
PRECEDING, PREVIOUS
forehead ... SINCIPUT, BROW
animal/bird ... FRONTLET
bone .... FRONTAL
hairy point ....
WIDOW'S PEAK
of the .... METOPIC
foreign ... OVERSEAS, EXOTIC,
ALIEN, PEREGRINE,
ECDEMIC, STRANGE
bill period of payment ...
USANCE
exchange .... VALUTA
exchange dealer ....
CAMBIST
lands .... OUTREMER
mission ...... LEGATION,
EMBASSY
opposed to .... DOMESTIC
origin .... EXOTIC
quarter ... ENCLAVE, PERA
trade discount ..... AGIO
foreigner .... ALIEN,
OUTLANDER, TRAMONTANE,
OUTSIDER, STRANGER
in Japan .... GAIJIN
in South Africa ....
UITLANDER
foreknowledge ... PRESCIENCE
foreland .... CAPE
forelimb part .... MANUS
forelock ...... COTTER PIN,
LINCHPIN
foreman .... GAFFER
foremost .... FIRST, PREMIER,
LEADING, CHIEF
part ... VAN, FRONT, BOW
forenoon .... MORNING
foreordain ..... (PRE)DESTINE
forerun .. PRECEDE, ANTECEDE,
FORESHADOW, HERALD

forerunner .... HERALD, PROGNOSTIC, ANCESTOR, PREDECESSOR, HARBINGER, PRECURSOR

foreshadow .... ADUMBRATE, PRESAGE, PREFIGURE

foresight .... VISION

foreskin .... PREPUCE

forest ... WOODLAND, WOODS, WEALD

  clearing .... GLADE

  cutting right in the ..... VERT

  debris .... SLASH

  decaying matter ... DUFF

  deity ..... NYMPH, FAUN, PAN

  fire locator .... ALIDADE

  floor layer ...... LITTER

  glade .... CLEARING

  green growth ..... VERT

  humus .... MOR

  keeper .... RANGER

  kind of .... PINERY

  of the .... SYLVAN

  open space ...... SLASH, CLEARING, GLADE

  outlying part ... PURLIEU

  ox .... ANOA

  pertaining to ... SYLVAN

  Philippine .... GUBAT

  soil .... PODZOL

  trees of certain area ..... SILVA

  trees, the .... SYLVA

  warden .... RANGER

forestall .... ANTICIPATE, PREVENT, AVERT

Forester's opera ...... LORLE

forests, coniferous .... TAIGA

foretell .... PREDICT, FORECAST, PROPHESY, AUGUR, VATICINATE, PROGNOSTICATE, PRESAGE, (FORE)BODE

foretoken .... OMEN, PROGNOSTIC, AUGURY

foretooth .... INCISOR

forever ... ETERN(E), ALWAYS, ETERNALLY, AY(E)

forewarning .... AUGURY, OMEN, PORTENT

foreword .... PREFACE, INTRODUCTION, FRONTISPIECE

Forfar .... ANGUS

forfeit .... FINE, PENALTY, GIVE, DEFAULT, LOSE

  for pious purpose .... DEODAND

forfeiture .... FINE, PENALTY, LOSS

  of right for cause .. LAPSE

for(e)gather ...... ASSEMBLE, MEET, ENCOUNTER

forge .... BLOOMERY, STITHY, IMITATE, SMITHY, FURNACE, FORM, COUNTERFEIT, SHAPE, FALSIFY

  apparatus ...... TROMPE

  fireplace of .... HEARTH

forget ..... LAPSE, OVERLOOK, NEGLECT

  me-not ..... MOUSE-EAR, PLANT, MYOSOTIS

forgetful one ..... AMNESIAC, LOTUS-EATER, PROF(ESSOR)

forgetfulness ..... OBLIVION, AMNESIA

  drug .... NEPENTHE

  fruit of .... LOTUS

  river of .... LETHE

forgive ...... EXCUSE, REMIT, PARDON, OVERLOOK, ABSOLVE

forgiving .... PLACABLE

forgo .. ABSTAIN, DO WITHOUT, WAIVE

fork .... BISECT, (BI)FURCATE, PRONG, TINE, BIGHT, BRANCH

forked .... CLEFT, PRONGED, ZIGZAG, FURCATE, BIFID

  organ/part ... FURCULUM

forlorn .... DESERTED, MISERABLE, WRETCHED, BEREFT

form .... CAST, BLANK, CONTOUR, MOLD, FIGURE, PATTERN, RITUAL, FORMALITY, SHAPE, OUTLINE, ORGANIZE, CEREMONY, FASHION, CREATE

  into fabric ...... WEAVE, KNIT

  of bust .... TAILLE

  of government ... POLITY

  of obeisance .... BOW, SALAAM, GENUFLECTION, KOWTOW

oval .... OVOID
take .... MATERIALIZE
formal .... CEREMONIOUS,
    PRIM, STIFF, METHODICAL,
    FRIGID
    artificially .... STILTED
    ceremony .... FUNCTION,
    RITE
    choice .... VOTE
    dance .... BALL
    entrance .... DEBUT
    march .... PROCESSION
    talk ... ADDRESS, LECTURE
formality .... CEREMONY,
    PROPRIETY
formation .... ARRANGEMENT,
    ORDER
    battle ... HERSE, PHALANX
    military .... ECHELON
    panlike .... PATELLA
    side of .... FLANK
formative ending of word .....
    DESINENCE
formed on earth's surface .....
    EPIGENE
former .... QUONDAM,
    ERST(WHILE), EX, ONE-TIME,
    WHILOM, EARLIER,
    PREVIOUS
    days/times .... PAST,
    YORE, AGO, ELD
    emperor .... KAISER,
    TSAR, CZAR
    opposed to ...... LATTER
formerly ...... ERST(WHILE),
    NEE, ONCE, ONE-TIME,
    WHILOM
    prefix .... EX
formic acid source .... ANT
formicary .... ANTHILL
formicid .... ANT
formidable .... MEAN,
    DREADFUL, DIFFICULT,
    AWESOME, FEARFUL
formless .... AMORPHOUS,
    ARUPA
    void .... CHAOS
Formosa .... TAIWAN
    capital .... TAIPEI
    strait port .... AMOY
    tea .... OOLONG
formula ..... CREED, RECIPE,
    SOLUTION, PRESCRIPTION
fornent .... FACING, OPPOSITE
forsake ... ABANDON, DESERT,
    RENOUNCE, LEAVE

forsaken ... LORN, DESOLATE,
    LEFT
forsooth ... INDEED, NO DOUBT
forswear ... RENOUNCE, DENY,
    PERJURE
fort ..... KEEP, (ARMY)POST,
    COTTA, CITADEL, GARRISON,
    PRESIDIO
    coastal .... MARTELLO
    of Moros .... COTTA
    small .... FORTALICE,
    SCONCE
    U.S. ... DIX, DONELSON,
    DUQUESNE, (MC)HENRY,
    SUMTER, ORD
    wall .... PARAPET
    wooden ... BLOCKHOUSE
Fortaleza .... CEARA
forte .... SPECIALTY,
    STRONG POINT, LOUD
    opposed to ...... FOIBLE
forth .... ONWARD, OUT,
    FORWARD
forthright .... DIRECT, FRANK
forthwith ... EFTSOON, ANON,
    AT ONCE, IMMEDIATELY, NOW
fortification ...... EARTHWORK,
    REDAN, OUTWORK,
    STRONGHOLD, FORTRESS,
    ABAT(T)IS, PALISADE, BAIL,
    BASTION, RAVELIN,
    REDOUBT, BULWARK, FORT
    ditch/moat ..... FOSS(E)
    material .... GABION
    outwork ..... TENAIL(LE),
    FLECHE, DEMILUNE
    part of .... PARAPET,
    RAMPART, EMBRASURE,
    BATTLEMENT,
    BREASTWORK, BAIL
    sloping embankment ....
    GLACIS, SCARP
    wall .... TALUS
fortified .... ARMED,
    STRENGTHENED
    hill .... MERLIN
    house .... PEEL
    line .... MAGINOT,
    SIEGFRIED, WESTWALL
    place ...... FORTRESS,
    CASTLE, PILLBOX,
    CITADEL, REDAN,
    GARRISON, PRESIDIO
    rampart ...... BULWARK
    tower .... DONJON,
    DUNGEON, PEEL

town ....BURG
fortify ....ARM, MAN,
STRENGTHEN
fortis .... SPEECH SOUND
opposed to ....LENIS
fortitude ....ENDURANCE,
PATIENCE, GRIT, GUTS,
PLUCK, COURAGE
fortnight ....TWO WEEKS
fortnightly ....PERIODICAL
fortress ....GIBRALTAR,
CITADEL, FORT, BASTILLE,
STRONGHOLD
flying ....SUPERFORT
impregnable, so-called ...
GIBRALTAR,
CORREGIDOR,
SINGAPORE
mobile ....TANK
fortuitous ......(BY)CHANCE,
ACCIDENTAL
Fortuna, Roman ......TYCHE
fortunate ....FAVORABLE,
BLESSED, HAPPY, LUCKY,
AUSPICIOUS
fortunately ....HAPLY,
HAPPILY
fortune ......RICHES, CHANCE,
STARS, LUCK, LOT, FATE,
WEALTH
hunter ....ADVENTURER
hunter's prize ......HEIR
slang ....PILE
teller ....ORACLE, SEER,
GYPSY, PALMIST,
AUGUR, SIBIL, SIBYL,
HARUSPEX
teller's cards ......TAROT
telling ....TAROT
forty days fast ......CARENE,
LENT
five degree angle .....
OCTANT
inches ....ELL
niner ....MINER,
ARGONAUT
rods ....FURLONG
winks ... DOZE, (CAT)NAP
winks of Spaniard ......
SIESTA
forum ....ASSEMBLY,
(LAW)COURT,
MARKET(PLACE), SQUARE
forward ... PERT, PRECOCIOUS,
FRONT, AHEAD, EAGER,
ADVANCE(D), EARLY,

TRANSMIT, BOLD, DISPATCH,
SEND
part ......FORE, FRONT,
BOW, ANTERIOR
fossa .. PIT, HOLLOW, CAVITY
fosse ....DITCH, MOAT
fossette .... DIMPLE, HOLLOW
fossil ....ROCK, MINERAL,
ANTIQUATED, PINITE
crinoid ....CRINITE
mollusk ....DOLITE
plants ....CALAMITE
resin ... AMBER, RETINITE
fossilize ....PETRIFY
foster ....REAR, SUCKLE,
NOURISH, PROMOTE,
CHERISH
child ....STEPSON,
FOUNDLING,
FOSTERLING
songwriter .....STEPHEN
foul ... FECULENT, STINKING,
LOATHSOME, PUTRID,
ROTTEN, OBSCENE,
INDECENT, UNFAIR,
ENTANGLE, UNCLEAN,
SQUALID
dirt ....FILTH
smelling ....FETID,
OLID, NOISOME, ROTTEN
smelling fruit ... DURIAN
smelling plant .. HENBANE
up .. BUNGLE, ENTANGLE
foulard .... (NECK)TIE, SCARF
foumart ....POLECAT
found .... BASE, ESTABLISH,
CAST
on earth's surface ......
EPIGENE
thing .. TROVE, DISCOVERY
foundation ....CORSET,
BASIS, BASE, ENDOWMENT,
FUND, BED(ROCK), RIPRAP
garment ....CORSET,
GIRDLE
founded ....FUSIL
abbreviation ....ESTAB,
EST
founder ......STUMBLE, FALL,
FAIL, COLLAPSE, LAMINITIS,
CASTER
foundling ....WAIF, EPPIE
place for ....CRECHE
foundry ....CASTING(S)
fount ....SOURCE, SPRING,
WELL

fountain .... WELL, SPRING, FONT, SOURCE
  drink .... SODA, POP
  drinking ...... BUBBLER
  Mt. Helicon ....
      HIPPOCRENE
  nymph .... EGERIA, NAIAD
  of youth .... BIMINI
  poetic .... FONT
fountainpen .... STYLOGRAPH
  tube .... BARREL
four-bagger ..... HOMER(UN)
  combining form ... TETRA
  dollar gold piece .. STELLA
  flush ...... BLUFF, BRAG
  footed .... TETRAPOD, QUADRUPED
  group of ..... TETRAD, H-CLUB
  H club's concern ....
    HEART, HANDS, HEAD, HEALTH
  hundred, the ..... ELITE
  in hand item ..... ASCOT, TEAM, COACH, NECKTIE
  inch measure ..... HAND
  o'clock, the ....
    MARVEL-OF-PERU, PLANT
  pecks .... BUSHEL
  poster ...... BED(STEAD)
  set of .... TETRAD
fourchette .... WISHBONE
fourflusher .... BLUFFER, PHONY, HUMBUG, BRAGGART
  game of a .... POKER
fourfold .... QUADRUPLE
fourgon .... WAGON, CAR, TUMBRIL, VAN
fourpence ..... GROAT, COIN
fourscore .... EIGHTY
foursome .... QUARTET
  gathering place of ... TEE
foursquare ..... FIRM, FRANK
14 days .... FORTNIGHT
  pounds .... STONE
1492 ship .... NINA, PINTA
fourth .... QUARTER
  dimension .... TIME
  estate .... PRESS
foussa .... CIVET
fouter .... FIG
foveola .... VARIOLE
fowl .... PHEASANT, TURKEY,

COCK, HEN, CHICKEN, GOOSE, DUCK
  castrated .... CAPON
  comb of ..... CARUNCLE
  dealer .... POULT(ER)
  disease .... PIP
  dish stewed in wine ....
    SALMI(S)
  domestic ..... DORKING, LEGHORN, MINORCA, COCHIN, POULTRY
  flesh below beak ....
    WATTLE
  forelimb .... WING
  leg joint .... HOCK
  meat, broiled ....
    CARBONADO
  outgrowth ..... WATTLE, JOWL, SPUR
  small .... BANTAM
  stuffing for .... FARCE
  table .... CAPON
  wattle .... JOWL
  young .... POULT
fowling piece .... GUN
fowls, domestic .... POULTRY
fox .... TOD, RE(Y)NARD
  African .... CAAMA, ASSE, FENNEC
  face of .... MASK
  female ..... VIXEN, BITCH
  flying .... KALONG
  head of .... MASK
  hunter .... PINK
  hunter's coat ..... PINK
  hunter's cry ... TALLYHO
  killer .... VULPECIDE
  like .... VULPINE, VULPECULAR
  male .... DOG
  tail .... BRUSH
  terrier .... WIREHAIR
  terrier, RCA's ... NIPPER
  young .... CUB
foxglove .. DIGITALIS, FIGWORT
foxtail .... GRASS
foxy ... CUNNING, CUTE, SLY, CRAFTY, SOUR, VULPINE
foy .... FEAST, PRESENT
foyer ..... VESTIBULE, LOBBY
fra ..... MONK, BROTHER, ABBE
  title of .... MONK, FRIAR
fracas ..... BRAWL, QUARREL, MELEE, RUMBLE
fraction .... FRAGMENT, DECIMAL, SCRAP, PART

fractious ..... UNRULY, CROSS,
PEEVISH, FRETFUL
fracture .... BREAK, CRACK,
SPLIT
fragile .... FRAIL, BRASH,
FINESPUN, FLIMSY, TENDER,
DELICATE, FRANGIBLE,
WEAK, BRITTLE
fragment ... PIECE, PART, BIT,
FLINDER, MORCEAU, SHRED,
FRACTION, CHIP, SIPPET,
SHIVER
  cloth ..... RAG, TATTER
  pottery ... SHARD, SHERD
fragrance .... SCENT, AROMA,
INCENSE, ODOR
  of wine/brandy ....
BOUQUET
fragrances: rare .... AROMATA
fragrant .... REDOLENT,
ODOROUS, BALMY, OLENT,
AROMATIC, SWEET, SPICY
  bark .... CANELLA
  flower ... ROSE, JASMINE,
LILAC
  gum resin .... MYRRH
  oil ..... BALSAM, ATTAR
  ointment ... (SPIKE)NARD
  plant .... PINESAP,
LAVENDER
  rootstock ...... ORRIS
  seed .... ANISE, DILL,
ANISEED
  shrub .... TIARA
  wood .... CEDAR
frail ...... DELICATE, WEAK,
BASKET, FLIMSY, SLIGHT,
FEEBLE, FRAGILE, SLENDER,
TENDER
  slang .... GIRL, WOMAN
frailty .... WEAKNESS,
FAILING, FAULT, DEFECT
fraise .... RUFF, COLLAR
framb(o)esia .... YAWS
frame ..... DEVISE, COMPOSE,
RACK, SHAPE, FORM,
FASHION, DESIGN,
CONSTRUCT
  automobile ..... CHASSIS
  bobbins' .... CREEL
  body .... BUILD
  building's boarding ....
SIDING
  carriage .... CHASSIS
  cloth-stretching .. TENTER
  counting .... ABACUS

  display .... EASEL
  drying .... HERSE, RACK,
TENTER
  for embroidery ....
TABO(U)RET
  for feeding animals ......
HAYRACK
  for holding things .. RACK
  in baseball ..... INNING
  of mind .... MOOD,
MORALE, TEMPER
  of ship .... HULL
  openwork .... CAGE
  set with spikes .... HERSE,
PORTCULLIS
  soap bar .... SESS
  stand ..... RACK, EASEL
  spiked .... HERSE
  supporting ..... TRESTLE
  torch .... CRESSET
framework ... FABRIC, SHELL,
TRUSS, CADRE
  bridge support ... TRUSS
  for carrying person ....
LITTER
  for traveling crane ......
GANTRY
  of animal body ....
SKELETON
  of rods, sticks, etc. ......
WATTLE
  on which to dry skins ....
HERSE
  over oil well .... DERRICK
  roof support ..... TRUSS
franc, 1/100 of ...... CENTIME
France (see French) .. GALLIA,
GAUL
  novelist .... ANATOLE
  Southern .... MIDI
  symbol of .... COCK
franchise ..... RIGHT, LICENSE,
CHARTER, SUFFRAGE,
PRIVILEGE, SOC
Franciscan ...... MINORITE,
FRIAR, CAPUCHIN
  friar .... MINORITE
  mission .... ALAMO
Franck, composer .... CESAR
Franco (dictator) title ....
(EL) CAUDILLO
francolin .... TITAR,
PARTRIDGE
francs, 20 .... LOUIS
frangible .... BREAKABLE,
FRAGILE

frangipani .... JASMIN(E)
    neckwear .... LEI
frank .... BLUNT, OPEN,
    CANDID, PLAIN, EXEMPT,
    OUTSPOKEN, HONEST,
    RIPUARIAN
Frankenstein novel authoress ..
    SHELLEY
frankfurter .... SAUSAGE,
    WIENER, WEENIE, HOTDOG,
    WEENY
    jurist .... FELIX
frankincense ...... OLIBANUM,
    GUM RESIN
Frankish king .... CLOVIS
    law .... SALIC
    peasant .... LITUS
franklin .... FREEHOLDER
frankness .... CANDOR,
    CANDIDNESS
Franks, ruler of ...... PEPIN,
    MARTEL
frantic .... FRENZIED,
    EXCITED, FRENETIC, FURIOUS
    make ... PANIC, FRENZY,
    MADDEN
    person .... FRENETIC
frap .... TIGHTEN
frappe .... DESSERT, ICED,
    DRINK
frater .... FRIAR, BROTHER,
    COMRADE
fraternity ..... BROTHERHOOD
    local .... CHAPTER
    meeting place .... LODGE
    to-do .. RUSH, INITIATION
fraternize .... ASSOCIATE
frau .... WIFE
fraud ..... DECEIT, DECEPTION,
    JAPE, IMPOSTOR, IMPOSTURE,
    HOAX, TRICK(ERY),
    ARTIFICE, SHAM, BUNCO,
    HUMBUG
    conspiracy to commit ...
    COVIN
fraudulent ... FAKE, DECEITFUL
fraught .... FILLED, BESET,
    CHARGED, LOADED, LADEN
fraxinella .... DITTANY
fray ...... FIGHT, CONFLICT,
    FRAZZLE, RAVEL, RAG,
    MELEE, BRAWL, RUMBLE
fraying, cord to stop ....
    MARLINE, MARLING
frazzle .... FRAY, SHRED

freak ..... CAPRICE, DAPPLE,
    WHIM, MONSTROSITY, QUEER,
    ABNORMAL, STREAK, FLECK,
    ATROCITY
    of nature .. SIAMESE TWIN,
    HUNCHBACK,
    BEARDED LADY
freckle .... LENTIGO
Frederick I of Germany ......
    BARBAROSSA
    the Great's palace ......
    SANS SOUCI
free .... ABSOLVE, LOOSE,
    GRATIS, CLEAR, OPEN,
    DISENGAGE, LIBERATE,
    LIBRE, RID, MANUMIT,
    RELEASE, FOOTLOOSE,
    EMANCIPATE, AT LARGE
    and easy ..... INFORMAL
    for-all ..... MELEE, FRAY,
    BRAWL, RHUBARB,
    CLEM, RUMBLE,
    BATTLE ROYAL
    from infection .. ASEPTIC
    lance .... MERCENARY
    speech restraint .... GAG
    swimming organism ......
    PROTOZOA
    ticket .... PASS
    ticket holder .. DEADHEAD
freebooter .... CATERAN,
    PIRATE, FILIBUSTER,
    BUCCANEER, PLUNDERER
freedman .. TIRO, LAET, THANE
freedom .... LIBERTY,
    EXEMPTION, INDEPENDENCE,
    FRANCHISE, LICENSE
    from doubt .. CERTITUDE,
    CERTAINTY
    from punishment ....
    IMMUNITY, IMPUNITY
    kind of .... LICENSE
    to enter .... ENTRY
freehanded ...... GENEROUS
freehold ..... ESTATE, OFFICE
freeholder .... YEOMAN,
    FRANKLIN
freeman .... CITIZEN, CHURL,
    THANE, CEORL, VILLEIN,
    BURGESS
    actress .... MONA
freemen's assembly ..... MOOT
freestone ...... PLUM, PEACH
freethinker .... ATHEIST,
    LIBERTINE
freewill .... VOLUNTARY

freeze ∼ ICE, CONGEAL, CHILL, GELATE, NIP
freezer ∼∙∼∙∼ REFRIGERATOR
freight .... CARGO, LADING
 boat ...... SCOW, BARGE
 car dumping apparatus ∼ TIPPLE
 steamer ∼∙ WHALEBACK
 surcharge ∼∙∼ PRIMAGE
 train car ...... CABOOSE
freighter ∼∙ TANKER, SHIPPER, LIGHTER, TRAMP
fremd ∼∙∙ FOREIGN, STRANGE, ALIEN
fremitus ∼∙∼∙∼∙ VIBRATION
French ....∼∙∼∙ GALLIC
 abbe ....∼∙ ABBOT
 according to ...∼∙ A LA
 actor ∼∙∼∙ FERNANDEL, CHEVALIER, BOYER
 administrative department INTENDANCE
 afoot ....∼∙ A PIED
 African lake .... (T)CHAD
 after ∼∙∙∙∙∙∙∙∙∙∙ APRES
 again .... ENCORE
 airplane ∼∙ SPAD, AVION
 airship .... AERONAT
 Algerian soldier ∼ TURCO
 all .... TOUT(E)
 Alp top ....∼∙ PIC
 Alpine sight ... ADROITE
 among ....∼∙ ENTRE
 angel ....∼∙ ANGE
 annual income ∼∙ RENTE
 anxiety ....∼∙ SOUCI
 aperitif ....∼∙ PERNOD
 April .... AVRIL
 architectural ornament ∼ OVE
 arm ∼∙∼∙∙∙∙∼∙∼ BRAS
 army sharpshooter ∼∙∼∙ TIRAILLEUR
 art center ....∼ BARBIZON
 art show ....∼∙ SALON
 article ...... LA, LE, DES, LES, UN(E), UNES, DE
 artist ∼∙ MONET, MATISSE, CHAGALL, DORE, DERAIN, DEGAS, COROT, RENOIR, MANET
 astronomer ... LAGRANGE
 aunt .... TANTE
 author ... CAMUS, ZOLA, GIDE, COCTEAU, STAEL, FRANCE, RENAN, DUMAS, HUGO, VERNE, SARTRE, LOTI

awl ∼∙∙∙∙∙∙∙∙∙∙ ALENE
axe ∼∙∙∙∙∙∼∙∼∙∙ HACHE
baby ∼∙∙∙∼∙∼∙∼ ENFANT
back ∼∙∙∼∙∙∼∙∼∙ DOS
bacteriologist .... PASTEUR
ballet member ∙∙ DANSEUR
banner ∼∙∼∙∼∙∙∼ FANION
basis .... FOND
bath .... BAIN
beach .... PLAGE, RIVAGE
bean ...... FEVE, PHASEL, HARICOT
beast ....∼∙ BETE
beauty .... NINON
bed ....∼∙ LIT, COUCHE
beef .... BOEUF
behold .... VOILA
being .... ETRE
Belgian river ... YSER
bench .... BANC
between .... ENTRE
bicycle .... VELO
biologist .... CARREL
bitter ...... AMER, ACRE
black ....∼∙ NOIR(E)
blessed .... SACRE
blue .... BLEU
"Bluebeard" .... LANDRU
boarding house/school .. PENSION
bodice .... GILET
bonds .... RENTES
book .... LIVRE
box .... BOITE
bread .... PAIN
broken .... CASSE
broth .... POTAGE
brown .... BRUN
but .... MAIS
cabbage .... CHOU
cafe .... ESTAMINET
cafe noir .... COFFEE
cake ... GATEAU, CIERGE
Canadian: sl. .. CANUCK
cap's decoration .... POMPOM, COCKADE
car .... RENAULT
card .... CARTE
care .... SOIN
carriage .... FIACRE, VOITURE
castle .... CHATEAU
cathedral city .. R(H)EIMS

cavalryman .. CARABINIER
chain ....,, .. SAUTOIR
chalk .. .. TALC
challenge .... DEFI
cheese .... BRIE
chemist .... PASTEUR,
          RAOULT
chestnut .... MARRON
chicken .... POULE,
          HOUDAN
child .... ENFANT
citizen .... CITOYEN
city .... RIOM, LILLE,
      AMIENS, CALAIS,
      CLICHY, BLOIS,
      CAMBRAI, CANNES,
      CASTRES, CHARTRES,
      NANTES, AVIGNON,
      NIMES, CAEN, COLMAR,
      CHAUMONT, PARIS,
      AGEN, ARLES, LIMOGES,
      DOUAY, DOUAI,
      BELFORT, DIJON,
      NANCY, ORLEANS,
      LYON(S), LISLE,
      VERDUN, VICHY,
      TROYES, TOURS,
      TOULON, SOISSONS,
      SEDAN, NEUILLY, PAU,
      R(H)EIMS, RENNES,
      METZ, ROUEN
cleric .... ABBE, PERE
cloth .... TOILE
clothes .... DRAP
cloud .... NUAGE
coach for hire .... FIACRE
cognac .... MARTELL
coin .... OBOLE, ECU, SOU,
      FRANC, DENIER,
      CENTIME, LIVRE,
      TESTON, LOUIS (D'OR)
colony .... (T)CHAD
combining form .. GALLO
comfort .... AISE
company .... CIE
composer ...... RAVEL,
      BIZET, BERLIOZ, LALO,
      (D)INDY, RAMEAU
concrete .... BETON
conqueror ...... CLOVIS
corn .... BLE
count .... COMTE
country dance ... BRAWL
couturier .... DIOR,
          BALMAIN
critic .... TAINE

crown princess ....
          DAUPHINE
crude .... CRU
crusader ..... MONTFORT
cry for help .... AMOI
cup .... TASSE
curse .... ANATHEMA
dance .. GAVOT, CANCAN,
      APACHE, BAL, BRAWL,
      COURANTE, QUADRILLE,
      RONDE, GALLIARD,
      COTILL(I)ON
daughter ......:.. FILLE
dear .... CHER(I)
decree .... ARRET
deed ...... ,, ... FAIT
delightful ... CHARMANT
department ..... ARLES,
      OISE, ORNE, NORD,
      VENDEE, HAUT-RHIN,
      EURE, ARIEGE, SOMME,
          GIRONDE
department head ....
          PREFECT
depot .... GARE
detective force ... SURETE
devil .... DIABLE
dialect .... PATOIS,
      LANGUE D'OC
district .... PERCHE
diversion .... JEU
donkey .... ANE
down .... BAS
down with ..... ABAS
dramatist ..... MOLIERE,
      ETIENNE, COCTEAU,
      DUMAS, LESAGE,
      VOLTAIRE, RACINE
dream .... REVE
droghiere ...... GROCER
dry .... SEC
duchy ...... AQUITAINE,
      ANJOU, VALOIS
dugout .... ABRI
duke .... DUC
dungeon ...... CACHOT
east .... EST
edict .... ARRET
egg ... OEUF, OVALE, OVE
elder .... AINE
eleven .... ONZE
emblem .... LILY
emperor .... LOUIS,
          NAPOLEON
empress .... EUGENIE,
          JOSEPHINE

enamel .... EMAIL
enamelware .... LIMOGES
end .... FIN
entertainer ..... DISEUSE
equal ..... EGAL, PAREIL
equality .... EGALITE
evening .... SOIR
exist .... ETRE
explorer ... CADILLAC,
LA SALLE
eye .... OEIL
fabric .... GROS, ETOILE,
DRAP, LAME
fabulist ... (LA) FONTAINE
fascist organization .....
CAGOULARD
fat .... GRAS
father .... PERE
"FBI" .... DST
fear .... PEUR
feudal tax .... TAILLE
fighter plane ...... SPAD
finally .... ENFIN
fine bearing .... BEL AIR
fire .... FEU
five .... CINQ
flag .... TRICOLOR
flax .... LIN
forest .... BOIS
fortification ... PARADOS
foundation .... FOND
fox .... REYNARD
friar .... FRERE
fried potatoes .... CHIPS
friend .... AMI(E)
from .... DES
froth .... BAVE
fund .... FOND
game .... JEU(X)
gauze .... LISSE
general .... KLEBER
geologist ...... CORDIER
gift .... CADEAU
gingerbread ....
PAIN D'APICE
girl .... FILLE
glance.......... APERCU
glass .... VERRE
glove .... GANT
go .... ALLER
god .... DIEU
good .... BON
goodby .... ADIEU,
AU REVOIR
gopher .... GAUFRE
gossip .... ONDIT

grape-growing area .....
MEDOC
gravy .... JUS
gray .... GRIS
ground .... TERRE
guerrillas ...... MAQUIS
Guiana capital ....
CAYENNE
hack .... FIACRE
hair style .... GOULUE
hairdresser .... MARCEL,
FRISEUR
half .... DEMI
half-mask .... LOUP
hall .... SALLE
handle .... ANSE
hat designer ..... DACHE
head .... TETE
headache ... MAL DE TETE
health .... SANTE
heaven .... CIEL
heavenly being ... ANGE
heir to throne .. DAUPHIN
helmet .... HEAUME
here ICI
hero in romance ......
AMADIS, BAYARD
heroic verse ....
ALEXANDRINE
hidden ... SECRE, PERDU
high society ....
HAUT MONDE
hill .... PUY
hillock .... MOTTE
his .... ALUI, SES
historian ...... MERIMEE,
RENAN, TAINE
holy .... SACRE
horn .... BRASSE
house .... MAISON
hunting match ..... TIR
husband .... MARI
in .... DANS
income .... RENTE
infantryman ... CHASSEUR,
ZOUAVE
infinitive .... AVOIR
ink .... ENCRE
inn .... AUBERGE
is .... EST
island .... ILE
island in Indian Ocean ...
REUNION
island off Newfoundland
MIQUELON
join .... UNIR

juice .... JUS
kind .... SORTE
king .... ROI
king's heir .... DAUPHIN
kingdom .... ARLES
lace ... ALENCON, CLUNY, FAL
lamb .... AGNEAU
land .... TERRE
land measure ... ARPENT
landscape artist .. COROT
language .... LANGUE
laugh .... RIRE
law .... LOI
lawyer .... AVOCAT
leather .... CUIR
leave .... CONGE
Legion of Honor member CHEVALIER
legislature .... SENAT
Lenten season .. CAREME
lexicographer .. LAROUSSE
life .... VIE
likewise .... DEMEME
liking .... GRE
lily .... LYS
little ...... PETIT(E), PEU
lodging place ...... GITE
love .... AIMER
loving .... TENDRE
maid (servant) ... BONNE, FILLE
mail .... POSTE
Manche capital .. ST. LO
mansion .... HOTEL
marshal .... FOCH, BAZAINE, VENDOME, MURAT, NEY, SAXE, RUEL, JOFFRE, MASSENA, TURENNE
mask .... LOUP
matchless .... SAN EGAL
matin lay ...... AUBADE
May .... MAI
meager .... MAICRE
measure .... MINOT
meat dish .... SALMI
merry .... GAI
military ensign .... ORIFLAMME
milk .... LAIT
minstrel ..... JONGLEUR
mirth .... GAITE
misdemeanor ..... DELIT
money of account .. LIVRE
month ... MAI, MOIS, JUIN

morning .... MATIN
Morocco capital .... MEKNES
mother .... MERE
mountain .... MONT
municipal official .. JURAT
museum .... MUSEE, CLUNY, RODIN, GUIMET, CARNAVALET, LOUVRE
muslin ..... MOUSSELINE
my .... MON
my dear ..... MA CHERE
nail .... CLOU
name ...... NOM, RENE, HENRI, JACQUES, MICHEL(LE), PIERRE, JEAN
national ...... CITOYEN
national anthem .... MARSEILLAISE
naturalist ..... LAMARCK
naval base .... BREST
navigator ..... CARTIER
near .... PRES
neat .... SOIGNE(E)
negative .... PAS
nerve .... NERF
news .... NOUVELLES
night .... NUIT
no .... NON
nobleman .. COMTE, DUC
noon .... MIDI
nose .... NEZ
nothing .... RIEN
notion .... IDEE
novelist .. LESAGE, LOTI, GARD, MAUROIS, SAGAN, ROMAINS, MALRAUX
nursemaid .... BONNE
oath .... VOIRE DIRE
obsession ..... IDEE FIXE
ogre .... HUGON
on .... ADROITE
on foot .... A PIED
one .... UN(E)
our .... NOUS
out .... HORS
over .... SUR
Pacific islands .... MARQUESAS
painter .... RENOIR, SEURAT, MANET, CEZANNE, MONET, INGRES, PISSARRO, DEGAS, COROT
pancake .... CREPE

pantomimist ... PIERROT
paper-maker .. PAPETIER
parent ...... PERE, MERE
parliament .... SENAT
pastry .. BABA, NAPOLEON
patron saint ...... DENIS
petticoat .... COTTE
philosopher ..... SARTRE,
    PASCAL, DIDEROT
phonetician ...... PASSY
physicist .... PERRIN,
    AMPERE
pilgrimage town ......
    LOURDES
plumcake .... BABA
pocket .... POCHE
poem .... VERS, DIT,
    VILLANELLE
poet .... LAMARTINE,
    TROUVEUR, TROUVERE,
    RACINE, RONSARD
police .... GENDARME
police official ....
    COMMISSARY
pond/pool .... MARE
porcelain .... SEVRES,
    LIMOGES
pork .... SALE
port ...... BREST, DIEPPE,
    CAEN, HAVRE, ROUEN,
    SETE
porter .... SUISSE,
    CONCIERGE
possessive ...... MES, SES,
    NOUS
pot au feu .... STEW
pout .... MOUE
premier .... TARDIEU,
    HERRIOT
president .... BLUM,
    (DE) GAULLE, CARNOT,
    POMPIDOU
president's residence ....
    ELYSEE
pretty .... JOLI(E)
priest .. ABBE, CURE, PERE
prize for literature ....
    GONCOURT
profession .... METIER
pronoun ... MOI, TOI, TU,
    VOTRE, JE, ILS, UNE,
    ELLE, MES, CES, VOUS
Protestant ... HUGUENOT
Protestant leader ....
    MORNAY

Protestant reformer ....
    CALVIN
Provencal poet .. MISTRAL
province ... LANGUEDOC,
    LYON(N)AIS, PICARDY,
    PROVENCE
punishment ...... PEINE
pupil .... ELEVE
queen .... REINE
rabbit .... LAPIN
racecourse ..... AUTEUIL
railroad station ... GARE
read .... LIRE
ready .... PRET
rebel .... JACOBIN
receipt .... RECU
refugee .... EMIGRE
relative ...... MERE, PERE,
    TANTE
Republic personified ....
    MARIANNE
resort .... ANTIBES,
    BIARRITZ, BAIN,
    CANNES, MENTON
revenue .... RENTE
Revolution refrain ......
    CAIRA
revolutionist ... DANTON,
    MARAT, CARMAGNOLE
ribbon .... SAUTOIR
rifle .... CHASSEPOT
river ...... RHONE, SEINE,
    ISERE, DOUBS, SAONE,
    AIRE, VESLE, LOIRE, OISE,
    SOMME, MARNE, MEUSE,
    ORNE, SAAR, YSER,
    LOT, AISNE
roast .... ROTI
Roman Catholic ....
    GALLICAN
room .... SALLE
royal edict .... ARRET
royal family ..... CAPET,
    VALOIS
royal standard ....
    ORIFLAMME
ruling family .... VALOIS
rumor .... ON DIT
sad(ness) .... TRISTE(SSE)
salt .... SEL
salt tax .... GABELLE
satin fabric ..... ETOILE
satirist .... VOLTAIRE,
    RABELAIS
saying .... DIT
school ..... ECOLE, LYCEE

sculptor .... HOUDON, RODIN
sea .... MER
seaport .... CALAIS, CHERBOURG, (LE)HAVRE, MARSEILLE(S), TOULON
seasoning .... SEL
secondary school .. LYCEE
secret intelligence .. SDECE
security .... RENTE
senior .... AINE
servant .... BONNE
she .... ELLE
sheep .... MOUTON
shelter ... ABRI, COUVERT, GITE
shepherd .... PATRE
shield ...... EGIDE, ECU, TARGE
shoot .... TIRER
shooting match ..... TIR
shoulder .... EPAULE
shrine .... LOURDES
sickness .... MALAISE
silk .... SOIE, GROS
silk center .... LYON
singer .... PIAF
sir .... SIEUR
site of Roman ruins ..... ORANGE
skater .... PATINEUR
ski champ .... KILLY
slang .... FROG
small .... PETIT(E)
smoking-room .... ESTAMINET
soap .... SAVIN
society .... MONDE
soldier ... POILU, SOLDAT, LEGIONNAIRE, CHASSEUR
soldier hero ..... BAYARD
Somaliland capital ...... DJIBOUTI, JIBUTI
son .... FILS
song .... CHANSON
soprano .... PONS
soul .... AME
soup .... POTAGE
south .... MIDI, SUD
spinster .... FILLE
spirit .. AME, ELAN, ESPRIT
square .... CARRE
star .... ETOILE
state .... ETAT
statesman ...... BRIAND,

MAZARIN, CARNOT, REYNAUD
stock exchange .. BOURSE
stoneware .... GRES
storehouse .... ETAPE
storm .... ORAGE
street .... RUE
student .... ELEVE
style .... TON
stylist .... DIOR
Sudan .... MALI
summer .... ETE
supply .... FOND
sweetbread .... RIS
sweetmeat ..... DRAGEE
taste .... GRE
tawny .... TANNE
tea .... THE
their .... LEUR
then ..... ALORS, DONC
there! .... VOILA
they .... ILS
think .... PENSER
thirty .... TRENTE
tidy .... SOIGNE(E)
tire .... PNEU
title of respect ..... SIEUR
tobacco .... TABAC
too .... TROP
town ..... AGEN, ST. CYR, CRECY, VALENCE, VIMY, NESLE, RIOM
true .... VRAI
Tuesday .... MARDI
twelve peers .. DOUZEPERS
uncle .... ONCLE
under .... SOUS
underground fighters .... MAQUIS
upon .... SUR
verse .... RONDEL, VIRELAY, ALBA
very .... TRES
vest .... GILET
vineyard .... VIGNE, CLOS
vogue .... TON
voucher .... RECU
wagon .... VOITURE
wall .... MUR
warehouse ... ENTREPOT
wartime capital .. VICHY
water .... EAU
watered silk ..... MOIRE
wave .... ONDE
wax .... CIRE
we .... NOUS

weapon .... ARME
weight ..... LIVRE, SOL, GRAMME
well .... BIEN
well groomed .. SOIGNE(E)
wheat .... BLE
wind .... MISTRAL
wine .... MEDOC, HERMITAGE, BORDEAUX, BURGUNDY, PINARD, VIN
wing .... AILE
winter .... HIVER
with .... AVEC
without .... SANS
wood .... BOIS
woodland .... FORET
world .... MONDE
World War I plane ...... NIEUPORT
writer .... MAUROIS, RENAN, HUGO, STAEL, DUMAS, VERNE, FRANCE, VOLTAIRE, HEINE, VILLON
yesterday .... HIER
your .... VOTRE
youth .... FILS
Frenchman .... GAUL, HUGUENOT
frenzied ..... BERSERK, AMOK, FRANTIC, RAVING, ENRAGED, MADDING
fighter ... AMUCK, AMOK, BERSERK, BARESARK
frenzy ...... FUROR, ORGASM, MANIA, RAGE
freon ..... GAS, REFRIGERANT
frequent .... HAUNT, OFT, CONSTANT, HABITUAL, OFTEN
frequenter of a kind .. HABITUE
frequently .... OFTEN
frere .... BROTHER, FRIAR
fresh ...... NEW, SASSY, PERT, CLEAN, RECENT, BRISK, DRUNK, TIPSY, RAW
clothes .... CHANGE
colloquial ... PERT, BOLD, SAUCY, IMPUDENT
talk .... LIP
water alga .... DESMID
water worm ...... NAID
freshener, skin .... LOTION
freshet .... FLOOD, SPATE, TORRENT

freshman .... NOVICE, BEGINNER, NEWCOMER
Annapolis .... PLEBE
slang .... FROSH
West Point .... PLEBE
fret ...... FUME, NAG, STEW, FUSS, VEX, CHAFE, CHAMP, GNAW, WORRY
British .... CHEVY
fretful ... PEEVISH, IRRITABLE, PETULANT
Freud, psychiatrist .. SIGMUND
Freya's dwelling ... FOLKVANG
friable ..... BRITTLE, MEALY, FRAGILE, FRAIL, CRISP, SHORT
friar ...... MONASTIC, LISTER, ABBOT, FRATER, FRA, MONK, CARMELITE, DOMINICAN, AUGUSTINIAN
beggar .... SERVITE
bird .... PIMLICO
head covering .... COWL, CAPUCHE
of fiction .... TUCK
robe of .... FROCK
friar's lantern .. IGNIS FATUUS
friary .... MONASTERY
fricative ...... SPIRANT, HISS
friction .... ERASURE, RUB(BING), DISAGREEMENT, ABRASION
air .... WINDAGE
match .... FUSEE
fried lightly .... SAUTE(E)D
slang .... DRUNK
friedcake .... CRULLER, DOUGHNUT
friend ... ALLY, QUAKER, PAL, AMIGO, SUPPORTER, SYMPATHIZER, BUDDY, CHUM, CRONY
boy's best ...... MOTHER, MAMA
close .... SIDEKICK
faithful .... ACHATES, DAMON, PYTHIAS
false .... IAGO
French .... AMI(E)
lion's ...... ANDROCLES, ANDROCLUS
man's best .... DOG
friendly .... AMICABLE, KIND(LY), AMIABLE
dwarf .... TROLL, LEPRECHAUN

hint .... TIP
Islands .... TONGA
relations .... AMITY
understanding .. ENTENTE
friendship .... AMITY
Friesian .... FRIESE
frieze square .... METOPE
frigate .... WARSHIP
bird .... IWA, ATAFA
Frigg's husband .... ODIN
fright ... PANIC, ALARM, AWE,
FEAR, TERROR
frighten ... DAUNT, STARTLE,
FEEZE, SCARE, TERRIFY,
ALARM, TERRORIZE
frightened ... AFEAR, AFRAID,
SCARED, ALARMED
frigid .... COLD, FORMAL,
STIFF, HYPERBOREAN
zone subsoil ....
PERMAFROST
frijol .... BEAN
frill .... RUFF(LE), JABOT
FURBELOW, ADORNMENT,
FALBALA, RUCHE
Friml (Rudolf) forte ....
OPERETTA
fringe ...... THRUM, BORDER,
MARGIN, EDGE, LOMA,
SKIRT
benefit ..... INSURANCE,
VACATION, BONUS
hairs, etc. ...... FIMBRIA
of Jew's scarf .... ZIZITH
frippery .... FINERY
useless .... FALLAL
friseur .... HAIRDRESSER
frisk .... FROLIC, CAPER,
GAMBOL, TITTUP
slang .... SEARCH
frisky ...... SPRY, KITTENISH
animal ..... GOAT, COLT,
KITTEN
Frisson of horror ...... GRUE
frith .... INLET, ESTUARY
fritter .... SHRED, PIECE,
CAKE, DALLY, DAWDLE,
WASTE
frivolity .... LEVITY
frivolous ... PALTRY, TRIVIAL,
GIDDY, TRIFLING, LIGHT,
PETTY, SILLY, FLIGHTY,
FLIPPANT
frizz .... SIZZLE, FRY
frizzed .... CRAPED, CRIMPED
fro ..... AWAY, BACK(WARD)

frock ... ROBE, TUNIC, GOWN,
MANTLE, SOUTANE, COAT,
SMOCK, OVERALL, JERSEY,
DRESS
froe .... CLEAVER
frog ...... POLLYWOG, TOAD,
ANURAN, PEEPER, FROSH,
RANA, PADDOCK,
SALIENTIAN
farm .... RANARIA
fish .... ANGLER
genus .... RANA
larva .... TADPOLE
like .... RANINE
slang .... FRENCHMAN
sound .... CROAK
young .... TADPOLE
froggery .... RANARIA
frolic ...... GAY, FUN, MERRY,
MERRIMENT, GAIETY,
GAMBOL, PLAY, ROMP,
(SKY)LARK, PRANK, CAPER,
FRISK, CAVORT, SPREE
from head to foot .. CAP-A-PIE
here .... HENCE
now on ..... HENCEFORTH
that time .... THENCE
there .... THENCE
where? .... WHENCE
fromenty .... PUDDING
Frome's (Ethan) wife ..... ITU,
ZEENA
frond .... LEAF
front .... OBVERSE, VAN,
FOREHEAD, FACE, FORE
boat .... PROW, BOW
hoof .... TOE
of building ..... FACADE
of coin/medal .. OBVERSE
page box .... EAR
page news .... CRIME,
SCANDAL, DISASTER,
CALAMITY
position ..... FIRING LINE
slang ... DUMMY, STOOGE
frontage .... FACADE
frontal .... METOPIC
frontier .... BOUNDARY
settlement ..... OUTPOST
frontiersman ... BOONE, EARP,
CODY, CARSON, LOGAN,
BOWIE, HICKOK
frontlet ... FOREHEAD, FILLET,
HEADBAND
frontispiece .... PREFACE,
FOREWORD

fronton .... JAI ALAI
frosh ...... FRESHMAN, FROG
Frost, Robert _____, poet .. LEE
frost .... ICE, RIME, HOAR,
CHILL, NIP
frosting .... ICING
equipment .... ICER,
FREEZER, REFRIGERATOR
frosty .... HOARY, ICY,
FREEZING, AUSTERE, FRORE,
RIMY
froth ...... SCUM, SUDS, FOAM,
YEAST, LATHER, SPUME
drink's .... HEAD
frothy .... SPUMY, FOAMY,
TRIFLING
froufrou ..... RUSTLE, SWISH
frounce ... CREASE, WRINKLE,
CURL
frow .... WIFE, WOMAN
frown ...... (G)LOWER, LOUR,
SCOWL, GRIMACE
frowzy .... MUSTY, UNTIDY,
DIRTY
woman .... DOWD,
SLATTERN
frozen .... CHILLY, ICY,
FRAPPE, GLACE, GELID,
CONGEALED
dessert ..... FRAPPE, ICE,
MOUSSE, SHERBET
dew .... RIME
partly .... FRAPPE
rain .... SLEET,
SNOW(FLAKES)
vapor .... FROST
fructify .... FERTILIZE
fructose ... SUGAR, LEVULOSE
fructuous .... FRUITFUL,
PRODUCTIVE
frugal .... ECONOMIC(AL),
THRIFTY, SPARING, SAVING,
CHARY
frugality ..... THRIFT(INESS),
PARSIMONY, ECONOMY
fruit ... DRUPE, YIELD, CROP,
PRODUCT, RESULT,
CONSEQUENCE, BERRY
aggregate ..... ETAERIO
apple-shaped .... QUINCE
basket .... POTTLE
bat .... PECA
bear .... FRUCTIFY
bearing no .... ACARPOUS
beech tree .... MAST
boat .... ORANGER

cactus .... FIG
cake .... SIMNEL
carbohydrate ... PECTIN
citrus ...... LIME, LEMON,
ORANGE
coating .... BLOOM
cocktail ..... MACEDOINE
collective ...... SYNCARP
combining form ....
CARP(O)
cordial .... RATAFIA
course .... DESSERT
covering.......... RIND,
EPICARP, CALYPTRA
cultivation, study of .....
POMOLOGY
date-like .... JUJUBE
dealer .... COSTER
decay .... BLET, ROT
dish .... COMPOTE,
COMPOTIER
dot(s) .... SORI, SORUS
downy bristles ... PAPPUS
dried .... PRUNE, RAISIN
drink .... ADE
dry .... ACHENE
eating ..... FRUGIVOROUS
eating bat .. FLYING FOX,
HAMMERHEAD, KALONG
elm .... SAMARA
enzyme .... PECTASE
filled crust ... DUMPLING
fir .... CONE
flesh .... PULP
fly .... DROSOPHILA
foul-smelling ... DURIAN
gourd ...... PEPO, SETON
growing, science of .....
POMOLOGY,
HORTICULTURE
hard-shelled ...... NUT,
GOURD
hawthorn .... HAW
hybrid .... POMA
injury .... BRUISE
inner layer ... ENDOCARP
juice .... MUST, STUM
juice, distilled ... BRANDY
juice drink ..... BRANDY,
LEMONADE, ADE, SHRUB,
SHERBET, SQUASH
juice squeezer ... REAMER
juicy part .... PULP
key .... SAMARA
knife .... CORER
lemon-like ...... CITRON

liquid .... JUICE
maple .... SAMARA
multiple ...... SOROSIS
oak .... ACORN
of discord .... APPLE
of forgetfulness ... LOTUS
oil tube .... VITTA
one-seeded .... NUT
palm .. DATE, COCONUT,
          BETEL NUT
part .... RIND, PULP,
          CORE, PIT
peel .... ZEST, RIND
picker .. OKIE, BRACERO
pie ...... TART, COBBLER
pine .... CONE
plant stem .... CANE
plum-like .... SLOE,
          PERSIMMON
preserve ..... COMPOTE,
          JAM
prune-like .. MYROBALAN
pulp ...... POMACE, PAP
pulpy ...... DRUPE, UVA
refuse .... MARC
rind ...... PEEL, EXOCARP,
          EPICARP, CALYPTRA
rosebush .... HIP
salad ...... MACEDOINE
sculptured ..... CORBEIL
seed .... PIP, KERNEL
seller .. COSTER(MONGER)
ship .... FRUITER,
          ORANGER
skin .... EPICARP, PEEL,
          RIND
small .... HAW, ACHENE,
          AKENE
sour .... LIME, LEMON
stew .... SASS, SAUCE
stone ... PIT, PIP, PYRENE,
          PUTAMEN, NUTLET
sugar .... FRUCTOSE,
          LEVULOSE
tomato-like .... POMATO
trees collectively ....
          ORCHARD
tropical ... MANGO, DATE,
          BANANA, AVOCADO,
          PAPAYA, PA(W)PAW
undeveloped .... NUBBIN
vineyard .... GRAPE
winged .... SAMARA
fruitcake .... SIMNEL
fruiter ...... SHIP, ORANGER
fruiterer .... COSTER

fruitful .... FERACIOUS,
    FRUCTUOUS, PRODUCTIVE,
    PROLIFIC, FERTILE,
    FECUND
  make .... FRUCTIFY
fruitless ... STERILE, BARREN,
          FUTILE, VAIN
  undertaking ...... FOLLY
fruits, study of .. CARPOLOGY
frustrate ... DEFEAT, DASH,
    HINDER, NULLIFY, FOIL,
    THWART, BAFFLE, BALK
frustration .... DEFEAT
frutescent .... SHRUBBY
fruticose .... SHRUBBY
fry ..... FRIZZ, FINGERLING,
    CHILDREN, YOUNG, FISH
  lightly/quickly ... SAUTE
frying-pan .. SKILLET, SPIDER
fub .... TRICK
fubsy .... PLUMP, SQUAT
fuchsia red ...... MAGENTA
fuchsin ... MAGENTA, DYE,
          SOLFERINO
fucoid .. SEAWEED, ROCKWEED
fucus .. PAINT, DYE, SEAWEED
fuddy-duddy .... DODO
fudge .... NONSENSE, CANDY,
          FAKE
Fuego island native ..... ONA
Fu(e)hrer .... HITLER, LEADER
fuel .... COMBUSTIBLE, PEAT,
    PEET, COKE, WOOD,
    (CHAR)COAL
  brick .... BRIQUET
  carrying vessel .. TENDER,
          OILER, TANKER
  dung .... CHIP
  liquid .. OIL, PETROL(EUM)
          ALCOHOL, GAS
  oil .... KEROSENE
  ship ..... OILER, TANKER
  turf .... PEAT
fugacious .... FLEETING,
    TRANSIENT, EPHEMERAL
fugitive ...... EXILE, FLEEING,
    FLEETING, ESCAPEE,
    ABSCONDER,
    RUNAGATE, RUNAWAY,
    DESERTER, REFUGEE
  Negro slave .... MAROON
fugue .... TONAL
  concluding passage .....
          STRETTA, STRETTO
fulcrum ..... PROP, THOLE
  oar .... THOLE

Fulda river .... EDER
fulfill .... OBEY, ACCOMPLISH,
     SATISFY, COMPLETE,
     PERFORM, IMPLEMENT,
     REDEEM
fulfillment .... FRUITION
fulgent .... RADIANT
full ...... FILLED, COMPLETE,
     CROWDED, OROTUND,
     REPLETE, SATED
  and rounded ..... PLUMP
  as a skirt ... BOUFFANT(E)
  attendance ..... PLENARY
  blooded ....
     THOROUGHBRED,
     PEDIGREED
  blooded horse .... ARAB
  blown .... OPEN,
     MATURE(D)
  dress ..... FORMAL, TAILS
  flavored .... MELLOW
  grown .... ADULT
  house: colloq. ...... SRO
  measure ..... AMPLITUDE
  meeting .... PLENARY
  of cracks .... RIMOSE
  of holes .... PITTED,
     POCKMARKED
  of life ...... LUSTY, SPRY
  of: suffix ..... ITOUS, OSE,
     ULENT
  of ups and downs ....
     CHECKERED
  stop .... PERIOD
fullness .... PLENUM,
     PLENITUDE, SATIETY,
     SURFEIT, REPLETION
fulmar ... PETREL, MALDUCK,
     NELLY, MALLEMUCK
fulminate .... DETONATE,
     EXPLODE, THUNDER
fulsome .... COARSE
Fulton's (Robert) invention ...
     STEAMBOAT
  boat .... CLERMONT
fumarole .... HORNITO
fumble ..... GROPE, BUNGLE
fume ... STEAM, VAPOR, RAGE,
     REEK, GAS, SMOKE, FRET,
     RAVE
fumigant .... PASTILLE
fumigate .... DISINFECT
fuming .... RAGING
fumy .... VAPOROUS
fun .... SPORT, JEST, JOLLITY,

PLAY, AMUSEMENT,
     MERRIMENT, JINKS
  Island seaport .. ODENSE
  of, make .... MOCK,
     RIDICULE
Funafuti .... ATOLL
funambulist ....
     TIGHTROPE WALKER
  kind of .... ACROBAT,
     AERIALIST
function .... OFFICE, DUTY,
     RITE, USE, PARTY, ROLE,
     WORK
  trigonometry ..... SINE,
     COSINE, TANGENT
functionary .... OFFICIAL
fund ... STOCK, STORE, SUPPLY,
     OUTLAY, COPPERS
  kind of ..... SLUSH, TRUST
  raiser .... TAGGER
fundament ... BUTTOCKS, ANUS
fundamental .... BASAL,
     ELEMENTAL, VITAL,
     ORGANIC, CARDINAL, BASIC,
     ESSENTIAL
funeral .. EXEQUIES, OBSEQUIES
  announcement ....
     OBIT(UARY)
  attendants ..... CORTEGE,
     PALLBEARERS
  bell .... KNELL
  box ..... COFFIN, CASKET
  "casket team" ....
     PALLBEARERS
  coach .... HEARSE
  director ..... MORTICIAN,
     UNDERTAKER
  fire .... PYRE
  hymn ...... EPICEDIUM,
     DIRGE
  music ... DIRGE, REQUIEM
  notice ...... OBIT(UARY)
  ode .... EPICEDIUM
  oration .. ELOGE, EULOGY
  pile .... PYRE
  procession ..... CORTEGE,
     EXEQUY
  pyre .... PILE, SUTTEE
  rite(s) .... EXEQUY,
     OBSEQUY, OBSEQUIES
  song ... LAMENT, ELEGY,
     DIRGE, NENIA,
     REQUIEM, THRENODY
funereal .... SAD, FERAL,
     DISMAL, LUGUBRIOUS,
     GLOOMY, MOURNFUL

fungi ...... SPORE, BOLETUS, YEAST
   native to region ....
    MYCOLOGY
   parasitic .... ERGOT
   pertaining to .... AGARIC
   spongy material ....
    AMADOU
   study of ...... MYCOLOGY
   tissue .... TRAMA
fungous .... SPONGY
fungus ..... SMUT, PUFFBALL, MILDEW, MOLD, AGARIC, EPIPHYTE, YEAST, (BLACK)KNOT, BLACKRUST, AMANITA, WART, RHIZOPUS, TUCKAHOE, LICHEN, MUSHROOM, RUST, TOADSTOOL
   cells/sacs .... ASCI
   combining form .. MYC(O)
   disease ..... ERGOT, SCAB, BRAND, ROT, MYCOSIS
   dots .... TELIA
   edible ...... EARTHNUT, TRUFFLE
   foul-smelling ....
    STINKHORN
   growth ... ERGOT, MOLD, MILDEW
   growth in body .. MYCOSIS
   parasitic on animal .....
    EPIPHYTE
   plant .... MOREL, MUSHROOM, UREDO, AMANITA
   poisonous ... TOADSTOOL, AMANITINE
   smut .... BUNT
   spores cluster .... SORUS
   thallus of .... MYCELIUM
funicle .... FIBER, CORD
funk ...... FEAR, FRIGHT(EN), PANIC, SHIRK, COWARD
funnel .... FLUE, CHIMNEY, SMOKESTACK
funny ..... DROLL, AMUSING, COMIC(AL), ABSURD, FARCICAL, HUMOROUS
   bone .... HUMERUS
   bone site .... ELBOW
   colloquial ..... KILLING
fur .... BUDGE, FITCH(ET), FITCHEW, CARACAL, KARAKUL, CARACUL, MINK, PELAGE, CRIMMER, VAIR,

GRIS, SKIN, PELT, MINEVER, CALABER
   bearing animal ... MINK, COYPU, GENET, VAIR(E), MARTEN, OTTER, SABLE, LYNX, WEASEL, POLECAT, RABBIT, CALABAR, SEAL, ERMINE, FITCH(ET), FITCHEW, CHINCHILLA
   bearing skins collectively
    PELTRY
   cape .... PELERINE
   coypu's .... NUTRIA
   garment .... WRAP, PARKA, ANORAK
   hat ...... BUSBY, CASTOR
   kid pelt .... GALYAK
   lamb pelt ...... GALYAC
   lynx .... CARACAL
   matted .... DAGLOCK
   neckpiece ... STOLE, BOA, CHOKER
   pertaining to ... PELISSE
   piece .. MUFF, BOA, STOLE
   rabbit .... LAPIN
   royal .... ERMINE
   scarf .... TIPPET
   seal .... SEECATCH
   squirrel ... VAIR, CALABER
furbelow .... FRILL, FALBALA, JABOT, FLOUNCE, RUFFLE
furbish .... BRIGHTEN, POLISH, BURNISH, RENOVATE
furcate ... FORK(ED), BRANCH
furculum .... WISHBONE
furfur .... DANDRUFF, SCURF
Furies, one of the ... ERINY(E)S, ALECTO, EUMENIDES, TISIPHONE, MEGAERA
furious ... FRANTIC, VIOLENT, MAD, FRENZIED
furl .... ROLL UP
furlough .... LEAVE
furnace ... SMELTER, SMITHY, STITHY, CRESSET, BLOOMERY, CUPOLA, BLAST, FORGE, OVEN, CREMATORY, KILN, CREMATORIUM, BELLOW
   air pipe of ..... TUYERE
   feed the .... STOKE
   for cremation ....
    (IN)CINERATOR
   opening ...... STOKEHOLE
   part ... BOSH, CRUCIBLE
   tender .... STOKER

vent .... TUE
furnish ..... CATER, ENDOW,
SUPPLY, PROVIDE, EQUIP,
OUTFIT, PLENISH
furnishings ...... GEAR, DECOR
furniture ..... GOODS, FIXTURE
decoration .... BUHL
inlaid wood .... BUHL
lace decoration ....
MACRAME
leg, kind of ... CABRIOLE
set .... SUITE
wood ...... KOA, WALNUT
furor ...... FLURRY, TUMULT,
FURY, RAGE, CRAZE, FRENZY
furrow ... GROOVE, WRINKLE,
RUT, CHASE, PLOW, SEAM,
STRIA, TRENCH, SULCUS,
RILL(E)
for seeds .... DRILL
for sugarcane planting . ..
WINDROW
of wheel .... RUT
furrowed .. SEAMED, RUTTED,
SULCATE
furry growth .... MOLD
tail .... SCUT
furs collectively ...... PELTRY
further ...... AID, MOREOVER,
PROMOTE, ADVANCE, AND,
ABET
furtive .... SURREPTITIOUS,
SECRET, STEALTHY, COVERT,
SLY, SNEAKY, SHIFTY, WARY
furuncle ...... BOIL, ABSCESS
fury ... RAGE, ANGER, WRATH,
IRE
furze ... GORSE, WHIN, GORST,
WHUN
fusain .... PENCIL
fuse .... ANNEAL, (S)MELT,

SOLDER, BLEND, WELD,
MIX, MERGE
kind of ...... CHEMICAL,
ELECTRICAL,
PERCUSSION
partly .... FRIT
fused .... FUSIL
fusee .... FLARE, MATCH,
VESUVIAN
fuselage .... NACELLE
fusiform .... ROUNDED
fusil .... FUSED, MELTED,
MUSKET
fusillade .... BARRAGE,
DRUMFIRE, SALVO, BURST
fusing .... SYMPHYSIS
fusion .... COALITION, MERGER
fuss ... ADO, PREEN, FIDGET,
FRET, TINKER, KICKUP,
BUSTLE, TO-DO, STIR,
POTHER, BOTHER
fussy ... FINICAL, FASTIDIOUS,
FINICKY, PER(S)NICKETY,
PRISSY, HOITY-TOITY
fustian .... CORDUROY,
VELVETEEN, POMPOUS,
BOMBAST
fustic .... DYE
fusty ... STALE, STUFFY, MOLDY
futile .... VAIN, IDLE, OTIOSE,
USELESS, FRUITLESS
future .... POSTERITY
kind of ...... HEREAFTER
futurity .... RACE
fuzz .... LINT, DOWN
fuzzball .... PUFFBALL
fuzzy ..... BLURRED, UNCLEAR
dog .... RAGS
fyke .... (FISH)NET
fylfot ..... SWASTIKA, CROSS,
EMBLEM
Fyn .... FUNEN, ISLAND

G

G, Greek .... GAMMA
Hebrew .... GIMEL
letter .... GEE
slang .... GRAND
string ...... LOINCLOTH,
BREECHCLOUT
gab ...... CHATTER, GABBLE,
TALK
gift of .... GLIBNESS,
ELOQUENCE, FLUENCY
gabble ..... JABBER, CHATTER

gabby .... TALKATIVE
gaberlunzie .... BEGGAR
gabion .... CYLINDER
gable .... PEDIMENT,
AILERON, PINION
ornament .... FINIAL
Gabon capital .... LIBREVILLE
city .... PORT GENTIL
ethnic group .. PONG-WE,
CHIRA, PAHOUIN,
PUNU, ADOUNA, LUMBU

Gabriel .... ARCHANGEL
what he sounded ....
TRUMPET
gaby .... FOOL, SIMPLETON
gad ..... OATH, EXCLAMATION,
SPIKE, PROWL, RAMBLE,
GALLIVANT,
TRAIPSE, ROAM, ROVE, GOAD
parent of .... JACOB,
ZILPAH
son of .... ERI, ARELI
gadabout .... ROAMER,
FLANEUR, PLAYBOY
gadfly .... PEST, TORMENTOR,
ANNOYER, TABANID
gadget .... DOODAD, DINGUS,
JIGGER, HICKEY,
THINGUMADOB, DEVICE,
CONTRIVANCE, GIMMICK,
JIMJAM
gadid .... COD, POLLACK,
HADDOCK, FISH, HAKE
gadoid, a .... CODFISH, HAKE,
HADDOCK, POLLACK
gadroon ... BEADING, REEDING,
FLUTING
gadwall .... DUCK
Gadzooks ... OATH, EXPLETIVE
Gaea .... TELLUS,
MOTHER EARTH, GODDESS,
GE
son ..... URANUS, TITAN
Gael .... CELT, SCOT
Gaelic .... ERSE, SCOT(CH),
CELT(IC), MANX, IRISH,
KELTIC
bard .... OSSIAN
game pole .... CABER
god .... LER, MIDER,
DAGDA
poem .... DUAN
sea god .... LER
spirit .... BANSHEE
warrior .... DAGDA
Gaels, of the ...... GOIDELIC,
GADHELIC
gaff ...... SPAR, HOAX, HOOK,
SPEAR, FLEECE, SPUR,
DANCEHALL
rope .... VANG
slang ..... HOAX, TRICK,
CHEAT
gaffe ... BLUNDER, FAUX PAS
gaffer .... FOREMAN, OLD MAN
gag ..... CHOKE, QUIP, HOAX,
SILENCE, JOKE, MUZZLE,

WISECRACK, MUFFLE, SCOB,
RETCH
overworked .... WHEEZE
gage .... SECURITY,
CHALLENGE, PLEDGE,
WAGER, ESTIMATE, PLUM
Gahlee native ...... GALILEAN
gaiety .... FESTIVITY, FINERY,
JOLLITY
Gaillard Cut, formerly ....
CULEBRA
gain .... EARN, REALIZE, NET,
WIN, GET, ATTAIN, LUCRE,
REAP, PROFIT
control .... MASTER
extra .... .. PERQUISITE
knowledge ...... LEARN
slang .... VELVET
strength .... RALLY
gainly ..... COMELY, SHAPELY,
GRACEFUL
gainsay ...... DENY, REFUTE,
OPPOSE, CONTRADICT,
FORBID, IMPUGN
Gainsborough's forte ....
PORTRAITS
gait .... PACE, RUN, LOPE,
WALK, RACK, STRIDE,
CANTER, GALLOP, STEP
circular .... AMBIT
easy/slow ... TROT, CRAWL,
CANTER, ROMP
fastest .... GALLOP
gaiter .... PUTTEE, SPAT,
LEGGING, SHOE, GAMBADE
gal .... GIRL
gala .... FIESTA, FESTIVAL,
CELEBRATION, FESTAL,
FESTIVE
galactic .... LACTIC
galacto: comb. form ... MILKY,
Galahad, describing .... PURE,
NOBLE
parent ...... LANCELOT,
ELAINE
quest of ... (HOLY) GRAIL
Galatea's beloved ...... ACIS
lover .... PYGMALION
galaxy ... MILKY WAY, BEVY,
COLLECTION
Galcha .... PAMIR(I)
gale .... BREEZE, SHRUB,
OUTBURST, WIND GUST
Gale (Zona), novelist .. BREESE
galena .... LEAD
Galilean .... CHRISTIAN

sea .... TIBERIAS
the .... JESUS
town ... MAGDALA, CANA,
NAZARETH
galilee ...... PORCH, PORTICO
galimatias .... GIBBERISH
galingale ...... SEDGE, ROOT
galiot .... GALLEY,
MERCHANT SHIP
galipot .... TURPENTINE,
OLEORESIN
gall .... NERVE, BILE,
AUDACITY, IMPUDENCE,
SORE, IRRITATION, ANNOY,
VEX, CHEEK, EFFRONTERY,
TEMERITY, FELL
bladder ..... CHOLECYST
bladder fluid .... GALL,
BILE
bladder, of the ... CYSTIC
bladder part ... CERVIX
combining form ....
CHOL(O), CHOLE
gallant ... STATELY, IMPOSING,
GRAND, CAVALIER, SQUIRE,
BRAVE, HERO, NOBLE,
LOVER, CIVIL, KNIGHT,
BULLY
galleon .... CAR(R)ACK,
ARGOSY, (WAR)SHIP,
TRADER
gallery .... BELVEDERE,
ARCADE, VERANDA, LOGGIA,
POY, SOLLAR, PIAZZA,
MUSEUM, LOFT, ART-ROOM,
CORRIDOR, PORCH,
PORTICO, COLONNADE,
BALCONY, SALON
art .... SALON
church .... JUBE
French .... LOUVRE
in mining ...... HEADING
Italian .... UFFIZI
London .... TATE,
GUILDHALL
gallet .... CHIP, SPALL
galley ... KITCHEN, ROWBOAT
armed ... AESC, DROMOND
bench .... BANK
Mediterranean ....
GAL(L)IOT
Roman ...... UNIREME,
BIREME, TRIREME
ship's .... CABOOSE
slave .... DRUDGE

work on .... EDIT,
PROOFREAD
Galli-Curci, soprano ......
AMELITA
Gallia .... GAUL
Gallic .... FRENCH
chariot .... ESSED
gallimaufry ..... HASH, OLIO,
HODGEPODGE, ASSORTMENT
gallinaceous ...... RASORIAL
bird .... TURKEY,
PEAFOWL, PHEASANT,
QUAIL
galling ... VEXING, CHAFING,
IRRITATING, BITTER
gallinipper .... MOSQUITO
gallinule ... RAIL, (MUD)HEN
gallipot .... JAR
gallivant .... GAD
galliwasp .... LIZARD
gallon, half .... POTTLE
gallons, 8 .... BUSHEL
31½ .... BARREL
galloon ..... BRAID, RIBBON
gallop ... GAIT, LOPE, HURRY,
TANTIVY, AUBIN, CANTER
Galloway ..... CATTLE, HORSE
gallstone ...... CHOLOLITH
galluses .... BRACES,
SUSPENDERS
gallows ... SCAFFOLD, GIBBET,
YARDARM, TREE
galop .... DANCE
galore .... PLENTIFULLY,
ABUNDANCE
galosh ... CLOD, (OVER)SHOE,
BOOT
galumph ..... PRANCE, STRUT
galvanize ... EXCITE, STARTLE
Galway Bay island ..... ARAN
gam ..... HERD, VISIT, CALL,
POD, SCHOOL
slang .... LEG
gamb(e) ..... LEG, SHANK
gambado .... GAITER,
PRANK, LEAP, LEGGING
Gambia's capital ... BATHURST
Gambier island ... MANGAREVA
gambit .... MANEUVER
gamble ... BET, STAKE, WAGER,
RISK
reckless ... FLIER, FLYER
gambler ..... DICER, BETTOR,
GAMESTER, GAMER, PLAYER
confederate of .... SHILL
kind of ...... TINHORN,

PLUNGER, SPECULATOR, PUNTER
gambler's accomplice ... SHILL
capital .... STAKE
concern .... ODDS
note .... IOU
gambling center .. LAS VEGAS, CASINO, MONACO, MONTE CARLO, RENO
table character .. BETTOR, CROUPIER, DEALER, RAKER, KIBITZER
gamboge ...... GUM RESIN, PIGMENT
gambol .... DIDO, CAPER, ROMP, FRISK, FROLIC, PLAY, CURVET
gambrel .... HOCK, ROOT
Gambrinus' invention ... BEER
game .... POLO, GOLF, LAMB, BINGO, BADMINTON, TAROT, PLOY, FUN, CRICKET, FOOTBALL, BEANO, AMUSEMENT, SPORT, PLAY, FROLIC, RECREATION, PLUCKY, SCHEME
anagrams ... LOGOMACHY
animal .... FOX
animal flesh ... VENISON
Basque .... PELOTA, JAI ALAI
big ... ELEPHANT, TIGER, LION, GORILLA, RHINO, BEAR
board .... CHESS, DARTS, HALMA, CHECKERS, PACHISI, PARCHESI
breeding place .. WARREN
card ... MONTE, BRIDGE, CASINO, TAROT, CANASTA, OMBER, FARO, POKER, WHIST, PAM, LOO, ECARTE
children's .... TAG, JACKSTONE
court .... TENNIS, BASKETBALL
dice .... CRAPS, LUDO
fish ..... SALMON, TROUT, MARLIN, BARRACUDA, BASS, TARPON
follow ... STALK, TRACK
guessing ..... CHARADE, MORA
handball: Eng. ...... FIVES
hockey .... SHINN(E)Y

hold scoreless in .. BLANK, SKUNK
like billiards .. BAGATELLE
lottery number ... POLICY
military tactics .... KRIEGSPIEL
ninepins-like ... SKITTLES
of chance .... BINGO, FARO, LOO, KENO, LOTTERY, LOTTO, RAFFLE, HAZARD
of forfeits ..... FILLIPEEN
of marbles ... TAW, MIGS, MIGGLES
of skill .... TENNIS, CHESS, POKER, DARTS, BOWLING, POOL
oriental .... FANTAN
parlor .... LOTTO
period ...... CHUKKER, QUARTER, SET
piece ... ROOK, KNIGHT, QUEEN, TILE, MAN, DOMINO, KING, PIN, DIE
pin .... BOWLING
point ...... GOAL, RUN
pointed missiles .. DARTS
preserve ..... SANCTUARY
rhyming .... CRAMBO
Scotch .... SHINTY
snare .... GIN
Spanish .... PELOTA, MONTE, OMBER
start of ...... KICKOFF, TOSS UP
tennis-like ...... FIVES
tossing .... DIABOLO
trail .... TRACK
trap .... GIN
with plastic disk ...... FRISBIE
gamecock ...... ROOSTER
spur of .... GAFF
gamekeeper ..... WARDEN, RANGER
gamete, female, immature ... OOCYTE
gametes' union ..... ZYGOSIS, SYNGAMY
gamic .... SEXUAL
gamin ..... ARAB, URCHIN, WAIF, TAD
gaming cube ... DICE, BONES
tile .... DOMINO
gamma .... MICROGRAM

gammon .... NONSENSE,
    BACON, HAM, HUMBUG
gamp .... UMBRELLA
gamut .... RANGE, SCALE
gamy .... PLUCKY
Gand .... GHENT
gander .... GANNET, GOOSE
    take a .... LOOK
Gandhi .... MAHATMA,
    MOHANDAS
    political doctrine ....
    SATYAGRAHA
ganef .... THIEF, GANOV
gang ..... CREW, SQUAD, SET,
    MOB, WALK
    criminals' ... MOB, RING
    fight .... RUMBLE
    head of ...... FOREMAN,
    RINGLEADER
    member .... MOBSTER
Ganges boat .... PUTELEE
    city on the .... VARANASI
    fish .... SOOSOO
gangland ..... UNDERWORLD
gangling .... LANKY
gangplank ... RAMP, CATWALK
gangrel .... BEGGAR
gangrene .... DECAY,
    MORTIFICATION
gangrenous state .... NECROSIS
gangster ... GOON, HOOD(LUM),
    TOUGH(IE), THUG, GORILLA,
    MUG, YEGG, MOBSTER,
    HIGHBINDER
    bodyguard .... TORPEDO
    chief ...... RINGLEADER
    girl of .... MOLL
    gun: sl. .... GAT, ROD,
    ROSCOE, EQUALIZER
gangue .... MATRIX
gangway's handrail .. MANROPE
gannet ..... SOLAN, GANDER,
    MARGOT, GOOSE
ganoid ..... GAR, STURGEON,
    BOWFIN, AMIA
gantlet .... GLOVE
Ganymede ...... CUPBEARER
gaol .... JAIL, BRIDEWELL
gap .... GULF, HIATUS,
    CHASM, LACUNA, CLEFT,
    SHARD, HOLE, OPENING,
    BREACH
    between peaks ...... COL
    credibility .... DISTRUST
gape .... STARE, DEHISCE,

OGLE, GAWK, YAWP, YAUP,
    YAWN, LOOK
gapes, the .... RICTUS
gaping ..... RINGENT, RICTUS
gar ..... NEEDLEFISH, GANOID,
    SNOOK, STURGEON
garage .... MEW, CARPORT
    way to ...... BREEZEWAY
Garand .... RIFLE
Garapan Island's capital ....
    SAIPAN
garb ..... CLOTHING, STYLE,
    ATTIRE, DRESS, GUISE
garbage ...... TRASH, SWILL,
    REFUSE, OFFAL
    collect .... SCAVENGE
garble .... CONFUSE, FALSIFY,
    DISTORT, MIX UP, MUDDLE,
    JUMBLE
Garbo, actress .... GRETA
garcon .... BOY, YOUTH,
    WAITER, SERVANT
garden ...... PITCH, HERBARY,
    PLEASANCE, ARBOR,
    ORCHARD, GARTH
    bed .... PLOT
    Biblical ... GETHSEMANE
    cultivation of ....
    HORTICULTURE
    fence .... HAHA
    first .... EDEN
    kind of ...... HOTHOUSE,
    GREENHOUSE,
    TERRARIUM
    kitchen .... OLITORY
    miniature ... TERRARIUM
    of golden apples ....
    HESPERIDES
    pest .... APHID, WEED
    plant .... ORACH(E)
    rock .... ROCKERY
    section .... BED, PLOT
    soprano .... MARY
    tool ...... HOE, TROWEL,
    RAKE, DIBBLE
    vegetable .... SASS,
    KAILYARD, KALEYARD
    wall .... HAHA
gardener's asset ....
    GREENTHUMB
    handtool .... TROWEL,
    DIBBLE
    plague ...... CUTWORM,
    WEED, APHID, BORER
gardenia ... FLOWER, MADDER
Gardner, Erle ____ .. STANLEY

garfish .... SNOOK
Gargantua ..... GIANT, KING
   creator of .... RABELAIS
   son .... PANTAGRUEL
gargantuan .... HUGE,
   GIGANTIC
gargle ...... RINSE, LISTERINE,
   WASH
garibaldi .... BLOUSE
garish ...... GAUDY, SHOWY,
   GLARING
garland .... FILLET, CHAPLET,
   LEI, FESTOON, WREATH,
   ANADEM
garlic ...... ALLIUM, MOLY,
   RAMSON
   part .... CLOVE
garment ... CLOTHING, DRESS,
   RAIMENT, COAT, VESTMENT,
   HABILIMENT, CLOTH(E),
   COVERING, WRAP, BLOUSE,
   ROBE, TEDDY
   Arabian .... AB(B)A
   bishop's ...... CHIMER(E),
   CHIMAR
   breast .... HALTER
   clergyman's ..... CASSOCK
   corsetlike .... GIRDLE
   East Indies .... SARI
   Eskimo .... PARKA
   fastener .... PATTE,
   AUTOMATIC
   flap/fold of ..... LAPPET
   Greek .... CHITON
   hooded .... ALMUCE,
   PARKA
   India ...... SARI, SAREE,
   BANIAN, BANYAN
   knight's .... TABARD
   knitted .... JERSEY
   leg .... CHAUSSES
   loose .... KIMONO,
   BLOUSE, ROBE, TOGA,
   CAMISE, DOLMAN,
   CYMAR
   Malay .. SARONG, BATIK,
   PAREUS
   Moslem .... IZAR
   outer .... CAPOTE, TOGA,
   SCAPULAR, SURTOUT,
   COAT, PALETOT,
   KIMONO, SMOCK
   patchwork .... CENTO
   Polynesian .... PAREU(S)
   priest's ... COPE, STOLE,
   AMICE, ALB, EPHOD

   rain .... PONCHO
   Roman .... ROBE, TOGA,
   STOLA, TUNIC
   scarflike .... TIPPET
   sleeveless .... CAPE,
   SCAPULAR
   tentlike .... CHADRI
   trade spy .... KEEK
   trimming ..... BEADING
   tunic-like ...... TABARD,
   CHITON
   Turkish .... DOLMAN
   under ... CHEMISE, SHIRT
garments .... COSTUME
garner .... GRANARY, GATHER,
   STORE, HOARD
garnet ..... RED, ALMANDITE,
   OLIVINE, CARBUNCLE,
   TACKLE, RHODOLITE,
   MELANITE, UVAROVITE,
   PYROPE, ESSONITE, GEM,
   TOPAZOLITE
garnish .... TRIM, RELISH,
   EMBELLISH, DECORATE,
   ADORN, DECK, OLIVE,
   ORNAMENT, LARD
garnishee .... TRUSTEE
garnishment .... LIEN
Garonne river tributary ... LOT
garret .... ATTIC, (COCK)LOFT,
   ATELIER, MANSARD
Garrick, actor .... DAVID
garrison .... (MILITARY)POST,
   PRESIDIO
garrote .... STRANGLE,
   STRANGULATION, SCRAG
garrulous .... TALKATIVE,
   VOLUBLE, LOQUACIOUS,
   GASSY
garter snake .... ELAP(S)
garth .... GARDEN, YARD
gas ... VAPOR, RADON, DRUG,
   BRAG, FREON, NEON,
   ARGON, ETHYL, FUEL,
   BUTANE, ETHER, FLATUS,
   STIBINE, PROPANE
   balloon .... HELIUM
   blue .... OZONE
   burner .... BUNSEN,
   WELSBACH
   charger .... AERATOR
   cigaret lighter .. BUTANE
   colorless .... OXAN(E),
   STIBINE, KETENE,
   ETHENE
   combining form .. AER(O)

container .... TANK
dirigible .... HELIUM
engine .... PETROL
fill with .... AERATE,
   INFLATE
fitter .... PLUMBER
garlic-odored .... ARSINE
in stomach/intestine ....
   FLATUS, FLATULENCE
inert .... ARGON
jet .... LAMP
marsh .... METHANE
mask part .... CANISTER
mine .... DAMP
non-inflammable ......
   HELIUM
pipe .... FLUE
radioactive .... RADON,
   NITON
step on the .... HURRY,
   ACCELERATE, GUN
gasconade ...... BRAG, BOAST,
   BLUSTER
gaseous .... AERIFORM
   cloud .... NEBULA
   combining form ... AERI
gash ...... CUT, HEW, HACK,
   SLASH
gasket .... LINING
gasoline .... PETROL
   air mixer ... CARBURETOR
   jellied .... NAPALM
   slang .... JUICE
gasp .... HEAVE, PANT
gast(e)ropod ...... W(H)ELK,
   MOLLUSK, SLUG, SNAIL,
   LIMPET
   marine .... MUREX
   mollusk ...... ABALONE,
   TRITON, WHELK
gastric digestion product ....
   CHYM
gastrin .... HISTAMINE,
   HORMONE
gastronome ...... EPICURE,
   GOURMET, GOURMAND
gastronomy .... EPICURISM
gat .... CHANNEL
gata .... SHARK
gate .. DOOR, WICKET, PORTAL
   bar .... PORTCULLIS
   give the .... DISMISS,
   SACK, DISCHARGE
   in metallurgy ... RUNNER
   joint .... HINGE
   keeper's dwelling .. LODGE

rear .... POSTERN
receipts: colloq. ... TAKE
revolving ..... TURNSTILE
tower .... BARBICAN
trellised .... LATTICE
water .... SLUICE,
   PENSTOCK
gatehouse .... LODGE
gatekeeper .... PORTER
gateway ... TORAN(A), PYLON
   bar .... PORTCULLIS
   Egyptian temple .. PYLON
   Persian .... DAR
   Shinto temple ..... TORII
gather .... REAP, (A)MASS,
   ACCUMULATE, CULL,
   COLLECT, INFER, ASSEMBLE,
   MUSTER, SHEAVE, FOLD,
   GLEAN, PUCKER, HARVEST,
   GARNER, SHIRR
gathering .... MEET(ING),
   RALLY, CROWD, BOIL,
   CONCOURSE, ASSEMBLAGE,
   ASSEMBLY
   of people .... TURNOUT
   social .... BEE, PARTY
gauche ... AWKWARD, CLUMSY,
   TACTLESS
gaucho ... COWBOY, LLANERO
   knife .... MACHETE
   milieu ... PAMPAS, LLANO
   place .... RANCHO
   rope of .... REATA
   weapon .... MACHETE,
   BOLA(S)
gaud ...... FINERY, TRINKET,
   ADORN, BAUBLE, ORNAMENT
gaudy ...... GARISH, SHOWY,
   FLASHY, TAWDRY, FLORID,
   GINGERBREAD, TAFFETA
   ornament .... TINSEL
gauffer ... CRIMP, PLEAT, FLUTE
gauge ... VALUE, RATE, TYPE,
   EXTENT, CAPACITY, FEE,
   MEASURE, APPRAISE,
   ESTIMATE
   face of .... DIAL
   rain .... UDOMETER,
   PLUVIOMETER
Gauguin's island home .. TAHITI
Gaul ... GALLIA, FRENCHMAN
   metal collar ..... TORQUE
gaunt ...... HAGGARD, SPARE,
   LANK, LEAN, EMACIATED,
   GRIM, SICKLY, BONY, THIN
gauntlet .. GLOVE, CUFF, GAGE

throw down the .... CHALLENGE, DEFY
Gautama .... BUDDHA
gauze .... BAREGE, CREPE, HAZE, MIST, TISSUE, LENO
   silk .... TIFFANY
gauzy .... FILMY, SHEER, DIAPHANOUS
   fabric .. CHIFFON, LACE, TULLE
   film in wine .. BEESWING
gavel .... HAMMER, MALLET
gavial .... CROCODILE
gawk ...... STARE, GAPE, CUCKOO, SIMPLETON
gawky ... CLUMSY, AWKWARD, UNGAINLY
gay .... MERRY, LIVELY, WANTON, BRIGHT, BOON, PERKY, RIANT, FESTAL, FESTIVE, JOLLY, JOVIAL, JOCUND, HILARIOUS
   and swaggering .. JAUNTY
   rake .... LOTHARIO
   tune .... LILT, JAZZ
Gay-Pay-Oo ...... GPU, OGPU
   successor .... NKVD
gaze ..... GAPE, STARE, LEER, GAWK, GLARE
gazebo .... BALCONY, TURRET
gazelle .... ANTELOPE, GOA, CORINNE, KUDU, CORA, ADDRA, SPRINGBOK, KORIN, MOHR, KEVEL, CHIKARA, ARIEL
   African ... ADMI, MOHR, SPRINGBOK, ORYX, KORIN, CORA
   Asiatic .... AHU
   black-tailed .... GOA
   Sudan .... DAMA
   Tibetan .... GOA
gazette .... NEWSPAPER
Gaziantep .... AINTAB
Gdansk .... DANZIG
Ge .. GAEA, GAIA, GERMANIUM
gear ..... CAM, KIT, TACKLE, COG, OUTFIT, OVERDRIVE, TOOLS, RIG(GING), HARNESS, BAGGAGE, GARB
gecko .... LIZARD, LACERT(IL)IAN, TARENTE
gee ... EXCLAMATION, EVADE, TURN RIGHT, GO AHEAD, JESUS
   opposed to .... HAW

geese, domestic ...... EMDENS
   fat .... AXUNGE
   flock ..... RAFT, GAGGLE
   genus .... ANSER
geest .... ALLUVIUM
geetas .... STINGY
Gehenna .... HELL
geisha .... DANCER, HOSTESS, DANCING GIRL
gel .... JELLIFY
   opposed to .... SOL
gelatin(e) ... ASPIC, COLLOID, AGAR, JELLY, GLUTIN
   case .... CAPSULE
   copying pad .... POLYGRAPH
   fish bladder ... ISINGLASS
gelatinous ... VISCOUS, VISCID
geld ... STERILIZE, CASTRATE, EMASCULATE
gelding .... EUNUCH
gelid .... COLD, FROSTY, FROZEN, ICY
gem .... STONE, JEWEL, CAT'S-EYE, OPAL, CHATOYANT, MUFFIN, LIGURE, TOPAZ, AGATE, EMERALD, AMETHYST, SARDONYX, BERYL, JADE, GARNET, RUBY, PERIDOT, SPINEL, SARD, ONYX, PEARL, DIAMOND
   artificial .... PASTE, RHINESTONE
   Biblical .... LIGURE
   blue .... HYACINTH
   carnelian ..... SARD(INE)
   carved .... CAMEO
   carving .... GLYPTICS
   cut .... BRIOLETTE
   cutter .... LAPIDARY
   cutting device ...... LAP
   dealer .... LAPIDARY, CARTIER, BEERS
   Egyptian .... SCARAB
   engraver ...... LAPIDARY
   engraving ..... GLYPTICS
   expert .... LAPIDARY
   facet ..... CULET, BEZEL, BEZIL
   flaw .... FEATHER
   green .... BERYL, EMERALD, AQUAMARINE
   green-like ... PERIDOTIC
   merchant ..... LAPIDARY
   polisher ...... LAPIDARY

red .... CARBUNCLE
relief .... CAMEO
rim of .... GIRDLE
ruby spinel .... BALAS
setting ... BEZEL, CHATON
simulated ..... DOUBLET
slang .... SPARKLER, ICE
State .... IDAHO
weight .... CARAT, KARAT
gemel .... HINGE
   part of ..... HOOK, LOOP
Gemini .... TWINS
   star ..... CASTOR, POLLUX
geminate .... COUPLED,
      DOUBLE, PAIRED
gemma .... BUD
gems collector/dealer ....
         LAPIDARY
gemsbok .... ANTELOPE,
         CHAMOIS, ORYX
gemstone .... IOLITE
gendarme(rie) ... POLICE(MAN)
gender .... MASCULINE,
      BEGET, SEX, FEMININE,
         BREED, NEUTER
   classification ....
      MASCULINE, FEMININE,
      NEUTER, NATURAL,
         GRAMMATICAL
   common .... EPICENE
gene .... FACTOR
genealogical record ..... TREE
genealogy ... HERALDRY, TREE,
   LINEAGE, PEDIGREE, DESCENT
general .... GENERIC,
   INCLUSIVE, ECUMENICAL,
   PANDEMIC, USUAL, COMMON,
   WIDESPREAD, UNIVERSAL
   arrangement ... GET-UP,
         FORMAT
   aspect .... TENOR
   Civil War .... GRANT,
      LEE, BRAGG, MEADE,
      SCOTT, SHERIDAN
   direction .... DRIFT,
         TREND
   man of a .... AIDE
   of the Armies .. PERSHING
   of the Army ....
         MACARTHUR,
         EISENHOWER
   opinion ..... CONSENSUS
   opposed to ....
      PARTICULAR, SPECIFIC,
         DETAILED
   paralysis .... PARESIS

pardon .... AMNESTY
welfare ... COMMONWEAL
Generalissimo ....
   CHIANG (KAI CHEK),
   SHOGUN, FRANCO
generate .. BEGET, PROCREATE,
   ORIGINATE, PRODUCE
generation .... AGE
generator .... DYNAMO
generic .... GENERAL,
   INCLUSIVE, UNIVERSAL
generous ... LIBERAL, LAVISH,
   AMPLE, OPEN-HANDED,
   GRACIOUS, UNSELFISH
   giving ...... LARGESS(E)
genesis ...... ORIGIN, BIRTH,
   CREATION, BEGINNING
genet .... JENNET, CIVET
genetic .... GENIC
genetics, subject of ....
         HEREDITY
geneva .... GIN
   lake .... LEMAN
genial ...... WARM, AMIABLE,
   DEBONAIR(E), JOCUND,
         JOVIAL
geniculate .... BENT
genie .... JINNI, DEMON,
      SPIRIT, JINNEE
genius ..... ABILITY, TALENT,
      DEMON, SPIRIT
Genoese city .... LIGURIA
   magistrate .... DOGE
genre ...... TYPE, KIND, SORT,
         STYLE
gens .... CLAN, TRIBE
gent .... PRETTY, GUY,
      GENTLE(MAN)
genteel .... REFINED,
   WELL-BRED, POLITE,
      ELEGANT, NICE
gentian .... ROOT, FLOWER,
   COLUMBO, AGUEWEED
gentile .... PAGAN, HEATHEN,
   GOY, NON-JEW
gentle ...... REFINED, POLITE,
   TAME, PLACID, TENDER,
   KINDLY, MILD, SOFT,
   DOCILE, LENIENT, LAMBLIKE
   breeze .... ZEPHYR
   craft, the ...... FISHING,
         SHOEMAKING
   heat .... TEPOR
   push .... NUDGE
   sex .... WOMAN,
         WOMANKIND

gentleman .... YOUNKER
    CAVALIER, GENT, COURTIER,
    SIR, GALLANT, MILORD,
        SIGNOR, RYE
    amateur in sports ....
        CORINTHIAN
    attendant .... DONZEL
    from Indiana ....
        TARKINGTON
    in waiting ..... COURTIER
    of fortune .. ADVENTURER,
        PIRATE
    Spanish .... CABALLERO
gentleman's gentleman ......
        VALET
"Gentlemen Prefer Blondes"
    author ..... (ANITA) LOOS
gentlewoman ..... (MI)LADY,
        MILADI
Gentoo .... HINDU
gentry .... NOBLE
genu .... KNEE
genuflect ...... KNEEL, BEND,
        CURTSY
genuine .... REAL, TRUE,
    AUTHENTIC, HONEST, LEGIT,
    PUREBRED, SIMON PURE,
        PUCKA
genus .... CLASS, VARIETY,
     SORT, ORDER, KIND
    birds .... CORVUS
    cats .... FELIS
    cattle .... BOS
    cetaceans .... INIA
    chestnuts .... CASTANEA
    cows .... BOS
    dogs .... CANIS
    ducks ...... ANAS, ANSER
    eels .... CONGER
    fishes .... ANABAS
    foxes .... VULPES
    frogs .... RANA, ANURA
    gannet .... SULA
    gastropods ...... HARPA,
    NERITA, OLIVA, TRITON
    grapes .... VITIS
    geese .... ANSER
    ginseng .... ARALIA
    goats .... CAPRIA
    goose barnacles .. LEPAS,
        ANATIFA
    gooseberry .... RIBES
    goshawks .... ASTUR,
        BUTEO
    grasses ..... POA, AVENA,
        STIPA, AIRA

griffon .... GYPS
gulls .... LARI, XEMA,
        LARUS
herbs ... RUTA, TOVERIA,
    ANEMONE, ARUM, RULAC,
    MANIHOT, ACARUM, CICER,
        NOLANA
herring .... ALOSA
hogs .... SUS
honeybee .... APIS
housefly .... MUSCA,
        FANNIA
insects .... CICADA
lemurs .... GALAGO
lily .... ALOE
man .... HOMO
maples .... ACER
mints .... NEPETA
mollusks .... NERITA,
    ANOMIA, TEREDO
monkeys .... ATELES
moose .... ALCES
nettles .... URTICA
oats .... AVENA
olives .... OLEA
oysters .... OSTREA
palms .... ARECA
peacocks .... PAVO
pigs .... SUS
primates .... HOMO
shads .... ALOSA
sheep .... BOS
shrubs ... FUCHSIA, ITEA,
    RHUS, OLEA, ERICA
swans .... OLOR
swine .... SUS
terns .... STERNA
thistles .... CARLINA
thrushes .... TURDUS
trees ... CORNUS, CELTIS,
        SAPOTA
turtles .... EMY
wasp .... VESPA
whales .... INIA
wrens .... NANNUS
geode ...... CAVITY, VUG(H),
    DRUSE, VUGG, VOOG
geographer ...... MERCATOR,
    PTOLEMY, VAREN
geography, work on ....
        ALMAGEST
geological age .... PLIOCENE,
        CENOZOIC
    angle .... HADE
    division ...... EON, LYAS,
        LIAS, ERA

epoch ..... UINTA, ECCA,
PLEISTOCENE, PLIOCENE,
MIOCENE, OLIGOCENE,
EOCENE, PALEOCENE,
DRIFT
era .... PALEOZOIC,
MESOZOIC, CENOZOIC
formation ..... TERRANE,
TRIASSIC, TERRENE,
IONE, TERRAIN
recent epoch .. HOLOCENE
ridge .... OSAR
system .... TERTIARY,
CRETACEOUS, JURASSIC,
PERMIAN, CAMBRIAN,
DEVONIAN, SILURIAN
geology on land structure .....
TECTONICS
geomancy .... DIVINATION
geometrical body ...... LUNE,
PRISM
curve .... PARABOLA
figure ... ELLIPSE, CONE,
RHOMB, CUBE, CIRCLE,
SQUARE, ANGLE, PRISM,
POLYGON, HELICOID
line ..... LOCUS, SECANT
point relating to curve ...
ACNODE
premise ...... POSTULATE
principle ..... THEOREM
ratio .... SINE, PI
solid ... CUBE, PYRAMID,
SPHERE, LUNE, PRISM,
CONE
study .... CONICS
term ..... SINE, TANGENT,
VERSOR, LOCUS,
SECANT, THEOREM
geometrid moth larva .. LOOPER
geometry, branch of ... CONICS
subject of .... POINT, LINE,
SOLID, PLANE
type ...... PLANE, SOLID
geoponic ... RURAL, BUCOLIC,
PASTORAL, RUSTIC,
AGRICULTURAL
George Eliot .... EVANS
georgette .... CREPE
Georgia, capital of .. ATLANTA
city ...... ROME, MACON
Negro .... GULLAH
peak .... KENNESAW
pine .... LONG-LEAF
river .... S(U)WANEE
seaport ...... SAVANNAH

Georgian seaport (Soviet) .....
BATUM
georgic .... POEM, RURAL,
AGRICULTURAL
Geraint .... KNIGHT
wife of .... ENID
geranium .... CRANESBILL
gerbil(l)e .... JERBOA
gerent ..... MANAGER, RULER
geriatrics .... NOSTOLOGY
germ ..... MICROBE, BACTERIA,
SPORE, ORIGIN, VIRUS,
BUG, SEED
fermenting .... ZYME
free .... ASEPTIC
German .... HUN, BOCHE,
KRAUT, TEUTON(IC), ALMAIN,
COTILLION, JERRY,
ALEMAN, JUNKER
above .... UBER
admiral .... SPEE,
RAEDER, TIRPITZ
adventurer ....
MUNCHAUSEN
again .... UBER
air .... LUFT
aircraft manufacturer ...
DORNIER
airplane ... STUKA, TAUBE
alas .... ACH
already .... SCHON
and .... UND
army ..... REICHSWEHR
art songs .... LIEDER
article .... DAS, EIN, DER
ass .... ESEL
at no time .... NIE
bacteriologist ..... KOCH,
LOFFLER
bank .... UFER
battleship ... BISMARCK,
TIRPITZ, (GRAF)SPEE
beautiful .... SCHON
because .... WEIL
bed .... BETT
beer ...... BIER, LAGER
blood .... BLUT
blue .... BLAU
bomber .... STUKA
bread ... BROT, BROTCHEN
but .... ABER
cake .... KUCHEN,
TORTE, STOLLEN,
SPRINGERLE
camp .... STALAG
canal .... KIEL

cathedral site .... ESSEN, COLOGNE
chancellor ... ADENAUER, ERHARD, BRANDT, BISMARCK
chap .... KERL
cheese .... KASE
chemist .... LIEBIG, BUNSEN
city ..... HAMELIN, JENA, EMDEN, EMS, CASSEL, COLOGNE, COBLENZ, SPEYER, TREVES, BONN, KOLN, KREFELD, MAINZ, HALLE, ESSEN, TRIER, HANOVER, DRESDEN, LEIPZIG, STUTTGART, GOTHA, WEIMAR, DESSAU, LUBECK, KARLSRUHE, ROSTOCK, ULM, MUNSTER, MEISSEN, MANNHEIM, MARBURG
coal region .... SAAR, AACHEN, RUHR
coffee cake ..... KUCHEN
coin .... T(H)ALER, GROSCHEN, GUILDER, GULDEN, PFENNIG, KRONE, KREU(T)ZER, MARK, HELLER
cold .... KALT
composer ...... BRAHMS, BACH, FLORIO, WAGNER, WEBER, STRAUSS
councillor .... RAT
count .... GRAF, LANDGRAVE
criminologist .... SAUER
critic .... LESSING
cry of surrender .... KAMERAD
dam .... EDER
dance .... COTILLION
day .... TAG
dear .... LIEB
defense force .... LANDSTURM
defense line .. SIEGFRIED, LIMES
dessert .... STREUSEL
district ..... SAAR, RUHR
dog .... HUND
dollar .... TALER
donkey .... ESEL
dramatist .... LESSING

dream .... TRAUM
drinking toast ... PROSIT
duchy .... HESSE, BADEN, LIPPE
east .... OST(EN)
eat .... ESSEN
eight .... ACHT
emperor ...... KAISER, WILHELM, OTTO
evening .... ABEND
everything .... ALLES
exclamation .... ACH, HOCH, HIMMEL
explorer .... BARTH
eye .... AUGE
fairytale writer .. GRIMM
far .... WEIT
fascist .... NAZI
fellow .... KERL
field .... FELD
five .... FUNF
folksong ..... VOLKSLIED
forest .... WALD
forest keep .. WALDGRAVE
four .... VIER
from .... VON
fruit .... OBST
full .... VOLL
gentleman .... HERR(EN)
Gestapo chief .. HIMMLER
girl .... FRAULEIN
glad .... FROH
god ..... WODEN, WODAN
good .... GUT(EN)
government ...... REICH
governor .... MARGRAVE
gypsy .... ZIGUENER
hair .... HAAR
hall .... AULA, SAAL
head .... KOPF
heart .... HERZ
heir .... ERBE
hero, legendary .... SIEGFRIED
high .... HOCH
highway .... AUTOBAHN
historian .... RANKE
home ...... HAUS, HEIM
hot .... HEISS
housewife ... HAUSFRAU
hunter .... JAGER
hypnotist ...... MESMER
ice .... EIS
iron .... EISEN
island ..... HELGOLAND, ALSEN

Kantian philosopher .... FICHTE
king .... KONIG
kingdom .... SAXONY, HANOVER, HESSE, PRUSSIA
knight ..... TANNHAUSER
leaf .... BLATT
league .... BUND
legend's site ... HAMELIN
legislative assembly ..... LANDTAG
letter .... RUNE
love .... LIEBE
lyric .... LIED
lyric poem .... LIEDER
married woman .... FRAU
master race .... HERRENVOLK
mathematician .... HESSE
measles .... RUBELLA, ROSEOLA, RUBEOLA
mercenary soldier .... LANSQUENET, HESSIAN
military governor .... MARGRAVE
military reserve .... LANDWEHR
mimist.. .... SCHARRE
minnesinger .... TANNHAUSER
mister .... HERR
money .... MARK
money, Soviet zone ..... OSTMARK
moon .... MOND
morning ...... MORGEN
mountain .... HARZ
mouth .... MUND
musician, legendary .... PIED PIPER
name prefix .... VON
nation .... VOLK
naval base .... EMDEN, KIEL
Nazi ideology .... HERRENVOLK
negative .... NEIN
new .... NEUE
night .... NACHT
nine .... NEUN
no .... NEIN
number .... DREI, ZWEI, FUNF, SECHS, NEUN, ZEHN, EIN(E), VIER
ocean .. MEER, NORTH SEA

one .... EIN(E)
only .... NUR
operatic soprano .... LEHMANN
painter .... HOLBEIN, GROSZ
parliament .... REICHSTAG
part .... TEIL
people .... VOLK
philosopher ...... KANT, HEGEL, FICHTE, HERDER, HERBART
physicist .... HERTZ, PLANCK
playwright-cobbler ...... SACHS
please .... BITTE
poet ...... RILKE, ARNDT, HEINE, SCHILLER
port .... BREMEN
POW camp ..... STALAG
president .... LUBKE, EBERT, TALER, HEUSS
prince's title .... LANDGRAVE, MARGRAVE
principality ...... LIPPE
printer ...... GUTENBERG
prison camp ... STALAG, DACHAU
pronoun ...... DU, ICH, SIE, UNS, WIR
republic .... LIPPE, WEIMAR
resort .... EMS, BADEN
rifleman .... YAGER, JA(E)GER
river ..... RHINE, RUHR, EDER, AAR, ISER, WESER, ODER, HUNTE, WERRA, ELBE, ALLE
roll .... BROTCHEN
robbery .... RAUB
roof .... DACH
royal family member .... GUELPH, GUELF
sacred place .... HIERON, ABATON
sausage .... WURST
scientist .... MACH
seaport ... KIEL, EMDEN, WISMAR
shore .... UFER
Sigurd .... SIEGFRIED
silver .... ELECTRUM
siren .... LORELEI, LURLE

I

six .... SECHS
sky .... TIU
slang ... JERRY, DUTCH
Slavic people .... WEND
snare .... SPRINGE
socialist .... LASSALLE
society .... VEREIN
soldier .. KRAUT, UHLAN,
HEINIE, BOCHE
song .... LIED(ER)
spa .... EMS, BADEN
spirit .... GEIST
sprite .... NIX
state .... BADEN, HESSE,
STAAT
state police ...... GESTAPO
steel .... STAHL
steeple .... TURM
street .... STRASSE
student, freshman ......
FROSH
students' hall .... BURSE
submarine ....
UNTERSEEBOOT
sun .... SONNE
superior .... OBER
tank, armored .. PANZER
ten .... ZEHN
the .... DER, DAS
three .... DREI
time .... ZEIT
title of nobility ... GRAF,
PRINZ, VON
title of respect .... GRAF,
HERR
toast .... PROSIT
today .... HEUTE
town .... STADT
train .... ZUG
true .... WAHR
two .... ZWEI
U-boat .... UNTERSEEBOOT
upper .... OBER
village .... DORF
water sprite .... NIX
watering place ..... EMS
weight .... LOTE
wheat .... SPELT
white .... WEISS
whole .... GANZ
wife .... FRAU, FROW
wine .... HOCK
with .... MIT
without .... OHNE
woman, unmarried ....
FRAULEIN

WWI plane ..... TAUBE
year .... JAHR
yellow .... GELB
yes .... JA
young .... JUNG
your .... DEIN, EUER
germane .... RELEVANT,
PERTINENT, AKIN
Germanic people .... CIMBRI
tribesman .... JUTE
germanium .... GE
Germany .... REICH
germinate .... SPROUT,
PULLULATE
Gernreich, fashion designer ...
RUDI
Geronimo .... APACHE
Gershwin, composer ..... IRA,
GEORGE
gesso ...... GYPSUM, PLASTER
Gestapo chief .... HIMMLER
gestation .... PREGNANCY,
CYESIS
gest(e) ...... DEED, EXPLOIT,
ADVENTURE, BEARING
gesture .... MOTION, ACTION,
TOKEN, GESTE, MOVEMENT
of contempt .. FICO, FIG
of indifference .... SHRUG
of respect .. OBEISANCE,
BOW, CURTSY
get .... OBTAIN, SECURE,
GAIN, ACQUIRE
aboard .... EMBARK
about .... CIRCULATE
ahead .... PROSPER,
SUCCEED
along ... MAKE OUT, FARE
along well .... CLICK,
PROSPER, THRIVE
around .... GAD, EVADE,
OUTWIT, CIRCULATE,
CIRCUMVENT
away .... LEAVE, ESCAPE
by ... MANAGE, SURVIVE
by trickery .... FINAGLE
in touch ...... CONTACT
in uninvited .... CRASH
on _____ .... BOARD
rid of .... LIQUIDATE,
DISPOSE
the idea .... SAVVY,
GRASP, SEE
to the bottom of ....
FATHOM

together .... AMASS,
    REUNION, BEE
    up ... COSTUME, OUTFIT,
        WEAR
    well .... HEAL
getaway .... ESCAPE
Gettysburg general ... MEADE,
    LEE
gewgaw ... BAUBLE, TRINKET,
    GIMCRACK, GAUD,
    FALDEROL, FOLDEROL,
    DOODAD, KICKSHAW
geyser .... (HOT)SPRING
    mouth of .... CRATER
Ghana, capital of .... ACCRA
    junta leader ..... ANKRAH
    "redeemer" ... NKRUMAH
    region .... ASHANTI
ghastly ..... MACABRE, PALE,
    GRIM, LURID, GRIS(T)LY,
    GRUESOME, PALLID
gha(u)t .... PASS, RANGE
ghee .... BUTTER
gherkin .... CUCUMBER
ghetto .... JEWRY
ghost ...... SPIRIT, INKLING,
    MANES, EIDOLON, KER,
    SHADE, LEMUR, SPOOK,
    WRAITH, PHANTOM, HANT,
    APPARITION, SPECTRE,
    SHADOW, LARVA, WAFF
    place of .... HAUNT
ghostly .... SPECTRAL,
    SPIRITUAL, EERIE, SPOOKY
ghoulish .... FIENDISH,
    LOATHSOME, VAMPIRIC,
    HORRIBLE
GI .. YANK, GOVERNMENT ISSUE
    address .... APO
    bed .... SACK
    ID .... DOGTAG
    insect repellent ..... DDT
    Joe ... DOGFACE, PRIVATE
    rifle ..... BAR, GARAND,
        ARMALITE
giant .... BANA, GOLIATH,
    BALDER, TROLL, TITAN,
    ANTAEUS, ASTERIUS, LOKI,
    ETEN, OGRE, JUMBO,
    GARGANTUA,
    PANTAGRUEL, MIMIR,
    BALDER, YMER, FAFNIR,
    JOTUN(N)
    Biblical .... ANAK
    fairy tale .... OGRE
    killer ...... DAVID, JACK

legendary .... ATLAS
one-eyed .... ARGES,
    CYCLOPS, ALEC
100-armed ... ENCELADUS
100-eyed .... ARGUS
Philistine .... GOLIATH
rime-cold .... YMER
underground .... TROLL
giantess ..... NORN, SKULD,
    GROA, URTH, NATT
giaour .... CHRISTIAN,
    UNBELIEVER
gib ..... (TOM)CAT, GILBERT,
    SALMON, GUT
gibbed .... CASTRATED
gibber .... CHATTER, JABBER
gibberish .. JARGON, CHATTER,
    MUMBO-JUMBO, JABBER
gibbet ... GALLOWS, SCAFFOLD
gibbon ... APE, LAR, PRIMATE,
    WAUWAU, WOUWOU
    Sumatran ...... SIAMANG
Gibbons, composer ... ORLANDO
gibbous .... HUMPBACKED,
    ROUNDED
gibe .... JEER, TEASE, SNEER,
    HECKLE, JAPE, FLEER,
    SCOFF, RIB, TAUNT, GIRD,
    DERIDE
giblet .... GIZZARD
Gibraltar, cape ... TRAFALGAR
    founder of .... GEBIR
Gibson, Charles ____ .. DANA
    girl .... MODEL
    tennis champ .... ALTHEA
gibus .... OPERA HAT
gid ...... STAGGERS, STURDY
giddiness .... VERTIGO
giddy .... DIZZY, WHIRLING,
    FICKLE, HOITY-TOITY,
    QUEER
Gide, critic .... ANDRE
gift .... PRESENT, TALENT,
    ABILITY, BOUNTY, TIP,
    DONATION, BENEFICENCE,
    INSTINCT, LARGESS(E),
    BONUS, DOLE, GRANT,
    LEGACY, BOON, ALMS, SOP,
    HANDOUT
    giver .... DONOR
    of gab .... GLIB,
        ELOQUENCE
    of money ..... GRATUITY
    recipient .... DONEE
    to bride .. DOWER, DOWRY
    to employee ..... BONUS

gifted .... TALENTED
gig ... CARRIAGE, (ROW)BOAT,
　　　DEMERIT, NAP, CHAISE
gigantic .... COLOSSAL, HUGE,
　　　TITANIC, ENORMOUS,
　　　IMMENSE, MAMMOTH
　　statue .... COLOSSUS
giggle ...... LAUGH, TITTER,
　　　SNICKER, CHUCKLE
gigot .... MUTTON, VEAL,
　　　　　SLEEVE
gigue .... JIG
Gil, writer .... BLAS
gila monster .... LIZARD
Gilbert and Sullivan actor/fan
　　　　　SAVOYARD
　　island .... MAKIN, BERII,
　　　　　TARAWA
gild ... AUREATE, GILT, ADORN
gill ... WATTLE, SWEETHEART,
　　　GIRL, CHOLLER, BRANCHIA,
　　　GLEN, BROOK, NOGGIN,
　　　　　QUARTERN
　　fungus .... AGARIC
gillie ... SERVANT, ATTENDANT
gills, 4 .... PINT
gillyflower .... STOCK
gilsonite .. UINTAITE, ASPHALT
gilt .... GILDING, DORE, SOW,
　　　　　PIG
gilthead ... CUNNER, SPAROID,
　　　PORGY, SCUP, BREAM
gimcrack ... CHEAP, DOODAD,
　　　SHOWY, GAUD(Y),
　　　(K)NICK(K)NACK, GEWGAW,
　　BAUBLE, TRINKET, NOVELTY
gimlet .... WIMBLE
gimmick .... GADGET
gimp .... ORRIS, FABRIC,
　　　NOTCH, GUIPURE
gin ... RUM(MY), TRAP, SLOE,
　　SNARE, BEGIN, NET, GENEVA,
　　WHETHER, IF, TOILS
　　liquor .... SCHNAPPS
　　mill .... SALOON
　　rummy debacle ... BLITZ
ginger .... SPICE, ROOTSTALK,
　　PEP, ENLIVEN, CARDAMOM,
　　ASARIUM, CURCUMA
　　ale-beer ... SHANDYGAFF
　　colloquial ...... VIGOR,
　　　　　SPIRIT
　　cookies .... SNAPS
　　wild .... ASARUM
gingerbread .... GAUDY,
　　　TAWDRY, CAKE

gingerly .... TIMIDLY,
　　　　CAUTIOUSLY
gingersnap .... COOKY
gingery ..... SPICY, PUNGENT
gingham ... CHAMBRAY, CLOTH
gingili .... SESAME
gingival .... ALVEOLAR
gingko ... ICHO, MAIDENHAIR
ginseng .... HERB, ROOT
　　genus .... ARALIA
"Gioconda, La" .. MONA LISA,
　　　OPERA, PORTRAIT
　　composer ... PONCHIELLI
　　painter .... DA VINCI
gip ...... CHEAT, SWINDLE(R)
gipon .... TUNIC, JACKET
gipsy (see gypsy) .... ROM
giraffe .... CAMELOPARD
　　like animal ...... OKAPI
　　long feature of .... NECK
girandole .... FIREWORKS,
　　CANDLEHOLDER, PENDANT,
　　　　　EARRING
girasol ..... OPAL, SUNFLOWER
gird ...... GIBE, JEER, SCOFF,
　　ENCIRCLE, FASTEN,
　　ENCLOSE, EQUIP, CLOTHE,
　　　　　ENDUE
girder ... TBAR, IBEAM, TRUSS,
　　　　　IBAR
girdle .... SASH, BELT, GIRT,
　　　SURCINGLE, CEST(US),
　　ZODIAC, ZONE, CINCTURE,
　　CORSET, SASH, RING,
　　CINGULUM, ZOSTER
India ..... CUMMERBUND
Japanese .... OBI
girdler .... BEETLER
　　world .... TOURIST,
　　　CIRCUMNAVIGATOR
girl ... MISS, SIS, MINX, BELLE,
　　MADCAP, LASS(IE), TIT,
　　JILL, DAMSEL, FILLE,
　　MAID(EN), CHIT
　　age of .... PUBERTY
　　beautiful ...... STUNNER
　　bold .... HOYDEN,
　　TOMBOY, QUEAN, SLUT
　　colloquial .. SWEETHEART,
　　　　　FILLY
　　flirtatious ...... FIZGIG
　　giddy .... FIZGIG
　　graceful .. NYMPH, SYLPH
　　group .... GSA
　　haircut .... BOB, BANGS,
　　　　　PAGEBOY

impudent .... QUEAN, SLUT
in uniform ...... NURSE,
 WAC, MAJORETTE,
 SPAR, WREN
in white .... NURSE
introduced to society ....
 DEB(UTANTE)
lively .... FILLY, HOYDEN
name meaning .. COLLEEN
 happiness .. FELICITAS
 hospitable .... ZENIA
 joyful .... ADA
 noble .... ADELA
 of song .... KATE, IRENE,
 DAISY, LOLA, ADELINE,
 IDA, LILI MARLENE,
 FANNY, SADIE, SALLY,
 RIO RITA
pert, saucy ..... HUSSY,
 CHIT, MINX, FRAIL
Scouts founder .... LOW
slang .... FLOSSY, FLOSSIE,
 TIT, SKIRT, BABE,
 TOMATO
society .... SORORITY
student .... COED
sulky look ... MOUE, POUT
young .... MOPPET
girls' group ... GSA, SORORITY
girth ...... ENCIRCLE, GIRDLE,
 STRAP, BAND, CINCH
 saddle .... CINCH
gisarme .... BATTLE-AX,
 HALBERD
gist ... CORE, NUB, ESSENCE,
 SUMMARY, CRUX, PITH,
 KERNEL, POINT
gitano .... GYPSY, NOMAD
gittern ..... CITHER, CITHARA
Giuba .... JUBA
give .... YIELD, CONCEDE,
 IMPART, HAND OVER, PAY,
 CONFER, GRANT, (EN)DOW
 and take ..... EXCHANGE,
 BANTER, REPARTEE,
 BANDY, HORSE-TRADE
 away ... DONATE, BETRAY,
 EXPOSE, REVEAL, BESTOW
 back ... RESTORE, RETURN
 birth .... KINDLE,
 FARROW, DELIVER,
 WHELP
 birth prematurely .. SLINK
 ear .... HEED, LISTEN,
 HEARKEN

 expression .... VOICE,
 ARTICULATE
 forth ..... EMIT, ISSUE,
 SPOUT, EXUDE
 in .... YIELD, CONCEDE,
 GRATIFY
 in law .... REMISE
 occasion .... INVITE
 off/out .... EMIT
 party .... THROW
 pleasure to .... GRATIFY,
 SATISFY
 Scottish .... GIE
 sparingly ... DOLE, STINT
 up ... CEASE, QUIT, CEDE,
 YIELD, SURRENDER,
 CAPITULATE, FORSAKE,
 LET GO, RENOUNCE
 way ..... BEND, YIELD,
 LET PASS
 with reluctance .. GRUDGE
given ...... PRONE, STATED,
 SPECIFIED, ASSUMED
 orally .... PAROL
 to fighting .. PUGNACIOUS,
 QUARRELSOME,
 COMBATIVE
giving attention ..... AUDIENT
 milk .... MILCH
 offense . ... INVIDIOUS
 satisfaction ..... HUNKY
gizzard ..... CROP, STOMACH,
 GIBLET
glabrous .... HAIRLESS, BALD,
 SMOOTH
glace ..... CANDIED, FROZEN,
 ICED
glacial .... ICY, FRIGID, COLD
 deposit .... ESKER,
 MORAINE, OSAR, ESKAR,
 ASAR, DILUVIUM,
 PLACER
 drift .... TILL, DRUMLIN
 epoch .... PLEISTOCENE
 fissure ...... CREVASSE
 formation ..... DRUMLIN,
 SERAC
 hill .... KAME, PAHA
 ice ... NEVE, FIRN, SERAC
 ice block .... SERAC
 period .... ICE AGE
 ridge ..... ESKAR, ASAR,
 DRUMLIN, OSAR, ARETE,
 ESKER, KAME, OS
 snowfield ... NEVE, FIRN
glaciate .... FREEZE

glacier .... ICECAP
    deposit of ...... MORAINE
    facing .... STOSS
    fissure .... CREVASSE
    ridge .... OS
    shaft .... MOULIN
glacis ... SLOPE, EMBANKMENT
glad .... FAIN, WILLING,
    PLEASED, HAPPY
    eye: slang .... OGLE
    rags: slang ..... FINERY,
    CLOTHES
    slang .... GLADIOUS
    tidings .... EVANGEL,
    GOSPEL
glade .... LAUND, DELL,
    VALLEY, LAWN
    combining form ... NEMO
gladiator .... RETIARIUS,
    LANISTA, WARRIOR
    school for .... LUDI
gladiolus ..... LILY, IRIS, IRID
    bulb .... CORM
gladly .... FAIN, READILY,
    WILLINGLY, LIEF
glair .... ALBUMEN
glaive .... (BROAD)SWORD,
    HALBERD
glamor ...... CHARM, ALLURE
    colloquial ... OOMPH, IT
glamorous .... ALLURING
glance .... GLIMPSE, LEER,
    OGLE, FLASH, APERCU,
    ONCE-OVER
    amorous ...... OEILLADE
    at book .... BROWSE
    off .... GRAZE
    quick ... SCAN, LOOK-IN,
    SKIM
    sideways .... SKEW,
    SQUINT
glancing blow .... SNICK
gland .... CAROTID, THYROID,
    PAROTID, PANCREAS,
    SPLEEN, PINEAL, FOLLICLE
    combining form ....
    ADEN(O)
    describing one ....
    DUCTLESS
    hormone, adrenal ....
    CORTISONE
    milk .... MAMMA
    organ .... THYROID,
    LIVER, KIDNEY
    reproductive cell ....
    GONAD

    secretion ..... HORMONE,
    ADRENALIN(E), BILE,
    URINE, SALIVA, GALL,
    SEBUM, CERUMEN
    surgical removal ....
    ADENECTOMY
glanders .... FARCY
glandlike .... ADENOID
glands inflammation ....
    ADENITIS
    study of .... ADENOLOGY
glandular ...... ADENOID(AL)
    disease .... GOITER,
    CRETINISM
    inflammation .. ADENITIS
    organ .... LIVER
    tumor .... ADENOMA
glare .... STARE, BLAZE, LOOK
glaring .... GARISH, FLAGRANT
Glasgow river .... CLYDE
glass ..... MIRROR, CRYSTAL,
    CALX, SMALTO, VERRE,
    MOUSSELINE, TACHYLITE,
    LENS, TUMBLER, CULLET,
    SMALT, LALIQUE, RUMMER
    artificial jewelry .. STRASS
    baking dish .. CASSEROLE
    bead .... BUGLE
    beer .... SCHOONER
    blowpipe ..... MATRASS
    blue .... SMALT
    bottle ... CRUET, CASTOR,
    CARBOY, CASTER,
    PHIAL, VIAL
    bowl .... AQUARIUM
    bubble .... BLEB
    coloring pigment ....
    SMALTINE, MAT(T)RASS
    combining form .. VITRO,
    HYAL(O)
    container .. PHIAL, VIAL,
    BEAKER, AMP(O)ULE
    container for distilling ...
    BALLOON, MATRASS
    cutter .... GLAZIER
    cutting tool .... LAP,
    DIAMOND
    drinking ..... TUMBLER,
    GOBLET
    for drinking toasts ......
    RUMMER
    fused .... FRIT(T)
    gem .... STRASS
    ground .... FRIT
    heat-resistant ..... SILEX
    jar ..... BOCAL, CLOCHE

lead .... STRASS
liqueur .... PONY
liquor .... SNIFFER
like ... VITRIC, VITREOUS
made of .... VITREOUS
maker .... GLAZIER
making material .. SILICA,
   SAND, POTASH, SILICON,
   ZAFFRE, ZAFFER, FRIT(T)
making, rod used in .....
   PUNTY, PONTIL
molten .... PARISON
mosaic(work) .. TESSERA,
   SMALTO
piece ..... PANE, SLIVER
polishing disk ...... LAP
roof .... BULL'S-EYE
scraps .... CULLET
Senator .... CARTER
set .... GLAZING
spangled ... AVENTURINE
toast-drinking .. RUMMER
translucent .... OPALINE
tube, graduated ....
   BURET(TE)
vial .... AMP(O)ULE
waste .... CULLET
window .... PANE
Glassboro "summit" figure ...
   JOHNSON, KOSYGIN
glasses: colloq. ...•...... SPECS,
   GOGGLES
glassmaker ...•....... GLAZIER
glassware articles ...•.. VITRICS
   cooking ...•...•... PYREX
glassworker ...•...... GLAZIER
glasswort ...•.. KALI, SAMPHIRE
glassy ...•...... TRANSPARENT,
   SMOOTH, LIFELESS,
   VITREOUS, HYALOID,
   VITRIC, HYALINE
   eyed ...•. DAZED, STUNNED
   sea ......•....•.. HYALIN(E)
   substance ...•...•. ENAMEL,
   FEL(D)SPAR
   volcanic rock .. OBSIDIAN
glaze ...... COAT(ING), FILM,
   ENAMEL, VENEER, GLOSS,
   POLISH
   metallic ...•...•.. REFLECT
   with stickum ...•..•...•. SIZE
glazier ....•.. PUTTIER
glazing machine ...•.. CALENDER
gleed ...•...•..........• COAL
gleam ...•...•..... GLINT, FLASH,
   GLISTEN, GLOZE

glean ...•...•.. REAP, COLLECT,
   GATHER
glebe ...• LAND, EARTH, LUMP,
   FIELD, SOIL, CLOD, TURF
glede ...•...•..•...•.... KITE
glee ...•...•..•.. MIRTH, GAIETY,
   MERRIMENT
gleed ...•...•..•. COAL, EMBER
Gleek ...•...•..•...•....• TIB
gleeman ...•...•.... MINSTREL
gleet ...•...•..•....... OOZE
gleg ...•.. KEEN, SHARP, ALERT
glen ...•...•.. DINGLE, VALLEY,
   VALE, DALE, DELL, GILL
Glengaries .... TAMS, CAPS
Glengary man .... SCOT
glib ...•...•.. FACILE, BLAND,
   FLUENT, OILY, SMOOTH,
   VOLUBLE
glide ...•...• FLOW, SKIM, SLIP,
   SKIP, SCUD, SKATE, SLIDE,
   SASHAY
   in music ...•...•.... SLUR
   on aircraft .... VOLPLANE
   snake's ...•...•..•. SLITHER
gliding across .... LABILE
   step .... GLISSADE
glim ...• CANDLE, LAMP, LIGHT,
   EYE
glimmer ...•..•. GLEAM, BLINK,
   FLICKER
glimpse ...•..•. GLANCE, FLASH,
   INKLING
glint ...• FLASH, DART, GLEAM,
   GLIMPSE
glioma ...•...•..•...•... TUMOR
glissade ...•...•.. SLIDE, GLIDE
glisten ...• SPARKLE, GLITTER,
   FLASH, GLEAM, SHINE
glitter ...•...•....• CORUSCATE,
   GLISTEN, SPARKLE, FLASH,
   BRILLIANCE
glittering ...•..•..•.. RUTILANT,
   BRILLIANT
glitters, it ...•...•....... GOLD
gloaming ...•. DUSK, TWILIGHT
global ...•..•... WORLD-WIDE,
   ROUND, SPHERAL
globe ...• EARTH, ORB, SPHERE,
   CLEW, BALL
   king's ...•...•...•. MOUND
   trotter ...•...•..•. TOURIST
globefish ...•...•..•... PUFFER
globin ...•...•....... HISTONE
globular ...•. SPHERICAL, ROUND
globule .. BLOB, PILL, SPHERULE

liquid ━━·━━· DROP, BEAD
glockenspiel, instrument like a
    XYLOPHONE, MARIMBA
glomerate ━━━━━━━ CLUSTERED
glonoin ━━━━━ NITROGLYCERIN
gloom ━━━━━ DARKNESS, BLUES,
    SADNESS, DUMPS, DIMNESS,
    MIRK, MURK
gloomy ━·. DREAR(Y), MOROSE,
    GLUM, DISMAL, BLUE,
    SATURNINE, RAYLESS,
    MOODY, SAD, DARK,
    MELANCHOLY, DOUR,
    FERAL, STYGIAN
gloria ━·━·━·· PRAISE, HALO
glorify ━·━·· EXALT, HONOR,
    PRAISE, BLESS
gloriole ━·━·━·━··· HALO
glorious ━·━·━·━·, SPLENDID,
    MAGNIFICENT
glory ━·━·━··· FAME, RENOWN,
    SPLENDOR, RADIANCE,
    EXULT, HALO, HONOR,
    REJOICE, KUDOS, ECLAT
  cloud of ━·━···· NIMBUS
  head's ━·. CORONA, HALO,
    LAUREL, HAIR, TOP,
    CROWN, TIARA
  light ━·━···━··· HALO
gloss ━━━━━━━ LUSTER, SHEEN,
    SHINE, ANNOTATE, POLISH
  over ━·━·━·━·· EXCUSE
glossary ━·━·· LEXICON, CLAVIS
glossing machine ·· CALENDER
glossy ━·· SPECIOUS, LUSTROUS,
    GLACE, SHINY, SILKEN,
    SLICK, SLEEK
  colloquial ━ PHOTOGRAPH
  fabric ━·. SATIN, SATEEN,
    SILK
  material ━·━·━·· ENAMEL
glot: comb. form ·· LANGUAGES
glottal stop ━·━·━·━·· STOSS
glove ━·━· MITT, CUFF, CESTUS,
    SUEDE, GA(U)NTLET
  fabric ━·━·━ LISLE, SUEDE
  leather ━·━·━· SUEDE, KID,
    MOCHA
  triangular piece of ━·━···
    GUSSET
glow ━·━·━·· RADIATE, FLUSH,
    FLASH, GLEAM, BLAZE,
    ARDOR, RUTILATE
glower ━·━·━·· GLARE, SCOWL,
    FROWN, GRIMACE, GAZE,
    STARE

glowing ━·· ARDENT, LAMBENT,
    CANDENT, LUMINOUS,
    FLUSHED
  thru/haze ━·━·━·· LURID
glowworm ━·━·━·━·· FIREFLY
Gluck, con.poser ·· CHRISTOPH
  opera ━·━·━·━·· ARMIDA
  soprano ━·━·━·━·· ALMA,
    (REBA) FIERSOHN
glucose ━·━· DEXTROSE, SUGAR,
    RUTIN, SIRUP
glucoside ━·━· SALICIN, RUTIN,
    GEIN, INDICAN, SAPONIN,
    SINIGRIN, SINALBIN
glue ━·━· GELATIN, GOO, GUM,
    MUCILAGE, AGAR, CEMENT,
    PASTE
gluey ━·━·━·· STICKY, PASTY
glum ━·· LONG-FACED, SULLEN,
    SULKY, GLOOMY, MOROSE
glume ━·━·━·━·· HUSK, BRACT
glut ━·. SURFEIT, GORGE, CLOY,
    FILL, SATIATE, SATE,
    PAMPER
gluten ━·. LOAF, BREAD, FIBRIN
glutenous material ━·━· FLOUR
glutin ━·━·━·━·━·· GELATIN
glutinous ━·━·· VISCID, GLUEY,
    SIZY, ROPY, STICKY
glutton ━·━·━·· WOLVERINE,
    EPICURE, GO(U)RMAND,
    CORMORANT, GARGANTUAN
gluttonous ━·━·━·━·· GREEDY,
    VORACIOUS, PIGGISH
  animal ━·━·━·━· PIG, HOG,
    MARTEN, WEASEL
  appetite/meal ━·· GORGE
gluttony ━·━·━·━·━·· VORACITY,
    EDACITY, GREEDINESS
glyph ━·━·━·━·━·· CARVING
gnarl ━·━·━· CONTORT, TWIST,
    SNARL, GROWL, SNAG,
    KNOT, NURR
gnash ━·. BITE, GRIND, GRATE
gnat ━·━· MOSQUITO, STINGER,
    MIDGE, PEST
gnaw ·· CHEW, BITE, CORRODE,
    TORMENT, HARASS, NIBBLE,
    FRET
gnawed, appear ━·━·━· EROSE
gnawer ━·━·━· RODENT, MOUSE
gnome ━·━·━ ELF, NIS, KOBOLD,
    BROWNIE, DWARF, GOBLIN,
    SAYING, GREMLIN, BOGIE,
    MAXIM, IMP

gnomon of sundial .. COLUMN, PIN, STYLE

gnosis: comb. form .... KNOWLEDGE

Gnostic sect member .... MANDEAN

GNP, part of .... GROSS, NATIONAL, PRODUCT

gnu ... ANTELOPE, WILDEBEST

go .... TRAVEL, PROCEED, OPERATE, DEPART, DIE, QUIT, RETIRE

about ..... TACK, GAD, CIRCULATE

after .... PURSUE, CHASE, FOLLOW

against .... OPPOSE

ahead .... GEE, PROCEED

along .... AGREE, COOPERATE, ACCOMPANY

around ... CIRCUMVENT, CIRCULATE, SKIRT

astray .... ERR, SIN, DEVIATE, ABERRATE

at high speed .... BARREL

away! ..... SCAT, SCRAM, SHOO

away suddenly .. DECAMP

back ... REGRESS, REVERT, RECEDE, RETURN, RETREAT, RETROCEDE

between ...... MEDIATOR, AGENT, MIDDLEMAN, ARBITRATOR, INTERMEDIARY

by .... PASS

by plane .... FLY

cart .... PRAM, STROLLER

devil .... SLED

down ... LOSE, SET, SINK

for ..... SUPPORT, LIKE, ADVOCATE

forth .... SALLY, FARE

getter ... HUSTLER, DOER, SALESMAN

off ... EXPLODE, HAPPEN, DEPART, DETONATE

on _____ .... AND ON

one better .... EXCEL, OUTDO, SURPASS

over the wall .... BREAK JAIL, ESCAPE

Scottish .... GAB

to bed .... RETIRE

to bed: colloq. .... HIT THE SACK, HIT THE HAY

wrong ... MISCARRY, SIN

goa .... GAZELLE, COLONY, ANTELOPE

capital of .... PANJIM

language ..... KONKANI

powder ..... ARAROBA

goad ..... SPUR, PROD, GAD, EGG, URGE, INCITE, NEEDLE, PRICK, STING, STICK, ANKUS

goal ...... INTENTION, POST, AIM, END, THULE, OBJECT, BOURN(E)

falls short of .... MANQUE

goat ..... ANGORA, PASANG, BEZOAR

Alpine .... IBEX

animal related to ...... GORAL, SHEEP

antelope .... SEROW, GORAL

constellation .... CAPRICORN

cry .... MAA

deity .... PAN

female ... NANNY, CAPRA

genus .... CAPRIA

get one's ... RILE, ANNOY, ANGER, IRK, IRRITATE

hair of .... MOHAIR

hair cloth ...... CAMLET, TIBET, CILICE, ABA, SACKCLOTH

hair cord .... AGAL

Himalayan ..... GORAL, TAHR

horn of ..... CORNUCOPIA

leap .... CAPRIOLE

leather ..... MOCHA, KID

like ... CAPRINE, HIRCINE

like animal ..... GORAL, CHAMOIS

male .... BUCK

man deity .... FAUN

mountain ...... TAHR, IBEX, GORAL

pertaining to .... CAPRIC

seller .... BUTCHER

sexual excitement ... RUT, HEAT, ESTRUS

shaped constellation .... CAPRICORN

sucker .... POTOO

wild .... TAIR, TEHR, IBEX,
TUR, THAR, KRAS
willow .... SALLOW
wool .... CASHMERE
goatee ...... BEARD, VANDYKE,
IMPERIAL
goatfish .... MULLET
goatish .... HIRCINE, CAPRINE
goatman .... FAUN
goats, group of ...... FLOCK
goatskin .... MOROCCO
bag ...... MUSSUCK
goatsucker ...... NIGHTHAWK,
WHIPPOORWILL, POTOO
gob ... MASS, LUMP, TAR, SAILOR
gobbet .... BIT, LUMP, CHUNK,
MASS, FRAGMENT
gobble .... EAT, SEIZE
gobbledygook .... TALK
coiner of word ....
MAVERICK
gobbler .... TURKEY, TOM
Gobbo .... LAUNCELOT
Gobi .. SHAMO, LAKE, DESERT
gobioid fish .... LOTER
goblet ...... GLASS, CHALICE,
CRYSTAL, TASS, BOCAL,
CUP, HANAP
drinking .... MAZARD,
MAZER
Eucharist ...... CHALICE
goblin .... ELF, SPIRIT, BOGIE,
NIS(SE), POOK, GNOME,
PUCK, PUCA, OUPHE,
KOBOLD, HOB, BOGY,
BROWNIE
doglike .... BARHEST
Egyptian ...... OUPHE
friendly .... NIS(SE)
habitat .... CAVE
helpful .... BROWNIE
Norse .... NIS(SE),
KOBOLD
goby .... MAPO, FISH
god ... DEITY, IDOL, CREATOR,
ALMIGHTY, BRAHMA, SIVA,
JEHOVAH, DEVI, ALLAH
agriculture .... SATURN,
FAUNUS, THOR, NEBO,
OSIRIS
air .... SHU
alcoholic drinks .... SIRIS
altar fire .... AGNI
appearance of ....
THEOPHANY
Arcadian .... PAN

avarice .... MAMMON
baboon-faced .... THOTH
beauty .... APOLLO
belief in (one) ....
(MONO)THEISM
caduceus-carrying ......
HERMES
combining form .... THEO
commerce .... MERCURY,
HERMES
cosmos .... VARUNA
creator .... ATUM
darkness ...... SETH, SIN
day .. JANUS, HORUS, HOR
dead .... YAMA, ANUBIS,
ORCUS, OSIRIS
defender .... ANSEL
discord ...... LOKI, LOKE
dog-headed .... THOTH
dreams .... MORPHEUS
earth ... BEL, DAGAN, GEB
east wind .... EURUS
elephant-headed ....
GANESHA
euphemism for .... GAD,
GOSH, GOLLY
falcon-headed .... HORUS
false .... BAAL, MOLOCH,
MAMMON
fearing ... PIOUS, DEVOUT
fertility .. OSIRIS, DAGAN,
FREY
fields ...... PAN, FAUN
fire .... AGNI, GIRRU,
VULCAN
fish .... DAGAN
flocks .... PAN
force .... PTAH, SHU
forest ...... FAUN, PAN
given food ...... MANNA
goat .... PAN
guide to Hades .. HERMES
Hades .. PLUTO, HERMES,
DIS, ORCUS
half man, half fish ....
DAGON
happiness ...... EBISU,
HOTEI
harvest .... CRONUS
health .... OSIRIS
heaven ...... BEL, ANU
herds .... PAN
horses ...... POSEIDON
ibis-headed ...... THOTH
image conveyance .. RATH

jackal-headed .. ANUBIS, WAPUET
justice .... RAMMAN
killer .... DEICIDE
learning .... THOHT
light ... BALDER, BALDUR, OSIRIS, SHU
lightning .... AGNI, JUPITER
like .... DEIFIC
love .... AMOR, EROS, KAMA, POTHOS, CUPID
lower world .... SERAPIS, PLUTO, HADES, DIS
marriage .... HYMEN
medicine .... IMHOTEP, ASCLEPIUS
Memphis .... PTAH
mirth ..... COMUS, KOMOS
mischief .... LOKI
moon ... THOTH, NANNAR
mountains .... ATLAS, OLYMPUS
music ...... APOLLO, BES
north wind ...... BOREAS
offering to ...... CORBAN
one-eyed .... ODIN
peace ... BALDER, FREY, FORSETI
pleasure .... BES(A)
poetry .... APOLLO
praise to ...... HOSANNA
prosperity ...... FREY
rain .. FREY, INDRA, ESUS, JUPITER
revelry .... COMUS, BACCHUS, KOMOS
river .... ALPHEUS
Saturday .... SAETER
science .... HERMES
sea ...... DYLAN, ATLAS, POSEIDON, NEPTUNE, NEREUS, TRITON, PONTUS, AEGER, YMIR
seven-armed ...... AGNI
shepherds .... PALES
sky ..... ANU, NUT, TYR, YMIR, JUPITER, DYAUS, TIU
sleep .... SOMNUS, MORPHEUS, HYPNOS
southeast wind ... EURUS
study of ...... THEOLOGY
sun ..... RA, SOL, FREY, NINIB, BELI, SHAMASH, AMEN-RA, PHOEBUS, APOLLO, AMON, BAAL, BALDER, HELIOS, HORUS, MITHRAS
thieves ...... MERCURY, HERMES
thunder ... THOR, DONAR, ZEUS, JUPITER, JOVE, PERUN
two-faced .... JANUS, AGNI
underworld ...... PLUTO, ORCUS
vegetation ... ESUS, ATTIS
victory ...... ODIN, ZEUS
visible appearance of .... THEOPHANY
war .. THOR, AS(S)UR, ER, TYR(R), ODIN, MENT, MARS, ARES, QUIRINUS, COEL, WODEN, IR(R)A, TIU
waters ... NEA, FONTUS, VARUNA
wealth .... PLUTUS
winds ... ADAD, AEOLUS, BOREAS, ADDU, EURUS, VAYU
wing-shod ...... HERMES, MERCURY
wisdom .... NEBO, ODIN, EA, GANESA, SABU, THOTH
woods ...... SYLVANUS, SILVANUS
youth .... APOLLO
God's acre .... CEMETERY
chosen people ....
ISRAELITE(S)
Little Acre author........
CALDWELL
Godden .... RUMER
goddess ...... DEA, BEAUTY, DEVI, SHRI, LACHESIS
abundance .... SRI
agriculture ... DEMETER, CERES, ISIS, OPS
air .... HERA
arts and sciences ....
ATHENA, MUSE, CLIO, CALLIOPE, EUTERPE, ERATO, THALIA, URANIA, MELPOMENE
astronomy ..... URANIA
avenging .. NEMESIS, FURY
beauty ... VENUS, FREYA
birth .... PARCA
cat-headed ...... PACHT

chance .... TYCHE
chase .. ARTEMIS, DIAN(A)
childbirth .... LUCINA
comedy .... THALIA
crops .... ANNONA
dawn .... EOS, AURORA,
          US(H)AS
death ..... DANU, HEL(A)
destiny ..... URD, URTH,
          MOIRA, NORN
destruction .. KALI, ARA
discord .... ERIS, ATE
doom ...... URTH, WYRD
earth ...... TELLUS, TARI,
          GAIA, TERRA, CERES,
          ARURU, ISHTAR, LUA,
          GAEA, GE, ERDA, OPS,
          SEB
faith .... FIDES
fate .... PARCA, NORN,
          NONA
fertility .... ASTARTE,
          FAUNA, ANNONA, ISIS,
          ISHTAR
fields ..... TELLUS, FAUNA
fire .. VESTA, HESTIA, PELE
flowers .... CHLORIS,
          NANNA, FLORA
fortune .... TYCHE
fountains .... FERONIA
fruits .... POMONA
ghosts .... HECATE
giant .... NORN, URTH
grains .... CERES
harvest ...... OPS, CARPO
healing .... EIR, GULA
health ... SALUS, HYGEIA,
          HESTIA
hearth .... HESTIA, VESTA
heaven .... NUT
history .... CLIO, SAGA
hope .... SPES
horses .... EPONA
hunting .... DIAN(A),
          VACUNA
invention .... MINERVA
justice .... THEMIS,
          ASTRAEA, MAAT
life ...... ISIS, LACHESIS
light .... LUCINA
love ... HATHOR, ASTARTE,
          SELENE, ARTEMIS,
          FREYA, APHRODITE,
          IS(H)TAR, VENUS
magic .... HECATE

marriage ..... GAEA, GE,
          JUNO, HERA
minor .... NYMPH
mischief ...... ATE, ERIS
moon .... CYNTHIA,
          SELENE, LUNA, DIANA,
          ARTEMIS, LUCINA,
          PHOEBE, HECATE, ISIS
music .... EUTERPE
nature .... ARTEMIS,
          CYBELE, NYMPH
night .... LETO, NOX, NYX
peace ...... PAX, IRENE,
          MINERVA, EIR
persons drowning .... RAN
plenty .... OPS
poetry .... ERATO,
          CALLIOPE
prosperity .... SALUS
rainbow .... IRIS
retribution ... ARA, ATE,
          NEMESIS
revenge .... NEMESIS
science .... MUSE
seas ..... DORIS, RAN(A),
          INO, SALACIA,
          AMPHITRITE
seasons ... HORA, HOUR
sky .... NUT, FRIGG
splendor .... UMA
spring .... VENUS, IDUN,
          ITHUN(N)
strife .... ERIS
trees .... POMONA
truth .... MAAT, MA
underworld .... HEL,
          HECATE, LARUNA, GAEA
vegetation .... CORA,
          CERES, FLORA, KORE
vengeance .... ARA,
          NEMESIS
victory .... NIKE
virtue .... FIDES
volcano .... PELE
war ... MINERVA, ANATU,
          ALEA, ATHENA, ENYO,
          BELLONA, ISHTAR,
          VACUNA
waters .... ERUA
welfare .... SALUS
wisdom .... MINERVA,
          PALLAS, ATHENA
womanhood ...... MUT,
          SATI, JUNO
woods .... DIAN(A),
          ARTEMIS

youth .... HEBE, IDUN, ITHUN(N)
goddesses of beauty/charm ... GRACES
 destiny .... FATES
 fate ..... NORNS, MOERAE
 nature .... HORAE
 seasons ...... HOURS, HORAE
godfather .... SPONSOR
godforsaken .... WICKED, DESOLATE, FORLORN, DEPRAVED
godhead .... DIVINITY
godless ..... PAGAN, WICKED, IMPIOUS, ATHEISTIC
godlike .... HOLY, DIVINE, OLYMPIAN
godliness .... PIETY
godly .... PIOUS, RELIGIOUS, DEVOUT
 person .... SAINT
godmother .... CUMMER
godparent .... SPONSOR
godown .... WAREHOUSE
gods' abode ... ASGARD, MERU
 battle against the .... THEOMACHY
 "blood" .... ICHOR
 cupbearer ... GANYMEDE, HEBE
 drink .... NECTAR
 king of .... WODEN
 messenger ...... HERMES, MERCURY, IRIS
 mother of .... RHEA
 origin of .... THEOGONY
 queen of .... SATI, HERA, JUNO
 race of .... VANIR
 strife among .... THEOMACHY
godsend .... MANNA
godspeed .... SUCCESS
Godwin Austen, Mount ...... DAPSANG
godwit .... SNIPE
Goebbels' (Joseph) forte ...... PROPAGANDA, BIG LIE
Goethe's hero .... FAUST, WERTHER
 heroine .... MIGNON
goffer ... CRIMP, PLEAT, FLUTE
Gog and _____ .... MAGOG
goggle ... STARE, BULGE, ROLL
goggler ..... CICHARRA, SCAD

goggles .... SPECTACLES, SUNGLASSES
Gogol hero .... (TARAS) BULBA
Goidelic language ...... ERSE, MANX
going ..... EXIT, DEPARTURE, WORKING, AVAILABLE, LEAVING
 get .... BEGIN, START
 in .... ENTRY, ENTRANCE
 on .... NEARLY, NEARING
 out ...... EXIT, EXODUS, EGRESS(ION)
goings on .... BEHAVIOR, CONDUCT
goiter .... STRUMA
Golconda .... MINE
gold ...... GILT, ORO, CYMB, MONEY, RICHES, WEALTH, AU(RUM), SOL
 alchemist's .... SOL
 alloy .... ASEM
 assaying cup ..... CUPEL
 band .... CARCANET
 black .... OIL
 braid .... ORRIS
 brick ...... SHIRK(ER), LOAF(ER)
 Bug author .... POE
 cast .... INGOT
 Coast .... GHANA
 Coast languages ... TSHI
 Coast river ...... VOLTA
 coat with .... GILD
 coating ... GILT, GILDING
 coin ..... DUCAT, KRONE, GUINEA, ANGEL, MOHUR, LOUIS, OBANG, LIRA, SCUDO, TOMAN, DARIC, LION, PISTOLE, IMPERIAL, DOUBLOON, BEDIDLIK, EAGLE
 collar .... CARCANET
 color .... YELLOW
 colored metal ... ORMOLU
 colored ore ..... PYRITE
 content ... CARAT, KARAT
 cover .... GILT
 deposit .... PLACER
 district, African ... RAND
 fineness ... CARAT, KARAT
 imitation ...... ORMOLU, PINCHBECK
 in alchemy .... SOL
 lace .... FILIGREE
 land .... OPHIR

leaf .... FOIL
leaf, imitation ....
        CLINQUANT, ORMOLU
like .... AURBATE
like alloy .... ASEM,
        OROIDE, ORMOLU
lump .... NUGGET
miner of 1849 ....
        FORTY-NINER
miner' camp: sl. ....
        DIGGINGS
mines region .. KLONDIKE
mosaic .... ORMOLU
native .... NUGGET
necklace ..... CARCANET
paint .... GILT
pertaining to ..... AURIC
product ... COIN, ALLOY,
        JEWELRY
rush partaker ....
        ARGONAUT
rush site .... YUKON
seeker .... MINER,
        ARGONAUT
separate gravel from ....
        PAN
sheet ..... FOIL, LATTEN
Spanish .... ORO
symbol .... AU
tinge .... GILD, GILT
vein .... LODE
wire work ..... FILIGREE
goldbrick .... LOAF, SHIRK
golden ..... AURIC, YELLOW,
        AUREATE
Age .... SATURNIAN,
        MILLENIUM
apples, guardian of .....
        IDUN, ITHUN, HESPERID
ball, king's ...... MOUND
ball, small .... GLOBE
calf .... IDOL
color ..... YELLOW, DORE
combining form ....
        CHRYS(O)
Fleece keeper ... AEETES
Fleece location .. COLCHIS
Fleece maiden .... HELLE
Fleece searcher ... JASON,
        ARGONAUTS
Fleece ship .... ARGO
Horn location ....
        BOSPORUS, ISTANBUL
king, legendary ... MIDAS
oriole ..... PIROL, LORIOT
robin .... ORIOLE

shiner ..... ROACH, DACE
Treasury item ...... ODE,
        SONNET, POEM
goldeneye ... BIRD, WHISTLER
goldenrod .... SOLIDAGO,
        YELLOWWEED
"Goldfinger" hero ..... BOND
goldfinch .... REDCAP,
        (YELLOW)BIRD
goldfinny .... CUNNER
goldfish ..... FANTAIL, COMET
goldilocks ...... BUTTERCUP
Goldsmith, poet ..... OLIVER
golem .... ROBOT, AUTOMATON
golf aid ...... CADDY, CADDIE
    ball material .... BALATA
    ball's position ...... LIE
    championship cup ......
        RYDER
    club ..... CLEEK, IRONS,
        (MID)IRON, BRASSIE,
        NIBLICK, JIGGER,
        WOOD, PUTTER, SPOON,
        BULGER, MASHIE,
        DRIVER
    club part .... NECK,
        HOSEL, TOE, HEAD
    course .... GREEN, LINKS
    course hazard ....
        (SAND)TRAP, STYMIE,
        POND, BUNKER
    feat ..... EAGLE, BIRDIE,
        HOLE-IN-ONE
    hole ...... CUP, DOGLEG
    holes unplayed ..... BYE
    partner, imaginary ......
        BOGEY
    position .... STANCE
    problem .... STYMIE
    score ...... PAR, BOGEY,
        BIRDIE, EAGLE
    stroke ...... PUTT, BAFF,
        SCLAFF, DRIVE, LOFT
    stroke, awkward ....
        FOOZLE
    stroke over par ... BOGEY
    term ... LIE, LOFT, BOGEY,
        TRAP, FORE, BIRDIE,
        EAGLE, BONE, BAFF,
        DIVOT, DORMIE, BISQUE,
        PUTT, FAIRWAY, GREEN,
        HOLE, HAZARD, ROUGH,
        SLICE, HOOK
    tourney ...... PRO-AM,
        OPEN
    turf .... DIVOT

golfer .... HOGAN, SNEAD, TEER, CASPER, LITTLER, PALMER, PLAYER, NICKLAUS, SANDERS, OUIMET, MANGRUM, DIVOT DIGGER, JONES
adviser of, sometimes .... CADDIE
attire of ... PLUS FOURS, KNICKERS
cry of .... FORE
goal of .... CUP
poor .... DUBBER
Golgotha .... CALVARY
goliard ..... JESTER, MINSTREL
Goliath ... GIANT, PHILISTINE
home of .... GATH
slayer of .... DAVID
golliwogg .... DOLL
gomeral ... SIMPLETON, DOLT, FOOL
gomuti ... SAGO, EJOO, PALM, ARENGA
palm .... ARENG(A)
product ... SUGAR, WINE, ROPE
gonad .... OVARY, TESTIS, SPERMARY
gonagra .... GOUT
gondola ...... (CANAL)BOAT, BARGE, CABIN
man ... POLER, BOATMAN
place of .... VENICE
race .... REGATTA
gondolier's song .. BARCAROLE
work ... ROWING, POLING
gone ...... LOST, DEAD, AGO, OUT, USED, UP, CONSUMED, OFF, AWAY
by .... PAST
"Gone with the Wind"
character .... MELANIE, (RHETT)BUTLER, (SCARLETT) O'HARA, ASHLEY
Goneril's father .... LEAR
sister .. REGAN, CORDELIA
gonfalon ...... FLAG, ENSIGN, BANNER
gong .... BELL, TAMTAM, TOM-TOM
Philippine .. KULINTANG
striker .... HAMMER
gonof/gonoph .... THIEF
gonorrhea .... CLAP
goo .... GLUE

goober .... PEANUT
good ... SUITABLE, EFFICIENT, UNSPOILED, VALID, GENUINE, REAL, SOUND, MORAL, BON, KIND, PUCKA, PUKKA
arrangement .... EUTAXY
Book .... BIBLE
by .... ADIEU, TATA, FAREWELL, AU REVOIR
cheer .... REVELRY, FEASTING
digestion .... EUPEPSIA
fellow (Robin) ... SPRITE
for-nothing fellow .... IDLER, LOAFER, WASTREL, VAGABOND, NE'ER-DO-WELL
harvest: archaic .. FOISON
health .... PEART
humored ..... CHEERFUL, JOLLY, AGREEABLE
looking .... COMELY, FAIR, BEAUTIFUL, HANDSOME
luck bringer .... MASCOT
luck present ... HANDSEL
management .... EUTAXY
natured .... AMIABLE, PLEASANT
news .. EVANGEL, GOSPEL
order .... EUTAXY
point! .... TOUCHE
sense ... JUDGMENT, WIT
Shepherd .... JESUS
taste, of .... ESTHETIC
time ...... BASH, SPREE
turn .... FAVOR
will .... GREE
"Goodbye, Columbus" author ROTH
player ... (ALI) MCGRAW
goodly ..... READILY, AMPLE, FINE, PLEASING
goodman ... HUSBAND, MASTER
title equivalent to .... MISTER
goodness ... VIRTUE, KINDNESS
goods .... FEE, STOCK, MERCHANDISE, WARES
British .... FREIGHT
cast overboard .. JETSAM, LIGAN, LAGAN, JETTISON, LAGEND
deliver the ....

COME ACROSS,
PRODUCE, FULFILL
movable .... CHATTEL
on hand ..... INVENTORY,
STOCK
sold together .... TIE-IN
goody .... CANDY
gooey .... STICKY
goof ...... BONER, BLUNDER,
FAIL, DOLT, ERR(OR)
on diamond ... FUMBLE,
MUFF
goofy .... STUPID, SILLY
gook ..... KOREAN, JAPANESE,
ORIENTAL, VIETCONG
goon .... THUG, HOOD(LUM),
RUFFIAN, ROUGH(NECK)
goop's inventor ..... BURGESS
goosander ...... MERGANSER,
DUCK
goose .... SOLAN, BARNACLE,
GRAYLAG, BERNICLE,
BRANT, IDIOT
berry .... FABES
colloquial ... DUPE, GULL
cry ..... YANG, CACKLE,
HONK
domestic, large .. EMDEN
eggs .... OOO, ZERO(S)
European wild ....
GRAYLAG
foot membrane ....
WEB(BING)
footless .... GANNET
genus .... ANSER
grease .... AXUNGE
Hawaiian .... NENE, NENI
male .... GANDER
of a .... ANSERINE
pygmy .... GOSLET
sea .... SOLAN
sound ..... HISS, CACKLE
stepper .... GERMAN
wild ... BERNICLE, BRANT
young .... GOSLING
gooseberry ...... FABES, POHA
goosefoot ..... BEET, SPINACH
gooseneck .... LAMP
gopher ... RODENT, SQUIRREL,
TORTOISE, MINNESOTAN,
SUSLIK, SPERMOPHILE
Mexican .... TUCAN
slang .... BURGLAR
state .... MINNESOTA
tortoise ...... MUNGOFA
gorcock .... GROUSE

Gordian knot cutter .. ..
ALEXANDER
tier .... GORDIUS
gore .... PIERCE, CRUOR,
BLOOD, GUSSET, STAB, HOOK
gorge ..... CLOUGH, CANYON,
RAVINE, GULLET, PASS,
GORMANDIZE, BARRANCA,
GULLY, CHASM, FLUME,
GLUT, POUCH,
CLOY, STUFF, COULOIR,
KLOOF
gorged .... REPLETE
gorgeous .... BEAUTIFUL,
RESPLENDENT, MAGNIFICENT,
SPLENDID
"Gorgeous Gussie" .. MORAN
gorget .... COLLAR
Gorgon ... MEDUSA, JEZEBEL,
EURYALE, STHENO
Gorgons, watchers for the ....
GRAEAE, GRAIAE
gorilla ..... APE, TROGLODYTE
slang .. THUG, GANGSTER,
GOON
Gorki, novelist .. .. MAXIM
gormandize .... GORGE, GUTTLE
gorse .. FURZE, WHIN, SHRUB
gory .... BLOODY
goshawk .... BUTEO
Goshen race .... TROT
gosling .... GOOSE
gospel ..... EVANGEL, TRUTH,
DOCTRINE, EVANGILE
preaching of ....
EVANGELISM
writer .... MARK,
MATTHEW, JOHN, LUKE
gossamer .... (COB)WEB,
FILM(Y)
gossamery ..... DIAPHANOUS,
GAUZY, THIN,
FILMY
gossip .... TATTLE(R), CAT,
BLAB(BER), TIDBIT, TITBIT,
BUSYBODY, HEARSAY,
SCUTTLEBUTT, CHAT(TER),
ONDIT, EME, QUIDNUNC,
TALK, BUZZ, CHITCHAT,
TALE(BEARER)
choice: colloq. .. EARFUL,
TIDBIT
female .... TABBY, CAT
malicious ..... SCANDAL
gossipy morsel .... TIDBIT
gossoon .... BOY

Goth .... BARBARIAN, ALARIC
Gothic .... MEDIEVAL,
            BARBAROUS
    arch .... OGIVE
    bard .... RUNER
    vault's groin ..... OGIVE
Goths' Christian bishop ......
                  ULFILA(S)
Gotland seaport .... VISBY
Gouda .... CHEESE
gouge .... ROUT, CHEAT,
    CHISEL, BENT, GROOVE,
    SWINDLE(R), (DE)FRAUD,
           IMPOSTOR
goulash ...... RAGOUT, STEW
Gounod opera ...... FAUST
    opera hero ...... ROMEO
gourd ...... MELON, SQUASH,
    CALABASH, PUMPKIN, PEPO,
          CURCURBIT(E)
    pod's substance .. LOOFAH
    rattle .... MARACA
    shaped rattle .... MARACA
    shell .... CALABASH
gourmand .... GLUTTON,
    GOURMET, EPICURE
gourmet ... TASTER, EPICURE,
    GASTRONOME, GO(U)RMAND
gout .... CLOT, BURSITIS,
    ARTHRITIS, PODAGRA,
          GONAGRA
    French .... TASTE
    remedy .... GUACO
govern .... DIRECT, RULE,
    REIGN, MANAGE, CURB, RUN
governess ... DUENNA, NANNY
government ... CONTROL, RULE,
    DIRECTION, STATE,
    REGIME(N), POLITY
    business .... OFFICIAL
    by gods ..... THEARCHY
    by men .... PATRIARCHY
    by military ....
          STRATOCRACY
    by priests ... THEOCRACY,
    HAGIARCHY, HIERARCHY,
        HIEROCRACY
    by saints ... HAGIARCHY
    by ten .... DECARCHY
    by three rulers ....
    TRIARCHY, TRIUMVIRATE
    declaration .. MANIFESTO
    fiscal problem ... BUDGET
    grant .... SUBSIDY,
          FRANCHISE
    mob's .... OCHLOCRACY

    of 2 rulers ...... DIARCHY
    report ..... WHITE PAPER,
          BLUE BOOK
    seat .... CAPITAL
    without .... ACRACY
    women's .... GYNARCHY,
        GYNECOCRACY
governor .... RULER,
    REGULATOR, BAN, REGENT,
    PILOT, NOMARCH, VICEROY,
    EPARCH, EXARCH,
        ETHNARCH
    Algerian .... DEY
    military ..... MARGRAVE
    Moslem .... HAKIM
    Persian .... SATRAP
    Roman ..... PROCONSUL
    subordinate ... TETRARCH
    Turkish .... BEY
gowan .... DAISY
gowk ... SIMPLETON, CUCKOO
gown .... DRESS, ROBE,
    NEGLIGEE, MANTUA, FROCK
    like garment .... TUNIC,
        TOGA
    outer .... SURCOAT
    skirt of .... LAP
goy .... GENTILE
Graafian follicle ..... OVISAC
grab .... SEIZE, SNATCH,
    TAKE, SHIP, HOG
grabble .... SEIZE, GROPE,
        SPRAWL
Gracchus' brother ..... GAIUS
grace .... BEAUTY, FAVOR,
    CHARM, DECENCY, PRAYER,
    DIGNIFY, TACT, ATTEND,
    ADORN, CHARISMA, HONOR,
    MERCY, TITLE
    Aglaia ..... BRILLIANCE
    Euphrosyne .... JOY
    kind of .... REPRIEVE,
    RESPITE, MORATORIUM
    note .... INCIDENTAL
    Thalia .... BLOOM
graceful .... BEAUTIFUL,
    WILLOWY
    animal .... GAZELLE
    bird .... SWAN
    dance ... BALLET, WALTZ
graceless .... CLUMSY,
    AWKWARD, INELEGANT
Graces, one of the ... THALIA,
    EUPHROSYNE, AGLAIA, JOY
    mother of .... AEGLE
gracile .... SLENDER, SLIM

gracious ... BENIGN, URBANE,
 POLITE, MERCIFUL
grackle ... BLACKBIRD, MINA,
 MYNA(H), DAW, TINKLING,
 TROUPIAL
gradate .... BLEND
gradation ... ABLAUT, STAGE,
 DEGREE, NUANCE, STEP,
 TRANSITION
grade .... STEP, DEGREE, MARK,
 RATING, INCLINE, CLASS,
 LEVEL, RANK, SORT
 "failure" .... FLUNK
grader .... PUPIL
gradient ...... WALKING, SLOPE
gradin ...... SHELF, STEP, SEAT
gradual fall .... DECLINE
graduate ... ALUMNUS, GRAD
graduated glass tube . BURETTE
graduation ceremony ....
 COMMENCEMENT
 certificate ..... DIPLOMA
gradus .... DICTIONARY
Graeae, one of the .... DEINO
 concern of the .. GORGONS
 describing the .. ONE-EYED
 parent of ..... PHORCUS
Graf .... EARL, COUNT
 battleship .... SPEE
graffiti .... SCRAWLS
graft ... CLAVE, TRANSPLANT,
 (S)CION, IMP, INARCH
grafted, in heraldry .... ENTE
grafter, petty ...... GRIFTER
grail ...... AMA, PLATTER,
 CHALICE, CUP
 Holy .... SANGREAL,
 SANGRAAL
grain ... SEED, CEREAL, WHEAT,
 RICE, OAT, RYE, BIT,
 KERMES, WALE, MEAL,
 SPELT, CORN, CURN,
 MILLET, KERNEL
 basket .... SCUTTLE
 batch of .... GRIST
 beard ..... AWN, ARISTA
 beetle .... CADELLE
 black .... URD
 bract .... GLUME
 building ..... GRANARY
 chaff .... BRAN
 combining form ... GRANI
 cracked .... GROATS
 cutter .... SCYTHE
 disease ... SMUT, ERGOT
 elevator .... SILO

 exchange .... PIT
 fungus .... ERGOT
 grindstone .... MANO
 ground .... GRITS, GRIST,
 SAMP
 hand mill .... QUERN
 hulled ... GROATS, GRITS
 husk ...... GLUME, BRAN
 in kernels .... CORN,
 MAIZE, MEALIES
 Indian ..... MAIZE, CORN
 loss thru spillage ......
 ULLAGE
 measure ...... BUSHEL,
 QUARTER, MOY, CAVAN,
 GANTA, CHUPA, SACK
 mill ... . QUERN
 outer covering ... HUSK
 pest .... CADELLE
 refuse .... SCOURINGS
 row, drying ... WINDROW
 shelter .... HUTCH
 skin .... BRAN
 small .... GRANULE
 sorghum ...... KAF(F)IR
 stack .... MOW
 storehouse .. ELEVATOR,
 SILO, GARNER, GRANARY
 stumps .... STUBBLE
grains .... SPEAR
 3.17 .... CARAT
grainy .... GRANULAR
gram ..... PLANT, CHICK-PEA
 molecule .... MOL(E)
grama .... GRASS
gramary .... MAGIC
gramercy .... THANKS
gramineous .... GRASSY
grammar causal connective ...
 FOR, SINCE, THEREFORE
grammarian ...... PROSODIST
grammatical case .... DATIVE
 construction ... SYNESIS,
 SYNTAX
 description ..... PARSE
 error .... SOLECISM
 mark .... ASPER
 term ..... CASE, GENDER,
 MOOD, PARSE, SUBJECT,
 TENSE
gramophone .... PHONOGRAPH,
 VICTROLA
grampus ... SPRINGER, ORC(A),
 WHALE, COWFISH
 relative .... DOLPHIN
Granada, king of ... BOABDIL

granary ..... SILO, ELEVATOR, GRANGE, CRIB, GARNER, STOREHOUSE, BIN, GOLA

grand ... GREAT, CHIEF, MAIN, MAGNIFICENT, IMPOSING, STATELY, AUGUST, NOBLE, PIANO, MAJESTIC

Canal bridge .... RIALTO
Coulee .... DAM
Coulee designer .. SAVAGE
duchess' relative .... TSARINA
jury's word .. IGNORAMUS
mal .... FIT, EPILEPSY
National site .... AINTREE
Old Party member ...... REPUBLICAN
Pre heroine .. EVANGELINE
slam .... JACKPOT, VOLE

grandam .... CRONE
grandchild .... OYE
Grande and others ...... RIOS
grandee ..... NOBLEMAN, PEER
grandeur ... GLORY, MAJESTY, EMINENCE, DIGNITY, NOBILITY, SPLENDOR
grandfather ...... PATRIARCH
pertaining to .... AVITAL, AVAL
grandfatherly .... KINDLY, BENIGNANT
grandiloquence ..... BOMBAST
grandiloquent .... MAGNIFIC, TURGID
grandiose ...... COSMIC, EPIC, IMPOSING, GRAND, HOMERIC, POMPOUS, IMPRESSIVE
Grandma Moses ...... ANNA
grandmother .... BELDAM(E), GRANDAM
grandmotherly .... FUSSY, INDULGENT
grandparents, having same ... GERMAN
of .... AVAL
grandson .... NEPOTE
grandstand .... BLEACHERS
play .... STUNT
grange ..... GRANARY, FARM
granger .... FARMER
granite ..... ROCK, PORPHYRY, APLITE, MUSCOVITE, BIOTITE
constituent .. FEL(D)SPAR, MICA, QUARTZ
imitation ... SCAGLIOLA

rock resembling .. GNEISS
granny ..... KNOT, GRANDMA
grant ..... APPANAGE, ADMIT, CONFER, ASSENT, AGREE, (CON)CEDE, AWARD, PATENT, (RE)MISE
by will .... DEMISE
of money ...... SUBSIDY, ENDOWMENT
U.S. president .. ULYSSES
granted without obligation .... GRATUITIOUS, GRATIS, FREE
grantee .... RECIPIENT
grantor .... DONOR
granular .... GRAINY
mineral ...... CORUNDUM
mow .... NEVE, FIRN
grape .... MUSCADINE, DELAWARE, CONCORD, CATAWBA, NIAGARA, ISABELLA, MALMSEY, MUSCAT, UVA, BERRY, TOKAY, ACINUS, MALAGA, SCUPPERNONG, WAMPEE, MALVASIA
acid, of ...... GLYCOLIC
coating, powdery .... BLOOM
conserve .... UVATE
crushed pulp ...... RAPE, POMACE
disease ...... COULURE, ESCA, ERINOSE
dried ..... RAISIN, PASA
fruit .... SHADDOCK, POMELO
fruit, dried .... CURRANT
jelly .... SAPA
juice ... DIBS, SAPA, STUM, MUST
juice deposit .... TARTAR
juice, in pharmacy .. SAPA
juice liquor ...... RAKI, RAKEE
like ...... POKE, UVA(L), UVIC
preserve .... UVATE
product .... WINE
pulp ..... POMACE, RAPE
refuse .... BAGASSE, MARC
seed .... ACINUS
Spanish .... UVA
sugar .... MALTOSE, DEXTROSE, GLUCOSE
unfermented ...... STUM
wine .... CATAWBA

grapefruit .... POMELO,
　　PUMELO, SHADDOCK
grapes, bunch .... BOB,
　　BOTRYOID
　of/like .... VINACEOUS
　powdery coating .. BLOOM
　pulp ..... RAPE, POMACE
　where grown .. VINEYARD
grapevine ... RUMOR, HEARSAY
　disease .... ERINOSE
　item ..... RUMOR, GOSSIP
graph ..... DIAGRAM, CHART
　meteorological event ....
　　ISOPLETH
graphic .... CLEAR, VIVID,
　　LIFELIKE, PICTORIAL
　art .... PAINTING,
　　DRAWING, ETCHING,
　　PHOTOGRAPHY,
　　DRYPOINT, OFFSET
　description ...... IMAGE
　granite...... PEGMATITE
graphite ... LEAD, PLUMBAGO,
　　CARBON, KISH
graplin ... GRAPNEL, CRAMPON
grapnel .... GRAPLIN(E),
　　ANCHOR, CREEPER, DRAG
grapple ..... WRESTLE, BIND,
　　GRIP, HOLD, CLUTCH, LOCK
grappler ... WRESTLER, HAND
grappling iron ..... GRAPNEL,
　　GRAPLIN, CRAMPON
grasp ... SEIZE, UNDERSTAND,
　　HOLD, CONTROL, REACH,
　　HENT, GRIP, GRAB, CLUTCH
grasping .... GREEDY,
　　AVARICIOUS, FELL, SORDID,
　　HENT, MISERLY
grass ..... POA, DARNEL, RIB,
　　ZACATON, GRAMA, SORGO,
　　HERB(AGE), BROME, REED,
　　BAMBOO, LAWN, PASTURE,
　　GRAZE, RYE, WHEAT,
　　BARLEY, OAT, AVENA,
　　QUITCH, FESCUE, VETIVER,
　　NARD, FOXTAIL
　African .... ALFA
　Algerian ...... ESPARTO
　Andean .... ICHU
　Asiatic .... MILLET,
　　CITRONELLA
　basketry .... OTATE,
　　REED, ESPARTO
　blade .... SPEAR
　blue .... POA
　bract .... GLUME

　brooms .... ZACATON
　bunch .... TUFT
　carpet ..... CHICKWEED
　cereal .... RICE, MILLET,
　　SORGHUM, RAGGEE,
　　RAG(G)I, OAT, RYE
　Ceylon . PATANA, CHENA
　chafflike bract ... GLUME
　cloth material .... RAMIE
　clump .... HASSOCK,
　　TUSSOCK
　coarse .... SEDGE, REED,
　　ESPARTO, COUCH,
　　SACATON
　cordage .... ESPARTO
　corn .... KAF(F)IR
　country .... VELD(T)
　covered soil .... TURF,
　　SWARD
　cutter ... (LAWN)MOWER,
　　REAPER, SCYTHE
　dried .... HAY
　East Indies ...... GLAGA
　family, of the .. POACEOUS
　flower part ...... PALEA,
　　BENT
　fodder .... TEOSINTE
　for thatch ... NETI, ALANG
　forage ... GAMA, MILLET,
　　REDTOP, SORGHUM,
　　SORGO, TEOSINTE
　genus .... AVENA, STIPA,
　　POD
　grain-yielding .. FETERITA
　grapevine ...... MESQUITE
　growth, new .... FOG
　hay .... TIMOTHY
　husk .... GLUME
　Indian cereal ..... RAGEE,
　　CORN
　jointed stem ...... CULM
　Kentucky .... POA
　killer .. DOWPON, ESTERON
　lawn .... REDTOP
　leaf ...... BLADE, SPEAR
　like Indian corn ....
　　TEOSINTE
　marsh ... SPART, SEDGE,
　　REED, FESCUE
　meadow ... POA, FESCUE
　mesquite .... GRAMA
　millet .... PANIC
　moor .... HEATH
　new growth .... FOG
　oat .... AVENA
　ornamental .... EULALIA

paper-making ... ESPARTO
pasture .. GRAMA, FESCUE, REDTOP
pertaining to .. POACEOUS
Philippine .... COGON, TALAHIB
plant like .... SEDGE
plot .... LAWN
poisonous .... DARNEL
quaking .... BRIZA
reedy .... BENT, DISS
rope-making .... MUNG
rope: Sp. .... SOGA
rug .... MAT
rye .. MARCITE, DARNEL
scale .... PALEA
second crop .... ROWEN
seed weight measure ... CARAT
shoot .... SPEAR
snipe .... SANDPIPER
sorghum .... SORGO
sour .... SORREL
Spanish .... ESPARTO
stem .... CULM
stemmy .... REED
swamp ..... SEDGE, REED
tuft .. TUSSOCK, HASSOCK
uncut/ungrazed .... FOG
wheat-like .... CHEAT, CHESS
widow .... DIVORCEE
wiry .... BENT, POA, ZACATON

grasshopper .. GRIG, LOCUST, KATYDID, CRICKET
military ..... AIRPLANE, SCOUTER

grassland ... SWARD, PASTURE, RANGE, LEA, CAMPO, SAVANNA(H), VELD(T), PRAIRIE, MEAD, PAMPA

grassy .... TURFY
plain .... CAMPO

grate ...... RUB, RASP, GRIND, ANNOY, FRET, CREAK, FIREPLACE, GRIDE, ABRADE, SCRAPE, IRRITATE, CHARK, JAR, SCROOP

grateful .... APPRECIATIVE, WELCOME, PLEASING, THANKFUL

grater ..... ANNOYER, VEXER, PEST

gratification ..... GRATUITY, SATISFACTION

gratify .... SATISFY, HUMOR, INDULGE, REWARD, PLEASE, SATE
vanity .... FLATTER

gratin .... CRUST

grating .. GRATE, IRRITATING, HOARSE, ANNOYING, RASPING, GRID(IRON), RASPY, GRILL(E), LATTICE(WORK), STRIDENT

gratis .... FREE, GRATUITOUS
gratitude ..... APPRECIATION
gratuitous ..... FREE, GRATIS
gratuity ...... TIP, PRESENT, BOON, CUMSHAW, VAIL, LAGN(I)APPE, PERQUISITE, FEE, GIFT

gratulation .... JOY

graupel .... SLEET, HAIL

gravamen .... GRIEVANCE, COMPLAINT, CHARGE, ACCUSATION

grave .... WEIGHTY, OMINOUS, MOUND, TOMB, SOLEMN, SOMBER, SCULPTURE, BARROW, SOBER, ETCH, SEDATE, DULL, SERIOUS, STAID, CARVE, SEPULCHER, SATURNINE
cloth .... CEREMENT, SHROUD
digger .... SEXTON
heap of earth/stone ..... BARROW, TUMULUS, MOUND
marker .... BARROW, STELE, HEADSTONE
robber .... GHOUL

gravel ..... CALCULUS, BEACH, SAND, HECKLE, GRIT
a boat .. BEACH, GROUND
between road ties ..... BALLAST
colloquial ..... IRRITATE, ANNOY
deposit .... GEEST
mound .... OS
shifter .... RIDDLE

graven .... CARVED, SCULPTURED, FIXED
image .. IDOL, ICON, IKON

Gravenstein .... APPLE

graver ...... BURIN, ETCHER, SCULPTOR, CARVER, CHASER, CHISEL

Graves' disease .... GOITER

gravestone ... MARKER, STELE,
STELA, MEMORIAL,
BARROW, SLAB
graveyard .... CEMETERY
gravid .... PREGNANT
graving tool .... STYLET,
CHISEL, BURIN
gravitate ...... DROP, FALL,
SINK, SETTLE
gravity .... SOLEMNITY,
SERIOUSNESS, WEIGHT
gravy ..... SAUCE, PROFIT, JUS
thickener .... ROUX
gray .... DULL, DREARY,
DISMAL, OLD, ASHEN,
GRIZZLE, HOAR(Y)
brownish ...... TAUPE
Friar ... .. FRANCISCAN
hair ...... GRIZZLE
matter ...... BRAINS,
THALAMUS
mole ...... TAUPE
mottled ...... GRISEOUS
parrot ...... JAKO
rock ...... SLATE
grayfish .... DOGFISH
grayish blue ..... TEAL, BICE,
AZURINE, PERSE, LIVID
brown ...... TAUPE, DUN
tan ...... BEIGE
white ...... HOARY
graylag ...... GOOSE
grayling .... UMBER,
BUTTERFLY, FISH, TROUT
graze .... PASTURE, RUB,
SCRAPE, SCRATCH, TOUCH,
GLANCE(OFF), FEED,
BRUSH, SHAVE, NICK,
BROWSE, AGIST
livestock ...... PASTURE
with bullet .... CREASE
grazing land ...... (G)RANGE,
RANCH(O), PASTURE
rope ... LARIAT, TETHER
grease .... FAT, LARD,
LUBRICANT, LUBRICATE,
BRIBE, TIP, AXUNGE, DAUB,
OIL, COOM
cosmetics ... COSMOLINE
monkey ..... MECHANIC
refuse .... SLUSH
sheep's wool .... SUINT
greasewood ...... ORACHE,
CHICO
greasy ... UNCTUOUS, SLIPPERY,
PINGUID, FATTY, OILY

great ...... HUGE, EMINENT,
SUPER(IOR), IMPOSING,
CLEVER, EXPERT, FINE,
NOBLE, UNCO, MAGNA,
BIG, TITANIC
amount ...... BARREL,
LOADS
artist .... MASTER
artistic work ....
MASTER(PIECE)
Barrier reef .... OTEA
Bear .... URSA
care .... PAINS
combining form .. MAGNI,
MEGA(LO)
Commoner ... BRYAN,
CLAY, PITT, STEVENS
Dane .... DOG
deal: colloq. ...... HEAP,
LOT
Desert ...... SAHARA
Divide ... DEATH, CRISIS
Emancipator ... LINCOLN
grandchild .... IER
Lakes ... ERIE, ST. CLAIR,
ONTARIO, HURON,
SUPERIOR, MICHIGAN
Lakes boat ... MACKINAW
Lakes fish ... TULLIBEE,
CISCO, PIKE,
MASKALONGE
Lakes steamer ....
WHALEBACK
Mogul ..... NABOB, VIP
northern diver .... LOON
number ... HORDE, LOTS,
HOST, LEGION, GALAXY,
HEAP, LAKH
omentum .... CAUL
Profile ...... BARRYMORE
Pyramid builder ... CHEOPS
Pyramid dweller ....
PHARAOH, KHUFU,
KHAFRE, MENKAURE
Pyramid site .... GIZA
Spirit, Indian ... MANITO
Tom of Oxford .... BELL
toe .... HALLUX
White Father .. PRESIDENT
White Way ... BROADWAY,
RIALTO
greatcoat .... PALETOT
Greater Antilles island .. CUBA,
PUERTO RICO, JAMAICA,
HISPANIOLA
greatest ..... UTMOST, VERIEST

greatly .... HIGHLY
greaves .... CRACKLINGS,
    ARMOR, CRACKNEL
grebe ...... DABCHICK, LOON,
   DUCKER, DIPPER, DIDAPPER
Grecian ... GREEK, HELLENIC,
    GRECO
Grecism .... HELLENISM
Greco-Egyptian deity ....
    SERAPIS
   Turkish dispute, object of
    CYPRUS
gree .... GOOD WILL
Greece .... ATTICA,
   (H)ELLAS, ACHAEA, ELIS
   of modern ...... ROMAIC
greed(iness) .... EDACITY,
   CUPIDITY, AVARICE,
   GLUTTONY, AVIDITY
greedy .... GRASPING,
  AVARICIOUS, ACQUISITIVE,
  VORACIOUS, GRIPPLE,
  RAVENOUS, ESURIENT,
  AVID, COVETOUS,
  INSATIABLE
  person ... PIG, GLUTTON,
  GO(U)RMAND, HARPY,
  CORMORANT
Greek ..... CRETAN, ARGIVE,
  HELLENE, AEOLIAN, ATTIC,
  ACHAEAN, IONIAN,
  HELLENIC
  abbess .... AMMA
  actor's boot ...... BUSKIN
  after piece .... EXODE
  alphabet ... MU, PI, TAU,
  RHO, ALPHA, BETA, ETA,
  NU, XI, KAPPA, THETA,
  ZETA, OMEGA, IOTA
  alphabet first letter ......
    ALPHA
  alphabet last letter ......
    OMEGA
  apartment ...... ANDRON
  architect .... ICTINUS
  aristocrat ..... EUPATRID
  assembly .. AGORA, BOULE
  athlete .... MILO
  athletic contest ... AGON
  author ... AESOP, HOMER,
  PINDAR, ZENO, SAPPHO,
  PLATO, PLUTARCH,
  TIMON
  avenging spirit .. ERINYS,
  ATE, FURY

basket of fruits ....
    CALATHUS
bee .... MELISSA
belt .... ZOSTER
bestman ... PARANYMPH
beverage ..... OENOMEL
bishop .... EPARCH
boatman .... PHAON
bottle .... AMPULLA
boxing-wrestling bout ...
    PANCRATIUM
bridesmaid .. PARANYMPH
buckle .... FIBULA
cape ... PAPAS, MATAPAN,
  ARAXOS, MALEA
capital .... ATHENS
Catholic .... UNIAT(E)
centaur .... NESSUS
channel .... EURIPUS
choral dance movement ..
    STROPHE
church diocese ....
    EPARCHY
Church, father of ....
   GREGORY, ORIGEN
Church hermits'
  community .... SKETE
circus arena ....
    HIPPODROME
citadel .... ACROPOLIS
city ..... NEMEA, SPARTA,
  ARGOS, SALONIKA,
  CORINTH, CHALCIS,
  PIRAEUS, MYCENAE,
  JANINA, THERMA,
  LARISSA, ELIS, ARTA,
  ERETRIA, SICYON,
  ELEUSIS
city in Asia Minor ......
    MELETUS
city in Italy .... SYBARIS
city in Turkey ....
    PERGAMUM
clan .... OBE
clasp .... FIBULA
classical name ... DANAI
coin ... OBOL, DRACHMA,
  OBOLUS, LEPTON,
  STATER
colony ...... ELEA, IONIA
column ... DORIC, IONIC
comic poet ... MENANDER
commander ... NAVARCH,
  HIPPARCH, CHILIARCH
concubine ..... HETAERA,
  HETAIRA

commonalty ..... DEME,
DEMOS
concert hall ...... ODEUM
contest .... AGON
counselor .... NESTOR
country .... ELIS, EPIRUS
courtesan .... THAIS,
HETAERA
cross, design like ....
SWASTIKA
cry of sorrow ..... AI AI
cup .... SCYPHUS, DEPAS
dance .... PYRRHIC
devoted wife: myth. ......
BAUCIS
dialect .... (A)EOLIC,
DORIC, IONIC
dirge .... LINOS
district ... AONIA, ATTICA,
ARGOLIS, LOCRIS,
MEGARIS
drink .... NECTAR
earth .... GEOS
enchantress ...... CIRCE,
MEDEA
epic poem ..... ODYSSEY,
ILIAD, RHAPSODY
fabulist .... AESOP
faction .. ELAS, EAM, EDES
farce .... MIME
fate .... LACHESIS
feather .... PTERON
female worshipper ......
ORANT
festival ... DELIA, AGON,
DIONYSIA
fillet .... TAENIA
flask .... OLPE
galley .... BIREME,
TRIREME
garden: myth. ....
HESPERIDES
garment .... PEPLOS,
CHITON, CHLAMYS
geographer ..... STRABO
geometer .... HERON
ghost .... KER
giant ..... ARGUS, ORION,
CYCLOPS, BRIAREUS,
ARGUS, TITAN, CACUS
giant wrestler .. ANTAEUS
girdle .... ZOSTER
god ..... APOLLO, ARES,
ARTEMIS, EOS, CHAOS,
ONIROS, HYMEN,

BACCHUS, LETO, EROS,
ZEUS, HELIOS
earth .... BEL
festivity ...... COMUS
fire .... VULCAN
flocks .... PAN
heaven(s) .... URANUS,
ZEUS, BEL
hunter .... ORION
love .... EROS
marriage ..... HYMEN
medicine ... ASCLEPIUS
mockery ...... MOMUS
north wind ... BOREAS
rain .... ZEUS
revelry ..... BACCHUS,
COMUS
river .... ERIDANUS
sea .... NEREUS,
POSEIDON
sky ..... ARGUS, ZEUS
sleep .... HYPNOS,
HYPNUS
sun .. HELIOS, APOLLO,
PHOEBUS
supreme .... ZEUS
vegetation .. DIONYSUS
wealth .... PLUTUS
winds .. AEOLUS, EURUS
wine ...... DIONYSUS
war .... ARES
goddess .... DEA
agriculture ... ARTEMIS,
DEMETER
air .... HERA
arts .... ATHENA
beauty ..... APHRODITE
chance .... TYCHE
chase .... ARTEMIS
dawn .... EOS
destruction .... ARA
discord .... ERIS
earth .... GAEA, GAIA,
HECATE
fate .... MOERA
flowers .... CHLORIS
ghosts .... HECATE
goblins ...... ARTEMIS
health .... HYGEIA
hearth .... HESTIA
heavens .... HERA
hunting ...... ARTEMIS
justice .... THEMIS
love .... APHRODITE
marriage ... DEMETER,
GAIA, HERA

memory ... MNEMOSYNE
mischief ..... ATE, ERIS
moon .... SELENE,
HECATE, ARTEMIS,
ASTARTE
nature .... ARTEMIS
night ...... LETO, NYX,
LEDA
peace .... IRENE
retribution ... ARA, ATE
seas ...... INO, DORIS
sky .... INO
sorcery ...... HECATE
strife .... ERIS
vegetation ...... CORA,
COTYS
vengeance .... NEMESIS,
ARA
victory .... NIKE
war .... ATHENA,
BELLONA
weaving ...... ERGANE
wisdom ...... ATHENA,
PALLAS
witchcraft .... HECATE
women .... HERA
youth .... HEBE
gods, queen of ..... HERA
governor .... EPARCH,
NOMARCH
grave marker ..... STELE
guerrilla ...... ELAS, EDES,
EAM, KLEPHT
guest .... XENOS
gulf .... AEGINA,
SALONIKA, CORINTH,
PATRAS
gymnasium ...... XYST,
PAL(A)ESTRA
half man, half dragon ...
CECROPS
hat ... PETASUS, PETASOS
headband ...... TAENIA,
MITER
headland .... ACTIUM
heart .... KARDIA
hedgehog ...... ECHINOS
hemp .... KANNABIS
herald .... STENTOR
hermit .... GILES
hero .... AJAX, IDAS,
THESEUS, JASON,
ALCINOUS
historian .... XENOPHON,
DIONYSIUS, HERODOTUS
"holy hill" .... ATHOS

Hours .... HORAE
hunter: myth. ..... ORION
huntress ..... ATALANTA
hymn .... PAEAN
immigrant .... METIC
initiate .... EPOPT(A)
island ...... CHIOS, DELOS,
SALAMIS, LEMNOS,
LEUCADE, CRETE, ELIS,
KOS, RHODES, NAXOS,
MILO, NIO, MELOS,
PELION, SKORPIOS,
MYTILENE, SAMOS, IOS,
THASOS, SPORADES,
PATMOS, EVVOIA, PAROS
isthmus ...... CORINTH
jar ... CRATER, AMPHORA
jump .... HALMO
king ...... CONSTANTINE
king of Arcadia .. LYCAON
king of Corinth ....
SISYPHUS
king of Crete ....
IDOMENEUS
king of Mycenae ....
ATREUS
language .... KOINE
language, pertaining to ..
ROMAIC
legislative assembly ......
BOULE
leper .... LEPRA
leprosy .... ALPHOS
letter ...... ALPHA, BETA,
CHI, DELTA, ETA,
EPSILON, CAMMA, IOTA,
KAPPA, PHI, LAMBDA,
MU, NU, OMICRON, PSI,
RHO, SIGMA, TAU,
THETA, UPSILON, XI,
ZETA, OMEGA
liqueur .... OUZO
love feast .... AGAPE
lyric poet .... PINDAR,
ANACREON, ALCAEUS
magistrate .... DIMIURGE,
ARCHON, EPHOR
mantle .... CHLAMYS,
PALLIUM, PALLA,
HIMATION
market place .... AGORA
marriage ...... GAMOS,
HYMEN
masses .... DEMOS
mathematician .. EUCLID
measure .... BEMA

memorial of victory ..... TROPHY
metropolitan ..... EPARCH
milestone .... HERMA
military organization ....
BAM, ELAS, EDES
militia .... PALIKAR
Modern .... ROMAIC
monks' community .....
SKETE
money ... MINA, TALENT,
DRACHMA
monster: myth. .. SPHINX,
HYDRA, CHIMERA,
HARPY, LAMIA, TYPHON
moralist ..... PLUTARCH
mountain ...... PELION,
PARNASSUS, ATHOS,
OLYMPUS, HELICON,
HYMETTUS, IDA, OSSA
mountain chain ..... OETA,
PINDUS
mouse .... HYRAX
Muse .... CLIO,
EUTERPE, ERATO,
URANIA, CALLIOPE,
POLYMNIA, THALIA
Muses' home: myth. ....
AONIA
musician .... ARION
mythical flier ... ICARUS
mythical princess ......
EUROPA
native ... SCIOT, CYPRIOT
note in music ...... NETE
nymph ...... M(A)ENAD,
(HAMA)DRYAD,
SALMACIS, HESTIA,
NEMERTES, ARETHUSA,
OENONE
official .... EPHOR
orator ..... DEMOSTHENES
order of architecture ....
CORINTHIAN, IONIC,
DORIC
overseer .... EPHOR
painter .. GRECO, ZEUXIS
parliament .... BOULE
pastoral district ....
ARCADIA
pastoral poet ..... BION,
THEOCRITUS
patriarch .... ARIUS
patriot .... BOZZARIS
peasant-poet .... HESIOD
people .... DEMOS

peninsula .... MOREA,
PELOPONNESUS
philosopher ...... ZENO,
PLATO, DIOGENES,
EPICTETUS, HERACLITUS,
THALES, ARISTOTLE
physician .... GALEN
pillar .... HERMA
pitcher .... OLPE
place for discussions ....
EXEDRA
plain .... OLYMPIA
platform .... BEMA
poem ...... EPIC, EPODE,
ILIAD, ODYSSEY
poet ..... HOMER, ARION,
HESIOD, MENANDER,
PINDAR, ANACREON,
THESPIS, ALCAEUS
poetess .... SAPPHO
poetry in strophes ......
MELIC
populace .... DEMOS
port .... AULIS
portico ...... STOA, XYST
premier........ PAPAGOS
priest's helper .. PARASITE
priestess .... HERO
princess .... IRENE
province .... NOME
queen ...... ANNE-MARIE
queen-mother ......
FREDERIKA
race .... GENOS
racing course ....
HIPPODROME
regent .... ZOETAKIS
region .... DORIS,
THESSALY
resistance group .. EDES,
ELAS, EAM
retreat to the sea ......
KATABASIS
revolutionary leader .....
YPSILANTI
river .... PENEIOS,
SALAMBRIA
rose .... CAMPION
sacred grove ...... ALTIS
satirist .... LUCIAN
scarf .... PEPLOS,
PEPLUS, PEPLUM
scholar's specialty .....
ILIAD
sculptor .... MYRON,
PHIDIAS, LYSIPPUS

seagod .... TRITON
seaport .... ENOS,
    SALONIKA, PATRAS
senate .... BOULE
serf .... PENEST
serpent: myth. .. PYTHON
seven .... ZETA
shawl ... PEPLOS, PEPLUM
shepherd, legendary .....
    ENDYMION
shield .... PELTA
shipping tycoon ....
    ONASSIS, NIARCHOS,
    VERGOTTIS
signpost .... HERMA
skeptic .... PYRRHO
skirt for men ....
    FUSTANELLA
slab .... STELE
slaughter of cattle ......
    HECATOMB
slave .... PENEST,
    HETAERA, HIERODULE
soldier .... PELTAST,
    PALIKAR, HOPLITE
song .... MELOS
soothsayer ..... TIRESIAS,
    CALCHAS
sorceress .. CIRCE, MEDEA
soul .... PNEUMA
speaker's platform ......
    BEMA
spider .... ARACHNE
spirit .... PNEUMA
stage ...... PROSCENIUM
star .... ASTER
statesman ..... METAXAS,
    PERICLES
stoa .... PORTICO
Stoic philosopher ....
    EPICTETUS
street dress .... HIMATION
sungod .... HELIOS
sylvan deity ...... SATYR
symbol .... ORANT
symbol of abundance ...
    CALATHUS
talking horse .... ARION
temple part .... NAOS,
    CELLA
theater .... ODEON
theologian .... ARIUS
thread, legendary .. CLEW
time .... CHRONOS
titan .. CRONUS, OCEANUS
town .... SERES

township .... DEME
tragedian .... THESPIS
tragedy, father of .....
    THESPIS
tragic hero ...... ORESTE
tribe .... PHYLE
tribe subdivision ....
    PHRATRY
troop unit .... TAXIS
trumpet .... SALPINX
tunic .... CHITON
underground army ......
    ELAS, EAM, EDES
uterus .... METRA
valley .... TEMPE, NEMEA
vase ..... PELIKE, PYXIS
verb tenses ..... AORISTS
village, battlesite ....
    MARATHON
war cry .... ALALA
war dance ...... PYRRHIC
warrior ...... DIOMEDES,
    AJAX, ACHILLES,
    ACAMAS, ODYSSEUS
wedding song/poem ....
    HYMEN(EAL)
weight ... MINA, OBOL(US)
wine .... OENOMEL
wing .... PTERON
wise man .... THALES
woman .... GYNE
women's headband .....
    MITER
word .... LOGOS
wrestling school ....
    PAL(A)ESTRA
green .... NEW, LEAFY, MILD,
    ACTIVE, BILIOUS, UNRIPE,
    VERT, SIMPLE, RAW, NILE,
    CALLOW, BICE, FRESH,
    NAIVE, VERDANT, OLIVE,
    EMERALD, RESEDA, JADE
becoming .... VIRESCENT
bright .... EMERALD
chalcedony ..... JASPER
cheese .... SAPSAGO
colloquial ..... JEALOUS
color .. JADE, VERT, BICE,
    OLIVE, EMERALD
eyed .... JEALOUS,
    ENVIOUS
film on copper .. PATINA
fly .... APHID
gage .... PLUM
garnet .... OLIVINE
golden .... AENEOUS

growing plants ....
    VERDURE
Hat author .... ARLEN
heraldic .... VERT
land .... ERIN
light: colloq. ....
    PERMISSION, PERMIT,
    AUTHORIZATION
Mansions character .....
    ABEL, RIMA
manure .... CLOVER
monkey .... GRIVET,
    VERVET, GUENON
mountain state ....
    VERMONT
onion .... SCALLION
room .... FOYER
room occupant ... ACTOR
sand .... MARL
shade ... LIME, OLIVE, PEA
sickness .... CHLOROSIS
stamp name ...... EIRE
stone .... PERIDOT, JADE
tail .... GRANNOM
tea .... HYSON
vegetation .... VERDURE
vitriol .... COPPERAS
greenery .... VERDURE,
    HOTHOUSE
greenfinch .... LINNET,
    GROSBEAK, SPARROW
greenheart ... WOOD, BEBEERU,
    TREE
greenhorn .... NOVICE,
    BEGINNER, DUPE, ROOKIE,
    GULL, TYRO
greenhouse ...... HOTHOUSE,
    VINERY, VIVARIUM
vine .... SMILAX
greening .... APPLE
greenish .... VIRIDISCENT,
    VIRESCENT
blue .... TORQUOISE
white .... RESEDA
yellow ... OLIVE, SULPHUR
Greenland base .... ETAH
capital .... GODTHAAB
discoverer .... ERIC
fish ...... LING, BURBOT
native .... ITA
town .... ETAH
greenlet .... SONGBIRD,
    VIREO
greenness .... VIRIDITY,
    VERDANCY, VERDURE
greens ..... VEGETABLES, KALE

greenshank ...... SANDPIPER
greensickness .... ANEMIA,
    CHLOROSIS
greenstone ..... JADE, WHIN,
    DIORITE
greensward .... TURF
greet ..... ACCOST, WELCOME,
    MEET, HAIL, ADDRESS
greeting ... AVE, SALUTATION,
    WELCOME, SALUTE, ALOHA,
    HAIL
card .... VALENTINE
Indian .... NETOP
Oriental .... SALAAM
gregarious .... SOCIABLE,
    OUTGOING
grego .... CLOAK
Gregory of ____, Saint ....
    NYSSA, TOURS
gremlin .... MEDDLER, GNOME
grenade .... SHELL, BOMB
grenadier ...... INFANTRYMAN,
    FISH
grenadine ...... SIRUP, CLOTH
Grendel .... MONSTER
Grenoble river .... ISERE
Gretchen .... MARGARET
Gretna Green arrivals ....
    ELOPERS, SWEETHEARTS
Grey, author .... ZANE
greyhound ... DOG, STEAMSHIP,
    BUS, WHIPPET, SALUKI
gribble .... BORER
grid .... GRATING, ELECTRODE,
    FOOTBALL
slang .... FOOTBALL
griddle .... PLATE, PAN
cake ... SCONE, FLAPJACK
gride .... SCRAPE, RASP,
    GRATE, JAR
gridiron .... GRILL(E), GRATING,
    FOOTBALL FIELD
scores, briefly .... TDS
grief .... TEEN, WOE, SORROW,
    PAIN, SADNESS, MISERY,
    DOLOR
grievance .... GRAVAMEN,
    COMPLAINT, RESENTMENT,
    SCORE
colloquial .. BEEF, GRIPE
grieve .... RUE, DISTRESS,
    SADDEN, LAMENT, MOURN,
    CRY
grievous .... SEVERE,
    ATROCIOUS, SAD,
    HEINOUS, LAMENTABLE

griff(e) .... MULATTO, SPUR
griffon .... DOG, GYPS
grifter .... CONMAN
   assistant .... SHILL
grig ...... EEL, GRASSHOPPER,
               CRICKET
grill ... RESTAURANT, BROIL,
   GRID(IRON), QUIZ, RACK,
   INTERROGATE, HIBACHI
   meat-roasting ....
              BUCCANEER
grilse .... SALMON, FISH
grim .... FIERCE, SAVAGE,
   CRUEL, STERN, DOUR,
   MACABRE, RESOLUTE,
   SINISTER, GHASTLY,
             MERCILESS
   Reaper .... DEATH
grimace ...... SCOWL, FLEER,
   POUT, MOUE, MOP, FROWN,
   GLOWER, MOW(E), MOUTH,
         MUG, SNOOT
grimalkin ...... CAT, WOMAN
grime ..... SOOT, DIRT, COLLY
Grimes (Golden) ...... APPLE
grimy .... DINGY
grin .... SMILE
grind ..... MASTICATE, GRATE,
   PULVERIZE, CRUSH, MULL,
   CHEW, GRIT, BRAY, MILL,
   TRITURATE, CRUNCH,
   LEVIGATE, SHARPEN,
   HONE, RUB, SAND,
   DRUDGERY, TASK, WHET
   harshly .... GRIDE
   the teeth ... GNASH, GRIT
grinder ...... MOLAR, HONER,
   TOOTH, CRUSHER, MILL
grinding device .... MILL,
   MOLAR, MULLER, MORTAR,
   PESTLE, MILLSTONE,
   WHETSTONE, METATE
   substance .... SAND,
   EMERY, ABRASIVE
grindstone ...... HONE, MANO,
           METATE
gringo .... AMERICANO,
        FOREIGNER
grinning .... RIDENT
grip ..... HOLD, GRASP, CLASP,
   CLUTCH, CLAMP,
   CONTROL, HANDLE,
   BAG, VALISE, STAGEHAND
gripe .... PINCH, DISTRESS,
   CLUTCH, AFFLICT,
   CONTROL, HANDLE

slang ..... COMPLAIN(T),
   GRUMBLE, BEEF
grip(pe) .... COLD, FLU,
        INFLUENZA
gripping device .... VISE, VICE,
   CLAMP, DOG, CLUTCH
gripple .... AVARICIOUS,
         MISERLY
gripsack .... VALISE
Griqua .... MULATTO
Griselda, like .... PATIENT,
           MEEK
griseous .... GRAY
grisette .... SHOPGIRL
griskin .... LOIN
grisly .... HORRIBLE, MORBID,
   GHASTLY, GRUESOME
grist ... MEAL, LOT, QUANTITY
   for the _____ ...... MILL
gristle .... CARTILAGE
grit .... PLUCK, SAND(STONE),
   NERVE, COURAGE,
   FORTITUDE, GRAVEL
grith ..... SANCTUARY, PEACE,
        SECURITY
grits ... MEAL, HOMINY, KASHA
gritty ...... SANDY, PLUCKY,
   BRAVE, SABULOUS
grivet ...... GUENON, WAAG,
   TOTA, MONKEY
   kin .... VERVET
grizzle ... GRAY, FRET, WORRY,
        COMPLAIN
grizzly ..... GRAYISH, BEAR
groan .... MOAN
groat .... COIN
grocer .... STOREKEEPER
grog .... RUM, RUMBO
groggery/grogshop ... SALOON
groggy ...... TIPSY, DRUNK,
        DIZZY
groin, of or near ... INGUINAL
   swelling .... BUBO
grommet ...... EYELET, RING,
        BECKET
gromwell .... FLOWER
Gromyko, Soviet diplomat ....
        ANDREI
groom .... MANSERVANT,
   DEVELOP, CURRY, NEATEN,
   (H)OSTLER, TRAIN,
   ATTENDANT, BRUSH,
   TIDY(UP), EQUERRY, SICE
   horse ... COISTREL, SYCE
grooming process ... TOILETTE

groove .... CULLIS, ROUTINE,
FLUTING, FURROW, FLUTE,
RUT, CREASE, CHASE,
STRIA(E), SCARF, FILLISTER,
SULCUS
    barrel .... RIFLING,
CROZE
    in architecture ... GLYPH
    in iron .... FULLER
    made by plow ... FURROW
    masonry .... RAGLET,
RAGGLE
    minute .... STRIA
grooved ..... LIRATE, STRIATE,
SULCATE, STRIGOSE
grooves ...... RIFLINGS, SCORES,
SPLINES
grope ...... PROBE, FEEL, TAY,
FEEDL, FUMBLE
    for words .... HAW
Gropius .... GROPE
    architectural school .....
BAUHAUS
grosbeak .... MORO,
(HAW)FINCH
gross ... COARSE, FAT, BURLY,
CORPULENT, GLARING,
FLAGRANT, DENSE, THICK,
RANK, ENTIRE, CRASS,
VULGAR, RUDE, CRUDE
    1/12 of .... DOZEN
    opposed to .... NET
grot .... CAVE, SHRINE
grotesque .... BIZARRE,
FANTASTIC, ABSURD,
BAROQUE
Groton product ... SUBMARINE
grotto .... CAVE, SHRINE,
SUMMERHOUSE
grouch ... SULK, GRUMBLE(R)
Groucho _____ .... MARX
ground ...... EARTH, LAND,
SUBJECT, TOPIC, BASIS,
FOUNDATION, CAUSE,
MOTIVE, REASON, TERRAIN
    above .... ALIVE
    beam .... SLEEPER
    break .... START, DIG
    corn .... MEAL, SAMP,
FARINA
    cover .... TRAVERSE,
TRAVEL
    dig in the .... GRUB
    elevation .... RISE
    gain .... PROGRESS
    give .... YIELD, RETREAT

grain ...... MEAL, SAMP,
GRIST
hog ...... WOODCHUCK,
MARMOT
hog day .... CANDLEMAS
meal .... FARINA
nut ..... GOBBE, PEANUT
parcel of .... SOLUM
pulverizer ...... SPIDER
rising .... HURST
squirrel ..... CHIPMUNK,
HACKEE, GOPHER, SUSLIK,
SPERMOPHILE
unplowed, solid ....
HARDPAN
grounder ...... DAISY CUTTER
groundhog .... MARMOT,
WOODCHUCK
groundless .... BASELESS,
IDLE, UNJUSTIFIED
groundling .... CREEPER
grounds ... DREGS, SEDIMENT,
BASIS, REASON, LAWNS,
GARDENS, LEES, RESIDUE,
GROUT
    around building .. CLOSE,
COMPOUND
    college .... CAMPUS
groundsel .... RAGWORT
groundwork ..... BASIS, BASE,
FOUNDATION
group ... UNIT, BAND, CREW,
MASS, CLUSTER, SCHOOL,
SWARM, BLOC, BODY, HERD,
FLOCK, DROVE, BEVY,
COVEY, GENUS, CADRE,
CLASS, CORPS, NYE
    advisers' ... BRAINTRUST,
CAMARILLA
    discussion .. BULL SESSION
    of admirers ..... CLAQUE
    animals/plants ....
GENUS
    buildings .... PILE
    buses, etc. ...... FLEET
    eight .... OCTAD,
OCTET(TE)
    families .... CLAN
    fishes .... SCHOOL
    five .... PENTAD,
QUINTET(TE),
QUINARY
    fliers .... FLIGHT
    flora or fauna .. GENUS
    girls .... BEVY

houses, country ...... HAMLET

lions .... PRIDE

modeled figures ...... DIORAMA

nine .... ENNEAD, NONUPLET

paid applauders ...... CLAQUE

performers .... CAST, TROUPE

seven .... HEPTAD, SEPTET(TE)

ships .... FLEET, FLOTILLA

speech sounds .... PHONEME, DIAPHONE

ten .... DECADE

trees ... GROVE, WOODS, FOREST

20 priests ...... FETIAL

singing ... HOOTENANNY, CHOIR, TRIO, CHORUS

slang .... CABOODLE

small .... KNOT

grouped ... AGMINATE, BANDED

grouper .... MERO, BONACI, SEABASS, WARSAW

grouse .... HEATHBIRD, PTARMIGAN, SAGE HEN, PINTAIL, PHEASANT, BLACKCOCK

female .... GORHEN

male .... GORCOCK, BLACKCOCK

red .... MOOR COCK, MUIRFOWL

slang .... COMPLAIN(T), GRUMBLE, CRAB

grout .... MEAL, GROUNDS, LEES, SEDIMENT, DREGS, PORRIDGE

grove .... BOSCAGE, COPSE, TOPE, NEMUS, BOSK(ET), WOOD(S), HOLT, SPINNEY

near Athens ... ACADEME

pines .... PINETUM

prairie .... MOTT(E)

sacred .... NEMUS

where Aristotle taught ... LYCEUM

grovel .... CRAWL, CREEP, CRINGE, FAWN

grow ... SPROUT, CULTIVATE, ACCRUE, DEVELOP, BREED, FLOURISH, RAISE, ACCRETE, THRIVE, WAX, MATURE

dim/faint .... WANE

hot/red .... FLAME

rapidly ..... MUSHROOM, BOOM

tired ...... FLAG, WEARY

grower .... FARMER

growing in couples ... BINATE

in high altitude .. ALPINE, ALPESTRINE

in pairs ...... GEMINATE, DIDYMOUS

on .... EPIGEOUS

one side only .... SECUND

out .... ENATE

together ...... ACCRETE

under water .. IMMERSED

growl .. RUMBLE, COMPLAIN(T), GRUMBLE, YAR(R), GNAR, SNARL, GIRN

growler .... DOG, BEAR

growler's content ...... BEER

grown .... MATURE

up .... ADULT

growth ...... DEVELOPMENT, CORN, SHOOT, WATTLE, POLYP, WEN, SPUR, ACCRETION

abnormal body .. TUMOR, CANCER

body ...... WART, MOLE

facial ... BEARD, WHISKER

new .... SHOOT

place of rapid ... HOTBED

process .... NACENCY

skin ... WEN, WART, MOLE

stunted in ..... SCRUBBY, RUNTY

together ..... SYMPHYSIS

grub .... DIG, DRUDGE, RUMMAGE, ASSART, UPROOT, LARVA, MAGGOT

axe .... MATTOCK

slang ..... EAT(S), FEED, FOOD

street .... MILTON

street habitues ... HACKS

to ... SLAVE, MOIL, SPUD

grubble .... FEEL, GROPE

grubby .... DIRTY, UNTIDY, MESSY

Gruber, composer .... FRANZ

grubstake recipient .... PROSPECTOR

grudge .... ILLWILL, MALICE,

ENVY, SPITE, ANGUUS,
INQUE, PEEVE
grue ....•....•... SNOW, ICE
gruel ...•...•... BROTH, ATOLE,
EXHAUST, CAUDLE,
PORRIDGE, BURGOO,
LOBLOLLY
grueling ...••... EXHAUSTING
gruesome ...•...•... MORBID,
GRISLY, GHASTLY,
FEARSOME, MACABRE,
HORRIFYING, GRIM
gruff ...•...•... HOARSE, BLUNT,
HARSH, RUDE, SURLY
throat sound ...•.•... GRUNT
grugru ...•...•.. PALM, LARVA
grume ...•...•...•... CLOT
grumble ...•. GRIPE, COMPLAIN,
GROUCH, GROUSE, GROWL,
RUMBLE, MUTTER,
FRET, REPINE, KICK
grumbler ...•...•...•... GROUCH,
COMPLAINER
grumpy ...•.•... SURLY, PEEVISH
Grundy, Mrs. ...•...•... PRUDE
grunion ...•...•... SILVERSIDE
grunt and groaner ... WRESTLER
sound ...•...•...•.. OINK
grunter ...•...•...•... PIG, HOG
former ...•...•... INDIAN
Grus ... CRANE, CONSTELLATION
Gruyere ...•...•...•... CHEESE
g-string ...•...•... LOINCLOTH
guacharo ...•... GOATSUCKER,
(OIL)BIRD
Guadalcanal town ...•... AOLA
guaiac ...•.. TONKA BEAN, SEED
Guam capital ...•...•... AGANA
governor ...•...•... GUERRERO
illness ...•...•.. GUHA, GUJA
native/tribe ... CHAMORRO
tree ...•...•...•...•... IPIL
guama ...•...•... INGA, GUAVA
guana ...•...•...•... MAJAGUA
guanaco-like animal ...•.. LLAMA,
CAMEL
guanay ...•...•... CORMORANT
droppings ...•...•.. GUANO
guano ...•.. TUATARA, MANURE,
FERTILIZER
source of ... BATS, GUANAY
Guarani ...•...•...•...•... TUPI
guarantee ...•.. VOUCH, PLEDGE,
ASSURANCE, ASSURE,
ENDORSE, WARRANT(Y),
AFFIRM, SURETY, BOND

guarantor ...•...•...•.. SURETY
guaranty ...•...•...•... SECURITY
guard ...•...•.. DEFEND, SHIELD,
PROTECT(OR), WATCH,
SHIELD, OSTIARY, PATROL,
PICKET, CONVOY
armed ...•...•...•.. SENTRY,
SENTINEL
Asgard's ...•.... HEIMDALL
car's ...•...•...•.. FENDER
Freemason's ...•...•.. TILER
Hades ...•...•.. CERBERUS
Io's ...•...•...•...•.. ARGUS
night ...•...•.. BIVOUAC
of the bed ...•... EUNUCH
on ...•. ALERT, VIGILANT
post ...•...•...•... WATCH
ship ...•...•...•... CONVOY,
CORVET(TE)
troops' ...•...•.•.. PICKET
guarded ... CAUTIOUS, CAREFUL
guardhouse ... BRIG, HOOSEGOW
guardian ...•...•... CUSTODIAN,
TRUSTEE, CUSTOS, KEEPER,
WARDEN, TUTELAR,
DRAGON
concern of ...•...•.. WARD,
INCOMPETENT
function of ...•... TUTELAGE
legendary ...•.•.. ARGUS,
CERBERUS
minor's ...•...•.. CURATOR,
TUTOR
of an incompetent ...•...
CURATOR
of portals ...•...•.. JANUS
spirit ... GENIUS, DAEMON,
LARES
guardianship ...•... TUTELAGE,
TUITION
guarding against attack ...•..•..
DEFENSE
Guatemala grass ...• TEOSINTE
Indian ...•...•...•.. MAYA
insect ...•...•...•... KELEP
money ...•...•... QUE(T)ZAL
plain ...•...•...•... PETEN
president ...•...•... MENDEZ,
ARBENZ, AREVALO,
PONCE
volcano ...•...•... FUEGO,
ATITLAN
guava ...•...•...•... ARACA
guayule ...•...•...•...•... SHRUB
gude ...•.•...•...•... GOOD
gudgeon ...•. MINNOW, TRICK,

GULL, BAIT, DUPE, GOBY, TRUNNION

Gudrun, brother of .. GUNNAR

husband of ⁓ .. ⁓ SIGURD, ATLI

rival of ⁓ . ⁓ ⁓ BRYNHILD

guenon .... TALAPOIN, MONKEY, GRIVET, MONA

guerdon .... REWARD, RECOMPENSE, CROWN, PRIZE

Guernsey .... ⁓ CATTLE, SHIRT, SWEATER

guerrilla ... MAQUI, PARTISAN, REBEL, RAIDER, BUSHWACKER, FEDAYEEN, CHETNIK

Philippine ⁓ .... HUK

Serbian .... CHETNIK

Vietnamese ... VIETCONG

guess ...... SURMISE, THEORY, CONJECTURE, ESTIMATE

guessing game ... ⁓ CHARADE

guesswork .... SURMISE

guest ..... VISITOR, COMPANY, CALLER, LODGER

paying .... BOARDER

guff .... NONSENSE

guffaw ...... HEEHAW, BRAY, LAUGH(TER), HORSELAUGH

Guiana hut .... BENAB

native .... BONI

tree .... MORA

guide ... KEY, MARON, PILOT, COURIER, SCOUT, CLUB, CLEW, STEER, LEAD, CONDUCT, TRAIN, CONVOY, MERCURY

to solution ⁓ . CLUE, KEY, HINT

tourist's ⁓ . ⁓ CICERONE, DRAGOMAN

traveler's .... DRAGOMAN

guidebook .... BAEDEKER, MANUAL, ITINERARY

guided missile ... IRBM, ICBM

guiding ... DIRIGENT, POLAR, LEADING

example ⁓ .... PRECEDENT

ideal .... LODESTAR

light .... BEACON, LODESTAR, NORTH STAR

rule ... MOTTO, PRINCIPLE

star .... LODESTAR

guidon ...... FLAG, PENNANT

Guido, musical note of ... UT, ELAMI

highest note .... ELA

guild ... CRAFT, UNION, HANSE

Hall statue .. GOG, MAGOG

in plant ecology .... PARASITES, LIANAS, EPIPHYTES

guilder . ⁓ ..... COIN, GULDEN

guile ... ⁓ . ⁓ CUNNING, DECEIT, WILE, CRAFT

guileful .... ⁓ .... TRICKY

guileless .... NAIVE, CANDID, ARTLESS, FRANK, OPEN, HONEST, SINCERE

guillemot ... BIRD, COOT, AUK, MURR(E), DOVEKIE, DOVEKEY

guillotine ... BEHEAD, MAIDEN

wagon .... TUMBREL, TUMBRIL

guilt ... CULPABILITY, CULPA, CRIME, SIN

guiltless .... INNOCENT, PURE, CLEAR

guilty .... CULPABLE, NOCENT

guimpe .... BLOUSE, CHEMISETTE

Guinea .... COIN, FOWL

capital .... CONAKRY

city .... KANKAN

corn ..... DURRA, MILLET

fowl .... PINTADO

native .... SUSU, FULANI, MALINKE

pig .... RAT, CAVY, PACA

pig, animal like .... PIKA

pig kin .... AGOUTI

pig, male .... BOAR

president .... TOURE

seaport .... CONAKRY

squash ...... EGGPLANT

young .... KEET

Guinevere's husband .... (KING) ARTHUR

lover .... LANCELOT

guipure .... LACE, GIMP

guise .... CLOAK, GARB, SEMBLANCE, PRETENSE, MIEN, APPEARANCE

guitar, ancient .... LUTE

Hawaiian .... UKE(LELE)

India .... VINA

Japanese .... KOTO

like instrument .. CITOLE, BANDORE, BALALAIKA, PANDORE, SAMISEN,

GITTERN, CITHER(N),
CITTERN, ROTE
oriental .... SITAR
plucking implement .....
    PLECTRUM, PLECTRON
small .... UKE(LELE)
strumming tool ....
    PLECTRUM
guitarist, famed .... SEGOVIA
guitguit .... BIRD,
    HONEY CREEPER
Guitry, playwright .... SACHA
gula .... GULLET, THROAT
gulch .... RAVINE, VALLEY,
    ARROYO, CANYON, COULEE
gulden .... COIN, GUILDER
gules .... RED
gulf .... BIGHT, GAP,
    CLEAVAGE, EDDY,
    WHIRLPOOL, ABYSS
    Greek .... AEGINA
    Lepanto .... CORINTH
    of Bothnia ...... ALAND
    of Finland (sea)port .....
        LENINGRAD, KRONSTADT
    state .... FLORIDA, TEXAS,
        LOUSIANA, ALABAMA
    weed .... SARGASSO,
        SARGASSUM
gull .... DUPE, CHEAT,
    GUDGEON, CULLY,
    KITTIWAKE, PEWEE,
    PEWIT, ALLAN, MEDRICK,
    GOSLING, BURGOMASTER,
    COB(B), XEMA
    bird like .... TERN
    like a .... LARINE
    of a .... LARINE
    robber .... JA(E)GER
    sea .... COB, MEW, SKUA,
        KITTIWAKE
gullet .... MAW, FAUCES,
    GORGE, NECK, CRAW,
    ESOPHAGUS, THROAT
gullible ... CREDULOUS, NAIVE
    person .... GULL, DUPE,
        CONY
"Gulliver's Travels" author ...
    (LEMUEL) SWIFT
    dwarf .... LILLIPUTIAN
    land .. LAPUTA, LILLIPUT,
        BROBDINGNAG
    people ... LILLIPUTIANS,
        YAHOOS
gully ..... RAVINE, CHANNEL,
    DONGA, GUT, ARROYO,

COULOIR, SIKE, WADI, NULLAH
gulp ..... SWALLOW, REPRESS,
    SWIG
    down .... BOLT
gum ... CAROB, LATEX, RESIN,
    ADHESIVE, CHICLE, KINO,
    MATTI, ASA, STORAX, GLUE,
    MUCILAGE, RUBBER,
    BALATA, BENJAMIN,
    CAMPHOR, KAURI
    arabic .... ACACIA,
        ACACIN(E)
    astringent .... KINO
    benzoin .... BENJAMIN
    elastic .... RUBBER
    for golf balls ... BALATA
    leaves eater .... KOALA
    pharmacy .. TRAGACANTH
    plant .... ULE
    resin .... AMMONIAC,
        CAMBOGE, OLIBANUM,
        FRANKINCENSE,
        TACAMAHAC, ASAFETIDA,
        CAMBOGIA, BALM,
        BALSAM, MYRRH,
        STORAX, TACMAHACK,
        BDELLIUM, GALBAN,
        LOBAN, ELEMI, COPAL,
        COPALM
    resin, bad-smelling ......
        GALBANUM
    resin in alcohol ....
        LACQUER
    resin narcotic .. HASHISH
    resin poison ..... ANTIAR
    resin solvent ... HEXOME
    tree .... EUCALYPTUS,
        ACACIA, KARRI,
        XYLAN, NYSSA, TUPELO,
        TUART, BALATA,
        COPALM
gumbo ... PATOIS, OKRA, SOUP,
    SOIL, OCRA, GOMART
gumboil ... ABSCESS, PARULIS
gumma .... TUMOR
gummed paper ...... STICKER
gummy ...... STICKY, VISCID
    substance ...... GUTTA,
        DEXTRIN(E)
gumption .... COURAGE,
    ENTERPRISE, COMMON SENSE
gums, abscess ..... GUMBOIL
    inflammation of .....
        GINGIVITIS
    pertaining to .. GINGIVAL,
        ULETIC

source .... FERULA
the .... ULA
gumshoe .... RUBBER
   slang ... TEC, DETECTIVE,
            SNEAK
gun ... COLT, MAUSER, LUGER,
   MAXIM, CARBINE, GATLING,
   JINGAL, JEZAIL, PISTOL,
   REVOLVER, BAZOOKA,
   AUTOMATIC, RIFLE,
   CANNON, FIREARM,
            MORTAR
   ancient .... MUSKET,
     HARQUEBUS(E),
     BLUNDERBUSS,
     BLUNDERBORE
   attachment ... SILENCER
   barrel sight .... BEAD
   barrel's end ... MUZZLE
   British ..... STEN, BREN
   brush .... SWAB
   butt .... STOCK
   caliber .... BORE
   carriage .... CAISSON,
            GALLOP
   carriage part .... LIMBER,
            RACER
   carriage rope .. PROLONGE
   case .... HOLSTER
   chamber .... GOMER
   crew's shield ....
     MANT(E)LET, TURRET
   dog ... POINTER, SETTER,
         RETRIEVER
   emplacement ... PILLBOX
   for .. HUNT, SEEK, ATTACK
   house on warship ....
            TURRET
   make ... COLT, MAGNUM,
   HARRINGTON, MAUSER,
   WINCHESTER, LUGER
   muzzle plug ... TAMPION,
         TOMPION
   part ... BORE, BUTT, BOLT,
   COCK, LOCK, HAMMER,
   GOMER, STOCK, BARREL,
   BREECH, CYLINDER,
   TRIGGER, PIN, SIGHT,
   CHAMBER, MAGAZINE
   pointer ... SIGHT, DOTTER
   position of ....
     EMPLACEMENT
   ship's .... CHASER
   sight .... BEAD
   slang ... THROTTLE, GAT,
   ROD, IRON, BARKER,

     ROSCOE, BETSY
   small .... DERRINGER
   strap .... SLING
   tube .... BARREL
   turret ... BLISTER, CUPOLA
gunboat .... TINCLAD
guncock .... NAB
guncotton plus picric acid .....
      MELINITE
gunfire ...... VOLLEY, SALVO,
   DRUMBEAT, FUSILLADE
gung ho ... WORK TOGETHER,
      SLOGAN
gunlock catch .... SEAR
   tumbler .... NUT
gunman ... THUG, GANGSTER
   female accomplice ......
        MOLL
Gunnar's brother-in-law ......
      SIGURD
   sister .... GUDRUN,
      GUTHRUN
   wife .... BRYNHILD
gunnel .... FISH, BLENNY,
      GUNWALE
gunners' platform ....
      BANQUETTE
gunnery .... ARTILLERY,
      CANNONS
gunny .... BAG, SACK
gunpowder ...... TEA, NITER
"Gunpowder Plot" figure .....
      FAWKES
gunrunner .... SMUGGLER
guns .... WEAPONS, ARMS,
   FIREARMS, ARTILLERY,
     ORDNANCE
   set of heavy ... BATTERY
   warship's ..... BATTERY
gunstock .... BUTT
Gunther's wife .... BRUNHILD
gunwale .... GUNNEL
guppy .... MINNOW
gurgitation ...... WHIRLING,
      SURGING
gurgle ...... BICKER, BUBBLE,
      BURBLE
gurglet .... GOBLET
gurgling sound producer ......
     BABY, BROOK
gurnard ... GURNET, ROCHET,
      BATFISH
gurnet .... GURNARD
gush ..... POUR(OUT), SPOUT,
   OUTFLOW, SPURT, JET,
     SLOP OVER

gusher, kind of ... OIL WELL, GEYSER
  sometimes ...... CRITIC, REVIEWER, VOLCANO, WRITER
gushing ... EFFUSIVE, POURING
gushy .... EFFUSIVE, SENTIMENTAL
gusset .... GORE
gust ...... WIND, OUTBURST, RUSH, SAPOR, FLURRY, BLAST, SAVOR, FLAVOR, TANG, RELISH
gusto .... TASTE, LIKING, RELISH, ZEST, ENJOYMENT, PALATE, ELAN
gusty ...... WINDY, BLUSTERY
gut ...... INTESTINE, GULLY, EVISCERATE, DESTROY, CATGUT, SNELL
guts ...... ENTRAILS, BOWELS, INTESTINES, PLUCK, COURAGE, IMPUDENCE
gutta .... DROP, MINIM
gutter .... TROUGH, SLUM, VALLEY, CULLIS, DITCH, KENNEL
guttersnipe .... URCHIN, ARAB, GAMIN
guttle ... GORMANDIZE, GORGE
guttural ... GULAR, RASPING, VELAR, DRY, HUSKY, THROATY
guy ... ROPE, CHAIN, FELLOW, CHAP, JOSH, TEASE
  rope ... STAY, VANG, STAT
guzzle ... DRINK, SWIG, SWILL
guzzler .... TOPER, SOT
Gwyn, king's mistress .. NELL, ELEANOR
gymkhana performer .. RIDER, ATHLETE, EQUESTRIAN
gymnast ... ACROBAT, TURNER, TUMBLER, ATHLETE
  club of ..... TURNVEREIN
  feat of ..... HANDSPRING
  suit .... MAILLOT
gymnastics ...... ATHLETICS, CALISTHENICS, TUMBLING
  apparatus .... BUCK

gymnosophist .... NUDIST
gynoecium .... PISTIL(S)
gyp ..... SWINDLE(R), CHEAT, SERVANT
gypsum .... SELENITE, ALABASTER, GESSO, TERRE ALBA, YESO
gypsy ..... ROAMER, NOMAD, BAZIGAR, CALO, BOHEMIAN, ROMANY, ZINGARA, ZINGARO, TSIGANE
  book LIL
  boy/husband ...... ROM
  devil .... BENG
  Dutch .... BAZIGAR
  French ...... BOHEMIAN
  gentleman .... RYE, ROM
  German ...... ZIGEUNER
  girl .... CHAI
  Hindu .... KARACHEE
  horse .. GRI, GRY, GRASNI
  Italian .... ZINGABI
  language ...... ROMANY
  non .... GAJO
  opera .... MANERICO
  Persian .... SISECH
  Rose _____ .... LEE
  Scottish .... CAIRD
  sea .... BADJAO
  Spanish .... GITANO, ZINCALO
  thief .... CHOR
  tongue .... CHIB
  village .... GAV
  wagon .... CARAVAN
  winch .... CRAB
  woman ...... ZINGARA, RANI, ROMI
gyrate ...... ROTATE, WHIRL, SPIN
gyrating toy .... TOP
gyrator .... PILOT
gyratory .... WHIRLING, SPIRALLING
gyre .... WHIRL, VORTEX
gyrene: sl. .... MARINE, LEATHERNECK
gyve ..... FETTER, SHACKLE, IRON

H

H, letter .... AITCH
  -shaped ... AITCH, ZYGAL
  sound of ...... ASPIRATE
habanera .... DANCE
habeas corpus ... WRIT, ORDER
habergeon .. JACKET, HAUBERK

haberdashery ...... TOGGERY
habile . .. APT, DEXTEROUS, FIT,
 ABLE, CLEVER, HANDY, ROBE
habiliment ..... ATTIRE, DRESS,
 GARMENT, CLOTHING
habilitate ...... EQUIP, OUTFIT
habit .... COSTUME, DRESS,
 DISPOSITION, PRACTICE,
 CUSTOM, USAGE, GARB,
 WONT, ROUTINE, ATTIRE,
 RUT
 prefix .... ECO
 riding .... JOSEPH,
 JODHPURS
habitable .... LIV(E)ABLE
habitant .. RESIDENT, DWELLER
habitation · · · ·· HOME, LAIR,
 DWELLING, ABODE
habitual ..... WONTED, USUAL,
 CUSTOMARY, STEADY,
 CHRONIC
habitually silent ... TACITURN,
 RETICENT, RESERVE
habituate ... FREQUENT, INURE,
 ENURE, ACCUSTOM, DRILL
 to weather ... ACCLIMATE
habituated .... USED
habitue .... FREQUENTER, USER
 tavern .... BARFLY
hachure .... LINES
hacienda ...... FARM, ESTATE,
 RANCH, PLANTATION, MINE
hack .. CHOP, AX, HOE, COUGH,
 MATTOCK, GASH, TAXI(CAB),
 TRITE, STALE, DRUDGE
 driver .... CABBIE
 literary .... DEVIL,
 SCRIBBLER, POETASTER
 worker .... JOBBER
hackbut .... HARQUEBUS
hackle .... HATCHEL, HAGGLE,
 FEATHERS, MANGLE, CUT,
 COMB
hackmatack .. LARCH, JUNIPER,
 TAMARACK
hackney .... FIACRE, FLY
 driver .... JARVEY
hackneyed ...... STALE, TRITE,
 BANAL, DRAB, STOCK
 expression ...... CLICHE,
 COMMONPLACE, PLATITUDE
haddock ... COD, FISH, GADID,
 GADOID
Hades .. ABADDON, DIS, ORCUS,
 PIT, HELL, PLUTO, SHEOL,
 ARALU, TARTARUS, AVERNUS

abyss below ... TARTARUS
 guard of ...... CERBERUS
 related to .. LIMBO, ABYSS
 river .... ACHERON, STYX,
 PHLEGETHON, LETHE
 way place to ..... EREBUS
 wheel-turner in .... IXION
hadj .... PILGRIMAGE
Hadrian's favorite .. ANTINOUS
haft .... HILT, DUDGEON, BAIL,
 HANDLE
hag .... WITCH, ENCHANTRESS,
 DEMON, MARSH, HARPY,
 VIRAGO, CARLINE, FURY,
 HARRIDAN, VIXEN, FELLING,
 CRONE, JEZEBEL, BELDAM(E)
haggard .... GAUNT, DRAWN,
 WILD, UNRULY, WAN, HAWK
 novel of .... SHE
hagfish .... CYCLOSTOME
haggle .... CHOP, HACK,
 MANGLE, WRANGLE, CAVIL,
 BARGAIN, QUIBBLE, PRIG,
 CHAFFER
haha ... FENCE, WALL, LAUGH
haiku .... POEM
hail .. GREET(ING), SLEET, AVE,
 AHOY, GRAUPEL, SALVE,
 METEOR, SIGNAL, CHEER,
 SALUTE, SHOWER, POUR,
 RAINDROPS
Hailey novel .... HOTEL,
 AIRPORT, WHEELS
hair .. TRESS, DOWN, FUR, NAP,
 THATCH, SHAG, PILE, ROACH,
 CRINE, FILAMENT
 arrange .... COIF
 band .... FIL(L)ET
 braid .... CUE, PLAIT,
 QUEUE, PIGTAIL, TRESS
 bunch of .... WHISK
 caterpillar .... SETA
 cheek ...... BURNSIDES,
 SIDEBURNS
 cloth .... ABA, CILICE
 coarse .... SETA
 coat .... MELOTE
 comb the .... COIF
 combining form .. PIL(O),
 CHAET(O), PILI, TRICHO
 covered with .... PILOSE,
 TOMENTOSE, LANATE,
 SHAGGY, FLOCCOSE
 curl of ... LOCK, RINGLET
 curlylike .... CIRROSE
 cut short .... CROP

disease .. MANGE, XERASIA, TRICHOSIS, SYCOSIS
diseased condition of .... PLICA
do the ..... MARCEL, SET, COIF
dresser .... FRISEUR, COIFFEUR, CURLER
dresser's term ....
PERM(ANENT), SET, MARCEL, COIF, (COLD)WAVE, RINSE
dressing .... POMADE, BANDOLINE
dressing style ..... CHAR
dye .... HENNA
dyer .... ANCIETTE
face .. BEARD, MUSTACHE, WHISKER
falling out of .... PSILOSIS
false .. PERUKE, JANE, RAT, TOUPEE, WIG
feeler .... PALP(US)
fetus .... LANUGO
fillet .... SNOOD
fine .... FUZZ, PILE
follicles disease .. SYCOSIS
girl's .... TRESS
head .... CRINE, MOP
hooked .... BARB
knot ..... CHIGNON, BUN, BOB
lock ... TRESS, CURL, TAG
mass of .... SHOCK
matted .. SHAG, DAGLOCK
matted condition ....
TRICHOMA
neck ..... MANE, HACKLE
net .... LINT, SNOOD
nostril .... VIBRISSA
not curly .... LANK
of head .... LOCK, POLL, THATCH
ointment .... POMADE
on abdomen ...... PUBES
ornament .. RIBBON, CLIP, COMB, BOW
pad .... RAT
piece .... RUG
pigment .... MELANIN
pin .... BODKIN
plait .... BRAID, PIGTAIL, QUEUE, TRESS
plant ...... PILUS, VILLUS
prefix .... CRINI
raising ..... HORRIFYING, EERIE, FEARSOME

remove .. EPILATE, BOB, DEPILATE, TRIM, TONSURE
ribbon .... BANDEAU
rigid .... SETA
ringlet .... CURL
roll ..... PUFF, CHIGNON, RAT, BUN, WATERFALL
rough .... SHAG
sensitive ...... TENTACLE
shedding of ..... ECDYSIS
sheep's .... WOOL
shirt .... CILICE
shreds .... NOIL
soft, fine .... PILE, FUZZ, DOWN
standing .... ROACH
strip .... EPILATE, DEPILITATE
substance ...... KERATIN
tuft .... FLOCCUS
unruly .... COWLICK
wash the ...... SHAMPOO
wave .... MARCEL, PERMANENT
hairbreadth .. CLOSE, NARROW
haircloth .... CILICE, ABA
haircut .... SHINGLE
hairdo ..... COIFFURE, BANGS, POMPADOUR, PAGEBOY, POODLE, TETE
hairdresser .... COIFFEUR, FRISEUR, CURLER, COIFFUSE
haired .... PILIFEROUS
hairiness .... VILLOSITY, PILOSITY
hairless ..... GLABROUS, BALD, PELON
state .... ALOPECIA
hairlike .... TRICHOID
process .... CILIA, CILIUM
hairline point .... PEAK
hairpiece .... WIG, TOUPEE, PERUKE
hairpin .... BODKIN
hairs, bunch of .. TUFT, PINICIL
covered with stiff .. HISPID
hairsplitter .... QUIBBLER
hairy ...... PILOSE, BARBATE, COMATE, COMOSE, HIRSUTE, PILAR(Y), CILIATE, PILEOUS, NAPPY, CRINITE, VILLOSE, VILLOUS
Ape .... YANK
covering, having ....
LANATE
tuft .... FLOCCUS

Haiti .... HISPANIOLA
Haitian bandit .... CACO
  capital .. PORT-AU-PRINCE
  city .... GONAIVES,
                 LES CAYES
  coin .... GOURDE
  dictator .... MAGLOIRE
  evil spirit ...... BAKA, BOKO
  hunter (ox) .. BUCCANEER
  king .... CHRISTOPHE
  liberator .... DESSALINES
  lord .... CACIQUE
  monetary unit ... GOURDE
  president ..... DUVALIER,
           ESTIME, MAGLOIRE
  rebel .... TOUSSAINT
  seaport .... CAYES
  sweet potato .... BATATA
  voodoo deity .. ZOMBI(E)
  voodoo priest ... PAPALOI
  voodoo priestess ....
                MAMALOI
hake .... WHITING, GADID,
               GADOID
  kin of .... COD
hakeem/hakim ...... DOCTOR,
               PHYSICIAN
halberd ... SPEAR, (BATTLE)AX,
     PARTISAN, PARTIZAN,
     GLA(I)VE, GISARME,
     POLE-AX(E), SPONTOON
halcyon .... HAPPY, TRANQUIL,
              PEACEFUL
hale .... WELL, HEARTY, HAUL,
     HEALTHY, ROBUST, DRAG
half .. HEMI, MOIETY, DEMI, SEMI
  an em .... EN
  and half part .... ALE
  baked ...... AMATEURISH,
           SOPHOMORIC
  boot .... BUSKIN, PAC
  breed .. METIS(SE), MESTEE,
     GRIFF(E), MESTIZO, HYBRID,
        LADINO, MESTIF(F),
     MULATTO, MULE, MUSTEE
  caste .... METIS
  farthing .... MITE
  gainer .... (BACK)DIVE
  hearted ..... RELUCTANT,
     UNWILLING, SPIRITLESS,
          LUKEWARM
  hitch .... KNOT
  man, half bull ....
            BUCENTAUR
  man, half dragon ....
            CECROPS

  man, half fish .. MERMAN,
            DAGON
  man, half goat ..... PAN,
            FAUNUS
  man, half horse ....
            CENTAUR
  mask ..... LOUP, DOMINO
  moon .... CRESCENT,
          ARC, LUNE
  note, in music .... MINIM
  one's better ... HUSBAND,
            WIFE
  penny .... MAG
  prefix ... HEMI, SEMI, DEMI
  step, in music .. SEMITONE
  turn of horse ....
           CARACOL(E)
  way .... MID
  wit .. DOLT, FOOL, IDIOT
  witted .. SILLY, IMBECILIC,
     MORONIC, STUPID
  year's income .... ANNAT
halfway .... PARTIAL,
           INCOMPLETE
  meet .... COMPROMISE
halibut .. SOLE, FLATFISH, BUTT
Halicarnassus' wonder ....
           MAUSOLEUM
halicore .... DUGONG, SEACOW,
           MANATEE
halidom(e) .... HOLINESS,
           SANCTUARY
halite .... (ROCK)SALT
halitus ... EXHALATION, AURA,
       BREATH, VAPOR
hall .... VESTIBULE, CORRIDOR,
     DORM, SAAL, SALLE, AULA,
     ATRIUM, SALA, LYCEUM
  concert .... ODEUM
  heroes' .... VALHALLA
  hotel ..... FOYER, LOBBY
  Odin's .... VALHALLA
  reception .. COURT, SALON
  round .... ROTUNDA
Halley, astronomer .. EDMUND
  discovery .... COMET
halloo .... SHOUT, YELL
hallow .... SANCTIFY, HOLY,
     CONSECRATE, BLESS
hallowed ...... HOLY, SACRED
  place .... SHRINE
Hall's (C. F.) concern .. ARCTIC
halluces .... DIGITS
hallucination ...... DELUSION,
  ALUSIA, FANTASY, CHIMERA,
           AUTISM

kind of .... VISUAL,
AUDITORY
product of ...... MIRAGE
hallucinogen .. LSD, MESCALINE,
AMPHETAMINE, SEDATIVE
drug: sl. .... ACID
source ... PEYOTE, FUNGI,
CAAPI
hallux .... (GREAT) TOE
hallway .... CORRIDOR
Halmahera .... GILOLO
halo .... AURA, NIMB(US),
AUREOLE, CORONA, GLORIA,
AUREOLA, GLORY, GLORIOLE
halogen .... IODINE, ASTATINE,
BROMINE, CHLORINE,
FLUORINE
compound ...... HALIDE
Hals, painter .. .. FRANS
halt .... PAUSE, STOP, LIMP,
HOBBLE, WAVER, LAME
the .... CRIPPLES
halter .... NOOSE, STRAP
halting place ..... ETAPE, INN,
OASIS, CARAVANSARY
halve .. DIVIDE, BISECT, DISSECT
ham ..... MEAT, HOCK, ACTOR
hog's .... GAMMON
it up ... EMOTE, OVER-ACT
parent of, Biblical .. NOAH
slang .... AMATEUR,
OVERACT
slice for frying ... RASHER
son of .... CUSH
hamal .... PORTER,
(HOUSE)SERVANT
Hambletonian ...... TROTTER,
HORSE
gait .... TROT
race, site of ..... GOSHEN
hamburg .... CHICKEN
hamburg(er) ... STEAK, PATTY,
SANDWICH
Hamilcar's son .... HANNIBAL
Hamite ..... BERBER, LIBYAN,
SOMAL(I), MASAI, AFAR
Hamitic language .. NUMIDIAN
hamlet .... VILLAGE, TRAGEDY,
TREF, BURG, DORP, MIR,
THORP(E), CLACHAN, WICH
and others ...... DANES
home of .... ELSINORE
locale of ...... ELSINORE,
ELSINGOR
uncle of ...... CLAUDIUS

Hammarskjold, UN secretary ..
DAG
hammer .... MALLET, BRAT,
MALLEATE, BANG, KEVEL,
FULLER, BEETLE, MAUL,
POUND(ER), SLEDGE, OLIVER
auctioneer's ...... GAVEL
and sickle flag .... SOVIET
blow .... POUND
chairman's ...... GAVEL
companion of .... TONGS
ear .... MALLEUS
end .... PEEN, POLL
firearm's .... COCK
head of ..... PEEN, POLL
heavy ..... SLEDGE, MAUL
kind of ..... CLAW, TRIP,
BALL PERN, DROP
large .... SLEDGE
lead .... MADGE
lock .... HOLD
part .. PEEN, CLAW, HEAD
percussion ...... PLEXOR,
PLESSOR
piano .... MALLET
presiding officer's ......
GAVEL
soft-headed ..... PLEXOR,
PLESSOR
stone-breaking .... KEVEL
striking part .... TUP
to .... MALLEATE
trip .... OLIVER
hammerhead .... SHARK, FISH,
BAT, BIRD, UMBRETTE
hammock ...... BED, COUCH
lines .... CLEWS
hamper ... HINDER, ENCUMBER,
IMPEDE, FETTER, MANACLE,
HANAPER, CRATE, MAUND,
TRAMMEL, HOBBLE, SEROON,
CRAMP, BASKET
Hampshire .... HANTS
Hampton Roads protagonist ..
MONITOR, MERRIMAC
hamster .... RODENT
hamstring .. TENDON, CRIPPLE,
DISABLE, LAME, MAIM
Hamsun, novelist ...... KNUT
hamulus .... HOOK
Han .... DYNASTY
cities .. WUHAN, HANKOW,
HANYANG, WUCHANG
hanaper ..... BASKET, HAMPER
hand .... NIEVE, MANUS, PAW,
PUD, DEAL, HOLDING, FIST,

GIVE, SIGNATURE, APPLAUSE,
AID, HELP, POINTER,
WORKER
at .... READY, NEAR
baby's .... PUD
below full house .. FLUSH
by .... MANUAL
care .... MANICURE
cart .... BARROW
clapping to music ... TAL
clenched .... FIST
clock .... POINTER
combining form .. CHIRO
done by .... MANUAL
down .... DELIVER,
BEQUEATH
drum ...... TAMBOURINE,
TOMTOM
first ..... NEW, ORIGINAL
give a .... APPLAUD
glass .... MIRROR
grenade .. EGG, PINEAPPLE
grinding device .. MULLER
in .... GIVE, SUBMIT,
PRESENT
in hand .... COOPERATION
jurist .... LEARNED
me-down .. SECONDHAND,
USED, CHEAP, READY-MADE
measure .... SPAN
mill .... QUERN, MANO
on .... PASS, READY,
TRANSMIT, AVAILABLE,
PRESENT
organ .... HURDY-GURDY
out .... DEAL, DISTRIBUTE
over .... SHELL, DELIVER,
CONSIGN
palm of .... VOLAR, LOOF,
THENAR
pick .... SELECT, CHOOSE
reared by .... CADE
screw .... JACK
second .... USED
slang .... PAW, HAM, FIN,
FLIPPER, MITT, GRAPPLER
sore on ...... CHILBLAIN
terminal part .... MANUS
upper .... ADVANTAGE
whist .... TENACE
without trumps ....
CHICANE
written .... MANUSCRIPT
handbag ... ETUI, PURSE, GRIP,
VALISE, RETIC(U)LE, SATCHEL,
CASE

handball ...... FIVES, PELOTA
handbill ..... DODGER, FLYER,
FLIER, THROWAWAY, POSER,
NOTICE, LEAF
handbook .. CATECHISM, TOME,
MANUAL, ENCHIRIDION
kind of ...... BAEDEKER
handcar .... VELOCIPEDE
handcart .... BARROW
handclasp .... SHAKE
handcuffs .... BRACELETS,
NIPPERS, DARBY, FETTER,
MANACLE, WRISTLET
Handel opus .. MESSIAH, LARGO,
NERO, BERENICE
place of birth .... HALLE
handful .... PLENTY, FEW,
FISTFUL
of hay/straw ...... WISP
handicap .. ODDS, HINDRANCE,
(DIS)ADVANTAGE, HINDER,
IMPEDE, RACE
handily ...... DEFTLY, EASILY
handkerchief ...... VERONICA,
MALABAR, SCARF, FOULARD,
SUDARY, SUDARIUM,
MOUCHOIR
colloquial ...... HANKIE,
WIPE(R)
large .... BANDAN(N)A,
MADRAS
handle .... HELVE, HAFT, HILT,
WIELD, EAR, GRIP, HANK,
TAKE CARE, ANSE, MANAGE,
OPERATE, DIRECT,
MANIPULATE, PLY, DEAL,
LUG, HEFT, ANSA, TREAT,
SWIPE
as middleman ...... JOB
awkwardly/clumsily ....
PAW, FUMBLE
bar: colloq. .. MUSTACHE
boat's .... TILLER
clumsily .... PAW
colloquial .. NAME, TITLE
cup's .... EAR
door .... KNOB
having .... ANSATE
hoop-shaped ...... BAIL
pail .... BAIL
printing press ... ROUNCE
roughly .... MAUL, PAW
rudder .... TILLER
scythe .. SNATH(E), SNEAD
slang .. NAME, MONICKER
sword .... HILT

whip's .... CROP
with .... ANSATE
handled .... PALMED, ANSATE,
MANAGED
handmade .... MANUAL
handmaiden ..... ATTENDANT,
SERVANT
handout .... GIFT, DOLE
handrail, kind of ... MANROPE
hands, clean: colloq. ....
INNOCENT, CLEAR
expertness with ....
HANDICRAFT
having two .... BIMANOUS
join .... COOPERATE
on hips .... AKIMBO
pertaining to .... MANUAL
warmer .... MUFF
without .. .. AMANOUS
handsel .... PRESENT, EARNEST,
TOKEN
handsome .... LARGE, COMELY,
IMPRESSIVE, BONNY, SHARP
man .... APOLLO, ADONIS
handspring .... TUMBLE
handstone .... MANO
handwriter, wall .... AGITPROP
handwriting ..... SCRIPT, FIST,
PENMANSHIP
bad .... CACOGRAPHY
expert ... CHIROGRAPHER
on the wall .... MENE,
TEKEL, UPHARSIN, GRAFFITI
pertaining to ... GRAPHIC
study of ... GRAPHOLOGY
style .... CHARACTER
handwritten document/will ...
HOLOGRAPH
handy ... CONVENIENT, READY,
DEFT, ADROIT, DEXTEROUS,
HABILE
man ...... JACK-OF-ALL-
TRADES, MOZO
bang ...... SUSPEND, EXECUTE,
EXHIBIT, HOVER, DANGLE,
DRAPE, SWAG, DROOP,
(IM)PEND, LOLL, STRING
around: colloq. .. LOITER,
LINGER, HOVER, LOAF
back .... LAG
down .... LAVE, PERPEND,
DROOP, LOP, SAG
fire .... PEND
jury .... DEADLOCK
loosely .... LOP, LOLL,
DANGLE, DRAPE

on .... WAIT, HOLD,
PERSEVERE
out .... HAUNT
over .... HOVER
slang ..... SCRAG, STRING
hangar .... (AIR)DROME, SHED,
SHELTER
area .... APRON
hangbird .... ORIOLE
hangdog .... MEAN
hanger ..... EXECUTIONER
on ...... TOADY, HEELER,
TRENCHER, SYCOPHANT,
PARASITE, FAVOR-SEEKER,
HABITUE, LEECH,
HENCHMAN
hanging .. .. SUSPENDED,
PENDULOUS, UNSETTLED,
PENDENT, PENSILE, SESSILE
apparatus .... GIBBET,
GALLOWS
cloth cover .... DRAPE
crookedly .... ALOP
down(ward) .... CERNOUS
nest maker ...... ORIOLE
piece/rag .... TAG
unevenly .... ALOP
hangings ..... ARRAS, DRAPES,
DRAPERY, TAPESTRY, WASH
hangman's noose ..... HALTER
rope .... HEMP
hangnail .... WHITLOW
hangnest .... ORIOLE
hangout ...... HAUNT, DEN,
RETREAT
hangover feeling .... NAUSEA,
HEADACHE
hank .. SKEIN, LOOP, COIL, RAN
hanker .. ITCH, CRAVE, LONG,
YEARN
hankering .... ITCH
hanky-panky .... TRICKY,
DECEPTIVE, TRICKERY,
JUGGLERY
Hannibal's conqueror .. SCIPIO
father .... HAMILCAR
defeat .... ZAMA
surname .... BARCA
victory site ..... CANNAE
Hanover beer .... BOCK
hanse .... GUILD, LEAGUE
Hanseatic League ..... HANSE
member .... BREMEN,
LUBECK, HAMBURG
Hansen's disease .... LEPROSY

hansom ... CARRIAGE, CAB, HACK
handspring ...... CARTWHEEL
hap .... CHANCE, LUCK, FORTUNE
haphazard ... RANDOM, CASUAL,
HIT-OR-MISS, AIMLESS
hapless ...... LUCKLESS, UNLUCKY
happen ..... TRANSPIRE, BEFALL,
FARE, OCCUR, CHANCE,
BETIDE, EVENTUATE
again .... RECUR
in the end .... EVENTUATE
together .... COINCIDE,
CONCUR
happening .... EVENT, INCIDENT,
OCCURRENCE, TIDING,
OCCASION, CASUS
before due ... PREMATURE,
RATH(E)
by chance .... FORTUITOUS
happiness ...... BLISS, FELICITY
happy ..... JOYOUS, GLAD, COSH,
LUCKY, BLITHE, FAUST
go-lucky ...... EASYGOING
medium ... AVERAGE, MEAN
hara-kiri ..... SUICIDE, SEPPUKU
harangue .... TIRADE, DIATRIBE,
EXHORT(ATION), SPIEL,
PERORATE, RANT, ORATE,
SCREED
Haran's brother ..... ABRAHAM
daughter .... MILCAH
father .... TERAH
harass .... TORMENT, RIDE,
TROUBLE, HARRY, HECKLE,
NAG, BOTHER, ANNOY, VEX,
IRK, MOLEST, BESET, TEASE,
OBSESS, PESTER, JADE,
PLAGUE
harbinger .... FORETELL, OMEN,
USHER, HERALD, PRECURSOR,
FORERUNNER
harbor .... SHELTER, HAVEN,
ANCHORAGE, CONCEAL,
CHERISH, COVE, PIER,
PORT, BAY
boat .... TUG
city .... SEAPORT
laborer .... STEVEDORE
small .... MARINA
sound .... CHUG(CHUG),
TOOT, (FOG)HORN, CHURN,
BELL
wall .... JETTY
hard .... FIRM, RIGID, SOLID,
VIOLENT, DIFFICULT, HARSH,
CALLOUS, NEAR, PETROUS,

STERN, ARDUOUS, ADAMANT,
DOUR, PETROSAL, SCLEROID,
SCLEROUS, MARBLY
bed .... PALLET
biscuit ... TACK, CRACKNEL
bitten ..... TOUGH, DOGGED
boiled .... TOUGH, CALLOUS
cash .... SPECIE
coal .... ANTHRACITE
covering .... SHELL, ARMOR
drawn .... TAUT, TENSE
fat .... SUET
hearted .... CRUEL, PITILESS
heartwood .... DURA
prefix .... DIS
problem .... POSER,
DILEMMA
roll .... BAGEL
rubber .... EBONITE
shell .... LORICA, CARAPACE
to bear .... GRIEVOUS
to grasp .... ELUSIVE
to understand ...... DEEP,
OBTUSE
very ..... STEEL, CASTIRON
water .... ICE
working ..... INDUSTRIOUS
hardboard .... MASONITE
harden .... STIFFEN, INURE, GEL,
ENURE, TEMPER, STEEL,
PETRIFY, SEAR, OSSIFY, SET,
INDURATE
by heat .... BAKE
hardfisted ..... STINGY, MISERLY
hardhack ..... SPIR(A)EA, ROSE,
SHRUB
hardhanded .... SEVERE,
RUTHLESS
hardhead .... MENHADEN,
SCULPIN
hardheaded ...... PRACTICAL,
STUBBORN, SHREWD
animal .... MULE, ASS,
DONKEY
hardihood .... DARING,
INSOLENCE
hardly ...... BARELY, SCARCELY
hardship .... RIGOR, TRIAL
hardtack .... BREAD, WAFER,
TOMMY, PANTILE
hardware dealer ....
IRONMONGER
hardwood ..... TEAK, OAK, ASH,
ELM, EBONY, YAKAL,
HICKORY, MAHOGANY
hardy ..... DARING, BOLD, RASH,

ROBUST, CHISEL, DURABLE,
TOUGH
Hardy novel character ... TESS,
JUDE
locale .... WESSEX
hare .. CONY, RODENT, RABBIT,
LEPUS, LEPORIDE, PIKA,
MALKIN, PUSS, LAGOMORPH
dialect .... WAT
family .... LEPORID
female .... DOE
genus .... LEPUS
hunting dog .... HARRIER
like .... LEPORINE
like animal ..... AGOUTI,
HYRAX
male .... BUCK
rabbit hybrid .. LEPORIDE
Scottish .... MALKIN
tail .... SCUT
track .... SLOT, SPOOR
young .... LEVERET
harebrained ... STUPID, GIDDY,
RASH
harem ...... SERAGLIO, SERAI,
ZENANA
dweller/slave ....
ODALISQUE, ODALISK
room .... ODA
hari-kari ... SUICIDE, SEPPUKU
haricot .. STEW, (KIDNEY) BEAN
hark .... LISTEN, HEAR
back .... REVERT
harl ...... FILAMENT(S), BARB
harlequin ...... CLOWN(ISH),
COMIC, LUDICROUS,
COLORFUL, (PANTO)MIME,
BUFFOON
girl of ...... COLUMBINE
Harlem painter .... HALS
harlot .... RAHAB, STRUMPET
harm ... SCATHE, EVIL, INJURY,
DAMAGE, HURT, WRONG,
MALEFIC, INJURE, MAR,
BALE, BANE, MALIGNANT
harmattan .... WIND
harmful .... ILL, NOXAL,
INJURIOUS, NOXIOUS,
NOCENT, BANEFUL, NOISOME,
NOCUOUS
gas in mine ...... DAMP
harmless .... INNOCUOUS,
INOFFENSIVE, INNOCENT,
NAIVE
harmonic ...... CONSONANT,
AGREEING

harmonica ..... MOUTH ORGAN
harmonious ..... CONSONANT,
CONGRUOUS, IN ACCORD,
ORDERLY
harmonist .... MUSICIAN, POET,
COMPOSER
harmonium .... ORGAN,
MELODEON
harmonize .... ATTUNE, AGREE
harmony .. AGREEMENT, MUSIC,
TUNE, PEACE, CHORD,
UNISON, RAPPORT, TONE,
BALANCE, CHIME, CONCORD,
CONSONANCE, COSMOS,
ORGANUM, SYMMETRY
of voices ...... CONCENT
harness ... GEAR, INSPAN, RIG,
EQUIP, GRAITH, DRAFT
bull .... COP
course site ...... GOSHEN
horse........ HEADGEAR,
TACKLE
men's .... BRICOLE
part ..... BLIND(ER), BIT,
COLLAR, TRACE, HAME,
HALTER, TERRET, REIN,
SADDLE, TUG, BILLET,
BRIDLE
ring .... TERRET
strap .... CRUPPER,
MARTINGAL(E)
harnessed horses .. TEAM, SPAN
Harold, diminutive of .... HAL
harp .... LYRE, KOTO, NANGA,
TRIGON
constellation ...... LYRA
like instrument ....
DULCIMER, SAMBUKE,
PSALTERY
slang .... IRISHMAN
Harper's Ferry event ... RAID,
BATTLE
Harpies, one of the ... AELLO,
CELAENO, OCYPETE
harpoon ...... SPEAR, JAVELIN
barb .... FLUKE
missile like a .. HURLBAT
harpsichord .... SPINET,
VIRGINAL
Harpy .. WITCH, EAGLE, AELLO,
MONSTER, BUZZARD,
OCYPETE, CELAENO
harquebus .... HACKBUT,
HAGBUT, FIREARM
fork .... CROC

harridan .. SHREW, FURY, NAG, VIRAGO, HAG, JEZEBEL

harrier .. FALCON, DOG, HAWK

Harriet, diminutive of .. HATTIE

harrow .... DRAG, BRAKE, WOUND, LACERATE, VEX, TORMENT

    rival of .... ETON

harry .... RAID, HARASS, TORMENT, PILLAGE, PESTER, PLUNDER

    Old .... DEVIL, SATAN

harsh .... STERN, DISCORDANT, BITTER, COARSE, CRUDE, ROUGH, SEVERE, CRUEL, RASPING, DRASTIC

    and dry .... HACKING

    critic .... SLATER

    sound ... STRIDOR, ROAR, GRUFF

    sounding ...... STRIDENT

    taste ...... ACERB, BITTER

    voiced person ... STENTOR

harshness .... ASPERITY

hart .... DEER, STAG

Harte, author .... BRET(T)

    character ...... AH SIN

hartebeest ... ANTELOPE, ASSE, BONTEBOK, CAAMA, TORA, LECAMA

    kin of .... SASSABY

hartshorn .... ANTLERS

hartstongue .... FERN

harum-scarum ... WILD, RASH, RECKLESS, AMOK

haruspex .... SOOTHSAYER, PRIEST

Harvard educator ..... PUSEY, CONANT, LOWELL

    newspaper ..... CRIMSON

harvest ... CROP, REAP, YIELD, RABI, KIRN

    bug ...... CHIGGER, TICK, MITE

    feast .... KIRN

    festival .... LAMMAS

    fly .... CICADA

    home .... KIRN

    last sheaf .... KIRN

    leftover .. STUBBLE, STUMP

harvestman .... DADDY-LONGLEGS

hash ... CHOP, MINCE, BUNGLE, MIXTURE, HODGEPODGE, RAMEKIN, RAMEQUIN, MULLIGAN

house: sl. ... RESTAURANT, JOINT

    mark: military .... STRIPE

hashish .. B(H)ANG, NARCOTIC, MARIJUANA, CANNABIS

    source .... HEMP

hasp .... SKEIN, CATCH

hassle .... FRAY, MELEE, SQUABBLE, DISCUSSION, RUCKUS, BRAWL

Hasso, actress .... SIGNE

hassock .. SEAT, MAT, CUSHION, KNEELER, FOOTSTOOL, TUSSOCK

haste .... SPEED, HURRY

hasten ..... HURRY, DISPATCH, SPEED(UP), ACCELERATE, APACE, HIE, SCAMP

hasty .. QUICK, HURRIED, FAST, IMPETUOUS, IMPATIENT, IMPULSIVE, CURSORY, RASH, ABRUPT, BRASH, TEARING

    pudding ... MUSH, SEPON, HASH

hat ... SCONCE, TOQUE, BERET, HEADGEAR, CAP, CAUBEEN, PETASOS, PETASUS, FELT, TAM, TOPPER, CHAPEAU, BONNET

    beaver fur .... CASTOR

    brimless ..... TOQUE, FEZ

    collapsible .... GIBUS

    crown .... POLL

    cylindrical .... SHAKO

    decoration .... COCKADE, POMPON

    ecclesiastic ...... BIRETTA

    felt ... HOMBURG, FEDORA

    fur .... CONEY

    high .... TILE, BEAVER

    holder .... BANDBOX

    hunter's .... TERAI

    lining leather .... SKIVER

    maker .... MILLINER

    making fiber ... BUNTAL, RAFFIA

    man's silk .... BEAVER

    material ..... VELOUR(S), FELT

    opera .... GIBUS

    part .. BRIM, BAND, LINING

    pith .... TOPEE, TOPI, HELMET

    plant .... SOLA

    rabbit fur .... CASTOR

    silk .... BEAVER

slang .... LID
small .... COIF
soft .... FEDORA, PORKPIE
soldier's ..... HAVELOCK,
    SHAKO, KEPI, BUSBY,
    BERET
straw .... PANAMA,
    LEGHORN
take off ...... DOFF, VAIL
tasseled .... FEZ
three-cornered .. TRICORN
trimming ...... ROULEAU
turned up brim ....
    COCKUP, BRETON
under one's .... SECRET,
    CONFIDENTIAL
woman's .... PILLBOX,
    CLOCHE, TURBAN
batch ...... CONCOCT, DEVISE,
    PLAN, PLOT, TRAPDOOR,
    FLOODGATE, FISHTRAP,
    ENGRAVE
hatchel .... HECKLE, TEASE
hatchery .... INCUBATOR
hatchet ...... AX, TOMAHAWK
    handle .... HELVE
    man .... GOON
    stone .... MOGO
    type ... CLAW, SHINGUNG,
        LATHING
hatchway .... SCUTTLE
hate .... DETEST, LOATHE,
    DESPISE, DISLIKE, ABHOR,
    ABOMINATE, AVERSION,
    PHOBIA, MALICE, ODIUM
    combining form ... MIS(O)
    of foreigners ....
        XENOPHOBIA
hateful ... EXECRABLE, ODIOUS,
    REPUGNANT, OBNOXIOUS,
    LOATHSOME, REPULSIVE,
    ABOMINABLE, HEINOUS
    person ...... CAD, TOAD
Hatfield enemy .... MCCOY
hating, combining form ......
    MIS(O)
hatred .... ODIUM, ENMITY,
    AVERSION, ILL WILL, HATE,
    ANIMOSITY, DISLIKE
    combining form .. MIS(O)
    of change ..... MISONEISM
    of debate/argument .....
        MISOLOGY
    of mankind ....
        MISANTHROPY
    of marriage ... MISOGAMY

of women .... MISOGYNY
hats, women's ..... MILLINERY
hatrack .... TREE
hatter, woman ...... MILLINER
hauberk .. ARMOR, HABERGEON
haughtiness .... HAUTEUR,
    ARROGANCE
haughty .. ARROGANT, PROUD,
    SNOOTY, STUCK-UP, SNOTTY,
    CAVALIER, SUPERCILIOUS,
    PROUD, LOFTY
haul .... PULL, DRAG, TUG,
    CATCH, BOOTY, TRICE, LUG,
    BOUSE, ROUSE, DRAW, HALE,
    SWAG, TOW, CART, DRAG,
    HEAVE, TOTE
haulage ... CARTAGE, PORTAGE
hauling car .... VAN
haulm ... STALK, STEM, STRAW,
    HAY, CULM
haunch .. HIP, HANCE, HUCKLE
    bone .... ILIUM
    part ...... HIP, BUTTOCK,
        THIGH, LOIN, LEG
haunt .. HANG-OUT, FREQUENT,
    PERVADE, DEN, RETREAT,
    OBSESS, LAIR, NEST, LIE,
    RESORT, SPOOK, PURLIEU
    animal ...... LAIR, DEN
    dialect .... GHOST
    in mind .... OBSESS
    low .... DEN, DIVE
    of literary hacks ....
        GRUB STREET
hausfrau .... HOUSEWIFE
haustellum .... PROBOSCIS
haustorium .... SUCKER
hautboy .... OBOE
haute monde .. HIGH SOCIETY
hauteur ..... SNOBBERY, PRIDE,
    ARROGANCE
Havana .... CIGAR,
    (LA) PARASITA
    castle .... MORRO
have at .... ATTACK
    done .... FINISH, STOP
    effect .... TELL
    feeling .... SENTIENT
    feet .... PEDATE
    flavor ..... TASTY, SAPID
    limits .... FINITE
    no worries .... CAREFREE
    offensive smell ..... OLID
    ribs .... COSTATE
    rough edges ..... EROSE,
        RAGGED

same origin ... CONNATE, COGNATE
Scot .... HAE
scruples .... DEMUR
spikes .... SPINED, TINED, PRONGED
strong desire for .... HUNGER, COVET
title to .... OWN
haven ...... REFUGE, SHELTER, ASYLUM, SANCTUARY, PORT, HITHE, LEE, HARBOR
animal's .... PRESERVE
ship's .... ANCHORAGE
haversack ...... (CANVAS)BAG
havoc .... DESTRUCTION, DEVASTATION
haw ..... BERRY, HOI, EYELID, SLOE, FRUIT, COMMAND, FALTER
companion of ...... HEM
inflammation .... STY
opposed to .... GEE
Hawaii .... OWYHEE
author of book .... MICHENER
Hawaiian .... POLYNESIAN, KANAKA
acacia .... KOA
apple .... MAILE
association .... HUI
bathing resort ... WAIKIKI
bird ...... IO, OOAA, IIWI, MAMO, KOAE, NOIO, NUKUPUU, OMAO
blueberry .... OHELO
bonito .... AKU
breech cloth ...... MALO
bush .... OLONA
canoe .... WAPA
capital .... HONOLULU
chant .... MELE
city .... HONOLULU, HILO
cliff .... PALI
club .... HUI
cloak .... MAMO
cloth .... TAPA, KAPA
coffee .... KONA
crater .... KILAUEA
dance .... HULA
dancer .... WAHINE
dress .... MUUMUU
drink .... KAVA
emblem .... LEHUA

farewell .... ALOHA
feast .... LUAU
fern .... IWAIWA, HEII
fiber .... WAUKE
fish .. ULUA, LANIA, AKU, PALANI, AHI
floral emblem .... LEHUA
floral wreath .... LEI
flower .. LEHUA, HIBISCUS
food .... POI, TARO
food fish ... ULUA, LANIA, UKU
foreman .... LUNA
frigate bird .... IWA
fruit .... POHA
game .... HEI
garland .... LEI
god .... KANE, KUPO
goddess of fire/volcano .. PELE
goggler .... AKULE
goose .... NENE, NENI
grass .... HILO
greeting .... ALOHA
harbor .... PEARL
herb .... NOLA
honeyeater .... OO
hula dancer ..... WAHINE
island ... MAUI, MOLOKAI, NIIHAU, HAWAII, KAUAI, LANAI, OAHU, KAHOOLAWE
Islands .... SANDWICH
Islands discoverer ...... GAETANO
language .... POLYNESIAN
lava .... AA
like bird .... KITE
liquor ...... AWA, KAWA
lizard fish .... ULAE
loincloth .... PAU, MARO, MALO
love .... ALOHA
mountain ...... KEA, LOA
mulberry bark ..... TAPA
musical instrument ..... UKE(LELE), PUA
national park .... HALEAKALA
native .... KANAKA
neckpiece .... LAI, LEI
newcomer ...... MALHINI
noble .... ALII
noddy .... NOIO
nut .... LITCHI
octopus .... HEE

pa.percloth .... OLONA
party .... LUAU
pepper .... AVA
pit for baking .... IMU
plant ...... KALO, OLONA
plantation boss .... LUNA
porch .... LANA(I)
port .... HILO
precipice .... PALI
press .... LOMILOMI
range .... KOOLAU
raven .... ALALA
royal chief .... ALII
rub .... LOMILOMI
salutation .... ALOHA
seaweed .... LIMU
shampoo ...... LOMILOMI
shrub .... AKIA
song .... MELE
starch .... APII
state flower .... HIBISCUS
taro, fermented .... MOD
taro paste .... POI
tern .... NOIO
thrush .... (OL)OMAO
town .... HILO
tree .... LEHUA, AALII,
AULU, ALANI, KOA,
ILIAHI, OHIA
tree fern ..... PULU, AMAU
valley .... MANOA
volcano ... KILAUEA, LOA,
MAUNA, HALEAKALA
windstorm .... KONA
woman .... WAHINE
wood .... MILO, KOU
wreath .... LEI
yam .... HOI
hawfinch .... GROSBEAK
Hawhaw of WWII ..... LORD
hawk ...... CHEATER, SPREAD,
SWINDLER, PEDDLE, ELANET,
HARRIER, FALCON, KITE,
BUZZARD, CARACARA, IO,
MORTARBOARD, HAGGARD,
ACCIPITER, MERLIN, OSSIFRAGE
Australian .... KAHU
bill of .... PAWL
blind .... SEEL
cage .... MEW
carrier .... CAD
claw .... TALON
European .... FALCON
eyed ...... KEEN-SIGHTED
falconry .... BATER
fish .... OSPREY

genus .. BUTEO, ACCIPITER
head cover .... SEEL
headed god .... HORUS, RA
hunt with .... FLY
leash of ...... LUNE, JESS
leg's feather .... FLAG
like bird ... OSPREY, KITE
male .... TERCEL
moth .... SPHINX
moth caterpillar ......
HORNWORM
nemesis of the .. HOUBARA
nest .... AERIE, AERY
parrot .... HIA
small .... EYAS, KITE,
ELANET
sparrow .... NISUS
stomach of ...... PANNEL
swoop of .... SOUSE
vulture-like ... CARACARA
weed .... MOUSE-EAR
young ...... AERIE, EYRIE,
EYAS
hawker .. PEDDLER, HUCKSTER,
COSTER, CADGER, CHAPMAN,
FALCONER, PEDLAR
route of .... WALK
spot/talk of ...... PITCH
Hawkeye .... IOWAN
state .... IOWA
Hawkshaw .. DETECTIVE, DICK,
SLEUTH
hawkweed .... DINDLE
hawser frame .. BITT, BOLLARD
iron .... CALKING
knot .... BEND
post .... BOLLARD
hawthorn ...... MAY(FLOWER),
COCKSPUR, AZAROLE
fruit .... HAW, BERRY
Hawthorne's birthplace ......
SALEM
hay .. GRASS, CLOVER, ALFALFA,
DANCE, FODDER, TIMOTHY
bale of .... TRUSS
bird .... BLACKCAP
box .... MANGER
bundle of .... TRUSS
fever ...... POLLINOSIS,
ROSE COLD
fever, cause of ... POLLEN
fever characteristic ......
SNEEZING, ASTHMA
fever remedy .. BENADRYL
fine cut .... CHAFF
fodder .... CHAFF

for thatching ... HA(U)LM
grass .... REDTOP
hit the ..... RETIRE, SLEEP
lifting implement ....
PITCHFORK
pile .... COCK
plant .... SAINFOIN
row, drying ... WINDROW
second crop .... ROWEN
spread the .... TED
stack of ...... RICK, MOW
storage place .... MOW,
LOFT
haycock .... RACK, COB, RICK
Hayden, ballerina .... MELISSA
haying job .... TED
hayseed .... RUSTIC, HICK
haystack ...... RICK, MOW, COB,
COIL, PIKE, GOAF
haywire .... CRAZY, AMOK,
DISORDERLY, CONFUSED
Hayworth, actress ...... RITA
role ... SADIE (THOMPSON)
hazard .... RISK, CHANCE,
JEOPARDY, DANGER, STAKE,
VENTURE, PERIL, JUMP
hazardous ... RISKY, PERILOUS,
DANGEROUS, UNSAFE
haze .. FILM, FOG, BRUME, MIST,
SMOG, VAPOR, SMAZE, GLIN,
PALL
composition of ..... FOG,
SMOKE, DUST
fellow student .. INITIATE
thin .... GAUZE
hazel .... TREE, SHRUB, NUT,
WOOD, BIRCH
hazelnut .... FILBERT
hazy .... VAGUE, OBSCURE
hd. .... HEAD
he .... PERSON, ANYONE
carved it .... SCULPSIT
combining form ... MALE
in chemistry ..... HELIUM
Latin .... IPSE
man, describing a ....
VIRILE
painted it .. PNXT, PINXIT
speaks .... LOQUITUR
wrote it .... SCRIPSIT
head .. PATE, TETE, MIND, VAN,
POLL, LEAD(ER), CAPITA,
PASH, NOB, MAZARD, WITS,
CAPUT, CONK, SKULL, TOP,
APTITUDE, FRONT, CHIEF
and shoulders ..... BUST

and shoulders cover ......
NUBIA
armor .... MORION
back part ...... OCCIPUT,
POLL
band .... FILLET
beer .... FROTH
cold ... CORYZA, SNIFFLES
colloquial ...... NODDLE,
PATE, WITS, SCONCE
combining form ....
CEPHAL(O)
convent .... ABBESS
cord .... AGAL
counting .... CENSUS,
CAPITATION
cover .. HAT, CAP, SHAWL,
HELMET, COWL, HOOD,
HAIR, WIMPLE,
TURBAN, BURNOOSE
crown of ... PATE, VERTEX
effervescent beverage ....
FROTH
enlarged at the ....
CAPITATE
garland .... CHAPLET
gear ...... WIMPLE, HAT,
BERET, BEANIE, MITRE,
CAP, HELMET
hair of .... POLL
like structure ..... CAPUT
membrane covering .....
CAUL, OMENTUM
money .... POLL TAX
monastery .... ABBOT
nautical slang .... TOILET
newspaper ..... CAPTION
of foreign mission ......
NUNCIO, AMBASSADOR
of the .... PARIETAL,
CEPHALIC
off ...... INTERCEPT, AVERT,
BLANCH
pain .... HEMIALGIA,
HEMICRANIA
protective covering .....
HELMET, MASK, MORION
shaped like .... CAPITATE
shaved .... TONSURE
ship's .... BOW
shrinker .... ANALYST
side of .... MALAR
skin of .... SCALP
skull .... SCONCE
slang ..... BEAN, NOGGIN,
NOB, DOME, NUT

start .... LEAD
to foot .... CAP-A-PIE
to shave .... TONSURE
top of .... PATE, CROWN,
        VERTEX
wrap .. BURNOOSE, NUBIA,
        TURBAN, TARBOOSH,
        SHAWL
wreath .... CHAPLET,
        LAUREL
headache .... MEGRIM,
        HEMIALGIA, MIGRAINE
    colloquial ...... WORRY,
        TROUBLE, PROBLEM
headband ...... AGAL, FILLET,
        TAENIA
headcheese .... BRAWN
headdress .. COIFFURE, DIADEM,
        MITER, MITRE, BIRRETTA, WIG,
        COMMODE, TIAR(A), POUF,
        TOUPEE
    bishop's .... MITER, MITRE
    capelike .... PINNER
    cobra .... URAEUS
    cowl-like .... ALMUCE
    Indian .... BONNET
    maker .... MILLINER
    military ... SHAKO, BUSBY
    nun's ... CORNET, WIMPLE
    of feathers ..... TOPKNOT
    Sister of Carmelite's ....
        CORNET
    widow's .... BANDORE
    women's .... POUF,
        POMPADOUR, MILLINERY
header .... DIVE
headgear .. HAT, CAP, HELMET,
        HARNESS, HOOD, TOQUE, TAJ,
        SHAKO, TIAR(A), TOPI, FEZ
headhunter .... DAYAK
heading ...... TITLE, CAPTION,
        GALLERY, DRIFT
    of subject matter .. TROPE
headland .. CAPE, NESS, BLUFF,
        PROMONTORY, HOOK
headless .. ACEPHALOUS, ETETE,
        LEADERLESS
    man of fiction ....
        (BROM)BONES
headline .. BANNER, SCREAMER,
        STREAMER, TITLE
headliner .... STAR
    of 1898 .... MAINE
    of 1909 .... PEARY
    of 1914 ..... WORLD WAR
    of 1917 .. AEF, DOUGHBOY,

        ARMISTICE
    of 1934 .... DIONNE
    of 1945 .... A-BOMB,
        HIROSHIMA
    of 1950 .... BRINKS
    of 1957 .... SPUTNIK
    of 1959 .... CASTRO
    of 1969 ... MAN ON MOON
headlong ...... RECKLESS(LY),
        RASH(LY), PELLMELL,
        TANTIVY
    fall .... CROPPER
    flight .... LAM
headman .... CHIEF, BOSS,
        LEADER, HETMAN,
        RINGLEADER
headmaster ...... PRINCIPAL,
        RECTOR
headpiece ...... CAP, HELMET
headquarters .... MAIN OFFICE,
        BASE
headrest .... PILLOW
headset part ..... EARPHONE
headsman ..... EXECUTIONER,
        LEADER
headspring ... SOURCE, ORIGIN,
        FOUNTAIN
headstone ..... STELE, BARROW
headstrong ..... SELF-WILLED,
        RASH, WILLFUL, WAYWARD,
        STUBBORN
headwaiter .... CAPTAIN
headway .... PROGRESS
heady .... RASH, NAPPY
heal .... CURE, REMEDY,
        GET WELL, RECONCILE,
        RECUPERATE, MEND
healer ..... DOCTOR, SHAMAN,
        PHYSICIAN
    kind of ... FAITH, QUACK,
        MEDICINE MAN
healing .. CURATIVE, REMEDIAL,
        MEDICINAL, THERAPEUTIC
    substance ..... MEDICINE,
        PANACEA, BALM,
        NOSTRUM, DRUG,
        OINTMENT, BALSAM
health .... WELL-BEING,
        SOUNDNESS
    condition ...... WELFARE
    drinking toast .. PROSIT,
        SALUD, MABUHAY
    in good ...... FIT, HALE
    resort .... SPA
    science of ..... HYGIENE,
        HYGIENICS

healthful .... SALUTARY, SALUBRIOUS, WHOLESOME
healthy .. SOUND, WELL, HALE, ROBUST
heap ..... MOW, RUCK, STACK, PILE, MOUND, (A)MASS, COB, RAFT, CONGERIES, RAFF
  colloquial .... LOTS, GREAT DEAL
  of a .... ACERVAL
  of rock fragments ..... DEBRIS
  piled by wind ..... DRIFT
  slang .... CAR
  stone ..... MOUND, SCREE, CAIRN
hear .... LISTEN, LEARN, HEARKEN, HARK(EN), HEED
  ye .... OYEZ, OYES
hearer .... AUDITOR, LISTENER
hearing ..... OYER, AUDITION, AUDIENCE, INTERVIEW, TRIAL, INQUEST
  act/sense of ... AUDITION
  aid .... AUDIPHONE, EAR(PHONE)
  hard of .... DEAF
  in court .... TRIAL
  instrument .... AUDIOMETER, STETHOSCOPE
  keen .... HYPERACUSIA, HYPERACUSIS
  of .... AURAL, OTIC, AUDITORY, ACOUSTIC
  organ .... OTOCYST
  range .... EARSHOT
  science of .... AUDIOLOGY
hearken ...... LIST(EN), HEED, HEAR, HIST, ATTEND
Hearn, writer ...... YAKUMO, LAFCADIO
hearsay ..... REPORT, RUMOR, GOSSIP, TALK
  means of spreading ..... GRAPEVINE
hearse .... BIER
  cover .... PALL
heart ...... GIST, PITH, COR(E), BREAST, BOSOM, ESSENCE, CARDIA, SPIRIT
  action record .... CARDIOGRAM
  ailment .... ANGINA, CARDITIS
  attack ...... OCCLUSION, STROKE, SHUTDOWN
  attack cause .... THROMBOSIS
  auricle .... ATRIUM
  beat ...... PULSE, STROKE
  beat condition .. FLUTTER, PALPITATION, ARRHYTHMIA
  beat regulator .... PACEMAKER
  bleeding ...... DICENTRA
  blood vessel ...... AORTA
  booster ...... PACER, LVB
  cavity .... AURICLE, CAMERA, ATRIUM
  colloquial .... TICKER
  contraction ..... SYSTOLE
  deposit .... PLAQUE, CHOLESTEROL
  enlargement .... MEGALOCARDIA
  inflammation... CARDITIS
  leaf .... MEDIC
  muscular substance ..... MYOCARDIUM
  of the .... CARDIAC
  part .... AURICLE, VENTRICLE
  point .... FESS
  shaped .... CORDATE, CARDIOID, CORDIFORM
  sound .... MURMUR
  stimulant ... SPARTEIN(E), DIGITALIS, CORDIAL, HELLEBOREIN
  study of .... CARDIOLOGY
  transplant patient ...... BLAIBERG, BLOCK, KASPERAK, WASHKANSKY
  transplant surgeon ...... WADA, COOLEY, SHUMWAY, BARNARD
  trouble......... ANGINA, CONDITION
heartache ..... GRIEF, SORROW
heartbeat ...... PULSE, THROB, TACHYCARDIA, PALPITATION, PULSATION
  condition ...... FLUTTER
heartburn ..... PYROSIS, ENVY, JEALOUSY, CARDIALGIA, WATER BRASH
hearten .... ENCOURAGE, CHEER (UP)
heartfelt .... GENUINE, SINCERE

hearth .. FIRESIDE, HOME, LING
goddess of the .... VESTA,
HESTIA
heartless ..... CRUEL, PITILESS,
SARDONIC, MERCILESS
heartdeaf .... MEDIC
hearts/diamonds ... (RED)SUIT
heartsease .... PANSY,
PERSICARY, WALLFLOWER
heartsick ... DESPONDENT, SAD
heartwood .... DURA(MEN)
heartworm .... NEMATODE
hearty .... HALE, SINCERE,
CORDIAL, GENIAL, LUSTY,
VIGOROUS, FELLOW,
COMRADE, ROBUST, SAILOR
heat .. CALOR, HOTNESS, FEVER,
WARM(TH), EXCITEMENT,
ANGER, TEPOR, ARDOR, FIRE,
ZEAL, CAUMA, INTENSITY,
INFLAME
animal ..... RUT, ESTRUS
bubble up with ....
INTUMESCE
caused by ...... THERMIC
combining form ....
THERMO, THERMY
decomposition by ....
PYROLYSIS
exhaustion ... SUNSTROKE
gentle .... TEPOR
great .... BROIL
lightning ...... WILDFIRE
liquify with .... MELT
measuring device ....
CALORIMETER
oppressive ..... SWELTER
pertaining to .... CALEFY,
CALORIC, THERMAL,
THERMIC
pervious to ....
TRANSCALENT
production of ....
DIATHERMY
prostration ... SUNSTROKE
rash .... MILIARIA
resistant .... STABILE
resistant material ....
ASBESTOS, COPPER
sexual ...... ESTRUS, RUT
source .... SUN, FUEL
to liquid state ..... MELT
unit .. THERM(E), CALORIE,
CALORY, BTU
heated .... HOT, ANGRY
chamber .... STOVE

to whiteness ... CANDENT
wine .... REGUS
heater .. ETNA, BURNER, BUNSEN,
OVEN, STOVE, CHAUFFER
hot-water/gas ... GEYSER
portable ...... CHAUFFER
slang....... GUN, PISTOL
heath ..... MOOR, BENT, ERICA,
AZALEA, WASTELAND, PIPE
heathbird .... GROUSE,
BLACKCOCK
heathen ..... PAGAN, INFIDEL,
GENTILE, ETHNIC, PAYNIM,
IRRELIGIOUS
deity .... IDOL
heather ... GORSE, ERICA, LING,
BILBERRY, CROWBERRY
heating .... CALEFICIENT,
CALEFACTION
device .... RETORT, ETNA,
BOILER, STOVE, OVEN,
BURNER
heaume .... HELMET
heave ..... HEFT, CAST, FLING,
KECK, HURL, RAISE, LIFT,
HAUL, SWELL, BULGE, PANT,
GASP
heaven .. PROVIDENCE, GLORY,
CIEL, WELKIN, ZION, EDEN,
ELYSIUM, SKY, FIRMAMENT,
OLYMPUS
arch of .... SKY
combining form .. URANO
edge of .... HORIZON
flier to .... ETANA
personified ..... URANUS
heavenly .. EDENIC, CELESTIAL,
ETHEREAL, SUPERNAL, HOLY,
URANIC, DIVINE
being .... ANGEL, CHERUB,
SERAPH(IM)
city .... SION, ZION
body ..... COMET, MOON,
STAR, SUN, PLANET,
METEOR
bread .... MANNA
path .... ORBIT
heavens, imaginary belt of ...
ZODIAC
description of the ....
URANOLOGY
heaves .... BROKEN WIND
heavily .... CLUMSILY, SLOWLY
heavy .... GRAVE, SERIOUS,
BURDENSOME, PONDEROUS,
SAD, LEADEN, GLOOMY,

WEIGHTY, ROUGH, THICK, MASSIVE
blow .. .. ONER, HAYMAKER
boat .... .. STOGY, BROGAN
demand .. .. DRAFT
duty . .. . TOUGH
earth .. .. BARYTA
footed .. .. PLODDING
hammer .. .. SLEDGE
handed .. .. CRUEL, ARBITRARY, OPPRESSIVE
hang .. .. DRAG
hearted .. .. SAD
hydrogen .. .. DEUTERIUM
load .. .. BURDEN
nail .. .. SPIKE
role .. .. VILLAIN
spar .... BARITE, BARYTES
step/walk .. .. TROD, SLOG, CLUMP
wire .. .. CABLE
with child .. .. PREGNANT
hebdomad .. .. .. WEEK, SEVEN
hebephrenia .. .. DEMENTIA
hebetate .. .. DULL, STUPID, BLUNT
Hebraism .. .. JUDAISM
Hebrew .. .. .. ZION, ISRAELITE, S(H)EMITE
  acrostic .. .. AGLA
  alien resident .. .. GER
  alphabet . .. . ALEPH, ALEF, AIN, NUN, MEM, JOD, VAU, WAW, PE, TAV, TAW, RESH, TETH, CHETH, BETH, GIMEL, DALETH, ZAYIN, YODH, CAPH, KAPH, LAMED(H), SAMEKH, AYIN, SADHE, KOPH, SHIN
  ancestor .. .. EBER
  ascetic .. .. ESSENE, NAZARITE
  bible books .. .. .. NEBIIM
  bread .. .. AZYM
  bride .. .. KALLAH
  brotherhood .. .. .. ESSENE
  canonical lawbook .. .. .. TALMUD
  city .. .. KIRJATH
  coin .. .. .. GERAH, SHEKEL
  day .. .. YOM
  deity .. .. BAAL
  divine presence .. .. SHEKINAH
  drum .. .. TOPH

dry measure .. EPHA, KAB
ear of corn .. .. ABIB
father .. .. ABRAM
festival . .. .. PURIM, SEDER
first month .. .. TISHRI
flute .. .. NEHILOTH
god .. .. EL, ELOHIM, JEHOVAH
greeting .. .. SHALOM
Hades .. .. SHEOL
healer .. .. ASA
hello .. .. SHALOM
herdsman .. .. AMOS
high priest . .. .. ELI, EZRA
high priest, first .. AARON
horn .. .. SHOFAR, SHOPHAR
household idols .. .. TERAPHIM
hymn .. .. KADDISH
instrument .. .. ASOR
judge .. . .. HALAKIST, ELI, HALACHIST, ELON
king .. .. .. DAVID, SAUL
kind of demons .. .. ASMODEUS
kingdom .. .. ISRAEL
language .. .. .. RABBINIC
law of Moses .. . TORA(H)
letter .. PE, DALETH, MEM, AYIN, RESH, TETH, YOD, VAU
lyre .. .. ASOR
marriage custom .. .. LEVERATE
measure .. .. .. KOR, KAB, (H)OMER, EPHA(H), HIN
month .. .. .. TISHRI, ELUL, ADAR, BUL, AB, ZIV, ABIB, SEBAT, KISLEV, NISAN, TEBET, SHEBAT, VEADAR, IYAR, SIVAN, TAMMUZ
name for God .. .. EL, ADONAI, ELOHIM
name for Syria .. .. ARAM
order .. .. ESSENE
Passover month .. .. ABIB
precept .. .. TORA
priest .. .. LEVITE
princess .. .. SARAH
prophet .. HOSEA, DANIEL, ELIAS, ISAIAH, NAHUM, JOEL, HAGGAI, NASI, JEREMIAH, MALACHI

AMOS, ELISHA, EZRA, MICAH, JONAH
prophetess ..... DEBORAH
psalms of praise .. HALLEL
quarter .... GHETTO
religion .... JUDAISM, HEBRAISM
sanctuary .... BAMAH
scarf .... ABNET, TALLITH
scholar .... HALAKIST, HALACHIST
scripture marginal notes .. MASORA
seer ..... BALAAM, ISAAC, MOSES
son .... BEN
songs of praise ... BALLEL
stringed instrument ..... ASOR
sun god .... BAAL
teacher .... RAB
ten .... YOD(H)
trader .... BANIAN
tribe .... DAN, LEVITES
universe .... OLAM
weight .... GERAH, OMER, SHEKEL
word .... SELAH
Hebrides Island .. LEWIS, UIST, HARRIS, MULL, IONA, SKYE
hecatomb .... SACRIFICE, SLAUGHTER
heck! ..... HELL, INTERJECTION
heckle ..... HATCHEL, ANNOY, TAUNT, BAIT, NEEDLE
heckler .... TAUNTER, HOOTER, HISSER, BOOER, TEASER
hectic .... CONSUMPTIVE, HOT, FEVERED, FEVERISH, FLUSHED, FEBRILE
hector ..... BULLY, BRAWLER, TEASE, PESTER, BROWBEAT, BAIT, HUFF
   parent of .... PRIAM, HECUBA
   wife of .... ANDROMACHE
Hecuba's children ... HECTOR, TROILUS, CASSANDRA, PARIS
   husband .... PRIAM
heddle .... CAAM
hedge ...... TEMPORIZE, HAW, HEM, REW, BUSH, THICKET, BOMA, EQUIVOCATE, QUICKSET, SHILLY-SHALLY, FENCE, BARRIER, WAVER, HEM AND HAW, ROW

debris .... BRASH
form a .... PLASH
laurel .... TARATA
pant .... PRIVET
trimmer .... PLASHER, SHEAR
hedgehog .... PORCUPINE, URCHIN
   Greek .... ECHINOS
   like animal ..... TENREC, TENDRAC
   spine of .... QUILL
hedgerow .... REW
Hedin, explorer .... SVEN(ANDERS)
hedonist .... VOLUPTUARY
heebie jeebies .... JITTERS, NERVOUSNESS
heed .. HEAR(KEN), OBEY, CARE, ATTENTION, NOTE, LISTEN, MIND, RECK, NOTICE
heedful .... VIGILANT, ATTENT(IVE)
heehaw ...... BRAY, GUFFAW, LAUGH(TER)
heel ... LOUSE, TAP, BOUNDER, CAD, CHASE, LIST, SLANT, TILT, LEAN, CAREEN, CANT, CALX
   boot's .... DUCE
   bone .... CALCANEUS, FIBULA
   combining form ... TALO
   down at the ...... SEEDY, SHABBY
   over .. TIP, CAREEN, TILT, CAPSIZE
heeled: sl. .... MONEYED, RICH, ARMED
heeler ..... COCK, HANGER-ON
heeling .... ALIST, ATILT
Heflin, actor .... VAN
heft ... INFLUENCE, PULL, LIFE, WEIGHT, HEAVE, BULK
hefty ...... HEAVY, WEIGHTY, POWERFUL
Hegel, philosopher .... GEORG
hegemonic .. RULING, LEADING
hegira ...... FLIGHT, JOURNEY
   destination ...... MEDINA
hegumen .... ABBOT
Hehe crop ..... MAIZE, MILLET
Heidelberg memento .... SCAR
heifer .... COW, STIRK
   maid changed to ..... IO
height ..... EXTREME, CLIMAX,

ALTITUDE, ELEVATION, ACME, PINNACLE, TOP, SUMMIT, STATURE, EMINENCE, APEX

of great .... SKYEY

of play's action ....
CATASTASIS, CLIMAX, DENOUEMENT

heighten .... INTENSIFY, INCREASE, ENHANCE

heinous .. ODIOUS, ABOMINABLE, WICKED, HATEFUL

heir .... LEGATEE, (IN)HERITOR, SCION, SON, HERES

joint .... PARCENER

kind of .... APPARENT, PRESUMPTIVE, FORCED, LEGAL

legal .... HERES

to a throne ....
CROWN PRINCE

heist: sl. .. HOLDUP, ROBBERY

Hejaz capital .... MECCA

holy city .... MECCA, MEDINA

Hel .. GODDESS, UNDERWORLD

held ..... DETAINED, GRIPPED

capable of being ....
TENABLE

in music .... TENUTO

in trust ...... FIDUCIARY

Helen .. EILEEN, ELAINE, ELENA, AILEEN

dimunitive of .... NELL(Y), LENA

Mitchell Armstrong .....
MELBA

of Troy's abductor ....
PARIS

daughter .... HERMIONE

husband .... MENELAUS

mother .... LEDA

son .... DORUS

suitor ..... PARIS, AJAX

heliacal .... SOLAR

helianthus .... SUNFLOWER

helical .... SPIRAL, TORSE

helico: comb. form .... SPIRAL

helicoid ...... COILED, SPIRAL

Helicon ..... MOUNTAIN, TUBA

dweller .... MUSE

helicopter: colloq. ....
WHIRLYBIRD, GIRO, CHOPPER

kin .... AUTOGIRO, GYROPLANE

Heliopolis ...... BAALBEK, ON

Helios ...... APOLLO, SUN GOD, HYPERION

daughter of .... CIRCE

father of ...... HYPERION

sister of .... ARTEMIS

heliotrope ...... BLOODSTONE, (SUN)FLOWER, TURNSOLE

helix .. SPIRAL, MOLLUSK, SNAIL

hell .. HADES, SHEOL, ABADDON, TARTARUS, ABYSS, PIT, INFERNO, GEHENNA, AVERNUS, TOPHET(H)

border of ...... LIMBO

capital of .. PANDEMONIUM

diver .... DABCHICK

euphemism for.... HECK

in New Testament..........
GEHENNA

Hellas .... GREECE

hellbender ... SPREE, DEBAUCH, SALAMANDER

hellbent ..... DETERMINED, SET, RESOLVED

hellcat ...... VIRAGO, SHREW, WITCH, VIXEN

Hellene .... GREEK

Hellenism .... GRECISM

Hellespont ..... DARDANELLES

nightly swimmer ....
LEANDER

victim .... LEANDER

hellhound .... CERBERUS, FIEND

hellish .... FIENDISH, STYGIAN, INFERNAL

helm ... RUDDER, WHEEL, STEER, TILLER

Helmer, Mrs. .... NORA

helmet .. HAT, ARMET, SALLET, BAS(I)NET, CASQUE, MORION, BURGONET, SCONCE, HEAUME

crested, hatlike .. MORION

decoration ..... PANACHE

eye cover .... VISOR

faceguard .... VISOR

front .... VENTAIL

lower part ...... BEAVER

nosepiece .... NASAL

opening .... VUE

part ...... BEAVER, VISOR

pith ..... TOPI, TOPEE

plume .... PANACHE

Roman .... GALEA

shaped .... GALEATE

shaped part ...... GALEA

visored .... ARMET

helminth .... (TAPE)WORM, (ROUND)WORM, PARASITE
helmsman ... TILLER, CONNER, PILOT, STEERSMAN, COX(ON), COXSWAIN
Heloise, husband of .. ABELARD
helot .... SERF, ESNE, SLAVE
help .. ASSIST, WAIT ON, HAND, SERVANT, EMPLOYEES, STAFF, SUCCO(U)R, AID, SECOND, ABET
   me signal .. SOS, MAYDAY
   of any kind .... LIFT
   over .... TIDE
helpless .... WEAK, FEEBLE, SPINELESS, IMPOTENT, LOST
helpmate .... WIFE, HUSBAND, SPOUSE
Helsingfors ... ... HELSINKI
Helsingor .... ELSINORE
helter-skelter ...... HURRIED, DISORDERLY
helve .... HANDLE, HAFT, ANSE, HILT
Helvetia ...... SWITZERLAND
hem .. BORDER, MARGIN, EDGE, SEW, SHUT, ENCIRCLE
   and haw .. HEDGE, FALTER
   in .. FENCE, CROWD, BESET, INVEST
   stiffening cloth ... WIGAN
hematin .... HEME
hematite .. LIMONITE, IRON ORE
hematoma .... TUMOR
heme .... HEMATIN
Hemingway, author ... ERNEST
   character ... PILAR, BRETT
   soubriquet .... PAPA
hemiplegia .... PARALYSIS
hemipterous insect ... BEDBUG, LICK, APHID
hemlock .. YEW, WEED, POISON, VALERIAN, CONIUM
   alkaloid .... CONIN(E)
   poison .... BENNET
hemoglobin product .... BILIRUBIN
hemophiliac .... BLEEDER
hemorrhage .... BLEEDING
hemorrhoid .... PILES, TUMOR
hemostatic .... STYPTIC
hemp ...... PITA, TOW, FIBER, PLANT, RAMIE, IFE, RINE, HASHISH
   African .... IFE

cleaning tool .. SWINGLE, HATCHEL
cloth .. CANVAS, SACKING
dampen .... RET
drug .... HASHISH
E. Indies .... SUNN
fabric ... BURLAP, GUNNY
fiber .. TOW, AGAVE, SISAL
fiber from ropes .. OAKUM
filament .... HARL
Greek .... KANNABIS
Indian .. B(H)ANG, K(I)EF, RAMIE, DAGGA
leaves .. KEF, KIEF, BHANG
Manila .... ABACA
narcotic .... HASHISH, CHARAS, MARIJUANA
plant .. MARIJUANA, SUNN
refuse ..... TOW, HURDS, HARDS
resin ... CHARAS, HASHISH
sisal .... HENEQUEN, HENEQUIN
shrub .... PUA
soak .... RET
source .... CANNABIS
hempen cloth .... HESSIAN
hen ...... CHICKEN, CACKLER, LAYER, PULLET
   brooding .... SITTER
   chickens of ...... BROOD
   cry of .. SQUAWK, CACKLE
   extinct .... HEATH
   hawk .... REDTAIL
   mud .... RAIL
   roost .... PERCH
   slang .... WOMAN
   sound .. CACKLE, CLUCK, CHUCK(LE), SQUAWK
   spayed .... POULARD
   young .... POULARD, CHICKEN
henbane .... NIGHTSHADE, HYOSCYAMUS
henbit .... PLANT, MINT
hence .... THUS, ERGO, AWAY, THEREFORE, OFF, THEN, SO
henchman .... ADHERENT, SQUIRE, ATTENDANT, FOLLOWER, HANGER-ON, PAGE
henequen ...... FIBER, AGAVE, (SISAL)HEMP
Hengist's brother ..... HORSA
   kingdom .... KENT
henhouse .... COOP

henna ... ALCANA, DYE, SHRUB
henpeck ...... NAG, DOMINEER
Henrietta, diminutive of ......
    ETTA, NETTY, NETTIE, HETTY
Henry, diminutive of ... HAL,
    HENNY, HANK
    IV's family ... LANCASTER
    Kaiser .... NOAH
    VIII's wife ..... ARAGON,
    BOLEYN, SEYMOUR,
    CLEVES, HOWARD,
    PARR
hent .... GRASP(ING), PURPOSE,
    APPREHEND, CONCEPTION
hep: sl. .... ON TO, INFORMED,
    FAMILIAR, CONVERSANT,
    AWARE
hepatic(a) ...... LIVERWORT,
    LIVER-SHAPED
hepcat ...... (SWING)DANCER,
    HIPSTER, BEATNIK
    cry of .... SOLID
Hephaestus .... VULCAN
heptachord .... LYRE
Hera, husband of ...... ZEUS,
    JUPITER
    mother of .... RHEA
    of Romans .... JUNO
    rival of .. LETO, IO, LEDA,
    EUROPA, THEMIS
    son of .... ARES
Herakleion .... CANDIA
Herakles .... HERCULES
herald .... MESSENGER, CRIER,
    FORERUNNER, HARBINGER,
    USHER, PROCLAIM, BLAZON,
    ANNOUNCE(R), FORETELL
    coat of .... TABARD
    god ... HERMES, MERCURY
    morning .... COCK, LARK
    of good news ... GABRIEL
    staff of ...... CADUCEUS
heraldic ...... ARMORIAL, BAY
    band ...... FESS(E), ORLE,
    TRESSURE, FILLET
    bearing ... FESS(E), ORLE,
    GIRON, GYRON, ENTE,
    BEND, SALTIRE, PHEON,
    LAVER
    cross ...... PATTE, PATEE
    design .... SEME
    device .... CREST
    fillet .... ORLE
    mastiff .... ALAN
    shield border ...... ORLE,
    BORDURE

shield boss .... UMBO
shield division ..... ENTE,
    CANTON
shield horizontal band ...
    FESS
shield side segments .....
    FLANCH
shield stripe .... PALE
star .... ESTOILE
term .... PATTE, SEME
triangle .... GIRON
wreath ..... TORSE, ORLE
heraldry ...... ENTE, ARMORY
    animal partly visible ....
    ISSUANT
    bar, horizontal .... LABEL
    bastardy mark .... BATON
    bear .... GRISE
    bearing ... ORLE, SALTIRE,
    TRESSURE
    bend .... COTISE
    bird .... MARTLET
    black tincture ..... SABLE
    blood-red ...... MURREY
    blue .... AZURE
    chaplet .... ORLE
    checkered .... VAIR
    cherub .... SERAPH
    circle .. ANNULET, BEZANT
    colter .... LAVER
    creature ..... LION, BISSE,
    CANNET, GRIFFON,
    PARD, MARTLET,
    WYVERN, WYVER
    crest .... MARTLET
    cross ... SALTIRE, SALTIER,
    CRUX
    diamond-shaped figure ..
    MASCLE
    division ...... PALE, PALY
    dog .... ALAN(T)
    duck .... CANNET(TE)
    face-to-face ... AFFRONTE
    fillet .... ORLE
    flower strewn ...... SEME
    flying in air .... FLOTANT
    footless bird .... MARTLET
    foreleg of beast ... GAMB
    fur tincture .... PEAN,
    VAIR(E)
    grafted .... ENTE
    green tincture ..... VERT
    headless .... ETETE
    horizontal band .... FESS,
    FILLET
    iris .... LIS

laver .... COLTER
leaves, having .... POINTE
left side .... SINISTER
line .. UNDE, URDY, UNDY,
     NEBULY, DEXTER,
     SINISTER
lozenge ... MASCLE, FUSIL
manacle .... TIRRET
orange tincture ... TENNE
ornament of headpiece ..
     CREST
pointed .... URDE
position of animal ......
     GARDANT, SEJANT,
     PASSANT
purple tincture ....
     PURPURE
red tincture ...... GULES
row of squares ....
     COMPONY
running .... COURANT
sheaf of grain ... GERB(E)
shield .... PAVIS
shield bar .... GEMEL
shield-shaped ... PELTATE
shield's center ...... FESS
shield's corner .. CANTON
silver .... ARGENT
sitting ..... SEJANT, ASSIS
sleeping position ....
     DORMANT
snake .... BISSE
spangled .... SEME
standing .... STATANT
strewn .... SEME
subject of .. COAT OF ARMS,
     ARMORY, GENEALOGY
triangle ... GYRON, GIRON
two-winged .... VOL
vertical division .... PALY
voided escutcheon .. ORLE
walking .... PASSING
wavy .... ONDE, UNDE(E),
     NEBULE
winged .... AILE, VOL
wreath ..... ORLE, TORSE
herb .... SAGE, GRASS, CATNIP,
RUE, MOLY, WORT, RUTA,
GALAX, CARAWAY, OREGANO,
THYME, SEDGE, PARSLEY,
PARSNIP, SEDUM, CHERVIL,
QUINOA, TARRAGON,
YARROW, CLINTONIA
aromatic .. GINGER, MINT,
GINSENG, BERGAMOT,
ROSEMARY, ANISE, DILL,

ANET, BASIL, DITTANY,
     FLEAWORT
aromatic root .... NONDO
aster family ..... ARNICA
bean family .. PEA, LOTUS
bennet .... AVENS
bitter .. ALOE, RUE, TANSY,
     GENTIAN
bulbous .... GARLIC
carrot family ... LOVAGE,
     PARSLEY, ERINGO,
     ERYNGO, FENNEL, DILL
chicory family ... ENDIVE
cloverlike .... MEDIC,
     LUCERNE
coarse ..... ELECAMPANE,
     IVA, ERYNGO
concoction ...... TISANE
crowfoot family ....
     CLEMATIS, COHOSH
decoction .... PTISAN,
     TISANE
dill .... ANET
eve .... IVA
evergreen .... GALAX
fabulous .. MOLY, PANACE
flowering ...... HEPATICA
forage .... SULLA
fragrant .... BALM
genus ...... RUTA, GEUM,
     ALETRIS
ginger .... ALPINIA,
     CARDAMOM, CARDAMUM
goose foot family .. BLITE
gourd family .... MELON,
     SQUASH
Himalayan .... ATIS
laxative .... SENNA
lily family .... COLICROOT
magic .... MOLY
medicinal ..... ALOE, RUE,
     BONESET, TANSY, FENNEL
mint family ...... BALM,
     CATNIP, BASIL, HYSSOP
mustard family .... CRESS
mythical .... MOLY
nettle family ...... HEMP
nightshade .... HENBANE,
     TOMATO
of grace .... RUE
onion .... CHIVE
parsley family .... CICELY
pea family ...... MIMOSA,
     CASSIA, LOTUS, LOTOS,
     FENUGREEK
perennial ... SEDUM, SEGO

pink family .... CAMPION
pod .... OKRA, OCRA
purslane family ....
    CLAYTONIA
root .... GINSENG, CHOY,
    CHAY, NONDO
scented .... CATNIP
seasoning ...... PARSLEY,
    SAGE, THYME, BASIL
snake charm .... MUNGO
spinach-like ..... ORACHE
starch yielding ...... PIA
strong smelling ....
    YARROW, RUE
symbol of grief ..... RUE
tonic .. .. BONESET,
    CORIANDER
tropical .... GINSENG,
    GINGER, LOOFA
use of ... MEDICINE, FOOD,
    SEASONING
with aromatic seeds .....
    ANISE
with stinging hairs ......
    NETTLE
woolly .... POLY
herbage .... GRASS
herbivore .. VEGETARIAN, TAPIR
Hercules .... HERAKLES,
    STRONG MAN, ALCIDES,
    CONSTELLATION
captive .... IOLE
monster slain by .. HYDRA
parent of ...... ALCMENE,
    ZEUS
queen served by ....
    OMPHALE
tutor .... CHIRON
victim of .... NESSUS
wife of ... HEBE, DEIANIRA
woman saved by ....
    HESIONE
herd .. CROWD, PUBLIC, FLOCK,
    SHOAL, DROVE, RABBLE,
    POD, CORRAL
animals together .... POD
of horses .... CAVIYA,
    HARRAS
of whales ..... GAM, POD
herd's grass .... REDTOP,
    TIMOTHY
herds, living in ... GREGARIOUS
herdsman .... VAQUERO,
    SHEPHERD, COWBOY,
    RANCHERO, GAUCHO,
    DROVER

constellation ..... BOOTES
stick of .... GOAD
here .... ICI, HITHER, NOW,
    EXCLAMATION, PRESENT
and ____ ... NOW, THERE
and there .... ABOUT
lies: inscription ....
    HIC JACET
opposed to .... THERE
hereafter .... FUTURE
heredes .... HEIRS
singular of .... HERES
hereditary .... ANCESTRAL,
    LINEAL, INNATE, GENETIC
factor .... GENE
right .... UDAL
ruler .... DYNAST
heredity .... GEN(E), GENETICS
theoretician on .. MENDEL
Hereford .... CATTLE
heres .... HEIR
plural of .... HEREDES
heresy .... HERETODOXY
heretic ..... DISSENTER, ARIUS
garment of ... SANBENITO
public burning of ....
    AUTODAFE
heretofore .... ERENOW
heritable land .... ODAL
heritage .... PATRIMONY, LOT,
    LEGACY, BIRTHRIGHT,
    ISRAELITES
heritor .... HEIR
herl .... FLY, BARB
herma ... MILESTONE, SIGNPOST
hermaphroditic ... EFFEMINATE
hermaphroditism .. GYNANDRY
hermeneutic .... INTERPRETIVE
Hermes ...... GOD, MERCURY,
    HERALD, MESSENGER
footwear .... TALARIA
gift to Odysseus ... MOLY
hat, winged .... PETASOS,
    PETASUS
parent of .... MAIA, ZEUS
son of .... PAN
staff of .... CADUCEUS
hermetic .. MAGICAL, AIRTIGHT,
    ALCHEMICAL, SEALED
Hermione's brother ... DORUS
husband .... ORESTES
parent .... HELEN,
    MENELAUS
hermit .. ANCHORITE, EREMITE,
    RECLUSE, TROGLODYTE,
    SOLITAIRE, ASCETIC, SANTON,

ANCHORET, MARABOUT,
COOKY, HUMMINGBIRD,
CRAB, THRUSH
crab .. PAGURIAN, PAGURID
hermitage .... RETREAT, WINE,
CLOISTER, MONASTERY
Russia's .... MUSEUM
hermitic .. SECLUDED, SOLITARY
hern .... HERON
hernia ..... RUPTURE, BREACH,
CYSTOCELE
support .... TRUSS
Hero ... IDOL, STAR, DEMIGOD,
PALADIN, DEFENDER,
CHAMPION, PRIESTESS, LION,
PROTAGONIST
animal .... AKELA,
RIN TIN TIN
Crusades ..... TANCRED
Filipino ... RIZAL, MABINI
legendary ..... TRISTRAM,
TRISTAN, AMADIS,
PALADIN, LEONIDAS,
(EL)CID
lover of .... LEANDER
of old .... KNIGHT
opposed to ..... VILLAIN
Persian .... RUSTUM
Spartan .... LEONIDAS
Herodias' daughter ... SALOME
husband .... ANTIPAS
heroic .... BOLD, BRAVE,
VALIANT, GALLANT,
SPARTAN, EXALTED, DARING,
EPIC(AL)
events .... EPOS
narrative .. SAGA, ODYSSEY
poem ...... EPIC, EPOPEE,
EPOS, ILIAD
verse ...... ALEXANDRINE
heroics .... CLAPTRAP
heroin ...... NARCOTIC, HORSE
addict .... SNOWBIRD
slang ...... SNOW, SMACK
heroine .... JOAN OF ARC
heron .... BITTERN, RAIL, SOCO,
AIGRET(TE), EGRET, HERN,
CRANE, BOATBILL, SHOEBILL
brood .... EDGE
green .... POKE
kin .... HAMMERHEAD
night ..... QUA, SQUAWK
herpes .. SHINGLES, COLD SORE,
TETTER
designating one .. ZOSTER,
LABIALIS

herpetology subject ... REPTILE
herring ..... SPRAT, PILCHARD,
CISCO, BLUEFIN, ANCHOVY,
PILCHER, SARDINE
canned .... SARDINE
cured .... BLOATER
keg .... CADE
kin .... SHAD
lake ...... MELBA, CISCO
like fish .... SPRAT, SHAD,
ANCHOVY, ALEWIFE,
CISCO
measure .... CRAN
pertaining to .. CLUPEOID
pond .... OCEAN
red .... BAIT
sauce .... ALEC
slang .... ALEWIFE
that recently spawned ...
SHOTTEN
tub .... CADE
young .. SMELT, SPARLING,
BRIT
Herriot, premier .... EDOUARD
Herschel's discovery .. URANUS
herse .... PORTCULLIS
Hersey novel town .... ADANO
hesitant .... RELUCTANT,
WAVERING, VACILLATING,
TIMID, UNCERTAIN, CHARY
hesitate ... WAVER, VACILLATE,
FALTER, HAW, HEM, PAUSE,
DEMUR, TEETER
in speaking .... STUTTER,
STAMMER, HEM
hesitation .... INDECISION,
RELUCTANCE
sound of ...... ER, UM
Hesperia .. BUTTERFLY, ITALY,
SPAIN, WESTERN LAND
Hesperian .... WESTERN,
OCCIDENTAL
Hesperides .... AEGLE, HESTIA,
NYMPHS, GARDEN
treasure ....
(GOLDEN) APPLES
Hesperus ..... (EVENING) STAR,
VENUS
fate of .... WRECK
parent .... EOS, ASTRAEUS
Hess, a Nazi .... RUDOLF
pianist .... MYRA
Hessian .... MERCENARY,
GERMAN
hessite .... TELLURIDE

hest .... ORDER, PLEDGE, BID(DING)
Hestia ...... VESTA, GODDESS, NYMPH
  parent of .. RHEA, CRONUS
Hesychast .... MYSTIC
het up: sl. .... EXCITED, AGOG
hetaera ... COURTESAN, SLAVE, CONCUBINE, THAIS
hetaerism ...... CONCUBINAGE
hetero: comb. form ....
  (AN)OTHER, DIFFERENT
  opposed to .... HOMO
heterodox .... HERETICAL
  opposed to ..... ORTHODOX
heterogeneous ..... FOREIGN, VARIED, DISSIMILAR, MOTLEY
heterogynous insect .. ANT, BEE
hetman .... ATAMAN, COSSACK, COMMANDER, CHIEF
hew ... CHOP, CUT, HACK, AX, GASH
hex .... (BE)WITCH, JINX, SORCERER, HOODOO
hexad ..... SESTET, SEXTET(TE)
Hexham's river .... TYNE
hexapod .... SIX-FOOTED
hexapody .... HEXAMETER
hexastich ...... STANZA, POEM
hexose .... SUGAR
heyday .... PRIME, MAY
hiatus .. GAP, LACUNA, BREAK, PAUSE, COL, OPENING
Hiawatha's bark ...... CANOE
hibachi .... GRILL, BRAZIER
hibernal .... WINTRY, HIEMAL, BRUMAL
hibernate .... SHACK, WINTER, SLEEP
  opposed to .. GESTIVATE
hibernating animal ..... BEAR, WOODCHUCK, LEMMING
Hibernia ...... ERIN, IRELAND
hibiscus .. PLANT, SHRUB, TREE, MALLOW, GUMAMELA
hic jacet .. HERE LIES, EPITAPH, INSCRIPTION
hick .... RUSTIC, HAYSEED
hickey ...... GADGET, DEVICE
hickory .. PECAN, WOOD, CANE, SWITCH, TREE, (WAL)NUT
  fruit .... PIGNUT
  nut ...... PECAN, TRYMA
  tree .... SHAGBARK, SHELLBARK
  wattle .... ACACIA

hidalgo .... NOBLEMAN
  state capital ... PACHUCA
hidden ...... LATENT, COVERT, INNATE, ARCANE, CRYPTIC, OBSCURE, SECRET, INNER, PERDU
  provision .. JOKER, RIDER
hide ...... SECRETE, CONCEAL, COVER, BURY, FLOG, PELT, SKIN, THRASH, VEIL, MASK, FELL, CLOAK, STOW, SCREEN
  behind words .... HEDGE
  calf/lamb .... KIP
  for safekeeping ... CACHE
  raw ...... KIP, SHAGREEN
  softening solution .. BATE
hideaway .. LAIR, DEN, RETREAT
hideous ..... SCABROUS, UGLY, GRUESOME, REVOLTING, AWFUL, GRIM, REPULSIVE
  monster .... MEDUSA, GORGON
hideout ... LAIR, DEN, RETREAT
hiding, in .... PERDU
hidrosis .... SWEATING, PERSPIRATION
hidrotic .... SUDORIFIC
hie .... HASTEN, HURRY, SPEED
hiemal .... WINTRY, HIBERNAL, BRUMAL
hierarch .... HIGH PRIEST
hierarchy .... ANGELS
hieratic .... PRIESTLY, SACERDOTAL
hiero: comb. form .... SACRED, HOLY
hieroglyph ...... PICTOGRAPH
hieroglyphic ..... EMBLEMATIC, SYMBOLICAL
hieroglyphics, pillar with ..... OBELISK
hierophant .... HIGH PRIEST
higgle .... CHAFFER, WRANGLE, BARGAIN
higgledy-piggledy .. DISORDER, JUMBLE
high .... TOWERING, LOFTY, TALL, SUPERIOR, EXPENSIVE, SHRILL, DRUNK, ALT, DEAR, ALOFT
  abode ...... AERIE, AYRIE
  and dry ...... STRANDED
  and low .... EVERYWHERE
  and mighty ... HAUGHTY, ARROGANT

and piping ...... TREBLE

blood pressure ....
HYPERTENSION

brow ..... INTELLECTUAL,
CULTURED, CULTIVATED,
CIVILIZED

class .... QUALITY, TONY,
PLUSH, RITZY, SUPERIOR

colloquial .... STIFF

colored .... VIVID, LURID,
FLORID

combining form .... ALTI

crime .... TREASON

explosive .... TNT

flown .... EUPHUISM,
BOMBASTIC

hat .... SNOB(BISH), SNUB,
STYLISH, STOVEPIPE,
SNOOTY

hole .... FLICKER,
WOODPECKER

jinks ... PRANKS, CAPERS,
REVELRY, MERRIMENT

Mass celebrant .. DEACON

pitched ... SHRILL, TREBLE

priest .... ELI, AARON,
ANNAS, HIERARCH,
PONTIFF, HIEROPHANT

sign .... SIGNAL, CUE

society .... HAUTE MONDE

sounding ..... SONOROUS

spirited .... FIERY, PROUD

strung .... EXCITABLE,
TENSE, SENSITIVE,
NERVOUS

tail .... SCURRY, RUSH

time ..... NONE TOO SOON

toned .. STYLISH, MODISH,
LUXURIOUS, LOFTY,
QUALITY

waters .... FLOOD

wind .... GALE

highball ...... DRINK, STINGER

highbinder .... GANGSTER,
HOODLUM, RUFFIAN

highboy ...... BUREAU, CHEST

highbrow .... LONGHAIR,
INTELLECTUAL

highest ...... SUPREME, SUMMA

combining form ... ACRO

heaven .... EMPYREAN

mountain .... EVEREST

note, in music ...... ELA

number of die ...... SISE

point ..... FINIAL, NOON,
APOGEE, PEAK, CLIMAX,
APEX, ZENITH, VERTEX,
PINNACLE

possible .... MAXIMAL,
MAXIMUM

highfalutin ..... HIGH-FLOWN,
POMPOUS, PRETENTIOUS,
FLIGHTY

highhanded .... OVERBEARING,
ARBITRARY

highland rock ... MONADNOCK

highlander ..... TARTAN, SCOT,
GAEL, PLAIDMAN

breeches .... TREWS

pouch .... SPORRAN

sword of ..... CLAYMORE

wear of .... KILT

Highlands robber ... CATERAN

highly ...... EXTREMELY, VERY

colored .. FLORID, LURID,
VIVID

decorated .... GAUDY

wrought ...... D(A)EDAL

highway ...... ROAD, AVENUE,
THOROUGHFARE, ITER,
FREEWAY, (TURN)PIKE

Alaska–Canada .. ALCAN

German ...... AUTOBAHN

pest .... ROADHOG

Roman ..... ITER, AVIAN

highwayman .. PAD, BRIGAND,
HIJACKER, LADRONE

Hiiumaa .... DAGO

hijack(er) ...... HOLDUP(PER)

hike ... WALK, TRAMP, MARCH,
RAISE, BOOST

hiker's bag ..... HAVERSACK,
KNAPSACK

hilarious .... GAY, MERRY

hilarity .. GAIETY, MIRTH, GLEE,
MERRIMENT

hilding .... WRETCH

hill ... MOUND, PILE, BARROW,
BUTTE, DJEBEL, FELL,
CUESTA, KOP(JE), MOUNT,
MONTICULE, HEAP

builder .... ANT

cone-shaped .... BRAE

dugout .... ABRI

flat-topped .... MESA

fortified .... MERLIN

glacial .... KAME

go over the .... DIE

in a plain .... BUTTE

isolated .... INCH

of glacial drift .. DRUMLIN

pointed .... TOR

Rome .... PALATINE, AVENTINE
rounded .. MORRO, KNOB, HUMMOCK
sand .... DENE, DUNE
signal .... BEACON
small .... MOUND, DOWN, HILLOCK, DUNE
South African ..... KOP, BULT
top ... TOR, KNAP, CREST, COP, BROW
U.S. ...... LOMA, LOMITA
wood .... HOLT
Hillary's conquest ... EVEREST
other work .. APICULTURE
hillbilly ..... BACKWOODSMAN, RUSTIC
food .... TATERS
hillock .. MOUND, TOFT, TUMP, KNOLL, KOPJE
hills, land between ....
INTERVALE
range of .... SIERRA
hillside .... BRAE, SLOPE
hollow ... CORRIE, SLACK
rubble .... SCREE
hilltop .... KNAP, TOR
hilt .... HAFT, HANDLE, HELVE
wooden .... DUDGEON
Himalayan animal .... OUNCE, PANDA
antelope .. GORAL, SEROW
bearcat .... PANDA
broadmouth ...... RAYA
capital ...... GANGTOK, KATMANDU
cedar .... DEODAR
country ... SIKKIM, NEPAL
forest .... BHABAR
goat .. KYL, GORAL, TAHR, KRAS, TAIR
grassland .... TARAI
herb .... ATIS
marmot .... PIA
massif ...... ANNAPURNA
monkshood .... ATIS
mountains, personification of .... HIMAVAT
Mts. state ...... BHUTAN
peak .... NEPAL, EVEREST, MASHARBRUM, HUMP, API
river .... INDUS
sheep .... NAHOOR
tea .... AUCUBA

tree ...... DEODAR, TOON
walnut .... CORYLUS
wild goat .... KYL, THAR, TAHR, TAIR, KRAS
Himalayas: sl. ... (THE) HUMP
himself: Lat. .... IPSE
hind .. BACK, POSTERIOR, REAR, DEER, ROE, PEASANT, TAIL, RUSTIC
brain .... CEREBELLUM
leg of animal ...... HAM
red .... CABRILLA
hinder .... IMPEDE, BLOCK, OBSTRUCT, PREVENT, DETER, DELAY, EMBAR, HAMPER, RETARD, CUMBER
hindmost .... LAST
hindquarter .... HAUNCH
hindrance .... RUB, CLOG, LET, OBSTACLE, IMPEDIMENT, HITCH, BAR
Hindu .. GENTOO, JAIN(A), SER, KOLI, TAMIL, SIKH, BABU, BANA
acrobat .... NAT
age of the world ... YUGA
ancestor .... MANU
Anglicized .... BABU
ascetic .. YATI, YOGI, JOGI, FAKIR, SADHU, MUNI
avatar .... RAMA
bandit .... DACOIT
banker .... SOWCAR, SOUCAR
barber .... NAPIT
bear .... BHALU
beggar .... NAGA
betelnut .... SUPARI
bible .... VEDA
boat .... YARAHA
brook .... NALA
bulbul .... KALA
butter .... GHI
call to prayer ..... AZAN
caste .. PASI, SUDRA, TELI, JAT, MAL, KORI, RAJPUT
caste, military ....
KSHATRIYA
caste, priestly .. BRAHMAN
cavalry .... RISALA
charitable gift ..... ENAM
city .... ABAD
city, holy ...... BENARES
congregation ..... SAMAJ
cottage .... BARI
court officer ..... AMALA

cremation of a widow ... SATI
cultured .... BRAHMIN
cultured person ....
    BRAHMAN
cymbal .... TAL, DAL
dance drama ...... RASA
dancing girl .. BAYADERE,
    BAYADEER
deity .... KRISHNA, DEVA,
    UMA, KAMA, VARUNA,
    AGNI, DEWA, VAYU,
    YAMA, BHAGA, SIVA,
    VISHNU, MANU, RAMA,
    AKAL
demon ..... ASURA, RAHU
destiny .... KARMA
Devi .... MAYA
Devi's father ... HIMAVAT
disciple .... SIKH
divorce law ...... TALAK
drinking pot ...... LOTA
ejaculation .... OM
epic .... RAMAYAMA
epic hero .... ARJUNA
essence .... AMRITA
exchange rate ..... BATTA
evil spirit .. ASURA, MARA
fair .... MELA
fate .... KARMA
female slave .... DASI
festival ... PUJA, DEWALI,
    HOLI
flying beings .... GARUDAS
gardener .... MALI
garment .... DHOTI, SARI,
    SAREE
gentleman .. BABOO, BABU
giant: myth. .... BANA
gnome .... YAKSHA
god .. DEVI, BRAHMA, SIVA,
    AKAL, INDRA, KA,
    JAGANNATH
    cosmos ...... VARUNA
    elephant-headed ......
        GANESHA
    fire .... AGNI
    heaven .... DYAUS
    love ... KAMA, BHAGA
    nature .... DEVA
    rain .... INDRA
    sky .... DYAUS
    supreme .. SIVA, VISHNU
    trinity ..... TRIMURTI,
        BRAHMA, SIVA,
        VISHNU

underworld ..... YAMA
goddess ...... UMA, VAC,
    USHAS, MAYA, SAKTI,
    LAKSHMI
    beauty/luck .... SHREE,
        S(H)RI
    dawn .... US(H)AS
    destruction/evil .. KALI
    mothers .... MATRIS
    speech .... VAC(H)
    splendor .... UMA
    wealth .... SRI
gods' abode .... MERU
groom .... SYCE
guitar .. SITAR, VINA, BINA
gypsy ...... KARACHEE
handkerchief ... MALABAR
hell .... NARAKA
hero ..... RAMA, NALA,
    ARJUNA
holy book .. SASTRA, VEDA
holy city .... BENARES
holy destination ......
    HARDWAR, VARANASI
holy man ..... SADH(U)
idol .... SWAMI
illusion .... MAYA
immortality .... AMRITA
incarnation .... AVATAR
kingdom, last .... NEPAL
kismet .... KARMA
kneeling rug ...... ASAN
land grant .. INAM, ENAM,
    SASAN
language ..... SANSKRIT
lawgiver .... MANU
leader ... GANDHI, SIRDAR
loincloth ...... DHO(O)TI
lord .... SWAMI
low-caste .... MAL, KORI
magic .... MAYA
margosa .... NEEM
master .. SAHIB, SWAMI,
    SWAMY, MIAN
Maya ..... SAKTI, DEVI
meal .... ATA
measure .... KOS, RYOTS
mendicant ...... NAGA
merchant .... BANIAN
military caste .... RAJPUT
monastic philosophy ....
    VEDANTA
money .... ANNA
month ...... SA(RA)WAN,
    ASIN, BAISAKH, JETH,
    KUAR, KA(R)TIK,

AGHAN, MAGH, CHAIT, PHA(L)GUN
mountain . . . . MERU
mountain pass . . . GHAUT
mountaineer . . . . BHIL
musical instrument . . . . . SITAR, VINA, SAROD
mystic word . . . . OM
Nobel Prize winner . . . . . TAGORE
noble . . . . RAJAH
nursemaid . . . . AYAH
patriarch . . . . PITRI
peasant . . . . RYOT
philosophy . . . . YOGA, SANKHYA, VEDANTA
pillar . . . . LAT
poet . . TAGORE, KALIDASA
police station . . . . THANA
policeman . . . . SEPOY
pot . . . . LOTA
prayer carpet/rug . . ASAN
priestly caste . . BRAHMAN
prince . . . . MAHARAJA, RAJA(H), RANA
princess . . . . . MAHARANI, RANEE, RANI
private apartment . . . . . . MAHAL
puce . . . . UDA
pundit . . . . SWAMI
queen . . . . . . RANEE, RANI
ravine . . . . NALA
religious book . . . SASTRA
religious creed . . . JAINISM
religious observances . . . DHARMA
religious devotee . . MUND
religious sect . . . . SIKHISM
religious teacher . . . . PIR, SWAMI, GURU
rites . . . . ACHAR
rug for prayer . . . . . ASAN
ruling caste . . . . . RAJPUT
sacred literature . . . VEDA
sacred river . . . . . GANGA, GANGES
sacred tree . . . . PIPAL, BO
sacred word . . . . OM
sage . . . . GAUTAMA, MAHATMA
Sakti . . . . MAYA
Sanskrit school . . . . . TOL
savant . . . . PANDIT
scarf . . . . SAREE
school of philosophy . . . .

MIMANSA, VEDANTA
scripture . . . . AGAMA, TANTRA, SASTRA
seclusion of women . . . . . PURDAH
sect . . . . JAINA
sect member . . SIKH, SEIK, SADH
serpent . . . . NAGA
servant . . . . CELA
social class . . . . CASTE
soldier . . . . SEPOY
sorceress . . . . USHA
soul . . . . ATMA(N)
spirit . . . . MARA
summer house . . . MAHAL
supreme deity . . . VARUNA
swan . . . . HANSA
teacher . . . MULLA(H), PIR, GURU
temple . . . . DEUL
temple tower . . . . SIKHRA
timber tree . . . . DAR
title . . . . MIR, SIDI, SRI, RAJA(H), NAIK, SAHIB, RAO
title for European . . . . . . SAHIB
title of respect . . . SWAMI, SWAMY, SAHIB, MIAN, BAHADUR
trader . . BANIAN, BANYAN
tree . . . . DAR
trinity . . . . BRAHMA, SIVA, TRIMURTI, VISHNU
turban . . . . PAGRI
turban cloth . . . . . LUNGI, LUNGEE
underworld king . . . YAMA
veranda . . . . PYAL
water nymph . . . . . . APAS
weaver . . . . TANTI
weight . . . . TAEL, MAUND, SER, TOLA
widow . . . . . SATI, SUTTEE
woman personified . . . . . . MAYA
woman's dress . . . . SAREE, SARI
writings . . . . VEDA
Hinduism . . . . ANIMISM
cosmic principle . . KARMA
ego . . . . . ATMAN, JIVATMA
elixir . . AMRITA, AMREETA
fate . . . . KARMA
pilgrim's city . . VARANASI

sacred literature .. .. VEDA
universal soul .... ATMAN
Hindustan hillman ..... TODA
magic .... JADU
Mogul emperor .. AKBAR,
AURANGZEB
state .... PUNJAB
Hindustani ...... HINDI, URDU
hinge ..... JOINT, AXIS, PIVOT,
KNEE, ELBOW, DEPEND,
GIMMER
type of .... BUTT, SPRING,
STRAP
hinny .. MULE, WHINNY, NEIGH
parent of .... HORSE,
DONKEY
hint ... INTIMATION, INTIMATE,
SUGGEST, ALLUDE, CUE,
IMPLY, INKLING, POINTER,
INNUENDO, CLEW, CLUE,
ALLUSION, TIP(OFF)
kind of .... WINK, NUDGE
hinterland .... BOONDOCKS,
BACK COUNTRY, INLAND,
BACKWOODS
hip .... FRUIT, COXA, HUCKLE,
HAUNCH, ILIA
boots .... WADERS
bone .. ILIA, PELVIS, ILIUM
joint .... COXA
joint disease ... COXALGIA
pains .... SCIATICA
pertaining to the ....
SCIATIC, ILIAC
slang .. INFORMED, ON TO,
AWARE
width of: sl. .... BEAM
hipbone .... ILIUM
part of ... PUBIS, ISCHIUM
hippo: comb. form ..... HORSE
hippocampus .... SEA HORSE
hippocras ..... CORDIAL, WINE
Hippocrates' birthplace .. COS
Hippocratic ____, doctors' ....
OATH
hippodrome .... ARENA,
(RACING) COURSE
hippopotamus ..... BEHEMOTH,
PACHYDERM, SEACOW
hips supporter .... GIRDLE
width .... BEAM
hipster ..... HEPCAT, BEATNIK
hircine .... GOATLIKE
hire ... EMPLOY, ENGAGE, LET,
RENT, CHARTER, LEASE, FEE
hired assassin/killer ....

HIGHBINDER, BRAVO,
CUTTHROAT
hireling .... MERCENARY,
PENSIONARY
hirsute .... PILOSE, HAIRY,
SHAGGY, BRISTLY
Hispania .... SPAIN
former part of ....
PORTUGAL
Hispanic .... SPANISH
Hispaniola .... HAITI
hispid ..... STRIGOSE, SPINY,
HAIRY
hiss .... SIBILATE, SISS
sign of .... DISAPPROVAL,
HATRED
hisser .. ... GOOSE, SNAKE,
HECKLER
hissing ... SIBILANT, SIBILANCE,
FIZZY, FIZ(Z)
drink ...... SODA WATER,
CHAMPAGNE, FIZ(Z)
sound .. SIBILATION, PSST,
FIZZLE, SSH, SIZZLE,
WHIZ(Z), SWISH
hist .... SHUSH
histamine .... GASTRIN
histone ...... PROTEIN, GLOBIN
historian .... ANNALIST,
CHRONICLER, RECORDER
historical ..... FACTUAL, REAL,
AUTHENTIC
period .... ERA
records .... CHRONICLES,
ANNALS
history .... ANNALS, PAST,
RECORD, CHRONICLE, STORY,
NARRATIVE, TALE, ACCOUNT,
LORE, MEMOIRS
famous in ...... STORIED
Muse of .... CLIO
person's life .. BIOGRAPHY
histrionic .... THEATRICAL,
ARTIFICIAL, AFFECTED,
OVERACTING
histrionics .... DRAMATICS,
THEATRICALS, AFFECTATIONS
hit ... BOP, ACE, STRIKE, SMITE,
SOCK, CUFF, BIFF, KNOCK,
BUMP, SUCCESS, CLOUT,
SLUG, POMMEL
aloft .... LOB
baseball ... SINGLE, BUNT,
HOMERUN
colloquial .. WED, MARRY,
SUCCESS

direct .... BULL'S-EYE
hard .... SLUG, SLOG
lightly .... TAP
on the head .. CONK, BOP,
BEAN
or miss .... AIMLESS,
HAPHAZARD, RANDOM
sign .... SRO
hitch .... HOBBLE, LIMP, JERK,
HINDRANCE, FASTEN, TIE,
TUG, SNAG
hitchhike .... THUMB A RIDE
hitchpost .... PICKET
hither .... HERE, NEARER
hitherto .... UNTIL NOW,
TO NOW, HERETOFORE
Hitler's occupation ....
HOUSE PAINTER
rank .... CORPORAL
title ..... (DER)FU(E)HRER
wife .... (EVA) BRAUN
Hitlerite .... NAZI
Hittite .... SYRIAN
hive .. SWARM, BOX, GUM, SKEP,
APIARIA
hives .... URTICARIA
cement for .... PROPOLIS
characteristic of ... ITCH,
WHEAL
nettle .... UREDO
remedy for ... BENADRYL
"Hizzoner": sl. ...... MAYOR,
HIS HONOR
"HMS Pinafore" character ...
BUTTERCUP
ho! .... WHOA, HALT, STOP
hoactzin .... BIRD
hoar .... WHITE, GRAY
hoard ... AMASS, ACCUMULATE,
RESERVE, CACHE, STORE(UP),
SUPPLY
hoarder ...... MISER, SQUIRREL,
ANT, BEE
hoarding ... BILLBOARD, FENCE
time, usually .. SHORTAGE
hoarfrost .... RAG, RIME
hoarse ... HUSKY, GRATING,
RAUCOUS, GRUFF, THROATY,
ROUPY
hoarseness .... ROUP
hoary .. WHITE, GRAY, FROSTY,
OLD, CANESCENT, ANCIENT
hoatzin .... BIRD
hoax ..... BAM, HOCUS, SPOOF,
SHAM, GAFF, KID, CANARD,
TRICK, FRAUD, JOKE, RUSE

hob ..... RUSTIC, LOUT, PUCK,
ELF, GOBLIN, PEG
hobble .... LIMP, HAMPER,
HINDER, FETTER, ROPE, HITCH
hobbledehoy ..... YOUTH, BOY,
ADOLESCENT
hobby .... HORSE, AVOCATION,
PASTIME, FALCON, FAD
British colloquial ....
CUP OF TEA
of kings, alleged ....
PHILATELY
hobgoblin .... PUCK, BUGBEAR,
SPRITE, ELVE, ELF, BOG(E)Y,
IMP
hobnail .... RUSTIC
hobnob ... ASSOCIATE, MINGLE,
RUB ELBOWS, PAL
hobo ..... STIFF, VAGRANT, BO,
TRAMP
bundle/bedding of ......
BINDLE
camp .... JUNGLE
stew .... MULLIGAN
hobo's city hangout ....
SKID ROW
Hobson's choice .. TAKE-IT-OR-
LEAVE-IT
hock ...... HAM, HOX, PAWN,
JOINT, WINE
joint ailment ..... SPAVIN
of humans .... ANKLE
slang .... PAWN
hockey .... SHINNY
cup .... STANLEY
disk .... PUCK
field .... BANDY
goal .... CAGE
player .... GOALIE
stick .... CAMAN
hockshop .... PAWNSHOP
sign .... BALL
hocus .... DRUG, DUPE, HOAX,
FRAUD, CHEAT
pocus .... TRICK(ERY),
LEGERDEMAIN, GIBBERISH
hod .... TROUGH, SCUTTLE
hodgepodge .. STEW, POTTAGE,
HASH, FARRAGO, MESS,
CENTO, MEDLEY, MELANGE,
OLIO, MISHMASH
hoe .... TILL, HACK
hog .... PIG, SWINE, GRUNTER,
BABIRUSA, PORK(ER), GRAB
British dialect ..... SHEEP
cholera .... ROUGET

cured side .... FLITCH
deer .... AXIS
disease .... MEASLES
fat .... LARD, ADEPS
female .... SOW, GILT
food .... MAST
ground .... MARMOT
hind leg .... HAM
kind of .... ROAD
leg: sl. .. REVOLVER, COLT
like animal .... TAPIR
male .... BOAR
peanut .... EARTHPEA
plum ....AMRA
salted side .... FLITCH
thigh .... HAM
uncastrated .... BOAR
vital organ ...... HASLET
wild .... BOAR, PECCARY,
    DENE, BOSCHVARK,
    RAZORBACK
young .... GILT, SHOAT,
    SHOTE
hogback .... RIDGE
hogfish .... PORPOISE
hoggish ..... FILTHY, GREEDY
hognose .... SAND VIPER
hognut .... PIGNUT
hogs genus .... SUS
hogshead ...... BARREL, CASK
    content of .... BEER
hogtie .... TRUSS
hogwash .... SWILL, BALONEY,
    REFUSE
hoi polloi .... MASSES,
    COMMON PEOPLE
hoiden .... TOMBOY
hoist .... RAISE, PULL UP,
    ELEVATOR, TACKLE, REAR,
    JACK, HEAVE, LIFT, CAT,
    WINCH, BOUSE
    anchor .... WEIGH
hoisted just off bottom .. ATRIP
hoisting device .... CRANE,
    WINCH, WINDLASS, BOOM,
    FORKLIFT, DERRICK, SLING,
    DAVIT, PARBUCKLE, GIN,
    CAPSTAN, SHEER LEGS
hoity-toity ..... GIDDY, FUSSY,
    PETULANT, CAPRICIOUS,
    ARROGANT, PATRONIZING,
    SNOOTY, HUFFY
    person .... SNOB
hokeypokey ...... TRICK(ERY),
    ICECREAM, HOCUS-POCUS

Hokkaido, capital of ....
    SAPPORO, YEZO
    city .... OTARU
    native .... AINU
Hoko Gunto ..... PESCADORES
hokum ..... BUNK, NONSENSE,
    HUMBUG, CLAPTRAP,
    BALONEY, APPLESAUCE
hold .... GRASP, CLUTCH,
    SUSTAIN, KEEP BACK, BIND,
    OCCUPY, CONTAIN, REGARD,
    PRISON, MAINTAIN, RESTRAIN,
    DAM, STAY, DETAIN, GRIP
    attention ...... INTEREST
    back .. RESTRAIN, DETAIN,
        DAM, DETER, STEM
    dear .... CHERISH
    due to war ...... INTERN
    fast .. GRIP, CLING, BELAY
    forth .... OFFER, PREACH,
        LECTURE
    in custody ...... DETAIN,
        IMPOUND
    in law .... DECIDE,
        ADJUDGE, BIND
    off .... AVERT
    on .... PERSIST, CONTINUE
    out .. LAST, ENDURE, OFFER
    over ... DELAY, POSTPONE
    scoreless ... BLANK, BLITZ
    session .... SIT
    ship's .... HATCH
    up ... HIJACK, ROB(BERY),
        DELAY, STOPPAGE
holder .... OWNER, PAYEE,
    POSSESSOR, CONTAINER, DOP
    benefice ..... INCUMBENT
    lease .... LESSEE, TENANT,
        RENTER
holding ... TENURE, PROPERTY,
    CLASP
    device ...... CLAMP, VISE,
        TONGS
holdings ... PROPERTY, BONDS,
    STOCKS, POSSESSIONS
holdout .... RESISTER
holdup: sl. .... HEIST
holdup man .... FOOTPAD,
    BRIGAND, BANDIT, HIJACKER
hole .... CAVITY, EXCAVATION,
    COVE, BAY, INLET, GAP,
    HOLLOW, BORE, ORIFICE,
    OPENING, LILL, DEFECT,
    FLAW, PREDICAMENT, WELL,
    PIT, EYE, VENT(AGE),
    APERTURE

ace in the ⌐⌐ CLINCHER, ADVANTAGE
air .... SPIRACLE
animal's ⌐⌐⌐ LAIR, DEN, BURROW
automat's .... SLOT
cloth .... EYELET
coin .... SLOT
embankment .... GIME
enlarger tool ...... REAM
for cable .... HAWSE
for molten metal .. SPRUE
gangster's .... HIDEOUT
golf game .... CUP
in garment ... TEAR, RENT
in-one, golf .... ACE
in mold .... GEAT
of tube, etc. ...... BORE
skin .... PORE
sleeve's .... SCYE
stopper ⌐⌐ PLUG, SPILE, SPILL, CORK
up ⌐ HIBERNATE, DIG IN, HIDE
water ⌐⌐⌐ POND, POOL
holed up .... ENSCONCED
holes, full of .... PERFORATED
holiday ⌐ FESTIVAL, VACATION, RECESS, FERIA, FIESTA
kind of ⌐ ROMAN, EASTER, WEEKEND
of a .... FERIAL
Roman .... FERIA
holiness .... SANCTITY
Holland ⌐⌐⌐ DUTCH, CLOTH, NETHERLANDS
capital ..... (THE) HAGUE
capital (North) .... HAARLEM
city ...... EDE, ARNHEIM, (THE) HAGUE, LEYDEN
dialect ⌐⌐⌐ FRANKISH, FRISIAN
gin .. GENEVA, SCHNAP(P)S
merchants' league ....⌐⌐ HANSE
painter ⌐⌐⌐ (VAN) EYCK
province .... ZEELAND
river ...... EMS, SCHELDT
seaport ....⌐ EDAM
village .... EDE
Hollandia ⌐⌐⌐⌐ KOTABARU
hollands ⌐⌐⌐⌐⌐⌐ GIN
holler .... YELL, SHOUT
hollow ⌐⌐ CONCAVE, SUNKEN, EMPTY, CAVITY, HOLE,

VALLEY, FOSSA, FOVEA, FOSSETTE, BIGHT, FALSE, CAVERNOUS, CAPSULAR
boggy .... SLAK
cheek/chin's ⌐⌐⌐ DIMPLE
circular ⌐⌐⌐ CORRIE
cylinder .... TUBE
formed by curve ... SINUS
long, narrow ⌐ TROUGH
narrow ⌐⌐⌐ DINGLE
opposed to ⌐⌐⌐ SOLID
pipe's ⌐⌐⌐⌐⌐ BORE
sound ⌐⌐⌐⌐⌐ HOOT
tile .... KEY
holly ⌐ HOLM, ILEX, INKBERRY, WINTERBERRY, YAUPON, ACEBO, ASSI, ERYNGO
hollyhock ⌐⌐⌐⌐ ALTH(A)EA, MALLOW
Hollywood award ⌐⌐⌐ OSCAR
columnist ⌐⌐⌐ GRAHAME, LOUELLA, (HEDDA) HOPPER, RONA
industry ⌐⌐⌐⌐⌐ MOVIE
landmark ⌐⌐⌐⌐⌐ CIRO'S
name .... GABLE, GARBO, HARLOW, KEATON, BARA, NEGRI, MENJOU, PICKFORD, SWANSON, DEMILLE, FORD, FONDA, COOPER
street ⌐⌐⌐ VINE, SUNSET
writer .... SCENARIST
holm ⌐ HOLLY, OAK, AIT, ISLET, BOTTOMS
oak .... ILEX
Holmes, Sherlock ⌐ DETECTIVE
alter ego ⌐⌐⌐⌐ WATSON
brother of ⌐⌐⌐ MYCROFT
creator of ⌐⌐⌐⌐⌐⌐ (CONAN) DOYLE
favorite word ⌐⌐⌐⌐⌐ ELEMENTARY
holograph ⌐⌐⌐ HANDWRITTEN, (MANU)SCRIPT
holothurian ⌐⌐⌐⌐⌐ TREPANG
Holstein .... CATTLE
holt ..... COPSE, GROVE, HILL, COPPICE, WOODS, WILLOWS
holy .. SANTA, CHASTE, BLESSED, SACRED, SINLESS, SAINTLY, HALLOW(ED), DIVINE
city .... ROME, MECCA, JERUSALEM, LHASA, VARANASI, HARDWAR
communion .. EUCHARIST

cross .... ROOD
Father .... POPE
Grail .... SANGR(E)AL,
   CHALICE, SANGRAAL
Grail finder ... GALAHAD
Grail knight ...... BORS,
   PERCIVAL, PARSIPAL,
   AMFORTAS
Grail knights' enemy ....
   KLINGSOR
Innocents' Day ....
   CHILDERMAS
Land .... PALESTINE
Land Pilgrim's badge ...
   SCALLOP
Land visitor .... PILGRIM,
   PALMER
man .. FAKIR, MARABOUT,
   MAHATMA
of holies ...... SANCTUM
   SANCTORUM
office .... INQUISITION
oil .... CHRISM
person .... SAINT
picture .... ICON
place .... SANCTUARY,
   CHURCH, TEMPLE,
   SANCTUM, SHRINE,
   HALIDOM(E)
prefix ..... HAGIO, HIERO
Scriptures .... BIBLE
Sepulcher visitor .. HADJI,
   PILGRIM
Spirit .... PNEUMA,
   PARACLETE
Thursday island ....
   ASCENCION
War: Moslem ..... JIHAD
water container ... FONT,
   CRUET, STOUP, STOOP
water sprinkling ....
   ASPERGES
Writ .... BIBLE
homage ..... TRIBUTE, HONOR,
   REVERENCE
to saints .... DULIA
hombre ... OMBER, CARD GAME
slang ..... FELLOW, MAN,
   GUY
Homburg .... (FELT) HAT
home .... RESIDENCE,
   HOUSEHOLD, INSTITUTION,
   DWELLING, DOMICILE, ABODE,
   HEARTH, ROOF
animal's ..... DEN, LAIR,
   HABITAT

base, baseball .... PLATE,
   PLATTER
bird's ...... NEST, AERIE
bred .. DOMESTIC, NATIVE,
   CRUDE
figuratively .... ROOF
grown .... NATIVE, LOCAL
for poor/sick ... HOSPICE
in a jiffy/instant .. PREFAB
Indian .. TEPEE, WIGWAM
of gods .. OLYMPUS, MERU,
   ASGARD
of Golden Fleece ....
   COLCHIS
of mentally ill ... ASYLUM
of the .... DOMESTIC
screen . TV, VIDEO, TELLY,
   TELEVISION
Sweet Home" composer ..
   PAYNE

homecoming, alumni ....
   REUNION
homeground .. BAILIWICK, BASE
homeless child .... WAIF, ARAB
homelike ..... COZY, FAMILIAR
homely .. PLAIN, SIMPLE, UGLY,
   CRUDE, INTIMATE
homemaker .... HOUSEWIFE
Homer .... KOR, HOMERUN
enchantress .... CIRCE
epic of ... ILIAD, ODYSSEY
sea nymph ..... CALYPSO
swineherd of ... GUMAEUS
translator of ... CHAPMAN
writings of .. EPICS, SAGAS,
   NARRATIVES
Homeric .... EPIC(AL)
homerun with bases full ......
   GRAND SLAM
homesickness ..... NOSTALGIA
excessive ... NOSTOMANIA
homespun ... PLAIN, HOMELY,
   UNPRETENTIOUS, SIMPLE
cloth .... RUSSET
homestead ... MESSUAGE, TOFT
outbuildings ... STEADING
single farm ..... ONSTEAD
site .... TOFT
homesteader .... SOONER
homestretch .... LAST LAP
homework .... LESSONS
homey ...... COZY, FRIENDLY,
   FAMILIAR
homicidal .... MURDEROUS
homily .... SERMON, LECTURE,
   TALK

homing faculty .. ORIENTATION

hominy .... SAMP, GRITS

homo .... MAN, PRIMATE
  combining form ... SAME,
    LIKE, EQUAL
  sapiens .... MAN

homologate ... CONFIRM, AGREE,
    RATIFY

homonym .... NAMESAKE

homopterous insect ... CICADA,
    APHID

homosexual ... ... INVERT,
    LESBIAN

homunculus .... DWARF

Honan's capital ..... KAIFENG

Hondo .... HONSHU

Honduras capital ....
    TEGUCIGALPA
  hero .... LEMPIRA
  monetary unit .. LEMPIRA
  seaport ... TELA, LA CEIBA

hone .. SHARPEN, WHET(STONE),
    MOAN, STROP, OILSTONE,
    GRUMBLE, YEARN, GRIND(ER)

honest ...... FAIR, TRUTHFUL,
    PURE, UPRIGHT, VERACIOUS,
    WHITE

honesty ...... HONOR, PROBITY,
    INTEGRITY, PLANT,
    MOONWORT, VERACITY

honewort .... PARSLEY

honey .. DEAR, DARLING, SWEET
  and water mixture ......
    MEAD, HYDROMEL
  and mulberry juice ......
    MORAT
  badger .... RATEL
  bear .... KINKAJOU
  bee .... APIS, DINGAR,
    DESERET
  buzzard ...... KITE, PERN
  container ... COMB, CRUSE
  creeper .... GUITGUIT
  drink ..... MEAD, MORAT
  eater ... IAO, MOHO, BEAR,
    MANUAO
  fermented .... MEAD,
    METHEGLIN
  pharmacy .... MEL
  plant .... FIGWORT
  pollen mix .... BEEBREAD
  prefix .... MELI
  producing .. MELLIFEROUS
  source .. NECTAR, FLOWER
  weasel .... RATEL

honeybee genus .... APIS

honeycomb eater .... BEEMOTH
  material .... BEESWAX
  part .... CELL

honeycombed .... FAVOSE,
    ALVEOLATE, FAVEOLATE

honeydew .... NECTAR

honeyed ...... MELLIFLUOUS,
    SWEET, SACCHARINE,
    SUGARY
  drink ...... MEAD, MORAT
  words .... FLATTERY

honeysuckle .... AZALEA, VINE,
    CLOVER, WOODBINE,
    EGLANTINE

hong ... FACTORY, WAREHOUSE

Hongkong capital ... VICTORIA
  peninsula ..... KOWLOON

honk .... YANG

honky-tonk: sl. .... DIVE,
    SALOON, CABARET

Honolulu airbase ... HICKHAM
  exclusive section ....
    KAHALA
  greeting .... ALOHA
  native dancer ... WAHINE
  swimming resort ....
    WAIKIKI

honor ... GLORY, FAME, CREDIT,
    CHASTITY, DIGNITY,
    DECORATION, AWARD,
    ESTEEM, VENERATE, EXALT,
    RESPECT, ENNOBLE, HOMAGE,
    REVERE(NCE)
  mark of .... CHAPLET,
    LAUREL

honorable .... UPRIGHT
  mention .... CITATION

honorarium .... TIP

honorary commission, military
    BREVET

honors ..... DIGNITIES, TITLES,
    TRIBUTES, COMPLIMENTS,
    ACCOLADE, AWARDS

Honshu .... HONDO
  bay .... ISE, TOYAMA
  city .... HIMEJI, KURE,
    KYOTO, SENDAI, KOBE,
    OKAYAMA
  historical city ....
    HIROSHIMA
  port .... KOBE

hooch ..... WHISKEY, LIQUOR,
    BOOTLEG

hood .... BIGGIN, CAMAIL
  airplane's ...... NACELLE
  bird's .. CREST, CALOT(TE)

carriage's .... CAPOTE
cloak .... CAPOTE
folding .... CALASH,
               CALECHE
hanging part ..... TIPPET
monk's .... AMICE, COWL,
        CAPOUCH, CAPUCHE
movable .... CAPOTE
part .... CAMAIL
slang ... GANGSTER, THUG
tail of .... LIRIPIPE
woman's folding ....
                CALASH
hooded .. CUCULLATE, COWLED
garment ... PARKA, CAPE,
                CAPOTE
seal .... BLADDERNOSE
snake .. COBRA, PUFFING,
                ADDER
woman's cloak ....
                CAPUCHIN
hoodlum .. HOOLIGAN, ROWDY,
PUNK, GANGSTER, LARRIKIN
hoodoo ... BAD LUCK, VOODOO,
BEWITCH, JINX, HEX
hoodwink .. BLINDFOLD, DUPE,
DECEIVE, CHEAT, SEEL
hooey ...... NONSENSE, BUNK
hoof .... FOOT, PAW, UNGULA
colloquial .... TRAMP,
                WALK
like a .... UNGUAL
on the .... ALIVE
paring tool .... BUTTERIS
shaped .... UNGULATE
slang .... DANCE
hoofbeat .... CLIP-CLOP
hoofed ... UNGUAL, UNGULATE
hoofer: sl. ..... (TAP) DANCER
hook ... BEND, CROOK, CLEEK,
HAMULUS, CLEVIS, GAFF,
HEADLAND, GRAMPON,
TACH(E), SWINDLE, GORE,
       GRAPNEL, JIGGER
and eye .... FASTENER
and loop .. GEMEL, HINGE
colloquial .. LAND, CATCH
engine .... GAB
in baseball .... CURVE
like .. FALCATE, UNCINAL,
            UNCINATE
like mark ...... CEDILLA
longshoreman's .. BALING
money .... LARI(N)
on a pole .... GAFF
part .... BARB

pot .... CLEEK
shaped .... UNCINAL,
UNCIFORM, HAMULATE
stretcher .... TENTER
hooka(h) .... NARGILEH, PIPE,
NARG(H)ILE, HUBBLE-BUBBLE
hooked .... UNSCINATE,
AQUILINE, ADUNC(OUS),
      GAFFED, FALCATE
nose, describing a ......
              AQUILINE
hookey player .... TRUANT
hooklike .. UNCINATE, FALCATE
process .... UNCUS
hookup .... TIE-UP
hooligan .... RUFFIAN, ROWDY,
       HOODLUM, SPIV
hoop .. .. [EAR]RING
shaped handle ..... BAIL
hooper .... COOPER, SWAN
hoopla .. EXCITEMENT, BUSTLE,
            FUROR
hoosegow: sl. ... JAIL, PRISON,
            CLINK
Hoosier humorist ...... ADE
novelist .... TARKINGTON
poet .... RILEY
State .... INDIANA
hoot ... SHOUT, EXCLAMATION,
SASS, WHOOP, BOO, CRY,
            ULULATE
sign of a .... SCORN,
           DISAPPROVAL
hooter ... FAN, OWL, HECKLER
Hoover, _____ ... JOHN, DAM,
           HERBERT
blankets" ... NEWSPAPERS
Dam lake .... MEAD
flag" .... (EMPTY) POCKET
hop ... CAPER, SPRING, DANCE,
LEAP, VINE, FRISK
airplane .... FLIGHT
kiln .... O(A)ST
of ball/stone .... DAP
o'-my-thumb .... DWARF
plant .... LUPULUS
stem .... BINE
hope ...... LOOK FOR, DESIRE,
ASPIRE, ANTICIPATION, LONG
hopeful .... OPTIMISTIC,
EXPECTANT, SANGUINE,
ASPIRANT, CONTENDER,
          CANDIDATE
Hopei .... HOPEH, CHIHLI
capital of ...... TIENTSIN

hopeless .. DESPERATE, FUTILE, VAIN
  position .... CHECKMATE, RATTRAP
hophead .... ADDICT
Hopi .... MOKI, MOQUI
  room of .... KIVA
hoplite weapon .... SPEAR
hopped up ...... STIMULATED, CHARGED
hopper .. TOAD, FROG, LOCUST, FLEA, CRICKET, CICADA, KANGAROO
  columnist .... HEDDA
  short for a .... ROO
hops drier .... OAST
  kiln .... O(A)ST
  mellowed .... OLDS
  resinous powder .... LUPULIN
  stem .... BINE
hora .... FOLKDANCE
Horae ...... EIRENE, EUNOMIA, HOURS
horary .... HOURLY
horde .. SWARM, HOST, SWARM, LEGION, CROWD, DROVE, THRONG, ARMY, PACK
Horeb .. (MT.) SINAI, MOUNTAIN
horizon ...... LIMIT, SKYLINE
  arc of the ...... AZIMUTH
  designating kind of .....
    APPARENT, TRUE, VISIBLE, SENSIBLE, CELESTIAL
horizontal .... LEVEL, PLANE, FLUSH, FLAT
  band: heraldic .... FRIEZE
  position .... PRONE
  rudder ...... HYDROFOIL
hormone .. ESTRADIOL, PROLON, ESTRONE, ADRENALIN, CORTISONE, ESTROGEN, ESTRIOL, INSULIN, SECRETIN, GASTRIN, THEELIN, THEELOL, PROLACTIN, ANDROGEN, PROGESTIN
  for blood pressure ......
    ADRENALIN
horn ..... BUGLE, SIREN, TUBA, CORNU, PRONG, DAG, CROCKET
  bell-like part ..... FLARE
  bird beak's .... EPITHEMA
  blare .... FANFARE, TOOT, TANTARA

  blow one's: colloq. .....
    BOAST
  crescent .... CUSP
  deer .... CROCHE, ANTLER
  hollow ...... CAVICORN
  hunting .... BUGLE
  in ... MEDDLE, INTERVENE
  insect's .... ANTENNA
  Jewish .... SHOPHAR, SHOFAR
  like ... CORNEOUS, CORNU
  moon's .... CUSP
  musical .. CORNET, TUBA, TRUMPET
  of a ____ ...... DILEMMA
  of plenty ... CORNUCOPIA
  part of .... MUTE
  pierce with .. GORE, HOOK
  pout .... CATFISH, BULLHEAD
  quicksilver ..... CALOMEL
  rani's .... SHOFAR
  shaped thing .... CORNU
  snail's .... TENTACLE
  sound .... MORT, BLARE
  stag's .... ANTLER
  tissue .... KERATIN, SCUR
  tone .... MOT
  unbranched .... DAG
hornbeam .... IRONWOOD
hornbill ...... TOCK, HOMARI
Hornblower of fiction ....
    HORATIO
hornbook .... PRIMER
Horne, singer .... LENA
horneblende .... EDENITE
horned .. CORNICULATE, GORED
  animal .. GNU, RAM, STAG, RHINO, DEER, BUFFALO, BULL, IBEX
  animal, fabled .. UNICORN
  devil .... SATAN
  horse .... UNICORN
  pout .... BULLHEAD, CATFISH
  problem .... DILEMMA
  toad .... LIZARD
  viper ..... ASP, CERASTES
hornet .... WASP, STINGER, VESPID, YELLOW JACKET
Hornie .... SATAN
hornless ... POLLED, ACEROUS
  animal .... POLLARD
  cow .... MUL(L)EY
  dialect .... NOT
  stag .... POLLARD

hornlike .... CERATOID,
KERATOID, CORNEOUS,
CORNU
hornpipe-like ...... MATELOTE
horns of a deer ...... BALCON
hornswoggle: sl. .... HUMBUG,
SWINDLE
horntail ...... SAWFLY, INSECT
hornworm ...... CATERPILLAR
horny ... CORNEOUS, CALLOUS,
CERATOID, KERATOID
growth .... WART, CORN,
KERATOSIS, NAIL
scale .... NAIL, SCUTE,
SCUTUM
plate .... SCUTUM, SCUTE
plates, covered by ......
SCUTATE
skin ...... CORN, CALLUS
substance. .. KERATOSE,
KERATODE
tissue .... CERATIN
horologe ..... CLOCK, WATCH,
SUNDIAL, HOURGLASS,
TIMEPIECE
horologist ..... WATCHMAKER
horrendous .... HORRIBLE,
FRIGHTFUL
horrent .... BRISTLING
horrible .... DIRE, GRIM,
TERRIBLE, DREADFUL,
HIDEOUS, GRIS(T)LY
colloquial .... UGLY,
SHOCKING
horrid ..... UGLY, REVOLTING,
REPULSIVE, HATEFUL,
DREADFUL
horrified .. AGHAST, APPALLED
horrify ...... DISMAY, SHOCK,
FRIGHTEN, APPAL(L), SCARE
horrifying .... GRUESOME
horror ...... TERROR, AVERSION,
DREAD, LOATHING
hors de combat ..... DISABLED
d'oeuvre ..... APPETIZER,
OLIVE, CANAPE
horse .... BIDET, ARAB, BEAST,
EQUINE, PADNAG, SORREL,
BOLLARD, ZAIN, TURK,
MOUNT, DOBBIN, PRAD,
COB, STEED, JENNET,
BAYARD, CAVALIA
Alexander the Great's ...
BUCEPHALUS
ambling .... PADNAG
ancestor of .... EOHIPPUS

ankle .... HOCK
armor .... BARD(E)
Australian ...... WALER,
BRUMBIE
back of .... WITHERS
back tumor ..... WARBLE
backward movement ....
PASSADE
baggage .... SUMPTER
Barbary .... BARB
belly band .... GIRTH
blacksmith ..... FARRIER
blanket .... MANTA,
HOUSING, TRAPPING
blinder .... WINKER
body .... BARREL
breaking rope ... .
HACKAMORE
box of .... STALL
breaker .... ROUGHRIDER
breed .... MORGAN
broken-winded ....
WHISTLER
brown .... SORREL, ROAN,
BAY
buyer .... KNACKER
callus, foreleg ....
CHESTNUT
care for pay of ... LIVERY
caretaker ...... HOSTLER,
GROOM
castrated ...... GELDING
cavalry .... WALER
chestnut .... BUCKEYE
clean coat of ..... CURRY
colloquial .... BANGTAIL,
RIP
color .. PIED, PINTO, ROAN,
DAPPLE, BAY, SORREL
comber .... CURRIER,
GROOM
combining form ....
HIPP(O), KERAT(O),
HIPPUS
command to .. GEE, HAW,
WHOA, GIDDAP
covering, ornamental ....
TRAPPINGS
curvetting .... GAMBADE,
GAMBADO
dancing .... LIPPIZAN
dealer .. KNACKER, COPER
desert .... ARAB
dialect .... HOBBY
disease .... HEAVES, BOTS,
MAL(L)ANDERS, GID,

LAMPERS, ROARING, SPAVIN, SURRA(H), LAMPAS, NAGANA, LOCO, FARCY, DISTEMPER, STRANGLES, DOURINE, EMPHYSEMA, STAGGERS, WHISTLING, QUITTOR, THRUSH, VIVES
dishonestly entered in race ..... RINGER
dock-tailed ..... CURTAL
doctor ..... FARRIER, VET
donkey offspring .. HINNY
Don Quixote's .... ROSINANTE
draft .... SHIRE, SUFFOLK, PERCHERON, CLYDESDALE
dried intestine ...... GUT
easy paced .... PAD
eczema ...... MALANDERS
exercise before race ..... SWEAT
exercise place .. PADDOCK
eye cover .... BLINDER, WINKER
eyelid inflammation . HAW
famous .... TRIGGER, CHAMPION, TRAVELLER, MAN O' WAR, BUCEPHALUS, CITATION, SEA BISCUIT, WHIRLAWAY
farm .... RANCH
feed ...... FODDER, OATS
feeder .... GROOM
feeding for a fee .. LIVERY
female .... MARE, DAM
fictional ...... ROSINANTE, BAYARD
fetlock growth .... GRAGE
fetlock inflammation .... GREASE
foot disease .... QUITTOR, THRUSH, FOUNDER, LAMINITIS, GREASE
foot pad .... FROG
for hire .... HACK
forehead of ... CHANFRIN
fresh .... REMOUNT
from Medusa's body .... PEGASUS
gait of ...... RACK, LOPE, (FOX) TROT, GALLOP, CANTER, WINDING
gentian ...... FEVERROOT
genus .... EQUUS

glandular inflammation .... VIVES
goader .... SPUR
golden .... PALOMINO
graceful .. ARAB, COURSER
growth .... GRAGE, FUSSE
guide rope .... LONGE
Gulliver's Travels .... HOUYHNHNM
gypsy .... GRAS, GRI, GRY
hadit .... VICE
hair .... SETON
half turn ...... CARACOLE, DEMIVOLT
halter .... HACKAMORE
herd of stud .... HARRAS
hock .... GAMBREL
hoof's hollow .... COFFIN
hoof's inflammation .... LAMINITIS
horned .... UNICORN
hybrid .... ZEBRULA
incisor .... NIPPER
Indian ... PINTO, CAYUSE, PAWNEE, MUSTANG, PONY
inferior .... NAG, PLATER, SLEEPER, PLUG, COCKTAIL
joint .... HOUGH, FETLOCK
lame a .... GRAVEL
laugh .... GUFFAW
lead .... PACER
leap .. CURVET, CARACOLE, GAMBADO, GAMBADE, BUCK, VAULT, CAPRIOLE
leg eczema .... MAL(L)ANDERS
leg growth .... FUSSE
leg part ... HOUGH, HOOF, FETLOCK, PASTERN, SHANK, HOCK, GASKIN
longshot .... OUTSIDER, SLEEPER
mackerel .. SAUREL, CERO, SCAD, TUNA, TUNNY, CAVALLY
magic .... BAYARD
male .... GELDING, COLT, STALLION, STEED
man: myth. .... CENTAUR
mane of .... CREST
master of the . MARSHAL
mettle .... PRIDE
mint .... MONARDA

mouth disease ⁓ LAMPAS, LAMPERS

muscles atrophy ⁓⁓⁓⁓⁓ SWEENY

nearest wheels ⁓⁓ POLER

nervous condition ⁓⁓⁓⁓ STAGGERS

nettle ⁓⁓⁓⁓⁓⁓⁓ WEED

old .... JADE, SKATE, RIP, PADNAG, PLUG, HACK

opera ⁓ WESTERN, MOVIE, OATER

ornamental covering .... CAPARISON

pack ⁓ SUMPTER, DRUDGE

parasitic larva ⁓ BOTFLY, WARBLE

pedigreed ⁓⁓⁓⁓⁓⁓⁓⁓ THOROUGHBRED

pen ⁓⁓⁓⁓⁓⁓⁓⁓ CORRAL

piebald ... CALICO, PINTO

position of ... PESANTE

race ... PLATER, TROTTER, PACER, STEEPLECHASE

race board ⁓⁓⁓⁓⁓ TOTE

race, fixed ⁓⁓⁓⁓⁓⁓⁓ BUILDER PLAY

race "triple crown" winner OMAHA, CITATION, GALLANT FOX, COUNT FLEET, WHIRLAWAY, SECRETARIAT, WAR ADMIRAL

racing ⁓⁓⁓⁓⁓⁓⁓⁓ TURF

bet ⁓⁓⁓⁓⁓ FORECAST, QUINELLA

course ⁓⁓ HIPPODROME

fan ⁓⁓⁓⁓⁓ TURFMAN

meet ⁓⁓⁓ DERBY, ASCOT

official ⁓⁓⁓⁓ STEWARD

radish tree ⁓⁓⁓⁓ BEHEN

rawhide ⁓⁓⁓⁓⁓ SHAGREEN

rearing of ⁓⁓⁓⁓⁓ PESADE

reddish brown ⁓⁓⁓ BAY, SORREL, CHESTNUT

relief ⁓⁓⁓⁓⁓⁓⁓ RELAY

rider ⁓⁓⁓⁓⁓ EQUESTRIAN, CAVALRYMAN

rider's fall ⁓⁓⁓⁓⁓ SPILL

rider's seat ⁓⁓⁓⁓⁓ SADDLE

riding ⁓ STEED, PALFREY, MOUNT, STEED

river ⁓⁓⁓⁓⁓⁓⁓⁓ HIPPO

round-up ⁓⁓⁓⁓⁓⁓ RODEO

rump ... CROUP, CRUPPER

runaway ⁓⁓⁓⁓⁓⁓ BOLTER

saddle ⁓ MOUNT, PALFREY, NAG

seat on ⁓⁓⁓⁓⁓ SADDLE

shackle ⁓⁓⁓⁓⁓ TRAMMEL

shelter ⁓⁓⁓ STALL, STABLE

shoer ⁓⁓⁓⁓⁓⁓ FARRIER

short ⁓⁓⁓⁓⁓⁓⁓⁓⁓ COB

side ⁓⁓⁓⁓⁓⁓⁓⁓ FRANK

sideways step of ... VOLT

skin disease ⁓⁓⁓ CALORIS

slang ⁓⁓⁓⁓⁓⁓⁓⁓ SKATE

small .... BRONCO, BIDET, PONY, COB, GEN(N)ET, GENET(TE), SHETLAND, GALLOWAY, JENNET, TIT

sound ⁓⁓⁓ NEIGH, SNORT, WHINNY, NIE

spirited ⁓ STEED, COURSER

spotted ⁓⁓⁓ APPALOOSA

stall ⁓⁓⁓⁓⁓⁓⁓⁓ BOX

stand on hind legs ⁓ REAR

stocky ⁓⁓⁓⁓⁓⁓⁓⁓ COB

sweat ⁓⁓⁓ FOAM, LATHER

swift ⁓⁓⁓ PACER, RACER, ARAB, CLIPPER, SPANKER

talking ⁓⁓⁓⁓⁓⁓⁓ ARION

tamer ⁓⁓⁓⁓ ROUGHRIDER

tender ⁓⁓⁓⁓⁓⁓ GROOM

tooth ⁓⁓⁓⁓ TUSH, NIPPER

toy ⁓⁓⁓⁓ SHETLAND, PONY

training rope/place ⁓⁓⁓ LONGE

trappings ⁓⁓⁓⁓ HARNESS

trotting ⁓⁓⁓⁓⁓⁓ MORGAN

tumor ⁓ WARBLE, SPLINT

turn of ⁓⁓⁓⁓⁓⁓ MANEGE, CARACOLE, (DEMI)VOLT

upward leap ⁓⁓ CAPRIOLE

urine ⁓⁓⁓⁓⁓⁓⁓⁓ STALE

useless ⁓⁓⁓⁓⁓⁓⁓ WEED

vertigo ⁓⁓⁓⁓ GID, MEGRIM

war ⁓ CHARGER, COURSER, BUCEPHALUS

whip ⁓⁓⁓⁓⁓⁓⁓⁓ CROP

white-flecked ⁓⁓⁓⁓⁓ ROAN

wild .. MUSTANG, TARPAN, BRUMBIE, BRONC(H)O

winged ⁓⁓⁓⁓⁓⁓ PEGASUS

winless ⁓⁓⁓⁓⁓⁓ MAIDEN

winning gait ⁓⁓⁓⁓ ROMP

woman's ⁓⁓⁓⁓⁓ PALFREY

work .... GARRAN, HACK

worn out: sl. ⁓⁓⁓⁓⁓ SKATE, JADE, YAUD, PLUG, SCREW, HACK

worthless ... WEED, JADE, NAG, RIP
young ...... COLT, FOAL, FILLY, YEARLING
horseback .... HOGBACK
on .... A CHEVAL
horsefly ..... GADFLY, BOTFLY, TABANID
horsehair .... SETON, SNELL
horsehide ball ...... BASEBALL
leather .... ELK
horselaugh .... GUFFAW
horseman .. EQUESTRIAN, RIDER, CAVAL(I)ERO, CABALLERO
armed .... CAVALIER
in bullfighting .. PICADOR
horsemanship .... MANEGE, EQUESTRIAN, EQUITATION
movement in .... PIAFFER
horsemen .... CAVALRY
horsemen's parade ....
CAVALCADE
horsemint .... MONARDA
horseplay ... PRANK, COMEDY, FUN, JINKS
horses, art of riding .. MANEGE, EQUITATION
collection of ...... STUD, STABLE
herd of .... HARRAS
left behind in race .. RUCK
of .... EQUESTRIAN
of one owner .... STABLE, STRING
pertaining to ..... EQUINE
relief .... RELAY
school for ...... MANEGE
string of .... STABLE
troops on ...... CAVALRY
horseshoe .... RINGER
gripper .... CALK
points .... LEANERS
horseshoeing enclosure ....
TRAVE
horsetail .... EQUISETUM
leaves .... STROBIL(E)
to a pasha .... STANDARD
horsewhip .. LASH, CROP, FLOG, CHAB(O)UK
horsewoman ... EQUESTRIENNE
hortatory .. URGING, ADVISING, ADVISORY
horticultural lot ...... GARDEN
hortus siccus ..... HERBARIUM
Horus .... RA, SUN GOD
head of .... HAWK

parent of ..... OSIRIS, ISIS
hosanna ...... SHOUT, PRAISE, EXCLAMATION
hose .... SOCKS, STOCKINGS
spout .... NOZZLE
Hosea .... OSSE
wife of .... GOMER
hosiery .... STOCKINGS, SOCKS
hospice .. POORHOUSE, REFUGE, ASYLUM, INN
oriental .... IMARET
hospitable .... RECEPTIVE, ENTERTAINING
hospital .... INFIRMARY, LAZARETTO
attendant ...... ORDERLY
dispensary .... CLINIC
division .. WARD, CLINIC, PAVILION
for foundlings ... CRECHE
for mentally sick ....
BUGHOUSE, BOOBY HATCH
for the poor ..... SPITAL, LAZARET(TE)
kind of .... LYING-IN, MENTAL, MATERNITY, SANATORIUM
vehicle ...... AMBULANCE
hospitality for all ....
OPEN HOUSE, OPEN HAND(ED)
hospitium .... INN, HOSPICE
host ..... MULTITUDE, HORDE, THRONG, ARMY, BREAD, ENTERTAINER, LANDLORD, INNKEEPER, LEGION
heavenly .... ANGEL
receptacle ... PYX, PATEN, TABERNACLE
hostage .... PLEDGE, PAWN
hostel .... INN, TAVERN
hostelry .... INN, HOTEL
hostess .... ENTERTAINER
famed .... (PERLE) MESTA, HOWAR
hostile .... ANTAGONISTIC, WARLIKE, ADVERSE, INIMICAL, BELLICOSE
feeling .... ANIMUS, GRUDGE, RANCOR
hostilities .... WAR(FARE), CONFLICT
hostility ..... ANIMUS, ENMITY, BELLICOSITY, ANTAGONISM, ILL-WILL
hostler .... GROOM
hot .. THERMAL, HEATED, FIERY,

EXCITABLE, HECTIC, ANGRY, VIOLENT, ARDENT, TORRID, SULTRY, PEPPERY

air .... HUMBUG, BOMBAST

and bothered .... UNEASY

and damp .... MUGGY

baths .... THERME

blooded .... ARDENT, LUSTY, PASSIONATE, RECKLESS

cargo ...... CONTRABAND

dog .. WIENER, SANDWICH, FRANKFURTER

foot .... PRANK

goods — ... CONTRABAND, SWAG

iron treatment .. CAUTERY

plate .... STOVE

property, literally .... GOLDMINE

rod: sl. ... JALOPY, RACER

rods' race .... DRAG

slang .. NEW, FRESH, GOOD

spring ... GEYSER, THERME

springs deposit .... GEYSERITE

springs, of ..... THERMAL

taste .... PEPPERY

tempered .... TESTY, IRRITABLE, IRACUND, PEPPERY

water: colloq. .. TROUBLE, FIX, JAM

wind .... SIROCCO

hotchpotch .... STEW, MESS, JUMBLE

hotel .... SUITE, PUB, TAVERN, HOSTEL, INN

boy ...... PAGE, BUTTONS

chain .... HILTON, SHERATON

cheap .... FLOPHOUSE

dining room ...... GRILL

employee .... VALET

entrance hall ..... FOYER, LOBBY

floor .... MEZZANINE, ENTRESOL

foyer .... LOBBY

guest .... TRANSIENT, TRAVELER

keeper ... BONIFACE, HOST

page .... BUTTONS

public room .... LOUNGE

reception center .... DESK

resident .... GUEST

hotfoot: colloq. .. HURRY, HIE, HASTEN

hothead .... YANIGAN, FIREBRAND

hotheaded ...... RASH, HASTY, TESTY, IMPETUOUS

hothouse ... STOVE, GREENERY, VIVARIUM

hotrod .... RACER, JALOPY

hotrods, race of .... DRAG

Hottentot ...... NAMA, NEGRO

land .... NAMAQUA

language .... NAMA, BUSHMAN

race .... NEGROID

tribe .... NAMA

village . ... KRAAL

Houdini, magician .... HARRY, (EHRICH) WEISS

hound .... NAG, FOLLOW, CERBERUS, (HUNTING) DOG, HUNT, CHASE, AFGHAN, BRACHET

female .... BRACH

hunting .... HARRIER, SETTER, BEAGLE, BASSET

wolf .... ALAN

hour .... MATIN

hourglass .... HOROLOGE

houri .... NYMPH

hourly .. FREQUENT(LY), OFTEN, HORAL, CONTINUAL

Hours .... PRAYERBOOK

house ..... DWELLING, HOTEL, INN, FAMILY, THEATER, CHURCH, TEMPLE, LODGE, PALACE, CASINO, COTTAGE, HOME, ROOF, APARTMENT, DOMICILE, AERIE

bees' .... HIVE

bird's .... NEST, AERIE

correctional .... BRIDEWELL, REFORMATORY

country ...... HACIENDA, VILLA, CASINO

Eskimo ..... IGLOO, IGLU

flat roof of ..... TERRACE

fortified .... PELE

French .... MAISON

ground around .... CURTILAGE

ice ...... IGLOO, IGLU

instant .... PREFAB

Indian .... TEPEE, HOGAN, WIGWAM, LODGE

kind of . . . . . PENT, POOR,
HASH
legislative . . . . CONGRESS,
DIET, PARLIAMENT
log . . . . IZBA, CABIN
mud . . . . TEMBE
of the . . . . DOMESTIC
of two family units . . . . .
DUPLEX
organ . . . . PERIODICAL
pertaining to a . . . DOMAL
pigeon . . . . COTE
plant . . . . FERN
poor man's . . . . . . SHACK,
HUT, HOVEL
portable . . . . TENT, TEPEE,
WIGWAM
porter . . . . JANITOR
ranch . . . CASITA, GRANGE,
HACIENDA
side covering . . . SHINGLE,
SIDING
slang . . . . JOINT, HOLE
slippers . . . . SCUFF
small, dingy . . . . HOLE
Spanish . . . . CASA
state visitor's (U.S.) . . . . .
BLAIR
stately . . PALACE, MANSION
summer . . . . CASINO,
GAZEBO, RANCH, VILLA,
MAHAL
with its outbuildings . . . .
MESSUAGE
work for pay . . . CHAR(E)
houseboat . . . . BARGE
housebreak . . . . TAME, SUBDUE
housebreaker . . . . BURGLAR
housefly genus . . . . . . FANNIA,
MUSCA
of the . . . . MUSCID
household . . . MENAGE, FAMILY,
DOMESTIC, HOME, MAINPOST
animal . . . . PET
feudal . . . . MEINIE, MEINY
food supply . . . . LARDER,
PROVISIONS
gods . . . . . LARES, PENATES
linen . . . . NAPERY
mallet . . . . BEETLE
sprite . . . . KOBOLD
task . . . . . CHORE, CHAR(E)
things, discarded . . . .
LUMBER
housekeeping . . . . MENAGE
housel . . . . EUCHARIST

houses, buyer of old . . . .
KNACKER
housesite . . . . TOFT
housetop . . . . ROOF
housewarming . . PARTY, INFARE
housewife . . HAUSFRAU, HUSSY,
SEWING KIT, VROUN
concern of . . . SOOT, DIRT,
WASH, MENU
housing . . . . . . PAD, SHELTER,
COVERING, LODGING
engine . . . . NACELLE
horse's . . . . BLANKET,
TRAPPING(S)
hovel . . . . . SHELTER, DWELLING,
SHED, HUT, SHACK, HUTCH
hover . . FLUTTER, LINGER, FLY,
WAVER, LIBRATE
how . . . . METHOD, MANNER
-de-do . . . . ; . MESS
howdah . . . . SEAT
howdy . . . . . . GREETING, HELLO
however . . YET, NEVERTHELESS,
BUT, THO(UGH)
howitzer . . . . CANNON
howl . . WAIL, ULULATE, WAUL,
YIPE
howler . . . . OWL, MONKEY
colloquial . . . . . BLUNDER
howling monkey . . . . . . ARABA
slang . . . . . . GREAT, HUGE
howly . . . . HORARY
hoy . . . . BARGE
hoyden . . . . TOMBOY
hr., part of . . . . MIN, SEC
huaraches . . . . SANDALS
hub . . . . NAVE, CENTER
the . . . . BOSTON
Hubbard . . . . SQUASH
hubble . . . . HUMP
bubble . . . PIPE, HOOKAH,
UPROAR, HUBBUB
hubbly . . . . . . ROUGH, UNEVEN
hubbub . . . UPROAR, DIN, ADO,
TURMOIL, STIR, BROUHAHA,
NOISE, TUMULT
hubby . . . . HUSBAND
hubris . . . . ARROGANCE,
INSOLENCE
huckle . . . . HAUNCH, HIP
"Huckleberry Finn" composer
GROPE
hucklebone . . HIPBONE, TALUS,
ANKLEBONE
huckster . . . . TRADESMAN,
PEDLAR, PEDDLER, HAWKER

colloquial .... ADMAN
huddle .. JUMBLE, CONFERENCE,
    CAUCUS
"Hudibras" author ... BUTLER
Hudson cliffs .... PALISADES
    River city ...... YONKERS,
    TROY
hue ...... COLOR, SHADE, TINT,
    TINGE, CRY, DYE
    and cry .... SHOUTING
Huey P., the kingfish ... LONG
huff .. BULLY, OFFEND, HECTOR,
    PUFF, MIFF, TIFF, TANTRUM
huffy ..... TOUCHY, PETULANT
bug .... EMBRACE, CUDDLE,
    CLASP
    kind of .... BEAR, BUNNY
    me-tight .... VEST
huge .. GIGANTIC, VAST, LARGE,
    ENORM(OUS), IMMENSE,
    MAMMOTH, OUTSIZE, TITANIC,
    LEVIATHAN
huggermugger .... JUMBLE,
    SECRET, MUDDLE
Hugo, novelist .... VICTOR
Huguenot .... PROTESTANT
    leader ... ADRETS, CONDE
hula hula .... DANCE
    dancer .... WAHINE
hull ...... HUSK, POD, SHUCK,
    SHELL, CALYX
hullabaloo ... UPROAR, HUBBUB,
    CLAMOR
hulled grain ...... SAMP, GROAT
hum ... DRONE, CROON, BUZZ,
    WHIR(R)
human .. HOMO, ADAMITE, MAN,
    BIPED, MORTAL, PERSON,
    WIGHT
    body ... CARCASS, CORPUS
    body model ... MANIKIN,
    MANAKIN
    flesh eater ..... CANNIBAL
    limb .... ARM, LEG
    race .... MANKIND
    soul .... PSYCHE
    trunk .... TORSO
humane ..... KIND, MERCIFUL,
    TENDER
humanities .... LANGUAGES,
    LITERATURE, (FINE)ARTS
humanity .. MANKIND, PEOPLE,
    MERCY, KINDNESS
humanize .... REFINE, CIVILIZE
humankind .... PEOPLE
humble .... MODEST, LOW(LY),

UNPRETENTIOUS, DEGRADE,
    STOOP, SUBMISS, ABASE,
    CHASTISE, MEEK, DEMEAN
pie ..... NUMBLES, CROW,
    NOMBLES
humbug .. FRAUD, HOAX, SHAM,
    IMPOSTOR, DUPE, DECEIVE,
    CHEAT, GAMMON, BOSH,
    FLAM, HOKUM, SLAVER,
    HORNSWOGGLE
humdinger: sl. .. ONER, AONE,
    LULU, EXCELLENT, SNORTER
humdrum .... DULL, DRAB,
    COMMONPLACE, ROUTINE,
    MONOTONOUS
humerus .... BONE
humid ... DAMP, MOIST, DANK,
    WET, SULTRY
humidity measuring device ....
    HYGROMETER
humiliate .... DEGRADE, ABASE,
    MORTIFY, SHAME, ABASH
humility .. MODESTY, MEEKNESS
humming ..... BUZZING, BRISK,
    DRONING, ACTIVE
    sound ... WHIR(R), CHIRM,
    DRONE
hummingbird .. HERMIT, TOPAZ,
    SYLPH, RACKETTAIL,
    TROCHILUS, SWORDBILL,
    COLIBRI, COSTA, SAPPHO,
    STAR, AVA, BLUET
hummock ... KNOLL, HILLOCK,
    HILL, MOUND, HUMP
humor ... CAPRICE, BLOOD, BILE,
    CHOLER, PHLEGM,
    TEMPERAMENT, DISPOSITION,
    FANCY, WHIM, LYMPH,
    INDULGE, BABY, GRATIFY,
    CODDLE, SALT, MOOD, WIT
    bad .... TIFF
    body .... BILE
    out of ... CROSS, IRRITABLE,
    MOODY
    quaint .... DROLLERY
    slang .... CORN
humoresque .... CAPRICE
humorist ... WIT, WAG, JOKER,
    RABELAIS, COBB, ROGERS,
    BENCHLEY, NASH, ADE,
    FARCEUR
humorous .... FUNNY, JOCOSE,
    DROLL, COMICAL, JOCULAR,
    WITTY, AMUSING
    play ..... COMEDY, FARCE
    slang suffix .... EROO

hump .... HUBBLE, HUMMOCK, ARCH, HUNCH, BULGE
    animal with ...... CAMEL
    of a humpback .. KYPHOS
    the .... HIMALAYAS
humpback .. WHALE, KYPHOSIS
humpbacked .... GIBBOUS
humped animal .. CAMEL, ZEBU, DROMEDARY
Humpty Dumpty, describing .. SQUAT
    personification ..... EGG
humus .... MULCH, MOLD, SOIL
Hun ...... GERMAN, VANDAL, SAVAGE, ATTILA, ATLI, BOCHE, ETZEL
bunch .. HUMP, LUMP, CHUNK, HUNK, PREMONITION
hunchback of Notre Dame .... QUASIMODO
hundred .... CENTUM
    combining form .. HECTO, CENTI
    dollar bill: sl. ... C-NOTE, CENTURY
    lacs .... CRORE
    years .... CENTURY
hundredfold .... CENTUPLE
hundredth .... 100TH, CENTISIMAL
    abbreviation of ..... PCT
hundredweight .... CENTNER, CENTAL, QUINTAL, KANTAR
Hungarian .... MAGYAR
    capital .... BUDAPEST
    cavalryman ...... HUSSAR
    city ..... BUDAPEST, PECS, MISKOLC, DEBRECEN, SZEGED
    chocolate party ... DOBOS
    coin ...... FILLER, PENGO
    composer .. LISZT, LEHAR, BARTOK
    Communist leader ...... KADAR, (BELA)KUN
    dance .... CZARDAS
    designer .... BALAZS
    dessert .... STRUDEL
    dog .... PULI
    dramatist .... MOLNAR
    dynasty .... ARPAD
    gypsy .... TZIGANE
    hero .... HUNYADI, NAGY
    king .... BELA
    kingdom .... SERBIA
    lake .... BALATON
    language .... MAGYAR
    leader .... (BELA)KUN
    legislator ...... MAGNATE
    monetary unit ... FORINT, GULDEN, PENGO
    patriot .... KOSSUTH
    pianist .... LISZT
    plain .... PUSZTA
    premier ... KALLAI, FOCK
    president ..... LOSONCZI, DOBI
    Red leader ... (BELA)KUN
    regent .... HORTHY
    river .... PECS, DRAVE, THEISS, TISZA, DRAVA, DRAU
    shepherd's food .... GOULASH
    slang .... HUNKY, HUNKIE
    violinist .... AUER
    wine .... TOKAY
    writer .... JOKAI
hunger .... APPETITE, CRAVING, DESIRE, STARVE, PINE, YEN, ACORIA, ESURIENCE
    continuous ..... BULIMIA
    for home/country ...... NOSTALGIA
    greedy .... RAVENOUS
    politician's ... PUBLICITY, PRAISE
    striker, famous .. GANDHI
hungry ... FAMISHED, STARVED, RAVENOUS, ESURIENT, AVID
    go .... FAST
hunk ...... LUMP, SLICE, SLAB, PIECE, CHIP, HUNCH
hunks ...... MISER, TIGHTWAD
hunky .... SQUARE, WELL, HUNGARIAN
Huns, king of the ..... ETZEL, ATTILA, ATLI
hunt .... SEARCH, PURSUE, HOUND, HARRY, SEEK, CHEVY, FERRET, QUEST, BATTUE, CHASE, SCOUR, TRAIL, SHIKAR
    actress .... MARSHA
    African .. SAFARI, SHIKAR
    critic, poet ...... LEIGH
    for lost scent ...... CAST
    goddess of the ... DIANA, ARTEMIS
    illegally .... POACH
    on private property ..... POACH
    with hawk .... FLY

hunted animals .... GAME
hunter ...... TRAPPER, YAGER,
 FOWLER, CHASSEUR, JAGER,
 NIMROD, ORION, PREDATOR,
 STALKER, SHIKARI
 actor .... TAB
 actress .... KIM
 aid of .... RETRIEVER
 bait of .... DECOY
 cap of .... MONTERO,
 DEERSTALKER
 clue to ... SPOOR, TRACKS
 cry of .... TALLYHOO
 kind of ...... TREASURE,
 FORTUNE
 screen of .... BLIND
 sea .... WHALER
hunters, collectively ... CHASE
 help to .... BATTUE
hunting, art of ...... CHASE,
 VENERY
 bird .... FALCON
 call .. HALLOO, TALLYHOO,
 YOICK, CHEVY, TANTIVY
 dog .... BASSET, ALAN(D),
 SETTER, BEAGLE, HOUND,
 POINTER
 dog's chase .... RAKE
 dog's clue .... SCENT
 dog's cry .... TONGUE
 dog's stance ... DEADSET,
 POINT
 dogs, set of .... PACK
 event .... MEET
 expedition ...... SHIKAR,
 SAFARI
 fond of .... VENATIC
 ground .... PRESERVE
 hat .... TERAI
 horn .... BUGLE
 horn note .... MORT
 hounds, set of ..... PACK
 knife .... BOWIE
 living by .... VENATIC
 party member ... BEATER,
 GUN-BEARER
 pertaining to ....
 VENATIC(AL)
 preserve, royal .... PARK
 sport .... CHASE, VENERY
huntress: myth. ... ATALANTA,
 DIANA, ARTEMIS
hup, sergeant's .... ONE
hurdle .... BARRIER, SLED,
 OBSTACLE, SURMOUNT,
 WATTLE

fence on horseback .....
 LARK
hurds .... TOW
hurdy-gurdy .. (BARREL) ORGAN
hurl .... LAUNCH, HURTLE,
 THROW, FLING, CAST DOWN,
 TOSS, PITCH, CATAPULT
 in baseball .... PITCH
hurlbat .... HARPOON, JAVELIN
hurly-burly .... HUBBUB,
 DISORDERLY, TUMULT,
 UPROAR, TURMOIL,
 CONFUSION
Hurok, impresario .... SOL
Huron ..... WYANDO(TE), LAKE,
 IROQUOIS
hurrah ...... VIVA, ULE, CHEER,
 SHOUT, APPLAUSE
hurricane ... STORM, CYCLONE,
 TORNADO, TYPHOON
 center .... EYE
hurried .... HASTY, SPED
 in music .... AGITATO
hurry .. RUSH, URGENCY, DASH,
 HUSTLE, FLURRY, SPEED, HIE,
 HASTE(N), ACCELERATE,
 BRUSH
 colloquial .... HOTFOOT
Hurst, novelist .... FANNIE
hurt .... WOUND, DAMAGE,
 OFFEND, INJURE, ACHE, HARM,
 PAIN(ED), DERE
hurtful .... MALEFIC
hurtle ... CLASH, COLLIDE, DASH,
 FLING, CAST, HURL
husband ... SPOUSE, HELPMEET,
 CONSERVE, GROOM, CONSORT,
 GOODMAN, HELPMATE, LORD,
 FERE, YOKEFELLOW
 and wife .... COUPLE
 authority of ...... MANUS
 bereaved ...... WIDOWER
 brother of .... LEVIR,
 IN-LAW
 having one ... MONANDRY
 prospective: colloq. .....
 INTENDED
husbandman .... GRANGER,
 FARMER
husbandry .. THRIFT, FARMING,
 FRUGALITY, TILLAGE,
 GEOPONICS
hush .. SILENCE, CALM, SOOTHE,
 LULL, QUIET, SHUSH
 up .... SILENCE, SUPPRESS

husk .... HULL, SHELL, CHAFF, BRAN, SHUCK
   of grain ... BRAN, GLUME
   rice in the .... PADDY
husky .... HOARSE, ESKIMO, BURLY, ROBUST, DOG
   command to a ... MUSH
hussar .... CAVALRYMAN
   jacket .... DOLMAN
   monkey .... PATAS
Hussites' leader .... ZIZKA
hussy ... MINX, WOMAN, GIRL, ETUI, TART, SLUT, DOXY, QUEAN, CASE, SEWING KIT, HOUSEWIFE
hustings ... ASSEMBLY, COURT, PLATFORM, BOONDOCKS
hustle .. JOSTLE, SHOVE, HURRY, DRIVE, PUSH
hustler .... GO-GETTER
hut .... BARI, CABANA, (COTE), SHANTY, SHACK, CABIN, HOVEL, LEANTO, JACAL, MIMI, MIAM(IA)
   army .... QUONSET
   dome-shaped ..... IGLOO
   icy .... IGLOO, IGLU
   kind of .. QUONSET, NISSEN
   leanto .... SHED
   prefab .. NISSEN, QUONSET
   Swiss .... CHALET
hutch .. BIN, CHEST, HUT, PEN, TROUGH, COOP, WARREN
Huxley, writer ...... ALDOUS, JULIAN
huzza .... CHEER, SHOUT, HURRAH
Hwang Hai ...... YELLOW SEA
hyacinth .. GEM, MUSK, STONE, FLOWER, BULB, BIRD
   gem ... ZIRCON, GARNET, TOPAZ, JACINTH
   wild .... CAMAS
hyaline .... GLASSY, TRANSLUCENT
hyalite .... OPAL
hyaloid .... GLASSY, VITREOUS
hybrid .... CROSS, MULE, HALFBREED
   animal ... HINNY, CATALO
   cattle .... CATTABU
   citrus tree ...... TANGELO
   dog .... MONGREL
   language .... JARGON
   sterile .... MULE
hybridize .... CROSS

hydatid .... CYST
Hyderabad city ... GOLCONDA
   ruler .... NIZAM
hydra .... POLYP, SERPENT, CONSTELLATION, HYDROZOAN, COELENTERATE
hydrangea .... SHRUB
hydrant .... FIREPLUG
   attachment .... HOSE
hydranth .... ZOOID
hydrargyrum .... MERCURY
hydrate .... SLAKE
   of aluminum ... DIASPORE
hydraulic device .. RAM, TREMIE
hydrocarbon .... BENZENE, (M)ETHANE, BUTANE, OCTANE, TOLANE, CYMENE, PROPANE, MELENE, PINENE, TERPENE, RETENE
   aromatic .... CARANE, CHRYSENE
   coal tar .... PYRENE
   compound .... IMINE
   gaseous ...... FLUORINE, ETHANE
   inflammable .... BUTANE
   isotope .... PROTIUM
   liquid .... TOLUENE
   mixture .... MALTHA, OZOCERITE
   oily .... ETHERIN, OCTANE
   pine tar .... RETENE
   radical ..... ETHYL, AMYL
   resins .... RETENE
   wax .... MONTAN
hydrocephalus victim ... WATERHEAD
hydroid .... POLYP
   colony branch ... ZOOID, HYDRANT
hydromedusa ...... JELLYFISH
hydromel, fermented ... MEAD
hydrometer .... SPINDLE
   scale .... BAUME
hydropathy .... WATER CURE
hydrophobia ... LYSSA, RABIES, LYTTA
hydroponics ... TANK FARMING
hydrous .... WATERY
   silicate .... TALC
   wool fat ....·.... LANOLIN
hydrozoan .... POLYP, HYDRA, JELLYFISH, MILLEPORE
   covering of .... PERISARC
   stinging cell .... NEMATOCYST

hyena-like animal ...... WOLF
hygienic .... SANITARY,
                 HEALTHFUL
Hyksos .... HIQ SHASU
hyla .... TREETOAD
hylophagous ... WOOD-EATING
hymen ...... MARRIAGE, POEM,
       SONG, MAIDENHEAD
hymenopter ... BEE, WASP, ANT
hymeneal .... NUPTIAL
hymn .... PSALM, PAEAN, ODE,
CANTICLE, CHORALE, INTROIT,
     TE DEUM, ASPERGES
     book .. PSALTER, HYMNAL,
                GRADUAL
     for the dead .... REQUIEM
     in God's praise ....
                KADDISH
     of praise ... ... ANTHEM,
       LAUD, MAGNIFICAT
     praising God .... GLORIA,
     ALLELUIA, ALLELUJAH
     sacred .... ANTHEM
     thanksgiving ..... PAEAN
     tune .... CHORAL
hymnist ...... NEALE, WATTS,
     WESTLEY, HEBER, DOONE
hymnoptera .... BEES
hyoscyamus .... HENBANE
hyp .... MELANCHOLIA,
          HYPOCHONDRIA
hypaethral .... ROOFLESS
hyperbole .... EXAGGERATION,
          AUXESIS, ELAS
hyperbolic function ..... COSH
hyperborean .... FRIGID, COLD,
                GELID
Hyperion .... TITAN
     daughter of .... EOS
     parent of ...... URANUS,
                GAEA
     son of .... HELIOS
hyperpnea .... PANTING
hypethral .... ROOFLESS
hyphen .... DASH
hypnosis .... TRANCE
hypnotic .. SOPORIFIC, ACETAL,
     LUMINAL, ECTENIC
     URETHAN(E), MESMERIC

compound ...... AMYTAL
drug .... VERENOL,
     TRIONAL NEMBUTAL
force .... OD, ODYL(E)
state .... TRANCE
hypnotism .... MESMERISM
     founder of ...... MESMER
hypnotist .... MESMERIST
hypnotize .. ENTRANCE, CHARM
hypochondria .. HYP, ANXIETY,
          MELANCHOLY
hypochondriac ....
     VALETUDINARIAN,
          NOSOMANIA
hypocrisy .... PHARISAISM,
     PRETENSE, INSINCERITY
     example of ....
     CROCODILE TEARS
hypocrite .. PRETENDER, SHAM,
     PHARISEE, TARTUF(F)E
hypostasis .... SEDIMENT,
     DEPOSIT, ESSENCE
hypothecate .... PLEDGE,
          MORTGAGE
hypothermal .... TEPID,
          LUKEWARM
hypothesis ...... THEORY, ISM,
PROPOSITION, SUPPOSITION,
          ASSUMPTION
hypothesize .. SUPPOSE, ASSUME
hypothetical .... ASSUMED,
          CONDITIONAL
     force ... IDANT, OD, ELOD,
          ODYL, BIOD
     primordial substance ....
          PROTYLE
hyrax ... RABBIT, HYRACOID,
          CONY, DAMAN
hyson .... TEA
hyssop .... MINT, THISTLE
hysteria .... EXCITABILITY,
ANXIETY, JITTERS, PANIC, FIT,
      FRENZY, TARASSIS
     symptom ... AEROPHAGIA,
          AURA
hystricomorphic animal ......
     RODENT, CAVY, AGOUTI,
          PORCUPINE

I

I .... EGO, SELF
     am to blame .. MEA CULPA
     big .... EGO
     don't care pose ....

          INSOUCIANT
     excessive use of ....
          IOTACISM
     have found it! .. EUREKA

letter .... IOTA
pray thee .... PRITHEE
used in wires .... AYE
Iago's master ...... OTHELLO
wife .... EMILIA
iamb ...... (METRICAL) FOOT
Iasi .... JASSY
coin .... LEU
iatric .... MEDICINAL,
MEDICAL
Ibanez, novelist ...... BLASCO,
VICENTE
Iberia ...... SPAIN, PENINSULA
author of ..... MICHENER
Iberian region .... LUSITANIA
ibex .... GOAT, TUR, ZAC,
KAIL, WALIE, TEK, SAKEEN
habitat ... MOUNTAIN,
ALPS, APENNINES,
PYRENEES
ibid(em) .... SAME
ibis .... HERON, JABIRU
Ibo .... NIGERIAN
Ibsen, dramatist ... HENDRICK
character .... (A)ASE,
HEDDA, GYNT, NORA,
ELLIDA
Icarian .... RASH, DARING,
FOOLHARDY
Icarus's daughter ... ERIGONE
parent .... DAEDALUS
ice ..... DESSERT, FROST(ING),
FREEZE, SHERBET, GRUE,
CHILL, FIRN
breaker ..... PICK, ATKA
breaking in water ....
DEBACLE
coat .... RIME
cream ... BISQUE, SUNDAE
cream freezer rotator ....
DASHER
cream holder ...... CONE
cream treat .... SODA
crosser .... ELIZA
field bump .... HUMMOCK
flakes .... SNOW
floe .... PACK, PAN
fragments .... BRASH
hockey disc ...... PUCK
mass ... SERAC, GLACIER,
FLOE, BERG, PACK
of .... GLACIAL
partly melted .... SLUSH
pinnacle .... SERAC
rain .... SLEET, HAIL
runner .... SKI, SKATE

sheet .... GLACIER
slang ...... DIAMOND(S)
iceberg .... FLOE, LETTUCE
piece from .... CALF
small .... GROWLER
iceboat .... SKIFF
equipment ... RUNNERS,
SAIL
icebox ...... REFRIGERATOR
items .... LEFTOVERS
iced .... GLACE, FRAPPE
Iceland bay .... FAXA
capital ...... REYKJAVIK
city .... VIK
epic .... EDDA
god ... LOKI, THOR, AESIR,
WODEN, BALDER, ODIN
HEIMDALL
hot spring .... GEYSIR
king .... ATLI
language ...... NORSE
literature .... EDDA
measure ...... FET, ALEN,
KORNTUNNA
monetary unit .... KRONA
narrative ... SAGA, EDDA
parliament ...... ALTHING
poet .... SKALD
queen of story ....
BRUNHILD
volcano .... HECKLA,
ASKJA
Iceni, queen of ...... BOADICEA
Ichabod Crane's rival .. BROM
work .... PEDAGOGUE
ichneumon ... FLY, MONGOOSE
ichnology subject .. FOOTPRINTS
ichthyic .... PISCINE
ichthyosis ...... XERODERMA
icing .... FROSTING
icon .... IMAGE, FIGURE,
PICTURE
Ictalurus punctatus ... CATFISH
icterus .... JAUNDICE
ictus ... FIT, STROKE, ACCENT,
UPBEAT, ARSIS
icy .... COLD, GLACIAL,
GELID, FRIGID, ALOOF
coating .... RIME,
HOARFROST
id. ... SAME, IDAHO, IDEM, EGO
Idaho .... POTATO STATE
capital .... BOISE
city ...... POCATELLO,
NAMPA, TWIN FALLS,
BOISE

county .... ADA
nickname ... GEM STATE
state bird ...... BLUEBIRD
state flower .... SYRINGA
state gem .... GARNET
town .... MOSCOW
idant .... CHROMOSOME
idea ...... THOUGHT, IMAGE,
NOTION, OPINION, PLAN,
AIM, INKLING, FANCY,
EIDOS, IMPRESSION,
CONCEPT(ION)
combining form .... IDEO
main .... MOTIF
utopian .... BUBBLE
worthless .... BILGE
ideal ... MODEL, ARCHETYPE,
VISIONARY, PERFECT,
PARAGON, HERO,
FAULTLESS, UTOPIAN
guiding ...... LOADSTAR
state ... UTOPIA, OCEANA
idealist .... DREAMER,
VISIONARY
idealize .... DEIFY
ideals of citizenship ... CIVISM
ideas, sentimental ..... CORN
worthless .... BILGE
ideate ...... IMAGINE, FANCY,
CONCEIVE, THINK
idee fixe .... OBSESSION
idem .... (THE) SAME
identical .... ALIKE, EQUAL,
ONE, (SELF)SAME
identification, means of .....
CHECK, LABEL, BRAND,
(DOG)TAG, NOTCH,
MARKER
identify .... EARMARK
identity .... ONENESS,
INDIVIDUALITY
of origin .... ISOGENY
ideologist .... VISIONARY,
THEORIST, DREAMER
ideology ..... DOCTRINE, ISM,
PRINCIPLE, THEORY, DOGMA
Ides, date before ..... NONES
of March victim .. CAESAR
idiocy .... STUPIDITY,
AMENTIA, FOLLY, ANOESIA,
MONGOLISM, FATUITY
idiom ... DIALECT, LOCUTION,
CANT, SLANG, ARGOT,
PARLANCE
idiophone ... CELESTA, CHIMES,
TRIANGLE

idiosyncrasy .. ECCENTRICITY,
ODDITY
idiot .... DULLARD, OAF,
AMENT, SIMPLETON, NITWIT,
DUNDERHEAD, CRETIN,
CHANGELING, MOONCALF
better than an .. IMBECILE,
MORON
idle .... USELESS, FUTILE,
VAIN, POINTLESS, BASELESS,
INACTIVE, LAZE, LOITER,
OTIANT, LOAF, OTIOSE,
LAZY
talk .... GOSSIP, GAB,
PATTER, CHITCHAT,
GAS
idleness ... INDOLENCE, SLOTH,
LAZINESS
idler ... LOAFER, LAZYBONES,
ROUNDER, SPIV, BUM,
DRONE, LOUNGER
ido, creator of .... JESPERSEN
idocrase .... VESUVIANITE
idol ..... IMAGE, ICON, EFFIGY,
LION, EIDOLON, CELEBRITY
Chinese .... JOSS
household god ....
TERAPHIM
in logic .... FALLACY
social .... LION
idolater ... ADORER, ADMIRER,
PAGAN
idolism .... SOPHISM,
SOPHISTRY
idolize .... ADORE, ADMIRE
idolatry, object of ...... GOD,
HERO
Idum(a)ea .... EDOM
Idun .... ITHURN(N)
idyl(l) ...... POEM, PASTORAL,
ECLOGUE
idyllic .... PASTORAL,
PICTURESQUE
i.e. .... ID EST, THAT IS
Ieperen .... YPRES
if .... SUPPOSITION, PROVIDED
not ... NISI, UNLESS, ELSE
ign. ...... UNKNOWN, IGNITION
igneous ..... FIERY, PLUTONIC
rock .... DIABASE,
BASALT, BOSS, LAPILLUS,
MARGARITE,
MONZONITE, MELAPHYRE
rock formation ....
LACCOLITH

ignis fatuus .... DELUSION, WILL-O'-THE-WISP

ignite ... LIGHT, KINDLE, FIRE, BURN, EXCITE

igniter ..... FUSE, DETONATOR

ignoble .... HUMBLE, LOW, BASE, MEAN

ignominious ..... DEGRADING, SHAMEFUL, DISGRACEFUL

ignominy .... INFAMY, SHAME, DISGRACE

ignoramus ... DUNCE, NITWIT, KNOW-NOTHING

ignorance .... TAMAS, INNOCENCE, NESCIENCE

ignorant .... UNLETTERED, ILLITERATE, UNTUTORED, UNAWARE, NESCIENT

ignore .... DISREGARD, NEGLECT, OMIT, ELIDE, SNUB, OVERLOOK, CUT

Igraine's husband ...... UTHER

iguana ..... LIZARD, GOANNA

"Il Trovatore" gypsy .... MANRICO

ileus .... COLIC

   cause of .. CONSTIPATION

ilex .... HOLLY, OAK

"Iliad," ascribed author of ... HOMER

   character ..... STENTOR, ACHILLES, AJAX, CALCHAS, HECTOR

Ilion .... TROY

ilium .... HIPBONE

ilk .... KIND, SORT, CLASS, FAMILY, BREED, STRIPE

ill .... BAD, SICK, EVIL, ADVERSE, INDISPOSED, QUEER

   advised .... UNWISE

   at ease .... UNEASY, RESTIVE

   bred ... RUDE, IMPOLITE, LOUT, BOOR, CARL(E)

   combining form ..... MAL

   considered ..... UNWISE

   disposed .... HOSTILE, UNFRIENDLY

   fated .... UNLUCKY, UNFORTUNATE, STAR-CROSSED

   favored .... UGLY

   gotten gain .... LOOT, LUCRE

   humored .... CROSS, SULLEN

   mannered .... RUDE, CADDISH, LOW-BRED

   prefix .... MAL

   starred .... UNLUCKY

   temper .... BILE, SPLEEN, PET

   tempered ...... CROSS, PEEVISH, SULLEN, SURLY, CRANKY, VINEGARY, WASPISH

   tempered person .... CURMUDGEON

   use ... ABUSE, MALTREAT

   will .... ENMITY, HATE, MALICE, DISLIKE, GRUDGE, RANCOR, SPITE, ANIMUS, HATRED

illation .... INFERENCE, CONCLUSION

illative word ...... THEREFORE

illegal ...... FOUL, UNLAWFUL, ILLICIT

   blow in boxing ... FOUL

   liquor .... BOOTLEG

illegible .... UNREADABLE

illegitimate .... BASTARD, ILLEGAL, MISBEGOT(TEN)

Illinois, capital ... SPRINGFIELD

   city ... CHICAGO, PEORIA, ROCKFORD, ALTON, ELGIN, DECATUR, CAIRO, PEKIN, GRANITE, JOLIET, MOLINE, QUINCY, URBANA

   greatest son .... LINCOLN

   river ... SPOON, WABASH

   state bird .... CARDINAL

   state flower ..... VIOLET

   state tree .... OAK

illiterate .... IGNORANT, UNLETTERED, UNEDUCATED

illness .... DISEASE, INDISPOSITION, MALADY

   feign .... MALINGER

illume .... LIGHT

illuminant .... LIGROIN(E)

illuminate ...... ENLIGHTEN, LIGHT(UP) ELUCIDATE, EXPLAIN

illumination .... LIGHT, INSTRUCTION

   unit .... LUX

illusion .... DELUSION,

HALLUCINATION, TULLE
FANTASY, CHIMERA,
MIRAGE, FANCY
illusionist, kind of .. MAGICIAN
illusive ... DECEPTIVE, UNREAL
illustrate ..... CITE, PICTURE,
EXEMPLIFY, EXPLAIN,
DRAW, ADORN
illustration .... DRAWING,
DIAGRAM, GRAPH,
EXEMPLUM, SAMPLE,
INSTANCE, EXAMPLE
illustrious .... EMINENT,
CELEBRATED, NOBLE,
FAMOUS, DISTINGUISHED,
NOTED
illy .... BADLY
image ...... COPY, LIKENESS,
IDEA, EMBODIMENT,
(E)IDOLON, ICON, IDOL,
STATUE, IKON, REPLICA,
SIGIL, EFFIGY
deceptive ...... CHIMERA,
ILLUSION
destroyer ... ICONOCLAST
mental ... RECEPT, IDEA,
CONCEPT(ION)
imagery .... STATUES
imaginary .... UNREAL,
VISIONARY, FANCIFUL,
MYTHICAL, FICTIVE
ailment .... CRUD
land of sleep .... NOD
imagination .... DREAM,
FANCY, NOTION, IDEA
imagine ..... GUESS, SUPPOSE,
SURMISE, WEEN, CONCEIVE,
FANCY, IDEATE, WIS,
VISUALIZE
imagist ...... POET, DREAMER,
VISIONARY
imam .... PRIEST, CALIPH
imaret .... INN, SERAI
imbecile .... CRETIN, FOOL,
ANILE, MORON,
FEEBLE-MINDED, STUPID,
AMENT, DOTARD
imbecility .... STUPIDITY,
FATUITY, IDIOCY
imbibe ...... DRINK, INHALE,
ABSORB, SIP, BIB
imbricate .... OVERLAP
imbroglio ... ENTANGLEMENT,
CONFUSION, PLOT
DISAGREEMENT

imbrue ... WET, STAIN, SOAK,
STEEP
imbue .... TINCT, INGRAIN,
STAIN, INSPIRE, PERVADE,
DYE, SATURATE, INFUSE,
PERMEATE, TINGE
imitate ..... DUPLICATE, ECHO,
EMULATE, SIMULATE,
MIMIC, APE, MIME, COPY,
MOCK
imitation .... COPY,
COUNTERFEIT, MIMICRY,
BOGUS, SHAM, MIMESIS,
PARODY
gem .... PASTE
gold ... OROIDE, ORMOLU
gold leaf ... CLINQUANT
ludicrous .... TRAVESTY,
CARICATURE
of behavior/speech ......
MIMESIS
pearl .... OLIVET
imitative ..... MIMETIC, APISH
animal ..... APE, MONKEY
imitativeness .... APERY
imitator ...... COPIER, APER,
MIMIC
immaculate ...... UNSOILED,
CLEAN, PRISTINE, SPOTLESS,
PURE, SINLESS, INNOCENT
immanent .... INHERENT
OMNIPRESENT, UBIQUITOUS
immaterial .... SPIRITUAL
immature ...... YOUNG, RAW,
CALLOW, GREEN, UNRIPE,
PUERILE
immaturity, period of ....
NONAGE
immeasurable .... VAST,
BOUNDLESS
immediate .... NEAR(EST),
CLOSE(ST), ADJACENT,
INSTANT, DIRECT
immediately ...... AT ONCE,
FORTHWITH, INSTANTLY,
AS SOON AS, PROMPTLY
slang .... PDQ
immemorial .... ANCIENT,
(AGE)OLD
immense ... LIMITLESS, HUGE,
ENORM(OUS), INFINITE
immensity .... VASTNESS,
INFINITY
immerse .... ABSORB, DOUSE,
DUNK, SUBMERGE, ENGROSS,

DIP, PLUNGE, BAPTIZE, DUCK, STEEP

immersed ... ABSORBED, RAPT, BAPTIZED

immersion .... BAPTISM

immigrant .... ALIEN
describing one .... ALIEN, STRANGER, FOREIGNER
illegal .... WETBACK
newly arrived ... GRIFFIN, GREENHORN

immobile .... FIXED, FIRM, STABLE, MOTIONLESS, SET, STILL, SESSILE

immoderate ...... EXCESSIVE, UNDUE, EXTRAVAGANT

immodest .... IMPUDENT, FORWARD, BOLD, INDECENT, BRAZEN

immolate .... SACRIFICE

immoral ... INDECENT, LEWD, WICKED, OBSCENE, WANTON

immorality .... VICE

immortal .... DEATHLESS, DIVINE, ENDURING, PERPETUAL, AMBROSIAL

immortality ..... ATHANASIA, AMRITA

immortelle ..... EVERLASTING

immovable ...... STATIONARY, SET, IMPASSIVE, FIXED

immune .. EXEMPT, PROTECTED
render ...... VACCINATE, INOCULATE

immunity .... EXEMPTION, PROTECTION
kind of ..... DIPLOMATIC, CONGRESSIONAL

immunization method .... INOCULATION

immunizer .... SERUM

immunizing substance .... TOXOID, SERUM, ANTITOXIN, VACCINE, HAPTEN(E)

immure ... CONFINE, IMPRISON, ISOLATE, SECLUDE, SHUT UP

immutable ..... UNCHANGING, CHANGELESS, ETERNAL

imp ...... CHILD, DEMON, ELF, PUCK, SPRITE, BRAT, TROLL

impact .... WEDGE, COLLISION, SHOCK, PACK, DINT, FORCE, CONTACT

main .... BRUNT

impair ...... INJURE, REDUCE, DAMAGE, MAR, VITIATE, SPOIL

impairment .... INJURY, DETERIORATION
speech .... DYSPHASIA

impale .... FENCE IN, TRANSFIX, PIERCE, SPIT

impalpable .... SUBTLE, INTANGIBLE

impart ... GIVE, REVEAL, TELL, SHARE, COMMUNICATE, CONVEY, LEND, BESTOW

impartial ... JUST, UNBIASED, FAIR, EVEN(HANDED)

impasse .... DEADLOCK, STALEMATE, BLIND ALLEY

impassioned ... FIERY, ARDENT

impassive ..... CALM, SERENE, PLACID, STOIC, STOLID, APATHETIC, INSENSIBLE, PHLEGMATIC

impasto .... PAINTING

impatience ..... RESTLESSNESS, EAGERNESS

impatiens ...... JEWELWEED, TOUCH-ME-NOT

impatient .... EAGER, RESTIVE, INTOLERANT

impeach .... DISCREDIT, CHALLENGE, IMPUGN, INDICT, ACCUSE

impeccable ...... FAULTLESS, FLAWLESS, BLAMELESS

impecunious ... POOR, BROKE

impede ..... BLOCK, RETARD, HINDER, OBSTRUCT, DELAY, HAMPER, STYMIE
legally .... ESTOP

impediment ...... OBSTACLE, BARRIER, HITCH, HINDRANCE
speech ... LISP, STAMMER, STUTTER

impedimenta ...... BAGGAGE, ENCUMBRANCE

impel ... PUSH, PROPEL, FORCE, INCITE, COMPEL, CONSTRAIN, ACTUATE, MOVE, MOTIVATE, DRIVE, URGE

impending .... IMMINENT, OVERHANGING

impenetrable ..... IMPERVIOUS, DENSE

impennate bird ...... PENGUIN

imperative .... URGENT, ORDER, COMPELLING

imperator .... EMPEROR

imperceptible .... UNSEEN, INVISIBLE

imperfect .... FLAWED, DEFECTIVE, FAULTY

imperfection ... FLAW, FAULT, DEFECT, BLEMISH, VICE

imperial .... MAJESTIC, SOVEREIGN, AUGUST, MAGNIFICENT, BEARD, REGAL, GOATEE

   color .... PURPLE

   decree .... RESCRIPT

   palace officer .. PALATINE

   domain .... EMPIRE, EMPERY

imperil .... ENDANGER, JEOPARDIZE

imperious .... ARROGANT, DICTATORIAL, URGENT, MAGISTRAL

impersonal ...... DETACHED, OBJECTIVE

impersonate .... EMBODY, MIMIC, IMITATE, ACT

impersonator ..... IMPOSTOR, ACTOR

impertinence ..... INSOLENCE, IRRELEVANCE, IMPUDENCE

impertinent .... SAUCY, PERT, FLIP(PANT), INSOLENT, IMPUDENT, SASSY, MALAPERT

   talk .... LIP, SASS

impetuous .... RUSHING, IMPULSIVE, RASH, TEARING, HOT, HASTY

impetus .. INCENTIVE, IMPULSE, MOTIVE, DRIVE, FORCE, MOMENTUM

impi .... ZULU, KAFFIR, WARRIOR

impiety .... IRREVERENCE

impinge .... ENCROACH, TRESPASS

impious ... GODLESS, PROFANE, IRREVERENT

impish .... MISCHIEVOUS, ELVAN

implacable ...... RELENTLESS, INEXORABLE, INFLEXIBLE, PITILESS, MORTAL

implant ..... EMBED, INSTILL, INCULCATE, GRAFT, (EN)ROOT

implement .... FULFILL, ACCOMPLISH, ENFORCE, UTENSIL, KIT, TOOL, EFFECTUATE, INSTRUMENT, DEVICE

   hay spreading .. MULCHER

   household .... APPLIANCE

   kitchen .... UTENSIL

   pounding .... PESTLE

   threshing .... FLAIL

implicate .... INVOLVE, ENTANGLE, INCLUDE, INCRIMINATE

implication .... OVERTONE

implicit .... TACIT, ABSOLUTE, IMPLIED, INHERENT

implied ..... TACIT, IMPLICIT

implore ..... PLEAD, BESEECH, ENTREAT, BEG, PRAY

imply .... HINT, SUGGEST, INTIMATE, CONNOTE

impolite .... RUDE, DISCOURTEOUS

impolitic ... UNWISE, TACTLESS

impone ...... WAGER, STAKE

import ...... INTRODUCE, SIGNIFY, TENOR, DRIFT, INTENT, SENSE, MEANING

   tax .... TARIFF

important .... VITAL, MOMENTOUS

importance .... WEIGHT, MOMENT, VALUE, CONSEQUENCE, HEFT

importune ... ENTREAT, PRAY, URGE, ASK, PLEAD, BESEECH, PRESS

impose ...... INFLICT, FORCE, FOIST, ENTAIL, PALM OFF, FOB, LEVY

   by fraud .... FOIST

imposing .... IMPRESSIVE, NOBLE, GRAND(IOSE), AUGUST, MAGNIFIC

imposition .... OBTRUSION, INFLICTION

impost .... DUTY, LEVY, TAX, SPRINGER

impostor ..... FRAUD, CHEAT, QUACK, IMPERSONATOR, CHARLATAN, SHAM, FAKER, GOUGE, HUMBUG, PHON(E)Y

imposture .... FRAUD, SHAM, DECEPTION

impotent .... POWERLESS, STERILE, HELPLESS

impound .... POIND

impractical one ... DREAMER, IDEALIST

imprecation ..... CURSE, OATH

impregnable .. INVULNERABLE, FIRM

impregnate .... FERTILIZE, FILL, FECUNDATE, SATURATE

impresario ... ENTREPRENEUR, PROMOTER

    Sol .... HUROK

impress .... DRAFT, LEVY, STAMP, (IM)PRINT, AFFECT, MARK

impressed clearly .... GRAVEN

impression .. EFFECT, INKLING, PRINTING, MARK, STAMP, IMPRINT, IDEA

    on coin .... MINTAGE

    trial .... PROOF

impressionist composer ...... DEBUSSY, RAVEL, FAURE

    painter .... MONET, MANET, DEGAS, RENOIR, PISSARRO

imprest .... LOAN, (CASH)ADVANCE, LENT

imprimatur ...... SANCTION, LICENSE, APPROVAL

imprint .... PRESS, STAMP, MARK

imprison ...... IMMURE, JAIL, CONFINE, INCARCERATE, CAGE

imprisonment .... LIMBO, INCARCERATION

improbable .... UNLIKELY

impromptu ...... EXTEMPORE, EXTEMPORANEOUS, OFFHAND, IMPROVISED

improper .... UNFIT, INDECOROUS, UNSEEMLY, UNBECOMING, INDECENT, AMISS, WRONG, UNDUE

improperly .... UNDULY

impropriety ... MISBEHAVIOR, MISCONDUCT

improve ..... BETTER, EMEND, REVISE

improvisation on stage .... AD LIB, ASIDE

improvise ...... EXTEMPORIZE, MAKE-DO, AD LIB, INVENT, VAMP, CONTRIVE

    in music .... VAMP, RIDE

improvised .... OFFHAND, IMPROMPTU

imprudent .... CARELESS, INDISCREET, RASH

impudence .... CHEEK, NERVE, GALL, BRASS, INSOLENCE, LIP

impudent .... INSOLENT, SAUCY, BOLD, IMPERTINENT, SASSY, IMMODEST, BRASH, RUDE, MALAPERT, PERT, FORWARD, SNOTTY, FRESH, AUDACIOUS

impugn .... CRITICIZE, CHALLENGE, ASPERSE, BLAME, DENY, ATTACK

impulse ...... PUSH, IMPETUS, THRUST, URGE, FORCE, MOTIVE, ESTRO, NISUS

    to steal ... KLEPTOMANIA

impulsive ... RASH, IMPETUOUS, CAPRICIOUS, SNAP

impunity .... EXEMPTION, FREEDOM

impure ...... DIRTY, DEFILED, MIXED, ADULTERATED

impute .... ATTRIBUTE, ASCRIBE, CHARGE

in ... AMIDST, WITH, ENCLOSE, AMONG, AT, AT HOME

    a body ...... EN MASSE, ALTOGETHER

    a group ...... EN MASSE

    a hurry ..... POSTHASTE

    a manner of speaking .... SO TO SAY

    a series .... EN SUITE

    abundance ..... GALORE, TEEMING

    accord .... EN RAPPORT

    accordance with .... PURSUANT

    addition ...... ALSO, TOO

    agreement .... UNITED

    any case .... AT ALL

    as-much-as .... SINCE

    bad faith ..... MALA FIDE

    bad taste ...... COARSE, RANK

    circulation ..... ABROAD, ABOUT

    clover ...... PROSPEROUS

    due manner ...... DULY, ACCORDINGLY, REALLY, TRULY

    fact .... DE FACTO

favor of .... FOR, PRO
good time .. EARLY, SOON
high spirits .. EBULLIENT
hoc signo ____ .. VINCES
line .... AROW
love .. GAGA, INFATUATED
name only ..... NOMINAL,
    TITULAR
no manner ..... NOWISE
one's element .. AT HOME
place of ...... FOR, LIEU,
    (IN)STEAD, ELSE, VICE
progress ..... (ON)GOING,
    CURRENT
re ... CONCERNING, ANENT
row ... ALINED, ALIGNED
spite of .... MAUGER,
    MAUGRE, DESPITE,
    NOTWITHSTANDING
status quo .... AS IS
that case .... THEN
the capacity of ..... QUA
the course of ... DURING
the end .... FINALLY,
    EVENTUALLY,
    ULTIMATELY
the name of Allah ....
    BISMILLAH
the same place .. IBID(EM)
the whole ...... IN TOTO
time, musically, ...
    ATEMPO
Ina, actress .... CLAIRE
inaction ... IDLENESS, INERTIA
inactive .... IDLE, INERT,
    PASSIVE, DORMANT, LATENT,
    STATIC
inadequate .... MEAGER,
    SCANTY, NOT ENOUGH,
    LACKING
inadvertence ...... OVERSIGHT
inamorata .... MISTRESS,
    SWEETHEART
inane ..... PUERILE, FATUOUS,
    INEPT, SILLY, EMPTY,
    VACANT, FOOLISH, VACUOUS
inanimate .... DEAD,
    SPIRITLESS, DULL, LIFELESS
inanity .... VACUITY
inappropriate ... MALAPROPOS
inapt .... INEPT, UNSUITABLE,
    AWKWARD
inarch .... GRAFT
inarm .... EMBRACE
inarticulate ..... DUMB, MUTE,
    VOICELESS, APHONIC

inasmuch ...... SINCE, BECAUSE
as .... SEEING
inattention ..... NEGLIGENCE
inattentive .... LOST
inaugurate .... INDUCT, BEGIN,
    DEDICATE, OPEN
inauspicious ...... UNLUCKY,
    ILL-OMENED, UNFAVORABLE,
    ILL, ADVERSE, UNTIMELY
inbeing .... ESSENCE
inborn .... NATURAL, INNATE,
    INBRED, INDIGENOUS,
    INHERENT, NATIVE,
    ORGANIC, CONGENITAL,
    CONNATE
character .... NATURE
inbreeding ...... ENDOGAMY
incalculable .... UNTOLD
Incan .. QUECHUA(N), PERUVIAN
empire capital ... CUSCO,
    CU(Z)CO
king .... ATABALIPA,
    ATAHUALPA, HUASCAR
incandescence .... GLOW
incandescent ...... RED-HOT,
    WHITE-HOT, GLOWING
incantation ...... CHANTING,
    MAGIC, SORCERY,
    CONJURATION, INVOCATION
incapacitate .... DISABLE,
    DISQUALIFY
incarcerate .... IMPRISON,
    CONFINE, JAIL
incarnadine .... PINK, RED
incarnate .... RED, ROSY,
    PERSONIFIED
incarnation ..... EMBODIMENT,
    PERSONIFICATION, AVATAR
incendiary .... ARSONIST,
    FIREBUG, AGITATOR,
    PYROMANIAC
bomb material ....
    THERMIT(E)
incense ..... ENRAGE, ANGER,
    IRK, ODOR, PERFUME,
    OLIBANUM, GUM, STACTE,
    MATTI, MASTIC,
    SANDARAC, BENZOIN
burner .... THURIBLE
Chinese ...... JOSS STICK
incensed ...... IRATE, ANGRY,
    WROTH
incentive .... ENCOURAGEMENT,
    INDUCEMENT, IMPULSE,
    MOTIVE, STIMULUS
incept .... INGEST

inception ..... ORIGIN, START
inceptive .... INITIAL
incertitude .... DOUBT, INSECURITY
incessant .... CONTINUAL, CONSTANT
inch ...... TRIFLE, BIT, HILL, ISLAND
.001 of an .... MIL
1/12 .... LINE
inches, eighteen .... CUBIT
nine .... SPAN
thirty .... PACE, STEP
twelve .... FOOT
inchoate .... INCIPIENT, RUDIMENTARY
Inchon .... CHEMULP(H)O
incident .... OCCURRENCE, HAPPENING, EPISODE, EVENT, ATTENDANT(ON)
incidental .... MINOR, SECONDARY, BYE, ODD, CASUAL, CHANCE, RANDOM, PASSING
in music ... GRACE NOTE
opinion .. OBITER DICTUM
incidentally .... OBITER
incinerate .... CREMATE, BURN (UP)
incinerator ..... CREMATORY, CREMATORIUM, FURNACE, DESTRUCTOR
incipient ... INCHOATE, INITIAL
incise .. ENGRAVE, CARVE, CUT
incision ..... CUT, GASH, SLIT
incisive .... KEEN, SHARP, PIERCING, ACUTE, CUTTING, BITING, TRENCHANT
incisor .... TOOTH
incite .... INSTIGATE, FOMENT, INDUCE, EXHORT, GOAD, EGG, AGITATE, SPUR, ABET
inciter .... INSTIGATOR, PROVOCATEUR, AGITATOR, EGGER
inclement .... SEVERE, ROUGH, HARSH, STORMY, PITILESS
inclination ... GRADE, SLANT, BEND(ING), LEAN(ING), SLOPE, BIAS, TASTE
incline ... SLOPE, SLANT, BEND, GRADE, CANT, TEND, LEAN
downward .... DIP
inclined ... WILLING, DISPOSED, ALIST, PRONE, PRONATE,

APT, OBLIQUE, MINDED
chute/trough .... FLUME
walk .... RAMP
inclose ... HEM(IN), SURROUND, SHUT IN
inclosure ...... FENCE, YARD, CORRAL, WALL, PEN
include ... INVOLVE, ENCLOSE, COMPRISE, EMBRACE, CONTAIN
inclusive .... GENERIC
incognito .... DISGUISE
incoherent .... RAMBLING, DISJOINTED
income ... EARNING, REVENUE, ANNUITY, RENTE, USANCE
from lease ..... RENT(AL)
incommode .... BOTHER, PUT OUT, INCONVENIENCE
incomparable ...... PEERLESS, MATCHLESS
incomplete ... LACKING, PART
incomprehensible: slang .. GREE
inconclusive ...... UNCERTAIN, DOUBTFUL
incondite .... CRUDE, UNPOLISHED
incongruous ... INCOMPATIBLE, UNFIT, INAPPROPRIATE, INCONSISTENT
inconsequential ..... TRIVIAL
inconsiderable ...... TRIVIAL, SMALL
inconstant .... UNSTABLE, VOLATILE, FICKLE, CAPRICIOUS, MUTABLE
inconvenience .... BOTHER, TROUBLE, INCOMMODE
incorporate .... INCLUDE, EMBODY, MIX, MERGE
incorporeal right .. COPYRIGHT, PATENT
incorrect .... INACCURATE, UNTRUE, FAULTY, WRONG, ERRONEOUS
incorrect epithet/naming .....
MISNOMER
incorruptible .... HONEST
increase ... GROW, MULTIPLY, ENLARGE, AUGMENT, ACCRETE
bet on .... RAISE
incredible ... UNBELIEVABLE
incredulity .... DOUBT, SKEPTICISM, UNBELIEF
cry of .... WHAT, OH NO

incredulous ...... SKEPTICAL

increment .... ACCRUAL,
INCREASE, GROWTH, GAIN

incretion, product of ....
HORMONE

incriminate .... INVOLVE,
CHARGE, IMPLICATE,
ACCUSE

incrustation .... SCAB

incubate ... BREED, HATCH, SIT,
BROOD

incubator .... HATCHERY

incubus ..... SPIRIT, BURDEN,
DEMON, NIGHTMARE

inculcate .. INSTIL(L), IMPRESS,
IMBUE

incumbency ... TENURE, DUTY

incumbent .... IMMINENT

incumbrance ... LIEN, BURDEN

incunabula .... INFANCY

incur .... RUN

incurable ..... IRREMEDIABLE

incursion .... INVASION,
INTRUSION, INROAD, FORAY,
RAID

incus .... ANVIL

indecency .... FILTH

indecent .... OBSCENE,
IMMODEST, IMMORAL, FOUL,
COARSE, RANK, LEWD,
RACY, OFF-COLOR, RISQUE

indecision ...... VACILLATION,
HESITATION

indecisive ...... VACILLATING,
WAVERING

indecorous .... IMPROPER,
UNSEEMLY

indeed ... TRULY, CERTAINLY,
FORSOOTH, REALLY

indefatigable ..... UNTIRING,
TIRELESS

indefensible ..... UNTENABLE,
UNJUSTIFIABLE

indefinite .... UNSURE,
HAZY, NEBULOUS, OBSCURE,
AMBIGUOUS, VAGUE,
INDISTINCT, NUBILOUS

amount ..... ANY, SOME

article .... AN

pronoun ..... (ANY)ONE

indelible .... LASTING,
PERMANENT

indelicate ... COARSE, ROUGH,
CRUDE, GROSS

indemnify ..... PAY, INSURE,
REDEEM, REIMBURSE

indent .... NOTCH, IMPRESS,
REQUISITION

indentation .... NOTCH,
DINGE, JAG, CUT, MARGIN,
CRENELET

on a blade .... CHOIL

on glass bottle .... KICK

independent, an ...... LONER,
MUGWUMP

indescribable .... UNTOLD

indeterminate .... VAGUE,
UNDECIDED, INDEFINITE

in botany ..... RACEMOSE

index .... FOREFINGER,
POINTER, INDICATOR,
SIGN, LIST, CATALOG(UE),
EXPONENT, MARK

India .... BHARAT, TAMIL,
HINDUSTAN

aborigine ...... BENGALI

acrobat .... NAT

adjutant ...... MARABOU,
ARGALA

alcoholic drink .. ARRACK

animal ..... DHOLE, ZEBU

antelope ..... NILG(H)AI,
CHIRU, SASIN,
NILG(H)AU

ape .... GIBBON

army officer .... JEMADAR

army servant .... LASCAR

artilleryman ...... LASCAR

astrologer .... JOSHI

attendant ... AYAH, PEON

audience .... DURBAR

banker .... SOWCAR,
SARAF, SHROFF, SOUCAR

bear .... BALOO

bearer .... SIRDAR

bedstead ...... CHARPOY

Bihar capital ..... PATNA

bird .... ARGALA,
MARABOU, JACANA,
SHAMA, KOEL,
AMADAVAT, RAYA

bison ...... GAUR, TSINE,
GAYAL

black buck ...... SASIN

boat ..... DONGA, DUNGA

bodice .... CHOLI

bond .... ANDI

boycott of foreign goods
SWADESHI

bread .... CHAPATI

bride's neck wear .. TALIS

buck .... SASIN

buffalo ... ARNA, ARNEE
building .... MAHAL
bulbul .... KALA
burrowing animal ......
                     RATEL
bush .... KANHER
business suspension .....
                     HARTAL
butter .... GHEE
cake .... CHAPATI
calico .... SAL(I)OO
canoe .... TANEE
cap .... TOPEE, TOPI
cape ..... COMORIN, DIVI
capital .... (NEW) DELHI
capital, summer .. SIMLA
carpet .... AGRA
carriage .... RATH,
        GHARRY, TONGA
cashmere .... ULWAN
caste ...... JAT, GADDI,
    MEO, PARIAH, SUDRA,
    MAL(I), SHIR, LOHANA,
               RAJPUT
caste mark .... TILKA
caterpillar .... SUGA
cattle ... BRAHMA, ZEBU,
        GAUR, GOUR
cavalryman ..... SOWAR
cedar .... DEODAR
chamois .... SARAU
chief ... RAJA(H), SIRDAR
cigarette .... BIRI
church .... SAMAJ
city ... GOLCONDA, GAYA,
    SHOLAPUR, MUTTRA,
    LUCKNOW, MEERUT,
    BENARES, SURAT,
    BANGALORE, SIBI,
    SIMLA, SALEM, AGRA,
    HYDERABAD, HOWRAH,
    PATNA, PATIALA,
    MORADABAD, LASHKAR,
    LAHORE, BARODA,
              MADURA
civet .... ZIBET(H)
clerk ..... BABOO, BABU
cloth ... SALU, SAL(L)OO,
        SURAT, ULWAN
cloth strip .... PATA
coin ...... MOHUR, HOON,
    FELS, FANAM, ANNA,
    PICE, PI(E), RUPEE
combining form ... INDO
condiment .... CURCUMA
corporal .... NAIK

cot .... CHARPOY
cotton cloth ..... CALICO
courthouse .. CUTCHERRY
cow .... GAEKWAR
crane .... SARUS
crocodile ...... GAVIAL,
    MUGGER, MUGGAR
cuckoo .... KOEL
curtain .... PURDAH
custom .... DASTUR
dancing girl .. BAYADEER,
            BAYADERE
dancing girl's act ....
               NAUTCH
deer ...... CHITAL, AXIS
desert .... THAR
devil's tree .... DITA
dialect .... PUSHTU
diamond cutting center ..
           GOLCONDA
diamond, famous ....
    KOHINOOR, KOHINUR
dill .... SOYA
disciple .... CHELA
district .. AGRA, MALABAR
district ruler ..... NABOB,
               NAWAB
division .... OUDH
dog ..... DHOLE, KOLSUN
dormitory ..... GHOTUL
drama .... NATAKA
Dravidian ..... GOND(I)
Dravidian language .....
        TELUGU, TELEGU
drink .... SOMA
drug .... BHANG
dugout .... DUNGA
dust storm ..... PEESASH
dye .... CURCUMA
elephant .... HATHI
elephant driver .. MAHOUT
elk .... SAMBAR
emperor ... BABER, ASOKA
empress of .... VICTORIA
entertainment .. TAMASHA
epic .... RAMAYAMA,
       MAHABHARATA
estate, inherited ... TALUK
Eurasian in .... FERINGI,
    SAHIB, FERINGHEE
European lady in ....
          MEMSAHIB
extra pay .... BATTA
falcon .... BAS(A)RA,
        SHAHEEN,
        SHASHIN

fan .... PUNKA(H)
farmer .... RYOT, MEO
feathered headdress ......
 BONNET
festival .... DEWALI
fiber tree .... BAOBAB
fig tree ... PIPAL, BO TREE
fighter bird .. AMADAVAT
flute ... PUNGI, MATALAN
foot soldier .... PEON
footman .... PEON
footstool .... MORA
forage plant ...... GUAR
founder .... IVAN
fowl .... BRAHMA
fruit .... BEL
game .... PACHISI
garment .... BANIAN,
 DHOTI, KURTA
gateway .... TORAN
gazelle .... CHIKARA
ghost .... BUHT
girl leader ...... BELOSA
goat, wild .... TAHR
gold coin ...... MOHUR
gorge .... TANGI
gossip .... GUP
government estates .....
 AMANI
government official .....
 DEWAN, DIWAN
granary .. GOLA, GUNJ,
 GUNGE
grant .... ENAM
greeting ...... NAMASTE
groom .... SYCE, SICE
guide .... SHIKARI,
 SHIKAREE
guitar .... VINA
gully .... NULLAH
guru ...... MAHARISHI
harem .... ZENANA
harvest .... RAB(B)I
hat .... TOPEE, TOPI
hawk .... SHIKRA,
 BADIUS
headman ...... PATEL,
 MOKADDAM
head servant .... SIRDAR
helmet ...... TOPI, TOPEE
hemp ... B(H)ANG, KEF,
 GANJA, RAMIE, KEEF
hemp drug .... HASHISH
hemp shrub ...... PUA,
 POOA(H)
hill .... GARO

hill dweller ...... DOGRA
Hindu banker ... SOUCAR
hog deer ... AXIS, ATLAS
holy city ...... HARDWAR,
 NASIK, BENARES
holy man .... FAKIR,
 SADHU, YOGI
home rule ...... SWARAJ
horse disease .... SURRA
hunter .... SHIKAR(I),
 SHIKAREE
hunt(ing) ...... SHIKAR
hunting guide .... SHIKARI
hut .... BARI
inheritance ...... TALUK
intoxicant ...... SOMA
island .... CEYLON,
 MAURITIUS, NICOBAR,
 ANDAMAN
islands near .... MALDIVE
jacket .... KOLA
Jesuit in ...... PAULIST
jungle .... SHOLA
kingdom ...... NEPAL
knife .... DAO
laborer .... PALLI
lace .... GOTA
lacs, 100 .... CRORE
lady ...... BEGUM, BIBI,
 MEMSAHIB
lady's maid ...... AYAH
land grant ...... SASAN
land grant tenant ....
 ENAMDAR
landing place ...... GHAT
landowner .. ZAMINDAR
language ...... SANSKRIT,
 ASSAMESE, BENGALI,
 BIHARI, GUJARATI
learned man .. PUNDIT,
 PANDIT
leguminous plant .. GUAR
levee .... DURBAR
license .... CHOP
licorice .... ABRIN,
 JEQUIRITY
lieutenant governor ......
 NAIB
litter ...... MUNCHEEL,
 DOOLEE, DOLY
litter bearer ...... SIRDAR
loam .... REGUR
loincloth .... LUNGI,
 LUNGEE
low class .... BHAT
lunch .... TIFFIN

macaque .... RHESUS
magnolia tree ....
     CHAMPAC, CHAMPAK
mahogany .... TOON
mail .... DA(W)K
marijuana .... GANJA
market .... PASAR
master ..... SAHIB, MIAN
matting .... TATTA
meal .... AT(T)A
measure of distance .....
     KOS, GUZ
merchant ..... SOUDAGUR
midwife .... DHAI
military caste ... RAJPUT
military post ....
     CANTONMENT
millet ... DHOOR, DURRA,
     DOURA(H), JOAR,
     CHENA
minstrel .... BHAT
mistress ...... MEMSAHIB
mogul dynasty founder ..
     BABER, BABAR, BABUR
monetary unit ... RUPEE,
     LAC, LAKH
money lender .. MAHAJAN
monkey .... RHESUS,
     WANDEROO
Moslem .... SWAT
Moslem princess .. BEGUM
Moslem language ....
     URDU, HINDUSTANI
mountain ...... ABIL,
     DAPSANG, NILGIRI
mountain chain ....
     GHA(U)T, MUSTAGH,
     KARAKORAM, GHATS
mountain pass .. GHA(U)T
mulberry ... (A)AL, ACH
murder .... THUGGEE
musical instrument ......
     RUANA, SAROD, SARON,
     VINA
musket ball .... GOLI
muslin .... GURRAH,
     DOREA
mystic .... GURU
Naga capital ... KOHIMA
narcotic .... BHANG,
     HASHISH
national mourning ......
     HARTAL
native .... BENGALI
native cavalryman ......
     SOWAR

native chief ..... SIRDAR
native clerk, in English ..
     BABOO, BABU
native's inheritance .....
     TALUK
Negro .... HUBSHI
news by relays ..... DAK,
     DAWK
Nilgiri .... BADAGA
northern ..... HINDUSTAN
novice .... CHELA
nurse ...... AMAH, AYAH
Occidental just arrived in
     GRIFFIN
official ... DEWAN, NAZIR
official seal .... CHOP
oil plant .... RAMTIL
oil tree .... BEN
100 lacs .... CRORE
ox .... GAUR
oxlike animal ..... ZEBU
pageant ...... TAMASHA
pagoda .... CHORTEN
palanquin ...... PALKEE
palm .... NIPA
palm sap .... TODDY
panda .... WAH
parliament lower house ..
     LOK SABHA
part of .... DECCAN
partridge .... KYAH
paymaster .... BUXY
peasant .... RYOT
peninsula ... HINDUSTAN
people in Bombay ......
     MARATHA, MAHRATTA
pepper plant ..... BETEL
permit .... CHOP
physicist ... BOSE, RAMAN
pigeon .... TRERON
pillar .... LAT
plum .... AMRA
poetic .... IND
poison ...... BISH, BIKH
police station .... THANA
policeman .... PEON,
     SEPOY
political party .. SWARAJ,
     SWATANTRA
political protest .. HARTAL
Portuguese district .....
     DAMAO
powder .... ABIR
prayerlike gesture ......
     NAMASTE
president .... PRASAD

priest .... SHAMAN
priest's garment .. DHOTI
prime minister .. NEHRU,
   GANDHI, SHASTRI
prince .... RAJA(H),
   MAHARAJA(H)
princess .... RANI, BEGUM,
   RANEE, MAHARANEE,
   MAHARANI
property .... DHAN
protectorate ..... SIKKIM
province .... PUNJAB
queen .... BEGUM, RANI,
   RANEE, MAHARANI
queen mother .. RAJMATA
race .... TAMIL, JAT
rat .... BANDICOOT
ravine .... NULLAH
reception (hail) .. DURBAR
region .... CARNATIC,
   MALABAR, CANARA
religious fanatic ... THUG
religious sect .... SAMAJ
republic .... BHARAT
resort .... SIMLA
revenue collector ....
   ZAMINDAR
rice .... BORO
rich man .... NABOB,
   NAWAB
rifle pit .... SANGAR
river ..... INDUS, GUMTI,
   JUMNA, GANGES,
   GODOVARI, KISTNA,
   JAMUNA, NARBADA,
   NERBUDDA
river landing place ......
   GHAT
road .... PRAYA
roast meat ...... CABOBS,
   KABOBS
robber ... THUG, DACOIT
robe of distinction ......
   SEERPAW
root .... ATIS
rope dancer .... NAT
rug .... DRUGGET
rule .... RAJ
ruler .... NAWAB, NABOB,
   NIZAM, RAJA(H), RANI,
   RANEE, RAO
ruling caste ..... RAJPUT
sacred city .... BENARES,
   NASIK, HARDWAR
sacred word .... OM
sacrificial victim .. TRAGA

sailor .... LASCAR
salute with palms ....
   NAMASTE
salvation ...... MOKSHA
sash ...... CUMMERBUND
savant .... PUNDIT
scholar .. PANDIT, PUNDIT
screen ... PURDAH, TATTY
seal .... CHOP
seaport .... SURAT
servant .... AMAH, MATY,
   AYAH, HAM(M)AL,
   HAMAUL
shawl .... CHUDDAR,
   CHUDDER
sheep ..... OORIAL, SHA,
   URIAL, SNA
shell money ...... ULO,
   UHLLO
shirt .... BANIAN
show .... TAMASHA
shrine .... DAGOBA
shrub ..... MADAR, ODAL
silk ..... MUGA, ROMAL,
   RUMAL, CABECA, ERI
silk cloth ...... PONGEE
sir .... SAHIB
skipper .... SERANG
snake ... KRAIT, DABOIA,
   BONGAR, KATUKA,
   COBRA
snake fighter ....
   MONGOOS(E)
soldier .... PEON, SEPOY,
   GURKHA
songbird .... SHAMA,
   WHITE EYE, KOEL,
   AMADAVAT
sorghum .... CUSH
sovereign(ty) ...... RAJ
spectacle ..... TAMASHA
spinning wheel ....
   CHARK(H)A
spittoon .... PIGDAN
stairs to river landing .....
   GHAT
stamp .... CHOP
state ... SIKKIM, MYSORE,
   ASSAM, BOMBAY,
   GUJARAT, KERALA,
   BENGAL, MADRAS,
   COORG, TRIPURA,
   ORISSA, MARWAR,
   MANIPUR JODHPUR,
   BIHAR, KASHMIR,
   AJMER, PUNJAB, JAIPUR

state capital ..... PATNA, IMPHAL, CALCUTTA, MERCARA

state revenue lands ...... AMANI

stone .... LINGAM

storehouse .... GOLA

stork .... ARGALA, ADJUTANT

sugar .... GUR

sun helmet .. TOPI, TOPEE

suspension of work, etc. .. HARTAL

tax collector .. TAHSILDAR, ZAMINDAR

tax collection area ...... TALUK

tea .. PEKOE, DARJEELING, ASSAM, NILGIRI

teacher .... GURU

temple .... PAGODA

temple girl ... BAYADERE, BAYADEER

temple tower .. SHIKARA

tenant .... ENAMDAR

tenant farmer ..... RYOT

term of address ... SAHIB

territory ... GOA, DAMAN, DIU, ANDAMAN, NICOBAR, TRIPURA, MANIPUR

timber tree .... DAR, SAL

title ...... AGA, NAWAB, SAHIB, RAJA(H)

title of respect .. PANDIT, S(H)RI, SHREE, SAHIB, HUZOOR

tower ... SHIKARA, MINAR

tracker ... PUGGE, PUGGI

tree .... NEEM, BEL, DAR, AMRA, SAL, CHAMPAC, CHAMPAK, BANYAN, PIPAL, ENG, GORAN, SAJ, MYXA, AMLA, RAMTIL, PALMYRA, MARGOSA

tree bark .... NIEPA

tribal community ...... MURIA

tribesman .... NAGA, KHOND

turban ..... PUG(G)REE, PUGGRY

turban cloth ..... LUNGI, LUNGEE

turmeric ..... CURCUMA

twilled cotton ..... SALOO, SALU

two-wheeled carriage .... TONGA

umbrella .... CHATTA

valley .... DHOON

vehicle ... GHARRY, RATH, TONGA

veranda .... PYAL

vernacular .... PRAKRIT

vessel .... LOTA(H), PATAMAR

vetch .... AKRA

viceroy .... CURZON

village .... ABADI

vine .... ODAL, SOMA

viol .... RUANA

violin ... SAROD, RUANA

waistband .... CUMMERBUND

warrior .... SINGH, GURKHA

watchman .... MINA

water carrier .. BHEESTY, BHEESTIE

water course .... NULLAH

wayside stop ..... PARAO

weasellike animal .... MONGOOSE, ICHNEUMON

weight ...... TOLA, PICE, POLLAM, CHITTAK, MAUND, RAT(TI), SER

Westerner in ... GRIFFIN

wheat .... SUJI

wild cat .... CHAUS

wild dog .... DHOLE, BUANSU

wild hog ..... BABIRUSA

wild sheep ..... OORIAL, SHA, NAROOR, SHABO

woman's house .. ZENANA

xylophone .... SARON

yellow .... P(I)URI, PURREE

Zoroastrian ..... PARSEE, PARSI

Indian ...... HOPI, MOHAWK, OTOE, UTE, INCA(N), ERIE, AMERIND, CREE, CHIPPEWA, KIOWA, PEQUOT, SAC, SEMINOLE, REDSKIN, ONEIDA, DELAWARE, SIOUX, APACHE, MAYAN, IROQUOIS

Alabama .... CREEK

Alaska .... ALEUT,
TLINGIT, TLINKIT
Aleutian island .: AKKHAS
Algonquian .. CHIPPEWA,
ARAPAHO(E),
OJIBWA(Y), MAHICAN,
MOHEGAN, DELAWARE,
CREE, MOHICAN,
KICKAPOO, SAC, SAUK,
SANNUP, MICMAC, FOX,
PEQUOT
Antilles .... CARIB
Argentine ....
ARAUCAN(IAN)
Arikara .... REE
Arizona .... APACHE,
HOPI, YUMA, NAVAJO,
PIMA, PAPAGO
arrow poison ... CURARE
Athapascan .... APACHE,
TAKU, DENE, NAVAHO,
NAVAJO
ax .... TOMAHAWK,
HATCHET
baby .... PAPOOSE
ball game .... LACROSSE
battle-ax .... TOMAHAWK
bead money ... WAMPUM
blanket ...... MACKINAW
boat .... CANOE
Bolivia .... AYMARA,
CHARCA, MOXO,
MAROPA, OTUKE
brave, young ....
TENDERFOOT
Brazil ... GUARANI, TUPI,
CARIB, TAPUYA
bread .... TUCKAHOE
British Columbia .. HAIDA
British Honduras ....
MAYA(N)
Caddoan ...... PAWNEE,
ARIKARA, REE
California ... SERI, YUKI
Canadian .... HAIDA,
DENE, CREE
ceremonial pipe ....
CALUMET
ceremony .... POWWOW
challenge sign ....
SCALP LOCK
chick pea .... GRAM
chief ... COCHISE, LOGAN,
SACHEM, TECUMTHA,
TECUMSEH, HIAWATHA,
PONTIAC, SAGAMORE,

BRANT, GERONIMO,
MASSASOIT, POWHATAN
chief, Apache ....
GERONIMO, COCHISE
chief, Delaware ....
TAMMANY
chief, Seminole .. OSCEOLA
Chile .... ARAUCAN
Chippewa .... OJIBWA(Y)
clan symbol ..... TOTEM
Colorado .... UTE
communal home ....
LONG HOUSE
conference ... POWWOW
corn ... MAIZE, MANDAN,
KANGA, ZEA, SAMP,
MEALIES, MEALY,
NUBBIN, FLINT
council hall ....
LONG HOUSE
council room ...... KIVA
Creek .... ALABAMA,
MUSKHOGEAN
Dakota .... SIOUX,
ARIKAREE, REE
Delaware .... LENAPE
dwelling .. HOGAN, TEPEE,
WIGWAM, LODGE,
WI(C)KIUP
Ecuador .... CANELO,
CARA
Eskimo .... AMERIND
feast .... POTLATCH
female .... MAHALY,
PURIS
fetish .... TOTEM
Flathead .... SALISH(AN)
Florida ...... SEMINOLE,
CALUSA
food .... PEMICAN
footwear ..... MOCCASIN
Georgia .... CREEK
Gila River .... PIMA
girl in poem ....
MINNEHAHA
god .... MANITOU
great spirit ... MANITO(U),
MANITU
greeting .... NETOP, HOW
Guatemala .... MAYA(N)
halfbreed ..... METIF(F)
headdress .. WAR BONNET
hero in poem ....
HIAWATHA
Hopi ...... MOKI, MOQUI

horse ...-...-... MUSTANG,
CAYUSE, PINTO
Huron .... WYANDOT
hut ... LODGE, WI(C)KIUP,
HOGAN, TEPEE
Illinois ...-...-. KICKAPOO
Iowa ....-... SAC, SAUK
Iroquoian ..... MOHAWK,
WYANDOT, ERIE,
CAYUGA, CHEROKEE,
ONEIDA, HURON,
SENECA, MINGO,
TUSCARORA, ONONDAGA
Kansas ... PANI, PAWNEE
Lake Erie .... CHIPPEWA
maize ....-...-... CORN
male, married ... SANNUP
Manitoba .... CREE
medicine man .. POWWOW
memorial post ... TOTEM,
XAT, XYST
mestizo .... GRIFF(E),
HALF-BREED, METIF(F)
Mexican .... APACHE,
OTOMI, YAQUI, AZTEC,
MAYA(N)
Michigan ...-... SAC, SAUK
Missouri ...... MANDAN
mixed blood .. METIF(F),
METISSE, HALF-BREED
moccasin ..-...-... PAC
money ...-...-... PEAG(E),
SE(A)WANT(T),
WAMPUM, PIMAN
mystic symbol ......-...
SWASTIKA
Nebraska ...-... PAWNEE,
OMAHA, PONCA
Negro ...-......-... ZAMBO
New Mexico ... PUEBLO,
ZUNI, TANO
New York ..... CAYUGA,
IROQUOIS, SENECA
nomadic ......-... APACHE
North Dakota ...-...-...
CHIPPEWA, PAWNEE,
CADDOAN
Ocean continent ...-...-...
LEMURIA
Ocean vessel ...-... DHOW
Oklahoma .... CREEK,
PONCA, ARAPAHO(E),
SAC, SAUK
Oregon .. YANAN, CAYUSE
Panama ...-...-... CUNA
peace pipe ...-... CALUMET

Penutian ...-...-. CHINOOK,
CHINUK
Peru ...-...-. PANO, INCA,
CANA, AYMARA,
CHANCA
pierced nose ... NEZ PERCE
poison ...-...-... CURARE
pole ...-...-...-... TOTEM
pony .... CAYUSE, PINTO
prayer stick .. BAHO, PAHO
priest .... POWWOW
princess ...-. POCAHONTAS
Pueblo ...-... HOPI, ZUNI,
TANO
Quechuan ...-...-... INCA
room for religious service
KIVA
Salishan ...-...-. TULALIP,
FLATHEAD
seafaring ...-...-. TLINGIT
Seneca Lake ...-. CAYUGA
Shoshonean ...-...-... HOPI,
COMANCHE, PAIUTE,
UTE
Sioux ... . PONCA, DAKOTA,
MANDAN, OMAHA,
SAPONI, KAW, OTOE,
OSAGE, TETON
sled dog ...-...-...-... HUSKY
sledge ...-...-. TRAVOIS(E)
slipper .... MOCCASIN
South American ...-...-...
GUARANI, TUPI, CARIB,
OTA, TAPUYA(N),
AYMARA, ONA,
ARAWAK, ANETO,
ARAUCAN(IAN)
Sonora ...-...-. YAQUI, SERI
spirit .... MANITOU
supplanted by Incan ...-...
AYMARA
tepee ...-. WIGWAM, LODGE
tent ...-. TE(E)PEE, LODGE,
WIGWAM
Tierra del Fuego ...-... ONA
trophy .......-...-... SCALP
unit of money ...-. PIMAN
Utah ......-...-...-... UTE
Uto-Aztecan ...-... YAQUI
village ...-...-...-... PUEBLO
wampum ... SE(A)WAN(T)
war ceremony ...-...-...-...
POWWOW
war cry ...-...-... WHOOP
war trophy ...-...-. SCALP
warrior ...-...-... BRAVE

weapon ..... TOMAHAWK
West Indies ...... CARIB
Western ..... UTE, ZUNI,
        OTO(E), HOPI
whisky to an .. FIREWATER
white person to an ......
        PALEFACE
wife .... SQUAW
wigwam ...... TE(E)PEE,
        LODGE
winter festival ....
        POTLATCH
Wisconsin ... SAC, SAUK,
        KICKAPOO
woman .... SQUAW
yell .... WHOOP
"yes" of .... UGH
young .... BUCK
Yucatan .... MAYA(N)
Indiana capital .. INDIANAPOLIS
    city ... GARY, EVANSVILLE,
        KOKOMO, MUNCIE,
        MARION, MISHAWAKA
    county .... OWEN, CASS,
        CLAY, WELLS, KNOX,
        PIKE
    native .... HOOSIER
    river .... MAUMEE,
        TIPPECANOE, WABASH
    state bird .... CARDINAL
    state flower ...... PEONY
    state nickname .. HOOSIER
    state tree .... TULIP
    university .... PURDUE
    village ..... SANTA CLAUS
Indic dialect .... PALI
Indica(avis) .... APUS
indican .... GLUCOSIDE,
        UROXANTHIN
indicate ...... SHOW, POINT,
    INTIMATE, SIGNIFY, EVINCE
indication(s) .. SIGNS, INDICIA,
        TOKEN
indicator ... GAUGE, REGISTER,
    POINTER, INDEX, ARROW,
        DIAL, CLUE, SIGN
    wind .... VANE
indict ... IMPEACH, ARRAIGN,
    ACCUSE, CHARGE
indictment .... CHARGE,
        ACCUSATION
indifference .... APATHY,
        LETHARGY
indifferent ...... APATHETIC,
    FAIR, AVERAGE,
    UNCONCERNED, DETACHED,

COOL, ALOOF, SOSO,
    LANGUID, COLD
to pain/hardship ....
        STOIC(AL)
indigence ...► POVERTY, NEED,
    WANT, PENURY
indigenous .... INHERENT,
    INBORN, ENDEMIC, INNATE,
    NATIVE, EDAPHIC
indigent ... POOR, DESTITUTE,
        NEEDY
indigestion ....► DYSPEPSIA,
        APEPSIA
indignant ...... ANGRY, IRATE,
        WROTH
indignation ... ANGER, SCORN,
        IRE, WRATH
indignity ... INSULT, AFFRONT,
        HUMILIATION
indigo ...... DYE, BLUE, ANIL
    bale of .... SEROON
    berry .... RANDIA
    blue .... INDIGOTIN
    Chinese .... ISATIS
    compound .... ISATIN
    derivative ..... KETOLE,
        INDOL(E), ISATIN
    dye .... ISATIN
    forming substance ......
        INDICAN
    plant .... ANIL
    oxidized .... ISATIN
    source of .... ANIL
    wild .... BAPTISIA
indirect ... ROUNDABOUT,
    SECONDARY, DEVIATING,
        OBLIQUE
    expression ....
        CIRCUMLOCUTION,
    AMBAGE, PERIPHRASIS,
        PERIPHRASE
indiscreet ...►...►.. UNWISE,
        IMPRUDENT
indiscrete .... COMPACT
indispensable ..... NECESSARY,
    VITAL, ESSENTIAL
    one .... KEYMAN
indisposed .... SICK, ILL,
    UNWILLING, AVERSE
indisposition .... MALAISE,
    AVERSION, ILLNESS,
    AILMENT, PIP
indisputable ....
    UNQUESTIONABLE,
    APOD(E)ICTIC

indistinct ... FAINT, OBSCURE, DIM, VAGUE, HAZY

indite .... COMPOSE, PEN, WRITE, INSCRIBE

individual ..... PARTICULAR, PERSON, SELF, ONE, SINGLE, SOLE

  biological development ~ ONTOGENY

  combining form ~.. IDIO

  performance ... ~ ~ SOLO

individualism .... EGOISM

Indo-China, part of ... BURMA, MALAYA, THAILAND, CAMBODIA, LAOS, VIETNAM

  Chinese .. LAO, TAI, SHAN

  European .... ARYAN, CROAT

  European language . ~ ~ AVESTAN, HITTITE

  Iranian .... KAF(F)IR

indoctrinate .... TEACH, BRAINWASH, INSTRUCT, BRIEF

indolence .... IDLENESS, LAZINESS, INERTIA, SLOTH

indolent .... IDLE, LAZY, LISTLESS, SUPINE, SLOTHFUL, OTIOSE

Indonesia .... EAST INDIES

  capital of ...... JAKARTA

  part of ... JAVA, BORNEO, SUMATRA, CELEBES, WEST IRIAN

Indonesian ... BATTAK, DYAK, LAMPONG, ATTA

  bird .... PEAFOWL, HORNBILL, BULBUL

  city .... JAKARTA, SURABAJA, BANDUNG, MACASSAR

  island ... JAVA, MADURA, MOLUCCAS, BANGKA, TIMOR, BALI, LOMBOK, BORNEO, CELEBES, SUMATRA, CERAM, MADOERA

  knife .... PARANG

  language ..... JAVANESE, SUDANESE, MADURESE, MALAY

  monetary unit ... RUPIAH

  news agency .... ANTARA

  ox .... BANTENG

  premier .... HATTA

  president ..... SUKARNO

  puppeteer ~ (TO)DALANG

  rhino .... BADAK

  shadow-play .... WAYANG PURWA

  volcano ...... TAMBORA, KRAKATAO

  xylophone ...... GENDER, GAMBANG

indorse ... ATTEST, SANCTION, APPROVE

indri .... LEMUR

indubitable .... SURE, EVIDENT, DOUBTLESS, UNQUESTIONABLE, CERTAIN

induce .... PERSUADE, CAUSE, EFFECT, DRAW, URGE, PREVAIL, LEAD

inducement ... . INCENTIVE, MOTIVE

induct ... INSTALL, INTRODUCE, INITIATE

inductance, measure of ~..... HENRY

induction ceremony ~ . ~ . ~ .. INAUGURAL

indulge ... . HUMOR, SPOIL, BABY, CODDLE, PET, PAMPER, YIELD, SATISFY, GRATIFY

indulgence ~ . ~ . ~ .. FAVOR, PRIVILEGE

indulgent ~ ~ LENIENT, KIND, TOLERANT

indurate ~ . ~ . ~ ... HARDEN

Indus .... CONSTELLATION

  River tributary ... SUTLEJ

  tribesman ... . GOR

industrial giant ~.. MAGNATE, TYCOON

  spy ... .. ~ . ~ . ~ .. KEEK

  Workers of the World member ... ~ WOBBLY

industrialist .... TYCOON

industrious ... DILIGENT, BUSY, HARD-WORKING, ASSIDUOUS, OPEROSE

inearth ~ . ~ . ~ .. INTER, BURY

inebriate .... INTOXICATE(D), EXCITE, DRUNK(ARD), SOT, TOPER

ineffectual ~ . ~ ... IDLE, VAIN, FUTILE

inelastic ~ . ~ .. STIFF, RIGID, INFLEXIBLE

inelegant ~ ~ CRUDE, COARSE

ineligible ..... UNSUITABLE, UNQUALIFIED

ineluctable .... CERTAIN, INEVITABLE, UNAVOIDABLE, DOOM, FATE

inept .... ABSURD, FOOLISH, ·CLUMSY, AWKWARD, PUERILE, UNFIT

inerrant .... INFALLIBLE

inert .... DULL, SLOW, INACTIVE, NEUTRAL, LATENT, SUPINE, TORPID

inescapable ...... INEVITABLE

inevitable ...... DUE, CERTAIN

inexorable ..... HARD, STERN, UNYIELDING

inexperienced ... RAW, GREEN

inflexible .... INERRANT

infamous .... NOTORIOUS, OUTRAGEOUS, SCANDALOUS, VICIOUS

infamy .... DISGRACE, NOTORIETY, ODIUM, SHAME, OBLOQUY

infancy .... BABYHOOD, MINORITY, INCUNABULA
   to puberty .. CHILDHOOD

infant ... MINOR, BABY, CHILD, TOT, BABE, BAIRN, CHRISOM
   doctor of .... PEDIATRIST
   room of .... NURSERY

infanta .... PRINCESS

infante .... PRINCE

infantile .... CHILDISH
   paralysis ....
      POLIO(MYELITIS)

infantryman .. (FOOT)SOLDIER, DOUGHBOY, DOGFACE, TURCO
   firearm of .... MUSKET
   mounted ...... DRAGOON

infantrymen's formation ......
      PHALANX

infatuate .... CHARM, ENAMOR

infatuated .... FOOLISH, GAGA, ENAMORED

infatuation ... PASSION, FOLLY, CRUSH, RAVE

infect .... CONTAMINATE, CORRUPT, IMBUE, TAINT, AFFECT

infected ... DISEASED, TAINTED

infection ..... DISEASE, TAINT
   source .... NIDUS

infectious ..... CONTAGIOUS, CATCHING

infecund .... BARREN

infer ...... DEDUCE, GATHER, CONCLUDE, PRESUME, DERIVE

inference ...... COROLLARY, DEDUCTION, CONCLUSION, ILLATION

inferior ...... SUBORDINATE, MEDIOCRE, LOW(ER), POOR, LESS, MINOR, PETTY, LOUSY, EXECRABLE, SHODDY
   diamonds .... BORTS
   horse .. PLATER, TIT, NAG
   lawyer .... SHYSTER, PETTIFOGGER
   poet .... RHYMESTER, RIMESTER, VERSIFIER, POETASTER
   writer .... HACK

infernal ... HELLISH, FIENDISH, DIABOLICAL, HATEFUL, DEVILISH, SATANIC
   abyss .... TARTARUS
   region .... AVERNUS

inferno ... HELL, ABYSS, HADES, GEHENNA
   Hebrew .... SHEOL

infertile .... BARREN

infest ...... OVERRUN, SWARM

infidel ...... PAGAN, ATHEIST, HEATHEN, SARACEN, MISCREANT

infielder .... SHORTSTOP, BASEMAN

infiltrate .... FILTER

infinite .... ENDLESS, ETERNAL, VAST, BOUNDLESS, IMMENSE

infinitesimal .... MINUTE

infirm .... WEAK, FEEBLE, DECREPIT, UNSTABLE, LAME, SENILE, ANILE

infirmary .... HOSPITAL, DISPENSARY

infirmity .... DEFECT, FRAILTY, WEAKNESS

inflame .... EXCITE, FIRE, IGNITE, FAN, RANKLE, MADDEN

inflammable ... COMBUSTIBLE, PICEOUS, FIERY
   material .. TINDER, PUNK, AMADOU, ACETONE

inflammation .... ITIS, ANGINA
   bone .... OSTEITIS, ARTHRITIS
   bone marrow .. MYELITIS

breast ......-...... MASTITIS
cornea ......-... KERATITIS
eyelid ....- STY
glandular ...... ADENITIS
intestinal ...-...... COLITIS,
ENTERITIS
iris ..-.... IRITIS, UVEITIS
respiratory passages ...-...
CROUP
throat ...-...-... CATARRH
tissue .... CELLULITIS
udders of cow ..- GARGET
urinary bladder ...-...-...
CYSTITIS
inflate ...... DILATE, EXPAND,
INCREASE, DISTEND, SWELL,
PUFF, AERATE
inflated .... BOMBASTIC,
POMPOUS, HIGHFLOWN,
TUMID, SWOLLEN, BLOATED,
TURGID
condition ...-..- TYMPANY
in finance ..... WATERED
inflect ...-. TURN, BEND, CURVE,
MODULATE
inflection ...-..-... CADENCE
inflexible ... FIRM, ADAMANT,
UNSHAKABLE, FIXED, SET,
UNALTERABLE, IRON, RIGID,
STIFF, OBDURATE
inflict ...-...-.. DEAL, IMPOSE,
WREAK
inflorescence ...-..... FLOWER(S),
FLOWERING, CYME, RACEME,
WHORL
influence ...- WEIGHT, EFFECT,
AUTHORITY, POWER,
INDUCE, AFFECT, DRAG,
HOLD, PULL, IMPEL,
SWAY, HEFT
in electricity ..- INDUCTION
influential ...-....- EFFECTIVE,
POWERFUL
influenza ...-.... GRIPPE, FLU,
CATARRH, CORYZA
influx ...-..........- INFLOW
inform ...-....... APPRISE, TELL,
ACQUAINT, NOTIFY,
ADVISE, WARN, ALERT
against .... DELATE,
BETRAY, DENOUNCE
slang .. RAT, SQUEAL, SING
informal ....:.. CASUAL
talk .... CHAT, CAUSERIE
information ... NEWS, WORD,
INTELLIGENCE, DATA,

FACTS, LEARNING, AVISO
bit of .... ITEM
file .... DOSSIER
in law ...... ACCUSATION
slang .. DOPE, LOW-DOWN
informative ..... INSTRUCTIVE,
EDUCATIONAL, NEWSY,
FACT-FULL
informant ...-...-.. REPORTER,
APPRISER
informed ...-......- HEP, WISE,
AWARE, ON TO, HIP,
CONVERSANT
informer ..... STOOL(PIGEON),
SQUEALER, REPORTER, RAT,
NARK, SPY, DELATOR,
SNITCH, BIRDIE, FINK, NOSE
turn ...-... PEACH, SING,
STOOL, SQUEAL
infract ...-.....-... VIOLATE
infrequent ..... RARE, SELDOM
infringe ...-...-...- VIOLATE,
ENCROACH, BREAK,
TRESPASS
infringement, copyright/patent
PIRACY
infuriate ...- ENRAGE, MADDEN
infuse .... INSTILL, SOAK,
IMPART, IMBUE, FILL, STEEP,
INGRAIN
infusion ...-..-..-... TINCTURE,
ADMIXTURE, TEA
infusoria ...-...-... PROTOZOA,
VORTICELLA
infusorian's stinger ....
TRICHOCYST
ingenious ...-....... CLEVER,
INVENTIVE, ORIGINAL,
D(A)EDAL
ingenue ... ACTRESS, STARLET
ingenuity .. SKILL, CLEVERNESS
ingenuous ...... NOBLE, OPEN,
CANDID, ARTLESS,
INNOCENT, GUILELESS,
FRANK, NAIVE
ingest ..- INCEPT, SWALLOW,
EAT
ingle .... BLAZE, FIRE(PLACE)
ingot ...... PIG, (METAL)BAR,
BULLION
silver ....- SYCEE
zinc .... SPELTER
ingrain ... DYE, INFUSE, IMBUE
ingratiate .... INSINUATE
ingredient .... ELEMENT,
COMPONENT, CONSTITUENT

ingress .... ENTRY, ACCESS, ENTRANCE

ingressive, in grammar .... INCEPTIVE

ingrown ...... INNATE, NATIVE, INBORN

inhabit .. LIVE, DWELL, PEOPLE

inhabitant ..... RESIDENT, ITE, DENIZEN, CIT(IZEN), INMATE

castle's ...... CASTELLAN

inhabiting the shore .... LIMICOLINE

inhalant ...... BENZEDRINE, VICKS

inhale .... BREATHE, DRAW, INSPIRE, SUCK, RESPIRE

sharply .... SNIFF

inhere .... STICK, CLEAVE

inherence .... IMMANENCE

inherent .. INDIGENOUS, BASIC, IMMANENT, INNATE, INBORN, INTRINSIC, ORGANIC

inheritance .... LEGACY, HERITAGE, BEQUEST, BIRTHRIGHT, PATRIMONY, PARCENARY

law .... SALIC

tax .... DEATH DUTY

unit of .... GENE

inheritor ...... DEVISEE, HEIR, LEGATEE

inhibit .... FORBID, CHECK, WITHHOLD, RESTRAIN, PROHIBIT, SUPPRESS, ENJOIN, BAR

inhospitable .... HOSTILE, FORBIDDING

inhuman ..... BESTIAL, CRUEL

inhume .... INTER, BURY

inimical .... UNFRIENDLY, ADVERSE, HOSTILE, UNFAVORABLE

inimitable ...... MATCHLESS, PEERLESS

iniquitous .... WICKED, VICIOUS, UNJUST

iniquity ... EVIL, WICKEDNESS, SIN, INJUSTICE

initial ..... INCEPTIVE, FIRST, INTRODUCTORY

ornamental letter .... PARAPH

initials .... MONOGRAM

woven together .. CIPHER

initiate ...... INDUCT, START, INTRODUCE, ADMIT, OPEN, BEGIN, INSTITUTE, FOUND, HAZE

initiative ... ENTERPRISE, LEAD

inject .. INTERJECT, INOCULATE

injector .... SYRINGE

injection .... CONGESTION, INOCULATION, SHOT

set .... SYRETTE

injunction .. ORDER, COMMAND, ENJOINING, MANDATE

injure ...... HURT, DAMAGE, HARM, SPOIL, IMPAIR, SCATHE, MAR, WRONG, TEEN

injurious ... NOXIOUS, NOISOME, DAMAGING

injury ..... OFFENSE, DAMAGE, TRAUMA, HARM, WOUND, TEEN

compensation for .... DAMAGES, SOLATIUM

done in retaliation ...... REPRISAL

injustice ... WRONG, INEQUITY

ink ... BLACKEN, DAUB, SIGN, COLOR

berry .... POKEWEED

fish .... CUTTLE

ingredient ...... TANNIN

spreader .... BRAYER, ROLLER

inker ... ROLLER, DABBER, PAD

inking pad, printer's .. DABBER

inkle ... TAPE, YARN, THREAD

inkling ... IDEA, HINT, NOTION, SUSPICION, INDICATION, INTIMATION

inky .... DARK, BLACK

inlaid work ... MOSAIC, BUHL, TARSIA, NIELLO, MARQUETRY, PARQUETRY

inland .... INTERIOR

body of water ..... LAKE

sea ..... ARAL, CASPIAN

Sea island ...... KYUSHU, HONSHU, SHIKOKU

inlay ... FILLING, INSERT, INSET

material .... NIELLO, TILE

inlet ...... CREEK, BAY, ZEE, FIORD, ARM, RIA, BAYOU, BIGHT, COVE, FIRTH, FJORD, ESTUARY

inmate .... OCCUPANT, INHABITANT, PRISONER

inmost .... DEEPEST
part ...... CORE, HEART,
DEPTHS
inn ... LODGING, RESTAURANT,
KHAN, SERAI, CARAVANSARY,
AUBERGE, IMARET,
HOSPITIUM, TAMBO,
POTHOUSE, PUB, TAVERN,
HOTEL, MOTEL, HOSTEL,
HOSPICE, FONDA,
ROADHOUSE
Canterbury Tales' ....
TABARD
worker .... POTBOY,
TAPSTER, BARMAID
innards .... ENTRAILS,
NUMBLES, VISCERA, GUTS
innate .... INDIGENOUS,
INBORN, INHERENT,
INBRED, HEREDITARY,
CONGENITAL, NATIVE,
NATURAL
inner ... INTERIOR, INTERNAL,
ENTAL, BEN
bark .... BAST
coat of eye .... RETINA,
UVEA
combining form ... ENTO
man .... SOUL, STOMACH,
PALATE
Mongolian province ....
JEHOL, CHAHAR,
NINGSIA
parts .... INNARDS
sole .... RAND
wheel member ....
(ROTARY)ANN
Innisfail ...... ERIN, EIRE,
IRELAND
innkeeper .... BONIFACE,
PADRONE, PUBLICAN,
(H)OSTLER, HOST(ELER),
LANDLORD
wife of .... HOSTESS
innocence .... SIMPLICITY,
BLUET, NAIVETE
innocent .... GUILTLESS,
ARTLESS, SIMPLE, NAIVE,
IGNORANT, FOOL, PURE
innocuous .... HARMLESS
innominate ...... ANONYMOUS
bone ... HIPBONE, ILIUM,
ISCHIUM, PUBIS
innovation .... CHANGE,
IMPROVEMENT
innuendo .. HINT, INSINUATION,

SLUR, ASPERSION
innumerable ...... COUNTLESS,
MANY, MYRIAD
Innuit's home ... IGLOO, IGLU
inoculate .... INJECT,
VARIOLATE, INFECT
Inonu, Turkish president .....
ISMET
inopportune ...... UNTIMELY,
INAUSPICIOUS, MALAPROPOS
inordinate .... EXCESSIVE,
IMMODERATE, UNDUE
inordinately .... OVERLY
input, computer's ...... DATA
inquest .... INQUIRY,
INVESTIGATION, ASSIZE
official .... CORONER
inquiline .... COMENSAL
inquiry .... EXAMINATION,
INVESTIGATION, QUERY,
QUESTION
inquisition ... INVESTIGATION,
HOLY OFFICE, INQUIRY
inquisitive .... CURIOUS,
PRYING, SNOOPY, NOS(E)Y
inroad ...... RAID, INVASION,
ENCROACHMENT
insane .. DEMENTED, SENSELESS,
FOOLISH, DAFT, BUGS,
PHRENETIC, BATTY, MAD,
CRAZY
asylum ..... BUGHOUSE,
MADHOUSE
make ...... DERANGE,
DEMENT
person .... LUNATIC,
MADMAN, NUT
insanity ... MADNESS, LUNACY,
DEMENTIA, PSYCHOSIS,
MANIA
near .... FRENZY
insatiable .... GREEDY,
VORACIOUS
inscribe ...... MARK, ENROLL,
DEDICATE, ENGRAVE, WRITE
inscription ..... DEDICATION,
LETTERING, RUNE, GRAFFITO
bookplate .... EX LIBRIS
on book .... ENVOY,
COLOPHON
on coin .... LEGEND,
EXERGUE
tomb's .... EPITAPH
inscrutable ...... ENIGMATIC,
MYSTERIOUS, ABSTRUSE,
INCOMPREHENSIBLE

expression .. POKERFACE,
IMPASSIVE, DEADPAN
one .... SPHINX
insect .... BEETLE, BEE, WASP,
FLY, MOSQUITO, SPIDER,
TICK, MITE, NIT, ANTLION,
APHID, COCCID, CHALCID,
BUG, EARWIG
adult .... IMAGO
eating animal ....
AARDVARK, MOLE,
HEDGEHOG, SHREW,
DESMAN
back of .... NOTUM
blood-sucking ....
CONENOSE
bodies, dried ... KERMES
body part ..... THORAX,
CLAVA, COXA, NOTUM,
ACRON
burrow of .... MINE
colonists .... BEES, ANTS
combining form ....
ENTOMO
dipterous ..... MOSQUITO,
GNAT
eating animal .. TENREC,
TENDRAC
egg ...... NIT, OOTHECA
exudation .... LAC
eyes .... OCELLI
feeding ant ...... KELEP
feeler .... PALP(US),
ANTENNA
flylike ... CICADA, CICALA
form between molts .....
INSTAR
four-winged .... BEETLE
guest of another ....
INQUILINE
hard covering .... CHITIN
immature .... LARVA,
PUPA
jaw .... MANDIBLE
larva .... MAGGOT, GRUB
leaping ... FLEA, LOCUST,
CRICKET,
GRASSHOPPER,
FROGHOPPER,
SPRINGTAIL
leg part .... TARSUS
leg segment ...... COXA,
TIBIA
lepidopterous..... MOTH,
BUTTERFLY
life stage .. PUPA, LARVA,

IMAGO, MAGGOT, EGG,
INSTAR
like .... ENTOMOID
limb .... PROLOG
lip .... LABIUM, LABRUM
migratory .... LOCUST
molting .... ECDYSIS
nest .... NIDUS
noisy .... CICADA
order of .... ACARID,
LOCUST, DIPTERA
plant juice sucker ....
THRIPS, APHID
poison .... VENOM
poison remedy ....
SABADILLA
powder .... PYRETHRUM
resin .... LAC
scale .... COCCID
segment .... SOMITE,
TELSON
shieldlike process ....
CLYPEUS
slim-waisted ...... WASP
small .... CHALCID
smelly ...... STINK BUG
social .... ANT, BEE,
TERMITE
sound ... CHIRP, CHIRR,
DRONE, HUM, BUZZ,
STRIDOR
stick .... EMESA
stinger of .... DART
stinging .. GADFLY, BEE,
WASP, HORNET, GNAT
sucking .... SAPPER
sucking organ ....
HAUSTELLUM,
PROBOSCIS
tree .... KATYDID
twig-like ....
WALKING STICK
wing cover .... ELYTRON,
ELYTRUM
wing, rib in .... NERVURE,
NERVE
wing spot .... ISLE
winged .... WASP, GNAT,
BEE, HORNET,
MOSQUITO, COCKROACH
wingless .... APTERA
with incomplete metamor-
phosis .... NYMPH
young .... NIT
insecticide ... DDT, PESTICIDE,
ROTENONE

insectivore ..... SHREW, MOLE, VIREO, HEDGEHOG, DESMAN, TENREC

insects, kind of .... LACEWING

    moving mass of .. SWARM

    pertaining to ... ENTOMIC

    swarm of .... NEST

insecure ...... UNRELIABLE, UNSTABLE, UNSAFE, UNCERTAIN, RISKY

inseminate .... IMPREGNATE, SOW

insensate ...... COLD, STUPID, FOOLISH, UNFEELING

insensibility ...... ANALGESIA, COMA

insensible .. NUMB, UNFEELING, IMPASSIVE, STOIC

insert ... PUT IN, INTRODUCE, INTROMIT, INGRAFT, INSET, IMMIT

    slyly .... FOIST

insertion ... AD(VERTISEMENT), INSET, INTRODUCTION

    sign .... CARET

inset .... INSERT, INFLUX, INLAY, PANEL

inside ... INTERIOR, INTERNAL, INDOOR(S), SECRET, WITHIN

    clinch .... KNOT

    colloquial ...... STOMACH, INTESTINES

    combining form ... INTRA

    out, turn .... EVERT

insidiate .... PLOT, SCHEME

insidious .... WILY, SLY, CUNNING, CRAFTY

insight .... ACUMEN, KEN, DISCERNMENT, INTUITION

insigne .... STAR

insignia .... EMBLEM, REGALIA, BADGE, CROWN, SCEPTER

insignificant .... TRIVIAL, SMALL, PALTRY, PUNY, MINOR, PETTY

    person ..... INSECT, SNIP, SHRIMP

insincere .... HYPOCRITICAL, UNTRUE

insinuate ...... IMPLY, HINT, INTIMATE, SUGGEST, FOIST

insinuation .... INNUENDO, HINT

insipid ...... BANAL, TASTELESS, DULL, LIFELESS, DRY, STALE, VAPID, FLAT, JEJUNE, TAME, WASHY

insipient ..... STUPID, UNWISE

insist ...... URGE, MAINTAIN, DEMAND, AFFIRM, PERSIST, PRESS

insolation .... SUNSTROKE

insolence .... ARROGANCE, HUBRIS, IMPUDENCE, IMPERTINENCE

insolent .... AUDACIOUS

insolvent .... BANKRUPT

insomnia .... VIGILANCE

insouciant ...... COOL, CALM, CAREFREE, INDIFFERENT

inspan ...... YOKE, HARNESS

inspect .... EXAMINE, SCRUTINIZE, PRY, SCAN

inspection, brief ... LOOK-SEE

inspector .... OVERSEER, EXAMINER

inspiration .... INHALING, IDEA, STIMULUS, INHALATION

inspire .. BREATHE, INFLUENCE, AROUSE, CAUSE, STIR, ANIMATE, INHALE, IMBUE, EXCITE, UPLIFT

inspired .... DEMONIC

inspirit .... CHEER

inspissate .... THICKEN, CONDENSE

instability .... INCONSTANCY, INSECURITY

install ...... INSTATE, INVEST, INDUCT, FIX, SET UP, ESTABLISH

instance .... INSTIGATION, OCCASION, SUIT, ILLUSTRATION, PLEA, SOLICITATION, EXAMPLE, CASE, BEHEST, REQUEST

instant .. URGENT, PRESSING, IMMEDIATE, IMMINENT, TRICE, QUICK, WINK, TIME, MOMENT, JIFFY, TICK

    drink .... COFFEE, TEA, COCOA, ADE

instar ... LARVA, PUPA, IMAGO, MAGGOT

instead .... ELSE, LIEU, RATHER, VICE

instigate ...... URGE, FOMENT, CAUSE, EGG, PROMPT, ABET, INCITE, SPUR

instigation .... INSTANCE

instigator, kind of ... PLOTTER,
AGITATOR, DEMAGOGUE,
PROVOCATEUR

instill ..... INFIX, INCULCATE,
INFUSE, IMPLANT

instinct .... BENT, GIFT,
TALENT, KNACK

institute ...... SET UP, FOUND,
ESTABLISH, INITIATE, START,
SCHOOL

institution .. SCHOOL, CHURCH,
ESTABLISHMENT, HOME,
REFORMATORY

instruct ...... COACH, TEACH,
BRIEF, EDUCATE, EDIFY,
TUTOR

instruction ...... EDUCATION,
LESSON, ORDER, TUTORSHIP,
TUTELAGE, TUITION
art of .... DIDACTICS
in teaching methods .....
PEDAGOGY

instructive .... DIDACTIC

instructor ... TEACHER, COACH,
MENTOR, PEDAGOGUE,
LECTOR

instrument ... AGENT, MEANS,
TOOL, IMPLEMENT, DEVICE,
DEED, AGENCY
board .... PANEL
boring .... JUMPER,
AUGER, GIMLET
Hebrew .... TIMBREL
in law ...... DOCUMENT,
DEED, CONTRACT
lutelike .... BANDORE
measuring ...... OCTANT
nautical .... SECTANT
of punishment ... STOCKS
stringed musical ....
GUITAR, UKE,
MANDOLIN, BANJO,
LYRE, VIOLIN, VIOLA,
SAMISEN, CITTERN,
REBEC, KOTO
surveyor's ..... TRANSIT,
ALIDADE
torture ... WHEEL, RACK,
STRAPPADO

instrumental introduction .....
INTRADA

instrumentality ...... AGENCY,
MEANS, MEDIUM

instruments, for all .... TUTTI

insubordinate .... DISOBEDIENT,
REBELLIOUS

insufferable ..... UNBEARABLE,
INTOLERABLE

insufficient .... LACKING,
INADEQUATE, SCANTY

insular .... NARROW-MINDED,
DETACHED

insulate .... SET APART,
SEGREGATE, ISOLATE

insulating material .. ASBESTOS,
BAGASSE, CELOTEX,
KERITE, OKONITE

insulin discoverer ..... BEST,
BANTING
disease treated with .....
DIABETES

insult ... AFFRONT, INDIGNITY,
ASSAIL, OFFEND, FLOUT,
SLUR, RUFFLE, OUTRAGE

insurance agent ....
UNDERWRITER
contract .... POLICY
protection ... COVERAGE
term .... TONTINE, RISK,
ANNUITY, POLICY

insure .... GUARANTEE,
SECURE, PROTECT,
UNDERWRITE

insurer .... UNDERWRITER

insurgence .... UPRISING,
INSURRECTION

insurgent .... MUTINEER,
REVOLTER, REBEL,
REBELLIOUS, RISER

insurrection ..... REBELLION,
UPRISING, REVOLT

intact ..... COMPLETE, WHOLE

intaglio ...... DIE, ENGRAVE,
GEM
opposed to ...... CAMEO

intangible .... VAGUE,
INCORPOREAL
asset ...... GOOD WILL,
PRESTIGE

intarsia .... MOSAIC

integer ...... ENTITY, WHOLE
odd .... GNOMEN

integral .... ESSENTIAL,
NECESSARY, COMPOSITE,
WHOLE, ENTIRE

integrate .... UNIFY

integrity .... SINCERITY,
UPRIGHTNESS, VIRTUE,
SOUNDNESS, HONESTY,
HONOR

integument ..... SHELL, HIDE,

RIND, HUSK, TESTA, COAT,
DERM, SKIN, ARIL
intellect ...... INTELLIGENCE,
INWIT, BRAIN, MENTALITY,
NOUS
of the .... NOETIC
intellectual .... MENTAL,
INTELLIGENT, EGGHEAD,
HIGHBROW, NOETIC
identification ... EMPATHY
liking .... PALATE
intellectuals, collectively ......
CLERISY, INTELLIGENTSIA
intelligence ... NEWS, TIDINGS,
INFORMATION, REPORT,
INTELLECT, MIND, WIT,
SENSE, ACUMEN, BRAINS
lively .... ESPRIT
intelligencer ..... INFORMANT,
SPY, NEWSLETTER
intelligent .... SMART,
BRILLIANT, CLEVER, SHARP,
ASTUTE, APT, BRIGHT,
SENSIBLE
intelligentsia .. INTELLECTUALS
intelligible .... CLEAR,
UNDERSTANDABLE
intemerate .... PURE
intemperance .. DEBAUCHERY,
EXCESS, CRAPULENCE
intemperate ...... EXCESSIVE,
SEVERE, VIOLENT,
IMMODERATE
intend .... PLAN, MEAN,
PROPOSE, CONSTRUE
intended .... MEANT
colloquial .... FIANCE(E),
BETROTHED
intensify .... HEIGHTEN,
DEEPEN, ENHANCE
intensity .... DEPTH,
VEHEMENCE
intent ... EARNEST, ENGROSSED,
SET, PURPOSE, OBJECT,
EAGER, DETERMINED
intention .... PURPOSE, GOAL,
OBJECT(IVE), AIM, END
intentional ...... DELIBERATE,
VOLUNTARY
inter .... BURY, INHUME,
INURN, ENTOMB
companion of .... ALIA,
ALIOS
interbreed .... CROSS
intercalation ...... EMBOLISM
intercede .... INTERVENE,

MEDIATE, INTERPOSE
intercept ..... CUT OFF, STOP,
PREVENT
intercessor .... MEDIATOR,
PLEADER, ADVOCATE,
BISHOP, PARACLETE
interchange ... SWAP, TRADE,
EXCHANGE, ALTERNATE
intercom .... TALKBACK
interdict ... BAN, PROSCRIBE,
FORBID, PROHIBIT, RESTRAIN,
ENJOIN, VETO, BAR
in Scottish law ....
INJUNCTION
interest .... CLAIM, RIGHT,
BENEFIT, CONCERN, BEHALF,
SHARE, WEAL, ZEAL, STAKE,
PIQUE, USANCE
excessive .. USURY, MANIA
interested ...... CONCERNED,
BIASED
interfere .... COLLIDE,
INTERVENE, MEDDLE,
INTERPOSE, MOLEST
interim .... MEANWHILE,
PROVISIONAL, TEMPORARY,
INTERVAL, MEANTIME,
DIASTEM
interior ...... INSIDE, INNER,
INLAND
interject ... INTERPOSE, INSERT
interjection ... EXCLAMATION,
OH, AH, EGAD, AW,
OUTCRY, HECK, GEE, GOSH
interlace ..... WEAVE, BRAID,
PLEACH, TWINE
interlard .... DIVERSIFY
interlock ... KNIT, LINK, MESH
interlocution ..... DIALOGUE,
CONVERSATION
interlope(r) ..... MEDDLE(R),
INTRUDE(R)
interlude .... OVERTURE,
INTERMISSION, EPISODE,
INTERVAL, VERSET
intermediary ... GO-BETWEEN,
MEDIATOR, MEANS, AGENCY,
MEDIUM, MIDDLEMAN
intermediate .... MESNE,
MIDDLE, BETWEEN, MEDIAN
interment .... BURIAL,
SEPULTURE
intermezzo .... INTERLUDE
interminable .... ENDLESS,
CEASELESS, LASTING
intermingle ..... MIX, BLEND

intermission ... RECESS, PAUSE, INTERLUDE, INTERRUPTION, ENTR'ACTE, INTERVAL

intermittent ..... RECURRENT, PERIODIC, OFF AND ON, FITFUL, SPASMODIC

intermix .... BLEND

intern ... DOCTOR, CONFINE, DETAIN

internal ... DOMESTIC, INNER, INTERIOR, INWARD, INTRINSIC

combustion apparatus ... CARBURETOR

fruit decay .... BLET

organs .... VISCERA, VITALS

international agreement ...... TREATY, PACT, ENTENTE

business combine .... CARTEL

exhibition ... EXPOSITION

language ...... IDO, RO, ESPERANTO, VOLAPUK

sports .... OLYMPICS

writers' group ..... PEN

"Internationale" author ...... POTTIER

internecine .... DEADLY, DESTRUCTIVE

interoffice note .... MEMO

interpolate ... INSERT, CORRUPT, FOIST

interpose .... INSERT, INTRODUCE, INTERVENE, INTERCEDE, MEDIATE, INTERRUPT

interpret .... EXPLAIN, ELUCIDATE, CONSTRUE, TRANSLATE, READ, REDE, RENDER

dreams .... REDE

falsely .... GLOSS

interpretation .. EXPLANATION, EXPOSITION, TRANSLATION, CONSTRUCTION, RENDITION, READING, REDE

Biblical .... EXEGESIS

false .... WRENCH

interpretative ... EXPLANATORY, HERMENEUTIC

interpretation, science of ..... HERMENEUTICS

interpreter ...... TRANSLATOR, EXEGETE

of sacred mysteries ...... HIEROPHANT, MYSTAGOGUE

travelers' ... DRAGOMAN

interred .... BURIED

interregnum .... PAUSE, INTERVAL

interrex .... REGENT

interrogate ... ASK, QUESTION, EXAMINE, QUIZ

interrogation mark .. EROTEME

interrogative word, usually ... WHAT, HOW, WHEN, WHERE, WHO

interrogator .... PROBER, QUESTIONER, INQUIRER, QUERIST

interrupt .... BREAK INTO, CUT OFF, OBSTRUCT

interruption ... INTERMISSION, BREAK, OUTAGE

intersect ... DECUSSATE, CROSS, CUT, MEET, JOIN

intersecting lines ... SECANTS

interstice .... CHINK, SLIT, AREOLA, CREVICE, PORE

intertwine ..... LACE, PLEACH, WEAVE, TANGLE

interval .... GAP, INTERLUDE, BREAK, LACUNA, HIATUS, CAESURA, INTERREGNUM, INTERIM

intervene .... INTERPOSE, INTERFERE, MEDDLE, BUTT IN

intervening ... MESNE, BETWEEN

period .... INTERVAL

intervention ... INTERFERENCE

interweave ..... (INTER)LACE, BLEND, ENTWINE, PLAIT, PLAT, SPLICE, RADDLE

interwoven ... LACED, NETTED, RETICULAR

intestinal .... ENTERIC

deposit .... BEZOAR

fortitude ... GRIT, GUTS, PLUCK

griping .... CRAMPS

not .... PARENTERAL

pains ... CRAMPS, COLIC

parasite ..... TRICHINA, PINWORM, NEMATODE, ASCARIS, TRICHURIS, HOOKWORM, TAPEWORM

pouch .... C(A)ECUM

worm purgative ...... SANTANIN(E)

intestine(s) .... COLON,
BOWEL(s), GUTS, ENTRAILS,
VISCERA
  combining form .. ENTERO
  inflammation of ....
ENTERITIS,
(ENTERO)COLITIS
  membrane .... CAUL,
PERITONEUM
  obstruction of .... ILEUS,
VOLVULUS
  of the ... ENTERIC, ALVINE
  part ... ILEUM, ENTERON,
COLON, DUODENUM,
JEJUNUM
  process, hairlike .. VILLUS
intimacy .... FAMILIARITY,
CLOSENESS
intimate ..... HINT, PRIVATE,
CLOSE, IMPLY, CRONY,
FRIEND, SUGGEST
  wear .... STEP-IN(S),
PANTY, SLIP-IN
intimately ..... INLY, CLOSELY
intimation .... NOTICE,
SUGGESTION, DECLARATION,
INKLING, CUE, HINT,
ANNOUNCEMENT
intimidate ... COERCE, DAUNT,
BULLY, COW, (OVER)AWE,
FRIGHTEN, BUFFALO,
BAMBOOZLE
intolerable ..... UNBEARABLE,
UNENDURABLE
intolerance .... BIGOTRY
intolerant .... IMPATIENT,
BIGOTED
  person ... BIGOT, ZEALOT
intone .. CHANT, RECITE, SING
intort .... TWINE, COIL, CURL,
TWIST
intoxicant ..... LIQUOR, GROG,
RUM, GIN, WHISKY, SOMA
intoxicate .... INEBRIATE,
ELATE, EXCITE, SOUSE
  in medicine ..... POISON
intoxicated .. LIT, DRUNK(EN),
SOUSED, POTTED, FRIED,
GROGGY, NAPPY,
PLASTERED, LOADED, JAG
intoxicating .... HEADY
  effect .... KICK
intractable .... UNRULY,
STUBBORN, UNMANAGEABLE,
WILD
intransigent ...... STUBBORN,
UNCOMPROMISING
intrepid .... BOLD, BRAVE,
FEARLESS
intrepidity .. COURAGE, NERVE,
VALOR
intricacy .... COMPLEXITY
intricate .... INVOLVED,
COMPLICATED, INVOLUTE,
KNOTTY, KNOTTED,
DA(E)DAL, MAZY,
COMPLEX, TRICKY
  knot .... GORDIAN
  points/plots, etc. .. NODI
intrigue ..... CABAL, SCHEME,
FASCINATE, PERPLEX, PLOT,
CONSPIRACY, AMOUR,
AFFAIR, BRIGUE
intriguer ...... MACHINATOR,
SCHEMER
intrinsic .... INTERNAL,
ESSENTIAL, INHERENT,
TRUE, REAL
intrinsically .... PER SE
introduce ... INDUCT, INITIATE,
INSTITUTE, INSERT,
PRESENT, OPEN,
INTERPOLATE, USHER,
INFUSE, BEGIN, BROACH,
LAUNCH, IMMIT, INTERJECT
introducer, kind of ... EMCEE,
USHER, TOASTMASTER
introduction .... FOREWORD,
PRESENTATION, PRELUDE,
PREFACE, PROEM
  musical ...... OVERTURE
  to branch of study ......
ISAGOGE
  to constitution ....
PREAMBLE
  to play/poem ....
PROLOGUE
  to society .... DEBUT
introductory ... PRELIMINARY,
INITIAL, EXORDIAL,
PREFATORY
  remark .... PREFACE,
FOREWORD
  study .... ISAGOGICS
introit .... PSALM, HYMN
intromit ..... ADMIT, LET IN,
INSERT, ENTER
intrude .... INTERLOPE,
BUTT IN, TRESPASS,
ENCROACH
intuition ... HUNCH, INSIGHT,
PERCEPTION

intuitive ... ... INSTINCTIVE,
NOUMENAL
intumesce ... SWELL, EXPAND,
BUBBLE, ENLARGE
inulase ... ... ENZYME
inulin ... ... ALANTIN
hydrolyzed ... LEVULOSE
inundant ... ... OVERFLOWING
inundate ... FLOOD, OVERFLOW,
DELUGE, OVERWHELM,
SWAMP
inundation ... ... DELUGE,
SPATHE, FLOOD,
OVERFLOW
inure ... HABITUATE, ACCUSTOM
inurn ... BURY, ENTOMB, INTER
inutile ... ... USELESS,
UNPROFITABLE, IDLE
invade ... INTRUDE, VIOLATE,
RAID, TRESPASS, CROWD,
THRONG
invaders' foothold ... ...
BEACHHEAD
invalid ... ... INFIRM, WEAK,
SICKLY, NULL, VOID, SICK,
NUGATORY
invalidate ... NULLIFY, VOID,
ANNUL, VITIATE, OUTLAW
invaluable ... ... PRICELESS,
PRECIOUS, COSTLY, DEAR
invar, for one ... ... ALLOY
invariable ... ... UNIFORM,
CONSTANT, UNCHANGING
invariably ... ... ALWAYS
invasion ... ... INTRUSION,
INFRINGEMENT, TRESPASS,
INROAD, INCURSION
craft ... ... LST
invective ... ... VITUPERATION,
DENUNCIATION, CURSE,
ABUSE
inveigh ... ... RAIL, DENOUNCE,
CENSURE
inveigle ... ... LURE, TRICK,
ENTICE, LEAD ON,
CAJOLE, COAX, SEDUCE,
TEMPT
invent ... ... FABRICATE,
ORIGINATE, DEVISE,
CONCOCT, COIN
new word ... ... COIN,
NEOLOGIZE
invention ... ... FIGMENT,
FABRICATION, INGENUITY,
FALSEHOOD, DEVICE,
CONCOCTION

kind of ... ... FALSEHOOD,
LIE
inventor ... ... ARTIFICER
automobile ... ... DAIMLER
camera ... ... EASTMAN
celluloid ... ... HYATT
cotton gin ... ... WHITNEY
decimal measurement ...
STEVIN
dynamite ... ... NOBEL
dynamo ... ... FARADAY,
GRAMME
elevator ... ... OTIS
escape-lung ... ... MOMSEN
fountain pen ... ...
WATERMAN
harp ... ... JUBAL
machine gun ... GATLING
motion pictures ... EDISON
motor ... ... TESLA
new words ... NEOLOGIST
phonograph ... ... EDISON
protection of ... PATENT
radar ... ... TUVE, BREIT
radio ... ... MARCONI
revolver ... ... COLT
sewing machine ... HOWE
steam engine ... ... WATT
steamboat ... ... FULTON
tank (military) ... SWINTON
telegraph ... ... MORSE
telephone ... ... BELL
thermometer ... GALILEI
tractor ... ... HOLT
training airplane ... LINK
transistor ... ... BARDEEN,
BRATTAIN
typewriter ... ... SHOLES
safety lamp ... ... DAVY
inventory ... ... STOCK, STORE,
CATALOG(UE), LIST
official ... ... INDENTURE
Inverness ... OVERCOAT, CAPE
inverse ... ... OPPOSITE
opposed to ... ... DIRECT
inversion ... ... REVERSAL
invert ... ... REVERSE,
HOMOSEXUAL
invertebrate ... ... SPINELESS
covering of ... TEST, SHELL
hearing organ of ... ...
OTOCYST
sense organ of ... ...
STATOCYST
inverted state ... TOPSY-TURVY
invest ... ... CLOTHE, ADORN,

ENVELOP, COVER, INSTALL, DON, BESIEGE, ARRAY, ENDOW, ENDUE, SPEND, BELEAGUER, ORDAIN, SURROUND
investigate ... EXAMINE, PROBE
investigation .... PROBE, RESEARCH, INQUEST
investigator .... PROBER, TRACER, INQUISITOR, EXAMINER
investiture .... INDUCTION, INSTALLATION, VESTURE
investment .... COVERING, SIEGE, CLOTHING, CAPITAL
kind of .... CAPITAL, EBOND, BLUE CHIPS
rash .... PLUNGE
investor .... CAPITALIST
list/securities of .... PORTFOLIO
inveteracy ..... FEUD, ENMITY
inveterate .... CHRONIC, DEEP-ROOTED, HABITUAL, OBSTINATE
invidious .... OFFENSIVE
invigorate .... ENLIVEN, ANIMATE, STRENGTHEN, BRACE
invigorating .. TONIC, BRACING
invincible ... UNCONQUERABLE
inviolable .... SACRED, SACROSANCT
inviolate .. UNBROKEN, SACRED
invisible .... UNSEEN, IMPERCEPTIBLE
emanation .... AURA
invitation .... BID, CARD
invite ..... BEG, ASK, REQUEST, ENTICE, CALL, ALLURE, BID
inviting .. TEMPTING, ENTICING
invocation ..... INCANTATION, PRAYER, CONJURATION, MARANATHA
opening ..... AGNUS DEI
invoke ... CONJURE, ENTREAT, BEG, PRAY, IMPLORE
involucre .... BRACTS
secondary .... INVOLUCEL
involuntary ..... ACCIDENTAL, AUTOMATIC, UNINTENTIONAL
action .... REFLEX
involute .... INVOLVED, INTRICATE, ROLLED UP

involve ... ENTAIL, IMPLICATE, INCLUDE, EMBROIL, COMPLICATE, REQUIRE
involved .... INVOLUTE, COMPLICATED, COMPLEX, INTRICATE, IMPLICATED
get .... THICKEN
invulnerable ... UNASSAILABLE
inward ..... INTERNAL, ENTAD
Io, lover of .... ZEUS
rival of .... HERA
watcher of .... ARGUS
iodine antiseptic ...... IODOL, IATROL
source .... KELP
Iolanthe .... PERI
iolite .... CORDIERITE
ion, negative .... ANION
positively charged ...... CATION
Ionian gulf .... PATRAS
island ... ITHACA, CERIGO, CORFU, CORCYRA, KAI, LAUT, LET(T)I, PAXOS, ZANTE
Ionic capital's volute ... HELIX
iota... JOT, WHIT, DOT, TITTLE
IOU, part of ...... OWE, YOU
Iowa, capital of ... DES MOINES
college .... COE
city .... WATERLOO, DAVENPORT, SIOUX, DUBUQUE, CLINTON, KEOKUK
college city .... AMES
county .... POLK, TAMA, ADAIR, CASS, LINN, LYON
native .... HAWKEYE
religious society .. AMANA
state bird ... GOLDFINCH
ipecac .... EVEA, MADDER
product .... EMETINE
Iphigenia's brother .. ORESTES
sister .... ELECTRA
ipse _____ .... DIXIT
ipsissima _____ .... VERBA
ipso _____ .... FACTO, JURE
IQ, part of .... INTELLIGENCE, QUOTIENT
iracund .... CHOLERIC, IRASCIBLE, TESTY
irade .... DECREE
Iran .... PERSIA
Iranian .... TUDAH, PERSIAN, KURD, SOGDIAN

angel .... MAH
bird .... BULBUL
capital .... TEHERAN
carpet .. HAMADAN, KALI
chief .... MIR
city ... ISFAHAN, MESHED,
   TABRIZ, TEHERAN, AMOL,
   HAMADAN, RESHT,
   KERMAN, YEZD,
   PERSEPOLIS, SHUSHAN,
   SUSA, SHIRAZ
coin .... RIAL, LARI,
   P(O)UL, DINAR, DARIC,
   MOHUR
desert .... LUT, KAVIR
empress ... FARAH (DIBA)
evil spirit ..... AHRIMAN
fairy .... PERI
gate .... DAR
gazelle .... CORA
governor .... SATRAP
hero ..... RUSTAM, YIMA
in Russia ..... TA(D)JIK,
   TADZHIK
island .... QUISHM
lake .... URMIA
language ..... KURDISH,
   AFGHAN, PUSHTU,
   PERSIAN, PASHTO,
   ARYAN, AVESTAN,
   PAHLAVI, GALCHA,
   PAMIR
lower house ..... MAJLIS
monetary unit ..... RIAL
moon .... MAHI
mystic .... SUFI
official .... KHAN
oil center ...... ABADAN
poet .... OMAR
port .... ABADAN
premier .... HOVEIDA,
   RAZMARA, MOSSADEGH,
   ZAHEDI
province .... FARS
queen .... SORAYA
river — KARUN, TAB, ZAB,
   SAFID RUD
rug .... SENNA,
   KURDISTAN
ruler ..... SHAH, PAHLEVI
sacred cord ...... KUSTI
sacred writings .. AVESTA
screen .... PURDAH,
   PARDAH
shah .... PAHLEVI
sir .... AZAM

tiara .... CIDARIS
tile .... KAS(H)I
trading center .... ISPAHA
Turk .... SART
water vessel .... AFTABA
water wheel ..... NORIA
weight .... MAUND
Iraq .... MESOPOTAMIA
capital .... BAGDAD
city ... BAGHDAD, MOSUL,
   BASRA
district .... AMARA
gnostic .... MANDEAN
king ...... FAISAL, GHAZI
monetary unit ... DINAR
president ..... ARIF
prime minister .. YAHYA
province .... AMARA
seaport .... BASRA,
   MOSQUES
irascible .... IRACUND,
   IRRITABLE, WRATHFUL,
   CROSS, BRASH, TESTY
irate — ... ANGRY, INCENSED,
   WROTH, MAD
IRBM, part of ....
   INTERMEDIATE, RANGE,
   BALLISTIC, MISSILE
ire — WRATH, ANGER, CHOLER,
   RAGE, FURY, DISPLEASURE
Ireland — . IRENA, EIRE, ERIN,
   EIRANN, HIBERNIA,
   IRISH FREE STATE, ERSE,
   IERNA
capital of North ....
   BELFAST
emblem of ... SHAMROCK
patron saint ... PATRICK
settlers in ...... OSTMEN
Spenser's .... IRENA
Irene .... PAX
actress ... DUNNE, RICH
parent of .. ZEUS, THEMIS
irenic — . PEACEFUL, PACIFIC,
   SERENE
iridescent .... RAINBOWLIKE,
   OPALESCENT, LUSTROUS,
   PAVONINE, VERSICOLOR,
   NACREOUS
gem .... OPAL
iridiscence .... REFLET
iris ... IXIA, GODDESS, ORRICE,
   FLEUR-DE-LIS, EYE, RAINBOW,
   (BLUE)FLAG
combining form .. IRIDO

inflammation of ⁓ ⁓ ⁓ ⁓ UVEITIS, IRITIS

layer of ⁓ ⁓ ⁓ ⁓ UVEA

plant ⁓ ⁓ TILEROOT, FLAG, IXIA, ORRIS

plural of ⁓ ⁓ ⁓ ⁓ IRIDES

root ⁓ ⁓ ⁓ ⁓ ⁓ ORRIS

Irish ⁓ ⁓ ⁓ ERSE, MILESIAN, CELTIC, HIBERNIAN

accent ⁓ ⁓ ⁓ ⁓ BROGUE

alas ⁓ ⁓ ⁓ ⁓ OCHONE

alphabet ⁓ ⁓ ⁓ OGUM, OG(H)AM

ancestor, legendary ⁓ ⁓ ⁓ MILESIAN

assembly signal ⁓ SLOGAN

assessment ⁓ ⁓ ⁓ CESS

ballad hero ⁓ ⁓ ⁓ RORY

battle cry ⁓ ⁓ ABU, SLOGAN

bay ⁓ ⁓ GALWAY, SLIGO

beauty: legendary ⁓ EMER

buxom ⁓ ⁓ ⁓ ⁓ SONSIE

capital ⁓ ⁓ ⁓ ⁓ DUBLIN

capital (former) ⁓ ⁓ TARA

castle ⁓ ⁓ ⁓ ⁓ TARA

cattle ⁓ ⁓ ⁓ ⁓ KERRY

cheese ⁓ ⁓ ⁓ ⁓ KEBBOK

chieftain's follower ⁓ ⁓ ⁓ GALLO(W)GLASS

chisel ⁓ ⁓ ⁓ ⁓ CELT

city ⁓ ⁓ DUBLIN, BELFAST, CORK, LIMERICK, TARA, COBH, SLIGO

church ⁓ ⁓ ⁓ ⁓ KIL

clan ⁓ ⁓ ⁓ SEPT, SIOL

clansman ⁓ ⁓ ⁓ AIRE

club/cudgel ⁓ SHILLELAH, SHILLALA, ALPEEN

coin, fake ⁓ ⁓ ⁓ RAP

colloquial ⁓ ⁓ ⁓ TEMPER

county ⁓ ⁓ ⁓ DONEGAL, MONAGHAN, GALWAY, KERRY, KILKENNY, CORK, MAYO, SLIGO, CLARE, KILDARE

cudgel ⁓ ⁓ ⁓ ⁓ ALPEEN

dagger ⁓ ⁓ ⁓ ⁓ SKENE

dandy ⁓ ⁓ ⁓ ⁓ BUCKEEN

dialect ⁓ ⁓ ⁓ ⁓ OGHAM

dirge ⁓ ⁓ ⁓ ⁓ KEEN

doctor ⁓ ⁓ ⁓ ⁓ OLLAM

dissident ⁓ ⁓ ⁓ FENIAN

district ⁓ ⁓ ⁓ ⁓ BIRR

dramatist ⁓ ⁓ ⁓ O'CASEY, SHAW, YEATS, STEELE, BEHAN

early kingdom ⁓ MUNSTER

emblem ⁓ ⁓ ⁓ SHAMROCK

endearment term ⁓ ⁓ ⁓ ⁓ MACHREE

epic ⁓ ⁓ ⁓ ⁓ TANA

essayist ⁓ ⁓ ⁓ ⁓ LECKY

exclamation ⁓ ⁓ ARRA(H), AROO

export ⁓ ⁓ ⁓ ⁓ LINEN

fairy ⁓ ⁓ LEPRECHAUN, SHEE

family ⁓ ⁓ ⁓ ⁓ CINEL

farmer ⁓ ⁓ ⁓ ⁓ COTTAR, COTTIER

fish ⁓ ⁓ ⁓ ⁓ POLLAN

fishing boat ⁓ ⁓ HOOKER

floral emblem ⁓ ⁓ ⁓ ⁓ SHAMROCK

folklore character ⁓ LIMER

foot soldier ⁓ ⁓ ⁓ KERN

fortification ⁓ ⁓ ⁓ LIS

Free State ⁓ ⁓ IRELAND, SAORSTAT

freebooter ⁓ ⁓ RAPPAREE

freeman ⁓ ⁓ ⁓ ⁓ AIRE

garment ⁓ ⁓ INAR, LENN

general ⁓ ⁓ ⁓ ⁓ SHEA

girdle ⁓ ⁓ ⁓ ⁓ CRISS

girl ⁓ ⁓ COLLEEN, LASSIE

god ⁓ ⁓ ⁓ DAGDA, LER

god of poetry ⁓ ⁓ OGMA

handsome ⁓ ⁓ ⁓ SONSIE, SONSY

hero ⁓ ⁓ FINN, FIONN, RORY, FENIAN, FERGUS

heroine ⁓ ⁓ ⁓ ⁓ EMER

hill ⁓ ⁓ ⁓ ⁓ INCH

historian ⁓ ⁓ ⁓ LECKY

hockey ⁓ ⁓ ⁓ HURLING

hood ⁓ ⁓ ⁓ COCHULL

initials ⁓ ⁓ ⁓ ⁓ IRA

island ⁓ ⁓ ACHILL, INCH

island group ⁓ ⁓ ARANN

jargon ⁓ ⁓ ⁓ SHELTA

John ⁓ ⁓ ⁓ SEAN, EOIN

king ⁓ ⁓ ⁓ ENNA, AED, BRIAN, BORU

laborers ⁓ ⁓ ⁓ AIRE

lake ⁓ ⁓ KILLARNEY, LOCH, REE, DERG, CONN, LOUGH, NEAGH, CORRIB

lake dwelling ⁓ CRANNOG

lament ⁓ ⁓ ⁓ KEEN, CORONACH, WIRRA

landholding system ⁓ ⁓ RUNDALE

legislature .... DAIL,
   EIREANN
lighthouse rock .. FASTNET
limestone .... CALP
lord .... TANIST
love .... GRA
lower house .... DAIL
Lowlander .. SASSENACH
luck .... CESS
lucky ..... SONSIE, SONSY
moss ..... CARRAG(H)EEN
mountain ..... DONEGAL,
   SPERRIN, WICKLOW
musical festival .... FEIS
musical instrument ......
   CRUT, TIMPAN
nationalist ...... EMMET,
   PARNELL
novelist . . REID, SHAW,
   MOORE
outlaw .... PAPIST
Papist .... TORY
parliament .. OIREACHTAS
party .... SINN FEIN
patriot .... EMMET,
   PARNELL
patriotic group ..... IRA
patron saint .... PATRICK
peasant .... KERN(E),
   COTTAR, COTTIER
pipe (tobacco) .. DUDEEN
playwright .... SHAW,
   MOORE
poet .... YEATS, COLUM,
   JOYCE, WILDE
policeman .... PEELER
potato .... YAM
pretender .... BUCKEEN
priest .... DRUID
prime minister ... LYNCH,
   LEMASS, DE VALERA
princess .... ISEULT,
   ISOLDE, DEIRDRE
proprietor ...... TANIST
province ...... MUNSTER,
   LEINSTER, CONNAUGHT,
   ULSTER
rascal .... SPALPEEN
rebel ... FENIAN, FIANNA
river .. SHANNON, CAVAN,
   NORE, LAGAN, BOYNE,
   SUIR, FOYLE
Royalist .... TORY
saint ... AIDAN, PATRICK
saloon .... SHEBEEN
Saxon .... SASSENACH

scamp .... SPALPEEN
sea god .... LER
seaport .... CORK,
   LIMERICK, DUBLIN,
   TRALEE, COBH, BELFAST
secret organization .. IRA,
   MOLLY MAGUIRES
secret society member ...
   ORANGEMAN
shield .... SCIATH
shillaly .... LAH
shoe .... BROGUE
slang .... MICK
smack .... HOOKER
society ...... FEINN, AOII
soldier .. .... KERN(E),
   GALLOGLASS, RAPPAREE
song .... RANN
sorrow .... WIRRA
spirit .... BANSHEE
sprite .... SHEE
statesman .... GRATTAN
steward ...... ERENACH
sweetheart . ... GRA
symbol .... DEIRDRE
tax .... CESS
tenant .... SAER
tobacco pipe .... DUDEEN
tobacco pouch ....
   SPLEUCHAN
tribe ... CINEL, SIOL, SEPT
Ulster county ..... DOWN
verse .... RANN
wail .... KEEN
whiskey ... USQUEBAUGH,
   POT(H)EEN
white .... BAWN
woman revolutionary ...
   GONNE
young man ... BUCKEEN
Irishman ... MICK, HIBERNIAN,
   PADDY, CELT, PAT,
   MILESIAN, TEAGUE, HARP
irk .... ANNOY, DISGUST,
   TIRE, IRRITATE, VEX,
   TROUBLE, NETTLE, BOTHER
irksome ... TEDIOUS, TIRESOME
iron .... PRESS, POWER, FIRM,
   FERRITE, FERRUM, SMOOTH,
   MANGLE
alloy .... STEEL
bar .... BLOOM, JOINTER
chancellor: sobriquet ....
   BISMARK
coated .... TERNE
collar .... GARROTE

combining form .... SIDER(O)
disulfide .... PYRITE
hand .... CONTROL
horse .... LOCOMOTIVE, BICYCLE, TRICYCLE
in golf .... CLUB, MASHIE, NIBLICK
lung .... RESPIRATOR
meteorite ...... SIDERITE
ore .... HEMATITE, SIDERITE, MAGNETITE, TURGITE, TACONITE, LIMONITE
out .... SMOOTHEN, STRAIGHTEN, ELIMINATE
oxide .... MAGNETITE
oxide powder .... CROCUS
oxidized .... RUST
peg used in quoits .. HOB
pertaining to .... FERROUS, FERRIC
pig .... SPIEGEL
prefix .... FERRO
pyrite .... MARCASITE
ready for rolling .... LARGET
sheet ...... TERNEPLATE
slang .... FIREARM
sulfide .... PYRITE
symbol for .... FE
weed genus .... VERNONIA
wood .... ACLE, HELE, COLIMA
ironbark .... EUCALYPTUS
ironclad .... MONITOR, MERRIMAC, WARSHIP, UNBREAKABLE, FOOLPROOF, IRONSIDES
ironer .... MANGLE
ironic(al) ...... SATIRIC(AL), SARCASTIC
writing .... LAMPOON
irons ..... CHAINS, SHACKLES, FETTERS, GYVE
Ironsides .... CROMWELL
ironwood ..... TITI, COLIMA, ACLE, HORNBEAM
ironworks .... SMELTERY
irony ...... MOCKERY, SATIRE, SARCASM
Iroquoian .... HURON, SENECA, WYANDOT, ONEIDA, MOHAWK, CAYUGA, TUSCARORA, CHEROKEE, ONONDAGA, ERIE

irrational .... SENSELESS, INANE, ABSURD, W(H)ACKY
number .... SURD
Irrawaddy tributary .... CHINDWIN
irreconcilable .. CONFLICTING, INCOMPATIBLE
irredenta ...... UNREDEEMED
irrefragable .... INDISPUTABLE
irregular ...... ANOMALOUS, DISORDERLY, UNEVEN, ABNORMAL, ATYPIC(AL), DESULTORY, SPOTTY, ERRATIC, EROSE, FITFUL, SPORADIC
in shape ...... BAROQUE
irregularity .... ANOMALY
irregularly edged ..... EROSE
irreligious .... PROFANE, IMPIOUS, GODLESS, PAGAN
irreproachable .... FAULTLESS, BLAMELESS, IMPECCABLE, ABOVEBOARD
irresistible ..... COMPELLING, OVERPOWERING
irresolute .... HESITANT, UNDECIDED, INDECISIVE
irrespective ..... REGARDLESS
irreverence ...... DISRESPECT
irrevocable .... FINAL, UNALTERABLE
irrigate .... WATER, FLUSH
irrigation ditch ...... SLUICE, ACEQUIA
irritability ...... ERETHISM, IMPATIENCE
irritable .. IRASCIBLE, TOUCHY, TESTY, CROSS, CRANKY, EDGY, TE(T)CHY, GRUMPY, IRACUND, SPLENETIC
irritable person .... TARTAR, CURMUDGEON, GROUCH, CRANK
irritate ...... NETTLE, PEEVE, EXASPERATE, PROVOKE, VEX, CHAFE, RANKLE, PIQUE, RASP, ANNOY, IRK, ITCH, NEEDLE, TEASE, GRATE, GRAVEL, RILE, GALL
irritation .. ITCH, ANNOYANCE, PIQUE
irruption .... BURSTING, INVASION
is .... EXISTS
Isaac .... PATRIARCH

parent of ――.―― ABRAHAM, SARAH
son of ――..... ESAU, EDOM, GAD, JACOB
Isadora, dancer ..... DUNCAN
isagoge ...... INTRODUCTION
Isaye's pupil ..... MENUHIN
Iscariot ..... JUDAS, TRAITOR
ischemia .... ANEMIA
Iseult .... ISOLDE
husband of .... MARK
love of ..... TRIST(R)AM
Ishmael ... OUTCAST, PARIAH
parent of ..... ABRAHAM, HAGAR
son of .... DUMAH
Isidore, diminutive of ... IZZY
isinglass .―.. GELATIN, AGAR, CARLOOL, MICA
source of ..... STURGEON
'isio' brother/husband .. OSIRIS
sister .... NEPHTHYS
Islam adherent ...... MOSLEM, MUSLIM, MUSLEM
canonical law .... SHARIA
convert .. ANSAR, MURED
founder/prophet ......·. MOHAMMED
school .... MADARA
supreme deity ... ALLAH
Islamic teacher ―.... MULLAH, ALIM
island ....― ISLE, AIT, ALT
Alaskan ... KISKA, ATTU, PRIBILOF, ALEUT
at earth's center ... MERU
Beautiful ...... FORMOSA
Caroline .... YAP
city .... AMOY
coral .... ATOLL
country ... JAPAN, ERIN
Danish .... AERO
empire .... JAPAN
enchanted .... BALI
French .... ILE
Greek .... CRETE
Hebrides .... IONA
in a lake .... HOLM
isolated .... INCH
Italian ..... ELBA, CAPRI, SICILY
largest (world's) .... GREENLAND
legendary ...... ATLANTIS
low .... KEY
mythical .... NAXOS

near bigger one .... CALF
Philippine .... PANAY, SAMAR, MINDANAO, LUZON, MINDORO, PALAWAN, SULU
river ..... AIT, EYOT, HOLM
small ..... AIT, CAY, KEY, ISLE, ISLET
Spanish .... ISLA
islands, group of .... ARCHIPELAGO
of Langerhans secretion INSULIN
isle .... AIT, KEY
of Man capital .. DOUGLAS
of Man judge . DEEMSTER
of Wight channel .... SOLENT
of Wight town ... COWES
islet ..... CAY, KEY, AIT, ALT, HOLM
ism ―....... DOCTRINE, SYSTEM, THEORY, BELIEF, DOGMA, TENET, DOXY
isolate ――...... SET APART, SEGREGATE, ENISLE, INSULATE, IMMURE, SECLUDE
isolated ...... QUARANTINED, (EN)ISLED, SEGREGATED
rock .... SCAR
isolation............ SOLITUDE
Isolde .... ISEULT
love of .... TRISTRAM
isomer .... METAMER, MALEIC
isomeric terpene ..... PINENE
isometric .... CUBIC
isopiestic .... ISOBAR
isopod .... CRUSTACEAN
isopyre .... OPAL
Israel(i) ... SION, ZION, JACOB
ancient capital .. SAMARIA
ancient city .... SAMARIA, TIRZAH
battlesite .... ESDRAELON
camp .... ETHAM
capital ...... JERUSALEM, TEL AVIV
city ...... HAIFA, JAFFA, TEL AVIV, JOPPA
coin .... MIL
dance .... HORA
defense line ..... BARLEV
desert .... NEGEV
foreign minister ... EBAN
general .... DAYAN

hero .... GIDEON
high priest .... ELI
king .. AHAB, OMRI, SAUL,
    ELAH, NADAB, SOLOMON,
    JEHU, JEROBOAM
lake .... HULEH
legislature ..... KNESSET
peace .... SHALOM
plain .... SHARON,
    ESDRAELON, JEZREEL
political party ... MAPAM
port ...... ELATH, ACRE,
    HAIFA, JAFFA
premier .... ESHKOL,
    BEN GURION,
    (GOLDA) MEIR
president .... SHAZAR,
    WEIZMANN
prophet of ...... ELISHA,
    ELIJAH, ELIAS
region .... NEGEV
seaport ... JAFFA, JOPPA
strip .... GAZA
town .... EILAT
Israelite ...... JEW(ISH), SION,
    HEBREW, ZION
judge .... ELON
king .... DAVID
land in Egypt ... GOSHEN
leader ... JOSHUA, JOSUE
paid curser ..... BALAAM
strong man .... SAMSON
tribe ... GAD, LEVI, DAN,
    AS(H)ER, GAD,
    MANASSEH, NAPHTALI
Israelites, biblical .. HERITAGE
issei's kin of a sort .... NISEI,
    KIBEI
issue .... EXIT, OUTFLOW,
OUTLET, RESULT, UPSHOT,
OFFSPRING, CHILD, POINT,
QUESTION, EMANATE, EMIT,
ARISE, EDITION, EMERGE,
DEAL OUT, PUBLISH,
PROGENY, OUTCOME
minor point of ....
    TECHNICALITY
take ... DIFFER, DISAGREE
Istanbul .... STAMBOUL,
    BYZANTIUM,
    CONSTANTINOPLE
foreign quarter .... PERA,
    FANAR, BEYOGLU
inn ...... SERAI, IMARET
section .... BEYOGLU,
    SCUTARI, USKUDAR,

    STAMBOUL
suburb .... GALATA
isthmus .... STRAIT, PANAMA,
    BALK, NECK, KRA
Corinth .... MEGARIS
Panama .... DARIEN
istle .... FIBER, PITA, PITO
ita .... NEGRITO
itacolumite ...... SANDSTONE
it doesn't pay .... CRIME
is legal .... LICET
is silent, in music .. TACET
reads same both ways ...
    PALINDROME
Italian .... ROMAN, LATIN,
    PICENE, SABINE
actress .... ANGELI,
    MAGNANI, LOREN,
    DUSE, LOLLOBRIGIDA
adventurer ... CASANOVA
anatomist ..... FALOPIUS
ancient .... ROMAN,
    PICENE, SABINE, OSCAN
ancient city .... CAPUA,
    CANNAE
anew .... DE NOVO
art period ...... SEICENTO,
    TRECENTO
astronomer ...... GALILEO
author .... DANTE,
    PETRARCH
baby .... BAMBINO
baked shrimp ... SCAMPI
bandit .. BRIGANTE, CACO
bathhouse ...... BAGNIO
bell .... CAMPANA
bell town .... ATRI
bowl .... TAZZA
breed of cattle .. MODICA,
    PADOLIAN
capital ...... ROME, ROMA
car .... FIAT
cathedral .... DUOMO
cathedral city .... MILAN
Celt .... SENONE
cheer .... VIVA
cheese .... GRANA,
    GORGONZOLA, PARMESAN
chest .... CASSO(NE)
chief .... DUCE
city .... MILAN, NAPLES,
    GENOA, PALERMO,
    SIENA, TARANTO,
    TRIESTE, ASTI,
    RIMINI, RAVENNA,
    PERUGIA, LUCCA,

PAVIA, MODENA,
MONZA, FOGGIA, FORLI,
LODI, TORINO,
NOVARA, UDINE, PISA,
MASSA, GORIZIA,
OSTIA, ANCONA,
CREMONA, TRENT(O),
ROME, SPEZIA, PARMA,
PADUA, BRESCIA,
CARRARA, LEGHORN,
BARI, VENICE, TURIN,
FERRARA, VERONA
civil government .... QUIRINAL
coin ..... LIRA, SOLDOS,
LIRE, SOLDI, ZECHIN,
ZECCHINO, SCUDO,
SEQUIN
comedy character ......
SCARAMOUCH(E),
PANTALOON
commune .... MEDA,
ESTE, TRIBA, ASOLA,
ALBA
composer .... GUIDO,
ROSSINI, TOSTI,
MENOTTI, LULLY,
MASCAGNI, PAGANINI,
VERDI
condiment ..... TAMARA
conductor ... MANTOVANI,
TOSCANINI
country, ancient ....
LATIUM, ETRURIA
countryside .. CAMPAGNA
cup .... TAZZA
cupid .... AMORINO,
AMORETTO
customs house .. DOGANA
dance .. PAVIN, PAVAN(E),
CALATA, VOLTA,
TARANTELLA,
SALTARELLO
dear .... CARO, CARA
department ... LIGURIA,
CALABRIA, PIEDMONT,
UMBRIA, EMILIA,
LOMBARDY, LUCANIA,
APULIA
dessert .... SPUMONI,
SPUMONE
"Detroit" .... TURIN
dialect .... LIGURIAN
dictator ... MUSSO(LINI)
dish ... PIZZA, RISOTTO,
PASTA

dough .... PASTA
dramatist ...... ALFIERI
drink .... BEVERE
duchy .... PARMA
dynasty .... SAVOY
eight .... OTTO
enclave, Swiss ....
CAMPIONE
enough .... BASTA
evening .... SERA
faction ... BIANCHI, NERI
family ...... ASTI, DORIA,
ESTE, DONATI, MEDICI,
CENCI
farewell .... ADDIO
Fascist gangster ......
DUMINI
Fascist leader ...... RAS,
MUSSO(LINI)
feast .... FESTINO, FESTA
festival .... RIDOTTO
field .... CAMPO
first .... PRIMO
flower .... FIORE
fortress .... ROCA
fountain, famous .. TREVI
gallery .... UFFIZI
game ..... BOCCE, MORA
gentleman ... SIGNOR(E),
SIGNORINO, SER
goodby .... ADDIO
good morning ....
BUON GIORNO
goose .... OCA
governor ...... PODESTA
Greek city ....
PAESTUM (PESTO)
Greek colony .... ELEA
guessing game .... MORA
gulf ... GENOA, SALERNO,
TARANTO, VENICE
gypsy .... ZINGABI
hair .... PELO
hamlet .... BORGO,
CASAL(E)
hammer ...... MARTELLO
hand .... MANO
harbor .... PORTO
harp .... ARPA
hat .... LEGHORN
hate .... ODIO
headland .... SCILLA
health resort ... AGNONE
helmet .... ELME
historian .... CANTU
holiday .... FESTE, FESTA

house .... CASA
innkeeper .... PADRONE,
OSTE
island ... CAPRI, CORSICA,
ELBA, LINOSA,
PANTELLERIA,
LAMPEDUSA, LIDO,
LIPARI, SARDINIA,
SICILY, COS
islander .... SARD
judge .... PODESTA
king .... EMMANUEL,
HUMBERT(O)
kiss .... BACIO
labor contractor ....
PADRONE
lady ... DONNA, SIGNORA,
SIGNORINA
lake ...... COMO, LAGO,
MAGGIORE, AVERNO,
VICO, AVERNUS,
GARDA, ALBANO
language .... TUSCAN,
OSCAN, LADIN
leader .... DUCE
little .... POCO
love .... AMORE
lover .... AMOROSO
magistrate .... PODESTA,
DOGE
man .... SIGNOR(E)
marble .... CIPOLIN,
CAR(R)ARA
marshy land .. PONTINE,
MAREMMA
mayor .... PODESTA
measure .... BRACCIO
meat balls ...... RAVIOLI
millet ...... BUDA, MOHA,
TENAI
miss .... SIGNORINA
mister .... SIGNOR
mother .... MADRE
mountain ..... ALBANITA,
CENIS, APENNINES,
CAVO, CHIANTI
movie director ....
(DE)SICCA
music ..... TARANTELLA
musical suite .... PARTITA
musical theorist .. GUIDO
musician .... GUIDO
muslin ..... MUSSOLINO
name .... ESTE
name for Italy ... ITALIA
nationalist .... MAZZINI

naval base ... TARANTO,
POLA, BRINDISI
night .... SERA
nine .... NOVE
noblewoman ....
MARCHESA, CONTESSA,
MARCHIONESS, MARQUIS,
MARCHESE
not only .... NONCHE
novelist .... MANZONI
one .... UNO
opera ..... NORMA, AIDA
opera house ...... SCALA
opera singer .... CARUSO,
PATTI, TEBALDI,
ALDANESE, CORELLI,
PINZA, AMATO, GIGLI
otto in French ..... HUIT
painter .... LIPPI, VINCI,
GIOTTO, SPADA,
TITIAN, RENI, ANDREA,
VASARI, RAPHAEL,
ROSSI
patriot ...... GARIBALDI,
MAZZINI, CAVOUR
patriotic organization ...
RISORGIMENTO,
CARBONARI
peak .. CIMA, MARMOLADA
people .... OSCAN,
SARDS, SABINES
philosopher .... BRUNO,
DION
physicist .... ROSSI,
VOLTA, MARCONI
pie .... PIZZA
plague........ PELLAGRA
plain .... CAMPAGNA
plateau .... SILA
poet .... LEOPARDI,
PETRARCH, MANZONI,
DANTE, ARIOSTO,
TASSO, REDI
police ..... CARABINIERI
political party ....
IRREDENTIST
political party member ..
GUELF, GUELPH
porridge ...... POLENTA
port .... BARI, GENOA,
TRIESTE
pottery .... FAENZA,
MAJOLICA
premier .... MORO,
CRISPI, CAVOUR, PARRI,
RUMOR, ORLANDO

prima donna .... DIVA,
    TEBALDI
province ... ESTE, COMO,
    PISA, PARMA, MANTUA
public entertainment ...
    RIDOTTO
public square ... PIAZZA
region ...... CALABRIA,
    VENETO, SICILIA,
    LIGURIA, (LE)MARCHE,
    LUCANIA, PIEMONTE
republic .... GENOA
resort ..... CAPRI, LIDO,
    COMO, SORRENTO,
    SAN REMO
restaurant .... PIZZERIA
rifleman .. BERSAGLIERE
river ... ORCO, PO, ARNO,
    RENO, TEVERE, TREBBIA,
    LIVENZA, PIAVE, ADIGE,
    TIBER
Romance language ....
    LADIN
sausage .... SALAMI
sculptor .... CANOVA,
    DUPRE, CELLINI,
    LEONI, PISANO
seacoast .... MARINA
seaport .... GENOA,
    NAPLES, PALERMO,
    VENICE, (LA)SPEZIA,
    POLA, SAN REMO, TRANI,
    SALERNO, TRIESTE,
    GENOVA
seashore .... RIVA
secret society ..... MAFIA,
    CAMORRA, CARBONARI
ship .... POLACCA
shrimp dish ..... SCAMPI
sign .... SEGNO
silk .... SETA
sir .... SIGNOR(E)
sky .... CIELO
slang .... GUINEA
somewhat .... POCO
song .... VILLANELLA,
    CANZONE
songbird ..... BECCAFICO
soprano ..... ALBANESE,
    TEBALDI, PATTI
spa .... AGNONE, ABANO
spider .... TARANTULA
strait .... MESSINA
street .... CALLE, VIA,
    CORSO
tender .... PIA

tenor .... CORELLI,
    CARUSO, SCHIPA
that .... CHE
the .... GLI
three .... TRE
time .... TEMPO
title ... CONTE, MARCHE,
    MARQUIS, DONNA,
    SIGNOR, CONTESSA
tobacco ..... CAPORALE
today .... OGGI
town .... CASAL(E),
    CASSINO, MEDA, ELEA,
    ITRI, ASTI, POLA, ATRI
tractor .... PICCOLINO
tribe .... SABINE
under .... SOTTO
university city .. PADUA,
    PISA, BARI
valley .... SACCO
vase .... TAZZA
verse .... RANN
violin .... CREMONA,
    STRAD(IVARIUS), AMATI
violin maker ....
    GUARNERI, AMATI
    STRADIVARI
violinist ...... TARTINI,
    PAGANINI
voice .... VOCE
volcano .... ETNA,
    STROMBOLI, VESUVIUS
waterway .... CANALE
weight ..... LIBRA, ONCIA
well .... BENE
what .... CHE
wind ..... ANDAR, SOVER,
    SIROC(CO)
wine .... ASTI
wine measure ..... ASTI,
    ORNA, ORNE
winter .... INVERNO
woman's title .. MADONNA
woods .... PINETOS
woodwork ..... TARSIA
you .... TU
Italic type inventor .. MANUTIUS
Italy .... AUSONIA, HESPERIA
   barbarian ruler of ....
    ODOVACAR, ODOACER
itch ...... PRURITUS, PSORA,
    SCABIES, HANKERING,
    URGE, CRAVE, RIFF
   barber's .... SYCOSIS
Item ..... UNIT, PARTICULAR,

THING, ENTRY, ARTICLE, DETAIL
itemize .... LIST
iterate .... REPEAT
Ithunn .... IDUN
itinerant .... TRAVELER, NOMADIC, VAGRANT, HOBO, TRAMP
   vendor .... PEDDLER
itineration .... CIRCUIT, TOUR, JOURNEY
itinerary .. ROUTE, ROADBOOK, GUIDEBOOK
itself .... PER SE
iva .... YELLOW BUGLE
"Ivanhoe" author ..... SCOTT
   character ...... ROWENA, CEDRIC, GURTH, WAMBA, ULRICA, ISAAC, CRONE, BOUEF
Ives, actor .... BURL
   composer ..... CHARLES
   partner of ..... CURRIER

ivied .... VINY
ivories .... DICE, KEYS, TEETH
ivorine .... WHITE
ivory ... DENTINE, TUSK, TUSH
   animal with ... ELEPHANT, WALRUS, WARTHOG
   Coast capital .. ABIDJAN
   Latin .... EBUR
   like .... DENTINE
   source .. NARWHAL, TUSK, ELEPHANT
   synthetic ...... IVORIDE
   tickler .... PIANIST
   time-beaters .. CASTANETS
ivy .... VINE
   clump .... TOD
   of the .... HEDERAL
istle .... IXTLE, PITA
Iwo _____ .... JIMA
   Jima mount .. SURIBACHI
ixia .... IRIS
Ixion offspring ..... CENTAUR
Izmir .... SMYRNA

J

J, in physics .... JOULE
   letter .... JAY
ja .... YES
jab .... THRUST, POKE, BLOW, DIG, PUNCH
jabber .... BABBLE, PRATE, GIBBER(ISH), CHATTER, SPUTTER, YAP
jabberwocky .... RIGMAROLE
jabiru ..... STORK, IBIS, BIRD
jabot .... FRILL, RUFFLE, STONE, LIGURE
jack ... JUG, HOIST, OPENER, RABBIT, CLOWN, KNAVE, NOB, FELLOW, SAILOR, DONKEY, SALMON, TORCH, MULE, BOWER, MUG
   and _____ .... JILL
   Benny's stock in trade ... VIOLIN, GAGS
   Ketch .... HANGMAN
   in cribbage .... NOB
   in-the-pulpit ...... ARAD, AROID, WAKEROBIN
   Leonard's forte .. INSULT
   of-all-trades .... TINKER
   of clubs .... PAM
   part of .... DETENT
   slang .... MONEY

Sprat's favorite .... LEAN
   pudding ...... BUFFOON, FOOL
   rabbit .... HARE
   tar .... SAILOR
   tree .... JACA
   up .... RAISE, HIKE
jackal .... DIEB, KOLA, THOS, CHEAT(ER), SWINDLER, (WILD)DOG, SCAVENGER
   headed deity .... ANUBIS
jackanapes .... MONKEY, UPSTART, IMP
jackass ...... DONKEY, FOOL, NITWIT, DOLT
   and mare offspring ... MULE
   rarely one ... WISE GUY, SMART ALECK
jackdaw, bird like ..... CROW
jacket ... ETON, REEFER, RIND, BOLERO, SACK, SPENCER, SACQUE, DOUBLET, CASING, WRAPPER, JERKIN, SKIN, NORFOLK, ROUNDABOUT, COAT(EE), JUPE
   ad on book ...... BLURB
   Arctic region ... ANORAK
   armor ... ACTON, JUPON, GIPON

children's ...... PALETOT
cold wear .... PARKA, ANORAK
cowboy's ..... CHAQUETA
dinner .... TUX(EDO)
Eskimo .... PARKA
fur .... PARKA
hooded .... JUMPER, ANORAK, PARKA
knitted .... JERSEY
leather .... ANORAK
Levant .... GREGO
life-saving ..... MAE WEST
mail .... HAUBERK, HABERGEON
Malay .... BAJU
outer .... WAM(M)US, WAMPUS
sailor's .... PEACOAT
sleeveless .... VEST, BOLERO, TABARD, WAISTCOAT
sports... WINDBREAKER
women's ... JUPE, JUPON, CAMISOLE, PALETOT
woolen ...... CARDIGAN, LUMBERJACK
jackknife ...... (FANCY) DIVE, STAB
jacksnipe .... SANDPIPER
Jackson, Andrew ....
        OLD HICKORY, ANDY
Jacob .... ISRAEL
brother of .. EDOM, ESAU
diminutive of ..... JAKE, JACK
father of .... ISAAC
father-in-law ..... LABAN
in French ...... JACQUES
son of ... JUDAH, ASHER, DAN, GAD, LEVI, REUBEN, JOSEPH, BENJAMIN
twin .... ESAU
variant of .... JAMES
wife of ... LEAH, RACHEL
Jacobin .... DOMINICAN, FRIAR, RADICAL, PIGEON
jaconet ... NAINSOOK, COTTON
jac(ti)tation .... BRAGGING, BOAST
jade .... TIT, NEPHRITE, MARE, YAUD, MURRHINE, PLUG, GREEN, WOMAN, WEARY, ROSINANTE, TIRE, HUSSY, SLUT, HARASS, STONE, NAG

jaeger .... SHOOI, TEASER, ALLAN, SKUA, SEABIRD
Jaffa .... JOPPA
jag ..... BARB, NOTCH, PINK, TEAR, SPREE, SNAG
Jaga .... BANTU
jager .... RIFLEMAN
jagged .... EROSE, SERRATED, RAGGED, ROUGH, CLEFT, NOTCHED
jaguar .. PANTHER, TIGER, CAR
Jahve(h) .... JEHOVAH
jai-alai .... PELOTA
court .... FRONTON
game like .... HANDBALL
player .... PELOTARI
racquet .... CESTA
stroke .... REBOTE
jail ...... BRIDEWELL, LIMBO, LOCK UP, CELL, (IM)PRISON, GAOL, CAGE, COOP, PEN, QUOD
not in ..... FREE, LOOSE, AT LARGE
official .... WARDER, WARDEN
ship's .... BRIG
slang ..... JUG, COOLER, CALABOOSE, STIR, CLINK(ER), POK(E)Y
jailbird .. PRISONER, CONVICT, LAWBREAKER
with privileges ... TRUSTY
jailer ..... PROVOST, WARDEN, TURNKEY, GAOLER
Jakarta .... BATAVIA
jake .... SATISFACTORY
jakes .... PRIVY, TOILET
jalap........... ROOT, PLANT
jalopy .... CRATE, HOTROD
jalousie ...... BLIND, SCREEN, SHADE
jam ... BLOCK, CRAM, WEDGE, SQUEEZE, SHOVE, CROWD, PRESERVES
colloquial .... PREDICAMENT, SPOT, FIX
like preparation .... PRESERVE(S), JELLY
material ...... CURRANT
jama .... TUNIC
Jamaican bird .... TODY, TINKLING, GRACKLE
capital .... KINGSTON
export .... RUM
grackle ...... TINKLING

island .... CAYMAN
jamb(e) .... (SIDE) POST,
  JAMBEAU
James Bond's creator ....
  FLEMING
direction normally given ..
  HOME
father of disciple ....
  ZEBEDEE
the outlaw .... JESSE
the Second supporter ....
  JACOBITE
Jamshid subjects ...... PERIS
Jane, mate of ...... TARZAN,
  ROCHESTER
of history .... GREY
singer .... FROMAN
jangle ..... QUARREL, BICKER
Janis ____, popsinger .. JOPLIN
janitor ... PORTER, DOORMAN,
  CONCIERGE, SUPER, SEXTON
Janus, describing ....
  TWO-FACED, DECEITFUL
Japan ..... ENAMEL, VARNISH,
  LACQUER, NIPPON, NIHON,
  CIPANGO, ZIPANGU
foreigner in ..... GAIJIN
Japanese .... NIPPONESE
aborigine .... AINO, AINU
admiral ...... ITO, TOGO,
  YAMAMOTO, NOMURA
adviser .... GENRO
alien to a .... GAIJIN
American .... ISSEI,
  SANSEI, KIBEI, NISSEI
apricot .... UME
army reserve ..... HOJU
automobile ..... TAJURI,
  DATSUN, TOYOTA
badge .... (KIRI)MON
bamboo ..... WHANGEE
banjo .... SAMISEN
baron .... HAN
battle cry .... BANZAI
bay .... OSAKA, ISE,
  YED(D)O
bean .... ADSUKI
beer ... SAKE, SAKI, ASAHI
beriberi .... KAKKE
board game ... GOBAN(G)
boat .... SAMPAN
box .... INRO
brazier .... HIBACHI
bream .... TAI
Buddha .... AMIDA
Buddhism .... ZEN

Buddhist festival .... BON
Buddhist monastery .....
  TERA
camellia .... JAPONICA
cape ... OKI, MINO, SUZU,
  MELA, OMA, SADA,
  DAIO, NOMO
capital ... TOKIO, TOKYO,
  YED(D)O
capital, former .... NARA,
  KYOTO
carp .... KOI
carriage .... SADOS,
  RICKSHA(W.)
caste .... SAMURAI
cedar .... SUGI
charcoal stove .. NIBACHI
cheer .... BANZAI
cheer leader .... OENDAN
cherry .... FUJI
chest .... TANSU
chicken dish ... YAKATORI
chinaware ...... KUTANI,
  IMARI
church .... TERA
city ... OTARU, OKAYAMA,
  MOJI, IWAKUNI,
  MIYAJIMA, OSAKA,
  TOKYO, NAGOYA,
  KYOTO, SENDAI,
  YOKOHAMA, NAGASAKI,
  NARA, FUKUOKA,
  KAWASAKI, HIMEJI,
  SASEBO, KOBE
clan .... GEN, HEI,
  TOKUGAWA
clogs .... GETA
clover .... HAGI
coin ..... SEN, YEN, RIN,
  OBAN(G), ITZEBU
commoner ..... HEIMIN
confection .... AME
conveyance .... KAGO
councilor .... KARO
court .... DAIRI
crash pilot ... KAMIKAZE
crest .... MON
Crown Prince .. AKIHITO
dancing girl ..... GEISHA
date plum .... KAKI
deer .... SIKA
deity ...... AMIDA, AMITA
dish .... SUKIYAKI,
  TERIYAKI, YAKATORI,
  SUSHI
divine wind .. KAMIKAZE

dog .... TANATE
door .... FUSUMA
drama .... KABUKI,
    NOGAKU, NOH
drink .... SAKE
earthquake, 1923 .. KANTO
eating tool .. CHOPSTICKS
emperor .... MIKADO,
    HIROHITO, JIMMU,
    TENNO, YOSHIHITO,
    MUTSUHITO
emperor's reign .. MEIJI,
    SHOWA, TAISHO
Empire .... EDO
empress .... NAGAKO
engraver .... HOKUSAI
"Enlightened Peace" era..
    MEIJI
factory .... HONG
family .... BATSU
family emblem .... MON
fan .... OGI
festival .... BON
fighter plane ...... ZERO
fish ..... FUGU, TILAPIA,
    TAI, AYU, GOURAMI
flag .... RISING SUN
flower arrangement ....
    IKEBANA
foreign ministry ....
    GAIMUSHO
foreigner to a .... GAIJIN
game .... GOBAN(G)
garment ...... KIMONO
gateway .... TORII
general ... ARAKI, TOJO,
    YAMASHITA
generalissimo ... SHOGUN
gift .... OMIYAGE
glue .... AME
god .... KAMI
god of happiness .. EBISU,
    HOTEI
goldfish .... FUNA
government system .....
    SHOGUNATE
grill .... HIBACHI
guitar .... KOTO
hanging .... KAKEMONO
heart transplant surgeon ..
    WADA
herb .... UDO
house .... MITSUI,
    MITSUBISHI, SUMITOMO
immigrant ...... ISSEI,
    NISSEI

imperial badge .. KIRIMON
industrial family ....
    ZAIBATSU, MITSUI,
    YASUDA
Inland sea .... NAIKAI,
    SETO
island .... HONSHU,
    SAISHU, HONDU, IZU,
    KURIL(E), KYUSHU,
    SADO, HOKKAIDO,
    SHIKOKU
Kurile islands ... CHISHIMA
legislature .... DIET
lily .... AURATUM
litter .... NORIMONO
lord .... DAIMIO
lute .... BIWA
measure ... RIN, CHO, RI,
    MO, SHO
mile .... RI
military caste .. SAMURAI
military code ... BUSHIDO
military governor ......
    SHOGUN
military service .... YOBI
monastery ...... TERA
money ...... SEN, YEN
monk .... BONZE
monopolies ... ZAIBATSU
mountain ... FUJI(YAMA),
    USU, WASHU
musical instrument .....
    SAMISEN, KOTO
mystic symbol ....
    SWASTIKA
naval base ...... KURE,
    SASEBO
news agency .... DOMEI,
    KYODO, JIJI
newspaper ... SHIMBUN,
    MAINICHI, YOMIURI
nobility ...... SAMURAI,
    HATAMOTO
nobleman ...... KUGE,
    DAIMIO, DAIMYO,
    KAMI
opera .... YUZURU
outcast ...... RONIN,
    A(E)TA, YETA
outer garment .. KIMONO,
    HAORI, MINO
outlaw .... RONIN
pagoda .... TAA
painter ..... HIROSHIGE
painting school ... TOSA,
    KANO, SESSHU, SHIJO

palanquin .... KAGO,
NORIMONO
paper art ...... ORIGAMI
parliament .... DIET
paste .... AME
peach .... MOMO
peninsula .... IZU
persimmon .... KAKI
pine .... MATSU
"Pittsburgh" .. YAWATA
plant ..... AUCUBA, UDO
play .... NOH, KABUKI
plum ..... KELSEY, KAKI,
SUMOMO
plumlike fruit .. LOQUAT
poem .... HAIKU
porgy .... TAI
pottery .... AWATA,
SATSUMA
prefecture .... FU, MINO,
KEN, OWARI
premier .... KISHI,
KONOYE, TOJO, SATO,
IKEDA
primitive ... AINU, AINO
province ...... KUNI, ISE,
UGO
puppet emperor of ......
PU-YI
puppet show .. BUNRAKU
puppet state ....
MANCHU(O)KUO
quince ...... JAPONICA
radish .... DAIKON
raincoat .... MINO
rattle-trap ... GATAKURI
religion .... SHINTO(ISM),
BUDDHISM
religious dance ...... NO
religious festival ... BON
resort area .... NIKKO,
HAKONE
rice beer ..... SAKE, SAKI
rice paste .... AME
river boat ...... SAMPAN
robe .... KIMONO
room-divider .... SHOVI
rose .... AINO
sake-like wine ... SHOCHU
salmon .... MASU
salad plant .... UDO
samurai's code .. BUSHIDO
sash .... OBI
sauce .... UDO
screen .... SHOVI, BYOBU
scroll ...... KAKEMONO

sculptress ... (YOKO) ONO
seal, business .... HANKO
seaport .... KOBE, MOJI,
SAKATA, NAGASKI,
KURE, TOYAMA,
YOKOHAMA, OTARU
seaweed .... NORI
seaweed food .... KOMBU,
KOBU
sect .... ZEN
self-defense forces ......
JIEITAI
self-defense system ......
JUDO, KARATE,
JUJITSU, JUJUTSU
ship .... MARU
shoe .... GETA
shogun .. GENERALISSIMO,
TYCOON
shoot, edible ...... UDO
shrine ..... OYAMA-ZUMI
shrub .... QUINCE,
JAPONICA
signature stamp .. HANKO
slang .... NIP
sliding door .... FUSUMA
social reformer ....
KAGAWA
sock .... TABO, TABI
song .... UTA
spirit .... GANBARO
spruce .... YEDDO
stamp .... HANKO
statesman .... GENRO,
ITO, TANAKA
stew .... CHANKO
strait .... TSUSHIMA
straw cape .... MINO
street, famed ..... GINZA
style of painting ... KANO
suicide .... SEPPUKU,
HARAKIRI, HARI-KARI
suicide attack ....
KAMIKAZE
sun tree .... HINOKI
sword .... CAT(T)AN,
KATANA
syndicate ...... ZAIBATSU
temple gate .... TORII
tidal wave ...... TSUNAMI
teacher .... SENSEI
temple .... PAGODA
10,000 years .... BANZAI
title .... KAMI
town .... TOI, MACHI

tree ━.━.━ KIRI, LOQUAT,
GINGKO, SUGI, HINOKI
umbrella ....━ AMA-GASA
varnish ━.━.━ RHUS
vegetable ... UDO, GOBO
vehicle, man-drawn ━.━
RICKSHA
verse ━.━.━ HOKKU, HAIKU
village ....━ MURA
volcano ━.━.━.━ ASOSAN,
FUJI(YAMA),
ASAMA(YAMA),
ADZUMAYAMA
walking stick ━ WHANGEE
warehouse ...━.━ HONG
warplane ....━ ZERO
warrior ....━ SAMURAI
watermelon .... SUIKA
way of the warrior ━.━.
BUSHIDO
weight ━.. RIN, SHI, MO,
CATTY
whisky ━.━.. SUNTORY,
NIKKA
wild dog ━.━.━ TANATE
wind ━........... MONSOON
wine ...━ SHOCHU, SAKE
wisteria ..━.━.....━ FUJI
wood oil ...━.━.━ TUNG
wooden shoes .... GETA
wrestler's foot exercise .━
SHIKO
wrestling ━.━.━ SUMO
wrestling champion ━.━
YOKOZUNA
writer ━.━.━ KAGAWA
writing ━.━.━ KANA,
KATAKANA
yeast ━.━.━.━ KOJI
zaibatsu ....━ MITSUI,
SUMITOMO, YASUDA
zither ....━ KOTO
jape ━.... JOKE, JEST, MOCK,
FOOL, TRICK, JEER, FRAUD,
GIBE
japery ....━.. RIBALDRY
Japheth's father ...━.━ NOAH
son ....━ GOMER
japonica ━ QUINCE, CAMELLIA,
SHRUB
jar ━..........━ GRATE, SHAKE,
VIBRATE, BANGA, EWER,
JUG, PELIKE, HYDRIA,
RATTLE, SHOCK, JOG, JOLT,
CLOCHE, DISCORD, CLASH,
TURN, URN, CRUSE,

AMPHORA, DISCONCERT,
OLLA
bell-shaped ━.━ CLOCHE
clay stone ━.━.━ STEEN
druggist's ....━ GALLIPOT
earlike projection ━ LUG
earthenware ━ TERRINE,
CROCK, GOGLET
like glass container ━.━.
BEAKER
long-necked .... GOGLET,
GURGLET
porcelain ━.━.━ POTICHE
table ....━ TERRINE
wide-mouthed ━. OLLA,
EWER
with moist sponge ━.━.
HUMIDOR
jara ━.━.........━ PALM
jardiniere ... POT, URN, VASE,
BOWL, STAND
jargon ━.━.━ LINGO, SLANG,
SHELTA, CANT, PATOIS,
PATTER, ABRACADABRA,
ZIRCON, DRIVEL, ARGOT,
GIBBERISH, DIALECT
jargonel(le) ....━ PEAL
jarl ━.━.━ EARL, CHIEFTAIN,
NOBLEMAN
jarovize ━.━.━.━ VERNALIZE
jasmine ━.━.━.━ JESSAMY,
JESSAMINE, BELA
Jason, father of ━.━. AESON
men of ....━ ARGONAUTS
quest of .. GOLDEN FLEECE
ship of ....━ ARGO
sorceress who helped ━.
MEDEA
uncle of ━.━.━ PELIAS
wife of .. CREUSA, MEDEA
jasper ━ MICA, QUARTZ, PARK
jaundice ━.━.━ ICTERUS,
PREJUDICE
cause of ━.━.━ ENVY,
JEALOUSY
remedy ━.━.━ ICTERIC
jaundiced ━.. YELLOW, BIASED,
PREJUDICED
jaunt ━.━.━ EXCURSION,
(SIDE)TRIP, SALLY
jaunty ━.━.. AIRY, DAPPER,
SPRUCE, RAKISH,
DEBONAIR(E), STYLISH,
CHIC, PERKY, COCKY,
MODISH

Java .... CHICKEN, COFFEE,
ISLAND, HOOD
   capital of ..... JAKARTA
Javanese ...... INDONESIAN,
SUNDANESE
   almond .... KANARI
   badger ... RATEL, TELEDU
   bat .... KALON
   burrowing animal ......
TELEDU
   carriage .... SADO
   city .... SEMARANG,
BANDUNG, BANDOENG
   civet ..... RASSE, DEDES
   cotton .... KAPOK
   language ... KAWI, KAVI
   man .. PITHECANTHROPUS
   measure .... PALEN
   mountain .... AMAT
   ox .... BANTENG
   pepper .... CUBEB
   plum .. JAMAN, JAMBOOL,
LOMBOY
   port .... TEGAL
   resin .... BENZOIN
   rhinoceros ...... BADAK
   silk .... IKAT
   skunk .... TELEDU
   sparrow ...... RICEBIRD
   tree .... UPAS, KAPOK,
ANTIAR(IN)
   upas .... ANTIAR
   village .... DESSA
   volcano .... SEMERU,
RAUN, GEDE
   weight ..... TALI, AMAT
javelin .... LANCE, DART,
ASSEGAI, SPEAR, SHAFT,
JER(R)EED, JER(R)ID, PILUM
   throwing device ....
AMENTA
   with a line .... HURLBAT,
HARPOON
jaw .. MAW, CHAP, MANDIBLE,
JOWL, CHOP, CHAT
   angle of .... GONION
   combining form ....
GNATHOUS
   cover .... GUM(S)
   device with .... VISE
   flesh .... GILL
   lower .... MANDIBLE,
GONION, CHIN
   muscle .... MASSETER
   of the .... GNATHIC
   slang ..... TALK, SCOLD

   upper .... MAXILLA
   without ..... AGNATHIC
jawbone ..... JOWL, MAXILLA
jawbreaker .... CANDY
   in boxing .... HAYMAKER
jay ..... CROW, PIE, JACKSON,
JOIN, CHATTERBOX
   bird like a ..... MOTMOT
   talk .... CHATTER
Jayhawk state .... KANSAS
jazz ..... SWING, RAG(TIME),
BOOGIEWOOGIE (BE)POP
   composer ....
(DUKE) ELLINGTON
   dance .... SHIMMY
   ensemble .... COMBO
   fan .. HEPCAT, JITTERBUG,
HIPSTER
   fan jargon .... JIVE
   melodic phrase .... RIFF,
LICK
   music .... SWING
   up .... ENLIVEN
jealous .... ENVIOUS,
GREEN(EYED)
Jeanneret, architect ....
(LE) CORBUSIER
jeans .... OVERALLS,
TROUSERS, LEVIS, DENIMS
jeep .... PEEP
jeer ... TAUNT, FLOUT, SNEER,
SARCASM, GIRD, JIBB,
MOCK, SCOFF, GIBE, JEST,
BOO, JAPE, DERIDE
jeers .... TACKLE
Jeeves, creator of ....
WODEHOUSE
   position of ..... BUTLER
Jefferson's (President) home ..
MONTICELLO
Jeffries, prize-fighter .... JIM
Jehol .... CHENGTEH
Jehovah .... (THE) LORD,
YAHWE(H), GOD, JAH,
YAHVE(H)
   prophet of .... ELIAS
Jehovah's Witnesses founder ..
RUSSELL
jejune ...... ARID, BANAL, DRY,
STALE, BARREN, DULL,
FLAT, INSIPID
Jekyll's (Dr.) alter ego ....
(MR.) HYDE
jell .... CRYSTALLIZE, SET,
CONGEAL, SOLIDIFY
jellied gasoline ...... NAPALM

jelly ...... ASPIC, PRESERVES, JAM, DESSERT, SPREAD
  animal .... GELATINE
  bean .... CANDY
  delicacy .... ASPIC
  fruit .... JAM, GUAVA
  ingredient .... PECTIN
  like candy .... PASTE
  like substance ...... GEL, GELATIN, COLLOID
  material .... CURRANT
  meat juice .... ASPIC
  petroleum .... VASELINE
  tomato juice ...... ASPIC
  vegetable .... PECTIN
jellybean .... CANDY
jellyfish .... HYDROZOAN, MEDUSA, PLANOBLAST, QUARL, ACALEPH(E)
  disk .... PILEUS
  like a .... MEDUOID
  stinging cell .... NEMATOCYST
jellyroll .... CAKE
jennet ....ASS, DONKEY, HORSE
Jenny, singer .... LIND, WREN
jeopardize .... IMPERIL, ENDANGER
jeopardy ...... HAZARD, RISK, PERIL, DANGER
jerboa ... GERBIL(LE), RODENT
jeremiad .... TALE, WOE, LAMENT(ATION)
Jeremiah's scribe .... BARUCH
Jerez .... XERES
Jericho's betrayer .... RAHAB
jerk ... TWITCH, FLIP, TWEAK, TWIST, PUSH, SODA MAN, MEAT, YANK, BOB, HITCH, BEEF
jerked beef .... CHARQUI
jerkin .... JACKET, VEST, (WAIST)COAT
jerkwater ...... TRAIN, SMALL
Jerry .... GERMAN, HUN
Jersey ..... CATTLE, SWEATER, CLOTH, SHIRT, SINGLET
Jerusalem ...... (HOLY) CITY, ARIEL
  artichoke ... SUNFLOWER, TUBER, GIROSOL, GIRASOL(E)
  captor of .... SALADIN
  hill .... ZION, SION
  mosque .... OMAR
  oak .... AMBROSE

pool .... BETHESDA
ravine .... KEDRON
ridge .... OLIVET
spring .... SILOAM
stream .... KEDRON
theater .... KHAN
thorn tree ...... RETAMA
Jespersen's language ..... IDO
jess .... STRAP, LEASH
  user of ...... FALCON(ER)
jessamine .... JASMINE
jest .... JAPE, WAGGERY, BADINAGE, RAILLERY, QUIP, TRIFLE, WIT, JIBE, TAUNT, JOKE, WITTICISM, RIDICULE, FUN, JEER, MOCK, BANTER, SALLY
jester ..... BUFFOON, CLOWN, MIME, WAG, ZANY, JOKER, FOOL
  ancient .... GOLIARD
  cap of .... COXCOMB, COCKSCOMB
  garment of ..... MOTLEY
  wandering ..... GOLIARD
Jesuit .... CASUIST, SCHEMER
  order, founder of .... LOYOLA
  saint .... REGIS
Jesus ..... SAVIO(U)R, LOGOS
  agony and sufferings .... PASSION
  brother of .. JUDAS, JAMES
  Christ, _____ SUPERSTAR
  life's event ..... MYSTERY
  monogram .... IHS
  of _____ ...... NAZARETH
  sayings of .... LOGIA
jet ... SPURT, EBON(Y), SQUIRT, RAVEN, STREAM, GUSH, SPOUT, NOZZLE, BLACK, LIGNITE, SPRAY
  engine ...... ATHODYD, TURBO PROP
  fuel .... HYDRAZINE
  plane ... SABRE, SCORPION
jetsam .... LIGAN, LAGAN, LAGEND, JETTISON
jettison .... JETSAM, DISCARD
jetty .... MOLE, BLACK, STARLING, PIER, WHARF
jeu .... DIVERSION, GAME
  de mots .... PUN
  d'esprit ..... WITTICISM
jeune fille .... GIRL

Jew ...... ISRAELITE, HEBREW, JUDEAN, TOBIT, SEMITE
born in Israel ..... SABRA
bread .... MATZOS, MATZOTH
legendary .... GOLEM
not a .... GENTILE, GOY(IM), GOI
Portuguese ... SEPHARDIM
pseudo-christian .... MARRANO
Shakespearean ... TUBAL, ISAAC
Spanish ...... SEPHARDIM

jewel ...... BRILLIANT, GEM, NAIF, STONE, BIJOU, OPAL, TRINKET
Biblical ...... BDELLIUM
setting ...... BEZEL, PAVE, MOUNT(ING)

jeweler's magnifying glass .... LOUPE
weight .... KARAT, CARAT

jewelry .... BROOCH, PIN, QUOIN, JEWELS, BIJOUTERIE
artificial .... PASTE, STRASS
cheap .... PASTE
expert .... APPRAISER
item ..... PIN, (EAR)RING, PENDANT, BROOCH, DIADEM, TIARA, NECKLACE, BRACELET, TRINKET
making material .... TOMBAC(K), OROIDE, ORMOLU, CORUNDUM, TOPAZ, AMETHYST
set of .... PARURE

jewels, adorn with ..... BEGEM

jewelweed .... CELANDINE, IMPATIENS

Jewett, writer .... SARAH (ORNE)

jewfish ...... (SEA)BASS, MERO, TARPON

Jewish ... HEBREW, YIDDISH, JUDEAN, JUDAIC
ascetic ...... ESSENE
battle trumpet .. SHOFAR, SHOPHAR
benediction ...... SHEMA
bread .... MATZOS, MATZOTH

breastplate gem .. LIGURE, SARDIUS
bride .... KALLAH
calendar month .. TISHRI, CHESHVAN, KISLEV, TEBET, SHEBAT, ADAR, NISAN, IYAR, (ZIF), SIVAN, TAMMUZ, AB, ELUL, ABIB
cantor ...... CHAZ(Z)AN
captive .... MESHACH, ABEDNEGO, SHADRACH
Christians .... DIASPORA
commentaries on Scriptures ... MIDRASH
council/court .... SANHEDRIN
day .... YOM
Day of Atonement .... YOM KIPPUR
demon ...... ASMODEUS
evil spirit .... ASMODEUS
family of patriots .... MACCABEES
Feast of Lots ..... PURIM
festival ... SEDER, PURIM
Festival of lights ...... HANUKKAH
high priest ... ELI, EZRA
holiday .... YOM KIPPUR, PASSOVER, SUKKOTH, HANUKKAH, PURIM, PESACH, SABUOTH, CHANUKAH, SUCCOS
holy of holies ... ORACLE
language ...... YIDDISH
law .... TALMUD, TORAH
liturgy's first word ...... SHEMA
living place ..... GHETTO
marriage broker .... SCHATCHEN
month, extra .... VEADAR
mystic .... ESSENE
New Year .... ROSH HASHANA
occult philosophy ...... CABALA
Passover ...... PESACH
Pentecost ..... SABUOTH
people .... ZION, ISRAEL, SION
place for worship ...... SYNAGOGUE
prayer book ... MAHZOR, SIDDUR

priest's girdle ... ABNET
priest's headdress ....
　　　　　　　MITRE, MITER
priest's vestment .. EPHOD
quarter .... GHETTO
ram's horn ...... SHOFAR
rebel in Jerusalem ....
　　　　　　　ZEALOT
religion .... JUDAISM
religious philosophy .....
　　　　　　　CABALA
religious service .. HALLEL
scarf .... ZIZITH
scholar .... RAB(BI)
school .... YESHIVA,
　　　　　　　CHEDER
scribe .... MASORITE,
　　　　　　　MASORETE
sect member .. PHARISEE,
　　　　　　　SADDUCEE
seminary ...... YESHIVA
shawl .... ZIZITH
skullcap .... YAMILKE
slang .... YIDDISH
tabernacle wood ....
　　　　　　　SHITTIM
tassels .... ZIZITH
teacher .... RAB(BI),
　　　　　　　SCRIBE
temple builder ... MICAH
title of honor ..... GAON,
　　　　　　　RAB
trumpet ...... SHOPHAR,
　　　　　　　SHOFAR
undergarment .. TALLITH
vestment .... EPHOD
weight .... GERAH, OMER
Jews' dispersion ... DIASPORA
cloak .... GABERDINE
evensong ...... MINHAN
harp ...... CREMBALUM
massacre .... POGROM
of the........... JUDAIC
parchment on doorpost ..
　　　　　　　MEZUZA(H)
savior .... MORDECAI
section of city ... GHETTO
Jezebel .... VIRAGO
describing .... EVIL,
　　　　　　　WICKED
husband of ...... AHAB
victim of .... NABOTH
jib .... BALK, BOOM, SAIL,
　　SIDLE, SHY, START, SPAR
boom's stay ....
　　　　　MARTINGAL(E)

jibe ..... AGREE, HARMONIZE,
　JEST, JEER, SCOFF, TAUNT,
　　　　　　　FIT, RIB
jiffy .... INSTANT, TRICE,
　　　　　MOMENT, SECOND
jig .... DANCE, FISHHOOK,
　　　　　　　GIGUE
jigger ... FLEA, CHIGOE, TICK,
　CUP, GADGET, SAIL, TACKLE
jiggle ... ROCK, JERK, TEETER
jihad ... CRUSADE, HOLY WAR,
　　　　　　　DEFENSE
jill .... SWEETHEART, WOMAN,
　　　　　　　GIRL
Jim Crow .... NEGRO
jimjams .... DELIRIUM,
　　　　　　　JITTERS
jimmy ..... (CROW)BAR, PRY,
　　　　　　LEVER, JACK
Valentine, of fiction .....
　THIEF, SAFE-CRACKER
jimson weed .... DATURA,
　STINKWEED, THORN APPLE
jingal ...... CANNON, MUSKET
jingle .... CLINK, VERSE,
　　TINKLE, DOGGEREL
jingo .... CHAUVINIST,
　RADICAL, (SUPER)PATRIOT,
　　MILITARIST, WARRIOR
jingoism .... MILITARISM
jink .... ELUDING
jinks .... HORSEPLAY, PRANKS
jinn(i) .... GENIE, DEMON
jinrikisha .... RICKSHA(W)
Jinsen .... CHEMULPHO,
　　　　　　　SEAPORT
jinx .... HEX, HOODOO,
　EVIL EYE, BAD LUCK
personification of ....
　　　　　　　JONAH
jipjapa hat .... PANAMA
jitney .... NICKEL, BUS
jitter .... FIDGET
jitters ...... DITHERS, NERVES,
　NERVOUSNESS, HYSTERIA
the ... JIMJAMS, FIDGETS,
　(BIG)SCARE, WILLIES,
　　　　　　　CREEPS
jittery .... EDGY, JUMPY,
　NERVOUS, HECTIC, SCARED
jiujutsu .... JUDO
jivatma .... ATMAN, EGO
jive .... JAZZ
jo(e) .... SWEETHEART
Joan of Arc, name for .....
　　　　　　　PUCELLE

place of execution .... ROUEN

scene of triumph .... ORLEANS

Joan's spouse (in a song) ...... DARBY

job ..... CHORE, CHARE, DUTY, WORK, POSITION, STINT, TASK

do inferior .... SCAMP

easy .... SNAP, WHISTLE, SINECURE

kind of .... SINECURE, PARTTIME

opening .... VACANCY

Job's comforter ..... BILDAD, ELIHU, ELIPHAZ, ZOPHAR

tears .... GRASS, COIX

jockette .... TESTA, RUBIN, CRUMP, KUSNER

jockey .... SLOAN, ARCARO, DODSON, HARTACK, BAEZA, SHOEMAKER, BROOKS, SANDE, CHEAT, SWINDLE, RIDER, MANEUVER

uniform .... SILKS, COLORS

woman .... KUSNER, RUBIN, CRUMP

jocko .... CHIMP(ANZEE), MONKEY

jocose .... MERRY, DROLL, PLAYFUL, FACETIOUS, HUMOROUS, WITTY

jocular ..... JESTING, WAGGISH, WITTY, HUMOROUS, FACETIOUS

jocund ..... GAY, GENIAL, AIRY, MERRY

Jodhpur .... MARWAR

jodhpurs .... BREECHES

joe .... SWEETHEART

pye weed ... EUPATORIUM

joey .... PAL, KANGAROO

jog .... REMIND, TROT, PROJECTION

John ____, actor .... BARRYMORE, GILBERT PAYNE, IRELAND

Birch society founder ..... WELCH

Brown's Body" author ... BENET

Bull .... ENGLAND, ENGLISHMAN

Dory .... FISH

Dos ____ .... PASSOS

father of disciple .... ZEBEDEE

Hancock .... SIGNATURE

Irish .... IAN

Mannering .... BARON

Smith's savior .... POCAHONTAS

johnnie ..... LOTHARIO, DANDY, FOP, MAN, BOY

Johnny jumper .... VIOLET, PANSY

johnnycake .... HOECAKE, PONE, CORN BREAD

Johnson, (Mrs.) hunter ..... OSA

Samuel birthplace .... LICHFIELD

U.S. President ... ANDREW, LYNDON

join ..... YOKE, MERGE, RABBET, ENROLL, ENLIST, MORTISE, LOCK, COALESCE, MEET, WELD, SPLICE, SOLDER, CONNECT, FASTEN, UNITE, ACCOMPANY, COMBINE, LINK, MELD

corners ..... MITER, MITRE

in marriage ...... SPLICE

the colors .... ENLIST

joiner ..... FOLLOWER, ENLISTEE

joint .... TENON, HIP, SEAM, LINK, HINGE, TOGGLE, SCARF, RABBET, ELBOW, CONCURRENT, NEXUS, JUNCTURE, MUTUAL

arm's ..... WRIST, ELBOW

carpal .... KNEE

carpenter's .... MITER, MITRE

cavity .... BURSA

deposit .... TOPHUS

door's .... HINGE

finger .... KNUCKLE

fluid .... SEROSITY

grass .... CULM

in marriage ...... SPLICE

L-shaped .... ELL

leg's .... KNEE

mutton .... HAUNCH

of stem ..... KNOT, NODE

out of .... DISLOCATED

piping .... ELL

put out of ..... LUXATE, DISLOCATE

rheumatic pain .... LUMBAGO

right angled .... ELL
rule ..... CONDOMINIUM
slang ... SALOON, HOUSE,
    RESTAURANT, REEFER,
    DIVE
stem .... NODE
tighten .... STEM
tubing .... ELL
venison .... HAUNCH
jointly .... TOGETHER,
    HAND IN HAND
joke ... JOSH, QUIP, SALLY,
    JAPE, TWIT, PUN, PRANK,
    WHEEZE, JEST, WAGGERY,
    WISECRACK, GAG, DIDO,
    SPOOF, KID, WITTICISM,
    RIB, HOAX
    said as a .... JOCULAR
joker .... CLOWN, JESTER,
    FLOP, GAG, CUTUP, CARD,
    WAG, WIT, BUFFOON,
    FARCEUR
    in a bill, etc. ...... RIDER
joking ..... JOCOSE, JESTING,
    FACETIOUS
jollity ... FUN, GAIETY, MIRTH
jolly .... BUXOM, GAY, MERRY,
    CONVIVIAL, VERY, JOVIAL,
    BOAT, YAWL
Jolson, Al .... ASA
jolt ...... SHAKE, JAR, JERK,
    SHOCK, SURPRISE, BUMP,
    JOUNCE, BOUNCE
Jonah (Jonas) ..... PROPHET
    dislikers of ..... SAILORS
    swallower of .... WHALE
    to all people .. BAD LUCK,
    JINX
Jonathan .... APPLE
    father of .... SAUL
Jones, bandleader ..... SPIKE
    spirit of sea ...... DAVY
jongleur .... MINSTREL
jonquil .... NARCISSUS
    plant like ..... DAFFODIL
Joplin, pop singer ..... JANIS
Joppa .... JAPPA
Jordan .... POT, RIVER,
    KINGDOM
    ancient name .... EDOM,
    MOAB
    capital of .... AMMAN
    city .... AMMAN,
    JERUSALEM, PETRA,
    JERICHO
    king .... HUSSEIN

language ...... ARABIC
monetary unit ... DINAR
mountain .... GILEAD
port .... AQABA
prime minister ... JUMAA
valley .... GHOR
village .... JERICHN
Joseph .... HABIT
    native place of ....
    ARIMATHEA
    parent of .... JACOB
    son of .... MANASSEH
    wife of .... MARY
josh .... JEST, BADINAGE,
    BANTER, KID, RIDICULE,
    TEASE, RIB, RAG
Joshua, people of .. ISRAELITES
    predecessor of .... MOSES
    tree .... YUCCA
Josip Broz ... TITO, DICTATOR
joss .... IDOL
    house .... TEMPLE
jostle .. ELBOW, RUSH, NUDGE,
    SHOVE, PUSH, BUFFET,
    HUSTLE, MAUL
jot .... BIT, NOTE, TITTLE,
    MINIM, MITE, PARTICLE,
    MOTE, POINT, WHIT, SPECK,
    IOTA
jota .... DANCE
jotting .... MEMO, NOTE
Jotun(n) .... GIANT
joule, part of .... ERG
jounce .... JOLT, BOUNCE,
    SHAKE
journal ..... RECORD, DIARY,
    EPHEMERIS, REGISTER,
    PAPER, LOGBOOK,
    MAGAZINE, PERIODICAL,
    NEWSPAPER, DAYBOOK,
    ANNALS, TRUNNION
journalism .... PRESS
journalist .... EDITOR,
    REPORTER, CORRESPONDENT,
    DIARIST, NEWSPAPERMAN,
    PUBLICIST, SCRIBE,
    NEWSMAN
    budding ...... COPY BOY,
    CUB (REPORTER)
    kind of .... LEGMAN,
    STRINGER
journey ... TREK, FARE, TOUR,
    TRIP, TRAVEL, HIKE,
    JUNKET, SAFARI, RUN
    extended ..... ODYSSEY,
    TOUR

for adventure .... QUEST
forced .... HEGIRA, FLIGHT, EXODUS
in circuit .... EYRE
of a .... VIATIC(AL)
of solon abroad .. JUNKET
on foot .... HIKE, TRAMP
over snow .... MUSH
stage of .... LEG
stopping place ... STAGE, INN
to shrine ... PILGRIMAGE
water .... VOYAGE, PASSAGE
journeyman .... WORKER, JOBBER
joust .... COMBAT, TILT, TOURNAMENT, TOURNEY, BOUT
Jove .... JUPITER
jovial ... GAY, GENIAL, JOLLY, MERRY
friar .... TUCK
jowl .... CHAP, CHEEK, JAW(BONE), CHOP, DEWLAP, WATTLE
joy ... BLISS, ECSTASY, GLEE, DELIGHT, PLEASURE, RAPTURE
ride, of a sort .... SPIN
song of . CAROL, P(A)EAN
joyful and triumphant ....
JUBILANT
joyous .... MERRY, BLITHE, ELATED, GAY, GLAD, FESTAL, FESTIVE, RIANT
JP, part of .. JUSTICE, PEACE, JET, PROPULSION
jube .... LOFT, GALLERY
jubilate .... EXULT
juca ...... CASSAVA, MANIOC
Judah, city of .... AMAM, ENAM, ADAR
king of ... ADAD, AMON, AHAZ, OBIJAH, JOSIAH, JOSIAS, ASA, MANASSEH
parent of .... JACOB
son .... ONAM, ER, ZARA
tree .... REDBUD
Judaism .... HEBRAISM
commandment ....
MITSVAH, MITZVAH
convert to .... GER
hymn of praise .. KADDISH
mourners' prayer ....
KADDISH

scriptures ...... TORA(H)
Judas ... BETRAYER, TRAITOR, ISCARIOT
brother of .. JESUS, JAMES
replacement .. MATTHIAS
tree .... REDBUD
Judea procurator .... PILATE
judge ..... (A)EDILE, CRITIC, TRY, ARBITRATOR, SETTLE, ARBITER, UMPIRE, DEEM, RATE, REFEREE, CRITICIZE
Athenian .... DICAST
of lower world .. AEACUS, MINOS, RHADAMANTHUS
quality/worth .. APPRAISE, EVALUATE, RATE
judge's assistant ... ASSESSOR, MASTER
bench ... BANC, TRIBUNAL
challenge .... RECUSE
chamber .... CAMERA
court .... BENCH
decision ...... VERDICT, SENTENCE
entry after verdict ....
POSTEA
jurisdiction .. JUDICATURE
lower rank ...... PUISNE
Moslem .... CADI, HAKIM
order ... WRIT, SUBPOENA, INJUNCTION
position/rank ... ERMINE
robe .... GOWN
room .... CHAMBER
seat ...... BENCH, BANC
Spanish .... ALCALDE
symbol of authority .....
MACE, GAVEL
judges collectively .... BENCH
said of .... PUISNE
judgment ...... DOOM, SENSE, ARRET, DECISION, OPINION, SENTENCE, VERDICT, AWARD, VIEW
against person ....
IN PERSONAM
against property .. IN REM
await .... PEND
Day .... DOOM(SDAY)
suspension of ... EPOCHE
judicatory .. COURT, TRIBUNAL
judicial assembly ..... COURT
inquiry .... INQUEST
order .... WRIT
judicious .... WISE, POLITIC, PRUDENT, WISE

judo ..... JUJITSU, J(I)UJUTSU
Judy, (puppet) husband of ....
PUNCH
jug ~ RANTER, EWER, FLAGON,
THERMOS, TOBY
slang ~............. JAIL
jugal ~............. MALAR
jugate ....~ PAIRED
Juggernaut ....~ KRISHNA
incarnation .... VISHNU
juggle ~..~..~. MANIPULATE,
WANGLE, RIG
juggler ~..~... MANIPULATOR,
CHEATER
jugulate ~..~.....~ STRANGLE
juice ~...... ESSENCE, LIQUID,
FLUID, JUS, SAP, SURA,
MUST, STUM, RHOB, LIQUOR,
WINE, AL
meat ... GRAVY, DRIPPING
plant/tree ~. SAP, MANNA,
CHICLE, LATEX
slang ~.~.~. ELECTRICITY,
GAS(OLINE), OIL
juicy ~..~... PIQUANT, RACY,
SUCCULENT, SPICY
Juilliard school degree: abbr. ~
DMUS
specialty ...~.~~ MUSIC
jujitsu (jiujutsu) ....~ JUDO
juju ... FETISH, TABOO, CHARM
jujube ~.~. LOZENGE, JELLY,
ELB; BER
juke box ~.~.~. PHONOGRAPH
julep .... DRINK
ingredient ...... BRANDY,
MINT, SIRUP
Jules Verne's captain .. NEMO
vessel .... NAUTILUS
Juliana's (Queen) domain ~..
NETHERLANDS
house ~.......... ORANGE
mother ~... WILHELMINA
people ~........ DUTCH
spouse ~..... BERNHARD
julienne .... SOUP
Juliet's confessor ....~
(FRIAR) LAURENCE
cousin ~......... TYBALT
family .... CAPULET
love .... ROMEO
suitor .... PARIS
July 15, Roman calendar .....~
IDES, IDIBUS, IDUS
4th day ... INDEPENDENCE
7th day of .... NONES,

NONAS, NONIS
jumble ~. MEDLEY, MIX, MESS,
FARRAGO, MISHMASH,
CLUTTER, LITTER, HASH,
COOKY, MUDDLE, CONFUSION,
PI(E)
jumbled type ~.~..~.~ PI(E)
jumbo ~.~. LARGE, ELEPHANT
jump ~.... HOP, LEAP, START,
VAULT, BUCK, SPRING,
BOUNCE, BOB, BOUND, SKIP
about ... FRISK, PRANCE
in music ....~. SALTO
playful .... CAVORT,
CAPER, PRANCE, FRISK
jumper .... SLED, PAWL,
DELIVERY BOY, JACKET,
ROMPER, BLOUSE
jumping ~. SALTANT, LEAPING,
SALTATION
amphibian ~.~..~ FROG,
TOAD
animal ~.~.~ KANGAROO,
JERBOA, GOAT
bean dweller ~.~. LARVA
dance ~.~.~.~.~ JIG
insect ~.~. FLEA, LOCUST,
GRASSHOPPER
stick ~.~.~.~.~ POGO
jumpy ~.~.~ EDGY, NERVOUS,
TENSE, SKITTISH
junco ~.~. FINCH, SNOWBIRD
junction ~.~.~.~ CROSSING,
UNION, MEETING
line ~.~.~.~.~ SEAM
juncture ~.~.~. CRISIS, POINT,
JOINT
June bug ~.~.~. DOR, BEETLE,
FIGEATER
event ~.~.~.~ WEDDING,
MARRIAGE
13, Roman calendar ...~.~
IDES
21 ...~.~.~.~. SOLSTICE
juneberry ~.~.~.~ SHADBLOW,
SHADBUSH
jungfrau ~.~.~.~....... ALPS
jungle ~.~........ WILDERNESS
Book's wolf ...... AKELA
fever ~.~.~.~... MALARIA
junior ~.~.~.~ CADET, PUISNE,
YOUNGER
French ~.~.~.~.~ FILS
leaguer ....~ DEB
weekly "take" of ....
ALLOWANCE

juniper ...... CEDAR, RETEM,
GORSE, SAVIN(E), SHRUB,
EZEL, CADE, HACKMATAK
junk ... CABLE, ROPE, TRASH,
RUBBISH, DISCARD, SCRAP,
SHIP, SOMA
junker .... PRUSSIAN, GERMAN
junket .... FEAST, PICNIC,
EXCURSION
junkie: sl. ...-...... ADDICT,
(DOPE) FIEND
junkman .... SCRAPPER
Juno .... HERA, GODDESS
husband of .... JUPITER
messenger of .... IRIS
junta ..-.. COUNCIL, MEETING,
ASSEMBLY
junto ...-.. FACTION, CLIQUE,
CABAL
Jupiter ... ZEUS, PLANET, JOVE
consort of ... JUNO, HERA
daughter of ... MINERVA,
HEBE
Egyptian .... AMMON
giver of rain .... PLUVIUS
moon of ... IO, EUROPA,
CALLISTO, GANYMEDE
nurse of .... GOAT
son of ... ARCAS, CASTER,
TANTALUS, HERMES,
HEPHAETUS
temple .... CAPITOL
jupon .... JACKET, TUNIC
jura .... LAW
jural .... LEGAL
jurant .... SWEARING
Jurassic, strata below .. TRIAS
system strata ...... LIAS
jurel .... FISH, RUNNER
jurisdiction ...... SOKE, SOC,
VENUE, SPHERE, DOMAIN
bishop's .... SEE
jurisprudence .... LAW
jurist .... TANEY, HAND
juror ... TALESMAN, VENIREMAN
challenge a ...... RECUSE
guard of .... BAILIFF
jurors collectively ..... PANEL
one of the .... POLL
jury .... PANEL
finding of ...... VERDICT
head ...-..-... FOREMAN

illegally influence ...-..~
EMBRACE
kind of .... GRAND
member ..... TALESMAN
summons to .... VENIRE
juryman ... JUROR, TALESMAN
jus ...... JUICE, GRAVY, LAW
just .-..... FAIR, RIGHTEOUS,
EQUITABLE, IMPARTIAL,
UPRIGHT, ONLY, BARELY,
MORAL, SIMPLY
begun .... INCHOATE
clear of bottom ....
AWEIGH, ATRIP
right .... JAKE
think! .... IMAGINE
justice .... DOOM, EQUITY,
RIGHT, FAIRNESS, JUDGE
Supreme Court ... CHASE,
VINSON, WARREN,
FORTAS, STONE,
HUGHES, MARSHALL,
TAFT, TANEY,
CARDOZO, JAY
justification .... DEFENSE,
VINDICATION, EXCUSE,
EXPLANATION, WARRANT
justify ... EXCUSE, WARRANT,
ACQUIT, ABSOLVE,
VINDICATE
jut ...-..-.... ABUT, PROJECT,
PROTRUDE, STICK OUT,
OVERHANG
jute ..-..-.... FIBER, PLANT
chief .... HENGIST
cloth .... SACKING,
GUNNY
product .... BURLAP,
(GUNNY)SACK, MAT,
ROPE
refuse ..... HURDS, TOW
Jutland seaport ..... AARHUS
Jutlander .... DANE
jutting land .... HEADLAND,
PROMONTORY, NESS, CAPE
rock .... CRAG, TOR
jutty ..... JETTY, PIER, MOLE
Juvenal .... POET, SATIRIST
juvenile ..- . YOUTHFUL, YOUNG,
CHILD, INFANTILE
hero .... ROLLO
story writer ..... MILNE,
OUIDA, RAMEE, SEUSS

K

K, Greek .... KAPPA
    Hebrew .... KAPH
    in assaying ...... CARAT,
                 KARAT
    chemistry .... KALIUM,
               POTASSIUM
    chess .... KING
    electricity .... CAPACITY
    mathematics ....
               CONSTANT
    meteorology .... SMOKE
    nautical usage .... KNOT
ka .... SOUL
kabobs .... (ROAST)MEAT
kaddish .... DOXOLOGY,
        HYMN, PRAYER
kadi ..... JUDGE, MAGISTRATE
Kaffir ...... INFIDEL, BANTU,
    SORGHUM, FODDER, CORN
    language .... XOSA
    tribe .... ZULU
    war club .... KIRI
    warriors .... IMPI
kago ..... PALANQUIN, LITTER
kail .... KALE, COLE
kailyard .... GARDEN
kaiser ... WILHELM, EMPEROR
    Biblical .... NOAH
kaka(po) .... PARROT
kakemono .... SCROLL,
            HANGING
kaki .... PERSIMMON
kala-azar ...... BLACKFEVER
Kalahari .. DESERT, PLATEAU
    nomad .... BUSHMAN
kale ... BORECOLE, CABBAGE,
    COLE(WORT), BROCCOLI,
    COLLARD, GREENS, BROTH
    slang .... MONEY
kaleyard .... GARDEN
kali ... GLASSWORT, SALTWORT
    by-product .... SODA ASH
Kalinin .... TVER
Kaliningrad .... KONIGSBERG
kalinite .... ALUM
Kallikaks, the .... JUKES
kalmuck .. MONGOL, ELEUT(H)
kalong .... BAT
kalpak .... CAP
kamala .... POWDER
kame .... HILL, RIDGE
kamerad .... COMRADE
kamsin .... WIND
kanae .... MULLET

kanaka .... HAWAIIAN
kanari .... ALMOND
kangaroo .... WALLAROO,
    MACROPODIAN, MARSUPIAL,
    ROO, WOLABA, WOLARU,
            WALLABY
    female .... DOE, GIN
    male .... BOOMER
    pouch .... MARSUPIUM
    rat .... POTOROO
    young .... JOEY
Kansan .... JAYHAWKER
    famous .... EISENHOWER
Kansas, capital of ... TOPEKA
    city ... TOPEKA, SALINA,
        WICHITA, EMPORIA,
            ABILENE
    guerrilla .... JAYHAWKER
    native ...... JAYHAWKER
    river .... OSAGE
    state animal ... BUFFALO
    state bird .... LARK
    state flower .. SUNFLOWER
    state tree .. COTTONWOOD
Kansu, capital of ... LANCHOW
kantar ..... HUNDREDWEIGHT
kaoliang .... SORGHUM
kaolin(e) .. CLAY, LITHOMARGE
kaph in Greek .... KAPPA
kapok .... CEIBA, COTTON
kaput ..... RUINED, DEFEATED,
       LOST, DONE FOR
Kara Kum .... DESERT
Karachi is its capital .... SIND
Karafuto .... SAKHALIN
karakul ... SHEEP, FUR, OVINE
Karelian .... FINN
    lake ..... SEG, LADOGA
Karloff, actor .... BORIS
Karlovy Vary ..... KARLSBAD,
            CARLSBAD
karma .... DESTINY, FATE
Karnak city .... THEBES
    feature .... TEMPLE
kar(r)oo .... TABLELAND
karyo, as comb. form ... NUT,
            KERNEL
karyotin .... CHROMATIC
Kashmir, capital of ....
         SRINAGAR
    claimant of .... INDIA,
         PAKISTAN
    district .... LADAKH
    pagoda .... CHORTEN

river .... JHELUM
wool .... CASHMERE
katabasis .... RETREAT
Katanga leader .... TSHOMBE
katchung .... PEANUT
Katherine, diminutive of ......
    KIT(TY), KAY, KATE
Katmandu is capital of ....
    NEPAL
native .... NEPALI
katydid kin ..... GRASSHOPPER
kauri ..... PINE, WOOD, RESIN,
    GUM
kava .... SHRUB, PEPPER,
    DRINK, AVA
kayak .... CANOE, UMIAK
kayo .... KNOCKOUT
Kazak(h) .... KIRGHIZ
Kazan, movieman ...... ELIA
kea .... PARROT
favorite prey of ... SHEEP
Keats' name by Shelley ....
    ADONAIS
keck .... RETCH, HEAVE,
    BELCH, VOMIT
keddah .... TRAP
kedge .... ANCHOR
keek .... PEEP, SPY
keel .... SHIP, RUDDLE,
    LIGHTER, BARGE, CAREEN,
    TILT, LIST, CARINA
like .... CARINAL
like structure ... CARINA
over ..... CAPSIZE, UPSET,
    TURN OVER
part .... SKEG
shaped ...... CARINATE
without .... RATITE
Keeling Islands .... COCOS
keen .... ASTUTE, INCISIVE,
    SMART, TART, SNELL, GARE,
    GLEG, SUBTLE, SHARP,
    CUTTING, PIERCING, ACUTE,
    WAIL, DIRGE, EAGER,
    PUNGENT, PENETRATING,
    PERCEPTIVE, SHREWD,
    TRENCHANT
eyed animal .. LYNX, CAT
keenness .... ACIES, EDGE,
    ACUITY
of mind .... ACUMEN
keep ... TEND, GUARD, SAVE,
    DONJON, DETAIN, RETAIN,
    DEFEND, PRESERVE,
    (WITH)HOLD, CONCEAL,
    CUSTODY, FORT,

STRONGHOLD, CASTLE,
    LIVELIHOOD, RESERVE
close to .... HUG
company .... CONSORT,
    HOBNOB
from flying ..... GROUND
house for oneself .. BACH
out ..... EXCLUDE, BAR
tally .... SCORE, RECORD
up .... CONTINUE,
    MAINTAIN
keeper .... GUARD(IAN),
    PROTECTOR, CUSTODIAN,
    CARETAKER
castle .... CONSTABLE
forest .. RANGER, WARDEN
fortress ...... CONSTABLE
game .... WARDEN
jail .. TURNKEY, WARDEN
museum ...... CURATOR
keepers, usually .... FINDERS,
    BROTHERS
keeping .... CUSTODY, CARE,
    CHARGE, OBSERVANCE
horses for hire ... LIVERY
keeps course .... CAPES
keepsake ...... RELIC, TOKEN,
    SOUVENIR, MEMENTO
keeve ...... TUB, VAT, KIVER,
    KEIR
kef .... HEMP, NARCOTIC
Kefauver, senator ..... ESTES
keg .... CADE, CASK, FIRKIN,
    TUN, VAT, BARREL
cork .... BUNG
of beer .... GROWLER
open a .... UNHEAD
stopper .... BUNG
water .... BREAKER
kegler .... BOWLER
Keijo .... SEOUL
keir .... VAT
keitloa .... RHINO(CEROS)
Kelantan capital ....
    KOTA BHARU
kelep .... ANT
Keller, Miss .... HELEN
keloid .... TUMOR
Kelly, performer .... EMMETT,
    GENE, PATSY
kelp ..... SEAWEED, WRACK,
    VARIC, ASH
derivative ...... IODINE
kelpie .... (WATER) SPIRIT
kelter ..... CONDITION, ORDER

Kemal, Turkish leader ...... ATATURK

Kemble, actress ...... FANNY

ken .... LORE, PRESCIENCE, DESCRY, SEE, RECOGNIZE, SIGHT

kench .... BOX, BIN

content of ... FISH, SKIN

Kennedy Space Center site ... CANAVERAL

kennel ..... DOGHOUSE, PACK, GUTTER, SEWER, DRAIN

sound ... YIP, BARK, YELP

keno, game like .... LOTTO, BINGO, BEANO

Kent county seat .. MAIDSTONE

resort/seaport .. MARGATE

Kentuckian .... LINCOLN

Kentucky capital .. FRANKFORT

city .... PADUCAH, COVINGTON, LEXINGTON, OWENSBORO

college .... BEREA

county .... OWEN, BOYD, TODD, LYON, HART, KNOX, PIKE

event .... DERBY

explorer .. JOLIET, BOONE

honorary title .. COLONEL

personage ..... COLONEL

pride of .... HORSES, WHISKY

state bird ..... CARDINAL

state flower .. GOLDENROD

state nickname .... BLUEGRASS

tobacco .... BURLEY

tourist attraction .... MAMMOTH CAVE

tree .... CHICOT

Kenya capital ... NAIROBI

city.. MOMBASA, NAIROBI

language .... HINDU, BANTU, SWAHILI

monetary unit .. SHILLING

Olympic champ .. KEINO, TEMU, BIWOTT

president ..... KENYATTA

seaport ...... MOMBASA

secret society .. MAUMAU

Kenyatta, Kenya president .... JOMO

Keos .... ZEA

kepi .... CAP

Kepler, astronomer .... JOHANNES

keratinous .... HORNY

formation .. HAIR, HORN, NAIL

keratoid .. HORNY, HORNLIKE

keratosis .... WART

kerchief .... BABUSHKA, BANDAN(N)A, SCARF, MADRAS, CURCH

kerf ...... CUT(TING), NOTCH

Kerkyra .... CORFU

kermes .... DYE, OAK

kermess .... FAIR, CARNIVAL

kern(e) .... PEASANT, (FOOT)SOLDIER

kernel .... GIST, SEED, GRADI, PIT, NUT(MEAT), NUCLEUS, BARREL, CORE, HEART, PITH, ESSENCE, CORN

combining form .. KARYO, CARYO

having .... NUCLEATE

kerosene .... OIL

source of .... COAL, PETROLEUM

Kerry ..... CATTLE, COUNTY

blue .... TERRIER

kersey .... CLOTH

kestrel .. FALCON, WINDHOVER

ketch .. JACK, SHIP, HANGMAN, YAWL

Levantine .... SAIC

ketchup ..... CATSUP, SAUCE

ketone .. ACETONE, BUTYRONE, IRONE, CARONE

ketosis, cause of ... DIABETES MELLITUS

Kett, comic strip's ..... ETTA

kettle ... BILLY, CA(U)LDRON, POT(HOLE), BOILER

coating inside .... SCALE

handle .... BAIL

in the South ...... SIROP

repairer .... TINKER

stand .... TRIVET

kettledrum .... TIMPANO, TIMPANI, AT(T)ABAL, NAKER, TIMBAL

cavalry ...... ANACARA

player .... TIMPANIST

kevel .... CLEAT, PEG

key .... COTTER, CLAVIS, PIN, BOLT, WEDGE, PITCH, TONE, REEF, ISLE(T), CLEW, CODE, CAY, ISLAND, SOLUTION

blade of .... WEB
emergency .... PICK
false .... GLUT
filler .... ULLER
fruit .... SAMARA
instrument ..... MANUAL
locksmithing ..... WARD
part ..... BIT, PIN, STEM
pertaining to ..... TONAL
repairer ..... LOCKSMITH
shaped ... URDE, CLECHE
signature in music ......
           SHARP, FLAT
substitute .... PICK
telegraph .... TAPPER
keyboard .... CLAVIER
instrument (musical) ...
     CELESTA, PIANO,
     ORGAN, SPINET,
     HARMONIUM,
     MELODEON, CLAVIER,
     CLAVICHORD,
     HARPSICHORD,
     VIRGINAL
machine ... LINO(TYPE),
     TYPEWRITER, TELETYPE,
     TELEX
shaped .... URDE
keyed up ...... AGOG, EAGER,
           EXCITED, TENSE
keyhole guard .... TAPPET
ridge .... WARD
keynote ...... TONIC, THEME
sign .... ISON
keystone .. SAGITTA, SUPPORT,
           WEDGE
characters .... COPS
prop .... PIE
State ..... PENNSYLVANIA
state founder ...... PENN
keyway .... SLOT
khaki color .... DUN
khamsin .... WIND
khan .... INN, ALY,
     CARAVANSARY, AGA, CHAM
Khania .... CANEA
Khartoum is capital of .. SUDAN
khedah .... TRAP
khedive's estate .... DAIRA
Khmer .... CAMBODIAN
emperor ... JAYAVARMAN
temple ..... ANGKOR VAT
Khotan .... HOTIEN
Khrushchev, USSR premier ...
           NIKITA
Khufu .... CHEOPS

Kiangsi, capital of ....
           NANCHANG
Kiangsu, capital of .. NANKING
city .... SOOCHOW
kibblings .... BAIT
kibbutz .... SETTLEMENT
kibe .... CHILBLAIN
kibitz ..... MEDDLE, HORN IN
kibitzer .... SPECTATOR,
     MEDDLER, ONLOOKER
kibosh ...... NONSENSE, VETO,
           SQUELCH
kick ..... BOOT, CALCITRATE,
     KEVEL, RECOIL, GRUMBLE,
     COMPLAIN(T), SPURN,
     EXCITEMENT, OBJECT(ION),
           THRILL
in .... DIE, PAY
in football .. PUNT, HACK
off .... DIE, START
Kickapoo .... ALGONQUIN,
           INDIAN
kickback, usually ..... BRIBE,
     PAYOLA, REBATE
kickshaw .... TIDBIT, TRIFLE,
     TRINKET, GEWGAW,
     DELICACY, BAUBLE, TOY,
           FOOD
kickup .... ROW, FUSS
kid ..... BANTER, JOSH, JOKE,
     RIB, (Y)EARLING, GOAT,
     SUEDE, ANTELOPE, LEATHER,
     TEASE, DECEIVE, LAD
colloquial .... CHILD
prepared for slaughter ...
           FATLING
sailor's .... TUB
slang .... HOAX
undressed .... SUEDE
Kidd, Captain .... PIRATE,
           PRIVATEER
kidder .... TEASER
kidderminster .... CARPET
kiddy: colloq. .... CHILD
wear .... ROMPER
kidnap ..... ABDUCT, SNATCH,
           SHANGHAI
kidney ...... GLAND, CLASS,
           SORT, NEER
ailment remedy ....
           NEPHRITE
bean .... BON, HARICOT,
           PHASEL
combining form ... RENI,
     RENO, NEPHRO
concretion ...... GRAVEL

condition .... NEPHRISM, NEPHROSIS
duct .... URETER
external layer ... CORTEX
of the .... RENAL, NEPHRITIC, NEPHRIC
protein .... RENIN
shaped .... RENIFORM
shaped fruit ... CASHEW
stone .... JADE, NEPHRITE
substance .... MEDULLA
tube .... URETER
kidskin parchment ... VELLUM
kier .... VAT
Kilauea, goddess of .... PELE
kilderkin ..... CASK, BARREL
Kilimanjaro peak ...... KIBO
kill ...... BLAST, DISPATCH, LIQUIDATE, SLAY, DESTROY, RUIN, CANCEL, CHANNEL, STREAM, CREEK
bill .... VETO
by drowning .... NOYADE
by hanging .. STRING UP
by mob action ... LYNCH
by stoning ..... LAPIDATE
by suffocation .... BURKE
in printing ..... DELE(TE), CANCEL
in tennis .... SMASH
joy .... WET BLANKET, SPOILSPORT
legally .... EXECUTE
unlawfully .... MURDER, ASSASSINATE
Killarney land .... ERIN
killdeer ...... PLOVER, BIRD
killer .... SLAYER, MURDERER
hired ... BRAVO, ASSASSIN
of a god .... DEICIDE
political ...... ASSASSIN
whale .... ORC(A), DOLPHIN, GRAMPUS
killick .... ANCHOR
killing .... CARNAGE, FATAL, DEADLY, SLAUGHTER
deliberate ...... MURDER
mass .... MASSACRE, BATTUE, PURGE, CARNAGE, POGROM, GENOCIDE, BUTCHERY
of fetus .... ABORTICIDE
of a king ...... REGICIDE
of old men ..... SENICIDE

political .... PURGE, ASSASSINATION
killock .... ANCHOR
Kilmer poem .... TREES
poet .... JOYCE
kiln .... O(A)ST, STOVE, OVEN, TILER(Y), FURNACE, DRYER, DRIER, LEER
kilograms, 100 ...... QUINTAL, CENTAL, CENTNER
1,000 .... MILLIER
kiloliter .... STERE
kilt ...... FILIBEG, PHILIBEG, TUCK, PLEAT, SKIRT
undergarment ... TREWS
kilting .... PLEATS
kiltie .... SCOT(SMAN)
Kim _____ ....O'HARA, NOVAK, HUNTER
friend of .... LAMA
kimono ...... DRESSING GOWN
sash .... OBI
kin .... FOLKS, FAMILY, RELATIVE(S), RELATED, SIB(S)
kind .... RACE, VARIETY, GENTLE, GENEROUS, BENIGN, ILK, SPECIES, CLASS, SORT, GENUS
in ..... GOODS, PRODUCE
of ... SOMEWHAT, ALMOST
of a ... ALIKE, MEDIOCRE
of this/that ... SUCH(LIKE)
kindergarten .. SCHOOL, CLASS
activity .... GAMES, EXERCISES
pioneer .... FROEBEL
kindle .... BURN, ROUSE, IGNITE, LIGHT, EXCITE, TIND, FIRE, SPUNK, LUNT
kindled .... LIT
kindling ..... PUNK, AMADOU
kindling brick .... BRIQUET(TE)
kindly ..... BENIGN, GENIAL, PLEASE
kindness .... GOOD WILL, LENITY, GRACE
kindred ... COGNATE, ALLIED, AKIN, BLOOD, KITH, TIE, SIB, KINSHIP, RELATIVES, FAMILY
kine .... CATTLE, COWS
king .... SOVEREIGN, ROI, REGULUS, PADISHAH, RANK, REX, MONARCH, RULER, SIRE

and jack ..... TENACE
Albanian .... ZOG
Ammonite ..... HANUN
Arthur's birthplace ......
   TINTAGEL HEAD
capital ..... CAMELOT
chronicler .. GEOFFREY
clown .... DAGONET
court .... CAMELOT
death place ... CAMLAN
fairy sister ....
   MORGAN LE FAY
father .... UTHER
.father-in-law ....
   LEOGADAN
fictitious visitor ......
   YANKEE
fool/jester ... DAGONET
foster brother .... KAY
half-sister ....
   MORGAN (LE FAY)
knight (see round table)
   GARETH, GAWAIN,
   GALAHAD, LANCELOT,
   MODRED
knights .. ROUNDTABLE
lance .... RON(E)
magician ..... MERLIN
mother ...... IGRAINE,
   YGERNE, IGERNE,
   IGERNA
nephew ..... GAWAIN,
   KAY, GARETH,
   MO(R)DRED
place .... ASTOLAT
queen ...... GUINEVERE
realm .... BRITAIN
resting place .. AVALON
seneschal .... KAY
shield name .. PRIDWIN
step-sister ....
   MORGAN (LE FAY)
sword ..... EXCALIBUR
wife .... GUINEVERE
Canute's consort .. EMMA
changed to mountain ....
   ATLAS
Cole .... NAT, OLD
crab .... LIMULOID,
   LIMULUS, XIPHOSURAN
David's daughter .. TAMAR
faithful friend ... ITAI
father .... JESSE
general .... REI, IGAL,
   ABNER, AMASA,
   ABIGAIL, SHAMAH

son .. ABSALOM, AMNON
during Christ's time .....
   HEROR
Egyptian ...... PHARAOH
fairyland .... OBERON
Ferdinand ...... BOMBA
Gath .... ACHISH
great .... PADISHA
Iranian .... SHAH
killer ...... REGICIDE
Lear's daughter ....
   GONERIL, REGAN,
   CORDELIA
dog .... TRAY
legendary .... MIDAS
maned .... LION
Midian .... REBA
Mongkut's country .....
   SIAM
morning reception of ....
   LEVEE
of a ...... ROYAL, REGAL
of Amalek .... AGAG
Arcadia ..... LYCAON
Argos .... DANAUS
Assyria .... PUL,
   SENACHERIB
Athens .... THESEUS,
   CODRUS
Attica .... CECROPS
Babylon .. HAMMURABI,
   BELSHAZZAR,
   SELEACUS
Bashan .... OG
beasts .... LION
Belgium ... BAUDOIN,
   LEOPOLD
birds .... EAGLE
Bohemia ..... WENZEL,
   WENCESLAUS
Britain ..... ARTHUR,
   UTHER, LEAR,
   ARTEGAL, BELINUS, LUD
Bulgaria .... BORIS
Burgundy ... GUNTHER
Bythinia ... NICOMEDES
Colon .... GASPAR
Corinth ..... POLYBUS
Crete .... MINOS
Cyprus ... PYGMALION
Damascus ... ARETUS
Denmark .. VALDEMAR,
   WALDEMAR
dwarfs ...... ALBERICH
Egypt .. FUAD, FAROUK
elves .... ERLKING

England .... STEPHEN, ETHELRED
England and Denmark KNUT, CNUT
Epirus ..... PYRRHUS
Ethiopia .... CEPHEUS
fairies .... OBERON
Franks .... PEPIN
"golden touch" ..... MIDAS
hobbies, alleged ...... PHILATELY
Huns ... ATLI, ATTILA, ETZEL
Ioclus .... AESON
Iran .... XERXES
Iraq .... FEISAL
Israel .... AHAB, JEROBOAM, NADAB, HOSHEA, JEHU, ELAH, OMRI, SAUL, SOLOMON, DAVID
Israel, last .... HOSHEA
Jews .... HEROD
Judah/Judea .. ABIJAH, AHAZ, MANASSEH, HEROD, ASA, UZZIAH, JOSIAH, JOSIAS
Kent .... ETHELBERT
Langobards .. ALBOIN
Ligurians .... CYGNUS
Lydia .... CROESUS
Moab .... EGLON
Mycenae ..... ATREUS
Myrmidons .. PELEUS
Naples .... MURAT
Norway .... OLAF, OLAV, HAAKON
Numidia ... JUGURTHA, MASINISSA, SYPHAX
Peris ...... JAMSHID
Persia .... CYRUS, XERXES, DARIUS
Phrygia ...... MIDAS, GORDIUS
Pontus .. MITHRIDATES
Rome .... TARQUIN
Salem ... MELCHIZEDEK
Scotland ...... BRUCE
Siam .... ANANDA, MONGKUT
Sodom .... BERA
Spain .... REY, ALFONSO, JUAN
Sparta .... MENELAUS, LEONIDAS

Syria .... HAZAL
Thebes .. LAIUS, CREON
Thessaly ... ADMETUS, PELIAS
Thrace .... TEREUS, LYSIMACHUS
Troy .... PRIAM
Tyre .... HIRAM
Ulster ... CONCHOBAR
Visigoths ..... ALARIC
Volsunga ...... ATLI
Zulus ..... CETEWAYO
Saul's commander ...... ABNER
sculptor ..... PYGMALION
snake .... COBRA
Solomon's country ...... OPHIR
with ass' ears ..... MIDAS
with eternal thirst, hunger TANTALUS
kingbird ..... FLYCATCHER, BEE MARTIN, PIPIRI
kingcup .... MARIGOLD
kingdom .. REALM, REGALITY, ESTATE, DOMAIN, MONARCHY, EMPIRE, LESOTHO
African .... NUBIA, NUMIDIA
ancient .... EDOM, CROATIA, IDUMBA, ELAM, MACEDONIA
Asiatic .... SIAM, THAILAND, KOREA, NEPAL
Caspian ...... PARTHIA
cause of loss of .... NAIL, HORSE
come ...... HEREAFTER, HEAVEN
kind of .... ANIMAL, PLANT, VEGETABLE
kingfish ...... BARB, OPAH, PINTADO, WHITING, HAKU, SIERRA, CERO
kingfisher .... HALCYON, KOOKABURRA
kingfisher's kin ...... MOTMOT
kinglet ..... WREN, SONGBIRD
kingly ..... LEONINE, ROYAL, AUGUST, REGAL, MAJESTIC, NOBLE
authority/power .. .. DIADEM
kingmaker: soubriquet ..... WARWICK

King's chamber ... CAMARILLA
  clover .... MELILOT
  color .. ORPIMENT, PURPLE
  evil .... SCROFULA
  Peak range ...... UINTA
  robe .... DALMATIC
  rod .... WARDER
  steward ... CHAMBERLAIN
  symbol ..... ORB, MOUND
kingship ... ROYALTY, MAJESTY
kink .. BUCKLE, KNOT, SNARL,
  CURL, CRICK, TWIST,
  CROTCHET, QUIRK, WHIM
  thread .... BURL
kinkajou ... POTT(O), MAMMAL
  animal like a .. RACCOON
kinky .... CURLY
kino .... GUM, ASTRINGENT
kinsfolk ... RELATIVES, FAMILY
kinship ... AFFINITY, ENATION,
  AGNATION
kinsman .... RELATIVE, SIB,
  RELATION
kiosk .... PAVILION,
  SUMMERHOUSE, BANDSTAND,
  NEWSSTAND
kip .... HIDE, BED,
  ROOMING HOUSE
Kipling's heroine ..... MAISIE
  novel .... KIM
  "Shere Khan" .... TIGER
  title .... SAHIB
  wolf .... AKELA
Kirghiz ... KAZAK(H), MONGOL
  mountains .... ALAI
  tent .... YURT
kirk .... CHURCH
Kirman .... RUG
kirmess ...... FAIR, CARNIVAL
kirn .... FEAST
kirtle ... SKIRT, COAT, TUNIC
Kish's father .... NER
  son .... SAUL
kismet .... DESTINY, FATE,
  DOOM
kiss .... OSCULATE, CANDY,
  BUSS, SMACK, CARESS,
  SUGARPLUM, PECK
  and _____ .... TELL
"Kiss" sculptor .... RODIN
kisser: sl. ...... MOUTH, LIPS,
  FACE
kissing game .... POST OFFICE
kist ..... BOX, LOCKER, CHEST,
  TOMB
kit ...... TUB, BUCKET, PACK,

  SET, LOT, COLLECTION,
  GEAR, VIOLIN, OUTFIT
  and _____ ..... CABOODLE
kitchen ... CUISINE, COOKERY,
  SCULLERY
  chief .... CHEF
  garden .... OLITORY
  help .... SCULLION
  leftovers .... PEELINGS
  of the .... CULINARY
  police for short ...... KP
  ship's .... GALLEY,
  CABOOSE
  table .... DRESSER
  tool ..... CORER, DICER,
  GRATER, SIEVE
  waste .... SLOPS
  wear .... APRON
  worker .... SCULLION
Kitchener ..... STOVE, RANGE
  statesman ...... HORATIO
kitchenware .... POTS, PANS,
  UTENSILS
kite .... MILAN, ELANET,
  GLED(E), HAWK, BIRD,
  ROGUE, SHARPER, SOAR,
  FALCON
kith and kin ...... RELATIVES
kitsch .... TRASH
kittenish ... FRISKY, PLAYFUL
kittens: colloq: ... HYSTERICS
kittiwake .... GULL, WAEG
kittle .... PUZZLE, TICKLE
kitty ...... CAT, ANTE, POOL,
  STAKES, POT, WIDOW
kiva ...... DWELLING, ROOM
kiwi ..... ROA, MOA, APTERYX
Klausenburg .... CLUJ
klaxon .... HORN
klepht .... BRIGAND
kleptomaniac .... THIEF,
  FILCHER, SHOPLIFTER
Klingsor .... MAGICIAN
klipspringer .... ANTELOPE
Klondike road .... ALCAN
kloop ...... GORGE, VALLEY
knack ... HANG, FLAIR, SKILL,
  ART, TALENT, APTITUDE,
  INSTINCT, DEVICE, TRICK,
  DEXTERITY, TRINKET, FEAT
knaggy ...... ROUGH, KNOTTY
knap ..... HILL, KNOCK, RAP,
  NIBBLE, SNAP, BITE,
  SUMMIT
knapsack ...... (DUFFLE)BAG,
  PACK, KIT, MOCHILA

knar .... KNOT
knarl .... NODE
knave ...... SERVANT, SCAMP,
   COISTREL, VARLET, LOREL,
   · LOSEL, ROGUE, RASCAL,
             CHURL
   game cards' .... JACK
   in cribbage .... NOBS
   of clubs .... PAM
   playing cards' ..... JACK
knead .... MALAX, MOLD,
   PETRIE, MASSAGE, ELT
kneading material .... DOUGH,
             CLAY
knee .... JOINT, GENU
   ailment ...... GONAGRA
   bend the .... GENUFLECT
   bone .... DIB
   flexure .... GENU
   inflammation ... GONITIS
   joint ... HOCK, KNUCKLE
   like part .... GENU
   tendon ..... HAMSTRING
kneecap ... PATELLA, ROTULA
kneel .. GENUFLECT, KOWTOW
kneeling, act of .... KOWTOW
   desk .... PRIE DIEU
kneepan .... PATELLA
knell ...... TOLL, RING, OMEN
knickerbocker(s) ....
   NEW YORKER, TROUSERS,
           PLUS FOURS
knickknack ...... GIMCRACK,
   TOY, DOODAD, NOVELTY,
   TRIFLE, TRINKET, GEWGAW,
      GAUD, BAUBLE
knife ...... CUT, STAB, BLADE,
   CHIV, SNEE, SNY,
   MACHET(T)E, BARLOW,
   PARANG, BOWIE, BOLO,
          GENEFE
   Burmese ...... DAH, DOW
   combining form ... DORI
   cord .... LANYARD,
         LANIARD
   dealer .... CUTLER
   Dyak .... PARANG
   Eskimo woman's ... ULU
   for opening veins ....
      LANCET, FLEAM
   handle .... HAFT
   Hindu .... KURRI
   Irish .... SKEAN
   kind of .... PEN, BOWIE,
   FAN, SWITCHBLADE,
   TRIVET, TREVET

   large .... COUTEAU
   like tool .... SLITTER
   Malay ..... CREESE, KRIS
   Maori .... PATU
   Moro .... KRIS
   part .... TANG, HAFT
   Philippine .. ITAK, BOLO
   sharpener .... STEEL
   surgical .... SCALPEL,
     CATLIN, LANCET
   thrust ... STAB, STOCCADO
   tosser .... JUGGLER
knight .... SIR, CAVALIER,
   BAYARD, EQUITE, EQUES,
   PALADIN, TEMPLAR,
   CHAMPION, EREC,
         RITTER
   arena of the ...... LISTS
   armor bearer of ....
         ARMIGER
   attendant .... SQUIRE,
   ARMIGER, PAGE,
         DONZEL
   challenge .... GAGE
   cloak of .... TABARD
   Crusader ...... TEMPLAR
   ensign .... PENNON
   errand of a ...... QUEST
   errant .... PALADIN
   fight of a ... TILT, JOUST,
        TOURNEY
   groom of ..... COISTREL
   in chess .... HORSE
   lance target ... QUINTAIN
   mantle of .... TABARD
   medieval .... BEVIS
   of the road .... HOBO,
        TRAMP
   of the "Round Table" ...
   BORS, GARETH, BALAN,
   BALIN, BORT, GALAHAD,
   LANCELOT, KAY,
   GERAINT, GAWAIN,
   PELLEAS, MO(R)DRED,
   BEDIVERE, TRISTAN,
   MORGA(I)N, PERCIVAL,
      TRISTRAM
   page of .... VARLET
   pledge .... GAGE
   protective cover of ......
        ARMOR
   Templar .... MASON
   title of .... SIR
   to .... DUB
   vocation ..... CHIVALRY
   weapon of ...... LANCE

without armor ....
    BARESARK
knighthood ... CHIVALRY, HOST
knightliness .... CHIVALRY
knightly .... CHIVALROUS
knit .... PURSE, PUCKER,
    INTERLOCK, COUPLE, SEAM,
    UNITE, JOIN
knitted goods dealer .. HOSIER
knitting ... BROCADE, CROCHET
    machine guide ..... SLEY
    stitch .... PURL
knives, seller of ...... CUTLER
    tosser of .... JUGGLER
knob ..... NUB(BLE), KNURL,
    NODE, UMBO, HILL, KNOLL,
    HANDLE, KNOP, STUD,
    FINIAL
    like .... NOPAL
    like ornament .... KNOP
    medical .... TUBERCLE
    ornamental .. BOSS, STUD
    pertaining to a .... ORLET
    projecting .... BOSS
knobbed .... TOROSE, NODOSE,
    TOROUS
knobby .... TUBEROSE,
    TUBEROUS, NUBB(L)Y
knobkerrie .... CLUB, KIR(R)I,
    KERRI
knobs, decorate with .... BOSS
knobstick .... RAT, SNOB
knock ... RAP, BLOW, CLASH,
    BUMP, HIT, CRITICIZE,
    STRIKE, KNAP
    about ... ROAM, HUSTLE,
    WANDER
    down .. FLATTEN, FLOOR
    kneed ..... BOWLEGGED,
    WOBBLY, VALGUS
    lightly .... RAP, TAP
    out ... KAYO, DEFEAT, KO
knockabout ... YACHT, NOISY,
    ROUGH, HUSTLE
knocker .... RAPPER,
    FAULTFINDER, NAGGER,
    CRITIC
knockout blow .... HAYMAKER
knoll ... HILLOCK, HUMMOCK,
    TOFT, MOUND, KNAP
Knossos .... CRETE
knot ..... NODE, JOINT, TUFT,
    NODUS, HITCH, TIE, SNAG,
    COCKADE, NODULE, NUB,
    BOW, EPAULET,
    CLUSTER, BOND, KNUR,

    SANDPIPER, PROBLEM,
    LUMP, ENTANGLE
    cloth .... BURL
    fiber .... NOIL, NEP
    fibrous .... NEP
    hair ..... NOIL, CHIGNON
    kind of ...... OVERHAND,
    THIEF, LOOP, REEF,
    BOWLINE, GRANNY,
    PROLONGE, TREFOIL,
    CAT'S-PAW,
    SHEEPSHANK, MOUSE
    lace .... TAT(T)
    loose .... GRANNY
    nautical .... MILE
    pertaining to a .... NODAL
    rope .... CLINCH
    running .... NOOSE
    silk .... NOIL
    thread .... BURL
    tree .... GNARL
    wood ...... BURL, KNAR,
    NURL, GNARL, KNOR
    wool .... NOIL
    yarn .... SKEIN
knots, full of .... NODOUS
    rid of .... ENODATE
knotted .... NODATED,
    TANGLED, INTRICATE,
    NODED
knotty ... KNAGGY, NODOSE,
    NODOUS
knotweed ...... PERSICARY,
    ALLSEEDS
knout .... WHIP, FLOG
know ...... REGARD, REVEAL,
    KEN, WOT, AWARE, WIS(T)
    all: colloq. ... WISEACRE,
    SMART ALECK,
    QUIDNUNC
    beforehand .... FORESEE
    how .... SKILL
    it-all .... WISEGUY,
    WISEACRE
    long ago .... WOT
    nothing ..... IGNORAMUS,
    AGNOSTIC
knowing ...... HEP, SCIENT,
    GNOSTIC, SHREWD, CLEVER,
    DELIBERATE
knowledge ...... LORE, KITH,
    NOESIS, EXPERTISE, KEN,
    COGNITION, WISDOM,
    SCIENTIA, AWARENESS,
    INFORMATION
    branch of .... OLOGY

has .... AWARE
lack of ...... IGNORANCE
means to ..... ORGANON
of .... GNOSTIC
source of .... LAMP
spiritual .... GNOSIS
surface ...... SCIOLISM,
            SMATTER(ING)
universal ... PANTOLOGY,
            PANSOPHY
knowledgeable ...... HEP, HIP,
            WISE, INTELLIGENT,
            SAPIENT, INFORMED
known as ... YCLEPT, YCLEPED
knuckle .... JOINT
    down under ..... YIELD,
            GIVE IN
knucklebone ...... KNOB, BIB
knur .... KNOT
knurl .... RIDGE, KNOT, KNOB,
            NODULE
KO: sl. .... KNOCKOUT
koa .... ACACIA
koala .... BEAR
Kobenhavn ..... COPENHAGEN
kobold .. GNOME, (HOB)GOBLIN,
    BROWNIE, SPRITE, NIS(SE)
kodak .... CAMERA
kodok .... FASHODA
koel .... CUCKOO
Koheleth .... SOLOMON
Kohinoor .... DIAMOND,
            (CROWN) JEWEL
kohl .... COSMETIC
kohlrabi .... CABBAGE
kok-sagyz ...... DANDELION
Kok's (Adam) settlers ....
            GRIQUA
kokama .... GEMSBOOK
Koko's weapon .... SNEE
kokoon .... GNU
Kol dialect .... MUNDARI
kola .... NUT
    nut content .. CAFFEIN(E)
kolinsky .... MINK, FUR
koodoo .... KUDU
kook .... CUCKOO
kookaburra ..... KINGFISHER
kooky .... CRAZY, SILLY,
            ECCENTRIC
kop .... HILL, MOUNTAIN
kopje .... HILL(OCK)
kor .... HOMER
Koran chapter ..... ALCORAN,
            SURA(H), SURO
    interpreter ...... ULEMA

memorizer ...... HAFIZ
paradise bridge ....
            AL SIRAT
scholar .... ULEMA
supplement to the ....
            SUNNA(H), SHIITE
teacher of ...... ALFAQUI
Korea .... CHOSEN
    founder of ..... TANGUN
Korean capital, North ....
            PYONGYANG
    capital, South ... SEOUL,
            KEIJO
    city ..... FUSAN, TAEGU,
            GENSAN, WONSAN
    coin .... WON
    dynasty .... SILLA
    kingdom .... SILLA
    island .... KOJE
    monetary unit ..... WON,
            HWAN
    mount .... SORAK
    port .... GENSAN, FUSAN
    premier ....
            KIM IL SUNG (NORTH),
    CHUNG IL KWON (SOUTH)
    president ....
            (CHUNG HEE) PARK,
            RHEE
    river .... YALU, HAN
    seaport .... JINSEN,
            CHEMULP(H)O,
            INCHON, WONSAN,
            PUSAN
    soldier .... ROK
    stockade .... JKOJE
    true faith ..... AL SIRAT
    weight .... KON
    women's blouse .. CHIMA
    women's skirt .. CHOGORI
Korina wood .... AFARA
koruna, 1/100 of ...... HELLER
kosher .. CLEAN, FIT, PROPER
    opposed to .... TREF
Kosygin, Russian premier ....
            ALEKSEI
Kotabaru .... HOLLANDIA
Kovno .... KAUNAS
kowtow .... SALUTATION,
            HOMAGE, RESPECT
kr. .... KRONA, KRONOR,
            KRONER, KRONE(N),
            KRYPTON, KREUTZER
kraal ... ENCLOSURE, VILLAGE,
            PEN
kraft ...... WRAPPING PAPER

Kreisler, violinist ...... FRITZ
Kremlin .... CITADEL
Kriembild's husband ....
    SIEGFRIED, ETZEL, ATTILA
krimmer .... LAMBSKIN
kris .... CREESE, DAGGER
Kriss Kringle .. SANTA (CLAUS)
krona .... CROWN
Kronos' wife .... RHEA
Kronstadt ..... BRASOV, PORT
Kropotkin, anarchist ..... PETR
Kruger, Transvaal president ..
    OOM PAUL
Ku Klux Klan official ....
    KLEAGLE
Kublai Khan dynasty ... YUAN
kuchen .... COFFEECAKE
kudos ...... FAME, GLORY,
    CREDIT, PRAISE, PRESTIGE
kudu ...... ANTELOPE, KOODOO
kulak .... FARMER
kulun .... ULAN BATOR
Kumasi is capital of .. ASHANTI
    is in .... GHANA
kumiss .... OMEIRIS
kummel .... LIQUEUR
Kung Fu-tse ...... CONFUCIUS

Kuomintang .... YUAN
    founder ... SUN YAT-SEN
    leader .. CHIANG KAI-SHEK
kurrajong .... CALOOL
Kurdistan .. .. RUG
Kuril(e) island ...... ITURUP,
    CHISHIMA, ETORO
kust .... NODE
Kuwait .... SHEIKDOM
    export .... OIL
    monetary unit .... DINAR
kvass .... BEER
Kwangchow .... CANTON
Kwangsi capital ... NANNING
Kwantung capital ... CANTON
    city .... SWATOW
    seaport .... DAIREN
kyack .... PACKSACK
Kymric .... WELSH
kyphos .... HUMP
kyphosis .... HUMPBACK
Kyser, bandleader .... KAY
Kyushu base .... SASEBO
    city .... KUMAMOTO,
    NAGASAKI, SASEBO,
    MOJI
    volcano ...... ASO(SAN)

L

L, Greek .... LAMBDA
    in chemistry ....
    LANTHANUM
    in geodesy ... LONGITUDE
    letter .... ELL, EL
    shaped .... ELL
"La Boheme" character ......
    MIMI, MUSETTA, RODOLPHO
"La Gioconda" ... MONA LISA
La Guardia, Mayor ....
    FIORELLO
La Rochefoucauld's forte .....
    MAXIMS
laager .... CAMP
Laban's daughter ...... LEAH,
    RACHEL
labarum .... STANDARD
labdanum .... RESIN
Labe .... ELBE
labefaction ...... DOWNFALL
label ... FILLET, TAG, LAPPET,
    CLASSIFICATION, STICKER,
    TAB, NAME, TALLY, PASTER,
    DESCRIBE, MARK, STAMP,
    BRAND, DOCKET
labellum .... LIP, PETAL

    flower with ..... ORCHID
labia .... LIPS
    minora ...... NYMPHA(E)
labial .... (ORGAN) PIPE
labiate .... LIPPED
labile ... UNSTABLE, SKIMMING
labium ...... LIP, LABELLUM
labor .... WORK, TRAVAIL,
    TOIL, PARTURATION,
    STRIVE, CHILDBIRTH,
    TASK, MOIL
    group .... UNION
    leader ... LEWIS, GREEN,
    MEANY, HOFFA,
    PETRILLO, REUTHER
    omnia ____ ...... VINCIT
    organization, international
    ILO
    throes, pains ... TRAVAIL
    resources .... MANPOWER
    spy recruiter ... HOOKER
    strike placard carrier ....
    PICKET
    union .... CIO, AFL,
    ILGWU, ARTEL
    union branch .... LOCAL

union negotiation ...... COLLECTIVE BARGAINING
laboratory burner ..... ETNA, BUNSEN
need ... ACIDS, OLEATES, TEST TUBES
labored ... OPEROSE, DIFFICULT
breath ...... PANT, GASP
laborer .... WORKER, NAVVY, PROLE, TOTY, HAND, SERF, SEGGON
Chinese .. COOLIE, COOLY
Egyptian .... FELLAH
India .... TOTY
Mexican .... PEON, BRACERO
migratory .... OKIE
oriental .... COOLIE
Spanish .... OBRERO, PEON, TRABAJADOR
underground .. SANDHOG
unskilled .... NAVVY, BOHUNK
transient .. ROUSTABOUT, FLOATER
laborious .... DIFFICULT, INDUSTRIOUS, TOILSOME
labra .... LIPS
Labrador .... PENINSULA
tea .... LEDUM
labradorite .... FELDSPAR
labroid fish .... WRASS
labrum .... LIP
laburnum ... SHRUB, PEA TREE, SANDALWOOD
labyrinth .... MAZE
builder of .... DAEDALUS
dweller, legendary ...... MINOTAUR
labyrinthine ...... INTRICATE, MEANDROUS
lace .... MACRAME, GIN, EDGING, EMBROIDER, WEAVE, NOOSE, SNARE, GUIPURE, LACIS, WHIP, THRASH, BEAT, ADORN, FILET, TATTING, MALINES, VAL, STRING, RIBBON, BRAID, NETTING, INTERTWINE, FILIGREE, LASH
cape .... MANTILLA
collar .... BERTHA
edging .... FRILL
French .... ALENCON, CLUNY
frilled .... R(O)UCHE

into .... ATTACK, ASSAIL, SCOLD, CRITICIZE
loop(s) .... PURL
make .... TAT
metal tip of ... A(I)GLET, TAG
opening .... EYELET
pattern .... TOILE
shoe/sandal .... LATCHET
silk bobbin ..... BLONDE
three-cornered ... FICHU
thread .... MACRAMB
trimming .. JABOT, FRILL
Lacedaemon .... SPARTA
lacer .... TIER
lacerate .... RIP, TEAR, MANGLE, DISTRESS, REND, HURT, TORN, CUT
lacert(il)ian .... LIZARD, CHAMELEON, GECKO
lacet .... BRAID
Lachesis .... FATE, GODDESS, WEIRD
companion of .. ATROPOS, CLOTHO
lachrymose .... TEARFUL, MOURNFUL, TEARY
lady .... NIOBE
lacing .... THRASHING, CORD, TRIMMING, BRAID, BEATING
laciniate .... FRINGED
lack ...... REQUIRE, DEARTH, NEED, SHORTAGE, DEFICIENCY, WANT(ING)
desire ..... INAPPETENCE
of stress .... ATONY
lackadaisical .... LISTLESS, SPIRITLESS, LANGUID, INDOLENT
lackey .... FLUNK(E)Y, FOOTMAN, SLAVE, TOADY, (MAN)SERVANT, FOLLOWER, ATTENDANT
uniform of ...... LIVERY
lacking .... (DE)VOID, SHORT, DESTITUTE, IN NEED, DEFICIENT, SHY
brightness .. LACKLUSTER
enthusiasm ... LUKEWARM
grace .... CLUMSY, AWKWARD, CRUDE, GAUCHE
refinement ...... COARSE, GROSS, CRUDE, INCONDITE
reverence .... IMPIOUS

lackluster ...... DULL, DRAB
Laconia is capital of .. SPARTA
    people of .... SPARTAN(s)
laconic ⌐⌐... CONCISE, TERSE,
             BRIEF, PITHY
    answer .... UGH
    person .... INDIAN
lacquer ⌐⌐... DUCO, VARNISH,
      JAPAN, ENAMEL, LAC
    plus pigment ... ENAMEL
lacs, 100 .... CRORE
lactary .... DAIRY
lactase .... ENZYME
lactate .... SUCKLE
lacteal .... MILKY
lactescent .... MILKY
lactose .... SUGAR
lacuna ⌐.. GAP, HIATUS, SPACE,
           CAVITY
lad ⌐⌐.. STRIPLING, SHAVER,
  YOUTH, SONNY, YOUNGSTER
ladanum .... RESIN
ladder ⌐⌐..... STEE, SCALADE,
             SCALE
    accommodation ....
           GANGWAY
    attack using ... ESCALADE
    part ..... RUNG, STAVE,
      SPOKE, STEP, ROUND,
      RUNDLE
lade ⌐.. LOAD, BAIL, LADLE,
      DIP, BURDEN
ladida: sl. ⌐⌐..... FLOSSY,
      FOP(PISH)
ladies' man ⌐⌐.... SHEIK(H)
Ladin .... ROMANSH
Ladino .... MESTIZO, DIALECT
ladle ... DIPPER, BOWL, SCOOP,
    SPOON, BAIL, DIP
    dip/pour with ..... LAVE
    spout .... GEAT
ladore .... CASCADE
ladrone ⌐⌐.... THIEF, ROBBER,
      BANDIT
    Island(s) .... GUAM,
      MARIANAS
lady ⌐.. MADAM, FEMALE, BIBI,
    BURD, MISTRESS, WIFE,
    SWEETHEART,
    (GENTLE)WOMAN, DAME
    Churchill .. CLEMENTINE
    Godiva, he saw ....
      PEEPING TOM
    Hamilton .... EMMA
    Italian .... DONNA,
    SIGNORA, SIGNORINA

killer: sl. ⌐⌐... DON JUAN,
    CASANOVA
    of the Lake ...... ELLEN,
    VIVIAN, NIMUE
    silk habit .... PELISSE
    Spanish .. DONA, SENORA,
    SENORITA
ladybird ⌐... BEETLE, VEDALIA
ladybug .... BEETLE
ladyfinger ... COOKIE, COOKY
ladylike ⌐⌐...⌐ WELL-BRED,
    REFINED
ladylove .... SWEETHEART
lady's maid ⌐⌐..... ABIGAIL,
    SOUBRETTE
    slipper .... ORCHID
    smock ⌐⌐....... CRESS,
    CUCKOOFLOWER
    tresses .... ORCHID
Laertes' sister ...... OPHELIA
    son .... ODYSSEUS
lag ⌐⌐... DELAY, TRAIL, IDLE,
    LOITER, LINGER, STAVE,
    DRAG, FALTER, ARREST,
    CONVICT, DALLY, TARRY
lagan ...... JETSAM, FLOTSAM
lager .... BEER, CAMP
Lagerlof .... SELMA
laggard .... LOITERER,
    BACKWARD, SLOWFOOT
lagn(i)appe ⌐⌐.⌐⌐ GRATUITY,
    PRESENT
lagomorph ⌐⌐.... HARE, PIKA,
    RABBIT, RODENT
lagoon ⌐⌐..⌐.. LAKE, POND,
    LIMAN, HAFF
    islands .... ELLICE
    site of ..... CORAL REEF,
    ATOLL
Lahr, comedian .... BERT
laic .... CIVIL, TEMPORAL,
    LAY(MAN), SECULAR
lair ... CAVE, DEN, LIE, HAUNT,
    HANGOUT
    hare's .... FORM
laity ...... LAYMEN, PEOPLE
Laius's son .... OEDIPUS
lake ⌐⌐.. LOCH, ERIE, LAGOON,
    POOL, PIGMENT, SHAT,
    SHOTT, SALINA
    African .. NYASSA, CHAD,
    VICTORIA
    artificial ...... RESERVOIR
    Australian .. EYRE, FROME
    basin .... PLAYA
    bird .... LOON

Blue Nile .... TANA
Chad tributary .... SHARI
city .... ERIE
Erie city .... LORAIN,
                  LACKAWANNA
Erie port .... TOLEDO
Erie tributary .. MAUMEE
fish .... POLLAN
Geneva .... LEMAN
Great ... ERIE, ONTARIO,
        SUPERIOR, MICHIGAN,
                  HURON
herring .... CISCO
Hoover Dam ..... MEAD
in an atoll ...... LAGOON
Irish .... LOUGH
Island in a .... HOLM
Maggiore town ....
                  LOCARNO
Michigan city ....
        MILWAUKEE, GARY,
                  KENOSHA
mountain .... OHILD
Nyassa country .. MALAWI
of a ...... LACUSTRINE,
                  LACUSTRAL
of Constance ....
                  BODENSEE
outlet .... BAYOU
poet .... COLERIDGE,
        SOUTHEY, WORDSWORTH
resort .... TAHOE
salt .... SALINA
Scottish .... LOCH
shallow .... LAGOON
small ...... MERE, POND
trout .... POGY, SALMON,
                  NAMAYCUSH
world's lowest .. DEAD SEA
lakes, found in/on ....
                  LACUSTRINE
    study of .... LIMNOLOGY
lakh .... LAC
laky .... DARK-RED
Lal Bahadur ____ ... SHASTRI
lalique .... GLASS
lallation ...... LAMBDACISM
Lalo, composer ... EDOUARD
lam ...... BEAT, FLOG, FLEE,
        VAMO(O)SE, THRASH,
                  FLIGHT, ESCAPE
lama ... MONK, PRIEST, NUN,
                  TESHU
    chief ..... DALAI, BLAMA
lamasery .... MONASTERY
lamb .... (Y)EAN, SHEEP,

CHILD, COSSET,
    (Y)EANLING, FATLING
breast .... CARRE
Charles .... ELIA
fur .... KARAKUL
hide .... KIP
holy .... AGNUS
leg of .... GIGOT
like a .... TIMID(LY),
    MEEK(LY), INNOCENT
mother of .... EWE
of God .... JESUS
pet ...... CADE, COSSET
skin .... BUDGE
slice .... CHOP
stew .... HARICOT
lambast(e) .... THRASH, BEAT,
                  SCOLD
lambda in Hebrew .. LAMED(H)
lambdacism .... LALLATION
lambent .... GLOWING,
                  FLICKERING
lambkin .... OHILD
lamblike ..... MEEK, GENTLE,
                  INNOCENT
lambrequin .... DRAPERY
lambskin .... BUDGE, VELLUM
lame ..... CRIPPLE(D), HALT,
        MAIM, DISABLE(D),
        CLAUDICANT, SPAVINED,
        HALTING, PLATE, FEEBLE
    duck, kind of ....
                  SPECULATOR
Lamech, son of ...... JABAL,
                  JUBAL, NOAH
    wife of .... ADAH
lamed(h) ...... ELL, LAMBDA
lamelli as prefix ...... PLATE,
        SCALE, LAYER, LEAF
lamellibranch ...... MOLLUSK,
                  OYSTER, CLAM
lamelliform ..... PLATELIKE,
                  SCALELIKE
lamellirostral bird ..... DUCK,
                  SWAN, GOOSE
lament ... DEPLORE, (RE)PINE,
        GRIEVE, ELEGIZE, RUE,
        MOURN, ELEGY, DIRGE,
        (BE)WAIL, (BE)MOAN
lamentable ..... DEPLORABLE,
                  WRETCHED
lamentation ...... JEREMIAD,
                  WAILING, PLAINT
lamia .... SORCERESS,
        VAMPIRE, DEMON(ESS),
                  WITCH

lamiaceous plant ...... MINT,
BERGAMOT, ROSEMARY
lamina .... FLAKE, SCALE,
BLADE, LAYER, PLY, LEAF,
PLATE
   brain .... OBEX
laminated ...... LAYERED,
SHEETED
   material ..... PLYWOOD
   rock .... SHALE
lamination ...... PLY, LAYER
laminitis .... FOUNDER
Lammas .... FESTIVAL
lammergeier ...... VULTURE,
OSSIFRAGE
lamp .... ETNA, LUCERNA,
GEORDIE, ARGAND, TORCH,
GOOSENECK, LANTERN,
BULB, GAS JET, GLIM,
LUMINAIRE
   automobile .. TAIL LIGHT
   black .... SOOT
   chain .... PENDANT
   cord/tape .... WICK
   decorative ..... LAMPION
   fuel .... KEROSENE,
PETROLEUM
   heating .... ETNA
   holder .... CRESSET
   lighter ..... SPILL, TAPER
   miner's .... DAVY
   oil .... LAMPION
   part .... WICK, BURNER,
CRESSET
   poetic ...... SUN, STAR,
MOON
   slang ...... EYES, GLIM
   waving .... ARATI
lampas ..... LAMPERS, CLOTH
lampblack ..... GRIME, SOOT,
PIGMENT
lamper eel .... LAMPREY
lampers .... LAMPAS
lampoon ...... PASQUINADE,
LIBEL, SATIRE, CARICATURE,
SQUIB, RIDICULE, SKIT
lamprey ... EEL, CYCLOSTOME
lanai .... PORCH
lanate .... WOOL(L)Y
Lancashire city .... WIGAN
   county seat ... LANCASTER
   seaport ...... LIVERPOOL,
MANCHESTER
Lancaster, actor .... BURT
lance .... JAVELIN, SPEAR,
DART, CUT, (SEA)FISH,

PIERCE
   barb .... FLUKE
   corporal in reality ....
PRIVATE
   flag of ..... BANDEROL(E)
   part ...... REST, MORNE
lancelet .... AMPHIOXUS
Lancelot .... KNIGHT
   liege of .... ARTHUR
   love of .... ELAINE
   mistress of .. GUINEVERE
   uncle of .... BORS
lancer ...... HUSSAR, U(H)LAN
lancers ..... (SQUARE)DANCE,
QUADRILLE
lancet .... (SURGICAL) KNIFE,
SCALPEL, FLEAM,
PHLEBOTOME
   point .... NEB
lancewood .... YAYA
Lanchester, actress ..... ELSA
lancinate .... STAB, TEAR,
PIERCE
land ...... COUNTRY, REGION,
SOIL, GROUND, ESTATE,
CATCH, DISEMBARK,
ALIGHT, EARTH, TERRA,
DEBARK, TRACT, TERRENE
   along river .... HOLM,
BOTTOMS, INTERVALE
   and sea fighter ... MARINE
   barren .... DESERT,
WASTE, GALL
   between hills .. INTERVALE
   border .... RAND
   church ... GLEBE, CLOSE
   cleared .... FIELD,
ASSART, CUTOVER
   close .... GARTH
   colloquial .... WIN, GET,
SECURE, HOOK
   conveyance ...... DEED
   cultivated ...... ARADO,
TILLAGE, TILTH, ARADA
   disputed .... MARCH
   east of Eden .... NOD
   ecclesiastical benefice ...
GLEBE
   eroded ...... PENEPLAIN,
PENEPLANE
   grabber of a sort ....
STAKE JUMPER
   grant .... HOMESTEAD
   grassy ... DOWN, VELDT
   held in fee simple .. ALOD,
ODAL

holder ..... THANE, THEGN
holdings, record of ......
    TERRIER
irrigated to excess ....
    WATER-SICK
marshy ...... MAREMMA
meadow .... LEA
measure ... ACRE, AR(E),
    HECTARE, RO(O)D,
    MORGEN,
    VIRGATE
mine .... CLAYMORE
of dwarfs ..... LILLIPUT
of leprechauns .... EIRE
of Office Machines,
  alleged .... SWEDEN
of plenty .... GOSHEN
of shrubs, etc. .. BARRENS
of song .... ARABY
owner of adjacent ......
    ABUTTER
ownership, restricted ....
    FEE TAIL
ownership, unrestricted ...
    FEE SIMPLE
pertaining to .. GEOPONIC,
    AGRARIAN
piece of ... PARCEL, LOT,
    PLAT
plaster .... GYPSUM
pledged as security ......
    WADSET
plowed ... ARADA, ARADO
point of low .... SPIT
power ..... (RED) CHINA
promised ...... CANAAN
reverting to the state ....
    ESCHEAT
reclaimed ...... POLDER,
    INNINGS
relating to ... AGRARIAN
rental .... FEU
rented .... HOLDING
strip of .... NECK
tenure ...... LEASEHOLD
tenure system .. SOCAGE
tilled .... ARADO, ARADA
title .... PATENT
treeless .... TUNDRA,
    SAVANNA(H), STEPPE
triangular piece .. DELTA,
    GORE
turtle .... TORTOISE
valued for taxes ....
    CADASTRE

wet ..... SWAMP, MARSH,
    MAREMMA
with heaviest rainfall ....
    ASSAM
with hardwoods ....
    HAMMOCK
landau .... CARRIAGE,
    AUTOMOBILE
landed ... TITHES, PRAEDIAL,
    ALIT, ALIGHTED
estate ... DOMAIN, MANOR
property .... ESTATE
landfall .... ISLE
landgrave .... COUNT
landing ground, aircraft ....
    STRIP, RUNWAY
passage .... GANGPLANK,
    RAMP
place .... AIRPORT, PIER,
    HELIPORT, DOCK,
    GHAT, LEVEE, QUAY,
    JETTY, TARMAC, WHARF,
    QUAI
place of the Ark ....
    ARARAT
Landis, baseball czar ......
    KENESAW
landloper ...... VAGABOND,
    VAGRANT, TRAMP
landlord .... BONIFACE,
    HOST, LAIRD
landmark .... MOUNTAIN,
    MONUMENT, MILESTONE,
    CAIRN, SENAL
landowner .... LAIRD
landscape .... PAYSAGE,
    SCENE(RY)
landscapist .... TOPIARIST
landslide .... VICTORY,
    AVALANCHE
landsman .... SAILOR
landtag ..... DIET, ASSEMBLY
lane .... PATH, COURSE,
    STREET, ALLEY, WYND
langrage .... SHOT
Langtry, actress .... LILY
language ...... LIP, TONGUE,
    SPEECH, DIALECT, IDIOM,
    DICTION, PARLANCE
artificial .... ESPERANTO,
    VOLAPUK, IDO, RO
beggars' .. ARGOT, LINGO
classical ... LATIN, GREEK
colloquial .... SLANG
dead .... LATIN
dialect .... LINGO, IDIOM

difficulty of understanding .... DYSPHASIA
gypsy .... ROMANY
hybrid .... JARGON, LINGUA FRANCA
hypothetical .... URSPRACHE
kind of .. GESTURE, SIGN
mixed .... PIDGIN
of .... LINGUISTIC, LINGUAL
of special vocabulary ..... LINGO, ARGOT
of the soul, so-called .... MUSIC
of the street ..... SLANG
ordinary .... PROSE, DIALECT
outlandish ..... JARGON
pompous .. HIGHFALUTIN
pretentious ... CLAPTRAP
Romance ...... SPANISH, FRENCH, CATALAN, PROVENCAL, ITALIAN, ROMANIAN, PORTUGUESE
science/study of .... LINGUISTICS
slang .... ARGOT
thieves' ... ARGOT, FLASH
using click sounds .... NAMA
languages, he speaks/writes several .... POLYGLOT, LINGUIST
Languedoc's capital .... TOULOUSE
languid ... DROOPING, WEAK, LISTLESS, DULL, SLOW, LACKADAISICAL, WAN, DREAMY
languish .... WASTE, PINE(AWAY), FLAG, FADE, SWOON
languor .... LASSITUDE, KAIF, WILT, WEAKNESS, INDIFFERENCE, DULLNESS, BLUES, HEAVINESS, LETHARGY, STILLNESS, ENNUI
langur .... MONKEY, MAHA, WANDEROO, SIMPAI
laniard .... CORD
laniary .... CANINE
Lanier, poet .... SIDNEY
laniferous .... FLEECY

lank(y) .... LEAN, GANGLY, SLENDER, SPINDLING, GANGLING
lanner(et) .... FALCON
lanose .... WOOL(L)Y
lansquenet .... SOLDIER, MERCENARY
lantana .... VIBURNUM, MAJORANA
lantern ... LAMP, LANTHORN, CRESSET
    feast .... BON
    roof's .... LOUVER
    wheel .... TRUNDLE
lanthorn .... LANTERN
Lantsang .... MEKONG
lanuginose .... DOWNY
lanugo .... DOWN, HAIR
lanyard ...... THONG, CORD, ROPE
Lanza, singer .... MARIO
Laocoon .. PRIEST, SCULPTURE
Laodicea .... LATAKIA
Laomedon's kingdom ... TROY
    son .... PRIAM
Laos .... KINGDOM
    capital (administrative) .. VIENTIANE
    capital (royal) .... LUANG PRABANG
    fortress town .. NAM BAC
    king of ...... (SAVANG) VATHANA
    monetary unit ...... KIP
    language .... FRENCH, LAOTIAN
    rebels ..... PATHET LAO
lap .... WRAP, (EN)FOLD, CIRCUIT, LICK
    dog .... PET, POM
    robe .... RUG
lapel ...... REVER(S), FACING, FOLD, FLAP
    stiffener .... WIGAN
    thing pinned on .... BUTTON, BADGE, BOUTONNIERE
lapidary .... ENGRAVER, JEWEL(L)ER, GEM-CUTTER, ARTIFICER
lapidate .... STONE
lapidify .... PETRIFY
lapillus .... ROCK
lapin .... RABBIT, FUR
lapis .... STONE

lazuli .... SAPPHIRUS, AZURE-BLUE
lazuli pigment .... ULTRAMARINE
Laplander .... LAPP
   sledge of .... PULK(H)A
lapper .... DOG, CAT
lappet ...... FLAP, WATTLE, FOLD, LOBE, DEWLAP, LABEL
lapse .... ERR(OR), FALL, LAPSUS, INTERVAL, MISSTEP, SLIP, FAULT
lapsus .... SLIP, LAPSE, ERROR
lapwing ... PLOVER, TREUTERO, PEWIT, PEWEE, WEEP
lar .... SPIRIT
larboard ... PORT(SIDE,) APORT
larceny .... THEFT
   describing kind of ...... PETTY, GRAND
larch .... TAMARAC(K), TREE, PINE, SPRUCE, HACKMATACK
lard .... FAT, GREASE, GARNISH, ENRICH
   tub for .... FIRKIN
larder .... BUTTERY, SPENCE, PROVISIONS, PANTRY, CUPBOARD
Lardner, humorist .... RING
large .... OUTSIZE, MAN-SIZE
   amount .. OODLES, SCADS,
   at .... LOOSE, FREE, ABROAD
   prefix .... MEGA, MACRO, MAGNI
   scale .... EXTENSIVE
   very .... DECUMAN
largely .... MAINLY
largess(e) ... GIFT(S), BOUNTY
lariat .... LASSO, ROPE, TETHER, RIATA, REATA, NOOSE
   eye of ... HONDA, HONDO
larine bird .... GULL
lark .... ADVENTURE, PRANK, SONGBIRD, WAGTAIL, PIPIT, FROLIC, TEASE, HURDLE, SPREE, OSCINE, LAVEROCK
   genus .... ALAUDA
larkspur .. PLANT, DELPHINIUM
larrigan .... MOCCASIN
larrikin ... HOODLUM, ROWDY
larrup ... FLOG, BEAT, WHIP, THRASH
larva .... PLANULA, GRUB, MAGGOT, CATERPILLAR,

LOA, BOT(T)
   butterfly ... CATERPILLAR
   beetle's .... GRUB, CADELLE, WOLF
   botfly .... WABBLE
   case enclosing .. INDUSIUM
   final stage of .. CHRYSALIS
   flea's .... CHIGOE, CHIGGER
   fly .... GENTLE
   frog's .... TADPOLE
   mite's ... JIGGER, LEPTUS
   moth's .... EGGER, CATERPILLAR, WOLF
   next form of ...... PUPA
   of antlion ... DOODLEBUG
   of horsefly .... BOT
   of tapeworm .. COENURUS
   of trematode .. CERCARIA
   six-legged .... LEPTUS
   weevil's .... GRUGRU
   wingless .... CREEPER
larval tapeworms ..... MEASLES
laryngeal clearing sound ..... AHEM
larynx, rod for clearing ..... PROBANG
lasagna .... MACARONI
lascar .... SAILOR, ARTILLERYMAN
lascivious .... LEWD, WANTON, LUSTFUL, LIBIDINOUS, LICENTIOUS
laser inventor .... TOWNES
lash ... QUIRT, SPLICE, STROKE, FASTEN, DASH, SCOURGE, WHIP, SWITCH, FLOG, CENSURE, REBUKE, BIND, SMITE, WALE, TIE
   with words ..... BLISTER
lashing ... REBUKE, SCOLDING, WHIPPING, ROPE, TYING
lashings .... LOADS
lass ...... GIRL, SWEETHEART, MAID, SERVANT
lassie .... COLLEEN, GIRL, SWEETHEART
   of the movies ..... COLLIE
lassitude .... LANGUOR, LETHARGY, WEARINESS
lasso ... LARIAT, REATA, LASH, ROPE, NOOSE, THONG, RIATA
last .. END, ENDURE, ENDMOST, OMEGA, HINDMOST, FINAL(E), LATEST, NEWEST,

ULTIMATE, GO ON, CONTINUE, DURE, REARMOST
act .... FINALE
at .... FINALLY
chance of —— ....
          MONTANA
but one .. PENULT(IMATE)
Goth .... RODERICK
in succession ....
          LATTERMOST
Judgment ... DOOMSDAY
mentioned of two ......
          LATTER
Mohican .... UNCAS
month .... ULTIMO
resort .... PIS ALLER
will and —— ....
          TESTAMENT
person in a race ....
          TAILENDER
supper .... CENA
supper cup/platter ......
          GRAIL
syllable of word .. ULTIMA
word of comedian ......
          PUNCHLINE
word, usually ..... AMEN
lastex .... THREAD
lasting ... DURABLE, LIFELONG
effect .... SCAR
lastly .... ENFIN, FINALLY
Latakia .... LAODICEA, TOBACCO
latch .... HOOK, FASTEN(ING), (SPRING)LOCK, LASKET
latchkey notch .... WARD
latchet ... STRAP, LACE(T), TAP
late ...... OVERDUE, RECENT, NEW, FORMER, DEAD, TARDY, NEO
lateen .... VESSEL, DHOW
latent .... DORMANT, QUIESCENT, POTENTIAL, CONCEALED, HIDDEN, DELITESCENT
later ... AFTER, SUBSEQUENTLY
lateral .... SIDEWAYS, SIDEWISE
opposed to ..... MEDIAL
laterally .... SIDEWISE
laterite .... CLAY
latest .... LAST
combining form ... CENE, NEO
latex, plant's .... MILK

plural of .... LATICES
source of .... POPPY, MILKWEED, RUBBER TREE
lath ..... SLAT, SPLINT, SPALE
lathe clamp .... CHUCK
operator .... TURNER
lather ... FOAM, FROTH, SWEAT, FLOG, SUDS, FRENZY, SCUM, SPUME
lathing shop .... TURNERY
Latin ...... ROMAN, ITALIAN, SPANIARD, LANGUAGE
abbot .... ABBAS
above .... SUPRA
after .... POST
alas .... VAE, EHEU
all .... TOTO
alone .... SOLUS
always .... SEMPER
am present ...... AD SUM
America, foreigner in ...
          GRINGO
American measure ......
          VARA
and .... ET
and others .... ET AL
anger .... IRA
art .... ARS
band .... FASCIA
bear ..... URSA, URSULA
before .... ANTE
behold .... ECCE
being .... ESSE
between .... INTER
bird .... AVIS
blessed .... BEATA
book .... LIBER
born .... NATUS
both .... AMBI
bronze .... AES
brother .... FRATER
bug .... CIMEX
but .... SED
city .... URBIS
copper .... CUPRUM
day .... DIEM, DIES
day of wrath .. DIES IRAE
discourse .... SERMO
dog .... CANIS
duct .... VAS
earth .... TERRA
earth exhalation ....
          MEPHITIS
egg .... OVUM, OVA
epic .... AENEID

equal .... PAR
error .... LAPSUS
everywhere ..... UBIQUE
evil ...... MALA, MALUM
fate .... NONA
fillet .... FASCIA
fire .... IGNIS
fish .... PISCES
fly .... MUSCA
force .... VIS
gentle .... LENIS
god .... DEUS
god willing
.... DEO VOLENTE
goddess .... DEA
gold .... AURUM
good .... BONUM
grape .... UVA
great .... MAGNA
he .... ILLE, IPSE
head .... CAPUT
heat .... CALOR
hence .... ERGO
highest .... SUMMA
himself .... IPSE
holidays .... FERIA
holy .... SANCTUS
honey .... MEL
hour .... HORA
house .... DOMUS
hut .... TABERNA
in passing ...... OBITER
is .... EST
itself .... IPSO
knee .... GENU
lamb .... AGNUS
laughter .... RISUS
law ..... JUS, LEX, JURA
leisure .... OTIUM
light .... LUX, LUMEN
magpie .... PICA
man .... HOMO
mass .... MISSA
members .... SOCII
mine .... MEUM
mint .... MONETA
month .... MENSIS
mountain .... MONS
name .... NOMEN
needle .... ACUS
net .... RETE
not .... NON
number .... UNUS
observe .... NOTA
onion .... CEPA
order .... ORDO

other .... ALIA
our .... NOSTER
peace .... PAX
peacock .... PAVO
people .... POPULI
place(s) .... LOCUS, LOCI
poet .... OVID
power .... VIS
quarter site ...... PARIS
quarter dwellers ....
.... ARTISTS, STUDENTS
same .... IDEM
sash .... FASCIA
see .... VIDE
shed .... TABERNA
sister .... SOROR
skin .... CUTIS
snow .... NIVIS
soft .... LENIS
star .... STELLA
stone .... LAPIS
strength .... VIS
table .... MENSA
that is .... ID EST
thing .... RES
this .... HOC
thread .... FILUM
throat .... GULA
throughout ...... PASSIM
thus .... SIC
tile .... TEGULA
time ... TEMPUS, TEMPORA
toad .... BUFO
total .... SUMMA
twice .... BIS
under .... SUB
unless .... NISI
voice .... VOX
wasp .... VESPA
waste away ...... TABERE
water .... AQUA
wax .... CERA
we .... NOS
well .... BENE
where .... UBI
wife .... UXOR
within .... INTRA
without .... SINE
wolf .... LUPUS
wool .... LANA
yawn .... HIARE
year ...... ANNO, ANNUS
latite .... LAVA
latitude ... WIDTH, BREADTH,
.... EXTENT, SCOPE

latitudinarian of a sort .... DEMOCRAT
Latium people .... VOLSCI
Latona .... LETO
   progeny of ...... APOLLO, DIANA
latria .... WORSHIP
latrine .... TOILET, PRIVY
latten .... opposed to ..... BRASS
latter, opposed to ..... FORMER
Latter-day Saint ... MORMON
lattice .... ESPALIER, GRILLE, TRELLIS, SCREEN
latticework .... ESPALIER, TRELLIS, PERGOLA
Latvian .... LETT(IC)
   capital .... RIGA
   city ..... RIGA, LIEPAJA, LIBAU
   coin .... LAT
   monetary unit .... LAT(U)
   river .... DVINA
   rulers .... RUSSIANS
   seaport .... LIEPAJA
   state, ancient .. LIVONIA, COURLAND
laud .... EXTOL, PRAISE, HYMN, GLORIFY, EXALT
laudable ..... PRAISEWORTHY, COMMENDABLE
laudanum .... RESIN
laudation .... PRAISE, EULOGY
laudatory .... EULOGISTIC, PRAISING
laugh ..... CHORTLE, DERIDE, CHUCKLE, GIGGLE, TITTER, FLEER, SNICKER, GUFFAW, TE-HEE, HAW-HAW, CACKLE, HEEHAW, BRAY, NICKER, ROAR
   able to .... RISIBLE
   at .... RIDICULE, DISREGARD, MOCK
   coarse .... FLEER
   down .... SILENCE, EMBARRASS
   off ...... SCORN, REJECT
   too much ... CACHINNATE
laughable ... DROLL, RISIBLE, FUNNY, COMICAL, AMUSING, RIDICULOUS, ABSURD
laughing ...... RIANT, RIDENT
   gas ..... NITROUS OXIDE
   jackass ..... KINGFISHER, KOOKABURRA, BIRD
laughingstock .... BUTT

laughs, he never ..... AGELAST
laughter (see laugh)
   causing .... RISIBLE
   pertaining to ... GELASTIC
   sound of .... PEAL
la(u)nce .... EEL
Launcelot, the clown .. GOBBO
Launce's dog .... CRAB
launch ... HURL, START, BEGIN, MOTORBOAT, DISCHARGE, SEND OFF
   Malay .... LANCA
   Spanish/Portuguese ..... LANCHA
launder .... WASH
laundress .... WASHERWOMAN
laurdress .... WASHERWOMAN
lauraceous tree .... AVOCADO, NUTMEG, LAUREL, CAMPHOR
laurel .... BAY, DAPHNE, IVY, SHRUB, TREE, AZALEA, RHODODENDRON, CAJEPUT
   actor .... STAN
   bark .... COTO
   bay .... MAGNOLIA
   California ..... CAJEPUT, CAJUPUT
   family .... HEATH, KALMIA
   mountain ...... CALICO, BUSH
   woven sprigs of .... LAUREATE
laurels .... HONOR, FAME
Lausanne canton ...... VAUD
La(u)wine .... AVALANCHE
lava .... TAXITE, MAGMA, COULEE, LATITE, OBSIDIAN, ASH
   cinder .... SCORIA
   cooled .... AA
   fragment ..... LAPILLUS
   lava .... LOINCLOTH, WAISTCLOTH
   pieces of .. SLAG, SCORIA
   stream of .... COULEE
lavabo ... WASHBOWL, BASIN, TOWEL, LAVATORY
lavage .... WASHING
Laval, premier .... PIERRE
lavalier(e) .... PENDANT
lavatory .... (WASH)BOWL, BASIN, LAVABO, RESTROOM
lave ...... ABSTERGE, BATHE, WASH, FLOW, DIP, POUR, REMAINDER

lavender .... ASPIC, MINT,
PURPLE
product ... OIL, PERFUME
laver ... BASIN, FONT, SEAWEED
laverock .... LARK
lavish .... PRODIGAL,
MUNIFICENT, WANTON,
UNSPARING, UNSTINTED,
GENEROUS, LIBERAL,
PROFUSE
law .... CANON, CODE,
ORDINANCE, REGULATION,
STATUTE, RULE, PRINCIPLE,
LEX, JUS, EDICT, ACT
and order .... PEACE
appendix, in ..... CODICIL
break the .... INFRACT
breaker .... FELON,
SINNER, CRIMINAL,
JAILBIRD
court .... FORUM, BENCH
courts of ..... JUDICIARY
decree having force of ...
UKASE
degree .... LLB
denying throne to women
SALIC
expert .... JURIST
fictitious name in ....
(JOHN) DOE
imperial .... UKASE
intervening .... MESNE
kind of .... STATUTE,
COMMON, (UN)WRITTEN
like for like ...... TALION
making ..... LEGISLATION
municipal ... ORDINANCE
not enforced ....
DEAD LETTER
of Moses .... TORA(H),
PENTATEUCH
of Moses book .. GENESIS,
NUMBERS, EXODUS
of the place ... LEX LOCI
offenses against ... MALA
pertaining to .. FORENSIC,
CANONIC, LEGAL,
JURAL
points in ...... LIS, RES
Roman .... LEX, JUS
the: colloq. ....
POLICE(MAN)
unwritten ...... COMMON
usance .... USAGE
violate the ..... INFRACT
volume .... CODEX

written .... STATUTE
lawful .... LEGITIMATE, LEGAL,
LICIT, JUST
lawgiver ...... SOLON, DRACO,
MINOS, MOSES
Lawine .... AVALANCHE
lawless .... UNRULY
lawlessness .... ANARCHY,
LICENSE
lawmaker ...... LEGISLATOR,
SOLON, SENATOR,
COUNCILOR
lawmaking ..... LEGISLATION,
ENACTMENT, LEGISLATIVE
lawn ...... CAMBRIC, GLADE,
GRASS PLOT, BATISTE
Lawman .... LAYAMON
Lawrence of ____ ... ARABIA
laws, body of .... CODE,
PANDECTS, DECALOG(UE)
describing some ....
DEAD LETTER, ARCHAIC
what some lack ... TEETH
lawsuit .... CASE, LITIGATION,
ACTION
expenses .... COSTS
grounds .... GIST
party to ...... LITIGANT,
LITIGATOR, SUER
lawsuits, habitual .. BARRATRY
prone to ...... LITIGIOUS
lawyer .... BARRISTER,
COUNSEL(OR), ATTORNEY,
SOLICITOR, LEGIST,
ADVOCATE, LEGALIST,
MOUTHPIECE, JURIST
cap of .... COIF
fee of .... RETAINER
of fiction .... TUTT,
PERRY MASON
profession of .... BAR
stock objection of ......
LEADING, IRRELEVANT,
INCOMPETENT
unscrupulous .. SHYSTER
woman .... PORTIA
lawyers' bag ...... BRIEFCASE
Bible .... BLACKSTONE
concern ... BRIEF, CASE,
TRIAL, HEARING,
EVIDENCE
patron saint .... IVES
lax .... LOOSE, SLACK,
CARELESS
laxative ... PHYSIC, APERIENT,
PURGATIVE, CATHARTIC,

BLUE PILL, ALOIN, CASSIA, MAGNESIA
drug .... ALOES
leaf .... SENNA
pulp .... DITTY, BET, BALLAD, CASSIA

lay .... DITTY, BET, BALLAD, PLACE, LAIC, SECULAR, DEPOSIT, SET, ASCRIBE, RECLINE, POEM, SONG, MELODY
aside .... SAVE, PEND, TABLE
down ...... BET, WAGER
down arms .. SURRENDER, CAPITULATE
figure ... PUPPET, DUMMY
into .... BEAT, SCOLD
it on .... EXAGGERATE, FLATTER
off .... DISCHARGE, STOP, CEASE
open .... EXPOSE
out .... SPEND
siege .... INVEST
up ...... STORE, HOARD, PILE, HEAP
waste .... RAVAGE, DEVASTATE
Layamon's verse chronicle ....
BRUT
layer .... COAT, VENEER, LAMINA, TIER, THICKNESS, FOLD, STRATUM, SHOOT, TWIG, DESS, PATINA, PLY
feathered .... BIRD, HEN
of iris .... UVEA
product of .... EGG
layers, form in ...... STRATIFY
layette, part of ...... BOOTEE, BEDDING
layman .... LAIC, AMATEUR
layout .... ARRANGEMENT, MAKE-UP, FORMAT
lazar .... LEPER, BEGGAR
Lazarus ...... BEGGAR, LEPER
poet and essayist .. EMMA
sister of .. MARTHA, MARY
laze .... LOAF, LOUNGE
laziness ... SLOTH, INDOLENCE
lazy ... INDOLENT, SLOTHFUL, IDLE, SLUGGISH, OTIOSE
fellow ... DRONE, IDLER, LOAFER, DEADBEAT
Susan ..... TURNTABLE, TRAY

lazybones .... IDLER, LOAFER, BUM, DRONE
lazzarone .... BEGGAR
Le Gallienne, actress .... EVA
lea ..... MEAD(OW), PASTURE, GRASSLAND
measure of .... YARN
leach ..... LIXIVIATE, EXTRACT
leaching product .... LYE
leachy .... POROUS
lead .... GUIDE, CONDUCT, PLUMBUM, PROMPT, HEAD, MINIUM, CLUE, HINT, CUE, GALENA, BULLET, PILOT, CONDUCE
astray .... MISGUIDE
black .... GRAPHITE, PLUMBAGO
color .... LIVID
glass for gem making ....
STRASS, PASTE
in alchemy ..... SATURN
off .... BEGIN
on ... ENCOURAGE, LURE
ore ... GALENA, SULPHIDE
oxide .... LITHARGE
pellets .... SHOT
poisoning ... PLUMBISM, SATURNISM
red .... MINIUM
rope .... LONGE
shot .... PELLET
up to .... PAVE
white .... CERUSE
writing implement ......
PENCIL
leaden .... DULL, SLUGGISH, HEAVY, GLOOMY
sky .... CLOUDY
leader .... CHIEF, HEAD, COMMANDER, OVERMAN
Argonauts' ...... JASON
chorus .... CANTOR, CORYPHEUS
in music .... CONDUCTOR
in printing .... DOTS, DASHES
Italian .... DUCE
of Israelites ..... MOSES, JOSHUA
racing contest early .....
PACER, PACESETTER
sheep ...... BELLWETHER
Spanish ...... CAUDILLO
leadership quality, special ....
CHARISMA

leading ...... CHIEF, AHEAD, PRINCIPAL, FOREMOST, STELLAR, MAIN
   actor/actress .... STAR
   lady .... PREMIERE
leads .... BULLETS
leaf ... PHYLLOME, LAMELLA, PAGE, TENDRIL, FROND, SPATHE, PETAL, LAMINA
   attachment .... STEM, PETIOLE, STIPEL, TWIG
   beverage .... TEA
   book .... FOLIO, PAGE
   bud .... GEMMA
   central vein ...... MIDRIB
   combining form .... PHYLL(O)
   cutter .... ATTA, ANT
   disease .. MOSAIC, RUST
   division of calyx .. SEPAL
   drug ... HEMP, HASHISH, MARIJUANA
   fern .... FROND
   floating .... PAD
   flower ...... SEPAL, BRACT
   fodder .... RAPE
   form ... SIMPLE, PINNATE, PALMATE, DENTATE, CRENATE, SERRATE, UNDULATE, LOBED
   front side of ..... RECTO
   gland .... LENTICEL
   grass .... BLADE
   large .... FROND
   like .... PHYLLOID
   like part ...... STIPULE, BRACT
   lily .... PAD
   metal .... FOIL
   miner beetle ...... HISPA
   modified .... BRACT, PALEA, CARPEL, PISTIL
   of calyx .... SEPAL
   palm ...... OLA, FROND
   part ... STOMA, LAMINA, STIPEL, STIPULES, BLADE, PETIOLE, STALK, VEIN, (MID)RIB
   pitcher-like ... ASCIDIUM
   poetic .... FROND
   point .... MUCRO
   pores .... STOMA
   rib ...... VEIN, NERVURE
   rudimentary .... CATAPHYLL
   side of ... VERSO, RECTO

   stalk .. PETIOLE, RHUBARB
   stem angle .... AXIL
   through book ... RIFFLE
   tip .... MUCRO
   tissue .... MESOPHYLL
   tobacco ..... CAVENDISH
   type .... LILYPAD
   vein ..... RIB, NERVURE
   water lily .... PAD
leafage .... FOLIAGE
leafless .... APHYLLOUS
   plant .... CACTUS
leaflet ...... PINNA, FOLDER, TRACT, HANDBILL, PINNULE, THROWAWAY
leaflets, ring of ...... BRACTE, EPICALYX
leaflike design in windows ... FOIL
   part .... SPATHE
leafstalk ... PETIOLE, CHARD, PHYLLODE, RHUBARB
leafy .... FOLIOSE
   shelter .... BOWER
league ... FEDERATION, BUND, ALLIANCE, ASSOCIATION, BLOC
   in .... ALLIED
   merchants' ...... HANSE
leaguer .... (BE)SIEGE
Leah's father .... LABAN
   husband .... JACOB
   sister .... RACHEL
   son .... LEVI
leak ... LET, SEEP, OOZE, DRIP
leal .... LOYAL, TRUE
lean ... SPARE, LANK(Y), POOR, BONY, CANT, TILT, SCRAGGY, HEEL, SLIM, INCLINE, TEND, SLANT, GAUNT, SCRAWNY, SKINNY, THIN, MEAGER
   make .... EMACIATE
   pocket .... POOR
   sideways .... CAREEN
   to ... SHED, SHACK, ROOF
Leander's love .... HERO
leaning .... PENCHANT, INCLINATION, BENT
   tower of —— ..... PISA
leap ...... SPANG, LOUP, DIVE, LUNGE, SPRING, JUMP, BOUND, VAULT, HOP
   ballet .... ENTRECHAT
   goat's .... CAPRIOLE

horse's .... CURVET, CAPRIOLE
over .... SKIP
playful .... GAMBOL, CAPER, CAVORT
year .... BISSEXTILE
year gainer ..... FEBRUARY
year hope .... PROPOSAL
leapfrog .... GAME
leaping ... SALIENT, SALTANT, SALTATION
Lear, daughter of ..... REGAN, GONERIL, CORDELIA
dog of .... TRAY
forte of Edward .... LIMERICK
learn .... KNOW, ASCERTAIN, DISCOVER, UNEARTH, HEAR
by heart ...... MEMORIZE
superficially ... SMATTER
learned .... ERUDITE, LETTERED, WISE, EDUCATED, INFORMED, LITERATE
man .... PANDIT(A), PUNDIT, SCHOLAR, INTELLECTUAL, SAGE, PEDANT, SAVANT, MULLA(H)
people .... LITERATI, CLERISY
learning .... WISDOM, ERUDITION, KNOWLEDGE, LORE, CULTURE, EDUCATION
branch of .... OLOGY, SCIENCE
shallow .... SCIOLISM
lease ... DEMISE, REMISE, LET, CONTRACT, HIRE, RENT, CHARTER, TENURE
consideration .. RENT(AL)
grant .... DEMISE
party to a ...... LESSOR, LESSEE, LANDLORD, TENANT
leaseholder .... LESSEE
leash .... CONTROL, ROPE, CURB, BRACE, JESS, SLIP, THONG, REIN, LUNG, LONGE, TETHER
hound .... LIMER
ring .... TERRET
least ... SMALLEST, SLIGHTEST, MINIMUM, FEWEST
likely .... LAST, MINIMAL
leastwise .... ANYWAY

leather .... SUEDE, KID, CALF
armor .... GAMBESON
bag .... POUCH
bookbinding .... SKIVER
bottle .... MATARA
convert into ... TAW, TAN
cordovan .... CORDWAIN
cutter .... SKIVER
decorated ...... DICING
factory .... TANNERY
fine ... VELLUM, CALFSKIN
flask ... OLPE, MATARA
glove .... NAPA, SUEDE, KID, MOCHA, MITTEN
heel (shoe) ...... RAND
kind of .... CHAMOIS, MOCHA, SHAGREEN, KIP, CALF, OXHIDE, LEVANT, NAPA, ROAN, COWHIDE, ELK
like ...... CORIACEOUS
maker .... TANNER
pouch, Highlanders' .... SPORRAN
prepare ...... TAN, TAW
saddle .... MOCHILA
sheepskin ...... ROAN
shoe repair .... FOXING
soft ... CHAMOIS, SUEDE, NAPA, ROAN, MOCHA
softener .... DUBBIN(G)
strap .... THONG
strip ..... RAND, WELT, STRAP, THONG
thong .... BRAIL
velvety .... MOCHA
waterproofer .. DUBBIN(G)
worker ... CORDWAINER, TANNER
worker's tool .. GRINDERY
leatherback .... TURTLE
leatherette ...... MOROCCO
leatherfish .... LIJA
leatherneck .. MARINE, GYRENE
leatherwood .... WICOPY
leave ... BEQUEATH, ENTRUST, COMMIT, FORSAKE, SET OUT, DEPART, PERMISSION, RETIRE, EXEAT, VAMOSE, QUIT, SKIDDOO
hurriedly ..... HIGHTAIL, DECAMP, LAM, SKIDDOO
kind of ..... SABBATICAL
military ...... FURLOUGH
off ... DESIST, CEASE, STOP

out .... OMIT, IGNORE, ELIDE, EXCEPT
port .... OUTSTAND
secretly .... DECAMP
stage ...... EXIT, EXEUNT
taking ... CONGE, ADIEU, FAREWELL
leaven .... BARM, YEAST, (EN)ZYME, SOURDOUGH
leaves ...... FOLIAGE, PAGES, DEPARTS
circular arrangement of .. VERTICIL
cluster .... ROSETTE
collectively ..... FOLIAGE
covered with .... FOLIOSE
fragrant .... THYME
having .... FOLIACEOUS, FOLIAGED, PETALED
having two ... BIFOLIATE
laxative .... SENNA
numbering of .... FOLIATION
of .... FOLIAR
seasoning .... LAUREL, THYME
spread around plant ..... MULCH
vegetable .... SLAW
leaving(s) .... CHAFF, REFUSE, WASTE, RESIDUE, DRAFF, DREGS, REST, ORTS, REMNANTS, OFFAL
pick up .... GLEAN
Lebanon capital ...... BEIRUT
city/town ...... HERMEL, BAALBEK, ZAHLE, TRIPOLI, BEIRUT, SAIDA
monetary unit ... POUND
native ...... LEVANTINE
premier .... KARAME
president .... HELOU
seaport ... TYRE, SAIDA, TRIPOLI
Valley river ... ORONTES
lebensraum .... LIVING SPACE
lebistes .... GUPPY
lecher .... SATYR, DEBAUCHEE
lecherous .... LUSTFUL, RANDY, SENSUAL
lechery .... LEWDNESS
lectern .... AMBO, PULPIT, (READING) DESK, STAND
lection .... READING
lector .... READER, LECTURER

lecture ... SCOLD(ING), TALK, PRELECT(ION)
hall .... LYCEUM
kind of .... SERMON
moralizing .... SERMON, HOMILY
lecturer .... DOCENT, (PRE)LECTOR, READER
foreign .... LECTOR
stand of .... LECTERN
Leda's daughter ...... HELEN, CLYTEMNESTRA
husband .... TYNDAREUS
lover: mythology .. SWAN, ZEUS
son ..... CASTOR, POLLUX
ledge .... LODE, BERM(E), RIDGE, SHELF, SILL
altar .... RETABLE
ledger entry ... CREDIT, DEBIT, LOSS, RENT, INTEREST
lee .... SHELTER, PROTECTION
opposed to .... STOSS, WEATHER, WINDWARD
leech .... ANNELID, PARASITE, WORM, BLEED, PHYSICIAN, HEAL
like .... HIRUDINOID
sucker of .. ACETABULUM
leek .... ALLIUM, VEGETABLE, BULB, ROCAMBOLE, SCALLION
relation .... ONION, GARLIC
leer ...... SCOFF, SNEER, EYE, OGLE, STARE, MOCK
leery ..... WARY, SUSPICIOUS, DUBIOUS
lees .... DRAFF, DREGS, GROUNDS, RESIDUE
leet .... COURT
Leeward islands ...... NEVIS, ANTIGUA, ST. KITTS, MONTSERRAT
leeway ... MARGIN, SAG, ROOM
left ... LARBOARD, DEPARTED, WENT, PORT, GONE, SINISTER
after expenses ...... NET
aground .... NEAPED, BEACHED, STRANDED
combining form .... L(A)EVO
hand ..... LEVO, SINISTER
hand of page ..... VERSO, LEVO

handed ..... SOUTHPAW, CLUMSY, AWKWARD, DUBIOUS, INSINCERE, SINISTRAL, MORGANATIC
lonely .... BEREFT
on the .... NIGH
opposed to ...... RIGHT
over .... REMNENT
political ...... LIBERAL, RADICAL
side of bow ... LARBOARD
side, on the .... APORT, NEAR
turn .... HAW
leftist .... RED, RADICAL, LIBERAL
leftover ... ORT, MANAVELIN, MORSEL, SCRAP
lefty .... SOUTHPAW
leg .... LIMB, PROP, PIN, GAMB(E), SHANK
armor .... GREAVES, JAMB(EAU)
bone ..... FIBULA, TIBIA
colloquial .. PIN, STUMP, GAM, PEG
covering .... LEGGINGS, PUTTEE, PEDULE, CHAUSSES, GAITER, PUTTY
fleshy part .... CALF
fowl's .... DRUMSTICK
front of .... SHIN
from knee to ankle ..... CRUS, SHANK
in heraldry ...... GAMB
irons .... NIPPERS
joint ...... KNEE, ANKLE, HOCK
journey's .... TREK
lamb's, cooked .. GIGOT
mutton .... GIGOT, AVINE
part .. SHIN, SHANK, HAM, CALF, CRUS
pertaining to ... CRURAL, SURAL
protuberance, bird's ... SPUR, CALCAR
shake a .... HURRY, DANCE
thigh .... FEMUR
triangle's .. HYPOTENUSE
vein .... SAPHENA
wooden .... STUMP
work .... WALK(ING)

legacy .... BEQUEST, INHERITANCE, GIFT, PATRIMONY
receiver of .... LEGATEE, HEIR(ESS)
legal .... LAWFUL, VALID, LEGITIMATE, LICIT, LICET, JURAL
abstract .... PRECIS
action ...... (LAW)SUIT, CASE, LITIGATION, RES, REPLEVIN
arrest .... CAPTION
attachment ...... LIEN
charge .... FEE
claim .... LIEN, DEMAND
code .... PANDECT
contestant .... LITIGANT
defense .... ALIBI
delay .... MORA
fee ..... DUE, RETAINER
force, lose ...... STALE
hearing .... OYER, TRIAL
instrument ...... DEED
matter .... RES
notice .... MONITION
offense ... DELICT, DELIT, CRIME
order .... WRIT
paper .... DEED
point .... RES
possession .... SEIZIN, SIESIN
profession .... BAR, LAW
record ... ESTREAT, ACTA
redress .... REMEDY
right .... DROIT
site .... VENUE
substitute .... SURROGATE
summons .... SUBPOENA
tender .... MONEY
thing .... RES
warning ...... CAVEAT
wrong .... TORT
legalism in relation ... NOMISM
legalist .... LAWYER
legalize .... SIGN
legally bound .... LIABLE
competent ... SUI JURIS
legate ... ENVOY, AMBASSADOR
Papal .... NUNCIO
Roman ..... GOVERNOR
legatee .... HEIR, INHERITOR
legation ... MISSION, EMBASSY
legato, opposed to .. STACCATO

legend ... MYTH, FABLE, SAGA, MOTTO, TALE, CAPTION, STORY, INSCRIPTION, TITLE
legendary ..... TRADITIONAL, FABULOUS, FICTITIOUS, EPIC, STORIED
   bird .... ROC
leger .... LIGHT
legerdemain .... DECEIT, SLEIGHT OF HAND, TRICKS, MAGIC, HOCUS-POCUS
   practice .... CONJURE
leges, singular of .... LEX
legging(s) .... GAITER, GAMBADO, PUTTIE, GAMBADE, PUTTEE
leggy .... LONG LIMBED
Leghorn .... LIVORNO, CHICKEN, HAT
legible .... READABLE, DECIPHERABLE
legion .... ARMY, HORDE, MULTITUDE
   unit ... COHORT, MANIPLE
legislate .... ENACT
legislation .... LAW(S)
legislative body .... DIET, HOUSE, SENATE, CONGRESS, CORTES, DAIL, FOLKETING, BUNDESTAG, STORTING, PARLIAMENT, ASSEMBLY, COUNCIL
   building .... CAPITOL
legislator .... LAWMAKER, SOLON, SENATOR
legislature .... DIET, PARLIAMENT, CONGRESS, SENATOR
   lameduck .... RUMP
   two-chambered .... BICAMERAL
legist .... LAWYER
legit: sl. ..... THEATER, STAGE
legitimate .... LAWFUL, LICIT, LEGAL, ALLOWED, REASONABLE
legless amphibian .. CAECILIAN
legree ..... MASTER, OVERSEER
   fictional .... SIMON
legume ..... POD, BEAN, PEA, PLANT, SEED, LOMENT, LENTIL, SOY
legumin .... GLOBULIN, CONGLUTIN
leguminous seed ..... LOMENT, PULSE, PEA, BEAN

Lehar, composer ..... FRANZ
Lehmann, soprano ..... LILLI, LOTTE
lehua .... TREE, MYRTLE
lei ...... GARLAND, WREATH
   singular .... LEU
Leicester .... SHEEP
leister ...... SPEAR, TRIDENT
leisure .... EASE, OTIOSE
leisurely .... SLOW(LY), UNHURRIED
leman .... MISTRESS, SWEETHEART, LOVER
Lemberg ...... LWOW, LVOV
lemming ...... RODENT, RAT
lemon ...... CITRUS, FRUIT
   juice squeezer ... REAMER
   juice vitamin ..... CITRIN
   like fruit .... LIME, CITRON
   peel .... RELISH
   yellow .... CITRINE, CITREOUS
lemons, of .... CITRIC
lemur ...... AYEAYE, MONKEY, POTTO, MACACO, SIFAKA
   arboreal .... LORIS
   Asiatic .... LORI(S)
   Ceylon .... LORI
   flying .. COLUGO, GALAGO
   kin of .... TARSIER
   Madagascar ...... INDRI
   nocturnal .... LORIS
Lemuria .... CONTINENT
lemuroid .... POTTO
Lena, singer .... HORNE
   tributary .... ALDAN
lenard .... LINNET
Lenape .... INDIAN
lend ...... LET OUT, IMPART
length .... EXTENT
   abbreviation ..... LGTH
   at .... FINALLY
   finger to elbow ... CUBIT
   great .... LONG
   having .... LINEAR
   in time .... DURATION
   of day's march ... ETAPE
   unit ...... MICRON, MIL, METER, YARD
lengthen ... STRETCH, EXTEND, PROLONG, ELONGATE, DISTEND, PROTRACT
lengthwise .... LONGWAYS
lengthy ...... PROLIX, LONG, DRAWN OUT, EXTENDED

colloquial ‒‒•‒•‒•• TALL
lenient •••• GENTLE, CLEMENT,
MILD, MERCIFUL, AUDIENT
Lenin, premier ••‒•‒•‒••
NIKOLAI (ULIANOV)
Leningrad ‒•‒•‒ PETROGRAD
river ••‒•‒ NEVA
lenis ••••‒ SMOOTH, SOFT, MILD
opposed to ‒•••‒ FORTIS
lenitive ‒•‒•‒••‒ SOOTHING,
SOFTENING, LAXATIVE
lenity ••‒• MILDNESS, MERCY
leno ‒•‒•‒ WEAVE, FABRIC
lens ••‒••‒•• MENISCUS
hand •••‒•‒••• READER
kind of ‒•••‒ CONCAVE,
CONVEX
shaped ‒•‒•‒• LENTOID,
LENTICULAR
type of ‒•‒•‒ MENISCUS,
TORIC
lent ••‒•‒•‒•‒• IMPREST
observance ‒• PENITENCE,
FASTING
revelry before •• CARNIVAL
Lenten ‒•‒ MEAGER, CHEERLESS,
QUADRAGESIMAL
lentiginous ‒•‒•‒••• FRECKLY
lentigo ••‒•‒••• FRECKLE
lentil ••••‒ PEA, SEED, PLANT,
ERVUM, LEGUME, PULSE
l'envoi ‒• POSTSCRIPT, STANZA,
VERSE, DEDICATION,
INSCRIPTION
Leonard's (Jack) forte •••‒•••
INSULT
Leonardo da ____ ••‒•• VINCI
Leoncavallo, composer ••••••
RUGGIERO
opera by ‒• PAGLIACCI,
ZAZA
Leonidas' scene of defeat •••••
THERMOPYLAE
leopard ‒•‒•‒• OCELOT, CAT,
PANTHER, OUNCE
like animal ••‒•• JAGUAR
pet •••••••••• CHEETAH
young ‒•‒•‒• WHELP
leotard ••••••••••• TIGHTS
leper ‒•‒•‒• OUTCAST, LAZAR,
LAZARUS, PARIAH
colony •••• LEPROSARIUM
hospital •••••••••• SPITAL
patron saint of •••• GILES
lepidolite ••••••••••• MICA

lepidopteron ‒•‒•‒•••• MOTH,
BUTTERFLY
lepidosiren ‒•‒•‒•••• DOKO
lepidate ‒•‒•• SCALY, FLAKY,
SCURFY
Lepontine Alps peak ‒• LEONE
leporid (leporine) animal ‒•‒••
HARE, RABBIT
leprechaun ‒•‒•‒ ELF, GOBLIN,
FAIRY
leprose ‒•‒•• SCALY, SCURFY
leprosy ‒•‒•‒•••••• LEPRA
leprous ‒•‒•‒••••• UNCLEAN
beggar ‒•‒•‒••• LAZAR(US)
leptons, 100 ‒•‒•‒••• DRACHMA
leptus ‒• LARVA, MITE
lepus ‒• HARE, CONSTELLATION
lerot ••••••••••• DORMOUSE
"Les Miserables" author ••••‒
HUGO
character ‒•‒•• FANTINE,
JAVERT, VALJEAN
Lesage, novelist ‒•‒•• ALAIN,
RENE
lesbian ‒•‒•‒•‒•‒•• EROTIC,
HOMOSEXUAL, SAPPHO
Lesbos ••••••••••• MYTILENE
poet ‒• ARION, LESCHES,
ALCAEUS, SAPPHO
lese majeste ‒•‒•‒•••• TREASON
lesion ‒•‒•‒ INJURY, DAMAGE,
HURT
less ‒•‒•‒•• MINOR, MINUS,
FEW(ER), SMALLER
in music ‒•‒•‒•• MENO
lessee ‒•‒•‒•‒•‒•• TENANT,
LEASEHOLDER, RENTER
lessen ‒•‒•‒ (A)BATE, REDUCE,
MINIFY, MITIGATE, THIN,
DIMINISH, TAPER, DECREASE,
DISPARAGE, MINIMIZE
lesser ‒•‒•‒•••• SMALLER, MINOR
Antilles islands •••••••••••
LEEWARD
Bear ‒•‒• URSA (MINOR)
lesson ‒•‒•‒•• INSTRUCTION,
EXERCISE, ASSIGNMENT
from fable ••••••‒ MORAL
music ‒•‒•‒••• ETUDE
lessor ‒•‒•‒••••• LANDLORD
let ‒• ALLOW, LEASE, PERMIT,
RENT, LEAVE, ABANDON,
FORSAKE, HIRE (OUT),
ASSIGN, OBSTACLE, SUFFER
bait drop •••••••• DAP
down ••••• DISAPPOINT,

RELAX, SLACKEN,
LOWER
fall .... DROP
go .... UNHAND, RELEASE,
LOOSE
in ..... ADMIT, INTROMIT
it be given .... DETUR
it stand ...... STET, STA
on ...... PRETEND, HINT
out ..... RELEASE, EMIT,
LEASE, DISMISS
sink .... VAIL
up .... CEASE, RELAX,
SLACKEN, ABATE, EASE
letdown ..... DISAPPOINTMENT
lethal .... FATAL, DEADLY
lethargic ..... INERT, TORPID,
COMATOSE, DULL, SLUGGISH
sleep .... SOPOR
lethargy .... TORPOR, STUPOR,
LANGUOR, LASSITUDE,
INERTNESS, DROWSINESS,
INERTIA, APATHY,
INDIFFERENCE, COMA
Lethe .... OBLIVION,
FORGETFULNESS, RIVER
lethiferous .... DEADLY
Leto .... LATONA
daughter of .... ARTEMIS,
DIANA
son of .... APOLLO
Lett ..... LATVIAN, LIVONIAN
letter ...... MESSAGE, EPISTLE,
MISSIVE, INSCRIBE, BREVE,
CREDENCE
addresser of ..... MAILER
airmail ...... AEROGRAM
beginning a word ....
INITIAL
bishop's ...... PASTORAL
capital, in printing ......
UPPER CASE
carrier .... POSTMAN,
MAILMAN, POSTBOY,
COURIER
cross stroke ...... SERIF
cut off last ..... APOCOPE
for letter ..... LITERATIM,
LITERALLY
illuminated ... MINIATURE
large .... MAJUSCULE,
CAPITAL, UNCIAL
main stroke .... STEM
of challenge ..... CARTEL
of credence .. CREDENTIAL
official .... BULL

opener .... CENSOR,
MADAM, SIR
Papal .... BULL
perfect .... CORRECT
representing a word .....
LOGOGRAM
resignation ...... DEMIT
short ... MISSIVE, MEMO,
NOTE, LINE
silent .... MUTE
small, in printing ....
LOWER CASE, MINISCULE
to _____ .... GARCIA
to host .... GRACENOTE,
BREAD-AND-BUTTER
to the .... EXACTLY,
PRECISELY, LITERAL
lettered .... LEARNED,
EDUCATED, LITERATE
letterhead detail .... ADDRESS,
NAME
letterpress .... TEXT
letters ..... LITERATURE, MAIL
capital, in printing ......
UPPER CASE
collection/delivery of ....
MAIL, PAPERS
men of .... LITERATI,
INTELLECTUALS,
SCHOLARS
of credence .. CREDENTIAL
slanting up ..... ITALICS
woven in design ....
MONOGRAM
lettuce .... MINION, ROMAINE,
SALAD, COS, BIBB
slang .... (PAPER)MONEY
letup .... LESSENING,
ABATEMENT, STOP, PAUSE,
CEASE
leucorrhea .... WHITES
leukemia ..... TUMOR, CANCER
Levantine .... SILK, SHIP
garment .... CAFTAN,
GREGO
ketch .... XEBEC, SAIC,
SETTEE
land .... ISRAEL
port ...... ACRE, ELATH
region .. SYRIA, LEBANON,
PALESTINE
state ... SYRIA, LEBANON
levee .... DIKE, DURBAR,
LANDING, QUAY,
EMBANKMENT, RECEPTION
break in ...... CREVASSE

level ..... RASE, EVEN, GRADE,
RAZE, HEIGHT, ALTITUDE,
DEMOLISH, LAY LOW, AIM,
PLANE, SMOOTH, FLAT(TEN)
combining form ... PLANI
headed .... SENSIBLE
on the .... FAIR, HONEST
plot .... TERRACE
leveling slip .... SHIM
lever ... SWIPE, TAPPET, PEDAL,
CRANK, PRISE, PRY,
(CROW)BAR, SAMSON,
PRIZE, PEAV(E)Y,
PEEV(E)Y, LAM
foot .... TREADLE
leveret .... HARE
Levi's parent .... JACOB, LEAH
leviathan ..... WHALE, HUGE,
MONSTER
author of .... HOBBES
levigate .... MIX, GRIND
levin ..... LIGHT, LIGHTNING
levis .... OVERALLS
levitate ... FLOAT, RISE, SOAR
levity .. BUOYANCY, FRIVOLITY,
FICKLENESS
levulin .... CARBOHYDRATE
levulose .... FRUCTOSE
levy .... COLLECT, ASSESS,
TAX, IMPRESS, IMPOSITION,
DRAFT, IMPOSE, TRIBUTE,
FINE, IMPOST, ENLIST,
WAGE, CESS, MUSTER,
TITHE, SCOT
en masse, for example ...
MOBILIZE
Lew Wallace hero .. (BEN) HUR
lewd .... LUSTFUL, CADGY,
INDECENT, UNCHASTE,
LASCIVIOUS, LIBIDINOUS
Lewis Carroll character ......
MADHATTER, ALICE, SNARK
companion-explorer ....
CLARK
Gantry of Sinclair ......
ELMER
lex .... LAW
lexicographer .... WORDMAN,
COMPILER, ROGET
lexicographic work .....
DICTIONARY, THESAURUS
lexicon .... DICTIONARY,
VOCABULARY, WORDBOOK
Leyte, capital of .. TACLOBAN
Lhasa holy man ....
(DALAI) LAMA

is capital of ...... TIBET
liability .. OBLIGATION, DEBT,
DUTY, HANDICAP,
RESPONSIBILITY
opposed to ...... ASSET
liable .... APT, OPEN, BOUND,
SUBJECT, RESPONSIBLE,
ANSWERABLE, LIKELY
liaison .... LINKING (UP),
LOVE AFFAIR, AMOUR,
SANDHI
officer ...... COORDINATOR
liana ... CIPO, VIBURNUM, SIPO
liang .... TAEL, WEIGHT
liar .... FIBSTER, CHEAT,
FIBBER, SAPPHIRA,
ANANIAS, DISSEMBLER,
PREVARICATOR
tall ...... MUNCHAUSEN,
ANGLER
lias .... ROCK
libation .... DRINK
Liban .... LIEBAJA
libel ... ROORBACK, SLANDER,
MALIGN, DEFAME,
CALUMNY, MUD
libelous .... VILLIFYING,
DEFAMATORY, SLANDEROUS
liber .... BOOK
diminutive of ..... LIBEL
plural of .... LIBRI
liberal .. LEFTIST, FRANK,
AMPLE, GENEROUS,
ABUNDANT, FREE,
BROADMINDED, LICENTIOUS,
PROGRESSIVE, RADICAL
arts subject ..... HISTORY,
LITERATURE, LOGIC,
RHETORIC
liberate .... FREE, REDEEM,
RANSOM, RELEASE, UNTIE,
MANUMIT
military slang ..... LOOT
slang .... DEPRIVE
Liberian capital .. MONROVIA
coast .... KRU
native .... VAI, TOMA
president ...... TUBMAN
tribe .... KRA, KRU,
GOLA, GORA
"Uncle Shad" .. TUBMAN
libertine ..... RAKE, SKEPTIC,
LICENTIOUS, DEBAUCHEE,
ROUE
liberty .... FREEDOM,

EXEMPTION, FAMILIARITY, PERMISSION
abuse of .... LICENSE
at .... FREE, ALLOWED
Island .... BEDLOE'S
libidinous .... LEWD, LASCIVIOUS, LUSTFUL
libido .... SEX
library .... BIBLIOTHECA
newspaper ..... MORGUE
reading place .. CARREL(L)
supervisor ..... CURATOR
librate ..... OSCILLATE, HOVER, POISE
libretto ... BOOK, TEXT, WORDS
libri .... BOOKS
Lybia .... KINGDOM
Libyan capital (joint) ....
TRIPOLI, BENGASI
city .... BENGASI
gulf .... SIDRA
king .... IDRIS
premier .... (EL) BADRI
port .... TRIPOLI
strongman ..... GADAFFI
lice .... VERMIN
infested .... LOUSY
of .... PEDICULAR
license .... PATENT, AUTHORIZATION, PERMIT, FREEDOM, AUTHORIZE, FRANCHISE, PERMISSION, LIBERTY
licentious .... LIBERTINE, DISSOLUTE, LASCIVIOUS, LEWD
licet .... LEGAL
lich .... CORPSE
lichee .... LITCHI, NUT
lichen .... PARELLA, ALGA, FUNGUS, MOSS, PARELLE, RATMARA, ORCHIL, ARCHIL, ORCHAL, EPIPHYTE, LUNGWORT
bearded .... USNEA
genus ... EVERNIA, USNEA
product .... LITMUS, CUDBEAR, ORCIN(OL)
licht .... LIGHT
licit .... LAWFUL, LEGAL, DUE, JUST, PERMITTED
lick ... LAP, WHIP, THRASH, BEAT, VANQUISH, BLOW, CLIP
plural: sl. ...... CHANCE, TURN

licking: colloq. ..... BEATING, DRUBBING, WHIPPING
lickspittle .... TOADY, FLATTERER
licorice ... ABRIN, JEQUIRITY, PEA
seed .... GOONCH, JEQUIRITY
lid ... CAP, CASE, COVER, TOP
colloquial .... CURB, RESTRAINT
joint .... HINGE
slang .... HAT, CAP
lie .... FLAM, PERJURE, PLUMPER, NESTLE, SPRAWL, TALE, FIB, MENDACITY, RECLINE, STRETCH, EXIST, ENTOMB, FALSEHOOD, EQUIVOCATE, ADMISSIBLE, LAY, LAIR, CORKER, REST, LIGE, PREVARICATE, FABRICATE
anchored ...... MOORED
at anchor .... RIDE
big: colloq. ... WHOPPER
describing one ... WHITE
detector ..... POLYGRAPH
in warmth .... BASK
U.N. Secretary General ..
TRYGVE
waiting .... LURK, SKULK
Liechtenstein's capital ....
VADUZ
king .... JOZEF II
peak .... FALKAIS
premier .... BATLINER
lied .... LYRIC, SONG
lief .... GLADLY, DEAR, WILLING(LY), VALUED, BELOVED
Liege .... LUIK, LOYAL, FAITHFUL, LORD, SOVEREIGN, VASSAL, SUBJECT, DEVOTED
liegeman .... VASSAL
lien .... CLAIM
lienectomy, objective of ......
SPLEEN
lientery .... DIARRHEA
Liepaja .... LIBAU
lier .... RECLINER
lierne .... RIB
lieu .... PLACE, STEAD
lieutenant ..... AIDE, DEPUTY
command of ... PLATOON
slang ...... LOOIE, LOOEY, SHAVETAIL

life ⋯⋯⋯ DAYS, ANIMATION, BIOTA, EXISTENCE, BREATH
  account of one's ⋯⋯⋯ BIOGRAPHY, MEMOIRS
  after death ⋯ HEREAFTER
  belt, kind of ⋯ MAE WEST
  destruction of ⋯ BIOLYSIS
  French ⋯⋯⋯ VIE
  insurance ⋯⋯ TONTINE
  Latin ⋯⋯ VITA, ANIMA
  long ⋯⋯ LONGEVITY
  of ___ ⋯⋯⋯ RILEY
  of the party ⋯⋯ CUTUP
  pertaining to ⋯ BIOTIC(AL)
  plant and animal ⋯ BIOTA
  prefix ⋯⋯⋯ BIO
  preserver ⋯⋯ MAE WEST
  principle ⋯⋯⋯ ATMAN, PRANA, JIVA, SPIRIT
  prolonger, alleged ⋯⋯⋯ ELIXIR
  relating to ⋯ BIOTIC(AL)
  saving fluid ⋯⋯ PLASMA
  saving jacket ⋯ MAE WEST
  size, larger than ⋯ HEROIC
  without ⋯⋯⋯ AZOIC, AMORT, DEAD
  work ⋯⋯⋯ CAREER
lifeless ⋯⋯⋯ DEAD, DULL, LISTLESS, AMORT, INERT, AZOIC, VAPID
lifelike ⋯⋯⋯ NATURAL, GRAPHIC
lifesaver ⋯⋯⋯ LIFEGUARD
lifetime ⋯⋯⋯ AGE, DAYS
lift ⋯⋯ HEFT, SWIPE, PERK, RAISE, HOLD UP, ELEVATE, EXALT, PLAGIARIZE, STEAL, HOIST, BOOST
  British ⋯⋯ ELEVATOR
  colloquial ⋯ PLAGIARIZE
  slang ⋯⋯⋯ STEAL
  with effort ⋯⋯ HEAVE
lifting muscle ⋯⋯ ERECTOR, LEVATOR
ligament ⋯⋯⋯ TENDON, TAENIA
  combining form ⋯ DESMO
  like a ⋯⋯⋯ DESMOID
  twist a ⋯⋯⋯ SPRAIN
ligan ⋯⋯ FLOTSAM, JETSAM
ligate ⋯⋯⋯ BANDAGE
ligature ⋯⋯⋯ TAENIA, TIE, BANDAGE, BOND, THREAD
light ⋯ LAND, ILLUME, AIRY, SLEAZY, GLIM, LEGER, (IL)LUMINE, ILLUMINATION, NEON, MILD, IGNATE, FAIR, ASPECT, LAMP, KLIEG, TAPER, WHERRY
  again ⋯⋯⋯ RELUME
  amplifier ⋯⋯ LASER
  anchor ⋯⋯⋯ KEDGE
  around sun ⋯ AUREOLA
  beacon ⋯⋯⋯ FANAL
  burning ⋯ TORCH, CRESSET
  carrying case ⋯ LANTERN
  celestial ⋯⋯⋯ CORONA, HALO, NIMBUS
  circle of ⋯⋯⋯ AUREOLA, HALO, NIMB(US), AUREOLE, CORONA
  feeble ⋯⋯⋯ TAPER
  fingered gentry member ⋯ DIP, PICKPOCKET
  flooded with ⋯ LUMINOUS
  footed ⋯ NIMBLE, SPRY
  fuse ⋯⋯⋯ SPIT
  game luring ⋯⋯ JACK
  giving device ⋯ TORCH, LAMP, LANTERN
  giving of ⋯⋯ LUCENT, LUMINOUS
  giving substance ⋯⋯⋯ PHOSPHOR
  guiding ⋯⋯⋯ BEACON
  handed ⋯⋯⋯ DEFT
  headed ⋯⋯ GAY, SILLY
  holding case ⋯ LANTERN
  Horse Harry ⋯⋯ LEE
  measure ⋯⋯ LUMENS
  of reflected ⋯ CATOPTRIC
  opera ⋯⋯⋯ OPERETTA
  pertaining to ⋯ PHOTIC
  providing ⋯ LUCIFEROUS
  put out ⋯⋯⋯ DOUSE
  reflecting ⋯⋯ RELUCENT
  ring of ⋯⋯⋯ CORONA
  science of ⋯⋯ OPTICS, PHOTICS
  source of ⋯ SUN, LAMP
  streak in sky ⋯ METEOR
  surrounding saint ⋯⋯⋯ NIMBUS
  touch ⋯⋯⋯ TAP, PAT
  type of ⋯⋯ KLIEG, ARC, NEON
  unit ⋯⋯⋯ LUX, PHOT, LUMEN, PYR, HEFNER
  up ⋯⋯⋯ KINDLE

very .... ETHEREAL
without ...... APHOTIC
wood ... BALSA, POPLAR
lighted: poetic .... LITTEN
lighten .. ILLUMINATE, FLASH,
GLADDEN, RELIEVE, EASE
lighter ... KEEL, SCOW, BARGE,
BOAT, HOY
lamp .... SPILL
than-air craft ... AEROSTAT
lightfingered person ....
PICKPOCKET, DIP
lightheaded ... GIDDY, DIZZY,
FRIVOLOUS, FLIGHTY,
DELIRIOUS
lighthearted ... GAY, CAREFREE
lighthouse ... BEACON, PHARE,
FANAL, PHAROS
appurtenance ....
BEACON (LIGHT)
lighting fixture .... SCONCE
means of ... SPILL, MATCH
lightly .... AIRILY
lightning ... LEVIN, IGNITION,
FLASH, FIREBALL
bug .... FIREFLY
flash of .... BOLT
rod .... ARRESTER
without thunder ....
WILDFIRE
lights .... LUNGS
out signal ...... TAPS,
CURFEW
lightsome ..... NIMBLE, GAY,
LIVELY, LUMINOUS, BRIGHT
lignaloes .... ALOES
ligneous ...... WOODY, XYLOID
lignite ...... JET, (CHAR)COAL
lignose .... EXPLOSIVE
ligulate ...... LORATE, THONG
ligule .... COROLLA
ligure .... JACINTH, STONE
Ligurian Sea city ...... GENOA,
LEGHORN, LIVORNO,
LA SPEZIA
like ...... SIMILAR, AS, COPY,
ENJOY, COGNATE,
RESEMBLING, CHOOSE,
AKIN, RELISH
bear .... URSINE
better .... PREFER
combining form ....
HOME(O), OID, INE
hare .... LEPORINE
ladder .... SCALAR
tail .... CAUDAL

wing .... PTERIC
likelihood ..... PROBABILITY,
CHANCE
likely .... APT, LIABLE,
PROBABLE, CREDIBLE,
PRONE, SEEMLY
liken .... COMPARE
likeness .... EFFIGY, ICON,
IMAGE, GUISE, SIMILARITY,
(RE)SEMBLANCE
bad .... CARICATURE
show .... MIRROR
likes ... TASTES, PREFERENCES
likewise ... ALSO, DITTO, TOO,
MOREOVER, BESIDES
not .... NOR
likin: Chinese .... TAX
liking ..... FONDNESS, GUSTO,
TASTE, PREFERENCE,
PALATE, AFFECTION,
FANCY, PENCHANT
lilac ...... FLOWER, SYRINGA,
SHRUB
lilaceous plant ... ALOE, ONION,
LEEK
Liliom .... CAROUSEL
Lilith ..... DEMON, VAMPIRE,
WITCH
husband of ...... ADAM
Lillie, Miss .... BEA(TRICE)
Lilliputian ..... MIDGET, TINY,
DWARF(ISH), SMALL
republic ... SAN MARINO
lilt ... RHYTHM, SONG, SWING
lily .... ARUM, ALOE, IXIA,
LOTUS, YUCCA, LIS, CALLA,
SEGO, TULIP, ONION, LYS
bulb .... SQUILL
butterfly ..... MARIPOSA,
SEGO
calla .... ARUM
family .... ALOE, SQUILL,
GARLIC, CAMAS(S),
QUAMASH
family, of the ....
LILACEOUS
leaf .... PAD
"Maid of Astolat" ......
ELAIN(E)
palm .... TI
plant .. CAMAS(S), CAMMAS
livered ..... COWARDLY
relative .... ONION
sand .... SOAPROOT
sea .... CRINOID
shaped .... CRINOID

water .. LOTUS, NELUMBO,
LOTOS, NYMPHAEA
Lima, money in .... SOL
limacine mollusk .. SLUG, SNAIL
limax/limacis .... SLUG
limb ...... BRANCH, LEG, FIN,
BOUGH, ARM, WING, IMP,
DISJOINT, MEMBER, EDGE,
MARGIN, BORDER
joint ..... KNEE, ELBOW
muscle .... FLEXOR,
LEVATOR
limber .... PLIANT, AGILE,
FLEXIBLE, LITHE, SUPPLE,
LISSOM(E)
limbo .... JAIL, PRISON,
IMPRISONMENT
Limburg(er) .... CHEESE
limbus .... EDGING, BORDER
lime ... CALX, CATCH, CEMENT,
LINDEN, CITRON, FRUIT
bush .... SNARE
combining form ... CALCI
fruit like .... CITRON
harden with ... CALCIFY
mixture .... CEMENT
powder .... CONITE,
KONITE
product .... APATITE,
CALCIC
remove ..... DECALCIFY
sulfur, use of ..... SPRAY
tree ...... LINDEN, TEIL,
BASS(WOOD), TUPELO
limelight .... SPOTLIGHT
limen .... THRESHOLD,
STIMULATION
limerick man .... LEAR
limes .... DEFENSES,
FORTIFICATION
limestone .... TUFA, PISOLITE,
TRAVERTIN(E), DOLOMITE,
CALCITE, MALM, LIAS,
CHALK, CALP, OOLITE,
COQUINA
crystallized .... MARBLE
limey .... SAILOR, SOLDIER,
ENGLISHMAN
limicoline bird ...... CURLEW,
PLOVER, SNIPE, SANDPIPER,
KILLDEER
limit ..... MARGIN, BOURN(E),
TERM, BOUND(ARY),
RESTRICT, CURB, CONFINE,
DEMARCATION, BUTTING,
PALE, SPAN, FIX,

CIRCUMSCRIBE, METE,
STINT, STENT
limitation to inheritance .. TAIL
limited ..... SCANT, NARROW,
CIRCUMSCRIBED, FINITE
limitless ...... VAST, INFINITE,
UNBOUNDED, BOUNDLESS,
IMMENSE
limits .... BOUNDS
limn ... DEPICT, DRAW, PAINT,
PORTRAY, DESCRIBE, SKETCH
Limoges .... PORCELAIN,
CHINAWARE
limonene .... TERPENE
limousine ..... AUTO(MOBILE),
SEDAN
limp ... HITCH, FLABBY, HALT,
SOFT, LAX, WILTED,
HOBBLE, FLIMSY, FLACCID
limpet ... SHELLFISH, LAMPREY
limpid .... CLEAR, PELLUCID,
TRANSPARENT
limpkin .... COURLAN
limuloid .... KING CRAB,
LIMULUS
limulus .... KING CRAB
limy .... STICKY
linage .... ALIGNMENT
linchpin .... FORELOCK
Lincoln's hat ..... STOVEPIPE
sobriquet .. RAILSPLITTER,
(HONEST) ABE
son ..... WILLIE, ROBERT
wife ..... (MARY) TODD
Lind, soprano .... JENNY
soubriquet ....
NIGHTINGALE
linden .... TEIL
tree ... LIME, BASSWOOD,
LINN
Lindsay, poet .... VACHEL
line .... ROUTE, CORD, CERIF,
ROW, ROPE, STRING, WIRE,
REIN, DEMARCATION,
CORDON, OCCUPATION,
TRADE, BUSINESS, VECTOR,
FILE, PATTER, QUEUE, RANK,
SERIF
ancestral .... LINEAGE
battle .... FRONT
control .... REIN
cutting .... SECANT
draw the .... LIMIT
family .... ANCESTRY,
BLOOD, TREE
fine ... SERIF, CERIF, STRIA

hair ...... CERIPH, SERIF
imaginary ...... VECTOR
in .... AROW
in prosody ...... STICH
in trigonometry ....
SECANT, SINE, TANGENT
inside of .... CEIL
intersecting .... SECANT,
VECTOR
joining barometric points
ISOBAR
junction .... SEAM
nautical .... MARLINE,
EARING
of action ...... DEMARCHE
of color .... STREAK
of persons ...... QUEUE
pertaining to .... LINEAL,
LINEAR
reference .... AXIS
roof .... CEIL
ship side ...... PLIMSOLL
the inside .... CEIL
threadlike .... STRIA
toe the .. OBEY, CONFORM
waiting ...... CUE, QUEUE
walls of .... CEIL
with bricks ...... REVET
with stone ...... STEAN(E)
without angle ... AGONE
lineage ... STEM, GENEALOGY,
BLOOD, STRAIN, DESCENT,
ANCESTRY, FAMILY,
PEDIGREE, STOCK
lineal .... HEREDITARY
lineament ... FEATURE, MARK,
(OUT)LINE, CHARACTERISTIC
lineate .... STREAKED
lined ...... RULED, STRIATE(D)
linen ...... CRASH, TOILE,
LINGERIE, STATIONERY,
FLAXEN, NAPERY, BYSSUS,
HOLLAND, BATISTE
and wool cloth ... LINSEY
articles of ...... LINGERIE
closet item ...... TOWEL,
SHEET, NAPKIN
cloth ...... SEERSUCKER,
DUCK
cloth for bookbinding .
BUCKRAM
cloth, mummy's .. BYSSUS
coarse ...... DOWLAS,
DRABBET
fabric ...... VELOUR(S),
SCRIM, CRASH

fiber .... FLAX
fine ... BATISTE, CAMBRIC,
DAMASK, LAWN, TOILE
household ...... NAPERY
measure .... CUT
plant .... FLAXEN
room .... EWERY
scraped/softened .. LINT
sheer .... TOILE
source of .... FLAX
tape .... INKLE
table ... NAPERY, RUNNER
vestment ... ALB, AMICE
liner ...... STEAMER, VESSEL,
(STEAM)SHIP
lines on map ...... HACHURE
on optical lens .. RETICLE
ling .... BURBOT
linger ...... DELAY, DWELL,
DALLY, HOVER, LAG,
TARRY, LOITER, WAIT,
DAWDLE
lingerie ... UNDERWEAR, SLIP,
LINEN, UNDIES
lingo ...... CANT, JARGON,
PATOIS, LANGUAGE, DIALECT
lingua ... TONGUE, PROBOSCIS,
GLOSSA
linguiform ...... LINGULATE
linguist .... POLYGLOT
linguistic form ...... PHRASE,
WORD, SENTENCE
linguistics branch ....
MORPHOLOGY, SYNTAX,
SEMANTICS, PHONOLOGY,
PHILOLOGY
liniment ...... LOTION,
INUNCTION, ARNICA
linin .... CATHARTIC
lining .... GASKET, BUSHING,
BUCKRAM, DOUBLURE
link .. NEXUS, TORCH, YOKE,
CONNECT(ION), JOIN, LOOP,
RING, TIE, COPULA,
ATTACH, CATENATE, CHAIN
train cars ...... COUPLE
linked series .. CHAIN, CATENA
Linkletter, TV man ...... ART
links .... GOLF COURSE,
CAT(ENA)
connect in series ......
CATENATE
man ... CADDY, CADDIE
linn ...... LINDEN, CASCADE,
WATERFALL, RAVINE, POOL
linne .... CRATER

linnet .... SONGBIRD, FINCH, LINTWHITE

linotypist .... COMPOSITOR, TYPESETTER

linseed oil, hardened .... LINOLEUM

   mixture .... MEGILP(H)

   source .... FLAX

   refuse .... MILKCAKE

lint ...... FLAX, FLUFF, FIBER, LINEN, NAP, RAVELINGS, FUZZ

lintel .... CROSSPIECE, SQUINCH, TRANSOM, SUMMER

   counterpart of ..... SILL

lintwhite .... LINNET

linty .... FLUFFY

liny .... THIN

lion .... LEO, CAT, FELINE, CELEBRITY, SIMBA, IDOL

   female .... LIONESS

   group .... PRIDE

   mane of .... CREST

   mountain .... PUMA, COUGAR, PANTHER

   neck hair .... MANE

   of God .... ARIEL

   of Judah .... SELASSIE

   pride of .... MANE, CREST

   young of a .... WHELP, LIONET, CUB

lioness of story/movie ... ELSA

lionet .... CUB

lionheart .... RICHARD I

lionhearted .... BRAVE

lip .... LABIUM, LABRUM, LABELLUM, KISS, LABIAL, SUPERFICIAL, IMPERTINENCE

   adornment ...... PELELE, LABRET

   combining form .. CHIL(O)

   cup's .... BRIM

   ladle .... GEAT

   like edge .... LABRUM

   like organ ...... LABIUM

   of the .... LABIAL

   ornament ...... PELELE, LABRET, M(O)USTACHE

   service, of sorts .... MALARK(E)Y, HYPOCRISY

   slang .... INSOLENCE, IMPERTINENCE

   sound .... LABIAL

   touch with .... KISS, OSCULATE

liparoid ..... FATTY, FAT-LIKE

lipase .... ENZYME

lipide .... FATS, LIPOID

lipoid .... FAT-LIKE

lipoma .... TUMOR

Lippe, capital of .... DETMOLD

lipped .... LABIATE

lipper .... SPRAY, RIPPLE, BLUBBER

Lippi, painter ...... FILIPPO, FILIPPINO

lips .... LABRA, LABIA, KISSER

   combining form ... LABIO

   of the .... LABIAL

lipstick ..... ROUGE, POMADE

liquefied .... FUSIL(E)

liquefy .. FUSE, MELT, THAW

   opposed to ..... SOLIDIFY

liquescent .... MELTING

liqueur ... RATAFIA, KUMMEL, CORDIAL, POUSSE, CURACAO, COGNAC, CREME, ABSINTH(E), CHARTREUSE

   glass .... PONY

   sweet .... GENEPI, ANISETTE, CURACAO, MARASCHINO

liquid .... FLUID, CLEAR, TRANSPARENT

   becoming ... LIQUESCENT

   body tissue ...... LYMPH

   change into ..... LIQUEFY

   fatty oil .... OLEIN

   fire substance ... NAPALM

   food ...... SOUP, BROTH

   in pharmacy ...... AQUA

   made .... FUSIL(E)

   measure ... PINT, QUART, GALLON, GILL, BARREL, HOGSHEAD, MINIM, TUN

   measuring device .... DOSIMETER, JIGGER

   medicated, for sores ..... LINIMENT

   mouthful of .... SUP

   oily .... FURFURAL

   opposite .... SOLID

   oxygen .... LOX

   pickling .... BRINE, SOUSE

   rock .... MAGMA

   solvent .... MENSTRUUM

   strained .... FILTRATE

   thick .... DOPE, TAR

   waste .... SLOPS

liquidambar ... BALSAM, TREE, SWEETGUM

liquidate ...... CASH, SETTLE, PAY, KILL, DISPOSE (OF)
liquify by heat .... MELT
liquor ... TIFF, RAKI, MASTIC, RUM, RYE, JUICE, DRINK, MEAD, BITTERS, CREME, WHISKY, GIN, GROG, POTATION, TAP, RAKEE, POTTLE, ALE, ANISETTE
alcoholic .... LUSH, MESCAL
bad ...... BOUSE, BOWSE
bitter .... ABSINTH(E)
bottle .... MAGNUM
cabinet .... CELLARET
cheap .... SLIPSLOP
colloquial .... BOOZE
drink .... DRAM, TIFF
drink, drugged .... MICKEY (FINN)
fruit juice ...... BRANDY
glass .... SNIFTER
intoxicating ...... TODDY
leftover in glass .... HEELTAP
loss thru leakage, etc. .... ULLAGE
malt .... STOUT, ALE, PORTER
measure ...... NIP, DRAM, GILL, PINT, NOGGIN
Oriental .... ARRACK
pick-me-up .... STIM
rice .... SAKE
sap .... NIPA
sold here ...... SALOON, BARROOM, CANTINA
sugarcane ..... TAF(F)IA
tonic .... BITTERS
weak .... SLIPSLOP
lira, 1/20 of .... SOLDO
liriodendron .... TULIP, MAGNOLIA, WHITEWOOD
liripipe .... TIPPET
Lisbon river .... TAGUS
Lisle .... LILLE, THREAD, FABRIC, GLOVES, STOCKINGS
lissom(e) ...... LITHE, SUPPLE, NIMBLE, SVELTE, LIMBER
list ... CALENDAR, HEEL, TIP, CANT, TABLE, CAREEN, LEAN, ITEMIZE, SCROLL, SELVAGE, BOUNDARY, INVENTORY, SLATE, CATALOG(UE), ROLL, PLOW, REGISTER, TILT,

ROTA, TARIFF, TABULATE, INDENTURE, INDEX, SCHEDULE
actors' .... CAST
ancestors' ..... PEDIGREE
business meeting .... AGENDA
candidates' .... SLATE, TICKET
jury .... PANEL
of bonds, etc. .... PORTFOLIO
details .... TABLE
goods .... INVOICE
legal decisions .... DOCKET
officers .... ROSTER
persons .... ROSTER, ROLL
saints ..... HAGIOLOGY, CANON
the dead .... BEADROLL
titles ... CATALOG(UE)
team players' ... LINEUP
listen ...... HIST, EAVESDROP, HARK(EN), OBEY, HEARKEN, HEED, HEAR
listener .... AUDITOR
surreptitious .... EAVESDROPPER, BUGGER
listening .... AUDIENT
device ... BUG, MONITOR
post, usually ... EMBASSY
lister .... PLOW
listing .... TABLE, SELVAGE
listless ...... LACKADAISICAL, LANGUID, SPIRITLESS
listlessness ... ENNUI, APATHY
lists ... ARENA, TOURNAMENT, TILTS, ROLLS
Liszt, pianist .... FRANZ
lit .... LANDED, ALIGHTED
litany .... PRAYER
litas .... LIT
litchi ..... LICHEE, TREE, NUT
literal .... WORD-FOR-WORD, ETYMOLOGICAL, TEXTUAL, PROSAIC, REAL, MATTER-OF-FACT, ACCURATE, UNVARNISHED, VIRTUAL, PLAIN, EXACT
quotation, indication of .. SIC
translation .. METAPHRASE
literally .... VIRTUALLY, LITERATIM

literary ... LETTERED, LEARNED
bits .... ANA, ANALECTA
collection .... ANA,
   MISCELLANEA,
   MISCELLANY
composition .... PARODY,
   VIGNETTE
criticism ..... EPICRISIS,
   REVIEW, CRITIQUE
drudge .... HACK
effort .... LUCUBRATION
extracts .... ANALECTA,
   ANALECTS
form ...... POEM, VERSE,
   ESSAY
hack .... GRUB
hacks, of ... GRUBSTREET
initials .... RLS, GBS
invention ...... FORGERY
man .... LITTERATEUR
movement leaders ......
   AVANT GARDE
patchwork .... CENTO
pseudonym ... ELIA, SAKI
quotation, brief .. SNIPPET
review .... CRITIQUE
scholar ...... HARMONIST
scraps ... ANA, ANALECTS
society .... LYCEUM
study .... GRAMMAR
style ..... PEN, ROCOCO
work, inferior .. SCRIBBLE,
   POTBOILER
literate .... LEARNED,
   EDUCATED, CULTURED,
   LETTERED
literati ..... MEN OF LETTERS,
   SCHOLARS, INTELLECTUALS
literatim .... LITERALLY,
   LETTER FOR LETTER
literature .... WRITINGS
lithe .... SLIM, LISSOM(E),
   SVELTE, LIMBER, SUPPLE,
   FLEXIBLE, AGILE
lithograph ... PRINT, CHROMO
lithoid .... STONELIKE
lithology, subject of ... ROCKS
lithomarge .... CLAY, KAOLIN
lithophyte ..... CORAL, PLANT
lithopone .... PIGMENT
Lithuanian .... BALT, LETT
capital .... KAUNAS,
   KOVNO, VILNA
city ... VILNIUS (WILNO)
coin ...... LIT(AS), RUBLE
river port .... KAUNAS

seaport .... MEMEL
territory .... MEMEL
litigant ... SUER, DEFENDANT,
   COMPLAINANT
litigate .... SUE
litigation .... LAWSUIT
litigious .... QUARRELSOME
litotes .... MEIOSIS
litten .... LIGHTED
litter ... BIER, COFFIN, DOOLI,
   FALL, PALANQUIN,
   PALANKEEN, DOOLEE,
   STREW, MULCH, SCATTER,
   JUMBLE, DISORDER, MESS,
   STRETCHER, RUBBISH,
   CLUTTER
bearer ... PIG, CAT, DOG
last-born of ....
   WALLYDRAG
of pigs .... FARROW
litterateur ... MAN OF LETTERS,
   WRITER, AUTHOR
little ... PUNY, WEE, PALTRY,
   SMALL, BRIEF, TRIVIAL,
   YOUNG, MINUTE, TINY,
   POCO
Bear .... URSA MINOR
Big Horn protagonist ....
   SITTING BULL, CUSTER
"big" man ....
   COCKALORUM
bit .... MORSEL, FIG
Boy Blue" author .. FIELD
by little ..... PIECEMEAL
combining form ....
   MICR(O)
Corporal .... NAPOLEON
fellow .... BUB
Flower, mayor ....
   LA GUARDIA
Fox .... VULPECULA,
   CONSTELLATION
hours ..... SEXT, TIERCE,
   PRIME, NONE
Miss Muffet's food ......
   WHEY
people .... FAIRIES
piece .... FLINDER
ring .... ANNULET
Russia .... UKRAINE
Tibet .... LADAKH
littleneck .... QUAHOG, CLAM
littoral ..... SHORE, COAST(AL)
litu, singular of .... LITAS
liturgical singer ..... CANTOR
vestment .... AMICE, ALB

liturgy ... RITE, RITUAL, MASS
litus .... SERF
Litvinov, Russ. statesman .....
                         MAXIM
livable .... HABITABLE,
                      ENDURABLE
live .... INHABIT, BREATHE,
     DWELL, EXIST, ENDURE,
     SUBSIST, RESIDE,
     ENERGETIC, VIVID
  able to .... VIABLE
  alone .... BACH
  coal .... EMBER
  it _____ .... UP
  oak .... ENCINA
  together .... COHABIT
  under false pretenses ....
             MASQUERADE
  wire: colloq. ... HUSTLER,
             GO-GETTER
livelihood ...... SUBSISTENCE,
    SUPPORT, SUSTENANCE,
    LIVING, KEEP,
  (DAILY)BREAD, MAINTENANCE
liveliness .... VIVACITY
livelong ...... ENTIRE, WHOLE
lively ..... SPRY, AGILE, GAY,
    CANTY, BRISK, SPIRITED,
    VIVID, KEEN, ANIMATED,
    SPRIGHTLY, VIVACIOUS,
    ACTIVE, PE(A)RT, PERKY
  air .... LILT
  dance .... REEL
  music ... ANIMATO, VIVO
  person .... GRIG
liven .... CHEER(UP)
liver .... HEPAR
  disease ..... CIRRHOSIS,
    PORPHYRIA
  function of .. METABOLISM
  inflammation .. HEPATITIS
  is supposed seat of ......
    DESIRE, EMOTION
  lobster's ...... TOMALLEY
  pertaining to .. HEPATIC,
          VISCERA
  secretion .... BILE, GALL
  shaped like .... HEPATIC
  substance in ... HEPARIN
livered, yellow .... COWARDLY
liveried servant .... FLUNK(E)Y
liverish ...... BILIOUS, CROSS,
         PEEVISH
liverwort .... AGRIMONY,
  HEPATICA, BRYOPHYTE
  genus .... RICCIA

lettuce .... PYROLA
liverwurst .... SAUSAGE
livery .... UNIFORM, STABLE
  wearer of ...... SERVANT,
    RETAINER, LACKEY,
    FLUNK(E)Y
liveryman .... RETAINER,
         LACKEY
livestock ..... CATTLE, COWS,
         STEERS
  farm .... RANCH
  round up ..... WRANGLE
livid ...... BLACK-AND-BLUE,
    WAN, PALE, ASHEN,
    DISCOLORED
living .... BEING, QUICK,
  EXTANT, ALIVE, LIVELIHOOD,
    ANIMATE
  capable of ...... VIABLE
  close to ground ....
      EPIGEAL
  corpse .... ZOMBI(E)
  ecclesiastical ... BENEFICE
  inside animals ....
    ENTOZOIC,
    ENTOPHYTIC
  on land or in water ......
    AMPHIBIAN
  on river bank .. RIPARIAN
  picture .. TABLEAU VIVANT
  prefix LIVI
  room ..... SALA, PARLOR
  space ..... LEBENSRAUM
  thing ..... ORGANISM
  wild, loose .... RIOT
  within ...... IMMANENT
Livonian .. ESTH(ONIAN), LETT
Livorno .... LEGHORN
livre, replacement of .. FRANC
lixiviate .... LEACH
lixivium .... LYE, LEACH
lizard ..... AGAMA, GUANA,
  BASILISK, ADDA, GECKO,
  SAURIAN, LACERT(IL)IAN,
  MONITOR, EFT, SKINK,
  GILA, NEWT, SWIFT, UTA,
  GALLIWASP, MOLOCH, SEPS,
  IGUANA, REPTILE,
  CHAMELEON
  amphibious ...... NEWT,
    SALAMANDER
  chameleon-like ... AGAMA
  climbing .... IGUANA
  color-changing .. AGAMA,
    CHAMELEON

combining form ‿ SAURO, SAURUS
crested ‿‿‿‿ BASILISK
fish ‿‿‿‿‿ SAURY, ULAE
genus ‿‿‿‿ AGAMA, UMA
legless ‿‿‿‿ BLINDWORM, SLOWWORM
like ‿‿‿‿‿‿‿ SAURIAN
monitor ‿‿ URAN, VARAN
Old World ‿‿‿‿‿‿ SEPS, AGAMA
wall ‿‿‿‿‿‿‿‿ GECKO
with winglike membranes DRAGON
Lizette of poetry ‿‿‿‿ REESE
llama ‿‿ VICUNA, RUMINANT, ALPACA
habitat ‿‿‿‿‿‿ ANDES
hair of ‿‿‿‿‿‿ WOOL
relative ‿‿‿‿‿‿ CAMEL, GUANACO
llanero's weapon ‿‿‿‿ BOLA
llano ‿‿‿‿‿‿‿‿ PLAIN, STEPPE
lo ‿‿ ECCE, SEE, BEHOLD, LOOK
companion of ‿ BEHOLD
loa ‿‿‿‿‿‿‿‿‿‿ LARVA
loach ‿‿‿‿‿‿‿‿‿‿ CARP
load ‿‿‿‿ ENCUMBER, LADING, FILL, FREIGHT, ONUS, SADDLE, CARGO, BURDEN, WEIGHT, LADE
a gun ‿‿‿‿‿‿‿‿ CHARGE
transported ‿‿‿‿ HAUL
loaded ‿‿‿‿‿‿‿‿‿ WEIGHTED
slang ‿‿‿‿‿ INTOXICATED, DRUNK, IN THE MONEY, MONEYED
loader, dock ‿‿‿‿ STEVEDORE
loadstar ‿‿‿ POLARIS, LODESTAR
loadstone ‿‿‿‿‿‿‿ MAGNET(ITE)
loaf ‿‿‿‿ IDLE, LOUNGE, LOLL, BREAD, LOITER, BAP, CAKE, GOLDBRICK
white bread ‿ MANCHET
loafer ‿‿‿‿ IDLER, LOUNGER, SHOE, DRONE, BUM
loam ‿‿‿‿ MARL, SOIL, LOESS, REGUR, EARTH, DIRT, MALM
constituent ‿‿ CLAY, SAND
loan ‿‿‿‿‿‿‿‿ PREST, TOUCH
ask for a ‿‿ BRACE, TOUCH
of money ‿‿‿‿‿‿ IMPREST
note: colloq. ‿‿‿‿‿‿ IOU
privilege ‿‿‿‿‿‿‿‿ CREDIT
shark ‿‿‿‿‿‿‿‿‿ USURER
loath ‿‿‿‿‿‿‿ AVERSE, HOSTILE,

UNWILLING, RELUCTANT, HESITANT
loathe ‿‿‿‿‿ ABHOR, DETEST, HATE, ABOMINATE
loathsome ‿‿‿‿ CLOYING, VILE, DETESTABLE, DISGUSTING, FOUL, REPULSIVE, ABHORRENT
lob ‿‿‿‿‿‿‿‿ COP, LOP, LOFT
lobby ‿‿‿‿‿ HALL, ANTEROOM, VESTIBULE, FOYER, LOUNGE
lobbyist ‿‿‿‿‿‿‿ RAINMAKER
lobe ‿‿‿‿‿‿ LOBULE, LAPPET
ear ‿‿‿‿‿‿‿‿ EARLOP
whale tail's ‿‿‿‿‿ FLUKE
lobelia ‿‿‿‿‿‿‿‿ CAMAS(S)
loblolly ‿‿‿‿‿‿ PINE, GRUEL, MUDHOLE, PUDDLE, BROTH
lobo ‿‿‿‿‿‿‿‿‿‿ WOLF
lobscou(r)se ‿‿‿‿‿‿‿‿ STEW
lobster ‿‿‿‿‿‿‿ CRUSTACEAN, MALACOSTRACAN, MACRURAN
appendage ‿‿‿‿ UROPOD
claw ‿‿‿ NIPPER, CHELA, PINCER
coral ‿‿‿‿‿‿‿‿‿ ROE
egg(s) ‿‿‿‿ ROE, SPAWN, BERRY
feeler of ‿‿‿‿ PALP(US), ANTENNA
first legs of ‿‿‿‿ PINCERS
liver ‿‿‿‿‿‿‿ TOMALLEY
ovaries of ‿‿‿‿‿‿ CORAL
part of a ‿‿‿‿‿‿‿ THORAX, TELSON, CHELA
protective covering ‿‿‿ MAIL
spawn of ‿‿‿‿‿‿‿‿ CORAL
trap for ‿‿‿‿‿‿‿‿‿ POT
lobworm ‿‿‿‿‿‿‿‿ LUGWORM
local ‿‿ RESTRICTED, BRANCH, CHAPTER, TOPICAL, WAY TRAIN, REGIONAL, VICINAL
relationship ‿‿‿‿ UBIETY
locale ‿‿‿‿‿‿‿ SCENE, VENUE, PLACE, LOCALITY, SITE
locality ‿‿‿‿‿‿‿ AREA, PLACE, SITUS, SPOT, LOCUS, HABITAT, LOCALE, DISTRICT, NEIGHBORHOOD, VENUE
restricted to a ‿‿ ENDEMIC, INDIGENOUS
locate ‿‿‿ MARK OFF, SETTLE, SPOT, PLACE, FIND,

location .. POSITION, SITUATION,
    SITE, SPOT, PLACE(MENT)
  person's ... WHEREABOUTS
loch ...... LAKE, POND, BAY
loci, singular of ...... LOCUS
lock .... TRESS, DETENT,
    COTTER, CURL, JAM, HASP,
    CONFINE, LINK, RINGLET
  away .... STORE
  brand .... YALE
  hair ...... CURL, TRESS,
    RINGLET, TAG
  mechanism ..... DETENT
  of wool .... FLOCK
  out .... BAR
  part ..... BOLT, TUMBLER,
    CYLINDER, STUMP
  ship .... COFFER
  up .... JAIL
locker ...... CHEST, CLOSET,
    COMPARTMENT, AMBRY,
    KIST
locket's content .... PICTURE,
    HAIR, MINIATURE
lockjaw ... TETANUS, TRISMUS
lockup ...... CALABOOSE, STIR,
    JUG, JAIL, PEN
loco ...... CRAZE, DEMENTED,
    CRAZY
locofoco ...... CIGAR, MATCH
locomotion, form of ....
    WALKING
locomotive .... MOGUL,
    SWITCHER, DOLLY, DINKEY,
    DUMMY, IRON HORSE
  coal car .... TENDER
  cowcatcher ..... FENDER
  driver .... ENGINEER,
    MOTORMAN
  driver's place ...... CAB
  on a mission ... WILDCAT
  pulling power .. TRACTION
  safety device .... PILOT,
    COW-CATCHER
  stopping place ....
    TANKTOWN
  sound ..... CHOO, CHUFF
locoweed .... PLANT
locum tenens ..... SUBSTITUTE
locus .... PLACE, POINT
locust .... CICADA, CICALA,
    TREE, INSECT, ACACIA
  kin .... CRICKET,
    GRASSHOPPER
  tree ...... ACACIA, CAROB,
    HONEY

locution ... EXPRESSION, WORD,
    PHRASE, IDIOM
lode ...... VEIN, ORE DEPOSIT
  cavity ... VUG(G), VUGH
  mining .. VUG, VEIN, REEF
lodestar .... POLARIS
lodge ...... HOUSE, CHAPTER,
    DEN, HUT, BILLET, BOARD,
    QUARTER, ROOM, CABIN
  Indian ..... TENT, TEPEE,
    WIGWAM
lodger .... ROOMER, GUEST
  temporary ... TRANSIENT
lodging .... QUARTERS, ABODE,
    BILLET, PIED-A-TERRE
  house ...... HOTEL, INN,
    HOSTEL(RY)
  house bed .... DOSS
loess .... LOAM
loft .... ATTIC, GALLERY,
    JUBE, LOB, GARRET,
    MANSARD
lofty .... HIGH, GRAND,
    ARROGANT, HAUGHTY,
    NOBLE, SUBLIME, SKYEY
  dwelling .... AERIE, AERY
log .... DIARY, RECORD,
    TIMBER
  barrier .... BOOM
  birling contest ... ROLEO
  float .. RAFT, CATAMARAN
  holder .... PEAV(E)Y,
    CANT HOOK
  house .... CABIN
  measure ...... SCALAGE
  roller .... DECKER
  sling ..... PARBUCKLE
  spin a .... BIRL
  splitter .... WEDGE
  turner .... PEAV(E)Y
loganberry .... BRAMBLE
logarithm decimal part ....
    MANTISSA
  inventor .... NAPIER
  unit .... BEL
loge..... BOX, COMPARTMENT,
    STALL
logger .... LUMBERJACK,
    WOODCUTTER
  boots of .... PACS
  sled of .... TODE,
    GO-DEVIL, TRAVOIS
loggerhead .. TURTLE, DUNCE
  bird .... SHRIKE
loggia ..... ARCADE, GALLERY,
    PORTICO

logging, evade work in .... SNIB
sled ..... GO-DEVIL, TODE,
TRAVOIS
tool .... PEAV(E)Y
logia .... MAXIMS, SAYINGS
logic .... REASONING
deductive ..... SYLLOGISM
major premise ....
SUMPTION
logical .... REASONABLE
logically connected ....
COHERENT
logion .... MAXIM, SAYING
plural of .... LOGIA
logistic .... ARITHMETIC,
CALCULATIVE
logistics, concern of ....
TRANSPORTATION, SUPPLY,
QUARTERS
logogriph .... ANAGRAM,
WORD PUZZLE
Logos .... REASON, WORD
logroller ... DECKER, BIRLER,
POLITICIAN
logrolling .... BIRLING
subject of .... BILL
logs floating in mass .. DRIVE
passage down slope .....
SLUICE, FLUME
pile of .... ROLLWAY
logy .... DULL, SLUGGISH
Lohengrin's bride .... ELSA
composer ..... WAGNER
father .... PARSIFAL
opera character .... ELSA,
ORTRUD, TELRAMUND
loin .... CHUMP, RACK,
BEEFCUT
combining form ....
LUMB(O)
muscle .... PSOAS
section of ...... GRISKIN
loincloth ..... MARO, LUNGI,
LUNGEE, MALO, DHOTI,
PAGNE, LAVA-LAVA,
SARONG, G-STRING
loins .... HIPS
pertaining to the ....
LUMBAR
Loire River city ...... ORLEANS,
BLOIS, NANTES
loiter .... LOUNGE, LOAF,
LINGER, DAWDLE, IDLE,
DALLY, LAG, TARRY,
SAUNTER

loiterer .... LAGGER, IDLER'
LAGGARD
Loki's daughter ...... HEL(A)
son .... NARE
victim .... BALDER
wife .... SIGYN
loll ... DROOP, LOUNGE, HANG,
LOP, LAZE
lollapaloosa .... LULU,
KNOCKOUT
Lollard leader ... WYCLIFFE
lollipop ..... SUCKER, CANDY
Lollobrigida, actress ... GINA
Lombard capital ...... PAVIA
Lombardy capital .... MILAN
city .... PAVIA
ruler .... ALBOIN
Lome, location of ..... TOGO
loment .... LEGUME
London, ancient name of .....
AGUSTA
art gallery .... TATE
barrister .... TEMPLAR
bobby's beat ..... POINT
borough ... KENSINGTON,
GREENWICH, STEPNEY,
CHELSEA, BATTERSEA,
ISLINGTON,
WESTMINSTER, LAMBETH
botanical gardens site . .
KEW
city company member . .
LIVERYMAN
cleaning woman .. CHAR
club .... KITCAT
coach builder .. TILBURY
court .... HUSTINGS,
MARSHALSEA
dialect .... COCKNEY
district .... SOHO,
LAMBETH, MAYFAIR,
CHELSEA, ADELPHI,
BANKSIDE, LIMEHOUSE,
WHITEFRIARS,
WHITECHAPEL
fashionable section .....
MAYFAIR, BELGRAVIA
foreign quarter ... SOHO
hair style .... ONION
hawker .... COSTER, MUN
hooligan .... SPIV
horse market ....
TATTERSALL'S
landmark .... BRIDGE,
TOWER
mental hospital .. BEDLAM

native .... COCKNEY
park .... HYDE
place of execution ......
TYBURN
prison .... NEWGATE,
MARSHALSEA
ship of Jack ..... SNARK
royal stables ..... MEWS
ruffian .... MOHOCK,
MOHAWK
statue ..... MAGOG, GOG
street .... SOHO, STRAND,
FLEET, PALLMALL,
LOMBARD
streetcar .... TRAM
student of law .. TEMPLAR
suburb .... EALING,
WEMBLEY, KEW
subway .... TUBE
theatre .... DRURY LANE
underwriters ... LLOYD'S
West End .... SOHO
writer .... JACK
Londoner .... COCKNEY
Londres .... CIGAR
lone .... SOLITARY, ISOLATED,
SOLO, SOLE
Ranger's pal .... TONTO
Star State .... TEXAS
loneliness .... MELANCHOLIA
kind of ...... NOSTALGIA
lonely ..... DESOLATE, LORN,
SOLITARY, ISOLATED
loner, kind of .... HERMIT,
MUGWUMP
lonesome .... DESOLATE
long .... HANKER, PROLIX,
EXTENDED, SLOW, PINE,
CRAVE, YEARN, LENGTHY,
ASPIRE, ACHE
ago .... LANG SYNE
before .... SOON
cut .... SLASH, GASH
discourse ..... DESCANT
distance contest ......
MARATHON
dozen .... THIRTEEN
drawn ..... PROLONGED,
EXTENDED
faced ...... GLUM, SAD,
DISCONSOLATE
fish .... GAR, EEL
for ...... HANKER, PINE,
CRAVE
green: sl. .. (PAPER)MONEY
headed .... SHREWD

Island county .. QUEENS,
KINGS, NASSAU, SUFFOLK
Island racetrack ......
BELMONT
journey ... ODYSSEY, TREK
knife .... YATAGAN
leaf .... PINE
legged bird ...... HERON,
EGRET, STORK, STILT,
RAIL, CRANE, CURLEW
life .... LONGEVITY
limbed .... RANGY,
LEGGY
live! .... VIVE, VIVA
necked animal .. GIRAFFE
necked bird ...... SWAN,
STORK, HERON
opposite of ...... BRIEF,
SHORT
seat ...... SETTEE, BENCH
since .... LANG SYNE
shot race horse .. SLEEPER,
PLATER
shot, what it isn't ....
FAVORITE
spear .... LANCE
step .... STRIDE
suffering .... PATIENT,
MEEK
tongued .... TALKATIVE,
GOSSIPY
tooth ...... FANG, TUSK
tramp .... TREK
winded .... PROLIX,
WORDY, VERBOSE
longanimity ... FORBEARANCE,
PATIENCE
longeron .... SPAR
longevity .... LONG LIFE
Longfellow bell town .... ATRI
longhair ...... INTELLECTUAL,
HIGHBROW
longhand reporting ......
LOGOGRAPHY
writing .... SCRIPT
longhorn .... CATTLE
longing ... YEN, YEARNING
longshoreman ...... DOCKER,
STEVEDORE, DOCKHAND,
LUMPER
longshot winner ..... SLEEPER
longspur .... BIRD, FINCH,
SPARROW
longways ...... LENGTHWISE
loo .... PAM, CARD GAME
looby .... LUBBER, LOUT

loofah ·····•·••·•· SPONGE
looie (looey) ··•·· LIEUTENANT
look ······· CON, PORE, HIST,
    MIEN, GANDER, PRY, SEE,
    SEARCH, SEEM, APPEAR(ANCE),
    GLANCE, SEEK, ASPECT,
    GAZE, GAPE, PEER, EYE,
    SKEW, SCAN
  alike ··•·•·•·• RINGER
  amorous ·····•··· OGLE
  askance ···•·•··· LEER
  back ··•··· RECOLLECT,
    RECALL
  dagger ···•··•·• GLARE
  forward to ·· ANTICIPATE,
    EXPECT
  frowning ··•··•·• LOUR,
    SCOWL, (G)LOWER
  in ··•··•··········· VISIT
  into ··•··· INVESTIGATE,
    PROBE, INQUIRE
  obliquely ·· SKEW, SQUINT
  over ···•··•·•· INSPECT,
    EXAMINE
  over: sl. ··•··•·•·· CASE
  prying ··•·· PEEK, KEEK,
    PEEP, SPY
  quick ··· PEEK, GLIMPSE,
    GLANCE
  scornful ··•··•·· SNEER
  see: sl. ··•· GLANCE, PEEK
  sly ·········•· LEER, PEEK
  steady ··•··· GAZE, STARE,
    GAPE
  threatening ··•·· LOWER
  up to ··•··•·•·· ADMIRE
looker-on ··•··•· SPECTATOR,
    OBSERVER, BYSTANDER
looking glass ··•·•· MIRROR
lookout ··•··•··•· CONCERN,
    PROSPECT, WORRY,
    WATCHER, ESPIER, GUARD,
    OBSERVER, SPOTTER
  nautical usage ···•··••·•·
    CROW'S NEST
  ship's ··•··•·•· CONNER
  turret ··•··•· BARTIZAN,
    BARTISAN
loom ··•··•·•· APPEAR, LOON,
    TAKE SHAPE, WEAVE
  frame ··•·•· BATTEN
  part ··•·• HEDDLE, PIRN,
    SHUTTLE, REED,
    TREADLE, WARP,
    PICKER, HARNESS,
    BEAM, ROLLER, SLEY,

    CAAM, EASER, BATTEN,
    HEALD
  remnant ··•··•··· THRUM
loon ··•··•··•· DIVER, GREBE,
    (DIVING)BIRD, LOUT, DOLT
  archaic ··•··•··· SERVANT,
    SCAMP, ROGUE
  Scottish ··•··•··•· BOY
loony ··•··•·· CRAZY, LUNY,
    DEMENTED, DAFT
loop ··•·• TAB, BRIDE, TERRY,
    CIRCUIT, EYE(LET), RING,
  NOOSE, PICOT, LAP, FOLIUM,
    GROMMET
  edging ··•··•·•· PICOT
  in electricity ··•· CIRCUIT
  in lace ··•··•··•· PICOT
  in lariat ··•·••··· HONDOO
  in physics ··•·•· ANTINODE
  like structure ··•·• ANSA
  of rope, nautical ··•··•·•·
    PARREL, PARRAL
  on boot/garment ··· TAG
  on lace's edge ··•·• PURL
  rope ··•··•· BIGHT, NOOSE
  running ··•··•··•·•· NOOSE
  thread's ··•··•··•· EYE
looper ··· (MEASURING)WORM,
    LARVA
loophole ··•··•· PLEA, ESCAPE,
    EYELET, JOKER, M(E)USE
loops, edge with ··•··•· PURL
Loos, writer ··•··•··•·· ANITA
loose ··•··•· FREE, AT LARGE,
  UNBOUND, INEXACT, LEWD,
  UNBIND, (RE)LAX, RELEASE
  cut ··•··•··· FREE, UNTIE,
    ESCAPE
  end ··•··•··•··· TAGRAG
  jointed ··•··•·· LIMBER,
    LANKY
  let ··•··•··•··•· RELEASE
  set/turn ··•· RELEASE, FREE
  tongued ··•· TALKATIVE
  woman ··•··•·· WANTON
loosen ··•··•· SLACKEN, UNTIE,
  RELEASE, FREE, RELAX,
  EASE, UNDO
loot ··•··•·· PLUNDER, RIFLE,
  SPOILS, DESPOIL, PILLAGE,
  BOOTY, (RAN)SACK
lop ··•· TRIM, CUT OFF, SNIP,
  HANG, LOLL, PRUNE, POLL,
  CHOP, SNED, SNATHE
lope of sorts ··•··•·· CANTER
lopobranch ··•··•·· SEA HORSE

loppy .... DROOPING
lopsided .... UNEVEN,
    UNBALANCED, ASKEW,
    ALIST, ALOP
loquacious ...... TALKATIVE,
    GARRULOUS, VOLUBLE
    bird ...... JAY, MAGPIE
    opposite .... TACITURN,
        RETICENT
loquacity ...... GARRULITY,
    LERESIS, TALKATIVENESS
loquitur ...... HE/SHE SPEAKS
loran, part of ... LONG, RANGE,
    NAVIGATION
lord ..... SEIGNOR, SEIGNEUR,
    LIEGE, PEER, EARL, RULER,
    MASTER, NOBLEMAN,
    DOMINEER, BARON, RULE,
    BISHOP, VISCOUNT, MARQUIS
    companion of ... MASTER
    humorous usage ....
        HUSBAND
    Marmion's horse ... BEVIS
    of Hosts .. JEHOVAH, GOD
    privileged ..... PALATINE
    Scottish .... LAIRD
    the .... GOD
    wife of .... LADY
Lord's Day....... SUNDAY
    land ... DEMESNE, MANOR
    manor .... DEMESNE
    Prayer, first word(s) .....
        PATERNOSTER,
        OUR FATHER
    Supper ....
        HOLY COMMUNION,
        EUCHARIST
lordly .... OVERBEARING,
    HAUGHTY, NOBLE
lordship ..... RULE, DOMINION
lore .... WISDOM, ERUDITION,
    LEARNING, KNOWLEDGE
    creature with ..... BIRD,
        SNAKE
Lorelei .... SIREN, LURLEI
    golden possession of ....
        COMB
    victims of .... SAILORS,
        MARINERS
Lorenz, ethologist ... KONRAD
lorgnette .... LORGNON,
    EYEGLASSES, OPERA GLASS
lorgnon .... MONOCLE,
    PINCENEZ, LORGNETTE
lorica ... CARAPACE, LORLEA,
    SHELL, CORSELET, CUIRASS

lorikeet .... PARROT, LORY
loris .... LEMUR
lorn .... FORSAKEN, DESOLATE,
    BEREFT
Lorna, heroine ...... DOONE
    Doone author ....
        BLACKMORE
    Doone character ... RIDD
lorry .... TRUCK, WAGON
lory ..... PARROT, LORIKEET
Lortzing's opera .... UNDINE
Los Angeles football team ....
    RAMS
    suburb ...... TORRANCE,
        LYNWOOD
lose .... MISPLACE, MISS,
    FORFEIT, MISLAY, WASTE,
    SQUANDER
    ardor .... PALL
    color ...... FADE, PALE,
        WHITEN
    footing .... SLIP
    forward speed .... STALL
    one's head ...... PANIC
    one's way ...... WILDER
    purposely .... THROW
loser, poor/bad .... CRYBABY,
    SOREHEAD
loss .... FORFEITURE,
    DEPRIVATION, DEFEAT,
    DECREMENT, PERDITION
    at a .... PUZZLED
        BEWILDERED
    cause of, sometimes .....
        LEAKAGE, SPILLAGE
    compensation for ....
        SOLATIUM
    describing one ....
        IRREPARABLE
    from container ....
        SPILLAGE, LEAKAGE
    gambling, ultimate ......
        SHIRT
    of consciousness ....
        SYNCOPE, SYNCOPATION
    of feeling .... INSENSATE,
        ANESTHESIA
    of hair .... ALOPECIA
    of memory .... AMNESIA
    of mental power ....
        DEMENTIA
    of reading ability ....
        ALEXIA
    of sense of smell ....
        ANOSMIA

of speech ..... APHASIA, ALALIA
of the soul ... PERDITION
of voice .... APHONIA
of will power .. AB(O)ULIA
unexpected ...... UPSET
lost — MISLAID, GONE, MISSING, WASTED, BEWILDERED, RUINED, ENGROSSED
 animal .... STRAY
 Horizon author .. HILTON
 Horizon, site of ....
  SHANGRI-LA
 often, figuratively .. SHIRT
lot ..... SHARE, BUNCH, FATE, PARCEL, SCAD, RAFT, SLEW, SLUB, CABOODLE, DESTINY, FORTUNE, PORTION, PLOT, GRIST
 city of .... ZOAR
 colloquial .... SORT
 father of .... HARAN
 feast of .... PURIM
 uncle of ..... ABRAHAM
 sister of .... MILCAH
 son of .... MOAB
loth ... HATE, DETEST, ABHOR
Lothario .... RAKE, SEDUCER
Loti, Pierre .... VIAUD
lotion ... COLOGNE, OINTMENT, FRESHENER, CALAMINE
lots .... MUCH, PLENTY
 divination by .. SORTILEGE
 of something .. HEAP, PILE
lottery ...... GAME, CHANCE, TOMBOLA, DRAWING,
 kin ...... RAFFLE, KENO, NUMBERS, BINGO, LOTTO
 ticket .... BLANK
 winning ... PRIZE, TERN
lotto kin .... BINGO, KENO
lotus ...... NELUMBO, SHRUB, HERB, WATER LILY, CHINQUAPIN, LOTE, SADR
 enzyme .... LOTASE
 tree ...... JUJUBE, SADR
loud ...... NOISY, CLAMOROUS, INSISTENT, VIVID, FLASHY, SHOWY
 colloquial ...... VULGAR, UNREFINED
 in music .... FORTE
 speaker ...... AMPLIFIER, WOOFER, TWEETER, MONITOR

loudmouthed ... THERSITICAL, BLATANT, STENTORIAN
 person ...... STENTOR, THERSITES
lough .... LAKE
Louis of trumpet fame ......
  PRIMA
 XIII's minister ....
  RICHELIEU
Louiseville event ...... DERBY
Louisiana .. PELICAN (STATE)
 boat .... BATEAU
 capital of — BATON ROUGE
 city ...... SHREVEPORT, MONROE, NEW ORLEANS
 county .... PARISH, WINN, CADDO, ACADIA
 farmer ...... HABITAN(T)
 land measure ... ARPENT
 native .... CREOLE, ACADIAN, CAJUN, CAIJAN
 Negro patois ..... GUMBO
 nickname ..... PELICAN, CREOLE, SUGAR
 patois .... CREOLE
 parish .... ACADIA
 river .... AMITE
 state bird ...... PELICAN
 state flower .. MAGNOLIA
 tobacco .... PERIQUE
lounge — LOAF, LOITER, LOLL, COUCH, SOFA, DIVAN, SETTEE, LAZE, LOBBY
lounger .... IDLER, LOAFER
lounging suit .... PAJAMAS
loup .... (HALF)MASK
 garou .... WEREWOLF
lour .. LOWER, FROWN, SCOWL
Lourdes miracle .... CURE
Lourenco ____, Mozambique capital .... MARQUES
louse .... NIT, APHID, INSECT, PARASITE, COOTIE, SLATER, RAT
 plural of .... LICE
 up ...... BUNGLE, SPOIL, BOTCH
lousy .... DIRTY, DISGUSTING, INFERIOR, POOR, PEDICULAR, PEDICULOUS
lout .... GAWK, APE, HOB, LOOBY, BOOR, LOB, LOON, BUMPKIN
 archaic ... CURTSY, BOW, STOOP, BEND

louver ..... LANTERN, TURRET, WINDOW, SLAT, TRANSOM
lovage .... PARSLEY
love .... AMO(R), GRA, AFFECTION, LIKING, SWEETHEART, ATTACHMENT, DOTE, WOO, ENAMOR
  affair ... AMOUR, LIAISON, INTRIGUE, ROMANCE
  apple .... TOMATO
  feast .... AGAPE
  foolish .... INFATUATION
  foolishly .... DOTE
  full of .. EROTIC, AMATIVE
  god of ... AMOR, CUPID, EROS
  goddess of ...... FREYA, VENUS
  in .... ENAMORED
  in tennis .... ZERO
  knot .... AMORET
  letter ..... BILLET-DOUX
  lies-bleeding ..... PLANT, AMARANTH
  lightly ...... PHILANDER
  make ...... WOO, COURT
  note .... VALENTINE
  of country .. PATRIOTISM
  of fine arts ...... VIRTU
  potion .... PHILTER, PHILTRE
  pertaining to ... EROTIC, AMATORY
  seat .... SOFA
  set, in tennis ... SIX-ZERO
  song .. SERENA, SERENADE
  story .... ROMANCE
lovebird .... PARROT
lover ... BEAU, SWAIN, ROMEO, LEMAN, SPARK, SWEETHEART, FLAME, MINION, PARAMOUR
  boy .... AMORIST
  silly .... SPOONER
lovers' lane frequenters ...... SWEETHEARTS, TRYSTERS
  meeting .... TRYST
  song .. SERENADE, SERENA
loving ... AMOROUS, AMATIVE, EROTIC, DOTING, FOND, DEVOTED, AMATORY
  combining form .. PHILE
  cup .... TIG, TROPHY
low .... MENIAL, SCURVY, SCALY, MOO, ORRA, SHALLOW, DEEP, WEAK, HUMBLE, COARSE, VULGAR, INFERIOR, VILE, BASE, POOR
  birth-weight infant ...... PREEMIE
  bow .... CURTSY
  brow .... PLEBEIAN
  comedy ..... HORSEPLAY, FARCE, BURLESQUE, SLAPSTICK
  country .... BELGIUM, NETHERLANDS, LUXEMBURG
  down: colloq. .... MEAN, DESPICABLE
  down: sl. .... FACTS, DOPE, INFO(RMATION)
  lay .... KILL, HIDE
  necked ..... DECOLLETE
lowan .... LEIPOA, MALLEE
lowbred .... COARSE, VULGAR, CRUDE, ILL-MANNERED, BASE
Lowell, poet ... AMY, ROBERT
lower ... DIP, DEBASE, DEMIT, NETHER, DEMOTE, SCOWL, LOUR, GLOWER, FROWN, VAIL, LOOM, INFERIOR, REDUCE, WEAKEN, ABASE
  Alsace .... BAS-RHIN
  California capital ...... LAPAZ, MEXICALI
  Canada ...... QUEBEC
  classman .... FRESHMAN, SOPHOMORE
  House member .... REPRESENTATIVE
  in architecture ..... VAIL
  in geology ..... EARLIER
  in rank .. JUNIOR, PUISNE
  in value .... DEBASE, DEPRECIATE
  on one side ... LOPSIDED
  World ..... HELL, SHEOL, HADES, EARTH, DIS
  World gods ..... MANES
lowering .. OVERCAST, CLOUDY, FROWNING
lowery ... OVERCAST, CLOUDY
lowest .... LOWERMOST, MEANEST, LAST
  animal life ..... AM(O)EBA
  deck .... ORLOP
  form of wit .... PUN
  part .... BOTTOM
  point .... NADIR, NETHERMOST, BOTTOM
  point of planet's orbit ... PERIGEE

Lowin role .... HAMLET
lowland .... HOLM, PLAIN
Lowlander ...... SASSENACH
Lowlands dialect ..... LALLAN
lowly .... HUMBLE, MEEK(LY),
　　　　　　　　　HUMBLY
lox .... SALMON, OXYGEN
loxia .... WRYNECK
loyal ...... LEAL, STA(U)NCH,
　　　　TRUE, FAITHFUL, DEVOTED
　　friend .... ACHATES,
　　　　　　　　　DAMON
　　wife .... PENELOPE
loyalty ..... FIDELITY, FEALTY,
　　　HOMAGE, ALLEGIANCE,
　　　　　　　　　TROTH
lozenge ... CATECHU, CACHOU,
　　　JUJUBE, MASCLE,
　　PEPPERMINT, PASTIL(LE),
　　TROCHE, DIAMOND, CANDY,
　　COUGH DROP, RHOMB
LP .... LONG PLAY(ING)
LSD source .... ERGOT
　　term .... ACID, TRIP,
　　　　　　　　TURN ON
lu, in chemistry ... LUTETIUM
Luanda is capital of .. ANGOLA
luau .... FEAST
　　dish .... POI
lubber ... LOOBY, LOB, SAILOR
lube .... OIL, LUBRICANT
Lublin extermination camp ...
　　　　　　　　MAIDENEK
lubricating oil .... LUBE
lubricant .. OIL, GREASE, DOPE,
　　　　CASTOR, VASELINE
lubricate .... OIL, GREASE,
　　　　　　　SMOOTHEN
lubricator ...... OILER, DOPER
lubricous .... SLIPPERY
Lucan's work .... PHARSALIA
luce .... PIKE, FISH
Luce (Clare Booth) estate ....
　　　　　　　　HALENAIA
lucent .... SHINING
Lucern(e) .. FODDER, ALFALFA,
　　CANTON, LAKE, MEDIC
luces .... LIGHTS
　　singular of .... LUX
Lucian the _____ .... SKEPTIC
lucid .... BRIGHT, SANE,
　　CLEAR(HEADED), SHINING,
　　RATIONAL, TRANSPARENT,
　　　　　　　LUCULENT
lucida .... STAR

lucidity ... SANITY, CLARITY,
　　CLEARNESS, TRANSPARENCY
Lucifer .. DEVIL, MATCH, SATAN
　　poetic .... VENUS
lucite .... RESIN
luck .... FORTUITY, HAP, LOT,
　　FORTUNE, FATE, CHANCE
　　bad .... DEUCE, WANION,
　　HOODOO, JINX, CESS,
　　　　　　　　　ACE
　　of .... ALEATORY
　　of Roaring Camp author..
　　　　　　　　　HARTE
luckily .... HAPLY,
　　　　　　FORTUNATELY
lucky .... CANNY, WITCH,
　　　　　　FORTUNATE
　　piece .... AMULET
　　stroke .... FLUKE
lucrative ...... FAT, PAYING,
　　PROFITABLE, GAINFUL,
　　　　REMUNERATIVE
lucre ..... PELF, EMOLUMENT,
　　PROFIT, MONEY, RICHES
　　descriptive word for .....
　　　　　　　　　FILTHY
Lucrezia _____, poisoner .....
　　　　　　　　　BORGIA
lucule .... SUNSPOT
luculent .... LUCID, CLEAR
ludicrous .... FARCICAL,
　　ABSURD, RIDICULOUS,
　　COMIC(AL), LAUGHABLE
Ludwig, biographer .... EMIL
lues .... SYPHILIS
luetic .... SYPHILITIC
Luftwaffe divebomber .. STUKA
　　leader .... GOERING
lug ...... EAR, DRAG, CARRY,
　　PULL, HAUL, TOW
luggage ...... BAGGAGE, TAN,
　　　　BAGS, TRAPS
　　carrier .... PORTER
　　item .... SUITCASE,
　　　　VALISE, TRUNK
lugger .... VESSEL, TOTER,
　　　　　　　　FALCON
lugubrious ... SAD, MOURNFUL,
　　DOLEFUL, DISMAL
lugworm .... ANNELID
Luik .... LIEGE
Luish .... LUWIAN
Luke .... EVANGELIST
lukewarm .... TEPID,
　　　　　INDIFFERENT
lull .... MITIGATE, CALM,

SOOTHE, ALLAY, QUIET, RESPITE, ROCK, HUSH, SLACK
lullaby ...... (CRADLE)SONG, BERCEUSE
lulu: sl. ⇁ ONER, OUTSTANDING, WHIZ
lumbago ⇁⇁⇁ BACKACHE, RHEUMATISM
lumber ⇁⇁ CLUTTER, BOARDS, RUMBLE, WOOD
British .... TIMBER
dressing machine .... TRIMMER
marker .... KEEL
lumberjack .... LOGGER, WOODCUTTER, JACKET, SAWYER
blanket of ... MACKINAW
climbing iron of .... SPUR
warning cry .... TIMBER
lumberman .... LOGGER, SAWYER, GIRDLER, HEWER
boot of ..... PAC, OVER, LARRIGAN
hook of ⇁⇁⇁ PEAV(E)Y, PEEV(E)Y
lodging of .... CAMP
tool of .. AXE, ADZE, SAW
sled .... TRAVOIS
lumbricoid ..... ROUNDWORM
lumen .... LUX
luminal .... SEDATIVE, HYPNOTIC, PHENOBARBITAL
luminary ... STAR, SUN, MOON
luminescence ... COLD LIGHT
luminous .... BRIGHT
energy .... LIGHT
radiation .... AURA
lummox .... LOUT, LOON, LOOBY, LUBBER, DUNCE, LUNKHEAD, DUMBBELL
lump .... WAD, CLOT, NUB(BIN), MASS, NODE, SWAD, HUNK, BURL, HUNCH, KNOT, GOB(BET), BAT, NODULE, DOMINO, SWELLING, COLLECTION, NUGGET, NUBBLE
butter ⇁⇁⇁⇁ PAT
clay .... CLOD
of earth .... CLOD
round, small ..... BOLUS, KNOB
lumper ⇁⇁⇁⇁ STEVEDORE, DOCKER

lumpish ⇁⇁⇁ DULL, STUPID' HEAVY
lumpy ..... CLUMSY, KNOBBY
Lumumba, Congo premier .... PATRICE
Luna ⇁⇁⇁⇁ SELENE, MOON
in alchemy .... SILVER
lunacy ⇁⇁⇁ MADNESS, MANIA, INSANITY
lunar ⇁⇁⇁⇁ PALLID, PALE, CRESCENT-SHAPED
crater .... LINNE
month ...... LUNATION, MOON
phenomenon ⇁⇁ ECLIPSE
spaceship .... APOLLO
lunate ..... CRESCENT-SHAPED, LUNAR
lunatic ..... INSANE, MADMAN
lunch(eon) ⇁⇁⇁⇁ SNACK, DEJEUNER, BITE, REFECTION, TIFFIN, MEAL
lune ⇁⇁⇁⇁ LEASH, LUNULA
lung disease ⇁ TUBERCULOSIS, CONSUMPTION, PHTHISIS, SILICOSIS, TB, SIDEROSIS
membrane ... PLEURA
pus-filled cavity ⇁ VOMICA
sound .... RALE
lunge ⇁⇁⇁ THRUST, LONGE, LEAP, FOIN, PASSADO
lungee ⇁⇁ LUNGI, LOINCLOTH
lunger ⇁⇁⇁⇁ TUBERCULAR, CONSUMPTIVE
lungfish ⇁⇁⇁⇁⇁ DIPNOAN, MUDFISH
lungi .... LOINCLOTH
lungs used as food ⇁⇁ LIGHTS
lungwort .... LICHEN
lunkhead ⇁⇁ DUMBBELL, LOON, DUNCE, LUMMOX
lunt ⇁⇁⇁⇁⇁ MATCH, KINDLE, TORCH, SMOKE
lunula ⇁⇁⇁⇁ LUNE, LUNULE
lunule ..... LUNE, HALFMOON
luny .... LOONY
Lupercus .... FAUNUS
Lupin, thief .... ARSENE
lupine .... WOLFLIKE, PLANTRAVENOUS, WOLFISH
animal ⇁⇁⇁⇁ WOLF
Lupino, actress .... IDA
Lupus .. WOLF, CONSTELLATION
lurch ⇁⇁ ROLL, PITCH, SWAY, CHEAT, LURK

lurcher ..... THIEF, POACHER, (HUNTING)DOG
lure .... ATTRACT, TEMPT, ENTICE, DECOY, INVEIGLE, BEGUILE, BAIT, FLY, SPINNER, TREPAN, SEDUCE, INDUCE(MENT)
lurer .... SIREN, SEDUCER, BAITER, DECOY, TEMPTRESS
lurid ..... RED, SENSATIONAL, STARTLING, GLOWING, GARISH, VIVID
lurk .... SKULK, SNEAK, PROWL
Lurlei .... LORELEI, SIREN
luscious ... DELICIOUS, TASTY, SWEET, CLOYING
lush ..... JUICY, SUCCULENT, LUXURIANT
Lusitania, now .... PORTUGAL
lust .... DESIRE, APPETITE
luster ..... SCHILLER, SHEEN, GLORY, GLOSS, RADIANCE, BRILLIANCE, LUSTRUM, REFLET, NAIF, SHINE, GLAZE, POLISH
lusterless .... DULL, WAN, DRAB, MAT(TE)
lustful .... LEWD, SENSUAL, RANDY
lustrate .... PURIFY
lustring .... LUTESTRING, SILK CLOTH
lustrous ... NACREOUS, NITID, SILKY, SHINING, RADIANT, SATINY, GLOSSY, BRILLIANT
lustrum .... FIVE-YEAR(PERIOD), LUSTER
lusty .... ROBUST, STURDY, STRONG, VIGOROUS
lute ...... CEMENT, SEAL, CLAY, INSTRUMENT
composer for the .... LUTANIST, LUTENIST
obsolete ...... THEORBO
oriental .... TAR
relative of ...... GUITAR, MANDOLIN, ASOR, PANDORE, UKELELE
lutestring .... LUSTRING
Lutetia .... PARIS
Luther, theologian ... MARTIN
Lutheran .... PROTESTANT
luthern .... DORMER, WINDOW
Luwian .... LUISH

luting .... CEMENT
lux .... LUMEN, LIGHT
luxate .. DISLOCATE, DISJOINT
luxe .... ELEGANCE, RICHNESS
Luxemb(o)urg capital .. ARLON
luxuriant .... RANK, FERTILE, LUSH, PROFUSE
luxuriate .... BASK, WALLOW
luxurious ...... TONY, RICH, PLUSH, POSH
luxury-lover ...... SYBARITE, LUCULLUS
Luzon battlesite ..... BATAAN, MANILA BAY, CORREGIDOR
city ... PASAY, CALOOCAN, DAGUPAN, QUEZON, MANILA, CAVITE, ANGELES, LAOAG, OLONGAPO
island .... MINDORO, CORREGIDOR, LUBANG
falls .... PAGSANJAN
mountain ...... ARAYAT, CORDILLERA, CARBALLO, ZAMBALES
mountain capital .... BAGUIO
mountain people .... IGOROTS
native ... NEGRITO, AETA
peninsula ..... BONDOC, BICOL
people of .... BICOLANOS, PAMPANGOS, TAGALOGS, ILOCANOS, ZAMBALENOS
province .... TARLAC, PAMPANGA, QUEZON, BULACAN, PANGASINAN, BATAAN, ABRA, CAGAYAN, BATANGAS
rare animal .... TAMARAU
volcano ..... TAAL, MAYON
walled city .. INTRAMUROS
water buffalo .. CARABAO
wild buffalo ... TAMARAU
world wonder .... RICE TERRACES
Lwow .... LVOV, LEMBERG
lycanthrope ..... WEREWOLF
lycanthropy, product of .... WOLF
lycee .... (SECONDARY)SCHOOL
lyceum ...... LECTURE HALL, LYCEE
Lycian city .... MYRA
king .... SARPEDON
leader .... PANDARUS

lycopod .... CLUB MOSS
Lydia, capital of .... SARDIS
Lydian .... EFFEMINATE,
    GENTLE, SENSUAL,
    VOLUPTUOUS
  king .... CROESUS
  language .... ANATOLIC
lye .. LIXIVIUM, BUCK, CAUSTIC
  soak in ..... BATE, BUCK
  source of ... (WOOD)ASHES
lying .... MENDACIOUS,
    DECUMBENT, FALSE,
    DISHONEST, RECLINING,
    RECUMBENT
  downward ..... PRONE,
    PRONATED, ACUMBENT,
    DECUMBENT
  flat .... PROSTRATE
  on one's back .. SUPINE
  under oath ..... PERJURY
lymph .... HUMOR, SERUM,
    SPRING, WATER
  and fats .... CHYLE
  gland swelling ..... BUBO
  vessel .... VARIX
lymphatic .... PLASMIC,
    SLUGGISH
  glands tuberculosis ......
    SCROFULA
  vessels .... LACTEAL
lymphoid tissue back of mouth
    TONSIL
lyncean .... KEEN-EYED
  animal .... LYNX
lynching, usual end of ....
    HANGING

lynx ... CARACAL, WILDCAT,
    BOBCAT, CONSTELLATION,
    CARCAJOU, CATAMOUNT,
    PISHU
  fur .... CARACAL
  of a .... LYNCEAN
Lyra .. HARP, CONSTELLATION
lyre .... HARP, TRIGON
  like instrument .... ASOR,
    CITHARA, SACKBUT
  shaped .... LYRATE,
    LYRIFORM
  player .... LYRIST
lyrebird .... MENURA
lyric .... LIED, SONGLIKE,
    MELIC; ALBA
  muse .... ERATO
  ode .... EPODE
  poem .... MELIC,
    RONDEAU, SONNET,
    ELEGY, HYMN, ODE,
    RONDEL, CANZONE,
    EPODE
  poet .... ODIST, LYRIST,
    SAPPHO, MINSTREL
  solo .... MONODY
lyrics of opera/oratorio ......
    LIBRETTO
lyriform .... LYRATE
lysin .... ANTIBODY
  of .... LYTIC
lysol .... ANTISEPTIC,
    DISINFECTANT
  constituent ..... SOAP,
    CRESOL
lytic .... LYSIN
lytta .... WORM

M

M, Greek .... MU
  letter .... EM(MA)
ma .... MOTHER, MAMMA
  chere .... MY DEAR
Maas .... MEUSE
mabolo .... PLUM
macabre .... GHASTLY, GRIM,
    LURID, GRUESOME, HORRIBLE,
    EERIE
  part of a title .... DANSE
macaco .... LEMUR, MONKEY,
    MACAQUE
macadam ..... ROAD, STONES
  material .. TAR, ASPHALT
Macao coin .... AVO
  island .. TAIPA, COLOANE

MacArthur, general ....
    ARTHUR, DOUGLAS
macaque ..... KRA, RHESUS,
    MACACO, MONKEY,
    WANDEROO
macaroni .... DANDY
  flour paste like ....
    SPAGHETTI
  ingredient .... SEMOLINA,
    DURUM
  strip .... LASAGNA
macaroon .. COOKY, RATAFIA,
    BISCUIT
Macassar .... MALAYAN
Macau island .... TAIPA,
    COLOANE

macaw .. ARA(RA), MARACAN, PARROT
"Macbeth" character ....
.... DUNCAN, ROSS, BANQUO, HECATE, MACDUFF
maccaboy .... SNUFF
mace .. STAFF, STICK, CLUB, SPICE, MAUL
 bearer .. BEADLE, MACER
 reed .... DOD
 royal .... SCEPTRE
 source of ...... NUTMEG
 wielder .... KNIGHT
macedoine .. SALAD, MEDLEY
Macedonia capital .... PELIA, SKOPJE
 city ..... BEREA, EDESSA, PYDNA
 region .... PIERIA
 seaport ...... SALONIKA
macer .... BEADLE
macerate .... STEEP, SOFTEN, RET, TORMENT, WASTE AWAY, SOAK
Mach, physicist ...... ERNST
machete .... KNIFE, BOLO
Machiavelli, Florentine ......
.... NICCOLO
Machiavellian ...... CRAFTY, DECEITFUL
machina, ___ ...... DEUS EX
machinate ...... PLOT, PLAN, SCHEME, DEVISE
machination(s) ...... DESIGN, ARTIFICE, INTRIGUE, CABAL, PLOT, SCHEME
machine ...... MOTOR, TOOL, AUTOMATON, ENGINE, MECHANISM, DEVICE, GADGET
 cloth smoothing ....
.... MANGLE
 cotton-cleaning .... GIN
 crushing .... PRESS, MILL
 cutting .... CROPPER
 duplicating ..... RONEO, XEROX
 finishing .... EDGER
 flying .... AIRPLANE, AIRCRAFT
 glazing ...... CALENDER
 grass-cutting ...... MOW
 grass-spreading .. TEDDER
 grinding .... MILL
 gun ...... GATLING, BREN, STEN, MAXIM, POM POM
 gunner .... MITRAILLEUR

 gunner's post ..... NEST
 hoisting ..... GIN, CRAB
 nap-raising .. TEASEL(LER)
 ore-dressing .... VANNER
 part .. CRANK, SOLENOID, GEAR, COG, CAM, ROTOR, PISTON, VALVE, PAWL
 parts adjusting device ...
.... TRAMMEL
 political .... PARTY
 printing .... PRESS
 repairer ...... MECHANIC
 shearing ...... CROPPER
 spinning .... MULE
 threshing ..... COMBINE
 tool .... LATHE
 weaving .... LOOM
 weighing .... TRONE
 wood-turning .... LATHE
machinist's groove .... TSLOT
machree .... MY HEART
Mack, of baseball .... CONNIE
Mackenzie river tributary ....
.... LIARD
mackerel .... TUNA, FISH, SCOMBROID, SAUREL, BONITO, ALBACORE
 cured .... BLOATER
 like fish .... CERO, SCAD, SIERRA, PINTADO, PLAINTAIL, TUNNY, CAVALLA, BESHOW
 net .... SPILLER
 of the ..... SCOMBROID
 young .... SPIKE, TINKER
Mackinaw .. BLANKET, COAT, BOAT
 trout ...... NAMAYCUSH
Mackintosh .... RAINCOAT
mackle .. BLUR, MACULE, BLOT
MacLeish, poet .. ARCHIBALD
macrocosm .... UNIVERSE, WORLD
macrural crustacean .. PRAWN, SHRIMP, LOBSTER
maculate ..... STAIN, DEFILE, IMPURE, SPECKLE, SPOT(TED), BLOTCH
macule .... BLUR, BLOT
mad ... INSANE, SORE, RABID, CRAZY, FRANTIC, FRENZIED, IRATE, FRENETIC, SENSELESS, ANGRY, FURIOUS
 monk .... RASPUTIN
Madagascar animal .. LEMUR,

TENREC, TENDRAC, AYEAYE, TEMEE
civet .... FOSSA
fiber .... RAFFIA
lemur .. INDRI(S), AYEAYE
native .... HOVA
palm tree ...... RAFFIA
tribe .. HOVA, MALAGASY
madam ...... LADY, WOMAN, MISTRESS, MILADY
Italian .... MADONNA
"Madame Butterfly" composer PUCCINI
name of .. CIO-CIO (SAN)
madame, English equivalent .. MRS
Spanish .... SENORA, SRA
madcap .... RASH, IMPULSIVE, RECKLESS, HOTSPUR
madden ... INCENSE, ENRAGE, ANGER
madder .... VINE, CRIMSON, PLANT, DYE, ALIZARIN(E), COFFEE, RUBIA, GARDENIA, IPECAC, EVEA, CHINCHONA
made .... SUCCESSFUL, INVENTED, CONSTRUCTED
of wood .... XYLOID
to order .. CUSTOM-BUILT
up ... INVENTED, FALSE, FABRICATED, COSMETIZED
Madeira ... WINE, ISLAND, RIVER
capital .... FUNCHAL
Island wind ...... LESTE
town .... FUNCHAL
wine .... TINTA
mademoiselle .... LADY, MISS, WOMAN, GIRL
abbreviation .... MLLE
madhouse ... BEDLAM, CHAOS, BABEL, ASYLUM
madman ... LUNATIC, MANIAC
madness .. FRENZY, DEMENTIA, FURY, MANIA, DELIRATION, FOLLY, RABIES, RAGE, LUNACY
fits of .... LUNES
kind of .... INFATUATION
Madonna .... MARY
madras .... KERCHIEF, CLOTH
city .... CALICUT, SALEM
state .... COCHIN, TRAVANCORE
state, part of .. CARNATIC

weight .... POLLAM
madre .... MOTHER
madrepore .... CORAL
formation .. ATOLL, REEF
Madrid boulevard/park/ museum ...... PRADO
madrigal .. POEM, SONG, GLEE
Madrileno ...... SPANIARD
madrona .. EVERGREEN, BERRY
madwort .... ALYSSUM, SHRUB
Mae West ...... LIFEBELT, LIFE-PRESERVER
maelstrom ...... WHIRLPOOL
maenad .. NYMPH, BACCHANTE
maestro .... TEACHER, CONDUCTOR, COMPOSER, MASTER
Mafeking native .... BOER
Maffei work ... --- MEROPE
maf(f)ia .. BLACK HAND
nemesis of .. FEDS, NARCO
magazine ..... STORE(HOUSE), WAREHOUSE, DEPOT, PUBLICATION, PERIODICAL, JOURNAL
classy .... SLICK
content .... MUNITION(S), AMMO
inferior .... PULP
leaves .... SHEETS
part of .... SPREAD
work .... JOURNALISM
Magdalen college scholar .... DEMY
mage .... WIZARD, MAGICIAN
Magellan, navigator .... FERDINAND
ship of .... VICTORIA, TRINIDAD, SANTIAGO
magenta .. FUCHSIN, DYE, RED
maggot .. GRUB, LARVA, WHIM, NOTION, MAWK, BOT(T)
bluebottle fly ... GENTLE
Magi ... BALTHASAR, MAGUS, MELCHIOR, GASPAR
magic .... OBEAH, ART, GRAMARY(E), WITCHCRAFT, WIZARDRY, THEURGY, THEURGIC, RUNE, JUJU, CONJURATION
black .. VOODOO, SORCERY
formula .. ABRACADABRA
hammer, owner of ...... THOR
horse .... BAYARD
image .... SIGIL

lamp finder ... ALADDIN
Mountain author ... MANN
potion .... PHILTER, PHILTRE
practice .... CONJURE
sign .... SIGIL
spell ..... CONJURATION, ABRACADABRA, CANTRIP
symbol .... PENTACLE
word .... SESAME
magical .... RUNIC, HERMETIC
herb .... MOLY
piece ... CHARM, AMULET
magician .. WARLOCK, MAGE, MERLIN, HOUDINI, MAGUS, MEDICINE MAN, SHAMAN, MAGI(AN), WIZARD, SORCERER, THEURGIST, KLINGSOR, CONJURER, ARCHIMAGE
device of ..... GIMMICK
skill of .... SLEIGHT OF HAND, LEGERDEMAIN
stick of .... WAND
talk of .... PATTER
tricks of .. LEGERDEMAIN, HOCUS-POCUS
word of .... PRESTO
Magindanao .... MORO
Maginot line, opposed to .... LIMES, SIEGFRIED
magisterial ..... MASTERFUL, POMPOUS
magistral .... IMPERIOUS
magistrate .. JUDGE, JUSTICE, CADI
Athenian .... ARCHON
civil .... SYNDIC
Genoese/Venetian ...... DOGE
Greek .... EPHOR
Roman ...... DUUMVIR, PR(A)ETOR
Spanish .. ALCALDE, JUEZ
town .... REEVE
magnanimous ...... GENEROUS
magnate ... BIGWIG, TYCOON, MOGUL, NABOB
magnesia .... ANTACID, LAXATIVE
magnesium silicate .... TALC
magnet .... LOADSTONE, LODESTONE
alloy .... ALNICO

end .... POLE
magnetic ...... ATTRACTIVE, MESMERIC, ELECTRIC
direction .. NORTH, SOUTH
flux, unit of .. MAXWELL, WEBER
force .... OD, ODYL(E)
resistance .... RELUCTANCE
magnetism ...... MESMERISM, ATTRACTION, ALLURE
magnetite .... LOADSTONE
magneto .... DYNAMO
magnific .... POMPOUS, GRANDILOQUENT, IMPOSING
magnificat ...... HYMN, SONG, POEM
magnificence .. STATE, POMP, SPLENDOR, GLORY, GRANDEUR
magnificent .. GRAND, STATELY
array .... PANOPLY
magnify .... ENLARGE, EXALT, EXAGGERATE
magnifying instrument .... TELESCOPE, MICROSCOPE
magniloquent ...... POMPOUS, LOFTY, GRANDIOSE, BOMBASTIC
magnitude ..... SIZE, EXTENT
magnolia .... SHRUB, FLOWER, SWEET BAY
state .... MISSISSIPPI
magnum .... BOTTLE
opus .... WORK, MASTERPIECE
magnus hitch .... KNOT
magpie .. PIET, CROW, MAG(G), PICA
kin .... JAY
Latin .... PICA
maguey .. ALOE, AGAVE, FIBER
magus .. SORCERER, MAGICIAN, ASTROLOGER
Magyar .... HUNGARIAN
Magyarorszag ..... HUNGARY
maharaja's wife .. MAHARANI, MAHARANEE
Mahatma, famous ... GANDHI
Mahdi follower ..... DERVISH
Mahican .... MOHEGAN
mahjongg playing piece ...... TILE
wind ..... NORTH, EAST, SOUTH, WEST
mahogany ..... (HARD)WOOD,

TOON, TREE, CAOBA,
BAYWOOD, NARRA
of the ...... MELIACEOUS
pine .... TOTARA
Mahomet ...... MOHAMMED,
PROPHET
burial place of .. MEDINA
Mahound .. DEVIL, MOHAMMED
Mahren .... MORAVIA
Maia .... PLEIADE, MAY
maid ... VIRGIN, FILLE, LASS,
WENCH, GIRL, DOMESTIC,
SLAVEY
lady's .... ABIGAIL
of Astolat ...... ELAINE
of Orleans ....
JOAN OF ARC
old .... SPINSTER, TABBY
servant .... BONNE,
SOUBRETTE
maiden .. VIRGIN, GUILLOTINE,
UNMARRIED, NEW, FRESH,
FIRST, DAMOSEL, NYMPH,
DAMSEL, LASS, COLLEEN
appearance ...... DEBUT,
INTRODUCTION
changed to heifer .... IO
changed to spider ......
ARACHNE
in song .... CHLOE
name .... NEE
maidenhair .... FERN, GINKO
maidenhead ..... VIRGINITY,
HYMEN
maidenly .... GENTLE, MODEST
mail .. POST, LETTERS, ARMOR,
DAWK, SEND, DA(U)K
bag .... POUCH
boat .... PACKET
carrier .... POSTMAN,
PONY EXPRESS
coat of .... ARMOR,
HAUBERK, BYRNIE
examine ...... CENSOR
India .... DA(W)K
mark .. CACHET, STAMP,
INDICIA
pertaining to .... POSTAL
Mailer, author .... NORMAN
mailing charge ..... POSTAGE
right .... FRANK
maillot ...... SWIMMING SUIT
mailman .... POSTMAN,
LETTER CARRIER
maim .... LAME, CRIPPLE,

MANGLE, MUTILATE, DISABLE,
SCOTCH
main ...... CHIEF, FOREMOST,
DUCT, FORCE, POWER,
PRINCIPAL, LEADING
action of drama ....
EPITASIS
body .... TRUNK
bounding ... SEA, OCEAN
course .... ENTREE
in the .. MOSTLY, CHIEFLY
part ...... BODY, TRUNK
point .. GIST, CRUX, NUB
stress .... BRUNT, ACCENT
Maine admiral ..... SIGSBEE
bay .... CASCO
capital .... AUGUSTA
city .. BANGOR, LEWISTON,
AUBURN, SACO, BATH
college .... BATES, COLBY
lake .... SEBAGO
motto .. DIRIGO, I GUIDE
mountain ... KATAHDIN
native .... DOWN-EASTER
peak .... KATAHDIN
river .... SACO
state bird .... CHICKADEE
state symbol ...... PINE
town ..... MILO, ORONO,
BANGOR
trout .... OQUASSA
Mainland .... POMONA
mainly .... CHIEFLY, MOSTLY,
LARGELY
mainspring ...... INCENTIVE,
MOTIVATION
maintain .. CARRY ON, KEEP,
CONTINUE, PRESERVE,
DEFEND, (UP)HOLD, AFFIRM,
CLAIM
maintenance .... UPKEEP,
SUPPORT, LIVELIHOOD
divorcee's ..... ALIMONY
Mainz .... MAYENCE
maison de sante ....
SANITARIUM, HOSPITAL
maitre d'hotel .... BUTLER,
STEWARD, MAJOR-DOMO,
HEADWAITER
maize .... CORN, CEREAL,
YELLOW, MEALIE, MEALY
ground .... GRITS, SAMP,
HOMINY
majestic .... AUGUST, NOBLE,
GRAND, STATELY, EPIC,
IMPERIAL, KINGLY

majesty .... DIGNITY,
GRANDEUR, NOBILITY
majolica .... POTTERY
major .. MAIN, CHIEF, OF AGE,
SPECIALIZE
Barbara author .... SHAW
domo ...... SENESCHAL,
STEWARD, BUTLER,
MAITRE D'HOTEL
opposed to .... MINOR
premise ...... SUMPTION
suit, in bridge ... SPADES,
HEARTS
Majorca .... MAJOLICA,
MALLORCA, ISLAND
city .... PALMA
majority .... AGE, BULK,
SENIORITY, PLURALITY
age .... ADULTHOOD
opposed to ... MINORITY
rule .... DEMOCRACY
majuscule .... CAPITAL, UNCIAL
make .. CREATE, BUILD, STYLE,
DEVISE, BRAND, FASHION
airtight ...... SEAL, LUTE
believe ..... ACT, FEIGN,
PRETEND, PRETENSE,
SHAM, MIMETIC
black .... NEGRIFY
capable .... ACTIVATE
capital of ...... EXPLOIT
cheeselike ...... CASEFY
choice .... OPT
cross sign .... SAIN
dainty .... PRETTIFY
do .... EKE
eyes at ...... OGLE, FLIRT
fast ..... SECURE, BELAY,
TIGHTEN
for .... ATTACK
haste ...... HIE, HURRY
hit .... CLICK
indistinct .... BLUR
insane .... DEMENT,
DERANGE
into law ...... ENACT,
LEGISLATE
into leather ... TAN, TAW
intricate .... COMPLICATE
it .... SUCCEED, ACHIEVE
laws .... LEGISLATE
less .... (DI)MINISH,
DECREASE
level ...... EVEN, PLANE
like .... IMITATE,
IMPERSONATE

member ... . ENROLL
merry .... REVEL
nervous .... FLUSTER
out .... FARE, DESCRY,
ESPY, DISCERN
out the meaning ....
DECIPHER
over .. RE-DO, RENOVATE,
REVAMP, CHANGE
position secure ....
ENTRENCH
possible .... ENABLE
public .... AIR, BARE,
ANNOUNCE, VENTILATE
quiet ..... (S)HUSH, MUTE,
MUFFLE
ragged .... FRAY
ready .. PRIME, PREPARE
resentful ..... EMBITTER
room ...... MOVE OVER
safe .... SECURE
selection .. PICK, CHOOSE,
OPT
sense .... ADD UP
small(er) ...... MINIFY,
MICRIFY, MINISH
smooth ...... SLICK(EN),
POLISH, PREEN
stupid .... HEBETATE
unfriendly ... DISAFFECT,
ANTAGONIZE
unnecessary .... OBVIATE
up ... INVENT, COMPOSE,
FORM, RECONCILE,
COSMETICS, LAYOUT,
NATURE
up material ..... ROUGE,
COSMETICS, LIPSTICK,
MASCARA
use of .. AVAIL, EXERCISE,
UTILIZE
watertight .... CALK
whole ..... MEND, HEAL,
INTEGRATE
wine .... VINT
young ...... REJUVENATE
maker: archaic .... POET
makeshift .... STOPGAP,
PROVISIONAL, EXPEDIENT
makeup, newspaper .. FORMAT
mako .... SHARK
makua .... KUA
mal de mer .... SEASICKNESS
Malabar monkey .. WANDEROO
Malacca .... CANE, STRAIT
malachite .... BICE, VERDITER

maladroit .... CLUMSY, AWKWARD
malady .... ILLNESS, DISEASE, AILMENT, SICKNESS
Malaga .... GRAPE, WINE
Malagasy capital ....
    TANANARIVE
   city .... TAMATAVE, MAJUNGA
   ethnic group ... MERINA, BETSILEO, SAKALAVA
   French ...... MALGACHE
   president ... TSIRANANA
   seaport ...... TAMATAVE
malaise .... DISCOMFORT
malamute ...... HUSKY, DOG
malanders .... ECZEMA, PUSTULES
malapert ...... BOLD, SAUCY, IMPUDENT
Malaprop's (Mrs.) creator ...
   SHERIDAN
malapropos .. INAPPROPRIATE, INOPPORTUNE
malar .... CHEEKBONE
malaria .. MIASM(A), QUARTAN, PALUDISM
   carrier ...... MOSQUITO, ANOPHELES
   characteristic ..... CHILLS
   drug ...... PLASMOCHIN, ATABRINE, ATEBRIN
   organism ... SPOROZOAN
malarial .... PALUDAL
malark(e)y ...... NONSENSE, BALONEY, LIP SERVICE, BUNCOMBE
Malawi .... NYASALAND
   capital .... ZOMBA, LILONGWE
   city .. LILONGWE, ZOMBA
   language .... BANTU
   president .... BANDA
Malay ape ...... LAR, MIAS
   apple .... OHIA
   archipelago .. INDONESIA
   beverage .... TAFIA
   bird .... MEGAPOD
   canoe ..... PRAH, PRAU, PROA, PRAO
   chief ..... DATO, DATU
   cloth .... BAT(T)IK
   coin .... TAMPANG, ORA, TRA(H)
   dagger ...... KRIS, CRIS, CREESE

   dish .... SATAY
   dress .... SARONG
   dyeing method ....
   BAT(T)IK
   English trade language ..
   BECHE-DE-MER
   fiber .... TERAP
   fruit .... KANARI
   garment .... SARONG
   gibbon .... LAR
   island .... JAVA, TIMOR, BORNEO, SABAH, SUMATRA
   isthmus .... KRA
   jacket .... BAJU
   jumping disease ... LATA
   knife .... PARANG
   law .... ADAT
   leather .... KULIT
   measure .... PAU
   motorcar ..... MOTOKAR
   mountain ..... TAHAN
   negrito .... A(E)TA, ITA
   nervous disease .... LATA
   nut .... KANARI
   orangutan .... MIAS
   outrigger .... PROA
   palm .. ARENG, GOMUTI, ARECA, BETEL, GEBANG
   Peninsula city ....
   KUALA LUMPUR
   puppeteer .. (TO)DALANG
   rattan .... SEGA
   sea cucumber .. TRIPANG
   seaweed product ....
   AGAR(AGAR)
   self-defense art ....
   KURIPAN
   shadow play .. WAYANG
   sir .... TUAN
   stage .... PANGGONG
   state .... KEDAH, PERAK, PAHANG, SELANGER, KELANTAN, PENANG, TRENGGANU, PERLIS, JOHORE
   station .... STESHEN
   telephone ...... TALIPON
   tic .... LATA
   title .... TUAN
   tree .. TERAP, RAMBUTAN, DURIAN, UPAS
   tribe .... ARIPAS
   tribesman .... MACASSAR, MAKASSAR
ungulate .... TAPIR

verse form ...... PANTUN
village .... KAMPONG
warehouse .... GODON
warrior ...... KURIPAN
weapon .... PARANG
weight .... KATI, CADDY
wild ox .... BANTENG
xylophone .... GAMBANG,
GENDER
yam .... UBI
Malayan .... TAGALOG
Malaysia capital ....
KUALA LUMPUR
city ..... IPOH, KLUANG,
MALACCA
crocodile ...... MUGGER
flower ...... GUMAMELA,
HIBISCUS
flying bat ...... KALONG
head of state ....
NASIRUDDIN SHAH
plant .... RAFFLESIA
prime minister .. RAHMAN
river .... PERAK
seaport .. GEORGE TOWN,
MALACCA
shadow play ... WAYANG
state .. MALAYA, SABAH,
SARAWAK
title for man .... TUN
title for woman ....
TOH PUAN
malcontent .... REB(EL),
REBELLIOUS, DISSIDENT
Maldive Islands .. SULTANATE
capital .... MALE
prime minister .... NASIR
sultan ...... FARID DIDI
male .... HE, MANLY, VIRILE,
MASCULINE
animal ..... STAG, RAM,
BULL, BOAR
attendant ... HENCHMAN
bee .... DRONE
bird ...... TERCEL, TOM,
LANNERET, COCK
castrated human ....
EUNUCH
cat .... TOM, GIB
chicken .. ROOSTER, COCK
deer .... STAG, PRICKET,
BUCK, HART
donkey .... JACK(ASS)
duck, wild .. MALLARD,
DRAKE
ferret .... HOB

figure of column .....COB
TELAMON, ATLANTES
fish .... MILTER
fish reproductive gland ..
MILT
hog .... BOAR
horse .... STALLION
kangaroo .... BOOMER
line of family ....
SPEAR SIDE
plant .... MAS
salmon .... JACK
seal .... SEECATCH
servant .... VALET, MAN,
BOY, KNAVE, LACKEY
sex .... MANKIND
sex hormone ....
ANDROGEN
sheep ...... TUP, RAM,
WETHER
swan .... COB
swine .... BOAR
turkey .... TOM
young .... BUCK
maledict .... ACCURSED
malediction .... CURSE,
ANATHEMA, MARANATHA,
MALISON, SLANDER,
DAMNATION
malefaction .... CRIME
malefactor .... CRIMINAL,
FELON, EVILDOERS
malefic ..... EVIL, HARMFUL
malevolence .... ILL WILL,
MALICE
malevolent .. EVIL, MALICIOUS,
SPITEFUL, VICIOUS
malfeasance ... MISCONDUCT,
WRONGDOING
malformed ...... MISSHAPEN
human ... HUNCHBACK
Mali capital .... BAMAKO
city ..... SEGOU, KAYES
ethnic group ..... PEULS,
BAMBARA, TOUAREG,
MALINKES, MARKAS
president ....
(MODIBO) KEITA
malic acid salt ...... MALATE
malice ...... RANCOR, SPITE,
ILL WILL, ENVY, SPLEEN,
VENOM, MALEVOLENCE,
GRUDGE
malicious .. SPITEFUL, CATTY,
VINDICTIVE, NASTY, VICIOUS
burning .... ARSON

malign .... DEFAME, ASPERSE, BALEFUL, ABUSE, VILIFY, TRADUCE, SLANDER, SINISTER, LIBEL, REVILE

malignant .. DANGEROUS, EVIL, VICIOUS, HARMFUL, VIRULENT
opposed to ..... BENIGN
spirit .... KER
tumor .... CANCER

Malines ...... MECHLIN, LACE

malinger ..... SHIRK, SKULK

malison .. CURSE, MALEDICTION

malkin .. DOWDY, MOP, HARE, SCARECROW, CAT

mall .... LANE, PROMENADE, WALK, AVENUE, ALLEE

mallard .... DRAKE, (WILD)DUCK
genus .... ANAS

malleable .. PLIABLE, DUCTILE, AMENABLE, TENSILE, SOFT

malleate .... POUND

mallee .... EUCALYPTUS

mallemuck .. PETREL, FULMAR, ALBATROSS

mallet .... GAVEL, MAUL, HAMMER, BEETLE, PESTLE, TUP, MADGE
game played with .... CROQUET, POLO
presiding officer's .... GAVEL
striking part of .... TUP
tamping .... BEETLE

malleus .... HAMMER

Mallorca .... MAJORCA

mallow ... ALTHEA, HIBISCUS, COTTON, OKRA, (HOLLY)HOCK

malm ..... LIMESTONE, LOAM, MARL

Malmo man .... SWEDE

malmsey .... MADEIRA, WINE, GRAPE, MALVOISIE
grape .... MALVASIA, MALVOISIE

malodorous .. FETID, STINKING

malt .... BARLEY, LIQUOR
liquor .... ALE, BEER, PORTER, STOUT
liquor's yeast ..... BARM
product ...... ALE, BEER, VINEGAR, ALEGAR
sugar .... MALTOSE

Malta capital ...... VALETTA
defender .... GORT
island .... GOZO, COMINO
prime minister .. OLIVIER
wind .... GREGALE

Maltese .... CAT, DOG, CROSS

maltha .. CEMENT, OZOCERITE, BITUMEN, TAR

maltose .... SUGAR

maltreat(ment) .... ABUSE

malty .... DRUNK

malvasia .... GRAPE
product ...... MALMSEY

mama .... MOTHER, MAW, MOM(MY)

mamba ..... COBRA, ELAPINE, SNAKE

mambo .... RIFF, DANCE

mameluke .... SLAVE

mamey .. MAMMEE, SAPODILLA

Mamie's maiden name .. DOUD

mammal .. SUCKLER, PRIMATE
aquatic .... DESMAN, MANATEE, OTTER, SEAL, DUGONG, SEACOW, WHALE, DOLPHIN, PORPOISE
"armored" .. ARMADILLO
cetacean ...... DOLPHIN, WHALE, NARWHAL, PORPOISE
egg-laying .... PLATYPUS, DUCKBILL
extinct ...... MASTODON
flesh-eating .... MINK, OTTER, WEASEL
fur .... PELAGE
hairless water ... WHALE, CETACEAN, DOLPHIN, PORPOISE
lowest order .... MONOTREME
mouselike .... SHREW
nocturnal ... LEMUR, BAT
plant-eating .... RHINO(CEROS)
ring-tailed .... RACCOON
snouted ...... DOLPHIN, DESMAN, PORPOISE
two-handed .... BIMANE

mammals, of certain MUSTELINE

mammary gland ...... UDDER
inflammation .. MASTITIS
gland secretion .... COLOSTRUM

mammee .. SAPODILLA, MAMEY, MARMALADE

mammet .. DOLL, IDOL, PUPPET

mammilla ...... NIPPLE, TEAT
mammock ...... SCRAP, SHRED,
   FRAGMENT
mammoth .. ELEPHANT, HUGE,
   ENORMOUS, GIGANTIC
  like animal ... MASTODON
mammy ..... MAMA, MOTHER,
   NEGRESS
man (see person/fellow) ......
  FORTIFY, PERSON, HUSBAND,
  BRACE, MALE, OPERATE,
  HOMO SAPIENS, BIPED, STAFF,
  SERVANT, HOMBRE, GEEZER,
  GUY, FELLER, RUN
  among men ...... HERO
  and ___ .... WIFE
  at-arms .... SOLDIER
  bald-headed .. PILGARLIC
  child .... BOY
  country, old ... GAMMER,
   GAFFER
  dashing, gay .... SPARK
  eater .. CANNIBAL, SHARK,
   CROCODILE, LION,
   TIGER, LAMIA
  elderly ...... CRONE, FOGY,
   DOTARD
  Friday .... SERVANT,
   FOLLOWER
  Genesis .... ONAN
  gentleman's ...... VALET
  handsome ...... ADONIS,
   APOLLO
  handy .... FACTOTUM
  hideous .... OGRE
  Isle of, capital of ....
   DOUGLAS
  kind of .... STRAW
  lanky .... BEANPOLE
  Latin .... HOMO
  lecherous .... SATYR
  like .... ANDROID
  little .... MANIKIN
  long-suffering ...... JOB
  nautical usage ...... SHIP
  newly-married ....
   BENEDICT
  of brass.......... TALOS
  of Destiny, alleged .....
   NAPOLEON
  of figures .... CPA,
   BOOKKEEPER
  of Galilee .... JESUS
  of God .. SAINT, HERMIT,
   PRIEST, RABBI
  of learning ..... SAVANT,

   PUNDIT
  of letters .... SAVANT,
   SCHOLAR, LITTERATEUR
  of the world ....
   SOPHISTICATE
  old .. GEEZER, GRAYBEARD
  on a beat .... COP,
   REPORTER
  patient .... JOB
  prehistoric ....
   ZINJANTHROPUS
  recently married ....
   BENEDICT
  sea .... SAILOR, TAR,
   MARINER
  servant .. VALET, LACKEY
  single .... BACHELOR
  strong .. SAMSON, ATLAS
  to a .... ALL, EVERYONE
  unmanly ...... MILKSOP,
   SISSY
  unmarried ..... CELIBATE,
   BACHELOR
  wise ..... SOLON, NESTOR
  without a country ......
   NOLAN, STATELESS
  who annoys women ......
   MASHER
  young, gay ...... SPARK
manacle .. FETTER, HANDCUFF,
   SHACKLE, HAMPER
manage .... WIELD, HANDLE,
  CONTROL, CONDUCT, TEND,
  ADMINISTER, CONTRIVE,
   OPERATE, RUN
  frugally .... HUSBAND,
   NURSE
  to live .... SCRAPE
manageable .. DOCILE, RULY,
  TRACTABLE, GENTLE, TAME,
   WIELDY
management of household ....
   MENAGE
manager .. GERENT, DIRECTOR,
  STEWARD, OPERATOR, SYNDIC
  opera .... IMPRESARIO
Managua is capital of ....
   NICARAGUA
manakin ..... DWARF, MODEL,
   BIRD
mañana .... TOMORROW
manatee .. DUGONG, SEA COW,
  HALICORE, SIRENIAN,
   COWFISH
manavelins .. LEFTOVERS, ORTS,
   ODDS AND ENDS

Manchester native .... MANCUNIAN
manchet .... BREAD
Manchu .... MONGOLIAN, TUNGUS
  dynasty ...... TA CH'ING
  dynasty, revolt against .. TAIPING
Manchukuo .... MANCHURIA
  emperor of .... PU-YI
Manchuria capital ....
    FENG-TIEN, M(O)UKDEN
  city .. JEHOL, CHENGTEH, TALIEN, DAIREN
  port of .... HARBIN, ANTUNG
  river .... SUNGARI
manciple .... SLAVE, STEWARD
mandamus .... WRIT, ORDER
Mandan ...... SIOUX, INDIAN
mandarin .... ORANGE, COAT, TANGERINE, DUCK
  residence of .... YAMEN, YAMUN
  tea .... CHA
mandate .. ORDER, COMMAND, COMMISSION
mandatory ...... OBLIGATORY
mandible .... BEAK, JAW
Mandingo .... NEGRO
mandolin strumming piece ... PLECTRUM
mandragora ...... MANDRAKE
mandrake ..... MANDRAGORA, MAY APPLE
mandrel ...... LATHE, SPINDLE
mandrill ...... BABOON, APE
manducate .... CHEW, MASTICATE
mane .... JUBA, CREST
maned ..... LEONINE, JUBATE
  king ...\........... LION
manege ...... HORSEMANSHIP
manes .... SOUL
maneuver .... PLOY, ARTIFICE, TRICK, STRATAGEM, JOCKEY, MANIPULATE
manganese spar .. RHODONITE
mange .... SCAB
  cause of .... MITE
  loss caused by .... HAIR
mangel .... BEET
manger ..... BIN, CRIB, RACK, TROUGH, CRATCH, STALL
mangle .... GARBLE, MAR, HACKLE, HAGGLE, MUTILATE,

DISFIGURE, LACERATE, CALENDER
mangler .... MUTILATOR
mango .... MUSKMELON, FRUIT
mangonel kin ...... CATAPULT
mangy ...... SCURVY, MEAN, SORDID, SQUALID, SCURFY, SCALY, SCABBY, SCABROUS
manhandle .... MAUL
Manhattan hotel .... CHELSEA, AMERICANA, DELMONICO'S, WALDORF, WARWICK, PLAZA
  purchaser of ... MINUIT, MINNEWIT
manhunters' group .... POSSE
mania .... CRAZE, OBSESSION, DELIRIUM
  for dancing .. TARANTISM
maniac ... MADMAN, LUNATIC
maniacal ...... MAD, RAVING
manifest ..... SHOW, ATTEST, SIGNIFY, PATENT, LIST, OVERT, TESTIFY, WAYBILL, APPARENT, EVIDENT, OBVIOUS, CLEAR, PLAIN, EVINCE, REVEAL, OPEN
manifestant .. DEMONSTRATOR
manifesto ..... DECLARATION, PROCLAMATION, EDICT
manifold .... MULTIFARIOUS, MANY, VARIED, MULTIPLE
manihot ...... CASSAVA, MANIOC
manikin .. PHANTOM, DWARF, MODEL, MANNEQUIN
Manila .... PAPER, HEMP, CIGAR, CITY
  Acapulco trading ship .. GALLEON
  Bay hero .... DEWEY
  Bay island .. CORREGIDOR
  hemp source .... ABACA
manioc .. CASSAVA, MANIHOT, STARCH, YUCA, JUCA
maniple .... ORALE, FANO(N), FANUM
maniples, three .... COHORT
manipulate .... HANDLE, MANEUVER, JUGGLE, RIG
manipulator .... JUGGLER
Manipur capital .... IMPHAL
Manitoba capital .. WINNEPEG
mankind .... HUMANITY
manlike .... MASCULINE
manly .... VIRILE, MASCULINE
manna .. FOOD, SUSTENANCE, LERP

mannequin .... MODEL, MAN(N)IKIN
manner ..... AIR, MIEN, SORT, MODE, FASHION, BEHAVIOR, BEARING, HABIT, DEPORTMENT, METHOD
  of dress .... GUISE
  of running .. LOPE, JOG, CANTER, TROT
  of speaking .... DICTION
  of walking .... GAIT, WADDLE, SWAGGER
mannerism .... POSE, AFFECTATION
mannerist .... STYLIST
mannerly .... POLITE, COURTEOUS
manners .. MORES, BEHAVIOR, CONDUCT
  study of ...... ETHOLOGY
mannish .. MASCULINE, VIRILE, MANLY
manor ~ MANSION, DEMESNE, ESTATE
manorial court .. ~ .. ~ .. LEET
manque .... DEFECTIVE
manrope .... HANDRAIL
mansard ~ ~ GARRET, ATTIC, ROOF
manse .... ~ ..... PARSONAGE
manservant .. FOOTBOY, VALET, YEOMAN, LACKEY, FLUNK(E)Y
mansion .. ~ .. ~ HOUSE, DOME, MANOR
manslaughter ..... HOMICIDE
  premeditated .. MURDER
mansuetude ~ .. ~ .. TAMENESS, GENTLENESS
manta .. ~ .. SHAWL, CAPE, RAY, DEVILFISH, BLANKET
manteau .... CLOAK, MANTLE
mantel .. ~ .. ~ .. SHELF, LEDGE, LINTEL
  ornamental band ....
                FRIEZE
mantelet ~ SHELTER, SCREEN, CAPE, CLOAK
mantic .... PROPHETIC
mantilla ~ SCARF, VEIL, CAPE, CLOAK
  user .. SENORITA, SENORA
mantis crab/shrimp .. SQUILLA
mantle .. CAPE, CLOAK, COVER, PALLIUM, COPE, CHLAMYS, FROCK
  armor .. ~ ...... TABARD

  having a ...... TUNICATE
Mantua .. MANTOVA, CLOAK, MANTLE
Mantuan, the .... VIRGIL
manual .... HANDBOOK, GUIDEBOOK, TEXTBOOK
  art .... CRAFT
  training .... SLOYD, SLOID
  workers, all ..... LABOR
manufacture ...... PRODUCE, INVENT, CONCOCT, MAKE, FABRICATE
manufacturing left-overs ....
                SHORTS
manumission .... LIBERATION, EMANCIPATION
manumit .. ~ .. ~ FREE, LIBERATE, EMANCIPATE
manure .. FERTILIZE, GUANO, DUNG, MUCK, ORDURE
manuscript .... MS., HANDWRITTEN
  copier .. ~ .. ~ ..... SCRIBE
  leaf of .... FOLIO
  mark, ancient ... OBELUS
  rolled .... SCROLL
  to be set in type .. COPY
  volume .... CODEX
manx ...... CAT, CELT, GAEL
many .. NUMEROUS, MANIFOLD, MULTIFARIOUS, LOADS, INNUMERABLE, LOTS, MYRIAD, SCORES
  a time .... OFT(EN)
  combining form .. POLY, MYRIA
  headed monster .. HYDRA
manyplies .... OMASUM
Mao Tse ___ .... TUNG
  daughter of .. ~ .. LI-NA, MAU-MAU
  son .. ~ .. ~ ...... AN-YING
  wife .... CHIANG CHING
Maori canoe .... WAKA
  clan .. ~ .... HAPU
  club .... MARREE
  human flesh .. LONG PIG
  parrot .... TUI
  raft .. ~ .. ~ .. , ... MOKI
  tattoo .... MOKO
  village .... KAIK(A)
  wages .... UTU
  weapon .... PATU
  wood .... RATA
map .. CHART, CARTE, ORRERY,

PLAT, COROGRAPHY, PLAN,
GRAPH
book .... ATLAS
extra in a .... INSET
line(s) .... HACHURE,
ISOBAR, OSOCHEIM,
ISOTHERM, ISOTHERE
maker .... MERCATOR,
CARTOGRAPHER
maker's abbreviation ...
ISL, RD, RTE
maker's machine ....
OROGRAPH
marker .... PUSHPIN
of lines ..... CARTOGRAM
slang .... FACE
maple .. TREE, SIRUP, SUGAR,
WOOD, ACER, BOX ELDER
chat of .... SAMARA
fruit .... SCHIZOCARP
leaf land .... CANADA
samara of .... CHAT
seed .... SAMARA
tree .... BOX ELDER,
SYCAMORE
tree tap/spout .... SPILE
maps .... ATLAS
maquis .... GUER(R)ILLA
mar .. BLEMISH, SCAR, INJURE,
DAMAGE, SPOIL, IMPAIR,
DISFIGURE, DEFACE
marabou .... ARGALA, STORK,
ADJUTANT
marabout ... HERMIT, TOMB,
HOLY MAN
maraca .... RATTLE
Maracanda ...... SAMARKAND
maranatha .... CURSE,
MALEDICTION, INVOCATION
marasca .... CHERRY
product .. MARASCHINO,
LIQUEUR, CORDIAL
marasmus .... WASTING
Marat, (Jean) killer of ......
CORDAY
marathon .... FOOTRACE,
NONSTOP
victorious general at ....
MILTIADES
maraud .. PLUNDER, PILLAGE,
RAID, FORAY
marauder .... RAIDER
marble ...... AGATE, RANCE,
SHOOTER, ALLEY, RANSE,
ALAY, CARRARA, DOLOMITE,
MIB, LIMESTONE, MIG(GLE),

TAW, COLD, CALCITE,
CIPOLIN, AGGIE, HARD
flooring ...... TERAZZO
game .... TAW, MIGS,
MIGGLES
glass, small, square .....
TESSERA
imitation .... SCAGLIOLA
like/of ... MARMOREAL,
MARMOREAN
players' line .... TAW
stone resembling ......
SODALITE
worker's tool .... BURIN
marc ...... BRANDY, REFUSE
marcel ...... HAIRDRESSER
March .. FILE, ADVANCE, HIKE,
PROGRESS, WALK, BORDER,
FRONTIER, BORDERLAND
date .... IDES
day's .... ETAPE
for dead .... DIRGE
organized .. .. PARADE
style .... GOOSESTEP
triumphantly .. GALUMPH
marchen .... TALE, STORY
marches, king of ..... SOUSA
marchese .... MARQUIS
marchioness ...... MARQUISE,
LADY, MARCHESA
Marco ____, traveler ... POLO
Marconi, physicist ....
GUGLIELMO
marconigram .... RADIOGRAM
Mardi Gras ..... CARNIVAL,
FESTIVAL
day .... TUESDAY
home of .. NEW ORLEANS
king .... REX
scene of .... PARIS,
NEW ORLEANS
mare .... YAUD, HORSE, SEA,
JADE
milk of ..... KOUMIS(S),
KUMISS
nostrum ..... OUR SEA,
MEDITERRANEAN
tail of .... CLOUD
young .... FILLY
Margaret, diminutive of .....
MEG, PEG, GRETA, MARGE,
PEGGY, MAGGIE, MADGE
margarin(e) .... OLEO
margarite .... PEARL
margay .... CAT, OCELOT

marge ...... MARGIN, BORDER, EDGE, SHORE

margin .... MARGE, RAND, LEEWAY, MARGENT, EDGE, BRINK, BORDER, VERGE, LIMIT, LIP

marginal note .... SCHOLIUM, MARGENT, APOSTIL(LE)
notes of Old Testament .. MASORA(H)

margrave .... GOVERNOR
territory of .... BORDERLAND, MARCH, MARQUISATE

marguerite .... DAISY, CHRYSANTHEMUM

Maria .... LING

Marian, contralto .. ANDERSON

Marianas Island .... ROTA, LADRONES, GUAM, TINIAN, PAGAN, AGUIJAN, AGRIHAN, GUGUAN, SAIPAN

Marie Antoinette ...... REINE
Wilson role ...... IRMA

marigold ... ASTER, COWSLIP, (MAY)FLOWER, KINGCUP, CAPER

marijuana .. HEMP, NARCOTIC, CIGARETTE, WEED, GANZA, POT, HASHEESH
cigarette .... REEFER
cigarette holder .... ROACH CLIP
form of .... HASH

marimba-like instrument ..... XYLOPHONE

marina .. HARBOR, BOAT BASIN, DOCK

marinade ..... VINEGAR, WINE, SALT, PICKLE

marinate .... PICKLE

marine ... NAVAL, NAUTICAL, MARITIME, FLEET, LEATHERNECK, THALASSIC, GYRENE
British: sl. .... JOLLY
glow .... SEAFIRE
organism, phosphorescent NOCTILUCA
plant .... SEAWEED
plant cast ashore .... WRACK
plant group .... BENTHOS
worm .... SYLLID, NEMERTIAN, NEMERTEAN

mariner .... SAILOR, SEAMAN, JACK-TAR, GOB
colloquial .... TAR, SALT
domain of .... SEA, SPACE
victim of (fictional) ..... ALBATROSS

Marion, actress ..... DAVIES
Civil War general ...... FRANCIS, SWAMP FOX

marionette .... PUPPET, DOLL
man ...... (TONY) SARG

mariposa flower .. LILY, TULIP

marish .... SWAMP(Y)

marjoram ..... ORIGAN, MINT, OREGANO

mark .. VESTIGE, STAIN, SIGN, TOKEN, BRAND, SCAR, MACRON, DENOTE EVANGELIST, SYMBOL, SCRIBE
adverse .... DEMERIT
aimed at by throw ...... COCKSHY
Antony's wife .. OCTAVIA
authentication .... SEAL, CACHET
black .... STIGMA
cattle .... BRAND
critical .... OBELUS
diacritical ...... BREVE, TILDE, ACCENT, CEDILLA, UMLAUT, ABLAUT
dirty .... SMUT, SMUTCH, SMUDGE, BLOT
down .... RECORD, NOTE
footnote ..... ASTERISK, STAR, OBELISK, DAGGER
for identification .... DAGGER, DOGTAG, MOLE, LABEL, BRAND
for doubtful passages ... OBELUS
kind of ...... DOT, SPOT, LINE, STAIN, SCRATCH, BLEMISH, DENT, BRUISE, PUNCTUATION
missile's .... TARGET
of bondage ...... YOKE, BRAND
of disgrace ..... STIGMA, BRAND
of omission ... ELLIPSIS, DELE, CARET
of word addition .. CARET
of wound .... SCAR

one hundredth of .... PFENIG

over syllable ..... BREVE

over vowel .... MACRON, BREVE, TILDE, UMLAUT

postal .. STAMP, CACHET

pronunciation .... TILDE, UMLAUT, CEDILLA, BREVE, MACRON

proofreader's .... CARET, DELE, STET

question .... QUERY

reference .... OBELUS, ASTERISK, OBELI, DIESIS, DAGGER

VI .... TIGER, TANK

skin ...... MOLE, NEVUS

skin with color .. TATTOO

thin .... LINE

Twain .... CLEMENS

up .. .. HIKE, RAISE

with line ...... STRIATE

with spots ..... MOTTLE, DOT, DAPPLE, SPECKLE

markdown .... DISCOUNT

marked .. DISTINCT, OBVIOUS, NOTICEABLE

marker .. MONUMENT, SCORER, GRAVESTONE, MILESTONE, LINER, STELE, PEG, PICKET

air-race .... PYLON

channel .... BUOY

grave .... BARROW

slang ...... IOU, PLEDGE

stone .... CAIRN, MONUMENT

market .. MART, STORE, SHOP, SELL, BAZA(A)R

bond ... CURB, EXCHANGE

place ... FORUM, AGORA, EMPORIUM, PLAZA, RIALTO

stock .. EXCHANGE, CURB

town .... BOURG

marking instrument ... SCRIBE

marksman .. SHARPSHOOTER, SHOT

hangout .... GALLERY, RANGE

hidden .... SNIPER

target of .... BULL'S-EYE

marl .... MALM, EARTH, STRATUM

marlin .... SPEARFISH

kin .... SAILFISH, SWORDFISH

marlinspike .... FID

marmalade ..... CONFECTION, PRESERVE, JAM

material .... RIND, PEEL(ING)

tree .... SAPODILLA, MAMMEE, SAPOTA, MAMEY, CHICO

"Marmion" character .... LOCHINVAR

marmoreal ..... MARBLELIKE, COLD, SMOOTH

marmoset .... MONKEY, MICO, TAMARIN

marmot .... RODENT, WOODCHUCK, PRAIRIE DOG, WHISTLER

Maroc .... MOROCCO

maroon ..... SLAVE, ISOLATE, CHESTNUT, STRAND, LOITER, LOAF, ENISLE

Marpessa's abductor .... IDAS

Marquand's sleuth .... (MR.) MOTO

marque .... REPRISAL

marquee .. AWNING, MARQUISE, TENT, CANOPY, SHELTER

marquetry .... MOSAIC, PARQUETRY

material .. TILE, PARQUET, IVORY, WOOD

Marquette, explorer .... JACQUES, PERE

Marquis, humorist ...... DON

Marquisate, ruler of .... MARGRAVE

marquise .... MARQUEE, RING

British equivalent ...... MARCHIONESS

Marrakech .... MOROCCO

marriage .... WEDLOCK, MATRIMONY, WEDDING, HYMEN, NUPTIALS

bond .... KNOT

broker ...... SCHATCHEN

contract ..... HANDFAST

dowry .... DOT

gift .... DOWRY

hater of .... MISOGAMIST

hatred of .... MISOGAMY

kind of .... MORGANATIC, CONVENIENCE, MONOGAMY

notice .... BAN(N)S

obstacle annulling ...... DIRIMENT

outside the tribe .... EXOGAMY
pertaining to ... MARITAL
proclamation ... BAN(N)S
second .... BIGAMY
settlement .. DOWRY, DOS
song .... NUPTIAL, HYMNEAL
unsuitable .. MISALLIANCE
vow .... TROTH
with one of lesser status . MESALLIANCE
within the tribe .... ENDOGAMY
marriageable woman .. NUBILE
married .... CONJUGAL, CONNUBIAL
marron .... CHESTNUT
marrow ...... PITH, ESSENCE, MEDULLA
bones .... KNEES
fat .... PEA
Marruecos .... MOROCCO
marry .. WED, UNITE, ESPOUSE, WIVE, ADOPT, HITCH
Mars .... ARES, WAR, PLANET
combining form ... AREO
in alchemy .... IRON
moon of ...... PHOBOS, DEIMOS
of .... MARTIAN
sister of ...... BELLONA
son of .... REMUS
"Marseillaise" composer .... (DE) LISLE
marsh .. SLUE, LERNA, MOOR, BOG, SLOUGH, OOZE, WETLAND, MORASS, SALINA, QUAG, SWAMP, MUSKEG, FEN
bird .. RAIL, COOT, SORA
danger spot ... QUAGMIRE
elder ..... RAGWEED, IVA, GUELDER-ROSE
fever .... HELODES
gas .... METHANE
grass ...... REED, SEDGE
hen .... RAIL, COOT
hollow .... SWALE
mallow .... ALTHEA
marigold ..... COWSLIP, MAYFLOWER, CAPER
plant .. BULRUSH, TULE, MOORWORT, CATTAIL, FESCUE
salt .... SALINA

marshal .... GUIDE, ARRANGE, ARRAY, ASSEMBLE
famous ..... NEY, FOCH, PETAIN, MONTGOMERY, GORT, ROMMEL
Marshall Islands group ...... RALIK, RATAK
island .... MILI, MAJURO, WOTJE, MALOELAP, LIKIEP, JALUIT, WOTHO, BIKINI, KWAJALEIN, ENIWETOK
marshmallow .. CONFECTION, CANDY
marshy .. PALUDINE, PALUDAL, PALUDIC, FENNY, BOGGY
ground hollow .... WALE
inlet/outlet ...... BAYOU
land .... MAREMMA
marsupial ...... KOALA, TAIT, (O)POSSUM, DASYURE, YABBI, PHALANGER, POUCHLIKE, BANDICOOT, WOMBAT, KANGAROO
marsupium formation .. POUCH
Marta, actress .... TOREN
Martell .... COGNAC
marten ...... SABLE, MAMMAL
describing a .. MUSTELINE
fur .... BAUM
kin .... GLUTTON
like animal .... WEASEL
martial .. WARLIKE, MILITARY, SOLDIERLY
opposed to .. CIVIL(IAN)
martin ...... BIRD, MARTLET, SWALLOW
martinet .... DISCIPLINARIAN
martini .... COCKTAIL
extra .... OLIVE
ingredient .... GIN, VERMOUTH
Martinique capital .... FORT-DE-FRANCE
music .... BEGUINE
volcano .... PELEE
Martinmas to X'mas .... ADVENT
martlet .... MARTIN
marvel ... PRODIGY, WONDER, MIRACLE
of-Peru .... PLANT, FOUR-O'CLOCK
marvelous ..... MIRACULOUS, SPLENDID
Marwar .... JODHPUR

Marx .... CHICO, HARPO, GROUCHO, KARL
co-worker of Karl .... ENGELS
Marxism .... SOCIALISM, COMMUNISM
Mary, mother of Jesus ... MADONNA
picture/statue of .... MADONNA
Maryland capital ... ANNAPOLIS
city .... BALTIMORE, CUMBERLAND, ROCKVILLE
founder .... CALVERT
governor .... AGNEW
seaport .... BALTIMORE
state bird .... ORIOLE
state fish .... ROCKFISH
state sport .... JOUSTING
swamp .... POCOSON
symbol .... ORIOLE
Mascagni, composer ... PIETRO
mascara .... COSMETIC
mascle .... LOZENGE VOIDED
masculine .... MALE, VIRILE, MAN(LY), MANNISH
Masefield work .... ODTAA
mash .... PAP, CRUSH
masjid .... MOSQUE, MOSK
mask .... VISOR, VIZARD, VISARD, HELMET, SCREEN, LOUP, LARVE, DISGUISE, MASQUE, CONCEAL, CAMOUFLAGE
grotesque .... MASCARON
half .... DOMINO, LOUP
lacy .... VEIL
wearer .... MASQUER, MUMMER, KLANSMAN
maskalonge .... FISH, PIKE
masked .... DISGUISED
ball .... MASQUE, MASQUERADE
in botany .... PERSONATE
masker .... MUMMER
masochism .... SADISM
mason .... STONECUTTER
bench .... BANKER
chisel of .... BROACH, TOOLER
companion of .... DIXON
hammer of .... GAVEL
mortar board .... HAWK
Masonic doorkeeper .... TILER
Masonite .... HARDBOARD

masonry .... BRICKWORK, STONEWORK
broken pieces .... RUBBLE
wedge .... SHIM
Masqat .... MUSCAT
masque .... MASQUERADE, BALL, COMUS
masquerade .... DISGUISE, RIDOTTO, MUM(M), MASQUE, BALL
costume .... DOMINO
mass .... SQUASH, BOLUS, GOB(BET), FLAKE, CLOT, LUMP, BULL, MAGNITUDE, MAJORITY, LARGE-SCALE, WAD, LITURGY, ASSEMBLE, GATHER, MUSH
book .... MISSAL
for the dead .... REQUIEM
killing .... MASSACRE, CARNAGE, BATTUE
loose, downy .... FLUE
meeting .... RALLY
movement, kind of .... STAMPEDE, MIGRATION, EXODUS
of bacteria .... CLUMP
of dusts, etc. .... CLOUD, FOG
of inferior things ... RUCK
shapeless .... LUMP
solidified .... CONCRETION
Massachusetts cape .... ANN, COD
capital .... BOSTON
city .... CHICOPEE, CHELSEA, TAUNTON, LYNN, MALDEN, QUINCY, REVERE, MELROSE, SALEM, CAMBRIDGE, SPRINGFIELD, ATHOL, WORCESTER, HOLYOKE
county .... DUKES, SUFFOLK
famous hall .... FANEUIL
nickname .... BAY STATE
state bird .... CHICKADEE
state flower .... ARBUTUS, MAYFLOWER
state tree .... ELM
massacre .... CARNAGE, POGROM, SLAUGHTER
organized .... POGROM
massage .... KNEAD, SHAMPOO, RUB(DOWN)
massager; man .... MASSEUR

woman ...... MASSEUSE
Massenet, composer .. JULES
opera by .. MANON, THAIS
masses, the .. PLEBS, PEOPLE,
HOI POLLOI, MULTITUDE
masseur ... RUBBER, MASSAGER
Massey, performer ... ILONA,
RAYMOND
Massine, ballet dancer ....
LEONIDE
massive .. PONDEROUS, BULKY,
SOLID, IMPOSING, HEAVY,
HUGE
mast .... ACORNS, SPAR, POLE,
(CHEST)NUTS, BEECHNUTS
iron band of ...... TRUSS
platform ..... MAINTOP,
LOOKOUT, CROW'S NEST
support .... BIBB
mastaba(h) ... TOMB, CHAPEL
master .... MAIN, CHIEF,
CONTROL, SUBDUE, DOM,
BOY, EFFENDI, SAHIB,
PADRONE, EMPLOYER, TUTOR,
EXPERT
builder ...... ARCHITECT
cruel .... LEGREE
hand .... EXPERT
in any art ..... MAESTRO
music .... MAESTRO
of ceremonies ...... MC,
EMCEE, COMPERE
of household .. GOODMAN
pertaining to a .. HERILE
race ideology ....
HERRENVOLK
ship's .. SKIPPER, CAPTAIN
stroke .... COUP
workman ...... ARTIST,
CRAFTSMAN, FOREMAN,
OVERSEER
masterly .... EXPERT(LY)
mastermind .... PLANNER,
DIRECTOR
masterpiece .. CHEF-D'OEUVRE,
MAGNUM OPUS
mastership .. RULE, CONTROL,
DOMINION
mastery .. GRIP, SWAY, SKILL,
ASCENDANCY, CONTROL,
UPPER HAND
masthead .... LOOKOUT
mastic .... CEMENT, RESIN,
LIQUOR
tree .... ACOMA

masticate ..... CHEW, GRIND,
CRUNCH, MANDUCATE
masticating animal .... GOAT,
CAMEL, CATTLE, RUMINANT,
DEER, LLAMA, ANTELOPE,
GIRAFFE, BISON
mastication product ..... CUD
mastiff .. (WATCH)DOG, ALAN,
BULLDOG
mastodon, animal resembling ..
ELEPHANT, MAMMOTH
mat ...... SHAG, DOILY, PAD,
DULL, CUSHION, SNARL,
MATRIX, INTERWEAVE,
CARPET
leaf .... YAPA
making material .. RUSH,
REED, BAST, VETIVER
protecting dike or embankment .... MATTRESS
sleeping .... PETATE
Mata Hari .... SPY
Matabele .... ZULU
matador ...... BULLFIGHTER,
TOREADOR, TORERO
dart with flag of ....
BANDERILLA
garment of .... CAPE
queue of .... COLETA
red cloth used by ....
MULETA, MULETILLA
sweet sounds to a .. OLES
sword of .... ESTOQUE
match .... LUNT, VESUVIAN,
MATE, TEAM, EQUAL, FIT,
TALLY, PARALLEL, MARRIAGE,
CONTEST, COUNTERPART,
PAIR, SUIT
boxing ..... SETTO, BOUT
cockfighting ...... MAIN
friction .. FUSEE, LUCIFER,
FUZEE, LOCOFOCO
in dice .... MAIN
stick .... LINSTOCK
tycoon .... KREUGER
wax .... VESTA
wooden .... VESTA
matching piece .... MATE
matchless .... PEERLESS,
UNEQUALED, INIMITABLE
matchmaker ..... SCHATCHEN
indefatigable ...... EROS,
CUPID
matchwood .... SPLINTERS
mate .... MARRY, MATCH,
COMRADE, HUSBAND, WIFE,

FERE, HOLLY, TEA, COUPLE, SPOUSE
mateless .... AZYGOUS
mater .... MOTHER
    dolorosa .. VIRGIN MARY
material .. MATTER, PHYSICAL,
    SUBSTANCE, PERTINENT,
    ESSENTIAL, CORPOREAL,
    SENSUAL, WORLDLY, DATA
    inner surface .... LIMING
maternal .... MOTHERLY
    relationship .... ENATION
maternity ...... MOTHERHOOD
    hospital ...... LYING-IN
matey .. CHUM(MY), FRIENDLY
matgrass .... MARRAM, NARD
mathematical ...... PRECISE,
    EXACT, ACCURATE
    arbitrary number ....
        RADIX
    arc .... RADIAN
    figure .... GRAPH, CONE,
        DIAGRAM
    formula .... LAW
    function ...... (CO)SINE
    instrument .... VERNIER,
        CALCULATOR,
        COMPUTER
    line .... VECTOR
    proposition .... THEOREM
    ratio .... SINE
    symbol .... DIGIT, POINT,
        DOT, FACIEND,
        OPERAND,
        MULTIPLICAND
    term ..... FACIEND, COSH,
        CONSTANT, FACIENT,
        SURD, (CO)SINE
mathematician ...... EUCLID,
    NEWTON, DESCARTES,
    PASCAL, PTOLEMY, GAUSS,
        VERNIER
    of the earth .... GEODETE
mathematics subject ....
    TRIGONOMETRY, ARITHMETIC,
    ALGEBRA, GEOMETRY,
        CALCULUS
matin ...... MORNING(SONG),
    (CANONICAL)HOUR, AUBADE
    canticle .... VENITE
    singer .... LARK
matinee ...... LEVEE, SOIREE,
    RECEPTION, PERFORMANCE
    idol of old .. VALENTINO,
        GABLE, BARRYMORE
matrass .... BOLTHEAD, FLASK

matriculate .... ENTER,
    ENROL(L), REGISTER
matriculation fee ... TUITION
matrimonial .... CONJUGAL,
    NUPTIAL, MARITAL
matrimony .... MARRIAGE
matrix ...... MO(U)LD, CAST,
    UTERUS, WOMB, MAT, DIE,
        GANG(UE)
matron ...... WIFE, WIDOW
matronly .. SEDATE, DIGNIFIED
matted .... CESPITOSE
matter ...... COPY, PUS, PITH,
    SUBSTANCE, CONTENT, AFFAIR
    classification of ....
        ANIMAL, MINERAL,
        VEGETABLE, ORGANIC
    in law .... RES
    of course ...... ROUTINE
    of fact .... LITERAL,
        CASUAL, PROSAIC,
        DRY, PRACTICAL
    of opinion ...... MOOT,
        DEBATABLE
Matterhorn ... MONT CERVIN,
        MOUNTAIN
matters of faith .. CREDENDA
Matthew .... EVANGELIST,
        APOSTLE
Matto Grosso capital ......
        CUYABA
mattock .... PICK(AX), HACK
        TWIBIL(L)
    like tool ..... ADZ, AXE
mattress .. PALLET, PAILLASE
    case .... TICK
    stuffing material ....
        KAPOK, FLOCK, CEIBA
maturate .. RIPEN, SUPPURATE
maturation .... MEIOSIS
mature ...... AGE, RIPE(N),
    FULL-GROWN, DEVELOPED
    note ..... DUE, PAYABLE
Mau Mau land ...... KENYA
maud .. RUG, SHAWL, PLAID,
        WRAP
    wearer of .... SHEPHERD
maudlin .... SENTIMENTAL,
    TEARFUL, MUSHY, WEEPY,
        TEARY
    sentiment .... MUSH
Maugham (W. Somerset)
    heroine ....
        SADIE (THOMPSON)
    play .... RAIN

maul .... BEETLE, MALLET,
MANGLE, HAMMER, MACE,
CLUB, CLOBBER, BRUISE, PAW
mauler .... WRESTLER, BOXER
Manassas: soubriquet ...
(JACK) DEMPSEY
maumet .. IDOL, DOLL, PUPPET
Mauna Loa crater .. KILAUEA
volcano ...... LOA, KEA
maund ..... BASKET, HAMPER
maunder .... DRIVEL
Maurer, Rumanian premier ..
ION
Mauriac, Fr. novelist ....
FRANCOIS
Maurois, novelist .... ANDRE,
HERZOG
work on George Sand ..
LELIA
work on Shelley ... ARIEL
Mauritania capital ....
NOUAKCHOTT
city .... ATAR, KAEDI
ethnic group ..... MOOR,
NEGRO, BERBER
president ...... DADDAH
Mauser .... RIFLE, PISTOL
mauve .... MALLOW, DYE,
PIGMENT, PURPLE
maverick .. CALF, DOGIE, WAIF
mavis .... THRUSH, BIRD
maw .... CRAW, STOMACH,
GULLET, THROAT, CROP
dialect ..... MA, MAMMA,
MOTHER
mawkish .... SPOON(E)Y,
SICKENING, NAUSEATING,
SENTIMENTAL
max., opposite of .... MIN
maxilla .... JAW(BONE)
segment of ...... STIPES
maxim .... MOTTO, PROVERB,
ADAGE, REDE, TRUISM,
APHORISM, MORAL, SAW,
AXIOM, PRINCIPLE, PRECEPT,
SAYING, GNOME
invention of ....
EXPLOSIVES,
(MACHINE)GUN
Maximalist ...... BOLSHEVIK
maxims, collection of .. SUTRA
religious leader's .. LOGIA
Maxwell .... ELSA, WEBER
May .. HEYDAY, SPRINGTIME,
PRIME, MAIDEN

apple ─.─.─. MANDRAKE,
PLANT
Day folk dance .. MORRIS
Day signal .... SOS,
M'AIDEZ
fifteen ....─. IDES
first .... BELTANE
fly .... DUN, EPHEMERID,
EPHEMERA, DRAKE,
EPHEMERON
tree .... HAWTHORN
VIPs .... MOTHERS
Maya .. SAKTI, DEVI, GODDESS,
INDIAN
consort of .... SIVA
Mayan .... INDIAN
city .. CALAKMUL, UXMAL
maybe .. PERHAPS, PERCHANCE,
MAYHAP, POSSIBLY
Mayday .... SOS, M'AIDEZ,
SIGNAL
Mayence .... MAINZ
Mayflower .... ARBUTUS,
HAWTHORN, COWSLIP,
ANEMONE, MARIGOLD
passengers of the ....
PILGRIMS
mayor ...... BURGOMASTER,
HIZZONER
mayor's domain ...... TOWN,
CITY, MUNICIPALITY
title of address: sl. ......
HIZZONER
mazard .. HEAD, SKULL, FACE,
MAZER
Mazarin, statesman ... JULES,
CARDINAL
maze .... STUPEFY, BEWILDER,
LABYRINTH
exit aid .... CLEW
mazed .... MEANDERED
mazer .. MAZARD, CUP, BOWL,
GOBLET
mazurka ...... DANCE, POLKA
mazzard .... CHERRY
MC's asset .... WIT
McCambridge, actress ....
MERCEDES
McCoy, the real .... GENUINE
McIntosh .... APPLE
McLaglen's role .. INFORMER
mdse. .... MERCHANDISE
mead .... LEA, HYDROMEL
meadow .... LEA, GRASSLAND,
MEAD
barley .... RIE

bird ... BOBOLINK, LARK
grass .... POA, FESCUE
lark .... TROUPIAL
mouse .... VOLE
plant .... INNOCENCE
poetic .... MEAD
rue .... CROWFOOT
meadowsweet ...... SPIR(A)EA
meager .. BARE, SPARE, LEAN,
  THIN, LENTEN, SPARING,
  POOR, INADEQUATE, SPARSE,
  SCANT(Y), EMACIATED
meal .. FARINA, MESS, SPREAD,
  SUPPER, DINNER, BREAKFAST,
  CHOW, FOOD, CORN, GRIST,
  FEED, REPAST, FARE, FLOUR,
  BRAN, PINOLE, AGAPE, MASH
  boiled in milk .... MUSH
  boxed, field ... K RATION
  coarse .... GROUT, SAMP,
    GRITS, HOMINY,
    GROATS
  corn ...... SAMP, HOMINY
  end's serving .... DESSERT
  family .... POTLUCK
  light .... SNACK, LUNCH,
    COLLATION, REFECTION
  main course .... ENTREE
  noon ...... LUNCH(EON)
  oat .... GROATS
  part of .... HELPING,
    SERVING
  table .... BOARD
  wheat .... GROATS
mealies .... MAIZE, CORN
meals .... BOARD
mealy .. FARINACEOUS, PALE,
  POWDERY, SPOTTY, FARINOSE
  mouthed .. EUPHEMISTIC
mean .. LOW-DOWN, AVERAGE,
  CAITIFF, PITIFUL, PITIABLE,
  SCALY, NASTY, BASE, CRUEL,
  SNIDE, CATTY, SIGNIFY,
  DENOTE, POOR, INFERIOR,
  HUMBLE, PALTRY, IGNOBLE,
  INTEND, PETTY, MISERLY,
  VICIOUS, MEDIUM, MIDDLING,
  EVIL
  person .... CAITIFF
meander .. RAMBLE, WANDER,
  ROAM
meandrous .... WINDING,
  TORTUOUS, LABYRINTHINE
meaning ...... SENSE, IMPORT,
  PURPORT, SIGNIFICANCE,
  INTENT

ambiguous in .. CRYPTIC
meaningless .... IDLE, FUTILE
means ..... AGENCY, RICHES,
  WEALTH, RESOURCES, WAY,
  METHOD, TOOL,
  WHEREWITHAL
  by all ...... CERTAINLY,
    OF COURSE
  by any ...... SOMEHOW
  for communicating knowl-
    edge ...... ORGANON
  of defense .... MUNIMENT
  of entry .... DOOR, GATE,
    PORTAL, INGRESS
  of escape .... LOOPHOLE
  of expression ... OUTLET,
    MEDIUM
  of living .... LIVELIHOOD
meantime ... INTERIM, WHILST
measles .. RUBELLA, MORBILLI,
  RUBEOLA, ROSEOLA,
  (ROSE)RASH
  mark .... SPOT
measly ...... SCANTY, SKIMPY,
  MISERLY
measure .. LITER, STEP, METE,
  CRITERION, POLE, PERCH,
  GAUGE, STANDARD, INCH,
  YARD, BUSHEL, FOOT, LAW,
  STATUTE, APPRAISE
  cloth .... ELL
  combining form .. METRO
  depth of .... FATHOM
  distance .... MILE,
    KILOMETER
  dry .... ROTL, BUSHEL
  equality of ... ISOMETRY
  grain .... BUSHEL, PECK
  land .... MORGEN, ACRE,
    AR(E), HECTARE
  length ..... CUBIT, YARD,
    FOOT, ROD, METER,
    STEP, ELL
  liquid .. QUART, TIERCE,
    LITER, TUN, GALLON,
    PINT, GILL, DRAM
  medicine .... DOSE
  metric .... MICRON, TON,
    STERE
  metrical foot ....
    ANAP(A)EST
  nautical .... KNOT
  of .... MENSURAL
  of astronomical distance..
    SECPAR, PARSEC
  of capacity .. CASK, PINT,

PECK, BUSHEL, QUART, STERE, BARREL, TUN
of earth ‥‥‥ GEODESY
of energy ‥‥‥ ENTROPY
of length, ancient ‥‥‥ CUBIT
of wood ‥‥‥‥ CORD
of work, in physics ‥‥‥ ERGON
out ‥‥‥‥‥‥ METE
paper ‥‥‥ REAM, QUIRE
poetry ‥‥‥‥‥ SCAN
sound volume ‥ DECIBEL
speed ‥‥‥‥‥ KNOT
swords ‥ DUEL, CONTEND
time ‥‥‥‥‥ CLOCK
type ‥‥‥‥‥‥ EM, EN
weight ‥‥ GRAIN, GRAM, METAGE, CARAT
wine ‥‥‥‥‥‥ BUTT
wire ‥‥‥‥‥‥ MIL
yard ‥‥‥‥‥‥ VERGE
yarn ‥‥‥‥ LEA, SPINDLE
measured medicine ‥‥ DOSE, DOSAGE
measurement ‥ MENSURATION, DIMENSION, METERAGE
contents/weight ‥‥‥‥ METAGE
end to end ‥‥ LENGTH
standard/unit of ‥‥‥‥ MODULE
measurer ‥‥ METER, GAUGER
measuring instrument ‥‥‥‥ TRANSIT, STADIA, CAL(L)IPER, STADIOMETER, GA(U)GE, METER, SEXTANT
standard ‥‥ YARDSTICK
stick ‥‥‥‥‥ RULE, ROD
unit, sound volume ‥‥‥ DECIBEL
worm ‥‥‥ LOOPER, LARVA
meat ‥‥‥ PORK, FOOD, FLESH, BEEF, MUTTON, VEAL, STEAK, VENISON, TRIPE
and vegetable dish ‥‥‥‥ RAGOUT, OLLA, HASH
ball ‥‥‥ RISSOLE, PINDA
carving board ‥‥‥‥‥‥ TRENCHER
covering, jellylike ‥‥‥‥‥ GLAZE
cured ‥‥‥‥‥‥ HAM
cut ‥‥‥ CHOP, BRISKET, RUMP, FIL(L)ET, RIB, CHUCK, LOIN, STEAK,

ICEBONE, HAM
dish ‥‥‥‥‥ RAVIOLI, SALMAGUNDI, RISSOLE, STEW
dried ‥‥ BILTONG, JERK, PEM(M)ICAN, CHARQUI
eater ‥‥‥‥ CARNIVORE
hard, salted ‥‥‥ JUNK
in gravy ‥‥‥‥ AU JUS
jelly ‥‥‥‥‥‥ ASPIC
juice ‥‥‥‥‥ GRAVY
leg ‥‥‥‥‥‥ CUTLET
paste ‥‥‥ PEM(M)ICAN
pie ‥‥‥ RISSOLE, PATE, PASTY
piece ‥‥ COLP, CHUNK, FIL(L)ET, COLLOP
pickle ‥‥‥‥‥ CORN
pickled ‥‥‥ MARINADE
pig ‥‥‥‥‥‥ PORK
product ‥‥‥‥‥ HAM
restaurant ‥ ROTISSERIE
rib ‥‥‥‥‥ CUTLET
roast ‥ CABOBS, KABOBS, BAR, FRICANDO, FRICANDEAU
roasting device ‥‥‥‥ SKEWER, GRILL, SPIT, BUCCANEER, BROACH
roll ‥‥ RISSOLE, ROULADE
salted, smoked ‥ BACON, HAM
seasoned ‥ BAR, CABOBS
seller ‥‥‥‥ BUTCHER, KNACKER
shop ‥‥‥‥ SHAMBLES, ROTISSERIE
slice ‥‥‥‥‥ COLLOP
spiced ‥‥‥ BOLOGNA, SALAMI, SAUSAGE
stew ‥ HARICOT, RAGOUT, GOULASH, FRICASSEE, OLLA
strips ‥‥‥‥ BILTONG
stuffed ‥‥‥‥ SAUSAGE
thick piece ‥‥‥ CHUNK
meatball ‥‥‥ PINDA, RISSOLE
meatless ‥‥‥‥ MAIGRE
meatman ‥‥‥‥ BUTCHER
meatus ‥‥ OPENING, PASSAGE, FORAMEN, DUCT
mechanical contrivance ‥‥‥ DEVICE, GADGET
game ‥‥‥‥‥ PINBALL
Mecca black stone location ‥ KIBLAH

chief magistrate .. SHERIF
Moslem who visited ....
               HADJI
pilgrimage .... HADJ
pilgrim's dress ... IHRAM
shrine ... KAABA, CAABA
son of ...... MOHAMMED,
              MAHOMET
to Medina journey .....
        HEJIRA, HEGIRA
mechanic, military ....
           ARTIFICER
mechanical .... INVOLUNTARY,
  AUTOMATIC, SPONTANEOUS
bar .... LEVER
man .... ROBOT,
          AUTOMATON
mechanics .... DYNAMICS,
    STATICS, WORKINGS
Mechlin ...... MALINES, LACE
medal .... BADGE, MEDALLION
back of .... VERSO
face of .... OBVERSE
give .. DECORATE, AWARD
space .... EXERGUE
medallion .... CAMEO
medals, collector of ....
        NUMISMATIST
of .... NUMISMATIC
meddle .. TAMPER, INTERFERE,
  INTERVENE, INTRUDE, PRY,
  BUTT IN, INTERLOPE, MELL
meddler .... BUSYBODY,
  KIBITZER, GREMLIN
meddlesome .... CURIOUS,
  OFFICIOUS, INTERFERING
man .... PAUL PRY
Medea .... SORCERESS
consort of .... JASON
father of .... AEETES
victim of .... CREUSA,
    CREON, GLAUCE
Medean king of Persia ......
        CAMBYSES
Medes' language .... AVESTAN
media, part of mass .. PRESS,
    TELEVISION, RADIO
medial ..... MIDDLE, AVERAGE,
       ORDINARY
median .... AVERAGE, MIDDLE,
  MESAL, MEAN, MESNE, MESIAL
priests .... MAGI
mediate .... INTERVENE,
      CONCILIATE
mediator ...... INTERCESSOR,
  ARBITER, ARBITRATOR,

        REFEREE
medic ...... DOC, CORPSMAN,
  SURGEON, PHYSICIAN,
      ALFALFA
medicable .... CURABLE,
      CURATIVE
medical .... IATRIC, CURATIVE
assistant ...... INTERN(E)
combining form .. IATRO
examiner ...... CORONER
group .... AMA
profession symbol ......
      CADUCEUS
science branch ....
  GERIATRICS, THERAPY,
    NEUROLOGY
student .... MEDIC(O),
      INTERN(E)
suffix .... ITIS, OMA
treatment ...... THERAPY
treatment: comb. form ..
      IATRY
medicate .... TREAT
medicated candy .. LOZENGE,
    COUGH DROP
cloth .... STUPE
liquid .... LOTION
medication .... DOSAGE
medicinal .... IATRIC
bark .... PEREIRA,
  VIBURNUM, CINCHONA
capsule .... CACHET
cigarette .... CUBEB
gum .... KINO
herb .... SENNA, ARNICA,
      ALOE
lozenge .... TROCHE
plant .... RUE, COHOSH,
  ALOE, HERB, TANSY,
  SPURGE, SIMPLE,
  URENA, BONESET,
    IPECAC
root .. ZEDOARY, JALAP,
  ARTAR, GINSENG
shrub .... ALEM
tablet .... LOZENGE,
  TROCHE, TABLOID
medicine .... DRUG, REMEDY,
      CURE
capsule .... CACHET
chest .... CABINET
cure-all .... ELIXIR,
     PANACEA
dropper .... PIPETTE
drugs with syrup ......
    ELECTUARY

man ～～～(～(WITCH)DOCTOR, MAGICIAN, ANGEKOK, MUMBOJUMBO, PEAI, QUACK .... SHAMAN,

measure ～～～～ DOSE
mock .... PLACEBO
patent/quack ～ NOSTRUM
pertaining to .... IATRIC
science of .... IATROLOGY
treat with ...... MEDICATE
vomit .... EMETIC
medieval catapult ... ONAGER, MANGONEL, TREBUCHET
coat ...... GAMBESON
empire ...... TREBIZOND
fortification .... CASTLE
galley ～～ AESC, BIREME, GALIOT
household official ...... SENESCHAL
judicial council ... CURIA
knight ～～～ PENNON
lyric .... ALBA
lyric poet .... MINSTREL
musical instrument ～～ ROT(T)E, LUTE, LYRE, REBEC(K)
servant ～～～～ SEWER
shield ...... ECU, PAVIS
ship .... DROMON
singer ～～～ MINSTREL, TROUBADOUR
sport ～～～ TILT, JOUST, TOURNEY
town ～～～～ BOURG
trading vessel .... NEF
tunic ～～ JUPON, GIPON
vassal ～～～ VAVASOR
village .... BOURG
war engine ～～～ BOAR, TREBUCHET
warship ～～～ DROMON
weapon .... MACE, ONCIN
wind instrument ～～～ SACKBUT
mediocre ～～ SO SO, INFERIOR, ORDINARY, AVERAGE, MIDDLING
meditate ～～～ MUSE, BROOD, PORE, PONDER, REFLECT, CONTEMPLATE, RUMINATE, MULL
meditative ～ PENSIVE, MUSING
Mediterranean ～.... INLAND, LANDLOCKED

bush ～～～～～ CAPER
city .... ORAN
country .... TUNISIA
evergreen .. LAURUSTINE
fish .... OMBER
galley .. BIREME, TRIREME, GAL(L)IOT
grass .... DISS
gulf ～～ TARANTO, TUNIS
island ..... CAPRI, LIDO, ELBA, RODI, SICILY, GOZO, MALTA, CRETE, SARDINIA
pine ～～～～～ PINASTER
pirate ～～～～ XEBEC
plant ～～～. MANDRAKE, TURNSOLE
principality ～～. MONACO
raisin ～～～～ SULTANA
regions ～～～～ LEVANT
resin ～～～～.... MASTIC
resort ～～～ NICE, LIDO, RIVIERA, MENTON
river to the ～ EBRO, NILE, RHONE
sailboat ～～～ LATEEN, CAIQUE
seaport ～～～～ TETUAN, TOULON, TRIPOLI, PORT SAID
ship ～～～ XEBEC, SETEE, FELUCCA, SAIC, TARTAN, LATEEN, ZEBEC(K), POLACRE
ship master ～. PADRONE
shrub ...... LAURUSTINE
sparoid ...... GILTHEAD
trading ship ... PADRONE
tree .... CAROB
tributary .... TIBER, TEVERE, ORONTES
vessel .... FELUCCA, LATEEN, GALLEASS
volcanic island .. LIPARI
warship .... BIREME, TRIREME
wind ～～～ LEVANTER, MISTRAL, PTESIAN, SOLANO, SIROCCO
medium ～ AGENCY, MEAN(S), AVERAGE
artist's .... CANVAS, OIL, CLAY, BRONZE, MUSIC, PAINTING, STONE, VIOLIN, PIANO

exchange .... MONEY, CURRENCY
in music .... MEZZO
response of a .... ORACLE
session with a ... SEANCE
size .... MIDDLING
spiritualistic .... PSYCHIC
with deities ..... ORACLE
medley .. MIXTURE, FANTASIA, MACEDOINE, FARRAGO, OLIO, POTPOURRI, MELANGE, PASTICHE, CENTO, SALMAGUNDI, HODGEPODGE, PASTICCIO
race .... RELAY
medulla ...... MARROW, PITH
oblongata .... BULB
medullary sheath .... MYELIN
Medusa .. GORGON, JELLYFISH
hair of .... SNAKE(S)
sister of .... STHENO, EURYALE
slayer of ...... PERSEUS
medusan .... JELLYFISH
meed .. REWARD, RECOMPENSE
meek .. SPINELESS, LAMBLIKE, HUMBLE, LOWLY, SUBMISSIVE
meerschaum .... SEPIOLITE, PIPE, MINERAL, SEAFOAM
meet ...... EQUAL, CONVENE, RENDEZVOUS, MATCH, SEEMLY, ENCOUNTER, CONFRONT, FACE, ASSEMBLE, FIT(TING), SIT
by appointment ... DATE, RENDEZVOUS
companion of ... PROPER
face to face ... CONFRONT
meeting .... RALLY, HUDDLE, CAUCUS, DATE, SESSION, ASSEMBLY, GATHERING, BEE, CONFERENCE, CONCLAVE, SYMPOSIUM
clandestine .... RENDEZVOUS, TRYST
full attendance .... PLENARY
hostile .... DUEL, RENCONTRE, RENCOUNTER
lovers' .... TRYST, RENDEZVOUS
place of "Big Three" ... POTSDAM, YALTA, CASABLANCA
point .... JUNCTION

room .... CAMARILLA
to elect Pope .. CONCLAVE
megalomania ...... DELUSION
megalomaniac's delusion ....
POWER, GRANDEUR, WEALTH
megapod .... MALEO
mound-building .. LEIPOA
megalith ..... STONE, MENHIR
structure using ....
DOLMEN, CROMLECH, MONUMENT, TOMB
megaphone of a kind ....
LOUDSPEAKER
megass(e) .... BAGASSE
Megiddo ..... ARMAGEDDON
megrim(s) ..... VERTIGO, WHIM, HEADACHE, MIGRAINE, FANCY, FAD, BLUES
Mehitabel .... CAT
Mehta, conductor ... ZUBIN
Meiji emperor .... MUTSUHITO
"Mein Kampf" author ......
HITLER
meinie (meiny) .... RETINUE, RETAINERS, HOUSEHOLD
meiosis .... LITOTES, MATURATION, REDUCTION
Meir, Israeli premier ... GOLDA
Mekong .... LANTSANG
mel .... HONEY
actor .... FERRER
baseballer .... OTT
singer .... TORME
melancholia .... GLOOM, DEPRESSION
melancholic spell ...... HUMP
melancholy .... DREAR, SAD(NESS), ATRABILIOUS, GLOOMY, PENSIVE, BLUE, HIPPED, SOMBER
fit of .... HYP(S), HUMP, HYPOCHONDRIA
Melanesian islands .... FIJI, SOLOMON, ADMIRALTY
native .... FIJI
melange ...... MIXTURE, OLIO, HODGEPODGE
melanin .... PIGMENT
melanite .... GARNET
melanoma .... TUMOR
melanous, opposed to ....
XANTHOUS
Melba, soprano ...... NELLIE
Melchior, tenor ..... LAURITZ
meld .. BLEND, MERGE, UNITE
Meleager .... ARGONAUT

animal killed by ... BOAR
mother of ...... ALTHEA
melee .... FREE-FOR-ALL,
RUMBLE, MIX-UP, SCUFFLE,
BRAWL, (AF)FRAY, RUCKUS,
HASSLE, SKIRMISH
melic .... LYRIC
melicocca .... GENIP
melilot .... CLOVER
melinite .. LYDDITE, EXPLOSIVE
mell .... MEDDLE, MIX
melli: comb. form .... HONEY
mellifluous .... HONEYED
mellow .... RIPE(N), SOFT,
MATURE, LOAMY, TIPSY,
GOOD, AGE
melodeon .... ACCORDION
like .... HARMONIUM
melodic .... LYRICAL, ARIOSE
embellishment ....
GRACE NOTE, CADENZA
phrase .... OSTINATO
melodious .... CANOROUS,
DULCET, ORPHEAN, TUNEFUL,
ARIOSO, MUSICAL
melodrama ..... HISTRIONICS
melodramatic ... HISTRIONIC
melody .. ARIA, LAY, STRAIN,
CAVATINA, ARIETTA, AIR,
TUNE, SONG
counterpoint to main ...
DESCANT
meloid .... BEETLE
melon .. PEPO, CANTALOUP(E),
GOURD, CAS(S)ABA
dessert .... BOMB
pear .... PEPINO
slang .... PROFITS
Melpomene .... MUSE
melt ... RUN, FUSE, DISSOLVE,
SOFTEN, THAW, LIQUEFY,
FUZE, VANISH
fat .... RENDER
into mold ...... FOUND
ore .... SMELT
melted .... FUSIL(E)
melting pot .... CRUCIBLE,
AMERICA
Melville, novelist ... HERMAN
character .... AHAB,
WHALE, MOBY DICK,
BILLY BUDD
novel ..... TYPEE, OMOO,
MOBY DICK
member .. ORGAN, LIMB, LEG,
ARM, AFFILIATE, PART

academy .... FELLOW
club ... ROTARIAN, LION,
JAYCEE
embassy staff .. ATTACHE
fraternity ...... BROTHER
sorority .... SISTER
membership .... AFFILIATION,
SEAT
charge .... DUE
membrane .... PIA, WEB,
COVERING, VELUM, VELAMEN,
PELLICLE, TELA
animal eye .... TAPETUM
bird's beak .... CERE
brain .... MENINGES,
PIA MATER,
DURA MATER,
ARACHNOID
combining form ....
HYMEN(O)
diffusion thru .. OSMOSIS
egg yolk .... VITELLINE
embryo's sac ... AMNION
enclosing .... CAUL
eye .... UVEA, CORNEA
eyeball .... SCLERA
fetus .... CHORION, CAUL
fold of mucous ... PLICA
lining abdominal cavity ..
PERITONEUM
nictitating .... HAW
uniting toes/fingers .....
WEB(BING)
membranous covering ....
INVOLUCRE
layer .... TAPETUM
Memel River city ..... TILSIT
Memmon, killer of .. ACHILLES
memento .. RELIC, KEEPSAKE,
TOKEN, PRAYER, SOUVENIR,
REMEMBRANCE, TROPHY
memo .... NOTE, CHIT
memoir ...... REMINISCENCE,
BIOGRAPHY, MONOGRAPH
memorabilia .... ANA
memorable ... NOTABLE
period ...... EPOCH, ERA
memorandum .... CHIT, NOTE,
BRIEF, MINUTE
pad .... TICKLER
memorial .... SHRINE, STATUE,
COMMEMORATIVE,
MONUMENT, TROPHY
of a sort ...... PETITION
post .. XAT, TOTEM, XYST
memory ...... REMINISCENCE,

REMEMBRANCE, RECOLLECTION
book ... DIARY, MEMOIR, ALBUM
helping the .. MNEMONIC
loss of .... AMNESIA
of .. MNESIC, MNEMONIC
pertaining to .... MNESIC
pill .... CYCLERT, RIBAMINOL
science to improve ...... MNEMONICS
testing device .... TACHISTOSCOPE
Memphis god .... PTAH
high priest .... RANOFER
river .... NILE
ruler .... PHARAOH
men in blue suits .. UMP(IRES)
in white ...... DOCTORS
of .... MASCULINE
of letters ..... LITERATI
party for .... STAG, SMOKER
men's affair ... STAG, SMOKER
menace .... THREAT(EN)
menacing .... MINATORY, MINACIOUS
menad .. NYMPH, BACCHANTE
menage .... HOUSEHOLD, HOUSEKEEPING, DOMICILE
menagerie .... ZOO
mend .... COBBLE, PATCH, DARN, REPAIR, IMPROVE, FIX
in tailoring ..... BUSHEL
mendacious .... FALSE, LYING
mendacity ... LIE, FALSEHOOD
Mendel, botanist .... GREGOR
forte of ...... GENETICS, HEREDITY
Mendelssohn, composer ...... FELIX
mender .... REPAIRER
pots/pans ...... TINKER
shoe .... COBBLER
socks .... DARNER
tear .... DARNER
mendicant .. BEGGAR, BEGGING
kind of .... FRIAR
Moslem .... FAKIR
Menelaus' brother .... AGAMEMNON
daughter .... HERMIONE
father .... ATREUS
wife .... HELEN
menhaden ..... YELLOWTAIL,

FISH, HERRING, WHITING, POGY, MOSSBUNKER, HARDHEAD, OLDWIFE
menhir .... MEGALITH, MONUMENT
menial .... SERVILE, SERVANT, DOMESTIC
meninges .... ARACHNOID, PIA MATER
meniscus .... LENS, CRESCENT
Menlo Park inventor .. EDISON
Mennonite .... AMISH
menopause ...... CLIMATERIC
Menotti, composer .... GIAN-CARLO
heroine .... AMELIA
mensal .... MONTHLY
menstrual .... MONTHLY
discharge .... CATAMENIA
mental .... INTELLECTUAL, PHRENIC
attitude ..... VIEWPOINT
bias .... WARP
communication .... TELEPATHY
concept .... IDEA
condition .... DEMENTIA
deficiency ...... IDIOCY, IMBECILITY, AMENTIA, MORONITY, MONGOLISM
discipline .... YOGA
disorder ..... PARANOIA, SCHIZOPHRENIA, NEUROSIS, DISTEMPER
drug .... METRAZOL
effort .... HEADWORK, CEREBRATION
hospital ..... BUGHOUSE, BEDLAM
patient ...... BEDLAMITE
perception .... KEN
picture ..... IDEA, VISTA, PHANTASM, FANTASM, RECEPT, VISION, FANCY
quirk .... WARP
reservation .... QUALIFICATION
reservation, dishonest ... SALVO
state .... MORALE, MOOD, DISPOSITION
strain .... TENSION
training .... EDUCATION
view .... OUTLOOK
mentality .. MIND, ATTITUDE, DISPOSITION

mentally alert .... ACUTE
   deficient person .. IDIOT,
      IMBECILE, MORON
   sound ..... LUCID, SANE
   wandering ... DELIRIOUS
mention .... CITE, ALLUDE,
  SPECIFY, REFER(ENCE), NAME
mentor ... ADVISER, TEACHER,
      COACH
mentum .... CHIN
menu .. CARTE, BILL (OF FARE)
  item .... ENTREE
Menuhin, violinist .. YEHUDI
  teacher of ...... ENESCO
Mephisto(pheles), debtor of ..
      FAUST(US)
Mephistophelean .... CRAFTY,
  DIABOLICAL, FIENDISH
mephitic .... NOXIOUS,
      POISONOUS
mephitis ..... MIASMA, DAMP,
      STENCH
mercantile ...... COMMERCIAL
  paper .... DRAFT, CHECK
mercaptan .... THIOL
Mercator ... CARTOGRAPHER,
  GEOGRAPHER, MAPMAKER
mercenary .... HIRED, VENAL,
  GREEDY, HIRELING, SORDID,
      POTHUNTER
  soldier .... HESSIAN,
  CONDOTTIERE, SWISSER
mercery .... TEXTILES
merchandise .. COMMODITIES,
    WARE(S), GOODS
merchant .. TRADER, COSTER,
  SHOPKEEPER, DEALER
  fleet captain ....
      COMMODORE
  of .... MERCANTILE
  of Venice character .....
    ANTONIO, SHYLOCK,
    TUBAL, PORTIA,
    JESSICA, NERISSA,
    BASSANIO, SOLANIO,
    GOBBO, SALERIO
  ship ... TRADER, ARGOSY,
      GAL(L)IOT
  ship captain ... MASTER
  ship, India-England .....
      INDIAMAN
  ships collectively ....
      MARINE
merchants, guild of ... HANSE
merci .... THANKS
merciless .... GRIM

Mercouri, actress ... MELINA
mercurial .. VOLATILE, FICKLE,
      SWIFT
mercuric chloride ... CALOMEL
  sulfide .... CINNABAR,
      VERMILION
Mercury ... HERMES, PLANET,
  QUICKSILVER, MESSENGER,
      AZOTH
  cap of .... PETASUS
  ore .... CINNABAR
  shoes of .... TALARIA
  staff of ...... CADUCEUS
mercy .... HUMANITY, GRACE,
  CHARITY, CLEMENCY,
  COMPASSION, LENITY
  grant .... SPARE
  in military usage ....
      QUARTER
  killing ..... EUTHANASIA
mere .. ONLY, NOTHING MORE,
  LAKE, SEA, MARSH, POND,
  BOUNDARY, SIMPLE
  nonsense .... FALDERAL
  nothing .... FIDDLESTICK
merely .. ONLY, PURELY, JUST,
      SIMPLY
meretricious .... TAWDRY
merganser ..... HARLE, SMEE,
  GOOSANDER, SMEW, DUCK,
      SHELDRAKE
merge .. MELD, MELT, UNITE,
  MIX, FUSE, BLEND, ABSORB
merger ..... FUSION, COMBINE
Merida is capital of ....
      YUCATAN
meridian .... NOON, APEX,
  ZENITH, PRIME
merino .. WOOL, SHEEP, YARN
merit .... VIRTUE, EARN,
  WORTH, DESERT, VALUE,
  EXCELLENCE, DESERVE, MEED
merits .... QUALITIES
Merkel, actress .... UNA
merl(e) .... BLACKBIRD
  actress ...... OBERON
Merlin ..... SEER, MAGICIAN,
  FALCON, PIGEON-HAWK
  mistress of ..... VIVIAN
Mermaid Tavern habitue .....
  (BEN) JONSON, SHAKESPEARE
Meroe's location ...... NILE,
      ETHIOPIA
meros ...... THIGH, SURFACE
Merovingian king .... CLOVIS

Merrimac .... IRONCLAD,
FRIGATE
merriment ... MIRTH, GAIETY,
GLEE, FROLIC
merry .. JOCOSE, GAY, FESTIVE,
MIRTHFUL, JOLLY, FESTAL
Andrew .. JOKER, JESTER,
MIME, CLOWN,
BUFFOON
go-round .... WHIRLIGIG,
TURNABOUT, WHIRL,
CAR(R)OUSEL,
CAR(R)OUSAL
maker .... REVEL(L)ER
making, riotous ... ORGY
making time .. CARNIVAL,
FESTIVAL
monarch .... COLE
person .... ANDREW
thought ...... WISHBONE
Widow composer ....
LEHAR
mesa ... FLATRAIL, TABLELAND,
BUTTE
mescal ...... CACTUS, AGAVE,
LIQUOR, PEYOTE
mescaline .... ALKALOID
mesh ...... NET(WORK), WEB,
INTERLOCK, TISSUE,
ENTANGLE, ENGAGE, NETTING
knot ...... SHEET BEND
meshed ..... SHRINE, GEARED
fabric .... NET, LACE
is in ___ .... IRAN
mesial plane .... MESON
mesmeric .... MAGNETIC,
HYPNOTIC
force .... OD
mesmerism ...... MAGNETISM,
HYPNOTISM
mesmerist .... HYPNOTIST
mesne .... MIDDLE,
INTERMEDIATE
meson .... TETRACHORD,
BARYTRON, PENETRON
Mesopotamia .... IRAQ, IRAK
boat .... GUFA
city ...... EDESSA, URFA,
NIPPUR
wind .... SHAMAL
mesquit(e) ...... ALGARROBA,
SCREWBEAN
bean flour ...... PINOLE
mess .. FOOD, MEAL, JUMBLE,
MUDDLE, BOTCH, BUNGLE,
CHOW, HODGEPODGE, HASH,

MEDDLE, PUTTER, MUSS
message .... COMMUNICATION,
REPORT, WORD
messenger .. NUNCIO, ENVOY,
ERRAND BOY, HARBINGER,
HERALD, PAGE
of the gods ... MERCURY,
HERMES
Messiah ... JESUS, DELIVERER
composer ...... HANDEL
Messina, rock in the Straits of
SCYLLA
Messrs. .. MESSIEURS, MISTERS
messuage .. TOFT, HOMESTEAD
messy ...... UNTIDY, DIRTY
mestee .... MUSTEE
mestizo ...... METIS, LADINO
metabolism .. METAMORPHOSIS,
TRANSFORMATION,
METASTASIS
metal .... IRON, TIN, LEAD,
ALUMINUM
alloy .... BRONZE, BRASS,
MONEL(L), NIELLO,
STEEL, SOLDER
assaying vessel .... TEST,
CUPEL
band .... COLLET
bar .. OFFSET, INGOT, FID
block .... DIB
bolt .... RIVET
casting(s) ... PIG, INGOT,
FOUNDRY
coat with .... PLATE,
TERNE
coating ... PATINA, RUST
"coin," slot machine ....
SLUG
comb .... CARD
cutting tool ... HACKSAW
decorative alloy .. NIELLO
disk .... MEDAL, PATEN,
MEDALLION, SEQUIN
dross .... SLAG
extracting apparatus ....
SMELTER
eyelet .... GROMMET
fabric .... LAME
fastener .... TNUT
filings .... LEMEL
for coinage ...... FLAN,
PLANCHET
hard-tipped end .... TAG
heavy .... LEAD
in furnace, molten ......
BATH

leaf .... FOIL
lightest .... LITHIUM
line of type .... SLUG
lining .... BUSH(ING)
loop of .... EYE
marker ..... DIE, STAMP,
SWAGE
mass from outer space ..
METEOR(ITE)
mixture .... ALLOY
patching/joining alloy ..
SOLDER
peg/pin .... SPILL, BOLT,
GUDGEON
piece .... SHIM
plate .. PATEN, PATIN(A),
HORSESHOE
plate, cut .... TREPAN
plate on scabbard ......
CHAPE
plate, thin .. SHIM, LAME
purify .... SMELT
rare-earth .. LANTHANUM
rattle .... SISTRUM
refine .... SMELT
refuse ..... SLAG, DROSS,
SCORIA, SCUM
ring ..... BEE, GROMMET
rod .... BOLT
scum .... DROSS
shaped for coinage ......
FLAN
shaper ...... SWAGE, DIE,
STAMP, LATHE
shavings .... WOOL
sheet cutter ...... SHEAR
sheet of .. FOIL, LAMINA,
TAGGERS, LATTEN
spacer, in printing ......
SLUG
strip ...... SLAT, SPLINT
suit ...... MAIL, ARMOR,
HAUBERK
thread ..... WIRE, LAME
threads, cloth made of ..
LAME
waste ..... SPRUE, SLAG,
CALX, CALCES
welding .... SOLDER
white .. ALUMINUM, TIN
worker .. SMITH, WELDER
works .... FOUNDRY,
SMITHY
Metalious, novelist ... GRACE
work .... PEYTON PLACE
metallic rock .... ORE

sound .. CLASH, CLANK,
CLINK
sulfide .... PYRITE
wire .... LAME
metalloid .. SILICON, ARSENIC
metals, melting and molding of
FOUNDRY, CASTING
metalware, enameled ... TOLE
metalworker .... WELDER,
(TIN)SMITH, RIVETER
metamer .... ISOMER
metamere .. SOMITE, SEGMENT
metamerism .. SEGMENTATION
metamorphose ... TRANSFORM
"Metamorphoses" author ....
OVID
character ...... THISBE,
PYRAMUS
metamorphosis ....
TRANSFORMATION, CHANGE,
METASTASIS
metaphorlike figure of speech ..
TROPE, SIMILE
mixed ...... CATACHRESIS
metaphorical ..... FIGURATIVE
metaphrase .... TRANSLATION,
TRANSLATE
metaphysical ...... ABSTRACT,
SUBTLE, ABSTRUSE
poet .. DONNE, CRASHAW,
COWLEY
metastasis ...... METABOLISM,
TRANSFORMATION
metathesis .... TRANSPOSITION
Metaxas, Gr. general ....
JOANNES
mete .. DOLE, ALLOT, MEASURE,
APPORTION, LIMIT,
BOUNDARY
metencephalon .... HINDBRAIN
meteoric .... DAZZLING, SWIFT
phenomenon ..... HAIL
shower .. LEONID, PERSEID
meteor .... BIELID, FIREBALL,
SHOOTING STAR, HAIL,
RAINBOW, LEONID, PERSEID
exploding .. BOLIDE, BOLIS
train of .... TAIL
meteorite .... AEROLITH,
AEROLITE, SIDERITE,
ANIGHITO, TEKTITE,
WILLIAMETTE
meteorologic prefix ... STRATO
meteorologist's concern .....
CLIMATE, WEATHER

meteors, shower of ... ...
   ANDROMID, LEONID, PERSEID
meter .... RHYTHM, CADENCE
   cubic .... STERE
   face of .... DIAL
   millionth part of ......
       MICRON, MIKRON
meters, 100 square .... AR(E)
   10,000 square ... HECTARE
methane ... ... PARAFFIN,
       HYDROCARBON
metheglin ... ... MEAD, LIQUOR
   material ... ... HONEY
method ...... SYST(EM), WAY,
   PROCEDURE, PROCESS,
   MANNER, MODE, TECHNIQUE
   of making .... FACTURE
   of procedure ....
       TECHNIQUE
methodical .... ORDERLY,
   SYSTEMATIC, FORMAL
Methodism, founder of ......
       WESLEY
Methodist Church, of the ...
       WESLEYAN
   preacher ..... ROUNDER
Methuselah's claim to fame ..
       AGE
   father ... ... ENOCH
   grandson .... NOAH
meticulous .... FINICAL,
   CAREFUL, SCRUPULOUS
metier .. TRADE, OCCUPATION,
   PROFESSION, FORTE, WORK,
   SPECIALTY
metif(f) .. HALFBREED, MESTEE
metis .... MULATTO
metopic .... FRONTAL
metric measure .... HECTARE,
   DECIARE, DECASTRE, AR(E),
   LITER, STERE, KILO, DECARE,
       GRAM
   ton .... MILLIER
metrical accent .... ICTUS
   beat .... ICTUS
   composition ... ... POEM,
       VERSE
   foot .. ANAPEST, DACTYL,
   IAMB(US), TROCHEE,
   CHORIAMB(US),
   TRIBRACH, PYRRHIC
   stress .... ICTUS
   time unit .... MORA
   writing .. VERSE, POETRY
metrify .... VERSIFY
metro .... SUBWAY

metropolis ... ... CITY, CAPITAL,
       SEE, SEAT
metropolitan ... (ARCH)BISHOP,
   URBAN, EPARCH
   Opera man ... ... BING,
       MEHTA
mettle ... ... COURAGE, SPIRIT,
   ARDOR, SPUNK, PLUCK
mettlesome .. BRAVE, SPUNKY,
   COURAGEOUS, GAME
Metz's river ... ... MOSELLE
Meuse ... ... MAAS, LESSE
   River city .... SEDAN
mew ... GARAGE, BARN, SHED,
   CAGE, STABLE, (SEA)GULL,
       MOLT, DEN
   cat's ... ... MIAOW, MEOW,
       MIAU
mewl ... ... WHIMPER, WHINE
mews ... ... STABLES
Mexican ... ... NAHUATL
   agave .... PULQUE
   alcoholic drink ... ...
       PULQUE, MESCAL,
       TEQUILA
   American to a ... GRINGO,
       YANQUI
   Aztec emperor ....
       MONTEZUMA
   bandit ... ... LADRONE,
       BANDIDO
   basket grass ... ... ISTLE
   battlesite .. BUENAVISTA
   bean beetle ... LADYBUG
   beverage ... ... OCTLI,
       PULQUE, TEQUILA,
       MESCAL
   beverage seed ... ... CHIA
   bird .. TINAMOU, VERDIN
   blanket .... SERAPE
   bread ... ... TORTILLA
   brick .... ADOBE
   cactus ... MESCAL, PEYOTE,
       CHAUTE
   cake ... ... TORTILLA
   cat, wild, spotted ... ...
       MARGAY, EYRA
   city ... ... MONTERREY,
   PUEBLA, JUAREZ,
   COLIMA, TAMPICO,
   JALAPA, OAXACA,
   PACHUCA, ORIZABA,
       GUADALAJARA
   coin ... ... PESO, CENTAVO
   conqueror ...... CORTEZ
   corn cake ..... TORTILLA

corn mush ...... ATOLE, AMOLE
cottonwood ..... ALAMO
cypress .... AHUEHUETE
dance .... RASPA
dish .... TAMALE, TACOS, ENCHILADA
district .... TEQUILA
dog .... CHIHUAHUA
dollar .... PESO
drink .. TEQUILA, PULQUE, MESCAL
emperor .. MAXIMILIAN, MONTEZUMA
fascist movement ....
    SINARCHISM, SINARQUISM
fiber plant .. DATIL, PITA, ISTLE, IXTLE, SISAL
food .... TAMALE
gopher .... TUZA
grass .... OTATE, TUCAN, TEOSINTE, ZACATON
grinding stone .. METATE
gruel .... ATOLE
handyman .... MOZO
hut .... JACAL
illegal migrant ....
    WETBACK
Indian .... OTOMI, ZUNI, SERI, TOLTEC, OPATA, MAYAN, AZTEC, LIPAN, YAQUI, ALAIS
Indian craft .... OJOS
intoxicating drink ......
    MESCAL, PULQUE, TEQUILA
laborer .. PEON, BRACERO
liquor .... TEQUILA, PULQUE, MESCAL
man .... HOMBRE
mat .... PETATE
mescal .... PEYOTE
minnow ...... MOONFISH
mix-blood ...... MESTIZO
monetary unit ..... PESO
mountain .... PARICUTIN, TOLUCA, ORIZABA, COLIMA
mullet .... BOBO, LISITA
muralist .... RIVERA, OROZCO
mush .... ATOLE
musical instrument .....
    CLARIN
native .. AZTEC, MAYA(N)
noble .... HIDALGO

onyx .... TECALI
painter .... OROZCO, RIVERA
patriot .... JUAREZ
peasant .... PEON
peninsula .... YUCATAN
persimmon .... CHAPOTE
pine .... OCOTE
plant .... CHIA, MAGUEY, SOTOL, AGAVE, PULQUE, MESCAL, OCOTILLO, CACTUS, JALAP, DATIL, AMOLE
plantation .... HACIENDA
policemen ..... RURALES
poppy .... CHICALOTE
president ..... MADERO, ALEMAN, DIAZ, CALLES, MATEOS, GIL, HUERTA, CARDENAS, CAMACHO, JUAREZ, ORDAZ, CARRANZA, OBREGON
pyramid ..... TEOCALLI
raccoonlike animal ....
    CACOMISTLE
race ..... MAYA, TOLTEC, AZTEC
ranch .... HACIENDA
reed .... OTATE
resin tree .... DRAGO
revolutionary ....
    (PANCHO) VILLA
river .. RIO BRAVO, FUERTE, SALADO, YAQUI
robber .... BANDIDO
rodent .... TUCAN
rubber tree ... (GUAY)ULE
ruins, site of .. PALENQUE
salamander ... AXOLOTL
saloon .... CANTINA
sandals ..... HUARACHES
sauce .... TABASCO
scarf .... TAPALO
scorpion .. VINEGARROON
seaport ...... ACAPULCO, TAMPICO, MATAMOROS
shawl .... SERAPE
shrub .... GUAYULE
"spitfire" actress ....
    (LUPE) VELEZ
state .... SINALOA, VERACRUZ, CHIAPAS, CHIHUAHUA, COLIMA, HIDALGO, PUEBLA, ZACATECAS, DURANGO,

JALISCO, SONORA, TABASCO, YUCATAN
state capital . . . . . JALAPA, OAXACA, CULIACAN, TOLUCA, TUXTLA, MERIDA, GUADALAJARA, HERMOSILLO
statesman . . . . JUAREZ
sugar . . . . PANOCHA, PENUCHI, PENUCHE, PANOCHE
tea . . . . APASOTE
temple . . . . TEOCALLI
tennis star . . . . OSUNA
thong . . . . ROMAL
tree . . . ABETO, GUAYULE, DRAGO, RETAMA, MESQUIT(E), AHUEHUETE, ULE
volcano . . . . ORIZABA, PARICUTIN, COLIMA, POPOCATEPETL, BOQUERON, TOLUCA
weight . . . . ARROBA
wild oat . . . . EYRA
wind instrument . . . . . . CLARIN
wood . . . . LINALOA
Mexico City district . . . . . . TACUBAYA
empress of . . CARLO(T)TA
Meyerbeer, composer . . . . . . GIACOMO, JAKOB
opera by . . . L'AFRICAINE
mezereon . . . . DAPHNE
mezuzah, name on . . SHADDAI
mezzanine . . . . ENTRESOL
mezzo . . . . HALF, MEDIUM, MODERATE, SOMEWHAT
mho, reciprocal of . . . . . OHM
Miami county . . . . . DADE
miasma . . . . METHANE
disease . . . . MALARIA
mlb(s) . . . . MARBLE(S)
mica . . . . . BIOTITE, NACRITE, TALC, SILICATE, MINERAL, MUSCOVITE, PARAGONITE, LEPIDOLITE
transparent . . . ISINGLASS
Micah . . . . PROPHET, MICHEAS
Micawber, Dickens' . . . . . . WILKINS
what he has plenty of . . . OPTIMISM
mice . . . . VERMIN
of . . . . MURINE

Michael . . . . . (ARCH)ANGEL, ORANGE
Michaelmas daisy . . . . ASTER
miche . . . . PILFER, SKULK
Micheas . . . . MICAH, PROPHET
Michener (James) novel . . . . . . HAWAII, IBERIA
Michigan capital . . . LANSING
city . . . . DETROIT, FLINT, DEARBORN, LANSING, GRAND RAPIDS, IONIA, KALAMAZOO, SAGINAW, PONTIAC
county . . . ALGER, CASS, CLARE, IOSCO
lake city . . . MILWAUKEE, MUSKEGON
lake port . . . . . . RACINE
nickname . . . . WOLVERINE STATE
river . . . . CASS
state animal . . . . WOLVERINE
state bird . . . . ROBIN
state fish . . . . TROUT
Mick of "Rolling Stones" . . . . JAGGER
Mickey . . . . FINN, MOUSE, ROONEY
mickle . . . . MUCH
micra, singular of . . . MICRON
miscrastur . . . . HAWK
micrify . . . . MINIMIZE
microbe . . BACTERIUM, GERM, MICROORGANISM, VIRUS, PATHOGEN
microcosm . . . WORLD, MAN, UNIVERSE
microgram . . . . GAMMA
Micronesia island . . . NAURU, PONAPE
microorganism(s) . . . . . VIRUS, PROTOZOA, BACTERIA, AM(O)EBA
microphone . . . . MIKE
range of . . . . BEAM
microscope glass plate . . SLIDE
microscopic . . . . MINUTE
microspores . . . . POLLEN
Midas' touch, product of . . . . GOLD
midday . . . . NOON
middle . . . . . MESIAL, MEDIAN, MESNE, MEDIAL, MID, MEAN, WAIST, CENTER, MIDST, HUB
Ages, of the . . MEDIEVAL

Ages, the .... MOYEN AGE
class .... BOURGEOIS(IE),
        BOURGEOISE
combining form ....
        MEDI(O)
ear ... TYMPANUM, DRUM
East country ..... IRAN,
        IRAQ, INDIA, TIBET,
        BURMA
in law .... MESNE
kingdom .... CHINA
part .... DEEP
toward the .... MESAD
way .... VIA MEDIA
West product ..... CORN
middlebreaker .... LISTER
middleman .... BROKER,
        INTERMEDIARY, GO-BETWEEN
middling .... AVERAGE, SOSO,
        MEDIOCRE, ORDINARY,
        MEDIUM, PORK
middy .. MIDSHIPMAN, BLOUSE
Midgard .... EARTH
to Asgard ..... BIFROST
midge .. FLY, GNAT, MIDGET,
        BANTAM, DWARF, PUNKIE
midget ...... MIDGE, DWARF,
        MINIATURE
Midianite king ... HUR, REBA
midland .... INTERIOR
dialects .... MERCIAN
midmorning .... TEN, ELEVEN
midnight sun, land of ....
        NORWAY
midriff .... DIAPHRAGM
midshipman .. REEFER, MIDDY,
        PLEBE
"Midsummer Night's Dream"
        character .... THISBE,
        PUCK, OBERON, HERMIA,
        TITANIA
tinker .... SNOUT
midterm event ...... EXAM(S)
midway features .. SIDESHOWS
island .. SAND, EASTERN
Islands discoverer ......
        BROOKS
midweek .... WEDNESDAY
midwifery ...... OBSTETRICS,
        TOCOLOGY
mien ... LOOK, AIR, BEARING,
        APPEARANCE, MANNER
miff ..... HUFF, TIFF, OFFEND
miggle ..... TAW, MIBS, MIGS
might .. POWER, VIGOR, FORCE,
        STRENGTH

and _____ .... MAIN
mightily .... AMAIN
mighty .... VERY, POWERFUL,
        PUISSANT, EXTREMELY,
        STRONG, GREAT, HUGE,
        POTENT
mignon ..... DAINTY, PRETTY
mignonette .. RESEDA, PLANT,
        WELD, WOLD
migraine .. HEADACHE, MEGRIM
migrate .... MOVE, TREK
migration ..... EXODUS, TREK
birds/animals' ....
        VISITATION
migratory .... NOMADIC,
        ROVING, WANDERING,
        PEREGRINE
bird .. TERN, WI(D)GEON,
        SHOVELER, KUTSARA
butterfly ..... MONARCH
creature ...... LEMMING,
        LOCUST
horde .... SWARM
worker .. JOAD, BRACERO,
        OKIE, PEON, WETBACK,
        ARKIE, HOBO
Mikado ... EMPEROR, OPERA
character .... YUM YUM,
        KOKO
court of the ..... DAIRI,
        DAIRO
mike ..... LOAF, MICROPHONE
milady's concern .. HAIRDO,
        FIGURE, DIET, WEIGHT,
        WAISTLINE
Milan opera house ....
        (LA) SCALA
mild .. PLACID, SOFT, GENTLE,
        TEMPERATE, MODERATE,
        BLAND, LENIENT
drink after hard one ....
        CHASER
oath .. EGAD, DRAT, GEE,
        GOSH
mildew .... BLIGHT, MOLD,
        FUNGUS, RUST
mile, nautical .... KNOT
⅛ of .... FURLONG
⅛ of LI
Miled, son of .... EBER
Milesian .... IRISH
milestone ... STELE, LANDMARK,
        PILLAR, EVENT, HERMA
milfoil ...... YARROW, PLANT
miliaria .... HEAT RASH,
        STROPHULUS

milieu are are are ENVIRON(MENT), SURROUNDINGS, AMBIENCE

militant .... WARLIKE, COMBATIVE, AGGRESSIVE, FIGHTING

militarist are b:e a:e a:e a:e.... JINGO

military ... MARTIAL, SOLDIERS, ARMY

   academy site .... WEST POINT

   address .... FPO, APO

   assistant .... AIDE

   banner are are a:e a:e ENSIGN, STANDARD

   cap .... KEPI, SHAKO, BUSBY, PERSHING

   chaplain .... PADRE

   coat, buffalo skin ... BUFF

   depot a:e a:e a:e a:e ARSENAL, MAGAZINE

   engine ... ONAGER, TANK, CATAPULT

   engineer are a:e a:e PIONEER, PONTONIER

   equipment, heavy .... HARDWARE

   expedition are... ANABASIS, CRUSADE

   force a:e... ARMY, LEGION, MILITIA

   formation a:e a:e PHALANX

   governor ...... MARGRAVE

   greeting .... SALUTE

   group ...... ARMY, CORPS, DIVISION

   guardhouse a:e a:e a:e BRIG

   headdress are a:e a:e SHAKO, BUSBY

   horn .... BUGLE

   landing point .... BEACHHEAD

   messenger a:e.... ESTAFET

   movement .... DEPLOYMENT, MARCH, MANEUVER

   occupation, lift .... EVACUATE

   officer .... BRASSHAT

   police .... MP, REDCAP

   post ... GARRISON, BASE, STATION, PRESIDIO, FORT

   prisoner ... are a:e a:e a:e POW

   punishment .... GA(U)NTLET

   rank, temporary ....

BREVET

roll .... are a:e a:e: a:e... MUSTER

salute .... SALVO

school .... ACADEMY

school site ... WEST POINT, ANNAPOLIS

school student ... CADET

science .... SOLDIERY

science subjects ...... TACTICS, STRATEGY, BALLISTICS, LOGISTICS

signal for parley/retreat .. CHAMADE

station a:e a:e... GARRISON

store .... EXCHANGE, CANTEEN, PX

storehouse ...... ETAPE, ARSENAL, ARMORY, DEPOT, MAGAZINE

student ... CADET, PLEBE

supplies .... MUNITIONS

tactical exercises .... WAR GAMES

truck ... CAMION, AMTRAC

unit ... SQUAD, PLATOON, CADRE, COMPANY

unit roll .... MUSTER

weapons :..a:e. ORDNANCE

militate .... FIGHT

militia ... SOLDIERY, RESERVES, (CITIZEN)ARMY

   member ...... RESERVIST

milk .... LAC, EMULSION, EXTRACT, LACTOSE, BLEED, SUCK

   beverage ...a:e a:e a:e SHAKE

   camel .... KUMISS

   coagulated part ... CURD

   coagulating enzyme ..... RENNIN

   combining form .... LACT(O)

   constituent ...... CASEIN

   cow's .... KOUMIS(S), KUMISS

   curd .... CASEIN

   curdled .... (BONNY)CLABBER

   curdler .... RENNET

   curdling substance ...... RENNET, RENNIN

   curds .... LACTARENE

   farm ... DAIRY, LACTARY

   fermented ... K(O)UMISS

   food from fermented .... YOG(H)URT

giving .... MILCH
gland .... MAMMA
like .... LACTEOUS
mare's .... KUMISS
not giving .... YELD
obtained from ... LACTIC
part of .... CURD, WHEY,
    CASEIN, PLASMA,
    SERUM, LECITHIN
pertaining to ... LACTIC,
    LACTARY, LACTEAL
protein .... CASEIN
run .... AVERAGE,
    ORDINARY
secrete .... LACTATE
secreting ... LACTESCENT
separator .. CENTRIFUGE
shake .... FRAPPE
sickness ...... SHAKES
sour ... CURD, CLABBER,
    WHIG
store .... DAIRY
sugar .... LACTOSE
synthetic fabric ....
    LANITAL
watery part ...... WHEY
with .... AU LAIT
yielding .... LACTIFEROUS
milkfish .... SABALO, TARPON,
    AWA
milking, kept for ...... MILCH
milkless .... YELD
milksop .. SISSY, MOLLYCODDLE
milkweed .. SPURGE, STAPELIA
juice .... LATEX
milkwort .... SENEGA
milky .. LACTEAL, LACTEOUS,
    LACTESCENT
liquid .... LATEX
way .... GALAXY
Way black area ....
    COALSACK
Way, of the ... GALACTIC
mill ..... GRIND(ER), FACTORY
dam .... WEIR
hand .... QUERN
owner's fee ... MULTURE
slang ... FIST FIGHT, BOX
Millay, Edna ___ ....
    ST. VINCENT
milldam .... WEIR
millenary .... THOUSAND
millepore .... CORAL,
    HYDROZOAN
miller .... MOTH
Miller's salesman .... LOMAN

millesimal ...... THOUSANDTH
millet .. PANIC, JUAR, GRAIN,
GRASS, PEARL, HIRSE, DURRA,
    DOURA(H)
seed(s) like .... MILIARY
sorghum-like ..... MILO
milliard .... BILLION
milliner .... HATTER
millinery .. HATS, HEADDRESSES
milling charge .... TOLL,
    THIRLAGE, MULTURE
refuse .... TAILING
millimeter, 1/1,000 of a ......
    MICRON, MIKRON
million electron volts ... MEV
hardest to earn ... FIRST
times: comb. form ......
    MEGA
ton explosive force ......
    MEGATON
millipede .... MYRIAPOD,
ARTHROPOD, WIREWORM
it has plenty of .... LEGS
millpond .... DAM, DIKE
Mills bomb .... GRENADE
millstone .... BURDEN
part .... RYND, INK
Milo .... MELOS, SORGHUM
milord .... NOBLEMAN,
    GENTLEMAN
Milquetoast .... CASPAR
creator of ...... WEBSTER
where he appears ....
    COMIC STRIP
milreis, antecedent of ...:..
ESCUDO, CRUZEIRO
milt .... SPLEEN, ROE
mim .... QUIET, SHY, DEMURE
mime .... IMITATE, FARCE,
CLOWN, JESTER, BUFFOON,
    MIMIC
mimeograph .... STENCIL,
    DUPLICATE
mimesis .... IMITATION,
REPRESENTATION, MIMICRY
mimetic .... IMITATIVE,
    MAKE-BELIEVE
mimic ...... MIME, IMITATIVE,
MAKE-BELIEVE, MOCK, COPY,
SIMULATE(D), IMITATE,
    APE(Y)
female .... MIMA
mimicking .... APERY
mimicry .. MIMESIS, IMITATION
mimosa .... HERB, SHRUB,
ACACIA, SOAPBARK

descriptive word for .... SHRINKING
mimosaceous tree ...... SIRIS
mina .... STARLING
   New Testament .. POUND
minacious .... MENACING
minaret .... TOWER
   caller from a ... MUEZZIN
   part of .... MOSQUE
minatory .... MENACING
mince .... HASII, DICE, CHOP, SUBDIVIDE
minced meat .... RISSOLE
   oath .. GEE, GAD, DRAT, EGAD, HECK
mincing .... MINIKIN
   bite .... NIBBLE
mind .... REASON, HEED, LOOK AFTER, PURPOSE, CARE, NOUS, MOOD, MENTALITY, TEND, MEMORY, OPINION, INTELLECT, PSYCHE
   bear in ...... REMEMBER
   call to ...... RECOLLECT
   drug .. LSD, MESCALINE, SEDATIVE, AMPHETAMINE
   of the .... MENTAL, PHRENIC
   vagueness of ..... HAZE
Mindanao city ...... DAVAO, ZAMBOANGA, BUTUAN
   inhabitant ..... MUSLIM, MORO
   province ...... AGUSAN, DAVAO, SURIGAO, COTABATO
   volcano .... APO
minded .. INCLINED, DISPOSED
mindful .... AWARE, CAREFUL
mine .... PIT, DIG, EXPLOSIVE, TUNNEL, SOURCE
   arch .... OVERCAST
   car .... HUTCH
   ceiling .... ASTEL
   channel ...... TAILRACE
   claim .... STAKE
   coal .... PIT
   compartment .... PANEL
   drain pit .... SUMP
   entrance .... ADIT
   excavation, steplike .... STOPE
   gas ..... DAMP, MEPHITIS
   gold .... BONANZA
   gunpowder ...... NITER
   kind ...... COAL, GOLD,

      DIAMOND, SILVER
   partition .... SOLLAR
   passage .. STULM, WINZE
   pit/pool .. STOPE, SUMP, ARROYO
   product .... ORE
   prop ..... STULL, SPRAG, NOG
   railway car .... TRAM
   refuse .... MULLOCK, TAILING
   rich .... BONANZA
   rubbish .... ATTLE
   shaft ... WINZE, ARROYO, DOWNCAST
   shaft lining .... TUB
   sieve .... JIG(GER)
   step .... LOB
   support against cave-ins . STULL, SPRAG, NOG
   sweeper ...... PARAVANE
   thrower .... MORTAR
   truck .... HUTCH
   tunnel .... ADIT
   vein .... LODE
   ventilating shaft .... DOWNCAST
   wall .... ASTEL
   waste .... TAILING
   waterway ..... TAILRACE
   winch .... WHIM
   worker .... COLLIER, PITMAN
miner ..... PITMAN, COLLIER, GOLDDIGGER, SAPPER
   compass of .... DIAL
   disease of .... SILICOSIS
   safety lamp of .... DAVY
mineral ...... TALC, GYPSUM, CALCITE, DIAMOND, ORE, TRONA, EPIDOTE, APATITE, SPALT, SPINEL(LE), QUARTZ, TOPAZ, FLUORITE, URALITE, ELATERITE, PYRITE, LEUCITE, BARITE
   amorphous ..... PINITE
   black .. COAL, GRAPHITE
   blue .. IOLITE, LAZULITE
   concretion ... CALCULUS
   crystalline .. SPAR, MICA, FELDSPAR
   deposit .. PLACER, LODE, SINTER, MASS, VEIN, BED
   glassy .... SILICA
   hard .... SPINEL(LE)
   hardest .... DIAMOND

jelly .... PETROLEUM,
            VASELINE
  luster of .... SCHILLER
  lustrous .... RUTILE
  magnetite .... LOADSTAR,
            LODESTAR
  mixture .... MAGMA
  native .... ORB
  oil .... KEROSENE,
            PETROLEUM
  pitch ..... ASPHALT, TAR,
            BITUMEN
  radioactive .... CARNOTITE
  salt .... ALUM
  silicate .... MICA
  softest .... TALC
  spot in a .... MACLE
  spring .... SPA
  tar .. MALTHA, BITUMEN,
            ASPHALT, BREA
  truck/wagon ...... CORF
  vein .... LODE
  water ... SELTZER, VICHY
  wax .... OZOCERITE
  worthless ...... GANGUE
miners' group: abbr. ..... UMW,
            MFD
Minerva .... ATHENA, AZALEA,
            GODDESS
  shield of .... (A)EGIS
minestrone .... SOUP, TUREEN
minesweeper ...... TRAWLER
minever .... FUR, ERMINE
mingle .... MELL, MIX, BLEND,
            COMBINE, JOIN
Minhow .... FOOCHOW
miniature .. MODEL, PAINTING,
            PORTRAIT, SMALL,
            DIMINUTIVE
  aquarium .. TANK, BOWL
  garden ...... TERRARIUM
  tree .... BONSAI
minify .. REDUCE, MINIATURIZE
  opposed to .... MAGNIFY
minikin .... DIMINUTIVE,
            DARLING
minim .. DROP, TINIEST, DASH,
            SMALLEST
  in music .... HALF NOTE
minimal .... LEAST
minimize .... LESSEN
minimum .. LEAST, SMALLEST,
            LOWEST
mining bar .... GAD
  basket .... CORF
  bed of ore .... REEF

car .... TRAM, HUTCH
  chisel .... GAD
  claim .... STAKE
  excavation .... STOPE
  kind of .... PLACER
  nail .... SPAD
  refuse .... MULLOCK,
            ATTLE, TAILING
  tool ...... GAD, JUMPER
  trough .... HUTCH
minion ..... FAVORITE, TYPE,
  FOLLOWER, DAINTY, MISTRESS
  of the law .. POLICEMAN
minister .. SHEPHERD, CURATE,
  SERVE, REVEREND, CATER,
  AGENT, DIPLOMAT, VIZIER,
  (AT)TEND, CLERGYMAN,
            PASTOR
  assistant of ...... DEACON
  home of .... MANSE,
            RECTORY,
            PARSONAGE
  title of ...... REVEREND
ministry .... CLERGY, PULPIT
  admit to the .... ORDAIN
minium .... VERMILION
miniver .... FUR, ERMINE
mink .. FUR, MAMMAL, VISON,
            KOLINSKY
  kin of .... SKUNK
  like animal ..... WEASEL
Minnehaha's love .. HIAWATHA
minnesinger ...... MINSTREL,
            TROUBADOUR
Minnesota capital .. ST. PAUL
  city ...... DULUTH, ELY,
  WINONA, MINNEAPOLIS,
    ST. PAUL, MANKATO,
            HIBBING
  lake .... ITASCA
  native .... GOPHER
  nickname ....
            GOPHER STATE
  state bird .... LOON
Minnesotan .... GOPHER
minnow .... MINNY, GUDGEON,
  SILVERSIDE(S), MOONFISH
minor ...... PETTY, YOUTH,
  LESS(ER), UNDER-AGE
  details ...... MINUTIAE
  in law .... PUPIL
  offense .... MISDEMEANOR
  planet .... AMOR, CERES,
            EROS, HERMES
  suit .. DIAMONDS, CLUBS
minorate .... CURTAIL

Minorca ... CHICKEN, ISLAND
minoress .... CLARE
Minorite .. FRIAR, FRANCISCAN
minority .. NONAGE, PUPILAGE
   group's persecution .....
                POGROM
Minos' co-judge .... AEACUS
   daughter ...... ARIADNE
   kingdom .... CRETE
   monster ...... MINOTAUR
   parent .... ZEUS, EUROPA
   structure .... LABYRINTH
   wife .... PASIPHAE
Minotaur's dwelling ....
             LABYRINTH
   killer .... THESEUS
minster .... CHURCH,
             CATHEDRAL
minstrel ... BARD, MUSICIAN,
   RIMER, SKALD, TROUBADOUR,
         (MINNE)SINGER
   musical instrument .....
           HARP, LUTE
   show end man ... BONES
   show entertainer ....
         INTERLOCUTOR
   song .... LAY
   wandering .... GLEEMAN,
   GOLIARD, JONGLEUR
mint .... BASIL, COIN, HYSSOP,
   STAMP, INVENT, FABRICATE,
   PLANT, CANDY, THYME,
   MARJORAM, DITTANY, CLARY,
   SAGE, CATNIP, SAVORY, HERB
   charge .... BRASSAGE
   drink .... JULEP
   genus .... MENTHA
   plant .... BASIL, CATNIP,
          OREGANO
   product .... COIN(S)
mintage .... COINAGE
minuet .... DANCE
Minuit's bargain ....
          MANHATTAN
minus ...... LESS, NEGATIVE,
          WITHOUT
minuscule ...... SMALL, TINY,
          MINUTE
minute .... WEE, NOTE,
   MICROSCOPIC, MINUSCLE,
   MOMENT, INSTANT, SMALL,
   TINY, MEMORANDUM, PETTY
   account .... DETAIL
   combining form .. MICRO
   distinction ...... NICETY
   groove .... STRIA

organism ..... MICROBE,
   GERM, AM(O)EBA,
        BACTERIUM
orifice .... STOMA, PORE
minutiae .... DETAILS
minutes ...... ACTA, RECORD
   15 .... QUARTER
minx .... HUSSY, GIRL, TART,
      MALAPERT, JADE
   play the .... FLIRT
miracle .... MARVEL, WONDER
   bread .... MANNA
   scene of ...... LOURDES,
          CANA
   worker .. THAUMATURGE
miracles, study of ....
        THAUMATOLOGY
miraculous .. SUPERNATURAL,
   MARVELOUS, WONDERFUL
mirage .... ILLUSION, VISION,
         DELUSION
mire .... OOZE, MUD, BOG,
       SLUSH, MUCK
Miriam's brother ..... MOSES,
         AARON
mirror ..... (LOOKING)GLASS,
   REFLECT, CRYSTAL,
        SPECULUM
   back coating .... SILVER
   star .... SIDEROSTAT
   tinfoil of .... TAIN
mirrors, of .... CATOPTRIC
mirth ..... GLEE, MERRIMENT,
   HILARITY, JOLLITY, GAIETY
mirthless .... HUMORLESS, SAD
miry .. OOZY, BOGGY, MUDDY,
        SWAMPY
misadventure .... MISHAP,
   BAD LUCK, ACCIDENT
misalliance .... MISMATCH
misanthrope .... (MAN)HATER
   of a sort .... CYNIC
misbegotten .... BASTARD,
       ILLEGITIMATE
misbehavior ..... MISCONDUCT
miscarriage .... ABORTION
miscarry ...... FAIL, ABORT
miscegenation, product of ....
   MESTIZO, MULATTO, HYBRID,
        MESTEE
miscellanea .... ANA,
       MISCELLANY
miscellaneous .... VARIED,
   MIXED, ASSORTED, SUNDRY
miscellany .. OLIO, POTPOURRI,
   MELANGE, MIXTURE

mischief ... DEVILTRY, HARM, INJURY, PRANK, TRICK, DIDO, WRACK
  maker ... ERIS, LOKI, IMP, DEVIL, PEST, PRANKSTER, PUCK, INTRIGUER, PLOTTER
mischievous .. IMPISH, PESKY, NAUGHTY, TROUBLESOME, PRANKISH, ELFIN, DEVILISH, PUCKISH, ROGUISH, ARCH
miscreant .. VILLAIN, INFIDEL, CRIMINAL, HERETIC
miscue ..... MISTAKE, ERROR
misdeed .. CRIME, SIN, FAULT
misdemeanor .... OFFENSE, MISCONDUCT, DELICT
mise ...... PACT, AGREEMENT
miser .... NIGGARD, WRETCH, MUCKWORM, HOARDER, HUNKS, SKINFLINT, TIGHTWAD
  of fiction ...... MARNER, SCROOGE
miserable .. FORLORN, ABJECT, PITIABLE, WRETCHED, UNHAPPY
misericord .... DAGGER
  place of a .. MONASTERY
miserly .... SORDID, CRIPPLE, TIGHT, STINGY, GREEDY, NIGGARD(LY), PENURIOUS
  person ..... TIGHTWAD, SKINFLINT, CHURL, NIGGARD
misery ..... GRIEF, DISTRESS, PAIN, AGONY, DOLOR, WOE
misfortune .... FARDEL, BAD LUCK, ADVERSITY, WOE, MISHAP, AFFLICTION
misgiving ...... DOUBT, FEAR, QUALM, APPREHENSION, SCRUPLE
misguided .... MISLED
mishandle .. ABUSE, MALTREAT
mishap .. BAD LUCK, ACCIDENT
  awkward .. CONTRETEMPS
mishmash .... OLIO, JUMBLE, HODGEPODGE, MELANGE
misinform .. LIE, MISREPRESENT
mislay ...... LOSE, MISPLACE
misle .. MIST, MIZZLE, DRIZZLE
mislead .... DELUDE, DECEIVE
mismanage ... BUNGLE, BOTCH
mismatch ...... MISALLIANCE
misogynist ... WOMAN-HATER

misplace .... MISLAY, LOSE
misplay .... ERR(OR)
misrepresent .... LIE, DISTORT, GARBLE
miss .... FAIL, OVERLOOK, AVOID, ESCAPE, GIRL, LADY
  a catch .... MUFF
  intentionally ...... BALK
  something .... MUFF
  the bus .... FAIL
"Missa Solemnis" composer .. BEETHOVEN
missal .... PRAYERBOOK
missel .... THRUSH
misshape .. DEFORM, CONTORT, DISTORT
misshapen ...... MALFORMED, DEFORMED
missile ..... ARROW, BULLET, LANCE, SHELL, PROJECTILE, SHAFT, DART, ICBM, MIRV, SPEAR, ROCKET, GRENADE
  detecting device .. RADAR
  guided .. IRBM, ROCKET, SAM, TALOS, NIKE
  part of ...... WARHEAD
  pit .... SILO
  returning ... BOOMERANG
  square-headed .. QUARREL
  tip of .... WARNOSE
  type .... BALLISTIC
  whaler's .... HARPOON
missing .... ABSENT, LOST, LACKING
mission ... EMBASSY, ERRAND, CALLING
missionary ...... EVANGELIST, APOSTLE
Mississippi capital .. JACKSON
  city .. MERIDIAN, BILOXI, JACKSON, HATTIESBURG
  county ... CLAY, LAMAR, YAZOO
  explorer ...... JOLIET
  nickname .... BAYOU
  river ..... YAZOO, PEARL
  steamboat quarters .. TEXAS
  Valley pike .... MUSKELLUNGE, MASKALONGE
Mississippian, any .. TADPOLE
missive ..... LETTER, MESSAGE
Missouri caverns ... MERAMEC
  city .... ST. LOUIS, SPRINGFIELD, SEDALIA,

INDEPENDENCE, JOPLIN, KANSAS

county .... KNOX, LINN, OZARK, ADAIR, DADE, HOLT

guerrilla ... JAWHAWKER

mountains .... OZARK

notable ...... PERSHING

river .... OSAGE

state flower .. HAWTHORN

state tree .... DOGWOOD

tributary .... PLATTE

misspelling ..... CACOGRAPHY

misspend ... WASTE, SQUANDER

misstep .... ERROR, FAUX PAS, TRIP

missy: colloq. .... GIRL

mist .... BRUME, MISLE, SMOG, SEREIN, SMUR, GAUZE, VAPOR, HAZE, FOG

rain like .... DRIZZLE,

mistake ...... BONER, FAULT, MISCUE, ERROR, BLUNDER, LAPSE, SLIP, SOLECISM

in conduct ..... FAUX PAS

in printing .... ERRATUM

mistaken .... ERRONEOUS, INCORRECT, WRONG

mister .. SIR, HERR, MONSIEUR, SENOR, SIGNOR, GOSPODIN, GOODMAN

mistletoe berry eater .. MISSEL

mistral .... WIND

poet .... FREDERIC

mistreat .... ABUSE

mistress ..... LEMAN, MINION, MISSUS, INAMORATA, MOLL, MRS., MADAM, MISSIS, PARAMOUR

mistrial, cause of, sometimes .. TECHNICALITY

mistrust ... DOUBT, SUSPICION

misty .. NUBILOUS, BRUMOUS, NEBULOUS

rain .... SEREIN, MIZZLE

misunderstanding ... QUARREL, IMBROGLIO

misuse ...... ABUSE, MISTREAT

of words, ridiculous .... MALAPROPISM

Mitchell (Helen) singer ...... MELBA

mite .. SPIDER, ACARID, MOTE, ACARUS, TICK, ARACHNID, ATOMY

larva .. JIGGER, CHIGOE,

CHIGGER, LEPTUS

miter .... TIARA, HEADDRESS, HEADBAND, BISHOPRIC

mithridate .... ANTIDOTE

mitigate .... EXTENUATE, TEMPER, SOFTEN, MODERATE, ASSUAGE, EASE

mitosis .... CELL DIVISION

stage of ...... ANAPHASE, PROPHASE, TELOPHASE

mitrailleur .. MACHINE GUNNER

mitt .... GLOVE

slang .... HAND

mitten .... GLOVE

mittimus ... DISMISSAL, WRIT, WARRANT

mitzvah .... COMMANDMENT, PRECEPT

mix ...... LEVIGATE, JUMBLE, BLEND, SCRAMBLE, ADDLE, STIR, COMBINE, MINGLE, MERGE, FUSE, COALESCE

up ..... FIGHT, TANGLE, SNAFU, EMBROIL, GARBLE, COMPOUND

mixed, capable of being ..... MISCIBLE

language ...... PIDGIN, JARGON

type .... PI

mixer, drink ...... SHAKER, BARTENDER

mixture ...... HODGEPODGE, FARRAGO, POTPOURRI, COMPOUND, (MISH)MASH, HASH, AMALGAM, MELANGE, OLIO, BLEND

flour, milk, etc. .. BATTER

jumbled ... HODGEPODGE

musical .... MEDLEY

Mizar .... ALCOR

Mize, baseball player ...... BIG JAWN

mizzen .... SAIL

mizzle .... DRIZZLE, RAIN

mnemonic subject ... MEMORY

Mnemosyne's daughter(s) .... MUSE(S)

concern ...... MEMORY

moa .... RATITE

relative .. APTERYX, KIWI, OSTRICH

Moab .... KINGDOM

father of .... LOT

giant ..... EMIM, ZUZIM

king .... MESHA

mountain .... NEBO
Moabite stone, name on .....
　　　　　　　　　　　AMRI
moan ～ CRY, LAMENT, GRIEVE,
　　　COMPLAIN, (BE)WAIL
　　sound like ...... GROAN
moat .... FOSS(E), DITCH
　　structure surrounded by ..
　　　　　　FORTRESS, CASTLE
mob .... THRONG, CANAILLE,
　　GANG, BOODLE, RIFFRAFF,
　　RABBLE, CROWD, MASSES
mobile ..... MOVABLE, FLUID,
　　　VARIABLE, FLEXIBLE
　　field hospital ....
　　　　　　　　　AMBULANCE
mobilize .. ORGANIZE, MUSTER
mobster: sl. ......～ GANGSTER,
　　　　　　　　　　　GOON
　　girl ....～ MOLL
Moby Dick .... PELEG, WHALE
　　author of .... MELVILLE
　　hunter of ...... AHAB
moccasin .... SLIPPER, SNAKE,
　　LARRIGAN, FLOWER, PAC
　　flower ～......... ORCHID
　　sport shoe like .. LOAFER
mocha ...～～ COFFEE, LEATHER
mochila .... KNAPSACK
mock .. DERIDE, FLEER, JAPE,
　　FLOUT, TAUNT, JEST, MIMIC,
　　SCOFF, IMITATION, JEER,
　　RIDICULE, DEFY, IMITATE,
　　COUNTERFEIT, SNEER, JIBE
　　attack ～～～....... FEINT
　　combat .... JOUST
　　orange ～ SERINGA, SHRUB,
　　　　　　　　　SYRINGA
　　sea battle ～. NAUMACHY,
　　　　　　　　NAUMACHIA
　　sun ～～～～ PARHELION
　　up ～..... MODEL, DUMMY
mockery ～ TRAVESTY, FARCE,
　　　BURLESQUE, JOKE
　　god of ～～～～～ MOMUS
modal auxiliary verb ... MAY,
　　MIGHT, WOULD, MUST,
　　　　　　　　SHOULD
mode ～.. FAD, VOGUE, STYLE,
　　METHOD, MOOD, WAY,
　　　　　　　FASHION
model ～～ SIT(TER), PATTERN,
　　EXAMPLE, (ARCHE)TYPE,
　　STANDARD, MANIKIN,
　　MOCK-UP, DESIGN, POSE,

PARADIGM, EXEMPLAR,
　　　　　　MANNEQUIN
　　for imitation .. LODESTAR
　　of human being ....
　　　　　　　HOMUNCULUS
　　of perfection .. PARAGON,
　　　　　　　　　IDEAL
　　original ～～ ARCHETYPE,
　　　　　　　PROTOTYPE
　　small scale .. MINIATURE
moderate ... MITIGATE, MILD,
　　TEMPERATE, RESTRAIN, BATE,
　　　　　　　　PRESIDE
　　in music ～～...... MEZZO
moderation ..... TEMPERANCE
modern ... NEO, NEW, LATEST,
　　　　　　UP-TO-DATE
　　city sight ～. SKYSCRAPER
　　person .... NEOTERIC
modernize ～...... RENOVATE,
　　　RETOOL, UPDATE
modest ～ SHY, DEMURE, COY,
　　VERECUND, UNASSUMING,
　　RESERVED, DECENT, HUMBLE
modicum .... BIT
modified leaf .... BRACT
modifier ～ ADVERB, ADJECTIVE
modify ..... ALTER, QUALIFY,
　　CHANGE, AMEND, ENODATE,
　　　　　　　　VARY
modish ～ FASHIONABLE, CHIC,
　　　　　　　STYLISH
modiste ～～～... DRESSMAKER
modulate .... ADJUST, ADAPT,
　　ATTUNE, INFLECT, (IN)TONE
modulation .... CADENCE
modus operandi .. PROCEDURE
　　vivendi ....～ COMPROMISE
moguey .... RAFT
mogul ～ NABOB, MONGOL(IAN),
　　LOCOMOTIVE, VIP
　　dynasty founder .. BABER,
　　　　　　BABUR, BABAR
　　emperor .. BABER, AKBAR,
　　HUMAYUN, JEHAN,
　　　　　BABAR, BABUR
　　ruler ～........ NAWAB
mohair ～～ FABRIC, GARMENT,
　　　　　　　MOREEN
　　source of ～～. ANGORA
Mohammed ...... MAHOMET,
　　MAHOUND, MUHAMMAD,
　　　　　　　PROPHET
　　birthplace of .... MECCA
　　burial place of .. MEDINA
　　daughter of ..... FATIMA

descendant of ... SHERIF, SAYID, SEID
destination .... MEDINA
flight of .. HEGIRA, HEJIRA
follower of ..... ISLAM, MUSLIM, MOHAMMEDAN
religion founded by ..... MOSLEM, ISLAM
sister of .... JINNAH
son-in-law .... ALI
successor of ..... CALIF, CALIPH, K(H)ALIF
wife of .... AISHA, AYESHA(H)
Mohammedan angel ... AZRAIL, AZRAEL
beggar/ascetic ... FAKIR
bible .. KORAN, ALCORAN
bier .... TABUT
blacksmith .... LOHAR
call to prayer .... AZAN, ADAN
canonical law ... SHARIA
caravansary ..... IMARET
crusade .. JIHAD, JEHAD
cup .... LOTAH
day of fasting ... ASHURA
demon .... JINNI(E)
devil ... EBLIS, SHAITAN, SHEITAN
fasting period ..... RAMADAN, ASHURA
festival .... BAIRAM
Filipino .... MORO
god .... ALLAH
hermit .... SANTON
holy war .. JEHAD, JIHAD
infidel .... KAFIR
inn .... IMARET, CARAVANSARY
judge .... CADI
law .... SUNNA(H)
leader .... IMAM
magistrate .... CADI
Malay .... MORO
messiah .... MAHDI
monk .... SANTON
month .. RAJAB, JUMADA, RABIA, RAMADAN, SAFAR, SHABAN, SHAWWAL
mystic .... SUFI, SUNNITE
mysticism .... SUFISM
noble ...... AMIR, EMIR, AMEER, SHERIF, EMEER
non .... KAF(F)IR

nymph .... HOURI
orthodox ...... SUNNITE
prayer hour ..... AZAN
priest .... IMAM
prince .... AMIR, AMEER
prince's title ..... NAWAB
principle .... IJMA
religion .... ISLAM
ruler .. SULTAN, CALIPH, AMIR, AMEER
ruler's decree .... IRADE
sacred book ... ALCORAN, KORAN
saint .... PIR
salutation ...... SALAAM
Satan .... EBLIS, SHAITAN
savior .... MAHDI
scholars .... ULEMA
sect member .. SUNNITE, SHIITE, SHIAH, SUFI
shrine .... KAABA
slave .... MAMELUKE
teacher ...... MOLLAH, MULLA(H)
title .. EMIR, EMEER, AMIR, AGA, NAWAB, CALIPH, SAY(Y)ID
unbeliever ..... KAF(F)IR
uncle .... ABBAS
veil .. YASHMAK, YASHMAC
woman's clothing .. IZAR, ISAR
Mohave .... YUMA(N)
Mohawk .... INDIAN, RIVER, IROQUOIAN
chief .. HIAWATHA, BRANT
city on the ..... UTICA
mohur, 1/15 of ...... RUPEE
moiety ... HALF, PART, SHARE
moil .... DRUDGE(RY), CONFUSION
and ____ ...... TOIL
moire .. FABRIC, SILK, TABBY, TAFFETA
moist .... WET, DANK, DAMP, HUMID, IRRIGUOUS
to the touch ... CLAMMY
moisten .. (BE)DEW, DAMPEN, WET, WASH, BATHE
with oil .... EMBROCATE
moisture .... DEW
combining form ....
HYGR(O)
condensed ... MIST, DEW
moke .. DONKEY, IDIOT, DOLT
Moki .... HOPI

molar ... GRINDER, CHOPPER, TOOTH
molasses ...... SIRUP, SYRUP, THERIACA, TREACLE
 beverage ... RUM, TAFIA, ARRACK
 candy ... TOFFEE, TAFFY
 rum .... TAF(F)IA
 source .... SORGO
 tobacco leaf mixture .... CAVENDISH
molave ... VITEX, TREE, WOOD
mold .. CAST, MILDEW, KNEAD, SOIL, MOULAGE, MATTER, SHAPE, FORM, FUNGUS, MATRIX, PATTERN
 core .... NOWEL
 opening for molten metal SPRUE, GEAT, GIT
 poetic .... EARTH
 product .... CASTING
 slime ..... MYXOMYCETE
Moldavia, capital of .... KISHINEV
 prince's title .. HOSPODAR
 town .... JASSY
molded, can be ...... FICTILE
molder .... DECAY, CRUMBLE, DIE, STAMP
molding .. SHAPING, CORNICE, CYMA, REGLET, CONGE, OGEE, LISTEL, FILLET
 building's ..... CORNICE
 concave .... COVING, SCOTIA, CAVETTO, COVE
 convex .... REEDING, OVOLO, TORUS, BAGUET(TE)
 cornice .... CYMA
 curved .... NEBULE
 decoration .... GADROON
 edge .... ARRIS
 egg-shaped ...... OVOLO
 material .... ORMOLU
 narrow .... TRINGLE
 ogee .... TALON
 rounded .... REED
 S-shaped .... OGEE
 square .... LISTEL
 wall .... CORNICE
moldy .. MUSTY, STALE, MUCID, FUSTY, HOAR
mole .... JUTTY, PIER, QUAY, MAMMAL, STAR NOSE, N(A)EVUS, BREAKWATER,

ANCHORAGE, HARBOR, TALPA, PLATYPUS
animal resembling ...... DESMAN
 gray .... TAUPE
molecular film ... MONOLAYER
molecule .... PARTICLE
 component ...... ATOM, (AN)ION
moleskins .... TROUSERS
molest .... ANNOY, TROUBLE, DISTURB, PESTER
molestation ..... ANNOYANCE
Moliere character .... TARTUF(FE), ALCESTE
moll's friend ..... GANGSTER, MOBSTER
mollifier, baby's ..... SUCKER, RATTLE(R), PACIFIER, THUMB
mollify .... PLACATE, PACIFY, CONCILIATE, APPEASE, SOOTHE
mollusca .... MOLLUSKS, SLUG
molluscoid .... BRYOZOAN, BRACHIOPOD
 by-product .... PEARL
mollusk .. CLAM, SNAIL, SLUG, MUSSEL, MUREX, CHITON, ABALONE, WENTLETRAP, RETEPORE, OCTOPUS, SQUID, WHELK, LIMPET, COCKLE, OYSTER, SCALLOP, HELIX, NAUTILUS, PTEROPOD, TRITON
 arm of .... TENTACLE
 beaked .... OCTOPUS, SQUID, CEPHALOPOD, CUTTLEFISH
 bivalve .. CLAM, PIDDOCK, CHAMA, MUSSEL
 borer .... TEREDO, SHIPWORM
 burrowing ..... PIDDOCK
 counterfeit .... SLUG, QUEER
 edible part ..... SCALLOP
 egg(s) of .... SPAWN, OOTHECA
 genus .... MUREX, OLIVA
 gills .... CERATA
 light producing substance LUCIFERIN
 muscle of ..... SCALLOP
 shell .... CONCH, COWRY, COWRIE
 study of .. CONCHOLOGY

sucking organ .... PROBOSCIS
teeth .... RADULA
tentacled .... SQUID, OCTOPUS
two-gilled ..... SPIRULA
molly .... FISH
where seen usually ...... AQUARIUM
mollycoddle .. MILKSOP, PET, PAMPER
Molnar, dramatist .. FERENC
work .... LILIOM
Moloch .... GOD, LIZARD
sacrificial site ... TOPHET
Molotov .... PERM
cocktail: sl. ...... BOMB, GRENADE
molt .. SHED, CAST(OFF), MEW, EXUVIA(T)E
molten ... MELTED, LIQUEFIED
rock ...... LAVA, MAGMA
waste ..... SPRUE, SCUM, DROSS, SCORIA
Molucca island .... MALUKU, BANDA, CERAM, SERANG, TERNATE, HALMAHERA, GILOLO
moly .. GARLIC, MOLYBDENUM
mom: colloq. .... MOTHER
moment .. SEC, TRICE, FLASH, JIFF(Y), POINT, TICK, INSTANT, IMPORT(ANCE), CONSEQUENCE
of truth .... CRISIS
momentarily .. SHORTLY, SOON
momentary ...... TRANSIENT, PASSING, TRANSITORY
momentum .. IMPETUS, FORCE, SPEED
Momus .... FAULTFINDER
Mona Lisa .. (LA) GIOCONDA, PORTRAIT
painter .... DA VINCI
smile of ..... ENIGMATIC, CRYPTIC
monacero .... UNICORN
monachal .... MONASTIC
Monaco playground .... MONTE CARLO
ruler .... RAINIER
monad .... ATOM, UNIT, ELEMENT, RADICAL, MICROCOSM, MONATOMIC
monarch .. SHAH, CZAR, TSAR, KAISER, ROI, REY, REX,

POTENTATE, EMPEROR, KING, BUTTERFLY
golden ball of .. MOUND
jungle ...... LION, TIGER
of the sky .... EAGLE
monarchist .... ROYALIST
monarchy, type of .... ABSOLUTE, DESPOTIC, LIMITED, CONSTITUTIONAL
monarda .... HORSEMINT, OSWEGOTEA, BERGAMOT
monastery .. FRIARY, CLOISTER, HERMITAGE, MONKERY, PRIORY, HOSPICE, LAMASERY, ABBEY, NUNNERY
buyer of provisions ..... MANCIPLE
church of ...... MINSTER
dining hall ...... FRATER, REFECTORY
head of .. ABBOT, PRIOR, MANDRA, HEGUMEN, ARCHIMANDRITE
resident .... MONK, CENOBITE
room .... LOCUTORY, LAVABO
small .... CELL
subsidiary ... SUCCURSAL
monastic ..... OBLATE, MONK, ASCETIC, SELF-DENYING, MONACHAL
brother .... FRA
haircut .... TONSURE
life .... CLOISTER
monde ..... SOCIETY, WORLD
Monegasque territory .... MONACO
Monet, painter ...... CLAUDE
monetary .... PECUNIARY, FINANCIAL
unit for calculation ..... MILL.
money .... FUND, ORA, CASH, COWRY, TENDER, LUCRE, WAD, SPENSE, SILVER, COIN(S), BILLS, BANKNOTES
advance .... EARNEST, IMPREST, ARLES
bead .. WAMPUM, PEAG(E)
box .... ARCA, KIST, TILL
bribe .. SOAP, SLUSH FUND
bronze .... AES
certificate .. BOND, SCRIP, TENDER

changer .... SHROFF, CAMBIST
coin .... MINT
coined .... SPECIE
drawer for .... TILL
earnest ... ARLES, TOKEN, ADVANCE
exchange fee ...... AGIO
fishhook .... LARI(N)
for political purposes ... LUG
from public office .. PAP
function of .. EXCHANGE, MEASURE
handler .... CASHIER, TELLER
Indian .. WAMPUM, BEAD, PEAG(E), SEWAN
left by will ...... LEGACY
legalize as ... MONETIZE
lender .... SHYLOCK, USURER
making .... PROFITABLE, LUCRATIVE
manual .... CAMBIST
market .... BOURSE
metal .. SPECIE, COIN(AGE)
of .... PECUNIARY, FINANCIAL
on hand .... CASH
paid for injury .. DAMAGE
paid to slain man's kin .. WER(E)GILD
payer/receiver ... TELLER, CASHIER
political patronage .. PAP
pouch .... SPLEUCHAN
premium .... AGIO
project .... FUND
ready ...... CASH, FUND
received: sl. ...... TAKE
reserve .... FUND
resources .... FINANCES, FUNDS
roll of .. ROULEAU, WAD
sent by mail .... REMITTANCE
shell .. SE(A)WAN, COWRY, COWRIE
slang .. BOODLE, CABBAGE, MOOLA, DOUGH, LETTUCE, MAZUMA, SHEKEL, KALE, JACK, SCRATCH, SUGAR, WAMPUM, ROLL, DUST
small amount .. PITTANCE

stone .... FEI
substitute ..... COUPON, SCRIP
token .. EARNEST, ARLES, ADVANCE
tray .... TILL
moneyed .... RICH, WEALTHY
monger ..... TRADER, DEALER
Mongol ..... BURIAT, ESKIMO, INDIAN, ASIATIC, TA(R)TAR, ELEUT(H), MOGUL
conqueror .. TAMERLANE, TIMURLENK, GENGHIS(KHAN)
dynasty .... YUAN
emperor .. KUBLAI KHAN
Mongolian .... KALMUCK, KALMYK, TUNGUS
capital ..... ULAN BATOR
conqueror ...... KUBLAI, GENGHIS(KHAN)
desert .... GOBI, SHAMO
dynasty .... YUAN
monetary unit .. TUGRIK
monk .... LAMA
People's Republic capital KULUN, ULAN BATOR
premier ..... TSEDENBAL
presidium chairman ..... SAMBU
priest .... SHAMAN, LAMA
tent .... YURT
tribesman ...... BURYAT
weight .... LAN
Mongolism .... IDIOCY
Mongoloid ..... LAI, DURBAN, TURK, SHAN, SHAR(R)A, LAPP
Mongols, clan/tribe of ...... HORDE
mongoos(e) ..... ICHNEUMON, URVA
prey of .... SNAKE, RAT, COBRA
mongrel .. CUR, HYBRID, DOG, MUTT, TYKE
relative .... SURICATE
mongst .... MIDST
moni(c)ker ...... (NICK)NAME
monition .. WARNING, NOTICE, CAUTION, SUMMONS
monitor .. IRONCLAD, LIZARD, REMINDER, WARSHIP, RECEIVER, LOUDSPEAKER, CHECK, MENTOR
builder of the .. ERICSSON
lizard .... URAN

monk .. LAMA, SANTON, FRIAR,
BONZE, FRA, PRIOR, BEDE,
TALAPOIN, FRANCISCAN,
AUGUSTINIAN, CARMELITE,
CENOBITE, VOTARY,
DOMINICAN
ascetic .... FAKIR
Buddhist .... BONZE,
AR(A)HAT
cloak of .... COWL
Eastern Orthodox Church
CALOYER
ever silent .... TRAPPIST
Franciscan ... CAPUCHIN
head .... ABBOT
head cover ...... HOOD,
COWL, CAPUCHE,
CAPOUCH, AMICE
hermit .... ANCHORET
hood .. COWL, CAPUCHE,
CAPOUCH, AMICE
room for conversation ..
LOCUTORY
room of .... CELL
settlement .... SCETE
title .... FRA
monkey .. PRIMATE, TITI, ZATI,
CAPUCHIN, HOWLER,
TAMARIN, SIMIAN,
JACKANAPES, WANDEROO,
MONA, RHESUS, MARMOSET,
VERVET, TARSIER, JOCKO,
TOTA, FUR, RAM, TRIFLE,
FOOL, PLAY, LANGUR,
MACAQUE, NISNAS, MACHIN,
TALAPOIN
arboreal .... POTTO,
TARSIER, GRIVET, TITI,
SIME, TOTO
Asiatic .... LANGUR
astronaut .... BONNY
bearded ...... ENTELLUS
bonnet ..... SATI, TOQUE
bread .. BAOBAB, FRUIT,
TREE
business ... FOOLISHNESS,
MISCHIEF
capuchin .. SAPAJOU, SAI
flower .... FIGWORT
green .... GUENON
green-haired .... GRIVET,
VERVET
grivet .... TOTA, VERVET
howling .. ARABA, MONO,
STENTOR
marmoset .... TAMARIN

puzzle .... PINON
red .... PATAS
sacred .... RHESUS
space traveler ....
ASTROMONK, BONNY
spider .... ATELES, QUATA
squirrel .... SAMIRI
suit .... UNIFORM
wrench part ...... JAW
monkeyshine ... PRANK, JOKE,
MISCHIEF
monkish .... MONASTIC
title .... DOM
monkshood ... ATIS, ACONITE,
ATEES, WOLFSBANE
monochord .... SONOMETER
monocle .. EYEGLASS, LORGNON
monocotyledon plant .... LILY,
PALM, ORCHID
monody .. LYRIC SOLO, DIRGE,
ELEGY, THRENODY,
MONOPHONY
monogram .... CIPHER
composition of ....
INITIALS, LETTERS
monograph .. MEMOIR, PAPER,
TREATISE, THESIS
monolith ... PILLAR, OBELISK,
COLUMN, MENHIR, MEGALITH,
DOLMEN
monolithic ..... SOLID, SINGLE
monologue ...... SOLILOQUY
monologuist of a sort ....
SOLILOQUIST
monomachy .... DUEL
monomania .... CRAZE,
OBSESSION
monopolize .... CONTROL,
CORNER
monopoly .... CARTEL, TRUST,
SYNDICATE, POOL
maneuver ... COEMPTION
monosaccharide .. SUGAR, OSE,
GLUCOSE, PENTOSE
monosodium glutamate ......
AJINOMOTO, MSG
monostich .. VERSE, EPIGRAM,
POEM
monotone .... DRONE
monotonous .. TEDIOUS, DRAB,
FLAT, HUMDRUM, TIRESOME,
DREARY
talk .... DRONE
monotony .... TEDIUM
monotreme .... DUCKBILL,
ECHIDNA, ANTEATER

Monroe _____ ...... DOCTRINE
   actress .... MARILYN
   poet .... HARRIET
mons ...... PUBIS, VENERIS
   language .... PEGU
monsieur ... (GENTLE)MAN, SIR,
                MR
monsoon ...... (TRADE)WIND
   weather .... RAINY
monster .... CERBERUS,
   UNICORN, CENTAUR,
   ENORMOUS, HUGE, OGRE,
   GILA, TERATISM, FREAK,
   MONSTROSITY
   combining form ....
           TERAT(O)
   fabulous .... MINOTAUR,
   CHIMERA, BASILISK,
   COCKATRICE, HARPY
   female .... GORGON,
   MEDUSA, HARPY,
   CHARYBDIS, CHIMERA
   fire-breathing .. CHIMERA,
   DRAGON
   hundred-eyed .... ARGUS
   hundred-handed ....
          BRIAREUS
   hundred-headed ....
          TYPHOEUS
   many-headed .... HYDRA
   mythical .... BUCENTAUR,
   CENTAUR, SPHINX,
   HARPY, DRAGON,
   CHIMERA, HIPPOGRIFF,
   MINOTAUR, GRIFFIN,
   GRYPHON, GRIFFON,
   CHARYBDIS
   resembling a .. TERATOID
   sea ..... KRAKEN, WHALE
   snake-haired ... MEDUSA
   tiger-bodied .... SU
   winged .... GERYON
monstrosity .... FREAK,
   TERATISM, MONSTER
monstrous .. TERATOID, HUGE,
   ENORMOUS, HIDEOUS,
   ATROCIOUS, HORRIBLE
Mont Cervin .... MATTERHORN
montage .... ASSEMBLAGE
Montague Barstow .... ORCZY
   scion of .... ROMEO
Montaigne "Essays" translator
          FLORIO
Montana capital ..... HELENA
   city .. HELENA, MISSOULA,
   BUTTE, GREAT FALLS,

          BILLINGS
   county .. BLAINE, CARTER
   lake .... FLATHEAD
   motto .... ORO Y PLATA
   national park .. GLACIER
   river .... TETON,
         LITTLE HORN
   state flower .. BITTERROOT
Monte Carlo location ....
          MONACO
   Cristo author .... DUMAS
   castle .... D'IF
   hero .... DANTES
monteith .... PUNCHBOWL
Montenegro's former capital ..
         CETINJE
montero .... CAP
Montezuma's conqueror ......
         CORTES
month, by the ... PERMENSEM
   excess of calendar over
   lunar .... EPACT
   first day ..... KALENDS,
         CALEND(I)S
   last .... ULT(IMO)
   named after pleiad .. MAY
monthly ..... MENSAL, MENSES,
   PERIODICAL, MENSTRUAL
monticule .. HILL, MOUNTAIN
monument .... STATUE, CAIRN,
   CENOTAPH, DOLMEN, SHRINE,
   TABLET, OBELISK, STELE,
   (CROM)LECH, PILLAR,
   PANTHEON, MAUSOLEUM,
   TOMB, MENHIR, MEMORIAL,
   MILESTONE
   honoring the dead ......
         CENOTAPH
   inscription .... EPIGRAPH
   of stone(s) ...... CAIRN,
   MEGALITH, MENHIR,
   DOLMEN
monumental .... GREAT,
   COLOSSAL
moo .... LOW
mooch .. SNEAK, SKULK, LOAF,
   LOITER, PILFER, STEAL,
   CADGE, BEG
mood .. VEIN, HUMOR, TEMPER,
   MORALE, SPIRIT(S)
   describing a ....
   INDICATIVE, IMPERATIVE,
   SUBJUNCTIVE
   in logic .... MODE
moody .... SULLEN, GLOOMY,
   DEPRESSED

moon .... MONTH, ORB, LUNA,
SATELLITE, DIANA, LUMINARY
  apogee/perigree .. APSIS
  between half and full ...
                    GIBBOUS
  crater ..... COPERNICUS,
        TYCHO, COLOMBO,
    LANGENUS, GUTENBERG
  dark area on ..... MARE
  erratic movement .....
                   LIBRATION
  first on ... USA, ARMSTRONG
  flower .. MORNING-GLORY,
                    ACHETE
  goddess .. LUNA, PHOEBE,
        SELENE, ASTARTE,
        ARTEMIS, DIAN(A),
        CYNTHIA, LUCINA,
                    HECATE
  half-lighted ... QUARTER
  hole .... CRATER
  horn .... CUSP
  inhabitant ... LUNARIAN
  motion's variation ......
                   EVECTION
  mountain ..... PYRENESS
  of the .. LUNAR, SELENIC
  on the wane ....
                  DECRESCENT
  orbit closest to ....
                    PERILUNE
  orbiter .. APOLLO, COLLINS,
    GORDON, ROOSA, WORDEN
  personified .... LUNA
  pertaining to the ....
            LUNAR, SELENIC
  phase ...... NEW, FULL,
                    GIBBOUS
  poetic .... LAMP
  point ...... CUSP, HORN
  point farthest from earth
                    APOGEE
  point nearest earth .....
                    PERIGREE
  satellite .... ORBITER,
                  SURVEYOR
  science dealing with the ..
                SELENOLOGY,
      ASTROLOGY, ASTRONOMY
  sea .... RAINS, SERENITY,
        CRISES, NECTAR,
                  FERTILITY
  shadow .... UMBRA
  shaped .... ROUND,
        CRESCENT, LUNATE

  sun relationship ....
                  LUNISOLAR
  trench .... RILL(E)
  valley .... RILL(E)
  vehicle ...... ROVER, LEM
  walker .... ARMSTRONG,
        ALDRIN, CONRAD, BEAN,
        SHEPARD, MITCHELL,
        SCOTT, IRWIN, YOUNG,
        DUKE, CERNAN, SHIMITT
  watcher ... ASTROLOGER,
                  ASTRONOMER
mooncalf .... IDIOT, FOOL,
                    IMBECILE
moonling, fictional ... SQUAPS
moonshine .. FUSTIAN, WHISKY,
                    NONSENSE
moonshiner ..... BOOTLEGGER
moonstone .... FELDSPAR,
                    ADULARIA
moonstruck .... CRAZED,
                    LUNATIC
moonwort .... FERN, HONESTY
moor ...... SECURE, ANCHOR,
    HEATH, FEN, DOCK, MORISCO,
    MOSLEM, LANDE, BENT, FELL
  cock/fowl ..... GROUSE,
                    GORCOCK
  grass .... NARD
  grouse .... GORHEN
  hen .. GROUSE, GALLINULE
moorage .. DOCK, ANCHORAGE
mooring buoy/spar .. DOLPHIN
  fee .... WHARFAGE
  place ...... ANCHORAGE,
        DOCK, BERTH, MARINA,
                    PORT
  rope .... PAINTER
Moorish .... MORESQUE,
                    MORISCAN
  cloak .... BURNOUS,
                    BURNOOSE
  coin .... MARAVEDI
  fabric .... TIRAZ
  fortress .... ALCAZAR
  garment .... JUPON
  hermit ...... MARABOUT
  kettledrum .. AT(T)ABAL
  king of Granada ....
                    BOABDIL
  palace/fortress ....
        ALCAZAR, ALHAMBRA
  sailboat .... SAPIT
  tabor .... AT(T)ABAL
moose ..... ALCES, ELK, DEER
  feeding place ..... YARD

kin .. REINDEER, CARIBOU
male .... BULL
pouch .... BEL
territory .... MAINE
moot .. ASSEMBLY, DEBATABLE
place of .. LAW SCHOOL,
MOCK COURT
mop ...... WIPE, WASH, RUB,
SWAB, GRIMACE, SWOB,
MALKIN, MAUKIN
cannon .... SWAB
mope .... MOON, SULK
moppet .. CHILD, DOLL, GIRL,
(SMALL)FRY
Moqui .... HOPI
mora, in law .... DEFAULT,
DELAY
moraceous tree ... MULBERRY
moral ..... CHASTE, ETHICAL,
VIRTUOUS, MAXIM, LESSON,
RIGHTEOUS, DECENT
allegorical story with ...
FABLE, APOLOGUE
constitution ....
CHARACTER
decay .... DRY ROT
distinction ...... RIGHT,
WRONG
fault .... VICE
law .... DECALOG(UE)
obligation .... DUTY
philosophy ...... ETHICS
poem .... DIT
slip .... LAPSE
talk .... HOMILY, SERMON
teachings .... PRECEPTS
weakness ...... FRAILTY
morale ...... MOOD, TEMPER,
SPIRIT
morality .... ETHICS,
RIGHT CONDUCT
talk on .... HOMILY,
SERMON
moralized tale .... EXEMPLUM
morally corrupt .... PUTRID,
ROTTEN, VENAL
instruct .... EDIFY
instructive ... DIDACTIC
unrestrained ....
LICENTIOUS, LIBERTINE
weak .... FRAIL
morals, pertaining to .. ETHICS
supervisor ...... CENSOR
morass ...... SLACK, FEN, BOG,
MARSH, SWAMP, QUAGMIRE
moratorium .... GRACE

Morava river .... MARCH
Moravia .... MAHREN
capital .... BRNO
writer .... ALBERTO
moray .. CONGER, EEL, ELGIN
morbid .... DISEASED,
UNHEALTHY, PATHOLOGICAL,
GRISLY, GRUESOME
morbilli .... MEASLES
morceau .... BIT, MORSEL,
FRAGMENT
mordant .... EROSIVE, BITING,
CAUSTIC, CUTTING, ACRID,
ACID, SARCASTIC, CORROSIVE
Mordecai's cousin .... ESTHER
mordent .... TRILL
more .. AGAIN, PLUS, GREATER,
FURTHER
cry for .... ENCORE
in music .... PIU
than enough .... AMPLE,
SURPLUS, EXCESS
than one/once ....
MULTIPLE
work .... UTOPIA
moreen .... FABRIC, TABBY
morel .... MUSHROOM,
NIGHTSHADE
morello .... CHERRY
moreover .... AND, ALSO,
BESIDES, ELSE, LIKEWISE,
FURTHER
morepork .... RURU
mores .. FOLKWAYS, CUSTOMS
singular of .... MOS
Moresque .... MOORISH
Morgan .. STALLION, TROTTER,
BUCCANEER
morganatic union ....
MESALLIANCE
morganite .... BERYL
morgue .... MORTUARY,
LIBRARY
moribund .... DYING
moringa .... BEN
morion ..... HELMET, QUARTZ
Morisco .... MOOR
Mormon .... DANITE
church founder .. SMITH
church head, U.S. ......
YOUNG
not a .... GENTILE
priest .... ELDER
sacred instrument .. URIM
state .... DESERET
Mormonite .... DANITE

morning .... EOS, AURORA,
MATIN, DAYBREAK, DAWN,
MORROW
   canticle .... VENITE
   delivery .... MAIL, MILK,
(NEWS)PAPER
   glory .. SUNRISE, PLANT,
IPOMEA
   music .. AUBADE, MATIN
   of .... MATUTINAL,
MATIN(AL)
   poetic .... MORN
   prayer .... MATINS
   reception .... LEVEE
   song .. MATIN, MATTINS,
ALBA
   star ≈≈ PLANT, PLANET,
SATURN, VENUS,
PHOSPHOR
Moro cannon ...... LANTAKA
   chief .... DATO, DATU,
MAGINDANAO
   Island ..... MINDANAO
   Ital. premier ...... ALDO
   musical instrument .....
KULINTANG
   priest .... PANDITA
   sailboat .... VINTA
Moroccan ...... BERBER, RIFF,
MOOR
   soldier .... ASKAR
   wife .... SHERIFA
Morocco ...... MARRAKECH,
LEATHER, MAROC, KINGDOM
   capital .... RABAT
   city ...... CASABLANCA,
MARAKECH, RABAT, FEZ
   coin .... RIAL
   district .... RIFF
   dynasty founder ..... ALI
   French name .... MAROC
   hat .... FEZ
   international zone ......
TANGIER
   leather, imitation .. ROAN
   monetary unit .. DIRHAM
   mountain .. JEBEL MUSA
   mountainous region ....
RIF
   native ...... BERBER, RIF,
CLEUH, MOOR
   premier ....
BENHIMA (MOHAMED)
   region ..... TAFILET, RIF
   ruler ... SULTAN, HASSAN,
KING

   seaport .. RABAT, CEUTA,
MOGADOR, TETUAN,
CASABLANCA, TANGIER
   Spanish name ....
MARRUECOS
moron ...... IDIOT, IMBECILE,
NITWIT, AMENT
morose .. GLUM, BLUE, SOUR,
DOUR, SATURNINE, GLOOMY,
SULLEN, SURLY
Morpheus, god of ____
DREAMS
morphine addicts' analgesic
   drug ..... METHADONE
   refined .... HEROIN
morro ..... HILL(OCK), BLUFF
morrow .. MORNING, NEXT DAY
Mors .... THANATOS
Morse invention .. TELEGRAPH
morsel .. TIDBIT, BIT(E), PIECE,
MORCEAU, DISH, SCRAP, ORT
mort .... DEAD, DEATH
mortal .. FATAL, DEADLY,
IMPLACABLE, EXTREME,
PERSON, LETHAL, HUMAN
   opposed to ...... VENIAL
   remains .. CORPSE, DUST,
CADAVER
mortality ...... DEATH(RATE)
mortar ...... BOWL, CANNON,
PLASTER, CEMENT, COMPO
   and .... PESTLE
   crush in a .... BRAY
   for filling .... GROUT
   mixer .... RAB
   patch with ...... SLUSH
   sound-proofing ....
PUGGING
   tray .... HOD
mortarboard .... HAWK, CAP
   part .... TASSEL
mortgage ..... PLEDGE, DEED,
LIEN, WADSET
mortgagee .... LIENOR
mortician ...... UNDERTAKER
mortification ..... GANGRENE,
CHAGRIN, SHAME,
HUMILIATION
   example of ... FAST(ING),
SELF-DENIAL,
FLAGELLATION
mortify .. HUMILIATE, SHAME,
EMBARRASS, DECAY, ABASH
Mortimer, the dummy ....
SNERD
mortise .... JOIN, FASTEN

mortmain ...... DEAD HAND
mortuary ...... CINERARIUM,
    MORGUE, CREMATORY,
    CHARNEL
morvin .... MALLEIN
mos, plural of ...... MORES
mosaic ...... INLAY, COLLAGE
    gold .. ORMOLU, PIGMENT
    law .... TORA(H),
    PENTATEUCH
    law reading .. PARASHAH
    material .. TESSERA, TILE,
    SMALTO
    work .... TESSERA,
    INTARSIA
moschate .... MUSKY
Moscow .... MOSKVA
    chief rabbi ...... LEVIN
    citadel .... KREMLIN
    square .... PUSHKIN
Moselle .... WINE
    city on .. METZ, TREVES,
    TRIER
    tributary .... SAAR
Moses ... LAWGIVER, LEADER
    brother of .... AARON
    death place .... NEBO
    father-in-law of .. JETHRO
    people led by ....
    ISRAELITES
    saw Canaan there ......
    NEBO, PISGAH
    sister of .... MIRIAM
    spy of .... CALEB, NAHBI
    successor of .... JOSHUA,
    JOSUE
    wife of ...... ZIPPORAH
mosey: sl. .... AMBLE, STROLL,
    SHUFFLE(ALONG), MOVE
mosk .... MOSQUE
Moslem (see Muslim) ....
    SARACEN, PAYNIM, ISLAM(IC),
    MOHAMMEDAN, BERBER,
    PATHAN, MUSLIM,
    MUSSULMAN
    beggar .. FAKIR, DERVISH
    bridge to paradise ......
    ALSIRAT
    caliph .... OMMIAD
    call to prayer .... AZAN,
    ADAN
    cap ..... FEZ, TARBOOSH
    Christian to a ... GIAOUR
    chronicle ...... SARSILA,
    TARSILA
    coin .... DINAR

    college .... ULEMA
    converts .... ANSAR
    crier .... MUEZZIN
    decree .... IRADE
    devil .... EBLIS
    doctor .. HAKIM, HAKEEM
    drinking cup .... LOTAH
    Egyptian .... FULA(H)
    era, start of .... HEGIRA,
    HEJIRA
    fasting period ....
    RAMADAN, RAMAZAN
    festival .... BAIRAM
    garment .... JUBBAH
    governor .... HAKIM
    head .... RAIS, REIS
    headgear ...... FEZ, TAJ,
    TARBUSH, TARBOUCHE,
    TARBOOSH
    hermit .... SANTON,
    MARABOUT
    hero .... GHAZI
    holy book ...... KORAN
    holy city .... MECCA,
    MEDINA, KAIROUAN
    holy man .... IMAM,
    MARABOUT
    holy war .. JIHAD, JEHAD
    idol .... MAUMET
    interpreter of religious
    laws .. MOLLAH, MUFTI,
    MULLA(H)
    judge ...... CADI, KADI,
    HAKIM, CAZI, KAZI
    lady .... BEGUM
    language .... URDU
    law .... SUNNA(H)
    lawyer .... MUFTI
    leader .... AGA, CALIPH,
    IMA(U)M
    marriage .... MUTA
    measure .... ARDEB
    mendicant ...... FAKIR,
    DERVISH
    messiah .... MAHDI
    minister .... VIZI(E)R
    "miracle" performer ....
    FAKIR
    monk .... SANTON
    month .... SAFAR, RABIA,
    RAMADAN, RAJAB,
    SHABAN, JUMADA,
    RAMAZAN
    mosque .. MASJID, MUSJID
    mystic .... SUNI

noble ‑‑ ‑‑ SHERIF, EMIR, EMEER, AMEER
nomad .... KURD
non ...... RAIA, RAYAH, KAF(F)IR, GIAOU, ZENDIK
nymph .... HOURI
official .... HAJIB
people .... PATHAN
Philippine .... MORO
philosopher .. AVICENNA, AVERROES
physician ‑‑ ‑‑ HAKIM, HAKEEM
pilgrim .. HA(D)JI, IHRAM
pilgrimage .... HADJ
pilgrim's costume . IHRAM
place for prayer .... MOSQUE
power emblem .... CRESCENT
prayer .... SALAT
prayer caller .. MUEZZIN
prayer's direction .... KIBLAH, KAABA
priest ‑‑ ‑‑ ‑‑ IMA(U)M
prince .... AMIR, AMEER, EMIR, EMEER, NAWAB
princess .... BEGUM
principle .... IJMA
prophet .... MAHDI
religion .... ISLAM
religious brotherhood ... SENUS(S)I
religious duty ..... HADJ
religious festival .... BAIRAM
religious person .. IMAM, HATIB, PAKIL, HADJI
rosary .... TASBIH
ruler ‑‑ SULTAN, HAKIM, CALIPH, CALIF
sacred book ..... KORAN
saint .... PIR, SANTON
Satan .... EBLIS
scholars .... ULEMA
school .... MADRASA
sect founder .. WAHHAB(I)
sect member .. SUNNITE, SUFI, WAHABI, WAHABEE
shrine .. KAABA, CAABA, MESHED
slave .... MAMELUKE
spirit .... JIN(N), JINNEE, GENIE, GENII, JINN(I)
summons to prayer ..... AZAN

sword ..... (Y)ATAGHAN, SCIMITAR
teacher .. ALIM, MULLA(H), MOLLAH
temple .... MOSQUE
theologian ...... ULAMA
title .... SHERIF, NAWAB, MULLA(H), MOLLA, AGA, HAFIZ, MAHDI, HADJI
title of respect .. SAYYID, AG(H)A, SA(I)YID, NAWAB
tomb ‑‑ ‑‑ TABUT
tribe .... BASHKIR
tunic .... JAMA(H)
Turkestan .... SALAR
Turko-Tartar ... BASHKIR
unbeliever ...... GIAOUR, KAF(F)IR
viceroy .. NAWAB, NABOB
weight .... ROTL
who memorized Koran .. HAFIZ
woman's dress .... IZAR
Moslems collectively .. ISLAM
mosque ...... TEMPLE, MOSK, MASJID, MUSJID
tower .... JAMI, MINARET
mosquito ... CULEX, CULICID, STEGOMYIA, GALLINIPPER, INSECT
bite injection .. ALLERGEN
carried disease .. DENGUE, MALARIA
genus .... CULEX, AEDES
hawk ...... DRAGONFLY
larva ...... W(R)IGGLER
yellow fever .. STEGOMYIA
moss .... LICHEN, BRYOPHYTE, CARRAGEEN, EPIPHYTE
filaments ...... RHIZOID
mossbunker ..... MENHADEN, POGY
mosstrooper ‑‑ ‑‑ RAIDER, MARAUDER
most .... GREATEST
is superlative of .. MANY, MUCH
mostly .... CHIEFLY
mot .... WITTICISM, REPARTEE
mote .... SPECK
motel .... INN
motet ...... SONG, ANTHEM
moth ..... EGGER, FORESTER, INSECT, IO, BROWNTAIL, GYPSY, LUNA, BOMBYCID,

MILLER, ARRINDA, CECROPIA, CLEARWING, SATURNIID, PYRALIDID, AGLOOSA
clothes .... TINEA
destroying apples .... CODLIN(G)
eaten .... WORN OUT, PASSE, GNAWED
hawk .... SPHINX
kin .... BUTTERFLY
larva .... LOOPER
proboscis ...... LINGUA
night-flying ... NOCTUID
repellent ..... CAMPHOR
spot in wing of .... FENESTRA
mother .... ABBESS, MATER, DREGS, AMMA
Carey's chicken .. PETREL
colloquial .. MAMA, MUM, MOM(S), MOMMY, MUMMY, MAMMY, MOMSY
combining form .. MATRI
country ...... HOMELAND
earth .... GAEA
Goose creator .... PERRAULT
Hubbard .... CRONE
killer .... MATRICIDE
nursery rhyme's .. GOOSE, HUBBARD
of Cities .... KIEV
of gods .. RHEA, CYBELE
of horse .... DAM
of many children .... MULTIPARA
of pearl .... NACRE
of presidents .. VIRGINIA
of quintets ..... ZAHRA
of the Gracchi .... CORNELIA
superior .... ABBESS
who rules family/tribe .. MATRIARCH
wit ..... COMMON SENSE, INTELLIGENCE
motherhood .... MATERNITY
motherly .... MATERNAL
moths, of a group of .... TORTRICID
motif ..... THEME, SUBJECT, FEATURE, IDEA
motion .. MOVEMENT, GESTURE, PROPOSAL, SUGGESTION
imparting ...... MOTOR, KINETIC

in .. MOVING, TRAVELING
neurosis .... TIC
pertaining to ... KINETIC, MOTIVE
picture .. CINEMA, MOVIE, PHOTOPLAY, FLICKER, FILM
picture, cheap .. QUICKIE
picture first prints ...... RUSHES
picture word .. FINIS, END
pictures collectively ..... SCREEN
producing ...... MOTILE
rolling/swelling .. SURGE
toward the left .... LEVODUCTION
motionless ...... INERT, STILL
motivate ...... IMPEL, INCITE
motivation ...... MAINSPRING
motive .. REASON, IMPELLENT, GROUND, INCENTIVE, CAUSE, GOAL, INDUCEMENT, SPUR
in art, music ..... MOTIF
power ...... STEAM, ELECTRICITY
motley ...... VARICOLORED, HETEROGENEOUS
motor ..... ENGINE, TURBINE
fuel substance ... BORON, ETHYL, OCTANE
speed up ..... REV, RACE
vehicle frame ... CHASSIS
motorboat .. LAUNCH, SCOOTER
motorcar ...... AUTOMOBILE
motorcyclist ...... HAILWOOD
motorman, what he drives ... LOCOMOTIVE, STREETCAR
mott(e) .... GROVE
mottle ...... DAPPLE, SPOT, STREAK, BLOTCH
mottled .... PIED, PINTO, DAPPLED, VARIEGATED, PIEBALD
gray .... GRISEOUS
motto .... DEVICE, ADAGE, GNOME, SAYING, MAXIM, CATCHWORD, SLOGAN, SAW
in a book .... EPIGRAPH
in a ring .... POSY
mouchoir .... HANDKERCHIEF
moue .... GRIMACE, POUT
mouflon .... SHEEP
mould ...... FORM, KNEAD, MATRIX, FASHION
moulding (see molding)

moulin .... SHAFT
Moulmein is in .... BURMA
mound .. TELL, DENE, GLOBE,
    TERP, HILLOCK, HUMMOCK,
    KNOLL, DUNE, TUMULUS,
    PILE, HEAP, BARROW, HUMP,
    HILL
   domelike .... STUPA
   formed by wind .. DOWN
   golfer's .... TEE
   of a burrowing animal ..
    MOLEHILL
mounds, full of .... TUMULOSE
mount .. HILL, CLIMB, ASCEND,
    HORSE, POST, FIX
   by ladder ...... ESCALADE,
    SCALE
   Cook .... AORANGI
   Etna town .... ENNA
   Hood's range .. CASCADES
   of Olives .... OLIVET
   Rainier .... TACOMA
mountain .... HEAP, PILE,
    MOUND, BUTTE, BARROW,
    MONTICULE, KOP
   antelope .. KLIPSPRINGER
   Apollo's .... PARNASSUS
   ash .... ROWAN, SORB
   ash, tree-like ... SERVICE
   Asia Minor .... IDA
   base .... PIEDMONT
   Biblical .... NEBO, SINAI,
    ARARAT, HOREB
   cat ...... COUGAR, PUMA
   chain .... RANGE, SIERRA
   climber ...... ALPINIST
   climber's aid ..... PITON,
    CRAMPON
   climber's slider ....
    GLISSADE
   climber's staff ....
    ALPENSTOCK
   combining form .... ORO
   crest ...... ARETE, SPUR
   defile .... PASS, COL
   dew .... WHISKY
   feature .... ARETE, SPUR,
    CRATER, SNOWCAP
   formation .... OROGENY,
    RIDGE, ARETE, SPUR
   gap .. PASS, DEFILE, COL,
    GATE
   goat .... IBEX, TAHR
   gorge/gully ... COULOIR
   high .... ALP
   highest .... EVEREST

lake .... TARN
legendary .... MERU
lion .... COUGAR, PUMA,
    PANTHER, PAINTER
main mass ..... MASSIF
measuring instrument ...
    OROMETER
movable .... OSSA
of light, so-called ......
    KOHINUR
pass — COL, GHAT, GAP,
    DEFILE
pass, historical ....
    THERMOPYLAE
peak .. CONE, HORN, BEN
Pennine Alps ......
    MATTERHORN,
    MONT CERVIN
pool .... TARN
prefix .... ORO
range .... SIERRA,
    CORDILLERA
ridge — SAWBACK, SIERRA,
    ARETE
ridge central mass ....
    MASSIF
ridge notch .. WIND GAP
road's bend .... LOOP
rocky .... TETON
rounded .... KNOB
rubble .... SCREE
sheep.. BIGHORN, MOUFLON
sickness .... PUNA, VETA
slope .... VERSANT
small ...... MONTICULE
spinach .... ORACH
spur .... ARETE
State .... MONTANA
sunrise/sunset light .....
    ALPENGLOW
system ..... CORDILLERA
system in Europe .. ALPS
Tagalog .... BUNDOK
top .... PEAK
top cover .... SNOWCAP,
    ICECAP
top light ... ALPENGLOW
trail marker ..... KARN
way .... TUNNEL
where Moses saw Canaan
    NEBO, PISGAH
youngest .... PARICUTIN
mountaineer .... ALPINIST,
    CLIMBER, SHERPA
   climbing aid of ... PITON

mountains, formation of ..... OROGENY
 range of .... SIERRA
 study of .... OROGRAPHY,
  OROLOGY
mountebank .... QUACK,
 CHARLATAN, EMPIRIC
mounted sentinel .... VEDETTE
 traveler .... RIDER
Mountie .... POLICE, TROOPER
 outfit of .... RCMP
mourn .... RUE, GRIEVE,
 LAMENT, (BE)WAIL
 in sympathy ... CONDOLE
mourner, hired .... MUTE,
 WEEPER
 revivalist church ....
  PENITENT
mourners' bench occupant ....
  PENITENT
mournful .. LUGUBRIOUS, SAD,
 MELANCHOLY, LACRIMOSE,
  GRIEVOUS
mourning band .... CRAPE,
 CREPE
 cloak .... BUTTERFLY
 clothes .. SABLES, WEEDS,
 SACKCLOTH, BOMBASINE
 song .... DIRGE
mouse ..... GIRL, BLACK EYE,
 RODENT
 bird .... COLY
 deer .... NAPUS,
 CHEVROTAIN
 ear .. PLANT, HAWKWEED,
 FORGET-ME-NOT
 he's not one .... MAN
 like animal ...... SHREW,
 SORICINE
 meadow .... VOLE
 relative .... JERBOA,
 GERBIL(LE)
mousse .... DESSERT
mousseline .... MUSLIN, GLASS
mousy .... TIMID, QUIET
mouth ...... LIPS, STOMA, OS,
 GRIMACE, OPENING, SAY,
 DECLAIM, ORIFICE
 and lower cheeks .. CHOPS
 away from ..... ABORAL
 by word of ...... ORAL,
 VERBAL
 channel's .... CHOPS
 combining form .... ORI,
 STOME
 condition .... NOMA

gag .... MUZZLE
gaping .... RICTUS
 inflammation ....
  STOMATITIS
 Latin .... ORIS, OS
 of the .. BUCCAL, ORAL,
 STOMATIC, OSCULAR
 opening .... RICTUS
 opening measurement ...
  GAPE
 organ ...... HARMONICA,
 (PAN)PIPE, OCARINA,
  BAGPIPE
 part ...... TONGUE, LIP,
 UVULA, VELUM
 pertaining to .. STOMATIC,
  BUCCAL
 river .. DELTA, ESTUARY,
  FRITH
 slang .. MUG, KISSER, YAP,
 PUSS, TRAP
 spoken by the ..... ORAL
 strap .... MUZZLE
 study of the ....
  STOMATOLOGY
 thru the .... ORAL
 to pharynx passage ....
  FAUCES
 toward the .... ORAD
 ulcerous condition ......
  NOMA
 volcano .... CRATER
 wash .... GARGLE,
 LISTERINE
mouthed, loud .. STENTOR(IAN)
 open .... AGAPE
mouthful .... GOBBET
 small .... MORSEL
mouthlike opening .... STOMA
mouthpiece ...... SPOKESMAN,
 BOCAL, REED, NOZZLE
 slang .... LAWYER
mouths .... ORA
mouthy .... BOMBASTIC,
 TALKATIVE
mouton .... FUR
movable .. MOBILE, PORTABLE
 defense structure ....
  BASTIL(L)E
 mountain .... OSSA
 shelter in siege ..... CAT
 support .... TRESTLE
move .... TOUCH, AFFECT,
PROMPT, PROPOSE, EVACUATE,
 TRANSFER, STIR, BUDGE,

(A)ROUSE, SHIFT, PUSH, CARRY
able to .... MOTILE
about slyly ..... SLINK, PROWL, LURK
aimlessly ...... DOODLE, MAUNDER
along .... MOSEY, SASHAY
back .. RETREAT, REGRESS, JIB
back and forth .. SEESAW, SHUTTLE, DIDDLE
clumsily .. LOB, LUMBER, LUMP, WALLOP
confusedly .... MILL
forward ...... ADVANCE, FORGE, NOSE
furtively .. SNEAK, LURK, SKULK
gradually .. EDGE, INCH
heavily ... LOB, LUMBER, LUG, WALLOP
in a line .... FILE
in and out ...... WEAVE
in circles .. PURL, EDDY, CIRCULATE, SWIRL, GYRATE, CURL, MILL
in little waves ..... LAP
like a bird/butterfly ..... FLIT
movie camera ..... PAN
nimbly .... WHISK, FRISK
on casters .... TRUCKLE, TRUNDLE
on wheels .... ROLL
over .... TRANSFER
side to side ..... WEAVE
sidewise .... EDGE, SIDLE, SKEW, SLUE, JIB
slightly .... BUDGE
slowly .... INCH, WORM, FILTER, CRAWL, CREEP
smoothly .... GLIDE
suddenly, fast .... DART
to and fro .... WAG, SHUTTLE, OSCILLATE, VIBRATE
toward something ...... GRAVITATE
TV camera .... PAN
uneasily .... FIDGET
unsteadily ...... WAMBLE
up and down ..... WAVE, SEESAW
with sudden turn .. JINK

movement .. MOTION, ACTION, TEMPO
in music .... TEMPO, RHYTHM
in prosody .... CADENCE
of charged particles .... CATAPHORESIS
of organism ...... TAXIS
of the sea .... TIDE
mover, slow .. SNAIL, TURTLE
movie .. CINEMA, PHOTOPLAY, MOTION PICTURE
award .... OSCAR
camera platform .. DOLLY
combining form .. CINE
early heroine ... PAULINE
fare .. WESTERN, MYSTERY, MELODRAMA, MUSICAL, CARTOON
film, 1,000 ft. ..... REEL
full length ..... FEATURE
immortal star .... VALENTINO
last word of a ..... END
low budget .... QUICKIE
operator .... EXHIBITOR
part .... ROLE, LEAD, INGENUE
part of a .. REEL, SCENE, CREDITS
process .. TECHNICOLOR, CINEMASCOPE
projector ..... BIOSCOPE
role, small .... BIT
script .... SCENARIO
short .... NEWSREEL, CARTOON
shot .. CLOSE-UP, CLINCH
studio worker .... GRIP, STAGEHAND
term for sound adjustment SYNC
theaterowner .. EXHIBITOR
with sound ...... TALKIE
moving .. STIRRING, PATHETIC, MOTILE, IMPELLING, TOUCHING, POIGNANT, AFFECTING
about .... AMBULANT
area around body .... PERIPHERY
combining form .. KINETO
engine .... LOCOMOTIVE
in circular path .. GYRAL, GYRATORY
picture award .... OSCAR

staircase ..... ESCALATOR
vehicle .... VAN
mow ...... CUT DOWN, DESS,
   DESTROY, MATH, REAP,
   HAYSTACK, (HAY)LOFT,
   GRIMACE
'em down ..... KILL 'EM
Mowgli, friend of ..... BEAR,
   AKELA, BALOO
   tiger of .... SHERE KHAN
mowing implement .. SCYTHE,
   SICKLE, REAPER
Mowrer, Edgar ____ .. ANSEL
moxa .. CAUTERANT, CAUTERY,
   PLANT
Mozambique native ... BANTU,
   YAO
   port .... BEIRA
Mozart, composer ....
   WOLFGANG
   opera .... SERAGLIO
   (ABDUCTION FROM),
   MAGIC FLUTE,
   MARRIAGE OF FIGARO,
   DON GIOVANNI,
   COSI FAN TUTTI
Mozart's city .... SALZBURG
mozetta .... CAPE
   wearer of .... POPE
Mr. Catastrophe, sobriquet ..
   TRIPP
   Europe, sobriquet ......
   MONNET
Mrs. .... MISTRESS
   Grundy .... PRUDE
   Montagu Barstow ......
   ORCZY
   Sairey or her umbrella ..
   GAMP
Ms. .... MANUSCRIPT, MIZZ,
   MISS, MRS
much ... LOT, MANY, ALMOST,
   NEARLY
   in music .... MOLTO
mucid .... MUSTY, MOLDY
mucilage ..... ARABIN, PASTE,
   GLUE, ADHESIVE, GUM
mucilaginous .. STICKY, SLIMY
muck .. MANURE, DIRT, MIRE,
   FILTH, FERTILIZER
mucker .... CAD
muckle .... MUCH
muckworm .... MISER
mucous: comb. form .. MYX(O)
   membrane disease ......
   LUPUS

membrane fold ... PLICA
membrane inflammation..
   CATARRH
membrane secretion ....
   MUCIN
membrane tumor ....
   PAPILLOMA
membrane watery
   discharge ..... RHEUM
mud ..... MIRE, SLIME, WASH,
   WARP, SLUDGE, MURGEON,
   OOZE, LIBEL, SLANDER,
   SLUSH, MUCK, SLOP
   animal living in .. SIREN
   bath .... WALLOW
   dauber .... WASP
   hen .... RAIL, COOT,
   GALLINULE
   living in .... LIMICOLOUS
   puppy .... SALAMANDER
   river .... SILT
   volcano .... SALSE
muddle ...... EMBROIL, MESS,
   ADDLE, HASH, JUMBLE,
   BUNGLE, MIX UP, CONFUSE,
   SNAFU
   headed .... STUPID,
   CONFUSED
muddled .... WOOZY
muddy .. ROILY, RILE, SLUDGY,
   CLOUDY, DULL, VAGUE,
   SLOPPY, TURBID
mudfish .... DIPNOAN, BOWFIN
mudguard .... FENDER
mudhole .... LOBLOLLY,
   WALLOW
mudslinger ...... MUCKRAKER
mudworm .... IPO
muezzin .... CRIER
   call of .... AZAN
   place of ...... MINARET
muff .... BUNGLE(R), FUMBLE,
   BOTCH
muffin .... GEM, BREAD, COB,
   POPOVER
muffle .. MUTE, OVEN, STIFLE,
   DEADEN, WRAP
muffler .... SCARF, BAFFLE,
   MUTE, SILENCER
mufti .... ULEMA
   slang .... CIV(V)IES
mug ..... SEIDEL, TOBY, CUP,
   NOGGIN, STEIN, MUNGO
   leather .... JACK
   slang .. FACE, GRIMACE,
   PHOTOGRAPH, ASSAULT

mugger .. CROC(ODILE), GOA,
ROBBER, ACTOR
muggins ..... DOMINO, DUPE,
CARD GAME, FOOL
muggy ...... HUMID, SULTRY
mugwump ...... REPUBLICAN,
INDEPENDENT
Muhammad Ali ....
(CASSIUS) CLAY
Mukden is capital of ....
MANCHURIA
mulatto .... CREOLE, GRIQUA,
METIS, GRIFF(E)
mulberry .... MURREY, TREE,
AAL, FUSTIC, SYCAMINE
bark .... TAPA
tree genus .... CECROPIA,
MORUS
mulct .... FINE, DEFRAUD,
AMERCE, BILK, PENALIZE
mule ..... SHAVETAIL, HINNY,
HYBRID, TRACTOR, SLIPPER
cry .... BRAY
disease .... DOURINE
driver .... SKINNER
female .... MARE
pack .... SUMPTER
parent .. MARE, DONKEY
skinner .... DRIVER
young .... FOAL
muliebrity ..... WOMANHOOD,
FEMININITY
opposed to ... VIRILITY
mulish .. STUBBORN, STERILE,
OBSTINATE
mull ...... PONDER, SWEETEN,
COGITATE, MUSLIN, FLAVOR,
THINK, CONSIDER
mulla(h) .... INTERPRETER,
TEACHER
mulle(i)n .. FIGWORT, PLANT,
FOXGLOVE
muller ..... GRINDER, PESTLE
mullet ...... LIZA, (GOAT)FISH
mulley .... POLLED COW
mulligan .... STEW, HASH
mulligatawny, for example ...
SOUP
multifarious .... DIVERSE,
MANIFOLD, MANY, VARIED
multiflora .... ROSE
multiped creature .. CENTIPEDE
multiple .... MANIFOLD
multiplicand .... FACIEND
multiplication result ....
PRODUCT

multiply number by itself ....
SQUARE
multitude ..... SWARM, HOST,
LEGION, RUCK, CROWD,
THRONG, MYRIAD, HORDE,
GALAXY
multitudinous .... MANY,
NUMEROUS, MANIFOLD,
CROWDED
mum ..... BEER, DEODORANT,
CHRYSANTHEMUM, MOTHER,
SILENT, ALE
is the ___ .... WORD
mumble ..... MUMP, MUTTER,
MURMUR, CHEW
mumbojumbo .. FETISH, IDOL,
MEDICINE MAN, GIBBERISH
mummer .... ACTOR, GUISER,
MASKER, MASQUER, PARADER
mummify ...... DRY, SHRIVEL
mummy .... CORPSE
cloth .... BYSSUS
mump .... MUMBLE, MUTTER,
CHEAT, BEG
mumps .... PAROTITIS
munch .... CHEW, CHAMP
Munchausen, specialty of ....
YARNS
tales, collector of ......
RASPE
title of .... BARON
weakness of ....
MYTHOMANIA
Munchen .... MUNICH
mundane .... TERRENE,
TERRESTIAL, TEMPORAL,
WORLDLY, EARTHLY
mundungo ...... TOBACCO
Mundy work .... OM
mungo cloth ... SHODDY, MUG
Munich .... MUNCHEN
municipal tax .... OCTROI
municipality .... CITY, TOWN,
PUEBLO
munificent .... LAVISH,
GENEROUS
muniment .... DEFENSE,
FORTIFICATION
munitions manufacturer .....
KRUPP, SKODA
plant/storehouse ....
ARSENAL
Munro, H. H. .... SAKI
Munsel, singer ..... PATRICE
muntjac ...... RATWA, DEER
mural .. WALL-LIKE, PAINTING

painter .... RIVERA
Murat, Fr. marshal .. JOACHIM
murder ..... HOMICIDE, SLAY,
           KILL, BUMP OFF
  by drowning .... NOYADE
  by suffocation ... BURKE
  king's .... REGICIDE
  parent's ..... MATRICIDE,
           PATRICIDE
murderer .... MANSLAYER,
  PARRICIDE, PATRICIDE,
  MATRICIDE, ASSASSIN
  Biblical .... CAIN
murderous frenzy .... AMOK,
           BERSERK
murex .... WHELK
murid .... DISCIPLE, RAT
murine .. RODENT, RATS, MICE
murk ... GLOOM, DARK(NESS),
           DIM
murmur .. HUM, CURR, PURL,
  COMPLAINT, MUMBLE,
           MUTTER
  cat's .... PURR
  dove's .... COO
  wind's .... SOUGH
murmuring sound .. SUSSURUS
murphy .... POTATO
murrain .. ANTHRAX, PLAGUE,
           PESTILENCE
murre .... AUK, GUILLEMOT
murrelet .... (SEA)BIRD
murrey .... MULBERRY
murrhine substance ... STONE,
  JADE, FLUORITE
mus .... RAT, RODENT
musaceous plant .... BANANA
musca .. FLY, CONSTELLATION
muscadine ..... GRAPE, WINE
Muscat .... GRAPE, WINE
  and ___ .... OMAN
  natives .... OMANI
muscatel .... WINE
muscid insect .... HOUSEFLY
muscle ..... BRAWN, LACERT,
  LEVATOR, TERES, TENSOR,
  RECTUS, SPHINCTER, SINEW,
  TISSUE, STRENGTH, ERECTOR,
           TRICEPS, BICEPS
  attachment ..... TENDON
  bending .... FLEXOR
  buttocks ...... GLUTEUS
  combining form ... MY(O)
  contraction .. TIC, SPASM,
           CRAMPS
  disease ...... MYOPATHY

injury .... SPRAIN
jaw .... MASSETER
like .... MYOID
loin .... PSOAS
of .... SARCOUS
pain .... MYALGIA
part of .. HEAD, T(A)ENIA
protuberance .... VENTER
spasm(s) ...... CLONUS,
  CLONOS, CRAMP(S),
           CRICK
tension .... TONUS
muscles ..... THEWS, BRAWN,
           PSOAS
  science dealing with ....
           MYOLOGY
  wasting of ... DYSTROPHY
muscovado .... SUGAR
Muscovite ... RUSSIAN, MICA,
  SERICITE, GRANITE
Muscovy ..... RUSSIA, DUCK
muscular .. BRAWNY, THEWY,
  BURLY, STRONG, TOROSE
  contraction .. TIC, CRAMP
  contraction, childbearing
  .... LABOR
  elasticity .... TONUS
  fatigue .... MYASTHENIA
  impotence ..... ATAXIA
  power .... THEWS, SINEW
  strength ...... BRAWN
  tissue tumor ..... MYOMA
muse .... PONDER, MULL,
  GODDESS, MEDITATE, THINK,
  MEDITATION, PIERIS
  astronomy ...... URANIA
  chief .... CALLIOPE
  comedy .... THALIA
  dance .... TERPSICHORE
  eloquence .... CALLIOPE
  epic poetry .... CALLIOPE
  history .... CLIO
  love .... ERATO
  lyric poetry .. EUTERPE,
           ERATO
  music .... EUTERPE
  pastoral poetry .. THALIA
  poetry .... ERATO
  sacred poetry ....
  POLYMNIA, POLYHYMNIA
  tragedy .... MELPOMENE
Muses, domain of the ....
  PARNASSUS, AONIA
  fountain of the ....
           HIPPOCRENE
  home of the .... HELICON

mountain of the ....⁓
   PARNASSUS, HELICON
of the .... PIERIAN
one of the .... CALLIOPE,
   CLIO, ERATO, EUTERPE,
   MELPOMENE, POLYMNIA,
   URANIA, THALIA
place where worshipped ..
   PIERIA
spring of the .. CASTALIA
musette ... BAGPIPE, MELODY,
   OBOE
museum ....⁓.⁓ GALLERY
   custodian ..... CURATOR
   part of .... COURT
mush .. ATOLE, PAP, PORRIDGE,
   SENTIMENTALITY, JOURNEY,
   SAMP
   to whom addressed .....
   (SLED)DOG, MALEMUTE,
   HUSKY, MALAMUTE
mushroom .. FUNGUS, AGARIC,
   MORIL, DEATH CUP, MOREL,
   CHAMPIGNON, CHANTERELLE,
   AMANITA
   alkaloid ⁓. MUSCARIN(E)
   cap .... PILEUS
   cap's part ...... LAMELLA
   covering .... VOLVA
   immature ...... BUTTON
   leaflike plates ... PILEUS
   poisonous .. TOADSTOOL,
   AMANITA, AGARIC
   stalk .... STIPE
   sugar extract ....
   TREHALOSE
   underground .. TRUFFLE
mushy .. SENTIMENTAL, PAPPY,
   SOFT
Musial, baseball player ......
   STAN, THE MAN
music .. HARMONY, AIR, TUNE,
   LAY
   adapter ..... ARRANGER
   aftersong .... EPODE
   appropriate to night ....
   SERENADE, NOCTURNE
   arranger ...... ADAPTER
   as is .... STA
   canto .... PASSUS
   clef .... TREBLE
   concluding passage .....
   CODA
   cradlesong .... LULLABY
   excerpt .... MORCEAU
   for nine .... NONET

for practice ... ETUDE
for two .... DUET
grace note ..... SANGLOT
hall ...... ODEUM, GAFF,
   AUDITORIUM, ODEON,
   ODEA
high in ....⁓⁓.. ALT
high part ...... TREBLE
highest singing voice ....
   SOPRANO
interval in ...... OCTAVE,
   TRITONE
lead in .... PRESA
leap in .... SALTO
lively .. GIOCOSO, GALOP
major scale ..... GAMUT
man .... PRESTON
mark in .... SLUR, SEGNO
measured beat ... PULSE,
   TEMPO, MOTO
melodious .... ARIOSO
moderately, slow ....
   ANDANTE
mute .... SORDINO
night .... NOCTURNE,
   SERENADE
note in Guido's scale ...
   ALT, ELA, ELAMI
nursery .... LULLABY
played on bells .. CHIMB,
   CHIMES, CARILLON
played outdoors ....
   SERENADE
playful .... SCHERZANDO
rate of speed .... TEMPO,
   ANDANTE, ALLEGRO,
   LENTO
sacred ...... CHORAL(E)
sentimental ...... CORN,
   SCHMALTZ
short song .... ODE
silent: direction .. TACET
sign ...... SEGNO, PRESA
slow in .. TARDO, LARGO,
   LENTO
smooth style in .. LEGATO
so much .... TANTO
soft in .... PIANO
solo .... ETUDE
stately .. MINUET, LARGO
sustained .... TENUTO
teacher .... MAESTRO
tempo .... ANDANTE,
   ALLEGRO, PRESTO, LENTO
theme .... MOTIV
time in .... TEMPO

timing device ....
    METRONOME
together in .... ADUE
too much .... TANTO
twice in .... BIS
unaccented ...... ARSIS
whole note .. SEMIBREVE
musical .. MELODIOUS, MELIC,
    LYRIC(AL), CANOROUS
accompaniment ....
    OB(B)LIGATO
ballad .... DERRY
beginning .... INTRO
bells .. CARILLON, CHIMES
burlesque .. COMIC OPERA
character .... CLEF, KEY,
    REST, SHARP
chord ... TRIAD, CATGUT
combination .... CHORD
comedy .... REVUE,
    EXTRAVAGANZA,
    BURLESQUE
comedy music ... SCORE
comedy that fails ....
    TURKEY
composition ..... FUGUE,
    ARIOSO, NOCTURNE,
    CONCERTO, MOTET,
    OPERA, SONATA,
    SYMPHONY, CANTATA,
    ORATORIO, MINUET,
    OCTET(TE), SERENADE,
    SERENATA, RONDO,
    ETUDE, BAGATELLE,
    CAPRICCIO,
    HUMORESQUE
concord .... CONCENT
consonance .... CONCERT
direction ..... STA, SOLI,
    TACET
disability ...... AMUSIA
drama .... OPERA
ending .... CODA
entertainment between acts
    INTERMEZZO
excerpt .... MORCEAU
exercise .... ETUDE
flourish .... FANFARE,
    CADENZA
group .... TRIO, CHORUS,
    CHOIR, GLEE CLUB,
    BAND, COMBO,
    ORCHESTRA, MAZURKA,
    SERENADE, QUARTET,
    OCTET, DUET
half step ..... SEMITONE

horn, comic ... BAZOOKA
instrument .... CALLIOPE,
    REED, OCARINA, PIANO,
    LYRE, LUTE, FLUTE,
    VIOL(IN), ROTTE,
    SPINET, SITAR,
    CORNET, MANDOLIN,
    GUITAR, CITHERN,
    CLAVICHORD
brass-wind ... CORNET,
    TROMBONE, TRUMPET,
    BUGLE
fingerboard .... VINA
flute-like ... FLAGEOLET
guitar-like ...... LUTE,
    GITTERN, UKULELE,
    MANDOLIN, BANJO
harp-like ... SAMEBUKE
inventor ...... JUBAL
keyboard .... CLAVIER,
    SPINET, PIANO,
    CLAVICHORD, ORGAN,
    CELESTA
lute-like ..... THEORBO
lyre-like .... CITHARA
muffler .... MUTE
organ-like .. CALLIOPE
player ...... HARPIST,
    PIANIST(E), VIOLINIST,
    GUITARIST, FLUTIST
range of .... DIAPASON
soundboard ... ZITHER
string .... CHORD,
    CATGUT
stringed ... DULCIMER,
    BANDORE, VINA, LUTE,
    GUITAR, REBEC,
    CLAVIER, LYRE, ROTE,
    BANJO, ASOR, CITOLE,
    ZITHER, CITHER(N),
    SAMEBUKE, SAMISEN,
    MANDOLIN, UKULELE,
    VIOLA, VIOL
thread .... CATGUT
tone/volume changer ..
    PEDAL
toy .... KAZOO
trumpet-like ....
    CLARION, TUBA
violin-like .. REBEC(K),
    CELLO, VIOL, VIOLA
wind ..... FLAGEOLET,
    FLUTE, OCARINA,
    CLARINET, REED,
    TUBA, SAXOPHONE,
    ORGAN

with finger holes .....
OCARINA, FLUTE, PIPE
instruments, collectively .
STRINGS, TRAPS, BRASS,
WINDS, PERCUSSION
interlude, short .. VERSET
interval .... TRITONE,
OCTAVE, REST
introduction .. OVERTURE
lines ...... STEM, STAFF
medley .... CENTO, OLIO,
PASTICCIO, PASTICHE
movement .... SCHERZO
notation .... TABLATURE
note of old .... ELK, UT,
ARE, FE
ornament .... ROULADE
passage ...... CADENZA,
MORCEAU
passage, brilliant ....
BRAVURA
passage performed in fast
tempo .... PRESTO
patchwork ...... CENTO,
MEDLEY
percussion instrument ...
MARIMBA, XYLOPHONE,
DRUM, CYMBAL
performance .. CONCERT,
RECITAL, REVUE
phrase ...... LEITMOTIF
pipe .. OAT, REED, OBOE,
CLARINET, FLAGEOLET,
FLUTE
pitch .... TONE
play .... OPERETTA
range .... GAMUT
reed .... PIPE, FLUTE
rhythm, unit of ... BEAT
show ~....... REVUE,
EXTRAVAGANZA,
VAUDEVILLE
show that fails .. TURKEY
sign ... ISON, PRESA,
SEGNO, CLEF, REST, DOT
signature ...... THEME
sound .... TONE
sound, make ... SING,
YODEL, WARBLE, TRILL
sounds, science of ......
HARMONICS
study .... ETUDE
syllable .. DO, RE, MI, FA,
SOL, LA, TI
symbol .... CLEF
trill .... TREMOLO

vibrato .... TRILL
work .... OPUS
musician ... ORPHEUS, JUBAL,
HARMONIST
musicians' patron saint ......
CECILIA
stand .... DESK
musing .... MEDITATION,
REFLECTIVE, REVERIE
musk cat .... CIVET
have smell of ....
MOSCHATE
product .... PERFUME
muskeg .... MARSH, BOG
muskellunge .... PIKE
musket ... FIREARM, DRAGON,
CULVERIN, JINGAL,
GINGAL(L)
flintlock .... FUSIL
musketeer of fiction .. ARAMIS,
ATHOS, PORTHOS,
D'ARTAGNAN
Muskhogean Indian ....
CHICKASAW
muskmelon .... ATIMON,
CANTALOUPE, CAS(S)ABA,
MANGO
muskrat .... MUSQUASH
kin .... VOLE
musky .... MOSCHATE
Muslim (see Moslem) ......
MOSLEM, MUSSULMAN
cap .... KOPIA
chronicle ..... TARSILA,
SARSILA
court .... AGAMA
fasting month ....
RAMADAN
maid .... HOURI
religious person .. HADJI,
IMAM, HATIB, PAKIL
muslin ...... BATISTE, MOSAL,
TARLETAN, MULL, ADATI,
TARLATAN, SHELA, NAINSOOK
bag .... TILLOT
gauze .... TIFFANY
striped .... DORIA
musquash .... MUSKRAT
muss .... DISHEVEL, ROW,
CREASE, RUMPLE, MESS,
TOUSLE, DISORDER,
COMMOTION
mussel .... MOLLUSK, UNIO
product .... PEARL
Mussolini, dictator .. BENITO
nickname .... MUSSO

son-in-law ...... CIANO
title of .... (IL)DUCE
Mussulman .... MOSLEM,
SARACEN
must...... JUICE, SAPA, STUM,
NECESSARY, MILDEW, ALBA,
MAUN, ESSENTIAL, WINE,
MOLD
elephant's ..... FRENZY
mustache ...... HANDLE BAR,
BEARD, WHISKERS
mustached sea animal ....
WALRUS
Mustafa Kemal ____ ....
ATATURK
mustang ...... HORSE, BRONCO,
PONY
mustard .. CONDIMENT, WEED,
WOAD, SEASONING, TURNIP,
CRESS, RADISH
application ... POULTICE
container ...... CASTER
dye .... WOAD
gas ...... YPERITE, VESICANT
glucoside ..... SINALBIN
plaster .... SINAPISM
pod .... SILIQUE
seed glucoside ....
SINALBIN, SINIGRIN
wild .... CHARLOCK
mustee .. OCTOROON, MESTIZO
musteline animal ...... MINK,
MARTEN, POLECAT, WEASEL,
WOLVERINE, RATEL, OTTER
muster .... GATHER, SUMMON,
ASSEMBLE, LEVY, COLLECT,
ROLL, LIST
in .... ENLIST
out .... DISBAND
musty .. FUSTY, STALE, DULL,
SMELLY, TRITE, ANTIQUATED,
FETID, HOAR, RANCID, RANK,
MUCID, MOLDY
mutable .... FICKLE,
INCONSTANT, CHANGEABLE,
VOLATILE
mutant .... SPORT
mutate ...... VARY, CHANGE
mutation .... EVOLUTION,
CHANGE, SALTATION
in linguistics .... UMLAUT
mute .. MUFFLE, DUMB, MUM,
DEADEN, DUMMY, VOICELESS,
SURD
consonant .... LENE
for trumpet ... SOURDINE

in linguistics .... SILENT
mutilate ..... DAMAGE, MAIM,
DISFIGURE, MAR, DEFORM,
MANGLE
mutineer .... REBEL
mutiny .... RISE, REVOLT,
REBELLION
Mutsuhito's realm .... JAPAN
reign .... MEIJI
son .... HIROHITO
mutt .... MONGREL, DOG, CUR
mutter .. MUMBLE, GRUMBLE,
COMPLAIN, MURMUR
mutton .... SHEEP, FLESH,
CABOB, (RED)MEAT
bird .... OII
cut .... SADDLE
chop .... CABOBS, KABOBS
chops .... WHISKERS,
SIDEBURNS, BURNSIDES
fish .... SAMA
head ...... DOLT, DUNCE
neck .... SCRAG
stew .... HARICOT
mutual .. JOINT, RECIPROCAL,
COMMON
aid, solons' ....
LOG-ROLLING
mutually destructive ....
INTERCINE
muzhik .... PEASANT
muzzle .... NOSE, GAG, SNOUT
muzzy .... CONFUSED, DAZED,
BEFUDDLED
my faith, literally .... MA FOI
fault .... MEA CULPA
Gal ____" .... SAL
heart, literally .. MACHREE
Sweetness ...... NAOMI
mycelium of fungi ..... SPAWN
myelencephalon .. AFTERBRAIN
myna(h) .... BIRD
kin of .... STARLING
Mynheer .... SIR, DUTCHMAN
myopic ...... NEARSIGHTED,
SHORTSIGHTED
Myra Breckinridge personified
(RAQUEL) WELCH
pianist .... HESS
myriad .... MULTITUDE,
COUNTLESS, TEN THOUSAND
myriapod .... CENTIPEDE,
MILLIPEDE, ARTHROPOD
segment .. TELSON, SOMITE
myrmicid .... ANT

Myrmidon ～～～ ～～ FOLLOWER,
   ADHERENT, SUBORDINATE
myrrh ～～～～～～～～ CICELY
myrtle .. PERIWINKLE, GUAVA,
   CAJEPUT, SHRUB, CAJUPUT
   berry ～～～～～ ALLSPICE
Mysore, capital of ～～～～～
   BANGALORE
mysterious .. WEIRD, CRYPTIC,
   ORACULAR, ARCANE, SECRET,
   ENIGMATIC, INSCRUTABLE,
   OCCULT, MYSTIC(AL), RUNIC,
   UNKNOWN, ESOTERIC
mystery ～～～～～ RIDDLE, CRAFT,
   CONUNDRUM, ARCANUM,
   ENIGMA, SECRECY, PUZZLE,
   RUNE
  in Christianity ～～ MASS,
   SACRAMENT, EUCHARIST
  story ～～～～～ WHODUNIT,
   MAIGRET
mystic ～～～～ ESSENE, EPOPT(IC),
   ORPHIC, OCCULT,
   MYSTERIOUS, ESOTERIC,
   ENIGMATIC, SUFIST, YOGA,
   YOGI(N), CABALIST
  art ～～～～ CABALA, MAGIC,
   ASTROLOGY, ALCHEMY,
   OCCULTISM, VOODOO,
   SORCERY, WITCHCRAFT
  cry ～～～～～～～ EVOE, OM
  Mt. Athos ～～ HESYCHAST
  practice ～～～～～～ YOGA
  symbol ～～～～～ CHARACTER
  union with God ～～～～～
   THEOCRASY
  word ～～～～～ ABRAXAS,
   ABRACADABRA
  writing ～～～～～～ RUNE
mystical ～～～～～～～ OCCULT,
   ALLEGORICAL, ENIGMATIC,
   MYSTERIOUS
  doctrine ～～ CAB(B)ALA,
   KABALA

  ecstasy ～～～ THEOPATHY
  interpretation .. ANAGOGE
mystify .. OBFUSCATE, PUZZLE,
   PERPLEX, BEWILDER, HOAX
myth .. FABLE, LEGEND, STORY
mythical ～～～～～～ IMAGINARY,
   LEGENDARY, FICTITIOUS,
   FABULOUS
  animal ～～～～～ GRIFFIN,
   GRYPHON, GRIFFON
  antelope ～～～～～～ YALE
  being ～～～～～ CENTAUR
  bird ～～～～～～～ ROC
  ferryman ～～～～ CHARON
  flyer ～～～～～ ICARUS
  giant ... CYCLOPS, YMIR,
   YMER, JOTUN, FAFNIR
  hero ～～～～～～ EGIL(E)
  horse ～～～～ UNICORN,
   PEGASUS
  hunter ～～～～～ ORION
  island/continent ～～～～～
   ATLANTIS
  king ～～～～ OLAF, ATLI
  land ～～～～～ LEMURIA
  maiden ～～～～ IO, DANAB
  man of brass ～～～ TALOS
  monster ～～～～ DRAGON,
   CHIMERA, SPHINX,
   MINOTAUR, GRIFFIN
  mountain ～～～～～ OSSA,
   HELICON, PARNASSUS
  musician ～～～～ ORPHEUS
  river ～～～～～～ STYX
  serpent .. APEPI, MIDGARD
  sisters ～～～～～ GORGONS
  trio ～～～ FATES, GORGONS
  watchdog ～～～～～ GARM,
   CERBERUS
  wolf ～～～～～～ FENRIR
  woman ～～～～～～ IDUN
mythologist ～～～～～～ MULLER
mythomania, victim of .. LIAR,
   MUNCHAUSEN, ANANIAS
Mytilene ～～～～～～ LESBOS

N

N.B. ～～～～～～～ NOTA BENE
  Greek ～～～～～～～ NU
  Hebrew ～～～～～～ NUN
  letter ～～～～～～ EN
na .... NO, NOT, NOR, SODIUM
NAACP, part of .. NATIONAL,
   COLORED, PEOPLE
nab .. SEIZE, SNATCH, CATCH,

   ARREST, NICK, SNAG,
   CAPTURE
Nabal's wife ～～～～～ ABIGAIL
nabob .... NAWAB, RICH MAN,
   DIVES
nacelle ～～～～～～ BASKET, CAR,
   FUSELAGE
nacl ～～～～～～～～ SALT

nacre .... SHELLFISH,
MOTHER-OF-PEARL
nacreous .... LUSTROUS
nacrite .... MICA
nadir .... DEPTHS, LOW POINT
  opposite of ..... ZENITH
nae .... NO, NOT
naevus .... FRECKLED
nag .. BADGER, ANNOY, PONY,
  HORSE, SHREW, VIRAGO,
  TERMAGANT, PESTER,
  TEASE, RIDE, SCOLD,
  HECTOR, TIT, HENPECK,
  PLAGUE
naga .... COBRA, SNAKE
nagana disease carrier ....
  TSETSE
Nagasaki, destroyer of ......
  A(TOM)BOMB
nagger .. SCOLD, TERMAGANT,
  SHREW, VIRAGO
Nagoya's bay .... ISE
Naha is capital of .. OKINAWA
nahoor .. SHEEP, BHARAL, SNA
Nahor's wife .... MILCAH
naiad ..... NYMPH, SWIMMER,
  OREAD
naif .... NAIVE, ARTLESS
nail .. BRAD, PIN, SPAD, SPRIG,
  TACK, SPIKE, UNGUIS,
  TENTER, TACH(E), CLAW,
  FASTEN, SECURE, FIX, CATCH,
  UNGULA
  biting .... PHANEROMANIA
  finishing .... BRAD
  having .... UNGUAL
  headless ..... SPARABLE,
  SPRIG
  horseshoe .... STUB
  like a .... UNGUAL
  polish .. ENAMEL, CUTEX
  shoemaker's .. SPARABLE
  short .... TACK
  size .... TENPENNY
  slang .... CIGARETTE
  slantingly .... TOE
  substance ..... KERATIN
  3-inch .... TENPENNY
  unit of weight ..... KEG
  wooden .... PEG
nailhead .... STUD
nails, 100 lbs. .... KEG
nainsook .... MUSLIN, COTTON
naive .... ARTLESS, INNOCENT,
  GUILELESS, GREEN, SIMPLE,
  INGENUOUS, CHILDLIKE
  girl .. INGENUE, INNOCENT
naivete .... INNOCENCE
naked .. BARE, NUDE, EXPOSED,
  STARK, PLAIN
  in law .... INVALID
namaycush .. TROUT, TOGUE,
  SALMONOID
namby-pamby .. INSIPID, SILLY,
  VAPID, WISHY-WASHY
  person nicknamed ......
  PHILIPS
name ..... DUB, COGNOMEN,
  NOMINATE, TERM,
  LABEL, EPITHET,
  APPELLATION, CITE, MENTION,
  (EN)TITLE, APPOINT,
  DESIGNATE, REPUTATION
  announcer ......
  NOMENCLATOR
  assumed .... ALIAS,
  PSEUDONYM, SOBRIQUET,
  INCOG
  bad .... NOTORIETY,
  ILL-REPUTE, CACONYM
  characteristic .. EPITHET,
  SOBRIQUET
  derivation of ... EPONYM
  fake .... ALIAS
  false .... ANONYM
  give a .... ENTITLE
  meaning beauty ..... ADA
  bright .... BERTA
  comfort .... NOAH
  daughter ...... INGA
  girl .... COLLEEN
  healer .... ASA
  high .... ELI
  holy .... OLGA
  life .... EVA
  little .... ETTA
  moon goddess .. DELIA
  noble ...... PATRICK
  peace .... IRENE
  pleasure ...... EDNA
  princess .... SARA
  rose .... RHODA
  serving .... OBED
  spring born ... VERNA
  weary .... LEAH
  of a place .... TOPONYM
  of thing, etc. ..... NOUN
  of two same terms ......
  TAUTONYM
  one by one .. ENUMERATE
  plate .... FACIA

slang ... ... MONI(C)KER,
    HANDLE
substitute ... ... DINGUS
    to an office ... NOMINATE
named ... ... CITED, YCLEPT,
    YCLEPED, MENTIONED,
    APPOINTED
nameless ... ... ANONYMOUS,
    UNKNOWN, UNIDENTIFIED,
    OBSCURE
    person ... ... ANONYM
namely ... SILICET, TO WIT, VIZ,
    VIDELICET
names list ... ... BEADROLL
namesake ... ... HOMONYM,
    EPONYM
nana ... AMAH, NURSE, NANNY
Nancy ... ... NARCISSUS
nankin ... ... BUFF, COTTON
nanny ... ... NURSE
    vehicle of ... ... PRAM,
    BUGGY, STROLLER
Naomi ... ... MARA
    daughter-in-law of ... ...
    RUTH
naos ... ... TEMPLE, CELLA
nap ... ... SIESTA, SLEEP, PILE,
    SHAG, SNOOZE, DOZE, WINK,
    RAS
    of a sort ... FORTY WINKS,
    SIESTA
    raising device ... TEASEL,
    TEAZEL, GIG, CARD
    shearer ... ... CROPPER
napalm inventor ... ... FIESER
nape ... SCRAG, SCRUFF, PALL,
    NUCHA, NUQUE
napery ... ... LINEN, DOILIES,
    NAPKINS, DAMASK
Napier's invention ... ...
    LOGARITHMS
napkin ... ... DIAPER, NAPERY,
    SERVIETTE, TOWEL, BIB,
    DOILY
Naples ... ... NAPOLI
    beggar in ... LAZZARONE
    bay island ... ... CAPRI
    king of ... ... MURAT
    lake near ... ... AVERNUS
    native of ... NEOPOLITAN
    patron saint ... JANUARIUS
Napoleon ... COIN, CARD GAME,
    PASTRY
    birthplace of ... AJACCIO
    brother of ... ... LUCIEN,
    JEROME

conqueror of ... ...
    WELLINGTON, KUTUZOV
    downfall of ... WATERLOO
    game like ... ... PAM
    isle identified with ... ...
    ELBA, CORSICA, HELENA
    marshal of ... NEY, MURAT
    scene of defeat ... ...
    WATERLOO
    scene of victory ... JENA,
    MARENGO,
    AUSTERLITZ,
    WAGRAM
    sister of ... ... ELISA,
    CAROLINE
    wife of ... ... JOSEPHINE
Napoli ... ... NAPLES
nappy ... ... WOOLLY, DOWNY,
    HAIRY, DISH, ALE, FOAMING
Naraka, Hindu ... ... HELL
narcissism ... ... SELF-LOVE
narcissus ... JONQUIL, FLOWER,
    DAFFODIL, EGOIST, NANCY
    composer ... ... NEVIN
    love of ... ... SELF
    nymph who loved ... ECHO
narcosis ... ... SLEEP, STUPOR
narcotic ... OPIATE, SEDATIVE,
    DOPE, MORPHINE, CODEINE,
    ANODYNE, HASHISH, OPIUM,
    HEROIN, COCAINE, DRUG,
    JUNK
    beechnut ... ... FAGINE
    cigarette ... REEFER, KEF,
    MARIJUANA
    dreamy tranquillity ... KEF
    drug, inject ... MAINLINE
    plant ... ... HEMP, POPPY,
    BHANG, MARIJUANA,
    K(H)AT, MANDRAKE,
    DUTRA, CUCA
    slang ... DOPE, SNOW, POT
    smoking effect ... ... KEF
    under influence of ... ...
    DOPEY, STONED
    user ... ... DOPE, ADDICT,
    FIEND, POT-HEAD
nard ... ... SALVE, OINTMENT,
    PLANT
nares ... ... NOSTRILS
narghile ... ... HOOKA(N), PIPE
narial ... ... RHINAL
narine ... ... NASAL
nark ... ... SPY, INFORMER,
    STOOL PIGEON

narrate ..... RECITE, RECOUNT, RELATE, TELL
narration ~ STORY, ACCOUNT, RECITAL
narrative .... TALE, ACCOUNT, STORY, SAGA, NOVELLA, CONTE
   poem ...... EPIC, ILIAD, ODYSSEY, BEOWULF, EPOS, LAY
narrow ... CONTRACT, CLOSE, LIMIT, ANGUST, STRAIT(EN)
   band .... FANON
   combining form .. STENO
   escape ...... CLOSE CALL
   minded .... BIGOTED, BIASED, PEDANTIC, SECTARIAN, PETTY
   opening .... SLOT
   street ..... ALLEY, LANE
narrower at the base .. OBTUSE
narrows .... STRAIT, SOUND
narthex .... VESTIBULE
narwhal .. WHALE, CETACEAN
nary .... NO, NOT ANY
nasal ...... RHINAL, NARINE
   catarrh .... CORYZA
   hemorrhage .. EPISTAXIS
   intonation ...... TWANG
   mucous ... SNOT, SNIVEL
   noise .... SNORT
   passage .. NARES, NOSTRIL
nascency .. BEGINNING, BIRTH, GENESIS, FORMATION
naseberry .... SAPODILLA
Nash, humorist .... OGDEN
Nasser, UAR president ...... GAMAL (ABDEL)
nasty ~. MEAN, FOUL, FILTHY, OBSCENE
natal ~ ~ ~. INNATE, INBORN, NATIVE
natant .. SWIMMING, FLOATING
natatorium .... POOL
nates .... BUTTOCKS
Nathan, George ___ .. JEAN
nation ..... STATE, COUNTRY, PEOPLE
   extermination of .... GENOCIDE
   temperance leader ...... CARRY
national .... CITIZEN
   character .... ETHOS
   Guard .... MILITIA
   hymn .... ANTHEM

native .. INDIGENOUS, NATAL, ENDEMIC, SON, INBORN, AUTOCHTHON, ABORIGINE, ENCHORIC, NATURAL, ENCHORIAL
   ability ~ ~ TALENT, GIFT, APTITUDE
   agent ..... ~ COMPRADOR
   animal .... INDIGENE
   chief .... CACIQUE, DATU
   inhabitant .... DENIZEN
   metal .... ORE
   original ~... ABORIGINE, ABORIGINAL
   plant .... INDIGENE
   salt .... HALITE
   suffix .... ITE
nativity .... BIRTH
natrium .... SODIUM
natty ~ SMART, SHARP, CHIC, TRIM, SPRUCE
natural .. WILD, INNATE, REAL, INBORN, NORMAL, UNPOSED
   ability .. APTITUDE, GIFT, KNACK, TALENT, FLAIR, GENIUS
   abode ... ~ ~ HABITAT
   philosophy .... PHYSICS
   science branch .. BOTANY, PHYSICS, GEOLOGY, ZOOLOGY, CHEMISTRY
naturalist ...... BEEBE, MUIR, BIOLOGIST, ANIMIST, AUDUBON, BURBANK, DARWIN, ANDREWS
naturalize .... DENIZEN
naturalized plant/animal ..... DENIZEN
naturally .... OF COURSE
nature .. ESSENCE, KIND, SORT, TYPE, CHARACTER
naught .. NOTHING, NIL, ZERO
   bring to .. VOID, NULLIFY, UNDO, CANCEL
naughty ~ MISCHIEVOUS, BAD, IMPISH, OBSCENE
nausea ~.~. QUALM, DISGUST, PALL, WAMBLE
   affected with ... QUEASY
nauseate .... SICKEN
nauseous .... SICKENING
Nausicaa's find ..... ULYSSES
   parent .... ALCINOUS
nautical .... MARINE, NAVAL, MARITIME, OCEANIC
   call .... AHOY

chain .... TYE
command .... AVAST
dick .... DEADEYE
fly .... BURGEE
mile .... KNOT
rope .. RATLINE, HAWSER,
   MARLINE, NETTLE
term .. ALEE, AWEATHER,
   ABEAM, ASTERN, ABAFT,
   AFORE, ATRY
nautilus .... ARGONAUT,
   MOLLUSK
Verne's commander of ..
   NEMO
Nauvoo, formerly .. COMMERCE
Navaho .... ATHAPASCAN,
   INDIAN
hut .... HOGAN
naval .... NAUTICAL, MARINE,
   MARITIME
  academy .... ANNAPOLIS
  cadet ..... MIDSHIPMAN,
    MIDDY
  commander ... CAPTAIN,
    ADMIRAL, SKIPPER
  force .... FLEET, ARMADA
  hero .... NELSON, DEWEY,
    FARRAGUT
  officer .. ENSIGN, YEOMAN,
    MATE
  pass of a sort .. NAVICERT
  protective/offensive device
    PARAVANE
  Reserve woman ... WAVE
  ships collectively ......
    MARINE
  title .... ADMIRAL,
    COMMODORE
  unit list/roll ... MUSTER
  vessel ...... DESTROYER,
    CORVETTE, FLATTOP,
    WARSHIP, UBOAT,
    CRUISER, TENDER
  War College site ....
    NEWPORT
nave .... HUB
navel .... UMBILICUS
  of Sicily .... ENNA
  point .... NOMBRIL
navigate .... AVIATE, SAIL,
   STEER, CRUISE
navigation detecting system ..
   LORAN, SONAR
navigator .... NAVVY, BERING,
   ERIC, TASMAN, COOK,
   MAGELLAN, BAFFIN

Navigators Island .... SAMOA
navvy .... LABORER
navy ...... FLEET, WARSHIPS,
   SEA FORCE
  bed .... SACK
  color .... BLUE
  group .... FLOTILLA,
    SQUADRON, ARMADA,
    TASKFORCE
  mascot of .... GOAT
  pharmacist ... CORPSMAN
  ration .... HARDTACK
  recruit .... BOOT
  scout boat .... VEDETTE,
    VIDETTE
nawab .... NABOB, TITLE
nay ...... DENIAL, NO, VOTE
Nazarene .... JESUS
Nazarite, he was one ....
   SAMSON
Nazi ...... FASCIST, HITLERITE
  airforce ..... LUFTWAFFE
  collaborator .. QUISLING,
    LAVAL
  concentration camp .....
    DACHAU, NORDHAUSEN,
    BUCHENWALD, BELSEN
  defector .... HESS
  district .... GAU
  district leader ....
    GAULEITER
  emblem .... SWASTIKA,
    FYLFOT
  extermination center ....
    BELSEN
  greeting .... HEIL
  ideology ... HERRENVOLK
  leader .... HITLER,
    GOERING, HIMMLER,
    GOEBELS, HESS, LEY,
    FUEHRER
  organization, U.S. ......
    BUND
  salute ..... HEIL HITLER
  state police ... GESTAPO
  symbol ...... SWASTIKA
Nazimova, actress ...... ALLA
NB .... NOTA BENE
NCO ..... SERGEANT, SARGE,
   CORPORAL
neap .... TIDE
near .. CLOSE, NIGH, ALMOST,
  APPROACH, INTIMATE, ABOUT
  by .. VICINAL, CLOSE TO,
   AROUND

East country ·· ··· SYRIA, LEBANON, TURKEY, ISRAEL, JORDAN, EGYPT
sighted ··· ··· ··· MYOPIC
sightedness ··· ··· MYOPIA
sighted person ··· MYOPE
nearby ··· ··· ··· NIGH, CLOSE, AROUND
nearest ··· ··· ··· ··· NEXT
nearly ··· ··· ABOUT, ALMOST, ALL BUT
neat ··· ··· NATTY, TRIG, SPIFFY, PURE, TAUT, SPRUCE, NET, TIDY, SOIGNE, ADROIT, CLEAN
neatherd ··· ··· ··· COWHERD
neb ··· ··· BEAK, BILL, SNOUT, NOSE, TIP, NIB
Nebraska capital ··· LINCOLN
  city ·· OMAHA, FREMONT, HASTINGS, ORD
  county ··· ··· KNOX, POLK, YORK, CASS
  Indian ··· ··· OMAHA, OTOE, PAWNEE
  river ··· ··· PLATTE, NEMAHA
  state flower ··· ··· ··· ··· GOLDENROD
Nebraskan ··· ··· CORNHUSKER
nebulous ··· ··· CLOUDY, MISTY, HAZY, VAGUE, INDEFINITE
necessaries ··· ··· ··· ESTOVERS
necessarily ··· ··· ··· PERFORCE
necessary ·· MUST, ESSENTIAL, MANDATORY, REQUISITE, VITAL, REQUIRED
necessitate ·· COMPEL, ENTAIL, REQUIRE, OBLIGE
necessity ·· FATE, COMPULSION, NEED, WANT
  of ··· ··· ··· ··· ··· ··· PERFORCE
neck ··· CHANNEL, CARESS, GULLET, STRAIT, KISS, PET, SPOON, CERVIX, SCRAG
  and neck ··· ··· ··· ··· CLOSE
  and shoulder covering ··· SHAWL, TUCKER
  animal with long ··· ··· ··· GIRAFFE
  armor ··· ··· ··· GORGET
  artery ··· ··· ··· CAROTID
  back of ·· NAPE, CERVIX, NUCHA, SCRUFF
  covering ·· MANE, RUFF, PARTLET
  cramp ··· ··· ··· ··· CRICK

hair ··· ··· ··· ··· MANE
  human ··· ··· ··· ··· SCRAG
  ligament ··· ··· ··· PAXWAX
  muscle ··· ··· ··· SPLENIUS
  of beef ··· ··· ··· ··· CLOD
  of land ··· ISTHMUS, SPIT
  of the ··· ··· ··· JUGULAR, CERVICAL
  part of horse ··· WITHERS
  piece ··· BOA, STOLE, TIE, CRAVAT, SCARF, COLLAR, FICHU
  scarf ··· ·· ASCOT, TIPPET
neckcloth ··· ··· ··· CRAVAT
neckerchief ··· ··· ··· SCARF
necklace ··· STRAND, CHAPLET, CARCANET, BEAD
  appendage ··· ··· LOCKET, LAVALIER
  colloquial ··· ··· CHOKER
  metal ··· ··· ··· ··· TORQUE
  of several strands ··· ··· ··· RIVIERE
  ornament ··· LAVALIER(E)
neckline, having low ··· ··· ··· DECOLLETE
  shape ··· ··· ··· ··· VEE
necktie ·· ASCOT, BOW, SCARF, CRAVAT, CHOKER, FOULARD
  ornament ··· ··· STICKPIN
  party ··· ··· ··· HANGING
neckwear ··· ··· ··· COLLAR, RUFF
necrology ··· ··· ··· OBIT(UARY)
necromancer ··· ··· DIVINER, WIZARD, SORCERER, CONJURER
necromancy ··· ·· (BLACK)MAGIC
necropolis ··· ··· ··· CEMETERY, GRAVEYARD
necropsy ··· ··· ··· ··· AUTOPSY, POST MORTEM
nectar ··· ··· DRINK, BEVERAGE, HONEYDEW
  of the gods ··· ··· AMBROSIA
  product ··· ··· ··· HONEY
nectarine ··· ··· ··· ··· PEACH
nee ··· ··· ··· ··· ··· ··· BORN
need ··· ··· LACK, NECESSITY, OBLIGATION, WANT, EXIGENCY, REQUISITE
needle ··· POINTER, INDICATOR, GOAD, PROVOKE, PROD, PRICK, TEASE, HECKLE
  blunt, thick ··· ··· BODKIN
  bug ··· ··· ··· ··· ··· NEPA

case .... ETUI, ETWEE
crystal like .... ACICULA
etching .... STYLE
like spine ..... ACICULA
pushing disk ...... PALM
shaped .... SPICULE,
 ACERATE, ACICULAR,
 ACEROSE, SPICULAR,
 ACUATE, ACIFORM
threading hole ...... EYE
needlefish .... GAR, PIPEFISH
needlelike .... SPICULATE
crystal .... ACICULA
needlewoman ... SEAMSTRESS,
 SEMPSTRESS
needlework ...... EMBROIDERY,
 SEWING
beginner's .... SAMPLER
needy ...... POOR, DESTITUTE,
 INDIGENT
neep .... TURNIP
nefarious ... WICKED, VICIOUS
Nefertiti's husband ....
 AKHENATON, PHARAOH
negate .. NULLIFY, DENY, VOID,
 COUNTERACT, NEUTRALIZE,
 ANNUL
negation .. DENIAL, NULLITY,
 NONENTITY
act of ...... VETO, REJECT
negative .... MINUS, NO
connective ...... NEITHER,
 NOR
emphatic .... NEVER
ion .... ANION
opposite of ....
 AFFIRMATIVE, POSITIVE
prefix .... NON
quality .... MINUS
slangy ...... NOPE, NIX,
 NO DICE,
 NO SOAP
terminal ...... CATHODE
vote .... NAY
neglect .. SHIRK, OMIT, IGNORE,
 DISREGARD, OVERLOOK,
 SLIGHT, FORGET
neglectful .. REMISS, DERELICT
negligee .... GOWN, PEIGNOR
negligence .... CULPA
negligent .... LAX, REMISS,
 CARELESS, DERELICT
negligible .. TRIFLING, TRIVIAL
amount .... PEANUTS,
 CHICKEN FEED
negotiate .. TREAT, BARGAIN,

DEAL, DISCUSS, PARLEY,
 TRANSACT
Negrillo .... BUSHMAN
Negrito ...... ITA, NEGROID,
 A(E)TA, TAPIRO, BALUGA
Negro ... BLACK, HOTTENTOT,
 BANTU, NUBIAN, IBO,
 HAUS(S)A, KAFFIR, SWAHILI,
 DAHOMAN, ETHIOP(IAN),
 NUBA, JIM CROW
 KROO, YORUBA,
 MANDINGO
and white offspring ......
 MESTEE, MUSTEE,
 MULATTO
black magic .... VOODOO
colloquial ...... DARKIE,
 DARK(E)Y
dance ...... JUBA, SAMBA,
 CAKEWALK
family servant .. MAMMY
fugitive .... MAROON
hairdo .... NATURAL
magic ...... OBEAH, OBI
mulatto offspring ......
 GRIFF(E)
pigmy .... AKKA
religious folk song ......
 SPIRITUAL
tribe ...... TEMBU, SERER
witchcraft ... OBI, OBEAH
woman servant .. MAMMY
young male ...... BUCK
Negroes, discrimination against
 JIM CROW
Negroid .... NUBIAN, KAFFIR,
 TEMBU, ETHIOP(IAN),
 PAPUAN, BANTU
negus, Ethiopia's ....
 (HAILE)SELASSIE
Nehru, India prime minister ..
 JAWAHARLAL
neigh ...... (S)NICKER, HINNY,
 WHINNY
neighborhood ..... VICINAGE,
 VICINITY, LOCALITY,
 PRECINCTS, PURLIEU,
 COMMUNITY
neighboring .... NEARBY,
 ADJACENT
neighbors' gathering ...... BEE
neither, companion of ... NOR
Nejd, capital of ..... RIYADH
robe .... ABA
Nellie ____, journalist ... BLY
Nelson, Admiral .... HORATIO

scene of victory ... ...
TRAFALGAR
"Nelson's blood" ... ... RUM,
GROG
nelumbo ... ... LOTUS,
(WATER)LILY
Neman .... NIEMEN, NEMUNAS
nemathelminth ... NEMATODE,
(HOOK)WORM
nemato: as comb. form ... ...
THREAD
nematode ...... (HOOK)WORM,
PINWORM, ASCARID,
ROUNDWORM
nembutal ... ... SEDATIVE,
HYPNOTIC
nemesis ... AVENGER, GODDESS,
RETRIBUTION
nemoral ... ... SYLVAN
neon ... ... LIGHT
neophyte .... CONVERT, TYRO,
BEGINNER, NOVICE, AMATEUR
neoplasm ... ... TUMOR
Neopolitan secret society ... ...
CAMORRA
neoteric ... ... NEW, MODERN,
RECENT
Nepal, capital of ... ...
KATMANDU
coin of ... ... MOHAR
inhabitant ... ... MAGAR,
GURUNG, NEWAR,
GURKHA, KHA
king ... ... MAHENDRA,
PRITHWI
language ... ... NEWARI,
BHUTIA
Mongoloid ... RAIS, LAPP,
LAI
mount .. EVEREST, LHOTSE
mountaineers ... SHERPAS
neighbor ... TIBET, INDIA,
CHINA
people ... ... GURKHA
premier ... RANA, SURYA
sect ... ... ACHAR(A)
warrior ... ... GURKHA,
RAJPUT
Nephele, daughter of .. HELLE
nephew ... ... NEPOTE, NEVE
nephric ... ... RENAL
nephrism, organ affected by ...
KIDNEY
nephrite ... ... JADE
nephritic ... ... RENAL
nepotism ... ... FAVORITISM

beneficiary of ... RELATIVE
subject of .. EMPLOYMENT
nepotists, first ... ... PRELATES
beneficiaries .. NEPHEWS
Neptune .. LER, POSEIDON, SEA,
PLANET
discoverer of ... ... GALLE
scepter of ... ... TRIDENT
son of ... ... TRITON
nereid ... (SEA)NYMPH, THETIS,
AMPHITRITE
Nereus' daughter ... NEREID,
THETIS
Nero ... ... TYRANT, DESPOT,
EMPEROR
band leader ... ... PETER
mother of .... AGRIPPINA
Poppaea of ... ... SABINA
start of his reign LIV
wife of ... ... OCTAVIA,
POPPAEA
Wolfe's creator .. STOUT
nerol ... ... ALCOHOL
neroli ... ... OIL
nervation ... ... VENATION
nerve ... ... TENDON, SINEW,
COURAGE, BOLDNESS,
TEMERITY, PLUCK
block ... ... ANESTHESIA
cell ... ... NEURON(E)
cell branch ... DENDRON,
DENDRITE
cell process ... DENDRITE,
AXON, NEURITE
colloquial .. GUTS, GALL,
FACE, AUDACITY,
CHEEK, CRUST, GALL
combining form ... ...
NEUR(O)
connective tissue ... ...
NEUROGLIA
fiber, sheath of ... MYELIN
fibers, bundle of ... ...
TRACT, PEDUNCLE
fibers network ... ... RETE
inflammation .. NEURITIS
layer ... ... ALVEUS
network ... ... RETIA
of a ... ... NEURAL
pain ... ... NEURALGIA
passage for ... ... HILUM
sending impulses ... ...
MOTOR
sensory ... ... AFFERENT,
EFFERENT
substance ... ... ALBA

surgical cutting of ‑‑ ‑‑‑ NEUROTOMY

tissue substance ‑‑‑‑‑‑‑ LECITHIN

tonic ‑‑‑‑‑‑‑ NERVINE, SEDATIVE

(w)racking ‑‑‑‑‑ TRYING

nerves ‑‑‑‑‑‑‑ HYSTERIA, FIT, JITTERS

network of ‑‑‑‑‑ PLEXUS

pertaining to ‑‑‑‑ NEURO, NEURAL, NERVINE

nervous ‑‑‑‑‑‑‑ EDGY, TENSE, JITTERY, SKITTISH, FEARFUL, TIMOROUS

condition ‑‑‑ NEURALGIA

disease ‑‑‑‑‑ TARANTISM, NEURITIS

disorder ‑‑‑‑‑ PARALYSIS, NEUROSIS, CHOREA, TIC

feeling ‑‑ JITTERS, JIMJAMS

prostration ‑‑‑‑‑‑‑‑‑‑ NEURASTHENIA

seizure ‑‑‑‑‑‑‑ ANEURIA, EPILEPSY, FRENZY, JITTERS, PANIC

state ‑‑‑‑‑‑‑‑‑ TIZZY

strain ‑‑‑‑‑‑‑‑‑ TENSION

twitch ‑‑‑‑‑‑‑‑‑ TIC

nescience ‑‑‑‑‑ IGNORANCE, AGNOSTICISM

ness ‑‑‑‑ CAPE, HEADLAND, PROMONTORY

Nessus ‑‑‑‑‑‑‑‑ CENTAUR

slayer of ‑‑‑‑‑‑ HERCULES

nest ‑‑ DEN, NIDUS, RETREAT, HAUNT, RESORT, NIDE

ants' ‑‑‑‑‑‑‑‑ FORMICARY

build a ‑‑‑‑‑‑‑‑ NIDIFY

eagle's ‑‑‑‑ AERIE, EYRIE, AERY, EYRY

egg ‑‑‑ MONEY, SAVINGS

of eggs ‑‑‑‑‑‑‑‑‑ CLUTCH

pheasant's ‑‑‑‑‑‑‑‑‑ NIDE

squirrel's ‑‑‑‑‑‑‑‑‑ DRAY

nestle ‑‑‑‑ SNUGGLE, SHELTER, CUDDLE, NUZZLE, SETTLE

nestling ‑‑‑‑‑‑‑ EYAS, OWLET, FLEDGLING, POULT, SQUAB, EAGLET

Nestor ‑‑‑‑ SAGE, COUNSELOR, WISE MAN

net ‑‑‑‑‑ MESH, SAGENE, GAIN, BALANCE, LEFT-OVER, CLEAR, RETICLE, FILET, GIN, (EN)TRAP, (EN)SNARE, TULLE

armed with a ‑‑‑ ‑‑‑ RETIARY

fishing ‑‑ SEINE, TRAMMEL, TRAWL

hair ‑‑‑‑‑‑‑‑‑‑‑ SNOOD

like a ‑‑‑‑‑‑‑ RETIFORM, RETICULATE, RETICULAR

making of ‑‑‑‑‑ RETIARY

ornamental ‑‑‑‑‑‑‑ FRET

silk ‑‑‑‑‑‑‑‑‑ MALINE(S)

trapping ‑‑‑‑‑‑‑‑‑‑ TOIL

nether ‑‑ DOWN, LOWER, UNDER-

world ‑‑‑‑‑‑ HELL, HADES

Netherlands (see Dutch) ‑‑‑‑‑ HOLLAND

anatomist ‑‑‑‑‑‑‑‑‑ RAU

Antilles capital ‑‑‑‑‑‑‑‑‑ WILLEMSTAD

Antilles island ‑‑‑ ARUBA, CURACAO

botanist ‑‑‑‑‑ (DE)VRIES

capital (commercial) ‑‑‑‑ AMSTERDAM

capital (political) ‑‑‑‑‑‑‑ (THE) HAGUE

carnival ‑‑‑‑‑‑‑ KERMIS, KERMESS

cheese market ‑‑‑‑ EDAM

city ‑‑‑‑ GOUDA, LEIDEN, UTRECHT, ROTTERDAM, HAARLEM, EINDHOVEN, ARNHEM, BREDA

coin ‑‑ GULDEN, GUILDER, RYDER

colonist ‑‑‑‑‑‑‑‑‑ BOER

commune ‑‑‑‑ EPE, EDE

cupboard ‑‑‑‑‑‑‑‑‑‑‑ KAS

duchy ‑‑‑‑‑‑‑ BRABANT

fair ‑‑‑‑‑‑‑‑‑‑‑ KERMIS

governor ‑‑‑‑‑‑‑‑‑‑‑‑ STAD(T)HOLDER

Guiana ‑‑‑‑‑‑ SURINAM

measure ‑‑‑‑‑‑‑ ROEDE, STREEP, MORGEN

merchants' league ‑‑‑‑‑‑ HANSE

monetary unit ‑‑ GUILDER

of the ‑‑‑‑‑‑‑‑‑ DUTCH

painter ‑‑‑‑‑ HALS, EYCK, LELY

premier ‑‑‑‑ ‑‑ (DE)JONG, ZIJLSTRA

province ‑‑‑‑‑‑ DRENTE, FRIESLAND, UTRECHT, ZEELAND, LIMBURG

queen of ‑‑‑‑‑ JULIANA, WILHELMINA

queen's consort ～～～～ BERNHARD
regime ～～～ MONARCHY
river ～～～～ EMS, MAAS, SCHELDE, RHINE, MEUSE, IJSSEL
ruling family ... NASSAU
seaport ～～ ROTTERDAM
ship .... GAL(L)IOT
theologian ...～ ERASMUS
tulip center ... HAARLEM
uncle ～～～～～ EME
viceroy ～～ STADHOLDER
weight ～～～ WIGT(JE)
woman ～～ FROW
youth gangs ～～ PROVOS
nethermost ～～～～ LOWEST
netted ～～～～～ GAINED
netting knot .... SHEET BEND
nettle ～ WEED, STING, ANNOY, VEX, IRRITATE
Latin ～～～～ URTICA
plant ～～ RAMIE, RAMEE
rash ～ HIVES, URTICARIA, UREDO
sting with ～～ URTICATE
network ～ WEB, RETE, PLEXUS, RETICULUM, MESH, LACE, TISSUE, TRELLIS, LATTICE, RESEAU
of blood vessels, etc. ～～ PLEXUS
ornamental ～～～ FRET
Neufchatel ～～～～～ CHEESE
neuk ～～～ CORNER, NOOK
neurad, opposed to ～ HAEMAD
neuralgia medicine ～～～～ VERATRIN(E)
neuralgic pain ～～ HEMIALGIA
neurasthenia ～～～ NEUROSIS
neurite ～～～～～ AXONE
neurons' contact point ～～～ SYNAPSE
neuropteron ～～～ ANT LION
neurotic ～～ PSYCHIC, NEURAL
neuter ～～～ GENDER, ASEXUAL
verbal noun .... GERUND
neutral ～ INDIFFERENT, ALOOF, NEUTER, NONPARTISAN
neutralize ～～～ COUNTERACT
magnetic field .. DEGAUSS
Nevada capital .. CARSON CITY
city .... ELKO, RENO, LAS VEGAS, SPARKS
county .. ELKO, WASHOE, LYON

Indian ～～～～ PAIUTE
lake .... TAHOE
state flower .. SAGEBRUSH
state tree .... PINON
neve .... SNOW, FIRN, ICE
never .... AT NO TIME
failing ...... FOOLPROOF
nevertheless .. YET, HOWEVER, STILL
Nevin's song ～～～ ROSARY, NARCISSUS
nevus ..... MOLE, BIRTHMARK
new .... NEOTERIC, DIFFERENT, FRESH, MODERN, LATE, NEO, ORIGINAL, NOVEL, RECENT, CENE
combining form ....～ NEO
Deal agency .. NRA, CCC, TVA
Deal president ～～～～～ ROOSEVELT, FDR
England boat .. SHARPIE
England state ... MAINE, VERMONT
Englander .... YANK(EE), DOWN EASTER
New Britain city ..... RABAUL
New Caledonia capital ......～ NOUMEA
New Guinea .... PAPUA
bird .... CASSOWARY
brain disease ...... KURU
capital .... RABAUL
city .... LAE
hog .... BENE
island .... ARU
kingfisher .. KOOKABURRA
native .. PAPUAN, KARON
Negroid .... PAPUAN
port .... DARU, LAE
"Stone Age" tribe ...... FORE
wild hog .... BENE
New Hampshire capital ...... CONCORD
city .... NASHUA, DOVER, KEENE, BERLIN
county .... COOS
lake .... SUNAPEE
river .... SACO
state bird ...... FINCH
state flower ..... LILAC
state tree .... BIRCH
New Hebrides capital ～ VILA
island .... TANA
New Jersey capital .. TRENTON

city .. NEWARK, CAMDEN,
　　　PATERSON, NUTLEY,
　　　BAYONNE, HOBOKEN,
　　　LINDEN, VINELAND,
　　　MONTCLAIR
colonizer ...... PATROON
county ... BERGEN, SALEM,
　　　MORRIS, MERCER,
　　　SUSSEX
river .... PASSAIC
state bird ... GOLDFINCH
state flower ..... VIOLET
town .... LAKEHURST
New Mexico artists' colony ..
　　　TAOS
canyon .... CHACO
capital .... SANTA FE
caverns ...... CARLSBAD
city ... ROSWELL, HOBBS,
　　　LAS CRUCES
county ..... OTERO, TAOS
Indian .... NAVAJO, UTE,
　　　APACHE, MESCALERO,
　　　SIA, ZUNI, NAVAHO
Indian pueblo .... ACOMA
resort town .... TAOS
river .... GILA,
　　　CIMARRON, PECOS
state .... YUCCA
state flower ..... YUCCA
state tree .... PINON
town ..... TAOS, RATON
New Orleans festival ....
　　　MARDI GRAS
music .... RAGTIME
native .... CREOLE
New South Wales capital ....
　　　SYDNEY
New Testament book ... LUKE
hell .... GEHENNA
in Syriac ...... PESHITO
language of ...... KOINE
New York capital ... ALBANY
city ...... OLEAN, UTICA,
　　　AUBURN, GOTHAM,
　　　TROY, ROME, ELMIRA,
　　　YONKERS, ITHACA,
　　　OSWEGO
City borough ... QUEENS,
　　　MANHATTAN, RICHMOND,
　　　BRONX, BROOKLYN
political machine .....
　　　TAMMANY
prison .... TOMBS
section ...... HARLEM
street .... BOWERY

subway .. IRT, IND, BMT
colonizer ...... PATROON
county .. TIOGA, GREENE,
　　　ESSEX, YATES,
　　　SARATOGA
fictitious name .... JUKES
Indian .... ONEIDA
island .... ELLIS
lake .. SARANAC, ONEIDA,
　　　SENECA, PLACID,
　　　CAYUGA
military post ....
　　　WEST POINT
motto .... EXCELSIOR
planetarium ..... HAYDEN
river .. MOHAWK, GENESEE
state prison .. SING SING
team .. METS, JETS, KNICKS
town .... OSSINING
New Zealand aborigine ......
　　　MAORI
bird .. MOA, MIRO, KIWI,
　　　LOWAN, TUI, KEA,
　　　MOREPORK, PEHO,
　　　NOTORNIS, APTERYX,
　　　WEKA
capital ..... WELLINGTON
caterpillar ...... AWETO,
　　　WERI
cattail .... RAUPO
city .... AUCKLAND,
　　　DUNEDIN
corn .... KANGA
demon .... TAIPO
discoverer ...... TASMAN
explorer .... COOK
fish .... IHI, HIKU,
　　　SCHNAPPER
governor general ....
　　　PORRITT
harbor .... OTAGO
hen .... WEKAS
island .... STEWART,
　　　CHATHAM, ANTIPODES,
　　　NIUE
lake .... TAUPA
locust .... WETA
mollusk .... PIPI
morepork .. RURU, PEHO
mountain climber ......
　　　HILLARY
mulberry .... AUTE
myrtle ...... RAMARAMA
native .... M(A)ORI
owl .... RURU
palm .... NIKAU

parrot ... ... KEA, KAKAPO, KAKA
pigeon .... KUKU
pine tree .. KAURI, KAURY
plant .... KARO
prime minister ....
    HOLYOAKE, COATES
raft .... MOKI
rail .... WEKA
robin .... MIRO
sandalwood ..... MAIRE
seaport ...... AUCKLAND
shark .... MAKO
sheep ...... CORRIEDALE
shrub ...... RAMARAMA, KARO, TUTU
smelt .... INANGA
soldier .... ANZAC
tree .. AUTE, MIRO PUKA, TOTARA, PELU, HINO(U), NAPAU, RATA, KAIKAKA, TATARA, GOAI, HINAU, MAIRE, WHAU, AKE, KOPI, TORU, TARATA, RAMARAMA
tribe .... RINGATU
volcano ...... RUAPEHU
wages .... UTU
war club .... MERI
weapon .... PATU
wild hog .... BENE
wineberry .... MAKO
wood hen .... WEKA
newborn .... YEANLING
Newcastle river .... TYNE
newcomer ...... TENDERFOOT
newel .... POST
Newfoundland airport ......
    GANDER
capital .... ST. JOHN'S
cod-fisher ...... BANKER
companion island ......
    LABRADOR
fishing grounds .. BANKS
floating ice ... CLUMPERS, CROWLERS
Indian .... MICMAC
seal .... MOTHER
seal hunter ...... SWILER
tea .... SWITCHEL
newlywed .... BRIDE(GROOM), BENEDICT
serenade to .. CHARIVARI, SHIVAREE
newmarket .... COAT
newness .... NOVELTY

news .... TIDINGS, WORD, REPORT, INFORMATION
agency .. WIRE SERVICE, UPI, TASS, REUTERS, ANETA, INS, DOMEI, KYODO, JIJI, HAVAS, CETEKA
beat .... SCOOP
bit .... ITEM
commentator ....
    BRINKLEY, CRONKITE, KALB, LAWRENCE, DOWNS, HUNTLEY
item .... OBIT
last minute ..... FUDGE, BREAK, FLASH
maker, (Time says) ..... NAME
medium ...... BULLETIN, RADIO, GRAVEVINE, GOSSIP
report .. FLASH, BULLETIN
source .... PIPELINE
stand .... KIOSK
newsboy's territory .... ROUTE
newsletter .... BULLETIN, INTELLIGENCER
newsman .. REPORTER, SCRIBE, JOURNALIST
newsmonger .... GOSSIP, TATTLER
newspaper .. GAZETTE, SHEET, JOURNAL, DAILY, TABLOID
bit .... FILLER, ITEM
columnist ...... RESTON, ALSOP, WINCHELL
extra leaf .... INSERT
feature .... HEADLINE, COLUMN, COMICS, SCOOP, ROTO(GRAVURE)
headline ..... STREAMER, BANNER
item .... FILLER, PARAGRAPH
issue ... EDITION, EXTRA, STARFINAL
makeup of ..... FORMAT, LAYOUT
official .... REDACTOR, EDITOR
page insert ...... FUDGE
stand .... KIOSK
style of writing ....
    JOURNALESE
two facing pages ....
    SPREAD

work ...... JOURNALISM
newspaperman .... REPORTER,
CUB, JOURNALIST,
COLUMNIST, SCRIBE,
INKSLINGER
achievement of ... SCOOP,
BEAT
report of ..... DISPATCH,
COPY, STORY
source of ..... CONTACT,
PIPELINE
territory of .... BEAT
newspapers in general .. PRESS
newsprint .... PAPER
roll of .... WEB
newsstand .... KIOSK
newt .... EFT, SWIFT, TRITON,
SALAMANDER
Newton, mathematician ......
ISAAC
next .. NEAREST, THEN, BESIDE
door resident .. NEIGHBOR
to last ... PENULT(IMATE)
nexus .... LINK, TIE,
CONNECTION
Ney, Marshal .... MICHEL
Nez Perce .... INDIAN
Niagara .... FALLS
Falls .... HORSESHOE
nib .... BEAK, BILL, POINT,
PRONG
nibble .... KNAP, PECK, BITE,
NIP, MORSEL, BROWSE
Nibelung .... DWARFS
guard .... FAFNIR
leader .... ALBERICH
Nibelungenlied king .. ETZEL
knight ..... HILDEBRAND
niblick .... IRON, (GOLF)CLUB
Nicaragua capital .. MANAGUA
city ..... LEON, GRANADA
coin .... CORDOBA
monetary unit ....
CORDOBA
president ...... SOMOZA
river .... TIPITAPA
nice ..... FINE, NEAT, NICAEA,
REFINED, FASTIDIOUS,
DELICATE, SUBTLE, PLEASANT,
DAINTY, PRETTY, FINICAL
discernment .... ACUMEN,
INSIGHT
figure .. LISSOM(E), SVELT
Nelly .... PRUDE
nicety .. DELICACY, SUBTLETY,
AMENITY

niche .... RECESS, NOOK, SLOT,
TABERNACLE, CORNER,
AMBRY, APSE
nick .... CHEAT, DEFRAUD,
SCORE, TALLY, NOTCH,
TRICK, ARREST, SLIT, CUT
actor .... ADAMS
Charles' dog ...... ASTA
Old ...... SATAN, DEVIL
the detective .... CARTER
nickel .. COIN, FIVE CENTS, NI
alloy .... INVAR
like metal ...... MONEL
silver .... ELECTRUM
slang .... JITNEY
sulfide .... MILLERITE
nicker .... NEIGH, LAUGH
nickname .... SO(U)BRIQUET,
MONI(C)KER, AGNOMEN,
COGNOMEN, AGNAME
feminine or masculine ...
LOU
Nicosia is capital of .. CYPRUS
nicotine .... TAR
nicotine acid .... NIACIN
nictitate .... BLINK, WINK
nide .... NEST
nidus .... NEST
Niemen .... MEMEL, NEMAN,
NEMUNAS
river .... RUSS
Nietzsche, philosopher .....
FRIEDRICH
superman of ....
UBERMENSCH
nieve .... FIST, HAND
niffer .... BARTER, TRADE,
EXCHANGE
nifty ...... STYLISH, SMART
Niger, capital of .... NIAMEY
city .... ZINDER, NIAMEY
people .... HAUSA, PEUL,
TOUAREG, IJO
president .... DIORI
river mouth .... NUN
Nigerian capital ...... LAGOS
city .... IBADAN, EDE,
KANO, OGBOMOSHO
dissident region .. BIAFRA
division .... SOKOTO
native ... IBO, HAUS(S)A,
EDO, ARO, BENI(N)
prime minister ....
BALEWA, IRONSI
seaport .. BONNY, LAGOS

secessionist state .... BIAFRA
    state ..... BIAFRA, NUPE
    tribal chief .... OBA
    tribe ...... YORUBA, IBO,
      HAUSA, FULANI, BENIN,
      ARO, EBOB, EDO
niggard ... STINGY, SKINFLINT,
    CHURL, MISER(LY)
niggardly .... MISERLY, FEW,
    SCANTY, STINGY
niggle .... PUTTER
nigh ..... NEAR(LY), ALMOST,
    ANEAR, CLOSE(BY)
night .. DARK(NESS), EVENING
    attack .... CAMISADO
    before .... EVE
    blindness .. NYCTALOPIA
    clothes .... PAJAMAS,
      NIGHTIE, NIGHTY
    club .... ROADHOUSE,
      BISTRO, CABARET
    combining form ....
      NOCT(I)
    flyer ... BAT, OWL, MOTH,
      FIREFLY
    letter .... TELEGRAM
    moth .... NOCTUID
    noise-maker .. ALLEYCAT
    of the ...... NOCTURNAL
nightcap .... DRINK
nightfall .... DUSK
    occurring at ....
    ACRONICAL, ACRONYCAL
nighthawk ..... GOATSUCKER,
    BULLBAT
nightingale .... PHILOMEL
    BULBUL, THRUSH, SONGBIRD
    note of .... JUG
    so-called ... (JENNY)LIND
nightjar .... POTOO, BIRD,
    GOATSUCKER
nightmare ... DREAM, INCUBUS
    demon .... MARA
nightrider .... VIGILANTE,
    TERRORIST
nightshade .. MOREL, DATURA,
    BELLADONNA, HENBANE,
    PLANT, MORIL, MANDRAKE,
    TOBACCO, SOLANUM, PETUNIA
    relative .... TOMATO,
    POTATO
nightsight .... NYCTALOPIA
nightstick .. TRUNCHEON, CLUB
    user .. POLICE(MAN), COP
nightwalker .... THIEF

nigrescence .... BLACKNESS
nihil .... NOTHING
Nihon .... JAPAN
Nike .... GODDESS, VICTORIA,
    ATHENA
nil .... NOTHING, NULL
Nile .... NILUS, HAPI
    bird ..... IBIS, SHOEBILL
    boat ... BARIS, DAHABEAH
    catfish .... BAGRE
    city .... ASWAN, THEBES,
      MEROE, KHARTOUM,
      TANTA, TANIS, SAIS,
      OMDURMAN
    dam .... ASWAN
    floating weeds .... SUDD
    goddess .... ISIS
    heron .... IBIS
    island .... RODA
    native .... NILOT
    negro .... SUK, JUR
    of the .... NILOTIC
    passenger boat ....
      DAHABEAH
    plant .... PAPYRUS
    queen of the ....
      CLEO(PATRA)
    reeds .... SUDD
    sailboat .... CANGIA
    ship's captain .... RAIS,
      REIS
    source of .... TSANA
    town .. ROSETTA, LUXOR
    tributary .... KAGERA
    valley hollow ...... KORE
    village on the ... KARNAK
    weeds .... SUDD
nilgai .... ANTELOPE
Nilus .... NILE
nim .... STEAL
nimble ...... DEFT, LISSOM(E),
    VOLANT, LIGHT, ALERT,
    AGILE, SPRY, QUICK
nimbus ..... CLOUD, AUREOLA,
    HALO, AURA, GLORIA
nimiety ... EXCESS, PLEONASM,
    REDUNDANCY
Nimitz, admiral ..... CHESTER
Nimrod .... HUNTER
    parent of .... CUSH
nincompoop ...... SIMPLETON,
    FOOL, DOLT, SOFTHEAD,
    NITWIT, IDIOT
nine: comb. form ..... ENNE
    days' devotion .. NOVENA
    group of .... ENNEAD

headed serpent ... HYDRA
inches .... SPAN
"ladies" .... MUSES
number .... ENNEA
part composition ....
           NONET
sided plane ... NONAGON,
           ENNEAGON
team of ...... BASEBALL
the .... MUSES
ninefold .... NENARY
ninepins ...... SKITTLE, GAME
nineteen XIX
nineteenth hole: colloq. ......
      LOCKER ROOM, BAR
ninetieth .... NONAGESIMAL
Nineveh founder ..... NINUS
ninny ... DOLT, FOOL, DUNCE,
    SIMPLETON, ASS, IDIOT
ninth day before the ides .....
        NONES
Ninus .... NINEVEH
Niobe, brother of .... PELOPS
fate of .... STONE
father of ..... TANTALUS
husband of .... AMPHION
Niobean .... WEEPING, WEEPY
nip .. BITE, PINCH, SEVER, CUT,
    CHECK, BLIGHT, DRAM,
    DRINK, SIP
and tuck .... CLOSE,
    NECK AND NECK
slang .. JAPANESE, CATCH,
    STEAL
nipa .... PALM, AT(T)AP
liquor .... TUBA
nipper ...... PLIERS, PINCERS,
    CLAW, TWEEZERS,
    FORCEPS
nippers .... HANDCUFFS,
    LEG IRONS
nipping ...... BITING, SHARP
nipple .... PAPILLA, TIT, PAP,
    TEAT, DUG, MAMMILLA
baby's toy .... PACIFIER
inflammation .. THELITIS
shaped like a .. MASTOID
Nippon .... JAPAN
nippy .. SHARP, BITING, NIMBLE
nis .... KOBOLD
Nishapur's famous son ....
    OMAR(KHAYYAM)
nisi .... UNLESS
Nissen .... PREFAB
nisus ..... EFFORT, ENDEAVOR
nit .... EGG, INSECT

niter .... SALTPETER, NITRATE,
    SALT
niton .... RADON
nitrate .... NITER, SALTPETER,
    FERTILIZER, SALT, ESTER
nitric .... AZOTIC
acid ...... AQUA FORTIS
nitrogen .. AZOTE, NONMETAL
containing .... AZO(TIC)
nitrogenize .... AZOTIZE
nitroglycerine .. GLONOIN(E),
    TNT, EXPLOSIVE
nitrohydrochloric acid ....
    AQUA REGIA
nitrous acid salt ..... NITRITE
nitrous oxide .. LAUGHING GAS
nitwit .... JACKASS,
  FOOL, IDIOT, MORON, BOOB(Y)
Niven, actor .... DAVID
niveous .... SNOWY, SNOWLIKE
nix(ie) .... NO, SPRITE, FAIRY
slang .. NO, NOT AT ALL
Nizam .... NABOB
domain .... HYDERABAD
Njorth .... VANIR
parent of ...... FREY(A)
no .... NAY, NOT SO
gentleman he .... BRUTE,
    BOOR, LOUT
longer existing ....
    EXTINCT, DEAD
more .... ENOUGH
more than .. MERE, ONLY
one .... NONE
slangy .. NOPE, NIX, NAW
Noah, boat of .... ARK
father of .... LAMECH
grandson of ...... ARAM
landing place of ....
    ARARAT
pertaining to .... NOETIC
son of .. JAPHETH, SHEM,
    HAM
nob .... HEAD, JACK
nobble .... CHEAT, BRIBE
nobby .. STYLISH, FIRST-RATE
Nobel, industrialist .. ALFRED
invention of .. DYNAMITE
laureate .... UREY
Prize winner, chemistry ..
  UREY, CURIE, SANGER,
  LANGMUIR, SEABORG,
  PAULING, WERNER,
  BAEYER, HAHN, ADLER
literature ...... MANN,
  CAMUS, STEINBECK,

PASTERNAK, JENSEN, FAULKNER, SARTRE, SACHS, SHAW, ELIOT

medicine .... BURNET, KOCH, RICHET, KREBS, GOLGI, ECCLES, LYNEN

peace .... ORR, MOTT, BUNCHE, WILSON, DUNANT, LANGE

physics ..... RAMAN, FERMI, CURIE, BOHR, TAMM, BRAUN, DALEN, YANG

nobility .... PEERAGE, GRANDEUR, ARISTOCRACY, NOBLESSE

rank just below .... GENTRY

noble ..... KINGLY, MAJESTIC, PATRICIAN, GRAND, LOFTY, STATELY, PEER, SUBLIME, BLUEBLOOD

birth .... HIGHBORN, EUGENY

nobleman ..... PRINCE, PEER, BARON, THANE, LORD, DUKE, EARL, HIDALGO, JARL, COUNT, MILORD, GRANDEE, YOUNKER, MARQUIS, MAGNIFICO

noblesse .... ARISTOCRATS

noblewoman .. LADY, PEERESS, DUCHESS, CONTESSA, MILADY

nobody ... NONENTITY, NONE, NO ONE

nocent ... INJURIOUS, HURTFUL, GUILTY

nock .... NOTCH

noctambulist ... SLEEPWALKER

nocti, as combining form ..... NIGHT

noctuid .... MOTH

noctule .... BAT

nocturnal bird .. OWL, KAKAPO

creature .... BAT, COON, LEMUR, RATEL, WEASEL, JACKAL, TAPIR, TARSIER, RAC(C)OON, (O)POSSUM

parrot .... KAKAPO

nocturne .... SERENADE

nocuous .. NOXIOUS, HARMFUL

nod .... BOW, BECK, DROWSE, DOZE, NUTATE

land of .... SLEEP

sign of .. YES, APPROVAL, AGREEMENT, ASSENT

nodding .. NUTANT, ANNUENT

noddle .... PATE, HEAD, GULL

noddy ..... FOOL, SIMPLETON

node .. DILEMMA, KNOT, KNOB, FOCUS, SWELLING, JOINT

nodose .... KNOTTY, KNOBBY

nodous .... KNOTTY

nodule .. KNOT, LUMP, JOINT

cartilaginous .. SESAMOID

tone's .... GEODE

nodus .... COMPLICATION

noel ..... CAROL, CHRISTMAS

Coward's song .... NINA

noesis .... PERCEPTION, COGNITION

noetic .... SCHOLAR

nog .... PIN, ALE, BRICK

noggin .... MUG, CUP, HEAD, GILL, PATE

noise .. CLAMOR, DIN, SOUND, BRUIT, (UP)ROAR, RACKET, STRIDOR, HUBBUB

maker at night .... ALLEYCAT

surf .... ROTE

noiseless ..... SILENT, QUIET, STILL, CATLIKE

noisome .... FETID, NOXIOUS, STINKING, HARMFUL

noisy .... BLATANT, LOUD, CLAMOROUS, CLAMANT

bird ..... (MAG)PIE, JAY

merry making .... REVELRY, CAROUSAL

revelry ...... JAMBOREE

nom de plume (see pen name) .. PEN NAME, PSEUDONYM

nomad .. WANDERER, GYPSY, ITINERANT, LAPP, ROVER, TRAMP, ROAMER

Afghan .... KUCHI

desert .. ARAB, BEDOUIN, SLEB, BUSHMAN, KURD

nomadic .... ITINERANT

tribe .... HORDE

nome .... NOMARCHY

is in .... ALASKA

nominal .... TOKEN, TITULAR, SLIGHT, SMALL

value .... PAR

nominate .... NAME, APPOINT, DESIGNATE, CALL

nomination .... NAMING, APPOINTMENT

nominee ... ... CANDIDATE, APPOINTEE

nomology, subject of ... ... LAWMAKING, LEGISLATION

non-believer ... ... PAGAN, INFIDEL, AGNOSTIC, ATHEIST

 Christian ... ... PAGAN, PAYNIM

 Jew ... ... GENTILE

 member ... ... OUTSIDER, MAVERICK

 Mormon ... ... GENTILE

 Moslem ... ... GIAOUR

nonage ... ... MINORITY

nonce ... ... MEANWHILE, MEANTIME

noncom ... . NCO, SERGEANT, SARGE, CPL

nonchalant ... . INDIFFERENT, COOL, INSOUCIANT

nonconformist ... . SECTARY, DISSENTER, HERETIC, REB(EL), RECUSANT, DISSIDENT

none ... ... NARY, NO ONE, NOT ANY, NOTHING

 too soon ... . HIGH TIME

nonentity ... NOBODY, CIPHER, STRAWMAN, UNPERSON

nonesuch ... PARAGON, APPLE, ONER, NONPAREIL

nonmetal ... CARBON, OXYGEN, FLUORINE, NITROGEN

nonmetallic element ... BORON, SILICON, IODINE, ASTATINE, FLUORINE

nonpareil ... ... UNRIVALED, SUPREME, NON(E)SUCH, PEERLESS

nonpartisan ... ... NEUTRAL

nonplus ... . MYSTIFY, STUMP, PERPLEX, PUZZLE, CONFUSE, CONFOUND

nonprofit organization ... . FOUNDATION

nonsense ... TWADDLE, BUNK, (TOMMY)ROT, SLAVER, DRIVEL, TRUMPERY, BLAH, TOSH, FLIMFLAM, BLATHER, FALDEROL, FOLDEROL, MALARK(E)Y, FUDGE, BILGE, FLAPDOODLE, HOKUM, POPPYCOCK, RUBBISH, BOSH, BAH, BALONEY, TRASH, HOOEY, BULL, RIG(A)MAROLE, BALDERDASH, KIBOSH, TOMFOOLERY

 deceitful ... ... GAMMON

 high-sounding ... FUSTIAN

nonsensical ... ABSURD, SILLY, FOOLISH, INANE, RIDICULOUS

 creature ... GOOP, SNARK, SMOO, NOIO, GOOF

 poem ... ... LIMERICK

nonstop ... ... MARATHON, CONTINUOUS

nonsuch ... ... PARAGON

noodle ... HEAD, FOOL, PASTA, FARFEL, FERFEL

 dish ... ... CHOW MEIN

nook ... . CORNER, RETREAT, RECESS, DEN, (AL)COVE

 and ___ ... . CORNER, CRANNY

noon ... . MIDDAY, MERIDIAN

 rest ... ... SIESTA

noose ... LOOP, TRAP, HALTER, (EN)SNARE

 trap ... ... SPRINGE

nopal ... ... CACTUS

nope ... ... NO, NIX

 opposite of ... ... YEP

Nordic ... ... TEUTON(IC), CAUCASIAN

Norfolk ... ... JACKET

Norge ... ... NORWAY

noria ... ... (WATER)WHEEL

norm ... STANDARD, RULE, MODEL, PATTERN, AVERAGE

normal ... NATURAL, REGULAR, USUAL, ORDINARY, MEAN, STANDARD, TYPICAL, AVERAGE

 breathing ... EUPN(O)EA

 school grad ... TEACHER

Norman crusade leader ... ... TANCRED

Normand, actress ... . MABEL

Normandy capital ... . ROUEN

 conqueror of ... . ROLLO

 department ... EURE, ORNE, MANCHE

 duke of ... ROLLO, HROLF

Norn ... ... SKULD, URTH, VERTHANDI, GODDESS

Norris, novelist ... . FRANK, KATHLEEN

Norse ... ... SCANDINAVIAN

 Adam ... ... ASKR

 chieftain ... JARL, ROLLO, YARL

 deities' home ... ASGARD

 deity ... ODIN, THOR, EIR

destiny .... NORN
earth: myth. ... MIDGARD
epic .... EDDA
explorer .. ERIC, ERICSSON
galley .... AESC
giant ..... ATLI, FAFNIR,
    YMER, MIMIR, EGIL,
    (H)YMIR, WATE, TROLL,
    JOTUN(N)
giantess .... NORN, GROA
goat .... HEIDRUN
god ... HEIMDALL, ODIN,
    HODER, HODUR, DONAR,
    ULL, LOKI, VALI, FREY,
    FORSETI, BALDER,
    AEGER, THOR, BRAGI,
    TYR, VANIR, AESIR,
    HOENIR
goddess .. FREYA, NORN,
    IDUN, ITHUN(N),
    URTH, SKULD,
    VERTHANDI, HEL(A),
    MOIRA, EIR, RANA,
    WYRD, SIF, FRIGG(A)
gods, abode of the ......
    ASGARD
gods, king of ... WODEN,
    ODIN
hall of heroes ....
    VALHALLA
hero .... EGIL(L)
home of gods .. ASGARD
king .... ATLI, OLAF
letter .... RUNE
lore .... RUNE
minstrel .... SCALD
mythology, summary of ..
    EDDA
navigator .... ERIC
Nibelung dwarf ....
    ALBERICH
nobleman .... JARL
plateau .... FJELD
poem .... RUNE
poet ...... SCALD, SKALD
poetry .. RUNE(S), EDDA
race of gods ...... VANIR
rainbow bridge .. BIFROST
river .... KLAR
saga .... EDDA
saint .... OLAF
serpent ...... MIDGARD
tale ...... SAGA, EDDA
underworld .... HEL
viking .... ROLLO
watchdog .... GARM

watchman of Asgard ... ...
    HEIMDALL
wolf .... FENRIR
woman, first .... EMBLA
world's destruction .....
    RAGNAROK
Norseman .... VIKING
north .... ARCTIC, BOREAL
  of the far ....
    HYPERBOREAN
North African city .. ALGIERS
  garment .... HAIK
  region .... SUDAN
  seaport .... ORAN
  sheep .... AOUDAD
North Atlantic fish .... LING,
    BURBOT, CAP(E)LIN,
    MACKEREL
North Borneo .... SABAH
North Carolina cape .. FEAR,
    HATTERAS, LOOKOUT
  capital .... RALEIGH
  city ...... GREENSBORO,
    DURHAM, CHARLOTTE
  college .... ELON
  county ..... ASHE, HOKE,
    NASK
  native/nickname ....
    TARHEEL
  resort town ..... TRYON
  river .... NEUSE, PEE DEE
  state bird .... CARDINAL
  state flower ... DOGWOOD
  university .... DUKE
North Dakota capital ....
    BISMARK
  city ...... MINOT, FARGO,
    JAMESTOWN
  county ..... CASS, DUNN
  mining town ...... ZAP
  nickname .. FLICKERTAIL
North Pole discoverer ....
    PEARY
North Sea port ..... BERGEN,
    KIEL, BREMEN, EMDEN
  serpent .... KRAKEN
  tributary .. THAMES, TEES,
    RHINE, ELBE, MEUSE,
    TYNE, SCHELDE, YSER,
    TAY, WESER, MAAS
  water .... KATTEGAT
North Star .... LODESTAR,
    POLARIS
  state .... MINNESOTA
Northern .... BOREAL
  Bear .... RUSSIA

Cross .... CYGNUS
Rhodesia .... ZAMBIA
sea bird .. SKUA, JAEGER,
PUFFIN
Spy .... (WINTER)APPLE
Northerner .... YANKEE,
COPPERHEAD
Northampton landmark ......
MT. TOM
Northman .. NORMAN, THULE,
NORSE(MAN),
Northumberland river .. TYNE
Northwest Territory settlement
MARIETTA
Norway (see Norse, Norwegian)
NORGE
Norwegian (see Norse) ....
NORSE(MAN)
capital .... OSLO
city .... BERGEN,
TRONDHEIM, STAVANGER,
NARVIK, ALESUND
coin ...... KRONA, ORA
composer .. GRIEG, OLSEN
dramatist .... IBSEN
explorer .... NANSEN,
AMUNDSEN
fish ...... LING, BURBOT
goblin .. NIS(SE), KOBOLD
haddock ...... ROSEFISH
inlet ...... FIORD, FJORD
king ...... OLAV, HAAKON,
OLAF
language .... RIKSMAAL,
LANDSMAAL
measure .. ALEN, MORGEN
monetary unit ... KRONE
mountain .... KJOLEN
native .... LAPP,
LAPLANDER
noble .... JARL
novelist .... NOJER,
HAMSUN
parliament .. LAGT(H)ING,
STORT(H)ING
poetry .... EDDA
port .... HAMMERFEST
prime minister .. BORTEN
region .... LAPLAND
river .... NANSEN, KLAR,
GLOMMEN, TANA
rodent .... LEMMING
saint .... OLAF
sea monster .... KRAKEN
seaport .... BERGEN,

TRONDHEIM, STAVANGER,
HAMMERFEST
soprano .... FLAGSTAD
Storthing section ......
LAGTING, ODELSTING
territorial subdivision ...
AMT
toast .... SKOAL
traitor .... QUISLING
whirlpool .. MAELSTROM
writer .... IBSEN, NOJER
nose .... CONK, BEAK, SCENT,
SNOUT, MUZZLE, SPOUT,
SMELL, NOZZLE, DEFEAT,
NEB, PROBOSCIS, PRY, SNIFF,
SNOOP
ailment .... CORYZA,
CATARRH
bone .... VOMER
combining form ....
RHIN(O)
counting .. CENSUS, POLL
describing one ...... PUG,
SNUB, AQUILINE, ROMAN,
TILTED, SHARP, SIMOUS
discharge .... RHEUM
dive .... PLUNGE
elephant's .... TRUNK
inflammation .. RHINITIS
Latin .... NASUS
long .. SNOUT, PROBOSCIS
of the .... NASAL, RHINAL
opening .... NARE, NOSTRIL,
NARIS
person with famous ......
CYRANO (BERGERAC),
DURANTE
point on .... ALARE
slang .... SPY, INFORMER,
SCHNOZZLE, SNOOT,
NOZZLE
turned up .... RETROUSSE
nosebleed .... EPISTAXIS
nosegay ...... POSY, BOUQUET,
CORSAGE
nos(e)y .. INQUISITIVE, PRYING
nostalgia ...... NOSTOMANIA,
HOMESICKNESS, LONGING
nostology .... GERIATRICS
subject of ..... OLD AGE
nostomania ...... NOSTALGIA,
HOMESICKNESS
Nostradamus .... SEER,
ASTROLOGER
nostril .... NARE
hairs .... VIBRISSA

of the .. NARIAL, NARINE
nostrum .. REMEDY, PANACEA
nosy .... PRYING, INQUISITIVE, CURIOUS
not any .... NARY, NONE
appropriate ...... INAPT, INEPT, IMPROPER, UNFIT
at home .. OUT, ABROAD
cautious .... RASH, RECKLESS
complex .. SIMPLE, EASY
compulsory ... OPTIONAL
divided .... WHOLE
handsome ..... HOMELY, PLAIN
in jail anyway ....
        AT LARGE, LOOSE
in style .... PASSE
mature .... GREEN
moving .... STILL, INERT, STATIC
now .... LATER
occupied .. IDLE, VACANT
often .. SELDOM, RARELY
one or the other ....
        NEITHER
planned .... CASUAL, HAPHAZARD, RANDOM
prefix ..... NON, MIS, DIS
pronounced ...... MUTE, ELIDED
quite .. HARDLY, BARELY
real .. SHAM, FICTITIOUS, IMAGINARY, FAKE
ripe .... GREEN
speaking .... MUM, MUTE
specific .... GENERAL, INDEFINITE
suitable .... UNFIT, INAPT
nota bene .... NOTE WELL
notable ...... UNCO, SIGNAL, EMINENT, STRIKING
act .. DEED, FEAT, GEST(E), HEROISM, EXPLOIT
personage .... LION, VIP, CELEBRITY, HERO
notarize .... ATTEST, CERTIFY
notary .... SCRIVENER
notch .. JAG, INDENTURE, PEG, NICK, DEGREE, TALLY, MARK, (IN)DENT, DEFILE, GAP, SCORE, RECORD
key .... WARD
made by ax/saw .. KERF
notched .... EROSE, CRENATE, SERRATE, DENTATE

bar .... RATCH
part .... JOG
wheel .... RATCHET
note .. DISTINCTION, EMINENCE, HEED, BILLET, OBSERVE, REMARK
an eighth .... QUAVER
equal to two others .....
        BREVE
explanatory ... SCHOLIUM, POSTIL
Guido's .... GAMUT
half .... MINIM
highest .... (A)ELA
marginal .... (A)POSTIL, APOSTIL(LE)
musical, accented ......
        THESIS
of comment ...... GLOSS
part of .... STEM
promissory .... IOU
short .. CHIT, MEMO, LINE
signaling attack ....
        WARISON
stem of .... TAIL
well .... NOTA BENE
notebook .... CAHIER
noted ... FAMOUS, RENOWNED, EMINENT
notes in Guido's scale ... ALT, ELA, ELAMI
noteworthy .... NOTABLE, SPECIAL, EMINENT
nothing .. NAUGHT, NIHIL, NIL, ZERO, NONE, NOUGHT
but ...... ONLY, MERELY
doing! .... NO, NO DICE, NO SOAP
for .... FREE, GRATIS
notice .... HEED, REGARD, DISCERN, SEE, BILLING, REVIEW, WARNING, OBSERVE, ADVICE
death .... OBIT
of payment due ....
        PROMPT
official .... BULLETIN, MONITION
to desist .... CAVEAT
to end treaty ....
        DENUNCIATION
notification .... AVISO, ADVICE
notify ...... APPRISE, ADVISE, WARN, INFORM, TELL, ACQUAINT
notion .. VIEW, BELIEF, FANCY,

DESIRE, IDEA, CURIO, WHIM,
INKLING, OPINION
counter item .. SHOELACE,
SAFETY PIN, THREAD
fallacious ...... IDOLISM
foolish ...... MOONSHINE
notions .... ARTICLES
notoriety .... REPUTE, ECLAT,
REPUTATION
notorious .... WELL KNOWN,
FAMED, INFAMOUS, ARRANT
notornis, relative of ... COOT,
RAIL
Notre Dame ...... OUR LADY,
CATHEDRAL
notwithstanding ... MAUGRE,
YET, INSPITE, MAUGER, THO,
(AL)THOUGH
nougat .. CANDY, CONFECTION
nought ...... NOTHING, ZERO,
CIPHER, USELESS
bring to .. NULLIFY, VOID
nomenal .... INTUITIVE
noun .... SUBSTANTIVE
form .... CASE
kind of .... APTOTE,
TRIPTOTE
of common gender .....
EPICENE
suffix .. ULE, ERY, ENCE,
IER, FER, ISE, ITE, ITIS
verbal .... GERUND
nourish .... FOSTER, SUSTAIN,
FEED, SUPPORT, ALIMENT
nourishing .... ALIBLE,
NUTRITIOUS, ALIMENTAL,
ALIMENTARY, NUTRIENT
nourishment .... ALIMENT,
NUTRIMENT, PABULUM,
FOOD
baby's ...... MILK, PAP
nous ...... MIND, INTELLECT,
REASON
nouveau riche ...... UPSTART,
PARVENU
nouveaute .... NOVELTY
nouvelles .... NEWS
nova .... STAR
Nova Scotia(n) ... ACADIA(N),
BLUENOSE
bay .... FUNDY
cape .... CANSO, BRETON,
SABLE
capital .... HALIFAX
inhabitant .... BLUENOSE,
ACADIAN

seaport .... TRURO
village ...... GRAND PRE
Novarro, actor .... RAMON
movie role .... BEN HUR
novel .... FRESH, SIMENON,
ROMANCE, NEW, STRANGE,
RARE, UNUSUAL
novella .... NARRATIVE
novelty ...... WRINKLE, FAD,
NEWNESS, INNOVATION,
TRINKET, BRIC-A-BRAC,
GIMCRACK
November 11 .... MARTINMAS
13, Roman calendar ....
IDES
novena .... DEVOTIONS
novice .... TENDERFOOT,
NEOPHYTE, CONVERT,
BEGINNER, ACOLYTE, CHELA,
TYRO, AMATEUR, TIRO,
APPRENTICE, GREENHORN
novitiate ... NOVICE, TRAINEE,
NEOPHYTE
novocaine .... ANESTHETIC,
PROCAINE
Novotna .... JARMILA
now .... AT ONCE, HERE
nowadays .... PRESENTLY,
AT PRESENT
noway .. NOWISE, NOT AT ALL
nowt .... OXEN, CATTLE
Nox .... NYX, GODDESS
brother of ...... EREBUS
husband of ...... CHAOS
is goddess of .... NIGHT
noxious ...... EVIL, NOCENT,
BANEFUL, NOISOME,
PERNICIOUS, HARMFUL,
MEPHITIC, MIASMIC,
MIASMAL
air .... MIASMA, MALARIA
vapor ..... FUME, REEK,
SMOG
Noyes, poet .... ALFRED
nozzle .. NOSE, SNOUT, SPOUT,
JET, ROSE
furnace .... TUYERE
thing with .. HOSE, PIPE,
TEAPOT, BELLOWS,
WHALE
nuance .... SHADE, VARIATION
nub .. KNOB, SNAG, LUMP, GIST
nubbin ...... LUMP, CORN
nubble .... KNOB, LUMP
nubia .... WRAP
Nubian .... NEGRO(ID)

harp .... NANGA
nubilous .... CLOUDY, FOGGY,
    MISTY, VAPOROUS, OBSCURE
nucellus .... NUCLEUS
nucha .... NAPE, SCRUFF
nuclear device ...... REACTOR
    division in germ cells .....
              MEIOSIS
    missile ...... ICBM, MIRV,
        A-BOMB, H-BOMB
    scientist .... BRAUN
nucleus .... KERNEL, CENTER,
        NUCELLUS
    atom's ...... DEUT(E)RON,
        PROTON
    cell .... MESOPLAST
    military unit's .... CADRE
nude .... BARE, NAKED,
        UNCLOTHED
nudge .... POKE, ELBOW, PUSH,
    JOG, JOSTLE, PROD
nudibranchiate .... SNAIL,
        MOLLUSK
nudist .... ADAMITE,
        GYMNOSOPHIST
Nuevo Leon capital ....
        MONTERREY
nugatory .... TRIFLING,
    TRIVIAL, INVALID
nugget .... LUMP
nuisance .... BANE, BORE,
    ANNOYANCE, TROUBLE,
        PLAGUE
    colloquial .. TERROR, PEST
    insect .... GNAT
null ..... VOID, INVALID, NIL
nullah .... RAVINE, GORGE,
    GULLY, WATERCOURSE
nullify ... INVALIDATE, UNDO,
    VOID, CANCEL, ABROGATE,
    NEGATE, REPEAL, OVERRIDE
nulliparous .... BARREN
nullipore .... SEAWEED
numb .... INSENSIBLE, DEADEN,
        UNFEELING
number .... TOTAL, COMPANY,
    COUNT, DIGIT, ENUMERATE
    added .... ADDEND
    astronomic ..... GOOGOL
    countless .... MYRIAD,
        HORDE, SWARM
    dividing evenly .. ALIQUOT
    8 iron .... NIBLICK
    5 iron ... MASHIE, MASHY
    four .... TETRAD
    irrational .... SURD

large ..... LEGION, RAFT,
    RAFF, SLEW
leaves of book .... FOLIATE
less than ten ...... DIGIT
lost .... TOLL, CASUALTY
magazine .... ISSUE
nine .... ENNEAD
one plus 100 zeros ....
    GOOGOL
page .... FOLIO
part of .... FRACTION
six .... SEXTET
subtracted .. SUBTRAHEND
without ..... NUMEROUS,
    COUNTLESS
whole .... INTEGER
numbers .... COLLECTION,
    QUANTITY, BOOK
    game ... LOTTO, LOTTERY
    in music ..... MEASURES,
        RHYTHM
    in poetry ... VERSES, FEET
    racket .... LOTTERY,
    POLICY GAME
numbfish ..... TORPEDO,
    (ELECTRIC)RAY
numbles .... INNARDS
numen .... DIVINITY, SPIRIT
numerate ..... COUNT, READ
numerous ... MANY, MANIFOLD,
    MYRIAD
    combining form ... MYRIA
Numidian crane ... DEMOISELLE
    king .... MASINISSA
    town .... ZAMA
numismatic object ...... COIN,
    MEDAL
numismatist ..... COLLECTOR
    concern of ...... COINS,
    MEDALS
nummular ...... COIN-SHAPED
numskull .. DOLT, BLOCKHEAD,
    DUNDERHEAD, NITWIT,
    MORON, DUNCE
nun .... VIRGIN, SISTER,
    PIGEON, SMEW, TITMOUSE,
    MONASA, CLARE, CARMELITE,
    VESTAL, VOTARY
    abode of ...... CONVENT,
    MONASTERY
    dress of .... HABIT
    head covering ... WIMPLE
    moth .... TUSSOCK
    throat cover ...... BARB
nunbird .... MONASE
nuncio .. AMBASSADOR, LEGATE

nuncupative . . . . ORAL,
   UNWRITTEN, VERBAL
nunnery . . . CONVENT, ABBEY,
   CLOISTER, PRIORY
   head of a . . . . ABBESS,
   SUPERIOR, PRIORESS
nuns, descriptive of some . . . . .
   CONTEMPLATIVE
   of . . . . MONASTIC
nuptial(s) . . . . WEDDING,
   MARRIAGE, MATRIMONIAL,
   HYMENEAL, BRIDAL,
   SPOUSAL
   participant . . . .
   RINGBEARER, BESTMAN,
   BRIDESMAID
   poem . . . EPITHALAMION
   principal . . BRIDE(GROOM)
   yes . . . . I DO
nuque . . . . NAPE, SCRUFF
Nuremberg war crimes
   defendant . . . . . . GOERING,
   KEITEL, HESS, RIBBENTROP
nurse . . . . AMAH, AYAH,
   SUCKLE(R), TEND, FOSTER,
   CARE, NANNY
   headcovering of . . WIMPLE
   part time . . . . SITTER
   shark . . . . GATA
nursemaid . . . . BONNE
nursery . . . . PLAYROOM,
   HOTHOUSE, GREENHOUSE,
   ASYLUM
   furniture . . . . . PLAYPEN
   public/day . . . . . CRECHE
   rhyme character . . . SPRAT
   rhyme opening words . . . .
   PAT-A-CAKE
   VIP . . . . BABY
   worker, part time . . . .
   (BABY)SITTER
nurture . . . FOOD, NUTRIMENT,
   FEED, NOURISH, FOSTER,
   REAR
nut . . . BETEL, BRAZIL, PECAN,
   FRUIT, ACORN, KOLA,
   COCO, KERNEL, CASHEW,
   PILI, PROBLEM, ALMOND,
   PINON, LI(T)CHI, LICHEE,
   HICKORY, TRYMA, PARA
   bearing . . . . . NUCIFEROUS
   combining form . . NUCI,
   CARYO, KARYO
   confection . . . . . PRALINE,
   MARZIPAN, NOUGAT
   covering . . . . SHELL,

meat . . . . KERNEL
off one's . . . . CRAZY
of a sort . . . . FANATIC
ridges . . . . KNURL
slang . . . HEAD, FOOLISH,
   QUEER, ECCENTRIC
three-cornered . . . . BEECH
turner . . . . SPANNER,
   WRENCH
nutant . . DROOPING, NODDING
nutcracker . . . . . BIRD, CROW,
   NUTHATCH
nuthatch . . . . . . NUTCRACKER,
   BIRD, TITMOUSE, CREEPER
nutlet . . . PYRENE, STONE, PIT
nutmeat . . . . KERNEL
nutmeg . . SPICE, KERNEL, MACE
nutria . . COYPU, RODENT, FUR
   animal like . . . . . BEAVER
nutrient . . . . NUTRITIOUS,
   NOURISHING
nutriment . . . . FOOD, ALIMENT,
   NOURISHMENT, MILK
nutrition, faulty . . . DYSTROPHY
   of . . . . TROPHIC
   study of . . . . . . DIETETICS,
   SITOLOGY
nutritionist . . . . DIETITIAN,
   DIETICIAN
nutritive . . . . ALIBLE
nuts . . . . CRAZY, FOOL, QUEER,
   ENTHUSIASTIC, GAGA
   collectively . . . . MAST
   pertaining to . . . . . NUCAL
nutty . . . ENTHUSIASTIC, GAGA,
   QUEER, FOOLISH, CRAZY
nux vomica . . . . . SEED, PLANT
   product . . . STRYCHNIN(E)
nuzzle . . PUSH, RUB, SNUGGLE,
   NESTLE
Nyasaland . . . . MALAWI
   capital . . . . (ZOMBA),
   LILONGWE
   president . . . . BANDA
nylghai . . . . ANTELOPE
nylon . . . . . . THREAD, BRISTLE,
   HOSE
   flow of . . . . . RUN, SNAG
   thread weight of . . DENIER
nylons . . . . . STOCKINGS, HOSE
nymph . . . . . . SYLPH, GODDESS,
   MAIDEN, WOMAN, LARVA,
   EGERIA, OENONE, PUPA,
   HOURI, OCEANID, ONDINE,
   SALMACIS, SYRINX, DAPHNE,
   MAENAD, AEGLE, HESTIA

adviser .... EGERIA
changed into bear .... CALLISTO
changed into laurel tree ... DAPHNE
changed into a rock ..... ECHO
changed into a stream ... ARETHUSA
fountain .... NAIAD
guards ..... HESPERIDES
mountain .... OREAD
pursuer of .... SATYR
river .... NAIAD, NAIS
sea ... NEREID, NEMERTES, SIREN
spring .... NAIAD
tree ..... (HAMA)DRYAD
water .... APAS
woodland ... ARETHUSA, (HAMA)DRYAD
nymphaea .. NUPAR, CASTALIA
nymphalid .... BUTTERFLY
nymphet .... LOLITA
nymphs, father of 50 .. NEREUS
spring/fountain ... CAMENAE
nyssa .... TUPELO
nystagmus, thing affected by .. EYEBALL
Nyx .... NOX
daughter of .... ERIS
is goddess of .... NIGHT

O

O .... CIPHER, ZERO, EXCLAMATION
Greek .... OMEGA, OMICRON
in baseball .. (PUT)OUTS
in chemistry .... OXYGEN
in pharmacy ..... PINT
in physics .... OHM
oaf ...... DULLHEAD, CHILD, BOOR, GAWK, RUSTIC, LOUT, DOLT, RUBE, DUNCE
variant of ...... OUPHE
Oahu city .... HONOLULU
oak .... WOOD, TREE, HOLM, WOOD(WORK), ROBLE, ENCINA, CERRIS, BLACKJACK, ALDER, BLUEJACK, DURMAS, ROBUR, EMORY
bark .. TAN, EMORY, CRUT
bark infusion ..... OOZE
black ...... QUERCITRON
British slang ..... DOOR
California ...... ROBLE ENCINA
evergreen .... ILEX
fruit ..... ACORN, MAST, CAMATA
genus .... QUERCUS
holm .... ILEX
Jerusalem ..... AMBROSE
live .... ENCINA
moss .... EVERNIA
of the .... QUERCINE
pin .... THOLE
Ridge work .... NUCLEAR
thicket ..... CHAPARRAL
white .... ROBLE
Oakley, rifle expert ... ANNIE
slang .... PASS
oaks, thicket of ... CHAPARRAL
oakum .... FIBER
seal with .... CALK
oar .... PADDLE, SCULL, SWEEP, BLADE, PROPEL, ROW(ER), SPOON
blade ..... PALM, WASH
fulcrum ...... THOLE
lock .... THOLE
part of ... LOOM, PALM, PEEL
shaped .... REMIPED
oarlock support ..... POPPET
oars, row of .... BANK
oarsman .... ROWER, STROKE
oasis .... WADI, WADY, SPRING, DOUMA
oast .... KILN, OVEN
oat ..... GRASS, CEREAL, REED
genus .... AVENA
grass, of the .. AVENACEOUS
rental .... AVENAGE
oatcake .... CAPER
oater .... HORSE OPERA
Oates of the Popish Plot .... TITUS
oath .... VOW, CURSE, SWEARWORD, PLEDGE, PLIGHT
breaking of ... PERJURY
mild ..... EGAD, DRAT, GOSH, ZOUNDS

solemn ... . SACRAMENT
strong ... DAMN(ATION),
HELL
take .... SWEAR, PROMISE
taker .... JURANT
testify under .... DEPOSE
oatmeal .... PORRIDGE
cake ...... SCONE, PONE
porridge .. .... BURGOO,
STIRABOUT
oats .... FEED, AVENA
hulled, cracked .. GROATS
Oaxaca is in .... MEXICO
Ob river is in .... SIBERIA
Obadiah .. ABDIAS, PROPHET
obbligato ... ACCOMPANIMENT
obdurate .... STUBBORN,
OBSTINATE, INFLEXIBLE,
MULISH, BULLHEADED,
DOGGED
obeah ... MAGIC, WITCHCRAFT,
FETISH, TALISMAN
obedience .. .. SUBMISSION
obedient .... AMENABLE,
DOCILE, TRACTABLE,
COMPLIANT, DUTIFUL
obeisance .... HOMAGE,
DEFERENCE, CONGE(E),
REVERENCE, CURTSY, BOW,
SALAAM, GENUFLECTION
obelisk ...... OBELUS, PILLAR,
NEEDLE, PYLON, SHAFT,
MONOLITH
characters on ....
HIEROGLYPH(IC)S
obelus .. .... OBELISK, MARK,
DAGGER
Oberammergau is in .. ....
BAVARIA
religious play .. PASSION
Oberon .... FAIRY, KING
actress .... MERLE
domain of ... FAIRYLAND
wife of .... TITANIA
obese .. .. STOUT, CORPULENT,
PUFFY, FAT, ADIPOSE,
LIPAROUS, PURSY, FLESHY,
PORTLY
obey ... MIND, HEED, SUBMIT,
COMPLY, CARRY OUT,
FOLLOW
obfuscate .. .. OBSCURE,
DARKEN, BEWILDER,
STUPEFY, CONFUSE
obi ... SASH, CHARM, OBEAH,
FETISH, MAGIC, TALISMAN

obit .. .. (DEATH)NOTICE
obiter dictum .... ASIDE,
COMMENT, REMARK
obituary .. .. NECROLOGY,
(DEATH)NOTICE
words ..... IN MEMORIAM
object ... AIM, OPPOSE, THING,
PURPOSE, PROTEST, TARGET,
INTENT, END, MIND, KICK,
GOAL, DEMUR, DISSENT
art ...... CURIO, BIBELOT
frivolously .... CAVIL
of attack .... TARGET
of manipulation ....
PUPPET, MARIONETTE
of pursuit .. .. GAME,
QUARRY
objection .. PROTEST, QUARREL,
OPPOSITION, CAVIL,
DEMURRER, KICK
objective .. .... REAL, ACTUAL,
DETACHED, GOAL, AIM,
FAIR, PURPOSE, TARGET
objector .. DISSENTER, REBEL,
DISSIDENT, OPPOSER
objet d'art ... FIGURINE, VASE
collector ..... VIRTUOSO
objurgate ... CHIDE, REBUKE,
REPROVE, BERATE, UPBRAID
oblate .. MONK, NUN, ASCETIC
opposite of ..... PROLATE
oblation .... OFFERING
obligate .... BIND, OWE
obligated .. .. BOUND,
INDEBTED
obligation .. DEBT, DUE, ONUS,
BURDEN, DUTY, BOND,
MUST
evade an .. .. WELSH
obligatory .. .. BINDING,
BOUNDEN
oblige .. COMPEL, CONSTRAIN,
FORCE
obliging .. HELPFUL, AMIABLE
oblique ... ASLANT, INCLINED,
INDIRECT, EVASIVE, SKEW,
AWRY, CANT
glance .. .. SQUINT
line .... BIAS
obliquely .. .. SIDEWAYS,
SIDEWISE
obliterate .... EFFACE,
EXPUNGE, RAZE, ERASE,
SPONGE, BLOT OUT, DESTROY
oblivion .... PARDON,
FORGETFULNESS, LETHE

drug of .... NEPENTHE
place of .... LIMBO
river of .... LETHE
oblivious .... FORGETFUL, HEEDLESS
oblong ... ... ELONGATED, ELLIPTICAL
obloquy ... CENSURE, INFAMY
obnoxious .... ODIOUS, UNPLEASANT, OFFENSIVE, HATEFUL, REPULSIVE
oboe ... ... WOOD WIND, REED, BASSOON, BOMBARDON, SHAWN, HAUTBOY
oboli, six .... DRACHMA
obol(us) .... COIN
Obote, Uganda president ..... APOLO
Obregon, Mex. president ..... ALVARO
obscene ... . LEWD, NAUGHTY, FILTHY, REPULSIVE, INDECENT, COARSE, FESCENNINE, SMUTTY, RAW, FOUL, GROSS
obscure ... NUBILOUS, DARK, MURKY, AMBIGUOUS, HIDDEN, OBFUSCATE, FOG, NAMELESS, ECLIPSE, GLOOMY, VAGUE, RECONDITE, OVERSHADOW, DIM, CRYPTIC, UNKNOWN
obscurity .... ANONYMITY
obsecration .... ENTREATY, PRAYER, PETITION
obsequies .... EXEQUY
obsequious .... SERVILE, SUBMISSIVE, FAWNING
observance .... CUSTOM, PRACTICE, RULE, RITE
for a dead .... WAKE
of formalities .. PUNCTILIO
observant .... WATCHFUL, ALERT, PERCEPTIVE, KEEN-EYED, ATTENTIVE
observation ...... ASSERTION, REMARK, COMMENT, ESPIAL
aircraft .... SCOUT
work .... SURVEY, RECONNAISSANCE
observatory, California ...... PALOMAR
concern of an ... PLANETS, STARS, WEATHER, MOON
observe .... NOTICE, SEE, CELEBRATE, ABIDE, REMARK, NOTE, DISCERN, EYE
secretly ... ... SPY, STAG, STALK
observer .. LOOKOUT, WATCHER
turned toward .. OBVERSE
obsess .... HAUNT, BESET, PREOCCUPY, HARASS
obsessed ... RIDDEN, HIPPED
obsession ...... (MONO)MANIA, IDEE FIXE, FIXATION
subject of .. IDEA, DESIRE, EMOTION
obsidian ... ... LAVA, ROCK, PERLITE, TEKTITE
obsolete ... . DISCARDED, PASSE, OUTMODED, ARCHAIC, OUT OF DATE, OLD, DISUSED, DATED
obstacle .... HITCH, IMPEDIMENT, HINDRANCE, LET, SNAG, BARRIER, BAR, HURDLE
course ... ... GANTLET
obstetrician .... ACCOUCHEUR
obstetrics, subject of ...... CHILDBIRTH, MIDWIFERY, TOCOLOGY
obstinate ... ... STUBBORN, MULISH, HARD(HEADED), DOUR, WILLFUL, PIGHEADED, DOGGED, BULLHEADED, UNBENDING, ORNERY
obstreperous ... ... NOISY, UNRULY, VOCIFEROUS, BOISTEROUS
obstruct .. DAM, BLOCK, CLOG, IMPEDE, STOP UP, HINDER, BAR, CHECK, OPPILATE, CHOKE
obstruction ... ... HINDRANCE, OBSTACLE, BARRIER
obstructionist's trick ... ... FILIBUSTER
obtain .... EARN, WIN, PROCURE, PREVAIL, GET, FANG, DERIVE, GAIN, SECURE
obtainable ... ... AVAILABLE
obtected thing .... PUPA
obtest .... BEG(FOR), BESEECH, ENTREAT
obtrude ... ... MEDDLE, EJECT, IMPOSE

obtund ... ... BLUNT, DULL, DEADEN
obturate ... ... STOP UP, PLUG, CLOSE
obtuse ... BLUNT, DULL, DENSE
obverse ... ... COUNTERPART, FRONT
   opposite of ... ... REVERSE, VERSO
obviate ... ... PREVENT
obvious ... ... EVIDENT, PLAIN, PATENT, PALPABLE
   not ... ... SUBTLE, SUBTILE
oca ... ... OXALIS
ocarina, shape of ... POTATO
O'Casey, Irish dramatist ... SEAN
occasion ... ... EVENT, OPPORTUNITY, TIME, HAPPENING, CAUSE, NONCE
occasional ... CASUAL, RARE, IRREGULAR, ODD, ORRA, SPORADIC
occasionally ... ... SOMETIMES, NOW AND THEN
occident ... ... WEST
   opposite of ... ... ORIENT
occidental ... ... HESPERIAN, WESTERN, PONENT
occipital protuberances .. INIA
occlude ... ... CLOSE, SHUT, BLOCK, ABSORB
occlusion ... ... SHUTDOWN
occult ... CRYPTIC, MYSTIC, ORPHIC, ESOTERIC, HIDDEN, SECRET, MYSTERIOUS
   art ... MAGIC, ASTROLOGY, ALCHEMY
   knowledge .. GRAMARY(E)
   religious philosophy ... ... CABALA
occultation ... ... ECLIPSE, LOST
occultism ... ... CAB(B)ALA, KABALA, MAGIC, NUMEROLOGY
occupancy ... TENANCY, TERM
occupant ... TENANT, INMATE, HABITANT
occupation ... ... PURSUIT, BUSINESS, METIER, TRADE, EMPLOYMENT, TENURE, WORK, CALL(ING)
occupational disease, miner's ... SILICOSIS
occupied ... BUSY, ENGROSSED
occupier ... ... TENANT

occupy ... ... ENGAGE, FILL, POSSESS, LIVE IN, USE, EMPLOY, INVEST
   attention wholely ... ... ENGROSS
   the whole of ... ... MONOPOLIZE
occur ... BEFALL, LIGHT, EXIST, HAPPEN, COME, BETIDE, PASS
   again ... RECUR, REPEAT
   at the same time ... COINCIDE
   irregularly ... SPORADIC
   yearly ... ... ANNUAL
occurrence ... ... OCCASION, EVENT, HAPPENING, INCIDENT, CASE
   degree/extent of ... ... INCIDENCE
occurring every 8th day ... ... OCTAN
   5th day ... ... QUINTAN
   4th day ... ... QUARTAN
   3rd day ... ... TERTIAN
ocean ... EXPANSE, SEA, DEEP, BRINE, MAIN, ATLANTIC, INDIAN, ARCTIC, ANTARCTIC, PACIFIC
   current ... UNDERTOW
   depression ... ... DEEP
   depth finder ... ... SONAR
   fish ... OPAH, SUNFISH, SHAD
   greyhound ... STEAMSHIP, LINER
   of the ... ... MARINE, THALASSIC
   of Storms' location ... ... MOON
Oceania island ... MICRONESIA, MELANESIA, POLYNESIA
oceanic ... ... VAST, PELAGIC
oceanid ... ... NYMPH
Oceanus ... ... TITAN, GOD
   domain of ... ... SEA
ocellated ... ... SPOTTED
ocellus ... ... SPOT, EYE(LET)
ocelot ... ... CAT
   cat like ... ... MARGAY
ocher ... ... CLAY, PIGMENT, YELLOW, SIL
   red ... RUBRIC, TIVER, REDDLE, RADDLE
ochone ... ... ALAS
ochre ... ... ALMAGRA

Ochs, newspaper publisher ..... ADOLPH
    folksinger ...-..-.... PHIL
ocotillo .... PINE, PLANT
ocrea .... SHEATH
octa, as combining form ...... EIGHT
octan ..-..-..-.--.- FEVER
octave ....-. EIGHT, OCTONARY, UTAS
Octavia's husband .. ANTHONY
octet(te) .... EIGHT
octo, combining form .. EIGHT
October 15 .... IDES
    flower .... COSMOS, CALENDULA
    Revolution leader ...... LENIN, TROTSKY
octogenarian .... DOTARD
    age of .... EIGHTIES
octonary .... EIGHT, OGDOAD, OCTAVE
octopod .... OCTOPUS
octopus ..... SQUID, OCTOPOD, DEVILFISH, MOLLUSK, POULPE
    arm of .... TENTACLE
    sucker of ... ACETABULUM
octoroon .....- METIS, MUSTEE, MESTEE
octroi ...-..-..-..-.- TAX
octuple .... EIGHTFOLD
ocular .-......., VISUAL, LENS, EYESIGHT, OPTIC(AL)
oculi ....-.- EYES
oculist's concern .... EYE
Ocypete .... HARPY
od, manifestation of .... MAGNETISM, HYPNOTISM
odalisque .... SLAVE, CONCUBINE
    place of .. ADA, ODA, IDA
odd ..... EXTRA, OCCASIONAL, INCIDENTAL, AZYGOUS, QUAINT, SINGULAR, PECULIAR, RUM, DROLL, ORRA, QUEER, ECCENTRIC, STRANGE
    notion ......-.- FREAK
    job .... CHAR(E)
    job man .... JACK
    slang ... BATTY, SCREWY
oddity ... FREAK, QUEERNESS, QUIRK, VAGARY
oddment ... SCRAP, LEFTOVER, REMNANT
odds .... ADVANTAGE

and ends ...-..-.- SCRAPS, REMNANTS, RUMMAGE, ETCETERAS, MANAVELINS
companion of .... ENDS
ode .... POEM, HYMN
    division of ...... STROPHE
odeon .... HALL, THEATRE
Oder, city on the ... BRESLAU, STETTIN
    tributary ...-.- WARTHE
odeum .... HALL
Odin ... WODEN, WOTAN, GOD
    concern of .. WAR, DEAD
    horse of .... SLEIPNER
    maiden of ... VALKYR(IE)
    parent of .... BOR
    son of ..... TIU, BALDER, TYR, THOR, VALI
    wife of .. FRIGG(A), JORD, FRIA
    wolf of ...-... GERE, GERI
odious .... HATEFUL, OFFENSIVE, DISGUSTING, REPULSIVE, DETESTABLE, HEINOUS
odium ... HATRED, DISGRACE, INFAMY, APPROBIUM
odograph, kind of .... TAXIMETER
    record ...-..- DISTANCE
odometer .... TAXIMETER
odontoid ......-. TOOTHLIKE
odontology .... DENTISTRY
    subject of .... TEETH
odontophore .... RADULA
odor .... SCENT, SMELL, AROMA, FRAGRANCE, NOSE
    disagreeable ..... STENCH, STINK, F(O)ETOR
    musty .... FUNK
    pleasant ...-..- INCENSE, FRAGRANCE
odorless ...-..-..- AOSMIC
odorous .... AROMATIC, REDOLENT, FRAGRANT, FETID
Odysseus ..... ULYSSES, KING
    captor of ... POLYPHEMUS
    father of .... LAERTES
    protection against Circe .. MOLY
    realm of ...-..- ITHACA
    wife of ...... PENELOPE
Odyssey ...-.- WANDERING, JOURNEY
    author of ...-... HOMER

enchantress in .... CIRCE
nymph .... CALYPSO
queen in ..... PENELOPE
Oedipus, daughter of ....
ANTIGONE
father .... LAIUS
mother of ...... JOCASTA
son of ...... POLYNICES,
ETEOCLES
wife of .... JOCASTA
oeil-de-boeuf ..... BULL'S-EYE,
WINDOW
oeillade .... OGLE
oenology, subject of ... WINES
Oenone .... NYMPH
husband of ...... PARIS
rival of .... HELEN
oeuvres .... WORKS
of .... FROM, THROUGH, BY,
HAVING, ABOUT
a reign .. REGIME, REGNAL
autumn .... FALL
course: of ...... MATCH
each .... PER
no ___ ...... MOMENT,
ACCOUNT, USE
old age ...... GERIATRICS
summer ...... (A)ESTIVAL
the world .... MUNDANE
off .... AGEE, AWAY, ABSENT,
WRONG, IN ERROR
color .... RISQUE,
INDECENT, OBSCENE
in nautical usage ....
SEAWARD
Offenbach, composer ....
JACQUES
offend .... INSULT, OUTRAGE,
AFFRONT, SLIGHT, MORTIFY,
MIFF, HURT, PIQUE, HUFF
offender .... CULPRIT
offense .... CRIME,
TRANSGRESSION, OUTRAGE,
FELONY, SIN, UMBRAGE,
RESENTMENT, DELICT
in law .... DELICT
minor .... MISDEMEANOR
official overlooking of ...
OBLIVION
offensive .... UNSAVORY,
NOISOME, UGLY, ODIOUS,
REPULSIVE, ATTACK,
FULSOME
for quick victory ....
BLITZ(KRIEG)
to morals ...... OBSCENE,

INDECENT
offer .... BID, PROFFER,
TENDER, PRESENT, PROPOSE,
SUGGEST(ION), PROPOSAL
final .... ULTIMATUM
offering ..... OBLATION, GIFT,
CONTRIBUTION, TRIBUTE
burnt .... HOLOCAUST
in performance of vow ...
CORBAN
to God .... CORBAN
offhand ... CASUAL, SLAPDASH,
EXTEMPORE, IMPROMPTU,
INFORMAL, CURT, AT ONCE
office ... SERVICE, DUTY, POST,
ROLE, FUNCTION, POSITION,
STAFF
holder ...... INCUMBENT
resign an .... DEMIT
wall sign .... THINK
officeholder .... IN
officer .... POLICEMAN,
CONSTABLE
abbreviation .... NCO,
COL, CAPT, MAJ, GEN, LT,
LIEUT, ADM
assistant to an ..... AIDE
kind of .... WARRANT,
TRUANT
medical .... CORONER
military .... LIEUTENANT,
CAPTAIN, MAJOR,
COLONEL, GENERAL,
ADMIRAL
military police .. PROVOST
subordinate ...... AIDE,
DEPUTY
officer's insignia .... INSIGNE,
EAGLE, BAR
official .... AUTHORIZED,
FORMAL, BUREAUCRAT
approval ... IMPRIMATUR,
VISA
course ...... CHANNEL(S)
decree .... UKASE, IRADE,
EDICT, RESCRIPT
denial .... DEMENTI
family, President's ......
CABINET
list .... CANON
notice .... MONITION
paper .... DOCUMENT
paper container ....
HANAPER, HAMPER
routine ...... RED TAPE
seal .... SIGNET

self-important .. BASHAW,
PANJANDRUM
snafu .... RED TAPE
statement ..... BULLETIN,
COMMUNIQUE
officialdom ... BUREAUCRACY
officiate ... PRESIDE, PERFORM
officious .... OBLIGING,
MEDDLESOME, PUSHING,
INFORMAL, GRATUITOUS,
PRAGMATIC
offish .... ALOOF
offscouring .... FILTH,
GARBAGE, REFUSE, RUBBISH
offset .... SPUR, BRANCH,
BALANCE, COMPENSATE,
(OFF)SHOOT
offshoot ...... BRANCH, SCION,
STEM, ISSUE
offshore .... SEAWARD
O'Flaherty, author ..... LIAM
offspring .... CHILD(REN),
PROGENY, ISSUE, RESULT,
PRODUCT
in womb .... FETUS
of mixed parentage ......
MUSTEE, MESTEE,
MESTIZO, MULATTO,
OCTOROON
oft .... OFTEN
Ogasawara island .... BONIN
Ogden ___ .... NASH
ogdoad ... EIGHT, OCTONARY
ogee .... MOLDING
molding .... TALON
ogle ... OEILLADE, EYE, LEER,
GLAD EYE
Ogpu .... GAYPAY-OO
predecessor of ... CHEKA
ogre .... MONSTER, GIANT,
BLUNDERBORE
Ohio capital ... COLUMBUS
city ... TOLEDO, AKRON,
CLEVELAND, ELYRIA,
CINCINNATI, PARMA,
BEREA, LIMA, LORAIN,
NEWARK, DAYTON,
CANTON, MARION
native .... BUCKEYE
river ...... SCIOTO, MIAMI,
WABASH
state bird ..... CARDINAL
state flower .. CARNATION
state gem stone ... FLINT
state nickname ....
BUCKEYE

Ohm, physicist .... GEORG
oikology expert ....
HOUSEKEEPER
oil ... IRONE, ACEITE, LUBE,
PETROLEUM, PAINTING,
ANOINT, ASARUM,
LUBRICANT, SMEAR,
SAFROL(E), LUBRICATE,
BRIBE, BENNE, TUNG
antiseptic ... CARVACROL
aromatic .... BALSAM,
ATTAR, LAVENDER
baptismal ...... CHRISM
billionaire ...... GETTY
bottle ... CRUET, CRUSE,
CASTOR, AMPULLA
burner .... LAMP,
CRESSET, CRAMMER
butter .... GHEE
colloquial .. FLATTER(Y)
combining form ... OLEO
container .. DRUM, CRUSE
country ... IRAN, KUWAIT
driller ..... WILDCATTER
drilling setup ...... RIG
essential ...... ESSENCE
flask .... OLPE
flower ... ATTAR, NEROLI,
ILANG-ILANG
fragrant .... ATTAR,
NARD, ILANG-ILANG
fruit rind ..... BERGAMOT
king, so-called ... GETTY
lamp .... LUCIGEN
lubricating ...... LUBE
of/obtained from .. OLEIC,
UNGUINOUS
orange .... NEROLI
painting .... CANVAS
painting, board for ......
PANEL
pan .... SUMP
perfume-making ... BEN,
ATTAR, BERGAMOT
plant ...... PATCHOULI,
RAMTIL
refining waste ... SLUDGE
resinous .... BALSAM
rich country ...... IRAN,
KUWAIT
rub with .... ANOINT
seed ...TIL, SESAME, RAPE,
POON, RAMTIL, BEN(NE)
ship .... TANKER
skin .... SEBUM
solvent .... ACETONE

source .... OLIVE,
       COD, PEANUT, BLUBBER
trap of engine ..... SUMP
tree ...... TUNG, EBU(E)
well ... GUSHER, GASSER
oilbird .... GUACHARO
oiler .... TANKER, SHIP
oilseed ...... SESAME, TIL, BEN
oily ... SOAPY, GREASY, SLEEK,
     SLICK, SMOOTH, OLEAGINOUS,
     SEBACEOUS, UNCTUOUS,
     SLIPPERY, FATTY, PINGUID
  hair liquid ....
                    BRILLIANTINE
ointment ...... SALVE, NARD,
     POMADE, BALM, CALAMINE,
     SALVE, VASELINE,
     INUNCTION
  base for .... LANOLIN(E)
Oise tributary .... AISNE
Ojibway .. CHIPPEWA, INDIAN
OK ... CORRECT, ALL RIGHT,
       ROGER, APPROVAL
Oka city .... OREL
okapi relative .... GIRAFFE
Okie is from ..... OKLAHOMA
Okinawa capital .... NAHA
Oklahoma city .. ENID, TULSA,
     LAWTON, MUSKOGEE, ADA,
                        CATOOSA
  emigrant .... OKIE
  Indian .... PONCA,
     PAWNEE, CHEROKEE
  migratory worker .. OKIE
  mountain .... OZARK
  native .... SOONER, OKIE
  part of ..... PANHANDLE
  product .... OIL
  state flower ... MISTLETOE
  state nickname .. SOONER
  state tree ...... REDBUD
Oklahoman ... OKIE, SOONER
okra ... GUMBO, PLANT, POD,
     SOUP, BENDY, MALLOW
old ..... WISE, AGED, SHABBY,
     YORE, ANTIQUE, ARCHAIC,
     DATED, SENILE, GRAY,
     WORN, ANCIENT, AULD
  age .... SENILITY
  age, study of ....
     NOSTOLOGY, GERIATRICS
  campaigner .. WARHORSE,
                        VET
  car's noise ...... RATTLE
  cloth measure ...... ELL
  colloquial .... DEAR

country .... NATIVE LAND,
                    MOTHERLAND
Dominion ..... VIRGINIA
dress .... RAG
fashioned .... PASSE,
     DATED, COCKTAIL,
     SQUARE, DEMODE,
                        FUSTY
fashioned person ....
                   FUDDY-DUDDY
Glory .... FLAG,
     STARS AND STRIPES
growing ..... SENESCENT,
                     AGING
hand .... EXPERT,
     VET(ERAN), STAGER
Harry .... SATAN, DEVIL
Hickory ....
     (ANDREW) JACKSON
lady: sl. ... WIFE, MOTHER
maid .... SPINSTER
man .... GAFFER,
     GEEZER, FATHER,
     HUSBAND, BOSS
movies .... SILENTS
salt .... TAR
Nick ... DEVIL, SATAN
Saxon poem ... HELIAND
Scratch ... SATAN, DEVIL
Sod .... ERIN
Testament addenda ......
                    APOCRYPHA
book .... JOB,
     JEREMIAH, PROVERBS,
     MICAH, TOBIT, JONAH,
     JUDGES, JOSHUA,
                       ISAIAH
in Syriac ....
     PESHITO, PESHITTA
marginal notes ....
                    MASORA(H)
Origen's edition ......
                    HEXAPLA
translation .... TARGUM
writer .... ELOHIST
timer .... VET(ERAN)
very ... HOARY, ANCIENT
woman .... CRONE,
     GAMMER, HAG
womanish .... ANILE
World lizard ...... SEPS
World, part of ..... ASIA,
     EUROPE, AFRICA
World plover .... PEWIT,
                    LAPWING
World swan .. WHOOPER

olden .... ANCIENT
older .... SENIOR
oldest member .... DEAN
　　of course .... FIRST BORN
　　son .... HEIR, SCION
oldtimer .... VET(ERAN)
oldwife .... MENHADEN,
　　　　　　　　TRIGGERFISH
oleaceous tree ... LILAC, ASH,
　　　　　　FORSYTHIA, OLIVE
oleaginous .. OILY, UNCTUOUS,
　　　　　　　　　　GREASY
oleander .... SHRUB, ROSEBAY
oleate .... ESTER, SALT
olefine .... ALKENE
olent .... FRAGRANT
oleo .... SPREAD, MARGARINE
oleoresin .... ANIME, ELEMI,
　　　　　　　BALSAM, TOLU
olfaction .... SMELLING
olfactory organ .... NOSE
olibanum ...... FRANKINCENSE,
　　　　GUM RESIN, INCENSE
Oligocene epoch animal ......
　　　　　　　　　MASTODON
olio .... STEW, MEDLEY,
　　　　MISCELLANY, OLLA,
　　　　MELANGE, MESS,
　　SALMAGUNDI, HODGEPODGE
olive ... WREATH, OLEA(STER),
　　　　　　TREE, RELISH
　　branch offering ... PEACE
　　drabs .... UNIFORM
　　genus .... OLEA
　　pimiento-stuffed ....
　　　　　　　　　　PIMOLA
　　refuse .... BAGASSE
"Oliver Twist" character .....
　　FAGIN, BUMBLE, SIKES,
　　　　DODGER, NANCY
olivine .... CHRYSOLITE,
　　　　GARNET, PERIDOT
olla ..... POT, JAR, STEW, JUG
ollapodrida ..... HASH, STEW,
　　OLIO, MEDLEY, ASSORTMENT
ology .... SCIENCE
oloroso .... SHERRY
olvinic .... PERIDOTIC
Olympian .... EXALTED,
　　GODLIKE, CELESTIAL,
　　MAJESTIC, GOD
　　cupbearer .... GANYMEDE
　　queen .... HERA
Olympus .... SKY, HEAVEN,
　　　　　　　　　MOUNT

mountain piled on ......
　　　　　PELION, OSSA
Oman, capital ...... MUSCAT,
　　　　　　　MASQAT
　　companion of ... MUSCAT
　　sultan .... TAIMUR
Omar ____, general ....
　　　　　　　　BRADLEY
　　Khayyam's birthplace ....
　　　　　　　　NISHAPUR
　　country .... IRAN
　　work .... RUBAIYAT
omasum .... PSALTERIUM,
　　　　　　　MANYPLIES
omber ... CARD GAME, HOMBRE
ombre, trump in ..... MANILLA
omega .... END
omelet(te) .... EGG DISH
omen .... SIGN, PORTENT,
　　AUGUR(Y), PRESAGE,
　　AUSPICE, PRECURSOR
　　death's .... KNELL
omers, ten .... EPHA
ominous .... SINISTER,
　　MENACING, FATEFUL,
　　PORTENTOUS, GRAVE
omission .... OVERSIGHT,
　　　　　　　NEGLECT
　　sign of .... CARET
　　syllable .... APOCOPE
　　vowel .... ELISION
　　word .... ELLIPSIS
omit .... SKIP, LEAVE OUT,
　　NEGLECT, IGNORE, DELETE,
　　PRETERMIT, ELIDE
Ommiad .... CALIPH
omnia vincit ____ ..... AMOR
omnibus .... (MOTOR)COACH,
　　　　　　　　　BUS
omnipotence .... GOD
omnipresent ...... IMMANENT,
　　　　　　　UBIQUITOUS
Omphale's domain .... LYDIA
　　servant .... HERCULES
Omri's son .... AHAB
on .... UPON, ABOVE, ABOUT
　　dit ...... RUMOR, GOSSIP,
　　　　　　　REPORT
　　Egyptian .... HELIOPOLIS
　　one's guard ..... ALERT,
　　　　　　　WARY
　　right hand ...... DEXTER
　　tap .... NEXT
　　the blue .... ASEA
　　the face of document ....
　　　　　　　EX FACIE

the other hand ... AGAIN
the way ...... PREGNANT,
   EN ROUTE, OFF,
   IN TRANSIT
time ... DULY, PUNCTUAL
to .... AWARE, HEP
windward side ....
   AWEATHER, LEE
your way! .. SCRAM, SCAT
onager ...... ASS, CATAPULT,
   DONKEY
Onassis, (A.) nickname of ...
   ARI, DADDY-O
wife of .... JACKIE
yacht of ...... CHRISTINA
once .... ANES, ONE TIME,
   FORMER(LY), QUONDAM,
   WHILOM, ERST(WHILE)
all at .... SUDDENLY
more ... AGAIN, ENCORE
over .... GLANCE
oncoming .... IMPENDING,
   APPROACH(ING)
one ... UNITED, UNDIVIDED,
   SAME, ACE, UNIT, SINGLE
against .... ANTI
and the other ...... BOTH
base hit .... SINGLE
behind another .. TANDEM
celled creature ....
   INFUSORIA, PROTOZOA,
   STENTOR, AM(O)EBA
combining form .. MONO,
   UNI
eyed giant .... CYCLOPS
eyed god .... ODIN
footed .... UNIPED
god, belief in .... THEISM
horned animal ....
   UNICORN, BADAK,
   RHINO
horse .... PETTY
horse town .... PODUNK
hundred: comb. form ....
   HECTO
hundred pounds ....
   CENTAL, CENTNER
hundred thousand, in
   India .... LAC
hundred years ....
   CENTURY, CENTENARY
legged .... UNIPOD
make ...... UNITE, WED
next to the last .. PENULT
of a trio ..... TOM, DICK,
   HARRY, CALM, COOL,

COLLECTED, ATHOS,
   PORTHOS, ARAMIS
of mixed blood ....
   MESTIZO, METIS,
   QUADRON
of two .... EITHER
or another .... ANY
pound sterling .... QUID
prefix ...... MONO, UNI
self: comb. form ... AUTO
sided .... EX PARTE,
   UNILATERAL, PARTIAL,
   PREJUDICIAL, BIASED,
   ROUT
spot .... ACE
square meter ....
   CENT(I)ARE
tenth are ...... DECIARE
thousand .... MIL
time .... FORMER
way sign ...... ARROW
eyed ...... MONOCULAR
eyed giant ..... CYCLOPS
one's public ...... AUDIENCE,
   FOLLOWING
strong point .... FORTE
Oneida .... INDIAN, IROQUOIS
oneirocritic's forte .. DREAMS
oneness ... UNITY, IDENTITY,
   SAMENESS
oner .... LONER
onerous .... OPPRESSIVE,
   BURDENSOME
onion .... SHALLOT, BULB,
   CIBOL, ALLIUM, ESCHALOT,
   LEEK, SCALLION, CEPA
plant ..... CHIVE, LEEK
sea .... SQUILL
onions, prepared with ....
   LYONNAISE
onionskin .... PAPER
onlooker ...... SPECTATOR,
   BYSTANDER
only .... LONE, SINGLY,
   SOLE(LY), MERE(LY), BUT,
   SIMPLY
onomasticon ..... DICTIONARY
onomatopoeia ...... ECHOISM
onomatopoeic .... ECHOIC
Onondaga .... INDIAN,
   IROQUOIS, LAKE
onrush .... FLOW, DASH,
   STAMPEDE, BIRR
onset ..... ASSAULT, ATTACK,
   START, BEGINNING

onslaught ..... ATTACK, RUSH, CHARGE, ONSET, ASSAULT
Ontario ..... LAKE, PROVINCE
capital of ..... TORONTO
city .... KINGSTON, LONDON
lake on .... OSWEGO
onto ... AWARE, COGNIZANT, HEP, CONVERSANT
onus .... BURDEN, DUTY, RESPONSIBILITY
onward ... ADVANCING, FORTH
onyx ... AGATE, GEM, NICOLO
oocyte .... GAMETE, EGG
oodles ... SCADS, LOTS, MANY, SLEWS
oolite .... LIMESTONE
oology, subject of .... (BIRD'S) EGGS
oolong .... TEA
Oom Paul .... KRUGER
oomiak ..... UMIAK, KAYAK, CANOE
oomph ... SEX APPEAL, VIGOR
oorial .... SHA
oosperm ... ZYGOTE, OOSPORE
ootheca ... EGG CASE, OVISAC
ooze .... LEAK, SLIME, BOG, MARSH, TRANSUDE, EXUDE, SLUDGE, MUD, PERMEATE, FLOW, PERCOLATE, GLEET, SWEAT, SEEP, SEDIMENT, EXUDATE, SOP, BLEED
oozy .... SLIMY, SLUDGY
opah ... SOKO, FISH, MOONFISH
opal ..... SILICA, GEM, RESIN, PITCH, HARLEQUIN, HYALITE, GIRASOL(E), ISOPYRE
fire ... GIRASOL(E), GIROSOL
opalescent ...... IRIDESCENT
opaline .... GLASS
opaque .... DARK, DULL, OBSCURE, OBTUSE
open ...... CLEAR, UNSEAL(ED), BARE, FREE, LIBERAL, GENEROUS, FRANK, CANDID, AVAILABLE, PUBLIC, UNFOLD, UNDO, BEGIN, START, DISCLOSE, EXPOSE(D), UNLOCK
air .... ALFRESCO, OUTDOOR(S)
and shut ...... OBVIOUS, SIMPLE
car .... PHAETON

country .... VELDT
eyed .... AWARE, AWAKE, WATCHFUL
handed .... LIBERAL, GENEROUS
hearted .... CANDID, KIND(LY), GENEROUS
minded .... PERVIOUS, AMENABLE
mouthed .... AGAPE
partly .... AJAR
sea .... MAIN
sesame .... PASSWORD
space in park .... CONCOURSE
to attack ... VULNERABLE
to choice ...... OPTIONAL
to debate .... MOOT
to the sky .... HYP(A)ETHRAL
wound .... SORE
opening ...... INAUGURATION, HOLE, GAP, APERTURE, CHANCE, START, ORIFICE, VACANCY, PORE, SLOT, MOUTH
in chess .... GAMBIT
small ..... OSTIOLE, PORE, ORIFICE, CRANNY
openings, in zoology ... STOMATA
opera .... NORMA, AIDA, LA BOHEME, MIKADO, RIENZI, THAIS, FIDELIO, FAUST, MANON, TOSCA, SALOME, ERNANI, CARMEN
box .... LOGE
comic .... BOUFFE
comic singer ..... BUFFO
company director .... IMPRESARIO
composer .... WAGNER, PUCCINI, VERDI, ROSSINI, BIZET, MENOTTI, MASSENET, GOUNOD, MOZART, HANDEL
describing an ... COMIC, HORSE, SOAP
glass .... LORGNETTE, BINOCULARS
hat ...... GIBUS, TOPPER
heroine .... ISOLDE, SENTA, ELSA, MIMI, CIO CIO SAN, AIDA, PAMINA
highlight .... ARIA

horse ......•.... OATER
house ...... MET, SCALA
singer ......•... CALLAS,
    NILSSON, PONS,
    CHALIAPIN, PINZA,
    TUCKER, STEVENS,
    MELBA, EAMES, ALDA,
    STEBER, GARDEN,
    TEBALDI, CABALLE
singular of ....• OPUS
solo ..... ARIA, CAVATINA
star .. DIVA, PRIMA DONNA
text of .... LIBRETTO
operate ... RUN, TEND, WORK,
    ACT, CONDUCT, MANAGE
against ......• MILITATE
operatic character ..•.. BUFFO
    prince ....• IGOR
    slave ....• AIDA
operation ..• PROJECT, ACTION
operative .... EFFECTIVE,
    DETECTIVE, SPY, WORKER
operator ....• AGENT
operculum .... FLAP, LID
operose ..•.... LABORED, BUSY
operetta composer ..•..• FRIML
Ophelia's love ..•..• HAMLET
    parent ...•..•• POLONIUS
ophidian ..... REPTILE, SNAKE,
    SERPENT, COBRA, ASP
Ophir's wealth .... GOLD
ophthalmologist ..... OCULIST
ophthalmology, subject of ..•..
    EYE, VISION, SIGHT
opinion ......• BELIEF, NOTION,
    CONVICTION, SENTIMENT,
    TENET, DOOM, JUDGMENT,
    IMPRESSION, EVALUATION,
    THOUGHT, PERSUASION
    general ..•.• CONSENSUS
    man ..•..•..• POLLSTER,
        POLL-TAKER
    opposing ..•..• HERESY
    united in ..• CONSENTIENT
opinionated ..•..• DOGMATIC,
    RABID
opium ..•.• DRUG, NARCOTIC,
    AFYON
    addict ..•.. (DOPE)FIEND,
        JUNKY, NOSCAPINE,
        PARAVERINE
    alkaloid ..•..•.• CODEINE,
        MORPHINE, CODEA
    derivative ..•.. HEROIN,
        MORPHINE, CODEINE
    seed .... MAW

seller ..•..•..•• PUSHER
source ..•....... POPPY
tincture of .. LA(U)DANUM,
    PAREGORIC
opossum ..•..•..• YAPO(C)K,
    MARSUPIAL, QUICA
place of young of ..•..•
    POUCH
play ..•.•... DEAD, FEIGN
oppidan ....• URBAN
oppilate ..• OBSTRUCT, BLOCK
opponent .... ADVERSARY,
    ANTAGONIST, FOE, ENEMY
opportune ......•• TIMELY,
    PROPITIOUS, APROPOS,
    SEASONABLE, WELL-TIMED,
    APT
opportunist ..•..•• TRIMMER,
    TIME-SERVER
opportunity ..•..•.• CHANCE,
    OCCASION
oppose ..•..• RESIST, FACE,
    WITHSTAND, OBJECT,
    OPPUGN, DEFY, DARE,
    REPUGN
opposed ..•.• AGAINST, ANTI,
    CONTRARY
opposite ..•..•..• FRONTING,
    ANTITHETIC, REVERSE,
    CONTRARY,
    ANTIPODE, VIS-A-VIS,
    FORNENT
    belief ..•..•..• HERESY
    directly .. DIAMETRIC(AL),
        INVERSE
    extremity ..•..•..• POLE
    number ..•. COUNTERPART
opposition ..... COMPETITION,
    RESISTANCE, HOSTILITY,
    CONTRAST
    in ... ANTI, AGAINST, CON
    party ..•..•.... MINORITY
oppress .. PERSECUTE, BURDEN,
    TYRANNIZE, DISTRESS, GRIPE
oppressive ..•..• TYRANNICAL,
    ONEROUS
    anything ..•..• INCUBUS
oppressor ....• TYRANT
opprobrious ..•..•..• ABUSIVE,
    INFAMOUS
opprobrium ... INFAMY, SCORN,
    DISGRACE, ODIUM, SHAME
oppugn ... DISPUTE, CRITICIZE,
    CONTROVERT, OPPOSE
Ops ..•..•..• RHEA, GODDESS
    concern of ..... HARVEST

daughter of ...... CERES
husband of ..... SATURN
opt .... CHOOSE, SELECT,
DECIDE
optic .... EYE
branch of ... CATOPTRICS
optical ...... OCULAR, VISUAL
aid .... MONOCLE,
LORGNETTE, LORGNON,
PINCENEZ
glass ... LENS, CONTACT
illusion .... MIRAGE
instrument .... ALIDADE,
PERISCOPE, MICROSCOPE,
TELESCOPE
instrument eyepiece .....
OCULAR
instrument lines ....
RETICLE
optician .... OPTOMETRIST
optimistic .... HOPEFUL, ROSY,
EXPECTANT, SANGUINE,
ROSEATE
optimum .... BEST
option .... CHOICE
optional .... ELECTIVE
optometrist .... OPTICIAN
opulence .... RICHES, WEALTH
opulent ..... RICH, WEALTHY
opuntia .... TUNA, CACTUS
opus .... WORK, SYMPHONY,
OPERA, COMPOSITION
plural of .... OPERA
oquassa .... TROUT
or ...... CONJUNCTION, GOLD,
YELLOW
ora .... MOUTHS, COIN
orach(e) .... SPINACH,
GOOSEFOOT
oracle ... SEER, HOLY OF HOLIES,
DELOS, AUGUR
giver .... FAUNUS
modern ..... COMPUTER
seat .... DODONA
site of .... DELPHI
woman ..... SYBIL, SIBYL
oracular .... SYBILLINE,
ORPHIC, PYTHONIC,
PROPHETIC, MYSTERIOUS,
WISE, VATIC
oral ...... STOMATIC, SPOKEN,
VERBAL, VOCAL
pledge .... PAROLE, WORD
orale .... FANON
orally ..... PAROL, VIVA VOCE
Oran is in .... ALGERIA

orange .... TANGERINE,
CITRUS, MANDARIN
flower oil .... NEROLI
genus .... CITRUS
juice squeezer ... REAMER
mock .... SYRINGA
of an .... CITRIC
peel .... ZEST
pekoe .... TEA
preserve .... MARMALADE
River tributary .... VAAL
seed .... PIP
variety .... MICHAEL
yellow .... LUTEOUS,
CROCUS, SAFFRON
orangewood .... HEDGE
orangutan .... APE, MIAS
habitat .... BORNEO,
SUMATRA
orate ... DECLAIM, SPEECHIFY,
MOUTH, PERORATE
oration ..... SPEECH, ADDRESS
orator ..... SPEAKER, CICERO,
OTIS, BRYAN, RHETOR
in law ...... PETITIONER,
PLAINTIFF
oratorio lyrics ...... LIBRETTO
part of ...... ARIA, DUET,
TRIO, CAVATINA
oratory ... CHAPEL, CHANTRY
fathers, founder of .. NERI
master of ..... RHETOR
orb ..... SPHERE, GLOBE, EYE,
SUN, MOON
orbit ...... PATH, EYE SOCKET
heavenly body's .. CYCLE
orbital point ... APSIS, APOGEE,
APSE, PERIGEE
orc .... GRAMPUS, WHALE
kind of .... DOLPHIN
orchard .... GARDEN
orchal .... LICHEN
orchestra .... BAND, PARQUET
circle .... PARTERRE
leader .... CUGAT,
DUCHIN, JAMES,
VALLEE, SHAW
platform ..... BANDSTAND
section ... BRASS, WINDS,
TRAPS, STRINGS,
PERCUSSION
space for .... PIT
theater's ... MAIN FLOOR
orchestral section .... WINDS,
STRINGS, BRASS, TRAPS,
PERCUSSION

orchid ..... SATYR, EPIPHYTE,
MOCCASIN, PUTTYROOT,
FLOWER, ORCHIS, POGONIA,
DICHEA, BUTTERFLY
climbing ...... VANILLA
genus .... DISA
petal .... LABELLUM
Philippine ....
WALING-WALING
symbol of an .... LUXURY
third petal of .... LIP
tuber .... SALEP
orchil .... DYE, LICHEN
orchis .... ORCHID
Orcus ..... HADES, DIS, PLUTO
ordain ...... DECREE, ORDER,
ENACT, PRESCRIBE, APPOINT
ordeal ... TRIAL, TRIBULATION,
HARDSHIP, CRUCIBLE,
EXPERIENCE
order .. SERIES, SYSTEM, CLASS,
METHOD, DIRECT(ION),
DID, INSTRUCT(ION), BEST,
COMMISSION, LODGE,
PRESCRIPT, PRESCRIBE,
COSMOS, MANDATE,
COMMAND
good .... EUTAXY
orderly .... TIDY, NEAT,
PEACEABLY, SYSTEMATIC,
ATTENDANT, AIDE, TRIM,
METHODICAL
orders, military ....
ANNOUNCEMENTS
ordinal .... NUMBER
number, ... FIRST,
SECOND, THIRD,
FOURTH, FIFTH
suffix .... (E)TH
ordinance ..... LAW, STATUTE,
CUSTOM, PRACTICE, RITE,
COMMAND
ordinary .... TAVERN,
CHAPLAIN, USUAL, NORMAL,
REGULAR, COMMON,
ROUTINE, VULGATE,
BICYCLE, CUSTOMARY,
MEDIAL, MEDIOCRE,
MILL-RUN, AVERAGE
ordnance ..... ARMOR, GUNS,
ARTILLERY, WEAPONRY
piece .... CANNON,
MORTAR
ordure .... FILTH, DUNG,
MANURE
ore .... MINERAL

analyze .... ASSAY
assaying ... CUPEL, TEST
bearing rock layer ......
LEDGE
bed of .... REEF
crushing machine .. STAMP
deposit ... LODE, POCKET
digger .... MINER
extract/refine ..... SMELT
fusing/extracting place ..
SMELTERY
ground .... PULP
iron ...... OCHER, OCHRE
layer .... SEAM, STOPE
mercury ..... CINNABAR
refiner .... SMELTER
screening sieve ....
TROMMEL
shovel for washing .. VAN
smelting product .. SPEISS
stratum of .... SEAM
test .... ASSAY
truck .... CORF
vein ...... LODE, STREAK
wagon .... CORF
washing container .. PAN
washing device ... DOLLY
washing trough .. STRAKE
worthless .... MATTE
oread .... NYMPH, NAIAD
oregano .... PLANT, MINT,
MARJORAM
Oregon capital .... SALEM
city .... MEDFORD,
PORTLAND, CORVALLIS,
EUGENE
dam .... BONEVILLE,
MCNARY
Indian .. KUSAN, CAYUSE,
NEZ PERCE
mountain ..... CASCADE
river .... COLUMBIA,
WILLAMETTE, KLAMATH
seaport .... ASTORIA
state nickname .. BEAVER
Trail users .... PIONEERS,
SETTLERS
Orestes, parent of ....
AGAMEMNON,
CLYTEMNESTRA
sister of .... ELECTRA
wife of ...... HERMIONE
organ .... INSTRUMENT,
PERIODICAL, MEANS,
BOMBARDON, HARMONIUM
atrophied ...... VESTIGE

barrel ... HURDY-GURDY
bass stop ...... BOURDON
connecting tissue .. PONS
device .... STOP, PIPE,
       REED, TREMOLO
dislocation ... PROLAPSE
falling of ..... PROLAPSE,
       PTOSIS
grinder's assistant ....
       MONKEY
keyboard ... MELODEON,
  HARMONIUM, ACCORDION,
      CLAVIER
loft .... GALLERY
matrix of .... STROMA
mouth ..... HARMONICA
of speech .... TONGUE
outgrowth ... APPENDIX
part ..... PIPE, CONSOLE,
   REED, PALLET, STOP
pipe .... FLUE, REED,
    MONTRE, LABIAL
pipe plug .... TAMPION
place in church .... LOFT,
    GALLERY
point .... MUCRO
seed-bearing ..... PISTIL
stop ..... MELODIA, OBOE,
  DIAPASON, VIOLONE,
  CLARABELLA, LARIGOT,
  MONTRE, SEXT, QUINT,
  TREMOLO, GEMSHORN,
  CARILLON, CELESTA,
  GAMBE, BOMBARDE,
  VIOLA, BOURDON,
  DOLCAN, BASSOON,
  DULCIANA, DULCET,
  OCTAVE, TUBA, FLUTE
tip .... MUCRO
touch .. BARBEL, PALP(US)
transplantation pioneer ..
  BARNARD, DEBAKEY
vital ..... HEART, LUNG,
  LIVER, KIDNEY, EYE
voice .... LARYNX
organic .. INHERENT, INBORN,
  CONSTITUTIONAL,
  FUNDAMENTAL
basis of bone .... OSSEIN
body .... ZOOID
compound ...... AMINE
in law ... FUNDAMENTAL
law .... CHARTER,
  CONSTITUTION
substance of ... MEDULLA

organism ... ANIMAL, PLANT,
  MONAD, MONAS
animal .... ZOOID
ductless .... SPLEEN
life cycle of ... ONTOGENY
living on another ....
  PARASITE
mode of formation ....
  MORPHOSIS
one-celled .... AM(O)EBA,
  PARAMECIUM
reaction to stimulus .....
  TAXIS
sea .... NEKTON
with parasite ..... HOST
organist .... BIGGS
organization .... CLUB,
  SOCIETY, UNION, CADRE,
  OUTFIT, SETUP
organize .... SYSTEMATIZE,
  INSTITUTE, ARRANGE,
  SET UP, FORM
organized movement ... DRIVE,
  CAMPAIGN, CRUSADE
orgeat .... SIRUP
orgy .... BINGE, REVELRY,
  CAROUSAL, BASH
oribi .... ANTELOPE
oriel .... (BAY)WINDOW
orient ...... ASIA, (FAR)EAST,
  PEARL, ADJUST, ADAPT
oriental ... EASTERN, BRIGHT,
  ASIAN, ASIATIC, CHINESE,
  JAPANESE
alcoholic drink .... SAKE,
  ARRACK
banker .... SHROFF
beverage ...... TEA, CHA
bow .... SALAAM
caravansary ... IMARET,
  SERAI, KHAN
cloth .... CAMLET
coin ... SEN, PICE, ANNA,
  DINAR, RIN
decree .... FIRMAN
destiny .... KISMET
drink ... ARRACK, SAKE,
  TUBA
dwelling .... DAR
gate .... TORII
greeting .... SALAAM
inn .... SERAI,
  CARAVANSARY, IMARET,
  KHAN
laborer .... COOLIE,
  SACADA

litter .... KAGO, DOOLEE, PALANQUIN
market ..... SOOK, SOUK
money-changer .. SHROFF
name .... ALI, OMAR
nurse ..... AMA(H), AYAH, EYAH
opposite of .... OCCIDENTAL, WESTERN
palanquin ...... DOOLEE
porter .. HAMAL, HAMAUL
potentate .... AGA
potentate's chamberlain .... EUNUCH
prince .... AMEER
prison .... BAGNIO
punishment .. BASTINADO
rice dish .... PILAU
ruler ...... SHAH, KHAN, SULTAN, RAJAH, NAWAB
ruler's decree ... FIRMAN
salute .... SALAAM, KOWTOW
seed .... SESAME
serai ...... IMARET, INN, KHAN
ship .... GRAB
tambourine ..... DAIRA
taxi .... RICKSHA
title ...... BABA, RAJAH
topaz ...... CORUNDUM
trousers ...... PAJAMAS, PYJAMAS
weight ..... CATTY, TAEL, ROTL, PICUL
wind .... MONSOON
orientate .... ADJUST, FAMILIARIZE
orientation of sorts .. BRIEFING
orifice ...... PORE, SPIRACLE, STOMA, OPENING, MOUTH, OUTLET, VENT, HOLE, OSTIOLE
oriflamme .... STANDARD, ENSIGN, BANNER
origan .... MARJORAM
Origen, for one .. THEOLOGIAN
origin .... SOURCE, BIRTH, PARENTAGE, ANCESTRY, LINEAGE, SEED, BEGINNING, ROOT, CAUSE, GERM, GENESIS
having single .... MONOGENIC
of the .... GENETIC

original ..... FIRST, EARLIEST, NOVEL, NEW, INITIAL, NATIVE, PRISTINE
native ...... ABORIGINE
sin .... REBELLION
sinner, alleged .... ADAM, EVE
originally .. CHIEFLY, INITIALLY
originate ... CREATE, INVENT, START, BEGIN, (A)RISE
Orinoco River tributary ...... APURE
oriole ...... TROUPIAL, BIRD, LORIOT, HANGBIRD, HANGNEST, GOLDENROBIN
kin of .... STARLING
Orion .... HUNTER, CONSTELLATION
lover/killer of ... DIANA
star ... RIGEL, BETELGEUSE
orison(s) .... PRAYER
Orkney county seat ...... KIRKWALL
fishing waters ..... HAAF
inlet .... VOE
island .... POMONA
Islands channel .... SCAPA FLOW
Orlando .... ROLAND
servant of, in *As You Like It* .... ADAM
orle .... BEARING
Orleans heroine .. JOAN OF ARC
orlon .... FIBER, FABRIC
orlop .... DECK
ormer .... (EAR)SHELL
ormolu .... GOLD MOSAIC, ALLOY
ornament .... ADORN(MENT), DECORATION, SPANGLE, EMBOSS, DECOR(ATE), BEAUTIFY
by engraving .... CHASE
cheap .. GAUD, GEWGAW, BAUBLE, TRINKET
drop-like .... GUTTA
in low relief ... ANAGLYPH
metal .... CHASE, EMBOSS, ETCH, ENGRAVE
perforated ...... PINK
showy ... GAUD, BAUBLE, GEWGAW
with needlework .... EMBROIDER
ornamental ...... DECORATIVE, FANCY

altar cloth ..... DOSSAL, DOSSEL
article, small .... KNICKNACK
band .... SASH
belt .... SASH
border .... DADO
bracket .... CONSOLE
braid .... LACE
button .... STUD
clasp ...... CHATELAINE
collar .... CARCANET
dish .... EPERGNE
garden area ... PARTERRE
lacing .... PICOT
metal foil .... TINSEL
needlework .... EMBROIDERY
plasterwork .... PARGET
ribbon .... SASH
shrub .... HENNA
tuft of cords .... TASSEL
tuft of silk ..... POMPON
upholstery ..... DOSSAL, DOSSEL
vessel .... VASE
ornate .. SHOWY, ELABORATE, BAROQUE, FLAMBOYANT, FLORID, FLOWERY, FANCY, PURPLE, AUREATE
ornery .... OBSTINATE, ORDINARY, STUBBORN, MULISH, TESTY, BASE, QUARRELSOME
person .... CURMUDGEON
ornis .... AVIFAUNA, BIRDS
ornithologist .... AUDUBON
ornithology, subject of .. BIRDS
ornithopod ...... DINOSAUR
ornithorhynchus ... PLATYPUS, DUCKBILL
oro .... GOLD
as combining form ...... MOUNTAIN
de _____ .... PLATA
orogeny, result of .. MOUNTAIN
orographical subject .... MOUNTAINS
oroide .... ALLOY
orology, subject of .... MOUNTAINS
orotund .... RESONANT, BOMBASTIC, POMPOUS, MELLOW, SHOWY
orphan .... WAIF
Jane's family .... EYRIA

orphanage .... ASYLUM
Orpheus, for one .. MUSICIAN
instrument of ..... LYRE
wife of .... EURYDICE
orphic ... OCCULT, ORACULAR, MYSTIC
orpiment .... PIGMENT
orpin(e) .... STONECROP
orra .... ODD, EXTRA
orrery .... PLANETARIUM
sight ...... PLANET, STAR, MOON, COMET
orris, orrice ..... PLANT, IRIS
Orson, actor ..... WELLES
ort ...... CRUMB, FRAGMENT, LEFTOVER, SCRAP, REMNANT
orthodox ... CONVENTIONAL, PROPER
Eastern church diocese .. EPARCHY
opposite of .. HETERODOX
orthoepy .... PHONOLOGY
orthographer .... SPELLER
orthopedist's concern .. BONES
orthopteron .... INSECT, COCKROACH, CRICKET
ortolan ..... BUNTING, SORA, BOBOLINK
oryx .... ANTELOPE, GEMSBOK
os ... BONE, MOUTH, OPENING, ESKER
Osage .... INDIAN, SIOUX
Osaka Bay port .... KOBE
location of ...... HONSHU
Oscar .... STATUETTE, AWARD
sister of ... EMMY, TONY
Osceola's tribe .... SEMINOLE
oscillate ..... VIBRATE, SWING, SWAY, WAVE, LIBRATE, WAG
oscillating device .... ELECTRIC FAN
oscillation transformer .... JIGGER
oscine .... FINCH, LARK, BUNTING, SHRIKE, TANAGER, CROW
oscitancy ... APATHY, STUPOR, DROWSINESS
oscitate .... YAWN, GAPE
osculate ... KISS, TOUCH, BUSS, SMACK
osculation .... KISS(ING), CONTACT
osier ..... SALLOW, WILLOW, DOGWOOD, ROD, WAND
twig .... WITHE

Osiris' brother ...... ISIS, SET
   emblem .... APIS
   husband .... ISIS
   son .... HORUS
Oslo .... CHRISTIANIA
Osman soubriquet ....
              CONQUEROR
   empire founded by ......
              OTTOMAN
Osmanli ..... OTTOMAN, TURK
osmund .... FERN
osprey ..... HAWK, OSSIFRAGE
Ossa's companion .... PELION
osseous .... BONY, OSTEAL
ossicle .... (EAR)BONE
ossifrage ..... OSPREY, HAWK,
          LAMMERGEIER
Ossining institution ....
          SING SING
ossuary .... URN, VAULT
   content of .... BONES
osteal .... BONY, OSSEOUS
ostensible .... SEEMING,
          APPARENT
ostentation .... POMP,
  SHOWINESS, GLOSS, PARADE,
   SPLURGE, EXHIBITION,
          DISPLAY
ostentatious .... SHOWY,
   PRETENTIOUS, ARTY,
          GAUDY
   show ..... POMP, PARADE
osteo: comb. form ... BONE(S)
osteoid .... BONE-LIKE
ostiole .... STOMA, PORE,
   ORIFICE, OPENING
osteoma .... TUMOR
Osterreich .... AUSTRIA
ostiary .... GUARD
ostler .... STABLEMAN
ostracism .. EXILE, EXCLUSION,
        REJECTION
ostracize .... REJECT, BANISH,
  EXCLUDE, BAR, SHUT OUT
ostrich .... RHEA, RATITE,
          NANDU
   bird like ...... EM(E)U,
        CASSOWARY
   kin of .... TINAMOU
Oswego .... TEA
   tea .... MONARDA,
        BEE BALM
Otaheite .... TAHITI
otalgia .... EARACHE
Ot(h)ello ... MOOR, TRAGEDY,
          OPERA

opera composer .. VERDI
   tormentor of ...... IAGO
   wife of ...... DESDEMONA
other ..... ELSE, ADDITIONAL,
         DIFFERENT
   combining form ....
       HETER(O), ALLO
others, and ...... ET AL, REST
otherwise .. ELSE, DIFFERENTLY
Othin .... ODIN
Othman .... OTTOMAN, OSMAN
otic .... AURAL, AUDITORY
otiose .... IDLE, USELESS,
  FUTILE, INDOLENT, VAIN,
         STERILE
Otis ____, Cornelia .. SKINNER
otological subject .... EAR
otologist .... AURIST
   concern of ... EAR(ACHE)
Ottawa .. INDIAN, ALGONQUIN
Ottawan chief ..... PONTIAC
otter .... FUR, MAMMAL,
        BROADTAIL
   genus .... LUTRA
   relative of ..... WEASEL,
       MINK, SKUNK
ottoman .... OTHMAN, TURK,
  POUF, (FOOT)STOOL, SEAT,
   DIVAN, COUCH, FABRIC,
         SILK
   court .... PORTE
   Empire capital ....
      CONSTANTINOPLE
   Empire founder .. OSMAN
   leader .... OSMAN
   non-Moslem ...... RAIA
   official .... PASHA
   standard .... ALEM
   sultan .... SULEIMAN
   Turkish government ....
         PORTE
Ouachita River .... WASHITA
ouananiche .... SALMON
oubliette .... DUNGEON
ouch .... BROOCH,
  EXCLAMATION, BUCKLE,
         CLASP
ought ... ANYTHING, AT ALL,
   CIPHER, NAUGHT, ZERO
oui .... YES
ouija equipment .. PLANCHETTE,
         BOARD
   user of .... SPIRITUALIST
ounce ..... (SNOW) LEOPARD,
       WEIGHT, ONS
ouphe .... ELF, GOBLIN

Our Lady .... MARY, NOTRE DAME
ourari .... CURARE
oust .... EXPEL, EJECT, EVICT, DISPOSSESS, FORCE OUT, BOUNCE
ouster ... EVICTOR, DISMISSAL
out ..... EXTERNAL, BEGONE, NOT IN, NOT AT HOME, AWAY
    and-out .... ARRANT, COMPLETE, RANK, CONFIRMED, UTTER, SHEER
    of bed .... UP
    of .... BEYOND
    of date .... DEMODE
    of gear .... CRANKY
    of place .... INEPT
    of practice ...... RUSTY
    of sight .... PERDU(E)
    of sort .... MOODY, INDISPOSED
    of-the-way ... SECLUDED, REMOTE
    of-town play opening ... PREVIEW
    slang .... EXCUSE
    way ...... EXIT, EGRESS
outage .... INTERRUPTION
outbreak .... ERUPTION, OCCURRENCE, RIOT, RASH
outbreeding .... EXOGAMY
outbuilding .... GARAGE, BARN, SHED
outburst ... STORM, TANTRUM, ERUPTION, FLAREUP, GUST
outcast ...... PARIAH, LEPER, WRETCH, EXILE
    Biblical .... HAGAR, ISHMAEL(ITE)
outclass .... BEST, EXCEL, SURPASS
outcry .... SHOUT
outcome .... RESULT, UPSHOT, AFTERMATH, ISSUE, CONSEQUENCE, EFFECT
outcropping .... BASSET
outcry .... PROTEST, OBJECTION, CLAMOR, DIRDUM
outdated .... PASSE
outdo .... EXCEL, SURPASS, EXCEED
outdoor .... OPEN-AIR, ALFRESCO, ABROAD

bench .... EXEDRA
party ...... PICNIC, FETE
set .... LOCATION
stairs .... PERRON
theatre/restaurant ...... DRIVE-IN
time .... SUMMER
outer ..... EXTERNAL, ECTAL, EXTERIOR
    covering ... TESTA, SKIN, COAT, HUSK, SHELL, CRUST, RIND, WRAP, COCOON
    edge .... RIM, LIP
    garment .... DOLMAN, KIMONO, SURTOUT, PALETOT, ROBE, (OVER)COAT, WRAP
    layer of cells .. ECTODERM
Mongolia, capital of .... ULAN BATOR, URGA
    space explorer .... ASTRONAUT, COSMONAUT
outfit .... SUIT, GARB, TURN-OUT, CAPARISON, RIG, GEAR, PARAPHERNALIA, GETUP, EQUIP(MENT), ORGANIZATION
    bride's .... TROUSSEAU
    to .... ACCOUTER, ACCOUTRE
outflank ... OUTWIT, THWART
outflow .... EFFLUX
outgo .... EXPENDITURE
outgoing .... GREGARIOUS, SOCIABLE
outgrowth .... RESULT, OFFSHOOT
outhouse .... PRIVY
outing ... AIRING, CLAMBAKE, TRIP, PICNIC, EXCURSION
outlander .... ALIEN, FOREIGNER, STRANGER
outlandish .. STRANGE, ALIEN, ABSURD, PECULIAR, BIZARRE, FANTASTIC
outlaw ... FUGITIVE, CRIMINAL, BRIGAND, PROSCRIBE, BANDIT, DESPERADO, HIGHWAYMAN, BAN, PRESCRIBE
outlay ...... APPROPRIATION, FUND

outlet ... EXIT, VENT, PASSAGE, MARKET, AGENCY

outline ... SCHEMA, DELINEATE, SKETCH, DRAW, ADUMBRATE, SUMMARY, RUN-DOWN

outlive ..... SURVIVE, OUTLAST

outlook .. VISTA, VIEW(POINT), PROSPECT; EXPECTATION

outlying .... REMOTE, OFF-CENTER

   district .... SUBURB, PURLIEU

outmoded .... PASSE, OBSOLETE, DESUETE

outplay .... BEST, DEFEAT

outpost guard .... PICKET

outpour ..... RAIN, TORRENT

outpouring ... SPATE, TORRENT

output .... YIELD, PRODUCT(ION)

outrage ..... OFFENSE, INSULT, OFFEND, SCANDAL, ATROCITY

outrageous ...... ATROCIOUS, HEINOUS, FLAGRANT, DAMNED, MONSTROUS

outre ... BIZARRE, ECCENTRIC

outrigger ..... PROA, CANOE, PRAO, PRAU

outright ..... TOTAL, WHOLE, OPENLY, AT ONCE, COMPLETE

outrival .... ECLIPSE, SURPASS, EXCEL

outset ..... START, BEGINNING

outshine ..... EXCEL, ECLIPSE

outside: prefix .... ECTO

outsider ... ALIEN, STRANGER, NON-MEMBER

outsize .... LARGE

outskirts .... SUBURBS

outsmart .... OUTWIT

outspoken ... BLUNT, FRANK, OPEN, CANDID, ARTICULATE

outspread ... EXTEND, EXPAND

outstand .... SAIL

outstanding .... PROMINENT, UNPAID, UNSETTLED, NOTABLE, (E)SPECIAL, EXCEPTIONAL

outstrip .... BEST, EXCEL, SURPASS

outward ...... OUTER, VISIBLE, EXTERIOR, ECTAD

outwit ... OUTSMART, EUCHRE, FOIL, OVERCOME

outwork ... TRENCH, RAVELIN, FORTIFICATION, TENAIL(LE)

   between bastions .... TENAIL(LE)

ouzel ... BLACKBIRD, THRUSH

   water .... PIET

ova .... EGGS

oval .... EGG-SHAPED, ELLIPSOIDAL, ELLIPTIC(AL)

   figure .... ELLIPSE

ovary .... GONAD

   wall .... PERICARP, EPICARP, ENDOCARP, MESOCARP

ovate .... EGG-SHAPED

ovation ... APPLAUSE, PLAUDIT

oven ... OAST, KILN, FURNACE, LEER, MUFFLE

   part of .... BROILER

   portable .... BAKER

over ..... ABOVE, ATOP, UPON, MORE THAN, SURPLUS, FINISHED, ENDED, BEYOND, AGAIN, ACROSS

a _____ .... BARREL

again ... ENCORE, ANEW

combining form ... SUR, SUPRA, SUPER, HYPER

expose film ... SOLARIZE

nice .... FINICAL

the hill: colloq. ... AWOL

there: poetic .. YON(DER)

overabundance .... PLETHORA

overact .... EMOTE, HAM(FAT)

overacting .... HISTRIONIC

overadorned .... ORNATE

overage ..... SURPLUS, EXCESS

overall(s) .... SMOCK, DUNGAREES, LEVIS, JEANS

   shirtlike .... FROCK

overawe ...... COW, SUBDUE, OVERCOME, DAUNT, BUFFALO

overbearing ...... ARROGANT, PROUD, CAVALIER, DOMINEERING, IMPERIOUS

overbold ..... RASH, RECKLESS

overcast .. LOWERING, CLOUDY, DARK, SEW

overcharge .. GOUGE, HOLD UP

overcoat .... PALETOT, INVERNESS, BENNY, ULSTER, SURTOUT, RAGLAN, CAPOTE

   double-breasted .... REDINGOTE

   loose .... BALMACAAN

overcome .. SUBDUE, CONQUER, MASTER, OVERWHELM, WIN, BEST, SURMOUNT, DEFEAT, BEAT

overconfident ...... COCKSURE

overcrowd .... CONGEST

overdue .... LATE, TARDY, BELATED

   instalment ...... ARREAR

overfeed ..... GLUT, SURFEIT, SATIATE, GORGE, PAMPER, BATTEN

overfed .... GROSS

overflow ...... SPILL, FLOOD, RUN OVER, SPATE, DELUGE

overflowing ...... INUNDANT

   with good spirits .... EXUBERANT

overhang ...... PROJECT, JUT, BEETLE

overhanging part of roof ...... EAVES

overhaul .... REPAIR, GAIN ON, OVERTAKE

overhead .... UPKEEP, ALOFT, COSTS, ABOVE

   conveyor's car ..... TRAM

   item .... RENT

overheat .... PARBOIL

overindulge ... SURFEIT, SATE, GLUT

overindulgence .... EXCESS

overjoy ...... ELATE, DELIGHT

overlap ...... EXTEND(OVER), IMBRICATE

overlapping ...... IMBRICATE, EQUITANT

overlay ...... CEIL, COVERING, PAVE

overleap ... PASS OVER, OMIT, SKIP

overlook ... IGNORE, NEGLECT, CONDONE, MISS, PRETERMIT

overlord .... LIEGE, BAN

overly .... TOO MUCH, EXCESSIVELY, INORDINATELY

overman ... LEADER, REFEREE, ARBITRATOR, ARBITER

overmatch ... CRUSH, EXCEED, SURPASS

overnice .... PRECISE, FASTIDIOUS, FINICKY

overpass ...... BRIDGE, SPAN, EXCEED

overpower .... BEAT, MASTER, SUBDUE, CONQUER, CONTROL

   with light .... DAZZLE

overproud .... LOFTY

override .... NULLIFY, DISREGARD

overrule ... SET ASIDE, ANNUL, COUNTERMAND

overrun ...... INFEST, SWARM

overseas .... ABROAD, FOREIGN

oversee ...... WATCH, STEER, SUPERVISE, SUPERINTEND, SURVEY

overseer .... SUPERVISOR, TASKMASTER, REEVE, BAILIFF, BOSS, STEWARD, LEGREE

overshadow ... OBSCURE, DIM, ECLIPSE, DOMINATE

overshoe ... SANDAL, PATTEN, ZIPPER, ARCTIC, GALOSH(E), GOLOSH(E), RUBBERS

overshoes, rubber ...... GUMS

overshoot .... EXCEED

oversight ... LAPSE, SLIP(UP), MISTAKE

oversize .... LARGE, HUGE

overspend .... EXHAUST

overstate .... EXAGGERATE

overstrung ... TENSE, JITTERY, TAUT

overt .... OPEN, PUBLIC, OBSERVABLE

overtake .... CATCH UP, OVERHAUL

overthrow .... UPSET, OVERCOME, CONQUER, DEPOSE, DOWN, WORST, END, RUIN, TOPPLE, UNSEAT

overtones ..... IMPLICATIONS, SUGGESTIONS

overtop ..... EXCEL, SURPASS, TOWER

overtrained .... STALE

overture .... OFFER, PROPOSAL, PRELUDE

overturn ..... UPSET, CAPSIZE, TIP OVER

overweening ...... CONCEITED, ARROGANT

overwhelm ....CRUSH, DEFEAT, SWAMP, DELUGE

overwhelming desire ... ESTRUS

overwrought ...... FATIGUED, NERVOUS, EXCITED, ORNATE, ELABORATE

Ovid .... NASO
  work of ....
    METAMORPHOSES,
    ART OF LOVE
oviform .. EGG-SHAPED, OVOID,
    OVATE
ovine .... SHEEP(LIKE)
ovisac .... OOTHECA
ovoid ... EGG-SHAPED, OVATE,
    OVIFORM
ovolo ...... THUMB, MOLDING
ovule .... EGG, EMBRYO, SEED
  center of ...... NUCELLUS
  covering .... PRIMINE
  inner coat ... SECUNDINE
  stalk .... FUNICULUS
ovum .... EGG
  content .... YOLK
owed as a debt .... DUE
owing .... UNPAID, DUE
owl .... MOMO, RURU, BIRD,
    UTUM
  barn .... MADGE
  horned .... BUBO
  leg feathers ...... FLAG
  nocturnal ...... KAKAPO
  sound .... HOOT,
    ULULATION, WHOOP
  young .... OWLET
owlish appearance .... SOLEMN
own ... POSSESS, HOLD, HAVE,
  CONFESS, ADMIT, RECOGNIZE
owner .... PROPRIETOR,
  TITLEHOLDER, POSSESSOR
ownership .. TITLE, POSSESSION
  yield .... CEDE
ox .... BEEF, BULL(OCK),
  BOVINE, ANOA, STEER,
  BUFFALO, BANTENG
  Bunyan's .... BABE
  castrated ...... BULLOCK
  command to .. HAW, GEE
  disease .... GRAPE
  extinct ... URUS, AUROCHS
  eye .... DAISY
  eyed goddess ...... HERA
  hide thong.... RIEM, REIM
  hornless ...... POLLARD
  joint .... HOUGH
  like .... BOVINE
  like animal ...... ZEBU
  meat, sun-dried ....
    BILTONG
  Paul Bunyan's ..... BABE
  stomach .... TRIPE
  tuberculosis .... GRAPE

  wagon journey ..... TREK
  wild ... YAK, URUS, GAUR,
  GAYAL, REEM, ANOA,
  BUFFALO, AUROCHS,
    BISON
  young ..... STEER, STIRK
oxalis .... OCA
oxen .... KINE, NOWT
  stall .... CRIB
oxeye .. PLANT, DAISY, DUNLIN
oxeyed goddess .... HERA
oxford ...... SHOE, COTTON,
    BROGAN
  bell .... GREAT TOM
  fellow .... DON
  grad .... AUNT
  movement .. BUCHMANISM
  movement leader ....
    BUCHMAN, KEBLE
  officer .... BEDEL(L),
    BEADLE
  scholar ..... DEMY, DON
  University fine SCONCE
  University Day ....
    ENCAENIA
  University student ......
    OXONIAN
oxheart ... CHERRY, CABBAGE
oxide .... CALX
  cobalt .... AFFERZ
  lead .... MASSICOT,
    LITHARGE
oxidize .... CALCINE, RUST
oxlip ..... PRIMROSE, PLANT,
    FIVE-FINGER
oxpecker .... STARLING
oxter .... ARMPIT
oxtongue ... BUGLOSS, PLANT
oxygen, allotropic form ......
    OZONE
  compound ...... OXIDE
  lack .... ANOXIA
  liquid .... LOX
oxygenate .... OXIDIZE,
    AERATE
oyez ... HEAR(YE), ATTENTION
oyster ... BIVALVE, MOLLUSK,
  SCALLOP, BLUEPOINT
  bed .... LAYER
  bed material .... CUTCH,
    CULCH
  delicacy .... STEW
  fish .... TAUTOG
  gatherer ..... TONGMAN
  grounds .... BED
  joint .... HINGE

killing snail ...... DRILL
plant .... SALSIFY,
 LUNGWORT
product .... PEARL,
 NACRE
root .... SALSIFY
shell .... SHUCK, TEST
spawn ... SPAT, CULTCH

species ...... MOLLUSCA
 tank of .... STEW
 young .... SPAT
Oz, creator of .... BAUM
ozocerite ..... WAX, MALTHA
ozone .... AIR, OXYGEN,
 BLUE GAS
ozoniferous substance .. ETHER

P

P, Greek .... PI, RHO
 Hebrew .... PEH
 letter .... PEE
 38 .... (WAR)PLANE,
 LIGHTNING
pa .... FATHER
pabulum .. FOOD, SUSTENANCE
paca .... AGOUTI, CAVY,
 RODENT
pace ... STRIDE, RATE, SPEED,
 WALK, TEMPO, GAIT, STEP
 kind of ...... LOPE, TROT,
 AMBLE, RUN, SPRINT
 setter .... LEADER
Pacelli, Eugenio ... PIUS, POPE
pachyderm ...... ELEPHANT,
 RHINO(CEROS),
 HIPPO(POTAMUS)
 trap for .... KEDDAH,
 KHEDAH
Pacific .... OCEAN, CALM,
 TRANQUIL, PEACEFUL,
 IRENIC
 archipelago .... SULU
 coast evergreen ....
 REDWOOD, SEQUOIA,
 MADRONA
 discoverer ...... BALBOA
 island .... PALMYRA, YAP,
 TUTUILA, OAHU, TAHITI
 island group ..... SAMOA,
 SOLOMON, CAROLINE,
 PALAU, PELEW,
 HAWAII, RYUKYU,
 SAIPAN, PALAU,
 TUAMOTU,
 PAUMOTO OCEANIA,
 OCEANICA, MICRONESIA
 island tree .... LEHUA
 shrub .... SALAL
pacifier .... NIPPLE, SOP,
 (TEETHING) RING, APPEASER
pacifist: colloq. .... DOVE
pacify .... PLACATE, MOLLIFY,
 APPEASE, ALLAY,

 CONCILIATE, SOOTHE
pack .... STOW, WAD, GANG,
 TRUSS, LOAD, (EM)BALE,
 CRAM, BUNDLE, PRESS,
 SEND OFF, CROWD, MASS,
 BURDEN, GROUP,
COLLECTION, FARDEL, TAMP
 animal ...... MULE, ASS,
 BURRO, DONKEY, CAMEL,
 SUMPTER, LLAMA
 animal cover ..... MANTA
 animal basket ... DOSSER,
 PANNIER
 animal belly band ....
 GIRTH
 dishonestly ..... DEACON
 girth .... CINCH
 horse .... SUMPTER,
 DRUDGE
 mule .... SUMPTER
 of ___ .... LIES
 of cards .... DECK
 of dogs ...... CANAILLE,
 KENNEL
package .. PARCEL, BALE, BOX,
 CASE, CEROON, WRAP,
 BUNDLE, CARTON
packed tightly .... DENSE
packer .... CANNER
packet .... PARCEL, BOAT
 boat .... PAQUEBOAT
packing .... CANNING
 box .... CRATE
 house .... CANNERY
 material .. OAKUM, LUTE
packman .... PEDDLER
packsack .... KYACK
packsaddle .... APAREJO
pact ...... AGREEMENT, MISE,
 COVENANT, TREATY,
 COMPACT
 Atlantic .... NATO
pad .... MAT, TABLET, WALK,
 HIGHWAYMAN, ROAD, WAY,
 PATH, PILLOW, SADDLE,

CUSHION, FOOT(PRINT),
      STUFF
for dabbing powder ..... PUFF
gauze .... SPONGE
hippie's .. BED, APARTMENT
ink .... DABBER
medicated cloth ....
      COMPRESS
of hay .... WASE
silk .... VELURE
slang ... BED, APARTMENT
with powder ..... SACHET
padded cell inmate .. PRISONER,
      MADMAN
padding ...... COTTON, WAD,
  KAPOK, DOWN, FELT, STRAW
hair .... RAT
paddle .... ROW, PROPEL,
  SPANK, SPOON, BAT,
 TODDLE, WADE, SCULL, OAR
pingpong .. BAT, RACKET
paddlefish .... SPOONBILL,
      GANOID
paddock .. PARK, FIELD, TOAD,
      FROG
paddy .... IRISH(MAN),
     RICE(FIELD)
wagon ... BLACK MARIA
paddywack ... RAGE, BEATING
Paderewski .... PIANIST,
      IGNACE
padishah ..... EMPEROR, KING,
      SULTAN
padlock .... CLOSE
padnag .... HORSE
Padova .... PADUA
padre ...... FATHER, PRIEST,
     CHAPLAIN
padrone ... MASTER, PATRON,
     INNKEEPER
Padua .... PADOVA
Padus .... PO(RIVER)
paean .... HYMN, SONG
Paestum .... PESTO
pagan ... ETHNIC, IDOLATOR,
 PAYNIM, INFIDEL, HEATHEN,
   GENTILE, NON-MOSLEM
Paganini, violinist .... NICOLO
page ... LEAF, FOLIO, EPISODE,
  RECORD, (FOOT)BOY,
 HENCHMAN, ATTENDANT,
  SERVANT, SUMMON
boy .... BUTTONS
left hand .... VERSO
ledger .... FOLIO

lineson .... LINAGE
number .... FOLIO
ornamental design .....
      VIGNETTE
person served by ....
    KNIGHT, NOBLE
place of employment ....
   HOTEL, CONGRESS
right hand ...... RECTO
singer .... PATTI
size .... OCTAVO
slang .... BUTTONS
title .... RUBRIC
pageant ... EXHIBITION, POMP,
 SHOW, SPECTACLE, PARADE
pageantry .. SHOW, SPECTACLE,
      DISPLAY
pages .... RECORD
of history ...... ANNALS,
     CHRONICLES
set of 24 .... QUIRE
Paget, actress .... DEBRA
Pagliacci character, NEDDA,
 TONIO, CANIO, BEPPO, SILVIO
word .... RIDI
Pago Pago is in ...... SAMOA,
     TUTUILA
pagoda .... TAA, TEMPLE
pagurian ...... CRUSTACEAN,
 (HERMIT)CRAB, PAGURID
pah ..... EXCLAMATION, TUT,
      POOH
paid .... SETTLED, DISBURSED,
    DISCHARGED
pail .. BUCKET, PIGGIN, SKEEL,
  CANNIKIN, STOUP
paillasse .... MATTRESS
paillette .... SPANGLE
pain ...... DISTRESS, ACHE,
 THROE, AIL, PANG, PENALTY,
    HURT, AGONY
abdominal .... COLIC
in the side .... STITCH
minor .... FLEABITE
sharp ..... TWINGE, ACHE
pained ...... OFFENDED, HURT
painful ...... SORE, IRKSOME,
    ACHY, BITTER
painkiller .... TONIC, OPIATE,
 NARCOTIC, DEMEROL,
 SEDATIVE, ANALGESIC,
 ANODYNE, ANESTHESIA,
    PAREGORIC
pains, great ... CARE, EFFORT
partner of .... ACHES

painstaking ..... ELABORATE, DILIGENT, CAREFUL

paint ..... ADORN, LIPSTICK, ROUGE, PIGMENT, DAUB, LIMN, FUCUS, STAIN, DEPICT, PORTRAY, COLOR, PICTURE, STIPPLE
  badly .... DAUB
  by machine ...... SPRAY
  drier .... JAPAN
  face ... ROUGE, COSMETIC, FARD
  finishing oil ...... TUNG
  first coat of .... PRIMING, BASE
  grinder .... MULLER
  ingredient ...... BARITE, TUNG
  in dots .... STIPPLE
  laid on thickly ∴ IMPASTO
  remover ...... ACETONE
  spreader .... SPATULA
  wall .... PARGET

painted bunting .. NONPAREIL

painter .... STIPPLER, ARTIST, COUGAR, PANTHER, DALI, DEGAS, CEZANNE, VAN GOGH, MONET, PICASSO, TITIAN, RUBENS, GOYA, MIRO, REMBRANDT
  designating one .. SUNDAY
  handrest of .. MAULSTICK
  mediocre .... DAUBER
  of animals ... BONHEUR, LANDSEER
  of presidents ... STUART

painting .... CANVAS, OIL, IMPASTO, PORTRAIT, LANDSCAPE,
  board .... PALETTE, PALLET
  cult .... DADA(ISM)
  frame .... EASEL
  genre .... ABSTRACT, CUBISTIC, ORIENTAL, SURREALISTIC
  material .. DYE, PIGMENT, COSMETIC, ROUGE, CANVAS
  medium .... OIL, PASTE, WATER COLOR
  night scene ... NOCTURNE
  on a board .... PANEL
  on ceiling .... MURAL
  plaster ... FRESCO, SECCO
  small .... MINIATURE
  stand .... EASEL
  style ... GENRE, CLASSIC, DADAIST, ABSTRACT, GRISAILLE, GROTESQUE
  technique ..... TEMPERA, IMPASTO, SECCO, FRESCO
  tool .... BRUSH, ROLLER, SPRAY GUN
  wall .... MURAL
  water color .. AQUARELLE

paintings, collection of .... GALLERY

pair ... SPAN, BRACE, COUPLE, MATE, YOKE, TEAM, DUO, DUET, DUAD, DYAD
  of harnessed animals .... YOKE
  one of a ... MATE, MATCH

paired ..... TEAMED, COUPLED, MATED, GEMEL, JUGATE, MATCHED

paisley .... SHAWL

Paiute .... INDIAN

pajamas .... TROUSERS

Pakistan capital .... ISLAMABAD RAWALPINDI, ISLAMABAD
  capital (East) .... DACCA
  capital (West) ... LAHORE
  city .... KARACHI, MULTAN, LAHORE, DACCA, SIALKOT, HYDERABAD, PESHAWAR
  disputed territory .... KASHMIR
  district .... SWAT
  language ..... BENGALI, PUNJABI, URDU, HINDI
  native ... SIKH, PATHAN, BENGALI
  president .. AYUB, MIRZA, JINNAH
  province .. PUNJAB, SIND
  river ... CHENAB, SUTLEJ

Pakistani .... PATHAN
  U.N. president ... SHAHI

pal .... CULLY, HOBNOB

palace ...... COURT, VATICAN, MALACANANG, TUILERIES, SERAGLIO, EL PARDO, BUCKINGHAM
  of a .... PALATIAL, PALATINATE
  resident .. EMPEROR, KING, BISHOP, QUEEN, PRINCE(SS)

paladin .... PEER, KNIGHT, CHAMPION
paladins, Charlemagne's 12 ... DOUZEPERS
palaestra .... GYMNASIUM
pupil .... WRESTLER
palanquin ..... LITTER, JAUN, DOOLEE, KAGO
bearer .... SIRDAR, HAMA(U)L
palatable .... TASTY, FLAVORFUL, SAVORY, TOOTHSOME, SAPID, AGREEABLE
palatalized, in phonetics ...... MOUILLE
palate .... TASTE, LIKING, VELUM, UVULA
covering .... VELUM
palatial .... STATELY
Palatinate .... PFALZ
palatine .... CAPE, ROYAL
Palau Islands .... BELEW
palaver .... TALK, PARLEY, CHAT, CAJOLERY, WHEEDLE, FLATTER(Y), CONFERENCE, CHATTER
pale ... WAN, PALLID, FAINT, FEEBLE, STAKE, PICKET, FENCE, WHITE, BLANCH, SALLOW, ASHEN, LIVID, DIM, ORDINARY
face .... AMERICAN, WHITE MAN
yellow .... FLAXEN
palea .... DEWLAP, FOLD, BRACT, SCALE
paleface .... AMERICAN, WHITE(MAN)
paleness .... PALLOR
Paleolithic Age division ...... CHELLEAN
Palermo is in ____ .... SICILY
Palestine .... CANAAN, HOLY LAND, ISRAEL
animal .... DAMAN
capital .... JERUSALEM
city .... HAIFA, ACRE, SAMARIA, CANA, CAPERNAUM, MEGIDDO, GAZA, HEBRON
coin .... MIL
district ...... DECAPOLIS
division .... PERAEA, GALILEE, GILEAD
guerrilla ..... FEDAYEEN

guerrilla leader .. ARAFAT
guerrilla outfit ....
EL FATAH, AL FATEH
inhabitants .... JEWS
kingdom ...... SAMARIA
mountain ...... GILEAD, NEBO, CARMEL, EBAL
plain .... SHARON
port ...... ACRE, JAFFA, HAIFA
tiger cub .... ASHBAL
town ...... SILOH, CANA
tribesman ..... ADANITE
village .... BETHEL
palestra .. SCHOOL, GYMNASIUM
trainee .... WRESTLER
paletot ... JACKET, OVERCOAT, GREATCOAT
palette .... BOARD, COLORS
knife .... SPATULA
palfrey .... (SADDLE)HORSE
palimpsest .... TABLET, PARCHMENT
paling .... FENCING
palinode ... POEM, RETRACTION
palisade .... FENCE BAIL, ESPALIER
composition of ... STAKES
pall ... SATE, SATIATE, CLOAK, CLOY, WEARY, DISGUST, BORE, COVERING
Palladium of Rome ... ANCILE
Pallas ..... ATHENA, ASTEROID
statue .... PALLADIUM
pallbearer .... MOURNER
concern of ...... COFFIN
pallet ... BED, PATE, PALETTE, PLATFORM, PAWL, CLICK, MATTRESS
palliate .. ALLEVIATE, SOOTHE, EXCUSE, TEMPER, SALVE, EASE, EXTENUATE, MITIGATE
palliative .... BROMIDE, SEDATIVE, OPIATE
pallid ..... PALE, WAN, FAINT, SALLOW
pallium ... MANTLE, HIMATION
pallor .... PALENESS
palm ...... SAGO, NIPA, TREE, GOMUTI, TALIPOT, GRIGRI, ENG, ASSAI, COHUNE, PRIZE, VICTORY, TRIUMPH, COCO, NIKAU, COQUITO, JARA
African .... D(O)UM
Asiatic .. NIPA, PALMYRA, BETEL, CALAMI

betel ..... ARECA, BONGA
Brazilian .... ASSAI,
     BABASSU, JUPATI,
     CARNAUBA
bud .... CABBAGE
cabbage ...... PALMETTO
climbing .... RATTAN
cockatoo .... ARARA
coconut .... NIOG
crease .... LINE
drink ...... ASSAI, TUBA,
     NIPA, TODDY
fiber ...... GOMUTI, DOH,
     DATIL, BURI, RAFFIA
fruit .... DATE, DOUM,
     SASA, COCONUT
grease the .... BRIBE
leaf ... FROND, OLA, PAN,
     ATAP, NIPA
leaf fan .... TALIPOT,
     PUNKA(H)
leaf mat ... PETATE, YAPA
leaf's symbol ... VICTORY,
     TRIUMPH
leaves, plaited ... SENNIT
like plant .. CYCAD, ZAMIA
lily .... TI
liquor ..... TODDY, NIPA,
     BINO
Madagascar ..... RAFFIA
Malayan .... ARENG,
     GOMUTI
muscle ..... LUMBRICALIS
nipa .... AT(T)AP
nut .... COCO
of the hand ..... THENAR
of the hand's ..... VOLAR
off .... FOIST, FOB
palmyra .... TAL
pest .... GRUGRU
pith product ...... SAGO
plant resembling .. CYCAD
raised part of ... MOUNT
reader .... PALMIST,
     CHIROMANCER
sago .... GOMUTI, ARENG
sap liquor .. NIPA, TODDY
sap sugar ..... JAGGERY
shrub like .... ZAMIA
starch .... SAGO
stem ... CANE, RAT(T)AN,
     CAUDEX
stroke on the .... PANDY
sugar .... JAGGERY
tree .... PALMETTO,
     PALMYRA, DATE,

TODDY, SAGO, RAFFIA,
     ARENG, GRIGRI,
     TALIPOT, ROYAL,
     DOUM, CALAMUS
tree bud .... CABBAGE
wax .... CARNAUBA
wine ..... TUBA, TODDY,
     GOMUTI, TAREE
Palma, capital of ....
     SANTA CRUZ
palmate .... WEB-FOOTED
palmer .... PILGRIM
palmetto .... SABAL, SERENOA
palmistry ...... CHIROMANCY
Palmyra .... TADMOR
leaf .... TAL, OLA(Y)
leaf fan ...... PUNKA(H)
queen of .... ZENOBIA
palomino ..... HORSE, EQUINE
palp(us) .... FEELER, ANTENNA
palpable .... TANGIBLE,
     EVIDENT, OBVIOUS,
     MANIFEST
palpitate .... QUIVER, THROB,
     TREMBLE, FLUTTER, BEAT
palpitation .... THROB,
     SALTATION, BEATING
palpus ..... FEELER, ANTENNA
palsgrave .... COUNT
palsied .... PARALYZED,
     SHAKING
palsy ... PARALYSIS, PARALYZE
palter ... TRIFLE, QUIBBLE, LIE
paltry ... TRIVIAL, PICAYUNE,
     TRIFLING, PETTY, MEAN,
     SMALL
paludal .... MARSHY, BOGGY,
     SWAMPY, MALARIAL
paludism .... MALARIA
pam .... JACK, GAME
game like .... NAPOLEON
Pamir .... GALCHA
pampas .... PLAIN
country of ... ARGENTINA
native .... GAUCHO
weapon .... BOLAS
pampean .... INDIAN
pamper ..... COSHER, CODDLE,
     GRATIFY, FONDLE, PET,
     HUMOR, COSSET, SPOIL,
     GLUT, INDULGE
pampered .... SPOONFED
pampero .... WIND
pamphlet ... TRACT, FLYSHEET,
     TREATISE, BROCHURE
of poems .... CHAPBOOK

unstitched ..... FOLDER
Pamplona animal ...... TORO
Pan ...... FAUNUS, SKILLET,
 DISH, GOD, GRIDDLE,
 ROTATE, (ICE)FLOE
 concern of .. SHEPHERDS,
  FLOCKS
 oil .... SUMP
 out .... TRANSPIRE
 slang .... FACE,
  CRITICIZE, RIB, ROAST
 small .... PANNIKIN,
  PATELLA
 warming .. CALEFACTORY
 with perforated bottom ..
  COLANDER
panacea .... CURE-ALL,
 REMEDY, NOSTRUM, ELIXIR,
 CATHOLICON, MEDICINE,
  CURE
panache .... PLUME,
 FLAMBOYANCE, APLOMB
Panama ... HAT, CANAL, GULF,
 ISTHMUS, DARIEN
 Canal locks ..... GATUN,
  MIRAFLORES
 city ..... COLON, ANCON
 coin .... BALBOA
 explorer of ...... BALBOA
 hat material ... JIPIJAPA
 monetary unit ... BALBOA
 port .... COLON
 president .... ROBLES
 river .... CHAGRES
 town .... GATUN
 tree ...... COPA, CATIVO
Panamanian jockey ... ICAZA
panatella .... CIGAR
Panay city .... ILOILO
pancake .... SLAPJACK,
 FLAPJACK, FRITTER
 mix .... BATTER
 Tuesday ..... MARDIGRAS
 turner .... SPATULA
pancreas .... GLAND,
 SWEETBREAD
pancreatic enzyme .. AMYLASE,
 STEAPSIN
 secretion .... INSULIN
panda .... BEARCAT, WAH
 animal resembling the ...
  RACCOON
pandanus ... SCREW PINE, TREE
pandects .... LEGAL CODE
pandemic .... GENERAL,
 PREVALENT

pandemonium ... HELL, CHAOS,
 DISORDER, CONFUSION
 dweller of .... DEMON
pander .... PIMP, CATER,
 PROCURER
Pandora .... BANDORE
pandour .... SOLDIER
pandowdy .... APPLE PIE,
 PUDDING
pane, glass .... QUARREL
 round .... ROUNDEL
panegyric .... ELOGE,
 ENCOMIUM, PRAISE, EULOGY,
 TRIBUTE, LAUDATION
panegyrist ...... ENCOMIAST,
 EULOGIST
panel ...... SADDLE, VENIRE,
 JURY, JURORS
 sunken .... COFFER
panelist .... JUROR
panes, frame for .... SASH
panetella .... CIGAR
pang .... DOLOR, THROE,
 TWINGE, PAIN, AGONY,
  ACHE
pangolin ... ANTEATER, MANIS
pangs of childbirth ... THROES
panhandle .... BEG
panhandler .... BEGGAR
panic ... FEAR, SCARE, FUNK,
 TERROR, GRASS, MILLET,
  BUTTON
 result of ...... STAMPEDE,
  HYSTERICS
 slang .... DELIGHT
panicle ..... RACEME, CLUSTER
pannier ..... BASKET, DOSSER
panocha ..... CANDY, SUGAR
panoply .... ARRAY
 panorama .... VISTA,
  VIEW
Panpipe .... SYRINX
pansy ... VIOLA, HEARTSEASE,
 PENSE
 slang .... QUEER
pant .... GASP, THROB,
 PULSATE, PUFF, HEAVE,
  HUFF
Pantagruel .... GIANT
 companion of .. PANURGE
 father of ... GARGANTUA
pantalets .... DRAWERS
pantaloons .... TROUSERS
Pantelleria .... COSYRA
pantheon ..... TEMPLE, TOMB
panther ... COUGAR, LEOPARD,

JAGUAR, PARD, PUMA, PAINTER

panties .... DRAWERS, UNDERPANTS

raid for example .. PRANK

panting .... GASPING, HYPERPNEA, PUFFY

pantofle .... SLIPPER

pantomime .... MIMIST

game .... CHARADE

pantry .. BUTTERY, CUPBOARD, EWERY, AMBRY, CLOSET, SPENCE, SPENSE, LARDER

shelf item ... TEA CADDY

pants ... TROUSERS, DRAWERS, SLACKS

baby's .... SOAKERS

work .... LEVIS

pantywaist .... SISSY, WEAKLING

Panza, Don Quixote's squire .. SANCHO

panzer .... ARMORED

pap ..... NIPPLE, TEAT, MASH, PULP

papa ..... PAW, POP, FATHER, DAD(DY), PA

papain .... ENZYME

papal (see Pope) ... APOSTOLIC

ambassador ... NUNCIO, LEGATE

authority .... TIARA

bodyguards ...... SWISS

book of decrees .... DECRETALE

cape .... ORALE, FANO(N), FANUM, FANNEL, MOZ(Z)ETTA

chamberlain .... CAMERLINGO

Court .... CURIA, SEE

decree .... DECRETAL, BULL, RESCRIPT

envoy .... LEGATE

envoy, special .... ABLEGATE

letter .. ENCYCLICAL, BRIEF, BULL(A), BREVE, TOME

order .... RESCRIPT

palace .... VATICAN

rescript ...... MANDATE

scarf veil .... FANO(N), ORALE, FANNEL, FANUM

seal .... BULI(A)

skullcap ..... ZUCCHETTO

papaveraceous plant ... POPPY

papaverine .... OPIATE

papaw .... PAPAYA

papaya .... PA(W)PAW

enzyme .... PAPAIN

Papeete's location .... TAHITI

paper .... ESSAY, WRITING, TREATISE, MONOGRAPH, WRAPPER, PASS, DAILY, SHEET, PELURE, CASSE, PAPIER, TAPA, THESIS, TRACT

ancient .... PAPYRUS

box for .... PAPETERIE

candy holder ... CORNET

cutter .... SLITTER, GUILLOTINE

damaged .... CASSE, RETREE

drawing .... ATLAS

fastener ... STAPLER, CLIP

filler .... KAOLIN(E)

for curling hair .... PAPILLOTE

gummed .... PASTER

hanging .... COLLAGE

holder .... FOLDER

kind of .... PAPYRUS, BOND, LINEN, FOOLSCAP, MANILA, TISSUE, CREPE

making material ... PULP, CELLULOSE, ESPARTO

match .... SPILL

measure ... REAM, QUIRE

money ..... BILL, SCRIP, NOTE, KALE, LETTUCE

nautilus ..... ARGONAUT, MOLLUSK

official ...... DOCUMENT

on .... THEORETICAL, IN THEORY

once folded ...... FOLIO

pulp, pressed .... PASTEBOARD

quantity of ..... REAM, BUNDLE, QUIRE

roll of .... BOLT

scrap of, sometimes ..... TREATY

seller .... NEWSBOY, STATIONER

shell .... MARRON

size .... ATLAS, FOOLSCAP, ROYAL, CAP, POTT, POST, FOLIO, CROWN, DEMY, IMPERIAL

small town ..... WEEKLY
spoiled .... SALLE,
           CASS(I)E, RETREE
sugar holder .... CORNET
untrimmed edge ....
           DECKLE, DECKEL
waterproofing substance ..
           PARAFFIN
white .... REPORT
wrapping .... KRAFT
writing ..... STATIONERY
papers .... CREDENTIALS,
           WRITINGS
Paphian .... EROTIC
papilla .... NIPPLE
papilloma .... TUMOR, WART,
           CORN
papillon .... SPANIEL
papillote .... CURLPAPER
pappy .... FATHER, DADDY,
           MUSHY, SOFT
paprika .... CONDIMENT,
           PIMIENTO
   vitamin .... CITRIN
papule ...... BLISTER, PIMPLE
papyrus ..... SEDGE, BULRUSH
par ...... NORMAL, AVERAGE,
           STANDARD
   avion ..... (BY) AIR MAIL
   in golf .... BOGEY
   one under .... BIRDIE
   two under .... EAGLE
Para, capital of ...... BELEM
parable ... FABLE, SIMILITUDE,
           ALLEGORY, STORY,
           APOLOGUE
   Talmud ... HAGGADA(H)
parabolic .... ALLEGORICAL
Paracelsus' remedy .... AZOTH
parachute ...... PATAGUIUM,
           PARAFOIL
   gear .... HARNESS
   jumper .... PARAMEDIC,
           STUNTMAN,
           PARATROOPER
   release device .. RIP CORD
   shape of ..... UMBRELLA
paraclete .... PLEADER,
           ADVOCATE, HOLY SPIRIT
parade .. MARCH, SHOW(OFF),
           REVIEW, FLAUNT, STRUT,
           CAVALCADE, WALK,
           DISPLAY, PROCESSION,
           PROMENADE
   feature .... FLOAT
   item .... FLOAT

march ...... GOOSESTEP
of cars .... MOTORCADE
official .... MARSHAL
prefix .... CADE
parader .... MUMMER, MODEL
paradigm ... MODEL, PATTERN,
           EXAMPLE
paradisiac .... EDENIC
Paradise ..... HEAVEN, EDEN,
           ELYSIUM, UTOPIA
   imaginary .. SHANGRILA
   Lost character ....
           (ITH)URIEL, ADAM, EVE
paraffin .... WAX
parafoil .... PARACHUTE
   inventor of ..... JALBERT
paragon ...... IDEAL, MODEL,
           PATTERN, DIAMOND,
           NON(E)SUCH
paragonite .... MICA
paragraph ...... ITEM, NOTE,
           CLAUSE
Paraguay capital ... ASUNCION
   city .... VILLARICA,
           CONCEPCION
   explorer of ...... CABOT
   language ..... GUARANI
   monetary unit .. GUARANI
   plains .... GRAN CHACO
   president .... STROESSNER
   river ...... PARANA, APA
   tea .... MATE, YERBA
   territory .... CHACO
   wood .... QUEBRACHO
parakeet ...... BUDGERIGAR,
           PARROT, PAROQUET, BUDGIE
parallel .... COUNTERPART,
           MATCH, EQUAL
parallelogram ... RHOMB(US),
           RHOMBOID
   remains of a .... GNOMON
paralysis ... PARESIS, STROKE,
           PARAPLEGIA, PTOSIS, PALSY,
           HEMIPLEGIA
   combining form .. PLEGIA,
           PLEGY
   infantile .... POLIO
   partial, local .... CRAMPS
paralytic stroke ...... SHOCK
paralyze ...... NUMB, PALSY,
           SHOCK
Paramaribo is capital of ......
           SURINAM
paramo .... PLAIN
paramount .... CHIEF,
           DOMINANT, SUPREME

paramour .... LOVER, MISTRESS, SWEETHEART, LEMAN, INAMORATA, MINION

Parana river tributary .... IGUASSU, IGUAZU

parang .... KNIFE

paranymph .... BEST MAN, BRIDESMAID

parapet ..... RAILING, WALL, BRATTICE

opening .... EMBRASURE

part .... MERLON

paraph .... FLOURISH

paraphernalia .... OUTFIT, GEAR, BELONGINGS, TRAPPINGS, EQUIPMENT

paraphrase .... REWORD(ING)

paraplegic .... PARALYTIC

paraquet .... PARROT

parasite .. TOADY, HANGER-ON, LEECH, DRONE, MOOCHER, SPONGE(R), WABBLE, TRENCHER, SYCOPHANT

animal .... ENTOZOON

blood .... TRYP

concern of a ...... HOST, MEAL TICKET

feeder of .... HOST

fish .... REMORA

fungus .... LICHEN

intestinal .... HELMINTH, TAPEWORM

living inside plant/animal ENTOPHYTE, ENTEZOON

one-celled ... SPOROZOAN

outside body ... EPIZOON

plant ... LICHEN, APHID, MISTLETOE, BINE

root .... PINESAP

parasite's find .... HOST, MEAL TICKET

parasitic insect .... FLEA, MOSQUITO, LICE, GNAT, MITE, ACARID, CHIGOE, CHIGGER, APHID, LOUSE

fungus .... LICHEN

plant ... ORCHID, DODDER

worm .... LEECH, TRICHINA, NEMATODE, TREMATODE, FLUKE

parasol .... UMBRELLA, SUNSHADE

ant .... ATTA

paravane .... OTTER

parboil .... OVERHEAT, SCALD, CODDLE

Parcae .... FATES

parcel .... PACKAGE, LOT, BUNDLE, BUNCH, PART, (AP)PORTION, PACK(ET), PLAT

out .... METE, ALLOT

parch .... DRY, TORRIFY, TORREFY, HEAT

parched ...... TORRID, ARID, DRY, THIRSTY, ADUST, ANHYDROUS

parchment .... VELLUM, DIPLOMA, PAPYRUS, SHEEPSKIN, KIDSKIN, FOR(R)EL

inscribed twice .... PALIMPSEST

roll ...... SCROLL, PELL

scroll, Pentateuch .... TORA(H)

pard ... PANTHER, COMPANION, PARTNER

pardon ...... REMIT, EXCUSE, FORGIVE, OVERLOOK, ASSOIL, CONDONE, SPARE, INDULGENCE, ABSOLVE

general .... AMNESTY

kind of .... OBLIVION

pardonable .... VENIAL, EXCUSABLE

pare ..... CUT, REDUCE, SKIN, WHITTLE, SKIVE, TRIM, PEEL, SHAVE

Fr. surgeon ... AMBROISE

paregoric .... SOOTHING, SEDATIVE

parent ...... SIRE, ANCESTOR, MATER, SOURCE, DAM, PATER, MOTHER, FATHER

child murderer .. FILICIDE

parentage ..... BIRTH, ORIGIN, ANCESTRY, PATERNITY

person of mixed .... MESTEE, MUSTEE, OCTOROON, MULATTO, MESTIZO, GRIFF

parenthesis .... EPISODE, INTERLUDE

parenthetical remark .. ASIDE

parents, having same .. GERMAN

paresis .... PARALYSIS

paretic .... PARALYTIC

pareu .... SKIRT

parfait .... DESSERT

parfleche .... RAWHIDE
parget .... PLASTER
parhelic circle's halo .. SUNDOG
parhelion .... (MOCK)SUN,
    SUNDOG
pariah .... OUTCAST, LEPER,
    EXILE, WRETCH
paries .... WALL
parietal .... SOMATIC
Paris .... PAREE, LUTETIA
  airport near .... ORLY
  cathedral .. NOTRE DAME
  chief of police .. PREFECT
  district in ..... AUTEUIL
  father of .... PRIAM
  museum .... CLUNY,
    LOUVRE
  palace .... TUILERIES
  parent of .... PRIAM,
    HECUBA
  patron saint .. GENEVIEVE
  police inspector, fictional
    MAIGRET
  rival of .... ROMEO
  river .... SEINE
  section .... MONTMARTRE
  suburb .... CLICHY, ISSY
  subway .... METRO
  thug .... APACHE
  university .... SORBONNE
  victim of ..... ACHILLES
  war caused by ... TROJAN
  wife .... OENONE
  woman kidnapped by ...
    HELEN
parish .... CONGREGATION
  head of .... PARSON,
    PASTOR, RECTOR
  official .... OVERSEER
parity .... EQUALITY, PAR
park ...... STADIUM, DEPOSIT,
    SQUARE
  fence/wall .... HAHA
parka .... JACKET, SHIRT
Parkinson's disease ... PALSY
  drug for .... L-DOPA
  patient's lack .. DOPAMINE
  researcher ...... COTZIAS
parlance .... SPEECH,
    LANGUAGE, IDIOM
parlay .. BET, WAGER, EXPLOIT
parley .... PALAVER,
  CONFER(ENCE), TALK,
  NEGOTIATE, WAGER,
  CONVERSE, TREAT,
  DISCUSSION, POWWOW

trumpet signal ....
    CHAMADE
parliament ...... LEGISLATURE,
    DIET, SEJM
  report .... HANSARD
parliamentary move ....
    CLOTURE, CLOSURE
parlor ... SALON, SHOP, SALA,
    LIVING ROOM, DEN
Parnassus dweller ..... MUSE
  spring .... CASTALIA
parochial .... PROVINCIAL,
    NARROW
parodist ... APER, IMITATOR
parody .... SATIRE,
  CARICATURE, SKIT,
  BURLESQUE
parol(e) ...... ORAL, PROMISE,
    (PASS)WORD
paronomasia .... PUN
paronymous .... COGNATE
parotitis .... MUMPS
paroxysm .... FIT, SPASM,
  ATTACK, CONVULSION,
    OUTBURST
parquet .... ORCHESTRA,
    FLOORING
  circle .... PARTERRE
parr .... SALMON
parrot ..... COCKATOO, LORO,
  KEA, LORIKEET, LORY,
  VASA, PARAKEET, REPEAT,
  IMITATE, MACAW, KAKA,
  ARA(RA), JAKO, ECHO,
  POLLY, POPINJAY, BUGIE,
  KAKAPO, AMAZON
  cry of .... SQUAWK
  fever .... PSITTACOSIS
  fish ... SHANNY, COTORO,
    SCARID, LANIA
  hawk .... HIA
  like .... ARINE
  sheep-killing .... KEA
parry ...... DEFLECT, WARD,
  VOID, FEND, EVADE
  fencing .... SEPTIME
parse .... ANALYZE
Parsee .... ZOROASTRIAN
  priest .... MOBED
  sacred writings .. AVESTA
Parsi "baptismal" rite ...
    NAVJOT
  fried rice .... PULLAO
  language ..... GUJARATI
  "towers of silence" ......
    DAKMAS

undershirt .... SUDRA
"Parsifal" composer ....
.... WAGNER
   magican ..... KLINGSOR
   person healed by ....
.... AMFORTAS
   priest .... MOBED
   son of .... LOHENGRIN
   woman in ...... KUNDRY
parsimonious .... MISERLY,
   STINGY, CLOSE,
   NIGGARDLY
parsley ... SANICLE, LOVAGE,
   GARNISH, PLANT, POTHERB,
   DILL
parsnip .... PLANT
parson .... MINISTER,
   CLERGYMAN, PASTOR
   assistant of .... CURATE
   bird .... TUI, POE, KOKO
   concern of a ..... PARISH
parsonage .. MANSE, RECTORY
part .... ROLE, DIVIDE,
   SEPARATE, LEAVE, SECTION,
   SEGMENT, PORTION, PIECE,
   SHARE, DUTY, SEVER
   main .... KEYSTONE
   of speech ..... (AD)VERB,
   (PRO)NOUN, ADJECTIVE
   payment .... DEPOSIT,
   INSTAL(L)MENT
   song ... GLEE, MADRIGAL
   stage .... ROLE
   that separates .. SEPTUM,
   DIVIDER
partake ... PARTICIPATE, EAT,
   SHARE
partan .... CRAB
parted .... SPLIT, DIVIDED
Parthenon .... TEMPLE
   designer .... ICTINUS
   sculptor of ..... PHIDIAS
   site of ...... ACROPOLIS,
   ATHENS
Parthenope .... SIREN
Parthenos .... VIRGIN
partial ... BIASED, PREJUDICED
partiality ...... BIAS, FONDNESS,
   LIKING, PREJUDICE
participant .... PARTAKER,
   PLAYER
   in quarrel ...... FEUDIST
participate .... SHARE,
   PARTAKE, SIT IN
particle .... SPECK, SHRED,
   TITTLE, GRAIN, MOTE,

MITE, WHIT, IOTA, JOT,
SCINTILLA, FLECK, GRANULE
   atom .... PROTON,
   NEUTRON
   glowing ...... SPARK(LE)
particular .... DISTINCT,
   SPECIFIC, SPECIAL,
   DETAIL(ED), ITEM,
   FASTIDIOUS, EXACTING,
   FINICAL, FUSSY
   moment ..... JUNCTURE
particularize .... ITEMIZE,
   SPECIFY
parties, fast round of .. WHIRL
partisan .... FOLLOWER,
   ADHERENT, GUERRILLA,
   ZEALOT, STALWART,
   FANATIC, MAQUI,
   FACTIONAL, DEVOTEE,
   HALBERD, PIKE
   combining form .. CRAT
   group .... CAMP, SIDE
partite .... PARTED
partition ... DIVIDE(R), ALLOT,
   DIVISION, (AP)PORTION,
   WALL, SEPTUM, SCREEN
partlet .... BIDDY, COLLAR,
   RUFF, HEN
partly open .... AJAR
partner ... SHARER, ASSOCIATE,
   TEAMMATE
   in crime .... ACCOMPLICE
   slang .... PARD
partnership .... CAHOOTS,
   ASSOCIATION
partridge .... GROUSE,
   PHEASANT, YUTU,
   SEESEE, FRANCOLIN, QUAIL,
   TINAMOU, TITAR, BIRD
   call .... JUCK
   flock .... BEVY, COVEY
parturition ..... CHILDBIRTH,
   DELIVERY, LABOR
party .... SOCIAL, GROUP,
   GATHERING, SHINDIG, TEA,
   BASH, FACTION, CLIQUE,
   PERSON, SOIREE
   conservative section of ...
   RIGHT WING
   declaration .. MANIFESTO
   didoes ...... HIGHJINKS
   disciplinarian ..... WHIP
   drinking .... CAROUSAL,
   WASSAIL
   for bride-to-be .. SHOWER
   giver ... HOST(ESS), MESTA

goer .... GUEST
kind of ...... TEA, STAG,
SEND-OFF, DESPEDIDA,
SHOWER, HEN, SOCIAL,
BRIDAL, CAROUSAL,
PARTISAN, ADHERENT,
POLITICIAN
organization .. MACHINE
wild .... ORGY
withdraw from .... BOLT
parvenu .... UPSTART,
SNOB(BISH), CLIMBER
parvis ...... PORTICO, COURT,
YARD
pas .... STEP, DANCE,
PRECEDENCE
de Calais .... DOVER
Pascal, Fr. mathematician ....
BLAISE
Pasch ..... PASSOVER, EASTER
paschal lamb .... JESUS
pash .... HURL, HEAD
pasha .... DEY, DOWLAH
Pasiphae's husband ... MINOS
son .... MINOTAUR
pasquinade .... LAMPOON,
SATIRE, SQUIB
pass ... GAP, END, ELAPSE,
MOVE, CONDITION, OCCUR,
ABRA, STRAIT, GHAT,
OUTSTRIP, PROCEED,
DEPART, GO, NACIVERT,
GORGE, BRENNER, KHYBER
away .. DIE, CEASE, LEAVE,
(E)LAPSE
come to .... HAPPEN,
TRANSPIRE, OCCUR
holder .... DEADHEAD
in .... REEVE
in sports .... BYE
lightly .... FLIT
matador's .... FAENA
mountain .... GHAT,
DEFILE, COL
off .... FOIST, FOB, PALM
out ...... FAINT, SWOON
over .... OMIT, SKIP,
SKIM, IGNORE
pretty .... FIX, JAM
slang .... ANNIE OAKLEY
through .... REEVE
tongue over .. LICK, LAP
up ...... REJECT, LET GO
word carelessly .. BANDY
passable .... FAIR, SOSO,
TOLERABLE

passado ..... LUNGE, THRUST
passage ... ROAD, PATH, WAY,
TRAVEL, CROSSING,
OPENING, VENT,
MIGRATION, TRANSIT(ION),
JOURNEY, CLOSE, VOYAGE,
CORRIDOR, AISLES
between cliffs ...... GAT,
DEFILE
between house and garage
BREEZEWAY
between traincars ....
VESTIBULE
body .... MEATUS
closed at one end ....
IMPASSE, BLIND ALLEY,
COURT, DEAD END
covered .... ARCADE,
SLYPE, CLOISTER
in(to) .... ENTRY,
ENTRANCE
means of ..... CHANNEL,
DUCT
mine .... ADIT
mouth to anus .. ENTERO
open to ...... PERMEABLE
organ .... LUMEN
out .... EXIT
performed by all .. TUTTI
repeat a .... CITE
reproduce one ... QUOTE
sloping .... RAMP
smoke .... CHIMNEY,
STACK, FUNNEL
passageway .... HALL,
CORRIDOR, ALLEY, ARCADE,
CLOISTER, ADIT, CANAL,
GANGPLANK, RAMP, AISLE,
DUCT, CATWALK, CHANNEL,
SLYPE
underground ... TUNNEL,
SAP, TUBE, BURROW,
SUBWAY
passbook .... BANKBOOK
passe .... PAST, OBSOLETE,
OUT-OF-DATE
passed .... QUALIFIED
passenger ... FARE, TRAVELER,
RIDER
kind of .... TENDER,
CHANCE, STEERAGE
passerine .... SPARROW,
OVENBIRD, SONGBIRD
passible .... SENSIBLE
passing .... FLEETING,
MOMENTARY, CURSORY,

CASUAL, DEATH, TRANSIENT
away .... LAPSE
fancy .... FAD, WHIM
over .... LABILE
through .... VIA
passion ...... ARDOR, FERVOR,
ZEAL, FEELING, ANGER,
AGONY, EMOTION, HATE,
LOVE, FEAR, LUST, GRIEF,
JOY, RAGE, FURY
flower ..... GRANADILLA,
MAYPOP
for big things ....
MEGALOMANIA
fruit .... MAYPOP
passionate .... INTENSE,
ARDENT, AMOROUS,
FERVENT, TORRID
passionflower .... MAYPOP
passive .... QUIET, PATHIC,
INACTIVE, PATIENT, INERT,
DORMANT
resistance exponent .....
GANDHI
Passover ..... PASCH, PESACH,
SEDER
bread .... MATZOS,
MATZOTH
meal .... SEDAR
of the .... PASCHAL
passport ...... SAFE-CONDUCT
endorsement ...... VISA,
VISE
passus .... CANTO
password ..... COUNTERSIGN,
OPEN SESAME, SIBBOLETH,
PAROLE
use of a .. IDENTIFICATION
past .... AGO, SINCE,
PRETERITE, YORE, BEYOND,
AGONE, OVER, ENDED,
GONE BY, BYGONE
master .... EXPERT
middle age .... ELDERLY
pasta product .... MACARONI,
SPAGHETTI, DOUGH
ingredient ...... FLOUR
paste ... GLUE, PAP, PUNCH,
MUCILAGE, BLOW, HIT,
FASTEN, MASH, DOUGH,
CANDY, ADHESIVE, GEM,
STICK
alimentary ..... WANTON,
ZITONI
clay .... PATE
food ... POI, PEM(M)ICAN

jewelry .... STRASS
mineral matter .. MAGMA
pellet of aromatic ....
PASTILLE
pasteboard .... BRISTOL,
TICKET, (PLAYING)CARD
container .... CARTON
pastel .. DYE, WOAD, PASTILLE,
PLANT, TINT, CRAYON,
DRAWING
Pasteur treatment, object of ...
RABIES
pasteurize .... STERILIZE
pasticcio ..... CENTO, MEDLEY,
POTPOURRI, PASTICHE
pastiche ... MEDLEY, PASTICCIO
pastille .... TABLET, LOZENGE
pastime .... DIVERSION, SPORT,
RECREATION, HOBBY,
AMUSEMENT
pastor ... SHEPHERD, DOMINIE,
CLERGYMAN, PRIEST,
PARSON, MINISTER
pastoral ..... RURAL, CROSIER,
RUSTIC, BUCOLIC, IDYLLIC,
ARCADIAN
cantata ...... SERENATA
god .... PAN, FAUNUS
melody .... MUSETTE
pipe .... REED, OAT
place .... ARCADIA
poem .... IDYL(L),
ECLOGUE, BUCOLIC
poem name ... CORYDON,
AMARYLLIS
poetry, symbol of .. REED
sound .... LOW, MOO,
BLEAT, CANTATA
staff ..... CROSIER, PEDA
pastrami .... BEEF
pastry .... CAKE, ECLAIR,
FLAN, TORTE, PIE, STRUDEL,
TART(LET)
cook ...... ICER, BAKER
fried .... TIMBALE
shell ...... PUFF, CRUST,
ECLAIR
pasture ... GRASS, GRAZE, LEA
for pay .... AGIST
grass ... GRAMA, REDTOP,
SACATON
land .... LEA, LLANO,
ESTANCIA, RANCH
pasty ...... (MEAT)PIE, PATE,
DOUGHY

pat .... APT, OPPORTUNE,
TIMELY, DAB, FIT, TOUCH,
TAP, STROKE
patagium .... PARACHUTE
Patagonia is in .... CHILE,
ARGENTINA
Patagonian .... TEHUELCHE,
INDIAN
rodent ..... MARA, CAVY
patch ...... SCRAP, REMNANT,
DARN, COBBLE, COVERING,
DRESSING, REPAIR, VAMP,
PIECE, PLOT
of color .... FLECK
up ...... MEND, SETTLE,
RECONCILE, REVAMP,
TINKER
patcher .... MENDER
patchouli.... PERFUME, PLANT,
MINT
patchwork .... MOSAIC,
JUMBLE, CENTO, QUILT,
VAMP
composition .... CENTO,
MEDLEY
pate .... HEAD, NODDLE,
PASTE
de foie ____ ...... GRAS
patella .... KNEECAP, PAN,
ROTULA, KNEEPAN
patellar reflex .... KNEE JERK
paten .... DISC, HOST, PLATE,
DISH, DISK, PATIN(A), ARCA
patent ...... PLAIN, OBVIOUS,
EVIDENT, OPEN, PATULOUS,
LICENSE, TITLE, MANIFEST
patentee, usually ... INVENTOR
pater ...... FATHER, OLD MAN
companion of ... NOSTER,
FAMILIA
paternal .... FATHERLY
paternity .... PARENTAGE,
FATHERHOOD, ORIGIN,
AUTHORSHIP
paternoster .... PRAYER,
ROSARY
path .... COURSE, TRAIL, LANE,
TRACK, WAY, WALK,
ORBIT, ROUTE, FOOTWAY
finder .... PIONEER,
TRAILBLAZER
heavenly .... ORBIT
winding .... AMBAGE
Pathan ... PAKISTANI, MOSLEM
pathetic .... MOVING, PITIFUL
fallacy .... EMPATHY

pathogen .... VIRUS, MICROBE,
GERM
pathological .... MORBID
subject .... DISEASE
pathos .... SUFFERING,
POIGNANCY
false .... BATHOS
opposite of ...... ETHOS
pathway, winding .... AMBAGE
patience .... SOLITAIRE,
ENDURANCE, FORBEARANCE,
STOICISM
patient .... INVALID, CASE,
FORBEARING, TOLERANT,
STEADY
man .... JOB, STOIC
patina .... PLATE, PATEN,
CRUST, VERDIGRIS, FILM,
COATING, VERD ANTIQUE
patio .... TERRACE,
COURT(YARD)
patisserie .... BAKERY
patois ...... SPEECH, DIALECT,
LANGUAGE, GUMBO, GOMBO
patriarch ... NASI, NESTORIUS,
FATHER, PATER, BISHOP,
ELDER
Biblical .... ISAAC,
ABRAHAM, JACOB
patrician .... NOBLE,
ARISTOCRAT(IC)
patrimony ..... INHERITANCE,
HERITAGE
patriot, kind of .... JINGO,
CHAUVINIST, NATIONALIST
patriotism, fanatical ....
CHAUVINISM, JINGOISM
patrol ... SCOUT, RECONNOITER
wagon ... BLACK MARIA
patrolman .... (BEAT)COP,
POLICEMAN
patron .... PADRONE,
BENEFACTOR, PROTECTOR,
SPONSOR, CUSTOMER,
SAINT
animals' ... PAN, FAUNUS
art .... MAECENAS
beggars' .... GILES
Broadway .... ANGEL
Cornish .... COLIN
cripples' .... GILES
England's ..... GEORGE
husbandry ..... GRANGE
Irish .... PATRICK
largesse of a .... PENSION
lawyers' .... IVES

lepers' .... GILES
literature ..... MAECENAS
music .... CECILIA
Russia's ...... NICHOLAS
sailors' .... ELMO,
          NICHOLAS
shoemakers' ... CRISPIN
wine-growers' .. VINCENT
youths' .... NICHOLAS
patronage ... FAVOR, SUPPORT,
   SPONSORSHIP, CLIENTELE,
   (A)EGIS, AUSPICES
   solicitor .... RUNNER
patronize .... SPONSOR,
   SUPPORT, FAVOR
patronizing .... HOITY-TOITY,
   CONDESCENDING
patrons collectively ....
   CLIENTELE
patronymic .... SURNAME
patsy ... FALLGUY, SCAPEGOAT
patten .... CLOG, SANDAL,
   OVERSHOE, WOODEN SHOE,
   CHOPINE
patter .... TAPS, TALK, CANT,
   JARGON, CHATTER, GURGLE,
   BICKER
pattern ... PARADIGM, MODEL,
   SAMPLE, EXAMPLE,
   TEMPLATE, FORMAT, GUIDE,
   DESIGN, DIAGRAM
   of flow movement ....
   RHYTHM, TREND
Patti, singer ... ADELINA, PAGE
patty .... PIE, CAKE
patulous ... OPEN, SPREADING,
   PATENT
paucity ... DEARTH, FEWNESS,
   SCARCITY
Paul Bunyan ... LUMBERJACK
   Bunyan's ox .... BABE
   pry .... SNOOP(ER)
   the saint's birthplace ....
   TARSUS
   the singer ..... ROBESON,
   ANKA, MCCARTNEY
paunch .... ABDOMEN,
   (POT)BELLY, RUMEN,
   BAY WINDOW, STOMACH
paunchy .... POTBELLIED
pauper .... BEGGAR
paupers' institution ....
   POORHOUSE
pause ...... RESPITE, LET UP,
   BREAK, REST, STOP,

HESITATE, HESITATION,
   LULL
in music ...... FERMETA
in pronunciation ....
   HIATUS
in prosody ... C(A)ESURA
vocalized .... ER
pave ...... COVER, OVERLAY,
   STUD, TILE, ASPHALT,
   COBBLE
pavement ...... (SIDE)WALK,
   FLAGGING
   pounder ... PATROLMAN,
   BEAT COP
   walker ..... PEDESTRIAN
paver .... TUP
   of a sort .... PIONEER
pavid .... AFRAID, TIMID,
   FEARFUL
pavilion .... MARQUEE,
   BELVEDERE, TENT, KIOSK,
   SUMMERHOUSE, AURICLE,
   GALLERY
paving material ..... ASPHALT,
   MACADAM, TAR, CEMENT,
   TILE, FLAG(STONE),
   SETT, SLAB
pavis .... SHIELD
Pavlova, ballet dancer ... ANNA
pavo .... PEACOCK,
   CONSTELLATION
pavonine .... IRIDESCENT
paw ..... MAUL, FOOT, HAND,
   GAUM, PUD, FATHER,
   OLD MAN, PAPA, TOUCH
pawl ...... PALLET, TRIPPER,
   RATCHET, CLICK, DETENT,
   BOLT
pawn ..... HOSTAGE, WAGER,
   TOOL, DUPE, PIGNUS, GAGE,
   SPOUT, HOCK, PLEDGE,
   GUARANTY, STAKE,
   CHESSMAN
   queened .... FERS
   receipt .... TICKET
pawnbroker .. (MONEY)LENDER
   shop of .... SPOUT
   slang .... UNCLE
Pawnee .... INDIAN, CHAUI
pawnshop: sl. .... SPOUT
pawpaw .... PAPAYA
pax .... PEACE, GODDESS,
   TABLET
pay ...... FEE, REMUNERATE,
   RECOMPENSE, REMIT,
   COMPENSATE, DEFRAY,

SETTLE, WAGE, SALARY,
LIQUIDATE, STIPEND
attention .... HEED,
LISTEN
back .... REIMBURSE
dirt .... ORE
for injury suffered ....
DAMAGES
for loss incurred ....
INDEMNIFY
homage .... HONOR
load .... CARGO
one's share .... ANTE
off .... RECKONING,
REDEEM
something additional to ..
PERQUISITE
up .... PONY, ANTE,
COME ACROSS
payable .... DUE
paying guest .... BOARDER
paymaster .. PURSER, CASHIER
payment, advance ..... ANTES,
HANDSEL, HERIOT
back ...... REBATE
call for .... DUN
death .... CRO
forced .. EXACTION, LEVY
per capita .. CAPITATION
to atone for killing ......
WER(E)GILD,
BLOOD MONEY
token ... ARLES, HANDSEL
paynim ... HEATHEN, PAGAN,
MOSLEM
payola .... BRIBE
Pb in chemistry .... LEAD,
PLUMBUM
pea .... LEGUME, PEASE,
SENNA, LICORICE
chick .... CICER
covering .... POD
heath .... CARMELE
pod .... PEASECOD
seed .... PULSE
soup .... FOG
stalk/stem ..... HA(U)LM
tree .... AGATI, LABURNUM
peabody bird ...... SPARROW
peace .... GRITH; SHALOM,
CONCORD, HARMONY,
CALM, QUIET, SERENITY
agreement ...... TREATY
goddess of .. IRENE, PAX
officer .... SHERIFF,
CONSTABLE

pipe .... CALUMET
Prize winner .. ORR, ROOT,
BUNCHE, KING
symbol of .... DOVE
peaceable ... HENOTIC, IRENIC,
SOLOMON
peaceful .. CALM, IRENIC(AL),
PACIFIC, SERENE, HALCYON
person ...... PACIFICO
peacemaker ..... ARBITRATOR,
MEDIATOR
slang .... COLT
peach .... FREESTONE,
CLINGSTONE, NECTARINE,
VICTORINE, TREE, PAVY,
FRUIT, BRANDY
kind of .... CLING
slang .. BETRAY, SQUEAL,
SING, SNITCH
state .... GEORGIA
stone .... PUTAMEN,
NUTLET
peacoat .... JACKET
peacock ... PAVO, BIRD, PAON,
MAO
bird resembling .. ARGUS
butterfly .... IO
eyelike spot ... OCELLUS
feather's spot ... OCELLUS
female .... PEAHEN,
PEAFOWL
fish .... WRASSE
like a .... VAIN
neck feathers ... HACKLE
of a .... PAVONINE
ore .... BORNITE
symbol of the ... VANITY
walk .... STRUT
peag(e) .... WAMPUM
peak .... CREST, SUMMIT,
HEIGHT, MAXIMUM,
PITON, ALP, CROWN,
DROOP, FADE
of rock .... AIGUILLE
volcano's .... CONE
peaked .... POINTED
peal ...... CLAP, CHIME, RING,
RESOUND, CARILLON, TOLL
peanut .... EARTHNUT,
GOOBER, MANI
pear .... JARGONEL(LE),
SECKEL, BOSC, TREE, FRUIT,
BERGAMOT, POME, ANJOU,
BARTLETT, OPUNTA, NOPAL
autumn .... BOSC
fruit like ..... AVOCADO

juice drink .... PERRY
prickly ... TUNA, NOPAL, OPUNTIA
prince's ...... BERGAMOT
seed .... PYRENE
shaped .... PEG-TOP, PYRIFORM
shaped fruit ...... FIG, AVOCADO, SHADDOCK
stone .... PYRENE
pearl ...... GEM, MARGARITE, PURL, BEAD, OLIVET
biblical .... BDELLIUM
Buck heroine ...... OLAN
Harbor is in ...... OAHU
high quality ..... ORIENT
imitation .... OLIVET
mother-of .... NACRE
Mosque city ...... AGRA
of the Orient .... MANILA
producer ...... OYSTER, NACRE, MOLLUSK
quality of a ..... LUSTER
river .... CHU-KIANG
singer .... BAILEY
pearlweed .... SEALWORT, SAGINA
pearmain .... APPLE
Pearson, Canadian premier ... LESTER
peart ... CLEVER, PERT, LIVELY
Peary's discovery .... NORTH POLE
peas and beans .... LEGUMES
peasant .... FARMER, RUSTIC, RYOT, FELLAH, HIND, CEORL, COTTAR, TAO, SERF, TILLER, CHURL, PEON, CARL(E), CAMPESINO, VILLEIN, KASAMA, MUZHIK
farmer .... CROFTER
peasants' revolt ... JACQUERIE
pease .... PEAS
peat .... FUEL, TURF
bog .... MOSS
land .... TURBARY
moss .... SPHAGNUM
spade .... SLADE
peav(e)y .... CANTHOOK
pebble .... STONE, QUARTZ, SCREE
pecan ... NUT, TREE, HICKORY, NOGAL
tree related to .. HICKORY
peccadillo .... FAULT
peccant ..... SINFUL, SINNING

peccary .... JAVALI, BOAR
peck .... NAG, DAB, KISS, NIBBLE, PICK
1/4 of .... QUARTERN
pecker .... PICK
pecks, 4 .... BUSHEL
pectin .... CARBOHYDRATE
pectinoid bivalve ..... SCALLOP
peculate .... EMBEZZLE
peculiar .... ODD, UNIQUE, STRANGE, SPECIAL, DISTINCTIVE, SINGULAR, QUEER, SCREWY, EXCLUSIVE
to locality ..... ENDEMIC
peculiarity ... TRAIT, ODDITY, CHARACTERISTIC
pecuniary .... FINANCIAL, MONETARY
pedagogue ... TUTOR, TEACHER
pedagogy .... TEACHING, DIDACTICS
pedal .. TREADLE, (FOOT)LEVER
digit .... TOE
pedant ... TEACHER, SCHOLAR, TUTOR, EDUCATOR
pedantic .... ACADEMIC, DIDACTIC
pedate ..... FOOTLIKE, FOOTED
peddle ... HAWK, SELL, VEND
peddler .... HAWKER, HUCKSTER, PACKMAN, PEDLAR, COSTER, CHAPMAN
cheap jewelry .... DUFFER
clandestine/illegal ...... PUSHER
confederate of .... SHILL
trinket .... FAKER
vehicle of ..... PUSHCART
peddle .... HAWK, VEND, SELL
pederasty .... SODOMY
boy used in .... CATAMITE
pedestal ...... BASE, SUPPORT
part of ..... DADO, SOCLE, PLINTH
put on a .... IDOLIZE
pedestrian .... WALKING, PROSAIC, DULL, WALKER
pediatrist, concern of .... INFANTS, CHILDREN
pedicel .... PEDUNCLE, STEM, STALK, RAY
without .... SESSILE
pedicular .... LOUSY
pedicure .... CHIROPODIST, CHIROPODY

subject of ...... TOENAILS
pedigree .... LINEAGE,
ANCESTRY, GENEALOGY,
BLOODLINE
pedometer .... ODOGRAPH
pedro .. SEVEN UP, CARD GAME
peduncle .... STALK, PEDICEL,
STEM, PEDICLE, STIPE(S),
PETIOLE, SCAPE
without .... SESSILE
Pee Dee ..... YADKIN, RIVER
Pee Wee of baseball ... REESE
peek ... PEEP, PEER, GLANCE,
LOOK
peel ...... RIND, STRIP, PARE,
TRIM, SHED, SKIN, UNDRESS,
TOWER, EXOCARP, EPICARP,
FLAY
for flavoring ...... ZEST
skin off ...... EXCORIATE
peen, tool with ..... HAMMER
peep .... PEER, CHIRP, LOOK,
PULE, GLIMPSE, PEEK,
KEEK, JEEP, CHEEP, PRY
military slang ..... JEEP
show .... RAREE
peeper ...... SNOOP(ER), PRY,
TOM, FROG, NESTLING,
CHICK, EYE
peephole ... EYELET, KEYHOLE,
LOOPHOLE
Peeping Tom .... VOYEUR,
PEEKER
lady looked at by ....
GODIVA
peer .... NOBLE, DUKE,
VISCOUNT, MARQUIS, BARON,
SQUINT, EARL, EQUAL,
PALADIN, LOOK, PEEP
Gynt's mother ..... ASE
peerage .... NOBILITY
Peerce, operatic singer .. JAN
peeress ... DUCHESS, BARONESS,
LADY, MARQUISE
peerless .... UNRIVALED,
NONPAREIL
peetweet .... SANDPIPER
peeve .... GRUDGE,
ANNOY(ANCE), IRRITATE
peevish .... GRUMPY,
FRACTIOUS, CROSS,
SPLENETIC, TESTY,
TE(T)CHY, SOUR,
QUERULOUS, FRETFUL,
IRRITABLE, PET

peewee ...... DWARF, RUNT,
LAPWING
peg .... NOG, PIN, TRE(E)NAIL
SPILL, SPIGOT, DOWEL,
PLUG, BOLT, STEP, THOLE,
KEVEL, HOB
and rings game .. QUOITS
colloquial ... LEG, FOOT,
TOOTH
golf .... TEE
joining timbers ....
TRE(E)NAIL, TRUNNEL
quoits .... HOB
pega .... REMORA
Pegasus .... HORSE
Peggy .... MARGARET
pegs, set of .... SPILIKIN
Pegu, capital of ... RANGOON
ironwood .... ACLE
peignor .... NEGLIGEE
Peiping .... PEKING
pekan ..... WEJACK, WEASEL
pekin .... SILK, SATIN
Peking .... PEIPING
Pekingese .... DOG
pekoe .... TEA
pelage .... FUR, HAIR
pelagic ..... MARINE, OCEANIC
Pele, football star ..... EDSON,
NEGRAO
Peleg's father .... EBER
son .... REU
pelerine .... CAPE
Peleus, descendant of ....
ACHILLES
wife of .... THETIS
Pelew .... PALAU
pelf .... BOOTY, WEALTH
Pelias' nephew .... JASON
son .... ACASTUS
Pelides .... ACHILLES
Pelion, companion of ... OSSA
pelisse .... COAT, CLOAK
pelite .... SHALE
pellagra treatment ... NIACIN
pellet ...... PILL, BALL, SHOT,
BULLET
of medicine .... PILL,
PILULE
pellicle ..... FILM, MEMBRANE,
SCUM
pellmell .... HEADLONG,
JUMBLED, DISORDER(LY)
pellucid .... CLEAR,
TRANSPARENT, LIMPID,
SHEER

Pelop's father .... TANTALUS
son ... ATREUS, THYESTES
Peloponnesus city ... MESSENE
country .... LACONIA
promontory .. MATAPAN
Peloponnesian seaport ....
PATRAS
pelota .... JAI ALAI
basket .... CESTA
court .... FRONTON
player .... PELOTARI
pelt ...... HIDE, FELL, BEAT,
POUND, CAST, SKIN,
PEPPER, STONE
peltry .... FURS, SKINS
pelvic .... ILIAC, PUBIC
pemmican .... MEAT
pen ...... ENCLOSURE, YARD,
WRITE(R), INDITE, CORRAL,
BALLPOINT, QUILL, HUTCH,
KRAAL, COTE
name ... See PSEUDONYM,
NOM DE PLUME
pig .... STY
point .... NIB, NEB
poultry ... COOP, HUTCH
slang .... PENITENTIARY,
PRISON, JAIL
penal .... PUNITIVE
penalize ...... PUNISH, FINE
penalty ...... FINE, FORFEIT,
HANDICAP, PUNISHMENT
penance .... PUNISHMENT
for example .. SACRAMENT
penates .... LARES
penchant ...... FLAIR, TASTE,
INCLINATION, LIKING,
FONDNESS, LEANING
pencil lead .... GRAPHITE
pend .... HANG
pendant .... TASSEL,
GIRANDOLE, EARRING,
LAVALIER(E), FOB
pendent .... HANGING,
SUSPENDED, UNDECIDED,
PENDING, PENSILE
pending .... UNDECIDED,
DURING, UNTIL
pendulous .... SWINGING,
HANGING
pendulum, device with inverted
METRONOME
weight .... BOB
Peneios .... SALAMBRIA
Penelope .... WEAVER
father .... ICARIUS

husband of ... ODYSSEUS,
ULYSSES
son of ..... TELEMACHUS
penetrable .... PERVIOUS
penetralia .... SECRETS,
CONFIDENCES
penetrate .... PIERCE, ENTER,
PERMEATE, IMBUE, REACH
penetrating .... ACUTE,
INCISIVE, TRENCHANT,
DEEP, KEEN, SHARP,
PUNGENT
penetration .... INSIGHT,
INTRUSION
open to ..... PERMEABLE
penetron .... MESON
pengo, replacement of ....
FORINT
penguin ... AUK, BIRD, JOHNNY
breeding place .. ROOKERY
describing a .. IMPENNATE
peninsula ...... CHERSONESE,
BONDOC, NECK, IBERIA,
SINAI, KOLA, KOWLOON,
ISTRIA, LABRADOR, MALAY,
KAMCHATKA
penitence .... ATTRITION,
CONTRITION, REMORSE,
REGRET, REPENTANCE
penitent ... CONTRITE, SORRY,
REPENTANT, REMORSEFUL
wear of ..... SACKCLOTH,
SANBENITO
penitential period ...... LENT
penitentiary .... PRISON
penman ..... SCRIBE, WRITER,
CHIROGRAPHER, AUTHOR
penmanship .. HAND(WRITING),
SCRIPT
Penn, William ...... QUAKER
penna .... FEATHER
pennant .... BANNER, BURGEE,
ENSIGN, FLAG, PENNON,
STREAMER
pennies .... PENCE
penniless .. POOR, BROKE, FLAT
Pennine Alps peak ...... ROSA
pennon ...... FLAG, PENNANT,
WING, PINION, ENSIGN
Pennsylvania capital ....
HARRISBURG
city ... YORK, BRADFORD,
SHARON, PHILADELPHIA,
SCRANTON, LANCASTER,
ERIE, ALLENTOWN

LEBANON, PITTSBURGH, ALTOONA
insurrection, cause of ... WHISKY
river .... LEHIGH
sect .... AMISH
state nickname .... KEYSTONE
state tree ...... HEMLOCK
town .... ONO
penny ...... COPPER, SALTER, COIN, (RED)CENT, GROAT
a-liner ... HACK(WRITER)
candy .... LICORICE
dreadful ... DIME NOVEL
wise .... THRIFTY, ECONOMICAL
penpoint .... NIB, NEB
pensile .... HANGING, PENDENT
pension .... STIPEND, SUBSIDY
pensionary .... PUPPET, HIRELING, DEPENDENT
pensive .... MEDITATIVE
penstock ... TROUGH, SLUICE
pent .... PENNED, CONFINED
pentacle ..... STAR, SYMBOL, PENTAGRAM
pentad .... FIVE, QUINTET
pentagram .... PENTACLE
Pentateuch .... TORA(H)
lesson read from .... PARASHAH
Pentecost .... SHABUOTH, WHITSUNDAY
penthouse ...... APARTMENT, LEANTO
pentobarbital sodium .... NEMBUTAL
pentosan .... XYLAN
pentose ... SUGAR, ARABINOSE
penurious ..... POOR, STINGY, MISERLY
penury .... POVERTY, INDIGENCE
peon .... LABORER, FOOTMAN, SERF
peony .... MOUTAN
flower .... PIP
people ...... FOLK, POPULATE, DEMOS, RACE, PERSONS, MORTALS, NATION, CITIZENS, HUMANS, PUBLIC
characteristics of .. ETHOS
common ..... POPULACE, MASSES, PLEBE
dark-skinned ..... NEGRO

full of .... POPULOUS
mass killing of ....
GENOCIDE, NOYADE, HOLOCAUST, POGROM
non-clerical ...... LAITY
of all the ..... PANDEMIC
prehistoric ...... PELASGI
unimportant .. SMALL FRY
pep .... SNAP, VERVE
drug ... ELAVIL, TRIAVIL, TOFRANIL
pill in short ... LSD, DMT, STP
peplos .... SCARF, SHAWL, PEPLUM
peplum .... SKIRT, PEPLOS
pepo .... MELON, SQUASH, PUMPKIN, GOURD
pepper .... PIM(I)ENTO, SPRINKLE, BEAT, KAVA, CAYENNE, ARA, SPICE, CONDIMENT, PELT, BETEL, STRAFE, RIDDLE, CHILIDO, CAPSICUM
and-salt .... GRAY
berry .... CUBEB
beverage .... KAVA
fruit .... PAPRIKA
picker .... PIPER
plant .... BETEL, KAVA, PAPRIKA
pod .... CHILI
pot .... STEW
sauce .... TABASCO
shrub ..... KAVA, KAWA, CAVA
pepperidge .... TUPELO
peppermint .... CANDY, LOZENGE, PLANT, OIL
oil product ..... MENTHOL
peppery ... HOT, FIERY, TESTY, SPICY, SHARP, IRRITABLE, PUNGENT
peppy .... BRISK, SPIRITED
pepsin .... ENZYME
Pepys, Samuel ...... DIARIST
Pequod .... WHALER, WHALEBOAT
captain of .... AHAB
per ..... BY, THROUGH, EACH
annum .... ANNUALLY
diem .... DAILY
hundred ...... PER CENT
Pera .... BEYOGLU
peradventure .... PERHAPS, MAYBE, POSSIBLY

perambulate ... WALK, STROLL
perambulator ... PRAM, BUGGY
percale .... COTTON
perceive .... DISCERN, GRASP,
OBSERVE, RECOGNIZE, NOTE,
SENSE
percentage .... PORTION
perceptible .... PALPABLE,
VISIBLE, SENSIBLE,
TANGIBLE, TACTILE
perception .... NOESIS,
COGNITION, INSIGHT,
GRASP, EAR
perceptive ..... ACUTE, KEEN
perch ...... SIT, SEAT, ROOST,
FISH, SAUGER, PERCOID,
RUFF(E)
high .... AERIE, AERY
fish like .... ANABAS,
DARTER, CABRILLA
perchance .... POSSIBLY,
PERHAPS, MAYBE, MAYHAP
perched .... SAT, (A)LIT
percher .... BIRD
percheron .... HORSE
percoid .... FISH, PERCH
percolate ...... PERK, LEACH,
BREW, FILTER, DRAIN,
OOZE, PERMEATE, SEEP
percolator .... COFFEEPOT
percuss .... RAP
percussion ... IMPACT, SHOCK
cap .... PRIMER
hammer .... PLEXOR,
PLESSOR
instrument ...... TRAPS,
DRUM, CYMBALS, BELL,
PIANO, MARACA
section .... TRAPS
Percy, Sir Henry .... HOTSPUR
perdition .... RUIN, LOSS,
DAMNATION, HELL
perdu(e) .... CONCEALED
pere .... FATHER, SENIOR
peregrinate .... TRAVEL,
JOURNEY
peregrinator ..... TRAVELER,
PILGRIM
peregrine .... FOREIGN,
MIGRATORY, ALIEN, FALCON
falcon .... DUCK HAWK,
TERCEL
peremptory .... FINAL,
DECISIVE, DOGMATIC,
IMPERIOUS, ABSOLUTE

perennial .... LASTING,
PERPETUAL
plant .... DAHLIA
perfect .... FLAWLESS,
FAULTLESS, UTTER,
CONSUMMATE, IDEAL,
EXACT, PRECISE, PURE,
POLISH, REFINE, MODEL
blessedness .... NIRVANA
diamond ..... PARAGON
model .... IDEAL
perfection, model of ....
PARAGON, PRECISION
perfectly .... FULLY
perfecto .... CIGAR
perfidious .... FAITHLESS
perfidy .... BETRAYAL,
TREACHERY
perforate ..... PUNCH, BORE,
DRILL, PIERCE, RIDDLE,
PINK(Y), PINKIE
perforated .... FENESTRATE
thing ... SIEVE, STRAINER
perforator .... PUNCHEON
perforation ..... HOLE, PUNCH
perforce .... NECESSARILY
perform .... EXECUTE,
FULFILL, EFFECT, DO,
RENDER, (EN)ACT
performance .... SHOW,
EXHIBITION, RENDITION
between acts .. INTERLUDE
in person .... LIVE
performer ... ACTOR, PLAYER,
ARTIST(E), TALENT, DOER,
TROUPER
actuated by wires ....
PUPPET, MARIONETTE
balancing trick ....
EQUILIBRIST
stock of .... REPERTOIRE,
REPERTORY
performers, group of ....
TROUPE, CAST
perfume .. SCENT, FRAGRANCE,
ESSENCE, (IN)CENSE,
BOUQUET, AROMA, A(T)TAR
bag .... SATCHET
base .... MUSK
box/case ..... POMANDER
flask .... FLACON
making process ....
ENFLEURAGE
making substance ....
MUSK, MYRRH,
BERGAMOT,

CASTOR(EUM), IRONE, ATTAR, VERDIGRIS, ORRIS, ORRICE, AMBERGRIS, COUMARIN, IONONE, SAFROL(E)

oil .... ATTAR, CITRONELLA, BEN, NEROLI

old .... MUSK

pad .... SACHET

perfumer, room ..... INCENSE

perfunctory ..... SUPERFICIAL

pergola .... TRELLISWORK, ARBOR

perhaps .. HAPLY, PERCHANCE, POSSIBLY, MAYBE, MAYHAP

peri .... ELF, FAIRY

cousin of a .... NISSE

perianth .... CALYX

periapt .... AMULET

Pericles' mistress .... ASPASIA

peridot .... OLIVINE, CHRYSOLITE

peril .... JEOPARDY, RISK, HAZARD, DANGER, MENACE

perimeter .... BORDER, BOUNDARY

period ..... INTERVAL, STAGE, DOT, STREAK, POINT, TERM, TIME, SPELL

brief .... SEC, SNATCH, SNAP, SPELL

geological ...... EOCENE, ERIAN, MIOCENE, JURA, UINTA

inactive ..... LULL, REST, RESPITE, DORMANCY

of extension ..... GRACE

of quiet .... LULL

of seclusion .... RETREAT

of time .... (A)EON, ERA, EPOCH, AGE, DECADE, CENTURY, TRACT

of trial ...... PROBATION

of unemployment .... LAYOFF

of year .... SEASON

short ...... SNAP, SPELL

unbroken ...... STRETCH

woman's .... MENSES

periodic ..... INTERMITTENT, RECURRENT, ETESIAN, REGULAR

periodical .... GAZETTE, PICTORIAL, JOURNAL, MAG(AZINE)

peripatetic .... WALKER, ITINERANT

peripheral .... DISTAL, EXTERNAL, OUTER

periphery .... PERIMETER, ENVIRONS, RIM, AMBIT, CIRCUMFERENCE

periphrasis .... AMBAGE, CIRCUMLOCUTION

periphrastic .... VERBOSE

perique .... TOBACCO

periscope trail ...... FEATHER, WAKE

perish ...... DIE, END, EXPIRE

peristyle .. COLONNADE, COURT

peritoneum, fold of .... OMENTUM

periwig .... PERUKE

periwinkle ... MYRTLE, SNAIL, MUSSEL, SHELL

perjure .... LIE

perjury, induce to commit ..... SUBORN

perk .... PERCOLATE, BUBBLE, RAISE, LIFT

perky .... JAUNTY, GAY, SAUCY, SPIRITED

Perle, society hostess .. MESTA

perlite ...... ROCK, OBSIDIAN

permanence .... FIXITY

permanent.... LASTING, FIXED, PERPETUAL

permeable .... PERVIOUS

permeate .. IMBUE, PERCOLATE, PENETRATE, DIFFUSE, PERVADE

permissible ...... ALLOWABLE

permission ... LEAVE, LICENSE, CONSENT, GRACE

to enter .... ENTREE

permissive .... LENIENT, ALLOWING

permit .... ALLOW, SANCTION, LET, LEAVE, LICENSE, AUTHORIZE, WARRANT, CEDULA

reluctantly .... BEAR, SUFFER, BROOK, TOLERATE

to leave .... EXCUSE

permitted .... LICIT

permutation .... CHANGE

permute ... ALTER, REARRANGE

Pernambuco .... RECIFE

pernicious .. NOISOME, VICIOUS, NOXIOUS, BANEFUL,

DEADLY, FATAL, WICKED,
EVIL
pernickety .... FUSSY,
FASTIDIOUS
Peron's lady ..... EVA, EVITA
slogan .... CUMPLE
perorate .... HARANGUE,
SPEECHIFY, ORATE
perpend .... PONDER
perpendicular ...... VERTICAL,
SINE, UPRIGHT, STRAIGHT UP,
PLUMB
perpetrate ...... DO, COMMIT
perpetual .... LASTING,
PERMANENT, CONSTANT,
CONTINUAL, INCESSANT
perpetuate .... PRESERVE
perpetuity .... ETERNITY,
SERIAL
in .... FOREVER
perplex .. NONPLUS, INTRIGUE,
BAFFLE, ELUDE, CONFUSE,
PUZZLE, STUMP, MYSTIFY,
FLUMMOX
perquisite .... APPANAGE, TIP,
GRATUITY, BONUS
perron .... STAIRCASE
perry .... DRINK
perse .... BLUE
persecute ... HARASS, AFFLICT,
OPPRESS, ANNOY
persecution, victim of ....
REFUGEE, MARTYR, JEW
of minority group ......
POGROM
persecutor, kind of ... TYRANT,
OPPRESSOR
Perseid .... METEOR
Persephone ..... PROSERPINA,
CORA
husband/abductor of ....
HADES, PLUTO
parent of .... ZEUS,
DEMETER
Perseus, daughter of .. PERSEIS
mother of .... DANAE
victim of .... MEDUSA
wife of ..... ANDROMEDA
perseverance ...... TENACITY,
PERSISTENCE, PERTINACITY
persevere .... PERSIST
Pershing's command .... AEF
Persia .... IRAN
conqueror of ..... CYRUS
Persian ...... MEDE, ELAMITE,
IRANI(AN), PARTHIAN,

PAHLAVI
ally .... MEDE
almond .... BADAM
angel .... MAH
apartment ...... ZENANA
bird .... BULBUL
blinds ... PERSIENNES
capital ..... PERSEPOLIS,
ISFAHAN
carpet .... HAMADAN,
SENNA, KALI
city ... ARBELA, TABRIZ,
TEH(E)RAN, ERBIL
coin ...... TOMAN, ASAR,
PAHLAVI, DARIC,
DINAR, ASHRAFI, PUL,
STATER
dance .... SARABAND
deity, supreme .. ORMAZD
dynasty ...... SASSANID,
SELJUK
elf .... PERI
emigrees .... PARSIS,
PARSEES
empire, destroyer of ....
ALEXANDER
empire founder .. CYRUS
empire province .. EGYPT
evil spirit ...... AHRIMAN
fairy .... ELF, PERI
father .... BABA
fire worshipper ... PARSI
Gate of Faith ...... BAB
god of light .. MITHRA(S)
governor .... SATRAP
Gulf region ... CHALDEA
gypsy .... SISECH
hemp .... KANAB
hook money .... LARI
inn .... SERAI, SARAI
javelin .... JERID
judge .... CADI
king .... DARIUS,
(ARTA)XERXES,
CAMBYSES, CYRUS
king of peris .... JAMSHID
king's headdress .. TIARA,
DIADEM
language .... ZEND,
PAHLAVI, AVESTAN
lynx .... CARACAL
measure ...... PARASANG
monk .... DERVISH
mystic .... SUFI
mystic symbol ....
SWASTIKA

native .... LUR
nightingale ..... BULBUL
official .... HAMAN
pavilion .... KIOSK
people .... MEDES,
            ELAMITES
plant .... POPPY
poet ... HAFIZ, FIRD(A)USI,
            OMAR(KHAYYAM)
potentate .... SHAH
pottery ...... GOMBROON
potion .... SOMA PULARI
priestly caste ..... MAGI
prophet .... MANES
refugee ... PARSI, PARSEE
religion .... BABISM,
            MITHRAISM
rice dish ... PILAU, PILAW
ruby spinel .... BALAS
rug .... KALI, SENNA,
            HAMADAN
ruler .... SHAH, SULTAN,
            DARIUS, XERXES
boot .... BABI(SM)
screen .... PARDAH
servant .... BACHA
songbird .... BULBUL
spinel .... BALAS
sprite .... PERI
summerhouse .... KIOSK
teacher ...... MULLA(H)
tiger .... SHER
title .... MIR(ZA), SHAH,
        BAB, AZAM, KHAN
turban cloth ..... LUNGI
veil .... PARDAH
weight ...... ABBAS, SER
writings ... AVESTA, ZEND
persicary .... KNOTWEED,
            HEARTSEASE
persiennes .. SHUTTERS, BLINDS
persiflage ...... BANTER,
        BADINAGE, RAILLERY
persimmon .... EBONY
persist ...... INSIST, ENDURE,
        PERSEVERE, CONTINUE,
            REMAIN
persistence .... TENACITY
persistent ...... DOGGED,
        TENACIOUS, STUBBORN,
            CONTINUED
persnickety .... FUSSY,
            FASTIDIOUS
person (see fellow/man) ......
    INDIVIDUAL, SELF, FELLOW,
    WIGHT, ONE, EGG, BEING

abject ... WORM, WRETCH
alert .... LIVEWIRE
Anglo-Indian .. WALLA(H)
angry .... SOREHEAD
annoying ... CUSS, PEST,
            HUNKS
argumentative .. POLEMIST
authorized to practice ...
            LICENTIATE
awkward ...... GAL(L)OT,
        GALOOT, FOOZLE,
            DUFFER
bad luck .... JONAH,
        JONAS, HOODOO
beastly .... YAHOO
boastful .... GASCON
boorish .... LOUT, GOOP
burdensome .. DEADWOOD
called for jury service ....
            TALES
callow .... CALF
club-footed .... TALIPED
clumsy .... CHUMP,
    CHUKKER, DUD, JUMBO,
    LUMMOX, LOB, LUBBER,
    LOON, SWAB, SLOB,
            HULK
coarse ...... BOOR, LOUT,
        MUCKER, MUG
colorless .... ALBINO
comical .... WAG
common ..... PLEBEIAN
complaining ...... CRAB,
        CRANK, GROUSE,
            GROUCH
contemptible ..... TOAD,
        CAD, SCOUNDREL,
    LOUSE, WORM, SKUNK,
    BUGGER, ROTTER, SWINE,
    STINKER, INSECT, CUR,
            SNOT
courageous .... LION
cowardly .... CUR,
        POLTROON, CAITIFF
cowering in fear ... FUNK
crafty .... FOX
cunning .... WEASEL
dance-maniac ....
            TARANTIST
dark-skinned .... NEGRO
defeated in contest ......
            ALSO-RAN
demented .... NUT, LOCO
diabolical .... FIEND,
    MEPHISTO, HELLION
disgruntled ... SOREHEAD

disorderly ..... LARRIKIN

dissatisfied ....
MALCONTENT

dissolute ..... RAKE, RIP

drunken........... LUSH,
HELLBENDER

dull ... BORE, DULLARD,
DUNCE, LUMP,
LURDAN(E), JERK,
MOKE, PLODDER,
FOOZLE

easily cheated .... GULL,
DUPE

eccentric .... KOOK,
CRANK, NUT, JERK

eminent .... VIP,
NOTABLE, LUMINARY

energetic ..... LIVEWIRE,
HUSTLER, DYNAMO,
RUSTLER

entertaining .... SCREAM

evil .... MISCREANT,
YAHOO, CAITIFF

extraordinary .. PRODIGY,
ONER

famous ...... NOTABLE,
CELEBRITY

feeble-minded ... IDIOT,
AMENT

fiendish .... HELLKITE

fleeing from justice ......
FUGITIVE

fond of fighting ......
SCRAPPER

foolish .... GABY, JAY,
COOT, BOOB(Y)

foppish .... LADIDA

formal .... STIFF

freed from slavery ......
LIBERTINE

frenzied for a fight ......
AMOK, AMUCK,
BERSERK(ER)

fuzzy ...... HOITY-TOITY,
FUDDY-DUDDY

gifted ..... WIZ, TALENT

greedy ... VULTURE, KITE,
PIG, HARPY

gullible .... BABE

handsome ...... LOOKER,
ADONIS

head of .... COSTARD

high in society ..... NOB

high-born .... NOBLE,
PRINCE

high-ranking .. MAGNIFICO

holy .... MAHATMA

humorous .... WAG

ill-mannered ..... BOOR,
LOUT, GOOP, CRAB,
YAHOO

imaginary .... MYTH

important .... NIBS, VIP,
MAGNIFICO, MOGUL,
BASHAW

impractical .... DREAMER,
VISIONARY, IDEALIST,
FANTAST

impudent ... MALAPERT,
UPSTART, HUSSY

impulsive ...... MADCAP

ineffectual .... DUD

inquisitive ...... MOUSER,
BUSYBODY, SNOOP

insignificant ..... SHRIMP,
SQUIRT, NONENTITY,
SNIP

intellectual ... EGGHEAD,
SAVANT, NOETIC,
SCHOLAR, PUNDIT

lazy .... POKE, DRONE,
LOAFER, IDLER,
LURDAN(E)

learned .... PUNDIT,
SCHOLAR, SAVANT,
SAGE, SOPHIST, ORACLE

lively .... GRIG

living by his wits ... SPIV

living in town .. OPPIDAN

loud-voiced ... STENTOR,
THERSITES

maladjusted ..... MISFIT

mean ...... LOUSE, CAD,
CAITIFF

meddling .... BUTTINSKY

mentally deficient ....
MORON, IDIOT,
IMBECILE

miserly .... CHURL,
NIGGARD, TIGHTWAD,
SKINFLINT

mix-blooded .... MESTEE,
HALFBREED, HALF-CASTE,
MUSTEE, CREOLE,
METIF(F), GRIFF(E),
LADINO, MULATTO,
METIS, MESTIZO

modern .... NEOTERIC

much-admired .. PIP(PIN)

mythical ...... SANDMAN

naive ...... BABE, LAMB

name of .... HANDLE,
MONICKER
nameless .... ANONYM
nearsighted ..... MYOPE
Negro-Indian .. GRIFF(E)
nice .... TRUMP
noble .... GENTLEMAN
noble born ..... CHILDE
noisy .. YAP, JAY, MAGPIE
not of noble rank ....
COMMONER, ROTURIER
obnoxious .. FINK, HUNKS
obstinate ..... ASS, MULE
odd .. ECCENTRIC, QUEER
oddly dressed ...... GUY
of equal status ....
COMPEER, CONGENER
of great energy ... DEMON
old-fashioned .... FOSSIL,
MOSSBACK, FOG(E)Y,
100-year-old ....
CENTENARIAN
optimistic ... POLLYANNA
out of place ..... ESTRAY
overnice .... PRIG
overweight .... FATSO
pale-looking .. WHEYFACE
partly paralyzed ....
PARETIC
pedantic .... PRIG
pledged .... HOSTAGE,
BETROTHED
poor ... BEGGAR, PAUPER
popular .... LION,
CELEBRITY
powerful .... MOGUL,
TITAN, POTENTATE,
GIANT, PARAMOUNT
pretending to knowledge
SCIOLIST
prying .... BUSYBODY,
MOUSER
promising ...... COMER
prone to argue .. POLEMIC,
POLEMIST
pugnacious .. SCRAPPER,
BANTAM
puritanical .... BLUENOSE
quarrelsome .. SCRAPPER
queer ..... CHARACTER,
CODGER, DUCK,
GOOSE, CRANK, NUT
quick-tempered ....
HOTSPUR
rebellious ... MALCONTENT,
DISSIDENT

reckless ..... DAREDEVIL,
MADCAP, HOTSPUR,
PLUNGER
regarded with contempt ..
SKATE
resembling another .....
RINGER
rich .... MONEYBAG,
CROESUS, NABOB
rough ... LARRIKIN, MUG
sanctimonious ... GOODY
saucy .... MALAPERT
savage .... HUN, VANDAL
second .... YOU
self-centered .... EGOIST,
EGOTIST, EGOMANIAC
self-important .... NIBS,
BASHAW
servile .... FLUNK(E)Y,
SPANIEL
short, fat ..... DUMPLING,
SQUAB
sickly .... INVALID
silly ...... GOOSE, GOOP,
GOOF, KOOK, PINHEAD,
TOMFOOL
slovenly .... SLOP
slow-moving ..... POKE,
SNAIL, DAWDLER,
LAGGARD
sly .... WEASEL, SNEAK,
FOX
small .... DWARF, RUNT,
PYGMY, BANTAM,
SHRIMP, LILLIPUTIAN,
INSECT, BUB, PIPSQUEAK,
SNIP(PET), HALFPINT,
SQUIRT, MIDGE(T),
AGATE
small-teethed ....
MICRODONT
stateless .... REFUGEE
stingy .... MISER,
NIGGARD, SKINFLINT,
HUNKS
stubborn .... MULE
stupid .... CHUKKER,
DIMWIT, DULLARD,
PINHEAD, DUFFER,
SIMPLETON, DOLT,
GABY, MUTT, OAF,
NUMSKULL, LUMMOX,
BOOB(Y), DUNDERHEAD,
DUMBBELL, MOKE,
SAP, ZOMBI(E),
MUTTONHEAD, LOON,

SOFTHEAD, LUNKHEAD,
JACKASS, SLOB
stylish ...... DUDE, FOP,
SWELL
surly .... HUNKS
sweet-faced .... CHERUB
sworn legally .... JURAT
syphilitic .... LUETIC
talkative ... (POPIN)JAY,
MAGPIE
third ... SHE, THEY, HE, IT
timid ..... LAMB, MOUSE
tireless .... DYNAMO
tongue of ..... CLAPPER
tricky ..... FOX, SLICKER
tuberculous .... LUNGER,
CONSUMPTIVE
ugly ... ZOMBI(E), GOON,
OGRE, GOLLIWOG,
FRIGHT, GAL(L)OT,
SOURPUSS
under patronage ....
PROTEGE, WARD
ungrateful ..... INGRATE
unreasonable ....
MISOLOGIST
unwanted ..... OUTCAST,
PARIAH, LEPER
used as tool ..... PAWN,
FRONT, STOOGE
vain .... POPINJAY,
PEACOCK
verging on insanity ......
MATTOID
vulgar ..... BOOR, LOUT,
MUCKER
waist measure of .. GIRTH
weak .... GOODY
wealthy .... NABOB,
CROESUS, PLUTOCRAT
white .... CAUCASIAN
who destroys maliciously
VANDAL
who makes kids sleepy ...
SANDMAN
who never laughs ....
AGELAST, DEADPAN,
POKERFACE
who sells on installment ..
TALLYMAN
wise .... SOLON, SAGE,
MAHATMA
with free ticket ....
DEADHEAD
with insatiable thirst, etc.
TANTALUS

with poor eyesight ......
MYOPE
withered, thin ... MUMMY
working off a debt .. PEON
worthless .... BUM, LOSEL
young .... LAMBKIN,
TEENAGER, CALF, SLIP
personable .... COMELY,
HANDSOME
personage ... NOTABLE, NIBS,
BIGWIG, DIGNITARY,
MAGNIFICO
personal .... INDIVIDUAL,
PRIVATE, INTIMATE,
CORPORAL
appearance .... MIEN,
BEARING, PRESENCE
aura .... MYSTIQUE,
CHARISMA
belongings .... TRAPS
characteristic ..... TRAIT
charm .... CHARISMA
combining form ... IDIO
well-being .. CONVENIENCE
personality .... PRESENCE,
SELF, CHARACTER, EGO
test .... RORSCHACH
personate .... PORTRAY,
MASKED
personator .... IMPOSTOR
personified .... INCARNATE
personify .... EMBODY
personnel ...... EMPLOYE(E)S,
CREW, STAFF
persons .... FOLK
perspective .... VISTA,
POINT OF VIEW, STANDPOINT
perspicacious .... KEEN,
SHREWD, PERCEPTIVE
perspicacity .... ACUMEN,
INSIGHT
perspicuous .... LUCID
perspiration .... SWEAT,
HIDROSIS, SUDOR,
EGESTA
stimulator ..... BONESET
perspire .... SWEAT, EGEST
persuade .... INDUCE,
CONVINCE, PREVAIL ON,
URGE, COAX
persuasible .... AMENABLE
persuasion .... BELIEF,
CONVICTION, OPINION
art of .... SOFT SELL
persuasive .... COGENT,
CONVINCING

pert .... BRASH, FLIP, ARCH,
SAUCY, FORWARD,
BOLD, IMPUDENT, SASSY
  girl .... MINX, CHIT
  language .... SASS
pertain ..... BELONG, RELATE
Perth river .... TAY
pertinacious ...... STUBBORN
pertinence .... RELEVANT
pertinent .... RELEVANT,
GERMANE, APT
perturb .... DISTURB, ALARM,
UPSET, DISTRESS, RUFFLE,
AGITATE
perturbation .... FEEZE
pertussis .. (WHOOPING)COUGH
Peru, capital of .... LIMA
  conqueror of .. PIZARRO
peruke ... HAIR, (PERI)WIG
peruse ... READ, SCRUTINIZE,
STUDY, CON, SCAN
Peruvian, ancient .... INCA(N)
  animal .... LLAMA,
VICUNA, ALPACA
  bark .... CINCHONA
  beef .... CHARQUI
  bird .... YUTU, TINAMOU
  city .... CALLAO,
AREQUIPA, TRUJILLO,
ICA, PUNO, AYACUCHO,
CUSCO
  coin ..... LIBRA, PESETA,
SOL
  cormorant ..... GUANAY
  current .... EL NINO
  dance .... CUECA
  department ..... TACNA
  fox .... ATOC
  goddess .... MAMA
  hill .... LOMA, MEDANO
  Indian .... AYMARA,
COLLA, QUECHUA,
CHUNCHO, ANDE, INCA
  inn .... TAMBO
  junta leader .... VELASCO
  king .. INCA, ATAHUALPA,
ATABALIPA
  language ...... QUECHUA,
AYMARA
  llama ..... PACO, ALPACA
  monetary unit ...... SOL
  mountain .... ANDES,
MISTI, HUASCARAN
  plant .... OCA, TOLA
  plateau .... TABLAZO
  port .... CALLAO

president .... BELAUNDE
recording device .. QUIPU
river .... APURIMAC,
UCAYALI, ACARI,
RIMAC, MARANON,
JAVARI
  seaport .... CALLAO
  singer .... SUMAC
  tanager .... YENI
  tobacco .... SANA
  tree .... CINCHONA
  volcano ... MISTI, OMATE
  wind .... PUNA, SURES
pervade .... FILL, PERMEATE,
IMBUE, DIFFUSE
perverse ... WRY, UNTOWARD,
WICKED, CONTRARY,
DIFFICULT
pervert ... VITIATE, CORRUPT,
MISLEAD, MISUSE, DISTORT,
TWIST, DEBASE, WARP
pervious ..... PERMEABLE,
PENETRABLE, AMENABLE
Pesach .... PASSOVER
pesade .... REAR
Pescadores Islands ......
HOKO GUNTO
pesky .... MISCHIEVOUS,
ANNOYING, BOTHERSOME
peso .... DURO
  1/100 of ...... CENTAVO,
CENTIMO
pessimism, opposite of ....
OPTIMISM
pessimist .... WORRIER
  slang .... CRAPEHANGER
pessimistic ..... WORRISOME
pest ... IMP, BANE, PLAGUE,
NUISANCE, VERMIN
  colloquial ...... TERROR
pester .... HECTOR, VEX,
BADGER, HARASS, ANNOY,
BOTHER, HARRY, DUN
pesticide .... DDT
pestiferous .... NOXIOUS,
ANNOYING
pestilence .... SCOURGE,
EPIDEMIC, PLAGUE,
MURRAIN
pestle .... MULLER, BRAY,
POUNDER, BEETLE
  companion of ... MORTAR
pet ...... CODDLE, FAVORITE,
DARLING, DANDLE, FONDLE,
SULK, COSSET
  lamb ..... COSSET, CADE

name .... NICKNAME,
SOBRIQUET
Petain, Marshal ...... HENRI
petal .... LEAF, LABELLUM
base .... UNGUIS
protuberance ... CALCAR
spurred .... LABELLUM
petals, arrangement of ....
WHORL, ROSETTE
without ..... APETALOUS
petard .... FIRECRACKER,
EXPLOSIVE
petasus .... CUPALO,
(WINGED)HAT
petcock ...... VALVE, FAUCET
peter .... DWINDLE, WANE
actor ...... FALK, FONDA,
OTOOLE, USTINOV
Bull's subject ....
TEDDYBEAR, TEDDIES
Pan's author .... BARRIE
captain .... HOOK
dog .... NANA
loss .... SHADOW
pirate .... SMEE
Peter's tribute to Pope .. PENCE
petiole .... (LEAF)STALK,
PEDUNCLE, STIPE
petit .... PETTY
mal .... EPILEPSY
petite .... SMALL, DIMINUTIVE
petition ...... ASK, ENTREATY,
PLEA, REQUEST, PRAY(ER),
SOLICIT, APPEAL, SUIT,
APPLY
petitioner, in law ..... ORATOR
petits fours .... CAKES
Petrarch's lady .... LAURA
petrel ..... TITI, MALLEMUCK,
STINKER, FULMAR
describing one .. STORMY
petrified goddess ...... NIOBE
petrified substance .... FOSSIL,
COAL
petrify .... FOSSILIZE,
HARDEN, DEADEN, STUN
Petrograd .... LENINGRAD
petrol .... GAS(OLINE),
GASOLENE
petrolatum .... VASELINE
petroleum, jelly ....
PETROLATUM, VASELINE
product ..... NAPHTHA,
COKE, BUTANE,
LIGROIN(E), CYMOGENE,
GASOLINE, KEROSENE,

BENZENE, PARAFFIN'
PITCH, BITUMEN
Petrosian, chess champ ....
TIGRAN
Petruchio's wife ...... KATIE,
SHREW
petticoat ... BALMORAL, SLIP,
SKIRT, WOMAN, GIRL,
CRINOLINE
pettifogger .... SHYSTER
pettish ...... PEEVISH, CROSS
pettitoes .... FEET, TOES
petto .... BREAST
petty ...... PALTRY, TRIVIAL,
MINOR, PICAYUNE,
TRIFLING, MEAN, FIDDLING
fault ...... PECCADILLO
officer ... MATE, YEOMAN,
BOSUN
petulant .... FRETFUL,
HOITY-TOITY, IRRITABLE,
PEEVISH, CROSS, TESTY,
SHORT
petunia .... FLOWER,
NIGHTSHADE
pew .... STALL, BENCHES,
SLIP
end carving .. POPPYHEAD
pewee .. PHOEBE, FLYCATCHER,
PEWIT
pewit ..... LAPWING, PEWEE,
PHOEBE, GULL
pewter .... TRIFLE
peyote ...... CACTUS, MESCAL
"Peyton Place" author ....
METALIOUS
pfennig, 1/2 of .... HELLER
100 .... MARK
Phaedra's husband .. THESEUS
parent .... MINOS
Phaedrus' forte ...... FABLES
phagedena .... ULCER,
GANGRENE
phalanger ...... TAPOA, ARIEL
phantasm .... SPECTER,
GHOST, EIDOLON
phantom ... VISION, SPECTER,
ILLUSION, IDOL, (E)IDOLON,
GHOST
Pharaoh .... RAM(E)SES,
CHEOPS, SETI
residence ...... MEMPHIS
Pharisaic ...... HYPOCRITICAL
pharmacist ...... DRUGGIST,
APOTHECARY

pharmaceutical concoction .... TISANE
pharmacology, subject of ..... DRUGS
pharmacy .... DRUGSTORE
pharos .. BEACON, LIGHTHOUSE
builder .... SOSTRATUS
phase ... ASPECT, SIDE, PART, FACET, STAGE, ANGLE, PHASIS
pheasant .... TRAGOPAN, LEIPOA, CHIR, GROUSE, POULT, MONAL, RING-NECK
brood .... NID(E), NYE
nest .... NIDE
phenobarbital .... LUMINOL
phenomenon .... EVENT
phial .... VIAL, BOTTLE
philabeg .... KILT
philanderer: sl. .... WOLF
philanthropic .... CHARITABLE, ALTRUISTIC
philatelist's delight   STAMP
Philip II's naval fleet .. ARMADA
philippic .... TIRADE, HARANGUE, DIATRIBE, SCREED, ORATION, INVECTIVE
Philippine aborigine ... AETA, ATA, NEGRITO
alum .... TAWAS
animal .... TAMARAW, CARABAO, TARSIER
ant .... ANAY
archipelago .... SULU
barge .... CASCO
battlesite .... BATAAN, CORREGIDOR
boat ...... BATEL, CASCO
breadfruit .... RIMA
buffalo .... TIMARAU, CARABAO, TAMARAW
cannon .... LANTAKA
canoe .... BANCA
cape .... BOLINAO
capital .... MANILA, QUEZON CITY
child .... BATA
Chinese invader .... LIMAHONG
citizen .... FILIPINO, TAGALOG
city .... CAVITE, ILIGAN, DAGUPAN, MANILA, CEBU, DAVAO, ZAMBOANGA

civet .... MUSANG
coconut toddy ..... TUBA
coin ...... PESO, PESETA, CENTIMO
deer .... USA
dialect ...... PAMPANGO, TAGAL(OG), ILOCANO, BICOL, WARAY-WARAY
discoverer ... MAGELLAN
dissident .... HUK
drink ...... VINO, TUBA, LUMBANOG
duck .... ITIK, PATO
dwarf ... NEGRITO, AETA
eggplant .... TALONG
expeditionary force ..... PEFTOK, PHILCAG
fabric .... PINA, JUSI
farmer .... KASAMA
fetish .... ANITO
fiber ... MAGUEY, HEMP, ABACA, PINA, JUSI
flag .... WATAWAT
food staple .... RICE, BIGAS, CORN
fort .... COTTA
fruit, foul-smelling ...... DURIAN
fruit tree ..... LANZONES, IBA, GUAVA, SANTOL
gourd .... UPO
governor general .. TAFT, IDE, WOOD, MURPHY, STIMSON
grapes .... UBAS
grass ... COGON, TALAHIB
guerrilla .... HUK
hardwood .... NARRA, YAKAL, IPIL, MOLAVE
heart .... PUSO
hemp .... ABACA
hero ...... AGUINALDO, LAPU LAPU, ABAD SANTOS, RIZAL, BONIFACIO
house .... BAHAY
island ..... SAMAR, CEBU, LEYTE, LUZON, MINDANAO, CORREGIDOR, PANAY, MASBATE, PALAWAN, MINDORO
jar .... BANGA
knife .... BOLO, ITAK
lamb .... TUPA
language ..... TAGALOG

leper colony .... CULION, TALA
liver .... ATAY
lungs .... BAGA
mahogany ...... NARRA
maid .... ALILA
mallard .... DUMARA
meat, dried, salted .. TAPA
midwife .... HILOT
monetary unit ..... PESO
Moro boat ..... VINTA, LIPA, KUMPIT
Moro chief .. DATU, DATO
Moslem .... MORO, MUSLIM, MARANAW
mountain ...... ARAYAT, CORDILLERA, APO, ZAMBALES, BANAHAW
municipality ..... PUEBLO
native ... MORO, IGOROT, DUMAGAT, TAGALOG
negrito ... AETA, ATA, ITA
number ... ISA, DALAWA, TATLO, APAT, LIMA, ANIM
nut .... PILI
omelet .... TORTA
overskirt .... SAYA
oyster .... TALABA
palm .... NIPA, ANAHAW
peasant ... TAO, KASAMA
plum .... DUHAT
president .... QUEZON, OSMENA, ROXAS, QUIRINO, MAGSAYSAY, GARCIA, MACAPAGAL, MARCOS
province ... LANAO, CEBU, SAMAR, BULACAN, ILOILO, RIZAL, ALBAY, ISABELA, LEYTE, LAGUNA, ABRA
rebel .... INSURRECTO, KATIPUNAN, HUK
rice .... MACAN, WAGWAG, PAGA
river ...... PASIG, CHICO
sailboat ... VINTA, BATEL
sapodilla .... CHICO
sarong ..... PATADIONG
sea .... SULU
secret society .... KATIPUNAN
servant .... ALILA
sheep .... TUPA
shirt .... BARO

skirt .... SAYA
slave .... ALIPIN
soy sauce .... TOYO
soybean cake .... TAUSI, TAHURE
soybean curd ... TOKUA, TAHO, TOFU
spinach .... TALINUM
spleen .... LAPAY
statesman...... ROMULO, QUEZON, RECTO, OSMENA
sultanate .... SULU
summer capital .. BAGUIO
sweet potato .... CAMOTE
tail .... BUNTOT
taro .... GABI
territorial claim .. SABAH
thatch .... NIPA, COGON
tongue .... DILA
town .... PUEBLO
tree ... MOLAVE, YAKAL, IPIL, DAO, LANETE, LIGAS, SAMPALOC
tribesman .... KALINGA, IGOROT, TINGGIAN, BADJAO, TAUSUG, MARANAW, NEGRITO
tripe .... GOTO
tuna .... TULINGAN
village .... SITIO
volcano ..... APO, TAAL, MAYON, HIBOK HIBOK
water chestnut .. APULID
water buffalo .. CARABAO
weapon ..... BOLO, KRIS, KAMPILAN
weasel .... MUSANG
yam .... GABI, TUGI, UBI
Philippines, discoverer of the .. MAGELLAN
philistine .... BABBIT
city .. GAZA, GATH, GAYA
giant .... GOLIATH
Philo ____, dick ...... VANCE
philology ..... SCHOLARSHIP, LINGUISTICS
philomel ...... NIGHTINGALE
Philomela, sister of ... PROCNE
philopena .... NUT
philosopher ..... SAGE, CYNIC, SKEPTIC, HEGEL, KANT, HUME, PLATO, LOCKE, ZENO, SPINOZA
stone of .... ELIXIR

philosophy .... EGOISM, MONISM
philter .... POTION, CHARM
phiz .... FACE
phlebotome .. LANCET, FLEAM
phlegm is one .... HUMOR
phlegmatic .. DULL, IMPASSIVE, SLUGGISH, COOL
phloem ... BAST, TISSUE, BARK
phlogistic .... INFLAMMATORY
phlogosis .... ERYSIPELAS
phobia .... FEAR, HATRED, AGORA
Phoebe .... DIANA, MOON, PEWEE, PEWIT, SELENE, ARTEMIS, GODDESS
Phoebus ... SUN, APOLLO, SOL
Phoenician capital .... TYRE, SIDON
    founder of Thebes ......
        CADMUS
    god ..... BAAL, DAGON, MOLOCH
    goddess .... ASTARTE
    port ...... SIDON, TYRE
    princess .... EUROPA
Phoenix .... BENU
phonate .... VOCALIZE
phone call ...... BUZZ, RING
    cubicle .... BOOTH
    emergency .... HOTLINE
    system .... INTERCOM
phonetics, smooth ...... LENE
phonics .... ACOUSTICS
phonograph .... VICTROLA, GRAMOPHONE
    needle ... STYLUS, STYLE
    record ... PLATTER, DISC, LONG PLAY
    record mold ..... MASTER
    with coin slot .. JUKE BOX
phonolite .... CLINKSTONE
phonology .... PHONETICS, PHONEMICS, ORTHOEPY
phony .... FAKE, SHAM, FALSE, SPURIOUS, IMPOSTOR, CHARLATAN
phosphate .... APATITE
phosphor .... STAR, VENUS
photo ..... PIC(TURE), SNAP, MUG, PIX, SHOT
    finish .... DEAD HEAT
    solution ...... REDUCER, HYPO
photograph ... STILL, PICTURE, SHOT, PRINT, FILM
    book .... ALBUM
    enlarge a ...... BLOW UP
photographer's place ....
    DARKROOM
photographic camera .. KODAK, LEICA, CANNON, GRAFLEX
    developing powder ......
        METOL
    equipment ..... CAMERA
    material ... FILM, ORTOL, TONER
    solution .... HYPO, FIXER, DEVELOPER, TONER, REDUCER
photographs pieced together ...
    MOSAIC, MONTAGE
photoplay .... MOVIE
phrase .... EXPRESSION, LOCUTION
    in liturgy .... PARSE
    in song .... REFRAIN
phraseology ...... PARLANCE, WORDING, DICTION, EXPRESSION
phratry .... PHYLE, CLAN
phrenetic ..... WILD, INSANE, EXCITED, FANATIC, DELIRIOUS
phrenic .... MENTAL
Phrygian king .... MIDAS
phthisis .... CONSUMPTION
phylactery .... CHARM, REMINDER
phyletic .... RACIAL
Phillis .... SWEETHEART
phylloid .... LEAFLIKE
physic .... LAXATIVE, CATHARTIC, APERIENT, PURGATIVE
physical .. SOMATIC, NATURAL, MATERIAL, BODILY, SOMAL
    discomfort .. DYSPHORIA
    exercise .... DRILL
    science .... GEOLOGY, CHEMISTRY
    vigor .... VITALITY
physician .. DOC(TOR), GALEN, MAYO, LISTER, MEDIC(O), MESMER
    former .... LEECH
    symbol ...... CADUCEUS
physicist .... MACH, OHM, AMPERE, BOYLE, HAHN, EINSTEIN, CURIE, RABI
physics, branch of .. KINETICS, MECHANICS, OPTICS,

ACOUSTICS, STATICS,
DYNAMICS
theory in .... RELATIVITY
physiognomy .... FACE
phytology .... BOTANY
pi .. JUMBLE, MIXTURE, MIX UP
piacular .... ATONING,
EXPIATORY
pianist ..... CLIBURN, ITURBI,
HESS, ANDA, LEVANT
White House .... NIXON,
TRUMAN
piano .... SPINET
favorite .... NOLA
forerunner of ....
CLAVICHORD,
HARPSICHORD
in music .... SOFT
key .... IVORY
keyboard ...... CLAVIER
piece ...... BAGATELLE,
BALLADE, NOLA
white key ...... NATURAL
pianolike instrument ... SPINET,
CELESTA, CLAVICHORD
piaster, 1/120 of ...... ASPER
piazza ..... SQUARE, ARCADE,
GALLERY, PORCH,
VERANDA(H)
pibroch, instrument for a .....
BAGPIPE
pica .... TYPE
picador's prey ... BULL, TORO
picaresque character ....
VAGABOND
picaroon .... ROGUE,
ADVENTURER, THIEF,
PIRATE
Picasso, painter .... PABLO
picayune ..... PALTRY, PETTY,
TRIVIAL, CHEAP
Piccadilly in London .. STREET
piccolo .... FLUTE
pick ..... PECKER, MATTOCK,
GLEAN, PLECTRUM, CULL,
PROBE, PLUCK, ELITE,
SELECT, CHOOSE, BEST,
MANDREL, CHOICE(ST),
NIBBLE
at ...... NAG, FINGER
on .... ANNOY, TEASE
the .... ELITE
up ..... LEARN, IMPROVE
pickax ..... GURLET, MATTOCK
pickerel .... PIKE
picket .... FENCE, GUARD,

TETHER, PALE, STAKE, POST
station of a ..... OUTPOST
pickings ..... SCRAPS, SPOILS
pickle .... MESS, ACHAR,
GHERKIN, JAM, FIX, SOUSE,
MARINATE, ALEC, CORN,
DILL
pickled .... DRUNK
food .... SOUSE
meat .... SOUSE
pickles .... RELISH
pickling solution .. MARINADE,
BRINE, SOUSE
pickpocket .... DIP, PRIG,
CUTPURSE
trainer .... FAGIN
picnic ... OUTING, CLAMBAKE,
COOKOUT, JUNKET
author of .... INGE
several days' ... MAROON
picot .... PURL
picotee .... CARNATION
pictograph ..... HIEROGLYPH
pictorial ..... GRAPHIC, VIVID
picture ...... IMAGE, IMAGINE,
DEPICT, LIKENESS,
IMPRESSION, SLIDE, STILL,
CANVAS, PROFILE, PHOTO,
REFLECT, PORTRAY,
SCENE(RY), TABLEAU, PRINT
composite .... MONTAGE
frame .... EASEL
girl .... PIN-UP,
CHEESECAKE
in words ..... DESCRIBE,
DELINEATE
life .... STILL
longer than wider ....
PANEL
moving .... CINEMA,
FILM, MOVIE
person's ...... PORTRAIT,
BUST
poorly painted .... DAUB
pretty girl's ..... PIN-UP
puzzle .... REBUS
section .... ROTO
tube .... KINESCOPE
wall .... MURAL
writing .... PICTOGRAPH,
HIEROGLYPH(IC)
picturesque .... SCENIC,
GRAPHIC, QUAINT, IDYLLIC,
STRIKING, VIVID
piddle ...... TRIFLE, DAWDLE,
URINATE

piddling .... USELESS
pidgin .... JARGON, CHINOOK
pie .... PASTY, PATE, PASTRY,
      PATTY, DUMPLING,
   MIXTURE, JUMBLE, COBBLER,
                        JAY
   covering .... CRUST,
                   MERINGUE
   cut, shape of .... WEDGE
   deer's vitals .... HUMBLE
   filling   ... MINCE MEAT
piebald .... HORSE, PIED,
   PINTO, MOTTLED, DAPPLED,
                    CALICO
piece ... UNIT, COIN, FIREARM,
      BIT, PART, CHIP, SLIVER,
      SPLINTER, FRAGMENT,
      SLICE, CANTLE, SCRAP,
      HUNK, MORSEL, COLLOP,
      CHUNK, EKE, PORTION
   cut off .... CHIP, KERF
   de resistance .... ENTREE,
                  MAIN EVENT
   of eight .... REAL
   of paper .... SLIP
   of part music ... DESCANT
   of soap .... CAKE
   of turf ...... SOD, DIVOT
   out .... EKE
   together .... PATCH
   worker .... JOBBER
piecen .... SPLICE
pied ...... SPOTTED, PIEBALD,
      MOTTLED, VARIEGATED
   a-terre .... LODGING
   Piper's river ...... WESER
   Piper's town ... HAMELIN
Piedmont .... PIEMONTE
   city ... TURIN, OSTI, TRINO
   ruling family .... SAVOY,
                    SAVOIE
   village .... MARENGO
pieplant .... RHUBARB
pier .. BUTTRESS, WHARF, DOCK,
   ANTA, QUAY, MOLE, SLIP,
   PILASTER, LANDING, JETTY,
                    JUTTY
   landing ... DOCK, JETTY
   space .... SLIP
pierce ... THIRL, THRUST, STAB,
      PRICK, LANCE, BORE,
      PUNCH, GOUGE, IMPALE,
      SPEAR, GORE, GRIDE,
      PENETRATE, PUNCTURE,
      STICK, LANCINATE
piercing .... SHARP, KEEN,

SHRILL, INCISIVE
pieridine .... BUTTERFLY
Pierre .... PETER, PIETRO
piers, space between .... SLIP
piet ... MAGPIE, OUZEL, OUSEL
pig ..... SOW, SHOTE, DUROC,
      JACOBIN, SWINE, HOG,
      GRUNTER, PORK(ER)
   animal like ..... PECCARY
   castrated ...... BARROW
   dig like a .... ROOT
   disease .... BULLNOSE
   feet of .... TROTTERS
   female ...... SOW, GILT
   for slaughter ..... FATLING
   intestines .. CHITTERLINGS
   iron .... INGOT
   litter .... FARROW
   male .... BOAR
   pen .... STY
   uncastrated ...... BOAR
   vital organs of ....
                   HA(R)SLET
   weed .... GOOSEFOOT
   wild .... BOAR
   young ..... GILT, SHOAT,
      PIGLET, ELT, GRICE,
                    SHOTE
pigboat .... SUBMARINE
pigeon ...... PIDGIN, TURBIT,
      DOVE, NUN, TUMBLER,
      POUTER, RUFF, PIPER,
      FANTAIL, CULVER, BARB
   Barbary .... BARB
   call .... COO
   carrier .... HOMING
   crested ..... TRUMPETER
   hawk .... MERLIN
   hearted .... TIMID,
                   COWARDLY
   house ..... COLUMBARY,
                 (DOVE)COTE
   ID tag .... LEGBAND
   neck feathers ... HACKLE
   pea .... DAL
   slang .... DUPE
   tumbler .... ROLLER
   wood .... CUSHAT,
                  RINGDOVE
   young .... SQUAB
pigeonhole .... SHELVE
pigeonholes, row of ..... RACK
pigfish .... GRUNTER
piggery .... STY
piggin .... PAIL, PIPKIN
piggish .... FILTHY

piggyback .... PICKABACK
pigheaded .... STUBBORN,
        OBSTINATE
piglet .... GILT
piglike animal ..... PECCARY
pigment .. DYE, ANTHOCYANIN,
    AQUAMARINE, CINNABAR,
    ZAFFRE, ETIOLIN, UMBER,
    BICE, STAINER, SMALT,
    ZAFFER, LITHOPONE,
    GAMBOGE, ORPIMENT
  absence of .... ALBINISM,
    ALPHOSIS
  being without ... ALBINO
  black .... MELANIN
  blood's .... HEMACHROME
  blue ...... SMALT, BICE,
    ULTRAMARINE
  bluish green ... VIRIDIAN
  board .... PALETTE
  brown ... UMBER, SEPIA,
    BISTER, BISTRE
  calico printing .. CANARIN
  cochineal .... LAKE
  coal tar .... MAUVE,
    ANILIN(E), ALIZARIN,
    MADDER
  cuttlefish .... SEPIA
  dark brown .... BISTER,
    SEPIA
  earth ... SIENNA, UMBER
  grayish-blue ...... BICE
  green .... BICE
  iron ore .... OCHRE
  lack of ... LEUCODERMA,
    ALPHOSIS, ALBINISM
  red .... CARMINE,
    VERMILION, CINNABAR
  reddish brown ... SIENNA
  skin tissue ..... MELANIN
  soot .... BISTER,
    BISTRE, LAMPBLACK
  without .... ALBINO
  yellow ... OCHRE, OCHER,
    ETIOLIN, FLAVIN(E),
    QUERCETIN, RETINENE
pigmentation: comb. form ....
    CHROMAT(O)
  dark .... MELANISM
  lack of .... LEUCODERMA,
    ALPHOSIS
pigmented black ... MELANOID
pigmentless creature .. ALBINO
pigmy .... (See PYGMY)
pignus .... PAWN, PLEDGE
pigpen .... STY

sound ....---... OINK,
    GRUNT(LE)
pigs' feet .... PETTITOES,
    TROTTERS
  litter of ... FARROW, TEAM
pigskin ... FOOTBALL, SADDLE
pigtail .... QUEUE, BRAID,
    TOBACCO, PLAIT, CUE,
    COLETA
pigweed .... AMARANTH
pika .... CONY, RODENT,
    LAGOMORPH
pike ...---... PICK, MOUNTAIN,
    PARTIZAN, GATE,
    TOLL ROAD, PIERCE,
    SPONTOON, FISH, LUCE(T),
    SPEARHEAD, PICKEREL
  American explorer ......
    ZEBULON
  collection .... TOLL
  like fish ..... ARAPAIMA,
    ROBALO, GAR
  perch .... SAUGER
piker: sl. ...... CHEAPSKATE,
    TIGHTWAD
pilaf(f) .... PILAU
pilaster .... ANTA, PIER,
    COLUMN, ALETTE
  groove .... STRIA
  top of .... CAPITAL
Pilate, Rom. governor ......
    PONTIUS
pilau/pilaw .... PILAF(F)
pilchard .... SARDINE,
    HERRING, PILCHER, FUMADO
pilcher .... PILCHARD,
    SCABBARD
pile ... CONGERIES, HEAP, RICK,
    STACK, HOARD, NAP,
    ACCUMULATE, BUILDING,
    MASS, SPILE
  driver ....---... MAUL, RAM,
    TUP, OLIVER
  hay .. RICK, STACK, MOW
  slang .... FORTUNE
  velvet .... NAP
pileous .... HAIRY
piles .... HEMORROIDS
  wood for .... ALDER
pileus .... (SKULL)CAP
pilewort .... CELANDINE
pilfer .... STEAL, SWIPE, ROB,
    THIEVE, MICHE, MOOCH
pilferer .... THIEF
pilgrim .... WAYFARER,

SOJOURNER, WANDERER, PALMER, IHRAM, ALDEN
badge of .... SCALLOP
destination of ... MECCA, SHRINE, ROME, JERUSALEM
garment of .... IHRAM
Holy Land ..... PALMER
"Pilgrim's Progress" author .. BUNYAN
protector ...... TEMPLAR, CRUSADER
pilgrimage .... HADJ
pilgrims, Indian friend of ..... MASSASOIT, WAMPANOAG
settlement ... PLYMOUTH
ship of ..... MAYFLOWER
traveling together .... CARAVAN
pill .... PELLET, PILULE, (BASE)BALL, BOLUS, DRAGEE
like a .... PILULAR
slang .... BORE
sugar coated ... DRAGEE
vet's .... BOLUS
pillage ... SACK, FLAY, LOOT, SPOIL, RIFLE, FORAY, MARAUD, RAPINE, RAVAGE, PLUNDER, HARRY
pillar ..... COLUMN, SUPPORT, STELE, POST, LAT, PIER, MONUMENT, OBELISK
bottom support .... PEDESTAL
drawing on ... GRAFFITO
of —— .... SMOKE, STRENGTH
of Hercules .. GIBRALTAR, JEBEL MUSA
projecting ring .... CINCTURE
top inhabitant .. STYLITE
top of .... IMPOST
with figure ... CARYATID, ATLANTES, TELAMON
writing on .... GRAFFITO
pillbox .... HAT
pillory .... STOCKS, YOKE, CANGUE, EXPOSE, GIBBET
pillow ... BOLSTER, HEADREST, CUSHION, PAD
covering ..... SLIP, TICK
fight .... ROMP
stuffing .... CEIBA, KAPOK, COTTON
pilose .... HAIRY, HIRSUTE

pilot .... AVIATOR, FLYER, GUIDE, STEER(SMAN), LEAD, CONDUCT
biscuit ...... HARDTACK
boat .... HELMSMAN
cow .... PINTANO
fish .... REMORA
lifesaver for .. PARAFOIL, CHUTE
place of .... COCKPIT
test flight .... SOLO
pilotless plane .... DRONE, GLIDER
pilous .... HAIRY
Pilsudski, Polish president .... JOZEF
pilule .... PILL
Pima ...... INDIAN, COTTON
pimento .... (ALL)SPICE
pimiento ... PEPPER, PAPRIKA, RELISH
pimola .... OLIVE
pimp ... PANDER, PROCURER, RELISH
pimpernel .... PRIMROSE
pimple .... POCK, PAPULE, WHEAL, WHELK, PUSTULE, CARBUNCLE
scar .... POCK
pin ... DOWEL, TOGGLE, PEG, TRIFLE, FASTEN, ACUS, TACK, FID, RIVET, NAIL, FASTENER, COAG, NOG, LILL, BADGE, BOLT, BROOCH, COTTER
buckle's .... TONGUE
colloquial .... LEG
down ...... HOLD, NAIL
firing .... TIGE
flatheaded .... TACK
gunwale .... THOLE
in bowling .... CLUB
meat-cooking .. SKEWER, SPIT, BROACH
metal .... RIVET
money ..... ALLOWANCE
oar .... THOLE
pivot .... PINTLE
supporting .... FID
up .... CHEESECAKE
pina .... PINEAPPLE
pinaceous tree ... PINE, CEDAR, FIR
pinafore .... DICKEY, SLIP, APRON, SAVE-ALL, TIER
children's ..... TIER, SLIP

pince nez .... EYEGLASSES, LORGNON
pincer ...... NIPPER, GRIPPER, CLAW, TWEEZER, FORCEPS, TONGS, PLIERS, CHELA
pinch .... STEAL, FILFER, NIP, FILCH, DISTRESS, RAID, PUGIL, GRIPE, SQUEEZE, ARREST, CRAMP
and twist .... TWEAK
hit .... SUBSTITUTE
of something ..... DASH
pindaric .... ODE
pine .... CONIFER, CEDAR, LONG, KAURY, KAURI, LANGUISH, PONDEROSA, MOPE, PINON, WASTE, YEARN, LOBLOLLY, OCOTE
board/wood .... DEAL
colloquial ... PINEAPPLE
cone .... STROBILE
fruit .... CONE
nut .... PINON
product .... RESIN, GALIPOT
seed .... PINON
tar extract ...... RETENE
tree disease .... BLISTER, RUST
tree resin ...... DAMMER, DAMMAR
Tree state .... MAINE
wild .... PINASTER
wood .... DEAL
pineal body .... SPIPHYSIS
pineapple .... PINE, PINA, ANANA
plantation .... PINERY
slang .... BOMB, (HAND)GRENADE
topknot .... COMA
pinfold .... POUND
ping pong ..... TABLE TENNIS
racket ..... PADDLE, BAT
pinquid .... FAT, OILY, GREASY, UNCTUOUS, FERTILE
pinion ... COGWHEEL, PENNON, WING, FEATHER, SHACKLE
pink ..... SALMON, RADICAL, FOXHUNTER, STAB, PRICK, SHIP
color ... SALMON, ROSY, DAMASK, CORAL
Pinkerton .... DETECTIVE, PRIVATE EYE
pinkie .... SHIP, FINGER

Pinkster .... WHITSUNTIDE
flower .... AZALEA
pinna .... AURICLE, FEATHER, FIN, WING, LEAFLET, EAR
pinnace .... BOAT
pinnacle .... PEAK, ACME, SUMMIT, SPIRE
of ice .... SERAC
pinner .... HEADDRESS
pinniped ..... SEAL, WALRUS, SEALION
pinnule .... LEAFLET
pinochle .... (CARD)GAME
game like ...... BEZIQUE
lowest cards ..... NINES
score .... DIX
term ...... MELD, KITTY, DIX
pinole .... FLOUR
pinon .... PINE
pinpoint ...... DOT, LOCATE
pins and needles .... PARESTHESIA
pint, 1/4 .... NOGGIN, QUARTERM
1/2 .... SPLIT
pintado .... CERO, SIERRA, KINGFISH
pintail .... DUCK, GROUSE, SMEE
pintano ..... COWPILOT, FISH
pintle .... BOLT
pinto ..... SPOTTED, PIEBALD, MOTTLED, PONY
pinworm ... ASCARIS, ASCARID
Pinza, operatic singer ... EZIO
pioneer ..... PAVER, PLANTER
pious ...... SACRED, DEVOUT, RELIGIOUS, GODLY, SAINTLY
feeling .... PIETISM
person .... PIETIST
pip ... SEED, ROUP, SPOT, PEEP, CHIRP, HIT
pipa .... TOAD
pipal ..... (BO)TREE, FIG TREE
pipe ... TUBE, WHISTLE, FLUE, HUB(B), BRIER, BRIAR, CALUMET
air .... VENTIDUCT
bending tool ... HICKEY
bowl leaving ... DOTTEL, DOTTLE
clay ... DUDEEN, CHALAM
collar of ...... FLANGE
curve of .... OFFSET
down .... SHUT UP

fitting .... TEE
gas .... FLUE
hashish smoking ....
      CHALAM
joint .... ELL
joint ring ...... GASKET
line: colloq. ~ CONTACT,
      SOURCE
musical ..... OAT, FLUTE,
      FIFE
nozzled .... HOSE
oriental ... NARG(H)ILE,
   HOOKAH, REED
part .... STEM, BOWL
peace .... CALUMET
player .... FLUTIST
principal .... MAIN
shaped .... TUBULAR,
     FISTULOUS
shepherd's .... OAT,
   LARIGOT, REED
small .... TUBULE,
     PIPETTE
smoke .. TEWEL, DUDEEN,
   CALUMET, HOOKAH,
     NARGILE
tobacco .... CHIBOUK,
     DUDEEN
tobacco bag .... POUCH
pipefish .... GAR
pipelike .... TUBATE
piper .... TRILLER
piping .... HISSING, SIZZLING,
   FOLD, REEDY
joint .... ELL
pipit .... (TIT)LARK
pipkin .... PIGGIN, POT
pippin .... APPLE, SEED
pipsqueak .... SNIP
pipy .... SHRILL
piquancy .... NIP, ZEST
piquant ..... PUNGENT, SPICY,
  SALTY, SHARP, BITING, RACY
pique ... RESENTMENT, PEEVE,
  OFFENSE, EXCITE, NETTLE,
  PROVOKE, COTTON, OFFEND,
     FABRIC
piracy .... ROBBERY
literary .... PLAGIARISM,
     PLAGIARY
piragua .... CANOE, PIROGUE,
     BOAT
Pirandello, Italian dramatist ..
     LUIGI
piranha ..... CARIBE, PIRAYA,
     FISH

pirate ..... PICAROON, XEBEC,
  FREEBOOTER, CORSAIR,
  SEAWOLF, (SEA)ROVER,
     PRIVATEER
famed .. ROGERS, DRAKE,
   KIDD, MORGAN,
     CORNISH
flag .... ROGER
literary ..... PLAGIARIST
of old ..... KIDD, TEACH,
     MORGAN
ship .... PICAROON,
  BRIGANTINE, PRIVATEER,
     FRIGATE
state .... TUNISIA
pirn .... SPOOL, BOBBIN
pirogue ..... CANOE, PIRAGUA
Pisa feature .... TOWER
Pisces .... FISH
piscine lore name .... WALTON
Pisgah's biblical climber .....
     MOSES
summit .... NEBO
pishu .... LLNA
pismire .... ANT, EMMET
pisolite .... LIMESTONE
piss .... URINE, URINATE
Pissarro, Fr. painter ..... CAMILLE
pistachio .... CASHEW, NUT
pistil, part of ... OVARY, STIPE,
  STIGMA, CARPEL, STYLE
pistol .... DERRINGER,
  (SIDE)ARM, ZIP GUN,
  MAUSER, LUGER, REPEATER,
  FIREARM, REVOLVER,
  AUTOMATIC, DAG(G)
case .... HOLSTER
chamber ..... MAGAZINE
slang .... GAT, ROD,
  HEATER, EQUALIZER,
    PEACEMAKER
pistole .... COIN
piston ...... PLUNGER, VALVE
pit ..... CAVITY, ABYSS, HELL
  WELL, POCK(MARK), SEED,
  GRAVE, ARROYO, STONE,
  SNARE, TRAP, ARENA,
  FOVEA, (POT)HOLE
bottomless ...... ABYSS
in anatomy ...... FOSSA
mine .... SUMP
peach/plum ... PUTAMEN,
     ENDOCARP
theater .... PARQUET
pita .. AGAVE, FIBER, BROCKET
pitch ... BITUMEN, ASPHALTUM,

RESIN, ERECT, SET UP,
HURL, CAST, TOSS, FLING,
TAR, ALCHITRAN, THROW,
DIP, ENCAMP, PLUNGE,
LURCH, SWAY, ROLL, REEL,
KEY, CANT

black .... PICEOUS
in baseball ...... TWIRL
pipe .... DIAPASON
salesman's ...... PATTER,
LINE, SPIEL, PLUG
uncompleted ..... BALK
pitchblende ingredient ....
URANIUM
pitcher ...... EWER, HURLER,
OLLA, TOSSER, JUG, TOBY
and the catcher ....
BATTERY
leaf .... ASCIDIUM
left-handed ... SOUTHPAW
pitch of .. TWIRL, SPITTER,
SPITBALL, BEANBALL,
CURVE
plant .... FLYTRAP
plate of the ...... SLAB,
BOX, MOUND
preparatory motion of ...
WINDUP
shaped ..... URCEOLATE
water ..... CARAFE
pitchman .... HAWKER
pitchy .... BLACK
piteous .... PITIFUL, PATHETIC
pitfall .... TRAP, SNARE
pith .... GIST, SUBSTANCE,
MEDULIA, PULP, MARROW,
CORE
helmet ..... TOPEE, TOPI
Pithecanthropus erectus ......
JAVA MAN
pithy ...... LACONIC, TERSE,
CONCISE, FORCEFUL
pitiable .... MEAN
pitiful ... PATHETIC, PITEOUS,
MEAN
pitman .... MINER
pittance .. DOLE, ALLOWANCE
pitted ..... FOVEATE, STONED,
POCKMARKED
pitter patter .... PITAPAT,
DRUMBEAT
pituitary hormone .. PROLACTIN
secretion .... MUCUS,
HORMONE
pity ..... MERCY, COMPASSION,
SYMPATHY

pivot .... PINTLE, WHEEL,
SWIVEL, TURN, HINGE,
STATOR
City .... GEELONG
pivotal .... CARDINAL
pixilated .... DRUNK
pixy ..... FAIRY, ELF, SPRITE,
PIXIE
Pizzaro's conquest ..... PERU
pizzicato .... PLUCKED
placard ... BILL, POSTER, SIGN
placate .... MOLLIFY, APPEASE,
PACIFY, SOOTHE
place ... SPACE, ROOM, REGION,
APPOINT, PUT, SET, STEAD,
LOCALE, LOCUS, POSITION,
STANDING, SPOT, LIEU
accurately .... TRUE
apart .. ENISLE, ISOLATE,
SEGREGATE
between ...... INTERPOSE
camping .... ETAPE,
BIVOUAC
city's ... SQUARE, PLAZA
dancing .... CASINO,
CABARET, BALLROOM
for athletics .. GYMKHANA
for relics ..... SEPULCHER
for rubbish .... DUMP
frequented .. HANGOUT,
HAUNT, PURLIEU
give .... YIELD
hiding .... LAIR, DEN,
HANGOUT, HIDEOUT,
MEW, CACHE
in a benefice .... INDUCT,
INSTALL
in a row .... ALIGN,
ALINE, LINE UP
mat .... DOILY
meeting .... TRYST,
RENDEZVOUS
near .... APPOSE
noisy .... MADHOUSE
of .... LIEU, STEAD
abode .... RESIDENCE,
DWELLING, HOUSE,
HOME
accused in court ......
DOCK
agony ..... GOLGOTHA
confusion .. MADHOUSE
honor .... HEADTABLE,
PEDESTAL
oblivion ...... LIMBO
rapid growth .. HOTBED

religious seclusion .... CONVENT, ABBEY, NUNNERY, MONASTERY, PRIORY, CLOISTER

safety .... REFUGE, HAVEN, SANCTUARY, HARBOR

torment ..... GEHENNA

trial .... VENUE

secret .... MEW, DEN, HIDEOUT

set in .... POSIT, SITUATE

side by side .. COLLOCATE

snugly .... ENSCONCE

storage .... WAREHOUSE, CRIB, DEPOT, CACHE, SILO, CELLAR, CLOSET

take ... OCCUR, HAPPEN, TRANSPIRE

to stand on .... POU STO

trading .. MART, MARKET, EXCHANGE

under water ... IMMERSE, SUBMERGE

placid .... CALM, QUIET, SERENE, TRANQUIL, PEACEFUL, IMPASSIVE

placket .... POCKET

plagiarism ...... CRIB, PIRACY

plagiarist .... THIEF

plagiarize .... CRIB, STEAL, LIFT, PIRATE

plague ... SCOURGE, CALAMITY, VEX, TORMENT, PEST(ER), HARRY, MURRAIN, TEASE, HECTOR, WANION, NUISANCE, HARASS, ANNOY

plagues, one of the .... LOCUST

plaice .... (FLAT)FISH, FLOUNDER, SOLE

plaid .... MAUD, TARTAN

plaidman .... TARTAN, HIGHLANDER

plain ...... CAMPAGNA, FLAT, LEVEL, BARE, CLEAR, MERE, CAMPO, LLANO, PALPABLE, EVIDENT, SIMPLE, PATENT, HOMELY, OPEN, OBVIOUS

Arctic .... TUNDRA

barren, high .... PARAMO

dweller .... LLANERO, GAUCHO, LOWLANDER

grassy .... CAMPO, SAVANNA(H), LLANO, VELD(T), PRAIRIE

high ..... PARAMO, MESA,

WOLD, WEALD

hill on a .... BUTTE

spoken ... BLUNT, FRANK, CANDID

treeless .... STEPPE, TUNDRA, VELD(T), WOLD, PAMPAS, SAVANNA(H)

plains Indian .... PAWNEE

plainsman ...... WESTERNER

plaint .. LAMENT(ATION), GRIPE

plaintiff .... DEMANDANT, SUER, ACCUSER, ORATOR, COMPLAINANT, SUITOR

answer of .. REPLICATION

list of wrongs suffered ... LIBEL

withdrawal of case ...... NONSUIT

plaintive ... MOURNFUL, SAD, WISTFUL

plait .... PLEAT, BRAID, PIGTAIL, QUEUE, PLAT, PLEX, PLY, TRESS, WIMPLE, PLEACH

plaited .... PLICATE, BRAIDED

grass/leaves .... SENNIT

trimming .... RUCHE

plan .. OUTLINE, MAP, SCHEMA, SCHEME, ETTLE, PLAT, DRAFT, DESIGN, PROJECT

artfully ..... MACHINATE

of journey .... ITINERARY

spoiler .... MARPLOT

townsite .... PLAT

planch(e) ..... FLOOR, BOARD

plancher .... PALLET

plane ... FLAT, LEVEL, EVEN, SURFACE, AIRFOIL, TROWEL

geometry .. PLANIMETRY

inclined .... RAMP

smoothing .... TROWEL

10-sided ...... DECAGON

tree ... PLATAN, CHINAR

war ..... SPAD, SPITFIRE, STUKA, ZERO, NAPIER, SUPERFORT, SABREJET, MIG

planet .... VENUS, MARS, SATURN, JUPITER, MERCURY, PLUTO, URANUS, EARTH, NEPTUNE

between Jupiter and Mars PALLAS

erratic movement of ..... LIBRATION

largest .... JUPITER
minor .... ASTEROID
satellite .... MOON, RHEA,
    DIONE, MIMAS, HESTIA,
    NEREID, UMBRIEL,
    PHOBOS, DEIMOS
shadow of ...... UMBRA,
    PENUMBRA
planetoid .... ASTEROID
planetarium .... ORRERY
planing tool ...... SPOKESHAVE
plank ..... BOARD, PRINCIPLE,
    SLATE, DECK
  curve of .... SNY
  down .... PAY
planks above keel .. DEADWOOD
planoblast .... JELLYFISH,
    HYDROID
plant (see shrub) .. PLANTAIN,
    HYSSOP, MILL, BUGLE,
    WORT, AROID, SOW, TREE,
    SHRUB, HERB, FACTORY,
    STOCK, CLOVER, FREESIA
aconite ..... MONKSWOOD,
    WOLFSBANE
agave .... PITA
air ... EPIPHYTE, ORCHID,
    MOSS, LICHEN
Alpine ...... EDELWEISS
amaranth family ....
    COCKSCOMB
amaryllis family ....
    EUCHARIS, CRINUM
and animal classification
    LINNEAN
and animal life ... BIOTA,
    BIOS
apiaceous ...... CARROT,
    PARSNIP, ANISE
appendage ..... STIPULE,
    TENDRIL, STIPEL
artichoke's kin ....
    CARDOON
aromatic .... LAUREL,
    MINT, GUACO, ANISE,
    LAVENDER, THYME,
    MONARDA
arum family ..... AROID,
    TARO
aster family .... DAISY,
    C(H)AMOMILE,
    TARRAGON, TIDYTIPS,
    ZINNIA, FEVERFEW
axis .... STALK, CAUDEX
banana .... CANNA,
    PLANTAIN

base ... CAUDEX, CAULIS
beanlike ...... SAINFOIN
beech family .... OAK
beetle ... (COCK)CHAFER,
    SCARAB, ROSEBUG
berry .... CURRANT
Biblical ... HYSSOP, TARE
bitter .... RUE
blue-flowered ... BLUET,
    LUPINE
body .... THALLUS
borage family .. COMFREY,
    HELIOTROPE,
    LUNGWORT
branch ... SPRAY, SPRIG,
    TWIG
brassicaceous ..... COLE,
    TURNIP, CABBAGE,
    BROCCOLI
breathing pore ... STOMA
broom .... SPART
bryophytic .... MOSS
bud .... (S)CION
bug .... CHINCH
bulb ... NARCISSUS, SEGO,
    ATAMASCO, SQUILL,
    JONQUIL, GARLIC
burning bush ... WAHOO
bursting ..... PUFFBALL
cactus .... MESCAL,
    CEREUS, SAGUARO
caper family .... CLEOME
capsule .... POD
carbohydrate ....
    PENTOSAN(E)
carrot family ... ERINGO,
    ERYNGO, CHERVIL,
    HEMLOCK, CONIUM,
    CORIANDER, COWBANE,
    DILL, ANISE, CUM(M)IN
celery family .... CARROT
century .. AGAVE, MAGUEY
chili .... CAPSICUM
chrysanthemum ....
    PYRETHRUM
climbing .... SCAMMONY,
    RUNNER, LIANA, LIANE,
    VINE, RATTAN, YAM
clinging part of .. TENDRIL
clover-like ..... MELILOT,
    MEDIC
composite family ....
    MILFOIL, YARROW,
    COSMOS, COREOPSIS,
    ASTER, DAHLIA, DAISY,
    DANDELION, SUNFLOWER

covering ...... ARMATURE, PEAT, TUNIC
creeping ...... IPOMOEA, GROUNDLING, PYXIE, PERIWINKLE
cross-bred ..... HYBRID
crow family .... COLUMBINE, HELLEBORE
crowfoot family .... HEPATICA, MOUSETAIL
cruciferous ...... CRESS, MUSTARD
cutting .... SLIP
cycad family ... COONTIE
cyperaceous ..... SEDGE
daisylike .... OXEYE
decay .... ROT, NECROSIS
disease .... SCAB, MOSAIC, RUST, SMUT, ESCA, BRAND, BLET, ERGOT, PSOROSIS, NECROSIS, CLUBROOT, CANKER, ERINOSE, GALL, WILT, ICTERUS, (BLACK)ROT, SCALD, YELLOW, MILDEW, BLIGHT, CURL, BUNT
dodder .... AMIL
dry climate .. XEROPHYTE, CACTUS
dwarf .... ALYSSUM
dye .... AMIL
eating animal .... HERBIVORE
eating aquatic mammal .. DUGONG, MANATEE
emetic .... IPECAC
environment ... HABITAT
experimental garden .... NURSERY
exudation .... RESIN, GUM, COPAL
fiber ..... HEMP, ABACA, RAMIE, JUSI, SUNN, FLAX, ISTLE, SISAL, MAGUEY, AGAVE, PITA
figwort family .... COLLINSIA
floating .... WATER LILY, LOTUS
flowering ... ACANTHUS, ROSE, RHODORA, CALLA, ORCHID
flowerless .... LYCOPOD, FERN, LICHEN
fluid ... SAP, MILK, LATEX

fodder .... VETCH, SAINFOIN
forage .... GUAR
fossil .... CALAMITE, HORSETAIL
fragrant .... BASIL, ANGELICA, THYME, MARJORAM, (SPEAR)MINT, HYSSOP
fragrant-leafed .... TARRAGON, CAMOMILE
fragrant seed ...... ANISE
garden .... ORACH(E)
gentian family .... CENTAURY
genus ...... ARUM, AGAVE, ERINGO
geranium family .... ALFILARIA
ginger family .. CURCUMA, TURMERIC
goosefoot .... BEET, SPINACH
gourd family .... (MUSK)MELON, CANTALOUPE
gout medicine ... GUACO
grass .... AVENA
grasslike .... RUSH
growing from inside ..... ENDOGEN
growing in solutions ..... HYDROPHONICS
growing within another .. ENDOPHYTE, ENTOPHYTE
grown flat .... ESPALIER
growth on a ...... GALL
hair .... VILLUS
hairlike growth .... TRICHOME, BRISTLE, PRICKLE
hairy-leafed ... ANCHUSA
heath family .... AZALEA, LAUREL
hemp .... CANNABIS
herbaceous .... LOBELIA
honeysuckle family ...... ELDER
insect ..... SCALE, APHID
insect-catching .. FLYTRAP
insect-eating .. CARNIVORE
interior chaff ..... PALEA
iris family ..... CROCUS, ORRIS, ORRICE, FREESIA, IXIA
juice .... MILK, SAP

kind of .... ANNUAL
kingdom, part of ....
    PHYLUM
knotweed family ....
    PERSICARY
leaf, poisonous ....
    JABORANDI
leaves for salad ....
    ESCAROLE
leguminous ..... DERRIS,
    GUAR, LENTIL, PEA
lice genus .... APHIS
life .... FLORA,
    VEGETATION
lilaceous ... SEGO, LEEK,
    ONION, TULIP
lily family ... SABADILLA,
    CAMAS(S), GARLIC,
    ONION, LEEK, ALLIUM,
    ALOE, LOTUS, YUCCA,
    SQUILL, ASPHODEL,
    HELLEBORE
liquid .... SAP, JUICE,
    MILK, LATEX
louse ..... APHID, APHIS
madder family .. COFFEE,
    HOUSTONIA, IPECAC,
    CINCHONA, GARDENIA,
    CHAY
main axis ... STALK, STEM
male .... MAS
mallow family ....
    CHECKERBLOOM,
    HIBISCUS, HOLLYHOCK
marigold ...... KINGCUP,
    ASTER, CAPER
marsh .... CATTAIL
material spread around ..
    MULCH
matter, decaying ... PEAT
meadow ..... INNOCENCE
medicinal ... GENTIAN,
    SENNA, HERB, ALOE,
    BONESET, ARNICA,
    IPECAC, LOBELIA,
    SIMPLE
milkweed family ....
    STAPELIA
milkwort family .. SENEGA
milky liquid ..... LATEX
mint family .... COLEUS,
    BASIL, BETONY,
    DITTANY, OREGANO,
    HENBIT, MAJORAM,
    CATNIP, SAGE, THYME,
    SALVIA, HYSSOP,

    BERGAMOT, LAVENDER,
    ROSEMARY, BUGLE,
    GERMANDER, PATCHOULI,
    MONARDA, FRAXINELLA
moor .... HEATHER
mosslike ... TILLANDSIA,
    LIVERWORT, LICHEN
mulberry family ....
    CONTRAYERVA
mushroom-like ....
    PUFFBALL
musky smelling ....
    MOSCHATEL
mustard family .... COLE,
    CABBAGE, WOAD,
    STOCK, CRUCIFER,
    CRESS, RAPE, KALE,
    ALYSSUM, CHARLOCK,
    RADISH, MADWORT
narcotic ... HEMP, POPPY,
    MARIJUANA, HASHISH
nettle family ...... HEMP,
    PELLITORY
nightshade family ....
    SOLANUM, TOBACCO,
    POTATO, PETUNIA
non-flowering ..... FERN
not native ...... EXOTIC
noxious .... WEED
odorous .... BUGBANE
oil ...... RAPE, RAMTIL,
    BENNE
one-celled ..... PROTIST
one-seeded ... PSORALEA
onion family ..... CHIVE
ornamental .... BEGONIA,
    CLARY
palmlike .... CYCAD
parasite .... LICHEN,
    BLIGHT, APHID
parasitic ...... DODDER,
    ORCHID, MISTLETOE
parsley family ... CICELY,
    SANICLE
pea family ..... LICORICE,
    SENNA, GRAM,
    COCKSHEAD, VETCH,
    ALFALFA, LOCOWEED,
    LENTIGO, LEGUME,
    INDIGO, LUPINE
pepper .... KAVA,
    CAPSICUM, CAYENNE,
    BETEL
perennial .... IRIS,
    CROCUS, SEDUM,

COLUMBINE, THYME,
DOGBANE
pest .... CHINCH
pink family .... CAMPION,
CARNATION, DIANTHUS,
CAMPO
pith .... PULP
pithy .... SOLA
poisonous ..... ACONITE,
LOCO, HENBANE,
HEMLOCK, WOLFSBANE
poppy family ....
CELANDINE, CHICALOTE,
BLOODROOT
pore ... LENTICEL, STOMA
potato family ... DATURA
prickly .... BRAMBLE,
THISTLE, NETTLE,
CACTUS, TEASEL, BRIER
primrose family ....
FUCHSIA, COWSLIP,
CYCLAMEN, OXLIP
product .... FRUIT
ragweed ..... BURDOCK,
COCKLEBUR
receptacle .... TORUS
red-sapped .. BLOODROOT
rheumatism medicine ....
GUACO
rock ...... LICHEN, MOSS,
STONECROP, LITHOPHYTE
root .... RADIX, EDDO
root, edible ..... MANIOC,
CASSAVA
root, fragrant .... ORRIS
root ointment ..... NARD
root purgative ... JALAP
rose family ..... BURNET,
DROPWORT, SHADBUSH,
BENNET, AVENS,
POTENTILLA, CINQUEFOIL,
FIVE-FINGER
rue family .. FRAXINELLA,
LIME, LEMON, ORANGE
runner .... STOLON
rushlike .... SEDGE
sacred .... RAGTREE
sage family ...... CLARY
salad .... CHICORY,
(WATER)CRESS, ENDIVE
salty soil ... HALOPHYTE
saxifrage family ....
MITERWORT
scale .... PALEA, SQUAMA
sea .... ENALID

sea animal resembling ...
SPONGE
sea-bottom .... BENTHOS
secretion ... GUM, RESIN
sedge .... PAPYRUS
seed .... HERB
seed case .... POD
seed organ ...... PISTIL
seed yielding oil .. SESAME,
BENNE
sensitive .... MIMOSA
sesame .... TIL
shoot ... (S)CION, LAYER
shoots ..... ASPARAGUS
single-seeded .. PSORALEA
slang ... SWINDLE, TRAP,
TRICK, DECOY
smelly .... BURDOCK,
TANSY, STINKWEED,
HENBANE, RUE,
FIGWORT, BUGBANE,
YARROW, MILFOIL,
MULLE(I)N, RAFFLESIA
soap .... AMOLE
spiny .... CACTUS
sprout .... SPIRE
stalk ... HA(U)LM, STEM,
CAULIS, SPIRE
stand .... JARDINIERE
starch ... POTATO, TARO,
CASSAVA, MANIOC, CORN
stem .... CAUDEX, CORM,
BINE, CAULIS, HA(U)LM,
AXIS
stem joint .... NODE
stem spongy center ......
PITH, MEDULLA
stunted .... SCRAG
stunter ...... HERBICIDE
suckers .... APHID
sun-turning .. HELIOTROPE
swamp ...... MARIGOLD,
DIONAEA, COWSLIP
swelling on .... BLEB
tendril .... CIRRUS
thistle-like ... ARTICHOKE
thorny ... BRIAR, BRIER,
BRAMBLE, WAIT-A-BIT
tissue .... XYLEM
tissue cavity ... LOCULUS
trifoliate .... SHAMROCK
tropical .... PALM, TARO,
CASSAVA, UDO, BANANA,
LANTANA, CYCAD,
MANGROVE, PLANTAIN,

PAPAYA, QUASSIA, RAMTIL, CLEOME
trumpet ...... BIGNONIA
tumor .... GALL
twining .... IPOMOEA
underwater .. HORNWORT, BENTHOS
vegetable .... CELERY, CAULIFLOWER, ARTICHOKE
verbena family .. VERVAIN
violet family ... PANSY
water .... FANWORT, PAPYRUS, HYDROPHYTE
with aromatic seeds .... ANISE, CUMIN
bulblike root .... TUBEROSE
edible root .... SKIRRET
edible stalk .. CARDOON
fragrant seed .... ANISE
fruit .... BEARER
heart-shaped flowers .. DICENTRA
no seeds .... FERN
perennial stem .... ACROGEN
pungent pods .... CAPSICUM
sun-turning flowers ... HELIOTROPE, TURNSOLE
trumpet-shaped flower SEGO
underground buds .... GEOPHYTE
woody .... BUSH
woody tissue .... XYLEM
yielding hashish .... CANNABIS
young .... SAPLING
plantain .... FLEAWORT, WEED, RIBWORT
fruit .... BANANA
spike .... CHAT
plantation ... COLONY, ESTATE, BOWERY, HACIENDA
cacti .... NOPALRIE
coffee .... FINCA
Scarlett O'Hara's .. TARA
planter ... COLONIST, SOWER, PIONEER, SEEDER
planting tool .. DIBBLE, SEEDER
plantlike animal ...... CORAL, SPONGE, ZOOPHYTE
plants, book on ..... HERBAL
collector of ... HERBALIST

of .... VEGETAL
scourge of ..... BLIGHT, LOCUSTS
stand for .... JARDINIERE
study of ..... PHYTOLOGY
where sold .... NURSERY
plaque ..... BROOCH, TABLET, BADGE
plash .... POOL, PUDDLE
plasma ..... QUARTZ, WHEY, PROTOPLASM
plaster ..... PARGET, COVER, OVERLAY, GROUT, SMEAR, STUCCO, DAUB, COMPO
bandage .... SPICA
cement .... PUTTY
cover with .... CEIL
first coat .... RENDER
for broken limb ... CAST
mustard ...... SINAPISM
of ____ .... PARIS
of Paris .. GESSO, STUCCO, GYPSUM, YESO, HYDRATE
smoothing tool .. TROWEL
wall .... STUCCO
plastered: sl. .... DRUNK
plasterwork .... PARGET, SCAGLIOLA
plastic .... FICTILE, FLEXIBLE, PLIABLE
art .... MODELING, CERAMICS, SCULPTURE
clay .... PUG
material .... FORMICA, LIGNIN, LUCITE
synthetic .... LUCITE, BAKELITE, FORMICA, BUNA, NYLON
plastid .... CELL
plastron ...... BREASTPLATE, DICKEY, SHIRT FRONT
plat .... BRAID, PLAIT, PLAN, MAP
Plata river, city on .... MONTEVIDEO
plate ..... DISC, SHARD, DISK, DISH, SCUTE, COAT, PLATTER, PATIN(A), LAMINA, OVERLAY, LAMELLA
armor .... TASSE
baseball .... (HOME)BASE
battery .... GRID
bony ... SCUTE, SCUTUM
Eucharist .... PATEN
horny .. SCUTE, SCUTUM
hurler's .... DISCUS

metal .... LAMB
metal cooking .. GRIDDLE
ship-shaped .... NEF
with brass .... BRAZE
with zinc ... GALVANIZE
plateau ... MESA, TABLELAND,
PUNA, ALTIPLANO, KAROO
top cover .... ICECAP
plated .... COATED, ARMORED
platelet .... SCUTUM
platelike organ ..... LAMELLA
platen .... ROLLER
plater .... HORSE, NAG
platform ... STAGE, BALCONY,
GALLERY, BEMA, ESTRADE,
SOLLAR, DOLLY
article .... PLANK
car .... FLATCAR
election .... HUSTINGS
engineroom ... CATWALK
floating .... RAFT
food-drying ..... FLAKE
for execution ... SCAFFOLD
fort's gun ..... BARBETTE
house painter's ....
SCAFFOLD
kind of ... SKID, ALTAR,
HUSTINGS
on wheels ...... TRUCK
politician's ... HUSTINGS
portable .... PALLET
principle .... PLANK
raised .... TRIBUNE, DAIS,
PODIUM, STAND, PULPIT
revolving .... TURNTABLE
ship's .... MAINTOP,
CROW'S-NEST, DECK
speaker's ..... ROSTRUM,
TRIBUNE
streetcar ...... VESTIBULE
platina .... PLATINUM
platinum .... PLATINA
blonde actress .. HARLOW
platitude ... TRUISM, CLICHE,
BROMIDE
platitudinous ... TRITE, DULL
Plato's school ..... ACADEME
work .... DIALOGUES,
APOLOGY, CRITO,
PHAEDO, SYMPOSIUM,
REPUBLIC
platoon commander ....
LIEUTENANT
unit .... SQUAD
platter ... PLATE, (HOME)BASE,

RECORD, DISH, SALVER,
TRENCHER
platyhelminth ... FLATWORM,
FLUKE, TREMATODE,
PLANARIAN
platypus .... DUCKBILL
plaudit ... OVATION, APPLAUSE,
PRAISE
plausible .... SPECIOUS,
CREDIBLE
play .... FRISK, GAMBOL,
GAMBLE, PERFORM, ACT,
(MELO)DRAMA, SPORT,
TRIFLE, BET(ON), FROLIC
actors in a .... CAST,
PERSONAE
amateurs' ... DRAMATICS
around .... GAD
at love .... FLIRT, DALLY
backer of .... ANGEL
between acts .. INTERLUDE
boisterously ...... LARK
bridge .... FINESSE
dilemma in a ...... NODE,
NODUS
down .... MINIMIZE
fast and loose .... DALLY,
TRIFLE
first performance ....
PREMIERE
for one actor ....
MONOLOGUE
for stakes ...... GAMBLE
grandstand ...... STUNT
ground .... PARK,
SANDLOT, OVAL,
DIAMOND
heroine .... PREMIERE
instrument carelessly ....
TWEEDLE
introduction to a ....
PROLOGUE
joke on .... RAG
jokes .... CLOWN
on words .... PUN,
QUIBBLE
part in a ...... ROLE, BIT
part of a ..... SCENE, ACT
possum ... DEAD, FEIGN,
PRETEND
practical joke on ... RAG
silent .... PANTOMINE
that fails .... TURKEY
the beau .... GALLIVANT
the violin .... FIDDLE
tricks on .... JAPE

truant .... MICHE
unsuccessful .... TURKEY
up .... ADVERTISE
wrong card .... RENIG
playa .... BASIN, BEACH
playboy .... GADABOUT
bunny .... HOSTESS
club founder ... HEFNER
player ... THESPIAN, MUMMER,
ACTOR, PERFORMER, GAMBLER
at dealer's right ... PONE
dishonestly entered in race
RINGER
incompetent .... DUB,
PALOOKA
piano .... NICKELODEON
unwilling to sign ....
HOLDOUT
who cuts the cards .. PONE
with lowest score .. BOOBY
players' position ...... LINEUP
playful ... SPORTIVE, SKITTISH,
FRISKY, MERRY, JOCOSE,
KITTENISH
playground item ...... SWING,
SLIDE
playing card(s) extra .. JOKER
spot .... PIP
shuffle .... RIFFLE
suit .. HEARTS, DIAMONDS,
SPADES, CLUBS
playing field .... OVAL, ARENA,
DIAMOND
playlet .... SKIT, SKETCH
plays collectively ..... DRAMA
performed by amateurs ..
DRAMATICS
plaything ...... BAUBLE, TOY,
PAWN
playwright ...... DRAMATIST
plaza ...... SQUARE, MARKET
plea .... EXCUSE, APPEAL,
REQUEST, ENTREATY,
ALLEGATION, PETITION,
PRAYER
for dismissal .. DEMURRER
pleach ... PLAIT, INTERTWINE,
INTERLACE
plead ... ARGUE, APPEAL, BEG,
IMPLORE, ENTREAT
in law .... SHOW
pleader .... PARACLETE,
ADVOCATE
pleading, act of .... SUIT
pleasant ... GENIAL, AMIABLE,

GAY, MERRY, ENJOYABLE,
AGREEABLE
Island .... NAURU
pleasantries .... AMENITIES,
CIVILITIES
pleasantry .... JOKE, BANTER
please ...... GRATIFY, ELATE,
DELIGHT, SUIT, SATISFY,
WILL, WISH, GLADDEN,
PRITHEE
"Please Please Me" singers ...
BEATLES
pleased .... GLAD
pleasing ..... NICE, PLEASANT,
AGREEABLE
pleasure ... JOY, ENJOYMENT,
RELISH, LIKING, GRACE,
DELIGHT, WISH, WILL,
CHOICE
boat .... YACHT, BARGE,
CRUISER
craft harbor .... MARINA
ground ..... PLEASANCE,
RESORT
seeker .... HEDONIST,
SYBARITE
trip ... JUNKET, OUTING
voyage .... CRUISE
pleat .... PLAIT, FOLD, SHIRR,
PLICATE, RUFFLE
pleated .... PLICATE
pleating ... GOFFER, GAUFFER
plebe ..... FRESHMAN, FROSH
plebeian ... COMMON, COARSE,
VULGAR
plebiscite .... REFERENDUM
plebs .... MASSES
plectron .... PLECTRUM
plectrum ... PICK, PLECTRON,
QUILL
pledge .... PAWN, SWEAR,
PROMISE, PLIGHT, SPONSION,
EARNEST, TOKEN, TOAST,
GAGE, ENGAGE, VOW,
PIGNUS, BOND, DEPOSIT,
HEST, PAROLE
pledged ..... SWORN, BOUND
pledget .... SWAB, DRESSING,
WAD, DOSSIL
pledgor .... PAWNER
pleiades, one of the ... MAIA,
STEROPE, TAYGETA,
MEROPE, ELECTRA,
ALCYONE, CELAENO
parent of ...... PLEIONE,
ATLAS

Pleione's daughter ... PLEIAD, MAIA, TAYGETA, STEROPE
   husband .... ATLAS
plenary ..... FULL, ABSOLUTE, COMPLETE
plenipotentiary .... FULL, PLENARY, AMBASSADOR, ENVOY
plenitude .... FULLNESS
plenteous .... ABUNDANT, COPIOUS
plentiful ...... COPIOUS, FULL, REPLETE, BOUNTIFUL, ABUNDANT, AMPLE, RIFE
plenty ...... AMPLE, ENOUGH, OPULENCE
plenum .... FULL(NESS)
   opposite of ..... VACUUM
pleon .... TELSON
pleonasm ...... TAUTOLOGY, NIMIETY, VERBOSITY, REDUNDANCY
pleonastic ...... REDUNDANT
plessor ..... PLEXOR, HAMMER
plethora .... EXCESS
plexor .... PLESSOR
plexus ..... NETWORK, RETE, RETIA
pliable .... FLEXIBLE, SUPPLE, PLASTIC, MALLEABLE, PLIANT
pliant .... SUPPLE, LIMBER, LITHE, FLEXIBLE
pliers .... PINCERS
plight .... SITUATION, CONDITION, PLEDGE, ENGAGE, BETROTH
plinth .... ORLO, BASE, BLOCK
plod ..... DRUDGE, TRUDGE, SLOG, WALK, STEP
plop .... DROP, PLUMP
plot ... PATCH, PLAT, CHART, SCHEME, CONSPIRACY, CONSPIRE, LOT, CABAL, DRAW, MAP, INTRIGUE, MACHINATE
   of story/play ..... NODE, SCENARIO
plotter .... SCHEMER, INTRIGANT(E), INTRIGUER, MACHINATOR
plough .... PLOW
ploughshare .... CO(U)LTER
plover ...... KILLDEER, STILT, SANDPIPER, PEWIT, LAPWING, SURFBIRD, DOTT(E)REL
   bird like .... TURNIX
   kin of .... BUSTARD, COURSER
plow ... LIST(ER), ROVE, TILL, PLOUGH, FURROW
   blade .... SHARE, CO(U)LTER
   land .... ARABLE
   part ...... SLADE, SHARE, SOLE, CLEVIS, SHE(A)TH
plowed land ..... ARADO, ERD, FURROW
plowman ..... TILLER, RUSTIC
   shoe of ..... CLODHOPPER
plowshare part .. MOLDBOARD
ploy .... MANEUVER, STRATEGY, STRATEGEM
pluck .... FORTITUDE, SPUNK, STRUM, TWEEZE, VELLICATE, AVULSE, COURAGE, SPIRIT, GRIT, PICK, PULL(OUT), SWINDLE, GUTS, DEPLUME, NERVE, TUG
plucky .. GAME, BRAVE, SPUNKY
plug ...... TAP, NAG, PLATER, ADVERTISEMENT, PUBLICIZE, PLOD, SLOG, SPILE, SPIGOT, BUNG, STOPPER, STOP UP, SHOOT, DOSSIL
   absorbent ..... TAMPON
   colloquial ... PITCH, LINE
   for wound ...... DOSSIL
   gun .. TAMPION, TOMPION
   in radio/TV .... COMMERCIAL
   of dirt .... COMEDO
   organ pipe ..... TAMPION, TOMPION
   slang .. RECOMMENDATION
   tobacco .... PERIQUE
   ugly ..... ROWDY, GOON, GANGSTER, RUFFIAN, THUG
   wind instrument .. FIPPLE
plugger, kind of .... PRESS AGENT, BARKER
plum .... DAMSON, PRIZE, FRUIT, RAISIN, SLOE, DAMASCENE, DRUPE, GAGE, DAMASKEEN, KAKI, FREESTONE
   brandy ...... SLIVOVITZ
   cake .... BABA

disease ..... BLACKKNOT, BLACKRUST
fruit like ... PERSIMMON, LOQUAT
Java .... LOMBOY
pit of .... PUTAMEN, ENDOCARP
powdery coating .. BLOOM
stone .... NUTLET
wild ..... SLOE, BULLACE
plumage .... FEATHERS
plumb ... VERTICAL, WHOLLY, SOUND, FATHOM, PLUMMET
bob .... PLUMMET
plumbago ... GRAPHITE, LEAD
plumbeous .... LEADEN
plumber .... (GAS)FITTER, PIPEFITTER
tool of .... SNAKE
plumbum .... LEAD
plume ...... EGRET, MARABOU, PANACHE, PLUMAGE, AIGRET, CREST, FEATHER, DOWN
helmet .... PANACHE
heron's ...... AIGRET(TE)
plummet .. PLUMB, FALL, DROP
plumose .... FEATHERED
plump ...... FUBSY, FAT, PLOP, CHUBBY, BLUNT(LY), PLUNK, ROTUND, BUXOM
and short ... ROLY-POLY
plumule ...... BUD, FEATHER, PLUMELET
plunder ...... LOOT, RAVAGE, BOOTY, PREY, MARAUD, PILLAGE, (DE)SPOIL, STEAL, PROG, HARRY, RIFLE, SWAG, RAPINE, (RAN)SACK, FORAY, FORAGE
search for ...... RAVEN, RAVIN
plunderer .... RAPPAREE, FREEBOOTER
plunge ...... DIP, DIVE, SWIM, LUNGE, DUNK
headlong .... PITCH
into a liquid ... IMMERSE, DUNK, DOUSE, SOUSE
plunger ..... DIVER, GAMBLER, PISTON, DASHER
plunk ... BLOW, PLUCK, STRUM, PLUMP
slang .... DOLLAR
sound ... TWANG, THUD

plural marriage ... POLYGAMY, POLYANDRY
plurality .... MAJORITY
plus value .... ASSET
plush .... LUXURIOUS
cloth like .... BOLIVIA
Plutarch's forte ... BIOGRAPHY
Pluto ... DIS, HADES, PLANET, GOD, DOG, ORCUS
domain of ...... HADES, LOWER WORLD, SHEOL, HELL, INFERNO
voice of .... COLVIG
plutocrat ... CROESUS, NABOB
plutonic .... IGNEOUS
pluvial .... RAINY, SOPPY
ply ...... LAMINATION, FOLD, HANDLE, TWIST, LAYER
plywood layer .... VENEER
Plymouth Colony governor ....
BRADFORD, CARVER, WINSLOW
pneuma .... SOUL, SPIRIT, HOLY SPIRIT
pneumogastric nerve ... VAGUS
Po, city on the .... TURIN, TORINO
river ... PADUS, ERIDANUS
tributary .... TICINO, TREBBIA, TESSIN, ADDA
valley tribesman ....
LOMBARD
poach .... MIX, SHIRR, TRESPASS, TRAMPLE, STEAL
poacher .... LURCHER
dog of .... LURCHER
poachy .... SODDEN, SOGGY
Pocahontas' father ....
POWHATAN
husband .... ROLFE
pochard .... DUCK, SMEE
kin of .... REDHEAD, WIDGEON
pock ... PIMPLE, PUSTULE, PIT, SCAR
pocket .... CAVITY, SACK, POUCH, BAG, SAC, SMALL, FOB, POKE
billiards .... POOL
money .... CASH
shape of .... U-CUT
pocketbook .... WALLET, BILLFOLD, PURSE
pockmark .... PIT
poco .... LITTLE
pod ... SHELL, COCOON, GAM,

SCHOOL, FLOCK, ARIL,
 BOLL, BURR, GROOVE,
CHIL(L)I, SHUCK, SEEDCASE,
ACHENE, CYPSELA, POUCH,
BENDY, LEGUME, CAPSULE
 edible ...... OKRA, OCRA
 fodder .... CAROB
 gastric stimulant ....
  CAPSICUM
 like fruit bearers.. CAROB,
  CATALPA
 mustard plant .. SILIQUE
 tree .... LOCUST
podagra .... GOUT
podesta ..... MAYOR, JUDGE,
  GOVERNOR
Podgorny, USSR president ...
  NIKOLAI
podium ..... DAIS, PLATFORM
Poe, ___ Allan ...... EDGAR
 bird .... RAVEN
 character .... PYM
 foster father of ... ALLAN
 girl in poem ....
  ANNABEL(LEE), LENORE
 gold bug .... SCARAB
 work of .... RAVEN,
  TAMERLANE
poem ... VERSE, ODE, SESTINA,
 RONDEL, BALLAD(E), LAI,
 VIRELAY, RUNES, PALINODE
 concluding stanza ......
  ENVOY, (L)ENVOI
 dirgelike ...... REQUIEM
 division .... CANTO,
  STANZA, FIT, FYTTE
 epic .... ILIAD, ODYSSEY,
  EPOPEE, EPOS, EPODE
 four-line ..... QUATRAIN
 14-line .... SONNET
 handed down orally .....
  EPOS
 Icelandic .... EDDA
 introduction to a ....
  PROLOGUE
 love .... MADRIGAL
 lyric ... EPODE, CANZONE,
  ODE, RONDEAU,
  MADRIGAL, RONDEL
 mourning ...... MONODY
 narrative .... IDYL(L),
  EPIC, LAY, ILIAD,
  ODYSSEY
 nonsense ..... LIMERICK
 of lament .... ELEGY
 of praise ... MAGNIFICAT

of rural life .... GEORGIC
one-line .... MONOSTICH
oral .... EPOS
part of .... CANTO, PASSUS
pastoral .... IDYL(L),
 BUCOLIC, ECLOGUE,
 GEORGIC
play's .... PROLOGUE,
 EPILOGUE
postscript .... (L)ENVOY,
 (L)ENVOI
sacred .... PSALM
said at play's end ....
 EPILOGUE
satirical .... IAMBIC,
 EPIGRAM
short ..... TELESTICH(E),
 VIRELAY, VILLANELLE
with witty point ....
 EPIGRAM

poems collection ....
 ANTHOLOGY, GARLAND
poet .... ODIST, MINSTREL,
 MINNESINGER, ELEGIST,
 TROUBADOUR, LYRIST,
 BARD, RHYMER,
 METRIST
 and Peasant composer ...
  (VON)SUPPE
 inferior ...... POETASTER,
  RHYMESTER, VERSIFIER,
  RHYMER, RIMER,
  SONNETEER
 inspiration of ..... MUSE
 old English ...... SCOP
 singer ... BARD, MINSTREL
 unknown .... ANON
poetess ..... SAPPHO, MILLAY,
 PARKER, LOWELL
poetic foot .... DACTYL,
 IAMB(US), SPONDEE,
 CHORIAMB, TROCHEE
 inspiration .... PEGASUS
 measure .... METER
 pronoun .... THINE,
  THOU, THEE
 retraction ..... PALINODE
 trio .... NOD
 verb .. DOST, HATH, HAST
poetry, epic .... EPOPEE
 incomplete line of ......
  HEMISTICH
 line of .... STICH
 muse of ...... CALLIOPE,
  ERATO, THALIA
 of .... MELIC

short-excerpt .. MORCEAU
poets, collectively .. PARNASSUS
Pogo's friend .... OWL
pogonia .... ORCHID
pogonip .... FOG
pogrom .... MASSACRE,
    SLAUGHTER
pogy .... MENHADEN, FISH
poi source .... TARO
poignancy .... PATHOS
poignant ... KEEN, TOUCHING,
    MOVING, TART, PIQUANT
poilu .... SOLDIER
poind ... DISTRAINT, IMPOUND
point ... DOT, AIM, JOT, SPECK,
    PERIOD, CAPE, PRICK,
    PUNTO, ISSUE, PEAK, USE,
    OBJECT
    antler's .... SNAG
    beside the ... IRRELEVANT
    barbed .... FLUB
    blank .... STRAIGHT,
        BLUNT, PLAIN
    central ..... FOCUS, CRUX
    compass .... AIRT(H),
        RHUMB
    culmination ... SOLSTICE
    earthquake's starting ....
        FOCUS
    ending in a .. MUCRONATE
    essential .... CRUX
    farthest .... APOGEE,
        SOLSTICE
    having .... ACUATE,
        HEBETATE
    highest .... ZENITH,
        ACME, PEAK, CLIMAX,
        APEX, SUMMIT
    in ...... APT, PERTINENT
    in game .... SCORE
    in law .... RES
    joint .... JUNCTURE
    land ... SPIT, CAPE, NESS,
        PROMONTORY
    lowest ..... NADIR, ZERO
    magnet .... POLE
    make a .... SCORE
    meeting .... FOCUS
    of a curve ...... ACNODE
    of concentration ... NODE
    of debate .... ISSUE
    of difference ..... LIMEN
    of land .... MORRO
    of law: sl. ...... BUTTON
    of time .... JUNCTURE
    of view .... OPINION,
        ANGLE, SLANT
    orbital ... APSIS, APOGEE
    pen .... NIB
    spear .... PIKE, GAD
    starting .... POST
    to the ... APT, PERTINENT
    turning ... PIVOT, HINGE
    won .... SCORE, GOAL
pointed ... CONICAL, INCISIVE,
    PIKED, ACUATE, PEAKED,
    SHARP, TAPERING
    arch ..... OGIVE, GOTHIC
    dull .. HEBETATE, ACUATE
    missile ... SPEAR, LANCE,
        DART, HARPOON, BOLT
    stick .... GOAD
pointer .... DIAL, ARROW,
    SETTER, VANE, INDICATOR,
    WAND, HAND, INDEX,
    RETRIEVER, (GUN)DOG
    colloquial ... TIP, CLUE,
        HINT
    dial's .... STYLE
    printer's .... FIST
    sundial ...... GNOMON
    teacher's .... FESCUE
pointing out .... INDICANT
pointless .... INANE, SILLY,
    SENSELESS, DULL
poise ..... BALANCE, BEARING,
    SUSPEND, HOVER, STABILITY,
    CARRIAGE, APLOMB,
    LIBRATE
poison .... TOXIN, DRUG,
    HEMLOCK, GALL, ARSENIC,
    CORRUPT, DATURA, VENOM,
    TOXICANT, BANE
    antidote ... MITHRIDATE,
        TREACLE
    arrow ...... INEE, UPAS,
        CURARE, (C)URARI,
        (W)OURALI, WOORALI
    castor bean ...... RICIN
    caused by .... TOXIC
    deadly .... ARSENIC,
        CYANIDE, STRYCHNIN(E)
    food .... BOTULIN
    gas .. LEWISITE, MUSTARD
    hemlock ...... CONIN(E),
        BENNET, CONIUM
    ivy .... SUMAC
    ivy irritant .... URUSHIOL
    remedy for ..... TREACLE
    snake ..... VENOM, VIRUS
    weed ... LOCO, HEMLOCK,
        CONIUM

poisoner, alleged ..... BORGIA
poisoning .... BOTULISM,
                     TOXICATION
    blood .... TOXEMIA
poisonous .... VENOMOUS,
    TOXIC(ANT), VIRULENT,
    VIPERINE, MEPHITIC,
                     NOCUOUS
    air .... MALARIA
    alkaloid .... CONINE,
    TROPIN(E), NICOTINE
    bark .... UPAS, SASSY
    compound ..... TOXIN(E)
    fungus .... AMANITA
    lizard .... GILA
    oil .... TUNG
    plant .... CONIUM,
    HEMLOCK, HENBANE,
    NUX VOMICA, TUTU,
    MANDRAKE, BELLADONA,
                   NIGHTSHADE
    protein .... RICIN(E)
    resin .... CANNABIN
    seed .... CALABAR
    shrub .... TUTU
    snake .... COBRA, ASP,
    VIPER, ADDER, KRAIT,
    COPPERHEAD,
    BUSHMASTER, FER-DE-
                       LANCE
    spider ...... TARANTULA
    vine ...... BITTERSWEET
    weed ... LOCO, HEMLOCK
poke .... JAB, PROD, PRY,
    DAWDLE(R), SACK, POCKET,
    BAG, JOG, DUB, PUSH,
    THRUST, INTRUDE, GOAD,
                       PUNCH
    with elbow ...... NUDGE
poker counter ..... CHIP, DIB
    deal .... DRAW, STUD
    face .... DEAD PAN
    faced comedian .. KEATON
    game like .... BRAG
    hand ... STRAIGHT, PAIR,
    TRIO, FULL HOUSE,
    (ROYAL)FLUSH
    player ..... FOURFLUSHER
    stake ... ANTE, POT, KITTY
    term ... PIGEON, KICKER,
    HOLE, FOLD, BOBTAIL
    to call in .... SEE
    variety of ... STUD, DRAW
pokerface .... DEADPAN
pokeweed ... POCAN, INKBERRY
pok(e)y .... DULL, SLOW,

STUFFY, DOWDY, JAIL
    slang .... JAIL
Pola .... PULJ
    movie actress ..... NEGRI
Poland ... SARMATIA, POLSKA
    capital of ..... WARSAW
    dictator ..... GOMULKA
    Mrs. in .... PANI
    native of .. POLE, POLACK
    weight .... LUT
Polaris .... POLESTAR,
                   NORTH STAR
pole ..... MAST, SHAFT, THILL,
    CABER, POST, PUNT, STILT,
    ROD, CABER, SLAV
    boat .... QUANT
    carriage .... SHAFT
    fir .... UFER
    fish .... GAFF
    in Gaelic game ... CABER
    memorial .... XAT
    metal cap .... SHOE
    positive .... ANODE
    propelled watercraft .....
    CASCO, PUNT,
                   GONDOLA
    symbolic .... TOTEM
    to pole .... AXIAL
    tribal .... TOTEM
    vertical .... MAST
    with decoy bird ... STOOL
    with footrest ..... STILT
    wagon ..... THILL, SHAFT
    wooden .... TREE
poleax(e) .... HALBERD,
                     HALBERT
polecat .... FITCH(ET),
    FITCHEW, MUSANG, SKUNK,
    FOUMART, CARNIVORE
    animal like ... ZORIL(A),
    WEASEL, FERRET
polemic .... CONTROVERSIAL,
    MOOT, DEBATABLE,
    ARGUMENT
polemics .... DISPUTE
polenta .... PORRIDGE
poler .... GONDOLIER,
    OARSMAN, HORSE
poles, walking .... STILTS
polestar .... POLARIS,
                   NORTH STAR
police ...... CONSTABULARY,
    CARABINIERI
    inspector, fictional ......
                     MAIGRET
    line .... CORDON

military .... REDCAP, MP
record book .... BLOTTER
record, letters in .... AKA
state .... TROOPER
test .... PARAFFIN,
            POLYGRAPH
vehicle .... WAGON,
            BLACK MARIA
policeman .... MINION, BULL,
FLATFOOT, COP, TROOPER,
ZAPTIAH, BLUECOAT,
BOBBY, PEELER, CONSTABLE,
DICK, BULL, GENDARME,
            PEON, REDCAP
baton/club of ....
    TRUNCHEON, STICK,
            BILLY, MACE
mounted ...... TROOPER
policewoman .... MATRON
policy .... PRINCIPLE,
            PLATFORM, PLAN
polio vaccine man ..... SALK
treatment method ....
            KENNY
polish .... GLOSS, BUFF,
LEVIGATE, FINISH, SLEEK
BURNISH, VENEER,
FURBISH, GLAZE, WAX,
LUSTRE, BRIGHTEN,
REFINE, PERFECT, SHINE,
SAND, SCOUR, GRACE,
            SHEEN, RUB
by hammering .. PLANISH
up ...... EDIT, IMPROVE
polished .... ELEGANT, SLEEK,
POLITE, SUAVE, GLOSSY,
            REFINED, URBANE
polishing material .... EMERY,
PUMICE, BUFF, WAX, RABAT,
RUBIGO, CROCUS, LUSTER,
            ABRASIVE
Polish carriage ..... BRITSKA
city .... LODZ, BRESLAU,
WROCLAW, POZNAN,
LUBLIN, POSEN, TORUN,
TARNOW, CRACOW,
BROMBERG, LWOW,
KALISZ, STETTIN,
GDYNIA, KATOWICE,
LIGNICA, LEMBERG
coin .... GROSZ
commander ...... BOR,
ANDERS, HETMA
dance ...... POLONAISE,
            MAZURKA

dictator ...... PILSUDSKI,
            GOMULKA
diet member ... MAGNATE
dress .... POLONAISE
king .. SOBIESKI, CONTI
legislator ...... MAGNATE
marshy region ... PRIPET
monetary unit .... ZLOTY
music .... POLONAISE,
            MAZURKA
parliament .... SEJM
pianist .... RUBINSTEIN,
            PADEREWSKI
port .... GDYNIA
premier ... PADEREWSKI,
SIKORSKI, PILSUDSKI
president .... PILSUDSKI
region .... MASURIA
river .. PRIPET, VISTULA,
        BUG, NAREW,
SAN NAREV, SERET,
            WARTHE
seaport .... DANZIG
slang .... POLACK
soldier .... UHLAN
soup .... ZUPA
title of address .... PANI
polite ...... CIVIL, REFINED,
GRACIOUS, MANNERLY,
GENTEEL, URBANE,
COURTEOUS, POLISHED,
            CORRECT
act .... CIVILITY
politic .... DIPLOMATIC,
PRUDENT, TACTFUL,
EXPEDIENT, SHREWD
political casualty .. LAMEDUCK
division ...... HUNDRED
faction .... BLOC, RUMP,
            JUNTA
gathering ...... CAUCUS,
            POWWOW
henchman ....
        (WARD)HEELER
organization ..... STATE,
            PARTY
patronage .... PAP,
        PORK(BARREL)
radical .... JACOBIN
rostrum .... STUMP
science .... CIVICS,
POLITICS, GOVERNMENT
spoils .... MELON,
        PATRONAGE
system .... REGIME
politician ... POLITICO, HEELER

not reelected .. LAMEDUCK
politics of a ...... RIGHT, LEFT, CENTER, LIBERAL
unattached ... MAVERICK
polity .... STATE
polka-like dance ..... REDOWA, MAZURKA
poll ...... HEAD, JUROR, CUT, CROP, VOTE, SURVEY, CANVASS(ING)
taker ... HARRIS, GALLUP, ROPER
pollack ... COALFISH, GADID, SEY
pollard .... DEER, GOAT
polled .... HORNLESS, CANVASSED, MUL(L)EY
pollen .... DUST, MICROSPORES
bearing organ .. STAMEN
brush .... SCOPA
sac .... ANTHER
pollex .... THUMB, DIGIT
polling place .... BOOTH
pollinosis .... HAYFEVER
polliwog .... TADPOLE
pollock .... CODFISH
pollster .... GALLUP, HARRIS, ROPER
pollute .... DEFILE, DIRTY
Pollux and Castor ..... ANAX, DIOSCURI, GEMINI
Pollyanna for example .... OPTIMIST
Pollywog .... TADPOLE
polo play period .. CHUKKER, CHUKKAR
stick .... MALLET
Venetian traveler .... MARCO
Polonius' daughter .. OPHELIA
servant ..... REYNALDO
son .... LAERTES
Polska .... POLAND
poltergeist .... GHOST
poltroon ... CRAVEN, DASTARD, COWARD, CAITIFF
polyanthus .... OXLIP, PRIMROSE, NARCISSUS
polyglot .... LINGUIST
polygon .... NONAGON, HEXAGON, ISAGON, TETRAGON
polygraph, they swear by the .. POLICE
Polynesian ... MAORI, SAMOAN, TAHITIAN, KANAKA,

HAWAIIAN, NUKUORO
apple .... HEVI
baking pit .... UMU
beverage ... KAVA, KAWA
chestnut .... RATA
cloth .... TAPA
dress .... MALO
drink .... KAVA
god ... PELE, ATUA, TANE
herb .... PIA
hero .... MAUI
human food ... LONG PIG
island ... PITCAIRN, FIJI, SAMOA, TOKELAU
kingdom .... TONGA
language ...... TONGAN
louse .... KUTU
mound .... AHU
mulberry bark .... TAPA
oven .... UMU
sky .... LANGI
spirit .... ATUA
supernatural force ...... MANA
tree .... IPIL
wages .... UTU
yam .... UBE, UBI
polyp ...... HYDRA, SEA PEN, CORAL, SEA ANEMONE, HYDROZOAN
like a .... HYDROID
Polyphemus ... CYCLOPS, MOTH
captive ...... ODYSSEUS, ULYSSES
polyzoan .... BRYOZOAN, HYDRA, SEA ANEMONE, POLYP, SEA PEN
pomace .... PULP
pomaceous fruit ...... APPLE, POME
pomade .... OINTMENT, COSMETIC, BANDOLINE, POMATUM
pomatum .... POMADE
pome ... PEAR, APPLE, QUINCE
disease ..... BROWN ROT
like fruit ...... AZAROLE
pomelo .... GRAPEFRUIT, SHADDOCK, SUHA
pomegranate flower .... BALUSTER
syrup ...... GRENADINE
Pomeranian ...... SPITZ DOG
pommel .... KNOB, BEAT
pomp ..... STATE, SPLENDOR, PAGEANTRY, SHOW

and Circumstance
composer ..... ELGAR
empty .... PAGEANT
pompadour .... HAIRDO,
POISSON
base .... RAT
pompano ... ALEWIFE, SAUREL,
CARANGOID
Pompey's scene of defeat ....
THAPSUS
pompom fire .. ACK-ACK, FLAK
pomposity .... WIND
pompous .... STATELY,
BOMBASTIC, GRANDIOSE,
MAGNIFIC, HIGHFALUTIN,
TUMID, OROTUND, TURGID
speech .... BOMBAST
walk ... STRUT, SWAGGER
Ponca .... SIOUX, SIOUAN
Ponce de Leon's discovery ....
FLORIDA
Ponchielli opera ....
(LA)GIOCONDA
poncho ..... RAINCOAT, CLOAK,
CAMLET
pond ... LAGOON, POOL, MERE,
TARN, SALINA, LAGUNE,
WATER HOLE
kind of .... STEW
ponder .. PERPEND, MEDITATE,
PORE, REFLECT, MULL,
RUMINATE, WEIGH,
CONSIDER, MUSE
ponderosa .... PINE
ponderous ... DULL, LABORED,
HEAVY, MASSIVE, BULKY,
WEIGHTY
ponds, study of .. LIMNOLOGY
pone ..... BREAD, LOAF, MERE
poniard .... DAGGER
Pons, operatic singer .... LILY
pontiff .... BISHOP, POPE,
PONTIFEX, HIGH PRIEST
pontifical .... EPISCOPAL,
PAPAL
pontil .... PUNTY
Pontius _____, Roman governor
PILATE
pontlevis .... DRAWBRIDGE
pontoon .... FLOAT
pony .. BRONCO, NAG, CAYUSE,
HORSE, CRIB, PINTO,
SHELTY, SHELTIE
tail .... HAIRDO
up .... PAY
pooch .... DOG

poodle .... BARBET, DOG
pooh .... TIRE, EXHAUST,
EXCLAMATION
pooh .... DISMISS,
DISREGARD
pool ... POND, PUDDLE, PLASH,
POT, BILLIARDS, MONOPOLY,
CARR, MERE, LINN,
WATER HOLE
artificial .... TANK
ball .... RINGER
bettors' .... POT, KITTY
business firms' ....
MONOPOLY, TRUST
mine .... SUMP
mountain .... TARN
pouch .... POCKET
rod .... CUE
table pouch .... POCKET
triangle .... RACK
waterfall .... LINN
poon .... TELUGU, TREE,
DOMBA, DILO
poor ..... DESTITUTE, NEEDY,
PALTRY, INFERIOR,
INDIGENT, PENNILESS
player .... DUB, HAM
slang .... LOUSY
sport .... SOREHEAD
poorhouse .... HOSPICE
poorly ILL
born .... LOWBRED
done literary work ......
INCONDITE
pop ..... CRACK, BURST, SODA,
SHOT, SHOOT, SNAP,
FATHER
art .... FUNK
conductor ... WHITEMAN
singer .... JOPLIN
the question ... PROPOSE
Pope (see Papal) ... PONTIFF,
LEO, PIUS, JOHN, VICAR,
ADRIAN, PAUL, URBAN
cape of ..... MOZ(Z)ETTA
cathedral of the ....
LATERAN
collar of the ..... ORALE
crown of the ...... TIARA
decree of the ..... BULL,
DECRETAL, RESCRIPT
envoy .... (AB)LEGATE
first .... PETER
headdress of ..... MITRE,
MITER

meeting to elect......... CONCLAVE
of Video ..... SULLIVAN
palace of .... VATICAN
pertaining to the .. PAPAL
see of the .... ROME
tenure of the .... PAPACY
the .... PAPA
title of .... HOLINESS,
HOLY FATHER
vestment of ... FANO(N),
FANUM
Pope's (Alexander) love .....
GONNE
popes collectively .... PAPACY
Popeye, rival of ...... BRUTO
sweetheart of ....
OLIVE(OYL)
the ___ ... SAILOR(MAN)
popinjay .... FOP, PARROT,
WOODPECKER
poplar ... ABELE, LIARD, ASPEN,
ALAMO, COTTONWOOD
balsam .... TACMAHACK
glucoside from .. SALICIN
spike ... CATKIN, AMENT
popover .... MUFFIN
Poppaea, Nero's wife .. SABINA
poppy .... CHICALOTE,
CELANDINE, PAPAVER,
OPIUM, BLOODROOT,
SANGUINARIA, PLANT
sap .... LATEX
seed .... MAW
poppycock .... BOSH,
NONSENSE, ROT, BALONEY
populace ..... DEMOS, PEOPLE,
MASSES
popular .... COMMON,
PREVALENT, VULGATE,
ENCHORIAL, EXOTERIC,
DEMOTIC
beauty .... BELLE
no more ..... HAS BEEN
opinion ...... CONSENSUS
social figure ...... LION,
CELEBRITY
success .... HIT
popularity .... FAME
populate .... INHABIT, PEOPLE
population count ..... CENSUS
Poquelin, Fr. writer .. MOLIERE
porbeagle .... SHARK
porcelain ..... EARTHENWARE,
CHINA, SPODE, LIMOGES,
MING, CELADON, SEVRES,

FIGULINE, FAIENCE
art of making .. CERAMICS
clay... CHINA, KAOLIN(E),
PATE
fine .... CHINA
of .... CERAMIC
worker .... POTTER
porch .... STOA, PORTICO,
PIAZZA, GALILEE, STOOP,
PARVIS, VERANDA(H),
GALLERY, LAN(A)I
church .... GALILEE
seat .... GLIDER
porcine animal ..... HOG, PIG
disease .... BULLNOSE
porcupine .... HEDGEHOG
anteater ...... ECHIDNA
Canadian .... URSON
spine .... QUILL
pore .... STUDY, PONDER,
OSTIOLE, READ, MEDITATE,
CON, FORAMEN, CHANNEL,
OPENING
breathing .... STOMA
plant ... LENTICEL, STOMA
pores, block the .... OPPILATE
porgy .... FISH, PARGO, SCUP,
BREAM, SPAROID, TAI
poriferan .... SPONGE
pork ... PIG, HOG, LARDO(O)N
cut .. CHOP, BACON, LOIN,
HAM
loin .... GRISKIN
pie .... HAT
sausage .... BOLOGNA
shoulder .... CALA
porker .... ELT, HOG
porky .... FAT
pornographic ..... SALACIOUS,
OBSCENE
porous ...... LEAKY, LEACHY
porpoise .... DOLPHIN,
CETACEAN, SEA HOG, INIA,
HOGFISH
porridge ... GRUEL, OATMEAL,
POTTAGE, GROUT, ATOLE,
SAMP, STIRABOUT, POLENTA,
BROSE, MUSH, BURGOO
bowl .... PORRINGER
oat husks ...... SOWENS
Porsena, king .... LARS
Tarquin's ..... AVENGER
port .... HARBOR, LARBOARD,
WINE, GATEWAY, HAVEN,
ANCHORAGE
facilities ..... WHARFAGE

portable bridge .... BAILEY, PONTOON
chair .... SEDAN
float .... PONTOON
hut .... QUONSET
kitchen cart .... CHUCK WAGON
lamp .... LANTERN
oven .... BAKER
sanctuary ... TABERNACLE
serving stand .... DUMB WAITER
shelter .... TENT
stove .... CHAUFFER
portal .... DOORWAY, GATE, ENTRANCE, POSTERN
portance .. CONDUCT, BEARING
portas .... BREVIARY
portcullis .... HERSE, BAR
portend .... BODE, WARN, PRESAGE, FORESHADOW, AUGUR
portent ..... OMEN, PRODIGY, MARVEL, WARNING, SIGN
portentous .... OMINOUS, SINISTER
porter .... JANITOR, BEER, HAMAL, ALE, CARRIER, STOUT, CONCIERGE, GATEKEEPER, DOORMAN, REDCAP
musical .... ROSALIE
songwriter .... COLE
porterhouse .... STEAK, T-BONE, BEEF
portfolio ... BRIEFCASE, OFFICE
porthole .... EMBRASURE
Portia's maid .... NERISSA
portico .. VERANDA(H), PORCH, PARVIS, LOGGIA, COLONNADE, STOA, PROSTYLE, ARCADE, PIAZZA
portion .... SHARE, PART, DESTINY, BIT, LOT
marriage .... DOWRY
meal .... SERVING, HELPING
out .... DEAL, METE
slang .... DIVVY
tiny ... MINIM, MODICUM
portly .... OBESE, STOUT, FAT
portmanteau ...... SUITCASE, VALISE
Porto Rico (see Puerto Rico)
portrait ..... EFFIGY, PICTURE
portray .. PERSONATE, DEPICT, DELINEATE, LIMN, PICTURE, ENACT, REPRESENT, DESCRIBE

Portugal .... LUSITANIA
capital of .... LISBON
Portuguese cape .... ROCA
city ..... LISBON, EVORA, BRAGA, FARO, LAGOS, COIMBRA, SANTAREM
coin .... CENTAVO, CRUSADO, REI, MOIDORE, ESCUDO, JOHANNES
colony .... ANGOLA, MACAU, MACAO, TIMOR, MOZAMBIQUE, CAPE VERDE
colony, former ..... GOA
dictator .... SALAZAR
East Africa .... MOZAMBIQUE
folk song .... FADO
gentleman .... SENHOR
governess .... AIA
Guinea capital ... BISSAU
India district .... DAMAO
Indian .... FERINGI, FERINGHEE
islands .... MADEIRA, AZORES, TERCEIRA
lady .... DONA
legislature ...... CORTES
measure .... VARA
molasses ...... MELACO
monetary unit .. ESCUDO
mountain ranges ... SERRAS
navigator .... MAGELLAN, (DA)GAMA, DIAZ
nobleman .... GRANDEE
overseas territory .... ANGOLA, MOZAMBIQUE, CAPE VERDE, MACAO, TIMOR, SAO TOME
poet .... CAMOES
premier ...... SALAZAR, CAETANO
river ...... SADO, SABOR, DUERO, MINHO, TAGUS, DOURO, TEJO
sail .... LATEEN
seaport .... OPORTO
ship .... CARVEL, CARAVEL(LE)
Timor capital ..... DILI
title .... DOM, DONNA, SENHOR

weight ..... LIBRA, ONCA
West Africa .... ANGOLA
wine ... MADEIRA, PORTO
pose .... SIT, MANNERISM,
PRETENSE, PROPOUND,
PROPOSE, ATTITUDE,
POSTURE, PUZZLE
Poseidon ..... NEPTUNE, GOD
attendant of ... PROTEUS
realm of .... SEA
scepter .... TRIDENT
wife of ..... AMPHITRITE
Posen .... POSNAN
poser .... FACER, POSEUR,
TEASER, MODEL, SITTER,
IMPOSTOR, PROBLEM
posh .... ELEGANT, RITZY,
LUXURIOUS
posit .... SITUATE, ASSUME,
POSTULATE
position .... POST(URE),
ATTITUDE, SITUATION,
STAND, STATUS, OFFICE,
SITUS, STANCE, PLACE,
LOCATION, SITE, STATION,
JOB, LIE
secure .... FOOTING,
FOOTHOLD
positive .... CERTAIN,
ABSOLUTE, OUT-AND-OUT,
SURE, PLUS, PRECISE,
EXPRESS, SPECIFIC
answer ... AYE, YES, YEA
electrode .... ANODE
pole .... ANODE
sign .... PLUS
positively .... QUITE
positivism .... ASSURANCE,
DOGMATISM, CERTAINTY,
COMTISM
possess .... OWN, HAVE,
DOMINATE
possessed ...... CRAZED, MAD,
CHARMED
possession .... PROPERTY,
WEALTH, OWNERSHIP
in law ... SEISIN, MANUAL
possessor ... OWNER, HOLDER
posset .... DRINK
possible .... POTENTIAL,
FEASIBLE, PROBABLE
possibly .... MAYBE, PERHAPS
possum .... COON
play .... FEIGN, PRETEND
post ... MAIL, INFORM, ENTER,
DA(W)K, BOLLARD, MARKER,

PILLAR, STAKE, POLE,
STATION, PLACE, COURIER,
POSITION, ASSIGN,
GARRISON, JOB
box device ...... USMAIL
chaise .... COACH,
CARRIAGE
doorway .... JAMB(E)
exchange .. PX, CANTEEN
memorial .... XAT
mortem .... AUTOPSY,
NECROPSY
mortem conductor ......
AUTOPSIST, CORONER
office bank .... GIRO
staircase .... NEWEL
window frame .. JAMB(E)
wooden framework ....
PUNCHEON
postage stamp country ....
SAN MARINO
postal stamp .... CACHET
system .... MAIL
poster ... STICKER, PLACARD,
BILL(BOARD)
posterior ..... HIND, RETRAL,
REAR, DORSAL, BUTTOCK,
LATER
opposed to ... ANTERIOR,
PRIOR
posterity .... FUTURE
postern .... BACKDOOR,
BACKGATE, ENTRANCE
postfree mail .... FRANK
postiche .... ARTIFICIAL,
PRETENSE
postmark .... CACHET
substitute ...... INDICIA
postmeridian ... AFTERNOON,
PM
"postoffice" delivery .... KISS
postpone ... ADJOURN, TABLE,
DELAY, DEFER, PUT OFF,
SHELVE
postponing, in law .. MORATORY
postrider .... COURIER
postscript of poem ... LENVOY,
LIENVOI
postulant .... CANDIDATE,
PETITIONER
postulate ...... POSIT, AXIOM,
THESIS, CLAIM, ASSUME,
PRESUME, PREMISE
posture .... POSITION,
ATTITUDE, STANCE,
CARRIAGE, BEARING, POSE

posy .... NOSEGAY, BOUQUET, FLOWER, SPRAY, CORSAGE
pot ~ PIPKIN, CRUSE, LOTA(H), JARDINIERE, OLLA, POOL, KITTY, SHOOT, ALUDEL, KETTLE
au-feu .... (BEEF)STEW
coffee .... URN
go to .. ROT, DETERIORATE
herb .... CLARY
marigold ... CALENDULA
mender .... TINKER
slang .... MARIJUANA
stand .... TRIVET
tea .... SAMOVAR
user .... HIPPIE
user's feeling ..... HIGH
potable .... DRINKABLE
potage .... SOUP, BROTH
potash source .... SUINT
potassium .... ALUM
bitartrate ...... TARTAR
carbonate ...... POTASH
chloride .... SYLVITE, MURIATE
nitrate ..... SALTPETER, NITER, GROUGH
potation ..... DRINK, LIQUOR, DRAFT
potato ... SPUD, TUBER, OCA, IDAHO, TATER
bud .... EYE
disease .... CURL
flour .... FARINA
fried .... CHIP
meal .... FARINA
skin .... JACKET
slang .... MURPHY
starch .... FARINA
sweet ..... CAMOTE, YAM, BATATA
potatoes with onions .... LYONNAISE
potbelly .... PAUNCH, BAY WINDOW
potboiler .... LITERARY
poteen .... WHISKY
potency ... STRENGTH, POWER, VIS
potent ... STRONG, POWERFUL,
potentate .... RULER, MONARCH, (MAJA)RAJAH
potential ... LATENT, POSSIBLE
difference ...... TENSION
potentilla ...... FIVE FINGER, ROSE

potheen .... WHISKY
pother .... STIR, WORRY, UPROAR, FUSS, ADO, BUSTLE
potherb .... PARSLEY, CLARY, CHIVES
pothole .... PIT
pothook .... SCRAWL
user .... STENO
pothouse ...... INN, TAVERN
potiche .... VASE, JAR
potion .... DOSE, DRINK, NEPENTHE
love ... PHILTER, PHILTRE
potman .... WAITER
potpie .... STEW
potpourri ..... MEDLEY, STEW, MIXTURE, OLIO, ANTHOLOGY
Potsdam conference member .. STALIN, ATTLEE, TRUMAN
potsherd .... SHARD, CROCK
potshot .... SNIPE
pottage ... PORRIDGE, BROSE, HODGEPODGE, SOUP, STEW
potted .... DRUNK
potter's clay .... ARGIL, SAGGER, SEGGAR, PATE
field .... CEMETERY, GRAVEYARD
field of Judas .... ACELDAMA
tool .... PALLET
wheel .... LATHE
pottery ...... EARTHENWARE, DELFT(WARE), GOMBROON, MAJOLICA, WARE, CERAMICS, BASALT, FAIENCE, FIGULINE
before glazing ... BISCUIT
clay ..... KAOLIN, PATE, ARGIL
fragment .... SHARD, SHERD, CROCK
glaze on .... REFLET
glazed .... DELF(T)
making .... CERAMICS
making device .. SAGGER
of .... CERAMIC, FICTILE
pottle .... TANKARD
potto ..... LEMUR, KINKAJOU
potty .... PETTY
pouch .... SPORRAN, SPLEUCHAN, SAC, BURSA, POD, BAG, POCKET, CECUM
intestinal ..... C(A)ECUM
like a .... SACCATE, MARSUPIAL
pouf ... OTTOMAN, HEADDRESS

poulard .. HEN, FRYER, PULLET
poult .... PULLET, CHICKEN
poultice .... APPLICATION,
              CATAPLASM
poultry ...... FOWLS, DUCKS,
           GEESE, TURKEYS
  breeding place .. HENNERY
  disease .. PIP, ROUP, POX,
              GAPES
  man .... POULTER
  pen .... HUTCH
  shelter ...... HENHOUSE,
             HENNERY
pounce .. TALON, CLAW, SWOOP
pound .... TAMP, THUMP,
  PULVERIZE, CRUSH,
  NETTON, SOV, BRAY, QUID,
  THROB, BEAT, THUD,
  ENCLOSURE, CORRAL,
  PEN, MALLEATE, LIBRA
  dog .... MONGREL
  dweller .... STRAY
  poet ...... EZRA(LOOMID)
pounder .... CANNON, WAVE,
           TAMPER
pounds, 100 .... CENTAL,
           CENTNER
pounding implement .. PESTLE,
  GAVEL, HAMMER, MALLET
pour ... FLOW, RAIN, SWARM,
  TEEM, SERVE, GUSH,
  DECANT, EFFUSE
  forth .... WELL
  metal into mold ... CAST,
           FOUND
pourboire .... TIP, GRATUITY
pouring hole .... SPRUE
pourpoint ... DOUBLET, JUPON
pout ...... MOUE, SULK, FISH,
  GRIMACE, MOPE
pouter .... PIGEON
poverty .... WANT, SCARCITY,
  NEED, INDIGENCE, PAUCITY,
  PENURY, LACK
  stricken .... POOR
pow .... POLL, HEAD
powder .... TALC, POUNCE,
  PICRA, DUST, SPRINKLE,
  PULVERIZE, CRUSH
  burn to .... CALCINE
  clothes scenting ....
           SATCHET
  crush into .... BRAY
  dried fly ... CANTHARIDES
  explosive ...... CORDITE,
           TETRYL

  grind to .... BRAY,
           TRITURATE
  insect ...... PYRETHRUM
  perfumed .... SACHET
  polishing .... ROUGE
  pound into .... BRAY
  room .... LAVATORY
  skin .... TALC
  stain removing .. PUMICE
powdery .... FRIABLE, DUSTY
power ..... SWAY, AUTHORITY,
  MIGHT, VIS, CONTROL,
  ABILITY, CAPACITY,
  FORCE, VIGOR
  colloquial ...... STEAM
  kind of ... STEAM, SOLAR,
  MOTIVE, ELECTRIC
  loom inventor ....
          CARTWRIGHT
  source of ..... SUN, FUEL
  symbol of .... FASCES
  theoretical .... ODYL
  to survive ...... VITALITY
  unit .... VOLT, WATT
  world ..... RUSSIA, USA,
          AMERICA
powerful ... POTENT, MIGHTY,
  STRONG, PUISSANT
powerless .... IMPOTENT
Powhatan's daughter ....
          POCAHONTAS
powwow ...... MEDICINE MAN,
          CONFERENCE
  Zuluans' .... INDABA
pox .... SYPHILIS
Poznan .... POSEN
practicable .... FEASIBLE,
  USEFUL, POSSIBLE
practical .... PRAGMATIC(AL),
  UTILE, USEFUL, WORKABLE
  joke ...... HOAX, PRANK,
          TRICK
  person .... REALIST
practice .... DRILL, USAGE,
  USE, WORKOUT, CUSTOM,
  HABIT, EXERCISE, PRAXIS,
  REHEARSE
  composition ..... ETUDE
  dishonest .... RACKET
  established ...... PRAXIS,
  USAGE, CUSTOM
  firearms with blanks .....
          DRY RUN
  joke ...... PRANK, HOAX
  performance ... REHEARSE
  systematic ..... EXERCISE

practiced ..... SKILLED, DEFT
pragmatic .... PRACTICAL,
               OFFICIOUS
Prague .... PRAHA
   castle .... HRADCANY
   square ...... WENCESLAS
prairie ...... PLAIN, SAVANNA,
     GRASSLAND, PAMPA(S)
   dog .... MARMOT
   grove .... MOTT(E)
   hen .... GROUSE
   soil .... GUMBO
   squirrel .... GOPHER
   state .... NEBRASKA
   vehicle ...... SCHOONER
   wolf .... COYOTE
praise .... TOUT, PANEGYRIC,
   LAUD, EXTOL, EXALT,
   EULOGIZE, KUDOS, ACCLAIM,
   ENCOMIUM, TRIBUTE,
   ELOGE, COMMEND, BLESS,
   EULOGY, GLORIFY, GLORIA
   song of .... CAROL
   too much ...... FLATTER
   undue .... PUFF
praiseworthy ..... LAUDABLE
praline ... CONFECTION, CANDY
pram .... BUGGY,
     PERAMBULATOR
prance .... CAVORT, CAPER,
   STRUT, SWAGGER
prandial meal .... DINNER,
     SUPPER
prank ...... ANTIC, DRESS UP,
   MISCHIEF, ESCAPADE,
   CANTRIP, LARK, GAMBADO,
   JAPE, JOKE, HOAX, TRICK,
   CAPER, DIDO, FROLIC
   with lighted match ......
     HOTFOOT
pranks .... (HIGH)JINKS
prankster .... BUFFOON
prase .. CHALCEDONY, QUARTZ
prat .... BUTTOCKS
prate ... CHATTER, YAP, BLAB,
   TATTLE, PRATTLE, BABBLE,
     GAB
prattle .... BABBLE, BLAB,
   PRATE, CHATTER
prawn .... SCAMP,
   CRUSTACEAN, MACRURAN
praxis .... PRACTICE,
     CUSTOM
pray ..... ENTREAT, IMPLORE,
   BESEECH, BEG, APPEAL, ORA
prayer ... LITANY, ROGATION,

ORISON, PLEA, AVE, BENE,
SUIT, ENTREATY, REQUEST,
PETITION, GRACE, NOVENA
   bead .... ROSARY
   bones .... KNEES
   book .... BREVIARY, PORTAS(S),
     MISSAL,
     PRIMER,-ORDO, HOURS
   desk .... PRIEDIEU
   ending .... AMEN
   evening .... VESPER
   for another .. BEADSMAN,
     INTERCESSION
   hour .... VESPER, MATIN
   hour, Moslem ..... AZAN
   in gibberish .. GLOSSOLIA
   last of the day ....
     COMPLIN(E)
   meal .... GRACE
   morning .... MATIN
   nine-day .... NOVENA
   of supplication ....
     SUFFRAGE
   protect by .... SAIN
   rug .... ASAN
   shawl .... TALLITH
   short .... GRACE
   wheel user ... BUDDHIST,
     LAMA
prayerful .... DEVOUT
prayers, endowment for .....
     CHANTRY
praying figure .... ORANT
   Indians .... NATICKS
preach .... SERMONIZE,
   LECTURE, ADVOCATE
preacher .... PULPITEER,
   CLERGYMAN, EVANGELIST,
   HOMILIST, PREDICANT,
     MINISTER
   circuit .... ROUNDER
   talk of .... SERMON,
     HOMILY
   traveling .. EVANGEL(IST),
     MISSIONARY
preachers collectively .. PULPIT
preaching .... SERMON,
     PREDICANT
preamble .... PREFACE
precarious .... INSECURE,
   UNCERTAIN, RISKY
   state ... TOUCH-AND-GO
precede ..... FORERUN, HEAD
precedence .... LEAD,
     PRIORITY
precedent .... EXAMPLE

preceding .... PREVIOUS
  all others ..... FOREMOST, FIRST
precentor .... CANTOR
precept .... MAXIM, RULE, DOCTRINE, APHORISM, DICTUM
  Brahmanism ..... SUTRA
  in law ... WRIT, WARRANT
preceptor .... TEACHER
precepts, collection of .. SUTRA
precinct(s) .... ENVIRONS, NEIGHBORHOOD
precious ..... DEAR, COSTLY, BELOVED, ARRANT
  colloquial .... VERY
  stone .... CABOCHON, OPAL, TOPAZ, GARNET, RUBY, SARD, GEM, DIAMOND, BRILLIANT
  stone cutter ... LAPIDARY
precipice .... CRAG, BLUFF, CLIFF
precipitate .... ABRUPT, SUDDEN, HASTEN, HASTY, HEADY, RASH, BRING ON CONDENSE
precipitation .... SNOW, SLEET, RAIN, DEW, HASTE, RUSH, MIST
precipitator .... REAGENT, CATALYST, CATALYZER
precipitous .... SHEER, STEEP, RASH, HASTY
  rock .... SCAR, CRAG, CLIFF, BLUFF
precis .... DIGEST, RESUME, SYNOPSIS, ABSTRACT, SUMMARY
precise ...... PRIM, SPECIFIC, DEFINITE, EXACT, FORMAL, PARTICULAR, CORRECT, EXPLICIT, PRISSY
precisely .... EXACTLY
precision .... ACCURACY
preclude .. PREVENT, SHUT OUT, HINDER, ESTOP, INHIBIT, BAR
precocious child ..... PRODIGY
precursor .... HARBINGER, HERALD, OMEN, FORERUNNER
predatory .... PREYING, PREDACIOUS
  bird .... EAGLE, OWL, VULTURE
predecessor ..... PRECURSOR,

ANCESTOR
predestination .... FATE, ELECTION, DESTINY
predicament ..... PLIGHT, FIX, DILEMMA, JAM, SPOT, PICKLE, PASS, SCRAPE, RATTRAP, QUANDARY
predicant .... PREACHER
predicate .... BASE
predict ..... PORTEND, AUGUR, FORETELL, PROPHESY, FORECAST, (FORE)BODE
prediction .... PROPHECY, FORECAST
predictor .... SEER(ESS), PROPHET(ESS), FORECASTER
predilection .... PREFERENCE, TASTE, LIKING, FONDNESS, PREJUDICE, PARTIALITY, LEANING
predisposed .... PARTIAL, PREJUDICED, BIASED, INCLINED, PRONE
predominant .... REGNANT
preempt .... APPROPRIATE, SEIZE
preen ... DRESS, PRIMP, PRINK
prefab .... QUONSET(HUT), NISSEN
preface .... PREAMBLE, FOREWORD, INTRODUCTION, FRONTISPIECE, PROEM, PRELUDE, BEGIN, START
prefatory note..... FOREWORD
prefect .... DEAN
prefer ...... CHOOSE, PRESENT, FAVOR
preferably .... RATHER
preference .... CHOICE, LIKING
prefix .... BEFORE
  about .... PERI
  across .... TRANS
  against .... ANTI
  backward .... RETRO
  bad .... MAL
  before .... PRE, ANTE
  between .... META
  blood .... HEMO
  both .... AMBI
  distant .... TEL(E)
  eight .... OCT(O)
  equal .... ISO
  false .... PSEUDO
  far .... TEL(E)
  fire .... PYR(O)

half ... SEMI, DEMI, HEMI
many .... MULT(I)
mountain .... ORO
outer ...... EXO, ECT(O)
over .... SUPRA
single .... MONO
thought .... IDEO
under .... SUB
with .... SYN
within .... ENDO
wrong .... MIS
pregnable .... VULNERABLE
pregnancy .... CYESIS,
      FETATION, GESTATION
   outside uterus ... ECTOPIC
pregnant .... CHILDING,
      EXPECTING,
   ABOUNDING, ENCEINTE,
      GRAVID
prehistoric: comb. form ......
      PALE(O)
   human .... CAVEMAN
   upright stone ... MENHIR
prejudice .... HARM, BIAS,
   PARTIALITY, OPINION,
   IMPERIL, ENDANGER
prejudiced ... PARTIAL, BIASED
prelate ... BISHOP, CARDINAL,
      PRIMATE
prelect .... LECTURE
preliminary ..... PREFATORY
   meeting .... CAUCUS
   race .... HEAT
   statement ... PREAMBLE,
      FOREWORD, PREFACE
prelude .... PREFACE,
   OPENING, OVERTURE, PROEM
   of fugue :...... TOCCATA
premature .... UNTIMELY,
      EARLY, INOPPORTUNE
   baby .... PREEMIE
   development .. PRECOCITY
premeditated ...... PREPENSE,
      DELIBERATE
premier ..... FOREMOST, CHIEF
Preminger, movie director ....
      OTTO
premise .... PROPOSITION,
      BASIS, PREFACE
premises, series of ... SORITES
premium .... REWARD, PRIZE,
      BONUS, AGIO, FEE
premonition .... FOREBODING,
      HUNCH
preoccupation ..... OBSESSION,
      FIXATION

   with sex .... EROT(IC)ISM
preoccupied ...... ENGROSSED,
      ABSORBED, RAPT
preoccupy .... OBSESS,
      ENGROSS, ABSORB
preparation ...... READINESS
prepare .... FIT(OUT), PRIME,
   GIRD, TRAIN, READY,
   ADAPT, DISPOSE, ACCUSTOM
   copy ..... EDIT, REDACT
   for action .... UNLIMBER,
      GIRD
prepared ...... READY, YARE
preponderant ...... DOMINANT
preposition ...... FOR, ONTO,
   INTO, UNTO, FROM, OUT,
      AFTER
prepossessing .... ATTRACTIVE,
      PLEASING
prepossession .... BIAS
preposterous .... ABSURD,
   SENSELESS, RIDICULOUS
prerogative .... RIGHT,
      PRIVILEGE
   king's .... REGALIA
presage .... BODE, OMEN,
   PORTEND, SIGN, WARNING,
   PORTENT, FORETELL,
      AUGUR(Y)
presbyter .... ELDER,
   MINISTER, PRIEST, PRESTER
prescience .... FORESIGHT
prescribe ... ORDAIN, ORDER,
   SET(DOWN), DIRECT,
      OUTLAW
prescribed .... THETIC
prescript ...... RULE, ORDER
prescription .... RECIPE
presence .... GHOST,
   ATTENDANCE, COMPANY,
      APPEARANCE
   of mind .... WIT
present .... BESTOW, TENDER,
   AT HAND, GIFT,
   BOON, DISPLAY, NONCE,
   INTRODUCE, SHOW,
      DONATION
   at .... NOW
   charges against .. PREFER
   good luck ..... HANDSEL
   to departing person .. FOY
presentation ... PERFORMANCE,
   GIFT, OFFERING, EXHIBIT,
      SHOW, DISPLAY
presentiment ... FOREBODING,
      HUNCH

presently .. NOW, ANON, SOON,
SHORTLY, NOWADAYS
preservative .. VINEGAR, BRINE
preserve ... CURE, SMOKE, SASS,
JAM, SAVE, PROTECT, SALT,
CORN, PICKLE, PERPETUATE,
CONFITURE, CAN,
MARMALADE
by drying .... DESSICATE,
DEHYDRATE
game ...... SANCTUARY
with salt .... CORN
preserved dead body .. MUMMY
preshrink cloth .... SANFORIZE
preside .. MODERATE, CONDUCT
president, college ..... PREXY
yacht club .. COMMODORE
presidential monogram .. HST,
FDR, LBJ, JFK, DDE
nickname .... IKE, ABE,
TEDDY, CAL, JACK,
ANDY
disapproval .... VETO
reception .... LEVEE
presiding officer .. MODERATOR,
SPEAKER, CHAIRMAN,
PRINCIPAL
officer's vote ... CASTING
presidio ..... FORT, GARRISON
press .... WEDGE, SQUEEZE,
CROWD, SQUASH, PUSH,
IRON, COMPEL, JOURNALISM,
DRIVE, URGE, WRING,
CRAM, FORCE
agency (see news agency)
agent .... PUBLICIST,
JOURNALIST
agentry ..... PROPAGANDA,
PUBLICITY, BALLYHOO
dough .... KNEAD
down .... TAMP
with hands ..... MASSAGE
presser .... IRONER
pressing ... URGENT, EXIGENT
iron .... GOOSE
pressure .... STRESS,
INFLUENCE, URGENCY,
FORCE, DEMANDS, DURESS
group ..... LOBBY, BLOC
measuring device ....
MANOMETER
unit .... BARIE, BARAD
prest .... LOAN
prester ... PRIEST, PRESBYTER
prestidigitator ..... MAGICIAN

prestige .... REPUTATION,
RENOWN, FAME, KUDOS
presto .... QUICKLY
he says this word ......
MAGICIAN
Preston's milieu ...... YUKON
presume ..... VENTURE, DARE,
SUPPOSE, ASSUME
presumption ...... TEMERITY,
INFERENCE
presumptive .... BRASH,
ARROGANT
presumptuous .... FORWARD,
BOLD, ARROGANT
pretend ..... CLAIM, ALLEGE,
PROFESS, FEIGN, SIMULATE,
DISSEMBLE
pretended courage .. BRAVADO,
BLUFF
pretender .... IMPOSTOR,
IMPERSONATOR, CLAIMANT,
ASPIRANT, FAKER, SHAM
to knowledge ..... QUACK,
CHARLATAN, SCIOLIST
pretense .... ACT, AIR, RUSE,
GUISE, PRETEXT, SHAM,
CLAIM, FEINT
of virtue ..... HYPOCRISY
pretension ... CLAIM, PRETEXT,
AIR, BLUFF
pretentious .... POMPOUS,
ASSUMING, ARTY
art .... KITSCH
preterition .... OMISSION
pretermit .... NEGLECT, OMIT,
OVERLOOK
pretext ... PRETENSE, EXCUSE,
COVER
for war ..... CASUS BELLI
pretty ... COMELY, FAIR, NICE,
BONNY, BONNIE
and delicately formed ...
DAINTY, MIGNON
girl .... CUTEY
pretzel .... BISCUIT
Preussen .... PRUSSIA
prevail ..... DOMINATE, WIN,
TRIUMPH, SUCCEED
on ... PERSUADE, INDUCE
prevalent .... GENERAL,
PANDEMIC, REGNANT, RIFE,
PREVAILING, CURRENT,
WIDESPREAD, COMMON,
RAMPANT
prevaricate ..... LIE, QUIBBLE,
PALTER, EQUIVOCATE

prevarication .. LIE, FALSEHOOD
prevaricator .... LIAR
prevent ..... AVERT, OBVIATE,
PRECLUDE, HINDER, DETER,
STOP, THWART, BLOCK,
BALK, FORESTALL,
FRUSTRATE
   legally .... ESTOP
prevention, legal ... ESTOPPEL
preventive court order ....
INJUNCTION
   medicine ... ANTIBIOTIC
previous .. PRIOR, PRECEDING,
FORMER
previse .. FORECAST, FORESEE,
WARN
prexy .... PRESIDENT
prey ...... VICTIM, QUARRY,
PLUNDER, ROB, GAME
   high sea .... PRIZE
   search for .... HUNT,
RAVEN, RAVIN
Priam's children .. CASSANDRA,
PARIS, CREUSA, HECTOR,
TROILUS
   domain .... TROY
   father .... LAOMEDON
   wife .... HECUBA
price ... CHARGE, RATE, COST,
VALUE, WORTH, FEE
   go up in .... BULL
   list ...... CATALOG(UE)
   of ride .... FARE
prick .. STING, PIERCE, TINGLE,
SPUR, DOT, PUNCTURE,
PROD, GOAD, PINK, QUALM
pricket .... BUCK, DEER,
CANDLESTICK
prickle .... SPINE, THORN,
STING, TINGLE, BARB,
BUR(R), SETA, ACULEUS,
TRICHOME, BRIAR
prickly .... THORNY, BURRY,
ECHINATE, SMARTING,
TINGLING, STINGING,
BRIERY, SPINY
   bush ..... BRIER, ROSE,
BRIAR
   heat .. LICHEN, MILIARIA
   pear .... TUNA, CACTUS,
NOPAL, OPUNTIA
   seed coat .... BUR(R)
   shrub .... BRAMBLE,
DEWBERRY, RASPBERRY
   weed .... NETTLE
pride .. ARROGANCE, CONCEIT,

VANITY, VAINGLORY,
SELF-ESTEEM
   disdainful ..... HAUTEUR
   lion's ...... LITTER, MANE
   ruffled .... PIQUE
priest ... PRESBYTER, PRESTER,
SHAMAN, FRA, FLAMEN,
CLERGYMAN, MINISTER,
CURE
   armband .... FANON
   army .... PADRE,
CHAPLAIN
   assistant of ... ACOLYTE,
SACRISTAN
   Buddhist .... LAMA
   gift of ...... MORTUARY
   high .... PONTIFF,
AARON, ELI
   house of a ..... PRESBYTERY
   Indian ...... SHAMAN,
MEDICINE MAN
   neckpiece of ..... AMICE
   newly ordained ....
NEOPHYTE
   office of .. FROCK, MATINS
   salaried .... VICAR
   shaven head of .. TONSURE
   skullcap ..... ZUCCHETTO
   vestment ... ORALE, ALB,
SURPLICE, COPE
priestess .... AUGE, HERO
priestly .... SACERDOTAL,
HIERATIC
priests group of 20 .... FETIAL
prig .... PRUDE, PEDANT,
STUFFED SHIRT, PICKPOCKET,
THIEF
prim ..... DEMURE, FORMAL,
PROPER, PRIGGISH, PRISSY,
MODEST, PRUDISH
prima .... FACIE
   donna .... DIVA, CALLAS,
ALDA, STEBER, MELBA,
PONS, TEBALDI
primary .... ULTIMATE,
ORIGINAL, CHIEF,
PRINCIPAL, FIRST
primate .... APE, BONOBO,
GIBBON, (ARCH)BISHOP,
MONKEY, LEMUR, ORANG,
GORILLA, SIAMANG
prime .. FIRST(RATE), CREAM,
PICK, PREPARE, MAY
   in music .... UNISON
   minister .... PREMIER
   of life .... HEYDAY

primer .... HORNBOOK,
    (TEXT)BOOK, READER
primitive ..... WILD, CRUDE,
    BASIC, ANCIENT, BARBARIC
    combining form ....
                  PALE(O)
    fish .... COELACANTH
    tribesman's ornament ...
                  LABRET
primogenitor ...... ANCESTOR
primordial .... ORIGINAL
primp .... PREEN, PRINK,
                  PRUNE
primrose .... PRIMULA,
    FAIRYCUP, SPINK, COWSLIP,
                  OXLIP
primula .... PRIMROSE
prince ..... KING, MONARCH,
    RAIA, PRINCIPE, RAS
    consort's wife ... QUEEN,
               EMPRESS
    ecclesiastical .. CARDINAL
    Ethiopian .... RAS
    in India .. (MAHA)RAJAH,
               RANA
    look-alike of .... PAUPER
    Monaco's reigning ......
               RAINIER
    Moslem .. NAWAB, IMAM
    Norodom, Cambodian ..
              SIHANOUK
    of darkness .... SATAN
    of Peace ... JESUS(CHRIST)
    of the church .. CARDINAL
    of Wales' motto ....
        ICH DIEN, I SERVE
    operatic .... IGOR
princeling .... SATRAP
princely ...... REGAL, ROYAL,
    LAVISH, LIBERAL
princess .... INFANTA
    carried by bull .. EUROPA
principal ... CHIEF, PRIMARY,
    ARCH, MAIN, PREMIER
    actor .... STAR, LEAD
    crop .... STAPLE
principle ... DOCTRINE, RULE,
    MAXIM, THEOREM, TENET,
    POSTULATE, PRECEPT, IDEAL
    first .... RUDIMENTS
    main .... KEYSTONE
principles of citizenship ......
              CIVISM
princox ...... FOP, COXCOMB
prink .... PRIMP, PREEN,
    DRESS UP, PRUNE

print .... IMPRESSION,
    PICTURE, ETCHING, STAMP,
               PUBLISH
    blurred/double .. MACKLE
    in red letters .. RUBRICATE
printed books, early ....
            INCUNABULA
printer .... PUBLISHER,
            TYPESETTER
printer's apprentice .... DEVIL
    direction .... STET,
          DELE(TE), RESET
    helper .... DEVIL
    ink pad .... DABBER
    lock .... QUOIN
    mark ... DAGGER, CARET,
        ASTERISK, DIESIS
    measure ... EN, EM, PICA
    metal block ...... QUAD
    proof .... GALLEY
    roller .... BRAY
    shop spirit ...... RALPH
printing .... EDITION,
    art of .... PRESS
    error(s) ...... ERRATUM,
              ERRATA
    establishment ..... PRESS
    form ... DIE, MOLD, MAT
    mark .... FIST, DIESIS,
              DASH
    process .... OFFSET
    system for the blind .....
            BRAILLE
    term ... RESET, DELE(TE),
        CLOSE, STONE
    trial impression .. PROOF
    type channel ...... NICK
prior ..... PREVIOUS, EARLIER,
             FORMER
    superior of a .... ABBOT
    to .... BEFORE
priority .... PRECEDENCE
priory .... MONASTERY,
    NUNNERY, ABBEY
Priscilla's husband .... ALDEN
    suitor .. (MILES)STANDISH
prison .... PENITENTIARY,
    BRIDEWELL, BASTIL(L)E,
    GAOL, QUOD, QUAD, JAIL,
        CAGE, LIMBO
    cell .... HOLE
    chaplain ..... ORDINARY
    colloquial/slang ... STIR,
    CLINK, JUG, PEN, CAN,
    HOOSEGOW, CALABOOSE
    cubicle .... CELL

division .... WARD
employee ..... TURNKEY,
    JAILER, WARDER
federal ...... ALCATRAZ,
    SING SING
guard: sl. .... SCREW
head of a .... WARDEN
London ..... NEWGATE
priest .... CHAPLAIN,
    ORDINARY
sentence ...... STRETCH
ship's ...... HULK, BRIG
spy .... MOUTON
term .... RAP
underground .. DUNGEON
prisoner ... CAPTIVE, TERMER,
    CONVICT, JAILBIRD
at bar .... CULPRIT
bond of ... BAIL, PAROLE
guard of .... BAILIFF
privileged ...... TRUSTY
redeem a .... RANSOM
shackles of ...... BILBO
prissy .... PRECISE, PRIM,
    FUSSY, OVERNICE
pristine .... NEW, UNSPOILED,
    ORIGINAL, PURE, FIRST
prithee ... PLEASE, I PRAY THEE
privacy .... SECLUSION,
    SECRECY
private ... PERSONAL, SECRET,
    CONFIDENTIAL, INTIMATE
apartment ...... MAHAL
army .... PFC
entrance .... POSTERN
eye ...... DETECTIVE, TEC
information .... TIP
remarks .... ASIDES,
    AD LIBS
road .... DRIVEWAY
room .... CLOSET
teacher .. TUTOR, COACH,
wrong .... TORT
privateer ..... KIDD, CORSAIR,
    PIRATE, CORNISH, DRAKE,
    CAVENDISH, ANSON, ROGERS,
    SWAN
privilege ...... FAVOR, RIGHT
corporation's ....
    FRANCHISE
king's .... REGALITY
privileges, equality of ....
    ISONOMY
privy .... LATRINE, JAKES,
    OUTHOUSE, PRIVATE,
    TOILET, STOOL, CLOACA

council ..... CAMARILLA
to .... INFORMED
prize .... STAKE, AWARD,
    VALUE, ESTEEM, TROPHY,
    LEVER, PRY, TREASURE
award since 1917 ....
    PULITZER
donor .... NOBEL,
    PULITZER
fighter .... BOXER,
    PUG(ILIST), SLUGGER,
    BEAKBUSTER, RINGSTER
fighter's wear ..... SILKS
fighting program .. CARD
kind of .... BOOBY
money .... PURSE
pro ...... FOR, PROFESSIONAL
bono ____ ..... PUBLICO
tempore ..... TEMPORARY
proa .... CANOE, PRAU
probability ...... LIKELIHOOD,
    ODD
probable .... LIKELY,
    POSSIBLE
probate court's concern ......
    WILLS, ESTATES
judge .... SURROGATE
probation ..... TRIAL, TESTING
probe ...... SEARCH, EXPLORE
for examining wounds ..
    STYLET
surgical .... STYLET
probity .... INTEGRITY,
    HONESTY
problem .... KNOT, QUESTION,
    DIFFICULTY, TICKLER,
    CRUX, PUZZLE, DILEMMA,
    POSER, TASK
proboscidian ...... ELEPHANT,
    MASTODON
proboscis .... SNOUT, TRUNK,
    NOSE
butterfly/moth's ....
    LINGUA
insect ..... HAUSTELLUM
proceed ...... ISSUE, GO ON,
    ADVANCE, MARCH, CONTINUE
at great speed .. HIGHBALL
without power ... COAST
proceedings .... ACTA,
    TRANSACTIONS, ACTS
last part of .... TAG
proceeds ... PROFITS, INCOME,
    ISSUE
process .... COURSE,

OUTGROWTH, APPENDAGE,
TUBERCLE
fish .... BARBEL
in law .... SUIT, ACTION,
WRIT, PROSECUTE
of decline ... DECADENCE
of knowing ..... NOESIS,
COGNITION
server .... SHERIFF
steel-making .. BESSEMER
procession .. TRAIN, RETINUE,
CORTEGE, FILE, PARADE,
CAVALCADE
of cars ..... MOTORCADE
official .... MARSHAL
staff .... VERGE
staff bearer ..... VERGER
processional .... HYMN
prochein, in law ..... NEAREST
proclaim ...... ANNOUNCE,
DECLARE, HERALD,
ENOUNCE, TRUMPET, SING,
CRY
proclamation .... MANIFESTO,
BAN, EDICT, NOTICE,
UKASE, BAN(N)S
proclivity ...... INCLINATION
Procne, husband of .. TEREUS
parent of ...... PANDION
sister of ..... PHILOMELA
transformation of ....
SWALLOW
procrastinate ..... POSTPONE,
DEFER, DELAY, DILLY DALLY
procreate ... BEGET, PRODUCE
proctor .... AGENT
procumbent .... PRONE
procurator .. PROCTOR, PILATE
procure .... GET, OBTAIN,
SECURE
procurer ...... PIMP, PANDER
prod ...... GOAD, DIG, POKE,
THRUST, JAB, URGE, ROUSE,
EGG, DRIVE, PUNCH
prodder, elephant ... MAHOUT
prodigal ...LAVISH, WASTEFUL,
WASTREL, SPENDER,
GENEROUS, PROFUSE,
SPENDTHRIFT
prodigious .... HUGE,
ENORMOUS, AMAZING
prodigy ... WONDER, MARVEL
prodrome .... SYMPTOM
produce .... CAUSE,
ENGENDER, GENERATE,

BEAR, YIELD, CREATE,
BEGET, FETCH, ISSUE
produced on earth's surface ...
EPIGENE
producing abundantly ....
FERACIOUS
vinegar .... ACETIC
product .... OUTGROWTH,
FRUIT, RESULT, CROP,
YIELD
production .... OUTPUT
productive .... FERTILE,
PROLIFIC, RICH, FECUND,
FRUCTUOUS
source .... MINE
proem .... PREFACE,
INTRODUCTION, PRELUDE
prof .... PROFESSOR
profanation .... SACRILEGE
profane .... DEFILE,
IRREVERENT, BLASPHEME,
DEBASE, VIOLATE
profess .... AFFIRM, CLAIM
profession ... CAREER, METIER,
AVOWAL, VOCATION,
CALLING, PURSUIT, LINE,
TRADE
professed .... AVOWED,
PRETENDED
professional .... PRO
non .... LAY, LAIC,
AMATEUR
professor .... TEACHER
assistant of ..... READER
proffer .... OFFER, GIVE,
TENDER, PRESENT
proficient .... ADEPT, APT,
SKILLED, EXPERT, DEFT
profile .... SIDE VIEW,
OUTLINE, BIO-DATA, SKETCH,
SILHOUETTE
profit .... AVAIL, GAIN,
ADVANTAGE, BENEFIT, BOOT
clear ...... NET, VELVET
easy .... GRAVY
kind of extra .. PERQUISITE
sudden, great ... KILLING
profitable .. GAINFUL, PAYING,
LUCRATIVE
profiteer .... SCALPER
profits .... RETURNS, PROCEEDS
for distribution .. MELON
from lands, etc. ..... ISSUE
profligate .... DISSOLUTE,
WASTEFUL
person .... ROUE

profound ..... INTENSE, DEEP, ABYSS
profundity .... DEPTH
profuse ... PRODIGAL, LAVISH, LUSH, GENEROUS
prog ..... FORAGE, PLUNDER
progenitor .. ANCESTOR, PARENT
progeny ..... SEED, OFFSPRING, CHILDREN, ISSUE, SCION, BREED
prognosis ..... FORECAST(ING)
prognosticate .... PREDICT, FORETELL, PROPHESY
prognosticator ... PREDICTOR, DIVINER, SEER, PROPHET, FORECASTER
program .... CARD, SYLLABUS, PROSPECTUS, PLAN
progress .... ADVANCE, IMPROVE(MENT), GAIN
  planned .... TELESIS
progressing by tens .. DECIMAL
Progressive of 1912 ....
  BULLMOOSE
prohibit .... FORBID, HINDER, BAN, VETO, TABOO, (DE)BAR, TABU, ENJOIN
prohibited ..... TABOO, TABU
prohibiting .... VETITIVE
prohibition ...... TABOO, BAN
  trade .... EMBARGO
prohibitionist .... DRY
prohibitive price ...... DEAR, COSTLY
project .... PROTRUDE, PROPOSAL, SCHEME, PLAN, JUT, IDEA, ENTERPRISE
projectile ... BULLET, ROCKET, BOMB, MISSILE, SHELL, JAVELIN
  part of .... WARHEAD, WAR NOSE
  path of ..... TRAJECTORY
projecting corner ... COIGN(E)
  edge .... BRIM, EAVE
  knob .... BOSS
  part .... JOG, SOCLE
  point .... NEB
projection ...... EAR, BULGE, LOBE, LEDGE, FIN, NOB, TORUS, JOB, SOCLE, JAG
prolapse .... PTOSIS
prolegomenon .... FOREWORD
proletarian .... WORKER
proliferate .... MULTIPLY
prolific ... FRUITFUL, FERTILE, FECUND, PRODUCTIVE

prolix ...... LONG-WINDED, WORDY, VERBOSE, DISCURSIVE
prolocutor ..... MOUTHPIECE, CHAIRMAN, SPOKESMAN
prologue reciter ..... CHORUS
prolong ..... NURSE, STRETCH, EXTEND, LENGTHEN, PROTRACT
prolonged dry weather .... DROUGHT
prom ..... BALL, DANCE, HOP
  organizers .... JUNIORS
promenade ... WALK, AVENUE, BALL, PARADE, MALL, ESPLANADE, ALAMEDA, GALLERY, STROLL, PASEO
  along coast ...... FRONT
Prometheus' boon to man ..... FIRE
prominence .... EMINENCE
  between eyebrows ...... GLABELLA
  give .... HIGHLIGHT, SPOTLIGHT
promiscuous .... CASUAL
  woman .... COCOTTE
promise ..... VOW, ENGAGE, PAROLE, PLEDGE, WORD, GUARANTEE, SPONSION
  in marriage .... BETROTH
Promised Land ..... CANAAN, ZION, SION
promising ..... ROSY, BRIGHT
promissory note .... IOU
  signer .... MAKER
promontory .... CAPE, HEADLAND, SKAW, TOR, NESS
promote .... RAISE, ADVANCE, BOOST, FOSTER
promoter .... IMPRESARIO
promotion ..... ADVANCEMENT
prompt ... QUICK, URGE, EGG, INSPIRE, CUE, ADVISE, MOVE, LEAD, YARE, RATH(E)
prompter .... CUER
promptly ... PRONTO, AT ONCE
promulgate .... PUBLISH
prone ... SUPINE, RECUMBENT, PROSTRATE, INCLINED, APT
pronephros .... KIDNEY
prong ... NIB, TINE, TIP, PIERCE
pronged thing .. FORK, ANTLER, TRIDENT, RAKE

pronounce .... DECLARE,
ARTICULATE; UTTER
  imperfectly ....
LAMBDACISM
  indistinctly .... SLUR
pronounced using tongue .....
LINGUAL
pronto..... AT ONCE, QUICKLY
pronunciamento .. MANIFESTO
pronunciation of r like l ......
LALLATION
  pause .... HIATUS
  poor .... CACOLOGY
  rough .... BURR
  standard ..... ORTHOEPY
  study of ...... PHONOLOGY
  unit of .... SYLLABLE
proof .... EVIDENCE, EXHIBIT,
TRIAL
proofreader's mark .... DELE,
CARET, STET
prop ... BRACE, SUPPORT, GIB,
BUTTRESS, STAY, CRUTCH,
SHORE, HOLD UP, SUSTAIN
  one-legged ..... UNIPOD
propaganda .... BALLYHOO
propagate ...... RAISE, BREED,
MULTIPLY, SPREAD
propel ... PUSH, IMPEL, DRIVE
  with a pole .... PUNT
propeller ..... DRIVER, SCREW,
BLADE, ROTOR
  driving force of .. THRUST
  part of .... BLADE
propensity .... BENT,
INCLINATION, TENDENCY,
PENCHANT, FLAIR
proper ...... MEET, DECOROUS,
SUITABLE, CORRECT,
FIT(TING), SEEMLY, PRIM,
DECENT
  order .... EUTAXY
  slang .... KOSHER
properly .... DULY
property .... ATTRIBUTE,
CHATTEL, REALTY,
HOLDINGS, OWNERSHIP,
POSSESSION, ESTATE, ASSET
  absolute .... AL(L)OD
  act to regain ... REPLEVIN
  captured at sea .... PRIZE
  claim to .... LIEN
  delivery of ...... LIVERY
  endowed .... PATRIMONY
  illegal detention of ......
DETINUE

  landed .... ESTATE
  legally held ..... SEISIN,
SEIZIN
  movie-making .... PROP
  personal ..... CHATTEL,
CHOSE
  reverted ...... ESCHEAT
  stationary ..... PRAEDIAL
  willed to someone ......
LEGACY
prophecy .... PREDICTION,
FORECAST
  by lots .... SORTILEGE
prophesy ... AUGUR, PRESAGE,
PREDICT, FORETELL,
FORECAST, DIVINE
prophet .... AMOS, HOSEA,
ISAIAH, JEREMIAH,
EZEKIEL, DANIEL, JONAH,
JOEL, ORACLE, SEER
  Moslem ..... MOHAMMED
  of disaster ..... ALARMIST
prophetess .... ORACLE, SIBYL,
PYTHONESS
  discredited .. CASSANDRA
prophetic .... VATIC(INAL),
SYBILLINE, PYTHONIC,
VATIC(AL), MANTIC, FATIDIC
prophets, book of the .. NEBIIM
propinquity .... NEARNESS,
KINSHIP, AFFINITY
propitiate ... APPEASE, PACIFY
propitious .... GRACIOUS,
FAVORABLE, AUSPICIOUS
proponent ...... PROPOSER,
ADVOCATE, STALWART
proportion ...... RATIO, RATE,
QUOTA, BALANCE, SYMMETRY
proportions ...... DIMENSIONS
proposal ..... OFFER, TENDER,
SUGGESTION, BID, MOVE,
MOTION
  legislative .... BILL
  tentative .... FEELER
propose .... MOVE
  for office ..... NOMINATE
proposed international language
IDO, ESPERANTO
proposition ... THEORY, PLAN,
PROPOSAL, OFFER, THEOREM,
PROJECT, PREMISE,
(HYPO)THESIS
  secondary ...... LEMMA
propound ..... POSE, PROPOSE,
SET FORTH

proprietor .... OWNER, TITLEHOLDER
propriety .... FITNESS
prorogue .... ADJOURN
prosaic .... DULL, LITERAL, UNPOETIC
proscribe ...... FORBID, BAN, OUTLAW, INTERDICT, BANISH, EXILE
prosecute .... CARRY ON, FOLLOW UP, SUE
prosecuting attorney ..... DA, FISCAL
proselyte .... CONVERT
Proserpina .... CORA, PERSEPHONE
   husband of .... PLUTO
   mother of .... CERES
prosit .... TOAST
prosody .... SCANSION
   verse .... STICH
prospect .. SCENE, VIEW, HOPE, OUTLOOK, SEARCH
prospective .. LIKELY, FUTURE
prospector ...... SOURDOUGH
   advance to ... GRUBSTAKE
prospectus .... PROGRAM
prosper ... SUCCEED, THRIVE, FLOURISH, BATTEN
prosperity ... BOOM, BONANZA
Prospero's slave ..... CALIBAN
   sprite .... ARIEL
prosperous .... WEALTHY, WELL-OFF, WELL-TO-DO, FAT, PALMY
prostitute ... TART, TROLLOP, TRULL, TRAMP, WHORE, HARLOT, CHIPPY, FILLE, DRAB
   kind of ...... COURTESAN
prostrate .... PRONE, FALLEN, SUPINE, LAY LOW
prosy .... DULL, JEJUNE
protagonist ..... HERO, STAR, RIVAL, CONTENDER
protect ..... GUARD, SHIELD, DEFEND
protection .... PASS(PORT), TUTELAGE, DEFENSE, (A)EGIS
   against loss .. INSURANCE
   means of ... SPINE, QUILL, ARMOR, PAINT, MOAT, HELMET, CAMOUFLAGE
protective band, fencing ...... BRACER

   cover ... ARMOR, SHELL, SHIELD, SCREEN, CAMOUFLAGE
protector .... PATRON, GUARDIAN, DEFENDER, KEEPER
protege .... WARD
proteid(e) ... AMINE, PROTEIN
protein ... PROTEID(E), FIBRIN, AMINE, ALBUMIN, ALEURONE, RICIN, CASEIN, RICINE, GLOBULIN, HISTONE
   egg yolk .... VITELLIN
   muscle tissue .... MYOSIN
proteose .... ELASTOSE, ALBUMOSE
protest ..... ASSERT, OUTCRY, COMPLAINT, SQUAWK, OBJECT(ION), DISSENT
Protestant .... ANGLICAN, LUTHERAN, OBJECTOR
   Anglo-Saxon ..... WASP
   non-conformist .... SECTARY
proton .... ANLAGE
   accelerator .. COSMOTRON
protoplasm .. PLASMA, COLLOID
   granule in .... MICROSOME
   unit of .... PLASTID
prototype ... PATTERN, MODEL, ORIGINAL
protozoan .... AM(O)EBA, PROTIST, MONAD, EUGLENA
   organ of locomotion .... FLAGELLUM
protract .... STRETCH, LENGTHEN, PROLONG, EXTEND
protrude ... BULGE, PROJECT, JUT(OUT), EXSERT
protrusion of organ .. HERNIA
protuberance ... KNOB, HUMP, VENTER, LOBE, NODE, BULGE, SWELLING, UMBO, NUB, SNAG, EAR, INION
protuberant .... TOROSE, TOROUS, BULGING
proud .... ARROGANT, HAUGHTY, SPIRITED, BYRONIC
Proust, F. novelist .... MARCEL
prove .... TEST, TRY(OUT), VERIFY, DEMONSTRATE
   false ... REFUTE, DEBUNK
provenance .... ORIGIN, DERIVATION

Provencal poet ...... MISTRAL
provender ..... FODDER, HAY,
    OATS, CORN, FORAGE,
    FOOD, FEED
proverb .... ADAGE, PARABLE,
    APHORISM, AXIOM, SAYING,
    MAXIM, SAW, BY-WORD
provide .. FURNISH, STIPULATE,
    PURVEY, SUPPLY, CATER,
    AFFORD
   food .... CATER
   with means ..... ENABLE
providence .... PRUDENCE
provident ... THRIFTY, FRUGAL,
    PRUDENT
providential .... LUCKY,
    FORTUNATE
province .... REGION,
    TERRITORY, SPHERE
   ruler of ..... GOVERNOR,
    ETHNARCH
provincial .... RUSTIC, LOCAL,
    NARROW
   speech .... PATOIS,
    DIALECT, IDIOM
proving directly .... D(E)ICTIC
provision .... VICTUALS,
    CONDITION, FOOD STORE
provisional ...... TENTATIVE,
    INTERIM, TEMPORARY
provisioner ... SUTLER, GROCER
provisions .... LARDER,
    GROCERIES, CATES
   search for ...... FORAGE
   storage place .... CELLAR
proviso ... CLAUSE, CONDITION,
    STIPULATION
provisory ...... CONDITIONAL
provocation ...... INCITEMENT
provoke .... ANGER, IRRITATE,
    PIQUE, ANNOY, GOAD, BAIT,
    STIR, INCITE,
    EXCITE, NEEDLE, RILE
provost .... JAILER
prow .... BOW, NOSE
prowess .... VALOR, SKILL,
    ABILITY
prowl .... LURK, SKULK
proximal ..... NEXT, NEAREST
   opposed to ..... DISTAL
proximity .... NEARNESS
proxy .... AGENT, DEPUTY
prude .... PRIG
prudent ... CAREFUL, SENSIBLE,
    DISCREET, CAUTIOUS
prudery personified .. GRUNDY

prudish .... PRISSY
prune .... PLUM, SHEAR, TRIM,
    CLIP, SNED, LOP
prunella .... TEXTILE
prurient ...... LUSTFUL, LEWD
pruritus .... ITCHING
Prussian .... JUNKER, GERMAN
   cavalryman ..... U(H)LAN
   city .... AACHEN, ESSEN,
    EMDEN
   district .... STADE
   land measure ... MORGEN
   legislature ..... LANDTAG
   province .... SAXONY
   resort .... EMS
   river .... RUHR
   seaport ... EMDEN, KIEL,
    STETTIN
prussiate .... CYANIDE
pry ...... LOOK, PEER, LEVER,
    PRIZE, SNOOP(ER), NOSE,
    CROWBAR, JIMMY, INSPECT
prying .. CURIOUS, INQUISITIVE
   person .. SNOOP, PEEPER,
    PEEPING TOM, GOSSIP
psalm .... HYMN, SONG,
    CONTICLE, INTROIT, VENITE,
    LAUD, CANTATE
   word .... SELAH
psalterium .... MANYPLIES,
    OMASUM
psaltery .... DULCIMER
psammite .... SANDSTONE
pseudo .. BOGUS, COUNTERFEIT,
    SPURIOUS, SHAM, FALSE
   intellectual ..... PUNDIT,
    CHARLATAN, SCIOLIST
pseudonym .... ANONYM,
    PEN NAME, NOM DE PLUME,
    ALIAS, INCOGNITO
   Arouet .... VOLTAIRE
   Athorton .... LIN
   Austen .... DAPSANG
   Bronte .... (CURRER)BELL
   Clemens .. (MARK) TWAIN
   Dickens .... BOZ
   Dodgson ....
    (LEWIS) CARROLL
   Dudevant ....
    (GEORGE) SAND
   Evans .. (GEORGE) ELIOT
   Gardner, E. S. ..... FAIR
   Goodman ... ADAM SMITH
   Herzog ....
    (ANDRE) MAUROIS
   Lamb .... ELIA

Millay ... (NANCY) BOYD
Moir .... DELTA
Mrs. Humphrey ... RITA
Munro .... SAKI
Poquelin .... MOLIERE
Porter .... (O)HENRY
Pyeshkov, Aleksei ......
              (MAXIM) GORKI
Ramee, M. L. ... OUIDA
Rosegger .... PK
Stein ... (ALICE) TOKLAS
Thibault ....
          (ANATOLE) FRANCE
Viaud, L. M. ....
           (PIERRE) LOTI
Wright .. (S.S.) VAN DINE
pshaw .... POOH, TUT
Psiloriti, Mount .... IDA
  location of ...... CRETE
psilosis .... SPRUE
psoas .... MUSCLE, LOIN
psora .... SCABIES
psychasthenia ..... NEUROSIS
Psyche .... SOUL, MIND
  love of .... CUPID
psychedelic experience ... LSD
psychiatrist .... ALIENIST,
      MESMER, FREUD, ADLER
psyches, parts of ... IDS, EGOS
psychic disorder .... NEUROSIS
  energy .... LIBIDO
  person .... MEDIUM
psycho .... NEUROTIC
psychological .... MENTAL
psychologist .... BINET
psychopathic .... LOCO
psychosis .... INSANITY
psychotic .... CRAZY
Pt, in chemistry ... PLATINUM
ptarmigan ..... GROUSE, RIPA
pteric .... ALAR
pteridophyte .... FERN
pteris rootstock .... ROI
pterodactyl .... PTEROSAUB
pteropod ... MOLLUSK, CLIONE
pterygoid .... WINGLIKE
ptisan ... TEA, TISANE, DRINK,
              DECOCTION
ptomaine, liquid .... CHOLINE
ptosis .... PROLAPSE
ptyalin .... ENZYME
pub .... TAVERN, INN, HOTEL,
              BAR
  serving ...... BEER, ALE,
              PORTER
  worker .... TAPSTER,

              BARMAID
puberty, of .... HEBETIC
pubescence .... DOWN
public ... OVERT, COMMUNITY,
      PEOPLE, OPEN, COMMON,
              COMMUNAL
  announcer .... CRIER
  auction .... VENDUE
  baths .... THERMAE
  disclosure ...... EXPOSE
  enemy .... CRIMINAL,
      GANGSTER, RACKETEER
  funds, steal .... PECULATE
  good ..... COMMONWEAL
  house ...... INN, HOTEL,
          TAVERN, BAR
  land .... AGER
  life .... CAREER
  notice ... AD, BULLETIN,
      PUBLICITY, SPOTLIGHT
  opinion ..... CONSENSUS
  opinion-taker ... GALLUP,
          HARRIS, ROPER
  prosecutor ... DA, FISCAL
  recreation spot .... PARK
  square ... PLAZA, PIAZZA,
              FORUM
  utility ... BUS, (TAXI)CAB
  walk .... ESPLANADE
  welcome, enthusiastic ...
              OVATION
  worship, science of ......
              LITURGIES
publican .... BARKEEP(ER),
              TAXMAN
publication .. BOOK, ARTICLE,
      PERIODICAL, MAGAZINE,
      BULLETIN, JOURNAL
publicist .... WRITER,
      (PRESS)AGENT, JOURNALIST
publicity ... NOTICE, RECLAME
  exaggerated ... PUFFERY
publicize .... PLUG
publish ... BLAZON, PUT OUT,
          ISSUE, NOISE
publisher .. OCHS, SULZBERGER,
      FIELDS, HEARST, MERRIAM,
              MCKAY
publisher's announcement ....
              BLURB
  trademark .... COLOPHON
Puccini, composer .. GIACOMO
  heroine .... MIMI, TOSCA
  opera ... TOSCA, BOHEME,
      MANON LESCAUT,
              TURANDOT

puccoon .... BLOODROOT, DYE
puce .... PURPLE
puck ...... DISK, SPRITE, ELF,
      IMP, (HOB)GOBLIN
pucka ... REAL, GENUINE, GOOD
pucker .... PURSE, POUT,
      WRINKLE, KNIT, FOLD,
      CREASE, COCKLE, RUCK,
      TUCK
puckered .... BULLATE
puckish .. IMPISH, MISCHIEVOUS,
      ELFIN
pudding .... CUSTARD,
      FROMENTY, ROLY-POLY,
      CHARLOTTE, MUSH, SPONGE,
      SAUSAGE, DUFF, HOY
  flour .... DUFF
  ingredient .... SUET,
      TAPIOCA, SAGO,
      SEMOLINA
  sailor .... DUFF
puddle ..... PLASH(ET), POOL,
      MUDDY, WALLOW,
      LOBLOLLY
puddling tool .... RABBLE
pudency .... MODESTY
pudendum .... VULVA
pudgy ... DUMPY, FAT, STOCK,
      ROLY-POLY
Pueblo ..... VILLAGE, TOWN,
      INDIAN
  council room ...... KIVA
  Indian ..... HOPI, MOQUI,
      PIRO, ZUNI, TANO
  Indian dwelling .... KIVA
puerile ... INFANTILE, YOUNG,
      CHILDISH, SILLY, TRIVIAL
Puerto Rico beverage ... MABI
  capital .... SAN JUAN
  city .... PONCE, CAGUAS,
      ARECIBO
  conqueror .... MILES
  discoverer of .. COLUMBUS
  governor ...... MUNOZ,
      ALBERTO, SANCHEZ,
      MAYAGUEZ
  porkfish .... SISI
  seaport .... ARECIBO
puff ..... PAD, GUST, PRAISE,
      FLAM, WHIFF, WAFF,
      BREATH, SWELL(ING), PANT,
      INFLATE, BLOW
  adder .... SNAKE
  at a cigarette ...... DRAG
  ball .... FUNGUS
  bird ... BARBET, MONASA

headdress .... POUF
  of wind .... FLATUS
  out .... BOUFFANT
  small .... WHIFFET
  up ...... ELATE, BLOW,
      BLOAT, INFLATE, SWELL
puffed .... BAGGY
puffer .... (GLOBE)FISH
puffin .... BIRD
  kin of .... AUK
puffy ... OBESE, FAT, PANTING,
      SWOLLEN
pug ...... BOXER, (BULL)DOG,
      PUGILIST, FOOTPRINT,
      TRAIL, TRACK, CLAY
Puget Sound seaport .. TACOMA
pugging ...... CLAY, MORTAR,
      SAWDUST
puggree .... SCARF
pugh .... EXCLAMATION, BAH,
      PAH, PISH
pugilist .... PUG, BOXER,
      BEAKBUSTER, RINGSTER
  assistant of ..... SECOND,
      HANDLER
  encounter .... MILL
pugnacious .... QUARRELSOME,
      COMBATIVE, BELLIGERENT,
      BELLICOSE
  man .... BRUISER
puisne .... JUDGE, JUNIOR
puissant .... MIGHTY, STRONG
puke ...... VOMIT, THROW UP
pukka .... REAL, GENUINE
pulchritude .... BEAUTY
pulchritudinous ... BEAUTIFUL
  one ..... PIN-UP, VENUS
pule .... WHIMPER, WHINE
pulex .... FLEA
Pulj, former name of ... POLA
pull ... DO, (RE)STRAIN, MOVE,
      PLUCK, TOW, HAUL, DRAG,
      TUG, DRAW, PERFORM
  apart ... PAN, CRITICIZE,
      TEAR, REND, RIP
  back .... RETREAT,
      WITHDRAW
  by the root .... STUB
  down ... HUMBLE, REDUCE
  for .... CHEER, ROOT
  forcibly .. WRENCH, YANK
  off .... EFFECT,
      ACCOMPLISH, DOUSE
  over .... SWEATER
  slang .... INFLUENCE
  up .... STOP, HIKE, REIN

up stake .. LEAVE, DEPART
pullet .... HEN, POULARD
pulley ...... WHEEL, TACKLE, SHEAVE
pullman ...... SLEEPER, BERTH
pullulate ... BUD, GERMINATE, BREED, TEEM
pulmonary disease .. PHTHISIS
pulp ...... CHYME, PAP, PITH
apple/fruit ..... POMACE
grape .... RAPE
in mining .... SLIME
product .... PAPER
slang .... MAGAZINE
pulpit ...... ROSTRUM, BEMA, PLATFORM, MINISTRY, DESK, AMBO
preachings .... SERMONS, HOMILIES
pulpiteer .... PREACHER
pulpy .... FLESHY
pulpy fruit .. GRAPE, FIG, UVA, DRUPE, POMEGRANATE
pulque .... MESCAL, AGAVE
pulsate .... QUIVER, VIBRATE, BEAT, THROB, THRILL
pulsation ... THROB, BEAT(ING)
pulse .... BEAT, THROB, FEELING, SEED, SPHYGMUS
beat absence ... ACROTISM
of the .... SPHYGMIC
plant .... PEA, BEAN, LENTIL, SOY
split .... DAL
pulverize .... BRAY, POWDER, TRITURATE, GRIND, MILL, LEVIGATE, ATOMIZE, MULL, POUND, CRUSH
pulverized material .. POWDER, DUST
pulverizing device .... SPIDER
pulverulent .. DUSTY, POWDERY
puma .... CAT, COUGAR, FUR, (MOUNTAIN)LION, CATAMOUNT
pumice .... ROCK, POLISH
pummel .... BEAT
pump .... QUIZ, INFLATE, DRAW(OUT), QUESTION, SHOE
handle .... SWIPE
kind of .... SUCTION, PRESSURE, CHAIN, LIFT, FORCE, RAM
part .... RAM, VALVE
plunger of .... RAM
pumpernickel ... BROT, BREAD

pumpkin ...... PEPO, GOURD, MELON, FRUIT
pumpkinseed ...... (SUN)FISH
pun ... QUIBBLE, PARANOMASIA, EQUIVOKE
puna .... PLATEAU
punch ... DRINK, PERFORATE, PASTE, JAB, FORCE, BOP, DOUSE, PUPPET, PIERCE, BOX, POKE, PROD, GAD, BUFFET, BLOW, STAMP
and _____ .... JUDY
and Judy character ......
   PUPPET
and Judy dog ...... TOBY
bowl .... MONTEITH
drunk .... DAZED, DIZZY
engraver's ..... MATTOIR
weak .... TIFF
puncheon .... CASK, POST, TIMBER, DIE, PERFORATOR, AWL
punchinello .... CLOWN, BUFFOON
punctate ... DOTTED, SPOTTED
punctation .... DOT
punctilio .... NICETY
punctilious ... EXACT, STRICT, PRIM, SCRUPULOUS
person ..... PRIG, PRUDE
punctual ... PROMPT, ON TIME, MINUTE
punctuate ... MARK, INTERRUPT
punctuation mark ....
(SEMI)COLON, DASH, COLA, PERIOD, COMMA, HYPHEN, BRACKETS, DOT
puncture .... PERFORATE, PRICK, PIERCE, HOLE
pundit ... SAVANT, AUTHORITY, SCHOLAR
pung .... SLED, SLEIGH
pungent ... RACY, SPICY, TART, ACRID, TANGY, GINGERY, PEPPERY, PIQUANT, SALTY, SHARP, BITING, KEEN
bulb ... ONION, GARLIC, SHALLOT, LEEK, SCALLION
Punic citizen .. CARTHAGINIAN
War battlesite ..... ZAMA
War belligerent ... ROME, CARTHAGE
War general ..... SCIPIO
punish .... DISCIPLINE, CHASTISE, WREAK, FRAP,

CASTIGATE, CHASTEN,
CORRECT, AVENGE,
PENALIZE, FINE
by fine .... AMERCE
to correct .... CHASTISE,
CHASTEN
punishment ... PENALTY, RAP,
BASTINADO, FINE, TALION
divine .... PLAGUE
eye for an eye ... TALION
endless ...... DAMNATION
instrument of ... STOCKS,
PILLORY, RACK,
GARROTE, FERULE
of ..... PENAL, PUNITIVE
voluntary ...... PENANCE
punitive .... PENAL
Punjab, capital (India) ....
CHANDIGARH
capital (Pakistan) ....
LAHORE
city .... PATIALA, SIMLA,
AMBALA, JULLUNDUR,
SIALKOT
native .... JAT, SIKH
warrior .... SIKH
punk .... TOUCHWOOD,
TINDER, HOODLUM,
CATAMITE, AMADOU,
ASTRINGENT
punka(h) .... FAN
punkie ..... FLY, MIDGE, GNAT
punster .... WIT, WAG
punt .... KICK, PROPEL,
GAMBLE, KENT, QUANT
punty .... POINTIL
puny ... SLIGHT, WEAK, SMALL,
FRAIL
pup .... DOG, SEAL
name of .... FIDO
pupa ..... CHRYSALIS, NYMPH
covering of .... THECA,
COCOON
pupil ...... GRADER, DISCIPLE,
TRAINEE, TYRO, STUDENT
contraction of ... MYOSIS
dilatation of .. MYDRIASIS
dilator .... ATROPINE
French .... ECOLIER,
ELEVE
organ with .... EYE
pupilage .... NONAGE
puppet .... MARIONETTE,
PAWN, TOOL, DOLL, DUPE,
PENSIONARY, MAUMET,
MAMMET

maker .... SARG
show .... GALANTY
show character ... JUDY,
PUNCH(INELLO)
show dog .... TOBY
puppeteer .... SARG
puppy ... WHELP, DOG, SHARK
purchasable .... VENAL
purchase .... ORDER
or sale of office ....
BARRATRY
purdah .... SCREEN, CURTAIN
pure .... VIRGIN, CHASTE,
SHEER, NEAT, ABSOLUTE,
CLEAR, SIMPLE, MERE,
UTTER, PERFECT
puree .... SOUP
purfle ... BORDER, TRIMMING,
PURL
purgation .... CATHARSIS
purgative .... CATHARTIC,
JALAP, PHYSIC, LAXATIVE,
CALOMEL, APERIENT,
CASTOR OIL, HELLEBORIN
rectal .... ENEMA
purgatory ..... LIMBO, EREBUS
purge ... FLUX, EXORCISE, SOIL,
PHYSIC, CLEANSE, RID,
PURIFY, ABSTERGE
purification .... CATHARSIS
by holy water .. BAPTISM
purified, capable of being .....
FINABLE
purify .. CLEANSE, DISTIL(L),
DEPURATE, SANCTIFY,
PURGE, SUBLIMATE, REFINE
by distillation ... RECTIFY
by holy water .. BAPTIZE
Puritan .... BLUENOSE,
ROUNDHEAD
of a sort ...... WOWSER
purity ... SANCTITY, CHASTITY,
INNOCENCE
of color .... CHROMA
purl ...... SWIRL, LOOP, RIB,
EDDY, MURMUR, PEARL,
RIPPLE, PURFLE
purlieu ... HAUNT, ENVIRONS,
HANGOUT
purloin .... STEAL, FILCH
purple ..... ROYAL, IMPERIAL,
ORNATE, AMARANTHINE,
REGAL, MAUVE, AMETHYST
brown .... PUCE
Heart .... MEDAL,
DECORATION, ORDER

medic .... ALFALFA
red .. CARMINE, CRIMSON
shade ... LILAC, MODENA,
AMARANTH, MAUVE
purplish red .... CLARET,
MAGENTA, MURREY,
MULBERRY
purport .... SENSE, OBJECT
INTENTION, TENOR, PROFESS,
CLAIM, MEANING
purpose .... AIM, SAKE,
INTENT(ION), END, DESIGN,
GOAL
purposeful .... TELIC
purse .... MONEY, PRIZE
FINANCES, PUCKER, KNIT,
BILLFOLD, SPORRAN,
HANDBAG, POUCH, BURSE
purser .... BURSAR
purslane .... WEED
pursuant .... FOLLOWING
pursue ..... CHASE, FOLLOW,
SEEK, CARRY ON, CONTINUE,
DOG, HOUND, TRAIL
pursuit .. QUEST, OCCUPATION,
CHASE
pursy ... FAT, OBESE, PUDGY
purulence .... PUS
purulent .... PYIC
purvey ... CATER, PROVISION,
FURNISH
pus .... MATTER, SANIES
accumulation .. EMPYEMA
filled cavity ..... VOMICA
formation of .... PYOSIS
form .... FESTER,
SUPPURATE, MATURATE
of .... PYIC, PYOID
substance .... PYIN
push ... FORCE, IMPEL, PROPEL,
CLIQUE, THRUST, SHOVE,
PRESS, DRIVE, NUDGE,
HUSTLE, JOSTLE, ELBOW
along .... PLOD
off ...... LEAVE, DEPART
on .... PROCEED
over: sl. .... SETUP
with nose .... NUZZLE
pushcart operator ... PEDDLER,
VENDER
pusher .... PEDDLER
commodity of ..... DOPE,
HEROIN, NARCOTIC,
LSD, POT, MARIJUANA
pushing .... ARROGANT,
CONCEITED, BUMPTIOUS

pusillanimous .... COWARDLY,
IRRESOLUTE
puss .... CAT, GIRL, FACE,
MOUTH, HARE
pussy .... CATKIN, CAT
pustule ..... WHELK, FESTER,
WHEAL, PIMPLE, BLISTER,
BLAIN
on neck ..... MALANDERS
scar .... POCK
put ...... IMPEL, DRIVE, PUSH,
SET, LAY, PLACE, IMPOSE,
APPLY, STATE, EXPRESS,
WAGER
aside ..... DISCARD, DAFF
away ... KILL, CONSUME,
STORE, STOW
down .... PLUMP, CRUSH,
HUMBLE, RECORD,
QUASH
effort .... EXERT
forward .... PRESENT,
PROPOSE
film in camera ... LOAD
in .... INSERT, FOIST,
INTROMIT
in-Bay hero ...... PERRY
in irons ...... SHACKLE,
FETTER, MANACLE
off .... DOFF, POSTPONE,
DELAY, EVADE, DIVERT,
STALL, DEFER
off position .... LUXATE
on .. CLOTHE, DON, STAGE
on the block .... SELL,
AUCTION
out ..... DISMISS, EXPEL,
INCOMMODE, EVICT,
PUBLISH, OUST, DOUSE,
QUENCH
side by side .. JUXTAPOSE
to flight ..... ROUT(ED),
FEEZE
to work .... HARNESS
up ... POST, ERECT, SHOW,
BUILD, LODGE
up with .... BEAR,
TOLERATE, ENDURE
putamen .... STONE, PIT
putative .. REPUTED, SUPPOSED
Putnam, Revolutionary general
ISRAEL
putrefaction .... DECAY,
ROT(TING)
putrefy ... DECAY, DECOMPOSE,
ROT

putrescent .... DECAYING, ROTTING

putrid ..... ROTTEN, STINKING, DECAYED, FOUL

putsch .... REBELLION, UPRISING

puttee .... GAITER, PUTTY, LEGGING

putter ...... NIGGLE, DAWDLE, TINKER

puttier .... GLAZIER

putting area .... GREEN

putty .... CEMENT

puttyroot .... ORCHID

Putumayo river .... ICA

puzzle .... STUMP, DUM(B)FOUND, NONPLUS, CONFUSE, BEWILDER, BAFFLE, REBUS, PERPLEX, MYSTIFY, QUESTION, RIDDLE, ENIGMA, KITTLE, MYSTERY

word ...... LOGOGRAPH

puzzled .... STUCK

puzzler .... CRUX, POSER

puzzling ..... KNOTTING, ODD, ENIGMATIC

thing .... CRUX

pygarg .... ADDAX

Pygmalion's statue .. GALATEA

pygmy ... DWARF, NEGRILLO, ATOMY, NEGRITO, RUNT, MININ

antelope .... ORIBI

Pyle, newspaperman ... ERNIE

pylon ...... GATEWAY, TOWER, MARKER, POST, PYRAMID

pyralidid .... MOTH

pyramid, builder of largest ... KHUFU, CHEOPS

builders ..... EGYPTIANS

dweller ... DJOSER, UNAS

site of .... EL GIZA

Step, builder ... IMHOTEP

terraced ..... ZIGGURAT, ZIKURAT

truncated .... PYLON

pyre .... PILE

pyrene .... NUTLET, SEED, STONE

Pyrenees goat .... IBEX

highest point .. ANETHOU, ANETO

mammal .... DESMAN

republic ...... ANDORRA

pyretic .... FEVERISH

pyrexia .... FEVER

pyriform ...... PEAR-SHAPED

pyrite .... FOOL'S GOLD

pyrogenic .... IGNEOUS

pyromaniac .... FIREBUG, ARSONIST, INCENDIARY

pyrope .... GARNET

pyrosis ... HEARTBURN, BRASH

pyrotechnics ..... FIREWORKS

pyrrhic .... WAR DANCE

like victory ... CADMEAN

victory site .... ASCULUM

Pyrrhonism ..... SKEPTICISM

Pythagoras' birthplace .... SAMOS

forte ..... MATHEMATICS

Pythias' friend ...... DAMON

python .... SERPENT, ANACONDA, BOA, SNAKE

diety .... ZOMBI(E)

pythoness ...... SOOTHSAYER, PROPHETESS, PRIESTESS

pythonic .... ORACULAR, PROPHETIC

pyx .... BOX, CIBORIUM

pyxis .... CASE, BOX, VASE

Q

Q, Greek .... KAPPA

in chess .... QUEEN

Qara Qum's capital .... DOHA

Qatar's capital .... DOHA

QED, part of .... QUOD, ERAT

quack .... CHARLATAN, MOUNTEBANK, DEMAGOGUE, CROCUS, EMPIRIC(IST), SCIOLIST, WISEACRE, IMPOSTOR, FAKER, CRY

crier .... DUCK

doctor's aide .... TOADY,

TOADEATER

medicine ...... NOSTRUM, HERB

quad .... QUOD, PRISON, JAIL

quadragesima .... LENT

quadragenarian .... FORTYISH

quadragesimal .... FORTY, LENTEN

quadrangle ..... COURTYARD, SQUARE, TETRAGON

quadrant ..... ARC, FOURTH, SEXTANT, ALTIMETER

graduated edge of .. LIMB
quadrate ..... SQUARE, AGREE,
QUARTER, RECTANGULAR,
RECTANGLE, CONFORM
quadriga .... CHARIOT
quadrille ..... (SQUARE)DANCE,
LANC(I)ERS
  card .... MATADOR
  second highest trump ....
MANILLA
  sight .... VANE
quadrivium, part of ... MUSIC,
GEOMETRY, ASTRONOMY
quadroon .... MULATTO,
HYBRID
quadrumane ... BABOON, APE,
MONKEY, PRIMATE
quadruped .... MAMMAL,
FOUR-FOOTED, RHINO,
HIPPO, CAMEL, ZEBRA, ASS,
DONKEY, GIRAFFE, TAPIR
quadruple .... FOURFOLD
quaff ...... DRINK, SWALLOW,
GULP
quagga-like animal ... ZEBRA,
DONKEY
quaggy ... BOGGY, MIRY, SOFT
quagmire .... BOG, FEN
quahaug .... CLAM
quahog .... CLAM
  young ...... LITTLENECK
quail ...... RECOIL, COWER,
WINCE, COLIN, CRINGE,
BOBWHITE, PARTRIDGE,
BIRD, WILT
  flock .... COVEY, BEVY
quaint .. SINGULAR, FANCIFUL,
STRANGE, CURIOUS,
ANTIQUE, UNUSUAL
  humor ...... DROLLERY
quake ...... SHAKE, QUIVER,
SHIVER, DIVER, SHUDDER,
TEMBLOR, TREMBLE
Quaker .... FRIEND
  colonist .... PENN
  gray .... ACIER
  ladies ... BLUET, FLOWER
  midweek of a ....
WEDNESDAY
quaking tree ... ASPEN, POPLAR
quaky .... SHAKY
qualification ..... CONDITION,
ABILITY
qualified .... ABLE, FIT,
COMPETENT, LIMITED
qualify ..... LIMIT, DESCRIBE,

FIT, PASS, ENTITLE
qualifying word ..... ADVERB,
ADJECTIVE
quality ..... NATURE, CALIBER,
ATTRIBUTE, KIND, AURA,
FEATURE, TRAIT, GRADE,
PROPERTY, CHARACTER
  bad/poor .... PUNK,
INFERIOR, BUM
  colloquial .... CLASS
  distinguishing .... TRAIT
  of high ..... TONY, PLUSH
  of sound ... TIMBRE, TONE
  special .... (DE)LUXE
qualm ...... NAUSEA, DOUBT,
UNEASINESS, TWINGE,
MISGIVING, SCRUPLE,
COMPUNCTION
qualmish .... QUEASY, QUEER
quamash ..... CAMAS(S), LILY
quandary .... DILEMMA,
PREDICAMENT, STRAIT
quant ... POLE, PROPEL, PUNT
quantity ... DOSE, MASS, GRIST,
LOT, PORTION, AMOUNT
  indefinite ..... SOME, ANY
  large .... RAFT, RAFF,
SLEW, BUSHEL
  small .... LICK, SCRUPLE,
SCANTLING
Quantrill's men ..... RAIDERS
quantum ... AMOUNT, PORTION
  of heat energy .. PHOTON
quarantine .... ISOLATE
  building/ship ....
LAZARETTO
  signal ..... YELLOW JACK
quarrel .... SPAT, ROW,
SQUABBLE, PANE, CHISEL,
DISPUTE, WRANGLE, FEUD,
BICKER, BRUSH, MIFF, JAR,
ALTERCATION, FLITE,
RUN-IN, RUCTION, BRABBLE,
AFFRAY, STRIFE, BROIL,
MISSILE
quarrelsome ...... LITIGIOUS,
BELLIGERENT, PUGNACIOUS
quarry .... GAME, PREY,
EXCAVATE, VICTIM
quarrying tool .... TREPAN,
TRAPAN
quarryman .... STONECUTTER
quart(e) .... CARTE
quarter ...... FOURTH, SPAN,
DISTRICT, MERCY, LODGE,
BILLET, CANTON

note .... CROTCHET
of a circle .... QUADRANT
phase .... DIPHASE
round .... OVOLO
quartern .... GILL
quarters ..... BILLET, ABODE,
LODGINGS, ROOMS
slang .... DIGGINGS
quarts, 4 .... GALLON
quartz ...... ONYX, SINOPLE,
MORION, CRYSTAL, CACO,
AVENTURINE, SILICA, SILEX,
FLINT, PLASMA,
CHALCEDONY, SARD(INE),
CAIRNGORM, RUBASSE,
AGATE, JASPER, TOPAZ,
AMETHYST, CITRINE,
PRASE, CHRYSOPRASE,
CHERT, CARNELIAN
quartzite .... SANDSTONE
quash .... ANNUL, VOID,
SET ASIDE, QUELL,
SUFFRESS
in law .... ABATE
quasi .... AS IF, SEEMINGLY
quass .... KVASS
quaternion .... TETRAD
quatrain ...... STANZA, POEM
quaver ...... TREMOLO, SHAKE,
TREMBLE, TRILL
quavery .... TREMULOUS
quay ... LEVEE, PIER, WHARF,
LANDING
queachy .... SWAMPY, BOGGY
quean ..... JADE, SLUT, MINX,
HUSSY
queasy .... QUALMISH,
FASTIDIOUS
Quebec acre .... ARPENT
city ... HULL, MONTREAL,
VERDUN
part of .... UNGAVA
river .... SAGUENAY
Quechuan ... INDIAN, INCA(N),
PERUVIAN
Queen .... REGINA, REINA
ace combination ....
TENACE
Anne's lace .... CARROT
beheaded ... ANTOINETTE
Charlotte Island Indian ..
HAIDA
English .. VICTORIA, BESS,
ANNE
fairy ...... TITANIA, MAB,
UNA

Greek gods' .... HERA
it .... DOMINEER
legendary .... DIDO
Mab" author ... SHELLEY
Moslem .... BEGUM
of Calydon ..... ALTHEA
of gods ..... JUNO, HERA,
SATI
of Ithaca ..... PENELOPE
of Iceland ....
BRUN(N)HILD(E)
of Lydia ...... OMPHALE
of Palmyra ..... ZENOBIA
of the Antilles ..... CUBA
of the jungle ..... SHEENA
of the Nile .. CLEO(PATRA)
of the nymphs ..... MAB
of Thebes ...... JOCASTA
Olympian .... HERA
Roman gods' ..... JUNO
Sheba .... BALKIS
widowed .... DOWAGER
quooning .... APPLE
queen(ly) ... REGINA(L), REGAL
Queens .... BOROUGH
Queensland's capital ....
BRISBANE
Queenstown .... COBH
queer ... FUNNY, ODD, GIDDY,
BIZARRE, SINGULAR,
STRANGE, ECCENTRIC,
RUM, WEIRD, ERRATIC,
CRANKY
bird .... NUT, CRANK
notion .... KINK
person .... NUT
slang ..... COUNTERFEIT,
HOMOSEXUAL, SPOIL
quell .. ALLAY, QUIET, SUBDUE,
CRUSH, QUASH, END,
SUPPRESS
quelque chose .... TRIFLE
quench .... COOL, SLAKE,
SATISFY, EXTINGUISH,
DOUSE, PUT OUT
quercetin ..... DYE, FLAVIN(E)
quercitron .... OAK, DYE
quercus genus .... OAKS
querist .... ASKER
quern .... MILL, GRINDER
querulous .... PEEVISH,
FRETFUL, PETULANT
query ... INQUIRY, QUESTION,
ASK
quest .... SEARCH, HUNT,
SEEK(ING), PURSUIT

question ... DOUBT, PROBLEM, INTERROGATE, DISPUTE, POINT, POSE, ISSUE, QUERY, QUIZ, INQUIRY, ASK, GRILL
and answer teaching ..... CATECHESIS
  baffling .... POSER, DILEMMA
questionable .... MOOT, DEBATABLE, SHADY, DUBIOUS, DOUBTFUL, SUSPICIOUS, SUSPECT, FISHY
questioning .... ROGATORY
quetzal .... TROGON, BIRD
queue ...... LINE, (PIG)TAIL, FILE, CUE, BRAID, PLAIT, TRESS
  torero's .... COLETA
Quezon, Philippine president .. MANUEL
qui vive ... ALERT, CHALLENGE
quibble .... CAVIL, PUN, EVASION, QUIP, EVADE, CARP
quick ... READY, FAST, AGILE, FLEET, ALIVE, SNAPPY, YARE, VOLANT, APT, SWIFT, RAPID, PROMPT, PREGNANT
  assets .... CASH
  bread .... MUFFIN
  in learning .... APT
  look ... EYEBEAM, GLANCE
  response to helm .. YARE
  tempered ...... IRACUND, IRASCIBLE
  witticism .... SALLY
quicken ..... ANIMATE, SPEED, REVIVE, STIR, HASTEN, ROUSE
quickie, movie .... B-PICTURE
quickly ...... SOON, PRESTO, PRONTO, FAST, ANON, PDQ
  in music .... SUBITO
quicksand .... MORASS, SYRT(IS)
quickset ... HEDGE, CUTTING, SLIP
quicksilver .... MERCURY, AZOTH
quid ...... PLUG, SOVEREIGN, POUND, CUD
  pro quo ..... SUBSTITUTE
quidnunc .. GOSSIP, BUSYBODY, SNOOP
quien ____, who knows? .. SABE

quiescent ...... STILL, QUIET, LATENT, DORMANT
quiet ... STILL, CALM, HUSH(ED), SILENT, PACIFY, MUM, ALLAY, MIM, SILENCE, STILLNESS
  interval .... LULL
quietism, teacher of .. MOLINOS
quietude .... CALMNESS, STILLNESS, REST
quietus ... DEATH, DISCHARGE, RELEASE
quill ...... REMEX, FEATHER, CALAMUS, SPINE, PEN, PLECTRUM, BARREL
  feathers......... REMIGES, CALAMI
quillai .... SOAPBARK
quilt .... PATCHWORK, BEDCOVER, STITCH, CADDOW, DUVET
quilting party .... BEE
quince .... POME, BEL
quinia .... QUININ(E)
quinine .... KINA
  source ...... CINCHONA
  water .... TONIC
quinnat salmon .... CHINOOK
quint .... ORGAN STOP
quintessence .... CREAM, ELIXIR
quintuple .... FIVEFOLD
quintuplets ... DIONNE, FISHER
quip .... JEST, QUIBBLE, JOKE, WITTICISM, SALLY, MOT, (WISE)CRACK, GIBE
quire .... CHOIR
quirk ... PECULIARITY, TWIST, TURN, STROKE, ODDITY, KINK
quirt .... WHIP, ROMAL
quisling ..... COLLABORATOR, TRAITOR
  fifth columnist .. VIDKUN
quit .... RESIGN, LEAVE, RETIRE, FREE, STOP, REPAY, DISCHARGE, GIVE UP
quitch .... GRASS, WEED
quitclaim .... RELEASE
quite ...... ENTIRELY, TRULY, REALLY, WHOLELY, VERY, ALL, ENOUGH
Quito is capital of .. ECUADOR
quits .... EVEN
quittance .. RECEIPT, REPRISAL
quiver ...... SHAKE, SHUDDER,

TREMOR, NIMBLE, QUAKE, FLUTTER, THRILL, TREMBLE, VIBRATE
content of ..... ARROWS
quivering tree .... ASPEN, PALPITANT
Quixote's giant .... WINDMILL
horse .... ROSINANTE
love .... DULCINEA
squire .. SANCHO (PANZA)
title .... DON
quixotic .... CHIVALROUS, ROMANTIC, VISIONARY, ABSURD
quiz .... HOAX, JOKE, EXAM(INATION), ASK, TEST, PROBE
kid .... PRODIGY
quizzical ...... ODD, COMICAL
quod .... JAIL, PRISON
quoin ... CORNER, KEYSTONE, LOCK, BLOCK

quoit ...... DISCUS, RINGER
quoits pin .... HOB, PEG
target .... HOB, PEG, TEE
quondam .... ONCE, ONETIME, FORMER, ERSTWHILE, WHILOM
quonset hut .... PREFAB
British kind ..... NISSEN
quorum .... COMPANY
quota .... SHARE, ALLOTMENT
quotation ... CITATION, CITAL, EXCERPT, PRICE, EXTRACT
ending speech/story ..... TAG
opening chapter .... EPIGRAPH
reader .... STOCKHOLDER, SPECULATOR
quote ... CITE, REFER, REPEAT, ADDUCE
quoth .... SPOKE, SAID
quotidian .... DAILY

R

R, Greek .... RHO
Hebrew .... RESH
in chemistry ... RADICAL
in chess .... ROOK
in mathematics ... RATIO, RADIUS
pronunciation like l ..... LALLATION
Ra .... SUN GOD
crown of .... ATEN
in chemistry ... RADIUM
symbol of ...... SUNDISK
wife of .... MUT
raad .... CATFISH
Rabat is capital of .. MOROCCO
rabato .... RUFF, COLLAR
Rabbat Ammon .... AMMAN
rabbet .... JOINT, REBATE
rabbi ...... TEACHER, AMORA
seminary ..... YESHIVA
teachings .... MISHNA(H)
rabbit ... CONY, LAGOMORPH, HARE, ANGORA, RODENT, LEPORID, COTTONTAIL
breeding place .. WARREN
ears .... ANTENNA
family .... LEPORID
female .... DOE
fever .... TULAR(A)EMIA
foot ... CHARM, TALISMAN
fur ..... CON(E)Y, LAPIN

fur hat .... CASTOR
hunting dog ... HARRIER
hybrid .... LEPORIDE
like rodent .... MARMOT
male .... BUCK
pen .... HUTCH
pet name .... BUNNY
rock .... HYRAX
tail of............ SCUT
variety .... LOP
young .... BUNNY
rabbitry .... WARREN, HUTCH
rabble .... CROWD, DOGGERY, CANAILLE, MOB, (RIFF)RAFF, RAGTAG
rouser .... AGITATOR, RIOTER, DEMAGOGUE
the .... MASSES
Rabelais, Fr. satirist .... FRANCOIS
Rabelaisian .... EARTHY
rabid ..... VIOLENT, RAGING, FANATICAL, ZEALOUS
rabies .... MADNESS, HYDROPHOBIA, LYSSA
RCA trademark ..... NIPPER
raccoon-like animal .. PANDA, COATI
race ...... LINEAGE, FAMILY, PEDIGREE, STIRPS, FOLK,

CONTEST, CHANNEL,
MANKIND
black .... NEGROID
channel .... FLUME
contestant .... ENTRANT,
ENTRY
division .... NEGROID,
CAUCASIAN, MONGOLOID
easily won .... RUNAWAY
engine .... REV
hotrods' .... DRAG
kind of .... SWEEPSTAKE,
SWEEPS, RAT, TROT
of dwarfs .... NIBELUNG
pertaining to .... ETHNIC
prelims .... HEATS
short ...... DASH, SPRINT
start of ..... BREAKAWAY
track ..... HIPPODROME,
TURF, CINDER PATH,
OVAL
water .... ARROYO
white .... CAUCASIAN
yellow ...... MONGOLOID
racecourse .... CIRCUS,
HIPPODROME, TRACK,
OVAL, TURF
circuit .... LAP
combining form .. DROME
marker ... PYLON, LANE
name/site of ..... EPSOM,
HIALEAH, PIMLICO,
SARATOGA, ASCOT,
JAMAICA
official .... STARTER
section ... STRETCH, BEND
racehorse .... TROTTER
disability .... GLANDERS,
SPAVIN, STRINGHALT
enclosure ..... PADDOCK
exercise area ... PADDOCK
inferior .... PLATER,
SLEEPER
kind of .. MUDDER, PLATER
winless .... MAIDEN
raceme ... CLUSTER, PANICLE
racer .... HOTROD,
(BLACK)SNAKE, SPRINTER,
TRACKMAN
course of .... LANE
racetrack .... OVAL,
HIPPODROME, TURF
character ..... DOPESTER,
TOUT, TIPSTER
cover .... TANBARK
fence .... RAIL

raceway .... CHANNEL
Rachel's father .... LABAN
husband .... JACOB
son ... JOSEPH, BENJAMIN
rachis ..... SPINE, BACKBONE,
STEM
rachitis .... RICKETS
Rachmaninoff, composer/
pianist .... SERGEI
racial division, of .... ETHNIC
origin .... ETHNOGENY
Racine (Jean), Fr. poet ....
BAPTISTE
masterpiece .... PHEDRE
racing colors .... SILKS
course .... CAREER,
HIPPODROME
program ... CARD, FORM
scull .... WHERRY
racists, latest .... NAZIS
rack ... GIN, GRATING, FRAME,
TORMENT, UPHEAVAL,
TORTURE, WRECKAGE,
CLOUDS, STAND, SCORE
corn .... CRIB
display .... EASEL
fodder ...... CRIB, HACK,
CRATCH
food .... FLAKE
hat .... TREE
horse's ..... PACE, GAIT
racket ... BAT, NOISE, PADDLE,
SNOWSHOE, BABEL, DIN,
UPROAR, REVEL(RY)
hold on .... GRIP
slang .... BUSINESS,
PROFESSION, LINE
string .... CATGUT
rackets .... TENNIS
raconteur's forte .. ANECDOTES,
STORIES
racy .... PIQUANT, FRESH,
PUNGENT, RISQUE, LIVELY,
SPIRITED
Radames' love .... AIDA
radar device, for short ... TFR
image .... BLIP
like device .... SONAR
screen flash .... BLIP
part of word ..... RADIO,
DETECTING, RANGING
sound ..... BEEP, RACON
system .... SHORAN
raddle ... INTERWEAVE, OCHER
Radek, Soviet writer .... KARL
radian .... ARC

radiance .... GLORY,
REFULGENCE, BRIGHTNESS,
LIGHT
radiant ... BRIGHT, BEAMING,
AGLOW
combining form .. HELI(O)
look .... BEAM
radiate .... SHINE, EMIT, CAST
radiation measure .. ROENTGEN
radical ... BASIC, FIREBRAND,
JINGO, RED, PINK,
EXTREME, ULTRA, LEFTIST,
JACOBIN
with valence of two .....
DYAD
radicel .... ROOT(LET)
radicle .... ROOT, RADIX
radio .... WIRELESS
active shower .. FALLOUT
ad .... COMMERCIAL
aerial .... ANTENNA
broadcasting outfit .. VOA
cabinet .... CONSOLE
dash in .... DAH
detector .... RADAR
frequency band ....
CHANNEL
gear ... ANTENNA, AERIAL
interference ..... STATIC
news, brief ...... FLASH
newscaster ... MURROW,
HEATTER, SWING
operator, amateur .. HAM
performer ...... TALENT
receiver ... CRYSTAL, SET,
TRANSISTOR
reception disturbance ...
STATIC, STRAYS
signal for aviators .. BEAM
signoff .... ROGER
station ID .. CALL LETTERS
term .... ROGER
tube .... GRID
radioactive matter .. NOBELIUM,
CARNOTITE, RADON, NITON
particles .... GEIGERS
radioactivity, measure of .....
CURIE
radiotelephony term ... ROGER
radium F .... POLONIUM
discoverer .... CURIE
disease treated with .....
CANCER
emanation ...... NITON,
RADON

source of .. PITCHBLENDE,
URANITE
radius ...... SPOKE, EXTENT,
RAY, SCOPE, RANGE
radix .... BASE, ROOT,
RADICAL, ETYMON
radon .... NITON
RAF, part of .... ROYAL,
AIR, FORCE
raff .... RABBLE, TRASH
companion .... RIFF
raffish .... VULGAR, CHEAP,
TAWDRY, LOW,
DISREPUTABLE, FLASHY
raffle .... LOTTERY
ticket .... BLANK
raft .... BALSA, LOT,
CATAMARAN, COLLECTION
component of ..... LOGS,
BARRELS, BOARDS
log .... CATAMARAN
rafter .... SPAR, BEAM
rag ... TATTER, TEASE, SCOLD,
SLATE, SHRED, REMNANT,
BRAT, JOSH, RIB
baby .... DOLL
chew the ..... CONVERSE,
CHAT
ragamuffin .. TATTERDEMALION
rage .... FAD, FASHION,
SPREAD, VOGUE, CRAZE,
WRATH, FRENZY, RAVE,
FUROR, FURY, FUME, ANGER
ragged ..... UNEVEN, ROUGH,
RAMPAGE, FRAYED,
TATTERED, JAGGED,
SHAGGY, UNKEMPT,
SHABBY
raggee .... GRASS, RAGI
ragger .... TEASER
Raggedy doll ... ANNE, ANDY
raging .... RAMPANT,
RAMPAGING
raglan ... TOPCOAT, OVERCOAT
ragman .... JUNKMAN
ragout .... HARICOT, HASH,
TUCKET, STEW, GOULASH,
SALMI
ragpicker .... JUNKMAN
rags .... CLOTHES
ragtag .... RABBLE
ragtime .... JAZZ
ragwort .... JACOBY,
GROUNDSEL
ragweed ...... COCKLEBUR,
AMBROSIA

rah .... CHEER, HURRAH
raia .... NON-MOSLEM, RAYAH
raid ..... INVADE, INCURSION,
    FORAY, ASSAULT, FORAGE,
    SORTIE, ATTACK, INVASION,
    MARAUD
    slang .... PINCH
raider ... COMMANDO, UBOAT,
    RANGER
rail ..... COOT, CRAKE, SORA,
    FENCE, BIRD, COMPLAIN,
    WEKA, BAR, HERON,
    ORTOLAN, SCOFF, RANT,
    MUDHEN
    bird like .... COURLAN
    collar of .... FLANGE
    kin of .... NOTORNIS
railing .. FENCE, BALUSTRADE,
    PARAPET
    bridge .... PARAPET
raillery ..... SATIRE, BANTER,
    PERSIFLAGE, RIDICULE,
    BADINAGE
railroad .... RUSH
    baggage car .... VAN
    bridge .... TRESTLE
    car ..... COACH, DINER,
        CABOOSE, SLEEPER,
        SMOKER, PULLMAN
    car compartment ......
        DUPLEX
    center .... YARD
    crossing .... GATE
    elevated .... EL,
        MONORAIL
    engine ..... LOCOMOTIVE
    engine serviceman ......
        HOSTLER
    flare ...... FUSEE, FUZEE
    freight car .... GONDOLA
    handcar .... VELOCIPEDE
    industrial ..... TAPLINE
    line end .... TERMINUS
    side track .... SPUR
    siding .... TURN-OUT
    signal .... HIGHBALL,
        SEMAPHORE
    single track ... MONORAIL
    sleeping car .. WAGON-LIT
    station .... DEPOT
    stop for locomotives ....
        TANK TOWN
    supply car ...... TENDER
    switch device ... SHUNT,
        FROG
    tie .... SLEEPER

track section .. GANTLET
trunkline .... MAIN
underground ... SUBWAY,
    METRO
workers' vehicle ....
    HANDCAR
raiment .... ATTIRE, CLOTHING,
    APPAREL, DRESS
rails, of the .... RALLINE
    support ...... ROADBED
railway, amusement .. COASTER
    car .... TRAM
railways .... ROADS
rain ... SEREIN, SHOWER, FALL,
    (OUT)POUR, FLURRY,
    DOWNPOUR
    briefly .... SPIT
    character .... SADIE
    forest .... SELVA
    fine mist .... MIZZLE,
        SEREIN
    formed by ..... PLUVIAL
    frozen ..... SLEET, HAIL
    gauge .... UDOMETER
    heavy .... TORRENT
    mist .... SCUD
    shower .... BRASH
    sudden ... SPATE, BRASH
    sunset .... SEREIN
    tree ...... ZAMIA, SAMAN
rainbow .... IRIS, ARC(H),
    METEOR
    bridge .... BIFROST
    color like ..... PAVONINE
    trout ..... STEELHEAD
raincheck .... STUB
raincoat ...... MACKINTOSH,
    SLICKER, PONCHO,
    TRENCH COAT
raindrops, frozen ...... HAIL
Rainer, actress .... LUISE
    Maria ____, Ger. poet ....
        RILKE
rainfall .... SHOWER
    heavy .... DELUGE
    place of heaviest .. ASSAM
Rainier (Mount) site ....
    TACOMA
rainmaker: sl. ..... LOBBYIST
rainproof canvas ... TARPAULIN
rainy .... WET, PLUVIOUS,
    PLUVIAL, SOPPY
raise .... BREED, HIKE, HOIST,
    EXALT, REAR, (UP)LIFT,
    AROUSE, STIR, NURTURE,
    COLLECT, EAN, BOOST,

ELEVATE, ERECT, INCITE, PULL UP
in relief .... EMBOSS
nap .... TEASE(L)
rents exorbitantly .. RACK
to third power ..... CUBE
raised .... EMBOSSED
road .... CAUSEWAY
raisin ...... SULTANA, GRAPE
in pudding .... PLUM
raisins drink .... CORDIAL, ROSOLIO
raison ___ .... D'ETAT, D'ETRE
raj .... RULE
rajah's wife ..... RANEE, RANI
Rajasthan's capital .. JAIPUR
rake .... SCRAPE, SCOUR, DEBAUCHEE, SLANT, RANSACK, COMB, LOTHARIO, LECHER, ROUE, LIBERTINE
off .... REBATE, COMMISSION, KICKBACK
with gunfire ... ENFILADE, STRAFE
rakish ... DISSOLUTE, DASHING, JAUNTY
rale ..... RHONCHUS, RATTLE
ralline bird .... RAIL
rally ... COLLECT, GATHERING, ASSEMBLY, REVIVE, RESURGE, MEET, BANTER
ram ..... PRESS, DRIVE, STUFF, CRAM, POUND, TUP, SHEEP, PUMP, BATTER, TAMP
constellation ..... ARIES
headed god ...... AMMON
horn ... SHOPHAR, SHOFAR
kind of ... (BELL)WETHER
ship's .... BEAK
Rama .... KRISHNA
Ramadan .... FASTING
ramage .... BOUGH
Ramayana character .... SITA, HANUMAN
Ramazan .... FASTING
ramble ..... MEANDER, ROVE, SPREAD, GAD, SAUNTER, STROLL, ROAM
rambler ...... ROSE, TRUANT, TRAMP, NOMAD, ROVER
Rambouillet .. (MERINO) SHEEP
rambunctious .... WILD, UNRULY, DISORDERLY
ramekin/ramequin ..... HASH
Rameses .... PHARAOH

ramie .... FIBER, HEMP
ramification .... BRANCH, OFFSHOOT, RESULT
ramify ...... DIVIDE, SPREAD
ramjet ..... ATHODYD, ENGINE
rammer ...... BEAK, RAMROD
ramose .... BRANCHED
ramp ...... REAR, HELICLINE, RAGE, STORM, RUSH, PASSAGE, ROADWAY, STAND
rampage .... RAGE, RUSH, OUTBREAK
rampaging person ..... AMOK, BERSERK, JURAMENTADO
rampant ... RIFE, WIDESPREAD
rampart ... RAVELIN, PARAPET, BULWARK, VALLATION, EMBANKMENT, REDAN
rampion .... CAMPANULA, BELLFLOWER
Ramses .. PHAROAH, MONARCH
domain .... EGYPT
ramshackle .... RICKETY, SHAKY, RUN-DOWN
ramson .... GARLIC, ROOT
ramus .... BRANCH
ran, also .... COMPETED, LOST
rana .... FROG
rance .... MARBLE
ranch ...... FARM, ESTANCIA, HACIENDA, GRAZE, PLANTATION
event .. RODEO, ROUNDUP
hand .... COWBOY, COWPOKE
tyro .... DUDE
rancher .. COWBOY, STOCKMAN
rancho .... HUT
rancid ..... RANK, STINKING, SPOILED, SMELLY
rancor ...... ILL-WILL, GALL, SPITE, MALICE, HATRED, ENMITY
rand .... MARGIN, EDGE, BORDER
random .... HAPHAZARD, AIMLESS, CASUAL, CHANCE, DESULTORY, HIT-OR-MISS
randy .... CRUDE, COARSE, LUSTFUL, BEGGAR, VULGAR
range ...... ROW, RANK, GRASSLAND, SCOPE, STOVE, SIERRA, TRAIN, ROAM, REACH, GAMUT, LATITUDE, SWEEP

finder .... TELEMETER, STADIA
of emotion ..... GAMUT
of hills .... RIDGE
of vision .... SCAN, EYESHOT, EYESIGHT, SCOPE
over .... SCOUR
Rocky Mountains ...... UINTA, TETON
sighting for .... ZERO
ranger ... WARDEN, FORESTER, SOLDIER
concern of a .... FOREST
Rangoon is capital of .. BURMA
weight .... CATTY
rangy .... LANKY
rani/ranee .... QUEEN
husband of ..... RAJA(H)
Ranier's domain, Prince ...... MONACO
ranine .... FROGLIKE
rank ... EMINENCE, POSITION, FERTILE, RANCID, INDECENT, UTTER, FLAGRANT, GRADE, TIER, RANGE, ROW, LINE, COARSE, ARRANT, STANDING, REEKY
and file .... SOLDIERS, FOLLOWERS
having .... GENETIC
of lower .... PUISNE
rankle .... FESTER
ranks .... ARMY
ransack .... RIFLE, SEARCH, PILLAGE, RUMMAGE
ransom ...... RESCUE, REDEEM, BLOODMONEY
person held for .. HOSTAGE
rant ...... HARANGUE, BOAST, RAVE, DECLAIM, RAIL, TIRADE, BLUSTER, RAGE
ranunculaceous plant .. PEONY, ANEMONE, LARKSPUR
ranunculus ...... CROWFOOT, BUTTERCUP
rap .... TAP, PUNISHMENT, CUFF, KNAP, (TH)WACK, BOP, CLOUT, PERCUSS, KNOCK, BLAME, SENTENCE, BLOW
rapacious .... GREEDY, RAVENOUS, AVARICIOUS, VORACIOUS
bird .... SHRIKE
fish .... PIRANHA

rapacity ... VORACITY, GREED
rape ...... VIOLATE, RAVISH, PLUNDER, ASSAULT, PULP, CABBAGE, COLE, FODDER
soil .... COLZA
rapeseed .... COLZA
mass of crushed .... OIL CAKE
rapid .... SWIFT, ABRUPT, QUICK, FLEET, FAST, RIPPLE
combining form .. TACHY
fire .... STACCATO, FUSILLADE
rapidity ..... VELOCITY, SPEED
rapidly .... APACE
rapids .... DALLES, DELLS, CHUTE
rapier .. SWORD, BILBO, TUCK
rapine ... PILLAGE, PLUNDER, RAVIN
rapparee .... VAGABOND, ROBBER, PLUNDERER
rappee .... SNUFF
rapper ...... DOOR KNOCKER
rapping .... TATTOO
rapport ...... HARMONY, AGREEMENT, RELATIONSHIP
rapscallion ... ROGUE, RASCAL
rapt ...... ABSORBED, INTENT, ENGROSSED
raptorial bird ... EAGLE, OWL, HAWK, VULTURE, FALCON
rapture ...... ECSTASY, BLISS, TRANSPORT
rapturous .... ECSTATIC
Raquel Welch's pet name ..... BIRDLEGS
soubriquet ... SEX QUEEN
rara avis .. RARITY, ONER, BIRD
rare ... UNDERDONE, TENUOUS, UNCOMMON, UNUSUAL, SCARCE, THIN, ODD
rarebit .... RABBIT
raree .... (PEEP)SHOW
rarefy .... THIN, REFINE
rarely .... SELDOM
rareripe fruit .... PEACH
rarity ... TENUITY, SCARCITY, THINNESS
rascal ... SCAMP, SCOUNDREL, BEGGAR, SCALAWAG, YAP, CAD, VARLET, SCAPEGRACE, SPALPEEN, ROGUE
rascally .... BASE, MEAN, DISHONEST

rase .... LEVEL, DESTROY
rash ... RECKLESS, ERUPTION,
FOOLHARDY, WILD,
WANTON, HASTY, ROSEOLA,
EXANTHEMA, MEASLES
   person .... HOTSPUR,
PLUNGER
rasher .... HAM, BACON
rashness .... TEMERITY
Rasmussen, Arctic explorer ...
KNUD
rasorial .... GALLINACEOUS
   bird ...... HEN, CHICKEN
rasp ... GRATE, FILE, SCRAPE,
RUB, IRRITATE, ABRADE
raspberry .... ACINUS, SHRUB,
SASS, FRUIT
Raspe's character ....
MUNCHAUSEN
Rasputin, Russian monk ......
GRIGORI
raspy ...... IRRITABLE, ROUGH,
GRATING
rasse .... CIVET
rassle .... WRESTLE
rat ... GNAWER, VERMIN, VOLE,
APOSTATE, RODENT
   domesticated ....
GUINEA PIG
   genus .... MUS
   hair .... PAD
   kind of .... MOLE
   poison .... RATSBANE
   race .... SCURRY,
SCRAMBLE
   rodent resembling ......
MOUSE, HAMSTER
   slang .... DESERTER,
INFORMER,
STOOL(PIGEON)
ratable .... TAXABLE
ratal .... ASSESSMENT
ratafia ...... COOKY, LIQUEUR,
MACAROON
rataplan .... DRUMBEAT
ratchet .... PAWL, CLICK,
CATCH, WHEEL, DETENT
rate ..... RATIO, PROPORTION,
PRICE, CLASS, APPRAISE,
ESTEEM, DESERVE, SCOLD,
CHIDE
   at any .... ANYWAY
   exchange .... AGIO
   of mass to volume ....
DENSITY

rated .... VALUED, TAXED,
RANKED
ratel-like animal ..... BADGER
Rathbone, actor .... BASIL
rathe .... QUICK, EAGER,
EARLY, PROMPT
rather .... SOMEWHAT,
CERTAINLY, SOONER,
PREFERABLY
   than .... ERE
Ratibor river .... ODER
ratification .... SANCTION,
APPROVAL
ratify .. SEAL, PASS, SANCTION,
CONFIRM, APPROVE, ENDORSE
rating .... RANK, CLASS,
GRADE, SCORE, MARK,
REPRIMAND
ratio .... PROPORTION,
QUOTIENT
ratiocinate .... REASON
ration ... ALLOWANCE, SHARE,
ALLOTMENT, DISTRIBUTE,
METE
rational ...... SANE, SENSIBLE,
REASONABLE, SOUND, LUCID
rationale ...... REASON, BASIS
rationalize .... EXPLAIN
rations .... FOOD
   bag .... HAVERSACK
ratite .... MOA, EM(E)U,
OSTRICH, CASSOWARY, RHEA
ratoon .... SHOOT, SPROUT
rats, of .... MURINE
rattail .... GRENADIER
rattan ... PALM, CANE, REED,
SEGA
ratter .... DESERTER, BETRAYER,
DOG
rattle .... CHATTER,
DISCONCERT, UPSET, CLACK,
CLAPPER, NOISE, SISTRUM,
UPROAR, MARACA,
CREPITATE, RALE
rattlebrain .... IDIOT, ASS,
FOOL
rattlebrained .... SILLY,
FRIVOLOUS
rattlepate .... ASS, FOOL
rattlesnake .... VIPER,
CASCABEL, SIDEWINDER,
MASSASAUGA
   plantain .... ORCHID
   without rattle ....
COPPERHEAD
rattletrap ... MOUTH, JALOPY

rattling .... CREPITANT

rattrap .. JAM, PREDICAMENT, FIX

ratwa .... MUNTJAC

raucous ..... HARSH, HOARSE

ravage .... DEVASTATE, SACK, PLUNDER, HAVOC, DESPOIL, PILLAGE, RUIN

rave ...... RAGE, RANT, ROAR

ravel ..... INVOLVE, UNTWIST, UNDO, SLEAVE, FRAY, (EN)TANGLE

   stocking's .... RUN

ravelin .... OUTWORK, FORTIFICATION, REDAN

raveling .... LINT

raven .... DEVOUR, PREY, PLUNDER, CROW, BLACK(BIRD), CORBY, CORBIE

   Barnaby Rudge's .. GRIP

   cry of .... CAW

   like a .... CORVINE

   of a .... CORVINE

   quote of ..... NEVERMORE

ravenous .... VORACIOUS, HUNGRY, RAPACIOUS, LUPINE

ravin .... RAPINE, PLUNDER, PREY

ravine ...... CLOUGH, CHINE, WADI, WADY, GULCH, CANYON, BARRANCA, GILL, NULLAH, COOMB, COMB(E), GORGE, GULLY, DELL, LINN, FLUME, COULEE

raving .... DELIRIOUS, NOTABLE, FRENZIED

ravish ..... RAPE, ENRAPTURE, DELIGHT

ravishment .... ECSTASY, RAPTURE

raw .... SORE, UNCOOKED, BLEAK, BAWDY

   cotton .... LINT

   in the ..... NUDE, NAKED

   material .... STAPLE, STOCK, STUFF

   slang .... UNFAIR

rawboned ..... GAUNT, LEAN

Rawalpindi is capital of ...... PAKISTAN

rawhide ... WHIP, PARFLECHE

   kind of .... SHAGREEN

   whip ... THONG, KNOUT, QUIRT

ray ... BEAM, SKATE, TRACE, THORNBACK, BETA, GAMMA, ALPHA, GLEAM, STINGAREE, PETAL, MANTA, LASER, SAWFISH

   actor .... ALDO

   eagle .... OBISPO

   flower .... FLORET

   kind of ... BETA, GAMMA, LASER

   like part .... RADIUS

rayah .... RAIA, NON-MOSLEM

Rayburn, Speaker ...... SAM

rayless ...... DARK, GLOOMY

"Raymonda" ballet composer .. PETIPA

rayon ...... ACETATE, RATINE, FIBER, VISCOSE, JERSEY

   cellulose acetate .... CELANESE

   corded/ribbed .. REP(S), REPP, OTTOMAN

   making material .... CELLULOSE

   sheer .... VOILE

   twilled .... SERGE

raze ... SCRAPE, SHAVE, LEVEL, DEMOLISH, ERASE, DESTROY

razee .... SHIP

razor .... SHAVE(R)

   billed bird .... ALCA

   clam .... SOLEN

   seller .... CUTLER

   sharpen .... HONE, STROP

razorback .... HOG, FINBACK, (RORQUAL)WHALE

razz ..... HECKLE, RIDICULE, TEASE, DERIDE, SASS

razzle-dazzle ..... CONFUSION

Rb, in chemistry ... RUBIDIUM

re ..... ANENT, CONCERNING, REGARDING, ABOUT

   echoing .... REBOANT

   in chemistry .. RHENIUM

rea .... TURMERIC

reach ..... EXTEND, STRETCH, RANGE, SPAN, ATTAIN, ACHIEVE, GAIN, HEIGHT, GRASP

react ..... RESPOND, REDOUND

reacting easily/readily ...... RESPONSIVE

reaction .. RESPONSE, TROPISM, REFLEX

reactionary .... TORY, CONSERVATIVE, RIGHT(IST)

read ...... PERUSE, INTERPRET,
CONSTRUE, FORETELL,
UNDERSTAND, DECIPHER,
PORE, CON, STUDY,
REGISTER
   inability to ...... ALEXIA
   metrically .... SCAN
   numbers ..... NUMERATE
   out of ... EXPEL, DISMISS
readable .... LEGIBLE
reader ..... PRIMER, RECITER,
LECTURER, BOOK, PERUSER
   meter .... RECORDER
   scripture .... LECTOR
readily .... EASILY,
WILLINGLY, QUICKLY
readiness .... ALACRITY
reading ... LECTION, PERUSAL,
RECORD(ING)
   desk/stand ... LECTERN,
PRIE-DIEU, AMBO
   of Scriptures ... LECTION
reads alike forward or
backward ..... PALINDROME
ready .... PREPARE(D),
WILLING, LIKELY, APT,
INCLINED, AVAILABLE,
FAIN, SET, YARE, HANDY,
QUICK, OPEN, WARE,
PROMPT
   artillery ..... UNLIMBER
   made .... STOCK
   money .... CASH
real .... PUCKA, PUKKA,
ACTUAL, GENUINE,
SIMON PURE, FACTUAL,
COIN, CONCRETE
   estate ..... REALTY, LAND
   estate broker ... REALTOR
   plural of .... REIS
   thing .... MCCOY
realgar .... SANDARAC,
MINERAL
realism, opposite of .. IDEALISM
realistic .... PRACTICAL
   opposite of ... VISIONARY
reality .. VERITY, TRUTH, FACT
realize ... GAIN, UNDERSTAND,
ACHIEVE, APPREHEND,
OBTAIN
really ...... TRULY, INDEED,
ACTUALLY, QUITE
realm ..... KINGDOM, SPHERE,
DOMAIN, REGION, DEMESNE,
CLIME
ream .... ENLARGE

reamer ...... BORER, BROACH,
ENLARGER
reams .... LOTS
reanimate .... REVIVE
reap .... HARVEST, GAIN,
GATHER, MOW
reaper .... MOWER
   Grim .... DEATH
reaping tool .... SICKLE,
SCYTHE, TWIBIL(L)
rear ..... RAISE, RAMP, ERECT,
BUILD, GROW, RISE, SUCKLE,
BACK(PART), (BE)HIND,
BREED, NURSE, ARRIERE, AFT
   horse's .... PESADE
   young bird ...... FLEDGE
reared by hand .... CADE
rearmost .... LAST
rearrange .... PERMUTE
reason ...... SANITY, ARGUE,
DISCUSS, JUSTIFY, NOUS,
LOGOS, GROUND,
RATIOCINATE, MOTIVE,
CAUSE, EXPLANATION,
BASIS
   against .... OPPUGN
   deprive of ...... DEMENT
   for being .... END,
RAISON D'ETRE
   for ill-will ...... GRUDGE
   with .... RIGHTLY
reasonable ... RATIONAL, SANE,
SENSIBLE, JUST, LOGICAL
reasoning, correct .. LOGIC(AL)
   false .... IDOLISM,
SOPHISM
   faulty ..... PARALOGISM,
SYLLOGISM
   subtle, difficult ....
METAPHYSICS
reata ... LARIAT, LASSO, NOOSE
reave .... SEIZE, TEAR
rebate ... KICKBACK RAKE-OFF,
DEDUCTION, RABBET
rebec(k) ..... VIOLIN, FIDDLE
Rebecca's brother ..... LABAN
   diminutive of ...... REBA,
BECKY
   father .... ISAAC
   husband .... ISAAC
   son .... ESAU, JACOB
rebel .. DISSENTER, DISSIDENT,
OPPOSE(R), REVOLT(ER),
MUTINEER, RELUCT, RISE,
RESIST, INSURGENT,

INSURRECTO, DEFIER, RECUSANT, MALCONTENT

angel .... BELIAL

rebellion .... REVOLUTION, SEDITION, MUTINY, REVOLT, INSURGENCE, INSURRECTION, UPRISING

minor .... PUTSCH

rebellious .... DEFIANT

rebirth .... REVIVAL

rebound .... RICOCHET, RECOIL, CAROM, RESILE, BOUNCE

rebuff ...... REFUSE, REPULSE, REPEL, SPURN, SLAP, SNUB, REJECT

rebuke .... REPRIMAND, REPREHEND, SLAP, UPBRAID, DERIDE, CENSURE, REPROVE

rebus for example .... PUZZLE

rebut ...... REFUTE, DISPROVE, CONTRADICT

recalcitrant .... RESISTANT, DEFIANT, UNRULY, REBEL, RENITENT

recall ... REMEMBER, CANCEL, REVIVE, RECOLLECT, REPEAL, ANNUL, REVOKE, WITHDRAW

recant ... RENOUNCE, ABJURE, RETRACT, WITHDRAW

recap .... RETREAD

recapitulate .... REPEAT, SUMMARIZE, SUM UP

recapitulation ...... SUMMARY, REPRISE

recede ..... EBB, DRAW BACK

receipt ... QUITTANCE, RECIPE

receivable .... DUE

receive ...... HOLD, ACCEPT, ADMIT, ACQUIRE, TAKE

received, in radio ...... ROGER

receiver .... TREASURER, COLLECTOR, RECIPIENT

in baseball ..... CATCHER

stolen goods ..... FENCE

trust property ... BAILEE, TRUSTEE

receiving callers .... IN, AT HOME

recent .... NEW, MODERN, NEOTERIC

combining form ... NEO

recently ... LATELY, OF LATE, LATTERLY

receptacle ...... CONTAINER, VESSEL, BIN, BOX, BASKET, FONT, BASIN, CAN

flower .... TORUS

holy water ...... STOUP, FONT

reception ... WELCOME, LEVEE, SOIREE, AT HOME, DURBAR

receptive .. AMENDABLE, OPEN

receptor ..... EYE, EAR, NOSE

recess ... NICHE, BREAK, NOOK, HOLLOW, VACATION

recession ... RECEDING, SLUMP

business .... SLUMP

recessional .... HYMN

Recife .... PERNAMBUCO

recipe ... FORMULA, REMEDY, PRESCRIPTION, RECEIPT

recipient ... DONEE, RECEIVER

reciprocal .... MUTUAL

reciprocate .... EXCHANGE, RETURN

recital ... NARRATION, STORY, ACCOUNT, CONCERT, MUSICALE

recitation ... STORY, ACCOUNT

recite ..... NARRATE, RELATE, REPEAT, ENUMERATE

loudly .... DECLAIM

mechanically ... PATTER

monotonously ... CHANT, DRONE

reciter of literary works ...... READER

reck .... HEED

reckless ... MADCAP, WANTON, WILD, RASH, HEEDLESS, CARELESS, AUDACIOUS

courage ... DERRING-DO

person .... HOTSPUR, MADCAP, PLUNGER, DAREDEVIL

reckon .... FIGURE(UP), COUNT, CALCULATE, COMPUTE, CONSIDER, JUDGE, SUPPOSE

reckoning .... GUESS, CALCULATION, TAB, COUNT

reclaim ... RECOVER, RESTORE, REFORM

reclaimed land ...... POLDER

reclame .... PUBLICITY

recline ... LIE, REST, LAY, LEAN

reclining .... RECUMBENT

recluse ..... HERMIT, EREMITE, TROGLODYTE, SOLITAIRE,

MONK, SOLITARY,
ANCHORITE, ANCHORESS
recognition ...... ADMISSION,
NOTICE, AWARENESS,
GREETING
recognizance ... BOND, BADGE,
TOKEN
recognize ... IDENTIFY, ADMIT,
ACCEPT, OWN, PERCEIVE
recoil .... RESILE, COWER,
RETREAT, REACT(ION),
SHRINK, QUAIL, KICK,
DRAW BACK, REDOUND
recollect .... RECALL,
REMEMBER
recollection ..... ANAMNESIS,
MEMORY, REMEMBRANCE
recommend .... TOUT,
ENTRUST, COMMIT, ADVISE,
COUNSEL
recommendation .... PLUG
recompense .... REPAY,
REWARD, COMPENSATE
reconcile ... ATONE, COMPOSE,
ADJUST, HARMONIZE,
SYNCRETIZE
recondite .... ABSTRUSE,
OBSCURE, DEEP, PROFOUND
reconnaisance .... SURVEY
reconnoiter .... SCOUT,
SURVEY, EXPLORE
record .... TAB, ENTER,
SET DOWN, ENTRY, TAPE,
ACTA, FILE, NOTATE,
PLATTER, POST, ENROLL
copy of .... ESTREAT
formal .... MINUTES,
REGISTER, DOCUMENT
historical .... ANNALS
of arrests ...... BLOTTER
of past events ... HISTORY
of travel ..... ITINERARY
personal .... DIARY,
DOSSIER
police .... BLOTTER
ship .... LOG
recorded proceedings ... ACTA
recorder .... REGISTRAR,
FLUTE, SECRETARY, TAPER
recording device .... TAPE,
METER
records, place for public ......
ARCHIVES
recount ... RELATE, NARRATE,
TELL, RECITE

recoup .... REIMBURSE,
RECOVER, WIN BACK
recourse .... RESORT
recover .... RALLY, RETRIEVE,
REGAIN, RECOUP, RECLAIM,
RECUPERATE
from illness .. CONVALESCE
one's spirit ... PERK(UP),
RALLY
recreant .... CRAVEN,
COWARD(LY), TRAITOR(OUS),
DISLOYAL
recreation ..... AMUSEMENT,
PASTIME, PLAY
recrement .... REFUSE,
WASTE, DROSS
recruit .... DRAFT(EE),
CONSCRIPT, ENLIST(EE),
ROOKIE, MUSTER
rectangle .... QUADRATE
rectangular .... QUADRATE
rectifier .... ADJUSTER
tube .... DIODE
rectify .... AMEND, CORRECT,
ADJUST, REFINE, PURIFY,
REMEDY
rectitude .... HONESTY,
INTEGRITY
recto, opposed to ..... VERSO
rector .... MINISTER
assistant of ..... CURATE
dwelling of ...... MANSE
recumbent .... PRONE,
RESTING, LEANING
recuperate .... RECOVER
recuperation ...... RECOVERY
recur ... RETURN, COME BACK
recurrence .... RETURN,
REPETITION
recurring period ...... CYCLE
recuse .... CHALLENGE
red ... CERISE, CORAL, GARNET,
COLOR, RUBIOUS, RUBY,
RADICAL, COMMUNIST
admiral ..... BUTTERFLY
and blue color ... PURPLE
apple .... DELICIOUS
bird .... CARDINAL,
TANAGER, BULLFINCH
breast .... ROBIN,
SANDPIPER
breasted bream .. SUNFISH
bright .... MADDER,
CARDINAL, CERISE,
SCARLET
bug .... CHIGGER

cedar .... JUNIPER, SAVIN(E)
cent .... PENNY
corundum .... RUBY
country .... USSR
Cross' concern .... DISASTER, CALAMITY
Cross fund raiser .... TAGGER
deep ..... GARNET, RUBY, CARNATION
deer ......, STAG(GARD), STAGGART
Desert ... NEFUD, NEFUF
dye ...... AURINE, EOSIN, HENNA
eyed fish ... RUDD, CARP
flag signal ..... DANGER
fuchsia .... MAGENTA
haired .... CARROTY
hat .... BIRETTA
hat wearer ... CARDINAL
hind .... CABRILLA
hot ..... INCANDESCENT, SIZZLING
in heraldry .... GULES
in the .... LOSING, INDEBTED
hue ...... ROSE, BLOOD, PINK
inscribed in ...... RUBRIC
lattice ..... TAVERN, INN
lead .... MINIUM
letter ...... MEMORABLE
light signal ..... DANGER
man .... INDIAN
meat ..... BEEF, MUTTON
mineral .... RUTILE, GARNET
ocher .... REDDLE, RADDLE, RUBRIC, RUDDLE
pigment ... CHICA, ROSET
osier .... DOGWOOD
pepper .... CAYENNE
planet .... MARS
Polled .... CATTLE
purplish ...... CARMINE, AMARANTH, MAGENTA
River .... SONGKOI
Sea city ... JIDDA, JEDDA
Sea kingdom .... YEMEN
Sea seaport ...... MOCHA
Sea ship .... DHOW
shade .... TOMATO
Square figure ..... LENIN

Square landmark ......, KREMLIN
squirrel ..... CHICKAREE
star ..... ANTARES, MARS
stone ...... RUBY, SARD
suit ... HEARTS, DIAMONDS
wine .... CLARET
yellow .... ORANGE, TITIAN
redact .... REVISE, EDIT
redbreast ...... ROBIN, KNOT, BREAM
redbug ...... FLEA, CHIGGER
redcap .... PORTER, GOLDFINCH
redd .... TIDY-UP
redden .... BLUSH, FLUSH, COLOR
reddish .... RUFESCENT, RUFOUS, ERUBESCENT
brown .....:... AUBURN, MAHOGANY, BAY, CHOCOLATE, HAZEL, LUGGAGE, TITIAN, RUSSET, SORREL
yellow .... SANDY, AMBER, LUTEOUS, ORANGE, TANGERINE, TITIAN
rede ..... ADVISE, PLAN, TALE, COUNSEL, STORY, SCHEME
redeem ... RECOVER, RANSOM, RESCUE, FULFILL, ATONE, DELIVER
Redeemer ..... JESUS CHRIST, SAVIOR, GOEL
redemption ...... SALVATION
Redemptorist founder ...... LIGUORI
redeye .... VIREO, RUDD
redfin .... FISH, CARP
redhead .... DUCK, WOODPECKER, CARROT TOP
kin of .... POCHARD, WIDGEON
redingote ...... OVERCOAT
redness, excessive .. ERYTHRISM
of skin ..... RUBEFACTION
redo .... REVAMP
redolence ...... SCENT, ODOR
redolent .... SMELLING, SCENTED, FRAGRANT
redouble ... (RE)ECHO, REPEAT, INCREASE, REFOLD
redoubt ...., BREASTWORK, STRONGHOLD

redoubtable .... FEARSOME, DREAD
redound ...... REACT, RECOIL
redowa-like dance .... POLKA, WALTZ
redpoll .... FINCH
redress ... REMEDY, CORRECT
redskin .... INDIAN
    trophy of .... SCALP
redstart ..... BIRD, WARBLER, BRANTAIL
redtop .... GRASS
reduce .... LOWER, THIN, LESSEN, DIMINISH, CHANGE, DEGRADE, SUBDUE, CONQUER, DECREASE, SLASH
reduction .... CUTBACK
    in biology ...... MEIOSIS
redundancy .... NIMIETY, PLEONASM, TAUTOLOGY
redundant ...... PLEONASTIC, REPETITIOUS, EXCESS(IVE), WORDY
reduplicate, in botany .... VALVATE
redware .... SEAWEED
redwing .. SONGBIRD, THRUSH
redwood .... SEQUOIA
ree .... ARIKARA
reecho .... RESOUND
reechoing .... REBOANT
reed .... OAT, GRASS, RATTAN
    bird .... BOBOLINK
    buck .... NAGOR, ANTELOPE
    in architecture .. MOLDING
    instrument with .... CLARINET, OBOE, SAXOPHONE, BASSOON, ORGAN
    like .... FERULACEOUS
    loom .... SLEY
    mace .... CATTAIL
    poetic .... ARROW
    weaver's .... SLEY
reeding .... GADROON
reedy .... PIPING, THIN
reef ..... SHELF, KEY, SHOAL, RIDGE, LEDGE
    coral .... CAY, KEY
    mining ..... LODE, VEIN
reefer ... COAT, MIDSHIPMAN, MIDDY, CIGARETTE
    prototype of ..... JOINT
reek ... FUME, VAPOR, EXUDE, SMOKE, STINK

reel ..... SWING, FALL BACK, WHIRL, DANCE, SWAY, SWIFT, SPOOL, WAMBLE, TEETER, STAGGER, LURCH, TOTTER, WIND, WINCE
    for thread ..... FILATURE
reeling of cocoon silk .... FILATURE
reem .... UNICORN
Reese, baseball player .... PEEWEE
    Tears author ... LIZETTE
reeve ..... OVERSEER, BAILIFF, STEWARD, SLIP, PASS IN, SANDPIPER, THREAD
refection ..... REPAST, LUNCH, MEAL
refectory .... FRATER, DINING HALL, MESS(HALL)
refer ...... ASSIGN, ADVERT, ASCRIBE, ALLUDE, SUBMIT, POINT
    to .... VIDE
referee ... JUDGE, MODERATOR, UMPIRE, OVERMAN, ARBITER
reference .... REGARD, ALLUSION, MENTION, TESTIMONIAL
    book ... ATLAS, ALMANAC, MANUAL
    mark .... ASTERISK, DAGGER, OBELUS, DIESIS, STAR
    to a law .... CITATION
referendum ...... PLEBISCITE
refine .... POLISH, PURIFY, SUBLIMATE, CLARIFY, IMPROVE, PERFECT
    by distillation .. RECTIFY
    by melting .... SMELT
refined .... GENTEEL
refinement .... GENTILITY, POLISH, DELICACY, ELEGANCE
refinery .... SMELTERY
refining vessel .... CUPEL
reflect ...... MIRROR, PONDER, THINK, IMAGE
reflection ..... IMAGE, REFLEX, LIKENESS, MUSING, BLAME, DISCREDIT
reflective .... PENSIVE
reflet .... LUSTER
refluent ..... EBBING, REFLUX
reform ...... CORRECT, BETTER

reformer .... MORALIST, CRUSADER, RIIS
   religious .... LUTHER
reformatory ..... MAGDALENE
refract .... BEND
refractory .... OBSTINATE, UNRULY, STUBBORN, RESTIVE
refrain ... FORBEAR, ABSTAIN, CHORUS, HOLD BACK, VERSE, PHRASE, SONG, WHEEL, BURDEN, REPETEND
   short .... BOB
   song .... BURDEN
   syllable .... TRA
refresh .... COOL, REVIVE, RENEW
   with food/drink .. REFECT
refreshment ...... REFECTION, DRINK, SNACK
refrigerant ..... ICE, ETHANE, CRYOGEN, FREON
refrigerate ..... CHILL, COOL, FREEZE
refrigerator .... FREEZER, ICEBOX, FRIGIDAIRE
reft .... ROBBED
refuge ...... HAVEN, HARBOR, SANCTUARY, ASYLUM, SHELTER, RETREAT, CITADEL
refugee .... EVACUEE, ESCAPEE
   organization .... IRO
refulgent .... RADIANT, SHINING, GLOWING
refund .... REBATE, REIMBURSE, REPAY(MENT)
refurbish .... RENOVATE
refusal ...... OPTION, DENIAL, REJECTION
refuse .... NAYSAY, NILL, SPURN, REJECT, WASTE, RUBBISH, TRASH, OFFAL, SCUM, BALK, DECLINE, DRAFF, EJECTA, REBUFF
   cane .... BAGASSE
   consent to .... VETO
   grape .... MARC
   metal ..... DROSS, SCUM
   table ...... ORT, SCRAPS
   wine .... LEES
refusing to plead in court ..... MUTE
refutation .... DISPROOF
refute ...... REBUT, DISPROVE
regain ..... RECOVER, RECOUP

regal ..... QUEENLY, KINGLY, ROYAL, STATELY
regale .... ENTERTAIN, FEAST, TREAT
regalia .... FINERY, DECORATIONS, INSIGNIA
   king's .... SCEPTER, CROWN
Regan's father .... LEAR
   sister .... CORDELIA, GONERIL
regard ..... CONSIDER, LOOK, ESTEEM, GAZE, CONCERN, REFERENCE, RESPECT, OBSERVE
regarding ..... CONCERNING, IN RE, ABOUT
regards ..... EYES, AFFECTION
regatta .... BOAT RACE
   boat ..... YACHT, SCULL, SHELL
   sights .... CATBOATS
regent .... INTERREX
   of the sun .... URIEL
regicide's victim .... KING
regime .... GOVERNMENT
regimen ... DIET, SYSTEM, RULE
regiment commander ...... COLONEL
   part of .... BATTALION
regimental flag ...... PENNON
Regin, son of .... SIGURD, SIEGFRIED
Regina ____, monastery ...... LAUDIS
regina(l) .... QUEEN(LY)
region .... REALM, AREA, SPACE, PLACE, SPHERE, CLIME, TERRITORY
regional ... LOCAL, SECTIONAL
register ..... (EN)ROLL, LIST, RECORD, ENTER, METER, CALENDAR
   death .... NECROLOGY
regma ... SCHIZOCARP, MAPLE
regnant ... RULING, REIGNING, PREVALENT
regorge .... VOMIT
regress .... RETURN
regret .... RUE, REPENT, DEPLORE, PENITENCE, MOURN, REMORSE
regular ..... STABLE, STEADY, ORDERLY, USUAL, CUSTOMARY, UNIFORM, PROPER

patronage ..... CUSTOM
regulate ..... ADJUST, DIRECT, CONTROL
regulation .... RULE, LAW
regulator ... GOVERNOR, VALVE
  temperature .. CRYOSTAT
rehash .... REVISE
rehearsal .... PROLUSION, PRACTICE
  kind of .... DRYRUN, DRESS
rehearse ...... RECITE, DRILL, PRACTICE, TRAIN
Reich .... GERMANY
reign ... RULE, SWAY, PREVAIL, REGIME
  of a family ..... DYNASTY
reigning .... REGNANT
reimburse .... REFUND, PAY BACK, REPAY
rein .... CHECK, CONTROL, RESTRAIN, LEASH
  draw .... STOP
reindeer .... CARIBOU
  man .... LAPP
reine's husband .... ROI
reinstate ... RESTORE, REVEST
reiterate .... SAY AGAIN, REPEAT
reject .... VOMIT, REBUFF, DISCARD, REPEL, SPURN, DECLINE, REFUSE
  bill .... VETO
rejoice ... DELIGHT, GLADDEN, GLORY
rejoin .... ANSWER
rejoinder ..... REPLY, ANSWER
relapse .... BACKSLIDE, SLIP BACK, FALL BACK
relate .... TELL, PERTAIN, RECOUNT, NARRATE
related ... TOLD, CONNECTED, COGNATE, GERMANE, AKIN, ALLIED
  by blood .. SIB, KIN(DRED)
  on father's side .. AGNATE, AGNATIC
  on mother's side .. ENATE, ENATIVE
relation .... ACCOUNT, RECITAL, KIN(SHIP), KINSMAN
relationship .... CONNECTION, RELEVANCE, KINSHIP
  sympathetic .... RAPPORT
relative .... RELEVANT,

PERTINENT, KINSMAN, SIB, KIN(FOLK)
  for short ...... BROD, SIS
relatives, employment of ...... NEPOTISM
relator .... NARRATOR, COMPLAINANT
relax .... LOOSEN, EASE, REST, SOFTEN, REDUCE, SLACKEN
relaxation ...... RECREATION, AMUSEMENT, DIVERSION
relay .... SHIFT, REMOUNT
release .... FREE, RELIEVE, CLEAR, DISCHARGE, UNTIE, UNDO, LIBERATE, EXEMPT, LOOSE, LET GO, QUITCLAIM, RELIEF
  air .... DEFLATE
  claim ... REMISE, WAIVER
  hold .... DROP
  mass of ice .... CALVE
relegate .... EXILE, ASSIGN, CONSIGN, BANISH, COMMIT
relent ... SOFTEN, THAW, YIELD
relentless ..... PITILESS, GRIM, HARSH
relevant .... PERTINENT, GERMANE, RELATED, APPLICABLE, APT, APROPOS, APPOSITE
reliable .... DEPENDABLE, TESTED, TRIED, WORTHY, TRUSTY, SOLID
reliance .. TRUST, DEPENDENCE
relic .... CURIO, SOUVENIR, RUIN
  sacred .... HALIDOM
relics .... RUINS
relict ..... WIDOW, WIDOWED, SURVIVOR
relief ..... RELEASE, REMEDY, RELIEVO, RILIEVO, SUCCOR, EASING, AID
relieve .... EASE, LIGHTEN, REDUCE, FREE, REMOVE, ALLAY, COMFORT, ALLEVIATE, RID
  by talking ..... ABREACT
  thirst .... SLAKE
relievo .... RELIEF
religieuse .... NUN, SISTER
religieux .... MONK, PIOUS
religion .... BELIEF, FAITH
religionist .... FANATIC
religious ..... PIOUS, DEVOUT,

GODLY, SCRUPULOUS, MONK, NUN, DIVINE
beggar ... FAKIR, SERVITE
belief .... CREED
belief, antagonistic ......
HERESY
brotherhood ⏤ SODALITY, ORDER
devotee ⏤⏤⏤⏤ FAKIR
devotion .... NOVENA
emotion ..... THEOPATHY
expedition .... CRUSADE
festival .... HOLIDAY
group chief ... HIERARCH
journey ..... PILGRIMAGE
lay society .... SODALITY
leader .... SHEPHERD
leader's saying .... LOGIA
lore .... HIEROLOGY
man ...... MONK, LAMA
military order member ...
TEMPLAR
mysticism ⏤.. QUIETISM
observance ... FAST, LENT
offering ⏤.⏤.. OBLATION, SACRIFICE
order .... DOMINICAN, JESUIT, TEMPLAR, FRANCISCAN, MARIST
period .... LENT
person .. PIETIST, OBLATE
reformer .. LUTHER, HUSS
rites, of .... SACRAL
ritual .... CULT
school head ..... RECTOR
sect ...... DENOMINATION
vigil .... WATCH
war .... CRUSADE
worship, system of .. CULT
relinquish ... RELEASE, YIELD, FOREGO, WAIVE, ABANDON, LET GO, SURRENDER, RESIGN, RENOUNCE
reliquary ⏤...... SEPULCHER, CASKET, SHRINE
relish ... CONDIMENT, FLAVOR, PICKLES, ENJOY, GUSTO, ACHAR, SAVOR, ZEST, SAUCE, RADISH, TASTE, PLEASURE, CHUTNEY, CHUTNEE, SAPOR
fish egg .... CAVIAR(E)
meat juice .... ASPIC
relucent .... BRIGHT
reluct .... REVOLT
reluctant ... AVERSE, LO(A)TH,

UNWILLING, HESITANT
rely ...... COUNT(ON), BANK, DEPEND, TRUST, RECKON, LEAN
relying on experience ....
EMPIRICAL
remain ... STAY, LAST, ENDURE
balanced .... LIBRATE
firm .... STAND(PAT)
undecided ⏤...... PEND, HANG FIRE
remainder .... REMNANT, BALANCE, REST, RESIDUUM, LEFT-OVER, RESIDUE, RESIDUAL
remains .. CADAVER, VESTIGES, RUINS, REMNANT, TRACES
remand .. SEND BACK, RETURN
remark .... NOTE, WORD, OBSERVE, NOTICE, COMMENT(ARY), REMARQUE
correct: sl. .... MOUTHFUL
cutting ... SARCASM, NIP
indirect, derogatory .....
INNUENDO
clever ... NIFTY, BON MOT, WITTICISM, CRACK, SALLY
mocking ...⏤...... JEST
unfavorable ... BRICKBAT
remarkable .... UNCO, SIGNAL, UNUSUAL, NOTABLE
Remarque, Ger. novelist .....
ERICH (MARIA)
Rembrandt, Dutch painter ....
(VAN) RIJN, RYN
work ⏤......... TITUS
remedy .... CURE, RECIPE, REDRESS, RELIEF, HEAL, CORRECT, ANTIDOTE, REPAIR
any .... TREACLE
cure-all ⏤⏤.⏤. ELIXIR, PANACEA
in coinage ... TOLERANCE
quack .... NOSTRUM
secret ⏤.⏤. ARCANUM, ELIXIR
soothing .... LOTION, BALM, BALSAM, SALVE, UNGUENT, DEMULCENT
remember .... RECALL, RECOLLECT, REMIND, REMINISCE
remembrance ...... SOUVENIR, KEEPSAKE, MEMENTO, TOKEN, MEMORY

remex ... FEATHER, OARSMAN
remiges .... FEATHERS
reminder .... MEMENTO,
SOUVENIR, TICKLER, MEMO
reminiscence .... MEMORY
reminiscent ...... SUGGESTIVE
remiss ...... LAX, NEGLIGENT,
DERELICT
remission .... PARDON
remit .... PARDON, SEND,
FORGIVE, CANCEL,
SLACKEN, PAY
remnant .... RAG, TRACE,
FRAGMENT, REMAINDER,
RESIDUE, LEAVING,
ODDMENT, (TAG)END,
LEFT-OVER
remodel .... RECAST
remo(u)lade .... SAUCE
remonstrance ...... PROTEST,
COMPLAINT
remonstrate .... PLEAD,
PROTEST, OBJECT
remora ...... PEGA, SUCKFISH
favorite host of .. SHARK
remorse ...... REGRET, PITY,
PENITENCE, COMPASSION
remorseless .... CRUEL,
MERCILESS, PITILESS
remote ...... ALOOF, SLIGHT,
FAR(OFF), SECLUDED,
DISTANT, ULTERIOR
remount ...... RELAY, HORSE
removal ... OUSTER, DISMISSAL
of diseased tissue ....
ERASION
surgical ...... ABLATION
remove ... OUST, EJECT, EXPEL,
DEPOSE, TAKE OFF, KILL,
DISMISS, DELE
bark ...... DECORTICATE
clothes ... STRIP, UNDRESS
by popular vote .. RECALL
from grave ..... DISINTER
from office .... OUST,
DEPOSE
ice .... DEFROST
impurities ...... FILTER,
REFINE, RECTIFY, SMELT
in law .... ELOIGN, ELOIN
juice .... REAM
marks .... ERASE
tumor .... EXCISE
to another place ....
TRANSFER
water ...... DEHYDRATE

remunerate .... REWARD,
RECOMPENSE, PAY
remuneration .... EMOLUMENT,
PAY, REWARD
remunerative .... PAYING,
LUCRATIVE, GAINFUL
Remus' brother .... ROMULUS
parent ..... MARS, RHEA
renaissance .... REBIRTH,
REVIVAL
humanist ..... ERASMUS
sword .... ESTOC
renal .... NEPHRIC,
NEPHRITIC
Renard .... FOX
renascence .... REVIVAL,
REBIRTH
rend ... RIP, RIVE, TEAR, PULL,
SPLIT
render .... DEPICT, RECITE,
PERFORM, PLAY, ACT(OUT),
TRANSLATE, CONSTRUE,
DELIVER, SUBMIT, PRODUCE,
HAND OVER
fluid ..... FUSE, LIQUEFY
rendezvous ..... DATE, TRYST,
MEET(ING), APPOINTMENT,
ASSEMBLE
rendition ...... PERFORMANCE,
VERSION, TRANSLATION
renegade .... APOSTATE,
DESERTER, TURNCOAT,
TRAITOR, RAT
renege .... FINAGLE
renew ...... RESUME, REPEAT,
REFRESH, RENOVATE,
RESTORE
Reni, Ital. painter .... GUIDO
rennet .... RENNIN
Reno is in .... NEVADA
Renoir, painter ...... PIERRE
renounce ... RECANT, GIVE UP,
ABJURE, ABDICATE,
FORSWEAR, REJECT,
DENY, DISOWN, RELINQUISH
throne .... ABDICATE
renovate ...... FURBISH, RENEW,
REPAIR, REVIVE, REDO
renown ... FAME, REPUTATION,
ECLAT, NAME, REPUTE
person of ..... CELEBRITY
renowned .... FAMOUS
rensselaerite .... TALC
rent ... RIP, TEAR, LEASE, LET,
HIRE, SCHISM, HOLE, GAP
rente ..... REVENUE, ANNUITY

renunciation ..... ABDICATION, WAIVER

reopen .... RESUME

reorganization ...... REVAMP, SHAKE-UP

rep .... FABRIC

repair .... GO, MEND, FIX, RESTORE, REMEDY, BETAKE

   hole/tear .... DARN

repairman .... COBBLER, MECHANIC

reparable .... MENDABLE

reparation .... REDRESS, ATONEMENT, REPAIRS, SALLY

repartee ...... MOT, RETORT, GIVE-AND-TAKE, RIPOSTE, REJOINDER, DIALOGUE, BANTER

   engage in .... FENCE

   skilled in .... WITTY

repast ...... REFECTION, MEAL

repatriate .... RETURN, SEND BACK

repay .... RECOMPENSE, REIMBURSE, REFUND, REWARD

repeal ..... REVOKE, CANCEL, ABROGATE, RESCIND, ANNUL, ABOLISH, REVOCATION

repeat ...... RECITE, PARROT, BIS, RECUR, (RE)ITERATE

   gossip .... RETAIL

   performance ... ENCORE

repeatedly .... OFT(EN), FREQUENTLY

repeater ...... ECHO, PARROT, RIFLE, PISTOL, WATCH, CLOCK

repeating rifle inventor ...... MAUSER

repel ...... REPULSE, SPURN, REJECT, REFUSE

repellent .... REPULSIVE, WATERPROOF

repent .. RUE, GRIEVE, REGRET, CREEPING, CRAWLING

repentance ...... PENITENCE, REMORSE, REGRET, CONTRITION, ATTRITION

repercussion .... RECOIL, REBOUND, ECHO, REACTION

repertoire .... STOCK

repertory .... STOCK, COLLECTION, STOREHOUSE

repetend .... REFRAIN

repetition ...... RECITATION, COPY, ROTE, RECURRENCE

   in music .... REPRISE

   mechanical .... ROTE

   of performance .. ENCORE, REPLAY

repine ...... FRET, COMPLAIN

replace ... SUPPLANT, RETURN, RESTORE

replenish .... RESTOCK

replete .... FULL, STUFFED

repletion .... FULLNESS

replica .... REPRODUCTION, COPY, FACSIMILE

replicate .... FOLD

replication ..... FOLD, REPLY, ECHO, COPY(ING), ANSWER

reply ...... RETORT, ANSWER, RETURN, RESPONSE, RESPOND, COMEBACK, REJOIN(DER)

repondez s'il vous plait .. RSVP

report .... RUMOR, GOSSIP, BRUIT, SAY, DENOUNCE, TALK, HEARSAY, ACCOUNT, BROADCAST, CAHIER, HANSARD, TELL, BULLETIN, NOISE

   card entry ...... MARK, GRADE

   slanderous ..... SCANDAL

reporter .... JOURNALIST, SCRIBE, NEWSMAN, CRIER

   concern of ...... SCOOP, BEAT, FACTS, DATA, CONTACTS, DEADLINE, ACCURACY

   delight of .... BY-LINE

   paper of .... FLIMSY

   routine of .... LEGWORK

repose .... SLEEP, PEACE, (EN)TRUST, PLACE, RELY, REST, LAY, LIE, CALM

repository .... CHEST, CLOSET, VAULT, SAFE, CONFIDANT, MUSEUM, WAREHOUSE, SEPULCHER

reprehend .... CENSURE, REBUKE, REPROVE, BLAME

reprehensible .... CENSURABLE

represent .. EXHIBIT, PORTRAY, DEPICT, DESCRIBE, DENOTE, ENACT, TYPIFY, SYMBOLIZE

   graphically .... PLOT

representation ...... IMAGE,

LIKENESS, ALLEGATION,
ALLEGORY, MIMESIS
of heavenly bodies ......
ORRERY
ridiculous ..... TRAVESTY
representative .... AGENT,
DEPUTY, DELEGATE, ENVOY,
AMBASSADOR, PROXY,
TYPICAL, SOLON
repress .... CURB, STIFLE,
RESTRAIN, SUBDUE,
HOLD BACK
reprieve ... DEFER, POSTPONE,
GRACE, RESPITE
reprimand .. SCOLD, CENSURE,
BAWL, REBUKE, RATING,
REPROVE
reprint .... REISSUE
reprisal .... QUITTANCE,
RETALIATION, VENGEANCE,
MARQUE, REVENGE,
RETORTION
reprise .. REPETITION, SUMMARY
reproach ... CHIDE, REPROVE,
REBUKE, CENSURE, UPBRAID,
BLAME
reprobate .... VICIOUS,
DEPRAVED, ROGUE,
SCOUNDREL, ROUE, RAKE
reproduce .... REFLECT
reproduction ...... COPY
reproductive cell .... GAMETE,
GONAD
organ .... OVARY, TESTIS
reproof ... CENSURE, REBUKE
reprove .... REBUKE, CENSURE,
UPBRAID, CHIDE
reptant .... CREEPING,
CRAWLING, REPENT
reptile .... LIZARD, SAURIAN,
OPHIDIAN, SNAKE,
ALLIGATOR, TURTLE,
CROCODILE, LACERT(IL)IAN
carnivorous ... TUATARA
extinct ...... PTEROSAUR
eye tissue .... PECTEN
footless ... APOD, SNAKE
fossil ...... STEGOSAURUS
movement of ..... CREEP,
CRAWL, SLITHER
mythical ... SALAMANDER
Nile .... CROC
scale .. SCUTUM, PLATELET
reptiles, study of ....
HERPETOLOGY
republic .... DEMOCRACY

author .... PLATO
not quite one ... BANANA
of letters ...... LITERATI
Republican .... WHIG
mascot ...... ELEPHANT
Mr., soubriquet .... TAFT
Party .... GOP
recalcitrant ... MUGWUMP
repudiate ... RECANT, REJECT,
DISOWN, DENY
repugnance .... AVERSION,
DISTASTE, HATE
repugnant .... OFFENSIVE,
HATEFUL
repulse .... REPEL, REBUFF,
REJECT, REFUSE,
DRIVE BACK
repulsion .... AVERSION,
DISLIKE, DISTASTE
repulsive ...... UGLY, ODIOUS,
COARSE, LOATHSOME,
REVOLTING, DISGUSTING,
OFFENSIVE
reputation ..... REPUTE, NAME,
FAME
repute .... ESTEEM, ODOR
reputed .... SUPPOSED,
PUTATIVE, KNOWN
request .... APPEAL, SUIT,
PRAY, PETITION, ASK, BEG,
INSTANCE, ENTREAT(Y)
requiem ... MASS, DIRGE, HYMN
requiescat in ____ ...... PACE
require ..... DEMAND, COMPEL,
NEED, ORDER, INVOLVE
requirement .... NEED,
IMPOSITION
requisite ... NEED, ESSENTIAL,
REQUIRED
requite ...... PAY, RETALIATE,
ATONE, COMPENSATE
reredos ... SCREEN, PARTITION
reroute .... DETOUR
rerun ...... REPLAY, RESHOW
rescind ..... RECALL, REPEAL,
ABOLISH, CANCEL, ANNUL,
ABROGATE
rescript ...... DECREE, ORDER,
COPY
rescue .... RANSOM, SAVE,
DELIVER(ANCE), REDEEM,
SALVATION
research .... STUDY
center .... LAB(ORATORY)
reseau .... NETWORK
resect .... EXCISE

reseda .... MIGNONETTE
resemblance .... LIKENESS,
SIMILARITY
resentment .. HUFF, DUDGEON,
INDIGNATION, UMBRAGE,
OFFENSE, BAD BLOOD
reservation, in law ... SAYING,
SALVO
without .... OUTRIGHT
reserve ..... KEEP, SET ASIDE,
EARMARK, BACKLOG,
STORE, STOCK, RETICENCE,
SILENCE, CASH, RETAIN
reserved .... TACITURN,
RETICENT, QUIET, RETIRING,
SHY, ALOOF, DISTANT
reserves, armed forces ....
MILITIA
reservoir .... SUMP, STORE,
SUPPLY, CISTERN
overflow of ..... SPILTH
reset gem .... REMOUNT
reside ... DWELL, LODGE, LIVE
residence .... DOMICILE,
DWELLING, ABODE,
MANSION
king's .... PALACE
minister's .... MANSE,
PARSONAGE, RECTORY
papal .... VATICAN
place of .... ADDRESS
rural .... BOWER
stately .... MANSION
resident .... (IN)HABITANT,
INHERENT
doctor .... INTERN(E)
residential street .... TERRACE
residual .... REMAINDER
residue .... ASH, DREG,
REMAINDER, REST,
LEFT-OVER, REMANENT,
SHIFTINGS, BITTERN
resign .... QUIT, RELINQUISH,
ABDICATE, DEMIT
resignation ...... ABDICATION,
DEMISSION, SUBMISSION
resile .... REBOUND
resiliency .... ELASTICITY,
BUOYANCY
resilient .... ELASTIC,
FLEXIBLE, SUPPLE, BUOYANT
resin .... MASTIC, SHELLAC(K),
PITCH, ROSIN, ELATERITE,
AMBER, ANIME, COPAL,
ASAFETIDA, ALKYD,
COPAIBA, COPALM, TUPI,

GUM, KAURI, LA(B)DANUM
aromatic .... COPAIBA
cathartic ..... SCAMMONY
fossil ... RETINITE, AMBER
fragrant .... MYRRH,
ELEMI, FRANKINCENSE
gum .. MYRRH, RESINOID,
COPAL, MASTIC,
BDELLIUM, GAMBOGE,
AMMONIAC
hemp .... CHARAS,
HASHISH
incense .... SANDARAC,
MYRRH
perfume making ....
BENZOIN
pine ..DAMMAR, DANAMER
poisonous ... CANNABIN
solvent for ...... ETHER
synthetic ..... BAKELITE,
CATALIN, SILICONE,
LUCITE
thermoplastic ... SARAN
varnish ... COPAL, ANIME,
DAMMAR, DAMMER
resinous juice ..... LAUDANUM
powder, hops ... LUPULIN
secretion .... LAC
resist ... FIGHT, DEFY, BUCK,
FEND, OPPOSE, REPUGN,
WITHSTAND
resistance .... OPPOSITION,
DEFIANCE
fighter .... PARTISAN,
MAQUI, ELAS, EDES,
GUERRILLA, ACTIVIST
to authority .... MUTINY
resolute .... DETERMINED,
RESOLVED, GRIM
resolve ..... ANALYZE, DECIDE
resonance .... SONORITY,
SYNTONY, VIBRANCY
resonant .... SONOROUS,
REECHOING, VIBRANT,
OROTUND
resort .... RECOURSE, SPA
Riviera .... CANNES
resound ..... (RE)ECHO, PEAL,
EXTOL, RING, BOOM,
VIBRATE, REVERBERATE
resource(s) .... WEALTH,
CAPITAL, MEANS, ASSETS,
RESORT, EXPEDIENT
resourceful .... QUICK-WITTED
respect ...... ESTEEM, HONOR,
REGARD

respectable .... DECENT
respectful .... OBEISANT
Respighi, composer .. OTTORINO
respiration .... EUPN(O)EA,
    BREATHING, DYSPN(O)EA
   combining form .. SPIRO
   stimulant .... METRAZOL
respirator .... GAS MASK,
    IRON LUNG
respiratory disease ... HEAVES
   organ .... LUNG
respire .... BREATHE, INHALE,
    EXHALE
respite .... DELAY, LULL,
    REPRIEVE, GRACE
resplendent .... DAZZLING,
    SHINING, GRAND,
    SPLENDID, BRILLIANT,
    GORGEOUS
respond ..... REACT, ANSWER,
    REPLY, RETURN
respondent .... DEFENDANT
response ... REACTION, REPLY,
    ANSWER
responsibility ... DUTY, ONUS,
   LIABILITY, OBLIGATION
responsible .... LIABLE,
   ACCOUNTABLE, RELIABLE
responsive .... SENSITIVE
rest ... REMAINDER, BALANCE,
   SEAT, RECLINE, SLEEP,
   REPOSE, EASE, SUPPORT,
   STOP, OTHERS
   colloquial ... BREATHER,
    BREAK
   eternal .... DEATH
   in prosody ... C(A)ESURA
   midday .... SIESTA
restaurant ..... CAFE(TERIA),
   AUTOMAT, DINER, CABARET,
   EATERY, BISTRO
   bench .... BANQUETTE,
   compartment ..... BOOTH
restful ..... QUIET, PEACEFUL
resting .... DORMANT
restive ... BALKY, IMPATIENT,
   UNRULY, NERVOUS,
   RESTLESS, FRETFUL
restless .... RESTIVE, UNEASY,
   FRETFUL, AGITATO
restock .... REPLENISH
restorative .... ANODYNE
restore ...... RETURN, RENEW,
   REPAIR, REBUILD,
   RETROCEDE
   to health .... RECUPERATE

restrain ...... INHIBIT, STAY,
   BRIDLE, DETER, CHECK,
   HOLD, SUPPRESS, CURB
restraint ... CURB, LID, REIN,
   RESERVE, CONTROL
restrict .... LIMIT, CONFINE
restroom .... CLOSET,
   LAVATORY
result ... EFFECT, EVENTUATE,
   ISSUE, ENSUE, UPSHOT,
   OUTCOME, ANSWER,
   AFTERMATH
resume .. SUMMARY, ABSTRACT,
   REOPEN, REPRISE, PRECIS,
   RENEW, CONTINUE
resurge ...... RALLY, REVIVE
resurrect ... REVIVE, RESTORE
resurrection .... REVIVAL
   he experienced .... JESUS,
   LAZARUS
resuscitate .... REVIVE
resuscitation ...... ANABIOSIS
ret ...... SOAK, STEEP, DAMP,
   MACERATE
retable .... SHELF
retailer ...... DEALER, CLERK
retain .... HOLD, KEEP
retainer .... ATTENDANT,
   ADHERENT, FEE
retainers, body of ... RETINUE
retaining wall .... REVETMENT
retake .... RECAPTURE
retaliate .... REQUITE
retaliation .... TALION,
   REPRISAL, RETORTION,
   RETORSION, TIT-FOR-TAT
retard ...... HINDER, DELAY,
   IMPEDE, SLOW
retch ...... KECK, VOMIT, GAG
rete ...... NETWORK, PLEXUS
retem .... JUNIPER
retention .... MEMORY
retentive .... TENACIOUS
retepore .... MOLLUSK
retiarius .... GLADIATOR
retiary .... NETLIKE
reticence .... RESERVE
reticent .... TACITURN,
   RESERVED, SILENT
reticular .... NETLIKE
reticule .... (HAND)BAG,
   RETICLE
reticulum .... NETWORK
retinue ... TRAIN, ENTOURAGE,
   CORTEGE, ROUT, ESCORT,

SUITE, RETAINERS, MEINIE,
MEINY
retire ... WITHDRAW, RETREAT,
REST, REMOVE
retired ...... ABED, SECLUDED,
ASLEEP, EMERITUS
retiring .... SHY, MODEST,
RESERVED
retort .... REPARTEE,
WITTICISM, RIPOSTE,
REJOIN(DER), SQUELCH,
ALEMBIC, QUIP, SALLY,
REPLY
retortion .... REPRISAL
retract ... DISAVOW, REVOKE,
RENEGE, RECANT, ABJURE,
UNSAY, WITHDRAW
retraction .... PALINODE
retral .... POSTERIOR
retread .... RECAP
retreat .... ASYLUM, NEST,
WITHDRAW, BACK DOWN,
HIDEOUT, SHELTER, LAIR,
RETIRE, SANCTUM, REFUGE,
STUDY, PULLOUT, ARBOR,
KATABASIS
cozy .... DEN, NOOK,
ALCOVE
disorderly .... ROUT,
FLIGHT
kind of ..... MONASTERY,
CONVENT, HERMITAGE,
NUNNERY
shaded .... BOWER
signal .... CHAMADE
retrench ... CURTAIL, LESSEN
REDUCE, DECREASE,
CUT-DOWN, ECONOMIZE
retrenchment ...... RAMPART
retribution .... REQUITAL,
NEMESIS, REWARD
retributive justice .... NEMESIS
retrieve ... RECOVER, RESTORE,
REGAIN, REVIVE, SET RIGHT,
MAKE UP
retriever ... (GUN)DOG, SETTER,
POINTER
retrocede .... RESTORE
retrograde .... DECLINE,
REVERSE, INVERSE
retrogress .... DECLINE,
DEGENERATE
return ..... REPLY, RESPOND,
REPLACE, REQUITE, REELECT,
REPORT, RECUR, COME BACK,

RESTORE, YIELD, RESPONSE,
REVERT
in kind .... RECIPROCATE
returns ...... YIELD, REVENUE,
PROFIT
Reuben's father ...... JACOB
reunion .... GET-TOGETHER,
BOURBON
capital .... ST. DENIS
with Brahma ... NIRVANA
rev ...... ACCELERATE, RACE
Reval .... TALLINN
revamp .... REDO, PATCH,
RENOVATE, SHAKE-UP
reveal ...... EXHIBIT, MANIFEST,
TELL, BETRAY, JAMB, BARE,
DIVULGE, DISCLOSE, DISPLAY
reveille .. CALL, SIGNAL, ROUSE
revel ... DELIGHT, CAROUSAL,
FESTIVITY, ROISTER
revelation ...... DISCLOSURE,
ORACLE
revelations ...... APOCALYPSE
revel(l)er ..... MERRYMAKER,
CORYBANT
exclamation of a ....
WHOOPEE
revelry ...... FESTIVITY, RIOT,
SATURNALIA
revenant ..... EIDOLON, GHOST
revenge ... RETALIATE, AVENGE,
VENGEANCE, TALION
revenue .... INCOME
bishop's .... ANNAT
reverberate .... (RE)ECHO,
REFLECT, RESOUND,
REBOUND, RECOIL
revere .. VENERATE, WORSHIP,
ADORE, RESPECT
reverence .... OBEISANCE,
AWE, WORSHIP,
VENERATION, BOW, CURTSY,
ADORATION
gesture of .... OBEISANCE
lacking .... IMPIOUS
reverie .... MUSING, FANTASY,
(DAY)DREAM, NOTION
revers .... LAPEL
reversal .... ABOUT-FACE,
VOLTE-FACE, TURNABOUT,
ANNULMENT
reverse .... OPPOSITE,
CONTRARY, BACK, REVOKE,
ANNUL, INVERT
reversion .... RETURN
of property .... ESCHEAT

to primitive type ....
ATAVISM, THROWBACK
revert .... RETURN
revest .... REINSTATE
revet .... FACE
review ..... REPORT, ACCOUNT,
SURVEY, NOTICE, REVUE,
INSPECT, CRITICISM,
CRITIQUE, PARADE,
EPICRISIS
adverse .... PAN
enthusiastic .... RAVE
reviewer .... CRITIC
revile .... VILIFY, ABUSE,
ASPERSE, VILIPEND, SCOLD
revise .... EDIT, AMEND,
REWRITE, REHASH
revival .... REBIRTH, RENEWAL
revivalist .... EVANGELIST
revive ...... RALLY, RESURGE,
RESUSCITATE
memory .... REFRESH,
REMIND, JOG, RECALL
revocation ..... ANNULMENT,
REPEAL
revoke ..... ABJURE, REPEAL,
CANCEL, RESCIND, RENEGE,
ANNUL, RENIG, ADEEM
revolt .... UPRISING,
REBEL(LION), MUTINY,
DISGUST, RISE
revolting .... OFFENSIVE,
LOATHSOME, HORRID
revolution .... CYCLE,
ROTATION, REBELLION,
GYRE
fighter ...... MINUTEMAN
general of the ..... ASHE,
GATES, ARNOLD, GREENE,
LINCOLN, SULLIVAN
revolutionary .... RADICAL,
REBEL
revolutionist .... ANARCH,
REB(EL)
revolve ..... ROTATE, CIRCLE,
GYRATE, SPIN,
TURN, ORBIT
revolver .... PISTOL, COLT,
GAT, ROD, BULLDOG
revolving part .... ROTOR
revue .... SHOW, FOLLIES
revulsion .... AVERSION
reward ... TIP, PAY, GUERDON,
BONUS, RETURN, PRIZE,
AWARD
of a sort ..... SOP, WAGES

rewrite .... REVISE
rewriting .... RESCRIPT
rex .... KING
Reynard .... FOX
Rh factor .... RHESUS
rhabdomancy ...... DOWSING,
DIVINATION
rhapsodical .... ECSTATIC
rhea .... NANDU, EMU,
OSTRICH, CYBELE, OPS
husband of ..... CRONUS
parent of ....URANUS,
GAEA
progeny of .... ZEUS,
HADES, HERA, HESTIA,
POSEIDON, DEMETER
rheotrope ...... COMMUTATOR
rhesus .... MACAQUE, MONKEY
rhetor .... ORATOR
rhetorical device .. ANAPHORA
figure .... LITOTES
rheum ... RHINITIS, CATARRH,
COLD
rheumatic pain ..... LUMBAGO
person .... ACHER
rheumatism of back/loins ....
LUMBAGO
remedy .... GUACO
rhinal .... NASAL
Rhine .... RHEIN, RIJN, RIVER
branch .... WAAL
city on the ... MANNHEIM,
MAINZ, MAYENCE,
KOLN
siren ... LORELEI, LURLEI
tributary .... MAIN
wine ..... HOCK, MOSELLE
rhinitis .... RHEUM
rhino(ceros) ... ABADA, MONEY,
CASH, BORELE
for one ..... PACHYDERM
one-horned ..... BADAK
two-horned .... KEITLOA
rhinology, subject of .... NOSE
rhizoid .... ROOTLIKE
rhizome ..... STOLON, TUBER,
STEM, ROOTSTALK
(ROOT)STOCK
rhizopod .... TESTACEAN
rhizopus .... FUNGUS
Rhode Island capital ....
PROVIDENCE
city .... PAWTUCKET,
WARWICK, CRANSTON
founder ...... WILLIAMS
state flower ..... VIOLET

Rhodes .... RODI
    ancient wonder .. COLOSSUS
Rhodesia capital ... SALISBURY
    city ... GWELO, UMTAIL,
                BULAWAYO
    language .. BANTU, SHONA
    port .... BEIRA
    premier .... SMITH
    tribe .... ILAS
rhododendron ..... ROSEBAY,
                    LAUREL
    kin of .... AZALEA
rhodolite .... GARNET
rhomb ..... PARALLELOGRAM,
                    LOZENGE
rhombencephalon .. HINDBRAIN
    part ... PONS, CEREBELLUM
rhombus .... LOZENGE
rhonchus ..... RALE, SNORE,
                    RATTLE
Rhone tributary ..... ISERE,
                    SAONE
rhubarb .... (PIE)PLANT,
    ARGUMENT, DISCUSSION
rhyme ...... VERSE, CRAMBO
    and reason ...... SENSE
rhymer .... VERSIFIER,
                POET(ASTER)
rhymester .... VERSIFIER,
                POET(ASTER)
rhyming .... CRAMBO
rhythm .. TEMPO, BEAT, SWING,
    CADENCE, METER, MEASURE,
                    LILT, TIME
rhythmic rise and fall .. HEAVE
rhythmical accent ..... ICTUS
ria .... INLET
rial .... COIN
rialto .... BRIDGE, MART,
                    MARKET
riant .... GAY, BLITHE,
    CHEERFUL, LAUGHING,
                    SMILING
riata .... LARIAT
rib ... COSTA, VEIN, KID, WIFE,
    TEASE, TWIT, RIDGE
    in architecture ... LIERNE
    leaf .... NERVURE
    of 8 .... COSTAL
ribald ..... COARSE, VULGAR
ribaldry .... JAPERY
riband .... RIBBON
ribbed ..... COSTATE, RIDGED,
    TEASED, KIDDED
ribbon .... DECORATION,
    BADGE, STRIP, BAND

cutting, for example ....
                    CEREMONY
decorative ...... RIBAND
document's ...... LABEL
hair .... BANDEAU
knot .... COCKADE
like part ...... T(A)ENIA
of cotton, etc. ... FERRET
paper ... TICKER TAPE
seal .... LABEL
trimming ...... GALLOON
worsted .... CADDIS
ribbons .... TATTERS
ribs, having ...... COSTATE
ribwort .... PLANTAIN
rice ... CEREAL, PADDY, GRASS,
                    GRAIN
    alcoholic drink .. ARRACK,
                    SAKE
    boiled with meat .. PILAU,
                    PILAF(F)
    cooked with gravy ......
                    RISOTTO
    dish, spicy .... PILAU
    field .... PADDY
    husk .... BRAN
    in husk .... PADDY
    playwright ...... ELMER
    wine .... SAKE
riceball .... PINDA
ricebird .. SPARROW, BOBOLINK
rich ... WEALTHY, ABOUNDING,
    VALUABLE, OPULENT,
    WELL-TO-DO, LUXURIOUS,
    ABSURD, AFFLUENT
    man .... CROESUS, NABOB,
    PLUTO, MIDAS, DIVES
Richard I of England ....
    LIONHEART, COEUR DE LION
    unknown .... ROE
riches ... OPULENCE, WEALTH,
                    LUCRE
richest part ..... CREAM, FAT
richly ...... FULLY, AMPLY
richness .... LUXE, MEANS
ricin .... PROTEIN
rick .... STACK
Rickenbacker, American ace ..
                    EDDIE
rickets .... RACHITIS
rickety ...... FEEBLE, SHAKY
rickey .... DRINK
Rickover, Adm. ...... HYMAN
rickrack .. BRAID, TRIMMING
ricksha(w) ..... JINRIKISHA

ricochet ...... SKIP, REBOUND,
                          CAR(R)OM
rictus ..... GAPING, RINGENT
rid .... FREE, CLEAR,
          DISENCUMBER, RELIEVE
    of defect .... REAM
    of false ideas .. DISABUSE
Ridd's heroine ....
                    LORNA (DOONE)
ridden .... OBSESSED
riddle ...... ENIGMA, PEPPER,
     SIEVE, PERFORATE, PUZZLE,
        PROBLEM, CONUNDRUM,
                         MYSTERY
    bandleader .... NELSON
    picture .... REBUS
ride .... TEASE, HARASS, BAIT,
                          MOUNT
    pay for ... FARE, PASSAGE
    take for a .... DECEIVE,
                           KILL
    to hounds .... HUNT
rider .... CLAUSE, JOKER,
      AMENDMENT, EQUESTRIAN,
               PASSENGER, FARE
ridge .... RUGA, WALE, BACK,
         CREST, RANGE, CHINE,
        ARETE, RAND, CUESTA,
                         ARISTA
    between furrows ... LIST
    between peaks ... SADDLE
    glacial ... OSAR, DRUMLIN
    like part ... KEEL, CARINA
    of earth ..... HOGBACK,
                      HORSEBACK
    sand .... DUNE, DENE
    sandy .... LANDE
ridgepole .... ROOFTREE
ridicule .... DERISION, MOCK,
         DERIDE, TAUNT, JEER,
     SCOFF, SCOUT, JEST, ROAST,
                           TWIT
    playfully .... KID
ridiculous .... ABSURD,
       GROTESQUE, LUDICROUS,
                         FOOLISH
riding boot .... JEMMY
    breeches ..... JODHPURS
    academy .... MANEGE
    costume .... HABIT
    horse .... PALFREY,
               MOUNT, ROADSTER
    school .... MANEGE
    whip ...... QUIRT, CROP
Ricka .... FIUME
"Rienzi" composer .. WAGNER

rife ... CURRENT, PREVALENT,
       PREVAILING, WIDESPREAD
Riff .... BERBER
riffle .... SHOAL, REEF,
                        SHUFFLE
riffraff .... MOB, DOGGERY,
                          TRASH
rifle ... CARBINE, CHASSEPOT,
          BROWNING, PILLAGE,
      PLUNDER, ROB, MAUSER,
        REPEATER, FIREARM,
       GROOVE, RANSACK, BAR,
                         GARAND
    bullet ..... MINIE(BALL)
    chamber ..... MAGAZINE
    pin .... TIGE
    position .... READY
rifleman .... JA(E)GER, YAGER
    rating of ..... EXPERT,
                      MARKSMAN,
                   SHARPSHOOTER
rifler .... ROBBER
rift ..... CLEFT, CRACK, GAP,
       SPLIT, FISSURE, BREACH
rig ...... FIT, DRESS, CLOTHE,
        ATTIRE, EQUIP(MENT),
         CARRIAGE, COSTUME,
      DRESS, GEAR, MANIPULATE,
                   TACKLE, CART
Riga gulf island ...... OESEL
    native .... LATVIAN
Rigg's disease ..... PYORRHEA
Rigel .... STAR
rigger .... SCAFFOLD
rigging .... EQUIPMENT, GEAR
    part ..... ROPES, CHAINS,
      SPAR, SAILS, SHROUDS,
                         YARDS
right ...... TITLE, STRAIGHT,
         VIRTUOUS, CORRECT,
      SUITABLE, REDRESS,
     LICENSE, SOUND, NORMAL,
            FITTING, DEXTRAL
    and wrong decider ......
                         CASUIST
    by .... PROPERLY
    combining form .. RECT(I)
    exclusive .... PATENT
    hand side ...... DEXTER
    hand page ...... RECTO
    king's .... REGALITY
    legal ...... TITLE, DROIT
    now... PRONTO, AT ONCE,
                   IMMEDIATELY
    of expression ..... VOICE
    of way .... EASEMENT

on the .... OFF
side .... DEXTER
slang .... ROGER
special .... FRANCHISE,
      CHARTER
to choose ...... OPTION
to decide .... SAY-SO
to enter .... ENTREE,
      INGRESS
to mail free ...... FRANK
turn .... GEE
word .... MOTJUSTE
righteous ... VIRTUOUS, MORAL
rightfully .... DULY
righto .... YES, CERTAINLY
rights, equality of ... ISONOMY
      relating to .... JURAL
rigid ...... STRICT, STIFF, SET,
   SEVERE, RIGOROUS, AUSTERE
rigmarole .... NONSENSE,
      BLATHER
"Rigoletto" author ..... VERDI
rigor ... SEVERITY, HARDSHIP,
      RIGIDITY
   companion of ... MORTIS
rigorous .. STERN, STIFF, RIGID,
   HARSH, SEVERE, PRECISE,
      STRICT
Rigsdag, part of ... LANDSTING,
      FOLKETING
Riis, social reformer .. JACOB
Rijeka .... FIUME
Rijn .... RHINE
rile .... ANGER, IRRITATE,
      ROIL, VEX
rilievo .... RELIEF
Rilke, Ger. poet ..... RAINER
rill .... RIVULET, BROOK,
   TRENCH, VALLEY, FURROW
rim ..... BORDER, LIP, BRINK,
   VERGE, MARGIN, BRIM, EDGE
   cap's projecting ... VISOR
   cask's ..... CHINE, CHIMB
   rail/pipe's ...... FLANGE
   roof's .... EAVE
   wheel ..... FELLY, FELLOE
rime ... RHYME, (HOAR)FROST
rimer ..... BROACH, MINSTREL
rimple ..... CREASE, WRINKLE
rimy .... FROSTY
Rinaldo's magic horse ....
      BAYARD, BAJARDO
rind ... BARK, COATING, SKIN,
   CRUST, PEEL, CORTEX,
   EPICARP, EXOCARP
   candied .... CITRON

ring ... RESOUND, KNELL, RIM,
   ANNULET, SET, (EN)CIRCLE,
   SET, ARENA, DING, SIGNAL,
   CALL(UP), CLIQUE, CIRQUE
bell .... PEAL, TOLL,
   CHIME, KNELL
give a .... CALL,
   (TELE)PHONE
harness .... TERRET
jeweled ...... MARQUISE
metal .... BEE
neck .... PHEASANT
of guards .... CORDON
of leaves ... INVOLUCEL,
   INVOLUCRE
of light .... HALO
of neck feathers ... RUFF,
   TORQUES
of rope .... GROMMET
of rubber ...... GASKET
shaped .... ANNULAR
shaped cake .. DOUGHNUT
single gem of .. SOLITAIRE
stone setting ..... COLLET
tailed animal ..... COON
up ... (TELE)PHONE, CALL,
      DIAL
ringdove .... CUSHAT
ringent ..... GAPING, RICTUS
ringer .... QUOIT, HORSESHOE,
   LOOK-ALIKE
ringing, persistent .. CLANGOR
   sound in ear ... TINNITUS
ringlet ... CURL, TRESS, LOCK
ringworm .... TINEA, SERPIGO
rinse .... WASH, LAVE
rinsings .... DREGS
Rio ____ .... BRAVO, GRANDE,
   NEGRO, MUNI
de ____ ... ORO, JANEIRO
Grande, city on .. LAREDO
Grande tributary .. PECOS
Muni city .... BATA
seaport ..... MATAMOROS
riot ...... UPROAR, DISORDER,
   HUBBUB, ORGY, HIT, EMEUTE
riotous ..... WILD, DISSOLUTE,
   WANTON, LUXURIANT,
   NOISY, DISORDERLY
rip ... CUT, SPLIT, REND, TEAR,
      RIVE
colloquial ... NAG, HORSE
into .... ATTACK
roaring .... NOISY,
   BOISTEROUS

van Winkle author .... IRVING
riparian .... RIVERINE
ripe .... MATURE, READY, MELLOW, ADULT, DEVELOPED
ripen .... MATURE, AGE
ripening early .... RATH(E), RARERIPE
ripost(e) ..... RETORT, THRUST, RETURN
ripping .... FINE, EXCELLENT, SPLENDID
ripple ..... WAVE(LET), PURL, RAPID, LAP, UNDULATION, LIPPER
riptide .... UNDERTOW
Ripuarian .... FRANK
ris de veau ..... SWEETBREAD
rise .... OCCUR, HAPPEN, ASCENT, HILL, REBEL, STAND, GET UP, REVOLT, ASCEND, SOAR
  again .... RESURGE
  and fall .... WELTER, FLUCTUATE
  and float in the air ...... LEVITATE
  from the dead .... RESURRECT
  in the ground ..... LIFT
  of the tide .... FLOOD
  soprano .... STEVENS
risible .. AMUSING, LUDICROUS, LAUGHABLE, FUNNY
rising .. ANABATIC, MONTANT, BOIL, MOUNTING
risk ...... HAZARD, CHANCE, (EN)DANGER, PERIL, JEOPARDY
risque ..... RACY, OFF-COLOR, DARING, SCABROUS
rissole .... MEATBALL
rite ..... CEREMONY, LITURGY
  meaningless .... MUMBO-JUMBO
  public worship .. LITURGY
  washing .... LAVABO
Ritz, Swiss hotelman .. CESAR
ritzy ... ELEGANT, LUXURIOUS, TONY, CLASSY, POSH
rivage ... SHORE, COAST, BANK
rival ..... EMULATE, VIE, FOE, MATCH, COMPETITOR, EQUAL, OPPONENT, COMPETE

rivalry .... EMULATION, COMPETITION
rive ... REND, SPLIT, CLEAVE, TEAR
riven ..... RENT, SPLIT, TORN
river .... STREAM
  Avignon's ...... RHONE
  bank ...... RIPA, LEVEE
  bank, of a .... RIPARIAN
  barge .... GONDOLA
  barrier ..... WEIR, BOOM, BARRAGE
  "beautiful" ...... OHIO
  bed .... CHANNEL
  bend .... OXBOW
  blue, poetically .. DANUBE
  boat ..... FERRY, BARGE, PACKET, SAMPAN
  bottom .... BED
  branch .... ARM
  channel ...... FAIRWAY
  cross a ..... FORD, FERRY
  crossed by Caesar ... RUBICON
  curve in .... BEN, BIGHT
  dam .... WEIR
  deep, still spot of .. POOL
  deposit .... LOESS
  duck .... TEAL, SHOVEL(L)ER
  edge ...... BANK, LEVEE
  elbow .... BEND
  embankment .... LEVEE
  falls .... SAULTS
  famous ... NILE, RUBICON, AVON, DANUBE
  horse ... HIPPO(POTAMUS)
  inlet ... SLOUGH, BAYOU
  island .... HOLM
  isle .... HOLM, AIT
  land near .... HOLM, BOTTOMS
  landing ... LEVEE, GHAT
  large ..... AMAZON, NILE
  mouth ... EMBOUCHURE, ESTUARY, DELTA, BOCA
  nymph .... NAIAD
  of song ... VOLGA, OHIO, SWANEE, DANUBE
  of wailing ..... COCYTUS
  outlet .... BAYOU
  rapid .... SAULT
  sacred ... GANGES, ALPH
  sell down the .... BETRAY
  siren .... LORELEI
  soil .... DELTA

source .... HEAD
underworld .... STYX
valley ..... DALE, STRATH
wade across ...... FORD
widened part ..... LAKE
winding of .... ESS
Rivera, Mex. painter .. DIEGO
painting .... MURAL
Riviera beach .... PLAGE
resort .... CANNES
riviere .... NECKLACE
riverine .... RIPARIAN
rivet .... BOLT, FASTEN
holder .... DOLLY
washer of ...... BURR
riveter, female .... ROSIE
rivulet .... RILL, ARROYO,
BROOK, STREAM, RUN(D)LET,
RUNNEL
Riyadh is capital of ..... NEJD
riyal, where used ..... YEMEN
Rizal, Filipino patriot ... JOSE
Rn, in chemistry .... RADON
roach .... CARP, SUNFISH
movie producer ..... HAL
road .... MACADAM, PATH,
CAUSEWAY, (HIGH)WAY,
ITER, COURSE
agent .... HIGHWAYMAN
along embankment .....
STAITH
Canada to Key West .. USI
character ... HOBO, HOG,
TRAMP, (HITCH)HIKER
charge .... TOLL
curve .... ESS
fast .... SPEEDWAY
for locomotive .. RAILWAY
ledge .... BERM(E)
map abbreviation ... RTE
of a .... VIATIC(AL)
on the ..... TRAVELING,
ON TOUR
pavement ..... TELFORD
private ...... DRIVEWAY
runner ..... COCK, BIRD,
CUCKOO
shoulder ...... BERM(E)
sign ...... ESS, MILEPOST,
MILESTONE
surface .. TAR, MACADAM,
ASPHALT
toll .... (TURN)PIKE
worker .... NAVVY,
CAMINERO
roadblock .... BLOCKADE

roadhouse ..... INN, TAVERN,
NIGHT CLUB
roadside sign ... EATS, MOTEL
weed ...... DOG, FENNEL
roadster ... RUNABOUT, HORSE,
TWO-SEATER
seat .... RUMBLE
roadway, sloping ...... RAMP
roam .... ROVE, MEANDER,
RANGE, WANDER, RAMBLE,
GAD
roan .. HORSE, SHEEPSKIN, BAY
roar .... BELLOW, LAUGHTER,
GROWL, DIN, RUMBLE,
ROLL, BELL
roaring .... BRISK, NOISY
Twenties dance ....
CHARLESTON
roast .. BAKE, BROWN, PICNIC,
BARBECUE, BROIL, PARCH,
HEAT, PAN, CRITICIZE
meat ... CABOBS, KABOBS
turner .... JACK
roaster ... BROILER, CHICKEN,
PIG
roasting device/tool .... SPIT,
GRIDIRON, OVEN, PAN,
GRILL, BUCCANEER
rob ... PLUNDER, CLIP, FLAY,
LOOT, RIFLE, REAVE
a truck .... HIJACK
robalo .... FISH, SNOOK
robbed ...... REFT, DEPRIVED
robber .... RIFLER, THIEF,
SPOLIATOR, (FOOT)PAD,
YEGG, CATERAN, BANDIT,
RAPPAREE, BANDIDO,
LADRONE, BRIGAND
bird .... DAW, JA(E)GER,
SKUA, SHOOI
cattle .... RUSTLER
den of ... LAIR, HIDEOUT
highway ..... HIJACKER
sea .... PRIVATEER,
CORSAIR, PIRATE
robbery ..... THEFT, STICKUP,
HOLD-UP
robe .. TOGA, (DRESSING)GOWN,
WRAP, VESTMENT, CHIMAR,
CHIMER
bishop's .... CHIMER,
CHIMAR
girdle .... CAFTAN
long-sleeved ... CAFTAN,
KAFTAN
loose .... SIMAR

monk's .... FROCK
plural .... COSTUME, APPAREL, CLOTHES
woman's .... SIMAR
robed .... VESTED
robin ... THRUSH, REDBREAST, RUDDOCK
   Goodfellow .... HOB(GOBLIN), PUCK, ELF, FAIRY, SPRITE
   Hood .... OUTLAW
   Hood's companion ..... WILL (SCARLET), (FRIAR) TUCK
   Hood's sweetheart ...... (MAID) MARIAN
   Hood's weapon .... LONGBOW
Robinson Crusoe's man ..... FRIDAY
   model .... SELKIRK
   Ray .... SUGAR
roble ...... OAK, BEECH, TREE
roborant .... TONIC
robot .... AUTOMATON, GOLEM
robots, play about .... RUR
robust ...... HARDY, STURDY, HEALTHY, ROUGH, HALE, SOUND, MUSCULAR, LUSTY, WALLY, HUSKY
roc .... SIMURG, BIRD
   passenger of the .... SIN(D)BAD
rocambole .... LEEK
rochet ... VESTMENT, SURPLICE
rock ... SHAKE, STONE, CANDY, TOTTER, TEETER, SWAY, JIGGLE, GNEISS, PSEPHITE, GANISTER, DOLOMITE
   above a plain .... MONADOCK
   basaltic ..... WHIN(STONE)
   bass .... SUNFISH
   black .... BASALT
   boring tool ..... TREPAN, TRAPAN
   bottom .... LOWEST
   carving .... PETROGLYPH
   cavity ... GEODE, VUG(G), VUGH
   combining form ... SAXI, PETR(O), LITH(O)
   conglomerate .... GRAYWACKE

containing gem, fossil, etc. MATRIC
crushed .... BALLAST
decomposed .. SAPROLITE
dug out .... FOSSIL
easily split ...... SCHIST
ejected by volcano ...... LAPILLUS
eroded .... BOSS
face .... PRECIPICE
fine-grained ..... SHALE, SLATE
finely broken ..... SAND
formed by geyser .. SINTER
fragment(s) ...... SPALL, BRASH, DETRITUS
garden .... ROCKERY
granite-like ...... GNEISS
green .... OPHITE, VERD ANTIQUE
growths on ...... LICHEN
igneous ...... BASALT, PORPHYRY, TRAP, SYENITE, DIORITE, PERIDOT(ITE), PEGMATITE, PICRITE, GRANITE, PHONOLITE
in another rock .... XENOLITH
isolated .... SCAR
like .... PETROUS
like fish roe ..... OOLITE
mass .... HORST
metamorphic .... GNEISS
mica and quartz .. GREIN
molten.......... MAGMA
mottled .... OPHITE
of .... PETROUS
oil .... PETROLEUM, NAP(H)THA
pinnacle .... NEEDLE
plural: sl. ..... DIAMOND, GEM
porous .... TUFA, TUFF, TOPH(E)
projecting .. SCAR, LEDGE
rabbit .... HYRAX
ribbed ..... RIGID, FIRM
rose product .... LA(B)DANUM
salt .... HALITE
salt money .... EMOL
sedimentary ..... PELITE, MUDSTONE
siliceous ...... GANISTER
steep .... CLIFF

stratified .... SHALE
volcanic .. LAVA, BASALT,
WACK, LATITE,
PERLITE
weed ..... SEA OAK, TANG
rockaway .... CARRIAGE
Rockefeller, John____ ......
DAVISON
one other .... EDSEL,
NELSON
rocker .... CHAIR, CRADLE,
SKATE
rockery .... GARDEN
rocket .... PROJECTILE, ASROC
firing platform ....
LAUNCHING PAD
fuel ... LOX, HYDRAZINE
gun .... BAZOOKA
launcher ...... BAZOOKA
load .... WARHEAD
part of .... CAPSULE,
(NOSE)CONE
to get astronaut back ....
RETRO
rockfish ..... BASS, GROUPER,
RE(I)NA, BOCACCIO,
YELLOWTAIL
rockfoil .... SAXIFRAGE
Rockies' range .... TETON,
UINTA
Rockne, football coach ....
KNUTE
rocks at foot of cliff ... TALUS
bluish .... LIAS
living on ..... SAXATILE,
SAXICOLINE
of the oldest .. ARCHEAN
on the .... BANKRUPT
pile of ... TALUS, DEBRIS
slang .... MONEY, GEM,
DIAMOND
study of ..... PETROLOGY,
LITHOLOGY
rockweed .... FUCOID
rocky .... UNSTEADY, SHAKY,
WEAK, CRAGGY, DIZZY
cliff .... SCAR
hill .... TOR
mountain sheep ....
BIGHORN
mountain wind ....
CHINOOK
Mountains ..... ROCKIES
pinnacle .... SCAR, TOR,
ARETE

rococo .... FLORID,
TASTELESS, BAROQUE
rod ... POLE, TOGGLE, WAND,
PERCH, TWIG, WATTLE,
FERULE, VERGE, SHOOT,
SHAFT, BAR, STAFF,
STICK, SWITCH, SCEPTER
Biblical use ...... STOCK,
RACE, OFFSHOOT
billiards .... CUE
connecting ...... PITMAN
divination ..... DOWSING,
RHABDOMANCY
flogging .... SWISH
king's .... WARDER
royal .... WARDER,
SCEPTER
shaped ...... BACILLAR,
VIRG(UL)ATE
slang ..... GAT, PISTOL,
REVOLVER, GUN
steadying .... GUY
rodent ...... GNAWING, RAT,
MOUSE, BEAVER, SQUIRREL,
PIKA, CON(E)Y, MURINE,
RABBIT, LEPORID, CAVY,
HARE
aquatic .... BEAVER,
MUSKRAT
Belgian ...... LEPORIDE
burrowing ... VISCACHA,
CHIPMUNK, MARMOT,
GOPHER, VOLE,
GERBIL(LE), SUSLIK
eight-toothed .. OCTODON
largest extant ....
CAPYBARA
leaping .... JERBOA
Patsy winner .... BEN
pet .... HAMSTER
squirrel-like .. DORMOUSE,
GOPHER, SUSLIK,
CHIPMUNK
suicidal .... LEMMING
tailless .... PACA
water .. COYPU, MUSKRAT,
NUTRIA
rodents' disease ....
TULAR(A)EMIA
enemy .... RATTER
of .... MURINE
rodeo .... ROUNDUP
Rodi .... RHODES
Rodin, Fr. sculptor ....
AUGUSTE
work of .... THINKER

rodomontade ... BOAST(ING), BRAG(GING)

Rodrigo Diaz de Bivar .... (EL) CID

rods, 40 .... FURLONG

roe .. MILT, OVA, DEER, SPAWN, CORAL, (FISH)EGGS

roebuck .... DEER

Roentgen's discovery .... XRAY

rogation .... PRAYER

rogatory ...... QUESTIONING

Roger ..... RECEIVED, RIGHT, OK, OVER

Rogers, _____ ..... WILL, ROY

rogue .... PICAROON, SCAPEGRACE, BEGGAR, SCOUNDREL, KITE, KNAVE, VAGABOND, RASCAL

　animal .... ELEPHANT

rogues, of .... PICARESQUE

　gallery item .. ALIAS, MUG

roguish ... FUN-LOVING, ARCH

roi's heir .... DAUPHIN

　realm .... FRANCE

　wife .... REINE

roil ...... MUDDY, VEX, RILE, DISPLEASE, IRRITATE, IRK

roily .... MUDDY, TURBID, ANGRY

roister ..... REVEL, SWAGGER

Roland's magic possession .... HORN, OLIVANT

role ...... FUNCTION, OFFICE, PART, CHARACTER, PERSON

　without speech .... WALK-ON

roll .... BRIOCHE, ELAPSE, SCROLL, CATALOG(UE), CAKE, DRUMBEAT, PEAL, TRUNDLE, LIST, WRAP, ENFOLD, REGISTER, BUN, ROSTER, LURCH

　about .... WELTER, WALLOW

　along .... TRUNDLE

　back .... REPULSE

　hard .... BAGEL

　of bills .... WAD

　of bread .... MANCHET

　of cloth .... BOLT

　of coins .... ROULEAU

　of paper ..... WEB, BOLT

　of something .. ROULEAU

　out ... SPREAD, FLATTEN

　parchment ..... SCROLL

prevent .... TRIG

slang ..... ROB, MONEY, WAD

the eyes .... GOGGLE

Rolland, Fr. novelist .. ROMAIN

rolled backward ... REVOLUTE

roller .... WHEEL, SKATE, CYLINDER, WAVE, CANARY, WINCE, BRAYER, PIGEON

　coaster .... SWITCHBACK

rollick ...... ROMP, GAMBOL, CAPER, FRISK

rollicking .. LIVELY, CAREFREE

rolling stock ... LOCOMOTIVES

　Stones member .. JAGGER, WATTS, WYMAN

　sound .... RUMBLE

　sudden .... LURCH

Rollo .... VIKING

rolltop .... DESK

rollway .... CHUTE

roly-poly .... RUDGY, DUMPY, PUDDING

rom .... GYPSY

romaine .... COS, LETTUCE

Romains, Fr. novelist .. JULES

Roman ..... LATIN, ITALIAN, QUIRITE

　actor's boot .... BUSKIN

　administrator .... PATRICIAN

　agreement .... PACTA

　apostle .... NERI

　assembly .... FORUM, COMITIA

　awning .... VELARIUM

　basilica .... LATERAN

　bathhouses ... THERMAE

　bishop .... POPE

　bottle .... AMPULLA

　boxer's strap .... CESTUS

　boxing-wrestling contest .. PANCRATIUM

　bronze .... AES

　buckle .... FIBULA

　building for musical performances .. ODEUM

　cap .... PILEUS

　Catholic .... PAPIST, LATIN

　Catholic Church .. ROME

　Catholic festival .... LAMMAS

　Catholic, French .... GALLICAN

　census taker ..... CENSOR

chariot .... ESSED
circus arena ....
    HIPPODROME
circus fighter ....
    GLADIATOR
citizens .... EQUITES
civil law digest .. PANDECT
civilian .... QUIRITE
clan .... GENS
clasp .... FIBULA
cloak ... SAGUM, ABOLLA
coin ...... AES, AUREUS,
    SESTERCE, DENARIUS,
    TRIENS, SEMIS, SOLIDUS,
    BEZANT
commander ⌐ CENTURION
commoner .... PLEBEIAN
corselet .. LORICA, LORLEA
court(s) .. ATRIA, ATRIUM
cuirass .. LORICA, LORLEA
date ...... NONES, IDES
deity .... LAR
dictator .... SULLA
diviner .... AUSPEX
emperor .... TITUS,
    NERVA, OTHO, HADRIAN,
    GALBA, PROBUS, CARUS,
    OTTO, TRAJAN,
    CALIGULA
emperor's bodyguard ...
    PRETORIAN
emperor's decree ....
    RESCRIPT
emperor's standard .....
    LABARUM
Empire part .... HISPANIA
empire founder ....
    AUGUSTUS
entrance .... ATRIUM
epigrammatist .. MARTIAL
fable writer .. PHAEDRUS
farce .... MIME
farewell .... ADDIO
fates .... PARCAE
festival ... LUPERCAL(IA),
    SATURNALIA, OPALIA
fiddler .... NERO
foot soldiers .... VELITES
fountain, famed ... TREVI
frontier fortification .....
    LIMES
galley ⌐ BIREME, TRIREME
games .... LUDI
games official .. (A)EDILE
garment ⌐ TOGA, STOLE,
    TUNIC

general ... TITUS, SCIPIO,
    MARIUS, LUCULLUS,
    CASSIUS, AGRICOLA,
    SULLA, DRUSUS,
    AGRIPPA
girdle .... CESTUS
girl traitor ..... TARPEIA
gladiator ..... RETIARIUS
god, agriculture ... PICUS,
    SATURN
    chief ... JOVE, JUPITER
    festivity ...... COMUS
    fire .... VULCAN
    gates .... JANUS
    Hades.... ⌐ DIS, ORCUS,
        PLUTO
    herds .... ⌐⌐ PAN
    household ...... LAR,
        PENATES
    lightning .... JUPITER
    love ..... CUPID, AMOR
    lower world .. SERAPIS
    night .... SOMNUS
    pastoral ⌐. LUPERCUS,
        FAUNUS
    patron ⌐⌐. MERCURY
    rain .... JUPITER
    sea .... NEPTUNE
    season .... VERTUMNUS
    sleep ⌐⌐⌐. MORPHEUS,
        SOMNUS
    sun .... SOL
    thievery ..... MERCURY
    tutelary .... LAR
    underworld ..... DIS,
        ORCUS, PLUTO
    wine .... BACCHUS
    woods ...... SYLVANUS
    war ... MARS, QUIRINUS
goddess .... DEA
    agriculture ...... OPS
    beauty .... VENUS
    birth .... PARCA,
        LUCINA, MATUTA
    crops .... ANNONA
    crossroads .... TRIVIA
    dawn .... ⌐⌐ AURORA,
        MATUTA
    earth ⌐⌐⌐⌐⌐ TELLUS,
        TERRA
    faith ⌐⌐⌐⌐⌐⌐ FIDES
    fates .... PARCAE
    fertility .... FAUNA
    fields .... TELLUS
    fire .... VESTA
    flowers .... FLORA

fountain ..... FERONIA
fruits .... POMONA
harvest .... OPS
health .... SALUS
hearth .... VESTA
herds .... PALES
hope .... SPES
horses .... EPONA
hunting ...... DIANA,
VACUNA
light .... LUCINA
love .... VENUS
marriage .... JUNO
moon .... LUNA
night .... NOX
peace ... PAX, MINERVA
plenty .... OPS
sea .... MARE
summer .... AESTAS
underworld ....
PROSERPINA
vegetation ..... CERES
virtue .... FIDEO
war .... MINERVA,
BELLONA
wisdom ..... MINERVA
governor.... PROCONSUL,
PILATE, LEGATE
guard .... LICTOR
guardian spirits ... LARES,
PENATES
Hades .... AVERNUS
half boot .... CALIGA
hall ...... ATRIUM, OECUS
harvest festival ... OPALIA
headband .... VITTA
hell .... AVERNUS
helmet .... GALEA
highway ...... ITER, VIA
hill .... (See Rome)
historian ...... TACITUS,
NEPOS, LIVY
holiday .... FERIA
household gods ... LARES,
PENATES
jar .... AMPHORA
judge .... (A)EDILE,
QU(A)ESTOR
law .... LEX
lawmaker ..... SENATOR
legion commander ......
TRIBUNE
list .... ALBE
lower world ..... ORCUS,
HADES
magistrate ...... CONSUL,

PREFECT, DUUMVIR,
CENSOR, TRIBUNE,
PR(A)ETOR
magistrate's symbol .....
FASCES
maiden traitor .. TARPEIA
marble .... CIPOLIN
masses .... PLEBS
matron's garment .. STOLE
meal .... CENA, GENA
military unit ..... LEGION,
COHORT
monster: myth. ....
TYPHON, LAMIA
month's first day ....
CALENDS
name .... NOMEN
naturalist .... PLINY
noble .... PATRICIAN
nose .... NASUS
nymph: myth. .. EGERIA,
M(A)ENAD
officer for 10 men ......
DECURION
official .... EDILE,
PREFECT
official with the fasces ...
LICTOR
Optimus Princeps ....
TRAJAN
orator ... CATO, CICERO,
CAESAR
palace .... LATERAN
patron of literature ......
MAECENAS
people .... SABINES
philosopher .... SENECA
pin .... ACUS
plain .... CAMPAGNA
playwright .... TERENCE
poet ..... VERGIL, VIRGIL,
JUVENAL, LUCRETIUS,
CINNA, LUCAN, OVID
pontiff .... CAESAR
port .... OSTIA
portrait, wax ..... IMAGO
pound .... LIBRA
priest ... AUSPEX, AUGUR,
FLAMEN
procession .... TRIUMPH
province .... DACIA,
PANNONIA, PISIDIA,
MOESIA, NUMIDIA
public land .... AGER
racing course ....
HIPPODROME

river ...... TIBER, LETHE
road .... ITER, VIA
road, famous ... APPIAN
robe .... TOGA
room(s) .... ATRIUM,
            ATRIA
royal standard ....
            LABARUM
senator .... CATO,
       CICERO, PUBLIUS
serf .... COLONUS,
          COLONA
shield(s) ...... SCUTUM,
   EGIS, SCUTA, CLIPEUS
soldier .... VELITE,
        LEGIONARY
soldier's covering ....
         TESTUDO
soothsayer ... HARUSPEX
spirits .... LEMURES,
     MANES, LARES
standard ..... LABARUM
street .... CORSO
tablet .... TESSERA
taxman .... PUBLICAN
temple .... NAOS, CELLA
theater awning ....
        VELARIUM
theater's stage ....
     PROSCENIUM
ticket/token .... TESSERA
tragedian ...... SENECA
traitors' cliff .. TARPEIAN
treasurer ... QU(A)ESTOR
unit of weight .... LIBRA
urn .... CAPANNA
vase .... PYXIS
vestment ... TOGA, ROBE
war trumpet ...... TUBA
warrior ..... GLADIATOR
way .... VIA
weight ... SCRUPLE, BES,
        LIBRA
writer .... VARRO,
  TERENCE, LIVY, PLINY
writing tablet .. DIPTYCH
romance .... NOVEL, FICTION,
 (LOVE)AFFAIR, WOO, COURT
language ...... SPANISH,
   FRENCH, ITALIAN,
  PROVENCAL, ROMANIAN,
   CATALAN, LADIN
Romanian (see Rumanian)
capital .... BUCHAREST
Romanov, Russ. czar ....
     MIKHAIL

Romansh .... LADIN
romantic .... FANCIFUL,
   FABULOUS, VISIONARY,
  QUIXOTIC, SENTIMENTAL,
        BYRONIC
Romany .... GYPSY
Rome .... ROMA, RUM,
     ETERNAL CITY
conqueror of ... ALARIC
first emperor of ....
      AUGUSTUS
founder of ... ROMULUS
grandeur of ..... EMPIRE
hill of .... CAELIAN,
  AVENTINE, VIMINAL,
  PALATINE, QUIRINAL,
    CAPITOLINE
"pest" of ... PAPPAGALLO
port .... OSTIA
rebel against .. SPARTACUS
Romeo .... LOVER
and Juliet character .....
   ESCALUS, TYBALT,
  PARIS, MERCUTIO,
  CAPULET, ABRAM,
 MONTAGUE, LAURENCE
enemy of .... TYBALT
father of ..... MONTAGUE
kinsman of ... MERCUTIO
love of .... JULIET,
    ROSALINE
rival of .... PARIS
Rommel, Ger. marshal ....
     ERWIN
romp .... PLAY, ROLLICK,
     FROLIC
rompers .... JUMPERS
Romulus .... QUIRINUS
brother of .... REMUS
parent of .... MARS, RHEA
saver of ..... (SHE)WOLF
Ronald ____, actor .. REAGAN,
     COLMAN
rondeau ... POEM, RO(U)NDEL,
     RONDO
rondure ..... CIRCLE, SPHERE
ronin ..... OUTCAST, OUTLAW
rood .... CROSS, CRUCIFIX
roof .... CUPOLA, DOME,
 GAMBREL, TOP, SHELTER,
   LEANTO, MANSARD
arched .... VAULT
coach's .... IMPERIAL
covering ...... SHINGLE,
    SLATE, THATCH
drain .... GUTTER

edge .... EAVE
feature .... EAVES
figuratively ...... HOME, HOUSE
glass for light ....
    BULL'S-EYE
lantern .... LOUVER
of the World ..... PAMIR, TIBET
opening ..... SKYLIGHT, LUNET(TE), SCUTTLE
point finial .... EPI
raise the ..... COMPLAIN
raised border .. COAMING
rounded .. CUPOLA, DOME
sloped ... LEANTO, SHED
support .. TRUSS, RAFTER, SPRAG, PURLIN(E)
trough .... GUTTER
two-sloped .... MANSARD
window .... DORMER, SKYLIGHT
woven work ... WATTLE
roofing slate .... RAG
slate trimmer .... ZAX
tile ..... PANTILE, SLATE
roofless .... HOMELESS, HYPETHRAL
rooflike covering .... CANOPY
rooftree .... RIDGEPOLE, HOME, SHELTER
rook ..... CROW, SWINDLE(R), CASTLE, CHEAT
cry of .... CAW
rookery .... TENEMENT
inhabitant of .. PENGUIN, CROW, SEAL
rookie ...... RECRUIT, NOVICE
room ..... SALA, HALL, SALLE, CELL, CLOSET, STUDY, LODGE, QUARTER, SPACE, LEEWAY, CUDDY, ROTUNDA
band, ornamental ......
    FRIEZE
beneath roof ...... LOFT, ATTIC
conversation .. LOCUTORY
dressing ...... BOUDOIR
perfumer ...... INCENSE
harem .... ADA, ODA
hot bath .... CALDARIUM
inner .... BEN
private .... DEN, CLOSET, STUDY, SANCTUM
Pueblo Indian ..... KIVA
wine .... CELLAR

woman's sitting ....
    BOUDOIR
roomer .... LODGER
rooming house .... KIP
housekeeper .. LANDLORD
rooms .... QUARTERS, LODGINGS
roomy .... SPACIOUS
roorback .... LIE, LIBEL
roose .... PRAISE
Roosevelt, Mrs. ....
    (ANNA)ELEANOR, SARA
President .. FDR, TEDDY
roost .... PERCH, SIT
rooster .... COCK, BANTAM, CHANTICLEER
castrated .... CAPON
comb of ..... CARUNCLE
cry of .... CROW
fattened .... CAPON
feathers of ..... HACKLE
leg outgrowth ..... SPUR
young .... COCKEREL
root .... RADIX, RHIZOME, ORIGIN, SOURCE, BASE, CORE, PLUG, CHEER
aromatic ...... GINSENG, ORRICE
combining form ....
    RHIZ(O)
diuretic .... PAREIRA
dried .... RHATANY
dye .... CHOY, CHAY
edible ... TARO, RADISH, POTATO, YAM, PARSNIP, MANIOC, GIRASOL(E), EDDO, CASSAVA
emetic ...... MANDRAKE
expectorant .... SENEGA
flavoring .. SARSAPARILLA
for planting ...... SLIP
garlic .... RAMSON(S)
growth ...... TUBERCLE
hair ... FIBRIL, TRICHOME
medicinal ..... GINSENG, RHATANY
narcotic ..... MANDRAKE
of the .... RADICAL
part of .... RADICLE
perfume making .. ORRIS, ORRICE
purgative .... JALAP
relish .... RADISH
salad .... RAMSON(S), RAMPION
seasoning .... TURMERIC

shoot ... SUCKER, TILLER
small .... RADICEL
stock .... GINGER
substance ..... ZEDOARY
tip tissue ..... MERISTEM
U.S. statesman ... ELIHU
word .. ETYMON, RADICAL
rooting out .... EVULSION
rootlet .... RADICEL
rootlike .... RHIZOID
rootstalk .. RHIZOME, GINGER
rootstock ... RHIZOME, ORRIS,
PIP, ORIGIN, TARO, GINGER,
ORRICE
rope ... CORD, LASSO, STRAND,
TIE, FASTEN, MARLIN, CABLE
and pulley block ....
TACKLE
cattle catcher's .... BOLA
cord tied to .... MARLINE
cowboy's .... RIATA,
LASSO, LARIAT
dancer .... FUNAMBULIST
dancer's .... POY
fiber ...... IXTLE, ABACA,
HEMP, JUTE, MAGUEY,
GOMUTI, COIR, ISTLE,
BAST, SISAL
flag .... LANYARD
for cable's end .. MARLINE,
MARLING
for hanging .... HALTER,
HEMP, NOOSE
frayed end of .. FAG END
gaff to deck ..... VANG
guiding ... LONGE, GUY,
LUNGE, DRAGLINE
guy .... VANG
horse trainer's ... LONGE
in .... LURE, ENTICE
knotted at end ..... COLT
lead .... LONGE
loop ... BIGHT, FRAP, LAP
mooring .... PAINTER
old .... JUNK
pulling .... TUG
ship's .... SHROUD,
LANYARD, RATLINE,
PAINTER, VANG, GUY,
STAY, TYE, EARING
steadying ... GUY, VANG
tether .... LARIAT
thin ..... STRING, CORD
thread a .... REEVE
towing .... CORDELLE
walker ... FUNAMBULIST

wire .... CABLE
roped .... TETHERED, LASSOED
Roper, Elmo .... POLLSTER
ropy .... GLUTINOUS
roque .... CROQUET
Roquefort .... CHEESE
rorqual ..... FINBACK, WHALE,
RAZORBACK
rosaceous .... ROSY
plant ..... STRAWBERRY,
AGRIMONY
rosary ...... BEADS, CHAPLET,
GARDEN
prayer ... PATERNOSTER,
AVE, GLORIA PATRI
subject .... MYSTERY
rose .... RHODA, FLOWER
ERYSIPELAS, PERFUME,
NOZZLE, RAMBLER,
DAMASK
aborigine boxing champ
LIONEL
apple .... POMAROSA
Bowl players ...... UCLA
bush .... SHADBLOW,
SASKATOON
extract .... ATTAR
garden .... ROSARY
mallow .... HIBISCUS,
HOLLYHOCK
moss .... PORTULACA
of Sharon ...... ALTHEA
plant .... AVENS
petal oil .... ATTAR
rash .... ROSEOLA,
RUBELLA, MEASLES
straggling ..... RAMBLER
time .... JUNE, SPRING
under the ..... SECRETLY,
SUB ROSA
wild .. EGLANTINE, BRIER
roseate .... ROSY, BRIGHT
rosebay .... RHODODENDRON,
OLEANDER
rosebush fruit .... HIP
roseola ...... MEASLES, RASH,
RUBELLA
rosette .... COCKADE
rosin ..... RESIN, FLUX, ROZET
Rosinante ...... HORSE, JADE
master of ..... QUIXOTE
rosolio .... CORDIAL
Ross, flag-maker ...... BETSY
U.S. woman governor ...
NELLIE

Rossetti, poet ..... CHRISTINA, DANTE
Rossini's opera .... OTELLO
Rossiya .... RUSSIA
roster .... LIST, ROLL
rostrum .... DAIS, BEAK, TRIBUNE, PLATFORM, PULPIT, STAGE
rosy .... BRIGHT, RUDDY ROSACEOUS, PINK(Y)
fingered goddess .... AURORA
rot .... DECAY, PUTREFY, DECOMPOSE, SPOIL, RET
slang ... BOSH, NONSENSE, RUBBISH
rota .... LIST, COURT, ROUTINE, ROUND, ROSTER, CLASSIS
member ...... AUDITOR
Rotarian, female .... ANN
rotate ... SPIN, TWIRL, WHEEL, GYRATE, ROLL, PAN, TURN, REVOLVE
unevenly .... WOBBLE
rotating device .... CAM, AXIS, SPINDLE, ROTOR, AXLE, REEL, DASHER
rotation .... REVOLUTION
rotch(e) .... DOVEKIE, AUK, GUILLEMOT, DOVEKEY
rote .. ROUTINE, MECHANICAL
by .... MEMORY
rotenone source .... DERRIS
rotgut .... WHISKY
rotifer .... ANIMALCULE
rotisserie .... GRILL
pin .... SKEWER
rotor .... STATOR
rotl .... WEIGHT
plural of .... ARTAL
rotten ...... DECAYED, FOUL, SPOILED, TAINTED, PUTRID, BAD, NASTY, FETID, RANK, ADDLE
rottenstone .... TRIPOLI
rotund ..... PLUMP, SONOROUS
roturier .... COMMONER
roue .... LIBERTINE, RAKE, DEBAUCHEE, RAKEHELL
rouge .... COSMETIC
rough ...... UNEVEN, SHAGGY, STORMY, RIOTOUS, CRUDE, VIOLENT, RAGGED, RUGGED, AGRESTIC, HARSH, RUDE, COARSE, JAGGED, HUBBLY

and disorderly .... LARRIKIN
and-tumble .. DISORDERLY
and-tumble fight .. MELEE, BRAWL
cloth .... TERRY, DENIM, SHAG, DUFFEL, DUFFLE
combining form .... TRACHY
edged .... EROSE
in speech .... GRUFF
make .... FRET, FRAY
manner .... GRUFF
skin .... SHAGREEN
sounding ..... RAUCOUS
water .... SEA
roughen ... FRET, CHAP, FRAY
roughly .... ABOUT
roughneck ...... GOON, HOOD, THUG, BULLY, ROWDY
roughness .... ASPERITY
roughshod, go   .... TRAMPLE
rouleau .... ROLL
roulette color ... RED, BLACK
man .... CROUPIER
term ..... NOIR, ROUGE, MANQUE, BAS, PASSE
round .... COURSE, TOUR, SPHERICAL, GLOBULAR, CIRCULAR, PLUMP, ANNULAR, SALVO, GLOBOID
and plump ..... CHUBBY
make .... CIRCINATE
of applause ..... PLAUDIT
of duty ...... BEAT, TOUR
of play .... INNING
protuberance ..... UMBO, KNOB
Table knight .. LANCELOT, GAWAIN, BORS, KAY, BORT, BALIN, BALAN, GARETH, GERAINT, GALAHAD, MO(R)DRED, MORGA(I)N, TRISTRAM, TRISTAN, BEDIVERE, PERCIVAL, PARSIFAL, PELLEAS
trip .... EXCURSION
up .... RODEO, COLLECT, GATHER, RUSTLE, CORRAL
watchman's ...... TOUR
roundabout .... DEVIOUS, INDIRECT, CIRCUITOUS, JACKET, AMBAGIOUS

expression ..... AMBAGE, PERIPHRASIS
   way ... AMBAGE, DETOUR
rounded ... FUSIFORM, GIBBOUS
   projection .. LOBE, KNOB
rounder .... WATCHMAN, POLICEMAN, GUARD, SENTINEL, DRUNKARD
Roundhead .... PURITAN
roundly .... SEVERELY
roundup .... RODEO
roundworm .... LUMBRICOID, NEMATODE, ASCARID, PARASITE, STRONGYL(E)
roupy .... HOARSE
rouse ... WAKE, EXCITE, HAUL, REVEILLE, ROUST, STIR (UP)
rousing ...... STIRRING, BRISK
Rousseau, work by .... EMILE
roust ...... STIR (UP), ROUT, DRIVE (OUT)
roustabout ...... DECK HAND, LABORER
rout ... DEBACLE, ROUST, MOB, RABBLE, FLIGHT, DEFEAT
   in a way .... SKUNK
route .... COURSE, WAY, FORWARD, ITINERARY, RUN
   shortest .... BEELINE
routine ...... REGULAR, ROTA, ROT(T)E, CUSTOMARY, HUMDRUM
   task ...... CHORE, CHARE
rove .. .... WANDER, ROAM, RAMBLE, GAD, CARD, RANGE
   for plunder .... MARAUD, FORAGE
rover .... WANDERER, PIRATE, NOMAD, TARGET
roving for adventure .. ERRANT
row ..... LINE, OAR, PADDLE, SHINDY, SQUABBLE, FILE, BRAWL, DISPUTE, NOISE, QUARREL, CLAMOR, RUCKUS, KICK-UP
   form in a ...... ALINE, ALIGN
   of cut grass ..... SWATH
   of planted seeds .. DRILL
rowan .... ASH
rowboat .. CANOE, COBLE, GIG, GONDOLA, WHERRY, SKIFF, SCULL, SHELL, BANCA, CAIQUE
   racing ..... GIG, SCULL,

SHELL
   warship's .... GALLEY
rowdy .... HOOD(LUM), PLUG-UGLY, LARRIKIN, ROUGH(NECK)
   young .... HOOLIGAN
Rowe's (N.) rake ... LOTHARIO
rowel .... PRICK, SPUR
rowen .... GRASS, AFTERMATH, HAY
rower .... OAR(SMAN), GONDOLIER
   seat of .... THWART
rowing contest ..... REGATTA
rowlock ...... POPPET, THOLE
Roxas, Philippine president ... MANUEL
Roy Rogers' horse ... TRIGGER
royal ..... KINGLY, IMPERIAL, NOBLE, AUGUST, REGIUS, PRINCELY, REGAL, MAJESTIC
   authority ...... SCEPTER, SCEPTRE
   color .... PURPLE
   council, Oriental .. DIVAN
   crown .. TIARA, DIADEM, CORONET
   domain/realm .. KINGDOM
   flush, part of .... ACE, KING, QUEEN, JACK, TEN
   house .... TUDOR, PLANTAGENET, WINDSOR, STUART, HAPSBURG
   initials .... HRH
   palace .... COURT
   residence .... PALACE, BALMORAL
   seat .... THRONE
   staff ...... SCEPTER, ROD
   title .. DAUPHIN, ROI, REY, SIRE, EMPEROR, CZAR, TSAR, KING, PRINCE, INFANTA
royalist ..... CAVALIER, TORY
royalty .... SOVEREIGNTY
RSVP, part of ..... REPONDEZ, S'IL, VOUS, PLAIT
rub ...... MASSAGE, ABRADE, POLISH, SCOUR, RASP, GRATE, GRIND, SAND
   a-dub .... DRUMBEAT
   out ...... EXPUNGE, KILL, ERASE, SCRAPE, MURDER

the wrong way .... IRRITATE, DISPLEASE
to brightness .... POLISH, FURBISH
with nose ...... NUZZLE
with oil/liniment .... EMBROCATE
"Rubaiyat" author .... OMAR (KHAYYAM)
rhyming .... AABA
rubasse .... QUARTZ
rubber ... PARA, CAOUTCHOUC, GUMS, MASSEUR, MASSAGIST, ERASER, GUAYULE, EBONITE
band .... ELASTIC
boot .... WADER
City .... AKRON
filler in .... KAOLIN(E)
game, first .... LEG
hard .... EBONITE, VULCANITE
necking vehicle ... STAGE
plant ...... CAUCHO, ULE
product basis .... LATEX
ring .... GASKET
roller .... SQUEEGEE
sap .... LATEX
sheeting .... PLIOFILM
shrub .... GUAYULE
shoe .... GALOSH(E), GOLOSH(E)
stamp... APPROVE, DATER
stamp inker .... PAD
substance like .... GUTTA-PERCHA
synthetic ...... NEOPRENE, BUNA, BUTYLE, CARIFLEX
thread wound with cotton LASTEX
tree ...... ULE, SERINGA
rubberneck ...... SIGHTSEER, GAZE(R), CRANE
rubbers .... GUMSHOE, OVERSHOE, GALOSHES
rubbery .... ELASTIC
rubbing tool .... FILE
rubbish ... DEBRIS, DUST, JUNK, TRUMPERY, RAFF, DROSS, TRIPE, (TOMMY)ROT, TRUCK, REFUSE, TRASH, NONSENSE
collect .... SCAVENGE
mine .... STENT
pile .... DUMP
slang .... ROT

rubble .... DEBRIS, SCREE
rubdown .... MASSAGE
rube .... RUSTIC, YOKEL
rubefacient .. SALVE, PLASTER
rubella ...... MEASLES, RASH, RUBEOLA, ROSEOLA
rubellite .... TOURMALINE
rubeola ... MEASLES, RUBELLA
rubiaceous plant ...... COFFEE, GARDENIA, IPECAC, CINCHONA
Rubicon, he crossed the ...... CAESAR
rubicund ..... RUDDY, FLORID, REDDISH, ROSY
Rubinstein opera ... DEMONIO
pianist ... ARTUR, ANTON
rubious .... RED
ruble, 1/100 of a ... KOPE(C)K
rubric .... TITLE, HEADING, RED(DISH)
ruby ...... CORUNDUM, STONE, RED, SARDIUS
spinel .... BALAS
ruche ...... FRILL, TRIMMING
ruck ... STACK, HEAP, CREASE, PUCKER, FOLD, WRINKLE
ruckus ..... UPROAR, BRAWL, ROW, MELEE, FRAY, HASSLE
ruction ...... UPROAR, QUARREL
rudbeckia ..... (CONE)FLOWER
rudd ... CARP, RED-EYE, FISH, VIREO
rudder .... HELM
guide with .... STEER
handle ... TILLER, WHEEL
ruddle .... KEEL
ruddock .... ROBIN
ruddy ...... RUBICUND, ROSY, SANGUINE, RED(DISH), FLUSH(ED), FLORID
rude ..... CRUDE, UNCIVIL, COARSE, BOORISH, GROSS, UNCOUTH, ROUGH, SAUCY, HARSH, IMPOLITE, GRUFF
dwelling .... HOVEL, HUT
rudimentary ...... VESTIGIAL, INCHOATE
rudiment(s) ... ABC, ELEMENTS, BEGINNINGS, VESTIGE, FIRST
rue .... DEPLORE, HERB, REGRET, REPENT, GRIEVE, LAMENT, BEWAIL
plant ..... LEMON, LIME, ORANGE
rueful ..... SORRY, PENITENT

rufescent .... REDDISH
ruff ...... COLLAR, SANDPIPER,
    PIGEON, FRAISE
  female .... REEVE
  turned down ...... FALL
ruff(e) .... FISH, PERCH
ruffian ... PLUG UGLY, BRAVO,
    HIGHBINDER, THUG,
    TOUGH(IE), GOON,
    HOODLUM, HOOLIGAN
ruffle .... DISTURB, FRILL,
    FURBELOW, DERANGE,
    RIPPLE, WRINKLE,
    SHUFFLE, PLEAT, FLOUNCE
rufous .... REDDISH, RUSTY
rug .. MAT, RUNNER, DRUGGET,
    FOOTCLOTH, MAUD, CARPET,
    TOUPEE, WILTON
ruga .. FOLD, CREASE, WRINKLE
rugate ...... FOLDED, CREASED
rugby .... FOOTBALL
  football .... RUGGER
  formation .. SCRUM(MAGE)
  rival .... ETON
rugged ...... UNEVEN, STORMY,
    RUDE, STURDY, CRAGGY,
    HARDY, ROUGH, HARD,
    ROBUST
rugose/rugous ...... RIDGED,
    CORRUGATED
ruin ...... WRECK(AGE), BANE,
    SPOIL, HAVOC, DIDDLE,
    LOUSE UP, DOWNFALL,
    DESTROY
ruinous .... HARMFUL
ruins .... DEBRIS
rule ...... PRECEPT, DECISION,
    ORDER, NORM, REIGN, LAW,
    MAXIM, REGULATION,
    CUSTOM, PRESCRIPT, LINE,
    GOVERN, HABIT, STANDARD,
    CRITERION, REGIME(N),
    SWAY
  as a .... USUALLY
  book ... HOYLE, MANUAL
  Britannia composer ......
    ARNE
  of thumb basis ....
    PRACTICE, EXPERIENCE
  out ...... EXCLUDE, OMIT
ruler .... FERULE, EMIR,
    PRINCE, KING, MONARCH,
    GERENT, EMEER, QUEEN,
    POTENTATE, REGENT, TSAR,
    CZAR, RAJAH, GOVERNOR

  absolute .. SHAH, TYRANT,
    DESPOT
  amuser of a ...... CLOWN,
    JESTER
  cruel .... DESPOT
  hereditary ...... DYNAST
  length of a .... FOOT
  wife of .. .. EMPRESS,
    RANEE, QUEEN,
    TSARINA, CZARINA, REINA
rules of conduct .... CODE
  Order author ... ROBERT
ruling .... PREVALENT,
    DECISION, LINE
  party .... MAJORITY
Rum .... ROME, BAD, LIQUOR,
    TAF(F)IA, POOR, BACARDI
  dessert .... BABA
  source ...... MOLASSES,
    SUGAR CANE
Rumanian .... MAGYAR
  capital .... BUCHAREST
  city ...... BRASOV, CLUJ,
    PLOESTI, ARAD, IASI,
    ORADEA, YASSY, JASSY,
    TIMISOARA, LASI, GALATI
  coin ...... LEU, LEY, BAN
  composer ...... ENESCO
  district ...... DOBRUJA
  dramatist ...... IONESCO
  folk dance ...... HORA
  king .... CAROL,
    (MIHAI) MICHAEL
  monetary unit .. LEI, LEU,
    LEY
  native .... MAGYAR,
    MOLDAVIAN
  part of ...... WALACHIA
  premier ...... MAURER,
    CEAUSESCU,
    ANTONESCU
  river ...... ALUTA, ARGES,
    SERETH, CERNA
rumba .... DANCE
  exponent .. CUBAN, CUGAT
ramble ...... FREE-FOR-ALL,
    MELEE, LUMBER, ROLL
  seat .... DICKEY
rumdinger .... ONER
rumen ...... GULLET, CUD,
    PAUNCH
ruminant .. MEDITATIVE, GOAT,
    LLAMA, CATTLE, BISON,
    DEER, GIRAFFE, ALPACA,
    YAK, SHEEP, ANTELOPE,
    CAMEL

chew of .... CUD
stomach .... RUMEN,
(AB)OMASUM,
RETICULUM
ruminate .... PONDER, CHEW,
MUSE, MEDITATE, REFLECT
rummage .. RANSACK, SEARCH,
SALE, GRUB
rummer .... CUP, GLASS
rummy ...... GIN, ODD, QUEER,
STRANGE, DRUNKARD, SOT,
TOPER
bonus, sometimes ....
ROODLES
game like .... COONCAN
slang .... DRUNK
strategy .... KNOCK
rumor ..... GOSSIP, HEARSAY,
BRUIT, NOISE, REPORT,
ONDIT, GRAPEVINE
rump .. ARSE, CROUP, BREECH,
BUTTOCKS, CUT, FAG END
Rumpelstiltskin ..... DWARF
rumple ...... MUSS, TOUSLE,
DISHEVEL, CREASE, WRINKLE
rumpus .. DISTURBANCE, ROW,
UPROAR, POTHER, STIR
rumrunner .... SMUGGLER,
BOOTLEGGER
run ..... RACE, SCUD, LOPE,
TRIP, SPRINT, OPERATE,
SPEED, INCUR, LEAK,
SPREAD, CREEP, PUBLISH,
SMUGGLE, VIE WITH, TROT,
FLOW, HIE, SCORE, ROUTE
across .... MEET,
ENCOUNTER
after ..... CHASE, PURSUE
away .... ABSCOND, FLEE,
ELOPE, DECAMP, BOLT
baseball .... HOME
cricket .... BYE
down ...... SUMMARY,
OUTLINE
in ...... INSERT, FIGHT,
INCLUDE, ARREST
in the long .. ULTIMATELY,
EVENTUALLY
of-the-mill .. ORDINARY,
AVERAGE, SO-SO
off the tracks ... DERAIL
over .... SPILL
through .... PIERCE,
REEVE
runabout .... ROADSTER
runagate ..... DESERTER, RAT,

VAGABOND, FUGITIVE,
DRIFTER
runaround .... EXCUSES
runaway .... DESERTER,
FUGITIVE
slave .... MAROON
runcible spoon .... FORK
runcinate ...... SAWTOOTHED
rundle .... RUNG
rundlet ...... CASK, BARREL
rune ..... SONG, VERSE, POEM
rung .. RUNDLE, SPOKE, STAVE,
CROSSBAR, STEP
runic alphabet ..... FUTHARK
runnel ..... BROOK, RIVULET,
RUNLET, CHANNEL
runner .... AGENT, STOLON,
COURIER, SMUGGLER, GATE,
BLADE, FLAGELLUM, SKI,
SKATE, CONTENDER,
MESSENGER, RACER, SKEE,
ERRAND BOY
way of .... LANE
running ... MELTING, LINEAR,
CONTINUOUS, CURRENT,
EASY, FLOWING, CURSIVE,
CREEPING, CLIMBING
knot .... NOOSE
runt ... DWARF, PYGMY, CHIT
runway .... PATH, RAMP,
(AIR)STRIP, TRACK, CHUTE,
TROUGH, CHANNEL
rupee, newly minted ... SICCA
weight of .... TOLA
rupees, 15 .... MOHUR
rupture ...... BREAK, HERNIA,
BREACH, BURST
support .... TRUSS
"Rur" characters .... ROBOTS
rural ...... RUSTIC, GEOPONIC,
BUCOLIC, PASTORAL,
AGRESTIC, ARCADIAN
abode ... BOWER, VILLA,
HACIENDA
building .... BARN
opposed to ...... URBAN
poem .... ECLOGUE,
PASTORAL
sound .. MOO, LOW, BAA,
BLEAT, CROW
ruse ... STRATEGEM, ARTIFICE,
TRICK, DODGE
rush ... SURGE, DASH, CHARGE,
DRIVE, HURRY, RACE,
HASTE, SPATE, ONSLAUGHT,
PRESS, TORRENT, CANDLE,

REED, SCRIMMAGE, SPEED, HIE, HIGHTAIL, COURT, GUST

furiously ... ... RAMP

hour usually ... NINE(AM), NOON, FIVE(PM)

line (football) member . .... GUARD, TACKLE, CENTER

of water .... WASH

violently ..... RAMP(AGE)

rusk .... BREAD, CAKE, BISCUIT, ZWIEBACK

Russ ...... RUSSIAN, NIEMEN

Russell, Miss .... CONNIE, ROSALIND, GAIL, LILLIAN, JANE

philosopher ... BERTRAND

russet .. CLOTH, BROWN, APPLE

Russia .... ROSSIYA, MUSCOVY, RUTHENIA

capital .... PETROGRAD

founder of .... IVAN

Russian .... RED, COMMUNIST, COMMIE, MUSCOVITE

administrative body .. .... ZEMSTVO

airline ...... AEROFLOT

alcoholic drink .. KVASS, VODKA

anarchist .... KROPOTKIN

antelope .... SAIGA

aristocrat .... BOYAR(D)

assembly .... RADA

astronaut ...... GAGARIN

ballet dancer .. MASSINE, NUREYEV, PAVLOVA

capital .... MOSCOW, NOVGOROD, PETROGRAD

carriage ... TARANTAS(S), TROIKA, DROS(H)KY

cart .... TELEGA

cathedral ...... SOBOR

cereal .... EMMER

chalet .... DACHA

chess champion .... ALEKHINE, BOTVINNIK, TAL, PETROSIAN, SMYSLOV, SPASSKY

choreographer .. MASSINE

citadel ...... KREMLIN

city .... OREL, MOSCOW, KIEV, OMSK, TASHKENT, SAMARKAND, BOKHARA, GOMEL, PSKOV, KIEV

coin ...... CHERVONETS,

IMPERIAL, POLTINA, RUBLE, KOPE(C)K

collective farm .... KOLKHOZ

comedian ...... RAIKIN

community ...... MIR

composer .... BORODIN, STRAVINSKY, PROKOFIEV

cooperative ...... ARTEL

Cossack .... TATAR

council .. SOVIET, DUMA

country estate .. DACHA

dancer .. .... DANILOVA, PAVLOVA

dandelion .. KOK-SAGYZ

dramatist ...... GOGOL

drink .. VODKA, KVAS(S), QUASS

dwelling .... ISBA

edict .... UKASE

empress ...... TSARINA

exile's place .... SIBERIA

farmer .... KULAK

fur .. KARAKUL, CARACUL

greeting ...... BEAR HUG

guitar ...... BALALAIKA

guild ...... ARTEL

gulf .... AZOV

hemp .. RINE, KONOPEL

holy picture .. IKON, ICON

hood .... BASHLYK

horse team .... TROIKA

horseman ...... COSSACK

hut .... ISBA

ibex .... TEK

imperial order .... UKASE

inland sea .. ARAL, AZOV

James Bond .... ZAKHOV

lake .... BAIKAL, ARAL, NEVA, LADOGA, ONEGA, LACHA, TOPO, ILMEN

leather ..... YUFT, JUPTI

Little ...... UKRAINIAN

log hut ...... ISPA, ISBA

mammal........ DESMAN

marshal .... ZHUKOV, KUTUZOV

measure .... VERST, ARSHIN, ARCHINE, LOF

mister ...... GOSPODIN

monarchy founder ...... RURIK

monetary unit .... RUBLE

"mother of cities" .. KIEV

mountain .... ALAI, URAL

museum .... HERMITAGE
musical instrument .....
BALALAIKA
name for Russia ....
ROSSIYA
negative/no .... NYET
news agency ....NOVOSTI,
TASS
novelist .... TOLSTOI,
TOLSTOY, GORKI,
GORKY
oboe .... SZOPELKA
oil center .... BAKU
operatic singer ....
CHALIAPIN
painter .... CHAGALL
parliament .... D(O)UMA
peasant .... KULAK,
MUZHIK, MUZJIK
peasant cap ...... ASKA
peasants' district ....
VOLOST
peninsula ..... CRIMEA
physiologist ..... PAVLOV
pianist ..... RACHMANN
plain ... STEPPE, TUNDRA
plane .... MIG, ILYUSHIN
poet .... PUSHKIN
pound .... POOD
premier .... KOSYGIN,
STALIN, BULGANIN,
KHRUSCHEV, MALENKOV
president ..... SHVERNIK
prison .... ETAPE
region .... MARI, SIBERIA
resort ... YALTA, ODESSA,
SOCHI
revolutionary leader .....
LENIN, KERENSKY,
TROTSKY
river ...... VOLGA, NEVA,
ONEGA, DONETS, OREL,
LENA, URAL, DVINA,
UFA
ruling family ....
ROMANOFF, ROMANOV
saint .... OLGA
scarf .... BABUSHKA
sea .... ARAL
seaport .... PETSAMO
secret service ... CHEKA,
KGB, GAY-PAY-OO,
OGPU, NKVD, MVD
slang .... COMMIE
soup .... BORSCH
soviet, rural ..... VOLOST

spacecraft ..... SPUTNIK,
VOYUZ
squadron ..... ESKADRA
stockade .... ETAPE
teapot .... SAMOVAR
trade union ...... ARTEL
urn .... SAMOVAR
vehicle .... TROIKA
villa .... DACHA
village .... MIR
violinist......... ELMAN,
ZIMBALIST
wagon .... TELEGA
weight .. DOLA, POOD, PUD
wheat .... EMMER
whip .... KNOUT
windstorm .... BURAN
wolfhound .... ALAN,
BORZOI
yes .... DA
youth organization ....
KOMSOMOL
Russo-Japanese warship .....
MIKASA
rust .... OXIDE, ERODE,
VERDIGRIS, FUNGUS,
CORRODE, AERUGO
colored .... RUFOUS
fungus .... AECIA
life cycle of ..... TELIAL
on bronze .... PATINA
plant .... FERRUGO
sorus .... TELIUM
rustic ... YOKEL, CHURL, RUBE,
BUCOLIC, GEOPONIC,
CLOD, BOOR(ISH), HIND,
RURAL, BUM(P)KIN,
ARTLESS, ARCADIAN,
HAYSEED, HICK,
HOBNAIL
lover .... SWAIN
peasant ...... AGRESTIAN
pipe .... REED, CORN
rustle ..... SWISH, SUSURRATE
of silk skirt .. FROUFROU
up ... COLLECT, FORAGE
rustler ...... THIEF, ROBBER
object of .... CATTLE
rustling .... SUSURRANT,
SWISHING, FROUFROU
sound .... SUSURROUS,
SOUGH, SWISH
Rustum's son .... SOHRAB
rusty .... SHABBY
rut ...... GROOVE, FURROW,
TRACK, HEAT, ROUTINE

rutabaga ..... TURNIP, SWEDE
rutaceous plant .... RUE,
       ORANGE, LEMON, LIME
Ruth, husband of ...... BOAZ
    mother-in-law of .. NAOMI
    sister of .... EILEEN
    son of .... OBED
Ruthenia .... RUSSIA
Ruthenian .... UKRAINIAN
ruthless ...... PITILESS, CRUEL
rutilate ..... GLOW, GLITTER,
                GLEAM
Ruy Diaz de Bivar .. (EL) CID

Rwanda capital ...... KIGALI
    neighbor ...... BURUNDI
    people .... HUTU
    president ... KAYIBANDA
rye .... RIE, GYPSY, GRASS,
        CEREAL, WHISKY, GRASS,
               GENTLEMAN
    disease .... BLACKRUST,
               ERGOT
    grass .... DARNEL
    liquor .... WHISK(E)Y
ryot .... PEASANT
Ryukyu island ..... OKINAWA

S

S-curve .... OGEE, ESS
    Greek .... SIGMA
    Hebrew .... SIN
    letter .... ESS
    mark .... POTHOOK
    shaped .... SIGMATE,
          SIGMOID, ESS
    shaped molding .... OGEE
    shaped seat ....
       TETE-A-TETE, VIS-A-VIS
    shaped worm .... ESS
    sound .... HISS
Sa, in chemistry ... SAMARIUM
Saar capital ... SAARBRUCKEN
Saarinen, architect ..... EERO
Saba .... SHEBA
Sabah capital ..... JESSELTON,
       KOTA KINABALU
    part of .... LABUAN
    peak .... KINABALU
sabadilla alkaloid .. VERATRIA,
          VERATRIN(E)
Sabaist's object of worship ....
             STARS
sabalo .... MILKFISH
Sabatini, novelist ..... RAFAEL
Sabbath .. SATURDAY, SUNDAY
Sabbatical privilege ..... REST,
             LEAVE
saber ... SWORD, YATAG(H)AN
    toothed animal .... TIGER
sable ...... BLACK, FUR, FELT,
    DARK, MUSTELINE, SKUNK,
      SOBOL, LEMMING
    animal like ..... MARTEN,
         WEASEL
    fur .... ZIBEL(L)INE
    imitation ..... KOLINSKY
sablefish .... BESHOW
sabot .... (WOODEN)SHOE,

      PATTEN, CLOG, DINGHY
Sabrina river .... SEVERN
sabulous ..... SANDY, GRITTY
Sac .. INDIAN, SAUK, POUCH,
      VENTER, BURSA, CYST,
      VESICLE, ASCUS
    cavity like ...... BLISTER
    part of ... STRATEGIC, AIR,
           COMMAND
    small .... SACCULE
    spore .... ASCUS
sacaton .... GRASS, HAY
saccate .... POUCHLIKE
saccharine .. SWEET, HONEYED,
      SIRUPY, SUGARY
saccharize .... FERMENT
saccharose ... SUCROSE, SUGAR
saccule .... SAC, BOSS
sacerdotal .... PRIESTLY,
          HIERATIC
sachem .... CHIEF, SAGAMORE
sachet .... PAD, BAG, POWDER
Sacs, Ger. playwright .. HANS
    trade of .... COBBLER
Sachsen .... SAXONY
sack .... BAG, JACKET, SACQUE,
    DISMISS(AL), DISCHARGE,
    PLUNDER, RAVAGE, POKE,
    LOOT, BED, BASE, WINE,
    POUCH, GUNNY, PILLAGE
    making cloth .. OSNABURG
sackbut-like instrument ......
      LYRE, TROMBONE
sackcloth and ____ .... ASHES
    symbol of .... PENITENCE,
    MOURNING, REMORSE
sacking .... BURLAP
sacque .... JACKET, SACK
sacrament .... BAPTISM,
    PENANCE, MATRIMONY,

CONFIRMATION, EUCHARIST,
    MASS
sacrarium .. CHANCEL, SHRINE,
    SANCTUARY
sacred ..... HOLY, HALLOWED,
    VENERATED, INVIOLATE,
    DIVINE, SACROSANCT,
    INVIOLABLE, PIOUS,
    BLESSED, SAINT
  beetle .... SCARAB
  bird .... IBIS
  book ...... BIBLE, KORAN
  bull ...... APIS, HAPI
  chest .... CIST
  city ..... MEDINA, MECCA,
    JERUSALEM, BENARES
  College member ....
    CARDINAL
  combining form .. HIERO,
    HAGI(O)
  container ..... PYX, CIST,
    AMA
  cord .... RUSTI
  cow ...... UNTOUCHABLE
  fig tree .... PIPAL
  food .... MANNA
  fountain ... HIPPOCRENE
  hymn............ PSALM
  image ..... PIETA, ICON,
    IKON
  language .... PALI
  literature .... VEDA
  make .... SANCTIFY,
    CONSECRATE, BLESS,
    HALLOW
  melody .... CHORALE
  music .... MOTET
  object .... RELIC
  ode .... HYMN
  opposed to .... PROFANE,
    SECULAR
  picture .... ICON
  place .. SHRINE, SANCTUM
  plant .... RAGTREE
  poem ..... PSLAM, HYMN
  prohibition .... TABU,
    TABOO
  relic .... HALIDOM
  scriptures ...... KORAN,
    BIBLE
  shield .... ANCILE
  song ..... MOTET, PSALM
  things, traffic in .. SIMONY
  tree ..... PIPAL, BO(TREE)
  wine vessel .... AMA
  word .... LOGOS, OM

  writer .. HAGIOGRAPHER
  writing ..... SCRIPTURE,
    AVESTA
sacredness .... SANCTITY
sacrifice .... OFFERING,
    OBLATION, COST
  burning place of .... PILE
  by killing ..... IMMOLATE
  god demanding ....
    MOLOCH, MOLECH
  human .... SUTTEE
  object of .... HOMAGE,
    APPEASEMENT,
    ATONEMENT, EXPIATION
  place of .... ALTAR
  play, in baseball ... BUNT,
    FLY
sacrificial animal ..... LAMB
  block .... ALTAR
  fire .... IGNI
  offering .... IMMOLATION,
    HIERA, LAMB
  rite .... LIBATION
  table .... ALTAR
sacrilege .... DESECRATION,
    PROFANATION
sacrilegious .... PROFANE,
  IRREVERENT, BLASPHEMOUS
sacrist(an) .... SEXTON
sacristy .... VESTRY
sacrosanct ..... DIVINE, HOLY,
    SACRED, INVIOLABLE
sad .... BAD, DEJECTED,
    DOLEFUL, TRISTE,
    DOLOROUS, BLUE,
    DOLENT, DISMAL
  sack .... BOLO
saddle ..... LOAD, ENCUMBER,
    SEAT, PAD, PANEL
  attachment ..... HOLSTER
  bag .... ALFÓRJA
  band .... GIRTH
  blanket .... TILPAH
  bow .... POMMEL
  cloth ..... PANEL, MANTA
  colloquial ..... PIGSKIN
  cover for ..... MOCHILA
  footrest .... STIRRUP
  front part ..... POMMEL
  gaiter .... GAMBADO
  girth .... CINCH
  gun case .... HOLSTER
  horse .... NAG, PALFREY,
    REMUDA, HACK
  legging .... GAMBADO
  lining .... PANEL

pack .... APAREJO
pad .... CORONA
part ... GIRTH, POMMEL,
CINCH, STIRRUP, CANTLE,
LATIGO, PAD
rear part .... CANTLE
seat behind ..... PILLION
stirrup .... GAMBADO
strap ..... GIRTH, CINCH
Sadducee, opposite of ....
PHARISEE
sadness ... PATHOS, DOLENTE,
DOLOR
sadhi .... TSADI
sadiron .... FLATIRON
sadism .... MALTREATMENT
sadistic .... CRUEL
safari ...... JOURNEY, TREK,
EXPEDITION, CARAVAN
safe ... PRUDENT, CAUTIOUS,
VAULT, SECURE
conduct .. PASS, CONVOY,
PASSPORT
cracker ...... YEGG(MAN)
safeblower .. PETERMAN, YEGG
safeguard ... PROTECT, PASS,
CONVOY, GUARD
safekeeping .... CUSTODY,
STORAGE
safety .... SECURITY
device .... FENDER,
MAE WEST, BUMPER,
ARMOR, CATCH, VALVE
lamp .... DAVY
place of .... HAVEN,
REFUGE, SANCTUARY,
HARBOR, ISLAND
saffron .... DYE, PLANT,
SEASONING, YELLOW,
CROCUS
safrol(e) .... OIL
sag .... SINK, DROOP, CURVE,
HANG, WILT, DECLINE,
DRIFT, LEEWAY
saga ...... EPIC, EDDA, TALE,
LEGEND, ILIAD
sagacious .... PERCEPTIVE,
SHREWD, DISCERNING,
ASTUTE, WISE, SAPIENT
sagacity ... ACUMEN, WISDOM
sagamore .... SACHEM
sage ... WISE, SOLON, NESTOR,
PLANT, MINT, SCHOLAR,
SEER, SAPIENT, HERB
scarlet .... SALVIA
hen .... GROUSE

of Emporia .... WHITE
Sagebrush State .... NEVADA
sagger .... (FIRE)CLAY
Sagitta ... ARROW, KEYSTONE,
CONSTELLATION
sagittary .... CENTAUR
sago .... STARCH, PALM,
GOMUTI
saguaro .... CACTUS
Sahara ... DESERT, WASTELAND
fertile area ...... FEZZAN
like the .... ARID
wind .... LESTE
sahib .... SIR, MASTER
saiga .... ANTELOPE
Saigon Chinese district ......
CHOLON
sail .... CANVAS, GLIDE,
FLOAT, NAVIGATE, CRUISE,
LUG, KITE, VELA, VOYAGE,
SPANKER, JIGGER
around the world ....
CIRCUMNAVIGATE
bellying part of ... BUNT
close to the wind ... LUFF,
POINT
corner .... CLEW
edge of .... LUFF
fastener .... CLEW
fore-and-aft ... SPANKER,
MIZ(Z)EN
free edge of ...... LEECH
furl .... REEF
haul up .... TRICE
hoist .... CLUE-UP
ice .... SCOOTER
kind of .. JIB, FOREROYAL,
MAIN, ROYAL, LATEEN
loop .... CRINGLE
near the wind ..... LUFF
out to sea ..... OUTSTAND
part of .... REEF
poetic .... SHEET
reduce .... REEF
ring .... CRINGLE
rope ..... HALYARD, TYE
specified distance ... LOG
square .... LUG
tackle .... HALYARD
tapering cloth .... GORE
triangular .. LATEEN, JIB
sailboat ... VINTA, SAIC, SLOOP,
CAIQUE, SMACK, DHOW,
BARK, BARQUE, SKIFF,
YACHT, KUMPIT, YAWL,
KETCH

sailfish .. .... (BASKING)SHARK
   kin of .. .. MARLIN
sailing, oblique .. LOXODROMICS
   race .. .. REGATTA
   raft .. .. BALSA
   vessel .. .. SCHOONER,
      GALLEON, FRIGATE,
      KETCH, SLOOP, YAWL
sailor .. . MARINER, GOB, TAR,
   SALT, LASCAR, NAVYMAN,
   JACK, SEADOG, DECK HAND,
   SHIPMAN, SEAMAN, HAT,
      SARTOR
   bed of .. .. HAMMOCK
   clumsy .. .. LUBBER
   contentious .. SEA LAWYER
   drink of .. .. GROG
   experienced .. SHELLBACK
   jersey .. .. FROCK
   kidnap .. .. .. SHANGHAI
   inexperienced, new .. .. ..
      LANDSMAN, LUBBER
   prospective .. .. .. MIDDY
sailor's bad luck .. . .. JONAH,
      JONAS
   biscuit .. .. TACK
   call .. .. AHOY
   choice .. PORGY, PIGFISH
   church .. .. BETHEL
   cord .. LANYARD, LANIARD
   dish .. .. SCOUSE
   handicraft .. . SCRIMSHAW
   hat .. .. .. SOU(TH)WESTER
   jumper .. .. BLOUSE
   leave .. .. .' FURLOUGH
   mess tub .. .. KID
   patron saint .. .. .. ELMO
   patroness .. .. .. EULALIA
   quarters .. ..
      FO(RE)C(A)S(T)LE
   rebellion .. .. .. MUTINY
   social call .. .. GAM
   song .. .. .. SHANT(E)Y,
      CHANTEY
   sword .. .. CUTLAS(S)
   underwear .. .. SKIVY
   work song .. SHANT(E)Y,
      CHANTEY
   "yes" .. .. AYE-AYE
sain .. .. CROSS, BLESS
saint (see patron).. .. SACRED,
   CANONIZE, HOLY, BLESSED,
      SAN(TA)
   Anthony's fire .. ..
      ERYSIPELAS
   Bernard .. .. DOG

Andrew's Cross .. ..
      SATIRE, SALTIER
Bernard monk's concern ..
      TRAVELER,
      WAYFARER
declare person a .. ..
      CANONIZE
Elmo's fire .. .. CORPOSANT
homage to a .. .. DULIA
Joan character .. DAUPHIN
John's bread .. .. .. CAROB,
      ALGAROBA
John's evil .... EPILEPSY
Laurent, fashion stylist ..
      YVES
memorial of .. .. .. RELIC
Patrick's Day celebrant ..
      IRISH
sacred image of .. . ICON,
      (E)IKON
tomb of .. .. SHRINE
worshiper .. . HAGIOLATER
Vitus' dance .. CHOREA
Saint's day .. .. FIESTA
saintly .. .. PIOUS
saints, author of lives of .. .. ..
      HAGIOGRAPHER
catalogue/list of .. ..
   DIPTYCH, HAGIOLOGY,
      CANON
register .. .. .. MENOLOGY
rule by .. . HAGIOCRACY,
   HAGIARCHY, THEOCRACY
worship of .. HAGIOLATRY
sake .. . PURPOSE, END, CAUSE,
   BEHALF, BENEFIT, MOTIVE,
      ACCOUNT
saker .. .. FALCON
Sakhalin .. .. KARAFUTO
Saki .. .. MUNRO
Sakti .. .. MAYA
sal volatile .. .. .. HARTSHORN
salaam .. .. OBEISANCE,
      GREETING, BOW
salable .. .. VENDIBLE,
      MARKETABLE
salacious .. .. OBSCENE,
      LUSTFUL
salad .. . LETTUCE, (COLD)DISH,
      (COLE)SLAW
   days .. .. TEENS
   dressing .. MAYONNAISE,
      REMO(U)LADE
   fruit .. .. MACEDOINE
   green .. .. .. DANDELION,
   UDO, CRESS(E), ENDIVE

herb ..... CRESS, ENDIVE
kind of .... TOSSED
leaves .... ESCAROLE,
    SORREL
vegetable .... ENDIVE,
    CHICORY, SUCCORY
Saladin's foes .... CRUSADERS
salamander .... REPTILE, EFT,
    NEWT, TRITON, POKER,
    HELLBENDER, MUD PUPPY,
    LIZARD, WATER DOG,
    AXOLTL
Salambria .... PENEUS
salami .... SAUSAGE
salary ... EMOLUMENT, WAGE,
    COMPENSATION, PAY,
    STIPEND, SCREW
additional to .. PERQUISITE
increase .... RAISE
sale .... SELLING, DEAL,
    VENDITION, MARKET,
    BARTER
incentive .... REBATE
kind of .... AUCTION,
    INVENTORY, CLEARANCE,
    CASH, RUMMAGE, FIRE
Salem witchcraft trial judge ..
    SEWALL
salep .... TUBER
drink from ...... SALOOP
source of .... ORCHID
saleratus ...... BAKING SODA
sales talk .... PATTER, PITCH,
    LINE, SPIEL
salesman ... CLERK, DRUMMER
salicaceous tree ..... WILLOW,
    POPLAR
salicin .... GLUCOSIDE
saliferous ..... SALINE, SALTY
salient ... CAPERING, LEAPING,
    PROMINENT
salientian .... TOAD, FROG
salina ... POND, LAKE, MARSH
saline ...... SALTY, MARINAL
solution .... BRINE
Salish .... INDIAN, FLATHEAD
saliva ... SPIT(TLE), SPUTUM
enzyme .... PTYALIN,
    AMYLASE
excessive secretion of ....
    PTYALISM
resembling ..... SIALOID
running from mouth ....
    SLAVER, DRIVEL, DROOL
wet/smear with .. SLOBBER
salix ... ITEA, OSIER, WILLOW

salle .... ROOM
sallet .... HELMET
sallow ... PASTY, PALE,
    PARLOUS, WILLOW, OSIER
sally ... SORTIE, QUIP, RETORT,
    JAUNT, EXCURSION,
    WITTICISM, RIPOSTE,
    ISSUE, RUSH OUT, JEST,
    JOKE
Lunn .... TEACAKE
with the fan ...... RAND
salmacis .... NYMPH
salmagundi ...... POTPOURRI,
    MEDLEY, OLIO, MIXTURE
salmon .... GRILSE, MORT,
    CHINOOK, JACK, QUINNAT,
    SPROD, COHO, SOCKEYE,
    HOLIA, CHINUCK,
    OUANANICHE
chinook ...... QUINNAT
color .... PINK
dog .... CHUM, KETA
eggs .... ROE
eggs relish .... CAVIAR(E)
female ... BAGGIT, RAUN
gristle .... GIB
hook .... KIP, GIB
humpback ...... HADDO,
    HOLIA
male ..... COCK, KIPPER
net .... MAUD
one year old ... BLUECAP
quinnat ...... CHINOOK
red .... SOCKEYE
running up river ....
    ANADROMOUS
salted .... LOX
silver .... COHO
smoked .... LOX
trout ...... NAMAYCUSH,
    STEELHEAD, HARDHEAD
young ..... SMOLT, PARR,
    GRILSE, SAMLET
salmonoid ...... STEELHEAD,
    TROUT, NAMAYCUSH
Salome's parent ... HEROD(IAS)
salon .... GALLERY, HALL,
    LEVEE, DRAWING ROOM,
    ART SHOW, SHOP
Salonika .... THERMA
saloon .... BAR, HALL, SEDAN,
    GINMILL, BARRELHOUSE,
    DIVE, DRAMSHOP,
    GROGGERY, HONKY-TONK,
    TAVERN, CANTINA, OASIS,
    GROGSHOP

keeper ‑‑ ‑‑ ‑‑ PUBLICAN
saloop ‑‑ ‑‑ ‑‑ ‑‑ ‑‑ DRINK
Salop ‑‑ ‑‑ ‑‑ ‑‑ SHROPSHIRE
salpa ‑‑ ‑‑ ‑‑ ‑‑ ‑‑ TUNICATE
salt ‑‑ ‑‑ SAL, HUMOR, SAILOR,
    SEASON, TAR, BRINE,
    BORAX, PICRATE, WIT, NACL
away ‑‑ ‑‑ STORE, SAVE
acid ‑‑ ‑‑ ‑‑ ‑‑ OLEATE
alkaline ‑‑ ‑‑ ‑‑ BORAX
bed ‑‑ ‑‑ ‑‑ ‑‑ ‑‑ VAT
bottle ‑‑ ‑‑ CRUET, CASTER,
    CASTOR
chemical ‑‑ ‑‑ ‑‑ ESTER
crystalline ‑‑ ‑‑ NITER,
    NITRE
deposit ‑‑ ‑‑ ‑‑ ‑‑ LICK
factory ‑‑ ‑‑ ‑‑ SALTERN
lake ‑‑ ‑‑ ‑‑ ‑‑ SINK
malic acid ‑‑ ‑‑ MALATE
marsh ‑‑ ‑‑ ‑‑ ‑‑ SALINA
meat ‑‑ ‑‑ ‑‑ SALAMI
organic ‑‑ ‑‑ ‑‑ ESTER
pertaining to ‑‑ ‑‑ SALINE
pond ‑‑ ‑‑ ‑‑ ‑‑ SALINA
pork ‑‑ ‑‑ ‑‑ SOWBELLY
preserve with ‑‑ ‑‑ CORN
resembling ‑‑ ‑‑ HALOID
rheum ‑‑ ‑‑ ‑‑ ECZEMA
rock ‑‑ ‑‑ ‑‑ ‑‑ HALITE
soluble ‑‑ ‑‑ ‑‑ SALAR
spring ‑‑ ‑‑ LICK, SALINA
tax ‑‑ ‑‑ ‑‑ ‑‑ GABELLE
tree ‑‑ ‑‑ ATLE, TAMARISK
water ‑‑ ‑‑ ‑‑ ‑‑ BRINE
saltant ‑‑ LEAPING, DANCING,
    JUMPING
saltation ‑‑ ‑‑ ‑‑ PALPITATION,
    MUTATION, LEAP(ING),
    BEATING, DANCING
salted ‑‑ ‑‑ ‑‑ ‑‑ ‑‑ CORNED
saltpeter ‑‑ ‑‑ ‑‑ NITER, NITRE
saltworks ‑‑ ‑‑ SALTERN, SALINA
saltwort ‑‑ ‑‑ ‑‑ BARILLA, KALI
salty ‑‑ ‑‑ ‑‑ PUNGENT, WITTY,
    PIQUANT, SHARP, BRINY
    SALINE
salubrious ‑‑ ‑‑ ‑‑ SALUTARY
Salus ‑‑ ‑‑ ‑‑ ‑: ‑‑ HYGEIA
concern of ‑‑ ‑‑ HEALTH,
    PROSPERITY
salutary ‑‑ ‑‑ ‑‑ SALUBRIOUS,
    HEALTHFUL, BENEFICIAL,
    WHOLESOME, HEALTHY
salutation ‑‑ ‑‑ ‑‑ GREETING,

WELCOME, SALAAM, AVE,
    HAIL, BOW, ALOHA
salute ‑‑ ‑‑ GREET, WELCOME,
    BOW, TIP, HAIL, KISS,
    CURTSY
flag ‑‑ ‑‑ ‑‑ ‑‑ ‑‑ DIP
gun ‑‑ ‑‑ ‑‑ ‑‑ ‑‑ SALVO
salvage ‑‑ ‑‑ ‑‑ SAVE, RESCUE
salvation ‑‑ ‑‑ ‑‑ RESCUE,
    REDEMPTION
Army founder ‑‑ BOOTH
salve ‑‑ ‑‑ SOOTHE, PLASTER,
    BALM, UNGUENT,
    DEMULCENT, NARD, CHRISM,
    LOTION, HAIL, ASSUAGE,
    SMOOTH, OINTMENT, POMADE
salver ‑‑ ‑‑ ‑‑ TRAY, WAITER
salvia ‑‑ ‑‑ ‑‑ DEER, RUSA, SAGE
salvo ‑‑ ‑‑ ‑‑ BROADSIDE,
    FUSILLADE, VOLLEY, SALUTE,
    EVASION, EXCUSE
Samantha, actress ‑‑ EGGAR
samara ‑‑ ‑‑ KEY FRUIT, CHAT
tree bearing ‑‑ ‑‑ ASH, ELM
Samaritan magician ‑‑ MAGUS
sambar ‑‑ DEER, RUSA, MAHA
sambuke-like instrument ‑‑ ‑‑ ‑‑
    HARP
same ‑‑ ‑‑ ‑‑ DITTO, ALIKE,
    IDENTICAL, EQUAL, IDEM,
    SIMILAR
combining form ‑‑ HOMO
Samedi ‑‑ ‑‑ ‑‑ ‑‑ SATURDAY
samiel ‑‑ ‑‑ ‑‑ ‑‑ SIMOOM
samisen-like instrument ‑‑ ‑‑
    BANJO
samite ‑‑ ‑‑ ‑‑ ‑‑ LAMB
samlet ‑‑ ‑‑ PARR, SALMON
Samoa ‑‑ ‑‑ ‑‑ NAVIGATORS
Samoan ‑‑ ‑‑ ‑‑ POLYNESIAN
bird ‑‑ ‑‑ ‑‑ ‑‑ ‑‑ IAO
capital ‑‑ ‑‑ ‑‑ TUTUILA
city ‑‑ ‑‑ ‑‑ ‑‑ APIA
cloth ‑‑ ‑‑ ‑‑ ‑‑ TAPA
clothes ‑‑ ‑‑ ‑‑ PAREUS
costume ‑‑ ‑‑ PULETASI
council ‑‑ ‑‑ ‑‑ FONO
island ‑‑ SAVAII, UPOLU,
    TUTUILA
loincloth ‑‑ ‑‑ LAVA-LAVA
maiden ‑‑ ‑‑ ‑‑ TAUPO
mollusk ‑‑ ‑‑ ‑‑ ‑‑ ASI
seaport ‑‑ ‑‑ ‑‑ APIA
waist cloth ‑‑ LAVA-LAVA
warrior ‑‑ ‑‑ ‑‑ TOA
samovar ‑‑ ‑‑ TEAPOT, URN

samp .... GRITS, HOMINY, PORRIDGE, (CORN)MEAL
sampan .... BOAT
samphire .... GLASSWORT
sample ... SPECIMEN, PATTERN, EXAMPLE, TASTE, TEST
  cloth .... SWATCH
sampler .... TASTER
sampler item .... MOTTO
"Samson and Delilah"
  composer ... SAINT SAENS
Samson's deathplace .... GAZA
  mistress .... DELILAH
  vulnerable part ..... HAIR
Samuel .... PROPHET
  parent of ..... HANNAH, ELKANAH
  son of .... ABIA
  teacher .... ELI
samurai ..... WARRIOR, RONIN
San .... SAINT
  Antonio shrine ... ALAMO
  Francisco .... FRISCO
  Marino mount ... TITANO
  Marino rulers ... REGENTS
sanatory .... CURATIVE
sanbenito wearer .. PENITENT, HERETIC
Sancho Panza's master .... (DON) QUIXOTE
sanctify .... PURIFY, CONSECRATE, HALLOW, BLESS
sanctimonious .... DEVOUT
sanction .... APPROVAL, LAW, SUPPORT, FIAT, DECREE, RATIFY, AMEN, IMPRIMATUR, APPROVE, PERMIT, FIRMAN, ENDORSE
sanctity ... HOLINESS, PURITY
sanctuary ... CHURCH, REFUGE, HAVEN, TEMPLE, SHELTER, BEMA, ASYLUM, FANE, SHRINE, GRIT, HALIDOM(E)
  animal/bird .... RESERVATION
  portable ... TABERNACLE
sanctum .... STUDY, DEN, ADYTUM, SMOOTH, POLISH
sand .... GRIT, COURAGE, POLISH, SMOOTH, BEACH
  bank .... CAY, SHOAL
  bar .... SHOAL, SPIT, SHELF, REEF
  dab .... FLATFISH
  deposit .... ESKER

dollar .... SEA URCHIN
eel .... LA(U)NCE
flea ... CHIGOE, CHIGGER
George ..... DUDEVANT, DUPIN
hill .... DUNE, DENE
launce .... EEL
lily .... SOAPROOT
lot game .... BASEBALL
living in .. ARENICOLOUS
mound ..... DENE, DUNE
particles .... SILT, GRIT
ridge .... ESKER, ESKAR, DUNE, OSAR
slang ... GRIT, COURAGE
snake .... ERYX
trotter .... CAMEL
viper .... HOGNOSE
sandal .... (OVER)SHOE, SLIPPER, HUARACHE
  fastener ...... LATCHET, LACET
  wooden .... PATTEN
sandals, winged ..... TALARIA
sandalwood .... INCENSE, SANTAL, ALGUM, ALMUG, LABURNUM
  Island .. SUMBA, SOEMBA
sandarac ..... RESIN, INCENSE, ADAR, REALGAR, ARAR, ALERSE, MOROCCO
sandbank .... CAY, SPIT
  channel .... GAT
sandbar .. SHELF, SHOAL, SPIT
Sandburg, poet .... CARL
sander .. POLISHER, SMOOTHER
sandglass .... HOURGLASS
  what it tells ...... TIME
sandhog .... DIGGER
sandpaper .... ABRASIVE
sandpiper ...... YELLOWLEGS, BIRD, KNOT, STINT, GREENSHANK, JACKSNIPE, DUNLIN, TATTLER, RUFF, REE, STILT, PLOVER, STIB, TEREK
  Arctic .... PECTORAL
  beach ..... SANDERLING
  female .... REEVE
  relative ... PLOVER, SNIPE
  spotted ...... PEETWEET
sands ...... BEACH, MOMENTS
sandstone .... MEDINA, PSAMMITE, BEREA, PAAR, ITACOLUMITE, ARKOSE
sandstorm ... SIMOOM, SAMIEL

sandwich bread .... RYE
    filling ..... HAM, CHEESE,
              SALAMI
    Islands .... HAWAII
sandy .... ARENACEOUS,
        SHIFTING, SABULOUS,
        GRITTY, ARENOSE
    color .... GINGER
    mound .... DOWN
    soil .... LOAM, LOESS
    waste .... DESERT
sane ..... RATIONAL, SOBER,
        SENSIBLE, WISE,
    REASONABLE, LUCID, SOUND
sanforize .... PRESHRINK
sang froid ...... COMPOSURE,
    INSOUCIANCE, COOL, POISE
Sangraal ...... (HOLY)GRAIL
sanguinaria ... POPPY, PLANT,
        BLOODROOT
sanguine .... RED, RUDDY,
    CONFIDENT, HOPEFUL,
        OPTIMISTIC
    person .... OPTIMIST
Sanhedrin ... COURT, COUNCIL
sanicle .... PARSLEY
sanies .... PUS, DISCHARGE
sanitarium .... RESORT
    building ...... PAVILION
sanitary .... HYGIENIC
sannup .... INDIAN,
        ALGONQUIAN
sans .... WITHOUT
    culotte ....
        REVOLUTIONARY,
        RADICAL
    pareil .... PEERLESS
    souci ...... GAY, CASTLE
    Souci site ...... POTSDAM
Sanskrit .... VEDIC, INDIC
    dialect .... PALI
    epic .... RAMAYANA
    god .... INDRA, VAYU
Santa .... HOLY, SAINT
    ——— .... FE, ANITA,
        CLAUS, BARBARA
    Claus ... KRISS, KRINGLE
    Claus' sled runner ......
        REINDEER
    Claus' vehicle ..... SLED
    Claus' way ... CHIMNEY
    stand-in of .. PAPA, POP,
        DAD(DY)
Santiago de Cuba ... ORIENTE
santon .... HERMIT, MONK
santonica .... WORMWOOD,

        WORMSEED
Sao Salvador .... BAHIA
sap ... JUICE, TRENCH, FLUID,
        VIGOR, FOOL, DRAIN,
    UNDERMINE, DIG, EXHAUST,
        WEAKEN
    drain .. SPILE, TAP, SPOUT
    flow of .... LACTESCENCE
    tree .... LATEX, MILK,
        BALATA
sapajou .... CAPUCHIN,
        MONKEY, GRISON
saphead .... FOOL, DOLT
sapid .... SAVORY, TASTY,
        TASTEFUL
sapience .... WISDOM,
        SAGACITY
sapient ... WISE, DISCERNING,
        SAGE
sapindaceous plant ....
        SOAPBERRY
sapless .... DRY, INSIPID
sapling .... YOUTH
saponaceous .... SOAPY
saponin .... GLUCOSIDE
sapor .... SAVOR, FLAVOR,
        RELISH, TASTE, TANG
saporous ...... TASTY, SAVORY
sapota .... MARMALADE,
        SAPODILLA
sapper ... DIGGER, TRENCHER
Sapphira's husband .. ANANIAS
    weakness .... LYING
sapphire ... BLUE, CORUNDUM,
        STONE, GEM
sapphirine .... SPINEL
Sappho's home .... LESBOS
    work .... POETRY
sappy .... JUICY
    slang ... SILLY, FATUOUS,
        FOOLISH, INANE
saprophyte .... FUNGUS
sapsago .... CHEESE
sapsucker ..... WOODPECKER
sapwood .... ALBURNUM
saraband .... DANCE
Saracen ...... ARAB, MOSLEM,
        MOOR
    foe of .... CRUSADER
    leader .... SALADIN
Sarah, diminutive of ... SADIE,
        SAL, SALLY

handmaid of ..... HAGAR
husband of ... ABRAHAM
son .... ISAAC
saran .... RESIN
Sarawak rajah ...... BROOKE
sarcasm ... JEER, GIBE, IRONY,
SATIRE
sarcastic .... IRONIC(AL),
SATIRIC(AL), MORDANT,
CAUSTIC, SARDONIC,
VITRIOLIC
sarcoma .... TUMOR
sarcophagus ... TOMB, COFFIN
sard .... CHALCEDONY
sardine .. PILCHARD, HERRING,
LOUR
fish like .... BRISLING
Sardinian city ..... CAGLIARI
coin .... CARLINE
duchy .... SAVOIE
language ...... CATALAN
ruling house ..... SAVOY
seaport .... BOSA
sheep ..... MOUF(F)LON
sardius .... RUBY, SARD
sardonic .... SARCASTIC,
IRONIC(AL), SATIRIC(AL)
sardonyx product ..... CAMEO
Sarg, U.S. puppeteer ... TONY
sargasso ...... (GULF)WEED,
SEAWEED
sark .... CHEMISE, SHIRT
sarmentose plant ....
STRAWBERRY
sarong .... WAISTCLOTH,
PAREUS, LOINCLOTH
Sarpedon's parent ...... ZEUS,
EUROPA
sarsaparilla .... BEVERAGE,
SMILAX, MEAD
sartor .... TAILOR
sash .... WAISTBAND,
CUMMERBUND, FRAME,
SCARF, TOBE, GIRDLE, OBI,
BELT
pane holder ...... SPRIG
sashay .... GAD, GLIDE
sasin ...... BUCK, ANTELOPE
Saskatchewan capital .. REGINA
saskatoon .... (SHAD)BUSH,
SHADBLOW
sass ... DESSERT, PRESERVES,
VEGETABLE, TALK
sassaby .... ANTELOPE
sassafras drink ..... SALOOP,
ROOT BEER

oil .... SAFROL(E)
Sassenach .... SAXON,
ENGLISHMAN, LOWLANDER
Sassoon, poet ...... SIEGFRIED
sassy ..... IMPUDENT, SAUCY,
TREE
Satan .... DEVIL, DEIL,
LUCIFER, BELIAL, EBLIS,
MEPHISTO, APOLLYON,
ABADDON, (OLD)HARRY,
(OLD)NICK, SHAITAN,
HORNIE
co-rebel of ...... AZAZEL
satanic .... DIABOLICAL,
INFERNAL, WICKED
satchel .... ETUI, SCRIP,
ETWEE, VALISE, (HAND)BAG
sate ...... GRATIFY, SATIATE,
SATISFY, GLUT, SURFEIT,
FILL
satellite .... FOLLOWER,
DEPENDENT, MOON, PLANET
artificial .... SPUTNIK,
PLANETOID, LUNIK,
ECHO, EXPLORER,
PIONEER
path of .... ORBIT
shadow of ...... UMBRA
satiate ...... GRATIFY, GLUT,
SURFEIT, SATE, CLOY,
SATISFY, JADE
satin, adjective for ... SMOOTH,
SOFT, GLOSSY
fabric ...... RAYON, SILK,
NYLON, CYPRUS,
CYPRESS
fabric smooth like ......
VELVET
flower .... LUNARIA
imitation .... SATEEN,
SATINET(TE)
satiny .... LUSTROUS
satire .. IRONY, WIT, SARCASM,
PASQUINADE
Satirical .... IRONIC(AL),
SARCASTIC, CAUSTIC
work .... SKIT,
BURLESQUE, PARODY,
CARICATURE, LAMPOON
satirist .... JUVENAL
satirize .. RIDICULE, LAMPOON
in verse .... BERIME
satisfaction ..... ATONEMENT,
REPARATION, PAYMENT
for a killing .... CRO

for injuries ..... DAMAGES, GREE
satisfactory .... JAKE
satisfy .... GRATIFY, FULFILL, ANSWER, MEASURE UP, SOLVE, PLEASE
satisfying .... HUNKY
satrap ... GOVERNOR, TYRANT, SUBORDINATE
saturate .... SOAK, STEEP, SODDEN, SEETHE, DRENCH, SOP, IMBUE
saturaged state .. WET, SOGGY, SODDEN, SOAKED
Saturn ..... CRONUS, PLANET
in alchemy ...... LEAD
wife of .... OPS
saturnalia ... ORGY, REVELRY
saturniid .... MOTH
saturnine .... TACITURN, GLOOMY, GRAVE, MOROSE, GLUM
satyr ..... BUTTERFLY, DEITY, LECHER, FAUN, SILENUS
deity resembling a ..... SILENUS
god attended by ..... BACCHUS
staff of .... THYRSUS
Sau .... SAVA
sauce ..... DRESSING, SEASON, RELISH, SOY, CHILI, MELBA, SOUBISE, MORNAY, WORCESTER, MATELOTE, VELOUTE, CURRY, FLAVOR
and liqueurs .... CREMES
bean .... SOJA, SOY(A)
colloquial ... IMPUDENCE
flavoring material ...... CAPERS
fish .... ALEC
pepper .... TABASCO
spicy .... REMO(U)LADE
thickener .... ROUX
tomato .... CATSUP, KETCHUP
saucepan ...... POT, POSNET, CASSEROLE
saucer .... DISH
flying .... UFO
object likened to .... EYE
saucy ...... MALAPERT, RUDE, IMPUDENT, PERT, BOLD, INSOLENT, SASSY, PERKY, FRESH, COCKY,

IMPERTINENT, BRASH, FLIP(PANT), ARCH
girl ... MINX, MALAPERT, CHIT
talk .... LIP
Saudi Arabian capital .... MECCA, RIYADH
city .... MEDINA
desert ...... RED, NEFUD
inhabitant .... BEDOUIN
monetary unit ... RIYAL
port .... JIDDA
province .... HE(D)JAZ
principality ...... ASIR
religious center .. MECCA, MEDINA
ruler .... KING, FEISAL, (IBN)SAUD
state .... NEJD
sauger .... PERCH
Sauk .... SAC
Saul's father ...... KISH
general ...... ABNER
grandfather .... ABIEL, NER
kingdom ...... ISRAEL
shepherd .... DOEG
son .... JONATHAN
successor ...... DAVID
Sault Ste. Marie canals .. SOO
sauna ...... BATH(HOUSE)
saunter .... STROLL, LOITER, WALK, AMBLE, GAIT
across street ... JAYWALK
saurel ...... SCAD, SKATE
saurian ...... LIZARD, CROCODILE, DINOSAUR, REPTILE, ALLIGATOR
sauropod .... DINOSAUR
saury .. SKIPPER, LIZARDFISH
sausage ..... WEINER, WEENY, WEENIE, FRANKFURTER, SALAMI, PUDDING, (LIVER)WURST, BOLOGNA, SAVELOY
cover .... INTESTINE
shaped ...... ALLANTOID
saute .... FRY
sauterne ...... YQUEM, WINE
Sava ...... SAVE, SAU
savage ..... WILD, RUGGED, UNTAMED, FIERCE, FERAL, FEROCIOUS, HUN, FERINE, CRUEL, BARBARIAN, FELL, BESTIAL
Island .... NIUE
state .... FERITY

savanna(h) .... PLAIN, GRASSLAND
plain like .... PAMPAS, LLANO, STEPPE
savant .... SCHOLAR, SAGE, PUNDIT, PANDIT
save .... EXCEPT, RESCUE, SPARE, PRESERVE, BUT, SALVAGE, LAY BY, HOARD
all .... PINAFORE, OVERALLS
saveloy .... SAUSAGE
savin(e) ..... CEDAR, JUNIPER
saving ...... EXCEPT, FRUGAL
clause .... SALVO
in law .... EXCEPTION
savings bank .... SAVE-ALL
investments ..... LEGALS
savior .... REDEEMER, RESCUER, JESUS
savoir-faire .... TACT, DIPLOMACY
Savonarola, Ital. reformer .... GIROLAMO
savor ... SMACK, TASTE, SMELL, AROMA, TINGE, SEASON, FLAVOR, RELISH, SAPOR
savory ... SAPID, TOOTHSOME, MINT, SIPID, PIQUANT, YUMMY, TASTY, APPETIZING, SALTY, PALATABLE
smell .... AROMA
savoy .... CABBAGE
Savoyard show(man) ... RAREE
savvy .. UNDERSTAND, SHREWD, WISE, WISDOM
saw .... CUT, MOTTO, SAYING, MAXIM, PROVERB, ADAGE, REDE
blade .... WEB
cut of .... KERF
kind of ..... RIP, EDGER
notch .... KERF
sawfish's .... SERRA
surgical .... TREPAN, TREPHINE
toothed .... SERRATE
sawbones: sl. .... SURGEON
sawbuck: sl. .... TEN(SPOT)
sawdust .... COOM, SCOBS
sawfish .... RAY
snout .... SERRA
sawfly .... HORNTAIL
sawhorse ..... BUCK, TRESTLE
sawing frame .... HORSE
sawtooth .... SERRA

ridge .... SIERRA
sawtoothed ...... RUNCINATE
sawyer .. WOODCUTTER, BEETLE
Saxony's capital .... DRESDEN
Saxe _____ ... COBURG
Coburg and Gotha ...... WINDSOR
saxhorn .... TUBA
saxifrage ... SESELI, ROCKFOIL
Saxon ... SASSENACH, ENGLISH
Saxony ..... SACHSEN, YARN
capital of ...... DRESDEN, MAGDEBURG
city .... ERFURT
say .. AVER, UTTER, DECLARE, STATE, ALLEGE, REPORT, DICTUM, CHANCE, MOUTH
again ... ITERATE, REPEAT
repetitiously ..... CHANT, HARP
sayid .... SAID, FATIMID
saying .... ADAGE, SAW, PROVERB, MOTTO, EPIGRAM, MOT, MAXIM, DICTUM, APHORISM, AXIOM, GNOME
sayings attributed to Jesus .... LOGIA
Sb in chemistry ..... STIBIUM, ANTIMONY
scab .... CRUST, MANGE, SCOUNDREL, BLACKLEG, ESCHAR
scabbard ... CASE, SHEATH(E), PILCHER
plate .... CHAPE
what it sheathes .. SWORD, DAGGER, BAYONET, BOLO, SCIMITAR
scabby ... MANGY, MEAN, LOW, BASE, SCURVY, SCALY
scabbies .. ITCH, MANGE, PSORA
scabrous ..... MANGY, SCALY, RISQUE, SALACIOUS
scad .... SAUREL, SKATE
scads .... OODLES
scaffolding timber ... PUTLOG
scaffold ... GIBBET, PLATFORM, STAGE, GALLOWS, RIGGER
scalawag ..... RASCAL, SCAMP
scald .... BURN, HEAT
scale ..... CLIMB, ESCALADE, CLAMBER, GO UP, GAMUT, LAMELLA, PLATE, FLAKE, LAMINA
animal .... SQUAMA
chaffy .... PALEA

charges .... TARIFF
horny .... SCUTUM
insect's secretion .... LAC
measuring ..... VERNIER
model .... MOCK-UP
musical .... GAMUT
plant .... SQUAMA
pointer .... TONGUE
skin off .... BLANCH
weighing .... STEELYARD
scalelike part of animal/plant.. SQUAMA
scales .... BALANCE
covered with ..SQUAMATE, SQUAMOSE, SQUAMOUS, LEPIDOTE
the .... LIBRA
scaling ladder .... SCALOSE
of wall .... ESCALADE
scall .... SCURF
scallion .... ONION, SHALLOT, LEEK
scallop .... MOLLUSK, DADOE, CRENULATION, QUIN, CRENA, PINK
scalloped .... CRENATE
scalp ... CHEAT, ROB, DEFEAT
disease ... SCALL, FAVUS
to an Indian .....TROPHY
tumor .... WEN
scalpel ... LANCET, BISTOURY, KNIFE
scalper ... PROFITEER, INDIAN
scaly ..... LEPROSE, SCURFY, SCABROUS, SCABBY, MANGY, BASE, LOW, MEAN, SQUAMATE, SQUARROSE
bark .... PSOROSIS
coating .... SCURF
combining form .... LEPID(O)
Scamander .... MENDERES
scammony .... RESIN
scamp ... SCALAWAG, ROGUE, RASCAL, SCOUNDREL, SCAPEGRACE, SPALPEEN
scamper ...... BRATTLE, SCUD, SCURRY
scampi .... PRAWN
scan ...... ANALYZE, STUDY, GLANCE, RECITE, SCRUTINIZE
scandal .. DISGRACE, OUTRAGE, SHAME
scandalize .... OFFEND, OUTRAGE, SHOCK, MALIGN

scandalmonger .... GOSSIP(ER), TALEBEARER
scandalous .... LIBELOUS, SHAMEFUL, OFFENSIVE
scandent plant .... VINE
Scandinavian .... NORSE(MAN), LAPP, DANE, SWEDE, NORTHMAN, NORDIC, SQUAREHEAD, FINN
chieftain ... JARL, RURIK
coin .... ORE
country ...... NORWAY, SWEDEN, DENMARK, ICELAND
explorer .... ERIC
folklore being ..... TROLL
giantess ... URTH, WYRD
goblin .... NIS
god .... THOR, LOKI, ALFADIR
heaven: myth. .. ASGARD, ASGARTH
legend ...... SAGA, EDDA
legislature ..... T(H)ING
measure .... ALEN
monster .... KRAKEN
musician .... SKALD
name ...... SVEN, OLAF, NILS, ERIC
nation .... GEATAS
navigator .... ERIC
pirate/sea rover .. VIKING
plateau .... FJELD
poem .... RUNE
poet .... SKALD
settler .... VARANGIAN
territorial division .. AMT
weight .... LOD
scant .... MEAGER, EXIGUOUS, SLIGHT, STINT, FEW, INADEQUATE, SHORT, SPARSE
scantling .. TIMBER, BEAM, STUD
scanty ...... MEAGER, SPARSE, SHORT, SMALL, SPARING, SCARCE
scape .... STALK
bearing .... SCAPOSE
scapegoat ..... BUTT, VICTIM, WHIPPING BOY, PATSY, FALL GUY
scapegrace .. RASCAL, ROGUE, SCAMP
scaphoid .... BOAT-SHAPED
scapolite .... SILICATE, WERNERITE

scar .. .. .. MARK, CICATRIX,
NAVEL, BLEMISH, CICATRICE,
CLIFF
scarab .. .. .. BEETLE, CHARM
Scaramouche .. .. POLTROON,
RASCAL, BRAGGART
    author .. .. SABATINI
scarce .. .. RARE, UNCOMMON
scarcely .. .. HARDLY
scarcity .. .. .. PAUCITY, LACK,
RARITY, SHORTAGE, DEARTH
scare .. STARTLE, FRIGHT(EN),
FEAR, PANIC, ALARM
    up .. .. PRODUCE
scarecrow .. MALKIN, MAUKIN,
MAWKIN, JACKSTRAW,
STRAW MAN, BUGABOO
    stuffing .. .. STRAW
scarehead .. .. .. STREAMER,
BANNER
scaremonger .. .. .. ALARMIST,
TERRORIST
scarf .. .. .. ASCOT, NECKTIE,
(NEC)KERCHIEF, SASH,
TAPALO, MANTILLA,
MUFFLER, FOULARD,
BABUSHKA, SAREE, SARI,
TIPPET
    clerical .. . TIPPET, STOLE
    cloth .. .. LUNGI, LUNGEE
    pope's .. .. ORALE
    shoulder .. .. SASH
    sun helmet .. .. .. PUGGRY,
PUG(G)REE
    woman's .. .. STOLE,
MANTILLA, PEPLOS,
BOA
scarlatina .. .. FEVER
scarfskin .. .. CUTICLE,
EPIDERMIS
scarlet .. .. RED
    bird .. .. TANAGER
    fever .. .. SCARLATINA
Scarlett O'Hara's home .. .. ..
TARA
scarp .. .. SLOPE, DECLIVITY
scat .. .. TAX, SCRAM
scathing .. .. SEARING
scatter .. .. LITTER, SPRINKLE,
STREW, DISPERSE, DISPEL,
SHED, STUD, SOW, DISSIPATE
    by blowing .. .. .. WINNOW
    for lost scent .. .. .. CAST
    grass .. .. TED
scatterbrained .. .. GIDDY,
FLIGHTY, FRIVOLOUS

scattered .. .. SPORADIC,
STUDDED, STREWN
scattergood .. .. SPENDTHRIFT,
WASTREL, PRODIGAL
scattering of Jews .. DIASPORA
scaup .. .. DUCK, CANVASBACK,
REDHEAD, SHUFFLER, DOGS,
GRAYBACK
scavenger .. .. HYENA
scenario .. . SCRIPT, OUTLINE,
LIBRETTO
scend .. .. HEAVE, PITCH
scene .. .. LOCALE, SITE,
TABLEAU, SETTING, VIEW,
SPECTACLE
scenery .. .. DIORAMA,
PANORAMA, PICTURE, VIEW,
LANDSCAPE, VISTA
    chewer: sl. .. .. HAM
    mover .. .. .. PROP(MAN)
    natural .. .. LANDSCAPE
scenic .. .. PICTURESQUE,
DRAMATIC
    view .. .. SCAPE,
PANORAMA, VISTA
scent .. .. .. SMELL, PERFUME,
TRACK, FRAGRANCE, CLUE,
AROMA, NOSE, ODOR
    animal's .. .. FOIL
    kitchen .. AROMA, NIDOR
    left by animal .. .. DRAG
    of wine .. .. .. BOUQUET
    subtle .. .. AURA
scented .. .. OLENT
    water .. .. COLOGNE,
BAY RUM
scepter .. . FERULA, TRIDENT,
ROD, WAND, STAFF, MACE
Schacht, Ger. financier .. .. ..
HJALMAR
Scharre, mimist .. .. .. ROLF
schedule .. .. .. SLATE, LIST,
CATALOGUE, BOOK,
CALENDAR, INVENTORY,
(TIME,)TABLE, AGENDA
Scheherazade's life-saver .. .. ..
TALES
Scheldt .. .. ESCAUT
schema .. . OUTLINE, DIAGRAM
PLAN
scheme .. .. SYSTEM, PLOT,
INTRIGUE, PROJECT, CABAL,
OUTLINE, PLAN, PURPOSE,
DEVICE, PROJECT
    utopian .. .. BUBBLE
scheming .. CRAFTY, TRICKY

Schick, pediatrician .... BELA
Schicklgruber's son ....
(ADOLF) HITLER
schipperke .... DOG
schism ...... DIVISION, SPLIT,
SEPARATION, SECESSION,
CONCISION, SECT
schist .... ROCK, SLATE
schistosome .... FLUKE
schizocarp ... REGMA, MAPLE
schizophrenia treatment ......
PHENIGAMA
schizophrenic syndrome ......
CATATONIA
Schlesien .... SILESIA
Schleswig-Holstein capital ...
KIEL
schnapps .... GIN
schnauzer ... PINSCHER, DOG,
TERRIER
schnozzle .... NOSE
Schnozzola .... DURANTE
scholar ... SAVANT, STUDENT,
PUPIL, CLASSICIST, PUNDIT,
PANDIT
assistant/attendant .....
FAMULUS
inferior .... PEDANT
literary ...... HARMONIST
Moslem .... ULEM
scholarly .... STUDIOUS,
ERUDITE, LEARNED
paper .... THESIS
people .... LITERATI
scholars' association ....
ACADEMY
scholarship ...... LEARNING,
BURSE, PEDANTRY,
PHILOLOGY, ERUDITION
scholastic .... ACADEMIC,
DOGMATIC, PEDANT(IC)
scholiast .... ANNOTATOR
school .... TRAIN, TEACH,
COLLEGE, UNIVERSITY,
EDUCATE, ACADEMY, LYCEE,
ECOLE, SECT, ACADEME,
LYCEUM
assignment ..... LESSON
banner .... PENNANT
book ..... PRIMER, TEXT,
READER
boy, new .... SCUM
children's ....
KINDERGARTEN,
NURSERY

for training horses ......
MANEGE
grounds .... CAMPUS
group .... PTA
headmaster ..... RECTOR
honor society .... ARISTA
kind of .. PREP(ARATORY),
ELEMENTARY, COLLEGE,
MILITARY, SEMINARY
of birds .... POD
of fish ...... SHOAL, POD
of thought .... ISM
of whales ..... POD, GAM
official ...... PRINCIPAL
principal ... HEADMASTER
riding .... MANEGE
teacher .... MASTER
term .... SEMESTER
young women's ....
SEMINARY
schooling .... EDUCATION
schoolmaster .... PEDANT,
TEACHER, SNAPPER,
PEDAGOGUE, DOMINIE
rod of .... FERULE
schooner ...... WAGON, SHIP
schorl .... T(O)URMALINE
schottish, dance like ... POLKA
Schranz, Austrian skier ... KARL
Schubert, composer ... FRANZ
classic .... AVE MARIA
Schumann Heink, singer .....
ERNESTINE
Schweiz .... SWITZERLAND
sciatic area .... HIP
science ... ART, SKILL, OLOGY,
TECHNICS
applied .... TECHNOLOGY
combining form .. TECHNO
fiction writer ... ASIMOV,
VERNE
of boxing .... FISTICUFFS
causes ...... ETIOLOGY
crop production ......
AGRONOMY
deciphering documents
DIPLOMATICS
fruit cultivation ......
POMOLOGY
government .. POLITICS
heard sound ....
ACOUSTIC(S)
human behavior ......
PSYCHOLOGY
law-making ....
NOMOLOGY

medicine .. IATROLOGY
motion .. .... KINETICS,
DYNAMICS, KINEMATICS
mountains .. OROLOGY
musical sounds .. ...
HARMONICS
origins .. .... ETIOLOGY
plants .. .. BOTANY
public worship .. . ...
LITURGICS
soils .. . ... AGROLOGY
versification .. PROSODY
vital statistics .. ..
DEMOGRAPHY
words ..... SEMANTICS
on freezing points .. ..
CRYOSCOPY
on races .. .. .. EUGENICS
EUTHENICS
scientific quack .. ... EMPIRIC
research animal .. ..
HAMSTER
study of trees .. ..
DENDROLOGY
scientist .. .. SAVANT
scilicet .. ... NAMELY, TO WIT
scimitar .. SWORD, SAX, TURK
scincoid .. .. SKINK
scintilla ... SPARK, PARTICLE,
WHIT, IOTA, TRACE, BIT
scintillate ... SPARKLE, FLASH,
TWINKLE
sciolist .. QUACK, CHARLATAN,
PEDANT
scion .. .. SHOOT, BUD,
DESCENDANT, SPROUT, SON,
GRAFT, HEIR, SLIP, SPRIG
Scipio, Roman general .. .. ..
AFRICANUS
victim of .. .. .. CARTHAGE,
HANNIBAL
scirrhus .. .. .. TUMOR, CANCER
scission .. .. DIVISION, FISSION
scissorbill .. .. SKIMMER
scissors-like instrument .. .. ..
SHEARS
scissortail .. .. FLYCATCHER
sciurine animal .. .. .. RODENT,
MARMOT, SQUIRREL
sclerite .. .. SPICULE
scoff ... SNEER, GIBE, FLOUT,
JEER, DERIDE, TAUNT,
MOCK, RAIL, FLEER, JIBB,
GIRD
scold .. ... (BE)RATE, REPROVE,
REBUKE, RAIL, DERIDE,

UPBRAID, REVILE, CHIDE,
NAG, LAMBASTE, JAW,
FLITE, FLAY
scolder ... NAG(GER), MAGPIE,
BERATER
scolding .. .. BARFUL
scombroid .. .. MACKEREL
sconce .. .. SHED, HUT,
SHELTER, HEAD, HELMET,
SKULL, BULWARK, FORTIFY,
BRAINS, FORT, SCREEN
scone .. .. (TEA)CAKE
scoop .. LADLE, SHOVEL, BEAT,
DIG(OUT), GOUGE, TROWEL,
ROUT, DREDGE
scoot ... DART, SCURRY, HIE
scooter .. .. SAILBOAT,
MOTORBOAT
scop .. .. POET, BARD
scope .. .. AREA, RANGE,
EXTENT, AMBIT, LATITUDE
limited .. .. LOCAL
scopoline .. .. NARCOTIC
scopulate .. .. BRUSHLIKE
scorch .. .. .. BURN, SHRIVEL,
SINGE, CHAR, SERE, SEAR,
PARCH, BLISTER
score .. .. SCRATCH, DEBT,
ACCOUNT, GRUDGE, RATING,
TALLY, CHALK, TWENTY,
MARK, NOTCH, CRITICIZE,
TAB
scoreless, hold .. .. .. BLANK
scoria .. .. DROSS, SLAG, LAVA,
AA
scorn .. . DISDAIN, CONTEMPT,
SPURN, DESPISE, MOCK,
DERISION, CONTEMN
scorpine .. .. HOGFISH
Scorpio's brightest star .. .. ..
ANTARES
scorpion .. .. ARACHNID,
SCOURGE, WHIP,
VINEGARROON
claw .. .. CHELA
fish .. .. LAPON
Scot .. .. KILTIE, GAEL,
SCOTCHMAN, TAX, LEVY
Scotch .. .. .. STINGY, WHISKY,
SCORE, CUT, NOTCH, MAIM,
CRUSH, STIFLE, BLOCK,
WEDGE
scoter ... DUCK, EIDER, COOT
Scotia .. .. SCOTLAND
Scotland ... SCOTIA, MOLDING
capital .. .. EDINBURGH

scotoma .... BLIND SPOT
Scotsman ... BLUECAP, SANDY
Scott novel .... IVANHOE
   poem .... MARMION
Scottish .... CALEDONIAN
   absent .... AWA
   ache ...... WARK, STOUND
   active .... YAULD
   ago .... SYNE
   alas .... OCHONE
   alder tree .... ARN
   alderman .... BAILIE
   ale .... YILL, NAPPY
   alley .... WYND
   assembly signal .. SLOGAN
   attendant ' .... GILLIE,
               GILLY
   awl .... ELSEN
   awry .... AGL(E)Y
   bagpipe music .. PIBROCH,
           CORONACH
   bailiff .... REEVE
   bank .... BRAE
   barren .... YELD
   barter .... TROKE
   beer .... YILL, NAPPY
   beef cut .... SEY
   beg .... SORN
   beggar .... RANDY
   belly .... WAME
   biscuit .... SCONE
   blaze .... INGLE
   bold .... CROUSE
   boor .... TYKE
   bound .... STEND
   boundary .... MEAR
   box .... KIST
   boy .... LOON
   brandy .... ATHOLE
   breeches .... TREWS
   broadsword .. CLAYMORE
   brook .... SIKE
   broth ...... BROO, BREE
   brow of hill .... SNAB
   bucket .... STOOP, STOUP
   burden .... BIRN
   burn .... STREAM
   bushel .... FOU
   buxom .... SONSIE
   cake ... SCONE, BANNOCK
   cap .... BALMORAL,
         GLENGARRY,
       TAM(-O-SHANTER)
   cat ...: .... MALKIN
   catch .... KEP
   cattle .... NOWT

   charm .... CANTRIP
   cheese .... KEBBOK
   chemise .... SARK
   chest .... KIST
   chief .... THANE
   child ...... BAIRN, WEAN
   church .... KIRK
   churl .... CARLE
   city .... AYRS, GLASGOW
   clan chief .... THANE
   clothe .... CLEAD
   codfish .... GLASHAN
   coin .... BAWBEE, BAUBEE,
          DEMY, LION
   comb .... KAME
   congress .... MOD
   corner .... NEUK
   corpse .... LICH
   countrified ..... HODDEN
   county .... PEEBLES,
     ARGYLL, BUTE, AYR,
     BANFF, FIFE, ORKNEY
   court officer ..... MACER
   cow .... RUNT, CRUMMIE
   crab .... PARTAN
   cravat .... OVERLAY
   craw .... CRAG
   crowd ... MEINIE, MEINY
   cry of blame ... DIRDUM
   cuckoo .... GOWK
   cup .... TASS
   curlew .... WHAUP
   cut .... SNEG
   dagger .... SKEAN
   dairymaid .... DEY
   daisy .... GOWAN
   deception .... BROGUE
   dell .... SLACK
   devil ... DEIL, MOHOUND
   dining room .... SPENCE
   dirge .... CORONACH
   dish .... HAGGIS
   do .... DAE
   dog .... SEALYHAM
   dolt ... GOMERAL, GOWK
   donkey .... CUDDY
   dramatist ...... BARRIE
   dwarf .... BLASTIE
   ear .... LUG
   earnest money ... ARLES
   earth .... YIRD
   else .... ENSE
   empty .... TOOM
   endure .... DREE
   explorer .... RAE
   extent .... STENT

extra .... ORRA
fair .... TRYST
faithful .... LEAL
fall of rain .... ON-DING
farm worker ...... HIND, ORRAMAN
farmer ...... CROFTER, COTTAR, COTTER
fellow .... CARL(E)
festivity .... KIRN
few .... WHEEN
fine .... WALLY
fireplace .... INGLE
first rate .... WALLY
firth .... KYLE
fold .... WIMPLE
fool .... GOMERAL
fox .... TOD
friend .... EME
game .... SHINTY
garment .... SARK
girl .... CUMMER, LASSIE, QUEAN
go .... GAE, GANG
goblet .... TASS
godmother .... CUMMER
goldsmith .... GED
good .... GUDE
good-for-nothing .. ORRA
gooseberry ..... THAPRES
guillotine ...... MAIDEN
gulf .... BISM
gypsy .... CAIRD
hag .... CARLINE
haggle .... PRIG
hamlet .... CLACHAN
handsome .... SONSY, SONSIE
hare ... MAUKIN, MALKIN
hawk .... ALLAN
head .... POW
heir .... TEIND
Highlander .. GAEL, CELT
hill ...... DOD(D), INCH
hill(side) .... BRAE
hellside hollow .. CORRIE
historian .... HUME
hoe .... PADLE
hut .... BOTHY
inlet .... GIO
inventor .... WATT
island ..... ARRAN, BUTE, INCH, IONA, HEBRIDES, UIST, HARRIS
jackdaw .... KAE
jade .... YAUD

jail .... TOLBOOTH
keen .... GLEG
kilt .... FILIBEG
kindle ..... LUNT, TIND
kindred .... SIB
king .... BRUCE
kiss .... PREE
knowledge .... KENNING
laborer .... HIND
lake .... LIN, LOCH, KATRINE
lake dwelling .. CRANNOG
land, flat .... LINKS
land tax .... CESS
landholder ..... LAIRD, THANE, THEGN
lark .... LAVEROCK
light .... LICHT
little .... SMA
lively .... CROUSE
locker .... KIST
lord .... THANE
love .... LOE
lowlander ... SASSENACH
Lowlands ...... LALLAN
lucky .... SONSIE
magic spell ..... CANTRIP
magistrate ..... PROVOST, BAILIE
marauder ....
MOSS TROOPER, CATERAN
mare .... YAUD
market .... TRYST
match .... LUNT
mathe ... GRUB, MAGGOT
mathematician .. NAPIER
Mayday ...... BELTANE
measure .... CRAN
men's undergarment ....
TREWS
miscellaneous ..... ORRA
mist .... DROW
money .... SILLER
more .... MAIR
mortgage .... WADSET
mountain .. BEN, NEVIS
much ... MICKLE, MUCKLE
mud .... GLAR
municipal official .. BAILIE
musical instrument ....
BAGPIPE
must .... MAUN
myself .... MASEL
national emblem ....
THISTLE
native .... CALEDONIAN

neck	CRAG	require	NEID	
negative	DINNA, NAE	resort	OBAN	
New Year's eve		river	ESK, DEE, DEVON,	
	HOGMANAY	AYR, CLYDE, TAY, AFTON,		
nimble	YAULD		DOON	
no	NAE	river land	CARSE	
once	ANES	rivulet	RINDLE	
one	AIN, ANE, YIN	robber	CATERAN	
odd	ORRA	robbery	REIF	
outcry of blame	DIRDUM	rock	SKERRY	
own	AIN, ANE	rope	WANTY	
ox	NOWT, RUNT	rosin	ROZET	
oxter	ARMPIT	rowboat	COBLE	
pail	COGGIE, STOUP	rug	MAUD	
pain	WARK, STANG,	Satan	DEIL, HORNIE	
	STOUND	scholarship	BURSE	
parlor	BEN	schoolmaster	DOMINIE	
pay for a killing	CRO	scold	THREAP	
peak	NEVIS	scone	FARL(E)	
peasant	COTTAR,	scratch	RIT	
	CROFTER, COTTER	seaport	DUNDEE,	
peep	KEEK		GREENOCK	
pert	CROUSE	seize	VANG	
philosopher	HUME,	seldom	SINDLE	
	CAIRD	self	SEL	
physicist	BAIRD	servant	GILLY, GILLIE	
pig	GRICE	sharp	GLEG, SNELLY	
pipe	CUTTY	shawl	MAUD	
pirate	KIDD	shelter	BIELD	
plaid	TARTAN, MAUD	shirt	SARK	
plait	WIMPLE	silver	SILLER	
pleasant	DOUCE	simpleton	GOWK	
pocket	POUCH	since	SYNE	
poet	BURNS, EDINA,	sister	TITTY, TITTIE	
	HOGG, DUNBAR	skirt	KILT	
pole	CABER	small	SMA	
poll	POW, HEAD	smart	STOUND	
pool	LINN, CARR	smoke	LUNT	
porridge	BROSE,	snow	SNA	
	SOWENS	snow fall	ON-DING	
port	OBAN	soldier	KERN(E)	
pottage	BROSE	spell	CANTRIP	
pouch	SPORRAN,	spirit	BANSHEE	
	SPLEUCHAN	sponge	SORN	
praise	ROOSE	squall	BLEFFERT	
prank	CANTRIP	stomach	KYTE	
precipitation	SNA	stream	BURN	
prefix to names	MAC	student scholar	BURSAR	
prison	TOLBOOTH	suffer	DREE	
privateer	KIDD	supple	WANDLE	
pronunciation	BURR	sweetheart	JO(E)	
pudding	SAUSAGE	sword	SKEAN,	
puzzle	KITTLE		CLAYMORE	
ragged	DUDDY, DUDDIE	tap	TUCK	
reef	SKERRY	tartan pattern	SETT,	
relish	GUST		PLAID	

taste .... PREE, GUST
tatter .... TAVER
tea cake .... SCONE
tedious .... DREE
tenant .... CROFTER,
            COTTER, COTTAR
tern .... TARRET
terrier .... SEALYHAM,
            SKYE, CAIRN
theologian .... DUNS
thicket .... RONE
throat .... CRAG
thumb .... THOOM
tickle .... KITTLE
tinker .... CAIRD
toad .... TADE
tobacco pouch ....
            SPLEUCHAN
topper .... TAM
torch .... LUNT
tower .... PEEL
town .... BUR(G)H
toy .... WALLY
trade .... TROKE
tribal payment ..... CRO
trick .... BROGUE
trousers .... TREWS
true .... LEAL
turnip .... NEEP
tuyere .... TEW
twang .... TIRL
uncanny .... UNCO
uncle ...... EAM, (Y)EME
university scholar ......
            BURSAR
vagabond .... WAFF
vagrant .... CAIRD
valley ... SLACK, STRATH
vex .... FASH
vigor .... VIR
village .... REW
violet .... BLAVER
vulgar .... RANDY
walk .... GO
water spirit ..... KELPIE,
            KELPY
waterfall ... LIN(N), LYN
wear under kilts .. TREWS
weeds .... WRACK
weighing machine ....
            TRONE
weight .... TRONE
whaup .... CURLEW
whether .... GIN
whirlpool .... WEEL

whiskey ... USQUEBAUGH,
            ATHOL(E),
            MOUNTAIN DEW
witch .... CARLINE
woman .... CUMMER,
            RANDY, CARLINE
woman, unmarried ......
            QUEAN
womb .... WAME
world .... WARL
worse .... WAUR
worthless .... WAFF
wrap .... MAUD
wrestle ...... WARS(T)LE
yawn .... GANT
yell .... GOWL
scoundrel .. VILLAIN, RASCAL,
      SCAMP, BASE, ROGUE, CAD,
      VARLET, KNAVE, BEGGAR,
      SCAB, REPROBATE
scour .... FLUSH, PURGE,
      LOOK OVER, SEARCH,
      SAND, POLISH, SCRAPE,
      SCRUB, FURBISH, RAKE,
      RUB, SKIRR
scourer .... CATHARTIC
scourge .... BANE, WHIP,
      SCORPION, AFFLICTION,
      LASH, FLOG, TORMENT,
      PLAGUE
of God .... ATTILA
scouring rush ..... HORSETAIL
scout ..... SPY, RECONNOITER,
      SCOFF, REJECT, RIDICULE,
      FELLOW, GUY, DO-GOODER,
      TENDERFOOT
boat .... VEDETTE
group ..... TROOP, DEN,
      PATROL, PACK
scow ..... BARGE, FLATBOAT,
      LIGHTER
puller .... TOWBOAT,
      TUG(BOAT)
scowl .... (G)LOWER, FROWN,
      MOUE, GRIMACE, LOUR
scrabble .... PAW, SCRAPE,
      SCRAWL, DOODLE
scrag .... NECK, HANG,
      THROTTLE, GARROTE
scraggly .. UNKEMPT, JAGGED
scraggy .... BONY, LEAN,
      SKINNY
scram ..... VAMO(O)SE, SCAT,
      SHOO, BEAT IT, GET LOST,
      LAM
scramble ... CLIMB, CLAMBER,

SCUFFLE, MIX UP, TEAR, RAT RACE
scrambled .... PIED
scrap ..... TATTER, BIT, PIECE, DISCARD, ORT, LEFTOVER, ARGUMENT, SHRED, FRAGMENT, MAMMOCK, QUARREL, END, JUNK(RAG), FRACTION, FIGHT, MORSEL, ODDMENT
glass .... CULLET
hunt for ..... SCAVENGE
of paper only, sometimes.. TREATY, PACT
scrape ..~..~.. ABRADE, RUB, SCOUR, GRIDE, PREDICAMENT, SCRATCH, SCUFF, RAKE, RASP, GRAZE, SHAVE, FIX
bottom ... DREDGE, SOUR
ground in golf ... SCLAFF
scraped linen .... LINT
metal .... FILING
scraper, water ~..~. SQUEEGEE
scrapings .... SHAVINGS
scrappy ... PUGNACIOUS, GAME
scraps ~.~..~. SOUVENIRS, CLIPPINGS, MEMENTOS
literary .... ANA
scratch ..... GRATE, SCRAPE, CHAFE, RUB, SCRIBBLE
Old .... DEVIL
scratching ground for food ..~ RASORIAL
scratchy .... ITCHY
scrawl .... DOODLE, SCRIBBLE
scrawny ~.~.~.. LEAN, THIN, SCRAGGY
scream ~.~.~....... SCREECH
scream ..... SHRIEK, SQUALL, YELL, CATERWAUL, SCREECH
screamer .... HEADLINE
bird .... CHAJA
scree ~.~..~. TALUS, STONE, PEBBLE, RUBBLE
screech ~.~.~. SHRIEK, CRY, SCREAM
screechy .... SHRILL
screed ~.~..~.. HARANGUE, TIRADE, SPEECH
screen ... SCONCE, PARTITION, CURTAIN, PAVIS, SHIELD, SIFT, BLIND, GRILLE, MOVIES, SHADE, SHROUD, SECLUDE, PARAVENT
altar .... REREDOS

bar .... MULLION
bulletproof .. MANT(E)LET
canvas .... PAVESADE
chancel .... REREDOS
chimney .... BONNET
for concealment/ protection .. BLINDAGE
making material .... VETIVER
mesh .... SIEVE
wind .... PARAVENT
screw ~..~. PROPELLER, MISER, SALARY, TURN, TWIST, TIGHTEN
part .... THREAD
pine tree ..... PANDANUS
thread .... HELIX
threader .... CHASER
screwball .... NUT
screwy ~.~..~ ODD, PECULIAR, ECCENTRIC
scribble ~.~.. SCRAWL, WRITE, DASH, DOODLE
scribbler ~............ HACK
scribe ~.~..~. WRITER, AUTHOR, PENMAN, CLERK, SECRETARY, AMANUENSIS, SCRIVENER
Biblical .... BARUCH
scrimmage ~.~.. MELEE, FIGHT, TUSSLE, AFFRAY
scrimp ~.~..~.. SKIMP, STINT, SCANTY, ECONOMIZE
scrip ~.~..~. SATCHEL, WALLET, LIST, BAG, WRITING, CERTIFICATE
script ~.~..... HANDWRITING, SCENARIO, PENMANSHIP, LIBRETTO, RONDE, SERTA
scriptural .... BIBLICAL
analysis .... EXEGESIS
interpreter ..... EXEGETE
scripture(s) ... BIBLE, KORAN, ALCORAN, BOOK, TORAH, SUTRA, ITALA
interpretation of .... ANAGOGE
passage ~.~..~... TEXT
reader .... LECTOR
scrivener ~.~. NOTARY, SCRIBE, COPYIST, AMANUENSIS
scrobiculate .... PITTED
scrod .... CODFISH
scrofula ~.~..~.. KING'S EVIL, STRUMA

scroll .... LIST, ROLL, SCHEDULE
　of Ionic capitals .. VOLUTE
　shaped ...... TURBINATE
　tablet like .. CARTOUCH(E)
scromboid fish .... CERO
Scrooge .... MISER
scrouge .... CROWD, PRESS, SQUEEZE
scrounge .... PILFER
scrub ... MEAN, POOR, SMALL, RUB, BRUSH, SCOUR, MOP
scrubber ...... CHARWOMAN
scrubbing implement .... MOP
scruff .. NAPE, NUQUE, NUBIA
scrunch .... CRUSH, CHEW
scruple ... QUALM, MISGIVING
scrupulous ... EXACT, HONEST, UPRIGHT, POOR, CAREFUL, PRECISE, CORRECT, FINICAL, RELIGIOUS
scrutinize ..... INSPECT, SCAN, EXAMINE, CON, EYE, PROBE
scud ...... SKIM, GLIDE, RUN
scuff .... SCRAPE, BRUSH, SHUFFLE, SLIPPER
scuffle ..... SHUFFLE, BRAWL, FRAY, MELEE, TUSSLE, FIGHT
scull .... PADDLE, SHELL, OAR, (RACING)BOAT, WHERRY
sculler ... BOATMAN, OARSMAN
scullery, content of ... POTS, PANS
scullion ... SERVANT, WRETCH
sculpin .... BULLHEAD, SEA RAVEN, HARDHEAD
sculptor .... CARVER, STATUARY
　framework of ....
　　ARMATURE
　tool of .... CHISEL, GRAVER, CALIPER
sculpture head to chest .. BUST
　medium .. CLAY, BRONZE, MARBLE
　style of ...... GROTESQUE
sculptured .... GRAVEN, GLYPHIC
scum .... DROSS, REFUSE, SKIM, SPUME, PELLICLE
　rid of .... DESPUMATE
scup .... PORGY, BURGOO, BREAM, FISH, SPAROID
　kin of ... SNAPPER, GRUNT

scuppernong ... GRAPE, WINE, MUSCADINE
scurf .... SCALL, FURFUR, DANDRUFF
scurfy ... MANGY, LEPIDOTE, LEPROSE
scurrilous ... VULGAR, COARSE, THERSITICAL, ABUSIVE
scurry .. SCAMPER, RUN, DART, SCOOT, RACE, HIGHTAIL
scurvy ...... VILE, LOW, MEAN
scut .... TAIL
scutage .... TAX
Scutari ... USKUDAR, SHKODER, LAKE
scute .... SCUTUM
scutellate .... ROUND
scutter .... BUSTLE
scuttle ..... BASKET, BUCKET, SCURRY, SCAMPER, HATCHWAY, HOD, SINK
scuttlebut .... RUMOR, GOSSIP
scutum .... SHIELD, PLATELET
Scylla .... ROCK
　whirlpool opposite ......
　　CHARYBDIS
scye .... ARMHOLE
scyphozoan .... JELLYFISH
scythe bearer .... DEATH
　cut, one stroke ... SWATH
　handle .... SNATH(E), SNEAD, NIB
　sharpener ...... STRICKLE
　sweep of .... SWATH
sea ..... WAVE, SWELL, MAIN, OCEAN, DEEP, MARE
　anemone ...... ACTINIA, POLYP
　animal, fishlike ....
　　LANCELET, AMPHIOXUS
　arm ... GULF, BAY, FIORD, FRITH, LOCH, LOUGH
　bass .... JEWFISH
　bat .... DEVILFISH
　bird ..... ERN(E), GULL, ALBATROSS, SHAG, CORMORANT, PETREL, TERN, SOLAN, SCOTER, KESTREL, PUFFIN, MEW, FULMAR, EIDER, GANNET, NODDY, SKUA, SCAUP
　biscuit ...... HARDTACK
　born goddess ....
　　APHRODITE
　borne .... AFLOAT

bread .... HARDTACK
calf .... SEAL
coast ..... SHORE, STRAND
cow .... DUGONG,
 SIRENIAN, MANATEE,
 WALRUS, HIPPOPOTAMUS
creature, legendary ......
 MERMAID, MERMAN
cucumber .... TREPANG,
 HOLOTHURIAN
devil .... ANGELFISH,
 SHARK, OCTOPUS, RAY
disaster aid device ......
 SOFAR
dog ...... GOB, MARINER,
 TAR, SEAL, SAILOR
duck ..... SCAUP, COOT,
 SCO(O)TER, EIDER
eagle .... ERN(E), OSPREY,
 TERN
ear .... ABALONE
elephant .... SEAL
fan .... CORAL
farer .... MARINER, MAORI,
 SAILOR
foam ..... MEERSCHAUM,
 SPUME
fox .... SHARK
god ..... LER, NEPTUNE,
 NEREUS, TRITON,
 POSEIDON, AEGIR,
 PROTEUS
grave .... LOCKER
gull .... MEW, COB(B),
 KITTIWAKE
hog .... PORPOISE
holly .... ERYNGO,
 ERINGO
horse .... WALRUS,
 HIPPOCAMPUS
inhabitant: myth. ......
 MERMAN, MERMAID
inlet .. FIORD, FJORD, RIA
lands beyond the ......
 OUTREMER
lawyer .... SAILOR
lettuce ..... LAVER, ULUA
lily .... CRINOID
lion .... SEAL
marker ..... BUOY, DAN
mew .... GULL
mile .... KNOT, NAUT
monster .... KRAKEN,
 LEVIATHAN
near the ...... MARITIME
needle ...... GAR(FISH)

nettle .... MEDUSA,
 ACALEPH, JELLYFISH
nymph .... NEREID,
 THETIS, SIREN, NAIAD,
 CALYPSO
of the .... PELAGIC,
 THALASSIC, NAVAL,
 MARINE, NAUTICAL,
 MARITIME
on the .... MARITIME
onion .... SQUILL(A)
pen .... POLYP
personified .... NEPTUNE
poetic .... FOAM
prefix .... MARI
put to .... SAIL
raven .... SCULPIN
robber .... PIRATE,
 BUCCANEER, FOMOR
robin .... GURNARD
rover .... PIRATE
serpent .... ELOPS
shell .... MOLLUSK
slug .... TREPANG
snail .... W(H)ELK
soldier .... MARINE
spot at .... ISLE(T)
spray .... SPINDRIFT
squirt .... TUNICATE,
 ASCIDIAN
surface movement ......
 LIPPER
swallow .... TERN, PETREL
tangle .... SEAWEED
unicorn....... NARWHAL
urchin .... ECHINUS,
 ECHINOID
wall .... JETTY,
 BREAKWATER
water .... BRINE
with many islands ......
 ARCHIPELAGO
wolf .... BLENNY, PIRATE
worm ...... LURG, SAO
worthy .... STANCH
seabat .... DEVILFIHS
Seabee's concern ... AIRFIELD,
 HARBOR
seaboard .... COAST
seacoast .... SHORE
seaflower ... POLYP, ANEMONE
seagull .... KITTIWAKE, MEW,
 COB
seahorse .... HIPPOCAMPUS
seal ..... PINNIPED, INITIAL,
 BULLA, BLADDERNOSE,

STAMP, RATIFY, CLOSE, CACHET, SIGIL, SIGNET
bottle .... CAPSULE
cut skin of ...... FLENSE
eared ... SEA LION, OTARY
fur .... SEECATCH, URSAL
hooded ... BLADDERNOSE
hunter .... SWILER
kind of .... WAFER
large .... SEA LION
letter .... CACHET
male .... SEECATCH
off .... TRAP
Pope's .... BULL
rawhide ...... SHAGREEN
sound of .... BARK
tube .... CAPSULE
tusked .... WALRUS
with lead .... PLUMB
young .. PUP, HARP, CALF
sealed completely .. HERMETIC
sealer ..... SWILER, CALKER, PUTTY
sealing material ... MUCILAGE, PASTE, GLUE, TAPE, WAX(WAFER)
agent .... LUTE
seals, breeding place of ...... ROOKERY
flock of .... POD
pertaining to ... PHOCINE
seam ... WRINKLE, LINE, PURL, SUTURE, JUNCTURE
fill up .... CALK
filling material .. OAKUM, TAR
tapered .... DART
seamaid .... SIREN, MERMAID, NYMPH
seaman ... SAILOR, MARINER, GOB, RATING, JACKY, SALT, TAR
rating of .... ABLE
seamark ...... LIGHTHOUSE, PHAROS, BEACON, BUOY, DAN
seamen's chapel ...... BETHEL
seamstress ...... SEMPTRESS, SEWER
seance ..... SESSION, MEETING, SITTING
noise .... RAP
participant .... MEDIUM, SPIRITUALIST
recording device .. OUIJA
seaplane stabilizer ... SPONSON

sear .... WITHER, DRY(UP), BRAND, HARDEN, BURN, SERE, SCATHE
search ... EXPLORE, RUMMAGE, PROBE, SEEK, DELVE, GROPE, FORAGE, FERRET, QUEST, RANSACK, HUNT
for food .... FORAGE
for Holy Grail ... QUEST
for mineral .... PROSPECT
for talent .... SCOUT
party of a sort .... POSSE
person's person ... FRISK
steadily .... MOUSE
thoroughly ...... COMB
with divining rod ...... DOWSE
searching ...... KEEN, SHARP
searing .... BURNING
seashore ..... COAST, BEACH, STRAND
of the .... LITTORAL
seasickness ..... MAL DE MER
seaside strip .... BOARDWALK
season .... FALL, WINTER, SUMMER, SPRING, FLAVOR, SPICE, CURE, INURE, TEMPER, CORN, DEVIL, SALT
yield of .... VINTAGE
seasonable .... TIMELY, OPPORTUNE
seasonal .... PERIODIC
symbol .... HOLLY, PUMPKIN, SWALLOW, SNOW
seasoning ..... SPICE, GARLIC, SALT, CONDIMENT, MUSTARD
leaf .... BAY, LAUREL
pod .... CHILI
seasons .... HORAE
seat ... CHAIR, BENCH, STOOL, BUTTOCKS, CENTER, OTTOMAN, SEDILIA, PERCH, SOFA, SEDILE, GRADIN, VIS-A-VIS, SETTEE, INSTALL
bishop's .... METROPOLIS
chair's .... BOTTOM
coach .... DICKY
high .... ROOST
mobile .... WHEELCHAIR
of government .. CAPITAL
of judgment .. TRIBUNAL

on camel/elephant .... HOWDAH, HOUDAH
royal .... THRONE
seats, church .... PEW, SEDILIA
se(a)wan .... WAMPUM
seaward .... OFF
seaweed ... TANGLE, SARGASSO, SARGASSUM, VAREC, NULLIPORE, ALGA, KELP, LAVER, AGAR, REDWARE, FUCUS, FUCOID
edible ...... DULSE, LIMU, CARRAG(H)EEN, AGAR, TANGLE
extract .... AGAR
genus .... ALARIA
leaflike part ...... FROND
product ... AGAR(AGAR)
purple .... SION
soda ash .... BARILLA
washed ashore .... SEAWARE, WRACK
seaworm .... LURG, SAO
seaworthy .... STANCH
sebaceous .... OILY
matter ... TALLOW, FAT, SEBUM
sec ...... BRUT, DRY, INSTANT
secede .... WITHDRAW, SEPARATE
secern .... SECRETE
secesh ... REB(EL), WITHDRAW
Seckel .... PEAR
seclude ... ISOLATE, IMMURE, SCREEN
secluded .... REMOTE, SHUT OFF, ISOLATED, HERMITIC
spot .... NOOK
valley .... GLEN
seclusion .... PRIVACY, SOLITUDE, ISOLATION
second .... AID, MOMENT, INSTANT, TRICE, JIFFY, ASSISTANT, ABET, BACK
best .... RUNNER-UP
childhood .... DOTAGE, SENILITY
estate .... NOBILITY
growth crop ...... ROWEN
hand dealer ... JUNKMAN, RAGMAN, SCRAPMAN
lieutenant: sl. .... SHAVETAIL
mentioned ...... LATTER

nature .... HABIT
placer .... RUNNER-UP, ALSO-RAN
rate .... INFERIOR, MEDIOCRE
self .... ALTER EGO
story man ...... BURGLAR
team .... SCRUB
secondary .... MINOR, INFERIOR, BYE
secondhand ...... USED, WORN
secrecy .... PRIVACY
secret .... HIDDEN, MYSTERY, ARCANUM, ARCANE, OCCULT, COVERT, UNDERHAND, CRYPTIC, PRIVATE
action .... STEALTH
advisers' group .... CAMARILLA
agent .... SPY
agent's work ... ESPIONAGE
discussion .... HUDDLE
meeting .... CONCLAVE
most .... INMOST
place .... SANCTUM, HIDEOUT
remedy .... ELIXIR
service .... INTELLIGENCE
society .... CAMORRA, MAF(F)IA, TONG, KU KLUX, KLAN(KKK), PORO, BLACKHAND
watch .... ESPIONAGE, SPYING
writing .... CODE
secretary .... AMANUENSIS, DESK, ESCRITOIRE
abbreviation ...... SECY
public .... SCRIBE
secrete ... SECERN, CONCEAL, HIDE, STASH, CACHE
secretion .... SWEAT, SALIVA, SAP, MUCUS, LATEX, BILE, SUDOR, EXUDATION, CHALONE
secretive ...... SLY, STEALTHY, RETICENT
secretly ...... SUBROSA, SLYLY, UNDERHAND
secrets .... PENETRALIA
sect .... FOLLOWING, DENOMINATION, CULT, FACTION, PARTY, SCHOOL
sectarian .... BIGOTED, APOSTATE

sectary .... DISSENTER
section ...... PART, SEGMENT,
DIVISION
secular .... WORLDLY,
TEMPORAL, LAIC(AL), LAY
secund .... UNILATERAL
secundine .... AFTERBIRTH
secure ... SAFE, FIRM, STABLE,
SURE, GUARD, GET,
ACQUIRE, FAST(EN), MOOR,
BELAY, ANCHOR
place .... FASTNESS, FORT,
STRONGHOLD
security .... SAFETY,
SAFEGUARD, BOND, PLEDGE,
GUARANTEE, SURETY,
GRITH, GAGE
for payment .... LIEN,
COLLATERAL, BOND
sedan .... AUTOMOBILE,
(CLOSED)CAR, CHAIR,
LITTER, LIMOUSINE
sedate .... QUIET, SERIOUS,
CALM, GRAVE, SOBER,
STAID, DEMURE
sedative .... URETHAN(E),
DEMEROL, NEMBUTAL,
CODEIN(E), AMYTAL,
BARBITAL, BROMIDE,
ANODYNE, LUMINAL,
OPIATE, CALMATIVE
Seder, event commemorated by
EXODUS
sedge clump .... TUSSOCK
sediment ...... SILT, MAGMA,
SLUDGE, LEES, DREGS,
DRAFF, GROUT, FOOTS,
OOZE
sedimentary deposit layer .....
VARVE
sedition .... TREASON
seduce .... PERSUADE, TEMPT,
LURE
seducer .... SIREN, VAMP,
LOTHARIO, CASANOVA,
ENTICER
seductive .... CHARMING
sedulous ..... BUSY, DILIGENT
sedum .... STONECROP
see .... DISCERN, ESPY, VISIT,
DESCRY, BEHOLD, DIOCESE,
PERCEIVE, VIEW, WITNESS,
MEET, COMPREHEND
bishop's .... METROPOLIS
head of a .... BISHOP
slow to .... PURBLIND

seed .... SOW, GERM, OVULE,
SPERM, PIP(PIN), BEAN
aromatic .... ANISE(ED),
CUM(M)IN, GUAIAC,
TONKA
bearing organ .... PISTIL
bud .... PLUMULE
case .... POD, BUR(R),
CYPSELA
coat .... BRAN, ARIL,
TESTA, HULL,
TEG(U)MEN, HUSK
combining form .. SPERM,
SPERMAT(O)
container .... PIT, STONE,
POD
cover, false .... ARILLODE
edible .... PEA, BEAN,
LENTIL, PULSE,
SOY(BEAN), PISTACHIO,
PINON
flavoring ...... CARAWAY,
ANISE, CUM(M)IN
food ...... PEA, LENTIL,
SOY, BEAN, LEGUME,
SESAME, COQUITO
hole-making tool ....
DIBBLE
immature .... OVULE
leaf .... COTYLEDON
lense-shaped ... LENTIGO
like .... SEMINAL
oil ...... CHAULMOOGRA,
SESAME, GINGILI
oil-yielding ..... SESAME,
TILL, BENNE, GINGILI,
GINGELI
one-celled .... CARPEL
oyster .... SPAT
pear .... PIP
plant .... HERB, EXOGEN
pod .... CYPSELA
poisonous .. NUX VOMICA
prematurely produce ....
BOLT
remove .... GIN
remover ... GIN, RIPPLE
rudimentary ..... OVULE
scar .... HILUM
spice .... NUTMEG,
CARDAMON
stalk .... FUNICULUS
strong-smelling ....
CARAWAY
vessel .... PERICARP,

CAPSULE, BUR, POD,
SILICLE
seedless .... AGAMOUS
   plant .... FERN
seedling .... SAPLING
seeds: combining form .. CARPO
   row of planted .. DRILL
   study of ..... CARPOLOGY
seedsman .... SOWER
seedy ...... SHABBY, TACKY
seeing .... VISION, SIGHT
seek ...... EXPLORE, SEARCH,
INQUIRE, PURSUE
seel ...... HOODWINK, BLIND
seeled bird ... HAWK, FALCON
seem ...... APPEAR, LOOK
seeming ... APPARENT, SHOW,
QUASI, OSTENSIBLE
seemingly .... QUASI
seemly .... FAIR, COMELY,
SUITABLE, FITTING, PROPER,
MEET, DECENT
seen, can be ...... VISIBLE,
DISCERNIBLE, PERCEPTIBLE
seep .... LEAK, PERCOLATE,
OOZE, PERMEATE
seer .... SOOTHSAYER,
PROPHET, ARUSPEX
seeress .... SIBYL, CASSANDRA
seersucker ... FABRIC, LINEN
seesaw ... FLAP, TESTER, TILT,
WAG, VACILLATE,
CROSSRUFF, BASCULE
seethe .... BOIL, BUBBLE,
SIMMER, STEW, FERMENT
seething .... ABOIL
segment .... SECTION,
DIVISION, PART, PORTION,
SECTOR
   of crustacean ... TELSON
sego .... PLANT, LILY
segregate .... ISOLATE,
SEPARATE, SET APART
seidel .... MUG
seigneur ...... LORD, NOBLE
seine .... NET, RIVER
   city on the ..... ROUEN,
TROYES
   tributary ...... EURE,
OISE, MARNE
seism .... EARTHQUAKE
seismograph subject .. TREMOR,
TEMBLOR, QUAKE
seize .... GRAB, ATTACK,
ARREST, NAB, GRASP, LASH,
TAKE, CONFISCATE, COLLAR

first .... PREEMPT
for debt ..... DISTRAIN,
GARNISH
for official use ....
COMMANDEER
in law .... LEVY
power, etc. ...... USURP
seizure .... ATTACK, FIT
selachian ..... RAY, SHARK,
DOGFISH
Selassie, Emperor ..... HAILE
seldom .... RARELY
select ..... CHOICE, PICK(ED),
EXCLUSIVE, WALE, CULL,
ELITE, CHOOSE
selected .... INDUCTEE,
DRAFTEE
selection .... CHOICE
selective service ...... DRAFT
Selene ...... LUNA, MOON,
ARTEMIS, HECATE
   love of .... ENDYMION
selenite .... GYPSUM
self .... EGO
assurance .. CONFIDENCE,
POISE, APLOMB
centered ... EGOCENTRIC,
SELFISH
combining form ... AUTO
conceit ... VANITY, PRIDE,
EGOTISM
confidence ..... PANACHE
confident ..... ASSURED,
POISED, COCKSURE,
COCKY
conscious ... SHY, TIMID
control, power of .. WILL
cremation ..... SUTTEE
defense art ..... JUJUTSU,
KARATE, JUDO
denial ...... SACRIFICE
denying ...... MONASTIC
destruction ..... SUICIDE,
IMMOLATION
determination ....
FREE WILL
esteem ... PRIDE, VANITY,
EGOISM
evident ...... AXIOMATIC
explanatory .... OBVIOUS
fertilization ....
ORTHOGAMY
government .. HOME RULE
immolation ..... SUICIDE
important .... BUMBLING,
POMPOUS

important person .. NIBS
love ...... NARC(ISS)ISM
possessed ... COOL, CALM,
   COMPOSED
propelled .. AUTOMOTIVE
protection .... DEFENSE
reliant ...... DEPENDABLE
reproach ... REPENTANCE,
   REMORSE
restraint .. MODERATION,
   TEMPERANCE
righteous .... SMUG
satisfied .... SMUG
selfheal .... SANICLE
sell ... BETRAY, DUPE, TRADE,
   AUCTION, VEND, PEDDLE,
   BARTER, MARKET, HAWK
for .... FETCH
out sign .... SRO
seller .... VENDOR, PEDDLER,
   RETAILER, COSTER
on installment ....
   TALLYMAN
Selm .... LAGERLOF
selvage .... LIST
semantics, concern of ....
   MEANING
semasiology ...... SEMANTICS
semblance .... PRETENSE,
   LIKENESS, IMAGE, GUISE
seme .... DOTTED
Semele's father ..... CADMUS
son .... DIONYSUS
semester ... TERM, HALF YEAR
Seminole chief ...... OSCEOLA
semiology, subject of .. SIGNS,
   SYMPTOMS
Semiramis' husband ... NINUS
kingdom ...... BABYLON
semisolid substance .. GELATIN
Semite .. HEBREW, JEW, ARAB,
   BABYLONIAN, PHOENICIAN
god .... STERAPH
Semitic language ..... PUNIC,
   ARAMAIC, HEBREW, ARABIC,
   AMHARIC
people .... CHALDEAN,
   BABYLONIAN
tribe .... AMMON
vampire .... LILITH
semolina .... MEAL
semper .... ALWAYS
sempstress .... SEAMSTRESS,
   SEWER
sen, 1/10 of a .... RIN
senate house .... CURIA

send ... DISPATCH, TRANSMIT,
   REMIT, FORWARD
back .. REMAND, RETURN,
   REMIT, REPATRIATE
flying .... ROUT
for .... SUMMON
forth .... EMIT
out ..... ISSUE, DESPATCH
packing .... DISMISS,
   DRIVE
Seneca .. IROQUOIAN, INDIAN,
   CAYUGA
senega .... MILKWORT
Senegal, capital of ... DAKAR
city ... THIES, KAOLOCK,
   DAKAR
ethnic group .... WOLOF,
   PEUL, SERERE
president ..... SENGHOR
senescent .... AGING
seneschal .. MAJOR DOMO, KAY
senhor .... SIR, (GENTLE)MAN
senile ..... DOITED, ELDERLY,
   AGED
senility ... DOTAGE, OLD AGE
senior .... OLDER, ELDER
class publication ....
   ANNUAL, YEARBOOK
member of group .. DEAN,
   DOYEN
seniorita .... MISS, LADY
seniority .... PRECEDENCE
senna .. PLANT, PEA, LAXATIVE
source of .... CASSIA
sennet .... FLOURISH
sennight .... WEEK
sensate .. CONSCIOUS, ESTHESIA
sensation .... FEELING, HIT,
   EXCITEMENT, PERCEPTION
of smell ..... OLFACTION
of taste ..... GUSTATION
sensational .... LURID,
   STARTLING, EXCITING,
   SHOCKING
sense ... MEANING, FEEL(ING),
   PERCEIVE, SIGHT, TASTE,
   TOUCH, SAPIENCE, INTUIT,
   SMELL, HEARING
of sight, of the ... OPTIC
of smell ..... OLFACTION
of taste ..... GUSTATION
organ ... EYE, RECEPTOR,
   TASTE BUD, ANTENNA,
   FEELER, NOSE, EAR,
   PALP(US)
sixth .... INTUITION

sound .... LOGIC
senseless .... ABSURD, INEPT,
INANE, FOOLISH, STUPID,
FATUOUS, UNCONSCIOUS,
IRRATIONAL, WANTON
senses, one of the ..... SIGHT,
TASTE, SMELL, TOUCH,
HEARING, INTUITION
sensible ... SANE, REASONABLE,
RATIONAL, AWARE, WISE,
PASSIBLE, LEVEL-HEADED
sensitive .... TE(T)CHY, RAW,
TOUCHY, TENSE, TENDER,
SORE
plant .... MIMOSA
sensitivity .... ERETHISM
sensual .... CARNAL, LUSTFUL,
LYDIAN
sensualist .... SYBARITE
sensuous .... EPICURIAN
sentence .... DECISION,
OPINION, JUDGMENT, DOOM
break down ..... PARSE
mark ..... COLON, COMMA
part .... VERB, NOUN,
PREDICATE
reading same backward ..
PALINDROME
slang .... RAP
structure .... SYNTAX
sententious .... PITHY, TERSE,
POINTED
sentient .... CONSCIOUS
sentiment .... ATTITUDE,
FEELING, OPINION, EMOTION
sentimental .... MAWKISH,
MAUDLIN, GUSHY,
ROMANTIC, SOPPY, MUSHY,
SPOONY, NAMBY-PAMBY
sentimentalism .... SCHMALTZ
sentimentality .... MUSH
sentinel .... SENTRY,
WATCH(DOG), GUARD,
PICKET
mounted ..... VEDETTE,
VIDETTE, LOOKOUT
sentry ..... SENTINEL, WATCH,
GUARD, BIVOUAC
box .... BOOTH
challenge of ....
WHO GOES THERE
challenge of French .....
QUI VA LA
order of .... HALT
Seoul .... KEIJO
sepal .... LEAF, CALYX

separate .... (SET)APART,
DIVIDE, SEGREGATE,
SECEDE, SEVERAL,
DISCRETE, ISOLATE,
ALIENATE, SEVER,
PART, SORT, DISTINCT,
SPLIT, SECERN
forcibly .. REND, WRENCH
in botany .... SOLUTE
into parts ... DISMEMBER
separation ... BREAK, DIVORCE,
SCHISM, SECESSION,
AVULSION
in chemistry ... DIALYSIS
separatist .... DISSENTER
separator .... SEPTUM
Sephardic dialect .... LADINO
Sephardim .... JEWS
sepia ...... DUN, CUTTLEFISH,
PIGMENT
sepiolite .... MEERSCHAUM
seppuku .. HARAKIRI, SUICIDE
seps .... SKINK, SNAKE
sept .... CLAN, TRIBE
September 13, Roman calendar
IDES
septic .... INFECTIVE
septicemia .... SEPSIS
septime .... PARRY
septum .... PARTITION
septuple .... SEVENFOLD
sepulcher ...... TOMB, GRAVE,
BURY, RELIQUARY, VAULT,
CRYPT, SEPULTURE
sepulchral... DISMAL, GLOOMY,
TOMBLIKE
sepulture .. BURIAL, INTERMENT
sequel ... AFTERMATH, EFFECT,
UPSHOT
sequence ...... RUN, SEQUEL,
SUCCESSION, SERIES
sequester .... ISOLATE,
SET APART, SEGREGATE,
SEPARATE, SEIZE,
CONFISCATE, ENISLE,
SECLUDE
sequestered .... RETIRED,
SECLUDED
sequin .... SPANGLE,
ZECCHIN(O)
sequoia .... REDWOOD
seraglio ..... HAREM, PALACE,
SERAI, ZENANA
serai .. CARAVANSARY, IMARET,
INN, SERAGLIO
Serang .... CERAM

serape ...·... BLANKET, SKAWL
seraph ..·.. ANGEL, CHERUB
seraphic ...·.·.·.. ANGELIC
Serb ...·...·...·...·.··· SLAV
Serbian guerrilla ...· CHETNIK
sere ...·.. DRIED, WITHER(ED),
DRY
serein ...·.·.·.·.·.·.. RAIN
serenade ...·.·..· NOCTURNE
mock ...·.·.·. SHIVAREE,
CHARIVARI
serene ...·.·.. CALM, EQUABLE,
TRANQUIL, IMPASSIVE,
QUIET, COMPOSED
serenity ...· REPOSE, CALMNESS
serf ...·.. ESNE, SLAVE, THRALL,
BONDMAN, HELOT, VILLEIN,
LITUS
female ...·.·.·.·.· NEIF
liberate a ...·.. MANUMIT
serfdom .. BONDAGE, HELOTRY,
SLAVERY
sergeant ...·.. TOPKICK, SARGE,
NCO
at-law's cap ...·.. BIGGIN
fish ...·.·. ROBALO, COBIA
seric ...·.·.·.·.·.·.· SILKEN
sericeous ...·.·.. DOWNY, SILKY
series ...·.·.· SET, SEQUENCE,
SUCCESSION, CHAIN
of columns .. COLONNADE
of links ...·.·.·.·· CHAIN
of six ...·.·.·.·.·· HEXAD
of stairs ...·.·.·.· FLIGHT
of steps ...·.·.·.·.· SCALE
of trouble ... GA(U)NTLET
serin ...·.·.·.·.·.·.·.·.· FINCH
serious ...·.·· GRAVE, EARNEST,
SOLEMN, GRIM, SOBER,
SINCERE, CRITICAL, SEDATE
sermon ...·.· LECTURE, SPEECH,
DISCOURSE, HOMILY
sermonize ...·.·.·.·.·· PREACH
sermons, study of ...·.·.·.·.·
HOMILETICS
serous ...·.·.·.·.·.·.· WATERY
membrane .. PERITONEUM
serow ...·.·.· JAGLA, ANTELOPE
serpent ... FIREWORK, SATAN,
COCKATRICE, DRAGON,
OPHIDIAN, BASILISK,
SNAKE, SEPS, (A)BOMA,
BOA, ELOPS
monster ...·.·.·· HYDRA,
LAMIA, ELOPS
nine-headed ...·.·· HYDRA

worship ...·.·.·.·. OPHISM
serpentine ...·.·.·.· WINDING,
CUNNING, COILED,
OPHIDIAN, OPHITE,
SINUOUS
serpigo ...·.·.·.·.· RINGWORM
serranoid fish ...·.· CABRILLA,
REDHIND
serried ...·.·.·.·.·· COMPACT
serum ...·.· ANTITOXIN, WHEY
serval ...·.·.·.·.·.· WILDCAT
servant ...·.·.·.· SLAVE, MAN,
ANCILLARY, (BAT)MAN,
HIND, DOMESTIC, MAID,
MENIAL, GILLY, GILLIE
boy ...·.. PAGE, GOSSOON,
GARCON
college ...·.·.·.·.·.· GYP
devoted ...·.·.·.· FRIDAY
female ...· SLAVEY, WENCH
feudal ...·.·.·.· SERGEANT
head ...·.·.·.·.·· BUTLER
house of ...·.·.·.· LODGE
liveried ...·.·.·· FLUNKY,
LACKEY
male ...· LACKEY, VALET,
BUTLER
man's ...·.·.·.·.·· VALET
personal ...·.·.·.·.· VALET,
EQUERRY
seat in carriage .. RUMBLE
uniformed ...·.· CHASSEUR
serve ...·.·.·.· WAIT, SUPPLY,
DELIVER, (AT)TEND, SATISFY
food ...·.·· CATER, WAIT
server ...·.·.· WAITER, TRAY,
SALVER, ATTENDANT
alcoholic drinks ...·.·.·.·
BARTENDER
service .. EMPLOYMENT, WORK,
MASS, RITE, USE, SHADBUSH
club ...· ROTARY, KIWANIS,
LIONS, JAYCEE
stripe, military ...·.·.·.·.·
HASH MARK
tree ...·.·.·.·.·.·.· SORB
serviceable ...· USEFUL, USABLE,
UTILE
serviceman ...·.·.·.·.· SOLDIER
services, one of the .. ARMY,
NAVY, AIR FORCE
serviette ...·.·.·.·.·.· NAPKIN
servile ...·.·.·.· TAME, SLAVISH,
MENIAL, FAWNING, ABJECT
serving ...·.·.·.·.·.· PORTION
boy ...·.·.·.·.·.·.· KNAVE

man .... POTMAN
stand ..... DUMB WAITER
servite .... MENDICANT
servitor .... ATTENDANT,
ADHERENT, FOLLOWER,
SERVANT
servitude .... BONDAGE,
SLAVERY, YOKE, EASEMENT
symbol of .... YOKE
sesame ... TIL, BENNE, SEMSEM,
TEEL, GINGILI
grass .... GAMA
oil .... BENI, GINGILI
seed ... GINGILI, GENGELI,
GINGELLY
sess .... TAX
sessile .... IMMOBILE
session ... ASSEMBLY, SEANCE,
MEETING, SITTING
discontinue ... ADJOURN,
PROROGUE
sestet .... SEXTET(TE)
set ...... BATCH, JELLY, SEAT,
RECORD, FIX, WANE,
DECLINE, SCENERY, LAY,
POST, EMBED, PRESCRIBE,
RIGID, RESOLUTE, CLIQUE,
COLLECTION, COTERIE, KIT
afloat .... LAUNCH
all ... PREPARED, READY
apart .... ISOLATE,
SEGREGATE, RESERVE
aside .... ANNUL,
DISCARD, REJECT,
DEFER, PEND, QUASH,
EARMARK
down ..... RECORD, LAY
down as a fact .... POSIT
firmly .... INFIX
forth ..... START, STATE,
THETIC
free .... LIBERATE,
DELIVER, EXTRICATE
in competition ...... PIT,
MATCH
in motion ..... ACTIVATE,
EXCITE
in operation .. LAUNCH
in type .... COMPOSE
of clothes ..... COSTUME,
SUIT
of nine .... ENNEAD
of players .... TEAM
of rules .... CODE
of three .... TERNION
off ... EXPLODE, DETONATE

on fire ... KINDLE, IGNITE
on horse .... MOUNT
out .... DEFINE, PLAN,
LEAVE, DEPART, GO
playing cards ..... DECK,
PACK
right ..... REPAIR, ALIGN,
AMEND, CORRECT
sail .... CAST OFF
thickly .... STUD
to .... BOUT, FIGHT,
CONTEST
up ... FOUND, ESTABLISH,
PITCH, ERECT
upon ... ATTACK, SIC(K)
value on .... PRICE,
APPRAISE
seta .... BRISTLE, CHAETA
setback ..... UPSET, RELAPSE,
EDDY, REVERSE, REVERSAL
Seth's brother ..... CAIN, ABEL
parent ..... ADAM, EVE
son .... ENOS
setoff .... OFFSET
seton .... DISCHARGE
setose .... BRISTLY
settee .... SEAT, BENCH,
SOFA, LOUNGE
setter... (GUN)DOG, RETRIEVER
setting ...... SCENE, MOUNT,
LOCALE, MILIEU
jewels' .... PAVE
scheme .... DECOR
settle ...... BENCH, ARRANGE,
COLONIZE, DECIDE, PAY,
FIX, ALIGHT, SINK, REST,
SOFA, LIQUIDATE, COUCH,
CONCLUDE, END
argument ...... CLINCH
down ... ABATE, SUBSIDE
for the night .. BED DOWN
on land illegally .. SQUAT
settlement ...... COLONY,
VILLAGE, AGREEMENT,
PAYMENT, PLANTATION
settled, in law .... VESTED
settler .... SOONER,
HOMESTEADER, COLONIST,
BOOMER
land .... HOMESTEAD
settlers led by Kok ... GRIQUA
settlings .... DREGS, LEES,
SEDIMENT, DRAFF
Sevastapol is in ...... CRIMEA
seven ...... HEPTAD, VII, SEPT

against Thebes, one of ... TYDEUS
combining form .... HEPT(A)
days ...... HEBDOMAD
deadly sins, one of the ...
SLOTH, ENVY, LUST,
ANGER, PRIDE,
GLUTTONY
Dwarfs, one of ..... DOC,
DOPEY, BASHFUL,
HAPPY, SLEEPY, SNEEZY,
GRUMPY
group of .... HEPTAD
Hills of Rome, one of the
CAELIAN,
PALATINE, AVENTINE,
QUIRINAL, VIMINAL,
CAPITOLINE
of number .... SEPTIMAL,
SEPTENARY
series of .... HEPTAD
Wonders of the World ...
COLOSSUS, PYRAMIDS,
MAUSOLEUM, PHAROS
year period ..... TEENS
sevenfold .... SEPTUPLE
seventeen XVII
year locust ...... CICADA
seventh son .... SEER
sever ...... SEPARATE, CUT,
DIVIDE, BREAK(OFF)
several .... FEW, SEPARATE,
DIVERS(E)
severe .... ACUTE, DRASTIC,
HARSH, SERIOUS, STERN,
RIGOROUS
not .... BENIGN, LENIENT
Severn river .... USK
severity ... RIGOR, HARSHNESS,
AUSTERITY
sew .. STITCH, BASTE, SUTURE,
SEAM, FELL, QUILT, TACK
up ... MONOPOLIZE, CLOSE
sewage disposal ... SANITATION
hole .... CESSPOOL
Seward's "folly" .... ALASKA
sewan .... SHELLS
sewer .... DRAIN, PIPE,
SEAMSTRESS, GUTTER,
KENNEL
entrance ..... MANHOLE
sewing .... NEEDLEWORK
case .... ETUI, ETWEE
kit ... HUSSY, HOUSEWIFE
machine inventor .. HOWE

part .... LOOPER
sex appeal ... OOMPH, CHARM
hormone ...... STEROID
of a ... MASCULINE, MALE
FEMALE, FEMININE
sexes, common to both .....
EPICENE
sexless .... FRIGID
sext .... HOUR
sextant ...... QUADRANT,
ALTIMETER
sextet .... HEXAD
sexton ... GRAVEDIGGER,
BELLRINGER, SACRIST(AN)
sextuple .... SIXFOLD
sexual ...... CARNAL, GAMIC
continence .... CHASTITY
desire, of ..... EROTIC
excitement ...... HEAT,
(O)ESTRUS, RUT
inclination/urge .. LIBIDO
pervert .... DEVIATE
sexually cold .... FRIGID
sexy .... EROTIC
picture .... PINUP
Seychelles, capital of ....
VICTORIA
island .... MAHE
Sforza, Ital. statesman .....
CARLO
shabby ... UNKEMPT, RAGGED,
SEEDY, DOWDY, WORN,
MEAN, DINGY, MANGY,
TACKY, RATTY,
THREADBARE, DISGRACEFUL,
CRUMMY
woman ...... SLATTERN,
DOWD, SLOVEN
shack .... SHANTY, HOVEL,
CABIN, HUT
shackle .. MANACLE, TRAMMEL,
FETTER, GYVE, PINION,
BILBO, RESTRAIN, HAMPER,
LEG-IRON, IRON(S), CHAIN
shad ...... ALEWIFE, ALOSE,
ALOSA, ALLIS
fish like ..... MENHADEN
running upriver ....
ANADROMOUS
shadbush .... SERVICE,
SASKATOON, JUNEBERRY,
ROSE
shaddock .... POMELO
shade .... UMBER, UMBRA,
TRACE, TOUCH, SCREEN,

COLOR, TONE, HUE, TINGE,
BLIND, TINT, SHADOW
blue .... ALICE
cap's .... VISOR
lines .... HATCH
of difference ... NUANCE
of meaning ..... NUANCE
tree .... ELM, LIN
shaded walk ... MALL, ARBOR,
ALAMEDA, CLOISTER
shades, the .... HADES
shadow .. DOG, GLOOM, OMEN,
TAIL, TRAIL, GHOST, TRACE,
VESTIGE, SHADE, UMBER,
UMBRA, SPY, CLOUD
astronomer's ... UMBRA
fighting ..... SCIAMACHY
man without .... ASCIAN
The .. (LAMONT) CRANSTON
shadowbox .... SPAR
Shadrach's fellow-captive .....
MESHACH, ABEDNEGO
shady ⇒.... DOUBTFUL,
DISHONEST, DUBIOUS
retreat ... KIOSK, ARBOR,
NOOK
SHAEF commander ....
(IKE) EISENHOWER
theater ..... ETO, EUROPE
shaft .... ARBOR, HANDLE,
SPEAR, BOLT, BEAM,
OBELISK, SHANK, SPINDLE,
ARROW, FLAGPOLE, SPIRE,
POLE, THILL, CONDUIT,
MISSILE, FLUE, PILLAR,
COLUMN, JAVELIN,
ARROYO
bearing .... HOTBOX
column's .. VERGE, SCAPE,
FUST, TRUNK
feather's .... SCAPE
handle .... HELVE
mine .... PIT
part of .... JOURNAL,
BOSS, GUDGEON,
TRUNNION
shag ⇒. NAP, MAT, TOBACCO,
CORMORANT
shagbark ⇒....... WALNUT,
HICKORY
shaggy ...... HIRSUTE, NAPPY,
UNKEMPT, THRUMMY, HAIRY,
SCRUBBY, BUSHY
shagreen ..... RAWHIDE, SKIN
Shah Jahan's masterpiece ....
TAJ MAHAL

of Iran .... PAHLEVI
shaitan .. DEVIL, FIEND, SATAN
shake ...... WOBBLE, QUIVER,
TREMBLE, VIBRATE, QUAKE,
TREMOR, THRILL, SHIVER,
JOLT, UNNERVE, WAVE,
RID, JAR, MOMENT,
SUCCUSS, ROCK, CONVULSE
down ...... EXTORT(ION),
BLACKMAIL, BOGUS
due to cold ..... SHIVER
due to horror, fear ......
SHUDDER
up .... REVAMP
Shakespearean actor ....
GIELGUD, OLIVIER,
WILLIAMSON
Athenian .... TIMON
character .... ROMEO,
TYBALT, CASSIUS,
OTHELLO, IAGO,
ORLANDO, LEAR,
MERCUTIO, SHYLOCK,
SOLINUS, BENVOLIO,
BRUTUS, HAMLET,
PORTIA, KATE
clown .. GOBBY, COSTARD,
FESTE
elf .... PUCK
forest ...... SHERWOOD,
ARDEN
king ..... LEAR, HAMLET
seven .... AGES
songwriter .... ARNE
theatre .... GLOBE
villain .... IAGO
witch .... CYCORAX
shaking ...... ASPEN, PALSIED
shako decoration ... POMPON
shakti .... DEVI, POWER
shaky ⇒...... WEAK, DOTTY,
UNSOUND, CRANKY,
UNCERTAIN, QUAKY,
RICKETY
shale .... ROCK, PELITE
product .... TARE
shall .... MUST
shallop .... DINGHY, BOAT
shallot ..... ONION, SCALLION,
ESCHALOT, BULB
kin .... LEEK
shallow .... SUPERFICIAL,
SHOAL
lake ... LAGOON, LAGUNE
sham ... BASTARD, IMITATION,
FALSE, HUMBUG, FAKE,

FEIGN, COUNTERFEIT,
ARTIFICIAL, PHON(E)Y
fight ... . SCIAMACHY
shaman ... . PRIEST,
MEDICINE MAN
Shamash ... . SUN GOD
shamble ... SHUFFLE, LUMBER,
WALK, GAIT
shambles ... . ABATTOIR,
DISORDER
shame ... MORTIFY, DISGRACE,
FIE, DISHONOR, ABASH,
BLACKEYE
shamefaced ... . SHY, BASHFUL
shameful ... . INDECENT,
OFFENSIVE
shameless ... . BRAZEN
shammy ... . CHAMOIS
Shamo ... ... GOBI
shampoo ... .. MASSAGE, WASH,
SOAP, LOMILOMI
shamrock ... . CLOVER
country ... ... IRELAND,
ERIN, EIRE
Shan ... . T(H)AI
shandrydan ... .. CHAISE, CART
Shanghai ... . SEAPORT,
CHICKEN, KIDNAP
Shangri-la ... ... UTOPIA,
PARADISE
shank ... ... CRUS, LEG, SHAFT,
GAMB(E)
in botany ... FOOTSTALK
shanny ... ... BLENNY
Shantung ... ... TUSSA(H)
capital of ... ... TSINAN
city ... ... CHEFOO
shanty ... HOVEL, HUT, SHACK
shantytown ... ... SLUM
shape ... ... FIGURE, GUISE,
PHANTOM, FORM, STATE,
CONDITION, MO(U)LD,
MODEL
bust's ... ... TAILLE
shapeless ... ... AMORPHOUS
shapely ... ... SVELT, NEAT
shaping machine ... .. EDGER,
LATHE
shard ... .. POTSHERD, SHEEL,
PLATE, FRAGMENT
share ... (AP)PORTION, PARTAKE,
PART, RATION, BIT, LOT,
CUT, MOIETY, STAKE
in common ... ... JOINT,
MUTUAL
slang ... . DIVVY

shark ... THRESHER, SWINDLER
CHEAT, TOPE, MAKO,
SHOVELHEAD, GATA,
HAMMERHEAD, MAN-EATER,
DOGFISH, ANGELFISH,
PORBEAGLE
eating fish ... ... PEGA
loan ... ... USURER
nurse ... ... GATA
rider/sucker ... REMORA
skin ... ... SHAGREEN
young ... ... PUPPY
sharp ... KEEN, PEAKED, ACUTE,
CLEAR, DISTINCT, VITRIOLIC,
CLEVER, SMART, PIERCING,
PUNGENT, SEVERE, CUTTING,
GLEG, PUNGENT,
TRENCHANT, HANDSOME,
EDGED, ACERB, ACIFORM,
NIPPY, NIPPING, INCISIVE
at the end ... ... ACUATE
blade ... ... RAZOR
colloquial ... ... ADEPT,
EXPERT
combining form ... ...
ACET(O)
cry ... ... YELP
edged ... ... KEEN
end ... ... POINT
eyed one ... LYNX, EAGLE
in phonetics .. VOICELESS
northern seas ... ...
PORBEAGLE
pain ... ... STING
reply ... ... RETORT
taste ... ... TANG, TART
turn ... ... ZIG
witted ... ... KEEN
sharpen ... ... WHET, STROP,
EDGE, HONE, GRIND
sharpening device ... ...
WHETSTONE, STROP, HONE,
GRINDSTONE, STRAP,
GRINDER
sharper ... .. SWINDLER, KITE,
GYP, CHEAT
sharpness ... . EDGE, ACERBITY,
BARB
of temper ... ... ASPERITY
Shasta ... ... VOLCANO, DAISY
sharpshooter ... ... SHOT,
MARKSMAN, SNIPER,
RIFLEMAN
shatter ... . BREAK, WRECK,
BURST, SHIVER, DASH,
SMASH

shave .... SCRAPE, GRAZE,
TRIM, SKIVE, PLANE, SHEAR,
PARE, WHITTLE, CUT
shaver ..... BOY, RAZOR, LAD,
YOUTH, YOUNGSTER
shaveling .... MONK, PRIEST
shavetail .. MULE, LIEUTENANT
Shavian forte .... WIT
shaw .... COPSE, THICKET
shawl .... MANTA, MAUD,
PAISLEY, SERAPE, PEPLOS,
WRAP, TALLITH, CASHMERE,
MUFFLER
shawn .... OBOE
Shawnee .... INDIAN
bread .... PONE,
JOHNNYCAKE
chief .... TECUMSEH,
TECUMTHA
shay .... CHAISE, CARRIAGE,
STANHOPE, BUGGY
she .... FEMALE, FEMININE
carved it .... SCULPSIT
died .... OBIT
painted it ... PNXT, PINXIT
speaks .... LOQUITUR
wrote it ...... SCRIPSIT
sheaf .... BUNDLE, BALE,
BUNCH
shear ..... CLIP, CUT, FLEECE,
POLL, TRIM, STRIP, SHAVE,
CROP
shearing tool .... CLIPPER
Shearer, ——— .... NORMA,
MOIRA
shearing machine ... CROPPER
shears .... SCISSORS
sheatfish .... CATFISH
sheath ... CAPSULE, SCABBARD,
STALL, DRESS, OCREA,
(EN)CASE, COT, SLEEVE,
THECA, SPATHE
metalplate on .... CHAPE
sheathe ...... RETRACT, COVER
sheathed ... THECATE, OCREATE
sheaves of grain ...... STOCK,
SHOCK
Sheba .... SABA
people ...... SAB(A)EAN
queen of .... BALKIS
shebang ... BUSINESS, AFFAIR,
THING, MATTER
shed ...... SCONCE, LEANTO,
RADIATE, DISCARD, COTE,
MOLT, CAST(OFF), DIFFUSE,
DROP, FALL OUT

aircraft ..... AIRDROME,
HANGAR
animal .... HOVEL
chicken .... COTE
sheep .... COTE
skin/feathers ... MO(U)LT,
PEEL, MEW
shedding leaves annually ......
DECIDUOUS
Sheean, writer ...... VINCENT
sheen .... POLISH, GLOSS,
LUSTRE, LUSTER, SHINE
Bishop .... FULTON
Sheena's domain ..... JUNGLE
sheep ... CARACUL, KARAKUL,
MERINO, SHA, OORIAL,
URIAL, CHEVIOT, NAHOOR,
LEICESTER, BROADTAIL,
ARUI
brain ailment ...... GID
caretaker .... SHEPHERD
castrated ...... WETHER
cry of .... BAA, BLAT,
BLEAT, MAA
descriptive of .... MEEK,
TIMID
disease ... LOCO, SCRAPIE,
SHAKES, ROT, COE,
STAGGERS, WILDFIRE, GID,
STURDY, ANTHRAX
dog ... COLLIE, SHEPHERD,
SHELTIE, SHELTY
enclosure .... KRAAL
fat .... SUET, TALLOW
female .... EWE
flesh .... MUTTON, VEAL,
LAMB
flock ... FOLD, DRYBAND
flock leader ....
BELLWETHER
foot of .... TROTTER
fur .... CARACUL,
KARAKUL, MOUTON
genus .... BOS, OVIS
grease .... SUINT
group of ... FOLD, FLOCK
head .... JEMMY
intestinal disorder ......
BRAXY
kept together ..... FOLD
killing bird .... KEA
like .... OVINE
like animal ...... SAIGA
male .... RAM, TUP,
WETHER
mountain .... IBEX

mutton .... SUFFOLK
neck growth of .... POKE
parasite ...... COENURUS,
                  FLUKE
pen .... FOLD, KRAAL
pertaining to .... OVINE
sexual excitement ... RUT,
           HEAT, ESTRUS
shelter ...... COTE, FOLD
skin cap .... KALPAK,
            CALPAC(K)
skin dealer .. FELLMONGER
skin disease .... SCAB,
           MANGE
sound ..... BL(E)AT, BAA
stomach trouble .. BRAXY
tender .... SHEPHERD
unshorn .... HOG
walk .... SLAITH
white .... WILTSHIRE
white-faced .. CORRIEDALE
wild ... URIAL, ARUI, SHA,
      RASSE, OORIAL,
      MOUF(F)LON, AOUDAD,
      ARGALI, UDAD, SNA,
      NAHOOR
wool .... FLEECE
wool secretion .... YOLK
young .... HOG,
    (Y)EANLING, LAMB, TEG
sheepfold ...... COTE, KRAAL,
       REE, PEN
sheeplike ...... OVINE, MEEK,
       DOCILE
sheepshank .... KNOT
sheepshead .... SPAROID
sheepskin .... PARCHMENT,
   ROAN, SKIVER, DIPLOMA
   cap .. CALPAC(K), KALPAK
sheepwalk .. PASTURE, SLAITH
sheer .... VEER, SWERVE,
    DEVIATE, TURN, STEEP,
    STARK, PURE, THIN,
    UTTER, ABSOLUTE
  delight ...... RAPTURE,
     ECSTASY
  legs .... SHEARS
sheet ..... SAIL, NEWSPAPER,
    EXPANSE
  bend .... KNOT
  blurred .... MACKLE
  metal(piece) ..... PLATE,
    LATH, LEAF
  metal cutter .... SNIP
  of lava .... COULEE
sheeting material ... PERCALE

shekel .... MONEY
sheldrake .... DUCK,
          MERGANSER,
shelf .... REEF, LEDGE,
    MANTEL, BERM(E),
    GRADIN(E), RETABLE,
    SANDBAR, BEDROCK
  drapery ... LAMBREQUIN,
    VALANCE
shell ..... CARAPACE, MISSILE,
  MOLLUSK, BOMBARD, COVER,
    BIELD, LORICA, CONCH,
    TUNICA, SHARD,
  RACING BOAT, CARTRIDGE,
  INTEGUMENT, POD, SHUCK
  abalone .... ORMER
  artillery ...... SHRAPNEL,
    OBUS
  bean .... LIMA
  boat .... HULL
  corn .... HUSK
  crab, clam, etc. ..... TEST
  defective .... DUD
  dish, baking ... SCALLOP
  ear .... ORMER, ABALONE
  enclosed in a .. OBTECTED
  explosive .... BOMB,
    SHRAPNEL, GRENADE
  failing to explode .. DUD
  fish ... BARNACLE, NACRE,
    COCKLE
  fragments .... SHRAPNEL
  fruit .... RIND, PEEL
  game ...... THIMBLERIG
  hole .... CRATER
  hurling device ... MORTAR
  invertebrate's ...... TEST
  mollusk's .... CONCH
  money .. COWRIE, COWRY,
    PEAG(E), SE(A)WAN,
    WAMPUM
  of .... TESTACEOUS
  1/20 of .... GERAH
  out .... PAY, GIVE
  pastry .... TART
  seed ..... TEST(A), HUSK
  spiral .... CONCH
  that doesn't explode .....
    DUD
  tip of ...... WARNOSE
  trumpet .... CONCH
  turtle/tortoise ....
    PLASTRON
shellac(k) ... RESIN, VARNISH,
  BEAT, DRUB, LAC(QUER)

shellacking .... BEATING,
    WHIPPING
shellback .... SAILOR
shellbark .. WALNUT, HICKORY,
    SHAGBARK
Shelley, poet ... PERCY, ARIEL
   elegy by .... ADONAIS
shellfish ..... CLAM, LOBSTER,
    SHRIMP, CRAB, MOLLUSK,
    SCALLOP, ABALONE,
    MOSSBACK, NACRE,
    BARNACLE, COCKLE
   spawn .... SPAT
   trap .... CREEL
shelter ..... COVER(T), HAVEN,
    REFUGE, RETREAT, SHED,
    SCONCE, NESTLE, CABANA,
    BIELD, ROOF
   aircraft .... HANGAR,
    AIRDROME
   airraid ... ABRI, DUGOUT
   auto .... CARPORT
   canvas .... TENT
   cattle ... KRAAL, CORRAL
   collapsible .... TENT
   decorative ..... PAVILION
   dove's .... COTE
   hillside .... ABRI
   movable ... MANT(E)LET
   overhanging .... CANOPY
   rain .... UMBRELLA
   refugee's .... ASYLUM,
    SANCTUARY
   ship's .... HARBOR
   small .... COT
   soldier's ..... (PUP)TENT
sheltered side .... LEE
shelty ..... PONY, (SHEEP)DOG
shelve ..... DEFER, LAY ASIDE,
    RETIRE
Shem's descendants ....
    S(H)EMITES
   father .... NOAH
   son ... ELAM, ARAM, LUD,
    AS(S)HUR
shenanigan .... MISCHIEF,
    NONSENSE, TRICK(ERY)
Shensi, capital of .... SIAN
sheol ... UNDERWORLD, HELL,
    HADES
shepherd .... PASTOR,
   MINISTER, SHEEP DOG, LEAD,
   TEND, DAPHNIS,
   ENDYMION, CORYDON
   concern of .... SHEEP
   dog .... COLLIE

   kings .... HYKSOS
   pipe .... OAT, REED
   plaid .... MAUD
   staff of ... CROOK, KENT,
    PEDA
shepherdess ...... AMARYLLIS
shepherds, god of .... PAN,
    FAUNUS
   pertaining to .. PASTORAL,
    BUCOLIC
sherbet ... BEVERAGE, DESSERT,
    DRINK, ICE
Sheridan, Union general ......
    PHILIP
sherif .... EMIR
   ancestor of ..... FATIMA,
    MOHAMMED
sheriff ...... VISCOUNT, REEVE
   aide of .... BULLDOG,
    CATCHPOLL, BAILIFF,
    YEOMAN
   armed group of ... POSSE
   badge of .... STAR
   deputy .... BAILIFF
Sherlock Holmes, creator of ..
    DOYLE
   man of .... WATSON
sherry ..... JEREZ, OLOROSO,
    AMONTILLADO, WINE
Sherwood Forest hero ....
    ROBIN HOOD
Shetland .... PONY, WOOL
   fishing grounds ... HAAF
   island .... MAINLAND
   island tax .... SCAT(T)
   pony ... SHELTIE, SHELTY
   sheep dog ...... SHELTIE,
    SHELTY
shibboleth .... SLOGAN,
    PASSWORD, TEST WORD
shield ..... SCUTUM, (A)EGIS,
   PAVIS, TARGE, ARMOR,
   MANT(E)LET, DEFEND,
   PROTECT, SCUTA, ECU,
   BUCKLER, COVER, MULGA
   arm .... BUCKLER
   Athena's .... (A)EGIS
   band across .... FESS
   bar, heraldic ..... GEMEL
   bearer .... ARMIGER,
    SQUIRE
   boss/knob of ..... UMBO
   bulletproof .. MANT(E)LET
   center point .... FESS
   hand .... BUCKLER
   of shields ...... TESTUDO

rawhide ..... PARFLECHE
Roman .... TESTUDO
shaped .... SCUTATE,
PELTATE, CLYPEATE,
CLYPEIFORM
spike of .... UMBO
Zeus' .... (A)EGIS
shift ..... CHANGE, TRANSFER,
MOVE, SHUNT, ASSIGNMENT,
HAUL, VEER, DEVIATE,
SWITCH, CHEMISE, TRICK
shifty ..... EVASIVE, TRICKY,
FURTIVE
Shiite .... SHIAH, MOSLEM
opposed to .... SUNNITE
shikar .... HUNT(ING)
shikari ...... HUNTER, GUIDE
shill .... ACCOMPLICE,
CONFEDERATE
confederate of a ....
BARKER, GAMBLER
shillelagh ...... CUDGEL, CLUB
shillings, 21 .... GUINEA
shilly-shally .... HESITATE,
WAVER, VACILLATE, HEDGE
shimmer ..... GLIMMER, FLASH
shimmy .... WOBBLE, DANCE,
CHEMISE
shin .... CLIMB, SHANK
Shinar ... SUMER, BABYLONIA
shinbone .... TIBIA
shindig .... PARTY, DANCE
shindy ... ROW, DISTURBANCE,
RIOT, COMMOTION
shine .... LIGHT, GLEAM,
GLOW, EXCEL, GLOSS,
POLISH, LUSTER, FLICKER,
TWINKLE, RADIATE, GLITTER
shiner ... BLACKEYE, MINNOW
shingle .... SIGN(BOARD),
GRAVEL, CLIP, SLAT, FACIA,
SIDING, SHIM
man with ...... LAWYER,
DOCTOR
shingles ...... HERPES, ZONA
shining ...... RADIANT, BRIGHT,
EMINENT, LUCENT, NITID,
LUCID, LUSTROUS
shinleaf ...... WINTERGREEN
shinny .... HOCKEY
shinplaster ... POULTICE, SCRIP
Shinto .... SINTU
deity .... KAMI
temple .... SHA
temple gate .... TORII
text .... KOJIKI, NOHONGI

ship .... VESSEL, AIRCRAFT,
EMBARK, BRIG, BILANDER,
LINER, CARRACK, HULK,
DHOW, DROMON(D),
TARTAN, GALLEON, CLIPPER,
PINKIE, PINKY, YACHT,
HOOKER
abandoned .... DERELICT
afterpart of .... QUARTER
anchor rope ... HAWSER
anchorage ....
ROAD(STEAD), MARINA
balance of .... TRIM
ballast .... LASTAGE,
KENTLEDGE
beak .... ROSTRUM
biscuit .... (HARD)TACK,
PATILE
boat on ..... GIG, JOLLY,
YAWL, PINNACE,
DINGHY, LAUNCH
body of .... HULK, HULL
boom .... BUMPKIN
bow flag .... JACK
breadth .... BEAM
cabin .... CUDDY
canvas .... SAIL
capacity ...... TONNAGE
captain .... MASTER,
SKIPPER
captive .... PRIZE
carpenter .... CHIPS
chains .... TYES
change course of ... TACK
channel .... GAT
clean bottom of .. BREAM
clean hull of ..... GRAVE
cleaning tool .... HOG
clumsy .... TUB, ARK,
DROGHER
coal .... COLLIER
coal bin .... BUNKER
crane .... DAVIT
crew member .... HAND,
MATE, YEOMAN, STOKER
crosspiece .... BEAM
device for raising sunken
CAMEL, CAISSON
direct a .... NAVIGATE
drain hole ..... SCUPPER
fender .... SKID
fictional .... CAINE
flag ...... BURGEE, JACK
flat-bottomed ..... KEEL
forward part ...... BOW,
PROW, STEM

framework .... HULL,
    CARCASS
fraud .... BARRATRY
fuel tank of ..... BUNKER
galley .. CABOOSE, CUDDY,
    KITCHEN
gun platform .. SPONSON
heave of .... SCEND
hold .... BULK
hospital ...... SICK BAY
hunting .... RAIDER,
    SEALER, WHALER,
    WHALEBOAT
jail .... BRIG, HULK
kitchen .... GALLEY,
    CABOOSE
ladder .... RATLINE
land from ...... DEBARK
lateen-sailed .... TARTAN
left-side ..... LARBOARD,
    PORT
line on side .... PLIMSOLL
list .... MANIFEST
load ...... CARGO, BULK
logbook .... JOURNAL
lowest deck ...... ORLOP
made smaller ..... RAZEE
master .... CAPTAIN,
    SKIPPER
master's declaration ....
    PROTEST
merchant .... GAL(L)IOT,
    TRADER, GALLEON,
    ARGOSY
metal plating .... STRAKE
mooring place ....
    ANCHORAGE, MARINA,
    DOCK, BERTH
mythical .... ARGO
not seagoing ...... HULK
of the desert ..... CAMEL
of 1492 ..... NINA, PINTA
officer .... PURSER, MATE,
    MASTER, SKIPPER,
    BOS'N, CAPTAIN
opening .... HATCH(WAY)
part of .... DECK, SALON,
    POOP, GALLEY,
    STEERAGE, STERN, BOW,
    KEEL, RUDDER,
    PROMENADE
passage ... GAT, STEERAGE
passenger accommodation
    PASSAGE
passenger, clandestine ...
    STOWAWAY

path of .... LANE
peg .... KEVEL
permit .... PRATIQUE
personnel .... CREW,
    COMPLEMENT
petty officer .... BOS(U)N
pirate .... CORSAIR,
    FRIGATE, PRIVATEER
place for sick .... BAY
planking .... STRAKE
platform ...... SPONSON
poetic ...... KEEL, BARK
position finder ... LORAN
prison ...... HULK, BRIG
provisioner ... CHANDLER
prow's front .. CUTWATER
pull .... KEDGE
rear of .... AFT
record .... LOG
rib .... FUTTOCK
rigging ... GEAR, TACKLE
rope .... TYE
sailing .... TARTAN,
    SCHOONER, GALLEON,
    CLIPPER
sails .... KITES
scout .... PINNACE
side opening ... PORTHOLE
side scaffold ..... FLAKE
single-masted ... TARTAN
sink a .... SCUTTLE
skipper .... MASTER,
    CAPTAIN
slow .... BUCKET, TUB
smoke pipe ...... STACK,
    FUNNEL
space for provisions .....
    LAZARETTO
speed measuring device ..
    LOG
square-masted ..... BRIG
square-rigged .. CLIPPER
steer a .. NAVIGATE, CONN
stern section ...... POOP,
    BUTTOCKS
supplier ...... CHANDLER
supply .... TENDER,
    TRANSPORT, COLLIER
table railing ...... FIDDLE
tender .... COCKBOAT,
    PINNACE
tax on .... TONNAGE
timber .... KEELSON, SNY,
    CARLING, BITT,
    STEMSON, FUTTOCK

torpedoed May 1915 ...
        LUSITANIA
track .... WAKE
trading .... ARGOSY,
   GALLEON, GAL(L)IOT
troop .... TRANSPORT
two-masted .. BRIG, GRAB
water in the hold .. BILGE
waterline ...... PLIMSOLL
wheel .... HELM
whistle .... HORN, BLAST
widest breadth .... BEAM
windlass ...... CAPSTAN
"window" ... PORTHOLE
worm ... TEREDO, BORER
wrecked .... WRACK
shipbuilding peg .. TRE(E)NAIL,
      TRUNNEL
shipjack .... SHAD
shipping hazard ... REEF, FOG
  list .... MANIFEST
  news .... SAILINGS
ships, collectively ...... CRAFT
  group of .... FLEET,
      FLOTILLA
shipshape ... ORDERLY, NEAT,
     TRIM, TIDY
shipside scaffold .... FLAKE
shipworm .... TEREDO, BORER
shipwreck goods ... FLOTSAM,
      JETSAM
shipwrecked person ....
      CASTAWAY
shire .... COUNTY
shirk ...... NEGLECT, EVADE,
  SKULK, FUNK, GOLDBRICK,
   DODGE, SHUN, MALINGER
shirker ... TRUANT, SLACKER,
    DODGER, EVADER
shirt .... CHEMISE, CAMISE,
  SKIVVY, JERSEY, SARK,
   GUERNSEY, PARKA
  broadcloth .... PIMA
  collar stiffener ..... STAY
  front .... DICK(E)Y,
     PLASTRON
  front ornament .... STUD
  sleeve ...... HOMESPUN,
   PLAIN, SIMPLE
  sleeve button .. CUFFLINK
shittah .... ACACIA
shivaree .... SERENADE,
     CHARIVARI
shive .... SPLINTER, CORK
shiver .... SHAKE, QUAKE,
  BREAK, SHATTER, QUIVER,

  TREMBLE, SPLINTER,
  FRAGMENT, SHUDDER,
     CHITTER
shivery ...... BRITTLE, CHILLY,
     CHILLING
Shkoder .... SCUTARI
shoal ...... SHALLOW, MASS,
  SPIT, BANK, REEF, BAR,
   SCHOOL, RIFFLE
shoat .... PIG(LET), SHOTE
shock ... IMPACT, BLOW, STUN,
  APPAL(L), CONCUSSION,
   JOLT, JAR, BRUNT,
  STROKE, STARTLE,
  PARALYZE, TRAUMA
  absorber ...... CUSHION,
     SNUBBER
  dog .... POODLE
  gather into a ...... STOOK
  main .... BRUNT
  tactics ...... BLITZKRIEG
  therapy drug ... INSULIN,
     METRAZOL
  to action ..... GALVANIZE
shod .... CALCED
shoddy .... SHAM, CHEAP
shoe ... FOOTWEAR, BROGAN,
  BOOT, BROGUE, GALOSH(E),
  PUMP, OXFORD, STOG(E)Y,
  CLOG, GAITER, LOAFER,
    CLODHOPPER
  armor .... SOLLERET
  canvas .... SNEAKER
  cloglike .... PATTEN
  fastener .... LATCHET
  flap .... TONGUE
  form .... LAST
  front .... VAMP
  heavy .... GALOSH(E)
  house ..... MULE, SLIPPER
  lace tag .... AGLET
  leather .... SUEDE,
     FOXING
  low ...... PUMP, SANDAL,
     SLIPPER
  maker ..... CORDWAINER
  mender .... COBBLER
  moccasin-like ...... PAC
  model .... LAST
  ornament ...... BUCKLE
  oxford .... BROGAN
  part .... (IN)SOLE, RAND,
  INSTEP, UPPER, HEEL,
  LAST, VAMP, EYELET,
     WELT
  plate .... CALK, CREEPER,

CRAMPON, CLAMPER,
TRAMP
repair .... COBBLE
shape of .... LAST
sole addition ... HOBNAIL
sole part .... SHANK
spike .... CLIMBER
sport .... LOAFER
style .... PLATFORM
tennis .... SNEAKER
uppers material ....
PRUNELLA, FOXING,
LASTING
walking .... BALMORAL
woman's .... CHOPINE
wooden .. CLOG, PATTEN,
SABOT, GETA
wooden-soled .... CLOG,
SABOT
shoebill .... STORK, HERON
shoelace tip .... TAG
shoemaker .. COBBLER, SUTOR,
SNOB, CORDWAINER
awl of .... ELSEN
block of .... LAST
patron saint of .. CRISPIN
shoes, brown .... TANS
open-heeled ... STEP-INS
work .... BROGAN
shoestring .... LACE(T)
shogun ... GOVERNOR, TYCOON
Sholem, author .... ASCH
shoo .. SCAT, GET OUT, SCRAM,
DRIVE
shool .... JAEGER
shoot ... ROD, CAST, TWINGE,
BUD, SPRIG, TWIG, HURL,
FIRE, FILM, THROW, DART,
PLUG, FLAGELLUM, CHIT,
SPROUT, PROJECT
firearm .... FIRE
forth .... BURGEON
from cover .... SNIPE,
AMBUSH
game for food ..... POT
grafting .... (s)CION
lichen .... FROND
plant ... STOLON, (s)CION,
VIMEN, RAT(T)OON
root/stem ..... TILLER,
RAT(T)OON
scene again ..... RETAKE
seaweed .... FROND
shooter .... MARBLE, ALLEY,
TAW

shooting iron ... PISTOL, GUN,
FIREARM
match .... SKEET, TIR
star ... METEOR, LEONID,
BOLIDE, FIREBALL
shoots .... BROWSE
shop ...... STORE, BOUTIQUE,
FACTORY, PARLOR
girl .... GRISETTE
nameplate of ..... FACIA
shophar .... HORN
shoplifter .... STEALER,
BOOSTER
shopman .... CLERK
shoptalk .... SLANG
shoran .... RADAR
part of ... SHORT, RANGE,
NAVIGATION
shore ... COAST, BEACH, PROP,
RIVAGE, SAND, BANK,
WATERSIDE
along .... LITTORAL
bird ... CURLEW, RUFF,
SNIPE, AVOCET,
SANDPIPER, STILT,
PLOVER, RAIL,
DOWITCHER, DOTT(E)REL
of the .... LITTORAL,
COASTAL
poetic .... STRAND
short .... BRIEF, LOW,
CONCISE, CURT, ABRUPT,
SCANT, FRIABLE, LACKING,
SHY
and fat ... TUBBY, PODGY,
PUDGY, SQUAT
and stout .... SQUAB
and thick .... PODGY,
CHUNKY, SQUAB
branch .... SNAG
cake .... BISCUIT
combining form ....
BRACHY
comedy ... SKIT, SKETCH
fall .... LACK
for .... IN BRIEF
in .... BRIEFLY
in loan money ....
STRINGENT
lived .... TRANSIENT,
EPHEMERAL, TRANSITORY,
DECIDUOUS
musical passage ....
MORCEAU
of .... LACKING
race ...... DASH, SPRINT

rest .... NAP, SIESTA
ride .... SPIN
seller .... BEAR
shrift .... ABRUPT
skirt .... MINI
slang .... SHY
sighted .... MYOPIC
snort .... SHOT
song ...... ODE, DITTY,
ARIETTA
sound .... SNAP
spoken .... LACONIC,
CURT, BRIEF, TERSE
story .... CONTE
supply, in .... SCARCE
tail .... SCUT
tempered .... TESTY
visit .... CALL
winded ... PURSY, PUFFY
shortage .... DEFICIT, LACK,
DEFICIENCY, NEED
shortchange ...... CHEAT
shortcoming .. FAULT, DEFECT
shorten .... REDUCE,
ABBREVIATE, ABRIDGE,
CROP, CUT, DOCK, LOP,
REEVE, ELIDE, CONDENSE
mast/bowsprit ..... REEF
shortened ..... CURTATE, CUT
shortening .... LARD, FAT, OIL,
OLEO
shorthand ... GREGG, PITMAN,
STENOTYPE
character .... POT, HOOK
girl .... STENO
sign .... PHONOGRAM
shortly .... SOON, ANON,
RUDELY
shorts .... TROUSERS,
LEFT-OVERS
shortsighted .. MYOPIC, MYOPY
person .... MYOPE
shorty .... RUNT
Shoshonean Indian ..... OTOE,
UTE, P(A)IUTE, HOPI,
COMANCHE
Shostakovich, composer ......
DMITRI
shot ...... TRY, GUESS, SCOPE,
RANGE, PELLET, MARKSMAN,
DOSE, FLECKED, SHELL,
LANGRAGE, LANGREL
and shell .... AMMO,
AMMUNITION
that hits target ... CLOUT
shote .... SHOAT, PIG(LET)

shoulder .... CARRY, PUSH,
EPAUL
armor .... PAULDRON
belt .... BALDRIC
blade .... SCAPULA
blade part ... ACROMION
bone .... HUMERUS
combining form .... OMO
muscle .... DELTOID
of the .... SCAPULAR
ornament .. EPAULET(TE)
pack .... KNAPSACK
protection for ....
PAULDRON
road's .... BERM(E)
wrap ..... SHAWL, SCARF,
STOLE
shoulders, covering for ......
NUBIA
draw up .... SHRUG
fur piece ...... PALATINE
of the .... HUMERAL
shout ..... WHOOP, YELL, CRY,
CALL, HOLLER
down .... SILENCE
of joy/approval .... OLE,
HURRAH, VIVA, HEAR,
HUZZA, BRAVO
shove .... BUNT, JOG, THRUST,
NUDGE, PUSH, JOSTLE
off ...... LEAVE, DEPART
shovel ... SCOOP, SPADE, VAN,
PEEL
shovelhead .... SHARK,
STURGEON
show ...... EVINCE, EXHIBIT,
DISPLAY, REVEAL, GUIDE,
MANIFEST, PROVE, APPEAR,
FLASH, PARADE, PAGEANT,
EXPOSE, SIGHT, PRETENSE,
MUMMERY
anger .... FUME
bill .... PLACARD
empty .... FARCE
hypocritical .. MUMMERY
in .... USHER
indecision ..... WAVER,
FALTER, VACILLATE
in law ... PLEAD, ALLEGE
likeness .... MIRROR
of embarrassment ......
SQUIRM
off ..... PARADE, FLAUNT
peep .... RAREE
stage ... REVUE, FOLLIES

up ..... ARRIVE, COME, APPEAR

vain .... POMP

water .... AQUACADE

shower ... SLEET, HAIL, SPRAY, SPRINKLE, SCATTER, POUR, BATH, PARTY, FALLOUT, RAIN(FALL), PEPPER

fall in a .... CASCADE

of meteors .. ANDROMID, LEONID

rain .... BRASH

showing good taste .... DECOROUS

showman, famous ..... FLO, ZIEGFELD, BARNUM, RINGLING, CARROLL, ROSE

showpiece .. EXAMPLE, EXHIBIT, SAMPLE

showy .... FLASHY, OSTENTATIOUS, ARTY, FLAMBOYANT, GAUDY, SWANKY, LOUD, GARISH, ORNATE, TAWDRY

display .... BLAZON, SPLURGE

display in dress .... FRIPPERY

gaieties .... GAUDS

show ..... PAGEANT(RY), EXTRAVAGANZA, SPECTACLE

thing, worthless .... TRUMPERY

shrapnel .... SHELL

shred .... WISP, VESTIGE, FRAZZLE, TATTER, FRAGMENT, RAG, SNIP, PARTICLE, DAG, MAMMOCK

shrew .... SORICINE, TERMAGANT, ERD, SCOLD, VIXEN, HARPY, VIRAGO, NAG

like .... SORICINE

mouse .... HYRAX

name of Shakespeare's ... KATE

sister of Shakespeare's .... BIANCA

shrewd ..... CLEVER, ARTFUL, SAGACIOUS, FOXY, CANNY, WILY, ASTUTE, CAGEY, CUNNING, SMART, SLY, KEEN

person .. FOX, SMOOTHIE

shrewish .... NAGGING, TERMAGANT

shrews, of .... SORICINE

shriek .... CRY, SCREAM, YELL, SCREECH

shrieve .... SHERIFF

shrift .... ABSOLUTION

shrike .... WOODCHAT, BIRD, OSCINE

shrill .... HIGH-PITCHED, STRIDENT, PIPY

sound/voice .... TREBLE, PIPING, REEDY, SKIRL, SHRIEK, SCREAM

shrimp .... CRUSTACEAN, MALACOSTRACAN, MACRURAN

appendage ...... UROPOD

covering .... MAIL

kin .... GRIBBLE

like crustacean .. PRAWN

shrine .... TABERNACLE, DAGOBA, ALTAR, MARTYRY, GROTTO

for relics ...... FERETORY

visitor .... PILGRIM

shrink .... CONTRACT, COWER, CRINGE, RECOIL, SHRIVEL, WIZEN

from .... FUNK

shrinking .... TIMID, SHY

shrive .... ABSOLVE

shrivel ...... CURL, WITHER, WRINKLE, WIZEN, MUMMIFY

shroff .... BANKER, MONEYCHANGER

Shropshire .... SALOP

river .... SEVERN

shroud .... VEIL, PALL, COVER, CEREMENT, SCREEN, SHEET

Shrove Tuesday .. MARDI GRAS

shrub ... BUSH, LILAC, SALAL, ELDER, PLANT, OLEASTER, LAUREL, SMILAX, ALTHEA, BRAMBLE, GORSE, SENNA, SUMAC, ALDER, SPIREA, MISTLETOE, MAGNOLIA, CASCARILLA, RHODORA

aromatic ..... LAVENDER, MINT, BERGAMOT, ROSEMARY

bean family ..... RETEM, BROOM

berry .... CURRANT

birch family ...... HAZEL

bushy ...... CADE, TOD, SAVIN

climbing .... AMPELOPSIS,
CLEMATIS, LIANA
dwarfed .... BONSAI
evergreen .... LAUREL,
ERICA, LAURUSTINE,
OLEASTER, TOYON,
SAVIN, HEATH, MYRTLE,
JASMINE, TITI, YEW,
SALAL, JUNIPER, FURZE,
CAMELLIA, ILEX,
OLEANDER
fence .... HEDGE(ROW)
flowering ...... AZALEA,
JASMINE, SYRINGA
genus .... OLEA, ITEA,
RHUS, LANTANA,
SPIREA, SYRINGA,
ERICA, EVEA
grape family ....
AMPELOPSIS
grown flat ..... ESPALIER
heath family .... KALMIA
holly family .... ILEX
honeysuckle .. WEIGELA,
VIBURNUM
mallow family .. HIBISCUS,
ALTH(A)EA
mint family ... ROSEMARY
olive ..... OLEA, PRIVET,
JASMIN(E)
Pacific coast ..... SALAL
pea family .. MESQUIT(E),
CASSIA, LOTUS,
MIMOSA, LABURNUM,
LOTOS, WISTERIA
pepper family ... CUBEB,
KAVA
poisonous .... SUMAC(H),
OLEANDER
prickly .... BRAMBLE,
CAPER, CHICO
rose family .. HARDHACK,
SPIR(A)EA
rubber source .. GUAYULE
spiny ..... CHICO, FURZE,
GORSE
spurge family ....
CASCARILLA
stunted ... SCRUB, BONSAI
tea family .... CAMELLIA
tropical ... INGA, ABELIA,
LANTANA, JASMIN(E),
JESSAMINE, HENNA
shrubbery .... BOSCAGE, TOD,
COPPICE

shrubby ..... FRUTESCENT,
FRUTICOSE
shrubs, clump of ...... SCRUB
shuck ...... POD, HUSK, SHELL
shudder ..... QUAKE, TREMOR,
SHAKE, TREMBLE
shuffle .... SHIFT, SCUFF,
DECEIVE, MIX, RIFFLE,
TRICK, SHAMBLE
shuffler .... COOT, DUCK
Shufu .... KASHGAR
shun .... EVADE, DODGE,
AVOID
shunt ...... TURN OFF, SHIFT,
DIVERT, SWITCH, SIDETRACK
shush ... HIST, HUSH, SILENCE,
QUIET
Shushan .... SUSA
shut .... CLOSE, BAR, SECURED
eye: sl. .... SLEEP
in ... CONFINE, INVALID,
PENT(UP)
out ..... BAN, EXCLUDE,
OSTRACIZE
up ... IMPRISON, CLOSET,
IMMURE
with force .... SLAM
shutter .... BLIND, SLIDE,
PERSIENNE
shuttle, bobbin/spool .... PIRN
shuttlecock .... BIRD
shy ... COY, BASHFUL, WARY,
SHORT, DIFFIDENT, DEMURE,
BALK, RESERVED, RETIRING,
MIM, TIMID, MODEST,
RECOIL, START, CHARY,
TIMOROUS, VERECUND, JIB
Shylock .... USURER,
MONEYLENDER
daughter of ..... JESSICA
money of ..... DUCATS
shyster .... PETTIFOGGER
si: Sp. .... YES
sialid .... INSECT, DOBSON FLY
Siam .... THAILAND (see)
siamang .... GIBBON
Siamese (see Thailand)
capital .... BANGKOK,
THONBURI, AYUDHYA
coin ... BAHT, ATT, TICAL
dynasty......... CHAKRI
isthmus .... KRA
king........ ADULYADEJ,
MONGKUT,
CHULALONGKORN,
PRACHATIPOK, MAHIDOL

kingdom capital .... CHIENGMAI
measure ...... SOK, KUP, SISTI
monetary unit ..... BAHT, TICAL
premier ...... THANARAT
queen .... SIRIKIT
river .... MENAM, CHAUPAYA
tongue .... LAO, TAI
tribe .... MEO
twins, one of ... CHANG, ENG
weight .... PAI, TICAL
Sian .... SINGAN
sib ..... KIN(SMAN), RELATIVE, BROTHER, SISTER
Sibelius, composer ..... JEAN
  work .... FINLANDIA
Siberian .. VOGUL, SAMOYED(E)
  antelope .... SAIGA
  city .... OMSK, TOMSK
  forests .... TAIGA
  fur ... CALABAR, CALABER
  ibex .... TEK
  leopard .... OUNCE
  mountains .... ALTAI
  native ... TATAR, YAKUT, YUIT, KIRGIZ
  peninsula .. KAMCHATKA, TAIMIR
  plain .... STEPPE
  region .. OMSK, TA(R)TARY
  river ... AMUR, LENA, OB, IRTISH, YENISEI, KOLIMA, TOBOL
  sheep .... ARGALI
  squirrel .... CALABER, CALABAR, MINIVER
  tent .... YURT
  warehouse .... ETAPE
  wasteland .... STEPPE
  wild cat .... MANUL
  wild sheep ...... ARGALI
  windstorm ...... BURAN
sibilance .... HISS
sibilate .... HISS
sibling ... SIS(TER), BROTHER, KIN
sibyl .... SEERESS, ORACLE, SORCERESS, WITCH, FORTUNETELLER
sibylline .... ORACULAR
  sign .... OMEN
sic ... THUS, SO, SUCH, ATTACK

sicca .... SEAL
siccative ..... DRIER, DRYING
Sicilian .... TRINACRIAN, SICANIAN
  capital .... PALERMO
  city .... ENNA, GELA, RAGUSA, MAZZARO, PALERMO, CATANIA, TRAPANI
  evergreen .... MAQUIS
  hero .... ENTELLUS
  inhabitant, legendary .... CYCLOPS
  king .... RENE
  landmark .... ETNA
  resort .... ENNA
  river .... ACIS
  seaport .... PALERMO, MARSALA, MILAZZO, MESSINA, MESSENE
  secret society ..... MAFIA
  shotgun .... LUPARA
  volcano .... (A)ETNA
  whirlpool ... CHARYBDIS
  wine .... MARSALA
sick ... INDISPOSED, UNWELL, ILL, UNSOUND, SURFEITED, AILING, ATTACK
  person .... INVALID, PATIENT
sickbed, of a ...... CLINICAL
sicken .... AIL, NAUSEATE
sickle ... HOOK, SIVE, SCYTHE, BUSHWHACKER
  shaped .... FALCATE
sickness ... MALADY, DISEASE, NAUSEA
Sid _____ .... CAESAR
Siddhartha .... BUDDHA
side ...... ASPECT, FACTION, MINOR, FACET, FLANK
  arm .... PISTOL, SWORD, BAYONET, REVOLVER
  by side ...... ABREAST, COLLATERAL
  dish .... ENTREE, ENTREMETS, SALAD, SLAW, TRIMMING
  interest .... HOBBY, AVOCATION
  kick .... ALTER EGO, CONFEDERATE, PARTNER, PAL, FRIEND
  meat .... BACON
  of a .... LATERAL
  pain .... STITCH

portion ...·...·... RASHER
road ...·..·..·... BYWAY
step ...·..·... AVOID, EVADE,
  DODGE
trip ...·...·...·... SALLY
view ...·...·...·... PROFILE
sideboard ...·..·... CREDENZA
sideburns ... MUTTON CHOPS,
  WHISKERS
sideline ...·.. BENCH, BY-WORK
sidelong look ...·...·... SQUINT
sidereal ...·.. STARRY, STELLAR
siderite ...·..·... METEORITE,
  IRON(ORE)
sidero, as combining form ...·
  IRON, STAR
sides, unequal ...·..·... SCALENE
sideslip ...·...·..·... SKID
sidesplitting ...·.. CONVULSIVE,
  HEARTY
sidestep ...·..·.. AVOID, EVADE
sidetrack ... SHUNT, SWITCH,
  DIVERT, TURN, SIDING,
  AVERT
sidewalk ...·...·.. PAVEMENT,
  BANQUETTE
  entrepreneur ...· BEGGAR,
  HAWKER, PEDDLER,
  ARTIST, NEWSBOY
sideways, move ...·..·.. SIDLE,
  EDGE, SKID
  walker ...·..·...·... CRAB
sidewinder ...·.. RATTLESNAKE,
  CROTALUS
sidewise ...·...·..·... LATERAL
  move ...·..·.. SKEW, SIDLE
siding ..· CLAPBOARD, SHINGLE,
  SPUR
sidle ...·...·... EDGE, SKEW, JIB
Sidon's name now ...·.. SAIDA
siecle ...·..·...·... AGE, CENTURY,
  PERIOD
siege ...·..·..·...·.. INVESTMENT
  lay ...·..·.. INVEST, BESET
siegers' shelter ...·..·...·... CAT,
  MANTLET
Siegfried ...·..·..·...·... SIGURD
  follower ...·..·.. NIBELUNG
  Line ...· WESTWALL, LIMES
  sword of ...·..·... BALMUNG
  wife of ...·..·... KRIEMHILD
sienna ...·..·..·...·... PIGMENT
Sierra ...·..·.. RANGE, PINTADO,
  KINGFISH, MADRE, LEONE,
  NEVADA
  fish resembling ...·..·...·.

Leone capital ...·..·... MACKEREL
  ...·..·..·...
  FREETOWN
mountain ...·...·..·.. DANA
Nevada fog ...·.. POGONIP
Nevada lake ...·.. TAHOE
Nevada peak ... WHITNEY,
  MULHACEN
siesta ...·..·...·.. NAP, REST
sieur ...·..·..·...·.. SIR
sieve ...·..·... SIFTER, STRAINER,
  SCREEN, FILTER, LAUN,
  TROMMEL, RIDDLE, BOLTER,
  CRIBBLE
  like a ...·..·..·... ETHMOID
sift ...·..·..· WINNOW, SIEVE,
  WEIGH, SCREEN, FILTER,
  BOLT
sifter ...·..·.. SIEVE, STRAINER,
  BOLTER
siftings ...·..·..·...·.. RESIDUE
sigh ... YEARN, SUSPIRE, MOAN,
  SOUGH, SOB, SOUF
sight ...·..·... VIEW, SPECTACLE,
  LOOK, GLIMPSE, VISION,
  EYE, AIM, SCENE, PICTURE,
  ESPY
  by ...·..·..·... VISUAL(LY)
  colloquial ...·..·... UGLY
  come into ...·..·... LOOM
  gun ...·..·..·...·.. BEAD
  of ...·.. VISUAL, OCULAR
sightless ...·..·..·...·.. BLIND
sightly ...·..·..·... COMELY
sigil ...·..·... SIGNET, SEAL
sigmoid ...·..·.. ESS, SIGMATE
sign(s) ..· TOKEN, INDICATION,
  GESTURE, SYMPTOM, BADGE,
  EVIDENCE, INDEX, INDICIA,
  OMEN, SYMBOL, MARK,
  VESTIGE, PORTENT, INDEX,
  EARMARK
  affirmative ...·..·... NOD
  arithmetical ...·..·.. PLUS,
  MINUS
  away ...·..·..·... CONVEY
  Blue Eagle ...·..·... NRA
  display ...·..·.. PLACARD,
  SHINGLE
  homage ...· BOW, KNEEL,
  CURTSY, GENUFLECTION,
  SALAAM
  in magic ...·..·...· SIGIL
  in music ...·..·.. SEGNO,
  NEUM(E), CLEF, STAFF,
  PRESA

language science .... SEMIOLOGY

omission .... CARET

road/street ...... ARROW

up ... ENLIST, JOIN, HIRE, ENGAGE, EMPLOY, ENROL(L)

signal .. SIGN, TOKEN, NOTABLE, STRIKING, CUE, ALARM, BUZZ, WARN, FLAG

actor's .... CUB

assembly ...... REVEILLE

board .... SHINGLE

danger ...... RED FLAG, RED LIGHT, SIREN, SYMPTOM

entrance/exit ... SENNET

eye .... WINK

flag .... ENSIGN, WAIF, JACK

for parley ..... CHAMADE, WHITE FLAG

Indian .... SMOKE

light .... FLARE, BEACON

lights out .... TAPS

parley .... CHAMADE

railroad .... FUSEE

retirement ..... CURFEW, TAPS

retreat .... CHAMADE

seance .... TAP

set .... CODE, LORAN

stage ...... CUE, SENNET

warning ... ALARM, SIREN, WINK, RED LIGHT, ALERT, CAUTION

signaling apparatus .... SEMAPHORE, BEACON, HOWLER, FOGHORN, BLINKER

signature .... HAND, SEAL

flourish .... SCROLL, PARAPH

in radio .... THEME

of a sort .... THUMBMARK, CRISS-CROSS

musical .... THEME

signboard .... SHINGLE

signet .... SIGIL, SEAL

significance .... MEANING, MOMENT, IMPORT

significant ...... MEANINGFUL, IMPORTANT, MOMENTOUS

signify ..... MEAN, INDICATE, DENOTE, IMPLY, BODE

Signoret, actress ..... SIMONE

signpost .. CLUE, HERMA, GUIDE

signs, of .... SEMIOTIC

Sigurd .... SIEGFRIED

father of .... REGIN

victim of .... FAFNIR

Sikh religion founder .. NANAK

Sikkim capital ..... GANGTOK

inhabitants .... NEPALESE

king .... CHOGYAL

queen .... GYALMO

woman's dress ...... KHO

Sikorsky, airplane builder .... IGOR

silage .... FODDER

Silas Marner author ... ELIOT

ward of .... EPPIE

silence ... STILLNESS, REPRESS, THROTTLE, MUTE, (S)HUSH, HIST, QUIET(UDE), GAG, OYEZ, LULL, WHIST

silencer ... MUFFLER, HUSHER

silent ..... QUIET, STILL, MUM, MUTE, TACIT, INACTIVE, WHIST, NOISELESS

habitually ..... TACITURN

it is .... TACET

Silenus .... DEITY, SATYR

foster son of ... BACCHUS

Silesia .... SLASK, LINEN

silex ... SILICA, FLINT, QUARTZ

silhouette .... OUTLINE, PORTRAIT

silica .... SILEX, MINERAL, QUARTZ, SAND, MICA

deposit .... SINTER

silicate ... TREMOLITE, ESTER, MICA, CERITE, EPIDOTE

silique .... POD

silk .... ALAMODE, TULLE

and cotton cloth .... EOLIENNE

and wool cloth .... BARATHEA, EOLIENNE

cloth, damasklike .... LAMPAS

cloth for ribbons, etc. .... SARCENET

cloth, striped .. TABARET

coarse .... TUSSA(H), TUSSAR, TUSSER

cocoon .... BAVE

corded .... FAILLE, PADUASOY, REP(S), REPP, OTTOMAN

cotton (tree) ..... CEIBA, KAPOK

damask-like ... . LAMPAS
fabric .... SHANTUNG,
    SURAH, VOILE, PEKIN,
    PONGEE, CHARMEUSE,
    CAFFA, MOIRE, SATIN,
    SENDAL, BAREGE, GROS,
    MADRAS, MESSALINE,
    VELVET, VELOUR(S),
    SAMITE, TAFFETA
fiber ... . FLOSS
filament ... ... BRIN
finely woven ... .
    LANSDOWNE
for mourning ... ... ALMAS
for ribbons ... ... SARCENET
glossy ... ... LUSTRING,
    LUTESTRING
hat ... ... TILE, TOPPER
heavy ... ... GROS
hit the ... ... PARACHUTE
knitted ... ... JERSEY
like ... ... SERICEOUS
lining material ... ...
    SARCENET
net ... ... MALINE(S)
netting ... ... TULLE
producing moth ... ...
    AILANTHUS
raw ... GREGE, MARABOU
ribbed ... REP(S), FAILLE,
    REPP
ribbonlike ... ... GIMP
rough ... ... RAJAH
screen print ... SERIGRAPH
sheer ... ... VOILE
shreds ... ... NOIL
source of ... ... COCOON,
    AILANTHUS, ERIA
stocking ... ... ELEGANT,
    WEALTHY, WHIG
synthetic ... ... NYLON,
    ORLON, RAYON, DACRON
taffeta ... ... TABBY
thread ... TRAM, SLEAVE,
    FLOSS
threadmaker ... ...
    THROWSTER
twilled ... ALMA, SERGE,
    SURAH
twisted ... ... ROVE
veil ... ... TULLE
waste ... ... NOIL, FLOSS,
    KNUB, FRISON
watered ... ... MOIRE,
    TABBY, MOREEN
weight ... ... PARI

silken ... ... SOFT, SMOOTH,
    GLOSSY, SERIC
silky ... ... SMOOTH, SATINY
silkworm ... ERI(A), TUSSA(H),
    TUSSER, BOMBYX, TUSSORE
cocoon covering .. FLOSS
covering ... ... COCOON
disease ... ... UJI
food ... ... MULBERRY
leaves ... ... MULBERRY,
    AILANTHUS
moth ... ... BOMBYCID,
    CECROPIA
raising ... ... SERICULTURE
silky ... ... SERICEOUS, SOFT,
    LUSTROUS
furred animal .. TAMARIN,
    MARMOSET
sill ... ... LEDGE
counterpart ... ... LINTEL
projection ... ... DRIP
sillabub ... DESSERT, BEVERAGE
siller ... ... MONEY
Sills, singer ... ... BEVERLY
silly ... ... ASININE, IMBECILE,
    INANE, FATUOUS, SAPPY,
    ABSURD, SLAP-HAPPY,
    DAFFY, DAFT, PUERILE,
    KOOKIE, KOOKY
language ... ... BOMBAST
one ... ... GOOSE
silo ... ... PIT, TOWER
silt ... ... WASH, SEDIMENT,
    ALLUVIUM
silurid ... ... CATFISH
silva ... ... WOODS
silver ... SILLER, COIN, MONEY,
    ARGENT(UM), SYCEE
Age writer ... ... TACITUS,
    JUVENAL, MARTIAL
alloy ... BILLON, ALBATA
containing ... ... LUNAR
dollar: sl. ... CARTWHEEL
fluoride ... ... TACHIOL
fox fur ... ... PLATINA
gilded ... ... VERMEIL
in alchemy ... ... LUNA
ingot ... SYCEE, BULLION
lacework ... ... FILIGREE
like/of ... ... ARGENTINE
screen ... MOVIES, CINEMA
State ... ... NEVADA
telluride ... ... HESSITE
tongued ... ... ELOQUENT
tongued person ... ORATOR

unminted ...-.... BULLION,
SYCEE
wire work ..... FILIGREE
silverfish .... TARPON, SARGO
silverside(s) .... MINNOW,
TINKER, GRUNION
silverware decoration ....
GADROON
silvery ...-....... ARGENT(INE)
silviculture .... FORESTRY
simar .... JACKET, ROBB
Simenon, author ... GEORGES
detective .... MAIGRET
novel .... MAIGRET
simian .... APE, MONKEY
astronaut ...-.... BONNY,
ASTROMONK
similar ... AKIN, LIKE, AGNATE,
ANALOGOUS, SUCH
combining form .. HOMEO
similarity .... LIKENESS
similarly .... LIKEWISE
simile .... METAPHOR
similitude ...-..... FACSIMILE,
IMAGE, LIKENESS
simmer ... BOIL, SEETHE, STEW
down ..... COOL, SUBSIDE
simnel ... FRUITCAKE, BISCUIT
simoleon .... DOLLAR
Simon ...... APOSTLE, PETER
pure ...-... REAL, GENUINE,
AMATEUR
the overseer .... LEGREE
simoon ...-..... TEBBAD, WIND,
SAMIEL
simp ...-.. DOLT, SIMPLETON
simper .... SMIRK, SMILE
simple ... MERE, SNAP, SINGLE,
PLAIN, EASY, BARE,
ARTLESS, GREEN, STUPID,
COMMON, LOWLY, NATURAL
in law .... ABSOLUTE
machine ... LEVER, AXLE,
WHEEL, PULLEY, SCREW
minded .... STUPID,
FOOLISH
organism ...-.... AMOEBA,
MONAD
simpleton ... MORON, IMBECILE,
GOOSE, NITWIT, SAP, OAF,
NINCOMPOOP, FOOL, DOLT,
BOOBY, DIMWIT, COOT,
DAW, GAUP, SOFTHEAD,
NINNY, NODDY, DOODLE,
GOMERAL, GOWK, GAWK,
GABY, ZANY

Simplon _____ .... PASS
simply ... MERELY, ONLY, JUST
simulacrum .... IMAGE,
TRAVESTY, SHAM
simular ...-......... FEIGNED
simulate .... FEIGN, ACT,
PRETEND, ASSUME, FAKE,
SHAM, IMITATE, AFFECT, APE
simulation ... FEINT, PRETENSE,
FEIGNING
simurgh ...-.......... ROC
sin .... FAULT, OFFENSE,
INIQUITY, TRESPASS, ENVY,
SLOTH, GREED, VICE,
TRANSGRESS, EVIL, GUILT
capable of .... PECCABLE
petty ...... PECCADILLO
repentance for ....
CONTRITION, ATTRITION,
PENITENCE, REMORSE
Sinai ...-...... MOUNT, HOREB
sinalbin .... GLUCOSIDE
Sinaloa capital ..... CULIACAN
sinapism .... PLASTER
Sinatra, former Mrs. ... AVA,
MIA
Sinbad the _____ ...-... SAILOR
transport of .... ROC
since .... SITH, AGO, HENCE,
INASMUCH AS, BEFORE NOW
sincere ... FAITHFUL, HONEST,
EARNEST, OPEN, FRANK,
CANDID
sinciput .... FOREHEAD
Sinclair, novelist ..... UPTON,
MAY, CATHERINE,
LEWIS
character .... DOREMUS,
CASS, BABBITT
Sind, capital of ..... KARACHI
sine ....-.... WITHOUT
prole .... CHILDLESS
qua _____ .... NON
sinecure .... SNAP
sinew(s) ..... TENDON, FORCE,
THEWS, MUSCLE
sinewy ...-.. TOUGH, MUSCULAR,
BRAWNY, WIRY
sinful ...-.... WICKED, IMMORAL,
EVIL, PECCANT
sing ..... BUZZ, HUM, CHANT,
WARBLE, CAROL
in certain way ... CROON,
YODEL, HUM
slang .. CONFESS, SQUEAL
Singapore founder ... RAFFLES

garment .. .. SAMFOO,
KEBAYA, SARI,
CHEONGSAM
old name .. .. TEMASEK
president .. .. YUSOF
prime minister .. .. .. LEE
soup .. .. SOTO
singe .. .. BURN
singer .. .. CAROLER, VOCALIST,
CHORIST(ER), YODELER,
BIRD, POET, CANTOR,
MINSTREL
choir .. .. ALTO
female .. .. DIVA, SOPRANO,
CHANTEUSE,
CANTATRICE,
COLORATURA, LIND,
CHANTRESS, PRICE,
STEVENS
male .. .. TENOR, BARITONE,
MINSTREL, LANZA
opera ... MELBA, CALLAS,
ALDA, PONS, PATTI,
TAUBER, CARUSO,
TIBBET, GLUCK, NILSSON,
PINZA, TUCKER,
TEBALDI, TRAUBEL
stock of .. .. REPERTOIRE,
REPERTORY
wandering .. .. .. BUSKER,
MINSTREL
singers' group .. .. CHOIR,
TROUPE, ENSEMBLE
singing voice .. .. SOPRANO,
TENOR, BARITONE,' ALTO,
FALSETTO, COLORATURA,
BASSO
single .. .. INDIVIDUAL,
SOLITARY, UNMARRIED,
SOLE, (A)LONE, ACE, SOLO,
UNWED
combining form .. MONO,
UNI, HAPLO
file .. .. TANDEM
foot .. .. RACK
footed .. .. MONOPODE
handed .. .. UNAIDED
in biology ... UNIVALENT
in telegraphy ... SIMPLEX
man .. .. BACHELOR
out .. .. PICK, SELECT,
CHOOSE
point .. .. ACE
sticker .. SAILBOAT, SLOOP
thing .. .. UNIT
track railway .. MONORAIL

singlet .. . JERSEY, UNDERSHIRT
singly .. .. SOLO, ALONE,
UNAIDED, ONE BY ONE
singsong recitation .. .. CHIME
singular .. .. SOLE, UNIQUE,
INDIVIDUAL, STRANGE,
QUEER, UNUSUAL, ODD,
RARE
opposed to .. .. PLURAL
sinigrin .. .. GLUCOSIDE
sinister .. .. EVIL, OMINOUS,
WICKED, BALEFUL,
LEFT(SIDE), PORTENTOUS,
GRIM
opposed to .. ... DEXTER
sink .. .. FALL, SUBSIDE,
RECEDE, DECLINE, LOWER,
SEWER, CESSPOOL, BASIN,
DIP, DESCEND, SETTLE,
SAG, BOWL, SLUMP
ship deliberately .. ..
SCUTTLE
sinker .. .. DOUGHNUT
Sinkiang capital .. .. URUMCHI
Sinn ____, Irish society .. FEIN
sinople .. .. CINNABAR
sinuate .. .. WAVY, SINUOUS
sinuous .. ... WAVY, WINDING,
DEVIOUS, SLITHERY,
SERPENTINE
sinus .. .. CAVITY, BEND, CURVE,
ANTRA, ANTRUM
Sioux .. CROW, OSAGE, PONCA,
TETON, MANDAN, IOWA,
CATAWBA, DAKOTA, OTO(E)
chief .. .. SITTING BULL
sip ... DRINK, NIP, TASTE, TIFF
siphon .. .. DRAW, STRAW
sipid .. .. SAVORY
sipper .. .. STRAW
sippet .. .. TOAST, CROUTON,
FRAGMENT
sipping tube .. .. STRAW
sir .. ... SEIGNOR, (MON)SIEUR,
SAHIB, SENOR, EFFENDI,
TUAN, SRI
sire .. ... BEGET, (FORE)FATHER
siren .. WITCH, CIRCE, NYMPH,
ENCHANTRESS, CHARMER,
LORELEI, (FOG)HORN,
WHISTLE, VAMP,
PARTHENOPE
Rhine ... LORELEI, LURLEI
sirenian .. .. MANATEE, SEA COW,
DUGONG
Sirius .. .. CANICULA, DOG STAR

of .... SOTHIC
sirloin, beef .... BARON
sirocco .... WIND
    Madeira Island .... LESTE
sirup (see syrup) .... TREACLE,
    ORGEAT, GRENADINE,
    SORGHUM, MOLASSES
sirupy .... SACCHARINE
sisal .... FIBER, HEMP, AGAVE,
    HENEQUIN
Sisera's enemy .... BARAK
    murderer .... JAEL
    soldiers ..... CANAANITES
siskin .... FINCH, TARIN
sissy ... PANTYWAIST, MILKSOP
    like a .... EFFEMINATE
sister .... TITTY, TITTIE,
    NUN, SOROR, WOMAN,
    NURSE, SIB
    British .... NURSE
    fictional .... CARRIE
    headdress of a ... CORNET
Sistine Chapel feature ....
    FRESCOES
    Madonna painter ....
    RAPHAEL
sistrum .... RATTLE
sit ...... ROOST, POSE, PERCH,
    BROOD
    in .... ATTEND
    on .... REPRESS
site .... SEAT, SCENE, LOCALE,
    LOCATION, STEAD
sitology .... DIETETICS
Sitsang .... TIBET
sitter .... BROODER, NURSE
sitting ..... SESSION, MEETING,
    SEATED
    Bull's antagonist ....
    CUSTER
    room .... PARLOR, SALA,
    BOUDOIR
    spiritual .... SEANCE
situate .... LOCATE, POSIT,
    PLACE
situation ..... STATE, POSITION,
    PLACE
    difficult .... JAM, STRAIT,
    PLIGHT, FIX
situs ..... LOCATION, POSITION
Sitwell, poet .... EDITH,
    OSBERT
Siva's wife .... DEVI, MAYA,
    SA(K)TI
six .... HEXAD, SESTET
    combining form ... HEXA

footed .... HEXAPOD
group of .... HEXAD,
    SEXTET(TE), SESTET,
    SEXTUPLET, SENARY
    in dice game .. SICE, SISE
    of .... SENARY
    pointed figure ..... STAR
    prefix .... HEXA
    shooter .... REVOLVER
    years, lasting .. SEXENNIAL
16 1/2 feet .. ROD, POLE, PERCH
sixth day, occurring every ....
    SEXTAN
    sense .... INTUITION
sizable .... BIG, SUBSTANTIAL,
    HUGE
size .... MAGNITUDE, BULK
    of hole .... BORE
    of paper .... DEMY,
    FOOLSCAP, ROYAL
sizy .... GLUTINOUS, VISCOUS
sizzle .... HISS, FRIZZ(LE)
sizzling .... (RED)HOT
skate ..... RAY, HORSE, CHAP,
    ROCKER
    blade .... RUNNER
skating arena .... RINK
    sign .... REDBALL
skean ...... DAGGER, SWORD
skedaddle .... BOLT, DECAMP,
    BLOW
skee .... SKI
skein ...... HANK, MESH, RAP
    of yarn .... HASP
skeletal disease ..... RICKETS,
    RACHITIS
skeleton ...... FRAME(WORK),
    ATOMY, CARCASS, BONES
    copy in printing .. DUMMY
    force .... CADRE
    hiding place of .. CLOSET
    sea animal .... CORAL
Skelton, comedian ...... RED
skep .... BASKET, BEEHIVE
skeptic .. DOUBTER, AGNOSTIC,
    CYNIC, PYRRHO, LUCIAN
    Biblical .... THOMAS
skeptical .... DUBIOUS
skerry .... REEF
sketch ... DESIGN, DRAW(ING),
    OUTLINE, DRAFT, SKIT,
    MAP, PLAYLET, AFTERPIECE
    out .... DELINEATE
skete member .. MONK, HERMIT
skew .... SIDLE, SWERVE,
    SQUINT, OBLIQUE, TWIST

skewer .... PIN, SKIVER, SPIT,
BROACH, BROCHETTE, TRUSS
ski .... RUNNER
run ..... SCHUSS, SLALOM,
DOWNHILL, JUMP
skid ..... (SIDE)SLIP, RUNNER,
BRAKE, SLIDE, TRIG
row character ....
VAGRANT, HOBO,
DERELICT
skiddoo .... LEAVE, DEPART
skiff ...... CAIQUE, ROWBOAT
skiing race .... SLALOM
skill .... TALENT, GIFT,
PROFICIENCY, CRAFT,
DEXTERITY, KNOW-HOW,
PROWESS, FINESSE,
SCIENCE, ADROIT, EXPERTISE
combining form ....
TECHNO
manual ..... HANDICRAFT
skillet .... (FRYING)PAN,
SPIDER
skillful .... EXPERT, DEFT,
APT, DEXT(E)ROUS, ADROIT,
HANDY, HABILE, ADEPT,
ABLE, ACCOMPLISHED
one .... PRO
workmanship .. D(A)EDAL
skim ..... SCUD, SCUM, COAT,
GLANCE, GLIDE, FLIT
skimmer .... SCISSORBILL
skimp ..... SCANTY, SCRIMP,
ECONOMIZE
skimpy ... STINGY, NIGGARDLY
skin ..... CUTIS, (EPI)DERMIS,
BARK, COAT, DERM(A),
SHELL, STRIP
abscess .... FURUNCLE
animal ...... PELT, HIDE,
FUR, SUEDE, KID,
PELLAGE, FELL
blemish .... WART,
FRECKLE, MOLE
bulge .... INION
cast off .... SLOUGH
colloquial ...... CHEAT,
SWINDLE, DEFRAUD
coloration .... CYANOSIS
combining form ....
DERMAT(O), DERM(O),
DERMA
condition .... RASH,
URTICARIA, HIVES,
UREDO, LENTIGO
container .... KENCH

covering .... HAIR, FUR
cut away .... PEEL, PARE
dark .... MELANIC
decoration ..... TATTOO
deep ...... SUPERFICIAL,
SHALLOW
deer antler's .... VELVET
design on ..... TATTOO
discoloration ..... BRUISE
disease .... TINEA,
TETTER, LEPROSY,
PURPURA, PRURIGO,
ARAKIS, ERYSIPELAS,
ACNE, ECZEMA,
RINGWORM, PSORA,
MANGE, HIVES, PINTA,
PSORIASIS, SCABIES,
IMPETIGO, ITCH,
SERPIGO, YAWS,
MILIARIA, LICHEN,
LUPUS, HUMOR, HERPES,
SCALL, SCURF, FAVUS,
VITILIGO
disease drug .. NEOMYCIN
disease, oil for .. CAJUPUT
diver's aid .... SCUBA
diving device ....
AQUALUNG
drying frame ..... HERSE
dryness .... XEROSIS
duct dirt .... COMEDO
elevation ...... BLISTER,
PAPULE, PIMPLE,
PUSTULE, WHEAL,
WALE, WELT
eruption ... EXANTHEMA
flaw .... WRINKLE
fold .... PLICA
fruit ... RIND, PEEL, ZEST
horny growth ..... CORN,
KERATOSIS
inflammation ... PIMPLE,
PAPULE, PUSTULE,
BOIL, CARBUNCLE
injury ...... CONTUSION,
BRUISE
Latin .... CUTIS
layer .... DERMIS,
DERM(A), CUTIS
like .... DERMATOID,
DERMOID
lotion .... CALAMINE
nodule .... MILIUM
of the .. DERMIC, DERMAL,
CUTANEOUS
oil .... SEBUM

opening .... PORE
outer layer ..... EPICARP
peel off ...... EXCORIATE
person with abnormal
  white .... ALBINO
pertaining to ....
            CUTANEOUS
redness .... RUBOR,
            ERYTHEMA
scales .... SCURF
scar .... VACCINATION,
            BRAND
shed .... MOLT
shed by snake ... SLOUGH
ship's ... PLATE, ARMOR,
            SHELL
sore .... GALL
specialist ....
        DERMATOLOGIST
spot .... N(A)EVUS
strip the .... FLAY
swelling .... BLEB
treat .... TAW, TAN
tree .... BARK, RIND
tumor .... WEN
untanned ... SHAGREEN,
            KIP
whip mark .. WELT, WALE,
            STRIPE, WHEAL
skinflint ... MISER, NIGGARD,
            TIGHTWAD
skink ... SEPS, LIZARD, ADDA
  like/of the ..... SCINCOID
skinless .... APELLOUS
skinner .... SWINDLER,
        (MULE)DRIVER, STRIPPER
  actress/writer ....
        CORNELIA (OTIS)
skinny .... SCRAGGY,
    EMACIATED, THIN, LEAN
skip ...... SPRING, RICOCHET,
    ABSCOND, DECAMP,
    PASS OVER, CAPER, DAP,
    OMIT, LEAP, JUMP, HOP,
            SKITTER
skipjack ...... BEETLE, FISH,
            ELATER
skipper .... SAURY, RAIS, RAS,
    CAPTAIN, MASTER,
            BUTTERFLY
skirmish ...... BRUSH, MELEE,
    BATTLE, (AF)FRAY
skirr .... SCOUR, GLIDE
skirt .... BORDER, FRINGE,
    DIRNDL, PANNIER,
    KIRTLE, CHOGORI,

HOBBLE, PETTICOAT
armor .... TASSE
ballet dancer's ..... TUTU
he wears one ...... SCOT
men's .... KILT
slang ..... WOMAN, GIRL
slit .... PLACKET
swish of silk ... FROUFROU
triangular part ..... GORE
waist .... PEPLUM
skit .... GIBE, SKETCH,
    SLAPSTICK, PARODY,
            PLAY(LET)
skitter ...... SKIP, SCAMPER
skittish ..... NERVOUS, JUMPY,
    FICKLE, PLAYFUL
skivvy .... SHIRT
skittle(s) .... BOWLS, PIN,
            NINEPINS
skive ..... SHAVE, PARE, SLICE
skivvy .... UNDERWEAR,
            UNDERSHIRT
skoal .... TOAST
skua .... JAEGER, GULL
skulduggery .... TRICKERY
skulk ... LURK, MICHE, SLINK,
    SHIRK, MALINGER, PROWL
skull ...... HEAD, CRANIUM,
    SCONCE, MAZARD
  back part ..... OCCIPUT
  bulge .... INION
  cavity ..... FOSSA, SINUS
  domed part .... CALVARIA
  of the ... CRANIAL, INIAL,
            CEPHALIC
  part of ...... BRAINPAN,
    CRANIUM, BREGMA,
            CALVARIA
  protuberance ..... INION
  study of the ....
        CRANIOLOGY
  surgical saw for .. TREPAN,
            TREPHINE
skullcap ... CALOT(TE), PILEUS,
    IVETTA, BEANIE, COIF,
            ZUCCHETTO
skunk ... CONEPATE, POLECAT,
    MEPHITIS, STINKER,
    CHINCHE, TELEDU
  animal resembling ....
        ZORIL(A), TELEDU
  kin of ..... MINK, OTTER
  spray of .... MUSK
sky ..... FIRMAMENT, HEAVEN,
    CLIMATE, VAULT, OLYMPUS,
    EMPYREAN, COPE

bear .... URSA
blue ... AZURE, CERULEAN
curved vault of .. WELKIN
highest point .... ZENITH
of the .... CELESTIAL
pilot .... AVIATOR,
CHAPLAIN, CLERGYMAN
prefix .... SCIO
skylark .... FROLIC
genus .... ALAUDA
skylight .... DORMER
skyline .... HORIZON
skyways .... AIR LANES
slab ..... CHUNK, TILE, STELE,
PIECE, VISCID, SLICE,
DALLE, TABLE(T)
atop column .... ABACUS
slack ..... IDLE, LOOSE, SLOW,
SLUGGISH, DULL, REMISS,
MORASS, LAZE, RELAXED,
LAX, WEAK, LULL, DELL,
DUFF
slacken .... SLOW DOWN,
LOOSEN, EASE, ABATE,
LET UP, RELAX
slacker ... TRUANT, SHIRKER,
SPIV, IDLER, LOAFER
slacks .... TROUSERS
slag ... DROSS, LAVA, SCORIA,
CINDER
slake ..... QUENCH, SATISFY,
HYDRATE
slalom .... SKI
slam ... SHUT, HIT, PAN, VOLE,
BANG
slander ..... DEFAME, ASPERSE,
TRADUCE, LIBEL, SMEAR,
REVILE, MALEDICTION,
MALIGN, CALUMNY, MUD
slanderous story ... ROORBACK
slang ... CANT, ARGOT, JARGON,
PATOIS, SHOPTALK,
DIALECT, LINGO
suffix .... EROO
slant .... TILT, INCLINE,
OPINION, KEEL, CANT,
RAKE, SLOPE, SKEW, BIAS,
ANGLE, GLANCE, HEEL
combining form .. CLINO
line .... SOLIDUS
slanted edge .... BEVEL
slanting ..... OBLIQUE, ATILT,
ASKEW
type .... ITALIC
slap ..... SPAT, CUFF, WHACK,
BIFF, THWACK, RAP, SMACK,

BLOW, REBUFF, SPANK
happy ... SILLY, FOOLISH
slapdash .... OFFHAND
slapjack .... PANCAKE
slapstick .... COMEDY,
HORSEPLAY
slash .... CUT, GASH, JAG,
SCOURGE, SLIT, LASH
Slask .... SILESIA
slat ...... STRIP, LATH, FLAP,
BEAT, SPLINE
barrel .... STAVE
movable .... LOUVER
slate .... TABLET, BALLOT,
TICKET, LIST, ABUSE,
ENROLL, BOOK,
SCOLD, RAKE
ax/trimmer ...... ZAX, SAX
excavation site .. QUARRY
roofing .... RAG
slater .... WOOD LOUSE
slattern ...... TROLLOP, SLUT,
SLOVEN, DRAB
slaughter .... BUTCHER(Y),
MASSACRE, CARNAGE,
POGROM, HECATOMB
slaughterhouse ..... ABATTOIR,
SHAMBLES
waste .... TANKAGE
Slav .... CROAT, VENED,
BULGAR, SLOVENE, POLE,
SLOVAK, CZECH, SERB(IAN)
slave .... BONDMAN, SERVANT,
TOIL, HELOT, DRUDGE,
SERF, THRALL, VASSAL
Biblical .... HAGAR
block .... CATASTA
driver ...... TASKMASTER
educated .... HETAERA
female .... ODALISK,
ODALISQUE, HETAERA,
HETAIRA
liberate .... MANUMIT
mark of .... STIGMA,
BRAND
Moslem ..... MAMELUKE
runaway ...... MAROON
ship .... SLAVER
soldier ...... MAMELUKE
temple .... HIERODULE
slaver .... DRIVEL, DROOL,
SLOBBER, HUMBUG,
NONSENSE
slavery .... BONDAGE,
THRAL(L)DOM, SERVITUDE,

SERFDOM, HELOTRY,
DRUDGERY
free from .... MANUMIT,
EMANCIPATE
slaves, dealer in ..... MANGO
tied together .... COFFLE
slavish .... SERVILE
slaw .... SALAD
slay .. DESTROY, MURDER, KILL
sleave .... THREAD, FLOSS,
TANGLE
sleazy ...... TAWDRY, FLIMSY
sled ..... SLEIGH, TOBOGGAN,
SLEDGE, BOBSLED, LUGE,
DOUBLE-RIPPER, JUMPER,
HURDLE, TRAVOIS(E),
PUNG, TODE, GO-DEVIL
dog .... HUSKY
dog, command to .. MUSH
logging .... TODE
slider .... RUNNER
sledge .... HAMMER, DRAG,
TRAVOIS(E), SLED, SLEIGH
sleek .. GLOSSY, OILY, SMOOTH,
POLISH, UNCTUOUS, SLICK
sleep .... REST, REPOSE,
SLUMBER, NOD, DOSS,
BUNK, SHUTEYE
combining form .. HYPNO
deep .... STUPOR, SOPOR
drugged ...... NARCOSIS
god of .... SOMNUS,
HYPNOS, HYPNUS
inability to ... INSOMNIA
inducing drug ....
NARCOTIC, OPIATE
last .... DEATH
lightly .... DOSE
midday .... SIESTA
short .. (CAT)NAP, WINK,
DOZE, SIESTA, SNOOZE,
SNATCH
unnatural .. SOPOR, COMA,
LETHARGY, STUPOR,
TRANCE
winter ...... HIBERNATION
sleeper ... RACE HORSE, BEAM,
TIE
long .... RIP, SLUGABED
sleepiness ...... SOMNOLENCE
sleeping bag .... SACK
car part .... BERTH
compartment ... CUBICLE
dress ...... NIGHTGOWN,
PAJAMAS

pill .... VERONAL,
BARBITAL, GOOFBALL
place .. DOSS, PAD, BUNK,
COT, BERTH, BED,
FLOP, LODGING
sickness carrier .. TSETSE
sickness cause ....
TRYPANOSOME
sickness remedy ....
SURAMIN
sleepless one ...... INSOMNIAC
sleeplike state .... COMA,
TRANCE
sleepwalker .. SOMNAMBULIST
sleepy .... DROWSY,
SOMNOLENT, OSCITANT,
DOZY
sleet ... HAIL, RAIN, GRAUPEL
sleety .... BRUMAL
sleeve .... ARM, GIGOT
bar on .... CHEVRON
end of .... CUFF
hole .... SKYE, SCYE
kind of .... DOLMAN
sleeveless garment ..... CAPE,
CLOAK, ABA, MANTLE
sleigh .... SLEDGE, SLED,
CUTTER
boxlike .... PUNG
puller .... REINDEER
rider .... SANTA
slider .... RUNNER
sleight ..... SKILL, TRICK(ERY)
of hand .. LEGERDEMAIN,
HOCUS-POCUS, MAGIC
of hand artist .. JUGGLER,
MAGICIAN
slender .... WISPY, TENUOUS,
FEEBLE, SLIGHT, LANK,
LEAN, FRAIL, SVELT, SLIM,
MEAGER, THIN, LITHE,
WILLOWY, GRACILE
finial .... EPI
in phonetics ...... CLOSE
waisted .... WASPISH
sleuth ..... DETECTIVE, TEC,
HAWKSHAW, PRIVATE EYE
fictional .... NERO, CHAN,
HERCULE, TRENT,
MOTO, HOLMES
slew ... SWAMP, SLOUGH, SLUE,
LOT
Slezsko .... SILESIA
slice ..... SKIVE, GASH, PIECE,
PORTION, SPATULA, HUNK,
LAYER, SHAVE, CHUNK,

CUT, SLAB, CANTLE,
COLLOP, CHIP
bacon .... RASHER
slick .... SLEEK, GLOSSY,
SMOOTH, OILY, UNCTUOUS,
CLEVER, SMART, SUAVE
slang .... MAGAZINE
slicker .... COAT
slide ..... GLIDE, SLIP, CHUTE,
PLATE, SLUE, COAST,
LAWINE, SKID, SLIPSTICK,
AVALANCHE
fastener .... ZIPPER
slight ..... WISPY, TENUOUS,
SNUB, SLIM, FAINT, IGNORE,
AFFRONT, GO-BY, CUT,
NEGLECT, FRAIL, FRAGILE,
THIN
slightest .... LEAST
amount .... GRAIN
slim .... SLENDER, SLIGHT,
MEAGER, SCANT, THIN,
SVELTE, SPARE, GRACILE
slime .... MUD, SLUDGE,
SEDIMENT, OOZE, MUCK
combining form .. MYX(O)
slimsy ...... FLIMSY, SLIGHT,
SLENDER
slimy .... VISCID, VISCOUS
matter .... GLEET, OOZE,
SLUDGE, GOB
sling ..... CAST, FLING, HURL,
DRINK
barrel/log ... PARBUCKLE
slingshot .... CATAPULT
killer with .... DAVID
slink ... SNEAK, LURK, SKULK,
CREEP, STEAL
slinky ... SINUOUS, STEALTHY
slip ...... ERR(OR), MISTAKE,
LAPSE, SCION, GAFFE,
LEASH, SLIDE, CUTTING,
TRIP, PETTICOAT, FAULT,
SKID, BONER, LAPSUS,
REEVE, TUMBLE
away .... ELAPSE
back .... RELAPSE
knot .... NOOSE
on garment ... SWEATER
out of place ... PROLAPSE
stream ..... RACE, WASH
up .... OVERSIGHT, ERROR
slipcase, book .... FOREL
slipover .... SWEATER
slipper ...... SCUFF, STEP-IN,
PANTOF(F)LE, MULE

flat-heeled .... MARY JANE
strap .... SANDAL
slippery .... EELY, SLICK,
SHIFTY, EVASIVE, SLIMY,
GREASY, ELUSIVE
customer ... EEL, DEBTOR
slipshod ..... WISHY-WASHY,
CARELESS, SLOVENLY, SLOPPY
slipstream ...... (PROP)WASH
slit ... SLASH, CUT, SPLIT, GASH
slither ..... SLIDE, SLIP, GLIDE
sliver .... SPLINTER, FIBER
slobber ...... DROOL, SLAVER
sloe ...... HAW, BLACKTHORN,
PLUM, GIN
slog ...... SLUG, TOIL, PLOD
slogan .... SHIBBOLETH,
CATCHWORD, MOTTO,
(BATTLE)CRY, CATCH PHRASE
sloop ..... SAILBOAT, DANDY,
CUTTER
of war .... FRIGATE
vessel like a .... HOY
slop ..... SLUSH, MUD, SNOW,
SWILL, SPILL, SLOSH
over .... SPILL, GUSH
slope .. SCARP, TALUS, SLANT,
INCLINE, DECLIVITY GRADE,
BRAE, GRADIENT, SPLAY,
GLACIS
combining form .. CLINO
sloping edge ..... BEZEL, BEZIL
sloppy ...... MUDDY, UNTIDY,
MESSY, CARELESS, SLIPSHOD
slops ... TROUSERS, BREECHES
slosh .... WADE, SLOP
slot .... GROOVE, TRACK,
KEYWAY, TRAIL
machine coin ...... SLUG
machine windfall ....
JACKPOT
sloth .... INDOLENCE,
LAZINESS, INERTIA,
SLOWNESS, EDENTATE
three-toed .... AI
two-toed .... UNAU
slouch ... DROOP(ING), HULK
slough .... SHED, DISCARD,
CAST OFF, SWAMP, MARSH
Slovakian city ..... KOSICE
slovenly .... SLOPPY, UNTIDY,
SLIPSHOD, FROWZY,
UNKEMPT, DOWDY
Slovensko .... SLOVAKIA
slow ...... SLACK, SLUGGISH,
GRADUAL, RETARD

footed creature .. TURTLE, SLOTH, UNAU, SLUG, LAGGARD, LORIS

in music .... LENTO, TARDO, LARGO, ANDANTE

leak .... DRIP

learner .... DUNCE

paced .... TARDIGRADE

train .... LOCAL

witted ..... DULL, DENSE

witted person ... DUNCE, DOLT, DOPE

slowpoke ..... SNAIL, SLOTH, SLUGGARD

slubber .... SMEAR, STAIN, DAUB, BOTCH

sludge .... MIRE, MUD, OOZE, SLEET, (DRIFT)ICE, SEDIMENT, SLUSH, FLOE

slue ... PIVOT, SLEW, SLOUGH, LOT

slug ... TOKEN, BLOW, SNAIL, HIT, BULLET, TREPANG, MOLLUSK, CATERPILLAR, PELLET, SWAT, GASTROPOD

genus .... LIMAX

sluggard ..... DRONE, IDLE(R), LOAFER, LAZY

slugger ... PRIZE FIGHTER, PUG

sluggish ... LETHARGIC, LAZY, DULL, TORPID, LANGUID, INERT, SLOW, LEADEN, LOGY, TARDIGRADE

slugs, of or like .... LIMACINE

sluice .... CHANNEL, (FLOOD)GATE, FLUME, PENSTOCK, SOW

slum .... GHETTO

kid .... GUTTERSNIPE

slumber ...... SLEEP, REPOSE

slump ... FALL, SINK, DECLINE

business ..... RECESSION

slur .... BLUR, DISCREDIT, DISPARAGE, ASPERSE, ELIDE, SMEAR, STAIN, SULLY, SMIRCH

slush ..... MIRE, MUD, DRIVEL, SLOP, PATCH

fund's use ..... BRIBE(RY)

slut ...... BITCH, DOG, DRAB, JADE, TROLLOP, QUEAN, SLATTERN

sly .... CAGEY, TRICKY, INSIDIOUS, FURTIVE, WILY, CRAFTY, FOXY, CUNNING

on the .... SECRETLY, COVERTLY

Slye, pathologist .... MAUD

smack ... SAILBOAT, FLAVOR, TRACE, SAVOR, SLAP, BLOW, BUSS, TASTE, KISS, WHACK, THWACK, PLAP

slang .... HEROIN

small ... LITTLE, LOW, TRIVIAL, PETTY, MEAN, MINIATURE, LIL, MINUTE, MINUSCULE, DINKY, WEE, PETIT(E), BANTAM, TINY, TEENY, PUNY

allowance ..... PITTANCE

and active .... DAPPER

animal .... RUNT

amount ...... FRACTION, MITE, MODICUM, IOTA, MORSEL, GRAIN, MINIM, PINCH, DRAM

anything .... PINHEAD

arms .... PISTOLS, RIFLES, CARBINES, REVOLVERS

bite .... NIP

bottle ...... VIAL, PHIAL

bright object ... SPANGLE

bunch .... WISP

car .... COMPACT

change .... COIN(S)

combining form .... MICR(O), STENO, LEPTO

cube .... DICE

fish ...... FRY, MINNOW, SARDINE, ID(E), SMELT, FINGERLING

flag ... FANION, PENNANT

fry .... CHILDREN, YOUNGSTERS, KIDS

handbills ...... DODGER, FLYER

hollow .... AREOLA

horse ..... PONY, BIDET, SHETLAND

in law .... PETIT

man ..... BANTAM, RUNT

minded ... PETTY, MEAN

part .. DETAIL, FRACTION, BIT

person .... MIDGE, DWARF, RUNT, BANTAM, SHRIMP

pest .... GNAT, IMP

piece .... SNIP(PET)

point .... DOT

portion .... MODICUM
quantity ... SPOT, IOTA, BIT
role in movie/play .. BIT
shield .... ECU
space .... AREOLA
talk .... CHITCHAT
time ..... PETTY, MINOR
town .... BURGH
town paper ..... WEEKLY
violin .... KIT
smallage .... CELERY
smallest ...... TINIEST, LEAST, MINIM
liquid measure .. MINIMUM
planet .... MERCURY
smallpox ...... VARIOLA, VARICELLA
disease of ..... ZYMOTIC
mark .... POCK
resembling ... VARIOLOID
smalt ...... PIGMENT, GLASS, BLUE, BICE
smalto .... ENAMEL
smaragd .... EMERALD
smart .. STING, SUFFER, SHARP, BRISK, CLEVER, NEAT, CHIC, APT, STYLISH, SLICK, DASHING, NIFTY, DAPPER, CLEAN, QUICK, WITTY, SPRUCE, SWANKY
aleck .. WISE GUY, QUACK
alecky .... FLIP
as a ____ .... WHIP
blow .... RAP
guy .... SLICK
set ..... ELITE, LITERATI
slang .... SPIFFY
smartly dressed ...... NATTY
phrased .... NEAT
smash ......SHATTER, WRECK, BREAK, CRASH, ROUT, DEFEAT, DASH,
smashup .. COLLISION, WRECK, RUIN, DISASTER
smaze, relative of ...... SMOG
smear .... SLUBBER, SOIL, SLANDER, SPOT, DAUB, MALIGN, DEFAME
smearcase .... CHEESE
smee .... POCHARD
smell ... SCENT, SENSE, SNIFF, FLAVOR, ODO(U)R, WHIFF, NOSE
fats' .... RANCID
goatlike .... HIRCINE

loss of .... ANOSMIA
of the sense of .... OLFACTORY
offensive .... STENCH, OLID, FETOR, RANK, FOUL, STINK, REEK, ODOR
organ of .... NOSE, OLFACTORY
pleasant .... AROMA
savory .... AROMA
stale ...... MUSTY, FUSTY
smeller .... FEELER, NOSE, ANTENNA
smelling .... REDOLENT
salts .... INHALANT
smelt ..... FISH, REFINE, FUSE, CAP(E)LIN, SPARLING
fish like .... TROUT
smelter .... FURNACE, FORGE, BLAST
smelting by-product .. SPEISS, SLAG, DROSS
waste .... TUTTY
smew ..... DUCK, MERGANSER, SCOTER
smidgen .... BIT, IOTA
smilax ... VINE, SARSAPARILLA
smile ... LAUGH, GRIN, SMIRK, SIMPER, SNEER, BEAM, GRIMACE
Mona Lisa ... ENIGMATIC, CRYPTIC
smiling ...... RIDENT, RIANT
smirch ..... DIRTY, DISCOLOR, SMEAR, STAIN, SULLY, SMUDGE, BLOT, SMUT(CH), TARNISH
smirk ...... SMILE, GRIN, LEER, SIMPER
smite .. HIT, DEFEAT, DISTRESS, STRIKE, ENAMOR, AFFLICT
smith .... METALWORKER, FORGE, VULCAN
block of .... ANVIL
furnace of .... FORGE
invisible ...... WAYLAND
smithereens ...... BITS, PIECES, FRAGMENTS
smithsonite .... CALAMINE
smithy .... FORGE, STITHY
smitten .... STRICKEN, AFFLICTED, ENAMORED
smock .... FROCK, CAMISE, CHEMISE
smog .... MIST, SMAZE

ingredient ──.──.── SMOKE,
　　　　　SOOT
smoke ... VAPOR, FUME, MIST,
　　CIGAR(ETTE), REEK, SMOG,
　　　　　LUNT, FLOC, CURB
a pipe .... WHIFF
and mist ... SMOG, SMAZE
country boy's .. CORNSILK
fragrant ──.──.── INCENSE
good ──.──.──.── CIGAR
meat .... REEST
out .... FLUSH
pipe ..... STACK, FUNNEL
screen ..... CAMOUFLAGE
tree ..... YELLOWWOOD
smokeless power ──.── FILITE,
　　　　　CORDITE
smoker ──.──.── PARTY, STAG
smokestack ──.──.── FUNNEL,
　　　CHIMNEY, FLUE
worker .... STEEPLEJACK
smoking pipe ──.── HOOKAH,
　　BRIAR, NARGHILE, CALUMET
room .... DIVAN
smoky quartz .... CAIRNGORM
smolder ──.──.──.── BURN
Smollett, novelist .... TOBIAS
smolt ──.──.──.── SALMON
smooch ──.──.──.── SMUTCH
smooth ──.── VELVETY, SAND,
　　BLAND, EVEN, CALM,
　SERENE, POLISH(ED), SUAVE,
　SOOTHE, OILY, SLEEK, SLICK,
　IRON, GLABROUS, URBANE,
　　REFINE, SOFT, GRIND
and white .... ALABASTER
consonant .... LENE
feathers .... PREEN
in mechanics ──.──.──
　　　　FRICTIONLESS
in music .... LEGATO
in performance .. DOLCE
in phonetics ..... LENE
over .... GLOSS
pated .... BALD
tongued ..... GLIB, OILY
with beak .... PREEN
smoothing rock ...... PUMICE
smorgasbord treat ...... EELS
smother .... SUFFOCATE,
　　WELTER, STIFLE, CHOKE
smudge ... STAIN, SPOT, BLUR,
　　SOIL, SMUTCH, SMEAR,
　　SMOKE, BLOT, SLUR
smug ──.──.──.── TRIM, NEAT,
　　　　COMPLACENT

smuggle ... SNEAK IN, BOOTLEG
smuggled goods ──.──.──.──
　　　　CONTRABAND
whisky ──.──.── MOONSHINE
smuggler ...... GUNRUNNER,
　　BOOTLEGGER, (RUM)RUNNER
ship of .... RUNNER
smut .... SOOT, CROCK,
　　OBSCENITY, BUNT, FUNGUS
Smuts, S. African statesman ──
　　　　　JAN
smutty ──.──.──.── OBSCENE
Smyrna ──.──.──.── IZMIR
fig .... ELEME
snack ──. TIFFIN, BITE, LUNCH,
　　　　　CANAPE
snaffle ──.──.──.── BIT, CURB
snafu ──.──.── BOOBOO, MUDDLE,
　　　　MIXED UP
snag ──.──.── TOOTH, TEAR,
　　OBSTACLE, HITCH
snail ──.──.── HELIX, WHELK,
　　NERITA, ESCARGOT,
　GASTROPOD, MOLLUSK,
　　SLUG(GARD),
genus ──.──.──.── NERITA,
　　　OLEACINA
oyster-killer ──.──.── DRILL
shell ──.──.── PERIWINKLE,
　　　CARACOLE
snails, of or like ... LIMACINE
snake ──.── REPTILE, SERPENT
　　(A)BOMA, VIPER, LORA,
　PYTHON, OPHIDIAN
big ──.──.── BOA, PYTHON,
　　CONSTRICTOR,
　　ANACONDA
bird ──.──.──.── DARTER
bite remedy ──.── GUACO,
　　　CEDRON
black ──.──.── RACER
burrowing ──.── GOPHER
castoff of .... SLOUGH
charmer's flute .... PUNGI
common ──.──.── ADDER
crusher .... BOA,
　　CONSTRICTOR, PYTHON
deity ──.──.── ZOMBI
eyes .... AMBSACE
fish like .... EEL, LAMPREY
garter .... KLAP
haired woman ── MEDUSA,
　　　GORGON
hooded .... COBRA
horned ..... SAND VIPER
like ──.──.──.── SINUOUS,

COLUBRINE, ANGUINE, APADAL

movement ..... SLITHER
poison ... VENOM, VIRUS
poisonous ... MOCCASIN, SEPS, KRAIT, COBRA, ASP, BONGAR, HABU, VIPER, CERASTES, MAMBA, COTTONMOUTH, ADDER
root .... STEVIA, SANICLE
sand .... ERYX
sea .... KERRIL
skin shedding .. ECDYSIS
sound ..... HISS, RATTLE
space on head of ... LORE
warning of .... HISS, RATTLE
water .... MOCCASIN

snakebird .... WRYNECK, DARTER, PLOTUS
snakehead .... FIGWORT
snakemouth .... ORCHID
snakes, study of .. OPHIOLOGY
snakestone .... AMMONITE
snaky ... ANGUINE, WINDING, SERPENTINE
snap ... BITE, SNATCH, BREAK, SPELL, COOKY, SINECURE, EASY, SIMPLE, FLIP, FLICK, KNAP, CLIP, FASTENER, WAFER, CRACK, FILLIP
snapdragon .... FIGWORT
snapper .... TURTLE, SESI, BEETLE, TAMURE
  kin of .... SCUP
snappish ..... CROSS, UNCIVIL, RUDE, IRRITABLE, TESTY, EDGY
snappy .. BRISK, SHARP, SMART, STYLISH, CROSS
  make it .... HURRY
snare .... CATCH, (DRAG)NET, GIN, WEB, RATTRAP, PIT(FALL), MESH, SPRINGE, BENET, (EN)TRAP
snark .... BOOJUM
snarl ..... COMPLICATE, KNOT, GIRN, TANGLE, GNAR(L), GROWL
snatch .... GRASP, GRAB, KIDNAP(PING), WREST, SEIZE, SPELL, BIT, TAKE, SWIPE
sneak .... STEAL, SKULK, MOOCH, LURK, SLINK

sneakers ..... (CANVAS)SHOES, GUMSHOES
sneaking .... COWARDLY, FURTIVE
snee .... DIRK
sneer .... SMILE, SCOFF, FLEER, SCORN, MOCK
sneering .. DERISIVE, SCORNFUL
sneeze .... SNUFF
  sound .... ACHOO
sneezewort .... YARROW
snell .... LEADER, ACUTE, SMART, SEVERE, QUICK, KEEN, HARSH, SNOOD, GUT
Snerd, dummy .... MORTIMER
snick ..... NICK, NOTCH, CUT, CLICK
  and ____ .... SNEE
snicker .... NEIGH, TEHEE, TITTER, LAUGH, GIGGLE
snickersnee .... KNIFE
snide .... SLY, MALICIOUS, MEAN
sniff .... INHALE, SMELL, SCENT, SNORT, NOSE
sniffles .... (HEAD)COLD
sniffy .... SCORNFUL, DISDAINFUL
snifter ...... DRINK, SIP, NIP
snigger .... SNICKER
snip .... SHEAR, CUT, SHRIMP, BIT, PIECE, CLIP
snipe .... CIGAR, BIRD, WOODCOCK, GODWIT
sniper .... AMBUSHER
snippet ... SCRAP, FRAGMENT, TAG
snit .... TIZZY
snitch .... STEAL, PILFER, TELL, PEACH, INFORMER, SQUEAL
snivel ..... SNIFF, SNUFFLE, FRET, WHINE, COMPLAIN
snob .... HIGH-HAT, PRIG, PARVENU, PRUDE
snobbery .... HAUTEUR
snobbish ..... RITZY, UPPISH, HIGH-HAT, STUCK-UP, PROUD, UPPITY, SNOOTY
snood .... RIBBON, SNELL, (HAIR)NET, FILLET
snook .... ROBALO
snoop .... PRY, SKULK, LURK, PROWL
snoot ... FACE, NOSE, GRIMACE
snooty .... SNOBBISH, HAUGHTY, PROUD

snooze ... NAP, DOZE, DROWSE
snore ... STERTOR, RHONCHUS, SNIFF
snorer, loud .... GRAMPUS
snort ... LAUGH, DRINK, SNIFF, SNUFF, NIP
snorter .... HUMDINGER
snotty .. OFFENSIVE, IMPUDENT
snout ... NEB, NOSE, NOZZLE, MUZZLE, ROSTRUM, JAWS, BEAK, SERRA
    dig with ..... ROOT, ROUT
    elephant's .... TRUNK
    push/rub with ... NUZZLE
    tapir's .... PROBOSCIS
snouted creature ...... TAPIR, DESMAN, PIG, ELEPHANT, ECHIDNA, ANTEATER, AARDVARK
snow .. FIRN, SLEET, SNA, PASH
    bird ...... JUNCO, LERWA
    briefly .... SPIT
    bunting .... FINCH
    field .... NEVE
    granular ..... FIRN, NEVE
    growing under .... NIVAL
    gust of ...... FLURRY
    house ..... VOLE, IGLOO, IGLU
    leopard .... OUNCE
    of .... NIVAL
    on a glacier .... NEVE
    runner .... SKI, SKEE, (BOB)SLED, TOBOGGAN
    shoe .... SKI
    slang ... HEROIN, COCAINE
    slide, mass ... AVALANCHE
    travel over ...... MUSH
    watery .... SLOP
    White's friends .. DWARFS
snowbird ..... JUNCO, LERWA, FINCH, ADDICT
snowbird's need ..... HEROIN, COCAINE, DOPE, DRUG
snowdrop .... ANEMONE
snowfall .... SLEET, HAIL
snowflake ... BUNTING, FINCH
snowlike .... NIVEOUS
snowshoe ... PAC, RACKET, SKI
snowstorm .... BLIZZARD
snowy .... NIVEOUS, SPOTLESS, WINTRY, WHITE, BRUMAL
    weather need ... MUFFLER, OVERSHOES, EARMUFF
snub .... HIGH-HAT, CUT, SLIGHT, SCORN, AFFRONT, TURNED-UP, REBUFF, UPSTAGE
nose(d) .... PUG
snubber .... SNOB
snuff ... SMELL, SNIFF, SNORT, SCENT, ODOR, RAPPEE, PINCH, PUT OUT, MACCOBOY
    out .. EXTINGUISH, DOUSE
snuffle .... SNIFF, TWANG, SNIVEL
snug ..... TAUT, WARM, COZY, SECURE, TRIM, NEAT, COSY, COMFORTABLE
    as a bug ___ .. IN A RUG
    retreat ...... NEST, DEN
snuggle ..... NESTLE, CUDDLE
so .... ERGO, THEREFORE, SIC, HENCE, VERY, THUS, LIKEWISE, THEN, TRUE
    and so .... SOMEONE, SOMEBODY
    be it ... AMEN, ALTERCATE
    Big author ...... FERBER
    Big heroine ...... SELINA
    long .... GOOD-BY
    Red the ___ ...... ROSE
    so .... AVERAGE
soak .... SATURATE, WET, MACERATE, DRENCH, STEEP, SOG, SOP, SODDEN, SOUSE, RET, IMBRUE
    colloquial .... DRINK
    fiber .... RET
    flax .... RET
    in brine/vinegar .... MARINATE
    slang ... HIT, BOX, PAWN, DRUNKARD
    to soften .... RET, MACERATE, STEEP
    up .... SORB
soaked...... SODDEN, SOGGY
soap .... DETERGENT, SAPO, CLEANSER, CASTILE
    convert into .... SAPONIFY
    cresol mixture .... LYSOL
    foam .... SUDS
    frame bar .... SESS
    ingredient .... LYE
    material .... TALLOW
    oil .... CITRONELLA
    olive oil .... CASTILE
    opera .... MELODRAMA
    plant .... AMOLE
    slang .... MONEY
    substitute ...... QUILIAI

vine .... GOGO
soapbark .... QUILIAI, MIMOSA
   glucoside ... SAPONIN(E)
soapberry ... LICHEE, LITCHI,
    RAMBUTAN
soapbox character .. AGITATOR,
   ORATOR, DEMAGOGUE,
    QUACK
soapstone ..... TALC, STEATITE
soapsuds ...... FOAM, BUCK,
    LATHER
   bleach in .... BUCK
soapy .... SAPONACEOUS, OILY,
   SUAVE, UNCTUOUS
   water .... SUDS
soar .... FLY, RISE, TOWER
soaring .... HIGH, TOWERING
sob .... WEEP, CRY, SIGH
sober ... TEMPERATE, SOLEMN,
   SERIOUS, GRAVE, SEDATE,
   PLAIN, QUIET, STAID
sobriety .... TEMPERANCE,
    MODERATION
sobriquet .... AGNAME,
   NICKNAME, ALIAS
soccer .... FOOTBALL
   player, famed ..... PELE,
    CHARLTON
Soche .... YARKAND
sociable .... FRIENDLY,
   OUTGOING, AFFABLE, NICE,
    FOLKSY
social ... PARTY, GATHERING,
   CIVIC, BEE
   affair ..... SHINDIG, TEA,
   MUSICALE, SOIREE
   appointment ...... DATE
   asset .. TACT, DIPLOMACY,
    GRACE
   call .... GAM
   class .... CASTE
   climber ... TUFTHUNTER,
   UPSTART, SNOB
   Contract author ....
    ROUSSEAU
   contract theorist .. LOCKE,
   HOBBS, ROUSSEAU
   disease in short ...... VD
   error .... SOLECISM,
   FAUX PAS
   finesse .... TACT
   gathering for men ....
   SMOKER, STAG
   grace, lacking .. GAUCHEE
   insect .. ANT, BEE, VESPID,
   WASP, TERMITE

order .... REGIME
   outcast ... PARIAH, LEPER
   outdoors .... FRY
   reformer, American .....
    MOTT
   register .... BLUEBOOK
   science ..... SOCIOLOGY
   standing .... STATION
   system ... CASTE, REGIME
   unit .... FAMILY
   virtue .... TACT
   visit .... GAM, CALL
   wasp .... VESPID
socialist ..... MARX, FOURIER,
   ENGELS
society .... COMPANY,
   ASSOCIATION, COMMUNITY,
   VEREIN
   bigwig .... NOB
   bud .... (SUB)DEB,
    DEBUTANTE
   combining form ... SOCIO
   doings .... SOCIALS
   entrance into ..... DEBUT
   fashionable .... BONTON
   for animals .... SPCA
   Islands' capital .. PAPEETE
   Islands, one of the ......
    TAHITI
   of Friends .... QUAKERS
   of Friends founder .. FOX
   of Jesus founder ....
   IGNATIUS (OF LOYOLA)
   of the learned .. ACADEMY
   with government ....
    POLITY
socials .... PARTIES
sociology .... DEMOTICS
sock ..... WALLOP, COMEDY,
   SHOE, STOCKING, BOX,
    BLOW
sockdolager .. FINISHER, ONER
socket .... MORTISE, PAN
   bit .... POD
   roof beam .... OPA
sockeye .... SALMON
socks .... SOX, HOSE
Socrates' disciple ..... PLATO
   wife .... XANTHIPPE
sod ..... TURF, SWARD, GLEBE,
   PEAT, DIRT, EARTH, SOIL
soda —— .... JERK, POP,
    FOUNTAIN
   ash ..... BARILLA, ALKALI
   ash source .... SEAWEED
   caustic .... LYE

fountain order .... MALT, SHAKE, SUNDAE
water .... FIZZ
sodality .... FELLOWSHIP
sodden ..... SOAKED, SOGGY, STEEP, POACHY
sodium .... NATRUM
carbonate ...... NATRON, TRONA, SODA(ASH), SAL SODA
combining form .. NATRO
hydroxide .... LYE, CAUSTIC SODA
nitrate .... SALTPETER, CALICHE, SALTPETRE, NITER
oxide .... SODA
thiosulfate .... HYPO
Sodom's neighbor .. GOMORRAH
sodomite .... BUGGER
sodomy, form of ... PEDERASTY
sofa .... COUCH, SETTLE, LOUNGE, CHESTERFIELD, DAYBED, SQUAB, SETTEE, DIVAN, DAVENPORT, VIS-A-VIS
covering .... TIDY
soft ...... VELVETY, SMOOTH, BLAND, MILD, TEMPERATE, WEAK, EASY, PAPPY, GENTLE, HUSH, SUBDUED, LOW, TENDER, SMOOTH, FOOLISH
and limp .... FLABBY
drink ... ADE, POP, MEAD, COLA, SODA
fabric ..... SILK, PANNE, VELVET
feathers ... DOWN, RIDER
food .... PAP, SOUP
hair .... VILLUS
ice .... LOLLY
in music .... PIANO
in phonetics .... SIBILANT
job ..... SINECURE, SNAP
mass .... PULP
metal .... TIN, LEAD
mineral .... TALC
palate .... VELUM, UVULA
pedal ...... TONE DOWN, EASE, MODERATE, PLAYDOWN
roll .... BUN
saddle .... PANEL
shoulder .... BERM(E)

soap .... FLATTER, BLARNEY, CAJOLE
spoken .... SUAVE
sound .... SIGN, MURMUR
sweet and .... DOLCE
tissue .... BREI
toned organ stop .. DOLCE
soften ..... MITIGATE, TEMPER, RELENT, EASE, LOOSEN
by soaking .... RET, MACERATE, STEEP
softening .... LENITIVE
of the brain.... DEMENTIA
softhead .... SIMPLETON
softie ...... SISSY, WEAKLING
softly .... LOW
Sogdian .... IRANIAN
soggy .... WET, SOAKED, SODDEN, POACHY
Soho feature ... RESTAURANTS
soigne .... TIDY, NEAT
soil ... LAND, SULLY, DEFILE, PURGE, CLAY, LOESS, MARL, SOD, GLEBE, GUMBO, LOAM, COUNTRY, EARTH, GROUND, DIRTY, SMIRCH
hard layer of .... PAN
hole-making tool .... DIBBLE
in combination ... AGRO
infertile .... PODZOL
organic part of ... HUMUS
poetic .... GLEBE
restorer .... VETCH
unfruitful ...... BARREN
wind-deposited ... LOESS
soja .... SOY(BEAN), SAUCE
sojourn ..... STAY, VISIT, TARRY
sojourner .... PILGRIM, TRUTH
Sol ... SUN(GOD), GOLD, NOTE
impresario ...... HUROK
sola .... ALONE
solace .... COMFORT, RELIEF, ALLAY, CONSOLE, CHEER
solan goose .... GANNET
solanum .... NIGHTSHADE
solar .... HELIACAL
deity ...... HELIOS, SOL, LLEU
disk .... ATEN
furnace site .... ODEILLO
phenomenon ... ECLIPSE, CORONA
spot/streak ..... FACULA
system model ... ORRERY
solarium .... SUNROOM

solder ... BORAX, BOND, ROSIN,
JOIN, PATCH, FUSE, BRAZE,
CEMENT
soldier ...... WARRIOR, POILU,
MAN-AT-ARMS, TERMITE
bag of ..... HAVERSACK,
KNAPSACK, MUSETTE
brutal .... PANDOUR
call to quarters .. TATTOO
cap of .... SHAKO
cavalry ... UHLAN, SPAHI
fellow .... BUDDY
food of ..... CHOW, MESS,
K-RATION
freebooting ... RAPPAREE
from Down Under ......
ANZAC
headgear ...... HELMET,
CAP, BERET
killed .... CASUALTY
kind of ..... MERCENARY,
LANCE(R), LEGIONARY,
TERRITORIAL
Korean .... ROK
mercenary ..... HESSIAN,
SWISSER, SWITZER
mounted ..... CAVALRY,
SPAHI
of fortune .. ADVENTURER
old .... VET(ERAN)
pack of .... KIT
shelter of ...... FOXHOLE
slang ...... DOUGHBOY,
DOGFACE, SADSACK
trainee .... CADET
with musket .. DRAG(O)ON
wounded in battle ....
CASUALTY
soldierly .... MARTIAL
soldiers, collectively ....
MILITARY, ARMED FORCES
rebellion of .... MUTINY
Three author .... KIPLING
sole ...... SINGLE, ONLY, ONE,
(FLAT)FISH, PLAICE,
HALIBUT, MERE, ALONE,
SOLITARY
foot's .... PLANTAR, VOLA
of the foot's ...... VOLAR
plow's .... SLADE
solecism ...... IMPROPRIETY,
BARBARISM
solely .. MERELY, ONLY, ALONE
solemn ..... SACRED, FORMAL,
SERIOUS, SOBER, GRAVE,
SOMBER

wonder .... AWE
looking .... OWLISH
word .... OATH, VOW,
PLEDGE, TROTH,
PAROL(E)
solemnity .... FORMALITY,
GRAVITY
solemnize .... CELEBRATE
solfatara emission ...... GAS,
VAPOR
solferino .... FUCHSIN, DYE
solicit ...... ENTREAT, APPLY,
ASK, BEG, SEEK, BID
customers .... TOUT
solicitation .... ENTREATY,
PETITION
solicitor .... LAWYER
solicitude ... CARE, CONCERN
solid ...... COMPACT, SOUND,
FIRM, GENUINE, THICK,
HARD, MASSIVE, MASSY
ground ... TERRA FIRMA
six-sided .... CUBE
solidago .... GOLDENROD
solidarity .... UNITY
solidified lava .... COULEE
solidify ..... GEL, SET, JELL,
CONGEAL, HARDEN, CAKE
solidity .... FIRMNESS
solidus ... BEZANT, SLANT LINE
soliloquy .... MONOLOGUE
solitaire .... RECLUSE,
PATIENCE, HERMIT,
CANFIELD, GEM, CARD GAME
solitary .... SINGLE, ONLY,
LONE(LY), REMOTE, HERMIT,
ALONE, CONFINEMENT,
HERMITIC
solitude .... ISOLATION,
SECLUSION
sollar ... BRATTICE, GALLERY
solo ... (A)LONE, SURAKARTA,
ARIA
Solomon .... SAGE, KING,
WISEMAN
father of .... DAVID
island .... MALAITA,
CHOISEUL,
GUADALCANAL
Islands' capital .. HONIARA
Islands' city ...... KIETA,
AUKI, SOHANO
sayings of ...... MAXIMS,
PROVERBS
solon ... LEGISLATOR, SENATOR,

LAWGIVER, LAWMAKER, SAGE, WISEMAN
soluble salt .... SALAR
solus .... ALONE
solution .... EXPLANATION, ANSWER, SEPARATION, BREAK
  in pharmacy .... AQUA
  part of .... SOLUTE, SOLVENT
  strength of .. TITER, TITRE
solve ..... UNRAVEL, EXPLAIN
solvent ..... DILUENT, WATER, ACETONE, MENSTRUUM, HEXONE
  wood tar ...... FURAN(E)
soma .... TRUNK, BODY
Somalia capital .. MOGADISHU
  city .... HARGEISA, BERBERA
  monetary unit .. SOMALO
  premier .... EGAL
Somaliland antelope ... BEIRA
somatic .... PHYSICAL, CORPOREAL, BODILY, PARIETAL
somber ..... SOLEMN, GLOOMY, SAD, DISMAL, GRAVE
sombrero .... HAT
some .... ANY, ABOUT
  time ... LATER, ONE DAY
somersault .... TUMBLE, SOMERSET, FLIP(FLOP)
something done for effect ....
  EYEWASH
  easy .... PIE
  imagined .... FIGMENT
  monstrous ..... PRODIGY, FREAK
  notable/outstanding ....
  DAISY
  that links .... COPULA
  to stand on ..... FOOTING
sometime .... ONCE, FORMER, ERST(WHILE)
sometimes ...... OCCASIONALLY
somewhat .... RATHER
  suffix .... ISH
somite .... TELSON, MATAMERE, SEGMENT
somnambulist .. SLEEPWALKER
somniferous ...... SOPORIFIC
somnolence ...... SLEEPINESS, DROWSINESS
somnolent ... SLEEPY, DROWSY

son .. HEIR, PROGENY, SCION, JUNIOR
  favorite .... BENJAMIN
  in law .... GENER
  of: prefix ..... FITZ, MAC
  of a .... FILIAL
  rey's .... INFANTE
  roi's .... DAUPHIN
  younger .... CADET
sonance .... SOUND, TUNE
sonant ... VOICED, SOUNDING
  opposed to .... SURD, VOICELESS
sonata, part of .... CODA, RONDO, MOVEMENT, SCHERZO
sonderclass .... YACHT
song ...... DITTY, MELODY, CHANSON, CHANT, CANTICLE, POETRY, VERSE, LYRIC, BALLAD, RUNE, CANZONE, LIED(ER)
  accompaniment ... VAMP
  after .... EPODE
  and-dance performer ....
  DISEUSE
  baby's .... LULLABY
  Christmas .. CAROL, NOEL
  combining form ....
  MALACO
  dirgelike ...... REQUIEM
  evening .... VESPERS
  flourish .... CADENZA
  gay .... LILT
  identification .... THEME, SIGNATURE
  improvisation .... VAMP
  joyful .... P(A)EAN
  kind of ... BLUES, TORCH, SOUL, FOLK
  last words .... TAG
  like .... ARIOSE, CANOROUS, CANTABILE
  lively .... CANZONET
  love ... SERENADE, SERENA
  merry ...... GLEE, LILT
  minstrel's .. LAY, BALLAD
  morning .... MATIN
  of .... MELIC
  of joy .... CAROL
  of lamentation ....
  THRENODY, DIRGE
  of praise ... (H)ALLELUIA, PAEAN, HALLELUJAH, HYMN, LAUD, MANIFICAT
  of Solomon .. CANTICLES

of Songs ..... CANTICLES
of triumph ...... PAEAN
operatic .... ARIA
part .... MADRIGAL
poetic .... RUNE
prefix .... MELO
radio program ... THEME,
                    SIGNATURE
refrain .... BURDEN,
            CHORUS, FALLA
sacred ... MOTET, PSALM,
            HYMN, ANTHEM
sad .... BLUES, DIRGE
sailor's ...... CHANT(E)Y
section .... FIT
set of verses of ... STAVE
short .... DITTY, ODE,
            CAVATINA, ARIETTA,
            CANZONET
thrush .... MAVIS, MAVIE
words of .... LYRICS
writer .... LYRICIST
songbird .... MAVIS, LARK,
            THRUSH, CANARY, ORIOLE,
            PIPIT, WHINCHAT, WREN,
            REDWING, BULBUL, VIREO,
            VEERIE, ROBIN(ET),
            NIGHTINGALE, LINNET,
            REDSTART, BOBOLINK,
            THRASHER, SPARROW,
            BUNTING, GOLDFINCH,
            CARDINAL, TANAGER
mewing .... CATBIRD
of the .... TURDINE
vocal organ ..... SYRINX
songlike ...... MELIC, ARIOSE,
            CANOROUS, LYRIC,
            CANTABILE
songs, anthology of ..GARLAND,
songster ... SINGER, WARBLER
sonnet's last six lines .. SESTET
Sonora, capital of ....
                    HERMOSILLO
    Indian .... YAQUI
sonority .... RESONANCE
sonorous .... RESONANT,
                    ROTUND
sonsy ..-...-. BUXOM, LUCKY,
                    HANDSOME
soon .... ANON, ERELONG,
            PRONTO, QUICKLY,
            EARLY, READILY, SHORTLY,
            BETIME, ENOW
afterward .... THEN
sooner .... HOMESTEADER,
            OKLAHOMAN, RATHER

than ..-...-...-... ERE
soosoo .... DOLPHIN
soot ... CROCK, GRIME, SMUT,
            COOM, CARBON, BISTRE,
    BISTER, COLLY, LAMPBLACK
full of .... FULIGINOUS
pigment .. BISTRE, BISTER
sooth ... FACT, REAL, SMOOTH,
                    TRUTH
soothe .... SALVE, CALM,
            APPEASE, MOLLIFY, EASE,
            ALLAY, RELIEVE, COMFORT,
            LULL, PLACATE, PACIFY
soother .... ANODYNE,
            CONSOLER, SOLACER
soothing ... EASING, CALMING,
                    LENITIVE
soothsay .. FORETELL, PREDICT
soothsayer ..... (H)ARUSPEX,
            PROPHET, AUGUR, SEER,
            MANTIS, ORACLE, DIVINER,
                    TIRESIAS
brew of a ... HELLBROTH
soothsaying .... AUGURY
sooty .. DARK, DUSKY, BLACK
matter .... SMUT
sop ..... BRIBE, SOAK, STEEP,
            OOZE, MORSEL, CONCESSION
Sophia Scicolone ...... LOREN
sophism ... IDOLISM, FALLACY
sophist .... CASUIST
sophisticate .... CORRUPT,
            ADULTERATE, FALSIFY
sophisticated ... HEP, REFINED,
            HIP, SUBTLE, COMPLEX,
            BLASE, INTELLECTUAL
sophistry .. IDOLISM, FALLACY,
                    CHICANERY
sopor .... STUPOR, LETHARGY
soporific ... SOMNIFIC, OPIATE,
                    SULFONAL
sopping ...... WET, DRENCHED
soppy ... RAINY, SENTIMENTAL
soprano ..... VOICE, TREBLE,
            PONS, ALBANESE, FARRAR,
                    NILSSON
Sopwith plane ...... TABLOID
sora .... RAIL, ORTOLAN,
                    CRAKE, BIRD
Sorata .... ILLAMPU
Sorb .... SLAV, APPLE
descendants .... WENDS
Sorbonne, the .... PARISU
sorcerer .... WARLOCK,
            MAGICIAN, WIZARD,

CONJURER, MAGUS, CHALDEAN, HEX
attendant ..... FAMULUS
sorceress .... SYBIL, WITCH, CIRCE, LAMIA, MEDEA
sorcery .... WITCHCRAFT, THEURGY, MAGIC, OBE, VOODOO, SORTILEGE, DIABLERIE, DIABOLISM, CONJURATION, WIZARDRY
sordid .. FILTHY, DIRTY, MEAN, BASE, SQUALID, WRETCHED, IGNOBLE
sordino .... MUTE
sore .... TENDER, PUSTULE, PAINFUL, FESTER, ACHING, TOUCHY, ANGRY, RESENTFUL, LESION
dressing .. PATCH, GAUZE
inflamed .... BLAIN
mustard application on ... POULTICE
open .... ULCER
ulcer-like ...... CANCER
sorehead .... LOSER, GRIPER, MALCONTENT
sorghum ...... GRASS, SIRUP, FODDER, MILO, FETERITA, KAF(F)IR
grain .... SORGO, KAOLIANG, DURRA, MILLET, DOURA(H)
millet-like .... MILO
soricine animal ...... SHREW
sorority .... SOROSIS
sorosis .... SORORITY, MULBERRY, FRUIT
sorrel .... PLANT, HORSE
wood .... OCA
sorrow .... GRIEF, WOE, SADNESS, GRIEVE, ANGUISH, DOLOR
sorrowful expression ... ALAS, ALACK(ADAY), WOE IS ME
sinner .... PENITENT
sorry .... POOR, INFERIOR, MISERABLE, DISMAL, REGRETFUL, PENITENT, REMORSEFUL, SAD, CONTRITE
sort ...... KIND, CLASS, TYPE, NATURE, ILK, CLASSIFY, KIDNEY
of .... SOMEWHAT
sortie ... RAID, SALLY, FORAY
sortilege .... SORCERY, DIVINATION, PROPHECY

sorts, out of ... ... CROSS, ILL, INDISPOSED
sotol, plant like ...... YUCCA
sot ...... DRUNKARD, TOPER, SOUSE, BLOAT, RUMMY
soubise .... SAUCE
soubrette .... MAID(SERVANT)
soucar .... BANKER
souchong .... TEA
souffle .. PUFFY, SPOONBREAD
sough .... RUSTLE, SIGH, MURMUR, MOAN
soul .... EMBODIMENT, ATMAN, SPIRIT, AME, ANIMA, ESPRIT, ESSENCE, PNEUMA
dead person's ...... MANES
dwelling place .... TABERNACLE
personified .... PSYCHE
singer .... (ARETHA) FRANKLIN
timid .... LAMB
sound NOISE, SEEM, APPEAR, SANE, WELL, TRIG, SOLID, SAFE, SECURE, FATHOM, HEALTHY, STABLE, RELIABLE, VALID, STRAIT, INLET, PLUMB, AUDIO, PURL, HONK, STRIDOR
amplifier ..... RESONATOR
auto horn .... HONK
bee's ...... DRONE, HUM
bell's .. DING, PEAL, TOLL, CLANG, JINGLE
bird ...... TWEET, CHIRP, PEEP, TWITTER
bomb .... WHINE
breathing ...... STRIDOR
bullet .... ZIP, PING
buzzing .... WHIR(R)
cat's ...... PURR, MEOW, MEWL
chuckling .... CHORTLE
combining form .... PHON(O)
cooing .... CURR
deep ..... CAVERNOUS, BOOM, RUMBLE
depth .... PLUMB
discordant ...... JANGLE
donkey's .... BRAY, HEEHAW
dove's ...... COO, CURR
dull .... THUD
elephant's .... ROAR, TRUMPET

from cold ...... CHATTER
gleeful .... CHORTLE
grating .... SCROOP, JAR
guttural .... GRUNT,
    GRATE
harsh .. GRIDE, JAR, RASP
heard .... ACOUSTIC
hissing .... ZIP, SIZZLE,
    FIZZLE, FIZ(Z),
    SIBILATION, SIBILANCE,
    SWISH
hog's .... GRUNT
in harmony ...... CHIME
insect .... CHIRRUP,
    DRONE, HUM
lung .... RALE
menacing ...... GROWL,
    SNARL, GR-R-R
mournful .... KNELL
murmuring .... SOUGH,
    COO, CURR, HUM
of ...... SONIC, SONANT,
    TONAL, PHONIC
of contentment ... PURR
of delight .... SQUEAL
of disapproval .... HOOT,
    HISS, BOO, CATCALL
of footsteps ..... TRAMP,
    CLUMP
of goose .... HISS
of gunfire .... PEAL
of laughter .... PEAL
of pain ... GROAN, MOAN,
    OUCH, SHRIEK, YELL
of surprise .... GASP
of warning ...... TOCSIN,
    ALARM, HISS, SIREN,
    RATTLE
of whale .... SQUEAL,
    CLICK, MEW, CHIRRUP
of yearning .... SIGH
off .... SPEAK, ORATE
pensive .... SIGH
proofing material .. PUG
reverberating ..... ROLL
ringing .... TANG
rolling .... RUMBLE
rooster's .... CROW
rustling .... SWISH
science of ... ACOUSTIC(S)
shrill ...... SKIRL, ZING
sleeper's .... SNORE
snake ..... HISS, RATTLE
soft, rubbing ..... SWISH
steam .... HISS
strident .... SCROOP

surf .... ROTE
thin, sharp ...... SQUEAK,
    SQUEAL
thunder ...... (G)RUMBLE,
    ROLL, PEAL
trumpet .... BLARE
unit of measurement ....
    MACH, DECIBEL
voiceless ...... CEDILLA
warbling .... CHIRM
wave, bend ..... REFRACT
whiplash .... WHISH
whirring .... BURR, BIRR,
    ZIZZ
soundless .... ASONANT,
    SILENT, MUTE, STILL
soundproof, make ... DEAFEN,
    PUG
sounds in ear .... TINNITUS
soup ...... BISQUE, JULIENNE,
    CONSOMME, POT(T)AGE,
    GUMBO, CHOWDER, STEW,
    BOUILLON, BORSCHT
bread .... CROUTON
content .... NOODLE
dish .... TUREEN
flavor .... CHIVE
ingredient .... LENTIL,
    NOODLE, MACARONI
meat ... BISQUE, BURGOO
plant .... LEEK
slang ... NITROGLYCERIN,
    OVERCAST
spoon .... LADLE
thick .... PUREE, BISQUE,
    GUMBO, POTTAGE
thickening mixture ......
    ROUX
thin .... BROTH
to ____ .... NUTS
to nuts ..... MEAL, MENU
vegetable ...... OKRA,
    BISQUE, BURGOO,
    MINESTRONE
soupcon ... SUSPICION, TRACE
sour .... TART, ACID(ULOUS),
    ACETOUS, RANK, RANCID,
    CROSS, BITTER, ACETOSE,
    ACIDIC
ale ... VINEGAR, ALEGAR
disposition, of ... GROSS,
    TESTY, PEEVISH,
    LIVERISH
gourd .... BAOBAB
grass .... SORREL
gum .... TUPELO, NYSSA

milk drink .... LEBAN
puss .... PRUNE
source ...... SPRING, ORIGIN,
ROOT, FOUNT(AIN),
HEADSPRING
of genius/inspiration ....
MUSE
sourdine .... MUTE
sourdough .... LEAVEN,
SETTLER, PROSPECTOR
sourpuss .... CRAB
Sousa's employment .. MARINE,
BANDLEADER
soubriquet .. MARCH KING
souse ..... BRINE, DRUNKARD,
PICKLE, SOAK, STEEP,
INTOXICATE, SWOOP
soused .... DRUNK, TIPSY
soutache .... BRAID
soutane ..... CASSOCK, TUNIC
South Africa, foreigner in ....
UITLANDER
South African .... BOER,
AFRIKANER
animal ...... SURICATE,
QUAGGA
antelope .... GNU,
BUSHBUCK, SASSABY
assembly .... RAAD
beverage .... MATE
camp .... LAAGER
capital ..... CAPE TOWN,
PRETORIA
city .... CAPE TOWN,
DURBAN
dialect ..... AFRIKAANS
district .... RAND
Dutch ...... BOER, TAAL
farmer .... BOER
fox .... ASSE
golfer .... PLAYER,
SEWGOLUM
grassland .... VELD(T)
hill .... KOP
javelin .... ASSAGAI
legislature .... RAAD
monetary unit ..... RAND
monkey .... VERVET
mountain .... KOP
mulatto .... GRIQUA
native ... BANTU, KAFFIR,
ZULU
plain .... VELD(T)
plateau .... KAROO
polecat .... MUSANG
policeman .... ZARP

policy ...... APARTHEID
president .... DONGES
prime minister .. VORSTER,
VERWOERD, SMUTS,
HERTZOG
province ... NATAL, CAPE,
TRANSVAAL
racial policy .. APARTHEID
republic .... TRANSVAAL
river ..... VAAL, ORANGE,
KUBANGO, OKAVANGO
road .... KLIP
settler .... BOER
spear .... ASSAGAI
swamp .... VLEI
tableland ..... KAR(R)OO
thong .... RIEM
town .... STAD
tribal council .... INDABA
valley ...... KLOOP, VAAL
village .... KRAAL
weapon ..... KNOBKERPIE
workmen .... VOLK
South American animal ......
VICUNA, ALPACA, LLAMA,
TAYRA, TAPIR
alligator .... CAIMAN,
CAYMAN
arid ground .... ESPINAL
armadillo .... TATOUAY,
MATACO, POYOU
bean .... TONKA
bird .... SERIEMA,
TINAM(O)U, AGAMI,
RHEA, SCREAMER,
TURCO, JACU, TOPAZ,
MANAKIN, HOA(C)TZIN,
JACANA, GUACHARO,
CURASSOW, ARACARI,
GUAN
butternut .... SOUARI
city .... LIMA
coin .... CONDOR
crocodile ...... YACARE
dance .... BEGUINE,
CARIOCA, SAMBA,
TANGO
deer .... GEMUL
desolate region ... PUNA
duck .... PATO
fish .... CHARACIN,
ARAPAIMA, PIRANHA
guinea pig .... PACA
hare .... TAPETI
hat .... JIPIJAPA
hawk .... CARACARA

herdsman ..... LLANERO
hog .... TAPIR
hummingbird .. WARRIOR
Indian ..... CARIB, INCA,
    MAYAN, ONA, GUARANI,
    PATAGONIAN,
    TEHUELCHE
knife .... MACHETE
laborer .... PEON,
    BRACERO
lapwing ..... TREUTERO
lizard .... TEJU
mammal ..... KINKAJOU,
    GRISON
missile weapon .... BOLA
monkey .... SAPAJOU,
    CAPUCHIN, MARMOSET,
    ARABA, ACARI, TITI,
    TETEE
nightbird .... GUACHARO
opossum ..... YAPO(C)K,
    QUICA
ostrich .... RHEA
palm ...... GRUGRU, ITA
parrot .... MACAW,
    AMAZON
plain ... PAMPA(S), LLANO,
    PARAMO, CAMPO
plant .... PAREIRA,
    COPAIBA, RHATANY,
    GUACO, JABORANDI,
    JIPIJAPA
raccoon .... COATI
river ... AMAZON, PLATA,
    PARA, ORINOCO
rock .... TALPATATE
rodent ... TAPETI, PACA,
    TAPIR, RATEL,
    GUINEA PIG, NUTRIA,
    AGOUTI, CAPYBARA,
    COYPU, AGOUTY
ruminant .... LLAMA
seed ..... GUAIAC, TONKA
snake ...... ABOMA, BOA,
    BUSHMASTER
tanager ..... YENI, LINDO
tea leaf .... MATE
tick .... CARAPATO
tortoise ..... MATAMATA
toucan .... ARACARI
tree ... CAROB, CEBIL,
    BALSA, MORA, BEBEERU,
    TOLU
trumpeter .... AGAMI
tuber .... OCA
turtle .... MATAMATA

ungulate .... TAPIR
weapon .... BOLAS
wild cat .. MARGAY, EYRA
wind .... PAMPERO
wood sorrel .... OCA
South Carolina capital ....
    COLUMBIA
county .... JASPER, HORRY
river .... PEE DEE
    SANTEE, CATAWBA
South Dakota capital .. PIERRE
city ... ABERDEEN, HURO
state animal .... COYOTE
state flower ..... PASQUE
"South Pacific" star ... PINZA
South Pole explorer .....
    AMUNDSEN
South Sea canoe .. PROA, PRAU
garment .... SARONG
island ...... BALI, SAMOA,
    TA(H)TI, ARU, OTAHEITE
island drink ....
    KAVA(KAVA)
loincloth ..... LAVA-LAVA
native ..... POLYNESIAN,
    KANAKA, BALINESE,
    SAMOAN, TAHITIAN
novel .... OMOO
shrub ...... KAVA(KAVA)
South wind .... NOTUS,
    AUSTER
southerly .... AUSTRAL
southern .... AUSTRAL
Cross .... CRUX
France .... MIDI
States .... DIXIE
southpaw .... LEFT-HANDED,
    LEFTY
souvenir .... MEMENTO,
    KEEPSAKE, FAVOR, RELIC,
    SCRAP
sovereign ... SUPREME, CHIEF,
    MONARCH, RULER, KING,
    EMPEROR, PRINCE, LIEGE,
    SOVRAN, ROYAL, POUND,
    QUID
dignity .... MAJESTY
female .... QUEEN,
    EMPRESS, TSARINA
of a .... REGNAL
power .... SWAY
sovereignty ...... DOMINION,
    RULE, THRONE, EMPERY,
    SCEPTRE, ROYALTY
Soviet (see Russian) .. COUNCIL

administrative body ..... PRESIDIUM
government ... KREMLIN
news agency .... TASS
newspaper ...... PRAVDA
poet ...... YEVTUSHENKO
president ..... MIKOYAN, PODGORNY, KALININ
republic .... UZBEK, KAZAKH, LATVIA, TADZHIK, KIRGHIZ, UKRAINE, MOLDAVIA, TURKMEN
Russia .... USSR
Union founder ... LENIN
sovran .... SOVEREIGN
sow ..... PIG, SLUICE, PLANT, PROPAGATE, SEED, SWINE, SCATTER, BROADCAST, DISSEMINATE, STREW
bug .... SLATER, WOOD LOUSE, ISOPOD
young .... GILT
sowens .... PORRIDGE
sox .... SOCKS
soy(a) .... SOJA, SAUCE, BEAN
soybean enzyme ...... URASE
cake .... TAHURE
product ... MISO, NAT(T)O, SUFU, TAHO, TOKUA, TAUSI, TEMPLA
sauce .... SOJA, TOYO
spa ... SPRING, BATH, RESORT
space .... ROOM, EXPANSE, EXTENT, AREA, GAP
Age initials .... NASA
Age launcher ... SPUTNIK
agency: abbr. ...... NASA
beacon .... QUASAR, PULSAR
between .... DISTANCE
between bird's eye and bill LORE
blank .... LACUNA
craft capsule ...... SPECS
craft part .... MODULE
craft to moon .. APOLLO
craft to Venus .. MARINER
dog .... STREIKA
empty ... VOID, VACUUM, BLANK
filled with matter .... PLENUM
filler .... SHIM
in biology ...... LACUNA
in from margin .. INDENT

monkey .... ENOS, ASTROMONK
of time .. SPAN, INTERVAL
pertaining to ... SPATIAL
ship blister .... MODULE
traveler .... ASTRONAUT, COSMONAUT
vehicle .... SPUTNIK, APOLLO, SATELLITE, EXPLORER
void .... VACUUM
spacious ...... ROOMY, VAST, LARGE
spade ...... SCOOP, SAM, DIG
tool like .... SPUD, SHOVEL
spadefoot .... TOAD
spades .... SUIT
spaghetti, food like .... MACARONI
ingredient ...... DURUM
spahi, spahee ... CAVALRYMAN
Spain .... ESPANA, IBERIA, HESPERIA
capital of .... MADRID
district of ... GRANADA, ASTURIAS, GALICIA, NAVARRE, ANDALUSIA
kingdom of ... ARAGON, CASTILE, LEON
Spalato .... SPLIT
spale .... LATH
spall .... GALLET, CHIP, FLAKE, SPLIT
spalpeen .... SCAMP, RASCAL
span ... WINGSPREAD, BRIDGE, TEAM, CROSS, PAIR, PERIOD, QUARTER
in inches .... NINE
spang ... DIRECTLY, ABRUPTLY
spangle ... PAILLETTE, SEQUIN, GLITTER
Spaniard .... IBERIAN, CASTILIAN, SENOR
spaniel .... DOG, SPRINGER, PAPILLON, CLUMBER, COCKER
kind of ... TOY, WATER
Spanish abbot .... ABAD
afternoon .... TARDE
almond .... JORDAN
America mestizo .... LADINO
American country ...... MEXICO
American town .. PUEBLO

American War soldier ... ROUGHRIDER
another .... OTRO
apron .... DELANTAL
article ... EL, LAS, LA, LOS
as .... COMO
asphalt .... BREA
aunt .... TIA
baby .... NINA, NENA
barrel .... TONEL
bayonet .... YUCCA
bear .... OSO
berry, dried .... PASA
blanket .... PONCHO, SERAPE, MANTA
blind .... CIEGO
blue .... AZUL
bonnet .... GORRA
booth ... CASILLA, TIENDA
botanist ..... MONARDES
boy .... NIÑO
breech .... BRAGA
brush .... CEPILLO
buffoon .... GRACIOSO, COMICO
bull .... TORO
business firm ..... CASA
cape .... TRAFALGAR
capital .... MADRID
card game .... OMBRE, MONTE, OMBER
castle .... ALCAZAR, ALHAMBRA, TORRE
cathedral city ..... AVILA, SEVILLA
cellist .... CASALS
chaperon ..... DUEN(N)A
cheer ...... OLE, BRAVO
cigar .... ROPO
city ..... CADIZ, CIUDAD, LEON, IRUN, CORUNNA, ALMERIA, JEREZ, MURCIA, GUERNICA, BILBAO, LORCA, MADRID, TOLEDO, PAMPLONA, SEGOVIA, CORDOVA, BADAJOZ, CARTAGENA, OVIEDO, VITORIA, ZARAGOZA
cloak ...... CAPA, MANTA
clothing .... ROPA
clown .... GRACIOSO
club(house) .... CASINO
coffeepot ..... CAFETERA
coin .... DOUBLOON, CENTAVO, PESETA, PESO, DOBLA, CENTEN, REAL, MARAVEDI, PISTOLE
collar .... CUELLO
colony in Africa ... IFNI
composer .... FALLA
conquistador ... CORTEZ, PIZARRO
cot .... CATRE
cough .... TOS
council .... JUNTA
court .... PATIO, JUZGADO
cow .... VACA
cowboy ...... GAUCHO, VAQUERO
cup .... TAZA
cupid .... AMORINO, AMORETTO
dance .... FLAMENCO, TANGO, VALSE, SARABAND, JOTA, CARIOCA, PAVIN, BOLERO, DANZA, BAILE, GUARACHA, PAVAN(E), CANARY, CACHUCHA
daughter-in-law .. NUERA
Davis Cupper .. SANTANA, GISBERT, ARILLA, GIMENO
day .... DIA
dear .... CARO
dialect ...... ARAGONESE, CASTILIAN, ASTURIAN, ANDALUSIAN
dictator .... FRANCO
dish ... OLLA, BACALAO, PAELLA
district .... GRANADA
dollar ... PIASTRE, DURO, PESO, PIASTER
dramatist .... TELLEZ
dress .... TRAJE
dressing gown .... BATA
drink .... VINO
each .... CADA
east .... ESTE
event .... CASO
execution ..... GARROTE
expensive .... CARO
explorer ..... MAGELLAN, BALBOA, DESOTO, CORONADO, MENENDEZ
face .... CARA
farm .... HACIENDA, RANCHO, GRANJA

fascist .... FALANGIST
feast .... FIESTA
fleet .... ARMADA, FLOTA
flesh .... CARNE
fly .... CANTHARIS
forest .... MONTE
fortress official .. ALCAIDE
friend .... AMIGO
game ... PELOTA, JAI ALAI
general .... ALVA
gentleman .. CABALLERO,
    GRANDEE, SEÑOR, DON,
    CAVALI(E)RO
girl .... NIÑA, CHICA
god of love ..... AMADIS
governess ...... DUENNA
grape .... MALAGA
grass .... ESPARTO
guitarist .... SEGOVIA
gypsy dance .. FLAMENCO
habit ... SIESTA, MANANA
half-breed ..... LADINO
hall .... SALA
hamlet .... ALDEA
harbor .... PUERTO,
    ASILO
hard .... DURO
hat .... SOMBRERO
headdress .... MANTILLA
Hebrew dialect .. LADINO
herdsman ...... PASTORES
hero ... (EL) CID, AMADIS
hill .... ALCOR, ALTO
holiday .... FIESTA
horse .... CABALLO,
    GENET, JENNET
horseman .... JINETE,
    CAVAL(I)ERO
hour .... HORA
house .... CASA
housecoat .... BATA
hunter's cap .. MONTERO
Inquisition prey ....
    HERETIC
island .... CANARY
inn ..... POSADA, MESON,
    FONDA, VENTA
jacket .... CHAQUETA
jail .... CALABOZO
jar ...... TARRO, JARRO,
    OLLA, TINAJA
kettle ... CALDERA, OLLA
kettledrum ..... TIMPANO
king ...... REY, ALFONSO,
    MILESIAN, JUAN

kingdom .... ARAGON,
    LEON, CASTILE,
    NAVARRE
knapsack ..... MOCHILA
knife .... CUCHILLO
knight .... CABALLERO
lady ... DOÑA, SEÑORITA,
    SEÑORA
lame .... COJO
landlady .... DUENA
landmark .... ALHAMBRA,
    ESCORIAL
lasso .... REATO, RIATA
legislature ...... CORTES
letter .... CARTA
lighthouse ...... FARO
linen .... CREA, HILO
little .... POCO
lounging robe ..... BATA
love .... AMOR
lover .... AMADOR
mackerel .... SIERRA
Madrid boulevard ....
    PRADO
Main .... CARIBBEAN
man .... HOMBRE
manager ...... GERENTE
mantle .... CAPA
marry .... CASAR
matter .... CASO
mattress ...... COLCHON
mayor .... ALCALDE
measure .... VARA,
    CANTARA, LINEA
meat .... CARNE
merchantship .. GALLEON
mestizo .... LADINO
mole .... TOPO
monetary unit ... PESETA
Moorish capital ....
    CORDOBA
Morocco seaport ....
    TETUAN
moss .... TILLANDSIA
mother .... MADRE
mountain ... MONTANA,
    MONTE, GUARA,
    MULHACEN
mountain pass .... ABRA
mountain range .. SIERRA
mounted soldier .. JINETE
moviehouse .... CINE
muffler .... BUFANDA
muralist .... SERT
my .... MIO
nobleman .... HIDALGO,

GRANDEE, DON, CONDE, DUQUE
none .... NADA
nothing .... NADA
novelist .... CERVANTES, IBANEZ, BAROJA
now .... AHORA
pack saddle ... ALBARDA
painter ... DALI, PICASSO, SERT, MIRO, GOYA, MURILLO
palace .... ESCORIAL
paprika ...... PIMIENTO
park .... ALAMEDA
peak .... MULHACEN
pedestal .... BASA
penal colony .. PRESIDIO
peninsula .... IBERIA
pianist .... ITURBI
pitch .... BREA
plantation .... HACIENDA
plowed land .... ARADA
poem .... ODA
police .... RURALE
porridge .... ATOLE
port ...... CADIZ, PALOS
post office ...... CORREO
pot .... OLIA
prefix .... HISPANO
pretty .... LINDO
priest ..... PADRE, CURA
prince .... PRINCIPE
princess .... INFANTA
prison .... CALABOZO
promenade ...... PASEO
province ... AVILA, YESTA, LERIDA, CATALUNA, CATALONIA, ASTURIAS, MALAGA, LEON, JAEN
purse .... BOLSA
queen .... ELENA, REINA
rabbi ...... MAIMONIDES
raisin .... PASA
region .... ASTURIAS
ribbon .... CINTA
river ...... EBRO, TAGUS, MINO, DUERA, RIO, DOURO, ARGA, ADAJA, TAJO
robber .... LADRON
rubber .... CAUCHO
ruler .... FRANCO
ruling house ... BOURBON
Sahara ..... RIO DE ORO
sailing vessel .. GALLEON, CARVEL, CARAVEL(LE)

sale .... VENTA
saltwort .... BARILLA
seaport .... PALOS, ALMERIA, ADRA, BILBAO, MALAGA, ALGECIRAS, VIGO
seaport in Africa .. CEUTA
shawl .... MANTA, SERAPE, MANTILLA
she .... ELLA
sheep ... MERINO, OVEJA
sheepfold .... REDIL
sheepskin .... ZALEA
sheet ..... SABANA, HOJA, PLIEGO
shepherd ...... PASTORES
sherry .... JEREZ
ship .... BARCO
shirt .... CAMISA
shirtwaist .... BLUSA
shoe ..... ZAPATO, BOTIN
shoot .... TIRAR
shop ... TALLER, TIENDA
shrimp .... CAMARON
shy .... TIMIDO
sick ..... MALO, ENFERMO
sickle .... HOZ
side .... LADO, CARA
sidewalk .... ACERA
sign(al) .... SENAL, SENA
signature .... FIRMA
silk .... SEDA
silly ...... TONTO, BOBO
silver .... PLATA
sitting room .. (ANTE)SALA
skin .... CUTIS
skipper .... PATRON, CAPITAN
skirt .... FALDA
sky .... CIELO
smoke .... FUMAR
snow .... NIEVE
some .... UNOS
something .... ALGO
song .... FLAMENCO
statesman ...... AZANA
steel .... ACERO
stock farm ..... RANCHO
stopover .... PARADA
stopper .... TAPON
storeroom ...... BODEGA
strawberry ...... FRESA
street .... CALLE
streetcar ...... TRANVIA
sun .... SOL
sweet .... DULCE

sword .. ESPADA, TOLEDO
tablecloth ...... MANTEL
teakettle .... TETERA
tennis star ...... GIMENO,
SANTANA, ARILIA,
GISBERT
thank you ...... GRACIAS
the .. EL, LA, LO, LOS, LAS
they .... ELLAS
thick .... ESPESO
thief .... LADRON
thimble .... DEDAL
thin .... FINO
thirst .... SED, ANSIA
this .... ESTE, ESTA,
ESTO
title .... DON, DOÑA,
SEÑOR(A), CONDE,
DUQUE
tomorrow ...... MAÑANA
tower .... TORRE,
MIRADOR, MINARETE
town ... PUEBLO, ALDEA,
CIUDAD
town official .... ALCALDE
ugly .... FEO
uncle .... TIO
until .... HASTA
vessel .... GALLEON
walking cane ... BASTON
warehouse ..... BODEGA
watch .... RELOJ
watchman ...... SERENO
watchtower ... MIRADOR
watchword .... LEMA
water .... AGUA
waterfall ...... CASCADA,
CATARATA
watermelon ..... SANDIA
wave .... OLA
wax .... CERA
wealthy .... RICO
weapon ..... ARMA, BOLA
weather .... TIEMPO
web .... TELA
wedding .... BODA
weight ...... PESO, PESA,
CARGA, ARROBA, MARCO,
TONELADA
well .... BIEN, POZO
whale .... BALLENA
wheat .... TRIGO
wheel .... DISCO
white .... PURO, BLANCO
who .... QUIEN
who knows ... QUIEN SABE

wine ... MALAGA, TINTO,
VINO, SHERRY
wine-making center ......
JEREZ
woman .. MUJER, SEÑORA
wool .... LANA
work .. OBRA, TRABAJO
writer .... IBAÑEZ,
ALARCON
spank .... SMACK, PADDLE,
SLAP, CUFF
spanker .... SAIL, DRIVER
spanking .... RAPID, BRISK,
QUICK
spanner .... WRENCH
spar ...... POLE, YARD, GAFF,
SPRIT, BEAM, RAFTER,
BARITE, (SHADOW)BOX,
MAST, BOOM, DISPUTE,
WRANGLE, LONGERON
branch of service .. USCG,
COAST GUARD
for stowing ..... STEEVE
lower a .... REEF
part of .... SEMPER,
PARATUS
spare .... SAVE, RESERVE,
EXTRA, SCANT(Y), MEAGER,
THIN, LANKY, LEAN
sparge ..... SPLASH, SPRINKLE
sparing ... FRUGAL, THRIFTY,
SCANTY, MEAGER
spark .... WOO, BEAU, COURT,
ACTIVATE, ARC, TRACE,
SCINTILLA, PARTICLE,
KINDLE, LOVER
gives off ...... IGNESCENT
stream .... ARC
sparked .... ARCED
sparkle ... GLITTER, GLISTEN,
FLASH, VIVACITY, GLEAM,
EFFERVESCE, BRILLIANCE,
CORUSCATE
sparkler .... DIAMOND,
FIREWORK, EYE, BRILLIANT
sparkling water .. SODA WATER,
FIZZ
Sparky, baseballer ...... LYLE
sparling ..... SMELT, HERRING
sparoid .... GILTHEAD,
(SEA)BREAM, GAR, TAI,
SCUP, PORGY
sparrow .... DONEY,
WEAVERBIRD, FINCH,
PASSERINE, RICEBIRD,
CHIPPY

sparry .... SPATHIC, SPATHOSE
sparrowgrass ..... ASPARAGUS
sparse ..... SCANTY, MEAGER, SCARCE
   opposite of ...... DENSE, CROWDED
Sparta .... LACEDAEMON
Spartan ... HARDY, WARLIKE, STOIC(AL), SEVERE, BRAVE, HEROIC
   admiral .... LYSANDER
   bondman .... HELOT
   king .... TYNDAREUS, LEONIDAS, CLEOMENES, AGESILAUS
   lawgiver ...... LYCURGUS
   magistrate .... EPHOR
   queen .... LEDA
   serf/slave .... HELOT
spasm .... TIC, CONVULSION, THROE, CHOREA, FIT, KINK
   muscle .... CRICK, CRAMP
   of distress .... PANG
   of pain .... SHOOT
   twitch .... TIC
spasmodic .... FITFUL, INTERMITTENT
spasms, series of ..... CLONOS
Spassky, chess champ .. BORIS
spat .... GAITER, SLAP, DISPUTE, ROW, TIFF, QUARREL, OYSTER, SPAWN
spate .... FLOOD, DOWNPOUR, OUTPOURING, FLOOD, FRESHET, DELUGE, INUNDATION
spathe .... GLUME
   enclosure .... SPADIX
spathic .... SPARRY
spatter ... SCATTER, SPRINKLE, SPRAY, SPLASH, DEFAME
spatterdash .... LEGGING
spatterdock .... LILY
spatula ..... SLICE, BLUNGER
spavined .... LAME
spawn ... PRODUCE, EGGS, ROE, SPAT
spay ..... STERILIZE, CASTRATE
spayed hen .... FOULARD
speak .... UTTER, TALK, DISCOURSE, ADDRESS, ORATE
   angrily .... SNARL
   at length ..... EXPATIATE
   evasively .. HEDGE, STALL

   imperfectly .... LISP, STUTTER, STAMMER
   in silly way ..... DROOL, SLOBBER
   inability to ...... ALALIA
   incoherently .... GIBBER
   irreverently .. BLASPHEME
   lengthily ...... PERORATE
   loudly .... EXCLAIM
   noisily ...... RANT, RAVE, BLUSTER
   of .... MENTION
   sharply ..... SNAP, SNARL
   softly .... WHISPER, MURMUR
   unable to ... DUMB, MUTE
   under the breath ...... MUTTER
speakeasy .... BLINDPIG, BLIND TIGER
speaker, bete noire of .... HECKLER
   loud .... STENTOR
speaking many tongues ...... POLYGLOT
   style .... PARLANCE, PERSIFLAGE, DELIVERY
spear .. ASSAGAI, PIERCE, STAB, DART, PIKE, GAFF, JAVELIN, HARPOON, SHAFT, LANCE, BLADE, SHOOT
   body of a .... SHAFT
   fish .. GIG, GAFF, LEISTER
   Neptune's ..... TRIDENT
   of grass .... BLADE
   point .... PIKE
   shaped .... HASTATE
   three-pronged .. TRIDENT, LEISTER
   thrower .... WOMERA
spearfish .... MARLIN
spearhead .. VANGUARD, LEAD, VAN
spearwort .... CROWFOOT
special ... UNIQUE, PECULIAR, UNUSUAL, SPECIFIC, PARTICULAR
specialist, foot diseases .... PODIATRIST
specialized ...... TECHNICAL
specialty .... FORTE, LINE, METIER
specie .... COIN
   factory .... MINT
species ...... VARIETY, CLASS, SORT, KIND

specific ... PRECISE, DEFINITE,
EXPLICIT, SPECIAL,
CONCRETE
specify ...... DEFINE, DETAIL,
STIPULATE, NAME
specimen ... EXAMPLE, SAMPLE,
MODEL
specious .... PLAUSIBLE
reasoning ...... IDOLISM,
SPHISM, SYLLOGISM
speck ... MOTE, BIT, SPOT, JOT,
STAIN, MARK, PARTICLE,
FLECK
speckle .... DOT, MOTTLE,
DAPPLE, FLECK, SPOT,
MACULATE
specs .... EYEGLASSES
spectacle ...... SIGHT, SHOW,
EXHIBITION, SCENE, VIEW,
PAGEANT
spectacles ...... SPECS, LENSES,
SUNGLASSES
part .... RIM, ARM, LENS
spectacular .... STRIKING
spectator .... ONLOOKER,
WATCHER, OBSERVER,
LOOKER-ON
specter .... APPARITION,
GHOST, WRAITH, SHADOW,
BOGEY, SPIRIT, SPOOK,
PHANTOM, PHANTASM(A),
FANTASM
spectral .. PHANTOM, GHOSTLY,
EERY
speculate .. PONDER, MEDITATE,
CONJECTURE, GUESS,
GAMBLE, THINK
speculation reckless ... FLIER,
FLYER
speculative ..... THEORETICAL
speculator .... PLUNGER,
GUESSER, GAMBLER
inexperienced ..... LAMB
welshing ..... LAME DUCK
speculum .... MIRROR
speech .... TONGUE, TALK,
EXPRESSION, UTTERANCE,
OENOMEL, EPILOGUE,
DIALECT, LIP, SERMON,
ORATION, DECLAMATION,
WHISPER
abusive .... TIRADE
art .... ORATORY,
RHETORIC
blustering .... HARANGUE
brevity of ... LACONISM

combining form .. LOG(O)
defect ... LISP, STUTTER,
APHASIA, STAMMER, ALOGIA,
DYSPHONIA, DYSPHASIA,
IMPEDIMENT
delirious .... RAVING
ecstatic ..... RHAPSODY
emphatic .... BIRR
exalted to trivial .. BATHOS
farewell ... VALEDICTORY
figure of ...... LITOTES,
SIMILE, METAPHOR,
TROPE
formal ...... ADDRESS,
ORATION
graduation ....
VALEDICTORY
human ...... LANGUAGE
incoherent .. GIBBERISH,
JARGON
ill-tempered ... VINEGAR
last words .... TAG
loss of .... APHASIA,
ALALIA, ANEPIA
loud, wild .... RANT
manner of .... DRAWL
narrative part ....
CATASTASIS
noisy, blustering ....
TIRADE, HARANGUE
opening part .. EXORDIUM
of praise .... PANEGYRIC
ornamental ending .. TAG
part of ..... (PRO)NOUN,
(AD)VERB, ADJECTIVE
pompous ...... BOMBAST
slang .... SPIEL
sound ..... PHONE, LENIS,
FORTIS, PHONEME
style of ...... LOCUTION,
EUPHUISM
surplusage ..... PADDING
tiresome .... SCREED
wild .... RANT
speechless .... SILENT,
VOICELESS, SURD, DUMB,
MUTE, TONGUE-TIED,
APHONIC, APHASIC
speed ..... VELOCITY, HASTE,
REV, TEAR, RATE, FLY,
RUSH, HIE
drug ...... METHEDRINE,
AMPHETAMINE
full .... AMAIN
measuring device ....
TACHOMETER

of sound .... MACH
unit, proposed ..... VELO
up .... ACCELERATE,
HASTEN, HURRY
writing ..... SHORTHAND
speedily ... APACE, POSTHASTE
speedwell ... VERONICA, PLANT
speedy .. SWIFT, RAPID, QUICK,
APACE, PROMPT, FAST
spelean .... CAVE-LIKE
speleology, subject of .. CAVES
spell .... CHARM, TRANCE,
MEAN, SIGNIFY, PERIOD,
HEX, FIT, TURN, STREAK
of activity ...... SPRINT,
SPURT
out .... READ, INTERPRET
spellbind .... ENCHANT,
ENTRANCE, HOLD,
FASCINATE, CHARM
spellbinder .... ORATOR
spelling ——— .... BEE
incorrect ... CACOGRAPHY
spelt .... WHEAT
spelter .... ZINC, INGOTS
spence ..... LARDER, PANTRY
spencer .... JACKET, TRYSAIL
spend ... CONSUME, WEAR OUT,
EXHAUST, DISBURSE, PASS,
LOSE
lavishly .... DISPEND,
SQUANDER
the night ..... SHACK UP
the summer .... ESTIVATE
spendthrift ... SCATTERGOOD,
ROUNDER, WASTREL,
PRODIGAL, SQUANDERER,
WASTEFUL
Spengler, philosopher ....
OSWALD
Spenser, poet .... EDMUND
spent ..... WORN, EXHAUSTED,
ALL IN, WEARY, TIRED,
FAGGED, CONSUMED
sperm ~ SEMEN, WHALE, SEED,
MILT
whale .... CACHALOT
spermary ..... GONAD, TESTIS
spermatozoid .... GAMETE
spermophile .... SUSLIK,
GOPHER, CHIPMUNK
spew ...... THROW UP, VOMIT,
EJECT, SPUB
Speyer .... SPIRES
sphacelate .... MORTIFY
sphagnum .... (PEAT)MOSS

sphene .... TITANITE
sphere ... ORBIT, BALL, GLOBE,
STAR, PLANET, SKY, FIELD,
PROVINCE, DOMAIN, REALM,
RONDURE
spherical .. GLOBULAR, ROUND,
GLOBOUS, GLOBOSE, OVOID,
GLOBATE, GLOBOID
spheroid, example of a ....
EARTH, BALL
spherule .... GLOBULE
sphery ... STARLIKE, CELESTIAL
sphincter .... CONSTRICTOR
sphinx ...... MOTH, MONSTER
head of ..... RAM, HAWK
query of .... RIDDLE
site of ...... GIZA, GIZEH,
THEBES
sphragistics' subject .... SEALS
sphygmus .... PULSE
spica .... STAR, SPIKE
spice .... CINNAMON, AROMA,
FLAVOR, MULL, CHILE,
TURMERIC, GINGER,
SASSAFRAS, CHIL(L)I,
SPEARMINT, STACTE,
SEASON, CLOVE, MACE,
PEPPER, NUTMEG,
CANELLA
bud .... CLOVE, CAPER,
SAFFRON
Island(s) ...... TERNATE,
MOLUCCAS
leaf ... ANGELICA, BASIL,
BORAGE, BURNET,
CHERVIL, CHIVES, MINT,
PARSLEY, SORREL, SAGE,
THYME, TARRAGON,
SAVORY, ROSEMARY
seed ... ANISE, CARAWAY,
CUMIN, DILL, SESAME,
MACE, FENNELL, POPPY,
CORIANDER, CARDAMON,
CELERY
spiceberry .... WINTERGREEN
spiced ale .... WASSAIL
dish .... SALMI,
CHILI CON CARNE,
TAMALE, OLLA
spick and span .... NEAT,
TRIM, FRESH, CLEAN
spiculate .... NEEDLELIKE
spicule .... SPIKE, SCLERITE,
ACTINE
spicy ... AROMATIC, PUNGENT,

PIQUANT, FRAGRANT, RACY,
RISQUE, GINGERY, JUICY
sensation .... HEAT
spider ... TRIVET, ARACHNID,
MITE, ARTHROPOD, SKILLET,
(FRYING)PAN
class .... ARACHNIDA
crab .... MAJA, MAIA,
THORNBACK
girl turned into ....
ARACHNE
job of ...... WEAVING,
SPINNING
monkey .. ATELES, QUATA
nest of .... NIDUS
poison .... VENOM
poisonous .. TARANTULA
trap of .... WEB
spiegel .... PIG IRON
spiel .... SPEECH, TALK
spiffy ... NEAT, SMART, SPRUCE
spigot ..... SPILE, TAP, PLUG,
PEG, FAUCET, VALVE
spike .... NAIL, ANTLER,
MACKEREL, PIERCE, TINE,
IMPALE, FOIL, BROB, THWART,
SPINE, GAD
cereal .... EAR
fork's ..... PRONG, TINE
lavender .... MINT
like .... SPINATE
mountain climber's ....
PITON
of flowers .... SPADIX,
AMENT
of plantain .... CHAT
shield's .... UMBO
spikelet .... SPINULE
spikenard ... OINTMENT, PLANT
spile ..... SPIGOT, PLUG, TAP,
STAKE, SPOUT
spill .... SLOP, OVERFLOW,
FALL, SPILE, SPLINTER,
PEG, PLUG, TUMBLE,
ROD, PIN
the beans .... TELL,
DIVULGE, SQUEAL,
DISCLOSE, CONFESS, SING
Spillane's hero ...... HAMMER
spin ... ROTATE, BIRL, WHIRL,
RIDE, TURN, GYRATE,
WEAVE, REVOLVE, REEL,
TWIRL
a—— ...... YARN, TALE,
WEB
spinaceous plant .... SPINACH

spinach .... ORACH(E),
GOOSEFOOT, GREENS,
TALINUM
spinal .... RACHIDIAN
column .... SPINE,
BACKBONE, R(H)ACHIS
column, having ....
VERTEBRATE
cord .... MYELON
cord cut .... PITH
cord inflammation ......
MYELITIS, RACHITIS
cord membrane ....
EPENDYMA
cord sheath .. MYELIN(E),
MATER
cord tumor ...... GLIOMA
marrow .... NUCHA
spindle .. ARBOR, HYDROMETER,
DISTAFF, BUFF, TRIBLET,
MANDREL, ROD, PIN, SHAFT,
AXIS, AXLE
flywheel .... WHARVE
shaped like ... FUSIFORM
weaver's .... QUILL
spindling .... GANGLING,
GANGLY, LANKY
spindrift ... (SEA)SPRAY, SCUD,
FOAM
spine ... THORN, SPIKE, QUILL,
RAY, CHAETA, NEEDLE,
BACKBONE, CHINE, RACHIS,
PRICKLE
curvature of .. KYPHOS(IS),
LORDOSIS
spinel ...... SAPPHIRINE, STONE,
BALAS
ruby .... BALAS
spines, covered with ... HISPID
spinet ...... PIANO, VIRGINAL,
HARPSICHORD
spinnaker .... SAIL
spinner ... LURE, TOP, SPIDER,
WEAVER, SILKWORM
of life's thread ... CLOTHO
spinney ..... GROVE, THICKET
spinning machine ..... JENNY,
MULE, THROSTLE
mule inventor ....
CROMPTON
toy .... TOP
wheel .... CHARK(H)A
wheel part .... TREADLE,
DISTAFF
spinster .... (OLD) MAID,
FEME SOLE, FILLE

spiny ..... SPINOSE, ACICULAR, THORNY, ACANTHOID, PRICKLY, HISPID
spiracle .. BLOWHOLE, AIR HOLE
spiraea .... HARDHACK, MEADOWSWEET
spiral .... HELICAL, HELIX
  combining form .. HELICO
  like a .... SPIROID
  motion .... GYRE
  of wire .... COIL
  shaped .... HELICOID, TURBINATE
  shell whorl ..... VOLUTE
spiraled .... VOLUTE
spirant .... FRICATIVE
spire .... STEEPLE, COIL, SPROUT, STALK, PEAK, FLECHE, SHAFT
  ornament .... FINIAL
spirit ..... SOUL, MIND, LIFE, WILL, GHOST, VIVACITY, MORALE, HEART, VIM, SPUNK, ARDOR, BOGEY, BOGIE, VIGOR, VERVE, COURAGE, PEP, DEVA, BANSHEE, ELAN, AHRIMAN, METTLE, MARA
  heralding death .... BANSHEE, BANSHIE
  living in fire .... SALAMANDER
  mischievous ... ERLKING, GOBLIN
  of chivalry .... ERRANTRY
  of the sea ... DAVY JONES
  presiding .... NUMEN
  the .... GOD, HOLY GHOST
spirited ... ANIMATED, LIVELY, VIGOROUS, ENERGETIC, SPUNKY, ARDENT, FIERY, BRISK, PERKY
spiritless .... LISTLESS, DEPRESSED, DULL, COLD, LACKADAISICAL
spirits .... MOOD, TEMPER, DISPOSITION, LIQUOR, ETHANOL, LIQUEURS
  believer .... ANIMIST
  night-walking .. LEMURES
  of the dead ... MANES
  of hartshorn ... AMMONIA
  of wine .... ALCOHOL
  out of .... SAD
spiritual .... FOLK SONG
  being .... ENS, ANGEL
  guide .. PRIEST, CONFESSOR

  knowledge ...... GNOSIS
  mother .... AMMA
  opposite of .. CORPOREAL
  sitting .... SEANCE
spiritualism, third party in .... MEDIUM
spiritualist's equipment .. OUIJA
spirituous drink .... WINE
spiritus frumenti ..... WHISKY
spirochete .... TREPONEMA
  disease .... YAWS
spirogyra .... ALGA
spirt .... SPURT, GUSH
spirula .... MOLLUSK
  kin of .... SQUID, CUTTLEFISH
spiry .... CURLED, COILED
spit .... SKEWER, BROACH, SHOAL, SANDBANK, IMPALE, EMIT, EXPECTORATE, RAIN, SNOW, SALIVA
spital ..... HOSPITAL, SHELTER
spitchcock .... EEL
spite ...... MALICE, ILL WILL, RANCOR, VENOM, GRUDGE, SPLEEN
spiteful ... VIPERINE, VIPEROUS, VENOMOUS, VINDICTIVE, MALICIOUS, SPLENETIC, CATTY, SNIDE
  woman .... CAT
spitefulness .... SPLEEN
spitfire, Mexican .... (LUPE)VELEZ
spitter .. BROCK, SPITBALL, DEER
spitting image ...... LIKENESS
spittle .... SALIVA
  insect ..... FROGHOPPER
spittoon .... CUSPIDOR
spitz dog .... POMERANIAN
spiv .... IDLER
splanchnic .... VISCERAL
splash ... DAUB, SPARGE, LAP, SPRINKLE, SPLATTER, SPLOTCH, SPATTER, DASH, SWASH
splashboard ...... MUDGUARD
splat .... SLAT
splatter ... SPLASH, SPRINKLE, SPATTER, DAB
splay ... BEVEL, AWRY, FLAN, AWKWARD, DISLOCATE, SPREAD(ING)
spleen .... SPITE, MALICE, MELANCHOLY, WHIM, MILT

surgery ‑‑.... LIENECTOMY, SPLENECTOMY

splendid .... LUSTROUS, GORGEOUS, GRAND, GLORIOUS, SUPERB, FINE, EXCELLENT, RIPPING

splendor ... BRILLIANCE, POMP, GLORY, ECLAT, GLITTER, GRANDEUR, LUSTER

splenetic ... PEEVISH, SPITEFUL, IRRITABLE

splice ‑‑ WED, MARRY, JOIN(T), UNITE

splint ...‑‑.......... LATH

splinter ...... SHIVER, SLIVER, FLINDER, SPILL, SPLIT

splinters .... MATCHWOOD

split ...... SEPARATE, DIVIDE, BURST, RIVE, REND, CLEAVE, RIFT, CHAP, SCHISM, SPALATO, BREAK, BREACH, SLIVER, CLEFT

   capable of being .. FISSILE

   open .... DEHISCE, BREAK

   pulse .... DAL

   rattan .... CANE

   slang ‑.. PEACH, SQUEAL, SHARE

splitting ...... ACHING, SEVERE

   apart .... FISSION

splotch ‑‑ BLOT, STAIN, SPLASH, SPOT

splurge .‑.‑‑.‑‑. OSTENTATION

spode ‑.‑.‑‑.‑‑. PORCELAIN, CHINAWARE

Spohr, composer ... LOUIS

   opera by ...... JESSONDA

spoil ...... TAINT, DAMAGE, IMPAIR, ROT, VITIATE, DECAY, INDULGE, LOOT, MESS, ROB, SACK, PILLAGE, PLUNDER, SWIZE, MAR, LOUSE UP

   liable to ‑‑.. PERISHABLE

spoliation .... RAPINE

spoiled ... PAMPERED, WASTED

spoils ‑‑. BOOTY, LOOT, PRIZE, TROPHY

spoilsport .... MARPLOT, KILLJOY, WETBLANKET

spoke .... RUNG, BAR, PIN

spoken ‑‑.‑‑ UTTERED, ORAL, VOCAL

   merely ‑‑.‑‑.......... LIP

spokes .... RADII

spokeshave .... PLANE

spokesman ..... MOUTHPIECE

spoliate ...‑‑.. ROB, PLUNDER, DESPOIL

sponge ...... PARASITE, BUM, CAKE, ASCON, TRENCHER, PUDDING, MOOCH, SWAB, CADGE, PORIFERAN

   cake .... JELLYROLL

   gourd .. LOOF(A), LOOFAH

   opening .... OSCULUM

   slang .... DEAD BEAT

   spicule ‑‑...... ACTINE, OXEA, TOXA

   substitute .... LOOFAH

   throw the .... YIELD, SUBMIT, SURRENDER, GIVE UP

sponger ‑‑ CADGER, MOOCHER, LEECH, PARASITE

spongy ‑.. ABSORBENT, ELASTIC, POROUS

sponsor .. SURETY, GODFATHER, PATRON, BACKER, ANGEL

   beneficiary of .. PROTEGE

   slang .... ANGEL

sponsorship ‑‑.‑.‑ AUSPICES, (A)EGIS

spontaneous ‑‑.‑.‑ IMPULSIVE, AUTOMATIC

spontoon ‑‑..‑.‑ PIKE, HALBERD

spoof ‑‑.‑‑ HOAX, JOKE, FOOL, TRICK, DECEIVE

spook ...‑‑.‑ GHOST, SPECTER

spooky ‑‑.‑‑.‑ WEIRD, EERIE, GHOSTLY, SPECTRAL

spool ‑‑... BOBBIN, REEL, COP, PIRN

spoon ‑‑. SCOOP, PET, CARESS, NECK

   large ....‑‑. LADLE

   like implement .... OAR, PADDLE, SPATULA

   shaped ...... SPATULATE

spoonbill ‑‑..‑.‑ PADDLEFISH, AJAJA, AIAIAI

spoonfed ‑‑.‑‑.‑ PAMPERED, CODDLED

spoony ‑‑..‑ MAWKISH, SILLY, FOOLISH, SENTIMENTAL, AMOROUS

spoor ‑‑.‑.‑‑.‑ TRAIL, TRACK

Sporades island .... SAMOS

sporadic .... OCCASIONAL, DESULTORY, IRREGULAR

sporangium ..... SPORE CASE

spore ... GERM, SEED, ZYGOTE

case .... SPORANGIUM,
 ASCI, THECA, SORI,
 ASCUS
cluster(s) ... SORUS, SORI
producer .... FERN, MOSS
sac .... ASCUS, THECA
small .... SPORULE
sporran ...... PURSE, POUCH
sport .... PASTIME, DIVERSION,
 PLAY, FUN, DISPLAY, WEAR,
 FROLIC, JEST, MUTANT,
 GAME, PLAY, TRIFLE
group .... TEAM
official .. UMPIRE, REFEREE
shirt .... TEE
shoe .... LOAFER
team .... FIVE, NINE,
 ELEVEN, CREW,
 FOURSOME, SQUAD
sporting .... FAIR
house ... CASINO, ALLEY,
 HALL
sports attendance ...... GATE
meet .... GYMKHANA,
 OLYMPICS
site .... RINK, OVAL,
 ARENA, LINKS, FIELD,
 COURSE, TRACK,
 STADIUM, COLISEUM,
 GRID, DIAMOND,
 COURT, GREEN
sportscaster .. COSELL, GOWDY,
 GIFFORD
sportsman's vest .. TATTERSALL
sporty .... FLASHY, SHOWY
spot .... STAIN, MARK,
 BLEMISH, BIT, SMUT(CH),
 FLECK, (FLY)SPECK,
 MACULA(TE)
colloquial .... JAM,
 TROUBLE
in mineral .... MACLE
on animal's face .. BLAZE
on lunar halo ....
 PARASELENE
on solar halo ....
 PARHELION
playing card .... PIP
skin ... STIGMA, MACULA
small .... FLECK,
 (PIN)POINT, PRICK, DOT
spotless ..... PURE, INNOCENT,
 CLEAN
spotlight .... FOCUS
spotted .... MACULATE,

DAPPLE(D), MOTTLED,
 PIED, EYED
animal ..... (LEO)PARD,
 DAPPLE, CHEETAH,
 CAVY, GENET(TE),
 OCELOT, CHITAL, PACA
fever .... TICK, TYPHUS
with drops ...... GUTTATE
spotter .. DETECTIVE, LOOKOUT
spotty ... IRREGULAR, UNEVEN
spousal .... NUPTIAL
spouse ..... WIFE, HUSBAND,
 CONSORT, MATE
spout ..... NOZZLE, SPILE,
 SNOUT, STREAM, ELEVATOR,
 JET, GUSH
slang ...... PAWN(SHOP)
steam .... JET
water .... GARGOYLE
whale's .... BLOWHOLE
spraddle .... SPAN
sprag ...... TRIG, WEDGE,
 CHOCK, BLOCK
sprain ...... WRICK, WRENCH
sprat ...... HERRING, BRIT,
 BRISLING
sprawl ... SPREAD, LOLL, LIE,
 CRAWL
spray ... ATOMIZE(R), SHOWER,
 SPRINKLE, SPRIG, MIST,
 BOUQUET, LIPPER, SPUME,
 NEBULIZE, TWIG
spread .... OLEO, SPLAY,
 UNFOLD, UNFURL, EXHIBIT,
 EXTEND, DISPERSE, SCATTER,
 COVER, FEAST, STRETCH,
 PROPAGATE, BRUIT, JAM,
 BUTTER, FAN, JELLY,
 OVERLAY
awkwardly ...... SPRAWL
colloquial .... MEAL,
 DISPLAY
false rumors .... ASPERSE
for drying .... TED
grass .... TED
here and there .. SCATTER,
 STREW
out ...... FAN, DEPLOY,
 EFFUSE, FLARE
rapidly ..... MUSHROOM
rumors .... HAWK
thick .... SLATHER
thin .... BRAY
troops .... DEPLOY
spreading .... PATULOUS
from the center .. RADIAL

implement .... MULCHER,
SPATULA, TEDDER
spree .... BINGE, FROLIC,
CAROUSAL, BUM, LARK,
WASSAIL, BAT, TEAR, JAG,
(HELL)BENDER, TOOT,
FROLIC, ORGY, BUST(ER)
sprig ... TWIG, BRAD, SPRAY,
STRIPLING, FELLOW
sprightly ...... GAY, LIVELY,
BRISK, BLITHE, TID,
CHIPPER, AGILE, ANIMATED,
PERT, JAUNTY
spring .... LEAP, BOUND,
DART(LE), VAULT, SOURCE,
(A)RISE, SEASON, STEM,
BOLT, WELL, JUMP,
FOUNT(AIN)
  Apollo's ...... CASTALIA
  artificial ...... FOUNTAIN
  back .. RECOIL, REBOUND,
RESILE
  Biblical .... AIN
  chicken .... BROILER,
FRYER
  deposit ... TRONA, TUFA,
TRAVERTIN
  festival .... MAYDAY
  flower ... CROCUS, TULIP
  guard .... MIMIR
  holiday .... EASTER
  like .... VERNAL
  mineral .... SPA
  month .... APRIL, MAY,
MARCH
  of .... FONTAL
  poet's .... CASTALIA
  poetic .... FONT
  sign of .. BUDS, SWALLOW
  slang ..... FREE, RELEASE
  small .... GEYSER
  tide .... FLOOD
  water ... SELTZER, LYMPH
springboard .... BATULE
springbok .... GAZELLE,
SPRINGER
springe .... SNARE, TRAP
springer ... SPANIEL, GRAMPUS,
IMPOST
springhead .... SOURCE
springing back ..... RESILIENT,
ELASTIC
springs .. THERMAE, SPA, BATHS
springtime .... MAY
springy .... ELASTIC,
FLEXIBLE

sprinkle ... SHOWER, SPARGE,
STREW, SCATTER, SPLASH,
DUST, DEG, DREDGE, RAIN,
SPRAY
  water to purify .. BAPTIZE
  with flour ...... DREDGE
  with sieve .... SIFT
sprinkling .... ASPERSION
  with holy water ....
ASPERGES
sprint ...... DASH, RACE, RUN
sprinter .. DASHER, TRACKMAN
sprit .... SPAR, BOOM
sprite ..... ELF, FAIRY, GHOST,
PIXIE, PIXY, NIX, ARIEL,
FAY, HOB, BROWNIE
  helpful .... KOBOLD
  mischievous .. PUCK, IMP,
GOBLIN, KOBOLD
  water ... NIX, UNDINE, NIS
sprout .... GERMINATE, GROW,
SHOOT, (S)CION, BURGEON,
CHIT, BUD, PULLULATE
  root/stem .... TILLER,
RAT(T)OON
spruce ... TRIG, LARCH, TRIM,
NEAT, NATTY, EPINETTE,
DAPPER, SMART,
CONIFER
  fruit .... CONE
  slang .... SPIFFY
  up .... TITIVATE
sprue .... PSILOSIS
spry .... AGILE, NIMBLE,
ACTIVE, BRISK
spud .... POTATO
  tool like .. SPADE, CHISEL
spue .... SPEW
spume ... FOAM, FROTH, SCUM
spun .... WOVE(N)
spunk ...... AMADOU, PUNK,
SPARK, KINDLE, TINDER,
GRIT, SPIRIT, PLUCK,
METTLE, COURAGE
spunky ...... GAME, BRAVE,
SPIRITED
spur .... STIMULUS, ERGOT,
RIDGE, GRIFFE, PRICK,
SIDING, GOAD, ROWEL,
STRUT, BRACE, INCITE,
URGE, HURRY, CALCAR
  gamecock's .... GAFF
  mountain .... ARETE
spurge .... MILKWEED,
EUPHORBIA
spurious .... FAKE, FALSE,

COUNTERFEIT, ARTIFICIAL, SHAM, BASTARD, TIN, FORGED, BOGUS, PHON(E)Y

spurn .... REJECT, REFUSE, SCORN, DECLINE, KICK

spurr(e)y ...... (CHICK)WEED

spurt ...... JET, SPOUT, GUSH, STREAM, SQUIRT, BURST, DART

of energy .... LICK

sputnik .... SATELLITE

sputter ... SPLUTTER, JABBER, SPIT

sputum .... SPIT(TLE), SALIVA

spy .... FINK, OPERATIVE, PRY, SEE, PERCEIVE, WATCH, AGENT, UNDERCOVERMAN, KEEK, NOSE, PRIVATE EYE, SCOUT, FUCHS, (MATA)HARI, ARNOLD, ANDRE, CAVELL, ROSENBERG, INFORMER, STEIBER, CICERO, GEISLER, RINTELEN

spying .... ESPIONAGE

Spyri's heroine .... HEIDI

squab .... PIPER, PIGEON, COUCH, SOFA, CUSHION

squabble .... WRANGLE, QUARREL, ROW, DISPUTE, SPAT, MUSS, HASSLE, HASSEL

squad leader .... SERGEANT

squadron of airplanes .... ESCADRILLE

squalid ... SORDID, UNCLEAN, FOUL, FILTHY, MANGY

squall ... SCREAM, CRY, GUST, GALE, (WIND)STORM, TROUBLE, FLAW, WAUL, WAWL

squally ...... GUSTY, STORMY

squalor .... FILTH

squama .... SCALE

squamate .... SCALY

squander .... WASTE, DISSIPATE, (DI)SPEND

square .. PLAZA, PARK, SETTLE, RECONCILE, HONEST, FAIR, BALANCED, FORUM, QUADRATE, EVEN (UP), TALLY, AGREE, FIT, CUBICAL, PIAZZA

column .... PILASTER

dance .... HOEDOWN, QUADRILLE, REEL, LANC(I)ERS

dance need ...... CALLER

root of nine ..... THREE

shooter ..... FAIR DEALER

slang ..... BRIBE, HUNKY, WHITE

squared circle .... ARENA, (PRIZE)RING

squarehead .... GERMAN, SCANDINAVIAN, BOCHE

squaring circle .. CYCLOMETRY, CYCLOTOMY

squarrose .... SCALY

squash ... PEPO, PRESS, CRUSH, SILENCE, GOURD, SQUISH, FLATTEN, SPORT, QUELL, CASHAW, ZUCCHINI, CUSHAW

winter .... HUBBARD

squashy .... MUSHY

squat .... DUMPY, FUBSY, TUBBY, CROUCH, PUDGY

squatter .... SETTLER

squaw ...... WOMAN, MAHALA

Indian .... WIFE

squawbush .... SUMAC

squawk ..... CRY, COMPLAIN, PROTEST, HERON

squeak .... CREAK, CRY

squeal .... INFORM, SING, CRY, PEACH

squeamish .... QUEASY, FASTIDIOUS, DAINTY, FINICAL

person .... PRUDE

squeeze ...... SQUASH, WRING, CRUSH, JAM, NIP, EKE, EXTORT, (COM)PRESS, EXTRACT, HUG

chin .... CHUCK

squeezer, juice ...... REAMER

squelch .... CRUSH, (S)QUASH, KIBOSH, SUPPRESS, SUBDUE, SILENCE

squeteague .... CROAKER, GRUNT(ER)

squib .... FIRECRACKER, LAMPOON, DETONATOR, PASQUINADE

squid .... MOLLUSK, CUTTLEFISH, CALAMARY

arm of .... TENTACLE

relative .... SPIRULA

shell of .... PEN

squilgee .... SQUEEGEE

squill .... SEA ONION, LILY

squilla .. CRUSTACEAN, PRAWN,
SHRIMP, MANTIS CRAB,
STOMATOPOD
squinch ... CORBELING, LINTEL
squint .... SKEW, STRABISMUS,
GLANCE, PEER
eyed .... CROSS-EYED
squire .. ARMIGER, ATTENDANT,
GENTLEMAN, ESCORT,
GALLANT, ARMOR-BEARER,
DONZEL, HENCHMAN
squirm ... WIGGLE, WRIGGLE,
WRITHE
squirrel .... MARMOSET,
TAMARIN, RODENT,
CHIPMUNK, WOODCHUCK,
PHALANGER, SPERMOPHILE,
CHICKAREE, PENTAIL,
CALABAR, CALABER, XERUS
burrowing ..... GOPHER
flying .... ASSAPAN
flying aid ..... PATAGIUM
fur ... CALABAR, CALABER,
VAIR
ground .... GOPHER,
SUSLIK, SISEL
like rodent ... DORMOUSE
nest .... DREY, DRAY
parasite of ..... WABBLE
shrew .... TANA
skin .... CALABER, VAIR,
CALABAR
skin fold ... PARACHUTE,
PATAGIUM
squirt ... SPURT, SPIRT, SHOOT,
JET, STREAM
gun .... SPRAY
sri .... MISTER
SRO, part of ..... STANDING,
ROOM, ONLY
charge ...... STANDAGE
sign .... SOLDOUT
SS, Nazi .... BLACK SHIRTS
head .... HIMMLER
St. (see Saint) .... SAINT
Anthony's fire ....
ERYSIPELAS
Elmo's fire ... CORPOSANT
Francis' birthplace ......
ASSISI
John's bread ..... CAROB
Laurence river discoverer
CARTIER
stab ..... SPIT, PIERCE, GORE,
WOUND, THRUST, PUNCH,
PINK

colloquial .... TRY,
ATTEMPT
stabile .... STATIONARY
opposite of ..... LABILE
stabilize(r) .... BALLAST
stable .... STEADY, FIRM,
FIXED, CONSTANT,
STEADFAST, SECURE, BARN,
ENDURING, PADDOCK, MEW,
LODGE
compartment ..... STALL
field .... PADDOCK
member .... BOXER,
FIGHTER, RACEHORSE
part .... HAYMOW,
HAYLOFT
sound ... NEIGH, SNORT,
(W)HINNY
stableman .... (H)OSTLER,
GROOM, CURRIER
stables, royal .... MEWS
staccato, opposed to .. LEGATO
stack ...... RICK, PILE, HEAP,
CHIMNEY, SCINTLE, MOW,
RUCK
base of .... STADDLE
stacte .... SPICE
staddle .... SUPPORT, BASE,
CRUTCH, FRAME
stadia .... TRANSIT, ROD,
RANGEFINDER
stadium .... BOWL, ARENA,
PARK
passageway .... RAMP
staff ...... TRUNCHEON, ROD,
POLE, STICK, CLUB, WAND,
BATON, STAVE, RETINUE,
CUDGEL, ANKUS, CANE,
OFFICE, VERGE
bearer .... VERGER
bishop's ... ROD, CROSIER,
CROOK
in music .... STAVE
member .... AIDE
metal cap .... SHOE
mountain climber's .....
ALPENSTOCK
officer, in short ..... ADC
officer's .... CADRE
plural of .... STAVES
shepherd's ...... CROOK
symbol .... CLEF
symbol of authority .....
WARDER, MACE
teaching ...... FACULTY
winged .... CADUCEUS

Stafford, singer .... JO
stag ...... HART, (RED)DEER,
                    POLLARD
   horn's tine ..... BROCKET
   mate of .... HIND
   party .... SMOKER
stage ...... DOCK, PLATFORM,
   SCAFFOLD, PRESENT, DAIS,
   SHOW, LEGIT, PRODUCE,
   PHASE, STEP, FOOTLIGHTS,
   (THE) BOARDS, THEATER,
                DRAMA
   assignment .. PART, ROLE
   assistant ..... PROMPTER
   call, trumpet .... SENNET
   curtain ...... BACKDROP
   device .... SLOTE
   direction ... EXIT, SENNET,
   ENTER, EXEUNT, MANET
   extra .... SUPE(R)
   footlights ...... FLOAT(S)
   front .... APRON,
              ORCHESTRA
   group: abbr. ...... ANTA
   name ..... DUSE, COHEN
   overact on .... HAM
   part .... ROLE, LEAD
   part of .... WING,
   PODIUM, PROSCENIUM,
   BOARDS, COULISSE,
              APRON
   players .... CAST
   profession ...... ACTING
   prop ... CURTAIN, DROP,
           FOOTLIGHTS
   remark ... ASIDE, AD LIB
   settings ...... SCENERY
   show ...... VAUDEVILLE,
   REVUE, MUSICAL
   side scene ..... COULISSE
   slang .... LEGIT
   trumpet call .... SENNET
   whisper ... AD LIB, ASIDE
stagecoach .... CONCORD
stagehand ... GRIP, CALLBOY
stager ... VETERAN, OLD HAND
Stagg, Amos ____ ... ALONZO
stagger ...... WAMBLE, LURCH,
   STARTLE, TOTTER, REEL,
   SWAY, OVERWHELM
staggered arrangement ....
             ZIGZAG
staggering condition ...... GID
stagger(s) ...... GID, (A)REEL,
            VACILLATE
   cause of ..... COENURUS

Stagirite .... ARISTOTLE
stagnant .... DULL, STANDING,
   SLUGGISH, TORPID, FOUL,
               STALE
stagnation .... STASIS
stagy .... THEATRICAL,
            AFFECTED
staid .... SOBER, FIXED,
   SETTLED, SEDATE, STEADY
stain ..... TARNISH, SLUBBER,
   SPLOTCH, TAINT, DISCOLOR,
   DYE, TINGE, SULLY,
   MACULA(TE), BLOT, SMUDGE,
   SPOT, SPOIL, CORRUPT,
   TINT, IMB(R)UE, DISHONOR
   remover .... PUMICE
stainer for microscope ....
           SAFRANIN(E)
staining art .... MARBLING
stair .... STEP, STILE
   face .... RISER
   post .... NEWEL
staircase .... PERRON
   bend .... RAMP
   guard .... HANDRAIL
   landing ...... HALFPACE
   post ... BALUSTER, NEWEL
   spiral .... CARACOLE
   step .... WINDER
stairs pillar .... NEWEL
   plane .... RAMP
   set of .... FLIGHT
   shaft .... WELL
stairway, mechanical ....
           ESCALATOR
   step .... FLIER
stake ... SPILE, POST, INTEREST,
   SHARE, GAMBLE, FINANCE,
   ANTE, POT, PALE, PICKET,
   HITCH, PILE, TETHER, BET,
   WAGER, RISK, IMPONE
   fence .... WEIR
   for foundation .... SPILE
   played for .... MAIN
   wooden .... TREE
stakes .... BETS, WAGERS,
         PRIZE, KITTY
   driver .... MAUL
   fence of .... PALISADE
stalag inmate .. POW, PRISONER
stale ..... VAPID, FLAT, BANAL,
   DRAB, MUSTY, HACK, HOAR,
   STAGNANT, TASTELESS,
   TRITE, HACKNEYED, FUSTY
stalemate .... DEADLOCK,
   CHECK, DRAW, IMPASSE, TIE

Stalin's daughter ....
   (SVETLANA) ALLILUYEVA
Stalinabad .... DUSHANBE
Stalingrad .... VOLGOGRAD
Stalino, former .... DONETSK
stalk ...... SCAPE, FILAMENT,
   HAULM, STEM, PEDICEL,
   CULM, PEDICLE, STRIPE(S),
   PETIOLE, STOVER, CAULIS
  eyed crustacean .. PRAWN,
   LOBSTER, SHRIMP
  flower .... PEDUNCLE
  grass ... HA(U)LM, STRAW,
   CULM
  having a ..... PETIOLATE
  leaf .... PETIOLE
  like structure ... PEDICEL
stalking horse .... BLIND,
   PRETEXT, DECOY
stall .. STABLE, COMPARTMENT,
   COT, CRIB, SEAT, STAND,
   MANGER, BOOTH, LOGE,
   TEMPORIZE, HEDGE, PUT OFF,
   DELAY
  covering .... TILT
  shop's front .... BULK
stallion .... (STUD)HORSE,
   STEED, ENTIRE, MORGAN
stalwart ...... FIRM, ROBUST,
   SUPPORTER
Stamboul .... ISTANBUL
stamen, part of ..... ANTHER,
   FILAMENT, STALK,
   POLLEN SAC
stamina .... ENDURANCE
stammer ...... STUTTER, HEM
stamp .... IMPRINT, MARK,
   CACHET, BRAND, DIE, SIGN,
   SIGIL, TAMP, IMPRESS
  Chinese .... CHOP
  mail .... POSTAGE
  official/ornamental .....
   SEAL
  on coin .... MINTAGE
  out .... SCOTCH
stampede .. FLIGHT, ROUT, RUN
stamper .... DATER
stamping ground .... HAUNT,
   HANG OUT
  device .... DATER,
   PUNCHEON
stamps, substitute for .. INDICIA
Stan, the Man .... MUSIAL
stance .... POSTURE, POSITION
stanch .... STEM, CHECK,
   WATERTIGHT, FAITHFUL,
   LOYAL, TRUE, FIRM,
   STOP
stanchion .... BRACE, POST
stand ... POSITION, ATTITUDE,
   BOOTH, STALL, FACE,
   TANTALUS, CASTER, BEAR,
   RESIST, RACK, HALT,
   ENDURE, TOLERATE,
   UNDERGO, STATION, VIEW,
   OPINION
  against .... OPPOSE
  artist's .... EASEL
  by .... MAINTAIN
  conductor's ...... PODIUM
  for .... REPRESENT, MEAN
  for election .... RUN
  high .... TOWER
  in .... SUBSTITUTE
  kind of .... LAST,
   ONE NIGHT, NEWS
  on hind legs ..... RAMP,
   REAR
  orator's .... SOAPBOX
  ornamental ... PEDESTAL,
   TABORET
  out .... PROJECT,
   DISSENTER
  painter's .... EASEL
  priest's .... PULPIT
  sacrificial .... ALTAR
  stockstill .... FREEZE
  three-legged .... TRIPOD,
   TRIVET, TEAPOY
  two-legged ...... BIPOD
standard ... BANNER, ENSIGN,
   CRITERION, REGULAR,
   ORDINARY, UNIFORM,
   NORMAL, GONFALON, FLAG,
   COLORS, MODEL, EXAMPLE,
   TYPICAL, YARDSTICK,
   CLASSIC
  battle .... ORIFLAMME
  bearer .... CANDIDATE,
   CHAMPION, LEADER,
   CHIEF, ENSIGN,
   VEXILLARY
  of excellence ...... IDEAL
  pasha's ..... HORSETAIL
standee, subway, etc. ....
   STRAPHANGER
standing .... STATUS,
   POSITION, RANK,
   REPUTATION, STAGNANT,
   PRESTIGE, ERECT, UPRIGHT
  order .... SOP
  out .... SALIENT

room area .... AISLES
room charge .. STANDAGE
with feet on ground .....
STATENT
Standish, colonist ..... MILES
standoffish .. ALOOF, RESERVED,
WITHDRAWN
standoff .... TIE, DRAW
standpat(ter) .. CONSERVATIVE,
TORY, DIEHARD
standstill .... HALT, STOP,
CESSATION, DEADLOCK
stang .... PAIN
stanhope .... CARRIAGE, SHAY
stannum .... TIN
Stanovoi mountain ... KOLYMA,
YABLONOI, ANADYR
stanza .... VERSE, STAVE,
STROPE, ENVOI, STROPHE,
DISTICH, (L)ENVOY
eight-line ...... TRIOLET,
OCTAVE, OCTONARY
four-line ... TETRASTICH,
QUATRAIN
seven-line ... HEPTASTICH
six-line .... SEXTAIN,
HEXASTICH
stapelia .... MILKWEED
stapes .... (STIRRUP)BONE
staple ... FLOUR, SALT, SUGAR,
PRINCIPAL, FIBER, CHIEF,
COMMODITY
star .... SUN, ASTERISK,
PLANET, ACE, EXCEL,
LEADING, RIGEL, MIRA, NOVA
apple .... CAIMITO
binary .. ANTARES, ALGOL,
ALBIREO
blue .... VEGA
brightest ... COR, LUCIDA,
SIRIUS
Chamber .... COURT,
TRIBUNAL
cluster .... ASTERISM,
GALAXY, MILKY WAY
combining form .. ASTRO,
SIDER(O)
Cygnus .... DENEB
Draconis' tail ..... JUZA
evening ..... HESPER(US),
VESPER, VENUS
fallen .... ALGA
five-pointed ... PENTACLE
group .... DIPPER,
CONSTELLATION
like a ... ASTRAL, STELLAR

Lyra .... VEGA
morning ..... PHOSPHOR,
VENUS
neutron .... PULSAR
new .... NOVA
of a .... STELLAR
of David .... HEXAGRAM
Orion .... RIGEL
path of .... ORBIT
pertaining to a .. SIDEREAL
poetic .... LAMP
pulsing .... PULSAR
red .... ANTARES, RUSSIA
Scorpio .... ANTARES
shaped .... STELLATE,
ASTERIATED, ASTEROID,
ASTROSE
shell .... FLARE
shooting .... METEOR
six-pointed ... HEXAGRAM
spangled, in heraldry ....
SEME
sports ... ACE, CHAMPION
thistle .... CALTRAP,
CALTROP, WEED
yellow .... CAPELIA
starch .... AMYLUM,
CARBOHYDRATE, AMYLOSE,
ARROWROOT, CASSAVA,
SAGO, TAPIOCA, GLYCOGEN,
AMIDINE, MANIOC
food .... FARINA
grain nucleus .... HILUM
grain part ... GRANULOSE
like .... AMYLOID
pudding .... SAGO
source ... TARO, CASSAVA,
SAGO, MANIOC, ARUM,
COONTIE, CURCUMA, CANNA
starchy .... FORMAL, STIFF
food .... AMYLOID
plant .... AROID
root .... TARO
substance ...... AMYLOID
stare ..... GAZE, LOOK, GAPE,
GLARE, OGLE, GAWK,
GOGGLE
down .... OUTFACE
starfish ... ASTEROID, SUNSTAR,
FIVE-FINGER
limb of .... RAY
relative ...... COMATULID
starflower .... PRIMROSE
stargazer ...... ASTRONOMER,
ASTROLOGER
stark ... STIFF, RIGID, BARREN,

BLEAK, DESOLATE, SHEER,
UTTER(LY)

mad .... RAVING
starlet .... INGENUE
starlike .... ASTEROID,
ASTRAL, STELLAR
starling .... MINO, BIRD,
OXPECKER
kin of .. MYNA(H), ORIOLE
starnose .... MOLE
Starr of comic strips .. BRENDA
starry .... SIDEREAL,
STELLAR
stars .... FATE, DESTINY,
FORTUNE
dotted with .... SEME
group of ....
CONSTELLATION
of the .. ASTRAL, SIDEREAL,
STELLAR
worshiper of .... SABAIST
start ...... SHY, JERK, ROUSE,
LAUNCH, OPEN, SHOOT,
FRIGHT, COMMENCE(MENT),
LEAD, EDGE, ONSET,
INCEPTION, JIB
card game .... DEAL
starting point .. GATE, SCRATCH
startle ...... ALARM, SHOCK,
SURPRISE, AFFRIGHT,
SCARE, GALVANIZE
starvation, widespread ....
FAMINE
starve ...... FAMISH, HUNGER
starved .. HUNGRY, FAMISHED
starwort ...... ASTER, ALGA
stash ... HOARD, HIDE, CACHE,
SECRETE
state .... CONDITION, STATUS,
SPECIFY, FETTLE, ETAT,
AVER, SITUATION, DECLARE,
SAY, MOOD, POLITY
attorney .... DA
Beaver .... OREGON
Beehive .... UTAH
Cornhusk ..... NEBRASKA
Cotton .... ALABAMA
council .... SENATE
dependent ..... SATELLITE
Fair author ..... STONG
Hawkeye .... IOWA
Hen .... DELAWARE
house .... CAPITOL
Lone Star .... TEXAS
Mountain .... MONTANA
of affairs .... CASE

of balance .... EQUIPOISE
of excitement ... FERMENT
of mind ... MORALE, MOOD
of suspended animation ..
ANABIOSIS
treasure .... MONTANA
treasury .... FISC
troops .... MILITIA
under oath ...... SWEAR,
DEPOSE
without proof .. ALLEGE,
CLAIM
statehouse .... CAPITOL
stately .... MAJESTIC,
DIGNIFIED, GRAND, ROYAL,
AUGUST, REGAL, IMPOSING
house ... MANSION, DOME,
PALACE
music .... LARGO
statement .... ACCOUNT,
DECLARATION, TESTIMONY,
BILL, BULLETIN, PRECIS,
ASSERTION
authoritative ... DICTUM
ex-employer's ....
REFERENCE
formal .... AFFIDAVIT,
DEPOSITION,
COMMUNIQUE
in belief .. CREDO, CREED
of facts .... CASE
preliminary .... PREFACE
unsupported .... SAY-SO
stater .... COIN
stateroom .... CABIN
static .... STATIONARY,
INACTIVE, STRAYS
opposed to ..... KINETIC,
DYNAMIC
station .... DEPOT, POST,
POSITION, LOCATION,
RANK, STATUS, STOP,
TERMINUS, TERMINAL,
PLACE
stationary ... STABILE, STATIC,
FIXED, AT REST, IMMOBILE
combining form ... STAT
stationer .... BOOKSELLER
stationery .. PAPETERIE, LINEN
item ... PAPER, ENVELOPE
statistician .... STATIST
statoscope .... BAROMETER
statuary .... STATUES,
SCULPTOR
statue ... CARVING, ACROLITH,

SCULPTURE, NIKE, EFFIGY,
FIGULINE, FIGURINE
base of .... PEDESTAL,
PLINTH
gigantic ...... COLOSSUS
ledgelike foundation ....
SOCLE
London .... GOG, MAGOG
mold ..... (PLASTER)CAST
of ___ .... LIBERTY
of Liberty poetess ....
LAZARUS
of Liberty sculptor ......
BARTHOLD
of Mary ...... MADONNA
statuesque .... STATELY,
GRACEFUL
woman .... JUNO
statuette .... FIGURINE
award .... OSCAR
stature .... HEIGHT
status .... CONDITION, STATE,
STANDING, RANK, POSITION
symbol ... MINK, YACHT,
ROLLS ROYCE, DIAMOND
statute ... RULE, LAW, EDICT,
ACT
part of .. TITLE, ARTICLE
stave ... STAFF, STICK, RUNG,
STAP, LAG, VERSES, STANZA,
PUNCTURE
off ... WARD, HOLD OFF,
FEND, AVERT, STALL
staves, bundle of ..... SHOOK
hold .... HOOP
stavesacre .... LARKSPUR
stay .... (A)BIDE, REMAIN,
RESIDE, HALT, TARRY,
CHECK, STOP, DELAY, WAIT,
GUY, TACK, PROP, SUPPORT,
KEEP, DWELL, LIVE, LINGER,
BRACE
longer .... TARRY
staying power ...... STAMINA,
ENDURANCE
staylace .... A(I)GLET
stays .... CORSET, ABIDES
Ste. (see Saint) ...... SAINT(E)
stead .... LIEU, SERVICE,
PLACE, SITE
steadfast .. STABLE, CONSTANT,
FIRM, FIXED
steady .... FIRM, STABLE,
FIXED, CONSTANT, EQUABLE,
REGULAR, STAID, UNIFORM,
CALM, EVEN

colloquial .... BEAU,
SWEETHEART,
BOY FRIEND
opposite of ..... ASTATIC,
JERKY, UNSTABLE
steak .... T-BONE,
PORTERHOUSE, SIRLOIN
steal ... PINCH, THIEVE, PILFER,
NIM, FILCH, PURLOIN,
LOOT, ROB, HOOK, SNITCH,
CRIB, BURGLE, MOOCH, PRIG
cattle, etc. ...... RUSTLE
colloquial ..... BARGAIN,
CRIB
ideas, writings .... CRIB,
PLAGIARIZE, PIRATE
slang .... SWIPE, LIFT
trust money ... PECULATE
stealer .... THIEF, ROBBER,
BURGLAR
stealthy .... SECRET,
SURREPTITIOUS, FURTIVE,
SLY, CLANDESTINE,
SNEAKY, FELINE
steam ..... VAPOR, GAS, FUME
boiler safety device ......
HYDROSTAT
burn with .... SCALD
colloquial .... FORCE,
ENERGY, POWER
engine ..... LOCOMOTIVE
give off .... REEK
roll ... CRUSH, OVERRIDE
steamboat stateroom ... TEXAS
steamer .... SHIP, LINER,
WHALEBACK
steamship .... LINER,
GREYHOUND
smokestack of ... FUNNEL
stearin .... SUET, TALLOW
steatite .... TALC, SOAPSTONE
steed .... HORSE, CHARGER,
STALLION
steel ...... TOUGHEN, METAL
alloy .... INVAR
beam/bar .... IBAR,
IRAIL, GIRDER
change to ..... ACIERATE
kind of ..... TOLEDO,
DAMASK, TEMPERED
making plant ....
(RE)FINERY
making process ....
DUPLEX, CEMENTATION
poetic .. SWORD, DAGGER
with inlaid gold .. DAMASK

steelhead .... TROUT, SALMONOID
steelyard ... SCALE, BALANCE
Steen, painter .... JAN
steenbok .... ANTELOPE
steep .... PRECIPITOUS, EXCESSIVE, LOFTY, ABRUPT, SOAK, MACERATE, IMBUE, SOP, SHEER, RET, SATURATE, IMMERSE
slope .... SCARP
steeple ...... TOWER, BELFRY, MINARET, FLECHE
part of ... BELFRY, SPIRE, EPI
steeplebush .... HARDHACK
steeplechase ..... HORSERACE
steer .... DIRECT, GUIDE, CATTLE, OX, YAK, HELM, BEEF, BULLOCK, BOVINE, PILOT, STIRK, STOT
clear off .... AVOID
ship .... CONN
slang .... TIP
zigzag course .. PLY, YAW
steering gear .... WHEEL, RUDDER, HELM, TILLER
steersman .. PILOT, HELMSMAN, WHEELER, COX(SWAIN), NAVIGATOR
steeve ... STOW, SPAR, DERRICK
stegomyia .... MOSQUITO
stein .... MUG
writer .... GERTRUDE
steinbok .... ANTELOPE
stele ...... HEADSTONE, LAT, PILLAR, MONUMENT
stella .... STAR
stellar .... CHIEF, LEADING, SIDEREAL, ASTRAL
stellate .... STARRY
stem ...... STALK, PETIOLE, PEDICEL, PEDUNCLE, CHECK, STOP, AXIS, ARISE, BINE, SPRING
angle .... AXIL
climbing .... BINE
covering .... OCREA
fleshy .... TUBER
for grafting .... SLIP
hollow .... CANE
joint .... NODE
leaf's .... FOOTSTALK
main .... TRUNK
of arrow .... STELE
palm .... CAUDEX

plant ..... AXIS, CAULIS
raceme's ...... R(H)ACHIS
rootlike ...... RHIZOME
rudimentary .. CAULICLE
ship's........BOW, PROW
shoot .... TILLER
trailing .... RUNNER
twining .... BIND
underground ..... TUBER, CORM
stench .... ODOR, SMELL, F(O)ETOR, STINK, REEK, MEPHITIS
Stendhal hero .... SOREL
Stengel, baseball's ..... CASEY
steno, combining form .. THIN, NARROW, SMALL
stenosis .... STRICTURE
stenography .... SHORTHAND
Stentor .... HERALD
stentorian .... LOUD
step .... GAIT, TREAD, FOOTBALL, FOOTPRINT, RUNG, PACE, STAIR, STRIDE, GRADIN, STAGE, RANK, WALK
dance .... PAS, CHASSE
down .... RESIGN, ABDICATE, REDUCE
fence .... STILE
in .... INTERVENE
ins ...... UNDERPANTS, SLIPPERS
ladder .... RUNG
lightly .... TRIP
mincingly .... SASHAY
on heavily .... TRAMPLE, PLOD
on it .... HURRY, HASTEN
projecting part .. NOSING
softly .... PAD, TIPTOE
up .... INCREASE, ACCELERATE
stepmother, of/like a .... NOVERCAL
steppe .... PLAIN, WASTELAND
plain like a ..... PAMPAS, LLANO, SAVANNA(H)
stepper .... DANCER
steps, outdoor .... PERRON, STILE
sterculiaceous tree ... CACAO, KOLA
stere .... CUBIC METER
stereo .... BINAURAL
stereotype plate ..... CLICHE

stereotyped .... TRITE,
HACKNEYED
sterile ... BARREN, INFERTILE,
UNFRUITFUL, ACARPOUS,
MULISH, OTIOSE, EFFETE
   in botany ..... ACARPOUS
sterilize .... GELD, CASTRATE,
EMASCULATE
sterlet .... STURGEON
sterling ... PENNY, EXCELLENT
stern ... FIRM, SEVERE, HARD,
GRIM, REAR, DOUR, STRICT,
FORBIDDING, AUSTERE,
HARSH, AFT
   toward the ...... ABAFT,
AFT, REAR
   wheeler ..... STEAMBOAT
sternum .... BREASTBONE
   attachment .... RIB
sternutation .... SNEEZING,
SNEEZE
sternutatory .... ERRHINE
   substance .... SNUFF
stertor .... SNORE
stet .... LET IT STAND
Stettin river .... ODER
stevedore ... DOCKER, LUMPER,
DOCK WORKER, STOWER,
(UN)LOADER, LONGSHOREMAN
Stevens, singer .... RISE
Stevenson, statesman .. ADLAI
stew .... SIMMER, DISH, BOIL,
POTPIE, HARICOT, TANK,
OLIO, FRET, TERRINE,
HODGEPODGE, POTPOURRI,
OLLA, RAGOUT, HASH,
GOULASH, BURGOO,
POTTAGE, CURRY
   colloquial ...... WORRY,
MULLIGAN
   flavor .... CHIVE
   pan .... SKILLET
   sailors' ... LOBSCOU(R)SE
steward .... MAJOR DOMO,
SENESCHAL, REEVE, BUTLER,
BAILIFF, MAITRE D'HOTEL,
MANAGER, FACTOR
   college/monastery ......
MANCIPLE
stewardess, airplane ... HOSTESS
stewardship .... MANAGEMENT
stewed .... DRUNK
   fruit .... FOOL
stibium .... ANTIMONY
stich .... LINE, VERSE
stick .. WAND, STAFF, BATON,
ROD, CANE, CLUB, STAB,
ADHERE, PUNCTURE, PIERCE,
POKE, COHERE, CLING,
ABIDE, CLEAVE, IMPALE,
FAGOT, PADDLE, PASTE,
BAT, FERULE
   around .... STAY
   celery .... STALK
   conductor's ...... BATON
   fairy's .... WAND
   for leveling grain ....
STRICKLE
   insect .... EMESA
   jumping .... POGO
   match .... LINSTOCK
   metal cap ...... FERRULE
   out ..... EXTRUDE, JUT,
PROJECT, PROTRUDE
   pointer .... FESCUE
   policeman's ....
TRUNCHEON, BILLY
   sharp-pointed .... GOAD
   slang ... GREAT, DEFRAUD
   stirring .... MUDDLER
   throwing ...... DINGBAT
   up for .... DEFEND
sticker ...... BUR(R), THORN,
LABEL
stickler ..... DISCIPLINARIAN,
MARTINET
stickpin's place ..... NECKTIE,
CRAVAT
sticks, the .... COUNTRY,
BOONDOCKS
sticktight (fruit) ....
(COCKLE)BUR
stickum .... GLUE
sticky .... TACKY, VISCID,
TREACLY, ADHESIVE,
GOOEY, GLUEY, HUMID,
GUMMY, GLUTINOUS
   substance ... GOO, GLUE,
PASTE, GUM
stiff ...... WIRY, RIGID, FIRM,
TAUT, TENSE, TIGHT,
HARSH, HIGH, FORMAL,
WOODEN
   necked .... STUBBORN,
OBSTINATE
   slang ... HOBO, CORPSE
stiffen .... BRACE, TAUTEN
stiffening material ..... STAY
stifle .... SMOTHER,
SUFFOCATE, SUPPRESS,
REPRESS, CHECK, SCOTCH,
CHOKE

stigma ... BRAND, SCAR, STAIN, BLOT, PORE, MARK

stigmatize ..... BRAND, MARK

stile .... STEP(S)

stiletto ...... STYLET, DAGGER

still ... WITHAL, QUIET, SILENT, STATIONARY, HUSHED, DISTILLERY, PLACID, WHIST, YET, INERT, MOTIONLESS, EVEN, SERENE, CALM, PHOTO, ALEMBIC

existing .... EXTANT

"Stillenacht" composer ...... GRUBER

stillness ...... SILENCE, HUSH, QUIETUDE

stilt .... PLOVER, BIRD, POLE, POST, SANDPIPER

stilted .... POMPOUS, BOMBASTIC, PEDANTIC

stiltlike toy ..... POGO STICK

stilton .... CHEESE

Stilwell's nickname .... VINEGAR JOE

stimulant ... EXCITANT, COFFEE

stimulate ..... WHET, EXCITE, (A)ROUSE, SPUR, FAN, ANIMATE

by electric shock .... GALVANIZE

stimulus ... INCENTIVE, SPUR, MOTIVE, DRIVE, IMPULSE, INDUCEMENT, FILLIP, STING, GOAD, INCITEMENT

sting .... PAIN, STIMULUS, BITE, SMART, PRICK, NETTLE, URTICATE

in zoology ..... ACULEUS

ray .... STINGAREE, BATFISH

slang ...... CHEAT, DUPE

stinger .... WASP, HORNET, GNAT, BEE, GADFLY

stinging ...... CAUSTIC, NIPPY

ant .... KELEP

creature ...... RAY, BEE, WASP, HORNET, ANT

hair .... NETTLE

sensation ... URTICATION

taste .... PUNGENT

stingaree .... RAY

stinger .... WASP, HORNET, VESPID, YELLOW JACKET, NETTLE, HIGHBALL

stingo ... ALE, BEER, ZEST, VIM, ENERGY

stingy ...... MISERLY, CLOSE, NIGGARDLY, PENURIOUS, SKIMPY, NEAR

stink .... STENCH, ODOR, SMELL, REEK

stinker .... PETREL

stinking ..... BAD-SMELLING, SMELLY, MALODOROUS, PUTRID, RANK, RANCID, MUSTY, FETID, NOISOME, FOUL

smut .... BUNT

stint .... DUTY, RESTRICT, LIMIT(ATION), SANDPIPER, ASSIGNMENT, BOUT, CHORE, TASK

stipe ... STEM, PETIOLE, STALK

stipel .... STIPULE

stipend ...... SALARY, WAGE, PENSION, ALLOWANCE, PREBEND

stipes ...... STALK, PEDUNCLE

stipulate ... SPECIFY, DEMAND, ARRANGE, PROVIDE

stipulation ...... AGREEMENT, CONDITION, PROVISION, CLAUSE, PROVISO

stipule, secondary .... STIPEL

stir .... AGITATE, SHAKE, (A)ROUSE, EXCITE, INCITE, ADO, PROVOKE, FUSS, MOVE(MENT), INFLAME, ROIL, ROUST, (A)WAKEN, TUMULT, TO-DO, CHURN

slang ...... PRISON, JAIL

up ... FOMENT, ROIL, RILE

stirabout .... PORRIDGE

stirk ...... HEIFER, BULLOCK

stirps ... RACE, STOCK, FAMILY

stirring ... MOVING, ROUSING, BUSY, ACTIVE

stirrup ... FOOTREST, GAMBADO

bone .... STAPES

cup ...... TOAST, DRINK

stitch ... SEW, CRICK, FASTEN, PAIN, ACHE, SUTURE, QUILT, TACK, BASTE, BIT

bird .... IHI

colloquial .... BIT

line .... SEAM

stitching material ...... GUT, THREAD, WIRE, STAPLE

stitchwort ...... CHICKWEED

stithy .. SMITHY, FORGE, ANVIL

stoa .... PORTICO, WALK

stoat .... ERMINE

like animal .... MINK, WEASEL, MARTEN, OTTER
stoccado .... STAB, THRUST
stock .... STIRPS, TRUNK, RHIZOME, LINEAGE, ANCESTRY, RACE, BUTT, SUPPLY, STORE, CAPITAL, , BREED, PROVIDE, TRITE, ORDINARY, GOODS, INVENTORY, REPERTORY, PLENISH, FUND
exchange .... BOURSE
dealer ... JOBBER, BEAR, BULL, BROKER
member(SHIP) ... SEAT, TRADER
speculator .. LAMEDUCK
telegraphic device ..... TICKER
trick ...... WASH SALE
farm ...... STUD, RANCH
in .... ON HAND
in trade ... LINE, STAPLE
keep in .... CARRY
market ..... EXCHANGE, BOURSE, CURB
market event .... CRASH, PANIC
market gamble ... FLYER
market maneuver .. RAID
of inferior ..... LOWBRED
replace ...... REPLENISH
still .... MOTIONLESS
take .... INVENTORY, APPRAISE
stockade .... ENCLOSURE, CORRAL, PEN, ETAPE, BARRIER, BOMA
stockfish .... HADDOCK, COD
stocking .. HOSE, SOCK, NYLON
stockish .... DULL
stockman .... RANCHER
stockpile ..... SUPPLY, STORE, RESERVE, HOARD
stockroom .... STORAGE
stocky .... PLUMP, THICKSET, CHUNKY, STURDY, STOUT, STUBBED, STUBBY, DUMPY
stodgy .... DULL, TEDIOUS, BULKY
stogie ..... CIGAR, BOOT, SHOE
stoic ... IMPASSIVE, SPARTAN, PATIENT, EPICTETUS
first .... ZENO
philosopher .... SENECA
stoker ..... FIREMAN, TEASER

Stokowski, conductor .... LEOPOLD
stola .... PALLA
stole .... SCARF, ROBBED, BOA
stolen goods buyer .... FENCE
property ... LOOT, SWAG, PELF
stolid .... PHLEGMATIC, IMPASSIVE, WOODEN, DULL
stolon .... RHIZOME, RUNNER
stoma .. PORE, MOUTH, ORIFICE
stomach .... CRAW, ABDOMEN, BELLY, APPETITE, DESIRE, TOLERATE, BEAR, CROP
ache .... GASTRALGIA, CARDIALGIA
animal's .... PAUNCH, CRAW, OMASUM, MAW
colloquial .... TUMMY, GIZZARD
disorder .... NAUSEA, BRASH, PYROSIS
gas .... FLATUS, FLATULENCE
inflammation .. GASTRITIS
opening .... PYLORUS
pertaining to ... GASTRIC
protruding .. BAYWINDOW
ruminants' .. PSALTERIUM, TRIPE, OMASUM, PAUNCH, MAW
stony concretion .... GASTROLITH
upset .... DYSPEPSIA, INDIGESTION
wall movement .... PERISTALSIS
washing out of ... LAVAGE
stomachache reliever .... ANTACID, ASPIRIN
stomatic .... ORAL
stomatopod .... SQUILLA, CRUSTACEAN
stomp .... STAMP
stone ..... ROCK, GEM, PELT, DENTRITE, DORNICK, LAPIS, PEBBLE
Age human .... CAVEMAN
Age period ... EOLITHIC, NEOLITHIC
Age tools ... (N)EOLITH
author .... IRVING
azure-blue .. LAPIS LAZULI
bladder .... CALCULUS
broke .... PENNILESS
cameo .... ONYX

carver .... GRAVER
carved in relief .. CAMEO
cavity .... GEODE
change into .... PETRIFY
cherry .... PIT
Chief Justice ... HARLAN
chip ...... SPALL, GALLET
chisel .... CELT
clay .... SHALE
combining form ....
    LITH(O), PETR(O), LITE,
    LYTE
crop ..... ORPIN, SEDUM
cubic measure for ......
    PERCH
cutter ....→ MASON
cutter's disease ....
    CHALICOSIS, SILICOSIS
cutter's chisel ..... DROVE
dress .... NIG, SCABBLE,
    TRIM
dressing tool .... ADZ(E),
    HACKHAMMER
drupe .... NUTLET
engraved on ... LAPIDARY
engraving ..... INTAGLIO
excavation site .. QUARRY
fire-starting ...... FLINT
flake .... SPALL
flint-like ... HORNSTONE
for throwing .. DORNICK,
    DINGBAT
fragments ──... BRASH,
    DEBRIS
fruit ... DRUPE, CHERRY,
    PUTAMEN, PLUM, PIT,
    PYRENE, PIP, SEED
gall .... CALCULUS
green .... OLIVINE
grinding .... MANO
hammer .... MASH
hard ... FLINT, ADAMANT
headed ax ... TOMAHAWK
heap ... CAIRN(E), SCREE,
    CARN(E)
huge .... MENHIR,
    MEGALITH, BOULDER
hurling apparatus ......
    ONAGER, CATAPULT,
    MANGONEL, TREBUCHET
implement ...... EOLITH,
    MANO
jar ....→ CROCK
kidney .... CALCULUS
Latin .... LAPIS
lifting device .. LEWIS(SON)

like .... LITHOID(AL)
measure .... PERCH
monument ..... MENHIR,
    DOLMEN, CROMLECH,
    STELE, CAIRN
ornamental ...... JADE,
    SODALITE
parsley ..... HONEWORT
particles .... GRIT
paving .... SLAB,
    MACADAM, SETT, FLAG
peach .... PIT
pertaining to .... LITHIC
pestle .... MULLER
philosopher's ... CARMOT
piece(s) .. RUBBLE, SPALL,
    GALLET
pile .... TALUS
pillar .... STELE
precious .... GEM,
    DIAMOND, JEWEL,
    RUBY, PEARL, OPAL,
    EMERALD, SAPPHIRE
prefix .... LITHO
red .... SPINEL
roller ...... CARP, TOTER,
    DACE
roller, eternal .. SISYPHUS
semi-precious .. PERIDOT,
    TOPAZ, CHRYSOLITE,
    CHRYSOPRASE, ZIRCON,
    CORAL, ONYX, AGATE,
    OLIVIN, SARD, GARNET,
    TOURMALINE, AMETHYST
sharpening .. HONE, WHET
slab .... STELA, STELE,
    TABLET
spark-producing .. FLINT
square hewn .... ASHLAR,
    ASHLER
tablet .... STELE
throwing device ....
    ONAGER, CATAPULT,
    SLING(SHOT), MANGONEL
to death ...... LAPIDATE
tool .... NEOLITH,
    PALEOLITH
trim .... NIG, DRESS
turn to .... LAPIDIFY,
    PETRIFY
upright prehistoric ......
    MENHIR
wall-facing ..... ASHLER,
    ASHLAR
with lined cavity .. GEODE
woman turned to .. NIOBE

stonechat ..... THRUSH, BIRD
stonecrop .... SEDUM, PLANT,
ORPIN(E)
stonecutter .... MASON,
LAPIDARY, LAPICIDE
stones, heap of .... SCREE,
CAIRN, TALUS
  roadbuilding .. MACADAM
"Stonewall ____," general ....
JACKSON
stoneware .... POTTERY, GRES
stonework .... MASONRY
stony .... PITILESS, HARD,
PETROUS, PETROSAL
  deposit in body ....
CALCULUS
stooge .... HECKLER, FOIL,
UNDERLING, TOOL, PAWN,
DUMMY, MOE
stook .... SHOCK
stool ..... TABO(U)RET, STUMP,
FOOTREST, PRIVY, LURE,
DECOY
  foot .. CRICKET, OTTOMAN
  pigeon ...... INFORMER,
PEACHER, NARK, DECOY,
SPY
stoop ... DEIGN, CONDESCEND,
SWOOP, BEND, PORCH,
VERANDA(H), STOUP, LOUT
stop ... STANCH, BLOCK, PLUG,
CLOSE, INTERCEPT, CEASE,
END, PULL UP, DESIST,
ARREST, WHOA, HALT,
CHECK, DEFEAT, LET UP,
BELAY
  football carrier .. TACKLE
  hole .... PLUG
  legally .... ESTOP
  nautical .... AVAST
  resisting .... YIELD,
SURRENDER, CAPITULATE
  short .... BALK
  talking .. DRY UP, SHUT UP
  temporarily ..... PAUSE
  watch .... TIMER
stopcock ...... FAUCET, VALVE
stopgap .... MAKESHIFT,
SUBSTITUTE
stoppage of body fluid .. STASIS
  debate .... CLOTURE,
CLOSURE
  hostilities ..... RESPITE,
TRUCE, ARMISTICE
  operation ... SHUTDOWN
stopped diapason .... MELODIA

stopper .... TAP, SPILE, CORK,
PLUG, BUNG, SHIVE,
STOPPLE, TAMPION, TOMPION
stopple .... STOPPER
storage place ..... STOREROOM,
CRIB, CELLAR, ARSENAL,
LOFT, BIN, DEPOT, HUTCH,
CACHE, SILO, GRANARY,
BARN, MAGAZINE
storax .. STYRENE, GUMRESIN,
BALSAM
store .... STOCK, RESERVE,
SUPPLY, HOARD, CACHE,
STOW, DEPOSIT, BOUTIQUE,
SHOP, WAREHOUSE, SAVE,
LAY-UP, OUTLET, FUND,
GARNER
  army ...... CANTEEN, PX,
COMMISSARY
  fodder .... ENSILE
  helper .... CLERK
  kind of .... DRUG,
GROCERY, FIVE-AND-TEN
  small articles .... NOTIONS
storehouse .. ETAPE, GRANARY,
DEPOT, BARN, REPERTORY
  weapons ..... ARSENAL,
ARMORY, MAGAZINE
storekeeper .... GROCER
storeroom .. BUTTERY, CELLAR,
CLOSET
storied ... FAMOUS, LEGENDARY
stork .. ADJUTANT, MARABOU,
JABIRU, AYAYA
  delivery of .... BABY
  kin of ...... HERON, IBIS,
HAMMERHEAD
stork's bill .... GERANIUM
storm .... RACE, ASSAULT,
RANT, ATTACK, OUTBURST,
FUME, TEMPEST, RIPSNORTER,
STOUR
  accompaniment .. SNOW,
SLEET, HAIL, RAIN,
THUNDER
  center .... EYE
  cloud formation ....
WATERSPOUT
  Country girl .... TESS
  cyclonic ...... TYPHOON,
HURRICANE
  with rotating winds .....
CYCLONE, TORNADO
stormy .... WILD, RAGING,
VIOLENT, INCLEMENT
Storting .... PARLIAMENT

sits in _____ .... OSLO
story .. ACCOUNT, NARRATION,
 NARRATIVE, RUMOR,
 REPORT, FLOOR, FABLE,
 MARCHÉN, TALE, REDE
 animal .... FABLE
 bedtime .... YARN
 colloquial .... FIB
 complication in a .. NODE,
 NODUS
 correspondent's ....
 DISPATCH
 exaggerated .... YARN
 exclusive ... SCOOP, BEAT
 false .... HOAX, CANARD,
 FABLE
 heroic .... SAGA
 long .... NOVEL
 part of .... PASSUS
 romantic .... GEST(E)
 short .. CONTE, PARABLE
 tell a .... SPIN
 teller ..... RACONTEUR,
 SCHEHERAZADE,
 MUNCHAUSEN
 traditional ...... MYTH,
 LEGEND
 with moral lesson ......
 PARABLE, FABLE,
 ALLEGORY
storyteller: colloq. ... FIBBER,
 LIAR
stoss, opposite of .... ALEE
stound .... PAIN, ACHE, SMART
stoup .... TANKARD, PAIL,
 BUCKET, FONT
stour .... STORM, TURMOIL,
 COMBAT
stout ... BRAVE, STURDY, FAT,
 CORPULENT, OBESE, PORTER,
 BEER, ALE, THICKSET,
 STOCKY, PORTLY, HUSKY,
 BOCK
 hero .... NERO(WOLFE)
 novelist .... REX
stouthearted .... BRAVE
stove .... ETNA, HEATER,
 RANGE, OVEN, CHAUFFER,
 KITCHENER
stovepipe ... FLUE, (SILK)HAT
stover ... FODDER, CORNSTALKS
stow ..... STORE, PACK, STEEVE
 cargo .... STEEVE
Stowe, author .... HARRIET
 character .... TOPSY, EVA,
 LEGREE

strabismic .... CROSS-EYED
strabismus .... SQUINT,
 CROSS-EYE
"Strad" .... VIOLIN
straddle .... BESTRIDE
 colloquial .... HEDGE
Stradivarius .... VIOLIN
strafe ...... BOMBARD, RAKE
straggle .... STRAY, WANDER,
 RAMBLE, TRAIL
straggler .. STRAY, WANDERER
straight ... (UP)RIGHT, ERECT,
 DIRECT, HONEST, FRANK,
 PURE, UNMIXED, ALIGNED
 away .... AT ONCE
 combining form .. RECT(I)
 edge ...... RULER, LINER
 faced .... IMPASSIVE
 jacket .... CAMISOLE
 liner .... BEE, RULER
 man .... FOIL, STOOGE
 man's companion ......
 COMEDIAN
 out .... DIRECT
 passage ...... ENFILADE
 route .... BEELINE
 row .... RANK
 up .... VERTICAL
straightforward .... OPEN,
 FRANK, CANDID, HONEST
strain .... STRIVE, PULL,
 TENSION, HEAVE, PRESS,
 BREED, TAX, STRETCH,
 FILTER, LINEAGE, FILTRATE,
 RACE, SIFT, SIEVE, TRACE,
 STOCK, LINE
strained .... TENSE
strainer .... SIEVE, SIFTER,
 FILTER, COLANDER, TAMIS,
 STRUM
strains .... TUNE, AIR
strait ... LEPANTO, MALACCA,
 MAGELLAN, MACKINAC,
 MESSINA, MENAI, EURIPUS,
 NECK, ISTHMUS, GIBRALTAR,
 NARROW, TIGHT, CHANNEL,
 KERCH
 laced .... PRIGGISH,
 STUFFY
straiten .... CONTRACT, LIMIT,
 DISTRESS
straits .... DIFFICULTY,
 DISTRESS
 of Messina rock .. SCYLLA
 Settlement, part of ......
 PENANG, MALACCA

Settlement weight .... CATTY, CHEE

strand .... SHORE, BEACH, GROUND, THREAD, STRING, ROPE, MAROON, NECKLACE

strange .... UNCANNY, UNKNOWN, ODD, EXOTIC, UNCO, NOVEL, UNUSUAL, OUTRE, FREMD, ALIEN, PECULIAR, QUEER, QUAINT, SINGULAR

strangely beautiful ... EXOTIC

stranger .... EMIGRE, TRAMONTANE, ALIEN, NEWCOMER, OUTSIDER, FOREIGNER, GUEST, NOVICE, OUTLANDER

strangle .... THROTTLE, SUFFOCATE, CHOKE, STIFLE, REPRESS, GARROTE, SMOTHER, SCRAG, JUGULATE
  hold .... DEATH GRIP

strangler .... THUG

strangulate .... CHOKE, THROTTLE, GARROTE

strangury .... URINATION

strap ... TAB, LEASH, THONG, FASTEN(ER), REIN, BELT
  falcon's .... JESS
  for leading animal ...... HALTER
  shaped .... LIGULATE, LORATE
  shoulder .... HALTER

straphanger .... STANDEE

strapping ...... WELL-BUILT, ROBUST

strass .... PASTE, (LEAD)GLASS

stratagem ... TRICK, TREPAN, TRAPAN, SCHEME, DECEPTION, RUSE, MANEUVER, TACTIC, PLOY

strategic position .. VANTAGE

strategy .... TACTICS, MANEUVER, PLAN, ARTIFICE

stratified .... LAMINATED, LAYERED

stratum .... LAYER, LEVEL
  horizontal, in geology ... TABLE
  of mineral ...... STREAK
  soft, crumbly ..... MARL

Straus, composer ..... OSKAR

Strauss work .... SALOME

Stravinsky, composer ... IGOR
  work .... FIREBIRD

straw ... CULM, STALK, STEM, TRIFLE, FODDER
  bale of .... TRUSS
  bed .... PALLET
  boss .... ASSISTANT
  bunch of ... WHISK, WISP, TRUSS
  coat .... MINO
  colored .. FLAXEN, BLOND
  cover around plant ..... MULCH
  fine-cut .... CHAFF
  for fodder .... CHAFF
  for pointing ...... FESCUE
  hat .... PANAMA, SAILOR
  in the wind .... OMEN, SIGN, PORTENT
  like .... STRAMINEOUS
  man .... SCARECROW, JACKSTRAW, NONENTITY, DUMMY
  plaited .... SENNIT
  stack .... RICK, MOW
  thatching ..... HA(U)LM
  vote .... POLL
  vote man .... GALLUP, HARRIS, ROPER, POLLSTER

vote objective .... CONSENSUS
  worm .... CADDIS

strawberry bush ..... WAHOO
  like fruit .... ETAERIO

stray ... WANDER, STRAGGLE, ROAM, ROVE, DEVIATE, MEANDER, ERR, DIGRESS, LOST
  animal .. WAIF, MAVERICK
  animal's place ... PINFOLD

strays .... STATIC

streak ...... STRIPE, STRAIN, TRAIT, SPELL, HURRY, VEIN, TEAR, STRIA, FREAK, MOTTLE

streaked .... STRIGOSE, LINEATE

streaks, full of .... LIN(E)Y

stream ... RIVER, FLOW, RUSH, BROOK, POUR, TORRENT, RUNNEL, BECK, CREEK, ARROYO, BOURNE, KILL, RILL
  bed .. CHANNEL, RUNWAY
  fence .... WEIR

limestone deposit .. TUFA
of lava .... COULEE
overflow .... FRESHET
rocky obstruction ......
.... RIFFLE
sound ... PURL, MURMUR
source .. FOUNTAIN, HEAD
swift, violent ... TORRENT
streamer ..... FLAG, BANNER,
HEADLINE, SCAREHEAD,
PENNANT
streamlet .. RUNNEL, RIVULET
street .... CALLE, ROAD,
AVENUE, RUE, VIA, LANE
Arab ... GAMIN, URCHIN,
WAIF, MUDLARK
designating a .. DEAD END,
ONE-WAY, EASY, MAIN
ditch .... GUTTER
hydrant .... FIREPLUG
market .... CURB
musicians' employer ....
.... PADRONE
musicians' organ ......
.... HURDY-GURDY
of shops ...... BAZ(A)AR
short .... COURT
show .... RAREE
stray ..... URCHIN, ARAB,
GAMIN, WAIF
urchin ...... MUDLARK,
GAMIN, ARAB, WAIF,
GUTTERSNIPE
with houses both sides ...
.... ROW
streetcar ... TRAM, TROLL(E)Y
cowcatcher ..... FENDER
driver .... MOTORMAN
streetwalker ... URCHIN, ARAB,
GAMIN, PEDESTRIAN
Streisand, Miss ..... BARBRA
sister of ...... (ROZ)KIND
strength ...... POWER, VIGOR,
MIGHT, MAIN, ENERGY,
POTENCY, FORCE
source of .... SINEW
strengthen .... FORTIFY, PROP,
BRACE
with alcohol ..... NEEDLE
strenuous .... VIGOROUS
streptomycin discoverer ......
.... WAKSMAN
stress .... STRAIN, PRESSURE,
EMPHASIS, URGENCY,
TENSION, ACCENT,
EMPHASIZE

in music ... ACCENT, ARSIS
metrical .... ICTUS
stretch ...... TRACT, EXTEND,
SPREAD, STRAIN,
EXAGGERATE, EXPANSE,
SWEEP
of water .... RIFFLE
stretched out .... PROLATE
stretcher .... LITTER,
CROSSPIECE, TENTER
stretching muscle .... TENSOR
strew ...... SPREAD, SCATTER,
SPRINKLE
stria .... GROOVE, FILLET,
RIDGE, STREAK
stricken .. STRUCK, AFFLICTED
strict ...... RIGOROUS, RIGID,
STRINGENT, PUNCTILIOUS,
STERN, EXACT, ACCURATE,
PRECISE
adherence to law ....
.... LEGALISM
stricture .... CENSURE,
CRITICISM, STENOSIS
stride .... PACE, STEP,
STRADDLE, LOPE
strides .... PROGRESS,
ADVANCEMENT
strident ..... SHRILL, GRATING
sound .... STRIDOR
strife .... WAR, CONFLICT,
DISCORD, FEUD,
CONTENTION, STRUGGLE,
CONTEST, QUARREL
strigil .... PLUTING
strigose .... HISPID
strike ...... SMITE, BITE, HIT,
BLOW, HUELGA, IMPRESS,
HOOK, DAB, IGNITE,
ATTACK, LASH, FIND,
OCCUR, HAULDOWN,
DISMANTLE
demonstrator, etc. ......
.... PICKET
dumb .. AMAZE, ASTOUND
feature .... LOCKOUT
gently .... PAT, TAP
kind of .. SIT-IN, HUNGER,
SYMPATHY, SLOW-DOWN
of a sort .... BOYCOTT
off ..... ERASE, EXPUNGE,
DELETE
out ...... FAN, CANCEL,
EXPUNGE, DELETE
weapon .... PICKET
with closed fist ... PUNCH

with open palm .... SLAP
strikebreaker ... GOON, FINK, SCAB, BLACKLEG
strikebreakers' leader .. NOBLE
striker .... HARPOONER, CLAPPER, HAMMER, MALLET, BAT
striking .. REMARKABLE, VIVID
string .... CORD, THREAD, ROPE, TWINE, LINE, HANG, LACE, HOAX, JOSH, FOOL, CATGUT
   attached: colloq. .... CONDITION
   in horse racing .. STABLE
   of beads .... CHAPLET, STRAND
   quartet member .. VIOLA, VIOLONCELLO
   up .... HANG
   tipped end .... TAG, A(I)GLET
stringed instrument .... LYRE, MANDOLIN, VIOL(A), GUITAR, ZITHER, PANDORA, CELLO, HARP, SAMISEN, LUTE, KOTO, CITHARA, CITHER(N), REBEC, PSALTERY, DULCIMER, BANJO, CITOLE, CLAVICHORD, CITTERN, UKE(LELE)
   instrument player ...... LUTANIST
   instrument ridge ... NUT
   toy .... YOYO
stringency .... SCARCITY
stringent ...... STRICT, SEVERE, TIGHT
stringy ..... LONG, FIBROUS, ROPY, VISCOUS
strip .... UNDRESS, SPOIL, BARE, DISMANTLE, TAB, FASCIA, DIVEST, DENUDE, SWATH, BATTEN, DISARRAY, FLENSE, LATH
   from tree trunk .. FLITCH
   landing .... RUNWAY
   metal/wood ... SLAT, LIST
   of land .... NECK
   of leaves ..... DEFOLIATE
   skin .... EXCORIATE, FLAY
stripe ... CHEVRON, BAND, BAR, FILLET, TYPE, SORT, STREAK
   of color .... LIST

on skin ... WHEAL, WALE, WELT
striped ..... STRIATE, ZONATE
   animal ... ZEBRA, BONGO
   cloth .... MADRAS
   lengthwise ..... VITTATE
   squirrel ...... CHIPMUNK
stripling ... SPRIG, YOUTH, LAD
stripped ... SHORN, DEPRIVED, DIVESTED
stripteaser .... ECDYSIAST, (SALLY) RAND
   covering for ...... FAN, G-STRING
strive .... STRUGGLE, ENDEAVOR, TRY, FIGHT, VIE, COPE
strobil(e) .... CONE
stroke ... STRIPE, BLOW, MARK, CARESS, PET, SHOT, FIT, FONDLE, ICTUS
   brilliant ..... COUP, ACE
   cutting ..... CHOP, SLICE
   finishing .... COUP DE GRACE, COPESTONE
   indirect .... BRICOLE
   lucky ..... COUP, FLUKE
   oblique .... BRICOLE
   of luck .... WINDFALL
   on hand's palm .. PANDY
   tender .... CARESS
stroll .. WANDER, PROMENADE, SAUNTER, WALK
stroller .... VAGRANT
Stromboli .. ISLAND, VOLCANO
strong ..... INTENSE, STOUT, STURDY, VIRILE, FORCEFUL, ATHLETIC, PUISSANT, LUSTY, POWERFUL, ROBUST, HALE, TOUGH, FIRM
   arm man .... GOON, GANGSTER, BOUNCER
   articulation ...... FORTIS
   current .... RIPTIDE, UNDERTOW
   drink ... SPIRITS, LIQUOR
   feeling ... PASSION, FIRE, HATRED
   man ... ATLAS, HERCULES, SAMSON, TITAN, DICTATOR
   muscled .... THEWY, BRAWNY, HERCULEAN
   passion .... FLAME
   point .... FORTE

scented .... OLID
strongbox ...... SAFE, VAULT,
              CHEST, COFFER
stronghold .... CITADEL,
    CASTLE, REDOUBT, FORT,
    FORT(RESS), AERIE,
    FASTNESS, KEEP
strongroom .... VAULT
strongyl(e) ...... ROUNDWORM
strontium sulfite .. CELESTITE
strop .... STRAP, SHARPEN
strophe .... STANZA
strophulus .... MILIARIA
struck .... SMOTE, SMIT,
             SHUTDOWN
structural .... TECTONIC
   order .... TEXTURE
structure ... BUILDING, EDIFICE
strudel .... PASTRY
struggle ...... STRIVE, LABOR,
    CONTEST, WRESTLE,
    EXERTION, TUSSLE,
    STRIFE, CONFLICT, TRY
strum ... TIRE, PLUCK, FINGER,
            THRUM
struma .... GOITER, SCROFULA
strummer .... GUITARIST
strumpet .... HARLOT
strut .... SPUR, SWAGGER,
         BRACE, GAIT
struthious bird .. RHEAL, EMU,
         OSTRICH
struts .... CABANE
strychnine source ....
        NUX VOMICA
stub .... STUMP, UPROOT,
           BUTT
stubble .... BEARD, STUMP
stubborn .... ORNERY,
    OBSTINATE, WILLFUL,
    OBDURATE, DOGGED,
    HARDHEADED, MULISH,
    FROWARD
   animal .... ASS, MULE
   hair tuft .... COWLICK
stubby .... STOCKY
stuckup .... SNOBBISH,
    HAUGHTY, MIRED,
    ARROGANT
stud ... BOSS, KNOB, NAILHEAD,
    PAVE, BUTTON, ADORN
   horse .... STALLION
   shoe .... HOBNAIL
student ..... PUPIL, DISCIPLE,
    TRAINEE, COLLEGIAN,
    COED, SCHOLAR

Annapolis .. MIDSHIPMAN
first year ..... FRESHMAN,
            PLEBE
former .... DROPOUT
group ... CLASS, SEMINAR
in charge ...... MONITOR
initiate .... HAZE
international law ....
         PUBLICIST
military school ... CADET
population .. ENROLMENT
second year .. SOPHOMORE
third year ..... JUNIOR
university .. VARSITARIAN
West Point ...... CADET
students' scrimmage .... RUSH
studies .... EDUCATION,
         SCHOOLING
studio ... ATELIER, WORKSHOP
study .. READ, EXAMINE, PORE,
    WEIGH, ESSAY, CON,
    CONSIDER, SCRUTINIZE,
    PONDER, DEN, ROOM
   assignment ..... LESSON
   by candlelight ....
         LUCUBRATE
   group ... SEMINAR, CLASS
   hard ...... BONE, CRAM
   layout of .... CASE
   musical .... ETUDE
   of the Bible ... ISAGOGICS
   private .. DEN, SANCTUM
   superficially ... SMATTER
stuff .... ESSENCE, THINGS,
    JUNK, PACK, FILL, SATIATE,
    CRAM, PLUG
stuffed ... REPLETE, CRAMMED
stuffing ...... COTTON, KAPOK,
         WAD
stuffy .... CLOSE, DULL, PRIM,
    STRAIT-LACED
Stuka .... (DIVE)BOMBER
stulm .... ADIT
stum .... GRAPE, JUICE, MUST
stumble .. TRIP, BLUNDER, SLIP
stumbling block .. HINDRANCE,
        OBSTACLE
stump ... STUB, BUTT, STUBBLE,
    LOP, PUZZLE, PERPLEX,
    BAFFLE, FOIL, NONPLUS,
        ZUCHE
stumps: sl. .... LEGS
stun .... DAZE, STUPEFY,
    SHOCK, ASTOUND
stunning .... REMARKABLE
stunt ... FEAT, DWARF, TRICK

flying tour .. BARNSTORM
stunted tree ... SCRUB, SCRAG,
BONSAI
stuntman .... ACROBAT,
DAREDEVIL
stupa .... MOUND
stupe .... COMPRESS
stupefacient .... NARCOTIC
stupefy ... STUN, AMAZE, PALL,
DAZE, ASTONISH, DOPE,
ASTOUND, BEWILDER,
OBFUSCATE
stupendous ... OVERWHELMING,
IMMENSE
stupid ...... TOMFOOL, DULL,
FOOLISH, INEPT, DENSE,
SILLY, TIRESOME, ASININE,
DOPEY, CRASS, DUMB,
INSIPIENT
from overdrinking ......
SOTTISH
person ..... GOOSE, IDIOT,
ASS, COOT, FATHEAD, LOON,
DOLT, MORON, DUNCE, CLOD
stupor .... TRANCE, NARCOSIS,
TORPOR, SOPOR, COMA,
LETHARGY, OSCITANCY
combining form .. NARCO
in a .... DOPEY
sturdy .... FIRM, STOUT, HARDY,
STRONG, GID
sturgeon ...... SHOVELHEAD,
HAUSEN, STERLET, BELUGA,
GANOID
eggs .... ROB
eggs relish ..... CAVIAR(E)
roe .... CAVIAR(E)
stutter .... STAMMER
sty .... PEN, HAW, BOIL
Stygian ..... HELLISH, DARK,
INFERNAL, GLOOMY
style .... STYLUS, NEEDLE,
POINTER, DESIGN, MANNER,
FASHION, MODE, FAD,
BRAND, MAKE, TON, VOGUE,
ENTITLE, GENRE, TECHNIQUE,
NAME, CALL
architectural .... ROCOCO
artistic .... GUSTO
bombastic .... TUMID
dress .... COSTUME
furniture .... EMPIRE
literary .... ROCOCO
out of ..... PASSE, DATED
painting ... GENRE, DADA,
CUBISM

type ..... ROMAN, IONIC,
ITALIC, GOTHIC
styled ...... YCLEPT, CALLED,
NAMED
stylet ...... STILETTO, PROBE,
LANCET, DAGGER
surgical ...... PROBE,
TROCAR
stylish ... DRESSY, TONY, CHIC,
NIFTY, JAUNTY, NOBBY,
MODISH, SMART,
FASHIONABLE, A LA MODE
dresser ... FOP, BRUMMEL,
TOFF, DUDE, SWELL,
DANDY
ostentatiously ....
SWANK(Y)
stylist .. DESIGNER, MANNERIST
stylite .... ASCETIC
stylized flower .... LIS
stylograph .... PEN
stylus ... SCRIBER, NEEDLE, PEN
stymie (stymy) .... OBSTRUCT,
HINDER, IMPEDE, BLOCK,
BALK, FOIL
styptic .... ASTRINGENT,
AMADOU, ALUM
action of .... STYPSIS
substance .... ALUM
Styx .... LETHE, RIVER
ferryman of .... CHARON
suave ..... GRACIOUS, POLITE,
POLISHED, SOAPY, URBANE,
BLAND, AULIC, COURTLY,
SMOOTH
subaltern .. AIDE, SUBORDINATE
subaqueous .... UNDERWATER
subcontinent .... INDIA
subcontract .... SUBLET,
SUBLEASE
suberose .... CORKLIKE,
SUBEROUS
subdue .. CONQUER, VANQUISH,
TAME, OVERCOME, SOFTEN,
SUBJUGATE, OVERPOWER,
QUELL, CALM
subgum dish ..... CHOW MEIN
subject .... TEXT, LIABLE,
CONTINGENT, OCCASION,
VASSAL, NOUN, LIEGE,
THEME, TOPIC, SERVANT,
TRIBUTARY
change to another ......
METASTASIS
main .... MOTIF

to discussion ..... MOOT, DEBATABLE
to third degree ... SWEAT
subjoin .. APPEND, ADD, ANNEX
subjugate .... CONQUER, VANQUISH, OVERCOME, TAME
subjugation .... CONQUEST
sublimate ..... REFINE, PURIFY
sublime ... NOBLE, EXALTED, HIGH, MAJESTIC, LOFTY
submachine gun .... THOMPSON
submarine .... PIGBOAT, TUB, U-BOAT, SUBMERSIBLE
   chaser ..... CORVET(TE)
   device against ....
        PARAVANE
   "eye" of ...... PERISCOPE
   locator .... SONAR
   nuclear .... GATO
submaxilla .... JAW(BONE)
submerge ... HIDE, SINK, DIP, SUDMERSE, SWAMP, WHELM
submerged continent ....
       ATLANTIS
submersible ...... SUBMARINE, U-BOAT
submission .... SURRENDER, RESIGNATION
   sign/act of .... VAIL, KNEEL, BOW, CURTSY
submissive .. TAME, OBEDIENT, PASSIVE, DOCILE, PROSTRATE, MEEK
submit .... SURRENDER, PROPOSE, SUCCUMB, OBEY, YIELD, BOW, GIVE IN
subordinate ..... SECONDARY, INFERIOR, AIDE, ASSISTANT, MYRMIDON
suborn ...... BRIBE, CORRUPT
subpoena ..... SUMMON, WRIT
subrogate .... SUBSTITUTE
subrosa .... SECRETLY
subscribe .... SIGN, SUPPORT, PLEDGE, AGREE, CONSENT
subsequently .. AFTERWARD, LATER
subservience ...... SERVILITY
subservient .... SERVILE
subside ... ABATE, SINK, WANE, FALL, SETTLE, EBB
subsidiary .... TRIBUTARY, AUXILIARY, SUCCURSAL,
subsidy .. GRANT, SUBVENTION, AID, PENSION, SUPPORT

subsist .... LIVE, FARE, EXIST, ABIDE, FEED
subsistence ..... LIVELIHOOD, BEING
substance ..... GIST, ESSENCE, MATTER, MATERIAL, REALITY, PITH, MEANING, PURPORT, STUFF, WEALTH
   drying .... DESSICANT
substandard .... POOR, INFERIOR
substantial .... REAL, SOLID, AMPLE
substantiate .... CONFIRM, PROVE, VERIFY
substantive ... ACTUAL, NOUN, SOLID
substitute .... VICE, REPLACE, ALTERNATE, SUPPLANT, PROXY, SUBROGATE, EXCHANGE, FILL-IN
   food .... ERSATZ
   for .... PINCHHIT
   for a name ..... DINGUS
   temporary ..... STOPGAP
substitution of obligation .....
       NOVATION
subterfuge .... ARTIFICE, DECEPTION, BLIND, DEVICE, EVASION, TRICK, PRETENSE
subterranean .. UNDERGROUND, HIDDEN, SECRET
subtile ... SUBTLE, THIN, RARE, TENUOUS, KEEN
subtitle .... SUBHEAD
subtle .... RARE, THIN, ACUTE, KEEN, DEFT, SLY, (SUPER)FINE, NICE, FINESPUN, ARTFUL, DELICATE, WILY, ARTFUL, SUBTILE
   emanation .... AURA, ATMOSPHERE
   variation ...... NUANCE, SHADE
subtlety ...... FINESSE, CRAFT, ART, QUILLET
subtract ... DEDUCT, DETRACT, LESSEN
suburb ..... TOWN, OUTSKIRT, BARRIO, ENVIRON, FAUBOURG
suburban residence .... VILLA
   society .... VILLADOM
subvention ..... AID, GRANT, SUBSIDY

subversive .... DISSIDENT, REBEL, RED
subvert .... UNDERMINE, CORRUPT, RUIN
subway .... TUBE, METRO, TUNNEL
   entrance .... KIOSK, COVER, TURNSTILE
   stairway .... ESCALATOR
succeed ..... FOLLOW, ENSUE, PROSPER, FLOURISH, THRIVE, SUPERSEDE, SUPPLANT
success ... TRIUMPH, VICTORY
   colloquial .... HIT
succession .. SEQUENCE, SERIES
   of rulers .... DYNASTY
successive ...... CONSECUTIVE
successor .... HERES, HEIR, HERITOR
succinct ..... CONCISE, BRIEF, TERSE, PITHY, LACONIC, SHORT
succor .... HELP, AID, RELIEF, ASSIST(ANCE)
succory .... CHICORY
succubus .... DEMONESS
succulent .... JUICY
succumb ... SUBMIT, FALL, DIE, YIELD
succursal .... SUBSIDIARY
succuss .... SHAKE
such .... SIC
suck .. DRAW, ABSORB, INHALE, SIP
sucker ...... DUPE, LOLLIPOP, ALL-DAY, MUG, BABY, LEECK
suckers, having .... SURCULOSE
suckfish .... REMORA
suckle .... NURSE, REAR, FOSTER, LACTATE
suckler .... MAMMAL, NURSE, BABY, BOB
suckling .... CHILD, BOB, MAMMAL
sucrose ... SUGAR, SACCHAROSE
suction device .... LEECH
sud .... LATHER
Sudan, capital of .. KHARTOUM
   chief of state .... AZHARI
   city .... OMDURMAN, ELOBEID
   lake ..... CHAD, T(S)ANA
   prime minister ....
      MAHGOUB, SADIG, KHALIL
   province .... DARFUR

   region .... GEZIRA, SEGU
   river .... ATBARA
   town ... KODOK, FASHODA
Sudanese ..... MOSSI, FULAH, HAUSSA
   antelope .... OTEROP
   medicine man ....
      MUMBO JUMBO
Negros, of the .. NILOTIC
   sultanate .... WADAI
Sudanic language ...... TOSHI, YORUBA, MANDINGO
sudarium/sudary ... VERONICA, HANDKERCHIEF
sudden .. ABRUPT, PRECIPITATE, HASTY
sudor ... SWEAT, PERSPIRATION
sudorific .. SWEATER, HIDROTIC
suds ..... FOAM, FROTH, BEER
sue ...... WOO, APPEAL, PETITION, PLEAD, LITIGATE
   ——— Langdon ...... ANE
suede .... LEATHER
   source .... CALF, KID
suet .... FAT, TALLOW
Suez Canal builder ... LESSEPS
suffer ..... DREE, UNDERGO, BEAR, ENDURE, EXPERIENCE, LET, ALLOW, TOLERATE, PERMIT
sufferance ...... TOLERATION
suffering ..... DISTRESS, PAIN
   martyr's .... PASSION
suffice ... SERVE, DO, SATISFY
sufficient .... ADEQUATE, ENOUGH, ENOW, AMPLE
suffix .... POSTFIX, SUBINDEX, DESINENCE
   action .... ANCE
   adjective .... ENT, IAL, ISH, IST, OUS
   carbohydrate .... OSE
   chemical ...... ANE, ENE, OLE, ENOL, OLIC, ITOL
   condition .... SION, STER, ANCE, EMIA
   comparative ... IER, IOR
   diminutive ... ULE, ETTE
   follower .... ITE, IST
   inflammation ...... ITIS
   inhabitant of .... ITE
   lacking .... LESS
   one who ...... IST, STER
   skin .... DERM
   superlative .... EST

suffocate ... SMOTHER, CHOKE, STIFLE, ASPHYXIATE
suffocation, temporary ...... APN(O)EA
suffragan .. BISHOP, AUXILIARY
suffrage .... VOTE, FRANCHISE, VOTING
suffragist, U.S. .... CATT
suffuse ... BATHE, OVERSPREAD, COLOR
suffusion ...... BLUSH, FLUSH, TINT
Sufi disciple .... MURID
   wandering dervish ...... CALENDER
sugar .... SACCHAROSE, (LACT)OSE, MALTOSE, GLUCOSE, FLATTERY, SWEETEN, MANNOSE, MUSCOVADO, ARABINOSE, HEXOSE, DEXTROSE, FRUCTOSE
   alcohol .... SORBITOL
   beets .... SUCROSE
   beets refuse .... BAGASSE
   burnt .... CARAMEL
   cane .... SUCROSE
   cane, crushed .. MEGASS(E)
   cane cutting tool .... MACHETE
   cane disease ...... ILIAU
   cane refuse .... BAGASSE, TRASH
   cane sprout ..... RATOON
   combining form .... SACCHAR(O)
   convert into .... SACCHARIZE
   crude .... GUR
   crystalline .... FRUCTOSE, MALTOSE, GLUCOSE, LACTOSE
   cube .... LUMP
   flavoring ...... CARAMEL
   foundation for candy .... FONDANT
   fruit .... KETOSE, LEVULOSE, FRUCTOSE
   lump .... LOAF
   milk .... LACTOSE
   mushroom ... TREHALOSE
   palm sap ..... JAGGERY
   pentose .... RIBOSE
   plum .... BONBON
   raw .... MUSCOVADO, CASSONADE

slang .... MONEY
solution ... SYRUP, SIRUP
source of ... CANE, MAPLE, BEET
sprinkler .... DUSTER
substitute ... SACCHARIN
yeast .... TREHALOSE
sugarplum ..... BONBON, KISS
sugary ..... HONEYED, SWEET
suggest ... PROPOSE, INTIMATE, HINT, IMPLY, INSINUATE
suggestion .. PROPOSAL, HINT, TRACE, INDICATION
   open to ...... AMENABLE, PERVIOUS
sui ____ ...... GENERIS, JURIS
suicidal charge ...... BANZAI
   dive, bomber's .... KAMIKAZE
suicide .... HARA-KIRI, HARA-KARI, SEPPUKU
   in law ...... FELO-DE-SE
   Hindu widow's ... SUTTEE
   sacrificial ... IMMOLATION
suint .... GREASE
   derivative ...... POTASH
Suisse .... SWITZERLAND
suit .... AGREE, PETITION, WOOING, (BE)FIT, ADAPT, PLEASE, SATISFY
   bring .... SUE
   court ..... ACTION, CASE
   of armor ...... PANOPLY
   of mail .... ARMOR
   playing card .... SPADES, DIAMONDS, HEARTS, CLUBS
   tarot card ...... SWORDS, WANDS, CUPS, PENTACLES
   to a ____ .... TEE
suitable .... MEET, APT, FIT(TING), APPROPRIATE, BECOMING, PROPER
suitcase .... VALISE, GRIP
suite .... RETINUE, TRAIN, STAFF, FLAT
suited to ____ .... A TEE
suitor ..... WOOER, ADMIRER, PETITIONER, SUER, FELLOW
Sulawesi .... CELEBES
sulcate ... GROOVED, FLUTED, FURROWED
sulcus ...... FURROW, GROOVE
Suleiman soubriquet .... MAGNIFICENT
sulfate ..... COPPERAS, ALUM

sulfide mixture .... MATTE
sulfonal .... SOPORIFIC
sulfur .... BRIMSTONE
   alloy .... NIELLO
   combining form ... THI(O)
sulfuric acid .... VITRIOL
sulk .... MOPE, POUT, PET,
   GROUCH
sulky ...... SULLEN, CARRIAGE,
   GLUM, GIG
sullage .... SILT, SEWAGE
sullen .... GLUM, SURLY,
   MOROSE, SULKY, DULL,
   BALEFUL, DOUR, MOODY,
   DORTY
Sullivan, _____ ...... ED, BARRY
Sullivan brothers .... FIVE,
   SAILORS
Sullivan's collaborator ....
   GILBERT
   forte .... COMIC OPERA
sully ... TARNISH, SOIL, STAIN,
   BLEMISH, BLOT
sulphate, barium .... BARYTE
   calcium .... GYPSUM
   double .... ALUM
sulphide, arsenic ... ORPIMENT
   lead .... GALENA
   zinc .... BLENDE
sulphur .... BUTTERFLY
   alloy .... NIELLO
   bottom .... WHALE
sulphuric acid ...... VITRIOL
sulphurous ... FIERY, HEATED,
   HELLISH, INFERNAL,
   PASSIONATE
sultan ... CHICKEN, SULEIMAN,
   SALADIN, SELIM, MURAD,
   PADISHAH
   chamberlain of .. EUNUCH
   decree of .... IRADE
   of Swat .... BABE (RUTH)
   palace .... SERAI
   wives' apartment .. HAREM
sultana .... GRAPE, RAISIN
sultanate ..... KUWAIT, OMAN,
   MUSCAT
sultry ..... HOT, CLOSE, FIERY,
   PASSIONATE, MUGGY,
   TORRID, HUMID,
   SWELTERING, TROPICAL
Sulu capital .... JOLO
   Moslem .... MORO
sum ... AMOUNT, AGGREGATE,
   ADD, TOTAL, GIST, SUBSTANCE
   subtracted ... DEDUCTION

   up a speech .... PERORATE
sumac ..... RHUS, TEREBINTH
Sumatra burrowing animal ...
   TELEDU
   city .... PADANG, MEDAN,
   PALEMBANG
   deerlike animal ... NAPU,
   CHEVROTAIN
   gibbon .... SIAMANG
   gutta .... SIAK
   island near .... NIAS
   native of ..... MALAYAN,
   BAT(T)AK
   shrew/squirrel .... TANA
   volcano .... MERAPI
   wild cat .... BALU
Sumbara volcano .. TAMBORA
Sumerian god .... ABU
summary ...... GIST, DIGEST,
   RESUME, EPITOME,
RUN-DOWN, PRECIS, BRIEF,
   COMPEND(IUM),
   ABRIDGMENT, SYNOPSIS
   of main points ....
   SYLLABUS
summer ailment .... HEATRASH
   beverage .... ADE
   French .... ETE
   headliner .... HEATWAVE
   house .... COTTAGE,
   BELVEDERE, CASINO,
   ALCOVE, PAVILION, KIOSK,
   MAHAL, GROTTO
   insect .... GNAT
   pertaining to .. (A)ESTIVAL
   suit fabric .. PALM BEACH
   theater .... STOCK
   time .... DST
summit ...... APEX, PEAK,
   PINNACLE, ACME, TOP,
   KNAP, ZENITH
summon ... CALL, SUBPOENA,
   SEND FOR, EVOKE, ROUSE,
   CONVENE, BID, CITE
   by calling name ... PAGE
   by incantation .. INVOKE
   by magic .... CONJURE
   demon .... CONJURE
   for roll call ...... MUSTER
   spirit .... CONJURE
   to a meeting ... CONVOKE
summons ... EVOCATION, CALL,
   WRIT, CITAL, MONITION
sump .... (CESS)POOL, PIT,
   WELL, OIL
sumpter ... PACKHORSE, MULE

sumptuous ... LAVISH, COSTLY,
SPLENDID, RICH, DE LUXE
sun ... STAR, TAN, DRY, SOL,
LUMINARY
  bittern .... HELIAS
  bow ...... RAINBOW, IRIS
  burn .... TAN
  Chinese president ......
YAT-SEN
  combining form .. HELI(O)
  darkening of the .. ECLIPSE
  disk .... ATEN
  dried brick ..... (A)DOBE,
DOBIE
  dog .... PARHELION
  fish ...... OPAH, BREAM
  for drying ..... INSOLATE
  god ..... APOLLO, HELIOS,
RA, HYPERION, PHOEBUS,
AMON, VARUNA,
MARDUK, SOL,
MITHRA(S), HORUS, SHU,
ATEN, TUM, SHAMASH,
TITAN
  greatest distance from ...
APSIS
  halo of .... CORONA
  helmet ..... TOPI, TOPEE
  helmet scarf .. PUGGREE,
PUGGRY
  mirror .... HELIOSTAT
  mock .... PARHELION
  of the ... SOLAR, HELIACAL
  orbit/path .... ECLIPTIC
  personification of .. TITAN
  pertaining to the .. SOLAR,
HELIACAL
  poetic ... PHOEBUS, LAMP
  point farthest from ......
APHELION
  radiation .... INSOLATION
  room/porch ... SOLARIUM
  shadow .... UMBRA
  shield ... PARASOL, VISOR
  spot ... FACULA, MACULA,
FRECKLE
  spurge ...... TURNSOLE
  streak .... FACULA
  vitamin, so-called ......
(COD) LIVER OIL
  worship ... HELIOLATRY
Sun Yat-sen's party ......
KUOMINTANG
sunbeam .... RAY
  sunburn .... TAN
sunburnt .... ADUST

Sunda island .... BALI, JAVA,
SUMATRA, FLORES, LOMBOK
sundae .... ICE-CREAM
Sunday .... SABBATH,
LORD'S DAY
  evangelist .... BILLY
  supper treat ... MEATPIE
sunder .... PART, SEVER,
SEPARATE, SPLIT, RIVE,
CLEAVE, DIVIDE
sundial .... HOROLOGE
  pointer .... GNOMON
sundog .... PARHELION
sundry ..... MISCELLANEOUS,
DIVERS
sunfish ..... BREAM, CRAPPIE,
ROACH, BLUEGILL, MOLA,
CROPPIE, CICHLID
sunflower .... GIRASOL(E),
HELIOTROPE, TURNSOLE,
HELIANTHUS
  state .... KANSAS
sunken .... HOLLOW
  fence .... HAHA
  place .... SAG
Sunkiang capital .... HARBIN
sunn .... HEMP
sunny ...... CHEERFUL, WARM
sunrise ... DAWN, DAYBREAK,
AURORA
sunroom .... SOLARIUM
sunset, occurring at ....
ACRONICAL
sunshade .... PARASOL,
UMBRELLA, AWNING, VISOR
sunshine, bit of .... RAY
sunspot .... MACULA, FACULA
  dark part .... UMBRA
sunstroke ..ICTUS, INSOLATION
sunwise .... CLOCKWISE
Suomi .... FINLAND
sup ... DINE, DRINK, SIP, EAT
super .... ACTOR, EXTRA
  patriot .... JINGO,
NATIONALIST
superabundance .... PLETHORA
superannuate .... RETIRE
superannuated .. ANILE, AGED,
RETIRED, OBSOLETE,
OUTDATED
superb ..... GRAND, ELEGANT,
EXCELLENT, RICH
supercilious .... PROUD,
HAUGHTY, SNOOTY,
ARROGANT, SCORNFUL
superficial ...... SQUARE, LIP,

SHALLOW, CURSORY, EXTERNAL, SKIN-DEEP
polish .... VENEER
superfine ... OVERNICE, SUBTLE, DELICATE, DE LUXE
superfluous .... SURPLUS, EXCESSIVE, DE TROP, REDUNDANT, OTIOSE
superhighway ..... AUTOBAHN, FREEWAY, SPEEDWAY
superhuman .... DIVINE
superintend .... OVERSEE, SUPERVISE, MANAGE, DIRECT
superintendent ... SURVEYOR, MANAGER
superior ...... HIGHER, BOSS, BETTER, UPPER, EXCELLENT
superiors ... BETTERS, CHIEFS, MASTERS
superlative .... EXTREME, SUPREME, ACME, EXCESSIVE, ULTRA
absolute .... ELATIVE
ending .... EST
supernal .... HEAVENLY, CELESTIAL, DIVINE, ETHEREAL
supernatural .... OCCULT, DIVINE, MIRACULOUS, UNEARTHLY, MAGIC
force .... MANA
happening ..... MIRACLE
supernumerary .... EXTRA, FIGURANT(E), ACTOR
superpower, a ..... USA, USSR
superscribe .... ADDRESS
supersede .... SUCCEED, SUPPLANT, REPLACE
supersensitive .... SORE, THIN-SKINNED
supersonic noise .... BOOM
supervene .... ENSUE, HAPPEN
supervise ... OVERSEE, DIRECT, MANAGE
supervisor .... DIRECTOR, OVERSEER, MANAGER
college .... PROCTOR
morals .... CENSOR
supine ..... LISTLESS, PASSIVE, INACTIVE
opposite of ...... PRONE
supper .... DINNER, MEAL
supplant .... REPLACE, SUPERSEDE, DISPLACE, OUST
supple ..... LITHE, LISSOM(E), LIMBER, PLIANT, FLEXIBLE

supplement .... ADD
in law .... CODICIL
supplicate .... PETITION, APPEAL, PLEAD, PRAY, REQUEST, ENTREAT
supplicant .... PLEADER, BEGGAR
supplication .... PETITION, PRAYER, PLEA, REQUEST, ROGATION, ENTREATY
supplies ..... STORES, ISSUES, PROVISIONS
supply ..... STOCK, FURNISH, PROVIDE, EQUIP, STORE
food .... CATER, PURVEY, PROVISION
ship ...... OILER, TENDER, VICTUAL(L)ER
support .... BUTTRESS, SHORE, BACK(UP), UPHOLD, BEAR, MAINTAIN, SUSTAIN, ABET, KEEP, SECOND
chief .... MAINSTAY
idea/cause ..... ESPOUSE
kind of ...... LEG, PROP, LIMB, PEDESTAL, PEG, BASE, MORAL, FINANCIAL, PILLAR, UNIPOD
main .... PILLAR
supporter .... PARTISAN, ABETTOR, SECOND, FOLLOWER, ROOTER, FAN, PATRON, ADHERENT, BACKER
supporting framework .... TRESTLE, TRELLIS, SKELETON, EASEL
member ..... LEG, MAST
suppose ...... TROW, ASSUME, IMAGINE, PRESUME, THINK, WEEN, OPINE, CONJECTURE, SURMISE, RECKON
supposed .... REPUTED, PUTATIVE
supposition .... THEORY, HYPOTHESIS, IF
suppository .... PESSARY
suppress .... QUELL, SUBDUE, CHECK, QUASH, CRUSH, CONCEAL, STOP, THROTTLE
news story .... KILL
suppurate .. FESTER, MATURATE
suppuration ..... PUS, PYOSIS
supra .... ABOVE
supreme .... DOMINANT,

ULTIMATE, CHIEF, FINAL,
UTMOST, HIGHEST
being .... GOD
Court nickname ....
NINE OLD MEN
power .... IMPERIUM
Surakarta .... SOLO
Surat river .... TAPTI
surcease .... STOP, END
surcingle .... GIRDLE
surcoat .. JUPON, GIPON, CLOAK
surd ... IRRATIONAL, RADICAL,
VOICELESS
sure ... POSITIVE, CONFIDENT,
CERTAIN, UNERRING
grip .... CINCH
thing: sl. ... IN THE BAG,
CINCH, PIPE
surely .... OF COURSE, YES,
CERTAINLY
surety .... ASSURANCE, BOND,
SECURITY, HOSTAGE, BAIL,
SPONSOR, GUARANTEE
surf .... WAVES, SWELLS
duck .... SCOTER
noise .... ROTE, THUNDER
surface .... EXTERIOR
antique .... PATINA
curve .... CAMBER
front .... OBVERSE
gem's .... FACET
in aeronautics ... AIRFOIL
main .... OBVERSE
slanting/sloping ... CANT
surfbird .... PLOVER
surfeit .... SATE, SATIATE,
CLOY, JADE, SATIETY, GLUT,
EXCESS
surfeited ...... FED-UP, SATED,
BLASE
surge .... SWELL, BILLOW,
HEAVE, WAVE
of water/wave .... WASH
surgeon: colloq. .... SAWBONES,
MEDICO
hammer of ..... PLESSOR
knife of .... LANCET,
SCALPEL, BISTOURY
probe of .... STYLET
saw of .... TREPAN,
TREPHINE
surgery .... OPERATION,
NEOPLASTY
lip defect ... CHILOPLASTY
surgical compress ...... STUPE
instrument .. OSTEOTOME,

TREPAN, BISTOURY,
TROCAR, LEVATOR,
SCALPEL, LANCET
knife .... BISTOURY,
SCALPEL, LANCET,
FLEAM, PHLEBOTOME
operation .... RESECT,
LOBOTOMY
operation: comb. form ..
TOMY
pad .... SPONGE
pincers .... FORCEPS
removal of body part ....
ABLATION
removal of breast ....
MASTECTOMY
sewing .... SUTURE
thread ... SETON, CATGUT
treatment ... OPERATION
Suribachi, site of .... IWO JIMA
suricate, kin of .... MONGOOSE,
CIVET
Surinam capital ... PARAMARIBO
governor of ...... VRIES
prime minister ... PENGEL
toad .... PIPA
tree .... BALATA
surly ... GRUFF, SULKY, RUDE,
SULLEN, CRUSTY, GRUMPY,
ARROGANT, UNCIVIL, CROSS,
BOORISH, CHURLISH
surmise .... OPINE, GUESS,
CONJECTURE, IMAGINE,
INFER
surmount .... OVERCOME,
CONQUER, GET OVER,
EXCEED, HURDLE, TOP
surname .... AGNOMEN,
PATRONYMIC, COGNOMEN
surpass ...... EXCEED, EXCEL,
TOP, ECLIPSE, BEST, OUTDO,
CAP, TRANSCEND
surplice .... COTTA
vestment like ... ROCHET
surplus .... EXTRA, SPARE,
EXCESS, OVERAGE
surprise .. ASTOUND, ASTONISH,
AMAZE, STARTLE, JOLT
surrealist painter .... DALI
surrender ...... YIELD, CEDE,
CESSION, REMISE, GIVE UP,
SUBMIT, SUBMISSION, RESIGN
conditionally ....
CAPITULATE
sign of ... WHITE FLAG,
HANDS UP

surreptitious .. CLANDESTINE, SLY, SECRET, STEALTHY, FURTIVE, SNEAKY

surrey .... CARRIAGE

village .... KEW

surrogate ... DEPUTY, JUDGE, SUBSTITUTE

concern of .... WILLS

surround .... ENCOMPASS, (EN)CIRCLE, ENCLOSE, INVEST, BESET, GIRD, RING, ENVELOP, HEM, ENVIRON, BELEAGUER

surrounding .... MILIEU, ENVIRONMENT, AMBIENT

surtout .... (OVER)COAT

surveillance .... WATCH, OBSERVATION

survey ... INSPECT, VIEW, POLL, LOOK AT, CANVASS

surveying instrument .... ALIDADE, TRANSIT, LEVEL, STADIA, VERNIER, THEODOLITE, CALIPER, TACHYMETER

method .. DIALING, STADIA

surveyor's assistant .. RODMAN, LINEMAN

transit .... STADIA

survive .... (OUT)LIVE, WEATHER

survivor .... RELICT

Susa, location of .. IRAN, ELAM

Susan, diminutive of ... SUE, SUSIE, SUZY

susceptibilities ...... FEELINGS

susceptible ..... RESPONSIVE, LIABLE, SOFT, RECEPTIVE

to mistake ..... FALLIBLE

suslik ...... SISEL, SQUIRREL, GOPHER, SPERMOPHILE

suspect ... DISTRUST, PRESUME, IMAGINE, SURMISE

suspend ... HANG, HALT, STOP, HOLD, DEFER, EXCLUDE, ADJOURN

suspended .... PENSILE, PENDENT, HANGING, PENDANT

suspenders .... GARTERS, BRACES, GALLUSES

suspension .... DELAY, STOPPAGE, PENDENCY

of court sentence .... PROBATION

of hostilities ..... TRUCE, ARMISTICE

of proceedings .... ADJOURNMENT, RECESS

suspicion ...... TRACE, HINT, INKLING, MISTRUST, FEAR, HUNCH

suspicious .... LEERY, SKEPTICAL

suspiration .... SIGH

Susskind, TV man .... DAVID

sustain ... MAINTAIN, SUFFER, UPHOLD, CONFIRM, SUPPORT

sustenance ... FOOD, SUPPORT, BREAD

susu .... DOLPHIN

susurrant .... RUSTLING, MURMURING, WHISPERING

susurration .... MURMUR, RUSTLE, WHISPER

sutler .... VICTUAL(L)ER

customer of .... SOLDIER

sutor .... COBBLER, SYRUP

suttee ... SUICIDE, IMMOLATION

suture ... STITCH, SEW, SEAM, JUNCTION, RAPHE

suzerain ...... RULER, LIEGE, LORD

svelte ...... LITHE, LISSOM(E), SLENDER

Sverige .... SWEDEN

neighbor of ..... NORGE

swab ..... MOP, WIPE, BRUSH, SPONGE, MALKIN

swaddle ..... SWATHE, WRAP

swaddling clothes .... DUDS

swag .... SWAY, LURCH

slang .... LOOT, PLUNDER, BOOTY

swage ... DIE, STAMP, DOLLY, UPSET

swagger .... STRUT, BLUFF, BLUSTER, RUFFLE, ROISTER

swaggering .... SWASH

Swahili cheer word .... HARAMBEE

swain .... SUITOR, LOVER, YOUTH, GALLANT

swallow .... ABSORB, GULP, RETRACT, BEAR, TAKE IN, BIRD, TERN, BOLT, QUAFF, INGEST

bird like a .... SWIFT, MARTIN, CRAN

greedily .... GORGE

like .... HIRUNDINE

swallowing, difficulty in ......
     DYSPHAGIA
swallowtail .. BUTTERFLY, COAT
swallowwort ..... CELANDINE
swami ... LORD, MASTER, FAKIR
swamp ... INUNDATE, MARSH,
    SLOUGH, FEN, MORASS,
    BOG, OVERWHELM, FLOOD,
    MARISH
  air .... MALARIA
  fever .... MALARIA
  Fox, soubriquet .. MARION
  plant .... COWSLIP, SOLA,
    MARIGOLD
  trees .... MANGROVE
  vapor .... MIASM(A)
swampland ...... EVERGLADE
swamps ..... WETLAND, SLEW
swampy ... PALUDAL, MARSHY
  area .... SLASH
swan ... WHOOPER, POET, BIRD,
  SWEAR, TRUMPETER, ANSA
  constellation ... CYGNUS
  female .... PEN
  genus .... OLOR
  lover .... LEDA
  male .... COB
  song ...... VALEDICTORY
  young .... CYGNET
swanky ...... STYLISH, POSH,
  SHOWY, PLUSH
swap ...... BARTER, TRADE,
  EXCHANGE
swaraj .... HOME RULE
sward ..... SOD, LAWN, TURF
swarm ... TEEM, THRONG,
  CROWD, NEST, INVEST,
  OVERRUN, HIVE, SHIN,
  HORDE, MULTITUDE
swarmer ... BEE, LOCUST, ANT,
  INSECT
swarming .... TEEMING
swart(hy) ...... DARK, DUN,
  DUSKY
swash .... SPLASH, DASH
swastika .... FLYPOT
swat ...... BLOW, CLOUT, RAP
  king of ..... (BABE) RUTH
swath ..... ROW, TRACK, STRIP
swathe ..... BANDAGE, BIND,
  WARP(PING), ENVELOP
sway ..... OSCILLATE, SWING,
  ROCK, RULE, VEER,
  FLUCTUATE, DOMINION,
  CONTROL, POWER, LURCH
swear .. VOW, DEPOSE, CURSE,

CUSS, PLEDGE, AFFIRM
  falsely .... PERJURE
  off .... RENOUNCE
  word ...... PROFANITY,
    CURSE, OATH
swearing .... JURANT
sweat ..... EXUDE, PERSPIRE,
  PERSPIRATION, FERMENT,
  SUDOR, TRANSUDE, EXPLOIT,
  HEAT, EXERCISE, SWELTER,
  UVERWORK, LATHER, OOZE,
  EGESTA
  causing .... HIDROTIC
  shirt .... JERSEY
sweater .... PULL-OVER,
  SUDORIFIC, JERSEY, SLIP-ON,
  CARDIGAN, GUERNSEY
Sweden .... SVERIGE
Swedish capital ... STOCKHOLM
  city .. GOTEBORG, MALMO,
    UP(P)SALA
  clover .... ALSIKE
  coin .... KRONA, KRONE,
    ORE, CROWN
  district .... LA(E)N
  dwelling .... CHALET
  explorer .... HEDIN
  hero .... WASA
  hut .... CHALET
  island .. GOTLAND, OLAND
  king ..... ERIC, GUSTAV,
    BERNADOTTE
  lake .... MALAR
  manual training .. SLOYD
  measure .... STANG
  monetary unit ... KRONA
  mountain range .. KJOLEN
  name .. NILS, SVEN, GRETA
  native .... LAPP
  "nightingale" ....
    (JENNY) LIND
  Nobel Prize winner .....
    LAGERLOF
  noble's title .... GRAF
  novelist ..... LAGERLOF
  painter .... ZORN
  parliament .... RIKSDAG
  prime minister ....
    ERLANDER
  seaport .... KALMAR,
  HALSINBORG, MALMO,
  VISBY, GOTEBORG
  singer ...... YODEL(L)ER,
    YODLER
  soprano .... LIND
  turnip .... RUTABAGA

sweeny .... ATROPHY
sweep ... BROOM, DUST, BRUSH,
CLEAR, OAR, DRAG, RAKE,
TRAIL, RANGE, STRETCH
sweeping .... EXTENSIVE
   blow .... SWIPE
   movement .... SWOOP
sweepstakes .... LOTTERY,
(HORSE)RACE
sweet ..... PLEASANT, CANDY,
LUSCIOUS, HONEY, DULCET,
SUGARY
   actress .... BLANCHE
   and soft .... DOLCE
   bay .... MAGNOLIA
   cicely ... MYRRH, PARSLEY
   clover .... MELILOT
   drink .... NECTAR
   flag ...... CALAMUS, SEDGE
   gum .... COPALM,
LIQUIDAMBAR, BILSTED
   liqueur .... RATAFIA,
CORDIAL
   natured .... DOUCE
   pepper .... PIMIENTO,
PAPRIKA
   potato ... YAM, OCARINA,
BATATA, CAMOTE
   sap source ..... GOMUTI
   smelling .... OLENT,
FRAGRANT, ODOROUS
   sound ... MUSIC, MELODY
   sounding .... DULCET,
MELODIOUS
   tempered .... AMIABLE
sweetbread .. RUSK, PANCREAS
sweetbriar ... EGLANTINE, ROSE
sweeten .... DULCIFY
   and spice .... MULL
sweetened drink .... FLIP
sweetener .... CYCLAMATE,
SUCARYL, SUGAR,
SACCHARIN, SYRUP,
sweetening ..... SUGAR, SIRUP,
HONEY
sweetheart .... JILL, LASS(IE),
LADYLOVE, VALENTINE,
LOVER, BEAU, LEMAN,
JO(E), PHILLIS, PHYLLIS,
AMOUR, POPSY, GILL
   colloquial .... STEADY,
BOY FRIEND, SWEETIE,
FLAME
   idealized ...... DULCINEA
sweetmeat ...... CONFECTION,
CAKE, CANDY, PRESERVE,

NOUGAT, DRAGEE, CARAMEL
sweetsop .... ATES, ATTA
swell .... DILATE, BULGE,
SURGE, WAVE, PUFF(UP),
TUMEFY, INFLATE, DISTEND,
EXPAND, BLOAT, HUFF,
HEAVE, INTUMESCE
   colloquial ..... STYLISH,
EXCELLENT, FOP
   dresser .... TOFF, FOP,
DANDY, BRUMMEL,
DUDE
   in the ground ...... LIFT
   sea .... SURF
   with water .... BLOAT
swelled ..... TUMID, TURGID
swellfish .... PUFFER
swellhead .... BRAGGART
swellheaded ..... CONCEITED,
BOASTFUL
swelling .... BLEB, NODE,
TUMESCENT, TURGESCENCE,
BULGE, PUFF, LUMP, EDEMA,
TORUS, BUMP, GOITER
   armpit/groin ..... BUBO
   combining form .. C(O)ELE
   foot .... CHILBLAIN
   harmony ...... DIAPASON
   wave .... ROLLER
swelter .... PERSPIRE, HEAT,
ROAST, SWEAT
sweltering ..... SULTRY, HOT
swerve .... SHIFT, SKEW,
DEVIATE, SHEER, VEER,
CAREEN, DEFLECT
swift ... TANTIVY, FLEET, FAST,
RAPID, BIRD, TOM
   combining form .. TACHY
   footed animal .... DEER,
GAZELLE
   footed maiden ....
ATALANTA
Swift's "flying island" ....
LAPUTA
   hero .... GULLIVER
   pen name ..... DRAPIER
swiftness ... SPEED, VELOCITY
swig .... DRINK, GULP
swiler .... SEALER
swill ... SLOP, DRINK, QUAFF,
GULP, (HOG)WASH,
GARBAGE
swim .... DIP, DIZZY
swimmer ...... FISH, MERMAN,
NAIAD, MERMAID
swimming ... NATANT, CTENE

act of .... NATATION
bird .. SWAN, DUCK, LOON
pool ...... NATATORIUM,
                    TANK
stroke/style ...... CRAWL,
                    BREAST
suit .... MAILLOT
Swinburne, poet ... ALGERNON
swindle .... CHEAT, (DE)FRAUD,
    TRICK, SKIN, BILK, GIP,
    GYP, COZEN, GOUGE,
    WELSH, DIDDLE, BUNCO,
    CON, BUNKO, FLEECE, CLIP,
    HORNSWOGGLE
swindler ... TREPAN, SHARPER,
    CONMAN, FORGER, COZENER,
    GOUGE, JACKAL, HAWK,
    SHARK, CHEAT, GYP, GIP,
    SKIN(NER), (C)ROOK
swindling scheme ..... PLANT
swine .... HOG, PIG, PORCINE
    breed .... DUROC
    disease .... NOUGHT,
                    GARGET
    feeding of ..... PANNAGE
    female .... SOW
    flesh .... PORK
    genus .... SUS
    male .... BOAR
    young ... PORKER, PIGLET
swinelike .... PORCINE
swing ..... OSCILLATE, SWAY,
    HANG, STRETCH, BRANDISH,
    RHYTHM, SWITCH
    fan .... HEPCAT
    music .... JAZZ, JIVE
swinging .... PENDULOUS
swingle .... SWIP(P)LE
swink .. DRUDGE, LABOR, TOIL
swipe ... BLOW, STEAL, PILFER,
    HANDLE, LEVER
swipes .... BEER
swip(p)le .... FLAIL, SWINGLE
swirl ... EDDY, WHIRL, TWIST,
    CURL, WHORL
swirly ... TANGLED, KNOTTED
swish ... RUSTLE, FLOG, WHIP,
                    CANE
Swiss architect ....
                (LE) CORBUSIER
    army .... LANDWEHR
    canton .... LUCERNE,
    TICINO, BASEL, BERN,
    ANE, ZURICH, VALAIS,
    URI, VAUD, GRISONS,
    SCHWYZ, LUZERN,

    THURGAU, FRIBOURG
capital .... BERN(E)
castle .... CHILLON
cheese .... GRUYERB
city .... ZURICH, BASEL,
    BASLE, THUN, GENEVA,
    BERN, LAUSSANNE,
                    GENEVE
cottage .... CHALET
district .... CANTON,
                    OBERLAND
Family Robinson author ..
                    WYSS
federal council ....
                BUNDESRAT
herdsman .... SENN
Italian enclave ....
                CAMPIONE
Italian-speaking canton ..
                    TICINO
lake .... LEMAN, ZUG,
    ZURICH, NEUCHATEL,
    LUCERNE, MAGGIORE,
    GENEVA, THUN, BRIENZ,
                    BIENNE
language ... ROMANS(C)H
man of story ...... TELL
mathematician ... EULER
measure ... ELLE, IM(M)I
mercenary soldier ....
                SWITZER, SWISSER
mountain .... RIGI, JURA,
    JUNGFRAU,
    WETTERHORN
mountain pass .. SIMPLON,
    BERNINA, GEMMI,
                    KINZIG
mountaineer's horn .....
                ALP(EN)HORN
native .... BRISON,
                    VAUDOIS
painter .... KLEE
pass ... SIMPLON, GEMMI,
                    BERNINA
patriot .... ZWINGLI
plant .... EDELWEISS
political division ....
                    CANTON
president .... BONVIN
Protestant .... HELVETIC
psychologist ...... JUNG
resort ..... INTERLAKEN
Rhine port .. BASEL, BASLE
river .. REUSS, TICINO, AAR
scientist .... HALLER
shepherd .... SENN

sled .... LUGE
song .... YODEL
state .... CANTON
state council .. STANDERAT
town ... THUN, LOCARNO
union ...... SONDERBUND
wind .... BISE
Swisser .... SWITZER
switch .... SHUNT, ROD, TWIG,
STICK, SHIFT, LASH, DIVERT,
TRANSFER, (EX)CHANGE,
HICKORY, RAT(T)AN,
TOGGLE
blade knife .... SHIV
switchback .. ROLLER COASTER
switchman .... SHUNTER
Switzerland ...... HELVETIA,
SUISSE
swivet, in a .... AGOG
swollen ..... TOROSE, TOROUS,
BULGING, EDEMIC, TUMID,
BOLLEN, VARICOSE, BLOATED,
TURGID, TURGENT, BLOWN,
DISTENDED
swoon .. FAINT(ING), SYNCOPE
swoop .... POUNCE, DESCENT,
DESCEND
sword ..... RAPIER, SCIMITAR,
BLADE, CUTLAS(S), ESTOC,
ATAGHAN, SKEAN, GLA(I)VE,
FALCHION
Archaic .... TUCK, BILBO
belt .... BALDRIC
blade, weaker part of ....
FOIBLE
bulfighter's .... ESTOQUE
cavalry ... SABER, SABRE
curved .. SCIMITAR, SABER,
CUTLASS, SCIMITER
fencing .... EPEE, FOIL
fine-tempered ... TOLEDO
grass .... SEDGE
handle ...... HAFT, HILT
Highlander's .. CLAYMORE
hilt's knob ..... POMMEL
knob .... POMMEL
legendary .... BALMUNG,
EXCALIBUR
lily .... GLADIOLUS
poetic .... STEEL
put to the .... KILL,
SLAUGHTER
short .... SKEAN
shaped .... ENSATE,
ENSIFORM, XIPHOID,
GLADIATE

Siegfried's .... BALMUNG
St. George's .... ASCALON
strongest part of .. FORTE
thin ...... RAPIER, TUCK
swordfish ...... DORADO, AUS
saw of .... SERRA
swordplay .... FENCING
swords, cross ... FIGHT, DUEL
swordsman ... FENCER, BLADE
sworn ..... PLEDGED, BOUND,
PROMISED
word .... VOW, OATH
swound ...... FAINT, SWOON
sybarite .... EPICURE,
SENSUALIST, VOLUPTUARY
sycamine .... MULBERRY
sycamore ..... BUTTON WOOD
syce .... GROOM
syconium .... FIG
sycophant ..... BOOTLICKER,
FLUNK(E)Y, TOADY,
YES-MAN, HANGER-ON,
TOADEATER, PARASITE,
FLATTERER, SPANIEL
sycosis victim .... BEARD
Syene .... ASWAN
syllabic .... SONANT
syllable, accented/unaccented
THESIS, TONIC
contraction of a ....
SYNALEPHA
last .... ULTIMA
metrical stress on .. ICTUS
musical .... TRA, LA
omission of last ....
APOCOPE
short .... MORA
shortening of a .. SYSTOL
syllables, contraction of ......
SYNERESIS
syllabus .... SUMMARY,
ABSTRACT
syllogism .... LOGIC,
REASONING
middle term of .... MEAN
syllogisms, elliptical series of ..
SORITES
sylph .... UNDINE, FAIRY
sylphlike .... GRACEFUL,
SLENDER
sylvan .... WOODED
area .... WOODS, FOREST
diety .... SATYR, PAN,
FAUN(US)
symbol (see emblem) ....

EMBLEM, TOKEN, SIGN, TOTEM, MARK
American ..-.. UNCLE SAM, EAGLE
bad luck .... OPAL
British .. JOHN BULL, LION
of achievement .. RIBBON
authority .... ROD, STAFF, SCEPTER, MACE, CROWN, BADGE, ENSIGN, GLOBE, FASCES
birth .... STORK
bondage .... YOKE
comedy .... SOCK
death ..:... CROSS BONES
fortune ..... RAINBOW
grief .... RUB
hardness .... NAIL
immortality ....
PH(O)ENIX
mourning ..-.. CREPE, CYPRESS
office .... VERGE
SEMIOLOGY, SEMIOTIC
peace .... DOVE
plain speaking .. SPADE
purity .... LILY
royal power ..... ORB, SCEPTER
saintliness ..-.... HALO
servitude .... YOKE
sovereignty .... MOUND
strength ..-..-.. ATLAS, SINEW
success ..-... RAINBOW
sun .... ATEN
universe ... MANDALGA
victory ..-..-... PALM, LAUREL
war ...-..-.. MARS, ARES
wisdom .... OWL
phallic .... LINGA(M)
remembrance ....
ROSEMARY
status ..-.. MINK, YACHT
symbolic .... TYPICAL
light .... HALO
representation ....
ICONOLOGY
symbolize .... TYPIFY
symmetrical ..-..... SPHERAL, BALANCED
symmetry ...... PROPORTION, HARMONY, BALANCE
sympathetic ...... CONGENIAL, TENDER, AGREEABLE
response .... ECHO

sympathize ..-... COMMISERATE, CONDOLE
sympathy ..... CONSENT, PITY, AFFINITY, HARMONY, ACCORD, COMPASSION
expression of ....
CONDOLENCE, CLEMENCY
symphonic jazz leader ......-.
WHITEMAN
symphony form ..-... SONATA
division of ... MOVEMENT
intended for Napoleon ..
EROICA
third section of .. SCHERZO
symposium, kind of ....
CONSENSUS
symptom ... INDICATION, SIGN, PRODROME, WARNING, FEVER, TEMPERATURE
symptoms appearing together
SYNDROME
pertaining to ....
SEMIOLOGY, SEMIOTIC
synagogue ..-... SHUL, TEMPLE, CONGREGATION
figure ..-.....-... RABBI
officer ..-..-..-.. PARNAS
singer .... CANTOR
syncope ..-... SWOON, ELISION, FAINT
syncretize ..-..-.. RECONCILE, COMBINE
syncrisis ..-..-..-.. CONTRAST
syndic ..-..-..-... MANAGER, MAGISTRATE
syne ..-.--..-..-.. AGO, SINCE
synod ... COUNCIL, ASSEMBLY
synopsis .... SUMMARY, GIST, ABSTRACT, DIGEST, RESUME, BRIEF
synthetic ..-.. ARTIFICIAL, SHAM
fabric .. DACRON, RAYON, ORLON, NYLON, ACETATE
rubber ..-..-.. NEOPRENE, BUNA
silk ..-.... RAYON, NYLON
syntony .... RESONANCE
syphilis .... POX, LUES
lesion .... CHANCRE
remedy ..... SALVARSAN
test for .... HAHN
syphilitic .... LUETIC
Syria .... ARAM
Syrian .... ALAWITE, LEVANTINE, HITTITE
antelope .... ADDAX

bear .... DUBB
capital ...... DAMASCUS,
    ANTIOCH
city ...... ALEPPO, HOMS,
    PALMYRA, KADESH,
    HELIOPOLIS, SELEUCIA
goddess .... ASHTORETH
head of state .. AL-ATASSI
king .... ANTIOCHUS
mountain ..... HERMON
political party ... BAATII
premier .... ZAEYEN
religious follower .. DRUSE
river .... ORONTES
ruler .... ATASSI
seaport .... TRIPOLI
sect member ..... SUNNI,
    SHIITE
tribe ... AMALEK, SARACEN
tribesman .... DRUSE,
    SARACEN
weight .... COLA
syringa .... LILAC,
    MOCK ORANGE
syringe .... INJECTOR

syrinx .... PANPIPE
syrphus fly .... GNAT
syrup ...... SORGHUM, MAPLE,
    TREACLE, ORGEAT, MOLASSES
system .... METHOD,
    ARRANGEMENT, ORDER, ISM
betting .... PARIMUTUEL
of rule .... REGIME
of weights .... TROY
of worship ...... CULT
orderly .... COSMOS
political/social
    REGIME(N)
signals .... CODE
voting .... BALLOT
systematic .... ORDERLY,
    REGULAR, METHODICAL
arrangement ... SCHEMA
systematics .... TAXONOMY
systematize .... ARRANGE,
    ORGANIZE
syzygy .... DIPODY
Szczecin .... STETTIN
Szechwan capital ... CHENGTU
szopelka .... OBOE

T

T-bone steak .. PORTERHOUSE
Greek .... TAU
Hebrew ..... TAW, TETH,
    TAV, TAU
letter .... TEE
shaped .... TAU
ta, in chemistry .. TANTALUM
taa .... PAGODA
Taal .... AFRIKAANS
tab .. FLAP, LABEL, TAG, LOOP,
    STRAP, ACCOUNT, PAN,
    CHECK, BILL
colloquial ...... RECORD,
    RECKONING
in aeronautics ... AIRFOIL
shoe .... LATCHET, STRAP
tabanid .. (HORSE)FLY, GADFLY
tabard ...... JACKET, CLOAK,
    CAPE, MANTLE
tabaret ...... CLOTH, TABBY
tabasco .... SAUCE
capital of ....
    VILLAHERMOSA
tabby ..... MOREEN, TAFFETA,
    MOIRE, CAT, GOSSIP(ER),
    BRINDLED, SILK
taberna .. HUT, SHED, TAVERN
tabernacle .. TENT, DWELLING,

    SANCTUARY, SHRINE, HILET,
    TEMPLE, NICHE
tabes .... PHTHISIS,
    CONSUMPTION, ATROPHY,
    TUBERCULOSIS, EMACIATION
tabescent .... WASTING,
    WITHERING
tabetic .. CONSUMPTIVE, TABID
Tabitha .... DORCAS
table .... FURNITURE, BOARD,
    FOOD, POSTPONE, SHELVE,
    PEND, LIST(ING), DEFER,
    FARE, COMPILATION, FREEZE
centerpiece ... EPERGNE
cloth ... TAPIS, RUNNER,
    SPREAD
communion .... ALTAR,
    CREDENCE
companion .. MESSMATE
cover .... SCARF, BAIZE,
    SPREAD
decoration .... EPERGNE,
    DOILY, PLACEMAT
decorative cloth
    RUNNER
d'hote .... MEAL
game .. POOL, PINGPONG
in architecture ....

CORNICE, MOLDING,
PANEL
linen .. NAPERY, NAPKIN,
DAMASK
napkin ...... SERVIETTE
of content .... INDEX
of the .... MENSAL
on wheels .. TEA WAGON
scrap .... ORT
server .... WAITER
subject with junior .....
SPINACH
tennis .... PINGPONG
three-legged ..:. TRIVET
top's section ..... LEAF
with drawers ...... DESK
writing .... ESCRITOIRE,
SECRETARY
tableau ..... PICTURE, SCENE
tableland ... KAR(R)OO, MESA,
PLATEAU, PUNA
tablet .... PAD, SLAB, TESSERA,
STELE, FACIA, PILL, SLATE
blank ..... TABULA RASA
medicinal ...... TABLOID,
TROCHE, LOZENGE,
COUGH DROP
religious .... PAX
reused ...... PALIMPSEST
scroll-like .. CARTOUCH(E)
writing .. TRIPTYCH, SLATE
tableware item .. DISH, KNIFE,
FORK, SPOON
tabloid .. TROCHE, NEWSPAPER
taboo .. BAN, TABU, VERBOTEN,
PROHIBITION, PROHIBITED,
FORBID(DEN)
opposite of .... NOA
tabor ...... DRUM, TIMBREL,
TABOURET, AT(T)ABAL
taboret ...... STOOL, STAND
Tabriz native ..... IRANI(AN)
tabu ...... TABOO, VERBOTEN,
FORBIDDEN
tabular .... FLAT
tabulate .... LIST
tacamahac ...... GUM RESIN,
POPLAR
tache .... BUCKLE, HOOK
tachina .... FLY
tacit ...... STILL, SOUNDLESS,
UNSPOKEN, IMPLIED, IMPLICIT
taciturn ..... SILENT, RETICENT,
RESERVED, SATURNINE
one ...... INDIAN, CLAM
opposite of ....

GARRULOUS,
TALKATIVE, LOQUACIOUS
tack ...... NAIL, PIN, STITCH,
ZIGZAG, FOOD, ATTACH,
ADD, JIBE, SEW, BASTE,
BRAD
room item .... SPUR
SADDLE, STIRRUP
tackle .... GEAR, APPARATUS,
SEIZE, UNDERTAKE, CAT,
GRASP, LUFF, RIG
hoisting .. CAT, GARNET
in football ..... THROW,
STOP
ship's .... JEERS
small .... JIGGER
tacky ...... DOWDY, SHABBY,
SEEDY, STICKY,
Tacoma mount ..... RAINIER
tact ...... POISE, DIPLOMACY,
SAVOIR-FAIRE, DELICACY,
FINESSE
tactics .... MANEUVERS,
STRATEGEM, STRATEGY, PLOY
tactile .... TANGIBLE
taction .... TOUCH, CONTACT
tactless ..... RUDE, IMPOLITE,
GAUCHE
act .... GAUCHERIE,
FAUX PAS
tad .. CHILD, TOT, YOUNGSTER
Tadmor .... PALMYRA
tadpole .. POLLIWOG, LARVA,
POLLYWOG
Tadzhik's capital ....
STALINABAD
taels, 16 .... CATTY
taenia .... FILLET, HEADBAND,
TAPEWORM
taffarel .... TAFFRAIL
taffeta .... TABBY, FLORID,
DAINTY, GAUDY, SAMITE
taffrail .... TAFFEREL
taffy .... CANDY, TOFFEE
colloquial .... FLATTERY
tafia .... RUM
Taft, sculptor ...... LORADO
tag .... LABEL, A(I)GLET,
QUOTATION, TAIL END, LOCK,
FOLLOW, TALLY, APPEND
end .... REMNANT
game chaser .... IT
Tagalog (see Philippines) .....
MALAYAN, FILIPINO
Tagore's forte ...... POETRY
Tagus .... TEJO, TAJO

city on the ..... TOLEDO
Tahiti, capital of ... PAPEETE
   former name .. OTAHEITE
   god .... ORO
Tahitian .... POLYNESIAN
   canoe .... PAHI
   god ...... TAAROA, ORO
   peaks .... MOOREA
   people ..... POLYNESIAN
   seaport .... PAPEETE
Tai .... THAI
taiga .... FORESTS
Taihoku .... TAIPEH
tail .. BUSH, SCUT, FLEE, HIND,
    REAR END, CUE, BUNT,
    QUEUE, RETINUE, SHADOW,
    FOLLOW, TAG
   bushy .... BRUSH
   coin's .... VERSO
   colloquial ... DETECTIVE,
    SHADOWER
   combining form .... URO
   deer's/hare's .... SCUT
   docked .... BOB
   end .... TAG, REAR
   ender .... LAST
   feathers .... TRAIN
   having .... CAUDATE
   hood .... LIRIPIPE
   like .... CAUDAL
   pertaining to a .. CAUDAL
   plane .... STABILIZER
   rabbit's .... SCUT
   solid part .... DOCK
   turn .... FLEE, RETREAT
   word with ... BOB, HIGH,
    CAT
tailing ...... WASTE, REFUSE
tailless .. ACAUDAL, ANUROUS,
    ACAUDATE
   amphibian .. TOAD, FROG,
    BATRACHIA
tailor .... FIT, FASHION,
    BUSHELMAN, CLOTHIER,
    SNYDER, SARTOR
   concern of .. FIT, STYLE
   pattern of .. DELINEATOR
   pressing iron of .. GOOSE
   vent of .... SLIT
   work of ...... SARTORIAL
tailors, of .... SARTORIAL
tain .... (TIN)FOIL, TIN PLATE
taint ... INFECT, SPOIL, STAIN,
  INFECT(ION), SULLY, COLOR,
  DYE, CONTAMINATE, TINGE,
    POLLUTE

Taipeh .... TAIHOKU
Taisho emperor .. YOSHIHITO
Taiwan .... FORMOSA
   capital of ...... TAIPEH,
    TAIPEI
   city .... TAINAN
   deer .... SIKA
   government ....
    KUOMINTANG
   islands ...... PESCADORES
   legislature .... YUAN
   port .... KEELUNG
   premier .... YEN
   president ...... CHIANG
   tea .... OOLONG
Taj Mahal ..... MAUSOLEUM
   builder .... (SHAH) JAHAN
   site of .... AGRA
take .. OCCUPY, WIN, GRASP,
  CHARM, OBTAIN, ACQUIRE,
  ASSUME, EAT, DRINK, BUY,
  ABSORB, RENT, LEASE, USE,
  ADOPT, ACCEPT, RECEIVE,
    PRESUME
   a breather .... REST
   a liking to ...... COTTON
   amiss .. MISTAKE, RESENT
   as one's own ..... ADOPT
   back .. RETRACT, RECANT,
    RETURN
   by force ...... CAPTURE,
    GRAB, USURP, WREST,
    COMMANDEER, SEIZE,
    CATCH, SNATCH
   down .... NOTE, RECORD,
    WRITE
   edge off ... DULL, BLUNT,
    OBTUND
   effect .... INURE
   exception .... DEMUR
   forcibly .. WREST, REAVE
   in ...... ADMIT, CHEAT,
    RECEIVE
   into custody .. IMPOUND
   it on the lam ... ESCAPE,
    FLEE
   off ...... DEDUCT, FLEE,
    START, LEAVE, DOFF,
    REMOVE, DEPART
   offense .... RESENT
   on .... ASSUME, EMPLOY,
    OPPOSE, HIRE
   out .. EXTRACT, REMOVE,
    ABSTRACT, DELE(TE),
    EXPUNGE, ELIDE
   over .... ASSUME

part ...... PARTICIPATE
place ... OCCUR, HAPPEN,
    SUPERVENE
potshot at .... SNIPE
shape .... LOOM
slang .... CHEAT, TRICK,
    RECEIPT, PROFIT
the character of ......
    IMPERSONATE
time ..... DELAY, LINGER,
    LOAF
to ___ .... TASK
umbrage .... RESENT
unfair share .... HOG
up again .... RESUME
up dare .. CONTEND, VIE,
    FIGHT, DEFY
taken aback ...... STARTLED,
    SURPRISED, DUMBFOUNDED
taking .. WINNING, INFECTIOUS
takings ... PROFITS, RECEIPTS
talapoin ... GUENON, MONKEY,
    MONK
talaria, location of ... ANKLES
    of Hermes .... SANDALS,
    WINGS
talc .... STEATITE, POWDER,
    SOAPSTONE, AGALITE
talcum ...... POWDER, TALC
tale .... NARRATIVE, GOSSIP,
    FICTION, MARCHEN, REDE,
    FALSEHOOD, YARN, LEGEND
adventure ...... CONTE,
    GEST(E)
bearer ...... GOSSIP(ER),
    BUSYBODY,
    SCANDALMONGER
epic .... SAGA, ILIAD,
    AENEID
medieval .... LAI
of lamentation/woe .....
    JEREMIAD
of Two Cities heroine ...
    LUCIE
tall ... FISH STORY, YARN
talent .... GIFT, GENIUS,
    ABILITY, ENDOWMENT,
    APTITUDE, KNACK, SKILL,
    FACULTY, FLAIR
natural .. DOWER, DOWRY
talented ...... GIFTED, ABLE
tales .. WRIT, JUROR(S), VENIRE
talesman .... JUROR
Talien(wan) .. DAIREN, DALNY
taliera .... TARA

talion .... REVENGE,
    PUNISHMENT
taliped .... CLUBFOOTED
talipes .... CLUBFOOT
talipot .... PALM
talisman .... OBEAH, OBI,
    AMULET, CHARM, FETISH,
    GRIGRI
beetle .... SCARAB
talk .. CONVERSATION, UTTER,
    CONSULT, DISCUSS, YABBER,
    CONFER(ENCE), JAW, CHIN,
    SPEECH, BLAT, PALAVER,
    SPEAK, LECTURE
abusive .... JAW
back ..... SASS, RETORT,
    RIPOSTE, COMEBACK,
    REJOINDER
big .... BRAG, BOAST
boastful .... GAS, BRAG,
    BLUSTER, CRACK,
    GASCONADE
chatty ..... GOSSIP, GAB
childishly ...... DROLL,
    SLOBBER
down .... SILENCE
effusively .... GUSH
empty .. CHATTER, CANT,
    PATTER, BUNCOMBE,
    BULL, HUMBUG, GAS,
    HOGWASH, MOONSHINE,
    CLAPTRAP, FUDGE
evil ...... MALEDICTION,
    CURSE
excited ..... RANT, RAVE
flippant .. PERSIFLAGE
foolish .. TATTLE, BABBLE,
    BLAB(BER), DROOL,
    BLATHER, GAB, DRIVEL,
    TWADDLE, PRATTLE,
    BULL, CHATTER,
    TWATTLE, FAPDOODLE,
    MOONSHINE, PRATE,
    POPPYCOCK
fresh .... LIP
friendly ..... COSE, COZE
from pulpit .... SERMON,
    HOMILY
glib .. PALAVER, PATTER
hearsay .. GOSSIP, RUMOR
impudent ..... SASS, LIP
incoherent(ly) ....
    GIBBER(ISH), JABBER,
    MAUNDER
informal .... (CHIT)CHAT,
    CAUSERIE

insincere .... BUNCOMBE
insincerely ...... PALTER
light .... CHAFF, BANTER,
     RAILLERY, PERSIFLAGE
made for effect ....
     BUNCOMBE
meaningless .... CANT,
     MALARK(E)Y, PATTER,
     PIFFLE
melodramatic ... HEROICS
moral .. SERMON, HOMILY
noisily .... YAUP, YAWP,
     YAP
noisy .. YAP, RANT, BLAT,
     JANGLE
nonsensical ..... PIFFLE,
     JABBER
offensive .... JAW
out of .... PERSUADE,
     DISSUADE
over .... DISCUSS
peevishly .... CARP
persistently on something
     HARP
pert .... LIP
pointless .... TWADDLE,
     SLIPSLOP
pompous ...... FUSTIAN,
     BOMBAST
quiet(ly) ...... WHISPER,
     MURMUR
rapid .. CHATTER, PATTER
sales ..... SPIEL, PATTER
senseless ... BALDERDASH
sentimental ...... SLUSH
silly ..... CACKLE, BULL,
     DROOL, FLUMMERY
small ... PATTER, GOSSIP
solemn .... SERMON,
     HOMILY
stupid .... DROOL
to oneself .. SOLILOQUIZE
vernacular .... CANT,
     JARGON, LINGO
while crying .. BLUBBER
with another .. CONVERSE,
     CONVERSATION,
     DIALOGUE
talkative .... GARRULOUS,
     LOQUACIOUS, VOLUBLE,
     MOUTHY, GASSY, GABBY
bird .. MAGPIE, (BLUE)JAY
person .... JAY, MAGPIE,
     CHATTERBOX
talked about .... NOTORIOUS
talker, incessant .... GASBAG,

     CHATTERBOX, MAGPIE
talking dummy ...... SNERD
fond of .... LOQUACIOUS,
     GARRULOUS
picture .... TALKIE
to ... SCOLDING, REBUKE
tall .... HIGH, EXAGGERATED,
     HUGE, HIGHFLOWN, LOFTY,
     TAUNT
and lean .. LANKY, LATHY
chest .... HIGHBOY
tale .... YARN
tailboy .... CHEST
Tallchief, ballerina ... MARIA
tallest animal .... GIRAFFE
tallier .. SCORER, SCOREKEEPER
Tallinn .... REVEL, REVAL
tallith .... SHAWL, SCARF
tallow .... FAT, SUET, STEARIN
product .. CANDLE, SOAP
tree .... CERA, ROKA
tally ...... SCORE, ACCOUNT,
     LABEL, TAG, AGREE, JIBE,
     CORRESPOND, NOTCH, TAB,
     SQUARE, MATCH, REGISTER,
     CHALK UP
tallyho .... COACH, CRY
crier .... HUNTER
Talmud, part of .... GEMARA,
     MISHNA(H), HALAKAH,
     HALACHA, HAGGADA(H)
Talmudic anecdote/parable ..
     HAGGADA(H)
talon .. OGEE, POUNCE, CLAW,
     NAIL, STOCK, FANG, ZIPPER,
     HALLUX
Talos ... WATCHMAN, MISSILE
killer of ..... DAEDALUS
make of .... BRASS
talus .... SCREE, ANKLE(BONE),
     ASTRAGALUS, SLOPE,
     HUCKLEBONE
tam-o'-shanter .... CAP
tam .... GONG
tamandu(a) ...... ANTEATER
tamarack ...... LARCH, TREE
tamarau .. BUFFALO, CARABAO
tamarin .... MARMOSET
tamarind, Philippine ......
     SAMPALOC
tamarisk salt tree ... ATLE(E)
tambour .... DRUM, TABORET,
     EMBROIDERY
tambourine .... DRUM, DAIRA,
     TABOR, TIMBREL, RIKK,
     DAIRE, TAAR

tame .. BREAK, DOMESTICATE, DOCILE, GENTLE, SERVILE, DULL, SUBDUE, BUST

tameness ...... MANSUETUDE, GENTLENESS, DOCILITY

tamer, wild horse .. COWBOY, BRONC(H)OBUSTER

Tamerlane ...... TIMURLENK
    author of book .... POE

Tamil .... DRAVIDIAN

Tamiroff, actor .... AKIM

Tammany Society official .... SACHEM

tamp .. PACK, POUND, THUMP

tamper .... PLOT, BRIBE, CHANGE, TINKER, MEDDLE, POUNDER, ALTER, CORRUPT

Tampico man .... SENOR

tampion ..... STOPPER, PLUG

tampon .... PLUG

tan .... BARK, TANNIN, FLOG, WHIP, BEIGE, DUN, TAW, ROAN, TAWNY, (EM)BROWN, SUNBURN, ECRU, BUFF
    believe it or not! .... LUGGAGE

tanager .. SONGBIRD, REDBIRD

tanbark .... NAPA, ROSS

tandem .. BICYCLE, CARRIAGE

tang ...... TASTE, GUST, NIP, ODOR, TOUCH, TRACE, FLAVOR

Tanganyika merged with
    Zanzibar .. TANZANIA
    mountain .. KILIMANJARO
    town .... UJIJI

tangent .... TOUCHING, ADJACENT

tangerine.......... ORANGE, MANDARIN
    crossed with grapefruit/ pomelo .... TANGELO

tangible .. TACTILE, DEFINITE, PERCEPTIBLE, PALPABLE

tangle .. TRAP, SNARL, SLEAVE, KNOT, MUDDLE, WEAVE, INTERTWINE, SEAWEED, EMBROIL, MIX-UP

tangled mass .... SHAG, MAT, RAVEL

Tanis .... ZOAN

tank ...... POOL, STEW, VAT, POND, CISTERN
    destroyer .... BAZOOKA, HALF-TRACK
    farming ... HYDROPONICS
    fish .... AQUARIUM
    gunner's place .. TURRET
    hot water .... BOILER
    military .... MARK, SHERMAN
    oil .... BUNKER
    rainwater ...... CISTERN

tankard .. CUP, MUG, POTTLE, STOUP

tanker .... OILER, BUNKER

tanned hide .. LEATHER, CROP

tanning bark .... ALDER, KOA
    material ..... SUMAC(H), CATECHU, CATECHIN, CASHOO, KINO, FURAN, QUEBRACHO, GAMBIER
    powdered leaves .... SUMAC(H)

tantalize .. TITILLATE, TEASE, BEWITCH

Tantalus .... STAND
    daughter of ...... NIOBE
    father of .... ZEUS
    punishment of .. THIRST, HUNGER
    son of .... PELOPS

tantamount ..... EQUIVALENT

tantara .. FANFARE, FLOURISH, BLAST

tantivy .. SWIFT, FAST, GALLOP, HEADLONG

tantrum ..... OUTBURST, FIT, RAVE, CONNIPTION, RAGE, HUFF

Tanzania capital .... DAR ES SALAAM
    city/seaport .. ZANZIBAR
    island .... PEMBA
    part of .... TANGANYIKA, ZANZIBAR
    president ...... NYERERE

tap ...... PLUG, CORK, BAR, BROACH, SPILE, RAP, KNOCK, FAUCET, STOPPER, LIQUOR, DRAW, TIT, COCK, SPIGOT, DECANT, DRAFT, FLIP
    chin .... CHUCK
    dancer .. HOOFER, ASTAIRE

tapa cloth source .. MULBERRY
    wearer .... POLYNESIAN

tape ..... BAND, STRIP, DEMO
    braided .... INKLE

taper .. CANDLE, WANE, WICK, LIGHT, DECREASE, LESSEN

tapered ..... TERETE, CONOID

tapering object .... CONE,

PYRAMID, SPIRE, VOLCANO, SHIM
to a point .... SUBULATE
tapestry .... DOSSEL, DOSSAL, GOBELIN, ARRAS, TAPIS, DOSSER
tapeworm .. CESTODE, CESTOID, T(A)ENIA
drug .... TENIACIDE, TENIAFUGE
head of .... SCOLEX
infestation .. T(A)ENIASIS
larva .... COENURUS, CYSTICERCUS, MEASLES
sucker .... OSCULUM
taphouse ... INN, BAR(ROOM), TAVERN
tapioca source .... CAS(S)AVA, MANIOC, MANIHOT
tapir .... UNGULATE, DANTA
animal resembling .. HOG
pride of a .... SNOUT
tapis .... TAPESTRY
tapper .... TELEGRAPHER
tappet .... CAM
tapping sound .. TICK, DRUM
tappings .... SAP
taproom ...... BAR, SALOON
taps instrument ...... BUGLE, DRUM
series of .... PATTER
tapster .. BARMAID, BARTENDER
Tapuyan .... INDIAN, GES
tar .... SAILOR, BREA, PITCH, MALTHA, GOB, MARINER, SALT, ALCHITRAN
tarantas(s) .... CARRIAGE
tarantula .... SPIDER
tarboosh .... CAP, FEZ
tardy .. BELATED, LATE, SLOW, OVERDUE, DELAYED
tare ..... DEDUCTION, VETCH, WEED
allowance additional to .. TRET
Tarentum .... TARANTO
targe ...... BUCKLER, SHIELD
target .... AIM, MARK, BUTT, CLOUT, OBJECTIVE, GOAL
center of .... BLANK, EYE
circle .... INNER
easy ...... SITTING DUCK
finder .... RADAR, SONAR
get on .... ZERO
knight's ...... QUINTAIN
mound behind .... BUTT

of blame .... SCAPEGOAT
practice place ... RANGE
range .... BUTTS
shooting gallery .. DUCK
shooting post .... MANT(E)LET
towed .... DROGUE
white cloth ...... CLOUT
Tarheel .... CAROLINIAN
tariff .... TAX, LIST, DUTY
Tarkington, novelist .. BOOTH
tarlatan .... MUSLIN
tarn .... LAKE, LOCH
location ..... MOUNTAIN
tarnation .... DAMNED, DAMNATION
tarnish .... DULL, SULLY, BESMIRCH, STAIN, BLEMISH, SOIL
taro dish .... POI
fermented in pit .... MOD
root ..... ED(D)O, GABI, KALO
sprouts .... DASHEEN
tarot .... CARD
tarpaulin .... CANVAS
tarpon .. MILKFISH, GAMEFISH, SABALO, SILVERFISH
Tarquin's avenger ... PORSENA
tarradiddle .... FIB
tarry .. LOITER, LINGER, WAIT, STAY, SOJOURN, BIDE
tarsal bone .... CALCANEUS
tarsus .... ANKLE, HOCK
tart ..... FLAN, SOUR, SHARP, HUSSY, KEEN, ACID(ULOUS), CUTTING, (FRUIT)PIE, PASTRY, WANTON, TRAMP
tartan .... PLAID, SHIP, HIGHLANDER
trousers .... TREWS
Tartar .... TATAR, TURK
emetic ...... MORDANT, EXPECTORANT
wine cask .... ARGAL, ARGOL
Tartarus .... HADES, HELL
Tartuf(f)e ...... HYPOCRITE, COMEDY
author .... MOLIERE
Tarzan's mate ...... JANE
task ...... JOB, STINT, ONUS, ASSIGNMENT, DUTY
force .... COMMANDO
menial ...... DRUDGERY
routine .... CHORE

take to ... SCOLD, REBUKE
tedious .... GRIND
taskmaster .... OVERSEER
SLAVE DRIVER, LEGREE
Tasman, Dutch navigator ....
ABEL
Tasmanian capital ... HOBART
devil .... DASYURE
discoverer ...... TASMAN
phalanger .... TAPOA
pine .... HUON
river .... DERWENT
tiger/wolf ... THYLACINE
tass .... GOBLET, CUP, DRAFT
tassel ...... TUFT, CORNSILK,
TERCEL, ZIZITH
taste ... PALATE, EXPERIENCE,
FLAVOR, BENT, SAPO(U)R,
GUSTO, TANG, DEGUST,
SAVOR, LIKING, PREFERENCE,
PENCHANT
daintily .... SIP
distinctive .... TANG,
SMACK, FLAVOR
for something ... TOOTH
having ...... SAPOROUS
kind of ... SOUR, SWEET,
BITTER, SALTY
offensive .... RANK
try the .... SAMPLE
tasteful ..... REFINED, SAPID,
TASTY, DISCRIMINATING,
ELEGANT
luxury ...... ELEGANCE
tasteless ...... FLAT, INSIPID,
STALE, VAPID
taster .... SAMPLER, SIPPER
STATE, VAPID
taster ...... SAMPLER, SIPPER
tasty .... LUSCIOUS, SAVORY,
PALATABLE, SAPID,
TOOTHSOME, FLAVORFUL,
DELICIOUS
colloquial ...... YUMMY
Tatar .. TARTAR, MONGOLIAN,
TURK
capital .... KAZAN
drink .... KUMISS,
KOUMIS(S)
ruler .... CHAM
tater .... POTATO
tatouay .... ARMADILLO
tatter ... RAG, SCRAP, SHRED,
DAG, TAG
tattered .... DUDDY, DUDDIE,
RAGGED

tatterdemalion .. RAGAMUFFIN
tattersall .... CHECKERED
tatters .... RAGS, RIBBONS
tuttle ...... CHATTER, GOSSIP,
BLAB, PEACH
tattler .... SANDPIPER, GOSSIP
tattoo .. DOT, MARK, SIGNAL,
SUMMON, PINK
tau .... TEE, TAV
cross ...... ANKH, CRUX
taunt ... TALL, MOCK, SCOFF,
RIDICULE, NEEDLE, GIBE,
TWIT, JEER, REPROACH, JEST,
JAPE
taupe .... GRAY
taurine animal .... BULL
Taurus .... BULL,
CONSTELLATION
cluster .... HYAD(E)S
taut ..... FIRM, SNUG, TENSE,
TIDY, TIGHT, TRIM, EDGY,
STIFF, NERVOUS
tautog .... BLACKFISH, CHUB,
MOLL
tautology .... PLEONASM,
REDUNDANCE
tav .... TEE, TAU
tavern .... SALOON, INN, PUB,
HOSTEL, BISTRO, KHAN,
TAPROOM, ALEHOUSE,
ROADHOUSE, ORDINARY,
POTHOUSE
character .. BARFLY, SOT,
TOPER
server .... POTBOY,
BARMAID
taw .... MIB, AGATE, MARBLE,
ALLEY
tawdry ..... SLEAZY, GAUDY,
SHOWY, CHEAP, RAFFISH,
GINGERBREAD
tawny .. TAN, DUSKY, SWART,
RUBIATE
tax .... TITHE, LEVY, IMPOST,
CESS, SCOT, SCAT(T), ASSESS,
EXCISE, SESS
church .... TITHE
collector ...... OCTROI,
CATCHPOLL, CATCHPOLE
commodity ..... OCTROI,
DUTY, TARIFF, EXCISE
evader's nemesis .. TMAN
export/import ... TARIFF
feudal .... TALLAGE
man .... PUBLICAN
municipal .... OCTROI

official .... ASSESSOR
on ship ...... TONNAGE
privilege .... TOLL
protection ..... TRIBUTE
schedule .... TARIFF
substitute ...... SCUTAGE
taxable .... RAT(E)ABLE
taxi .... CAB, HACK
driver .. HACK, CABMAN,
CABETTE
2-wheeled .... HANSOM
taxicab .... HACK
parking space .... STAND
taxman .... PUBLICAN
taximeter for one ....
ODOGRAPH, ODOMETER
taxonomy subject ....
CLASSIFICATION, SYSTEMATICS
Taygeta ...... PLEIAD, STAR
Taylor, actress .... LIZ
composer, critic .. DEEMS
poet, writer .... BAYARD
U.S. president ....
ZACHARY
tazza ...... CUP, VASE, BOWL
Tchaikovsky opus ....
PATHETIQUE
Te Deum .... HYMN
hee .... TITTER, SNICKER,
GIGGLE
tea ...... RECEPTION, PEKOE,
PARTY, PARAGUAY, HOLLY,
MATE, CHA(A), LAPSANG,
TSIA, TCHA, LEDUM, YERBA,
PTISAN, OSWEGO, CAMBRIC
add liquor to ...... LACE
alkaloid .... CAFFEIN(E)
beverage like ....
CAMOMILE, BEEF
bitter principle .. THEINE
black .... PEKOE, BOHEA,
CONGO(U), OOLONG,
OOPAK, SOUCHONG
bowl .... CHAWAN
box ... CANISTER, CADDY
brand .. LIPTON, TETLEY,
SALADA
caffeine .... THEINE
cake .... SCONE
container .... CADDY
decoction .... TISANE
drink .... CAMBRIC
green .... HYSON
plant .... THEA
pot ...... URN, SAMOVAR,
KETTLE

serve .... POUR
substitute ...... YAUPON
table .... TEAPOY
waterboiler for .... POT,
URN, KETTLE, SAMOVAR
teaberry .... WINTERGREEN
teacake .... SCONE
teach ..... TRAIN, INSTRUCT,
EDUCATE, DRILL, COACH,
SCHOOL, TUTOR, DRILL,
EDIFY
Edward ... BLACKBEARD,
PRIVATEER, PIRATE
teacher .. TUTOR, PROFESSOR,
MENTOR, INSTRUCTOR,
RABBI, MULLA(H), PUNDIT,
PEDAGOG(UE), DON, GURU,
PRECEPTOR
bird .... WARBLER, VIREO
gift to .... APPLE
movie ...... (MR.) CHIPS
narrow-minded .. PEDANT
of music, great ....
MAESTRO
of the deaf ..... ORALIST
pointer of ...... FESCUE
unattached ..... DOCENT
teachers' group .... NEA
teaching .. TUITION, TUTELAGE,
INSTRUCTION, PEDAGOGY
science of ... DIDACTICS,
PEDAGOGY
teachings .... PRECEPT,
DOCTRINE
teak ..... TREE, WOOD, TEGA
teakettle spout ...... NOZZLE
teal .... DUCK, BLUE
team (see baseball, football) ...
JOIN, PAIR
athletic .... SQUAD
baseball .... NINE
basketball .. FIVE, QUINTET
cricket .... ELEVEN
football .... ELEVEN
of two animals ... SPAN,
YOKE
rowing .... CREW
second placer ....
RUNNER-UP
working ... CREW, GANG
teamster .... DRIVER, CARTER,
CARRIER
teapot .... SAMOVAR, KETTLE
cover .... COS(E)Y
tear .. REND, RIP, LACERATE,

SPLIT, DISRUPT, RIVE, RENT,
TATTER, JAG, LANCINATE
down .... WRECK,
DEMOLISH, DISMANTLE,
RAZE
gas ...... LAC(H)RIMATOR
into ...... ATTACK, RIP
jerker .... SAD,
SENTIMENTAL
limb from limb ....
DISMEMBER
slang .. SPREE, CAROUSAL
teardrop diamond cut ......
BRIOLETTE
tearful .... SAD, CRYING,
WEEPING, LAC(H)RYMOSE
mother .... NIOBE
tearing apart .... DIVULSION
for .... LANIARY
tears, of .... LACHRIMAL,
LACHRYMAL
teary lady .... NIOBE
Teasdale, poetess ..... SARA
tease ...... TANTALIZE, COMB,
CARD, ANNOY, MOCK, RIDE,
NEEDLE, HECTOR, RIB,
HARASS, IMPORTUNE, VEX,
TWIT, KID
teasel .... FLOWER, BURR,
BONESET, HERB
teaser ..... PUZZLE(R), POSER
teasing, good-natured .. CHAFF
teat .. NIPPLE, TIT, MAMMILLA,
PAP, DUG
Tebaldi, Met star ... RENATA
technetium .... MASARIUM
technical .... SPECIALIZED
technician .... EXPERT
technique ..... METHOD, ART,
PROCEDURE
techy .... PEEVISH, IRRITABLE,
SENSITIVE, TOUCHY
ted .... SPREAD, SCATTER
teddy .... BEAR
tedious ... BORING, TIRESOME,
MONOTONOUS, HUMDRUM,
IRKSOME, DREARY,
WEARISOME
tedium .... BOREDOM, ENNUI,
MONOTONY
tee .... TAU, MOUND
hee .... TITTER, SNICKER,
GIGGLE
shaped thing .... ANKH,
CRUX
to green .... HOLE

teem ...... ABOUND, SWARM,
EMPTY, POUR
teenager ...... BOBBY SOXER,
YOUTH
favorite record of ....
TOP TEN
teeny .... TINY, WEE
teepee .... LODGE, WIGWAM,
WICKIUP
teeter ...... SEESAW, WAVER,
WOBBLE, VACILLATE, SWAY
teeth (see tooth) .... INCISORS,
MOLARS, CUSPIDS, GRINDERS
arrangement .. DENTITION
artificial.... DENTURE,
PLATE
cleaning substance ......
DENTIFRICE
click of .... CHATTER
coating .... ENAMEL
colloquial .... GRINDERS
combining form ....
DENT(I), ODONT(O)
decay .... CARIES
deposit .... TARTAR
doctor .... DENTIST
extraction .. EXODONTIA
hard part of .. DENTIN(E),
IVORY
having .... DENTATE,
TOOTHED
having large ....
MACRODONT
having small ....
MICRODONT
long pointed ... TUSHES,
TUSKS, FANGS
of .... DENTAL
science dealing with ....
DENTISTRY,
ODONTOLOGY
set of .... DENTURE
shaped .... DENTIFORM,
DENTOID
sharp .... FANGS
slang .... IVORIES
small .... DENTICLES
sockets .... ALVEOLI
sound .. GNASH, CHATTER
tearing .... LANIARY
without ..... EDENTATE
teething process .. DENTITION
toy .... CORAL
teethridge .... ALVEOLUS
teetotaler .... NON-DRINKER,
ABSTAINER, DRY, NAZARITE

teetotalism ..... TEMPERANCE, ABSTINENCE
teetotum .... TOP
tegmen .... COVERING, TEGUMENT
Tegucigalpa is capital of ..... HONDURAS
tegula .... ALULA, TILE
tegular .... TILE-LIKE
tegument ..... TEGMEN, SKIN, ARIL
Tehuelche ...... PATAGONIAN
teil .... LINDEN
Tejo .... TAGUS
Tel Aviv greeting ... SHALOM
tela .. MEMBRANE, TISSUE, WEB
telar .... WEBLIKE
telamon .. ATLANTES, BEARER
    son of .... AJAX
telecast .... TELEVISE
telegram ..... MESSAGE, WIRE
    slower ...... DAYLETTER
telegraph .... CABLE
    code .... MORSE
    jungle .... TOM-TOM
    kind of ...... GRAPEVINE
    lever .... KEY, TAPPER
    part .... KEY, TAPPER
    signal .... DOT, DASH
    wire support .... PYLON
telegraphic device for quotations
        TICKER
Telemachus' parent ....
    PENELOPE, ODYSSEUS/ULYSSES
telemeter ... RANGE FINDER
teleost fish .... EEL
telephone ... CALL, RING(UP)
    diaphragm .. TYMPANUM
    exchange ..... CENTRAL, SWITCHBOARD
    inventor .... BELL
    main line ...... TRUNK
    operator .... CENTRAL
    wire .... LINE
telescope .... FIELD GLASS, BINOCLE, BINOCULAR, TUBE, SPYGLASS
    attached to another ..... FINDER
    measuring device ..... MICROMETER
    opening ...... APERTURE
telescopic .... FARSEEING
telestic(h) .. ACROSTIC, POEM
television (see TV) ... VIDEO, TELLY

ad .... COMMERCIAL
"magic" .... COLOR
radar air navigation .... TELERAN
tube .... ICONOSCOPE
tell ...... RELATE, RECOUNT, NARRATE, REPORT, REVEAL, RECITE, INFORM, ORDER
    it to ____ ..... SWEENEY
    it to the ____ .. MARINES, JUDGE
    off ...... REBUKE, SCOLD
    on .... INFORM, TIRE, PEACH, SQUEAL
    privately ...... WHISPER
    slang .... RAT
teller ...... NARRATOR, CLERK, CASHIER
    place of .... CAGE
    window of ..... WICKET
telling .. STRIKING, FORCEFUL, COGENT, EFFECTIVE
telltale .. TATTLER, INDICATOR
tellurian .... EARTHMAN, EARTHLY, TERRESTIAL
telluride .... HESSITE
Tellus' domain .... EARTH
telson ...... SOMITE, SEGMENT
Telugu .... DRAVIDIAN
temblor ...... (EARTH)QUAKE, TREMOR
temerarious .. RASH, RECKLESS
temerity .. AUDACITY, NERVE, GALL, EFFRONTERY, CHEEK, RASHNESS, BOLDNESS
temper .... MODERATE, MOOD, DISPOSITION, COMPOSURE, RAGE, DANDER, (AN)NEAL, PET, SPIRIT, TANTRUM, QUALITY, CHARACTER, TONE
    bad .... SPLEEN
    kind of .... IRISH
    of ugly .... ORNERY
tempera painting ...... SECCO
temperament .... DISPOSITION, NATURE, MOOD
    condition of .. CHOLERIC, SANGUINE, BILIOUS, PHLEGMATIC, MELANCHOLIC
temperamental .. EXCITABLE, MOODY, TESTY
temperance ..... MODERATION, ABSTINENCE, SOBRIETY
temperate .. MODERATE, MILD, ABSTEMIOUS, SOBER

temperature regulator .... THERMOSTAT, CRYOSTAT
tempest ..... STORM, TUMULT
tempestuous .... VIOLENT, TURBULENT, STORMY
Templar .. CRUSADER, KNIGHT
temple ..... CHURCH, CELLA, NAOS, FANE, SANCTUARY, PAGODA, RATH(A), MOSQUE, BASILICA, TABERNACLE, JOSS HOUSE
   Aztec .... TEOPAN
   chamber .... NAOS, CELLA
   Chinese .... PAGODA
   for all gods .. PANTHEON
   gateway .... TORII
   girl .... BAYADERE, BAYADEER
   Jupiter's ...... CAPITOL
   innermost parts .... PENETRALIA
   shrine .... ADYTUM
tempo .... PACE, SPEED, RATE, RHYTHM, TIME, BEAT, TAKT
temporal .. CIVIL, TRANSITORY, TRANSIENT, WORLDLY, SECULAR, MUNDANE
temporary .. INTERIM, ACTING, PROVISIONAL
   amnesia .... FUGUE
temporize ...... STALL, HEDGE
tempt .... LURE, ENTICE, INDUCE, PROVOKE, SEDUCE
tempter .... DEVIL, SATAN
tempting .... SEDUCTIVE, ATTRACTIVE
temptress .. EVE, SIREN, CIRCE, LORELEI, ENCHANTRESS, DELILAH
ten .... 10, DECAD(E)
   ares .... DECARE
   cents .... DIME
   combining form .... DEC(A), DEKA
   Commandments .... DECALOG(UE)
   cubic meters .. DECASTERE
   decibels .... BEL
   dollar gold piece .. EAGLE
   gallon hat .... SOMBRERO
   group of .... DECADE
   legged crustacean .... LOBSTER, PRAWN, MACRURAN, SHRIMP
   per center .... AGENT
   pfennig coin .. GROSCHEN

rins .... SEN
   sided ...... DECAGONAL
   square meters .. DECIARE
   thousand .... MYRIAD
   times as large .. DECUPLE
   year period ... DECADE, DECENNIAL, DECENNIUM, DECEN(N)ARY
tenace .... QUEENLACE, KING-JACK
tenacious .... RETENTIVE, PERSISTENT, STUBBORN, CLINGY
   animal .... BULLDOG
   follower .. TAIL, SHADOW
tenancy .... OCCUPANCY
tenant .. VILLEIN, OCCUPANT, INHABITANT, VASSAL, LESSEE, RENTER, INMATE, RESIDENT
tench .... CARP
tend ..... MINISTER, OPERATE, CARE, MIND, MANAGE, SERVE, INCLINE, BE APT
tendency .. BIAS, PROPENSITY, BENT, TREND, TENOR, DRIFT, INCLINATION, DISPOSITION
tender ...... DELICATE, SOFT, FRAGILE, FEEBLE, FRAIL, YOUNG, BID, PRESENT, BOAT, SHIP, OFFER, SORE, PROFFER, LIGHT, GENTLE, SENSITIVE
   feeling ...... SENTIMENT
   ship's .... PINNACE, COCKBOAT
   yacht .... DINGHY
tenderfoot .... NEWCOMER, NOVICE, BOY SCOUT
tenderloin .... STEAK
tenderness of mood .... LANGUOR
tending .... APT
tendon ...... SINEW, MUSCLE, TISSUE, THEW, LEADER, HAMSTRING
   division of ... TENOTOMY
   nodule .... SESAMOID
tendrac .... TENREC
tendril .. STIPULE, BINE, CURL
   having ..... CAPREOLATE
tenebrous ..... SAD, GLOOMY
tenement ..... HOUSE, ADOBE, APARTMENT, FLAT
   district/house .. ROOKERY
Tenerife mountain .... TEYDE
tenet ... PRINCIPLE, OPINION,

DOCTRINE, MAXIM, DOGMA, CREED, ISM

tenfold .... DECUPLE, DENARY

Tennessee capital .. NASHVILLE

city ⌐ MEMPHIS, JACKSON, CHATTANOOGA, KNOXVILLE

federal agency in ... TVA

Indian ...... CHICKASAW

mountain inhabitant .... MELUNGEON

state flower .... IRIS

tennis .... RACKETS

champ ...... ROSEWALL, PERRY, BUDGE, BETZ, MARBLE, BUENO, KRAMER, SANTANA, KING, ASHE, GONZALES, WILLS, HOAD, LAVER, GIMENO, STOLLE, TRABERT, GIBSON, COURT, SMITH, KODES, LACOSTE, RIGGS, TILDEN

competition .... TOURNAMENT

equipment ...... RACKET, PADDLE, NET, BAT, RACQUET

first ball .... SERVICE

ground .... COURT

handicap .... BISQUE

modified .... HANDBALL, SQUASH

racket string .... CATGUT

scoring system .... VASS

stroke .... LOB, CUT, VOLLEY, SMASH, SERVICE, DRIVE, BAT, SLICE, CHOP

table .... PINGPONG

term .... DEUCE, SET, MATCH, ADVANTAGE, SERVICE, LINER, SINGLES, DOUBLES, BYE, LOVE SET, LET, ACE FAULT, VANTAGE

uncounted service ... LET

world championship cup DAVIS

Tennyson heroine ..... ISOLT, ENID, ELAINE

heroine's home .... ASTOLAT

tenon, companion of .... MORTISE

tenor ⌐⌐⌐ DRIFT, TENDENCY, MEANING, GIST

great .... CARUSO, MELCHIOR

kind of ...... FALSETTO

violin ...... ALTO, VIOLA

tenpins .... BOWLING, BOWLS

tenrec .... TENDRAC

habitat ... MADAGASCAR

tense .. TIGHT, STRAINED, FLEX, TAUT, DRAWN, RIGID, STIFF, ELECTRIC

oppostie of .. LAX, SLACK, LOOSE

tensile ⌐⌐ DUCTILE, PLASTIC, FLEXIBLE

tensimeter ...... MANOMETER

tension ...... STRAIN, STRESS

tent .. TABERNACLE, SHELTER, MARQUEE, YURT, ENCAMP

circus .... BIGTOP

dweller .. INDIAN, ARAB, BEDOUIN, SCENITE, KEDAR, NOMAD

flap .... FLY

Indian .... LODGE, TE(E)PEE, WIGWAM

large .... PAVILION

maker .... OMAR

show .. CIRCUS, MARQUEE

show man ...... CARNIE

surgical .. PLUG, DOSSIL

tentacle ...⌐⌐ FEELER, PALP, ANTENNA

feature .... SUCKER

tentacles, creature with ...... OCTOPUS, CEPHALOPOD, CUTTLE(FISH), SQUID

tentative .... PROVISIONAL

tenterhook .... NAIL

tenterhooks, on ..... ANXIOUS, TENSE

tenth muse ...⌐⌐... SAPPHO

part .... TITHE

wave .... DECUMAN

tenths, pertaining to .... DECIMAL

tentmaker .. OMAR (KHAYYAM)

tenuity .. THINNESS, FINENESS, FAINTNESS, RARITY

tenuous ..... SLIGHT, FLIMSY, THIN, SLENDER, RARE

tenure ...... HOLDING, TERM

land .... SOCAGE

of office .... INCUMBENCY

teocalli .... TEMPLE

teosinte .... GRASS
tepee .. TENT, WIGWAM, LODGE
tepid .... (LUKE)WARM
tequilla ..... MESCAL, AGAVE,
　　　　　　　PULQUE, LIQUOR
　　drinker ...... MEXICAN(O)
teraphim .... IDOLS
teratism ...... FETUS, FREAK,
　　　　　　　MONSTROSITY
teratoid .... MONSTER,
　　　　　　　MONSTROUS
tercel ...... HAWK, PEREGRINE
tercet .... TRIPLET
terebinth .. SUMAC, TEIL, TREE,
　　　　　　　LINDEN
　　yield ...... TURPENTINE
teredo .. SHIPWORM, MOLLUSK,
　　　　　　　BORER
tergal .... BACK, DORSAL
tergiversate ..... APOSTATIZE,
　　　HEDGE, LIE, EQUIVOCATE
tergiversation .... APOSTASY,
　　　　　　　EVASION
tergum .... BACK
term .. DURATION, EXPRESSION,
　　　　　　　PERIOD, NAME
　　of endearment ....
　　　HON(EY), DEARIE, TOOTS
　　of office .... TENURE
　　plural ...... CONDITIONS,
　　　　　　　STIPULATIONS
　　school .... SEMESTER
termagant .. SHREW, HELLCAT,
　　　　　　　VIXEN
termer .... PRISONER
terminal .... FINAL, STATION,
　　LAST, DEPOT, EXTREMITY,
　　　　　　　END
　　negative ..... CATHODE
　　positive ...... ANODE
terminate .. CONCLUDE, STOP,
　　CEASE, END, CLOSE
termination .... FINISH, END,
　　CONCLUSION, EXPIRY,
　　　　　　　EXPIRATION
　　in grammar .. DESINENCE
　　of right .... LAPSE
terminology ..... WORDING
termite .... ANAY, WHITE ANT
terms .... CONDITIONS,
　　　　　　　STIPULATIONS
　　come to .... AGREE
　　make .... TREAT,
　　　　　　　NEGOTIATE
tern ...... (SEA)BIRD, NODDY,
　　(LOTTERY)PRIZE, MEDRICK

ternary ...... THIRD, TRIAD,
　　THREEFOLD, TRIPLE
terpene alcohol ... LINALOOL
　　derivative .... CAMPHOR
　　isomeric ..... LIMONENE
Terpsichore .... MUSE
　　concern of ...... DANCE,
　　　　　　　DANCING
terra .... EARTH
　　alba .. KAOLIN, GYPSUM,
　　　　　　　MAGNESIA
　　cotta .... CLAY
　　firma .... EARTH
terrace .. GALLERY, PLATEAU,
　　PORTICO, PATIO, BALCONY,
　　　　　　　BERM(E)
　　staircase ...... PERRON
terrain .... GROUND
terramycin ...... ANTIBIOTIC
terrapin ...... TURTLE, EMYD,
　　　　　　　CHELONIAN
terrene ..... EARTH(Y), LAND,
　　MUNDANE, WORLDLY
terrestrial .... EARTHLY,
　　WORLDLY, MUNDANE, GEAL
terret .... RING
terrible .... DIRE, SEVERE,
　　DREADFUL, FEARFUL, AWFUL,
　　　　　　　INTENSE
terribly: colloq. ..... VERY,
　　　　　　　EXTREMELY
terrier ...... AIREDALE, DOG,
　　SCHNAUZER, WIREHAIR
　　kind of ..... FOX, BULL,
　　BOSTON, IRISH, SKYE,
　　SCOTCH, SEALYHAM
terrific: colloq. ... EXCELLENT,
　　　　　　　GREAT
terrify .... APPAL(L), DAUNT,
　　ALARM, FRIGHTEN, DISMAY
terrifying .... GRIS(T)LY,
　　DREADFUL, HORRID
terrigenous ..... EARTHBORN
terrine .... STEW
territorial division ...... AMT
territory .. TERRENE, DOMAIN,
　　REGION, DISTRICT
　　disputed ..... KASHMIR,
　　CHENPAO, DAMANSKY,
　　　　　　　SABAH
terror .. FEAR, PANIC, DREAD
　　colloquial .... PEST,
　　　　　　　NUISANCE
terrorist ..... OGRE, ALARMIST,
　　GOON, NIGHTRIDER,
　　　　　　　VIGILANTE

terrorize ... FRIGHTEN, SCARE
terse .... CONCISE, SUCCINCT, CRISP, PITHY, LACONIC
tertiary .... THIRD
tessellate .... INLAY, TILE, MOSAIC, CHECKER
tessellation .... MOSAIC
tessera .... TILE
test .... TRIAL, TRY(OUT), WORKOUT, CHECK, PROVE, EXAMINE
   colloquial .... EXAM, MIDTERM
   clam/crab's ...... SHELL
   flight .... TRIAL RUN
   operation ... SHAKEDOWN
   ore .... ASSAY
   paper .... LITMUS
   print .... PROOF
   quality of .... SAMPLE
   severe .... ORDEAL, CRUCIBLE
   vessel ...... CRUCIBLE, CUPEL
testa .... INTEGUMENT, SHELL
testacean .... RHIZOPOD
testament .... COVENANT, WILL
testator .... LEGATOR
   beneficiary of ....
      HEIR(ESS), (IN)HERITOR
tester .... CANOPY, CIEL, ASSAYER, SIPPER
testifier .. WITNESS, DEPONENT
   statement of .. AFFIDAVIT, DEPOSITION
testify ...... DEPOSE, SWEAR, DEPONE, AFFIRM, MANIFEST
testimonial ...... CERTIFICATE, REFERENCE, COMPLIMENT, TRIBUTE
testimony .... DECLARATION, PROOF, EVIDENCE
testis .... GONAD
teston .... COIN
testudinate .... TORTOISE
testudo .... TORTOISE, SHIELD
testy .... TOUCHY, IRRITABLE, PEEVISH, PEPPERY, WASPISH, HOTHEADED
tetanus .. LOCKJAW, TRISMUS
tetched .... LOCO, DEMENTED
tetchy .... PEEVISH, IRRITABLE
tete-a-tete .... SEAT, CONVERSATION, FACE TO FACE
teth .... TEE
tether .... LEASH, FASTEN, LONGE, ROPE, LARIAT

Tethys .... TITANESS
   father of ...... URANUS
   husband of ... OCEANUS
tetrachord .... MESON
tetrad .... FOUR
tetragon ...... QUADRANGLE
Tetragrammaton ... YAHWEH, JEHOVAH, ADONAI
tetrarch .... HEROD
tetter ...... ECZEMA, HERPES, LICHEN
Teucrian .... TROJAN
Teuton(ic) ..... DUTCH, ENGLISH, NORDIC, GERMAN(IC)
   god .. WODEN, ODIN, ULL, AESIR, TYR, THOR, BALDER
   goddess .... MERTHUS
   hero .... OFFA
   metal collar ..... TORQUE
Tevere .... TIBER
tewel .. BORE, FUNNEL, TUYERE
Texas .. CADDOAN, LONE STAR
   capital .... AUSTIN
   city .. DALLAS, HOUSTON, LAREDO, EL PASO, WACO, ARLINGTON, ABILENE, AMARILLO, PASADENA, TYLER, LUBBOCK, ODESSA
   fever victim .... CATTLE
   leaguer .. HIT, FLY BALL
   mission .... ALAMO
   mounted police .... RANGER
   nickname .... LONE STAR
   plant .... LOCO
   river .. NECHES, BRAZOS, NUECES, PECOS
   seaport ...... GALVESTON
   shrine .... ALAMO
   shrub .... GUAYULE
   state flower .... BLUEBONNET
   state tree .... PECAN
   strip of land .... PANHANDLE
   university ...... BAYLOR, BAYARD
   winter wind ... NORTHER
text .. WORDING, LETTERPRESS, TOPIC, BOOK, SUBJECT
textile ...... WOVEN, CLOTH, FABRIC, FLAX, LINEN, WOOL, COTTON, DRAPERY

dealer ﹏﹏﹏﹏ MERCER
goods .... MERCERY
making apparatus .. LOOM
printing material ....
CATECHIN
shop ﹏﹏﹏﹏ MERCERY
worker .... DYER
textual .... LITERAL
texture ...... FABRIC, WOOF,
WEAVE, COMPOSITION, WEB,
GRAIN, WALE
kind of .. PINE, COARSE,
TWILLED, RIBBED
TFR, part of ...... TERRAIN,
RADAR, FOLLOWING
Thai(land) .. SIAM(ESE), SHAN
airbase ....KORAT
canal .... KLONG
capital .... BANGKOK
city ﹏﹏﹏﹏ THONBURI,
AYUTHIA
coin ﹏﹏﹏ BAHT, TICAL,
ATTIA, SATANG
king .... ANANDA,
BHUMIBOL, NARESUAN
language .... LAO, SHAN
monetary unit .... BAHT
native .... LAO
palace ...... OHITRA LADA
premier .. KITTIKACHORN,
THANARAT
queen ﹏﹏﹏ SIRIKIT
resort ﹏﹏﹏ HUA, HIN,
PATTAYA
river .... (ME)NAM
state guesthouse ....
BOROMABIMAN
temple .... WAT
throne room .... CHAKRI
weight .... KATI, CATTY
Thais ..... OPERA, COURTESAN
composer of .. MASSENET
thalamus ﹏﹏﹏﹏ TORUS
thalassic .... MARINE
Thalia ﹏﹏﹏ MUSE, GRACE
sister of ... ERATO, CLIO,
EUTERPE, URANIA,
POLYMNIA, CALLIOPE,
AGLAIA
sphere of ﹏﹏ COMEDY,
POETRY, BLOOM
thallophyte .. ALGA, FUNGUS,
LICHEN, BACTERIA
Thames landmark ﹏﹏ ETON,
BRIDGE
Thanatos personified .. DEATH

thane ..... FREEMAN, THEGN
latter-day equivalent of ..
BARON, KNIGHT
thankless .... UNGRATEFUL
person .... INGRATE
Thant, U .... SITHU
nationality .... BURMESE
Thapsus, victor at .... CAESAR
that ... WHICH, WHO, WHOM,
WHEN
is ......﹏﹏ ID EST, VIZ
place .... THERE
thatch ..... ROOF(ING), PALM,
HAIR
thatching material ... STRAW,
PALM, RUSHES, NIPA, GRASS,
COGON, HA(U)LM
thaumatology subject ....
MIRACLE(S)
thaumaturge's working ......
MIRACLE
thaumaturgy .... MAGIC
thaw ﹏﹏﹏ MELT, DISSOLVE,
LIQUEFY, SOFTEN, RELENT,
EASE
subject of a .. SNOW, ICE,
RESERVE, BERG
the Book .... BIBLE
"Enlightened One" .....
BUDDHA
Fair Penitent author ....
ROWE
king ﹏﹏﹏ LE ROI
same .... IDEM
seducer ...... LOTHARIO
Word .... LOGOS
theaceous tree .... TEA
thearchy .... THEOCRACY
theater .. STAGE, MOVIEHOUSE,
PLAYHOUSE, OPERA(HOUSE),
DRAMA, BOARDS
audience ﹏﹏﹏ HOUSE
awning .... MARQUEE
box/compartment .. LOGE
call .... CURTAIN
central stage .... ARENA
cheapest seat .. GALLERY
cheap .... GAFF
club .... LAMBS
curtain ... TEASER, DROP
district ... RIALTO, SOHO,
BROADWAY
entrance hall ﹏ LOBBY,
FOYER
fixture ﹏﹏﹏ MARQUEE,
CALLBOARD

goer on free ticket ...... DEADHEAD
ground floor ...... PIT, PARQUET, ORCHESTRA
group .... ASCAP
lobby .... FOYER
of war, 1945 .... ETO
part below balcony ..... PARTERRE
presentation ... CONCERT, PLAY, DRAMA, MUSICAL, REVUE, LECTURE, MOVIE
program .... BILL
seat .... LOGE, GALLERY, STALL
sign .... SRO, EXIT
slang .... LEGIT, GAFF
stage scenery .. COULISSE
street .... BROADWAY
the ..... STAGE, BOARDS, FOOTLIGHTS
theatrical .... HISTRIONIC, DRAMATIC, POMPOUS, AFFECTED, STAGY
company .... STOCK
curtain .... DROP
employee .... STAGEHAND
extra .... SUPER
financier: colloq. .... ANGEL
group .... TROUPE, CAST, ANTA
itinerary ... TOUR, TRIP, ROAD
nickname .... FLO, BILLY
producer .. ROSE, COHAN, ZIEGFELD
production ...... PLAY, REVUE, EXTRAVAGANZA
profession .... STAGE
role .... INGENUE, LEAD, HEAVY, STAR
show .... REVUE, EXTRAVAGANZA
sketch .... SKIT
Theban blind soothsayer ..... TIRESIAS
deities .... CABIRI
general ..... PELOPIDAS
god .... AMUN-RE
goddess .... MUT
king ...... CREON, LAIUS
POET .... PINDAR
queen .... JOCASTA
town .... LUXOR

Thebes .... LUXOR
founder of .... CADMUS
one of 7 against .... TYDUES
site of .... KARNAK
theca .... SAC, COCOON, CASE, CAPSULE
content .... SPORE, PUPA
thecate .... SHEATHE
Theda, actress .... BARA
theelin ... ESTRONE, HORMONE
theelol .... ESTRIOL, HORMONE
theft ..... ROBBERY, LARCENY, BURGLARY, THIEVERY
describing one .. GRAND, QUALIFIED
theine .... CAFFEINE
theme .. SUBJECT, ESSAY, TEXT, TOPIC, (LEIT)MOTIF
in a design ...... MOTIF
in art/music, etc. .. MOTIF
in radio .... SIGNATURE
Themis .... GODDESS
concern of .... JUSTICE, LAW
parent of .... GAEA, URANUS
what she holds .. SCALE
thenar .... PALM, SOLE
then ...... ALORS, THEREFORE
thence .... THEREFROM
thenceforth ..... THEREAFTER
theodolite .... TRANSIT
user of a .... SURVEYOR
theologian .... AQUINAS, LUTHER, CALVIN, ORIGEN, DIVINE, BEDE
theorbo .... LUTE
theorem .... PROPOSITION
expression of a .... FORMULA, EQUATION
theoretical ...... ACADEMIC, HYPOTHETICAL, SPECULATIVE, ABSTRACT
force .. OD(YLE), ODYL(E)
opposed to .. PRACTICAL, APPLIED
theorize ... GUESS, SPECULATE
theory ... IDEA, CONJECTURE, LAW, ISM, THESIS, HYPOTHESIS, SUPPOSITION, DOCTRINE
Darwin's .... EVOLUTION
Einstein's .. RELATIVITY
Malthusian .... POPULATION

Newton's ~~ ~~ ~~ GRAVITY
therapeutic .... CURATIVE
therapy ... CURE, TREATMENT
there .... YON(DER), AT,
  TOWARD, THITHER, THEN
thereafter .... ~~ THENCEFORTH,
  SINCE
therefore ..... ERGO, HENCE,
  THEN, CONSEQUENTLY,
  ARGAL
therefrom .... THENCE
therlac(a) .... TREACLE,
  ANTIDOTE
theranthropic being ....
  CENTAUR, HARPY, MERMAID,
  THOTH, TRITON
therm .... CALORIE
Therma .... SALONIKA
thermae .... BATHS
thermion .... ELECTRODE
thermometer, type of ....
  CENTIGRADE, FAHRENHEIT,
  REAUMUR, ODLOIUO,
  CRYOMETER
Thermopylae protagonist(s) ...
  PERSIANS, SPARTANS, XERXES,
  LEONIDAS
thermos .... JUG, FLASK
theroid .... BEASTLIKE
thersitical .... ABUSIVE, LOUD,
  SCURRILOUS
thesaurus .... TREASURY,
  LEXICON, DICTIONARY,
  STOREHOUSE
  compiler .... ROGET
Theseus' father ...... AEGEUS
  friend .... PIRITHOUS
  mother .... AETHRA
  victim .... MINOTAUR
  wife .... PHAEDRA
thesis .. THEORY, PROPOSITION,
  DISSERTATION, POSTULATE,
  TREATISE, ESSAY, MONOGRAPH
Thespian .... ACTOR, PLAYER,
  TRAGEDIAN, PERFORMER
Thespis' forte ..... TRAGEDY
Thessalian city ...... LARISSA
  mountain .. OSSA, PELION
  river .... SALAMBRIA
  tribe .... MYRMIDON
  valley .... TEMPE
  warrior ..... MYRMIDON
thetic .... PRESCRIBED
Thetis .... NEREID
  husband of ..... PELEUS
  son of .... ACHILLES

theurgist ... ~~ ~~ .... MAGICIAN
theurgy .... MAGIC
thews ..... MUSCLES, SINEWS
thewy .... MUSCULAR
they speak for themselves ....
  FACTS
thiamine deficiency disease ...
  BERIBERI
thick ...... DENSE, COMPACT,
  LUXURIANT, DULL, STUPID,
  CRASS, TURBID, CROSS, FAT
  as thieves .... CLOSE
  colloquial ... FRIENDLY,
  INTIMATE
  end .... BUTT
  headed .... DENSE,
  HEBETATE
  lay .... EXAGGERATE
  lipped .... LABROSE
  skinned .... SHAMELESS,
  CALLOUS
  slice .... SLAB
  soup .... PUREE
  sticky fluid ...... GRUME
thicken .. COAGULATE, DEEPEN,
  CURDLE, SOLIDIFY,
  INSPISSATE
thicket ..... SPINNEY, BRAKE,
  (UNDER)BRUSH, TOD, RONE,
  BUSH, BOSCAGE, COPPICE,
  CHAPARRAL, SHAW, COPSE,
  BOSK
thickhead ~~ ~~ DUNCE, IDIOT,
  FOOL
thickheaded ...... ~~ .. STUPID,
  FOOLISH
thickness ~~ LAYER, STRATUM,
  PLY
thickset ~~ ~~. STOUT, STOCKY,
  BEEFY, CHUNKY
thief ..... STEALER, PILFERER,
  FILCHER, GANEF, GANOV,
  GONOF, GONOPH, LURCHER,
  PICAROON, PRIG, LARCENER
  buyer of his loot .. FENCE
  cattle .... RUSTLER
  compulsive ....
  KLEPTO(MANIAC)
  discards of a ..... WAIF
  literary ..... PLAGIARIST,
  PIRATE, LIFTER
  store .... SHOPLIFTER
  trainer .... FAGIN
  wallet ...... PICKPOCKET
thieve .. STEAL, PILFER, SWIPE,
  FILCH

thieves' language ..... SLANG, ARGOT, CANT, JARGON
thigh, animal's .... HAM
and buttock .... HAM
armor plate ..... TUILLE
back of .... HAM
bone .... FEMUR
muscle ...... SARTORIUS
of the .... FEMORAL
part .... FLANK
pains .... SCIATICA
upper .... HIP
thill .... SHAFT, POLE
thimble .... THUMBSTALL
thimblerig .... SHELL GAME
bettor .... SUCKER
thimblerigger .... CHEAT, SWINDLER
thimbleweed ...... ANEMONE, RUDBECKIA, CONEFLOWER
thin ... TENUOUS, LEAN, SLIM, SLENDER, SPARSE, RARE, SLIGHT, MEAGER, SCANT, LANKY, SHEER, SPARE, FINE, FLIMSY, SUBTLE, LIN(E)Y, REEDY, HAIRLINE
cake .... WAFER
coating ... FILM, VENEER
combining form .. STENO
glue .... SIZE
layer ...... VENEER, FILM
man .... SLATS
Man's dog .... ASTA
man's nickname .. SLIM, SLATS, LANKY
paper .... TISSUE
skinned ...... SENSITIVE
soup .... BROTH
thine .... YOUR(S)
thing .. ENTITY, BEING, OBJECT, ITEM, MATTER, AFFAIR, CONCERN
easy to do ...... CINCH
emitted ..... EMANATION
hard to handle ....
HOT POTATO
imaginary .... MYTH
ineffectual .... DUD
in law .... RES
of same class ....
CONGENER
of small value ... STIVE, TRIFLE
of value .... ASSET
out of place .... ESTRAY
worthless .... CHIP

things, one thousand ....
CHILIAD
to be done ..... AGENDA
to be sold .... WARES
thingumajig .... THINGUMBOB, GADGET, CONTRIVANCE, DEVICE
thingumbob .. DEVICE, GADGET
think ..... CONCEIVE, IDEATE, JUDGE, CEREBRATE, TROW, RECKON, WEEN, DEEM, BROOD, SURMISE, REFLECT, OPINE, COGITATE, REASON
of ... CONSIDER, RECALL, RECOLLECT
over ..... PONDER, MULL
up .... INVENT
thinness .... RARITY, TENUITY
thiol .... MERCAPTAN
thiosulfate .... HYPO
third .... TERNARY, TERTIARY
degree user ....
INVESTIGATOR, POLICE, INTERROGATOR
estate .... COMMONS, BOURGEOISIE
every .... TERTIAN
in music .... TIERCE
International ....
COMINTERN
man, the ..... REF(EREE)
power .... CUBE
rate ..... POOR, INFERIOR
widow's .... DOWER
thirl .... PIERCE, THRILL
thirst ...... CRAVING, DESIRE
quencher .... POP
relieve .... SLAKE
Thirkell, writer ..... ANGELA
thirteen ... LONG DOZEN, XIII
"30" on copy .... END
this minute .... NOW, AT ONCE, PRONTO
Thisbe's love ...... PYRAMUS
thistle .. ARNICA, BURR, ASTER, COSMOS, HYSSOP
like plant ... ARTICHOKE, CARDOON
plant .... SAFLOWER
thistledown .... PAPPUS
thither .... THERE, YON
thole .... PIN, OARLOCK
purpose of ... FULCRUM
Thomas, Fr. composer ......
AMBROISE
opera by ...... MIGNON

thong ‥ WHIP(LASH), STRAP,
    RIEM, KNOUT, LEASH
    strangling ‥‥ GAROTTE,
                GARROTE
Thor ‥‥‥‥‥‥‥ SISECH
Thor's father ‥‥‥‥‥ ODIN
    noise ‥‥‥‥‥ THUNDER
    sphere ‥‥‥‥‥ WAR
    weapon ‥‥‥‥ HAMMER
    wife ‥‥‥‥‥‥‥ SIF
thorax ‥‥‥‥‥‥‥‥ CHEST
    insect's ‥‥‥‥‥ TRUNK
thorn ‥ TORUN, TREE, NETTLE,
STOB, SPINE, PRICKLE, BRIAR,
                BRIER
    apple ‥‥ DATURA, HAW,
                METEL
thornback ‥ RAY, SPIDER CRAB
Thorne novel ‥‥‥‥ TOPPER
thorny ‥‥‥ SPINATE, SPINY,
PRICKLY, BRAMBLY, SPINOSE
    plant ‥‥‥ BRIAR, DRIER
thorough ‥‥‥ COMPLETE,
    OUT-AND-OUT, ABSOLUTE
thoroughbred ‥‥ PEDIGREED,
    BLUEBLOOD, HIGHBORN
thoroughfare ‥ (PASSAGE)WAY,
STREET, HIGHWAY, AVENUE,
             CONCOURSE
thoroughwort ‥‥‥ BONESET,
              PLANT
thorp(e) ‥‥ HAMLET, VILLAGE
those in office ‥‥‥‥‥ INS
Thoth, representation of ‥‥‥
              IDIS
thou ‥‥‥‥‥‥‥‥‥ YOU
though ‥ NOTWITHSTANDING,
              HOWEVER
thought ‥‥ INTELLECT, IDEA,
    CONCEPT, HEED
    transference of ‥‥‥‥‥
            TELEPATHY
thoughtless ‥ RASH, RECKLESS,
            STUPID
    act ‥‥‥‥‥‥‥ FOLLY
thousand dollars: sl. ‥ GRAND
    prefix ‥‥‥‥‥‥ MILLI
    years ‥‥‥ MILLENNIUM,
            CHILIAD
thousandth ‥‥‥ MILLESIMAL
    anniversary ‥ MILLENARY
    of an inch ‥‥‥‥‥ MIL
Thracian king ‥‥‥‥ TEREUS
    slave ‥‥‥‥ SPARTACUS
    soldier ‥‥‥‥ MYRMIDON
thrall ‥‥‥ (EN)SLAVE, ESNE,

SERF, BONDMAN
thralldom ‥‥‥‥‥ SLAVERY,
    SERVITUDE, BONDAGE
thrash ‥‥‥ WALLOP, WHALE,
FLOG, CANE, TAN, BEAT,
ROUT, DEFEAT, LASH, DRUB,
LAM, TROUNCE, BELABOR,
WHIP, FLAIL, HIDE, LACE,
LAMBAST(E), LARRUP
thrasher ‥‥‥‥ (SONG)BIRD
thrasonical ‥‥‥‥ BOASTFUL
thread ‥‥‥‥ INKLE, CORD,
LINEN, LISLE, STRAND,
FILAMENT, STRING, FILUM
    a needle ‥‥‥‥ REEVE
    appendage like ‥‥ CIRRUS
    ball of ‥‥‥‥‥‥ CLEW
    bits ‥‥‥‥‥‥‥ LINT
    combining form ‥‥‥‥
            NEMAT(O)
    cotton ‥‥‥‥‥ LISLE
    cutters, screws ‥‥‥ TAP
    discharge ‥‥‥‥ SETON
    end ‥‥‥‥‥‥ THRUM
    fine ‥‥‥‥‥‥‥ FILM
    holder ‥‥‥‥‥ SPOOL,
        SHUTTLE, BOBBIN
    knot ‥‥‥‥‥‥‥ BURL
    like ‥‥‥‥ FILOSE, FILAR,
            FIBROID
    like part ‥‥‥‥‥ FILUM,
            FILAMENT
    linen ‥‥‥‥‥‥ INKLE
    lump ‥‥‥‥ KNOT, BURL
    material ‥‥ COTTON, FLAX,
    YARN, LINEN, SILK
    metal ‥‥‥‥‥‥ WIRE
    quantity ‥‥‥‥‥ SKEIN
    rubber ‥‥‥‥‥ LASTEX
    separate ‥‥‥‥ SLEAVE
    silk ‥‥‥‥‥‥‥ TRAM
    skein of ‥‥‥‥‥ HASP
    surgical ‥‥‥‥ CATGUT,
            SETON
    thick ‥‥‥‥‥‥ STRING
    use of ‥‥‥‥‥ SEWING,
    SUTURE, WEAVING
    used in labyrinth ‥ CLEW
    weight ‥‥‥‥‥ DENIER
threadbare ‥‥‥ WORN, STALE,
TRITE, SHABBY, RAGGED,
            SEEDY
threadworm ‥‥‥‥ NEMATODE,
    FILARIA
thready ‥‥‥ STRINGY, FIBROUS
threap ‥‥ ARGUE, CHIDE, SCOLD

threat .... WARNING, MENACE
    empty ... BLUSTER, BLUFF
threaten ... MENACE, HECTOR
threatening .... MINATORY,
    MINACIOUS, OMINOUS,
    MENACING, SULLEN
three .... TRIO, TRIAD, TER,
    THRIN
    angled .... TRIGONOUS
    banded armadillo .. APAR
    base hit .... TRIPLE
    card's .... TREY
    cut into .... TRISECT
    cornered .... TRIGONOUS,
    TRIGONAL, TRIANGULAR
    decker .... TRIREME
    dimensional .... CUBIC,
    STEREO
    feet .... YARD
    group of .... TRINE,
    TRINARY, TRIAD,
    TRINITY, TRIPLE(T),
    TRIPLEX, TRIPLICATE,
    TRIO
    hand card game .... SKAT
    in dice/domino .... TREY
    in one .. TRIUNE, TRINITY
    in sequence, same suit ...
    TIERCE
    leafed .... TRIFOLIATE
    leafed clover ... TREFOIL
    legged seat .... STOOL
    legged stand ... TEAPOY,
    TRIPOD, EASEL
    legged table ..... TRIVET
    lobbed .... TRIFID
    month period ....
    TRIMESTER, QUARTER
    prefix .... TRI
    pronged ...... TRIDENT,
    TRIDENTATE
    pronged spear .. TRIDENT,
    LEISTER
    ribbed ..... TRICOSTATE
    seeded ..... TRISPERMOUS
    set of .... TERNION
    shakes .... SECS
    song for .... TRIO
    times ... TRIPLE, TREBLE,
    THRICE
    toed sloth .... AI
threefold .... TERNARY,
    TREBLE, TRIPLE, THRICE,
    TRINE, TRINAL, TRIPARTITE,
    TRIPLEX
threes, arranged in .. TERNATE

threescore .... SIXTY
threnody .. CORONACH, DIRGE,
    SONG, REQUIEM
thresh ...... BEAT(OUT), FLOG
    out .... DISCUSS
thresher ...... SHARK, FLAIL
    shark .... SEAFOX
threshing implement ... FLAIL,
    COMBINE
threshold .... LIMEN,
    (DOOR)SILL, ENTRANCE, EVE
threw ... TOSSED, CAST, FLUNG,
    HURLED
thrice ..... THREEFOLD, VERY
thrift .... ECONOMY, FRUGALITY
thrifty ..... FRUGAL, SPARING,
    PROVIDENT, ECONOMICAL
    person .... HOARDER,
    MISER, NIGGARD,
    PENNY-PINCHER,
    SKINFLINT
thrill ... EXHILARATE, FLUSH,
    THIRL, ELECTRIFY, KICK,
    EXCITE, QUIVER, VIBRATE,
    TREMOR
thrilling .. ELECTRIC, EXCITING
thrips .... WOODWORM
thrive .... FLOURISH, PROSPER,
    GROW, SUCCEED, WAX,
    ADDLE, FATTEN, BATTEN
throat ... WEASAND, GULLET,
    CRAG, GORGE, MAW,
    THROTTLE, FAUCES
    armor .... GORGET
    clearing ..... HAWK, HEM
    condition ...... GOITER
    cut the .... JUGULATE
    disease .. CROUP, ANGINA,
    THRUSH, GARGET
    lozenge .... PASTIL(E)
    of the ...... (JU)GULAR,
    GUTTURAL
    part .... ESOPHAGUS,
    LARYNX, TRACHEA,
    PHARYNX
    skin, animal .... DEWLAP,
    WATTLE
    sore .... PHARYNGITIS
    sound .... CROAK
    wrapper ...... MUFFLER
throaty ... HOARSE, GUTTURAL
throb .... PULSATE, BEAT,
    VIBRATE, PALPITATE,
    THUMP, POUND, PUMP,
    PULSATION
throbber .... HEART

throbbing ꟷ.ꟷꟷ PALPITANT,
SALTATION, BEATING
throe(s) ..... SPASM, AGONY,
(LABOR)PAINS, PANG, RACK
thrombosis ..... COAGULATION
thrombus ...... CLOT, FIBRIN
throne ....ꟷ.. SOVEREIGN(TY),
CHAIR, RULER
bishop's ..... CATHEDRA
covering .... CANOPY
seat of a .... TRANSOM
sitter ... EMPEROR, TSAR,
POPE, CARDINAL, QUEEN
throng ... CROWD, MULTITUDE,
PRESS, HORDE, SWARM,
HOST, CONCOURSE
throstle .... THRUSH
throttle .... VALVE, STRANGLE,
CHOKE, SUPPRESS, SILENCE,
GAG, SCRAG
engine .... GUN
through .. PER, VIA, BY WAY OF,
AMONG, FINISH, OVER, DONE
throw .... HURL, DASH, UPSET,
SHED, FLING, TOSS, PITCH,
CAST, HEAVE
at a mark ..... COCKSHY
away .... DISCARD
dice .. ROLL, CAST, MAIN
football opponent ......
TACKLE
into confusion ....
DEMORALIZE
lava .... ERUPT
light back ...... REFLECT
of ball .... DELIVERY
out ... REJECT, DISCARD,
EJECT, OUST, BOUNCE
over ..... JILT, ABANDON
overboard ..... JETTISON
stones at ...... LAPIDATE
the towel ... QUIT, YIELD
together .... ASSEMBLE
up .. VOMIT, SPEW, RETCH,
PUKE, REJECT, REGORGE
throwaway ꟷ.ꟷ.ꟷ.. LEAFLET,
HANDBILL
throwback .... ATAVISM
thrown ... PITCHED, UNSEATED
thrum ꟷ.ꟷꟷ FRINGE, STRUM,
DRUM, TIRL
thrummy ꟷ.ꟷ.ꟷ.... SHAGGY
thrush ...... OUZEL, ROBIN,
APHTHA, MAVIS, THROSTLE,
(SONG)BIRD, BLUEBIRD,

VEERY, MISSEL, REDWING,
NIGHTINGALE, PITTA
disease .... APHTHA
of the .... TURDINE
water .... WAGTAIL
thrust ... JAB, LUNGE, SHOVE,
DRIVE, STAB, PIERCE, PUSH,
TILT, FOIN, EXSERT, DARTLE,
POKE
aside ..... SHOVE, BRUSH
down .... DETRUDE
fencing .... PASSADO
out lips .... POUT
Thsombe, Congo premier .....
MOISE
thud .... BLOW, THUMP
thug ... CUTTHROAT, ASSASSIN,
DACOIT, TOUGH, GORILLA,
STRANGLER, GOON, RUFFIAN
thuja ... CEDAR, ARBORVITAE,
PINE
Thule, part of ... NORWAY,
ICELAND
thumb ....ꟷ.ꟷ POLLEX, DIGIT
a ride .... HITCHHIKE
fleshy bulge of .. THENAR
in architecture ... OVOLO
index .... TAB
protector ꟷ.ꟷ. THIMBLE,
STALL
thumbnail ꟷ.ꟷ. BRIEF, SMALL
thumbstall .... THIMBLE
thump .... POUND, THUD,
CUDGEL, THRASH, POMMEL,
BEAT, THROB
thumping: colloq. ꟷ WHOPPING,
LARGE
thunder ...ꟷ.ꟷ.ꟷ.. PEAL
at the beach .... SURF
forth .... FULMINATE
god .... THOR
sound ... CLAP, RUMBLE,
CRASH, ROLL, PEAL,
MUTTER
thunderbolt ꟷ.ꟷ.. LIGHTNING
thunderer ..... ZEUS, JUPITER
thunderfish ... LOACH, RAAD
thunderstone ꟷ.ꟷ. BELEMITE,
CUTTLEFISH
thurible ꟷ.ꟷ.ꟷ. CENSER
thurifer ...ꟷ.ꟷ. ACOLYTE,
ALTAR BOY
thurify .... CENSE
Thuringian capital ... WEIMAR
castle .... WARTBURG
city .... GOTHA, JENA

thus ..... HENCE, THEREFORE, SIC, SO, ERGO
far .... YET
thwack ...... WHACK, SLAP, SMACK
thwart .... OBLIQUE, FRUSTRATE, DEFEAT, FOIL, HINDER, BALK, BAFFLE
Thyestes' brother .... ATREUS
parent .... PELOPS
thyme .... MINT, HERB
thymus .. GLAND, SWEETBREAD
thyroid disease ...... GOITER, CRETINISM, GOITRE
thysanuran .... BRISTLE TAIL
ti, in chemistry .... TITANIUM
tiara .... HEADDRESS, CROWN, CORONET, DIADEM
wearer ... PEERESS, QUEEN, DUCHESS, PRINCESS
Tiber .... TEVERE
Tiberias Sea .... GALILEE
Tibet .... SITSANG
mountain pass ..... NITI, LIPU LEKH, MANA
Tibetan antelope ... SUS, GOA, CHIRU
capital .... LHASA
chief lama ...... DALAI, PANCHEN
deer .... SHOU
gazelle .... GOA
general .... CHANG
goat wool ... CASHMERE
high priest ..... BLAMA
monastery .... LAMASERY
monetary unit ..... SANG
monk .... LAMA
mountain ...... NANSHAN
ox .... YAK
oxlike animal ..... ZEBU
priest .... LAMA
religion .... LAMAISM
river .... SUTLEJ
wild sheep .... SHA, NAHOOR, BHARAL
zoo animal .... PANDA
tibia ...... SHIN(BONE), FLUTE, CNEMIS
Tibur .... TIVOLI
tic .. LATA(H), SPASM, TWITCH
tical's replacement ..... BAHT
Ticino .... TESSIN
tick ...... ACARID, PARASITE, MITE, CLICK, CHECK, MARK, MOMENT, INSECT,

PILLOW CASE, ARACHNID, JIGGER
British ... CREDIT, TRUST
host of ... CATTLE, MAN, SHEEP
off ... COUNT, ENUMERATE
ticker .... TAPPER
slang .... HEART, CLOCK, WATCH, TIMEPIECE
tape figures .. QUOTATIONS
ticket ...... LICENSE, LABEL, TAG, PASS, DOCKET
candidates' ...... SLATE, BALLOT
free .. ANNIE OAKLEY, PASS
losing .... BLANK
of leave .... PAROLE
part .... STUB
slang ... DUCAT, DUCKET, PASTEBOARD
stub .... RAIN CHECK
tickle ...... GRATIFY, AMUSE, STIR, TINGLE, TITILIATE, EXCITE
tickler ... PUZZLE, REMINDER
ticklish ... TOUCHY, DELICATE, FICKLE
tickseed ... DAISY, COREOPSIS
tid plus two .... BITS
tidal flow .... EBB, NEAP
wave ... TSUNAMI, EAGRE, BORE
tidbit ...... MORSEL, GOSSIP, CANAPE, CATE, KICKSHAW
tide, designation of a .. EBB, NEAP, FLOOD, SPRING, RIP
tidings .. NEWS, INFORMATION, REPORT, EVANGEL, WORD, GOSPEL
tidy ... TAUT, ORDERLY, TRIM, NEAT, SPRUCE, SHIPSHAPE, CONSIDERABLE, LARGE, TRIG
tie ...... BIND, FASTEN, KNOT, EQUAL, LINK, BOND, CRAVAT, BEAM, STATEMATE, NEXUS, FOUR-IN-HAND, UNION, TACH(E), ASCOT, LASH, TRUSS, STANDOFF, HITCH
beam .... BALK
boat .... MOOR
connecting ... LIGAMENT
contest .... DRAW
down ... CONFINE, HOLD
fabric .... REP
game to break .. RUBBER

in a race ...... DEAD HEAT
up .... STOP, HINDER,
CONNECTION
tieback .... SASH
Tientsin river .... HAI
tier .. ROW, RANK, PINAFORE,
LACER, BANK
tierce .... HOUR, CASK
Tierra del Fuego Indian .. ONA
ties .... OXFORDS
support .... ROADBED
tiff .... HUFF, QUARREL,
LIQUOR, SPAT, ARGUMENT,
MIFF
tiffany .... GAUZE, MUSLIN
tiffin .... LUNCH, TEA, SNACK
tiger ...... JAGUAR, LEOPARD,
SABERTOOTH
eat ... OCELOT, MARGAY,
SERVAL, CHATI
of Malaya, so-called .....
YAMASHITA
Persian .... SHER, SHIR
young ..... CUB, WHELP
tigerish ... FEROCIOUS, CRUEL,
FIERCE
colloquial ...... STINGY,
MISERLY
place .... JAM, FIX, SPOT
slang .... DRUNK, TIPSY
tight ...... TAUT, COMPACT,
SEVERE, TENSE, CLOSE,
SNUG, STINGY, MISERLY
place ..... JAM, FIX, SPOT
slang ..... TIPSY, DRUNK
tighten .... FRAP, TAUTEN,
STRAITEN, SCREW
tightfisted ... STINGY, MISERLY
tightlipped .... SECRETIVE,
TACITURN
tightrope walker .... ACROBAT,
EQUILIBRIST, AERIALIST,
FUNAMBULIST
tightwad ...... MISER, PIKER,
SKINFLINT, NIGGARD, HUNKS
til .... SESAME
tilbury ..... CARRIAGE, COACH
tile ...... PANTILE, QUARRY,
TESSERA, DALLE, BRICK,
TEGULA, CERAMIC
like .... TEGULAR
making art .. CERAMICS
tiler .... DOORKEEPER
tiles, pertaining to ... TEGULAR
till .... UNTIL, UNTO,
CULTIVATE, FARM,

CASH (REGISTER), PLOW
land .... SUBDUE
tilled land ...... ARADA, FARM,
TILTH
tiller .... HELM, FARMER,
CULTIVATOR, PLOWMAN,
SHOOT
Tillie the ____ ...... TOILER
tilt ... SLANT, INCLINE, SLOPE,
LIST, JOUST, HEEL, DEBATE,
SEESAW, CANOPY, TIP,
TOURNAMENT, TOURNEY
tilted .... ACOCK
tilth .... ARADA, FARM
tilting arena .... LISTS
target .... QUINTAIN
tournament ....
CAR(R)OUSEL
timarau .... BUFFALO
timbal .... KETTLEDRUM
timber ...... WOOD, LUMBER,
TREES, LOG, BITT
above keel ... DEADWOOD
arched .... CAMBER
borer .... GRIBBLE
crack .... ANEMOSIS
deciduous ... HARDWOOD
down bend .... SNY
dressed ...... PUNCHEON
foundation .... SPILE
grooved ...... COULISSE
heartwood ..... DURAMEN
hewn piece .... BALK
hitch .... KNOT
joining peg .. TRE(E)NAIL,
TRUNNEL
rot .... DOAT
sawn .... LUMBER
small ..... SCANTLING
soak .... RET
standing ...... STUMPAGE
state .... OREGON
support ...... CORBEL
tree .... YEW
wolf .... LOBO
Timberlane, Judge ..... CASS
timbre .... TONE
timbrel .... TAMBOURINE, TABOR
time ...... PERIOD, INTERVAL,
OCCASION, MOMENT, DATE,
CLOCK, INSTANT, DURATION,
ERA, EPOCH
beating device ....
METRONOME
between ...... INTERIM,
INTERVAL

combining form .... CHRON(O)
extension .... GRACE
free .... LEISURE, BREAK
honored .. TRADITIONAL
in music ... TEMPO, BEAT, VOLTA
incalculable ...—.. EON
indicating device .... SUNDIAL, CLOCK, WATCH, HOURGLASS, CLEPSYDRA
limit ....—.. DEADLINE
of day .... MORNING, (AFTER)NOON
of greatest vigor .... HEYDAY
of imprisonment .. TERM
of life ... TEENS, NONAGE, DOTAGE
of rejoicing .... JUBILEE
out ...—.. REST, RECESS, BREAK
pass the .... WHILE
pertaining to .... HORAL
poetic .... EVENTIDE
prosperous .... HEYDAY
science of .... HOROLOGY
spend .... WHILE
waster —.. LOAFER, IDLER, SLACKER
timely .... OPPORTUNE, SEASONABLE, PROMPT
timepiece ... CLOCK, WATCH, HOROLOGE
art of making .... HOROLOGY
timer ......—.. STOP WATCH
timeserver ...—... TRIMMER, OPPORTUNIST
timetable ...—.... SCHEDULE
timid .... SHY, TIMOROUS, SHEEPISH, RESERVED, RETIRING, CHICKEN, PAVID
timidity, symbol of ... MOUSE
timing .... PACE
device —.. METRONOME, STOPWATCH
timon .... HELM, TILLER
Timor Archipelago, part ..... SUMBA, SUMBAWA, FLORES
capital —.. KUPANG, DILI
coin .... AVO
timorous —.. TIMID, FEARFUL, SHY, TREPID

Timoshenko, Soviet Marshal .. SEMYON
timothy .... GRASS, HAY
timpani .... KETTLEDRUMS
tin ...—.—.. CAN, STANNUM, PRESERVE
alloy .... PEWTER
and lead alloy .... TERNE
box .... TRUMMEL
coated sheet metal ...... TAGGER
fish .... TORPEDO
foil .... TAIN
hat .... HELMET
metal sheet ..... LATTEN
mine .... STANNARY
of .... STANNOUS
Pan Alley character ..... COMPOSER, PROMOTER
Pan Alley group .. ASCAP
plate .... FOIL, TAIN
pyrite .... STANNITE
sheet .... LATTEN
slang .... MONEY
smeltery ..... STANNARY
strips .... TINSEL
threads, decorative ...... TINSEL
tinamou-like bird ..... QUAIL
tincal .... BORAX
tinct ...—.. TINGED, TINT(ED), COLOR
tincture .. TINT, TINGE, SHADE, VESTIGE, TRACE, COLOR, VERT, ELIXIR
tind .—.—.......... KINDLE
tinder .... AMADOU, PUNK
tinderbox, like a .... POWDER KEG
tine —.. PRONG, SPIKE, ANTLER, TYND, BIT
tinea .—.—.. RINGWORM, MOTH, LARVA
tinge ... TAINT, TOUCH, COLOR, TRACE, SHADE, DYE, TINT, FLAVOR, DASH
tinged .—............. TINCT
tingle ..— NIP, PRICKLE, THIRL, DIRL, DINDLE
tiniest .—.—........ MINIM
tinker ...... BUNGLER, CAIRD, SILVERSIDES, MACKEREL, PUTTER, FUSS, MENDER
jargon of .... SHELTA
Shakespearean ... SNOUT
tinkle .... CLINK, JINGLE

tinkling .... GRACKLE
tin(s)man .... SMITH
tinsel .... SHOWY, GAUDY
tinseled .... CLINQUANT
tinstone .... CASSITERITE
tint ...... COLOR, TINGE, HUE,
    SHADE, STAIN, DYE
Tintagel Head's famous son ...
    ARTHUR
tinted .... TINCT
tintinnabula .... BELLS
tinware .... POTS, PANS
tiny .... MINUTE, SMALL,
    DIMINUTIVE, WEE, PETITE,
    TEENY, MINUSCLE
  bit .... MORSEL
  creature .... ATOMY,
    DWARF, RUNT
  gold particles ...... DUST
  opening .... PORE
tip .... APEX, FEE, LIST, TOP,
    TAP, UPSET, NEB, CANT,
    HEEL, VAIL, GRATUITY,
    CUMSHAW, POINT(ER), TILT,
    HINT, SLANT, TOPPLE,
    STEER, GREASE
  pen's .... NEB, NIB
  off .... WARNING,
    HINT
tippet .... LIRIPIPE, FUR,
    AMICE, ALMUCE, SCARF,
    CAMAIL
tipple .... DRINK, LIQUOR, BIB
tippler .... TOPER, SOT
tips seller .... TOUT
tipstaff .... BAILIFF,
    CONSTABLE
tipster .... TOUT(ER)
tipsy .... AWRY, DRUNK,
    INTOXICATED, CROOKED,
    HIGH, LOADED, GROGGY
tiptop .... FIT, AONE,
    SHIPSHAPE
tirade .... HARANGUE,
    PHILIPPIC, SPEECH,
    DIATRIBE, SPATE
tirailleur .... MARKSMAN,
    SHARPSHOOTER
tire ...... WEARY, FAG, PNEU,
    JADE, CLOY, BORE
  burst .... BLOWOUT
  casing .... SHOE
  iron .... STRAKE
  out .... EXHAUST
  part of .... CASING,
    SHOE, TUBE, TREAD, RIM

puncturer .... CALTRAP,
    CALTROP
tread mold .... MOULAGE
tired .... JADED, WEARY
  feeling .... ENNUI,
    WEARINESS, FATIGUE
  very .... ALL IN
Tiresias .... SOOTHSAYER
tiresome .... TEDIOUS, BORING,
    DREARY, DULL
  person .... BORE
tirl .... THRUM, STRUM
tisane .... PTISAN, TEA,
    DECOCTION
Tisiphone .... FURY
tissue .... CLOTH, GAUZE, MESH,
    NETWORK, TELA, BAST,
    WEB, PAPER, PHLOEM,
    GRISTLE
  animal .... CARTILAGE
  area of dead .... INFARCT
  cavity .... LOCULUS,
    VACUOLE
  change in ... CATAPLASIA
  combining form .. HIST(O)
  connecting ..... TENDON,
    PONS
  cutting instrument ......
    MICROTOME
  decay .... CARIES,
    GANGRENE
  hardening .... SCLEROMA,
    SCLERIASIS
  inflammation ....
    CELLULITIS
  like .... HISTOID
  nerve .... ALBA
  plant ..... PHLOEM, BAST
  study of ..... HISTOLOGY
  under epidermis ....
    HYPODERMA
Tisza .... THEISS
tit ...... BIRD, TEAT, NIPPLE,
    BREAST, HORSE, NAG, BLOW,
    GIRL, JADE, TAP
Titan .... HELIOS, ZEUS,
    CREUS, COEUS, CRONUS,
    ATLAS, EPIMETHEUS,
    IAPETUS, HYPERION,
    OCEANUS, PROMETHEUS,
    GIANT
  female ..... DIONE, LETO,
    TETHYS, RHEA, THEIA,
    MAIA, EURYNOME,
    PHOEBE

parent of .... GAEA,
    URANUS, GAIA
place of consignment ....
    TARTARUS
Titania .... FAIRY, QUEEN
    husband of ..... OBERON
titanic .... GIGANTIC
titanium dioxide ..... RUTILE
titanite .... SPHENE, MINERAL
Titans' war with Olympians ...
    TITANOMACHY
tithe .... LEVY, TENTH, TAX
tithing .... DECENARY
Tithonus' love .... EOS
    parent ...... LAOMEDON
    transformation ....
        GRASSHOPPER
titi .... MONKEY, TREE,
        IRONWOOD
titian .... AUBURN
titillate ... EXCITE, TANTALIZE,
        STIMULATE, TICKLE
titivate ... SPRUCE, DRESS(UP)
titlark .... PIPIT
title .... PARENT, LEGEND,
        CLAIM, RIGHT, NAME,
        CAPTION, APPELLATION,
        MUNIMENT, HEADING,
        DESIGNATION
    descriptive ...... EPITHET
    holder .. TITLIST, OWNER,
        CHAMPION
    of a noble .... RAS, LORD,
        EARL, COUNT, DUKE,
        BARON, MARQUISE,
        PRINCE
    ownership .... DEED
    pages .... ODDMENTS
    sports ... CHAMPION(SHIP)
    surbordinate .. SUBHEAD
    to property ... MUNIMENT,
        DEED
    transfer .... CEDE
titled person .... NOBLE
titmouse ... CHICKADEE, NUN,
        TAT, PARUS, VERDIN,
        BLUECAP, MAG
Tito, Marshal .. (JOSIP) BROZ
    resistance followers .....
        PARTISANS
titter .... TEHEE, SNICKER,
        LAUGH, GIGGLE
tittie .... SISTER
tittle ... IOTA, DOT, JOT, WHIT,
        PARTICLE
    tattle .. GOSSIP, CHATTER

tittup ... FRISK, FROLIC, CAPER,
        PRANCE
titular .... NOMINAL
Tiu .... TYR
Tivoli .... TIBUR
tizzy .... EXCITEMENT,
        DISTRACTION, DITHER, SNIT
Tlingit .... TONGA, INDIAN
tmesis .... DIACOPE
TNT .... TROTYL
to .... WITH, THITHER,
        AS FAR AS, UNTIL
    do .... STIR, FUSS,
        COMMOTION
    the point that ..... UNTIL
    the point ..... PERTINENT,
        RELEVANT, GERMANE,
        APT, RELATED
    wit .... NAMELY, SCILICET
    your health ..... PROSIT,
        SKOAL
toad .... FROG, PEEPER,
        NATTERJACK, PADDOCK,
    ANURAN, BUFO, SALIENTIAN,
    SPADEFOOT, AGUA, PIPA,
        BATRACHIA, HYLA
    back "wart" of ....
        VERRUCA
    larva .... TADPOLE
    sound .... CROAK
toadeater ...... SYCOPHANT,
        PARASITE
toadfish .... SAPO
toadflax .... WEED
toadstone's use .... CHARM
toadstool .... MUSHROOM,
    FUNGUS, BOLETUS, AGARIC
toady .. TRUCKLE, FLATTERER,
        SYCOPHANT, PARASITE,
        FLUNK(E)Y, LACKEY,
        LICKSPIT(TLE)
toast ..... COMPLIMENT, LEEP,
        SIPPET, BROWN, WARM,
        DRINK, SALUTE
    British .... CHEERS
    German .... PROSIT
    Norwegian ...... SKOAL
    object of a ..... HONOREE,
        CELEBRANT, LION,
        CELEBRITY, BELLE,
        AWARDEE, HERO
    Spanish .... SALUD
    type of .... MELBA
toastmaster ..... EMCEE, MC,
        SYMPOSIARCH
tobacco ... BROADLEAF, WEED,

SHAG, BURLEY, PERIQUE, LATAKIA, MUNDUNGO, DACCHA, MUNDUNGUS
and paper ...... MAKING
bit of .... SCREW
box .... HUMIDOR
cake of .... PLUG
chewing ..... QUID, PLUG
corporal's ..... CAPORAL
Cuban .... VUELTA, CAPA
kiln .... OAST
leaf alkaloid .. NICOTINE
leaf bundle ...... HAND
left in pipe ...... DOTTEL, DOTTLE
odor .... FUNK
pipe .. DUDEEN, CHIBOUK, CHIBOURUE, MEERCHAUM, CORNCOB
plant pest .... THRIPS
pouch .... SPLEUCHAN
product .... CIGAR(ETTE), SNUFF, PLUG
rolled, twisted .. PIGTAIL
shredded .... SHAG
smoke .... WHIFF
snuff .... RAPPEE
soldier's ...... CAPORAL
Turkish .... LATAKIA
use of .... CHEWING, SMOKE, SNUFF
toboggan ..... SLED, COASTER, DECLINE
like vehicle ..... BOBSLED
runway of .... CHUTE
toby ...... CIGAR, MUG, JUG
content of .... ALE
tock .... HORNBILL
tocology ...... OBSTETRICS, MIDWIFERY
tocsin .... BELL, ALARM
tod .... CLUMP, BUSH, FOX
toddle ...... WADDLE, TOTTER, PADDLE
toddler .... CHILD, BABY, TOT
toddy .. SAP, DRINK, BEVERAGE
toe ...... DIGIT, DACTYL(US)
bird's .... HALLUX
dance .... PIROUETTE
dancer .... BALLERINA
hold .... FOOTING
infection .... FELON, WHITLOW
membrane ... WEB(BING)
sore .... AGNAIL
the line ... BEHAVE, OBEY,

CONFORM
toenails, work on ... PEDICURE
toes, on one's .... ALERT
whirling on the ....
PIROUETTE
toffee/toffy .... CANDY, TAFFY
toft .. HOMESTEAD, MESSUAGE, KNOLL, HILLOCK
tog(s) ...... COAT, CLOTHES, DUDS, DRESS
toga .... ROBE, GOWN
together .... ASSOCIATED
toggery .. CLOTHES, CLOTHING, HABERDASHERY
toggle ... PIN, COTTER, BOLT, ROD
Togo, capital of ...... LOME
language .... EVHE
president ..... EYADEMA, OLYMPIO
tribe .... MINA, EWE
Togoland plus Gold Coast ....
GHANA
toil ... SNARE, LABOR, WORK, TRAVAIL, SLOG, DRUDGE
toile .... CLOTH, LINEN, CRETONNE
toilet ... COMMODE, LAVATORY, JOHN
case ...... ETUI, ETWEE, MUSETTE
outdoor .... JAKES
water .... COLOGNE, BAYRUM, LAVENDER
toiletry item .. SOAP, COLOGNE, POWDER, COSMETICS
toils ..... SNARES, TRAPS, GIN
toilsome .... LABORIOUS
Tojo, Japan premier .. HIDEKI
tokay .... WINE, GRAPE
token .... KEEPSAKE, PLEDGE, SCRIP, SLUG, SYMBOL, INDICATION, INDEX, SIGN, EARNEST
of servitude ...... YOKE
payment ...... ADVANCE, EARNEST, ARLES
tokens .... INDICIA
Tokyo .... YEDO, EDO
center .... SHIMBASI
Fifth Avenue of .. GINZA
tole .... ALLURE, ENTICE
Toledo .... SWORD, BLADE
tol(l)booth ..... JAIL, PRISON
tolerable .... BEARABLE, ENDURABLE, PASSABLE, SOSO

tolerably .... FAIRLY,
MODERATELY
tolerance .... MARGIN,
ALLOWANCE
tolerate ..... STAND, BROOK,
ALLOW, PERMIT, BEAR,
ENDURE, SUFFER
toll .. TAX, CHARGE, EXACTION,
KNELL, RING
collector ..... PUBLICAN
road .... (TURN)PIKE
toller ..... BELL RINGER, DOG
German poet ..... ERNST
Tolstoy, Russian novelist .....
LEO, LEV
Toltec .... NAHUATL(AN)
tom ...... MALE, CAT, TURKEY
Dick and Harry ....
ANYONE, EVERYONE
Thumb .... DWARF
tom .... DRUM
tomahawk .... HATCHET,
(BATTLE)AX
tomalley .... LIVER
tomato ...... BERRY, WOMAN,
GIRL, FRUIT, LOVE APPLE
juice jelly .... ASPIC
sauce .. CATSUP, KETCHUP
tomb .... SARCOPHAGUS,
SEPULCHER, MASTABA(H),
VAULT, GRAVE, CIST,
OSSUARY, DOLMEN,
CROMLECH, TAJ MAHAL,
CRYPT
commemorative ....
CENOTAPH
cover .... PALL
empty ...... CENOTAPH
flag .... BANDEROL(E)
for absent dead ....
CENOTAPH
heroes' .... PANTHEON
imposing ... MAUSOLEUM
inscription on .. EPITAPH,
IN MEMORIAM, HERE LIES,
HIC JACET
mummy's ... MASTABA(H)
rock .... CIST
royal .... PYRAMID
saint's .... SHRINE
stone over ...... LEDGER,
MEGALITH
tomboy ..... HOYDEN, HOIDEN
tombstone .... STELE
marshal ... (WYATT)EARP
tomcat .... GIB

tome .... BOOK, VOLUME
tomentose .... MATTED
tomfool .... STUPID, SILLY
tomfoolery .... NONSENSE,
SILLINESS
Tommy, Brit. soldier .. ATKINS
tommyrot .... RUBBISH,
NONSENSE
tomorrow .... MANANA
tomtit ... WREN, CHICKADEE,
BIRD
ton .... STYLE, VOGUE
toncan .. ARACARI, TEAN, TOCO
tone ... SOUND, PITCH, STYLE,
TINT, HUE, KEY
arm .... PICKUP
color .... TIMBRE
down .... SOFTEN
lack of .... ATONY
shade of .... NUANCE
toneless .... ATONY
tong member .... CHINESE
Tonga capital ... NUKUALOFA
king .... TUPOU
tongs .... CLAMP, FORCEPS,
PINCERS
tongue — SPEECH, LANGUAGE,
GLOSSA, IDIOM, TAB,
DIALECT, LINGUA
bell's .... CLAPPER
bone of .... HYOID
buckle's .... PIN
coating .... FUR(RING)
combining form .. ..
GLOSS(O)
curbing device .. BRANKS
elevation on .... PAPILLA
inflammation .. GLOSSITIS
lashing ...... REPRIMAND,
REPROOF
like organ ...... LINGUA,
PROBOSCIS
of the .... GLOSSAL,
LINGUAL
part of .... BLADE
shaped .... LANGUET(TE),
LINGULATE
shoe's .... TAB
tied .... SPEECHLESS
use of .... TASTE,
ARTICULATION,
INGESTION
wagon's ..... POLE, NEAP
tongueless ...... MUTE, DUMB
tonic .... INVIGORATING,
BEVERAGE, MEDICINE,

PICKUP, FILLIP, ROBORANT,
 BRACER, BRACING, ELIXIR
 bark .... CANELLA
 in medicine .... IRON
tonka bean .... GUAIAC
 flavor .... COUMARIN
tonkin .... BAMBOO
 capital .... HANOI
tonneau, later ...... CHASSIS
tonsil .... AMYGDALA
 inflammation ... QUINSY
 instrument for ....
      GUILLOTINE
tonsorial artist ...... BARBER
tonsured person .... PRIEST,
      MONK
tontine .... ANNUITY
tonus .... TONICITY
tony ..... STYLISH, LUXURIOUS
too .... ALSO, BESIDES,
 AS WELL, OVERLY, VERY,
 EXTREMELY, LIKEWISE
 large .... OUTSIZE
 many/much .... DE TROP
 much, in music ... TANTO
tool .... IMPLEMENT,
 INSTRUMENT, UTENSIL,
 MEANS, DEVICE, GADGET
 adz-shaped .... MATTOCK
 bookbinding .... GOUGE
 boring .. TREPAN, AUGER,
 DRILL, GIMLET, JUMPER,
     AWL
 carpenter's .... SAW,
  BEVEL, PLANE
 case .... KIT
 cobbler's .... AWL
 cutting ... BOLO, ADZ(E),
 MACHETE, SAW, SHEARS,
 SCISSORS, KNIFE,
 SICKLE, SCYTHE
 engraver's .... BURIN
 garden .... TROWEL,
 RAKE, HOE, SPADE
 handle .... HELVE
 hole enlarging .. REAMER
 hole-making ..... DIBBLE
 mason's .... CHISEL
 molding .... DIE
 person as a .... DUPE,
 PAWN, STOOGE, FRONT,
 DUMMY, PUPPET
 pipe-bending .... HICKEY
 pruning ...... BILLHOOK,
     SHEARS
 reaper's .... FLAIL

set .... KIT
shaving .... RAZOR
toothed .... SAW
trimming .... SHEAR,
   SCISSOR
toolmaker ...... MACHINIST
tools, set of .... KIT
toon .... TREE, WOOD
toot .... WHISTLE, HORN
 sound ... BLAST, WHISTLE,
   HONK
tooth .... IVORY, TUSK, TUSH,
 INCISOR, CUSPID, MOLAR,
 GAM, PEG, TASTE, APPETITE
 ache .... ODONTALGIA
 and .... NAIL
 boar's .... TUSK
 canine ... FANG, CUSPID,
   LANIARY
 combining form ....
  ODONT(O), DENT(I)
 crooked .... SNAG
 crust .... CEMENT
 decay .... CARIES
 deposit .. TOPHUS, CRUST
 doctor .... DENTIST
 dog's .... FANG
 elephant .... TUSK
 filler .... CEMENT
 for a tooth ...... TALION
 gear .... COG
 growth on .... EXOSTOSIS
 hollow in .... CAVITY
 horse canine ..... TUSH
 like .... ODONTOID
 long, projecting ... TUSK
 long, sharp ...... FANG
 of the .... DENTAL
 part .... DENTIN(E),
 CROWN, PULP, CEMENT
 paste ...... DENTRIFICE,
   ZIRCATE
 puller .... DENTIST
 shaped ...... DENTOID,
   DENTIFORM
 small .... DENTIL,
   DENTICLE
 snake's .... FANG
 socket .... ALVEOLUS
 substance .... PULP
 use of ..... GNAW, BITE,
   PIERCE
 walrus .... TUSK
 wheel ...... COG, GEAR
toothache ...... ODONTALGIA
toothed .... DENTATE, DENTED

wheel .... GEAR
toothlike part ...... TINE, COG,
        PRONG
    projection ...... DENTIL,
        DENTICLE, DENT(ATION)
toothless .... EDENTATE
toothpaste .... ZIRCATE,
        DENTRIFICE
toothsome .... TASTY,
        PALATABLE, SAVORY
tootle .... WHISTLE
toots .... DEAR, DARLING
tootsy .... FOOT
top ... ROOF, LID, COP, COVER,
    ZENITH, HIGHEST, OUTDO,
    TOY, APEX, HEAD, LEAD,
    EXCEL, SURPASS
    altar .... MENSA
    blow one's .... ERUPT
    bottle ..... CROWN, CAP
    carriage's .... CAPOTE
    cover .... LID, CAP
    flight ...... BEST, AONE,
        FIRST RATE
    hat .... GIBUS
    hill .... COP, BROW
    hole .... FIRSTRATE
    kick: sl. ..... SERGEANT
    of head .... CROWN
    of mountain ..... CREST,
        SUMMIT
    of wave .... CREST
    secret .... CLASSIFIED
    shaped .... TURBINATE
    spun with the fingers ....
        TEETOTUM
topaz .... GEM, QUARTZ,
        HUMMINGBIRD
    author of .... URIS
topazolite .... GARNET
topcoat .... RAGLAN
tope .. SHARK, SHRINE, DRINK
topee ..... CAP, HELMET, HAT
toper .... DRUNK(ARD),
    RUMMY, TOSSPOT, SOT,
    SOUSE, BIBBER
tophat .... GIBUS
toph(e) .... TUFA, TUFF
Tophet(h) .... HELL
topi .... HELMET, CAP
topic ...... SUBJECT, THEME,
    HEAD(ING), TEXT
topical .... LOCAL
topkick .... SARGE, SERGEANT
topknot ... HEADDRESS, TUFT
topnotch ... BEST, AONE, ONER

toponym .... NAME
topper .... COAT
topping .... CRUST
topple ...... FALL, OVERTURN,
        TOTTER
topsail .... RAFFE
topside .... DECK
topsy-turvy ...... INVERTED,
        DISORDERLY
toque .... HAT
tor .... CRAG, HILL
tora(h) .... TETEL,
        PENTATEUCH
torch .... FLAMBEAU,
    FLASHLIGHT, LUNT, CRESSET,
        LINK
    bearer ...... LINKBOY,
        LINKMAN
    for lure .... JACK
    material ... TOW, PITCH,
        TALLOW
tore .... TORUS
toreador .... BULLFIGHTER
    assistant of .... PICADOR
torero .... BULLFIGHTER
    queue of .... COLETA
torii .... GATEWAY
Torino .... TURIN
Torme, singer .... MEL
torment .... AGONY, RACK,
    SUFFERING, PAIN, ANGUISH,
    ANNOY, TEASE, BADGER,
    BAIT, VEX, PLAGUE, HARASS,
        TORTURE, HAGRIDE
torn .. RENT, RIVEN, TATTERED,
        REFT
tornado .... WHIRLWIND,
    HURRICANE, CYCLONE,
        TWISTER
tore .... COWFISH, BULL,
        TRUNKFISH
torose ... SWOLLEN, KNOBBED,
    BULGING, CYLINDRICAL
torpedo ... PROJECTILE, RAY,
    NUMBFISH, CRAMPFISH
    colloquial ... SABOTAGE,
        EGG
    part of ..... WAR HEAD,
    PROPELLER, TRIGGER,
        FIN, RUDDER
    slang .... FISH,
    BODYGUARD, GUNMAN
torpid ... DORMANT, SLUGGISH,
    DULL, NUMB, INERT
torpor ... STUPOR, LETHARGY,
        APATHY

torquate .... COLLARED
torque .... TWIST, COLLAR,
                NECKLACE
torques .... RUFF
torrefy .... PARCH, DRY
torrent .. RAPID, RUSH, FLOOD,
              SPATE, DOWNPOUR
torrid ..... ARID, SCORCHING,
     PARCHED, PASSIONATE,
     HOT, ARDENT, SULTRY,
              TROPICAL
torsion .... TWISTING
torsk ...... CUSK, CODFISH
torso .... TRUNK
tort .... WRONG, DAMAGE
torte .... CAKE
torticollis .... WRYNECK
tortile ..... COILED, TWISTED
tortilla ... CORN CAKE, BREAD,
               FLAT
tortoise ...... EMYD, TESTUDO,
    TESTUDINATE, GALAPAGO,
    HICATEE, CHELONIAN,
            TURTLE
  burrowing/land .. GOPHER
  of .... CHELONIAN
  shell .... CARAPACE,
             BUTTERFLY
tortoises, of ..... TESTUDINAL,
          TESTUDINATE
Tortue .... TORTUGA
tortuous .. CROOKED, DEVIOUS,
            WINDING
torture ..... AGONY, ANGUISH,
    TORMENT, RACK, PAIN,
        THIRD DEGREE
  for information .. SWEAT
  instrument of ..... RACK
  method of ... KEELHAUL,
          WATERCURE
torus ... THALAMUS, MOLDING,
            TORE
Tory .... CONSERVATIVE,
         REACTIONARY
Tosca's love .... MARIO
Toscana .... TUSCANY
Toscanini, conductor ......
            ARTURO
toss ..... CAST, FLING, PITCH,
    THROW, BUFFET, FLIP,
    HURL, SNAP, LOB
  about .... BANDY
  side to side ..... CAREEN
tossing expert ..... JUGGLER
tosspot ... DRUNKARD, TOPER,
        DRINKER, SOT

tot ... CHILD, TOTAL, ADD UP,
            DRINK
total ..... UTTER, COMPLETE,
  ENTIRE, WHOLE, SUM, ADD,
    AMOUNT, OUTRIGHT
totalitarian ruler ... DICTATOR
totality .... ENTIRETY
totalizator ...... PARI-MUTUEL,
        TOTE BOARD
tote ...... HAUL, CARRY, LOAD
totem .... XAT, POLE
toter .... LUGGER
totipalmate bird ..... GOOSE,
      DUCK, PELICAN,
      CORMORANT
totter ..... STAGGER, TODDLE,
     ROCK, SHAKE
toucan .... ARACARI, TOCO
touch .... TINGE, ADJOIN,
  CONTACT, TINT, MENTION,
  PAT, TAP, FINGER, AFFECT,
  LOAN, FEEL, TRACE, ABUT
  and go .... HASTY,
    UNCERTAIN, CASUAL
  at .... STOP
  closely .... OSCULATE
  clumsily .... PAW
  doctor's .... PALPATE
  examine by .... FEEL
  for medical diagnosis ....
          PALPATE
  ground with forehead ...
          KOWTOW
  having sense of .. TACTILE
  light, passing .... BRUSH
  lightly .... KISS
  me-not ...... IMPATIENS,
      JEWELWEED
  of ...... TANG, TACTILE,
    TACTIC, HAPTIC
  off .... START, FIRE
  perceptible by .. TACTILE
  system worker .. STENO,
    TYPIST, TYPER
  the feelings .... MOVE
touchable .... TACTILE
touchdown ..... GOAL, SCORE
touched ... MOVED, AFFECTED,
      DEMENTED
touching ... TACTION, MOVING,
      TANGENT
touchstone ... TEST, CRITERION
touchwood ... AMADOU, PUNK,
      TINDER
touchy .. TICKLISH, IRRITABLE,
  SENSITIVE, SORE, HUFFY

tough ...... COHESIVE, ROUGH, THUG, RUFFIAN, GLUTINOUS, STICKY, VISCOUS, HARDY, HARDBOILED, WIRY
   guy ...... BUTCH, GOON
   street .... HOODLUM
toughen .... ANNEAL
Toulouse, painter ... LAUTREC
toupee ...... WIG, HAIRPIECE, PERUKE, RUG
   slang .... RUG
tour ... SHIFT, TRIP, CIRCUIT, ROUND, EYRE
   de force .... FEAT
touraco kin .... CUCKOO
tourbillion .... FIREWORK, WHIRLWIND
tourist .... SIGHTSEER, TRAVELER, TRIPPER
   guide of ..... CICERONE, DRAGOMAN
   stopping place ... MOTEL, INN, HOSTELRY, HOTEL
   travel schedule .... ITINERARY
tourmaline .... GEM, SCHORL, RUBELLITE
tournament .... CONTEST, TOURNEY, COMPETITION, JOUST
   kind of ...... OPEN, PRO, AMATEUR, CAROUSEL
   knights' ..... TILT, JOUST
tourney .... TOURNAMENT, JOUST
tourniquet ... BANDAGE, PAD, GARROT
tousle .... DISHEVEL, RUMPLE, MUSS
tout ... SOLICITOR, BALLYHOO, TIP(STER), PUFF, SPY, PRAISE
tovarisch .... COMRADE
tow ..... PULL, DRAG, FIBER, HARDS, HURDS
   and pitch torch ... LINK
toward .... FACING, ABOUT
   center .... ENTAD
   exterior .... ECTAD
   mouth .... ORAD
towboat .... TUG, MULE
towel .... DRY, WIPE(R), ABSORBENT, DIAPER, NAPKIN
   church service ... LAVABO
   small .... SERVIETTE
tower .... BASTIL(L)E, SOAR,

REAR, SPIRE, TURRET, TOURELLE, PULLER, DRAGGER, ZIGGURAT
   a kind of .... IVORY
   bell .... BELFRY, CAMPANILE
   Biblical ... BABEL, EDAR
   bridge .... BARBICAN
   canal boat's ...... MULE
   castle .... DONJON, BARBICAN
   church .... STEEPLE
   fodder .... SILO
   fortified .... DONJON, DUNGEON, PEEL
   gate .... BARBICAN
   mosque .... MINARET
   of Babel ..... MADHOUSE
   of confusion ..... BABEL
   pointed .... SPIRE
   portable .... TURRET, BASTIL(LE)
   signal .... BEACON
   tapering ... SPIRE, STEEPLE
towering .... HIGH
towhead .... BLOND
towhee ..... CHEWINK, FINCH
   kin .. BUNTING, SPARROW
town ..... HAMLET, VILLAGE, CITY, BOROUGH, BURG(H), PUEBLO, WICK
   fortified/walled ... BURG, BURH
   imaginary ..... PODUNK
   league .... HANSEATIC
   magistrate .... REEVE
   map .... PLAT
   near castle ...... BOURG
   section .... WARD
   square ... PLAZA, CAMPO
   street .... MAINDRAG
   "Too Tough to Die" .... TOMBSTONE
township .... DEME
townsman .... CIT(IZEN), RESIDENT, OPPIDAN
Towser's treat .... BONE
toxic .... POISONOUS
toxicant .... POISON(OUS)
toxin ..... VENOM, POISON
   canned food ... BOTULIN
toxophilite .... ARCHER
toy .... PLAYTHING, FLIRT, DALLY, TEETOTUM, TRIFLE, TRINKET, BAUBLE, PLAY
   bear .... TEDDY

dog .... TERRIER,
CHIHUAHUA, PEKE
musical instrument ......
KAZOO
stilt-like ..... POGO STICK
stringed .... YOYO
with string ... TOP, YOYO,
DIABOLO
tra la la .... REFRAIN
trace ... TANG, TINGE, TOUCH,
MARK, SIGN, ENGRAM,
TRACK, VESTIGE, TRAIL,
FOLLOW, DELINEATE, DRAW,
SLOT
trachea .... WINDPIPE,
WEASAND
trachoma ... CONJUNCTIVITIS
track .... TRACE, VESTIGE,
TRAIL, PATH, ROUTE,
COURSE, WAY, CIRCUIT,
FOLLOW, RUNWAY
circuit .... LAP
down .... HUNT, SEARCH
game ...... SPOOR, PUG
horse racing ..... TURF
mark .. RUT, FOOTPRINT,
SPOOR, SLOT, SPUR
racing ...... SPEEDWAY,
CINDER PATH
ship's .... WAKE
train .... RAILS
tracker .... HUNTER, HOUND,
TAIL, DETECTIVE
tract ...... STRETCH, STEPPE,
AREA, EXTENT, LEAFLET,
PAMPHLET, TREATISE,
ENTERON
tractable ..... EASY, DOCILE,
COMPLIANT, OBEDIENT
tractate .... TREATISE
tractile .... DUCTILE, TENSILE
traction ... DRAWING, PULLING
tractor .... BULLDOZER,
AIRPLANE, MULE
and trailer .... SEMI
caterpillar .... CAT
trade .. DEAL, SWAP, BUSINESS,
SELL, CLIENTELE, EXCHANGE,
METIER, CRAFT, WORK,
OCCUPATION, BARTER,
COMMERCE, CUSTOMERS
agreement ...... CARTEL
association ..... CARTEL,
SYNDICATE
center .... MART, MARKET,
EXCHANGE, PIT

of .... MERCANTILE
questionable .... TRAFFIC
union strategy .. RATTEN
unlawful .. CONTRABAND
wind .... MONSOON
trademark .... BRAND
trader ... MONGER, MERCHANT,
SHIP
unauthorized ....
INTERLOPER
tradesman .... HUCKSTER,
ARTISAN, STOREKEEPER
trading .... COMMERCE,
COMMERCIAL
center ..... RIALTO, PIT,
EXCHANGE, EMPORIUM
grains .... PIT
place, stocks .. EXCHANGE
settlement ..... FACTORY
ship .... CRAY
stamp .... PREMIUM
tradition .. CUSTOM, PRACTICE,
USAGE, (FOLK)LORE
traditional ...... CUSTOMARY,
CONVENTIONAL, LEGENDARY
traduce .... VILIFY, SLUR,
DEFAME, SLANDER, MALIGN,
REVILE
traffic .... COMMERCE, TRADE,
BUSINESS
direction ...... UTURN,
ONEWAY
light .... BLINKER, RED,
GREEN, AMBER
stopper .... SIREN
violator .... JAYWALKER
trafficker ... TRADER, DEALER,
MERCHANT
tragacanth .... GUM
tragedian ... ACTOR, THESPIAN,
SHAKESPEARE
tragedy ...... DRAMA, PLAY,
DISASTER, CATASTROPHE
tragic .... SAD, FATAL,
CALAMITOUS, PATHETIC
tragopan .... PHEASANT
trail ... DRAG, TRACK, HUNT,
PATH, TRAIPSE, HOUND,
HEEL
along .... TAG, FOLLOW
animal ... SPOOR, SCENT,
SLOT, PUG, FOIL
behind ... LAG, STRAGGLE
blazer .... PIONEER
of scent .... DRAG
secretly ... SHADOW, TAIL

thru mud .... DAGGLE
trailer .... TAIL, TRACKER,
 VAN, WAGON, TRACER
 arbutus ..... MAYFLOWER
 branch .... STOLON,
 RHIZOME, RUNNER
trailing .... DECUMBENT
train ..... SUITE, PROCESSION,
 SERIES, INSTRUCT, AIM,
 TEACH, DRILL, CHAIN,
 JERKWATER, RETINUE
 designating a .. SPECIAL,
 LOCAL, EXPRESS,
 FREIGHT, FLIER,
 LIMITED
 for position ..... GROOM
 of attendants ... CORTEGE,
 SUITE, RETINUE,
 ENTOURAGE
 overhead ...... MONORAIL,
 EL
 rider with free ticket .....
 DEADHEAD
trainee .... APPRENTICE,
 PUPIL, NOVITIATE
trainer .. COACH, INSTRUCTOR,
 TEACHER, HANDLER,
 GYMNAST
trainmen's car ...... CABOOSE
traipse ... GAD, TRAMP, TRAIL,
 WANDER
trait .... QUALITY,
 CHARACTERISTIC
traitor .... BETRAYER,
 APOSTATE, RENEGADE,
 RECREANT
 American .... HISS,
 CHAMBERS
 Austrian .... REDL
 Czechoslovak ....
 GOTTWALD
 Finnish ...... KUSIINEN
 French ..... ESTERHAZY,
 LAVAL, PETAIN
 Hungarian ...... RAKOSI
 Norwegian ... QUISLING
 Romanian ..... PAUKER
traject .... CAST, THROW
trajectory .... ARC
tram ... STREETCAR, TROLLEY
 coal mine .... TUB
trammel .. POTHOOK, HAMPER,
 CONFINE, RESTRAIN,
 SHACKLE
tramontane ..... FOREIGNER,
 STRANGER, ALIEN

tramp .... HOBO, BUM,
 VAGABOND, VAGRANT,
 HIKE, RAMBLE, PLOD, TART,
 TRUDGE, HOOF, YEGG,
 CLUMP
 identification mark ......
 MONI(C)KER
 offering to .... HANDOUT
trampolin(e) .... NET
 user .... ACROBAT,
 TUMBLER
trance .... SPELL, DAZE,
 STUPOR, HYPNOSIS
tranquil .... CALM, PLACID,
 QUIET, SERENE, STILL
tranquility ..... POISE, PEACE
 Base site .... MOON
 of the spirit ... QUIETISM
tranquilize(r) ... CALM, QUIET,
 SOOTHE, RESERPINE,
 DEPRESSANT, SEDATIVE,
 OPIATE, ATARAXIC
transact .. DEAL, NEGOTIATE,
 TREAT
transaction .. DEAL, BUSINESS,
 SALE
transcend .... OVERSTEP,
 EXCEED, EXCEL, SURPASS
transcribe .... COPY
transcriber .... STENO,
 COPIER, COPYIST
transcript(ion) ... COPY,
 REPRODUCTION
transeunt, opposed to ....
 IMMANENT
transfer .... SEND, PASS,
 CEDE, REMOVE
 blood .... TRANSFUSE
 by will .... DEMISE
 of court suit ... REMOVER
 of lands, etc. .. MORTMAIN
 property .... DEED,
 CONVEY, GRANT
 residence .... MOVE
 sovereignty ..... DEMISE
transference .... SWITCH
transfix ..... NAIL, PIERCE,
 PIN, IMMOBILIZE, IMPALE
transform .... CONVERT,
 CHANGE, METAMORPHOSE,
 TRANSMUTE, TRANSFIGURE
transformation ...... CHANGE,
 METASTASIS, TRANSITION,
 METAMORPHOSIS
transformer, type of ....
 STEP-UP, STEP-DOWN

transfuse ..... INSTILL, IMBUE
transgress ...... SIN, VIOLATE,
INFRACT, OVERSTEP,
TRESPASS
transgression ... SIN, TRESPASS,
VIOLATION, OFFENSE
transgressor ...... OFFENDER,
SINNER
transient .... TEMPORARY,
MOMENTARY, FLEETING,
EPHEMERAL
laborer .... FLOATER
transit ...... PASSAGE, RAPID,
THEODOLITE, CONVEYANCE
transition .. PASSAGE, PASSING,
TRANSFER, CHANGE
transitive .... TRANSEUNT
transitory .... FLEETING,
EPHEMERAL, TEMPORARY,
BRIEF, MOMENTARY
translate .... INTERPRET,
CHANGE, TRANSFER,
DECODE, RENDER,
METAPHRASE
translation ... VERSION, PONY,
PARAPHRASE, RENDITION,
INTERPRETATION
translator ...... INTERPRETER
translucent .... CLEAR,
TRANSPARENT, PELLUCID
transmit ..... SEND, FORWARD,
CONVEY, CARRY
transmute .... CONVERT
transom .. LINTEL, CROSSPIECE,
LOUVER, SLAT, TRAVE
transparent ..... DIAPHANOUS,
SHEER, GAUZY, OPEN,
CANDID, OBVIOUS, CLEAR,
LIQUID, PELLUCID, HYALINE,
TRANSLUCENT, HYALOID,
LUCID, LIMPID
combining form ....
HYAL(O)
not .... OPAQUE
transpire ... HAPPEN, OCCUR,
LEAK OUT, PASS
transplant .... RESETTLE,
RELOCATE, GRAFT
transport .... BANISH,
(TROOP)SHIP, CARRY,
ENTRANCE, ENRAPTURE,
AIRPLANE
transporting, act of .. PORTAGE
transportation .... FARE,
DEPORTATION, CONVEYANCE
charge .... FARE

route .... LINE, AIRLANE
service/system .... LINE
transported .... RAPT,
CARRIED, ENTRANCED
transpose ...... INTERCHANGE,
REVERSE, INVERT
transposition .... METATHESIS
transude .... SWEAT, OOZE,
EXUDE
Transvaal capital .. PRETORIA
city .... BENONI
gold region .... RAND
transverse .... CROSSWISE
Transylvania city .... CLUJ
trap .... NET, SNARE, CATCH,
GIN, NAIL, TREPAN, TOIL,
PIT(FALL), CARRIAGE,
CAPARISON, WHIN,
LUGGAGE
fish .... WEIR, GIN
game .... GIN
kind of .... AMBUSH
slang .... MOUTH
trapan .... TRICK
trapdoor .... HATCH, DROP
trapper ..... SNARER, TREPAN
trappings .. DUDS, CAPARISON,
ADORNMENTS, REGALIA
Trappist .... MONK
monk .... MERTON
traps, orchestra ..... DRUMS,
CYMBALS, BELLS
trapshooting .... SKEET
target .... (CLAY)PIGEON
trash ..... REFUSE, RUBBISH,
NONSENSE, COLLAR,
RESTRAIN(T), TRIPE,
(RIFF)RAFF, JUNK
gaudy .... KITSCH
receptable ... (DUST)BIN
trashy .... WORTHLESS
trauma ..... WOUND, INJURY,
SHOCK
travail .. TOIL, PAIN, AGONY,
WORK, ANGUISH
trave .... CROSSBEAM
travel .... TOUR, JOURNEY,
TRIP, TRAFFIC, PAD
by car .... MOTOR
by ox wagon ...... TREK
in circle .... ORBIT
of .... VIATIC
on foot over snow .. MUSH
to holy place ....
PILGRIMAGE

what it does .. BROADENS, EDUCATES
traveler .... TOURIST, VOYAGE(U)R, WAYFARER, VIATOR, TRIPPER,
  aid of .... COURIER, CICERONE
  guidebook for .... BAEDEKER
  kind of .... HOBO, VAGABOND, SALESMAN, TRAMP, NOMAD, PILGRIM
  refuge ... OASIS, HOSPICE
  stopping place of .... INN, SERAI, HOSPICE
travelers, company of .... CARAVAN
traveling bag .... VALISE, HOLDALL, GRIP(SACK)
  actors' group ... TROUPE
  companion ... CHAPERON, COURIER, ESCORT
  show .... CIRCUS
  yen for .... WANDERLUST
traverse ...... PIVOT, SWIVEL, COURSE, CROSS(PIECE)
travertine .... LIMESTONE
travesty ... MOCKERY, PARODY, BURLESQUE, CARICATURE, SATIRE
travois .... SLEDGE
trawl .... (DRAG)NET
trawler .... BOAT
tray .... SERVER, SALVER, COASTER, TILL
  agriculture .... HYDROPONICS
  dish ..... WAITER, SALVER
  for types .... GALLEY
  liquids .... CAPSULE
treacherous ..... PERFIDIOUS, DISLOYAL, FAITHLESS, DECEITFUL
  person .... TRAITOR, RENEGADE, TURNCOAT, BETRAYER
treachery .. DECEIT, PERFIDY, BETRAYAL
treacle .. MOLASSES, ANTIDOTE, REMEDY
treacly .... STICKY
tread ... STEP, WALK, TRAMPLE, CHALAZA, PAD, CICATRICLE
  sound .... CRUNCH
treadle .... PEDAL, LEVER
treadmill .... WHEEL

treason .... TREACHERY, SEDITION
  kind of .... LESE MAJESTE
treasure ..... HOARD, VALUE, TROVE, CHERISH, PRIZE, WEALTH, APPRECIATE
  container .... CHEST
  isle of fiction .... MONTE CRISTO
  state .... MONTANA
treasurer ... BURSAR, PURSER
treasury ... VAULT, BURSARY, FISC, COFFERS, THESAURUS, EXCHEQUER
  agent .... TMAN
treat .... USE, BARGAIN, NEGOTIATE, DEAL, DELIGHT, ENTERTAIN, HANDLE, REGALE
  badly ..... ABUSE, SCORN, INSULT, ILL USE
  insolently ... ABUSE, HUFF
  lightly .... PALTER
  tenderly ... PET, CODDLE
  with contempt .. CONTEMN
  with warm application ... FOMENT
treatise ... DISCOURSE, PAPER, MONOGRAPH, THESIS, ESSAY, DISSERTATION
  opening part .. EXORDIUM
treatment ...... USAGE, CARE, HANDLING, MANAGEMENT, APPROACH, USE
  before doctor's arrival ... FIRST AID
  sprain .... ARNICA
treaty .... AGREEMENT, PACT, MISE, PROTOCOL, COVENANT, COMPACT, CONCORDAT
  kind of .... PEACE, ALLIANCE, ENTENTE, CONCORD
Trebizond .... TRABZON, SEAPORT
treble .. SOPRANO, THREEFOLD, TRIPLE, SHRILL
trebuchet's kin .... CATAPULT
  missile .... STONE
tree ...... STAKE, POST, POLE, GALLOWS, HATRACK, CORNER, ARBOR, GALLOWS
  balsam .... TOLU
  bark .... CORTEX
  bark remover .. SPUDDER
  beech .... ROBLE

betelnut .... ARECA
biblical ...... OLIVE, FIG
birch family .. HORNBEAM,
 HAZEL
boxwood .... SERON
branch(es) ..... RAMAGE,
 SPRAY, SPRIG, TWIG
buckwheat .... TITI
bully .... BALATA
butter .... SHEA
coffee .... CHICOT
combining form ....
 DENDR(I), DENDR(O)
cone-bearing ...... FIR,
 CEDAR, YEW, PINE,
 SPRUCE
cottonwood ..... ALAMO,
 POPLAR
covering .... BARK
crook .... KNEE
custard apple .. SWEETSOP,
 SOURSOP
cutting ...... LOP(PING)
decay .... NECROSIS
disease ... KNOT, MOSAIC
dogwood .... TUPELO,
 ASSAGAI
dwarf(ing) ...... BONSAI
dwelling creature ....
 OPOSSUM
ebony family ...... KAKI
evergreen .... FIR,
 EUCALYPTUS, CAROB,
 THUJA, OLIVE, YEW,
 PINE, BAY
exudation ...... BALATA,
 GUM, COPAL, LATEX,
 ROSIN, RESIN, SAP,
 MILK
fiber .... BAST, BASS,
 BAOBAB
flowering ...... CATALPA,
 TITI, MAGNOLIA
fragrant wood ....
 BASSWOOD
fraxinus .... ASH
frog ...... TOAD, PEEPER,
 HYLA
fustic .... MORA
gamboge family .. CALABA
giant .... SEQUOIA,
 REDWOOD
gingko .... ICHO
grown flat ..... ESPALIER
gum ... ACACIA, BALATA,
 EUCALYPTUS, ICICA,
 CHICLE, BUMBO,
 SAPOTA, XYLAN,
 RUBBER, SAPODILLA,
 TUPELO, PEPPERIDGE
gum resin .... ANTRA
hardwood ... TEAK, OAK,
 MOLAVE, ASH, IPIL
head of .... CROWN
heart-shape leafed ......
 CATALPA
hive .... BEEGUM
holly family .... ILEX
icy coating of ..... SLEET
iron .... ACLD
ironwood .... TITI
juice .... CHICLE, MANNA
kapok .... CEIBA
knot .... BURL
lemon .... CITRUS
light wood .... BALSA
like a .... ARBOREAL,
 DENDROID, DENDRITIC
lime .... CITRUS
linden .. BASSWOOD, LIMB,
 LINN, TEIL
lily family ... DRACAENA
locust .... ACACIA
lotus .... SADR
madder family .. BANCAL
magnolia .... CHAMPAK,
 CHAMPAC, TULIP,
 WHITEWOOD
marmalade ...... MAMEY,
 SAPODILLA, CHICO,
 MAMMEE
mark on .... BLAZE
Mediterranean ... CAROB
mimosa family .. ACACIA
moss .... USNEA
mulberry family .. FUSTIC
myrtle family ... CAJEPUT,
 CAJUPUT, LEHUA
oak ...... ENCINA, ROBLE
oil .... BEN
of a .... CEDARN
of heaven ... AILANTHUS
of life ...... ARBORVITAE
olive .... OLEA
palm .... CALAMUS
palm-like .... ZAMIA
pea family ...... CASSIA,
 DIVI-DIVI, MIMOSA,
 LABURNUM
pear .... NOPAL
Philippine ...... YAKAL,

MOLAVE, IPIL, SANTOL,
SAMPALOC
pine .... PINON, CYPRESS,
HEMLOCK, JUNIPER,
LARCH
plum .... DAMSON
poisonous .... SASSY,
UPAS
pomegranate .. BLAUSTINE
powder .... ARAROBA
pulse family .... LOCUST
rain ..... SAMAN, ZAMIA
remnant ... STUB, STUMP
resin ... PINE, BALSAM, FIR
rose family ..... LOQUAT,
MEDLAR
sapodilla .... BUSTIC
screw pine ... PANDANUS
shade ... ASH, ELM, LINN
shaped ... DENDRIFORM,
DENDROID
shoots .... BROWSE,
TWIGS
silk .... SIRIS
silk-cotton .... CEIBA
soapberry .... LITCHI
source of balsam ... TOLU
stock ..... STEM, TRUNK
stump .... SNAG, RUNT,
STOOL
stub .... STUMP
stunted .... SCRAG
stunting .... BONSAI
sumac ...... TEREBINTH
toad .... PEEPER
toad genus .... HYLA
top .... CROWN
"trembling" ..... ASPEN
trimmings ...... BRASH
tropical .... LEHUA,
TAMARISK, PAPAYA,
PALM, CINCHONA
trunk ... BOLE, STOCK
trunk, growth on ....
LICHEN
trunk knot ...... BURL
trunk protuberance ....
KNAR
trunk ring ...... GIRDLE
trunk strip ...... FLITCH
trunk wood ... DURAMEN
walnut family .. HICKORY
wide-spreading .. CEDAR,
JUNIPER
with applelike fruit ......
MEDLAR

with plumlike fruit ......
LOQUAT
with striped wood ....
ARAROBA
with winged fruit ... ASH,
ELM, MAPLE, SAMARA
young .... SAPLING,
SEEDLING
treeless plain .... WOLD,
SAVANNA, PAMPAS,
TUNDRA, STEPPE
treelike .... DENDRITIC
in form ...... DENDROID
treenail .... PEG, TRUNNEL,
SPIKE, PIN
trees .... FOREST, WOODS,
TIMBER
book on .... SILVA, SYLVA
clump of ... TUFT, GROVE,
BOSK, SCRUB
grove of pine ... PINETUM
of .... ARBOROUS
of a region .... SILVA
pertaining to .. ARBOREAL
place where sold ....
NURSERY
study of ... DENDROLOGY
stunted .... SCRUB
treatise on .... SILVA
trefoil .... CLOVER,
TRIFOLIUM, SHAMROCK
trek ...... TRAVEL, JOURNEY,
MIGRATION
trellis ..... LATTICE, BOWER,
ARBOR, ESPALIER
part .... LATH
trelliswork .... PERGOLA,
LATTICEWORK
trematode .... FLATWORM,
FLUKE
larva .... CERCARIA
tremble ...... SHIVER, QUIVER,
TOTTER, VIBRATE, SHUDDER,
WOBBLE, QUAKE, SHAKE
trembling .... PALPITANT
tremendous .... GREAT,
ENORMOUS, EXTRAORDINARY
tremolite .... AMPHIBOLE
tremolo ..... QUAVER, TRILL,
VIBRATO
tremor ..... QUAKE, SHAKING,
THRILL, TREPIDATION,
SHIVER
tremulous .... QUIVERING,
FEARFUL, SHAKY, ASPEN,
TREMULANT, QUAVERY

trenail .... TREENAIL
trench .... CUT, FURROW,
             DITCH, SAP, FOSSE
    embankment ... PARADOS
    knife .... BAYONET
    moon .... RILL(E)
    strengthener ... FASCINE
trenchant ..... SHARP, KEEN,
       INCISIVE, PENETRATING,
       FORCEFUL, CLEAR-CUT
trencher .... PLATTER, BOARD,
       SAPPER, DIGGER
trencherman .... EATER,
       PARASITE, SPONGER,
       HANGER-ON, GLUTTON
trend ...... DRIFT, TENDENCY,
       TENOR, COURSE
trepan ...... TREPHINE, AUGER,
       TRICK(STER)
trepang ..... SEA CUCUMBER,
       ECHINODERM
trephine .... TREPAN, SAW
trepidation ... ALARM, DREAD,
       FEAR, TREMOR
treponema .... SPIROCHETE
trespass .... SIN, TRANSGRESS,
       OFFEND, OFFENSE, INVADE,
       INFRINGE, ENCROACH,
       POACH
trespasser .... POACHER,
       INTRUDER, INVADER
tres ____ .... BIEN, CHIC
tress ... LOCK, PLAIT, BRAID,
       CURL, PIGTAIL, QUEUE,
       RINGLET
Treves .... TRIER
trews .... TROUSERS
trey, thing with .... DIE, DICE,
       CARD, DOMINO
triad .... TRINITY, TRINE,
       TRIUNE
trial ...... AFFLICTION, ESSAY,
       TEST, PROBATION,
       EXPERIMENT, HEARING,
       INQUEST
    ancient method of ......
       ORDEAL
    balloon ... FEELER, KITE
    by ____ .... COMBAT,
       JURY, FIRE
    performance ....
       PROLUSION, REHEARSAL
    scene of .... COURT
    severe .... ORDEAL,
       CRUCIBLE
    site .... VENUE

trials and ____ .. TRIBULATIONS
triangle .... TRIGON, SCALENE
    for example .. IDIOPHONE
    kind of ...... ISOSCELES,
       ETERNAL
    part .... SIDE, BASE,
       HYPOTENUSE
    side of .... LEG
    word for a love .. ETERNAL
triangular .. THREE-CORNERED,
       TRIGONAL, TRIGONOUS,
       DELTOID, TRIQUETROUS
    brace .... GUSSET
    flag ... PENNANT, PENNON,
       BUNTING
    insert in seam .... GUSSET
    muscle of shoulder ......
       DELTOID
    piece in a sail ...... GORE
    piece of land ...... GORE
    sail .... LATEEN,
       SPINNAKER, JIB
triarchy .... TRIUMVIRATE
tribe ... CLAN, GENE, FAMILY,
       FOLK
    leader ...... CHIEFTAIN,
       PATRIARCH
    wandering .... HORDE
tribal sign .... TOTEM
tribulation .... DISTRESS,
       SORROW, MISERY,
       AFFLICTION, TRIAL, WOE
tribunal ... BENCH, ROTA, BAR,
       SEAT, FORUM, COURT
tribune ... MAGISTRATE, DAIS,
       PLATFORM
tributary .... SUBJECT,
       SUBSIDIARY, RIVER, STREAM
tribute ..... HOMAGE, PRAISE,
       EULOGY, GIFT, TAX,
       OFFERING, OVATION
    to dead person .. EULOGY,
       EPITAPH
trice ...... INSTANT, MOMENT,
       SEC(OND), TIE
tricentennial .... TERCENTARY
trichoid .... HAIRLIKE
trichome ... PRICKLE, BRISTLE,
       ROOT HAIR
trichord .... LYRE
trick ..... ENTRAP, FUB, FOB,
       (FLIM)FLAM, GULL, CHEAT,
       STUNT, GAFF, ARTIFICE,
       TREPAN, DUPE, DIDO,
       DODGE, HOODWINK, JAPE,
       DECEPTION, FRAUD,

RUSE, GAG, PRANK, JOKE,
CHICANE(RY), WILE, KNACK,
STRATEGEM, HOAX,
ASSIGNMENT, SHIFT,
GIMMICK, DEVICE, NICK
device .... GIMMICK
easy to .... GULLIBLE
person easy to .... GULL,
DUPE, CULLY, GOOF
trickery .... ARTIFICE, FRAUD,
DECEPTION, ART, CRAFT,
CHICANE(RY)
trickle .... DRIP, SEEP, DROP,
FLOW
tricks, win all .... CAPOT
trickster .... TREPAN,
MAGICIAN, PRANKSTER,
JOKER, CHEAT, SWINDLER
tricktrack .... BACKGAMMON
tricky ... DECEITFUL, CRAFTY,
INTRICATE, SLY, CATCHY,
SMART, DECEPTIVE
and sly .... DEEP
condition .... CATCH
tricolor .... FLAG
tricorn .... HAT
tricycle .... VELOCIPEDE,
IRON HORSE
trident ...... SPEAR, LEISTER
bearer .... NEPTUNE,
POSEIDON
warrior with ... RETIARUS
tridentate .... TRIFID
Tridentum .... TRENT
tried ..... TESTED, RELIABLE,
PROVED
trierarch's command .. GALLEY,
TRIREME
trifid .... TRIDENTATE
trifle .... LITTLE, DESSERT,
PEWTER, TOY, DALLY, PLAY,
FLIRT, DOIT, FICO,
KICKSHAW, DIDDLE,
PALTER, FALDERAL,
FOLDEROL
trifles .... TRIVIA
trifling ..... PALTRY, TRIVIAL,
PETTY, PIDDLING, FRIVOLOUS
amount ... PEANUTS, FIG
objection ...... CAVIL,
QUIBBLE
trifoliate .... TERNATE,
THREE-LEAFED
plant .... SHAMROCK,
CLOVER, TRIFOLIUM,
TREFOIL, TRILLIUM

trifolium .... CLOVER,
SHAMROCK, TREFOIL
trig ..... NEAT, SMART, WELL,
SPRUCE, SOUND, FIT, TRIM,
PROP, WEDGE, CHOKE
trigeminal .... TRIFACIAL
trigger .... INITIATE, LAUNCH,
FIRE, TRIP
triggerfish .... OLDWIFE
trigo .... WHEAT
trigon ..... TRIANGLE, LYRE,
TRINE, HARP
trigonal .... TRIANGULAR
trigonometric function ....
(CO)SINE, SECANT
line ... SECANT, TANGENT
trigonous ..... TRIANGULAR,
THREE-CORNERED
trilateral .... THREE-SIDED
trill .... VIBRATO, WARBLE,
TIRALEE, ROLL, TREMOLO,
MORDENT
trilogy writer ...... ASCH,
GALSWORTHY
trim ... TIDY, TRIG, TAUT, CUT,
DECORATE, CLIP, DEFEAT,
LOP, CHEAT, ORDERLY,
NEAT, NIFTY, PRUNE,
DAPPER, NATTY, DRESS,
SCOLD, CHIDE, DOCK, PARE,
FETTLE, DECK
beard/hair .... BARBER,
CLIP
coin .... NIG
feathers .... PREEN
in curves ...... SCALLOP,
ESCALOP
lumber .... DRESS
shrubbery/wool ... SHEAR
trimmer ...... TIMESERVER,
OPPORTUNIST
trimming .... DEFEAT,
RICKRACK, GIMP, BEATING,
RUCHE, DECORATION,
EDGING, ORNAMENT,
GUIPURE,
braid/ribbon .. GALLOON
tool ... SHEARS, CLIP(PER),
SCISSORS, ZAX
Trimurti .... TRINITY
Trinacrian .... SICILIAN
trinal .... TRIPLE, THREEFOLD
trinary .. TERNARY, THREEFOLD
trine ... TRIGON, THREEFOLD,
TRIPLE, TRIAD, FAVORABLE,
TRINITY

Trinidad city .... ARIMA
 dance .... CALYPSO
 fish .... GUPPY
 music .... CALYPSO
 of Hindu gods .. TRIMURTI
 partner of ...... TOBACCO
Trinity College scholar ....
       SIZER, SIZAR
trinitrotoluene .... TNT,
    EXPLOSIVE, TROTYL
trinket .... TRIFLE, TOY,
  ORNAMENT, JEWELRY,
  GEWGAW, KNICKNACK,
  GIMCRACK, KICKSHAW,
     BIJOU, GAUD
 seller .... FAKER
trio, mythical .. FATES, GRACES,
      FURIES
 of fiction .... MUSKETEERS
 one of a ... HOPE, FAITH,
  CHARITY, CALM, COOL,
  COLLECTED, LACHESIS,
  ATHOS, PORTHOS, ARAMIS,
  TOM, DICK, HARRY,
  CLOTHO, ATROPOS
trioxide, of arsenic .. RATSBANE
trip ... STUMBLE, CAPER, SKIP,
  ERR, JOURNEY, TILT,
  OUTING, ERR, EXCURSION,
  JAUNT, VOYAGE, TUMBLE
tripartite .... THREEFOLD
tripe .... RUBBISH, TRASH
triple ... THREEFOLD, TERNARY,
  TREBLE, TRIAD, TRINAL,
  TRINE, TRIPLICATE
 alliance .... AXIS,
     DREIBUND
 crown .... TIARA
 crown winner ....
     SECRETARIAT
 time .... TRIPLEX
triplet .... TRISTICH
 in music .... TERCET
tripod .... TRIPOS, CAT,
  TRIVET, SPIDER
 part .... LEG
tripoli ..... ABRASIVE, ROCK,
    ROTTENSTONE
 badmen, former ....
      PIRATES
 ruler .... DEY, PASHA
 where it is .... LIBYA,
     LEBANON
tripos .... TRIPOD
tripper .. PAWL, CAM, TOURIST,
     DETENT

trippet .... CAM
triptych .... TABLET
triquetrous ...... TRIHEDRAL,
    TRIANGULAR
trireme .... GALLEY
 commander .. TRIERARCH
Tris, baseball player .. SPEAKER
trisaccharide .... TRIOSE
trismus .... LOCKJAW,
    TETANUS
triste .... SAD
tristesse .... SADNESS
tristful .... SAD, SORROWFUL
tristich .... TRIPLET
Tristram's beloved ... ISEULT,
    ISOLDE
trite .... HACK(NEYED), STALE,
  COMMONPLACE, CORNY,
  JEJUNE, STOCK, MUSTY
 expression ...... CLICHE,
  BANALITY, PLATITUDE,
    CORN
triton .... NEWT, SNAIL,
  (SEA)GOD, SALAMANDER, EFT
 lower extremity of .. TAIL
 parent of ..... POSEIDON,
   AMPHITRITE
 trumpet .... CONCH
triturate ... CRUSH, RUB, BRAY,
  GRIND, PULVERIZE
triumph ... SUCCESS, PREVAIL,
  VICTORY, EXULT(ATION),
  REJOICE, WIN
triumphant ...... EXULTANT,
   JUBILANT
triumvirate .... TRIARCHY
triume .... TRINITY, TRIAD
trivet .... TRIPOD, SPIDER
trivia .... TRIFLES
trivial ..... TRIFLING, PETTY,
  UNIMPORTANT, PALTRY,
  LITTLE, SLIGHT, BANAL,
    FLIMSY
 objection .... CAVIL
trivium, part of .... LOGIC,
  GRAMMAR, RHETORIC,
  MUSIC, GEOMETRY,
  ARITHMETIC, ASTRONOMY
troche .... LOZENGE,
  COUGH DROP,
  PASTIL(LE), ROTULA
trochee .... TROCHAIC
 and iamb ..... CHORIAMB
trochilus .... SCOTIA,
  HUMMINGBIRD, WARBLER
troglodyte .... CAVE MAN,

RECLUSE, HERMIT, GORILLA, APE, CHIMPANZEE
trogon ...... QUE(T)ZAL, BIRD
troika .... VEHICLE
Troilus' father .... PRIAM
killer .... ACHILLES
love .... CRESSIDA
mother .... HECUBA
Trojan ..... ILIAN, TEUCRIAN, DARDAN(IAN)
commander ... ANTENOR
country .... TROY
epic .... ILIAD
hero .... (A)ENEAS
horse builder .... EPEUS
king .... PRIAM
peace offering ....
(WOODEN)HORSE
War allies ...... DARDAN
War cause .... HELEN
War hero ...... MEMNON
War protagonist .. PARIS, HECTOR, AGENOR, ACHILLES, (A)ENEAS, DARDAN
War warriors ....
MYRMIDONS
troll .. GNOME, GIANT, DWARF, IMP, ROLL, SING, CHANT, FISH, SPIN
trolley ..... CART, STREETCAR, TRAM
car .... DINKEY
trollop ...... SLATTERN, SLUT
trombone ... HORN, SAMBUKE
forerunner of .. SACKBUT
mouthpiece ..... BOCAL
part .... SLIDE
trommel ...... SIEVE, SCREEN
trona .... URAO
Trondheim .... NIDAROS
troop .... BAND, COMPANY, TROUPE, FLOCK, GROUP
barracks ..... CASERN(E)
disposition .. DEPLOYMENT
formation .... ECHELON, HERSE
member .... SOLDIER, BOY SCOUT
quarters ..... BARRACKS, BILLET, CANTON(MENT), CASERN
trooper .... CAVALRYMAN, POLICEMAN, MOUNTIE
troops' halting place .. ETAPE

quarters .... CANTON, BILLET
screen .... BLINDAGE
spread .... DEPLOY
station .. POST, GARRISON
stationed in a fort ....
GARRISON
temporary encampment ..
BIVOUAC
turning movement ......
WHEEL
troopship .... TRANSPORT
trop ...... MANY, TOO (MUCH)
trope .... METAPHOR
trophy ... MEMORIAL, AWARD, MEMENTO, PALM, LAUREL, PRIZE, SPOILS, (LOVING)CUP
athletic contest ... MEDAL
Indian .... SCALP
matador's .... EARS
war ..... ARMS, BANNER, FLAG
tropic .... CIRCLE, SOLAR
circle .... CAPRICORN, CANCER
tropical .... TORRID, HOT, SULTRY, FIGURATIVE, WARM
animal .... TAPIR
disease .... AGUE, MALARIA, BERIBERI, BUBA, DENGUE, SPRUE, PSILOSIS, YAWS, FRAMB(O)ESIA,
evergreen ..... CASHEW
fever .... CALENTURE
fish .... OPAH
fruit .. PAPAYA, PAWPAW, TAMARIND, DATE, MANGO, GUAVA
herb .... LOOFA
lizard .... SKINK, SCINCOID
snake ..... FER DE LANCE
tree ... CASSIA, CASHEW, PALM, GUAVA, TAMARIND, PAPAYA, BALSA, SAPOTA, COLIMA
trot .. JOG, RUN, AMBLE, GAIT, CANTER
troth .... PLEDGE, FAITH
Trotsky, Russian revolutionist
LEON
trotter .... MORGAN
trotyl .... TNT
troubadour ..... BALLADEER, JONGLEUR, MINNESINGER,

(LYRIC)POET, MUSICIAN, MINSTREL

song .... SERENADE

theme of .... LOVE, CHIVALRY

traveling ..... JONGLEUR

trouble .... ILL, VEX, ANNOY, DISTURB, WORRY, HARASS, AFFLICT, BOTHER, PAINS, FASH, OBSESS, IRK, INCOMMODE, PESTER, DISORDER, AILMENT

troublemaker ..... PEST, IMP, AGITATOR, PROVOCATEUR, ERIS, HELLION

trough ... BOSH, HOD, GUTTER, CHUTE, VALLEY, SLUICE, MANGER, SHOOT, DRAIN, RUNWAY

fodder .... CRIB

for logs .... FLUME

mining .... HUTCH

ore washing ... LAUNDER

washing ore .... BUDDLE

water wheel .. PENSTOCK

trounce .... BEAT, FLOG, THRASH, DEFEAT

troupe .... BAND, GROUP

trouper .... ACTOR

troupial ... ORIOLE, COWBIRD, GRACKLE, CACIQUE

trousers ..... PEGTOPS, PANTS, SLACKS, PAJAMAS, SLOPS, JEANS

bottom fold .... CUFF

cotton .... DUCKS

leather .... CHAPS, CHAPARAJOS

trousseau .... BUNDLE

item .... STEELHEAD, LINGERIE

trout ... STEELHEAD, CHAR(R), NAMAYCUSH, DOLLY VARDEN, BLUEBACK, SALMONOID, OQUASSA

family .... SALMON

fish like .... SMELT

flap .... FLY

sea .... KIPPER

trowel .. DARBY, FLOAT, PLANE

Troy ... ILIUM, ILION, WEIGHT

founder of .... ILUS, LAOMEDON

tale of .... ILIAD

truant .... SHIRKER, SLACKER, ERRANT, TRIVANT, VAGRANT

play .... MICHE

truce ...... ARMISTICE, RESPITE, CEASEFIRE

signal ..... WHITE FLAG

Trucial Coast region ... OMAN

truck ...... BARROW, BARTER, EXCHANGE, TRUNDLE, CAMION, VAN, LORRY, DEALINGS, RUBBISH, BOGIE, BOGY

army ...... HALF-TRACK

artillery .... CAMION

dump .... TILLER

farm product .... VEGETABLES

rail .... LORRY

Truckee City .... RENO

truckle ..... CASTER, TOADY, CRINGE, YIELD, SUBMIT, TRUNDLE

truculent .... CRUEL, SAVAGE, HARSH, MEAN, RUDE, FIERCE, BELLIGERENT

trudge .... PLOD, ANKLE, WALK, TRAMP, SLOG, TRAIPSE

true .... RIGHT, CORRECT, EXACT, LAWFUL, RIGHTFUL, REAL, GENUINE, ALINE, ACTUAL

blue ..... LOYAL, STANCH

copy .... ESTREAT

level .... GEOID

love .... SWEETHEART

truffle ... MUSHROOM, FUNGUS, TUCKAHOE, EARTHNUT

Truk island .... TOL

truism ..... FACT, PLATITUDE, COMMONPLACE, AXIOM

trull .... TART, TROLLOP

truly .... REALLY, INDEED, IN FACT, SOOTH, QUITE, FAITHFULLY, ACTUALLY

Truman, cabinet member .... ACHESON, STIMSON, SNYDER, KIMBALL

playwright .... CAPOTE

president .... HARRY

trump in card game ..... RUFF

trumpery .... NONSENSE, RUBBISH, PALTRY

trumpet .... HORN, PROCLAIM, CLARION

belt .... BALDRIC

blast ... BLARE, FANFARE

call ... REVEILLE, SENNET, TAPS

caller .... GABRIEL
flourish .... FANFARE,
　　TUCKET, TANTARA
muffler .... MUTE
shell ..... TRITON, CONCH
signal .... CHAMADE,
　　FLOURISH
sound .... BLARE
trumpeter .... HERALD,
　ELEPHANT, SWAN, PIGEON,
　BUGLER, AGAMI, GABRIEL
trumps, five of ..... PEDRO
truncate ... LOP, TRIM, STUMP
truncheon ..... CUDGEL, CLUB,
　　STAFF, BATON, MACE
trundle ...... CASTER, CART,
　　WHEEL, ROLL, RULL
trunk ... STEM, SNOUT, COFFER,
　PROBOSCIS, BOX, CHEST,
　COMPARTMENT, MAIN LINE
　　STOCK
animal's .... SOMA
human .... TORSO
insect's .... THORAX
knot .... BURL
tree .... BOLE, BURL
trunkfish ..... TORO, COWFISH,
　　CHAPIN
trunks .... BREECHES, SHORTS
trunnel .... TRE(E)NAIL
trunnion .... GUDGEON,
　　JOURNAL
truss ...... BUNDLE, PACK, TIE,
　PROP, BRACE, BIND
trust .... RELY, CUSTODY,
　DUTY, CHARGE, CREDIT,
　CARTEL, MONOPOLY, HOPE,
　FAITH, RELIANCE,
　　CONFIDENCE
betrayal of ..... PERFIDY
of/like a ...... FIDUCIAL,
　　FIDUCIARY
territory .... MANDATE
to the British ...... TICK
trustee .... GARNISHEE,
　　WARDEN, CUSTODIAN
trustworthy ... TESTED, TRIED,
　RELIABLE, STA(U)NCH, SAFE
trusty .... CONVICT
truth .... REALITY, FACT,
　ACTUALITY, VERACITY,
　VERITY, VERITAS, FACT
assumed in theology .....
　　MYSTERY
drug .... PENTOTHAL
personified .... UNA

truthful .... HONEST,
　　VERACIOUS
boy .... WASHINGTON
try ...... TEST, MELT, REFINE,
　AFFLICT, EXPERIMENT,
　ATTEMPT, STRIVE, STAB,
　　ESSAY
to do .... TACKLE
trying .... IRKSOME, PAINFUL,
　　ANNOYING
experience ..... ORDEAL
tryma ...... DRUPELET, NUT,
　　HICKORY
tryout .... TEST, TRIAL,
　　AUDITION
trypsin .... ENZYME
trysail .... SPENCER
tryst .... DATE, MEETING,
　　RENDEZVOUS
Tsaritsyn ...... STALINGRAD
tsaritza ... CZARINA, TSARINA
Tschaikowsky, composer .....
　　PET(E)R
tsetse ... FLY, KIVU, MUSCID,
　　MAU
caused disease .. NAGANA,
　　SLEEPING SICKNESS
Tse-tung, Chinese leader .. MAO
tsine .... OX, BANTENG
Tuareg .... BERBER
tub .... CASK, TRAM, BUCKET,
　FIRKIN, VAT, KID, BATH,
　KEELER, DAN, KIT, GYLE,
　KEEVE, KNOP, HOD, SKEEL,
　　HOGSHEAD
2-handled .... COWL
tuba .... SAXHORN,
　　BOMBARDON
instrument resembling ...
　　EUPHONIUM
mouthpiece ..... BOCAL
tubby .... SQUAT
tube .... DUCT, PIPE,
　CYLINDER, HOSE,
　(ELECTRIC)RAILROAD,
　TELESCOPE, HUMIDOR
cannon/gun ..... BARREL
draining ..... CATHETER
electric wires' .. CONDUIT
for gas, smoke, etc. ......
　　FLUE
glass .... PIPET(TE)
graduated .. HYDROMETER
joint of .... ELL
tapering .... BURETTE

underground —. TUNNEL,
 SUBWAY
vacuum .... DIODE
tuber .... CASSAVA, MANIOC,
 RHIZOME, ONION, TARO, OCA,
 YAM, JALAP, CORM, BULB,
 EDDO, POTATO
 dried orchid ..... SALEP
tubercle .... PROCESS,
 PROJECTION
tubercular —.—.... LUNGER,
 CONSUMPTIVE
tuberculosis —..... PHTHISIS,
 CONSUMPTION,
 WHITE PLAGUE
 bovine .... GRAPE
 lymphatic gland ....
 SCROFULA
tuberculous —. CONSUMPTIVE,
 PHTHISIC
tuberous .... KNOBBY
tubular .... FISTULOUS
tuck .... FOLD, WRAP, COVER,
 CRAM, PUCKER, SWORD,
 RUCHE, PLEAT, TAP, LAP
 companion of ...... NIP
tuckahoe .... PORIA, TRUFFLE,
 FUNGUS
tucker .. COLLAR, CHEMISETTE,
 WEARY, TIRE
 companion of ...... BIB
tucket ... TANTARA, FLOURISH
tufa ...... LIMESTONE, TUFF,
 TOPH(E)
tuff .... ROCK, TUFA
tuft .... CLUSTER, CLUMP
 having a .... COMOSE
 of feathers ...... PLUME,
 CREST, COP, TOPKNOT
 of grass, etc. .... TUSSOCK
 of seed hairs ...... COMA
 of threads, etc. .. TASSEL
 on woman's hat .. POMPON
tufted ..... COMOSE, COMATE
tufthunter .... SNOB,
 SYCOPHANT, TOADY
 SOCIAL CLIMBER
tug ..... DRAG, PULL, HAUL,
 STRAIN, TOW(BOAT), TOIL
 boat pulled by ... BARGE,
 SCOW, SHIP
Tuileries .... PALACE
tuition ..... INSTRUCTION, FEE
tule .... BULRUSH
tulip .... FLOWER, BULB
 tree .... POPLAR

tulle —.—.. LACE, NET(TING),
 ILLUSION
tullibee .... WHITEFISH
Tully .... CICERO
tumble ... TRIP, SOMERSAULT,
 FALL, FLOP, SPILL, PLASH
tumbler ...... ACROBAT, DOG,
 PIGEON, (DRINKING)GLASS,
 TURNER, DOVE
 net of ..... TRAMPOLIN(E)
tumbleweed .... THISTLE,
 AMARANTH
tumbling box ..... RUMBLE(R)
tumbrel .... (DUMP)CART,
 WAGON, CAISSON
tumefy .... SWELL
tumescence .... SWELLING
tumid ... SWOLLEN, BULGING,
 BOMBASTIC, POMPOUS
tummy .... STOMACH
 ache .... COLIC
tumor .. SWELLING, NEOPLASM,
 MELANOMA, HEMATOMA,
 ANGIOMA, CYST, YAW,
 GUMMA, SCIRRHUS,
 NEUROMA
 anal .. PILES, HEMORRHOID
 benign ... ADENOMA, WEN
 blood vessel ... ANGIOMA
 bony tissue ..... OSTEOMA
 brain .... GLIOMA
 cartilaginous ....—
 CHONDROMA
 classification .... BENIGN,
 MALIGNANT
 combining form ....
 C(O)ELE
 epithelial ... CARCINOMA
 fat tissue .... LIPOMA
 fibrous .... FIBROMA,
 FIBROID, KELOID,
 CHELOID
 glandular —.—. ADENOMA
 malignant ..... CANCER,
 EPITHELIOMA, SARCOMA
 not malignant ... BENIGN
 scar tissue ..—.. CHELOID,
 KELOID
 skin ... PAPILLOMA, WEN
 tendon .... GANGLION
tumult .... COMMOTION,
 UPROAR, CONFUSION, RIOT,
 TURMOIL, BABEL, DIN,
 STIR, HUBBUB
tumultuous —.—...... RIOTOUS,
 TURBULENT

tumulus ... BARROW, MOUND
tun .... CASK, VAT
tuna .... TUNNY, CACTUS,
    MACKEREL, PEAR, OPUNTIA
    like fish ...... ALBACORE,
                    BONITO
tundra ... PLAIN, WASTELAND
    dweller .... LAPP
    like wasteland ... STEPPE,
                    PAMPAS
tune .... LILT, ARIA, TONE,
    MELODY, AIR, HARMONY,
                 CONCORD
tunesmith .... COMPOSER,
               SONGWRITER
tungsten .... WOLFRAM,
              CARBOLOY
    mineral ..... SCHEELITE,
              WOLFRAMITE
tungstite .... OCHER
Tungus .... MANCHU,
             MONGOLIAN
tunic ... COAT, ROBE, CHITON,
    STOLE, TOGA, GIPON,
    JUPON, KIRTLE, JAMA,
    BASQUE, FROCK
tunicate .... ASCIDIAN, SALPA
    bulb .... ONION
tunicle .... VESTMENT
tuning fork .... DIAPASON
Tunisian capital ...... TUNIS
    Berber .... KABYLE
    city ...... SFAX, SOUSSE,
      KAIROUAN, BIZERTE
    diplomat .. (MONGI) SLIM
    measure .... SAA(H)
    money .... DINAR
    oasis .... GAFSA
    president ... BOURGUIBA
    ruler ... BEY, PASHA, DEY
tunnel ... FLUE, BURROW, SAP,
    DIG, TUBE, SIMPLON,
              SUBWAY
tunneler .... SAPPER,
      BURROWER, ANT
tunny ..... MACKEREL, TUNA,
    ALBACORE, AMIA
tup .... RAM, SHEEP
tupelo .... DOGWOOD,
    PEPPERIDGE, NYSSA,
    WATER GUM, LIME(TREE)
Tupi .... INDIAN, GUARANI
tuque .... CAP
turban ...... HEADDRESS, HAT,
             MANDIL
    cloth ... LUNGEE, LUNGI

turbid ... CLOUDY, MUDDLED,
          MUDDY, ROILY
turbine ...... MOTOR, ENGINE
turbit .... PIGEON
turbot .. FLATFISH, BRILL, BUTT
    flatfish like .... SOLE,
      HALIBUT, FLOUNDER
turbulence .... DISORDER,
    TUMULT, COMMOTION
turbulent ..... WILD, UNRULY,
           AGITATED
Turco .... TURK
turdine bird .... THRUSH
tureen .... (SOUP)DISH
turf ...... SOD, PEAT, SWARD,
             TRACK
    of/like .... CEPITOSE
    piece of .... DIVOT
turfy .... GRASSY
turgid ...... SWOLLEN, TOROSE,
    TOROUS, TUMID, BLOATED,
           BOMBASTIC
Turin .... TORINO
Turk ... OSMANLI, OTTOMAN,
    TATAR, TURCO, MOSLEM,
    HORSE, TA(R)TAR
Turkestan inhabitant ... SART
    Moslem .... SALAR
    mountain ...... PAMIRS,
              ALAI
    river ILI
    tribe ... KIRGHIZ, USBEG
Turkey, Asiatic ... ANATOLIA
    bird like ..... CURASSOW
    buzzard .... VULTURE,
              AURA
    capital of ...... ANKARA,
             ANGORA
    chin adornment of ......
      WATTLE, CARUNCLE
    cock .... TOM
    male .... TOM, GOBBLER
    red dye ...... ALIZARIN,
             MADDER
    slang .... FAILURE
    sound .... GOBBLE
    trot .... DANCE
    wild .... BUSTARD
    young .... POULT
Turki .... TURKOMAN,
            OSMANLI
Turkic people ..... UZBEG,
            UZBEK
Turkish bathhouse .. BAGNIO
    cab .... ARABA

cap ..... FEZ, KALPAK, CALPAC
capital ...... ANKARA, ANGORA
caravansary .... IMARET
cavalryman ..... SPAHI, SPAHEE
chamber ...... ODA(H)
chieftain .... ZAIM
city ... ISTANBUL, IZMIR, SMYRNA, ADANA, BURSA, EDIRNE, TARSUS, GALLIPOLI, AYADIN, AIDIN, AINTAB, EDESSA, KONIA, SIVAS, EBZURUM, GAZIANTEP, CAESAREA, KAYSERI, MANIS(S)A, URFA
coin .. LIRA, PARA, ASPER, ALTUN, PIASTER, PIASTRE, YUZLUK
college .... ULEMA
commander ..... SIRDAR
confection ...... HALVAH
court .... PORTE
decree .... IRADE
delight .... CANDY
dialect .... JAGATAI
dispute with Greece ..... CYPRUS
district ...... VILAYET
dulcimer .... CANUN
dynasty .... SELJUK
emblem .... CRESCENT
emissary .... CHIAUS
ensign ..... HORSETAIL, CRESCENT
father .... BABA
flag ..... ALEM, CRESCENT
float .... KALAK
foreign quarter .... PERA, BEYOGLU
garment ...... CAFTAN, KAFTAN
general .. KEMAL, INONU
government ..... PORTE
governor ... MALI, PASHA, WALI, BEY
harem resident .. KADEIN
hat .... FEZ
hell .... DAGH
house for men .... SELAM LIK
inn ...... IMARET, KHAN, SERAI
island .... TENEDOS

javelin ..... JER(R)EED, JER(R)ID
judge ..... CADI, KADI
liquor .... MASTIC
magistrate .... CADI
master .... EFFENDI
measure ...... ARSHIN, DRA(H), KHAT, ALMUD, PIK, KILE
messenger ...... CHIAUS
military district ... ORDO
milk food .... YOG(H)URT
minister .... VIZI(E)R
mock battle .... JER(R)ID, JER(R)EED
monetary unit ... PIASTER, PIASTRE
money of account .. ASPER
monk .... DERVISH
mountain ...... ARARAT, TAURUS
non-Moslem .... GIAOUR, RAYAH, RAIA
oak .... CERRIS
official .... BASHAW, EMEER, EMIR, PASHA, PACHA
opium .... AFYON
oxcart .... ARABA
palace .... SERAI, SERAGLIO
parade .... ALAI
pasha's standard ...... HORSETAIL
pavilion .... KIOSK
peasant .... RAYA
peninsula .... GALLIPOLI
people ...... OSMANLI, KURD, TURKI
policeman ..... ZAPTIAH
pound .... LIRA
prayer rug .... MELAS
premier .... DEMIREL
president .... ATATURK, INONU, BAYAR, SUNAY
province .... VILAYET
regiment .... ALAI
region .... EREGLI, ESKISEHIR, KURDISTAN
rice dish .. PILAU, PILAW
river .... MARITSA, ARAS, TIGRIS, ZAB, MESTA, SARUS
robe .. DOLMAN, KAFTAN, CAFTAN
ruler ... SULTAN, CALIPH

saber .... YATAG(H)AN
scholar .... ULEMA
school .... ULEMA
sea .... MARMARA,
BOSPORUS
seaport .... TRABZON,
TREBIZOND
sergeant .... CHIAUS
sir .... EFFENDI
slave ...... MAMELUKE,
JANIZARY, JANISSARY
soldier .... NIZAM,
JANIZARY, JANISSARY
standard .... ALEM,
HORSETAIL
strait ...... DARDANELLES
sultan .... PADISHAH,
SELIM, CALIF, CALIPH
sultan's guard .. JANIZARY
sultan's palace .. SERAGLIO
sultan's visit to mosque ..
SELAM LIK
summerhouse .... KIOSK
sword ...... YATAGHAN,
SCIMITAR
teacher ...... MULLA(H)
title .... GHAZI, EFFENDI,
EMIR, EMEER, AG(H)A,
PACHA, PASHA, BEY
tobacco .... LATAKIA
tower .... MANARAT
tribesman ...... TATAR
veil .... YASHMAK,
YASHMAC
viceroy .... KHEDIVE
"victorious warrior" ....
GHAZI
vilayet subdivision ......
SANJAK
weight .. ROTL, OKE, OKA,
MAUND
whip .... KURBASH
zither .... CANUM
Turko-Tartar tribe .. BASHKIR
turmeric ..... CURCUMA, REA
turmoil ... TUMULT, UPROAR,
COMMOTION, STOUR,
HUBBUB, WELTER
turn .... BEND, CURVE,
REVOLVE, CANT, ROTATE,
AVERT, BLUNT, DIVERT,
SPIN, TREND, REPEL, PIVOT,
DEVIATE, VOLUTE, SCREW,
SWITCH
a new leaf ...... CHANGE,
REFORM

around ...... SLUE, PIVOT
aside ...... BRUSH, FEND,
SWERVE, SHUNT,
BLANCH, DEFLECT,
DAFF
away ... ESTRANGE, SHOO
back ... REPEL, REPULSE,
PUSH, REFLEX
combining form .. TROPO
course .... YAW
down ..... REJECT, VETO,
SPURN
equestrian .... CARACOLE
horsemanship ....
CARACOLE
in ...... DELIVER, ENTER
in music .... VOLTA
inside out ...... EVERT
into money ... (EN)CASH
left .... HAW
loose .... LIBERATE,
RELEASE, FREE
of mind .... CAPRICE
off course .... YAW
on an axis .... ROLL
one side .... DEFLECT
out ..... BECOME, DISMISS,
GATHERING, OUTPUT,
EQUIPAGE, ARRAY
outward .... EVERT
over .... TRANSFER,
CAPSIZE, KEEL
over a new leaf .. REFORM
over by tossing .... FLAP
page over .... LEAF
right .... JEE, GEE
ship's .... YAW, TACK
single .... WINDING
to .... CONSULT
unfriendly .... ESTRANGE,
ANTAGONIZE
up .... APPEAR
white .... PALE, BLANCH
turnabout ...... VOLTE-FACE,
REVERSAL
turncoat ... TRAITOR, BOLTER,
DESERTER, RENEGADE,
RUNAGATE, APOSTATE, BAT
turned back piece ... REVERSE
in mathematics .. VERSED
up .... SNUB, ACOCK,
TILTED
turner ... TUMBLER, GYMNAST,
ACROBAT
actress .... LANA
turning joint .... HINGE

machine .... LATHE,
SPANNER
point ..... PIVOT, CRUX,
CRISIS, CLIMAX,
SOLSTICE
turnip ...... ROOT, SWEDE,
RUTABAGA, NEEP
shaped .... NAPIFORM
turnix .... (GAME)BIRD
turnkey ..... JAILER, WARDER
turnout .... ATTENDANCE
turnover .... TART, PIE, UPSET
turnsole .... HELIOTROPE,
SUNFLOWER, DYE
turnpike .. TOLLGATE, HIGHWAY
turnstile .... GATE
turntable operator ....
DISC JOCKEY
Turnverein member .. TURNER,
GYMNAST, TUMBLER
turpentine .... OLEORESIN,
OIL, GAL(L)IPOT
substance like .... FLEMI
tree ... PINE, TEREBINTH,
TARATA
turpeth .... EMETIC
turquoise .... GEM
turret ...... TOWER, BARTIZAN
gun .... CUPOLA
opening .... LOUVER
tower .... BARTISAN,
BARTIZAN
viewing .... GAZEBO
turtle .... SNAPPER,
HAWK(S)BILL, ARRAU,
JURARA, TERRAPIN,
CHELONIAN, REPTILE,
EMYD, LEATHERNECK,
MOSSBACK, LOGGERHEAD
descriptive of a ....
SLOW(FOOT)
enclosure for .... CRAWL
genus ... CARETTA, EMYS
land .... TORTOISE,
TESTUDO
of the ...... CHELONIAN
old .... MOSSBACK
protective covering ....
MAIL
shell .... CARAPACE,
PLASTRON, PEE
shell substance .. CALIPEE,
CALIPASH
turn .... CAPSIZE
Tuscan city .... FLORENCE,
TOSCANA

wine .... CHIANTI
Tuscany island .... ELBA
river .... ORCIA
wine .... CHIANTI
tush .... CANINE, TOOTH
tusk .... FANG, IVORY, TOOTH
tusker ..... ELEPHANT, BOAR,
WALRUS, WARTHOG,
NARWHAL, PECCARY
tussah .... SHANTUNG,
SILKWORM
tussis .... COUGH
tussle ... GRAPPLE, WRESTLE,
SCUFFLE, FIGHT, STRUGGLE
tussock ..... THICKET, CLUMP,
TUFT
tut .... TSK
tutelage .. CARE, PROTECTION,
TEACHING, INSTRUCTION,
GUARDIANSHIP
tutelary deity .... LAR(ES),
PENATES, GENIUS
tutor .... TEACH(ER),
DISCIPLINE, INSTRUCT(OR),
MENTOR, COACH, MASTER
tutto .... ALL, ENTIRE
Tutuila city ...... PAGO PAGO
tux(edo) .... JACKET
tuyere ... NOZZLE, PIPE, TEW,
TEWEL
TV (see television) ..... TELLY,
VIDEO
award .... EMMY
broadcast ..... TELECAST
cabinet .... CONSOLE
camera move .... PAN
camera plate .... MOSAIC
camera platform .. DOLLY
commercial cat .. MORRIS
dragon .... OLLIE
emcee .... COMPERE
gossip columnist ....
RONA (BARRET)
horse .... MISTER ED
interference ...... SNOW
lines on tube .... RASTER
name .... IMOGENE
pickup tube .. ORTHICON
plug .... COMMERCIAL
producer ..... SUSSKIND
room .... DEN
show, kind of ..... QUIZ,
PANEL, LIVE,
GIVEAWAY, RERUN,
MOVIE
stand .... ROLLAWAY

street for tots .... SESAME
time .... SLOT
Tver .... KALININ
twaddle ... BUNK, NONSENSE,
PRATTLE, ROT, DRIVEL,
FUSTIAN
twain .... TWO
character .... SAWYER
humorist .... MARK
twang .... PLUNK, TANG
tweak ...... PINCH, PLUCK,
TWIST, TWITCH
Tweeddale .... PEEBLES
tweeg .... HELLBENDER
tweet .... CHIRP
tweeter .... LOUDSPEAKER
tweeze .... PLUCK
tweezers .... PINCERS
Twelfth Night ..... EPIPHANY
character .... VIOLA,
ORSINO, FESTE,
MALVOLIO
composer ...... AMRAM
twelve .... DOZEN, XII
Biblical .... APOSTLES
by twelve .... GROSS
dozen .... GROSS
twelvemo ...... DUODECIMO
twentieth .... VIGESIMAL
twenty .... SCORE
combining form ... ICOS,
VIGINTI
dinars .... BISTI
fifth anniversary ....
JUBILEE
five pounds .... PONY
minute walk ...... MILE
of .... VICENARY,
VIGESIMAL
one .... BLACK JACK
one merit badge wearer ..
EAGLE SCOUT
quires .... REAM
twibill .... MATTOCK,
(BATTLE)AX
twice ... DOUBLY, TWO TIMES,
BIS
prefix .... BI, DI
twiddle ... TWIRL, TOY, TRIFLE
twig ... ROD, SHOOT, BRANCH,
SPRIG, (S)CION, LAYER
and branch angle .. AXIL
Brit. slang ...... NOTICE,
OBSERVE
broom .... BARSOM

flexible ... OSIER, WICKER,
WILLOW, SWITCH,
WITHE
for grafting .... SLIP
willow .... SALLOW
twiggy ... SLENDER, DELICATE,
VIRGATE
Britain's .... MODEL
twigs, bunch of ...... WHISK,
FAGOT
clump of .... TUSSOCK
having .... VIRGATE
of .... VIMINAL
twilight ...... DUSK, GLOAM,
EVENTIDE, EVE, EVENFALL,
CREPUSCLE
of the Gods .. RAGNAROK
sleep inducer ....
SCOPOLAMIN
twill .... PRUNELLA
twilled fabric .... SERGE,
DENIM, REP
twin .... DOUBLE, COUPLE,
PAIR(ED), TWO, DIDYMOUS,
GEMEL
Biblical .... ESAU
crystal .... MACLE
twinberry ...... HONEYSUCKLE
twine .... CORD, WREATHE,
STRING, THREAD, SNARL,
INTERLACE
material ... ABACA, HEMP,
MAGUEY
twinge ...... SHOOT, QUALM,
TWITCH, PAIN, PANG
of conscience ....
COMPUNCTION,
SCRUPLE, QUALM
twining stem .... BINE
twinkle ... SPARKLE, GLIMMER,
FLICKER, WINK, GLINT,
BLINK
twinkling .... INSTANT
twins .... GEMINI
twirl .... SPIN, ROTATE,
WHIRL, FLOURISH
twist ...... WRICK, WRENCH,
TWINE, WIND, SPRAIN,
SKEW, CONTORT, SCREW,
TIC, WRITHE, SQUIRM,
TURN, CURVE, WARP
and turn ..... W(R)IGGLE
around ...... CURL, COIL
given to a ball ...... SPIN
in a tree .... GNARL
into thread ...... THROW

twisted ... CONTORTED, WRY,
　　　SKEW, AWRY, TORTILE
　　roll of cotton ..... SLUB
　　roll of tobacco .. PIGTAIL
　　thread .... LISLE
twister ... TORNADO, CYCLONE
twisting .... SPIRAL
　　pinch/pluck ...... TWEAK
twit .... UPBRAID, TAUNT,
　　　TEASE, RIB, JOSH,
　　REPROACH, MOCK, RIDICULE
twitch .. JERK, PLUCK, SNATCH,
　　PULL, TWEAK, TIC, TWINGE,
　　　VELLICATE
twitter ... CHATTER, FLUTTER,
　　CHIRRUP, TITTER,
　　　CHIRP(ING)
two ... BRACE, TWAIN, COUPLE,
　　　PAIR, DUO
　　aces in dice ...... CRAPS,
　　　CRABS
　　base hit .... DOUBLE
　　bells .... ONE O'CLOCK
　　bit: sl. .... CHEAP,
　　　WORTHLESS
　　by two .... BINAL
　　celled .... BILOCULAR
　　consisting of .. DYAD(IC)
　　cups .... PINT
　　edged .... ANCIPITAL
　　faced .... BIFACIAL
　　faced being .. HYPOCRITE,
　　　JANUS
　　fisted .... VIRILE,
　　　VIGOROUS
　　footed animal .. BIPED(AL)
　　forked .... BIFURCATE
　　handed .. AMBIDEXTROUS,
　　　BIMANOUS
　　handed animal .. BIMANE
　　horned .... BICORN
　　horse chariot ...... BIGA
　　hundred milligrams .....
　　　CARAT
　　leaf paper sheet ... FOLIO
　　legged .... BIPED
　　month period .. BIMESTER
　　of .... DUAL
　　plus tid .... BITS
　　seater .... TANDEM,
　　　ROADSTER
　　shillings .... FLORIN
　　sided .... BILATERAL
　　song for .... DUET
　　spot .... DEUCE
　　step .... DANCE

thousand pounds ....
　　　NETTON
toed sloth .... UNAU
together .... DUAD
week period .. FORTNIGHT
wheeled cab .... HANSOM
wheeled carriage ....
　　　CALECHE, TILBURY,
　　HANSOM, GIG, CALASH,
　　　CART
year-old sheep .... TEG(G)
twofold ..... BINAL, DUPLE(X),
　　　BINARY, DOUBLE
twosome .... COUPLE
Ty, baseball great ..... COBB
Tyburn event .... EXECUTION,
　　　HANGING
Tyche ... FORTUNA, GODDESS
tycoon ... SHOGUN, FINANCIER,
　　　BARON, MOGUL
tyke .... MONGREL, CUR, DOG,
　　　BOOR, CHILD
Tyler, English rebel ..... WAT
tympan .... DRUM
tympanic membrane ....
　　　EARDRUM
tympanist .... DRUMMER
tympanum .... EARDRUM
tympany .... CONCEIT
Tyndareus .... SPARTAN
　　wife of .... LEDA
Tyne river city ...... JARROW
type ... TOKEN, EMBLEM, SIGN,
　　CLASS, MODEL, CLASSIFY,
　　　SORT, KIND, BREED,
　　　VARIETY
　　assortment of .. FO(U)NT
　　blank .... QUAD(RAT)
　　body measure .... POINT
　　break in .... BATTER
　　case ...... UPPER, LOWER
　　disarrange ... SQUABBLE
　　face like writing ....
　　　CURSIVE
　　face projection .... KERN
　　jumbled .... PI(E)
　　kind of .. ITALIC, ROMAN,
　　　BOLDFACE, CONDENSED
　　line of .... SLUG
　　measure .... EM, EN
　　metal .... QUAD
　　mixed .... PI(E)
　　mold .... MATRIX
　　ornamental line .... SERIF
　　part .... KERN
　　set .... COMPOSE

size ⸺ PICA, AGATE, FONT,
ROMAN, BREVIER,
ELITE, NONPAREIL,
MINION
slanting .... ITALIC
style ... BODONI, CASLON,
GARAMOND, CLOISTER,
GOTHIC, ROMAN
tray .... GALLEY
typescript .... COPY
typesetter ...... LINOTYPIST,
PRINTER, COMPOSITOR
typesetting .... COMPOSING
machine: colloq. ... LINO
typewriter, kind of .. TELETYPE,
TELEX
part ⸺.... ROLLER, KEY,
SPACER, PLATEN,
CARRIAGE
type .... PICA, ELITE
typhlosis .... BLINDNESS
typhoon ⸺. STORM, HURRICANE

typhus carrier ... LOUSE, FLEA
cause of ..... RICKETTSIA
typical ..... CHARACTERISTIC,
SYMBOLIC
typify .... EXEMPLIFY
typographer .... PRINTER
typographical error .. ERRATUM
Tyr .... TIU
parent of .... ODIN
tyrannical .... DESPOTIC,
CRUEL, OPPRESSIVE
tyrannize .... OPPRESS
tyranny .. DESPOTISM, CRUELTY
tyrant ... DESPOT, OPPRESSOR
Tyre, king of .... HIRAM
princess of .... DIDO
tyro ... AMATEUR, BEGINNER,
NOVICE
Tyrolean city ⸺. INNSBRUCK
patriot .... HOFER
river .... ISAR
singer .... YOD(E)LER
tzigane ⸺⸺⸺⸺ GYPSY

U

U-boat .... SUBMARINE
boat locator ..... SONAR
Greek .... UPSILON
in chemistry .. URANIUM
letter .... EU
shaped bone ..... HYOID
turn, describing a ....
HAIRPIN
Ubangi tributary ...... UELE
Ubermensch ...... SUPERMAN,
OVERMAN
ubique .... EVERYWHERE
ubiquity .... OMNIPRESENCE
Ucayali tributary ... APURIMAC
udder inflammation .. GARGET
product .... MILK
protuberance ⸺... TEAT,
NIPPLE
Uganda capital ..... KAMPALA
city .... JINJA
kingdom ..... BUGANDA
president .... OBOTE
ugly ..... CROSS, UNGAINLY,
HIDEOUS, UNSIGHTLY,
VILE, REPULSIVE, OMINOUS,
DANGEROUS
duckling once ..... SWAN
sight .... EYESORE
uhlan .... SOLDIER,
CAVALRYMAN, GERMAN

uintaite ⸺⸺⸺ ASPHALT,
GILSONITE
uitlander .... FOREIGNER
ukase .... DECREE
Ukrainian capital ...... KIEV
city .... KHARKOV,
KHERSON
farmer ⸺⸺⸺ KULAK
holy city .... KLEV
legislature .... RADA
money of account .....
GRIVNA
native ⸺⸺⸺ COSSACK
ukelele .... UKE
instrument like .. GUITAR
player .... HAWAIIAN
Ulan Bator ⸺. KULUN, URGA,
KHOTO
ulcer .... SORE, CANKER
discharge ⸺. ICHOR, PUS,
SANIES
venereal ...... CHANCRE
ulcerate .... FESTER
ule .... CAUCHO
fluid .... LATEX
ulema .... MUFTI
Ulianov, Vladimir ..... LENIN
ulmaceous tree .... ELM
ulmus .... ELM
ulna projection ... OLECRANON

Ulster .... OVERCOAT
   lake .... ERNE
ult. ...... ULTIMATE, ULTIMO
Ultima Thule .... ICELAND
ultimate .... FARTHEST,
   EVENTUAL, FINAL, PRIMARY,
              MAXIMUM
ultimatum ...... LAST OFFER,
              DEMAND
ultra .... EXCESSIVE,
   RADICAL, EXTREME
   modern ... AVANT GARDE
   nationalist .... JINGO,
            CHAUVINIST
ultramarine .... PIGMENT
ulu .... KNIFE
ululant .... HOWLING
ululate ...... HOWL, WAIL,
   LAMENT, BAY, CRY, PULE
Ulysses .... ODYSSEUS
   author of .... JOYCE
   country of .... ITHACA
   father of .... LAERTES
   kingdom of ..... ITHACA
   name given to Cyclops ...
            NOMAN
   son of ..... TELEMACHUS
   wife of .... PENELOPE
umbelliferous plant .. CARROT,
           PARSLEY
umber ..... PIGMENT, SHADE,
   SHADOW, GRAYLING
   bird .... UMBRETTE
umbilical cord .... FUNICULUS
umbilicus .... NAVEL
umbles .... ENTRAILS
umbo ..... BEAK, BOSS, KNOB
umbra ...... SHADOW, SHADE
umbrage ... OFFENSE, FOLIAGE,
   RESENTMENT, SHADOW
umbrella .... COVER, PARASOL,
   (SUN)SHADE, GAMP, CHATTA
   cloth for .... GLORIA
   like flower .... UMBEL
   like fungus .. MUSHROOM
   part .... RIB
   of leaves .... TALIPOT
   style .... BUBBLE
   thing like ...... CANOPY,
         (PARA)CHUTE
   tree .... MAGNOLIA
umbrette .... UMBER,
       HAMMERHEAD
Umbria town .... ASSISI
umiak .... CANOE, KAYAK
umlaut .... DIERESIS

in linguistics .. MUTATION
umpire ..... ARBITER, JUDGE,
   REFEREE, DAYSMAN
UN agency .... WHO, UNESCO,
   FAO, IDA, ICAO, GATT,
          UNRRA
   president .... SPAAK,
   ARANHA, ARCE, EVATT,
   ROMULO, NERVO,
   PANDIT, MAZA, MUNRO,
   MALIK, MANESCU, SLIM
   secretary-general ...... LIE,
         (U)THANT
una .... CATBOAT
unaccented .... ATONIC,
       STRESSLESS
   vowel sound ..... SCHWA
unadorned ..... PLAIN, STARK,
       BALD, BARE
unadulterated .... NEAT, PURE
unaffected .... NATURAL,
   SIMPLE, NAIVE, SINCERE,
       ARTLESS
Unalaskan .... ALEUT
unalloyed .... PURE
unanimous .... SOLID
   opinion ..... CONSENSUS
unapproachable .... ALOOF,
   DISTANT, INACCESSIBLE
unarmed .... DEFENSELESS
unassuming .... MODEST, SHY,
   RETIRING, NATURAL
unattached .... SINGLE, FREE,
   LOOSE, LONE, VAGILE
unau .... SLOTH
unavailing .... FUTILE
unavoidable ..... INEVITABLE
unawares, take ..... SURPRISE
unbalanced .... DERANGED,
   LOPSIDED, UNEVEN
unbecoming .... IMPROPER,
       INDECOROUS
unbeliever .... DOUBTER,
   ATHEIST, PAGAN, SKEPTIC,
   AGNOSTIC, HERETIC,
   INFIDEL, MISCREANT
unbelieving .... INCREDULOUS
unbend ...... YIELD, RELENT,
   RELAX, STRAIGHTEN
unbending ..... RIGID, STIFF,
   FIRM, RESOLUTE, SET,
       ADAMANT
unbiased .... OBJECTIVE,
       IMPARTIAL
unbleached .... ECRU
   fabric .... BEIGE

unblemished ...... SPOTLESS, CLEAN, STAINLESS
unborn young in uterus .. FETUS
unbosom ...... TELL, REVEAL
unbounded .... LIMITLESS
unbranded cow .... MAVERICK
unbroken ..... INTACT, WILD, WHOLE, CONTINUOUS
unburden ...... RELIEVE, RID
unburnt brick .... ADOBE
uncalled for .... IMPERTINENT, GRATUITOUS, UNNECESSARY
uncanny .... WEIRD, EERIE, STRANGE, MYSTERIOUS, UNCO, EERY
unceasing ...... CONTINUOUS, ENDLESS, PERPETUAL
unceremonious ...... ABRUPT, INFORMAL, CURT
uncertain ... DOUBTFUL, VAGUE
uncertainty .. DUBIETY, DOUBT
unchaste .... WANTON
unchecked ...... LOOSE, RIFE, RAMPANT
unchristian .... WICKED
unciform ...... HOOK-SHAPED
uncinate .... HOOKLIKE, HAMATE, HOOKED
uncle .... NUNCLE, NUNKS, OOM, EAM
   American .... SAM
   cry ... YIELD, SURRENDER
   of fiction .... REMUS
   pertaining to .... AVUNCULAR
   Remus' author ... HARRIS
   Remus' rabbit ..... BRE'R
   slang ..... PAWNBROKER
   Tom's ____ ...... CABIN
unclean .... DIRTY, FOUL, FILTHY, OBSCENE, VILE, SQUALID, LEPROUS
   one, biblical ...... LEPER
unclose .... REVEAL, OPE(N)
unclothe ... UNCOVER, DIVEST, STRIP, UNDRESS
unclothed partially .... DISHABILLE
unco .... WEIRD, NOTABLE, NEWS, UNCANNY, STRANGE, UNKNOWN, VERY
uncoil .... UNWIND
uncoined metal ..... BULLION
uncombed .... UNKEMPT
uncommitted .... UNPLEDGED, FREE

uncommon .... RARE, ODD, SINGULAR, SCARCE, STRANGE, UNUSUAL, EXOTIC
uncommunicative ..... SILENT, RESERVE, TACITURN, RETICENT
uncompromising .... SET, DETERMINED, ADAMANT
unconcerned ..... INSOUCIANT, INDIFFERENT, ALOOF
unconditional ..... ABSOLUTE, TOTAL, TERMLESS
unconfined ..... FREE, LOOSE
unconfirmed news .. HEARSAY, RUMOR, GOSSIP, REPORT
unconnected .... DISCRETE
unconquerable .... INVINCIBLE
unconscious ...... MINDLESS, UNAWARE, UNWITTING, BLOTTO
   state ... COMA, NARCOSIS, SWOON, TRANCE, HYPNOSIS, SYNCOPE
unconstrained .... DEGAGE, FREE
unconventional .... UNUSUAL, INFORMAL, OUTRE
   one .... REBEL
uncooked .... RAW
uncouth .... VULGAR, GAUCHE, AWKWARD, GAWKY, CRUDE, CLUMSY, AGRESTIC
   person ..... BUM(P)KIN, LOUT, CODGER, RUSTIC, GAWK, YOKEL, BOOR
uncover ...... REVEAL, BARE, OPEN, EXPOSE
   hat .... DOFF
uncovered .... NUDE, EXPOSED, NAKED, BARE
unction ...... OINTMENT, OIL, UNGUENT
   give extreme ..... ANELE
unctuous ..... OILY, PLASTIC, SMOOTH, SUAVE, GREASY, PINGUID, SLEEK, SOAPY
   substance ...... CERATE, GREASE, OINTMENT, UNGUENT, LANOLIN
uncultivated .... VIRGIN, FALLOW, WILD, COARSE
uncultured .... ILL-BRED, COARSE
und so weiter .. ETC, ET CETERA
undaunted .... INTREPID, FEARLESS, UNDISMAYED

unde, in heraldry .... WAVY
undecided .... HESITANT,
PENDENT, PENDING,
IRRESOLUTE, WAVERING,
UNCERTAIN
undeniable .... TRUE,
IRREFUTABLE
under ...... (BE)NEATH, BELOW,
LOWER, NETHER
obligation ...... OWING,
INDEBTED, BOUND
par .... ILL, SICK
prefix .... SUB, HYP
underage ... MINOR, IMMATURE
underbrush .... THICKET
undercover man .... SPY,
SLEUTH, DETECTIVE
undercroft .... CRYPT
underdone .... RARE
undergarment .... SLIP,
CHEMISE, SHIRT
undergo ...... EXPERIENCE,
ENDURE, SUFFER
undergraduate .... FROSH,
SOPHOMORE, JUNIOR, PLEBE
underground .. SECRET, HIDDEN
being ... TROLL, GNOME,
DWARF
burial place ...... CRYPT,
CATACOMB
drain .... SEWER
fighter .... PARTISAN,
ELAS, MAQUI, EDES
fungus ...... TUCKAHOE,
EARTHNUT, TRUFFLE
organization ..... MAFIA
passage .... TUNNEL,
BURROW, TUBE, SAP
railway .... SUBWAY,
TUBE, METRO
resident .... GNOME,
DWARF, TROLL
stem .... TUBER,
POTATO, CASSAVA,
MANIOC, SALEP, ONION,
STOCK, RHIZOME
worker .... MINER,
SANDHOG
underhand ..... SLY, COVERT,
SECRET, CLANDESTINE
underhanded ... SLY, TRICKY,
DECEITFUL
underline .. STRESS, EMPHASIZE
underling ...... SUBORDINATE,
AIDE, SUBALTERN, SLAVE
underlying .... BASIC,

FUNDAMENTAL
principle .... ELIXIR
undermine .. SAP, WEAR AWAY,
ERODE, WEAKEN, SUBVERT
undernourish .... FAMISH,
STARVE
underpin .... PROP
underpinning .... SUPPORT
colloquial .... LEGS
underrate .... BELITTLE
underscore .... STRESS,
EMPHASIZE
undersea craft ... SUBMARINE,
UBOAT
explorer .... PICARD
undershirt ..... VEST, JERSEY,
SKIVVY, PETTICOAT, SINGLET
undersigned, the ..... WRITER
undersized .... SMALL,
SCRUBBY, RUNTY
being ..... DWARF, RUNT,
PIGMY
understand .... PERCEIVE,
COMPREHEND, SEE, KEN,
INFER, ASSUME, GRASP,
APPRECIATE
colloquial .... SAVVY,
DIG, GET
understanding .... NOUS,
AGREEMENT, DISCERNMENT,
SENSE, ACCORD
between nations, etc. .....
ENTENTE
understood ... TACIT, AGREED,
SENSED, PRESUMED,
ASSUMED, IMPLIED
readily ... CLEAR, LUCID,
LUCULENT
understrapper .. SUBORDINATE
understudy ...... SUBSTITUTE,
APPRENTICE
undertake .... PROMISE,
PLEDGE, CONTRACT, OFFER,
VOLUNTEER, TRY, ASSUME,
TACKLE
undertaker .... MORTICIAN
undertaking .... TASK,
ENTERPRISE, PROMISE,
GUARANTEE, JOB, VENTURE,
PROJECT
undertow .... RIPTIDE
underwaist .... BRA
underwater ...... SUBMARINE
apparatus .... SCUBA,
SNORKEL, BATHYSPHERE,
CAISSON, BATHYSCAPH

craft .... SUBMARINE, UBOAT, PIGBOAT
eye of sort .. HYDROSCOPE
ledge .... REEF
plant .... BENTHOS
prefix .... HYP(O)
projectile ...... TORPEDO
sound detection device ... SOFAR, SONAR
swimmer ..... FROGMAN, (SKIN)DIVER
worker .... SANDHOG
underwear ... LINGERIE, SLIP, SHORTS, PANTY, UNDIES, SCANTY, FLANNELS
underworld ... EARTH, HADES, SHEOL, HEL, EREBUS, ANTIPODES, GANGLAND
king .... YAMA
queen .... HEL
underwrite .... SUBSCRIBE, AGREE(TO), ASSUME, FINANCE, INSURE
underwriter .... INSURER, INSURANCEMAN
undeserving .... INDIGN
undesirable ... OBJECTIONABLE
person ...... BORE, BOOR, LOUT, LEPER, FELON
undeveloped .... LATENT
quality ...... POTENTIAL
undies ... PANTIES, LINGERIE, UNDERWEAR
undiluted ...... NEAT, SHEER, STRAIGHT, PURE
undine ..... NYMPH, SEAMAID, SYLPH
undisguised .... OPEN, OVERT, FRANK
undivided ... WHOLE, ENTIRE, INTACT
undomesticated .... WILD, UNTAMED, FERAL
undone .... UNFINISHED
undoubtedly ..... CERTAINLY, ADMITTEDLY
undraped .... BARE, NUDE
undress ..... STRIP, DISARRAY
stage of ..... DISHABILLE
undressed skin ..... PELT, KIP
Undset, Norwegian novelist ... SIGRID
undue .... IMPROPER, EXCESSIVE, INORDINATE
undulant fever ... BRUCELLOSIS
undulate ...... WAVE, RIPPLE

undulating ... . WAVY
object ... WAVE, RIPPLE, SNAKE, WORM
undulation ...... PULSATION, SURGE, WAVE, HEAVE, RIPPLE
unduly ....,.... UNJUSTLY, IMPROPERLY, EXCESSIVELY
undued ...... PLAIN, TINTLESS
undying .... ETERNAL, IMMORTAL, ABIDING
unearth ... DIG UP, DISCLOSE, DISCOVER, EXHUME
unearthly ..... EERIE, WEIRD, GHOSTLY
uneasy ..... FRETFUL, RESTIVE, ANXIOUS, RESTLESS, CONCERNED, FIDGETY, NERVOUS
feeling .... MALAISE
uneasiness ... MALAISE, UNREST, DISCOMFORT, ANXIETY
uneducated .... UNLETTERED, UNLEARNED, ILLITERATE
unemployed .... IDLE, AVAILABLE
unending ...... CONTINUOUS, CEASELESS
unenthusiastic ... COOL, COLD, INDIFFERENT
unequal .. UNEVEN, IRREGULAR, INADEQUATE
angled .... SCALENE
unequalled .... MATCHLESS, SUPREME, PEERLESS, NONPAREIL
unequivocal ... CLEAR, PLAIN
unerring .... EXACT, SURE, CERTAIN, ACCURATE
uneven .... EROSE, ROUGH, IRREGULAR, CROOKED, UNEQUAL, ODD, RUGGED, RAGGED, SPOTTY, HUBBLY
contest .... LOPSIDED
unexciting ..... ' TAME, DULL, VAPID
unexpected ...,..... SUDDEN, UNFORESEEN
meeting ..... ENCOUNTER
unexploded .... LIVE
unexpressive .... DULL, BLAND
unfading .... FAST
flower ..... AMARANTH, EVERLASTING
unfailing ..... REGULAR, SURE, CERTAIN

unfair ...... PARTIAL, BIASED, DISHONEST, FOUL
unfaithful .... DISLOYAL, UNTRUE
unfavorable .... ADVERSE, CONTRARY, BAD, ILL, INIMICAL
unfeeling .... INSENSATE, INSENSIBLE, NUMB, CALLOUS, CRUEL, STONY
unfermented grape juice ...... STUM
unfit .... INEPT, INAPT
to eat .... INEDIBLE
unfix ...... DETACH, LOOSEN
unflattering ... FRANK, BLUNT, DEROGATORY
unfledged .... CALLOW
bird ..... EYAS, NESTLING
unflinching ... FIRM, RESOLUTE
unfold ..... REVEAL, DISCLOSE, EVOLVE, UNFURL, OPEN, SPREAD
unforeseen ...... UNEXPECTED, SUDDEN
unfortunate .... HAPLESS, LUCKLESS
unfounded .... BASELESS, IDLE
unfrequented ..... SOLITARY, LONELY
unfriendly ... ANTAGONISTIC, ILL, COLD, HOSTILE, INIMICAL
unfruitful .... BARREN, STERILE
unfurl ...... UNFOLD, SPREAD, UNROLL
ungainly ..... UGLY, CLUMSY, AWKWARD
ungodly ... IMPIOUS, WICKED, DREADFUL
ungovernable .. UNRULY, WILD, REBELLIOUS
ungracious .. RUDE, IMPOLITE, AWKWARD
ungual growth ... NAIL, HOOF, CLAW, TALON
unguent .... BALM, SALVE, OINTMENT, POMADE, CHRISM
unguis ... NAIL, HOOF, CLAW, TALON, UNGULA
ungula ... CLAW, NAIL, TALON, UNGUIS, HOOF
ungulate ...... TAPIR, HORSE, COW, CATTLE, HOOFED
unhappy .... ILL-CHOSEN,

UNFORTUNATE, SAD, BLUE, MOROSE
unharmed .... SAFE
unhealthy ... SICKLY, MORBID
unhitch ... DETACH, UNFASTEN, RELEASE
unholy ..... WICKED, IMPIOUS, PROFANE
unhorse .... OVERTHROW, SPILL, UPSET
unicellular animal .. AM(O)EBA, PROTOZOAN
unicorn ... MONOCERO, REEM, LIN
fish .... UNIE
whale .... NARWHAL
unidentified flying object .. UFO
uniform ... EVEN, UNVARYING, STANDARD, OUTFIT, STEADY, EQUABLE
servant's .... LIVERY
shoulder ornament .... EPAULET(TE)
unify ... UNITE, CONSOLIDATE, WELD, INTEGRATE
unilateral .... ONE-SIDED
unimpeachable .... CLEAN, BLAMELESS, RELIABLE
unimportant .... PETTY, TRIVIAL
things .... TRIVIA
uninhabited .... DESOLATE, TENANTLESS
unintelligible chatter .... GIBBER(ISH)
unintentional .... UNWITTING
union ..... FUSION, JUNCTION, MARRIAGE, LIAISON, MERGER, ALLIANCE, LEAGUE, COALITION
business .... CARTEL, SYNDICATE
dues deduction .... CHECKOFF
from birth .. CONNATION
jack .... FLAG
labor .... ARTEL
member ... CARDHOLDER
merchants' ...... HANSE
of South Africa town .... MAFEKING
political .... BLOC, COALITION
soldier .... YANKEE
trade .... GUILD

unionist .... TORY,
CONSERVATIVE, FEDERALIST
unique ..... SINGULAR, RARE,
SOLE, SINGLE, UNUSUAL,
PECULIAR
unisexual .... DECLINOUS
unison .. CONCORD, HARMONY,
AGREEMENT
utter in .... CHORUS
Unisphere, part of ...... ASIA
unit .... ONE, STANDARD,
ITEM, PIECE
caloric .... THERM
charge .... RATE
electrical ... VOLT, WATT,
AMPERE
factor .... GENE
in medicine .... DOSE,
DOSAGE
of astronomical distance
LIGHT YEAR,
SECPAR, PARSEC
of brightness, c g s ......
LAMBERT
of capacity .... LITER,
LITRE
of electrical resistance ...
OHM
of energy ... ERG, JOULE
of force .. DENE, DYNE, OD
of heat .. CALORIE, THERM
of instruction .... LESSON
of length ..... ANGSTROM,
MICRON, CUBIT, METER
of light ..... LUMEN, LUX
of magnetic intensity ....
OERSTED
of metrical time ... MORA
of pressure .... BARAD
of reluctance .... REL
of value .... POINT
of weight ... TON, GRAM,
BUSHEL, KEEL, KEG,
MAUND, CARAT
of work .... ERG(ON),
JOULE, KILERG
of work energy ... JOULE
ultimate .... MONAD
wire .... MIL
unite ... COMBINE, COALESCE,
FEDERATE, FUSE, WELD,
JOIN, PIECE
United Arab Republic .. EGYPT
Kingdom national flag ..
UNION JACK
Nations (see UN)

United States (see American
/US) .... UNCLE SAM,
AMERICA, USA
unity ...... ONENESS, CONCORD,
HARMONY, SOLIDARITY
univalent .. SINGLE, UNPAIRED
univalve ...... SNAIL, MOLLUSK
shell's edge ..... LABRUM
universal .... PANDEMIC,
ENTIRE, GENERIC, GENERAL,
GLOBAL, CATHOLIC,
ECUMENIC(AL)
language .... ESPERANTO,
IDO, VOLAPUK
remedy .... AZOTH
universe .... COSMOS, CREATION,
WORLD, EARTH,
MACROCOSM
of the .... COSMIC
university business agent .....
SYNDIC
composition of ....
SCHOOLS, COLLEGES
grounds .... CAMPUS
group .... FRAT(ERNITY),
SORORITY
lecturer ...... PRELECTOR
official .... DEAN,
REGISTRAR, RECTOR,
TRUSTEE, REGENT,
BURSAR, BEADLE,
PROCTOR, PROVOST
professorship .... CHAIR
program of studies ......
CURRICULUM
rank .... DEGREE
teacher ...... PROFESSOR,
INSTRUCTOR
team .... VARSITY
unjust ...... PARTIAL, UNFAIR,
BIASED
unjustly .... UNDULY
unkempt ... MESSY, SLOVENLY,
UNTIDY, SHAGGY, SHABBY,
UNCOMBED, CRUDE, ROUGH
unkind .... CRUEL, HARSH
unknown .... UNCO, STRANGE,
OBSCURE
person .... JOHN DOE
unlace .... LOOSEN, UNTIE,
UNFASTEN
unlawful ... ILLICIT, ILLEGAL
goods/trade ....
CONTRABAND
hunting ...... POACHING
importation .. SMUGGLING

intrusion ...... TRESPASS
liquor .... BOOTLEG
unlearned .... IGNORANT, ILLITERATE
unleash ...... RELEASE, LOOSE, SET FREE
unleavened .... AZYMOUS
unless .... SAVE, EXCEPT
unlettered .... IGNORANT, ILLITERATE, UNEDUCATED
unlike .... DIFFERENT, DISSIMILAR
unload ... UNBURDEN, DUMP, REMOVE, RID
unlock .... OPEN, REVEAL
unloose ...... UNDO, RELEASE, UNTIE
unlucky .. ILL-FATED, HAPLESS, ILL-STARRED
unman ... UNNERVE, CASTRATE
unmannerly .... RUDE, DISCOURTEOUS, IMPOLITE
unmarried .... CELIBATE, SINGLE, UNWED
  in law .... SOLE
  man .... BACHELOR, CELIBATE
  state .... CELIBACY, MAIDENHOOD
  woman .... SPINSTER, MAIDEN
unmentionables .. UNDERWEAR
unmistakable .... CLEAR, OBVIOUS, APPARENT
unmitigated .... ARRANT
unmoved .... UNAFFECTED, INSENSATE
unnatural .... ARTIFICIAL, AFFECTED
unnerve .... UNMAN, SHAKE, SHOCK
unoccupied ... VACANT, IDLE, EMPTY
unorganized ...... DISORDERLY
unpaid .... OWING, DUE
unpaired .... UNIVALENT, SINGLE, ODD
unpleasant .... OFFENSIVE, DISAGREEABLE, UNSAVORY, DISTASTEFUL
unpleasantness .... SPAT, QUARREL
unplowed .. UNTILLED, FALLOW
unpolished .... AGRESTIC, CRUDE, COARSE
unprecedented ... NOVEL, NEW

unpredictable .... CASUAL, CAPRICIOUS
unprejudiced ...... IMPARTIAL, FAIR, UNBIASED
unpremeditated .... SPONTANEOUS
unpressed ..... BAGGY, SEEDY, RUMPLED
unprincipled .... IMMORAL, UNSCRUPULOUS
unprintable usually .. OBSCENE, OBSCENITY, VULGAR(ITY)
unpropitious ... INOPPORTUNE
unqualified .... ABSOLUTE, COMPLETE, SHEER
unravel .... FEAZE, SOLVE, UNTANGLE, TEASE
unreadable .... ILLEGIBLE
unreal .. FANCIFUL, IMAGINARY
unreasonable .... UNDUE, SENSELESS, INANE, IRRATIONAL
unreasoning devotion .. FETISH
unredeemed territory .... IRREDENTA
unreel .... UNWIND
unrefined .... CRUDE, COARSE, CRASS, GROSS
unrelenting .... STERN, ADAMANT
unremitting ...... INCESSANT, NON-STOP, PERSISTENT
unrest .... FERMENT, DISQUIET, AGITATION
unripe ..... GREEN, IMMATURE
unrivaled .... PEERLESS, MATCHLESS, NONPAREIL
unroll ..... DISPLAY, UNFURL
unroot .... STUB
unruffled ..... COOL, SMOOTH, UNFAZED, SERENE, CALM
unruly ... DISORDERLY, WILD, INTRACTABLE, FRACTIOUS, RESTIVE
  child .... BRAT
  hair .... COWLICK
unsavory .... TASTELESS, OFFENSIVE, DISAGREEABLE, UNPLEASANT
unsay .... RETRACT
unscramble .... UNRAVEL, SOLVE, STRAIGHTEN, CLEAR UP
unscrupulous ...... DISHONEST, UNPRINCIPLED

person .... CHEAT(ER),
SWINDLER
unseal .... OPEN
unseat ..... DISLODGE, OUST,
UNHORSE
unseemly ...... INDECOROUS,
IMPROPER, UNDUE
unsettle ... DISTURB, DISTRESS
unsettled .... UNCERTAIN,
UNSTABLE
unsheathe .... DRAW
unsightly ... UGLY, UNGAINLY
unskilled .... INEPT, CLUMSY,
AWKWARD
unsophisticated ..... ARTLESS,
NAIVE, SIMPLE, INGENIOUS,
SQUARE
unsparing ... LAVISH, LIBERAL,
PROFUSE, SEVERE
unspoiled .... FRESH
unspeakable ... WICKED, VILE
unspoken .... TACIT, SILENT,
UNSAID
unstable .... FICKLE,
CHANGEABLE, ERRATIC,
ASTATIC, INCONSTANT,
VARIABLE, LABILE
unsteady ... SHAKY, UNSTABLE,
WAVERING, ERRATIC
unsuccessful ...... ABORTIVE
unsuitable ..... INAPT, UNFIT
untamed ...... FERAL, WILD,
UNRULY, FERINE
state .... FERITY
untangle .... (UN)RAVEL
untanned hide .... KIP,
SHAGREEN, PELT
untenanted .... VACANT
untended .... UNCARED,
NEGLECTED
unterseeboot ..... SUBMARINE,
U-BOAT
untidy .... SLOVENLY,
UNKEMPT, SLOPPY,
SLIPSHOD, DOWDY, MESSY,
LITTERY, MUSSY
animal .... PIG
person ... SLOVEN, SLOB,
SLATTERN
place .... (PIG)STY
untie .... LOOSE(N), UNDO, FREE
until ... BEFORE, UNTO, UP TO,
PENDING, TILL
untimely .... PREMATURE,
INOPPORTUNE
unto .... TILL, UNTIL

untold .... COUNTLESS,
INCALCULABLE,
INDESCRIBABLE
untouchable ...... BRAHMAN,
LEPER, SACRED COW
untouched ... PURE, PRISTINE,
VIRGIN
untoward ...... UNFORTUNATE
untreated .... RAW
untrue ...... DISLOYAL, FALSE,
UNFAITHFUL
untruth ... LIE, FIB, FALSEHOOD,
CANARD, MENDACITY
untwine .... (UN)RAVEL
untwist ... FEAZE, (UN)RAVEL,
STRAIGHTEN
unusual ... UNIQUE, RARE, ODD,
NOVEL, OUTRE, UNCOMMON,
SINGULAR
unvarnished ... PLAIN, SIMPLE,
LITERAL
unvarying sound ... MONOTONE,
DRONE
unveil .... REVEAL, UNMASK
unvoiced ...... SURD, ELIDED,
MUTED
unwary .... CARELESS
unwholesome ...... NOXIOUS,
UNHEALTHY, DISTASTEFUL,
HARMFUL
unwieldy .... AWKWARD,
CLUMSY, HULKING
ship .... HULK, ARK
unwilling .... LOATH,
RELUCTANT, AVERSE
unwind ..... UNREEL, UNCOIL
unwise .... IMPOLITIC,
FOOLISH, UNSOUND,
TACTLESS
unwitting ..... UNCONSCIOUS,
INNOCENT
unwonted .... RARE,
UNACCUSTOMED, UNUSUAL
unworthy ..... UNDESERVING,
UNDESERVED, INDIGN
unwrinkled .... SMOOTH
unwritten .... BLANK
but understood ... TACIT
law .... TRADITION,
CUSTOM
unyielding ... ADAMANT, FIRM,
SET, GRIM, OBDURATE,
HARD, IRON
up .... ABOVE, OVER, ALOFT
and about .... ASTIR
and-coming ... PROMISING

in arms —. ANGRY, IRATE
prefix .... ANA
to-the-minute .. RED HOT
Upanishad .... ISHA
upas tree/poison ...... ANTIAR
upbeat .... ARSIS
upbraid ...... SCOLD, CHIDE,
REPROVE, REBUKE, SCORE,
TWIT, CENSURE, REPROACH
upbringing .... BREEDING
upcountry .... INLAND
Updike novel —..... COUPLES,
RABBIT REDUX
upend .... INVERT
upheaval .... STORM,
CONVULSION
uphold —. SUPPORT, SUSTAIN,
BACK
upholstery —. DOSSEL, DOSSAL,
GOBELIN
material ..... MOQUETTE,
VALANCE, TABARET,
FRISE, MOREEN,
VELOUR(S), MOHAIR,
LAMPAS, SCRIM, VELURE
stuffing .... FLOCK
upkeep —..— MAINTENANCE,
REPAIR
upland ...... PLATEAU, MESA
country .... TIBET
plover —..... SANDPIPER
uplift —..... RAISE, ELEVATE,
BRASSIERE
Upolu town/seaport .... APIA
upon .. ATOP, UP AND ON, OVER
upper —.—.... VAMP, BERTH,
HIGHER
air —..— OZONE, ETHER
Amazon ..... MARANON
case .... CAPITAL
class —. JUNIOR, SENIOR,
ELITE
crust —.—.—.... ELITE
hand —..... ADVANTAGE,
LEAD, MASTERY
house —.—...... SENATE
limit .... CEILING
Volta president ....
LAMIZANE, YAMEOGO
uppermost .... FIRST
uppish/uppity .... PROUD,
SNOBBISH, ARROGANT,
HAUGHTY
upright ..... ERECT, HONEST,
JUST, HONORABLE, VERTICAL

uprise —..—.— ASCEND, SWELL,
REBEL
uprising ... REVOLT, (E)MEUTE,
REBELLION, PUTSCH, MUTINY
uproar —..... COMMOTION,
DISTURBANCE, TUMULT,
RIOT, BABEL, HUBBUB,
RUCKUS, DIN, NOISE,
BROUHAHA, RACKET,
TURMOIL, CLAMOR
uproot —..— STUB, ERADICATE,
SUPPLANT, GRUB,
DERACINATE
upset ... CAPSIZE, OVERTURN,
DISTURB, TOPPLE, TOP OVER,
DEFEAT, DISTRESS,
DISORDER, SWAGE
upshot —... OUTCOME, RESULT
upside down .... TOPSY-TURVY
upsilon-shaped bone ... HYOID
upstage —..... SNOOTY, ALOOF,
CONCEITED, SNUB
upstart —..—. PARVENU, SNOB,
WHIPPERSNAPPER
upturned nose .... SNUB, PUG
upward movement —.. SCEND,
LIFT
Uraeus —.—..... ASP, COBRA
place of an ... HEADDRESS
symbol .... ASP
Ural Altaic branch .... TATAR
Urania .... APHRODITE, MUSE
sphere of .... ASTRONOMY
uranic .... CELESTIAL
Uranus' discoverer .. HERSCHEL
mother ....: GAIA, GAEA
offspring .... TITANS,
FURIES, CYCLOPES,
CRONUS, RHEA, SATURN
satellite .... ARIEL
wife .... GAEA
urban .... OPPIDAN
urbane —.. POLISHED, SMOOTH,
AFFABLE, SUAVE
urbanize —.—.. CITIFY, REFINE,
POLISH
urchin —.—.. HEDGEHOG, IMP,
GAMIN, MUDLARK,
(STREET)ARAB
urd —.—.—.—.... PYROL
urde —.—.—..... CLECHE
Urdu .... HINDUSTANI
uredo ...... HIVES, URTICARIA
urethane —.—...... SEDATIVE,
HYPNOTIC
uretic —. URINARY, DIURETIC

Urfa .... EDESSA
Urga .... ULAN BATOR
urge ... INCITE, PRESS, ALLEGE,
    PLEAD, EXHORT, EGG,
    GOAD, IMPORTUNE, COAX,
    PROD, SPUR, ENTREAT, YEN
urgency .... EXIGENCY
urgent ..... GRAVE, PRESSING,
    INSISTENT
Uriah .... HEEP
    wife of .... BATHSHEBA
urial .... CORIAL, SHA
Uriel .... ARCHANGEL
urinate .... PIDDLE
urination, difficult ....
    STRANGURY, DYSURIA
    excessive ..... POLYURIA
    involuntary ... ENURESIS
urinary ... URETIC, DIURETIC,
    URIC, URINOUS
    calculus ...... UROLITH
    duct ... URETER, URETHRA
    inflammation .. CYSTITIS
urine .... PISS
Uris, author .... LEON
urn .... KIST, STEEN, VASE,
    VESSEL
    figurative .... GRAVE
    for bones ..... OSSUARY
    shaped ...... URCEOLATE
uroxanthin .... INDICAN
Ursa .... BEAR
ursine animal .... BEAR
    howler .... MONKEY,
    ARAGUATO
Urth .... NORN
urticaria ...... HIVES, UREDO
urticate .... STING
Uruguay's capital ....
    MONTEVIDEO
    city ... PAYSANDU, SALTO
    cowboy .... GAUCHO
    discoverer .... DIAZ
    first colony .... COLONIA
    language ...... SPANISH
    monetary unit ..... PESO
    president ...... GESTIDO
urus ...... AUROCHS, TUR, OX
US (see American) ....
    UNITED STATES, AMERICA
    capitol lobbyist ....
    RAINMAKER
    coin .... DIME, CENT,
    NICKEL, QUARTER,
    EAGLE
    expatriate in Paris .. STEIN

flag .... OLD GLORY
Great White Father .....
    PRESIDENT
imaginary town ....
    PODUNK
insurance capital ......
    HARTFORD
marine .... GYRENE,
    LEATHERNECK
marines' slogan ....
    GUNG HO
national military park ...
    SHILOH
newspaper, oldest ....
    COURANT
paper money ....
    GREENBACK,
    LONG GREEN
patron saint (humorously)
    TAMMANY
president's wife ....
    FIRST LADY
soldier, WWI ... SAMMY,
    DOUGHBOY
volcano .... SHASTA,
    LASSEN
winter fog ...... POGONIP
usage .... TREATMENT,
    CUSTOM, PRACTICE, HABIT
usance .... USAGE, USE
use .... AVAIL, UTILITY,
    HABIT, EMPLOY, PURPOSE,
    WORTH, FUNCTION, UTILIZE,
    EXERCISE, CONSUME,
    SERVICE, TREAT
    as example .... CITE
    divining rod ...... DOWSE
    efforts .... EXERT, STRIVE
    of another's property ....
    USUFRUCT
    up .... EXPEND
    wastefully .... SQUANDER
used .... SECONDHAND
    up ... SPENT, EXHAUSTED,
    DEPLETED
useful .... UTILE,
    SERVICEABLE, HELPFUL,
    PRACTICAL
useless ... FUTILE, WORTHLESS,
    VAIN, IDLE, NEEDLESS,
    OTIOSE, INUTILE
user .... CONSUMER, UTILIZER
usher ... ESCORT, DOORKEEPER,
    FORERUN, INTRODUCE,
    HERALD
Uskudar .... SCUTARI

Usnach, son of .... NOISE
Uspallata Pass ... LA CUMBRE
   location .... ANDES
usquebaugh .... WHISKY
USSR (see Russian/Soviet)
ustulate .... BLACKENED,
    DISCOLORED
usual .... CUSTOMARY,
   HABITUAL, WONTED,
    NORMAL
usually .... COMMONLY,
   GENERALLY, ORDINARILY,
   AS A RULE, NORMALLY
usurer .... MONEYLENDER,
   SHYLOCK, VAMPIRE
usurp .... ASSUME, SEIZE,
    ARROGATE
Utah .... BEEHIVE (STATE)
   asphalt .... UINTA(H)ITE,
    GILSONITE
   city ...... PROVO, OREM,
   OGDEN, LOGAN
   Indian .... NAVAJO,
   PAIUTE, NAVAHO
   mountain .... UINTA,
    PEALE
   natives .... MORMONS
   nickname ...... BEEHIVE
   river ..... WEBER, PROVO
   state bird ..... SEAGULL
   state emblem ... BEEHIVE
   state flower .... SEGO
   state tree .... SPRUCE
utensil ..... TOOL, IMPLEMENT
   maker .... COPPERSMITH

uterus .... WOMB, MATRIX
   growth .... MOLE
   inflammation .. METRITIS
   pain .... METRALGIA
   part .... CERVIX
   swelling .... MOLE
Uther's son .... ARTHUR
utile .... PRACTICAL
utilize .... USE
utmost ..... EXTREME, BEST,
   VERIEST, MAXIMUM,
   REMOTEST, GREATEST
Uto Aztecan Indian ... YAQUI
"Utopia" author .... MORE
   imaginary .. SHANGRI-LA
Utopian .... EDENIC,
   IDEALIST(IC), VISIONARY
   scheme .... BUBBLE
utricle .... SAC, VESICLE
Uttar Pradesh capital ......
    LUCKNOW
   city .... MEERUT
   part of .... OUDH
utter ...... SHEER, COMPLETE,
   TOTAL, VOICE, BROACH,
   EXPRESS, SPEAK, STARK,
   ABSOLUTE, EMIT, RANK
   defeat .... ROUT
   in unison ...... CHORUS
utterance .... EXPRESSION
utterly .... COMPLETELY,
   ENTIRELY, FULLY
uvarovite .... GARNET
uxorial .... WIFELY
Uzbek capital ..... TASHKENT
   city .... KHIVA

V

V, author of ...... PYNCHON
   formation flyers ... GEESE
   Greek .... UPSILON
   Hebrew .... VAV
   letter/shaped ...... VEE
   shaped cut ...... NOTCH
   shaped piece .. WEDGE, PIE
   symbol .... VICTORY
vaca .... COW
vacancy ...... GAP, OPENING,
   EMPTINESS, BLANK, BREAK,
   VACUITY
vacant ... FREE, HOLLOW, VOID,
   EMPTY, IDLE, UNOCCUPIED
vacate ... LEAVE, VOID, ANNUL,
    QUIT
vacation .... RECESS, RESPITE,

   REST, HOLIDAY
vaccinate .... INOCULATE
vaccination pioneer .... JENNER
vaccine .... VIRUS
vaccinia .... COWPOX
vaccillate .... HESITATE,
   WAVER, TEETER, FALTER
vacuity ... INANITY, EMPTINESS,
   VOID, VACUUM
vacuous .... EMPTY, INANE,
   STUPID, IDLE
vacuum .... VOID
   opposed to .... PLENUM
   tube .... DIODE,
   ELECTRODE
vade mecum .... MANUAL
vagabond .... BUM, DRIFTER,

TRAMP, WANDERER, WANDERING, VAGRANT, RASCAL, VAG, LOREL, TRUANT, (HO)BO, WAFF, LANDLO(U)PER, RUNAGATE

vagabondage ...... VAGRANTS

vagary ..... ODDITY, CAPRICE, WHIM, FANCY

vagrant ... WAYWARD, ROVER, WANDERER, VAGABOND, BEGGAR, NOMAD(IC), TRAMP, CAIRD, BUM, HOBO, SPIV

greeting of ...... HOBO, HOBEAU

jargon of .... SHELTA

place in city .. SKID ROW

vague ...... HAZY, OBSCURE, NEBULOUS, INDEFINITE, UNCERTAIN, SKETCHY, LOOSE

vail ..... TIP, GRATUITY, DOFF

vain ... EMPTY, IDLE, USELESS, FUTILE, FRUITLESS, CONCEITED, PROUD, SMUG, OTIOSE

and affected .... FOPPISH

bird .... PEACOCK

manners .... AIRS

person ..... DANDY, FOP, COXCOMB, COCKSCOMB

quest .... WILD GOOSE CHASE

vainglory ..... VANITY, PRIDE

vair .... FUR

valance ... DRAPERY, CURTAIN

vale .... DALE, DINGLE, GLEN, VALLEY, FAREWELL, ADIEU

valediction .... FAREWELL, GOODBY, ADIEU

valedictory .... ORATION

Valence's river ...... RHONE

valentine ...... SWEETHEART, GREETING CARD

figure on a .. CUPID, EROS

Valera (Eamon de) nickname .. DEV

valerian .... BENNET, ALLHEAL, HEMLOCK, PLANT

valet ... MANSERVANT, DRESSER

valetudinarian ..... INVALID, SICKLY, HYPOCHONDRIAC

Valetta native ...... MALTESE

valgus .... KNOCK-KNEE(D)

Valhalla maiden .. VALKYR(IE)

presider at .... ODIN

valid .... SOUND, COGENT,

DEFENSIBLE, LEGAL

not .... NULL, VOID

validate ... CONFIRM, ATTEST, SEAL

validity .... SOUNDNESS

valise .... SUITCASE, PORTMANTEAU, GRIP(SACK)

Valkyrie ... BRUN(N)HILD(E), BRYNHILD

love of .... SIGURD

vallancy .... WIG

vallation .... RAMPART, EARTHWORK, WALL

valley .... VALE, CANYON, KLOOF, DALE, GLADE, SWALE, WADI, DINGLE, DELL, GUTTER, GLEN, COMB(E), COOMB, BOLSON, GULCH, STRATH, HOLLOW

Apollo's .... TEMPE

Argolis .... NEMEA

between cliffs .... CAN(Y)ON

entrance of ...... JAWS

moon .... RILL(E)

valor .... HEROISM

valorous .... BRAVE

valse .... WALTZ, TRISTE

valuable ...... DEAR, PRIZED

discovery .... FIND

valuation .... APPRAISAL

value ... ESTEEM, APPRECIATE, ADMIRE, ASSESS, WORTH, PRIZE, TREASURE

beyond amount owed .. EQUITY

highly .... CHERISH

more .... PREFER

of little .... TRIFLING, TRIFLE, TRIVIAL

valve ..... FLOODGATE, SPIGOT, PLUG, COCK, DAMPER, POPPET, STOPCOCK, PETCOCK

engine .... CHOKE, THROTTLE

sliding .... PISTON

vamo(o)se ... DEPART, LEAVE, GO, SCRAM, DECAMP, LAM

vamp .... FLIRT, SEDUCE, BEGUILE, UPPER, PATCH(WORK), REPAIR, ACCOMPANIMENT

vampire .... SIREN, LAMIA, FLIRT, BAT, BLOODSUCKER, LILITH

kind of .... USURER, BLACKMAILER
van ... FRONT, WING, WAGON, TRUCK, TRAILER, FORE, LORRY
Diemen's land .... TASMANIA
Doren, critic ...... MARK, CARL
man .... MOVER
Vance, sleuth .... PHILO
vandal .... HUN
Vandyke ... BEARD, COLLAR, GOATEE
forte of .... PORTRAITS
vane .... WEATHERCOCK
of feather ..... VEXILLUM
vanguard .... FRONT
vanilla ... ORCHID, FLAVORING
vanish .... MELT, FADE, DISAPPEAR, EVANESCE
vanity ... CONCEIT, EGO(T)ISM, FUTILITY, VAINGLORY, PRIDE
case .... ETUI
vanquish ... DEFEAT, CONQUER, SUBDUE, OVERCOME, BEAT, SUBJUGATE, LICK, BEST
vantage point .... COIGN
vapid ...... LIFELESS, INSIPID, STALE, FLAT, INANE, TASTELESS, DULL
vapor ... SMOKE, HALITUS, FOG, REEK, MIST, STEAM, FUME, BRAG, BLUSTER, BRUME, CLOUD
aircraft's ...... CONTRAIL
combining form ... ATMO
in air ... MIST, FOG, HAZE, SMOG
mass of .... WRACK
pressure measuring device TONOMETER
vaporizer .... ETNA
vaporous ..... FOGGY, MISTY, HALITOUS, FUMY
vaquero .... COWBOY
Varangian ... SCANDINAVIAN
Vargas, Brazilian president ... GETULIO
variable ... MUTABLE, FICKLE, ABERRANT, PROTEAN, VOLATILE, CHANGEABLE
variation .. CHANGE, DEVIATION
slight ... NUANCE, SHADE
varicella .... CHICKEN FOX

varicolored .... MOTLEY
phenomenon .. RAINBOW
varicose ..... VARIX, SWOLLEN, CIRSOID
varied .... D(A)EDAL
variegate .... DIVERSIFY
variegated ...... PIED, DAPPLE
variety ... SORT, KIND, CLASS
act .... TURN
show .... VAUDEVILLE
variola .... SMALLPOX
scar .... POCKMARK
variole .... FOVEOLA
various .... SEVERAL, MANY, DIFFERENT
varlet ...... KNAVE, RASCAL, SCOUNDREL, PAGE, COISTREL
varmint .... VERMIN
varnish ... ENAMEL, LACQUER, SHELLAC(K), JAPAN, GLOSS, EMBELLISH
and linseed oil mix ...... MEGILP
material .... COPAL, TURPENTINE, OLEORESIN, SHELLAC, ELEMI, RESIN, MASTIC, TUNG(OIL)
varsity .... TEAM, COLLEGIATE
eight member ... STROKE
varus .... BOWLEG(GED)
opposite of ...... VALGUS
vary .... DIFFER, MODIFY, ALTER, DIVERSIFY, DIVERGE
vas .... DUCT, VESSEL
vascular organ ..... PLACENTA
vase .... TAZZA, POTICHE, JAR, URN, AMPHORA, LACRIMAL, JARDINIERE
making material .... MURRHINE
support .... PEDESTAL
vaseline ... JELLY, OINTMENT, PETROLATUM, LUBRICANT
vassal .... SUBJECT, SERVANT, LIEGE(MAN), BONDMAN, SLAVE
tax paid by .... TRIBUTE
vassalage ... FIEF, SERVITUDE
Vassar's pride .... MILLAY
vast ...... HUGE, ENORMOUS, IMMENSE, COSMIC, OCEANIC
vat .... TUB, CASK, TUN, BAC, TANK, KIER, KEEVE, CISTERN
vatic .... PROPHETIC

Vatican art gallery .... BELVEDERE

chapel .... SISTINE

guard's nationality ...... SWISS

vaticinate .... PROPHESY, FORETELL, PREDICT

vaticinator ..... ORACLE, SEER, PROPHET

Vaud .... CANTON

capital of ..... LAUSANNE

vaudeville .... BURLESQUE, VARIETY(SHOW)

vault ..... LEAP, COPE, SPRING, CATACOMB, BOUND, ARCH, SAFE

burial .... TOMB, CRYPT

concave .... COVE

for bones ...... OSSUARY

horse's ...... CURVET

inside curve/surface ..... INTRADOS

underground ... DONJON, DUNGEON

vaulted .... ARCHED

roof .... DOME

vaunt .... BRAG, BOAST, CROW

vavasor .... VASSAL

veal .... GIGOT

of/like .... VITULINE

neck .... SCRAG

sausage .... BOLOGNA

slice .... SCHNITZEL

stew .... GOULASH

Veda, part of .. YAJUR, SAMA, ATHARVA, RIG

vedette .... SENTINEL, SCOUT(BOAT)

Vedic .... SANSKRIT, PALI

god .... DYAUS, AGNI

goddess .... USHAS

sky serpent .... AHI

vee .... FIVER, FIN

veer .... SHIFT, DEVIATE, SWERVE, TURN, SLUE, SHEER

veery .... THRUSH

Vega, for one .... STAR

constellation ...... LYRA

vegetable ... PLANT, LETTUCE, CABBAGE, TOMATO, OKRA, BEET, SASS, SAUCE, POTATO, CARROT, LEEK, PEA, BEAN, LEGUME, ENDIVE

basket .... SCUTTLE

boiled, buttered .. VICHY

decaying matter ... DUFF

farmer .... TRUCKER

garden .... TRUCK, KALEYARD, KAILYARD

gas .... METHANE

growing art .... HORTICULTURE

leafstalk .... CHARD

marrow .... SQUASH

oyster .... SALSIFY

poison ...... PTOMAIN(E)

root ... TURNIP, PARSNIP

vegetables grown for sale .... TRUCK

vegetarian .... VEGAN

sea mammal ... SEACOW, DUGONG, MANATEE

vegetation, covered with green VERDANT

green .... VERDURE

luxuriant .... LUSH

vehemence ... FERVOR, FORCE, PASSION, ARDOR, FIRE, FURY

vehement .... FERVENT, PASSIONATE, ARDENT

vehemently .... EARNESTLY

vehicle .... CART, SLED(GE), CONVEYANCE, CARRIAGE, CAR, VAN, TRAIN, WAGON

armored ... HALF-TRACK

covered ...... CARAVAN, SCHOONER, SEDAN

decrepit ... SHANDRYDAN

hospital .... AMBULANCE

"last ride" ...... HURDLE, TUMBRIL, TUMBREL

man-drawn .... (JIN)RICKSHA

on runners ..... SLED(GE), SLEIGH, TOBOGGAN

parade .... FLOAT

slow moving ...... SLUG

veil .... MANTILLA, CLOAK, MASK, SCREEN, YAS(H)MAK, CURTAIN, CAUL, CONCEAL

having a .... VELATE

in botany .... VELUM

material .... TULLE, ILLUSION, BAREGE

papal .... ORALE

veiled ... DISGUISED, HIDDEN, COVERED, VELATE

veiling .... CURTAIN

vein ... MOOD, BLOOD VESSEL, TENOR, VENA, STREAK, INTIMA

branch .... VENULE
heart .... VENA CAVA
inflammation .. PHLEBITIS
kind of .... JUGULAR
leaf .... RIB
mine ...... LEDGE, LODE,
REEF
mineral .... LODE
rich ore .... BONANZA
swollen .... VARIX
varicose .... VARIX
veining, art of ..... MARBLING
veinless .... AVENOUS
veins collectively ... VENATION
having .... VENOSE,
VENOUS, NERVATE
veinstone .... GANGUE
velamen .... MEMBRANE
velar .... GUTTURAL
veld(t) .... GRASSLAND
Velez, actress .... LUPE
velleity .... DESIRE, VOLITION,
WISH
vellicate ..... TWITCH, PLUCK
vellication .. TWITCH(ING), TIC
vellum .... PARCHMENT
velocipede .... BICYCLE,
TRICYCLE, HANDCAR
velocity ..... SPEED, RAPIDITY,
SWIFTNESS, RATE
measuring device ....
TACHOMETER
velum .... SOFT PALATE
velure .... VELVET, PAD
velutinous .... VELVETY
velvet ...... WINNINGS, GAIN,
PROFIT, VELOUR, SILK,
PANNE
velveteen .... FUSTIAN
velvety .... SMOOTH, MELLOW,
SOFT
vena .... VEIN
venal .... CORRUPT,
MERCENARY, VENDIBLE
vend .... SELL, PUBLISH
vendace .... WHITEFISH
vendee .... BUYER
vender .... ALIENOR, SELLER
vendetta .... FEUD
vendible ... VENAL, SAL(E)ABLE
vendition .... SALE
vendor ...... SELLER, PEDDLER
route of a .... WALK
vendue .... AUCTION
veneer .... ENAMEL, OVERLAY,

LAYER, BURL, VARNISH,
COATING
venerable .. OLD, HOARY, AGED
man ... SAGE, PATRIARCH
monk .... BEDE
venerate ..... REVERE, ADORE,
WORSHIP, HALLOW
venerated .... SACRED
veneration ... AWE, ADORATION,
HOMAGE, REVERENCE,
WORSHIP
venereal infection: sl. ... DOSE,
CLAP
sore/ulcer ..... CHANCRE
venery ...... CHASE, HUNTING
venesection .... PHLEBOTOMY
Venetia .... VENETO
Venetian barge .. BUCENTAUR
boat .... GONDOLA
boatman .... GONDOLIER
bridge .... RIALTO
business center .. RIALTO
canals .... RII
chief magistrate ... DOGE
gondolier's song ....
BARCAROLE
island .... RIALTO
magistrate .... DOGE
nobleman ... MAGNIFICO
painter .... TITIAN,
TINTORETTO, VERONESE,
TIEPOLO
red .... SIENA
resort .... LIDO
ruler .... DOGE
song ...... BARCAROL(L)E
state barge .. BUCENTAUR
street .... CANAL
traveler ... (MARCO) POLO
Venezia .... VENICE
Venezuela capital ... CARACAS
city ... MARACAIBO, CORO,
VALENCIA
dam .... GURI
discoverer of .. COLUMBUS
fish .... GUPPY
Indian ... CARIB, TIMOTE
language .... SPANISH
mining town ...... AROA
monetary unit .. BOLIVAR
patriot .... BOLIVAR
plain .... LLANO
president ...... LEONI,
CALDERA
river ..... PAO, ORINOCO,
APURE, CARONI

seaport ...... MARACAIBO
snake .... LORA
state .... LARA
tree .... BALATA
Venezuelan god ...... TSUMA
vengeance ...... REPRISAL,
REQUITAL, REVENGE,
TALION, WANION
vengeful .... VINDICTIVE,
SPITEFUL
veni, vidi, _____ VICI
venial .... PARDONABLE,
EXCUSABLE
opposed to ...... MORTAL
Venice, "Little" .. VENEZUELA
race in .... REGATTA
state barge .. BUCENTAUR
venireman .... JUROR
Venite ..... PSALM, CANTICLE
venom .... MALICE, VIRUS,
GALL, POISON, SPITE, BANE
venomous .... BANEFUL,
POISONOUS, MALIGNANT,
VIPERINE, VIPERISH,
VIPEROUS, VIRULENT
venous .... VEINY
vent .... HOLE, ISSUE, OUTLET,
PASSAGE, ESCAPE,
EXPRESSION, FLUE, ORIFICE,
APERTURE, OPENING
in earth's crust ....
VOLCANO, GEYSER
tailor's .... SLIT
whale's .... SPIRACLE,
BLOWHOLE
ventage ...... (FINGER) HOLE
venter .... BELLY, ABDOMEN,
WOMB, WAME
ventilate .... AIR, AERATE, FAN,
EXPOSE
ventilating shaft .. DOWNCAST
ventilation .... AIRING
opening .... LOUVER
ventilator ..... FAN, BLOWER
ventral .... ABDOMINAL,
STERNAL, H(A)EMAD
opposite of ..... DORSAL
ventriloquist .... BERGEN
Bergen's dummy .. SNERD,
CHARLIE
medium of ...... DUMMY,
PUPPET
venture .. BRAVE, ENTERPRISE,
CHANCE, RISK, DARE(SAY),
HAZARD
Venus .... PLANET, PHOSPHOR,

APHRODITE, CYTHEREA
as morning star .. LUCIFER
beloved of ...... ADONIS
flytrap .... DIONAEA
girdle .... CESTUS
in alchemy ...... COPPER
island .... MELOS
Milo's .... STATUE
planet .... VESPER
poetical ...... LUCIFER,
HESPERUS
son of .... CUPID
tree sacred to ... MYRTLE
Venus's flytrap ...... DIONAEA
veracious .... HONEST,
ACCURATE, TRUTHFUL, TRUE
veracity ..... TRUTH, HONESTY
veranda(h) .... LANAI, PORCH,
PORTICO, PIAZZA, BALCONY,
LOGGIA
in Dixie .... GALLERY
verb, expression of a .. ACTION,
EXISTENCE, OCCURRENCE
verbal .... ORAL, SPOKEN,
VOCAL
attack .... TIRADE,
INVECTIVE, OBLOQUY
noun .... GERUND,
INFINITIVE, PARTICIPLE
thrust .... DIG
verbatim ... WORD FOR WORD,
LITERAL
verbenaceous plant .. LANTANA,
VERBENA, VERVAIN
tree .... TEAK
verbiage .... PROLIXITY,
WORDINESS
verbose ...... PROLIX, WORDY,
WINDY
verboten .... FORBIDDEN,
TABOO, TABU
verbs, derived from ....
RHEMATIC
verd .... GREEN
antique ...... VERDIGRIS,
MARBLE, PATINA
verdancy .... GREENNESS,
INEXPERIENCE, VIRIDITY
verdant .... GREEN
Verdi, composer ... GUISEPPE
work .... OTELLO, AIDA,
ERNANI, (IL)TROVATORE,
NABUCCO, DON CARLO,
FALSTAFF
verdict .... JUDGMENT,
DECISION, FINDING

verdigris ...... RUST, PATINA, VERD ANTIQUE
verdin .... TITMOUSE, BIRD
verditer .... BICE
verdure .... GREENERY, GREENNESS
verecund ...... MODEST, SHY, BASHFUL
verein .... SOCIETY
verge .... BRINK, EDGE, MARGIN, STAFF, ROD, MARGE
Vergil's birthplace ... MANTUA
    hero .... (A)ENEAS
    queen .... DIDO
    work .... (A)ENEID
veriest ... UTMOST, GREATEST
verify ...... CONFIRM, CHECK, AFFIRM, ATTEST
verily ..... REALLY, IN FACT, TRULY, INDEED, CERTES
veritable ...... ACTUAL, REAL
veritas .... TRUTH
verity .... FACT, TRUTH, REALITY
vermeil .... VERMILION
vermiform .... WORM-SHAPED
    process .... APPENDIX
vermilion ..... VERMEIL, RED, PIGMENT, CINNABAR, MINIUM
vermin ... VARMINT, VARMENT, LICE, BEDBUG, RAT, WEASEL, PEST
Vermont capital .. MONTPELIER
    city ... BARRE, RUTLAND, BURLINGTON
vermouth .... WINE
vernacular ... DIALECT, IDIOM
vernal .... SPRINGLIKE, YOUTHFUL
Verne, author .... JULES
    character .... NEMO
    submarine .... NAUTILUS
veronal .... BARBITAL
veronica .... SUDARIUM, SPEEDWELL, FIGWORT, SUDARY
verruca .... WART
verrucose .... WARTY
versant .... SLOPE
versatile ...... MANY-SIDED, TALENTED
verse ...... ALBA, LINE, POEM, TROCHEE, OCTAMETER, TRIPODY, DIMETER, STANZA, RUNE, (MON)STICH

accented .... ARSIS
analysis .... SCANSION
comic .... DOGGEREL
form .... COUPLET, DIMETER, IAMB, (DI)STICH, SONNET, PANTOUM, PANTUN, ANAPEST, VIRELAY, SPONDEE
free .... VERS LIBRE
half line of ... HEMISTICH
inside ring .... POSY
kind of ...... DOGGEREL, LIMERICK, JINGLE
musical .... STAFF
satirical .... IAMBIC
set to music ..... LYRICS
two-feet .... DIMETER, DIPODY, SYZYGY
two-line .... DISTICH, COUPLET
unit .... FOOT
with nosegay ...... POSY
versed .... LEARNED, PROFICIENT, ADEPT, SKILLED, TURNED, FAMILIAR
verses, set of .... STAVE, STANZA, STROPHE, PANTUN
versifier .... POET(ASTER), RHYMER, RHYMESTER
versify ...... METRIFY, RHYME
version .... TRANSLATION, ACCOUNT, RENDITION
of Bible .... VULGATE, DOUAY
verso, opposed to .... OBVERSE, RECTO
versus .... AGAINST
vertebra: comb. form .... SPONDYL(O)
    body of .... CENTRUM
    top .... ATLAS
vertebral bone .... SACRUM, COCCYX
vertebrate ..... FISH, REPTILE, AVIS, MAMMAL
vertex .... APEX, TOP, ZENITH, SUMMIT
vertical .... UPRIGHT, PERPENDICULAR, PLUMB
verticil .... WHORL
vertiginous .... DIZZY
vertigo .... DIZZINESS,

GIDDINESS, MEGRIM, DINUS, GID, STAGGERS

Vertumnus' wife .... POMONA

verve .... VIGOR, ELAN, ENTHUSIASM, PEP, SPIRIT

vervet .... MONKEY

relative .... GRIVET

very .... REAL, EVEN, ACTUAL, TRULY, SAME, GENUINE, TRES, QUITE

colloquial ..... TERRIBLY

in English slang .. BALLY

large .... DECUMAN

light ...... FLARE, SIGNAL

new .... REDHOT

well .... FINE, FIRST RATE

vesica .... BLADDER

vesicant ...... MUSTARD GAS, EPISPASTIC

vesicate .... BLISTER

vesicle ...... CYST, BLEB, SAC, CAVITY, BLISTER, BULLA, UTRICLE

vespa ... WASP, YELLOWJACKET

vesper .... STAR, EVENING, EVENTIDE, HESPERUS, VENUS, EVE

vespers .... CANONICAL HOUR, EVENSONG

vespertilione .... BAT

vespiary inhabitant ..... WASP, HORNET, VESPID

vespid .... HORNET, WASP, YELLOWJACKET

vespine insect .... WASP

vessel .... UTENSIL, CASK, CANAL, VAS, BOWL, DUCT, SHIP, CRAFT, FRIGATE, GALLEON, GALLEY, AIRSHIP, DUCT, TUBE, PAN, LATEEN, LUGGER, (CAT)BOAT, CAR(R)ACK

anti-smuggling .. CUTTER

assayer's .... CUPEL

cargo .... OILER, FREIGHTER, TANKER, BARGE

Chinese .... JUNK, SAMPAN

clumsy ... ARK, DROGHER

combining form ... VASO

cooking .... PAN

Ecclesiastical .. AMA, PYX

fishing .... TRAWLER, SEALER, SMACK

Levantine ...... KETCH,

SAIC

Malay ..... PRAU, PROA

merchant ...... ARGOSY

supply .... TENDER, COALER

three-masted ..... BARK, ZEBEC

vessels, having ..... VASCULAR

vest .... WAISTCOAT, UNDERSHIRT, CLOTHE, EMPOWER, ENDOW, BOLERO, TATTERSALL

pocket .... SMALL

Vesta .... HESTIA, MATCH

vestal ...... VIRGIN(AL) PURE, CHASTE, NUN

virgin .... TUCCIA, PRIESTESS

vested .... ROBED, FIXED, ABSOLUTE, SETTLED

vestibule ...... HALL, LOBBY, FOYER, HALL(WAY)

vestige(s) .. MARK, BIT, TRACK, RELIC, NARTHEX, SIGN, TRACE, SHRED, REMAINS, SHADOW

of burn .... ESCHAR

vestment .... GARMENT, RQBE, GOWN, TUNICLE

clerical ...... ALB, TIPPET, AMICE, CASSOCK, SURPLICE, CHASUBLE, COPE

eucharistic .... MANIPLE

Jewish priest's ... EPHOD

papal .... FANON

place for .... AMBRY

vestry .... SACRISTY

Vesuvius .... VOLCANIC, FUSEE, MATCH

vesuvianite .... IDOCRASE, EGERAN

Vesuvius .... VOLCANO

city destroyed by .... POMPEII

vetch .... TARE, AKRA, SATIVA, ERS

vet(eran) .... TROUPER, STAGER, OLD HAND, OLDTIMER

of battles ... WAR HORSE

veterinarian .... DOCTOR, FARRIER, LEECH, VET

vetiver .... GRASS, BENA

veto .... PROHIBIT, FORBID, KIBOSH, DISAPPROVE

vex .... ANNOY, DISTURB, IRRITATE, TORMENT, TROUBLE, GALL, ROIL, ACERBATE, FASH, HARASS, IRK, NETTLE, NEEDLE, CARK, RILE

vexatious .... ANNOYING, TROUBLESOME, IRRITABLE, PESKY

via ... BY WAY OF, THROUGH

viaduct ..... BRIDGE, TRESTLE

vial .... PHIAL, BOTTLE, AMP(O)ULE

viand(s) ... DISH, FOOD, FARE, VICTUALS

viaticum .... EUCHARIST

viator .... TRAVELER, WAYFARER

Viand's pseudonym ..... LOTI

vibrant .... QUIVERING, RESONANT, PULSING, ENERGETIC

vibrate .... QUIVER, OSCILLATE, RESOUND, THRILL, JAR, TIRL, TREMBLE, FLUTTER, THROB, DINDLE, SHIMMY, RESONATE

vibration ...... QUIVER, THRILL, TREMOLO, FREMITUS

check .... DAMP

vibrator .... OSCILLATOR

vibrissa .... WHISKERS

viburnum .... SHRUB, HONEYSUCKLE, LANTANA, LIANA, LIANE

vicar .... DEPUTY, PRIEST, MINISTER, VICEGERENT

assistant of ..... CURATE

Christ's .... POPE

vicarious .... DEPUTY, SUBSTITUTE, DELEGATED

vice ...... SIN, STEAD, FAULT, ADDICTION, INSTEAD(OF), WEAKNESS

chairman, public dinner .. CROUPIER

president .... VEEP

versa .... CONVERSELY

vicegerent ..... VICAR, DEPUTY

vicenary number ..... TWENTY

viceroy .... BUTTERFLY, VICEGERENT, REGENT

of a .... VICEREGAL

wife of a ..... VICEREINE

Vichy and others ... WATERS, EAUX, SPAS

vicinage ..... NEIGHBORHOOD, VICINITY

vicinal .... LOCAL

vicinity ..... NEIGHBORHOOD, ENVIRONS

vicious ..... WICKED, UNRULY, MEAN, MALICIOUS

act .... OUTRAGE

vicissitude .... CHANGE

victim .... PREY, QUARRY, MARK, DUPE, LAMB

accident ..... CASUALTY

of Bellerphon ... CHIMERA

of Cain .... ABEL

victor ... CONQUEROR, WINNER

actor ..... JORY, MATURE

character .... LENA, AXEL HEYST

victoria ... WATERLILY, QUEEN, EMPRESS, CARRIAGE, AUTO(MOBILE)

capital (Australia) ...... MELBOURNE

goddess .... NIKE

Victorian vice ..... PRUDERY, BIGOTRY

victorious .... PALMARY, TRIUMPHANT

victory ...... LAUREL, PALM, TRIUMPH, CONQUEST, SUCCESS

author of ...... CONRAD

costly .... PYRRHIC

crown of .... LAUREL, ANADEM

easy .... WALKAWAY, RUNAWAY

goddess of .... NIKE, ATHENA

kind of .... CADMEAN, PYRRHIC LANDSLIDE, ROUT

symbol of .... PALM, CHAPLET, LAUREL

Victrola ...... PHONOGRAPH

kin of .... GRAMOPHONE

victual(s) .... EAT, FEED, FOOD, VIAND, VITTLE, PROVISIONS

victualer .... SUTLER, INNKEEPER, CATERER

vicuna .... ALPACA

vide .... SEE

videliet .... NAMELY

video .... TELEVISION, TV

vie ... COMPETE, CONTEND, LIFE
Vienna .... WIEN
    park .... PRATER
    Woods composer ....
            STRAUSS
Viennese dress ...... DIRNDL,
           LEDERHOSEN
Vietnam (North) capital ......
           HANOI
    city .... HAIPHONG
    monetary unit ..... DONG
    native .... MEO
    newspaper .... NHANDAN
    premier ....
        (PHAM VAN) DONG
    president ....
        (HO CHI) MINH
Vietnam (South) Buddhist sect
       CAO DAI, HOA, HAO
    capital .... SAIGON
    city ....DANANG, DALAT,
         HUE
    guerrillas ...... VIETCONG
    holiday .... TET
    monetary unit ... PIASTRE
    New Year .... TET
    premier .... KHANH,
         CAO KY
    president .. THIEU, DIEM
view ... VISION, SIGHT, VISTA,
    SCENE, OPINION, GOAL,
    PANORAMA, SCAPE, NOTION,
    GLIMPSE, PROSPECT, SURVEY
viewpoint .... OPINION
         OUTLOOK
vigesimal .... TWENTIETH
vigil ..... WATCH, EVE, WAKE
vigilance, in medicine ....
        INSOMNIA
vigilant .... ALERT, WARY,
        WATCHFUL
vigilante .... NIGHTRIDER
vigor ... VITALITY, INTENSITY,
    ENERGY, SNAP, DASH, FORCE
vigorous .... ROBUST, STRONG,
    FORCEFUL, ENERGETIC
Viking ...... PIRATE, ROVER,
        NORSEMAN
    famed .... ERIC, ROLLO,
        OLAF
    poet .... SKALD
vilayet .... EYALET
    subdivision of .. SANJAK
vile .... MEAN, WICKED,
    DEPRAVED, BASE, EVIL,
    SCURVY

vilify .... DEFAME, ABUSE,
    SLANDER, ASPERSE,
    REVILE, TRADUCE, MALIGN,
    CALUMNIATE, LIBEL
vilipend .... VILIFY, BELITTLE,
    DISPARAGE, REVILE
Villa, Mexican leader ....
        PANCHO
village ..... MUNICIPALITY,
    BARRIO, HAMLET, CASALE,
    KAIK, STAD, WICK, DORP,
    THROP(E), KRAAL, BURG,
    BURH, TOWN, CLACHAN
    Biblical .... CANA
    near castle ...... BOURG
villain ... SCOUNDREL, ROGUE,
    CRIMINAL, MEANIE,
    MISCREANT, KNAVE, FELON
    movie .... HEAVY
    of story .... LEGREE,
        RASSENDALE
villainy .... CRIME
villatic ...... RURAL, RUSTIC
villein .... PEASANT, CARL(E),
    ESNE, SERF, TENANT
Villon, Fr. poet .... FRANCOIS
Vilnius .... VILNA, WILNO
vim .... PEP, ZIP, ELAN,
    ENERGY, VIGOR, SPIRIT,
    STINGO
vimen .... SHOOT
vin .... WINE
vina .... ZITHER
vinaceous ...... VINOUS, RED
    fruit .... GRAPE
Vinci's patron .... SFORZA
vincible .... BEATABLE
vincit omnia ____ VERITAS
vindicate .... CLEAR, JUSTIFY,
    ABSOLVE
vindictive ..... (RE)VENGEFUL,
    SPITEFUL, MALICIOUS
vine ..... LIANA, GRAPE, BINE,
    CREEPER, LIANE, IVY,
    WISTERIA, PEA, HOP,
    ANGLEPOD, COW(H)AGE
    coil of .... TENDRIL
    gourd ..... COLOCYNTH
    support .... RISEL,
        TENDRIL, TRELLIS
    tuberous .... TAMUS
    woody .... SMILAX
vinegar ...... ACETUM, EISEL,
    ALEGAR
    bottle .... CRUET, CASTER,
        CASTOR

change to ...... ACETIFY
dregs .... MOTHER
eel .... NEMATODE
formation in ...... ROPE,
    MOTHER
from ale .... ALEGAR
kind of ..... PALM, CIDER
like/of .... ACETIC,
    ACETOUS, ACETOSE
pickling .... MARINADE
preserve in .... MARINATE
producing ..... ACETOUS
spiced .... MARINADE
stringy substance ....
    MOTHER
worm .... EEL
vinegarroon .... SCORPION
vinegary .... SOUR,
    ILL-TEMPERED
vinery .... GREENHOUSE
vineyard .... CLOS
vingt et un ...... BLACKJACK,
    TWENTY-ONE
vinous ..... VINACEOUS, WINY
vintage .... WINE, MODEL,
    CHOICE, CROP
vintner's assistant .. GOURMET
viol .... SARINDA
viola ... VIOLET, PANSY, PLANT
clef .... ALTO
violate .... BREAK, RAPE,
    RAVISH, DESECRATE,
PROFANE, ABUSE, INFRACT,
    INFRINGE
trust .... BETRAY
violation .... BREACH,
DESECRATION, INFRACTION
violator .... LAWBREAKER
violence ..... SEVERITY, FORCE
violent ...... ROUGH, FURIOUS,
    STRONG, FORCEFUL,
    TEARING
anger .... FURY
blow .... BASH
contact .... IMPACT,
    COLLISION
violet ...... MAUVE, PURPLE,
    FLOWER
blue .... INDIGO
violin ...... FIDDLE, CELLO,
VIOLA, VIOL(ONCELLO)
border .... PURFLING
bow .... ARCO,
    FIDDLESTICK
bow's knob .... NUT
companion of ..... BOW

E-string .... QUINT
famous ... AMATI, STRAD,
    CREMONA
forerunner of the ......
    REBEC(K)
inlaid border .. PURFLING
instrument resembling ...
    REBEC(K)
part of ... NECK, SCROLL,
PEG, NUT, BRIDGE,
PEG(BOX), WAIST,
    BUTTON
piano piece ..... SONATA
player .... FIDDLER
rare ... KIT, STRAD, AMATI
small .... KIT
stroke .... UPBOW
violinist .... ELMAN, AUER,
KREISLER, YSAYE, STERN,
HEIFETZ, MENUHIN
comedian .... BENNY
direction to ... SPICCATO
Roman .... NERO
so-called .. (JACK) BENNY
violone .... CONTRABASS
VIP ..... TOPBRASS, BIGSHOT,
    CELEBRITY
viper .... ADDER, ASP,
FER-DE-LANCE, SNAKE,
REPTILE, COPPERHEAD,
RATTLESNAKE, BUSHMASTER
horned .... CERASTES
viper's bugloss .... BUGWEED
viperine .... VENOMOUS
viperous .... VENOMOUS,
MALICIOUS, SPITEFUL
virago ... TERMAGANT, VIXEN,
FURY, SCOLD, AMAZON,
    HELLCAT
virelay .... VERSE, POEM
vireo .... GREENLET,
(SONG)BIRD, REDEYE, RUDD
virescent .... GREENISH
virgate .... TWIGGY,
    ROD-SHAPED
Virgil (see Vergil)
virgin .. VESTAL, VIRGO, NUN,
CHASTE, UNTOUCHED,
PURE, PARTHENOS,
MAID(EN), INITIAL,
    MADONNA
Islands' discoverer ......
    COLUMBUS
queen .... ELIZABETH
the .... MARY
unblemished ... CAMILLA

vestal .... RHEA
virgin's-bower ..... CLEMATIS
virginal ...... HARPSICHORD,
 MAIDENLY, PURE
 membrane .... HYMEN
Virginia capital .... RICHMOND
 city .... ROANOKE,
 PORT NEWS, NORFOLK
 cowslip .... BLUEBELL
 creeper .... IVY,
 WOODBINE, VINE
 dance .... REEL
 mount .... VERNON
 pine .... LOBLOLLY
 river .... JAMES, RAPIDAN
 seaport .... NORFOLK
 settlement .. JAMESTOWN
 state bird ..... CARDINAL
 truffle ...... TUCKAHOE
virginity .... MAIDENHOOD
Virgo .... VIRGIN,
 CONSTELLATION
 star .... SPICA
virgulate .... ROD-SHAPED,
 VIRGATE
viridian .... PIGMENT
viridity .... VERDANCY,
 GREENNESS
virile .... MANLY, MASCULINE,
 MALE
virtu .... CURIO, BIBELOT,
 RARITY
virtual .... LITERAL
virtually .... ALMOST, NEARLY,
 LITERALLY
virtue .... CHASTITY,
 EXCELLENCE, MERIT,
 QUALITY
virtues, one of the .. PRUDENCE,
 JUSTICE, HOPE, FAITH,
 CHARITY
virtuosity .... SKILL
virtuoso .... MAESTRO,
 CONNOISSEUR, ARTIST,
 AESTHETE
virtuous ..... CHASTE, MORAL
virulence .... DEADLINESS,
 VENOM, MALIGNANCY
virulent .... DEADLY,
 VENOMOUS, RABID,
 MALIGNANT, INFECTIOUS
virus ...... POISON, VENOM,
 VACCINE, PATHOGEN
 disease ...... MEASLES,
 SMALLPOX, CHICKEN POX,
 VARICELLA, HERPES,

VIROSIS, VARIOLA,
 RABIES, FLU, GRIP(PE),
 INFLUENZA, SHINGLES,
 POLIO, COLD
vis .... POWER, FORCE,
 STRENGTH
 a-vis ...... FACE TO FACE
visage .... FACE, MAP,
 COUNTENANCE
viscera .... INTESTINES,
 INNARDS, VITALS, GUTS,
 ENTRAILS
viscid ..... VISCOUS, STICKY,
 SIRUPY, VISCOSE, GUMMY
viscount .... SHERIFF
 heir of .... MASTER
viscous ...... VISCID, STICKY,
 SYRUPY, GLUEY, PASTY,
 SIZY
 product .... PASTE, GLUE,
 GUM
 substance ... PITCH, TAR,
 RESIN, SLIME,
 MOLASSES, SYRUP
vise ..... CLAMP, CLAM, DIAL
 part of .... JAW
Vishinsky, Soviet diplomat ....
 ANDREI
Vishnu ..... (THE) PRESERVER
 avatar of .... KRISHNA
 incarnation of .. KRISHNA,
 RAMA
 wife of .... SRI
visible .... PERCEPTIBLE,
 EVIDENT, DISCERNIBLE,
 IN SIGHT, VISUAL
 to naked eye ....
 MACROSCOPIC
Visigoth .... TEUTON
 king .... ALARIC
vision .... IMAGE, DREAM,
 FANCY, PICTURE, (EYE)SIGHT
 defect .... MYOPIA,
 DIPLOPIA, ANOPIA
 double .... DIPLOPIA
 pertaining to .. OPTIC(AL)
 range .... EYESIGHT,
 EYESHOT
 scope .... SCAN
 tri-dimensional ....
 STEREOPSIS
visionary .... ILLUSIONIST,
 DREAMER, IMAGINARY,
 IMPRACTICAL, UTOPIAN,
 IDEALIST, QUIXOTIC,
 FANTAST

visit ... CALL, STAY, SOJOURN, GO TO, INFLICT
   between whalers .... GAM
   kind of .... SOCIAL, PROFESSIONAL, OFFICIAL
   short ..... CALL, LOOK-IN
   social .... GAM
visitant ...... VISITOR, GUEST
visitation .... ∴ DISASTER, AFFLICTION
visitor ..... VISITANT, GUEST, CALLER, COMPANY
visor .... MASK, VIZARD, BRIM, EYE-SHADE, VISARD
vista ... VIEW, OUTLOOK, SCENE
Vistula River .... WISLA
   city on .... TORUN
   tributary .... SAN
visual ...... VISIBLE, OPTICAL, OCULAR
   disorder ... STRABISMUS, SQUINT, SCOTOMA
   purple ...... RHODOPSIN
   yellow .... RETINENE
visualize .... IMAGINE
vita .... LIFE
   Nuova author .... DANTE
vital .... FATAL, DEADLY, ESSENTIAL, IMPORTANT, MORTAL
   fluid .... BLOOD, SAP
   organ .... HEART, LUNG, LIVER
   principle .... SOUL
   statistics of beauty contestant ....
      MEASUREMENTS
vitality ... ZEST, VIGOR, LIFE, ZING, ENERGY
vitalize .... ANIMATE
vitamin B .... CHOLINE
   H .... BIOTIN
vitelline .... EGG YOLK
vitellus .... YOLK
vitiate ...... SPOIL, CORRUPT, PERVERT, INVALIDATE, TAINT, DEBASE
vitreous ... GLASSY, HYALINE, HYALOID
vitrics .... GLASSWARE
vitrify .... BAKE
vitrine .... SHOWCASE
vitriol .... SULFATE, SORY, BLUEJACK, BLUESTONE
vitriolic ..... SHARP, CAUSTIC, SARCASTIC, BITING

vitta ...... HEADBAND, RIBBON
vittle .... VICTUAL, FOOD
vituline animal .... CALF
vituperate ..... ABUSE, SCOLD, REVILE, BERATE
vituperation ...... INVECTIVE, ABUSE
viva .. ACCLAIM, EXCLAMATION, CHEER
   voce .... ORALLY
vivacious .... GAY, LIVELY, SPIRITED
vivacity ... ELAN, DASH, VERVE, ANIMATION, GAIETY, BRIO
vivandiere .... SUTLER
vivarium .... HOTHOUSE, GREENHOUSE
vive le .... ROI
vivid .... LIVE(LY), BRIGHT, GRAPHIC, STRIKING
vivify .... ANIMATE
vixen .... SCOLD, VIRAGO, TERMAGANT, HELLCAT, SHREW, FOX
viz. .... VIDELICET, NAMELY
vizard .... VISOR, MASK
Vladimir Ilich Ulianov .. LENIN
   pianist ...... HOROWITZ
vocabulary .... GLOSSARY, DICTIONARY, LEXICON, ARGOT, JARGON, SLANG
   of a .... LEXICAL
vocal ...... VERBAL, SONANT, ORAL, SPOKEN, UTTERED, SUNG, VOICED, ARTICULATE
   chords site ..... LARYNX
   composition ...... SONG
   ornament ..... ROULADE
   solo ...... ARIA, ARIOSO
vocalist .... SINGER
vocalize .... PHONATE
vocation .... TRADE, OCCUPATION, PROFESSION, CAREER, WORK, CALLING
voces .... VOX, VOICE
vociferation ... CLAMOR, RANT
vociferous ...... CLAMOROUS, BLATANT, BOISTEROUS
vodka mixture .. SCREWDRIVER
vogue ... MODE, FAD, FASHION, STYLE, TON
voice .... ARTICULATE, UTTER, SAY, VOX
   colloquial ... SPOKESMAN, MOUTHPIECE
   female ... ALTO, SOPRANO

impairment .. DYSPHONIA
kind of ..... BASS, ALTO,
    BASS(O), TENOR,
    SOPRANO, BARITONE,
    FALSETTO
loss of .... APHONIA
loud, strident .. FOGHORN
male ..... TENOR, BASSO
objection .... DEMUR,
    PROTEST, COMPLAIN
organ .... LARYNX
person with loud ....
    STENTOR
pertaining to .... VOCAL,
    PHONETIC
practice ...... SOLFEGGIO
quality .... TIMBRE
range .... DIAPASON
roaming .... VAGANS
voiced sound .... VIBRANT,
    SPEECH, SONG, SONANT,
    UTTERANCE
stop .... MEDIA
voiceless .. SURD, DUMB, MUTE,
    SILENT, SPEECHLESS, SPIRATE
sound ..... SURD, TENUIS
sound sign ..... CEDILLA
voices, for all .... TUTTI
void ...... VACATE, VACANT,
    EMPTY, LACKING, VACUUM,
    INVALID, CANCEL, ANNUL,
    NULLIFY, NULL, NULLITY
of infinite space .... INANE
voidance .... ANNULMENT
voided escutcheon ...... ORLE
voila .... BEHOLD, LO, SEE
voile .... FABRIC
voiture ... CARRIAGE, WAGON
volant .... FLYING, NIMBLE,
    QUICK, AGILE
Volapuk, inventor of ....
    SCHLEYER
volatile .... MUTABLE,
    MERCURIAL, FICKLE
liquid ... ETHER, ALCOHOL
volcanic .... VESUVIAN,
    EXPLOSIVE, EXTRUSIVE
activity ...... ERUPTION,
    BELCHING
ash .... TUFF
cinder .... SCORIA
dust .... TUFF
earth .... TRASS
ejection .... BELCH,
    LAPILLUS, LAVA,

PUMICE, SCORIA,
    COULEE
glass .... OBSIDIAN
island .... LIPARI,
    IWO(JIMA), FAROE
mud .... SALSE
opening ..... FUMAROLE
rock .... PERLITE,
    RHYOLITE, TUFF,
    LAPILLUS, WACK,
    OBSIDIAN, TALPATATE,
    TAXITE, PROPYLITE,
    TEPHRITE, TRACHYTE,
    PUMICE, BASALT, LATITE
rock cavity ...... VESICLE
slag .... SCORIA, CINDER
soil .... TALPATATE
vent .... CRATER,
    SOLFATARA
volcano, cone of ... MONTICULE
crater-like basic ....
    CALDERA
island .... IWO JIMA
kind of .... ACTIVE,
    DORMANT, EXTINCT
molten rock ..... LAVA,
    MAGMA
mouth of ... FUMAROLE,
    CRATER
well known ...... PELEE,
    TAAL, ETNA, VESUVIUS,
    ASAMA, FUJI
vole .... RODENT, MOUSE, RAT,
    SLAM
volery .... AVIARY
Volga figure ...... BOATMAN
tributary .... KAMA
volition ...... VELLEITY, WILL
volk .... NATION, PEOPLE
volley ..... SALVO, FUSILLADE,
    BURST, BROADSIDE
volplane ...... GLIDE, COAST
Volstead Act dissenters .. WETS
supporters .... DRYS
Volsunga Saga dwarf ....
    NIBELUNG
hero .... SIGURD,
    SIEGFRIED
king .... ATLI
volt-ampere .... WATT
volta, in music ... TURN, TIME
Voltaire .... AROUET
character ..... PANGLOSS
novel by ...... CANDIDE
volte-face ...... ABOUT-FACE
    REVERSAL

voluble .... TALKATIVE, GLIB,
    GARRULOUS
volume .... BOOK, BULK,
    CUBAGE, MASS, QUANTITY,
    TOME, CUBATURE
    of sound unit .. DECIBEL
voluminous ..... BULKY, FULL,
    LARGE
voluntarily .... FREELY
voluntary .... WILLFUL
volunteer ...... ENLIST, OFFER
    opposed to .... DRAFTEE,
    CONSCRIPT
voluptuary .... SYBARITE,
    SENSUALIST, HEDONIST
voluptuous .... SENSUAL,
    SENSUOUS, LYDIAN
volute .... WHORL, TURN,
    SPIRALED
volution ...... COIL, ROLLING
vomica .... PUS
vomit ..... REGORGE, EMETIC,
    THROW UP, PUKE, BELCH,
    SPEW, REJECT
    effort to .... RETCH
vomiting .... EMESIS
voodoo ... WITCHCRAFT, OBI,
    BEAH, HOODOO
    deity .... ZOMBI(E)
voracious .... EDACIOUS,
    GREEDY, RAVENOUS,
    INSATIABLE, RAPACIOUS,
    ESURIENT
voracity ..... GREED, EDACITY,
    RAPACITY
Voroshilov, USSR president ..
    KLEMENTI
vortex .... EDDY, WHIRLPOOL,
    WHIRLWIND, GYRE
votary .... NUN, MONK,
    CELIBATE, FAN, DEVOTEE
vote ...... SUFFRAGE, BALLOT
    by gesture .. THUMBS-UP,
    THUMBSDOWN
    counting .... POLL
    in .... ELECT
    in opposition ...... CON
    kind of .. STRAW, HAND,
    PROXY, SECRET, CON
    non-candidate's ....
    WRITE-IN
    of assent ... PLACET, AYE
    presiding officer's ....
    CASTING
    right to ...... SUFFRAGE,
    FRANCHISE

    solicitation for a bill .....
    LOBBY
    survey .... POLL
    voiced ... YEA, AYE, NAY
voter .... ELECTOR
voting method .. BALLOT, VOICE
vouch ... ATTEST, GUARANTEE,
    AFFIRM, SPONSOR, ASSURE
voucher .... CHIT, DEBENTURE
vouchsafe .... BESTOW,
    CONCEDE, DEIGN,
    GUARANTEE
vow .... OATH, PROMISE,
    PLEDGE, SWEAR
    taker .... MONK,
    CELIBATE, NUN, VOTARY,
    WITNESS
vowel .... LETTER
    change in sound ....
    UMLAUT
    contraction of .. SYNERESIS
    gradation ...... ABLAUT
    mark ,,, MACRON, BREVE,
    TILDE, DI(A)ERESIS,
    UMLAUT, CIRCUMFLEX
    slurring .... ELISION
vox .... VOICE
voyage ... JOURNEY, PASSAGE,
    TRIP
    pleasure .... CRUISE
voyager .... SAILOR
voyageur .... TRAVELER,
    BOATMAN
voyeur .... PEEPING TOM
vrouw ... HOUSEWIFE, WOMAN
vs. .... VERSUS
Vulcan .... HEPHAESTUS,
    HEPHAISTOS
    Star Trek .... (MR) SPOCK
vulcanite ... EBONITE, RUBBER
vulgar ... COMMON, COARSE,
    CRUDE, LOW-BRED, RANDY,
    BOORISH, PLEBEIAN, GROSS,
    OBSCENE
Vulgate, author of the .. JEROME
vulnerable .... ASSAILABLE,
    WEAK
Vulpecula ...... LITTLE FOX,
    CONSTELLATION
vulpine .... FOXY, TRICKY,
    VULPECULAR, CUNNING
vulture ...... CONDOR, URUBU,
    LAMMERGEI(E)R, ATRATA
    food .... CARRION
    hawk resembling ....
    CARACARA

W

W, Arabic .... WAW
   in chemistry ... TUNGSTEN
   old English .... WEN
Waadt .... VAUD
Wabash River city ....
               TERRE HAUTE
   tributary ... TIPPECANOE
wabble ...... LARVA, WOBBLE
wacker .... QUAKER
wacky .. ERRATIC, ECCENTRIC,
               ODD, QUEER
wad ..... MASS, CRAM, LUMP,
    STUFF, BUNDLE, PLUG,
    PLEDGET, BAT, DOSSIL, PAD
   of paper money .... ROLL
wadding material .... COTTON,
             KAPOK, HEMP
waddle .... TODDLE, WAG,
               WOBBLE
waddler ...... DUCK, GOOSE,
           TODDLER, BABY
waddy .... CANE,
    WALKING STICK, CLUB
wade ..... FORD, SLOSH, SLOG,
              PADDLE
wader ... HERON, EGRET, IBIS,
    CRANE, RAIL, COOT, SNIPE
waders .... BOOTS
wadi ..... CHANNEL, RAVINE,
      VALLEY, OASIS,
      WATERCOURSE
wading bird (see bird) ... IBIS
wadset .... MORTGAGE
wafer .... CRACKER, CAKE,
    CANDY, DISK, SNAP
   container ..... PYX, PIX
waff ..... GUST, PUFF, WAVE,
    WHIFF, GHOST, SOLITARY,
          VAGABOND
waffle .... (BATTER) CAKE
waft ..... WAIF, CARRY OVER,
  TRANSPORT, FLOAT, BREATH,
              GUST
wag ...... FARCEUR, JESTER,
    SHAKE, WIT, WAVE, JOKER,
   PUNSTER, WAGGLE, WIGGLE
wage .... HIRE, STIPEND,
    CARRY ON, PAY, ENGAGE,
    SALARY, EMOLUMENT
   boost .... RAISE
   deduct from ...... DOCK
   earners collectively ......
               LABOR
   war .... LEVY

wager ... BET, ANTE, PARLAY,
    VIE, IMPONE, GAMBLE,
    GAGE, STAKE, HAZARD
wages .... REWARD,
  RECOMPENSE, EMOLUMENT,
            STIPEND
   after deductions ....
           TAKE-HOME
   describing some .. LIVING,
          STARVATION
   payment in kind .. TRUCK
wagged, thing that's .. FINGER,
  TAIL, TONGUE, FLAG, HEAD
wagger .... DOG, PIPIT
waggery .... JEST, WIT, JOKE
waggish .... JOCULAR,
    SPORTIVE, PLAYFUL,
    MERRY, ROGUISH
waggle .... TOTTER
   dancer .... BEE
Wagner, composer .. RICHARD
   father-in-law of ... LISZT
   forte of .... OPERA
   wife of .... COSIMA
Wagnerian earth goddess .....
               ERDA
   music festival city ....
          BAYREUTH
   opus .... RIENZI,
  PARSIFAL, LOHENGRIN
   role .... WOTAN, ELSA,
    ISOLDE, TRISTAN,
    SENTA, HAGEN
   soprano .... NILSSON
wagon .... TRAM, TRAILER,
    DRAY, WAIN, VOITURE,
  CAMION, (T)CART, TUMBREL,
           TUMBRIL
   ammunitions ... CAISSON
   baggage ...... FOURGON
   battle ... DREADNAUGHT
   builder .... WAINWRIGHT
   Charlemagne's .... WAIN
   driver .... CARTER
   freight charge .. CARTAGE
   horse .... POLER
   oriental .... ARABA
   pin .... CLEVIS
   police ..... BLACK MARIA
   prairie .... SCHOONER
   repairer ... WAINWRIGHT
   shaft .... THILL
   tongue .... NEAP
   track .... RUT

yoke .... INSPAN
wagoner .... AURIGA
wagtail ... PIPIT, LARK, BIRD
wahoo ...... BURNING BUSH,
   SHRUB, ELM, BASSWOOD
fish .... ONO, PETO
waif ... GAMIN, ARAB, STRAY,
   FOUNDLING, WAFT, SIGNAL,
   MAVERICK
wail .... HOWL, (CATER)WAUL,
   YOWL, ULULATE, CRY,
   MOURN, LAMENT, WAWL,
   SOB
Wailing Wall chore .. PRAYER,
   LAMENTATION
devotee .... JEW
site .... JERUSALEM
wain .... WAGON, CART
wainscot .. CEIL, PANEL(ING),
   WALLBOARD, LINING
waist .... BODICE, BLOUSE,
   BASQUE
circumference ...... GIRTH
garment .... SARONG,
   LOINCLOTH
molding garment ......
   GIRDLE
of dress .... TAILLE
waistband .... BELT, SASH,
   GIRDLE, CINCTURE, OBI
waistcloth ... SARONG, PAREUS,
   LAVA-LAVA
waistcoat .... VEST, GILET,
   JACKET
waistline .... GIRTH
wait ... STAY, TARRY, REMAIN,
   BIDE, ATTEND
in ambush ...... COUCH
lie in .... AMBUSH, TRAP
on ..... SERVE, ATTEND,
   VISIT
waiter .... TRAY, SALVER,
   SERVER, GARCON, STEWARD,
   POTMAN
drive-in .... CARHOP
female .... WAITRESS
portable .... DUMB
waiting line ..... QUEUE, CUE
waitresses, chief of .. HOSTESS
waive ... RELINQUISH, GIVE UP,
   DEFER, FOR(E)GO, RENOUNCE
wake ... VIGIL, WATCH, TRACK
Island .... OTORI
periscope's ..... FEATHER
robin ..... PLANT, SARAH,
   ARUM, CUCKOOPINT,

TRILLIUM,
   JACK-IN-THE-PULPIT
submarine's .... FEATHER
up from this ...... SLEEP,
   TRANCE, DREAM, COMA,
   STUPOR
wakeful .... SLEEPLESS
waken .... STIR, ROUSE
Waldorf .... SALAD
room .... SERT
wale ..... RIB, WELT, WHEAL,
   TEXTURE, SELECT, CHOICE,
   BLOW
Waler .... HORSE
Wales city .... SWANSEA,
   CARDIFF
floral emblem ..... LEEK
mountain ..... SNOWDON
patron saint ..... DAVID
poetic name ... CAMBRIA
river .. SEVERN, USK, WYE
seaport .... SWANSEA
walk .. TRAMP, TREAD, PLOD,
   HIKE, AMBLE, STOA, ALLEY,
   HOOF
about .... AMBULATE
baby's .... WADDLE,
   TODDLE
beach .... ESPLANADE
clumsily .... LUMBER
coating .... PARGET,
   PLASTER
covered ...... CLOISTER,
   ARCADE, STOA, PORTICO
daintily .... MINCE
kind of .... WADDLE,
   PRANCE, LIMP, TRAMP,
   STRUT, TODDLE,
   LAMBETH, STRIDE,
   LUMBER, WOBBLE,
   SWAGGER, MINCE
leisurely ...... STROLL,
   PROMENADE, TRAIPSE,
   TRUDGE, SAUNTER
long ...... MARCH, HIKE
off .... LEAVE
on stilts ..... TRAMPOLIO
out on ... DESERT, LEAVE
public .... PARADE,
   PROMENADE
shaded .... MALL,
   ALAMEDA
softly ...... TIPTOE, PAD
through mud ..... SLOSH,
   SQUELCH
through water .... WADE

to and fro .... PACE
vain ... STRUT, SWAGGER,
PEACOCK
walker .... PEDESTRIAN,
AMBULANT
idle .... FLANEUR
walking .... AMBULANT,
GRADIENT, PEDESTRIAN,
adapted for .. GRESSORIAL
idle .... FLANERIE
papers .... DISMISSAL
shoes .... BALMORAL
stick ... CANE, MALAGA,
STILT, RATTAN, STAFF,
POGO, SUPPLEJACK,
MALACCA, WADDY
vendor .... PEDDLER
walkout .... STRIKE
wall .... PARAPET, PARIES,
SEPTUM, BULKHEAD, BARRIER
band .... CORDON
bench .... PODIUM
binder .... PERPEND
border .... DADO
bracket .... SCONCE
coating .... PLASTER
column .... PILASTER
cover .... KEIL,
LAG(GING), MANTLE
dividing .... SEPTUM
end of .... ANTA
eyed fish ... PIKE, DORY,
DORE
facing .... VENEER,
REVETMENT
garden .... HAHA
hanging cloth .... ARRAS,
TAPESTRY
indentation .. CRENEL(LE)
inscription .... GRAFFITO
kind of ... JETTY, RIPRAP
lining .... STEEN,
WAINSCOT
lizard .... GECKO
loophole .... CRENEL(LE)
mine .... BRATTICE
opening ... BAY, SCUTTLE,
CRENEL(LE), EMBRASURE
painter .... MURALIST
park .... HAHA
pertaining to .... MURAL
pier .... ANTA
recess .... BAY
river .... LEVEE,
EMBANKMENT

sea .... MOLE, PIER,
BREAKWATER
section .... PANEL
step .... STILE
stone .... ASHLAR
Street operator .... BEAR,
BULL, BROKER,
SPECULATOR
tapestry .... ARRAS
top layer .... COPING
top slab ...... CAPSTONE
wood lining .. WAINSCOT
wooden pin .... NOG
writing .... GRAFFITO
wallaba ... APA, ARAWAK, TREE
wallaby .... KANGAROO
Wallace, novelist .... LEW,
IRVING
work .... BEN HUR,
THE WORD
Wallach, actor .... ELI
wallaroo .... KANGAROO
wallboard .... WAINSCOT
walled town .... BURG
wallet .... POCKETBOOK,
BILLFOLD, KNAPSACK, SCRIP
walleye .... ALEWIFE
walleyed .... DRUNK
fish ...... PIKE, PERCH,
POLLACK, ALEWIFE
slang .... DRUNK
wallflower .... HEARTSEASE
walloper .... WHOPPER
wallow .... FLOUNDER,
PUDDLE, ROLL ABOUT,
LUXURIATE, MUDHOLE,
WELTER
walls, behind the .. IN PRISON
dividing .... SEPTA
wally ... FIRSTRATE, FINE, TOY
walnut .. HICKORY, SHAGBARK,
TREE, BROWN, WOOD,
TRYMA
Walpurgis Night revelers .....
WITCHES
walrus ... BRUT, SEAL, MORSE,
SEACOW, SEAHORSE,
PINNIPED, TUSKER
herd .... POD
male .... BULL
tooth .... TUSK
tusk .... IVORY
Walrus' list item ..... SHIP(S)
Walton, fisherman .... IZAAK
waltz .... DANCE, MUSIC,
VALSE, BOSTON

dance like ..... REDOWA
king .... STRAUSS
wamble .... REEL, STAGGER
wame .... BELLY, WOMB,
        VENTER
wampum ... BEADS, SE(A)WAN,
     PEAG(E), MONEY
wamus ... CARDIGAN, JACKET
wan .... PALLID, PALE,
     COLORLESS, ASHEN
wand .... STAFF, SCEPTER,
    BATON, WITHE, ROD,
    VERGE, SHOOT, SWITCH,
    WATTLE, MACE
   shaped like a ... VIRGATE
wander .... STROLL, STRAY,
    MEANDER, DRIFT, ROVE,
    STRAGGLE, GAD, TRAIPSE,
    RAMBLE, ROAM, DIGRESS,
    DIVAGATE
wanderer .... PILGRIM,
    LANDLO(U)PER, ARAB,
    ROVER, GYPSY, HOBO,
    VAGABOND, BEDOUIN,
    ITINERANT, VAGRANT,
    NOMAD, TRAMP
wandering .... ERRATIC,
    VAGRANT, NOMADIC,
    FOOTLOOSE, ERRANT,
    ODYSSEY
   beggar .... FAKIR,
    VAGABOND, ROGUE
   dervish .... CALENDER
   extended .... ODYSSEY
   minstrel .... GOLIARD
   student .... GOLIARD
   tribe .... GYPSY
wanderings .... ODYSSEY,
    TRAVELS
wanderoo .... MACAQUE,
    MONKEY, LANGUR
wandle .. SUPPLE, AGILE, LITHE
wane .... ABATE, EBB,
    DECLINE, SUBSIDE
wangle .... GET, JUGGLE,
   OBTAIN, FINAGLE, FALSIFY,
    W(R)IGGLE, WHEEDLE
wanigan .... ARK
want ... LACK, CRAVE, NEED,
    DESIRE, WISH,
   REQUIRE(MENT), DESTITUTION,
    POVERTY, SCARCITY,
    SHORTAGE
wanted man ..... DESPERADO,
    OUTLAW, ESCAPEE
wanton ... TRAMP, TART, RASH,

WILD, LEWD, UNCHASTE,
   PLAYFUL, FROLICSOME,
   RECKLESS, SENSELESS
   destroyer ...... VANDAL
wapiti .... DEER, ELK
war .... STRIFE, CONFLICT,
   BELLIGERENCE, HOSTILITY
   acquisitions ...... SPOILS
   against abuse .. CRUSADE
   agency .... OSS
   agreement .... CARTEL
    TRUCE, CEASEFIRE
   and Peace author ....
    TOLSTOI
   and Peace heroine ......
    NATASHA
   at .... BELLIGERENT
   bonnet wearer ... INDIAN
   chariot .... ESSED
   chief, name meaning ....
    CEDRIC
   cry .... WHOOP, YELL,
    BANZAI, SLOGAN,
    AMORT, ALALA
   dance .... PYRRHIC
   engine, stone-throwing ..
    CATAPULT, TREBUCHET
   fleet .... ARMADA
   galley beak .... ROSTRUM
   games .... MANEUVERS
   gas .... MUSTARD,
    YPERITE, ADAMSITE
   god ... MARS, ARES, TYR,
    IRRA
   holy .... JIHAD, CRUSADE
   horse .... CHARGER,
    VET(ERAN), COURSER,
    DESTRIER
   horse head armor ......
    CHAMFRON, CHAMFRAIN
   operation ..... CAMPAIGN
   paint; sl. .... COSMETICS,
    REGALIA
   participant ....
    ANTAGONIST,
    BELLIGERENT
   pertaining to ... MARTIAL
   preparation ....
    MOBILIZATION
   pretext for .. CASUS BELLI
   provoking event ....
    CASUS BELLI
   religious ...... CRUSADE
   symbol of .... MARS
   vessel .... CORVETTE,
    PTBOAT, UBOAT,

CRUISER, FLATTOP, DESTROYER, SUB, TRIREME, DREADNAUGHT

word .... DEBATE

warble .... YODEL, CAROL, SING, TRILL, BABBLE, LARVA, TUMOR

warbler (see songbird) .... BECCAFICO, SONGSTER, REDSTART, TROCHILUS

warbling .... CHIRM

ward .... FEND, GUARD, DISTRICT, AVERT, PARRY, CHARGE, PROTEGE(E)

  kind of .... MINOR, INCOMPETENT

  part of a ...... PRECINCT

  person (entrusted) with a TRUSTEE, GUARDIAN, PATRON

  politician ...... HEELER

warden .... PEAR, KEEPER, CUSTODIAN, TRUSTEE, GATEKEEPER, GUARDIAN, CONSTABLE, ALCAIDE, JAILER, JAILOR

  forest .... RANGER

  kind of .. GAME, FOREST, AIR-RAID, FIRE, PRISON

warder .... TURNKEY, WATCHMAN, CUSTODIAN, ROD, STAFF, GUARD

wardrobe ... CLOTHES, CLOSET, TROUSEAU

wardship .... CUSTODY

ware ..... CONSCIOUS, READY, PRUDENT, MERCHANDISE, DISHES, POTTERY

warehouse ... STORE, BODEGA, DEPOT, GODOWN, CAMARIN, ELEVATOR, ETAPE, HONG, ENTREPOT, MAGAZINE

  for candles .. CHANDLERY

  platform .... PALLET

  receipt .... QUEDAN, WARRANT

  weapons ...... ARSENAL

wares ... MERCHANDISE, GOODS

warfare ... STRIFE, STRUGGLE, POLEMY, CONFLICT

  temporary stoppage of ... TRUCE, ARMISTICE, CEASE-FIRE

Warfield, now a duchess ... WALLIS

warhead of missile .. PAYLOAD

warlike .... BELLICOSE, BELLIGERENT, MARTIAL, MILITANT, HOSTILE

warlock .... SORCERER, CONJURER, MAGICIAN

warm ..... ARDENT, LIVELY, HEAT(ED), CORDIAL, SUNNY, THERMAL, FRESH

  baths .... THERMAE

  compress .... STUPE

  make moderately ...... TEPEFY

  moderately ...... TEPID

  springs .... THERMAE

warmonger .... JINGO, MILITARIST

warmth .... ARDOR, ENTHUSIASM, ZEAL

  increasing in .. CALESCENT

warn ...... ADVISE, CAUTION, ADMONISH, FLAG, SIGNAL, ALERT, PORTEND

warning ...... OMEN, ALARM, PORTENT, PRESAGE, AUGURY, TIP-OFF

  in law .... CAVEAT

  signal ... ALAR(U)M, HISS, TOCSIN, SIREN, BEACON, ALERT

  signal device .. FOGHORN, SIREN

  snake's .... HISS, RATTLE

  system, for short .. DEWS

  weather ...... ADVISORY

  word of .... FORE, BEWARE, LOOK OUT, OFF LIMIT

warp .. DEFORM, DISTORT(ION), ABERRATION, BIAS, SILT, MUD, CONTORT, PERVERT

  thread ends ...... THRUM

warplane ..... SPAD, SPITFIRE, ZERO, FLYING FORTRESS, STUKA

warplanes, fleet of .. ARMADA

warrant ..... JUSTIFY, PLEVIN, AUTHORIZATION, GUARANTEE, MERIT, PRECEPT, VOUCHER, WRIT, ORDER

  convict's ...... MITTIMUS

  officer .... BOSUN

  royal .... BERAT

warren .... RABBITRY, HUTCH

  Chief Justice ...... EARL

inhabitant ..... RABBIT, GAME
warrigal .... DINGO
warring nations' agreement ... CARTEL, TRUCE, ARMISTICE
warrior .... FIGHTER, SOLDIER, COMBATANT, KURIPAN, SINGH, JINGO
  arena .... GLADIATOR
  Algerian .... SPAHI
  female .... AMAZON
  frenzied for battle .... BERSERK(ER)
  Indian .... BRAVE
  Japanese .... SAMURAI
  Philippine .. MAHARLIKA
warsaw .... FISH, GROUPER
warship .... MAN O'WAR, CRUISER, DREADNOUGHT, GALLEON, DESTROYER, FRIGATE, RAZEE, TRIREME, GALLEY, BATTLEWAGON, FLATTOP, IRONCLAD
  armored .... IRONCLAD, MERRIMAC, MONITOR
  boat on .... DINGHY, LAUNCH
  convoy ..... CORVET(TE)
  deck, lowest .... ORLOP
  eating quarters .... WARDROOM
  gun emplacement .... TURRET
  gun shield ..... CUPOLA
  kitchen .... GALLEY
  prison .... BRIG
  ram .... BEAK
  station for wounded ..... COCKPIT
  tower .... TURRET
warships, fleet of .... ARMADA
wart .... TUMOR, PAPILLOMA, VERRUCA, KERATOSIS
Wartburg's important resident LUTHER
wartime detainee ... INTERNEE
  detention ... INTERNMENT
warts, covered with .... VERRUCOSE
wary ... CANNY, LEERY, ALERT, CAG(E)Y, CHARY, SHY, CAUTIOUS, CAREFUL, SUSPICIOUS, CIRCUMSPECT
wash .... BATHE, DRIFT, ELUTE, SLOP, SWILL, LAVE, PURIFY, MOISTEN, RINSE

and iron ...... LAUNDER
basin/bowl ...... LAVER, LAVATORY, LAVABO
by rubbing .... SCRUB
hair/scalp ..... SHAMPOO
kind ... LOTION, MOUTH, HAIR
out with water ... FLUSH
washbowl in church . LAVABO
washerwoman .... LAUNDRESS
washing ... LAVAGE, LAVATION
  board .... DOLLY
  out of an organ .. LAVAGE
  lye/soapsuds ..... BUCK
  water for .... LAVATION
Washington art gallery .. FREER
  bloomer .... CHAT
  capital of ..... OLYMPIA
  city .... YAKIMA, SEATTLE, TACOMA, SPOKANE, EVERETT
  dam ... GRAND COULEE, WANAPUM
  educator ..... BOOKER (T)
  football team .. REDSKINS
  hostess .. HOWAR, MESTA
  Moscow telephone ...... HOTLINE
  motto .... AL-KI
  peak .... ALTA
  river .... COLUMBIA
  seeress .... DIXON
washout ..... FAILURE, FIASCO
washroom .... LAVATORY
washstand .... COMMODE
wasp .... HORNET, DIGGER, MUDDAUBER, WHAMP, VESPID, YELLOW JACKET, STINGER, COW KILLER
  like a .... VESPINE
  nest .... VESPIARY
  prick of .... STING
waspish ...... BAD-TEMPERED, TESTY, IRRITABLE, SLIM-WAISTED
wassail ... CAROUSE, TOAST, REVELRY, CAROUSAL, DRINKING SONG
Wasserman test subject ...... SYPHILIS
waste .... FRITTER, OCEAN, CHAFF, DESERT, SPOIL, WILD(ERNESS), RUIN, WEAR AWAY, DECAY, EXCRETION, LEFTOVER, SQUANDER, BARREN, REFUSE

allowance .... TRET
arctic .... TUNDRA
away .... PEAK,
  EMACIATE, ROT,
  DECAY, GNAW,
  MO(U)LDER, MACERATE
cause of .... HASTE
deposit .... SLUDGE
drain .... SEWER
fiber .... NOIL, FLOSS
glass .... CULLET
lay .... RAVAGE, RAZE
maker .... HASTE
matter ... REFUSE, EJECT
metal ...... SLAG, DROSS
pipe ..... SEWER, DRAIN
product ...... RUN-OFF
sugar cane/beets ....
  BAGASSE, MEGASS(E)
time .... IDLE, LOAF,
  LOITER, DAWDLE,
  FIDDLE, DIDDLE,
  FRIBBLE, FRIVOL
wasted ... GAUNT, EMACIATED
wasteful .... PRODIGAL,
  SPENDTHRIFT, EXTRAVAGANT
wasteland ... TUNDRA, STEPPE,
  DUST BOWL, DESERT,
  WILDERNESS, FOREST, MOOR,
  HEATH
reclamation .... INNING
wasting away .... MARASMUS,
  TABETIC, TABID, TABESCENT,
  EMACIATION, ATROPHY
disease .... TABES,
  CONSUMPTION,
  TUBERCULOSIS, TB,
  LEUKEMIA
disease, pertaining to ....
  HECTIC
wastrel .... PRODIGAL,
  SPENDTHRIFT,
  GOOD-FOR-NOTHING
wat .... HARE, HOT
watch .... LOOK, OBSERVE,
  TEND, GUARD(ING),
  LOOKOUT, SENTRY, EYE,
  VIGIL, HOROLOGE, TIMEPIECE
bearing .... JEWEL
chain .... FOB
covering ...... CRYSTAL
death ..... VIGIL, WAKE
during exams ....
  INVIGILATE
duty ...... PATROL, VIGIL
kind of .... REPEATER

mounted ...... VEDETTE
night .. NEW YEAR'S EVE
part ..... DETENT, HAND,
  DIAL, STUD, CLICK,
  PAWL, PALLET, STEM
pawl .... JUMPER
pocket .... FOB
secretly .... SPY
slang .... TICKER
soldier on ...... SENTRY,
  SENTINEL
sound .... TICK
time .... HOROLOGE
undercover .. ESPIONAGE,
  SPYING
watchdog .... GUARDIAN,
  MASTIFF, CERBERUS,
  DANDOG
watcher ... SPOTTER, LOOKOUT
ballroom .. WALLFLOWER
secret .... TAIL, SHADOW
watchful ... ALERT, VIGILANT,
  OBSERVANT, ATTENTIVE,
  OPEN-EYED
man .... IRA
watchmaker .... HOROLOGIST
watchman .. GUARD, SENTRY,
  SENTINEL, WARDER,
  WARDEN, LOOKOUT,
  VEDETTE
mythological .. HEIMDALL,
  ARGUS, TALOS
watchtower ...... BARBICAN,
  BEACON, MIRADOR
watchword ... SLOGAN, MOTTO,
  SHIBBOLETH, BATTLECRY,
  PASSWORD, CRY
person concerned with ...
  SENTRY, GUARD,
  SENTINEL
water ...... AQUA, SPRINKLE,
  IRRIGATE, DILUTE, EAU
animal ... POLYP, HYDRA,
  SEA ANEMONE,
  POLYZOAN ROTIFER,
  BRYOZOAN
as source of power ......
  WHITE COAL
baptismal .... LAVER
barely above .... AWASH
barrier ..... DAM, DIKE,
  LEVEE, BOOM, WEIR,
  MOLE, EMBANKMENT
bearer, in astronomy ....
  AQUARIUS

borne .... AFLOAT, FLOATING
bottle .... CARAFE, DECANTER
brain in sheep ...... GID
brash .... PYROSIS, HEARTBURN
buffalo .. CARABAO, ARNEE
bug .... COCKROACH, BEETLE
carrier bird .. ALBATROSS
channel .... FLUME, SLUICE, DRAIN, GUTTER, AQUEDUCT, RACEWAY, GULLY, GULLET
chestnut ..... CALTRAP, CALTROP, LING
chinquapin ...... LOTUS
clock .... CLEPSYDRA
closet ... TOILET, STOOL, CLOACA
cloud .... RAIN
color .... AQUARELLE, PAINTING
color painting ... FRESCO
combining form .... HYDR(O)
conduit ...... AQUEDUCT
container .... BREAKER, CISTERN, GOGLET, GURGLET
containing .... HYDROUS
corral .... CRAWL
crake .... OUZEL
cress .... POTHERB, MUSTARD
cure ...... HYDROPATHY, HYDROTHERAPY, TORTURE
current .... RACE
deposit ... SILT, SEDIMENT
dog .... SPANIEL, SALAMANDER
excursion .... CRUISE
exhibition ... AQUACADE
fairy .... NIX
floating on ...... AWASH
gate .... SLUICE, WICKET
gauge .... UDOMETER
glass .... GOBLET, TUMBLER
gum .... TUPELO
heater .... SAMOVAR
hemlock ...... COWBANE
hen .... COOT
hole .... POOL, POND

hunger for .... THIRST
ice .... SHERBET
jar .... BANGA, OLLA, EWER, HYDRIA
jet, revolving .... GIRANDOLE
journey .... PASSAGE, VOYAGE
jug .... OLLA, EWER
keg .... BREAKER
like .... AQUEOUS
lily ...... LOTUS, LOTOS, NELUMBO, VICTORIA, WOCAS, FANWORT
lily leaf .... PAD
living in .... AQUATIC
logged .... SWAMPY, SOGGY
marker ..... DANDY ROLL
mill .... CLOW
moccasin .... SNAKE, VIPER, COTTONMOUTH
movement ... EBB, TIDE, SEICHE
nymph .... NAIAD, NEREID, OCEANID
of .... AQUEOUS
opossum .... YAPOK
ouzel ... DIPPER, THRUSH, PIET
parting .... DIVIDE
passage .... SLUICE, STRAIT, CHANNEL
pepper ..... SMARTWEED
pimpernel .. BROOKWEED
pipe ... HOSE, AQUEDUCT, HOOKA(H), NARGHILE, MAIN, DRAIN
plant ..... CHINQUAPIN, CALTROP, LOTUS
plant leaf .... PAD
plant leaf walker .... JACANA
pump .... RAM
raising device ...... RAM, NORIA, TABUT
rat .... THIEF, VOLE, MUSKRAT
rodent .... NUTRIA
sapphire .... IOLITE
scented ...... COLOGNE, BAYRUM
science of .. HYDROLOGY
search for .... DOWSE
snake .... MOCCASIN
soak .... SATURATE

soluble stuff .. HYDROGEL
sound .... (S)PLASH
spirit ... ARIEL, UNDINE,
NIX(IE), KELPIE, KELPY
sports .... AQUATICS
spout .... SPATE,
GARGOYLE, GEYSER,
GUSH
spring .... LYMPH
sprite .... KELPIE,
NIX(IE), KELPY, NYMPH,
NAIAD, NEREID
storage .... CISTERN,
TANK, RESERVOIR
surface .... RYME
thrush .... OUZEL
transportation .... FERRY
trough, mining ....
LAUNDER
tube .... HOSE
vessel .... LOTA
washing ..... LAVATION
wave .... BILLOW
wheel ... TURBINE, NORIA
witch ... DOWSER, GREBE
without ... ANHYDROUS,
DRY, ARID, PARCHED
worm .... NAID
waterbuck ... ANTELOPE, KOB
watercourse .... CANAL,
CAN(Y)ON, FIORD, GORGE,
RAVINE, CHANNEL, DIKE,
NULLA, RUNNEL, BROOK,
GULLY
watercraft ...... BOAT, SHIP,
RAFT
watercress .... POTHERB
watered .... INFLATED,
DILUTED, SPRINKLED
fabric .... MOIRE, TABBY
Wateree .... CAWTABA
waterfall ... CASCADE, LIN(N),
CATARACT, CHIGNON, FOSS,
CHUTE
waterfinder .... DOWSER,
DIVINING ROD,
DOWSING ROD
waterfront laborer ....
ROUSTABOUT, STEVEDORE
watering place ... OASIS, SPA,
WELL, SPRING
waterless ... ANHYDROUS, DRY,
ARID, BARREN
Waterloo, victor of ....
WELLINGTON

waterproof covering ....
RAINCOAT, TARP(AULIN),
GOSSAMER, PONCHO
to .... CALK, PAY
watershed .... DIVIDE
waterside .... COAST, SHORE,
BEACH
watertight box ...... CAISSON,
COFFERDAM
make .... CA(U)LK
waterworks: sl. .... TEARS
waterwort .... ELATINE
watery ..... WASHY, AQUEOUS,
THIN, SEROUS, HYDROUS,
SOGGY
discharge .... RHEUM
grave .... SEA
wattle .... GILL, DEWLAP,
LAPPET, WAND, TWIG, ROD
birds' .... CARUNCLE,
GILL(S), JOWL
fish .... BARBEL
tree .... BOREE
Waugh, novelist ..... EVELYN
waul .... SQUALL, WAIL
waur .... WORSE
wave .. RIPPLE, FLAP, FLUTTER,
SURF, FLOURISH, WAFF,
UNDULATION, BRANDISH,
CURVE, ROLLER, SWELL,
SURGE, SEESAW, BILLOW,
BREAKER, COMBER
back and forth .... WAG
channel .... BORE, EAGRE
heave of a .... SCEND
hollow of ...... VALLEY
large .. DECUMAN, SWELL,
SEA, ROLLER
little .... RIPPLE
movement .... CHOP,
UNDULATION
signaling .... WAFF
tidal .... EAGRE, BORE
to and fro ... WAG, FLAP
top of .... CREST
with foamy crest ....
WHITECAP
wavelet .... RIPPLE
Wavell, Earl .... ARCHIBALD
waver .... TEETER, SWAY,
FLUTTER, VACILLATE,
FALTER, QUAVER, TREMBLE,
HESITATE
wavering sound .... TREMOLO
waves breaking on shore .....
SURF

move in ..... UNDULATE, RIPPLE
    sound of .... ROAR
    space between .. TROUGH
    tossing and tumbling .... WELTER
wavy .... UNDATE, SINUOUS, SINUATE
    edged .... REPAND, UNDULATE
    form ...... UNDULATION
    in heraldry .... UNDE(E)
wax ...... GROW, PARAFFIN, CERA, CERE, PELA, CERESIN, CERUMEN, CERATE
    and pitch mixture .... MALTHA
    candle ...... PARAFFIN, CIERGE, TAPER
    cloth treated with .... CERECLOTH, CEREMENT
    cobbler's .... CODE
    combining form .. CER(O)
    covered with .. CERATED
    figure .... CEROPLAST
    like secretion .. CERUMEN
    match .... VESTA
    mineral ...... OZOCERITE
    modeled in .. CEROPLASTIC
    myrtle ...... BAYBERRY
    ointment .... CERATE
    palm .... CARNAUBA
    producing ... CERIFEROUS
    source .... CARNAUBA
waxbill .... WEAVERBIRD
waxed runner .... SKI
waxwing .... CEDARBIRD
waxwork artist ...... TUSSAUD
waxy .... CERACEOUS
    substance .... CUTIN, SUBERIN
way ..... PATH, MODE, ROAD, STREET, LANE, ROUTE, COURSE, METHOD, WONT
    easy/direct ... HIGHROAD
    give .... YIELD
    of walking/running ..... GAIT
    on the .... MOVING, PROCEEDING
    out .... EGRESS, EXIT
    under .... MOVING, PROCEEDING
    station town .... WHISTLE STOP

    train .... LOCAL
    up .... STAIRS
waybill .... MANIFEST
wayfarer ... VIATOR, TRAVELER
    shelter for .. SPITAL, INN
wayfaring tree ... VIBURNUM, HOBBLEBUSH
waylay .... AMBUSH, AMBUSCADE
wayward .... HEADSTRONG, WILLFUL, ERRATIC, CAPRICIOUS, VAGRANT
weaverbird .... WAXBILL
weak .... DECREPIT, FRAGILE, DELICATE, VULNERABLE, INEFFECTIVE, PUNY, ANILE, WAN, FEEBLE, INFIRM, FAINT, FLACCID, FLABBY, FRAIL, EFFETE
    drink .... TIFF
    kneed ...... TIMID, SOFT
    minded ... DAFT, STUPID, IMBECILE, FOOLISH, INDECISIVE
    morally .... FRAIL
    point ..... DEFECT, FAULT
weaken .. UNDERMINE, DILUTE, ENERVATE, ATTENUATE, VITIATE, FLAG, DEBILITATE, SAP, ABATE, ENFEEBLE
    morally .... VITIATE
    spirit of ..... DEMORALIZE
weakening .... SAPPING
weakfish ... TOTUAVA, ACOUPA
weakling ...... WALLYDRAG, SISSY, CRYBABY, PANTYWAIST, SOFTIE
weakness .... DEFECT, LIKING, FETISH, FONDNESS, FRAILTY, DELICACY, INFIRMITY, FAULT
    bodily .... ASTHENIA, ATONY
    in character ..... FOIBLE
    moral .... FRAILTY
    of an organ ..... ATONY
    small ... FOIBLE, FRAILTY
weal ...... STRIPE, WELFARE, WALE, WELT, WHEAL, WELL-BEING
weald .... FOREST
wealth ...... ASSETS, RICHES, MEANS, ABUNDANCE, ASSET, OPULENCE, AFFLUENCE, FORTUNE
    benefits from ... USANCE

god of .... PLUTUS
income from .... USANCE
mere .... PELF
personified .... MAMMON,
CROESUS
wealthy ..... RICH, MONEYED,
PROSPEROUS, OPULENT,
WELL-TO-DO
government by ....
PLUTOCRACY
person ..... PLUTOCRAT,
CROESUS, NABOB,
MIDAS
wean .... CHILD, BABY,
WITHDRAW
weapon ...... CLUB, SWORD,
ARQUEBUS, CROSSBOW, ARM,
SLINGSHOT, LANCE, MACE
animal's ... TUSK, HORN
bird's ..... TALON, BEAK,
CLAW
gaucho's .... BOLA(S)
hoplite .... SPEAR
Indian ..... TOMAHAWK
medieval ...... GISARME,
HALBERD, CATAPULT
pampas .... BOLAS
plant's .... SPINE
war .... CANNON, GUN
weaponry .... ORDNANCE
weapons: colloq. .. HARDWARE
wear .... CHAFE, DON,
CLOTHES, ERODE, SPORT
away ... ABRADE, ERODE,
CORRODE, FRET
down ..... EXHAUST, TIRE
out .... HACK
ragged ... FRAY, FRAZZLE
to tatters ...... FRAZZLE
well .... LAST
wearied .... TIRED, JADED,
FAGGED
weariness ... ENNUI, FATIGUE,
TEDIUM, BOREDOM,
LASSITUDE
wearing apparel .... CLOTHES,
GARMENTS, CLOTHING
away .... EROSION,
ATTRITION
wearisome .... TEDIOUS,
TOILSOME, BORING
grow .... PALL, BORE
person .... BORE
weary .. TIRE(D), CHAPFALLEN,
FAG, JADE, WORNOUT,

BORE(D), TEDIOUS, IRKSOME,
TUCKER
weasand .... TRACHEA,
WINDPIPE, THROAT,
ESOPHAGUS
weasel ...... ERMINE, STOAT,
VARE, MUSTELINE, PEKAN,
SABLE, FERRET, ZORIL(A),
VERMIN
family .... MUSTELA
like animal .... SABLE,
MARTEN
relative .. STOAT, MARTEN,
OTTER, MINK, FERRET
words ..... AMBIGUITIES,
EQUIVOCATIONS
weather ... SURVIVE, SEASON,
SKY
condition ..... CLIMATE
indicator .... BAROMETER
item .... MOISTURE,
TEMPERATURE
map line ...... ISALLOBAR
personified .. JACKFROST
phenomenon ..... SMOG,
SLEET, SMAZE,
HAIL(STONE)
prolonged dry ....
DROU(G)HT
report .... ADVISORY
study of ... METEOROLOGY
under the ..... ILL, SICK,
AILING, TIPSY
warning .... ADVISORY
word ..... WARM, SLEET,
WINDY, RAIN, STORMY
weathercock ..... VANE, FANE
weathered .... SURVIVED
weatherglass ..... BAROMETER
weathervane figure ..... COCK
weave .... ENTWINE,
INTERLACE, TWIST, KNIT,
PLAIT, MAT, BRAID
kind of .... LENO
weaver .... WEBSTER
bobbin of .... PIRN
girl .... IRENE
material of .... REED,
WICKER, FIBER, YARN,
SLEY
weaverbird .... WAXBILL,
WHIDAH, TAHA, MAYA,
SPARROW
weaving art .... LOOM
contestant .... ARACHNE
frame .... LOOM

machine .... LOOM
occupation .. HANDICRAFT
reed .... SLEY
yarn .... WEFT, WARP,
              WOOF
web ..... TISSUE, NET(WORK),
    TRAP, SNARE, GOSSAMER
feather's ...... VEXILLUM
footed .... PALMATE
footed bird ...... SWAN,
    AVOCET, DUCK, GOOSE
footed creature .. OTTER,
    BEAVER, TOAD, FROG,
    MUSKRAT
in anatomy ..... TISSUE,
    MEMBRANE
like membrane ..... TELA
pertaining to ... RETIARY
spinner .... SPINER,
    ARACHNE
toed .... PALMATE
webbed .... PALMATE
webber .... MAXWELL
wed .... ESPOUSE, MARRY,
    UNITE, WIVE
wedding .... MARRIAGE,
    NUPTIALS, BRIDAL
announcement .. BAN(N)S
day designation ....
    (1st YEAR) PAPER;
    (25th) SILVER;
    (30th) PEARL;
    (50th) GOLDEN;
    (75th) DIAMOND
March bride ...... ELSA
party member .. RINGBOY,
    BRIDESMAID, BESTMAN,
    SPONSOR
song .... OH PROMISE ME,
    HYMEN(EAL)
wedge .... COTTER, KEY, JAM,
    TRIG, SHIM, QUOIN,
    COIGN(E), CLEAT
driver .... MAUL, BEETLE
shaped ..... CUNEIFORM,
    CUNEATE, SPHENOID,
    SPHENIC, CUNEAL
shaped piece ... PIE, VEE,
    CHOCK, QUOIN
to prevent rolling ....
    SCOTCH, CHOCK, SPRAG
wedlock .... MATRIMONY,
    MARRIAGE
Wednesday .... MIDWEEK
Wednesday's god ...... ODIN
wee .... LITTLE

hours .... DAWN
weed .... BUR, COCKLE,
    SANDBUR(R), SPURR(E)Y,
    NETTLE, PLANTAIN, REMOVE,
    RID, TOADFLAX,
    PURSLANE, DOCK,
    CHARLOCK, QUITCH,
    DANDELION, BROME
Biblical .... TARE
buckwheat .... DOCK
colloquial .... CIGAR,
    TOBACCO
digging tool .... SPUD
herbicide .... DOWPON
mourning .... CRAPE,
    WEEDER
narcotic ..... MARIJUANA,
    MARIHUANA
noxious .... TARE
out .... UPROOT
poison(ous) ...... LOCO,
    DARNEL, HEMLOCK
    JIMSON
roadside ... DOGFENNEL
weeding tool ... SPUD, HOE
weeds ...... CRAPE, WEEPER,
    WRACK
wearer .... WIDOW
weedy plant ..... CELANDINE
week .... HEBDOMAD,
    SENNIGHT
weekday .... FERIA
weekly .... HEBDOMADAL,
    PERIODICAL
newsmagazine ....
    NEWSWEEK, TIME
weeks, 52 .... YEAR
two .... FORTNIGHT
Weems, preacher .... PARSON
ween .... THINK, SUPPOSE,
    IMAGINE
weenie/weeny ...... SAUSAGE,
    WIENER(WURST)
weep ..... LAMENT, LAPWING,
    BLUBBER, CRY, MOURN,
    BEWAIL, SOB, BAWL
weeping goddess ...... NIOBE
philosopher .. HERACLITES
weevil .... CURCULIO, KIS,
    BEETLE, BORER, BOLL
larva .... GRUGRU
wing cover ...... SHARD
weft .... WOOF, YARN,
    FILLING
Weichsel .... VISTULA

weigh ...... CONSIDER, HOIST, PONDER, BEAR, BURDEN, HEFT, POISE, REFLECT, RAISE
down .... BURDEN
weighing device .... TRONE, SCALE, BALANCE, STEELYARD, FAIRBANKS
weight .. ROTL, OBOLUS, LOAD, HEFT, TON, STRESS, HEAVINESS, BURDEN, VALUE, EMPHASIS, IMPORTANCE, INFLUENCE, POWER
allowance .... TRET, TARE
balance .... RIDER
balloon's ...... BALLAST
boxer's .... FEATHER, LIGHT, BANTAM, MIDDLE, HEAVY
clock .... PEISE
coal .... KEEL
colloquial .... HEFT
deduction .... TARE
diamond .... CARAT
for wool .... TOD
4,000-pound .... LAST
hundred pounds .... CENTAL, CENTNER
leaden .... PLUMB
leg .... CLOG
lifting machine .. CRANE
measure .. TON, METAGE, KILO
metric ... KILO, CENTNER, QUINTAL
on animal's leg .... CLOG
pertaining to ..... BARIC
stabilizer .... BALLAST
system .... TROY, AVOIRDUPOIS, METRIC
3.17 grains .... CARAT
200 milligrams ... CARAT
unit ...... SHEKEL, TON, ROTL
watcher .... DIETER, MILADY, BOXER
with lead .... PLUMB
wool .... TOD
weights and measures, science of .... METROLOGY
weighty ... ONEROUS, SERIOUS, MOMENTOUS, BURDENSOME, OPPRESSIVE, HEAVY
weir .... BARRIER, FENCE, GARTH, TRAP, (MILL)DAM
weird ...... QUEER, SPOOKY,

UNCO, EERIE, EERY, MYSTERIOUS, UNCANNY, ELDRITCH, ODD, UNEARTHLY
sister ..... FATE, CLOTHO, LACHESIS, TROPOS
wejack .... PEKAN, WEASEL
weka .... RAIL
welcome .... GREET(ING), AGREEABLE, RECEIVE, HAIL
weld .... FUSS, UNITE, MIGNONETTE, SOLDER
welding material ... THERMIT, SOLDER
welfare ... WEAL, WELLBEING, PROSPERITY
organization .. RED CROSS, CARE, YMCA, YWCA
welkin .... HEAVEN, SKY
well ..... SPRING, HALE, TRIG, FOUNT(AIN), FIT, SHAFT, FLOW, GUSH, SUMP, EXPERTLY, PROPER, HEALTHY
along .... FAR
balanced .... POISED, SANE, SENSIBLE
being ... WELFARE, WEAL
bred .... GENTEEL, EDUCATED
doer ...... (BOY) SCOUT
done ..... BRAVO, BULLY
favored ..... HANDSOME, PRETTY
fed .... PLUMP, FAT
feeling .... EUPHORIA
groomed .... SLEEK, SOIGNE, SLICK
grounded ...... INFORMED
heeled ... RICH, WEALTHY, MONEYED
known ...... FAMOUS, NOTORIOUS, FAMILIAR
lining ..... STEAN, STEEN
mannered .. COURTEOUS, POLITE
nigh ... ALMOST, NEARLY
off ... PROSPEROUS, RICH
ordered .... NEAT
pit .... SUMP
proportioned ..... TRIM
read person .. BOOKWORM
supplied with money .... LOADED
thought of .... ESTEEMED, REPUTABLE

timed ...... OPPORTUNE,
AUSPICIOUS,
SEASONABLE
to-do .... RICH, WEALTHY
watered .... IRRIGUOUS
worn ... TRITE, OVERUSED
Welland .... CANAL
wellaway ...... ALAS, ALACK
Welle river .... UELE
Welles, actor .... ORSON
diplomat ...... SUMNER
Wellington's soubriquet ......
IRONDUKE, OLD NOSY
wellspring .... FOUNTAINHEAD
Welsh ...... CYMRIC, CYMRY,
CAMBRIAN, TAFFY, CELT(IC)
astronomer .... MEE
boat .... CORACLE
buccaneer ...... MORGAN
cheese dish ..... RABBIT
dog .... CORGI
god of sea .... DYLAN
onion .... CIBOL
rabbit .... RAREBIT
slang .. CHEAT, SWINDLE
welsher ... CHEAT, DEADBEAT,
SWINDLER
Welshman .... CAMBRIAN,
CELT
welt .... LASH, WALE, W(H)EAL,
THRASH, BEAT
welter .... ROLL, WALLOW,
SOAKED, TURMOIL,
CONFUSION
wen ... TALPA, TUMOR, CYST,
MOLE
wench ...... MAID, SERVANT,
WANTON, WOMAN, HUSSY,
DOXY
wend ..... JOURNEY, TRAVEL,
GO, PROCEED
Wendell, presidential candidate
WILLKIE
Wendy's dog .... NANA
wer(e)gild .... BLOOD MONEY,
CRO
werewolf .... LOUP-GAROU,
LYCANTHROPE
wernard .... LIAR
wernerite .... SCAPOLITE
Wesley, (John) follower ......
METHODIST
West .... OCCIDENT
West African .... ASHANTI
baboon ..... (MAN)DRILL
fetish .... JUJU

Gold Coast city ....
ACCRA, AKKRA
magic .... JUJU
taboo .... JUJU
tribe .... IBO
weaverbird .... WHIDAH
West Bengal capital ....
CALCUTTA
West, English novelist ......
REBECCA
West Flanders capital .. BRUGES
West German capital ... BONN
chancellor ... ADENAUER,
KIESINGER, BRANDT
president .... LUBKE
West Indies bird .... TODY,
COURLAN, LIMPKIN
capital ....
ROSEAU (DOMINICA),
CASTRIES (ST. LUCIA),
KINGSTOWN
(ST. VINCENT)
coin .... PISTAREEN
egret .... GAULIN
fish .... BACALAO,
TESTAR, PEGA, BANG,
CABRILLA, CERO,
BOGA, SESI
flea .... CHIGOE,
CHIGGER
grouper .... BONACI
heron .... GAULIN
hog plum .... AMRA,
JOBO
Indian .... TAINO,
CARIB, ESTERON
island .... BAHAMA(S),
HISPANIOLA,
ANTILLES, JAMAICA,
NEVIS, CURACAO,
TRINIDAD, CAICOS,
CUBA, HAITI,
BARBUDA, LEEWARD,
TOBAGO
liquor ...... MOBBY, RUM
lizard .... ARBALO,
GALLIWASP
magic ...... OBEAH, OBI
mahogany .... CAOBA
music .... CALYPSO
native .... CARIB,
CREOLE
native chief .... CACIQUE
Negro .... EBO(E),
MAROON
patois .... GUMBO

plant .... ANIL
rodent .... AGOUTI
rum .... TAF(F)IA
sailboat ...... DROGHER
shark .... GATA
shrub .... ANIL,
    CASCARILLA
state .... ANTIGUA,
    GRENADA, DOMINICA,
    (ST.) LUCIA,
    (ST.) VINCENT
talisman .... OBEAH
taro .... TANIA
tree .... CALABA,
    GENIP(AP), ARALIE,
    BONACE, BALATA,
    GREENHEART
vessel .... DROGHER
volcano .... PELEE
"white man" .... BUCKRA
witchcraft ...... OBEAH,
    OBI

West Irian capital ....
    KATABARU, HOLLANDIA
West, newcomer to the ....
    TENDERFOOT
West, of Broadway ..... MAE
West Pointer ...... YEARLING,
    PLEB(E), CADET
West Virginia capital ....
    CHARLESTON
    city .... WHEELING,
        WEIRTON
    state bird .... CARDINAL
    state nickname ....
        PANHANDLE
West wind .... ZEPHYR
    of the .... FAVONIAN
western .... OCCIDENTAL,
    HESPERIAN, MOVIE
    Australia capital .. PERTH
    Dvina .... RIVER
    Islands .... HEBRIDES
    land .... HESPERIA
    lawman .... SHERIFF,
        MARSHAL
    movie character ....
        COWBOY, DESPERADO,
        FRONTIERSMAN, INDIAN,
        SCOUT
    ocean .... ATLANTIC
    soil .... GUMBO
Westerner ...... PLAINSMAN
Westminster Abbey ....
    PANTHEON
    landmark .... ABBEY

rite .... CORONATION
street .... WHITEHALL
wet ..... DAMP, DANK, BATHE,
    SOAK, RET, RAINY, FOGGY,
    MOIST, SOPPING, ASOP,
    EMBRUE
    all .... WRONG, MISTAKEN
    blanket .... KILLJOY,
        SPOILSPORT
    combining form .. HYGRO
    plaster painting .. FRESCO
wetback ..... BRACERO, PEON
    nationality of .. MEXICAN
wether .... SHEEP
wetland(s) .... MARSHES,
    SWAMPS
wetter .... CHILD, BABY
Weygand, Fr. general ....
    MAXIME
whack .... BEAT, WHANG,
    SLAP, BLOW, THWACK,
    SMACK
    slang ...... SHARE, TRIAL,
        ATTEMPT, TRY
whacky ... WILD, ECCENTRIC,
    FOOLISH, MADCAP
whale ... CETE, THRASH, WHIP,
    SPERM, CACHALOT,
    CETACEAN, FINBACK,
    BOWHEAD
    Arctic .... NARWHAL
    baby .... CALF
    biggest .... BLUE
    blowhole ...... SPIRACLE
    carcass .... KRENG
    cut blubber of ... FLENSE
    dolphin .... ORCA
    fat .... BLUBBER
    female .... COW
    finback ...... RORQUAL,
        PORPOISE
    food ...... BRIT, SHRIMP
    food strainer ... BALEEN
    grampus .... ORC
    growth on jaw .. BALEEN
    hunter of fiction ... AHAB
    killer .. GRAMPUS, ORC(A),
        DOLPHIN
    kind of ...... FIN(BACK),
        BLUE, SEI, HUMPBACK
    male .... BULL
    mammal resembling .....
        DUGONG, MANATEE
    Melville's ... MOBY DICK
    morbid secretion ....
        AMBERGRIS

river .... DOLPHIN
shark .... MHOR
small .... PORPOISE,
  HOGFISH, DOLPHIN,
  BLACKFISH
sound ...... BARK, MEW,
  SQUEAL, CLICK,
  WHISTLE, CHIRRUP,
  WHINE
sperm .... CACHALOT
strip blubber from ......
  FLENSE
tail part .... FLUKE
tusked .... NARWHAL
white ... BELUGA, HUSO,
  HUSE
young .... CALF
whaleback .... FREIGHTER
whalebone .... BALEEN
  decorative article ....
  SCRIMSHAW
whaleman ...... HARPOONER
whaler's spear ...... HARPOON
whales, pertaining to .. CETIC,
  CETACEAN
  school/herd of ..... GAM,
  POD
  skin .... SCULP
whaling ship .... PEQUOD
  post ...... LOGGERHEAD
whammy ..... JINX, EVIL EYE
whang ...... STRIKE, WHACK,
  THRASH
whangee ...... BAMBOO, CANE,
  WALKING STICK
wharf ... DOCK, JETTY, QUAY,
  PIER, LANDING, QUAI
  loafer .... RAT
Wharton, novelist ..... EDITH
whatnot .... ETAGERE,
  CABINET
whaup .... CURLEW
wheal ... WELT, STRIPE, WALE,
  PUSTULE, PIMPLE
wheat .... CORN, DURUM,
  CEREAL, GRASS, GRAIN,
  SPELT, TRIGO, DURRA
  beard ..... AWN, ARISTA
  beer .... WEISS
  coat .... BRAN
  cracked .... GROATS
  disease ... ERGOT, BUNT,
  AECIA, SMUT, RUST
  flour foodstuff ....
  MACARONI, SPAGHETTI
  flour substance .. GLUTEN

grass resembling .. CHEAT,
  CHESS
ground .... FLOUR, MEAL
hard-grained ..... SPELT,
  DURUM
head .... EAR
hulled .... GROATS
liquor ...... WHISK(E)Y
meal .... SEMOLINA
milling by-product ......
  SHORTS
wheatear ...... CHACK, CHAT,
  WHITETAIL
wheedle ... WANGLE, CAJOLE,
  COAX, BLARNEY
wheel .... TURN, ROTATE,
  REVOLVE, PIVOT, PULLEY
  RUNDLE, HELM
  animalcule .... ROTIFER
  band .... STRAKE
  block ... SPRAG, WEDGE,
  TRIG
  break .. SKID, TRIG, DRAG
  center of ..... HUB, NAVE
  collar .... FLANGE
  furniture .... CASTER
  grooved .... SHEAVE
  horse .... POLER
  hub .... NAVE
  like .... TROCHAL
  little .... CASTER
  motion ..... ROTATION,
  ROLL
  part ... HUB, SPOKE, RIM,
  CAM, HOB, FELLY,
  AXLE, TIRE
  projection .... CAM
  pulley .... SHEAVE
  resembling a ... TROCHAL
  rim ...... FELLY, FELLOE,
  FLANGE
  shaft .... AXLE
  shaped .... ROTATE,
  ROTIFORM
  small .... TRUCKLE,
  TRUNDLE, CASTER
  spindle ..... AXLE, ARBOR
  spoke .... RADIUS, RUNG
  spur .... ROWEL
  swivel .... CASTER
  tire .... STRAKE
  tooth .... SPROCKET
  toothed .... COG
  turner in Hades ... IXION
  water .... NORIA
wheeler ... PILOT, STEERSMAN

wheelman .... CYCLIST, PILOT
wheels, move on .... ROLL
    set of swiveled .. CASTER
    shoe with .... SKATE
wheen .... FEW
wheeze ..... GAG, JOKE, GASP
wheezy breather ... ASTHMATIC
whelk ...... MUREX, PAPULE,
    PIMPLE, PUSTULE,
    GASTROPOD, SNAIL
whelp ... PUPPY, CHIT, YOUTH,
    BEAR
when ...... WHEREAS, WHILE,
    MOMENT, TIME
whenever .... ANYTIME
whereabouts .... LOCATION
whereas .... WHILE
wherefrom .... WHENCE
whereness .... UBIETY
wherewithal .... MEANS,
    RESOURCES, MONEY, CASH
wherry ..... ROWBOAT, SCULL,
    BARGE, LIGHTER
whet .... SHARPEN, HONE,
    STIMULATE, GRIND
whetstone .... HONE, BURR,
    BUHR
whether ... EITHER, IF, IN CASE
whey of milk .... SERUM
which .... WHATEVER
whichever .... ANYONE
whidah .... WEAVERBIRD,
    WIDOW BIRD
whiff .... BREATH, SMELL,
    PUFF, GUST, WAFT, SMOKE,
    WAFF
whiffet .... DOG, PUFF
whiffle ... VEER, SHIFT, BLOW,
    VACILLATE
Whig, opposed to .... TORY
while .... AS, UNTIL, YET,
    OCCUPY, ALBEIT
whilom .... FORMER(LY),
    ERST(WHILE), ONCE,
    QUONDAM
whim ...... CAPRICE, CRANK,
    KINK, CAPRICCIO, VAGARY,
    FANCY, NOTION
   wham ...... GIMCRACK,
    TRINKET
whimper ...... MEWL, WHINE,
    YAMMER, PULE
whimsical .... FLIGHTY,
    FANTASTIC, FREAKISH,
    CAPRICIOUS, QUAINT

whimsicality .... CAPRICE,
    ODDITY
whimsy .... NOTION, CAPRICE,
    HUMOR, FANCY
whin ..... FURZE, ROCK, TRAP,
    GORSE, GREENSTONE
whinchat .... SONGBIRD
whine ...... PULE, WHIMPER,
    COMPLAIN, MEWL, YAMMER
whinny .... HINNY, NEIGH,
    FURZY
whip ...... WHALE, PULLOUT,
    BEAT, FLAY, DEFEAT, WHISK,
    WALE, LASH, FLAP, FLOG,
    KURBASH, COWHIDE,
    SCOURGE, FLAIL, SWISH,
    KNOUT, LARRUP, LICK,
    LACE, BELABOR,
    FLAGELLATE
   Biblical .... SCORPION
   blow .... FLICK
   handle ... CROP, STOCK,
    BUTT
   leather .... KURBASH,
    KNOUT
   mark ...... WELT, WALE,
    STRIPE, W(H)EAL
   riding ..... QUIRT, CROP
   severely ...... TAN, FLOG
   stroke .... FLICK
   to a froth .... MILL
   up ...... EXCITE, ROUSE
whipcord .... CATGUT
whiplash ...... FLOG, THRASH,
    THONG
   snapper .... COSAQUE
   sound .... WHISH
whippersnapper ..... UPSTART,
    SQUIRT
whippet ... GREYHOUND, DOG
whipping boy ..... SCAPEGOAT
   stick ...... ROD, SWITCH,
    CANE
whippoorwill .... GOATSUCKER
   feathers .... VIBRISSA
whir .... BUZZ, VIBRATE,
    BIRR
whirl .... GYRATE, EDDY,
    CIRCLE, ROTATE, SPIN,
    STIR, UPROAR, REEL,
    PIROUETTE, SWIRL, GYRE
whirler and howler ... DERVISH
whirligig ... MERRY-GO-ROUND,
    CAROUSEL, BEETLE
whirling ____ ...... DERVISH
   man .... DERVISH

motion .... SWIRL
on toes .... PIROUETTE
wind .... CYCLONE, TORNADO
whirlpool ..... EDDY, VORTEX, MAELSTROM, WEEL, CHARYBDIS, GULF
whirlwind .... CYCLONE, TORNADO, HURRICANE, EDDY, TOURBILLION
Faroes .... OES
whirlybird .... HELICOPTER, AUTOGYRO, CHOPPER
whirr .... BIRR
whish .... SWISH, WHIZ
whisk ... WHIP, BEAT, BROOM, EGG-BEATER, CARRY, BRUSH
broom ..... RINGE, WISP
whiskers .... MUSTACHE, BEARD, SIDEBURNS, BURNSIDES
cat's .... VIBRISSA
chin .... GOATEE
side ..... CHOPS, MUTTON
whisk(e)y .... MOONSHINE, HOOCH, POT(H)EEN, ROTGUT, SCOTCH, REDEYE, RYE, MOUNTAIN DEW
storeroom ..... BUTTERY
to an Indian . FIREWATER
whisper .... MURMUR, BREATH(E)
actor's .... ASIDE
whispered, something ....
RUMOR, SECRET, HINT, CONFIDENCE
whist .... SILENT, STILL, SILENCE, CARD GAME
game series ...... RUBBER
game similar to .. BRIDGE, RUFF
term .... SLAM, MORT, MISERE, VOLE
whistle ...... FOGHORN, TOOT, PIPE, TOTTLE
whistler ..... MARMOT, OUSEL, GOLDENEYE
whistling sound ..... STRIDOR, WHIZZ
in the ears ..... TINNITUS
whit .... BIT, IOTA, JOT, PARTICLE, DOIT, TITTLE
white .... SILVER, HOAR(Y), PALE, WAN, ASHEN, SNOWY
admiral ...... BUTTERFLY

alkali .... SODA ASH
animal .... ALBINO
ant .... ANAY, TERMITE
bait .... BRIT, SPRAT, HERRING
bear .... POLAR
cedar ...... ARBORVITAE
cliffs site .... DOVER
clouds .... CERRI
coal .... WATER
collar employe ... CLERK
colored person ....
CAUCASIAN
combining form ....
LEUK(O)
creamy .... IVORY
earth .... GYPSUM, MAGNESIA, KAOLIN, TERRA ALBA
egg's ... ALBUMEN, GLAIR
eye .... SONGBIRD
fish .... ATINGA, MENHADEN, BELUGA, CISCO, POLLAN, TULLIBEE
flag signal .... TRUCE, SURRENDER
Friar .... CARMELITE, ALSATIAN
gum .... EUCALYPTUS
haired .... HOARY
Hart .... INN
hot ..... INCANDESCENT
House resident ....
PRESIDENT
lead .... CERUSE, CERUSSITE
lie .... FIB
livered person .. COWARD
make ... BLANCH, BLEACH
man .... BUCKRA
man's burden ....
IMPERIALISM
meat .... VEAL
men in .... DOCTORS
oak .... ROBLE
person ...... CAUCASIAN, PALEFACE
plague ... TUBERCULOSIS
race ...... CAUCASIAN
Rose house .... YORK
Sea gulf ..... ARCHANGEL
slang ..... HONEST, FAIR
spruce .... EPINETTE
thorn .... MAYFLOWER
turning ..... ALBESCENT

whale .... BELUGA
women in .... NURSES,
NUNS
whitebait .... BRIT
whitecap .... WAVE
whitefish ... VENDACE, BELUGA,
POLLAN, MENHADEN, CISCO,
TULLIBEE, ATINGA
whiten ... ETIOLATE, BLEACH,
BLANCH
whitening .... CANESCENT
whitetail .... DEER, WHEATER
whitewall .... TIRE
whitewash .. PLASTER, PARGET
whitewood .... LINDEN, TULIP
whither .... WHERE,
WHEREVER
whiting .... WEAKFISH,
DRUMFISH, MENHADEN,
HAKE, COD, CHALK
whitlow ..... AGNAIL, FELON
Whitman, poet .... WALT(ER)
Whitney, cotton gin inventor ..
ELI
Whitsunday ...... PENTECOST
Whitsuntide .... PINKSTER
whittle ... PARE, CUT, REDUCE,
SHAVE
whittling refuse ..... SHAVINGS
whiz(z) ...... WHIR(R), HISS,
SPEED BY, BARGAIN, EXPERT
kid .... PRODIGY
kin .... LULU
who goes there? .. CHALLENGE,
QUI VA LA
whoa .... STOP, HOLLA
whodunit .... MYSTERY
character .... DICK,
SLEUTH, DETECTIVE,
BUTLER, VICTIM
coiner of .... GORDON
movie .... CHILLER
staple .. MURDER, CLUES,
CRIME
whoever .... ANYONE
whole .... UNCUT, TOTO,
INTACT, ENTIRE, COMPLETE,
TOTAL(ITY)
as a .... ALTOGETHER
combining form ... HOLO
costume .... ENSEMBLE
note .... SEMIBREVE
number .... INTEGER
wholesale .... GROSS
opposed to ...... RETAIL
wholesome .... HEALTHY,

SALUTARY, SOUND
wholly .... ALL, ENTIRELY,
PLUMB
whoop ... CALL, SHOUT, CRY,
HOOT
whooper .... SWAN
whooping cough ... PERTUSSIS,
CHINCOUGH
whop .... BEAT, THRASH,
STRIKE, FLOP
whopper .... (BIG)LIE
whore .... HARLOT
whorehouse .... BROTHEL
whorl ... VERTICIL, VOLUTION,
FLYWHEEL, VOLUTE
fingerprint ...... RIDGE
wicked ..... EVIL, NAUGHTY,
SINFUL, IMPIOUS, GODLESS
act .... MISDEED, SIN
city .... SODOM,
GOMORRAH, BABYLON
wicker .... WITHE, TWIG
basket .... SKEP, HAMPER,
KIPSEY, PANNIER, KISH,
CREEL, CRATE, CORF
cradle .... BASSINET
tree ..... OSIER, WILLOW
wickerwork material ... OSIER,
WITHE, RAT(T)AN,
WILLOW
wicket .... DOOR, GATE,
WINDOW, ARCH, HOOP
in cricket .... INNING
in croquet ... HOOP, ARCH
part .... BAIL
wickiup ..... TEPEE, WIGWAM
wicopy .... BASSWOOD
wide .... BROAD, ROOMY,
AMPLE
eyed .... ASTARE
open .... AGAPE
widen ..... SPREAD, BROADEN
widespread ..... PREVALENT,
RIFE, RAMPANT, REGNANT
disease .... EPIDEMIC
fear .... PANIC
widgeon .. GOOSE, BALDPATE,
DUCK, SMEW, SMEE, ZUISIN,
MARECA
kin .. REDHEAD, POCHARD
widow ...... RELICT, BEREAVE,
SUTTEE, FEME SOLE, MATRON
bird .... WHIDAH
inheritance of ... DOWER
titled, wealthy ....
DOWAGER

widowhood .... VIDUAGE
widow's mites .... LEPTA
   third ... DOWER, DOWRY
width ... BREADTH, BROADNESS,
   WIDENESS, LATITUDE
wield ...... HANDLE, EXERCISE
Wien .... VIENNA
wiener .... SAUSAGE,
   FRANKFURTER, HOTDOG
wienerschnitzel .... VEAL
Wiesbaden's location .. HESSE
wife .... FERE, BRIDE, SPOUSE,
   RIB, BETTER HALF,
   BALL AND CHAIN, MRS.,
   FEME, YOKEFELLOW, MISSIS,
   MISSUS, MATRON, FROW,
   HELPMEET, HELPMATE
   bequest to .... DOS
   common-law .. MISTRESS
   dowry of .... DOT
   German .... FRAU
   in law .... FEME
   Indian .... SQUAW
   killer .... UXORICIDE
   king's ... CONSORT, QUEEN
   knight's .... DAME
   man's prospective ....
      INTENDED
   of a .... UXORIAL
   one .... MONOGAMY
   rajah's ..... RANI, RANEE
   submissive to one's ......
      UXORIOUS
   take to .... MARRY
wig ...... PERUKE, TO(U)PEE,
   TETE, GRIZZLE, GIZZ,
   PERIWIG
wigeon .... WIDGEON
wiggle .... WAG, WANGLE,
   WRIGGLE
wiggler ... LARVA, WRIGGLER
wigwag .... CODE, SIGNAL
wigwam ..... LODGE, TE(E)PEE,
   WICKIUP
wild .... PRIMITIVE,
   LICENTIOUS, UNBRIDLED,
   STORMY, DISORDERLY,
   RECKLESS, UNTAMED,
   GAGA, FERAL, FERINE,
   WASTE, DESOLATE, SAVAGE,
   FIERCE, PHRENETIC,
   HARUM-SCARUM, RIOTOUS
   animal .... BEAST
   apple ... CRAB, CREEPER
   ass .... ONAGER
   Bill ____ .... HICKOK

   brier .... DOG ROSE
   cat .... EYRA, LYNX,
   BOBCAT, OCELOT,
   SERVAL, MARGAY,
      MARGOT
   cattle .. GAUR, BANTENG
   celery .... SMALLAGE
   country .... WEALD
   cry ...... EVOE, WHOOP,
   SCREAM, SHRIEK,
      SCREECH
   dog ..... DHOLE, DINGO,
      CUON
   duck .. MALLARD, SCAUP,
   REDHEAD, CANVASBACK,
   GOLDENEYE, GADWALL
   Duck author ...... IBSEN
   eyed .... HAGGARD
   fowl ... PHEASANT, QUAIL,
   PARTRIDGE, DUCK
   fowl flock .... SKEIN
   goat ... IBEX, TAHIR, TAIR
   goose .... DRANT
   goose's call ...... HONK
   guess .... STAB
   hog .... BENE, BOAR,
      PECCARY
   honey source ... BEETREE
   horse .... MUSTANG,
   BRONC(H)O, CAYUSE,
   TARPAN, BRUMBIE
   Huntsman .... ODIN
   hyacinth ..... BLUEBELL
   life .... GAME
   life preserve ... WETLAND
   madder ..... BEDSTRAW
   mustard ..... CHARLOCK
   olive .... OLEASTER
   ox ..... ANOA, BANTENG,
      REEM
   ox hunter ... BUCCANEER
   parsley .... LOVAGE
   pig .... BOAR
   plum .... SLOE
   revelry .... ORGY
   rose ...... (SWEET)BRIER,
      EGLANTINE
   sheep ..... ARGALI, SHA,
   ARUI, URIAL, UDAD,
   MOUFLON, NAHOOR,
   AOUDAD, BIGHORN
   sown .... OATS
   state of being .... FERITY
   swan .... ELKE
   the .... NATURE
   West show ...... RODEO

wildcat ...... LYNX, OCELOT, MARGAY, MARGOT, SERVAL
Wilde, dramatist ..... OSCAR
  ballad's subject ... GAOL
  play .... SALOME
wildebeest ... GNU, ANTELOPE
wilderness .. JUNGLE, TUNDRA, WASTE(LAND), STEPPE, WILD(S), BOONDOCKS, DESERT
wildfire .... LIGHTNING, ERYSIPELAS
wildlife preserve .. WETLAND, SANCTUARY
wildness .... FERITY
wile .... ART, ARTIFICE, TRICK(ERY), DECEIT, LURE, BEGUILE
wiles .... CHARM
will .... BEQUEATH, VOLITION, WISH, DESIRE, POWER, DECREE
  addition to a ... CODICIL
  bequeathed by .... TESTAMENTARY
  convey by .... DEMISE
  exercise of the .. VOLITION
  handwritten .... HOLOGRAPH
  having made a .. TESTATE
  having no ... INTESTATE
  in law ...... TESTAMENT
  maker .... TESTATOR, DEVISOR
  o'-the-wisp ... WILDFIRE, IGNIS FATUUS
  power .... SELF-CONTROL
  power, loss of ... ABULIA
Willard, boxing champion ... JESS
  organization of Mrs. .... WCTU
  temperance leader ...... FRANCES
Williams, ballplayer ..... TED
Williamson, Shakespearean actor .... NICOL
willful .... HEADSTRONG, WAYWARD, STUBBORN, OBSTINATE
willies .... JITTERS, NERVOUSNESS, CREEPS
willing .... BAIN, MINDED, DISPOSED, CONSENTING, LIEF
  reluctantly .... FAIN

willingly ...... GLADLY, LIEF, READILY
Willkie, presidential candidate WENDELL
  utopian dream of .... ONE WORLD
willow .... OSIER, SALLOW, ITEA, SALIX
  ament .... CHAT
  bark, glucoside from .... SALICIN
  basket .... PRICKLE
  catkin .... CHAT
  herb .... ROSEBAY
  of the .... SALICACEOUS
  shoot .... WAND
  spike .... CHAT, CATKIN, AMENT
  twig .... WITHE, SALLOW, OSIER
  twigs, woven ... WICKER
willowy .... SVELT, SLIM, SLENDER
willy-nilly ...... INDECISIVE, IRRESOLUTE
Wilson, President .. WOODROW
Wilson's thrush .... VEERY
wilt .... DROOP, LANGUISH, WITHER, SHRIVEL
Wilt the _____ .... STILT
wily ...... SLY, CRAFTY, FOXY, SUBTLE, ASTUTE, ARTFUL, INSIDIOUS
wimble ...... GIMLET, AUGER
Wimbledon event ..... TENNIS
wimple .... RIPPLE
  wearer of .... NUN
win .. TRIUMPH, PREVAIL, EARN
  all games .... SWEEP
  all tricks .... VOLE, SLAM
wince ...... FLINCH, GRIMACE, RECOIL, REEL, ROLLER
winch .... CRANK, WINDLASS, HOIST, WHIM
Winchester .... RIFLE
wind .. ZEPHYR, STORM, GALE, HINT, NONSENSE, SCENT, COIL, LEVANTER, BUSTER, NOSER, BLAST, DUSTER, PAMPERO, REEL, SIMOOM, SAMIEL
  away from .... ALEE
  breath of .. WAFT, FLATUS
  combining form .. ANEMO
  cone .... SLEEVE

crack in timber made by ANEMOSIS
deposit .... LOESS, SEDIMENT
desert .... SIROCCO, SAMIEL, SIMOON
direction recorder .... ANEMOGRAPH, ANEMOSCOPE
driven clouds ..... SCUD
dry .... FOEHN
east .... EURUS
equatorial .... TRADE
gauge ..... ANEMOMETER
gentle .... ZEPHYR, BREEZE, AURA
gust of ...... PUFF, WAFT
high, strong ...... GALE
Indian Ocean .. MONSOON
indicator ... CONE, SOCK, (WEATHER) VANE, SLEEVE
instrument .. HORN, REED, SHAWN, PIPE, OCARINA, BASSOON, TROMBONE, CORNET, FLUTE, CLARINET, OBOE, TUBA, HARMONICA, BUGLE, SACKBUT
instrument finger hole ... VENTAGE
instrument mouthpiece .. LIP
mythical .... SANSAR
north ... BOREAS, AQUILO
northeast .... EURAQUILO, EUROCLYDON
puff .... FLATUS
Rocky Mountain .... CHINOOK
run before the ..... SCUD
scale .... BEAUFORT
science of the .... ANEMOLOGY
shake .... ANEMOSIS
shifting ...... VARIABLE
side away from ...... LEE
side toward .... WEATHER
sound ...... SOB, SOUGH, ROAR
south .... AUSTER
strong .... TEMPEST, STORM, GALE, PAMPERO
sudden, brief .... FLURRY, FLAW
up .... END, CONCLUDE, FINISH

warm .... FOEHN
wave .... RIPPLE
west ...... ZEPHYR(US), FAVONIAN
whirling .... CYCLONE, TORNADO
with snow/rain .... FLAW
windbag .... BRAGGART
windblown dust .... STOUR
windbreaker .... JACKET
winder pear .... WARDEN
windfall ..... VAIL, BONANZA, BOON, FORTUNE
windflower .... ANEMONE
windhover .... KESTREL, FALCON
winding .... MEANDROUS, AMBAGE, SPIRAL, MAZY, LABYRINTHINE, TORTUOUS
pathway .... AMBAGE
sheet .... SHROUD, CEREMENT
staircase ...... CARACOLE
windjammer .... SAILBOAT, SAILING SHIP
windlass ..... CAPSTAN, WINCH, HOIST, REEL
cylinder .... BARREL
windmill fighter .... (DON) QUIXOTE
part .... SAIL, VANE
pump .... GIN
window bar .... MULLION
bay .... ORIEL
cleaned ..... SQUEEGEED
door .... TRANSOM
dormer .... LUTHERN
drapery .... VALANCE, LAMBREQUIN
dressing .... TRIM
fastener ... HASP, LATCH
frame .... CASEMENT
frame piece ...... STILE
of a .... FENESTRAL
part ..... PANE, JAMB(E), SILL, SASH, LINTEL, GRILL(E), GRATING
roof .... DORMER, SKYLIGHT
round .... ROUNDEL
shade ... BLIND, SHUTTER
ship's ...... DEADLIGHT
small ...... FENESTELLA, WICKET
trellised .... LATTICE

windpipe .... WEASAND, TRACHEA, THROTTLE
  part of .... LARYNX
windrow ... FURROW, SWATH
winds, annual ...... ETESIAN
  god of .... AEOLUS
  study of ... ANEMOLOGY
windshake .... ANEMOSIS
windstorm .... BLIZZARD, BLOW, GALE, TYPHOON, BURAN, SQUALL, TWISTER
Windward Island ... GRENADA, MARTINIQUE, (ST.) LUCIA, DOMINICA, (ST.) VINCENT
  opposed to .... LEEWARD
windy ...... STORMY, GUSTY, VERBOSE, AIRY, BOASTFUL, BLOWY
wine .... VINTAGE, PORT, CATAWBA, MUSCATEL, SHERRY, CANARY, MADEIRA, YQUEM, MUSCADEL
  addicted to ...... VINOUS
  addiction to ... VINOSITY
  age of .... VINTAGE
  and dine .... TREAT, ENTERTAIN
  beverage .... NEGUS, SILLABUB
  bottle .... DECANTER, MAGNUM
  bottle indentation .. KICK
  Burgundy ..... CHABLIS
  burning of .. USTULATION
  cask ... BUTT, PIPE, TUN, BOSS, PUNCHEON
  cask deposit ..... ARGOL, ARGAL, TARTAR
  choice .... VINTAGE
  colored ...... VINACEOUS
  combining form ... BINI, OENO
  cup .... BEAKER
  deposit .... GRIFFE, LEES
  disorder .... CASSE
  distillate .... COGNAC, BRANDY
  drink, cold .. SANGAREE, COBBLER, SILLABUB
  dry ... SEC, SACK, BRUT, VERMOUTH, CHIANTI, CHABLIS, CLARET, TUSCANY
  effervescent .... CHAMPAGNE
  film on .... BEESWING

flavor .... MULL
flavoring ...... DOSAGE, DOSE
formation in ...... ROPE
fragrance of ... BOUQUET
glass .... RUMMER
god .... BACCHUS
grapes harvester .... VINTAGER
grower's patron .... VINCENT
jug .... OLPE
kind of .. BRANDY, CIDER, CORDIAL, PORT, VERMOUTH, PERRY, MUSCATEL
like .... VINACEOUS
loss of color ..... CASSE
merchant ..... VINTNER
mixture .... NEGUS
new .... MUST
of .... VINOUS, VINACEOUS, VINIC
pitcher .... OLPE
receptacle .... AMA
red ..... CLARET, MEDOC, PORT, TINTA, CHIANTI, BURGUNDY, DUBONNET, TUSCANY
refuse ...... LEES, DREGS
revived .... STUM
Rhine ... MOSELLE, HOCK
sauterne .... YQUEM
seller .. VINTNER, BISTRO
sherry .. OLOROSO, JEREZ
shop .... BISTRO, ESTAMINET, TABERNA
spiced .... BISHOP, SANGAREE, NEGUS, HIPPOCRAS, MARINADE
stock .... CELLAR
storage place .... CELLAR, BUTTERY
strength .... SEVE
strengthen .... DOSE
sweet ...... MUSCATEL, TOKAY, CANARY, MADEIRA, PORT, VERMOUTH, ALICANTE, MALMSEY, SAUTERNE
sweeten .... MULL
taster .... GOURMET
term ... BODY, BOUQUET, DRY, SEC, BRUT, VINTAGE, FLINTY
unfermented ...... MUST,

vessel .... TUN, AMA
CHALICE, AMPULLA
white .... MOSELLE
MALAGA, VERMOUTH,
SAUTERNE, MADEIRA,
MALMSEY, HOCK,
CHABLIS, SACK, BARSAC,
BURGUNDY, MARSALA
with honey ..... MULSE
wines, study of .... OENOLOGY
winesap ..... (WINTER)APPLE
wing .... PINNA, PINION,
PENNON, ALA
bastard .... ALULA
bind the .... PINION
building .... BAY
combining form .. PTERO
cover .... ELYTRUM,
ELYTRON, SHARD
footed ... ALIPED, SWIFT
footed creature ..... BAT,
LEMUR
feather .... PINION
furnish with .... IMP
in anatomy .... ALA
length .... SPAN
movement .. BEAT, FLAP,
FLUTTER
of building .. ELL, ALETTE,
ANNEX
protuberance ... CALCAR
shaped .... ALAR(Y),
ALIFORM
small .... ALULA
span of airplane .. SPREAD
support of airplane ......
CABANE
three-quilled ..... ALULA
winged .... ALATE(D),
PENNATE, FEATHERED,
FLEW, ALAR
being .... ANGEL,
SERAPH(IM), AMOR
figure .... ICARUS,
IDOLON, IDOLUM
goddess .... NIKE
fruit .... SAMARA
hat ... PETASUS, PETASOS
hat wearer ....
HERMES (MERCURY)
horse .... PEGASUS
monster: myth. ... HARPY
sandals .... TALARIA
sandals wearer ....
MERCURY (HERMES)
staff .... CADUCEUS

two .... DIPTERAL,
DIPTEROUS
wingless .... APTEROUS,
APTERAL
bird .... APTERYX,
KIWI, EMU
winglet .... ALULA
winglike .... ALA(R),
PTERYGOID
wings, flap the ...... WINNOW
furnish .... IMP
having .... ALATE(D)
having two ... BIPENNATE
wingspread .... SPAN
wink .... BAT, BLINK,
INSTANT, SIGNAL, HINT,
TWINKLE, NICTATE
winker .... EYE(LASH),
BLINDER
winkle .... SNAIL
winks, forty .... NAP, DOZE
winner .... VICTOR
longshot/surprise ......
SLEEPER
Winnie was his nickname .....
CHURCHILL
the Pooh author .. MILNE
winning .... CHARMING,
ATTRACTIVE, TAKING
disposition ...... SWEET
lottery combination .....
TERN
point .... ACE
winnings: sl. ...... VELVET
winnow ... SIFT, FAN, SCATTER
winsome .... ENGAGING,
BONNY, CHARMING
winter ... SEASON, HIBERNATE
apple .... DELICIOUS,
RUSSET
cap .... TUQUE
festival ...... POTLATCH
fodder .... SILAGE
of/like .... HIEMAL,
BRUMAL, HIBERNAL
product ... FROST, SNOW
sleep ..... HIBERNATION
solstice festival ....
SATURNALIA
spend the .... HIBERNATE
sport .... SKIING,
SLALOM
squash .... CUSHAW
torpid in ...... DORMANT
vehicle .... SLEIGH,
TOBOGGAN, SLED(GE)

wear .... EARMUFF, SNOWSHOES
weather .... SLEETY
winterberry .... HOLLY
wintergreen ... SHINLEAF, OIL, TEABERRY
    false .... PYROLA
"Winter's Tale" shepherdess .. MOPSA, DORCAS
wintry ..... BRUMAL, HIEMAL, HIBERNAL, COLD, SNOWY
winze .... SHAFT
wipe ..... MOP, DRY, EFFACE, SWAB, JEER
    out .... ELIMINATE, LIQUIDATE, ERASE, KILL, REMOVE, EXTERMINATE, ERADICATE
wiper .... TOWEL, DUSTER, DISHRAG, CAM
    finger/lip .... NAPKIN, SERVIETTE
wire .... TELEGRAPH, TELEGRAM, CABLE(GRAM)
    brush .... CARD
    coil .... SPRING
    cutting tool ...... PLIERS
    drum's .... SNARE
    light bulb .... FILAMENT
    measure .... MIL, STONE
    nail .... BRAD
    pen .... CAGE
    rope .... CABLE
    service .... UPI, INS, REUTERS
    spiral of .... COIL
    tapper ... BUGGER, TOUT
wiredancer .... AERIALIST
wirehair ...... (FOX) TERRIER
wireless .... RADIO
    adjunct ...... ANTENNA, AERIAL
wirepuller .... PUPPETEER
wirework .... GRILLAGE
wireworm .... MILLIPEDE
wiry .... STIFF, SINEWY
Wisconsin capital .. MADISON
    city .... MILWAUKEE, RACINE, KENOSHA, OSHKOSH, WAUSAU, APPLETON
    footballers .... BADGERS
    Indian .. SAC, WINNEBAGO
    lake .... WINNEBAGO
    motto .... FORWARD
    native .... BADGER

state animal .... BADGER
state bird .... ROBIN
state fish .... MUSKY
state flower ..... VIOLET
wisdom .... SAPIENCE, SAGACITY, LEARNING, LORE, WIT, ERUDITION, KNOWLEDGE
    goddess of .... MINERVA, ATHENA
    source of .... LAMP
    symbol of .... OWL
    tooth .... MOLAR
    universal .... PANSOPHY
wise ..... SAPIENT, JUDICIOUS, INFORMED, SHREWD, CUNNING, SAGE, DEEP, ERUDITE, SAGACIOUS, LEARNED
    adviser .... MENTOR
    and pithy ..... GNOMIC
    guy .... SMARK ALECK
    leader ...... STATESMAN
    man .. NESTOR, SOLOMAN, MENTOR, SAVANT, SAGE, SOLON, MAHATMA
    men, Biblical ..... MAGI
    saying .... ADAGE, SAW, REDE, PROVERB, MAXIM
    slang .... CONCEITED, KNOWING, FRESH, SAVVY
wiseacre .... QUACK, SMART ALECK, KNOW-IT-ALL
wisecrack ..... GIBE, RETORT, JOKE, GAG, QUIP
wish ..... DESIRE, CRAVE, BID, BEHEST
    mere .... VELLEITY
wishbone .... FURCULUM, FOURCHETTE
wishy-washy ...... SLOVENLY, SLIPSHOD, WEAK, THIN, INSIPID, WATERY, NAMPY-PAMBY
Wisla .... VISTULA
wisp .... BUNCH, SHRED, BUNDLE, TATE
wispy ...... SLIGHT, SLENDER
wisteria .... SHRUB, PEA, FLOWER, VIOLET
wit .... SENSE, WAG, MIND, HUMOR(IST)
    descriptive of .... QUICK, NIMBLE
    graceful, piercing .... ATTIC SALT

lively .... ESPRIT
lowest form of ..... PUN
sharp .... SALT
soul of .... BREVITY
sting of .... BARB
witch .... SORCERESS, HEX,
HAG, CRONE, ENCHANTRESS,
HARPY, WARLOCK, HELLCAT,
SIREN, LAMIA, CARLINE,
BELDAM(E), SYBIL
brew of ...... HELLBROTH
city .... SALEM
doctor ... MEDICINE MAN
folklore .... LILITH
Homer's .... CIRCE
means of transportation ..
BROOM
Shakespeare's ... DUESSA
witchcraft ... SORCERY, MAGIC,
WIZARDRY
talisman ..... OBI, OBEAH
witchery ... SORCERY, CHARM,
FASCINATION
witches' broom .. HEXENBESEN
with .... AMONG, CUM
cruel tendencies ....
SADISTIC
force .... AMAIN
spirit, in music .. CON BRIO
withal ... STILL, BESIDES, ALSO
withdraw ..... SECEDE, RECANT,
RETRACT, QUIT, WEAN,
PULLOUT, EVACUATE,
RETIRE, RETREAT, RECALL
withdrawn ..... RESERVED, SHY
withe .... WICKER, OSIER
wither .. FADE, SHRIVEL, WILT,
DRY UP, DECAY, WIZEN,
SCATHE
withering away .. TABESCENT
withhold .... RESTRAIN,
KEEP(BACK), REFUSE,
CHECK, DENY
within ...... INNER, BEN, INSIDE
without ..... LACKING, SANS,
BEREFT, OUTSIDE, SINE, EX
charge ..... GRATIS, FREE
combining form ... ECTO
delay .... FORTHWITH,
IMMEDIATELY
feet .... APOD
fluid .... DRY, ANEROID,
DEHYDRATED
legal force .... NULL
life .... AZOIC

passengers: colloq. ......
DEADHEAD
preparation .. EXTEMPORE,
IMPROMPTU
sound .... MUTE, SILENT
teeth .... EDENTATE
withstand .... ENDURE, RESIST,
OPPOSE, BEAR
witless ...... FOOLISH, STUPID
witness ...... TESTIFY, ATTEST,
TESTIFIER, OBSERVE(R),
SEE, TESTE, ONLOOKER
bear ... TESTIFY, ATTEST
perjured ...... STRAWMAN
place in court .... STAND
witticism .... JOKE, GAG,
WISECRACK, (BON)MOT,
SALLY, QUIP, PUN
Witt's planetoid .... EROS
witty .... DROLL, JOCOSE,
FACETIOUS, HUMOROUS,
JOCULAR, SALTY
exchange ..... REPARTEE
poem .... EPIGRAM
reply .... RETORT, SALLY
wive .... MARRY
wivern .... DRAGON
wizard ..... SAGE, MAGICIAN,
CONJURER, SHAMAN,
SORCERER, PELLAR,
ARCHIMAGE, MAGIAN,
MAGE
of Menlo .... EDISON
wizardry ... SORCERY, MAGIC
wizen ..... WITHER, SHRIVEL,
DRY(UP)
woad .... DYE, MUSTARD,
PASTEL
woald .... WELD
wobble .... WADDLE, SHIMMY,
SHAKE, VACILLATE
"Wobblies" of 1905 ..... IWW
wobbly .... SHAKY
Woden .... ODIN, OTHIN
woe ..... AFFLICTION, GRIEF,
MISERY, SORROW, TROUBLE,
DOLOR
woebegone ... SAD, DESOLATE
wolaba .... KANGAROO
wold ... MIGNONETTE, PLAIN,
FLOWER
wolf ... PHILANDERER, LARVA,
LUPUS
bound with magic rope ..
FENRIR
cry of .... HOWL

female .... BITCH
foot(print) .... PAD
male .... DOG
of a .... LUPINE
prairie .... COYOTE
timber .... LOBO
young .... WHELP
Wolfe, fiction detective .. NERO
victim of ...... MONTCALM
Wolfert, writer .... IRA
wolfhound ..... BORZOI, ALAN
wolfish .... RAPACIOUS,
RAVENOUS
wolflike ..... THOOID, LUPINE,
RAVENOUS
wolfram(ite) .. TUNGSTEN, CAL
wolfsbane .... ACONITE,
MONKSHOOD
Wollaston .... CRATER
wolverine .... CARCAJOU,
GLUTTON
woman .... EVE, DISTAFF, FRAU,
FEMALE, WIFE, LADY,
SHE, MULIER, MUJER,
SQUAW, JILL, MS
adviser .... EGERIA
annoyer .... MASHER,
OGLER
attendant ...... MATRON
bad-tempered .. VIRAGO,
SHREW, HELLCAT, VIXEN,
SPITFIRE, TERMAGANT
bearing second child ....
MULTIPARA
beautiful .. VENUS, SIREN,
VISION, HOURI,
BELLE, STUNNER,
HELEN
birth control advocate ...
SANGER
blouse .... BASQUE
bold .... QUEAN
bonnet .... CAPOTE
British sl. .... BIRD
cape of .... BERTHA,
MANTEAU, PELERINE
chaste ... VIRGIN, VESTAL
childless ..... NULLIFARA
cloak ...... CARDINAL,
MANTEAU, MANTUA,
CAPUCHIN
coat ... MANDARIN, MINK
collar .... BERTHA
colloquial (see slang) ....
PETTICOAT, HEN, FILLY,
FRAIL, BROAD

combining form ... GYN
companion .... CUMMER
conductor ...... QUACH
coronet .... TIARA
country ...... GAMMER,
GAFFER
dirty ... SLATTERN, DRAB,
MALKIN
domineering .. BATTLE-AX
dowdy .... FRUMP
dowry .... DOT
drawers .. PANTALET(TES)
dressing gown ....
CAMISOLE, KIMONO
elderly .... MATRON,
DOWAGER, GRANNY
escort of ..... (E)SQUIRE,
CHAPERON
evening dress .... FORMAL
evil ..... HAG, HELLCAT,
JEZEBEL
fairest .... HELEN
fascinating ...... WITCH
flyer .... AVIATRIX
frenzied ...... M(A)ENAD
graceful .... SYLPH
guard .... MATRON
hairstyle .... BOB, BANGS,
SHINGLES, CHIGNON,
UPSWEEP, PAGEBOY
half fish .... MERMAID
hat of ... TOQUE, TURBAN,
PILLBOX, BRETON,
CLOCHE
hater ...... MISOGYNIST
head and shoulder
covering ...... NUBIA
headdress ...... PINNER,
FRET, POUF
hideous .... BELDAME,
WITCH, MEDUSA
homosexual ..... LESBIAN
houseworker .... MARTHA
in uniform .. WAC, WREN,
WAVE, SPAR, NURSE
jacket of .. SACK, SACQUE,
SIMAR, CAMISOLE,
PALETOT
jungle .... SHEENA
killing .... FEMICIDE
little ... WIFE, SPOUSE, JO,
BETH, MEG, AMY
loose ..... TART, WENCH,
QUEAN, HUSSY, TRULL
mantle .... MANTEAU

married .... MATRON,
  MADAM(E), MISSUS,
  MRS, MS
masculine traits of .....
  VIRILISM
meek .... GRISELDA
model ...... MANNEKIN,
  MANNEQUIN
nagging .... SHREW
neckwear .... STOLE
noble .... COUNTESS,
  DUCHESS, BARONESS
of poor repute .. DEMIREP
of song ..... AMY, LOUISE
old ... HAG, GRANDAM(E),
  GAMMER, WITCH,
  CRONE, CARLINE
old, unmarried .. SPINSTER
opera comic ..... BUFFA
origin of .... RIB
pants .... CULOTTES
patient .... GRISELDA
performer ..... DISEUSE,
  ACTRESS, ARTISTE
pert .... MINX
popular .... BELLE
pretty .. LOOKER, STUNNER
quarrelsome .... VIRAGO,
  SHREW, HARRIDAN,
  XANTHIPPE, TERMAGANT
religious .... NUN, SISTER
repulsive .... GORGON
riding costume ... HABIT,
  JOSEPH
robe .... SIMAR
ruler ...... MATRIARCH,
  REINE, QUEEN, EMPRESS
scarf .... MANTILLA
scolding .... VIRAGO,
  HARRIDAN, SHREW, NAG,
  XANTHIPPE, TERMAGANT,
  FISHWIFE
seducer .... VAMPIRE,
  SIREN
shameless ..... JEZEBEL
shoe of .... CHOPINE
shoe style of .... WEDGIE
singer .... SOPRANO,
  CHANTEUSE, CHANTRESS,
  CANTATRICE
skirt .... KIRTLE
slang ...... DAME, SKIRT,
  FLOSSIE, FLOSSY, BABE,
  FRAIL, BROAD, SQUAW

soothsayer ..... SEERESS,
  PYTHONESS
spiteful .... CAT
spy .... MATA HARI
stately .... JUNO
suckling baby ....
  WET NURSE
tongue's curb ... BRANKS
ugly ... BELDAM(E), HAG,
  WITCH, GORGON
unfruitful .... BARREN
untidy .. SLATTERN, DRAB,
  MALKIN
vest of .... JERKIN
violent .... FURY
warrior .... CAMILLA,
  AMAZON
wicked .... JEZEBEL
womb of ... WAME, BELLY
  MATRIX, UTERUS,
  VENTER
work of a .... DISTAFF
wrap of .. NUBIA, DOLMAN
yellow-haired ... BLONDE
young .... MISS,
  BABE, NYMPH
Zodiac .... VIRGO
womanhood ..... MULIEBRITY
womb .... WAME, MATRIX,
  BELLY, VENTER, UTERUS
women, club of ...... SOROSIS,
  SORORITY
government by ....
  MATRIARCHY
organization of .... NOW,
  WCTU
preoccupation of .. DIET,
  WEIGHT, STYLE,
  PRICES, MAKE-UP
reformatory ....
  MAGDALENE
seclusion of .... PURDAH
undergarment ...... BRA,
  SLIP, BLOOMERS,
  TEDDY, UNDIES,
  LINGERIE, CHEMISE,
  KNICKERS, STEP-INS
vest .... JERKIN
wombat .. BADGER, MARSUPIAL
wonder .... MIRACLE,
  AMAZEMENT, MUSE, MARVEL
boy .... PRODIGY
world's .... PHAROS,
  PYRAMID
wonderwork .... MIRACLE
Wonson, in Japanese .. GENSAN

wont .... ACCUSTOMED, CUSTOM, HABIT
wonted .... USUAL
woo .... COURT, SUE, SEEK, ENTREAT, SPARK
wood .... FOREST, GROVE, XYLEM, LUMBER, TIMBER, MAHOGANY
  alcohol ...... METHANOL
  anemone .. THIMBLEWEED
  aromatic .... LINALOA
  ash oxide .... POTASH
  ashes extract .... LYE
  axe breaker .. QUEBRACHO
  bar .... FID
  batted for distance ...... TIPCAT
  bend in ..... SNY, WARP
  betony ..... LOUSEWORT
  bits .... KINDLING
  black ...... TEAK, EBONY, DOOK
  block .... NOG, SPRAG, TRIG, WEDGE
  borer .... TEREDO
  burning piece .... FIREBRAND
  charred .... BRAY
  coal .... LIGNITE, CHARCOAL
  combining form .... LIGN(O), XYL(O), HYL(O), LIGNI
  cutter .... RIPSAW
  cutting .... HAG
  destroying insect .... TERMITE, ANAY
  destroying mollusk ...... TEREDO
  dressed .... TIMBER
  dresser .... ADZ(E)
  drug .... QUASSIA
  dust .... COOM(B)
  easily burned .... SPUNK
  eater .... ANAY, TERMITE
  elastic .... YEW
  engraving ... XYLOGRAPH
  flat piece .... SPLAT
  fluting .... CHAMFER
  for bows .... YEW
  for bridges/piles .. ALDER
  for dagger hilt .... DUDGEON
  for furniture ..... EBONY, WALNUT, CALAMANDER

fragrant .... CEDAR, ALOES
groove .... CHAMFER
gum .... XYLAN
hard .... NARRA, MAHOGANY, EBONY, LOCUST, HICKORY, MOLAVE
hyacinth .... BLUEBELL, HAREBELL
ibis .... JABIRU
inlaid .... BUHL
knot .... KNAR
layer .... VENEER
light .... BALSA
louse .. SLATER, SOW BUG
made of ...... XYLOID
make into ..... LIGNIFY
mark .... ROE
measure .... CORD, FOOT
nymph ... HUMMINGBIRD, MOTH, BUTTERFLY, (HAMA)DRYAD
of ... LIGNEOUS, XYLOID
oil .... TUNG
partially burned .. CINDER
piece of .... BOARD, PLANK, SLAT, STAVE, BILLET
pigeon .... RINGDOVE, CUSHAT, CULVER
pin ..... NOG, FID, PEG
pin in boat .... THOLE
preservative .. CREOSOTE
resinous ..... LIGNALOES
shoe .... PATTEN, SABOT, CLOG
small .... GROVE
sorrel ..... OXALIS, OCA
stand, top of ..... CRISS
strip ..... BATTEN, SLAT, LATH, SPLINT, SPLIT, SLIP, STAVE, LIST
striped .... ARAROBA
tar distillate ... CREOSOTE, PITCH
twist in .... WARP
veneer .... BURL
warbler .... WAGTAIL
wheel brake ..... SPRAG, TRIG, NOG, WEDGE
winds .... OBOE, FLUTE, CLARINET, BASSOON
worker ..... CARPENTER
worm .... THRIPS

woodbine ...... IVY, CREEPER,
    HONEYSUCKLE, PERIDOT
woodchat .... SHRIKE
woodchuck .... MARMOT,
    GROUNDHOG, WEJACK
woodcock relative .... SNIPE,
    SANDPIPER, PEWEE
woodcraft .... HUNTING,
    TRAPPING
woodcutter .... LUMBERJACK,
    LOGGER, SAWYER
wooded .... SYLVAN
   area .... BOONDOCKS,
    WEALD
   hill .... HOLT
wooden ...... STOLID, DULL,
   STIFF, INSENSITIVE, TREEN
   bar .... TREE
   bench .... SETTLE
   board for meat-carving ..
    TRENCHER
   bowl ..... KITTY, MAZER,
    MAZARD
   brick .... DOOR
   bucket .... CANNIKIN
   club .... BILLET
   collar .... CANGUE
   hammer .... MALLET
   horse giver ..... TROJAN
   Indian's place ....
    CIGAR STORE
   limb .... PEG LEG
   pail .... PIGGIN
   peg/pin ... THOLE, SPILE,
   NOG, FID, TRE(E)NAIL,
    DOWEL
   pole/post .... TREE
   seat .... BENCH
   shoe ..... CLOG, SABOT,
    PATTEN
   spool toy ..... DIABOLO
   stake .... TREE
   time-beaters .. CASTANETS
woodland ..... FOREST, GROVE
   clearing .... GLADE
   deity ...... PAN, SATYR,
   FAUN, SILENUS,
    SILVANUS
woodluck .... ARI SPONSA,
    DUCK
woodman .. FORESTER, RANGER
woodpecker ...... FLICKER,
   YELLOWHAMMER, CHAB,
   SAPSUCKER, HIGH-HOLE,
   POPINJAY, COLY, REDHEAD
   genus .... YUNX

woods .... GROVE, SILVA,
    FOREST
   deity of the ..... SYLVAN
   out of the .. SAFE, CLEAR
woodsia .... FERN
woodsman .... TRAPPER,
   HUNTER, VOYAGEUR
woodbine .... IVY
woodwaxen .... DYEWEED
woodwind .... OBOE, BASSOON,
   CLARINET, FLUTE
woodworm .... THRIPS
woody .... LIGNEOUS, XYLOID
   fiber .... BAST
   fiber substance .. LIGNIN
   plant ..... SHRUB, TREE
   tissue .... XYLEM
   vine .... CLEMATIS
wooer .... SUITOR
woof ..... WEFT, BARK, ABB,
   FILLING, FABRIC, TEXTURE,
    CLOTH
woofer ... LOUD SPEAKER, DOG
wooing ..... SUIT, COURTSHIP
wool .... ALPACA, MERINO,
   PILE, LANA, ANGORA,
    FLEECE
   and cashmere .... CASHA
   and silk cloth .. CAMLET,
    EOLIENNE
   animal with ...... SHEEP,
   ALPACA, GOAT,
   VICUNA, MERINO
   bearing .... LANIFEROUS
   blanket .... SERAPE
   blemish .... MOTE
   cleaning machine ....
    WILLOW(ER)
   cloth .... FRIEZE
   cluster .... NEP
   coarse .... SHAG
   comb .... CARD
   combed knot of .... NOIL
   combining form .... LANI
   covered with .. FLOCCOSE,
    LANATE
   fabric ... DELAINE, CASHA,
   ETAMINE, BEIGE,
   LANSDOWNE, FRISCA,
   VELOUR(S), REPP,
   REP(S), STAMMEL,
   CHALLIS, CHALLIE,
   FRIEZE, BEAVER,
   HODDEN, TARTAN
   fat .... LANOLIN(E)
   felted .... CASHA

fiber .. NOIL, SLIVER, PILE, FLOCK
fiber, batted ... BATTING
goat's .... CASHMERE
grease .... SUINT
knitted .... JERSEY
knot .... NOIL, BURL
like fabric ..... LANITAL
lock of .... TAG
matted .... DAGLOCK
measure .... HEER
oily substance ... GREASE
particles ...... DOWN
piece of .... NOIL
produced one year .. CLIP
roll of .... SLUB
rug fibers .... NAP, PILE
salvage .... MUNGO
sheared at one time .....
CLIP, FLEECE
sheep .... MERINO
sheer .... VOILE
shreds of .... NOIL
spinning machine ....
THROSTLE
synthetic .... LANITAL
thread .. WORSTED, YARN
tuft .... FLOCCUS,
FLOCCULE, LOCK
twisted .... ROVE
unravel ... TEASE, CARD
waste ... MUNGO, FLOCK,
FUD
watered .... MOREEN
weight .... TOD
yarn .... WORSTED
woolen cloth .... TARTAN,
ETAMINE, JERSEY, CASHA,
MOREEN, WORSTED, FRIEZE,
MUNGO, CAMLET, SHODDY,
HODDEN, MELTON, DOESKIN,
KERSEY, RATINE, RATTEEN,
TRICOT(INE), MERINO,
PETERSHAM, DUFFLE, DUFFEL,
CASIMIRE, CALAMANCO
jacket .... CARDIGAN
material .... CADDIS
shawl .... PAISLEY
twilled fabric ....
SHALLOON, SERGE,
CAS(S)IMERE
woolly ..... FLEECY, LANOSE,
LANATE, FLOCCULENT
bear .... CATERPILLAR
haired people ....
ULOTRICHI

tuft .... FLOCCULUS
woorali ..... CURARE, URARI
woozy .. MUDDLED, BEFUDDLED
word ...... REMARK, PLEDGE,
PROMISE, NEWS, TIDINGS,
PAROLE, SIGNAL, TALK,
ORDER, INFORMATION,
LOCUTION
action .... VERB
addition to end of ....
PARAGOGE
airmail envelop ....
PAR AVION
appropriate .. MOT JUSTE
blindness .... ALEXIA
book .... LEXICON,
DICTIONARY,
THESAURUS, LIBRETTO
change in a .. METAPLASM
derivation .... PARONYM
dropping of middle sound
of .... SYNCOPE
dropping of last sound/
letter of ..... APOCOPE
exact .... MOT JUSTE
figurative .... TROPE,
METAPHOR, SIMILE
final .. AMEN, ULTIMATUM
first of doxology ....
GLORIA
for word .... LITERAL,
VERBAL, VERBATIM,
TEXTUAL, METAPHRASE
formative ending ....
DESINENCE
four-letter .. TETRAGRAM
game .... ANAGRAM,
CHARADE, ACROSTIC,
CONUNDRUM
hard to pronounce ......
JAWBREAKER
in a ... BRIEFLY, IN SHORT
inventor ..... NEOLOGIST
inversion .. ANASTROPHE
last .... AMEN
last syllable of .. ULTIMA
long: colloq. .. MOUTHFUL
meaning, study of ....
SEMANTICS, SEMASIOLOGY
misused ..... BARBARITY
new .... NEOLOGISM
new meaning of ....
NEOLOGISM
of assent ..... YES, YEA,
AMEN

of honor .... PLEDGE,
PAROLE, PROMISE
of mouth .... ORAL
of only one .. MONOMIAL
of opposite meaning ....
ANTONYM
of similar meaning ......
SYNONYM
of warning ... CAUTION,
BEWARE
ordinary meaning ....
LITERAL
origin of a .. ETYMOLOGY
original form ... ETYMON
prisoner's ...... PAROLE
puzzle ..... LOGOGRIPH,
ACROSTIC, CHARADE,
CROSSWORD, REBUS
reading same backward ..
PALINDROME
same pronunciation,
different meaning .....
HOMONYM, HOMOPHONE
same spelling, different
meaning ....
HOMOGRAPH,
HETERONYM
shorten a ...... SYNCOPE
square .... PALINDROME
substitute .... METONYM
symbol ...... LOGOGRAM
the .... BIBLE, LOGOS
unprintable, usually .....
FOUR-LETTER
vowel omission .. APHESIS
with tail .. CAT, BOB, HIGH
wordiness .... PLEONISM,
PROLIXITY, VERBIAGE,
VERBOSITY
wording .... PHRASING,
PHRASEOLOGY, DICTION,
TEXT
words .... TEXT, LYRICS,
DISPUTE
argument about ....
LOGOMACHY
attack with ...... BASTE,
ABUSE
author's .... TEXT
battle of .... LOGOMACHY
choice of .... DICTION
clever exchange of ......
REPARTEE
doctrine of ... NEOLOGY
eat one's .... RETRACT
few of .... LACONIC

incorrect use of ....
CATACHRESIS
manner of expression ....
ENUNCIATION, DICTION
misuse of .. MALAPROPISM
of .... VERBAL
of few .... LACONIC,
TERSE, CURT
play on .... PUN
prefix .... LOGO
ridiculous user of ....
(MRS.) MALAPROP
wordy ..... PROLIX, VERBOSE,
WINDY, REDUNDANT
work ... JOB, EFFORT, LABOR,
TOIL, EMPLOYMENT,
OCCUPATION, CRAFT,
BUSINESS, TASK, OPUS,
GRIND, ERGON
against .... MILITATE
aimlessly .... PUTTER,
POTTER
amount of .... LOAD
art .... PAINTING,
SCULPTURE, MUSIC,
CARVING, ETCHING,
OIL, OPUS,
COMPOSITION
artist's .... MASTER
assignment ...... SHIFT,
BEAT, STINT, TASK,
JOB, TRICK
at .... PLY
avoid .... SHIRK, SKULK,
MALINGER
clothes cloth .. OSNABURG,
DRILL, DENIM
energetically .... HUSTLE
evade .... MALINGER
fussily .... NIGGLE
great .... MASTER
group .... CREW, GANG,
TEAM, DETAIL
hard .... TOIL, SWEAT,
GRUB, PLUG, HUSTLE
in .... INSERT
incentive .... BONUS, TIP
life .... CAREER
of wonder ..... MIRACLE
out .... SOLVE, DEVELOP,
EVOLVE, EXERCISE,
PRACTICE
pants .... LEVIS
patiently ... PLOD, TOIL,
PLUG, PLY
shift .... TRICK

shoes .... BROGAN
suitable .... METIER
tedious ... CHORE, GRIND,
    TRAVAIL, DRUDGERY
time-out from ... BREAK,
    RECESS
trainee ..... APPRENTICE
trousers .... DUNGAREES
together: slogan ....
    GUNG HO
unit of .... ERG(ON)
unskillfully ..... DABBLE
with lead .... PLUMB
workable .... FEASIBLE
workaday .... COMMONPLACE,
    ORDINARY, PROSAIC, DRAB
workbag .... KIT
workbook .... MANUAL
workbox .... (TOOL)KIT, ETUI
worker .... LABORER,
    EMPLOYE, WAGE-EARNER,
    HAND
  agricultural ... FARMER,
    OKIE
  class ..... PROLETARIAT
  coal mine ..... COLLIER
  farm .... PEON, HIND
  gem .... JEWELER
  hard .... SCRUB
  menial .... SERVANT,
    DRUDGE, DOMESTIC
  migratory ... HOBO, PEON,
    BRACERO, OKIE
  odd job .... JACK
  restless .... FLOATER
  skilled .... ARTISAN,
    CRAFTSMAN
  stone ... MASON, JEWELER
  transient ...... FLOATER,
    HOBO, OKIE
  unskilled .... TINKER,
    COBBLER
  white collar ...... CLERK
  who replaces striker .....
    RAT, SCAB
working .... RUNNING,
    OPERATING
workhorse ... SLAVE, DRUDGE,
    TOILER
Workman, explorer ... FANNY
workmanship ...... ARTISTRY
works .... OEUVRES
workshop ..... LAB, ATELIER,
    STUDIO
workout ..... PRACTICE, TEST,
    EXERCISE

world .... COSMOS, UNIVERSE,
    EARTH, GLOBE, MANKIND,
    DOMAIN, REALM
  bearer of the ..... ATLAS
  domain .... ANIMAL,
    VEGETABLE, MINERAL
  of the .... TERRESTIAL,
    TEMPORAL, SECULAR,
    MUNDANE
  out of this .... OUTRE
  War I machinegun ......
    POMPOM
  War I plane ..... TAUBE,
    NIEUPORT, SPAD
  War II title .... SCAP
  wide .... UNIVERSAL,
    PANDEMIC, CATHOLIC,
    ECUMENIC, GLOBAL
  wonder .... PYRAMID,
    PHAROS, COLOSSUS
worldly .... MUNDANE,
    SECULAR, TERRENE,
    TERRESTIAL, EARTHLY,
    TEMPORAL
  wise .... SOPHISTICATED,
    KNOWING
worm ... NAID, ESS, ANNELID,
    ASCARID, HELMINTH,
  NEMATODE, WRETCH, TINEA,
    LOA
  bait .... LURG
  bloodsucking .... LEECH
  combining form .. VERMI
  drug .... VERMICIDE
  eaten .... RAGGED,
    WORN-OUT
  feeler of a .... PALP(US)
  flat .... TREMATODE,
    FLUKE
  in zoology ...... LYTTA
  larva ..... CATERPILLAR,
    MAGGOT, GRUB,
    CERCARIA
  marine .... NEMERTEAN
  move like a ..... CREEP,
    CRAWL
  out .... EXTRACT
  parasitic ...... CESTODE,
    CESTOID, FLUKE
  round .... ASCARID
  sand .... NEMERTEAN
  sea .... SAO
  segment .... SOMITE,
    METAMERE
  shaped ...... VERMIFORM
  ship ..... BORER, TEREDO

silk .... ERIA
snail resembling .. SLUG
sucker .... LEECH
sucking organ of ....
                    PROBOSCIS
threadlike ...... FILARIA
track .... NEREITE
water .... LEECH, TEREDO
worms, medicine for intestinal
                    SANTONINE(E)
  of the Nile .... ASPS
  parasitic .... FILARIA
wormseed .... SANTONICA
wormwood .... MOXA,
  MORTIFICATION, BITTERNESS,
                    ABSINTH(E)
worn ..... TATTERED, SHABBY,
  SPENT, RAGGED, EROSE,
                    JADED
  by friction ..... ATTRITE
  clothes .... RAGS
  end .... FRAZZLE
  look .... HAGGARD
  out .... EXHAUSTED,
    TIRED, SPENT,
    DECREPIT, JADED,
    SEEDY, EFFETE
worried .... CAREWORN,
                    ANXIOUS
worrier's crop .... ULCERS,
                    WRINKLES
worry ...... HARASS, PESTER,
  ANNOY, DISTRESS, ANXIETY,
  CARE, FRET, STEW, GRIZZLE
  colloquial ..... LOOKOUT,
                    CONCERN
worship .... VENERATE,
  IDOLIZE, ADORE, REVERE,
  HOMAGE, ADORATION,
                    DEIFY
  animal .... ZOOLATRY
  combining form .. LATRY
  due God alone .. LATRIA
  object of ... IDOL, HERO,
                    SWEETHEART
  of all gods ... PANTHEISM
  of idols .... IDOLISM
  of saints ... HAGIOLATRY
  place of .. ALTAR, SHRINE,
    TEMPLE, SYNAGOGUE,
    CHAPEL, PAGODA
  system of .. FETISH, CULT
worshipper .... ADORER,
  ADMIRER, VENERATOR,
  IDOLIST, IDOLATER
  stars .... SABAIST

worst .... BEAT, DEFEAT,
                    POOREST
  Dressed Woman Awards
    creator .... BLACKWELL
worsted cloth .... SERGE,
  ETAMINE, WOOL
  ribbon/yarn ..... CADDIS
wort .... HERB, PLANT
worth ... MERIT, PRICE, VALUE,
                    IMPORTANCE
  having ...... DESIRABLE,
                    ASSET
  of little .... TRIFLE,
                    TRIFLING
worthless .... USELESS,
  GOOD-FOR-NOTHING, VAIN,
  NUGATORY, LOSEL, RIP
  almost .... PALTRY,
    PETTY, PIDDLE
  fellow ...... BUM, IDLER,
                    LOSEL
  horse .... NAG, JADE,
                    PLATER
  ideas .... BILGE
  remains .... CARCASS,
    CARCASE, DREGS,
                    SCRAPS
  scrap .... ORT
  thing .... TRIPE, FICO,
                    CHIP
worthwhile .... OF VALUE
worthy .... DESERVING,
  MERITORIOUS, VALUABLE
Wouk, author ...... HERMAN
  ship .... CAINE
wound ...... LESION, PIERCE,
  GASH, TRAUMA, INJURY,
  SORE, STAB, HURT
  blood shed from ... GORE,
                    SANIES
  discharge from a .. ICHOR,
                    PUS, SANIES
  dressing .... PATCH
  edge of .... LIP
  jagged ...... LACERATION
  mark .... SCAR
  plug .... TENT, DOSSIL
woven double ..... TWO-PLY
  goods dealer .... HOSIER
  with raised design ....
                    BROCHE
wow ..... INTERJECTION, HIT,
                    AMUSE
wowser .... PRUDE
wrack ...... SEAWEED, RUIN,
  WRECKAGE, CLOUDS

wraith ... GHOST, APPARITION, SPECTRE, FETCH

wrangle ... QUARREL, ARGUE, BICKER, DISPUTE, ROW, HIGGLE

wrangler ... COWBOY, ARGUER

wrap .... SWATHE, COVER, ENVELOP, CLOAK, PELISSE, SWADDLE, NUBIA

   around .... LOINCLOTH, SARONG

   in burial cloth ..... CERE

   shoulder ... CAPE, SHAWL

   snugly .... TUCK

   to deaden sound .... MUFFLE

   up ..... FINISH, ENFOLD, ENVELOP

   woman's ...... DOLMAN

wrapper .... VESTURE

   book's .... JACKET

   candy's .... TINFOIL

wrapping material .... CELLOPHANE, PAPER, LEAF, KRAFT, MATTING

wrasse .... CUNNER, FISHES

wrath .... ANGER, FURY, CHOLER, RAGE, IRE

wreak .... INFLICT, EXACT

wreath .... ANADEM, LEI, CHAPLET, GARLAND, ORLE, TORSE

   bridal .... SPIREA

   for achievement .... CORONA

   for head .... ANADEM, CHAPLET, LAUREL

   hanging .... FESTOON

   victor's .... LAUREL, CROWN

wreathe .... COIL, TWIST, ENCIRCLE, ENVELOP

wreck ... RUIN, DESTRUCTION, DESTROY, DAMAGE, RAZE, SMASH(UP)

   building ... TEAR DOWN

wreckage .... FLOTSAM, JETSAM, (W)RACK

wren ..... SONGBIRD, TOMTIT, JENNY

wrench .... SPRAIN, SPANNER, TWIST, JERK, WREST, WRICK

   kind of ...... STILLSON, MONKEY

wrest ...... WRENCH, TWIST, USURP, WRING, EXTRACT, EXTORT

wrestle .... CONTEND, TUSSLE, GRAPPLE

wrestler ... MATMAN, MAULER, GRAPPLER

wrestling hold .... (HALF) NELSON, WRISTLOCK, (HEAD) LOCK, SCISSORS

   match division .... FALL

   oriental .... SUMO

   place/school .... PAL(A)ESTRA

   score .... FALL

   sound .... THUD, GRUNT, GROAN

   trick throw .... CHIP

wretch .... PARIAH, OUTCAST, MISER, WORM, HILDING, CAITIFF, SCULLION

wretched .... MISERABLE, WOEFUL, SAD, DISMAL, MEAN, FORLORN, ABJECT

wriggle ... WANGLE, WIGGLE, SQUIRM, DODGE

wriggler .... LARVA, HULA DANCER

Wright, airplane inventor ..... ORVILLE, WILBUR

wring ...... WREST, WRENCH, SQUEEZE, TWIST, EXTRACT, EXTORT, PRESS

   neck of .... SCRAG

wrinkle .... RIMPLE, FURROW, RIDGE, CREASE, TWIST, CRIMP, SEAM, COCKLE, FOLD, RUCK, RUGA, RUMPLE, SHRIVEL, PUCKER, NOVELTY

wrinkled .... LINED, RUGATE, RUGOSE

wrist ..... CARPUS, CARPAL(E)

   bone .... CARPAL(E), TRAPEZOID

   bone, of a .... SCAPHOLD

   guard .... BRACER

wristband ..... CUFF, BRACER

wristlet .... BRACELET, HANDCUFF

writ .... PROCESS, VENIRE, WARRANT, DOCUMENT, OYER BREVE, INJUNCTION, PRECEPT

   Holy .... BIBLE

   judicial .... TALES

of ____ ...... EXECUTION, PROHIBITION, CERTIORARI, VENIRE, RIGHT, MANDAMUS
of execution ..... ELEGIT
of right's issue ..... MISE
order of arrest ... CAPIAS
to serve in court .... SUBPOENA, SUMMONS, VENIRE
write ...... SCRAWL, INDITE, PEN, SCRIBBLE, COMPOSE, INSCRIBE, SCRIVE, LUCUBRATE
at length ...... EXPATIATE
effusively .... GUSH
hurriedly ..... DASH(OFF)
into law .... ENACT
one's name .... SIGN
up ...... SKETCH, REPORT
writer ..... SCRIBE, AUTHOR, PENMAN, AMANUENSIS, CLERK, COPYIST, POET, JOURNALIST
inferior .... HACK, POETASTER, SCRIBBLER
kind of ... GHOST, COPY, COPYIST
of trilogies .... ASCH
play .... DRAMATIST
unscrupulous .... PLAGIARIST
verse ..... POET, RHYMER
writers' group .... PEN
writhe ..... SQUIRM, CONTORT, TWIST
writing .... BOOK, POEM, DOCUMENT, LETTER, ARTICLE, DIARY, MONOGRAPH, TREATISE
as a profession ...... PEN
cipher ... CRYPTOGRAPHY
combining form .... LOG(UE)
desk .... SECRETARY, ESCRITOIRE, BUREAU
exalted to trivial .. BATHOS
flippant style of .... PERSIFLAGE
flourish ...... CURLICUE, TAG, CURLYCUE
foolish ...... TWADDLE, HOGWASH
implement .. PEN, STYLUS, QUILL, CHALK, BRUSH, PENCIL

mark .... CHARACTER
material, box for .... PAPETERIE
mystic .... RUNE
paper ..... STATIONERY, TALIPOT, PAPYRUS
paper size .... DEMY, IMPERIAL
parchment ..... VELLUM
pompous ...... FUSTIAN
preliminary ...... DRAFT
pretentious ..... KITSCH
secret ..... CIPHER, CODE
senseless ... BALDERDASH
sentimental ...... SLUSH
stroke .... SERIF
table .... ESCRITOIRE, DESK, BUREAU
tablet .... DIPTYCH
wall .... GRAFFITO
wedge-shaped .... CUNEI
writings .... LITERATURE
collection of ..... PAPERS
unpublished ... REMAINS
written, not ... ORAL, VERBAL, TACIT
order .... PRECEPT
plans, for short ... SKEDS
wrong .... EVIL, AMISS, ERRONEOUS, ABUSE, WICKED, IMMORAL, INCORRECT
act .... MISDEED, MISCONDUCT
civil .... TORT
do woman ..... SEDUCE, ABUSE
name .... MISNOMER
prefix .... MIS, MAL
wroth ..... IRATE, INCENSED, ANGRY
wrought .... FASHIONED, SHAPED, DECORATED, D(A)EDAL
up ..... EXCITED, TENSE, DISTURBED
wry .... TWISTED, DISTORTED, CONTRARY, PERVERSE
wryneck .... LOXIA, WEET, (SNAKE)BIRD
Wyandot .... HURON
Wycliffe disciple .... LOLLARD
Wylie, novelist ...... ELINOR
Wyoming capital ... CHEYENNE
cavern .... SHOSHONE
city ... LARAMIE, CASPER, SHERIDAN

mountain .... TETON,
MORAN, LARAMIE
peak .... GANNETT

state tree .. COTTONWOOD
Wystan Hugh ——— ... AUDEN
wyvern .... DRAGON

X

X ..... TEN, MARK, SIGNATURE
Greek XI
letter .... EX
marker, usually ....
ILLITERATE
marks the ——— .... SPOT
shaped .... EX
xanthic .... YELLOW
Xanthippe's husband ....
SOCRATES
prototype ...... NAGGER,
TERMAGANT, SHREW,
VIRAGO
xanthous .... YELLOW
Xavier, saint .... FRANCIS
Xe, in chemistry ..... XENON
xebec .... SHIP
common users .. CORSAIRS
xema .... GULL
xeno .... GUEST
as prefix ...... FOREIGN,
STRANGE
Xeres .... JEREZ

xerophilous plant/animal ....
CACTUS, CAMEL, XEROPHTYE
xerotic .... DRY
Xerxes I, father of .... DARIUS
wife .... ESTHER
xiphoid .... ENSIFORM,
SWORD-SHAPED
xiphosuran ...... KING CRAB,
ARACHNID
Xmas .... YULE(TIDE),
CHRISTMAS
Xtian. .... CHRISTIAN
xylan .... PENTOSAN
xylem ...... WOOD, HADROME
xyloid .... WOODY, LIGNEOUS
xylonite .... CELLULOID
xylophone-like instrument ...
MARIMBA, SARON
xylotomous insect ... TERMITE,
ANAY
xyst .... PORTICO
xyster ...... (BONE)SCRAPER

Y

Y, Greek .... UPSILON
Hebrew .... YOD(H)
in mathematics ....
ORDINATE
letter .... WYE
men .... ELIS
yabber ...... TALK, CHATTER,
GIBBER
yacht .... CRUISE(R),
KNOCKABOUT, CUTTER
club president ....
COMMODORE
flag .... BURGEE
racing .... SONDERCLASS
racing champion ....
INTREPID
sail .... SPINNAKER
tender .... DINGHY
yachting center ...... COWES
yachtsman .... LIPTON,
CORINTHIAN
Yadkin .... PEEDEE, RIVER
yaffle .... WOODPECKER
yager .... RIFLEMAN

yahoo ...... BRUTE, BUMPKIN,
LOUT
creator .... SWIFT
Yahwe(h) ..... GOD, JEHOVAH
yak .... SARLAK, OK
where found ...... TIBET
yaki .... CAYMAN
Yakutsk river .... LENA
Yale .... ELI, UNIVERSITY,
LOCK
Bowl sound ...... BOOLA
Mr. .... (ELIHU) ROOT
Yalta conference member ....
STALIN
native .... CRIMEAN
yam ..... ROOT, POTATO, UBE,
UBI, HOI
bean .... BONIATA, KAMA
Yamashita, Jap. general ......
TOMOYUKI
sobriquet .... TIGER
yamen resident ... MANDARIN
yammer ... WHINE, COMPLAIN,
YELL, WHIMPER, CLAMOR

Yangtze River city .... WUHU, NANKING
Yank ...... AMERICAN, JERK
Yankee .... AMERICAN, NORTHERNER
yap ..... YELP, JABBER, TALK, YAWP, YIP, BARK
   slang .... MOUTH, ROWDY, HOODLUM
Yaqui .... RIVER, INDIAN
yard .... SPAR, GROUNDS
   enclosed .... GARTH
   in law ...... CURTILAGE
   kind of ... PATIO, COURT, QUAD
yards, 220 .... FURLONG
yarn ..... STORY, TALE, SLUB, MERINO, THREAD, FIBER, SPINEL, INKLE, GARN, BOUCLE, ANGORA
   ball of .... CLEW
   count .... TYPP
   560 yards .... HANK
   flax .... LINEN
   knot .... BURL
   knitting .... SAXONY
   machine .... MULE
   measure .... CLUE, CLEW, LEA, SPINDLE, COP, HANK, SKEIN
   quantity .... SKEIN
   roll of .... COP
   skein of .... HASP
   teller ..... MUNCHAUSEN, ANGLER
   twilled .... CREWEL
   twisted .... CREWEL
   warp .... ABB
   waste .... THRUM
   winder .... PIRNER
   woolen, inferior .... SHODDY
   worsted .... CADDIS
yardstick .... STANDARD, CRITERION
yarrow .... MILFOIL, HERB
yashmak .... VEIL
yatag(h)an .... SABER
yaud .... MARE, JADE
yaupon ..... CASSINE, HOLLY, CASSENA
   use of .... TEA
yaw ...... TUMOR, DEVIATE, VEER
yawl .... JOLLYBOAT, SAILBOAT, KETCH, DANDY

yawn .... GAPE, CHASM, OSCITATE
   aloud ..... YAWP, YAUP
   meaning of, usually ....: FATIGUE, BOREDOM, DROWSINESS, ENNUI
yawner .... SLEEPYHEAD
yawning, fit of .... GAPES
yawp ...... YAP, GAPE, CRY, YAWN
yaws .... FRAMB(O)ESIA
   cause of ..... SPIROCHETE
Yb, in chemistry .. YTTERBIUM
yclept .... CALLED, NAMED, KNOWN (AS)
ye .... THEE, THOU
yea(h) ... YES, INDEED, TRULY
yean .... REAR, BRING FORTH
yeanling .... LAMB, KID, NEWBORN
year .... AGE, TIME, ANNO
   designating a .... LUNAR, SOLAR, NATURAL, TROPICAL, SIDEREAL, LEAP, FISCAL, CALENDAR
   every .... ANNUALLY, PER ANNUM
   half .... SEMESTER
   of plenary indulgence .... JUBILEE
yearbook .... ANNUAL, ALMANAC, ANNAL
yearling ..... LEVERET, COLT
yearly .... ANNUALLY, ETESIAN
   calendar ...... ALMANAC
yearn .... HANKER, LONG, ACHE, SIGH, CRAVE, PINE
years, 1000 .... CHILIAD
yeast .... BARM, LEAVEN, FERMENT, FOAM, FROTH, ANAMITE, BEES
   enzyme .... ZYMASE
Yed(d)o .... EDO, TOKYO
yegg .... CRIMINAL, SAFECRACKER, BURGLAR, TRAMP
yell .... YAMMER, SHOUT, SCREAM, SHRIEK, OUTCRY, CHEER, HOLLER, HALLOO
   college ..... CHEER, RAH
   ending cheers ..... TIGER
yellow ...... CHROME, DYE, PIGMENT, MELINE, ECRU, XANTHOUS, GAMBOGE

bird .... FOLDFINCH, WARBLER, CANARY, MELINE, ORIOLE
brown ..... DUN, SORREL
bugle .... IVA
calla .... AROID
clay ...... OCHER, OCHRE
colloquial ... COWARDLY
color .. XANTHIC, ALOMA, AMBER, GOLD, OCHER, SAFFRON
colored fruit .... MANGO, LEMON, AZAROLE
combining form .... CHRYS(O), XANTH(O), LUTEO
compound ... LUTEOLIN
daisy .. BLACK-EYED SUSAN
dark .... OCHRE
dye stuff .... MORIN
egg's .... YOLK
fever .... VOMITO
fever carrier .... AEDES, MOSQUITO
fever mosquito .... STEGOMYIA
flag signal .. QUARANTINE
gum resin .... CAMBOGIA
jacket .... WASP, VESPID, HORNET
journalism staple .... SCANDAL
lead ore ..... WULFENITE
metal ...... GOLD, BRASS
orange .... SAFFRON
pale ..... FLAXEN, BUFF
Peril harbinger .. CHINESE, MONGOLIANS
pigment .... FLAVIN, QUERCETIN, ORPIMENT, OCHRE, OCHER, ETIOLIN, SIL
quartz .... CITRINE
race .... CHINESE, MONGOL(IAN)
red .... CORAL
reddish .... SANDY
river .... HWANG HO
Sea .... HWANG HAI
Sea gulf .... POHAI
Sea port ..... TSINGTAO
Sea, river into .... YALU
skin, cause of .. JAUNDICE
turning .... FLAVESCENT
yellowbird .... WARBLER, GOLDFINCH

tree, per song ... BANANA
yellowhammer .... BIRD, FLICKER, WOODPECKER, YITE, VERDIN
state .... ALABAMA
yellowish brown .. CINNAMON, HAZEL, DRAB, KHAKI, FAWN
complexion .... SALLOW
red .... RUFOUS
yellowlegs .... SANDPIPER
Yellowstone sight ...... FALLS, LAKE, PARK
yellowtail ...... CARANGOID, ROCKFISH, MENHADEN
relative .... CAVALLA, POMPANO
yellowthroat .... WARBLER, BIRD
yellowweed ..... GOLDENROD, RAGWORT, CROWFOOT
yelp .... BARK, YAP, CRY, YAWP, YIP
Yemen capital .... SANA
city .... TAIZ, SANA
dynasty .... RASSITE
king ... (AL)BADR, IMAM
monetary unit .... RIYAL
neighbor of .... OMAN
president/premier ..... (AL)SALAL
seaport .... MOCHA
seat of government .. TAIZ
sect .... ZAIDI
town .... DAMAR
Yemenite .... ARAB
yen ... DESIRE, URGE, YEARN, LONG(ING), LIKING
where used ...... JAPAN
yenite .... LIVAITE
yeoman .... MANSERVANT, ASSISTANT, FREEHOLDER
yep .... YES
opposite of .... NOPE
yes .... AYE, YEP, YUP, AGREEMENT, YEA(H)
man .... SYCOPHANT
yeso .... GYPSUM
yet ... STILL, NOW, HOWEVER
yeti .. (ABOMINABLE) SNOWMAN
yew .... CONIFER, TREE
fruit .... BERRY, CONE
Yezd is in .... IRAN
Yiddish .... JEWISH, LANGUAGE
noodles .... FERFEL, FARFEL

synagogue .... SHUL
thief ..... GANEF, GANOF
yield .... GRANT, SUBMIT,
PRODUCT, RELENT,
CAPITULATE, DEFER,
GIVE(IN), SUCCUMB,
RETURN, PRODUCE,
SURRENDER, (CON)CEDE
farm .... CROP
gold .... PAN OUT
point .... CONCEDE
yill .... ALE
yip .... YELP, BARK
Ymir .... GIANT
yo-heave-ho, for example .....
CHANT
yodel .... WARBLE
yodeler .... SWISS, TYROLEAN
yoga need .... CONCENTRATION
yogi .... ASCETIC, MYSTIC,
SWAMI
ballplayer .... BERRA
yoke ..... CANGUE, HARNESS,
BONDAGE, SERVITUDE,
INSPAN, ENSLAVE, COUPLE,
HALTER
part of .... OXBOW
yokefellow .... PARTNER,
ASSOCIATE, HUSBAND, WIFE
yokel ..... RUSTIC, BUMPKIN,
HICK, RUBE
Yokum's creator .... CAPP
yolk, egg .... YELLOW,
VITELLUS
of the egg ..... VITELLINE
protein .... VITELLIN
yolked .... LECITHAL
yom .... DAY
Jewish holiday ... KIPPUR
yon(der) .... THERE
yore .... ELD, LONG AGO
yorker, game associated with ..
CRICKET
Yorkshire native ... DALESMAN
port ..... HULL, WHITBY
river .... AIRE
Yoruba .... NEGRO
Yosemite sight .... PARK,
CLIFFS, FALLS, REDWOOD
Yoshihito's empire ..... JAPAN
reign .... TAISHO
son .... HIROHITO
title .... EMPEROR
young .... YOUTHFUL, GREEN,
RAW, IMMATURE,
ADOLESCENT, JUVENILE

animal .... SUCKLING,
TOTO
cat .... KITTEN, PUSSY,
KITTY
bird .... FLEDGLING,
NESTLING, OWLET
blood .... YOUTH
branch .... SHOOT
bull .... CALF
chicken .... FRYER
cod .... SCROD
cow .... CALF, HEIFER
deer .... DOE, FAWN
dog .... PUP(PY), WHELP
eel .... ELVER
fish ..... PRY, FINGERLING,
PARR, SMELT, GRILSE
fowl .... POULT
fox .... CUB
frog .... TADPOLE
girl ...... MISS, MOPPET,
LASS, MAIDEN
goat .... KID
goose .... GOSLING
hare .... LEVERET
hawk ...... EYAS, EYRIE,
AERIE
hen ... PULLET, POULARD
herring .... BRIT,
SARDINE
hog .... GILT, SHOAT,
PORKER, SHOTE
horse ...... COLT, FILLY,
FOAL
kangaroo .... JOEY
lion ...... WHELP, CUB,
LIONET
male .... BUCK
man .... MASTER, YOUTH
Mormon church head ...
BRIGHAM
oyster .... SPAT
ox .... STEER
pigeon .... SQUAB
salmon ... PARR, GRILSE
seal .... PUP
sheep .... LAMB
squab .... PIPER
swan .... CYGNET
tiger ...... CUB, WHELP
Turks, so-called .. REBELS
whale .... CUB
with ...... PREGNANT,
ON THE WAY
wolf .... WHELP
younger son .... CADET

youngster .... SHAVER, BANTLING, SMALL FRY, TOT, TAD, LAD, YOUTH, KID, MINOR, URCHIN, TEENAGER
yours truly .... ME
youth .... LAD, STRIPLING, SHAVER, SHAVELING, SAPLING, CHIEL(D), TEENAGER, YOUNGSTER, ADOLESCENCE, WHELP, MINOR
  beautiful .... NARCISSUS
  group: abbr. ... BSA, GSA
  of a .... MINOR
youthful ... JUVENILE, VERNAL
  works .... JUVENALIA
yow .... OUCH
yowl ...... WAIL, CRY, YELL
yperite .... MUSTARD GAS
  where used in battle ..... YPRES
Yquem ... WINE, SAUTERNE(S)
Yseult .... ISOLDE
Yuan .... TAEL, DYNASTY
yuca .... MANIOC, CASSAVA
Yucatan capital ..... MERIDA
  Indian .... MAYA
  leaf fiber .... SISAL
  Mayan city .... USMAL
yucca ...... LILY, FLAT, PITA
  fiber .... ISOTE
  plant like .... SOTOL
Yuga .... ERA, AGE
  period ..... TRETA, KALI, KRITA, DVAPARA
Yugoslav(ia) capital .... BELGRADE, BEOGRAD
  city .... SENTA, ZAGREB, SKOPJE, SARAJEVO, NOVI SAD, NIS, AGRAM, SERAJEVO
  coin .... DINAR, PARA

Commune .... STIP
  district ... YUPA, BANAT
  guerrillas .... CHETNIKS, PARTISANS
  language .... SLOVENE
  monetary unit ... DINAR
  native .. CROAT, SLOVENE, SERB
  news agency .... TANJUG
  part of .... CROATIA, BOSNIA, MONTENEGRO, MACEDONIA, SLOVENIA
  peninsula .... ISTRIA
  port .... RIJEKA
  premier .... SPILJAK
  president .... TITO (BROZ)
  region .... DALMATIA, BANAT
  republic .. MONTENEGRO, SERBIA, CROATIA
  river ...... DRAU, DRINA, SAVA, DRAVA, PULJ, MORAVA, USKUB, TISZA
  seaport ..... POLA, PULJ, ZARA, SPALATO
  town .... CETINJE, CAPORETTO
Yukon capital .. WHITEHORSE
  mining town .. SKAGWAY
  mountain .... LOGAN, LUCANIA
  peak .... LOGAN
  region ...... KLONDIKE
  tributary .... TANANA
yule .... CHRISTMAS
  short for .... XMAS
  symbol .. LOG, MISTLETOE
Yum yum's friend ..... KOKO
Yuma ...... MOHAVE, INDIAN, MOJAVE
yummy ... TASTY, DELECTABLE
Yunnan capital .... KUNMING
Yutang, writer .... LIN

Z

Z, Arabic .... ZE
  English .... ZED
  Greek .... ZETA
  Hebrew .... ZAYIN
  letter .. IZZARD, ZEE, ZED
Zabrze is in .... POLAND
zac .... IBEX
  Starr father of .... RINGO
zacaton .... GRASS
Zaccur's father .... IMRI

Zambal .... MALAY
Zambezi tributary ..... SHIRE
Zamenhof's invention .... ESPERANTO
Zambia capital ...... LUSAKA
  city .... LUSAKA, KITWE, NDOLA
  language ...... BAMBA, TONGA, LOZI
  president ...... KAUNDA

river .... ZAMBEZI
zany ..... BUFFOON, CLOWN,
DOLT, SIMPLETON, FOOL
Zanzibar island ...... PEMBA
Zarathustra ...... ZOROASTER
zarf .... CUP
Zasu ___, comedienne .. PITTS
Zea .... KEOS, ISLAND
zeal .... ARDOR, FERVOR,
PASSION, ENTHUSIASM,
ELAN, VERVE
Zealand city .... COPENHAGEN
fiord .... ISSE
zealot ...... DEVOTEE, BIGOT,
FAN, PARTISAN, FANATIC,
ENTHUSIAST
zealotry .... FANATICISM
Zealots' conqueror .... TITUS,
VESPASIAN
zealous ... FERVENT, ARDENT,
RABID
zebec(k) .... SHIP
Zebedee's son .. JOHN, JAMES
zebra and horse offspring .....
ZEBRULA
and ass offspring ....
ZEBRASS
animal resembling .. ASS,
HORSE, QUAGGA
extinct .... QUAGGA
of the .... ZEBRINE
wood .... ARAROBA
young .... COLT
zebu .... BRAHMA
and yak offspring .. ZOBO,
BO(H)
zebuder .... IBEX, ZAC
zecchin(o) ...... COIN, SEQUIN
zed, equivalent of .... ZEE,
IZZARD
zee .... IZZARD
Zeeland, capital of ....
MIDDELBURG
island ...... WALCHEREN
zenana ..... HAREM, SERAGLIO
factotum ...... EUNUCH
resident .... ODALISK,
ODALISQUE, CONCUBINE
zenith .. APEX, PEAK, SUMMIT,
TOP, ACME, HEIGHT, VERTEX
opposed to ...... NADIR
sun's .... NOON
Zeno philosophy ... STOICISM
follower ... STOIC, CYNIC
Zenobia .... QUEEN
domain of ..... PALMYRA

zephyr .... BREEZE, WIND
Zephyrus ...... WEST, WIND,
DEITY
zeppelin .... DIRIGIBLE, BLIMP
zero .... CIPHER, NIL,
(N)AUGHT, NOTHING,
(N)OUGHT, NULLITY
on a compass .... NORTH
Zerulah's son ...... ABISHAI
zest ... BRIO, STINGO, FLAVOR,
RELISH, PEEL, ZING, GUSTO,
VITALITY, TASTE, PIQUANCY,
ZEAL
zestful ...... SAPID, PIQUANT
zeta .... ZEE, ZED, IZZARD
Zeus .... JUPITER
attendant of .... NIKE
beloved to .... IO,
EUROPA, LEDA
breastplate of ... (A)EGIS
brother of .... HADES
changed her to stone ....
NIOBE
daughter of .. IRENE, HEBE
disguise of .... SWAN
Egyptian's ..... AMMON
epithet ... SOTER, AMMON
festival .... NEMEAN
gift to Minos ..... TALOS
messenger of .... IRIS
monster killed by ....
TYPHOEUS
nurse of .... GOAT
oracle seat ..... DODONA
parent of .. RHEA, CRONUS
punishment to mankind of
PANDORA
shield of .... (A)EGIS
sister of .... HERA
son of .... AMPHION,
HEPHAESTUS, TANTALUS,
SARPEDON, ARES,
AEACUS, APOLLO,
PERSEUS, HERMES,
ARGUS, MINOS, ARCAS
surname of ..... ALASTOR
wife/lover of ... DEMETER,
JUNO, CERES, LATONA,
CALLISTO, THEMIS,
AEGLE, LEDA, DANAE,
HERA, LETO, DIONE,
METIS, EUROPA, SEMELE,
ALCMENE, AEGINA,
EURYNOME, ANTIOPE,
MAIA
Zhukov, marshal ..... GRIGORI

Zibeline .... (SABLE)FUR
Ziegfeld show ..... RIO RITA,
             SHOWGIRL
   theatrical producer ......
             FLO(RENZ)
ziggurat .... PYRAMID
zigzag .... CRANK(LE), TACK,
        STAGGER, FORKED
   course .... TACK, PLY
   road ..... SWITCHBACK
   skiing race ...... SLALOM
   what it has plenty of .....
            ANGLES
Zilpah's son ..... GAD, ASHER
Zimbalist, violinist .... EFREM
zinc .... SPELTER
   alloy ..... BIDRI, OROIDE,
      TOMBAK, TOMBAC(K)
   blende ..... SPHALERITE
   carbonate ....CALAMINE,
          SMITHSONITE
   ingots .... SPELTER
   oxide .... TUTTY
   ore .... BLENDE
   silicate ...... CALAMINE
zing ..... ZEST, VITALITY, PEP
zingara, zingaro ...... GYPSY
zingel .... PERCH
zinnia .... ASTER
Zion ..... HILL, HEAVEN, JEW
   site of .... JERUSALEM
Zionism, founder of ... HERZL
zip .. HISS, VIM, ENERGY, WHIZZ
   and ____ .... ZING
Zipangu ..... CIPANGO, JAPAN
   namer of .. (MARCO) POLO
zipper ..... (SLIDE) FASTENER,
     BOOT, OVERSHOE, TALON
zircon .... AZORITE, JACINTH
zither, instrument like .. LYRE,
     ROTA, CITHARA, VINA
zizany .... COCKLE, TARES
zizith .... TASSELS
zloty is money of .... POLAND
zoa, singular of .... ZOON
Zoan .... TANIS
zodiac .... GIRDLE, CIRCLE
   sign ... CRAB, LEO, LIBRA,
     PISCES, GEMINI, ARIES,
       RAM, VIRGO
zodiacal chart .... HOROSCOPE
Zola, ____ .... EMILE
   defender of .... DREYFUS
   heroine .... NANA
   novel ..... NANA, VERITE
          GERMINAL

zombi(e) .... COCKTAIL,
     PYTHON, SNAKE
   subject of ...... CORPSE
zone .... BELT, AREA, GIRDLE,
            CLIME
   designation ..... TORRID,
     TEMPERATE, FRIGID
zoo .... MENAGERIE
   floating .... ARK
zooid .... CORAL, POLYPITE,
         HYDRANTH
zoological region ... NOTOGAEA
zoologist's concern ......
          ANIMAL(IA)
zoology branch on shells ......
        CONCHOLOGY
zoophyte .... SPONGE, CORAL,
         RETEPORE
zoot ____ .... SUIT
"Zorba the Greek" composer ..
        THEODORAKIS
zoril(a) ... POLECAT, MARIPUT,
         WEASEL
   animal like a .... SKUNK
Zoroaster ..... ZARATHUSTRA
Zoroastra's birthplace ....
        AZERBAIJAN
Zoroastrian ... PARSEE, PARSI,
         YEMA
   demon .... DEVA
   evil spirit .... AHRIMAN
   fire worshipper .. CHEBER,
         PARSI
   god ...... AHURA, MAZDA
   sacred writings ....
     (ZEND)-AVESTA
   supreme deity .. ORMAZD,
        ORMUZD
   teaching ...... HUMATA,
    HUKHATA, HUVARSHTA
Zoroastrianism, commentary on
        ZEND
zoster .... BELT, GIRDLE
zuccetto .... SKULLCAP
zucchini .... SQUASH
Zug .... CANTON
Zuider ____ .... ZEE
zuisin .... WIDGEON
Zulu ..... MATABELE, BANTU,
      KAFFIR, ISLAND
   band of warriors ... IMPI
   headman .... INDUNA
   language .... BANTU
   spear ... ASSAGAI, ASSEGAI
Zululand capital .... ESHOWE

Zuni .... PUEBLO
Zweig, novelist ...... ARNOLD,
STEFAN
zygodactyl bird .... PARROT

zygote .... OOSPERM
zymase .... ENZYME
zymone .... GLUTEN
zythepsary .... BREWER

Notes

Notes

Notes

Notes

Notes

Notes

Notes

Notes

Notes